THE
GROVE
CONCISE
DICTIONARY
of
MUSIC

THE
GROVE
CONCISE
DICTIONARY
of
MUSIC

Edited by Stanley Sadie

Assistant Editor Alison Latham

© 1988 Macmillan Press Ltd, London

All rights reserved. No part of this publication
may be reproduced or transmitted, in any form or by any means,
without permission.

First published in the UK by
MACMILLAN PRESS LTD
Stockton House, 1 Melbourne Place, London WC2B 4LF
and Basingstoke

British Library Cataloguing in Publication Data

The Grove concise dictionary of music
1. Music – Encyclopaedias
I. Sadie, Stanley, *1930–*
780'.3'21

ISBN 0-333-43236-3

First American edition published 1988 as
The Norton/Grove Concise Encyclopedia of Music by
W.W. NORTON & COMPANY
500 Fifth Avenue, New York, NY 10100

ISBN 0-393-02620-5

Typeset by August Filmsetting, Haydock, St Helens
Printed in Great Britain by Bath Press, Avon

Preface

The name of Sir George Grove has always been identified, in the world of musical lexicography, with works that are both large and authoritative. The present work aims to retain the authority but within more modest dimensions. It does not represent an attempt to pour ten quarts into a pint pot: it should not be regarded as a concise version of the 20-volume *New Grove Dictionary of Music and Musicians* (1980). This dictionary was conceived and written for a different readership from that of *The New Grove*. It may, and I hope will, also be consulted by the same readership, for speedy reference or for information on events too recent for *The New Grove*; but our expectation is that it will chiefly be used by a broad sweep of music-lovers and students, and it is with their needs in mind that it was written.

Why, then, call it 'Grove' at all? There are two reasons. First, it is published by the same publishers, and edited by the same editor, as prepared *The New Grove*, and in its compilation *The New Grove* was its primary source book. Secondly, it was put together along broadly the same principles as informed *The New Grove*. Its articles were drafted by specialists, covering each subject area (and so bringing to it a specialist knowledge of recent events and recent research), before they were passed on to the editor and his assistants, who have aimed to ensure some degree of uniformity in style and approach and a proper balance between them. Further, the dictionary has aimed to maintain, as far as is practical within the constraints of a more limited scale, the sense of values and their literate expression traditional to Grove dictionaries.

The scope of the present dictionary, too, is as close to that of *The New Grove* as its scale permits. It does not, of course, carry the exhaustive bibliographical articles that *Grove* does, nor even concise equivalents of them, because the essence of their usefulness lies in their comprehensiveness and because the needs they serve are essentially academic. But it does cover, besides the central ground of composers, performers, instruments, terminology and genres, such topics as music publishing and publishers, instrument makers, acoustics and non-Western music (both in articles on important non-Western instruments and in general articles surveying national or regional music traditions). The dictionary also includes, unlike *The New Grove*, more than 1000 entries under the names or nicknames of individual works.

*

Broadly speaking, the lexicographical policies in this dictionary follow those of *The New Grove*. Entry headings are alphabetized as if continuous (ignoring spaces, hyphens, apostrophes, accents, modifications etc) up to the first mark of punctuation, then again thereafter if that mark is a comma. British terminology is generally preferred (crotchet rather than quarter-note, etc), but American is also given in specialized contexts. Transliteration systems follow those of *The New Grove*, with the same recognized exceptions (Tchaikovsky, Prokofiev); where a familiar form is not favoured, a cross-reference will be found leading to the preferred form (for example Chaliapin/Shalyapin).Cross-references are indicated by the printing of words in small capitals, with an initial large capital for the word under which the entry is to be found. For titles of works, English forms are normally preferred for other than western European languages; English forms are also used for works well known under accepted English titles. Lists of works in composer entries are, necessarily, selective. Oblique strokes indicate alternatives. We have generally used modern place-names rather than historical ones, but found ourselves unable to pursue such a policy rigorously (it is difficult, for example, to refer to Leningrad rather than St Petersburg or Petrograd, especially in relation to a time before Lenin was born; that is not the only exception that common sense has demanded). The dates given in lists of works are dates of composition (completion where composition – as opposed to minor revision – continued from one year to another) except for stage works, where dates of first performance are given. The dictionary aims to be up-to-date to early 1988.

A large team of writers and advisers has helped in the preparation of the work. Among the most prolific writers have been Malcolm Boyd, David Cummings, Paul Griffiths, Leanne Langley and Fiona Little, along with myself and the assistant editor; others who have contributed substantially include Elisabeth Agate, Tess Knighton, Helen Myers, Judith Nagley, Ian Payne, David Roberts, Sarah Roberts, Ian Rumbold, Alyn Shipton and Audrey Twine, while help has also been received from Christina Bashford, Andrew Clements, Ann Lewis, Theresa Lister, Anthony Marks, Jeremy Sams and Lilija Zobens. Claire Brook, of W.W. Norton (New York), gave valuable advice on aspects of editorial policy. Above all I am grateful to my assistant editor, Alison Latham, for her untiring work on the editorial preparation of articles and her efforts to give them clear expression and consistent usage. I would like to express my warm gratitude, too, to the numerous users of (and contributors to) *The New Grove* who have written to me over the years with corrections and other suggestions, many of which have helped us to improve the accuracy of the present work. The process continues: letters (sent c/o Macmillan Press, Little Essex Street, London WC2R 3LF) with information on any errors or other shortcomings found in the present work will be gratefully received and noted for the future.

STANLEY SADIE
London, July 1988

Abbreviations

A	alto, contralto [voice]	Chin.	Chinese
a	alto [instrument]	chit	chitarrone
ABC	American Broadcasting Company; Australian Broadcasting Commission	Cie	Compagnie
		cimb	cimbalom
acc.	accompaniment, accompanied by	cl	clarinet
AD	anno Domini	clvd	clavichord
ad lib	ad libitum	cm	centimetre(s)
amp	amplified	CNRS	Centre National de la Recherche Scientifique (F)
AMS	American Musicological Society		
Anh.	Anhang [appendix]	Co.	Company; County
anon.	anonymous(ly)	collab.	in collaboration with
appx	appendix	conc.	concerto
arr.	arrangement, arranged by/for	cond.	conductor, conducted by
attrib.	attribution, attributed to	cont	continuo
aut.	autumn	Corp.	Corporation
		c.p.s.	cycles per second
B	bass [voice]	Ct	countertenor
b	bass [instument]	Cz.	Czech
b	born		
BA	Bachelor of Arts	D	Deutsch catalogue [Schubert]; Dounias catalogue [Tartini]
bap.	baptized		
Bar	baritone [voice]	*d.*	denarius, denarii [penny, pence]
BBC	British Broadcasting Corporation	*d*	died
BC	British Columbia (Canada)	Dan.	Danish
BC	before Christ	db	double bass
bc	basso continuo	DBE	Dame Commander of the Order of the British Empire
bk	book		
BMus	Bachelor of Music	dbn	double bassoon
bn	bassoon	DC	District of Columbia (USA)
Bros.	Brothers	ded.	dedication, dedicated to
bur.	buried	Dept	Department
BVM	Blessed Virgin Mary	dir.	director, directed by
BWV	Bach-Werke-Verzeichnis [Schmieder, catalogue of J. S. Bach's works]	DMus	Doctor of Music
		DPhil	Doctor of Philosophy
c	circa [about]	ed.	editor, edited (by)
cap.	capacity	edn.	edition
carn.	Carnival	e.g.	exempli gratia [for example]
CBC	Canadian Broadcasting Corporation	elec	electric, electronic
CBE	Commander of the Order of the British Empire	EMI	Electrical and Musical Industries
		Eng.	English
CBS	Columbia Broadcasting System (USA)	eng hn	english horn
CBSO	City of Birmingham Symphony Orchestra	ens	ensemble
cel	celesta	esp.	especially
CH	Companion of Honour	etc	et cetera [and so on]
chap.	chapter	ex., exx.	example, examples

F ...   Fellow of the ...
f, ff   following page, following pages
f., ff.   folio, folios
f   forte
facs.   facsimile
fig.   figure [illustration]
fl   flute
fl   floruit [he/she flourished]
fp   fortepiano
Fr.   French

Ger.   German
Gk.   Greek
glock   glockenspiel
govt.   government [district in USSR]
grad   gradual
GSM   Guildhall School of Music and Drama, London
gui   guitar

H   Hoboken catalogue [Haydn]; Helm catalogue [C.P.E. Bach]
Heb.   Hebrew
HMS   His/Her Majesty's Ship
HMV   His Master's Voice
hn   horn
Hon.   Honorary; Honourable
hpd   harpsichord
Hung.   Hungarian
Hz   Hertz [c.p.s.]

ibid   ibidem [in the same place]
i.e.   id est [that is]
IFMC   International Folk Music Council
IMS   International Musicological Society
Inc.   Incorporated
inc.   incomplete
incl.   includes, including
inst(s)   instrument(s), instrumental
int   introit
ISCM   International Society for Contemporary Music
ISM   Incorporated Society of Musicians (GB)
It.   Italian

Jap.   Japanese
jr   junior

K   Kirkpatrick catalogue [D. Scarlatti]; Köchel catalogue [Mozart; no. after/is from 6th edn.]
kbd   keyboard
KBE   Knight Commander of the Order of the British Empire
kHz   kilohertz
km   kilometre(s)

L   Longo catalogue [D. Scarlatti]
£   libra, librae [pound, pounds sterling]
Lat.   Latin
lib   libretto
LittD   Doctor of Letters/Literature
LlB   Bachelor of Laws

LlD   Doctor of Laws
LP   long-playing record
LPO   London Philharmonic Orchestra
LSO   London Symphony Orchestra

M.   Monsieur
MA   Master of Arts
mand   mandolin
mar   marimba
MBE   Member of the Order of the British Empire
Met   Metropolitan Opera House, New York
Mez   mezzo-soprano
Mlle   Mademoiselle
mm   millimetre(s)
Mme   Madame
MMus   Master of Music
movt   movement
MP   Member of Paliament (GB)
MS(S)   manuscript(s)
Mt   Mount
MusB   Bachelor of Music
MusD   Doctor of Music
MusM   Master of Music

NBC   National Broadcasting Company (USA)
n.d.   no date of publication
no.   number
Nor.   Norwegian
n.p.   no place of publication
nr.   near

ob   oboe
obbl   obbligato
OBE   Officer of the Order of the British Empire
OM   Order of Merit
op., opp.   opus, opera
opt.   optional
orch   orchestra, orchestral
orchd   orchestrated (by)
org   organ
orig.   original(ly)
ORTF   Office de Radiodiffusion-Télévision Française
ov.   overture

P   Pincherle catalogue [Vivaldi]
p., pp.   page, pages
p   piano
p.a.   per annum
perc   percussion
perf.   performance, performed (by)
pf   piano
PhD   Doctor of Philosophy
pic   piccolo
pl.   plate; plural
PO   Philharmonic Orchestra
Pol.   Polish
Port.   Portuguese
posth.   posthumous(ly)
pr.   printed
PRO   Public Record Office, London
prol   prologue

PRS	Performing Right Society (GB)	str.	string(s)
Ps	Psalm	sum.	summer
pseud.	pseudonym	suppl.	supplement, supplementary
pt.	part	Swed.	Swedish
pubd	published	sym.	symphony, symphonic
pubn	publication	synth	synthesizer
qnt	quintet	T	tenor [voice]
qt	quartet	t	tenor [instrument]
		timp	timpani
R	Ryom catalogue [Vivaldi]	tpt	trumpet
R	photographic reprint	Tr	treble [voice]
r	recto	trans.	translation, translated by
RAI	Radio Audizioni Italiane	transcr.	transcription, transcribed by/for
RAM	Royal Academy of Music, London	trbn	trombone
RCA	Radio Corporation of America		
RCM	Royal College of Music, London	U.	University
rec	recorder	UK	United Kingdom of Great Britain and
recit	recitative		Northern Ireland
red.	reduction, reduced for	unacc.	unaccompanied
repr.	reprinted	unattrib.	unattributed
Rev.	Reverend	UNESCO	United Nations Educational, Scientific and
rev.	revision, revised (by/for)		Cultural Organization
RMCM	Royal Manchester College of Music	unperf.	unperformed
RNCM	Royal Northern College of Music,	unpubd	unpublished
	Manchester	US	United States [adjective]
RO	Radio Orchestra	USA	United States of America
Rom.	Romanian	USSR	Union of Soviet Socialist Republics
RPO	Royal Philharmonic Orchestra (GB)		
RSO	Radio Symphony Orchestra	v, vv	voice, voices
Rt Hon.	Right Honourable	v., vv.	verse, verses
RTE	Radio Telefis Eireann (Ireland)	*v*	verso
Russ.	Russian	va	viola
		vc	cello
S	San, Santa, Santo, São [Saint]; soprano	vib	vibraphone
	[voice]	viz	videlicet [namely]
$	dollars	vle	violone
s	soprano [instrument]	vn	violin
s.	solidus, solidi [shilling, shillings]	vol.	volume
SABC	South African Broadcasting Corporation		
sax	saxophone	wint.	winter
ser.	series	woo	Werke ohne Opuszahl [works without opus
SO	Symphony Orchestra		number]
SPNM	Society for the Promotion of New Music	WQ	Wotquenne catalogue [C. P. E. Bach]
	(GB)		
spr.	spring		
SS	Saints	ww	woodwind
Ss	Santissima, Santissimo		
SSR	Soviet Socialist Republic	xyl	xylophone
St	Saint, Sint, Szent		
Ste	Sainte	z	Zimmerman catalogue [Purcell]

A

A. (1) Name of a note, or a PITCH CLASS; *see also* PITCH NAMES. It is the 6th degree in the scale of C major, and is usually taken as the standard for tuning, $a' = 440$ cycles per second (or Hz) being the normal concert level; *see* PITCH.

(2) The Italian word *a* is used in music as a preposition, e.g. 'a 2', to mean 'in two voices'. In early music it refers to the number of voices in a polyphonic work; in scores after 1700 'a 2' means that two instruments play a single line together. The French equivalent is *à*.

Aaron [Aron], **Pietro** (*b* Florence, *c*1480; *d* ?Bergamo, *c*1550). Italian music theorist and composer. He was *cantor* at Imola Cathedral from *c*1515 to 1522, when he went to Venice. In 1536 he entered a monastery in Bergamo. In his valuable treatises, his ideas on modes, counterpoint, temperaments etc are always practical and often extend traditional ones: *Toscanello* (1523) is important for its clear, progressive discussions of musical practice. His correspondence with other musicians is also informative.

Aaron Copland School of Music. Name given in 1981 to the music department of Queens College, City University of New York.

Aaron Scotus (*b* ?Scotland, late 10th century; *d* Cologne, 18 Nov 1052). Benedictine abbot and theorist. As abbot of St Martin at Cologne, he decreed that his monks should sing the Office of St Gregory the Great composed by Pope Leo IX (1049–54) instead of the Common of Confessors. He wrote three treatises, dealing with singing, the Gregorian psalm tones and consonances.

Abaco, Evaristo Felice dall'. *See* DALL'ABACO, EVARISTO FELICE.

Abbado, Claudio (*b* Milan, 26 June 1933). Italian conductor. He studied under his father, at Milan and in Vienna, won several competitions and appeared widely in Italy. He conducted the Vienna PO at Salzburg in 1965, and made his New York and London débuts in the 1960s. He has worked at La Scala (1968, musical director, 1972–86), was principal guest conductor of the Chicago SO (1982–5), principal conductor (1979) and music director of the LSO (1983–8) and of the Vienna Staatsoper (from 1986). Besides the Romantic repertory and especially Verdi, he is noted for his vivid conducting of 20th-century music.

Abbatini, Antonio Maria (*b* Città di Castello, 1609-10; *d* there, *c*1678). Italian composer. He held several positions as *maestro di cappella*, mainly in Rome (notably at St John Lateran and S Maria Maggiore) but also at Orvieto Cathedral and the Santa Casa, Loreto. His most important work is the comic opera *Dal male il bene* (1653 – Acts 1 and 3; Act 2 by Marazzoli), which includes much *secco* recitative and two early ensemble finales. He wrote two further operas, but his output consisted mainly of sacred music. Most of the surviving works are small-scale concertato *sacre canzoni*, but he also cultivated the massive polychoral style.

Abbellimenti (It.). Embellishments.

Abbott, Emma (*b* Chicago, 9 Dec 1850; *d* Salt Lake City, 5 Jan 1891). American soprano and impresario. She studied in New York, Milan and Paris and made her opera début in London in 1876 but her contract was cancelled when she refused to sing *La traviata* on the grounds that it was immoral. She made her New York début the next year but was criticized for interpolating hymns into operas. She formed her own opera company in 1878 and did much to popularize opera and operetta in the USA.

Abbreviations. In musical notation, abbreviations are often used to save tiresome repetitions or leger lines. Repetitions of entire sections of a piece may be notated by two dots (occasionally four), arranged vertically in front of a double bar, to signify the repetition of a passage ending at that double bar or bounded by two double bars so marked (the first of such a pair has the dots following). Smaller-scale abbreviation includes slashes through a note stem, to indicate repetition (the number of slashes indicates the rate of repetition, the note head its duration) and the joining of notes by an oblique stroke to indicate oscillation (the stroke indicates the rate of oscillation, the note head its duration). Verbal abbreviations include 'col 8va', to indicate that a passage should be played in octaves (adding the octave above or below, according to the placing of the rubric); '8va' by itself indicates that the passage should be played an octave higher or lower (according to its placing). Another common abbreviation is *a 2*, to indicate either that two instruments play a passage together or that the instruments should be divided into two groups.

Abduction from the Seraglio, The. *See* ENTFÜHRUNG AUS DEM SERAIL, DIE.

Abe, Kōmei (*b* Hiroshima, 1 Sept 1911). Japanese composer. He studied the cello, composition and conducting at Tokyo Music School and has taught at the music college and the Academy of Arts in Kyoto. His music, spirited and firmly constructed, includes nine string quartets (1935–55), a Clarinet Quintet (1942) and a Piano Sextet (1964) as well as a Cello Concerto (1937) and two symphonies (1957, 1960).

Abegg Variations. Schumann's op.1, for piano (1830): the principal theme is based on the notes A–Bb–E–G–G.

Abel, Carl Friedrich (*b* Cöthen, 22 Dec 1723; *d* London, 20 June 1787). German composer. By 1743 he was a bass viol player in the Dresden court orchestra. He left in 1757–8 and went to London, where he directed his first joint concert with J.C. Bach in 1764; both men became chamber musicians to Queen Charlotte about this time. The Bach–Abel series, begun in 1765 and comprising 10–15 concerts each year, was given in their own rooms in Hanover Square from 1775. Abel directed alternate concerts, including many of his own works, often playing himself and introducing performers from Germany and Paris (where he visited regularly). He and Bach also gave concerts elsewhere, including at court. After Bach's death (1782) Abel spent two years in Germany but was active in the 1785–7 series, the Grand Professional Concerts.

Abel was one of the last professional bass violists; his expressive Adagios were especially praised. As a composer he was most prolific in symphonies and overtures (over 40 works), sonatas for two and three instruments, and bass viol pieces. His works, mostly in three movements, are generally genial and energetic but use a rich harmonic style, often unusual phrase-lengths, and melodies of instrumental character.

Abel was one of a long line of musicians. His grandfather Clamor Heinrich (1634–96) was a composer, organist and bass violist who worked at Celle, Hanover and Bremen. His father, Christian Ferdinand (1682–1761), also a bass violist, was a colleague of J.S. Bach at Cöthen, and his elder brother, Leopold August (1718–94), was a violinist at north German courts and composed several instrumental works. Johann Leopold (1795–1871), a grandson of Carl August, was a pianist and composer who taught music at German courts and later lived in London.

Abelard, Peter (*b* Le Pallet, 1079; *d* St-Marcel, 21 April 1142). French philosopher, poet and musician. He studied and taught in Paris and was famous for his love-songs (now lost) for Heloise, whom he married secretly in 1118; he was later castrated. His six biblical *planctus* (laments) are highly original and influenced the later French LAI.

Abendmusik (Ger.). 'Evening music': term used for Sunday evening concerts, mainly of sacred music, held in the Marienkirche, Lübeck; they began in the 1640s, flourished under Buxtehude in the late 17th century, and ceased soon after 1800.

Abert, Hermann (*b* Stuttgart, 25 March 1871; *d* there, 13 Aug 1927). German musicologist. He studied in Berlin and Halle, and taught in those universities and Leipzig, where his pupils included Blume, Fellerer and his daughter Anna Amalie Abert (*b* 1906). He was a wide-ranging scholar whose central achievements were his opera studies and his standard biography (after Jahn) of Mozart (1919–21).

Abingdon, 4th Earl of [Bertie, Willoughby] (*b* Gainsborough, 16 Jan 1740; *d* Rycote, 26 Sept 1799). English patron and composer. He was associated with J.C. Bach and C.F. Abel in London, and met (and was influenced by) Haydn, who began to set *The Invocation of Neptune* at his suggestion. He composed mostly songs and other vocal works, including a choral *Representation of the Execution of Mary Queen of Scots in Seven Views* (1790).

Abondante, Giulio (*fl* 1546–87). Italian lutenist and composer. He may have worked in Venice. His three extant books of solo lute music (two more are lost) include dance movements (e.g. galliards, passamezzos), fantasias and arrangements of vocal works.

Abos, Girolamo (*b* La Valetta, 16 Nov 1715; *d* Naples, Oct 1760). Maltese composer. He was a pupil of Durante in Naples and became *maestro* of the S Onofrio conservatory there; Paisiello was among his pupils. He was a respected composer of operas, mainly serious; several were staged in London. His church music, like Durante's, combines homophonic writing with the polyphonic tradition.

Abraham, Gerald (Ernest Heal) (*b* Newport, Isle of Wight, 9 March 1904; *d* Midhurst, 18 March 1988). English musicologist. He worked first as a writer, then for the BBC, and as professor at Liverpool University. Much of his finest work was on Russian and east European music and Romantic music generally; but his range was wide and his writings are informed by a broad cultural sympathy and perceptive critical judgment.

Abraham and Isaac. Britten's Canticle II (1952) for alto, tenor and piano on a text from the Chester miracle play.

Sacred ballad by Stravinsky for baritone and chamber orchestra (1963).

Abrahamsen, Hans (*b* Kongens Lyngby, 23 Dec 1952). Danish composer. He studied at the Royal Danish Academy with Bentzon and at the Jutland Academy with Nørgård and Gudmundsen-Holmgreen. His early works cultivate a detached simplicity; later ones tend to be frenetic on a miniature scale. They include *Walden* for wind quintet (1978) and string quartets.

Ábrányi, Kornél (*b* Szentgyörgyábrány, 15 Oct 1822; *d* Budapest, 20 Dec 1903). Hungarian writer on music. As a teacher and editor (1860–76) of the first Hungarian music periodical, *Zenészeti lapok*, he campaigned for a native musical idiom and the improvement of musical life and education. He did much to strengthen Liszt's connections with Hungary and wrote books on 19th-century Hungarian music.

Abravanel, Maurice (de) (*b* Thessaloniki, 6 Jan 1903). American conductor. He studied in Germany with Weill and left for the USA in 1936, conducting at the Met and on Broadway; in 1947 he became conductor of the Utah SO.

Abschiedsymphonie. *See* FAREWELL SYMPHONY.

Absil, Jean (*b* Bon-Secours, 23 Oct 1893; *d* Uccle, 2 Feb 1974). Belgian composer. He studied as an organist and then with Gilson for composition (1920–22). He taught at the Brussels Conservatory, 1939–59. At first he followed the late Romantic style of his teacher (e.g. in *Rhapsodie flamande*, 1928) but concerts by the Pro Arte Quartet introduced him to Berg, Milhaud, Hindemith, Schoenberg and others. In the mid-1930s he spent time in Paris, which prompted him to adopt a Milhaud-influenced polytonal style, which he applied to clear forms; admiration for Bartók also led him to work with folk music. His output includes 162 works with opus numbers in every genre except opera and ballet.

Absolute music. Term first used by German Romantic writers for an ideal of 'pure' music independent of words, drama or representational meaning (*see* PROGRAMME MUSIC); it has been suggested that it must be understood as objective structure without expressive content.

Absolute pitch. The ability to name the pitch of a note, or to sing a named note, without reference to a previously sounded one. It is sometimes called 'perfect pitch'.

Abt, Franz Wilhelm (*b* Eilenburg, 22 Dec 1819; *d* Wiesbaden, 31 March 1885). German composer. He studied in Leipzig at the University and the Thomasschule. He was Kapellmeister of several German cities and a conductor of international reputation. His huge output (over 3000 items) is mostly of choral music in a popular, pleasing style.

Abu Hassan. Singspiel in one act by Weber to a libretto by F.C. Heimer after *The 1001 Nights* (1811, Munich).

Abyndon [Abyngdon], **Henry** (*b* c1420; *d* 1497). English musician. He was a singer at Eton College and the Chapel Royal, where he was Master of the Choristers (1455–78); he also had connections with Wells Cathedral. No compositions are known, but he is thought to be the first person to have taken a music degree (MusB, Cambridge, 1464).

Abzug (Ger.). Term with several meanings: SCORDATURA tuning (usually of a lute), or by extension the addition of open lower strings; a decrescendo from an appoggiatura into the main note, or an inverted mordent (or *Schneller*); and in organ building, a rank of pipes from a compound stop that is used independently.

Academic Festival Overture. Brahms's op.80 (1880); composed for Breslau University, it incorporates student songs.

Académie de Musique. The original title of the Paris OPÉRA.

Academy. Term used in music for an institution at which the study and/or performance of music was cultivated. The earliest arose in Italy during the Renaissance; at these the classics, philosophy and literature were often studied too. They were widely imitated elsewhere. In Paris, the opera-giving organization under Lully was the Académie Royale de Musique; in 18th-century Germany the term

Akademie became synonymous with concert, and in 1791 a choir in Berlin was called 'Singakademie'. Later the term came to be used mainly for formal music schools like the Royal Academy of Music, London.

Academy of Ancient Music. Society formed in London in the early 18th century as the Academy of Vocal Music. It aimed to revive early church music and gave seasons of fortnightly concerts. Pepusch was director until his death (1752) and Handel and Geminiani played at meetings; it was disbanded in 1792.

English ensemble, named after the above. It was founded in 1973 by Christopher Hogwood to perform Baroque and Classical music on period instruments, has recorded a substantial repertory of music by Purcell, Handel (including *Messiah* and much theatre music), Mozart (the complete symphonies) and Beethoven, and has toured widely.

Academy of Music. New York theatre opened in 1854; it had the largest stage in the world at that time and seated 4600. Regular seasons of opera were given there until 1886.

Academy of St Martin-in-the-Fields. British chamber orchestra founded in 1959 in London by Neville Marriner. Early performances were at the church of St Martin. It soon gained an international reputation through recordings of classical and modern works.

Academy of Vocal Music. London society of aristocratic amateur and eminent professional musicians founded in 1725 in 'an attempt to restore ancient church music'.

A cappella [alla cappella] (It.). 'In the chapel': term for choral music sung without instrumental accompaniment.

Accademia di S Cecilia. Society founded in Rome c1566 as the Congregazione dei Musici di Roma; it held meetings to discuss and perform music. It was renamed c1839 and in 1877 became Italy's principal conservatory (Conservatorio di Musica 'Santa Cecilia').

Accademia Filarmonica. Society established in Bologna, Italy, in 1666. Meetings were held to discuss theory and to perform new music. G.B. Martini (elected 1758) was its most influential member; composers associated with it include Mozart (1770), Wagner (1876) and Ravel (1922).

Accardo, Salvatore (*b* Turin, 26 Sept 1941). Italian violinist. He studied in Naples and Siena, toured widely and is admired for his brilliant technique and his interpretative range from Bach and Paganini to contemporary music.

Accelerando (It.). Quickening.

Accent. The prominence given to a note or notes in performance usually by a marked increase in volume or prolongation.

Acciaccatura (It.). A 'crushed note': an ornament consisting of an accessory note adjacent to (usually a semitone below) the main note, sounded with it and at once released.

Accidental. A sign placed (in modern practice) before a note to alter its previously understood pitch by one or two semitones. The sharp (♯) raises a note by one semitone, the double sharp (✕) by two; the flat (♭) lowers a note by one semitone, the double flat (♭♭) by two. The natural (♮) cancels a previous sharp or flat. In present-day notation an accidental holds good for the bar in which it appears, except in some highly chromatic music where an accidental applies only to the note to which it is prefixed (as in notation up to the 17th century).

Acclamation. A formula pronounced or sung corporately, expressing a common sentiment, such as those in ancient Rome; acclamations such as 'Hosanna', 'Amen', 'Alleluia' and the Kyrie eleison occur in many liturgies.

Accompagnato (It.). Accompanied; it sometimes stands for *recitativo accompagnato*, i.e. recitative accompanied by the orchestra.

Accompanied sonata. Term for a type of keyboard sonata popular in the late 18th century in which the accompanying instrument or instruments (violin, sometimes flute, sometimes with cello) play a secondary and occasionally *ad libitum* role.

Accompaniment. The subordinate parts of a musical texture.

Accordatura (It.). The tuning of an instrument, especially a string instrument.

Accordion. A portable reed organ. It consists of a treble keyboard (with piano keys or buttons) and casework, connected by bellows to the bass casing and button keyboard. The player 'puts on' the instrument by means of its shoulder-straps; the right hand plays the treble keyboard and the left the bass keyboard buttons while controlling the bellows movement. The usual 120-button 'fixed bass' keyboard consists of two rows of bass notes, arranged in 5ths, and four rows of chord buttons (major, minor, dominant 7th and diminished triads respectively; with full coupling the bass notes sound in five octaves and chord buttons in the upper three). Accordions are made in smaller sizes. On some models the treble keyboard produces different notes on inward and outward movement of the bellows. There is a large repertory of educational music for the instrument. Solo works have been composed for it by Alan Hovhanness, Virgil Thomson and others; Berg, Prokofiev and Gerhard are among those who have included parts for it in their works.

Accorimboni, Agostino (*b* Rome, 28 Aug 1739; *d* there, 13 Aug 1818). Italian composer. A pupil of Rinaldo da Capua, he wrote mainly stage works; except for the heroic opera *Nitteti* (1777, Florence), all were comic and most were staged in Rome. *Il regno delle Amazzoni* (1783) enjoyed particular success. He also wrote an oratorio and religious pieces.

Acis and Galatea. Masque in two acts by Handel to a libretto by John Gay and others after Ovid (1718, Cannons), distinct from his *Aci, Galatea e Polifemo* (1708, Naples).

Ackté, Aïno (*b* Helsinki, 23 April 1876; *d* Nummela, 8 Aug 1944). Finnish soprano. She studied with her mother, a soprano, and in Paris, making her Opéra début as Gounod's Marguerite; she made her Met début, in French roles and as Wagner's Eva, in 1903–4, appeared at Covent Garden in 1907 and was the first English Salome in 1910, under Beecham. She had a strong, dramatic voice. Her remaining career was mainly in Finland.

Acoustics. The science of sound and hearing. It treats the sonic qualities of rooms and buildings, and the transmission of sound by the voice, musical instruments or electric means.

Sound is caused by vibration, which is communicated by the sound source to the air as fluctuations in pressure and then to the listener's ear-drum. The faster the vibration (or the greater its 'frequency'), the higher the pitch. The greater the amplitude of the vibration, the louder the sound. Most musical sounds consist not only of regular vibration at one particular frequency but also vibration at various multiples of that frequency. The frequency of middle C (*c*′) is 256 cycles per second (or Hertz, abbreviated Hz); but when one hears middle C there are components of the sound vibrating at 512 Hz, 768 Hz etc (*see* HARMONICS). The presence and relative strength of these harmonics determine the quality of a sound. The difference in quality, for example, between a flute, an oboe and a clarinet playing the same note is that the flute's tone is relatively 'pure' (i.e. has few and weak harmonics), the oboe is rich in higher harmonics and the clarinet has a preponderance of odd-numbered harmonics. Their different harmonic spectra are caused primarily by the way the sound vibration is actuated (by the blowing of air across an edge with the flute, by the oboe's double reed and the clarinet's single reed) and by the shape of the tube. Where the player's lips are the vibrating agent, as with most brass instruments, the tube can be made to sound not its fundamental note but other harmonics by means of the player's lip pressure.

The vibrating air column is only one of the standard ways of creating musical sound. The longer the column the lower the pitch; the player can raise the pitch by uncovering holes in the tube. With the human voice, air is set in motion by means of the vocal cords, folds in the throat which convert the air stream from the lungs into sound; pitch is controlled by the size and shape of the cavities in the pharynx and mouth. For a string instrument, such as the violin, the guitar or the piano, the string is set in vibration by (respectively) bowing, plucking or striking; the tighter and thinner the string, the faster it will vibrate. By pressing the string against the fingerboard and thus making the operative string-length shorter, the player can raise the pitch. With a percussion instrument, such as the drum or the xylophone, a membrane or a piece of wood is set in vibration by striking; sometimes the vibration is regular and gives a definite pitch but sometimes the pitch is indefinite.

In the recording of sound, the vibration patterns set up by the instrument or instruments to be recorded are encoded by analogue (or, in recent recordings, digitally) in terms of electrical impulse. This information can then be stored, in mechanical or electrical form; it can then be decoded, amplified and conveyed to loudspeakers which transmit the same vibration pattern to the air.

The study of the acoustics of buildings is immensely complicated because of the variety of ways in which sound is conveyed, reflected, diffused, absorbed etc.

The design of buildings for performances has to take account of such matters as the smooth and even representation of sound at all pitches in all parts of the building, the balance of clarity and blend and the directions in which reflected sound may impinge upon the audience. The use of particular materials (especially wood and artificial acoustical substances) and the breaking-up of surfaces, to avoid certain types of reflection of sound, play a part in the design of concert halls, which however remains an uncertain art in which experimentation and 'tuning' (by shifting surfaces, by adding resonators etc) is often necessary.

The term 'acoustic' is sometimes used, of a recording or an instrument, to mean 'not electric': an acoustic recording is one made (normally before 1926) before electric methods came into use, and an acoustic guitar is one not electrically amplified.

Action. The mechanism by which the strings or pipes of a keyboard instrument are sounded when a key is depressed; in the harp, the mechanism for changing the pitches of the strings.

Act tune. Music played between the acts of a play or opera in the 17th- and 18th-century English theatre. Purcell wrote act tunes for about 11 plays.

Actus musicus. Term used between 1650 and 1750 in Germany for a sacred work similar in function and structure to the HISTORIA but like oratorio in its non-biblical interpolations and its emphasis on drama.

Actus tragicus. Name by which Bach's cantata *Gottes Zeit ist die allerbeste Zeit* BWV106 (1707) is also known.

Adagietto (It.). Less slow or lighter in style than Adagio.

Adagio (It.). 'At ease', 'leisurely'; a movement in slow tempo.

Adam, Adolphe (Charles) (b Paris, 24 July 1803; d there, 3 May 1856). French composer. He studied at the Paris Conservatoire with Reicha (counterpoint) and Boieldieu (composition). A prolific composer, he wrote more than 80 stage works, some of which, especially those produced for the Opéra-Comique such as *Le chalet* (1834) and *Le postillon de Longjumeau* (1836), had considerable and lasting success. Other notable works, showing a natural sense of theatre, fresh invention and graceful melody, include the opera *Si j'étais roi* (1852) and the well-known ballet *Giselle* (1841).

Ádám, Jenő (b Szigetszentmiklós, 12 Dec 1896; d Budapest, 15 May 1982). Hungarian composer, conductor and teacher. He studied at the Budapest Academy with Kodály (1920–25) and worked there as a teacher and choirmaster (1929–57), helping in Kodály's educational reforms. As a conductor he championed Purcell and Handel in Hungary. He used folktunes in his operas and many choral works.

Adam, Theo (b Dresden, 1 Aug 1926). German bass-baritone. He made his début at the Dresden Staatsoper (1949) and joined the Berlin Staatsoper (1952); he sang Wotan at Bayreuth in 1963 and at Covent Garden in 1967. Other roles include Don Giovanni (1972, Vienna) and Sachs (1969, Met). He is noted too as a Bach interpreter.

Adamberger, (Josef) Valentin (b Munich, 6 July 1743; d Vienna, 24 Aug 1804). German tenor. Trained in Italy, he lived from 1780 in Vienna and sang in the German National Singspiel, creating Belmonte in *Die Entführung aus dem Serail* (1782). He retired in 1793 and became a singing teacher.

Adam de la Halle (b Arras, 1245–50; d Naples, ?1285–8, or ?England, after 1306). French poet and composer (trouvère). He probably studied in Paris, returning to Arras c1270. He later served Robert II, Count of Artois, and Charles of Anjou, both in Italy. A tribute of 1288 refers to his death, but he was also reported in England in 1306, among musicians at the knighting of Edward, Prince of Wales (later Edward II). His musical and literary works encompass virtually all genres of the time and he is one of the few medieval musicians to be credited with both monophonic and polyphonic music. There are monophonic *chansons* and jeux-partis, motets and polyphonic rondeaux as well as three plays with musical inserts. The monophonic works continue the tradition of the courtly lyric and *chanson de geste,* while the three-voice rondeaux and the dramatic works are more progressive. Of the plays, *Le jeu de Robin et de Marion* contains the most music, combining speech with extensive sung parts, some possibly borrowed from popular song, while the autobiographical *Le jeu d'Adam* includes allegory and social criticism.

Adams, John (Coolidge) (b Worcester, MA, 15 Feb 1947). American composer. He studied at Harvard with Kirchner, Kim, Del Tredici and Sessions, and in 1972 began teaching at the San Francisco Conservatory. He became interested in electronics (*Onyx,* 1976), then, influenced by Reich, turned to minimalism. His works, in an elegant minimalist style, include *Shaker Loops* for strings (1978), *Harmonium* for orchestra with choir (1981), the exuberant, parodistic *Grand Pianola Music* (1982) and the opera *Nixon in China* (1987), a summary of his musical languages over ten years.

Adams, Thomas (b London, 5 Sept 1785; d there, 15 Sept 1858). English organist and composer. Organist at several London churches from 1802, he gave recitals that included arrangements of orchestral music. His compositions, mostly for organ and piano, are remarkable for their use of learned devices.

Adam von Fulda (b Fulda, c1445; d Wittenberg, 1505). German composer and theorist. He was a Benedictine monk, then served Frederick the Wise of Saxony, becoming his Kapellmeister in 1498. From 1502 he was professor of music at the new University of Wittenberg. He wrote a notable treatise, *De musica* (1490), and sacred music, mostly settings of chorale melodies for four voices.

Adaskin, Murray (b Toronto, 28 March 1906). Canadian composer. He was a professional violinist before studying composition with Weinzweig (from 1944) and Milhaud. The most important of his works (e.g. Algonquin Symphony, 1958) are buoyantly composed for orchestra. He taught at the University of Saskatchewan (1952–72).

Added sixth chord. A subdominant chord with an

added major 6th above the bass.

Addinsell, Richard (*b* London, 13 Jan 1904; *d* there, 14 Nov 1977). English composer. After study at the RCM and in Vienna he visited the USA (1933), where he wrote for films. Most of his music was for the theatre and cinema; his Warsaw Concerto, in the style of Rakhmaninov, was used in the film *Dangerous Moonlight* (1941).

Additional accompaniments. Term for the extra instrumental parts added to scores, usually by Handel or Bach, to make them conform to a later taste for fuller textures. The practice had begun by 1784, with the Westminster Abbey Handel Commemoration; Mozart is one of those who wrote them, for *Messiah* (1789) and other works. In the 20th century similar additional accompaniments were provided for operas by Monteverdi.

Adelaide Festival of Arts (Australia). Biennial festival (March), established in 1960; local organizations are featured in concerts, opera, drama and ballet.

Adieux, Les. Publisher's title for Beethoven's Piano Sonata no.26 in E♭ op.81*a* (Beethoven preferred 'Das Lebewohl') which refers to the farewell, absence and return to Vienna of Archduke Rudolph.

Adler, Guido (*b* Ivančice, 1 Nov 1855; *d* Vienna, 15 Feb 1941). Austrian musicologist. He studied law at Vienna University, then music history, which he taught in Prague (from 1885) and Vienna (1898). He was noted for organizing musicological enterprises (editions, congresses, institutions) and for his work on Austrian music history, but is chiefly important for his profound thinking about the nature of music studies and his role in creating the discipline of musicology.

Adler, Kurt Herbert (*b* Vienna, 2 April 1905; *d* Ross, CA, 9 Feb 1988). American conductor and opera director. He studied in Vienna and made his début as a theatre conductor in 1925, then conducting in various European centres and assisting Toscanini at Salzburg in 1936. He went to the USA and joined the San Francisco Opera in 1943, becoming artistic director (1953) and general director (1963); as an administrator he has done much towards making San Francisco an important operatic centre.

He should not be confused with Kurt Adler (1907–77), the Czech-born conductor who held posts in Europe, went to New York in 1938 and conducted at the Met, 1951–73.

Adler, Larry (*b* Baltimore, 10 Feb 1914). American harmonica player. He is the first to achieve recognition for his instrument in classical musical circles and his virtuosity and skill have drawn concertos from many composers, including Vaughan Williams and Milhaud.

Adler, Peter Herman (*b* Jablonec, 2 Dec 1899). American conductor. He studied in Prague and held posts in Berlin and Kiev before going to the USA in 1939; there he worked with Toscanini at the NBC, conducted the Baltimore SO (1959–68), made his début at the Met in 1972 and did much for television opera, commissioning new works.

Adler, Samuel (Hans) (*b* Mannheim, 4 March 1928). American composer, conductor and teacher of German origin. He arrived in the USA in 1939 and studied at Boston University (1943–7) and Harvard (1946–8, with Piston, Thompson and Hindemith). He has taught at North Texas State University (1958–66) and the Eastman School. His large output exhibits great rhythmic vitality and includes five symphonies (1953–75) and six string quartets (1945–75).

Adlgasser, Anton Cajetan (*b* Inzell, 1 Oct 1729; *d* Salzburg, 22 Dec 1777). German composer. Trained at the Salzburg choir school, he was court and cathedral organist there from 1750 and later also organist at the Trinity church. In 1764–5 he studied in Italy. He collaborated with Michael Haydn and the young Mozart in the oratorio *Die Schuldigkeit des ersten Gebotes* (1767) and wrote some 20 other oratorios for Salzburg as well as many liturgical works, which use both modern and contrapuntal styles and long remained in use there. He also wrote an Italian opera, several German stage works and instrumental music.

Ad libitum (Lat.). 'At liberty': it may be used, for example, to indicate that a part so marked may be left out, or that the performer may depart from strict tempo.

Adlung, Jakob (*b* Bindersleben, 14 Jan 1699; *d* Erfurt, 5 July 1762). German scholar. From 1727 until his death he was an organist in Erfurt; he was also a teacher and built keyboard instruments. He published a vast collection of information on practical and theoretical music (1758) and a study of organs in Germany (1768).

Admeto. Opera in three acts by Handel to a libretto after A. Aureli (1727, London).

Adolfati, Andrea (*b* Venice, 1721–2; *d* Padua, 28 Oct 1760). Italian composer. A pupil of Galuppi, he worked mainly at the Modena court (1745–8) and the Annunziata church in Genoa (1748–60). He had ten operas staged, 1741–55, mostly with librettos by Metastasio; he also wrote cantatas, sacred works and six sonatas for strings and wind.

Adorno, Theodor W(iesengrund) (*b* Frankfurt, 11 Sept 1903; *d* Visp, 6 Aug 1969). German music sociologist. He began as a music critic and composer, then left Germany for Oxford and Los Angeles in the 1930s, returning to Frankfurt in 1949. He was a leader of historical-idealist musico-sociological thinking.

Adriaenssen, Emanuel (*b* Antwerp, *c*1554; *d* there, bur. 27 Feb 1604). South Netherlands lutenist and composer. After studying in Rome he returned to Antwerp in 1574 and opened a school for lutenists. He was well known as a virtuoso and fine teacher and was famous abroad for two books of lute music (fantasias, dances and arrangements of vocal pieces).

Adriana Lecouvreur. Opera in four acts by Cilea to a libretto by Colautti after a play by Scribe and Legouvé (1902, Milan).

Adson, John (*b* late 16th century; *d* London, 1640). English composer. He was a court musician and from 1634 music teacher to Charles I. His *Courtly Masquing Ayres* (1611) contains 31 five- and six-part dances for various instruments.

Adventures of Mr Brouček, The. *See* EXCURSIONS OF MR BROUČEK, THE.

Aeolian. Name given by Glarean (*Dodecachordon*, 1547) to one of the additions to the eight traditional church modes, the authentic mode on A, range *a–a'*. It is identical with the modern minor scale in its descending melodic form. *See* MODE.

Aeolian harp. A string instrument sounded by natural wind; normally four to 12 strings are stretched over one or two hardwood bridges mounted on a wooden soundbox, up to 3 metres long. Legends from Homer's time onwards describe instruments of this type. The Aeolian harp became fashionable as a domestic instrument in England in the 1780s; on the Continent it was usual to place instruments in grottos, gardens and summerhouses. Aeolian harps are also known in Ethiopia, Java, China and Guyana.

Aeolian-Skinner Organ Co. American firm of organ builders. It was founded in South Boston, Massachusetts, in 1901 by Ernest M. Skinner (1866–1961). He improved the 'Pitman' windchest, still used in electro-pneumatic-action organs, and developed organ stops imitating orchestral instruments. His firm merged with the organ department of the Aeolian Co. in 1931 (Skinner withdrew *c*1933) and continued to rise in popularity, moving away from orchestral tonal practices. It closed in 1973. Among its organs are those at Grace Cathedral, San Francisco (1934), the Mother Church, Boston (1952), Riverside Church, New York (1955), and the Kennedy Center, Washington, DC (1969).

Aerophone. Term for a musical instrument that produces its sound by using air as the primary vibrating agent; aerophones form one of the four main classes of instruments.

Afanas'yev, Nikolay Yakovlevich (*b* Tobolsk, 12 Jan 1821; *d* St Petersburg, 3 June 1898). Russian violinist and composer. He held orchestral posts in Moscow, Viksa and St Petersburg (1838–53) and toured as a soloist. A prolific composer, he was at his best in small-scale works showing the influence of Russian folk music.

Affections, Doctrine of the (Ger. *Affektenlehre*). Term used to describe a theoretical concept of the Baroque era, derived from classical ideas of rhetoric, holding that music moved the 'affections' (or emotions) of the listener according to a set of rules relating particular musical devices (rhythms, figures etc) to particular emotional states.

Affekt (Ger.). Term used in Germany in the Baroque period for the predominant expressive character of a piece or a passage; *see* AFFECTIONS, DOCTRINE OF THE. The theory of 'Affekt' was called *Affektenlehre*.

Affetuoso [affettuoso] (It.). Tenderly, affectingly.

Affrettando (It.). Hurrying.

Africaine, L'. Opera in five acts by Meyerbeer to a libretto by Scribe and Fétis (1865, Paris).

African music. Africa, home to 350 million people belonging to some 3000 tribes and speaking some 800 to 1000 distinct languages, is one of the most musically diversified regions of the world. The geographical variety of the continent – from the mountains and the vast desert of the north to the wide savannah belt, the central rain forests and the fertile southern coast – is reflected in a multiplicity of musical styles.

In spite of this diversity, unifying features may be identified. African music is primarily percussive. Drums, rattles, bells and gongs predominate, and even important melodic instruments such as xylophones and plucked strings are played with percusive techniques. African melodies are based on short units, on which performers improvise. Though melodies are often simple, rhythms are complex by European standards, with much syncopation (accents on beats other than the main one), hemiola (juxtaposition of twos and threes) and polyrhythm (simultaneous performance of several rhythms). While Western rhythms are classified as 'additive' (time span divided into equal sections, e.g. 12 beats divided $4 + 4 + 4$), African rhythms are usually 'divisive' (unequal sections, e.g. 12 beats divided $5 + 7$ or $3 + 4 + 5$). An unusual aspect of African rhythm is what has been called the 'metronome sense', the ability of many musicians to perform for long periods without deviating from the exact tempo. Group performances are most typical, and the 'call-and-response' style with a solo leader and responsorial group is used throughout the continent. Most African music is based on forms of diatonic scales, closely related to European scales; so the Western listener may find it more familiar, more accessible than the music of Asia.

These characteristics apply to the cultures south of the Sahara Desert, often referred to as 'Black Africa'. North African music is more closely allied to the music of other Arab countries of West Asia and is characterized by solo performance, monophonic rather than polyphonic forms, the predominance of melody over rhythm, a tense and nasal vocal style and non-percussive instruments including bowed rather than plucked strings. While the North as well as portions of West Africa and the east coast have been influenced by Islam, a distinctive sub-region is formed by Ethiopia, whose music has been influenced for centuries by Coptic Christianity, reflected in the ritual melodies, modes and liturgical chant (which is notated). Ethiopian instruments include the small *krar* lyre and the large, ten-string *beganna* lyre, claimed to be a descendant of David's harp.

In sub-Saharan Africa, music is an integral part of daily life. Songs accompany the rites of passage, work and entertainment. They were also important in the life of the traditional African courts, and are still used for political comment, especially in West Africa. Although the claims that all members of African communities participate in musical activities are now discredited, studies have shown that communal music-making is more common than in the West. And although musicians are generally accorded low social status, skilled professional musicians (called *griots* in some regions), employed by rich patrons, are common in many African societies. Musical notation is rare in Africa; skills and knowledge are passed from master to pupil in oral tradition.

The most celebrated African instruments are membrane drums. The famous 'talking drums' of West Africa, such as the *atumpan* of Ghana, can imitate speech tones and are sometimes used to signal messages. Speech is also imitated by bells, gongs and wind instruments of the horn, trumpet and flute types. Harps are played mainly north of the Equator, in a broad band extending from Uganda to the western savannah. Harp-lutes, such as the Gambian *kora*, are popular in West Africa. Other string instruments include fiddles in East Africa and the musical bow, fashioned like a hunting bow and played, with varying techniques and great sophistication, throughout the continent. Wind instruments of the trumpet and horn types are played in orchestras, in hocket fashion, with each instrument supplying its one note to the melodic whole. The *algaita*, an oboe-type instrument of West Africa, is probably of Islamic influence. Xylophones are common, particularly in the East where the Chopi xylophone orchestras of Mozambique perform polyphonic dance suites of uncommon beauty. An instrument unique to African and Afro-American music is the *mbira* or *sanza* (called thumb piano in earlier writings); it consists of a set of thumb-plucked metal tongues mounted on a board, often with a gourd resonator.

In recent decades, traditional African music has tended to be overshadowed by new hybrid urban forms such as highlife (Ghana), *juju* (Nigeria), Congolese (Zaire) and *kwela* (southern Africa) which blend elements from Western pop and disco idioms with local features.

Afro-American music. The music of black Americans is characterized by a style that fuses African and European elements. The 15 million and more Africans taken as slaves to the New World from the 16th century to the 19th were cut off from their own cultures. Despite their dispersal, music united them in a way that transcended barriers of language and custom, for example, at festive gatherings. The first black church congregations were formed in the late 18th century. Music for formal worship consisted of psalms and hymns; spirituals were performed after worship or at midweek services. With the singing went 'the shout', a form of religious dancing with hand-clapping and foot-stamping.

The first black musician known to have written in the European tradition was the former slave Newport Gardner (1746–1826), who gained his freedom and became a singing-school teacher and song composer. The first 'school' of black composers evolved in the second decade of the 19th century, led by the composer and bandmaster Frank Johnson. Members included James Hemmenway, Aaron J.R. Connor, William Appo and Henry F. Williams.

After the Civil War, Afro-American music came to be more widely heard. From 1872 amateur student groups, such as the Fisk Jubilee Singers and the Hampton Institute Singers, toured abroad. Black choral groups that sang 'genuine' plantation songs were widely used in white stage shows of the late 19th century. Lightly disguised, plantation songs also appeared on the minstrel stage. Celebrated minstrel-songwriters included Horace Weston, Sam Lucas, James Bland and Gussie Lord Davis.

New folk styles evolved in black communities in the late 19th century. The piano rag, originally played in black honky-tonk cafés and gambling saloons, re-flected the coalescence of European marches and quadrilles with elements of plantation dance music; Scott Joplin wrote numerous piano rags, a ragtime ballet and two operas. A second folk style, the vocal blues, obscure in origin, probably dates back at least to the 1880s. The minstrel bandleader W.C. Handy was first to popularize the blues with his *Memphis Blues* (1912) and *St Louis Blues* (1914). (*See* RAGTIME and BLUES.)

During the early 20th century the various types of Afro-American music – spirituals, shouts, rags, blues and syncopated music played by brass bands and dance orchestras – began to fuse into what was later known as JAZZ. Jelly Roll Morton is credited with being the first to notate a jazz arrangement (*Jelly Roll Blues*, 1915). Black musical nationalism reached its peak in the works of William Grant Still, the first composer to use all the folk idioms known to his generation, from the spiritual to the blues, in symphonic music. Nationalist feeling was also evident in the musical comedies produced by blacks from the 1920s.

Jazz groups now began to attract attention. New Orleans was established as the capital of jazz; but the tradition was soon carried to Chicago, and New York became the major centre for the big bands, one of the first of which was organized in 1923 by Fletcher Henderson. During the 1920s and 1930s a new kind of religious music, later called GOSPEL, appeared in black churches; its style, a direct heir to the shouts and jubilee songs, was disseminated through oral tradition at gatherings such as the meetings of the National Baptist Convention. Jazzmen of the 1940s experimented with new ideas, resulting in a new style called bebop, then simply BOP.

Several black composers continued to work in the European-based art-music tradition in the 1940s and 1950s; some used neo-classical techniques, including Howard Swanson, Ulysses Kay, George Walker and Julia Perry. In the 1960s, plantation songs and gospel were adopted for marches of the civil rights movement. After the assassination of Martin Luther King, composers produced memorial works drawing on black musical elements. The Society of Black Composers was founded in 1968, the Black Artist Group in 1972 and the *Black Music Research Journal* in 1980.

Afro-Cuban. A musical style that arose in Cuba, reflecting the African traditions of the black population: it stresses percussion instruments, improvisatory procedures, response patterns and especially rhythm and dance. The traditions have given rise to many dance types, such as the rumba, the mambo and the cha cha cha, that have become popular in the USA and Europe. Afro-Cuban jazz, created from bop and Latin American elements, arose in the late 1940s; its chief American exponent was Dizzy Gillespie, influenced by his collaboration with the Cuban composer and percussionist Chano Pozo.

After-dance. The second dance of a pair, usually faster than the first and in a different metre, but often thematically linked to it. A typical example was the *gagliarda*, following a *pavana*.

Agazzari, Agostino (*b* Siena, 2 Dec 1578; *d* there, ?10 April 1640). Italian composer and writer. He held posts as *maestro di cappella* in Rome, then in 1607 returned to Siena as organist of the cathedral and then reputedly *maestro di cappella*. His valuable *Del sonare sopra 'l basso con tutti li stromenti e dell'uso loro nel conserto* (1607), one of the earliest treatises on thoroughbass, describes styles for various instruments and how to play in ensemble. Of his works, 17 books of sacred music, five of madrigals and a moralizing *dramma pastorale, Eumelio* (1606), survive.

Age of Anxiety, The. Leonard Bernstein's Symphony no.2 (1949), after Auden.

Age of Enlightenment, Orchestra of the. English orchestra, founded in 1986 to play music of the Baroque, Classical and early romantic periods on original instruments. It has appeared under S. Kuijken, Mackerras and Rattle in London and at Glyndebourne and Salzburg festivals.

Age of Gold, The [Zolotoy vek]. Ballet in three acts by Shostakovich (1930, Leningrad).

Age of Steel, The [Stal'noy skok]. Ballet in two scenes by Prokofiev (1927, Paris).

Aggh«zy, Kßroly (*b* Pest, 30 Oct 1855; *d* Budapest, 8 Oct 1918). Hungarian composer and pianist. A pupil of Liszt, he toured as a pianist (1878–81) before turning to composition and teaching. The best of his piano music unites a Hungarian idiom, under a French influence, with Baroque stylistic features and links Liszt with 20th-century Hungarian music.

Agincourt Song. Song for two voices and three-part chorus commemorating the English victory at the Battle of Agincourt in 1415, when it was probably written.

Agitato (It.). Agitated, restless.

Agnesi, Maria Teresa (*b* Milan, 17 Oct 1720; *d* there, 19 Jan 1795). Italian composer. She wrote several theatrical works which were staged in Milan, Venice and Naples, and dedicated collections of her compositions to the rulers of Saxony and Austria. She also composed songs, concertos and keyboard music.

Agnus Dei. Fifth section of the Ordinary of the Mass in the Roman rite; the text is taken from *John* i.29 ('Behold the lamb of God'). It was added in the late 7th century to accompany the breaking of the bread. Between the 10th and 12th centuries a threefold form evolved with a contrasting middle section. It is often used in the Anglican service of Holy Communion.

Agogic. Term for a type of accent based on duration (the lingering on a note in order to stress it) rather than on volume; it is important in music for instruments (e.g. the harpsichord or the organ) where volume cannot be instantly varied and other means of accentuation have to be found. The term 'agogics' is sometimes used for any type of departure from strict rhythm.

Agon. Ballet by Stravinsky, choreographed by Balanchine (1957, New York).

Agostini, Lodovico (*b* Ferrara, 1534; *d* there, 20 Sept 1590). Italian composer. He studied music early (possibly in Rome) and then became a priest. From the 1570s until his death he served the Ferrarese court. His many madrigals and other secular vocal works, some lightweight and witty, others serious or virtuoso, reflect the richness of Ferrarese musical life.

Agostini, Paolo (*b* Vallerano, *c*1583; *d* Rome, 3 Oct 1629). Italian composer. A pupil of G.B. Nanino, he held church appointments in Vallerano and Rome before becoming *maestro di cappella* of the Cappella Giulia at St Peter's (1626). His output consists of church music, especially masses, which display his contrapuntal mastery; his polychoral works were also admired. He used newer styles in his solo motets.

Agostini, Pietro Simone (*b* Forlì, *c*1635; *d* Parma, 1 Oct 1680). Italian composer. He led a notorious, swashbuckling life. After studying in Ferrara under Mazzaferrata he had an unsettled existence, including military service and residence in Genoa and Rome, where he became director of music at S Agnese; from 1679 until he was murdered he was *maestro di cappella* at the Parma court. He wrote eight dramatic works, but several are lost; his finest music is in his *c*30 secular cantatas, which are akin to Stradella's.

Agrell, Johan Joachim (*b* Löth, 1 Feb 1701; *d* Nuremberg, 19 Jan 1765). Swedish composer. By 1734 he was a violinist at the Kassel court, also travelling in England, France, Italy and elsewhere. From 1746 he was Kapellmeister in Nuremberg. He wrote occasional vocal works and numerous symphonies, harpsichord concertos and sonatas, many of which were published. He was a fluent composer in the north German *galant* style of the time.

Agréments (Fr.). Embellishments.

Agricola, Alexander (*b* ?1446; *d* Valladolid, late Aug 1506). Franco-Netherlandish composer. His career centred mainly on Italian courts (Milan, Florence, Naples) and the French court, and from 1498 until his death he served Philip the Handsome of Burgundy at home and abroad. His travels brought him renown as a singer and composer. His works include eight masses, over 20 motets and other sacred pieces, nearly 50 *chansons* and *c*25 instrumental works. His style is predominantly northern, akin to Ockeghem's, using long, rhythmically complex contrapuntal lines built from short, decorative motifs and linked with frequent yet unobtrusive cadences.

Agricola, Johann Friedrich (*b* Dobitschen, 4 Jan 1720; *d* Berlin, 2 Dec 1774). German composer and writer. He was a pupil of J.S. Bach at Leipzig, then studied under Quantz at Berlin. After the success of his first intermezzo, *Il filosofo convinto in amore* (1750, Potsdam), he became a court composer to Frederick the Great and from 1759 was musical director at the Berlin Opera; he continued writing Italian operas until 1772 but lost royal favour. Among his other works, the keyboard music shows the influence of J.S. and C.P.E. Bach. With C.P.E. Bach he wrote an influential obituary of J.S. Bach (1754).

Agricola's wife, Benedetta Emilia (née Molteni, 1722–80), was a leading soprano at the Berlin Opera, 1743–74.

Agricola [Sore], Martin (*b* Schwiebus, 6 Jan 1486; *d* Magdeburg, 10 June 1556). German music theorist and composer. He claimed to be self-taught in music.

He taught in Magdeburg from c1519, and from 1525 or 1527 until his death he was choirmaster of the Lateinschule there. An enthusiastic Lutheran, he wrote treatises for scholars and amateurs, notably *Musica instrumentalis deudsch* (1532), on instruments. His *Sangbuchlein* (1541) is one of the earliest collections of German Protestant songs; he also composed Latin motets and instrumental pieces.

Agrippina. Opera in three acts by Handel to a libretto by Grimani (1709, Venice).

Aguado (y García), Dionysio (*b* Madrid, 8 April 1784; *d* there, 29 Dec 1849). Spanish guitarist. He perfected his technique in Spain before establishing himself as a performer and teacher in Paris (1825–38). There his popular guitar method was translated into French and he gave many concerts with Sor.

Aguiari, Lucrezia ['La Bastardina', 'La Bastardella'] (*b* Ferrara, 1743; *d* Parma, 18 May 1783). Italian soprano. She made her début in Florence in 1764 and sang at the Parma court from 1768, concentrating on the operas of the *maestro di cappella*, Giuseppe Colla, whom she married. Much praised by the Mozarts (who heard her in 1770) and Burney, she was one of Europe's most sought-after sopranos, with a fine tone throughout her unusually wide range.

Aguilera de Heredia, Sebastián (*b* ?Saragossa, c1565; *d* there, 16 Dec 1627). Spanish composer. He was organist of Huesca Cathedral, 1585–1603, and then of the cathedral of La Seo, Saragossa. All his music was for the church. His 23 extant organ works are in the traditions of Cabezón and Santa Maria yet include enough that was new to prompt developments found in Cabanilles and others, notably in the use of dissonance, unexpected harmonic progressions, false relations, variation techniques, virtuoso figuration and the like. His most significant pieces are those employing *medio registro*, where each half of the keyboard is capable of independent registration. His *Canticum Beatissimae Virginis deiparae Mariae* (1618) comprises 36 Magnificat settings, 32 of them in four cycles, each of settings on all eight tones; the others are double-chorus settings in a grand, contrapuntal manner.

Agus, Giuseppe (*b* c1725; *d* c1800). Italian composer. Working in England from c1750, he wrote ballet music for the London Italian opera and published numerous dances as well as sonatas and trios in the Tartini idiom. The violinist and composer Joseph Agus (1749–98), a pupil of Nardini who worked in London (1773–8) and later France, becoming *maître de solfège* at the Paris Conservatoire in 1795, was probably his son.

Ägyptische Helena, Die. Opera in two acts by Richard Strauss to a libretto by Hofmannsthal (1928, Dresden).

Ahern, David (*b* Sydney, 2 Nov 1947). Australian composer. He studied with Meale and Butterley and with Stockhausen in Germany (1968–9). His *After Mallarmé* for orchestra (1966) absorbs European avant-garde influences; some later works include electronics and improvisation.

Ahle, Johann Georg (*b* Mühlhausen, bap. 12 June 1651; *d* there, 2 Dec 1706). German composer and theorist, son of J.R. Ahle. At 23 he succeeded his father as organist of St Blasius, Mühlhausen, and held the post until his death (he was succeeded by J.S. Bach). Much of his surviving music consists of songs in his anecdotal novels named after the Muses; he also wrote occasional works for local use. His theoretical works include four *Musikalische Gespräche*, invaluable in the history of music theory.

Ahle, Johann Rudolf (*b* Mühlhausen, 24 Dec 1625; *d* there, 9 July 1673). German composer. After being Kantor at Erfurt he returned to Mühlhausen in 1650 as organist of St Blasius from 1654. He held municipal posts, including that of mayor. In his large output, mainly sacred vocal music, his tendency to popularization shows Hammerschmidt's influence, and his music has the variety of forms and styles typical of the chorale tradition and Italian trends. His vocal concertos are for up to 24 voices and continuo, but he is best remembered for his sacred songs to texts from the Bible or by leading poets: many of his tunes were popular and some have proved durable – like *Es ist genug*, known in Bach's harmonization and from Berg's use of it in his Violin Concerto.

Åhlström, Olof (*b* Åletorp, 14 Aug 1756; *d* Stockholm, 11 Aug 1835). Swedish composer and publisher. He was an organist in Stockholm and, as a composer, most esteemed for his songs. He also published native and foreign compositions and music journals.

Ahrens, Joseph (Johannes Clemens) (*b* Sommersell, 17 April 1904). German composer and organist. He studied in Büren, Münster and Berlin and at Benedictine abbeys and taught at the Berlin Hochschule from 1934, also serving as organist of St Hedwig. He has composed much organ music as well as masses and Passions.

Ahronovich, Yuri (*b* Leningrad, 13 May 1932). Israeli conductor. He studied in Leningrad, then under Sanderling and others, and held posts including the conductorship of the Moscow Radio SO (1964). He left Russia for Israel in 1972 and has since conducted widely in the West, making his Covent Garden début in 1974 (*Boris Godunov*) and becoming conductor of the Cologne Gürzenich Concerts in 1975.

Aiblinger, Johann Kaspar (*b* Wasserburg, 23 Feb 1779; *d* Munich, 6 May 1867). German composer. He went to Italy as a pupil of Simon Mayr, then in 1819 returned to Munich, where he became Kapellmeister of the Italian Opera House. He is noted mainly for his traditional sacred music (over 100 works).

Aichinger, Gregor (*b* Regensburg, 1564–5; *d* Augsburg, 20/21 Jan 1628). German composer. In 1578, at the University of Ingolstadt, he met members of the Fugger family who engaged him in 1584 as household organist in Augsburg. On one of his many study visits to Italy he was a pupil of Giovanni Gabrieli in Venice. His works are mainly sacred. The early polychoral pieces show Gabrieli's influence and the vocal concertos Viadana's, but many are in a more conservative polyphonic style. The *Cantiones ecclesiasticae* (1607) is the first significant German publication with thoroughbass and includes an important treatise on its notation and performance. He ranks with Leo Hassler among the most important and prolific composers in southern Germany in the late 16th and early 17th centuries.

Aida. Opera in four acts by Verdi to a libretto by Ghislanzoni (1871, Cairo), commissioned to celebrate the opening of the Suez Canal.

Air [ayre]. Term apparently originating in France and England in the 16th century and often used synonymously with 'tune' or 'song'. It was first applied mainly to lighter pieces, but from 1571 *air de cour* was used in France for solo lute-songs and ensemble songs, both light and serious. The vogue of the English lute ayre began in 1597 with the publication of the first of Dowland's four books. Other composers included Campion, Rosseter and Alfonso Ferrabosco (ii). Campion preferred the simple 'light ayre', while Dowland led towards the declamatory Italian style (*see* ARIA). After the decline of the lute ayre, in the mid-17th century, the term was often used in England more generally for a simple, unpretentious song quite different from the Italian aria. With the *air à boire* ('drinking-song') in the 1670s the more serious type of French song was called simply *air*. Even before this the word was applied to instrumental pieces; there are several airs in Purcell's stage works and in later Baroque suites, often in bourrée rhythm but sometimes simply meaning 'melody'.

Air column. The body of air inside the tube of a wind instrument.

Air de cour (Fr.). 'Court air': term used in France for secular songs sung to entertain the king and his courtiers. The first collection, published in 1571, contained solo *airs* with lute; later ones were for several voices. Both types appeared in great numbers in the reign of Louis XIII (1610–43).

Air on the G string. Title of the arrangement by August Wilhelmj (1845–1908) of the Air from Bach's Suite no.3 in D; it is transposed down a major 9th, to be playable exclusively on the violin's G string.

Aix-en-Provence Festival (France). Annual festival (July), established in 1948. Opera, especially Mozart, is featured; performances are in the courtyard of the archiepiscopal palace. Other events take place at the Cathedral of St Sauveur and in castles and abbeys.

A Kempis, Nicolaus (*b* c1600; *d* Brussels, bur. 11 Aug 1676). Flemish composer. He was organist of Ste Gudule, Brussels, from 1627. His four books of *Symphoniae* provide some of the earliest-known sonatas in the Low Countries; they are for various numbers and combinations of instruments and some include popular melodies. He was succeeded at Ste Gudule by his son Joannes Florentius (1635–after 1711), who was also a composer, as was his son Thomas (1628–88).

Akhnaten. Opera in three acts by Glass to a libretto by himself and others (1984, Stuttgart).

Akutagawa, Yasushi (*b* Tokyo, 12 July 1925). Japanese composer. He studied with Ifukube at the Tokyo Music School and developed contacts with composers in the USSR: these, and Prokofiev, have influenced his music, which is mostly orchestral or for the stage (e.g. the opera *Orpheus in Hiroshima*, 1967).

Alain, Jehan (*b* St Germain-en-Laye, 3 Feb 1911; *d* Petit-Puy, 20 June 1940). French composer and organist. He studied with Dupré and Dukas at the Paris Conservatoire (1927–39) and was organist of St Nicolas de Maisons Lafitte in Paris (1935–9); he was

killed in action. He shared Messiaen's enthusiasms for Debussy and Asian music, reflected in the modalities, rhythmic irregularities and ecstatic ostinatos of his works, which are mostly for the organ or the Catholic Mass. His organ works include *Deux danses à Agni Yavishta* (1934), two *Fantaisies* (1934, 1936), *Litanies* (1937) and *Trois danses* (1937–9).

His brother Olivier (*b* 1918) is a composer and teacher in Paris; his sister Marie-Claire (*b* 1926) is an organist who specializes in 17th- and 18th-century music.

Alaleona, Domenico (*b* Montegiorgio, 16 Nov 1881; *d* there, 28 Dec 1928). Italian composer. He studied at the Liceo di S Cecilia in Rome, where he was professor from 1916; a student of the Italian oratorio, he did much to establish Italian musicology. His works, including the opera *Mirra* (1920, Rome), sometimes use new divisions of the octave, for example into five equal parts.

Alamire, Pierre [Peter van den Hove] (*b* c1470–1475; *d* after 1534). Flemish music scribe. He mainly served the Netherlands courts at Mechlin and Brussels, with a period in Antwerp. His 40 surviving MSS cover much of the contemporary Franco-Flemish polyphonic repertory and range from large decorated choirbooks to more modest partbooks. He was also a diplomatic courier and even a spy, notably for Henry VIII.

Alard, (Jean-)Delphin (*b* Bayonne, 8 March 1815; *d* Paris, 22 Feb 1888). French violinist. He studied at the Paris Conservatoire, won fame as a soloist and chamber music player and held a court post. As a professor at the Conservatoire (1843–75) he transmitted the great Italian-French tradition of Viotti to a generation of violinists.

Alba (Provençal). Term for a troubadour poem in which lovers part at dawn after a furtive nocturnal meeting. Among the few such poems that survive only two have music, by Giraut de Bornelh and Cadenet.

Albanese, Licia (*b* Bari, 22 July 1913). American soprano. She made her début in Milan in 1934 as Butterfly, which she also sang at her Met début (1940). She had a large repertory (Mozart, French opera, Italian opera, especially Puccini) and sang under Toscanini.

Albani, Emma (*b* Chambly, 1 Nov 1847; *d* London, 3 April 1930). Canadian soprano. She studied in Paris and made her London début in 1872 as Amina, later singing major Wagner and Verdi roles at Covent Garden as well as oratorio; she also toured widely. She retired in 1911.

Albéniz, Isaac (Manuel Francisco) (*b* Camprodón, 29 May 1860; *d* Cambô-les-Bains, 18 May 1909). Spanish composer and pianist. One of the most important figures in Spanish musical history, he helped create a national idiom and an indigenous school of piano music. He studied at the Brussels Conservatory and with Liszt, Dukas and d'Indy; other important influences were Felipe Pedrell (who inspired him to turn to Spanish folk music), 19th-century salon piano music and impressionist harmony. But he was not simply a follower of the French school and exchanged ideas with Debussy and Ravel in Paris. Most of his many works are for piano solo, the best known being the *Suite Iberia* (1906–8), distinguished by its complex technique, bold harmony and evocative instrumental effects. He also wrote a notable opera, *Pepita Jiménez* (1896). He was a virtuoso pianist with a highly personal style.

Albergati (Capacelli), Pirro (*b* Bologna, 20 Sept 1663; *d* there, 22 June 1735). Italian composer. Born of noble parents, he was a musical patron in Bologna, where serenatas, oratorios, cantatas, and other works of his were performed at the Albergati palace. Between 1682 and 1721 he published 15 sets of instrumental works, sacred music and cantatas; he also wrote 15 oratorios.

Alberghi, Paolo Tommaso (*b* Faenza, bap. 31 Dec 1716; *d* there, 11 Oct 1785). Italian composer. He studied with Tartini and served at Faenza Cathedral, becoming *maestro di cappella* in 1760. He wrote mainly instrumental music in Tartini's style; the ornate violin writing reflects his virtuoso reputation. He also wrote sacred works. His son Ignazio (1758– after *c*1836), an operatic tenor and church composer, was *maestro di cappella* at Faenza Cathedral (1787– 96) and served at the Dresden court.

Albert, Prince Consort [Prince of Saxe-Coburg-Gotha] (*b* Rosenau, 26 Aug 1819; *d* London, 14 Dec 1861). German musician, consort of Queen Victoria. He was a capable singer, played the piano and organ and, after 1840, took an active part in organizing concerts at Windsor Castle and Buckingham Palace. As a composer he left church music and *c*40 German songs in a Mendelssohnian style.

Albert, Eugen [Eugène] **(Francis Charles) d'** (*b* Glasgow, 10 April 1864; *d* Riga, 3 March 1932). German composer and pianist. He attended the New Music School in London and gained the support of Liszt, becoming one of the great pianists of his day, renowned for his Beethoven, Brahms, Liszt and Bach. He wrote many charming character-pieces for piano as well as a Sonata in F♯ minor (1893) and two concertos; but he had greater success as a composer of operas, both tragic (*Tiefland*, 1903, a *verismo* work of some power) and comic (*Die Abreise*, 1898; *Flauto solo*, 1905). Musically he belonged much more to German and Italian than to British culture.

Albert, Heinrich (*b* Lobenstein, 8 July 1604; *d* Königsberg, 6 Oct 1651). German composer. He studied law and was a musician only from 1630; he spent these years in Königsberg, becoming organist of the cathedral. His main achievement lies in his eight books of *Arien* (1638–50) – 170 short songs, sacred and secular, written for occasions such as weddings, funerals and anniversaries, reflecting Königsberg political and artistic life. The poems, some Albert's own, are fine examples of the Königsberg school. At least 25 of his melodies became chorales. He included important rules for figured basses and other guidance for performers.

Albert, Stephen (Joel) (*b* New York, 6 Feb 1941). American composer. He studied under Milhaud, Rochberg and others in Rochester and Philadelphia and has held posts as composer-in-residence. His works, which include settings of Joyce and 10th-century Icelandic texts, a symphony *RiverRun*

(1984) and works for string quartet, use electronic as well as traditional means and incorporate neo-classical and neo-romantic elements.

Albert Herring. Chamber opera in three acts by Britten to a libretto by Eric Crozier after Maupassant (1947, Glyndebourne).

Alberti, Domenico (*b* Venice, *c*1710; *d* Rome, 1740). Italian composer. Although an amateur musician (he latterly served in the household of Marquis Molinari in Rome), he achieved fame as a performer and had several operas staged in Venice. He is remembered for his harpsichord sonatas, of which 14 survive complete, each in two movements and in an attractive *galant* idiom featuring the arpeggiated left-hand figuration, 'Alberti bass', that is named after him.

Alberti, Gasparo (*b* Padua, *c*1480; *d* Bergamo, *c*1560). Italian composer. He spent most of his life in Bergamo, first as a singer at S Maria Maggiore, later as *maestro di cappella*. His works, all sacred, include masses, double-choir Magnificats, psalms and three dramatic Passions; their textual clarity shows that he was influenced by current humanistic ideas.

Alberti, Giuseppe Matteo (*b* Bologna, 20 Sept 1685; *d* there, 1751). Italian composer. He played the violin at S Petronio, Bologna, and was several times president of the Accademia Filarmonica. He composed chiefly instrumental works; his concertos, which had the most success (particularly in England), were among the first by an Italian to show Vivaldi's direct influence.

Alberti bass. In keyboard music, a left-hand accompaniment figure consisting of broken triads, usually with the notes played in the order: lowest, highest, middle, highest; it takes its name from Domenico Alberti (*c*1710–1740), the first composer to use it regularly.

Albicastro [Weissenburg], **Henricus** (*fl* 1700–06). ?Swiss composer resident in the Netherlands. He pursued a military career and later lived in Amsterdam, where nine collections of music by him appeared *c*1700, mostly of sonatas for one or two violins and continuo. They are up-to-date in style, with sophisticated harmony and skilful counterpoint as well as virtuoso violin writing.

Albinoni, Tomaso Giovanni (*b* Venice, 8 June 1671; *d* there, 17 Jan 1751). Italian composer. Born of wealthy parents, he was a dilettante musician, never seeking a church or court post, though he had contact with noble patrons. He concentrated on instrumental and secular vocal music and had early successes with his opera *Zenobia* (1694, Venice) and 12 trio sonatas op.1 (1694). His reputation grew, with operas staged in other cities, beginning with *Rodrigo in Algeri* (1702, Naples); later operas, such as *I veri amici* (1722, Munich), were staged abroad. In all he wrote over 50 operas, several other stage works and over 40 solo cantatas; few works date from after 1730.

Albinoni's instrumental works, mostly for strings, were especially popular; ten sets were published in his lifetime. Bach based four keyboard fugues on subjects from the op.1 sonatas. While Albinoni's concertos were less adventurous and soloistic than

Vivaldi's, they were probably the earliest consistently in three movements, and his oboe concertos op.7 (1715) were the first by an Italian to be published. The sonatas (for one to six instruments with continuo) are mostly in four movements. His music is individual, with a strong melodic character and, especially in the early works, formally well balanced.

Instrumental music 5 sets of 12 concs. opp. 2, 5, 7, 9, 10, str (opp.7 and 9 with obs); *c*30 other concs., sonatas, balletti, sinfonias; 42 trio sonatas, incl. opp.1, 3, 8; 29 vn sonatas, incl. opp.4, 6
Dramatic music over 50 operas etc (*c*10 survive)
Vocal music mass; over 40 solo cantatas

Alboni, Marietta (*b* Città di Castello, 6 March 1823; *d* Ville d'Avray, 23 June 1894). Italian contralto. She was coached by Rossini in the principal contralto roles in his operas and sang throughout Europe (1842–52).

Alborada (Sp.). 'Morning song': in Spanish folk music, an instrumental or vocal composition, or concert, performed at daybreak, often out of doors. The word has been used (e.g. by Ravel and Rimsky-Korsakov) as a title for pieces redolent of Spain.

Albrecht, Karl (Franzovich) (*b* Poznań, 27 Aug 1807; *d* Gatchina, 8 March 1863). German conductor. He studied in Breslau, and worked there and in Düsseldorf before settling in St Petersburg, where he directed the German, then the Russian, opera. He conducted the première of *Ruslan and Lyudmila* (1842). His sons, Konstantin Karl (1836–93) and Eugen Maria (1842–94), were eminent teachers and administrators, the former a friend of Tchaikovsky and the latter a leading figure in St Petersburg musical life.

Albrechtsberger, Johann Georg (*b* Klosterneuburg, 3 Feb 1736; *d* Vienna, 7 March 1809). Austrian composer, teacher, theorist and organist. He served as organist in provincial localities including Melk Abbey (1759–65), then settled in Vienna, and from 1772 held posts at the Carmelite church and in the court orchestra. In 1791 he became assistant to the Kapellmeister at St Stephen's Cathedral, Leopold Hofmann, succeeding him in 1793. His prolific output (over 600 works) includes oratorios, church music and many instrumental works, of which the earliest (mainly divertimentos) are the most modern and original. His music of 1772 onwards reflects his growing interest in fugues: these appear in chamber works for various combinations (many entitled 'sonata') as well as in sacred vocal works. Though widely famous as an organist, Albrechtsberger was even more influential as a teacher and theorist. His pupils included Beethoven (1794–5), and his composition treatise *Gründliche Anweisung zur Composition* (1790) was especially popular.

Albrici, Vincenzo (*b* Rome, 26 June 1631; *d* Prague, 8 Aug 1696). Italian composer. He studied with Carissimi and held appointments in Rome, in the service of Queen Christina of Sweden, as a Kapellmeister at Dresden, at the English court, as organist of the Leipzig Thomaskirche and finally in Prague. Most of his surviving music consists of motets and cantatas. His brother Bartolomeo (*c*1640–after 1680), also a keyboard player, settled in London by 1666.

Albright, William Hugh (*b* Gary, IN, 20 Oct 1944). American composer. He studied at the University of Michigan, where he began teaching in 1970, and attended Messiaen's courses at the Paris Conservatoire. Much of his work, in a grand, allusive style, has an improvisatory spirit; he has written many organ pieces.

Albumleaf (Ger. *Albumblatt*). A composition written in the album of a friend or patron; later this meaning was lost sight of, and during the 19th century *Albumblatt* (or 'Blatt') was used as a convenient title, usually for piano pieces.

Alceste. Opera in three acts by Gluck to a libretto by Calzabigi after Euripides (1767, Vienna); Gluck made a revised, French version (1776, Paris). In the preface to the score he expounded his ideas for operatic reform. Several other composers wrote music relating to Euripides' story, among them Lully (1674), Handel (1727, 1749–50) and Wellesz (1924).

Alcina. Opera in three acts by Handel to a libretto after Ariosto (1735, London).

Alcock, John (*b* London, 11 April 1715; *d* Lichfield, 23 Feb 1806). English composer. He was a chorister of St Paul's Cathedral and then apprenticed to John Stanley. After holding two parish church posts he became vicar-choral and organist of Lichfield Cathedral (1750–1765) and remained in Lichfield, with organist's posts nearby. He took the Oxford BMus (1755) and DMus (1766). Besides liturgical music, his works include anthems (several, such as *We will rejoice*, with orchestra), catches and canons, harpsichord suites (1741), organ voluntaries (1774), six concertos (1750) and an opera. He also wrote a semi-autobiographical novel. His eldest son, John (1740–91), organist at Walsall from 1773, contributed anthems to a set of six published by his father *c*1790.

Alcock, Sir Walter (Galpin) (*b* Edenbridge, 29 Dec 1861; *d* Salisbury, 11 Sept 1947). English composer and organist. He studied under Sullivan and Stainer and held posts at the Chapel Royal, Westminster Abbey and (from 1917) Salisbury Cathedral. Much esteemed as teacher and recitalist, he played at three coronations.

Alda, Frances (Jeanne) (*b* Christchurch, 31 May 1883; *d* Venice, 18 Sept 1952). New Zealand soprano. She sang in Australia then went to Paris where she made her Opéra-Comique début as Manon (1904), singing at Covent Garden in 1906 and La Scala in 1908. That year she sang at the Met, remaining until her retirement in 1929 (in 1910 she married the director, Gatti-Cassazza). She had a pure, lyrical voice, ideal for such roles as Gilda and Mimì, and a fine technique.

Alday. French family of musicians, principally violinists. The most celebrated members were François (*c*1761–after 1835), a music teacher and concert director in Lyons, and his brother Paul (*c*1763–1835), who studied with Viotti and wrote violin concertos popular in Paris and Berlin. The family's collective achievement is represented by the *Grande* *méthode élémentaire pour le violon dédiée à leur père et composée par les fils Alday* (Lyons, *c*1824), which became widely known.

Aldeburgh Festival (UK). Annual festival (June) founded in 1948 to provide a focus for cultural activities in East Anglia. It was established around Benjamin Britten, who helped give it a distinctive character and whose music is featured (26 premières, 1948–76). Later festivals became international in outlook. The English Opera Group helped establish the festival; the ECO is the resident ensemble. Larger events take place at Snape Maltings (opened 1967), which also houses the Britten-Pears School of Advanced Musical Studies (established 1977).

Aldrich, Henry (*b* Westminster, Jan 1648; *d* Oxford, 14 Dec 1710). English music collector and composer. From 1662 his career was bound up with Christ Church, Oxford, and he was vice-chancellor of Oxford University, 1692–5. As a musician he is best remembered for his collection of music, the basis of the Christ Church music library, consisting of English and Italian music from the 16th century on. He himself wrote a good deal of music, most of it sacred but also including catches and items for Oxford degree ceremonies.

Aldrich, Richard (*b* Providence, RI, 31 July 1863; *d* Rome, 2 June 1937). American critic. He studied at Harvard under Paine and held posts in Providence and Washington, later joining the *New York Tribune* and then serving as music editor of the *New York Times*, 1902–23. He was noted for his urbane style, broad knowledge and sound judgment.

Aldrovandini, Giuseppe Antonio Vincenzo (*b* Bologna, 8 June 1671; *d* there, 9 Feb 1707). Italian composer. He studied with Perti and became *principe* of the Accademia Filarmonica, Bologna. From *c*1702 he was honorary *maestro di cappella* to the Duke of Mantua and later *maestro* of the Accademia del Santo Spirito, Ferrara. His habits may account for his lack of professional preferment; he drowned when drunk. Stylistically he belonged to the late 17th-century Bolognese school of vocal and instrumental composers. His operas were widely performed. Three of the first four are important in *opera buffa* history since they point to an independent regional development (the music is mostly lost); the libretto of the first, *Gl'inganni amorosi scoperti in villa* (1696), shows greater dramaturgical sophistication than its Neapolitan counterparts. Aldrovandini's serious operas were successful and, though not innovatory, include impressive music. He also composed oratorios, motets, cantatas, concertos and sonatas.

Aleatory. Term applied to music in which certain choices in composition or realisation are, to a greater or lesser extent, left to chance or to whim. Typical aleatory devices include giving the performer a choice in the order of sections; using random or chance elements; or using indeterminate symbolic, graphic, textual or other notations which the performer may interpret as he wishes. John Cage is the leading composer of aleatory music but many others, including Boulez, Stockhausen, Globokar and La Monte Young, have used aleatory tech-niques; more conservative ones, like Henze, Lutosławski and Maxwell Davies, have used aleatory passages in otherwise determined works.

Aleko. Opera in one act by Rakhmaninov to a libretto by Nemirovich-Danchenko after Pushkin (1893, Moscow).

Aleotti, Raffaella (*b* Ferrara, *c*1570; *d* after 1646). Italian composer. She was director of the 'concerto grande' at the convent of S Vito, Ferrara, for which she no doubt wrote her *Sacrae cantiones* (1593). Her sister Vittoria (*c*1573–after 1620), in the same convent, published a set of madrigals (1591) to texts by Guarini.

Alessandri, Felice (*b* Rome, 24 Nov 1747; *d* Casinalbo, 15 Aug 1798). Italian composer. He had over 20 operas staged in Italy, 1767–84, and travelled widely; in London he performed on the harpsichord and presented comic operas (*La moglie fedele*, 1768), and in Paris (1777–8) he directed the Concert Spirituel with Joseph Legros and composed for the Concert des Amateurs. In 1786 he went to St Petersburg. A period (1789–92) as assistant director of the Berlin court opera ended in failure, but he remained popular in Italy, and his serious operas *Zemira* and *Armido* (both 1794, Padua) received great applause.

Alessandro. Opera in three acts by Handel to a libretto by Paolo Rolli after Mauro (1726, London).

Alexander, Haim [Heinz] (*b* Berlin, 9 Aug 1915). Israeli composer of German birth. He studied in Berlin and with Irma and Stefan Wolpe at the Palestine Conservatory (1936–45). His earlier works are in an Israeli nationalist style, later modified by his encounter with serialism at Darmstadt in 1958; the two styles are integrated in *Patterns* for piano (1973).

Alexander, Meister (*fl* late 13th century). Poet-composer from south Germany. He was an important composer of secular song, mainly *Sprüche* and Minnesang. In some of his *Sprüche* he criticized the times in which he lived; his Minnesang poetry follows the classical theme of chivalry. His melodies are often individual and forward-looking.

Alexander Balus. Oratorio by Handel to a text by Thomas Morell (1748).

Alexander Brothers. German firm of wind instrument makers. It was founded in Mainz in 1782 by Franz Ambros Alexander (1753–1802) and taken over (1802) by his sons Philipp and Kaspar Anton. From *c*1900 it produced only brass instruments, its German, wide-bore orchestral horns being particularly esteemed.

Alexander Nevsky. Cantata by Prokofiev (op.78) to a text by the composer and V. Lugorsky (1939), derived from the film score Prokofiev wrote for Eisenstein's film of the same name.

Alexander's Feast. Handel's setting of Dryden's *Ode for St Cecilia's Day* with additions from Newburgh Hamilton's *The Power of Music* (1736, London).

Alexandre, Charles-Guillaume (*b c*1735; *d* Paris, 1787–8). French composer. He briefly held several posts as a violinist, but from the mid-1760s worked as a composer, arranger and violin teacher. His output includes stage works and many arrangements (particularly for string quartet) of opera airs for amateurs; he also wrote violin concertos using opera airs and six symphonies (1766) which combine Italian, Mannheim and French traits.

Alexandrov, Alexander Vasil'yevich (*b* St Petersburg, 1 April 1883; *d* Berlin, 8 July 1946). Soviet composer and conductor. He studied with Glazunov and Lyadov at the St Petersburg Conservatory and with Vasilenko at the Moscow Conservatory, where he taught from 1918. He was also founder-director of the Soviet Army Song and Dance Ensemble, for which he wrote songs and folksong arrangements; other works include the national anthem of the USSR.

His son Boris (*b* 1905), also a composer and conductor, studied with Glier at the Moscow Conservatory and used 12-note techniques in some early pieces; his well-known musical comedy *Wedding in Mahnovka* (1937) exploits Ukrainian folk harmonies.

Alexandrov, Anatoly Nikolayevich (*b* Moscow, 25 May 1888; *d* there, 16 April 1982). Russian composer. He studied with Taneyev and Vasilenko at the Moscow Conservatory (1910–16), where he taught from 1923. His colourful works include operas, many songs, four string quartets (1921–53) and much piano music (including 14 sonatas) in a Russian Romantic style.

Alfano, Franco (*b* Posillipo, 8 March 1875; *d* San Remo, 27 Oct 1954). Italian composer. He studied in Naples and with Jadassohn in Lepizig (1895–6), then moved to Berlin and Paris (1899–1905). He gained his first success with *Risurrezione*, a Tolstoy adaptation in the Puccini tradition (1904), followed most notably by *La leggenda di Sakuntala* (1921), which inclines more to Debussy and Strauss. Its rich orientalism made him the obvious choice to complete Puccini's *Turandot*, though his ending was drastically cut by Toscanini and not heard in full until 1982. His other works include more operas, songs (including four groups of Tagore settings), three string quartets, two symphonies (1910, 1932) and violin and cello sonatas.

Alfieri, Pietro (*b* Rome, 29 June 1801; *d* there, 12 June 1863). Italian musicologist and composer. A priest, he edited the first large modern collection of Palestrina's music (1841–6), composed church music on the Palestrina model and wrote manuals for improving the performance of Gregorian chant.

Al fine (It.). 'To the end': an indication to return to the start of a piece but to repeat it only to the point marked 'fine' (or otherwise indicated as the end).

Alfonso el Sabio [Alfonso X] (*b* Toledo, 23 Nov 1221; *d* Seville, 4 April 1284). Spanish monarch, patron and poet. His enlightened court attracted many scholars and artists. In 1254 he founded the chair of music at Salamanca University. He oversaw the compilation of the *Cantigas de Santa Maria*, a famous MS collection of songs by Spanish and other composers.

Alfonso und Estrella. Opera in three acts by Schubert (D732) to a libretto by F. von Schober (1854, Weimar). Its overture was also used for *Rosamunde* (but is not the piece known as *Rosamunde*

overture, which was composed for *Die Zauberharfe*).

Alford, Kenneth J. [Ricketts, Frederick Joseph] (*b* Ratcliff, 21 Feb 1881; *d* Reigate, 15 May 1945). British composer and bandmaster. He joined up as a bandboy in 1895 and spent his career as a military musician, publishing fine marches and other works under the name of Alford; *Colonel Bogey* is his best-known march.

Alfred. Masque by Arne to a libretto by David Mallett and James Thomson (1740, Cliveden, Bucks.); it contains the patriotic song 'Rule, Britannia'.

Alfvén, Hugo (Emil) (*b* Stockholm, 1 May 1872; *d* Falun, 8 May 1960). Swedish composer. He studied at the Stockholm Conservatory (1887–91) and privately with Lindegren, also training as a painter. Thereafter he worked as a choirmaster and Director Musices at Uppsala University (1910–39). His music is distinguished by orchestral subtlety and a painterly exploitation of harmony and timbre. It is almost all programmatic, often seeking to evoke the landscapes and seascapes of southern Sweden (e.g. *Midsummer Vigil*, 1903; *Shepherd-girl's Dance*, 1923). His main works include five symphonies, much choral music and songs.

Algarotti, Francesco (*b* Venice, 11 Dec 1712; *d* Pisa, 3 May 1764). Italian writer on opera. He held court posts in Berlin and Dresden, where he assisted in opera productions, then returned to Italy in 1753. His *Saggio sopra l'opera in musica* (1755) condemned the dominance of singers in serious opera in Italy, was critical of Metastasio and proposed the use of a unifying poetic idea, citing as a model C.H. Graun's *Montezuma*. His French libretto *Iphigénie en Aulide* was widely used as a model, by Gluck's librettist among others.

Alghisi, Paris Francesco (*b* Brescia, 19 June 1666; *d* there, 29/30 March 1733). Italian composer. He served briefly (*c*1681–3) at the Polish court, then entered the order of S Filippo Neri at Brescia, becoming *maestro di cappella* and organist. His compositions, mainly sacred, include oratorios (performed in Brescia and Bologna) and cantatas. Alghisi was famous as a teacher and, latterly, as a saintly ascetic.

Alice Tully Hall. *See* LINCOLN CENTER FOR THE PERFORMING ARTS.

Aliquot. A mathematical term used in music to refer to overtones or harmonics; an 'aliquot piano' has SYMPATHETIC STRINGS.

Alison, Richard (*fl* 1592–1606). English composer. In 1599 he was living in London and may have served the Earl of Warwick. The psalms he wrote for East's *Whole Booke of Psalmes* (1592) and those in his own *Psalmes of David* (1599) are mainly simple. He is also noted for elaborate consort music and pieces for solo lute.

Alkan [Morhange], **(Charles-)Valentin** (*b* Paris, 30 Nov 1813; *d* there, 29 March 1888). French pianist and composer. He was a leading piano virtuoso and an unusual composer, remarkable in technique and imagination yet largely ignored by his own and succeeding generations. A child prodigy, he studied at the Paris Conservatoire. Although he held no official appointment and rarely played publicly, he was known for the brilliance of his playing, his wide repertory of earlier music and as a champion of the pedal piano (for which he composed). His complex works include extra-musical elements; he favoured obscure titles and subject matter (often with a satanic, childish or mystical tone), bold tonal structures and unusual metres. He exploited brilliantly the keyboard's resources, often making great demands of technique and stamina, and used scrupulously exact notation. Many of his some 70 opus numbers are organized in long schemes of harmonic studies, such as the *25 préludes* in all the major and minor keys op.31 (1847) and the *12 études* op.39 (1857); his most famous and demanding works are his *Grande sonate* op.33 and the Concerto (for piano solo) from op.39. He was greatly admired by Liszt and Busoni.

Alla breve (It.). Term, deriving from a late medieval usage (then indicating that the breve was the unit of rhythmic measurement), to indicate, normally, two minim beats in a bar, and thus a quickish tempo (usually it stands for 2/2 time as opposed to 4/4).

Allargando (It.). Broadening.

Allegretto (It.). Less fast than Allegro; the term generally implies a certain lightness of style.

Allegri, Domenico (*b* Rome, *c*1585; *d* there, 5 Sept 1629). Italian composer. He was *maestro di cappella* at S Maria in Trastevere, Rome, from 1610 to his death. A collection of 1617 shows him among the first to write independent instrumental parts in vocal chamber music.

Allegri, Gregorio (*b* 1582; *d* Rome, 7 Feb 1652). Italian composer. He was a singer and composer at the cathedrals of Fermo and Tivoli and later *maestro di cappella* of Spirito in Sassia, Rome, and a singer in the papal choir. He composed many of his works for this choir and that of S Maria in Vallicella. His reputation rests on his *Miserere*, a psalm setting traditionally sung every Holy Week by the papal choir: it is basically a simple five-part chant, transformed by interpolated ornamented passages for a four-part solo choir which reaches top C (rare at that time). These passages were a closely guarded secret for many years; Mozart wrote out the work from memory when he was 14. Allegri was at his best in the *a cappella* style, as in his five masses; he also published three books of more up-to-date small-scale concertato church music.

Allegro (It.). Quick; a movement in lively tempo.

Allegro, il Penseroso ed il Moderato, L'. Secular choral work by Handel to a libretto by Jennens, partly after Milton (1740, London).

Alleluia [hallelujah] (Heb.: 'Praise Yahweh'). A popular acclamatory refrain or response. Traditionally the song sung by men and angels, it was used by Christians, Eastern and Western, by the 4th century. The third chant of the Roman Mass Proper, it is sung before the Gospel except in Lent. The alleluia and its repetition enclose a verse; the alleluia concludes with a long textless melisma, the jubilus, sung on the final vowel. The precentor and choir sing in alternation, so the alleluia is a responsorial chant.

Alleluia verses survive from the 8th century and melodies from the 10th; they were always associated with Easter. Early influences were psalmody and popular song. The alleluia repertory was extended in the following centuries and alleluia melodies were used in much of the late 12th-century Notre Dame polyphonic repertory. Only the solo sections of the responsorial chants were set in polyphony; the choral sections remained monophonic.

In the Byzantine rite, the alleluia comprises the singing of the word 'alleluia' followed by two or three psalm verses (the *allēluïarion*); this may have provided models for the Roman alleluia.

Alleluia Symphony. Haydn's Symphony no.30 in C (1765) in which part of an Easter plainsong Alleluia is quoted in the first movement.

Allemande [allemanda, almain, alman etc] (Fr.: 'German [dance]'). A popular Baroque dance and a standard movement of the suite. It originated in the 16th century as a moderate duple-metre dance in two or three strains. In the 17th century French composers for lute and keyboard developed it as a vehicle for motivic and harmonic exploration, using a wide range of tempo markings in quadruple metre with a short initial upbeat. French contributions to the allemande style were absorbed by German keyboard composers, including Froberger and Bach.

German ensemble allemandes were unaffected by this concern for textural and motivic interest, but Italian and English composers used more contrapuntal imagination; Corelli's vary widely in texture and in tempo (from *largo* to *presto*). In the late 18th century the title 'allemande' came into use for a new dance in triple metre; Weber's *Douze allemandes* op.4 (1801) are actually examples of the waltz-like GERMAN DANCE.

Allen, Sir Hugh (Percy) (*b* Reading, 23 Dec 1869; *d* Oxford, 20 Feb 1946). English organist. After holding posts in cathedrals, he went to Oxford as organist of New College in 1901, becoming professor there in 1918 and in the same year director of the RCM. He did much to reform English music education and was also noted as a conductor, especially of Bach.

Allen, Thomas (Boaz) (*b* Seaham Harbour, 10 Sept 1944). English baritone. After study at the RCM he joined the Welsh National Opera in 1969. He has sung at Covent Garden from 1971 and at Glyndebourne from 1973; among his best portrayals are Mozart's Figaro, Papageno and Don Giovanni, the role of his La Scala début (1987). He is also a noted concert singer.

Allende(-Sarón), Pedro Humberto (*b* Santiago, 29 June 1885; *d* there, 17 Aug 1959). Chilean composer. He studied at the Santiago National Conservatory (1899–1908) and in France and Spain. His works reflect his studies of indigenous music. His nephew Juan Allende-Blin (*b* 1928), also a composer, studied and worked in Germany and has edited music by Debussy.

All'ottava (It.). 'At the octave': an instruction to play an octave above or below the written pitch.

All'unisono (It.). 'At the unison': an instruction that any parts thus shown are to be taken as one part (at the same pitch or the octave above or below).

Alma Redemptoris mater (Lat.: 'Sweet mother of the Redeemer'). One of the four Marian antiphons, sung at the end of Compline from the first Sunday of

Advent to the Purification (2 February). There are settings by Dufay, Josquin, Palestrina and Victoria.

Almeida, Francisco António de (*b* c1702; *d* ?Lisbon, 1755). Portuguese composer. During his study years in Rome (1720–26) he wrote two Italian oratorios. He continued to use Italian styles in his later works, composed in Lisbon; these include the opera *La Spinalba* (1739), other theatrical works and sacred music.

Almenraeder, Carl (*b* Wuppertal, 3 Oct 1786; *d* Biebrich, 14 Sept 1843). German bassoonist. Self-taught, he played in orchestras and taught the bassoon. Influenced by Gottfried Weber, an acoustician, and after experimenting in the Schott factory, he made fundamental improvements to the bassoon. At Biebrich he established a manufacturing business with J.A. Heckel (1831), and he published a famous tutor (Mainz, 1843).

Almérie. A type of lute invented by Jean Le Marie (c1581–c1650).

Almira. Opera in three acts by Handel to a libretto by F.C. Feustking after a text by G. Pancieri (1705, Hamburg).

Almqvist, Carl Jonas Love (*b* Stockholm, 28 Nov 1793; *d* Bremen, 26 Sept 1866). Swedish author and composer. A poet, novelist and journalist, he opposed the current enthusiasm for virtuosos and instrumental music. His unaccompanied songs (*Songes*, c1830) and piano pieces (*Fria Fantasier*, 1847–9) are in a naive, folklike style.

Alpaerts, Flor (*b* Antwerp, 12 Sept 1876; *d* there, 5 Oct 1954). Belgian composer and conductor. He studied at the Antwerp Conservatory, and taught there from 1903 (director, 1934–41). He was an outstanding personality in Flemish musical life. His works include the opera *Shylock* (1913) and impressionist symphonic poems.

Alpenhorn. See ALPHORN.

Alpensinfonie, Eine. Tone poem by Richard Strauss (1915).

Alphorn [alpenhorn]. A long wooden trumpet of pastoral communities in the Alps. The name also covers similar instruments of Scandinavia, eastern Europe and the highlands of Germany. Alphorns are known best as herdsmen's calling instruments, but also serve to summon to church and formerly to war.

Al rovescio (It.). 'Upside-down', 'back-to-front': term that can refer either to inversion or to retrograde motion.

Al segno (It.). 'To the sign': an instruction to proceed, on repetition, only to the point at which a sign is placed.

Also sprach Zarathustra [Thus spake Zoroaster]. Tone poem by Richard Strauss (1896) after Nietzsche's poem.

Alta. A group of two or three shawms and a sackbut, a standard 15th-century instrumental ensemble.

Altenbergslieder. Berg's op.4 (1912), five songs for voice and orchestra to picture-postcard texts by Peter Altenberg.

Altenburg, Johann Ernst (*b* Weissenfels, 15 June 1734; *d* Bitterfeld, 14 May 1801). German trumpeter. After serving as a field trumpeter in the French army (1757–66) he was organist in Landsberg and from 1769 in the village of Bitterfeld. His treatise *Versuch einer Anleitung zur heroisch-musikalischen Trompeter- und Pauker-Kunst* (1795) is valuable for information on court and field trumpeters and their art.

Altenburg, Michael (*b* Alach, 27 May 1584; *d* Erfurt, 12 Feb 1640). German composer. He spent most of his life as a schoolmaster and clergyman at and near Erfurt. All his surviving music is sacred, and almost all appeared in the early 1620s; it ranges from simple chorale-based pieces to vocal concertos for large forces, and shows his concern for the simplification of Protestant church music. It was highly esteemed in his time; he was called a Thuringian Lassus.

Altered chord. In tonal harmony, a chord of which one or more notes is altered chromatically.

Alternatim (Lat.). 'Alternatively': term used for the manner in which alternate sections of liturgical items were performed by different forces. An early example is the alternating of polyphony and plainchant in responsories; this was extended to psalms, canticles, hymns, sequences and the Ordinary of the Mass. The alternation of choir with organ (*see* ORGAN MASS) or of fauxbourdon with plainchant gained currency in the 15th century.

Alternativo (It.). 18th-century term placed after a pair of dances to indicate that the first should be repeated after the second.

Althorn (Ger.). See ALTO HORN.

Altmeyer, Jeannine (Theresa) (*b* La Habra, CA, 2 May 1948). American soprano. She studied with Singher and Lotte Lehmann and in Salzburg and made her Met début in 1971, singing at Chicago (1972), Salzburg (1973) and Covent Garden (1975) and in the Stuttgart company (1975–9). She sang Sieglinde at Bayreuth (1979) and the Met (1986) and other Wagner roles as well as Strauss's Salome, and is noted for her radiant voice and intense expression.

Altnikol, Johann Christoph (*b* Berma bei Seidenberg, bap. 1 Jan 1720; *d* Naumburg, bur. 25 July 1759). German organist and composer. While a student at Leipzig, he assisted J.S. Bach as a bass singer and copyist. He worked at Naumburg from 1748. In 1749 he married Bach's daughter Elisabeth and after Bach's death (1750) took in his mentally handicapped son Gottfried Heinrich. His compositions, now mostly lost, include a Magnificat, cantatas, and keyboard music.

Alto (It.: 'high'). Term originally used for a high vocal part, lying above the tenor and sung by one or more male voices. It implied, from the 16th century to the 18th, a part roughly of the pitch *g*–*c"*, sung by men (falsettists, high tenors or castratos) or by boys, in church music, but sometimes by women in secular music. In English usage, 'alto' is usually applied to a male voice, 'contralto' to a female one, though the distinction is not rigid. In choral music, 'alto' is used for either sex (it is the 'A' in SATB).

In French and Italian, 'alto' is the term for the viola (its pitch relates to that of the violin as the alto voice does to the soprano). It is also used as an adjective for other instruments, especially wind: the alto clarinet is usually in E♭, a 5th below the standard soprano instrument; the alto flute is in G, a 4th below the standard. The alto recorder (an American term; in

English usage it is called the treble) is itself the standard instrument. The alto trombone, now largely obsolete, was pitched a 4th or 5th above the standard, tenor instrument in B♭. The english horn (cor anglais) is sometimes called an 'alto oboe'. The alto saxophone, in E♭ (occasionally F), is the standard instrument of the family.

The alto clef, used particularly by the viola, the viola da gamba (in high-lying music) and the alto voice, is shown with the sign for *c'* on the middle line of the staff.

Alto clarinet. A CLARINET pitched in E♭ (or F) and sounding a major 6th (or 5th) lower than written.

Alto flute. A FLUTE pitched in G, a 4th below the concert flute.

Alto horn [althorn]. American term for a valve brass instrument pitched in E♭, a 5th below the cornet or trumpet. It is equivalent to the English TENOR HORN.

Alto oboe. The ENGLISH HORN or cor anglais, also known as the tenor OBOE. It is pitched in F (a 5th below the oboe) and sounds a 5th lower than written.

Alto Rhapsody. Name by which Brahms's Rhapsody for alto, male chorus and orchestra op.53 (1869) is known in English; the text is from Goethe's poem *Harzreise im Winter*.

Alto saxophone. A SAXOPHONE pitched in E♭ and sounding a major 6th lower than written.

Altus (Lat.). 'High': a voice designation that originated in the mid-15th century as an abbreviation of 'CONTRATENOR altus'.

Alva, Luigi (*b* Lima, 10 April 1927). Peruvian tenor. He studied at Lima and Milan, where he made his European début as·Verdi's Alfredo (1954). He sang Paolino in *Il matrimonio segreto* at the Piccola Scala opening in 1955 and the next year made his début at the main house as Rossini's Almaviva. He sang at Covent Garden from 1960 and the Met from 1964. His elegant, refined style especially suited Mozart and Rossini.

Alvary [Achenbach], **Max(imilian)** (*b* Düsseldorf, 3 May 1856; *d* Grosstabarz, 7 Nov 1898). German tenor. He sang in Germany as well as New York and London, establishing himself as the outstanding Wagner tenor of his day. His most celebrated role was Siegfried (in *Siegfried*).

Alwyn, William (*b* Northampton, 7 Nov 1905; *d* Southwold, 11 Sept 1985). English composer. He studied with McEwen at the RAM (1920–23) and later taught there (1926–55); in 1961 he retired to Suffolk to compose. He disowned everything he wrote before the Divertimento for flute (1939), which opened a neo-classical phase, followed in the 1950s by a personal vein of English Romanticism. His music is characterized by precise workmanship. It includes five symphonies (1949, 1953, 1956, 1959, 1973) and two string quartets, opera (*Miss Julie*, 1976) and songs (often to his own words: he also published poems and essays); he wrote over 60 film scores.

Alyab'yev, Alexander Alexandrovich (*b* Tobolsk, 15 Aug 1787; *d* Moscow, 6 March 1851). Russian composer. He wrote comic operas, vaudevilles and songs, including the famous *Nightingale* (1823), be-

fore establishing himself as a serious stage composer in Moscow, where he wrote incidental music and operas, including two after Shakespeare.

Amabile (It.). Charming, gracious, amiable.

Amadei, Filippo (*fl* 1690–1730). Italian cellist and composer. He worked under the patronage of Cardinal Pietro Ottoboni in Rome, where he composed oratorios. By 1719 he was in London, where (as 'Sigr Pippo') he gave concerts and in 1720 played in the orchestra of the Royal Academy of Music. His few surviving works include Act I of *Muzio Scevola*, staged there in 1721 with Acts 2 and 3 by G. Bononcini and Handel. He returned to Ottoboni's service later in the 1720s.

Amadeus Quartet. English string quartet, led by Norbert Brainin. It was founded in 1947; the upper three players were pupils of Rostal. It ceased playing with the death of Peter Schidlof, the viola player, in 1987. The quartet, which toured widely and made many records, was noted for its polished interpretations of the Classical repertory, especially Mozart and Schubert.

Amadigi (di Gaula). Opera in five acts by Handel to a libretto by Haym after A.H. de la Motte (1715, London); J.C. Bach wrote an opera on the same subject (*Amadis de Gaule*), in three acts to a libretto by de Vismes after P. Quinault (1779, Paris).

Amadino, Ricciardo (*fl* Venice, 1572–1621). Italian printer. With Giacomo Vincenti, he published over 76 music books, 1583–6. Working alone, he issued many publications, including works by Gastoldi and Monteverdi (*Orfeo*, 1608), and printed theoretical volumes.

Amadis. *Tragédie lyrique* in a prologue and five acts by Lully to a libretto by P. Quinault (1684, Paris). J.C. Bach's *Amadis de Gaule* (1779, Paris) is based on a reworking of the same libretto. Handel's *Amadigi di Gaula* (1715, London) is on a similar plot.

Amahl and the Night Visitors. One-act Christmas opera by Menotti to his own libretto, the first television (NBC) opera (1951), staged in Bloomington, Indiana (1952).

Amati. Italian family of violin makers, active in Cremona. Andrea (*b* before 1511; *d* before 1580) originated and perfected the form of violin, viola and cello as they are known today; of his few surviving instruments, dated 1564 to 1574, most bear the coat-of-arms of Charles IX of France. His two sons Antonio (*b* c1540) and Girolamo (1561–1630), known as the Amati brothers, experimented with outline and arching and improved the form of the soundhole, but retained the elegance and a pleasing sound quality; besides violins in two sizes, they made many tenor violas and large cellos and were widely copied. Girolamo's son Nicolo (1596–1684), the family's most refined workman and highly regarded member, favoured a wider violin model (the 'Grand Amati'), well curved and long-cornered; with their golden orange colour, noble sound and ease of response, they are among the most sought-after violins. Nicolo's pupils included Andrea Guarneri and Antonio Stradivari.

Amato, Pasquale (*b* Naples, 21 March 1878; *d* Jackson Heights, NY, 12 Aug 1942). Italian baritone. He made his début in Naples in 1900 and sang at La Scala in 1907–8 under Toscanini; from 1908 to 1921 he sang leading baritone roles at the Met where his fine voice, polished style and dramatic powers were admired.

Ambros, August Wilhelm (*b* Vysoké Myto, 17 Nov 1816; *d* Vienna, 26 June 1876). Austrian music historian and writer. He was of wide cultural interests, much influenced by Hegelian thinking. His main achievement was the *Geschichte der Musik* (4 vols., 1862–78), based on original source studies in Austria, south Germany and Italy, which views music history as cultural history.

Ambrosian [Milanese] **rite, Music of the.** A chant repertory, distinct from Gregorian, found at and near Milan, a centre open to outside influences but essentially conservative; archaic forms of chants may thus survive. The rite gained independence through the prestige of the Milanese bishop St Ambrose (*c*340–97) although the earliest surviving sources date from the 11th and 12th centuries. Syllabic chants are more syllabic than their Gregorian counterparts, and melismatic chants are more melismatic. Individual categories of chant do not have well-defined musical styles, as Gregorian ones do. There is a lack of well-defined modality, but uniformity in cadence structure. Melodically, the music uses stepwise motion, sequential structure in melismas and frequent repetition of motifs.

Amelia al ballo [Amelia Goes to the Ball]. Opera in one act by Menotti to his own libretto (1937, Philadelphia).

Ameling, Elly [Elisabeth] (**Sara**) (*b* Rotterdam, 8 Feb 1934). Dutch soprano. Her teachers included Bernac. She gave her first recital in Amsterdam in 1961 and made her débuts in London in 1966 and New York in 1968. She is mainly known as a recital singer, bringing a special warmth and freshness to Schubert lieder and having an affinity for French song; she is also a natural interpreter of Bach and Mozart.

Amen (Heb.: 'So be it'). A liturgical acclamation used by Christians, Jews and Muslims especially as the seal or intensification of a doxology or other prayer. In the Western liturgies, it concludes the lesser doxology and most prayers; it is also used after the Gloria and Credo of the Mass. Polyphonic settings of the Gloria, Credo and Anglican Office responses often treat the amens separately. In the 17th century fugal amens became common; they were later used in the masses of Bach, Mozart and Beethoven and in the final chorus of Handel's *Messiah*. In Anglican traditions it is often sung to a plagal cadence after hymns.

Amen cadence [plagal cadence]. A CADENCE consisting of a subdominant chord followed by a tonic chord (IV–I), both normally in root position.

Amener (Fr.). A 17th-century dance in moderate triple metre, derived from the branle *de Poitou à mener*, in which one couple leads the other dancers.

American Guild of Organists. An educational and service organization for organists and choral conductors, founded in 1896 by John Knowles Paine and George Chadwick; it conducts examinations and publishes the *American Organist*.

American Indian music. The Mongoloid ancestors of modern American Indians migrated from Asia across the Bering Strait to the Americas during the last glacial period, 20 000–35 000 years ago. They migrated southwards, settling throughout the North and South American continents, reaching the extreme south in *c*6000 BC.

The indigenous music of the Americas includes styles of relative simplicity and, particularly in North America, of limited instrumentarium. Nevertheless the appeal of this music, and the contrast it presents with European idioms, gave impetus to the development of ETHNOMUSICOLOGY in the United States, beginning in the late 19th century and early 20th with the research of Jesse Walter Fewkes, Alice Cunningham Fletcher, Benjamin Ives Gilman and Frances Densmore.

North American Indian music is primarily vocal; instruments are limited mainly to frame and cylindrical drums, flutes and rattles, all used to accompany song. In the South there are more complex instruments including single-reed wind instruments in Venezuela and Brazil, and notched flutes and wooden and clay panpipes (some with pipes up to five feet tall) in the Andean region. Many South American Indian instruments have magico-religious significance, including the bullroarer, believed by some groups to divert storms, and clay, bark and bamboo trumpets, considered sacred and used as voice disguisers and megaphones.

Music is important in everyday life, accompanying nearly all social and religious gatherings, including dances, hunting and religious rites. The style varies from region to region. Most characteristic is the Plains style, extending from the Mississippi Valley westwards to the Rocky Mountains, including the Arapaho, Blackfoot, Comanche, Crow, Flathead, Kiowa, Pawnee and Sioux. Their music uses simple descending melodies, pentatonic scales and a high, tense vocal style rendered in distinctively hard pulsating tones. Songs are usually accompanied by drum and rattle. The tribes of the eastern woodlands, including the Iroquois, Wabanaki, Cherokee, Creek, Seminole and Chippewa, sing short songs in responsorial style with simple rhythmic organization and undulating melodies. The tribes of the north-west coast of the USA and Canada, including the Coast Salish, Kwakiutl and Bella Coola, have a more complex style with non-strophic, recitative-like songs using non-metrical rhythms, narrow melodic range and small intervals, especially minor 2nds. Indians have recently shown renewed interest in their traditional culture and music; the Plains style is the most conspicuous and may be heard at intertribal powwows and dances.

American in Paris, An. Tone poem for orchestra by Gershwin (1928).

American Musicological Society [AMS]. Organization founded in Philadelphia in 1934 to advance scholarly research. It holds meetings, gives awards and coordinates activities with other musical organizations; its publications include a journal (since 1948) and a newsletter (since 1971).

American Quartet. Nickname of Dvořák's String

Quartet in F op.96, so called because it was composed in America in 1893, inspired by black melodies.

Amériques. Work for large orchestra by Varèse (1921) that includes parts for fire siren, cyclone whistle etc.

Amfiparnaso, L'. Madrigal comedy in a prologue and 13 scenes by Orazio Vecchi to his own texts (1594), a quasi-dramatic work for five voices not intended to be staged.

Amico Fritz, L'. Opera in three acts by Mascagni to a libretto by P. Suardon (pseudonym of N. Daspuro) after Erckmann-Chatrian (1891, Rome).

Amiot, Jean Joseph Marie (b Toulon, 8 Feb 1718; d Beijing, 8 Oct 1793). French Jesuit missionary. While in Beijing (from 1751) he wrote several influential and pioneering works on Chinese music, notably a *Mémoire sur la musique des Chinois* (1779).

Amirov, Fikret (Meshadi Jamil') (b Kirovabad, 22 Nov 1922; d Baku, 20 Feb 1984). Soviet composer. He studied at the Azerbaijan State Conservatory (1939–48) and played a leading role in Azerbaijani musical life as a conductor and administrator. He wrote symphonies based structurally on the folk *mugam* form and operas, of which *Sevil'* (1953) was the first national lyrical-psychological opera.

Ammerbach, Elias Nikolaus (b Naumburg, c1530; d Leipzig, bur. 29 Jan 1597). German organist and arranger. He studied at the Leipzig University (1548–9) and probably abroad, and was organist at the Thomaskirche, Leipzig, 1561–95. His *Orgel oder Instrument Tabulatur* (1571), the first printed German organ tablature, introduced 'new German' notation in which pitches are expressed by letters with rhythm-signs above. It contains arrangements for organ or other keyboard instrument of vocal works and dances; some are lavishly decorated, as are the arrangements in his *Ein new künstlich Tabulaturbuch* (1575).

Ammon [Amon], Blasius (b Imst, c1560; d Vienna, 1–21 June 1590). Austrian composer. He studied in Innsbruck and Venice and served at the Cistercian monastery in Heiligkreuz and the Franciscan one in Vienna. He published five books of sacred music, showing Venetian influence with rich sonority and multiple-choir effects. He should not be confused with the Protestant hymn writer Wolfgang Ammon (1540–89).

Amner, John (b Ely, bap. 24 Aug 1579; d there, bur. 28 July 1641). English composer. From a family with connections with Ely Cathedral, he was *informator choristarum* at Ely from 1610 until his death. He studied at Oxford (BMus 1613) and graduated MusB of Cambridge in 1640. A contemporary of Gibbons and Tomkins, he wrote mainly English service music and anthems (mostly MS, some in *Sacred Hymnes*, 1615). His early pieces are simple and syllabic; later he used more intricate verse-anthem and polyphonic choral styles showing his skill in matching text with music. He also wrote a Pavan and Galliard for viols and keyboard variations.

Amor brujo, El [Love, the Magician]. Ballet in one act by Falla (1915, Madrid); the score includes songs and the 'Ritual Fire Dance'.

Amoroso (It.). Loving, affectionate.

Amram, David (Werner) (b Philadelphia, 17 Nov 1930). American composer and conductor. He developed an early interest in jazz and performed in a Dixieland band. An association with the New York Shakespeare Festival, from 1956, led to 18 incidental scores. He has written film scores as well as colourful pieces for orchestra (*Shakespearean Concerto*, 1959) and chorus.

Amy, Gilbert (b Paris, 29 Aug 1936). French composer and conductor. He studied with Milhaud and Messiaen at the Paris Conservatoire (1955–60) and with Boulez at the Basle Academy (1965). The main influence on his earlier works, including the Piano Sonata (1960), was Boulez, whom he succeeded as director of the Domaine Musical (1967–73). His later works include the orchestral pieces *Chant* (1969) and *D'un espace déployé* (with soprano, 1973) and music for smaller ensembles.

Ana, Francesco d' [Francesco Varoter] (b ?Venice, c1460; d there, late 1502 or 1503, before 6 Feb). Italian composer and organist. He was second organist at St Mark's, Venice, from 1490 until his death and an early and important composer of frottolas. Some of his 28 settings are syllabic, with many repeated notes, others are melismatic.

Anacreontic Society. Catch and glee club founded in 1766 in London. It held fortnightly meetings (Haydn was a guest performer in 1791) and disbanded in 1794. The tune of its constitutional hymn, John Stafford Smith's *To Anacreon in Heaven*, was adopted (1931) by the USA for its national anthem.

Anacrusis. Upbeat; term (borrowed from literary usage) for unstressed notes at the beginning of a phrase of music.

Analysis. That part of the study of music which takes the music itself, rather than any external factor, as its starting-point. It normally involves the resolution of a musical structure into relatively simpler constituent elements and the investigation of the roles of those elements in the structure. There are many different types and methods of analysis, including by fundamental structure (Schenker), by theme, by form (Tovey), by phrase-structure (Riemann) and by information-theory.

Ančerl, Karel (b Tučapy, 11 April 1908; d Toronto, 3 July 1973). Czech conductor. He studied under Scherchen and Talich and conducted for Prague radio, 1933–9 and 1947–50, then the Czech PO to 1968 and the Toronto SO from 1969. He appeared widely abroad and was admired for the warmth and lyricism of his conducting, especially in Czech music.

Anche (Fr.). REED.

Anchieta, Juan de (b ?Urrestilla, 1462; d Azpeitia, 30 July 1523). Spanish composer. He was related to Ignatius Loyola. He sang in the Castilian royal chapel from 1489 for most of his working life. From 1500 he was rector of the parish church at Azpeitia. His masses, Magnificats and motets, for large choirs, are chiefly graceful and sonorous, with few learned devices. One of his four secular songs, *Dos ánades*, was very popular.

Ancina, (Giovanni) Giovenale (*b* Fossano, 19 Oct 1545; *d* Saluzzo, 31 Aug 1604). Italian composer. He studied mainly at Turin University, graduating in 1567. In 1574 he went to Rome, studied theology and met Filippo Neri, at whose Oratory he was ordained in 1582. After ten years in Naples he returned to Rome in 1596 and was made Bishop of Saluzzo in 1603. Strongly influenced by Neri and the Counter-Reformation, he supplied popular secular pieces of his day with sacred texts. He also wrote texts for *laudi spirituali*; his *Tempio armonico* (1599) contains *laudi* by leading contemporaries and five by himself. He copied important MSS and may have written two music treatises.

Anda, Géza (*b* Budapest, 19 Nov 1921; *d* Zurich, 14 June 1976). Swiss pianist and conductor. He studied under Dohnányi and made his début in Brahms's Piano Concerto no. 2 under Mengelberg. He settled in Switzerland in 1943 and soon established an international reputation, being esteemed not only in the Romantic repertory but above all in Bartók and Mozart, whose concertos he recorded as soloist and conductor.

Andamento (It.). 'Walking': term for a leisurely type of fugue subject of some length, e.g. that of Bach's '48', i, 2. It may also mean a short motif repeated at various pitch levels.

Andante (It.). Moderately slow; a movement at a moderately slow or walking pace.

Andante favori. Slow movement written by Beethoven in 1803 for his Piano Sonata in C op.53 ('Waldstein') but then detached and issued as a separate work.

Andantino (It.). A little faster or more lighthearted than Andante.

Anderberg, Carl-Olof (*b* Stockholm, 13 March 1914; *d* Malmö, 4 Jan 1972). Swedish composer. He studied as a composer and conductor in Stockholm and abroad and was a conductor in Malmö. He developed an individual style from French neo-classical and Schoenbergian elements and wrote mostly chamber and orchestral works.

Anderson, June (*b* Boston, 30 Dec 1952). American soprano. She made her début at New York City Opera as Queen of Night in 1978, remaining in the company to 1984, singing the Italian lyrical and coloratura repertory. Her European début was at Rome as Rossini's Semiramide (1982) and she sang in *La Sonnambula* at La Scala. Her Vienna Staatsoper and Covent Garden stage débuts were as Donizetti's Lucia. She is possessor of a clear, ringing soprano, with a fine command of high and florid writing.

Anderson, Leroy (*b* Cambridge, MA, 29 June 1908; *d* Woodbury, CT, 18 May 1975). American composer. He studied with Enescu and Piston at Harvard (1926–30) and worked in Boston and New York as an arranger (1935–42) before revealing a talent for snappy, light orchestral music (e.g. *Sleigh Ride*, 1948; *The Typewriter*, 1950; *Blue Tango*, 1951).

Anderson, Marian (*b* Philadelphia, 17 Feb 1902). American contralto. She went to Europe in 1930, gave recitals and was much admired by Toscanini; her New York début followed in 1936. In 1955 she became the first black to sing at the Met (Ulrica). She had a large, rich voice and high artistic integrity.

An die ferne Geliebte [To the distant beloved]. Song cycle by Beethoven (op.98, 1816), settings for voice and piano of six poems by Alois Jeitteles.

André. German family of composers and music publishers, of French extraction. Johann (1741–99) was a dilettante composer of Singspiels and songs, whose success as a publisher of his own music and business experience in the family silk firm led him to found a music publishing house at Offenbach (1774). From 1784 he directed the firm, establishing relations with Pleyel, Haydn and Gyrowetz; by 1797 it had published its 1000th item. His son Johann Anton (1775–1842) studied in Mannheim and composed music in most of the classical forms but is more important as a publisher and for his editorial work on the 'Mozart-Nachlass', bought from the composer's widow in 1799. Apart from producing many reliable editions, he sorted Mozart's MSS, laying the foundations for later research. In 1799 he acquired the rights to the new lithographic process and set up plants in Paris and London. The firm was continued under his son August (1817–87) and his heirs, and still exists; two other sons, Carl August (1806–87) and Julius (1808–80), ran a branch in Frankfurt, and another, Jean Baptiste (1823–82), was a pianist and composer.

André, Maurice (*b* Alès, 21 May 1933). French trumpeter. At first a miner, he studied at the Conservatoire (where he taught from 1973) and played in Paris orchestras; in the 1960s, competitive successes launched him on a brilliant solo career, especially on a small trumpet which he played with great fluency in the Baroque repertory. Many composers have written for him.

Andrea Chenier. Opera in four acts by Giordano to a libretto by Illica (1896, Milan).

Andreae, Volkmar (*b* Berne, 5 July 1879; *d* Zurich, 18 June 1962). Swiss conductor and composer. He studied with Wüllner in Cologne (1897–1900) and in 1902 settled in Zurich, where he was conductor of the Tonhalle Orchestra (1906–49) and director of the conservatory (1914–41). He was guest conductor of leading European orchestras and an outstanding advocate of Bruckner and contemporary music. His works, in the German Romantic tradition, include operas, orchestral and chamber music and many male choruses.

Andreas de Florentia (*d* c1415). Italian composer and organist. He became a Servite monk in 1375 and was prior at Ss Annunziata, Florence (1380–97), where he knew Landini, and Pistoia (1393), and led the Tuscan Servites (1407–10). 30 Italian ballate by him survive in MS: some are lively, with striking use of imitation.

Andreozzi, Gaetano (*b* Aversa, 22 May 1755; *d* Paris, 21/24 Dec 1826). Italian composer and singing teacher. He studied in Naples, wrote successful though unremarkable works (44 operas, five oratorios) for Italian theatres and made a name as a singing teacher to the Neapolitan nobility.

Andriessen, Hendrik (*b* Haarlem, 17 Sept 1892; *d* Heemstede, 12 April 1981). Dutch composer and organist. He studied with Zweers at the Amsterdam Conservatory and in 1913 succeeded to his father's post as organist in Haarlem; in 1934 he moved to Utrecht Cathedral. He also had a distinguished career as a teacher at the conservatories of Amsterdam (from 1926), Utrecht (from 1937) and The Hague (from 1949). His works include much Catholic church music in a meditative, mystical style and four symphonies (1930–54), chamber music and many songs.

His pupils include his sons Jurriaan (*b* 1925), a fluent and diverse composer of orchestral, chamber, theatre and film music, and Louis (*b* 1939), a pupil of Berio and a leading figure in Dutch minimalism, whose works include *De Staat* (1976) for voices and orchestra.

Anerio, Felice (*b* Rome, *c*1560; *d* there, 26/7 Sept 1614). Italian composer, brother of G.F. Anerio. He sang in the Cappella Giulia and in 1594 succeeded Palestrina as composer to the papal chapel. He joined the priesthood and in 1611 was asked to reform the Roman Gradual. His works of the 1580s are mainly canzonettas and madrigals, but as papal composer he wrote masses, motets (1596, 1602), responsories (1606), psalms and other sacred works. Their style is conservative, enriched with expressive elements. He was one of the most important Roman composers of the late 16th and early 17th centuries.

Anerio, Giovanni Francesco (*b* Rome, *c*1567; *d* Graz, bur. 12 June 1630). Italian composer. He became a priest, then spent many years in Rome in *maestro di cappella* posts and was briefly at Verona Cathedral. He was also choirmaster at the Polish court in Warsaw (1624–8). A prolific, quite progressive composer, he is noted for his early oratorios, written in Italian for Filippo Neri's Oratory (*Teatro armonico spirituale*, 1619). His masses and motets are more conservative, but his *madrigali spirituali* include striking monodies and other madrigals and canzonettas are forward-looking.

Anet, Jean-Jacques-Baptiste (*b* Paris, 2 Jan 1676; *d* Lunéville, 14 Aug 1755). French violinist and composer, son of the violinist Jean-Baptist Anet (1650–1710) and generally known as 'Baptiste'. A pupil of Corelli in Rome, he served the exiled elector of Bavaria in Paris (until 1715) and Louis XIV. He played in concerts, including (from 1725) those at the Concert Spirituel. When his popularity faded he left the 24 Violons du Roi (*c*1735), and later served at the Lorraine court at Lunéville. He was the finest French violinist of his day, especially admired for his improvisation. His first book of violin sonatas (1724) shows Corelli's influence; his later sonatas and musettes are more French in character.

Anfossi, Pasquale (*b* Taggia, 5 April 1727; *d* Rome, ? Feb 1797). Italian composer. He was a violinist in Naples from *c*1752 and later trained as a composer under Sacchini and Piccinni. His first opera was staged in Rome in 1763; in the 1770s he worked there and in Venice, partly as *maestro di coro* at a girls' conservatory. His operatic ouput continued, notably with *L'incognita perseguitata* (1773, Rome). Moving to London, he was a music director for the King's Theatre, 1782–6; his first opera there was *Il trionfo della costanza* (1782). After the failure of his fifth London opera he returned to Venice, where his comic opera *Le pazzie de' gelosi* (1787) initiated a new period of popularity. He ceased writing operas in 1790 and became *maestro di cappella* at St John Lateran, Rome, in 1792.

Anfossi's operas, both heroic and comic, number over 60 and show a development from a style like Piccinni's to a more colourful idiom using freer structures. He also composed much church music and *c*20 oratorios.

Angel lute (Fr. *angélique*). A double-necked lute of the 17th and 18th centuries with ten single strings on the lower head and six or seven on the upper.

Angiolini,   (Domenico   Maria)   Gaspero (*b* Florence, 9 Feb 1731; *d* Milan, 6 Feb 1803). Italian choreographer. His teacher and model was the Viennese court ballet-master Hilverding, whom he succeeded in 1758. He collaborated with Gluck in ballet-pantomimes aiming to unite choreography and music, beginning with the highly successful *Don Juan* (1761) and the opera *Orfeo* (1762), and also wrote music for some ballets for St Petersburg (1766–72). After a further period in Vienna (1774–6), he worked mainly at St Petersburg and Milan. His nephew Pietro Angiolini (?1764–after 1830) was also a dancer and choreographer.

Anglaise (Fr.: 'English [dance]'). 18th-century term used on the Continent for various types of English dance. Pieces so titled may be in duple metre (including 6/8) and have a marked accent on the first beat of the bar. An example is in Bach's French Suite no.3.

Anglès, Higini (*b* Maspujols, 1 Jan 1888; *d* Rome, 8 Dec 1969). Catalan musicologist. He studied in Barcelona and in Germany and held posts at the library, the conservatory and the university in Barcelona; he also worked in Madrid and Rome. His early work was on folk music; later he became the leading authority on Spanish music of the Middle Ages and Renaissance.

Anglesi, Domenico (*b*? *c*1610–15; *d* after Aug 1669). Italian composer. He was a musician to the Medici court at Florence from 1638 and served Cardinal Giovan Carlo de' Medici. He wrote stage works, but virtually all his extant music is contained in his *Arie musicali* (1635), a fine collection of songs for voice and continuo, notable for their spaciousness, long-breathed melodies and clearcut tonalities.

Anglican chant. Harmonized formulae, derived from the pre-Reformation psalm-tone system, for the singing of psalms and canticles in the Church of England. A single chant consists of two sections, each a 'reciting' chord followed by other chords, usually on the metrical pattern of ex.1. Double

Ex. 1 Tallis

chants, to two verses of the psalm or canticle, repeat this formula. The most commonly used systems of 'pointing', or fitting the words to the chants, are those of the *Parish Psalter*, the *Oxford Psalter* and the *New Cathedral Psalter*.

Anhalt, István (*b* Budapest, 12 April 1919). Canadian composer of Hungarian birth. He studied with Kodály at the Budapest Academy (1937–41) and with Boulanger in Paris (1946–9), then moved to Canada, where he taught at McGill University (1949–71) and Queen's University, Kingston. Schoenbergian in its background, his music includes vocal and orchestral pieces, some with tape. His critical and analytical writings are informed and wide-ranging.

Animato (It.). Animated, lively.

Animuccia, Giovanni (*b* Florence, *c*1500; *d* Rome, *c*20 March 1571). Italian composer. After early training in Florence, where he moved in literary circles, by 1550 he was serving Cardinal Sforza in Rome. From 1555 he was *magister cantorum* at the Cappella Giulia, succeeding Palestrina, of whom he was an important contemporary. He composed *laudi spirituali* (1563, 1570) for the Oratory of Filippo Neri, many in a simple chordal style designed to aid the layman's participation. In his masses (1567) he made the text as intelligible as possible without loss of musical interest. His madrigals (1547, 1551, 1554) include extended cyclic pieces.

Paolo Animuccia (*c*1500–*c*1570), *maestro di cappella* at St John Lateran, Rome, and composer of motets and madrigals, was probably his brother.

Anna Amalia [Amalie], Duchess of Saxe-Weimar (*b* Wolfenbüttel, 24 Oct 1739; *d* Weimar, 10 April 1807). German musician and patron. She strongly influenced the Weimar court circle (including Goethe) and latterly devoted herself to the arts. Singspiels, including her own *Erwin und Elmire* (1776), were given at the court as was the 'first German opera', Schweitzer's setting of Wieland's *Alceste* (1773).

Anna Amalia [Amalie], Princess of Prussia (*b* Berlin, 9 Nov 1723; *d* there, 30 March 1787). German musician and patron. The youngest sister of Frederick the Great, she was an accomplished keyboard player; her compositions include a setting of Ramler's *Der Tod Jesu*. She built up a rich music collection (including many J.S. Bach autographs), now called the Amalien-Bibliothek and preserved in Berlin: the *c*600 works it contains reflect her conservative taste.

Anna Bolena. Opera in two acts by Donizetti to a libretto by Felice Romani (1830, Milan).

Anna Magdalena Bach Book. *See* CLAVIER-BÜCHLEIN.

Années de pèlerinage. Three volumes of piano pieces by Liszt: on Swiss subjects (1848–54), Italian subjects (1837–49) and an (unauthorized) posthumous collection (1867–77).

Ansatz (Ger.). In wind playing, EMBOUCHURE or (occasionally) MOUTHPIECE; in singing, the arrangement of the vocal apparatus or the attack of a note.

Ansbach Bachwoche (West Germany). Biennial festival (July), established in 1948. Concerts of J.S. Bach's music take place in the main churches and at the palace.

Anschlag (Ger.). A 'double appoggiatura', i.e. an ornament consisting of two notes rising by a leap and falling back by a step to the principal note. The term is also used to refer to piano touch.

Ansermet, Ernest (*b* Vevey, 11 Nov 1883; *d* Geneva, 20 Feb 1969). Swiss conductor. He was trained as a mathematician but made his conducting début in 1910 and became conductor of the Geneva SO in 1915; he also conducted the Ballets Russes, and in 1918 founded the Orchestre de la Suisse Romande which he conducted until his death. He was admired for his clear, precise performances, especially of Stravinsky and French 20th-century music.

Answer. In a fugal exposition, an entry of the theme at the pitch interval of (usually) a 4th or 5th from the SUBJECT. To preserve its tone–semitone relationships and to define the tonic key, a theme may be altered when it is 'answered'. An altered answer is called 'tonal', an unaltered 'real'.

Antarctic Symphony. *See* SINFONIA ANTARTICA.

Antecedent and consequent. A pair of musical statements that complement one another in rhythmic symmetry and harmonic balance.

Antegnati. Italian family of organ builders, composers and instrumentalists. They were active from the late 15th century to the second half of the 17th. The most outstanding members were Graziadio (*b* 1525), who built the organs of Asola Cathedral (1575) and S Giuseppe, Brescia (1581; extant); and his son Costanzo (1549–1624), a composer and cathedral organist in Brescia, an organ builder (he supervised the building of 144 instruments), and the author of a book that includes discussions of tuning and registration. The family built *c*400 organs, normally with a single manual, a pull-down pedal-board and a sound described as 'delicato' and 'dolce'. They typify the Italian Renaissance instruments for which Cavazzoni, Frescobaldi, the Gabrielis and Merulo composed.

Antes, John (*b* Frederick, PA, 24 March 1740; *d* Bristol, 17 Dec 1811). American Moravian composer. A minister and missionary and later warder of a Moravian community in England, he wrote three trios for two violins and cello (*c*1790; the earliest known chamber music by a native American composer), 31 anthems and songs, and 59 hymn tunes. His music is close to Haydn's in technique and spirit.

Antheil, George (*b* Trenton, NJ, 8 July 1900; *d* New York, 12 Feb 1959). American composer. He studied privately with Sternberg and with Bloch (1920) before moving to Berlin in 1922 to make his name as a modernist. Jazz, noise and ostinato were the means, worked into brutally simple designs in the *Airplane Sonata* (1922) and *Sonata sauvage* (1923) for piano, or the first two violin sonatas (1923), these last written after his move from Berlin to Paris. There he wrote the *Ballet mécanique* (1925) for an ensemble of pianos and percussion, including electric bells and propellers. In 1926 he turned to neo-classicism, then to opera: *Transatlantic* (1930, Frankfurt) was a satire on American political life. In 1936 he settled in Los Angeles, where he wrote symphonies, operas, vocal, chamber and piano music along more conventional lines.

Anthem. A choral setting of a religious or moral text

in English, usually for liturgical performance. The term is derived from ANTIPHON. In the 1662 Book of Common Prayer the anthem was formally acknowledged as an extra at the end of Matins and Evensong in the Church of England. Early anthems, from c1550 (by Tye, Tallis and others), are in four parts, predominantly imitative in note-against-note counterpoint. A significant development c1600 was the 'verse' style, in which verses for solo voices with instrumental accompaniment (normally organ) alternated with choral passages. This paralleled the CONCERTATO development abroad. Byrd's Easter anthem, *Christ rising again*, illustrates it at its best. Distinguished among his younger contemporaries were Morley (who considered it his task 'to draw the hearers ... to the consideration of holy things') and later Tomkins, Weelkes and Gibbons, who gave the anthem even greater dramatic impact.

After the Restoration (1661) a new style developed, with Cooke and Locke, in anthems for the Chapel Royal, showing homophonic textures and a succession of contrasting verses with occasional, often perfunctory choruses; French and Italian influence is evident. Strings were sometimes added for ritornellos. Locke, Humfrey and Blow used this new style; Purcell synthesized and developed these features, contributing to the verse anthem, the full anthem, and the newer orchestral type.

In the 18th century, anthems were written by Handel (including 11 for the Duke of Chandos, 1716–18, and some ten others), Greene, Boyce and others. In the period 1770–1817 adaptations and arrangements were used although Battishill and Samuel Wesley wrote effective anthems. The foundations of the Victorian revival were laid mainly by S.S. Wesley, many of whose best anthems were published in 1853. In the late 19th century, Stanford was particularly influential in church music: his anthems, reflecting an interest in new music abroad, are unmistakably English in style and structure. Vaughan Williams, Bax, Walton and Britten wrote isolated anthem-like compositions but few are practicable for daily cathedral use.

The American anthem of the late 18th century was modelled on English anthems from such collections as Tans'ur's *Royal Melody Complete* (1735) and Williams's *Universal Psalmodist* (1763). The centre of anthem composition during the 18th century was New England, where works by native composers, including the pioneer Billings, quickly outnumbered the available English models. Outside the mainstream were the Germanic immigrants, notably the Moravians who settled in Pennsylvania and North Carolina. Dudley Buck in the late 19th century and William Sowerby in the 20th have been among the most influential American anthem composers.

Anthology. A printed collection of musical works, usually by several composers, selected from a particular repertory. In the 16th century collections of separate popular forms are common, e.g. Petrucci's of French polyphonic *chansons* (*Odhecaton*, 1501), Attaignant's over 70 *chanson* collections (1528–52) and the vast number of madrigal collections (from 1530), notably the famous *Il trionfo di Dori* (1592) and *The Triumphes of Oriana* (1601). Collections of sacred vocal music became popular in the late 16th century and the early 17th, but the trend by the late 17th was for music for amateur domestic music-making, vocal or instrumental (*A Musicall Banquet*, 1651); many such collections extended to long series or were issued as periodicals (*Journal hebdomadaire*, 1764–1808). The first anthologies devoted to older music appeared in the later 18th century, flourishing in the 19th. Among anthologies of special interest are those commemorating individuals (Josquin, Belyayev, Fauré) or historical events (a royal wedding, a military victory).

Anthonello de Caserta (*b* ?Caserta, *fl* late 14th – early 15th centuries). Italian composer. The MSS containing his works suggest that he may have worked in northern Italy or Naples. He composed secular songs in Italian (six or seven ballate and a madrigal) and French (five ballades, two rondeaux and a virelai), all with courtly love lyrics. In the ballate the two voices largely declaim the text simultaneously; the French pieces are more complex contrapuntally and metrically.

Anticipation. In part-writing, an unaccented non-harmonic note that belongs to and is repeated in the harmony immediately following.

Antico, Andrea (*b* Montona, c1480; *d* after 1539). Italian music publisher. He worked as an engraver and publisher in Rome 1510–18, in Venice 1520–21 and (associated with the Scotto firm) 1533–9. He was the first music publisher in Rome and a competitor of Petrucci in Venice. His method differed from Petrucci's: he was an engraver of blocks that printed music and text together, whereas Petrucci used multiple impressions with movable type. His publications include frottolas, sacred works and madrigals; he also issued the first printed book of Italian keyboard music. He composed frottolas himself.

Antill, John (Henry) (*b* Sydney, 8 April 1904). Australian composer. He studied with Alfred Hill at the NSW State Conservatorium and worked for the ABC (1934–71). His orchestral *Corroboree* (1947) created a specifically Australian kind of music, based on his research into aboriginal music; he has written other orchestral pieces, operas, ballets and choral music.

Antimasque. Term, probably dating from 1609, for a comic or grotesque interlude in a MASQUE, normally preceding the terminal dances.

Antiphon. In the Roman rite, a liturgical chant with a prose text associated with psalmody sung by two choirs in alternation. It is usually a refrain to psalm or canticle verses and its melodies are often simple and syllabic. Categories include antiphons from the psalter, antiphons of Matins, Lauds and Vespers, antiphons to the *Benedictus* and Magnificat, and Mass antiphons for the Introit and Communion. Marian and processional antiphons are not associated with psalmody and rhymed antiphons evolved a style of their own during the 13th century. The Latin *antiphona* was borrowed from the Greek, where it meant the octave; it had appeared in the West by the 4th century.

Antiphonal. Term describing works, or the manner of performing them ('in antiphony'), in which an ensemble is divided into two or more distinct groups, performing in alternation and together; hence 'antiphonal singing', 'antiphonal psalmody' (*see* ANTIPHON; CORI SPEZZATI). The term is sometimes used synonymously with 'antiphoner', a Liturgical book containing antiphons (*see* LITURGICAL BOOK).

Antiphonel. An automatic player attachment for harmoniums and organs.

Anton (Clemens Theodor) of Saxony (*b* Dresden, 27 Dec 1755; *d* there, 6 June 1836). German prince and composer. He remained outside government for most of his life and composed numerous works, including operas and cantatas, songs and numerous instrumental works in a conservative, *galant* style.

Antoniou, Theodore (*b* Athens, 10 Feb 1935). Greek composer. He studied with Papaioannou at the Hellenic Conservatory in Athens (1956–61) and with Bialas in Munich. His large, varied output shows influences from Christou, Zimmermann and Penderecki.

Antonius de Civitate Austrie (*b* ?Cividale in Friuli; *fl* 1420–25). Italian composer. He was a Dominican friar and may have had connections with Florence and Forlì. His surviving works are three mass movements, five motets and five secular songs, four in French and one in Italian.

Antony and Cleopatra. Opera by Samuel Barber to a libretto by Zeffirelli after Shakespeare (1966, New York).

Antunes, Jorge (*b* Rio de Janeiro, 23 April 1942). Brazilian composer. He studied at the Federal University in Rio (1960–68) and with Ginastera (1969–70), continuing his studies of electronic music in Utrecht (1970) and Paris (1972–3). In 1973 he was appointed professor at the University of Brasilia. His works show concern with acoustics and music of the past and he is a leading figure in the Brazilian avant garde.

Anvil. A struck instrument of indefinite pitch; it may consist of one or two metal bars on a resonating frame, or an actual blacksmith's anvil. Its most famous use is in Wagner's *Das Rheingold*.

Apel, Willi (*b* Chojnice, 10 Oct 1893; *d* Bloomington, IN, 14 March 1988). American musicologist of German birth. He studied mathematics, then music, and took the doctorate in Berlin in 1936; he went to the USA in 1938, first to Harvard and then to the University of Indiana, Bloomington, where he taught, 1950–70. Most of his work was on medieval and Renaissance music, and his book on notation (1942), his study of Gregorian chant (1958), *Historical Anthology of Music* (1946–50) and his history of early keyboard music (1967) are standard works. Apel has also prepared numerous editions and is general editor of Corpus of Early Keyboard Music.

Apel Codex. German MS of the years around 1500. It was compiled by Nikolaus Apel and consists of 260 folios with 172 pieces, mainly liturgical music by composers from Germany and northern Europe. It is now in the library of Leipzig University.

Aperghis, Georges (*b* Athens, 23 Dec 1945). Greek composer. He studied in Athens and Paris, where he has remained. He was influenced by Xenakis and later by Kagel: most of his works are theatrical, often 'absurd', and many depend on visual effect.

Aperto (It.). 'Open': term used for open notes on the horn, open strings and undamped piano notes; it is also applied to first-time bars in medieval music, and was used by Mozart as a qualification to Allegro in several early works (his meaning is unclear).

A piacere (It.). 'At pleasure': an indication that the performer may use his discretion in the manner he performs a passage so marked (particularly in the matter of tempo).

ApIvor, Denis (*b* Collinstown, 14 April 1916). Irish composer of Welsh origin. He studied privately with Hadley and Rawsthorne and in the 1940s came under Lambert's influence. Serial interests led him towards an atonal, athematic style. His large output includes operas, ballets, instrumental and vocal music.

Apollonicon. A large, mechanical chamber organ including both keyboards and barrels; they were built in England, 1812–17.

Apollon musagète [Apollo Musagetes]. Ballet in two scenes by Stravinsky (1928, Washington, DC).

Apostel, Hans Erich (*b* Karlsruhe, 22 Jan 1901; *d* Vienna, 30 Nov 1972). Austrian composer of German birth. He moved to Vienna in 1921 and studied with Schoenberg and Berg, whom he followed in a long phase of atonal expressionism (e.g. in *Kubiniana* for piano, 1950) until in 1957 he became as absolute a serialist as Webern. His works include orchestral pieces but comprise mostly chamber music, sometimes with voice.

Apostles, The. Oratorio (op.49) by Elgar to his own biblical text (1903, Birmingham); its sequel is *The Kingdom*.

Apothéose. A form, current in Paris about 1725, with a programmatic element usually honouring a dead musician; examples are François Couperin's trio sonatas in memory of Corelli and Lully.

Appalachia. Work for choir and orchestra by Delius (1903), 'Variations on an Old Slave Song' from North America.

Appalachian dulcimer [Kentucky dulcimer, mountain dulcimer]. A partly- or fully-fretted zither of the USA, derived from north-west European forms. Its original use appears to have been for dance music; since the 1950s it has been used particularly for the accompaniment of ballads and dance-songs.

Appalachian Spring. Ballet in one act by Copland, choreographed by Martha Graham (1944, Washington, DC).

Appassionata Sonata. The publisher's title for Beethoven's Piano Sonata no.23 in F minor op.57 (1804–5).

Appassionato (It.). Impassioned.

Appenzeller, Benedictus (*b c*1480–88; *d* after 1558). ?Netherlands composer and singer. He was *maître de chapelle* to Mary of Hungary, regent of the Netherlands, in Brussels from 1537 until after 1551. He wrote *chansons* (23 published in 1542) and motets, and probably other works (in MSS where attributions may confuse him with Benedictus Ducis).

Appia, Adolphe (François) (*b* Geneva, 1 Sept 1862; *d* Nyon, 29 Feb 1928). Swiss stage designer. Reacting against socio-economic conditions, and influenced by Wagner's music and Jaques-Dalcroze's rhythmical gymnastics, he worked towards simplification of staging and a use of 'living space' that place him as father of non-illusionist musical theatre. In the 1920s he designed Wagner operas for La Scala and Basle, but only since World War II have his principles affected Bayreuth.

Applied dominant [secondary dominant]. The dominant of a degree other than the tonic, usually indicated by the symbol 'V/'.

Appoggiatura (It.). A 'leaning note', normally one step above (less often below) the main note. It usually creates a dissonance in the harmony and resolves by step on to the main note on the following weak beat. It may be notated as a small grace note or in normal notation. In early usage, the descending appoggiatura was called 'backfall', the ascending 'forefall' or 'beat'. Ex.1 shows some English 17th-century forms of notation. Ex.2 (D'Anglebert, 1689;

Ex. 1

Ex. 2

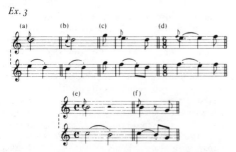

Dieupart, c1720) shows other notations and French names. The normal German name is *Vorschlag* or *Accent*. Ex.3 (Quantz, 1752) shows some possible interpretations of appoggiaturas; authorities, however, differ as to their realization (for example, that in ex.3*a*, shown as a crotchet, could be played as a quaver, and vice versa in ex.3*c*). In recitative in the late Baroque and Classical periods, and even into

Ex. 3

(a) (b) (c) (d)

(e) (f)

the 19th century, there was an understanding that an appoggiatura was normally to be added wherever a phrase ended on two repeated notes, the first on a strong beat; the first note should then be sung as the note immediately above (or very occasionally below) or at the pitch of the note preceding (see exx.4, from Handel's *Messiah*, and 5).

Ex. 4

Thou shalt break them with a rod of i-ron.

Thou shalt dash them to pieces like a potter's ves-sel.

Ex. 5

(a)   (b)

e non a-mo-re.   e non a-mo-re.

The acciaccatura, or 'crushed note', is sometimes called a 'short appoggiatura'; in modern notation, the stem of the grace note is struck through (in earlier notation it was normally notated as a short note, usually a semiquaver). A special case is the 'passing appoggiatura', where the extra note is interpolated between two main notes a 3rd apart and (normally) descending; its time may be deducted from the note preceding rather than the note following (ex.6).

Ex. 6

(a)

(b)

The double appoggiatura (Ger. *Anschlag*) consists of two preparatory notes, usually played rapidly: the second is usually the note above the main note.

Apponyi. Haydn's string quartets opp.71 and 74 (1793), dedicated to Count Franz Apponyi.

Apprenti sorcier, L'. *See* SORCERER'S APPRENTICE, THE.

Après-midi d'un faune, Prélude à l'. Orchestral work by Debussy (1894), an 'impression' of a poem by Mallarmé.

Aprile, Giuseppe (*b* Martina Franca, 28 Oct 1732; *d* there, 11 Jan 1813). Italian castrato singer. He began his career in Naples, sang at the most important Italian opera houses and in 1756–69 was at Stuttgart where he sang in Jommelli's works. He then returned, singing in Italy until he joined the Naples royal chapel in 1783. He was admired for his brilliance, his expressiveness and his acting. He composed songs and duets and was a famous singing teacher.

Apt MS. French MS, from the beginning of the 15th century. It consists of 45 folios containing 48 pieces preserving the repertory of the Avignon papal court (1377–1417), mainly mass movements, with motets and hymns. Composers include Cordier and Vitry; some of the music goes back to the early 14th century. Written by eight scribes, it is now at St Anne's Cathedral, Apt.

Arabella. Opera in three acts by Richard Strauss to a libretto by Hofmannsthal (1933, Dresden).

Arabesque. Term for various types of melodic, contrapuntal or harmonic decoration; it was used by Schumann, Debussy and others for piano pieces of a decorative character.

Arab music. The Arab world is a fairly homogeneous cultural and musical area, unified by the spread of Islam, from the 7th century AD, and by the predominance of the Arabic language. It includes countries of the Arabian peninsula (Saudia Arabia, Yemen and South Yemen), the Arabian Gulf (Bahrain, Kuwait, Qatar, United Arab Emirates and Oman) and contiguous countries (Iraq, Jordan, Lebanon and Syria); classical Iranian and Turkish music are closely related to Arab music, as is the music of North Africa. Branches of the Eastern Christian church in this region propagate their own religious music (e.g. the Syrian and Coptic churches); the art music of Israel, though related to Arab music, is closer to European tradition (see JEWISH MUSIC).

The fundamental characteristics of Arab classical music have been described over $c13$ centuries in historical, theoretical and poetical texts, including the writings of al-Kindī ($c801$–73) and al-Fārābī (d 950). Islamic musical scholarship treated melodic and rhythmic modes, the physics of sound, tunings and aesthetics. Although theory and practice did not always correspond, the fundamental features of classical Arab music may be extracted from these treatises since its establishment in the courts of the caliphs, from Central Asia to the Atlantic, after the spread of Islam. These include the predominance of vocal music, monophony (single melody) and heterophony (single melody with variations), melodic and rhythmic modes, highly developed melodies, sophisticated techniques of improvisation, preoccupation with subtle intonation, oral transmission and a close association with Arabic poetry. For Western listeners a marked 'oriental effect' is created by Arab scales, distinct from European diatonic forms, and by the characteristic preferred timbre of the region, resulting from ensembles of different instruments performing in unison.

Arab classical music is based on a system of melodic modes, known as *maqām*. Each mode has prescribed intervals, tonal emphases, cadence formulae, characteristic melodic contours and final tones. It also uses rhythmic modes (not unlike those of medieval Europe), based on short units derived from poetic metre.

Islamic religious music includes the chanting of the Koran, performed in varying styles throughout the region. Koranic chant is independent of the *maqām* system and more akin to Gregorian chant. The call to prayer, performed five times daily throughout the Islamic region, consists in most areas of seven or eight passages with repetition and variation. While classical Arab music and Islamic religious music are fairly homogeneous repertories, the folk music reflects the diversity of the many ethnic minorities including the Kurdish, Berber, Druze, Tuareg and Beduin peoples.

Classical Arab music is particularly rich in string instruments. Most important is the *'ūd*, a short-necked plucked lute, ancestor of the European lute whose name derives from the Arabic *al-'ūd* ('the lute'). It has a ribbed wooden body, often with elaborate decorations, and generally five courses of strings. The *rabāb* (*rabāba*) is the most common Arab spike-fiddle, an instrument whose neck extends through the body and protrudes as a spike at the bottom. The body has a rectangular or trapezoidal wooden frame with belly and back of animal skin. The *qānūn* is a plucked trapeziform-shaped box zither (psaltery) with 72–8 strings. The principal string instrument of Arab folk music is the *ṭanbūr*, a long-necked plucked lute with a pear-shaped body. The main wind instrument is the *nāy*, an oblique rim-blown cane flute with six finger-holes and one thumb-hole. Drums include the *duff* (*daff*), a single-headed frame drum, usually with rattles or jingles (like the European tambourine), and the *darabukka*, a single-headed goblet-shaped drum with a body of pottery, wood or metal.

Aragall, Giacomo (*b* Barcelona, 6 June 1939). Spanish tenor. He studied in Italy and made his La Scala début in the title role of *L'amico Fritz* (1963). His Covent Garden and Met débuts (1966, 1968) were as the Duke of Mantua; other admired roles include Alfredo and Cavaradossi. He is noted for his sensitive, idiomatic use of a forward, keen-edged voice.

Araia, Francesco (*b* Naples, 25 June 1709; *d* ?c1770). Italian composer. By the time he was 25 he had had operas given at the main Italian centres. In 1735–40 he was *maestro di cappella* to Empress Anne of Russia at St Petersburg; during a second spell there (1742–59), under Empress Elizabeth, he wrote heroic operas. His *Cephalus and Procris* (1755) is the first opera known to have been sung in Russian. In 1759 he retired to Italy, though he returned to his post during the brief reign of Peter III (1762).

Araiza, Francisco (*b* Mexico City, 4 Oct 1950). Mexican tenor. He studied in Munich and joined Karlsruhe Opera in 1974. He has sung widely (Met début as Belmonte, 1984) and is esteemed as a lyrical singer of Mozart.

Arakishvili, Dimitri Ignat'yevich (*b* Ordzhonikidze, 23 Feb 1873; *d* Tbilisi, 13 Aug 1953). Georgian composer. He studied with Il'yinsky in Moscow (1894–1901) and began an intensive period of field research into Georgian folk music, on which he drew in his operas and orchestral music. In 1918 he settled in Tbilisi as an influential composer, teacher and administrator.

Arányi, Jelly d' (*b* Budapest, 30 May 1895; *d* Florence, 30 March 1966). British violinist, sister of the violinist Adela Fachiri (1886–1962) and a great-niece of Joachim. She studied in Budapest and began her career in 1908, jointly with her sister; they played in England in 1909 and settled there in 1913. Her rhapsodic style and warm, accomplished playing suited her particularly to Bartók and Ravel; she inspired works too by Smyth, Vaughan Williams and Holst.

Arapov, Boris Alexandrovich (*b* St Petersburg, 12 Sept 1905). Soviet composer. He studied with Shcherbachov at the Leningrad Conservatory (1923–30), where he remained as a teacher. His works are mostly large-scale and colourful, sometimes using Asian materials (he made field studies in Georgia, China and Korea).

Araujo, Juan de (*b* Villafranca de los Barros, 1646; *d* Sucre, Bolivia, 1712). Composer of Spanish birth, resident in South America. He was choirmaster of the cathedrals at Lima (1672–6) and La Plata (now Sucre; from 1680) and a prolific and innovatory composer. Some 200 pieces by him survive, mostly polyphonic villancicos.

Arbeau, Thoinot [Tabourot, Jehan] (*b* Dijon, 17 March 1520; *d* Langres, 23 July 1595). French writer. After studying in Dijon, Poitiers and possibly Paris, he held ecclesiastical posts at Langres and became vicar-general there. His *Orchésographie* (1588), an illustrated dance manual, is invaluable, explaining the basic social dances of his time with a new tablature to correlate steps and music. It includes many tunes and reveals much about the way 16th-century dance music was performed.

Arcadelt, Jacques (*b* ?1505; *d* Paris, 1568). Flemish or French composer. He may have been an associate of Philippe Verdelot in France and in Florence, where he probably served the Medici after 1532. After 1537 he probably went to Venice, making contact with Willaert, then *maestro* at St Mark's. He was in papal service (1540–51) and until at least 1562 he served Charles of Lorraine in France. He may also have been associated with the French royal chapel. Much of his extensive output was published (and frequently reprinted) during his lifetime, establishing his great popularity in France and Italy. His sacred music (three masses, motets, Lamentations etc) is close to Josquin's but borrows new techniques from the *chanson*. His primary interest was secular music: 126 *chansons* and over 200 madrigals survive. A major figure in the early history of the madrigal, he stressed textual clarity and assimilated up-to-date techniques within a traditional framework. Some pieces, like *Il bianco e dolce cigno*, were enduringly popular. Many of his *chansons* are conventional, but with their sentimental rather than licentious texts they stand apart from the Parisian *chansons* of Sermisy and others.

Archduke Trio. Nickname of Beethoven's Piano Trio in Bb op.97 (1811), dedicated to Archduke Rudolph of Austria.

Archer, Violet (Balestreri) (*b* Montreal, 24 April 1913). Canadian composer. She studied with Clarke and Champagne at the McGill Conservatorium (1932–6), with Bartók in New York (1942) and Hindemith at Yale, and has pursued a career as a university teacher in the USA and Canada. Her two European teachers have had most influence on her music, which covers most genres; she has also been occupied with Canadian folksong.

Archilei, Vittoria (*b* Rome, 1550; *d* 1620s or later). Italian soprano, lutenist and dancer. She was the wife of the singer and lutenist Antonio Archilei (?*c*1550–1612) and probably his pupil. A protégée of Cavalieri, she served Ferdinando de' Medici in Florence from 1587 (as did her husband) apparently until her death. She was in sympathy with the vanguard of Florentine music and her virtuosity was praised by leading composers.

Archlute. A lute with two pegboxes, one of which houses unstopped bass strings; it usually had 13 or 14 courses (single or double). It was used for solo music and continuo playing from *c*1595 to 1730. In Italy it inherited the role of the Renaissance solo lute; in England it came into prominence as an alternative to the theorbo at the end of the 17th century.

Arcicembalo (It.). Term used by Nicola Vicentino (1555) for a harpsichord with many divided keys or a second manual.

Arco (It.). 'Bow': in playing string instruments; it is used after PIZZICATO to indicate that the player should resume playing with the bow.

Ardévol, José (*b* Barcelona, 13 March 1911; *d* Havana, 7 Jan 1981). Cuban composer and administrator. As conductor, journal editor, composer, teacher and national music director under Castro, he was largely responsible for reorganizing Cuban musical life in the 1960s. His output includes neo-classical orchestral and chamber works as well as more modern, post-Webernian vocal pieces.

Arditi, Luigi (*b* Crescentino, 22 July 1822; *d* Hove, 1 May 1903). Italian conductor and composer. He studied the violin, then worked in Milan, Havana and New York before settling in London as conductor at Her Majesty's (1858–69) and Covent Garden; he introduced important operas to London. Besides three early operas, he composed light orchestral music and popular songs.

Arena, Antonius de (*b* Solliès, late 15th century; *d* St Rémy or Solliès, 1544 or later). French judge, man of letters and dance theorist. His dance instruction manual *Ad suos compagnones studiantes* (1529, 32 edns. to 1770) contains a valuable study of the *basse danse* in the south of France, with 58 choreographed dances.

Arensky, Anton Stepanovich (*b* Novgorod, 12 July 1861; *d* Terioki, 25 Feb 1906). Russian composer, pianist and conductor. He studied at the St Petersburg Conservatory with Rimsky-Korsakov, then taught at the Moscow Conservatory (1882–95); in Moscow he directed Russian Choral Society concerts and wrote a successful opera, *A Dream on the Volga* (1888). He succeeded Balakirev as director of the imperial chapel in St Petersburg (1895–1901). An eclectic composer with a gift for melody, he wrote attractive songs and keyboard works as well as chamber music including a Piano Trio in D minor (1894).

Argento, Dominick (*b* York, PA, 27 Oct 1927). American composer. He studied with Rogers and Hovhaness at the Peabody Conservatory and the Eastman School, and with Weisgall privately; in 1959 he was appointed professor at the University of Minnesota. His most important works have been operas written for the Minnesota Opera (which he co-founded), including *Postcard from Morocco* (1971). He is distinguished as a composer for the voice, also seen in his song cycles and choral music.

Argerich, Martha (*b* Buenos Aires, 5 June 1941). Argentinian pianist. She made her début in 1946, later going to Europe and studying with Gulda, Magaloff and Michelangeli, winning Chopin prizes in Warsaw in 1965. She has a powerful technique and a fiery temperament, heard at their most persuasive in Chopin, Liszt, Bartók and Prokofiev.

Arghūl. A double clarinet of the Middle Eastern area; it consists of a melody pipe with finger-holes and a longer drone pipe, each with a single beating reed. It is used in the Arab countries and neighbouring regions.

Aria (It.: 'air'). Term for a song either independent or part of a larger work. The Italian word may be rendered as 'style' or 'manner', and in the 16th century 'aria' was used for simple settings of light poetry (e.g. 'aria napoletana'). Arias as melodies or schemes for songs were printed during much of the 16th century and well into the 17th in instrumental as well as vocal publications.

The aria had a central place in early opera, cantata and oratorio. Most Venetian opera arias before 1660 are in triple time or a mixture of triple and duple; many early arias have four or more verses, though after 1650 two became the standard in opera. Most arias have continuo accompaniment, with instrumental ritornellos between verses; a few from the 1640s onwards have instrumental sections between vocal phrases, but these remain a minority until well into the 18th century.

Most later 17th-century arias are in the form *ABB'* (the last line or group of lines rendered twice to similar music, with a tonic cadence only the second time), or *ABA* (sometimes *ABA'*), where the first line or couplet is repeated at the end. This became the standard *da capo* aria, which was dominant by 1680. In the early 18th century the accompaniment could vary in texture and instrumentation; the aria with continuo only became increasingly rare after the 1720s.

By then, longer arias were favoured. With the composers regarded as originators of the modern 18th-century style (Vinci, Hasse, Pergolesi etc), the proportions of the *da capo* structure changed. The middle section became shorter and often contrasted in tempo and metre; the corresponding enlargement of the first section later led to the practice of replacing the *da capo* with the *dal segno*, indicating a return not to the beginning but to a later point. In the 1760s and 1770s this gave way to a scheme close in outline to the contemporary symphony or sonata first movement, with a first section ending in the dominant, a middle section as development or contrast and a restatement of the first section as tonic recapitulation. Other important types of this time were the rondeau, *ABACA*, and the so-called rondò, which began with a slow section and ended with an allegro (*AB* or *ABAB*). By 1780 the latter (prototype of the early 19th-century cantabile–cabaletta) had largely replaced the one-tempo French variety. Arias in comic operas were more varied in form.

19th-century operas show a continuing reduction in the number of arias and an increase in their length. The sonata-form aria gave way to multi-tempo forms and there was a move from the older *bel canto* style towards a more dramatic one from the 1830s. Verdi's development exemplified the move towards free and fluid constructions that cannot readily be extracted from their context. In Puccini too the aria

tends to become part of the dramatic texture; and in Wagner's mature operas the extended sections for single voice cannot usually be extracted without mutilation.

Italian opera strongly influenced most other contemporary operatic genres, including French grand opera and Slavonic opera, in which the aria was accepted as a natural form of expression. Wagner's influence, however, was such that by the 20th century older traditions had been virtually discarded. Stravinsky, in *The Rake's Progress* (1951), revived the form but not the substance of the 18th-century aria; more recent tendencies have been towards highly integrated forms of music theatre from which the aria has usually been excluded.

In the early 17th century, and even as late as Bach's *Goldberg Variations*, an 'aria' sometimes served for a set of instrumental variations, and pieces called 'aria' (often in bourrée rhythm) were common in ensemble dance music in the Baroque.

Ariadne auf Naxos. Opera by Richard Strauss to a libretto by Hofmannsthal. The first version (1912, Stuttgart) incorporates a Molière play; the second (1916, Vienna), much more often performed, consists of a prologue and a one-act tragedy.

Ariane et Barbe-bleue. Opera in three acts by Dukas to a libretto by Maeterlinck (1907, Paris).

Arianna, L'. Opera in a prologue and eight scenes by Monteverdi to a libretto by O. Rinuccini (1608, Mantua); only the 'Lamento d'Arianna' survives. Handel's three-act opera *Arianna* (1734, London) is on the story of Ariadne in Crete.

Arienzo, Nicola d' (*b* Naples, 24 Dec 1842; *d* there, 25 April 1915). Italian composer. He wrote eight comic or semi-serious operas; *Il cuoco* (1873) was the most widely performed, *La figlia de diavolo* (1879), with its *versimo* tendencies, the most controversial. He taught history in Naples and published several historical studies, notably on *opera buffa*.

Arietta, ariette. The Italian and French terms, diminutives of 'aria' or 'air', for a short song in an opera or similar work. 'Arietta' has been used for instrumental pieces, e.g. by Beethoven in his Piano Sonata op.111. In 18th-century France 'comédie mêlée d'ariettes' meant a work of the *opéra comique* type.

Ariettes oubliées. Six songs by Debussy (1888), settings for voice and piano of poems by Verlaine.

Ariodante. Opera in three acts by Handel to a libretto by A. Salvi after Ariosto's *Orlando furioso* (1735, London). Méhul wrote a three-act opera on the same subject to a libretto by F.B. Hoffman (1799, Paris).

Arioso. Term indicating a singing as opposed to a declamatory style of performance. It was frequently used for a passage in regular tempo in or after a recitative, for example in 17th-century operas and Bach's cantatas. Handel and others sometimes used 'arioso' to mean a short aria, and the term is occasionally found in instrumental music (e.g. the last movement of Beethoven's Piano Sonata op.110).

Ariosti, Attilio (**Malachia [Clemente]**) (*b* Bologna, 5 Nov 1666; *d* England, ?1729). Italian composer, from an illegitimate branch of the noble Ariosti family. A skilled singer and instrumentalist, he was a monk (as Frate Ottavio), 1688–96; his works of this time include two oratorios. While briefly in the service of the Duke of Mantua he had two operas performed in Venice (1696–7). In 1697–1703 he was in Berlin as a friend of the electress, Sophie Charlotte; he wrote five operas there – the first in Italian staged in Berlin. He was next at the Austrian court in Vienna, but lost favour after Joseph I's death in 1711. By 1716 he was in London, and from 1722 (like Handel) a composer for the Royal Academy of Music, beginning with the successful *Coriolano* (1723). In 1724 he published six cantatas and six lessons for viola d'amore and continuo. His career then declined, and his sixth and last London opera was a failure. Ariosti's music is notable for its lyrical qualities. The London operas (none of which survives complete) favour slow expressive arias, most famously in the prison scene in *Coriolano*. Ariosti's brother, Giovanni Battista (1668–?), a monk in Bologna, is known for a set of 44 dances notated for 12-bar glockenspiel, *Modo facile di suonare il sistro* (1686).

Ariosto, Ludovico (*b* Reggio Emilia, 8 Sept 1474; *d* Ferrara, 6 July 1533). Italian poet and playwright. He studied law in Ferrara (1488–93) and served the Este court there from 1503. His famous epic poem *Orlando furioso* (1516) was drawn on by countless madrigalists throughout the century and inspired dramatic works by many later composers, notably Handel.

Aristides Quintilianus (*fl* *c*200). Author of a three-volume treatise *Peri mousikēs* ('On music'). Book 1 is concerned with harmonic, rhythmic and metrical theory and book 2 with the ethical and educational aspects of music; book 3 sets out the numerical and cosmological relationships in which music supposedly is involved, echoing neo-Pythagorean and neo-Platonic beliefs.

Aristoxenus (*b* Taranto, *c*375–60; *d* ?Athens). Greek theorist, a pupil of Aristotle. 453 works are attributed to him, on education and political theory, Pythagorean doctrine, biography, miscellanies and memoranda, but his greatest fame was as a musical theorist. Portions of three books on harmonics or the theory of scales have survived as *Harmonic Elements*; so does part of a treatise on *Elements of Rhythm*. He reduced the phenomena of Greek music to a coherent, orderly system, particularly in his doctrine on rhythm.

Arkhipova, Irina (Konstantinovna) (*b* Moscow, 2 Dec 1925). Soviet mezzo-soprano. She studied at the Moscow Conservatory, sang in the Sverdlovsk Opera from 1954 and in 1956 joined the Bol'shoy, making her début as Carmen. There she has sung Musorgsky's Marina and Marfa and such Verdi roles as Azucena and Eboli, also taking part in many new Soviet works. She has appeared widely abroad, with the Bol'shoy and as a guest; her Covent Garden début was as Azucena in 1975. She is noted for her polished and emotionally committed singing.

Arlecchino. Opera in one act by Busoni to his own libretto (1917, Zurich).

Arlen, Harold [Arluck, Hyman] (*b* Buffalo, 15 Feb 1905; *d* New York, 23 April 1986). American songwriter. Originally a ragtime pianist and dance-band arranger, by 1925 he arranged for Fletcher Henderson and by 1930 was writing revues for the Cotton Club, New York. In 1934 he turned to musical comedy and film-score composition, mainly with the lyricists E.Y. Harburg, Johnny Mercer and Ira Gershwin. His popular songs include *Get Happy* (1930), *Over the Rainbow* (1939) and *That Old Black Magic* (1942) and blend jazz with popular idioms. Among his film scores are *The Wizard of Oz* (1939) and *A Star is Born* (1954).

Arlésienne, L'. Bizet's incidental music for Daudet's play (1872, Paris), some of which was later incorporated into *Carmen*.

Arma, Paul [Weisshaus, Imre] (*b* Budapest, 22 Oct 1905). French composer of Hungarian birth. He studied with Bartók at the Budapest Academy (1921–4) and began his career as a pianist. In 1931 he moved to Germany, then to Paris, where he has worked on folksong and produced a varied creative output, noted for its experimentation.

Armide. Opera in five acts by Gluck to a libretto by Quinault after Tasso's *Gerusalemme liberata* (1777, Paris). Many composers based operas on Tasso's story, among them Lully (1686), Handel (*Rinaldo*, 1711), Salieri (1773), Haydn (1784) and Rossini (1817).

Armonica. A form of MUSICAL GLASSES, invented by Benjamin Franklin in 1761.

Armstrong, Louis ['Satchmo', 'Satchelmouth', 'Pops'] (*b* New Orleans, *c*1898; *d* New York, 6 July 1971). American jazz trumpeter, singer and bandleader. His career began in clubs and Mississippi river-boat orchestras in New Orleans, but in 1922 he joined Joe Oliver's Creole Jazz Band in Chicago. He made acclaimed recordings with Oliver then in 1924 went to New York, where he joined Fletcher Henderson. Returning to Chicago (1925) he began the series of recordings with his Hot Five and Hot Seven which confirmed his international reputation as the greatest and most creative jazz musician of his time. For almost 20 years he led a big band (usually that of Luis Russell), returning to a sextet in 1948 with the founding of his All Stars, which he led for the rest of his life. His best work dates from the period of the Hot Five, when he turned jazz from an ensemble to a soloist's idiom. His most notable recordings from 1925–7 include *Potato Head Blues, Hotter than That* and *West End Blues*.

Armstrong, Sir Thomas (Henry Ward) (*b* Peterborough, 15 June 1898). English organist and educationist. He studied at Peterborough, the RCM and Oxford, and held posts at Exeter and Windsor before becoming organist at Christ Church Cathedral, Oxford, and lecturer at the university (1933); in 1955 he became principal of the RAM. He was esteemed as teacher, educationist and all-round musician.

Arne, Michael (*b* *c*1740; *d* Lambeth, 14 Jan 1786). English composer, son of Thomas Arne. He published his first collection of songs, *The Floweret*, in 1750, and soon began a career as keyboard player and composer to the theatres and pleasure gardens, contributing songs to dramatic productions; his most famous song, *The Lass with the Delicate Air*, appeared in 1762. His biggest success was his setting

(1767) of Garrick's *Cymon*. In 1772 at Hamburg he conducted the German public première of Handel's *Messiah*. He was later in Dublin, then in London composing for Covent Garden (1778–83).

Arne, Thomas Augustine (*b* London, bap. 28 May 1710; *d* there, 5 March 1778). English composer. Son of an upholsterer, he was probably encouraged in his musical career by his violin teacher Michael Festing. In 1732–3 he and his sister Susanna (later Mrs Cibber) were associated with musicians, including Henry Carey and J.F. Lampe, who aimed to establish an Italian-style English opera. After the success of his masque *Dido and Aeneas* (1734), Arne was engaged at Drury Lane Theatre, where he was to produce his works until 1775. In 1737 he married the singer Cecilia Young, who appeared in his next production, *Comus* (1738); influenced by Handel's *Acis and Galatea*, it was his most individual and successful work. Also popular was the masque *Alfred* (1740) (including 'Rule, Britannia'). While in Dublin in 1742–4 Arne produced his oratorio *The Death of Abel* (1744) and music by Handel. His dialogue *Colin and Phoebe* established him as a leading composer at the London pleasure gardens; during the next 20 years he published annual song collections. Among his next major works were a miniature English *opera buffa*, *Thomas and Sally* (1760), the oratorio *Judith* (1761) and an English *opera seria* to a Metastasio libretto, *Artaxerxes* (1762), the first and only such work to achieve lasting fame. After his masque *The Arcadian Nuptials* (1764) Arne's career declined; *L'Olimpiade* (1765; now lost), his only Italian opera, was a failure. But his last years saw the production of many of his best works, notably *Shakespeare Ode* (1769), the masque *The Fairy Prince* (1771) and the afterpiece *May-day* (1775); he also wrote catches and glees for concerts at Ranelagh House.

One of the most significant English composers of his century, Arne wrote over 80 stage works and contributed to some 20 others. His essentially lyrical genius is obvious also in his instrumental music.

Dramatic music Comus, dialogue opera (1738); Alfred, masque (1740) (incl. 'Rule, Britannia'); Thomas and Sally, opera buffa (1760); Artaxerxes, opera (1762); Love in a Village, pasticcio (1762); The Fairy Prince, masque (1771); *c*50 other stage works (most inc.); contributions to other composers' works

Vocal music The Death of Abel (1744); Judith, oratorio (1761); sacred works; secular odes and cantatas; songs, many in Lyric Harmony (1746), Vocal Melody (1749–64); catches, canons, glees

Instrumental music overtures (2 sets); trio sonatas; kbd concertos and sonatas

Arnell, Richard (Anthony Sayer) (*b* London, 15 Sept 1917). English composer. He studied with Ireland at the RCM (1936–9) and has worked as a teacher and composer of film music, spending much time in the USA. His large output includes much orchestral music and the ballet *Punch and the Child* (1947).

Arnold, Denis (Midgely) (*b* Sheffield, 15 Dec 1926; *d* Budapest, 28 April 1986). English musicologist. He studied in Sheffield and held posts in Belfast,

Hull and (as professor) Nottingham and Oxford. A lively writer and teacher of wide scope, he specialized in Venetian music, especially Monteverdi and G. Gabrieli.

Arnold, Malcolm (Henry) (*b* Northampton, 21 Oct 1921). English composer. He studied with Jacob at the RCM and in 1941 joined the LPO as a trumpeter, leaving in 1948 to devote himself to composition. His most important works are orchestral (nine symphonies, 1951–82; numerous light and serious pieces). His language is diatonic, owing something to Walton and Sibelius, and the scoring is dramatically brilliant, Berlioz being his acknowledged model. A fluent, versatile composer, he has written scores for nearly 100 films.

Arnold, Samuel (*b* London, 10 Aug 1740; *d* there, 22 Oct 1802). English composer and editor. He was a Chapel Royal chorister and from 1764 harpsichordist at Covent Garden. His first pasticcio opera, *The Maid of the Mill* (1765), based on Richardson's *Pamela*, borrowed from French and Italian operas. In 1769–76 he owned Marylebone Gardens, where his summer concerts included in 1770 *The Servant Mistress*, based on Pergolesi's *La serva padrona*. Among his other works of the period were four oratorios and an ode. He took the Oxford DMus in 1773. In 1777 he began an association with the Little Theatre in the Haymarket, for which he wrote or contributed to over 50 stage works, among them *The Spanish Barber* (1777), after Beaumarchais's *Le barbier de Séville*, and *The Children in the Wood*, which uses folksong. He continued to compose in other genres, and was organist and composer to the Chapel Royal (from 1783), conductor of the Academy of Ancient Music (from 1789) and organist of Westminster Abbey (from 1793). As an editor he prepared a revision of Boyce's *Cathedral Music* as well as part of a proposed complete Handel edition.

Arnold, Yury (Karlovich) (*b* St Petersburg, 13 Nov 1811; *d* Karakesh, Crimea, 20 July 1898). Russian writer on music. He contributed to Russian journals and edited the *Neue Zeitschrift für Musik* in Leipzig (1863–70); his memoirs (1892–3) valuably record 60 years of Russian musical life.

Arnould, (Magdeleine) Sophie (*b* Paris, 13 Feb 1740; *d* there, 22 Oct 1802). French soprano. In 1757–78 she was the leading female singer at the Paris Opéra. The last great singer in the French style before Gluck, she was praised for both her acting and her sweet voice.

Aroldo. Opera in four acts by Verdi to a libretto by Piave (1857, Rimini), a revision of his earlier three-act opera *Stiffelio*.

Arpanetta. An upright double psaltery, with each main side of the trapeziform box acting as a soundboard.

Arpeggio (It.). The sounding of the notes of a chord in succession rather than simultaneously; in keyboard music, the breaking or spreading of a chord.

Arpeggione [guitar violoncello, bowed guitar]. A bowed string instrument, essentially a bass viol with guitar tuning (*E–A–D–g–b–e'*). It had a very brief existence, early in the 19th century, and is of note solely because of the fine sonata written for it by

Schubert: D821 (1824).

Arpichordum. A device used primarily on Flemish virginals in which a sliding batten brings metal hooks or wires close to the strings so that a buzzing sound is produced when the strings are plucked.

Arpicordo. An Italian 16th-century keyboard instrument, possibly a gut-string spinet.

Arrangement. The reworking or adaptation of a composition, usually for a different medium from that of the original.

Arrau, Claudio (b Chillán, 6 Feb 1903). Chilean pianist. After a début in Santiago at the age of five he went to study in Berlin. His international career began in 1918, with a London début in 1922 and a tour of the USA in 1923. He taught in Berlin (1925–40) and later settled in New York. While his thoughtful interpretations of the Romantic repertory are much admired, it is in Beethoven that his intellectually powerful playing has fullest scope.

Arresti, Giulio Cesare (b Bologna, 1625 (or 1617); d there, 1704 or later). Italian composer. He spent his life in Bologna, mainly as organist at S Petronio but also as *maestro di cappella* at S Salvatore and S Domenico. He was the leading Bolognese organ composer of his day and also wrote oratorios, masses and sonatas. He was involved for over ten years in a celebrated theoretical dispute with Cazzati.

Arriaga (y Balzola), Juan Crisóstomo (Jacobo Antonio) (b Bilbao, 27 Jan 1806; d Paris, 17 Jan 1826). Spanish composer. He studied under Baillot (violin) and Fétis (harmony) at the Paris Conservatoire; his music, which includes an opera (*Los esclavos felices*, 1820), a symphony and three fine string quartets, is elegant and accomplished and notable for its harmonic warmth. His death before he was 20 was a sad loss to Spanish music.

Arrieu, Claude (b Paris, 30 Nov 1903). French composer. She studied with Roger-Ducasse and Dukas at the Paris Conservatoire, then taught and worked for French radio. Her music, copious and in many genres, is in a French neo-classical style.

Arrigo, Girolamo (b Palermo, 2 April 1930). Italian composer. He studied at the Palermo Conservatory and with Deutsch in Paris, where he settled in 1954. In the late 1960s he abandoned a Boulezian style for one of passionate political commitment, for example in the opera *Orden* (1969) and the 'musical epic' *Addio Garibaldi* (1972).

Arrigoni, Carlo (b Florence, 5 Dec 1697; d there, 19 Aug 1744). Italian composer. He began his career in Florence, where two of his oratorios were performed. In 1732–6 he worked in London where he played and sang for Handel and presented his opera *Fernando* (1734). From 1737 he was chamber composer to the Grand Duke of Tuscany (the Empress Maria Theresa's husband), and his oratorio *Ester* (1738) and several cantatas were performed in Vienna.

Arroyo, Martina (b New York, 2 Feb 1936). American soprano. She sang at leading European opera houses in the 1960s (Zurich, 1963–8) and in 1965 sang Aida at the Met, where she has played all the major Verdi roles, to which she brings power and rich tone. She first sang in London in 1968, in Paris in 1973.

Ars Antiqua (Lat.). 'Ancient art': term used by early 14th-century writers in Paris to distinguish 13th-century polyphony from that of a 'new art' (Ars nova) as exemplified by, among others, Philippe de Vitry's treatise *Ars nova* (c1322). Jacques de Liège, a leading theorist and champion of the Ars Antiqua, defined it (*Speculum musice*, c1323–5), citing the authority of Franco of Cologne. Although in technical terms his definition covers only northern French polyphony, c1260–1320, it is now customarily extended to include the Notre Dame period, particularly Léonin and Pérotin, and thus sacred music, c1160–1320. The main musical forms of the Ars Antiqua period are organum, clausula, conductus and motet.

Arsis, thesis. Terms used respectively for unstressed and stressed beats, or Upbeat and Downbeat. The expression 'per arsin et thesin' has been used for the inversion of a theme or its displacement so that strong beats become weak and vice versa.

Ars Nova (Lat.). 'New art': term used to distinguish 14th-century polyphony from that of the 13th century or Ars antiqua period. The concept of a 'new art' is based on the wide range of musical expression made possible by the notational techniques explained in Philippe de Vitry's treatise *Ars nova* (c1322). The earliest examples are the motets in the Roman de Fauvel (copied c1316). The term has been loosely extended to include all music between this date and the Renaissance, but it is now customary to use it only to refer to French music from the Roman de Fauvel to the death of Machaut (1377). The main musical forms of the Ars Nova period are the isorhythmic motet and chanson.

Ars Subtilior (Lat.). 'More subtle art': term for the advanced musical style of the late 14th century. It is applied mainly to the music of French composers after Machaut (e.g. Cuvelier, Philippus de Caserta, Jacob de Senleches), who refined the notational features of the Ars Nova period to produce a more sophisticated and rhythmically more complex style.

Artaria. Austrian firm of music publishers. Founded in Mainz in 1765, it moved to Vienna in 1766. Its first music publications were issued in 1778. Notable among its composers were Haydn (from 1780, over 300 editions), Mozart (from 1781, 83 first and 36 early editions) and Beethoven (over 100 editions, including arrangements and reprints). Artaria was effectively Mozart's chief publisher. Other names in the firm's early catalogues are Boccherini, Clementi, Gluck and Salieri, and later, those of Cramer, Hummel and Moscheles. The music publishing side of the business closed in 1858.

Artaxerxes. Opera in three acts by Arne to his own translation of Metastasio's *Artaserse* (1762, London); other composers who wrote operas on the subject include Gluck (1741), Paisiello (1765), Piccinni (1766) and Cimarosa (1781).

Articulation. The separation of successive notes from one another, singly or in groups, by a performer, and the manner in which this is done; the term is more broadly applied to phrasing in general.

Art of Fugue, The [Die Kunst der Fuge]. Collection of keyboard pieces by J.S. Bach designed to demonstrate contrapuntal techniques; it was composed in the 1740s but left unfinished.

Artôt, Alexandre [Montagney, Joseph] (*b* Brussels, 25 Jan 1815; *d* Ville d'Avray, 20 July 1845). Belgian violinist. He studied at the Paris Conservatoire and made successful tours of Europe and the USA, being admired for the delicacy of his playing.

Artôt, (Marguerite-Joséphine) Désirée (Montagney) (*b* Paris, 21 July 1835; *d* Berlin, 3 April 1907). Belgian mezzo-soprano, later soprano. After a successful début in Meyerbeer's *Le prophète* (Paris, 1858), she concentrated on the Italian repertory, singing Rosina (*Il barbiere di Siviglia*) and Leonora (*Il trovatore*). Most of her career was spent in Germany.

Arts Florissants, Les. French early music ensemble. It was founded in 1979 in Paris by the American harpsichordist and conductor William Christie (*b* 1944); named after a work by M.A. Charpentier, it specializes in French Baroque music. It has performed and recorded many works of Charpentier, sacred and secular, as well as music by Lully and Rameau; notable are pioneer recordings of oratorios and the opera *Médée* by Charpentier and Lully's opera *Atys*. It also performs Italian music. The musicians give particular attention to authenticity in ornamentation, vocal techniques and pronunciation.

Art song. A song of serious artistic purpose, written by a professional composer, as opposed to a traditional or folk song. It is usually applied to solo songs, especially the 19th-century lied and *mélodie*.

Artusi, Giovanni Maria (*b c*1540; *d* Bologna, 18 Aug 1613). Italian theorist and composer. He was a canon in the Congregation of S Salvatore, Bologna, and wrote a little music, but it is as a controversial defender of the theories of his conservative teacher Zarlino that he is remembered. First, he defended him against the attacks of the progressive Vincenzo Galilei. Then he became embroiled in a related dispute with Ercole Bottrigari, who accused him of plagiarism – which proved to be unfounded, though Bottrigari's jealousy may have been aroused by Artusi's superior scholarship. He emerged in his first important theoretical work, *Seconda parte dell'arte del contraponto* (1589), as an independent theorist; this is the earliest published book devoted to the use of dissonances. He is rightly famous, though unjustly maligned, for criticizing in his *L'Artusi, overo Delle imperfettioni della moderna musica* (1600–03) certain contrapuntal licences taken by an unnamed composer, later identified as Monteverdi, in four as yet unpublished madrigals. This stimulated Monteverdi's famous reply in his fifth book of madrigals (1605) and his brother Giulio Cesare's gloss in *Scherzi musicali* (1607). The debate brought into focus the ideals of the new style (the *seconda prattica*, as Monteverdi called it); in a *Discorso* of 1608 Artusi answered the Monteverdi brothers point for point. The debate has tended to overshadow other important theoretical and practical matters discussed in *L'Artusi*.

Asaf'yev, Boris Vladimirovich [Glebov, Igor] (*b* St Petersburg, 29 July 1884; *d* Moscow, 27 Jan 1949). Soviet musicologist and composer. A pupil of Rimsky-Korsakov and Lyadov, he helped organize music studies in Petrograd after the Revolution and was professor at Leningrad Conservatory, 1925–43; he then went to Moscow, and finally was chairman of the Union of Soviet Composers. His compositions include operas, ballets and orchestral music, but he is remembered mainly for his influential writings on music, including a study of Stravinsky (1929), books on other Russian composers and above all *Music Form as a Process* (1947), in which he developed a theory about expressive aspects of musical form, which serves as a basis for several analytical studies.

Ascanio in Alba. Serenata in two acts by Mozart to a libretto by Giuseppe Parini (1771, Milan).

Ascension, L'. Orchestral work in four movements by Messiaen (1933), arranged for organ (1934).

Ashkenazy, Vladimir (Davidovich) (*b* Gorky, 6 July 1937). Icelandic pianist of Russian birth. He made his début in Moscow in 1945 and studied there under Oborin. After competition successes, he toured the USA in 1958; in 1963 he settled in England, moving to Iceland in 1968. A passionate interpreter of Russian music (notably Rakhmaninov), he also brings warmth and sincerity to the Romantic repertory and particular sensitivity and clarity to Mozart. He is also a perceptive conductor.

Ashley, John (*b* London, 1734; *d* there, 14 March 1805). English bassoonist and conductor. He was assistant at the 1784 Handel Commemoration in Westminster Abbey; his four sons took part. In 1788–93 he promoted *c*13 short 'Grand Musical Festivals' in provincial towns with sections of the orchestra led by his sons – Charles (1770–1818), a violinist, Charles Jane (1773–1843), a cellist, and Richard G. (1775–1836), a viola player, while John James (1772–1815) often played the organ. From 1795 he directed the Lenten Oratorios at Covent Garden, giving the English premières of Haydn's *Creation* (1800) and Mozart's *Requiem* (1801).

Ashley, Robert (Reynolds) (*b* Ann Arbor, 28 March 1930). American composer. He studied at the University of Michigan (1948–52, 1957–60) and at the Manhattan School of Music (1952–4), but was most influenced by contacts with Mumma and Cage. He and Mumma were founders of the ONCE Festival for experimental music (1961–8) and the Sonic Arts Union of composer-performers on electronic instruments. In the 1980s he began composing lengthy video operas (e.g. *Perfect Lives (Private Parts)*, 1983).

Asioli, Bonifazio (*b* Correggio, 30 Aug 1769; *d* there, 18 May 1832. Italian theorist and composer. Essentially self-taught, he began his career as a harpsichordist and opera composer and later wrote sacred music. After working in Correggio, Turin and Venice, he held a court appointment in Milan, becoming the first director of the new Milan Conservatory (1808–14). He produced several didactic works (1809–36).

Asola, Giammateo (*b* Verona, ?by 1532; *d* Venice, 1 Oct 1609). Italian composer. He probably studied under Ruffo in Verona. He was *maestro di cappella* at the cathedrals of Treviso (1577) and Vicenza (1578) and went to Venice in 1582. His 12 books of masses and over 30 volumes of other sacred works are in

Palestrinian style with freely imitative counterpoint; his pieces for multiple choirs show Venetian influence. He also composed madrigals.

Aspen Music Festival (USA). Annual (summer) festival and training course (the Aspen Music School), established in 1950; it grew out of the Goethe Bicentennial Convocation and Music Festival (1949). Events include concerts of chamber, choral, contemporary and electronic music and jazz, and teaching in an opera workshop, an audio-recording institute and master classes.

Asplmayr, Franz (*b* Linz, bap. 2 April 1728; *d* Vienna, 29 July 1786). Austrian composer. He was a violinist in the imperial Hofkapelle in Vienna, and a composer for the Kärntnertortheater there, 1761–1763. He later wrote ballets for Noverre, and one, *L'espiègle du village* (1774), for Angiolini. His *Pygmalion* (1776, Vienna) was the first melodrama performed in German-speaking lands. His instrumental music, chiefly chamber works mixing Baroque and Classical elements, is consistently pleasant and charming.

Asrael. Suk's Symphony in C minor op.27 (1906).

Assai (It.). 'Very', e.g. *allegro assai* (very fast).

Astarita, Gennaro (*b* ?Naples, *c*1745–9; *d* after 1803). Italian composer. He wrote over 40 operas, nearly all comic, staged in Naples, Venice and elsewhere in Italy, also in Bratislava and St Petersburg, where he was *maestro compositore* to an Italian company, 1795–1803.

Aston [Ashton], Hugh (*b c*1485; *d* ? Nov 1558). English composer. He graduated BMus at Oxford (1510) and was master of the choristers at St Mary Newarke Hospital and College, Leicester (*c*1525–48). His 'Hornepype' provides an early example of idiomatic keyboard writing; only four of his sacred works survive complete.

Aston, Peter (George) (*b* Birmingham, 5 Oct 1938). English composer. He studied at York University, where he was appointed lecturer in 1964; in 1974 he became professor at the University of East Anglia. He has been influenced by medieval, Renaissance and Baroque music in his works, which are mostly choral; they include *Haec dies* (1971).

Aston Magna Foundation for Music (USA). Organization founded in 1972 in New York for the study of 17th- and 18th-century music; it presents an annual (summer) festival of Baroque and Classical works played on original instruments.

Astorga, Emanuele (Gioacchino Cesare Rincón) d', Baron (*b* Augusta, 20 March 1680; *d* ?Madrid, ?1757). Italian composer of Spanish descent. His opera *La moglie nemica* (1698) was staged in his home town, Palermo; he later travelled widely, and his *Dafni* was given in Genoa and Barcelona in 1709. After serving briefly at Vienna he lived again in Palermo (1715–21) and later spent time in Lisbon, where a volume of his solo cantatas appeared (1726). His cantatas, which number over 150, are fluently written in a style like Alessandro Scarlatti's. His *Stabat mater* became very popular after his death.

A tempo (It.). 'At tempo': an instruction to return to the previous tempo after a deliberate deviation.

Athalia. Oratorio by Handel to a text by S. Humphreys after Racine (1733, Oxford).

Atherton, David (*b* Blackpool, 3 Jan 1944). English conductor. He studied at Cambridge and in 1968 became the youngest conductor to appear at Covent Garden. Though he has appeared widely in the standard repertory, it is chiefly as an interpreter of 20th-century music, notably Schoenberg and Stravinsky, that he is admired, particularly for his work with the London Sinfonietta; he conducted the Royal Liverpool PO, 1980–86, then the BBC SO.

Atkins, Sir Ivor (Algernon) (*b* Llandaff, 29 Nov 1869; *d* Worcester, 26 Nov 1953). English organist and composer. He studied in Truro and Hereford and became organist of Worcester Cathedral in 1897, retiring in 1950, conducting the Three Choirs Festivals over 50 years. He was closely associated with the music of Elgar, who worked with him on some of his influential English editions of music by Bach and others.

Atlanta Symphony Orchestra. American orchestra established in 1947 by Henry Sopkin from the Atlanta Youth SO (founded 1944); it became professional in 1967 under Robert Shaw. Its home is Symphony Hall (opened 1968, cap. 1762). It makes annual tours of the USA.

Atlántida. 'Scenic cantata' in a prologue and three parts by Falla on a Catalan text by Jacinto Verdaguer with his own additions; it was completed by Halffter (1962, Milan).

Atmosphères. Orchestral work by Ligeti (1961).

Atonal. Term applied to music that is not tonal, i.e. not in a key. The term is in some circumstances avoided for music that is serial; and it is sometimes reserved for the post-tonal but pre-serial music of the Second Viennese School (Schoenberg, Berg and Webern). The term 'pantonal' is occasionally used in the same sense.

Attacca (It.). 'Attack': an indication that no pause should be made between two movements.

Attaingnant, Pierre (*b* ?nr. Douai, *c*1494; *d* Paris, 1551/2). French music publisher. He was in Paris by 1514 and began publishing by 1525. He invented a new method of printing music in which staff-segments and notes were combined and printed in a single impression; for its economy and improved efficiency this method soon swept Europe. His success coincided with the flowering of the *chanson* and, with an extensive international network, he became the first music publisher to achieve mass production. As a printer of masses, motets and psalm settings he was equally adventurous, and was the king's music printer, 1537–47. His editions were unusually accurate for his time.

Atterberg, Kurt (Magnus) (*b* Göteborg, 12 Dec 1887; *d* Stockholm, 15 Feb 1974). Swedish composer. He worked in the patent office (1912–68), though he had lessons with Hallén at the Stockholm Conservatory (1910–11) and studied in Germany. He was also a conductor and critic. His large output, in the Alfvén tradition, includes operas, ballets and nine symphonies (1911–56).

Attila. Opera in a prologue and three acts by Verdi to a libretto by Solera and Piave after Werner (1846, Venice).

Attwood, Thomas (*b* London, bap. 23 Nov 1765; *d* there, 24 March 1838). English composer and organist. He studied in Naples and with Mozart in Vienna (1785–7; his book of studies with Mozart survives), then held important posts in London, including organist of St Paul's Cathedral and composer to the Chapel Royal (1796). Besides coronation anthems for George IV (1821) and William IV (1831), he composed music for over 30 stage productions, as well as glees, church and organ music and chamber works, the best being graceful and delicately polished and showing the influence of Mozart.

Atumpan. 'Talking drum' of West Africa, a large barrel drum with a tubular open foot at the base; it is played upright, usually in pairs (of different tones) by the master-drummer.

Atys. *Tragédie lyrique* in a prologue and five acts by Lully to a libretto by P. Quinault (1676, Saint Germain en Laye).

Atzmon, Moshe (*b* Budapest, 30 July 1931). Israeli conductor. He studied in Tel-Aviv and London and has held posts with the Sydney SO (1969–71), the North German RSO (1972–6) and the Basle SO; he made his operatic début at the Deutsche Oper, Berlin (*La Cenerentola*, 1969). He is noted for his vitality and his assured technique.

Aubade (Fr.). 'Dawn song': term for music to be performed in the morning; now simply a generic title.

Auber, Daniel-François-Esprit (*b* Caen, 29 Jan 1782; *d* Paris, 12/13 May 1871). French composer, the foremost representative of *opéra comique* in 19th-century France. He was a pupil of Cherubini and, from 1823, a devotee of Rossini's music. The synthesis of French *opéra comique* with Rossini's spirited writing is best seen in the light works Auber produced with the librettist Scribe, from *Fiorella* (1826) and *Fra Diavolo* (1830) to *La sirène* (1844); in a sparkling style, these works are characterized by triadic melodies, dance-like rhythms, light orchestration and homophonic texture. He also wrote more serious *opéras comiques* with Scribe as well as *La muette de Portici* (1828), important for inaugurating the epoch of French grand opera through its use of local colour, crowd portrayal and a modern revolutionary topic. He was director of the Paris Conservatoire (1842–70) and received many national honours.

Operas Le maçon (1825); Fiorella (1826); La muette de Portici (1828); Fra Diavolo (1830); Gustave III (1833); Lestocq (1834); La part du diable (1843); La sirène (1844); Haydée (1847); Manon Lescaut (1856); Le premier jour de bonheur (1868); 36 others
*Vocal music c*50 sacred works, incl. motets, hymns, mass sections, litanies; 6 secular cantatas, 28 romances, chansonettes
Instrumental music 3 vc concs. (1806–8); Vn Conc., D (1808); orch marches, dances, overture; str qt; pf sonata; variations
Other 7 pedagogical works

Aubert, Jacques (*b* Paris, 30 Sept 1689; *d* Belleville, 17/18 May 1753). French composer. At first a dancing-master and violinist, he entered the Duke of Bourbon's service in 1719 and composed music for stage works, given at the Fair Theatres as well as Chantilly and the Opéra. From 1727 to 1746 he played in the 24 Violons du Roi, from 1728 was first violinist at the Opéra and from 1729 to 1740 played at the Concert Spirituel. His instrumental music, which shows Italian influence while retaining French-style use of dance forms, includes five sets of violin sonatas, two of violin concertos (his op.17 of 1734 were the first published in France) and 12 suites of *concerts de simphonies*.

Aubert, Louis (*b* Paris, 15 May 1720; *d* after 1783). French violinist and composer, eldest son of Jacques. He joined the Opéra orchestra as a child, and by 1756 was first violinist and a principal conductor; from 1746 he also played in the 24 Violons du Roi. His sonatas (1750) use dance forms, and like the 6 *simphonies à quatre* (1755) are conservative in style.

His brother Jean-Louis (1732–*c*1810), a writer, was noted for his *Refutation suivie des principes de M. Rousseau de Genève touchant la musique françoise* (1754).

Aubéry du Boulley, Prudent-Louis (*b* Verneuil, 9 Dec 1796; *d* there, 28 Jan 1870). French composer and teacher. He studied under Méhul and Cherubini at the Paris Conservatoire and became a prolific composer, especially of works for guitar and strings or wind and for military band. He also wrote an introduction to music theory (1830). He is best remembered for encouraging provincial music-making.

Aubry, Pierre (*b* Paris, 14 Feb 1874; *d* Dieppe, 31 Aug 1910). French musicologist. He is known for his work on troubadour and trouvère song; he made 13th-century music available in edition and facsimile.

Auden, W(ystan) H(ugh) (*b* York, 21 Feb 1907; *d* Vienna, 29 Sept 1973). English poet, later naturalized American. He worked with Britten between 1935 and 1941 on songs, films, broadcasts, plays and the opera *Paul Bunyan*. Later he and Chester Kallman wrote librettos for Stravinsky (*The Rake's Progress*), Henze (*Elegy for Young Lovers, The Bassarids*) and others; he also wrote the words for Stravinsky's *Elegy for J.F.K.*

Audran, Edmond (*b* Lyons, 12 April 1840; *d* Tierceville, 17 Aug 1901). French composer. He studied at the Ecole Niedermeyer in Paris then became an organist in Marseilles before establishing himself in Paris as an operetta composer, notably with *Les noces d'Olivette* (1879), *La mascotte* (1880) and *La cigale et la fourmi* (1886).

Auer, Leopold (*b* Veszprem, 7 June 1845; *d* Loschwitz, 15 July 1930). Hungarian violinist. After a career as leader and chamber musician, he settled in St Petersburg where he taught, 1868–1917. There he exercised a profound influence on Russian violin playing; his pupils included Elman and Heifetz. He stressed purity of style and taste rather than virtuosity. Many Russians dedicated works to him, though he declined Tchaikovsky's Violin Concerto as technically awkward.

Aufforderung zum Tanz. *See* INVITATION TO THE DANCE.

Aufführungspraxis (Ger). PERFORMING PRACTICE.

Aufschnaiter, Benedict Anton (*b* Kitzbühel, bap. 21 Feb 1665; *d* Passau, bur. 24 Jan 1742). Austrian composer. After training in Vienna he became court Kapellmeister in Passau in 1705, succeeding Georg

Muffat, whose influence is apparent in his six orchestral suites, *Concors discordia* op.2 (1695). His many sacred works include vespers settings (1709, 1728) and masses (1712), with instruments and conservative in style.

Aufstieg und Fall der Stadt Mahagonny [Rise and Fall of the City of Mahagonny]. Opera in three acts by Weill to a libretto by Brecht (1930, Leipzig).

Auger, Arleen (*b* Los Angeles, 13 Sept 1939). American soprano. She studied in Long Beach and Chicago and made her début as Mozart's Queen of Night in Vienna in 1967, singing in the Staatsoper company till 1974; she made her New York début at the City Opera in the same role, 1969, and her Met début as Marzelline (*Fidelio*) in 1978. She has sung extensively in Germany and England and took part in recordings of early Mozart operas. Her clear yet full and warm tone and her perceptive musicianship, coupled with a commanding technique in florid music, serve well in such roles as Mozart's Countess and Handel's Alcina.

Augmentation. The statement of a theme in longer notes than when it was first heard; augmentation is often used in sacred music of the Middle Ages and the Renaissance and keyboard music of the Baroque (for example Bach's organ fugue in C, BWV 547).

Augmented interval. A perfect or major interval that has been increased by a chromatic semitone.

Augmented sixth chord. A chord built on the flattened submediant and containing the note an augmented 6th above (i.e. the raised subdominant), for example, in C, Ab–C–F♯. This is sometimes called 'Italian sixth'; *see also* FRENCH SIXTH CHORD and GERMAN SIXTH CHORD.

Augmented triad. A chord built of two successive major 3rds (e.g. C–E–G♯).

Auletta, Pietro (*b* S Angelo, Avellino, *c*1698; *d* Naples, Sept 1771). Italian composer. He was *maestro di cappella* at S Maria la Nova, Naples, by 1724, and in 1725–8 composed three operas there. His highly successful comic opera *Orazio* (1737) initiated a period of popularity and was widely performed. Notable for their lilting melodic style and subtle characterization, his surviving works include the two-act *La locandiera* (1738) which resembles Pergolesi's comic operas. His output fell sharply after 1740 and ended with the heroic opera *Didone* (1759), given in Florence.

His son Domenico (1723–53) was active in Naples as an organist and composer of sacred music (particularly psalm settings) and harpsichord concertos.

Aulin, Tor (Bernhard Vilhelm) (*b* Stockholm, 10 Sept 1866; *d* Saltsjöbaden, 1 March 1914). Swedish violinist, composer and conductor. He founded the first continuously active Swedish string quartet (1887), conducted several orchestras and composed violin concertos, chamber music and songs.

Aulos (Gk.). A Greek reed instrument consisting of a cylindrical or slightly conical tube generally about 50 cm long. Primitive examples were of reed or bone, but wood and ivory became common. Whether the instrument had single or double reeds has occasioned much controversy. The aulos is typically played in pairs: the two instruments, one held in each hand, project from the player's mouth to form an acute

angle. Homer's references to the aulos suggest that it was an instrument of the countryside and common people. It was played to accompany choirs, at marriages and funerals, and in celebration of famous men or victorious athletes. In the 4th and 5th centuries BC it fell out of favour (both Plato and Aristotle banned it from their ideal states), but later it continued as an indispensable element in musical practice and recovered its respectability.

Auric, Georges (*b* Lodeve, 15 Feb 1899; *d* Paris, 23 July 1983). French composer. He studied at the Paris Conservatoire and with d'Indy at the Schola Cantorum (1914–16), becoming acquainted with Satie, Milhaud and Honegger. He was a member of Les Six, wrote ballets for Dyagilev (*Les fâcheux*, 1923) and film scores for Cocteau and was a music critic. In the 1950s and 1960s he held administrative posts while maintaining his musical curiosity: some of the later pieces are serial.

Aurisicchio, Antonio (*b* Naples, *c*1710; *d* Rome, 3/4 Sept 1781). Italian composer. He made his début in Naples with a comic opera (1734) and later settled in Rome, working at S Giacomo degli Spagnuoli from 1751 and writing several operas. Latterly he was famous as a teacher. As a composer he was specially admired for his sacred music.

Aus den Sieben Tagen. A group of 15 works by Stockhausen (1968), for varying ensembles of three or more players, consisting of a text to suggest a mood but no musical notation.

Ausdrucksvoll (Ger.). With expression.

Aus Italien. Symphonic fantasia by Richard Strauss (1886).

Austin, Frederic (*b* London, 30 March 1872; *d* there, 10 April 1952). English baritone and composer. He sang in the English première of Delius's *Sea Drift* and was Gunther in the *Ring* at Covent Garden (1908) followed by other roles in the Beecham company. In 1924 he became artistic director of the British National Opera Company. He is chiefly remembered however for his version of *The Beggar's Opera*, which achieved great popularity in the 1920s. His son Richard (*b*1903) was a conductor and an active propagator of new music.

Austin, Larry (Don) (*b* Duncan, OK, 12 Sept 1930). American composer. He studied in California at Mills College and Berkeley, under Imbrie, Milhaud and Shifrin. He has taught at Davis, Tampa and Denton. His music uses group improvisations and 'open style' techniques as well as electronic and theatrical media. Among his works are *Improvisations*, for orchestra and jazz soloists (1961), *Walter* (a stage work involving tape and film, 1971) and a series of works based on Ives's sketches including two fantasies involving instruments and tape (1975–6) and *Life Pulse Music* for 20 percussion (1984).

Austin, William W(eaver) (*b* Lawton, OK, 18 Jan 1920). American musicologist. Educated at Harvard, he began teaching at Cornell University in 1947. He specializes in the music of Russia and the USA and in 20th-century music; his *Music in the 20th Century* (1966) is a broad survey up to 1950, notable for its francophone standpoint.

Austral, Florence (*b* Melbourne, 26 April 1894; *d* Newcastle, NSW, 16 May 1968). Australian soprano. She studied in Melbourne and New York and made her début as Brünnhilde (*Die Walküre*) at Covent Garden in 1922, going on to the other dramatic Wagner roles although her voice was lyrical rather than forceful. She toured widely in the USA and Australia, in recitals and opera, and made many recordings.

Australian music. *See* OCEANIC MUSIC.

Australian Opera. National company formed in Sydney in 1956. Activities include, besides a season at Sydney Opera House, performances in Melbourne and Adelaide.

Authentic cadence [full close; perfect cadence]. A CADENCE made up of a dominant chord followed by a tonic chord (V–I), both normally in root position.

Authentic mode. Any of the church modes of which the range includes the octave lying immediately above that mode's FINAL.

Auto (Sp.: 'act'). Term applied to a religious or allegorical composition, from the 16th-century *autos sacramentales*, performed in the streets at Corpus Christi until the late 18th century.

Autograph. In normal musical parlance, the MS of a work in the hand of its composer (as opposed to an MS copy or a printed edition). It may imply a complete copy in the composer's hand (in which case the term 'holograph' may, more precisely, be used); 'autograph' can also be used adjectivally ('a copy with autograph corrections'). Autographs may represent their composers' final thoughts on a work, but are not necessarily the ultimate authority as they may be superseded by (for example) a printed edition or a working copy incorporating later changes. No composers' autographs are known from earlier than the 16th century, though certain 15th-century MSS may contain autograph material. They survive in increasing profusion from later periods and many have been published in facsimile.

Autoharp. A zither-type instrument of German origin, popular in the USA from the late 19th century. The player strums the strings with his fingers, a finger-pick or a plectrum; damper bars controlled by buttons damp all strings except those that sound the required chord. It takes the form of a rectangular box (*c*30 × 45 cm), has 15–20 strings and a range of two to four octaves (*C–c'''*). Patented in 1882, it was used in social gatherings and by travelling preachers and gave rise to a folk tradition.

Automatic instrument. *See* MECHANICAL INSTRUMENT.

Auxiliary note [neighbor note]. In part-writing an unaccented non-harmonic note that lies a half or whole step away from the main note, which it ornaments by being approached from, and returning to, directly.

Avant garde (Fr.). 'Vanguard': term used for composers who adopt techniques or objectives radically different from those hallowed by tradition and generally accepted, with the implication that their work makes advances. The term came into use only after World War II, particularly with the adoption of such 'avant-garde techniques' as electronic sound, aleatory methods, total serialism etc.

Ave Maria (Lat.: 'Hail Mary'). A prayer, to words from St Luke's Gospel, adopted for use in the Roman rite in the 16th century. Numerous polyphonic settings survive by Renaissance composers, including Josquin and Victoria.

Aventures. Work by Ligeti for three singers and seven instrumentalists (1962), to which he added *Nouvelles aventures* (1965).

Ave regina caelorum (Lat.: 'Hail Queen of Heaven'). One of the four Marian antiphons, sung at the end of Compline from the Purification (2 February) until Wednesday in Holy Week. Dufay, Palestrina and Victoria are among those who made polyphonic settings.

Avery Fisher Hall. *See* LINCOLN CENTER FOR THE PERFORMING ARTS.

Avidom [Mahler-Kalkstein], **Menahem** (*b* Stanislav, 6 Jan 1908). Israeli composer of Russian birth. He studied with Rabaud at the Paris Conservatoire, but moved to Palestine in 1925 and was essentially self-taught. An active figure in Israeli musical life, he took part in the movement towards an Israeli nationalist style, rooted in Levantine culture; his works include operas and ten symphonies (1945–80).

Avignon Festival (France). Annual (summer) festival, established in 1946; events include concerts, opera and ballet.

Avison, Charles (*b* Newcastle upon Tyne, bap. 16 Feb 1709; *d* there, 9/10 May 1770). English composer. He was probably a pupil of Geminiani in London. He was organist of St Nicholas's Church, Newcastle, from 1736 until his death, refusing offers of posts elsewhere. From 1735 he organized and directed subscription concerts and later promoted them with John Garth in Durham; among the famous performers was the violinist Felice Giardini. His main literary publication (not all his own work) was *An Essay on Musical Expression* (1752), which discusses aesthetics, composers and performance. Its judgments, for instance that Geminiani and B. Marcello (whose psalms he edited) were better composers than Handel, led to controversy.

Avison was the most important English concerto composer of the 18th century. His 60 concerti grossi for strings, published between 1740 (op.2) and 1760 (op.10), are tuneful works modelled primarily on Geminiani's. His own arrangements of them included versions as organ concertos; he also arranged harpsichord sonatas by D. Scarlatti as 12 concerti grossi. In his sonatas opp. 5, 7 and 8 (1756–64) the two violins and cello are treated as accompaniments to the harpsichord; the harpsichord style is influenced by Rameau.

Avni, Tzvi (*b* Saarbrücken, 2 Sept 1927). Israeli composer of German birth. He studied with Ehrlich, Ben-Haim and Seter at the Tel-Aviv Academy, and in North America (1962–4). After an early nationalist phase he began to use avant-garde techniques, including electronics; among his works are large-scale religious tableaux.

Ax, Emmanuel (*b* Lwów, 8 June 1949). American pianist. He studied in Warsaw and in New York at the Juilliard School. After success in a competition in Israel in 1974, he made his New York début in 1975 and played in London two years later; he is a noted player of 20th-century music but is admired above all for his fluent, tasteful and often powerful readings of Chopin and Schumann.

Ayleward, Richard (*b* Winchester, 1626; *d* Norwich, 15 Oct 1669). English organist and composer. A chorister at Winchester Cathedral under Christopher Gibbons (1638–9) and Organist and Master of the Choristers at Norwich Cathedral (1661–4, 1666–9), he wrote service music and 20 verse anthems (some keyboard music attributed to him may be by his father).

Aylward, Theodore (*b c*1730; *d* London, 27 Feb 1801). English composer. From 1788 he was organist of St George's Chapel, Windsor, where he wrote several sacred works; but he also wrote many songs and other secular pieces, including a set of string quartets.

Ayre. *See* AIR.

Ayrton, Edmund (*b* Ripon, bap. 19 Nov 1734; *d* London, 22 May 1808). English composer. After serving as organist at Southwell Minister he became a Gentleman of the Chapel Royal (1764) and vicar-choral of St Paul's Cathedral (1767); in 1780–1805 he was Master of the Chapel Royal Children. He composed mainly sacred music, notably *Begin unto my God* (1784), an anthem with strong Handelian influences (sung at the thanksgiving after the War of American Independence in 1784). His brother William (1726–99) was organist of Ripon Cathedral from 1748.

Ayrton, William (*b* London, 24 Feb 1777; *d* there, 8 March 1858). English writer on music and impresario, son of Edmund Ayrton. He was a founder of the Philharmonic Society, contributed musical criticism to two London papers and edited the *Harmonicon* (1823–33). As director of the Italian opera, King's Theatre, he was the first to stage *Don Giovanni* in England (1817).

Azaïs, Hyacinthe (*b* Ladern-sur-Lauquet, 4 April 1741; *d* Toulouse, *c*1795). French composer. From 1756 he was *maître de musique* at the college in Sorèze. During a stay in Paris, 1770–71, two of his motets were performed at the Concert Spirituel. He lived in Toulouse from *c*1782. His instrumental music, including six symphonies (1770) and various chamber works, is light in tone. He was best known as a teacher and for his *Méthode de musique* (1776).

Azione sacra (It.). 'Sacred action': term for *sepolcri* (Easter oratorios set at Christ's sepulchre) composed for the Vienna court in the late 17th century. In the 18th century it was a synonym for 'oratorio'.

Azione teatrale (It.). 'Theatrical action': term for a type of stylized music theatre popular in the mid-18th century, especially at courts in and around Vienna.

B

B. Name of a note, or a PITCH CLASS; *see also* PITCH NAMES. It is the seventh degree in the scale of C major.

Baaren, Kees van (*b* Enschede, 22 Oct 1906; *d* Oegstgeest, 2 Sept 1970). Dutch composer. He studied in Berlin and with Pijper, and was director of the conservatories of Utrecht (from 1953) and The Hague (from 1958). In 1947, after a decade of creative silence, he began to write in a serial style influenced partly by Pijper but also by Webern, and in the 1950s he was influential in the training of the Dutch avant garde. His works are few, and mostly instrumental.

Babbi. Italian family of musicians. The most important members were Gregorio (1708–68), a tenor who sang in Naples and elsewhere and was renowned for his exceptional range, power and expressive capability; his son Cristoforo (1745–1814), a violinist and composer of orchestral and chamber music and operas, active·first at Bologna, then (from 1781) at Dresden, under whose direction the court orchestra became famous for its accuracy, precision and brilliant, full sound; and Cristoforo's son Gregorio (*c*1770–*c*1815), a singer, composer and organist who worked at the Dresden court and at Bologna.

Babbitt, Milton (Byron) (*b* Philadelphia, 10 May 1916). American composer. He studied at New York University with Marion Bauer and Philip James, and privately with Sessions, whom he followed to Princeton. There he taught intermittently from 1938 and permanently from 1948; he was largely responsible for the formation of a 'Princeton school' of 12-note composition, for in his lectures, essays and compositions he was able to combine extreme rigour with high enthusiasm. His own points of departure included Webern and, still more, the later serial music of Schoenberg, in which he detected a use of the 12-note set to create large forms dependent on the nature of the set, and particularly on the property of 'combinatoriality', by which different forms of the same set are related in having the same notes reordered within each of their two halves. It is symptomatic of his theoretical penetration and of his influence that much of the vocabulary of 12-note composition was introduced in his writings.

In his first published works he was most occupied with devising means by which rhythmic and timbral organization could be serial: solutions were offered in, respectively, the Three Compositions for piano

(1947) and the Composition for Twelve Instruments (1948). But the creation of a systematic 12-note rhythmic principle came only in the early 1960s with the innovation of 'time points', and at the same time Babbitt found an ideal instrument for determined colour control in the RCA Synthesizer. His works composed on it include *Ensembles for Synthesizer* (1962–4) and *Philomel* (1964) for soprano and tape. Until the early 1970s his music seemed to be created in tandem with his theory, each new work sprouting from some technical advance. Latterly he has been much more prolific and perhaps more relaxed – though wit was always a characteristic of his musical expression.

Orchestral music Relata I, II (1966, 1969); Ars combinatoria, 1981; Pf Conc. (1985)
Chamber music Composition for 4 Insts (1948); Composition for 12 Insts (1948); 5 str qts (1948, 1954, 1970, 1970, 1982); All Set, jazz ens (1957); Arie da capo, ens (1973–4); Paraphrases, 9 winds, pf (1979); Groupwise, ens (1983); Four Play, ens (1984)
Piano music Three Compositions (1947); Partitions (1957); Post-partitions (1966); Tableaux (1972); Canonical Form (1983)
Voice with instruments The Widow's Lament in Springtime (1950); Du (1951); A Solo Requiem (1977); The Head of the Bed (1982)
Tape Composition for Synthesizer (1961); Ensembles for Synthesizer (1964); Occasional Variations (1971)
Tape with voice Vision and Prayer (1961); Philomel (1964); Phonemena (1975)
Tape with instruments Correspondences (1967); Concerti (1976); Reflections (1975); Images (1979)

Babell, William (*b*?London, *c*1690; *d* Islington, 23 Sept 1723). English composer and harpsichordist of French descent. A pupil of Pepusch, he played in London concerts from 1711, and was also a church organist. He gained widespread fame as a harpsichordist through his virtuoso arrangements of operatic arias (especially Handel's), many of which were published; he also wrote solo sonatas and concertos. His works give insight into the performing practice of his day.

Babin, Victor (*b* Moscow, 13 Dec 1908; *d* Cleveland, 1 March 1972). American pianist and composer. He studied in Riga and Berlin (under Schreker and Schnabel), and in 1933 married Vitya Vronsky (*b*1909). They embarked on a piano-duo career, moving to the USA in 1937 and playing with much fluency and skill in a repertory from Bach to Stravinsky, including several works by Babin. Babin taught at the Aspen Music School (director, 1951–4), the Berkshire Music Center and the Cleveland Institute of Music (director from 1961 until his death).

Babi-Yar. Subtitle of Shostakovich's Symphony no.13 (1962), a setting of five poems by Yevtushenko.

Bacchus et Ariane. Ballet in two acts by Roussel to a libretto by A. Hermont (1931, Paris).

Baccusi, Ippolito (*b* Mantua, *c*1550; *d* Verona, 1609). Italian composer. After studying in Ravenna, he was *maestro di cappella* in Verona and Mantua and choirmaster of Verona Cathedral from 1592. His many masses, motets, psalms and madrigals are of high quality and show Venetian influence (Willaert, Gabrieli). He was an early advocate of doubling voices with instruments.

Bacewicz, Grażyna (*b* Łódź, 5 Feb 1909; *d* Warsaw, 17 Jan 1969). Polish composer and violinist. She studied with Sikorski at the Warsaw Conservatory and with Boulanger in Paris, simultaneously studying the violin: she was to write much for her own instrument, including seven concertos and solo and accompanied sonatas. Most of her music is neoclassical, but in the early 1960s she began to incorporate elements of the new Polish style exemplified by her contemporary Lutosławski, and in 1965 she adopted an avant-garde idiom. Her large output includes four symphonies, piano music, ballets and songs.

Bach. German family of musicians. They lived and worked in central Germany, mainly Thuringia, from the 16th century to the 18th, and represent the most remarkable and consistent concentration of musical talent ever recorded in a single family. Some were fiddlers and town musicians; others were organists, court musicians, Kantors and Kapellmeisters. Over 70 Bachs at some time earned their livelihoods through music.

The family's ancestry has been traced back to Veit Bach, in the 16th century, though some early details are uncertain. Veit, an amateur musician, lived in Wechmar but probably came from Moravia or Slovakia with the expulsion of Protestants in about 1545. Most of the musicians came from the main, Wechmar line and lived and worked in such small towns as Erfurt, Eisenach, Arnstadt and Ohrdruf, many of them in the Lutheran church. The musicians in the family are listed below, in alphabetical order; those calling for fuller discussion have separate entries, which follow. The numeral in parentheses after each name represents the individual's position in the family genealogy (see pp. 42–3), following the family tree drawn up in 1735 (with supplementary numbers; double numbers prefaced with 3 reflect an error in the 1735 genealogy).

46. Carl Philipp Emanuel (*b* Weimar, 8 March 1714; *d* Hamburg, 14 Dec 1788). Son of Johann Sebastian (*24*); see below.

3/56. Caspar (*b c*1570; *d* Arnstadt, after 1640). Possibly son of Hans (*54*). Court and town musician (bassoonist) in Gotha and Arnstadt.

3/58. Caspar (*b c*1600). Son of Caspar (*3/56*). Educated as a violinist at the courts of Bayreuth and Dresden; probably went to Italy.

5. Christoph (*b* Wechmar, 19 April 1613; *d* Arnstadt, 12 Sept 1661). Son of Johann (*2*). Court and town musician in Weimar, Erfurt and Arnstadt.

81. Ernst Carl Gottfried (*b* Ohrdruf, 12 Jan 1738; *d* there, 21 June 1801). Son of Johann Christoph (*42*). Kantor in Wechmar and Ohrdruf.

82. Ernst Christian (*b* Ohrdruf, 26 Sept 1747; *d* Wechmar, 29 Sept 1822). Son of Johann Christoph (*42*). Kantor in Wechmar.

10. Georg Christoph (*b* Erfurt, bap. 8 Sept 1642; *d* Schweinfurt, 24 April 1697). Son of Christoph (*5*). Kantor in Themar and Schweinfurt; composed a vocal concerto.

Georg Friedrich (*b* Tann, 17 March 1793; *d* Iserlohn, 2 Oct 1860). Not of the Wechmar line; son of Johann Michael. A flautist and composer, music teacher to the Crown Prince of Sweden, later music director in Elberfeld and Iserlohn.

74. Georg Michael (*b* Ruhla, bap. 27 Sept 1703; *d* Halle, 18 Feb 1771). Son of Johann Jacob (*68*). Kantor at Halle.

48. Gottfried Heinrich (*b* Leipzig, 26 Feb 1724; *d* Naumburg, bur. 12 Feb 1763). Eldest son of Johann Sebastian (*24*) and Anna Magdalena Bach. Feebleminded; but (according to C.P.E. Bach) he showed 'a great genius, which however failed to develop'.

76. Gottlieb Friedrich (*b* Meiningen, 10 Sept 1714; *d* there, 25 Feb 1785). Son of Johann Ludwig (*3/72*). Court organist and painter in Meiningen.

Hans: see under Johann below (unnumbered, 2 and 4).

3/62. Heinrich (*d* Arnstadt, bur. 27 May 1635). Son of Caspar (*3/56*). Musically educated in Italy, known as 'blind Jonas'.

6. Heinrich (*b* Wechmar, 16 Sept 1615; *d* Arnstadt, 10 July 1692). Son of Johann (*2*). Town musician in Schweinfurt, Erfurt and Arnstadt; composed chorales, motets, concertos, preludes and fugues.

Johann [Hans] (*b* Andelsbuch, *c*1555; *d* Nürtingen, 1 Dec 1615). Not a member of the Wechmar line. He was a violinist at the Stuttgart court and later at Nürtingen, and is known to have composed a song. He is traditionally regarded as a member of the family but any relationship remains uncertain.

2. Johann(es) [Hans] (*b c*1550; *d* Wechmar, 26 Dec 1626). Son of Veit (*1*). Baker, carpentmaker and fiddler, the earliest professional musician among the Wechmar Bachs. Studied in Gotha and travelled as a musician to various Thuringian towns.

3/59. Johann(es) (*b* 1612; *d* Arnstadt, bur. 9 Dec 1632). Son of Caspar (*3/56*). Town musician in Arnstadt.

4. Johann(es) [Hans] (*b* Wechmar, 26 Nov 1604; *d* Erfurt, bur. 13 May 1673). Son of Johann (*2*). Town musician and organist in Erfurt; composed motets.

67. Johann (*b* Themar, 1621; *d* Lehnstedt, 12 Sept 1686). Son of Andreas (*64*) (*b* 1587; *d* Thoman, 21 April 1637). Kantor in Ilmenau.

8. Johann Aegidius (*b* Erfurt, bap. 11 Feb 1645; *d* there, bur. 22 Nov 1716). Son of Johann (*4*). Violinist in Erfurt, also director of town music and organist.

36. Johann Aegidius (*b* Erfurt, bap. 4 Aug 1709; *d* Gross-Monra, 17 May 1746). Son of Johann Christoph (*19*). Kantor of Gross-Monra.

11. Johann Ambrosius (*b* Erfurt, 22 Feb 1645; *d* Eisenach, 20 Feb 1695). Son of Christoph (*5*). Married Maria Elisabeth Lämmerhirt (*b* Erfurt, 24 Feb 1644; *d* Eisenach, bur. 3 May 1694) in 1668. Town musician in Arnstadt, violinist in Erfurt, court trumpeter and director of town music in Eisenach.

44. Johann Andreas (*b* Ohrdruf, 7 Sept 1713; *d* there, 25 Oct 1779). Son of Johann Christoph (*22*). Oboist in the military band in Gotha, later organist in Ohrdruf.

71. Johann Balthasar (*b* Eisenach, 4 March 1673; *d* there, 11 June 1691). Son of Johann Ambrosius (*11*). Stadtpfeifer apprentice to his father.

18. Johann Bernhard (*b* Erfurt, bap. 25 Nov 1676; *d* Eisenach, bur. 5 April 1749). Son of Johann Aegidius (*8*). He was organist at Erfurt, then went to Magdeburg, and in 1703 became town organist and court harpsichordist at Eisenach (where he knew Telemann). He wrote organ music and French-style orchestral suites that were highly valued; some were copied by Johann Sebastian.

41. Johann Bernhard (*b* Ohrdruf, 24 Nov 1700; *d* there, 12 June 1743). Son of Johann Christoph (*22*). Organist in Ohrdruf and composer.

7. Johann Christian (*b* Erfurt, bap. 17 Aug 1640; *d* there, bur. 1 July 1682). Son of Johann (*4*). Violinist in Erfurt, then in Eisenach; director of Erfurt town music.

32. Johann Christian (*b* Erfurt, 1696). Son of Johann Christoph (*17*). Musician in Sondershausen.

50. Johann Christian (*b* Leipzig, 5 Sept 1735; *d* London, 1 Jan 1782). Son of Johann Sebastian (*24*); see below.

77. Johann Christian (*b* Halle, 23 July 1743; *d* there, 24 June 1814). Son of Georg Michael (*74*). Studied with W.F. Bach and taught in Halle.

13. Johann Christoph (*b* Arnstadt, bap. 8 Dec 1642; *d* Eisenach, bur. 2 April 1703). Son of Heinrich (*6*); see below.

12. Johann Christoph (*b* Erfurt, 22 Feb 1645; *d* Arnstadt, 25 Aug 1693). Son of Christoph (*5*). Town musician in Erfurt and Arnstadt.

22. Johann Christoph (*b* Erfurt, 16 June 1671; *d* Ohrdruf, 22 Feb 1721). Son of Johann Ambrosius (*11*). Organist in Erfurt and Ohrdruf; gave instruction to his brother Johann Sebastian (*24*).

17. Johann Christoph (*b* Erfurt, bap. 13 Jan 1673; *d* Gehren, bur. 30 July 1727). Son of Johann Christian (*7*). Kantor in Erfurt and Kantor and organist in Gehren.

28. Johann Christoph (*b* Eisenach, bap. 29 Aug 1676; *d*?). Son of Johann Christoph (*13*). Harpsichordist in Erfurt, travelled to England and Rotterdam.

19. Johann Christoph (*b* Erfurt, bap. 17 Aug 1685; *d* there, bur. 15 May 1740). Son of Johann Aegidius (*8*). Member, later director, of the Erfurt town music.

26. Johann Christoph (*b* Arnstadt, 13 Sept 1689; *d* Blankenhain, bur. 28 Feb 1740). Son of Johann Christoph (*12*). Organist in Keula and Blankenhain.

42. Johann Christoph (*b* Ohrdruf, 12 Nov 1702; *d* there, 2 Nov 1756). Son of Johann Christoph (*22*). Kantor in Ohrdruf.

49. Johann Christoph Friedrich (*b* Leipzig, 21 June 1732; *d* Bückeburg, 26 Jan 1795). Son of Johann Sebastian (*24*); see below.

83. Johann Christoph Georg (*b* Ohrdruf, 8 May 1747; *d* there, 30 Dec 1814). Son of Johann Andreas (*44*). Organist in Ohrdruf.

39. Johann Elias (*b* Schweinfurt, 12 Feb 1705; *d* there, 30 Nov 1755). Son of Johann Valentin (*21*). Lived with Johann Sebastian (*24*) as secretary, pupil and tutor of his later children; Kantor in Schweinfurt.

25. Johann Ernst (*b* Arnstadt, 5 Aug 1683; *d* there, 21 March 1739). Son of Johann Christoph (*12*). Organist in Arnstadt, succeeding Johann Sebastian (*24*). In 1705–6 he deputized for Johann Sebastian during the latter's journey to Lübeck.

34. Johann Ernst (*b* Eisenach, bap. 30 Jan 1722; *d* there, 1 Sept 1777). Son of Johann Bernhard (*18*). He studied at the Leipzig Thomasschule under Johann Sebastian; then he assisted his father at Eisenach, succeeding him and later serving as court Kapellmeister. He was also an administrator. His works include cantatas, motets, violin sonatas and pieces for organ and harpsichord.

29. Johann Friedrich (*b* Eisenach, *c*1682; *d* Mühlhausen, bur. 8 Feb 1730). Son of Johann Christoph (*13*). Succeeded Johann Sebastian (*24*) as organist in Mühlhausen; he wrote an organ fugue.

35. Johann Friedrich (*b* Erfurt, bap. 22 Oct 1706; *d* Andisleben, bur. 30 May 1743). Son of Johann Christoph (*19*). Organist in Quedlinburg and by 1735 schoolmaster in Andisleben.

78. Johann Georg (*b* Eisenach, bap. 2 Oct 1751; *d* there, 12 April 1797). Son of Johann Ernst (*34*). Succeeded his father as court and town organist and titular Kapellmeister in Eisenach.

Johann Georg (*b* Güstrow, *c*1786; *d* Elberfeld, 6 Dec 1874). Not of the Wechmar line, son of Johann Michael and music teacher in Elberfeld.

47. Johann Gottfried Bernhard (*b* Weimar, 11 May 1715; *d* Jena, 27 May 1739). Son of Johann Sebastian (*24*). A pupil of his father; organist in Mühlhausen and Sangerhausen; an unstable character who incurred debts.

15. Johann Günther (*b* Arnstadt, bap. 17 July 1653; *d* there, bur. 10 April 1683). Son of Heinrich (*6*). Assistant organist in Arnstadt, active as a keyboard and violin maker.

33. Johann Günther (*b* Gehren, 4 April 1703; *d* Erfurt, bur. 24 Oct 1756). Son of Johann Christoph (*17*). Town musician (tenor and viola player) in Erfurt.

43. Johann Heinrich (*b* Ohrdruf, 4 Aug 1707; *d* Oehringen, 20 May 1783). Son of Johann Christoph (*22*). Copyist at Leipzig Thomasschule, later assistant organist in Ohrdruf and appointed Kantor in Oehringen.

53. Johann Heinrich (*b* Hamburg, bap. 4 Nov 1709; *d*?). Son of Johann Christoph (*28*). According to genealogy, 'a good keyboard player'.

42

The Bach Family Tree

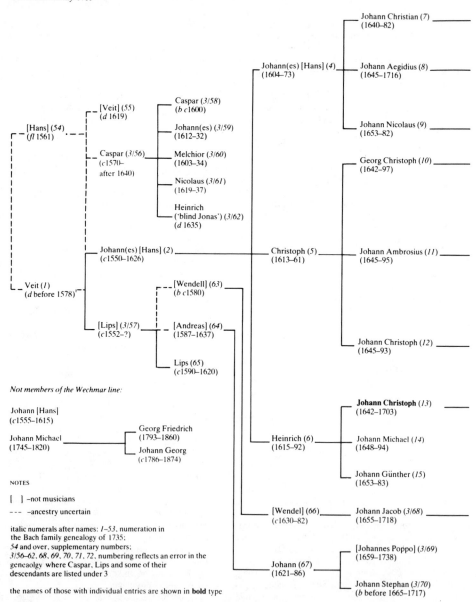

Not members of the Wechmar line:

Johann [Hans]
(*c*1555–1615)

Johann Michael
(1745–1820) ——————— Georg Friedrich
(1793–1860)
—— Johann Georg
(*c*1786–1874)

NOTES

[ ] –not musicians

- - - –ancestry uncertain

italic numerals after names: *1–53*, numeration in
the Bach family genealogy of 1735;
54 and over, supplementary numbers;
3/56–62, 68, 69, 70, 71, 72, numbering reflects an error in the
geneaolgy where Caspar, Lips and some of their
descendants are listed under 3

the names of those with individual entries are shown in **bold** type

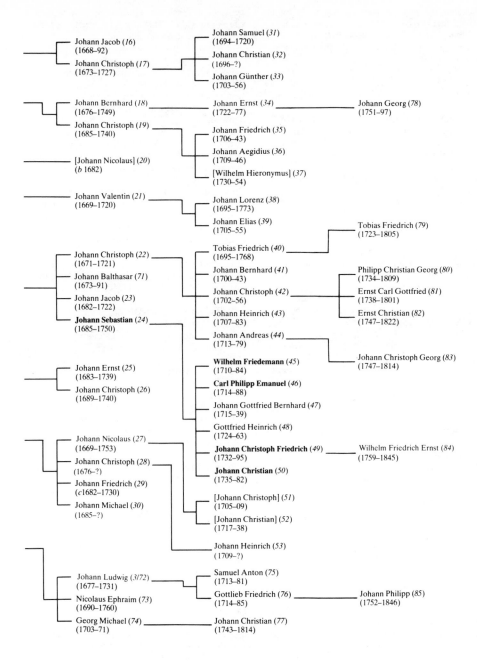

Johann Jacob (*16*)
(1668–92)

Johann Christoph (*17*)
(1673–1727)

Johann Samuel (*31*)
(1694–1720)

Johann Christian (*32*)
(1696–?)

Johann Günther (*33*)
(1703–56)

Johann Bernhard (*18*)
(1676–1749)

Johann Christoph (*19*)
(1685–1740)

[Johann Nicolaus] (*20*)
(*b* 1682)

Johann Valentin (*21*)
(1669–1720)

Johann Ernst (*34*)
(1722–77)

Johann Georg (*78*)
(1751–97)

Johann Friedrich (*35*)
(1706–43)

Johann Aegidius (*36*)
(1709–46)

[Wilhelm Hieronymus] (*37*)
(1730–54)

Johann Lorenz (*38*)
(1695–1773)

Johann Elias (*39*)
(1705–55)

Tobias Friedrich (*79*)
(1723–1805)

Johann Christoph (*22*)
(1671–1721)

Johann Balthasar (*71*)
(1673–91)

Johann Jacob (*23*)
(1682–1722)

Johann Sebastian (*24*)
(1685–1750)

Tobias Friedrich (*40*)
(1695–1768)

Johann Bernhard (*41*)
(1700–43)

Johann Christoph (*42*)
(1702–56)

Johann Heinrich (*43*)
(1707–83)

Johann Andreas (*44*)
(1713–79)

Philipp Christian Georg (*80*)
(1734–1809)

Ernst Carl Gottfried (*81*)
(1738–1801)

Ernst Christian (*82*)
(1747–1822)

Johann Christoph Georg (*83*)
(1747–1814)

Johann Ernst (*25*)
(1683–1739)

Johann Christoph (*26*)
(1689–1740)

Wilhelm Friedemann (*45*)
(1710–84)

Carl Philipp Emanuel (*46*)
(1714–88)

Johann Gottfried Bernhard (*47*)
(1715–39)

Gottfried Heinrich (*48*)
(1724–63)

Johann Nicolaus (*27*)
(1669–1753)

Johann Christoph (*28*)
(1676–?)

Johann Friedrich (*29*)
(*c*1682–1730)

Johann Michael (*30*)
(1685–?)

Johann Christoph Friedrich (*49*)
(1732–95)

Johann Christian (*50*)
(1735–82)

[Johann Christoph] (*51*)
(1705–09)

[Johann Christian] (*52*)
(1717–38)

Johann Heinrich (*53*)
(1709–?)

Wilhelm Friedrich Ernst (*84*)
(1759–1845)

Johann Ludwig (*3/72*)
(1677–1731)

Nicolaus Ephraim (*73*)
(1690–1760)

Georg Michael (*74*)
(1703–71)

Samuel Anton (*75*)
(1713–81)

Gottlieb Friedrich (*76*)
(1714–85)

Johann Christian (*77*)
(1743–1814)

Johann Philipp (*85*)
(1752–1846)

3/68. Johann Jacob (*b* Wolfsbehringen, 13 Sept 1655; *d* Ruhla, 11 Dec 1718). Son of Wendel (*66*) (*b* Wechmar, 1629–31; *d* Wolfsbehringen, 18 Dec 1682). Organist and Kantor in Thal, Steinbach, Wasungen and Ruhla.

16. Johann Jacob (*b* Erfurt, bap. 14 Aug 1668; *d* Eisenach, bur. 29 April 1692). Son of Johann Christian (*7*). Apprentice town musician in Eisenach.

23. Johann Jacob (*b* Eisenach, bap. 11 Feb 1682; *d* Stockholm, 16 April 1722). Son of Johann Ambrosius (*11*). Studied in Eisenach and became oboist with the Swedish guard; chamber musician at the Stockholm court. About 1704 Johann Sebastian (*24*) wrote a Capriccio (BWV992) on Johann Jacob's departure.

38. Johann Lorenz (*b* Schweinfurt, 10 Sept 1695; *d* Lahm in Itzgrund, 14 Dec 1773). Son of Johann Valentin (*21*). Pupil of Johann Sebastian (*24*), organist and Kantor in Lahm; wrote an organ fugue.

3/72. Johann Ludwig (*b* Thal, 4 Feb 1677; *d* Meiningen, bur. 1 May 1731). Son of Johann Jacob (*3/68*). He worked at the Meiningen court, becoming Kantor and later Kapellmeister. He wrote cantatas (several of which Johann Sebastian performed at Leipzig), motets and other sacred works; also orchestral music, most of which is lost.

14. Johann Michael (*b* Arnstadt, bap. 9 Aug 1648; *d* Gehren, 17 May 1694). Son of Heinrich (*6*). He studied under his father and Jonas de Fletin in Arnstadt, where he became organist; later he was organist and instrument maker at Gehren. He wrote motets and other sacred works, as well as many organ chorales; his chorale motets are notable for their word-setting and their command of both new and traditional styles, while his vocal concertos are richly orchestrated with virtuoso obbligato parts. His youngest daughter, Maria Barbara (1684–1720), was Johann Sebastian's first wife.

30. Johann Michael (*b* Eisenach, bap. 1 Aug 1685; *d*?). Son of Johann Christoph (*13*). Active in Stockholm as an organ builder.

Johann Michael (*b* Struth, 9 Nov 1745; *d* Elberfeld, 1820). Not of the Wechmar line but from a Hessian one thought to be linked with it. He travelled to the Low Countries, England and the USA, practised law, and became Kantor in Tann and later a teacher at Elberfeld. He published a theoretical work and six keyboard concertos and also wrote cantatas.

9. Johann Nicolaus (*b* Erfurt, bap. 5 Feb 1653; *d* there, bur. 30 July 1682). Son of Johann (*4*). Erfurt town musician (violist).

27. Johann Nicolaus (*b* Eisenach, 10 Oct 1669; *d* Jena, 4 Nov 1753). Son of Johann Christoph (*13*). He studied at Jena, travelled to Italy, and became organist of the town and eventually the university church in Jena; he was also an instrument maker. He was a skilful composer in various forms but little of his music is extant.

85. Johann Philipp (*b* Meiningen, 5 Aug 1752; *d* there, 2 Nov 1846). Son of Gottlieb Friedrich (*76*). Court organist and painter in Meiningen.

31. Johann Samuel (*b* Niederzimmern, 4 June

1694; *d* Gundersleben, 1 July 1720). Son of Johann Christoph (*17*). Musician and teacher in Sondershausen, and Gundersleben.

24. Johann Sebastian (*b* Eisenach, 21 March 1685; *d* Leipzig, 28 July 1750). See below.

3/70. Johann Stephan (*b* Ilmenau, before 1665; *d* Brunswick, 10 Jan 1717). Son of Johann (*67*). Kantor at the Cathedral in Brunswick.

21. Johann Valentin (*b* Themar, 6 Jan 1669; *d* Schweinfurt, 12 Aug 1720). Son of Georg Christoph (*10*). Town musician in Schweinfurt.

65. Lips [Philippus] (*b* Wechmar, *c*1590; *d* there, 10 Oct 1620). Son of the carpetmaker Lips (*3/57*) (*b c*1552) who was a son of Veit (*1*); he was a musician.

3/60. Melchior (*b* 1603; *d* Arnstadt, bur. 7 Sept 1634). Son of Caspar (*3/56*). Town musician in Arnstadt.

3/61. Nicolaus (*b* Arnstadt, 6 Dec 1619; *d* there, bur. 1 Oct 1637). Son of Caspar (*3/56*). Town musician in Arnstadt.

73. Nicolaus Ephraim (*b* Wasungen, bap. 26 Nov 1690; *d* Gandersheim, 12 Aug 1760). Son of Johann Jacob (*3/68*). Organist at Meiningen and Gandersheim.

80. Philipp Christian Georg (*b* Ohrdruf, 5 April 1734; *d* Werningshausen, 18 Aug 1809). Son of Johann Christoph (*42*). Kantor in Ohrdruf.

75. Samuel Anton (*b* Meiningen, bap. 26 April 1713; *d* there, 29 March 1781). Son of Johann Ludwig (*3/72*). Studied with Johann Sebastian (*24*), later court organist in Meiningen.

40. Tobias Friedrich (*b* Ohrdruf, 21 July 1695; *d* Udestedt, 1 July 1768). Son of Johann Christoph (*22*). Organist in Ohrdruf, later Kantor in Gandersleben, Pferdingsleben and Udestedt.

79. Tobias Friedrich (*b* Udestedt, 22 Sept 1723; *d* Erfurt, 18 Jan 1805). Son of Tobias Friedrich (*40*). Kantor in Erfurt.

1. Veit (*b* ?Bratislava; *d* Wechmar, before 1578). The earliest member of the family to show musical proclivities.

45. Wilhelm Friedemann (*b* Weimar, 22 Nov 1710; *d* Berlin, 1 July 1784). Son of Johann Sebastian (*24*); see below.

84. Wilhelm Friedrich Ernst (*b* Bückeburg, bap. 27 May 1759; *d* Berlin 25 Dec 1845). Son of Johann Christoph Friedrich (*49*). He studied with his father, lived briefly with his uncle Carl Philipp Emanuel in Hamburg and then with his uncle Johann Christian in London, where he taught and played the piano. After a concert tour, he became music director in Minden; later he moved to Berlin with court posts. He wrote much music, but its style is generally vapid. He was the last musician of the Bach family and lived to see the dedication of the Leipzig Bach monument in 1843.

B–A–C–H. In German nomenclature, the letters of Bach's name provide a motif (ex.1) which has been used as a germinal idea in compositions. It was used by Bach himself in *The Art of Fugue*; one of Bach's sons (Johann Christian) and his pupil J.L. Krebs wrote fugues on it, and it was often used in the 19th century after the Bach revival. Such composers as

Schumann, Liszt (in a major organ work), Busoni and Rimsky-Korsakov used it, as did Schoenberg and Webern.

Ex. 1

B   A   C   H

Bach, August Wilhelm (*b* Berlin, 4 Oct 1796; *d* there, 15 April 1869). German organist, teacher and composer. He was organist at Berlin churches, succeeded Zelter as director of the Institute for Church Music (1832) and taught at the Royal Academy of Arts. His output, mostly sacred and keyboard music, includes an organ method and a hymnbook. He is unrelated to the Bach family.

Bach, Carl Philipp Emanuel (*b* Weimar, 8 March 1714; *d* Hamburg, 14 Dec 1788). German composer [46 in Bach family genealogy], second son of J.S. Bach. He studied music under his father at the Leipzig Thomasschule and law at university. In 1738 he was summoned to become harpsichordist to the Prussian crown prince, moving to Berlin when his employer became King Frederick in 1740. There he was accompanist to the royal chamber music, with the particular task of accompanying the king's flute solos. The most important of his compositions of this period were his keyboard sonatas; he also wrote his famous *Essay on the True Art of Keyboard Playing* (1753–62), which established him as the leading keyboard teacher and theorist of his time. He was however discontented in Berlin, because of the poor salary, the want of opportunity and the narrow scope of his duties. Not until 1767 did he move, and then Frederick released him only reluctantly. He succeeded Telemann as Kantor and music director in Hamburg, with responsibility for teaching, for some 200 performances of music each year at five churches and for ceremonial music on civic occasions. He now produced much church music as well as keyboard music and sets of symphonies and concertos. But the openness of Hamburg intellectual life was agreeable to a man of his wide interests.

C.P.E. Bach, the best-known member of his family in his lifetime, was greatly respected for his treatise – which summarized the musical philosophy and the musical practices in north Germany at the middle of the 18th century – as well as for his music. His keyboard sonatas (he composed *c*150 as well as countless miscellaneous pieces) above all break new ground in their treatment of form and material, (e.g. in their 'varied reprises' and their handling of motifs); he also wrote improvisatory fantasias of intense expressiveness. His symphonies are in the fiery, energetic manner favoured in north Germany, with dramatic breaks, modulations and changes of mood or texture; usually the movements run continuously. He wrote *c*20. There are twice as many concertos (and more concerto-like sonatinas), also vigorous in style; all were written for harpsichord and some were adapted for other instruments. His chamber works are numerous; there are many songs, as well as choral works from his late years, including two

fine oratorios (*Die Israeliten in der Wüste, Die Auferstehung und Himmelfahrt Jesu*) as well as Passion settings and other church works which often include adaptations of his own and other composers' music.

*Keyboard music c*150 sonatas, incl. 6 Prussian Sonatas (1742–3); 6 Württemberg Sonatas (1744); 6 sonatas 'with altered repeats' (1760); fantasias, rondos, fugues, variations, minuets
Chamber music over 30 sonatas, duets with obbligato kbd; 3 kbd qts; 18 solo sonatas; *c*20 trio sonatas; duets, wind music
Orchestral music 20 syms.; *c*50 hpd concs.; concs. arr. from hpd concs. 12 sonatinas, hpd, orch
Vocal music Magnificat (1749); Die Israeliten in der Wüste, oratorio (1769); Die Auferstehung und Himmelfahrt Jesu, oratorio (1780); Morgengesang am Schöpfungsfeste, ode (1783); Passions; church cantatas, motets; occasional cantatas; *c*300 secular and sacred songs; chamber cantatas, arias

Bach, Johann Christian (*b* Leipzig, 5 Sept 1735; *d* London, 1 Jan 1782). German composer [50 in Bach family genealogy], youngest son of J.S. Bach. He probably studied first under his father, then on his father's death with his half-brother Carl Philipp Emanuel in Berlin. In 1754 he left for Italy, where he became Roman Catholic and took a post as organist at Milan Cathedral. He also embarked on an operatic career, with operas staged in Turin and Naples. He was then invited to compose for the King's Theatre in London, where he settled in 1762; his operatic career was patchy, but he was soon appointed royal music master and was successful as a teacher. He also promoted and played in a prominent concert series with his compatriot and friend C.F. Abel, bringing the newest and best European music to Londoners' notice. He befriended the boy Mozart on his London visit, 1764–5. Many of his works were published, including songs written for Vauxhall Pleasure Gardens. In 1772 and 1774 he visited Mannheim for performances of his operas *Temistocle* and *Lucio Silla*; in 1779 he wrote *Amadis de Gaule* for the Paris Opéra. But the success of these works, like that of his London operas, was limited. His popularity faded in the late 1770s, and after financial troubles his health declined; he died at the beginning of 1782, and was soon forgotten.

J.C. Bach's music blends sound German technique with Italian fluency and grace: hence its appeal to, and influence upon, the young Mozart. His symphonies follow the Italian three-movement pattern: the light, Italian manner of his earlier ones gave way to richer-textured and more fully developed writing by the mid-1760s. The peak of his output comes in the six symphonies of his op.18, three for double orchestra and exploiting contrasts of space and timbre. His interest in orchestral colour gave rise to several *symphonies concertantes*, for various soloists and orchestra, suitable material for his London concerts. At these he also played his piano concertos, attractive for their well-developed solo-tutti relationship though still modest in scale. Of his chamber music, the op.11 quintets (flute, oboe, strings and continuo) are particularly appealing for their charming conversational style and their use of colour. He also composed keyboard sonatas, with and without violin accompaniment, in a style accessible to his pupils and players of modest ability. His music is often leisurely in manner, and this must have militated against the operas' success as dramatic music. He also composed a quantity of Latin sacred music during his time in Italy. Though sometimes regarded as a decadently hedonistic composer by comparison with his brother Carl Philipp Emanuel, Johann Christian stands firmly as the chief master of the *galant*, who produced music elegant and apt to its social purpose, infusing it with vigour and refined sensibility.

Orchestral music over 40 syms. and ovs., incl. 6 each in op.3 (1765), op.6 (1770), op.8 (c1775), op.18 (c1782), 3 in op.9 (1773); 12 symphonies concertantes; 25 kbd concs., incl. 6 each in op.1 (1763), op.7 (1770), op.13 (1777); 2 ob concs.; 2 bn concs.
Chamber and wind music kbd sextet; 2 kbd qnts; kbd qt; 35 acc. kbd sonatas; 6 qnts op.11 fl, ob, vn, va, bc (1774); qts, str, fl and str, 2 fl and str; fl qts; 6 str trios op.2 (1763); over 20 trio sonatas, duets; wind sinfonias, wind qnts, marches
Keyboard music 6 sonatas op.5 (1766); 6 sonatas op.12 (1774); other sonatas, arrangements, duets
Dramatic music Orione (1763); Temistocle (1772); Lucio Silla (1774); La clemenza di Scipione (1778); Amadis de Gaule (1779); 6 others; contributions to other composers' works; Gioas, rè di Giuda, oratorio (1770)
Sacred vocal music c30 works, incl. Dies irae, c (1757)
Secular vocal music 6 cantatas and serenatas; 19 chamber duets; Vauxhall songs; arias, songs, folksong settings, transcrs

Bach, Johann Christoph (*b* Arnstadt, bap. 8 Dec 1642; *d* Eisenach, bur. 2 April 1703). German composer [13 in Bach family genealogy]. He studied under his father and in 1663 became organist of the Arnstadt castle chapel. In 1665 he was appointed town organist and court organist and harpsichordist at Eisenach, posts held for the rest of his life in spite of disputes with civic authority. J.S. Bach wrote that he 'was as good at inventing beautiful ideas as he was at expressing words'. He composed, as far as current taste allowed, in a *galant*, cantabile style, unusually full in texture'. His vocal works include motets and vocal concertos, the former in the tradition of the aria and chorale motet, with alternate imitative and chordal writing; he also wrote for keyboard, in a style akin to Pachelbel's.

Bach, Johann Christoph Friedrich (*b* Leipzig, 21 June 1732; *d* Bückeburg, 26 Jan 1795). German composer [49 in Bach family genealogy], son of J.S. Bach. He studied with his father and his relative Johann Elias (*39*), and on his father's death he took a post at the court of Count Wilhelm of Schaumburg-Lippe at Bückeburg, where he remained throughout his career, becoming *Concert-Meister* in 1759. He composed in most of the genres of the time; his chamber and keyboard music is lightweight, but his keyboard concertos and symphonies show Viennese Classical influence and some of the dramatic cantatas and oratorios (some to texts by Herder, for a time his colleague at the progressive Bückeburg court) show imaginative expression.

Bach, Johann Sebastian (*b* Eisenach, 21 March 1685; *d* Leipzig, 28 July 1750). German composer and organist [24 in Bach family genealogy]. He was the youngest son of Johann Ambrosius Bach, a town musician, from whom he probably learnt the violin and the rudiments of musical theory. When he was

ten he was orphaned and went to live with his elder brother Johann Christoph, organist at St Michael's Church, Ohrdruf, who gave him lessons in keyboard playing. From 1700 to 1702 he attended St Michael's School in Lüneburg, where he sang in the church choir and probably came into contact with the organist and composer Georg Böhm. He also visited Hamburg to hear J.A. Reincken at the organ of St Catherine's Church.

After competing unsuccessfully for an organist's post in Sangerhausen in 1702, Bach spent the spring and summer of 1703 as 'lackey' and violinist at the court of Weimar and then took up the post of organist at the Neukirche in Arnstadt. In June 1707 he moved to St Blasius, Mühlhausen, and four months later married his cousin Maria Barbara Bach in nearby Dornheim. Bach was appointed organist and chamber musician to the Duke of Saxe-Weimar in 1708, and in the next nine years he became known as a leading organist and composed many of his finest works for the instrument. During this time he fathered seven children, including Wilhelm Friedemann and Carl Philipp Emanuel. When, in 1717, Bach was appointed Kapellmeister at Cöthen, he was at first refused permission to leave Weimar and was allowed to do so only after being held prisoner by the duke for almost a month.

Bach's new employer, Prince Leopold, was a talented musician who loved and understood the art. Since the court was Calvinist, Bach had no chapel duties and instead concentrated on instrumental composition. From this period date his violin concertos and the six Brandenburg Concertos, as well as numerous sonatas, suites and keyboard works, including several (e.g. the Inventions and Book I of the '48') intended for instruction. In 1720 Maria Barbara died while Bach was visiting Karlsbad with the prince; in December of the following year Bach married Anna Magdalena Wilcke, daughter of a court trumpeter at Weissenfels. A week later Prince Leopold also married, and his bride's lack of interest in the arts led to a decline in the support given to music at the Cöthen court. In 1722 Bach entered his candidature for the prestigious post of *Director musices* at Leipzig and Kantor of the Thomasschule there. In April 1723, after the preferred candidates, Telemann and Graupner, had withdrawn, he was offered the post and accepted it.

Bach remained as Thomaskantor in Leipzig for the rest of his life, often in conflict with the authorities, but a happy family man and a proud and caring parent. His duties centred on the Sunday and feastday services at the city's two main churches, and during his early years in Leipzig he composed prodigious quantities of church music, including four or five cantata cycles, the Magnificat and the *St John* and *St Matthew Passions*. He was by this time renowned as a virtuoso organist and in constant demand as a teacher and an expert in organ construction and design. His fame as a composer gradually spread more widely when, from 1726 onwards, he began to bring out published editions of some of his keyboard and organ music.

From about 1729 Bach's interest in composing

church music sharply declined, and most of his sacred works after that date, including the B minor Mass and the *Christmas Oratorio*, consist mainly of 'parodies' or arrangements of earlier music. At the same time he took over the direction of the collegium musicum that Telemann had founded in Leipzig in 1702 – a mainly amateur society which gave regular public concerts. For these Bach arranged harpsichord concertos and composed several large-scale cantatas, or serenatas, to impress the Elector of Saxony, by whom he was granted the courtesy title of *Hofcompositeur* in 1736.

Among the 13 children born to Anna Magdalena at Leipzig was Bach's youngest son, Johann Christian, in 1735. In 1744 Bach's second son, Emanuel, was married, and three years later Bach visited the couple and their son (his first grandchild) at Potsdam, where Emanuel was employed as harpsichordist by Frederick the Great. At Potsdam Bach improvised on a theme given to him by the king, and this led to the composition of the *Musical Offering*, a compendium of fugue, canon and sonata based on the royal theme. Contrapuntal artifice predominates in the work of Bach's last decade, during which his membership (from 1747) of Lorenz Mizler's learned Society of Musical Sciences profoundly affected his musical thinking. The Canonic Variations for organ was one of the works Bach presented to the society, and the unfinished *Art of Fugue* may also have been intended for distribution among its members.

Bach's eyesight began to deteriorate during his last year, and in March and April 1750 he was twice operated on by the itinerant English oculist John Taylor. The operations and the treatment that followed them may have hastened Bach's death. He took final communion on 22 July and died six days later. On 31 July he was buried at St John's cemetery. His widow survived him for ten years, dying in poverty in 1760.

Bach's output embraces practically every musical genre of his time except for the dramatic ones of opera and oratorio (his three 'oratorios' being oratorios only in a special sense). He opened up new dimensions in virtually every department of creative work to which he turned, in format, musical quality and technical demands. As was normal at the time, his creative production was mostly bound up with the external factors of work and his employers, but the density and complexity of his music are such that analysts and commentators have uncovered in it layers of religious and numerological significance rarely to be found in the music of other composers. Many of his contemporaries, notably the critic J.A. Scheibe, found his music too involved and lacking in immediate melodic appeal, but his chorale harmonizations and fugal works were soon adopted as models for new generations of musicians. The course of Bach's musical development was undeflected (though not entirely uninfluenced) by the changes in musical style taking place around him. Together with his great contemporary Handel (whom chance prevented his ever meeting), Bach was the last great representative of the Baroque era in an age which was already rejecting the Baroque

aesthetic in favour of a new, 'enlightened' one.

Sacred choral music St John Passion (1724); St Matthew Passion (1727); Christmas Oratorio (1734); Mass, b (1749); Magnificat (1723); over 200 church cantatas, incl. no.80, Ein feste Burg (*c*1744), no.140, Wachet auf (1731); 7 motets, incl. Singet dem Herrn (*c*1727), Jesu meine Freude (?1723); chorales, sacred songs

Secular vocal music over 20 cantatas, incl. no.211, 'Coffee Cantata' (*c*1735), no.212, 'Peasant Cantata' (1742)

Orchestral music Brandenburg Concs. nos. 1–6 (1721); 2 vn concs., a, E (1717–23); 2-vn conc., d (1723); hpd concs. (*c*1738–9): 8 for 1 hpd (d, E, D, A, f, F, g, d), 3 for 2 hpd (c, C, c), 2 for 3 hpd (d, C), 1 for 4 hpd (a); 4 orch. suites, C, b (with fl), D, D

Chamber music 6 sonatas and partitas, vn (1720); 6 sonatas, vn, hpd (1717–23); 6 suites, vc (*c*1720); Musical Offering (1747); 7 fl sonatas (2 unacc.); 3 sonatas, viola da gamba, hpd; trio sonatas

Keyboard music 7 toccatas (*c*1708–10); Chromatic fantasia and fugue, d (*c*1720); Das wohltemperirte Clavier, '48' (1722, 1742); 6 English Suites (*c*1722); 6 French Suites (*c*1722); 15 Inventions, 15 Sinfonias (1723); 6 Partitas (1731); Italian Conc. (1735); French Ov. (1735); Goldberg Variations (1741–2); The Art of Fugue (*c*1745–50); suites, fugues, capriccios, 16 concertos

Organ music over 150 chorale preludes; preludes, fugues, toccatas, fantasias, sonatas, passacaglia

Bach, Wilhelm Friedemann (*b* Weimar, 22 Nov 1710; *d* Berlin, 1 July 1784). German composer [45 in Bach family genealogy], eldest son of J.S. Bach. He studied under his father at the Leipzig Thomasschule; his father put together a 'Clavier-Büchlein' for him and may have written book 1 of the '48' with him in mind. Friedemann also studied the violin with J.G. Graun. After university study, he became organist at the Dresden Sophienkirche in 1733; he moved to the Liebfrauenkirche, Halle, in 1746 but his years there were turbulent and he left in 1764. He later lived in Brunswick and then in Berlin, but with his difficult temperament and perhaps dissolute character found no regular employment though his organ playing was admired.

The volatility of his musical style is of a piece with his life. In his early years he wrote mainly for keyboard; at Dresden, for instruments; at Halle, church cantatas and some instrumental music; and in his late years, chiefly chamber and keyboard works. He vacillated in style between old and new, with *galant* elements alongside conservative Baroque ones, intense north German expressiveness alongside more formal writing. His keyboard music includes fugues and deeply-felt polonaises. His gifts are unmistakable here and in such works as the Concerto for two solo harpsichords or the often suite-like Sinfonia in F, but the final impression is of a composer whose potential was never fully realized.

Keyboard music 15 sonatas; Suite, g; Conc., G; *c*40 polonaises; fantasias, fugues, minuets; 7 chorale preludes, org; Conc., 2 kbds, F (*c*1773)

Instrumental music 5 hpd concs.; Conc. 2 hpds, E♭; sinfonias; 5 trio sonatas; 6 fl duets; 3 va duets

*Vocal music c*20 church cantatas; 2 secular cantatas

Bachauer, Gina (*b* Athens, 21 May 1913; *d* there, 22 Aug 1976). British pianist. She studied in Athens and under Cortot in Paris, also working under Rakhmaninov. She made her début in Athens in 1935, but was stranded in World War II and gave over 600 concerts for allied troops. She made her London and New York débuts in 1947 and 1950, and played widely in Europe and the USA after that. She was noted for her balanced musicianship and her commanding technique, particularly impressive in the late Romantic repertory.

Bach Choir. British choir formed in London in 1875 to perform Bach's Mass in B minor (1876). Otto Goldschmidt conducted for ten years; successors included Vaughan Williams (1920–26) and Adrian Boult (1926–32). From 1960, under David Willcocks, modern works have been given as well as Bach.

Bache, Walter (*b* Birmingham, 19 June 1842; *d* London, 20 March 1888). English pianist and conductor. He studied with Liszt in Rome (1862–5), then worked to establish Liszt's reputation by playing arrangements and giving orchestral concerts of his works. He was the younger brother of Francis Edward Bache (1833–58), a composer of pleasing piano pieces and songs.

Bach-Gesellschaft. A society founded in 1850, on the centenary of Bach's death, to publish a complete edition of his works. The 46-volume edition was completed in 1900 and was a model for subsequent editions of its kind. The society was reconstituted in 1900 as the Neue Bach-Gesellschaft, which has held festivals and published the *Bach-Jahrbuch*.

Bachianas brasileiras. Nine instrumental pieces by Villa-Lobos that combine elements of Brazilian folk music with Bachian counterpoint (1930–45); the first is for eight cellos, the fifth for soprano and eight cellos.

Bachmann, Sixt (*b* Ketterhausen, 18 July 1754; *d* Reutlingendorf, 18 Oct 1825). German composer. A child prodigy, he took part in an organ contest with the young Mozart in 1766; both emerged with credit. He later became a priest in Ober Marchthal, where he taught and composed keyboard, sacred and other works, many in a contrapuntal style.

Bachofen, Johann Caspar (*b* Zurich, 26 Dec 1695; *d* there, 23 June 1755). Swiss composer and teacher. Trained in theology, he taught singing in Zurich and from 1739 was Kapellmeister at the German School. In 1742 he became Kantor at the Grossmünster and director of the chapter house *collegium musicum*. He wrote cantatas, a Passion and numerous sacred songs, mostly for three voices and organ; the collection *Musicalisches Hallelujah* (1727) long remained popular.

Bach revival. The rediscovery of the music of J.S. Bach in the late 18th century and the early 19th. Bach's music had been set aside in a sense that the music of (for example) Palestrina or Handel had not; with the growing historicism of the early Romantic period, especially in England and Germany, Bach's music was revived, partly by his own disciples but also by historically aware musicians. A leader in the Bach revival was J.N. Forkel, who wrote a pioneering biography of him in 1802. In the early 19th century his music (especially the '48') began to be published and performed; a landmark was the performance by the Berlin Singakademie under Mendelssohn of the *St Matthew Passion* in 1829, the

supposed centenary of its first performance. In England Bach's music was propagated by Samuel Wesley and, later, Sterndale Bennett.

Bach trumpet. A misnomer still prevalent for a high trumpet with valves used in modern performances of Baroque music. The term was originally applied, in the late 19th century, to a straight trumpet in A or B♭ with two valves, then to a still shorter one in D with three (in fact half the length of the D trumpet of Bach's time).

Bacilly, Bénigne de (*b* ?Normandy, ?*c*1625; *d* Paris, 27 Sept 1690). French singing teacher and composer. He lived mainly in Paris. Although important as a composer and teacher – he published several books of chansons and secular and sacred airs – his most valuable legacy is the vocal treatise *Remarques curieuses sur l'art de bien chanter* (1668), a prime source of information on French 17th-century vocal practice.

Bäck, Sven-Erik (*b* Stockholm, 16 Sept 1919). Swedish composer. Like other Rosenberg pupils of his generation, during the 1940s and 1950s he came successively under the influences of Hindemith, Webern and Stockhausen. His works include operas, music for the Lutheran church and three string quartets (1945, 1947, 1962).

Backfall. A descending APPOGGIATURA.

Backhaus, Wilhelm (*b* Leipzig, 26 March 1884; *d* Villach, 5 July 1969). German pianist. He studied at the Leipzig Conservatory until 1899 and after further study with Eugen d'Albert began an international career. As the last exponent of the Leipzig tradition of pianism he was admired for the clarity and structural strength of his interpretations. Latterly he was heard most often in Beethoven and the Romantic repertory.

Bacon, Ernst (*b* Chicago, 26 May 1898). American composer. His teachers included Bloch for composition and Goossens for conducting; he made his career as a conductor, college teacher, pianist and composer. He is best known for his *c*250 songs, chiefly to American poems, which show unusual sensitivity to verbal inflection; he also wrote four symphonies (1932–63).

Bacon, Richard Mackenzie (*b* Norwich, 1 May 1776; *d* Costessy, 27 Nov 1844). English writer on music. He was proprietor and later editor of a newspaper in Norwich, where he helped establish a triennial music festival. He founded and edited the *Quarterly Musical Magazine and Review* (London, 1818–30), the first English journal devoted exclusively to writing on music. A strong proponent of serious, all-sung English opera, he also produced two treatises on singing.

Bacquier, Gabriel (*b* Béziers, 17 May 1924). French baritone. He studied at the Paris Conservatoire and after appearances at La Monnaie, Brussels, sang at the Opéra-Comique (1956) and the Paris Opéra (1958), notably as Boccanegra, Falstaff and Boris. He sang Mozart's Count at Glyndebourne (1962) and Riccardo in *I puritani* at Covent Garden (1964) and was also known in such comic roles as Dr Bartolo, Alfonso and Dulcamara.

Badia, Carlo Agostino (*b* ?Venice, 1672; *d* Vienna, 23 Sept 1738). Italian composer. After working at Innsbruck, he was court composer to the Viennese court from 1694. He enjoyed favour under Leopold I and Joseph I and by 1711 had written over 30 oratorios and 20 secular stage works, including *Ercole, vincitore di Gerione* (1708) and an opera for Dresden (1709). He also composed over 50 chamber cantatas and duets; a set of 12 cantatas was published (probably in 1699). He helped introduce Italian late Baroque style to the conservative Viennese court. His early works have both a lyricism and idiomatic instrumental writing; his oratorios and stage works make much use of ensembles, especially trios.

Badía [d'Agustí], **Conchita** (*b* Barcelona, 14 Nov 1897; *d* there, 2 May 1975). Spanish soprano. After study with Granados, Casals and Falla her career was devoted largely to Spanish song, in which her spontaneity and clear diction were admired. She sang in Paris, London and Vienna and was professor of singing at the Barcelona Conservatory; Montserrat Caballé was among her pupils.

Badinage, badinerie (Fr.). 'Jest', 'trifle': fanciful titles for a fast suite movement in the 18th century, used by Telemann and Bach (Orchestral Suite no.2 in B minor) and occasionally found in later music.

Badings, Henk (*b* Bandung, Java, 17 Jan 1907). Dutch composer. He was brought up in the Netherlands and studied at the Technical University in Delft, though he also studied music, notably with Pijper, who encouraged him to write his First Symphony (1930, played by the Concertgebouw). This and its successor made his reputation, and in 1934 he was appointed to teach at the Rotterdam Conservatory, later going to other institutions in the Netherlands and Germany. His works of the 1930s and early 1940s are in a sombre, polyphonic style owing something to Pijper, but his harmony became brighter and less tonal and more playful. He changed direction again *c*1952 when he began to use electronic resources, for instance in the radio opera *Orestes* (1954) and the wholly electronic ballet *Kain* (1956). He was a prolific composer whose output includes symphonies, numerous concertos, large-scale choral works, chamber music and songs.

Badura-Skoda, Paul (*b* Vienna, 6 Oct 1927). Austrian pianist. He studied at the Vienna Conservatory. After his début in 1948 he soon became widely known in the Viennese Classics and in contemporary music. With Jörg Demus he has been heard in piano duets. He has a collection of historical instruments, on which he has made some of his many recordings. Cadenzas for Mozart's concertos are among his compositions. His wife Eva (*b* 1929) is a musicologist whose work has centred on 18th-century topics; they are co-authors of *Mozart-Interpretation* (1957).

Baermann. German family of musicians, principally wind players. The most important members were Heinrich (1784–1847), a clarinettist known throughout Europe for his velvety tone and expressive playing, which inspired Weber's clarinet works, and his son Carl (1810–85), a clarinettist and basset-horn player who was a professor in Munich and the author of a valuable method (1864–75).

Bagatelle. A title, first found in Couperin, for a short, light piece. Most later examples, notably those by Beethoven and Bartók, are for piano solo; others include six by Webern for string quartet.

Bagge, Charles Ernest, Baron de (*b* Fockenhof, Kurland, 14 Feb 1722; *d* Paris, 24 March 1791). French dilettante and patron. A violin pupil of Tartini in Italy, he settled in Paris and from the 1760s was an influential concert organizer and patron of players (including Kreutzer); he also held a post at the Berlin court. He wrote chamber and orchestral music.

Bagpipe. A wind instrument which, in its simplest form, consists of a perforated tube (the chanter) provided with a reed and inserted into an airtight skin reservoir (the bag). The wind enters the bag through the blowpipe, a second tube with a no-return valve, and is supplied by the lungs of the player, who compresses the bag with his arm to gain the head of air required to cause the reed to vibrate. Additional pipes may be incorporated to provide drones.

The highly developed Scottish Highland pipe has been a martial instrument since at least the 16th century; it has found its way into almost every part of the world, sometimes supplanting local folk instruments. Irish forms include the mouth-blown war-pipe and the bellows-blown union pipe, suited only to indoor playing. The only English type is the bellows-blown Northumbrian pipe. In France, the bellows-blown musette was fashionable in the 17th and 18th centuries. The mouth-blown *gaita* of Spain and Portugal resembles the Scottish Highland pipe though it usually has only one drone. Old German types pictured by Praetorius include the *Bock, Schäferpfeife, Hümmelchen* and *dudy*. The native bagpipe of India consists of a single-reed cane pipe and a blowpipe tied in a goatskin.

Bahr-Mildenburg, Anna (*b* Vienna, 29 Nov 1872; *d* there, 27 Jan 1947). Austrian soprano. She studied with Rosa Papier and in 1895 was engaged at the Hamburg Opera. She formed a close professional and personal relationship with the music director, Mahler, and soon won renown for her forceful interpretations of Mozart, Wagner and Weber roles. In 1896 she joined Mahler at Vienna and until 1921 was successful there as Brünnhilde, Leonore and Donna Anna. She sang at Covent Garden in 1906 and 1913 and appeared at Bayreuth, 1897–1914, where she assisted Cosima Wagner.

Baïf, Jean-Antoine de (*b* Venice, 19 Feb 1532; *d* Paris, Oct 1589). French poet. He had a classical education and lived mainly in Paris. His output includes odes, sonnets, chansons and dramatic works, but he is chiefly important for his innovatory *vers mesurés à l'antique*, using quantitative metres as in ancient verse; he published at least three measured translations of the psalter. As a co-founder of the Académie de Poésie et de Musique, he promoted *musique mesurée* settings, which helped liberate the French *air* from the metrical conventions of the chanson. His verses were set by many composers.

Bailey, Norman (*b* Birmingham, 23 March 1933). English baritone. He studied at the Vienna Music Academy and sang widely in West Germany, 1960–67. His London appearance, as Sachs with the Sadler's Wells company in 1968 established him as a Wagnerian of international stature (his Sachs,

Gunther and Amfortas have been heard at Bayreuth). His clear declamation and strong musical intelligence have also been admired in Mozart, Verdi and Strauss.

Baillie, Dame Isobel (*b* Hawick, 9 March 1895; *d* Manchester, 24 Sept 1983). Scottish soprano. She studied in Manchester and Milan and made her London début in 1923; she was a leading oratorio singer, especially admired for her singing in *Messiah* and Brahms's *German Requiem*. After her retirement she taught, principally in Manchester.

Baillot, Pierre (Marie François de Sales) (*b* Passy, 1 Oct 1771; *d* Paris, 15 Sept 1842). French violinist and composer. He became professor at the Paris Conservatoire and, in the 1820s, led the Paris Opéra and Chapelle Royale orchestras. From 1805 to 1808 he toured Russia. With his noble, powerful tone, neat execution and pure style, he was the last representative of the classical Paris violin school and a noted chamber music player. His *L'art du violon* (1834) is a standard work, and with Viotti's other two greatest pupils, Rode and Kreutzer, he compiled a violin method (1803).

Baillou [Baglioni], Luigi de (*b* Milan, *c*1735; *d* there, *c*1809). Italian composer. He was a violinist at the Stuttgart court (1762–74), then settled in Milan as director (1779–1802) and principal violinist (from 1783) of the La Scala orchestra. His *c*20 ballets were given as entr'actes in operas; he also composed instrumental works.

Bainbridge, Simon (*b* London, 30 Aug 1952). English composer. He studied at the RCM and Tanglewood; American music, in particular Ives and Reich, has been a formative influence. There is a spatial element in some of his music, which is largely instrumental. Among his most characteristic pieces are the Viola Concerto (1976), *Concertante in moto perpetuo* (1983) and Fantasia for two orchestras (1984).

Baines, William (*b* Horbury, 26 March 1899; *d* York, 6 Nov 1922). English composer and pianist. He taught himself by studying the more advanced music of his time and experimenting at the piano (he worked as a cinema pianist). In his short life he wrote much music, including a symphony, chamber pieces and many impressionistic piano works.

Baini, Giuseppe (Giacobbe Baldassarre) (*b* Rome, 21 Oct 1775; *d* there, 21 May 1844). Italian scholar. A priest, he reorganized the papal chapel archives and was general administrator of the papal singers. His most important work was as a Palestrina scholar, his *Memorie storico-critiche* (1828) being the first attempt to give a full biographical and musicological view of the composer.

Bainton, Edgar (Leslie) (*b* London, 14 Feb 1880; *d* Sydney, 8 Dec 1956). English composer and teacher. A pupil of Stanford at the RCM, he taught at the Newcastle upon Tyne Conservatory (1901–33), then at the New South Wales Conservatorium, becoming a strong influence on musical life in Sydney. He wrote operas (including *The Pearl Tree*, 1944), three symphonies and other works in a late Romantic pastoral style.

Baird, Tadeusz (*b* Grodzisk Mazowiecki, 26 July 1928; *d* Warsaw, 2 Sept 1981). Polish composer. He studied at the Warsaw Conservatory with Rytel and

Perkowski, and began by following the party ideology in producing uncomplicated music. The cultural thaw of 1956 allowed him to work with 12-note serialism in his String Quartet (1957) and *Four Essays* for orchestra (1958). Later works, in a lyrical and dramatic, richly textured style, are mostly for orchestra, sometimes with solo voice (e.g. *Erotica* for soprano and orchestra, 1961).

Bairstow, Sir Edward C(uthbert) (*b* Huddersfield, 22 Aug 1874; *d* York, 1 May 1946). English composer, organist and conductor. He studied with Henry Farmer and, in 1913 was appointed organist at York Minster, where he remained until his death; from 1929 he was also professor of music at Durham University. He was well known as a conductor of choral societies and was an influential teacher. His compositions, influenced by Brahms, plainsong and the English Elizabethan–Jacobean school, include a Communion Service (1913), the anthem *Let all mortal flesh keep silence* (1925), secular vocal music and an Organ Sonata (1937).

Baiser de la fée, Le [The Fairy's Kiss]. Allegorical ballet in four scenes by Stravinsky based on music by Tchaikovsky (1928, Paris).

Baj, Tommaso (*b* Crevalcuore, *c*1650; *d* Rome, 22 Dec 1714). Italian composer. An alto or tenor in the Cappella Giulia, St Peter's, Rome, and ultimately its *maestro*, he is chiefly known for a nine-part *Miserere* in falsobordone style, long sung by the papal choir in Holy Week.

Bakala, Břetislav (*b* Fryšták, 12 Feb 1897; *d* Brno, 1 April 1958). Czech conductor. At Brno he studied composition with Janáček and conducting with František Neumann. From 1929 to 1931 he was conductor of Brno Opera, where he gave the posthumous première of Janáček's *From the House of the Dead* (1930). He was one of the finest conductors of Janáček and an influential conductor of the Brno SO.

Baker, David Nathaniel (*b* Indianapolis, 21 Dec 1931). American composer and jazz cellist. After study at Indiana University he played the cello with such jazz artists as Maynard Ferguson, Quincy Jones and Lionel Hampton. He has written extensively on black American music and many of his 2000 works draw on jazz, serial and electronic techniques, as well as gospel and folk materials.

Baker, Dame Janet (Abbott) (*b* Hatfield, Yorks., 2 Aug 1933). English mezzo-soprano. She studied with Helen Isepp and Meriel St Clair. Her Eduige in the Handel Opera Society *Rinaldo* (1959) established her in Handel and pre-classical opera. A long association with Britten began in 1963, with Polly in his realization of *The Beggar's Opera*; the role of Kate Wingrave was written for her (1971) and she made her Covent Garden début (1966) as Hermia (*Midsummer Night's Dream*). Her warm personality and richly expressive voice were admired in her Dorabella, Berlioz's Dido and Octavian for Scottish Opera. At Glyndebourne she sang in Leppard's versions of *Calisto* (1970), and *Il ritorno di Ulisse* (1972). After her retirement from the stage (her last role was Gluck's Alcestis, at Covent Garden, 1981) she continued to be heard as a recitalist and in oratorio and concert performances.

Baker, Theodore (*b* New York, 3 June 1851; *d* Dresden, 13 Oct 1934). American music scholar and lexicographer. He studied in Leipzig, worked on American Indian music and became literary editor and translator for Schirmer (1892–1926). He made many translations of books, librettos etc, but is best known for his biographical dictionary (1900, 7/1984).

Bakfark, Bálint [Valentin] (*b* Brassó, 1507; *d* Padua, 15 or 22 Aug 1576). Hungarian lutenist and composer. He was educated at the Buda court and later served the Polish court at Wilna (1549–66). After brief periods in Vienna and back in Transylvania, he settled in Padua. His extensive travels in Europe gained him great renown as he was celebrated as one of the great virtuosos of the age. His extant works, all for lute, require great technical mastery and include polyphonic fantasies, intricate arrangements of vocal works (sacred and secular) and a few dances.

Balakirev, Mily Alexeyevich (*b* Nizhny-Novgorod, 2 Jan 1837; *d* St Petersburg, 29 May 1910). Russian composer. At the Alexandrovsky Institute he studied with the German Karl Eisrich, who introduced him to the music of Chopin and Glinka and to the wealthy music patron and Beethoven enthusiast Ulibishev, who in turn introduced him (1855) to Glinka and the musical life of St Petersburg where he became known as a pianist and teacher. During an illness in 1858 he came under the care of Dimitry Stasov (brother of the critic) and met the young officer and amateur composer Musorgsky; both Musorgsky and another composing officer, Cui, soon accepted him as their mentor.

Though Balakirev produced the Overture on Three Russian Themes, several songs (notably *Selim's Song, Song of the Golden Fish* and *Georgian Song*) and incidental music for *King Lear* around this time (1858–61), he completed few big works, spending much time on his disciples (now including Rimsky-Korsakov and Borodin) and on the new Free School of Music. From 1862 he began collecting folktunes in the Caucasus, some of which he used in the Second Overture on Russian Themes (1864) and the Symphony in C, meanwhile editing and conducting Glinka's works. His fiery advocacy of musical nationalism gained him a prominent position in the Russian Musical Society by 1867, but his tactless, despotic character also gained him enemies, eventually straining relations within his own group. After completing the oriental fantasy for piano *Islamey* (1869) he withdrew from music, reappearing in the 1880s as director of the Imperial Court Chapel, then resuming composition during his reclusive retirement (from 1895).

Balakirev's importance in Russian orchestral music and lyrical song in the second half of the 19th century was equally as composer and leader: he expanded Glinka's orientalism, bright orchestral transparency and incessant variation technique and transmitted this idiom to Borodin, Rimsky-Korsakov, Musorgsky and even Tchaikovsky, partly by example and partly by direct interference in their compositions.

Dramatic music King Lear, incidental music (1861)
Orchestral music Sym. no.1, C (1897); Sym. no.2, d (1908); Tamara, sym. poem (1882); 2 ovs. on Russian themes (1858, 1864); 2 pf concs., inc.
Vocal music choral anthems; hymns; cantata; over 40 songs
Piano music 2 sonatas (1856, 1905); Islamey, oriental fantasy (1869); 7 mazurkas; 7 waltzes; *c*30 other solo pieces (scherzos, nocturnes etc); duets

Balalaika. A long-necked fretted lute with a triangular body, one of the most popular Russian folk instruments. It usually has three gut or steel strings, the tuning of which varies according to region and the genre of music: examples are piccolo $b'-e''-a''$, prime (the commonest size) $e'-e'-a'$, and bass $E-A-d$. A single balalaika often accompanies song and dance; large ensembles are also common.

Balancement (Fr.). 'Wavering': a term used mainly for the tremolo obtainable on a clavichord; also for the vibrato in vocal and string music.

Balanchivadze, Andrey (Melitonovich) (*b* St Petersburg, 1 June 1906). Georgian composer. He is son of the Rimsky-Korsakov pupil and pioneer Georgian composer Meliton Balanchivadze (1862–1937) and younger brother of the choreographer George Balanchin (1904–83). He studied at the conservatories of Tbilisi (with Ippolitov-Ivanov) and Leningrad (with Shteynberg), and has held official appointments in Georgian musical and political life. His works, using folk elements, include operas, ballets, symphonies and piano concertos. His First Symphony (1944) was a milestone in the evolution of Georgian music.

Balassa, Sándor (*b* Budapest, 20 Jan 1935). Hungarian composer. He studied with Szervansky at the Budapest Academy, and was soon winning international renown for large, fastidiously scored works such as the orchestral *Iris* (1971), though he is also capable of stark expressionism (as in the opera *The Man Outside*, 1978).

Balatka, Hans (*b* Olomouc, ?26 Feb 1825; *d* Chicago, 17 April 1899). Czech conductor and composer, active in the USA. An important figure in the development of music in the Midwest, he directed the Milwaukee Musical Society (1850–60, 1871–2) and German theatre (1855–60) as well as the Chicago Philharmonic Society (1860–69), and founded the Balatka Academy of Musical Art in Chicago (1879). He wrote orchestral, piano and vocal works.

Balbastre, Claude-Bénigne (*b* Dijon, 22 Jan 1727; *d* Paris, 9 May 1799). French organist and composer. He lived in Paris from the 1750s and held posts as organist, notably at the French court (from 1776). An internationally famous performer, he played often at the Concert Spirituel (until 1782), including his own concertos or opera transcriptions. He published several books of keyboard pieces, continuing the French harpsichord tradition, and six *Sonates en quatuor* for keyboard and accompaniment (1779).

Balbi, Lodovico (*b* Venice, *c*1545; *d* there, before 15 Dec 1604). Italian composer. A minorite friar, he studied with Costanzo Porta in Padua. He was *maestro di cappella* of the Cappella Antoniana, Padua (1585–91), and of Feltre (1593–7) and Treviso (1597–8) cathedrals. His sacred pieces (masses, motets, psalms), though accomplished, are unin-

spired; he also wrote madrigals. His nephew Luigi
(*fl* 1585–1621) was a church musician in Venice and
Padua.

Baldwin. American firm of instrument makers, notably of pianos and organs. It was started by Dwight
Hamilton Baldwin (1821–99), a piano and organ
dealer in Cincinnati, Ohio, from 1865. As D.H.
Baldwin & Co. (1873) it became one of the largest
dealers in the Midwest, agents for Bourne, Estey,
Fisher and Steinway. From 1889 it manufactured
reed organs and from 1891 low-priced upright
pianos. In 1947 it introduced the Baldwin electronic
organ, now chiefly two-manual domestic instruments. The Baldwin Piano and Organ Co. introduced a new concert grand piano in 1965; the parent
company acquired Bechstein (1963), which retains
its identity.

Baldwin, John (*b* before 1560; *d* London, 28 Aug
1615). English anthologist. The MS anthologies he
compiled, in a fine hand, include the valuable
Forrest–Heyther Partbooks (vocal music), My
Ladye Nevells Booke (keyboard pieces by Byrd) and
Baldwin's Commonplace-Book (including 20 of his
own compositions).

Balfe, Michael William (*b* Dublin, 15 May 1800;
d Rowney Abbey, 20 Oct 1870). Irish composer and
singer. He was the most successful composer of English opera in the 19th century and the only one
whose fame spread throughout Europe. Having developed his baritone voice and met Cherubini and
Rossini in Paris, he gained singing engagements
there and in Italy, returning to London in 1833; he
pursued his dual career until 1846, when he became
conductor at Her Majesty's Theatre. It was with
The Siege of Rochelle (1835) and *The Maid of Artois*
(1836) that he first scored unprecedented popular
success at Drury Lane, despite criticism from
academics who distrusted his Rossinian fecundity.
Italian Opera and Opéra-Comique commissions
followed and then his greatest triumph, *The Bohemian Girl* (1843), which ran for over 100 nights and
played in the principal capitals of Europe and North
and South America. A master of the simple English
ballad rather than of characterization, ensemble
writing or instrumentation, Balfe succeeded in
gauging precisely British public taste in his English
operas. He also produced distinctive art songs and
the first English Romantic opera without spoken
dialogue (*Catherine Grey*, 1837).

Ballabile (It.). 'Suitable for dancing': a movement,
usually in an opera, intended for dancing. The
'Galop con cori' in Act 2 of Verdi's *Ernani* is a *coro
ballabile*.

Ballad. A strophic folksong with a strong narrative
element, in stanzas of four (or more) lines, normally
without melodic repetition within a stanza. F.J.
Child's *English and Scottish Popular Ballads* (1882–
98) contains 305; the tradition is also strong in some
other European countries, notably Denmark. A
special category was the English 'broadside ballad',
originating in the 16th century and so called because
the texts were printed on large folio sheets (broad-
sides). Since the late 18th century such ballads have
been important in American popular music.

As a 19th-century art form, the ballad was cultivated in Germany in settings for voice and piano of
narrative poems, often imitations or translations of
traditional English ballads. One of the earliest significant ballad composers, J.R. Zumsteeg, served as
a model for Schubert and Loewe, who in turn
influenced Schumann, Brahms, Wolf and others. In
Victorian England and in the USA the word 'ballad'
was used for any kind of sentimental song, often
performed in an opera (e.g. Bishop's 'Home, sweet
home') or at a 'ballad concert'.

Ballade. (1) One of the three fixed forms, together
with the rondeau and the virelai, which dominated
French song and poetry in the 14th and 15th centuries. It originated as a song for dancing, but the
fully developed ballade consists of a poem of three
stanzas with the same metre, rhyme scheme and
concluding refrain. The music for each stanza follows the pattern I–I–II.

(2) Term, first used by Chopin, for a piano piece in
a narrative style or, later, for a piece of orchestral
programme music.

Ballad horn. A valved brass instrument, invented
*c*1870; it is akin to the B♭ baritone but circular in
shape and pitched a tone higher, in C.

Ballad opera. An English 18th-century dramatic
genre, usually comic, alternating spoken dialogue
with songs set mostly to traditional or popular
tunes. The first example was *The Beggar's Opera*, a
satire by Gay for which Pepusch arranged the music
(1728). Among its many successors was Coffey's *The
Devil to Pay* (1731), which in a German version
(1747) led to the creation of the Singspiel.

Ballard. French family of music printers. Their publications constitute a history of French musical taste
over 200 years. Robert (i) (?1525/30–1588), with his
cousin Adrien Le Roy, founded the firm Le Roy &
Ballard in 1551, receiving from Henri II the title of
music printer to the king in 1553. The firm's court
connections, knowledge of the repertory, printing
skill and the beauty of its editions gave it a virtual
monopoly on music printing in France during the
late 16th century. *Chanson* collections accounted for
much of its output, followed by motets, masses and
instrumental works.

Pierre Ballard (?1575/80–1639) carried on the business after Le Roy's death; his brother Robert (ii)
(*c*1575–*c*1650) became a lutenist and composer.
Pierre's son Robert (iii) (*c*1610–?1673) maintained
the firm's monopoly, undertaking orchestral scores
for the first time and initiating a series of song collections. Although his son Christophe (1641–?1715)
reached a highpoint in the firm's success by issuing
works by Lully, Campra, Charpentier, the
Couperins, Hotteterre and Marais, the new method
of printing from engraved plates became a threat.
His son Jean-Baptiste-Christophe (*c*1663–1750),
the publisher of Rameau's *Traité* (1722), and his
grandson Christophe-Jean-François (*c*1701–65)
witnessed the firm's decline.

Ballata. Italian dance-song, and poetic and musical
form, in use from the late 13th century until the
15th. Its typical form – *A* (*ripresa*), *BB* (two *piedi*),
A (*volta*), *A* (*ripresa*) – resembles that of the French

virelai. Landini's 141 polyphonic ballate offer a good cross-section of the musical styles used.

Ballet de cour (Fr.). 'Court ballet': a type of ballet danced at the French court from the late 16th century to the late 17th. *Circé ou le Balet comique de la Royne* (1581) was the first to combine poetry, music, décor and dance in a single scenario; most later *ballets de cour* consisted of dramatically separate *entrées*. Lully contributed to the genre from *c*1655, but it suffered an eclipse when Louis XIV ceased to dance (1670) and it was only briefly revived under Louis XV.

Ballets Russes. Ballet company launched in Paris in 1909 by Dyagilev. Noted for its exotic costumes (by Bakst), powerful choreography (Fokin) and Nizhinsky's dancing, it commissioned many works, among them Stravinsky's *The Firebird* (1910), *Petrushka* (1911) and *The Rite of Spring* (1913), Ravel's *Daphnis et Chloé* (1912) and Debussy's *Jeux* (1913).

Balletto. An Italian dance of the 16th and 17th centuries. The instrumental type, in binary form, appeared from *c*1561 to 1599 (for lute) and from 1616 to 1700 (for chamber ensemble). Many early ones indicate Germanic origin and show some connection with the allemande. The vocal *balletto* (English, ballett) is thought to have originated with Gastoldi's *Balletti a cinque voci* (1591), probably as part of a costumed dance. The texts are mostly strophic, set homophonically with 'fa-la' or similar interpolations. Later Italian *balletto* composers include Banchieri and Vecchi; Gastoldi's were imitated in Germany and in England, where the balletts of Morley and Weelkes were especially popular.

Ballif, Claude (André François) (*b* Paris, 22 May 1924). French composer. He studied with Messiaen at the Paris Conservatoire and with Blacher and Rufer in Berlin, then taught in Germany and France (at the Conservatoire from 1971). His works use his own 'metatonal' system, by which 11 of the 12 notes are kept in circulation; they include orchestral pieces, some incorporating sounds of the environment, and vocal music. His writings include a study of Berlioz (1968).

Ballo (It.: 'dance'). The term may refer to a social event, a choreography or a piece of music.

From the 13th century a distinction was made between the choreography of a ballo and of other types of dance, and in the 15th century the ballo assumed a definite shape: a sequence based on the four common musical metres (*bassadanza, saltarello, quadernaria* and *piva*). Every ballo shows the same pattern: an *intrada* followed by the ballo proper and a repeat of either the entire dance or the *intrada*. In the 16th century its dimensions increased; the *pavan, pavaniglia* and *bassa* replaced the *bassadanza* and *quadernaria* metres, and the *gagliarde, cascarda, tordiglione* and *canari* replaced the *piva* and *saltarello*. The ballo was prominent in 17th-century theatrical entertainments, Monteverdi's *Il ballo delle ingrate* being a well-known example.

Collections of balli, consisting of fashionable dances, began to appear *c*1520. Some 17th-century sources (e.g. Lorenzo Allegri's *Il primo libro di mu-*

siche, 1618) contain music for multi-movement balli presented as court entertainments. As dance music became increasingly stylized in 18th-century instrumental music, the term was used only occasionally to indicate the dance-like character of a composition.

Ballo in maschera, Un [A Masked Ball]. Opera in three acts by Verdi to a libretto by Somma based on Scribe's libretto for Auber's *Gustave III* (1859, Rome).

Ballou, Esther (Williamson) (*b* Elmira, NY, 17 July 1915; *d* Chichester, 12 March 1973). American composer. She studied under Luening, Wagenaar and Riegger and wrote some ballets; she taught in Washington, DC, devising methods for theory teaching. She was the first American woman composer to have a work (*Capriccio*, for violin and piano) given its première at the White House (1963). She wrote music in all media, particularly chamber and keyboard works.

Baltimore Symphony Orchestra. American orchestra founded in 1914 and first conducted by Gustav Strube (until 1930); its home is the Joseph Meyerhoff Symphony Hall (opened 1982). Activities include young peoples' concerts (from 1971) and summer series at Symphony Hall and Oregon Ridge Park, Baltimore County. Under Sergiu Commissiona (1970–84) a new American work was commissioned annually.

Baltsa, Agnes (*b* Lefkas, 19 Nov 1944). Greek mezzo-soprano. She studied in Athens and Munich. Her early career was at the Frankfurt Opera and in 1970 she came to prominence as Octavian at the Vienna Opera. Her American début was at Houston in 1971 as Carmen, a role with which she is particularly associated. She has also sung at Covent Garden, notably as Rossini's Italian Girl (1988).

Baltzar, Thomas (*b* Lübeck, *c*1630; *d* London, bur. 27 July 1663). German violinist and composer. After serving as a violinist at the Swedish court, he went to England in 1655, becoming a member of the King's Private Musick in 1661. He expanded English violin technique by using multiple stops, brilliant figuration and the instrument's highest register. Of his few surviving compositions some variations were printed in *The Division Violin* (1685).

Bamberg Symphony Orchestra. West German orchestra formed in 1946 from the Prague Deutsche Philharmonie (founded 1939), which left Prague in 1945. Conductors have included Herbert Albert (1947–8) and Eugen Jochum (1948–9, 1969–73).

Bampton, Rose (Elizabeth) (*b* Lakewood, OH, 28 Nov 1908). American mezzo-soprano, later soprano. She studied at the Curtis Institute and made her opera début as Siebel in *Faust* (1929, Chautauqua). Her Met début was in 1932. Five years later she became a soprano and sang Leonora (*Il trovatore*) at the Met, where she sang up to 1950, notably in Wagner roles (Sieglinde, Kundry); she also appeared in Europe and Buenos Aires.

Ban, Joan Albert (*b* Haarlem, 1597–8; *d* there, 27 July 1644). Dutch theorist and composer. He is important for his system of *musica flexanima* ('soul-moving singing'), whereby expressive word-setting is achieved through specific intervals, harmonies and rhythms, as seen in his song collection *Zanghbloemzel* (1642). These theories were further developed in *Kort sangh-bericht* (1643), but his work on tuning failed to gain acceptance.

Banchieri, Adriano (*b* Bologna, 3 Sept 1568; *d* there, 1634). Italian composer and theorist. A Benedictine monk, he was organist at the monastery of S Michele in Bosco for most of his life. Although a versatile composer of sacred and instrumental music, Banchieri is chiefly remembered for his treatises on performing practice and for his six books of spirited three-voice canzonettas; in these the pieces are textually linked to form works in the madrigal-comedy genre (the most famous is *La pazzia senile*). His treatise *L'organo suonarino* (1605) describes the realization of bass figures, giving instructions for accompanying liturgical chant, while *Cartella musicale* (1614) contains his writings on harmony, rhythm and vocal ornamentation.

Band. An instrumental ensemble. At its loosest 'band' is used for any ensemble bigger than a chamber group. The word may originate in the medieval Latin *bandum* ('banner'), the flag under which soldiers marched. Such origins seem to be reflected in its usage for a group of military musicians playing brass, woodwind and percussion instruments, ranging from a few fifes and drums to a full-scale military band. In 18th-century England 'band' was colloquially used for an orchestra. It is now often used for groups of related instruments, as in 'brass band', 'wind band', 'horn band' and 'steel band'. Several types were named by function rather than constitution (dance band, jazz band, rehearsal band, stage band). The marching band, which originated in the USA, consists of woodwind and brass instruments, a large percussion section, drum majorettes, flag twirlers etc. Another modern development is the American symphonic wind band, which derives from such groups as Gilmore's Band (1859) and the US Marine Band under John Philip Sousa (1880–92).

Bandmaster. The conductor or leader of a military band.

Bandoneon. A square-build button accordion or concertina, invented in the 1940s by Heinrich Band of Krefeld. It has been used in dance orchestras in South America and West Africa, and by some USA avant-garde composers.

Bandora [pandora]. A plucked string instrument of bass register with metal strings and scalloped and festooned body outline, said to have been invented in London in 1562. Besides having a considerable solo repertory, it was required to accompany some of the earliest printed English songs and was used in the classical mixed consort. There are many references to its use in the theatre and court entertainments in the late 16th century and the 17th; by the 18th it was falling into disuse. It had iron strings and brass wires, in twisted strands, running (usually) from lateral pegs over a glued bridge with a fret-like brass strip and hitch-pins. There were six or seven strings; tunings varied, but a typical one is

C–D–G–c–e–a. Composers who used it include Morley, Leighton and Barley.

Bandurria [mandurria]. A plucked string instrument, a hybrid of the guitar and cittern families, found in Spain and parts of Latin America. It had a cittern-shaped body and, in the 16th century, three strings; more recent examples may have up to five or six, tuned in 4ths.

Banister, John (*b* London, *c*1625; *d* there, 3 Oct 1679). English composer. He was a violinist in the King's Musick from 1660 until his death and from 1672 was host to some of the earliest public concerts recorded. As a composer he was most important for instrumental works, including grounds and dance movements; he also wrote songs for the Davenant–Dryden *Tempest* (1667) and other productions. His son John (*d* ?1725), who succeeded him in the King's Musick, was active in public concerts and composed small-scale works.

Banjo. A plucked string instrument with a long guitar-like neck and circular soundtable of tautly stretched parchment or skin (now usually plastic) against which the bridge is pressed by the strings (for illustration, *see* LUTE). The banjo and its variants have had long and widespread popularity as folk, parlour and professional entertainers' instruments. The name probably derives from the Portuguese or Spanish *bandore*. The modern banjo normally has raised frets and five steel strings tuned $g'-c-g-b-d'$ (C tuning) or $g'-d-g-b-d'$ (G tuning). The development of the modern banjo began in the second quarter of the 19th century as a commercial adaptation of an instrument used by West African slaves in the New World as early as the 17th century. After *c*1870 it was increasingly used in the USA as a genteel parlour instrument for popular music; in the 1920s and 1930s the tenor banjo (tuned $c-g-d'-a'$) was popular, but after World War II the original instrument regained favour, partly through the influence of Pete Seeger, who popularized rural southern styles.

Bánk bán. Opera in three acts by Erkel to a libretto by Egressy after Katona (1861, Budapest); the most successful Hungarian opera of the 19th century, it established with Erkel's earlier *Hunyady László* a native operatic style.

Banks, Don (*b* S. Melbourne, 25 Oct 1923; *d* Sydney, 5 Sept 1980). Australian composer. He studied in Melbourne, moved to London in 1950, and had lessons with Seiber, Babbitt, Dallapiccola and Nono. During the 1950s he wrote little, developing a serial style of strong, bold gestures and decisive forward movement. Then in the late 1960s came a rush of works, including concertos for horn (1965) and violin (1968), and pieces incorporating jazz styles. In 1972 he returned to Australia to teach in Canberra; in 1978 he became head of the School of Composition Studies at the Sydney Conservatorium. His later works include the String Quartet (1975).

Bantock, Sir Granville (*b* London, 7 Aug 1868; *d* there, 16 Oct 1946). English composer, conductor and teacher. He studied with Corder at the RAM (1889–93), then worked as a conductor and teacher (professor at Birmingham, 1908–34). He did much to promote the music of his English contemporaries and produced a large output of orchestral and large-scale choral works, influenced by early Wagner, a taste for the exotic, and Hebridean folksong. Though much performed at the beginning of the century, when he was at his most productive and a prominent figure in the English musical renaissance, his music has all but disappeared from the repertory; the oratorio *Omar Khayyám* (1906–9), the overture *The Pierrot of the Minute* (1908), the *Hebridean Symphony* (1915) and the *Pagan Symphony* (1928) have been admired for their undemanding lyricism.

Bar. A vertical line (often called bar-line) drawn through the staff to mark off metrical units; hence also the units so marked off. In American usage, the term 'measure' is usually preferred to 'bar'. Bar-lines are found occasionally in early polyphonic music, but first appear regularly in tablature for the keyboard or lute. They appear in solo parts and partbooks from the beginning of the 17th century, but bar-lines in early sources do not always immediately precede the main accented beat, as they do in later music.

Baranović, Krešimir (*b* Sibenik, 25 July 1894; *d* Belgrade, 17 Sept 1975). Yugoslav composer. He studied in Zagreb and Vienna, conducted the Zagreb Opera (1915–43) and the Belgrade PO (1952–61) and taught at the Belgrade Academy (1946–61). His colourful music, which uses Croatian folksong, includes the ballet *Gingerbread Heart* (1924).

Barbaia, Domenico (*b* Milan, ?1778; *d* Posilipo, 19 Oct 1841). Italian impresario. The most famous impresario of his day, he managed all the Neapolitan royal opera houses, the Viennese Kärntnertortheater and Theater an der Wien, and La Scala, Milan. He inaugurated a new *opera seria* tradition in Naples, was among the first to recognize Rossini's genius and gave early opportunities to Pacini, Bellini and Donizetti.

Barbarino, Bartolomeo (*b* Fabriano; *d* ?Padua, ?1617). Italian composer. He served under various patrons before becoming a musician of the Bishop of Padua in 1605. An early monodist, he used Caccini's principles of vocal expressivity and ornamentation in both sacred and secular works, writing *c*120 monodies in all. Some monodies are given in both simple and ornamented form. In his 1617 collection of three-part madrigals (half of them monodies), the continuo part is printed in each book, perhaps implying the use of more than one instrument.

Barbella, Emanuele (*b* Naples, 14 April 1718; *d* there, 1 Jan 1777). Italian violinist and composer. He played in Naples at the Teatro Nuovo, the royal chapel and (from 1761) S Carlo; he wrote mostly violin sonatas, duos and trio sonatas, in Tartini's style, some with unusual titles and tempo markings.

Barber, Samuel (*b* West Chester, PA, 9 March 1910; *d* New York, 23 Jan 1981). American composer. He studied as a baritone and composer (with Scalero) at the Curtis Institute (1924–32) and while there began to win acclaim with such works as *Dover Beach* (1931), written for himself to sing with string quartet. His opulent yet unforced Romanticism

struck a chord and during the 1930s he was much in demand: his overture *The School for Scandal* (1933), First Symphony (1936), First Essay (1937) and Adagio (originally the second movement of his String Quartet, 1936) were widely performed, the lyrical, elegiac Adagio remaining a popular classic. In the 1940s he began to include more 'modern' features of harmony and scoring. Of his operas, *Vanessa* (1958), praised as 'highly charged with emotional meaning', was more successful than *Antony and Cleopatra* (1966, for the opening of the new Met).

Dramatic music 2 ballets – Medea (1946), Souvenirs (1953); 3 operas, incl. Vanessa (1958), Antony and Cleopatra (1966)
Orchestral music The School for Scandal, ov. (1933); Adagio, str [arr. from Str Qt, 2nd movt] (1936); 2 syms. (1936, 1944); 3 Essays (1937, 1942, 1978); Vn Conc. (1940); Vc Conc. (1945); Pf Conc. (1962)
Vocal music 7 choral works, incl. Prayers of Kierkegaard (1954); 12 solo vocal works, incl. Dover Beach, Mez/Bar, str qt (1931); Knoxville: Summer of 1915, S, orch (1947); Hermit Songs (1952–3)
Chamber and instrumental music 11 works, incl. Vn Sonata (1931); Vc Sonata (1932); Str Qt (1936); Pf Sonata (1949)

Barberiis, Melchiore de (*fl* Padua, *c*1545–50). Italian composer and lutenist. His five volumes of music for lute or guitar (1546, 1549) include ricercares, fantasias and canzonas, arrangements of vocal works by Févin and Josquin and dances loosely grouped in suites.

Barberini. Italian family of music patrons in the 17th century. A Barberini pope, Urban VIII (1623–44), fostered Roman church music; but their chief importance lies in the creation of Rome's first large opera house in their palace in Via Quattro Fontane, which greatly influenced the early development of opera. It was opened in 1631 or 1632 with Landi's *Sant' Alessio*.

Barber of Seville, The. *See* BARBIERE DI SIVIGLA, IL.

Barbershop quartet singing. A style of singing that originated in the USA in the late 19th century, as a pastime of male quartets and choruses. The melody is carried by the lead (second) tenor, another tenor harmonizes above, the bass provides the foundation and the baritone completes the harmony (characterized by close, parallel part-writing).

Barbican Arts and Conference Centre. The Barbican Concert Hall (cap. 2025) opened in London in 1981. The LSO has its home at the Centre, which since 1977 has also housed the Guildhall School of Music.

Barbiere di Siviglia, Il. Opera buffa in two acts by Rossini to a libretto by Sterbini after Beaumarchais (1816, Rome). At its first performance it was called *Almaviva, ossia L'inutile precauzione* to differentiate it from Paisiello's opera of the same name, in four acts, to a libretto by Petrosellini (1782, St Petersburg).

Barbieri, Fedora (*b* Trieste, 4 June 1920). Italian mezzo-soprano. She studied at Trieste and Florence, at La Scala from 1946 and from 1950 at the Met (début as Eboli). She later sang at Covent Garden. Her powerful voice and strong stage presence, admired in a repertory of over 100 roles, were particularly suited to Verdi.

Barbieri, Francisco Asenjo (*b* Madrid, 3 Aug 1823; *d* there, 17 Feb 1894). Spanish composer and musicologist. From 1850 he concentrated on the zarzuela, writing more than 60 and infusing them with Spanish folk music; a few, such as *Pan y toros* (1864), *El barberillo de Lavapiés* (1874) and *Jugar con fuego* (1851), are still among the most popular. He was also important as a bibliophile, assembling the richest music library in Spain and publishing transcriptions of 15th- and 16th-century Spanish manuscripts.

Barbier von Bagdad, Der. Opera in two acts by Peter Cornelius to his own libretto (1858, Weimar).

Barbirolli, Sir John (*b* London, 2 Dec 1899; *d* London, 29 July 1970). English conductor. After studying the cello at the TCM and the RAM he made his recital début in 1917. He formed and conducted a string orchestra and was guest conductor at Covent Garden, 1929–33, returning in 1937. That year he succeeded Toscanini as conductor of the New York PO. In 1943 he returned to England as conductor of the Hallé Orchestra whose standards he raised immeasurably. He never pursued an operatic career. English music was at the centre of his repertory and he gave first performances of works by Britten and Vaughan Williams. He married the oboist Evelyn Rothwell in 1939.

Barbiton [barbitos]. Greek instrument, a type of lyre with long arms above which the yoke is fixed. It was popular in the 6th and 5th centuries BC.

Barcarolle (Fr.). A piece in 6/8 time with a lilting rhythm suggesting the songs sung by Venetian gondoliers. Famous examples are Chopin's Barcarolle in F♯ op.60 (1845) and the barcarolle at the beginning of Act 3 of Offenbach's *Les contes d'Hoffmann*.

Bardi, Giovanni de' (*b* Florence, 5 Feb 1534; *d* Sept 1612). Italian patron. An aristocrat, he served the Medici court in Florence for many years, creating lavish *intermedi* for court entertainment. A group of noblemen and musicians, later known as the CAMERATA, met at his house to discuss poetry, music and the sciences. As host to these gatherings and patron of Vincenzo Galilei and Giulio Caccini he was crucial in the movement that led to the first experiments in dramatic monody. Poems, plays and a few compositions by him survive.

Bárdos, Lajos (*b* Budapest, 1 Oct 1899). Hungarian composer, conductor and musicologist. He studied with Kodály at the Budapest Academy, where he later taught (1928–67). Through his work as a choral conductor he raised standards to an international level and toured widely abroad with his choirs. His works consist mostly of choral music; he has written extensively on Liszt, Bartók and Kodály.

Barenboim, Daniel (*b* Buenos Aires, 15 Nov 1942). Israeli pianist and conductor. After study at Salzburg, Rome and Paris he made his English début in 1955 and his New York début, under Stokowski, in 1957. From 1964 he appeared as conductor and soloist with the English Chamber Orchestra. Further engagements as a conductor came with the Berlin PO (1969), the New York PO (1970), and the Orchestre de Paris (1975). He conducted opera at the Edinburgh Festival (1973) and Bayreuth (1982).

He has accompanied Fischer-Dieskau and Janet Baker in lieder recitals and joined Zukerman and Perlman in chamber music. He married the cellist Jacqueline du Pré in 1967.

Bärenreiter. German firm of music publishers. It was founded in 1923 in Augsburg by Karl Vötterle. Its early output included folksong and educational and musicological works, extending to organ and early choral music (Schütz); in 1927 the firm moved to Kassel and in 1929 Vötterle founded the periodical *Musik und Kirche*. He helped found the Gesellschaft für Musikforschung and its periodical, *Die Musikforschung*; the firm also published the encyclopedia *Die Musik in Geschichte und Gegenwart* (*MGG*; 17 vols., 1949–87). Among important publications since the 1950s are *Acta musicologica*, several *RISM* volumes and collected editions of Bach, Mozart, Berlioz, Schubert and Liszt. More recently, works by avant-garde composers have been issued.

Bar form. Term for the three-part form *AAB*, consisting of two *Stollen* (forming an *Aufgesang*) and an *Abgesang*. It is particularly associated with the Meistersinger tradition, largely through its (in-correct) use in Wagner's *Die Meistersinger*, but the form has been used in other repertories dating back to the classical Greek ode.

Bargiel, Woldemar (*b* Berlin, 3 Oct 1828; *d* there, 23 Feb 1897). German composer and teacher. He studied at the Leipzig Conservatory with Moscheles (piano), Hauptmann, Rietz and Gade. He taught at the Cologne Conservatory and Berlin Hochschule für Musik, composing in the manner of his brother-in-law Schumann.

Baring-Gould, Sabine (*b* Exeter, 28 Jan 1834; *d* Lew Trenchard, 2 Jan 1924). English clergyman and folksong collector. He was a pioneer in the collection of English folksong and author of well-known hymns including *Onward, Christian Soldiers* (1865).

Bariolage (Fr.: 'odd mixture of colours'). A term used of various allied effects in playing bowed string instruments; generally it refers to a special effect in which the same note is played alternately on two strings, one stopped and one open.

Baritone. (1) A male voice of moderately low pitch, in the range *A–f'*. The term comes from the Greek, meaning 'deep-sounding'. It was first used ('baritonans') in the late 15th century but in its modern sense only from the 17th. The voice became important in opera in the late 18th century, particularly in Mozart's works (Don Giovanni, the Count in *Figaro*), though at this period the word 'baritone' was little used and 'bass' served for both voices. Verdi used it for a great variety of roles from the secondary heroic (Posa, *Don Carlos*), the comic (Falstaff) and the compassionate (Germont, *La traviata*) to the oppressed and suffering (Rigoletto) and the downright villainous (Iago, *Otello*). Other important baritone roles include Escamillo (*Carmen*) and Scarpia (*Tosca*); of Wagner roles, Wolfram (*Tannhäuser*) is a true baritone but Wotan and Sachs are closer to bass-baritone. Great exponents of the voice include the lied singer Julius Stockhausen, Victor Maurel, Verdi's original Iago and Falstaff, Tito Gobbi and Dietrich Fischer-Dieskau, a singer both of opera and lieder.

The term is also used adjectivally for an instrument of medium-low pitch, for example the baritone oboe and the baritone saxophone.

The baritone clef, either a C clef on the top line of the staff or an F clef on the middle line, is now little used.

(2) A valved brass instrument in B♭, pitched as the trombone (also known as the tenor SAXHORN). In Britain it has a narrower bore than the similarly pitched euphonium and is used in brass bands to fill the harmony rather than as a solo instrument; the compass sounds from *E* to *bb′*. In American band music, no regular musical distinction is made between two B♭ instruments of contrasting bore and timbre; 'bariton' is the normal term for the valved instrument of this pitch. In Germany, 'Bariton' signifies a larger-bore instrument, 'Tenorhorn' a smaller.

Baritone oboe. The deepest voice of the modern orchestral OBOE group, pitched an octave below the soprano or 'standard' instrument. It is now often replaced by the heckelphone.

Baritone saxophone. A SAXOPHONE in E♭, sounding an octave and a major 6th lower than written.

Barkin, Elaine (Radoff) (*b* Bronx, NY, 15 Dec 1932). American composer. She studied at Queens College, New York, at Brandeis and with Blacher in Berlin (1956–7), and has taught at Queens (1964–70), the University of Michigan (1970–74) and UCLA (1974–). Her works are serial and include chamber and mixed-media pieces; she has written extensively on 20th-century music.

Bar-line. A vertical line drawn through the staff to mark off metrical units; *see* BAR.

Barlow, David (Frederick) (*b* Rothwell, 20 May 1927; *d* Newcastle upon Tyne, 9 June 1975). English composer and teacher. He studied at Cambridge, with Jacob at the RCM and Boulanger, and lectured at Newcastle University. He began as an English Romantic (Second Symphony, 1959) but turned to lyrical serialism, his works including church operas and the String Quartet (1969).

Barlow, Fred (*b* Mulhouse, 2 Oct 1881; *d* Boulogne, 3 Jan 1951). French composer of English origin. He studied with Koechlin in Paris, and produced a small but varied output (operetta, ballets, songs, chamber music) of fastidious workmanship. In 1926 he became a Quaker, which had some influence on his music.

Barlow, Samuel L.M. (*b* New York, 1 June 1892; *d* Wyndmoor, PA, 19 Sept 1982). American composer and pianist. He studied at Harvard, in New York, in Paris and in Rome (with Respighi, 1923). His works, in a conservative style, include the opera *Mon ami Pierrot* (1935), the first by an American to be produced at the Opéra-Comique in Paris, and a piano concerto (1931).

Barlow, Wayne (Brewster) (*b* Elyria, OH, 6 Sept 1912). American composer and teacher. He studied with Hanson at the Eastman School, where he later taught (from 1937) and directed the electronic music studio, 1968–78. His works, in a free 12-tone style, include a Saxophone Concerto (1970), *Soundscapes* for orchestra and tape (1972), two ballets, chamber and organ music.

Barnard, John (*b* ?1591; *fl c* 1641). English music editor. He may have been a lay clerk at Canterbury Cathedral and was a minor canon of St Paul's Cathedral, London. His *First Book of Selected Church Musick* (1641), comprising ten vocal partbooks, is a valuable printed source of liturgical music by late 16th- and early 17th-century composers.

Barnby, Sir Joseph (*b* York, 12 Aug 1838; *d* London, 28 Jan 1896). English conductor and composer. He was indefatigable on behalf of choral music in England, first through developing lavish Anglican choral services at St Anne's, Soho, and subsequently through founding a choir (1867) which performed little-known choral masterpieces of Handel, Bach and Beethoven and new works by Gounod and Dvořák. His own music, influenced by Gounod and very popular in its day, includes numerous cathedral services, anthems, chants and hymn tunes.

Barn dance. A type of dance, originating in America and popular in Britain in the late 19th century and early 20th, derived from the SCHOTTISCHE.

Barnekow, Christian (*b* St Sauveur, 28 July 1837; *d* Frederiksberg, 20 March 1913). Danish composer. He studied in Copenhagen, where he played a leading role in the administration of several musical institutions. His choral and vocal music, chamber music and piano works are in the style of Hartmann and Gade.

Barnett, John (*b* Bedford, 15 July 1802; *d* Leckhampton, 16/17 April 1890). English composer. He studied the piano and composition, producing early piano sonatas, songs, masses and a grand scena and much light incidental music. His most important work, *The Mountain Sylph*, was produced for S.J. Arnold's new English Opera House in 1834. It replaced the customary spoken dialogue with recitative (thus being one of the first through-composed English operas), used fresh musical forms and, recalling Weber's music, succeeded in creating strong emotion and real dramatic tension; it had a long initial run and held the stage for the rest of the century. He wrote two further serious operas for Drury Lane but none of his later stage works repeated this success. He also wrote distinctive songs and an inventive string quartet. Quarrels with managers, failed attempts to establish a permanent English opera and a generally irascible disposition finally led to Barnett's withdrawal from the London stage in 1841, when he became a singing teacher in Cheltenham.

Barnett, John Francis (*b* London, 16 Oct 1837; *d* there, 24 Nov 1916). English composer, nephew of John Barnett. He became known as a piano teacher, popular composer of cantatas and oratorios (from *The Ancient Mariner*, 1867, to *The Eve of St Agnes*, 1913) and a conductor. He also produced several Mendelssohnian orchestral works and descriptive piano pieces and completed Schubert's Symphony in E from sketches (1883).

Baron, Ernst Gottlieb (*b* Breslau, 17 Feb 1696; *d* Berlin, 12 April 1760). German lutenist and composer. He worked at German centres including Jena (1720–22), finally joining the musical ensemble of Crown Prince (later King) Frederick of Prussia in

1737. He wrote a treatise on lutenists and lute playing (1727) and various lute pieces including suites and two concertos.

Baroque. Term used to designate the period or style of European music covering roughly the years 1600–1750. First used in French, it derives from a Portuguese word meaning a pearl of irregular shape; initially it was used to imply strangeness, irregularity and extravagance and was applied more to art than music. Only in the present century has it been used to refer to a period in music history.

Music of the Baroque period, which some authorities see as beginning as early as 1570 in Italy and ending during the second half of the 18th century, in such countries as England and Spain, has a number of characteristics in style and spirit, including the use of the basso continuo and the belief in the doctrine of the affections. The emphasis on contrast (of texture, pace, volume etc) in the music of the earlier Baroque, as compared with that of the late Renaissance, is also a distinguishing characteristic. Important early Baroque composers include Monteverdi, Giovanni Gabrieli and Schütz; of the middle Baroque, Alessandro Scarlatti, Corelli, Lully and Purcell; and of the late Baroque, Bach, Handel, Vivaldi, Domenico Scarlatti, Couperin and Rameau.

Barraqué, Jean (*b* Puteaux, 17 Jan 1928; *d* Paris, 17 Aug 1973). French composer. He studied at the Paris Conservatoire with Langlais and Messiaen (1948–51) and began his first two published works: the Piano Sonata (1952) and *Séquence* for soprano, piano and ensemble (1955), a monodrama after Nietzsche. The sonata lasts *c*40 minutes, in two roughly equal parts, the first with episodes solidly articulated, contrasted, polyphonic and generally fast, the second more discontinuous, stripped down and slow. 'Strict' and 'free' styles are contrasted in an aesthetic of violence and despair. In 1955 he encountered the French translation of Broch's *Death of Virgil*, to which his few later works – ... *au delà du hasard* for ensembles of voices and instruments (1959), *Chant après chant* for soprano, piano and percussion (1966), *Le temps restitué* for soprano, chorus and orchestra (1968) and the Concerto for clarinet, vibraphone and six trios (1968) – all relate as commentaries. He was opposed to musical developments which he saw as increasingly undisciplined; yet dissolution and catastrophe are central to his art.

Barraud, Henry (*b* Bordeaux, 23 April 1900). French composer. He studied with Dukas at the Paris Conservatoire and was head of music for Radiodiffusion Française (1945–65). His works, in most genres, are diverse, some elegant, others tackling profound religious experience.

Barré (Fr.). 'Barred': term for the technique in playing certain fretted plucked string instruments (e.g. guitar, lute, banjo) of stopping all or several of the strings at the same point by holding a finger (like a bar) across them.

Barrelhouse. A style of piano blues, dating from the early 20th century, which is a simple form of boogie-woogie, in regular 4/4 metre rather than with eight beats to the bar. The term, also used to mean 'crude' or 'rough', has been incorporated into the titles of tunes associated with the style.

Barrel organ. A mechanical organ in which a cylinder with protruding pins slowly revolves; the pins raise keys which operate a mechanism that allows wind to enter the required pipes. The wind is provided by bellows pumped by the same rotary motion of a handle that turns the barrel. Barrel organs were popular in English churches *c*1760–1840. The instrument is often confused with the barrel piano.

Barrel piano. A mechanical piano played by a pinned barrel or cylinder turned by a hand crank. It is also called 'street piano', 'cylinder piano' or, often, 'barrel organ', and is attributed to Joseph Hicks of Bristol who produced many between 1805 and 1850.

Barrière, Jean (*b* ?Bordeaux, *c*1705; *d* there, 6 June 1747). French composer and cellist. One of the finest cello virtuosos of his time, he wrote several sets of cello sonatas in an idiomatic style; those published after his Italian journey (1736–9) include italianate suite movements.

Barry, Gerald (b Clarecastle, 28 April 1952). Irish composer. He studied with Schat, Kagel and Stockhausen. His first large score was the ballet *Unkrautgarten* (1980), on which he drew for other theatre works; an opera *The Intelligence Park* was completed in 1987. He taught at University College, Cork, 1982–6. His music, harmonic rather than contrapuntal, is clear-textured and notable for vigorous orchestral writing and strong drama.

Barsanti, Francesco (*b* Lucca, 1690; *d* London, late 1772). Italian composer. He settled in London in 1714 as an orchestral player and returned after spending 1735–43 in Edinburgh. He wrote flute and recorder sonatas, overtures, antiphons and ten concerti grossi with attractively varied scoring.

Barshay, Rudolf (Borisovich) (*b* Labinskaya, 28 Sept 1924). Russian viola player and conductor. He studied at the Moscow Conservatory. In 1956 he founded the Moscow CO, which first appeared in Britain in 1962; it was admired for unity of phrasing and sweet tone. He emigrated to Israel in 1976 and became director of the Israel CO. An association with the Bournemouth SO began in 1982.

Barstow, Josephine (Claire) (*b* Sheffield, 27 Sept 1940). English soprano. She studied in Birmingham and at the London Opera Centre and joined Sadler's Wells Opera in 1967. She also sang with Welsh National Opera and from 1969 at Covent Garden. Her roles have included Mozart's Countess, Janáček's Jenůfa, Denise in Tippett's *Knot Garden* (which she created, 1970), Natasha (*War and Peace*), Violetta, Lady Macbeth and Salome. She has a vibrant, expressive, flexible soprano and is an actress of unusual intensity.

Bartay, András (*b* Széplak, 7 April 1799; *d* Mainz, 4 Oct 1854). Hungarian composer and folksong collector. One of the first to publish Hungarian folksongs, he was also director of the Hungarian National Theatre (1843–4) and composed operas, oratorios, songs and piano pieces. His son Ede (1825–1901) published important collections of Hungarian folkdances.

Bartei, Girolamo (*b* Arezzo, *c*1565; *d* ?1618). Italian composer and organist. A member of the Augustinian order he had an unsettled career which included appointments at monasteries in Rome and Orvieto. He was one of the best, most adaptable Augustinian musicians, his large output including sacred, secular and instrumental works ranging in style from rich and complex polyphony to monodies, such as the dramatic dialogue *Ave gratia plena* (1618) for soprano, tenor and continuo. His two-part ricercares (1618) are notable for their free and sinuous movement.

Bartered Bride, The [Prodana nevěsta]. Opera in three acts by Smetana to a libretto by Karel Sabina (1870, Prague); the original version (1866) was in two acts with spoken dialogue.

Barthélemon, François-Hippolyte (*b* Bordeaux, 27 July 1741; *d* London, 20 July 1808). French composer. After working in Paris he moved to London in 1764, and became a leading figure in musical life there, appearing as composer and soloist (on the violin and viola d'amore) in concerts and at the theatres and pleasure gardens, often with his wife, the singer Polly Young. He wrote and contributed to some 40 stage works, 1766–88, including the burletta *Orpheus* (1766), his first success, and later a series of ballets. He was a friend of Haydn's and may have suggested the subject of *The Creation*. His works, in style akin to J.C. Bach's, include sonatas, symphonies, violin concertos and songs.

Bartholomée, Pierre (*b* Brussels, 5 Aug 1937). Belgian composer and conductor. He studied at the Brussels Conservatory (1953–8). He was decisively influenced by meeting Pousseur in 1961 and since then he has worked towards new means of harmonic integration, sometimes with unconventional tunings, for example in *Tombeau de Marin Marais* (1967) which also reflects his Baroque interests.

Bartlet, John (*fl* 1606–10). English composer. He took the Oxford BMus in 1610 and is known as a composer of *A Book of Ayres* for one, two or four voices with lute or orpharion and bass viol.

Bartók, Béla (*b* Sînnicolau Mare, 25 March 1881; *d* New York, 26 Sept 1945). Hungarian composer. He began lessons with his mother, who brought up the family after his father's death in 1888. In 1894 they settled in Bratislava, where he attended the Gymnasium (Dohnányi was an elder schoolfellow), studied the piano with László Erkel and Anton Hyrtl, and composed sonatas and quartets. In 1898 he was accepted by the Vienna Conservatory, but following Dohnányi he went to the Budapest Academy (1899–1903), where he studied the piano with Liszt's pupil Istvan Thoman and composition with Janos Koessler. There he deepened his acquaintance with Wagner, though it was the music of Strauss, which he met at the Budapest première of *Also sprach Zarathustra* in 1902, that had most influence. He wrote a symphonic poem, *Kossuth* (1903), using Strauss's methods with Hungarian elements in Liszt's manner.

In 1904 *Kossuth* was performed in Budapest and Manchester; at the same time Bartók began to make a career as a pianist, writing a Piano Quintet and two Lisztian virtuoso showpieces (Rhapsody op.1,

Scherzo op.2). Also in 1904 he made his first Hungarian folksong transcription. In 1905 he collected more songs and began his collaboration with Kodály: their first arrangements were published in 1906. The next year he was appointed Thoman's successor at the Budapest Academy, which enabled him to settle in Hungary and continue his folksong collecting, notably in Transylvania. Meanwhile his music was beginning to be influenced by this activity and by the music of Debussy that Kodály had brought back from Paris: both opened the way to new, modal kinds of harmony and irregular metre. The 1908 Violin Concerto is still within the symphonic tradition, but the many small piano pieces of this period show a new, authentically Hungarian Bartók emerging, with the 4ths of Magyar folksong, the rhythms of peasant dance and the scales he had discovered among Hungarian, Romanian and Slovak peoples. The arrival of this new voice is documented in his String Quartet no.1 (1908), introduced at a Budapest concert of his music in 1910.

There followed orchestral pieces and a one-act opera, *Bluebeard's Castle*, dedicated to his young wife. Influenced by Musorgsky and Debussy but most directly by Hungarian peasant music (and Strauss, still, in its orchestral pictures), the work, a grim fable of human isolation, failed to win the competition in which it was entered. For two years (1912–14) Bartók practically gave up composition and devoted himself to the collection, arrangement and study of folk music, until World War I put an end to his expeditions. He returned to creative activity with the String Quartet no.2 (1917) and the fairytale ballet *The Wooden Prince*, whose production in Budapest in 1917 restored him to public favour. The next year *Bluebeard's Castle* was staged and he began a second ballet, *The Miraculous Mandarin*, which was not performed until 1926 (there were problems over the subject, the thwarting and consummation of sexual passion). Rich and graphic in invention, the score is practically an opera without words.

While composing *The Mandarin* Bartók came under the influence of Stravinsky and Schoenberg, and produced some of his most complex music in the two violin sonatas of 1921–2. At the same time he was gaining international esteem: his works were published by Universal Edition and he was invited to play them all over Europe. He was now well established, too, at home. He wrote the confident Dance Suite (1923) for a concert marking the 50th anniversary of Budapest, though there was then another lull in his composing activity until the sudden rush of works in 1926 designed for himself to play, including the Piano Concerto no.1, the Piano Sonata and the suite *Out of Doors*. These exploit the piano as a percussion instrument, using its resonances as well as its xylophonic hardness. The search for new sonorities and driving rhythms was continued in the next two string quartets (1927–8), of which no.4, like the concerto, is in a five-section palindromic pattern (*ABCBA*).

Similar formal schemes, with intensively worked counterpoint, were used in the Piano Concerto no.2 (1931) and String Quartet no.5 (1934), though now Bartók's harmony was becoming more diatonic. The move from inward chromaticism to a glowing major (though modally tinged) tonality is basic to the Music for Strings, Percussion and Celesta (1936) and the Sonata for Two Pianos and Percussion (1937), both written for performance in Switzerland at a time when the political situation in Hungary was growing unsympathetic.

In 1940 Bartók and his second wife (he had divorced and remarried in 1923) sadly left war-torn Europe to live in New York, which he found alien. They gave concerts and for a while he had a research grant to work on a collection of Yugoslav folksong, but their finances were precarious, as increasingly was his health. It seemed that his last European work, the String Quartet no.6 (1939), might be his pessimistic swansong, but then came the exuberant Concerto for Orchestra (1943) and the involuted Sonata for solo violin (1944). Piano Concerto no.3, written to provide his widow with an income, was almost finished when he died, a Viola Concerto left in sketch.

Opera Bluebeard's Castle (1918)
Ballets The Wooden Prince (1917); The Miraculous Mandarin (1926)
Orchestral music Kossuth (1903); 2 suites (1905, 1907); 2 Pictures (1910); 2 Portraits (1911); 4 Pieces (1921); Dance Suite (1923); Music for Strings, Percussion and Celesta (1936); Divertimento, strs (1939); Conc. for Orch (1943); 2 vn concs. (1908, 1938); 3 pf concs. (1926, 1931, 1945); Conc. for 2 Pf (1940)
Choral music Cantata profana (1930); other pieces and folksong arrs.
Chamber music 6 str qts (1908, 1917, 1927, 1928, 1934, 1939); 2 vn sonatas (1921–2); 2 rhapsodies, vn, pf (1928); 44 duos, 2 vn (1931); Sonata for 2 pf, perc (1937); Contrasts, vn, cl, pf (1938); Sonata, solo vn (1944)
Piano music Allegro barbaro (1911); Suite (1916); Sonata (1926); Out of Doors (1926); Mikrokosmos, 6 bks (1926–39); many other pieces
Songs 5 op.15 and 5 op.16 (1916); folksong arrs.

Bartolino da Padova (*fl* Padua and ?Florence, *c*1365–1405). Italian composer. He was contemporary with Landini and may have been a brother at the Carmelite monastery in Padua and a servant of the Carrara family; he may also have worked in Florence, 1388–90. Most of his 27 ballate and 11 madrigals show Jacopo da Bologna's influence, but some of the three-part works are more French in style with the contratenor and tenor providing a supporting duet for the upper voice.

Bartolomeo da Bologna (*fl* *c*1410–25). Italian composer. He may have been the Prior of S Nicolò, Ferrara, and cathedral organist there. His Latin ballade and a rondeau and virelai with Italian texts exploit complex rhythms but his two ballate are simpler. His two mass movements are parodies of his own ballate.

Bartolomeo degli Organi [Baccio Fiorentino] (*b* Florence, 24 Dec 1474; *d* there, 12 Dec 1539). Italian composer, organist and singer. Having been a singer at the Ss Annunziata, Florence, and in the baptistry's chapel, he served Lorenzo de' Medici, Duke of Urbino, and was organist at Florentine churches, becoming principal organist of the cathedral in 1509. His extant compositions include ten Italian secular works (mainly ballatas), a *lauda* and four instrumental pieces.

Bartolozzi, Bruno (*b* Florence, 8 June 1911; *d* Fiesole, 12 Dec 1980). Italian composer and theorist. He studied and taught at the Florence Conservatory and was a violinist. He is best known for his work on chords and unconventional sounds produced by wind instruments, on which he wrote an influential book (1967).

Bartoš, František (*b* Brněnec, 13 June 1905; *d* Prague, 21 May 1973). Czech composer and writer. He studied with Foerster at the Prague Conservatory but was more influenced by French neoclassicism. His output is modest; after 1945 he concentrated on musicology.

He should not be confused with František Bartoš (1837–1906), an important collector of Moravian folksong.

Bartoš, Jan Zdeněk (*b* Dvur Kralove nad Labem, 4 June 1908; *d* Prague, 1 June 1981). Czech composer and violinist. After graduating from the Prague Conservatory, to which he returned to teach in 1958, he played the violin in ensembles. His music is indebted to the nationalist traditions of Dvořák and Suk and includes operas, ballets and six symphonies (1949–78).

Barvynsky, Vasyl' Oleksandrovich (*b* Tarnopol', 20 Feb 1888; *d* L'vov, 9 June 1963). Ukrainian composer, pianist, musicologist and teacher. He studied in L'vov and Prague, and directed the Lisenko Music Institute in L'vov (from 1915), having a great influence through his works and teaching on the development of Ukrainian music, particularly chamber music.

Baryphonus, Henricus (*b* Wernigerode, 17 Sept 1581; *d* Quedlinburg, 13 Jan 1655). German theorist and composer. From 1605 he was Kantor of St Benedicti, Quedlinburg. His influential treatise *Pleiades musicae* (1615, expanded 1630) is the sole survivor of 17. He was one of the first to organize compositional theory on a harmonic rather than contrapuntal basis, and established an influential doctrine of intervals and their progression. Almost all his compositions are lost.

Baryton. A bass string instrument that is simultaneously bowed from above and plucked from behind. The few extant examples date from 1647 to 1799 and vary in size, decoration and number and disposition of strings. Most have six upper strings, tuned as a bass viol (*D–G–c–e–a–d'*), and ten to 15 underlying strings. The most noted composer for the baryton, which was particularly cultivated in Austria, was Haydn.

Bas-dessus (Fr.). 'Low treble': a second treble part; *see* DESSUS.

Basevi, Abramo (*b* Livorno, 29 Nov 1818; *d* Florence, 25 Nov 1885). Italian music critic. A prominent figure in Florentine cultural life, he founded two music journals and organized several concert series. He sought to reform Italian musical life by introducing classic Italian works and music in the German instrumental tradition. He was an early supporter of Wagner and a perceptive Verdi critic.

Basically Bach Festival. *See* MUSICA SACRA.

Basie, Count [William] (*b* Red Bank, NJ, 21 Aug

1904; *d* Hollywood, 26 April 1984). American jazz bandleader and pianist. His early career was in vaudeville after a brief stay in New York and informal lessons with Fats Waller. In the late 1920s he worked with the bands of Walter Page and Bennie Moten in Kansas City. After Moten's death (1935) Basie formed his own Barons of Rhythm, to become the Count Basie Orchestra by 1937. It was a leading band of the swing era and, apart from a brief interruption in the early 1950s, Basie led it until his death. It included many important jazz soloists, notably Lester Young (tenor saxophone) and Buck Clayton (trumpet), and was innovatory in using the rhythm section as a backdrop to the interplay of brass and reeds and as a foundation for soloists. Basie's early (and most influential) recordings include *One O'clock Jump* (1937) and *Jumpin' at the Woodside* (1938).

Basile, Andreana (*b* Posillipo, *c*1580; *d* Rome, *c*1640). Italian singer. Winning early fame as a contralto and performer on the *lira*, harp and guitar, she moved in 1610 to the service of the Mantuan court where she remained, though travelling extensively, until 1624. She was declared the finest singer of her time by Monteverdi, won honours from the Gonzagas, and was the dedicatee of an anthology by leading poets. Her later years were spent in Naples and Rome. Her daughter Leonora Baroni was a singer, and her brother Lelio (*c*1580–after 1623) composed a collection of madrigals.

Basili, Francesco (*b* Loreto, 31 Jan 1767; *d* Rome, 25 March 1850). Italian composer and conductor. He studied in Rome. While working as a conductor at Foligno, Macerata and Loreto, he produced 13 operas, notably *Gl' Illinesi* (1819); he became director of the Milan Conservatory (1827) and *maestro di cappella* of St Peter's, Rome (1837). With a style similar to Spontini's, he was best known for his church music.

Basiron, Philippe (*b* early 15th century; *d* before 6 Feb 1497). ?French composer. His extant works include three motets and five *chansons*. He may be the 'Philippon' to whom two mass cycles and three more chansons are attributed; a further mass (*Missa de Franza*) is assigned to Basiron in two sources but to Philippon in a third.

Basle Chamber Orchestra. Swiss chamber orchestra founded in 1926 by Paul Sacher to perform pre-Classical and modern works; it has given many first performances and commissioned works from Bartók, Britten, Stravinsky and Tippett.

Bass. The low part of the musical system. In a composition, it refers to the part standing lowest in any sonority, which in music since *c*1500 has played an important role in the sequence of harmonies. It applies to the bottom note of a chord, the lowest part in a polyphonic texture, the bottom register and the lowest male voice. The term – like the word 'base' – comes from the Latin *bassus* ('low', 'thick'), and first appeared in music *c*1450, when the lower contratenor part in four-part texture came to be called 'contratenor bassus'. In Baroque music, the existence of the basso continuo or thoroughbass (*see* CONTINUO) showed the importance of the bass part in governing the harmony.

The bass voice has a normal range of *F–e'*; it found a regular place in polyphony in the 15th and 16th centuries. In early opera it was used mainly for gods or mysterious figures, though later also for elderly fathers, generals and sometimes kings. In the 18th century the bass voice was much used for arias expressing rage, but by the mid-century the *basso buffo* (comic bass) was becoming popular; there are many examples in the operas of Pergolesi, Mozart and Rossini. In the 19th century the bass voice tended to be used for villains (Mephistopheles, Alberich) and figures of authority, such as Verdi's King Philip II and Grand Inquisitor (*Don Carlos*), Wagner's King Mark and Boris Godunov. These call for voices of the *basse-noble* and *basso profondo* type, particularly associated with Russian music. Another type, used in the earlier 19th century, is the *basso cantante* or *basse-chantante*, calling for a rather lighter voice.

The term 'bass' is sometimes used to signify any bass instrument, but particularly the double bass (in orchestral or jazz contexts) or the bass tuba (in band contexts). It is used to qualify other instrument names, to signify the lowest (or sometimes one from lowest) of a family of instruments. Examples are the bass flute (an instrument in C, an octave below the normal flute); the term is sometimes incorrectly applied to the alto flute in G); the bass clarinet, normally in B♭, an octave below the soprano; the bass saxophone, in B♭, an octave below the tenor; the bass trumpet, an octave below the normal trumpet; and the bass trombone, in G or F, a minor 3rd or a 4th below the tenor trombone. Bass tuba is simply another term for the tuba, already a bass instrument. The bass viol or viola da gamba is the normal bass instrument of the viol family. The term 'bass violin' has been used for the *basse de violon*, an instrument of *c*1700 tuned a whole tone below the cello; it has also been applied to the cello itself.

The bass clef, used by most instruments of bass and baritone pitch, shows the F below middle C on the second staff line from the top.

Bassadanza. *See* BASSE DANSE.

Bassani, Giovanni Battista (*b* Padua, *c*1657; *d* Bergamo, 1 Oct 1716). Italian composer, violinist and organist. He held appointments, chiefly at Ferrara and Bergamo, where he was *maestro di cappella* from 1686. His church music forms an interesting link between Monteverdi's and that of later composers such as Vivaldi, Durante and Pergolesi. Bassani's fame rests on his trio sonatas for strings, but he was a prolific composer in most genres, writing nine operas and 15 oratorios. His sacred and secular cantatas are noteworthy, and in his masses and psalm settings he was an important exponent of the concertato style.

Bassano, Giovanni (*b c*1558; *d* Venice, ?summer 1617). Italian cornett player and composer. As a member (and later head) of the instrumental ensemble at St Mark's, Venice, and singing teacher at its seminary, he was among the most respected virtuosos. His instruction books, notably on ornamentation, influenced Venetian composers (e.g. G. Gabrieli). His works include canzonettas and excellent motets for multiple choirs.

Bassarids, The. Opera with intermezzo by Henze to a libretto by Auden and Kallman after Euripides (1966, Salzburg).

Bass-bar. In bowed string instruments, a strip of wood glued under the belly to help sustain the downward pressure exerted by the tension of the strings on the bridge.

Bass-baritone. A male voice intermediate in compass between the baritone and the bass, of range approximately $Ab-f'$. Notable bass-baritone roles are those of Wotan in Wagner's *Ring* and Sachs in *Die Meistersinger*.

Bass clarinet. A CLARINET pitched in B♭, an octave below the soprano clarinet (for illustration, *see* WOODWIND INSTRUMENTS). Its range usually extends to E♭ on French and English instruments, and D on German ones. Early extant examples date from 1793 and were probably first intended to replace the bassoon in military bands. Meyerbeer scored for it orchestrally in 1836, and it was used from the later 19th century by such composers as Mahler, Wagner, Schoenberg and Stravinsky.

Bass drum. The largest orchestral drum of indeterminate pitch; it consists of a wooden cylindrical shell with two heads (hide or plastic) lapped on to hoops placed over the open ends and secured by counterhoops. It is normally struck with a large felt-headed stick between centre and rim. (For illustration, *see* PERCUSSION INSTRUMENTS).

Basse-chantante (Fr.). 'Singing bass': a bass singer with a particularly high or light voice; in the Baroque era a vocal bass as distinct from an instrumental bass or basso continuo.

Basse danse (Fr.; It. *bassadanza*). A graceful court dance of the 15th and 16th centuries, lacking the rapid steps and leaps of the 'alta danza' or 'saltarello'. The music was usually improvised over a *cantus firmus*.

Basse de musette. Name for an obsolete oboe, probably of Swiss 18th-century origin.

Basse de violon. A bass member of the violin family. It was tuned $Bb-F-c-g$ and was widely used in the later 17th century, notably in the French opera orchestra.

Basse fondamentale (Fr.). 'Fundamental bass': term used by Rameau for the bass line that would be produced by linking the roots of chords in a progression.

Basse-taille (Fr.). 'Low tenor': a Baroque term for the baritone voice.

Basset clarinet. Modern term for a soprano clarinet with a range extended downwards to written c, in the manner of the basset-horn. Several of Mozart's clarinet parts were for the basset instrument.

Basset-horn. Woodwind instrument, a member of the clarinet family, normally pitched in F but occasionally in G. Its compass extended downwards to written c (sounding F), a major 3rd below the lowest note of the conventional clarinet. Mozart used the basset-horn, particularly in masonic pieces. Some early basset-horns are sickle-shaped, others are sharply angled. The tone is apt to be rather thin and watery.

Basse-trompette. As distinct from *trompette basse* (bass trumpet), a type of upright SERPENT patented in 1810.

Bassett [basset]. Diminutive of BASS. In a passage or composition lacking a bass part, the lowest part, which executes the musical bass in a higher register. 'Bassetl' (diminutive of 'double bass') was the common term for cello in Austria and south Germany during the 18th century. 'Bassett' also specifies instruments in the baritone, tenor or alto range, (e.g. the basset-horn and basset clarinet). It is also an organ stop with flue pipes.

Bassett, Leslie (*b* Hansford, CA, 22 Jan 1923). American composer and teacher. He studied at the University of Michigan with Finney, whose influence is felt in his output, mostly of chamber and sacred choral music. In 1952 he returned to his alma mater as teacher, becoming head of the composition department in 1970. His Variations for Orchestra (1963) won a Pulitzer Prize.

Bass flute. A FLUTE in C, an octave below the concert flute; the term is occasionally used to denote the ALTO FLUTE in G.

Bass guitar. A large ELECTRIC GUITAR, usually with four heavy strings, invented in 1951. *See* GUITAR.

Bass-horn. A variety of upright serpent invented in the 1790s.

Bassi, Luigi (*b* Pesaro, 5 Sept 1766; *d* Dresden, 13 Sept 1825). Italian baritone. He sang in the Prague première of Mozart's *Le nozze di Figaro* and created the title role in *Don Giovanni* (1787). From 1815 he was producer with the Italian company in Dresden.

Bass oboe. A term for BARITONE OBOE, but sometimes used for a larger instrument in F, a 5th lower than the baritone OBOE.

Basso cantante (It.). 'Singing bass': a bass singer with a rather light and high voice.

Basso continuo. *See* CONTINUO.

Bassoon. A wooden conical wind instrument sounded with a double reed; in the orchestra, the tenor and bass to the woodwind (for illustration, *see* WOODWIND INSTRUMENTS). Formerly in a family of up to five different sizes, it survives in two: the bassoon and the double bassoon or contrabassoon, sounding one octave lower. The tenoroon, or tenor bassoon, pitched a 5th higher, is obsolete. Because of its wide compass and its range of characteristic tone-colours, from richly sonorous at the bottom to expressively plaintive at the top, it is one of the most versatile and useful members of the orchestra. A feature of its design is the doubling back on itself of the bore; the combination of wall thickness and bore conformation gives it its essential tone qualities. The standard compass of the present-day bassoon is from Bb' to e''. It is a non-transposing instrument, notated in the bass and tenor clefs. It is made up of four joints; the reed slides on to a metal tube or crook (usually S-shaped) which is inserted into the first. There are two standard fingering systems, and associated playing styles: the French, typified by Buffet's instruments, and the German, typified by Heckel's; the latter, smoother in tone and easier to control, has tended to oust the French.

The bassoon's early history is obscure. Its main predecessor is the dulcian, made in one piece and also known as the curtall. The French term 'fagot' ('bundle of sticks') was used by Afranio *c*1520 for his 'phagotus', the first instrument with a double-back tube; this provided the instrument's German and Italian names (*Fagott, fagotto*). The bassoon in joints appeared in early 17th-century France. By the late 17th, three-key bassoons going down to B♭' existed; further keys were added in the 18th, and changes early in the 19th made the upper register more accessible. Almenraeder, 'the Boehm of the bassoon', added some keys and adjusted others, and moved and enlarged tone holes, to improve intonation, evenness and fingering. He and Heckel opened a factory in 1831.

While the earliest use of the instrument was to strengthen the bass, it began in the early 17th century to assume a more independent role, particularly in compositions of Schütz and Bertoli. In Lully's operas it was used as bass to a wind trio; Vivaldi wrote 39 concertos for the instrument. Other 18th-century composers to use it in a solo capacity include Telemann, J.S. Bach, Boyce, Boismortier and J.C. Bach. Mozart's Concerto in B♭ K191/186*e* (1774) remains the most significant for solo bassoon. The modern repertory includes pieces by Elgar, Villa-Lobos, Strauss and Hindemith.

Basso profondo. A deep BASS voice.

Bass saxophone. A SAXOPHONE in B♭, sounding two octaves and a major 2nd lower than written.

Bass trombone. A TROMBONE in G or F, a minor 3rd or a 4th below the basic (tenor) in B♭.

Bass trumpet. A TRUMPET in C, sounding an octave lower than the normal valved trumpet in C.

Bass tuba. A TUBA in F or E♭.

Bassus (medieval Lat.). 'Low': the lowest voice in a polyphonic composition.

Bass viol. The bass instrument of the VIOL family, often called 'viola da gamba'. In 18th- and 19th-century American (and occasionally British) usage, 'bass viol' meant a four-string instrument tuned in 5ths like a cello.

Bastiaans, Johannes Gijsbertus (*b* Wilp, 31 Oct 1812; *d* Haarlem, 16 Feb 1875). Dutch organist and composer. He studied with C.F. Becker and Mendelssohn in Leipzig, and from 1838 held organ posts in Deventer, Amsterdam and Haarlem. His works, including numerous organ pieces and four-part chorales, show Mendelssohn's influence; he also wrote a harmony treatise (1867). His main importance lies in his propagation of Bach's music in Holland.

Bastianelli, Giannotto (*b* San Domenico di Fiesole, 20 June 1883; *d* Tunis, 22 Sept 1927). Italian critic, composer and pianist. Largely self-taught, he provided the analysis and encouragement for the new classicism in Italian music represented by Malipiero, Pizzetti and others (he taught in Florence). His works are few and mostly early.

Bastien und Bastienne. Singspiel in one act by Mozart to a libretto by Friedrich Wilhelm Weiskern and J.A. Schachtner after Rousseau (1768, Vienna).

Baston, John (*fl* 1711–33). English composer. A flautist and recorder player, he performed in his own 'interval music' concertos in London; several of these lively pieces were published.

Bataille, Gabriel (*b* ?Brie, *c*1575; *d* Paris, 17 Dec 1630). French composer, lutenist and poet. From 1619 he was a member of the royal musical establishment. He arranged six collections (1608–15) of polyphonic *airs de cour* by leading court composers for solo voice and lute; he also composed original songs, some for *ballets de cour*, and psalms as *musique mesurée*.

Bate, Stanley (Richard) (*b* Plymouth, 12 Dec 1913; *d* London, 19 Oct 1959). English composer. He studied with Vaughan Williams, Jacob and others at the RCM and with Boulanger and Hindemith. A prolific composer – he wrote three symphonies, three concertos each for violin and piano and one each for viola, cello and harpsichord as well as ballets, chamber and piano music – he was noted above all for his technical command and inventive handling of orchestral texture.

Bates, Joah (*b* Halifax, bap. 8 March 1740; *d* London, 8 June 1799). English organist and concert organizer. He was a Fellow of King's College, Cambridge, from 1770 and later held various civil service posts. A champion of 'ancient' (i.e. Baroque) music, he was a director of the Concert of Ancient Music, 1776–93, and the massive Westminster Abbey Handel commemoration of 1784. His wife Sarah (*c*1755–1811), a much-admired soprano, sang in many of his concerts.

Bates, William (*fl c*1750–*c*1780). English composer and singing teacher. He was well known for his music for London theatres and pleasure gardens, and also wrote other songs, chamber works and concertos.

Bateson, Thomas (*b* ?*c*1570–75; *d* Dublin, March 1630). English composer. Possibly from the Wirral, Cheshire, he was organist of Chester Cathedral from 1599 and from 1609 of Christ Church Cathedral, Dublin, where he graduated BMus (1612) and MA (1622) at Trinity College. His two madrigal books (1604, 1618), while not specially original, include elaborately scored, serious pieces in a distinctive vein.

Bath Festival (UK). Annual arts festival (May–June), established in 1948. It was first called 'The Bath Assembly', with concerts mainly of 18th-century music in buildings of the period. From the late 1950s new works were commissioned and since 1975 events have covered a wider range.

Bathyphone. A contrabass clarinet designed by Wilhelm Wiebrecht and manufactured from 1839; it was pitched in C with a range $E'-c'$, with a tube doubled back on itself.

Bati, Luca (*b* Florence, *c*1550; *d* there, 17 Oct 1608). Italian composer. He was *maestro di cappella* of Pisa Cathedral (1596) and then of the Medici court and Florence Cathedral (from 1598–9). His dramatic music for Medici weddings and Florentine carnivals is lost but his surviving madrigals (1594, 1598) and sacred works (in MS) are of high quality though not notably progressive.

Baton. The stick with which the conductor of an orchestra or similar ensemble beats the time. A thin, tapered stick, similar to the modern baton, was first used in the late 18th century, but the use of a roll of paper or a violin bow continued into the 19th century. *See* CONDUCTING.

Bâton, Charles (*b* Versailles, early 18th century; *d* Paris, after 1754). French composer and vielle (hurdy-gurdy) player. His father, Henri (*d* 1728), helped make the musette (bagpipe) and vielle from folk instruments into fashionable ones. Bâton extended the vielle's range further and wrote suites and sonatas for both instruments.

Battaglia (It.). A name used in the 16th–18th centuries for pieces describing a battle. They might be vocal (e.g. Janequin's *La guerre*) or instrumental (e.g. Byrd's *The Battell*), and often included imitations of gunfire and other such effects. Among orchestral battle-pieces of the early 19th century is Beethoven's *Wellingtons Sieg* or 'Battle Symphony', in which various national anthems are heard.

Battaglia di Legnano, La. Opera in four acts by Verdi to a libretto by Cammarano after Méry (1849, Rome).

Batten, Adrian (*b* Salisbury, bap. 1 March 1591; *d* London, 1637). English composer. He was a chorister at Winchester Cathedral, then a lay vicar at Westminster Abbey (1614–26) and vicar-choral at St Paul's Cathedral. His surviving works (all sacred) include services and over 40 anthems, competently crafted in a devotional, restrained style. He was probably also the copyist of the important 'Batten Organbook', an extensive source of English church music.

Batterie (Fr.). A signal or short march sounded by drums; *see* SONNERIE. *See also* BATTERY and RASGUEADO.

Battery. Term used for the Baroque practice of arpeggiating passages notated as chords.

Batteux, Charles (*b* Allenhui, 7 May 1713/1715; *d* Paris, 14 July 1780). French aesthetician, one of the clearest exponents of the precepts of the Age of Reason. His main work, *Les beaux arts réduits à un même principe* (1746), proposed that the arts (including music) are all imitations of nature, which in turn reveals truth, beauty and reason.

Battiferri, Luigi (*b* Sassocorvaro, 1600–10; *d* ?1682). Italian composer and organist. A priest, he held a succession of posts as *maestro di cappella*, principally at Urbino and Ferrara. His five extant volumes of music (mostly published in 1669) contain motets and impressive ricercares which mark the end of the Ferrara organ school. They were copied by Fux and Zelenka and were probably known to Bach.

Battishill, Jonathan (*b* London, May 1738; *d* Islington, 10 Dec 1801). English composer. A St Paul's chorister as a boy, he was a tenor soloist in London concerts and held organist's posts. From the 1750s he was conductor (from the harpsichord) at Covent Garden and wrote songs for Drury Lane Theatre. He later composed an opera, *Almena* (1765, with Michael Arne), further songs, and many popular anthems, notably *Call to Remembrance* (1797).

Battistini, Mattia (*b* Rome, 27 Feb 1856; *d* Colle Baccaro, 7 Nov 1928). Italian baritone. He made his début at the Teatro Argentina, Rome, in 1878. Appearances in London followed in the 1880s, but his British triumphs were in 1905–6 when his great agility and breath control were admired as Don Gio-vanni, Germont and Amonasro. In Russia he enjoyed great success, appearing from 1888 to 1914 as Onegin, Ruslan and Rubinstein's Demon and in Italian roles. Regarded as the leading Italian baritone of his time, he had an unusually high voice with a noble, clear quality.

Battle music. *See* BATTAGLIA.

Battle Symphony. English title for Beethoven's *Wellingtons Sieg oder Die Schlacht bei Vittoria* op.91 (1813) for panharmonicon and orchestra.

Battuta (It.). 'Beat', 'bar', 'measure': an instruction, in the form *a battuta*, to return to the strict beat.

Baudo, Serge (*b* Marseilles, 16 July 1927). French conductor. He studied at the Paris Conservatoire and made his début in 1950 with the Concerts Lamoureux; in 1959 he became conductor of the Nice-Côte d'Azur Orchestra. He was conductor of the Paris Opéra (from 1962) and of the Orchestre de Paris (1967–75). He has conducted Saint-Saëns and Offenbach at the Met and hs given premières of works by Messiaen, Milhaud and Dutilleux.

Baudrier, Yves (Marie) (*b* Paris, 11 Feb 1906). French composer. Self-taught, he had advice from Messiaen, with whom in 1936 he was a founder-member of the group La Jeune France. Honegger is the main influence on his few works, which include the orchestral *Le musicien dans la cité* (1937).

Bauer, Marion (Eugenie) (*b* Walla Walla, WA, 15 Aug 1887; *d* South Hadley, MA, 9 Aug 1955). American composer and teacher. She studied in Paris and Berlin, with Boulanger and others, and taught at New York University (1926–51). Her works, mostly instrumental, are in a Franco-American neo-classical style, and she has written extensively, notably on 20th-century music.

Bauld, Alison (Margaret) (*b* Sydney, 7 May 1944). Australian composer. She worked as an actress and singer, then studied music at Sydney and in York as well as with Lutyens and Hans Keller, and taught in Sheffield and York. Most of her music is theatrical, involving mime or dance as well as singing and instruments, for example *In a Dead Brown Land* (1971), a shadowy, poetic drama set in the Australian outback, *Dear Emily* (1973), a miniature theatre piece for soprano and harp, or *One Pearl* (1973), originally a narrative about a martyred woman for voice and string quartet, revised as a theatre piece with the singer dressed as a Buddhist monk.

Bauldeweyn, Noel (*b c* 1480; *d* Antwerp, 1530). Flemish composer. Choirmaster at St Rombaut's, Mechelen, from 1509 and later at Notre Dame, Antwerp, he was also much esteemed as a composer. His works, which include seven masses, at least ten motets and two or three songs, combine aspects of the obsolete late 15th-century Netherlands style and the newer style of Josquin and his immediate successors.

Baumgarten, Karl Friedrich (*b* Lübeck, *c* 1740; *d* London, 1824). German composer. He worked in London from *c* 1758 as an organist, teacher and violinist (he led the Covent Garden orchestra in 1780–94). He wrote and contributed to several stage works and composed chamber music (including quartets) and organ pieces.

Baumgartner, Wilhelm (*b* Rorschach, 15 Nov 1820; *d* Zurich, 17 March 1867). Swiss pianist, teacher and composer. After studying in Zurich and Berlin, where he accompanied Jenny Lind in song recitals, he settled in Zurich as a piano teacher and choirmaster. His works, mainly patriotic choruses and romantic solo songs with piano accompaniment, express personal moods and experiences.

Baur, Jürg (*b* Düsseldorf, 11 Nov 1918). German composer and teacher. He studied with Jarnach in Cologne and taught at the Düsseldorf Conservatory from 1946 (director, 1965–71) and in Cologne. Like his contemporary Zimmermann, he was stimulated by younger composers in the 1950s but remained conventional. His works, in most non-dramatic genres, include important settings of 20th-century poetry (Lorca, Celan, Ungaretti).

Bavarian Radio Symphony Orchestra. German orchestra founded in Munich in 1960; its conductors have included Jochum and Kubelik.

Bax, Sir Arnold (Edward Trevor) (*b* Streatham, 8 Nov 1883; *d* Cork, 3 Oct 1953). English composer. He studied at the RAM (1900–05) but was much more impressed by discovering the poetry of Yeats: thereafter he strongly identified with Irish Celtic culture. Drawing on many sources (Strauss, Debussy, Ravel, Elgar) he created a style of luxuriant chromatic harmony, rich ornament and broad melody, notably deployed in his tone poems *The Garden of Fand* (1916), *November Woods* (1917) and *Tintagel* (1919). Other important works of this period include his First Quartet (1918) and Second Piano Sonata (1919). In the 1920s his music became clearer in outline and more contrapuntal, though without losing its wide range of harmonic resource: Sibelius became an influence. His main works were now symphonies, seven written 1922–39, though he remained a prolific composer in all non-theatrical genres. In 1942 he was made Master of the King's Music, after which he composed little.

Bayle, François (*b* Tamatave, 27 April 1932). French composer. He studied with Messiaen and in 1960 joined the Groupe de Musique Concrète, which he directed when it was reorganized as the Groupe de Recherches Musicales (1968). His works are nearly all electronic.

Bayreuth Festival (West Germany). Summer festival (annual from 1951) of Wagner's operas, established in 1876 by the composer with the first complete performance of the *Ring*. Wagner, with the architect Otto Brückwald, designed the Festival Theatre specially for his works. In 1973 the Richard Wagner Foundation Bayreuth was created, taking over from the Wagner family the assets, including the Wagner Archives at Wahnfried, and the festival's administration.

Bazelon, Irwin (Allen) (*b* Evanston, IL, 4 June 1922). American composer. He studied with Milhaud at Mills College (1946–8) and has written much for orchestral and chamber resources, favouring brass and percussion. His concerto *Propulsions* (1974) is an important contribution to the percussion repertory.

Bazin, François (Emmanuel-Joseph) (*b* Mar-seilles, 4 Sept 1816; *d* Paris, 2 July 1878). French composer and teacher. He studied at the Paris Conservatoire (winning the Prix de Rome in 1840), where he later taught, becoming well known for his traditional views. His output consists mainly of *opéras comiques*, notably *Le voyage en Chine* (1865), but his theatrical career was gradually eclipsed by Massenet's.

Bazzini, Antonio (*b* Brescia, 11 March 1818; *d* Milan, 10 Feb 1897). Italian violinist, composer and teacher. After a successful concert career, spent partly in Germany, he devoted himself to composition, excelling in the classic forms of German chamber music. His pupils at the Milan Conservatory, where he was professor from 1873 (later director), included Mascagni and Puccini.

BBC. *See* BRITISH BROADCASTING CORPORATION.

Beach [née Cheney], **Amy Marcy** [Mrs H.H.A. Beach] (*b* Henniker, NH, 5 Sept 1867; *d* New York, 27 Dec 1944). American composer and pianist. She wrote much in a post-Brahms style comparable with that of Chadwick and Foote and toured Europe as a pianist and composer, 1911–14. Thereafter she spent many summers at the MacDowell Colony, coming under the influence of MacDowell and Debussy. She was the first American woman to succeed as a composer of large-scale art music and was celebrated as the foremost woman composer of her time in the USA. Her songs were widely sung and *The Canticle of the Sun* (1928) is still in the church repertory.

Bear. [L'Ours]. Nickname of Haydn's Symphony no.82 in C (1786).

Bearbeitung (Ger.). Arrangement, transcription.

Beard, John (*b* c1717; *d* Hampton, 5 Feb 1791). English tenor. He was a Chapel Royal chorister until 1734 and then sang frequently in Handel's Covent Garden company, appearing in ten operas, church music and most of the oratorios; he also sang in other composers' works (notably *The Beggar's Opera*) and eventually retired from the theatre in 1760. His heroic roles, such as Samson and Jephtha, helped establish the importance of the tenor voice at a time when castratos and women often still took leading male roles.

Beare. English family of violin dealers and restorers. John Beare (1847–1928), a dealer from 1865, divided his business in two in 1892: Beare & Son (now at Barnet) became wholesalers of new instruments; Beare, Goodwin & Co. (J. and A. Beare Ltd from 1954) specialized in early instruments of the violin family. In 1961 Charles Beare (*b* 1937) joined the firm, which maintains an international reputation for craftsmanship and restoration.

Beat. (1) The basic pulse underlying mensural music, i.e. the temporal unit of a composition; also the movement of the conductor's hand or baton indicating that unit. *See also* DOWNBEAT, UPBEAT, OFF-BEAT.

(2) A 17th-century English term for a lower appoggiatura, an inverted trill or a mordent.

(3) An acoustical phenomenon; *see* BEATS.

Béatitudes, Les. Oratorio by Franck to a text based on the Sermon on the Mount (1879).

Beatles. English pop group. Formed in Liverpool in 1956 by John Lennon (1940–80), Paul McCartney (*b* 1942) and George Harrison (*b* 1943), they were joined in 1962 by the drummer Ringo Starr (Richard Starkey) (*b* 1940). Their early work was an eclectic blend of blues, rhythm-and-blues and rock and roll, typified by the recordings *Love Me Do* (1962), *Please Please Me* and *She Loves You* (both 1963). They became the most popular group of their day. Most of their songs were written by Lennon and McCartney. In the mid-1960s they produced influential LP recordings, notably *Sergeant Pepper's Lonely Hearts Club Band* (1967), conceived as a self-contained, LP-length cycle; they also made films. After disbanding in 1970, the group's members composed and performed individually.

Beatrice di Tenda. Opera in two acts by Bellini to a libretto by Romani (1833, Venice).

Béatrice et Bénédict. Opera in two acts by Berlioz to his own libretto after Shakespeare's *Much Ado about Nothing* (1863, Baden-Baden).

Beats. The throbbing or 'beating' effect heard when two notes very close in pitch are heard simultaneously. This acoustical phenomenon results from the interference between two sound waves of slightly differing frequencies. The number of beats per second equals the difference in frequency, so the beats disappear if the two are in perfect unison. Beats are thus useful for the tuning of instruments; they can also be useful when they are audible between the harmonics of two notes for tuning a temperament exactly.

Beauchamp, Pierre (*b* 1636; *d* 1705). French dancer and choreographer. He was Louis XIV's dancing master for 22 years, and as choreographer to the Académie Royale de Musique (from 1671) collaborated with Lully. A key figure in developing the distinctive elements of French dance, he invented a dance notation published by Feuillet (1700).

Beaujoyeux, Balthasar de (*b* before *c*1535; *d c*1587). Italian violinist and ballet-master. In *c*1555 he led the string players sent from Italy to serve Catherine de' Medici in France. Among the works he produced as supervisor of court entertainment for several French monarchs was his own *Balet comique de la Royne* (staged 1581), the first known European work to combine dance, poetry and music into a coherent dramatic whole.

Beaumarchais, Pierre-Augustin [Caron de] (*b* Paris, 24 Jan 1732; *d* there, 18 May 1799). French writer. Objecting to the rules of classical French tragedy, he wrote serious plays in simple prose; his *Le barbier de Séville* was set as an opera by Paisiello, Rossini and others, and *Le mariage de Figaro* by Mozart. His libretto *Tarare* (set by Salieri) has a preface proposing the subordination of music to text in opera.

Beautiful Maid of the Mill, The. *See* SCHÖNE MÜLLERIN, DIE.

Beauvarlet-Charpentier, Jean-Jacques (*b* Abbeville, 28 June 1734; *d* Paris, 6 May 1794). French composer. One of the most celebrated organists of his day, he succeeded his father at the Hospice de la Charité, Lyons, and from 1763 played at the Académie des Beaux Arts there. He held posts in Paris from 1771, finally at Notre Dame (from 1783). Among his compositions are keyboard sonatas with violin (*c*1775) and organ pieces. His son Jacques-Marie (1766–1834), also an organist, composed vocal works to patriotic and sacred texts.

Beaux Arts Trio. American piano trio. Formed in 1955, it gave its first concert at the Berkshire Music Festival at Tanglewood. It has toured widely, has recorded most of the standard repertory (including all the trios of Haydn and Dvořák) and has been praised for its smoothness, precision and grasp of style.

Bebop. *See* BOP.

Bebung (Ger.). A trembling effect or vibrato obtained on the clavichord by varying the pressure of the finger on the key, so that the pressure of the tangent on the string varies and with it the volume of sound. It is usually indicated by dots above the note with a slur over them.

Becher, Alfred Julius (*b* Manchester, 27 April 1803; *d* Vienna, 23 Nov 1848). German critic and composer. He was an ardent revolutionary who worked as a lawyer, in journalism and as a theory teacher (Royal Music School, The Hague) before becoming a music critic for the *Allgemeine Wiener Musik-Zeitung* and the *Sonntagsblättern*. Admired by Mendelssohn, Schumann, Berlioz and Wagner, he wrote songs and piano pieces that achieved popularity. He was executed for his political views.

Bechet, Sidney (Joseph) (*b* New Orleans, 14 May ?1897; *d* Paris, 14 May 1959). American jazz clarinettist and soprano saxophonist. He went to Europe in 1919 (with Will Marion Cook's Southern Syncopated Orchestra) and travelled between Europe and the USA during the 1920s. He recorded with Louis Armstrong and played with Duke Ellington (1924–5) and was the pre-eminent clarinettist of his generation. During the New Orleans revival in the late 1930s he came to prominence again and recorded extensively. In 1949 he returned to Europe, settling in France in 1951.

Bechstein. German firm of piano makers. It was founded in Berlin in 1853 by Wilhelm Carl Bechstein (1826–1900), who won recognition from his first grand piano (inaugurated by Bülow), expanding output from 300 instruments a year in the 1860s to 5000 before World War I. In spite of large-scale production and marketing (notably in London, where in 1901 the firm opened a concert room, later called the Wigmore Hall) and mechanization, high standards were maintained. Bechstein's concert grand, the smaller, model B grand and the model 8 upright are among the finest pianos.

Beck, Conrad (*b* Lohn, 16 June 1901). Swiss composer. He studied in Zurich, Berlin and Paris, where he lived, 1923–32, associating with Honegger and Roussel. They influenced his move from a late Romantic style (five symphonies, 1925–30) to one of neo-Baroque seriousness. His works include oratorios (notably *Der Tod du Basel*, 1952), concertos and chamber pieces.

Beck, Franz Ignaz (*b* Mannheim, 20 Feb 1734; *d* Bordeaux, 31 Dec 1809). German composer. A pupil of J. Stamitz, he played the violin in Italy, and settled in France c1760. After a period in Marseilles he worked in Bordeaux, eventually as conductor of the Grand Theatre, composing several stage works. He was also a celebrated organist and conductor. Beck wrote symphonies, mostly early in his career, showing progressive traits such as thematic development, independent wind parts and (latterly) four movements. Among his other works are operas, sacred music (notably a *Stabat mater*, 1783), Revolutionary music and keyboard sonatas.

Becker, Carl Ferdinand (*b* Leipzig, 17 July 1804; *b* there, 26 Oct 1877). German organist and bibliographer. The first organ professor of the Leipzig Conservatory, he amassed an important collection of early music and musical literature; Bach was a special interest.

Becker, Cornelius (*b* Leipzig, 21 Oct 1561; *d* there, 25 May 1604). German theologian and poet. His rhymed version of the psalms, the 'Becker Psalter', was set by several Lutheran composers including Schütz (1628). In 1661 it was officially recognized as the standard psalter in Saxony.

Becker, Dietrich (*b* Hamburg, 1623; *d* there, 1679). German composer. One of the foremost north German violinists of his time, he was director of the Hamburg court orchestra from 1667 and of cathedral music there from 1674. His most interesting publication, *Musicalische Frühlings-Früchte* (1668), is a collection of sonatas and suites for three to five instruments with continuo.

Becker, Günther (*b* Forbach, 1 April 1924). German composer and teacher. He studied with Fortner, the main influence on his music of the 1950s along with his experience of Greece (reflected in *Epigramme*, 1961), where he lived, 1956–68. He has taught at Athens, Darmstadt and Düsseldorf. His later works, in which he abandoned serialism for Ligeti-style oscillating textures and then electronic modulation, include orchestral (*Stabil-instabil*, 1965), vocal and chamber pieces, many with tape; notable is *Meteoren* (1969, for organ, percussion and tape).

Becker, Jean (*b* Mannheim, 11 May 1833; *d* there, 10 Oct 1884). German violinist. A touring virtuoso nicknamed 'the German Paganini', he helped form the Quartetto Fiorentino (1865), the outstanding quartet of the day.

Becker, John (Joseph) (*b* Henderson, KY, 22 Jan 1886; *d* Wilmette, IL, 21 Jan 1961). American composer. He studied at the Cincinnati Conservatory and from 1917 taught at various Midwestern Catholic institutions. His early symphonies and songs look to the German mainstream, but in the 1920s his style changed radically, leading to the highly dissonant *Symphonia brevis* (1929). From this time he was in communication with Ives and Cowell, and in the 1930s produced much atonal, contrapuntal music – ballets (notably *A Marriage with Space*, 1935), concertos (including one for violin, 1948) and 'Soundpieces' for chamber forces.

Beckerath, Rudolf von (*b* Munich, 19 Feb 1907; *d* Hamburg, 20 Nov 1976). German organ builder. Based in Hamburg from 1949, he built over 100 organs, all with tracker action and renowned for their fine voicing. Among his most important are those in the Musikhalle, Hamburg, Johanniskirche, Düsseldorf, Oratoire St Joseph-du-Mont Royal, Montreal, and St Paul's Cathedral, Pittsburgh.

Beckwith, John (*b* Victoria, BC, 9 March 1927). Canadian composer and teacher. He studied in Toronto and with Boulanger in Paris (1950–52); in 1961 he began teaching at Toronto University. His large and eclectic output includes *Music for Dancing* (1948) and the opera *The Shivaree* (1982, Toronto). He has written extensively on Canadian music.

Beckwith, John 'Christmas' (*b* Norwich, 25 Dec 1750 (or 1749); *d* there, 3 June 1809). English organist and composer. He worked at Oxford and Norwich and was famous as an extemporizer. His compositions include anthems and keyboard music.

Bedford, David (Vickerman) (*b* London, 4 Aug 1937). English composer. He studied at the RAM with Berkeley and in Venice with Nono; he has also played and arranged pop music and written much for children. His large output shows a development from experimental simplicity (e.g. in *Music for Albion Moonlight* (1965) for soprano and sextet) to a style influenced by American minimalism (e.g. *Star's End* (1978) for rock group and orchestra).

Bedford, Steuart (John Rudolf) (*b* London, 31 July 1939). English conductor, brother of David Bedford. He studied at the RAM and Oxford and from the late 1960s worked at Glyndebourne and with the English Opera Group. He conducted the stage premières of Britten's *Owen Wingrave* (1973, Covent Garden) and *Death in Venice* (1973, Aldeburgh; 1974, Met), and taught at the RAM from 1965.

Bédos [Bedos] de Celles, François (*b* Caux, 24 Jan 1709; *d* St Denis, 25 Nov 1779). French organ builder and writer. He is best known for his *L'art du facteur d'orgues* (Paris, 1766–78), a valuable description of classical French organ building, including design, mixture compositions, pipe scales, tools, pipes and pipe making and details of performing practice.

Bedyngham, Johannes (*d* Westminster, 3 May 1459–22 May 1460). English composer. A member of the London Guild of Parish Clerks, he was towards the end of his life verger at St Stephen's, Westminster. He may have been the John Boddenham born in Oxford in 1422 and a scholar and chorister of Winchester College and later a scholar and fellow of New College, Oxford. His two mass cycles are unusually free in form, one of them parodying Binchois' ballade *Dueil angoisseux,* and his three motets are intricate pieces of great rhythmical complexity. Eight songs widely distributed in MS sources, often with alternative texts in different languages, are probably his, though some are also ascribed to other composers (e.g. the song *O rosa bella*, also ascribed to Dunstable). The dissemination of his music suggests he was a composer of stature.

Beecham, Sir Thomas (*b* St Helens, 29 April 1879; *d* London, 8 March 1961). English conductor. He studied with Charles Wood in London and

Moszkowski in Paris but was largely self-taught as a conductor. A family fortune enabled him in 1909 to found the Beecham SO and from 1910 he gave opera seasons at Covent Garden, His Majesty's and Drury Lane. Works new to Britain by Russian composers, Strauss and Delius were given and Beecham financed the first appearances in London of Dyagilev's Ballets Russes. In 1915 he formed the Beecham (later British National) Opera Company. By 1920 he could no longer finance opera seasons and turned increasingly to concert work. In 1932 he founded the LPO and took it on European tours. During the 1930s he returned to Covent Garden, as artistic director, and gave Ring cycles. During World War II he conducted in the USA. On his return to Britain in 1946 he founded the RPO. With his sure sense of rhythm and elegant phrasing Beecham established an easy mastery. His gifts were best displayed in the Viennese Classics, Delius and Berlioz.

Beecham Opera Company. Company formed by Thomas Beecham in London during World War I; after 1920 it became the nucleus of the British National Opera Company.

Beecke, (Notger) Ignaz (Franz) von (b Wimpfen am Neckar, 28 Oct 1733; d Wallerstein, 2 Jan 1803). German composer. He went to Wallerstein as an army lieutenant in 1759 and joined the court there, later becoming music director. An admired pianist and composer, he travelled widely (especially to Paris and Vienna), and from the 1770s recruited musicians such as F.A. Rosetti (Rössler) and built up a wide repertory. His vocal works, among them an opera, *Roland* (after 1770, Paris) and six Singspiels, such as *Claudine von Villa Bella* (1780, Vienna), were influenced by his teacher Gluck. Haydn (who visited Wallerstein in 1790) had a growing influence on his instrumental output, which includes some 20 symphonies, 12 string quartets, other chamber music and keyboard works.

Beer, Johann (b St Georg, 28 Feb 1655; d Weissenfels, 6 Aug 1700). Austrian-German composer and theorist. He was a singer at the ducal courts of Halle and Weissenfels (Konzertmeister, 1685). His music is unexceptional, but he was a versatile musician and author of lively treatises on the musicians and musical practices of his time, notably *Musicalische Discurse*.

Beer, (Johann) Joseph (b Grünewald, 18 May 1744; d Berlin, 28 Oct 1812). Bohemian clarinettist. The first important clarinet virtuoso, he toured widely and held posts in Paris, St Petersburg and (from 1792) Berlin. He composed several clarinet works. He is sometimes confused with the Austrian clarinettist Josef Böhr (1770–1819).

Beer-Walbrunn, Anton (b Kohlberg, 29 June 1864; d Munich, 22 March 1929). German composer and teacher. From 1901 he taught at the Munich Academy of Music, Furtwängler and Einstein being among his pupils. His compositions, many with a folklike quality, include chamber music, Shakespeare sonnet settings and the opera *Don Quijote* (1908).

Beeson, Jack (Hamilton) (b Muncie, IN, 15 July 1921). American composer and teacher. He studied at the Eastman School (1939–44) and privately with Bartók in New York (1944), then taught at Columbia University from 1945. His operas continue the tradition of Douglas Moore, with a feeling for lyricism and occasionally suggesting an American folk idiom; they include *Lizzie Borden* (1965).

Bee's Wedding, The. Nickname of Mendelssohn's *Lieder öhne Worte* no.34 in C for piano, also called 'Spinnerlied'.

Beethoven, Ludwig van (b Bonn, bap. 17 Dec 1770; d Vienna, 26 March 1827). German composer. He studied first with his father, Johann, a singer and instrumentalist in the service of the Elector of Cologne at Bonn, but mainly with C.G. Neefe, court organist. At 11½ he was able to deputize for Neefe; at 12 he had some music published. In 1787 he went to Vienna, but quickly returned on hearing that his mother was dying. Five years later he went back to Vienna, where he settled.

He pursued his studies, first with Haydn, but there was some clash of temperaments and Beethoven studied too with Schenk, Albrechtsberger and Salieri. Until 1794 he was supported by the Elector at Bonn: but he found patrons among the music-loving Viennese aristocracy and soon enjoyed success as a piano virtuoso, playing at private houses or palaces rather than in public. His public début was in 1795; about the same time his first important publications appeared, three piano trios op.1 and three piano sonatas op.2. As a pianist, it was reported, he had fire, brilliance and fantasy as well as depth of feeling. It is naturally in the piano sonatas, writing for his own instrument, that he is at his most original in this period; the *Pathétique* belongs to 1799, the *Moonlight* ('Sonata quasi una fantasia') to 1801, and these represent only the most obvious innovations in style and emotional content. These years also saw the composition of his first three piano concertos, his first two symphonies and a set of six string quartets op.18.

1802, however, was a year of crisis for Beethoven, with his realization that the impaired hearing he had noticed for some time was incurable and sure to worsen. That autumn, at a village outside Vienna, Heiligenstadt, he wrote a will-like document, addressed to his two brothers, describing his bitter unhappiness over his affliction in terms suggesting that he thought death was near. But he came through with his determination strengthened and entered a new creative phase, generally called his 'middle period'. It is characterized by a heroic tone, evident in the 'Eroica' Symphony (no.3, originally to have been dedicated not to a noble patron but to Napoleon), in Symphony no.5, where the sombre mood of the C minor first movement ('Fate knocking on the door') ultimately yields to a triumphant C major finale with piccolo, trombones and percussion added to the orchestra, and in his opera *Fidelio*. Here the heroic theme is made explicit by the story, in which (in the post-French Revolution 'rescue opera' tradition) a wife saves her imprisoned husband from murder at the hands of his oppressive political enemy. The three string quartets of this period, op.59, are similarly heroic in scale: the first, lasting some 45 minutes, is conceived with great breadth, and it too embodies a sense of triumph as the intense F minor Adagio gives way to a jubilant finale in the major, embodying (at the request of the dedicatee, Count Razumovsky) a Russian folk melody.

Fidelio, unsuccessful at its première, was twice revised by Beethoven and his librettists and successful in its final version of 1814. Here there is more emphasis on the moral force of the story. It deals not only with freedom and justice, and heroism, but also with married love, and in the character of the heroine Leonore, Beethoven's lofty, idealized image of womanhood is to be seen. He did not find it in real life: he fell in love several times, usually with aristocratic pupils (some of them married), and each time was either rejected or saw that the woman did not match his ideals. In 1812, however, he wrote a passionate love-letter to an 'Eternally Beloved' (probably Antonie Brentano, a Viennese married to a Frankfurt businessman), but probably the letter was never sent.

With his powerful and expansive middle-period works, which include the Pastoral Symphony (no.6, conjuring up his feelings about the countryside, which he loved), Symphonies nos.7 and 8, Piano Concertos nos.4 (a lyrical work) and 5 (the noble and brilliant 'Emperor') and the Violin Concerto, as well as more chamber works and piano sonatas (such as the 'Waldstein' and the 'Appassionata') Beethoven was firmly established as the greatest composer of his time. His piano-playing career had finished in 1808 (a charity appearance in 1814 was a disaster because of his deafness). That year he had considered leaving Vienna for a secure post in Germany, but three Viennese noblemen had banded together to provide him with a steady income and he remained there, although the plan foundered in the ensuing Napoleonic wars in which his patrons suffered and the value of Austrian money declined.

The years after 1812 were relatively unproductive. He seems to have been seriously depressed, by his deafness and the resulting isolation, by the failure of his marital hopes and (from 1815) by anxieties over the custodianship of the son of his late brother, which involved him in legal actions. But he came out of these trials to write his profoundest music, which surely reflects something of what he had been through. There are seven piano sonatas in this, his 'late period', including the turbulent 'Hammerklavier' op.106, with its dynamic writing and its harsh, rebarbative fugue, and op.110, which also has fugues and much eccentric writing at the instrument's extremes of compass; there is a great Mass and a Choral Symphony, no.9 in D minor, where the extended variation-finale is a setting for soloists and chorus of Schiller's *Ode to Joy*; and there is a group of string quartets, music on a new plane of spiritual depth, with their exalted ideas, abrupt contrasts and emotional intensity. The traditional four-movement scheme and conventional forms are discarded in favour of designs of six or seven movements, some fugal, some akin to variations (these forms especially attracted him in his late years), some song-like, some martial, one even like a chorale prelude. For Beethoven, the act of composition had always been a struggle, as the tortuous scrawls

of his sketchbooks show; in these late works the sense of agonizing effort is a part of the music.

Musical taste in Vienna had changed during the first decades of the 19th century; the public were chiefly interested in light Italian opera (especially Rossini) and easygoing chamber music and songs, to suit the prevalent bourgeois taste. Yet the Viennese were conscious of Beethoven's greatness: they applauded the Choral Symphony, even though, understandably, they found it difficult, and though baffled by the late quartets they sensed their extraordinary visionary qualities. His reputation went far beyond Vienna: the late Mass was first heard in St Petersburg, and the initial commission that produced the Choral Symphony had come from the Philharmonic Society of London. When, early in 1827, he died, 10 000 are said to have attended the funeral. He had become a public figure, as no composer had done before. Unlike composers of the preceding generation, he had never been a purveyor of music to the nobility: he had lived into the age – indeed helped create it – of the artist as hero and the property of mankind at large.

Orchestral music Sym. no.1, C, op.21 (1800); Sym. no.2, D, op.36 (1802); Sym. no.3, 'Eroica', E♭, op.55 (1803); Sym. no.4, B♭, op.60 (1806); Sym. no.5, c, op.67 (1808); Sym. no.6, 'Pastoral', F, op.68 (1808); Sym. no.7, A, op.92 (1812); Sym. no.8, F, op.93 (1812); Sym. no.9, 'Choral', d, op.125 (1824); Pf Conc. no.1, C, op.15 (1795); Pf Conc. no.2, B♭, op.19 (1798); Pf Conc. no.3, c, op.37 (c1800); Pf Conc. no.4, G, op.58 (1806); Pf Conc. no.5, 'Emperor', E♭, op.73 (1809); Triple Conc., C, pf, vn, vc, op.56 (1804); Vn Conc., D, op.61 (1806); 2 vn romances, F, G, opp.50, 40 (1798–1802); Choral Fantasy, c, pf, chorus, op.80 (1808); Battle Sym., 'Wellington's Victory' op.91 (1813); ovs. – Coriolan, op.62 (1807); Leonore no.1 (1807), no.2 (1805), no.3 (1806); Nameday op.115 (1815); Consecration of the House op.124 (1822); see also dramatic music

Chamber music without piano 17 str qts – op.18 nos.1–6, F, G, D, c, A, B♭ (1800); op.59 nos.1–3, 'Razumovsky', F, e, C (1806); op.74, 'Harp', E♭ (1809); op.95, 'Serioso', f (1810); op.127, E♭ (1825); op.132, a (1825); op.130, B♭ (1826); op.131, c♯ (1826); op.135, F (1826); Grosse Fuge, op.133, B♭ (1826); 3 str qnts – op.4, E♭ (1795); op.29, C (1801); op.104, c (1817); 5 str trios – op.3, E♭ (by 1794); op.8, Serenade, D (1797); op.9 nos.1–3, G, D, c (1798); Trio, 2 ob, eng hn, op.87, C (1795); Serenade, fl, vn, va, op.25, D (1801); Sextet, 2 hn, str, op.81b, E♭ (c1795); Septet, cl, bn, hn, vn, va, vc, db, op.20, E♭ (1800); Octet and Rondino, 2 ob, 2 cl, 2 bn, 2 hn, op.103, E♭ (c1793)

Chamber music with piano 3 pf qts, E♭, D, C (1785); Qnt, pf, ob, cl, bn, hn, op.16, E♭ (1796); 7 pf trios – op.1 nos.1–3, E♭, G, c (1795); op.11 (cl, vc, pf), B♭ (1797); op.70 nos.1, 'Ghost', and 2, D, E♭ (1808); op.97, 'Archduke', B♭ (1811); 5 vc sonatas – op.5 nos. 1–2, F, g (1796); op.69, A (1808); op.102 nos. 1–2, C, D (1815); 12 vn sonatas – op.12 nos.1–3, D, A, E♭ (1798); op.23, a (1800); op.24, 'Spring', F (1801); op.30 nos.1–3, A, c, G (1802); op.47, 'Kreutzer', a (1803); op.96, G (1812); hn sonata, op.17, F (1800); variations for vn, pf and vc, pf etc

Piano music 32 sonatas – op.2 nos.1–3, f, A, C (1795); op.7, E♭ (1797); op.10 nos.1–3, c, F, D (1795–8); op.13, 'Pathétique', c (1798); op.14 nos.1–2, E, G (1798–9); op.22, B♭ (1800); op.26, A♭ (1801); op.27 no.1, 'quasi una fantasia', E♭ (1801); op.27 no.2, 'Moonlight', c♯ (1801); op.28, 'Pastoral', D (1801); op.31 nos.1–3, G, d, E (1802); op.49 nos.1–2, g, G (sonatinas) (1795–7); op.53, 'Waldstein', C (1804); op.54, F (1804); op.57, 'Appassionata', f (1805); op.78, F♯ (1809); op.79, G (1809); op.81a, 'Les Adieux', E♭ (1810); op.90, e (1814); op.101, A (1816); op.106, 'Hammerklavier', B♭ (1818); op.109, E (1820); op.110, A♭ (1822); op.111, c (1822); variations, incl. 6 on original theme, F, op.34 (1802), Eroica Variations op.35 (1802), 32 in c (1806), Diabelli Variations op.126 (1823); Bagatelles 7 op.33 (1802), 11 op.119 (1822), 6 op. 126 (1824); rondos, dances; pf duets, incl. sonata op.6 (1797)

Dramatic music Fidelio [Leonore], opera (1805, rev. 1806, rev.1814 with ov. Fidelio); ov. and ballet The Creatures of Prometheus op.43 (1801); incidental music (incl. ov.) – Egmont op.84 (1810); The Ruins of Athens op.113 (1811); King Stephen op.117 (1811)

Choral music Mass, C, op.86 (1807); Missa solemnis, D, op.123 (1823); The Mount of Olives op.85, oratorio (1803); cantatas – on the death of Joseph II (1790), on the accession of Leopold II (1790), Calm Sea and Prosperous Voyage op.112 (1815); Der glorreiche Augenblick op.136 (1814); scenas etc

Songs c85, incl. Adelaide (1795), Ah! perfido (1796), An die Hoffnung op.32 (1805); 6 Gellert songs op.48 (1802), 8 songs op.52 (1790–96), 6 songs op.75 (1809), 4 ariettas and duet op.82 (c1809), 3 Goethe songs op.83 (1810), An die ferne Geliebte op.98, cycle (1816), many single songs, canons, musical jokes etc, c170 folksong arrs.

Beethoven Quartet. Soviet string quartet, led by Dmitry Tsïganov. It was founded as the Moscow Conservatory Quartet in 1923, and gave Beethoven's complete quartets on the 1927 centenary, changing its name in 1931. It was noted for its performances of contemporary music and gave the premières of all but the first and last of Shostakovich's 15 quartets.

Beggar's Opera, The. The first ballad opera, to a libretto by John Gay about London underworld characters, consisting of 69 short popular tunes for which Pepusch provided basses and an overture (1728, London).

Beggar Student, The. *See* BETTELSTUDENT, DER.

Beglarian, Grant (*b* Tiflis, 1 Dec 1927). American composer and administrator. After arriving in the USA in 1947 he studied with Ross Lee Finney at Michigan University; another major influence was Copland. He was an administrator at UCLA, 1969–82, then president of the National Foundation for Advancement in the Arts. His works include chamber music and *And all the Hills Echoed* for baritone, chorus, timpani and organ.

Behold the Sun. Opera in three acts by Alexander Goehr to a libretto by John McGrath (1985, Duisburg).

Behrens, Hildegard (*b* Oldenburg, 9 Feb 1937). German soprano. She studied in Freiburg, making her début there as Mozart's Count (1971), and later singing at Düsseldorf and Frankfurt in such roles as Fiordiligi, Musetta and Marie (*Wozzeck*). She made her début in 1976 at Covent Garden (Beethoven's Leonore) and the Met (Georgetta, *Il tabarro*) and sang Brünnhilde at Bayreuth in 1983, also singing that role and Isolde at the Met. She has a bright, incisive voice and an intense dramatic personality.

Behrman, David (*b* Salzburg, 16 Aug 1937). American composer. A nephew of Heifetz, he studied with Riegger, with Piston at Harvard and with Pousseur and Stockhausen in Europe. His works are nearly all electronic, using his own systems. From 1970 to 1976 he worked with Cage, Tudor and Mumma for the Merce Cunningham Dance Company.

Beiderbecke, (Leon) Bix (*b* Davenport, IA, 10 March 1903; *d* New York, 6 Aug 1931). American jazz cornettist, pianist and composer. His first recordings were with the Wolverines (1924). In 1925 he began an association with the saxophonist Frank Trumbauer, in Trumbauer's band and Jean Goldkette's. He joined Paul Whiteman's orchestra (1927–9) until alcoholism frequently prevented him from performing. His unique timbre and unorthodox cornet fingering gave his work an introspective character and influenced other white jazz musicians. His most famous solos are in Trumbauer's recordings of *Singin' the Blues* and *I'm coming Virginia* (both 1927). The few surviving examples of his piano playing display aspects of impressionism, notably *In a Mist* (1927).

Beijing opera. *See* PEKING OPERA and CHINESE MUSIC.

Beinum, Eduard (Alexander) van (*b* Arnhem, 3 Sept 1901; *d* Amsterdam, 13 April 1959). Dutch conductor. He became second conductor of the Concertgebouw Orchestra in 1931 and succeeded Mengelberg as principal conductor in 1945. He conducted the LPO, 1949–51, and made his American début in 1954 with the Philadelphia Orchestra. A champion of contemporary Dutch music, he was also admired for his balanced performances of Beethoven and Bruckner.

Beissel, (Johann) Conrad (*b* Eberbach, 1 March 1691; *d* Ephrata, PA, 6 July 1768). American composer. He emigrated from Germany in 1720 and established an austere Protestant monastic society at Ephrata in 1732. His anthems and hymns appeared in several collections, notably *Das Gesäng der einsamen und verlassenen Turtel-Taube* (1747), in which he explained his own method for singing and composition.

Beklemmt (Ger.). Oppressed, anguished.

Bel canto (It.). 'Beautiful singing': a term generally understood to refer to the elegant Italian vocal style of the 17th to 19th centuries, characterized by beautiful tone, florid delivery, shapely phrasing and effortless technique.

Beliczay, Gyula [Julius von] (*b* Komárom, 10 Aug 1835; *d* Budapest, 30 April 1893). Hungarian composer. He studied in Vienna, where he later worked (1857–71) and came to know leading musicians, among them Liszt and Wagner. Although his sacred works, chamber music and piano pieces owe much to Schubert, Schumann and Liszt, he was one of the best-known minor Hungarian composers of his day.

Bell. (1) A percussion instrument consisting of a hollow object, usually of metal (in some cultures clay or glass), which when struck emits a sound by vibration. Bells differ from gongs in that their zone of maximum vibration is towards the centre; bells are held at their vertex, or point farthest from their rim. The cup shape, the most common, appears in various forms, for example the modern European tower bell. Closed or crotal bells are exemplified by the sleigh-bell but include instruments made from shells and other materials. Bells may be sounded by a clapper, by a hammer, or by loose internal pellets.

The bell is found in many cultures, ancient and modern. Open and crotal bells were used in southeast Asia before 3000BC. Tuned bells were used in China from the Chou to Ming dynasties (1050BC to AD1644) as a means of fixing interval relationships in the system of music theory. In Greece clay bells were in use from about the 8th century BC and bronze bells from the 6th. From ancient times a great variety of bells has been used in all parts of sub-Saharan Africa; they are in both crotal and open forms, and mostly of hammered iron. The primary development of the bell in Europe was as a signalling device, first for the Christian church and later for secular uses. An early use of bells in orchestral music is in the cantata *Schlage doch, gewünschte Stunde* formerly attributed to Bach. Composers who have scored for bells include Rossini (*Guillaume Tell*), Meyerbeer (*Les Huguenots*) and Berlioz (*Symphonie fantastique*). *See also* TUBULAR BELLS.

(2) The terminal part of a wind instrument tube, opposite the mouthpiece, through which the air column contained in the instrument communicates with the ambient air.

Bella, Ján Levoslav (*b* Liptovský Svätý Mikuláš, 4 Sept 1843; *d* Bratislava, 25 May 1936). Slovak composer. He was a priest and church music director when he went to study in Germany and Prague, where he met Smetana. His output consists of songs in his native language and in German, a symphonic poem (*Fate and the Ideal*, 1874, conducted by R. Strauss in 1890) and other large-scale works, an opera (*Wieland der Schmied*, 1880–90) and many church works.

Bell Anthem. Purcell's verse anthem *Rejoice in the Lord Alway* (*c*1682–55), an allusion to the 'peals' of the introduction.

'Bell' is also a nickname for Haydn's String Quartet in D minor op.76 no.2 and for Khachaturian's Symphony no.2 in A minor.

Belle Hélène, La. Opera in three acts by Offenbach to a libretto by Meilhac and Halévy (1864, Paris).

Bell harp. A wire-strung psaltery, swung while being played; it commonly had 16 courses. It was invented in 18th-century England and was later popular as a street and domestic instrument, often as 'fairy bells'.

Belli, Domenico (*d* Florence, bur. 5 May 1627). Italian composer. He probably worked at the court in Parma, then at S Lorenzo, Florence (1610–13), before moving to the Medici court (1619). His surviving music (published in 1616) includes *Orfeo dolente*, a set of intermedi presented between the acts of Tasso's *Aminta*, and a collection of *Arie* whose elaborate bass lines and harmonic adventurousness prove Belli a radical early monodist.

Belli, Girolamo (*b* Argenta, 1552; *d* there, *c*1620). Italian composer. A pupil of Luzzaschi, he was a singer at the Mantuan court from 1583; he then moved to Rome before returning to Argenta. The pieces in his six surviving madrigal books (at least eight others are lost) show Luzzaschi's influence. He wrote much sacred music, of which five volumes survive.

Belli, Giulio (*b* Longiano, *c*1560; *d* Imola, in or after 1621). Italian composer. A Franciscan monk, he was twice *maestro di cappella* of Imola Cathedral (1582–90, 1611–13) and held similar posts at the Cà Grande, Venice, the Ferrarese court, Ravenna, Forlì and elsewhere, returning to Imola in 1621. His large sacred output includes 12 published books of masses, motets and psalms, many later reprinted.

Some of his early pieces are polychoral and show Palestrina's influence; later ones use smaller forces and include continuo. He also published five books of madrigals and canzonettas.

Bellincioni, Gemma (Cesira Matilda) (*b* Como, 18 Aug 1864; *d* Naples, 23 April 1950). Italian soprano. Her acclaimed portrayal of Santuzza in the first performance of *Cavalleria rusticana* (1890) made her much in demand for *verismo* roles and she created many ones, including Giordano's Fedora. At Covent Garden in 1895 she sang Santuzza and Carmen. She was the first Italian Salome (1906, Turin), a role she sang over 100 times.

Bellini, Vincenzo (*b* Catania, 3 Nov 1801; *d* Puteaux, 23 Sept 1835). Italian composer. He was given piano lessons by his father, and could play well when he was five. At six he wrote a *Gallus cantavit* and began studying composition with his grandfather. After a few years his sacred pieces were being heard in Catania churches and his ariettas and instrumental works in the salons of aristocrats and patricians. In 1819 he went to Naples to study at the conservatory, entering the class of the director, Nicola Zingarelli, in 1822. In 1825 his *opera semiseria*, *Adelson e Salvini*, was produced at the conservatory. Its success led to commissions from the Teatro S Carlo and from La Scala, Milan.

Bellini's first opera for Milan, *Il pirata* (1827), instantly laid the foundation of his career, and with it began his fruitful collaborations with the librettist Felice Romani and the tenor G.B. Rubini. From 1827 to 1833 Bellini lived mostly in Milan, and during this time his operas, including *La sonnambula* and *Norma*, earned him an international reputation, while he himself went through a passionate love affair with Giuditta Cantù, the wife of a landowner and silk manufacturer, Ferdinando Turina. Bellini's amatory entanglements have been romanticized in popular literature but the realities are less credible.

In 1833 Bellini visited London, where four of his operas were performed with great success at the King's Theatre and Drury Lane. He then proceeded to Paris, where he was commissioned to write *I puritani* for the Théâtre-Italien and formed a close acquaintance with Rossini and got to know Chopin and other musicians. *I puritani* enjoyed a genuine triumph in January 1835, and Bellini was appointed a Chevalier de la Légion d'honneur. He decided to remain in Paris and formulated several projects for his future there, but in August 1835 he fell ill and the following month he died, from 'an acute inflammation of the large intestine, complicated by an abscess of the liver' according to the post-mortem report.

Bellini's importance to posterity is as a composer of opera, especially *opera seria*; his other works can be ignored without great loss. His first influences were the folksong of Sicily and Naples, the teaching of Zingarelli and, above all, the music of Rossini. The Naples performance of Rossini's *Semiramide* in 1824 was one of the most decisive musical experiences of his student years, and the novel lyrical style of his early operas represented a sentimentalization and heightening of Rossinian lyricism, which in *Il pirata* broadens to include forceful and dramatic emotions. With this opera Bellini became one of Italy's most influential composers; Donizetti and Pacini, Mercadante and Verdi all learnt from him.

The quintessential feature of Bellini's operatic music is its close relationship with the text. He did not look for musical delineation of character, but the content and mood of each scene are given thoroughgoing musical interpretation and the text is precisely declaimed. His melodic style, of which the famous 'Casta diva' in *Norma* is a perfect example, is characterized by the building of broad melodic curves from small (usually two-bar) units. While his treatment of rhythm is more conventional, his melodies are supported by some colourful harmony and reticent though effective orchestration. More than any other Italian composer of the years around 1830, Bellini minimized the difference between aria and recitative by introducing a large number of cantabile, aria-like passages into his recitative. His expressive range goes far beyond the delicate, elegiac aspects of his art, which have been frequently overemphasized.

Operas Il pirata (1827); La straniera (1829); I Capuleti e i Montecchi (1830); La sonnambula (1831); Norma (1831); Beatrice di Tenda (1833); I puritani (1835); 3 others
Sacred music Mass; Magnificat; 5 Tantum ergo; 2 Te Deum; hymns, motets (all before 1825)
Other works ariettas; 6 sinfonie; Ob. Conc.; kbd pieces

Bellinzani, Paolo Benedetto (*b* Mantua or Ferrara, *c*1690; *d* Recanati, 25 Feb 1757). Italian composer. He held *maestro di cappella* posts at cathedrals including Urbino (1730–34) and Recanati (from 1737). His music, very popular in its day, includes liturgical works, two oratorios (now lost), secular vocal pieces, and sonatas in imitation of Corelli.

Bell-lyra [lyra-glockenspiel]. A portable glockenspiel in lyre form designed for use in marching bands; it had metal cups or steel bars (*c*15). It was used in German military bands in the 19th century.

Bellman, Carl Michael (*b* Stockholm, 4 Feb 1740; *d* there, 11 Feb 1795). Swedish poet. He was known as an entertainer and satirist in the 1760s and achieved fame through court patronage. A gifted poet and writer of *c*1700 poems, he was a parodist, re-using popular melodies, but his bold verses and his metrical patterns created a new song form. He generally drew on existing melodies, including French airs, dances etc, but recomposed them and may have written some of his own.

Bells, The. Rakhmaninov's op.35 (1913), a choral symphony to a text by Bal'mont after Edgar Allen Poe.

Bells of Zlonice, The. Dvořák's Symphony no.1 in C minor (1865).

Belly [table, soundtable]. The upper surface of the body of a string instrument.

Belshazzar. Oratorio by Handel to a biblical text by Charles Jennens (1745, London).

Belshazzar's Feast. Cantata by Walton to a text compiled by Osbert Sitwell from the Bible (1931, Leeds).

Belyayev, Mitrofan Petrovich (*b* St Petersburg, 22 Feb 1836; *d* there, 4 Jan 1904). Russian music publisher. Impressed by Glazunov's Symphony no.1, he decided to establish a firm for the publication of Russian music, setting up in Leipzig in 1885 under the name Belaieff. He issued over 2000 works by Russian composers including Balakirev, Rimsky-Korsakov, Taneyev, Borodin, Glazunov, Musorgsky and Lyadov.

Bemetzrieder, Anton (*b* Dauendorf, 1743/1748; *d* London, *c*1817). French theorist. He was a music teacher in Paris and from 1781 in London, where he also composed. His writings on music, notably *Leçons de clavecin, et principes d'harmonie* (1771), are mainly pedagogical.

Benatzky, Ralph (*b* Moravske-Budejovice, 5 June 1884; *d* Zurich, 16 Oct 1957). Austrian-Moravian composer. He took up a military career, then studied philology and music under Mottl. He worked in Munich and later Vienna, writing songs, operettas and (after a move to Berlin) revue-style works including *Casanova* (after J. Strauss, 1928) and *White Horse Inn* (1930), partly with other composers. In 1933 he left Germany and worked in Hollywood and elsewhere; his works include film scores and over 5000 songs.

Bencini, Pietro Paolo (*b c*1670; *d* Rome, 6 July 1755). Italian composer. He held *maestro di cappella* posts in Rome, from 1743 at the Cappella Giulia. He had several oratorios performed and wrote many sacred works. Two of his relations were composers; Antonio (*fl* 1730–42), also active in Rome, wrote mostly church music; Giuseppe (*fl* 1723–7), in Florence, composed cantatas etc.

Ben Cosyn's Virginal Book. English MS of keyboard music, probably compiled in 1620, with music by Bull, Byrd, Cosyn, Gibbons, Tallis and others; it is now in the British Library, London. Cosyn also copied part of a collection now in the Bibliothèque Nationale, Paris, in 1652. *See* COSYN, BENJAMIN.

Benda, Franz [František] (*b* Staré Benátky, bap. 22 Nov 1709; *d* Nowawes, 7 March 1786). Bohemian composer. Son of a village musician, he trained first as a singer. He served as a violinist at Warsaw in 1729–33, then entered the service of the Prussian crown prince at Potsdam – after his accession (1740), Frederick the Great. He became Konzertmeister in 1771. He studied composition with J.G. and C.H. Graun and wrote sonatas, other chamber works, concertos and symphonies, but few were published. He was best known for his expressive violin playing and his melodic embellishment.

Three of Franz Benda's brothers were musicians: GEORG BENDA, Johann (Georg) (1713–52), a violinist who played in crown prince Frederick's ensemble and composed (mainly for the violin), and Joseph (1724–1804), who joined Frederick's orchestra at Potsdam as a violinist and succeeded Franz as Konzertmeister (1786–97). Their sister Anna Franziska (1728–81) was a soprano. Among Joseph's sons were (Johann) Friedrich Ernst (1749–85), a violinist, harpsichordist and composer who served at Potsdam and in 1770 founded a concert series in Berlin.

Four of Franz's children became musicians: Maria Carolina (1743–1820) was a singer, pianist and composer at the Weimar court, where she married the composer E.W. Wolf. Both Friedrich (Wilhelm Heinrich) (1745–1814) and Karl Hermann Heinrich (1748–1836) were violinists at the Prussian court. Friedrich composed concertos, symphonies, chamber music and various vocal works; Karl Hermann Heinrich succeeded his uncle Joseph as Konzertmeister in 1802. Their sister (Bernhardine) Juliane (1752–83), a singer and composer, married J.F. Reichardt in 1776.

Benda, Georg (*b* Staré Benátky, bap. 30 June 1722; *d* Köstritz, 6 Nov 1795). Bohemian composer. He was a violinist with his brothers Franz, Johann and Joseph in the Prussian court orchestra, 1742–50, became Kapellmeister at the Gotha court, writing sacred cantatas, instrumental music and (in 1765) an Italian opera. In 1765–6 he visited Italy, and in 1770–72 was *Kapelldirector*. When Seyler's theatrical troupe arrived at Gotha, Benda began writing German stage works, particularly melodramas (works combining spoken text and music); his *Ariadne auf Naxos* and *Medea* (both 1775) were the first successful examples. His Singspiels *Walder* and *Romeo und Julie* (both 1776) were among the first with serious plots and longer, through-composed scenes.

Georg's son Friedrich Ludwig Benda (1752–92) was also a violinist and composer. He played for Seyler's troupe and later served at the Duke of Mecklenburg-Schwerin's court in Ludwigslust. He composed Singspiels, church music and instrumental works.

Bendinelli, Cesare (*b* Verona; *d* ?Munich, 1617). Italian trumpeter. In Vienna from 1567 and chief court trumpeter in Munich from 1580, he is important as compiler of the earliest known trumpet method, *Tutta l'arte della trombetta* (*c*1614), which contains the first dated pieces (1584–8) for the clarino register. He claimed to be the first to apply tonguing syllables to the trumpet.

Bendix, Victor (Emanuel) (*b* Copenhagen, 17 May 1851; *d* there, 5 Jan 1926). Danish composer and conductor. He established and conducted the Copenhagen Philharmonic Concerts (1897) and composed important piano works and symphonies, especially no.2, *Sommerklange fra Sydrusland* op.20 (1888), in graceful Slavonic folk style.

Bendl, Karel (*b* Prague, 16 April 1838; *d* there, 20 Sept 1897). Czech composer and conductor. He studied at the Prague Organ School. He was conductor of the Hlahol Choral Society, deputy conductor at the Prague Provisional Theatre, organist and choirmaster at St Nicholas and composition professor at the Prague Conservatory. With a style derived from Mendelssohn or Smetana, he wrote *c*300 choral works, mainly nationalistic choruses but including the popular cantata *Švanda the Bagpiper* (1881), and 140 songs; these and his 12 stage works, notably the Meyerbeerian *Lejla* (1868) and *The Montenegrins* (1881) and the tragic *The Child of Tabor* (1886–8), show his importance as a 19th-century Czech vocal composer.

Benedetti, Francesco Maria (*b* Assisi, 1683; *d* there, 1746). Italian composer. A Franciscan priest, he was *maestro di cappella* at the Basilica in Assisi (1713–16, 1729 onwards), at other times working at Turin and Aosta. His numerous sacred works, many on a grandiose scale, resemble Vivaldi's in style.

Benedetti, Piero (*b* Florence, *c*1585; *d* there, after 14 July 1649). Italian composer. He was a court chaplain in Florence, a member of the Accademia degli Elevati and from 1630 a canon of S Lorenzo. All his surviving compositions are songs. The extremes of style in his three books of *Musiche* (1611–17) are clear examples of musical mannerism: they are characterized by harsh, often unprepared dissonances, unusual harmonic progressions, erratic rhythms and striking declamatory passages.

Benedicite. A canticle, sung as a responsorial chant at Mass on the Ember Saturdays of Advent, Lent and September and at Sunday Lauds; it is used daily in Lent in the Anglican rite. The text, sung by three holy children in the fiery furnace (from the additions to *Daniel* in the Apocrypha), begins 'Benedicite omnia opera Domini Domino'.

Benedict, Sir Julius (*b* Stuttgart, 27 Nov 1804; *d* London, 5 June 1885). English composer and conductor of German birth. He studied with Hummel, Weber (1821–4) and Barbaia before becoming a conductor in Naples, finally settling in London in 1835. Although his main posts were at Drury Lane (1838–48), where he conducted successful English operas and staged three of his own, and Her Majesty's (from 1852), he also conducted successive Norwich festivals (1845–78), founded a Vocal Association and accompanied at the Monday Popular Concerts. Of his Rossinian English operas, *The Lily of Killarney* (1862) was extremely popular; he also wrote choral cantatas, notably *The Legend of St Cecilia* (1866), an oratorio, modest instrumental works and two piano concertos.

Benedictus (Lat.: 'blessed'). In the Roman rite, part of the Sanctus after the first Hosanna, consisting of the sentence 'Benedictus qui venit in nomine Domini' and followed by the second Hosanna. An adaptation from *Matthew* xxi.9, it is found in the Roman liturgy from the 7th century; it is also sung in various oriental rites. In Renaissance and later masses it is usually a separate section, often for fewer voices.

'Benedictus' is also the first word of four canticles (those of David, Azariah, the Three Young Men and Zachary), outside the psalter, which are used in various rites.

Benet, John (*fl* ?*c*1420–50). English composer. He was probably Master of the Choristers at St Anthony's Hospital, London, from 1443, and a member of the London Guild of Parish Clerks. His surviving works comprise three mass cycles (one also ascribed to Dunstable and Power, another of questionable ascription), other mass movements and three isorhythmic motets. The early pieces are rather awkward but he later achieved the harmonic clarity and smooth rhythmic flow of Dunstable's last works.

Beneventan rite, Music of the. A tradition of monophonic liturgical music in southern Italy during the 10th–13th centuries, perhaps predating the introduction there of Gregorian (Roman) chant. The name comes from Benevento, main source of the MSS; they contain rubrics, texts and melodies with variants from the standard 7th-century Roman liturgy, suggesting that they reflect a separate Beneventan (or Old Beneventan) rite. Many of the melodies have a range of only four or five notes, with much repetition and little development or division.

Benevoli, Orazio (*b* Rome, 19 April 1605; *d* there, 17 June 1672). Italian composer. He held posts as *maestro di cappella* at various churches in Rome before becoming a Kapellmeister in Vienna in 1644. By 1646 he had returned to Rome, soon becoming *maestro di cappella* of the Cappella Giulia at St Peter's. He was long held wrongly thought to be composer of the 53-part *Missa salisburgensis*. Benevoli's output consists entirely of sacred music, some in the Palestrina tradition but more in the modern polychoral idiom, with a tendency towards major-minor tonalities.

Bengtsson, (Lars) Ingmar (Olof) (*b* Stockholm, 2 March 1920). Swedish musicologist. He studied in Stockholm, Uppsala and Basle (1947) and was a music critic (*Svenska dagbladet*, 1943–59), a pianist, and from 1947 a lecturer at Uppsala University (professor, 1961). He has been involved in the publication of Swedish music and founded the Swedish Archive of the History of Music. He is author of a study of J.H. Roman and an important survey of musicology, *Musikvetenskap* (1973).

Ben Haim [Frankenburger], **Paul** (*b* Munich, 5 July 1897; *d* Tel-Aviv, 14 Jan 1984). Israeli composer. He studied at the Munich Academy (1915–20) and conducted in Augsburg (1924–31) before moving to Palestine, where he changed his name and began to attempt a synthesis of Middle Eastern music and Western tradition. His works include two wartime symphonies, concertos for violin (1960) and cello (1962), a String Quartet (1937) and choral pieces.

Benincori, Angelo Maria (*b* Brescia, 28 March 1779; *d* Belleville, 30 Dec 1821). Italian composer. He studied the violin in Parma and composition with Cimarosa and attempted to establish himself as a dramatic composer in Paris; of his seven operas, only *Aladin* (1821) achieved success. He was most admired for his chamber music, showing the influence of Haydn.

Benjamin, Arthur (*b* Sydney, 18 Sept 1893; *d* London, 10 April 1960). Australian-British composer and pianist. He studied at the RCM with Stanford and began teaching there in 1926. Through travels he came into contact with Caribbean music, which he used in his *Jamaican Rumba* (for two pianos 1938, later orchestrated) and other light pieces. His diverse output includes operas, concertante pieces, songs and chamber music, in a cheerful style; though the late works (e.g. *Concerto quasi una fantasia* for piano and orchestra, 1949) are darker. He was an accomplished pianist who gave several premières.

Benjamin, George (*b* London, 31 Jan 1960). English composer and pianist. He studied at the Paris Conservatoire with Messiaen and at Cambridge with Alexander Goehr: Ligeti and Boulez have been other influences. He first came to attention with the vividly imagined orchestral piece *Ringed by the Flat Horizon* (1980); this was consolidated with *A Mind of Winter* (1981) for soprano and small orchestra and *At First Light* for chamber ensemble (1982).

Bennet, John (*b* ?*c*1575–80; *fl* 1599–1614). English composer. He was probably from Lancashire. The pieces in his only publication, *Madrigalls to Foure Voyces* (1599), show great technical assurance; they range from light contrapuntal canzonets, like Morley's, to more solemn pieces recalling Dowland (e.g. the well-known *O sleep, fond fancie*). He contributed to the madrigal anthology *The Triumphes of Oriana* (1601).

Bennett, Joseph (*b* Berkeley, Gloucs., 29 Nov 1831; *d* there, 12 June 1911). English music critic. His work centred on the *Daily Telegraph*, but he contributed to other papers, edited two music journals and wrote several books, notably *Forty Years of Music* (1905).

Bennett, Richard Rodney (*b* Broadstairs, 29 March 1936). English composer and pianist. He studied at the RAM (1953–7) and with Boulez in Paris (1957–9), though his public career as a composer had begun before this. At 16 he was writing 12-note music, and the period with Boulez encouraged him towards Darmstadt techniques. But in the 1960s he recovered more conventional aspects to develop a style of Bergian expressionism (e.g. in his opera *The Mines of Sulphur*, 1965); his opera *Victory* was given at Covent Garden in 1970. His subsequent output is large, including many concertos, settings of English poetry, chamber music, and, notably, big Romantic film scores. A musician of great versatility, he has worked as a jazz pianist (several of his scores of the 1960s are in a sophisticated jazz style) and has played and arranged American popular music.

Bennett, Robert Russell (*b* Kansas City, MO, 15 June 1894; *d* New York, 18 Aug 1981). American orchestrator, conductor and composer. After study with Boulanger in Paris he worked as an orchestrator on Broadway, scoring *c*300 musicals in 40 years. His original music often shows a mastery of instrumentation on a higher level than the musical material itself. His opera on the life of Maria Malibran was staged in New York in 1935.

Bennett, Sir William Sterndale (*b* Sheffield, 13 April 1816; *d* London, 1 Feb 1875). English composer. He is the most distinguished English Romantic composer. Orphaned at the age of three, he went to live with his grandparents in Cambridge, became a chorister at King's College and studied the violin, piano and composition at the RAM. His First Piano Concerto (1832) made a remarkable impression and he received encouragement from many in high places, including Mendelssohn. He played two more piano concertos at the Philharmonic Society (1835, 1836) and made two visits to Germany, where he was enthusiastically lauded in print by Schumann and at the Leipzig Gewandhaus concerts played his Third Concerto and conducted two overtures (*The Naiads*, 1836; *Parisina*, 1835). From 1837 he taught at the RAM, though he continued to play at Philharmonic concerts, gave annual chamber music concerts and founded and directed the Bach Society (he conducted the first English performance of the *St Matthew Passion* in 1854). He succeeded Wagner as conductor of the

Philharmonic Society (1855) and became professor of music at Cambridge (1856); by 1866 he was principal of the RAM and in 1871 he was knighted. Several major works appeared in his later years, including choral commissions and a Symphony in G minor (1865). Bennett's music reflects a classical purity derived from Mozart (his confessed model) but also resembling Mendelssohn, the one Romantic composer he admired. The youthful piano concertos and concert overtures are his best work – charming and evocative and often surprising structurally; the piano works display a mastery of the instrument's potential. His solo songs, such as *Gentle Zephyr*, resemble the Leipzig Romantic style more than his other compositions. Bennett edited piano and choral music and had an incalculable if mainly conservative influence on a generation of RAM students.

Benoist, François (*b* Nantes, 10 Sept 1794; *d* Paris, 6 May 1878). French organist and teacher. He studied at the Paris Conservatoire (winning the Prix de Rome in 1815) where as organ professor (1819–75), he counted Alkan, Franck, Bizet and Saint-Saëns among his pupils.

Benoit, Peter (Leonard Leopold) (*b* Harelbeke, 17 Aug 1834; *d* Antwerp, 8 March 1901). Belgian composer, conductor and teacher. He studied with Fétis at the Brussels Conservatory, travelled in Germany and worked as a conductor in Paris, but settled at Antwerp, where he founded the Flemish Music School (later Royal Flemish Conservatory) and helped found the Flemish Opera. Aiming to stimulate national musical consciousness, he simplified his romantic style and incorporated national musical traits into his works (mainly cantatas, oratorios and sacred vocal pieces).

Bentzon, Niels Viggo (*b* Copenhagen, 24 Aug 1919). Danish composer. He studied at the Copenhagen Conservatory and began teaching there in 1949. Exceedingly prolific, he has cultivated a vigorous style owing something to Nielsen and to the Hindemith of the 1920s, composing in all forms, especially the symphony, concerto, piano sonata and string quartet.

Benucci, Francesco (*b c*1745; *d* Florence, 5 April 1824). Italian bass. From 1783 he was the leading *buffo* singer in Vienna. He sang Figaro at the première of Mozart's *Le nozze di Figaro* (1786) and Leporello at the Vienna première (1788) of *Don Giovanni*.

Benvenuto Cellini. Opera in two acts by Berlioz to a libretto by Léon de Wailly and A. Barbier after Cellini's autobiography (1838, Paris); Berlioz withdrew a revised, three-act version (1852).

Berardi, Angelo (*b* S Agata, *c*1636; *d* Rome, 9 April 1694). Italian theorist and composer, important for his writings on counterpoint. He was *maestro di cappella* at Tivoli (1673–9) and Spoleto cathedrals, and at S Maria in Trastevere, Rome. His first surviving treatise, *Ragionamenti musicali* (1681), discusses the origins and nature of music and the diversity of style. *Documenti armonici* (1687) and *Miscellanea musicale* (1689) describe 17th-century contrapuntal practice, the latter discussing the *seconda prattica*.

Berardi was also a prolific composer, almost entirely of church music.

Berberian, Cathy (*b* Attleboro, MA, 4 July 1925; *d* Rome, 6 March 1983). American singer. Her great vocal agility and striking platform presence (she was trained in mime and dance) caught the attention of avant-garde composers; in 1958 she gave works by Cage in Rome and on her American début (1960, Tanglewood) performed Berio's *Circles*. From 1950 to 1966 she was married to Berio, who wrote *Sequenza III*, *Visage* and *Recital I* for her.

Berceuse (Fr.). 'Lullaby': a quiet instrumental (especially piano) piece. Chopin's Berceuse in D♭ op.57 established compound metre, a 'flat' major key and simple, oscillating harmonies as its main features. *See also* LULLABY.

Berchem, Jacquet de (*b* Berchem-lez-Anvers, *c*1505; *d c*1565). Flemish composer. From the 1530s he was in Venice, where three volumes of his madrigals were published (1546, 1555, 1561). In 1546 he became choirmaster of Verona Cathedral, and he may have moved to Ferrara. He was an important figure in the early development of the 16th-century madrigal. His *Capriccio* is a setting of 91 stanzas from Ariosto's *Orlando furioso* (he may have originated the concept of a madrigal cycle). In his early five-part madrigals the Netherlands contrapuntal style predominates, but the later works (usually for four voices) employ syllabic, chordal declamation and more animated rhythms. His *chansons* and sacred music, which includes two masses and at least nine motets, are less progressive.

Berenice. Opera in three acts by Handel to a libretto by Antonio Salvi (1737, London).

Berezovsky, Maxim Sonzontovich (*b* Glukhov, 27 Oct 1745; *d* St Petersburg, 2 April 1777). Ukrainian composer. He studied in Italy with Padre Martini in 1765–75; his opera *Demofoonte* (1773, Livorno) was the first by a Russian composer given there. His sacred works are important in the Russian ecclesiastical repertory.

Berezowsky, Nicolai (Tikhonovich) (*b* St Petersburg, 17 May 1900; *d* New York, 27 Aug 1953). American composer and violinist. He studied at the imperial chapel in St Petersburg (1908–17) and in Vienna and moved to the USA in 1920, where he played in the New York PO. His works include four symphonies, concertos and the children's opera *Babar the Elephant* (1953).

Berg, Alban (Maria Johannes) (*b* Vienna, 9 Feb 1885; *d* there, 24 Dec 1935). Austrian composer. He wrote songs as a youth but had no serious musical education before his lessons with Schoenberg, which began in 1904. Webern was a pupil at the same time, a crucial period in Schoenberg's creative life, when he was moving rapidly towards and into atonality. Berg's Piano Sonata op.1 (1908) is still tonal, but the Four Songs op.2 (1910) move away from key and the op.3 String Quartet (1910) is wholly atonal; it is also remarkable in sustaining, through motivic development, a larger span when the instrumental works of Schoenberg and Webern were comparatively momentary. Berg dedicated it to his wife Helene, whom he married in 1911.

Then came the Five Songs for soprano op.4 (1912), miniatures setting poetic instants by Peter Altenberg. This was Berg's first orchestral score, and though it shows an awareness of Schoenberg, Mahler and Debussy, it is brilliantly conceived and points towards *Wozzeck* – and towards 12-note serialism, notably in its final passacaglia. More immediately Berg produced another set of compact statements, the Four Pieces for clarinet and piano op.5 (1913), then returned to large form with the Three Orchestral Pieces op.6 (1915), a thematically linked sequence of prelude, dance movement and funeral march. The prelude begins and ends in the quiet noise of percussion; the other two movements show Berg's discovery of how traditional forms and stylistic elements (including tonal harmony) might support big structures.

In May 1914 Berg saw the Vienna première of Büchner's *Woyzeck* and formed the plan of setting it. He started the opera in 1917, while he was in the Austrian army (1915–18), and finished it in 1922. He made his own selection from the play's fragmentary scenes to furnish a three-act libretto for formal musical setting: the first act is a suite of five character pieces (five scenes showing the simple soldier Wozzeck in different relationships), the second a five-movement symphony (for the disintegration of his liaison with Marie), the third a set of five inventions on different ostinato ideas (for the tragedy's brutally nihilist climax). The close musical structuring, extending to small details of timing, may be seen as an analogue for the mechanical alienness of the universe around Büchner's central characters, though Berg's music crosses all boundaries, from atonal to tonal (there is a Mahlerian interlude in D minor), from speech to song, from café music to sophisticated textures of dissonant counterpoint. *Wozzeck* had its première in Berlin in 1925 and thereafter was widely produced, bringing Berg financial security.

His next work, the Chamber Concerto for violin, piano and 13 wind (1925), moves decisively towards a more classical style: its three formally complex movements are still more clearly shaped than those of the op.6 set and the scoring suggests a response to Stravinskian objectivity. The work is also threaded through with ciphers and numerical conceits, making it a celebration of the triune partnership of Schoenberg, Berg and Webern. Then came the Lyric Suite for string quartet (1926), whose long-secret programme connects it with Berg's intimate feelings for Hanna Fuchs-Robettin – feelings also important to him in the composition of his second opera, *Lulu* (1929–35). The suite, in six movements of increasingly extreme tempo, uses 12-note serial along with other material in projecting a quasi-operatic development towards catastrophe and annulment.

The development of *Lulu* was twice interrupted by commissioned works, the concert aria *Der Wein* on poems by Baudelaire (1929) and the Violin Concerto (1935), and it remained unfinished at Berg's death: his widow placed an embargo on the incomplete third act, which could not be published or performed until 1979. As with *Wozzeck*, he made his own libretto out of stage material, this time choosing two plays by Wedekind, whom he had long admired for his treatment of sexuality. Dramatically and musically the opera is a huge palindrome, showing Lulu's rise through society in her successive relationships and then her descent into prostitution and eventual death at the hands of Jack the Ripper. Again the score is filled with elaborate formal schemes, around a lyricism unloosed by Berg's individual understanding of 12-note serialism. Something of its threnodic sensuality is continued in the Violin Concerto, designed as a memorial to the teenage daughter of Mahler's widow.

Operas Wozzeck (1925); Lulu (1935)
Orchestral music 5 Altenberg Songs, op.4 (1912); 3 Pieces, op.6 (1915); Chamber Conc. (1925); 7 Early Songs (1928); 3 Pieces from the Lyric Suite (1928); Der Wein, aria (1929); Vn Conc. (1935)
Chamber music Pf Sonata, op.1 (1908); Str Qt, op.3 (1910); 4 Pieces, cl, pf, op.5 (1913); Adagio, cl, vn, pf; Lyric Suite, str qt (1925)
Songs 4 op.2 (1910); many early songs

Berg, Gunnar (Johnsen) (*b* St Gall, 11 Jan 1909). Danish composer. He studied at the Copenhagen Conservatory (1936–7) and with Rosenberg. His first works were freely atonal, but in 1948 he went to Paris, and under the influence of Messiaen and Webern wrote the first Danish serial piece, his Cello Suite (1950). His later works comprise orchestral, chamber and piano pieces.

Berg, Josef (*b* Brno, 8 March 1927; *d* there, 26 Feb 1971). Czech composer. He studied with Petrželka at the Brno Conservatory (1946–50) and began as a neo-classicist, though in the 1950s he came under the influence of Moravian folk music and Janáček. He was then affected by new Western ideas and concentrated on chamber music and chamber operas of Brechtian alienation, leading to the 'happenings' of his last years.

Bergamasca. An Italian dance of the 16th–17th centuries, probably from Bergamo in northern Italy. Its melody and discants, in quadruple metre over recurrent I–IV–V–I harmonies, frequently served for variations.

Berganza (Vargas), Teresa (*b* Madrid, 16 March 1935). Spanish mezzo-soprano. She studied at the Madrid Conservatory and with Lola Rodriguez Aragon. In 1957 she sang Dorabella at the Aix-en-Provence Festival; she sang Cherubino at Glyndebourne in 1958, the year she made her American début (at Dallas). At Covent Garden (from 1960), she was admired as Rossini's Rosina and Cenerentola and as Carmen. She married the pianist Felix Lavilla, with whom she has given recitals.

Bergen International Festival (Norway). Annual (summer) arts festival, established in 1953. Events include symphony, church and jazz concerts and chamber music at Grieg's home.

Berger, Arthur (Victor) (*b* New York, 15 May 1912). American composer and teacher. He studied at New York University and with Piston at Harvard (1936) and has taught at various institutions, including Mills College and Brandeis University. His works of the 1940s were neo-classical, but his harmony became more spare and fragmented (Babbitt referred to 'diatonic Webern'; in 1957 he began using 12-note serialism, though this soon gave way to an individual cellular technique. His output is small and almost exclusively instrumental. He has been active as a music critic.

Berger, Ludwig (*b* Berlin, 18 April 1777; *d* there, 16 Feb 1839). German composer and pianist. After sojourns in St Petersburg and London, he settled in Berlin as an eminent teacher. His works include a piano concerto and Beethovenian sonatas and studies, some of which influenced Mendelssohn.

Berger, Theodor (*b* Traismauer an der Donau, 18 May 1905). Austrian composer. After study in Vienna, with Korngold and Schmidt, he went to Berlin. The romantic flavour of his music attracted Furtwängler, who conducted his works in Germany and abroad.

Berger, Wilhelm (Reinhard) (*b* Boston, 9 Aug 1861; *d* Jena, 15 Jan 1911). German composer and conductor. He studied at the Berlin Hochschule, becoming conductor of the Berlin Musikalische Gesellschaft in 1899, then court Kapellmeister at Meiningen. As a composer he followed Brahms in genre and style, gaining recognition for his choral and chamber music.

Bergerette (Fr.). (1) A tender French *air* of the 18th century in which constant reference is made to shepherds and shepherdesses.

(2) A 16th-century instrumental dance similar to the saltarello.

Berggreen, Andreas Peter (*b* Copenhagen, 2 March 1801; *d* there, 8 Nov 1880). Danish folklorist, teacher and composer. A self-taught organist and singing master, he collected and edited Danish and foreign folksongs and composed a notable set of hymn tunes; he also taught music theory. His works, mainly cantatas and partsongs, are indebted to Viennese Classical models.

Berglund, Paavo (*b* Helsinki, 14 April 1929). Finnish conductor. He studied the violin and joined the Finnish RSO in 1949. In 1952 he co-founded the Helsinki CO. He was chief conductor of the Finnish RSO (1962–72) and in 1965 gave Sibelius centenary concerts with the Bournemouth SO, becoming principal conductor in 1972. He has appeared widely with major orchestras and became musical director of the Helsinki PO in 1975.

Bergman, Erik (Valdemar) (*b* Uusikaarlepyy, 24 Nov 1911). Finnish composer. He studied in Helsinki, with Tiessen in Berlin (1937–9) and with Vogel in Ascona (1949–50), then worked as a music critic and teacher, notably at the Helsinki Academy (from 1963). His studies with Vogel led him from tonal Romanticism to 12-note music, deployed mostly in large-scale choral tableaux on God and nature; later he adopted a freer technique involving improvisation and aleatory writing.

Bergmann, Carl (*b* Ebersbach, 12 April 1821; *d* New York, 16 Aug 1876). German-American conductor and cellist. As a conductor of the New York Philharmonic Society orchestra, 1855–76, he helped shape the New York PO into a great orchestra; in particular, he championed Liszt, Berlioz, Wagner and Tchaikovsky.

Bergonzi, Carlo (i) (*b* ?Cremona 1683; *d* there, 1747). Italian violin maker. He was one of the greatest Cremonese makers, overshadowed only by his contemporaries Antonio Stradivari and Giuseppe Guarneri 'del Gesù'. Perhaps working alone from 1720, he built his finest instruments between 1730 and 1740. They have beautifully symmetrical scrolls and are made from unusually handsome wood; richly varnished, they are almost unsurpassed visually and tonally. His son Michel Angelo (*c*1722–after 1758) was a fine maker though he lost or abandoned his father's great varnish.

Bergonzi, Carlo (ii) (*b* Polisene, 13 July 1924). Italian tenor. He studied in Parma and at the Boito Conservatory. His début was as a baritone, at Lecce (1948), but after further study he sang the tenor role of Andrea Chénier at Bari (1951). In 1953 he appeared at La Scala and in London. He sang at Covent Garden as Verdi's Alvaro, Manrico and Riccardo and as Cavaradossi, and at the Met. He uses his beautiful voice with taste and discretion.

Bergsma, William (Laurence) (*b* Oakland, CA, 1 April 1921). American composer and teacher. He studied with Hanson and Rogers at the Eastman School (1940–44) and has taught at the Juilliard School (1946–63) and the University of Washington, Seattle. His imaginative works, in all genres, are essentially tonal while using some avant-garde principles; they include the opera *The Wife of Martin Guerre* (1956).

Beringer, Oscar (*b* Furtwangen, 14 July 1844; *d* London, 21 Feb 1922). English pianist and composer (his family settled in England in 1849). He made his début at 15, then studied further in Leipzig and Berlin before returning to England, where he taught at his own academy (1873–97) and at the RAM. He is remembered particularly for his piano exercises and methods as well as many editions.

Berio, Luciano (*b* Oneglia, 24 Oct 1925). Italian composer. He studied with his father and grandfather, both organists and composers, and with Ghedini at the Milan Conservatory in the late 1940s. In 1950 he married the American singer Cathy Berberian, and the next year at Tanglewood he met Dallapiccola, who influenced his move towards and beyond 12-note serialism in such works as his Joyce cycle *Chamber Music* for voice and trio (1953). Further stimulus came from his meetings with Maderna, Pousseur and Stockhausen in Basle in 1954, and he became a central member of the Darmstadt circle. He directed an electronic music studio at the Milan station of Italian radio (1955–61), at the same time producing *Sequenza I* for flute (1958, the first of a cycle of solo explorations of performing gestures), *Circles* (1960, a loop of Cummings settings for voice, harp and percussion) and *Epifanie* (1961, an aleatory set of orchestral and vocal movements designed to show different kinds of vocal behaviour). These established his area of interest: with the means and archetypes of musical communication.

For most of the next decade he was in the USA,

teaching and composing, his main works of this period including the Dante-esque *Laborintus II* for voices and orchestra (1965), the *Sinfonia* for similar resources (1969, with a central movement whirling quotations round Mahler and Beckett) and *Opera* (1970), a study of the decline of the genre and of Western bourgeois civilization. Two more operas, *La vera storia* (1982) and *Un re in ascolto* (1984), came out of his collaboration with Calvino. Other works include *Coro* (1976), a panoply of poster statements and refracted folksongs for chorus and orchestra, and numerous orchestral and chamber pieces.

Dramatic music Mimusique no.2 (1955); Allez-Hop! (1959); Passaggio (1962); Traces (1964); Opera (1970); Recital I (1972); Diario immaginario (1975); La vera storia (1982); Un re in ascolto (1984)
Ballets Per la dolce memoria di quel giorno (1974); Linea (1974)
Orchestral music Concertino (1949); Nones (1954); Variazioni (1954); Allelujah I, II (1955, 1957); Variazioni 'Ein Mädchen oder Weibchen' (1956); Tempi concertati (1959); Chemins I, IIb, IIc, III, IV, V (1965, 1967, 1969, 1972, 1975, 1980); Bewegung (1971); Conc., 2 pf, orch (1973); Eindrücke (1974); Points on the Curve to Find... (1974); Il ritorno degli Snovidenia (1977); Encore (1978); Accordo (1981); Requies (1984)
Vocal music El mar la mar (1950); Opus Number Zoo (1952); Chamber Music (1953); Circles (1960); Epifanie (1961); Sequenza III (1966); Laborintus II (1965); O King (1967); Sinfonia (1969); Questo vuol dire che (1969); Agnus (1971); E vo' (1972); Cries of London (1974); Calmo (1974); A-ronne (1975); Coro (1976); Duo (1982)
Chamber music Str Qt (1956); Serenata (1957); Différences (1959); Sincronie (1964); Chemins II (1967); Memory (1970); Musica leggera (1974); Chemins V (1980)
Solo instrumental music Sequenza I, fl (1958), II, harp (1963), V, trbn (1966), VI, va (1967), VII, ob (1969), VIII, vn (1975), IX, cl (1980), X, tpt (1984); Rounds, hpd (1965); Fa-Si, org (1975); Les mots sont allés, vc (1978)
Piano music Cinque variazioni (1953); Wasserklavier (1964); Sequenza IV (1966); Erdenklavier (1970)
Tape Thema (Omaggio a Joyce) (1958); Visage (1961); Chants parallèles (1975)

Bériot, Charles-Auguste de (*b* Louvain, 20 Feb 1802; *d* Brussels, 8 April 1870). Belgian violinist and composer. He studied under J.-F. Tiby, was encouraged by Viotti and briefly worked with Baillot. In the mid-1820s he made successful débuts in London and Paris and from 1829 travelled with the singer Maria Malibran giving concerts; she died soon after their marriage in 1836. He resumed his career in 1838 and taught at the Brussels Conservatory in 1843, retiring in 1852 with failing eyesight. He modernized the classical French violin style of Viotti and his followers by adapting Paganinian technique to Parisian elegance and piquancy, leading to a new Romantic approach and a 'Franco-Belgian school'. His playing and his music show a sweet melodic style, a sparkling technique and elfin grace (which influenced Mendelssohn's Violin Concerto); he wrote ten violin concertos, variations, duos and chamber works as well as instruction books. Henry Vieuxtemps was his pupil. His and Malibran's son Charles-Wilfrid (1833–1914) was a noted pianist and teacher.

Berkeley, Sir Lennox (Randall Francis) (*b* Boars Hill, 12 May 1903). English composer. He studied at Oxford and with Boulanger in Paris (1927–32), where he met Stravinsky and became friendly with Poulenc.

In 1928 he became a Roman Catholic. Back in London he worked for the BBC (1942–5) and taught at the RAM (1946–68). His official op.1 dates from after he was 30, but his output is large, including a full-length opera (*Nelson*, 1954), three one-acters (including the comedy *A Dinner Engagement*, 1954), four symphonies, sacred music (*Missa brevis* with organ, 1960), songs (Four Poems of St Teresa of Avila for contralto and strings, 1947; Five Auden Poems with piano, 1958), chamber and piano music. The earlier music looks towards Paris, with its suave neo-classicism, though his acquaintance with the young Britten was also important. In the 1960s his work became more complex and darker, including elements of 12-note serialism.

Berkeley, Michael (*b* London, 29 May 1948). English composer, son of Lennox Berkeley. He studied with George Malcolm, his father, and with Richard Rodney Bennett at the RAM. His music is conventional and includes the Fantasia Concertante (1977) and a Cello Concerto (1982), his best-known piece being the oratorio *Or shall we Die?* (1982).

Berkshire Music Festival (USA). *See* TANGLEWOOD.

Berlijn, Anton [Aron Wolf] (*b* Amsterdam, 2 May 1817; *d* there, 18 Jan 1870). Dutch composer. He studied under F. Schneider, Spohr and Finck and composed over 500 works, including operas, ballets, symphonic works and partsongs.

Berlin, Irving [Baline, Israel] (*b* Temun, 11 May 1888). American songwriter of Russian birth. Having settled in New York in 1893, he worked as a street singer, a singing waiter and a song plugger. He achieved international success with his song *Alexander's Ragtime Band* (1911) and contributed to New York revues and operettas. From 1935 he wrote songs for film musicals, his best known being *Top Hat* (1935), *On the Avenue* (1937) and *Annie Get your Gun* (1946). He has published *c*1500 songs and is one of the most versatile and successful popular songwriters of the 20th century.

Berlin, Johan Daniel (*b* Memel, 12 May 1714; *d* Trondheim, 4 Nov 1787). Norwegian organist and composer of German birth. He was Trondheim's leading musician, and an inventor and writer, publishing the first Danish-Norwegian music textbook (1744). Few of his *c*30 works, mostly instrumental, survive.

Berlin Festival (West Germany). Annual festival (Sept–Oct), established in 1951. Events include opera, concerts, ballet and jazz.

Berlin Philharmonic Orchestra. West German orchestra, originally the Philharmonic Orchestra, formed from members of the Bilsesche Kapelle (established 1867); its home is the Philharmonie (opened 1963), the city's largest concert hall (cap. 2397). It was first conducted by Joachim (1884) and Bülow (1887); under Nikisch (1895) it gained an international reputation, maintained by Furtwängler (1922–45, 1947–54) and his successor, Herbert von Karajan (1954–).

Berlioz, (Louis-)Hector (*b* La Côte-St-André, Isère, 11 Dec 1803; *d* Paris, 8 March 1869). French composer. As a boy he learnt the flute, guitar and, from treatises alone, harmony (he never studied the piano); his first compositions were *romances* and small chamber pieces. After two unhappy years as a medical student in Paris (1821–3) he abandoned the career chosen for him by his father and turned decisively to music, attending Le Sueur's composition class at the Conservatoire. He entered for the Prix de Rome four times (1827–30) and finally won. Among the most powerful influences on him were Shakespeare, whose plays were to inspire three major works, and the actress Harriet Smithson, whom he idolized, pursued and, after a bizarre courtship, eventually married (1833). Beethoven's symphonies too made a strong impact, along with Goethe's *Faust* and the works of Moore, Scott and Byron. The most important product of this time was his startlingly original, five-movement *Symphonie fantastique* (1830).

Berlioz's 15 months in Italy (1831–2) were significant more for his absorption of warmth, vivacity and local colour than for the official works he wrote there; he moved out of Rome as often as possible and worked on a sequel to the *Symphonie fantastique* (*Le retour à la vie*, renamed *Lélio* in 1855) and overtures to *King Lear* and *Rob Roy*, returning to Paris early to promote his music. Although the 1830s and early 1840s saw a flow of major compositions – *Harold en Italie, Benvenuto Cellini, Grande messe des morts, Roméo et Juliette, Grande symphonie funèbre et triomphale, Les nuits d'été* – his musical career was now essentially a tragic one. He failed to win much recognition, his works were considered eccentric or 'incorrect' and he had reluctantly to rely on journalism for a living; from 1834 he wrote chiefly for the *Gazette musicale* and the *Journal des débats*.

As the discouragements of Paris increased, however, performances and recognition abroad beckoned: between 1842 and 1863 Berlioz spent most of his time touring, in Germany, Austria, Russia, England and elsewhere. Hailed as an advanced composer, he also became known as a leading modern conductor. He produced literary works (notably the *Mémoires*) and another series of musical masterpieces – *La damnation de Faust*, the *Te Deum, L'enfance du Christ*, the vast epic *Les troyens* (1856–8; partly performed, 1863) and *Béatrice et Bénédict* (1860–62) – meanwhile enjoying happy if short-lived relationships with Liszt and Wagner. The loss of his father, his son Louis (1834–67), two wives, two sisters and friends merely accentuated the weary decline of his last years, marked by his spiritual isolation from Parisian taste and the new music of Germany alike.

A lofty idealist with a leaping imagination, Berlioz was subject to violent emotional changes from enthusiasm to misery; only his sharp wit saved him from morbid self-pity over the disappointments in his private and professional life. The intensity of the personality is inextricably woven into the music: all his works reflect something in himself expressed through poetry, literature, religion or drama. Sincere expression is the key – matching means to expressive ends, often to the point of mixing forms and media, ignoring pre-set schemes. In *Les troyens*, his grand opera on Virgil's *Aeneid*, for example, aspects of the monumental and the intimate, the symphonic and the operatic, the decorative and the solemn converge.

Similarly his symphonies, from the explicitly dramatic *Symphonie fantastique* with its *idée fixe* (the theme representing his beloved, changed and distorted in line with the work's scenario), to the picturesque *Harold en Italie* with its concerto element, to the operatic choral symphony cum tone poem *Roméo et Juliette*, are all characteristic in their mixture of genres. Of his other orchestral works, the overture *Le carnaval romain* stands out as one of the most extrovert and brilliant. Among the choral works, *Faust* and *L'enfance du Christ* combine dramatic action and philosophic reflection, while the Requiem and *Te Deum* exploit to the full Berlioz's most spacious, ceremonial style.

Though Berlioz's compositional style has long been considered idiosyncratic, it can be seen to rely on an abundance of both technique and inspiration. Typical are expansive melodies of irregular phrase length, sometimes with a slight chromatic inflection, and expressive though not tonally adventurous harmonies. Freely contrapuntal textures predominate, used to a variety of fine effects including superimposition of separate themes; a striking boldness in rhythmic articulation gives the music much of its vitality. Berlioz left perhaps his most indelible mark as an orchestrator, finding innumerable and subtle ways to combine and contrast instruments (both on stage and off), effectively emancipating the procedure of orchestration for generations of later composers. As a critic he admired above all Gluck and Beethoven, expressed doubt about Wagner and fought endlessly against the second-rate.

Operas Benvenuto Cellini (1838); Les troyens (1863, 1890); Béatrice et Bénédict (1862)
Orchestral music Les francs-juges (1826); Waverley, ov. (1828); Symphonie fantastique (1830); Le roi Lear, ov. (1831); Rob Roy, ov. (1831); Harold en Italie, va, orch (1834); Roméo et Juliette, with vv (1839); Rêverie et caprice, vn, orch/pf (1841); Le carnaval romain, ov. (1844); Le corsaire (1844)
Choral music La révolution grecque (1826); Chant sacré (1829); Méditation religieuse (1831); Lélio (1832); Sara la baigneuse (1834); Grande messe des morts (1837); Hymne à la France (1844); La damnation de Faust (1846); La mort d'Ophélie (1848); Te Deum (1849); L'enfance du Christ (1854)
Vocal music 9 works for solo v, orch, incl. Les nuits d'été (1841); over 30 songs, 1–4 vv, incl. Elégie en prose (1829)
Other works fugues, albumleaves, gui accs. for romances; arrs.
Writings Grand traité d'instrumentation (1834, 2/1855); Les soirées de l'orchestre (1852); A travers chant (1862); Mémoires de Hector Berlioz (1870); reviews, articles

Berman, Lazar (Naumovich) (*b* Leningrad, 26 Feb 1930). Soviet pianist. An infant prodigy, he studied at the Moscow Conservatory. His mature début was in 1940 and in 1958 he made his first foreign tour. He remained in Russia during the 1960s but from 1971 was acclaimed in the West with his bravura performances of Liszt, Tchaikovsky and Schumann. His American début was in 1976 (New York).

Bermudo, Juan (*b* Ecija, *c*1510; *d* Andalusia, *c*1565). Spanish theorist and composer. A member of the Observant Minorite order and a mathematician, he published three treatises on music; the most comprehensive, the *Declaración* (1555), incorporates many music examples and includes the first organ music printed in Spain.

Bernabei, Ercole (*b* Caprarola, 1622; *d* Munich, 5 Dec 1687). Italian composer. A pupil of Benevoli, he was *maestro di cappella* at St John Lateran, Rome, and director of the Cappella Giulia before moving to Munich as court Kapellmeister in 1674. Bernabei, though a master of the *stile antico*, also composed sacred music in the concertato idiom. His sons Giuseppe Antonio (?1649–1732) and Vincenzo (1660–*c*1735) also wrote sacred music and the former composed 13 operas.

Bernac [Bertin], Pierre (*b* Paris, 12 Jan 1899; *d* Villeneuve-les-Avignon, 17 Oct 1979). French baritone. After early encouragement by Caplet he gave his first recital in 1925. He gave the first performance of Poulenc's *Chansons gaillardes* (1926) and until 1960 was closely associated with that composer's music. His dry, high baritone and fastidious delivery were ideal for the French repertory.

Bernacchi, Antonio Maria (*b* Bologna, 23 June 1685; *d* there, 13 March 1756). Italian alto castrato. Renowned for his technical virtuosity, he sang in operas throughout Italy and also abroad, notably at Munich and for Handel in London (but he did not please English audiences). On retiring in 1736 he founded a singing school in Bologna.

Bernard, Matvey Ivanovich (*b* Mitau, 1794; *d* St Petersburg, 9 May 1871). Russian music publisher, pianist and composer. Through music journals, particularly *Nouvelliste* (1840–1916), his publishing house introduced much contemporary Russian and foreign music to St Petersburg.

Bernardi, Mario (Egidio) (*b* Kirkland Lake, 20 Aug 1930). Canadian conductor. He studied in Venice and Toronto as a pianist as well as conductor; he made his conducting début with the Canadian Opera Company in 1957, and conducted in London in 1963 where he was music director at Sadler's Wells, 1966–8, where he was particularly admired for his Verdi performances. He returned to Ottawa in 1969 as conductor of the new National Arts Centre Orchestra; there he presented many new Canadian works before he left in 1982.

Bernardi, Stefano (*b* Verona, *c*1585; *d* ?Salzburg, 1636). Italian composer and theorist. He was *maestro di cappella* in Rome and Verona and for the Archduke Carl Joseph before settling in Salzburg in 1624. Primarily a church composer, his style is transitional between the *a cappella* and concertato styles, the more modern idiom emerging in the motets and psalms of 1613. He wrote a counterpoint treatise (1615) and published books of madrigals and instrumental works for three to six players. The *Salmi concertati* (1637) are precursors of the solo concerto, contrasting a soprano voice with a four-part ripieno.

Bernart de Ventadorn (*b* Ventadorn, ?*c*1130–40, *d* ?Dordogne, *c*1190–1200). Troubadour poet and composer. A servant of the Viscount of Ventadorn, then of the Duchess of Normandy, Eleanor of Aquitaine and of Raimon V, Count of Toulouse, he later entered a monastery in Dordogne. 18 of the 45 poems attributed to him survive with complete melodies – more than of any other 12th-century poet. Through working in northern France, he may well

have played a leading part in stimulating the trouvère tradition there.

Bernasconi, Andrea (*b* ?Marseilles, ?1706; *d* Munich, ?27 Jan 1784). Italian composer. He was Kapellmeister at the Munich court from 1755, writing successful stage works (including some ten *opere serie*) in a conservative style. He also wrote symphonies and, after 1772, exclusively sacred music. His stepdaughter was the German soprano Antonia Bernasconi [Wagele] (*c*1741–?1803), who created the title role in Gluck's *Alceste* (1767, Vienna).

Berners, Lord (Sir Gerald Hugh Tyrwhitt-Wilson, Bart) (*b* Arley Park, 18 Sept 1883; *d* Faringdon House, 19 April 1950). English composer, writer and painter. Essentially self-taught, he was honorary attaché in Rome (1911–19), where he came to know Stravinsky and Casella. In 1919 he succeeded to the barony, and thereafter was an eccentric English gentleman. His early works are mostly small and ironical (chiefly songs and piano pieces), close to Les Six; later he wrote ballets, including *The Triumph of Neptune* (1926), *Luna Park* (1930) and *A Wedding Bouquet* (1936).

Bernhard, Christoph (*b* Kolobrzeg, 1 Jan 1628; *d* Dresden, 14 Nov 1692). German theorist, composer and singer. A pupil of Schütz, he visited Italy twice (possibly studying with Carissimi) and held a post at Dresden from 1655 before becoming Kantor of the Johannisschule, Hamburg, in 1663, and city director of church music. He worked with Weckmann in the weekly collegium musicum concerts, and composed a motet for Schütz's funeral at the latter's request. In 1674 he returned to Dresden, becoming Kapellmeister in 1681. He composed sacred vocal music to German and Latin texts; his published collection, *Geistliche Harmonien* (1665), contains 20 sacred concertos. Bernhard is chiefly important for his treatises, especially *Tractatus compositionis augmentatus* in which he classifies music into three styles: by the relationship of words and music, place of performance and types of dissonance used.

Bernier, Nicolas (*b* Mantes-la-Jolie, 5/6 June 1665; *d* Paris, 6 July 1734). French composer. He worked mainly in Paris, where he was *maître de musique* at the Sainte-Chapelle, 1704–26; from 1714 he also served at the king's chapel, Versailles. His output comprises sacred music (mainly motets) and secular cantatas and songs, generally conservative in idiom. He was a renowned teacher and wrote a composition treatise.

Bernstein, Leonard (*b* Lawrence, MA, 25 Aug 1918). American conductor, composer and pianist. He studied at Harvard and the Curtis Institute and was a protégé of Koussevitzky. In 1943 he made his reputation as a conductor when he stepped in when Bruno Walter was ill; thereafter he was associated particularly with the Israel PO (from 1947), the Boston SO and the New York PO (musical director, 1958–69), soon achieving an international reputation, conducting in Vienna and at La Scala. During his tenure the New York PO flourished as never before. A gifted pianist, he has often performed simultaneously as soloist and conductor. At the same time, he pursued a career as a composer, cutting across the boundaries between high and popular culture in his mixing of Mahler and Broadway, Copland and Bach. His theatre works are mostly in the Broadway manner: they include the ballet *Fancy Free* (1944) and the musicals *Candide* (1956) and *West Side Story* (1957). His more ambitious works, many of them couched in a richly chromatic, intense post-Mahlerian idiom, often have a religious inspiration, for example the 'Jeremiah' Symphony with mezzo (1943), 'Kaddish', with soloists and choirs (1963) and the theatre piece *Mass* (1971).

Operas Trouble in Tahiti (1952); A Quiet Place (1983)
Musicals On the Town (1944); Wonderful Town (1953); Candide (1956); West Side Story (1957)
Other dramatic music Fancy Free, ballet (1944); Facsimile, ballet (1946); On the Waterfront, film score (1954); Mass, theatre piece (1971); Dybbuk, ballet (1974)
Orchestral and choral music Sym. no.1, 'Jeremiah' (1942); Sym. no.2, 'The Age of Anxiety' (1949); Prelude, Fugue and Riffs, cl, jazz ens (1949); Serenade, vn, str, harp, perc (1954); Sym. no.3, 'Kaddish' (1963); Chichester Psalms (1965); Slava!, ov. (1977); Songfest (1977); Divertimento (1980); Halil (1981)
Chamber and instrumental music Cl Sonata (1942); Seven Anniversaries, pf (1943); Four Anniversaries, pf (1948); Brass Music (1948); Five Anniversaries, pf (1954); Touches, pf (1981)
Solo vocal music I Hate Music (1943); La bonne cuisine (1947); Two Love Songs (1949); Piccola serenata (1979)

Béroff, Michel (*b* Epinal, 9 May 1950). French pianist. He came to the attention of Messiaen and studied with Yvonne Loriod at the Paris Conservatoire. By the late 1960s his rhythmic control and awareness of the piano's percussive possibilities had won a wide audience in the music of Bartók, Stravinsky and Prokofiev. He has given memorable performances of Messiaen's *Vingt regards sur l'enfant Jésus*.

Berry, Walter (*b* Vienna, 8 April 1929). Austrian bass-baritone. He studied at the Vienna Academy and joined the Staatsoper in 1950; soon after, he appeared at the Salzburg Festival, singing in several first performances and as Mozart's Count, Leporello, Guglielmo and Papageno. At Covent Garden, the Met and elsewhere he has been admired as Barak.

Bersag horn. A type of valved bugle used by the Italian Bersaglieri corps from 1861; they were made in four different pitches (B♭ soprano, E♭ contralto, B♭ tenor and baritone, F bass) and each has a single valve lowering the pitch by a 4th, so that a diatonic scale can be played from the fourth partial upwards.

Bertali, Antonio (*b* Verona, March 1605; *d* Vienna, 17 April 1669). Austrian composer and violinist. He worked for the Archduke Carl Joseph from 1622 before moving to the service of the imperial court in Vienna in 1624, becoming Kapellmeister in 1649. He composed music for special occasions at court and was important for establishing Italian opera traditions in Vienna. Bertali's style is north Italian, and he composed in many genres including opera and oratorio; but his immediate posthumous reputation rested on two published instrumental collections (1671-2). Much of his music is lost.

Bertin, Louise(-Angélique) (*b* Les Roches, 15 Feb 1805; *d* Paris, 26 April 1877). French composer. Brought up in an artistic and literary milieu, she composed four operas, one to her own libretto; *Fausto* (1831) showed originality but *Esmerelda* (1836), to a libretto by Victor Hugo, was unsuccessful. She also published poetry.

Bertini, Gary (*b* Brichevo, 1 May 1927). Israeli conductor and composer of Russian birth. He studied in Milan and Paris. His conducting début was with the Israel PO (1955) which he took on a tour of the USA in 1960; he has appeared with the ECO (1965) and other British orchestras. He has given several first performances. His compositions include music for the stage and choral arrangements.

Berton, Henri-Montan (*b* Paris, 17 Sept 1767; *d* there, 22 April 1844). French composer, writer and teacher, son of Pierre-Montan Berton. He had little formal training but was helped by Sacchini. He wrote cantatas and successful operas, the most original of which, *Montano et Stéphanie* and *Le délire* (both 1799), show impressive use of motivic devices, adept characterization and ensemble writing and an Italianate lyricism; in later stage works he collaborated with Boieldieu, Cherubini and Kreutzer. He was professor at the Paris Conservatoire for nearly 50 years and produced a harmony treatise (1815) and some criticism. His son Henri (1784-1832) was a pianist and composer of *romances*.

Berton, Pierre-Montan (*b* Maubert-Fontaine, 7 Jan 1727; *d* Paris, 14 May 1780). French conductor, composer and tenor. He was a singer but became director of the Paris Opéra, eventually director-general, and superintendent of music at Versailles. He excelled in arranging older stage works, by such composers as Campra, Lully and Rameau, to suit contemporary taste and often interpolated his own material. He is remembered mainly for having raised orchestral standards at the Opéra and for helping to make possible the arrival in Paris of both Gluck and Piccinni.

Bertoni, Ferdinando (Gasparo) (*b* Salo, 15 Aug 1725; *d* Desenzano, 1 Dec 1813). Italian composer. After studying in Bologna with G.B. Martini, he settled in Venice, and had immediate success with his first comic opera, *La vedova accorta* (1745), and three *opere serie* (1746). Some 40 more operas followed; many, including *Le pesciatrici* (1751), were given abroad. As first organist at St Mark's from 1752 and *maestro di cappella* from 1785, he wrote masses, psalms and other sacred works. Many of his c40 Latin oratorios and over 80 solo motets were composed for the female voices and orchestra of the Mendicanti orphanage. He also wrote occasional works for Venice, including the cantata *L'isola reggia di Calipso* (1769), and remained popular as an opera composer, notably with *Orfeo ed Euridice* (1776), which uses the Calzabigi text earlier set by Gluck. In 1778-83 he directed performances of his operas in London. His last opera was given in Venice in 1791.

Bertouch, Georg von (*b* Helmershausen, 19 June 1668; *d* Oslo, 14 Sept 1743). Norwegian composer. After leaving his native Germany and visiting Italy, he joined the Danish army and was later commander of Akershus Castle, Oslo. As a composer he had contact with Mattheson, and wrote 24 sonatas modelled on Bach's '48'; his other works include church cantatas.

Bertrand, Anthoine de (*b* Fontanges, 1530–40; *d* Toulouse, 1580–82). French composer. From *c*1560 he lived in Toulouse and associated with the Ronsardist poets; late in life he came under Jesuit influence. His surviving works, 84 *chansons* (3 vols., 1576–8) and 27 sacred pieces (1582), probably represent only half his output. The *chansons*, mostly four-voice settings of Ronsard, combine structural clarity with Italianate verbal imagery; the sacred pieces are simple homophonic settings of Gregorian melodies.

Berwald, Franz (Adolf) (*b* Stockholm, 23 July 1796; *d* there, 3 April 1868). Swedish composer and violinist, the most individual and commanding musical personality Sweden has produced. He was the son of C.F.G. Berwald (1740–1825), a violinist of German birth who studied with F. Benda and played in the Stockholm court orchestra. Franz was a violinist or violist in the orchestra (1812–28) and probably studied composition with its conductor, J.B.E. Dupuy. He disowned all his early works, which in their bold modulations show Spohr's influence, except a Serenade for tenor and six instruments (1825) and the fine Septet (?1828). He cherished operatic ambitions but failed to stir much interest in any of his works except *Estrella de Soria* (1841, performed 1862) and *The Queen of Golconda* (1864); in fact he was never properly recognized in his own country.

He made his greatest contribution to the repertory in his orchestral compositions of the 1840s, above all the four symphonies: the *Sinfonie singulière* (1845) is the most original, but all share vigorous freshness, formal originality (he sometimes used cyclic forms) and warm harmony and textures, especially in slow movements. The chamber works (two piano quintets, four piano trios and two string quartets) which occupied his main attention from 1849 to 1859 are often Mendelssohnian in style and show a real command of form and idiom. Berwald pursued several business interests (he ran an orthopedic institute, a glassworks and a sawmill) and was active as a polemical writer on social issues from 1856. Although he was made professor of composition at the Swedish Royal Academy in 1867, the discovery of his work was a 20th-century phenomenon. His brother August (1798–1869) was also a violinist and composer, and a granddaughter, Astrid, a leading Swedish pianist and teacher.

Besard, Jean-Baptiste (*b* Besançon, *c*1567; *d* after 1617). Burgundian lutenist and composer. He studied law in Dôle and medicine in Rome before moving to Germany. His *Thesaurus harmonicus* (1603) contains 403 lute pieces, some with voice, representing 21 composers (including himself) and almost all the instrumental forms of the time; many pieces were copied into later collections. A smaller collection, *Novus partus*, appeared in 1617. Both are important for their size, catholicity of taste, influence and historical context. His extensive manual on lute playing, printed in *Thesaurus* and revised in *Novus partus*, concentrates on fingering techniques; it was later translated into English.

Besler, Samuel (*b* Brzeg, 15 Dec 1574; *d* Breslau, 19 July 1625). German composer, a leading light in the musical life of Breslau where he was Kantor of St Bernhard's. His compositions range from collections of carols and graces (1602–15) to grand works for double choir in celebration of state occasions. His Passion settings are transitional between the old and new styles; only the St Mark and St Luke of 1612 approach Schütz's more dramatic treatment of the chorus. His brother Simon (1583–1633) was a composer of simple church music.

Besozzi. Italian family of musicians. Alessandro (i) (*fl* 1680–1700) was a Milanese singer and opera composer and brother of Cristoforo (1661–1725), an oboist and bassoonist in the Duke of Parma's service. Cristoforo's oboist sons Giuseppe (1686–1760), Alessandro (ii) (1702–93) and Paolo Girolamo (1704–78) worked initially at Parma. Giuseppe was later at the Naples court, while Paolo Girolamo (also a bassoonist) and Alessandro (ii) joined the Turin court and gave concerts in Paris; Alessandro (ii) composed many sonatas etc.

Giuseppe's sons Antonio (1714–81) and Gaetano (1727–98), both oboists, travelled widely but worked mainly at Dresden and Paris respectively; Antonio's son Carlo (1738–after 1798) was also an oboist at Dresden. Louis-Désiré (1814–79), great-grandson of Gaetano, was a pianist and composer in France.

Besseler, Heinrich (*b* Dortmund-Hörde, 2 April 1900; *d* Leipzig, 25 July 1969). German musicologist. He studied under Gurlitt, Adler, Fischer and Ludwig and taught at Heidelberg, Jena and Leipzig (1956–65). He is noted especially for his monumental *Die Musik des Mittelalters und der Renaissance* (1931), which for the first time placed music history within the history of ideas; but he worked too on Bach, on the use of instruments and on musical iconography (he was co-editor of *Musikgeschichte in Bildern*). In his immense, multi-faceted learning and his understanding of the ethical functions of art and scholarship, he is one of the most original scholars of our time.

Besson. French and English firm of brass instrument manufacturers. It was founded in Paris (?1838) by Gustave Auguste Besson (1820–75), who in 1851 also opened a London factory. Among his improvements in brass-instrument making were the straight bore (1854), the full bore (1855) and the 'prototype' system of mandrels, assuring exact duplication of instruments (1856). From *c*1882 the French firm continued under the name Fontaine-Besson; its important instruments include the first piccolo G trumpet (1885), a bass trumpet in C for works by Wagner, the family of cornophones (1890) and the large-bore Bb trumpet (the first modern Bb trumpet).

Best, W(illiam) T(homas) (*b* Carlisle, 13 Aug 1826; *d* Liverpool, 10 May 1897). English organist. As organist to the Liverpool Philharmonic Society and at St George's Hall, Liverpool, and through many appearances elsewhere (he opened the Willis organ at the Royal Albert Hall, 1871), he was nationally known for his virtuoso performances. His powerful improvisations, which explored the full resources of the large-scale modern organ, and his fine pedal technique in the works of Bach and others were especially admired.

Besuch der alten Dame, Der [The Visit of the Old Lady]. Opera in three acts by von Einem to a libretto by Dürrenmatt (1971, Vienna).

Bethlehem Bach Festival (USA). Festival (May) inaugurated in 1900 and held annually from 1912. J.S. Bach's music is given in concerts by the Bach Choir of Bethlehem (PA), founded (1898) by John Frederick Wolle and conducted by him in 1900 and 1912–32.

Bettelstudent, Der [The Beggar Student]. Operetta in three acts by Millöcker to a libretto by F. Zell and R. Genée (1882, Vienna).

Betz, Franz (*b* Mainz, 19 March 1835; *d* Berlin, 11 Aug 1900). German baritone. His vast repertory included the Dutchman, Don Giovanni, Falstaff and King Mark (*Tristan und Isolde*); he sang Hans Sachs in the première of *Die Meistersinger* and Wotan in the first Bayreuth *Ring* cycle (1876).

Bevin, Elway (*b c*1554; *d* Bristol, bur. 19 Oct 1638). Composer of Welsh extraction. Possibly a pupil of Tallis, he was briefly at Wells Cathedral and then Master of the Choristers (1585) and organist (1589) at Bristol Cathedral. In 1605 he became a Gentleman Extraordinary of the Chapel Royal. He composed mainly sacred music, notably a Dorian or Short Service, and instrumental pieces. His *Briefe and Short Instruction in the Art of Musicke* (1631) contains ingenious canons.

Bewegt (Ger.). Agitated, moving onward.

Bialas, Günter (*b* Bielschowitz, 19 July 1907). German composer. He studied in Breslau (1925–7) and Berlin (1927–33). In 1933 he returned to Breslau and began to make a reputation as a neo-classical composer, though his development was interrupted by war service (1941–5). He taught at the academies in Detmold (1950–59) and Munich (from 1959) while widening his stylistic range to include 12-note serialism, African and medieval music. His main works are operas (including *Der gestiefelte Kater*, 1974), concertos and sacred choral pieces.

Bianchi, Antonio (*b* Milan, 1758; *d* after 1817). Italian singer and composer. In 1792–7 he sang in Berlin (where an opera of his was staged in 1794), and later in other German cities. He wrote many songs, perhaps including 'Vinqua Dorina bella', on which Weber wrote variations. Another composer of the same name (*c*1750–after 1816) worked in Venice and wrote sacred music.

Bianchi, Francesco (*b* Cremona, *c*1752; *d* Hammersmith, 27 Nov 1810). Italian composer. A pupil of Jommelli in Naples, he worked in Paris in 1775–8 as a harpsichordist and comic opera composer. He was *vicemaestro* at Milan Cathedral, *c*1782–1793, and second organist at St Mark's, Venice (1785–91, 1793–7), where he wrote oratorios for the Mendicanti orphanage in the 1780s. In 1779–84 he composed 60 operas, among them *La villanella rapita* (1783, Venice) and *Il disertore francese* (1784, Venice), a reform opera combining serious and comic elements. He presented his operas in London from 1794 (*La vendetta di Nino* of 1790 was especially suc-

cessful), and in 1802–7 worked in Paris, composing popular *opéras comiques* such as *Corali* (1804); he also wrote a theoretical treatise. His operatic output, some 90 works, is notable for its pleasing melodic style.

Biber, Heinrich Ignaz Franz von (*b* Liberec, bap. 12 Aug 1664; *d* Salzburg, 3 May 1704). Bohemian composer. He is important for his works for the violin, of which he was a virtuoso. In the mid-1660s he entered the service of the Prince-Bishop of Olomouc who maintained an excellent Kapelle at his Kroměříž castle. By 1670 Biber had moved to the Salzburg court Kapelle, becoming Kapellmeister in 1684. His formidable violin technique is best seen in the eight *Sonatae violino solo* with continuo (1681), where brilliant passage-work (reaching 6th and 7th positions) and multiple stopping abound in the preludes, variations and elaborate finales. Most of the Mystery (or Rosary) Sonatas (*c*1676, for violin and bass) require *scordatura* tuning: by linking the open strings to the key the sonority and polyphonic possibilities of the violin were increased. The unaccompanied Passacaglia here, built on 65 repetitions of the descending tetrachord, is the outstanding work of its type before Bach. Besides other violin works (which include a *Battalia*, with strings and continuo), Biber composed sacred music (in *a cappella* style as well as large-scale concertato works for solo and ripieno voices), 15 school dramas, three operas (only *Chi la dura la vince*, 1687, survives) and much instrumental ensemble music (often for unusual combinations including brass). Especially notable are the Requiem in F minor, the *Missa Sancti Henrici* (1701), the 32-part *Vesperae* (1693), the motet *Laetatus sum* (1676), and the *Sonata S Polycarpi* for eight trumpets and timpani. Biber may have composed the 53-part *Missa salisburgensis* (1628) formerly attributed to Benevoli.

Biches, Les. Ballet in one act by Poulenc (1924, Monte Carlo).

Bicinium (Lat.). Term applied by Lutherans in the 16th century to duos used as teaching material; it now signifies any two-part composition of the Renaissance or early Baroque.

Biedermeier. Term applied to bourgeois life and art in German and other north European countries from *c*1815 to 1848. Derived from the name of a caricatured, fictitious schoolmaster, for a satirical magazine, it is used of music in a derogatory sense to stand for conservative, middle-class philistinism towards the arts and the favouring by this public of music of an undemanding, trivial, sentimental character.

Bierey, Gottlob Benedikt (*b* Dresden, 25 July 1772; *d* Breslau, 5 May 1840). German composer. A pupil of Weinlig at Dresden, he became one of the most popular Singspiel composers at the beginning of the 19th century, producing *c*30 stage works.

Biggs, E(dward George) Power (*b* Westcliff, 29 March 1906; *d* Boston, 10 March 1977). American organist of English birth. He studied at the RAM and played in the USA from 1930, becoming an American citizen in 1937. From 1942 to 1958 he broadcast weekly recitals from Harvard University on an Aeolian-Skinner 'classic style' organ, introducing a wide audience to organ mixtures, mutations and Baroque reeds. In his recitals and recordings he performed a wide range of music.

Bihari, János (*b* Nagyabony, bap. 21 Oct 1764; *d* Pest, 26 April 1827). Hungarian violinist and composer of gypsy descent. Known primarily for his superb interpretation of the *verbunkos* (which originated in an 18th-century peasant dance), he performed for all social classes and had a lasting influence within the Hungarian folk tradition and, through Liszt, on Western art music. Many of his compositions, transcribed by others, were published during his lifetime; he is particularly associated with the Rákóczi March.

Bilitis, Chansons de. *See* CHANSONS DE BILITIS.

Billings, William (*b* Boston, 7 Oct 1746; *d* there, 26 Sept 1800). American composer and singing teacher, described as 'the father of our New England music'. A tanner by trade, and largely self-taught in music, he taught choral singing in Boston from 1769. He wrote over 340 pieces, chiefly psalm and hymn tunes but also 'fuging-tunes', anthems and set-pieces, for four-voice unaccompanied chorus; most appeared in his six tunebooks (1770–94). The initial book, *The New-England Psalm-singer*, was the first collection devoted exclusively to American music and to the music of a single American composer; despite its unevenness, it gave direction to American psalmody for decades and contains some of his best-known tunes ('Amherst', 'Brookfield', 'Chester' and 'Lebanon'). His second book, *The Singing Master's Assistant* (1778), was unusually popular; its musical quality and variety, humour and timely patriotic texts secured Billings's reputation. Subsequent volumes, some for specific audiences, were of less appeal, and his career declined after 1789. Of his few separate works, *An Anthem for Easter* remains the most popular anthem by an 18th-century American composer.

Billington [née Weichsell], **Elizabeth** (*b* London, ?1765–8; *d* nr. Venice, 25 Aug 1818). English soprano. A child prodigy, she studied with J.C. Bach and later James Billington, whom she married in 1783, the year of her début as Polly (*Beggar's Opera*) in Dublin. She made a reputation in England, then after the appearance of scurrilous 'memoirs' went to sing in Italian opera houses from 1794. She returned in 1801 and was in constant demand; she was also a close friend of the Prince of Wales. One of the finest English singers of her day, she had a wide range and remarkable accuracy. Her brother-in-law Thomas Billington (1754–*c*1832) was a composer.

Billy Budd. Opera, originally in four acts, by Britten to a libretto by Eric Crozier and E.M. Forster after Melville (1951, London); Britten's two-act revision (BBC broadcast 1960) is the one now staged.

Billy the Kid. Ballet in one act by Copland (1938, Chicago).

Bilson, Malcolm (*b* Los Angeles, 24 Oct 1935). American pianist. He studied in Berlin and Paris and has taught at Cornell University since 1968. He has been a pioneer in the use of period instruments, playing a fortepiano based on contemporary models in Viennese classical music. He formed the Amadé Trio in 1974, with Sonya Monosoff and John Hsu, and has made many recordings including (1983–8) a complete set of the Mozart piano concertos which has been much praised for its sense of style, its clarity of articulation and its musicianship.

Binary form. A musical structure, ubiquitous in Baroque dance movements and other pieces (e.g. Domenico Scarlatti's sonatas), consisting of two complementary parts, each normally repeated. In its most developed form the first section cadences in a related key (usually the dominant or relative major), the second in the tonic. Scarlatti provides numerous exceptions to the general rule that the second section is longer than the first, with a wider range of modulations. Long after the 'rounded' binary form (in which the second section includes a recapitulation of the first strain in the tonic) had led to Classical sonata form, simple binary structure continued to be used, especially for variations.

Binchois, Gilles de Bins dit (*b* ?Mons, *c*1400; *d* Soignies, 20 Sept 1460). Franco-Flemish composer. He was one of the three leading musical figures of the first half of the 15th century (with Dufay and Dunstable). Organist at Ste Waudru, Mons, from 1419, he was granted permission to move to Lille in 1423 and apparently entered the service of William Pole, Earl of Suffolk, soon after. Later in the 1420s he joined the Burgundian court chapel where he was much honoured and appointed a secretary to the court (*c*1437). He held prebends in Bruges, Mons, Cassel and Soignies, where he finally retired; there he was appointed provost of the collegiate church of St Vincent (1452), though he continued to receive a pension from the Burgundian court.

Although Binchois' name was mentioned in contemporary literature only alongside Dufay's, his works had a more independent reputation and, though less widely circulated than Dufay's, were very popular. Six of his songs survive in keyboard arrangements; tenor lines of two or three were used to make *basse danses*, and numerous compositions from the mid- and late 15th century, including three mass cycles (Ockeghem's *Missa 'De plus en plus'*, Bedyngham's *Missa 'Dueil angoisseux'* and the anonymous mass-motet cycle *'Esclave puist il devenir'*), were based on his works. The fact that many of his compositions survive in only one source, and that most of those were compiled in southern Europe, far from the Burgundian court, suggests that much of his work may be lost or survive only anonymously. His songs, mostly rondeaux, remain within the conventions of refined courtly tradition. They are nearly all for a single-texted upper voice supported by an untexted tenor in longer notes a 5th lower in range and a contratenor in the same range or a little lower. They are characterized by effortless, graceful melodies, uncomplicated rhythms and carefully balanced phrases. His sacred music tends to be more conservative. No complete mass cycle by him has survived, though some of the mass movements can be paired on the basis of similarity. He wrote only one isorhythmic motet, and many of his smaller sacred works are purely functional.

Sacred music 3 Gloria-Credo pairs; 5 Sanctus-Agnus pairs; 12 single mass movements; over 30 other works
Secular music c50 rondeaux; several ballades; Filles a marier, combinative chanson

Binder, Carl (*b* Vienna, 29 Nov 1816; *d* there, 5 Nov 1860). Austrian composer and conductor. He composed numerous scores for Viennese suburban theatres, including several for Nestroy plays; he also orchestrated operettas by Offenbach.

Binet, Jean (*b* Geneva, 17 Oct 1893; *d* Trélex, 24 Feb 1960). Swiss composer. He studied in Geneva and with Bloch in New York, then taught the Dalcroze method in Brussels (1923–9). Many of his works, in a refined French tonal style, were introduced by Ansermet; best known is the ballet *Le printemps* (1950).

Bing, Sir Rudolf (*b* Vienna, 9 Jan 1902). British opera impresario of Austrian birth. He worked in Berlin and Darmstadt and became general manager of Glyndebourne Opera (1936–48); he helped found the Edinburgh Festival (artistic director, 1947–9), and was general manager of the Metropolitan Opera, New York (1950–72), having great influence on the company and American opera through his uncompromising standards. His autobiography, *5000 Nights at the Opera* (London, 1972), relates some of the many vicissitudes of his career.

Bingham, Seth (*b* Bloomfield, NJ, 16 April 1882; *d* New York, 21 June 1972). American composer and organist. He studied at Yale under Parker and in Paris under d'Indy, Widor and others. He taught at Yale and at Columbia, 1919–54, and was music director at Madison Avenue Presbyterian Church. He was a prolific composer of church music and orchestral works, including several concertos and sonatas, in a conservative, lyrical style.

Bini, Pasquale (*b* Pesaro, 21 June 1716; *d* there, April 1770). Italian violinist and composer. A favourite pupil of Tartini, he worked in Rome, Pesaro (1747–54), at the Württemberg court (1754–*c*1759) and again in Pesaro. His compositions include violin concertos and sonatas.

Biniĉki, Stanislav (*b* Jasika, 27 July 1872; *d* Belgrade, 15 Feb 1942). Yugoslav composer and conductor. He helped found the Serbian School of Music and conducted the Belgrade Military Orchestra, various choirs and the first National Theatre operas. Besides composing the first Serbian national opera (*Dawn*, 1903), he wrote songs, folk-influenced choral music and many marches.

Binkerd, Gordon (*b* Lynch, NE, 22 May 1916). American composer. He studied with Rogers at the Eastman School and with Piston and Fine at Harvard; he was professor at the University of Illinois (1947–71). His works, in most forms, are chromatic but tonal, and generally contrapuntal; he is best known for his choral music.

Birchensha, John (*b* early 17th century; *d* ?London, bur. 14 May 1681). English theorist and composer. He taught the viol and composition in London, but his chief significance lies in the new rational, scientific attitude to music evident in his writings, *Templum musicum* (1664; his translation of J.H. Alsted's *Encyclopaedia*, xiv), and the preface to Salmon's *An Essay to the Advancement of Musick* (1672). He plan-

ned a book on the philosophical and mathematical as well as practical aspects of music. His fantasia-suites are jagged, declamatory music showing William Lawes's influence.

Bird. Nickname of Haydn's String Quartet in C op.33 no.3 (1781).

Bird instruments. Mechanical instruments that imitate birdsong; they include the bird organ (a small barrel organ), the bird flageolet (a pipe with piston operated by a clockwork wheel, driving the air and varying the sounding length), and the bird whistle (a tin vessel with an inflatable mouthpiece in which bubbling water changes the pitch).

Birds, The. *See* UCCELLI, GLI.

Birkenstock, Johann Adam (*b* Alsfeld, 19 Feb 1687; *d* Eisenach, 26 Feb 1733). German composer. One of Germany's leading violinists, he played at the Kassel court, becoming Konzertmeister in 1725; from 1730 he was court Kapellmeister at Eisenach. His compositions, including solo violin and trio sonatas, show both Italian and French influence and enjoyed considerable success.

Birmingham Symphony Orchestra. *See* CITY OF BIRMINGHAM SYMPHONY ORCHESTRA.

Birmingham Triennial Festival (UK). A festival was established in 1768 to raise funds for the recently founded General Hospital and held triennially 1784–1912 (with two exceptions); it was revived in 1968 (Sept). Until 1799 concerts centred on Handel's choral music. With the Town Hall opening (1834), forces were enlarged and new works were given. Premières include Mendelssohn's *Elijah* (1846) and Elgar's *The Dream of Gerontius* (1900), *The Apostles* (1903) and *The Kingdom* (1906).

Birtwistle, Sir Harrison (*b* Accrington, 15 July 1934). English composer. He studied at the Royal Manchester College of Music (1952–5), where Davies and Goehr were fellow students, interesting themselves in contemporary and medieval music. He then worked as a clarinettist and schoolteacher for brief periods; in 1975 he was appointed music director at the National Theatre. His works suggest comparison with Stravinsky in their ritual form and style, and sometimes with Varèse in the violence of their imagery (as in the opera *Punch and Judy*, 1968), a savage enactment of pre-social behaviour). In the 1970s, however, he began to work musical blocks into long, gradual processes of change (*The Triumph of Time* for orchestra, 1972), then to develop networks of interconnected pulsings beneath such processes (*Silbury Air* for small orchestra, 1977; ... *agm* ... for voices and orchestral groups, 1979). His biggest work of this period was the opera *The Mask of Orpheus* (1973–83, performed 1986), a multi-layered treatment of the myth.

Operas Punch and Judy (1968); The Mask of Orpheus (1986); Yan Tan Tethera (1986)
Other dramatic works Down by the Greenwood Side (music-theatre, 1969); Bow Down (music-theatre, 1977); incidental music
Orchestral music Chorales (1963); Tragoedia (1965); Nomos (1968); Verses for Ensembles (1969); An Imaginary Landscape (1971); The Triumph of Time (1972); Grimethorpe Aria, brass band (1973); Melencolia I, cl, harp, str (1976); Silbury Air (1977); Carmen arcadiae mechanicae perpe-

tuum (1977); Still Movement (1984); Secret Theatre (1984); Earth Dances (1986); Endless Parade, tpt, orch (1987)

Vocal music Monody for Corpus Christi, S, fl, hn, vn (1959); Entr'actes and Sappho Fragments, S, 6 insts (1964); Ring a Dumb Carillon, S, cl, perc (1965); Cantata, S, 6 insts (1969); Nenia: the Death of Orpheus, S, 5 insts (1970); Meridian, Mez, S chorus, 13 insts (1971); The Fields of Sorrow, 2S, chorus, 16 insts (1972); La plage, S, 5 insts (1972); ...agm..., chorus, small orch (1979); On the Sheer Threshold of the Night, 16vv (1980)

Other works Refrains and Choruses, wind qnt (1957); Précis, pf (1960); Verses, cl, pf (1965); Chronometer, tape (1972); For O, For O, the Hobby-horse is Forgot, 6 perc (1976); Cl Qnt (1980); Pulse Sampler, ob, claves (1981)

Bisbigliando (It.). 'Whispering': an effect used on the harp, consisting of constantly reiterated notes, generally played *pianissimo* in the upper and middle registers.

Bishop [née Riviere], **Anna** (*b* London, 9 Jan 1810; *d* New York, 18/19 March 1884). English soprano. She married Henry Bishop in 1831, eloped with the harpist Nicholas Bochsa in 1839 and spent the rest of her life making world concert tours, first with Bochsa and, after his death, alone. One of the most popular singers of her generation, she was noted for her masterly technique. She produced and sang in the first American performance of Flotow's *Martha* (New York, 1852).

Bishop, Sir **Henry R(owley)** (*b* London, 18 Nov 1786; *d* there, 30 April 1855). English composer. He received little formal education but studied harmony under Francesco Bianchi and had enough success with early ballets and stage works to be offered the musical directorship of Covent Garden in 1810. For 14 years he supervised the composition and performance of all kinds of dramatic musical works there, doing an immense amount of musical hack work. He also directed many of the Lenten Oratorio concerts from 1819 and was a founder–member of the Philharmonic Society and a harmony professor at the RAM. In 1824 he became musical director at Drury Lane, where his most ambitious work, the opera *Aladdin* (1826), was produced; soon after, he was at Vauxhall Gardens. He continued to write theatre music until 1840, when he became conductor of the Antient Concerts. He was knighted in 1842 and succeeded Crotch in the chair of music at Oxford in 1848.

The long list of Bishop's compositions (some 70 published stage works) suggests a greater productivity, especially during the years 1813–20, than he in fact achieved; most often he provided only incidental set pieces, many of which were adaptations of well-known airs, to spoken plays. His most popular songs, such as 'Tell me, my heart' (from *Henri Quatre*, 1820) and 'Home, Sweet Home' (*Clari*, 1823), outlived the works with which they were first associated; his glees, such as 'Blow, gentle gales', have remained among his most admired pieces.

Bishop-Kovacevich, **Stephen** (*b* Los Angeles, 17 Oct 1940). American pianist of Yugoslav parentage. He studied with Schorr and later Myra Hess, making his public début in San Francisco in 1951, his London début in 1961. He is noted as an assured and thoughtful interpreter of the Classical repertory

and an accomplished player of 20th-century music.

Bispham, David (Scull) (*b* Philadelphia, 5 Jan 1857; *d* New York, 2 Oct 1921). American baritone. He took up music when he was 30, studying in Milan and London where he made his opera début in Messager's *Basoche* in 1891; the next year he sang Kurwenal at Drury Lane and appeared in Covent Garden. He made his Met début as Wagner's Beckmesser in 1896, singing there until 1903. He had a wide repertory and was also admired as a recitalist and oratorio singer. He later organized a touring company in the USA, appeared as an actor and taught in Philadelphia.

Bitonality. The simultaneous use of two different keys.

Bittner, Julius (*b* Vienna, 9 April 1874; *d* there, 9/10 Jan 1939). Austrian composer. He followed a legal career and was mostly self-taught as a musician; but his works provoked a revival of interest in Austria in operas and operettas to fairytale and folktale librettos. He was also an influential critic.

Biwa. A pear-shaped Japanese lute, usually with four or five strings; it is held horizontally and plucked with a plectrum in an arpeggiated manner. It was brought from China to Japan in the late 17th century with other instruments of GAGAKU (court music), in which it is the bass instrument. Used in many strata of Japanese society, it is played solo, in the court ensemble and as accompaniment for Buddhist music and various forms of narrative.

Bizet, Georges (Alexandre César Léopold) (*b* Paris, 25 Oct 1838; *d* Bougival, 3 June 1875). French composer. He was trained by his parents, who were musical, and admitted to the Paris Conservatoire just before his tenth birthday. There he studied counterpoint with Zimmerman and Gounod and composition with Halévy, and under Marmontel's tuition he became a brilliant pianist. Bizet's exceptional powers as a composer are already apparent in the products of his Conservatoire years, notably the Symphony in C, a work of precocious genius dating from 1855 (but not performed until 1935). In 1857 Bizet shared with Lecocq a prize offered by Offenbach for a setting of the one-act operetta *Le Docteur Miracle*; later that year he set out for Italy as holder of the coveted Prix de Rome.

During his three years in Rome Bizet began or projected many compositions; only four survive, including the *opera buffa*, *Don Procopio* (not performed until 1906). Shortly after his return to Paris, in September 1861, his mother died; the composer consoled himself with his parents' maid, by whom he had a son in June 1862. He rejected teaching at the Conservatoire and the temptation to become a concert pianist, and completed his obligations under the terms of the Prix de Rome. The last of these, a one-act *opéra comique*, *La guzla de l'emir*, was rehearsed at the Opéra-Comique in 1863 but withdrawn when the Théâtre-Lyrique director, who had been offered 100 000 francs to produce annually an opera by a Prix de Rome winner who had not had a work staged, invited Bizet to compose *Les pêcheurs de perles*.

Bizet completed it in four months. It was produced

in September 1863, but met with a generally cool reception: an uneven work, with stiff characterization, it is notable for the skilful scoring of its exotic numbers. In the ensuing years Bizet earned a living arranging other composers' music and giving piano lessons. Not until December 1867 was another opera staged – *La jolie fille de Perth*, which shows a surer dramatic mastery than *Les pêcheurs* despite an inept libretto. It received a good press but had only 18 performances.

1868 was a year of crisis for Bizet, with more abortive works, attacks of quinsy and a re-examination of his religious stance; and his attitude to music grew deeper. In June 1869 he married Geneviève, daughter of his former teacher, Halévy, and the next year they suffered the privations caused by the Franco-Prussian war (Bizet enlisted in the National Guard). Bizet found little time for sustained composition, but in 1871 he produced the delightful suite for piano duet, *Jeux d'enfants* (some of it scored for orchestra as the *Petite Suite*), and he worked on a one-act opera, *Djamileh*. Both the opera and Daudet's play *L'arlésienne*, for which Bizet wrote incidental music, failed when produced in 1872, but in neither case did this have anything to do with the music.

Bizet was convinced that in *Djamileh* he had found his true path, one which he followed in composing his operatic masterpiece, *Carmen*. Here Bizet reaches new levels in the depiction of atmosphere and character. The characterization of José, his gradual decline from a simple soldier's peasant honesty through insubordination, desertion and smuggling to murder is masterly; the colour and vitality of Carmen herself are remarkable, involving the use of the harmonic, rhythmic instrumental procedures of Spanish dance music, to which also the fate-laden augmented 2nds of the Carmen motif may owe their origin. The music of Micaela and Escamillo may be less original, but the charm of the former and the coarseness of the latter are intentional attributes of the characters. The opera is the supreme achievement of Bizet and of *opéra comique*, a genre it has transformed in that Bizet extended it to embrace passionate emotion and a tragic end, purging it of artificial elements and embuing it with a vivid expression of the torments inflicted by sexual passion and jealousy. The work, however, was condemned for its 'obscene' libretto, and the music was criticized as erudite, obscure, colourless, undistinguished and unromantic. Only after Bizet's death was its true stature appreciated, and then at first only in the revised version by Guiraud in which recitatives replace the original spoken dialogue (it is only recently that the original version has been revived). The reception of *Carmen* left Bizet acutely depressed; he fell victim to another attack of quinsy and, in June 1875, to the two heart attacks from which he died.

Dramatic music Le Docteur Miracle (1857); Don Procopio (1858–9, perf. 1906); Les pêcheurs de perles (1863); Ivan IV (1865, perf. 1946); La jolie fille de Perth (1867); Djamileh (1872); Carmen (1875); L'arlésienne, incidental music (1872; also suites)

Orchestral music Ov., a–A (*c*1855); Sym., C (1855); Roma, sym., C (1860–68, rev. 1871); Petite suite (1871); Patrie, ov. (1873)
*Vocal music c*8 choral works; 47 songs, incl. Adieux de l'hôtesse arabe (1866); 3 duets
*Piano music c*18 works, incl. Trois esquisses musicales (1858); Variations chromatiques (1868); Jeux d'enfants, pf duet (1871)

Björling, Jussi [Johan] (**Jonatan**) (*b* Stora Tuna, 5 Feb 1911; *d* Stockholm, 9 Sept 1960). Swedish tenor. He studied at the Stockholm Conservatory, sang at the Royal Swedish Opera from 1930 and by the late 1930s was in demand in England and the USA for his elegant, thoughtful portrayals of such roles as Riccardo, Manrico and Don Carlos and Rodolfo, Cavaradossi and Des Grieux.

Blacher, Boris (*b* Niu-chang, 19 Jan 1903; *d* Berlin, 30 Jan 1975). German composer. He studied in Berlin at the Musikhochschule (1924–6), where he was later (1948–70) professor, and the university (1927–31), working thereafter as a composer and arranger. His works are mostly ironic in style, owing something to Stravinsky, Satie, Milhaud and jazz, the rhythmic life of which was perhaps the source of his 'variable metres'. Around 1950 he began to use 12-note serialism. His theatre works are particularly important; they include operas (*Romeo und Julia*, 1943 the wordless *Abstrakte Oper no.1*, 1953; *Zweihunderttausend Taler*, 1969) and ballets (*Hamlet*, 1949; *Tristan*, 1965). But his instrumental music is best known, notably the *Concertante Musik* for orchestra (1937) and the Paganini Variations (1947). In the 1960s he wrote electronic music.

Blachut, Beno (*b* Ostrava-Vitkovice, 14 June 1913; *d* Prague, 10 Jan 1985). Czech tenor. He studied at the Prague Conservatory and in 1939 sang Smetana's Jeník at Olomouc. From 1941, when he joined the Prague National Theatre, he was the leading Czech tenor and much admired as Janáček's Laca, the Prince in Rusalka and in Heldentenor parts. He visited Moscow, Berlin and Edinburgh with the National Theatre company.

Blackhall, Andrew (*b* 1535–6; *d* 31 Jan 1609). Scottish composer. Orginally a canon of the Abbey of Holyroodhouse, Edinburgh, he was later minister of several Scottish churches, notably Inveresk; in 1582 he was granted a pension by James VI. At least two five-part anthems, several psalm settings, a canticle in chordal style and a fine partsong by him survive.

Black Key Study. Nickname of Chopin's Etude in G♭ op.10 no.5 for piano.

Blackwood, Easley (*b* Indianapolis, 21 April 1933). American composer and pianist. He studied with Hindemith at Yale (1950–54) and Boulanger in Paris (1954–7); from 1958 he taught at Chicago University. His repertory as a pianist (Schoenberg, Boulez, Ives) indicates his own musical leanings; his complex and controlled works, mostly in standard forms, include five symphonies (1958–78).

Bladder pipe. A wind instrument in which a reed is enclosed by an animal bladder. The player blows through a mouthpiece into the bladder, which serves (like the bag of a bagpipe) as a wind reservoir. The bladder pipe was one of the principal medieval wind-cap instruments. It survives in Europe, but only as a toy or a folk instrument.

Blades, James (*b* Peterborough, 9 Sept 1901). English percussionist. He joined a circus band when he was 19, went on to dance bands, film music and recordings, and joined the LSO as principal percussion in 1940. He has worked with leading British orchestras and chamber ensembles and the English Opera Group, for which he devised special effects for Britten's church parables. He has lectured and broadcast widely and is author of standard works on percussion, notably *Percussion Instruments and their History* (1970).

Blagrove, Henry (Gamble) (*b* Nottingham, 20 Oct 1811; *d* London, 15 Dec 1872). English violinist. He was principal violin at both London opera houses and in Jullien's orchestra, was professor at the RAM and helped establish the first regular series of chamber music concerts in London (1835–6).

Blahoslav, Jan (*b* Přerov, 20 Feb 1523; *d* Moravský Krumlov, 24 Nov 1571). Czech theorist and hymnographer. A pupil of Listenius and Finck at Wittenberg University, he became a bishop (1557). His *Musica* (1558), though derivative, is probably the first music treatise in Czech, and was directed mainly at singers. He edited the *Szamotuly Kancionál*, a collection of over 450 hymn tunes and texts, including several of his own.

Blainville, Charles Henri de (*b* nr. Tours, *c*1710; *d* ?Paris, *c*1777). French theorist and composer. He wrote several theoretical works, and provoked controversy with his 'discovery' of a third mode between major and minor, in which he wrote a symphony (1751). His other works include an opera, songs, sonatas and symphonies.

Blake, David (Leónard) (*b* London, 2 Sept 1936). English composer. He studied at Cambridge and in Berlin with Eisler, whose influence has been profound. But his works reflect his interest in Far Eastern (the cantata *Lumina*, 1969) and Caribbean music (the opera *Toussaint*, 1977). Since 1963 he has taught at York University (professor from 1981).

Blanchard, Esprit Joseph Antoine (*b* Pernes, 29 Feb 1696; *d* Versailles, 19 April 1770). French composer. He held posts at cathedrals, including Amiens (1734–8), then worked at the king's chapel, Versailles (*maître*, 1761). His many sacred works were among the last in the French Baroque tradition but show more modern features and are notable for their imaginative sonorities and textures.

Blanchard, Henri-Louis (*b* Bordeaux, ?April 1791; *d* Paris, 18 Dec 1858). French composer and critic. He studied with Kreutzer (violin), Méhul and Reicha in Paris. He wrote popular vaudeville airs, plays and operas and was an editor of the *Revue et gazette musicale* (1836–58). (Blanchard claimed the birthdate above; 7 Feb 1778 is often given.)

Blanchet. French family of harpsichord and piano makers. They were active from the end of the 17th century to the mid-19th. Their shop was successful from the beginning – François Couperin's large harpsichord was a Blanchet – but reached its peak in the mid-18th century, when it became 'facteur des clavessins du Roi'. Third-generation members in particular, including François Etienne (ii) (*c*1730–

66) and his co-worker and successor Pascal Taskin, were renowned for craftsmanship and skilled reworking of 17th-century Flemish instruments. The firm built its first upright piano in 1827; its high-quality small uprights were widely imitated.

Bland. English family of singers. The most celebrated members were Maria Theresa (1769–1838), an Italian-born soprano in the Drury Lane company, who excelled in simple English and Italian songs, and her son Charles, a tenor who created the title role in Weber's *Oberon* (Covent Garden, 1826).

Bland, James A(llen) (*b* Flushing, NY, 22 Oct 1854; *d* Philadelphia, 5 May 1911). American songwriter. A professional minstrel performer, he wrote *c*60 songs, including ballads, dances, marches and comic and religious songs; the best known are *Carry me back to old Virginny* (1878) and *Oh, dem golden slippers* (1879).

Blangini, (Giuseppe Marco Maria) Felice (*b* Turin, 18 Nov 1781; *d* Paris, 18 Dec 1841). French composer and singing teacher of Italian birth. In Paris from 1799, he was fashionable as a singer, composer and teacher; between 1805 and 1830 he held appointments in Munich, Kassel and Paris, including one as private music director to Pauline Borghese, Napoleon's sister. Of his output (nearly 30 operas, church music, numerous *romances*, vocal nocturnes and canzonets), the vocal chamber music was most popular; his *romances* unite French and Italian tastes in their graceful form, simple texture and elegant melodic style.

Blankenburg, Quirinus Gerbrandszoon van (*b* Gouda, 1654; *d* The Hague, 12 May 1739). Netherlands composer and theorist. Organist at churches in Rotterdam, Gorinchem and The Hague, he was an expert on carillon and organ building. His printed music, for keyboard, includes a book (1732) of ornamented versions of 16th-century Dutch Protestant hymns and psalms. Three MSS contain vocal and harpsichord pieces, some of them arrangements; he also wrote a thoroughbass treatise, *Elementa musica* (1739).

Blaramberg, Pavel Ivanovich (*b* Orenburg, 26 Sept 1841; *d* Nice, 28 March 1907). Russian composer and writer. Self-taught, he was influenced by Balakirev and the Five. He composed elegant songs and popular stage works modelled on Meyerbeerian grand opera.

Blasius, (Matthieu-) Frédéric (*b* Lauterbourg, 24 April 1758; *d* Versailles, 1829). French composer. He was active in Paris as violinist and orchestral director, notably at the Comédie-Italienne (1790–1816). He wrote several stage works, Revolutionary music for wind band, concertos and numerous chamber works; his string quartets show a balance of parts rare in France at the time.

Blavet, Michel (*b* Bescançon, bap. 13 March 1700; *d* Paris, 28 Oct 1768). French flautist and composer. He rose to an unrivalled position in Parisian musical life, widely admired for his tone and technique, and played often at the Concert Spirituel. Later he also served the Count of Clermont and played in the Musique du Roi and at the Opéra. Many Italian features appear in his compositions, which include

12 flute sonatas and six flute duets (1728–40), concertos, arrangements for teaching, and four stage works; the pasticcio *Le jaloux corrigé* (1752) was the first work with recitative of the Italian type instead of the French.

Blech, Leo (*b* Aachen, 21 April 1871; *d* Berlin, 25 Aug 1958). German conductor and composer. He studied in Berlin (composition with Humperdinck) and from 1893 conducted at Aachen, then the German Theatre, Prague. From 1906 he was chiefly in Berlin, at the Hofoper, the Deutsche Opernhaus and the Volksoper; at the Staatsoper (from 1926) he distinguished himself in Verdi and Wagner until, being Jewish, he was obliged to stay in Riga in 1937. He was at the Stockholm Royal Opera during the 1940s and returned to Berlin in 1949 (Städtische Oper). Blech was also admired as an orchestral conductor. His own operas were successfully produced, notably *Versiegelt* (1908, Hamburg).

Blest Pair of Sirens. Cantata (1887) by Hubert Parry to words from Milton's *At a Solemn Music*.

Blewitt, Jonathan (*b* London, 19 July 1782; *d* there, 4 Sept 1853). English organist, conductor and composer. Son of Jonas Blewitt, he studied with Battishill and Haydn, then held organ and theatre posts in England and, between 1811 and 1825, Ireland. In a large output of stage works and songs, his Irish ballads were particularly popular.

Bleyer, Georg (*b* Tiefurt, bap. 28 Oct 1647; *d* ?after 1694). German composer. He was a musician at the Rudolstadt and Saxe-Lauenburg courts, failing to attain promotion anywhere. His compositions are chiefly sacred but he published *Lust-Music* (1670), a collection of French-style dances, and *Zodiacus musicus* (1683), 12 sonatas for two to four instruments.

Bleyer, Nicolaus (*b* Stolzenau, 2 Feb 1591; *d* Lübeck, 3 May 1658). German violinist and composer. He was a member of the Bückeburg court orchestra from 1617 and from 1621 a civic musician at Lübeck. He published collections of pavans, galliards etc; his violin writing shows lively figuration and rich double stopping.

Blind octaves. A way of writing passage-work for the piano to produce the effect of rapid scales or arpeggios in triple octaves. The notes are taken alternately by the right and left hands.

Bliss, Sir Arthur (Drummond) (*b* London, 2 Aug 1891; *d* there, 27 March 1975). English composer. He studied with Wood at Cambridge and served in the army in France. Immediately after World War I he made a mark with works using nonsense texts and brittle Les Six-style irony (*Rout*, 1920), but successive orchestral works (*A Colour Symphony*, 1922; Introduction and Allegro, 1926; Music for Strings, 1935) established him as Elgar's successor. His three ballets (*Checkmate*, 1937; *Miracle in the Gorbals*, 1944; *Adam Zero*, 1946) and a notable score for the film *Things to Come* (1935) express his feelings for high drama and atmosphere. Among his other works are concertos for piano (1938), violin (1955) and cello (1970), songs, chamber and piano music, and choral works (notably the choral symphony *Morning Heroes*, 1930). In 1953 he was appointed Master of the Queen's Music.

Blitzstein, Marc (*b* Philadelphia, 2 March 1905; *d* Fort-de-France, Martinique, 22 Jan 1964). American composer. He studied with Scalero at the Curtis Institute (1924–6), with Boulanger in Paris and with Schoenberg in Berlin. He was most influenced, however, by his encounter with Eisler and Brecht in New York in 1935, which led to his commitment to the doctrine of 'art for society's sake'. Out of that came his 'play in music' *The Cradle will Rock* (1937), on labour relations, followed by many less successful stage works. He was the first composer to develop a convincing music-theatre idiom representing American vernacular speech style. His main concert work was the 'symphony' *The Airborne* for soloists, men's choir and orchestra (1946), concerning the experience of flight and of victory against Nazism (he was in the US Army Air Force, 1942–5).

Bloch, Augustyn (Hipolit) (*b* Grudziądz, 13 Aug 1929). Polish composer. He studied at the Warsaw Conservatory and began as a neo-classicist, using more advanced techniques from the early 1960s, including noise-type sonorities. He has written several works for the stage.

Bloch, Ernest (*b* Geneva, 24 July 1880; *d* Portland, OR, 15 July 1959). American composer. He studied with Dalcroze in Geneva, in Brussels (1897–9) and with Knorr in Frankfurt (1900). In 1916 he went to the USA, thereafter spending most of his time there (he took citizenship in 1924). He also taught at Cleveland (1920–25), San Francisco (1925–30) and Berkeley (1940–52). His early works are eclectic: the opera *Macbeth* (1910) draws on Strauss, Musorgsky and Debussy. Then came a period of concern mostly with Jewish subjects (*Schelomo* for cello and orchestra, 1916), followed by a vigorous neo-classicism (Piano Quintet no.1, 1923; Concerto grosso no.1 for strings and piano, 1925). He returned to epic compositions in the 1930s with the Sacred Service (*Avodath hakodesh*, 1933) and the Violin Concerto (1937). His last works represent a summation of his career and lean towards a less subjective style.

Blockflöte (Ger.). RECORDER.

Blockwerk. The undivided chest of the medieval organ, based on a 'double Principal' (open and stopped 8' etc) without other 'stops' separated off.

Blockx, Jan (*b* Antwerp, 25 Jan 1851; *d* Kapellenbos, 26 May 1912). Belgian composer. He studied with Peter Benoit at the Flemish Music School and in Leipzig, eventually succeeding Benoit as director of the Royal Flemish Music Conservatory. His fame rests chiefly on his eight operas (1877–1908), national variants of the Romantic realism tradition showing the influence of Wagner yet also of Flemish folksong.

Blodek, Vilém (*b* Prague, 3 Oct 1834; *d* there, 1 May 1874). Czech composer, flautist and pianist. After studying at the Prague Conservatory, he worked as a private music teacher, pianist and choral conductor, eventually becoming flute professor at the conservatory. He wrote incidental music for 60 plays and collaborated with Smetana on music for the 1864 Shakespeare celebrations. His musical compositions, some Mendelssohnian, include a Symphony in D minor (1858–9), a flute concerto, songs, choruses, chamber music and, his best-known work, the opera *In the Well* (1867).

Blom, Eric (Walter) (*b* Berne, 20 Aug 1888; *d* London, 11 April 1959). English critic and editor of Danish origin. He held posts as critic for the *Manchester Guardian*, the *Birmingham Post* and *The Observer* and was editor of *Music and Letters* (1937–50, 1954–9) and *Grove 5* (1954). He was an excellent linguist and made several translations. His books include a sympathetic study of Mozart (1935) and a history of music in England (1942) and he was an essayist of grace and charm.

Blomdahl, Karl-Birger (*b* Växjö, 19 Oct 1916; *d* Kungsängen, 14 June 1968). Swedish composer. He studied with Rosenberg from 1935 and took a leading part in the Monday Group, studying Hindemith and the Second Viennese School from the mid-1940s onwards. Within his own music, Hindemith's influence gradually gave way to that of Berg and Bartók, his style remaining vigorous and dynamic. His works include the science-fiction opera *Aniara* (1959), unusual for its time in its stylistic diversity and electronic elements, as well as ballets (*Sisyphos*, 1954; *Minotauros*, 1957) and three symphonies (1943, 1947, 1950). He took a leading role in Swedish musical life and taught at the Royal Academy of Music in Stockholm (1960–64).

Blondeau, Pierre-Auguste-Louis (*b* Paris, 15 Aug 1784; *d* there, ?1865). French viola player and composer. Besides playing the viola in the Paris Opéra orchestra (*c*1818–42), he composed sacred vocal works, chamber and orchestral music and published studies of harmony, counterpoint and music history.

Blondel de Nesle (*fl* 1180–1200). French trouvère. The legend that he helped rescue Richard Coeur-de-lion from captivity is probably false. The dialect of his poems suggests that he was a native of Picardy, and his works are among the most widely circulated in the trouvère repertory.

Blow, John (*b* Newark, bap. 23 Feb 1649; *d* Westminster, 1 Oct 1708). English composer. He was trained as a Chapel Royal chorister and then worked as organist of Westminster Abbey, 1668–79. In 1674 he both became a Gentleman of the Chapel Royal and succeeded Pelham Humfrey as Master of the Children; from 1676 he was also an organist there. Henry Purcell served an apprenticeship under him and many others were influenced by his teaching. The 1680s and 1690s were his most productive years as a composer. While still active at the Chapel Royal (where he was named official composer in 1700), he was Almoner and Master of the Choristers at St Paul's Cathedral in 1687–1703, and in 1695 he returned to Westminster Abbey as organist, succeeding Purcell.

Blow was the most important figure in the school of musicians surrounding Purcell and a composer of marked individuality. His music uses a wide range of idioms and reflects his interest in structure. Foremost in his sacred output are *c*100 anthems, mostly verse anthems (some with instrumental move-ments); the powerful coronation work *God spake sometime in visions* (1685) combines features of both types. Blow also wrote several services and Latin sacred works. Most of his odes were written for court occasions; among the others are works for St Cecilia's Day such as *Begin the song* (1684). The highly original and poignant miniature opera *Venus and Adonis* (1685), also for the court, was his only dramatic work. A well-known part of his output was his secular vocal music, comprising *c*90 solo songs and several duets, catches etc; the *Ode on the Death of Mr Henry Purcell* (1696), a duet with instruments, is notable for its expressiveness. Blow's instrumental works include organ voluntaries and some 70 harpsichord pieces.

Dramatic music Venus and Adonis, masque (by 1685)
Sacred vocal music 12 services; *c*100 anthems, incl. God spake sometime in visions (1685); Latin works
Secular vocal music over 20 court odes; 10 odes for other occasions; over 120 songs, duets and trios, incl. Ode on the Death of Mr Henry Purcell (1696); catches
Instrumental music *c*30 org voluntaries; over 70 hpd pieces (some grouped in suites); 3 pieces for strs; sonata

Bluebeard's Castle. *See* DUKE BLUEBEARD'S CASTLE.

Blue Danube, By the Beautiful [An der schönen, blauen Donau]. Waltz (op.314) by Johann Strauss ii (1867).

Bluegrass music. A style of American country music that grew in the 1940s from the music of Bill Monroe and his group the Blue Grass Boys. It combines elements of dance, home entertainment and religious folk music of the south-eastern highlands. Bands have four to seven singers, who accompany themselves on acoustic string instruments. The repertory includes traditional folksongs and newly composed pieces. In the 1970s, 'newgrass' groups combined bluegrass style with rock songs and techniques.

Blues. A secular black American folk music of the 20th century, related to, but separate from, jazz. The term describes both a characteristic melancholy state of mind and the eight-, 12- and 32-bar harmonic progressions that form the basis for blues improvisation; the most common is 12 bars long. The other characteristic is the 'blue note', a microtonal flattening of the 3rd, 7th and (to a lesser extent) 5th scale degrees. Blues has had a decisive influence on Western popular music.

From obscure origins, the genre had developed by 1900 to its typical three-line stanza, with a vocal style derived from the field holler or shout of southern work songs. By the 1920s the first blues recordings were made, of the Mississippi delta 'country' tradition (and other southern regional variants) and the 'classic' vaudeville-based blues of such singers as Mamie, Clara and Bessie Smith, Sara Martin and 'Ma' Rainey. The migration north to Chicago during the 1920s led eventually to a new 'urban' blues tradition, coarser and fiercer than earlier styles. This in turn led in the late 1940s to the style known as rhythm-and-blues. All instruments were by this time amplified. The principal exponents were Muddy Waters and Howlin' Wolf. Blues influenced rock and roll and other genres, including skiffle and soul music. It has continued as an independent genre, latterly performed by B.B. King, Buddy Guy and Junior Wells, among others.

Blum, Robert (*b* Zurich, 27 Nov 1900). Swiss composer. He studied with Andreae at the Zurich Conservatory (1919–22) and Busoni at the Prussian Academy in Berlin (1923), then returned to Zurich as a choral conductor and teacher. His large output includes stage works in dialect, sacred and chamber music, orchestral pieces (six symphonies, 1924–69) and film scores.

Blume, Friedrich (*b* Schlüchtern, 5 Jan 1893; *d* there, 22 Nov 1975). German musicologist. He studied at Munich, Leipzig and Berlin, where in 1923 he became lecturer and later took charge of the musicology institute. In 1934 he went to the University of Kiel, where as professor he exercised great influence on international musicology until he retired in 1958. As a member of the State Institute for German Musicology he edited materials on German music history; he also edited the works of Praetorius, was general editor of an early choral music series (1929–38) and initiated and edited the encyclopedia *MGG* in 14 volumes (1949–68). He was also a first-rank scholar. His special field was the music of the Lutheran church, including Schütz and Bach. He was one of the great encyclopedic musicologists, able to survey music from the Renaissance to the 20th century and present his conclusions in four essays on Renaissance, Baroque, Classical and Romantic music, originally written for *MGG*, seeing music 'against the background of the history of the human spirit'.

Blumenfeld, Harold (*b* Seattle, 15 Oct 1923). American composer. He studied with Rogers at the Eastman School and with Hindemith at Yale, and in 1950 began teaching at Washington University, St Louis. As director of the Opera Theatre of St Louis (1962–6) and Washington University Opera Studio (1960–71) he presented an innovatory repertory that included Baroque and 20th-century works. His works, mostly post-1970, include operas and vocal works incorporating approaches from Berio, Crumb and Carter.

Blüthner. German firm of piano makers. It was started in Leipzig in 1853 by Julius Blüthner (1824–1910). His grand pianos achieved renown from 1873, when aliquot scaling (the addition of a fourth, sympathetic string to each trichord group in the treble) was introduced to enrich the upper register. Distinguished by a round, slightly romantic tone, the firm's instruments are still made largely by hand.

Boatswain's Mate, The. Opera in one act by Ethel Smyth to her own libretto after W.W. Jacobs (1916, London).

Bocca chiusa (It.). 'Closed mouth': singing without words and with the mouth closed; humming.

Boccherini, (Ridolfo) Luigi (*b* Lucca, 19 Feb 1743; *d* Madrid, 28 May 1805). Italian composer and cellist. The son of a cello or double bass player, he made his public début as a cellist at 13. After studying in Rome, he worked intermittently at the Viennese court, 1757–64. In 1760 he began to catalogue his compositions (though excluding cello sonatas, vocal music and certain other works). In 1764–6 he worked in Lucca, where he composed vocal music and in 1765 reputedly arranged the first string quartet performances in public. On tour with the violinist Filippo Manfredi in Paris, 1767–8, he had his six string quartets op.1 and six string trios op.2 published. In 1769 the duo arrived in Madrid, where Boccherini became composer and performer to the Infante Don Luis. Up to the time of Luis' death in 1785 he composed chamber music for his court, notably string quintets for two violins, viola and two cellos. From 1786, as chamber composer to Prince (later King) Friedrich Wilhelm of Prussia, he sent string quartets to the Prussian court, though probably never went there.

The chief representative of Latin instrumental music during the Viennese Classical period, Boccherini was especially prolific in chamber music: he wrote well over 120 string quintets, nearly 100 string quartets and over 100 other chamber works. At first he used a standard Italian idiom, but with unusually ornate melodies and frequent high cello writing. Later, reflecting his isolated position, his style became more personal, with delicate detail, syncopated rhythms and rich textures; he sometimes used cyclic forms. The orchestral music includes several virtuoso cello concertos and over 20 symphonies; the vocal works include an opera, two oratorios and a *Stabat mater* (1781).

Chamber music over 120 str qnts; *c*90 str qts; 48 str trios; over 100 sonatas, duets, flute quintets
Orchestral music over 20 syms.; 11 vc concs.
Sacred vocal music 2 oratorios (*c*1765); Stabat mater (1781); liturgical pieces; villancicos
Secular vocal music opera (1786); cantata

Bochsa, (Robert) Nicholas Charles (*b* Montmédi, 9 Aug 1789; *d* Sydney, 6 Jan 1856). French harpist and composer. He studied at the Paris Conservatoire and became harpist to the emperor, later to Louis XVIII, also composing seven operas for the Opéra-Comique and an immense requiem for the reinterment of Louis XVI. From a French indictment for forgery he took refuge in London in 1817, establishing himself as a brilliant concert artist and, for a time, professor at the RAM and music director at the King's Theatre. His musical reputation owed much to his many works for harp, which vastly expanded its technical and expressive range.

Böddecker, Philipp Friedrich (*b* Hagenau, 5 Aug 1607; *d* Stuttgart, 8 Oct 1683). German composer and bassoonist. He worked at the courts of Darmstadt and Durlach, becoming organist of Strasbourg Cathedral in 1642 and moving to the collegiate church at Stuttgart in 1652. He composed an interesting setting of the *Te Deum* for large forces, and his *Sacra partitura* contains vocal music showing the influence of Italian monody; his two sonatas (one each for violin and bassoon) are among the earliest German examples of the genre.

Bodenschatz, Erhard (*b* Lichtenberg, 1576; *d* Gross Osterhausen, 1636). German music editor and composer. After education in Dresden, Leipzig and Schulpforta he was a Kantor and pastor all his life.

He is best known for his *Florilegium Portense* (1603–21), an extensive and valuable anthology of German and Italian motets. His own works (all sacred) include a fine four-voice Magnificat (1599) and a set of 90 bicinia (1615).

Bodinus, Sebastian (*b c*1700; *d c*1760). German composer. He served at the Karlsruhe court and was Konzertmeister there for two periods. His compositions include concertos and symphonies but are mostly chamber works in the late Baroque style, including not only solo and trio sonatas but also quartets.

Bodky, Erwin (*b* Neman, 7 March 1896; *d* Lucerne, 6 Dec 1958). American pianist and composer of German origin. He studied at the Berlin Musikhochschule and with Busoni and Strauss and performed as a solo pianist; his compositions date from the 1920s. In 1938 he moved to the USA, taught at Brandeis University and worked on performing early keyboard music, notably Bach, on the harpsichord and clavichord.

Bodley, Seóirse (*b* Dublin, 4 April 1933). Irish composer. He studied in Dublin and with J.N. David in Stuttgart (1957–9) and has taught composition and Irish folk music studies at University College, Dublin, since 1959. His relatively small output absorbs several current European procedures, including since the early 1960s serial techniques, an interest in new timbres and aleatory methods and the incorporation of Irish folk elements, to form an individual, adventurous style capable of expressive intensity, as his *Configurations* for orchestra (1967) and his String Quartet (1969) show.

Boehm, Joseph (*b* Pest, 4 March 1795; *d* Vienna, 28 March 1876). Hungarian violinist and teacher. He studied briefly with Rode, made his début in Vienna in 1816, and in 1819 was appointed professor at the newly founded Vienna Conservatory. Considered the father of the Viennese violin school, he imparted to such pupils as Joachim and Reményi a sense of style and Classical tradition.

Boehm, Theobald (*b* Munich, 9 April 1794; *d* there, 25 Nov 1881). German flautist, goldsmith and ironmaster. He worked out the proportions and devised the mechanism of the modern flute, establishing a factory in Munich in 1828 and introducing his first prototype in 1832. It had a tapered bore larger than usual and was constructed on a system of 'open holes' controlled by interlinked keys with ring touchpieces encircling the finger-holes (the first Boehm keywork). Although opposition and his duties in the Bavarian steel industry (1833–46) slowed progress, he produced an improved design in 1847 (a cylinder flute with tapered head and revised hole positions), which has remained essentially unchanged.

Boehmer, Konrad (*b* Berlin, 24 April 1941). German composer. He studied composition, musicology and sociology at Cologne and moved in 1967 to Amsterdam. As a composer, he has used electronic means (in such works as *Position*, with voices and orchestra, 1961, and *Aspect*, 1967), and in his writings he has commented critically on developments in new music, including their relationship to popular culture.

Boëllmann, Léon (*b* Ensisheim, 25 Sept 1862) *d* Paris, 11 Oct 1897). French organist and composer. He studied at the Ecole de Musique Classique et Religieuse, Paris, and was organist of St Vincent-de-Paul; he also taught improvisation and contributed to *L'art musical*. His output is typified by the modal and liturgical organ works in *Douze pièces* op.16 (*c*1890), but his best-known piece is the *Suite gothique* (1895).

Boëly, Alexandre Pierre François (*b* Versailles, 19 April 1785; *d* Paris, 27 Dec 1858). French composer, organist and pianist. Largely self-taught, he followed a solitary career, becoming organist at St Germain l'Auxerrois only in 1840 and a piano teacher at the Notre-Dame choir school. He was unusual in France for his admiration of Bach, Haydn, Mozart and Beethoven and for the romantic bravura and audacious harmony of his compositions, which include two masses and many piano, organ and chamber works.

Boesmans, Philippe (*b* Tongeren, 17 May 1936). Belgian composer. He studied with Pousseur and others, and was later influenced by Berio and Boulez; he is noted for his use of intervallic patterns over static textures to create trance-like effects. His works include *Sonance I* and *II* for two and three pianos (1964–7), *Explosives* for harp and ten instruments, *Multiples* for two pianos and orchestra, *Attitudes* (music theatre, 1977), concertos for piano (1978) and violin (1979) and an opera *La Passion de Gilles* (1983).

Boësset, Antoine (de) (*b* Blois, 1586; *d* Paris, 8 Dec 1643). French composer. He held various appointments at the French court from 1613 and was widely recognized as the leading composer of *airs de cour* (nine books, 1617–42). He also wrote vocal music for *ballets de cour* and some sacred music. His son Jean-Baptiste (1614–85) was also a musician at the French court, writing *airs* and ballets.

Boethius, Anicius Manlius Severinus (*b* Rome, *c*480; *d c*524). Roman writer and statesman. He wrote on the mathematical disciplines (arithmetic, music, geometry and astronomy), logic, theology and philosophy. In *De institutione musica* he identified music as an all-pervading force in the universe (*musica mundana*) and a principle unifying the body and soul of man as well as the parts of his body (*musica humana*); music is also found in certain instruments (*musica instrumentalis*). Boethius provided a Perfect System of Greek theory with its tetrachord theory, the Pythagorean doctrine of consonances, the mathematics to rationalize musical consonances and the principles of monochord division. His treatise became the most widespread theoretical one on music in the Middle Ages.

Boeuf sur le toît, Le. Pantomimic spectacle, later a ballet, by Milhaud to a libretto by Cocteau (1920).

Bogatïryov, Semyon Semyonovich (*b* Khar'kov, 16 Feb 1890; *d* Moscow, 31 Dec 1960). Russian musicologist and composer. He studied with Shteynberg at the St Petersburg Conservatory (1912–15) and taught at the conservatories of Khar'kov and Moscow. He was the leading Russian authority on counterpoint and composed in an academic style; he completed Tchaikovsky's E♭ symphony.

Bogdanov-Berezovsky, Valerian Mikhaylovich (*b* Starozhilovka, 17 July 1903; *d* Moscow, 13 May 1971). Soviet critic and composer. He studied with Shteynberg and Shcherbachov at the Leningrad Conservatory (1919–27), where he was a close friend of Shostakovich and where he later taught (from 1940). He campaigned for new Western music and wrote important studies of Soviet opera. His works include operas, ballets and orchestral pieces.

Bohème, La. Opera in four acts by Puccini to a libretto by Giuseppe Giacosa and Luigi Illica after Henry Murger's *Scènes de la vie Bohème* (1896, Turin). Leoncavallo wrote a four-act opera on scenes from the same book (1897, Venice).

Bohemian Girl, The. Opera in three acts by Balfe to a libretto by Bunn (1843, London).

Böhm, Georg (*b* Hohenkirchen, 2 Sept 1661; *d* Lüneburg, 18 May 1733). German composer. He was organist of the Johanniskirche, Lüneburg, from 1698. He is important for his influence on J.S. Bach and for his development of the organ chorale partita (and variations) in which he used different compositional techniques in a synthesis of national styles. Böhm's keyboard works display his strongest gifts: among them are 11 suites and a Prelude, Fugue and Postlude in G minor which is one of the finest organ works of the period, combining French grace and charm with north German intensity. He also composed motets, cantatas, sacred songs, and a *St John Passion* (1704) formerly attributed to Handel.

Böhm, Karl (*b* Graz, 28 Aug 1894; *d* Salzburg, 14 Aug 1981). Austrian conductor. After study at Graz and Vienna he conducted at the Graz Opera from 1917. He moved to the Munich Staatsoper (1921), under Muck and Walter, and in 1927 became music director at Darmstadt. A long association with the Vienna PO began in 1933. The following year he became director of the Dresden Staatsoper, where he gave the premières of Strauss's *Die schweigsame Frau* and *Daphne*; in 1936 he took the company to Covent Garden. He was director of the Vienna Staatsoper (1943–5, 1954–6) and conducted at Salzburg, Bayreuth and the Met. As an orchestral conductor he was heard most in the Viennese Classics, Bruckner, Brahms and Berg. His interpretations were direct, fresh and well balanced, avoiding sentimentality and mannerism.

Böhner, (Johann) Ludwig (*b* Tottelstedt, 8 Jan 1787; *d* Gotha, 28 March 1860). German pianist, conductor and composer. He studied in Erfurt and with Spohr, then taught the piano and made concert tours. Winning praise for his Classical virtuoso piano pieces and orchestral works, he also anticipated Weber in his concert overtures and use of folk elements in opera. He was the model for E.T.A. Hoffmann's 'Capellmeister Kreisler'.

Boieldieu, (François-)Adrien (*b* Rouen, 16 Dec 1775; *d* Jarcy, 8 Oct 1834). French composer. A central figure in the *opéra comique* tradition, he was the leading opera composer in France during the first quarter of the 19th century. His musical training came principally from Charles Broche, the Rouen

Cathedral organist, and his inspiration from hearing *opéras comiques* by Grétry, Dalayrac and Méhul at the Théâtre des Arts. From 1791 he was organist at St André, Rouen, and as a concert pianist performed his own sonatas, potpourris and *romances*; he wrote his first *opéra comique* in 1793. He gained prominence in Paris with a series of successful stage works, from *La famille suisse* (1797) to *La calife de Bagdad* (1800) and *Ma Tante Aurore* (1803), also teaching the piano at the Paris Conservatoire. After holding a court post in St Petersburg (1803–11) he re-established himself in Paris and produced an especially inventive score in *Le petit chaperon rouge* (1818). He was a cautious admirer but not an imitator of Rossini, and upheld the French tradition with *La dame blanche* (1825), which won international success. His style is characterized by a natural melodic wealth; greater harmonic and orchestral richness is found in his later works, including *Les deux nuits* (1829). A son, Louis (1815–83), composed 11 operas and *romances*.

Boismortier, Joseph Bodin de (*b* Thionville, 23 Dec 1689; *d* Roissy-en-Brie, 28 Oct 1755). French composer. After moving to Paris *c*1723 he published over 100 sets of works, achieving great popularity and financial success. His output includes four stage works, including an opera *Daphnis et Chloé* (1747), motets, secular cantatas and numerous sonatas and concertos (many for flute), intended for amateurs. He introduced new instrumental combinations (e.g. three flutes alone), and wrote the first French solo concerto for any instrument (1729) and the first French flute sonatas with a fully realized harpsichord part (*c*1741–2). Works for the fashionable musette (bagpipe) and vielle (hurdy-gurdy) are also prominent. Boismortier's music is notable for its tunefulness, simplicity and elegance.

Boito, Arrigo [Enrico] (*b* Padua, 24 Feb 1842; *d* Milan, 10 June 1918). Italian librettist, composer and critic. He is best remembered for his one completed opera, *Mefistofele*, and for his collaborations with Verdi. He studied composition and aesthetics at the Milan Conservatory, then travelled, meeting Verdi in Paris. In Milan from 1862, and associated with the Scapigliatura, a radical literary movement, he wrote ironic poetry and erudite criticism decrying the state of Italian art. Although the first version of the five-act *Mefistofele* had a catastrophic première under his own direction in 1868, with revisions the work triumphed at Bologna, Venice and, in 1881, La Scala. It was through the efforts of the publisher Giulio Ricordi in 1879 that a successful Shakespearean collaboration, and what was to be a deepening friendship, began between Verdi and Boito. The librettos for *Otello* (1887) and *Falstaff* (1893), the second even more polished than the first, are remarkable for their fidelity to Shakespeare, sense of proportion, wit and vividness. His other well-known librettos include those for *La Gioconda* (set by Ponchielli, 1876) and for the 1881 revision of Verdi's *Simon Boccanegra*. In the 1890s Verdi encouraged Boito to complete his own second opera, *Nerone*, but he never did, lacking the confidence and musical proficiency to realize his ambitions (the work was performed in an edited version in 1924). As a music critic in the 1860s, he praised Mendelssohn and Meyerbeer and treated Verdi with respect; later he was less than enthusiastic about Wagner and showed antipathy for Richard Strauss.

Bokemeyer, Heinrich (*b* Immensen, March 1679; *d* Wolfenbüttel, 7 Dec 1751). German composer and theorist. He served at Husum, Schleswig and the Wolfenbüttel ducal palace (cantor from 1720). Widely respected as a theorist and composer, he wrote much music and three conservative treatises; his remarkable collection of books and music is still extant.

Bolcom, William (Elden) (*b* Seattle, 26 May 1938). American composer and pianist. He studied with Milhaud at Mills College (1958–61) and Leland Smith at Stanford (1961–4) and began teaching at the University of Michigan in 1973. As a pianist he has taken a leading part in the revival of ragtime and other American vernacular music. His works are polystylistic and concerned with momentous philosophical and religious themes: they include a monumental setting of Blake's *Songs of Innocence and Experience* for soloists, choirs and orchestra (1956–81).

Bolero. A Spanish dance and song, in moderate tempo and triple metre, popular at the end of the 18th century and throughout the 19th; its rhythms are closely related to the polonaise. The Cuban bolero, which superseded the Spanish in Latin America, is in duple time. Beethoven wrote a *Bolero a solo* WoO158,1:19; later examples in art music include those by Berlioz, Chopin and Ravel.

Boléro. Ballet in one act by Ravel (1928, Paris).

Bolet, Jorge (*b* Havana, 15 Nov 1914). American pianist of Cuban birth. He studied in Philadelphia; his teachers included Godowsky, Rosenthal and Serkin. He taught at the Curtis Institute, 1939–42, then military service took him to Japan (where he conducted the Japanese première of *The Mikado*). A powerful interpreter of Liszt in the grand Romantic tradition, his virtuosity has been widely recognized in the USA and Europe.

Bollius, Daniel (*b* Hechingen, *c*1590; *d* Mainz, *c*1642). German composer. Organist, then Kapellmeister, at the Mainz court, he is important primarily for his *Representatio* (*c*1620), an early German oratorio. Based on St Luke's account of John the Baptist's early life, it is marked by its expressive, declamatory solo writing and its varied instrumental interludes.

Bologna school. Term for the group of composers active in Bologna in the mid-late 17th century; most were associated with the church of S Petronio or the Accademia Filarmonica. They include Cazzati, Perti, G.B. Vitali, Torelli and Corelli (who had Bolognese links although he mainly worked in Rome); the school is associated with sacred music and particularly with the rise of the instrumental concerto and sonata, including music for trumpet and strings, a Bolognese speciality.

Bol'shoy Theatre. Moscow theatre, built in 1825 on the site of the Petrovsky Theatre (built 1780). In the 20th century it became the most important centre in Moscow for opera and ballet. Its companies have made visits abroad since 1964.

Bombardon. Tuba, especially in 12' F and 14' E♭, and particularly in a band; but it has been used of a variety of tuba-type instruments in different countries.

Bomtempo [Buontempo], João Domingos (*b* Lisbon, 28 Dec 1775; *d* there, 18 Aug 1842). Portuguese pianist and composer. He established himself as a pianist in Paris, met Clementi there and made visits to London before settling in Portugal, where he founded the Philharmonic Society (1822) and the conservatory (1833). Through his championship of the Viennese Classical repertory and his compositions (the earliest native symphonies, piano concertos and chamber music), he became a principal reformer of Portuguese music.

Bond, Capel (*b* Gloucester, bap. 14 Dec 1730; *d* Coventry, 14 Feb 1790). English composer. He was an organist in Coventry and organized many concerts in the Midlands. His compositions include six concertos (1766, among them one for bassoon) and anthems.

Bondeville, Emmanuel (Pierre Georges) de (*b* Rouen, 29 Oct 1898; *d* Paris, 27 Nov 1987. French composer. He studied at Rouen and at the Paris Conservatorie, also working with Dupré, and held posts at French Radio and in opera (director of the Paris Opéra, 1952–70). He wrote operas for the Opéra-Comique (*Madame Bovary*, 1951), piano works and symphonic poems as well as a *Symphonie lyrique* (1957) and *Symphonie choréographique* (1965).

Bondini, Pasquale (*b* ?Bonn, ?1737; *d* Bruneck, 30/31 Oct 1789). Italian impresario. He worked in Dresden, Leipzig and (from 1781) Prague, where he commissioned Mozart to write *Don Giovanni* – in which his wife Caterina created the role of Zerlina.

Bones. An ancient instrument of the CLAPPERS type, consisting of a pair of sticks and sounded by striking them together.

Bongos [bongo drums]. A pair of small Afro-Cuban single-headed drums with conical or cylindrical hardwood shells. Created in Cuba *c*1900, they are played in Latin American dance bands, rumba bands and Western rhythm bands. Composers who have used bongos in their scores include Varèse, Orff and Boulez.

Boni, Guillaume (*b* St Flour; *d* after 1594). French composer, *maître de chapelle* at Toulouse Cathedral. His motets (1573), psalms (1582) and settings of Ronsard's sonnets (2 vols., 1576) are mostly conservative in style and restrained in expression.

Bonini, Severo (*b* Florence, 23 Dec 1582; *d* there, 5 Dec 1663). Italian composer. A Benedictine monk, he studied with Caccini and published four collections of music (1607–9) in Florence while serving at nearby abbeys. From 1613 he was an organist in Forlì (where he published three further volumes), returning in 1640 to Florence as *maestro di cappella* of S Trinità. His compositions (motets, madrigals, canzonettas) show an assimilation of polyphonic, monodic and concertato styles. His treatise *Discorsi e regole* (1649–50) is an important source on the rise of monody and opera.

Bonne chanson, La. Song cycle by Fauré (op.61, 1894), settings for voice and piano of nine poems by Verlaine.

Bonno, Giuseppe (*b* Vienna, 29 Jan 1711; *d* there, 15 April 1788). Austrian composer of Italian origin. After studying with Durante and Leo in Naples (1726–36), he worked in Vienna, becoming imperial court composer in 1739 and Kapellmeister in 1774. In *c*1749–1761 he was also the prince of Saxe-Hildburghausen's Kapellmeister. A prominent conductor and teacher, he was highly esteemed in Viennese musical life and was a friend of the Mozarts. His output, mostly vocal, includes oratorios, church works and over 20 stage works (some written with Metastasio), in an idiom between the Italian Baroque style (still used in Vienna) and the Classicism of Gluck and Haydn. His church music shows an increasingly secular approach.

Bononcini. Italian family of musicians. Giovanni Maria (*b* Montecorone, bap. 23 Sept 1642; *d* Modena, 18 Nov 1678), a violinist for the Dowager Duchess Laura d'Este, was *maestro di cappella* at Modena Cathedral from 1673. He wrote mainly instrumental works (nine sets of sonatas and dance movements, 1666–78) but latterly turned to vocal genres, composing a chamber opera, madrigals and two sets of solo cantatas. His treatise *Musico prattico* (1673) was widely influential. His sonatas, among the finest of the late 17th-century Modenese school, show clearly his contrapuntal skill; the *sonate da camera*, showing both French and Italian features, were probably among the last to be used for dancing.

His son Giovanni (*b* Modena, 18 July 1670; *d* Vienna, 9 July 1747), composer and cellist, worked mainly at Bologna until 1691, publishing several instrumental collections, four masses and ten chamber duets (1691). From *c*1692 to 1696 he served the Colonna family in Rome, where he wrote stage works including the highly successful *Il trionfo di Camilla* (1696, Naples). At the Viennese court, 1698–1712, he presented *c*20 stage works; by 1706 his operas and cantatas were popular in Paris, London and elsewhere. After serving the Viennese ambassador at Rome, 1714–19, he went to London as a composer for the Royal Academy of Music, where his operas were extremely successful (more so than Handel's). In 1724–31 he was employed by the Duchess of Marlborough; he later spent time in Paris and Lisbon before returning to Vienna. His output was immense, including over 60 stage works (mostly operas), over 250 solo cantatas, and sacred pieces. Except in works such as the contrapuntal early chamber duets his idiom is simple and shows *galant* features; his arias, though praised for their grace and expressiveness, seldom achieve the dramatic vigour or depth of Handel's.

Dramatic music over 40 operas, serenatas incl. Il trionfo di Camilla (1696); oratorios
*Vocal music c*250 solo cantatas; 12 cantatas, 2 vv; 4 masses; Te Deum (1741)
*Instrumental music c*90 sinfonias, concs., trio sonatas, solo sonatas

His brother Antonio Maria (*b* Modena, 18 June 1677; *d* there, 8 July 1726), composer and cellist, worked with him in Bologna, Rome and Vienna, where in 1705–11 he wrote dramatic works as

Kapellmeister to the emperor's brother Charles. Returning to Italy in 1713, he lived mainly in Modena, where he became *maestro di cappella* in 1721. His compositions, including some 20 stage works, 40 solo cantatas and several sacred works, are more sophisticated than Giovanni's in texture and harmony but were less successful.

Their half-brother Giovanni Maria (1678–1753), a cellist at Modena and later a violinist in Rome, composed vocal works.

Bonporti, Francesco Antonio (*b* Trent, bap. 11 June 1672; *d* Padua, 19 Dec 1749). Italian composer. He was a priest at Trent Cathedral from 1697, moving to Padua in 1740. He published 12 sets of works, mainly solo and trio sonatas *da camera*. His idiom, based on Corelli's, has imaginative harmonies and lively part-writing, but also an unusual concentration on melodic detail. The inventions for violin and continuo op.10 (1712) may have influenced Bach; four were once attributed to him.

Bontempi, Giovanni Andrea (*b* Perugia, *c*1624; *d* Brufa, 1 July 1705). Italian composer. He sang at St Mark's, Venice, from 1643 but in 1650 went to the Saxon court at Dresden, becoming joint Kapellmeister (with Schütz and Albrici) in 1656. He is important for his two surviving operas and his *Historia musica* (1695) – the first history of music in Italian. The operas, typical of the mid-Baroque *bel canto* style, fuse German and Italian influences. *Il Paride* (1662) was a festival opera with ballets and comic intermezzos, while *Dafne* (1671; the libretto modelled on Schütz's, 1627) is the earliest German opera surviving in full score. Bontempi also wrote an important counterpoint treatise (1660).

Bonynge, Richard (Alan) (*b* Sydney, 29 Sept 1930). Australian conductor. He studied at the New South Wales Conservatorium and the RAM. He influenced the development of Joan Sutherland's career and conducted her performances from 1963 (they were married in 1954). They have appeared widely in the *bel canto* repertory, often with vocal parts ornamented by Bonynge. In 1976 he became musical director of Australian Opera.

Boogie-woogie. A style of piano blues, dating from the early 20th century, characterized by repetitive left-hand bass figures on standard blues chord progressions; the player's right hand plays an improvised part, independent of the steady rhythm maintained by the left.

Boosey & Hawkes. English music publishers and instrument manufacturers. Founded in London by Thomas Boosey (ii) in 1816, and originally foreign music importers, Boosey & Co. soon became the English publishers of Hummel, Rossini, Bellini and Verdi. From *c*1850 they also manufactured wind instruments and from 1868 brass. During the late 19th century their publishing centred on popular and educational music. Amalgamating with Hawkes & Son (1930), they continued to specialize in brass and military band music, meanwhile adding to the catalogue works by Stravinsky, Prokofiev, Bartók, Copland, Mahler, Britten and Maxwell Davies. A controlling interest in the firm was acquired by Carl Fischer in 1986.

Bop [bebop]. A style of jazz developed in New York in the early 1940s. It represented a considerable increase in complexity over earlier styles, with a more diversified rhythmic texture, an enriched harmonic vocabulary and an emphasis on the improvisation of rapid melodies full of asymmetrical phrases and accent patterns.

Borchgrevinck, Melchior (*b* ?*c*1570; *d* Copenhagen, 20 Dec 1632). Danish composer. An instrumentalist at the Danish court from 1587, he travelled to England and Italy (studying with G. Gabrieli) before becoming director of court music in 1618. His two anthologies (1605–6) of five-part madrigals were the first major music publications in Denmark. He also wrote an eight-voice mass, psalms and dances as well as two madrigals.

Bordes, Charles (Marie Anne) (*b* La Roche-Corbon, 12 May 1863; *d* Toulon, 8 Nov 1909). French scholar, teacher and composer. He was an organist and choirmaster before founding, with Guilmant and d'Indy, the Schola Cantorum of Paris (1894) for the revival of Gregorian chant and Renaissance polyphony. He published collections of early Basque and other French folk music, edited early music anthologies and wrote instrumental pieces, choruses and songs reflecting his scholarly interests.

Bordoni [Hasse], **Faustina** (*b* Venice, 1700; *d* there, 4 Nov 1781). Italian mezzo-soprano. She sang in operas in Venice in 1716–25, and from 1719 elsewhere, especially Vienna (1725–6). She then sang for three seasons (1726–8) in London, creating several roles in Handel's operas and becoming Cuzzoni's rival. As *virtuoso da camera* at the Dresden court, 1731–63, she sang in many works by her husband, Hasse (the Kapellmeister), and continued performing abroad until her stage retirement in 1751. Among the greatest singers of her age, Faustina had a strong and flexible voice and was a fine actress, at her best in heroic parts (such as Alcestis in Handel's *Admeto*).

Boréades, Les. *Tragédie en musique* in five acts by Rameau to a libretto probably by Cahusac; it is sometimes known as *Abaris*. Rameau died between the rehearsals in 1763 and the planned première.

Boretti, Giovanni Antonio (*b* Rome, *c*1640; *d* Venice, 17 Dec 1672). Italian composer and singer. His operatic style was varied and flexible. Five of his eight known operas (*c*1666–72) survive; their frequent, elaborate arias are typical of the exhibitionist style demanded by Venetian audiences from the mid-century onwards. The laments accompanied by strings are among his most attractive arias.

Borghi, Giovanni Battista (*b* Camerino, Macerata, 25 Aug 1738; *d* Loreto, 25 Feb 1796). Italian composer. He was *maestro di cappella* at Macerata Cathedral, 1759–78, and then at the Santa Casa of Loreto. He wrote many sacred works, *c*25 operas and occasional cantatas. He should not be confused with Luigi Borghi (*c*1745–*c*1806), a violinist and composer active in London.

Boris Godunov. Opera in four acts with a prologue by Musorgsky to his own libretto after Pushkin and Karamazin: second version (1874, St Petersburg),

original version (seven scenes) (1928, Leningrad), revised versions by Rimsky-Korsakov (1896) and Shostakovich (1959).

Bořkovec, Pavel (*b* Prague, 10 June 1894; *d* there, 22 July 1972). Czech composer and teacher. He studied with Suk at the Prague Conservatory (1925–7) but became more influenced by Stravinskian neo-classicism: his works include three symphonies, several concertos, five quartets and a nonet. He taught at the Prague Academy, 1946–63.

Borodin, Alexander Porfir'yevich (*b* St Petersburg, 12 Nov 1833; *d* there, 27 Feb 1887). Russian composer. As a youth he developed parallel interests in music and chemistry, teaching himself the cello and qualifying in medicine (1856); throughout his life music was subordinated to his research and his activities as a lecturer (from 1862) at the Medico-Surgical Academy in St Petersburg. His predilection for the music of Mendelssohn and Schumann, together with his acquaintance with Musorgsky, Cui, Rimsky-Korsakov, Liszt and above all Balakirev gave shape to his compositional efforts. It was mainly through Balakirev's influence that he turned towards Russian nationalism, using Russian folksong in his music; he was one of 'The Five', the group eager to create a distinctive nationalist school.

Borodin's earliest completed works include the First Symphony in E♭ (1867), showing a freshness and assurance that brought immediate acclaim, and no.2 in B minor (1876) which, though longer in the making, is one of the boldest and most colourful symphonies of the century, in the Russian context a mature, symphonic counterpart to Glinka's *Ruslan and Lyudmila*. The piece contributing most to his early fame, however, especially in western Europe, was the short orchestral 'musical picture' *On the Steppes of Central Asia* (1880; dedicated to Liszt). Among the important chamber pieces, including those works which give the lie most clearly to charges of inspired dilettantism still sometimes brought against him, are the early Piano Quintet in C minor (1862) – already showing the supple lyricism, smooth texture, neat design and heartfelt elegiac quality of his most characteristic music – and the two string quartets, the second famous for its beautiful Nocturne, with their craftsmanship and latent muscularity. His most substantial achievement was undoubtedly the opera *Prince Igor* (written over the period 1869–87; completed and partly orchestrated by Rimsky-Korsakov and Glazunov). Despite its protracted creation and weak, disjointed libretto (Borodin's own), it contains abundant musical richness in its individual arias, in its powerfully Russian atmosphere and its fine choral scenes crowned by the barbaric splendour of the Polovtsian Dances.

Dramatic music The Bogatïrs, opera-farce (1867); Prince Igor, opera, inc. (1887); one act of Mlada, opera-ballet (1872)

Orchestral music Sym. no.1, E♭ (1867); Sym. no.2, b (1876); Sym. no.3, a, inc. (1887); In the Steppes of Central Asia, musical picture (1880)

Chamber and piano music 2 str qts (1879, 1881); Pf Qnt, c (1862); *c*10 other chamber works; scherzos etc for pf solo and duet

Vocal music *c*16 songs

Boroni, Antonio (*b* Rome, 1738; *d* there, 21 Dec 1792). Italian composer. He studied under Padre Martini in Bologna and in Naples. In the 1760s his operas were given in Venice (notably *L'amore in musica*, 1763), Prague and elsewhere. While Kapellmeister at Stuttgart, 1770–7, he wrote *opéras comiques*; his last opera was given in 1778 in Rome, where he became *maestro di cappella* at St Peter's. He wrote much sacred music.

Borosini, Francesco (*b* Modena, *c*1690; *d* ?*c*1750). Italian tenor. A son of the tenor Antonio Borosini (*c*1660–after 1711), he sang in 1712–31 at the Viennese court, also appearing in Italy and in London (Bazajet in Handel's *Tamerlano*, 1724); he was the first great Italian tenor to sing there. His wife Rosa (*c*1693–after 1740), a soprano, sang at Vienna, 1721–40.

Borren, Charles (Jean Eugène) van den (*b* Ixalles, 17 Nov 1874; *d* Brussels, 14 Jan 1966). Belgian musicologist. He first studied law, practising as a barrister, then turned to musical studies; he became a music critic and a lecturer and in 1919 librarian of the Brussels Royal Conservatory. He also taught at the Free University and Liège University (1926–45). In his research he concentrated largely on Netherlands music from medieval to modern times; he wrote authoritative studies of such composers as Dufay and Lassus and contributed numerous articles to music dictionaries. He also worked on early English music.

Børresen, (Aksel Enjar) Hakon (*b* Copenhagen, 2 June 1876; *d* there, 6 Oct 1954). Danish composer. He studied with Svendsen, whose orchestral genius influenced him and whom he succeeded: his works include three symphonies and the opera *Den kongelige gaest* (1919).

Borris, Siegfried (*b* Berlin, 4 Nov 1906). German composer. He studied with Hindemith at the Berlin Musikhochschule (1927–9), where he began teaching in 1945. His large and diverse, essentially Hindemithian output includes much educational music, notably lively ensemble works and youth operas, some incorporating folk music.

Borromeo, Carlo (*b* Arona, 2 Oct 1538; *d* Milan, 3 Nov 1584). Italian prelate and patron. He was a powerful church reformer. A leading figure at the Council of Trent (1563), he influenced 16th-century sacred polyphony by advocating a strict chordal style that satisfied the requirement for textual intelligibility (e.g. Ruffo's masses, 1570).

Borrono, Pietro Paolo (*b* Milan; *fl* 1531–49). Italian composer and lutenist. He may have been at François I's court (1531–4) and at Milan *c*1550. His extant works, for one or two lutes, in three published collections (1536, 1546, 1548), include fantasias and toccatas, dances and arrangements of vocal works.

Bortnyansky, Dmitry Stepanovich (*b* Glukhov, 1751; *d* St Petersburg, 10 Oct 1825). Ukrainian composer. He studied in Italy from 1769; his first operas were given there, 1776–8. Returning to Russia in 1779, he became Kapellmeister at the St Petersburg court and in 1796 director. His many Russian sacred pieces (later edited by Tchaikovsky) are notable for their Italianate lyricism and skilful counterpoint. He also wrote operas, cantatas and instrumental pieces, notably a Sinfonia concertante (1790).

Bortolotti, Mauro (*b* Narni, 26 Nov 1926). Italian composer. He studied at the Rome Conservatory (1944–57) with Petrassi and at Darmstadt. In 1961 he was a founder-member of the Roman improvisation group Nuova Consonanza. His music, mostly instrumental, embraces serialism, aleatory procedures and electronics.

Borup-Jørgensen, (Jens) Axel (*b* Hjørring, 22 Nov 1924). Danish composer. He studied at the Copenhagen Conservatory (1946–50) and at Darmstadt (1959, 1962), coming under the influence of Ligeti, Fortner and Stockhausen. His large output covers most non-theatrical genres.

Boschi, Giuseppe Maria (*fl* 1698–1744). Italian bass. He and his wife, Francesca Vanini (*d* 1744), a contralto, both sang in Venice early in the century, and went to sing in London in 1710–11; he returned there (after singing in Dresden) in 1720–28, specializing in energetic roles (villains and tryants) in Handel's operas.

Bösendorfer. Austrian firm of piano makers. It was established in Vienna in 1828 by Ignaz Bösendorfer (1796–1859). Liszt's approval brought international renown, consolidated by the patronage of royalty and, in 1936, the BBC. Initially building only Viennese-action grands, it gradually changed to the English action in the late 19th century, its relatively modest output comprising 33 different models between 1828 and 1975. It has made a few fine uprights and builds grand pianos in five models, among the best modern instruments.

Boskovich, Alexander Uriah (*b* Cluj, 16 Aug 1907; *d* Tel-Aviv, 5 Nov 1964). Israeli composer. He studied in Vienna (1924) and Paris (1925) and worked in Cluj as a conductor and pianist before moving to Palestine in 1938. His most important works, of the 1960s, synthesize the Jewish spiritual and musical tradition with wider contemporary material. From 1955 he was music critic of the daily paper *Ha'aretz*.

Boskovsky, Willi (*b* Vienna, 16 June 1909). Austrian violinist and conductor. He studied at the Vienna Academy and joined the Vienna PO in 1932, becoming co-leader in 1939. He also led the Vienna Staatsoper Orchestra and in 1969 became conductor of the Vienna Strauss Orchestra. From 1954 to 1979 he conducted the Vienna New Year's Day Concerts.

Bossa-nova. A movement in Brazilian popular music from *c*1959 that effected changes in the classical urban samba. The style avoids emphasis on any single musical element: melody, harmony and rhythm are integrated; singers use a subdued tone like spoken language.

Bossi, Marco Enrico (*b* Salo, 25 April 1861; *d* Atlantic Ocean, 20 Feb 1925). Italian composer, organist and pianist. He studied with his father and with Ponchielli at the Milan Conservatory (1873–81). In 1881 he was appointed organist of Como Cathedral; later he was internationally renowned as an organist. He taught in Naples (1890–95), Venice

(1895–1902), Bologna (1902–11) and Rome (1916–23). One of those who sought to revive Italian non-operatic music, he was influenced by the German Romantics, Franck and Reger. His choral and organ works are best remembered. His son Renzo (1883–1965) studied in Leipzig and became an opera conductor and teacher; he wrote orchestral music and operas (including *Volpino il calderaio*, 1925).

Bossinensis, Franciscus (*b* ?Bosnia; *fl* 1510). Italian composer. Two collections of his lute music, containing 126 frottolas and 46 ricercares, were printed by Petrucci (1509, 1511). The frottolas are arrangements of four-voice works by other composers but each book concludes with a series of his own ricercares related to certain of the frottolas.

Boston [Boston dip]. A slow ballroom dance related to the waltz. It originated in the USA in the 1870s and was danced with the hands on the partner's hips.

Boston Symphony Orchestra. American orchestra founded in 1881 and first conducted by George Henschel (until 1884); its home is Symphony Hall (opened 1900). It provided players, administrators and teachers to other organizations in Boston. Summer Promenade Concerts (Boston Pops) were instituted in 1885. Its first recordings were made with Karl Muck in 1917. Under Serge Koussevitsky (1924–49) new works were introduced and commissioned and it took over the Berkshire (now Tanglewood) Musical Festival and founded (1940) a school for young musicians. Charles Munch (1949–62) instituted tours outside the USA. Erich Leinsdorf has been principal conductor (1962–9) and Seiji Ozawa (from 1972).

Bote & Bock. German firm of music publishers. It was founded in Berlin in 1838, when Eduard Bote and Gustav Bock purchased C.W. Froehlich & Co. It became the leading firm in north Germany for opera publication. Since 1945 it has concentrated mainly on new music.

Bottesini, Giovanni (*b* Crema, 22 Dec 1821; *d* Parma, 7 July 1889). Italian double bass player, conductor and composer. He studied at the Milan Conservatory, became principal bass at the Teatro S Benedetto, Venice, and toured in Europe and North America. Playing a three-string instrument tuned a tone higher than was usual, he was nicknamed the 'Paganini of the double bass' for his agility, pure tone and intonation. He was a lifelong friend of Verdi and held conducting appointments at theatres in Paris, Palermo, Spain, Portugal and London. Among his stage works, *Vinciguerra il bandito* (1870) and *Ero e Leandro* (1879, libretto by Boito) were well received. It is for his numerous technically demanding double bass compositions, expanding the instrument's compass, that he is best remembered.

Bottrigari, Ercole (*b* Bologna, 24 Aug 1531; *d* S Alberto, 30 Sept 1612). Italian writer on music. After a classical and humanistic education he joined the Ferrarese court (1576–86), then at its artistic height. His dialogue *Il desiderio* (1594) discusses Ferrarese musical life and instrumental tuning; his modernist approach contrasts strongly with that of some contemporary theorists (e.g. Artusi). He apparently composed madrigals.

Bouche fermée (Fr.). 'Closed mouth': singing without words and with the mouth closed; humming.

Boucher, Alexandre-Jean (*b* Paris, 11 April 1778; *d* there, 29 Dec 1861). French violinist. Although his virtuosity impressed all who heard him, including Boccherini, Spohr and Weber, a tasteless showmanship is reported to have dominated his performances. Beethoven wrote the seven-bar *Kleines Stück* WoO 34 (1822) for him.

Boucourechliev, André (*b* Sofia, 28 July 1925). French composer of Bulgarian birth. He studied in Sofia and at the Ecole Normale de Musique in Paris (1949–51). In 1954 he began to compose, later attending the Darmstadt courses. His works are mostly electronic and instrumental, including a series of aleatory *Archipels* (1967–70) for different instrumental combinations. He has written books on Chopin, Beethoven and Stravinsky.

Bouffons, Querelle des. A Parisian controversy over the respective merits of French and Italian music, in particular opera. It was sparked off in 1752 by performances of Pergolesi's *La serva padrona* by a troupe called the Bouffons. F.M. Grimm's *Lettre sur Omphale* (1752) favoured the 'natural' Italian idiom and criticized 'artificial' French works; Rousseau's *Lettre sur la musique française* (1753) expressed similar views. But the French style, supported by J.-B. Jourdan and other writers, remained popular, and the quarrel subsided, unresolved, when the Bouffons left Paris in 1754.

Boughton, Rutland (*b* Aylesbury, 23 Jan 1878; *d* London, 25 Jan 1960). English composer and writer. He studied briefly at the RCM but was mostly self-taught. While teaching in Birmingham (1905–11) he developed his ideas on the basis of Wagner and William Morris socialism, and put them into practice at his Glastonbury festivals (1914–27), where several of his operas were first produced, including *The Immortal Hour* (1914); this had immense success when staged in London in 1922. After the collapse of the Glastonbury venture he retired to farm, write and compose, and in 1945 completed his Arthurian cycle of five operas, in which Wagnerianism gives way to a simpler folksong manner.

Boulanger, Lili (Juliette Marie Olga) (*b* Paris, 21 Aug 1893; *d* Mézy, 15 March 1918). French composer, sister of Nadia. She studied at the Paris Conservatoire and won the Prix de Rome. Her composing life was short but productive: most important are her psalm settings and other large-scale choral works in a strong, subtle style.

Boulanger, Nadia (Juliette) (*b* Paris, 16 Sept 1887; *d* there, 22 Oct 1979). French teacher and conductor. She studied at the Paris Conservatoire and became the staunch, admiring friend of Stravinsky: his music and Fauré's provided the standards by which she taught, notably at the American Conservatory in Fontainebleau (from 1921). She was the most energetic, influential teacher, attracting pupils from all over the world; Copland and Carter were among them. As a conductor she was a pioneer in performing French Baroque and Renaissance music and she gave new works.

Boulevard Solitude. Opera in seven scenes by Henze to a libretto by Weil after Jökisch on the story of Manon Lescaut (1952, Hanover).

Boulez, Pierre (*b* Montbrison, 26 March 1925). French composer and conductor. He studied with Messiaen at the Paris Conservatoire (1942–5) and privately with Andrée Vaurabourg and René Leibowitz, inheriting Messiaen's concern with rhythm, non-developing forms and extra-European music along with the Schoenberg tradition of Leibowitz. The clash of the two influences lies behind such intense, disruptive works as his first two piano sonatas (1946, 1948) and *Livre pour quatuor* for string quartet (1949). The violence of his early music also suited that of René Char's poetry in the cantatas *Le visage nuptial* (1946) and *Le soleil des eaux* (1948), though through this highly charged style he was working towards an objective serial control of rhythm, loudness and tone colour that was achieved in the *Structures* for two pianos (1952). At this time he came to know Stockhausen, with whom he became a leader of the European avant garde, teaching at Darmstadt (1955–67) and elsewhere, and creating one of the key postwar works in his *Le marteau sans maître* (1954). Once more to poems by Char, the work is for contralto with alto flute, viola, guitar and percussion: a typical ensemble of middle-range instruments with an emphasis on struck and plucked sounds. The filtering of Boulez's earlier manner through his 'tonal serialism' produces a work of feverish speed, unrest and elegance.

In the mid-1950s Boulez extended his activities to conducting. He had been Barrault's musical director since 1946 and in 1954 under Barrault's aegis he set up a concert series, the Domaine Musical, to provide a platform for new music. By the mid-1960s he was appearing widely as a conductor, becoming chief conductor of the BBC SO (1971–4) and the New York PO (1971–8). Meanwhile his creative output declined. Under the influence of Mallarmé he had embarked on three big aleatory works after *Le marteau*, but of these the Third Piano Sonata (1957) remains a fragment and *Pli selon pli* for soprano and orchestra (1962) has been repeatedly revised; only a second book of *Structures* for two pianos (1961) has been definitively finished. Other works, notably *Eclat/Multiples* for tuned percussion ensemble and orchestra, also remain in progress, as if the open-endedness of Boulez's proliferating musical world had committed him to incompleteness. Only the severe memorial *Rituel* for orchestra (1975) has escaped that fate.

Since the mid-1970s Boulez has concentrated on his work as director of the Institut de Recherche et Coordination Acoustique/Musique, a computer studio in Paris where his main work has been *Répons* for orchestra and digital equipment.

Orchestral music Livre pour quatuor (1949); rev. as Livre pour cordes (1968); Poésie pour pouvoir (1958); Figures-Doubles-Prismes (1964); Eclat/Multiples (1970); Rituel (1975); Notations (1980); Répons (1981)
Chamber music Domaines (1968); Messagesquisse (1975)
Piano music 3 sonatas (1946, 1948, 1957); Structures I, II, 2 pf (1952, 1961)

Vocal music Le visage nuptial (1946); Le soleil des eaux (1948); Le marteau sans maître (1954); Pli selon pli (1962); Cummings ist der Dichter (1970)
Other works '... explosante-fixe...' (1971)
(*dates above show when works achieved substantially completed form; many have earlier versions and later revisions*)

Boult, Sir Adrian (Cedric) (*b* Chester, 8 April 1889; *d* Farnham, 22 Feb 1983). English conductor. He studied at Oxford and the Leipzig Conservatory, Nikisch being an early influence. He conducted at Covent Garden from 1914 and in 1918 began an association with contemporary English music, notably that of Holst, Elgar and Vaughan Williams. He was musical director of the CBSO (1924–30), then trained and conducted the newly formed BBC SO, which he rapidly brought to the front rank. He toured with it in Europe in the 1930s and was associate conductor of the Proms (1942–50); he was principal conductor of the LSO from 1951 to 1957. His controlled, undemonstrative technique was admired in a wide repertory, and he wrote two valuable handbooks on conducting.

Bourbon. French ducal, from 1589 royal, family; from 1700 also the Spanish royal family. Among the French Bourbon kings, Louis XIII and Louis XIV were especially important as patrons of music. The first two Spanish Bourbon monarchs, Philip V and Ferdinand VI, were also musical patrons.

Bourdon (Fr.). A term analogous to the English 'burden', used of the lowest drone on the hurdy-gurdy and of the free vibrating strings of the larger lutes such as the theorbo and bowed instruments such as the *lira da braccio*; also the lowest partial ('hum note') of tower bells.

Bourgault-Ducoudray, Louis (Albert) (*b* Nantes, 2 Feb 1840; *d* Vernouillet, 4 July 1910). French scholar and composer. He studied at the Paris Conservatoire, winning the Prix de Rome in 1862, and became interested in Renaissance polyphony, French folk music, Greek, Russian and oriental music. Although he published folksong collections and composed, it was through his lectures and writings advocating broader expressive means for the composer that he had most influence. Debussy was among his pupils.

Bourgeois, Derek (David) (*b* Kingston-upon-Thames, 16 Oct 1941). English composer. He studied at Cambridge and with Howells at the RCM; Walton and Britten have also been strong influences, and he has written much for educational use. Since 1971 he has lectured at Bristol University.

Bourgeois, Loys (*b* Paris, *c*1510–15; *d* in or after 1560). French composer and theorist. In 1545 he became *maître des enfants* at St Pierre and St Gervais, Geneva. He is chiefly remembered for his contribution to the Calvinist Psalter in which he may have supervised the adaptation of existing tunes and composed new melodies for the psalm translations by Marot and de Bèze (1551, 1554); his 'improvements' to psalm tunes led to a brief imprisonment in 1551 and the following year the Geneva council terminated his employment. He moved to Lyons and later to Paris. Two collections of four-voice psalms by him, one containing simple homophonic settings, the other more elaborate versions for voices or instruments, were published in 1547. His *Le droict chemin* (1550) was the first didactic manual in French on singing and sight-reading.

Bourgeois, Thomas-Louis (*b* Fontaine-L'Evêque, 24 Oct 1676; *d* Paris, 1750/51). French composer. He worked at Strasbourg and Toul and sang at the Paris Opéra 1708–11; in 1715–21 he served the Duke of Bourbon. His 40 cantatas contributed significantly to the genre in France and contain fine lyrical writing; he also wrote stage works.

Bourgeois gentilhomme, Le. *Comédie-ballet* with words by Molière and music by Lully (1670, Chambord).

Bournemouth Symphony Orchestra. British orchestra, originally the Bournemouth Municipal Orchestra (established 1897) and renamed in 1954. Its first conductor, Dan Godfrey, promoted British works and gave first English performances of Tchaikovsky. Under Constantin Silvestri (1961–9) it gained an international reputation. Conductors have included Rudolf Schwarz, Charles Groves, Paavo Berglund and Rudolf Barshay.

The Bournemouth Sinfonietta, founded in 1968, is its associated chamber orchestra.

Bournonville, Jean de (*b* Noyon, ?*c*1585; *d* Paris, 27 May 1632). French composer. From 1612 he was director of music at various choir schools, in his last months at the Sainte-Chapelle, Paris. He mainly composed *a cappella* church music but also wrote settings of French moral adages (1622). His lively, elegant counterpoint uses *chanson*-like melodic lines, and his psalm and Magnificat settings are interesting for their thematic unity. His son Valentin (*c*1610–*c*1663) was also a composer (his music, mainly sacred, is lost); another descendant, Jacques (*c*1675–after 1753), was a harpsichord teacher and composed sacred music.

Bourrée. A French dance in fast duple metre, popular in the 17th and 18th centuries. A crotchet upbeat and crotchet–minim syncopation on the third or seventh beat of a phrase are characteristic. Baroque composers included the bourrée as an optional dance in the suite after the sarabande. In England it was sometimes known as 'boree' or 'borry'.

Boutique fantasque, La. Ballet in one act by Respighi, with music arranged from Rossini's *Soirées musicales* and other pieces, choreographed by Massin (1919, London).

Boutmy, Josse [Charles Joseph] (*b* Ghent, 1 Feb 1697; *d* Brussels, 27 Nov 1779). South Netherlands composer. He served the Prince of Thurn und Taxis in Brussels from 1736, and in 1744–77 was court chapel organist. His harpsichord music (three books, 1738–*c*1750) combines French, Italian and German traits. Three of his sons became keyboard players and composers. Guillaume (1723–91), who served the Prince of Thurn und Taxis, and Jean-Joseph (1725–82), who worked at Ghent, Paris and The Hague, wrote italianate harpsichord music; Laurent-François (1756–1838) worked in France, the Low Countries and London and wrote light piano and chamber works, songs etc.

Bouzignac, Guillaume (*b* Narbonne, before 1592; *d* after 1641). French composer. He was a leading figure in early 17th-century church music. In 1609 he was *maître de musique* to the choirboys at Grenoble Cathedral, and may have held posts in the Languedoc region and at Rodez Cathedral. He was in the service of Gabriel de la Charlonye before 1634, probably moving on to Tours. Bouzignac's output, which survives in two MSS, comprises *chansons* and much church music (nearly 100 motets). His music, distinguished by its varied writing and bold juxtapositions, closely follows the sense of the text. He used a wide variety of expressive devices, was a skilled contrapuntist and excelled in handling the concertato style.

Bouzouki. Greek long-necked, plucked lute with three or four double courses of metal strings tuned *e–b'–e'* and *d–g–b'–e'* respectively. It is the most typical Greek urban instrument.

Bovicelli, Giovanni Battista (*b* Assisi; *fl* 1592–4). Italian music theorist. His treatise *Regole, passaggi di musica* (1594) is an important source of information on improvised vocal ornamentation and virtuoso singing in early Baroque Italy.

Bow. The use of a bow to draw sound from string instruments can be traced to the 10th century, when the bow was known throughout Islam and in the Byzantine empire. Up to *c*1600 bows were generally convex, like drawn hunting bows; the hair was strung on a shaft of elastic wood or bamboo, bent in an arc. During the late 17th century and early 18th, the European bow was gradually lengthened and straightened. About 1785 François Tourte (1747–1835) produced a bow so remarkably satisfactory that it became the model in his own time and, with a few changes, has continued as such. Tourte fixed the length of the violin bow at 74–5 cm, the playing hair at 65 cm and the balance point at 19 cm above the frog. Bows used for non-Western fiddles may be convex or straight.

Bowed guitar. *See* ARPEGGIONE.

Bowed keyboard instrument. A keyboard instrument in which a continuous bow (usually a rosined wheel) is applied to the strings, allowing sustained notes to be produced. *See* SOSTENENTE PIANO.

Bowles, Paul (*b* New York, 30 Dec 1910). American composer and writer. He studied in the late 1920s and early 1930s with Copland, Thomson and Boulanger. Most of his witty, evocative music, in many genres including opera, dates from before 1949, when he became more active as a writer.

Bowman, James (Thomas) (*b* Oxford, 6 Nov 1941). English countertenor. He studied at Oxford and in 1967 sang Britten's Oberon in London; the Voice of Apollo in *Death in Venice* was written for him. At Covent Garden he created roles in operas by Maxwell Davies and Tippett. He has sung with the Early Music Consort of London and his flexible, powerful voice has been much heard in Handel and Purcell.

Boyce, William (*b* London, bap. 11 Sept 1711; *d* Kensington, 7 Feb 1779). English composer. He was a St Paul's Cathedral chorister and an organ pupil of Maurice Greene, also studying with Pepusch. From 1734 he held organist's posts in London and from 1736 was a composer to the Chapel Royal, writing anthems and services. His oratorio *David's Lamentation over Saul and Jonathan* (1736) was followed by his first dramatic works, including a short opera, *Peleus and Thetis* (by 1740), *The Secular Masque* (1746) and the highly successful pastoral *The Chaplet* (1749), the first of a series of works for Drury Lane theatre. Increasing deafness hindered him – his last stage work was *Heart of Oak* (1759) – but his output in other vocal genres continued, and as Master of the King's Musick from 1757 he composed over 40 court odes. Among his few instrumental works are 12 trio sonatas (1747), *Eight Symphonys* (from ode and opera overtures, 1735–41, published 1760) and *Twelve Overtures* (1770). Boyce was among the finest and most respected English composers of his time, though his Baroque idiom had become old-fashioned by the end of his life. His music has a fresh vigour, especially evident in fugues, dance movements and expressive vocal writing. The owner of a valuable music library, he gained lasting fame for his *Cathedral Music* (1760–73), an edition of earlier English services by Orlando Gibbons, Purcell and others.

Sacred music 5 services; c60 anthems; hymns, sacred part-songs
Dramatic music Peleus and Thetis, masque (by 1740); The Chaplet (1749); The Shepherd's Lottery (1751); other stage works
Other vocal music David's Lamentation over Saul and Jonathan, oratorio (1736); Solomon, serenata (1742); over 50 birthday and New Year odes; cantatas, songs
Instrumental music 8 syms. (1760); 12 ovs. (1770); concs.; 12 trio sonatas (1747); kbd voluntaries

Boyd, Anne (Elizabeth) (*b* Sydney, 18 April 1946). Australian composer. She studied at Sydney University with Sculthorpe and at York University with Rands and Mellers. Her style is disciplined and cogent, reflecting an interest in the music of Southeast Asia and the Pacific. Since 1980 she has taught at Hong Kong University.

Boydell, Brian (*b* Dublin, 17 March 1917). Irish composer. He studied at Cambridge, at the RCM (1938–9) and in Dublin, where in 1962 he became professor of music. His music is tonal, influenced by Hindemith, and covers many forms; it includes a Violin Concerto (1953) and the choral pieces *Mors et vita* (1961) and *A Terrible Beauty is Born* (1965).

Boyd Neel Orchestra. British chamber orchestra founded in 1932 by Boyd Neel to perform Baroque music; it was conducted by him until 1953. It made European tours from the 1930s and gave premières of British works.

Boyhood's End. Cantata by Tippett (1943), a setting for tenor and piano of texts by W.H. Hudson.

Boykan, Martin (*b* New York, 12 April 1931). American composer. He studied with Piston at Harvard and Hindemith in Zurich and at Yale, and began teaching at Brandeis in 1957. His works, many of them long pieces for small ensembles and including three quartets, are in a 12-note style influenced by Webern and late Stravinsky but with a typically American long line.

Bozay, Attila (*b* Balatonfűzfő, 11 Aug 1939). Hungarian composer. He studied with Farkas at the Budapest Academy and in Paris (1967). He has composed mostly instrumental works in a strongly urged 12-note style. His String Quartet no.1 (1964) first brought him international recognition; his opera based on *Hamlet* was produced in Budapest in 1984.

Bozza, Eugène (*b* Nice, 4 April 1905). French composer. He studied at the Paris Conservatoire and has worked as a conductor (Opéra-Comique, 1939–48) and teacher. His works, in most forms, include much wind chamber music admired for its melodic fluency and elegance.

Brace. The bracket that joins the staves of a system at the left-hand end, indicating that the music on those staves should be played simultaneously.

Bradbury, William Batchelder (*b* York Co., ME, 6 Oct 1816; *d* Montclair, NJ, 7 Jan 1868). American composer and church musician. He worked mainly in New York, teaching children's singing classes and writing and compiling sacred music collections. His over 900 hymn tunes include *Jesus loves me, Just as I am*, *Sweet hour of prayer* and *He leadeth me*. In 1854 he set up a piano factory, in 1861 a publishing firm.

Brade, William (*b* 1560; *d* Hamburg, 26 Feb 1630). English instrumentalist and composer. He spent most of his life at German courts (Berlin, Bückeburg and, notably, Hamburg) and at the Danish court, and was acclaimed as one of the finest early violinists. His many published dances, in a popular melodic style, are more homophonic than traditional English ones of the period. By introducing dances new to Germany (e.g. branle, maschera, volta) he contributed to the development of the suite.

Braga, (Antônio) Francisco (*b* Rio de Janeiro, 15 April 1868; *d* there, 14 March 1945). Brazilian composer. He studied at the Paris Conservatoire with Massenet, then settled in Germany (1896–1900), where he absorbed Wagnerism. Back in Rio he worked as a composer, conductor and teacher (at the Instituto Nacional de Música, 1902–38). His music is mostly orchestral but he also wrote operas, church and chamber music.

Braga Santos, (José Manuel) Joly (*b* Lisbon, 14 May 1924). Portuguese composer. He studied with Luis de Freitas Branco, a great influence on him, and has worked in Lisbon as a composer, conductor, teacher (at the conservatory) and critic. At the end of the 1950s his music became affected by newer European trends; his works include operas, symphonies and concertos.

Braham, John (*b* London, 20 March 1774; *d* there, 17 Feb 1856). English tenor and composer. He was a boy soprano at Covent Garden, later studying with Rauzzini and winning acclaim on a continental tour, during which Cimarosa wrote *Artemisia* for him (1801). In English operas by Bishop, Attwood and others, he often wrote the music for his own part, his ballads, duets and patriotic songs, notably 'The Death of Nelson' (in *The Americans*, 1811), finding special popularity. As a showman he was capable of both tasteless ornament and fine singing; his voice was admired by contemporaries from Weber (who wrote Sir Huon in *Oberon* for him) to George IV.

Brahms, Johannes (*b* Hamburg, 7 May 1833;

d Vienna, 3 April 1897). German composer. He studied the piano from the age of seven and theory and composition (with Eduard Marxsen) from 13, gaining experience as an arranger for his father's light orchestra while absorbing the popular *alla zingarese* style associated with Hungarian folk music. In 1853, on a tour with the Hungarian violinist Reményi, he met Joseph Joachim and Liszt; Joachim, who became a lifelong friend, encouraged him to meet Schumann. Brahms's artistic kinship with Robert Schumann and his profound romantic passion (later mellowing to veneration) for Clara Schumann, 14 years his elder, never left him. After a time in Düsseldorf he worked in Detmold, settling in Hamburg in 1859 to direct a women's chorus. Though well known as a pianist he had trouble finding recognition as a composer, largely owing to his outspoken opposition – borne out in his D minor Piano Concerto op.15 – to the aesthetic principles of Liszt and the New German School. But his hopes for an official conducting post in Hamburg (never fulfilled) were strengthened by growing appreciation of his creative efforts, especially the two orchestral serenades, the Handel Variations for piano and the early piano quartets. He finally won a position of influence in 1863-4, as director of the Vienna Singakademie, concentrating on historical and modern *a cappella* works. Around this time he met Wagner, but their opposed stances precluded anything like friendship. Besides giving concerts of his own music, he made tours throughout northern and central Europe and began teaching the piano. He settled permanently in Vienna in 1868.

Brahms's urge to hold an official position (connected in his mind with notions of social respectability) was again met by a brief conductorship – in 1872-3 of the Vienna Gesellschaftskonzerte – but the practical demands of the job conflicted with his even more intense longing to compose. Both the *German Requiem* (first complete performance, 1869) and the Variations on the St Antony Chorale (1873) were rapturously acclaimed, bringing international renown and financial security. Honours from home and abroad stimulated a spate of masterpieces, including the First (1876) and Second (1877) Symphonies, the Violin Concerto (1878), the songs of opp.69-72 and the C major Trio. In 1881 Hans von Bülow became a valued colleague and supporter, 'lending' Brahms the fine Meiningen court orchestra to rehearse his new works, notably the Fourth Symphony (1885). At Bad Ischl, his favourite summer resort, he composed a series of important chamber works. By 1890 he had resolved to stop composing but nevertheless produced in 1891-4 some of his best instrumental pieces, inspired by the clarinettist Richard Mühlfeld. Soon after Clara's death in 1896 he died from cancer, aged 63, and was buried in Vienna.

Fundamentally reserved, logical and studious, Brahms was fond of taut forms in his music, though he used genre distinctions loosely. In the piano music, for example, which chronologically encircles his vocal output, the dividing lines beteen ballade and rhapsody, and capriccio and intermezzo, are vague; such terms refer more to expressive character than to musical form. As in other media, his most important development technique in the piano music is variation, whether used independently (simple melodic alteration and thematic cross-reference) or to create a large integrated cycle in which successive variations contain their own thematic transformation (as in the Handel Variations).

If producing chamber works without piano caused him difficulty, these pieces contain some of his most ingenious music, including the Clarinet Quintet and the three string quartets. Of the other chamber music, the eloquent pair of string sextets, the serious C minor Piano Quartet op.60 (known to be autobigraphical), the richly imaginative Piano Quintet and the fluent Clarinet Trio op.114 are noteworthy. The confidence to finish and present his First Symphony took Brahms 15 years for worries over not only his orchestral technique but the work's strongly Classical lines at a time when programmatic symphonies were becoming fashionable; his closely worked score led him to be hailed as Beethoven's true heir. In all four symphonies he is entirely personal in his choice of material, structural manipulation of themes and warm but lucid scoring. All four move from a weighty opening movement through loosely connected inner movements to a monumental finale. Here again his use of strict form, for example the ground bass scheme in the finale of the Fouth Symphony, is not only discreet but astonishingly effective. Among the concertos, the four-movement Second Piano Concerto in B♭ – on a grandly symphonic scale, demanding both physically and intellectually – and the Violin Concerto (dedicated to Joachim and lyrical as well as brilliant) are important, as too is the nobly rhetorical Double Concerto.

Brahms's greatest vocal work, and a work central to his career, is the *German Requiem* (1868), combining mixed chorus, solo voices and full orchestra in a deeply felt, non-denominational statement of faith. More Romantic are the *Schicksalslied* and the Alto Rhapsody. Between these large choral works and the many *a cappella* ones showing his informed appreciation of Renaissance and Baroque polyphony (he was a diligent collector, scholar and editor of old music) stand the justly popular *Zigeunerlieder* (in modified gypsy style) and the *ländler*-like *Liebeslieder* waltzes with piano accompaniment. His best-loved songs include, besides the narrative *Magelone* cycle and the sublime *Vier ernste Gesänge*, *Mainacht*, *Feldeinsamkeit* and *Immer leiser wird mein Schlummer*.

Orchestral music Sym. no.1, c (1876); Sym. no.2, D (1877); Sym. no.3, F (1883); Sym. no.4, e (1885); Serenade no.1, D (1858); Serenade no.2, A (1859); Pf Conc. no.1, d (1861); Pf Conc. no.2, B♭ (1882); Vn Conc., D (1878); Double Conc., vn, vc, a (1887); Academic Festival Ov. (1880); Tragic Ov. (1886); Variations on the St Antony Chorale (1873)

Chamber music 5 pf trios (op.8, B, 1854, rev. 1859); op.40, E♭, 1865 [vn, hn, pf]; op.87, C, 1882; op.101, c, 1886; op.114, a, 1891 [cl, vc, pf]; 3 pf qts (op.25, g, 1861; op.26, A, 1862; op.60, c, 1875); Pf Qnt, op.34, f (1864); Cl Qnt, op.115, b (1891); 3 str qts (op.51 nos. 1–2, c,a, 1873; op.67, B♭, 1876); 2 str qnts (op.88, F, 1882; op.111, G, 1890; 2 str sextets (op.18, B♭, 1860; op. 36, G, 1865); 2 vc sonatas (op.38, e, 1865; op.99, F, 1886); 3 vn sonatas (op.78, G, 1879; op.100, A, 1886; op.108, d, 1888); 2 cl/va sonatas (op.120, f, E♭, 1894)

Piano music sonatas, dance movts, studies, ballades, capriccios, intermezzos, fantasias, rhapsodies and variations (incl. Handel Variations, Bb, 1861; Paganini Variations, a, 1862–3); pf duets, incl. 21 Hungarian Dances (1868–80); pieces for two pfs

Vocal music 20 canons, mostly for female vv; *c*60 solo qts with pf acc., incl. Liebeslieder Waltzes, opp.52 and 65, Zigeunerlieder, op.103 (1888); 20 duets; *c*200 lieder, incl. 15 Romances from Tieck's 'Magelone' op.33 (1869), Vier ernste Gesänge, op.121 (1896)

Choral music German Requiem (1868); Alto Rhapsody (1869); Schicksalslied (1871); 13 unacc. motets, incl. Fest- und Gedenksprüche op.109 (?1886–9); 46 a cappella songs; 26 folksongs, arr. 4vv

Other 144 folksong arrs.; 10 arrs. of works by other composers; works for org, incl. 11 chorale preludes (1896)

Braille notation. The system of embossed dots to enable the blind to write and decipher, though not originally devised by him, was rationalized and made practical by Louis Braille (1809–52). Braille was also organist of a parish church, and in 1829 he devised a system expressing musical sound, as well as speech and numerals, with an embossed-dot system. Braille notation is founded on ten basic signs, using the six-dot cluster on which the Braille systems are based. Each pitch-class is represented, as a quaver (eighth-note), by the four upper dots, to which one or both of the two lower dots may be added to alter the rhythmic value. Further dot signs are used to signify octave, accidentals or intervals. The system has been developed to represent keyboard music, vocal music (choral as well as solo) and music for orchestral instruments and orchestral scores.

Brăiloiu, Constantin (*b* Bucharest, 26 Aug 1893; *d* Geneva, 20 Dec 1958). Romanian ethnomusicologist. He studied in Lausanne, Paris and Romania. At first a composer and music critic, he soon turned to musical folklore and did fieldwork in several Romanian provinces (1929–32). He held posts in Romania, Switzerland (where he founded the international folk music archives in Geneva, 1944) and Paris. His conviction that music in the oral tradition was being governed by a system, which the ethnomusicologist should define through analysis, led to important methodological, critical and theoretical writings.

Brain, Dennis (*b* London, 17 May 1921; *d* Hatfield, 1 Sept 1957). English horn player. Son of the hornist Aubrey Brain (1893–1955), he studied at the RAM with his father and made his début in 1938. He appeared with leading string quartets and was principal with the RPO (from 1946) and later the Philharmonia. His subtle phrasing and delicacy of execution were admired in Mozart and Strauss and in the works written for him by Britten (including the Serenade), Hindemith and others.

Brambilla. Italian family of singers. The most celebrated members were Marietta (1807–75), a contralto who specialized in travesty roles, notably Maffio Orsini in *Lucrezia Borgia* and others in Donizetti's works, and her niece, Teresa Brambilla-Ponchielli (1845–1921), a dramatic soprano who was a famous interpreter of the title role in her husband's opera *La gioconda*.

Brand, Max (*b* Lwów, 26 April 1896; *d* Langenzers-dorf, 5 April 1980). Austrian composer. He studied with Schreker in Vienna and experimented with 12-note technique in the 1920s. His opera *Maschinist Hopkins* (1929) was widely performed; a surrealist fantasy, it prefigures dramatic themes in Berg's *Lulu* and includes machines among the singing characters. Brand fled to the USA in 1940 and from the 1960s experimented with electronic media.

Brandenburg Concertos. Six concerti grossi for different instrumental combinations (1711–20) by J.S. Bach, dedicated to Margrave Christian Ludwig of Brandenburg.

Brando. The 16th-century Italian equivalent of the BRANLE; also a particular social and theatrical dance tenuously related to it.

Brandt, Jobst vom (*b* Waldershof, 28 Oct 1517; *d* Brand, 22 Jan 1570). German composer. Educated in Heidelberg, he was an administrator for the Palatinate. More than 50 secular polyphonic songs by him, in a motet style, were printed in contemporary collections (1549–58), and a book of psalms and sacred songs for up to nine voices and instruments appeared posthumously.

Brandts Buys. Dutch family of musicians. The most celebrated members were Jan Willem Frans (1868–1939), a composer living in Vienna who wrote a prize-winning piano concerto, lieder, eight operas, orchestral works and impressionistic chamber music, and his nephew Hans (1905–59), a musicologist and harpsichordist who published studies of Bach's Passions and *Das wohltemperirte Clavier*.

Branle. A French group dance popular over many centuries. Arbeau's *Orchésographie* (1588) mentions four types in various metres and tempos; others evolved, among them the 'branle de Poitou à mener', an ancestor of the minuet.

Brant, Henry (Dreyfuss) (*b* Montreal, 15 Sept 1913). American composer of Canadian birth. He studied at the McGill Conservatorium (1926–9) and in New York (1929–34), where he settled as a composer and arranger, later teaching at Columbia University (1945–52), the Juilliard School (1947–54) and Bennington College (1957–). His works include pieces for unusual combinations (*Angels and Devils* for solo flute and ten flutes, 1931), for spatially separated groups (*Antiphony 1* for five groups, 1953, and many later scores), in coexistent musical styles and with dramatic incidents (*The Grand Universal Circus*, 1956).

Brassart, Johannes (*b* ?Louwaige; *fl* 1420–45). Composer. He was in Liège, 1422–31, then at the papal chapel in Rome and at the Council of Basle in 1433. From 1434 until at least 1443 he was 'rector capelle' to the Emperors Sigismund, Albert II and Frederick III. Ten mass movements (including a Gloria–Credo pair), eight Introit settings and 14 other sacred works (including four isorhythmic motets) by him are known.

Brass band. A type of wind band, consisting solely of brass instruments and sometimes percussion, which originated in the 1820s. A typical band might consist of one soprano cornet in Eb; nine Bb cornets; one Bb flugelhorn; three Eb tenor horns; two Bb baritones; two Eb euphoniums; three tombones;

and four basses, two each in E♭ and BB♭. The growth of brass bands was closely linked to the rise of industry, and the success of the movement has been bound up with contests.

Brass instruments. Term used for lip-vibrated wind instruments (aerophones). Their air column is set in motion by the lips of the player, pressed against a cup-shaped (or funnel-shaped) mouthpiece. The category includes instruments made not only of brass but also of other metals and other substances, including wood or horn. Further, some instruments made of brass (such as the saxophone) do not rank as brass instruments as their air columns are set in vibration by reeds.

Brass instruments can sound only the natural HARMONICS corresponding to the active length of their tube (the harmonic sounded depends on the pressure of the player's lips against the mouthpiece); to obtain a further selection of notes the player must alter the length of the tube, which he or she does on modern instruments with valves (on certain earlier instruments, such as the cornett and the serpent, the length of tube could be altered by opening finger-holes).

The main brass instruments of the modern orchestra are the TRUMPET, occasionally the CORNET, the HORN, the TROMBONE and the TUBA; see illustration. *See also* BRASS BAND.

Brätel, Ulrich (*b c*1495; *d* Stuttgart, 1544–5). German composer. He probably studied with the humanist Vadian and was a composer and performer to the Viennese, Hungarian and Polish courts, as well as the court at Heidelberg. From 1534 he was in Duke Ulrich of Württemberg's service at Stuttgart, where his chief duty was to build up a new repertory for the Reformed church. He also wrote instrumental and secular vocal music, which, like his sacred works, reveal an old-fashioned approach.

Braun. German family of musicians. They were important in the history of wind playing. Anton (1729–98), an oboist, violinist and composer in Kassel, had several musical children, notably Johann (1753–1811), a violinist who served Queen Friedrike of Prussia and wrote concertos and chamber works; Johann Friedrich (1758–1824), an oboist at Ludwigslust; and Moriz (1765–1828), who toured as a bassoon virtuoso and served at Würzburg. Two of Johann Friedrich's sons became oboists. Carl Anton (1788–1835) served at Copenhagen and Stockholm; he composed symphonies, oboe pieces etc. Wilhelm Theodor Johannes (1796–1867) succeeded his father at Ludwigslust and wrote oboe pieces, keyboard works and string quartets.

Braunfels, Walter (*b* Frankfurt, 19 Dec 1882; *d* Cologne, 19 March 1954). German composer. He studied with Leschetizky in Vienna and with Thuille and Mottl in Munich. In 1925 he became founder-director of the Cologne Musikhochschule, to which he returned after his retirement during the Hitler years. As a composer he remained close to the Classical–Romantic tradition, owing much to Thuille's 'new German direction'. His operas, of which *Die Vögel* (1919) has been revived, are Wag-

nerian in form but lighter and clearer; he also wrote large-scale choral works (he was a Roman Catholic convert), songs and orchestral, chamber and piano pieces.

Bravura (It.). 'Skill', 'bravery': the element of brilliant display in vocal or instrumental music that tests the performer's skill.

Break. In jazz, a type of brief cadenza, performed by a solo singer or instrumentalist without rhythmic accompaniment, interpolated between ensemble passages; its effect is one of surprise and suspended time.

Breaking. English term used from the 16th century to the 18th to describe the ornamentation (usually improvised) of a melodic line by substituting groups of short notes for longer ones.

Bream, Julian (Alexander) (*b* Battersea, 15 July 1933). English guitarist and lutenist. After study at the RCM he made his London début in 1950, touring Europe from 1954 and the USA from 1958. He studied the Renaissance lute and in 1959 formed the Julian Bream Consort; with Peter Pears he performed Elizabethan lute-songs. His brilliant style and intense expression encouraged Britten, Walton and Henze to compose for him.

Brebis, Johannes (*fl* late 15th century). French singer and composer. A member of the court chapel of Ercole I d'Este in Ferrara (1471–8), he composed a motet in honour of the duke and several double-choir pieces in a simpler, homophonic style (among the earliest of their kind in north Italy).

Brecht, Bertolt (Eugene Friedrich) (*b* Augsburg, 10 Feb 1898; *d* Berlin, 14 Aug 1956). German writer. He collaborated with Weill (1927–30), Eisler and Dessau on works for the theatre; others to set his plays and poems include Sessions and Henze.

Bree, Johannes Bernardus van (*b* Amsterdam, 29 Jan 1801; *d* there, 14 Feb 1857). Dutch composer and conductor. After a brief career as a violinist, he directed choirs and orchestras and founded a string quartet, in all of which he stressed the German repertory. His masses reflect this preference, but most of his music, including two operas and orchestral works, remained close to the French style then prevailing in Amsterdam.

Breeches part [trouser role]. An operatic role (often a minor one) in which a female singer plays a male character, such as Cherubino (*Le nozze di Figaro*) or Octavian (*Der Rosenkavalier*).

Bregenz Festival (Austria). Annual (summer) festival, established in 1946. Events include concerts, ballet and open-air opera (particularly operetta) at Lake Constance.

Brehme, Hans (Ludwig Wilhelm) (*b* Potsdam, 10 March 1904; *d* Stuttgart, 10 Nov 1957). German composer and pianist. He studied at the Berlin Musikhochschule (1922–6) and with Kempff, then taught at the Stuttgart Musikhochschule from 1928. His works are traditional and in standard forms (three operas, two symphonies, two piano concertos etc), though some late pieces use 12-note series.

Breitengraser, Wilhelm (*b* Nuremberg, *c*1495; *d* there, bur. 23 Dec 1542). German composer. He studied at Leipzig University and became head-

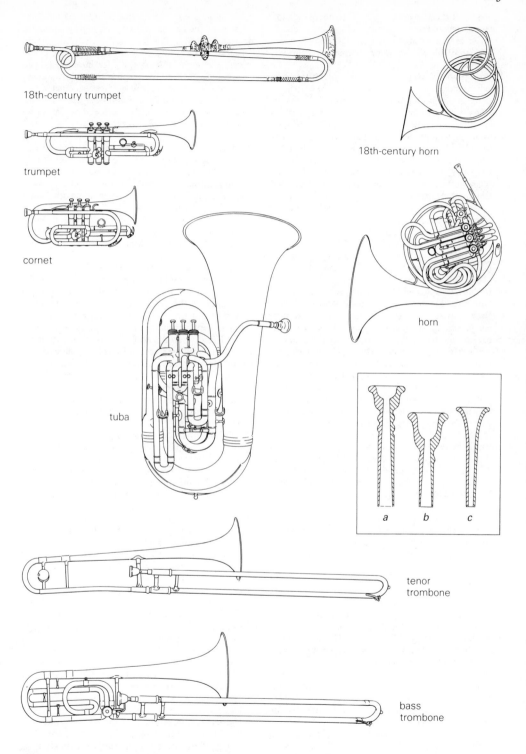

18th-century trumpet

trumpet

cornet

tuba

18th-century horn

horn

a   *b*   *c*

tenor
trombone

bass
trombone

Modern brass instruments and their 18th-century precursors; inset shows mouthpieces of (a) trumpet, (b) trombone, (c) horn

master of the Lateinschule in Nuremberg (*c*1520). He was one of the most popular of the more conservative German composers of his generation; more than 50 of his wide-ranging compositions survive, many in collections.

Breitkopf & Härtel. German firm of music publishers and printers. It was established in Leipzig in 1719 by the printer Bernhard Christoph Breitkopf (1695–1777). From 1745, under his son Johann Gottlob Immanuel (1719–94), it achieved renown for its efficient production and improved music typography (divisible and movable types introduced in 1754–5), as well as for its outstanding list of composers from Telemann to Haydn and C.P.E. Bach; its thematic catalogues remain invaluable. Gottfried Christoph Härtel (1763–1827) bought the firm in 1796; he used lithography, issued early collected editions, negotiated with Mozart's widow, courted Beethoven's favour (publishing the first editions of 25 of his works) and founded the *Allgemeine musikalische Zeitung* (1798–1848). Under his greatnephews Raymund (1810–88) and Hermann (1803–75) the firm issued works by Schubert, Brahms, Chopin and Berlioz, operas by Meyerbeer, Donizetti, Bellini and Lortzing and the complete Bach edition. Later it promoted modern German composers. Since 1945 the firm has been divided, one section in Leipzig, the other in Wiesbaden.

Brema, Marie [Fehrmann, Minny] (*b* Liverpool, 28 Feb 1856; *d* Manchester, 22 March 1925). English mezzo-soprano of German-American parentage. The first British-born singer to appear at Bayreuth (Ortrud in *Lohengrin*, 1894), she was associated particularly with the Wagner repertory; she created the part of the Angel in Elgar's *The Dream of Gerontius* (1900).

Brendel, Alfred (*b* Wiesenberg, 5 Jan 1931). Austrian pianist. He studied in Zagreb and Sofia and at the Vienna Academy; Edwin Fischer was an early influence. His début was in Graz (1948) and in 1962 he gave all the Beethoven sonatas in London; his American début was in 1963. He is most admired for his thoughtful, sensitive interpretations of Mozart, Beethoven, Schubert, complete cycles of whose sonatas he has given widely, and Liszt.

Brendel, Karl Franz (*b* Stolberg, 26 Nov 1811; *d* Leipzig, 25 Nov 1868). German music historian and critic. He succeeded Schumann as editor of the *Neue Zeitschrift für Musik* (1845–68) and elsewhere published influential articles advocating the New German School; he wrote an important history (1852) and taught at the Leipzig Conservatory.

Brendel, Wolfgang (*b* Munich, 20 Oct 1947). German baritone. He studied in Wiesbaden and became a member of the Munich Opera in 1971, making his début there as Papageno. He has sung at the Vienna Staatsoper, La Scala and the Met; he made his Covent Garden début in *Il trovatore* (1985). He possesses a smooth, firm and darkish baritone which serves well in Verdi and Strauss.

Brendler, (Frans Fredric) Eduard (*b* Dresden, 4 Nov 1800; *d* Stockholm, 16 Aug 1831). Swedish composer and flautist. He was a leading Swedish Romantic. His most important works, some showing Spohr's influence, include Variations for three bassoons and orchestra (1828) and two melodramas.

Brenet, Michel [Bobillier, (Antoinette Christine) Marie] (*b* Luneville, 12 April 1858; *d* Paris, 4 Nov 1918). French musicologist. Her interests ranged from Ockeghem to Berlioz, but she mainly studied the history of French music. Her principal works were *Les musiciens de la Sainte-Chapelle du Palais* (1900), *Les concerts en France sous l'ancien régime* (1900) and *La librairie musicale en France de 1653 à 1780* (1907).

Brentano, Clemens (Wenzeslaus Maria) (*b* Ehrenbreitstein, 9 Sept 1778; *d* Aschaffenburg, 28 July 1842). German poet. He was a leading lyric poet of the younger Romantic generation whose primary importance to music lies in his co-editorship, with Achim von Arnim, of the folk poetry collection *Des Knaben Wunderhorn* (i, 1805). Schubert, Schumann, Mendelssohn, Brahms, Wolf and Strauss wrote songs to Wunderhorn texts and Mahler based orchestral settings on them.

Bresgen, Cesar (*b* Florence, 16 Oct 1913). Austrian composer of German origin. He studied at the Munich Academy (1930–36) and in 1939 began teaching at the Salzburg Mozarteum. He knew Webern, for whom he wrote a Requiem (1945–72), but the influences on him have been Stravinsky, Hindemith, Bartók and Orff. His large output includes many stage pieces and music for young people.

Bretel, Jehan (*b c*1210; *d* Arras, 1272). French trouvère. He was associated with the abbey of St Vaast. Seven of his *chansons courtoises* survive, and he was a participant in no fewer than 89 jeux-partis. At the height of his fame he was designated 'Prince' of the Arras Puy.

Bretón, Tomás (*b* Salamanca, 29 Dec 1850; *d* Madrid, 2 Dec 1923). Spanish composer. He studied in Madrid and abroad, and worked in Madrid as a teacher and conductor. As a composer he strove for a sophisticated sort of Spanish lyrical drama; *La Dolores* (1895) was his most successful opera, the farce *La verbena de la paloma* his best-known work.

Bréval, Jean-Baptiste Sébastien (*b* Paris, 6 Nov 1753; *d* Colligis, 18 March 1823). French composer and cellist. He studied with J.-B. Cupis, became a cello teacher and played at the Concert Spirituel (from 1778) and with the Paris Opéra orchestra (*c*1801–14). His compositions are mostly attractive instrumental music reflecting contemporary Parisian taste; the most ambitious (string quartets, cello concertos and symphonies concertantes) include lyrical works of high calibre. He wrote important pedagogical material for the cello, principally the *Traité du violoncelle* op.42 (1804).

Breve. A note, in American usage called a double whole-note, that is half the value of a long and double that of a semibreve. It was the shorter of the two notes of early mensural music, hence its name, from the Latin *brevis* ('short'). The breve is first found in early 13th-century music; up to about 1600 its value could be a half or a third of a long. *See* NOTE VALUES.

Bréville, Pierre (Eugène Onfroy) de (*b* Bar-le-Duc, 21 Feb 1861; *d* Paris, 24 Sept 1949). French composer. He studied with Franck and became a member of his circle. He wrote an opera (*Eros vainqueur*, 1905), choral music and orchestral scores, but concentrated on songs, at first in a Wagnerian style, later influenced by Fauré and Debussy.

Brewer, Sir (Alfred) Herbert (*b* Gloucester, 21 June 1865; *d* there, 1 March 1928). English organist, conductor and composer. He held organ posts in Gloucester, Oxford, Bristol and Coventry, and from 1897 was an enterprising director of the Gloucester Three Choirs festivals. His many works range from cantatas to popular songs.

Brewster-Jones, (Josiah) Hooper (*b* Bute, 28 June 1887; *d* Adelaide, 1949). Australian pianist and composer. He studied in Adelaide and at the RCM with Bridge and Stanford (1902–8). His large output (four piano concertos, three symphonies, five opera-ballets, numerous instrumental works, 180 songs and over 200 keyboard pieces) reflects his appreciation of Debussy and Ravel and his enthusiasm for Australian themes.

Brian, Havergal (*b* Dresden, Staffs., 29 Jan 1876; *d* Shoreham, 28 Nov 1972). English composer. Largely self-taught, he won success at the beginning of the century as a composer of large-scale choral and orchestral pieces, but then was forgotten until a revival of interest began in the 1950s. Meanwhile, without prospect of performance, he had continued to write big works, including an opera *The Tigers* (1930), the 'Gothic' Symphony with soloists, choirs and brass bands (1927) and the four-hour concert opera *Prometheus Unbound* (1944). In his last years he became most productive, writing 27 symphonies after the age of 70, his heavy Romantic style growing more compact and elliptical.

Briccialdi, Giulio (*b* Terni, 2 March 1818; *d* Florence, 17 Dec 1881). Italian flautist and composer. He made technical improvements to the flute, was a professor at the Florence Conservatory from 1870 and composed much flute music, including pedagogical works and concertos.

Bridge. In string instruments, a wedge or bar, usually of hard wood, inserted between the belly and strings. Generally at right angles to the strings, the bridge raises the strings from the belly or fingerboard and transmits their vibrations to the soundboard.

Bridge, Frank (*b* Brighton, 26 Feb 1879; *d* Eastbourne, 10 Jan 1941). English composer. He studied with Stanford at the RCM (1899–1903) and made a reputation as a chamber musician (a violist) and conductor. His early works, including the orchestral suite *The Sea* (1911), the symphonic poem *Summer* (1914) and much chamber music, are close to Bax and Delius, but after World War I he developed rapidly. His Third (1926) and Fourth (1937) Quartets are highly chromatic, reflecting his admiration for Berg, though his music remained distinctively English. Also remarkable is the contrapuntal vigour and energy of his later orchestral works, which include the rhapsody *Enter Spring* (1927), *Oration* with solo cello (1930) and *Phantasm* with solo piano (1931). None of his more adventurous music was much regarded until the 1970s, his fame resting largely on his having been Britten's teacher.

Bridge, Sir (John) Frederick (*b* Oldbury, 5 Dec 1844; *d* London, 18 March 1924). English organist and composer. He studied with John Goss, became organist of Manchester Cathedral (1869) and at Westminster Abbey (1882), where he did much to facilitate the rebuilding of the organ. He played for state occasions, taught at the RCM and composed choral works.

Bridge [Bridges], Richard (*b* ?London; *d* London, 7 June 1758). English builder of organs, harpsichords and spinets. Probably apprenticed to Renatus Harris, he won Handel's approval and built important organs in the London area, 1730–57; among them were those for Christ Church, Spitalfields (1730; case and pipework survive), St Bartholomew-the-Great (1731), St Luke's, Old Street (1733; now at St Giles, Cripplegate), Marylebone Gardens (1740) and St Leonard's, Shoreditch (1757). He built new instruments in Rhode Island and Boston, and rebuilt those at Exeter and Worcester cathedrals.

Bridge passage. Term commonly applied to the section in a sonata exposition which modulates from the tonic to the dominant or relative major; it is also used more generally for any linking section.

Bridgetower [Bridgtower], George (Augustus) Polgreen (*b* Biala, Poland, 11 Oct 1778 ; *d* London, 28 Feb 1860). English violinist. He studied with Barthélemon and Attwood, played in the 1791 Salomon concerts and attracted the Prince of Wales's patronage. Through Prince Lichnowsky in Vienna he met Beethoven, who composed for him the Sonata in A op.30 no.1 (1803), subsequently dedicated to Rodolphe Kreutzer.

Briegel, Wolfgang Carl (*b* Königsberg, May 1626; *d* Darmstadt, 19 Nov 1712). German composer. From 1650 he was Kantor (eventually Kapellmeister) at the Gotha court and Kapellmeister at Hessen-Darmstadt from 1671. As well as composing many stage works (now lost) for Darmstadt, he revitalized the church music tradition there by writing a series of cantatas for the church year. He also wrote instrumental music (notably the lively *Tafelkonfekt*, 1672), solo sacred songs and dramatic dialogues.

Brier, Percy (*b* North Pine River, 7 June 1885; *d* Scarborough, Queensland, 9 May 1970). Australian musician. He studied at Trinity College, London (1902–6), and took a leading part in the development of music in Queensland as conductor, administrator, pianist and composer.

Brigg Fair. Orchestral work by Delius, subtitled 'An English Rhapsody' (1907).

Brighton Festival (UK). Annual (summer) festival, established in 1967. Events include orchestral concerts, chamber music, opera, exhibitions and tours. Drottningholm Opera is among its internationally known visiting performers.

Brillante (It.). Brilliant, sparkling, glittering.

Brindisi (It.). A song in which a company is called upon to drink; examples occur in Verdi's *Macbeth*, *La traviata* and *Otello*.

Brio (It.). 'Vivacity', 'energy', 'fire': a playing style of brilliance and dash.

Brioschi, Antonio (*fl c*1730–50). Italian composer. He probably worked near Milan. His large output, mostly for strings, includes trio sonatas (some of them published with G.B. Sammartini's in the 1740s) and some of the earliest Classical symphonies known (c1730 onwards), with clearly marked sonata forms.

Bristol Musical Festival (UK). Established in 1873, with Charles Hallé as conductor, it was held triennially until 1888, then less regularly until 1912. Lesser-known choral works were performed; Wagner's *Ring* was given in 1912.

Bristow, George Frederick (*b* Brooklyn, 19 Dec 1825; *d* New York, 13 Dec 1898). American composer. Once known as violinist, conductor, teacher and composer, he is now remembered for his advocacy of the native American musician. With Heinrich and Fry he tried to establish a distinctive style in American art music, choosing such subjects as *Rip Van Winkle* (opera, 1855) and *Columbus* (overture, 1861); but his music remained essentially European (Mendelssohnian). Of his over 120 compositions (including, unusually, chamber works), the five symphonies are noteworthy.

British Broadcasting Corporation. The BBC (up to 1927, British Broadcasting Company) was established in 1922; the first broadcast was on 15 November, the first music broadcast on 25 November, the first opera relay (*Die Zauberflöte*) from Covent Garden in January 1923. The BBC was soon active in promoting concerts for broadcasting, both of established repertory and of new music. In 1927 it took over the Proms and in 1930 the BBC Symphony Orchestra was founded, with 114 players under Adrian Boult; it performs regularly in London as well as on the radio, and often tours abroad. The BBC Philharmonic Orchestra BBC Philharmonic Orchestra (originally BBC Northern Orchestra; BBC Northern Symphony Orchestra, 1967–83) was founded in 1934, the BBC Scottish and Welsh Orchestras in 1935 (BBC Scottish and Welsh Symphony Orchestras from 1967 and 1974 respectively). These have worked from Manchester, Glasgow and Cardiff; other BBC groups have also worked from Birmingham, Belfast and Bristol. The BBC established several other groups specializing in different kinds of music, including the BBC Singers (an unaccompanied professional choir, formerly the BBC Wireless Chorus, then the BBC Chorus) and the BBC Symphony Chorus (an amateur group, formerly the BBC Choral Society, earlier the National Chorus).

The BBC has taken its responsibilities in cultural education seriously for many years, with regular programmes such as 'Music Magazine', contemporary and historical music programmes and talks, and especially with the foundation (1946) of the Third Programme, which became the Music Programme in 1964 and Radio 3 in 1970. It has had many distinguished music administrators, notably William Glock (Controller of Music, 1959–72) and has employed leading conductors for the BBC SO (including Sargent, Dorati, Colin Davis, Boulez, Kempe and Rozhdestvensky). BBC television transmissions began in 1936; many music programmes are transmitted, including biographical studies of composers and programmes about new music or music history, as well as performances, notably of opera (including the première of Britten's specially commissioned *Owen Wingrave*, 1971).

British National Opera Company. Established in 1922 from members of the Beecham Opera Company (1915–20), it performed in London and on tour until 1928, then as Covent Garden English Opera Company until 1931; its repertory included Debussy, Holst, Smyth, Vaughan Williams and Wagner. Its *Hänsel und Gretel* (1923) was the first complete opera to be broadcast in Europe.

Britten, (Edward) Benjamin (*b* Lowestoft, 22 Nov 1913; *d* Aldeburgh, 4 Dec 1976). English composer. He studied with Frank Bridge as a boy and in 1930 entered the RCM. In 1934 he heard *Wozzeck* and planned to study with Berg, but opposition at home stopped him. The next year he began working for the GPO Film Unit, where one of his collaborators was Auden: together they worked on concert works as well, Auden's social criticism being matched by a sharply satirical and virtuoso musical style (orchestral song cycle *Our Hunting Fathers*, 1936). Stravinsky and Mahler were important influences, but Britten's effortless technique gave his early music a high personal definition, notably shown in orchestral works (Bridge Variations for strings, 1937; Piano Concerto, 1938; Violin Concerto, 1939) and songs (*Les illuminations*, setting Rimbaud for high voice and strings, 1939).

In 1939 he left England for the USA, with his lifelong companion Peter Pears; there he wrote his first opera, to Auden's libretto (*Paul Bunyan*, 1941). In 1942 he returned and, partly stimulated by Purcell, began to concentrate on settings of English verse (anthem *Rejoice in the Lamb* and Serenade for tenor, horn and strings, both 1943). His String Quartet no.2 (1945), with its huge concluding chaconne, also came out of his Purcellian interests, but the major work of this period was *Peter Grimes* (1945), which signalled a new beginning in English opera. Its central character, the first of many roles written for Pears, struck a new operatic tone: a social outcast, he is fiercely proud and independent, but also deeply insecure, providing opportunities for a lyrical flow that would be free but is not. Britten's gift for characterization was also displayed in the wide range of sharply defined subsidiary roles and in the orchestra's sea music.

However, his next operas were all written for comparatively small resources (*The Rape of Lucretia*, 1946; *Albert Herring*, 1947; a version of *The Beggar's Opera*, 1948; *The Little Sweep*, 1949), for the company that became established as the English Opera Group. At the same time he began writing music for the Aldeburgh Festival, which he and Pears founded in 1948 in the Suffolk town where they had settled (cantata *St Nicolas*, 1948; *Lachrymae* for viola and piano, 1949). And in this prolific period he also composed large concert works (*The Young Person's Guide to the Orchestra*, 1946; *Spring Symphony* with soloists and choir, 1949) and songs.

The pattern of his output was thus set, though not the style, for the operas show an outward urge to ever new subjects: village comedy in *Albert Herring*, psychological conflict in *Billy Budd* (1951), historical reconstruction in *Gloriana* (1953), a tale of ghostly possession in *The Turn of the Screw* (1954), nocturnal magic in *A Midsummer Night's Dream* (1960), a struggle between family history and individual responsibility in *Owen Wingrave* (1971) and, most centrally, obsession with a doomed ideal in *Death in Venice* (1973), the last three works being intermediate in scale between the chamber format of *Herring* and *The Screw*, and the symphonic fullness of *Budd* and *Gloriana*, both written for Covent Garden. But nearly all touch in some way on the themes of the individual and society and the violation of innocence. Simultaneous with a widening range of subject matter was a widening musical style, which came to include 12-note elements (*Turn of the Screw*) and a heterophony that owed as much to oriental music directly as it did to Mahler (cycle of 'church parables', or ritualized small-scale operas: *Curlew River*, *The Burning Fiery Furnace*, *The Prodigal Son*, 1964-8).

Many of these dramatic works were written for the Aldeburgh Festival, as were many of the instrumental and vocal works Britten produced for favoured performers. For Rostropovich he wrote the Cello Symphony (1963) as well as a sonata and three solo suites; for Pears there was the Hardy cycle *Winter Words* (1953) among many other songs, and also a central part in the *War Requiem* (1961). His closing masterpiece, however, was a return to the abstract in the String Quartet no.3 (1975).

Operas Paul Bunyan (1941); Peter Grimes (1945); The Rape of Lucretia (1946); Albert Herring (1947); The Little Sweep (1949); Billy Budd (1951); Gloriana (1953); The Turn of the Screw (1954); Noye's Fludde (1958); A Midsummer Night's Dream (1960); Owen Wingrave (1971); Death in Venice (1973)
Church parables Curlew River (1964); The Burning Fiery Furnace (1966); The Prodigal Son (1968)
Ballet The Prince of the Pagodas (1957)
Orchestral music Sinfonietta (1932); Simple Symphony (1934); Variations on a Theme of Frank Bridge, strs (1937); Pf Conc. (1938); Vn Conc. (1939); Sinfonia da requiem (1940); The Young Person's Guide to the Orchestra (1946); Cello Sym. (1963)
Choral music A Boy was Born (1933); Ballad of Heroes (1939); Hymn to St Cecilia (1942); A Ceremony of Carols (1942); Rejoice in the Lamb (1943); Festival Te Deum (1944); St Nicolas (1948); Spring Sym. (1949); Cantata academica (1959); Missa brevis (1959); War Requiem (1961); Cantata misericordium (1963); Voices for Today (1965); The Golden Vanity (1966); Children's Crusade (1968); many others
Chamber music 3 str qts (1941, 1945, 1975); Lachrymae, va, pf (1949); Vc Sonata (1961); 3 vc suites (1964, 1967, 1972); many others
Solo vocal music Our Hunting Fathers (1936); Les illuminations (1939); Seven Sonnets of Michelangelo (1940); Serenade, T, hn, strs (1943); The Holy Sonnets of John Donne (1945); 5 canticles (1947, 1952, 1954, 1971, 1974); Winter Words (1953); Songs from the Chinese (1957); Nocturne (1958); Sechs Hölderlin-Fragmente (1958); Songs and Proverbs of William Blake (1965); The Poet's Echo (1965); Phaedra (1975); many others
Incidental music

Britton, Thomas (*b* Rushden, 14 Jan 1644; *d* London, 27 Sept 1714). English patron of music and amateur musician. From 1677 a coal dealer in Cler-

kenwell, he established weekly musical meetings in a room over his premises in 1678. The performers included such professionals as John Banister, Hart, Handel and Pepusch; the concerts were attended by leaders of fashionable London. Britton assembled a fine collection of music and instruments.

Brixi, František Xaver (*b* Prague, bap. 2 Jan 1732; *d* there, 14 Oct 1771). Czech composer. He held organist's posts in Prague and from 1759 was Kapellmeister of St Vitus's Cathedral. A popular and influential composer, he wrote *c*400 sacred works, several oratorios, cantatas etc, and orchestral and keyboard music in a simple, vivacious style. His father, Šimon (1693–1735), also a Prague organist, wrote mainly church music in the style of Fux and Caldara. Their relatives Jan Josef (?1712–1762) and his son Václav Norbert (1738–1803) were both organists, as was Viktorin (1716–1803), from another branch of the family; all three composed church music.

Brno International Festival (Czechoslovakia). Annual (autumn) festival and musicological symposium, established in 1966. Janáček's operas and early east European music are given.

Broadwood. English firm of piano makers. As son-in-law and partner of BURKAT SHUDI, John Broadwood (1732–1812) continued the business after Shudi's death (1773), becoming sole manager in 1782. He quickly made improvements to Zumpe's square pianos, then turned to designing grands (earliest surviving example, 1786). By the 1790s, with more evenness throughout the compass and increased dynamic flexibility, the Broadwood piano was widely used by leading musicians; by the 1820s annual output exceeded 100 squares and 400 grands (reaching 2500 instruments in the 1850s). Iron bracing was introduced on the grand to improve tuning stability and, later, to increase tension and power. After *c*1870 the firm declined.

Brockes, Barthold Heinrich (*b* Hamburg, 22 Sept 1680; *d* there, 16 Jan 1747). German poet. A leading literary figure of the Enlightenment, he wrote a Passion oratorio libretto, *Der für die Sünden der Welt gemarterte und sterbende Jesus* (1712), that was set by numerous composers including Telemann (1716) and Handel (1716–17); Bach used parts of it in his *St John Passion* (1724).

Brockes Passion. Title given to Handel's setting, probably written for Hamburg in 1716, of Brockes's Passion text.

Brockway, Howard (*b* Brooklyn, 22 Nov 1870; *d* New York, 20 Feb 1951). American composer and pianist. He studied in Berlin (1890–95), where his music made a great impression. On returning to the USA he taught at the Peabody Institute and in New York, notably at the National Institute of Musical Art (1910–40). His music, composed mostly before 1911 and covering orchestral, chamber, choral and piano works, is noted for its melodic and harmonic warmth (e.g. the Violin Sonata, 1894, and the Cello Suite, 1908). He also made popular arrangements of Kentucky folksongs.

Brod, Max (*b* Prague, 27 May 1884; *d* Tel-Aviv, 20 Dec 1968). Israeli writer and composer of Czech birth. He encouraged international interest in Janáček's operas, which he translated into German. He also wrote songs, piano music and incidental scores for his own plays.

Broderip. English family of musicians. William (1683–1727), his sons John (1719–70) and Edmund (1727–79), and John's son Robert (c1758–1808) were all organists in the West Country; Robert composed songs and keyboard music. Francis Fane Broderip (c1750–before 1807), probably also John's son, was a London music publisher associated with the firms of Longman & Luckey, Longman & Broderip and Broderip & Wilkinson.

Broken chord. The effect produced by performing the notes of a chord successively rather than simultaneously; thus a type of melodic figuration related to arpeggio.

Broken consort. A term for a consort of instruments of different kinds; *see* CONSORT.

Broman, Sten (*b* Uppsala, 25 March 1902; *d* Lund, 29 Oct 1983). Swedish composer. He studied with Finke and Zemlinsky at the German Conservatory in Prague, and worked in Sweden as an administrator, critic, chamber musician and conductor. His works from before 1962 are severely contrapuntal and Hindemithian in harmony; the later scores (notably a cycle of nine symphonies) include serial and electronic elements.

Bronner, Georg (*b* Hamburg, c1667; *d* there, early 1720). German composer. He was an organist in Hamburg (1689–1719); as co-director of the Hamburg opera he composed (with Mattheson and Schiefferdercker) a series of operas (1693–1702) and two oratorios (1705–1710), all now lost. His other sacred music includes a book of chorales (1715) in which each melody is set three times (with figured and unfigured basses and as vocal trios) and six sacred concertos (1696). Bronner used richly ornamented lines and colourful harmony allied to expressive word-setting.

Bronsart von Schellendorf, Hans (August Alexander) (*b* Berlin, 11 Feb 1830; *d* Munich, 3 Nov 1913). German composer, pianist and conductor. He studied in Berlin and with Liszt (1853–7), forming a close association with the New German School and becoming Intendant at Hanover and at Weimar. He was close to Bülow, who played his Piano Trio in G minor op.1 (1856) and the Second Concerto in Bb (op.18).

Brook, Barry S(helley) (*b* New York, 1 Nov 1918). American musicologist. He studied in New York but took the doctorate at the University of Paris in 1959 with a study of the 18th-century French symphony. In 1945 he began teaching in New York. He has done much to further international collaboration on music-bibliographical projects.

Brooklyn Conservatory of Music. Name given in 1971 to the music department of Brooklyn College, City University of New York; it is also the home of the Institute for Studies in American Music (founded 1971).

Broschi, Carlo. *See* FARINELLI.

Broschi, Riccardo (*b* Naples, c1698; *d* Madrid, 1756). Italian composer, brother of Farinelli. He was active by 1725 in Naples, where his only comic opera was

given. In 1728–35 he wrote at least six heroic operas, in some of which his brother sang. He served briefly at the Stuttgart court (1736–7), then returned to Naples before joining his brother in Madrid.

Brossard, Sébastien de (*b* Dompierre, bap. 12 Sept 1655; *d* Meaux, 10 Aug 1730). French lexicographer and composer. He was *maître de chapelle* at Strasbourg Cathedral, 1687–98, then held a similar post in Meaux, where he composed sacred music, chiefly motets. He was among the first in France to write violin sonatas, and his French cantatas are among the few based on biblical subjects. Of his writings on music the most important is his *Dictionnaire* (1701, rev. 1703), the first of its kind in France. His extensive library is now in the Bibliothèque Nationale, Paris.

Bros y Bertomeu, Juan (Joaquín Pedro Domingo) (*b* Tortosa, bap. 12 May 1776; *d* Oviedo, 12 March 1852). Spanish composer. He studied in Barcelona. *Maestro de capilla* at León and Oviedo cathedrals, he was one of the most admired Spanish church musicians of his day; his music was noted for its expressive fugal writing.

Brott, Alexander (*b* Montreal, 14 March 1915). Canadian composer, conductor and violinist. He studied at the McGill Conservatorium (1928–35) and the Juilliard School. In 1939 he founded the McGill CO, giving premières of many Canadian works. He was leader and assistant conductor of the Montreal SO (1945–58) and from 1948 toured as guest conductor with the Canadian Broadcasting Corporation. His many compositions derive largely from neo-classical procedures. His son Boris (*b* 1944) has conducted Canadian and regional British orchestras from the early 1960s.

Brouček, The Excursions of Mr. *See* EXCURSIONS OF MR BROUČEK, THE.

Brouwenstijn, Gré (*b* Den Helder, 26 Aug 1915). Dutch soprano. She studied in Amsterdam and joined Netherlands Opera in 1946, enjoying success as Tosca and Santuzza. She made her Covent Garden début as Aida (1951) and was Elisabeth in the 1958 *Don Carlos* there. Her beautiful voice, intelligence and sincerity served particularly well as Leonore in *Fidelio*.

Brouwer, Leo (*b* Havana, 1 March 1939). Cuban composer and guitarist. He studied in New York (1960–61) but was most influenced by the new music he heard at the 1961 Warsaw Autumn Festival. He has been occupied with being an artist in a revolutionary society; his early works are nationalist, the later ones adopting avant-garde techniques.

Brown, Christopher (Roland) (*b* Tunbridge Wells, 17 June 1943). English composer. He studied at the RAM with Berkeley and with Blacher in Berlin. His music is tonal and often religious in inspiration; it includes the cantata *David* (1970), an organ concerto (1979) and *The Vision of Saul* for soloists, chorus and orchestra (1983).

Brown, Earle (*b* Lunenburg, MA, 26 Dec 1926). American composer. He studied at the Schillinger School (1946–50) and in 1952 became associated with Cage. That year he began to use graphic notation, his *December 1952* being a design of slim black rectangles on a single page. Equally influential was his espousal of open form: *Twenty-five Pages* (1953) can be played in any order by any number of pianists up to 25. Later works, including *Available Forms I–II* for orchestra (1962) and his String Quartet (1965), exploit mobility in more sophisticated ways.

Brown, Howard Mayer (*b* Los Angeles, 13 April 1930). American musicologist. He studied at Harvard and in 1960 began teaching at the University of Chicago. His many writings are mostly on Renaissance music, instruments and performing practice.

Browne, John (*fl c*1490). English composer. He may have been the John (or William) Browne, clerk of Windsor, who died in 1479 or the lawyer and rector of West Tilbury who died in 1498. The Eton Choirbook originally contained 11 antiphons and four Magnificats by him, of which only nine antiphons (two incomplete) and a fragment of a Magnificat remain. The eight-voice *O Maria Salvatoris mater*, which opens the MS, shows contrapuntal expertise, but more remarkable are the six-voice settings of the *Stabat mater*, *Stabat virgo mater Christi* and *Stabat iuxta Christi crucem*.

Browne, Richard (*d* Lambeth, bur. 21 May 1710). English composer. He was an organist at St Lawrence Jewry (1686–1710) and elsewhere and taught at Christ's Hospital (1688, dismissed 1697). Best known for his catches and songs, he updated the Easter Psalms traditionally sung at Christ's Hospital by composing eight new ones in verse anthem style. There were two other composers of the same name: one (*fl* 1615) at Wells and Winchester cathedrals, one (*d* 1664) at Worcester Cathedral; both wrote anthems.

Bruce, (Frank) Neely (*b* Memphis, 21 Jan 1944). American composer and pianist. He studied with Ben Johnston at the University of Illinois and in 1974 began teaching at Wesleyan University. His works fall into three periods, exploiting serialism (1962–72), stylistic diversity (1971–6) and elements of American musical traditions (1976–); they include two series of *Grand Duos* (1971–83) for various solo instruments and piano. As a pianist he has given several premières.

Bruch, Max (Christian Friedrich) (*b* Cologne, 6 Jan 1838; *d* Friedenau, 20 Oct 1920). German composer. He studied with Hiller and Reinecke and had some success with his cantata *Frithjof* op.23 (1864) before taking posts in Koblenz, Sondershausen, Liverpool and Breslau. Official recognition came in 1891 when he became professor at the Berlin Academy. Although he composed three operas, his talent lay in epic expression; during his lifetime the secular choral works *Odysseus* op.41 and *Das Feuerkreuz* op.52, with their solid choral writing and tuneful style, sometimes showing affinities with folk music, were considered among his most significant works. Only his violin concertos and the *Kol nidrei* for cello and orchestra op.47 have remained in the repertory.

Bruck, Arnold von (*b* Bruges, ?1500; *d* Linz, 6 Feb 1554). Netherlands composer. He was a choirboy in Charles V's chapel until *c*1519 and became Kapellmeister at Archduke Ferdinand I's court in 1527. Having received a number of ecclesiastical honours, he retired in 1545, moving to Vienna then to Linz. He is one of the most important composers who worked in German lands in the first half of the 16th century. Sacred and secular German lieder predominate among his extant works, but his surviving Latin church compositions show him a master of liturgical *cantus firmus* treatment. The sacred German songs reflect the move towards the later motet-style chorales, but the secular songs (polyphonic arrangements of folksongs and court melodies, and quodlibets) are his greatest achievement.

Bruckner, (Joseph) Anton (*b* Ansfelden, 4 Sept 1824; *d* Vienna, 11 Oct 1896). Austrian composer. He was the son of a village schoolmaster and organist, with whom he first studied and for whom he could deputize when he was ten. His father died in 1837 and he was sent at 13 as a chorister to the St Florian monastery where he could study organ, violin and theory. He became a schoolmaster-organist, holding village posts, but in 1845 went to teach at St Florian, becoming organist there in 1851. During these years he had written masses and other sacred works. In 1855 he undertook a counterpoint course in Vienna with the leading theorist, Simon Sechter; the same year he was appointed organist at Linz Cathedral. He continued his studies almost to the age of 40, but more crucial was his contact, in 1863, with Wagner's music – first *Tannhäuser*, then *Tristan und Isolde*; these pointed to new directions for him, as the Masses in D minor, E minor and F minor, and Symphony no.1, all written in 1864–8, show.

In 1868, after Sechter's death, he was offered the post of theory teacher at the Vienna Conservatory, which he hesitantly accepted. In the ensuing years he travelled to Paris and London as an organ virtuoso and improviser. In Vienna, he concentrated on writing symphonies; but the Vienna PO rejected no.1 as 'wild', no.2 as 'nonsense' and 'unplayable' and no.3 as 'unperformable'. When no.3 was given, it was a fiasco. No.4 was successfully played, but no.5 had to wait 18 years for a performance and some of no.6 was never played in Bruckner's lifetime. He was criticized for his Wagnerian leanings during the bitter Brahms–Wagner rivalries. His friends urged him to make cuts in his scores (or made them for him); his lack of self-confidence led to acquiescence and to the formal distortion of the works as a result. Late in his life he revised several of his earlier works to meet such criticisms.

Bruckner taught at a teacher-training college, 1870–74, and at Vienna University – after initial opposition – from 1875. Only in the 1880s did he enjoy real success, in particular with Symphony no.7; his music began to be performed in Germany and elsewhere, and he received many honours as well as grants from patrons and the Austrian government. Even in his last years, he was asked to rewrite Symphony no.8, and when he died in 1896 no.9 remained unfinished.

Bruckner was a deeply devout man, and it is not by chance that his symphonies have been compared to cathedrals in their scale and their grandeur and in their aspiration to the sublime. The principal influences behind them are Beethoven and Wagner. Beethoven's Ninth provides the basic model for their scale and shape, and also for their mysterious openings, fading in from silence. Wagner too influenced their scale and certain aspects of their orchestration, such as the use of heavy brass (from no.7 Bruckner wrote for four Wagner tubas) and the use of intense, sustained string cantabile for depth of expression. His musical forms are individual: his vast sonata-type structures often have three rather than two main tonal areas, and he tends to present substantial sections in isolation punctuated by pregnant silences. Huge climaxes are attained by remorseless reiterations of motifs, or, in the Adagios, by the persistent use of swirling figural patterns in the violins against which a huge orchestral tutti is inexorably built up, often with ascending phrases and enriching harmonies. Secondary themes often have a chorale-like character, sometimes counterpointed with music in dance rhythms. Slow movements are often planned (as in Beethoven's Ninth) around the alternation of two broad themes. Scherzos are in 3/4, often with the kind of elemental drive of that in Beethoven's Ninth; they carry hints of Austrian peasant dances, and some of the trios show *ländler*-like characteristics. From no.3 onwards, Bruckner's symphonies each end with a restatement of the work's opening theme.

Because of their textual complications, Bruckner's symphonies have mostly been published in two editions: the *Sämtliche Werke* series (ed. R. Haas and others, in grey covers) usually give the work as first written, the *Gesamtausgabe* (ed. L. Nowak and others, in blue covers) the revised and cut versions.

Orchestral music Sym. no.'o', d (1864); Sym. no.1, c (1866, rev. 1891); Sym. no.2, c (1872, rev. 1876); Sym. no.3, d (1877, rev. 1889); Sym. no.4, 'Romantic', E♭ (1874, rev. 1880, 1888); Sym. no.5, B♭ (1876); Sym. no.6, A (1881); Sym. no.7, E (1883); Sym. no.8, c (1887, rev. 1890); Sym. no.9, d, unfinished (1896); ov., marches
Chamber and keyboard music Str Qnt, F (1879); 5 other chamber works; org preludes, fugues; pf pieces
Sacred vocal music Mass, b♭ (1854); Mass no.1, d (1864); Mass no.2, e (1866); Mass no.3, f (1878); mass movts; Te Deum, C (1884); c50 psalms, cantatas, choruses
Secular vocal music c40 cantatas, choruses; songs

Brüggen, Frans (*b* Amsterdam, 30 Oct 1934). Dutch recorder player, flautist and conductor. He studied at the Muzieklyceum, Amsterdam, and soon attracted notice for his fine tone, brilliant technique and knowledge of historical styles; his Boehm flute was exchanged for 18th-century flutes and recorders, or copies. He conducts his own ensembles, including the avant-garde group Sourcream, and founded the Orchestra of the 18th Century to play Classical music on period instruments.

Bruhns, Nicolaus (*b* Schwabstedt, 1665; *d* Husum, 29 March 1697). German composer and instrumentalist. From a prominent musical family in Schleswig-Holstein, he was a pupil of Buxtehude and worked briefly at Copenhagen as a composer and violin virtuoso before becoming organist at the Stadtkirche, Husum (1689). None of his instrumental chamber music survives, but five organ works and 12 cantatas are extant. His preludes and fugues, modelled on Buxtehude's, were known to Bach and use thematic transformation, echo devices and bril-

liant toccata-like passages. Bruhns's four small-scale sacred concertos brought the Italian-style solo cantata to new heights of virtuosity in Germany; he also wrote sacred madrigals and chorale ensemble concertos, works showing melodic beauty and formal strength. He usually favoured a five-part string ensemble with bassoon and continuo.

Brüll, Ignaz (*b* Prossnitz, 7 Nov 1846; *d* Vienna, 17 Sept 1907). Austrian pianist and composer. A close friend of Brahms, for and with whom he often played, he wrote chamber and orchestral music, many songs and ten operas, of which *Das goldene Kreuz* (1875) was his greatest success.

Brumby, Colin (James) (*b* Melbourne, 18 June 1933). Australian composer. He studied at Melbourne University, in Spain with Jarnach (1962) and in England with Goehr (1963). In 1964 he was appointed to the University of Queensland. His music is eclectic, and includes several operas (notably *The Seven Deadly Sins*, 1970), operettas for children and much choral music.

Brumel, Antoine (*b* c1460; *d* c1515). French composer. A singer at Notre Dame, Chartres, from 1483, he became Master of the Innocents at St Peter's, Geneva, by 1486. He was installed as a canon at Laon Cathedral by 1497 and the following year took charge of the choirboys at Notre Dame, Paris. In 1501–2 he was a singer at the Duke of Savoy's Court in Chambéry, and from 1506 to 1510 acted as *maestro di cappella* to Alfonso I d'Este. He was prominent among the composers who ranked, after Josquin Desprez, as the most eminent masters of the late 15th and early 16th centuries. He was primarily a composer of sacred music, notably masses (15 survive complete). They may be divided into three stylistic groups, the earliest depending primarily on a *cantus firmus*, the middle group (which includes the impressive *Missa 'Et ecce terrae motus'* for 12 voices) exhibiting greater rhythmic regularity, thinner textures and a closer relationship between text and music, and the later works tending towards concentration and brevity. He also wrote motets. The secular works also frequently use pre-existing melodies; the four-part pieces have texts but those in three parts are purely instrumental.

Brün, Herbert (*b* Berlin, 9 July 1918). German composer. He studied with Wolpe at the Jerusalem Conservatory (1936–8) and began teaching at the University of Illinois in 1963. There he has used computers in composing electronic and chamber pieces, a subject on which he has written extensively.

Bruna, Pablo (*b* Daroca, bap. 22 June 1611; *d* there, c26 June 1679). Spanish composer. Blinded as a child, he became organist of the collegiate church of Daroca in 1631 (choirmaster, 1674). Imbued with Spanish intensity, his music includes seven *Pange lingua* settings and 32 organ pieces (mostly tientos) characterized by suspensions, chromatic inflections, and fantastic figuration.

Bruneau, (Louis Charles Bonaventure) Alfred (*b* Paris, 3 March 1857; *d* there, 15 June 1934). French composer and critic. At the Paris Conservatoire he studied cello and composition (with Massenet). From 1887 he devoted himself mainly to composing for the stage. His *Le rêve* (1891) and *L'attaque du moulin* (1893), and the more symbolic *Messidor* (1897) and *L'ouragan* (1901), all to prose librettos by his friend Zola, were highly acclaimed. His music shows Italian *verismo* traits and the block triad sequences, whole-tone harmonies and use of plainsong that were to be developed in Debussy's works; it also displays a personal, not altogether happy, amalgamation of Wagnerian orchestration, suave, conventional lyricism and Berlioz-inspired harmonic boldness. Of his many songs, the *Chants de la vie* (1913) are his best. He was a regular contributor to French journals from 1890.

Brunelli, Antonio (*b* Pisa, *c*1575; *d* there, by 1630). Italian composer and theorist. He was an important figure in the period of stylistic transition in Florence in the early 17th century. A pupil of Nanino in Rome, he held posts as *maestro di cappella* at S Miniato, near Pisa (1603–4), Prato Cathedral (1607) and at Pisa in the service of the Grand Duke of Tuscany. In an early theoretical work, *Regole utilissime* (1606), he questioned the durability of the new monodic style, but nevertheless composed some of the most attractive of all Florentine monodies, duets and trios (1613, 1614). He collaborated with Peri on the music for the *Ballo della cortesia* (performed 1614) and, in addition to composing dance music for court entertainments, wrote sacred vocal music in the polyphonic tradition.

Brunette. A species of French *air*, popular in the 17th and 18th centuries, characterized by tender sentiments and often by references to young brunettes. Ballard issued volumes of *brunettes* between 1703 and 1711, and Chambonnières and D'Angelbert used *brunette* melodies in some of their harpsichord pieces. The name may derive from the refrain ('Ah, petite Brunette! Ah, tu me fais mourir') of the once famous song, *Le beau berger Tirsis.*

Brunetti, Gaetano (*b* ?Fano, 1744; *d* Colmenar de Orejo, 16 Dec 1798). Italian composer and violinist. Probably a pupil of Nardini in Livorno, he played in the Madrid royal chapel, from 1788 directing the newly formed chamber orchestra. He introduced music by Haydn and others there and wrote over 400 works for the court, including symphonies (mostly in four movements and with prominent wind parts), violin sonatas and string quartets. His style is generally graceful, with imaginative thematic work and detailed expression marks.

Brunetti, Giovan Gualberto (*b* Pistoia, 24 April 1706; *d* Pisa, 20 May 1787). Italian composer. Until 1754 he worked mostly in Naples, from 1745 at the Turchini conservatory. From 1754 he was *maestro di cappella* in Pisa, writing sacred works. He also composed operas (1733–76) and occasional cantatas. Of his sons, Antonio (i) (*c*1740–1786), a violinist, was Konzertmeister at the Salzburg court, where Mozart wrote music for him; Giuseppe (*c*1740–after 1780) worked at Pisa and Florence and composed sacred music and operas. Antonio (ii) (?1767–?1850), a son of Antonio (i), was *maestro di cappella* at Chieti, Urbino and Macerata and wrote operas and sacred works.

Bruni, Antonio Bartolomeo (*b* Cuneo, 28 Jan 1757; *d* there, 6 Aug 1821). Italian violinist and composer. He played in Paris from 1780 and later directed opera orchestras there. His 20 stage works of 1785–1801, mostly *opéras comiques*, were highly successful; he also wrote over 200 chamber works, including string quartets, trios and duos, violin sonatas and Revolutionary music. He compiled an inventory of the musical instruments confiscated during the Terror and pedagogical works.

Brunner, Adolf (*b* Zurich, 25 June 1901). Swiss composer. He studied in Berlin with Jarnach and Schreker (1921–5), then returned to Zurich, founding the Swiss Society for Protestant Church Music in 1955. His works, including orchestral, chamber and church music, are in a lean contrapuntal style looking back to the Italian concerto grosso and to Schütz.

Brusa, (Giovanni) Francesco (*b* Venice, *c*1700; *d* after 1768). Italian composer. His first four operas were staged in 1724–6, and in 1726–40 he was an organist at St Mark's, Venice. He resumed opera composition in the 1750s; he was choirmaster at the Ospedale degli Incurabili, *c*1766–8. Several stage works, four oratorios and sacred works from this period may be his or by a younger composer of the same name.

Bruscantini, Sesto (*b* Porto Civitanova, 10 Dec 1919). Italian bass-baritone. He sang at La Scala from 1949 (*Il matrimonio segreto*) and appeared at Glyndebourne (1951–61) as Mozart's Alfonso, Guglielmo and Leporello and Rossini's Figaro and Dandini. He sang in the USA from 1961 (Chicago and San Francisco) and his *buffo* artistry (as Dulcamara) was admired at Covent Garden in 1974.

Brusilovsky, Evgeny Grigor'yevich (*b* Rostov na Donu, 12 Nov 1905; *d* Moscow, 9 May 1981). Soviet composer. He studied with Shteynberg at the Leningrad Conservatory (1926–31) and in 1933 settled in Alma-Ata, using the music and legends of Kazakhstan in his operas, symphonies and other works, and teaching at the conservatory. His *Gulyandom* (1940) is the first Uzbek national ballet.

Bruson, Renato (*b* Este, 13 Jan 1936). Italian baritone. He studied in Padua and made his début in Spoleto as Luna (1961). He made his Met début, in *Lucia di Lammermoor*, in 1969, and in 1972 sang at La Scala and in Britain. He has sung in several Donizetti revivals but his reputation stands chiefly on his noble, well-focussed tone and eloquent phrasing in the great Verdi baritone roles, of which by the late 1970s and early 80s he was a leading exponent.

Brustad, Bjarne (*b* Oslo, 4 March 1895; *d* there, 22 May 1978). Norwegian composer and violinist. He studied in Oslo and abroad and was solo violinist in the Oslo Philharmonic Society Orchestra (1929–43), later concentrating on composition and teaching. His works include nine symphonies and four violin concertos in a neo-classical style admitting Norwegian folk elements.

Brustwerk (Ger.). A small organ-chest, usually with its own manual, encased compactly above the keyboards and below the *Hauptwerk*, in the 'breast' of the organ.

Bryars, Gavin (*b* Goole, 16 Jan 1943). English composer. He studied philosophy at Sheffield University and music privately; in the 1960s he played in jazz groups and since 1970 he has lectured at Leicester Polytechnic. A leading experimental composer, influenced by Cage and Satie, he first wrote for indeterminate forces (*The Sinking of the Titanic*, 1969), but more recently his music has been influenced by theories of literature; it is often repetitive and witty. His opera *Medea* was staged in 1984.

Brymer, Jack (*b* South Shields, 27 Jan 1915). English clarinettist. He became principal clarinet in 1947 in the RPO, under Beecham; later he played in the BBC SO and the LSO, and directed the London Wind Soloists. He is noted for his warm, flexible tone; he is also a popular broadcaster on music.

Bryne, Albertus (*b* ?London, *c*1621; *d* Westminster, 1671). English composer. He was organist at St Paul's Cathedral (1638–49, 1660–66) and Westminster Abbey (1666–8) and taught the harpsichord. As well as anthems and services, he composed influential harpsichord suites.

Bucchi, Valentino (*b* Florence, 29 Nov 1916; *d* Rome, 9 May 1976). Italian composer. He studied with Dallapiccola at the Florence Conservatory and became director of the Perugia (from 1957) and Florence conservatories (from 1974). His works, including operas, ballets and orchestral pieces, are in an immediate diatonic style, often with playful or grotesque features.

Buccin. A crude wind instrument, created during the French Revolution for use in outdoor music. None survives, but it was probably a straight conical tube, 1–1.5 m long, of brass alloy.

Buccina. A curved Roman brass instrument, originally made from an animal horn and later from brass; it was used for signalling.

Bucenus, Paulus (*b* Holstein, *fl* 1567–84; *d* ?Riga). German composer. He was a Kantor at Torún (*c*1570) and at Riga Cathedral (by 1576). A fluent and gifted composer of church music, he published 100 motets, 24 masses and many other liturgical works in a large two-volume collection (1583–4); his *St Matthew Passion* (1578) is one of the last Lutheran settings in Latin.

Buch der hängenden Gärten, Das. Songs by Schoenberg (op.15, 1909) for voice and piano, settings of 15 poems by Stefan George.

Buchla, Donald (Frederick) (*b* Southgate, CA, 17 April 1937). American instrument designer and composer. He has designed electronic instruments, for which he has composed, and studios (including those of IRCAM, Paris). In 1975 he co-founded a performing group for live electronic music.

Buchner, Hans (*b* Ravensburg, 26 Oct 1483; *d* ?Konstanz, 1538). German organist and composer. A pupil of Hofhaimer, he was organist to the imperial court choir and, from 1506, at Konstanz Cathedral. When the Reformation movement spread to Konstanz in 1526 he moved to Überlingen. His *Fundamentum* (*c*1520) deals with keyboard notation and the techniques of arranging vocal pieces for the organ and contains the first description of a method for handling a *cantus firmus* contrapuntally; its many music examples form the bulk of his output.

Bucht, Gunnar (*b* Stocksund, 5 Aug 1927). Swedish composer. He studied musicology at Uppsala University and composition with Blomdahl (1947–51) and others. In 1975 he was appointed professor of composition at the Musikhögskolan, Stockholm. He has been active in several Swedish national musical organizations. His works include an opera, symphonies and tape music.

Buck, Dudley (*b* Hartford, CT, 10 March 1839; *d* West Orange, NJ, 6 Oct 1909). American composer and organist. He worked in Hartford, Chicago, Boston and New York, chiefly as an organist and choirmaster. Besides a large amount of church music, he wrote large-scale secular cantatas including *The Centennial Meditation of Columbia* (1879), and significant organ works.

Buck, Zechariah (*b* Norwich, 10 Sept 1798; *d* Newport, Essex, 5 Aug 1879). English organist. At Norwich Cathedral for 58 years (1819–77), he had a formidable reputation as a choir trainer and organ teacher.

Budapest Quartet. String quartet of Hungarian origin. Its first concert was in 1917. Its first leader was Emil Hauser; he was succeeded by Joseph Roisman and by 1936 all the members were Russian or Ukrainian. The quartet won world fame for its warm, expressive interpretations of the classical repertory, particularly Beethoven. The quartet settled in the USA (1938) and until 1962 was in residence at the Library of Congress, Washington, DC; it disbanded in 1967.

Buffalo Philharmonic Orchestra. American orchestra, established in 1935 with Franco Autori as conductor; its home is the Kleinhans Music Hall (inaugurated 1940), which seats 2839. Conductors include Josef Krips (1953–63) and Lukas Foss (1963–70). Under Foss the repertory was mainly modern and recordings of Cage, Pederecki and Xenakis were made.

Buffoon, The Tale of the. *See* CHOUT.

Buff stop [harp stop]. A device on all harpsichords and some 18th- and 19th-century pianos. It mutes the strings by pressing a piece of buff leather against them at the nut, damping out high harmonics; the resultant sound is like pizzicato.

Bugle. A copper or brass natural trumpet with a wide conical bore; in Britain it has a pitch of B♭ (on the Continent often C). In the USA, the British type of bugle is known as the 'cavalry bugle', the ordinary bugle being a trumpet-like instrument with a piston valve. The bugle is used in the armed forces of most countries, usually to sound a set of formalized calls. *See also* KEYED BUGLE.

Buglhat, Johannes de (*fl* 1528–55). Music printer. He served Renée of France, Duchess of Ferrara. He and his associates Henrico de Campis and Antonio Hucher, rivals of Antonio Gardane, were among the first in Italy to use the single-impression method of music printing, introduced in Paris by Attaingnant in 1528.

Buhl, Joseph David (*b* nr. Amboise, 1781). French trumpeter. Besides holding posts in orchestras and military bands in Paris, he wrote an important method (1825) and revised the traditional French military signals (1803–29) still used by the French cavalry.

Buisine. Medieval name for a herald's trumpet; it was 1–2 m long and straight, of brass or silver, with a cylindrical or slightly conical bore.

Bukofzer, Manfred F(ritz) (*b* Oldenburg, 17 March 1910; *d* Berkeley, 7 Dec 1955). American musicologist. He studied at Heidelberg, Berlin and Basle. Emigrating to the USA in 1939, he became an American citizen and taught at the University of California, Berkeley, from 1941 until his death. His main research was on 14th- and 15th-century English music but he is equally remembered for his *Music in the Baroque Era* (1947), a standard survey; his style-based approach has become increasingly prevalent in musicological writing.

Bull, John (*b* Old Radnor, ?1562–3; *d* Antwerp, 12/13 March 1628). English composer, one of the leading keyboard virtuosos of his time. He served at Hereford Cathedral (chorister, 1573; Organist, 1582; Master of the Choristers, 1583) and the Chapel Royal, London (from 1574, Gentleman from 1586), and graduated MusD (Cambridge, 1589) and DMus (Oxford, 1592). As Public Reader at Gresham College, London (from 1597), he frequently fell foul of the authorities and was forced to resign in 1607, the year he married. Despite travels abroad as an organ consultant, he remained with the Chapel Royal as the king's organist. In 1613 he was charged with adultery and fled to the Netherlands, claiming religious persecution as the reason for his flight. The Archduke Albert employed him in Brussels until 1614, when diplomatic pressures hastened his dismissal. From 1615 until his last illness in 1626 he was at Antwerp Cathedral (organist from 1617).

Much of Bull's music was lost when he fled England, but there survive 120 canons, a dozen or so anthems and a vast body of outstanding keyboard music on which his fame mainly rests (most is in MS, some printed in *Parthenia*, 1613). His intricate plainsong settings and masterly hexachord fantasias, best suited to the organ, show strong continental influence. The virginal music includes elaborate variations (e.g. *Walsingham*), brilliant pavan and galliard pairs (e.g. *Quadran*) and highly embellished character-pieces; with their prodigious technical demands they have a dazzling brilliance lacking in his contemporaries' music. The remarkable canons, mostly on the *Miserere* chant (e.g. the six-part *Sphera mundi*), perfect the austere technique of Blitheman and Tallis; the surviving anthems are simple, direct and appealing.

Keyboard music over 30 In Nomines; fantasia, other pieces; *c*90 works for virginal, incl. variations on Walsingham, other variations, pavans and galliards, dances, character-pieces
Instrumental music 116 canons on Miserere; other canons; consort pieces
Sacred vocal music English anthems; Latin motet

Bull, Ole (Bornemann) (*b* Bergen, 5 Feb 1810; *d* Lysøen, 17 Aug 1880). Norwegian violinist and composer. A seminal figure in Norwegian music, he was one of the greatest 19th-century violinists. From the famous peasant fiddler 'Myllarguten', he learnt *slåtter* (folkdances), incorporated later in his improvisations, and from the Hardanger (peasant) fiddle, he came to modify his instrument, making the bridge flatter and the bow longer and heavier. He created his first public sensation in Bologna in 1833, playing his Concerto in A, followed by an equally successful appearance in Naples, showing in his Quartet for solo violin a remarkable ability to play polyphonically. From 1835, enthusiastic reports of concerts in Paris, London and throughout Europe and the USA made him a national hero in Norway. In the 1840s and 1850s he used his influence and flamboyance to draw attention to native Norwegian art, establishing a national theatre in Bergen, encouraging Ibsen, Bjørnson and the young Grieg and trying to establish a Norwegian colony in Pennsylvania. Until his death he performed with undiminished success and was well regarded by Thackeray, Twain, Liszt and Schumann, who thought him at least Paganini's equal. His compositions were criticized for lack of coherence but praised for affecting melody; *Et saeterbesøg* (1848) and the song *I ensomme stunde* are still often heard.

Bullant, Antoine (*b* ?nr. Amiens, ?*c*1750; *d* St Petersburg, ?June 1821). French composer and bassoonist. About 1771–2 he went to Paris, where he published four symphonies (1773) and several chamber works. He lived in St Petersburg from 1780 and from 1785 played in the imperial theatre orchestra. A major figure in musical life there and in Moscow, he produced Russian-language stage works up to 1789; his first comic opera, *The Merchant of Mead* (1783–4, St Petersburg), was among the most popular works of its kind.

Buller, John (*b* London, 7 Feb 1927). English composer. He studied with Milner and first came to notice with a series of Berio-like pieces based on *Finnegan's Wake*, including *Finnegan's Floras* (1972) and *The Mime of Mick, Nick and the Maggies* for vocal soloists, chorus, 12 instruments and tape (1977). Later works have included *Proença* (1977) and *The Theatre of Memory* for orchestra (1981).

Bullis, Thomas (*b* Ely, late 1657; *d* there, bur. 24 Aug 1712). English composer. A chorister and lay clerk under J. Ferrabosco at Ely Cathedral from 1677, he stood in as organist when required. He was a skilled contrapuntist and composed anthems and services in a lively rhythmic style. His father, Thomas Bullis (1627–1708), was also a composer at Ely.

Bullroarer. An instrument made from a spatulate piece of wood tied to a string which is knotted into a hole close to one end; the player whirls the blade through the air, holding it by the free end of the string.

Bülow, Hans (Guido) Freiherr von (*b* Dresden, 8 Jan 1830; *d* Cairo, 12 Feb 1894). German conductor and pianist. He studied with Wieck, Eberwein and Hauptmann, becoming a champion of the New German School and meeting Liszt at Weimar in 1849. He sought out Wagner in 1850, studied under Liszt from 1851 and made his first concert tour in 1853; he married Liszt's daughter Cosima in 1857. As conductor of the Munich Court Opera he gave the premières of *Tristan und Isolde* (1865) and *Die Meistersinger von Nürnberg* (1868). Cosima left him for Wagner in 1869. From 1872 he toured again as a pianist, giving the première of Tchaikovsky's First Piano Concerto (dedicated to him) in Boston (1875). He transformed the Meiningen court orchestra (1880–85) into one of the best in Germany. His playing was distinguished by its passionate intellectuality.

Bumbass. A bowed monochord consisting of a heavy gut string attached at each end to a long wooden pole and stretched over a pig's bladder. It is sounded with a notched stick or a horsehair bow and used in many parts of Europe to provide a droning rhythmic accompaniment to folksong or dance.

Bumbry, Grace (Melzia Ann) (*b* St Louis, 4 Jan 1937). American mezzo-soprano, later soprano. After study at Boston University and with Lotte Lehmann, she sang Amneris at the Paris Opéra in 1960. Wide attention came with her Venus at Bayreuth in 1961. At Covent Garden and the Met, her warm voice, commanding presence and acting ability have been admired as Eboli, Carmen, Tosca and Salome.

Bungert, (Friedrich) August (*b* Mülheim an der Ruhr, 14 March 1845/6; *d* Leutesdorf am Rhein, 26 Oct 1915). German composer. He studied at the Cologne Conservatory and in Paris and Berlin, achieving success with his Piano Quartet in Eb op.18. Besides songs, choruses, programmatic orchestral works and a comic opera, he wrote one impressive opera cycle, *Die Odyssee* (four parts, 1896–1903, modelled partly on Wagner's *Ring*), and planned another, *Die Ilias*, together to be entitled *Homerische Welt*.

Bunting, Edward (*b* Armagh, Feb 1773; *d* Dublin, 21 Dec 1843). Anglo-Irish organist and folksong collector. Through organ appointments and as a piano teacher, festival organizer and harp society founder, he became the leading musician in early 19th-century Belfast. His importance lies mainly in his systematic collection, from 1792, of traditional Irish folk melodies, published in three volumes as *A General Collection of Ancient Irish Music* (1796, 1809, 1840).

Buonamente, Giovanni Battista (*b* Mantua, late 16th century; *d* Assisi, 29 Aug 1642). Italian composer. Active at first at the Gonzaga court in Mantua, he was *musicista da camera* to the emperor in Vienna (*c*1626–9), and went briefly to Bergamo and Parma before being appointed *maestro di cappella* at S Francesco, Assisi (1633). As one of the first composers to cultivate the violin, he was partly responsible for introducing the new Italian violin style into northern Europe. Only the last four of his seven books of instrumental music survive (1626–37); they include sinfonias, canzonas, dances and sonatas, mostly in three parts. In some of these he explored the potential of violin technique and figuration. Most of his sacred music is lost.

Burck, Joachim a [Moller, Joachim] (*b* Burg, 1546; *d* Mühlhausen, 24 May 1610). German composer. Educated in Magdeburg and elsewhere, he was Kantor (1563) at the grammar school and organist

(1566) of St Blassius, Mühlhausen, and a public official there. After early polyphonic motet publications he became known as a prolific composer of sacred homophonic songs and odes in an up-to-date style. He also published several Passions, hymns, psalms and many occasional pieces.

Burden [burthen]. A refrain. The term has also been used for a drone or pedal note and for a shawm.

Burell, John. English composer. He is known from a Gloria and Credo in the Old Hall MS. A man of this name is listed as a royal chaplain in 1413, 1415 and 1421, and held canonries at Chichester, Hereford and York and, 1416–37, a corrody at Meaux Abbey. He was rector of Gilling East, Yorks., and a prebendary of York Minster.

Burghauser, Jarmil (*b* Písek, 21 Oct 1921). Czech composer. He studied composition and conducting at the Prague Conservatory (1933–46). His music has developed from the Dvořák–Novák tradition through neo-classicism to post-Webernian modernism. His works include many film scores.

Burghersh, Lord John Fane, 11th Earl of Westmorland (*b* London, 3 Feb 1784; *d* Wansford, 16 Oct 1859). English amateur musician. His career was political, military and diplomatic, but he devoted his leisure to music, often in connection with professional musicians in his foreign posts (Florence, Berlin, Vienna). A good violinist and a prolific though unoriginal composer (seven Italian operas, three symphonies), he was principal founder and first president of the RAM (1822), which he ruled autocratically for 37 years.

Burgmüller, (August Joseph) Norbert (*b* Düsseldorf, 8 Feb 1810; *d* Aachen, 7 May 1836). German composer and pianist. A son of Johann August Franz Burgmüller, founder of the Lower Rhine Music Festival (1818), he studied with Hauptmann and Spohr and produced lyric chamber works, piano sonatas, a piano concerto and two symphonies. He was admired by a close circle of artists and musicians, including Mendelssohn and Schumann, who likened the tragedy of his early death to Schubert's.

Burgon, Geoffrey (*b* Hambledon, 16 July 1941). English composer. After study with Berkeley at the GSM he worked as a jazz trumpeter. He uses a wide range of modern procedures and has been influenced by early English church music (*Think on Dredful Domesday*, 1969; *Veni spiritus*, 1979).

Burgundian school. Group of composers active at the ducal court of Burgundy in the period from 1384 (when the Burgundian chapel was organized) to 1477 (when the duchy was annexed to France). The court was at the Burgundian capital, Dijon, or at one of the northern cities (Brussels, Bruges, Lille) under Burgundian dominion during this period. Composers associated with the court include Tapissier, Grenon, Fontaine, Binchois, Morton, Hayne van Ghizeghem and Busnois; Dufay may also have been associated with the court. Composers of this group were noted for their sacred music and their *chansons*.

Burian, Emil František (*b* Plzeň, 11 June 1904; *d* Prague, 9 Aug 1959). Czech composer and writer. He studied with Foerster at the Prague Conservatory and before graduating in 1927 had already made a mark in the avant-garde theatre, producing works influenced by jazz, Les Six and dada. *The War* (1935) is a play with songs and dances suggesting Janáček and the Stravinsky of *The Wedding*; the cantata *May* (1936) is one of several works written for his own 'Voice Band', who made a feature of non-verbal vocalization. After the war he adopted the precepts of socialist realism.

Burkhard, Willy (*b* Evilard-sur-Bienne, 17 April 1900; *d* Zurich, 18 June 1955). Swiss composer. He studied in Berne, Leipzig, Munich and Paris, and taught at the conservatories of Berne and Zurich. He developed an individual post-Bachian style having some connections with Hindemith and Bartók, the most important works in his large output being the oratorios *Das Gesicht Jesajas* (1935) and *Das Jahr* (1942), and the Mass for soloists, chorus and orchestra (1951).

Burleigh, Cecil (*b* Wyoming, NY, 17 April 1885; *d* Madison, WI, 28 July 1980). American composer. He studied in Berlin (1903–5) and Chicago and performed as a violinist, 1909–11; in 1919 he resumed studies in New York (violin with Auer, composition with Bloch), and taught at Madison, 1921–55. His works, which include chamber music and songs, are heavily influenced by MacDowell's smaller pieces; from 1940 he used larger forms, e.g. the three symphonies of *c*1944, *Creation*, *Prophecy* and *Revelation*.

Burleigh, Harry T(hacker) (*b* Erie, PA, 2 Dec 1866; *d* Stamford, CT, 12 Sept 1949). American composer and singer. He studied in New York, 1892–5, where he was influenced by Dvořák among others. He sang in New York and worked as a music editor; he wrote 265 vocal works and made 187 choral arrangements of black spirituals as well as compiling a collection of minstrel melodies.

Burlesque. A humorous piece, usually involving parody or grotesque exaggeration. Bach called a movement of his Partita BWV827 'Burlesca'; later examples include Strauss's *Burleske* for piano and orchestra and Bartók's *Burlesque* op.2.

Burlesques (parodies) of serious plays and Italian opera were popular in 18th- and 19th-century London; the English form was followed in the USA until the 1860s, after which the term was increasingly reserved for variety shows including striptease.

Burletta. A type of English operatic comedy of the late 18th century and early 19th. It began as a satire on *opera seria*; when the musical content declined the term was retained as a means of evading the monopoly in legitimate drama enjoyed by Covent Garden and Drury Lane.

Burmeister, Joachim (*b* Lüneburg, 1564; *d* Rostock, 5 March 1629). German theorist. After studies in Lüneburg and at Rostock University he became a teacher and Kantor in Rostock. One of the most influential German theorists of his time, he developed a doctrine of musical-rhetorical figures to assist musical analysis. Of his theoretical works, the most comprehensive is *Musica autoschedastikē* (1601). His compositions comprise 91 simple hymntune harmonizations (1601) and four motets modelled on works by Lassus.

Burney, Charles (*b* Shrewsbury, 7 April 1726; *d* Chelsea, 12 April 1814). English music historian. Trained as an organist and violinist, he was apprenticed to Thomas Arne in London. After serving as music instructor to an aristocrat for two years, he settled in London as an organist and harpsichordist; his first sonatas and songs date from 1748. In 1760 he returned to London after nine years in King's Lynn, and made his name as a private teacher and writer. He took his two daughters (including Fanny, later a novelist) to Paris, then he made an English version (*The Cunning Man*, 1766) of Rousseau's *Le devin du village*. In 1770 and 1772 he toured Europe, collecting materials for a history of music, hearing many performances and meeting leading musicians; three important books resulted, *The Present State of Music in France and Italy* (1771) and *The Present State of Music in Germany, the Netherlands, and the United Provinces* (1773) as well as *A General History of Music* (4 vols., 1776–89). Among his other, prolific, writings were book and poetry reviews and dictionary articles, and among his friends, Padre Martini, Haydn, David Garrick and Samuel Johnson. As a composer he was undistinguished.

Burning Fiery Furnace, The. Britten's second church parable (op.77) to a text by William Plomer after the Book of Daniel (1966, Aldeburgh).

Burrows, (James) Stuart (*b* Pontypridd, 7 Feb 1933). Welsh tenor. He sang in concerts before appearing as Ismael in the Welsh National Opera's *Nabucco* in 1963. In 1967 he first sang at Covent Garden and in the USA. At the Vienna Staatsoper he sang Tamino (1970) and the following year Ottavio at the Met. His smooth, flexible lyric tenor is suited to lighter roles.

Burt, Francis (*b* London, 28 April 1926). English composer. He studied with Ferguson at the RAM (1948–51) and with Blacher in Berlin (1951–4), then remained in Germany and latterly Austria. He is best known for his operas, notably *Volpone* (1960).

Burton, John (*b* Yorks., 1730; *d* ?3 Sept 1782). English harpsichordist, organist and composer. A celebrated performer, he composed keyboard music and songs; his 10 sonatas of 1766, several movements from which became very popular, have the earliest known mention of the piano on an English titlepage, and he was among the earliest to play the instrument in public.

Bury, Bernard de (*b* Versailles, 20 Aug 1720; *d* there, 19 Nov 1785). French composer. He worked at the French court from 1741 as a keyboard player and from 1751 as *surintendant de la musique du roi*, writing stage works including one for the Opéra (1743) and several for the court; his dance music and treatment of the orchestra are notable. He also composed keyboard music, cantatas etc.

Busby, Thomas (*b* Westminster, Dec 1755; *d* London, 28 May 1838). English writer and musician. He held posts as organist in London and composed theatrical music and other vocal works. Among his writings are a history of music (1819), a book of anecdotes (1825) and biographies of his contemporaries.

Busch, Adolf (Georg Wilhelm) (*b* Siegen, 8 Aug 1891; *d* Guilford, VT, 9 June 1952). German violinist and composer, brother of Fritz Busch. He studied at the Cologne Conservatory and after early associations with Ferdinand Löwe and Max Reger cofounded the Busch Quartet. In England in the 1930s he formed the Busch Chamber Players, which he directed from the violin. He moved to the USA in 1939 and in 1950 established the Marlboro School of Music in Vermont. Though admired as a soloist, he was more remarkable in chamber music, to which his lucid, controlled playing was well suited. Yehudi Menuhin was among his pupils.

Busch, Fritz (*b* Siegen, 13 March 1890; *d* London, 14 Sept 1951). German conductor and pianist. After study at the Cologne Conservatory he conducted at Riga and Aachen and was music director at the Stuttgart Opera (1918–22). His period at the Dresden Staatsoper (1922–33) was notable for the first performances of operas by Strauss, Busoni (*Doktor Faust*) and Hindemith (*Cardillac*). After leaving Germany (1933) he conducted the Danish RSO and the Stockholm PO. An association with the producer Carl Ebert began in 1932: they were largely responsible for establishing opera at Glyndebourne. In the 1940s he conducted in the USA, returning to Glyndebourne in 1950. Busch was not markedly original, but thorough and decisive.

Busch, William (*b* London, 25 June 1901; *d* Woolacombe, 30 Jan 1945). English composer and pianist. He studied in the USA, Berlin and London and toured internationally as a pianist. His music combines an English lyricism with continental, especially Stravinskian, influences; it includes a Piano Concerto (1939) and songs.

Bush, Alan (Dudley) (*b* London, 22 Dec 1900). English composer. He studied at the RAM with Corder (1918–22) and privately with Ireland, going on to study musicology and philosophy at Berlin University (1929–31). In 1925 he began teaching at the RAM and in 1936, already a committed communist, founded the Workers' Music Association. His earlier works (*Dialectic* for string quartet, 1929; First Symphony in C, 1940) are progressive, using his own 'thematic' method, in which each note must be thematically significant. After the war he simplified his style and began a series of operas expressing his political beliefs: *Wat Tyler* (1953), *Men of Blackmoor* (1960), *The Sugar Reapers* (1966) and *Joe Hill* (1970), all produced in East Germany. He has also composed much choral, chamber and solo vocal music.

Bush, Geoffrey (*b* London, 23 March 1920). English composer. He studied at Oxford. He has written operas, symphonies, songs etc in a fluent and lively tonal style; as a scholar he has worked mainly on English 19th-century music.

Busnois [De Busne], Antoine (*b c*1430; *d* Bruges, 6 Nov 1492). French composer. Possibly a pupil of Ockeghem in Paris, he was a much-favoured singer in the chapel of Charles the Bold and then of his daughter, Mary of Burgundy. After her death in 1482 he became attached to the church of St Sauveur, Bruges. Two masses, a Credo, a Magnificat, eight motets, two hymns and 61 songs for three or four voices are attributed to him with reasonable certainty. His music typifies the Burgundian style in the third quarter of the 15th century and he occupies

a central position in the development of music between Dufay and Josquin. His works are characterized by triadic sonority, strong harmonic progressions, clear structure and extensive use of imitation. The *chansons*, for many of which he probably wrote the texts, are his most original works. Most are three-part rondeaux or bergerettes and some are based on popular melodies. Both his masses are four-voice *cantus firmus* structures and the motets, like the *chansons*, exploit a wide variety of contrapuntal technnniques.

Sacred music Missa 'L' homme armé'; Missa 'O crux lignum'; Credo; Magnificat; 8 motets; 2 hymns
Secular music 30 rondeaux; 13 bergerettes; 18 chansons

Busoni, Ferruccio (Dante Michelangiolo Benvenuto) (*b* Empoli, 1 April 1866; *d* Berlin, 27 July 1924). German-Italian composer and pianist. Born to musician parents, an Italian father and a German mother, he appeared from the age of eight as a pianist. In 1876 the family settled in Graz, where he had lessons with Wilhelm Mayer and produced his first published works. He then moved to Vienna, where he came to know Goldmark and Brahms, to Leipzig and eventually Berlin in 1894. Until he was 40 his output consisted mostly of piano and chamber music, including arrangements of Bach (these were eventually published in seven volumes). But in 1902 he began conducting concerts of modern music, including works by Debussy, Bartók, Sibelius and himself, and his music began to open itself to a wider range of influence. He adopted an aesthetic of 'junge Klassizität', by which he intended a return to the clarity and purely musical motivation of Bach and Mozart; yet such works as his *Elegien* (1907), the virtuoso *Fantasia contrappuntistica* (1910) and the Second Sonatina (1912), all for piano, show his awareness of the latest developments including Schoenberg's most recent music, along with his reverence of the past. His *Sketch of a new Aesthetic of Music* (1907) looks forward with enthusiasm to the use of microtones and electronic means.

The unresolved conflicts in his musical mind between futurism and classical recovery, Italian vocality and German substance, Lisztian flamboyance and Mozartian calm all inform his larger works, which include a Piano Concerto with choral finale (1904), several works on American Indian themes and operas – the E.T.A. Hoffmann fantasy *Die Brautwahl* (1912), a commedia dell'arte double bill of *Arlecchino* and *Turandot* (1917) and the unfinished *Doktor Faust* (1924), where the protagonist's search after knowledge and experience is finally assuaged when he gives birth to a new future.

Bussani, Francesco (*b* Rome, 1743; *d* after 1807). Italian bass. He appeared regularly in Italian operas in Vienna, 1783–94, creating the roles of Bartolo and Antonio in Mozart's *Le nozze di Figaro* (1786) and Don Alfonso in *Così fan tutte* (1790). His wife, Dorothea (née Sardi; 1763–after 1810), an Austrian soprano, created Cherubino in *Figaro* and Despina in *Così*. They later sang in Italy and Lisbon.

Büsser, (Paul-)Henri (*b* Toulouse, 16 Jan 1872;

d Paris, 30 Dec 1973). French composer and conductor. He studied with Widor and Guilmant at the Paris Conservatoire (1889–92) and had advice from Gounod; he became an opera conductor in Paris, from 1905 at the Opéra. His works include ballets, operas and Catholic church music, as well as orchestrations of Debussy's *Petite suite* (1907), *Printemps* (1912) and other works.

Bussotti, Sylvano (*b* Florence, 1 Oct 1931). Italian composer. He studied at the Florence Conservatory but gained more from contacts with Deutsch (1957), Metzger, Boulez and Cage (Darmstadt, 1958). His music at once exults in and criticizes the decadence of modernism: his notation is often flamboyantly virtuoso in its graphic style and fiercely demanding to perform; his works tend to abound in cross-references, to each other and to his personal life, which would seem colourful; he mixes a sensuousness amounting to eroticism with an extreme artificiality. His main works for the theatre include *La passion selon Sade* (1969), *Lorenzaccio* (1972) and *La racine* (1980). Among other compositions are Five Pieces for David Tudor for piano (1959), *The Rara Requiem* for voices and orchestra (1970) and *I semi di Gramsci* for string quartet and orchestra (1971).

Butler, Charles (*b* Wycomb, *c*1560; *d* Wooton St Lawrence, 28/9 March 1647). English musician. After a classical education at Oxford (BA 1583, MA 1587), he was vicar of Wooton St Lawrence until he died. His *Principles of Musik* (1636), a basic instruction manual with a discourse on music's role in sacred and secular life, is a valuable document of the period.

Butt, Dame Clara (Ellen) (*b* Steyning, 1 Feb 1872; *d* North Stoke, 23 Jan 1936). English contralto. She studied at the RCM and in 1892 was much praised as Orpheus in its production of Gluck's opera at the Lyceum Theatre; she also sang the role under Beecham at Covent Garden in 1920. Her powerful voice was heard most in concert; in 1899 at Norwich she gave the first performance of Elgar's *Sea Pictures*.

Butterley, Nigel (Henry) (*b* Sydney, 13 May 1935). Australian composer. He studied at the NSW State Conservatorium (1952–5) and with Rainier in London (1962) and has taught at the conservatories in Sydney and Newcastle, NSW. His early works are influenced by Bartók, Hindemith and Shostakovich, but in the mid-1960s he began to use newer techniques. Several of his works have Christian themes.

Butterworth, Arthur (Eckersley) (*b* Manchester, 4 Aug 1923). English composer. After study with Richard Hall at the Royal Manchester College of Music he worked as a trumpeter and freelance conductor. His music is conservative, influenced primarily by Sibelius and Elgar, and draws on the North Country for its inspiration; it includes three symphonies (1957, 1965, 1975).

Butterworth, George (Sainton Kaye) (*b* London, 12 July 1885; *d* Pozières, 5 Aug 1916). English composer. He was educated at Eton and Oxford and became associated with Vaughan Williams in collecting folksongs. His works include the orchestral rhapsody *A Shropshire Lad* (1912), based on his two

sets of songs from the same collection (1911–12).

Butting, Max (*b* Berlin, 6 Oct 1888; *d* there, 13 July 1976). German composer. He studied in Munich with Klose and Courvoisier, and at the university. In 1919 he returned to Berlin and became associated with socialist organizations and radio music. After the war he continued to compose and teach. His early works show Reger's influence, followed in the 1920s by newer trends, but keeping a clear contrapuntal treatment and close motivic working. He was prolific after 1945, becoming a leading musical figure in the DDR. His output includes ten symphonies, ten string quartets and choral works.

Buttstett, Johann Heinrich (*b* Bindersleben, 25 April 1666; *d* Erfurt, 1 Dec 1727). German composer and theorist. A pupil of Pachelbel, he was organist at Erfurt from 1684, composing sacred and keyboard works; the latter show Pachelbel's influence. He wrote a book (1716) condemning Johann Mattheson's progressive treatise *Das neu-eröffnete Orchestre* (1713). Franz Vollrath Battstedt (1735–1814), organist at Weikersheim and Rothaburg and composer of sacred music, was probably his grandson.

Buus, Jacques (*b* ?Ghent, *c*1500; *d* Vienna, 1565). Flemish composer. He may have been in France before becoming second organist at St Mark's, Venice (1541), and a member of Ferdinand I's court chapel in Vienna (1550). His instrumental ricercares (1547, 1549), some based on a single theme, exploit the devices of 'learned' Netherlands counterpoint and include some of the longest in existence. His motets (1549, some in anthologies) show Gombert's influence and some of his *chansons* (1543, 1550) are parodies of works by French composers.

Buxheimer Orgelbuch. German MS of *c*1470. It consists of 169 folios with more than 250 organ compositions, including liturgical works, dances and song arrangements, as well as C. Paumann's *Fundamentum organisandi*. It is now in the Bavarian State Library, Munich.

Buxtehude, Dietrich (*b* Hälsingburg or Oldesloe, *c*1637; *d* Lübeck, 9 May 1707). Danish (or German) composer. His first studies were under his father, who held posts as organist in Hälsingburg and Helsingør (Elsinore), as did Buxtehude himself between *c*1657 and 1668, when he became organist at the Marienkirche at Lübeck, one of the most important posts in north Germany; he was also appointed Werkmeister (general manager) of the church. Later that year he married Anna Margarethe Tunder, his predecessor's daughter. Besides his normal duties on Sundays and feast days, he reinstated the practice of giving *Abendmusik* concerts in the church on five Sunday afternoons each year. These events attracted much interest and drew J.S. Bach from Arnstadt in Advent 1705.

Surviving texts from the *Abendmusik* performances show that he composed a number of oratorio-like works, but none has survived. The bulk of his known sacred music consists of cantatas or sacred concertos, the latter often settings of psalm texts, consisting of contrasting sections in which each line of the text is treated with a new motif. He used a concertato style, for voices and continuo (sometimes with other instruments), in which the motifs are treated in dialogue in a manner related to the Venetian polychoral style; there are also arioso sections. Buxtehude wrote a number of chorale settings, commonly with the melody in the soprano but with instrumental accompaniment and interludes; in ensemble settings he used the chorale motet style, in the manner of a sacred concerto but with motifs from the chorale melody, and he also set chorales with the melody in one voice and instrumental counterpoints. His sacred arias are mostly in strophic or varied strophic form, with a fluent, sometimes Italianate melodic style. Some extended vocal works, akin to Bach's cantatas, combine movements in the sacred concerto style with others of the aria type.

Most of Buxtehude's instrumental music is for the organ: about half consists of freely composed music, often using a toccata-like section with several fugues and incorporating virtuoso passage-work, while half consists of chorale settings, some of the variation and fantasia types, but mostly highly unified settings of a single stanza of the chorale with a richly ornamented melody. He composed suites and other music for the harpsichord; his courantes are variations of the allemandes and the gigues are loosely fugal. French influence is noticeable. He also wrote several variation sets. The only works published in his lifetime were two collections each of seven sonatas, for violins, viola da gamba and harpsichord continuo (seven more sonatas survive in MS); they are closer to the German tradition of improvisatory viol playing than to the Corelli tradition, with movements in contrasting tempo and texture. They include ground bass movements and fugues, usually only in two parts as the viol part is not always independent of the bass. Especially in his sacred vocal works and his organ music, Buxtehude represents the climax of the 17th-century north German school, and he significantly influenced Bach.

Vocal music over 100 sacred works: German and Latin concs., chorale settings, arias, cantatas etc; 10 secular works
Organ music over 40 chorale settings (preludes, fantasias, variations); 2 chaconnes, passacaglia; over 40 preludes, canzonas, toccatas, fugues
Other keyboard music 19 suites; 6 variation sets incl. La Capricciosa
Chamber music 14 sonatas, 2 vn, va da gamba, hpd, op.1 (*c*1694), 7 other sonatas

Buzzolla, Antonio (*b* Adria, 2 March 1815; *d* Venice, 20 March 1871). Italian composer and conductor. He studied in Venice and with Donizetti and Mercadante and produced five operas, winning greater acclaim, however, for his graceful ariettas and canzonettas in Venetian dialect. From 1855 he was *maestro di cappella* at St Mark's, Venice.

BWV. Abbreviation for *Bach-Werke-Verzeichnis*; numbers following BWV identify works according to Wolfang Schmieder's thematic catalogue of the music of J.S. Bach (1950, 3/1961).

Byrd, William (*b* ?Lincoln, 1543; *d* Stondon Massey, 4 July 1623). English composer, the most versatile of his day. Brought up in London, he was a pupil of

Tallis. In 1563 he became Organist and Master of the Choristers at Lincoln Cathedral and married there in 1568. Though he remained at Lincoln until *c*1572 he was a Gentleman of the Chapel Royal from 1570 and its organist from 1575 (at first jointly with Tallis). In London he rapidly established himself as a composer, gaining influential friends and patrons and earning favour with Queen Elizabeth, who granted him a patent (with Tallis) in 1575 for the printing and marketing of part-music and MS paper. After his wife's death in the 1580s he remarried. He and his family were often cited as Catholic recusants, but he continued to compose openly for the Roman church. In 1593 Byrd moved to Essex, where he spent the rest of his life and was frequently involved in property litigation. His reputation was very high: he was described as 'Father of British Music'. Morley and Tomkins were among his pupils.

Much of Byrd's vast and varied output was printed during his lifetime. His sacred music ranges widely in style and mood, from the florid and penitential motets of the *Cantiones sacrae* to the concise and devotional ones in the *Gradualia* (motet sections intended to form an impressive scheme of complete Mass Propers). His secular songs predate the true madrigal; they use intricate, flowing counterpoint derived from an earlier English style (e.g. Tallis, Taverner) and range from solemn lamentations to exuberant jests. His instrumental music is specially important: the many consort songs greatly influenced the later lute ayre, while the virginal pieces are unparalleled in richness of invention and contrapuntal brilliance. In all the genres in which he wrote Byrd was both traditionalist and innovator, channelling continental ideas into a native English tradition, and his expressive range was unusually wide for his day. He wrote for both Catholic and Anglican churches with equal genius.

Sacred vocal music Cantiones sacrae, 5–8vv (1575) [with Tallis]; Cantiones sacrae, 5–6vv (2 vols.) (1589–91); 3 masses, 3–5vv, *c*1592–5; Gradualia, 3–6vv (2 vols.) (1605–7); 4 services, incl. Great Service, Short Service; anthems; Anglican liturgical settings
Vocal chamber music Psalmes, Sonets and Songs, 5vv (1588); Songs of Sundrie Natures, 3–6vv (1589); Psalmes, Songs and Sonnets, 3–6vv (1611); *c*50 consort songs
Instrumental music (viol consort) 14 fantasias, grounds, dances, 2 In Nomines, a 4–5; 10; hymn and Miserere settings, a 3–4
Keyboard music 11 fantasias; 14 variations; dances, incl. 20 pavans and galliards; grounds; descriptive pieces; some in Parthenia (1612–13), many in My Ladye Nevells Booke and the Fitzwilliam Virginal Book

Byström, Oscar Fredrik Bernadotte (*b* Stockholm, 13 Oct 1821; *d* there, 22 July 1909). Swedish composer. A teacher and church musician in Stockholm and an orchestral conductor in Turku, he wrote chamber works and a Symphony in D minor (1870–72) showing the influence of his friend Franz Berwald.

Byzantine rite, Music of the. Music of the liturgical rite of the Christian Roman Empire of the East from the time of the establishment of Constantinople (at the site of ancient Byzantium) in the early 4th century until the Ottoman conquest in 1453. The rite has remained the dominant liturgy of the Christian East during the past 1500 years. It is the only Eastern rite that fully survives in early MSS, in complete systems of musical notation, and is thus comparable to the repertories of the Roman and Milanese churches in the West. Chant MSS date from the 9th-century to the 15th, while lectionaries of biblical readings with EKPHONETIC NOTATION began in the 8th. Melodic notation comprises signs or digits and embodies a rich vocabulary of rhythmic and dynamic nuance. Most chants are assigned to one of the eight musical modes (OKTŌĒCHOS) with associated psalm tones (related to those of the West); many chants synthesize a large number of melodic formulae (CENTONIZATION). Hymnody far exceeded that of the psalmodic chants and most examples are strophic, with accentual rather than metric verse.

There are three main forms of syllabic Byzantine hymn writing: the *kontakion*, a long metrical sermon, often of 20–30 stanzas, cultivated in the 5th–6th centuries; the *kanon*, an elaborate nine-section poetic trope on the nine biblical canticles of the Byzantine Morning Service, used from the 7th century; and the *sticherarion*, choral interpolations in the concluding verses of the psalms, also from the 7th century. Two related classes of hymn are transmitted in a classic florid and formulaic style: the early *kontakia* (before its 9th-century simplification) and the *hypakoai* (shorter one-strophe hymns). From the 12th century, traditional styles gave way to a new, post-classic stylization, with extravagant embellishments (the 'kalophonic style').

The Divine Liturgy of the Byzantine rite corresponds to the Mass of the Roman rite. The term 'liturgy' is confined to the consecration prayers (anaphora), followed by the communion and dismissal rites. The Greek rite has three liturgies in normal use; two contain anaphora prayers attributed to St Basil (major feasts) and St John Chrysostom (ordinary feasts), almost identical in content and structure, and the third represents the Lent ceremonial when no consecration takes place.

C

C. Name of a note, or a PITCH CLASS; *see also* PITCH NAMES. It is the keynote of the scale in white notes on a keyboard; it is also taken as a standard because it represents the pitch class corresponding to powers of 2 in cycles per second (Hz) and vibrating lengths measured in feet also corresponding to powers of 2: thus middle C (the central note between the treble and bass staves) represents 256 Hz and a vibrating tube or string length of 2' (both only approximate by present-day pitch standards).

The letter C is used as a time signature to denote 4/4; this is not (as is sometimes said) an abbreviation for 'common' time but rather a relic of the broken circle of early mensural notation (*see* NOTATION and TIME SIGNATURES). C with a vertical line through it represents 2/2 time in modern usage.

Caamaño, Roberto (*b* Buenos Aires, 7 July 1923). Argentinian pianist and composer. He has appeared as a pianist throughout Latin America, Europe and the USA, and held posts at the Buenos Aires Conservatory (from 1956) and the Catholic University of Argentina (from 1966). In 1960–63 he was artistic director of the Teatro Colón. Besides numerous religious works and songs, he has written two piano concertos and prizewinning string pieces.

Cabaca. A rattle-type percussion instrument, consisting of a gourd covered with a network of beads, with a handle; it is used in the Latin American dance band and occasionally in orchestral music.

Cabaletta (It.). The concluding fast section of an extended ARIA or duet.

Caballé, Montserrat (*b* Barcelona, 12 April 1933). Spanish soprano. She studied at the Barcelona Liceo and made her concert début in 1954. After opera engagements at Basle and Bremen, and guest appearances in Milan, Vienna and Lisbon, she sang Donizetti's Lucrezia Borgia in a New York concert performance. Thereafter her pure legato, long-breathed phrases and ability to float soft, high notes have made her a leading Verdi and Donizetti soprano. She sang Gounod's Marguerite at the Met in 1965; her Covent Garden début was in 1972, as Violetta.

Cabanilles, Juan Bautista José (*b* Algemesi, 1644; *d* Valencia, 29 April 1712). Spanish composer. Organist at Valencia Cathedral from 1644, he represents the high point in the Iberian organ tradition

begun by Cabezón. Most of his organ pieces are tientos, often a series of imitative sections on different themes employing elaborate counter-point and using the upper and lower manuals independently to give a solo character to one hand. He excelled at an unornamented form featuring sharp dissonance with unusual melodic intervals and harmonies. Eight sacred choral works also survive.

Cabezón, Antonio de (*b* Castrillo de Matajudíos, 1510; *d* Madrid, 26 March 1566). Spanish organist and composer. Blind and of noble extraction, he was educated in Palencia, appointed organist to Queen Isabella and later performed in the Spanish chamber consort of Charles V. After Isabella's death in 1539 he served Philip II, whom he accompanied on numerous journeys abroad, both influencing and being influenced by foreign music. Cabezón ranked among the foremost keyboard performers and composers of his time. His compositions, most of them printed by his son Hernando in 1578, include tientos (short imitative works), glosas (keyboard versions of vocal pieces), *diferencias* (variation cycles mostly based on Spanish cancionero tunes), *falsobordone*, versos, canons and hymns. He created an idiomatic keyboard style, free of empty rhetoric and stereotyped figuration, and through the masterly use of dissonances, chromaticism and harmonic–melodic tension developed a language of expressive intensity, coloured by daring modulations. His brother Juan (1510/19–1566) and two sons, Augustín (*d* before 1564) and Hernando (1541–1602) were also musicians at the Spanish court.

Caccia (It.: 'hunt', 'chase'; pl. *cacce*). A poetic and musical genre cultivated in Italy in the 14th and early 15th centuries. The texts describe hunting scenes, occasionally of an allegorical nature (e.g. love pursuits). The music usually consists of a texted canon for the upper voices, reflecting the hunting theme, accompanied (unlike the French CHACE) by an independent tenor. Some, through their textual or musical structure, show a relationship with the trecento madrigal.

Caccini, Giulio [Giulio Romano] (*b* Rome/Tivoli, *c*1545; *d* Florence, bur. 10 Dec 1618). Italian composer and singer. He studied with Giovanni Animuccia and attracted the attention of Cosimo I de' Medici, who took him to Florence and supported his studies there with Scipione delle Palle. From the mid-1570s Caccini attended the meetings of Bardi's Camerata and developed a new style of song which led to his being acclaimed as the 'inventor' of the *stile recitativo*. In 1600 he succeeded Cavalieri as musical director of the Medici court and employed the new style in his opera *Euridice*, written in rivalry to Peri's *Euridice* but not performed until two years later, in 1602. In that year Caccini's most famous work also appeared – *Le nuove musiche*, a collection of madrigals and strophic songs for solo voice and figured bass (containing also some of his music for *Il rapimento di Cefalo*, a pastoral performed in 1600 on Henri IV's marriage to Maria de' Medici). *Le nuove musiche* contains an important essay on the techniques of composing and singing in the new style, methods of expression, ornamentation etc; its most popular song, *Amarilli mia bella*, was arranged by several other composers. In 1614 Caccini issued a second collection, *Nuove musiche e nuova maniera di scriverle*.

Caccini's inventiveness as a singer and his gifts as a teacher kept his name alive well into the 17th century, and *Le nuove musiche* inspired a large number of similar collections by other composers. Caccini's two daughters, Francesca ('La Cecchina', 1587–?1640) and Settimia ('La Flora', 1591–?c1683), were both singers and composers.

Stage works Il rapimento di Cefalo (1600); Euridice (1602); parts of J. Peri's opera *Euridice* (1600); intermedio
Songs over 70 songs, many in Le nuove musiche (1602) and Nuove musiche e nuova maniera di scriverle (1614)

Cachucha. A popular fast, triple-time dance of Andalusia, related to the FLAMENCO and the FANDANGO. Sullivan included one in *The Gondoliers* (1889).

Cadéac, Pierre (*b* ?Cadéac; *fl* 1538–56). French composer and choirmaster. He was master of the choirboys in Auch, Gascony. Most of his ten four-voice chansons were printed in anthologies (1538–41); one of them, *Je suis deshéritée*, was later widely used as a model for parody pieces. His sacred works (seven masses, a Credo, four Magnificat settings and 32 motets) were mainly published in Paris in the 1550s.

Cadence. The conclusion or punctuation point in a musical phrase; the formula on which such a conclusion is based. Cadences are the most effective way of affirming or establishing the tonality of a passage. Four forms are common in tonal music. The *perfect cadence* (also called authentic or final cadence or full close), at the end of a phrase, moves from a dominant chord to a tonic one (V–I), both normally in root position (ex.1); some theorists require that the uppermost voice must sound the tonic in the final chord if a cadence is to rank as perfect. The *imperfect cadence* (half cadence, half close) ends on the dominant and may be preceded by any chord, often the tonic (ex.2). The *plagal cadence* is one in which the tonic is preceded by the subdominant (IV–I: ex.3). The *interrupted cadence* (deceptive cadence, false close), the name of which speaks for itself, moves irregularly from the dominant to an unexpected final chord other than the tonic, usually the subme-

diant (V–VI: ex.4). In the Phrygian cadence, related to the minor-key imperfect cadence, the lowest part descends to the final or tonic by a semitone step (from a so-called upper leading note). A cadence in which the first chord is inverted is sometimes called a medial cadence (or inverted cadence) as opposed to a radical cadence with root-position chords.

Cadent. Term for an ornament between two notes in which the second is anticipated, as in the anticipation of the final note at a cadence. Typical uses are shown in ex.1 (Simpson, 1659; *b* represents a

Ex. 1

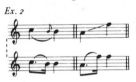

modern realization) and ex.2 (Marpurg, 1756). The German term is *Nachschlag*.

Ex. 2

Cadenza. A virtuoso passage near the end of a concerto movement or aria. The formal cadenza is a creation of the Baroque period. In *da capo* arias it was usually placed just before the final vocal cadence of the *A* section; aria cadenzas were usually brief, to be sung in a single breath. Instrumental cadenzas were mostly over a dominant pedal and in concerto movements they were usually inserted before the final ritornello (as in Bach's Harpsichord Concerto BWV1052).

In the Classical concerto the practice of indicating cadenzas by a fermata over a 6-4 chord became standard. Most early cadenzas were improvised and non-thematic, but in the 1780s Mozart began writing cadenzas thematically linked to the movement to which they belonged. With Beethoven thematic cadenzas became the norm, and in his Fifth Piano Concerto he wrote the cadenza into the score, a practice followed by most later composers (Brahms's Violin Concerto is an exception). Other later developments include the placing of cadenzas at other points (Mendelssohn's E minor Violin Concerto being an influential example) and the writing of accompanied cadenzas (by Schumann, Elgar, Walton and others).

Cadi dupé, Le (The Duped Cadi). Opéra comique in one act by Gluck to a libretto by Le Monnier (1761, Vienna); Monsigny had set the text in Paris earlier the same year.

Cadman, Charles Wakefield (*b* Johnstown, PA, 24 Dec 1881; *d* Los Angeles, 30 Dec 1946). American composer. He studied locally and *c*1909 became interested in American Indian music, which he recorded and arranged. In 1917 he settled in Los Angeles, and the next year his opera *Shanewis* was staged at the Met. His other works, within a conventional 19th-century style, include more operas and operettas, orchestral and chamber pieces and *c*180 songs, of which *At Dawning* was particularly popular.

Cadmus et Hermione. *Tragédie lyrique* in a prologue and five acts by Lully to a libretto by P. Quinault (1673, Paris): Lully's first *tragédie lyrique*.

Caduta de' giganti, La (The Fall of the Giants). Opera in two acts by Gluck to a libretto by Vanneschi (1746, London).

Caesar, Johann Melchior (*b* Saverne, *c*1648; *d* Augsburg, 18 Oct 1692). German composer. From 1683 he was Kapellmeister of Augsburg Cathedral, having held similar posts in Breslau and Würzburg. He wrote masses, psalms etc in the Italian concertante style, with instruments, and secular vocal pieces and dance suites showing marked French influence.

Cafaro, Pasquale (*b* S Pietro in Galatina, 8 Feb ?1716; *d* Naples, 25 Oct 1787). Italian composer. In 1745–71 he established himself in Naples as a respected composer of oratorios, operas, cantatas (some for court events) and church music. In 1771 he became *primo maestro* of the royal chapel and wrote only sacred works, notably a *Stabat mater* (1785). His seven operas, all serious, use a simple, graceful style akin to that of *opera buffa*.

Caffarelli [Majorano, Gaetano] (*b* Bitonto, 12 April 1710; *d* Naples, 31 Jan 1783). Italian mezzo-soprano castrato. He studied with Porpora at Naples and sang successfully in Italy from the late 1720s. From 1734 he was at the Naples royal chapel but also appeared in London (1737–8, creating roles in two Handel operas: 'Ombra mai fù' from *Serse*, 'Handel's Largo', was written for him), in Madrid, France, Lisbon and elsewhere; he was also a composer. As a singer he was ranked second only to Farinelli with an enchanting voice and fine execution, but his arrogance made him unpopular.

Caffi, Francesco (*b* Venice, 14 June 1778; *d* Padua, 24 Jan 1874). Italian music historian. He studied the history of Venetian music before 1797, notably through collecting and arranging authentic material, his subjects including Marcello, Lotti and Zarlino. His most important publication was the *Storia della musica sacra* (1854–5).

Cage, John (*b* Los Angeles, 5 Sept 1912). American composer. He left Pomona College early to travel in Europe (1930–31), then studied with Cowell in New York (1933–4) and Schoenberg in Los Angeles (1934): his first published compositions, in a rigorous atonal system of his own, date from this period. In 1937 he moved to Seattle to work as a dance accompanist, and there in 1938 he founded a percussion orchestra; his music now concerned with filling units of time with ostinatos (*First Construction (in Metal)*, 1939). He also began to use electronic devices (variable-speed turntables in *Imaginary Landscape no.1*, 1939) and invented the 'prepared piano', placing diverse objects between the strings of a grand piano in order to create an effective percussion orchestra under the control of two hands. He moved to San Francisco in 1939, to Chicago in 1941 and back to New York in 1942, all the time writing music for dance companies, nearly always for prepared piano or percussion ensemble. There were also major concert works for the new instrument: *A Book of Music* (1944) and Three Dances (1945) for two prepared pianos, and the Sonatas and Interludes (1948) for one.

During this period Cage became interested in Eastern philosophies, especially in Zen, from which he gained a treasuring of non-intention. Working to remove creative choice from composition, he used coin tosses to determine events (*Music of Changes* for piano, 1951), wrote for 12 radios (*Imaginary Landscape no.4*, also 1951) and introduced other indeterminate techniques. His *4' 33"* (1952) has no sound added to that of the environment in which it is performed; the Concert for Piano and Orchestra (1958) is an encyclopedia of indeterminate notations. Yet other works show his growing interest in the theatre of musical performance (*Water Music*, 1952, for pianist with a variety of non-standard equipment) and in electronics (*Imaginary Landscape no.5* for randomly mixed recordings, 1952; *Cartridge Music* for small sounds amplified in live performance, 1960), culminating in various large-scale events staged as jamborees of haphazardness (*HPSCHD* for harpsichords, tapes etc (1969). The later output is various, including indeterminate works, others fully notated within a very limited range of material, and pieces for natural resources (plants, shells). Cage has also appeared widely in Europe and the USA as a lecturer and performer, having an enormous influence on younger musicians and artists, and has written several books.

Orchestral music Conc., prepared pf, chamber orch (1951); Concert for Pf and Orch (1958); Atlas eclipticalis (1961); Renga (1976); 30 Pieces for 5 Orchs (1981); A Collection of Rocks (1984)
Instrumental music Amores, 2 prepared pf, 3 perc trios (1943); Str Qt (1950); Freeman Etudes, vn (1980)
Piano music Music of Changes (1951); Music for Pf 1–84 (1952–6); Water Music (1952); Winter Music (1957); Cheap Imitation (1969); Etudes australes (1975)
Prepared piano Bacchanale (1940); The Perilous Night (1944); Sonatas and Interludes (1948); many others
Percussion First, Second, Third Construction (1939, 1940, 1941); Credo in Us (1942); Imaginary Landscape no.2 (1942)
Electronic Imaginary Landscape nos.1, 3, 4, 5 (1939, 1942, 1951, 1952); Williams Mix (1952); Fontana Mix (1958); Cartridge Music (1960); Rozart Mix (1965); HPSCHD (1969); Roaratorio (1979)
Vocal music The Wonderful Widow of Eighteen Springs (1942); Aria (1958); Song Books (1970)
Indeterminate resources 4' 33" (1952); Variations I–VII (1958–66); Musicircus (1967)

Cagnoni, Antonio (*b* Godiasco, 8 Feb 1828; *d* Bergamo, 30 April 1896). Italian composer. He studied in Voghera and at the Milan Conservatory, where his inventive and fluent opera *Don Bucefalo* (1847) was a success. Among his later 15 operas, *Michele Perrin* (1864), *Claudia* (1866) and the well-received *Francesca da Rimini* (1878) show experiments with modern techniques, including mildly dissonant harmonies and the use of leitmotifs. He held church appointments and wrote a notable Requiem (1888).

Cahen, Albert [Cahen d'Anvers] (*b* Paris, 8 Jan 1846; *d* Cap d'Ail, 23 Feb 1903). French composer. One of Franck's first pupils, he wrote principally for the voice in a rich, melodic style, his best-known works being the opera *Le vénitien* (1890) and the song collection *Marines* (*c*1878).

Căianu, Ioan (*b* Leghea, 8 March 1627; *d* Estelnic, 1698). Transylvanian anthologist and organ builder. He held numerous administrative posts and is important for his *Cantionale Catholicum*, a collection of hymn texts (1676) which ran into many editions, and for the two MS organ anthologies he compiled, one with masses and litanies, the other (lost) with sacred and secular songs and dances, including music by western composers.

Caietain, Fabrice Marin (*b*?Gaëta, *fl* 1570–78). Italian composer. After studies in Italy he became choirmaster at Toul Cathedral (1570) and of the Duke of Lorraine's private chapel (1576), and possibly of St Georges, Nancy. He travelled extensively, meeting Baïf in Paris; his two books of *airs* (1576, 1578) show the influence of *musique mesurée*. He also wrote motets and *chansons* (both 1571).

Caimo, Gioseppe (*b* Milan, *c*1545; *d* there, ? by 31 Oct 1584). Italian composer. He was organist of S Ambrogio Maggiore, Milan (1564) and of Milan Cathedral from 1580, and visited the Bavarian court. Much of his music is lost; three books of madrigals (1564, 2 in 1584) and two of lighter secular works (1566, 1584) show Vicentino's influence.

Caix, François-Joseph de (*b* Lyons, late 17th century; *d* there, after 1751). French viol player. He played in the orchestra at Lyons until 1730, then entered the service of Louis XV with his five children (also violists), among them Marie-Anne Ursule (1715–51), Barthélemy (1716–?) and Paul (1717–?). Paul settled in Lyons as a teacher; Barthélemy, a *pardessus* player who composed six duet sonatas, went to Lyons (1738) but returned to royal service in 1748.

Caix d'Hervelois, Louis de (*b*?1670–80; *d c*1760). French composer. He worked in Paris and (with Marais and Forqueray) was one of the finest performer-composers of the French bass viol school. Most of his music for one and two bass viols was published in five collections (1719–48), the earlier pieces solidly in the French tradition while later ones attempted to incorporate elements of the new Italian manner. At his best in brief dance movements and character pieces, he combined to good effect a genuine melodic gift with the instrumental imagination of a virtuoso, though he rarely achieved the expressive depth of his peers.

Caja. Frame drum, sometimes with snare, of Spain and the New World.

Cajun music. The folk music of the French-speaking Acadians (i.e. 'Cajuns') of south-western Louisiana, largely from Canada; it was originally French but has absorbed elements of the music of southern whites and blacks. The fiddle and the accordion are favourite instruments.

Cakewalk. A dance of black American 19th-century origin, probably originated by slaves parodying their owners' behaviour. It featured a couple's prancing and strutting arm in arm and was popularized in blackface minstrel shows with syncopated, ragtime-like music. Debussy included a 'Golliwog's Cakewalk' in his *Children's Corner* (1908), for piano.

Calando (It.). 'Lowering', 'dropping': an instruction to make the music die away in volume and sometimes also in tempo.

Calata. An Italian dance, in use from the 15th century to the early 17th. Most of the surviving examples are in triple or compound metre.

Caldara, Antonio (*b* Venice, *c*1670; *d* Vienna, 28 Dec 1736). Italian composer. He was a chorister at St Mark's, Venice, and proficient on the viol, cello and keyboard. In the 1690s he began writing operas, oratorios and cantatas; his trio sonatas opp.1 and 2 (1693, 1699) are his only known instrumental chamber works. He served as *maestro di cappella da chiesa e dal teatro* to the Duke of Mantua, 1699–1707, and *maestro di cappella* to Prince Ruspoli in Rome between 1709 and 1716, meanwhile composing for other cities. From 1716 until his death he was vice-Kapellmeister at the Viennese court. He was much favoured there for his dramatic works, cantatas, liturgical music and oratorios; latterly he also composed stage works for the Vienna Carnival, for court celebrations and for Salzburg. His output (over 3000 works, almost all vocal) was one of the largest of his generation. His operas and oratorios make him a central figure in the creation of music drama in the tradition of Metastasio, many of whose texts he was the first to set.

Calegari, Antonio (*b* Padua, 17 Feb 1757; *d* there, 22/28 July 1828). Italian composer. The most popular Paduan composer of his time, he wrote successful stage works beginning with a *festa teatrale, Deucalione e Pirra* (1781), besides oratorios, cantatas and sacred music. As organist (1801–14) and then *maestro di cappella* at S Antonio, he also wrote church music. Among his writings are treatises on harmony, singing and composing by throwing dice. His brother Giuseppe (*c*1750–1812), a cellist in the S Antonio orchestra, composed stage works, oratorios and cantatas, and in 1787–1801 was intermittently impresario of Padua's Teatro Nouvo; Antonio's nephew Luigi Antonio (*c*1780–1849) wrote dramatic works including *Amor soldato* (1807) a successful comic opera, and a tragedy *Saul* (1821, Venice) for solo voices, chorus and two pianos.

Calegari, Francesco Antonio (*b* Venice, 1656; *d* there, 12 Nov 1742). Italian composer and theorist, probably unrelated to the foregoing. A Franciscan monk, he was a *maestro di cappella* in Venice (1701–3, 1727 onwards), and at S Antonio, Padua (1703–27). He wrote polyphonic sacred works and several treatises. His *Ampla dimostrazione degli armoniali musicali tuoni* (1732) expounds a harmonic theory similar to Rameau's; its daring treatment of dissonance is reflected in Calegari's later style.

Calestani, Vincenzo (*b* Lucca, 10 March 1589; *d c*1617). Italian composer. He worked at Pisa. His *Madrigali et arie . . . parto primo* (1617), for one and two voices and continuo, dedicated to his pupil Isabella Mastiani, is one of the most attractive and varied Italian songbooks of the time, with songs that are catchy or melodically sensuous and madrigals distinguished by expansive declamation and pliable rhythms.

Calife de Bagdad, Le. Opera in one act by Boieldieu to a libretto by Saint-Just (1800, Paris).

Calisto. Opera by Cavalli to a libretto by Faustini after Ovid (1651/2, Venice).

Calixtinus Codex. MS, probably from central France, of the period c1139–73. Of 195 folios, it contains liturgical music (connected with the feasts of St James) and conductus and is among the earliest sources of polyphony. It was largely written by one scribe, in Aquitanian neume notation. According to legend, it was prepared by Pope Calixtus II (1119–24): hence its name. It is now in the cathedral library at Santiago de Compostela, where practically all of it has been since 1173.

Callas [Kalogeropoulou], (Cecilia Sophia Anna) Maria (b New York, 2/4 Dec 1923; d Paris, 16 Sept 1977). Greek soprano. Greek by parentage, she left the USA in 1937 to study at the Athens Conservatory. She made her début as Tosca (1941, Athens) but wide acclaim did not come until she sang Gioconda at the Verona Arena (1947). Her early repertory included Wagner but she soon became identified with *bel canto* roles, singing Norma at her London (1952) and New York (1956) débuts. Her voice, with its penetrating individual quality and rich variety of colour, had great agility in florid music; she also had exceptional dramatic talent, a combination that made her pre-eminent. Her vocal powers declined, leading her to retire from the stage in 1965. She gave master classes in New York (1971–2) and made a final concert tour in 1973–4. During her marriage to G.B. Meneghini she was known as Maria Meneghini Callas.

Callcott, John Wall (b Kensington, 20 Nov 1766; d Bristol, 15 May 1821). English composer. He was an organist in London from the 1780s and a prolific, prizewinning composer of glees and other part-songs. He also wrote songs, anthems, music for a play and, less successfully, instrumental works; in 1791 he studied briefly with Haydn. Later he grew interested in earlier music, writing a Latin cantata (1800) and an Italian madrigal, and beginning a music dictionary; his *Musical Grammar* (1806) was a popular instruction book.

Calliope. A type of steam organ, invented in the USA in 1855 for outdoor use (on riverboats, at fairgrounds, on parades); a series of whistles is controlled either from a keyboard or on the barrel-organ principle.

Calm Sea and Prosperous Voyage [Meeresstille und glückliche Fahrt]. Overture (op.27) by Mendelssohn (1828).

Calvé [Calvet] (de Roquer), (Rosa-Noémie) Emma (b Decazeville, 15 Aug 1858; d Millau, 6 Jan 1942). French soprano. In the 1890s she was an international favourite, especially in London and New York, where her Santuzza and above all her Carmen were considered incomparable. Massenet

wrote Anita in *La navarraise* (1894) and Fanny in *Sapho* (1897) for her. Her voice was remarkable for its combination of steadiness with rich colour.

Calvin, Jean (b Noyon, 10 July 1509; d Geneva, 27 May 1564). French theologian. He was one of the leaders of the Reformation in Switzerland. He studied in France and was converted to reformed doctrines c1530. He was persuaded to help with church organization in Geneva, but in 1538 the city authorities forced him to leave because of his excessive zeal and strictness. He went to Basle and then to Strasbourg, where unison congregational singing had been established. An anthology of music for the Lutheran refugees there was published under his guidance in 1539, and a similar collection, the so-called First Genevan Psalter, appeared in Geneva in 1542, the year after he returned. Expanded editions, with translations by Marot and de Béze and music by Bourgeois, appeared in 1543 and 1551, the final version (sometimes called the Genevan or Huguenot psalter), with 125 tunes, appearing in Geneva, Paris, Lyons and elsewhere in 1562. Calvin insisted that all music in the service should be monophonic, since polyphony distracted the congregation from the words. Instrumental music was likewise excluded and the vernacular was to be used for all church worship. His musical ideals and his psalter rapidly gained support in other countries, and polyphonic psalm settings by such composers as Goudimel, Le Jeune, Clemens non Papa and Sweelinck gained in popularity.

Calvisius, Sethus (b Gorsleben, 21 Feb 1556; d Leipzig, 24 Nov 1615). German music theorist. He was one of the most influential of his time. Educated at the universities of Helmstedt and Leipzig, he was Kantor in Leipzig (1581–2 and from 1594 at St Thomas's), and Schulpforta (1582–94). His *Melopoeia* (1592) was one of the first German treatises to transmit Zarlino's ideas comprehensibly; his other writings are mainly pedagogical. He composed hymns, psalm settings and motets.

Calypso. A style of music, dance and song of the south and east Caribbean (particularly Trinidad), evolved from African and West Indian folk music. Calypso music resembles the Latin American samba.

Calzabigi, Raniero (Simone Francesco Maria) de (b Livorno, 23 Dec 1714; d Naples, July 1795). Italian writer and librettist. His first librettos, written in the 1740s, resemble those of Metastasio, whose works he began to edit in Paris in the 1750s. From 1751 he lived in Vienna, where he played a decisive role in Gluck's reforms, writing the librettos for *Orfeo ed Euridice* (1762), *Alceste* (1767) and *Paride ed Elena* (1770). With the choreographer Angiolini he also wrote a preface to Gluck's ballet *Don Juan* (1761). In c1773 he returned to Italy; in his last librettos, *Elfrida* and *Elvira* (both set by Paisiello), he reverted to the Metastasian style.

Camargo, La. *See* CUPIS DE CAMARGO family.

Cambefort, Jean de (b c1605; d Paris, 4 May 1661). French composer. A musician at the French court under Mazarin from 1642, and later in the service of Louis XIV, he was a skilled singer, and composer of *airs* remarkable both for their free, soaring lyrical qualities and for the way their melodies fit the rules of prosody (thus anticipating Lully). He wrote the music sung in the *Ballet de la nuit* (1653) and was one of the last composers of *airs de cour*.

Cambert, Robert (*b* Paris, *c*1627; *d* London, Feb/March 1677). French composer. He studied under Chambonnières and became organist of St Honore in 1652; ten years later he became a composer to the queen mother, Anne of Austria. Working with the poet Pierre Perrin (*c*1620–1675), he wrote dramatic works, notably *La pastorale* (1659), which was performed in the village of Issy and claimed as the 'Première Comédie Françoise en Musique' (in fact, another work of the kind dates from 1655). *Ariane* (written in the same year) followed, and then *Pomone*, given in 1671 and considered to be the first French opera; it was well received and was soon followed by *Les peines et les plaisirs de l'amour*. But in 1672, when Lully secured a royal privilege for dramatic music, Cambert was effectively barred from further work; he went to London in 1673, where *Ariane* was performed in 1674. *Pomone* and a ballet were given at Windsor before Charles II that year, but Cambert's position deteriorated. He may have been assassinated (by Lully's agent, it has been said), or if that term was used metaphorically he may have died from grief. Probably he wrote sacred and organ music, but all that is known other than his dramatic works is a handful of airs, duets and trios. His surviving dramatic music suggests a composer with a keen sense of the affective aspect of a text.

Cambiare (It.). 'To change': an instruction in orchestral parts for a woodwind player to change to another instrument, a brass player to another crook, a timpanist to another tuning.

Cambiata. *See* NOTA CAMBIATA.

Cambini, Giuseppe Maria (Gioacchino) (*b* Livorno, ?13 Feb 1746; *d* ?Paris, 1825). Italian composer and violinist. He performed at the Paris Concert Spirituel in 1773 and soon achieved great popularity as an instrumental composer, publishing over 500 works. He was also active in Parisian theatres, writing some 14 stage works in addition to oratorios and other vocal music. During the Revolution he composed popular hymns and odes; his career declined after 1800. Foremost in his output are over 150 string quartets (1773–1809) and over 80 *symphonies concertantes*, fluently written in the tuneful and brilliant French idiom of the time. His other instrumental music includes concertos, string quintets, trios, duos and sonatas, many for strings.

Camden, Archie [Archibald] (Leslie) (*b* Newark-upon-Trent, 9 March 1888; *d* Wheathampstead, 16 Feb 1979). English bassoonist. He studied in Manchester and joined the Hallé Orchestra in 1906, becoming principal in 1914. He played with the BBC SO (1933–45) and later as a soloist. He was an influential teacher and did much to raise standards of playing and popularize the bassoon.

Camden Festival (UK). Annual (Feb-March) festival established in 1953 as part of St Pancras Arts Festival (later Camden Festival) in London. Events included rarely performed operas, contemporary jazz and music in historic buildings. It ceased in 1987.

Camera (It.). 'Chamber': in Baroque sonatas and concertos the term 'da camera' normally indicated the inclusion of dance movements, in contrast to the 'da CHIESA' ('church') type.

Camerata. A group of noblemen and musicians who met at the home of Count Giovanni de' Bardi in Florence, *c*1573–87, to discuss poetry, music and the sciences. Caccini, Vincenzo Galilei and Piero Strozzi were among them. Their desire to re-create ancient Greek drama with music led to the earliest experiments in opera (e.g. *Dafne*, 1598; *Euridice*, 1600).

Camerloher, Placidus Cajetan von (*b* Murnau, 9 Aug 1718; *d* Freising, 21 July 1782). German composer. Kapellmeister at the Freising court from 1744, he served in the 1750s as director of chamber music at Liège. His instrumental output includes over 50 symphonies and chamber works, similar in style to Italian and Mannheim music; he also wrote Singspiels, meditations and sacred pieces. His expressive writing resembles that of the church music of Haydn and Mozart.

Camidge, Matthew (*b* York, bap. 25 May 1764; *d* there, 23 Oct 1844). English composer. His father was John Camidge (1734–1803), organist of York Minster and composer of harpsichord music and anthems. Matthew, who succeeded him, was famous as both performer and oratorio director at York festivals. Among his works are psalm and hymn tunes, other sacred music and keyboard sonatas (most with violin and cello accompaniment). His son John (1790–1859) and grandson Thomas (1828–1912) served as York Minster organists.

Cammarano, Salvatore (*b* Naples, 19 March 1801; *d* there, 17 July 1852). Italian librettist. Of a celebrated theatrical family, he collaborated with Donizetti (*Lucia di Lammermoor*, 1835, and others) and Verdi (*Luisa Miller*, 1849, most of *Il trovatore*, 1853), also producing *c*50 librettos for Pacini, Mercadante and many lesser composers; he was noted for his stagecraft and dramatic diction.

Cammer-Ton (Ger.). 'Chamber pitch': the pitch at which chamber music was performed in Germany in the Baroque period, probably around $a' = 410$–25. *See* PITCH.

Campagnoli, Bartolomeo (*b* Cento, 10 Sept 1751; *d* Neustrelitz, 7 Nov 1827). Italian violinist and composer. A noted player in Tartini's manner, he toured widely while in the service of German courts from 1776; in 1797–1818 he led the Leipzig Gewandhaus Orchestra. He wrote violin sonatas, duos etc and pedagogical works including fugues for violin solo, *41 caprices* for viola and a *Nouvelle méthode* for violin (1824).

Campanella, La. Liszt's *Transcendental Study* no.3 for piano, after Paganini, based on the third movement of Paganini's Violin Concerto no.2 in B minor.

Campion, Thomas (*b* London, bap. 12 Feb 1567; *d* there, bur. 1 March 1620). English composer and poet. A lawyer's son, he attended Peterhouse, Cambridge, and joined Gray's Inn in 1586. He also studied medicine, graduating at Caen University in 1605. By 1591 he was established in London as a writer and poet and from 1607 he supplied texts and music for James I's lavish court masques. He published c120 lute-songs, with his own texts, for solo voice with chordal accompaniment (1601, with P. Rosseter; 1613–14; 1617–18). The best of his melodies are elegant and distinctive and the matching of words and music is often exemplary. Campion also wrote a counterpoint treatise (1613–14).

Campioni, Carlo Antonio (*b* Lunéville, 16 Nov 1720; *d* Florence, 12 April 1788). Italian composer of French origin. *Maestro di cappella* at Livorno Cathedral and then at the grand ducal court in Florence, he composed many trio sonatas, requiems for the Austrian royal family and other sacred works.

Camp Meeting, The. Ives's Symphony no.3 (1904).

Campo (y Zabaleta), Conrado del (*b* Madrid, 28 Oct 1878; *d* there, 17 March 1953). Spanish composer. He studied at the Madrid Conservatory, where he was appointed professor of composition in 1915. His German interests (the late Beethoven quartets, Wagner and especially Strauss) are reflected in his many tone poems, operas and 12 string quartets.

Campos-Parsi, Héctor (*b* Ponce, 1 Oct 1922). Puerto Rican composer. He studied at the New England Conservatory (1947–50), with Copland and Messiaen at the Berkshire Music Center (1949–50) and with Boulanger at Fontainebleau (1951–3). He returned to Puerto Rico as a musical administrator and composer, of nationalist and internationalist (neo-classical, later aleatory and electronic) music.

Campra, André (*b* Aix-en-Provence, bap. 4 Dec 1660; *d* Versailles, 29 June 1744). French composer. He became a chaplain at Aix, then *maître de chapelle* at Arles (1681–3) and *maître de musique* at Toulouse (1683–94). Moving to Paris in 1694, he was *maître de musique* at Notre Dame Cathedral until 1700. Besides sacred music, he wrote for the Opéra, and with *L'Europe galante* (1697) created a popular new genre, the *opéra-ballet*. He became a 'conducteur' there in 1700, continuing to compose successful stage works until the 1730s. Louis XV granted him a pension in 1718; in 1722 he became music director to the Prince of Conti (for whom he wrote divertissements).

Campra's four *opéras-ballets*, notably *Les fêtes vénitiennes* (1710), show his musical style at its best, with strong, expressive characterization and imaginative dances. His ten *tragédies lyriques*, such as *Tancrède* (1702), have pictorial and dramatic effects which influenced Rameau. He expanded Lully's idiom with more orchestral and harmonic colour, Italianate melodic detail, concerto-like rhythms and da capo aria forms. Italian ideas also appear in his solo cantatas (three books, 1708–28), some of his motets (five books, 1695–1720) and other sacred works.

Campra's brother Joseph (1662–1744) played in the Opéra orchestra and later at Dijon, where two of his divertissements were staged; he also composed *airs*.

Canal, Marguerite (*b* Toulouse, 29 Jan 1890; *d* Cépet, 27 Jan 1978). French composer. She studied and later taught at the Paris Conservatoire

and was the first woman to conduct orchestral concerts in France (1917). She produced a small output of personally expressive songs and instrumental pieces.

Canale, Floriano (*b* Brescia, *c*1550; *fl* 1579–1603). Italian composer. An Augustinian monk, he was organist at S Giovanni Evangelista, Brescia (1581–1603). His publications include masses (1588), motets (1581, 1602, 1603) and psalms (1575), as well as secular and instrumental works (1600, 1601), all showing his skill and versatility.

Canary (Fr. *canarie*). A dance from the Canary Islands, popular in Europe during the Baroque period. Normally in 6/8 time, it resembled a fast gigue.

Cancan. A dance, apparently of Algerian origin, which came into vogue in Paris in the 1830s. The music, in a lively 2/4 time, is derived from the quadrille or galop. Offenbach was its most famous exponent.

Canción (Sp.: 'song'). From *c*1450 to *c*1530 the term was mainly used for a refrain song, like the VILLANCICO in form but often more contrapuntal and with a more serious poetic theme. During the 16th century the word was increasingly applied to settings of Italianate poems in Castilian, and sometimes to arrangements of French *chansons*. At other periods the term has been used interchangeably with other Spanish and Portuguese words for 'song'.

Cancionero (Sp.: 'songbook'). Term used from the 15th century for a collection or anthology of poems without music, whether intended for singing or not. The earliest is dated 1445. Most were compiled for learned or aristocratic readers; more mundane collections devoted to ballads (*romances*), dating from the mid-16th century, were for a wider public. The earliest songbooks with polyphonic music (now sometimes termed 'cancionero musical') were compiled *c*1480–1532 and contain partsongs based on pre-existent tunes. The most celebrated is the Cancionero Musical de Palacio (*c*1505–20), which represents the court musical repertory at the time of Ferdinand and Isabella.

Cancionero musical de Palacio. Spanish early 16th-century MS songbook, representing the court repertory at the time of Ferdinand and Isabella; 458 of its original 548 compositions survive, mostly villancicos for three or four voices, many by Juan del Encina. It is now in the Palacio Real Library, Madrid.

Cancrizans (Lat.). 'Crab-like': a part in a canon or other piece to be heard backwards. (Crabs in fact move sideways.)

Candeille, Pierre Joseph (*b* Estaires, 8 Dec 1744; *d* Chantilly, 24 April 1827). French composer. He was a choral singer in Paris in 1767–81 and from 1777 had stage works, motets and symphonies performed there. His *c*10 serious operas (e.g. *Pizarre*, 1785) have heroic subjects (unusual at the time) and include dramatic and spectacular effects; but only his revision of Rameau's *Castor et Pollux* (1791) achieved real success. He was choirmaster at the Opéra in 1800–02 and 1804–5, then retired to Chantilly.

His daughter and pupil Julie (1767–1834) appeared in Paris from the late 1770s as an opera singer, pianist and harpist; she composed a *symphonie concertante* (1786) and wrote words and music to several comedies including the successful *Catherine* (1792).

Candide. Comic operetta by Bernstein to a libretto by several authors after Hellman and Voltaire (1956, New York).

Canis, Cornelius (*b* Flanders, *c*1510–20; *d* Prague, 15 Feb 1561). Flemish composer. By 1547 he had succeeded Gombert as *maistre des enfans* of the imperial chapel, with which he had been connected at least since 1542; he may also have served Mary of Hungary. He seems to have left the court shortly before Charles V's abdication (1555–6) and in 1557 was appointed chaplain of St Martin and canon of Notre Dame, Courtrai, but apparently died while in Emperor Ferdinand I's service. His surviving works (mostly in MSS) include two masses, 32 motets for three to six voices and 29 *chansons*. The sacred music exploits a wide range of contrapuntal procedures; some of the *chansons* are based on pre-existent models, while others combine elements of the Parisian and Franco-Flemish styles.

Cannabich, (Johann) Christian (Innocenz Bonaventura) (*b* Mannheim, bap. 28 Dec 1731; *d* Frankfurt, 20 Jan 1798). German composer. He played the violin in the Mannheim court orchestra from 1744, went to study with Jommelli in the 1750s, and by 1758 was Mannheim court ballet composer and Konzertmeister. As court director of instrumental music (from 1774), he brought the orchestra to the height of its fame, training it in an even bowing style. He was influential as a violin teacher, and was a friend of the visiting Mozart, who wrote a piano sonata for his daughter. Moving with the court to Munich in 1778, he amalgamated the Mannheim and Munich orchestras. Financial problems later forced him to undertake concert tours.

Cannabich's *galant*, melodious style and rich orchestration serve well in his *c*40 ballets such as *Les mariages des Samnites* (1772). Of his *c*100 symphonies the later ones show a preference for minor keys. He also wrote various chamber works (quartets, duets etc).

His father, Martin Friedrich (?1675–after 1759), was a flautist in the Mannheim orchestra and composed flute pieces, while his son and pupil Carl (1771–1806), a violinist who played at Munich (from 1798 as Konzertmeister) and Frankfurt, wrote in a Mozartian style, violin concertos and other orchestral music, two operas and a cantata in Mozart's memory.

Cannon, (Jack) Philip (*b* Paris, 21 Dec 1929). English composer. He studied with Jacob at the RCM (1948–51), where in 1960 he was appointed professor. His works include *Oraison funèbre de l'âme humaine* for strings (1970).

Canon. Strictly, an inscribed formula by which polyphony is derived from a single line through strict imitation at fixed or (less often) variable intervals of pitch and time; since the 16th century the term has been used for the work itself. Special types include the 'rota' or ROUND, the CANCRIZANS and the MIRROR CANON.

In the 14th century canonic writing flourished in such genres as the CACCIA and the RONDELLUS, reaching an apex in Machaut's works. The Flemish masters of the 15th century employed it with increasing complexity, but its creative importance declined in the 16th century although its role as a subject for study began to grow. The teaching of counterpoint in the 17th century found expression in such collections as Thiele's *Kunstbuch*, a compendium of canonic art which points to the final phase of Bach's music. Canonic techniques had little place in the music of the symphonic era or in the Romantic period, but the neo-classical and serial schools of the 20th century have restored their place.

The word canon (or canun) was used in western Europe from the 12th century to the 14th for derivatives of the Perso-Arab plucked zither, *qānūn*.

Canso. Provençal term for 'song', used by troubadours of the 12th–13th centuries, particularly for strophic songs about courtly love.

Cantabile (It.). Singable, in a singing style.

Cantata. The most important genre of vocal chamber music in the Baroque period; the principal musical constituent of the Lutheran service. Since the late 18th century the term has been applied to a wide variety of works, sacred and secular, mostly for chorus and orchestra, from Beethoven's cantatas on the death and succession of emperors to the patriotic Soviet cantatas of Shostakovich.

In Italy the word 'cantata', first used for strophic variations in the *Cantade et arie* of Alessandro Grandi (i), soon came to be applied to pieces alternating recitative, arioso and aria-like sections. From *c*1650 this was the usual pattern, but the main cantata writers of the early 17th century, Luigi Rossi and Marazzoli, preferred the *arietta corte*, a single aria with changes of metre. Both these composers worked in Rome, the chief centre for the cantata in the 17th century, where Carissimi, one of the form's first great masters, was also active. In the early cantatas of his pupil, Alessandro Scarlatti, and those of Stradella and Steffani, the distinction between recitative and aria is clear and the number of sections usually smaller. By the end of the century historical, classical and humorous subjects were almost entirely swamped by Arcadian verses describing amatory feelings in a pastoral setting. The *cantata spirituale* set a sacred text in the vernacular.

In Scarlatti's cantatas after *c*1700, the structure is standardized as two or three da capo arias separated by recitative. Most are for soprano and continuo. This type was cultivated by other Italians, including Bassani, G. Bononcini, Vivaldi and B. Marcello, and by Handel during his Italian visit (1705/6–10). Many of Handel's cantatas, however, are distinguished from the Italians' in tonal structure and dramatic power. The later development of the Italian cantata was largely in the hands of such Neapolitan opera composers as Leo, Vinci and Pergolesi, in whose works full string accompaniment becomes the norm.

In Germany, the *Kantate* was primarily a sacred genre, though the term itself was not generally used during the Baroque period. A step towards the cantata as a multi-sectional form was taken in psalm compositions by Tunder, Buxtehude and others, whose chorale settings are akin to true cantatas since they use a closed form for each stanza. But it was the mixing of texts, especially biblical and poetic texts in what has been called the 'concerto–aria' cantata, that decisively established the German form.

Some of Bach's cantatas are retrospective in their use of a plain chorale text, but most show the effects of Neumeister's reforms of *c*1700, with recitative and *da capo* aria dominant constituents. Cantatas were composed in high numbers – Telemann and Graupner both wrote well over 1000 – and usually grouped into annual cycles. Bach's are untypical in their quality and their diversity. In the hands of lesser composers the genre became increasingly standardized, and in the later 18th century the petrifying of structures and the allegorical texts made it seem outmoded and fossilized.

Secular cantatas in German and Italian were composed by Keiser, Telemann, Bach and others, but this type was never cultivated to the extent it was in Italy.

In France and England the secular cantata was essentially an 18th-century genre, emulating the Italian type. J.B. Morin is credited with introducing the French *cantate* in his first book (1706). It set the pattern for French cantatas of the next two decades, with three arias, each introduced by recitative; mythological and amatory texts were favoured. Of later cantatas Clérambault's are among the finest. Rameau also wrote cantatas before 1733, after which the genre declined in favour of the new, shorter Rococo *cantatille*.

The English cantata arose largely from a desire on the part of 18th-century poets and composers to demonstrate the suitability of their language to Italianate recitative and aria styles. J.C. Pepusch claimed his *Six English Cantatas* (1710) as the first of their kind; his two sets are among the best. After 1740, the Italianate structure was relaxed and the English penchant for light, agreeable melody asserted itself. The change, seen in Stanley's cantatas, is complete in Arne's set of 1755 which, with their accompaniments of full strings and woodwind, mark the end of the cantata as a chamber form in England.

Cantata academica (Carmen basiliense). Choral work by Britten (1959); composed for the 500th anniversary of Basle University, it has a Latin text by Bernhard Wyss in praise of Basle.

Cantata profana. Choral work by Bartók to his own text after a Romanian hunting *colinda* (1930).

Cante hondo [cante jondo] (Sp.). Generic term for the oldest songs of the flamenco tradition, from the Andalusian region of southern Spain. 'Hondo' means deep or profound; *cante hondo* refers to a vocal timbre and is usually taken also to refer to a range of types.

Cantelli, Guido (*b* Novara, 27 April 1920; *d* Paris, 24 Nov 1956). Italian conductor. He studied at the Milan Conservatory. After conducting at La Scala he was invited by Toscanini to conduct the NBC SO (New York, 1949). His British début was with the La Scala orchestra, at the 1950 Edinburgh Festival, and in 1951 he began an association with the Philharmonia Orchestra. His Italianate verve was tempered by a sensitivity to nuance and balance of timbre.

Canteloube (de Calaret), (Marie) Joseph (*b* Annonay, 21 Oct 1879; *d* Gridny, 4 Nov 1957). French composer. He studied with d'Indy at the Schola Cantorum and collected and arranged folksongs from throughout France, especially from his native province (four volumes of *Chants d'Auvergne* for voice and orchestra, 1923–30). He also wrote two operas and other works.

Canti carnascialeschi (It.). 'Carnival songs': term for the songs sung out of doors during Carnival and the Calendimaggio (1 May–24 June) in Florence, *c*1480–*c*1515; *c*70 survive complete.

Canticle. A designation for hymns in the scriptures apart from the psalms. Three New Testament canticles are used in the Roman rite: *Benedictus* (*Luke* i.68–79) at Lauds, *Magnificat* (*Luke* i.46–55) at Vespers, and *Nunc dimittis* (*Luke* ii.29–32) at Compline. In the Anglican rite the name 'canticle' is also used for psalms and hymns (including the *Venite* and *Te Deum*) sung daily at Morning and Evening Prayer.

Canticum sacrum (ad honorem Sancti Marci nominis). Choral work by Stravinsky, a setting of a biblical text, first performed at St Mark's, Venice, in 1956.

Canti di prigionia. Choral work by Dallapiccola to texts by Queen Mary Stuart, Boethius and Savonarola (1941).

Cantiga. A Spanish and Portuguese medieval monophonic song. Apart from six love-songs by MARTIN CODAX, the only surviving music is a collection of over 400 songs made *c*1250–80 under the direction of Alfonso el Sabio and known as the *Cantigas de Santa Maria*. Most of them, with tunes probably of secular origin, are ballad-style accounts of miracles performed by the Blessed Virgin, but every tenth is a hymn in her praise. King Alfonso may have written some of the words and music himself. The texts and illustrations in the four surviving MSS provide valuable insight into methods of performance and other aspects of medieval life.

Cantilena. Latin term meaning 'song' or 'melody', used variously in the Middle Ages to refer to plainchant (especially chants with poetic texts rather than biblical prose) and non-ecclesiastical monophony. Because of its secondary meaning, the blending of two or more simultaneous melodic entities, it came to be applied to types of polyphony not based on a *cantus firmus*. These include English pieces of the late 13th and 14th centuries, characterized by harmony based on 3rds and 6ths and the techniques of voice-exchange and rondellus. The term is used in later music for a particularly sustained or lyrical vocal (usually solo) line; also an instrumental passage of similar character.

Cantillation. The musical or semi-musical chanting of sacred texts by a singer in a liturgical context; the term primarily refers to the Jewish synagogue tradition but is also used for comparable recitation in Christian and other rites.

Cantio. A monophonic Latin song of the later Middle

Ages, usually with a sacred text, but not strictly liturgical. Cantiones are strophic, usually with a repeating refrain rhyme, and combine features of chant and popular song.

Cantional. A collection of sacred songs; a hymnbook. The term is used especially for Czech collections (*kancionály*) and German Lutheran hymnbooks of the 16th and 17th centuries.

Cantiones sacrae (Lat.). 'Sacred songs': term used by many composers for their collections. Byrd used it for two books of motets (1589, 1591). He and Tallis jointly published a volume of *Cantiones sacrae* (1575) containing 17 pieces by each of them. Schütz also published collections under this title.

Canto (It., Sp.). Term for singing, the topmost part in a polyphonic work, a melody, a song or (sometimes 'cantino') the uppermost string of a bowed or plucked instrument.

Cantometrics. A system of analysis for studying aspects of folksong performance; musical factors relating to style are submitted to statistical analysis and correlated with social and cultural data to delineate the role of folksong in its cultural context.

Cantone, Serafino (*fl* 1580–1627). Italian composer. A Benedictine monk, he was organist at S Simpliciano, Milan. His many sacred works include double-choir motets (1599) and concertato pieces (1625); his command of counterpoint is a notable feature of his secular works.

Cantor. In Jewish and early Christian worship, the principal or solo singer. In Roman Catholic use, the cantor sang the solo portions of chant; in medieval cathedrals he was director of the choir. The leading singer in most Anglican cathedrals became known as the 'precentor'. In the Lutheran Church the KANTOR directed the music.

Cantoris. *See* DECANI, CANTORIS.

Cantus (Lat.). 'Song': the medieval and Renaissance word for melody; more specifically, the highest voice in a polyphonic composition.

Cantus coronatus (Lat.: 'crowned song'). A late medieval term, used by Johannes de Grocheo (*De musica*, *c*1300) to refer to a category of trouvère *chansons*. A few are described as 'couronnée' in trouvère MSS, but there is no clear musical distinction between these and other works in the same repertory. Perhaps they (or their composers) had been awarded a prize or 'crown'.

Cantus firmus (Lat.). 'Fixed melody': term normally used in the context of 14th–16th-century polyphony for a plainchant melody, often in long and equal note values, or for an existing melody used as a basis for polyphonic composition. In counterpoint manuals it often means 'given part'.

Canzo. *See* CANSO.

Canzona [canzone] (It.: 'song'). A type of instrumental composition of the 16th and 17th centuries (the word originally stood for an arrangement of a French polyphonic *chanson*). Canzonas typically begin with a dactylic rhythm (long–short–short) and are contrapuntal in texture. Among the earliest examples independent of vocal models are those of Merulo. The keyboard canzona, represented at its best by Frescobaldi, and the ensemble canzona, of

which Giovanni Gabrieli wrote some brilliant examples, led respectively to the fugue and the sonata.

In Italy the standard spelling was, and remains, 'canzone'. It also stands for a lyric poem by (or in imitation of) Petrarch and others, used for musical setting by frottola and madrigal composers of the 16th and 17th centuries, and for a simple tuneful song, e.g. Cherubino's 'Voi che sapete' in Mozart's *Le nozze di Figaro* (which begins with the characteristic rhythm).

Canzonetta [canzonet] (It.). A diminutive of CANZONA used for light secular vocal pieces of the 16th–18th centuries, of which Monteverdi and Morley wrote notable polyphonic examples. It later could signify a small-scale song in an opera; by Haydn and others the term was used for solo strophic songs with piano.

Caoine (Ir.: 'weeping'). Term for a lament sung over the dead in Ireland and other Celtic countries; it was probably semi-improvised and usually sung by four people.

Capdevielle, Pierre (*b* Paris, 1 Feb 1906; *d* Bordeaux, 9 July 1969). French composer. He studied at the Conservatoire and with d'Indy, and worked as an administrator and conductor. His works, which cover all genres, are highly charged but classically moderated somewhat in the manner of Roussel.

Cape, Safford (*b* Denver, 28 June 1906; *d* Uccele, 26 March 1973). American conductor, musicologist and composer. After studying in Belgium he devoted himself to the realization and performance of medieval and Renaissance music; he formed the Pro Musica Antiqua of Brussels, with which he toured widely and made many recordings. He established a European Seminar on Early Music at Bruges (1961).

Capecchi, Renato (*b* Cairo, 6 Nov 1923). Italian baritone. He made his début in *Aida* (1949) and at the Met in *La traviata* (1951), but is noted chiefly for his intelligence, clever timing and clear enunciation in comic roles such as Rossini's Bartolo and Schicchi.

Capella Rorantistarum. Polish choir of equal men's voices, founded in Kraków in 1540 and active until 1795. It sang daily in the cathedral and played an important part in continuing in Poland the *a cappella* tradition based on 16th-century polyphony.

Capirola, Vincenzo (*b* Brescia, 1474; *d* ? there, after 1548). Italian nobleman, lutenist and composer. An important MS of his music contains 43 pieces (arrangements of vocal pieces, dances and ricercares), of which some are for novices while others demand virtuoso technique; the preface offers practical advice on lute playing.

Caplet, André (*b* Le Havre, 23 Nov 1878; *d* Neuilly-sur-Seine, 22 April 1925). French composer and conductor. He studied at the Paris Conservatoire (1896–1901) and started his career as a conductor, in Paris and at the Boston Opera (1910–14). Debussy was a great influence on him, and a friend, Caplet being entrusted with the orchestration of *Le martyre de St-Sébastien* (1911), of which he conducted the first performance. His compositions became more individual, and even extraordinary in their melodic contours and effects of colour. His main works include the *Conte fantastique* after Poe for harp and strings (1919), the cello concerto *Epiphanie* (1923) and *Le miroir de Jésus* for women's voices, harp and strings (1923).

Capocci, Gaetano (*b* Rome, 16 Oct 1811; *d* there, 11 Jan 1898). Italian organist and composer. From 1855 to 1898 he was *maestro direttore di cappella* of St John Lateran, Rome, where his sacred works were in constant use; he wrote oratorios (*Battista*, 1833; *Assalone*, 1842) for the Oratorio Filippino. His son Filippo (1840–1911) was a concert organist.

Capo tasto. Term for the nut of a fretted instrument, or for a device to shorten the string length and facilitate upward transposition without affecting fingering.

Cappella (It.). CHAPEL; *see also* A CAPPELLA and MAESTRO. The Latin form is *capella*.

Cappuccilli, Piero (*b* Trieste, 9 Nov 1929). Italian baritone. He became prominent after his La Scala début (1964), appearing at Covent Garden as Germont (*La traviata*, 1967), in the Americas, and at the Salzburg Festival (*Don Carlos*, 1975). He is admired for his warm, ample voice and reliable musicianship.

Capriccio (It.: 'whim', 'caprice'). Term for a variety of compositions usually showing some freedom of manner; Frescobaldi and others used it for a keyboard piece in a fugal texture, Brahms for a short piano piece, Paganini for a virtuoso violin study, Tchaikovksy for an orchestral work and Strauss for an opera. In the 18th century it often indicated an improvised cadenza. 'A capriccio' ('following one's fancy') is a performance instruction permitting a free and rhapsodic approach to tempo, and even style.

Opera in one act by Richard Strauss to a libretto by Krauss (1942, Munich).

Capriccio espagnol. *See* SPANISH CAPRICE.

Capriccio italien. *See* ITALIAN CAPRICE.

Capricieuse. Berwald's Symphony no.2 in D (1842).

Capricornus, Samuel Friedrich (*b* Zerčiče, 21 Dec 1628; *d* Stuttgart, 10 Nov 1665). German composer of Bohemian birth. He worked at Reutlingen and Bratislava before becoming Kapellmeister to the Württemberg court in Stuttgart (1657). An admirer of Carissimi, he emulated his expressive style in his church music, which includes small sacred concertos and large concerted works. Most of his secular music, including ballets and operas, is lost.

Capriol Suite. Suite for string orchestra by Warlock (1926).

Caproli [Caprioli], **Carlo** (*b* Rome, 1615–20; *d* ?there, 1692–95). Italian composer. Chiefly important for his cantatas, he held posts as violinist and *maestro di cappella* in Rome. In the service of Prince Ludovisio Pamphili he wrote a successful opera for the French court, *Le nozze di Peleo e di Theti* (1654; now lost). Caproli's many cantatas fall into two groups: *ariette corte* (in closed form, for solo or ensemble), and the more numerous *arie di più parti* (combinations of recitative, aria and arioso). The solo cantatas are notable for their lyricism; stylistic features include chromatic alteration, unity of key, juxtaposition of major and minor over a com-

mon root and free treatment of the recurring text line at the close of a section.

Capuletti e Montecchi, I. Opera in two acts by Bellini to a libretto by Romani (1830, Venice).

Cara, Marchetto (*b* in or nr. Verona, *c*1470; *d* Mantua, ?1525). Italian composer, singer and lutenist. Having served the Mantuan court at least from 1494, he became *maestro di cappella* to Francesco and his son Federico Gonzaga in 1511 and was favoured by the duke and his wife, Isabella d'Este. Famous throughout northern Italy for his singing and playing, he was also, with Tromboncino, one of the two most important early 16th-century composers of frottolas, of which he wrote more than 100 (more published in anthologies); he favoured poems in *barzelletta* form and the basic texture consists of a simple harmonic pattern with passage-work added to the upper parts. His later works include madrigals in a more imitative style. He also wrote a three-voice *Salve regina* and seven *laudi*.

Caracciolo, Franco (*b* Bari, 29 March 1920). Italian conductor. After study in Naples and Rome he spent most of his time conducting the orchestras of Italian Radio and Television. At the Naples Festival he conducted operas by Cherubini, Cimarosa and Haydn; his repertory also included contemporary music.

Carafa (de Colobrano), Michele (Enrico-Francesco-Vincenzo-Aloisio-Paolo) (*b* Naples, 17 Nov 1787; *d* Paris, 26 July 1872). Italian composer. A nobleman, he trained for a military career but also studied music, in Naples and then with Cherubini. From 1814 he became one of the most prolific opera composers of his day. *Gabriella di Vergy* (1816), produced in Naples where he began a lifelong friendship with Rossini, was his first big success; it was followed by even more successful works at the Opéra-Comique in Paris, *Le solitaire* (1822), *Le valet de chambre* (1823) and above all *Masaniello* (1827). He became a French citizen (1834) and professor at the Conservatoire (1840). Competent but too often derivative and lacking in melodic sparkle, his music lost its popularity.

Cardew, Cornelius (*b* Winchcombe, 7 May 1936; *d* London, 13 Dec 1981). English composer. He studied at the RAM (1953–7) and in Cologne (1957–8), where he became Stockhausen's assistant in the scoring of *Carré* (1958–60). In 1961 he returned to London, where he worked as a graphic artist (and used the talent in his 193-page graphic score *Treatise*, 1967). The increasing freedom of his music (he had moved from post-Boulez to post-Cage in Germany) led naturally to his participation in the improvisation group AMM from 1966 and to his work with the Scratch Orchestra (of trained and untrained musicians) from 1969; in 1970 he completed *The Great Learning*. In 1971 he began seeking ways to make his music serve revolutionary struggle, writing protest songs and concert works and working with socialist groups. He died in a road accident.

Cardillac. Opera in three acts by Hindemith to a libretto by Ferdinand Lion after E.T.A. Hoffmann's *Das Fräulein von Scuderi* (1926, Dresden); Hindemith revised it with his own libretto (1952, Zurich).

Cardoso, Manuel (*b* Fronteira, bap. 11 Dec 1566; *d* Lisbon, 24 Nov 1650). Portuguese composer. He was at Évora Cathedral choir school and in 1588 joined the Carmelite convent in Lisbon, becoming choir director and organist. He also served the future King John IV at Vila Viçosa. His many published masses and motets show his mastery of the Palestrinian contrapuntal style; numerous other works were lost in the Lisbon earthquake of 1755.

Cardus, Sir (John Frederick) Neville (*b* Manchester, 2 April 1889; *d* London, 28 Feb 1975). English critic. Largely self-educated, he first wrote music criticism in 1913 and joined the *Manchester Guardian* in 1917, becoming chief music critic in 1927, at first in Manchester, later in London. He wrote for the *Sydney Morning Herald* (1939–47), rejoining the *Manchester Guardian* in 1951. His two main interests, music and cricket, interacted happily; avoiding technical jargon in both, he cultivated an easy but informed style that approached as near to fine writing as modern journalism will allow. He wrote with particular insight on Mahler, Strauss, Delius and Elgar.

Carestini, Giovanni (*b* Filottrano, *c*1705; *d*?there, *c*1760). Italian alto castrato. He had a strong, agile and expressive voice, and appeared (initially as a soprano) throughout Italy in the 1720s. He held court posts at Vienna, Parma, Munich, Dresden and Berlin. In 1733–5 he sang in Handel's operas and oratorios in London (creating Ruggiero in *Alcina* among other roles), returning there in 1739–40.

Carey, Henry (*b*?Yorkshire, 27 Aug 1687; *d* London, 5 Oct 1743). English composer. Working in London, he wrote words and music for short stage works such as *The Contrivances* (1729), in ballad opera style, the burlesque opera *Chrononhotonthologos* (1734), and *Nancy* (1739), an all-sung interlude on a contemporary subject. His librettos are mostly comic or satirical; several were set by other composers. Also among his works are poems, cantatas, hymn tunes and many songs. He committed suicide.

Caribbean music. *See* LATIN AMERICAN MUSIC.

Carillon. A set of stationary bells, normally in a tower or on a high outdoor frame. An average 18th-century carillon had two or three octaves; 20th-century instruments have up to six. The instrument, very popular in the Low Countries, is played either from a large keyboard or operated by a pegged barrel or paper rolls.

Carissimi, Giacomo (*b* Marini, bap. 18 April 1605; *d* Rome, 12 Jan 1674). Italian composer. Between 1623 and 1627 he was a singer and organist at Tivoli Cathedral. In 1628–9 he worked at Assisi and in 1629 he was made *maestro di cappella* at the Jesuit Collegio Germanico, Rome, where he remained until his death, training the students in music, educating the choirboys and organizing the music at the collegiate church of S Apollinare. In 1637 he became a priest.

The loss of Carissimi's autographs when the Jesuit order was dissolved in 1773 has left problems as to the authenticity and chronology of his works. A few authentic masses remain, showing him working in an old tradition and including probably the last work to be based on the medieval song *L'homme armé*. Most of the motets are for few voices with continuo, occasionally with obbligato instruments; they are unusually varied in structure but otherwise not distinguished above those of his contemporaries.

Carissimi's chief importance is as a composer of oratorios. Their narrative style is basically simple, with links to the *stile recitativo* of Monteverdi and Viadana's monodic motet style. Carissimi heightens its effect with rhetorical gestures, often involving the transposed repetition of a phrase to the same or different words. The oratorios also include stretches of aria-like writing, and a position of special importance is given to the chorus. The final chorus of *Jephte* was particularly esteemed (and was used by Handel in *Samson*). In his lifetime Carissimi also enjoyed a reputation as a composer of secular cantatas, which are distinguished by the variety of their musical structures and the diversity of their texts, which include some humorous ones.

Carissimi's pupils included not only several Italians (Bassani, Cesti, A. Scarlatti and Steffani may have been among them) but also the Germans J.K. Kerll and Christoph Bernhard and the Frenchman Charpentier. Carissimi's works, especially his motets, were held in high esteem in England throughout the 17th and 18th centuries.

Sacred music 4 masses; *c*100 motets; 14 oratorios, incl. Baltazar, Jephte, Jonas, Judicium Salomonis
*Secular music c*150 cantatas, incl. A pie d'un verde alloro, Ferma, lascia ch'io parli, Suonerà l'ultima tromba

Carl Rosa Opera Company. Founded by Carl Rosa to perform operas in English, it opened in Dublin in 1875 and in London the same year. First performances in English in the 1890s included works by Gounod, Verdi and Wagner, and new British operas were commissioned. After Rosa's death (1889) touring companies were set up; in 1930–40 it was the chief British touring company. Its last production was in London in 1960.

Carlton, Richard (*b c*1558; *d*?1638). English composer. He graduated at Cambridge (1577) and was Master of the Choristers at Norwich Cathedral. His five-part madrigal book (1601) includes well-known pieces (e.g. *When Flora faire*) and he contributed to *The Triumphes of Oriana* (1601).

Carmélites, Dialogues des [The Carmelites]. *See* DIALOGUES DES CARMÉLITES.

Carmen (Lat.: 'song'). Term used in the Middle Ages and the Renaissance for many types of song, usually to lyric poetry. It was also used for some German instrumental pieces in the late 15th century.

Opera in four acts by Bizet to a libretto by Meilhac and Halévy after Mérimée (1875, Paris).

Carmichael, Hoagy [Hoagland Howard] (*b* Bloomington, IN, 22 Nov 1899; *d* Rancho Mirage, CA, 27 Dec 1981). American songwriter, singer, pianist and bandleader. After qualifying as a lawyer he began his musical career as a jazz musician. His first piece, *Riverboat Shuffle* (1925), was written for Bix Beiderbecke. After playing and recording with various jazz musicians, he went to New York in 1930 to concentrate on songwriting. He collaborated with several lyricists, including Johnny Mercer, and over three dozen of his many songs became hits, including *Star Dust* (1929) and *In the cool, cool, cool of the evening* (1951). He contributed songs to motion pictures, as well as acting and appearing in 14 films.

Carmina burana (Lat.: 'Songs of Beuren'). Title given by J.A. Schmeller to his edition (1847) of a German MS of the early 13th century containing songs, some with music in neumatic notation. The MS was found at Benediktbeuren in 1803 but may have originated at Seckau; it is now at the Bavarian State Library, Munich. Carl Orff used the poems (but not the music) in his scenic cantata (1937, Frankfurt), the first part of his *Trionfi* trilogy.

Carnaval. Schumann's op.9, for piano (1835), a set of 21 pieces each with a descriptive title.

Concert overture, op.92, by Dvořák (1891), the second of his *Nature, Life and Love* cycle.

Carnaval des animaux, Le. 'Grand zoological fantasy' by Saint-Saëns, originally for two pianos and ensemble but also for two pianos and orchestra (1886); each of its 14 movements represents a different animal.

Carnaval romain, Le (Roman Carnival). Overture (op.9) by Berlioz (1844) using material from his opera *Benvenuto Cellini*.

Carnegie Hall. The name of several halls in the USA endowed by Andrew Carnegie. The most notable is in New York; it was built in 1891 (cap. 2784) and restored in 1986. The adjacent Carnegie Recital Hall (cap. 283) is used for début recitals and for chamber, modern and ethnic music.

Carnicer (y Batlle), Ramón (*b* Tárrega, 24 Oct 1789; *d* Madrid, 17 March 1855). Spanish composer. Working in Barcelona from 1816, he directed a theatre orchestra and composed for the Teatro de la Cruz three Italian *opere semiserie*, as well as substitute cavatinas and overtures for Paer and Rossini operas. In 1827 he settled in Madrid and wrote four more operas, of which *Cristoforo Colombo* (1831) is the most important. Many popular songs, church music and the Chilean national anthem (*Dulce patria*, 1828) are to his credit; he was founder-professor of the Spanish national conservatory.

Carol. A medieval strophic song in English or Latin, beginning with a burden (refrain) which is repeated after each stanza; in recent times, a strophic song associated with Christmas.

The carol, connected with the French CAROLE, originated as a dance-song in the 12th century. Most surviving medieval texts treat religious or moral subjects, often pertaining to Christmastide, but carols were appropriate also to secular feasts and processions. They were sung to popular melodies. The 15th-century polyphonic carol is marked by vigorous rhythms, transcribed in 6/8 or 3/4 time, somewhat angular melodies and simple two- or three-part harmonies. The carol declined after the Reformation, but carol-motets were composed by Byrd and others, and the older type continued in use. During the 19th century the tradition was diluted with new Christmas hymns in square, four-part harmony.

Carolan, Turlough (*b* nr. Nobber, 1670; *d* Ballyfarnon, 1738). Irish harper and composer. Blinded by smallpox at 18, he travelled throughout Ireland performing his songs and harp pieces. About 200 survive, many in dance rhythm: they show the influence of folk melody, traditional Irish harp music and, unusually, Italian music, by Vivaldi, Corelli, Geminiani and others.

Carole (Fr.). Courtly dance of western Europe in the 12th and 13th centuries. It may have been a round dance or a processional one and was always performed as a dance-song. The basse danse replaced it *c*1350 as the most fashionable courtly dance.

Caron, Leon Francis Victor (*b* Boulogne, 13 Jan 1850; *d* Sydney, 29 May 1905). Australian conductor and composer of French birth. He directed his own opera company in the 1880s, giving Australian premières of many operas in English, then joined the J.C. Williamson Royal Comic Opera Company. Besides pantomimes he wrote the cantata *Victoria* (1880).

Caron, Philippe (*fl* 2nd half of the 15th century). ?French composer. Possibly he was trained at Cambrai, knew Busnois, was in the service of Charles the Bold and spent time in Italy. His five masses include one based on *L'homme armé* and another on the tenor of one of his own *chansons*; they show a preference for two- and four-part textures rather than the more usual three-part polyphony. The *chansons* range from serious to frivolous; most are in duple metre, achieve a continuous melodic flow unusual for the time and make discreet use of imitation.

Caroso, Fabritio (*b* ?Sermoneta, *c*1527–35; *d* after 1605). Italian dancing-master. His two large dance manuals (*Il ballarino*, 1581; *Nobiltà di dame*, 1600) are significant sources for the study of late 16th-century dance music and steps.

Carpenter, John Alden (*b* Park Ridge, IL, 28 Feb 1876; *d* Chicago, 26 April 1951). American composer. He studied with Paine at Harvard, and had some lessons from Elgar, whom he much admired, in Rome in 1906. His works include songs and chamber music, but he is best remembered for orchestral pieces: the humorous *Adventures in a Perambulator* (1914), the jazz ballet *Krazy Kat* (1921) and the modish *Skyscrapers* (1924), intended for Dyagilev.

Carpentras [Genet, Elzéar] (*b* Carpentras, *c*1470; *d* Avignon, 14 June 1548). French composer. A chaplain in Avignon from 1505, he served the papal church in Rome as a singer (from 1508) and as master (from 1514), apart from brief periods as a member of the French royal chapel (before 1514) and in Avignon (1521–4); by 1526 illness had forced him to return to Avignon. After his retirement he prepared a four-volume edition of his sacred works containing most of his extant music: five masses, a set of Lamentations and collections of hymns and Magnificat sections. His Lamentations were performed annually in the Sistine Chapel until 1587. His sacred works explore the structural possibilities of pervading imitation but also combine relatively simple chordal sections with more contrapuntal writing to create clear structures with well-defined cadences. All his masses are based on *chansons* and, like his other sacred music, paraphrase borrowed melodies or use them as *cantus firmi*. Two *chansons* and four frottolas by him also survive.

Carr, Benjamin (*b* London, 12 Sept 1768; *d* Philadelphia, 24 May 1831). American publisher, composer and organist. He immigrated to Philadelphia in 1793, establishing a thriving music business there and in New York, and working as a church organist, concert promoter and conductor; he became known as the 'Father of Philadelphia Music'. He wrote *c*85 sacred and *c*275 secular works, many published in his own collections and periodicals. He is credited with the first American publication of *Yankee Doodle*. His brother Thomas (1780–1879), a Baltimore music publisher, was the first to issue F.S. Key's *The Star-Spangled Banner* set to J.S. Smith's *To Anacreon in Heaven*.

Carreira, António (*b* ?Lisbon, *c*1525; *d* there, *c*1589). Portuguese composer, a member of the Portuguese royal chapel, first as a singer then organist and finally *mestre de capela*. His 23 extant keyboard pieces, showing Cabezón's influence (among others), aided the expansion of idiomatic keyboard repertory and technique.

Carreño, (Maria) Teresa (*b* Caracas, 22 Dec 1853; *d* New York, 12 June 1917). Venezuelan pianist and composer. She studied with Gottschalk in New York and Anton Rubinstein in Paris. After success in Europe as a pianist, in 1875 she married the baritone Giovanni Tagliapietra, with whom in Venezuela she organised and conducted an opera company in which she also sang. She resumed her career as a pianist in 1889 and in 1892 married Eugen d'Albert.

Carreras, José (*b* Barcelona, 5 Dec 1946). Spanish tenor. After study at the Barcelona Conservatory he sang Ismaele in *Nabucco* in Barcelona. In 1971 he took part in a London concert performance of Donizetti's *Maria Stuarda*. His American début was in 1972; he subsequently sang with the Met, at Covent Garden and in other leading houses. His sweet timbre and pure phrasing have made him one of the most popular lyric tenors of his generation.

Carrillo(-Trujillo), Julián (Antonio) (*b* Ahualulco, 28 Jan 1875; *d* San Angel, 9 Sept 1965). Mexican composer. He studied in Mexico City and Europe (1899–1905, notably at Leipzig with Jadassohn) as a violinist and composer, and began to experiment with microtones. He returned to Mexico to teach, perform and compose, though not until 1924 did he begin to use microtones in his works: his Concertino for microtone sextet and orchestra (1927) was played by Stokowski and evoked great interest in the USA. In the 1930s he formed his own microtone orchestra, though he continued to write works in normal tuning as well as orchestral, vocal, chamber and instrumental pieces in quarter-tones and other divisions. Stokowski commissioned his Concertino for ⅓-tone piano (1962).

Carse, Adam (von Ahn) (*b* Newcastle upon Tyne, 19 May 1878; *d* Great Missenden, 2 Nov 1958). English instrument collector and composer. He studied at the RAM, where he taught, 1922–40. He wrote valuable studies on the history of the orchestra and left his collection of 350 early wind instruments to the Horniman Museum, London.

Carte, Richard D'Oyly (*b* London, 3 May 1844; *d* there, 3 April 1901). English impresario. He commissioned Gilbert and Sullivan's *Trial by Jury* (1875) for the Royalty Theatre, then formed the Comedy Opera Company and built the Savoy Theatre (1881) to produce their works; the partnership continued at the Savoy for ten years.

Carter, Elliott (Cook) (*b* New York, 11 Dec 1908). American composer. He studied at Harvard (1926–32), at the Ecole Normale de Musique in Paris (1932–5) and privately with Boulanger. Back in the USA he worked as musical director of Ballet Caravan (until 1940) and as a teacher. From boyhood he had been acquainted with the music of Schoenberg, Varèse, Ives and others, but for the moment his works leaned much more towards Stravinsky and Hindemith: they included the ballets *Pocahontas* (1939) and *The Minotaur* (1947), the Symphony no.1 (1942) and *Holiday Overture* (1944). However, in his Piano Sonata (1946) he began to work from the interval content of particular chords, and inevitably to loosen the hold of tonality. The development was taken further in the Cello Sonata (1948), already characteristic of his later style in that the instruments have distinct roles.

A period of withdrawal led to the First Quartet (1951), a work of complex rhythmic interplay, long-ranging atonal melody and unusual form, the 'movements' being out of step with the given breaks in the musical continuity: effectively it is a single unfolding of 40 minutes' duration. It was followed by exclusively instrumental works of similar complexity, activity and energy, including the Variations for orchestra (1955), the Second Quartet (1959), the Double Concerto for harpsichord and piano, each with its own chamber orchestra (1961), the Piano Concerto (1965), the Concerto for Orchestra (1969), the Third Quartet (1971) and the Brass Quintet (1974). At that point Carter returned to vocal composition for a triptych of works for soloist and ensemble: *A Mirror on which to Dwell* (1975), *Syringa* (1978) and *In Sleep, in Thunder* (1981), with words by Elizabeth Bishop, John Ashbery and Robert Lowell respectively. But he has also continued the output of large instrumental movements with *A Symphony of Three Orchestras* (1976), the piano solo *Night Fantasies* (1980), the Triple Duo (1983) and *Penthode* for small orchestra (1985). His String Quartet no.4 (1986) is in a simpler style.

Ballets Pocahontas (1939); The Minotaur (1947)
Orchestral music Sym. no.1 (1942); Holiday Ov. (1944); Variations (1955); Double Conc., hpd, pf, 2 chamber orch (1961); Pf Conc. (1965); Conc. for Orch (1969); A Sym. of Three Orchs (1976); Penthode, 5 inst qts (1985)
Voice and ensemble A Mirror on which to Dwell (1975); Syringa (1978); In Sleep, in Thunder (1981)
Chamber music Elegy, vc, pf (1943); Woodwind Qnt (1948); Sonata, vc, pf (1948); Eight Etudes and a Fantasy (1950); 4 str qts (1951, 1959, 1971, 1986); Sonata, fl, ob, vc, hpd (1952); Duo, vn, pf (1974); Brass Qnt (1974); Triple Duo, ens (1983)
Piano music Sonata (1946); Night Fantasies (1980)

Carter, (Charles) Thomas (*b* Dublin, *c*1740; *d* London, 12 Oct 1804). Irish composer. An organist in Dublin, he moved to London *c*1769, and composed stage works such as *The Birthday* (1787), a musical pastoral. Despite some impressive music they were unsuccessful. Some of Carter's songs (e.g. *O Nanny, wilt thou fly with me*) were more popular; he also wrote keyboard and other instrumental music. He should not be confused with the Irish composer Thomas Carter (1769–1800), active in London in the 1790s.

Cartier, Jean Baptiste (*b* Avignon, 28 May 1765; *d* Paris, 1841). French violinist and composer. A Viotti pupil and an orchestral musician for 40 years, he wrote *L'art du violon* (Paris, 1798), an imposing volume that reproduced from MSS and early editions several 17th- and 18th-century masterpieces, including Tartini's 'Devil's Trill' Sonata.

Carulli, Ferdinando (*b* Naples, *c* Feb 1770; *d* Paris, 17 Feb 1841). Italian guitarist, composer and teacher. He was the most prominent guitarist in Paris, 1808–23, and is known for his teaching works, chiefly his method op.27, and for his concertos, sonatas, studies, variations and transcriptions (over 300 opus numbers).

Caruso, Enrico (*b* Naples, 27 Feb 1873; *d* there, 2 Aug 1921). Italian tenor. He made his début at Naples in 1894 but his first real success came with Enzo in *La gioconda* at Palermo (1897). He sang Nemorino in *L'elisir d'amore* at La Scala (1900) and from 1902, when he made his début as the Duke of Mantua, to 1914 achieved great success at Covent Garden. But he sang most often at the Met (1903–20), where he was greatly loved and admired. His recordings made him universally famous. Caruso fused a natural baritone timbre with a tenor's smooth, silken finish. The brilliance of his high notes, exceptional breath control and impeccable intonation made his voice unique, and he was considered the greatest tenor of the century. He was a notable interpreter of Verdi and *grand opéra*; among the first performances in which he sang was *La fanciulla del West* (1910).

Caruso, Luigi (*b* Naples, 25 Sept 1754; *d* Perugia, 1822). Italian composer. He had over 60 operas, mostly comic, performed in Italian theatres, 1755–1810. From 1790 he held *maestro di cappella* posts, lastly (from 1810) at Perugia, where he wrote many sacred works.

Carvalho, Caroline [Miolan, Marie; née Félix-Miolan, Marie] (*b* Marseilles, 31 Dec 1827; *d* Château-Puys, 10 July 1895). French soprano. At the Theatre-Lyrique she created four roles by Gounod: Marguerite in *Faust* (1859), Baucis in *Philémon et Baucis* (1860), Mireille (1864) and Juliette (1867). She was married to the baritone and opera manager Leon Carvalho (1825–97).

Carver, Robert (*b c*1490; *d* after 1546). Scottish composer. His works are in the 'Scone Antiphonary', which may have belonged to the Scottish Chapel Royal. They combine elements of the English decorative style and the Flemish style of Josquin and Isaac. His earliest composition may be the ten-part festal mass *Dum sacrum mysterium*, possibly written for the coronation of James V in 1513. The other four surviving masses include the only setting based on *L'homme armé* by a British composer. He wrote two motets for five and 19 voices, the latter illustrating British composers' fondness for full sonorities.

Cary, Tristram (Ogilvie) (*b* Oxford, 14 May 1925). English composer. He became interested in electronic music while serving as a radio operator in the navy, then studied at Trinity College, London. Since 1968 he has taught at the RCM, where he founded the electronic studio, the first of its kind in the UK. His output of electronic and non-electronic music includes much for stage, films and television.

Caryll, Ivan (*b* Liège, 12 May 1861; *d* New York, 29 Nov 1921). Anglo-American composer and conductor of Belgian birth. He studied at the Liège Conservatory and became conductor at the Lyric Theatre in London, later working in the USA. He wrote *c*40 operettas and musical comedies, including *Little Christopher Columbus* (1893).

Casadesus, Robert (Marcel) (*b* Paris, 7 April 1899; *d* there, 19 Sept 1972). French pianist and composer. After study at the Paris Conservatoire he toured in Europe and the Americas. He became known for his performances of Mozart and French music; with his wife Gaby he formed a piano duo. Their son Jean (1927–72) was a successful pianist in North America. His uncles Francis (1870–1954), Henri (1879–1947) and Marius (1892–1981) were composers, conductors and string players; they published works of their own as unknown pieces by 18th-century composers (Handel, Bach's sons, Mozart).

Casals, Pablo (Paul) (*b* Vendrell, 29 Dec 1876; *d* Puerto Rico, 22 Oct 1973). Catalan cellist and composer. He studied at Barcelona from 1887 and made his début there in 1891. After further study in Madrid and Brussels his international career began in 1899, when he played Lalo's Concerto under Lamoureux in Paris. In 1905 he formed a trio with Thibaud and Cortot, recording works by Schubert and Beethoven. As a soloist Casals was renowned for his beautiful tone and intellectual strength. His playing did much to bring Bach's suites into the repertory. He formed the Orquestra Pau Casals in Barcelona in 1919 but his activities were curtailed by the Spanish Civil War. In 1950 at Prades he returned to music-making and later directed festivals at Perpignan and Puerto Rico. His many pupils included Guilhermina Suggia, with whom he formed a liaison. Casals wrote instrumental works and many choral pieces of a simple, devotional nature.

Casati, Gasparo (*b* Pavia, *c*1610; *d* Novara, 1641). Italian composer. He was *maestro di cappella* of Novara Cathedral from 1635. His surviving music is all sacred, chiefly in the concertato idiom, and includes motets in a nervous, highly charged style, characterized by varied rhythms, melismas, much triple-time arioso and marked contrasts. Girolamo Casati, (*b* Novara, 1590; *d* after 1657), *maestro di cappella* at Como (1635) and Pavia (1654) and a capable composer of small-scale concertato sacred pieces, may have been a relative of his.

Casavant Frères. Canadian firm of organ builders. Founded in 1845 by Joseph Casavant (1807–74) in

St Hyacinthe, Quebec, it was directed by his sons Claver and Samuel from 1879. In the 1890s it led the development of electro-pneumatic mechanisms and in the 1960s was one of the first in North America to revive the practice of building tracker-action organs.

Casavola, Franco (b Modugno, 13 July 1891; d Bari, 7 July 1955). Italian composer. He studied in Bari, Milan and Rome (with Respighi), and from 1920 was a futurist, writing ballets with Marinetti scenarios. In 1927 he reverted to a more traditional outlook, winning success with Il gobbo del califfo (1929), and from 1936 wrote much film music.

Cascarda (It.). Dance of the late 16th century, quick and in triple metre, often with dotted rhythms.

Case, John (b Woodstock, c1539; d 23 Jan 1600). English writer on music and philosopher. His Apologia musices (1588) is a brilliant, lucid synthesis of classical authorities on music (e.g. Boethius, Plato) and provides a thorough exposition of music theory in 16th-century England. The anonymous Praise of Musicke (1586) has wrongly been attributed to him.

Casella, Alfredo (b Turin, 25 July 1883; d Rome, 5 March 1947). Italian composer. In 1896 he was sent to Paris, where he studied with Fauré at the Conservatoire and became a friend of Enesco and Ravel. His musical enthusiasms, for Debussy, the Russian nationalists, Strauss and Mahler, are evident in the works of his 'first manner' (up to 1913), which include two symphonies, songs and piano pieces. But he felt a need to return to Italy, and in 1915 took a post at the Liceo di S Cecilia in Rome. There, as conductor, composer and organizer, he was an active propagandist for contemporary music; for since 1913 he had opened himself to the influences of Schoenberg, Stravinsky and Bartók and to new developments in the visual arts. Some works of this period have an ominous stillness (Notte di maggio for voice and orchestra, 1913; L'adieu à la vie for voice and piano, 1915; A notte alta for piano, 1917); others refer explicitly to the experience of war (Pagine di guerra for piano duet, 1915; Elegia eroica for orchestra, 1916). There is also a wrily humorous vein in such pieces as Pupazzetti for piano duet (1915) and the wilfully grotesque, fiercely dissonant Piano Sonatina (1916). The 'second manner' disappeared, however, c1920, and he became a neo-classicist, works of this period including the Concerto romano for organ, brass, timpani and strings (1926), Scarlattiana for piano and small orchestra (also 1926) and the opera La donna serpente (1928–31, after Gozzi). Some late works, including the Concerto for piano, percussion and strings (1943) and the large-scale Missa solemnis (1944), suggest a move towards quasi-serial chromaticism. He was the most influential figure in Italian music between the two world wars.

Casentini, Marsilio (b Trieste, bap. 3 Dec 1576; d Gemona, 16 June 1651). Italian composer. From 1600 he was maestro di cappella of the cathedral at Gemona, where he ran a music school. He wrote motets and madrigals, using both polychoral and concertato styles; in the dedication of his 1609 book of madrigals he wrote a lively defence of the new trends. His father Silao (c1540–1594) composed madrigals and a mass.

Casimiro Júnior [Casimiro da Silva], Joaquim (b Lisbon, 30 May 1808; d there, 28 Dec 1862). Portuguese composer. Although he was organist at Bemposta Palace, later at Lisbon Cathedral, and produced nearly 100 Latin sacred works, he was more active as a theatrical composer. Particularly successful among c200 stage works were his Batalha de Montereau (1850), an opera comica, and Opio e champagne (1854), an opereta closer to Auber.

Casini, Giovanni Maria (b Florence, 16 Dec 1652; d there, 25 Feb 1719). Italian composer. Serving in Florence in posts including cathedral organist and (in 1703–11) maestro di cappella, he wrote oratorios and church and organ music in a contrapuntal, often chromatic idiom. He was reputedly the greatest Italian organist of his time, and also played a five-manual harpsichord invented by Francesco Nigeti.

Casken, John (Arthur) (b Barnsley, 15 July 1949). English composer. He studied at Birmingham University with Joubert and Dickinson and in Warsaw with Dobrowolski and Lutosławski. He has been a lecturer at Durham University since 1981. His early works (Music for the Crabbing Sun for ensemble, 1971) make extensive use of aleatory counterpoint, but the governing factor in his later music is organization based on vertical aggregates (Firewhirl, 1980). Many of his pieces (e.g. Orion over Farne, 1984) draw inspiration from the Northumbrian landscape.

Cassadó (Moreu), Gaspar (b Barcelona, 30 Sept 1897; d Madrid, 24 Dec 1966). Spanish cellist. He studied under his father (the composer Joaquín Cassadó Valls, 1867–1926), at Barcelona Conservatory and with Casals in Paris. A fastidious artist with warm tone and sure technique, he was noted as a chamber-music player and a partner in Brahms's Double Concerto with Huberman and Szigeti. His compositions include an oratorio, a cello concerto and much chamber music.

Cassation. Term of uncertain derivation used by Haydn, Mozart and others for pieces resembling a serenade or divertimento.

Cassilly, Richard (b Washington, DC, 14 Dec 1927). American tenor. He studied at the Peabody Conservatory and made his début in 1954. Early roles include Tchaikovsky's Vakula in New York and Janáček's Laca in Chicago, the role of his Covent Garden début in 1968, by when he was a member of the Hamburg company. Other roles include Florestan, Tannhäuser (on his Vienna Staatsoper début, 1970), Othello (1970, Munich), Samson (1970, La Scala), Siegmund (1972, Paris Opéra) and Radamès (1973, Met), to which he brings intelligence and intensity.

Castaldi, Bellerofonte (b Modena, 1580–81; d there, 27 Sept 1649). Italian composer and poet. His bizarre personality is reflected in his two volumes of music. That of 1622 (which he engraved himself), though of no great distinction, is an interesting source of theorbo music. The 1623 volume is notable for its unusual presentation; besides strophic and dance-songs for one to three voices, it includes an echo madrigal and two elaborate sets of strophic variations for two voices. 15 songs are settings of his own poems.

Castaldi, Paolo (*b* Milan, 9 Sept 1930). Italian composer. He studied at the Milan Conservatory and at Darmstadt (1960–63). His aim has been to remove humanity from music, making it a mask to outline the lack of art in the present day. His means have included the 'composing' of performers' actions and attitudes, the distortion of old music (*Schoenberg* for orchestra, 1967) and the conversion of such music into a factitious and grotesque mechanism.

Castanets. Percussion instruments of indefinite pitch, associated with Spain. In Hispanic countries, and wherever they are used for accompanying dance, they consist of two pairs of small shallow cup-shaped pieces of wood; each pair is drilled to receive an ornamental cord, which is looped round the thumb (for illustration, *see* PERCUSSION INSTRUMENTS). They are also used to convey Spanish atmosphere, as in Bizet's *Carmen*.

Castel, Louis-Bertrand (*b* Montpellier, 5 Nov 1688; *d* Paris, 19 Jan 1757). French mathematician and theorist. A Jesuit priest and teacher, he had theories (built on Descartes) on the correspondence of sound and colour, and developed an 'ocular harpsichord' that coupled the sounding of pitches with analogous colour displays.

Castello, Dario (*fl* Venice, early 17th century). Italian composer and wind player. He is known for his two collections of sonatas (1621, 1629) for various instruments, in two to four real parts, through which he helped to develop a true instrumental idiom. They comprise 29 works mostly in the modern style (though traces of the older canzona are evident); some include a demanding concertante part for bassoon.

Castelnuovo-Tedesco, Mario (*b* Florence, 3 April 1895; *d* Los Angeles, 17 May 1968). Italian composer. He studied with Pizzetti at the Florence Conservatory and before 1918 had attracted the attention of Casella, who promoted his music. In 1939 he moved to the USA, where he taught at the Los Angeles Conservatory (from 1946) and wrote film music. His early songs and piano pieces are striking and he remained at his best in small forms, notably in his settings of all the songs from Shakespeare's plays (1921–5), and in his large output of guitar music. Other works include operas, Shakespeare overtures, concertos and oratorios.

Castiglioni, Niccolò (*b* Milan, 17 July 1932). Italian composer. He studied at the Milan Conservatory, the Salzburg Mozarteum (1952–3) and Darmstadt. After teaching in the USA (1966–9), illness obliged him to return to Italy and to compose more intermittently. His music shows a critical, intellectual growth through Webernian serialism to a style of highly polished artifice. His works include operas (*Attraverso lo specchio* for radio, 1961; *The Lords' Masque* and *Oberon*, 1980), orchestral pieces (*Aprèslude*, 1959; *Inverno In Ver*, 1972), instrumental and vocal music.

Castil-Blaze [Blaze, François Henri Joseph] (*b* Cavaillon, 1 Dec 1784; *d* Paris, 11 Dec 1857). French writer on music, librettist and composer. He studied law and harmony (at the Paris Conservatoire) but settled in Paris in 1820 writing musical articles for the *Journal des débats*, later for *Le constitutionnel*, *Le ménestrel* (of which he became the editor) and *La revue et gazette musicale de Paris*. He was knowledgeable and precise but conservative, preferring Rossini and Meyerbeer to Berlioz. His preoccupation was the translation and adaptation of popular Mozart, Weber and Rossini operas; he sucessfully produced French versions of these, some garbled or mutilated, at the Théâtre de l'Odeón (1824–9). His stage works were pastiches.

Castillon (de Saint-Victor), (Marie-)Alexis, Vicomte de (*b* Chartres, 13 Dec 1838; *d* Paris, 5 March 1873). French composer. Encouraged by Duparc, he studied with Franck and became a co-founder of the Société Nationale de Musique (1871). He was one of the first French composers of his generation to devote himself to chamber music and showed distinction in his orchestral works and songs; he died before reaching artistic maturity.

Castor et Pollux. *Tragédie en musique* in a prologue and five acts by Rameau to a libretto by Bernard (1737, Paris).

Castrato (It.). A male singer who has been castrated before puberty to preserve the soprano or contralto range of his voice; supported by a man's lungs, the voice was powerful, agile and penetrating. Castratos were used in the Roman Catholic Church for more than 300 years and occupied a dominant place in opera in the 17th and 18th centuries. *See* SINGING.

Castro, Jean de (*b* Liège, *c*1540; *d c*1600). South Netherlands composer. He went to Antwerp in the early 1570s, then to Germany and Lyons (1580), before joining the Düsseldorf and Cologne courts. One of the most prolific composers of his day, he published 27 volumes of chansons, odes, madrigals etc and eight of sacred works, mostly for two or three voices. Their style is bland, with free imitation and a patter technique, and they show harmonic influences from the Italian madrigal.

Castro, José María (*b* Avellaneda, 15 Dec 1892; *d* Buenos Aires, 2 Aug 1964). Argentinian composer, conductor and cellist. He studied in Buenos Aires, Paris and Rome. On his return to Argentina he was conductor of the Asociacion del Profesorado Orquestal PO. His music is neo-classical and includes a Concerto for Orchestra (1944) and three string quartets. His brother Juan José (1895–1968), also a composer and conductor, studied with d'Indy in Paris and conducted at the Teatro Colón and abroad; his music, including the orchestral *Allegro, lento e vivace*, combines Spanish idioms with a more cosmopolitan style.

Castrucci, Pietro (*b* Rome, 1679; *d* Dublin, 7 March 1752). Italian violinist and composer. A pupil of Corelli, he led Handel's opera orchestra in London for over 22 years and was a popular soloist. He invented the violetta marina (a type of viola d'amore), played by him and his younger brother Prospero (*d* 1760) in the sleep song in Handel's *Orlando*. His works include violin sonatas in a virtuoso style, flute sonatas and concerti grossi.

Casulana, Maddelena (*b c*1540; *fl* 1566–83). Italian singer and composer. She was renowned as a singer, notably in Vicenza and Venice, and several composers dedicated madrigal books to her. She published three such books of her own (1568, 1570, 1583), for four and five voices.

Catalani, Alfredo (*b* Lucca, 19 June 1854; *d* Milan, 7 Aug 1893). Italian composer. After studying in Lucca, Paris and Milan, he became associated with the Scapigliatura, an artistic and literary reform movement, and with the music publisher Lucca, for whom he wrote *Elda* (1876, rev. as *Loreley*, 1888), *Dejanice* (1883) and *Edmea* (1886). He achieved a personal style most successfully in *La Wally* (1892). Boito and Toscanini championed him but he was dismissed by Verdi, Puccini and the publisher Ricordi. He stressed orchestration and atmosphere over characterization and was old-fashioned in his high Romanticism. Yet his operas were among the most important in the period preceding the *verismo* school. He was professor at the Milan Conservatory from 1886.

Catalani, Angelica (*b* Sinigaglia, 10 May 1780; *d* Paris, 12 June 1849). Italian soprano. She made her London début at the King's Theatre (1806) in Portugal's *Semiramide*, soon receiving unprecedented fees and singing in operas by Pucitta, Piccinni and Paer; she was Susanna in the first London performance of *Le nozze di Figaro* (1812). In Paris she took over the direction of the Théâtre Italien (1814–17), then toured throughout northern Europe. Her superb voice was beautifully controlled, but her lack of dramatic involvement curtailed her career.

Catalogue d'oiseaux. Work by Messiaen for piano (1958), a cycle of 13 pieces, each based on the notated song of a different bird.

Catch. A light round or canon for male voices sung as convivial entertainment in England in the 16th–18th centuries. Judicious placing of rests in the music could give rise to *double entendres*.

Catch Club, The Noblemen and Gentlemen's. Organization founded in 1761 in London for dining and music, to encourage the composition and performance of canons, catches and glees. Early members included J.C. Bach and Thomas Arne. Composition prizes were awarded from 1763. A partsong was commissioned from Malcolm Arnold for the bicentenary.

Catel, Charles-Simon (*b* Laigle, 10 June 1773; *d* Paris, 29 Nov 1830). French composer and theorist. After studying with Gossec, he joined the National Guard, writing music for public functions and teaching harmony; he was répétiteur at the Opéra, professor at the Paris Conservatoire and a composer of Revolutionary hymns, marches and military symphonies. He is noted mainly for his theory manual, *Traité d'harmonie* (1802), and his ten stage works, from conventional *opéras comiques* and *Sémiramis* (1802), a *tragédie lyrique*, to the more modern *Les bayadères* (1810), a *tragi-comédie*; *Wallace, ou Le ménestrel écossais* (1817) is one of the first works with a Romantic Gothic and Scottish plot.

Catelani, Angelo (*b* Guastalla, 30 March 1811; *d* Modena, 5 Sept 1866). Italian musicologist and composer. After a brief career as a stage composer, he took up critical writing in Modenese journals; his most important work is a series of biographical and bibliographical studies (1850–66).

Cathédrale engloutie, La. Piano piece by Debussy, no.10 of his *Préludes* Book 1 (1910).

Cato, Diomedes (*b* Venice, before 1570; *d* ?after 1607). Italian composer and lutenist. He worked at the Polish court from at least 1588 to 1593 and again from 1602. More than 50 of his lute pieces survive – preludes, fantasias, dances and arrangements of vocal works. He also composed for voices, viol consort and keyboard.

Catoire [Katuar], Georgy (L'vovich) (*b* Moscow, 27 April 1861; *d* there, 21 May 1926). Russian composer and theorist of French descent. In Berlin he studied the piano with Klindworth and composition with Rimsky-Korsakov and Lyadov. In 1916 he was appointed professor at the Moscow Conservatory. His orchestral and chamber works are in the style of Tchaikovsky, with Wagnerian influence. He wrote important works on harmony and form.

Cat's Fugue. Harpsichord Sonata in G minor k30 by D. Scarlatti, so called because the strange fugue subject sounds as if it could have been improvised by a kitten on the keys.

Catulli carmina. Scenic cantata by Orff to medieval Latin lyrics (1943, Leipzig), the second part of the trilogy *Trionfi*.

Caturla, Alejandro García (*b* Remedios, 7 March 1906; *d* there, 12 Nov 1940). Cuban composer. A lawyer by profession (he was shot dead by a criminal), he studied music in Havana and with Boulanger in Paris (1928). Sharing Roldán's taste for Afro-Cuban rhythms, he wrote in an exuberant, primitive style that left a mark on Cuban music.

Caurroy, Eustache du. *See* DU CAURROY, EUSTACHE.

Caustun, Thomas (*b* ?*c*1520–25; *d* London, 28 Oct 1569). English composer. A Gentleman of the Chapel Royal from *c*1550, he composed three services and seven anthems (printed in Day's *Certaine Notes*, 1565), as well as many psalms for the first harmonized metrical English psalter (Day's *Whole Psalmes*, 1563).

Cavaccio, Giovanni (*b* Bergamo, *c*1556; *d* there, 11 Aug 1626). Italian composer. He was *maestro di cappella* of Bergamo Cathedral (1581–98) and of S Maria Maggiore there (1598–1626). He published at least 15 books of masses, Magnificats, psalms, hymns and motets, mostly for large forces in the Venetian polychoral style, as well as secular and keyboard works.

Cavaillé-Coll, Aristide (*b* Montpellier, 4 Feb 1811; *d* Paris, 13 Oct 1899). French organ builder. Of an established family of organ builders, he studied in Paris (1833), settling there with his father and brother and building his first organ at Notre Dame de Lorette (1838). He built nearly 500, among them those at La Madeleine, Ste Clotilde, Notre Dame, La Trinité and the Trocadéro (all now altered) and those at St Denis Abbey (1840), Bayeux Cathedral (1861) and Orléans Cathedral (1875) (all in their original state). He remained faithful to tracker action, took care over the wind supply and, by his disposition of elements and use of pedals to control the couplers, swell-boxes and reeds, introduced unprecedented flexibility in volume and expressiveness. Adding to the classical French organ overblown flutes, the Spanish swell-box and *chamade* Trumpets and the German string stops, he created the French Romantic instrument, which inspired the greatest French organ composers from Franck to Messiaen.

Cavalieri, Catarina (*b* Vienna, 19 Feb 1760; *d* there, 30 June 1801). Austrian soprano. She made her début in 1775 and was one of the finest singers of her day in Vienna, especially in German opera, creating Constanze in Mozart's *Die Entführung aus dem Serail* (1782) and singing Donna Elvira in the Vienna première (1788) of *Don Giovanni*.

Cavalieri, Emilio de' (*b* Rome, *c*1550; *d* there, 11 March 1602). Italian composer. Born into a noble, artistic family, he worked as organist and coordinator of Lenten music at the Oratorio del Crocifisso in S Marcello, Rome (1578–84). From 1588 he served Ferdinando de' Medici in Florence as a court overseer and diplomat, supervising and composing music for the famous, lavish *intermedi* given at Ferdinando's wedding (1589). He returned permanently to Rome in 1600. While in Florence he was, with Peri, Caccini and the poet Rinuccini, in the forefront of developments in dramatic monody. His *Rappresentatione di Anima, et di Corpo* (1600) was the first play set entirely to music; it includes highly expressive recitative, tuneful solo madrigals, strophic airs and dance-like choruses (the printed score was the first to use a figured bass). He also composed highly original sets of Lamentations and responses for Holy Week (?1599). Four secular dramatic works written for Florence are lost.

Cavalleria rusticana. Opera in one act by Mascagni to a libretto by Targioni-Tozzetti and Tenasci after Verga (1890, Rome). It is usually performed in a double bill with Leoncavallo's *Pagliacci*, hence the colloquial abbreviation 'Cav and Pag'.

Cavalli [Caletti Bruni], **(Pietro) Francesco** (*b* Crema, 14 Feb 1602; *d* Venice, 14 Jan 1676). Italian composer. He received musical instruction from his father, G.B. Caletti, and probably sang in Crema Cathedral choir. In 1616 the governor, Federico Cavalli, persuaded Caletti to allow him to take Francesco to Venice, where the boy (who adopted his patron's name) joined the *cappella* of St Mark's as a soprano and later tenor. In 1630 Cavalli made an advantageous marriage with a Venetian widow, Maria Sozomeno, and in 1639 he was appointed second organist at St Mark's. He began his opera career at the Teatro San Cassiano and in the 1650s was also active in other Venetian theatres and other Italian cities.

In 1660–62 Cavalli was in Paris, where his celebratory opera, *Ercole amante*, was played to a less than appreciative audience; when he returned to Venice he vowed never to work for the theatre again. In the event he composed six more operas, but his life centred more on St Mark's and in 1668 he succeeded Rovetta as its *maestro di cappella*. His wife had died in 1652; they had no children.

The modest quantity of Cavalli's extant sacred music is probably only a small part of a continuous production throughout his career. Most of it follows in the tradition of large concerted works for St Mark's, best represented by the Gabrielis and Monteverdi. The *Musiche sacrae* (1656) includes a mass and Magnificat for double choir with instruments as well as several motets, and the *Vesperi* (1675) consists of three Vespers services in eight parts with continuo. A requiem and another Magnificat are among other sacred pieces published during Cavalli's lifetime. He also left secular arias and cantatas, but his most important works were the nearly 30 operas composed for Venetian theatres. They run from the tentative beginnings of public opera to the establishment of Venice as the chief centre of Italian opera, and offer the only continuous view of Venetian operatic style over two decades. Modern revivals, notably of *Didone*, *Ormindo*, *Calisto* and *Egisto*, have shown Cavalli to be the most important opera composer in the quarter-century after Monteverdi.

Operas Gli amore d'Apollo e di Dafne (1640); Didone (1641); La virtù de' strali d'Amore (1642); Egisto (1643); Ormindo (1644); Giasone (1649); Rosinda (1651); Calisto (1651–2); Eritrea (1652); Xerse (1654); Statira (1655–6); Erismena (1655–6); Ercole amante (1662); Scipione affricano (1664); 13 others
Secular vocal music arias, cantatas
Sacred music Mass (1656); Vespers, 3 settings (1675); 2 Magnificats (1650); Requiem; psalms, hymns, antiphons; 6 inst works

Cavata (It.). 'Extraction': a passage extracted at the end of a recitative text and set, because of its particular significance, as an arioso or short aria. The term came into use in the later 17th century; there are examples in Bach's cantatas.

Cavatina (It.). In 18th-century opera a short aria without da capo, e.g. 'Porgi amor' in Mozart's *La nozze di Figaro*; in 19th-century Italian opera an elaborate aria, often ending with a faster cabaletta.

Cavazzoni, Girolamo (*b c*1525; *d* after 1577). Italian composer, son of Marco Antonio Cavazzoni. Having obtained a privilege from the Venetian senate, he published a book of ricercares in 1543 and by 1565 was associated with the Gonzaga family in Venice. Between 1565 and 1577 he was organist at S Barbara, Mantua. His highly imitative ricercares show the influence of Gombert's generation, and his 12 hymns and three Masses are for organ probably alternating with a choir.

Cavazzoni, Marco Antonio (*b* Bologna, *c*1490; *d* Venice, *c*1560). Italian composer. Having worked at Urbino (*c*1512), he may have been the singer called Marc'Antonio at St Mark's, Venice, as early as 1522. With the exception of a ricercare, all his extant keyboard music was published in one volume (1523); much of it is astonishingly mature for its time, featuring parallel 5ths and octaves and harsh dissonance, attesting its independence from vocal music.

Cavendish, Michael (*b c*1565; *d* London, ?5 July 1628). English composer. A member of the nobility, he published a book of 20 attractive ayres for voice and lute with eight madrigals (1598) and contributed to *The Triumphes of Oriana* (1601).

Cavos, Catterino (*b* Venice, 30 Oct 1775; *d* St Petersburg, 10 May 1840). Italian composer. He held a post at the Imperial Theatres, St Petersburg, and as a singing teacher. After successfully adapting a German Singspiel, he began an outstanding career as a composer of Russian opera. His best-known work is *Ivan Susanin* (1815), using folk melody and resembling in plot Glinka's *A Life for the Tsar*, the première of which he conducted in St Petersburg (1836). He also composed ballets, became director of all the imperial orchestras and was Kapellmeister of the Italian, Russian and German opera companies.

Cazden, Norman (*b* New York, 23 Sept 1914; *d* Bangor, ME, 18 Aug 1980). American composer. He studied at the Juilliard School and Harvard, and had lessons from Piston and Copland. While following a career as a pianist and teacher (at the University of Maine from 1969) he produced a large output of music in a widely expanded tonal style. *Songs from the Catskills* for band (1950) and *Woodland Valley Sketches* for orchestra (1960) reflect his interest in folk music.

Cazzati, Maurizio (*b* Lucera, *c*1620; *d* Mantua, 1677). Italian composer. His first posts were at Mantua and at Bozzolo (1647–8); next he was *maestro di cappella* of the Accademia della Morte, Ferrara, and at S Maria Maggiore, Bergamo. In 1657–71 he was *maestro di cappella* at S Petronio, Bologna; he reformed its musical establishment and, though unpopular with some, attracted fine instrumentalists (as well as singers) and encouraged instrumental music in the liturgy. As a composer too he was most significant for instrumental music, which makes up ten of his 66 publications. Especially notable are his three sonatas for trumpet and strings (1665), whose concerto-like manner influenced G.A. Perti, Torelli and others, and his solo violin sonatas (1670), the earliest published by a Bolognese composer. His 43 published sets of sacred works include psalms, hymns, Magnificats, solo motets etc. He also composed 11 oratorios, five operas and various secular vocal pieces.

Ceballos, Rodrigo de (*b* Aracena, *c*1530; *d* Granada, 1581). Spanish composer. He served the cathedrals in Seville (1553–56) and Córdoba (1556–61) and was *maestro de capilla* of the royal chapel, Granada. Some 40 motets and three masses by him survive, elegant and polished works placing him among the best Andalusian composers of his time.

Cebell. *See* CIBELL.

Cebotari, Maria (*b* Kishinev, 10 Feb 1910; *d* Vienna, 9 June 1949). Austrian soprano of Russian birth. After study in Berlin she sang at the Dresden Staatsoper in the 1930s, visiting Covent Garden with the company in 1936. She was best known in the operas of Strauss and Mozart.

Ceccato, Aldo (*b* Milan, 18 Feb 1934). Italian conductor. He studied at Milan and Berlin and made his début in 1964; his British and American débuts were in 1969. He was principal conductor of the Detroit SO, 1973–7. He is best known in the Italian repertory, and his detailed interpretations have been heard at Florence and Glyndebourne, in operas by Busoni and Strauss.

Cecchino, Tomaso (*b* Verona, *c*1580; *d* Hvar, 31 Aug 1644). Italian composer. He was *maestro di cappella* at the Cathedral of Hvar for most of his life, and composed secular and sacred music in a concise, restrained style. His secular songs show considerable charm; his motets are in the Venetian concertato manner, though his op.11 masses effectively combine the polyphony and a more modern, monodic style.

Cecilia. Saint and martyr of the early Christian church, honoured as patroness of music since the late 15th century. She was venerated as a saint from the late 5th century. Her status as patroness of music probably resulted from a misinterpretation of a phrase referring to musical instruments in the Acts of St Cecilia. She was celebrated in Cecilian festivals from the 16th century onwards (which gave rise to an English repertory of Cecilian court odes in praise of music, set by Purcell, Boyce and others); in the 19th century, the movement towards a simpler, more austere style of church music was named after her.

Cecilian festivals. St Cecilia's day (22 Nov) was traditionally celebrated with music. Societies were formed in Europe, the earliest recorded (1570) being at Evreux in France. From 1683 festivals in London included a church service followed by an entertainment, and odes for the occasion were composed by Purcell (1683, 1692), Handel (1736, 1739) and others; the day is now marked by a concert in aid of a musicians' charity. In Paris in the 19th century a solemn mass was held (Gounod composed for it in 1855).

Cecilian movement. A movement for the reform of Catholic church music in the 19th century, centred on the German-speaking countries and France. It favoured the development of a sober style of unaccompanied choral singing (including Renaissance polyphony), the re-creation of an 'authentic' tradition of Gregorian chant and the integration of music into the service.

Cédez (Fr.). 'Yield'; the French equivalent of RITENUTO.

Celesta. A keyboard instrument in the form of a small upright piano invented by Auguste Mustel in 1866; metal plates suspended over resonating boxes are struck by hammers and sustained after the manner of the piano action. Its compass is five octaves from *c*; it is written an octave below sounding pitch. Tchaikovsky included the celesta in *The Nutcracker* (1892) as did Bartók in his Music for Strings, Percussion and Celesta.

Celestina. A bowed keyboard instrument patented by Adam Walker of London in 1772. When the keys were depressed the strings were drawn against a continuous band of silk driven by a weight, spring or foot treadle. It could be added to a harpsichord as a special stop. None survives.

Celibidache, Sergiu (*b* Iaşi, 28 June 1912). Romanian conductor. He studied in Berlin and in 1945 became principal conductor of the Berlin PO. Much of his career has been with radio orchestras in Stuttgart, Stockholm and Munich. From 1983 he has conducted and taught at the Curtis Institute, Philadelphia. He is admired for his meticulously rehearsed performances of Russian music and the Viennese Classics.

Cellensis. Title attached to two masses by Haydn, both in C, HXXII:5 (1766) and 8 (1782); the former is also known as the Cecilian Mass, the latter as the Mariazell.

Cellier, Alfred (b London, 1 Dec 1844; d there, 28 Dec 1891). English organist, conductor and composer. He was a church organist in London, then director of theatres there and in Manchester; from 1877 he was associated with Richard D'Oyly Carte, Arthur Sullivan and the 'Savoy operas'. Among his own energetic operas and operettas, *Dorothy* (1886) was a major success.

Cello. *See* VIOLONCELLO.

Celtic harp. *See* CLÀRSACH.

Cembal d'amour. A keyboard instrument invented by Gottfried Silbermann in 1721. It is a clavichord with strings about twice the normal length and struck at their midpoint, so that the two segments vibrate independently.

Cembalo. The German and Italian term for HARPSICHORD. It also refers to an organ stop.

Cencerro (Sp.: 'cattle bell'). Clapperless animal bell of Spain and the New World, made of copper or bronze. *Cencerros* are specified by Messiaen in two works, but the range of the part requires cowbells.

Cendrillon [Cinderella]. Opera in four acts by Massenet to a libretto by Henri Cain after Perrault (1899, Paris).

Cenerentola, La [Cinderella]. Opera in two acts by Rossini to a libretto by Ferretti after Perrault (1817, Rome). Other composers who wrote Cinderella operas include Massenet (1899) and Wolf-Ferrari (1900); Prokofiev wrote a ballet on the story (1945).

Cento (Lat.). 'Patchwork': a literary or musical work made up of examples from different authors or pre-existing works. Musical examples include the QUODLIBET and its parallel types. It can also refer to a melody pieced together from pre-existing chant formulae; *see* CENTONIZATION.

Centonization (from Lat. *cento*: 'patchwork'). The composition of a work by the synthesis of pre-existing elements. The term (first used in 1934) has been applied mainly to liturgical chants that use melodic formulae shared by other chants. Centonate chants include the gradual, tract and responsory.

Central Park in the Dark. Work for small orchestra by Ives (1906), one of Two Contemplations (the other is *The Unanswered Question*).

Cents. Logarithmic unit used for expressing musical intervals; it is one hundredth of an equal-tempered semitone.

Ce qu'on entend sur la montagne [Bergsymphonie]. Symphonic poem by Liszt (1849) after Hugo, orchestrated by Raff and later Liszt.

Cercar la nota (It.). 'Seek the note': in singing, a slight anticipation of the following syllable, performed as if searching for the precise note. It was common in the 18th and 19th centuries but is now used only in commercial and popular music.

Ceremony of Carols, A. Britten's op.28 (1942), settings of carols in 11 movements for treble voices and harp.

Cererols, Joan (b Martorell, 9 Sept 1618; d Montserrat, 28 Aug 1676). Spanish composer and instrumentalist. He spent his entire life at the monastery of Montserrat, with responsibility for the musical life there. His most characteristic works are the engaging Spanish villancicos, though he excelled as a composer of sacred music for double chorus, often using bold rhythms with much syncopation and hemiola.

Čerha, Friedrich (b Vienna, 17 Feb 1926). Austrian composer and conductor. He studied composition with Uhl at the Vienna Academy, where from 1959 he has taught, and in 1958 founded the ensemble Die Reihe to perform 20th-century music. His works include an operatic setting of Brecht's *Baal* (1974–9) and orchestral music, notably the cycle of seven pieces *Spiegel* (1960–68); he also completed the third act of Berg's *Lulu*.

Černohorský, Bohuslav Matěj (b Nymburk, ?16 Feb 1684; d Graz, ?1 July 1742). Bohemian composer. He worked at monasteries in Prague and Horažďovice, and as cathedral organist at Assisi (1710–15) and Padua (1715–20, 1731–41). Regarded as influential in the development of Bohemian Classicism, he wrote sacred music and reputedly taught Tartini and Gluck.

Cerone, Pietro (b Bergamo, 1566; d Naples, 1625). Italian theorist. He served under Philip II and III in Madrid while studying Spanish music and theory; later he was a singer in Naples. His importance lies in his enormous, controversial treatise *El melopeo y maestro* (1613) which exerted a profound influence in Spain well into the 18th century: an introduction to musical theory, it describes the expressive and technical means appropriate to various sacred and secular forms.

Cerreto, Scipione (b Naples, c1551; d there, c1633). Italian theorist. His two published treatises, *Della prattica musica* (1601) and *Dell'arbore musicale* (1608), though conservative, throw much light on early 17th-century musical practices. Two MS counterpoint treatises and a few madrigals by him also survive.

Certon, Pierre (d Paris, 23 Feb 1572). French composer. He was matins clerk at Notre Dame, Paris (1529), and clerk at the Sainte-Chapelle (1532), where in 1536 he was appointed master of the choristers. Of his eight complete masses, six use parody technique and two are paraphrases; like his motets they show a feeling for structure and form. With *chansons* by Lassus and Costeley, his *Les meslanges* (1570) helped transform *chanson* style into a largely homophonic texture, with richer harmonies and more frequent syncopations; he published 285.

Ceruti, Roque (b Milan, c1683; d Lima, 6 Dec 1760). Italian composer active in Peru. He was palace composer in Lima, 1708–17, then *maestro de capilla* at Trujillo Cathedral, 1721–8, and Lima Cathedral, 1728–60. Besides serenatas and pastorales, he wrote brilliant, often theatrical, Spanish- and Latin-text sacred music that was circulated throughout South America.

Cervantes (Saavedra), Miguel de (b Alcalá de Henares, ?29 Sept 1547; d Madrid, 22 April 1616). Spanish writer. His plays, novels and poems include many illuminating references to music-making in his time. *Don Quixote* (1605–15) has inspired many composers from the 17th century onwards, notably Strauss (tone poem, 1897–8) and Ravel (songs, 1932–3); composers who have based operas on the story include Caldara (1727, 1730), Mendelssohn (1825), Donizetti (1833) and Massenet (1910).

Červený, Václav František (*b* Dubeč, 27 Sept 1819; *d* Hradec Králové, 19 Jan 1896). Czech maker and inventor of brass instruments. Prize-winning instruments from his factory (established 1842) were used in army bands and symphony orchestras throughout Europe. Among his inventions were the *cornon* (1846), from which the Wagner tuba was later developed; the *baroxyton* (1848), a type of euphonium; and the alto trumpet, still used in military bands. He introduced a new technique of drawing tubes into conical shape and a new mechanism for retuning brass instruments.

Cervetto, Giacobbe Basevi (*b* Italy, *c*1682; *d* London, 14 Jan 1783). Italian cellist and composer. Playing in London concerts from the 1740s, he helped to popularize the cello as a solo instrument in England, and composed cello and other chamber works in a *galant* style. His son and pupil James (1747/9–1837), prominent as a cellist in England, wrote similar works in a graceful style and later some more ambitious cello duets (*c*1795).

Cesare, Giovanni Martino (*b* Udine, ?*c*1590; *d* Munich, 6 Feb 1667). Italian composer. In 1615 he entered the service of Duke Maximilian of Bavaria as a cornettist. His music, the bulk of which is found in three publications (1611–21), includes motets, sacred concertos and pieces for cornetts and trombones in up to six parts that show the beginnings of a distinctive instrumental style.

Cesaris, Johannes (*fl c*1385–*c*1420). French composer. Described as one of the three composers who 'astonished all of Paris' with their music in the generation before Dufay, he was presented by Yolande of Aragon, Queen of Sicily, with a small organ for use at Angers Cathedral. Several of his seven or eight surviving *chansons* are rhythmically complex and three present two different texts simultaneously; others are much simpler and more modern in style. He also wrote a four-part isorhythmic motet.

Cesti, Antonio [Pietro] (*b* Arezzo, bap. 5 Aug 1623; *d* Florence, 14 Oct 1669). Italian composer (*not* 'Marc' Antonio Cesti'). After serving as a choirboy at Arezzo, he joined the Franciscan order and served his novitiate at S Croce, Florence. He spent a few years at the monastery in Arezzo before being elected organist of Volterra Cathedral (1644) and shortly afterwards its *maestro di cappella*. At Volterra he enjoyed the patronage of the Medici family and the friendship of the painter and writer Salvator Rosa.

With the successful performance of *Orontea* at Venice in 1649, opera became the centre of Cesti's professional life. In 1652 he secured a position with Archduke Ferdinand Karl at Innsbruck and in 1658 he obtained release from his monastic vows. On the death of Ferdinand Karl's successor in 1665 he was transferred to the Habsburg court at Vienna. His short period there was one of intense activity in opera,

including the composition of the colossal *Il pomo d'oro* to celebrate the Emperor Leopold I's marriage in 1668. Cesti was dissuaded from returning to Venice, where he had aroused resentment in other musicians, and spent his last year as *maestro di cappella* at the Tuscan court in Florence.

Cesti's early Venetian operas are quite modest in scope: most arias are accompanied only by continuo, there are few ensembles and instrumental pieces are consistently scored for two violins and continuo. Nearly all the later operas were composed as court entertainments on a more elaborate scale. His cantatas are mostly for solo voice and continuo; they display a highly flexible approach to form and are equally varied on subject matter and expression.

Operas Orontea (1649); La Dori (1657); Il pomo d'oro (1668); at least 8 others
Other vocal music over 60 cantatas incl. Aspettate, Pria chi'a-dori, Rimbombava d'intorno; 4 motets; Natura et quatuor elementa, sepolcro

Cesti, Remigio (*b* Arezzo, *c*1635; *d* Florence, 1710–17). Italian composer, nephew of Antonio Cesti. He entered the Dominican order in 1649 and was *maestro di cappella* at Pisa, Volterra, Arezzo and Faenza. He wrote sacred music and at least one opera, *Il principe generoso* (1665, Vienna) which shows him more progressive than his uncle in the emphasis on instrumental writing. He may also have composed a serenata *Io son la primavera* (usually attributed to Antonio) for Cosimo de' Medici's birthday in 1662.

Ceterone. A large CITTERN with extra bass strings in the manner of a theorbo or chitarrone; it was used in the late 16th century and throughout the 17th. It had nine to 14 wire strings, usually tuned in the manner of a cittern.

Cetra, La [The Lyre]. Title of Vivaldi's 12 concertos op.9 (1727).

Chabrier, (Alexis-)Emmanuel (*b* Ambert, 18 Jan 1841; *d* Paris, 13 Sept 1894). French composer and pianist. He was trained as a lawyer and worked in the Ministry of the Interior until 1880, meanwhile developing his talents as a pianist and improviser, studying composition, publishing piano pieces and writing light stage works. His friends included Verlaine, Manet, Fauré, Chausson, d'Indy and Duparc, who encouraged his admiration for Wagner. He produced several imaginative operas, among which the Wagnerian *Gwendoline* (1885) and the graceful *opéra comique Le roi malgré lui* (1887) were favourably received in Germany. He is best known for his sparkling orchestral rhapsody *España* (1883), but his natural talent for the lyric, the comic and the colourful is most apparent in his piano works, notably the *Impromptu* (1873), the ten *Pièces pittoresques* (1881), the *Bourrée fantasque* (1891) and the *Valses romantiques* (1883); they show free treatment of dissonance, modality, bold harmonic contrasts, rhythmic verve and dynamic inventiveness, and inspired subsequent generations of French composers, particularly Ravel.

Chace. French 14th-century term for canon, also used to describe a small repertory of two- and three-voiced canonic works imitating instrumental sounds, birdsong etc.

Cha cha cha. A social dance, popular in Europe and the USA in the late 1950s; it originated in Cuba *c*1953. Derived from the mambo, its characteristic rhythm – two crotchets, three quavers, quaver rest – gives it its name.

Chaconne (Fr.; It. *ciaconna*). A Baroque dance and variation form. It originated as a dance-song in Latin America and was popular in Spain and Italy in the 17th century, with music in triple metre and in the major mode. The chords most often used for refrains yielded a number of chaconne basses which were used as grounds for arias (by Monteverdi and others) and for instrumental pieces. Chaconnes occur frequently in the stage works of Lully and other French opera composers as well as in German keyboard music of the late 17th century and early 18th, by which time the distinction between chaconne and PASSACAGLIA became blurred. Bach's *ciaconna* for solo violin and Purcell's *Chacony* for strings are both in the minor mode.

Chadwick, George Whitefield (*b* Lowell, MA, 13 Nov 1854; *d* Boston, 4 April 1931). American composer. He studied with Jadassohn in Leipzig (1876–9) and in Munich (1879–80), then returned to Boston, where in 1897 he was appointed director of the New England Conservatory. His music is characteristic of the 'New England school' in its Germanic classicism, though he was influenced too by French music. A varied output includes operas (*Tabasco*, 1894; *Judith*, 1901; *The Padrone*, 1912), three symphonies and other orchestral works (Symphonic Sketches, 1895–1904), five quartets, choral music and songs. He was one of the most influential teachers in American music and one of its most versatile composers.

Chagrin, Francis (*b* Bucharest, 15 Nov 1905; *d* London, 10 Nov 1972). British composer. He studied with Boulanger and Dukas at the Ecole Normale de Musique (1933–4), Paris, and with Seiber in London, where he settled in 1936. He wrote orchestral works, songs and over 200 film scores and was primarily responsible for founding the Committee (later Society) for the Promotion of New Music (1943).

Chailley, Jacques (*b* Paris, 24 March 1910). French composer and musicologist. He studied with Boulanger (1925–7), at the Paris Conservatoire (1933–5) and at the Sorbonne (1932–6), and has taught at the Sorbonne, the Schola Cantorum (director from 1962) and elsewhere. His voluminous writings include studies of ancient and medieval music, Bach, *Tristan* and *The Magic Flute*; he has also written on ethnomusicology. His compositions are similarly heterogeneous, most written before 1960.

Chailly, Luciano (*b* Ferrara, 19 Jan 1920). Italian composer. He studied with Righini and Bossi at the Milan Conservatory (where from 1969 he has taught) and attended Hindemith's course at Salzburg (1948). His works include operas, chamber pieces etc, the later ones making cautious use of avant-garde techniques. His son Riccardo (*b* 1953), a conductor, has held a post at La Scala and (from 1982) with RIAS and the LPO, becoming director of the Concertgebouw Orchestra in 1986.

Chair [choir] organ. Term for a keyboard and chest secondary to the Great Organ when the chest has its own, separate case behind the organist's back or chair. *See* ORGAN.

Chaliapin, Fyodor Ivanovich. *See* SHALYAPIN, FYODOR IVANOVICH.

Chalumeau [salmoè]. A single-reed instrument of predominantly cylindrical bore, related to the clarinet. It was developed in the late 17th century and built in several sizes: the soprano had a range of $f'-c'''$, the lowest $F-c'$. The chalumeau was used by Vivaldi (who wrote concertos with 'salmoè'), Telemann, Handel, Graupner, Gluck, Dittersdorf and others. Towards the end of the 18th century 'chalumeau' came to be used as it is today, to signify the lowest register of the clarinet.

Chamaterò, Ippolito (*b* Rome, *c*1535–40; *d* after 1592). Italian composer. He was *maestro di cappella* at the cathedrals of Padua (early 1560s) and Udine (1569–75) and elsewhere in north-east Italy. He published six books of madrigals (1560–69) and four of sacred music (1569–75), two of which are important for his encouragement of the art of improvising vocal counterpoint.

Chamber music. Music suitable for performance in a chamber or room: the term is usually applied to instrumental music (though it can equally apply to vocal) for three to eight players, with one player to a part. The main genres are the PIANO TRIO, PIANO QUARTET, PIANO QUINTET, STRING TRIO, STRING QUARTET, STRING QUINTET and TRIO SONATA.

Chamber opera. Term for 20th-century operas of small proportions using a chamber orchestra, e.g. Britten's *The Turn of the Screw*. It has also been applied to 18th-century works such as Pergolesi's *La serva padrona*.

Chamber orchestra. A small ORCHESTRA.

Chamber organ [cabinet organ]. Term for an organ intended for domestic use. Such instruments, developed from the 16th-century POSITIVE, were popular in the 17th, 18th and early 19th centuries in Europe and in the USA. They commonly had a single manual and no pedals, and were blown from a single wedge-shaped bellows, operated by the player's foot below a weighted reservoir.

Chamber sonata. *See* SONATA DA CAMERA.

Chamber symphony. A work in symphonic form for chamber orchestra. The title probably originated with Schoenberg's op.9 for 15 instruments (1906).

Chambonnières, Jacques Champion, Sieur de (*b* Paris, 1601–2; *d* there, 1672, before 4 May). French composer and harpsichordist, son of Jacques Champion. Active at the French court by 1632, he gained a high reputation as a virtuoso harpsichordist and as a dancer; by 1643 he held the post of 'joueur d'espinette'. From 1641 he organized and performed in his own musical gatherings in Paris. He was also an important teacher, and influenced musicians such as Robert Cambert and Louis Couperin. After a decline in his fortunes he retired in 1662 and was succeeded by D'Anglebert.

Chambonnières was founder of the French classical school of harpsichord playing and composition and one of its most distinguished members. Composing exclusively for harpsichord, he was among the first to adopt an idiom based on the *style brisé* of the French lutenists. Most of his *c*140 pieces – those in his two published collections (1670) are grouped in suites – are dances (allemandes, courantes, sarabandes, gigues etc) in binary form; a few have character titles, and there are also several chaconnes. Chambonnières' pieces combine contrapuntal thinking with elaborate ornamentation and are distinctive for their formal balance and smooth melodic lines.

Chaminade, Cécile (Louise Stephanie) (*b* Paris, 8 Aug 1857; *d* Monte Carlo, 18 April 1944). French pianist and composer. She studied with Marsick and Godard, giving her first public concert when she was 18. She made many tours, notably in England from 1892, and wrote *c*200 charming piano pieces.

Champagne, Claude (Adonai) (*b* Montreal, 27 May 1891; *d* there, 21 Dec 1965). Canadian composer. He studied in Canada and in France (1920–28), where he discovered in Fauré, Debussy and Renaissance music the modal means for handling French-Canadian folk music. Back in Canada he taught at the McGill University Conservatorium (1930–42) and at the Montreal Conservatory from its foundation in 1942. His works include orchestral, chamber and choral pieces. Noteworthy are *Images du Canada français* (1943), sound pictures of outstanding mastery for chorus and orchestra, and *Altitude* (1959), a vast fresco for the same forces.

Champion, Jacques, called **La Chapelle** (*b* ?Paris, before 1555; *d* there, 1642). French composer. He was the son of Thomas Champion (*d c*1580; a musician in royal service) and member of a family of at least six musicians active in the 16th and 17th centuries. A keyboard player in the service of Henri III, he is described by Mersenne (*Harmonie universelle*, 1636–7) as having a 'profound knowledge and beautiful touch on the harpsichord'; the few keyboard pieces attributed to him suggest a rather conservative style.

Chancy, François de (*d* Aug 1656). French composer and lutenist. In the service of Cardinal Richelieu *c*1631–35, and then chamber musician to the king, he participated in *ballets de cour* and composed songs for one to four voices (usually with lute), and collections of dances and suites for mandora (1629) and lute (1631). He was highly regarded by Mersenne, who included Chancy pieces in his treatises.

Chandos Anthems. 11 anthems by Handel, composed 1717–18, when he was resident composer for James Brydges, Earl of Carnarvon, later the Duke of Chandos, at his palace Cannons (near Edgware, Middlesex).

Change ringing. An art of bell ringing, peculiarly English, that developed in the 17th century. Each member of a team of ringers pulls a rope controlling one of several church bells; the bells are sounded in prescribed sequences or 'changes'. On the Continent there was a parallel development in the CARILLON.

Changing note. An unaccented non-harmonic note that is quitted by a leap of a 3rd, most commonly downwards. *See* NOTA CAMBIATA.

Chanson (Fr.: 'song'). A lyric composition to French words; more specifically, a French polyphonic song of the late Middle Ages and Renaissance.

The first important *chanson* composer was Machaut, who may have invented the treble-dominated type of song in two, three or four parts, with its rhythmically irregular, decorated melodic lines. Machaut's *chansons* were succeeded by those of two overlapping generations: a 'mannerist' group delighting in rhythmic and notational complexity and a younger group whose simpler songs foreshadowed those of the early 15th-century Burgundian school, represented at its best by Dufay and Binchois. In their *chansons* the poems are mostly about chivalric love, and the music refines the treble-dominated three-part textures of earlier generations. Later in the century the *chansons* of Busnois and Ockeghem weld the three voices into a more homogeneous texture. About a third of those by Busnois are in four parts, which by *c*1500 became standard.

Towards the end of the 15th century a generation of Franco-Netherlands musicians, including Josquin and Obrecht, brought to the *chanson* a new technique of imitative counterpoint applied to equal but independent melodic lines. Not all composers were as ready as Josquin, however, to abandon the standard types or *formes fixes* (ballade, rondeau, virelai) and set the popular poems that circulated widely throughout France.

The so-called Parisian *chanson* of the 1530s and 1540s, as represented in the publications of Attaingnant and the songs of Sermisy and Janequin, were more varied, in subject matter and in musical style, which tended more towards simple chordal textures. Sermisy excelled in sophisticated lovesongs, Janequin in expressing a vivacious French spirit and in his long, descriptive *chansons*. After 1550 *chanson* composers such as Arcadelt, Lassus and Le Jeune were increasingly influenced by the Italian madrigal, but the simpler type, strophic and with the voices predominantly in the same rhythm, flourished as the 'voix de ville' or 'vaudeville'. The *chanson spirituelle*, a secular piece with moralistic or sacred words, reflected the religious conflicts in late 16th-century France.

Chanson de geste. A type of epic poetry in which (to judge by contemporary descriptions and the scraps that survive) each line was sung to the same melody. About 100 examples survive, mostly from the 12th century; they are northern French in origin. They treat heroic exploits or the lives of the saints; the most famous is *The Song of Roland* (*c*1080).

Chanson de toile (Fr.). Term used in 13th-century French sources for a spinning or weaving song. *Chansons de toile* normally tell of a young lady waiting, often spinning, in the absence of her noble lover. 20 examples survive, ten with melodies, of which six are by Audefroi le Bastart.

Chansonnier. An MS or printed book containing principally *chansons* (i.e. lyric poetry in French) or settings of such poetry. They range from 13th-century collections of the monophonic songs of the troubadours and trouvères to the small, elegantly decorated 15th-century miscellanies of secular French polyphony, often compiled for princes or courtiers in Italy and Germany as well as in France and the Low Countries. These also include Latin motets, pieces with non-French texts and even works apparently conceived for instruments. Well-known examples include the Mellon Chansonnier, copied *c*1476, which contains 57 pieces (now at the library of Yale University), the Laborde Chansonnier, copied *c*1470–80, with 103 pieces (Library of Congress, Washington, DC) and the Chansonnier Cordiforme, copied in Savoy before 1477, which contains 44 pieces and is famous for its heart-shaped format (Bibliothèque Nationale, Paris).

The term is also used of a songwriter who sings, in France (usually for a satirist) and in French Canada.

Chansons de Bilitis. Three songs by Debussy (1898), settings for voice and piano of prose-poems by Pierre Louÿs.

Chanter. The melody pipe of a BAGPIPE.

Chanterelle. The highest-pitched string of any instrument; today it is usually applied to the lute, the violin *e'* string and the melody string of the five-string banjo.

Chantilly MS. Southern French MS of the late 14th century, or an early 15th-century Italian copy. It consists of 64 folios containing 112 polyphonic works, 13 of them motets, the remainder ballades, rondeaux and virelais. The music dates from *c*1350–95, including ARS SUBTILIOR pieces of 1375–95 by papal singers from Avignon and musicians at the Foix and Aragon courts. There are two main scribes; the MS, famous for the complexity (and in some cases beauty) of its notation, was long in Florence and is now at the Musée Condé, Chantilly, near Paris.

Chants d'Auvergne. Traditional dialect songs of the Auvergne district of France. They have become known through Canteloube's four volumes of arrangements for voice and orchestra (1923–30), from which a suite of nine is often performed.

Chapel. In music, the term 'chapel' (and its equivalents in other languages, such as the Italian *cappella*, the French *chapelle*, the German *Kapelle*), means not only a place of worship or the clerics associated with it, but also a salaried group of musicians who served an ecclesiastical institution, or in the household or court of a prelate, monarch or nobleman in a sacred or a secular capacity. Such chapels might consist of a few singers, or a large body of singers and instrumentalists. Often they travelled abroad or to war with their rulers, for example when the English Chapel Royal was in France during the 15th century or when the Mantuan Chapel (in which Monteverdi served) was in Hungary early in the 16th century.

Among the most famous chapels in musical history are that of Henry V and VI of England, which had *c*30 members, including important composers; the Burgundian chapel under Philip the Bold, which included Dufay; the papal chapel, in Rome, during the late 15th century and the 16th, where Josquin and Palestrina served; the Habsburg chapels, including that of Maximilian I at the beginning of the 16th century and Leopold I in the second half of the 17th (the Viennese royal chapel was later to provide the basis for the Vienna PO and the Staatsoper); the Dresden Hofkapelle (court chapel), founded in 1648, from which the present orchestra of that name and the Dresden Opera House originate; and the

Chapelle Royale in Paris. The heads of these institutions bore such titles as *maestro di cappella* (Italian), *maître de chapelle* (French), *Kapellmeister* (German), *maestro de capilla* (Spanish) or *mestre de capela* (Portuguese); they were important and coveted posts, often filled by established composers. The English term 'chapelmaster' is rarely used.

Chapel master. *See* CHAPEL and MAESTRO.

Chapel Royal. The English royal chapel, attached to the court; the term denotes the liturgical musicians and the institution as a whole. Established by the 13th century, it travelled with the sovereign and for long had no permanent base. Its home since 1702 has been at St James's Palace. Tallis, Byrd, Gibbons, Purcell and Handel were among its most notable members.

Chapí (y Lorente), Ruperto (*b* Villena, 27 March 1851; *d* Madrid, 25 March 1909). Spanish composer. He studied at the Madrid Conservatory and in Rome, Milan and Paris, composing his first symphonic suite in 1873. A series of one-act operas followed, then over 1000 zarzuelas (beginning with *Música clásica*, 1880), many notable successes. He published four string quartets.

Chappell. English firm of music publishers, concert agents and piano manufacturers. It was started in 1810 by J.B. Cramer, Francis Latour and Samuel Chappell (*c*1782–1834). Chappell's son William (1809–88), a musical antiquarian, directed the firm only briefly (1834–44); under his brothers Thomas (1819–1902) and Samuel Arthur (1834–1904) its activities expanded greatly in the fields of popular music and light opera. In the early 20th century it led in the campaign against musical piracy, ran the Queen's Hall Promenade Concerts (1915–26) and published musical comedies by British and American composers, meanwhile continuing its vast trade in educational and band music.

Character-piece (Ger. *Charakterstück*). A piece, usually for piano, expressing a single mood or a programmatic idea.

Charivari [shivaree]. A mock serenade (e.g. for newlyweds) of loud, discordant noises using pots and pans, cowbells, guns and other noisemakers; by extension, any cacophony of out-of-tune noises.

Charleston. A lively, social dance of the 1920s, said to have originated in Charleston, South Carolina. It was fast, with a characteristic syncopated rhythm, as in the song *Charleston* (1923) by Cecil Mack and Jimmy Johnson.

Charpentier, Gabriel (*b* Richmond, Quebec, 13 Sept 1925). Canadian composer. He studied in Montreal and in France under Boulanger. He worked for the CBC in Montreal, 1953–79, and then became artistic director of the Pro Musica Society. He has written incidental music for the Shakespeare Festival at Stratford, including one of his two works based on the Orpheus myth and influenced by medieval religious drama (1969, 1972). He has also written music for films, chamber and choral music.

Charpentier, Gustave (*b* Dieuze, 25 June 1860; *d* Paris, 18 Feb 1956). French composer. He studied at the Lille Conservatory and with Massenet in Paris, developing a passion for the bohemian life of Montmartre and a distaste for authority, also winning the

Prix de Rome in 1887. In Rome he wrote the orchestral suite *Impressions d'Italie*, the symphony-drama *La vie du poète* and the first act of his most famous work, the opera *Louise* (1900). His growing reputation and the expected scandal of its theme of women's liberation made *Louise* a success; it anticipated Puccini's *verismo* works but also recalls Gounod and, in its leitmotifs and harmony, Wagner. In 1913 he had short-lived success with his last opera, *Julien*, further operas of the 'people' being projected but not completed. He was founder of the Conservatoire Populaire Mimi Pinson, which gave free musical tuition to midinettes from 1902.

Charpentier, Jacques (*b* Paris, 18 Oct 1933). French composer and organist. He studied Indian music in Bombay and Calcutta (1953–4) before his training under Aubin and Messiaen at the Paris Conservatoire. His works include *Etudes karnatiques* for piano (1961) and the *Livre d'orgue* (1973).

Charpentier, Marc-Antoine (*b* Paris, ?1645–50; *d* Paris, 24 Feb 1704). French composer. He studied in Rome, probably with Carissimi, whose oratorios he introduced into France. On his return to Paris he was employed as composer and singer by the Duchess of Guise and also collaborated with Molière in the theatre. In the early 1680s he entered the service of the grand dauphin, for which Louis XIV granted him a pension in 1683, and he was for a time music teacher to Philippe, Duke of Chartres (later Duke of Orleans and Regent of France). Perhaps also in the 1680s Charpentier became attached to the Jesuit church of St Louis in Paris, and from 1698 until his death he held the important post of *maître de musique* of the Saint-Chapelle, for which he wrote some of his most impressive works.

Charpentier's church music was based initially on mid-century Italian models, but soon incorporated French modes of expression – the 'official' grandeur of the *grand motet*; the declamatory manner of the court *air* and Lullian *récit*; the 'popular' simplicity of noëls; and an often elaborately ornamented melodic line. Charpentier was the only Frenchman of his time to write oratorios of any quality. His theatre compositions are even more indebted to French models, and he was an important composer of *airs sérieux* and *airs à boire*.

Sacred vocal music 11 masses; 10 Magnificats; Tenebrae lessons and responsories; 84 psalm settings; over 200 motets (incl. dramatic motets and oratorios); 9 Litany of Loreto settings; 4 Te Deum settings
Secular vocal music c30 airs, 8 cantatas
Dramatic music Les arts florissants (1686); David et Jonathas (1688); Médée (1693); 11 pastorals and divertissements; music for Le malade imaginaire (1685) and other plays
Instrumental music sacred ovs.; preludes; symphonies; suites, dances, sonata

Charton-Demeur [de Meur], **Anne** [Arsène] (*b* Saujon, 5 March 1824; *d* Paris, 30 Nov 1892). French mezzo-soprano. Noted by Berlioz for the warmth, delicacy and rare beauty of her voice, she sang the title role in the première of his *Béatrice et Bénédict* (1862) and Dido in his *Les troyens à Carthage* (1863).

Chase, Gilbert (*b* Havana, 4 Sept 1906). American music historian. He studied in New York, North Carolina and Paris. He was a music critic in Paris (1929–35), and Latin American specialist at the Library of Congress (1940–43), then worked for NBC. He has taught in Oklahoma, New Orleans, New York and Austin. His writings include *The Music of Spain* (1941) and *America's Music* (1955) as well as studies of Latin American music.

Chasse, La [The Hunt]. Nickname of Haydn's Symphony no.73 in D (?1781), so called because of the hunting-horn style of the last movement (originally the overture to *La fedeltà premiata*).

Chasseur maudit, Le [The Accursed hunter]. Symphonic poem by Franck (1882) after G.A. Bürger's ballad *Der wilde Jäger*.

Chastelain de Couci (*b* c1165; *d* May–June 1203). French trouvère. The hero of a largely fictitious *roman*, he was probably the crusader Gui IV de Coucy. At least 15 of his *chansons* survive.

Chaumont, Lambert (*b* ?Liège, c1630; *d* Huy, 23 April 1712). South Netherlands composer and Carmelite priest. His published eight organ suites (1695) are notable for their wide range of timbres, blend of sonorities and elegant counterpoint. The volume includes tuning instructions and essays on accompaniment and plainchant.

Chausson, (Amedée-)Ernest (*b* Paris, 20 Jan 1855; *d* Limay, 10 June 1899). French composer. He grew up in comfortable and cultured circumstances but turned to music only after being trained in law. Studying with Massenet at the Paris Conservatoire, he came under Franck's influence and visited Germany to hear Wagner. His friends in Paris included Mallarmé, Debussy, Albéniz and Cortot. He died prematurely in a cycling accident but his output reflects his growing maturity from dependence on Massenet, Franck and Wagner, seen in the prettiness of early songs and the orchestration of the symphonic poem *Viviane* (1882), to a more elaborate, intensely dramatic style in the *Poème de l'amour et de la mer* (1882–93) and the opera *Le roi Arthus* (1886–95), and finally to a period of serious melancholy which produced the Turgenev-inspired *Poème* op.25 for violin and orchestra (1896) and some concise chamber music. Once criticized for being vague and Wagnerian, his music took on a more classical expression from about 1890, when he turned towards older Gallic and Italian resources and to Couperin and Rameau.

Chautauqua Institution (USA). American organization founded in 1874 in Chautauqua, New York, as a training camp for Sunday school teachers; after its first assembly (1876) it rapidly expanded to become a summer programme of adult education at conservatory level, with lectures and seminars, in which performance was also important. It was widely imitated and many other such educational summer institutions were established.

Chávez (y Ramírez), Carlos (Antonio de Padua) (*b* Mexico City, 13 June 1899; *d* there, 2 Aug 1978). Mexican composer. He studied with Ponce (1910–14) and Ogazón (1915–20) but was self-taught as a composer, being most influenced by his experience of Indian culture. A visit to Europe in 1922–3 was unproductive, but his first trip to the USA (1923–4) began a close association: in 1926–8 he lived in New York and formed friendships with Copland, Cowell and Varèse. On his return to Mexico he became founder-director of the Mexico SO (1928–48) and director of the National Conservatory (1928–33), having a decisive influence on Mexican cultural life. His works include seven symphonies (the *Sinfonía india* is no.2, 1936) and two Aztec ballets (*El fuego nuevo*, 1921; *Los cuatro soles*, 1925). He was a master of orchestration, particularly of wind writing, and explored concerto writing; characteristic are the four *Soli* (1933–66) for small groups and orchestra.

Chaykovsky, Pyotr Il'yich. *See* TCHAIKOVSKY, PYOTR IL'YICH.

Checkmate. Ballet in one act by Bliss to his own libretto (1937, Paris).

Chédeville. French family of musette players, makers and composers, from Oulins. The chief members were the brothers Pierre (1694–1725), Esprit Philippe (1696–1762) and Nicolas (1705–82), great-nephews of Louis and Nicolas Hotteterre. All three worked in Paris, playing in the Opéra orchestra and the Grands Hautbois. Esprit Philippe and Nicolas were prolific composers of lightweight suites, dances etc, and arrangements for musette or vielle (hurdy-gurdy) intended for wealthy amateurs, and both also made musettes.

Chef (Fr.). 'Chief'; hence *chef d'orchestre* (conductor of an orchestra), *chef d'attaque* (leader), *chef de musique* (bandmaster).

Cheironomy. The doctrine of hand signs; the ancient form of conducting whereby the leading musician indicated melodic curves and ornaments by spatial signs. This method was particularly developed in traditions which had no equivalent in written musical notation, for example the music of Pharaonic Egypt, Indian music (in the teaching of Vedic chants), Jewish music and Byzantine and Roman chants.

Chekker. An instrument mentioned in various writings from the 14th century to the 16th; it has not yet been positively identified, though most sources refer to it as a keyboard instrument with strings.

Chelard, Hippolyte-André(-Jean)-Baptiste (*b* Paris, 1 Feb 1789; *d* Weimar, 12 Feb 1861). French composer and conductor. He studied at the Paris Conservatoire and in Italy, having success with *La casa da vendere* (1815) in Naples and *Macbeth* (1827), *Der Student* (1832) and *Die Hermannsschlacht* (1835) in Munich, where he had settled in 1830. He was Kapellmeister at Weimar from 1840 to 1852. Though he had a considerable reputation in Germany, he was overshadowed by Liszt and Berlioz, whose music his sometimes prefigured.

Chelleri, Fortunato (*b* Parma, 1686–90; *d* Kassel, 11 Dec 1757). Italian composer. He wrote some 18 operas for Italian cities, 1707–22, and one for Barcelona. After a period as court Kapellmeister at Würzburg (1722–4), he was the Landgrave of Hesse's Kapellmeister in Kassel (briefly in Stockholm). One of the finest Italian-trained composers then working in Germany, he wrote oratorios and sacred and instrumental music, and revised some of his Italian operas for performances there.

Chelleri visited London, 1726–7. The 'Pergolesi' *Concerti armonici*, now known to be by Wassenaer, have been attributed to him.

Chelsea Opera Group. Partly amateur group established in 1950 to give concert performances of Mozart operas, particularly in Oxford, Cambridge and London. Conductors have included Colin Davis (a founder) and Nicholas Braithwaite. Singers with the major London opera companies have tried out new roles with the group.

Cheltenham International Festival (UK). Annual (summer) series, mainly of orchestral, chamber and solo concerts, instituted in 1945 as the Cheltenham Festival (renamed 1974). It aimed to promote new British music; 291 premières were given in 25 years (Berkeley, Fricker, Hoddinott and Rawsthorne were most often represented). From 1966 contemporary works from abroad were included and since 1974 a smaller proportion of new works has been given.

Chemin-Petit, Hans (*b* Potsdam, 24 July 1902; *d* Berlin, 12 April 1981). German composer. He studied with Juon at the Musikhochschule in Berlin (1920–26), where he has worked as a composer, teacher and choral conductor. His works are predominantly vocal; the choral music is often polyphonically complex. He wrote several chamber operas after the success of his first, *Der gefangene Vogel* (1929).

Cheng. *See* ZHENG.

Cherepnin, Alexander Nikolayevich. *See* TCHEREPNIN, ALEXANDER NIKOLAYEVICH.

Cherkassy, Shura (*b* Odessa, 7 Oct 1911). American pianist of Russian birth. After study with Josef Hofmann at the Curtis Institute he made his début at Baltimore in 1922. From 1945 he has toured frequently in Europe. His remarkable technique and range of expression have made him much in demand in the Romantic repertory.

Cherubini, Luigi (Carlo Zanobi Salvadore Maria) (*b* Florence, 8/14 Sept 1760; *d* Paris, 15 March 1842). Italian composer and teacher. He was a dominant figure in French musical life for half a century. At 18, with 36 works (mainly church music) to his credit, he began a period of study with Sarti in Bologna and Milan (1778–80). The resulting Italian operas he produced in Italy and London (1784–5), and his work as an Italian opera director (1789–90) in Paris (where he had settled in 1786), pale in significance next to the triumphant première of his second French opera, *Lodoïska* (Paris, 1791). He was appointed inspector at the new Institut National de Musique (from 1795 the Conservatoire), his status soon being enhanced by the successes of *Médée* (1797) and *Les deux journées* (1800). As *surintendant de la musique du roi* under the restored monarchy, he turned increasingly to church music, writing seven masses, two requiems and many shorter pieces, all well received (unlike his later operas). National honours, a commission from the London Philharmonic Society (1815) and the directorship of the Conservatoire (1822) and completion of his textbook, *Cours de contrepoint et de fugue* (1835), crowned his career.

Cherubini's importance in operatic history rests on his transformation of merely picturesque or anecdotal *opéra comique* into a vehicle for powerful dramatic portrayal (e.g. *Médée's* depiction of psychological conflict) and for the serious treatment of contemporary topics (*Lodoïska's* realistic heroism; social reconciliation in *Les deux journées*). His best church music, notably the C minor Requiem (specially admired by Beethoven, Schumann, Brahms and Berlioz), unites his command of counterpoint and orchestral sonority with appropriate dramatic expression, while his non-vocal works, chiefly the operatic overtures, Symphony in D and six string quartets, make their effect through the creative use of instrumental colour.

Operas Lodoïska (1791); Médée (1797); Les deux journées (1800); Anacréon, opéra-ballet (1803); Faniska (1806); over 15 others
Vocal music Requiem, c (1816); Requiem, d (1836); 9 other masses; over 60 smaller sacred works; secular cantatas; ceremonial works; arias, duets, songs, canons
Instrumental music Ov., G (1815); Sym. D; orch dances, marches; 6 str qts (1814–37); other chamber works; pf pieces

Chest of viols. A term used, particularly in 16th- and 17th-century England, for a box of viols (usually six), matched in power, size and colour, and used for chamber music. It normally comprised two each of trebles, tenors and basses.

Chetham, John (*b* before 1700; *d* Skipton, bur. 26 June 1746). English psalmodist. His *A Book of Psalmody* (1718), a collection of psalm tunes and simple anthems from various sources, was highly popular in parish churches until the late 19th century.

Chevé method. *See* GALIN-PARIS-CHEVÉ METHOD.

Chevillard, (Paul Alexandre) Camille (*b* Paris, 14 Oct 1859; *d* there, 30 May 1923). French conductor and composer. He was associated with the Lamoureux concerts from the 1880s, promoting the music of Beethoven, Schumann, Wagner and the Russian nationalists; he became director of the Opéra in 1914. His compositions include chamber, orchestral and piano music and songs. His father was the Belgian cellist Pierre Chevillard (1811–77).

Chevreuille, Raymond (*b* Watermael-Boitsfort, Brussels, 17 Nov 1901; *d* Montignies-le-Tilleul, 9 May 1976). Belgian composer. Essentially self-taught, he began in the early 1930s to develop an individual 12-note style in which series are worked thematically in succession: the absence of formal unity is characteristic, but so is a fixed expressive tone, whether of lyrical pathos or exuberance. His large output includes eight symphonies, concertos, quartets, ballets, choral works and songs.

Chiabrera, Gabriello (*b* Savona, 8 June 1552; *d* there, 11 Oct 1638). Italian poet. He lived in Rome, Savona and Florence, where he was among those experimenting with early opera; his libretto *Il rapimento di Cefalo* (1600) was set by Caccini and others, who also set his lyric poetry.

Chiari, Giuseppe (*b* Florence, 26 Sept 1926). Italian composer. He studied engineering at Florence University and was associated with the Fluxus movement in New York from 1962, becoming one of the leading Italian practitioners of 'action music'.

Chiaula, Mauro (*b* Palermo, *c*1544; *d* there, *c*1603). Italian composer, a Benedictine monk. Apart from a brief period near Mantua, he spent his working life from 1561 at S Martino delle Scale, near Palermo. His extant music comprises masses (1588), motets (1590), Lamentations (1597) and some madrigals (lost). His music for a sacred drama in Palermo (1581), a mixture of double-choir motets and monody, was once popular but is now lost.

Chiavette (It.). Term used for one of the two groupings of clefs (the other is *chiavi naturali*) in which nearly all the vocal music of the golden age of *a cappella* polyphony was written. The chiavette system consists of treble, mezzo-soprano, alto and baritone clefs; *chiavi naturali* consist of soprano, alto, tenor and bass clefs. A third system, sometimes called 'low chiavette', is pitched a 3rd lower. It has been suggested that these systems represent differing pitch systems as opposed to differing vocal ranges.

Chicago Grand Opera Company. The city's first resident opera group, established in 1910; it was renamed in 1915 (Opera Association) and in 1922, and dissolved in 1932. It gave the première (1921) of *The Love of Three Oranges*, conducted by Prokofiev. Another Grand Opera Company existed in 1933–46.

Chicago Symphony Orchestra. American orchestra, originally the Chicago Orchestra, formed in 1891 by the conductor Theodore Thomas and named after him from 1906; it was renamed in 1912. Its home is Orchestra Hall (opened 1904, cap. 2566); summer concerts are given at Ravinia Festival. Under Frederick Stock (1905–42) many new works were presented and children's concerts instituted. The orchestra's international renown is based on its recordings, especially under Fritz Reiner (1952–63) and Georg Solti (music director from 1969), as well as on tours abroad. Other conductors have included Rafael Kubelik (1950–53), Jean Martinon (1963–8), Carlo Maria Giulini, Claudio Abbado and Henry Mazer.

Chichester Festival (UK). *See* SOUTHERN CATHEDRALS FESTIVAL.

Chichester Psalms. Choral work by Leonard Bernstein to a Hebrew biblical text (1965), written for Chichester Cathedral.

Chickering. American firm of piano makers. It was founded in Boston in 1823 by Jonas Chickering (1798–1853), in partnership with James Stewart. They made square pianos, uprights from 1830 and grands from 1840. The firm won greatest acclaim for Chickering's cast-iron frame for the grand piano (patented 1843), allowing higher string tension, hence thicker strings and a richer tone. Acquired by the American Piano Co. in 1908, the firm became part of the Aeolian American Corporation in 1932 and was acquired by Wurlitzer in 1985.

Chiesa (It.). 'Church': in the Baroque period the term 'da chiesa' indicated music suitable for performance in church; it distinguished the four-movement sonata or concerto (slow–fast–slow–fast, often with fugal textures) from the 'da CAMERA' ('chamber') type.

Chigi Codex. MS of the early 16th century. It consists of 289 folios with 20 masses, a Credo and 19 motets, by Ockeghem, Compère, Josquin and others. Copied in a well-known scriptorium in the Netherlands, it is exceptionally lavish, intended not for use but for presentation. It is now in the Vatican Library.

Chilcot, Thomas (*b* ?Bath, *c*1707; *d* there, 24 Nov 1766). English composer. Organist of Bath Abbey from 1728, he played in and directed concerts in the West Country. His compositions, clearly influenced by Handel, include a fine set of harpsichord suites and 12 harpsichord concertos.

Child, William (*b* Bristol, 1606/7; *d* Windsor, 23 March 1697). English composer. Probably a pupil of Bevin at Bristol Cathedral, he joined St George's Chapel, Windsor, in 1630, soon becoming organist. Though absent during the Civil War, he returned at the Restoration and also joined the Chapel Royal as an organist. He graduated BMus (1631) and DMus (1663) at Oxford. In addition to the 20 pieces in his *First Set of Psalmes* (1639), he composed *c*18 services and over 60 anthems, as well as mass sections, motets and a few secular and instrumental pieces. Long popular in English churches, his music has vitality and a sensitive feeling for words, and shows acknowledgment of the early Italian Baroque style.

Childhood of Christ, The. *See* ENFANCE DU CHRIST, L'.

Child of our Time, A. Oratorio by Tippett to his own text (1941); it uses black spirituals in the same way that Bach used chorales in his Passions.

Children's Corner. Set of six piano pieces (with English titles) by Debussy (1908), the last being the famous *Golliwogg's Cake-walk.*

Children's Overture. Orchestral work by Quilter (1914) based on nursery rhymes.

Childs, Barney (*b* Spokane, WA, 13 Feb 1926). American composer. He studied English at the universities of Nevada, Oxford and Stanford and was a private composition pupil of Carter. His music is frankly eclectic, sometimes incorporating indeterminate elements (e.g. *Interbalances* I–VI, 1960–63); it is also abundant, including numerous orchestral and ensemble pieces (two symphonies, 1954, 1956; eight string quartets, 1957–74).

Chilesotti, Oscar (*b* Bassano del Grappa, 12 July 1848; *d* there, 23 June 1916). Italian musicologist. An excellent lutenist, he examined the lute's structure, tuning and literature in numerous articles and editions.

Chilingirian Quartet. English string quartet, led by Levon Chilingirian. It was formed in 1971 and has played extensively in Europe, the USA and in Australia. Besides the standard repertory (they have recorded much Mozart and Schubert), the quartet has investigated fringe repertory, such as Arriaga, Berwald and Korngold, showing themselves accomplished players in a wide range of styles.

Chime bar. An instrument consisting of a bar of metal, wood or synthetic material mounted on a resonator and struck with a beater. Chime bars are made primarily for educational or therapeutic use and are available in sets of different pitch.

Chimes. A generic term for a set of instruments, normally percussion. In Western music the term is most commonly applied to a set of tuned, stationary bells, including clock chimes and the orchestral TUBULAR BELLS.

Ch'in. *See* QIN.

Chinelli, Giovanni Battista (*b* Moletolo, 24 May 1610; *d* Parma, 15 June 1677). Italian composer. He was *maestro di cappella* at Novara Cathedral (1631–4), at Parma Cathedral (1634–7, 1652–60) and in Venice (1637–52). His output consists mainly of sacred music in concertato style, often with strings, including one complete set of music for Compline (1639). He also wrote a collection of madrigals (1637).

Chinese music. Mainland China covers a vast area, inhabited by many culturally distinct ethnic groups which have interacted to varying degrees for more than 4000 years; Chinese musical genres are thus numerous and their styles varied. But throughout Chinese musical history a number of central themes dominate: a belief in the power of music, necessitating its control by the state; the juxtaposition of 'native' and 'foreign' (especially central Asian) idioms; and a fascination with theory, acoustics and metaphysical relation of music to the natural world, ideas which are enshrined in hundreds of treatises from the ancient to modern period.

Little is known about the sound of ancient Chinese music, but written documents provide information about music theory and music in society. Chinese musical history has been inextricably bound to politics. The bureau of music of each new administration established pitch standards and oversaw ceremonial and court music. Absolute pitch was regarded as an integral part of the system of weights and measures and new measurements were introduced with each new dynasty. Chinese philosophers (including Confucius) were early to recognize the power of music over the mind and emotions and its importance in education. Like the ancient Greeks, they recommended state control in view of its power over the morality of the masses. Although ancient music theory has little bearing on modern Chinese music, these fundamental views have persisted and can be witnessed in such movements as the Cultural Revolution.

From the time Confucianism became the state religion of China in the Han dynasty until the 1911 revolution, *yayue* ('elegant music', associated with Confucian ritual) was the state music; every dynasty tried to retain its ancient style. Court Confucianists were disturbed when *huyue* ('foreign music', particularly from the north and west) became fashionable (AD 386–589), and the predominance of *yayue* was restored in subsequent dynasties. After the disappearance of the imperial courts in China, however, *yayue* has been performed only in Confucian temples.

There are over 300 forms of regional theatre in China, the most famous of which is Beijing (Peking) opera. This developed in the late 18th century. Early companies performed in teahouses in an atmosphere of casual conversation and social mingling. The characters are categorized not by vocal range but by the type of person represented. There are four basic types: the main male characters, including bearded old men, court officials and generals (all usually in the baritone range); unbearded scholar-lovers, who sing in falsetto; the virtuous daughter or faithful wife, sung in high falsetto; and the flirtatious woman. The standard repertory consists of *c*30 aria melodies, each expressing a different mood. Accompanying instruments included bowed and plucked strings, drums, clappers, gongs, cymbals, bamboo flutes and oboes. After the establishment of the Chinese People's Republic (1949), Beijing opera was reformed according to the ideology of Mao Zedong and from 1964 traditional opera virtually disappeared. New texts and conventions emphasized patriotism and eliminated kowtowing and other gestures of humiliation; a new repertory was composed celebrating the triumphs of Marxist socialism.

Among the earliest instruments found in China are bronze bells, stone-chimes and ocarinas from the 2nd millennium BC. Stone reliefs from the beginning of the Christian era show panpipes, drums, bells, stone-chimes and zithers, being played in groups to accompany dances. Most famous of the classical Chinese instruments is the *qin*, a long zither with a history of 3000 years. The standard instrument has seven silk strings; the length is 3 'feet' 6.5 Chinese 'inches' (*c*120 cm) to symbolize the 365 days of the year; the 'dragon pond' sound opening in the bottom board measures 8 'inches' to symbolize the eight directions of the winds; the soundboard is convex to symbolize Heaven and the bottom board flat to symbolize Earth. Other classical string instruments include the *zheng*, a plucked half-tube zither used for personal and popular entertainment, and the *pipa*, a four-string plucked lute with frets, which probably originated·in central Asia. The Chinese traditionally classify instruments according to the material from which they are made. The eight main categories include wood (for example, the *muyu*, wooden fish clappers); skin (*gu*, drums); silk (*qin*, *pipa*), clay (vessel flutes and whistles), bamboo (oboes, panpipes, transverse and end-blown flutes) and gourd (*sheng*, free-reed mouth organ).

Chinese pavilion. *See* TURKISH CRESCENT.

Chinese woodblock. Term for the Western orchestral WOODBLOCK.

Chin rest. A device clamped to the lower part of the violin (or similar instrument played on the arm), generally at the left of the tailpiece. The chin rest separates the chin from contact with the instrument and gives the player a firmer grip.

Chishko, Oles' [Alexander] **Semyonovich** (*b* Dvurechnïy Kut, 3 July 1895). Soviet composer. He studied and worked as a singer before training as a composer at the Leningrad Conservatory (1931–4). His works include songs, folksong arrangements and 'song operas', notably the influential *Battleship Potemkin* (1937), produced throughout the USSR.

Chisholm, Erik (*b* Glasgow, 4 Jan 1904; *d* Cape Town, 8 June 1965). Scottish musician. He studied with Tovey at Edinburgh University and in the 1930s worked in Scotland as an opera and ballet conductor, presenting many works new to Britain (*Idomeneo*, *Les troyens* etc). In 1946 he became director of the South African College of Music. His

works bring Celtic elements into a moderately dissonant style: they include operas, ballets, two symphonies and two piano concertos.

Chitarra. *See* GUITAR.

Chitarrone. A name current from *c*1590 to *c*1655 for a theorbo-like instrument. It was usually strung in metal or gut, with six double courses over the fingerboard and eight single strings (basses); the stopped courses are turned like a lute's, but the two top strings are an octave lower. It was used primarily to accompany solo singing and was particularly popular *c*1600; there is also a small solo repertory. (For illustration, *see* LUTE.)

Chiuso (It.). 'Closed': in horn music, an instruction that notes should be fully stopped with the hand; this is countermanded by 'aperto'.

Chlubna, Osvald (*b* Brno, 22 June 1893; *d* there, 30 Oct 1971). Czech composer. A pupil of Janáček at the Brno Organ School (1914–15) and in master classes (1923–4), he worked as a bank clerk. An outstanding orchestrator, he scored the last act of Janáček's *Šárka* and with Bakala provided an optimistic end to *From the House of the Dead*. His own works include operas and symphonic poems, notably the cycles *Nature and Man* (1953) and *This is my Country* (1957).

Choir. A group of singers who perform together, usually in parts; the term is generally used for bodies of singers in a church or chapel in preference to the term 'chorus'. The word is also used for a homogeneous group of instruments within a larger group (e.g. 'a brass choir'). *See* CHORUS.

Choirbook. An MS or printed book large enough to allow an entire choir to sing from it. Choirbooks were used in the late 15th and early 16th centuries.

Choir organ. *See* CHAIR ORGAN.

C-hole. A type of SOUNDHOLE.

Chopin, Fryderyk Franciszek [Frédéric François] (*b* Żelazowa Wola, ?1 March 1810; *d* Paris, 17 Oct 1849). Polish composer. The son of French émigré father (a schoolteacher working in Poland) and a cultured Polish mother, he grew up in Warsaw, taking childhood music lessons (in Bach and the Viennese Classics) from Wojciech Żywny and Jósef Elsner before entering the Conservatory (1826–9). By this time he had performed in local salons and composed several rondos, polonaises and mazurkas. Public and critical acclaim increased during the years 1829–30 when he gave concerts in Vienna and Warsaw, but his despair over the political repression in Poland, coupled with his musical ambitions, led him to move to Paris in 1831. There, with practical help from Kalkbrenner and Pleyel, praise from Liszt, Fétis and Schumann and introductions into the highest society, he quickly established himself as a private teacher and salon performer, his legendary artist's image being enhanced by frail health (he had tuberculosis), attractive looks, sensitive playing, a courteous manner and the piquancy attaching to self-exile. Of his several romantic affairs, the most talked about was that with the novelist George Sand (Aurore Dudevant) – though whether he was truly drawn to women must remain in doubt. Between 1838 and 1847 their relationship, with a strong element of the maternal on her side, coincided with one of his most productive creative periods. He gave few public concerts, though his playing was much praised, and he published much of his best music simultaneously in Paris, London and Leipzig. The breach with Sand was followed by a rapid deterioration in his health and a long visit to Britain (1848). His funeral at the Madeleine was attended by nearly 3000 people.

No great composer has devoted himself as exclusively to the piano as Chopin. By all accounts an inspired improviser, he composed while playing, writing down his thoughts only with difficulty. But he was no mere dreamer – his development can be seen as an ever more sophisticated improvisation on the classical principle of departure and return. For the concert-giving years 1828–32 he wrote brilliant virtuoso pieces (e.g. rondos) and music for piano and orchestra; the teaching side of his career is represented by the studies, preludes, nocturnes, waltzes, impromptus and mazurkas, polished pieces of moderate difficulty. The large-scale works – the later polonaises, scherzos, ballades, sonatas, the Barcarolle and the dramatic Polonaise-fantaisie – he wrote for himself and a small circle of admirers. Apart from the national feeling in the Polish dances, and possibly some narrative background to the ballades, he intended notably few references to literary, pictorial or autobiographical ideas.

Chopin is admired above all for his great originality in exploiting the piano. While his own playing style was famous for its subtlety and restraint, its exquisite delicacy in contrast with the spectacular feats of pianism then reigning in Paris, most of his works have a simple texture of accompanied melody. From this he derived endless variety, using wide-compass broken chords, the sustaining pedal and a combination of highly expressive melodies, some in inner voices. Similarly, though most of his works are basically ternary in form, they show great resource in the way the return is varied, delayed, foreshortened or extended, often with a brilliant coda added.

Chopin's harmony however was conspicuously innovatory. Through melodic clashes, ambiguous chords, delayed or surprising cadences, remote or sliding modulations (sometimes many in quick succession), unresolved dominant 7ths and occasionally excursions into pure chromaticism or modality, he pushed the accepted procedures of dissonance and key into previously unexplored territory. This profound influence can be traced alike in the music of Liszt, Wagner, Fauré, Debussy, Grieg, Albéniz, Tchaikovsky, Rakhmaninov and many others.

Piano solo 31 mazurkas (opp.68, 6, 7, 17, 24, 67, 30, 33, 41, 50, 56, 59, 63); 14 nocturnes (opp.72, 9, 15, 27, 37, 48, 55, 62); 14 polonaises (opp.71, 26, 40, 44, 53); 19 waltzes (opp.69, 70, 18, 34, 42, 64); 4 ballades (opp.23, 38, 47, 52); 24 preludes (op.28); 27 studies (opp.10, 25); 4 impromptus (opp.66, 29, 36, 51); 4 scherzos (opp.20, 31, 39, 54); 3 rondos (opp.1, 5); marches; variations; Bolero (op.19); Sonata, b♭ (op.35, 1839); Fantasie, f/A♭ (op.49, 1841); Berceuse, D♭ (op.57, 1844); Sonata, b (op.58, 1844); Barcarolle, F♯ (op.60, 1846); Polonaise-fantaisie, A♭ (op.61, 1846)
Piano with orchestra Pf Conc. no.1, e (1830); Pf Conc. no.2, f (1829–30); 4 other works
Other Pf Trio; Vc Sonata; 2 chamber duos; c20 songs with pf acc.; arrs., transcrs.; 1 pf duet

Chorale. The congregational hymn of the Lutheran church. The texts and music of many early chorales were adapted from pre-Reformation hymns, antiphons etc, and from secular songs. Publications of numerous hymnbooks during and after Luther's lifetime helped to establish the chorale as a central item in the service and also stimulated the composition of new chorales. After 1600 melodies were written by J. Crüger and others, but chorale composition centred more on writing new texts to four-part versions of existing melodies in 'cantional' style, i.e. with the melody in the top part, simple supporting lines in the others and a regular harmonic tread. This style, initiated by the Calvinist theologian Osiander, reached its highest point of development in the chorale harmonizations of J.S. Bach. Chorales were much used as the melodic basis for other compositions. The chorale concerto is a sacred vocal piece based on a chorale; composers include Praetorius, Schein and Scheidt. There are large-scale examples of the period c1600–1620 with two or more vocal and instrumental choirs.

The chorale cantata is a cantata which is a setting of a chorale text (or partly a paraphrase of one, as in many of the cantatas of Bach's second cycle, 1724–5), generally using the chorale melody in various ways. An earlier type was the chorale motet, a vocal work often with instrumental doubling, where the chorale served as a *cantus firmus* in the 16th century and later served as a basis for fugal imitation.

Forms for organ include the chorale prelude, a short setting for organ of a chorale strophe, intended as an introduction for congregational singing. It was developed by 17th-century north German composers, notably Buxtehude, and is seen as its finest in Bach's *Orgelbüchlein*; later examples include those of Brahms and Reger. The term is often loosely applied to any organ piece, except variations, based on a chorale melody.

The chorale fantasia is a more extended organ piece based on a chorale (the term has also been used for the elaborate opening choruses in Bach's chorale cantatas); the chorale fugue is an organ fugue based on a chorale melody; the chorale partita or chorale variations is a set of variations on a chorale melody.

Choral Fantasia. Beethoven's op.80 for piano, chorus and orchestra to a text by Christoph Kuffner (1808).

Choral Symphony. Beethoven's Symphony no.9 in D minor (1824), of which the last movement is a setting for soloists, chorus and orchestra of Schiller's *Ode to Joy*.

Chord. The simultaneous sounding of two or more notes.

Chordophone. Generic term for instruments that produce their sound by means of strings stretched between fixed points. Chordophones form one of the four main classes of instrument.

Chorley, Henry F(othergill) (*b* Blackley Hurst, 15 Dec 1808; *d* London, 16 Feb 1872). English writer. A music reviewer for *The Athenaeum* (1834–68), he also wrote novels, plays and poetry, and wrote and translated librettos (he was a friend of Browning and Dickens). He is best remembered for his *Thirty Years' Musical Recollections* (1862), a lively chronicle of London musical life.

Choron, Alexandre(-Etienne) (*b* Caen, 21 Oct 1771; *d* Paris, 29 June 1834). French writer on music, teacher, publisher and composer. He wrote manuals on thoroughbass and counterpoint and essays on plainsong and church music, also publishing inexpensive editions of Reniassance and Baroque choral music and collaborating with Fayolle on the *Dictionnaire des musiciens* (1810–11). After holding public appointments, including the directorship of the Académie Royale de Musique, he founded the Institution Royale de Musique Classique et Religieuse. He composed chiefly sacred music and songs.

Chor-Ton (Ger.). 'Choir pitch': the pitch associated with church organs in Germany in the Baroque period, and sometimes known as 'Cornett-Ton' (after the instrument); probably it was nearly a semitone higher than modern pitch. *See* PITCH.

Chorus. A group of singers who perform together, usually in parts; also a piece of music written for such a group. In the performance of vocal part-music a distinction is generally made between a group of soloists (one singer to each part) and a chorus or choir (more than one singer to each). The designations 'chorus' and 'choir' are often used with qualifying terms (e.g. mixed choir, women's chorus, opera chorus etc). In English a distinction is often made between 'choir' and 'chorus': an ecclesiastical body of singers is normally called a choir, as is a small, highly trained or professional group; 'chorus' is generally preferred for large secular groups.

In ancient Greek drama, an all-male chorus played an essential part. In biblical times, choruses were used in Jewish worship. Western choral tradition begins with early Christianity, where patristic writers refer to antiphonal and responsorial singing in the 2nd and 3rd centuries. There are reasons for believing that some chant was chorally performed in the Middle Ages; not until *c*1430 was polyphony assigned to choirs. In medieval churches and monasteries, choirs were composed entirely of men, sometimes with boys, because of St Paul's prohibition of women's singing in church; women were permitted to sing only in convents. A typical cathedral choir might consist of four to six boys and ten to 13 men.

During the Renaissance, secular music continued to be sung by soloists, except in certain festive contexts (e.g. royal wedding festivities). Sacred polyphony began to be sung chorally, however, with choirs commonly in four basic voice parts, akin to the modern soprano–alto–tenor–bass (SATB) distribution. Soprano parts were normally assigned to boys until the 16th century, when castrato singers were introduced into Roman Catholic church choirs; the alto parts were sung by men with high voices, or in falsetto, or by boys. Later, castrato singers took over the alto as well as soprano parts. Choirs of 20–30 were used in the late 15th and early

16th centuries, though it is uncertain how many were used at any individual performance. But instances are recorded of larger choirs, for example 62 singers at Munich, under Lassus, *c*1570, and English performances with more than 70 when the Chapel Royal combined with another institution.

In the Baroque period these trends continued, for example at a feast in honour of S Petronio at Bologna in 1687, with a choir of 65, and at Handel's funeral in London, in 1759, where three choirs combined. In the late Baroque period, St Mark's, Venice, had a choir of 36; the English Chapel Royal had 34 to 38; there were 30 at Buxtehude's *Abendmusik* concerts at Lübeck; and Bach's choir at full strength numbered 36 (though in practice the number singing at any individual service was probably much smaller, even one or two to a part; in a plan for reforms Bach requested that some 12 singers be on call). Antiphonal effects were often used, for example in the traditional decani–cantores arrangement in English churches, the famous Venetian *cori spezzati* ('broken choirs', spatially apart) and similarly in Germany and in Rome where polychoral performance particularly flourished.

In early opera, the chorus played a structurally important part, but by *c*1640 it had virtually disappeared from Italian opera except at festive performances. It did, however, appear in Lully's *tragédie lyrique* and in English theatre music of the Restoration. It was also used in oratorio, in the works of Carissimi at Rome, Charpentier in Paris and Schütz at Dresden: it has been suggested that some of these performances, right up to Bach's time, were commonly sung one to a part. Handel's oratorio choruses were sung by groups of *c*25. In late Baroque opera, the items marked 'coro' were generally intended only for the assembled principals.

During the late 18th century and the early 19th a tradition of larger-scale performance developed, particularly in the Protestant countries. The commemoration of Handel at Westminster Abbey in 1784 brought 300 singers and 250 instrumentalists together; the number increased in successive years, to over 1000 by 1791. A chorus of 400 is reported as having sung in an oratorio in Vienna in 1773; the next year, 300 sang at Jommelli's funeral in Naples. In the special circumstances of late 18th-century France, a chorus of 2400 was assembled for a festival in 1794, celebrating the Revolution. In Germany, many new choirs were founded around the turn of the 18th century, often all-male, to sing convivial and patriotic music. With the industrialization of Britain, many new choral societies, with women as well as men, sprang up, to perform music by Handel and more recent composers. The growing festival movement fostered this development, as did the development of new technologies for printing music cheaply and new systems for teaching the reading of music. The Bach revival, affecting much of northern Europe in the early 19th century, should be seen in this context. But the concern for improvement in church music can be seen equally in the work of the Cecilian movement in the Roman Catholic countries of Europe and the growing popular traditions of choralism in the Methodist and other evangelical movements in the Protestant countries.

This applies equally in North America, where evangelical music played a large part in popular choral traditions, with hymns and gospel songs. An additional element was brought into religious choral music by the black population. The hymns of Moody and Sankey suited the revivalist tradition, which reached its apogee with Homer Rodeheaver's direction of mass singing by crowds estimated at between 60,000 and 250,000 at the beginning of the 20th century.

In Europe, the late 19th century saw the cultivation on a new scale of the oratorio and sacred cantata repertory. Characteristic developments at the time were the foundation of numerous Bach societies and Bach choirs, the monster Handel festivals (with 400 voices) at Crystal Palace, London, and the growth of choral festivals for children. In the early 20th century, the chorus's place at the centre of concert life became strengthened with the composition of many choral symphonies or works of similar kind, of which Mahler's Symphony no.8 ('Symphony of a Thousand') has claims to be regarded as the largest and most important. It was natural, too, that in the 19th century the chorus should have become increasingly important in opera, as plots moved from classical history and mythology towards themes which involved more recent or even contemporary history and dealt with the fate of communities and nations rather than the dilemmas of individuals; the trend is already to be seen in Beethoven's *Fidelio*, and more markedly in Meyerbeer's grand operas and in the works of Verdi. In the early 20th century, many nationalist composers wrote choral epics drawing on their own country's heritage and in its language, for example Kodály's *Psalmus hungaricus* and Janáček's *Glagolitic Mass*. 20th-century political movements also found a natural expression in choral music.

Many early choral foundations, such as those in Vienna, Dresden or Cambridge, survive and maintain their status in world music. Where older traditions prevail, these retain boy trebles with men singing alto, tenor and bass. But in Germany, Britain and the USA, arguably the countries with the strongest choral traditions, new chamber choirs have developed, offering performances of high precision and responsiveness and meeting the interest in the use of authentic forces in Baroque and Classical music.

Chorus is also used for that section of text and music which is repeated after each stanza or verse in a strophic composition. *See* REFRAIN.

It is also a term for various kinds of instrument: a 9th-century source refers to a simple bagpipe and a plucked string instrument; later it may be identified with a CRWTH, a string drum like the TAMBOURIN DE BÉARN, or a TABOR.

Chorzempa, Daniel (Walter) (*b* Minneapolis, 7 Dec 1944). American organist. He studied at the University of Minnesota and at Cologne, where he worked in the electronic music studio. He enjoyed success as a pianist in Germany and England, 1969–71, but became known as a virtuoso organist, in Europe and the USA, especially for his command in works by Liszt and Reubke.

Chouquet, (Adolphe) Gustave (*b* Le Havre, 16 April 1819; *d* Paris, 30 Jan 1886). French writer and music historian. He wrote for music journals in Paris, also becoming known as the author of song texts, a prizewinning music history (1864) and a pioneering history of French opera (1873); he catalogued the Conservatoire instrument collection.

Chout (The Tale of the Buffoon) [Skazka pro shuta]. Ballet in six scenes by Prokofiev to a libretto by Afanasyev (1921, Paris).

Chou Wen-chung (*b* Chefoo, 28 July 1923). American composer of Chinese birth. He studied with Varèse (1949–54), whose *Nocturnal* he completed. His music is a successful fusion of Chinese tradition and a sophisticated Western vocabulary and style. Two of his principal works, *The Willows are New* for piano (1957) and *Yü ko* for nine instruments (1965) are based on traditional works for the *ch'in*.

Chowning, John M. (*b* Salem, NJ, 22 Aug 1934). American composer. He studied with Boulanger in Paris (1959–62) and at Stanford, where he has taught and worked on computer-synthesized music since 1966. His few works include *Stria* (1977).

Chrétien de Troyes (*b* Troyes; *fl c* 1160–90). French trouvère. Author of the Arthurian romances *Perceval* and *Lancelot*, he is the earliest lyric poet in Old French. Five poems (two without music) are ascribed to him in trouvère MSS.

Christina (*b* Stockholm, 8 Dec 1626; *d* Rome, 19 April 1689). Queen of Sweden and patron of music, resident partly in Italy. She was a principal 17th-century patron of arts and learning and for 30 years a leading figure in Roman cultural life. Crowned in 1644, she brought French, German and English musicians to her Stockholm court where her early enthusiasm for French ballet was gradually supplanted by a preoccupation with Italian opera. In 1654 she abdicated, converting to Catholicism, and travelling to Rome where the extended welcome celebrations included a performance of Marazzoli's opera *La vita humana* (dedicated to her). She founded a literary academy in which musical performances occupied an important place, built a theatre in her home, the Palazzo Riario, and in 1671 opened the rebuilt Teatro di Tor di Nona as the first public opera house in Rome with a performance of Cavalli's *Scipione affricano*. Numerous musicians enjoyed her patronage and dedicated works to her, notably Pasquini, A. Melani, A. Scarlatti and Corelli.

Christmas Concerto. Corelli's Concerto grosso in G minor op.6 no.8, inscribed 'fatto per la notte di Natale' (1714).

Christmas Oratorio. Choral work by J.S. Bach to texts possibly by Picander relating to the Nativity; it comprises six cantatas for performance in Leipzig on the three days of the Christmas festival, New Year's Day, New Year's Sunday and Epiphany (1735). Schütz also wrote a Christmas Oratorio.

Christoff, Boris (*b* Plovdiv, 18 May 1914). Bulgarian bass. He studied at Rome and Salzburg. He made his Covent Garden début in 1949 and sang in the USA from 1956 (début at San Francisco, as Boris). His powerful stage presence and well-projected voice have contributed to his international identification with the roles of Boris Godunov and Verdi's Philip II. He was also a fine recitalist.

Christophe Colomb. Opera in two parts (27 scenes) by Milhaud to a libretto by Caudel (1930, Berlin).

Christou, Jani (*b* Heliopolis, 8 Jan 1926; *d* Athens, 8 Jan 1970). Greek composer. He studied philosophy at Cambridge (1945–8) while having private composition lessons from Redlich. In 1960 he settled in Greece, where he had a prominent position in avant-garde circles; he died in a car crash. His earlier works, up to the Second Symphony (with chorus, 1958), are freely atonal, drawing on Stravinsky, Berg and Mahler. Then he developed a style of ostinato patterning aimed at activating primordial emotions (as in the oratorio *Tongues of Fire*, 1964). Later works, called *Anaparastasis* ('Re-enactments'), move away from traditional notation to provide psychic rituals for the performers.

Christus. Oratorio by Liszt to a biblical and liturgical text (1867).

Unfinished oratorio by Mendelssohn, op.97, to a text by Chevalier Bunsen (begun 1844).

Christus am Ölberge [Christ on the Mount Olives]. Oratorio, op.85, by Beethoven to a text by F.X. Huber (1803, Vienna).

Chromatic (from Gk. *chrōmatikos*: 'coloured'). Based on an octave of 12 semitones, as opposed to a seven-note DIATONIC scale. A chromatic scale consists of an ascending or descending line of semitones. An instrument is said to be chromatic if throughout all or most of its compass it can produce all the semitones.

Chromatic Fantasia and Fugue. Keyboard work (BWV 903) by J.S. Bach (*c*1720).

Chrysander, (Karl Franz) Friedrich (*b* Lübtheen, Mecklenburg, 8 July 1826; *d* Bergedorf, 3 Sept 1901). German musicologist. A pioneer of 19th-century German musical scholarship, he wrote articles on Bach, Beethoven, Buxtehude, Dussek, Mendelssohn, Mozart, Pergolesi and Spohr, and on notation, church music, pedagogy and theory. In 1856 he co-founded the Händel-Gesellschaft; it was largely through his industry and finance that 48 volumes of Handel's music were published. He also edited the *Allgemeine musikalische Zeitung* (1868–71, 1875–82), other journals and works of Bach, Corelli and Carissimi.

Chueca, Federico (*b* Madrid, 5 May 1846; *d* there, 20 July 1908). Spanish composer. He wrote *c*37 zarzuelas, of which *La canción de la Lola* (1880) and *La gran vía* (1886) were successes. His ability to capture a regional flavour and to write appealing tunes was much acclaimed.

Chukhadjian, Tigran (*b* Constantinople, 1837; *d* Smyrna, 25 Feb 1898). Armenian composer and conductor. He studied in Constantinople and at the Milan Conservatory. The founder of Armenian national opera, he was the first to fuse European techniques, especially those of Italian opera and French operetta, with Armenian folk music, writing seven stage works, chamber and orchestral music and the earliest Armenian piano pieces.

His historical-heroic *Arshak II* (1868) is distinguished by its artistry, *The Pea Seller* (1876) by its comic liveliness.

Chung, Kyung-Wha (*b* Seoul, 26 March 1948). Korean violinist. She played in public from the age of nine and studied at the Juilliard School (1960–67). Since her New York and London débuts (1968, 1970) she has given warmly expressive interpretations of the standard repertory and concertos by Elgar and Walton. She often appears with her sister, the cellist Myung-Wha Chung (*b* 1944), and her brother, the pianist Myung-Whun Chung (*b* 1953).

Church mode [ecclesiastical mode]. A term used for the scalar and melodic categories into which Gregorian chant was classified from about the 8th or 9th century; Glarean (*Dodecachordon*, 1547) added four to the existing eight. *See* MODE.

Chute [cheute] (Fr.: 'fall'). Term used in French Baroque music for an appoggiatura or note of anticipation; it is also found in keyboard music for a passing note or acciaccatura used as an ornament in an arpeggiated chord.

Ciaccona (It.). *See* CHACONNE.

Ciampi, Vincenzo (Legrenzio) (*b* ?Piacenza, ?1719; *d* Venice, 30 March 1762). Italian composer. He studied with Leo and Durante in Naples, where his first six comic operas were staged, 1737–45. In 1747–8 he taught at the Ospedale degli Incurabili, Venice, writing oratorios and motets. He then worked in London as director of the first company to perform Italian comic operas there; it presented several of his own before he returned, in 1756, to Venice and later to the Incurabili. Besides instrumental works, he wrote *c*20 operas; of the comic ones, *Bertoldo* (1748, Venice) was especially popular and influenced *opéra comique*. He composed much instrumental music, notably trio sonatas and concertos. His idiom is tuneful, combining Baroque and *galant* elements.

Cibber, Susanna Maria (*b* London, Feb 1714; *d* there, 31 Jan 1766). English actress and mezzo-soprano singer, sister of T.A. Arne. She sang in English operas from 1732, and in Handel's oratorios, notably *Messiah* and *Samson*, in the 1740s, much admired for her sweet and expressive singing. She was a distinguished tragic actress.

Cibell [cebell, sebell]. An English instrumental or vocal piece of the period 1690–1710 modelled on a chorus in praise of the goddess Cybele in Lully's *Atys* (1676). True cibells are in duple metre, with gavotte-like rhythm, and have episodes with running figures in the bass. Some cibells take Purcell's *Trumpet tune, called the Cibell* as a starting-point.

Ciconia, Johannes (*b* Liège, *c*1335 or *c*1373; *d* Padua, 10 June–13 July 1412). Liégeois composer and theorist. Two men of the name are known. The elder was in service in Avignon in 1350, accompanied Cardinal Albornoz on an Italian campaign, 1358–67, and returned to Liège in 1372 as a priest at St John the Evangelist. A Liège document of 1385 however refers also to a choirboy called Johannes Ciconia, and recent opinion favours the younger Ciconia as the composer, which is more plausible on grounds of musical style. In 1401 this Ciconia received a benefice for a small Paduan church and from 1403 was *custos* and ccantor at Padua Cathedral. His music combines elements of the French Ars Nova with the Italian 14th-century style and strongly influenced other early 15th-century composers. His Italian songs, which include four madrigals and at least seven ballate, betray aspects of the French style then current in northern Italy, *chansons*, of which only two virelais and a canon survive, exploit the rhythmic complexities of the Ars Subtilior. Of his 11 motets, four are isorhythmic but others are closer in style to the Italian songs; most were written to celebrate important events or as eulogies. His mass music consists of 11 or 12 settings of the Gloria or Credo. He also wrote three theoretical treatises.

Cid, Le. Opera in four acts by Massenet to a libretto by d'Ennery, Blau and Gallet after Corneille (1885, Paris). Farinelli, Aiblinger and Cornelius also wrote operas on the subject.

Cifra, Antonio (*b* nr. Terracina, 1584; *d* Loreto, 2 Oct 1629). Italian composer. *Maestro di cappella* at Santa Casa, Loreto, from 1609, and at St John Lateran, Rome (1623–6), he was a prolific if uninspired composer of sacred music. His output is dominated by eight books of concertato motets and includes two volumes of masses (1619, 1621) in a more traditional style. His later polychoral music is more modern in outlook but still conservative. More inventive are the *Scherzi sacri* (1616, 1618) and secular *scherzi*. He also composed six books of five-part madrigals which show deft rhythmic and contrapuntal interplay.

Cikker, Ján (*b* Banska Bystrica, 29 July 1911). Slovak composer. He studied in Prague and attended Novák's master classes (1930–36) and has taught at the Bratislava Conservatory. He has composed fiercely expressive operas (*Resurrection*, 1962; *Coriolanus*, 1972) and is one of the most successful opera composers of his time in eastern Europe.

Cilea, Francesco (*b* Palmi, 26 July 1866; *d* Varazze, 20 Nov 1950). Italian composer. He studied at the Naples Conservatory (1881–9) and taught there (director, 1916–36) and elsewhere. His first opera, *Gina* (1889), made a good impression, but its successor, the *verismo* piece *La tilda* (1892), was less successful. *L'arlesiana*, given in Milan in 1897 with Caruso, won favour in spite of a weak libretto; Cilea revised it several times, and it has enjoyed modest success in Italy. His one unqualified triumph was *Adriana Lecouvreur* (1902, Milan), which won wide success with its appealing subject and rewarding title role. His last opera, *Gloria*, was given at La Scala under Toscanini (1907) but withdrawn after two performances.

Cima, Giovanni Paolo (*b* c1570; *fl* until 1622). Italian composer. He came from a musical family and was director of music and organist at S Celso, Milan, in 1610. His church music (1599, 1610) is mainly conservative, but in his instrumental works (1602, 1606) he made early use of the trio-sonata combination of two treble instruments and continuo.

Cimador, Giambattista (*b* Venice, 1761; *d* Bath, 27 Feb 1805). Italian composer and music publisher. In Venice he composed several works, notably the monodrama *Pimmalione* (1790) and a double bass concerto for Dragonetti. In London from 1791, he worked as a singer, violinist and pianist, becoming c1800 a partner of the publisher Monzani who issued his arrangements of works by Mozart and Cimarosa.

Cimarosa, Domenico (*b* Aversa, 17 Dec 1749; *d* Venice, 11 Jan 1801). Italian composer. He trained in Naples as a violinist, keyboard player and composer, and wrote mainly sacred works at first. He had comic operas staged there from 1772; his first serious opera was *Cajo Mario* (1780, Rome). By the mid-1780s he was established both in Italy and abroad. He became *maestro* c1782 at a Venetian conservatory, the Ospedaletto, holding this post with that of second organist at the Naples royal chapel from 1785. In 1787–91 he was *maestro di cappella* at the St Petersburg court (for which he wrote three operas), and in 1791–3 court Kapellmeister at Vienna, where his most famous opera, *Il matrimonio segreto*, was given in 1792 and encored *in toto* at its première. He then returned to Naples and was first organist of the royal chapel from 1796, the year of *Gli Orazi e i Curiazi*, his most widely praised serious opera; but he was imprisoned in 1799 for his republican sympathies and later moved to Venice, where he died – poisoned, accorded to rumours, which were officially denied.

Cimarosa's more than 60 operas, mostly comic, made him one of the most popular composers of his day, and some of his works were long in the repertory. Stendhal rated him alongside Haydn and Mozart. His writing in the operas shows a keen sense of drama and caricature, with much vivacity and light, clear textures; the later works show a warmer melodic style, with more colourful modulations and scoring. Among his other works are oratorios, keyboard sonatas, concertos and chamber music.

Operas Cajo Mario (1780), I due baroni (1783), L'impresario in angustie (1786), Il maestro di cappella (intermezzo, c1790), Il matrimonio segreto (1792), Gli Orazi ed i Curiazi (1796); c55 others
Vocal music 5 oratorios; Missa pro defunctis, g (1787); 18 masses; mass movts; sacred pieces; secular cantatas, hymns, songs
Instrumental music over 80 kbd sonatas; Hpd Conc., B♭; Conc., 2 fl, G (1793); 4 fl qts; other chamber works

Cimbalom. A Hungarian box zither, related to the English dulcimer. It usually takes the form of a trapeziform box across which the strings are stretched, and is played with a pair of hammers. The cimbalom has been used orchestrally by Liszt, Kodály (in *Háry János*) and Bartók.

Cimbasso (It.). A bass or contrabass valve trombone used by Verdi to replace the ophicleide in his scores up to and including *Aida* (1871). The name was also used for the early 19th-century RUSSIAN BASSOON.

Cimello, Tomaso (*b* Montesangiovanni, c1500; *d* after 1579). Italian composer. He was active as a poet-musician in the 1540s in Naples, where he later served the Colonna family; he then took minor orders and taught at Benevento (1571–3). He composed villanellas (1545) and madrigals (1548), many to his own verses, and wrote treatise on theory (MS).

Cimento dell'armonia e dell'invenzione, Il [The Contest between Harmony and Invention]. Title of

Vivaldi's 12 concertos op.8 (c1725), of which 'The Four Seasons' are nos.1–4.

Cincinnati May Festival (USA). Annual (from 1967) festival of choral and orchestral concerts established in 1873 by Theodore Thomas. Events are held in Music Hall, which opened with the third festival (1878). A permanent chorus was established after the fourth. Directors have included Eugene Goossens, Josef Krips, Max Rudolf and James Conlon (from 1979).

Cincinnati Symphony Orchestra. American orchestra established in 1895 with Frank van der Stucken as conductor; it disbanded in 1907 and reformed in 1909. Leopold Stokowski conducted 1909–12; later conductors include Thomas Schippers, Walter Susskind, Michael Gielen and Jésus López-Cobos (from 1986). Its home is Music Hall (opened 1878, cap. 3600; remodelled 1970–71); summer concerts are at River Bend Music Center (opened 1984). It was the first American orchestra to make a world tour (1967).

Cinderella. Ballet in three acts by Prokofiev (1945, Moscow). See also CENDRILLON; CENERENTOLA, LA.

Cinema organ. A type of organ designed to take the place of instrumental players in early 20th-century cinemas and theatres; it produced a warm sound, often with a large tremulant, and was designed to imitate the sound of orchestral instruments. In the USA the term 'theatre organ' is preferred.

Cinesi, Le. Opera in one act by Gluck to a text expanded from a libretto written by Metastasio for Caldara (1754, Vienna).

Cinque pas [sink-a-pace] (Fr.). 'Five steps': the basic step pattern of several dances (galliard, tourdion, saltarello); the term was sometimes used synonymously with galliard, notably in English Elizabethan literature.

Cinti-Damoreau [née Montalant], **Laure (Cinthie)** (b Paris, 6 Feb 1801; d there, 25 Feb 1863). French soprano. At the Paris Opéra (1825–35) she created the principal roles in Rossini's Le siège de Corinthe, Moïse, Le Comte Ory and Guillaume Tell and in Auber's La muette de Portici, being known for her pure tone and stylish ornamentation.

Ciphering. The sounding of an organ pipe without a key being depressed, due to mechanical fault or damage.

Circle of fifths. The arrangement of the tonics of the 12 major or minor keys by ascending or descending perfect 5ths, making a closed circle: C–G–D–A–E–B–F♯ = G♭–D♭–A♭–E♭–B♭–F–C (for illustration, see KEY SIGNATURE).

Circles. Work by Berio for female voice, harp and two percussionists (1960), settings of poems by E.E. Cummings; the singer moves to different positions on the platform.

Circus Polka (for a young elephant). Piece by Stravinsky composed for the Barnum and Bailey Circus (1942).

Cirillo, Francesco (b Grumo Nevano, Aversa, 4 Feb 1623; d after 1667). Italian composer and singer. He worked with the Febiarmonici, singers from northern Italy who produced the first operas in Naples. His music is Venetian in style, and though he composed music for some of the earliest Neapolitan operas (Orontea regina d'Egitto, 1654; Il rotto d'Elena, 1655), his importance rests primarily on certain forms of theatrical production and his role in the selection of repertory.

Cirri, Giovanni Battista (b Forlì, 1 Oct 1724; d there, 11 June 1808). Italian cellist and composer. After working in Bologna, he appeared in Paris and in London, where he lived, 1764–80, and was a popular performer and composer of chamber music (mostly for strings). He then returned to Forlì, later becoming maestro di cappella at the cathedral. His music has a tuneful style akin to Boccherini's.

Cithara. See KITHARA.

Cithrinchen. A cittern with a bell-like shape, popular in the second half of the 17th century, especially in Hamburg and northern Europe generally. It had five double courses of metal strings, tuned c–e–g–b–e' or a 4th higher. It was sometimes called the 'Bell Guittern'.

Citole. A plucked string instrument of the Middle Ages, particularly the period 1200–1350, related to the fiddle. It was made of one piece of wood, variously shaped; it evolved into the cittern in the 15th century.

Cittern. A plucked instrument, very popular in the 16th and 17th centuries. Unlike the lute and most other Renaissance and early Baroque plucked instruments, the cittern was played with a plectrum, which may partly account for its popularity, indicated by the many surviving books and MSS of idiomatic cittern music. The instrument, which is wire-strung, has a flat back and a pear-shaped body. The neck, with some 18 or 19 frets, is half cut away from behind the fingerboard on the bass side; the resulting overlap forms a channel along which the player's left thumb can slide, facilitating the rapid position shifts of the solo repertory. Citterns were made in several sizes: the most common for Italian instruments has a string length of c46 cm, larger ones c63 cm. There is evidence of a smaller cittern in England. (For illustration, see LUTE.)

Much cittern music was published. Lanfranco (1533) gave the Italian method of tuning, which (if the top course was e') was e'–d'd'–g'g–b–c'–a. In Italy a cittern revival began c1574, the year of Paolo Virchi's Il primo libro di tabolatura di citthara. Virchi demanded considerable virtuosity; his music, of the highest quality, includes fantasias, intabulations of pieces by Merulo, settings of madrigals, and pavans and galliards. He wrote for a new, fully chromatic cittern with six double courses tuned in unison, e'–d'–g–b–f–d. In France and northern Europe it became standardized as a four-course instrument.

City Center Opera Company. See NEW YORK CITY OPERA.

City of Birmingham Symphony Orchestra. British orchestra, originally the City of Birmingham Orchestra, founded in 1920 and renamed in 1948. Elgar conducted his own works at its first concert. From 1946 summer promenade concerts were given. From 1955 works were commissioned and from 1969, especially under Louis Frémaux, the repertory included contemporary music. Simon Rattle became conductor in 1980.

City of London Festival (UK). Biennial (summer) festival established in 1962. Musical events include concerts in City churches and other historic buildings; fringe events include open-air concerts and jazz.

Čiurlionis, Mikolajus Konstantinas (*b* Varéna, 4 Oct 1875; *d* Pustelnik, 10 April 1911). Lithuanian painter and composer. He studied with Noskowski in Warsaw and with Jadassohn and Reinecke at the Leipzig Conservatory (1901). His music makes use of invented modes, colourful harmony and autonomous rhythms; he wrote much for the piano as well as orchestral and chamber music. He was also famous as a painter.

Clagget, Walter (*b* ?Waterford, *c*1741; *d* 1798). Irish composer. In 1763–*c*1771 he was a cellist in Dublin, where his comic opera *The Power of Sympathy* was given in 1763. He later worked as an instrumentalist in London, and wrote music for two stage works besides instrumental solos, duets etc. Charles Clagget (1740–*c*1795), presumably his brother, was a violinist and inventor who devised improvements intended to make it 'almost impossible to . . . play out of tune' on the violin; he designed a piano with a 39-note octave and patented an early chromatic trumpet (1788).

Clair de lune. Third movement of Debussy's *Suite bergamasque* (1890) for piano. Song by Debussy to a poem by Verlaine, the third of his *Fêtes galantes*. Fauré set the same poem (op.43 no.3).

Cláirseach (Ir.). Term for the Celtic harp.

Clapisson, (Antoine-) Louis (*b* Naples, 15 Sept 1808; *d* Paris, 19 March 1866). French composer, curator and teacher. He studied at the Paris Conservatoire, played the violin professionally and wrote songs, comic chansonnettes and many popular *opéras comiques*, beginning with *La figurante* (1838). Defeating Berlioz for election to the Institute (Académie des Beaux-Arts), he became professor at the Conservatoire and in 1862 curator of its early instrument collection (most of which he had owned and restored).

Clapper. The tongue in an open bell that produces the sound by striking the side.

Clappers. An instrument consisting of two or more objects in the form of sticks, plaques or vessels of wood, bone, ivory, nutshells, marine shells etc. The playing of clappers is widespread and specimens have been found from prehistoric times. In Europe they were used as early as the 9th century. Various types are used in symphonic and operatic works (*see* CLAVES and WHIP).

Clari, Giovanni Carlo Maria (*b* Pisa, 27 Sept 1677; *d* there, 16 May 1754). Italian composer. He studied in Bologna, where the first of his two operas was given in 1695. He was *maestro di cappella* at Pistoia, 1703–24, and later at Pisa. His most famous works are his over 50 chamber duets and trios for voices and continuo (mostly written after *c*1730), which feature fugal and chromatic writing; Handel drew on five of them in his oratorio *Theodora* (1750). He also wrote liturgical works for Pistoia, using antiphonal writing, and 11 Italian oratorios.

Clarinet. A woodwind instrument of essentially cylindrical bore, played with a single beating reed; it has been made in a wide range of sizes and tonalities (for illustration, *see* WOODWIND INSTRUMENTS). The soprano instrument in B♭, with the 'Boehm' system of keywork and fingering, is the most widely used today; the high E♭ sopranino, the soprano in A, the E♭ alto and B♭ bass and contrabass clarinets, and occasionally the pedal clarinet (an octave below the bass) are also called for in orchestral and band compositions. A closely related instrument is the BASSET-HORN, essentially an alto clarinet in F or G. The basset clarinet is a soprano instrument with a downward extension of four semitones (as used by Mozart in several works). The modern Boehm-system clarinet was the product of a collaboration (*c*1839–43) between the clarinettist Hyacinthe Eléonore Kosé and the maker Louis-August Buffet (Boehm himself had nothing to do with the clarinet's design; it was not constructed according to the same acoustical ideals as the flute). The clarinet is generally made in five separate parts: mouthpiece, barrel, upper or left-hand joint, lower or right-hand joint, and bell; these are fitted together by tenon-and-socket connections. The weight of the instrument is taken by the right thumb, with a thumb-rest under the lower joint. The fingers and the left thumb control the seven open holes and 17 keys on a standard instrument. The lowest note of the standard Boehm-system clarinet is (written) *e*, sounding *d* for a B♭ instrument. The low register is known as the chalumeau (after the clarinet's predecessor); it overblows at the 12th to produce the singing 'clarion' register. At the top of the range the limit is less clearly defined; most tutors give fingerings to *c''''* and some virtuosos are prepared to perform a 3rd or more higher.

The earliest mention of the clarinet is in an order dated 1710 for a pair of clarinets from the maker Jacob Denner of Nuremberg. Handel wrote at least twice for the instrument, but it came into widespread use only after the middle of the 18th century. It quickly found its way into the military band and the wind ensemble and gradually found a regular place in the orchestra during the late 18th century. Burney reported favourably on what he deemed their first appearance in the London opera orchestra, in J.C. Bach's *Orione* (1763); Arne had already written for them, in 1760. In France, Rameau used them in *Zoroastre* (1749). The Mannheim and Paris orchestras deserve much of the credit for popularizing its orchestral use. Mozart composed his famous clarinet works for Anton Stadler, including the Trio K498 (for clarinet, viola and piano), the Quintet K581 and the Concerto K622; his Viennese serenades also use it. Beethoven supplied a Trio op.11 for clarinet, cello and piano, and used the instrument effectively in his Quintet op.16 for piano and wind. Weber and Spohr wrote concertos. Brahms made major contributions in his Trio op.114 for clarinet, cello and piano, Quintet op.115 and two sonatas op.120. In the 20th century the talents of specific players have inspired composers to extend the technique of the instrument, for example Benny Goodman (Bartók's *Contrasts* and concertos by Hindemith and Copland).

The B♭ clarinet once played a primary role in ragtime and jazz, though its significance has waned since *c*1945, except in 'Dixieland' jazz. Extended 20th-century compositions using the clarinet in imitation of jazz include Gershwin's *Rhapsody in Blue*, Stravinsky's *Ebony Concerto* and Bernstein's *Prelude, Fugue and Riffs*.

Clarinette d'amour. A late 18th-century member of the clarinet family, now obsolete. Usually pitched in A♭, G or F (though J.C. Bach appears to have written for one in D), it was distinguished by a globular or pear-shaped bell with narrow opening.

Clarino. The high register of a trumpet; also (in variants, such as 'clarion' and 'clairon') kinds of trumpet. The terms go back to the 12th century for long, straight trumpets; later they apparently refer to shorter, narrower-bore instruments. By the Baroque period, 'clarin' or 'clarino' (sometimes 'claret') came to stand for the uppermost trumpet part in an ensemble, and the term was occasionally used in that sense by Bach. It was also used by the Viennese Classical composers. 'Clarino' playing implied a singing style in the register from *c″* upwards. The same part of the clarinet compass is sometimes described as its 'clarino' register.

Clarke, Henry Leland (*b* Dover, NH, 9 March 1907). American composer. He studied at Harvard and with Boulanger in Paris (1929–31), and taught at various institutions in the USA, including the University of Washington, Seattle (1958–77). His music uses calculated limitation: invented scales and 'wordtones' (using the same pitch for a word throughout a composition). His works are mostly vocal and include the opera *Lysistrata* (1984) and the song cycle *William Penn Fruits of Solitude* (1972).

Clarke, Jeremiah (*b c*1674; *d* London, 1 Dec 1707). English composer and organist. He was a chorister at the Chapel Royal in the 1680s, then was organist at Winchester College (*c*1692–1695) and in 1699 became vicar-choral and organist of St Paul's Cathedral, London, advancing to Master of the Choristers in 1703. He was also a Gentleman of the Chapel Royal and from 1704 joint organist with Croft. He is thought to have committed suicide because of an unhappy love affair with a pupil of noble birth. Clarke is best known as a composer of the Trumpet Voluntary, long attributed to Purcell, but now known to be 'The Prince of Denmark's March' from an anthology of harpsichord music (1700); it also appears in a suite for wind instruments. His other works include some services and *c*20 anthems (mostly fairly slight), a number of odes for court occasions and other celebrations, and a quantity of songs and interludes for the theatre, which, along with his harpsichord pieces, best show his pleasing and tuneful style, not reflecting the 'melancholy cast' ascribed to him by contemporaries nor indeed the circumstances of his own death.

Clarke, Rebecca (*b* Harrow, 27 Aug 1886; *d* New York, 13 Oct 1979). English viola player and composer. After study with Stanford at the RCM she played in chamber groups, notably with Suggia and Myra Hess. She wrote songs, partsongs and much chamber music (Viola Sonata, 1919). She settled in the USA in 1939.

Clarke-Whitfeld, John (*b* Gloucester, 13 Dec 1770;

d Holmer, 22 Feb 1836). English organist and composer. Organist at Hereford Cathedral from 1820 and professor of music at Cambridge from 1821, he was one of the most respected church musicians of his generation, writing services and two Handelian oratorios.

Clàrsach. Scottish Gaelic term for the Celtic (or Irish) harp.

Classical. Term which, with its related forms such as 'classic' and 'classicism', has been applied to a variety of music from different cultures and is taken to mean any that does not belong to folk or popular traditions; it is also applied to any collection of music regarded as a model of excellence or formal discipline. But its chief application is to the Viennese Classical idiom which flourished in the late 18th century and the early 19th, above all in the hands of Haydn, Mozart and Beethoven. Among its musical characteristics are the use of dynamics and orchestral colour in a thematic way; the use of rhythm, including periodic structure and harmonic rhythm, to give definition to large-scale forms, along with the use of modulation to build longer spans of tension and release (most of the music is cast in sonata form or closely related forms); and the witty, typically Austrian mixture of comic and serious strains. It is no coincidence that this period was one of keen interest in classical antiquity; most of Gluck's 'reform' operas, composed at the beginning of this period, are based on classical subjects.

The term 'neo-classicism' has been applied to the 18th-century revival of interest in classical antiquity. In music it is more often applied to the early 20th-century movement, led by Stravinsky, which revived the balanced forms and clearly perceptible thematic processes of earlier styles to replace what seemed the increasingly exaggerated gestures and the formlessness of late Romanticism; *see* NEO-CLASSICAL.

Classical Symphony. Prokofiev's Symphony no.1 in D (1916–17), written in a neo-classical style.

Clausula (Lat.) Medieval term, denoting the concluding of a passage (or the passage itself thus concluded), used in medieval music theory with a similar range of meanings. It is now used almost exclusively for the settings in discant style of a fragment of plainchant, designed as more modern substitutes for passages of organum, in Notre Dame polyphony. The motet developed from the clausula *c*1200 through the addition of new texts to the upper voices.

Clavé, (José) Anselmo (*b* Barcelona, 21 April 1824; *d* there, 24 Feb 1874). Spanish choirmaster and composer. He helped organize the first Spanish choral society (1845) and composed male choruses, zarzuelas, cantatas and popular songs, many on politically inspired texts.

Clavecin (Fr.). HARPSICHORD.

Claves (Sp.). A percussion instrument of Cuban origin consisting of two cylindrical hardwood sticks measuring 20–25 cm long and up to 3 cm in diameter (for illustration, *see* PERCUSSION INSTRUMENTS).

Clavicembalo (It.). HARPSICHORD.

Clavichord. A stringed keyboard instrument used from the 15th century to the 18th. The usual shape is a rectangular box, with the keyboard set into or projecting from one of the longer sides (for illustration, *see* KEYBOARD INSTRUMENTS). As the player depresses the key, the tangent, a small brass blade driven into its end, strikes the string. The loudness, depending on the force with which the tangent strikes the string, is under the direct control of the player. As the tangent remains in contact with the string while it is sounding, the performer can influence the sound by altering the pressure on the key: the pitch can be altered, a vibrato (*Bebung*) can be produced, and the illusion of swelling the tone can even be provided.

For most of its history the clavichord was primarily valued as an instrument on which to learn, practice and occasionally compose. It appears as an alternative to the virginal and the harpsichord on title-pages of 16th-century collections. 16th-century clavichords are surprisingly loud and virginal-like – sensitive and exciting to play and ideal for early dance collections. There seems to have been little recognition of its special capabilities before the early 18th century, and no music specifically composed for it before the mid-18th. It was in the climate of the *Sturm und Drang* and *Empfindsamkeit* styles of the mid- to late 18th century that the clavichord had its greatest popularity and in which its special literature was created. C.P.E. Bach was the most important composer to conceive his music in its terms; his influential treatise *Versuch über die wahre Art das Clavier zu spielen* (1753–62) praises it. Later German writers regarded it as the ideal vehicle for intense personal expression. It fell out of use, however, in the Classical period. Its revival was initiated by Arnold Dolmetsch in the late 1880s.

Clavicor. A brass valved instrument of tenor pitch invented in France in 1837; it was used in military bands.

Clavicytherium. An upright harpsichord with a vertical soundboard.

Clavier. The keyboard of a piano, harpsichord, organ etc; also a generic, non-specific for a keyboard instrument. Bach's *Das wohltemperirte Clavier* does not specify the clavichord, and the title is best understood as 'The Well-tempered Clavier' or 'The Well-tempered Keyboard Instrument'. The term is sometimes applied to pianists' practice instruments with silent keyboards.

Clavierbüchlein (Ger.). 'Little keyboard book': title given by J.S. Bach to three collections he prepared of keyboard pieces, the first for his son W.F., in 1720, the other two for his second wife Anna Magdalena, the first begun in 1722 and completed in 1725, when he began the second. The book for W.F. contains early versions of the inventions and sinfonias and some preludes from Book 1 of the '48', as well as some pieces that may be by W.F. himself. The books for Anna Magdalena include French Suites nos.1–5 and Partitas nos.3 and 6 as well as other pieces by J.S. Bach, C.P.E. Bach and other composers.

Clavier-Übung (Ger.). 'Keyboard study': title of a four-volume collection of keyboard music published by J.S. Bach. The first volume (1731) contains six partitas for harpsichord; the second (1735) the Italian Concerto and French Overture, also for harpsichord; the third (1739) consists of organ music (21 chorale preludes, four duets, a prelude and fugue); and the

fourth (1741–2) the *Goldberg Variations* for harpsichord. The title was also used by earlier composers.

Clavijo del Castillo, Bernardo (*b* ?Navarre, *c*1549; *d* ?Madrid, after 1 Feb 1626). Spanish organist. He was *maestro de capilla* of the palatine chapel in Palermo (1569–87) and organist to the viceroy (1587–8). As organist of the cathedrals of Palencia (1589–92) and Salamanca (from 1592) he gained a high reputation, becoming professor of music at Salamanca University (1593) and succeeding Cabezón as *músico de tecla* of the Capilla Real (1603). A book of motets (1588) by him survives.

Claviorgan. A term applied since the 15th century to various types of keyboard instrument with strings and pipes.

Clayette, La. Name of a French music MS, probably of the 1260s, from the Ile de France area. It consists of 419 folios of which 22 contain music – 55 motets, mostly from the second quarter of the 13th century and all copied in the same hand. The MS, once owned by the Marquis of La Clayette, is now in the Bibliothèque Nationale, Paris.

Clayton, Thomas (*b* ?1660–70; *d* ?1720–30). English composer. He was intermittently a violinist in the King's Musick until 1706, and probably studied in Italy. His first stage work, *Arsinoe* (1705), was the first full-length opera in English, with Italianate *recitativo secco*, given in England. Trying later to maintain indigenous English music, he promoted concerts, some with his own vocal works, but with mixed success.

Clef. The sign placed at the beginning of a staff to denoting the pitch of one (and hence others) of its lines or spaces. They were first systematically used in 11th-century liturgical manuscripts. Letters denoting *F* and *c* were the most common; the *g* came increasingly into use in the 15th century. The *F* and *g* clefs have come to be known as the 'bass clef' and 'treble clef' respectively, in their normal situations on the fourth line up (for the bass) and the second line up (for the treble); the *c* clef, according to its placing, may be called the soprano clef (on the bottom line), or moving upwards, the mezzo-soprano, the alto, the tenor and the baritone.

Clemencic, René (*b* Vienna, 27 Feb 1928). Austrian recorder player. He studied in Nijmegen and at Vienna University. In 1958 he founded the Ensemble Musica Antiqua and from 1969 has directed the Clemenic Consort. In a repertory ranging from medieval to avant-garde music he has cultivated improvisatory techniques. In Vienna he has staged operas by Draghi, Leopold I and Peri.

Clemens (non Papa) [Clement, Jacob] (*b* *c*1510–15; *d* 1555–6). Franco-Flemish composer. He worked at Bruges Cathedral, 1544–5, and then may have been employed by Charles V or his general the Duke of Aerschot until 1549. From the next year he was employed by the Marian Brotherhood in 's-Hertogenbosch; after that he may have been at Ieper, Dordrecht and Leiden. He was a prolific composer, writing 15 masses, using a carefully applied parody technique, with themes from *chansons* or motets freely incorporated. Of his *c*233 motets, most are freely composed. He wrote 159 *souterliedekens* and *lofzangen*, three-voice polyphonic Dutch settings of the 150 psalms (published 1556–7). The metric texts were originally published with a popular song melody, and these he incorporated as *cantus firmi*. Some settings involved polyphonic imitation, others are homophonic. He also composed over 80 *chansons*, including love songs and drinking songs. His style is generally polyphonic, with note-against-note counterpoint, persistent imitation, parallel movement and shapely melodic parts. The 'non Papa' suffix, supposedly to distinguish Jacob Clement from Pope Clement VII (*d* 1534), seems to have been added jocularly.

Clément, (Jacques) Félix (Alfred) (*b* Paris, 13 Jan 1822; *d* there, 23 Jan 1885). French music historian and composer. Among his historical works, the *Dictionnaire lyrique, ou Histoire des opéras* (1867–9) remains valuable. He transcribed plainsong and composed two operas.

Clement, Franz (*b* Vienna, 17 Nov 1780; *d* there, 3 Nov 1842). Austrian violinist and conductor. Known for his technical skill and expressive tone, he was conductor of the Theater an der Wien. Beethoven wrote his Violin Concerto (1806) for him.

Clementi. English firm of instrument makers and music publishers. It was established in London in 1798, chiefly making square pianos. F.W. Collard was the main active partner and Muzio Clementi the European promoter of the firm's products, which from *c*1810 included a six-octave instrument; the firm introduced improvements in tone production in the 1820s. From 1832 it was Collard & Collard. Among its publications, besides Clementi's own piano music, were Haydn's *The Seasons* (1813) and several works by Beethoven.

Clementi, Aldo (*b* Catania, 25 May 1925). Italian composer. He studied with the Schoenberg pupil Sangiorgi, with Petrassi in Rome, and at Darmstadt (1955–62), having been guided towards serialism by Maderna. In three *Informels* (1961–3) he began to work with tangled textures of extreme density and essential changelessness; other works include the stage pieces *Blitz* (1973), *Collage 4* (1979) and *Es* (1981), all commemorating the end of music, which he sees as the art's only subject.

Clementi, Muzio (*b* Rome, 23 Jan 1752; *d* Evesham, 10 March 1832). English composer, keyboard player, publisher and piano manufacturer of Italian birth. He trained first in Rome, but in 1766–7 went to Dorset, England, to study the harpsichord. Moving to London in 1744, he became conductor at the King's Theatre and from 1770 gave concerts, often including his well-known keyboard sonatas op.2 (1779).

Clementi travelled widely as a pianist in 1780–85, and in 1781 took part in a piano contest with Mozart in Vienna. In 1785–1802 he was a frequent piano soloist in London (notably at the Grand Professional Concerts) and conductor of his own symphonies, but in the 1790s he was overshadowed by the visiting Haydn. He was in great demand as a teacher. In 1798 he established a music publishing and piano-making firm, touring Europe (initially with his pupil John Field) as its representative in 1802–10. Among the

firm's publications were major works by Beethoven. Clementi continued to conduct his symphonies in London and abroad; his last major works were three piano sonatas op.50 (1821).

Foremost in Clementi's large output are *c*70 keyboard sonatas, spanning some 50 years. Counterpoint, running figuration and virtuoso passage-work are constant elements. The earliest (some with violin) generally have two movements, but three are normal from *c*1782. Dramatic writing (which strongly influenced Beethoven) appears increasingly, and works such as op.13 (1785) feature motivic unity and powerful expression. The sonatas of after *c*1800 tend to be more diffuse. Only six of the symphonies and one piano concerto (1796) survive. Clementi also wrote keyboard duets, chamber music and two influential didactic works, *Introduction to the Art of Playing on the Piano Forte* (1801) and the comprehensive keyboard collection *Gradus ad Parnassum* (1817–26).

Keyboard music c70 solo sonatas; sonatinas, variations; pf duets
Chamber music over 40 acc. kbd sonatas; trio and nonet movts
Orchestral music 2 syms. (1787); pf conc.; minuet
Vocal music 2 canzonettas

Clemenza di Tito, La. Opera in two acts by Mozart to a libretto by Metastasio, revised by Caterino Mazzolà (1791, Prague). Many other composers set the same text, including Caldara (1734), Hasse (1735) and Gluck (1752).

Clérambault, Louis-Nicolas (*b* Paris, 19 Dec 1676; *d* there, 26 Oct 1749). French composer. Like his father Dominique (*c*1644–1704) and earlier members of the family, he served the French court. From 1714 he was organist of the Maison Royale de St Cyr (a school near Versailles) and at St Sulpice, Paris, and, from 1719, the Jacobins. He was considered one of France's finest players. His first harpsichord collection (1704) is wholly in the French style, but many of his other works combine French and Italian elements. Most notable are his 25 French cantatas (1710–43), some simple, others dramatic and intense. His other works include violin solo and trio sonatas, organ music and many motets. Clérambault's sons César-François-Nicolas (*d* 1760) and Evrard Dominique (1710–90) were both organists; the former succeeded to his father's posts and probably composed cantatas.

Clereau, Pierre (*fl* 1539–67). French composer. He was choirmaster at Toul until 1557. Three masses by him and a set of *Cantiques spirituels* survive. His sets of 29 *chansons* (2 bks, 1559), which show a new literary discernment and a preference for Ronsard's poems, include nine madrigals.

Cleve, Johannes de (*b* Kleve, 1528–9; *d* Augsburg, 14 July 1582). German composer. After early years in the Netherlands, he sang in the Vienna Hofkapelle from 1553. He was Kapellmeister at Graz (1564–70), then returned to Vienna, teaching at Augsburg from 1579. He composed for both the Catholic church (masses, 1559, and motets, 1559, 1579–80) and the Protestant (hymns, 1569–74); his late music shows declamatory, expressive passages and chromaticisms.

Cleveland Orchestra. American orchestra founded in 1918, with Nicolai Sokoloff as conductor. Its home is Severance Hall (1931, cap. 2000) and it gives a summer season at Blossom Music Center (opened 1968), Cuyahoga Falls. Under George Szell (1946–70) the orchestra was enlarged, its season was expanded and it achieved international acclaim. Lorin Maazel has been music director (1972–82) and Christoph von Dohnányi (1984–). Cleveland Orchestra Chorus was established in 1955; a children's chorus was formed in 1967.

Cleveland Quartet. American string quartet. It was founded in 1968, and has been in residence at the Cleveland Institute, the State University of New York, Buffalo, and the Eastman School, Rochester (from 1976). It has toured in Europe since 1974. The quartet, led by Donald Weilerstein, is noted for its vigorous and clearly defined performances of a wide repertory.

Cliburn, Van (*b* Shreveport, 12 July 1934). American pianist. In 1954 he appeared with the New York PO at Carnegie Hall but wider fame did not come until 1958, when he won the International Tchaikovsky Competition in Moscow. With his technical command and massive tone he gained a large following in the Romantic repertory but interpretative affectations led to a decline in his reputation.

Clicquot. French family of organ builders. The most celebrated members were Robert (*c*1645–1719), who as 'facteur d'orgues du Roy' was the leading builder in Paris, 1700–20, working on the instruments of Blois Cathedral, the great chapel at Versailles (1710–11) and the Palais des Tuileries (1719); and his grandson François-Henri (1732–90), whose work, notably the organ of St Sulpice (1781) and modernizations of 17th-century Parisian instruments, represents the climax of French classical organ building.

Clock, Musical. *See* MUSICAL CLOCK.

Clock Symphony. Nickname of Haydn's Symphony no.101 in D (1794), so called because of the 'tick-tock' accompaniment to the second movement's first subject.

Close position [close harmony]. The spacing of a chord in such a way that the upper voices lie as close together as possible or the interval between the highest and lowest is relatively small.

Cluster. A group of adjacent notes sounding simultaneously. Keyboard instruments are particularly suited to their performance since they may readily be played with the fist, palm or forearm.

Cluytens, André (*b* Antwerp, 26 March 1905; *d* Paris, 3 June 1967). French conductor of Belgian birth. His early career was in Antwerp and at French opera houses. He became musical director at the Opéra-Comique, Paris, in 1947 and conducted the Paris Conservatoire Orchestra from 1949. He conducted Wagner at Bayreuth and La Scala and gave unmannered performances of French music and the Viennese Classics.

Coates, Albert (*b* St Petersburg, 23 April 1882; *d* Cape Town, 11 Dec 1953). English conductor and composer. He studied at the Leipzig Conservatory and after an early career in Germany conducted at the Mariinsky Theatre, St Petersburg, 1911–16. He was heard in Wagner at Covent Garden in 1914 and from 1919 conducted the LSO: he gave first performances of Vaughan Williams, Bax and Holst (*The Planets*, 1920). From 1920 he appeared as guest conductor in the USA. Among his compositions was the opera *Pickwick*, staged at Covent Garden in 1936.

Coates, Edith (Mary) (*b* Lincoln, 31 May 1908; *d* Worthing, 7 Jan 1983). English mezzo-soprano. She sang at Sadler's Wells, London, from 1931 and in 1945 created Auntie in Britten's *Peter Grimes*. At Covent Garden (1937–67) she was heard in operas by Verdi and Bizet and in the premières of Bliss's *Olympians* (1949) and Britten's *Gloriana* (1953).

Coates, Eric (*b* Hucknall, 27 Aug 1886; *d* Chichester, 21 Dec 1957). English composer. He studied at the RAM, worked as an orchestral viola player, and wrote light orchestral music and *c*100 songs. He is best known for the suite *London* (1933) and *The Dam Busters* march from his film score.

Cobbett, Walter Willson (*b* London, 11 July 1847; *d* there, 22 Jan 1937). English amateur violinist, patron and lexicographer. He is best remembered for his invaluable *Cyclopaedia of Chamber Music* (1929, rev. and enlarged 1963).

Cobbold, William (*b* Norwich, 5 Jan 1560; *d* Beccles, 7 Nov 1639). English composer. Organist of Norwich Cathedral, 1595–*c*1610, he is best known for two settings of the 'Cries of London' for voice and viols, based on popular tunes. He also wrote psalms (for East's psalter, 1592) and consort songs.

Cocchi, Gioacchino (*b* ?Naples, *c*1720; *d* ?Venice, after 1788). Italian composer. He had over 30 operas performed in Italy, 1743–56; his greatest success was *La maestra* (1747, Naples). He also wrote oratorios as choir director at the Ospedale degli Incurabili, Venice, 1750–57. In 1757–62 he was music director at the King's Theatre, London, producing nine of his own operas. He worked as a singing teacher and concert director before returning to Venice *c*1772.

Coccia, Carlo (*b* Naples, 14 April 1782; *d* Novara, 13 April 1873). Italian composer. A pupil of Paisiello, he produced *c*22 operas (1808–20), succeeding mainly in the sentimental *opera semiseria*, of which his greatest success was *Clotilde* (1815). He was *maestro concertatore* at the S Carlos, Lisbon (1820), and conductor at the King's Theatre, London (1824–6); of his later, more serious works, *Caterina di Guisa* (1833) made a strong impression. In 1840 he succeeded Mercadante as *maestro di cappella* at S Gaudenzio, Novara, composing much church music.

Cockaigne (In London Town). Concert overture, op.40, by Elgar (1901).

Coclico, Adrianus Petit (*b* Flanders, 1499/1500; *d* Copenhagen, after Sept 1562). Flemish composer. Having become a Protestant, he emigrated to Germany and he taught music at Wittenberg (1545). After a period in Prussia (1547–50) he went to Nuremberg (1550), then to Copenhagen. His motet collection *Consolationes piae* (1552) is of interest because the words 'musica reservata' appear in the title, though the music is disappointing, with its crude harmony, lack of melodic sensibility and over-use of word-painting. He also wrote a theoretical treatise (1552).

Cocteau, (Clément Eugène) Jean (Maurice) (*b* Maisons-Laffitte, 5 July 1889; *d* Milly-la-Forêt, 11 Oct 1963). French poet. Associated with the Ballets Russes from their arrival in Paris in 1909, he collaborated with Satie and Picasso on *Parade* (1917) and with Stravinsky on *Oedipus rex* (1927). His polemic *Le coq et l'arlequin* (1918) provided an aesthetic for Les Six, whose guiding spirit he was: Milhaud, Poulenc, Auric and Durey all set his verse and Auric wrote music for his films of the 1930s and 1940s.

Coda (It.). 'Tail': the last part of a piece or melody; an addition to a standard form or design. In fugue the coda is anything occurring after the last entry of the subject, in sonata form anything coming after the recapitulation.

Codax, Martin (*fl c*1230). Galician composer and poet. He is known by seven poems, six with music, discovered in 1914, the only Portuguese-Galician secular medieval lyrics to survive.

Codetta (It). 'Little tail': in a fugal exposition, a link between two entries of the theme; in sonata form, the final section of the exposition, reinforcing the tonality at that point.

Codex (Lat.: 'manuscript'). Term often used in names assigned to medieval or Renaissance MSS. For descriptions of such MSS, see under the other name of the title (e.g. the MS sometimes called 'Codex Reina' is entered under REINA CODEX).

Coelho, Manuel Rodrigues. *See* RODRIGUES COELHO, MANUEL.

Coelho, Rui (*b* Alcacer do Sal, 2 March 1892; *d* Lisbon, 5 May 1986). Portuguese composer. He studied at the Lisbon Conservatory, with Humperdinck, Bruch and Schoenberg in Berlin (1910–13) and with Vidal in Paris. Strongly nationalist, his works include many operas, symphonies, suites, vocal music and ballets, of which *A princesa dos sapatos de Ferro* (1912) was the first Portuguese national ballet.

Coffee Cantata. Nickname of J.S. Bach's cantata no.211, *Schweigt stille, plaudert nicht*, to a libretto by Picander (*c*1735), referring to the growing fondness for coffee.

Cogan, Philip (*b* ?Cork, 1748; *d* Dublin, 3 Feb 1833). Irish composer. He lived in Dublin from 1772 and was organist at St Patrick's Cathedral, 1780–1810, gaining a high reputation as a player, composer and teacher. Notable among his works are keyboard sonatas, some with violin (1782–*c*1818). He also wrote piano concertos in the 1790s, stage works and songs.

Cohen, Harriet (*b* London, 2 Dec 1895; *d* there, 13 Nov 1967). English pianist. She studied at the RAM and quickly became identified with the English music of her time. She gave the first performance of Vaughan Williams's Concerto and was chosen by Elgar to record his quintet; Bax, an intimate friend, composed most of his piano works for her. Her memoirs are valuable for letters from friends in all walks of life.

Cohn, Arthur (*b* Philadelphia, 6 Nov 1910). American composer, conductor and writer. He studied at the Combs Conservatory, the University of Pennsylvania and the Juilliard School, Goldmark being his main composition teacher. His works include six string quartets (1928–45) and orchestral pieces; he has written books on 20th-century music and on the recorded repertory.

Colascione. A plucked string instrument, dating from the 17th century, with a long narrow neck and a small lute-shaped body. In its early forms, two or three strings are played with a plectrum. The *colachon* or *gallichone* seem to be variants, similar in shape, with six to eight strings (typically tuned $C–D–G–c–e–a$ or $D–G–c–f–a–d'$), used in the 18th century; there was also a smaller *colascioncino*.

Colbran, Isabella [Isabel] (**Angela**) (*b* Madrid, 2 Feb 1785; *d* Bologna, 7 Oct 1845). Spanish soprano. Admired for her vocal brilliance and dramatic stage presence, she influenced Rossini, whom she later married, in his operas for Naples, including *Otello* (1816), *Mosè in Egitto* (1818), *La donna del lago* (1819) and *Maometto II* (1820).

Cole, Hugo (*b* London, 6 July 1917). English composer and critic. He studied at Cambridge, at the RCM and with Boulanger in Paris; his works include operas and music for amateurs. In 1964 he became a critic for *The Guardian*.

Coleman, Charles (*b c*1605; *d* London, before 9 July 1664). English composer, singer and instrumentalist. A member of the King's Musick under Charles II, he succeeded Henry Lawes as 'composer in his Majesty's private music for the voices' in 1662. Though primarily an instrumental composer – pieces by him appear in well-known collections – his songs are more advanced. He performed in Shirley's masque *The Triumph of Peace* (1634), and composed for Davenant's *The Siege of Rhodes* (1656). His son Edward (*d* 1669) also served under Charles II and contributed music to various stage works and vocal anthologies.

Coleman, Ornette (*b* Fort Worth, 9 March 1930). American jazz saxophonist and composer. His early recordings, *The Shape of Jazz to Come* and *Change of the Century* (both 1959), were innovatory and he became the most important influence on avant-garde jazz during the 1960s. He performed as a trumpeter and violinist in the late 1960s and composed extended works for large ensembles, also exploring collective improvisation. In 1981 he founded Prime Time, an electric band. His improvisations are modal, independent of conventional harmonic sequences and melodic variations.

Coleridge-Taylor, Samuel [Taylor, Samuel Coleridge] (*b* London, 15 Aug 1875; *d* Croydon, 1 Sept 1912). English composer. His father was from Sierra Leone and his mother was English. He studied the violin, singing and composition (with Stanford) at the RCM, producing anthems, chamber music and songs. His fame rests mainly on the cantata *Hiawatha's Wedding Feast* (1898), once popular for its exotic flavour, and on choral works commissioned for provincial festivals, including further 'Hiawatha' scenes and *A Tale of Old Japan* (1911). He wrote incidental music for His Majesty's Theatre and was a composition professor and an excellent conductor, making three visits to the USA and maintaining contacts with prominent black Americans who shared his mission to establish the dignity of blacks. Stylistically close to the music of his idol Dvořák, some of his works are modelled on black American subjects and melodies, though some lack harmonic inventiveness. He was at his best in smaller pieces, including the *Petite suite de concert* for orchestra (1910).

Colgrass, Michael (*b* Chicago, 22 April 1932). American composer and percussionist. He studied with Milhaud, Riegger and Ben Weber. As a percussionist he has played with ensembles ranging from the Columbia SO to Dizzy Gillespie's band. His works are eclectic, reflecting his wide interests, and include operas, theatrical concert pieces and songs to his own texts, including *New People* (1969).

Colin, Pierre (*fl* 1538–65). French composer. Master of the choristers (*c*1539–61) and organist (1562–*c*1565) at St Lazarus Cathedral, Autun, he was a leading representative of the generation of composers after Josquin. His 36 imitative motets are among his best works, showing his concern for textual clarity. Most of his 26 masses are of the parody type; he also wrote ten Magnificats and eight *chansons*.

Coliseum. Theatre in London, built in 1904. Its seating capacity (2354) and stage are the largest in London and it was the first theatre to have a revolving stage. It is the home of English National Opera.

Colista, Lelio (*b* Rome, 13 Jan 1629; *d* there, 13 Oct 1680). Italian composer and lutenist. He worked at S Marcello and S Luigi dei Francesi, Rome, composing oratorios (now lost) and church sonatas for both, while taking part in the music at various Roman academies; he was the leading instrumental composer in Rome in the 17th century. His trio sonatas (Purcell's most important Italian models) are prophetic of Corelli in the rich cantilena of their slow movements, with chains of suspensions and 'walking' basses; his other works include cantatas and six symphonias for plucked instruments.

Colla parte (It.). 'With the part': an indication to play the same part as another (written-out) part, or to keep in tempo with another (flexibly performed) part; also *colla voce*.

Collasse, Pascal (*b* Rheims, bap. 22 Jan 1649; *d* Versailles, 17 July 1709). French composer. In 1677 he became Lully's secretary and *batteur de mesure* at the Paris Opéra, occupying a shared post at the royal chapel (1683–1704) and becoming (with Lalande) *compositeur* (1685) and *maître* (1696) *de la musique de la chambre du roi*. He also continued his association with the Académie Royale de Musique as an opera composer. Years of indoctrination under Lully hampered the development of his own style, though his orchestration could be more original. Among his many stage works the *tragédie lyrique Thétis et Pélée* (1689) excels; the 100-bar 'tempête' in Act 2 was probably the model for similar orchestral storms by Campra and Marais.

Collective compositions. Compositions written by two or more composers in collaboration. The history of such works goes back to the anthologies compiled as tributes in the 16th and 17th centuries (e.g. the *Triumphes of Oriana* (1601), madrigals written in praise of Elizabeth I). Several collaborative stage works were written in the 17th and 18th centuries. In the 19th, the Viennese publisher Diabelli put together a set of variations on a theme of his own by *c*50 composers, and six leading composers wrote a set called *Hexameron* (1837) on a theme by Bellini. A movement of Verdi's Requiem was written for what was planned as a collective requiem for Rossini. Brahms, Schumann and Dietrich wrote movements for a violin sonata in 1853, using the same motto theme, as did a group of Russian composers who wrote a string quartet in 1886.

Collegium Aureum. German early music group. It was founded in 1962 and is directed by Franzjosef Maier, from the leader's desk. It specializes in music from the late Baroque until the end of the Viennese Classical period and has worked towards the use of period instruments.

Collegium musicum (Lat.). Term, for a musical guild, that came to be used in 16th-century Germany for an association concerned with performance. Many such groups came into existence during the 17th and 18th centuries, especially in the German-speaking countries; North America followed in the 18th and 19th centuries. The term fell into disuse in Europe during the 19th century but has been revived recently to denote a group, usually at an academic institution, that favours period-style performances of early music.

Col legno (It.). 'With the wood': term in string playing meaning to set the strings of the instrument in motion with the wood of the bow rather than with the hair, giving a dry, staccato effect; the resumption of normal bowing is indicated by *arco*.

Colles, Henry Cope (*b* Bridgnorth, 20 April 1879; *d* London, 4 March 1943). English writer on music. He studied at the RCM and Oxford and in 1911 became chief critic of *The Times*. A wide-ranging and sympathetic writer, he was also editor of *Grove 3* (1927) and its revision *Grove 4* (1940).

Collin de Blamont, François (*b* Versailles, 22 Nov 1690; *d* there, 14 Feb 1760). French composer. He rose to favour at the French court, serving from 1719 as *surintendant de la musique de la chambre* and from 1726 *maître*. He wrote music for over 12 ballets, divertissments etc, mostly for royal occasions; with the successful *Les festes grecques et romaines* (1723, Paris) he and his librettist created the *ballet héroïque*. He also composed three books of cantatas (1723–9) and one of motets.

Collingwood, Lawrance (Arthur) (*b* London, 14 March 1887; *d* Killin, 19 Dec 1982). English conductor and composer. He studied at the St Petersburg Conservatory and after conducting at the Mariinsky Theatre returned to London in 1920. From 1931 he was principal conductor at the Sadler's Wells Theatre, giving early British performances of operas by Rimsky-Korsakov and Musorgsky. His opera *Macbeth* was produced at Sadler's Wells in 1934.

Colonna, Giovanni Paolo (*b* Bologna, 16 June 1637; *d* there, 29 Nov 1695). Italian composer. He studied in Rome with Benevoli and Carissimi, becoming organist at S Petronio, Bologna, in 1659 (*maestro di cappella*, 1674) and holding similar posts at other Bolognese churches. A founder member of the Accademia dei Filarmonici, he was an important composer of oratorios between Carissimi and Handel (though only six have survived). Skilful and lively counterpoint is a feature of most of his work, which includes collections of motets (1681) that anticipate Handel's chamber cantatas, and elaborate concerted settings of the mass and psalms, those of 1691 being among his best works.

Colonne, Edouard [Judas] (*b* Bordeaux, 23 July 1838; *d* Paris, 28 March 1910). French violinist and conductor. He studied in Bordeaux and at the Paris Conservatoire. He was an orchestral violinist during the 1860s and founded, with the publisher Hartmann, the Concert National in 1873. His performances of French works, especially those of Berlioz, at the Association Artistique concerts gained him recognition; the Concerts Colonne still exist in Paris. Besides making numerous European tours, he conducted the Odéon theatre orchestra and became the Opéra's artistic adviser and conductor (1892–3).

Color. A medieval Latin term used to signify the embellishment of a melody through repetition, ornamentation or chromatic alteration. It most frequently refers to melodic (as opposed to rhythmic) repetition in isorhythmic motets.

Coloration. Term in early notation for the use of colour (red or, later, black) to fill in notes; this indicated a change in rhythmic value. The term is also used for passages of 'music that are decorated in a florid style, with diminution.

Coloratura. Term for florid figuration or ornamentation, particularly in vocal music, for example the writing for the Queen of Night in Mozart's *Die Zauberflöte* or the music for Violetta that ends Act 1 of Verdi's *La traviata*. A coloratura soprano is one with a high, agile voice apt to such parts.

Colour organ. An instrument designed to relate music to colour, usually by projecting coloured light. Its most celebrated use is in Skryabin's *Prométhée: le poème du feu* (1908–10).

Coltellini, Marco (*b* ?Florence or Livorno, 13 Oct 1719; *d* St Petersburg, Nov 1777). Italian librettist. In Vienna by 1763, he wrote several librettos influenced by Calzabigi which were set by Traetta, Gluck, Mozart and others. From 1772 he worked at the Russian court. His daughter Celeste (1760–1829), a mezzo-soprano, sang in Italy and Vienna.

Coltrane, John (William) (*b* Hamlet, NC, 23 Sept 1926; *d* New York, 17 July 1967). American jazz saxophonist, bandleader and composer. He first became known as a soloist with Miles Davis (1955–7, 1958–60) and led his own bands from 1960. His solos were marked by great technical facility, expressed in rapid delivery (as in *Giant Steps*, 1959), systematic variation of motifs (*My Favorite Things*, 1960, and *A Love Supreme*, 1964) and radical developments in timbre. He mostly played the tenor saxophone, but from the early 1960s he also used the

soprano instrument. After Charlie Parker he was the most innovatory and widely imitated jazz saxophonist.

Combarieu, Jules (Léon Jean) (*b* Cahors, 5 Feb 1859; *d* Paris, 7 July 1916). French musicologist and critic. He founded the *Revue d'histoire et de critique musicales* (1901, from 1904 *Revue musicale*), published lectures on music history and contributed to several journals.

Combattimento di Tancredi e Clorinda, Il. Dramatic cantata by Monteverdi to a text from Tasso's *Gerusalemme liberata* (1624, Venice).

Combination tone. A sound that may be heard when two musical tones are sounded together; the frequency of a combination tone will normally be the sum or difference of the frequencies (or multiples of the frequencies) of the original tones.

Combinatoriality. In 12-note theory, the property of a set of pitches whereby when it is inflected (e.g. by inversion or retrograding) its pitches are replicated in analogous configurations in the inflected set.

Comédie-ballet (Fr.). A type of stage work devised by Molière and Lully in which music and dance were complementary to the main dramatic action.

Comédie mêlée d'ariettes (Fr.). A comedy made up of short arias, with spoken dialogue: a French 18th-century form. This title was generally used at the time for the genre now known as *opéra comique*.

Come prima (It.). 'As before': a direction to return to the previous tempo, to play in the same manner as in an earlier section, or to repeat a section.

Comes, Juan Bautista (*b* Valencia, 1582; *d* there, 5 Jan 1643). Spanish composer. He was *maestro de capilla* of Lérida Cathedral (1605–8), twice *maestro* of Valencia Cathedral (1613–18, 1632–8) and vice-*maestro* of the royal chapel in Madrid (1618–28). His 200 or so extant works, mostly sacred, are colourful and varied in texture and include polychoral pieces.

Come sopra (It.). 'As above': a direction used as a substitute for recopying a section; also used to mean COME PRIMA.

Come stà (It.). 'As it stands': an instruction to play without improvised ornamentation or rhythmic alteration.

Come ye Sons of Art. Ode by Purcell for the birthday of Queen Mary (1694); it contains the song 'Sound the Trumpet'.

Comissiona, Sergiu (*b* Bucharest, 16 June 1928). Romanian conductor. In 1959 he emigrated to Israel, founding the Israel CO in 1960. During the 1960s he was heard with the LPO and the Royal Ballet, Covent Garden. From 1965 he has been admired in the USA, giving colourful performances with orchestras in Philadelphia, Baltimore and New York.

Comma. A small interval, usually taken to be one-ninth of a whole tone; the commas used in temperament and tuning are of approximately 21.5 or 23.5 cents.

Commedia dell'arte (It.). A form of Italian comic theatre, involving masks, buffoonery and improvisation, which flourished in the period *c*1525–

*c*1750. Little is known about its music, but its stock characters (such as Harlequin and Scaramouche) influenced characterization in early comic opera and up to the time of Mozart, and was revived by Busoni, Strauss and Stravinsky.

Commedia per musica (It.). Term for comic opera, used in the 18th century, particularly in Naples.

Common chord. The familiar name for a major or minor triad (in American usage, only a major triad).

Common time. 4/4 time. It has been supposed, erroneously, that the time signature C, derived from the medieval half-circle designating the duple division of the breve and the semibreve, represented a 'C' standing for 'common time'. *See* TIME SIGNATURE.

Communion. In the Western Christian church, the final item of the Proper of the Mass, sung during Communion. It originated, by the 4th century, as a complete psalm sung antiphonally, but by the 12th only the Communion antiphon remained, except in the Requiem Mass. It comprises an antiphon, verse and Gloria Patri; as in the Introit, the verse and Gloria Patri are sung to the same psalm tone. The Communion ranges in style from short, syllabic pieces to longer ones melismatically ornamented. Texts are from the psalms or the Gospels; some are also Office Reponsories.

Comodo (It.). 'Comfortable', 'convenient': a tempo designation or qualification to other tempo marks, e.g. *andante comodo*.

Compenius. German family of organ builders. The most celebrated members were Esaias (*d* 1617), who built the organ at Hessen Castle (1605–10; now at Hillerød) under Praetorius's supervision and assisted Praetorius in writing his *Organographia*; his brother Heinrich the younger (*d* 1631), who built the organ at Magdeburg Cathedral (1604–5); and his nephew Johann Heinrich (*d* 1642), who built the organ for St Mauritius, Halle (1624–6), for Samuel Scheidt, under Scheidt's supervision. Compenius organs had a wealth of foundation stops and reeds and sometimes ivory and ebony pipes.

Compère, Loyset (*b* Hainaut, *c*1445; *d* St Quentin, 16 Aug 1518). French composer. He may have worked at Cambrai before he went to the ducal chapel in Milan in the 1470s; by 1486 he was a singer at the French court, in which capacity he was in Rome in 1495. Later he worked at Cambrai and Douai, remaining connected with the French court; finally he worked at St Quentin, with which he was connected from 1491. An able second-rank composer, he cultivated the late Burgundian style in his 16 surviving motets, which are based on the polarity between top part and tenor and on florid melodic lines; elsewhere he followed the *lauda* and frottola style, with equality and sometimes imitation between voices, syllabic melodies reflecting the words, and a bass providing harmonic support. Besides *chansons* and motets, he is known to have written three complete masses and six Magnificats.

Complement. The difference between an octave and a given simple interval, hence the INVERSION of that interval at the octave; the complement of a perfect 5th is a perfect 4th.

Compound interval. An interval greater than an octave; the sum of a simple interval (one less than an octave) and one or more octaves.

Compound time [compound metre]. A metre in which each beat is divisible by three (e.g. 6/8), as opposed to simple metre.

Comprimario (It.). A singer of a secondary part in opera.

Computers. The musical uses to which computers can be put fall into two main categories: musicological and compositional. The first includes techniques for processing and collecting musicological data, sorting and collating bibliographical material and preparing catalogues and indexes. Most important, however, have been experiments in using the computer as a tool for ANALYSIS. Many analytical methods lend themselves well to processing by computer, particularly distributional analysis and approaches based on information theory. Certain elements of 12-note techniques (e.g. the calculation of the intervallic permutations of a series) can be undertaken rapidly and efficiently by computer, as can any analytical task that can be rendered as an algorithm.

The composer can use the computer for the analysis and generation of compositional data, particularly in serial methods. For their *Iliac Suite* (1957) Hiller and Isaacson programmed a computer to compose to strict rules they had devised; Xenakis has used the computer to carry out stochastic processes based on mathematical formulae. Possibly the most widely explored application of computers is that of digital sound analysis and synthesis; a pioneer in this field was Max Matthews, an engineer at the Bell Telephone Laboratories in New Jersey, who in the late 1950s developed programs that enabled the composer to specify all the qualities of a sound and to store such data for future use. By the mid-1980s such facilities had become commonplace, both as part of home-computer systems and as the basis of the digital SYNTHESIZER. Sophisticated music-dedicated machines, such as the 4X at IRCAM in Paris and the Fairlight CMI, permit the storage, analysis and modification of huge quantities of data, and have become integral parts of the compositional processes of ELECTRONIC MUSIC.

Comte Ory, Le. Comic opera in two acts by Rossini to a libretto by Scribe and Lestre-Poirson (1828, Paris).

Comus. Masque by John Milton performed at Ludlow Castle in 1634 with music by Henry Lawes, who took part. Arne composed new music for J. Dalton's adaptation of Milton's verse (1738, London). Handel also set some numbers (1745).

Concentus Musicus. Early music ensemble, formed in Vienna in 1953 by Nikolaus Harnoncourt (*b* 1929), the cellist and bass viol player and conductor, and led by his wife Alice (*b* 1930). The group, which performs in period styles and on appropriate instruments, has made many recordings, notably of Monteverdi operas, Bach cantatas, Handel choral works and music of the Classical period; they first toured North America in 1966.

Concert. Term for a public musical entertainment, usually implying performance by an orchestra. Until the mid-19th century, a concert could be almost any type of non-theatrical entertainment. For a smaller-scale performance, the term 'recital' is usually preferred.

Performances at court by employed musicians have a long and obscure early history. In the 16th and 17th centuries, performances were given privately at meetings of academies or collegia musica, some open to guests. In England, concert-giving began in the late 17th century, usually in a tavern or private house; the earliest recorded such event was at the Mitre Inn, London, in 1664. Other well-known early concert-givers include John Banister, who gave subscription concerts in London from 1672, and Thomas Britton, whose Clerkenwell concerts date from 1768. The growth in the 18th century of musical societies, open to members and their guests and to visitors, led to a great increase in concert-giving. Concerts were held in the London pleasure gardens; the Bach–Abel concerts (1764) and the Concert of Ancient Music (1776) are two of the best known of many London series. In France, the most important early concerts were those given by the Concert Spirituel during Lent when the opera was closed; this series, begun in 1725, was important until the Revolution, though the Concert des Amateurs (later Concert de la Loge Olympique) had a more forward-looking musical policy. In Germany, concert life began early in the 18th century in Frankfurt, Hamburg and especially Leipzig, where the Gewandhaus concerts, founded in 1781, grew from an earlier series. The first known concert in North America was in Boston in 1731; series in Philadelphia and Charleston soon followed.

In the 19th century, the best-known concert series were organized by such institutions as the Gesellschaft der Musikfreunde of Vienna (1801), the Philharmonic Society of London (1813) and the Société des Concerts du Conservatoire in Paris (1828); but numerous concerts were organized by rival groups, smaller associations and such institutions as choirs (e.g. the Berlin Singakademie, 1791, or the Sacred Harmonic Society of London, 1832). More popular concert series, such as the Promenade Concerts in London (1895), arose towards the end of the 19th century. In the 20th, 19th-century traditions have broadly been continued; the predominant pattern in most large cities is of a local orchestra (often with a linked, amateur choir) giving regular concerts, sometimes arranged in subscription series, in a central concert hall.

For further information on concert institutions, see under individual names.

Concertante (It.). Term applied to music that is in some sense soloistic or 'concerto-like', e.g. the SYMPHONIE CONCERTANTE. *See also* QUATUOR CONCERTANT.

Concertato (It.). 'Concerted': term, derived from 'concerto', and used to mean 'in the manner of a concerto'. It is often applied to the 'vocal concerto' of the first half of the 17th century, in which a few voices were accompanied by organ (or other harmony instruments). The 'concertato motet' is a work in which the melody is shared between several voices, these voices also being deployed in groups to give textural variety. It was much used in Germany (notably by Schütz) as well as in Italy (where its practitioners included G. Gabrieli, Viadana and Monteverdi).

Concert band. Term used in America for a band largely of wind instruments; *see* MILITARY BAND.

Concertina. An accordion-type, free-reed instrument consisting of two hexagonal casings connected by bellows, each casing containing a small button keyboard. The English concertina, with a full chromatic scale of four octaves, has uniform tone, with the same note sounding on both extension and compression of the bellows; the German type sounds different notes on extension and compression.

Concertino. The solo group in a Baroque concerto; in later usage, a small-scale concerto.

Concerto. A term often applied in the 17th century to ensemble music for voices and instruments; since then it has usually denoted a work in which a solo instrument (or instrumental group) contrasts with an orchestral ensemble.

The *Concerti grossi* op.6 of Corelli, some of which probably date from the 1680s, resemble amplified trio sonatas and could be played by as few as three or four players or by orchestras of over 100. They were imitated by his pupils in Italy and by composers in Germany and England, where Handel's *Grand Concertos* op.6, while drawing also on other traditions, represent the summation of the Corelli type. Most were heard as interval music in oratorios, as were Handel's organ concertos, a form he seems to have originated and one which became popular among English composers.

The six Brandenburg Concertos of Bach derive less from this tradition than from the type of ripieno and solo concertos composed by Torelli and others at Bologna and by Vivaldi and others at Venice. It was the three-movement solo concerto of the Vivaldi type, with the quick movements usually in ritornello form, that survived the Baroque period and developed into the Classical concerto represented at its finest and most sophisticated in the 23 piano concertos of Mozart. Beethoven's are on a larger scale, but they adhere to the principles of the Classical design despite innovations such as the linking of movements, the participation of the soloist in the initial ritornello (adumbrated by Mozart in K271) and the writing of a cadenza into the score (Piano Concerto no.5).

While many early Romantic composers, including Chopin and Paganini, retained the ritornello design as an effective framework for virtuoso display, the 12 violin concertos of Spohr, dating from 1802–27, show structural innovations which anticipate Mendelssohn. Mendelssohn was influential in dispensing with the rigid solo–tutti division of the ritornello structure, in linking all the movements of a concerto and in the placing of cadenzas. Liszt treated the form even more freely, at the same time introducing an element of passionate rivalry between soloist and orchestra which established the expressive climate for concertos by Tchaikovsky, Rakhmaninov, Prokofiev and others.

A more conservative late Romantic tradition, retaining the ritornello design for the first movement but in a strongly symphonic manner, is represented by the concertos of Brahms, Dvořák (for cello) and Elgar (for violin). 20th-century composers such as Stravinsky and Bloch have turned to Baroque models for concertos, while others (Bartók, Tippett etc) have exemplified a new type of orchestral concerto in which different instruments or groups are highlighted in turn. But the traditional three-movement solo concerto inherited from the 19th century has proved remarkably resilient, and on the whole resistant to the programmatic elements that have often invaded the symphony.

Concert of Ancient [Antient] Music. London concert society, 1776–1848. It was founded by the Earl of Sandwich and others to preserve earlier music by presenting concerts of works more than 20 years old. Many works by Handel were given; later concerts were criticized for lack of variety because newer works were not included as they became eligible.

Concerto grosso. A type of concerto of the Baroque period in which a small group of instruments ('concertino') is contrasted with the main body 'ripieno' or 'concerto grosso'.

Concerts Colonne. Parisian concert association formed in 1873 as the Concert National; it was renamed in 1874 and later named after Edouard Colonne, who first conducted its concerts. They are given by the Orchestre de l'Ile-de-France.

Concerts Lamoureux. Parisian concert association, originally the Société des Nouveaux Concerts. It was founded in 1881 by the conductor Charles Lamoureux; in 1897 it combined with the Concerts de l'Opéra and was renamed. Concerts are given by the Orchestra de l'Ile-de-France.

Concerts Pasdeloup. See CONCERTS POPULAIRES DE MUSIQUE CLASSIQUE.

Concert Spirituel. Concert series (1725–90) founded in Paris by Anne Danican Philidor. At first instrumental and sacred Latin works were given; later, secular vocal works were introduced and the concerts became the centre of concert life in Paris. The name was revived and similar concerts were given elsewhere in Europe.

Concerts Populaires de Musique Classique. Parisian concert association, 1861–84, founded by the conductor J.E. Pasdeloup. It was revived in 1920 as Concerts Pasdeloup. Concerts are given by the Orchestra de l'Ile-de-France.

Conch-shell trumpet. A wind instrument made from a marine shell.

Concierto de Aranjuez. Guitar concerto by Rodrigo (1939).

Concitato. See STILE CONCITATO.

Concord. See CONSONANCE.

Concord Sonata. Ives's Second Piano Sonata (1915), named after the Massachusetts town in which the literary figures honoured in the work lived.

Conducting. The direction of a musical performance by visible gestures designed to secure unanimity of execution and interpretation. Modern conducting, with a lightweight baton, began in the early 19th century, but beating time to mark the rhythm goes back to the Middle Ages, even to ancient Greece.

There are accounts from the 16th century of a director stamping on the ground or striking a music book with a stick to mark out the rhythm; later, striking the ground with a stick was the normal practice (it may be assumed that this was Lully's practice when in 1687 he hit his foot with a staff and died of gangrene caused by the wound). There is evidence that, in the 16th and 17th centuries, the director of a performance indicated the rhythm with his hand or with a roll of music (or other paper).

In the 18th century, performances were directed from the harpsichord (or other keyboard instrument) or by the leading violinist. Mozart directed his operas from the keyboard; Haydn 'presided at the piano-forte' when his symphonies were performed in London. The violinist directing a performance was compelled to rely mainly on his bow, used to beat the time. Many conductors of the early 19th century were violinists. Spohr used a roll of paper when conducting a choir and orchestra in 1809; in 1816 he noted that the opera orchestra of Milan was conducted by the principal violin, and the next year he was persuaded by singers to use his violin, indicating the time with the bow – though once the performance was under way he laid his violin aside and 'directed in the French style, with a baton'. He produced his baton in London in 1820, to the orchestra's initial alarm but ultimate approval. It is often supposed that he was the first conductor to use a baton in the modern manner.

Notable 19th-century conductors include Mendelssohn, who used a white stick to maintain a steady tempo. Berlioz explained in a treatise the art of time-beating and held the tempo steady with a baton. Wagner, who also laid down principles on conducting, favoured more flexibility, and modern traditions of interpretation are indebted to his view of the conductor's responsibility for realizing, in his own way, the character of a work. Leading late 19th-century conductors were Hans von Bülow, Hermann Levi and Hans Richter. Mahler and Strauss were notable composer-conductors. Strauss, and his contemporary Nikisch, were noted for their unostentatious manner of conducting, followed too by such men as Boult and Kleiber. Others, for example Furtwängler and Beecham, developed highly individual styles; Furtwängler and Toscanini are widely considered the most influential conductors, at opposite poles of style, of the early 20th century. More recently, such conductors as Stokowski and Bernstein have been noted for their flamboyant approach, while Karajan stands unrivalled for the surface polish of his performances.

Conductor's part. A reduction of an orchestral score to two or a few more staves with the parts for transposing instruments notated at sounding pitch and all entrances of the different instruments cued. Band scores are printed in this form, which is also known as 'condensed score'.

Conductus (Lat., from *conducere*: 'to escort'). A medieval song with a serious, usually sacred text in Latin verse. The genre originated in southern France and was taken up by composers of the Notre Dame school c1160–c1240, when it flourished with great brilliance. Unlike other forms of the time, it was not based on a plainchant *cantus firmus*. Most examples are in syllabic style, though some end with a melismatic coda. It was superseded in the later 13th century by the motet.

Cone, Edward T(oner) (*b* Greensboro, NC, 4 May 1917). American critic and composer. He studied with Sessions at Princeton, where he began teaching in 1947; he later held professorships at the University of California at Berkeley (from 1972) and Cornell University (from 1979). His writings, intellectually curious and provocatively independent, are wide-ranging and include a book on form and performance (1968) and *The Composer's Voice* (1974). His few compositions include chamber, orchestral and vocal works.

Conforti, Giovanni Luca (*b* Mileto, *c*1560; *d* after 1607). Italian theorist and composer. A singer in the papal chapel (1580–85 and from 1591), he published two books (1601, 1607) showing how to ornament traditional psalm singing. His ornamentation treatise (1593) is a useful practical manual for singers.

Conga. (1) Afro-Cuban barrel drum played in the Latin American dance orchestra.

(2) A ballroom dance of Afro-Cuban origin introduced to Europe and North America in the 1930s; it is in duple time, with a continuously repeated two-bar rhythmic phrase and a syncopation anticipating the second beat.

Congolese music. A genre of popular African music in the former Belgian Congo (now Zaïre). It originated in the work camps of European companies, where people of many cultural groups were mixed; it is a fusion of native and foreign musical elements, based on dance forms of Latin-American origin, especially the rumba. It was typically played by ensembles including a frame drum, a marimba-type instrument and a bottle, with the addition of such Western instruments as the guitar, accordion, violins and brass instruments, and later more elaborate percussion sections and electric guitars.

Conjunct. A term applied to a melodic line that moves by step (i.e. in intervals of a 2nd) rather than in disjunct motion (by leap).

Conn. American firm of instrument manufacturers and distributors, primarily of band instruments. It was started in Elkhart, Indiana, in 1875 by Charles Gerard Conn and Eugene Dupont to produce cornets and a special type of mouthpiece. By the 1890s, known as C.G. Conn Co., it offered a range of brass instruments, flutes, clarinets and saxophones of its own make, and imported wind instruments. From 1915 it introduced assembly-line production and cultivated the new school-band market. The firm has expanded through affiliate companies (including Ludwig & Ludwig from 1930) and an electronic organ division (*c*1947).

Connell, Elizabeth (*b* Port Elizabeth, 22 Oct 1946). Irish soprano of South African birth. She studied at the London Opera Centre and began her career with Australian Opera (1975) and English National Opera (1975–80). She initially sang mezzo roles such as Eboli and Ortrud; later she turned to soprano ones, singing Fiordiligi, Leonora (*Il trova-*

tore) and Leonore (*Fidelio*); she has sung Lady Macbeth in the USA, a role in which her incisive soprano, with strong dramatic overtones, serves well.

Connolly, Justin (Riveagh) (*b* London, 11 Aug 1933). English composer. He studied at the RCM and at Yale (1963–6), where he effectively began as a composer, influenced by Carter. His works cover most non-theatrical genres; his sensitive word-painting is shown by his *Poems of Wallace Stevens I* (1967).

Conradi, Johann Georg (*d* Oettingen, 22 May 1699). German composer. Director of the Hamburg opera in the 1690s, he had earlier held posts at the courts of Oettingen-Oettingen (1671–83), Ansbach (1683–6) and Römhild (1687–90). Little survives of the sacred and ceremonial music written for these Protestant courts save a few sacred arias, concertos and cantatas. Of his nine known Hamburg operas, only *Die schöne und getreue Ariadne* (1691) is known: the lyrical music is an interesting expressive mixture of Venetian, German and French styles, French being dominant except in the highly dramatic recitatives. French dances are common, and the opera ends with a Lullian song and dance scene over a ground bass. Most of the 38 arias are in a kind of da capo form, and the orchestra plays a consistently active role.

His son Johann Melchior (1675–1756) sang under him at Römhild in 1687 and later succeeded him as Kapellmeister at Oettingen (1699–1732); he composed serenades and cantatas.

Consecration of the House, The [Die Weihe des Hauses]. Overture, op.124, and chorus by Beethoven, for Meisl's play opening a new theatre (1822, Vienna).

Consecutive fifths, consecutive octaves [parallel fifths, parallel octaves]. In part-writing, the simultaneous duplication of the melodic line of one voice by another at the interval of a perfect 5th or an octave, or any equivalent compound interval; such progressions are considered incorrect in classical harmony.

Conservatoire National Supérieur de Musique. *See* PARIS CONSERVATOIRE.

Conservatory (Fr. *conservatoire*; Ger. *Konservatorium, Hochschule für Musik*; It. *conservatorio*). A school for the study, usually towards a professional level, of music. The idea of the conservatory goes back to medieval church choir schools and the humanist view that music should be taught alongside other required subjects. In the late 16th and early 17th centuries, music became the predominant activity in certain orphanages in Venice and Naples. By the early 18th century, the Venetian conservatories (such as the Ospedale della Pietà, where Vivaldi taught) had a highly skilled choir and orchestra of orphan girls, who attracted substantial audiences; most of Vivaldi's concertos and his sacred music was written for these performers. In Naples, the four conservatories trained most of the many opera composers and singers who dominated music over much of Europe until the end of the 18th century.

These institutions declined later in the 18th century and most closed with the Napoleonic invasion in 1796. By this time, however, the conservatory movement had aroused interest elsewhere: Charles Burney in England and the clarinettist Anton Stadler in Vienna put forward plans for music schools. An early French one was the Ecole Royale de Chant (1783), which closed in 1795. That year the Conservatoire Nationale de Musique was founded, under national patronage; by 1806 it had 40 staff and over 400 students, with leading composers as professors. It was the model for many institutions elsewhere: conservatories opened in Prague (1811), Vienna (1817), London (the Royal Academy of Music, 1822) and Milan (1824). Of particular importance for its widespread influence in the 19th century was the Leipzig Conservatory (1843), which attracted students not only from Germany but from Scandinavia, Britain and the USA. Further conservatories were founded over the next three decades at Munich, Berlin, Dresden, Frankfurt, Weimar and Hamburg, and in Russia the St Petersburg and Moscow conservatories were founded in the 1860s, a time when many private institutions opened in the USA, notably at Chicago, Cleveland, Boston, Oberlin and Philadelphia. In the 1860s and 70s conservatories were founded in Florence, Turin, Venice and Rome. Further institutions were founded in Britain during the 1870s and 1880s, notably the Royal College of Music (1883); while Trinity College of Music (1872) spread its influence by examining pupils not only from Britain but throughout the Commonwealth. In the 20th century, the conservatory movement has often been closely linked with universities, particularly in the USA, for example at the large schools of music at Indiana University at Bloomington and at Yale University; the Juilliard School in New York follows a more traditional pattern. Many conservatories train pupils not only in instrumental excellence but also in musicianship, historical studies and a 'second study' instrument; many lay stress on opera classes, orchestral playing and ensemble work (some have given rise to professional ensembles, for example the Juilliard Quartet).

Consolations. Six piano pieces by Liszt (1850).

Console. The desk from which an organ is played, comprising keyboards, pedal, stop-knobs, switches etc (for illustration, *see* ORGAN).

Consonance. Acoustically, the sympathetic vibration of soundwaves of different frequencies related as the ratios of small whole numbers; psychologically, the harmonious sounding together of two or more notes. Theorists of different periods have disagreed about degrees of consonance; the octave and the 5th have normally been recognized as the purest consonances, but in some eras the 4th, and in others the 3rd (especially major), have been regarded as the more consonant. Descartes, noting simplicity of ratio and pleasingness as criteria for consonance, noted that the 4th was simpler but the 3rd more pleasing. Schoenberg saw degrees of consonance as dependent on the position in the harmonic series (*see* HARMONICS). *See also* DISSONANCE.

Consort. A small instrumental ensemble for playing music composed before *c*1700; the meaning can be extended to ensembles of voices, with or without instruments, and is sometimes applied to the music

itself. The word derives from the Italian 'concerto', which had the same meaning.

The term was originally applied to groups of different kinds of instruments; the term 'broken consort' is now used in that sense. Some early consort works were written specifically for flute, treble and bass viol, lute, bandora and cittern. The modern term 'whole consort' is now applied to a group of homogeneous instruments of different pitch. The consort repertory includes Lessons by Morley and Rosseter, for mixed ensemble; much of the viol fantasia repertory, by such composers as Byrd, Gibbons, Coperario, Jenkins and Purcell, can be played on a consort of viols.

Consort anthem. A CONSORT SONG with a sacred text, often adapted as a liturgical verse anthem with organ.

Consort of Musicke. English Renaissance music group. It is directed by the lutenist Anthony Rooley, who founded it in 1969 with the lutenist James Tyler; it specializes in English music (it has recorded the complete works of Dowland) and a substantial repertory of madrigals, including many of Monteverdi's; the vocal group is usually led by the soprano Emma Kirkby.

Consort song. Modern term for an English song form of *c*1575–1625 for solo voice or voices and instruments (normally viols), associated particularly with Byrd. An offshoot was the verse anthem.

Constant, Marius (*b* Bucharest, 7 Feb 1925). French composer and conductor. He studied in Bucharest before moving to Paris in 1944 to study at the Conservatoire with Messiaen, Aubin and Boulanger. In 1963 he founded the Ars Nova ensemble for modern music, with which he has toured. His compositions are instrumental, many of them ballet scores.

Constantinescu, Paul (*b* Ploieşti, 13 July 1909; *d* Bucharest, 20 Dec 1963). Romanian composer. He studied at the Bucharest Conservatory (1928–33) and in Vienna with Schmidt and Marx (1934–5), then returned to Romania to work on folk and church music, which he used in his works. These, including operas, orchestral and choral music, pointed the way for a new nationalist generation after Enescu.

Construction in Metal. Three percussion works by Cage (1939, 1940, 1941).

Consul, The. Opera in three acts by Menotti to his own libretto (1950, Philadelphia).

Contant, Alexis (*b* Montreal, 12 Nov 1858; *d* there, 28 Nov 1918). Canadian composer. Essentially self-taught, he was the first notable Canadian composer not to study in Europe. He was organist at St Jean-Baptiste, Montreal, for over 30 years. He wrote oratorios, orchestral masses etc; his *Caïn* (1905) is the first Canadian oratorio.

Contes d'Hoffmann, Les [The Tales of Hoffmann]. Opera in five acts by Offenbach to a libretto by Barbier, completed by Guiraud (1881, Paris).

Conti, Francesco Bartolomeo (*b* Florence, 20 Jan 1681; *d* Vienna, 20 July 1732). Italian composer. One of the leading theorbo players of his day, he served at the Viennese court, 1701–26; from 1713 he was court composer. He later spent several years in

Italy, returning to Vienna shortly before his death. He composed over 25 operas, 1706–32, mostly for Vienna; the comic works, notably *Don Chisciotte in Sierra Morena* (1719) were especially popular abroad. He also wrote ten oratorios, many cantatas and sacred works. All his music shows imagination and dramatic flair, foreshadowing Hasse and Jomelli. His son Ignazio Maria (1699–1759), also a theorbist, served at the Viennese court from 1719 and in 1727–39 composed operas, oratorios, cantatas and masses.

Conti, Gioacchino ['Gizziello'] (*b* Arpino, 28 Feb 1714; *d* Rome, 25 Oct 1761). Italian soprano castrato. He sang in Italian cities from 1730, notably in operas by Hasse, Vinci and Leo. He also appeared in Handel's operas in London (1736–7), and later in Lisbon and Madrid. A high soprano, he was one of the greatest castratos of the time, both brilliant and expressive. Nicola Conti (*fl* 1733–54), *maestro* at several Naples churches and composer of operas and sacred music, may have been his father.

Continuo. Term, short for 'basso continuo', to denote the continuous bass part – hence the term – that runs through a concerted work of the Baroque period (also the late Renaissance and the early Classical period) and serves as a basis for harmonies. The term 'thoroughbass' (or 'throughbass') has the same meaning. Continuo parts may be figured to indicate to the player what harmonies might appropriately be added above; often they are unfigured and the choice of harmonies is clear to a capable player. The practice of continuo playing arose at a time when music was coming increasingly to be conceived in terms of harmonic progression, with a melody line or lines underpinned by a bass line and supporting harmony.

The term probably came into use because of its coining by one of the early exponents of the practice, Viadana, in the title of his *Cento concerti ecclesiastici . . . con il basso continuo* (1602). The practice of continuo playing was closely linked with the growth of recitative and certain kinds of solo music, both vocal (monodies, arias) and instrumental (violin sonatas etc).

A continuo accompaniment may be 'realized' (the term for its interpretation and performance) in many different ways, depending on the kind of work and the context of its performance. Many theorists and composers of the Baroque period discussed in treatises and instruction books the ways in which accompaniments should be played: whether in full chords or more slender ones, whether in a contrapuntal style with imitation, in what register etc. The instrumental forces were often indicated by the composer. For sacred music, the use of an organ was often presumed. For chamber or orchestral music, a harpsichord was usually considered appropriate, though for small-scale ensembles, especially early in the period, and for the accompaniment of songs, a lute-type instrument (theorbo, chitarrone, archlute) would usually be preferred. In music where the bass part plays an active role in the contrapuntal texture, a sustaining instrument (particularly if an organ was not in use) would be appropriate – a cello, bass viol,

violone or a bassoon, for example, depending on the instruments used in the upper voices. Often more than one instrument capable of realizing the harmony would be used, particularly in a larger ensemble (e.g. a harpsichord and a theorbo together). The most famous example of a multiple ensemble is in Monteverdi's *Orfeo* (1607), where the composer specified two harpsichords, three chitarroni, harp, regals and two organs: this selection would allow the players to choose at any point instruments appropriate to the dramatic context. In a concerto of the late Baroque period, separate continuo instruments would generally be used for the ripieno and the concertino, for example an organ and a harpsichord or a harpsichord and a lute; the choice would be dictated by local traditions and circumstances.

The system of figures placed above (usually; sometimes below) the bass notes told a player, in general terms, what harmonies to play. These were indicated in terms of the intervals above the bass note. The absence of figures implied a root-position chord (which could be indicated $\frac{5}{3}$); the figure 6 (or $\frac{6}{3}$) meant a first inversion. Figures above 9 were used in the early Baroque period but were later abandoned in favour of their equivalents an octave lower (e.g. 4 would replace 11). Notes were realized diatonically unless otherwise indicated: this could be done with a flat or sharp sign, or sharpening could be specified by a stroke through part of a figure. Horizontal dashes meant that the last indicated harmony should be sustained. A simple flat or sharp sign meant that the 3rd above the bass should be flattened or sharpened.

By the mid-18th century, treatises indicated that continuo parts should generally be realized in four-part harmony; and the study of thoroughbass began to be used as a method of studying harmony (as it still is). With the increasing elaboration of orchestral and chamber writing during the Classical period, all the notes necessary for the harmony and the texture were written into the music and continuo playing became less important – though it should be noted that Mozart expected the pianist to play in the orchestral sections of his piano concertos, and Haydn directed his later symphonies (in the 1790s) from the piano. As late as 1849 Bruckner wrote figures to the organ part in his Requiem.

Contra-. A prefix meaning 'against', as in 'contrapunctus' and 'contratenor'; it may also mean 'lower octave'. The 'contra octave' is the one from *C'* to *B'*; instruments in that range are described as CONTRA-BASS instruments.

Contrabass. DOUBLE BASS.

Contrabassoon. DOUBLE BASSOON.

Contrafactum. Term used for the substitution in early vocal music of one text for another without substantial change to the music. It is applied to the practice of writing new words to existing melodies in late medieval song; in the Renaissance, it is chiefly used for the substitution of a sacred text for a secular one. For example, a Josquin *chanson*, *Plusieurs regretz* also exists as a contrafactum *O virgo genetrix*, a motet; and many *laude* (devotional songs) were written as contrafacta to frottola melodies. Contrafacta were used in the Reformation when Protestant psalmodists drew on *chanson* melodies or adapted Catholic texts to the Lutheran viewpoint. *See also* PARODY.

Contrafagotto (It.). *See* DOUBLE BASSOON and BASSOON.

Contralto. A voice with the approximate compass *g–e''*. The term denotes the lowest female voice; when it was first used it could also denote a falsetto male singer or a castrato. It originated as an abbreviation of the 15th-century 'contratenor altus'.

In early opera, the contralto range was used primarily for the representation of comic old women; later, it was favoured for female roles of tragic dignity, such as Handel's Cornelia (*Giulio Cesare*). It was used for prima donna parts in the early 19th century, particularly by Rossini (for example Cinderella in *La Cenerentola* and Rosina in *Il barbiere di Siviglia*). As the castrato voice fell into disfavour, composers often wrote heroic contralto roles. But more often a contralto is chosen for such roles as villainess, sorceress or older woman; Verdi's roles include the old gypsy Azucena (*Il trovatore*), and Wagner's sorceress Ortrud (*Lohengrin*).

Contrapunctus (Lat.). Term used, e.g. in Bach's *Art of Fugue*, for a fugue and for counterpoint generally.

Contrapuntal. Using counterpoint; the term describes music consisting of two or more melodic strands heard simultaneously.

Contrary motion. In part-writing, the simultaneous melodic movement of two voices in opposite directions.

Contrasts. Work for violin, clarinet and piano by Bartók (1938), written for Benny Goodman.

Contratenor (Lat.). 'Against the tenor': term for a polyphonic line in late medieval and early Renaissance music composed in the same range as the tenor (the given part). In three-voice *chansons* of the mid-15th century, the contratenor is usually a fairly florid part, filling in notes needed in addition to those of the melody (the superius) and the tenor. In *c*1450 the contratenor tended to be split into a contratenor altus and contratenor bassus, as composers came to favour four-voice music; this was to lead to the modern contralto and bass voices, as distinct from the top, melodic part and the (often pre-existing) tenor.

Contredanse. The most popular French dance of the 18th century. The tunes were often derived, like the name itself, from the English country dance; they were mostly in lively 2/4 or 6/8 rhythms and in major keys. Several examples were written by the Viennese Classical composers.

Converse, Frederick Shepherd (*b* Newton, MA, 5 Jan 1871; *d* Westwood, MA, 8 June 1940). American composer. He studied with Paine at Harvard (1889–93), with Chadwick, and with Rheinberger at the Munich Academy (1896–8). On returning to the USA, he became active in Boston musical life, teaching and composing. His *The Pipe of Desire* (1905) was the first American opera presented at the Met (1910); his second opera, *The Sacrifice*, was given in Boston in 1911. Other works include five symphonies and several symphonic poems, notably *The Mystic Trumpeter* (1904).

Conyngham, Barry (*b* Sydney, 27 Aug 1944). Australian composer. His early experiences were in jazz, but he had lessons with Raymond Hanson and Sculthorpe, then studied with Takemitsu in Japan (1970): that is reflected in the fragile beauty and delicacy of his orchestral pieces of the early 1970s (e.g. *Water . . . Footsteps . . . Time*, *Ice Carving*), though later works look more towards the modal emphaticness of Messiaen. His output is largely for orchestra, ensemble or dramatic forces. In 1975 he began teaching at the University of Melbourne.

Cooke, Arnold (Atkinson) (*b* Gomersal, 4 Nov 1906). English composer. He studied at Cambridge (1925–9) and then with Hindemith in Berlin, decisive in the formation of his lyrical, contrapuntal style. His works include an opera, six symphonies (1947–84), concertos and much chamber music.

Cooke, Benjamin (*b* London, 1734; *d* there, 14 Sept 1793). English organist and composer. He was a son of Benjamin Cooke (?*c*1700–1743 or later), a London music publisher 1726–43. He worked at Westminster Abbey as Master of the Choristers (from 1757) and organist (from 1762), and conducted the Academy of Ancient Music. A notable glee composer, he also wrote a Service in G, an *Ode on the Passions* (1784) and some 20 anthems, mostly conservative in style.

Cooke, Deryck (Victor) (*b* Leicester, 14 Sept 1919; *d* Thornton Heath, 26 Oct 1976). English writer on music. He studied at Cambridge and worked for the BBC music department (1947–59 and 1965–76). His main research was on 19th-century music (Wagner, Mahler, Bruckner and Delius) and musical semantics. He made a 'performing version' of Mahler's Tenth Symphony in 1960. His *The Language of Music* (1959) argues that tonal music is literally a language of emotions (those of the composer), its words being melodic phrases which have meaning through force of the intervals they comprise: his thesis is developed with energy and ingenuity.

Cooke, Henry (*b* ?Lichfield, *c*1615; *d* Hampton Court, 13 July 1672). English singer and composer. Active in London during the Interregnum, he entered royal service at the Restoration, quickly becoming Master of the Children of the Chapel Royal. He trained the choristers to a high standard, introducing the Italianate style of which he was a celebrated practitioner. As a composer he was less noteworthy: of his 32 known anthems and other sacred works only 13 survive, seven of them verse anthems with symphonies and ritornellos for strings. Although he used a wide harmonic vocabulary the ideas are little developed. He also wrote three court odes, secular songs, and some theatrical music for Davenant (now lost). It remained to his pupils Humfrey, Blow, Wise and Tudway to integrate the Italian style with greater artistry and thus consolidate the Baroque style in English church music.

Cooke, J(ohn) (*d* by ?25 July 1419). English composer. A member of the Chapel Royal from 1402, he may have been a pupil or associate of Leonel Power. At least five mass movements, two antiphons and an isorhythmic motet by him survive in the Old Hall MS.

Cooke, Thomas Simpson (*b* Dublin, 1782; *d* London, 26 Feb 1848). Irish singer, instrumentalist and composer. He first appeared in London at the English Opera House in 1813 and by 1815 was at Drury Lane, where he was a principal tenor for nearly 20 years and wrote music for over 50 productions (including an *Oberon* in opposition to Weber's of 1826). He was musical manager of Vauxhall Gardens, a Philharmonic Society member, a versatile instrumentalist (playing nine instruments in one concert) and a renowned singing teacher. His son Henry (Grattan) Cooke (1809–89) was a well-known oboist.

Coolidge, Elizabeth Sprague (*b* Chicago, 30 Oct 1864; *d* Cambridge, MA, 4 Nov 1953). American patron. She provided funds for music at the Library of Congress, by establishing a foundation named after her, and commissioned numerous works from Bartók, Schoenberg, Copland (*Appalachian Spring*) and Stravinsky (*Apollon-Musagète*) among others.

Coolidge Chamber Music Festival (USA). Occasional festival established in 1925 in Washington, DC; it was endowed by Elizabeth Sprague Coolidge and takes place in the Coolidge Auditorium (cap. 500) in the Library of Congress.

Cooper, Emil (*b* Kherson, 20 Dec 1877; *d* New York, 16 Nov 1960). Russian conductor. After study in Vienna he conducted in Odessa and Kiev from 1896. He conducted at the opera houses of St Petersburg and Moscow, 1905–22, giving the Russian première of the *Ring*. He appeared with Dyagilev's company in London and Paris and from 1929 conducted opera in North America, at Chicago (until 1932), the Met (1944–50) and Montreal (from 1950).

Cooper, Martin (Du Pré) (*b* Winchester, 17 Jan 1910; *d* Richmond, Surrey, 15 March 1986). English writer on music. He studied at Oxford and in Vienna under Wellesz (1932–4), then became a music critic, joining the *Daily Telegraph* in 1950 and serving as chief critic, 1954–76. He was editor of *The Musical Times* (1953–6). While his special interests lay in French and Russian music and German music of the early Romantic period, his work is distinguished by its breadth of cultural context and its urbanity of style. His books include *French Music from the Death of Berlioz to the Death of Fauré* (1951) and *Beethoven: the Last Decade* (1970).

His daughter Imogen (*b* 1949) is a pianist who studied with Kathleen Long, Brendel and at the Paris Conservatoire; she has shown herself a player of keen taste and perception, especially in Mozart and French music.

Cooper, Paul (*b* Victoria, IL, 19 May 1926). American composer. He studied at the University of Southern California and the Paris Conservatoire and has taught at various American institutions. His music ranges from the highly dissonant to the quiet and contemplative and includes five symphonies (1966–83), quartets and sacred choral pieces.

Copland, Aaron (*b* Brooklyn, 14 Nov 1900). American composer. He studied with Goldmark in New York and with Boulanger in Paris (1921–4), then returned to New York and took a leading part in composers' organizations, taught at the New School

for Social Research (1927–37) and composed. At first his Stravinskian inheritance from Boulanger was combined with aspects of jazz (*Music for the Theatre*, 1925) or with a grand rhetoric (*Symphonic Ode*, 1929), but then he established an advanced personal style in the Piano Variations (1930) and orchestral *Statements* (1935). Growing social concerns spurred him towards a popular style in the cowboy ballets *Billy the Kid* (1940) and *Rodeo* (1942), but even here his harmony and orchestral spacing are distinctive. Another ballet, *Appalachian Spring* (1944), brought a synthesis of the folksy and the musically developed, the score being a continuous movement towards a set of variations on a Shaker hymn.

Other works from the 'Americana' period include the *Lincoln Portrait* for speaker and orchestra (1942), the *Fanfare for the Common Man* (1942), the 12 Poems of Emily Dickinson for voice and piano (1950), two sets of Old American Songs (1950–52) and the opera *The Tender Land* (1954). But there were also more complex developments, especially among the chamber and instrumental works: the Piano Sonata (1941), Violin Sonata (1943), Piano Quartet (1950) and Piano Fantasy (1957). In the orchestral *Connotations* (1962) and *Inscape* (1967) he completed a journey into serialism, though again the sound is individual. Other late works, including the ballet *Dance Panels* (1963), the String Nonet (1960) and the Duo for flute and piano (1971), continue the cool triadic style. He was conductor, speaker and pianist, a generous and admired teacher, and author of several books, among them *Music and Imagination* (1952).

Operas The Second Hurricane (1937); The Tender Land (1954)
Ballets Billy the Kid (1940); Rodeo (1942); Appalachian Spring (1944); Dance Panels (1963)
Film scores The City (1939); Of Mice and Men (1939); Our Town (1940); North Star (1943); The Cummington Story (1945); The Red Pony (1948); The Heiress (1948); Something Wild (1961)
Orchestral music 3 syms. (1925, 1933, 1946); Music for the Theatre (1925); Pf Conc. (1926); Symphonic Ode (1929); Statements (1935); El salón México (1936); Quiet City (1939); Fanfare for the Common Man (1942); Music for Movies (1942); Lincoln Portrait (1942); Cl Conc. (1948); Connotations (1962); Music for a Great City (1964); Inscape (1967); 3 Latin American Sketches (1972)
Chamber music Vitebsk (1929); Vn Sonata (1943); Pf Qt (1950); Nonet (1960); Duo, fl, pf (1971)
Piano music Pf Variations (1930): Pf Sonata (1941); Danzón cubano, 2 pf (1942); Pf Fantasy (1957); Down a Country Lane (1962); Danza de Jalisco, 2 pf (1963); Night Thoughts (1972); Midsummer Nocturne (1977)
Choral music In the Beginning (1947); Canticle of Freedom (1955)
Songs 12 Poems of Emily Dickinson (1950); Old American Songs [arrs.] (1950, 1952)

Coppélia (La fille aux yeux d'émail). Ballet in two acts by Delibes to a libretto by Nuitter after E.T.A. Hoffmann (1870, Paris).

Coppola, Pietro (Antonio) (*b* Enna, 11 Dec 1793; *d* Catania, 13 Nov 1877). Italian composer. A melodist in the Bellinian vein, he first achieved success in Rome with the opera *La pazza per amore* (1835). After working as music director of the Lisbon opera house (1839–43, 1850–71), he returned to an Italian cathedral post and composed church music, including a famous *Salve regina*.

Coprario [Cooper], John [Giovanni] (*b* ?*c*1570–80; *d* ?London, *c*June 1626). English composer. He probably italianized his name after a visit to Italy. In 1603 he went to the Netherlands on behalf of Sir Robert Cecil, one of his chief patrons. From at least 1622 he served (and possibly taught music to) the Prince of Wales, who appointed him composer-in-ordinary on his accession as Charles I in 1625. William Lawes was among his pupils. In addition to his two published sets of songs (*Funeral Teares*, 1606; *Songs of Mourning: Bewailing the Untimely Death of Prince Henry*, 1613), he composed original, well-crafted works for strings: over 130 fantasias or suites for viol consort, violins with bass and organ, bass viols and organ or lyra viols. His treatise *Rules how to Compose* (MS) is a clear, practical guide. He was an original, influential and literate figure in the circle that included the younger Ferrabosco and Gibbons.

Copula, copulatio (Lat.). Medieval terms, used in the 11th–12th centuries, for the binding together of notes to form a melody (or, later, a group of notes in a ligature); they could also refer to the binding together of voices to form a composition. Later they referred to a style between organum and discant.

Coq d'or, Le. *See* GOLDEN COCKEREL, THE.

Coquard, Arthur(-Joseph) (*b* Paris, 26 May 1846; *d* Noirmoutier, 20 Aug 1910). French composer and critic. After a legal career he devoted himself to composing large-scale works for solo voice and orchestra, notably the expressive *Le songe d'Andromaque* (1884), and to opera (*La troupe Jolicoeur*, 1902). A member of Franck's circle, he contributed to *Le monde* and other journals.

Cor (Fr.). HORN.

Cor anglais. ENGLISH HORN.

Corbett, William (*b c*1675; *d* ?London, 7 March 1748). English composer. A popular soloist on the violin and other instruments, he led the Queen's Theatre orchestra, London, 1705–11, and wrote music for plays there. In 1716–*c*1740 he lived mainly in Italy, collecting music and violins. He wrote trio sonatas and a set of violin concertos, *Le bizzarie universali* (1728), that parody various musical styles.

Corbetta, Francesco (*b* Pavia, *c*1615; *d* Paris, 1681). Italian composer. He was guitar master to Louis XIV in Paris, following Charles II to London where he taught the royal family in the 1660s. He returned to Paris in 1671. Of his five extant collections for five-course Baroque guitar, three (1639–48) are in the Italian tradition, while the later books, both entitled *La guitarre royalle* (1671, 1674), represent the highpoint of French-style Baroque guitar literature. They include 14 suites, 12 duets and four arrangements for voices and guitar.

Corder, Frederick (*b* London, 26 Jan 1852; *d* there, 21 Aug 1932). English conductor, translator, teacher and composer. He studied at the RAM, and in Cologne and Milan, becoming conductor at the Brighton Aquarium and, with his wife Henrietta, producing influential English translations of Wag-

ner. From 1888, he was a professor at the RAM, of which he wrote a history (1922).

Cordero, Roque (*b* Panama City, 16 Aug 1917). Panamanian composer. He studied in the USA with Mitropoulos and Krenek, then became professor of composition at the National Institute of Music, Panama (1950–66). In 1966 he returned to the USA to teach at the Universities of Indiana (until 1972) and Illinois. His music is tonal and, from 1954, serial, using elements of Panamanian folklore; orchestral and chamber works form the bulk of his output, his mature 12-note writing at its most impressive in his Second and Third Symphonies (1946, 1965), Violin Concerto (1962) and three string quartets (1960, 1968, 1973).

Cordes avallées (Fr.). 'Lowered strings': term sometimes found in guitar, lute and mandore music to designate the alteration in tuning of at least one course of strings.

Cordier, Baude (*b* Rheims; *fl* late 14th or early 15th century). French composer. He may have been Baude Fresnel, a harp player and organist at the court of Philip the Bold from 1384. Many of his ten *chansons* (nine rondeaux and a ballade) are rhythmically and notationally complex (the rondeau *Tout par compas suy composés* is a canon notated in a circle, and another is heart-shaped); others, like his Gloria setting, are more modern and restrained in style.

Corelli, Archangelo (*b* Fusignano, 17 Feb 1653; *d* Rome, 8 Jan 1713). Italian composer and violinist. He studied in Bologna from 1666, and was admitted to the Accademia Filarmonica at 17. By 1675 he was in Rome, where he became the foremost violinist and a chamber musician to Queen Christina of Sweden, to whom he dedicated his 12 trio sonatas *da chiesa* op.1 (1681). His 12 trio sonatas *da camera* op.2 (1685) were dedicated to Cardinal Pamphili; Corelli was his music master, 1687–90. His next patron, Cardinal Pietro Ottoboni, received the dedication of the trio sonatas op.4 (1694). Corelli came to dominate Rome musical life, and also directed opera performances there and in Naples. After 1708 he retired from public view.

Corelli was the first composer to derive his fame exclusively from instrumental music. His works were immensely popular during his lifetime and long afterwards, and went through numerous reprints and arrangements (42 editions of the op.5 violin sonatas had appeared by 1800). They were seen as models of style for their purity and poise. His small output – six published sets and a few single pieces – contains innovations of fundamental importance to Baroque style, reconciling strict counterpoint and soloistic violin writing, and using sequential progressions and suspensions to give a notably modern sense of tonality. Distinctions between 'church' (abstract) and 'chamber' (dance) idioms are increasingly blurred in his sonatas. The op.6 concerti grossi (1714) resemble trio sonatas with orchestral reinforcement and echo effects. They were especially popular in England, preferred even to Handel's concertos well into the 19th century. There were many imitations of Corelli's music, notably of the folia variations in the violin sonata op.5 no.12 (1700), and some composers used his music as a springboard; Bach borrowed a theme from the trio sonata op.3 no.4 (1689) for an organ fugue. As a violinist Corelli was the finest, most influential teacher of his day; as an ensemble director he imposed high standards of discipline.

Chamber music trio sonatas, 6, op.1 (1681); 6, op.2 (1685); 6, op.3 (1689); 6, op.4 (1694); 6, op.5 (1700); other sonatas
Orchestral music 6 concerti grossi, op.6 (1714); ov.

Corelli, Franco [Dario] (*b* Ancona, 8 April 1921). Italian tenor. After study in Pesaro he sang in Italy from 1951, making his début at La Scala in 1954. He sang Cavaradossi at Covent Garden in 1957 and has appeared at the Met from 1961 (début as Manrico). His strong, dark voice has made him a favourite in such roles as Don José, Radamès and Calaf.

Corigliano, John (Paul) (*b* New York, 16 Feb 1938). American composer. He studied at Columbia, and with Giannini and Creston, then worked in radio and television. His works, in an accessible romantic style, with tonal harmony and brilliant orchestration, include *The Naked Carmen* (1970), an 'electric rock opera' after Bizet, *A Figaro for Antonio* (1985), commissioned by the Met, orchestral music (notably a Clarinet Concerto, 1977), vocal music and film scores. His father John (1901–75) was a violinist, mostly in New York.

Coriolan. Overture, op.62, by Beethoven, for H.J. von Collin's play (1807).

Cori spezzati (It.). 'Broken choirs': groups of singers placed in different parts of a building; the term is also applied to the technique of composing for them. The practice goes back to Jewish and early Christian music, but the term dates from the 16th century when music for multiple choirs became popular, particularly in Venice and elsewhere in northern Italy. Later, in the 17th century, the style was particularly favoured in Rome and in Germany and Austria. The technique depended essentially on the effect of sound coming from different directions, sometimes sound of different qualities (especially if instruments were used) or at different pitch levels. Composers particularly concerned with this tradition were, in Venice, Willaert and A. and G. Gabrieli; in Rome, Benevoli and Ugolini; and in Germany, Schütz, who made imaginative use of multiple choirs. Bach used two choirs in his *St Matthew Passion*.

Corkine, William (*fl* 1610–12). English composer. His two published books of ayres (1610, 1612) are of interest in containing added sections of dances etc for lyra viol and for bass viol.

Cornacchioli, Giacinto (*b* Ascoli Piceno, *c*1598; *d* ?there, after 1 Sept 1673). Italian composer. He held posts in Munich and Ferno, and had connections with the Barberini family in Rome, to whom his only known work, the opera *Diana schernita* (1629) is dedicated. It is one of the earliest comic operas, a parody of the Florentine conventions of myth and pastoral.

Cornago, Johannes (*fl* *c*1455–85). Spanish composer. At the Aragonese court of Naples throughout his life, he was by 1455 a member of the Franciscan Order and by 1475 a singer in the chapel of Ferdinand V of Spain. Most of his extant works, which include two masses, one of the earliest-known settings of the Lamentations and secular vocal pieces, were composed in Naples. He developed the distinctive Spanish style of the polyphonic courtly love-song and displays a personal style that proved influential.

Cornamusa. A straight wind-cap instrument, similar to the crumhorn, of the 16th century to the early 17th, known only in Italy; Praetorius described it as having a covered bell with small soundholes, and named five sizes. The term is also used in Romance languages to mean 'bagpipe'.

Cornelius, (Carl August) Peter (*b* Mainz, 24 Dec 1824; *d* nr. Copenhagen, 26 Oct 1874). German composer. Trained as actor and violinist, and friend of artists, poets and writers, he devoted himself to music from the 1840s, finding inspiration in Liszt and the New German School at Weimar in 1852. His first mature works were the lieder opp.1 and 2 and the song cycle *Trauer und Trost* op.3, followed by the comic opera *Der Barbier von Bagdad* (1855–8); all show his literary skill, refreshing simplicity and musical independence from the Liszt circle. In Vienna (1859–65), he wrote his second opera *Der Cid* and enjoyed fruitful relationships with Brahms, Carl Tausig and above all Wagner, who summoned him to Munich in 1865 as his private répétiteur and teacher at the Royal School of Music. His third opera *Gunlöd* was never finished. He continued to write poetry and essays defending Wagner and Liszt and translated vocal works by Pergolesi, Berlioz, Liszt and others. Although he revered Wagner, he stood ethically and artistically apart, his work (especially *Der Barbier*) thus representing an original achievement.

Cornelys, Teresa (*b* Venice, 1723; *d* London, 19 Aug 1797). Italian singer. She made her début in Venice, *c*1741, sang in Vienna, Hamburg, Copenhagen and the Low Countries, and settled in London (with support from Casanova) in 1759. There she organized concerts at Carlisle House, Soho Square, where the Bach–Abel series was inaugurated, 1765–7. She was also involved in opera performance, masquerades and other entertainments, but her reputation was justly dubious and she died in prison.

Corner, Philip (*b* New York, 10 April 1933). American composer. He was influenced by Messiaen at the Paris Conservatoire (1956–7), studied at Columbia with Luening and Cowell and became interested in Eastern music while serving in Korea (1959–60). Oriental features include improvisation, the calligraphy of his scores and his use of gamelan ensemble. He is one of the first to assimilate Cage's influence and is a pioneering minimalist.

Cornet. A valved brass instrument in B♭ in unison with the B♭ trumpet. The written compass is from *f*♯ normally up to *c'''*, though many players can reach up to an octave higher or more. The bore is wider than that of a modern trumpet and the mouthpiece is deeper, with the cup more gently shouldered into the throat (for illustration, *see* BRASS

INSTRUMENTS); the instrument's tone is accordingly softer, rounder and less brilliant than the trumpet's. The instrument first appeared in Paris *c*1828 with two valves and crooks to put it into every key from low D♭ up to C. In England, wind bands adopted it in place of the keyed bugle. It is now the staple treble instrument of the brass band and is also used in the military band; in the brass band a smaller model, in E♭, is also used. The instrument is capable of great agility and flexibility.

19th-century French composers from Berlioz onwards used the cornet for the sake of its valves (trumpets with valves were rare). In many leading orchestras of the late 19th century, especially in England and the USA, trumpet parts were played on cornets, a practice which deprived classical trumpet parts of their heraldic ring. Later orchestration, from Elgar and Stravinsky, occasionally includes cornet.

Cornet, Peeter (*b* ?Brussels, 1570–80; *d* there, 27 March 1633). Flemish composer. He is thought to have spent most of his working life in the service of the Brussels court and was a leading keyboard composer of his time. His works range from the profound *Salve regina* to animated courants, including imaginative fantasias that indicate his familiarity with other European music.

Cornett [cornetto]. A wooden, lip-vibrated wind instrument with finger-holes and a cup-shaped mouthpiece. The curved treble cornett, a more common type than the straight, has a range of *g* to *a″*, or up to *d‴*. The cornettino is pitched a 4th or 5th higher, the tenor cornett a 5th lower. In its heyday (*c*1550–1650), the cornett was used, often with trombones, for support in choral music, for 'tower music', in wind and mixed consorts; it was capable of virtuoso display (notably in works by Giovanni Gabrieli and Praetorius). Bach, Handel and Gluck also scored for it. (For illustration, *see* EARLY MUSIC.)

Corno di bassetto (It.). BASSET-HORN; also Bernard Show's pseudonym as a critic.

Cornu. A Roman brass instrument consisting of a long bronze tube, curved in a G shape. It was played in state processions.

Cornysh, William (*d* 1523). English composer. After being at court (from 1494) he became Master of the Children at the Chapel Royal, a post he held until his death. From 1509 he was the leading figure in the plays and entertainments that enlivened court life. In 1513 he made the first of several visits to France with the Chapel Royal, in Henry VIII's retinue. Several of his sacred vocal works are in the Eton Choirbook; their style ranges from the flamboyance of the *Stabat mater* to the simplicity of the *Ave Maria Mater Dei*. His notable secular partsongs (in MSS) are similarly versatile, *Yow and I and Amyas* being simple and chordal and *A robyn* a three-part canon apparently incorporating elements of pre-existent melody. Several other musicians with the surname Cornysh were active in the late 15th century and early 16th.

Coro. Work by Berio for chorus and orchestra, setting words by Neruda and using folksong (1976).

Coronaro, Gaetano (*b* Vicenza, 18 Dec 1852; *d* Milan, 5 April 1908). Italian composer, conductor and teacher. He studied, and later taught, at the Milan Conservatory, writing a successful short pastorale, *Un tramonto* (1873), and the Verdian grand opera *La creole* (1878). His brother Antonio (1851–1933) was cathedral organist at Vicenza, and his brother Gellio Benevenuto (1863–1916), a composer, pianist and conductor.

Coronation Concerto. Nickname for Mozart's Piano Concerto no.26 in D K537 (1788); it was performed at the Frankfurt celebrations of Leopold II's coronation. The name is also applied to Piano Concerto no.19 in F K459 (1784), also played at Frankfurt.

Coronation Mass. Nickname of Mozart's Mass in C K317 (1779), so called because of its possible association with the annual crowning of a statue of the Virgin near Salzburg, or because it was performed at Leopold II's coronation festivities in Prague (1791).

Coronation of Poppaea, The. *See* INCORONAZIONE DI POPPEA, L'.

Corradini, Francesco (*b* Naples, *c*1700; *d* ?Madrid, after 1749). Italian composer. He presented three operas (1724–5) in Naples, then settled in Spain, working in Madrid from 1731. He composed numerous Spanish operas. He was the first 18th-century Neapolitan composer to dominate the Spanish musical scene.

Correa de Arauxo, Francisco (*b c*1576; *d* Segovia, *c*31 Oct 1654). Spanish composer and theorist. He held appointments in Seville before becoming organist at the cathedrals of Jaén (1636–40) and Segovia (1640–53). His publication *Libro de tientos . . . Facultad organica* (1626), which combines organ music with a theoretical treatise, shows his importance in establishing the Baroque style in Spain. The compositions are arranged in order of difficulty and illustrate points made in the treatise on tablature, fingering, key signatures and ornaments; rhythmic complexities abound in the later pieces. 62 of the 69 compositions in the *Facultad organica* are tientos.

Corregidor, Der. Opera in four acts by Wolf to a libretto by Rosa Mayreder after Alarcón (1896, Mannheim); Falla's ballet *The Three-cornered Hat* is based on the same story.

Corrente. An Italian dance in quick triple metre; *see* COURANTE.

Corrette, Michel (*b* Rouen, 1709; *d* Paris, 22 Jan 1795). French composer and writer on music. A son of Gaspard Corrette (*d* by 1733), a Dutch or French composer and organist, he held various organist's posts in France and was well known as a teacher, composing, over some 75 years, stage and sacred works, cantatas, songs, many concertos (notably 25 *Concertos comiques*, 1732–60) and a variety of chamber music and keyboard pieces; most of his music is facile and inconsequential and many of his works use popular tunes. He also wrote at least 17 instruction books, notably *L'école d'Orphée* (1738), a violin treatise describing the French and Italian styles; these works give lucid insight into contemporary playing techniques.

Corri, Domenico (*b* Rome, 4 Oct 1744; *d* Hampstead, 22 May 1825). Italian composer and publisher. He studied with Porpora in Naples, 1763–6. In 1771 he moved to Edinburgh as a conductor and in *c*1779 set up a publishing firm, which his brother Natale

(1765–1822), also a composer, took over c1790. Moving to London, he established another firm (with his son-in-law J.L. Dussek from 1794), and presented his own stage works, notably *The Travellers* (1806). He also wrote keyboard music, songs and theoretical works and developed a new system for realizing figured basses (c1779).

Several of his children became musicians. Sophia (1775–1847), who married Dussek, was a singer, harpist and pianist. Philip Anthony (?1784–1832) emigrated to the USA and (as Arthur Clifton) wrote an American opera and other works. Montague Philip (c1784–1849) took over his father's London firm in 1804 and wrote stage music and piano pieces. Natale's daughter Frances (1795/1801–after 1833) was a singer.

Corroboree. An Australian aboriginal dance.

Corsaire, Le. Overture, op.21, by Berlioz after Byron (1844).

Corsaro, Il. Opera in four acts by Verdi to a libretto by Piave after Byron (1848, Trieste).

Corselli [Courcelle], Francesco (*b* Piacenza, c1702; *d* Madrid, 3 April 1778). Italian composer. He worked at Parma and composed two operas for Venice. In 1734 he went to Madrid as a royal *maestro de capilla*. He wrote over 400 sacred works, several operas and cantatas, villancicos etc. His style is in the vein of Durante and Pergolesi.

Corsi, Giuseppe (*b* Celano; *d* ?Modena, after 26 Dec 1690). Italian composer. A pupil of Carissimi, he was *maestro di cappella* at four Roman churches and worked for the dukes of Parma (1681–8) and Modena. He mainly composed church music, and was widely known for an eccentric cantata, *La stravaganza*, with oddities of pitch and rhythm designed to catch out his fellow composers.

Corsi, Jacopo (*b* Florence, 17 July 1561; *d* there, 29 Dec 1602). Italian patron and composer. A nobleman, he was a leading figure in musical circles in Florence. He was responsible for producing two of the earliest operas, Peri's *Dafne* (1598) and *Euridice* (1600); the first, given at his house, included at least two numbers composed by him.

Corteccia, (Pier) Francesco (*b* Florence, 27 July 1502; *d* Florence, 7 June 1571). Italian composer and organist. He was a singer at S Giovanni Battista, Venice (1515–22), and later organist of S Lorenzo, the Medici family chapel (1531). In 1540 he became *maestro di cappella* for the Duke of Florence, remaining there until his death. As an early madrigal composer he ranks with Arcadelt, Festa and Verdalot (he published 3 bks, 1544, 1547, and in collections); many were composed for court occasions. His sacred music includes a Passion, two volumes of music for Tenebrae services (1570), motets and hymns.

Cortellini, Camillo (*b* Bologna, c1560; *d* there, ?March 1630). Italian composer. A trombonist, he performed at S Petronio, Bologna, from 1593 and in the *concerto palatino*, becoming its director in 1613. His seven published books of sacred music include two early concerted masses with trombone parts (1617, 1626); he also published three madrigal books.

Cortese, Luigi (*b* Genoa, 19 Nov 1899; *d* there, 10 June 1976). Italian composer. He studied with Gédalge in Paris and Casella in Rome and from 1939 held posts in Genoa. His music is eclectic and may be compared with Martin, Pizzetti and French contemporaries. He wrote operas (*Prometeo*, 1945; *La notte veneziana*, 1955) and oratorios (*David*, 1938).

Cortot, Alfred (Denis) (*b* Nyon, 26 Sept 1877; *d* Lausanne, 15 June 1962). French pianist and conductor. At the Paris Conservatoire he studied first with Decombes, one of Chopin's last pupils, and soon appeared as soloist at the Colonne and Lamoureux concerts. After study at Bayreuth he conducted early French performances of Wagner and from 1902 gave concerts with the Societé de Festivals Lyriques, becoming a leading figure in French musical life. In 1905 the Cortot–Thibaud–Casals trio was formed. In 1919 he founded the Ecole Normale de Musique in Paris, where his interpretation courses became legendary. As a pianist he was remarkable for his understanding of Romantic music, especially Schumann and Chopin; he was also an ardent champion of new French music. He edited Chopin's piano music and was an avid and systematic collector.

Così fan tutte (ossia La scuola degli amanti). Opera in two acts by Mozart to a libretto by Da Ponte (1790, Vienna).

Cosme, Luiz (*b* Pôrto Alegre, 9 March 1908; *d* Rio de Janeiro, 17 July 1965). Brazilian composer. He trained at the Cincinnati Conservatory (1927–9) and spent several months in Paris before returning to Brazil, where he worked at the National Library. His compositions of the 1930s have links with impressionism and Brazilian folklore; those of the 1940s are freely serial. In 1950 he abandoned composition.

Cossetto, Emil (*b* Trieste, 12 Oct 1918). Yugoslav composer of Italian birth. He studied conducting at the Zagreb Academy (1941–5) and in 1945 became conductor of the Joža Vlahović Chorus, for which much of his nationalist, heroic music has been written.

Cossotto, Fiorenza (*b* Crescentino, 22 April 1935). Italian mezzo-soprano. She sang at La Scala, Milan, from 1957 and made her Met début in 1968, as Amneris. Her powerful, well-focussed voice and imposing stage presence have contributed to her international success in such roles as Eboli, Azucena and Bellini's Adalgisa.

Costa, Sir Michael (Andrew Agnus) (*b* Naples, 4 Feb 1808; *d* Hove, 29 April 1884). English conductor and composer of Italian birth. A pupil chiefly of Zingarelli, he arrived in London in 1829, and by 1833 was director and conductor of the Italian opera at the King's Theatre. His authoritative baton conducting, unprecedented discipline and dominant personality raised the standard of orchestral playing at the Royal Italian Opera, Covent Garden (which he founded in 1846), and the Philharmonic Society (1846–53, 1855–68). He returned to Her Majesty's in 1871 and, meanwhile, conducted Sacred Harmonic Society concerts, triennial Handel festivals and provincial festivals, for which he composed the oratorios *Eli* (1855) and *Naaman* (1864). He was knighted in 1869.

Costantini, Fabio (*b* Staffolo, *c*1570–75; *d* ?Tivoli, 1644). Italian music editor and composer. He sang under Palestrina at St Peter's, Rome (until 1610), and held posts as *maestro di cappella*, notably at Orvieto Cathedral (1610–14, 1618–22), Santa Casa, Loreto, Ancona and Ferrara Cathedral. His anthologies of polyphonic psalms (with other liturgical music; six books, 1614–39) and concertato motets (four books, 1616–34, one lost) were important in the dissemination of early 17th-century Roman music. As a composer he preferred the concertato style; the motets contain some of his best music.

His brother Alessandro (*c*1581–1657) succeeded Frescobaldi as organist of St Peter's in 1643; he also wrote concertato motets with a preference for duets and dialogues.

Costanza e Fortezza [Constancy and Courage]. Opera (or *festa teatrale*) by Fux, given on a huge scale at Prague in 1723 in celebration of the coronation there of the Habsburg emperor Charles VI.

Coste, Napoléon (*b* Doubs, 28 June 1806; *d* Paris, 17 Feb 1883). French guitarist and composer. He was probably the most significant 19th-century French guitar virtuoso, his pure and vigorous playing being compared with Sor's; his études op.38 are well known.

Costeley, Guillaume (*b* Fontanges, *c*1530; *d* Evreux, 28 Jan 1606). French composer. He was in Paris by 1554 and became court composer to Charles IX in 1560. He moved to Evreux in 1570 where from 1575 he was the first president of the St Cecilia society that ran the famous *puy* (song competition). He left his court post between 1577 and 1588. The chief composer of Parisian *chansons* of his generation, he wrote over 100 (1554–69, most published in a collected edn., 1570), adapting their customary form with graceful originality; they include a microtonal piece and a few *airs* that hint at *musique mesurée* (he was a member of Baïf's Académie).

Cosyn, Benjamin (*b c*1570; *d* ?London, after 1652). English composer. He was organist of Dulwich College (1622–4) and of Charterhouse (1626–43). At least 40 of his keyboard pieces survive, chiefly in 'Cosyn's Virginal Book' which he compiled, including voluntaries, elaborate plainsong settings, dances and genre-pieces; these show Bull's influence. John Cosyn (*d* 1508–9), composer of 57 extended five- and six-part psalm settings in *Musike* (1585), may have been his father.

Cotapos (Baeza), Acario (*b* Valdivia, 30 April 1889; *d* Santiago, 22 Nov 1969). Chilean composer. Self-taught, he lived in New York as an associate of Varèse, Cowell and Copland (1917–27), in France (1927–34) and Spain (1934–8), then returned to Chile. His music is dramatic, highly coloured and usually very dense in texture.

Cotillon (Fr.). An 18th- and 19th-century dance, in triple time, akin to the quadrille.

Cotrubas, Ileana (*b* Galati, 9 June 1939). Romanian soprano. After study in Bucharest and Vienna she sang in Frankfurt from 1968. The following year she was an appealing Mélisande at Glyndebourne. At Chicago and La Scala she has been a sympathetic Mimì and she is noted for her stylish portrayals of Violetta and Mozart's Susanna.

Couchet. Flemish family of virginal and harpsichord makers, descendants of the Ruckers family. The most important member was Joannes (1615–55), a grandson of Hans Ruckers, who worked under his uncle Joannes Ruckers until 1642. His instruments are identical in construction, decoration and sound to Ruckers', though he and three of his sons occasionally introduced an extended upper-manual compass, the unusual registration of two unisons (instead of one plus its octave) and three rows of jacks (instead of two). Some nine Couchet instruments survive.

Coulé (Fr.). SLIDE.

Coulthard, Jean (*b* Vancouver, 10 Feb 1908). Canadian composer. She studied with Vaughan Williams at the RCM (1929–31) and with other teachers, and taught at the University of British Columbia (1947–73). Her works are tonal and generally lyrical.

Counter-exposition. In fugue, a term for a second EXPOSITION immediately following the first.

Counter-fugue. Term for a fugue in which the first answer is an inversion of the subject; the inverted subject then features in the fugue as a whole. It may also, in works such as Bach's *Art of Fugue*, mean a fugue on a subject other than the main theme, which is then introduced as a counterpoint or *cantus firmus*.

Counterpoint. The art of combining two simultaneous musical lines. The term derives from the Latin *contrapunctum*, 'against note'. It was first used in the 14th century, when the theory of counterpoint began to develop from the older theory of discant. When one part is added to an existing one, the new part is said to be 'in counterpoint with' it. The term has sometimes been reserved for the theory or study of how one part should be added to another, but in most modern usage it is not distinct from 'polyphony' (literally meaning 'many-sounding'); there is however a tendency to apply the latter term to 16th-century usage (the period of Palestrina) and counterpoint to the early 18th century (the time of Bach).

Many early theorists discuss the rules for the addition of one line of music to one or more existing lines, for example Tinctoris (1477), Gaffurius (1496) and Zarlino (1558). The use of counterpoint in composition reached new heights in the late 15th century and the 16th with the works of such composers as Josquin, Palestrina, Lassus and Byrd. It persisted throughout the 17th century and much of the 18th, especially in church music, normally as imitative counterpoint (in which the voices imitate each other). Among the chief forms of contrapuntal music are the ricercar, canzona and fugue. A further highpoint in contrapuntal writing was reached in the music of J.S. Bach.

In Bach's time, the growing interest in music of the past led to the codification and idealization of what was supposed to be the style of Palestrina. Influential in this was J.J. Fux, who devised a system known as 'species' counterpoint in which the student learnt contrapuntal facility progressively.

He was given a part in long, even notes (the cantus firmus, or 'fixed song') to which he would first add another part in notes the same length, then two (or three) notes against each one, then four (or more) against each one, then a syncopated part (one against one, but moving alternately) and finally a combination of all these, so that the added part is free and florid. This may be done in two-part counterpoint or in three or more. The terms double (triple etc) counterpoint are used for counterpoint in which two (three etc) parts may be heard inverted, i.e. with either (any) as the upper part; this is also known as invertible counterpoint.

Composers of the Classical period were trained by such methods, and in the mature works of Mozart and Haydn counterpoint is extensively used to intensify the development sections of sonata-form movements. Beethoven used fugue in some of his profoundest music, such as the 'Hammerklavier' Sonata op.106 and his String Quartet in C sharp minor op.131. Schubert recognized, in his last months, the value of the study of counterpoint, and there is contrapuntal writing in some of his last works, such as the String Quintet in C. Among Romantic composers, Mendelssohn was a capable contrapuntist, much influenced by Bach; Brahms and Bruckner also used counterpoint in their symphonies, as did Wagner, often for dramatic purposes, in his operas. Berlioz, though opposed to academic counterpoint, wrote contrapuntal movements of individuality in several works. Italian composers had less use for counterpoint. In the 20th century, post-Wagnerian composers such as Strauss and Mahler, as well as Schoenberg and his school (following Brahms's model), have made much use of it. Stravinsky and Hindemith, more neo-classical in style, are more directly indebted to earlier examples, particularly Bach, while some English and French composers have gone back to 16th-century models.

Counter-subject. In fugue, a subsidiary theme heard against the subject; if it is used with all or most entries of the subject it is called a regular counter-subject.

Countertenor. Originally, English term for contra-tenor; later, a male voice at alto pitch. Counter-tenor singing has particularly flourished in England, where older choral foundations have continued to prefer male voices to sing alto parts. It has been argued that the countertenor voice is a natural continuation upwards of the tenor, to about *d''* or even higher, as distinct from the true male alto which is a falsetto voice. Others argue that the voices are really the same. It is a question for keen dispute and probably not susceptible of resolution. Countertenors are now often used for castrato parts in operas and other works, although their voices lack the castratos' power.

Country dance. An English dance popular in the 17th century. It spread to the rest of Europe, particularly France, where it became known as the CONTREDANSE.

Country music [Country and Western]. An American style of popular music, developed from the folk music of the rural southern USA and first known as

Hillbilly music. Until the 1920s it was performed largely at home, in church or at local functions, on fiddles, banjos and guitars. Later it developed towards a commercial industry, with local radio and gramophone cultivation of such artists as Fiddlin' John Carson, Jimmie Rodgers and the Carter Family. After World War II, Nashville became the centre of country music, and exponents like Roy Acuff, Ernest Tubb and Hank Williams became internationally known. The style broadened, with a fusion of south-western and south-eastern elements, to encompass other types of popular music in the 1960s and 1970s and became less regionally based. More recent performers include Johnny Cash and Willie Nelson. The subject matter for country songs has continued to be mother and home, the rambling man, prison, hard work, love and religion.

Coup d'archet (Fr.: 'bow stroke'). The term 'premier coup d'archet' was used in the late 18th century to refer to the emphatic unison bow-stroke traditionally used in Paris at the opening of a symphony to show the orchestra's excellence of ensemble playing.

Coup de glotte (Fr.: 'stroke of the glottis'). In singing, the sudden and complete interruption of the breath, and therefore of the sound.

Couperin, Armand-Louis (*b* Paris, 25 Feb 1727; *d* there, 2 Feb 1789). French composer, last important member of the Couperin family (for earlier members, *see* under Louis and François). He was a son of Nicholas, Louis Couperin's nephew. He inherited his father's position at St Gervais in 1748 and added several others (which his family and pupils maintained), including posts at the royal institutions and at Notre Dame. He died in a traffic accident when hurrying between churches. He was a noted improviser but a conservative composer who however was interested in style and experiment. He wrote motets, chamber works, harpsichord sonatas and trios, as well as *Symphonie de clavecins* and other works for two harpsichords in an early *galant* manner.

His son Pierre-Louis (1755–89) composed motets and other works and held posts as organist but died of grief on his father's death. Another son, Gervase-François (1759–1826), succeeded to their father's posts; he played before Napoleon at St Sulpice and also wrote a work commemorating the death of Louis XVI. He was criticized as a composer but his songs and piano pieces have been admired. His daughter Céleste-Thérèse (1793–1860) was the last musician in the family.

Couperin, François [le grand] (*b* Paris, 10 Nov 1668; *d* there, 11 Sept 1733). French composer. He was the central figure of the French harpsichord school. He came from a long line of musicians, mostly organists, of whom the most eminent was his uncle, Louis Couperin, though his father Charles (1638–79) was also a composer and organist of St Gervais. François succeeded to that post on his 18th birthday; his earliest known music is two organ masses. In 1693 he became one of the four royal organists which enabled him to develop his career as a teacher through his court connections. He was soon recognized as the leading French composer of his day through his sacred works and his chamber music and, from 1713, his harpsichord pieces. In 1716 he published an important treatise on harpsichord playing and the next year he was appointed royal harpsichordist.

Among the music Couperin composed for Louis XIV's delectation were his *Concerts royaux*, chamber works for various combinations. He had written works in his own elaboration of trio-sonata form in the 1690s following the Italianate style of Corelli but retaining French character in the decorative lines and rich harmony. Later, he published these alongside French-style groups of dances as *Les nations*; they include some of his emotionally most powerful music. He was much concerned with blending French and Italian styles; he composed programmatic tributes to Lully and Corelli and works under the title *Les goûts-réünis*. He also wrote intensely expressive pieces for bass viol.

But it is as a harpsichord composer that Couperin is best known. He published four books with some 220 pieces, grouped in 27 *ordres* or suites. Some movements are in the traditional French dance forms, but most are character pieces with titles that reflect their inspiration: some are portraits of individuals or types, some portray abstract qualities, some imitate the sounds of nature. The titles may also be ambiguous or metaphorical, or even intentionally obscure. Most of the pieces are in *rondeau* form. All are elegantly composed, concealing a complex, allusive and varied emotional world behind their highly wrought surface. Couperin took immense pains over the notation of the ornaments with which his harpsichord writing is sprinkled and animated. These, and his style generally, are expounded in his *L'art de toucher le clavecin*.

Couperin's children were also musicians: Nicholas (1680–1748) succeeded his father at St Gervais, and probably composed, while Marie-Madeleine (1690–1742) was probably an abbey organist and Marguerite-Antoinette (1705–*c*1778) was active as a court harpsichordist, *c*1729–1741.

Chamber music 12 trios, incl. L'apothéose de Corelli (1724), L'apothéose de Lully (1725), Les nations, 4 trios (1726); 4 Concerts royaux (1722); 10 'Nouveaux concerts' in Les goûts-réünis (1724); 2 bass viol suites
Harpsichord music Book 1, suites 1–5 (1713); Book 2, suites 6–12 (1716–17); Book 3, suites 13–19 (1722); Book 4, suites 20–27 (1730); 9 pieces in L'art de toucher le clavecin (1716)
Organ music 2 org masses (1690)
Sacred vocal music 18 versets (1703–5); 3 Tenebrae lessons (1713–17); 27 motets
Secular vocal music 9 airs, 3 trios

Couperin, Louis (*b* Chaumes, *c*1626; *d* Paris, 29 Aug 1661). French composer. He was the first important member of a major dynasty of French composers, influential for more than two and a half centuries. His grandfather Mathurin (1569–1640) and his father Charles (1595–1654) were both musicians; and his brothers François (*c*1631–*c*1710) and Charles (1638–1679) were known as keyboard players, while François' children Marguerite-Louise (*c*1676–1728) and Nicolas (1680–1748) were respectively a singer and harpsichordist and an organist (at St

Gervais, 1733–48). Louis settled in Paris and by 1653 was organist of St Gervais; he also held a post as treble viol player at the royal chapel. He wrote pieces for wind and strings, but most of his music is for keyboard: some 70 fugues, plainchant settings and other pieces for organ, notable for their vigorous counterpoint and expressive force, and some 135 for harpsichord, consisting of preludes and dances, longer than most from this period and remarkable for their lively ideas, their grandeur and their intensity.

Coupler. The mechanism in an organ or harpsichord whereby pipes or strings of one department or manual are made to sound on the keys of another.

Couplet (Fr.). Term used in the 17th and 18th centuries for the intermediate sections or episodes of a rondeau, as distinct from the recurrences of the opening section or refrain (which was sometimes called 'grand couplet').

Courante (Fr.: 'running'; Eng. corant, coranto; It. *corrente*). A Baroque dance, a standard movement of the suite. The Italian *corrente* was a fast dance in 3/4 or 3/8 time, homophonic in texture with a clear harmonic and rhythmic structure; the French *courante*, usually in 3/2 time, was steadier in tempo, with rhythmic ambiguities, especially hemiola, and a more contrapuntal texture. Bach used both forms in his keyboard suites.

Courses. Term for ranks of strings on a plucked instrument. A course may consist of one, two or three strings.

Courteville, Raphael (*fl* 1687–*c*1735). English composer. Appointed organist of St James's, Piccadilly, in 1691, he was a prolific writer of songs. Often showing Purcell's influence, they are in both the florid expressive style and in the tuneful idiom of the day; many appear in late 17th-century songbooks. Some were written for plays. Instrumental pieces by him are found in various instruction books. His father (*d* 1675) and his son (*d* 1772), both of the same name, were respectively a singer and an organist and composer.

Courting flute. Duct flute of the North American Indians. Used for serenading, it was made of wood or cane, with an external duct, and was found north of Mexico, mostly in the Plains–Plateau–south-west area of the USA.

Courtois, Jean (*fl* 1530–45). ?Franco-Flemish composer. He was *maître de chapelle* at Cambrai Cathedral in 1540 and a leading composer in the Low Countries. Two masses, 14 motets and 19 *chansons* by him survive.

Courville, Joachim Thibault de (*d* Paris, 8 Sept 1581). French composer. He was a bowed-lyre player at the French court. As co-founder with Baïf of the Académie de Poésie et Musique in 1570 he developed *vers mesurés* and composed melodies for Baïf's measured verse translation of the psalms. A few of his *airs* were published.

Cousineau. French family of harp makers and harpists, active in Paris. Remembered for their handsome pedal harps, Georges (1733–*c*1800) and his son Jacques-Georges (1760–1824) improved the harp's mechanism with their 'crutch' (*béquille*) system for shortening the strings, slide for the bridge pin and reorganization of connecting levers in the harp neck.

Coussemaker, Charles-Edmond-Henri de (*b* Bailleul, 19 April 1805; *d* Lille, 10 Jan 1876). French musical scholar. Although a lawyer by profession, he was deeply interested in music, becoming one of the first to investigate Gregorian chant, neumatic and mensural notation and medieval instruments, theory and polyphony. His approach of presenting in facsimile primary data was more scientific than Fétis's and his editions of liturgical dramas and the works of Adam de la Halle opened new paths of research. The *Scriptorum de musica* (4 vols., 1864–76), a compilation of early music theory, is his most important work.

Couture, Guillaume (*b* Montreal, 23 Oct 1851; *d* there, 15 Jan 1915). Canadian composer. He was the first Canadian to study at the Paris Conservatoire (from 1873) and in 1876 became choirmaster at Ste Clotilde, where Franck was organist. In Montreal from 1877 he founded concert societies, conducted and taught. He propagated a Canadian music that would reflect French origins.

Covell, Roger D(avid) (*b* Sydney, 1 Feb 1931). Australian critic, educationist and conductor. He became chief music critic of the *Sydney Morning Herald* in 1960. In 1974 he began teaching at the University of New South Wales. He has directed several Australian first performances of operas, including works by Monteverdi, Britten and Rossini. His book *Australia's Music* (1967) was the first serious attempt to outline and summarize music's part in Australian society. His later studies include nationalism in 19th-century music and 18th-century opera.

Covent Garden Theatre. London theatre, now also known as the Royal Opera House, built in 1858 (cap. 2117); it is the home of the ROYAL OPERA and Royal Ballet (formerly Sadler's Wells Ballet). Handel wrote many works for the first Covent Garden theatre (1732–1808); the second (1809–56) was known as the Royal Italian Opera from 1847.

Coward, Sir Noël (Pierce) (*b* Teddington, 16 Dec 1899; *d* Blue Harbour, 26 March 1973). English writer and composer. Essentially self-taught in music, he wrote plays and musicals including *Bittersweet* (1929).

Cowbell. A clapperless bell used in the orchestra; it is struck with a drumstick. Stockhausen and Cage have scored for a chromatic series of cowbells.

Cowell, Henry (Dixon) (*b* Menlo Park, CA, 11 March 1897; *d* Shady, NY, 10 Dec 1965). American composer. Before he had had any formal training in composition he wrote piano pieces using clusters and other new effects. He then studied in California and New York (1916–18), though continued an independent path as composer, publisher (through his New Music Edition, founded in 1927 and providing scores of Ives, Ruggles and others) and spokesman (through his book *New Musical Resources*, 1930). He taught at the Peabody Conservatory (1951–6) and Columbia University (1949–65). Apart from piano clusters (*Advertisement*, 1914), he

pioneered strumming on the instrument's strings (*Aeolian Harp*, 1923; *The Banshee*, 1925), complex rhythms, mobile form (*Mosaic Quartet*, 1935) and unusual combinations. But from 1936 he composed in a more regular, tonal style influenced by American and Irish folk music (18 *Hymns and Fuguing Tunes* for various forces, 1943–64). In his last 15 years he returned to clusters and other unconventional means while drawing on non-European musical cultures. His immense output includes over 140 orchestral works (including 21 symphonies and many concertos), *c*60 choral and *c*170 chamber works, over 200 piano pieces, and operas, incidental and film music, showing him to have been an indefatigable musical explorer.

Cowen, Sir Frederic Hymen (*b* Kingston, Jamaica, 29 Jan 1852; *d* London, 6 Oct 1935). English pianist, conductor and composer. He studied in Leipzig, where his teachers included Moscheles, Richter and Hauptmann, returning to London in 1868 and winning recognition for his Piano Concerto, First Symphony and especially his lyrical and colourful *Scandinavian Symphony* (1880). Later he was most successful in lighter orchestral works and songs (being described as 'the English Schubert' in 1898), but he is remembered as a popular ballad composer and an industrious conductor. Through his appointments with the Philharmonic Society (1888–92, 1900–07), the Hallé Orchestra, the Liverpool Philharmonic Society, the Scottish Orchestra and the Cardiff and Handel Festivals, he did much to dispel the prevalent idea that orchestral conducting was the job of a foreigner.

Cow horn. A bovine horn with the tip removed for blowing, used since antiquity by herdsmen and for sounding alarms. Wagner scored for the cow horn, to be sounded off stage, in *Der Ring des Nibelungen*, for the summoning of armed vassals.

Cowie, Edward (*b* Birmingham, 17 Aug 1943). English composer. He studied with Fricker and Goehr and worked at the universities of Leeds (1971–3), Lancaster (1973–83) and Wollongong, NSW (from 1983). His finely wrought scores attempt to convey the landscapes of England and Australia (he is also a painter). His works include a series based on the life of Ned Kelly and the opera *Commedia* (1978).

Craft, Robert (*b* Kingston, NY, 20 Oct 1923). American conductor and writer on music. He studied at the Juilliard School. From 1950 to 1968 he conducted in Los Angeles and the Ojai Festival; his main interests were older music (e.g. Monteverdi, Schütz, Bach and Haydn) and contemporary music (e.g. the Second Viennese School), and he directed the first recordings of the complete works of Webern and most of Schoenberg's. From 1948 he was closely associated with Stravinsky, sharing over 150 concerts with him and collaborating on seven books. He has written extensively on music and literature as critic and essayist; his works include *Chronicle of a Friendship* (1972) and other studies based on his special relationship with Stravinsky.

Cramer, Johann [John] Baptist (*b* Mannheim, 24 Feb 1771; *d* London, 16 April 1858). English composer, pianist and publisher of German descent. He was the eldest son of Wilhelm Cramer (1746–99), one of the finest violinists of his day, who settled in London in 1772. About the age of three the young Cramer was taken to London, where he studied with Clementi (1783–4) and C.F. Abel, soon establishing himself as a concert pianist, making continental tours and meeting prominent musicians. His performances of Bach and Mozart created great excitement and he helped introduce Beethoven's sonatas to English audiences, his expressive legato touch and refined improvisation being especially admired. He taught privately for many years and was a music publisher from 1805, establishing in 1824 the firm that still bears his name.

Cramer wrote 124 sonatas (all before 1820), nine piano concertos, influential didactic works (of which the most important was his two-part *Studio per il pianoforte*, 1804, 1810) and many pieces for the dilettante; though the quality varies, his music generally combines a Mozartian grace and clarity with a skilful ingenuity in passage-work. His brother Franz [François] (1772–1848) was a prominent violinist in London.

Craquer. In string playing, a bowing where two (or more) notes are played in one bowstroke but with each note distinctly articulated; it is indicated by dots under a slur.

Crawford (Seeger), Ruth (Porter) (*b* East Liverpool, OH, 3 July 1901; *d* Chevy Chase, MD, 18 Nov 1953). American composer. She studied in Chicago, in New York with Charles Seeger (later her husband) and in Berlin and Paris. Her few works exploit numerical systems and unusual effects in a remarkable, streamlined style; they include Three Songs (1932), Suite for Small Orchestra (1926), the String Quartet (1931), Violin Sonata (1926) and piano pieces. She transcribed, arranged and edited hundreds of American folksongs and taught children.

Craxton, (Thomas) Harold (Hunt) (*b* London, 30 April 1885; *d* there, 30 March 1971). English pianist and teacher. He studied under Matthay, then spent many years as an accompanist, notably to Clara Butt. He had a great reputation as a teacher and editor. His daughter Janet (1929–81) was a noted oboist, particularly active in contemporary music.

Creation, The [Die Schöpfung]. Oratorio by Haydn to a text by van Swieten based on an English original (1798, Vienna).

Création du monde, La. Ballet in one act by Milhaud to a libretto by Cendrars (1923, Paris).

Creation Mass. Haydn's Mass no.13 in B♭ (1801), so called because there is a quotation from *The Creation* in its Gloria.

Creatures of Prometheus, The. *See* GESCHÖPFE DES PROMETHEUS, DIE.

Crecquillon, Thomas (*b* between *c*1480 and *c*1500; *d* ?Béthune, ? early 1557). Franco-Flemish composer. He was a member (probably *maître*) of Emperor Charles V's chapel at least from 1540 until the early 1550s and held benefices in Termonde, Béthune and Louvain. He was a canon at St Aubin, Termonde and from 1555 at Béthune, where he may have died of the plague. His music, particularly the *chansons*

(almost 200), circulated widely in printed editions (one book of *chansons*, 1544, and two of motets, 1559, 1576) and he came to be ranked among the leading Franco-Flemish composers of the post-Josquin generation. All but one of his masses are based on polyphonic models. His music relies on imitative technique; smooth, continuous counterpoint is rarely disturbed by chordal passages, contrasting textures, harsh dissonances or dramatic gestures. He also wrote two Lamentations cycles.

Credo (Eng. Creed). The third item of the Ordinary of the Latin Mass, sung as an affirmation of Christian belief. The 'Nicene' version was introduced in the East in the early 6th century; by the 8th it had been introduced to the Mass and sung between the Gospel and the Offertory. It was incorporated into the Roman Mass in 1014. The celebrant begins 'Credo in unum Deum' and the choir continues with 'Patrem omnipotentem', with which most polyphonic settings usually begin. In later settings the Credo is often divided into several separate movements.

Credo Mass. Mozart's Mass in C K257, in which, in an Austrian tradition of 'Credo Masses', the word 'Credo' ('I believe') recurs many times.

Crescendo (It.). 'Growing': an instruction to become louder, sometimes expressed with a 'hairpin' or abbreviated *cresc. Decrescendo* means the opposite, i.e. *diminuendo.*

Crescentini, Girolamo (*b* Urbania, 2 Feb 1762; *d* Naples, 24 April 1846). Italian mezzo-soprano castrato. Known as 'l'Orfeo italiano', he sang in operas throughout Europe, most famously in Zingarelli's *Giulietta e Romeo* (1796, Milan), for which he wrote an aria. He was one of the last great castrato singers.

Crespin, Régine (*b* Marseilles, 23 March 1927). French soprano. After her Paris Opéra début in 1950, as Wagner's Elsa, she sang in the French provinces. She was Kundry at Bayreuth in 1958 and the following year appeared at Glyndebourne as the Marschallin; her exemplary diction and ability to shape a phrase have led to her identification with that role, which she sang at her Covent Garden (1960) and Met (1962) débuts. Latterly she has sung mezzo roles and is well known as a recitalist.

Creston, Paul [Guttoveggio, Giuseppe] (*b* New York, 10 Oct 1906; *d* San Diego, 24 Aug 1985). American composer. Untrained in composition, he came to notice with his First Symphony (1940). It was followed by much orchestral, choral and instrumental music in a brash, vital style, with long florid melodies, impressionistic harmony and full orchestration.

Cristofori, Bartolomeo (*b* Padua, 4 May 1655; *d* Florence, 27 Jan 1731). Italian keyboard instrument maker. He served at the Florentine court of Prince Ferdinand de' Medici from 1690. Although he experimented with harpsichord construction, he is best known for his invention of the piano, at least one of which was completed by 1700. The action consists of a pivoted lever set in motion by a key. When the lever rises, lifting the hammer, an underdamping mechanism is lowered simultaneously, allowing the string to vibrate; after the blow the leather-covered hammers fall back on to the silk strings crossed under them. Three Cristofori pianos survive, dated 1720 (now in New York), 1722 (Rome) and 1726 (Leipzig).

Criticism. The expression in words of judgments on aspects of the art of music. It embraces many kinds of writing about music, from historical and analytical discussion in books and periodicals to reviews in daily newspapers. The place of criticism (in the evaluative, as opposed to the style-analytical or historical, sense) in musicology is a vexed issue. Many scholars argue that an awareness of music as a vehicle of human expression is fundamental to the study of music and that evaluative criticism should accordingly have a place. Others prefer to limit their role to textual criticism, the preparation of faithful and accurate editions in which alternatives are considered and assessed and choices are made. At its best, scholarly criticism may communicate a view of a work or a repertory in a wide historical and social context, to show why it came into existence, how it relates to earlier and contemporary works, what techniques it uses and how effectively it uses them, and how it functions as a coherent work of art (this may involve some use of analysis) etc.

Criticism of the written text, the scholar's chief task, is different in many respects from criticism of the heard performance, the task of the journalist-critic, who may write for a magazine, a newspaper or a radio station. He is subject to certain editorial disciplines of space and time, imposed by his editors and arising from economic factors. He has to be aware of the public he is writing for and its degree of cultural sophistication. Nevertheless his first duty remains to the art of music itself, to encouraging the good and discouraging the bad (as he sees it) by bringing to it sympathy, receptiveness and a proper basis of knowledge. His second duty is to his readers, to attracting and holding their interest, to informing them, perhaps to entertaining them. Only after that does the critic have a duty to the performers he is reviewing: he should treat their work responsibly and take it seriously, but he is not their instructor. Any critical judgment is likely to include a subjective element and it is part of the critic's job to convey which elements are personal and which are not, so giving the reader some scope for forming his own opinions or at least for establishing limits within which his taste and judgment might lie. The critic should see his role as embodying some element of description and evaluation, when he is considering new music (for which he may wish to prepare himself by prior study of the score or attendance at rehearsals), or, when he is not, as describing the style, the technical adequacy and the musical insights of a performer (whose performance he may instinctively measure against some ideal of his own, possibly based on experience of previous performances). Extremes of approach in music criticism are represented, on the one hand, by what has been called the 'sensitized palate' approach, whereby the critic responds on an intensely personal plane by reporting his own reactions, which may say much

more about the critic than about the music and whose value must depend upon his response to any particular musical experience and the degree of interest attached to his subjective impressions; and on the other, by the critic who diligently describes, in terms as objective as possible, any work or performance while minimizing his personal response, which is apt to produce dull, objective writing. Unless the critic possesses a musical mind of exceptional interest and the capacity to express it felicitously, he will normally do best to steer a course between the Scylla of extreme subjectivity and the Charybdis of objective description. He may do best to regard himself as a professional, well-informed listener, drawing on his training, experience and love of music to arouse the enthusiasms and widen the experiential horizons of his readers.

The earliest criticism of Western art music is found in the work of late medieval theorists who criticized the innovations of their time; but it was only with the Renaissance that the discussion of music moved on to the question of the effect that music might have on the listener – a topic of concern to the humanist thinkers and religious reformers and counter-reformers of the time. The Baroque theory of expression, with its preoccupation over music as the provider of affective experience, also gave rise to a music-critical literature.

In the late 17th century, with the rise of periodicals and newspapers, the criticism of musical works and events could move into a wider arena. Some discussions in pamphlet form, however (always beloved of the French), may be ranked as music criticism, for example the early 18th-century disputes between the supporters of Italian opera and those of French. The writings of Addison in *The Spectator* in the second decade of the century inaugurated music criticism in England and greatly influenced that in Germany, when Mattheson imitated the style of Addison and Steele and then founded the first periodical wholly devoted to writings about music, *Critica musica* (1722–5). Others followed, including Scheibe's *Der critische Musikus* (1737–40) and the Berlin papers edited by Marpurg. It was no coincidence that music criticism appeared and flourished just at the time when concert life was starting, and in the same places: a middle-class public, eager to hear music, was also ready to read about it. French pamphlet wars continued during the 18th century, characteristically linked to operatic disputes, like the Querelle des Bouffons and the Gluck-Piccinni controversy, in the 1750s and 1770s. By this time specific criticism of new music publications, and discussions of other musical matters, were beginning to appear in general cultural journals, in London, Paris, Vienna and elsewhere. J.A. Hiller's weekly publication, issued in the late 1760s in Leipzig – rapidly becoming an important centre of musical commerce – was an early music periodical designed to appeal to a wide readership.

It was also in Leipzig that the *Allgemeine musikalische Zeitung* was founded, in 1798; in the ensuing years this was to be the leading periodical for the coverage of the Viennese Classical composers.

Literary figures such as E.T.A. Hoffmann, as well as its founder J.F. Rochlitz, wrote in this journal, inspired by idealistic notions linking the arts with social and political issues. Heine, too, wrote for a music periodical. Up to around this time, the daily press had carried reports on concerts and other musical events, though not reviews; but before the end of the 18th century critical comment had begun to appear. The first regular music critic on a daily paper is thought to have been appointed (to *The Times*, London) in 1845. Yet for the sheer quantity of published music criticism Paris prevailed, with such periodicals as Fétis's *Revue musicale* (1827), the publisher Heugel's *Le ménestrel* (1833) and the publisher Schlesinger's *Gazette musicale de Paris* (1834), which provided a platform for composers.

In its first issue, Liszt attacked critics as shallow and ignorant, and pressed the claims of composers to serve as critics. Many of the most interesting critics of the 19th century were in fact composers, which is not surprising since the holding of strong opinions about new music and the lack of need for judicious balance are bound to lead to interesting writing. Weber was a forceful and controversial critic, Berlioz a fine literary one with a command of the striking phrase, with keen insights on subjects that appealed to him even if purblind on others, and Schumann, who founded the *Neue Zeitschrift für Musik* in 1834 and edited it for ten years, showed himself a keenly discriminating writer, interested in aesthetic questions, acutely perceptive on promising young composers (he was the first to hail the genius of Chopin and Brahms, though also that of several now forgotten composers) and both equipped and ready to write long, detailed analysis–criticisms when necessary (for example on Schubert's Symphony no.9).

One leading and influential critic who was not a composer was Eduard Hanslick, the dominating figure in Viennese criticism for much of the latter part of the 19th century. A cultivated man, graceful writer and penetrating critic, he has been widely vilified for his resistance to Wagner (who was himself a prolific critic, though chiefly as a propagandist for his own thinking). London criticism in the mid-19th century was mostly conservative, ready to accept Rossini and Mendelssohn but not Verdi or Wagner, who were found vulgar and noisy. It was left to an Irishman, George Bernard Shaw, to counterbalance them with his eager advocacy of Wagner and his deprecation of Brahms, expressed trenchantly and wittily. Hugo Wolf, in Vienna, attacked Brahms and supported Wagner, in strongly polemical tones. In Prague, Smetana espoused the cause of Slavonic nationalism, as in St Petersburg did Cui and Stasov (in which he was opposed by the influential Serov). Tchaikovsky, a critic during the 1870s, found neither Brahms nor Wagner to his taste. In France the most important composer-critic was Debussy who was impatient of trivia (he called Grieg's piano miniatures 'pink bonbons stuffed with snow'), saw the danger of Wagner as a model (preferring Musorgsky) and stressed the need for French composers to be true to native tradition.

Debussy's criticism was written in the early years of the 20th century, but composer-critics have, in this century, generally been less prominent, partly no doubt owing to the changing nature of music criticism in an age of specialization and intense activity. The need (or perhaps simply the custom), in the English-speaking countries particularly, for newspaper criticism to be published the morning after a performance, which has prevailed for most of the 20th century, led to the development of a new form of journalism, which at its worst could be vacuous and inaccurate but at its best could convey the essence of an event judiciously, with immediacy and conveying a kind of enthusiasm that would be appropriate only to an instant product designed for instant consumption.

Distinguished practitioners of this medium in the USA have been W.J. Henderson, who wrote in New York between the 1880s and the 1930s and brought a fine knowledge of music and history to his reviews on the *New York Times* and later the *New York Sun*; he saw Wagner in a true perspective (though was disturbed by the morality of some of his operas), was conservative in taste yet had a ready sympathy for the best in new music, for example admiring Stravinsky's *Rite of Spring*. Among his successors was Olin Downes, a critic first in Boston and then for the *New York Times*, who despite a lack of traditional academic training formed a writing style of his own that conveyed his vigorous and unorthodox enthusiasms for then-unpopular contemporary causes, such as Sibelius, Prokofiev, Stravinsky and Shostakovich, as well as jazz. With Virgil Thomson, who wrote for the *New York Herald Tribune*, the tradition of the composer-critic was revived; though a believer in critical objectivity, and possessor of a cool, elegant and witty style, he could not always conceal his particular likes and dislikes. The most influential New York critic later in the 20th century has been Harold C. Schonberg, whose professional pianist's training and broad culture informed his writing for two decades. Criticism of a more scholarly kind is represented by the work of Joseph Kerman, in monthlies, quarterlies and books, who has endeavoured to use musicological method to serve critical ends and has brought a keen analytical and historically informed equipment to the task.

In England, the leading figure in criticism in the early 20th century was Ernest Newman, who was also a great Wagner scholar; his objective as a critic was complete scientific precision in the act of evaluation, involving closely reasoned argument based on a well-stocked mind and a readiness to respond to new stimulus. He wrote for daily newspapers in Manchester and Birmingham and for the London *Sunday Times*. Although not a newspaper critic, Donald Tovey has a place in any discussion of criticism for his brilliant series of analytical notes, with their numerous insights (those of a moderately successful composer) into the compositional process. Later noteworthy critics have included Frank Howes, critic for *The Times*, strongly in the tradition of English conservatism in his reactions to (for example) Stravinsky and Schoenberg but a keen champion of English music. The criticism of the Handel, Bizet and opera scholar Winton Dean, usually written for monthly journals, has led to an increased awareness of the interplay between literary and dramatic factors with musical ones. An outstanding practitioner of daily criticism in England was Andrew Porter, who through his work in the *Financial Times* was largely responsible for a change in the character of English criticism during the 1960s, whereby critics were assigned more space and thus encouraged to adopt a more literary manner; from the 1970s he was music critic of the *New Yorker*, where his elegant style, underpinned by sound scholarship and keen perception, exercised a substantial influence on American critical standards. English-language criticism has, broadly speaking, avoided the element of politicization that is found in much musical criticism in the European continent.

Crivelli, Arcangelo (*b* Bergamo, 21 April 1546; *d* Rome, 4 March 1617). Italian composer. He was a singer (1568) and *maestro di cappella* (1569–75) at the Steccata church in Parma. In 1578 he joined the papal choir in Rome and was twice papal composer (1590, 1595). His published masses (1615) and madrigals (1606) are conservative; motets and secular works survive in MSS and anthologies.

Crivelli, Giovanni Battista (*b* Scandiano; *d* Modena, March 1652). Italian composer. A musician in the service of Maximilian I of Bavaria, he was *maestro di cappella* at Milan Cathedral (1638–42) and S Maria Maggiore, Bergamo (1642–48). One of the most talented lesser composers to adopt the concertato style in motets and madrigals, he published a set of each in 1626, also contributing to the opera *La finta savia* (1643).

Croce, Giovanni (*b* Chioggia, *c*1557; *d* Venice, 15 May 1609). Italian composer. A pupil of Zarlino at St Mark's, Venice, he took holy orders in 1585. After working at S Maria Formosa he was made vice-*maestro* (1590) and *maestro di cappella* (1603) of St Mark's. A prolific and influential composer of the Venetian school, he published 14 volumes of masses and other sacred works which, though mostly conservative, include up-to-date concertato motets. His ten secular volumes are notable for their masterly canzonettas and madrigal comedies; several of his best madrigals were well known in England.

Croes, Henri-Jacques de (*b* Antwerp, bap. 19 Sept 1705; *d* Brussels, 16 Aug 1786). South Netherlands composer. A violinist, in 1729 he entered the service of the Prince of Thurn und Taxis at Brussels and in Germany. From 1744 he served in Charles of Lorraine's chapel in Brussels, becoming *maître* in 1746. Active as a composer from the 1730s, he wrote concertos, trio sonatas, divertissements etc and many sacred works.

Croft, William (*b* Nether Ettington, bap. 30 Dec 1678; *d* Bath, 14 Aug 1727). English composer. A Chapel Royal chorister and a pupil and protégé of John Blow, he was organist at St Anne's, Soho, 1700–12. From 1704 he was also an organist of the Chapel Royal. He succeeded Blow in 1708 as Chapel Royal composer, Master of the Children and organist of Westminster Abbey. In 1713 he took the Oxford DMus. His anthem collection *Musica sacra* (1724) was the first such publication in score. Croft was the first significant English composer consistently to use late Baroque style. In his *c*70 verse anthems, e.g. *O praise the Lord, all ye that fear him* (1709), he established a pattern of well-rounded movements; solos, duets and trios predominate. His other church works include full anthems, services and hymn tunes (notably 'St Anne'); he also wrote, mostly before *c*1710, songs, pieces for the theatre and harpsichord and organ music.

Croiza, Claire (*b* Paris, 14 Sept 1882; *d* there, 27 May 1946). French mezzo-soprano. She sang Delilah at the Théâtre de la Monnaie, Brussels, in 1906 and was later well known in operas by Berlioz, Gluck, Strauss and Bizet. Her musical intelligence and clarity of tone were valued in the *chansons* of Debussy, Fauré and Duparc. She taught at the Ecole Normale from 1922 and at the Paris Conservatoire from 1934.

Cromorne. A wind instrument of uncertain identity, used at the French court in the 17th century and early 18th. It is not a crumhorn but probably a type of bassoon or bass shawm. It was made in four sizes.

Crook. A detachable length of tubing inserted into a horn, trumpet or other brass instrument to change the tube length and hence the pitch.

Crooning. A type of quiet, sentimental popular singing current from the 1920s to the 1950s; it originated when the radio microphone enabled performers to sing softly and still be heard.

Cross, Joan (*b* London, 7 Sept 1900). English soprano and producer. She joined the chorus of the Old Vic in 1924 and was principal at Sadler's Wells, 1931–46, creating Ellen Orford in *Peter Grimes* (1945). Other Britten creations included the title role in *Gloriana* (Covent Garden, 1953). She sang with sincerity and technical skill, qualities she brought to her work as producer with the English Opera Group (from 1946) and the Norwegian National Opera.

Crosse, Gordon (*b* Bury, 1 Dec 1937). English composer. He studied with Wellesz at Oxford (1958–61) and briefly with Petrassi in Rome (1962), then taught at Birmingham University. His early works develop an expressionist style out of Webern and Davies: they include an operatic setting of Yeats's *Purgatory* (1966). Then, partly under Britten's influence, his music became smoother and more lyrical. The operas *The Grace of Todd* (1969) and *The Story of Vasco* (1974) both reveal skilful vocal writing and an underlying humanity of conception and feeling. Among his later works are a notable series of characterized chamber concertos (*Ariadne*, 1972; *Thel*, 1976; *Wildboy*, 1978), songs, choral works and music for children.

Cross flute. An older name for the flute (i.e. transverse flute), used to distinguish it from the end-blown recorder.

Crossley, Paul (Christopher Richard) (*b* Dewsbury, 17 May 1944). English pianist. He studied in Oxford, Leeds and under Messiaen and Loriod in Paris. He has specialized in contemporary music, being particularly admired for his performances of Tippett (who wrote his Third Sonata for Paul Crossley, 1973) and Messiaen. His virtuoso technique and thoughtful musicianship have also been heard in the Classical repertory and many new works.

Cross-relation. *See* FALSE RELATION.

Cross-rhythm. The regular shift of beats in a metric pattern to other than their normal positions; if every beat is shifted by the same amount it is called 'syncopation'.

Cross-strung. Term applied to a piano in which double-strung strings are formed from a single wire which crosses over itself when looped over a hitchpin or hook. The method (not to be confused with OVERSTRUNG) was patented in 1830.

Crotales. Small cymbals that can be tuned to a definite pitch; examples, of bronze, survive from ancient Egypt, Rome and Greece. The term has also been applied to the castanet-like ancient CLAPPERS (usually as 'crotala') and the 'antique cymbals' used by Debussy and Ravel.

Crotch, William (*b* Norwich, 5 July 1775; *d* Taunton, 29 Dec 1847). English composer. A child prodigy, he toured Britain as an organist from 1778, also playing the piano and violin and composing. He was an organist in Cambridge, 1786–8, then studied in Oxford, becoming organist of Christ Church in 1790. In 1797 he became professor of music; his lectures on the history of music (given at Oxford in 1800–04 and later at the Royal Institution) were the first of their kind. In 1806–7 he settled in London, where his *Palestine* (1812) was the first successful oratorio since Handel's day. As an organist he championed Bach's music. He was active as a conductor (from the piano), and famous as a teacher, becoming the first principal (1822–32) of the RAM. He retired in 1834.

Although Crotch did not fulfil his early promise, he wrote skilfully in a wide range of styles, especially in his three oratorios and his organ concertos. His finest work, *Palestine*, follows the Handelian model but has many modern and original touches. He also wrote odes, anthems, psalm tunes and chants, hymn tunes, songs and piano music, as well as the influential *Specimens of Various Styles of Music* (*c*1808–15) and manuals on harmony, composition and piano playing. He wrote on many scientific subjects and was a gifted painter.

Crotchet. The note, in American usage called a quarter-note, that is half the value of a minim and double that of a quaver. It is the equivalent of the semiminim and is first found in 14th-century music. In some early sources in black notation, it was shown as a minim with a crook; hence its name. In the 20th century, the crotchet is widely regarded as a convenient value for the standard pulse and is the denominator in the most frequently used time signatures. *See* NOTE VALUES.

Crouch, Frederick Nicholls (*b* London, 31 July 1808; *d* Portland, ME, 18 Aug 1896). English cellist, singer and composer. An orchestral musician and, in the USA from 1849, a singing teacher, he wrote two operas and hundreds of songs, notably *Kathleen*

Mavourneen (*c*1838).

Crown Imperial. March by Walton composed for the coronation of George VI (1937).

Crucifixion, The. Oratorio by Stainer to a text by J. Sparrow Simpson with extracts from the Bible (1887).

Cruft, Adrian (Francis) (*b* Mitcham, 10 Feb 1921; *d* Hillhead, Hants, 20 Feb 1987). English composer. He studied with Jacob and Rubbra at the RCM (1938–40, 1946–7) and produced a large amount of traditional, straightforward orchestral, choral and chamber music.

Crüger, Johannes (*b* Gross-Breesen, 9 April 1598; *d* Berlin, 23 Feb 1662). German composer and theorist. Kantor at the Nicolaikirche, Berlin, from 1622 until his death, he is important for his role in the revitalization of the Protestant chorale. He compiled, arranged and contributed melodies to several major chorale collections, including *Praxis pietatis melica*, the most influential of the 17th century, which appeared under various titles from 1640 in arrangements ranging from melodies with bass to settings for chorus with instrumental parts. He also wrote instruction manuals which drew together new theoretical ideas on composition and singing.

Crumb, George (Henry) (*b* Charleston, WV, 24 Oct 1929). American composer. He studied with Finney at the University of Michigan, and taught at the University of Colorado (1959–64) and the University of Pennsylvania (from 1965). He has produced a large output of music using numerology, unusual sounds and quotations to immediate illustrative ends. His works include many settings of Lorca (*Ancient Voices of Children* for soprano, treble and ensemble, 1970), several volumes of keyboard music published as *Makrokosmos* and orchestral pieces. He often calls for new playing techniques and his piano music is especially imaginative in its expansion of the colour palette. His vocal writing, too, is innovatory. His works typically unfold in a succession of opulent images, each complete, strung into a coherent whole through contrast, cross-reference and careful balance; many of his scores are graphic and visually striking.

Voice and ensemble Night Music I (1963); Madrigals, Bks I–IV (1965, 1965, 1969, 1969); Songs, Drones and Refrains of Death (1968); Night of the Four Moons (1969); Ancient Voices of Children (1970); Lux aeterna (1971); Apparition (1979)
Voice and orchestra Star-child (1977)
Orchestral music Echoes of Time and the River (1967); A Haunted Landscape (1984)
Chamber music 11 Echoes of Autumn, ens (1965); Black Angels, elec str qt (1970); Vox balaenae, ens (1971); Music for a Summer Evening, 2 amp pf, 2 perc (1974); Dream Sequence, ens (1976)
Keyboard music Makrokosmos I, II, amp pf (1972, 1973); Celestial Mechanics, pf 4 hands (1979); Pastoral Drone, org (1982); Processional, pf (1984)

Crumhorn. A double-reed wind-cap instrument with cylindrical bore and curved lower end to the body (for illustration, *see* EARLY MUSIC). The most important wind-cap instrument during the 16th and early 17th centuries, it is mainly associated with Germany, Italy and the Low Countries. It has three sections: the body, the cotton reel (or housing) and the wind cap; the reed is attached to a brass staple inserted into the top of the bore and enclosed by the cap. The crumhorn has a thumb-hole, seven finger-holes and one or more vent-holes in the curved lower section. Like most Renaissance wind instruments, they were made in different sizes: soprano (range $c'-d''$), alto ($g-a'$), tenor ($c-d'$), extended tenor ($G/A-d'$), bass ($F-g$), extended bass ($C-g'$), great bass ($Bb'-c$ or $C-d$) and extended great bass ($G'-d$). The most common were alto, tenor and extended bass.

The crumhorn probably developed in northern Italy in the late 15th century; it soon spread to Germany. It was played mainly by professional musicians at courts and in the larger town bands. Crumhorns were used at the wedding of Cosimo I de' Medici (1539). They remained in use into the 17th century, but rapidly lost ground in the middle of the century as taste changed and their limited compass and expressive range no longer met musical needs. Diderot included the crumhorn ('tournebout') in the context of *instrumens anciens* in his *Encyclopédie* (1765).

Crusell, Bernhard Henrik (*b* Uusikaupunki, 15 Oct 1775; *d* Stockholm, 28 July 1838). Finnish composer and clarinettist. He studied the clarinet from the age of eight and at 12 joined a military band in Sveaborg; in 1791 he went to Stockholm where he became a court musician two years later. He studied the clarinet in Berlin in 1798 with Tausch and in 1803 went to Paris to study composition with Gossec and Berton and the clarinet with Lefèvre. He later held posts as music director in the Swedish court chapel and royal regiment. His compositions include three clarinet concertos (1811, 1816, 1829), an air and variations for clarinet and a Concertante for clarinet, bassoon and horn (1816); he also wrote chamber music, including three clarinet quartets (1812, 1816, 1823), an opera *Den lilla Slafvinnan* (1824, Stockholm) and 12 songs. He was a fluent composer with a fresh vein of melody. He also made Swedish translations of operas by Mozart, Rossini and others.

Crustic, anacrustic. Terms used to distinguish a phrase that begins on the downbeat of a bar and ends at the end of one (crustic) from a phrase that begins and ends in the middle of a bar (anacrustic).

Cruz, Ivo (*b* Corumba, Brazil, 19 May 1901; *d* Lisbon, 8 Sept 1983). Portuguese composer. He studied in Lisbon and Munich and worked in Lisbon as a conductor (founder of the Lisbon PO, 1937) and teacher (director of the Lisbon Conservatory, 1938–71). His works, in a national impressionist style, include two symphonies, two piano concertos, songs and instrumental pieces.

Crwth. A Welsh and Middle English term for a plucked or bowed lyre.

Crystallophone. Term for instruments that sound through the vibration of glass or other brittle substances, such as the armonica and musical glasses.

Crystal Palace. Large iron-framed glass building erected in Hyde Park, London, for the 1851 Great Exhibition and moved to Sydenham in 1852. George Grove encouraged its use for music and appointed August Manns as conductor. It had the first permanent London orchestra which in 1855–1901 gave Saturday Concerts (Oct–April) at cheap prices. Other events included Handel festivals (mainly triennial, 1857–1926; forces ranged from *c*600 to 4000), choral festivals and brass band contests. It burnt down in 1936.

Csárdás. A Hungarian dance in vogue *c*1850–90, in simple duple time with syncopations and recurrent cadential formulas; it was related to the quick part of the VERBUNKOS.

Csermák, Antal György (*b c*1774; *d* Veszprém, 25 Oct 1822). Hungarian composer and violinist. A virtuoso player of the works of Haydn and Mozart and an admirer of the gypsy violinist Bihari, he became a famous interpreter of *verbunkos* music. From 1804 he was pioneer of a specifically Hungarian chamber music tradition, with his *Romances hongroises* and the string trio *Magyar nemzeti tánczok*. His works reflect his knowledge of the Viennese Classical style, an imaginative approach to harmony and the influence of Hungarian, Slovak and Romanian folk music.

Ctesibius [Ktesibios] (*fl* Alexandria, 3rd century BC). Inventor, probably active *c*270 BC. He was famous for his mechanical devices operated by the pressure of water or air, which were often elaborate toys, created to amuse the court. His most significant invention was the hydraulis, in which a lever-actuated piston forced air into a chamber partly filled with water and thence to the pipes.

Cuckoo and the Nightingale, The. Handel's Organ Concerto in F, no.1 of the Second Set (1740); the title comes from the falling minor 3rds and the trills that suggest birdsong.

Cuéllar y Altarriba, Ramón Félix (*b* Saragossa, 20 Sept 1777; *d* Santiago de Compostela, 7 Jan 1833). Spanish composer and organist. *Maestro de capilla* at Saragossa and Oviedo cathedrals, and later first organist at the basilica of Santiago de Compostela, he was renowned for his church music, above all for his 16 masses.

Cuenod, Hugues (Adhémar) (*b* Vevey, 26 June 1902). Swiss tenor. He studied in Basle and Vienna and began his career as a concert singer, taking part in the pioneer recordings of Monteverdi made by Nadia Boulanger (1937–9). His high, light voice was used with exquisite taste in lieder and French song. He sang character roles in opera from 1928, creating Sellem in Stravinsky's *The Rake's Progress* (1951, Venice); from 1954 his humorous interpretations were valued at Glyndebourne.

Cugley, Ian (Robert) (*b* Richmond, Melbourne, 22 June 1945). Australian composer. He studied with Sculthorpe and Maxwell Davies at Sydney University and has taught at the University of Tasmania, also working as a percussionist. His music, which includes choral, orchestral and chamber works, uses 20th-century techniques (serialism, electronics) with primitive elements.

Cui, César [Kyui, Tsezar Antonovich] (*b* Vilnius, 18 Jan 1835; *d* Petrograd, 26 March 1918). Russian composer and critic of French descent. A military engineer, he entered the musical life of St

Petersburg in 1856, when he met Balakirev, who encouraged his talent for opera and helped him with orchestration. He became friendly with the members of the 'Mighty Handful' and fervently advocated nationalist principles, both in his writings for Russian journals and newspapers, for the *Revue et gazette musicale de Paris* and in his book *La musique en Russie* (1880). His approach was often bigoted and his wit caustic, yet much of his own music contrasts strikingly with nationalist principles: the 15 stage works from *A Prisoner in the Caucasus* (1857–8) to the four children's operas (1905–14) reveal the influences of Auber and Meyerbeer, and the vast output of piano pieces and songs, for which he is best known, displays his fascination with Chopin and his ability to express succinctly a poem's sentiments.

Cuivré (Fr.). 'Ringing': the special brassy sound that can be produced from the horn when the player tenses his lips and articulates incisively; it can be done equally on the open or stopped horn.

Cummings, W(illiam) H(ayman) (*b* Sidbury, 22 Aug 1831; *d* London, 6 June 1915). English administrator, scholar and singer. As a boy he sang under Mendelssohn, and later at the Temple Church and the Chapel Royal, becoming a leading tenor in oratorio and a singing teacher at the RAM. He conducted the Sacred Harmonic Society, was principal of the Guildhall School of Music and helped organize the (Royal) Musical Association and the Purcell Society. His work on Purcell, Blow, Arne and Handel was aided by his own magnificent music library, a collection of some 4500 items.

Cunning Little Vixen, The [Příhody Lišky Bystroušky: The Adventures of the Vixen Bystrouška]. Opera in three acts by Janáček to his own libretto after R. Těsnohlidek (1924, Brno).

Cupid and Death. Masque by James Shirley, performed in 1653 with music probably by C. Gibbons; it was revived in 1659 with music by Gibbons and Locke.

Cupis de Camargo. Franco-Flemish family of musicians active in Brussels and Paris. The most celebrated members were Marie-Anne ['La Camargo'] (1710–70), a dancer at the Paris Opéra from 1726, who appeared in many important premières including Rameau's *Hippolyte et Aricie* (1733) and who, being the first to shorten her costume skirts to above the instep, influenced the aesthetics and technique of ballet; her brother Jean-Baptiste (1711–88), a famed horseman who extended violin-playing techniques and wrote violin sonatas and symphonies; and their brother François (1732–1808), a cellist in the orchestras of the Concert Spirituel and Opéra, who wrote sonatas, duos and a method for the cello.

Curlew River. Britten's first church parable (op.71) to a text by William Plomer after a Japanese Noh play (1964, Aldeburgh).

Curran, Alvin (*b* Providence, RI, 13 Dec 1938). American composer. A pupil of Carter, he went to Rome and was a founder member of the group Musica Elettronica Viva (1966). He has written intimate pieces as well as big environmental works, including *Monumenti* (1982) and *Maritime Rites* (1984), which uses ships, foghorns and boats full of singers.

Curschmann, Karl Friedrich (*b* Berlin, 21 June 1805; *d* Langfuhr, 24 Aug 1841). German composer. He studied in Kassel with Spohr and Hauptmann. He is remembered mainly for his 83 songs, popular in the early 19th century, which include settings of Goethe, Schiller, Uhland, Heine, Tieck and Müller; he also wrote a successful comic opera (1828).

Curtain tune. English 17th-century term for music played while the curtain was raised in the theatre.

Curtal. English name, used from the late 16th century to the early 18th, for the DULCIAN and the BASSOON.

Curtis Institute of Music. Conservatory founded in Philadelphia in 1924 by Mary Louise Curtis Bok. Its first director was Johann Grolle; among those who have taught there are Flesch, Martinů, Elisabeth Schumann, Rudolf Serkin and Stokowski.

Curwen. English family of music educationists and publishers. The most celebrated members were John Curwen (1816–80), a Congregational minister and proponent of the Tonic sol-fa system of teaching music to children and the poorer classes (he wrote several books on the subject as well as publishing journals); his son John Spencer Curwen (1847–1916), a trained musician who influenced the standard of educational material brought out by his father's publishing firm, J. Curwen & Sons (established 1863), and who became principal of the Tonic Sol-fa College (founded 1869); and his great nephew John Kenneth Curwen (1881–1935), head of the firm from 1919, who added orchestral music by Holst, Vaughan Williams and others to the catalogue. The firm was taken over by Faber in 1971.

Curzon, Sir Clifford (Michael) (*b* London, 18 May 1907; *d* there, 1 Sept 1982). English pianist. He studied at the RAM and in 1923 played at a Promenade Concert, under Wood. After further study with Schnabel in Berlin (1928–30) he toured widely in Europe and, from 1939, the USA. He was often heard in Schubert and the Romantics but his sensitivity and beauty of tone were most valued in Mozart.

Cusins, Sir William (George) (*b* London, 14 Oct 1833; *d* Remouchamps, 31 Aug 1893). English instrumentalist, conductor and composer. He was conductor of the Philharmonic Society (1867–83) and Master of Music to the queen (1870–93), and travelled widely. As well as composing, he wrote a monograph on Handel's *Messiah*.

Cutting, Francis (*fl* 1583–*c*1603). English composer and lutenist. Possibly from East Anglia, he lived in London in the 1580s. His output consists mainly of tuneful, close-textured dances and character-pieces for lute (most in MS).

Cuvelier, Jo(hannes) (*b* ?Tournai; *fl* 1372–87). French poet and composer associated with the French court. Three ballades by him survive, and he wrote the text of a fourth, set by Hymbert de Salinis.

Cuvelier d'Arras, Jehan le (*fl c*1240–70). French trouvère. He was associated with the poetic circle of Arras, being respondent in nine and judge in six others. Six *chansons* by him are known.

Cuzzoni, Francesca (*b* Parma, *c*1698; *d* Bologna, 1770). Italian soprano. She appeared in operas in Italy from 1716, and in 1723 made a sensational

London début as Teofane in Handel's *Ottone*. Admired for her versatile and beautifully expressive voice (her trill was famous), she had a leading role in every Handel opera until 1728 (notably Cleopatra in *Giulio Cesare*); Faustina Bordoni was her rival. She revisited London in 1734–6 and 1750, at other times singing in Florence, Hamburg etc, and (1745–8) Stuttgart. She died in obscurity and poverty.

Cyclic form. Term applied to musical works in which the same thematic material occurs in different movements. By the 19th century composers used cyclic principles for the sake of unity.

Cymbals. Percussion instruments, normally of indefinite pitch. The modern orchestral cymbals are a pair of large round plates of metal (an alloy of *c*80% copper and 20% tin), the exact constituents and processing of which are the makers' secrets. Diameters range from 30 to 65 cm (the cymbals of antiquity were much smaller). For orchestral purposes, cymbals of 40–50 cm are used, the desired tonal qualities being brilliance, resonance and a multiplicity of overtones. Orchestral cymbals are 'paired' with a slight difference in pitch. Each plate is slightly convex to ensure that only the outer edges meet; in the centre is a shallow, saucer-like recess forming a dome, with a hole through which the holding strap passes (for illustration, *see* PERCUSSION INSTRUMENTS). They are held vertically and clashed with a swift up-and-down movement; a sharper sound is obtained by striking a suspended cymbal with a hard drumstick.

Cymbals may have originated in Central Asia, from where they entered China. They were played in many ancient societies including Hittite Anatolia, Egypt, Greece and Rome. Cymbals from Pompeii range from small crotales to instruments 41 cm in diameter. Greek and Roman types appear in representations from the Middle Ages. They were prominent in Viennese janissary music of the late 18th century; Mozart (*Die Entführung aus dem Serail*), Haydn ('Military' Symphony) and Beethoven (Ninth Symphony) all used them. From the early 19th century they often appear in orchestral works; Berlioz scored for ten cymbals in his *Grande messe des morts* (1873). 20th-century composers have called for unusual effects, including Schoenberg who asked for a sustained note to be played by drawing a cello bow over a cymbal edge (Five Orchestral Pieces, 1909).

In jazz a variety of cymbals and cymbal effects are used, including the hi-hat pedal-operated cymbals and suspended cymbals: 'crash' (or 'splash'), 'ride', 'bounce' and 'sizzle'.

Cymbalum. Term designating two related musical instruments, a type of ancient cymbals and a medieval set of bells.

Czech Philharmonic Orchestra. Orchestra based in Prague. Its name was established in 1896 when concerts conducted by Dvořák were given by the National Theatre orchestra; it became independent in 1901. Under Talich (1919–39) it became an important ensemble. Subsequent conductors include Kubelík, Ančel and Neumann.

Czerny, Carl (*b* Vienna, 21 Feb 1791; *d* there, 15 July 1857). Austrian piano teacher, composer, pianist and writer on music. As Beethoven's pupil and Liszt's teacher he occupies a unique position among 19th-century pianists, both as a transmitter of ideas from one master to another and for his extraordinary productivity during a time of dramatic change in the piano and its literature. After early training from his father he was accepted as a pupil by Beethoven, who stressed material in C.P.E. Bach's *Versuch* and legato playing. He made his début in 1800, gaining renown for his interpretation of Beethoven, but was drawn to teaching rather than a career as a travelling virtuoso; among his pupils were Beethoven's nephew Karl, Döhler, Thalberg, Leopoldine Blahetka and Liszt, whose *Transcendental Studies* were dedicated to him. He was a remarkably prolific composer, with an output of over 1000 works, including chamber and orchestral music, sacred choral music and hundreds of arrangements in diverse styles; more significant are his wide range of studies and exercises and the treatises *School of Extemporaneous Performance* opp.200, 300 and *Complete Theoretical and Practical Pianoforte School* op.500 (1839).

Cziffra, György (*b* Budapest, 5 Nov 1921). French pianist of Hungarian birth. He studied in Budapest with Dohnányi and toured as soloist from 1933. His political beliefs led to imprisonment in the early 1950s. He escaped to the West, where his energy and dazzling technique soon earned him a wide following in the Romantic repertory.

D

D. Name of a note, or a PITCH-CLASS; *see also* PITCH NAMES. It is the second degree (or supertonic) of the scale of C.

Numbers prefixed by a D, in reference to works of Schubert, refer to the chronological numbering of the composer's works by O.E. Deutsch in his thematic catalogue (1951, 2/78).

Da capo (It.). 'From the head': an instruction, often abbreviated 'D.C.', placed at the end of a piece to indicate a return to the beginning. The word 'fine' (end) or a pause sign normally marks the end of the return. The instruction was regularly placed after the *B* section in the ternary (*ABA*) arias in the Baroque period and minuets in the Classical period to avoid having to write out the first section twice.

Daff. *See* DUFF.

Dafne. Opera in a prologue and six scenes by Peri to a libretto by Rinuccini (1597, Florence). The same libretto was set by Caccini (*c*1600), Gagliano (1608) and Schütz (1627). Operas on the same subject were composed by A. Scarlatti, Mulé and R. Strauss.

Dagincour [Dagincourt], **François** (*b* Rouen, 1684; *d* there, 30 April 1758). French composer. He worked as a church organist in Rouen from *c*1706. His music shows originality and variety of mood, especially the *Pièces de clavecin* (1733), in a style akin to F. Couperin's. He also wrote organ versets and songs.

Dahl, Ingolf (*b* Hamburg, 9 June 1912; *d* Frutigen, 6 Aug 1970). American composer of Swedish-German parentage. He studied with Jarnach at the Cologne Musikhochschule, with Andreae at the Zurich Conservatory and with Boulanger in California, where he settled in 1938 (teaching at the University of Southern California, 1945–70). Closely associated with Stravinsky's music as a writer, conductor and arranger (piano reductions of *Danses concertantes* and *Scènes de ballet*), he was influenced by Stravinsky in the leanness, vitality and serialism (from 1957) of his own music, which consists mostly of orchestral and instrumental works; notable are the Sinfonietta for concert band (1961) and the almost neo-Romantic *Aria sinfonica* (1965).

Dahlhaus, Carl (*b* Hanover, 10 June 1928). German musicologist. He studied at Göttingen and Freiburg, then worked as production adviser to the Deutsches Theater, Göttingen (1950–58), for the *Stuttgarter Zeitung* (1960–62) and then at Kiel University. In 1967 he became professor of music history at the Technical University, Berlin. His writings cover a broad spectrum, including theory, analysis and aesthetics. He has written on music from the 15th century to the present, notably on Josquin and Wagner; for the range and depth of his works he is one of the most influential musical thinkers of our time.

Dalayrac [D'Alayrac], **Nicolas-Marie** (*b* Muret, 8 June 1753; *d* Paris, 26 Nov 1809). French composer. From 1774 he was a sub-lieutenant at Versailles, where he studied composition and began writing chamber pieces; his string quartets were very popular. In 1782 he began a long series of works for Paris theatres, mostly *opéras comiques* – notably *Nina* (1786), perhaps the first of the sentimental type to exclude comic elements. He also adapted popular operatic tunes to Republican words. He remained famous in France and abroad after the Revolution, using gothic (e.g. *Camille*, 1791), oriental and chivalric subjects, and his work was accepted as the logical continuation of Grétry's. His *c*60 *opéras comiques* show his keen dramatic sense, with action and conversation in the ensembles, and his subtle melodic gift. Particularly influential were the *romances* (lyrical solo numbers). His style moved from one akin to Gluck's to a lighter, more Italianate idiom; some early works, such as *Sargines* (1788), anticipate Beethoven's style.

d'Albert, Eugen. *See* ALBERT, EUGEN D'.

Dalby, (John) Martin (*b* Aberdeen, 25 April 1942). Scottish composer. He studied at the RCM and has worked for the BBC. His works tend to be imaginative adventures, in a characterful atonal style, sparked off by old music and myth.

Dale, Benjamin (James) (*b* London, 17 July 1885; *d* there, 30 July 1943). English composer. He studied with Corder at the RAM and began impressively as a composer while there (e.g. Piano Sonata, 1902). But after 1912 he devoted himself to educational work.

D'Alembert, Jean le Rond (*b* Paris, 16 Nov 1717; *d* there, 29 Oct 1783). French philosopher. He wrote on many subjects and contributed articles, some on music, to Diderot's *Encyclopédie*. His main musical work was *Eléments de musique théorique et pratique* *suivant les principes de M. Rameau* (1752). In opera, he favoured the Italian musical style within the French dramatic structure.

Dalibor. Opera in three acts by Smetana to a libretto by Joseph Wenzig, translated into Czech by E. Spindler (1868, Prague).

Dall'Abaco, Evaristo Felice (*b* Verona, 12 July 1675; *d* Munich, 12 July 1742). Italian composer. A cellist, he worked first in Modena but by 1704 had joined the Bavarian court. He followed it to the Low Countries and France; after the return to Munich in 1715 he became Konzertmeister (he was also a violinist), remaining a favourite composer and player until the 1720s. His six published works, mostly for strings, are inventive and carefully written. The violin sonatas (*c*1708, 1716) and trio sonatas (1712) combine abstract and dance movements, later including some French types. Of the three sets of concertos, op.5 (*c*1719) includes one with two flutes and one with oboe, and op.6 (1735) has *galant* touches.

Dall'Abaco's son Joseph-Marie-Clément (1710–1805), a court cellist in Bonn, wrote nearly 40 cello sonatas, mainly in a conservative, Baroque style.

Dalla Casa, Girolamo (*b* ?Udine; *d* Venice, *c*Aug 1601). Italian composer and instrumentalist. With his brothers Giovanni and Nicolò he formed the first permanent instrumental ensemble at St Mark's, Venice (1568); Giovanni Gabrieli wrote concertante parts for them. He published an important ornamentation treatise (1584), as well as madrigals (1574, 1590) and motets (1597).

Dallam. English family of organ builders. Thomas (*c*1575–after 1629) established an unrivalled reputation, building new organs at, among other places, King's College, Cambridge (1605–6), St George's Chapel, Windsor (1609–10), Worcester Cathedral (1613; designed by Thomas Tomkins), Eton College (1613–14), Holyrood Palace, Edinburgh (*c*1615), Wells Cathedral (1620) and Durham Cathedral (1621). His son Robert (1602–65), besides building instruments at York Minster (1632–4), Magdalen College, Oxford (1630s), Jesus and St John's colleges, Cambridge (1634–8), and Gloucester Cathedral (1640–41), worked in Brittany as a recusant Catholic (1642–60), on his return constructing organs at St George's Chapel, Windsor (1660–61), Eton College (1662–3) and New College, Oxford (*c*1663). Through Robert's three sons and two grandsons French influence on English organs continued for 80 years.

Dallapiccola, Luigi (*b* Pisino d'Istria, 3 Feb 1904; *d* Florence, 19 Feb 1975). Italian composer. Interned with his family in Graz (1917–18), he was stimulated by Mozart and Wagner at the opera house, then studied with Antonio Illersberg in Trieste (1920–22): Debussy and early Italian music (Monteverdi, Gesualdo) became important influences. At the Florence Conservatory he studied composition with Casiraghi (1923–4) and Frazzi (1929–31), and he returned there to teach (1934–67). His musical horizons were widening as he came to know Schoenberg, Mahler, Webern and Berg, and in the mid-1930s he began to use 12-note series, though at first only as melodies within a relatively

diatonic style (6 *cori di Michelangelo*, 1936). The climax of this period was his first opera, the one-act *Volo di notte* (1940), about a night flier's experience of the infinite.

During the next decade Dallapiccola's works were concerned with taking up the cause of freedom (*Canti di prigionia*, 1941; the opera *Il prigioniero*, 1950), and his music became more atonal (closest to Berg). But as his 12-note serial practice grew more rigorous, so his music came nearer to Webern, especially in a sequence of works for solo voice and ensemble: *Goethe Lieder* (1953), *5 canti* (1956), *Preghiere* (1962), *Sicut umbra* (1970). The luminous, contemplative style of these works is that also of the opera *Ulisse* (1968), a projection of contemporary restlessness in the search for meaning.

Operas Volo di notte (1940); Il prigioniero (1950); Ulisse (1968)
Other dramatic works Marsia, ballet (1948); Job (1950)
Choral music 6 cori di Michelangelo (1936); Canti di prigionia (1941); Canti di liberazione (1955); Requiescant (1958); Tempus destruendi – Tempus aedificanci (1971)
Solo vocal music Divertimento in 4 esercizi (1934); 3 laudi (1937); 5 frammenti di Saffo (1942); 6 carmina Alcaei (1943); 2 liriche di Anacreonte (1945); Rencesvals (1946); 4 liriche di Antonio Machado (1948); 3 poemi (1949); Goethe Lieder (1953); An Mathilde (1955); 5 canti (1956); Concerto per la notte di Natale dell'anno 1956 (1957); Preghiere (1962); Parole di San Paolo (1964); Sicut umbra (1970); Commiato (1972)
Orchestral music Tartiniana (1951, 1956); Variazioni (1954); Piccola musica notturna (1954); Dialoghi (1960); Three Questions with Two Answers (1962)
Chamber music Ciaccona, intermezzo e adagio (1945); Quaderno musicale di Annalibera (1952)

Dall'Aquila, Marco (*b c*1480; *d* after 1538). Italian lutenist and composer. His surviving compositions (three fantasias, 14 ricercar-fantasias, six chanson arrangements, a prelude and a dance) – are exceptional for their exploitation of figures, idioms and sonorities suited to the lute.

Dallas Opera. Founded in 1957 as Dallas Civic Opera and renamed in 1981, it presents a wide repertory, including Handel, Vivaldi and new American works. Berganza, Caballé, Domingo, Sutherland and other international singers made their American débuts with the company.

Dallas Symphony Orchestra. American orchestra established in 1911 by Carl Venth; it became fully professional under Antal Dorati (1945–9). Later conductors include Georg Solti, Max Rudolf, Kurt Masur and Eduardo Mata (1977–). Its home from 1973 was State Fair Park Music Hall (cap. 4100); a new hall (cap. 2200) opened in 1988. The orchestra performs with Dallas Opera and presents an outdoor 'Starfest' summer season. The Dallas Symphony Orchestra Chorus was formed in 1977.

Dalla Viola, Alfonso (*b* Ferrara, *c*1508; *d* there, *c*1573). Italian composer and instrumentalist. Member of a family of musicians active at Ferrara, *c*1470–*c*1570, he served the Este family for 40 years as a performer and composer and was *maestro di cappella* at Ferrara Cathedral from *c*1563 to 1572. He provided music for plays, chiefly classical pastorals, most now lost, but his surviving madrigals (2 bks, 1539, 1540) show awareness of the style of Verdelot and Arcadelt and contain touches of individuality in declamation and tone colour. His relative, Francesco Viola (*d* 1568), sang at Ferrara Cathedral under Willaert, was also patronized by the Este family (he became *maestro di cappella* to Alfonso II in 1559) and wrote masses and motets as well as madrigals (1550).

Dallis Lute Book. English MS, copied in Cambridge, 1583. It consists of 254 pages with 288 compositions, 198 of them for lute solo (of which nearly 150 are dances, mainly passamezzos, pavans and galliards). There are also some lute songs, sacred pieces, *chansons*, madrigals etc. Its full title is 'Thomas Dallis Pupil's Lute Book'; it is now in Trinity College Library, Dublin.

Dal Pane, Domenico (*b* in or nr. Rome, *c*1630; *d* there, 10 Dec 1694). Italian composer. He was one of the best known soprano castratos of the late 1650s. He entered the Sistine Chapel in 1654 (*maestro di cappella* 1669–79). As a composer he was rooted in the Palestrina tradition, writing *a cappella* music for the papal chapel; but his experience of virtuoso singing is evident in his handling of concerted works, especially the *Sagri concerti* (1675), in which the balance between expressiveness and virtuosity and the precise declamation of the text are noteworthy. His two books of five-part madrigals (1652, 1678) show the survival of the polyphonic madrigal well into the 17th century.

Dal segno (It.). 'From the sign': an indication that the performer should repeat from the point at which the sign is placed; it is sometimes abbreviated D.S.

Damase, Jean-Michel (*b* Bordeaux, 27 Jan 1928). French composer. He showed talent as a pianist and composer from an early age and studied with Cortot, Büsser and Dupré. His works include ballets, concertos and chamber music of fluent elegance, characterized by idiomatic instrumental writing.

Dame blanche, La. Opera in three acts by Boieldieu to a libretto by Scribe after Scott (1825, Paris).

Damett, ?Thomas (*b* ?1389–90; *d* 15 July 1436–14 April 1437). English composer. The illegitimate son of a gentleman, he was a commoner at Winchester College until 1406–7 and became rector of Stockton, Wilts., in 1413. His name appears sporadically in the Royal Household Chapel accounts between 1413 and 1430–31. Nine works by him – six mass movements (including a Gloria–Credo pair based on a SQUARE) and three motets (one isorhythmic) – survive in the Old Hall MS and may be autographs.

Damnation de Faust, La. Cantata, op.24, by Berlioz to a text by G. de Nerval, A. Gandonnière and the composer, after Goethe (1846); it incorporates the earlier *Huit scènes de Faust* (1829).

Damoiselle élue, La [The Blessed Damozel]. Cantata by Debussy to G. Sarrazin's translation of Rossetti's poem (1888).

Damrosch. German-American family of musicians. Leopold (*b* Poznań, 22 Oct 1832; *d* New York, 15 Feb 1885), formerly Liszt's leading violinist in the Weimar court orchestra and conductor in Breslau, emigrated to New York in 1871 to conduct the Männergesangverein Arion; in 1873 he founded the

Oratorio Society and in 1878 the Symphony Society for orchestral concerts. He was instrumental in the establishment of German opera at the Met (1884).

His son Frank (1859–1937) worked as an educationist and choral conductor in New York, founding and directing the Institute of Musical Art (1905–26). His son Walter (1862–1950), who succeeded him as conductor of the Oratorio and Symphony Societies, also conducted German operas with his own company and at the Met; he persuaded Andrew Carnegie to build Carnegie Hall, and presented the American premières of works by Tchaikovsky, Wagner, Mahler, Elgar and Gershwin. From 1927 he was a musical advisor and director of broadcast orchestral music for the NBC.

Danby, John (*b* c1757; *d* London, 16 May 1798). English composer. A pupil of Webbe, he was a Roman Catholic and organist of the Spanish Embassy chapel. He is notable chiefly as a composer of glees, catches and other partsongs, of which he wrote nearly 100; he won eight Catch Club prizes and produced polished, graceful and sometimes original pieces. He also wrote masses, motets and vocal and instrumental tutors.

Dance. The present article outlines the history of dance and its music, social, theatrical and idealized, in Western society. (Information about particular dances will be found in their individual entries, indicated by cross-references.)

References to types of dance begin to appear in writings from the 12th century onwards, with such titles as CAROLE, *hovetantz*, ESTAMPIE and SALTARELLO; the *carole* (a line or circular dance) apart, little is known about their musical or choreographic features. The more formal, processional dance types led to the classical Burgundian BASSE DANSE and the more elaborate Italian bassadanza of the 15th century, and on to the Renaissance PAVAN. Most instrumental pieces for dancing at this period fall into short, repeated sections, between three and seven in number; sometimes dances are paired, with the second of a pair faster than the first and in a different metre. Nothing is reliably known, however, of the relationship of dance steps to surviving music.

With the 15th century, traditions of dance teaching and theory arose in Italy, and instruction manuals connect music and choreography. Court dances of the time, such as the CALATA and the *striana*, are known by name and by some salient features; a number of dances, such as the MORESCA (morris, *morisque*) and the BRANLE (brando), were considered inappropriate a for a gentleman. A new repertory arose after 1500 with the appearance of branles and moresche used in all parts of Europe for popular group dancing and professional solo dancing.

In the period 1550–1630 court dance is well documented and the sources reflect the popularity of dance, both social and theatrical. Vocal music of the time, though not necessarily intended for dance, reflects the rhythms of popular dance types such as the GALLIARD, the CANARY and the corrente (COURANTE, *coranto*). Traditionally, dance, often in triple metre, symbolized joy and requited love. At the same time dance, song and spectacle came together in the new dramatic forms including the *intermedio*, the *ballet de cour* and the masque, while dance rhythms permeated the development of the new instrumental idioms of the late 16th and early 17th centuries. At social gatherings, dances included the solemn processional pavane, circular branles and progressive longways dances; there were also individually choreographed dances for small groups and miming dances performed by couples in the embrace position which heightened the relationship between dance and the sport of love. Theatrical dance varied widely in scope; it comprehended formal processions for dignitaries, mock battles, horse ballets or stage works, sometimes with solo dances or small group dances (as in Monteverdi's *Ballo dell'ingrate*). There could also be geometrically figured dances for large groups such as formed the main items in the *intermedio*, *ballet de cour* and masque and persisted throughout the 17th century. Dance manuals of the period provide numerous specific choreographies for social dances, notably Fabritio Caroso's *Il ballarino* (1581) and *Nobiltà di dame* (1600), Thoinot Arbeau's *Orchésographie* (1588) and Cesare Negri's *Le gratie d'amore* (1602). Italy dominated dance in the 16th century and Italian dancing-masters worked in all parts of Europe. Surviving stage choreographies make it clear that group stage dances were elaborated versions of social dances of the time; in these, different types of movement followed in quick succession, with different numbers of dancers. It is clear that folkdance nourished court dance to some degree.

Music for dancing was supplied by any kind of instrument, but in Italy each kind of instrumentation was associated with a particular type of scene or personage: drums and double-reed instruments were used for peasants, for example. Much dance music of the time, especially in Italy, is constructed on ground basses and other variation patterns. The main types used were the ALLEMANDE, branle, corrente or courante, gagliarda or galliard, PASSAMEZZO (or *pass' e mezzo*), PAVAN and saltarello; there were local types, such as the English dump, and other popular ones – including the *ciaccona* (or CHACONNE) and SARABANDE – that were considered too crude or lascivious for courtly use. The 'dance-afterdance' pattern, with a slow duple dance followed by a fast triple (like the pavan–galliard or passamezzo–saltarello), is common in the musical sources.

From *c*1630 French influence became stronger in northern Europe while Italian influence persisted in the south. There was a multiplicity of dance types: the sarabande and chaconne became acceptable, the courante was developed and the minuet came into prominence. French dance spectacles grew in number and in scale, culminating in the theatrical dances in the operas of Lully and the favoured early 18th-century and Regency genre, the *opéra-ballet*, consisting of a series of divertissements in which dance was prominent. An English parallel is found in the use of dance in Purcell's semi-operas; in Italian opera, dance was generally used only in final scenes, though in certain courtly theatrical entertainments there was dancing between the acts, the music usually supplied by specialist composers.

Dance style changed markedly in the 17th century, though there is slender documentation until Playford's *English Dancing Master* (1651, many edns. to 1728), which treats primarily the English country-dance type. By the end of the 17th century the most popular dances included the allemande, branle, BOURRÉE, canary, chaconne, COUNTRY DANCE, courante, FORLANA, GIGUE, LOURE, MINUET, PASSACAGLIA, PASSEPIED, RIGAUDON and sarabande. In social dance, as in theatrical, these were often grouped into suites of increasingly standard pattern. In Germany, the instrumental ensemble suite flourished, with Schein, Peuerl, Krieger and Georg Muffat and the harpsichord suite with Froberger, Kuhnau and later Bach. In France, keyboard dances were collected in groups by Chambonnières, the Couperins and D'Anglebert, but the true suite appeared only late in the century. English composers of dance groups include Jenkins, Locke and Purcell. Italian dance collections fall into suite-like groupings or sonatas of the *sonata da camera* type, by such composers as Buonamente, Marini and later G.B. Vitali and Corelli.

By the early 18th century French domination of theatrical dance was widely acknowledged; it had also begun to play a part in the drama as well as being decorative. This process had already begun with Lully and continued in some degree in the *opéra-ballets* of Campra. The two most influential French dancers of the early 18th century were Marie-Anne Camargo (1710–70), famous for her virtuoso technique, and Marie Sallé (1707–56), more creative an artist in her expression of emotion; both were involved in the simplification of dance dress from the formality of the previous era to increase mobility. Camargo played a prominent part in the ballets of Rameau, the most inventive composer of theatrical dance of the early 18th century.

The major dance reformer, however, was Jean-Georges Noverre (1727–1810), who was influenced by Sallé, Rameau and the English actor David Garrick. He crystallized the vision of *ballet en action* (or *ballet d'action*) as music, drama, choreography and staging, all subordinated to a general scheme, and he demanded an end to virtuosity for its own sake and stereotyped, unpractical costumes. He worked with Jommelli and in Vienna with Gluck. Other important choreographers of this period were Franz Hilverding van Wewen (1710–68), a leading Viennese balletmaster who created fully developed pantomime ballets, some of them tragic, in place of decorative *divertissements*; he also worked at the Russian court, with the ballet composer Starzer, who later composed in Vienna for Noverre and his rival Gaspero Angiolini (1731–1803). Angiolini collaborated with Gluck on his 'reform' works, the ballet *Don Juan* (1761) and the opera *Orfeo ed Euridice* (1762).

Analagous with developments in opera at the time, a new type of ballet based on a middle-class view of peasant life was developed by Jean Dauberval (1742–1806), with *La fille mal gardée* (1789). Another development by a Noverre pupil, in London, was a ballet by Charles Louis Didelot (1767–1837) featuring machinery that enabled dancers to 'fly' on wires.

Social dance of the late 18th century centred on the minuet, the most important dance in the aristocratic divertimento (as well as the symphony and the string quartet) and the symbol of aristocratic dance in Mozart's *Don Giovanni*. There it is contrasted with the bourgeois CONTREDANSE (from the English country dance), usually in duple time, which later developed in different forms (ANGLAISE, ÉCOSSAISE, COTILLON and later the REEL) and was danced longways. In middle-class social dance, various types of round dance developed for couples in close embrace; this culminated in the waltz, which apparently developed from so-called German dances such as the DEUTSCHE and the LÄNDLER. They were introduced into the ballroom *c*1760. Vienna was the centre of the German dance and the waltz; Mozart and Beethoven later provided many of these for court balls, as did Schubert for bourgeois dancing. The waltz was much denounced as lascivious and immoral, but that did not prevent it from spreading (perhaps the contrary). Besides the minuet, other dances were used in art music, notably, in the mid-18th century, the polonaise, by such composers as W.F. Bach and Telemann, while the rhythms of others had an important place in vocal as well as instrumental music, lending a piece their particular expressive associations (such as the pathos of the SICILIANA, in A. Scarlatti and Handel and indeed up to Mozart).

The main development of the early 19th century was the rise of the Romantic ballet, a *ballet en action* based on expressive mime-dance and the dramatic use of a *corps de ballet*; influential in this is Dauberval's pupil Salvatore Viganò (1769–1821), choreographer of Beethoven's Prometheus ballet. Most ballets (*Prometheus* is an exception) were assembled by theatre staff musicians to the requirements of a choreographer. This tradition developed particularly at Paris, notably with Hérold, whose score for *La fille mal gardée* (1828) is still performed, and Halévy, whose *Manon Lescaut* (1830) used melody to identify character. Dance technique of the time emphasized lightness, grace and modesty, with the use of point-shoes for artistic effect. This style was inaugurated by *La sylphide* (1832, Paris), in which Marie Taglioni (1804–84), whose dancing reflected the early Romantic spirit, appeared. Her style contrasted with that of the Viennese Fanny Elssler (1810–84), notable for her strong dramatic character and virtuoso technique. Another important dancer was Carlotta Grisi (1819–99), who inspired Adam's *Giselle* (1841, Paris), a peak of Romantic ballet. These artists made London an important ballet centre in the 1840s; also important were Copenhagen and Russia, as they remain.

Within opera, ballet retained its largely secondary place, serving primarily a decorative function during much of the 19th century, though Glinka's operas are not alone in using it in scenes that grow out of the action, incorporating folkdance to dramatic ends. Meyerbeer also used dance dramatically in *Robert le diable* but in most of his operas it is ornamental. Verdi's operatic ballets, mostly added for Paris productions, make some token attempt at integration into the drama, as also does Wagner's for the production of *Tannhäuser* in Paris, where the inclusion of ballet was a traditional prerequisite.

The classical ballet, though influenced by the work of Delibes in Paris (*Coppélia*, 1870; *Sylvia*, 1876), was mainly the work of Tchaikovsky in Moscow, with his *Swan Lake* (1877), *Sleeping Beauty* (1890) and *Nutcracker* (1892). *Sleeping Beauty* was choreographed by the French ballet-master Marius Petipa (1818–1910), head of the Russian Imperial Ballet, who created 46 ballets which raised the style to a peak of spectacular grandeur. He mapped out in detail the sequence of dances which gave Tchaikovsky the practical help he needed. He also had some involvement in the other two and in ballets by Glazunov (*The Seasons*, 1900) and Minkus (*Raymonda*, 1898). The other leading Russian choreographer was Lev Ivanov (1834–1901), who worked on *Nutcracker* and the Polovtsian Dances in Borodin's *Prince Igor* (1890).

In social dance, however, Vienna's precedence remained because of the dominance of the waltz. Other important dances were the more complicated QUADRILLE and the lively, much simpler GALOP. The Bohemian POLKA also achieved great popularity towards the middle of the century, as did the SCHOTTISCHE. The quadrille fell into regular eight-bar patterns, but other forms allowed opportunity for greater development, especially the waltz with its extended introduction and the opportunities it allowed for melodic expansion and recapitulation. The Strauss family in Vienna were its best-known exponents. The waltz was one of the dances which, in idealized form, was used by piano composers, such as Chopin and Brahms; Chopin also drew on the rhythms of his native Polish dances such as the MAZURKA and the POLONAISE. Smetana and Dvořák, similarly, used such national dance forms as the FURIANT and the DUMKA.

The central figure in theatrical dance of the early 20th century was Sergey Dyagilev (1872–1929), whose genius changed the face and fortune of classical dance and determined its course, although he could neither choreograph nor compose. His company Ballets Russes, which first appeared in Paris in 1909, used music in three different ways: an anthology of works by one composer (for example the collection of Chopin pieces he assembled for *Les sylphides*, or the 'Pergolesi' ones that Stravinsky assembled for *Pulcinella*); a miscellany of works by different composers; or the use of an existing work to create a ballet quite distinct from the composer's intentions. But he also continued the practice of commissioning new music and thus created the basic repertory of modern ballet: Stravinsky's *Firebird*, *Petrushka* and *Rite of Spring*, Debussy's *Jeux*, Ravel's *Daphnis et Chloé*, Falla's *Three-cornered Hat* and Poulenc's *Les biches* are examples. He used such choreographers as Fokin, Massin and Balanchin; Picasso and Cocteau were among his designers. He trained the principal figures in British ballet as well as Balanchin, the most important in dance in New York. In Russia, the classical tradition was preserved and nurtured into the Soviet era, with the creation of new ballets by Glier (*The Red Poppy*, 1927) and Shostakovich (*The Age of Gold*, 1930) as well as Prokofiev (*Romeo and Juliet*, 1940; *Cinderella*, 1945). In the USA particularly, classical dance has been challenged by 'modern' dance, pioneered by Isadora Duncan (1878–1927), who took ancient Greek art as the inspiration for her free style of dancing (to any music that fired her), as well as Ruth St Denis (1877–1968), who drew on oriental sources and trained a new generation of American dancers, notably Martha Graham (*b* 1900). A pupil of Graham's, Merce Cunningham (*b* 1915), collaborated with John Cage, pioneering a dissociation of music and dance in which each aimed at self-sufficiency.

Social dance in the 19th century had originated in Europe and travelled to America; the traffic was reversed in the 20th. This was anticipated by the BOSTON (or *valse boston*) at the end of the 19th century; then followed the TANGO, immediately before World War I, along with ragtime dances such as the TWO-STEP and the CAKEWALK, and (after World War I) the CHARLESTON and the FOXTROT. In the 1930s, interest grew in Latin American dancing to bands including maracas, claves and Cuban drums; the RUMBA, SAMBA and TANGO were the most popular. The swing era of the 1930s saw the development of freer dances such as the JITTERBUG. In the 1940s and 1950s, as the bop and cool styles transformed jazz from dance music into concert music, Latin American bands popularized Caribbean and Latin American dances including the BOSSA-NOVA and the CHA CHA CHA; by the late 1950s the black dances associated with rhythm and blues, and later rock and roll, were preferred. Some rock dances, such as the TWIST, were variants of ragtime dances, but their execution depended less on the interaction of partners than on the individual as part of a group. In the 1970s and 1980s, the driving, propulsive beats of rock, funk and soul music, on guitars, brass and drums that threaten to overpower the melody, gave rise to a concept of never-ending dance with a constant stream of sound to which dancers can create any dance movements in sequences of their own choosing.

Dance of death (Fr. *danse macabre*; Ger. *Totentanz*). A medieval and Renaissance symbolic representation of death as a skeleton (or a procession of skeletons) leading the living to the grave; in more recent times, a dance supposedly performed by skeletons, usually in a graveyard. Goethe's poem *Der Todtentanz* lent impetus to the 19th-century tradition of the dance of death as a midnight revel by resurrected skeletons and inspired Liszt's *Totentanz* and, indirectly, Saint-Saëns's *Danse macabre*.

Dance of the Seven Veils. Popular name for Salome's dance before Herod in R. Strauss's opera *Salome* (1905); for orchestra alone, it is often performed as a concert item.

Dances of Galánta. Orchestral suite by Kodály (1933) based on gypsy tunes collected in the town of Galánta.

Dance Suite. Orchestral work by Bartók (1923), which he also arranged for piano (1925).

Danckerts, Ghiselin (*b* Tholen, *c*1510; *d* after Aug

1565). Flemish composer. A member of the Sistine Chapel (1538–65) in Rome, he achieved little fame as a composer, but in 1551 was a judge in the debate between Vicentino and Lusitano on chromaticism. He wrote a treatise (MS) revealing his conservative attitudes to contemporary musical practices.

Dancla, (Jean Baptiste) Charles (*b* Bagnères de Bigorre, 19 Dec 1817; *d* Tunis, 10 Nov 1907). French violinist, composer and teacher. The last exponent of the classical French school of violin playing, he studied at the Paris Conservatoire and gave chamber music concerts with his brothers Arnaud Phillipe (1819–62) and Leopold (1822–95) and his sister Laure (1824–80). From 1855 he taught at the Conservatoire, also producing 14 string quartets, and didactic works including the *20 études brillantes et caractéristiques* op.73.

Danco, Suzanne (*b* Brussels, 22 Jan 1911). Belgian soprano. She studied at the Brussels Conservatory and made her début at Genoa in 1941. A versatile artist, she was successful as Fiordiligi, Mélisande and Berg's Marie. In concert she was most often heard in the songs of Debussy, Ravel and Berlioz.

Dando, Joseph (Bourne Haydon) (*b* London, 11 May 1806; *d* Godalming, 9 May 1894). English violinist. Well known as an orchestral leader in London and the provinces, he organized the first public concert of string quartets in England (1835) and, with his chamber music colleagues, gave the English premières of works by Haydn, Mendelssohn and Schumann.

Dandrieu, Jean-François (*b c*1682; *d* Paris, 17 Jan 1738). French composer. He was an organist in Paris from 1704, from 1721 at the royal chapel. The most celebrated French harpsichord composer of the 18th-century after F. Couperin and Rameau, he published six harpsichord collections, *c*1704–1734. They include many character pieces. Several pieces in the later books are revisions of early works, written in a simpler, more modern style akin to Couperin's. The book of organ noëls (?1721–33) is based on music by his uncle Pierre (*d* 1733), who may also have written some of the *airs*. Jean-François also wrote trio sonatas (1705), violin sonatas (?before 1710) and an organ collection (1739).

D'Anglebert, Jean-Henri (*b* Paris, 1635; *d* there, 23 April 1691). French composer and keyboard player. In 1662 he succeeded Chambonnières as harpsichordist to Louis XIV, a post he officially held until his death. His *Pièces de clavecin* (1689) contains four suites of dances (three beginning with unmeasured preludes) complemented by transcriptions of popular tunes, arrangements of works by Lully, and five organ fugues that show a firm grasp of contrapuntal techniques. The volume contains a comprehensive table of ornaments, with many new signs that passed into general usage, and ends with a short treatise on keyboard harmony.

Daniel, Francisco (Alberto Clemente) Salvador (*b* Bourges, 17 Feb 1831; *d* Paris, 24 May 1871). French scholar and composer of Spanish descent. He worked and travelled in Algeria, Tunisia, Morocco, Egypt, Spain and Portugal (1853–64), collecting Arab folktunes which he introduced to the European public through piano fantasies, orchestral arrangements, a *Messe africaine*, lectures and writings. But his revolutionary political activities in Paris cut short his musical influence and prevented publication of his large Arab song collection.

Daniel-Lesur [Lesur, Daniel Jean Yves] (*b* Paris, 19 Nov 1908). French composer. He studied at the Paris Conservatoire (1919–29) and taught at the Schola Cantorum (1935–64). His works, in a rich but austere modal style, include the opera *Andrea del Sarto* (1969), orchestral pieces, cantatas, songs and piano music. In 1936 he was a founder-member of the group La Jeune France.

Danish Royal Orchestra [Kongelige Kapel]. The leading symphony orchestra in Denmark, founded during the reign of Frederick II (1559–88), it has had an international reputation since the 18th century; its home is the Royal Theatre, Copenhagen.

Dankworth, John [Johnny] **(Philip William)** (*b* London, 20 Sept 1927). English jazz musician. He studied at the RAM, went to the USA, and returned to become a leading figure of postwar modern jazz. He formed a group in 1950 and a large orchestra in 1953. His works include suites and other pieces for his own orchestra, an opera-ballet, combining jazz and symphonic music, and film scores. He has toured widely with the singer Cleo Laine (*b* 1927), whom he married in 1960.

Dannreuther, Edward (George) (*b* Strasbourg, 4 Nov 1844; *d* Hastings, 12 Feb 1905). English pianist and writer of German origin. He studied in Leipzig with Moscheles, Hauptmann and Richter, making his English début in 1863 with the first complete English performance of Chopin's F minor Piano Concerto (he later introduced to England concertos by Grieg, Liszt and Tchaikovsky). He became a prominent figure in London musical life, teaching at the RAM, contributing to early editions of *Grove*, writing on Romantic music for the *Oxford History of Music* and publishing a treatise on ornamentation (1893–5). He is also remembered for his role in founding the Wagner Society, his translations of Wagner's prose and his book on Wagner's operatic reform (1873).

Dannström, (Johan) Isidor (*b* Stockholm, 15 Dec 1812; *d* there, 17 Oct 1897). Swedish singer, teacher and composer. A colleague of Jenny Lind, he was noted for his Don Giovanni at the Stockholm Opera in the early 1840s and as a singing teacher and author of the important *Sång-method* (1849). Among his compositions, all vocal, the 'polskas' and the comic duet *Duellanterna* are best known.

Danon, Oskar (*b* Sarajevo, 7 Feb 1913). Yugoslav conductor and composer. He studied at the Prague Conservatory and conducted in Sarajevo from 1938. He became director of Belgrade Opera (1945) and took the company to Lausanne and Paris (1958). A visit to Edinburgh in 1962 and recordings of Borodin's *Prince Igor* and Glinka's *A Life for the Tsar* were important in re-establishing Slavonic opera in the West after World War II.

Danse macabre. Symphonic poem, op.40, by Saint-Saëns (1874) after a poem by Henri Cazalis. Liszt transcribed it for piano (1877). *See also* TOTENTANZ.

Dante Alighieri (*b* Florence, May–June 1265; *d* Ravenna, 14 Sept 1321). Italian poet. In the 1280s he led the development of a new style of vernacular poetry; this culminated in his *Divine Comedy*. Also a philosopher and politician, he became one of the six Priors of the Florentine republic in 1300, but was exiled soon after. No contemporary settings of his poems survive; a few 16th-century madrigalists set them (e.g. Luzzaschi, Marenzio) but it was not until the Romantic period that composers were inspired by his poetry, particularly by the Francesca da Rimini episode (Rossini, Donizetti, Verdi, Liszt).

Dante Sonata. Piano piece by Liszt, the seventh in Book 2 of the *Années de pèlerinage* (1837–49); its full title is *Après une lecture du Dante, fantasia quasi sonata*.

Dante Symphony. Orchestral work by Liszt (1857); its full title is *Eine Symphonie zu Dantes Divina Commedia*.

Danyel, John (*b* Wellow, bap. 6 Nov 1564; *d c*1626). English composer. He graduated BMus at Oxford (1603) and was a musician of the royal household from at least 1612 to 1625; he also directed plays in Bristol (1615) and at Blackfriars (1618). His single volume of lute-songs (1606) is well known.

Danzi, Franz (Ignaz) (*b* Schwetzingen, 15 June 1763; *d* Karlsruhe, 13 April 1826). German composer. Like his father Innocenz (*c*1730–98), he was a cellist in the Mannheim court orchestra. When the court moved to Munich in 1778 he stayed in Mannheim, playing at the National Theatre (for which he wrote his first stage works). In 1783 he joined the orchestra in Munich, where his Singspiel *Die Mitternachtsstunde* (1798) was popular; after touring Europe, he returned as deputy Kapellmeister (1798–1800). As Kapellmeister at Stuttgart, 1807–12, he was a close friend of Weber's; he was next Kapellmeister at Karlsruhe, and composed stage works for both courts.

Danzi wrote some 25 stage works, including Singspiels, incidental music, melodramas and a grand opera; he also wrote sacred music, songs, symphonies, concertos and numerous chamber works, notably wind quintets. Cantabile melodies, bold harmonies, chromatic inner parts and imaginative scoring characterize his style.

Daphne. Opera in one act by Richard Strauss to a libretto by Gregor (1938, Dresden).

Daphnis et Chloé. Ballet in three scenes by Ravel (1912, Paris).

Da Ponte, Lorenzo [Conegliano, Emmanuele] (*b* Vittorio Veneto, 10 March 1749; *d* New York, 17 Aug 1838). Italian librettist. He was first a professor and priest (he was a converted Jew) in Italy; after being banned from Venice in 1779 he went to Vienna, where he became librettist to the Italian theatre. His most notable librettos were for Mozart: *Le nozze di Figaro* (1786), *Don Giovanni* (1787) and *Così fan tutte* (1790); he also wrote for Salieri, Martín y Soler and others. In the 1790s he was librettist at the King's Theatre, London. He later emigrated to the USA (by 1805) and worked mainly as a teacher of Italian (ultimately at Columbia University); in 1823 he published his memoirs, which are racy, self-justificatory and unreliable. Most of his *c*50 librettos, many of them adaptations of other writers' works, are comic.

Daquin, Louis-Claude (*b* Paris, 4 July 1694; *d* there, 15 June 1772). French organist and composer. The finest player of his generation, he held organist's posts in Paris from the age of 12; in 1739 he became *organiste du roi*, and later he worked at Notre Dame. He composed four harpsichord suites (1735), including descriptive pieces such as 'Le coucou', and a book of noëls for keyboard or other instruments.

Darabukka. A goblet-shaped drum of the Arab countries; it is made from pottery, wood or metal, on to which a skin head is nailed or glued. Similar types of drum are found in Iran, Turkey and south-eastern Europe.

Dardanus. *Tragédie en musique* in a prologue and five acts by Rameau to a libretto by La Bruère (1739, Paris).

Dargomïzhsky, Alexander Sergeyevich (*b* Troitskoye, 14 Feb 1813; *d* St Petersburg, 17 Jan 1869). Russian composer. With Glinka, he established a tradition of national opera based on folksong and a concern for dramatic truth, and in his songs, ranging from expressive lyrical romances to powerful dramatic ballads, he made an important contribution to the repertory. Born into a wealthy aristocratic family that settled in St Petersburg in 1817, he received music lessons but chose government service for his career. An acquaintance with Glinka (1833–4) prompted him to compose his first opera, *Esmeralda* (1841), while he became a noted singing teacher and began writing songs. Resigning his official post in 1843, he travelled abroad and from 1845 experimented in his songs with characteristic Russian speech patterns, striving for direct expression of texts on everyday subjects through a declamatory vocal line and simple chordal accompaniment. The operas *Rusalka* (1855), with its colourful folk setting, and above all *The Stone Guest* (1866–9; completed by Cui and Rimsky-Korsakov, 1870) were the culmination of his quest for truthful musical expression of emotions. Although the latter has never been popular, even in Russia, it has been seen as a strong influence on Russian nationalist composers, particularly Musorgsky, and is the work by which Dargomïzhsky is chiefly known. His orchestral works, the folksong-based fantasies *Baba-Yaga* (1862) and *Kazachok* (1864), and the *Finnish Fantasy* (1863–7), are effective 'curtain-raisers' in the tradition of Glinka.

Darke, Harold (Edwin) (*b* London, 29 Oct 1888; *d* Cambridge, 28 Nov 1976). English organist. He studied with Parratt and Stanford at the RCM and was organist of St Michael's, Cornhill, London, for 50 years from 1916; he taught at the RCM for 50 years from 1919. He was a greatly admired organist in the central English tradition and composed a number of organ and choral works, carol settings etc.

Darmstadt, Internationales Musikinstitut. Information centre for contemporary music in Darmstadt, founded by Wolfgang Steinecke in 1946

(renamed 1949, 1963); summer courses in new music were instituted there in the same year and held annually to 1970 (then biennially). Many notable avant-garde composers have taught at them, including Messiaen, Stockhausen, Boulez, Nono, Berio and Pousseur. In the 1950s it attracted composers from all over the world, among them Cage, and has presented many important premières. Proceedings of the courses are published annually as *Darmstädter Beiträge zur Neuen Musik* (1958–).

Dart, (Robert) Thurston (*b* Kingston, Surrey, 3 Sept 1921; *d* London, 6 March 1971). English musicologist and performer. He was a chorister at the Chapel Royal and studied at the RCM and with van den Borren. In 1947 he was appointed to teach at Cambridge, where he was professor (1962–4) before leaving to found a music faculty at King's College, London. He also had a career as a harpsichordist. As a scholar, he worked mainly on keyboard and consort music of the 16th and 17th centuries and on Bull and Bach; but his adventurous mind was drawn to many other areas and he did perceptive work in source studies. He was a dynamic teacher and professor. Though a prolific writer, he wrote only one book, the modest but influential *The Interpretation of Music* (1954).

Dartington Summer School. Annual event (August) founded in 1948 at Bryanston School, Dorset; it moved to Dartington Hall, Devon, in 1953. It combines a summer school and concert festival, with coaching and performances by international and British musicians. The Dartington Quartet was formed originally (1958) for the summer school.

Darwish, Sayed [Sayyid] (*b* Alexandria, 17 March 1892; *d* there, 15 Sept 1923). Egyptian composer. The most popular figure in Egyptian music, he achieved fame as a singer-composer and wrote 26 immensely successful operettas.

Daser, Ludwig (*b* Munich, *c*1525; *d* Stuttgart, 27 March 1589). German composer. A member of the Munich Hofkapelle, he was Kapellmeister there (1552–63) and at the Stuttgart court (from 1572). An able composer with a lyrical gift, he wrote at least 22 masses, 24 motets, 34 German psalms and hymns and many other sacred works (all MS); a Passion setting was published in 1578.

Dash. A vertical dash placed above or below a note or chord indicates a reduced duration of the sound; the note is to be played staccato. The dash (or wedge) is now taken to represent a sharper, shorter staccato than the normal dot, though in 18th-century music it rather implied accentuation. A dash placed horizontally above a note indicates that the note is to be sustained to its full length (*tenuto*); used in a figured bass, it indicates the continuation of the preceding harmony (*see* CONTINUO).

Daughter of the Regiment, The. *See* FILLE DU RÉGIMENT, LA.

Dauprat, Louis François (*b* Paris, 24 May 1781; *d* there, 17 July 1868). French horn player, teacher and composer. He had considerable success as a soloist and orchestral player, was a remarkable teacher (his *Méthode pour cor alto et cor basse* is unsurpassed) and published five horn concertos.

Dauvergne, Antoine (*b* Moulins, 3 Oct 1713; *d* Lyons, 11 Feb 1797). French composer. He held court posts as a violinist and from 1744 also played at the Opéra, where he later presented his own works. But his greatest success, *Les troqueurs* (1753), was presented at a fair theatre: it was the first thoroughly French comic opera constructed on Italian models. He was a director of the Concert Spirituel from 1762 and from 1769 of the Opéra, where he tried unsuccessfully to discourage Gluck. Besides 18 stage works, he wrote Italianate violin sonatas (1739), *Concerts de simphonies* (1751), motets and other works.

Davaux, Jean-Baptiste (*b* La Côte-St André, 19 July 1742; *d* Paris, 2 Feb 1822). French composer. A composer and violinist in Paris from *c*1767, he held various government posts. He had two comic operas staged (1785) but was best known for his instrumental music, especially his 13 *symphonies concertantes* (*c*1772–1800). He also wrote 25 string quartets, other chamber works, symphonies, violin concertos and *ariettes*, in a simple, tuneful style. He invented a *chronomètre*, by 1784 – well before Maelzel's metronome.

Davenant, William (*b* Oxford, bap. 3 March 1606; *d* London, 7 April 1668). English dramatist, theatre manager and poet. He wrote the libretto of the first all-sung English opera with a unified heroic subject, *The Siege of Rhodes* (1656; music lost), and influenced the subsequent development of English opera through his use of incidental music in plays produced at the Duke's Theatre, London, particularly through his adaptations of Shakespeare's *Macbeth* (1663) and *Tempest* (with Dryden, 1667), using spectacular musical scenes.

Davico, Vincenzo (*b* Monaco, 14 Jan 1889; *d* Rome, 8 Dec 1969). Italian composer. He studied in Turin and with Reger in Leipzig, then lived mostly in Paris (1918–40), where Debussian tendencies in his music were reinforced, before returning to work for Italian radio. He is best remembered for his over 200 songs.

David, Félicien(-César) (*b* Cadenet, 13 April 1810; *d* St Germain-en-Laye, 29 Aug 1876). French composer. He may be regarded as second only to Berlioz among French composers of his time. He studied at the Paris Conservatoire. In 1831 he joined the Saint-Simonians and began composing choruses for their ceremonials; when the cult was disbanded (1832) he went to the orient to preach their gospel, finding a powerful source of musical inspiration in the customs and landscape of Egypt, where for nearly two years he gave music lessons, composed songs and piano pieces and explored the desert. This experience resulted in a series of successful descriptive works on exotic themes, from the novel *ode-symphonies* (*Le désert*, 1844; *Christophe Colomb*, 1847) to his masterpiece, *Lalla-Roukh* (1862), an *opéra comique* evoking Kashmir. Neither strictly oriental in inflection nor harmonically imaginative, much of his music won popularity for its tunefulness and its atmospheric orchestration (admired by Berlioz), and it influenced generations of later French composers, including Gounod, Saint-Saëns and Delibes.

David, Ferdinand (*b* Hamburg, 19 June 1810; *d* Klosters, 18 July 1873). German violinist, composer and teacher. He studied with Spohr and Hauptmann, eventually becoming leader of the Leipzig Gewandhaus orchestra under his friend Mendelssohn (1836) and head of the violin department at the Leipzig Conservatory (1843), where his pupils included Joachim and Wasielewski. Known for his intelligent musicianship, full tone and solid technique, he gave the première of Mendelssohn's Violin Concerto (1845), later dedicated to him. Besides writing five concertos, other works for solo violin and orchestra, chamber music and songs, he edited violin studies, concertos and chamber works by other composers and published a widely used *Violinschule* (1863).

Dávid, Gyula (*b* Budapest, 6 May 1913; *d* there, 14 March 1977). Hungarian composer. He studied with Kodály at the Budapest Academy, where he taught from 1950. His works move from folksong influence (as in the Viola Concerto, 1950, two wind quintets and two choral-orchestral cycles) to increased chromaticism, 12-note writing and greater concision (as in his unaccompanied choral works of the early 1960s and the Symphony no.3, 1960).

David, Johann Nepomuk (*b* Eferding, 30 Nov 1895; *d* Stuttgart, 22 Dec 1977). Austrian composer. He studied at St Florian, near Linz, and with Marx at the Vienna Academy (1920–23), then worked in Wels as a school teacher, organist and choirmaster (1924–34) before teaching at conservatories in Leipzig (1934–45), Salzburg (1945–8) and Stuttgart (1948–63). His early music is mostly lost or destroyed; that from 1927 to 1957 has connections with Hindemith in its contrapuntal energy, with Distler and Pepping in its renewal of Lutheran traditions (of organ and choral composition) and with Reger. His *Das Choralwerk*, 21 volumes of organ music (1932–74), is a compendium of polyphonic practice and organ technique from Reger onwards. He also wrote eight symphonies (1936–65) and two violin concertos (1952, 1957). His later works incorporate serial and more modern elements, sometimes derived from Dürer and Goethe. He achieved a masterly, distinctive blending of traditional and modern music thinking. His son Thomas Christian (*b* 1925) has composed concertos, church and chamber music.

Davidde penitente. Oratorio by Mozart, K469, to a text possibly by Da Ponte (1785); the music is largely drawn from his unfinished C minor Mass K427/417a.

Davïdov, Karl Yul'yevich (*b* Kuldiga, 15 March 1838; *d* Moscow, 26 Feb 1889). Russian cellist, composer and administrator. He studied with Hauptmann and Moscheles in Leipzig, where he worked from 1858 as a cellist and teacher, returning to Russia in 1862 as professor, later director, of the St Petersburg Conservatory; a superb soloist and chamber musician, he wrote four cello concertos.

Davïdov, Stepan Ivanovich (*b* 1777; *d* St Petersburg, 22 May 1825). Russian composer. He studied in St Petersburg. He is remembered principally for his contributions (parts 3 and 4, 1805,

1807) to a Russian adaptation of Kauer's highly successful Singspiel *Das Donauweibchen*, in which he made substantial use of Russian folk melodies. Besides ballets and other stage works, he composed church music.

Davidovsky, Mario (*b* Buenos Aires, 4 March 1934). American composer of Argentinian origin. He studied in Buenos Aires and moved to the USA in 1960, since when he has taught at various institutions, including the City University of New York (1968–80) and Columbia University (from 1981), where he directs the Columbia-Princeton Electronic Music Center. His works include chamber pieces and the *Synchronism* series of eight dialogues for live resources and tape (1963–74).

Davidsbündlertänze. Schumann's op.6 for piano, 18 character-pieces (1837).

Davies, Cecilia (*b* ?1756; *d* London, 3 July 1836). English soprano. She and her sister Marianne (1743/4–*c*1818) were gifted performers, from a very early age, notably on the glass harmonica. The two appeared in Ireland in 1763, then in London and on the Continent where they met the Mozart family, and Cecilia studied with Hasse in Vienna. Cecilia sang in Italy and England in the 1770s but their careers faded in the 1780s.

Davies, Fanny (*b* Guernsey, 27 June 1861; *d* London, 1 Sept 1934). English pianist. She studied at the Leipzig Conservatory and with Clara Schumann. After her London début (1885) she was often heard as a chamber musician, appearing with Casals, Joachim and the Bohemian String Quartet. Admired for her selfless dedication, she introduced works by Brahms and Debussy to Britain.

Davies, Hugh (Seymour) (*b* Exmouth, 23 April 1943). English composer. He studied at Oxford (1961–4) and was Stockhausen's assistant in Cologne (1964–6). His works include many for specially devised instruments and electronic resources.

Davies, (Albert) Meredith (*b* Birkenhead, 30 July 1922). English conductor. He studied at Oxford and was organist at St Albans (1947) and Hereford (1949) cathedrals. He studied conducting in Rome, 1954–6, and was organist of New College to 1960. Since then he has pursued a conducting career, in Birmingham, with the English Opera Group (1963–5), in Vancouver (1964–71) and elsewhere; he has achieved distinction as an interpreter of 20th-century British music (especially that of Britten, with whom he worked) and choral music generally.

Davies, Sir Peter Maxwell (*b* Manchester, 8 Sept 1934). English composer. He studied at the Royal Manchester College of Music (1952–6); his fellow students included Goehr and Birtwistle. They studied the music of Boulez, Nono and Stockhausen which, together with early English music, provided him with the roots of a style (Trumpet Sonata, 1955). He then studied with Petrassi in Rome (1957–9) and extended his range to orchestral works (*St Michael* for 17 wind, 1957; *Prolation*, 1958). But a period of teaching at Cirencester Grammar School (1959–62) encouraged him to reconsider not only school music (drawing out children's creative potential) but also his own: he began to write in a

more expressively focussed, dramatic way and to recover aspects of symphonic largeness, particularly as he found them in Mahler (second In Nomine Fantasia for orchestra, 1964). Much work was done at the universities of Princeton (1962–4) and Adelaide (1966).

Back in England, Davies and Birtwistle formed the Pierrot Players in 1967 (re-formed as the Fires of London, 1970) and Davies began a sequence of music-theatre pieces for them (*Eight Songs for a Mad King* and *Vesalii icones*, both 1969). These exploited a fiercely expressionist style that came out of *Pierrot lunaire* and from work on his opera *Taverner* (1967), concerning the war between creed and creativity in the mind of the Tudor composer. Another symptom of disintegration was his use of foxtrots in works of desperate seriousness (*St Thomas Wake* for orchestra, 1969), though at the same time he was working, in the big orchestral movement *Worldes Blis* (1969), towards a more integrated style.

Since 1970 he has pursued that style, with occasional expressionist throwbacks, while living remotely in Orkney, where in 1977 he founded the St Magnus Festival; there many of his works have been introduced, often reflecting on the landscapes, legend and literature of the islands (e.g. the opera *The Martyrdom of St Magnus*, 1977, children's operas, choral pieces). At the same time he has been writing large-scale symphonic works (three symphonies, 1976, 1980, 1983; Violin Concerto, 1985).

Operas Taverner (1972); The Martyrdom of St Magnus (1977); The Lighthouse (1980)
Children's operas The Two Fiddlers (1978); Cinderella (1980); The Rainbow (1981)
Ballets Nocturnal Dances (1970); Salome (1978)
Music-theatre Revelation and Fall (1968); L'homme armé (1968); Eight Songs for a Mad King (1969); Vesalii icones (1969); Blind Man's Buff (1972); Miss Donnithorne's Maggot (1974); Le jongleur de Notre Dame (1978); The Medium (1981); The no.11 Bus (1983)
Choral music Five Motets (1959); O magnum mysterium (1960); Veni Sancte Spiritus (1963); Westerlings (1976); Solstice of Light (1979)
Other vocal music Leopardi Fragments (1961); From Stone to Thorn (1971); Hymn to St Magnus (1972); Stone Litany (1973); Dark Angels (1973); Fiddlers at the Wedding (1974); The Blind Fiddler (1976); Into the Labyrinth (1983)
Orchestral music St Michael (1957); Prolation (1958); Sinfonia (1962); 2 In Nomine fantasias (1962, 1964); Worldes Blis (1969); St Thomas Wake (1969); 3 symphonies (1976, 1980, 1983); A Mirror of Whitening Light (1977); Sinfonia concertante (1982); Sinfonietta accademica (1983); Vn Conc. (1985)
Chamber music Alma Redemptoris mater (1957); Str Qt (1961); Shakespeare Music (1964); Antechrist (1967); Stedman Caters (1968); Eram quasi agnus (1969); Psalm cxxiv (1974); Ave maris stella (1975); Brass Qnt (1981); Image, Reflection, Shadow (1982); many arrs.
Instrumental music Hymnos, cl, pf (1967); Pf Sonata (1981); Org Sonata (1982)
Incidental music, film music

Davies, Sir (Henry) Walford (*b* Oswestry, 6 Sept 1869; *d* Wrington, 11 March 1941). English composer. He studied with Parry and Stanford at the RCM, where he joined the staff in 1895, also working as a conductor, organist (of St George's Chapel, Windsor, 1927–32) and, later, broadcaster. His works include church music. In 1934 he became Master of the King's Music.

Davis, Andrew (Frank) (*b* Ashbridge, 2 Feb 1944). English conductor. He was an organ scholar at King's College, Cambridge, and studied with Franco Ferrara in Rome. He first conducted the BBC SO in 1970 and was associate conductor of the NPO from 1973; he gave Strauss's *Capriccio* at Glyndebourne the same year. In 1975 he was appointed musical director of the Toronto SO.

Davis, Sir Colin (Rex) (*b* Weybridge, 25 Sept 1927). English conductor. He studied the clarinet at the RCM and gave Mozart performances with the Chelsea Opera Group in the early 1950s. He received wide acclaim for a London concert performance of *Don Giovanni* in 1959, and until 1965 was musical director of Sadler's Wells Opera. He conducted *Peter Grimes* at the Met in 1967 and that year became principal conductor of the BBC SO; his enthusiastic advocacy of Mozart, Berlioz, Stravinsky and Tippett won him a youthful following. He was musical director at Covent Garden, 1971–86. Davis has conducted the Boston SO from 1972 and the Bavarian RSO from 1981.

Davis, Miles (Dewey) III (*b* Alton, IL, 25 May 1926). American jazz trumpeter and bandleader. He played with Charlie Parker in the late 1940s and formed his first quintet in 1955. In 1957 he began making orchestral recordings with Gil Evans, with whom he had collaborated in 1949 on a series known as *Birth of the Cool*; his playing was marked by its lyricism. Davis's quintets with conventional jazz instrumentation and such players as John Coltrane, Sonny Rollins, Bill Evans and Ron Carter gave way in the late 1960s and early 1970s to a fusion with rock instruments and playing styles, and in the 1980s he performed on the synthesizer.

Davison, J(ames) W(illiam) (*b* London, 5 Oct 1813; *d* Margate, 24 March 1885). English critic. He had aspirations as a composer but turned to writing in the late 1830s, becoming editor of the *Musical World* (1843–85) and the influential music critic of *The Times* (1846–79). Though an early champion of Chopin in England, he was from 1850 increasingly conservative in his tastes.

Davy, Richard (*b c*1465; *d* ?Exeter, *c*1507). English composer. A scholar of Magdalen College, Oxford, from *c*1483, he became a choirmaster and organist there (1490–91) and was a vicar-choral at Exeter Cathedral (1497–1506). He was one of the most accomplished late 15th-century composers. His works include a four-part St Matthew Passion (in which, usually, the solo parts other than those of Christ and the Evangelist as well as the choruses are set to polyphony) and seven antiphons and a Magnificat in the Eton Choirbook.

Dawson, Peter (*b* Adelaide, 31 Jan 1882; *d* Harbord, 27 Sept 1961). Australian baritone. He studied in Glasgow and under Santley in London. He was best known as a ballad singer, making his first recording in 1904 and singing at ballad concerts; he made his Covent Garden début in 1909. He had several pseudonyms, recording Scottish songs as Hector Grant and composing as J.P. McCall.

Day, Alfred (*b* London, Jan 1810; *d* there, 11 Feb 1849). English theorist. Encouraged by his friend, the composer G.A. Macfarren, he produced a controversial *Treatise on Harmony* (1845, 2/1885) explaining all chords in a key as products of three fundamental combinations; his ideas greatly influenced later musical pedagogy in England through the writings of Macfarren, Ouseley and Prout.

De Amicis, Anna Lucia (*b* Naples, *c*1733; *d* there, 1816). Italian soprano. She sang in comic operas in Italy from *c*1754, and appeared in 1762 in London; she turned to serious singing in 1763, in an opera by J.C. Bach, and appeared as prima donna in Italy in the mid-1760s. After marriage, she resumed her career with further successes in Italy, 1768–78, notably in music by Jommelli, Mozart (*Lucio Silla*, 1772, Milan) and Gluck (*Alceste*, 1778, Bologna). She was remarkable for her vocal agility, her very high compass and her powerful characterization.

Dean, Winton (Basil) (*b* Birkenhead, 18 March 1916). English writer on music. At Cambridge he saw some of the Handel oratorio stagings of the 1930s, which implanted a deep feeling for Handel as a dramatic composer. His first book was a study of Bizet (1948), notable for its penetrating discussion of the composer as musical dramatist. He became a regular contributor of articles and reviews to periodicals and published on early 19th-century French and Italian opera. But his most important work lies in his Handel books, on the oratorio (1959) and the operas (1969; with J.M. Knapp, 1987), where he re-examined the background, sources and Handel's nature as a musical dramatist.

Death and the Maiden. Song by Schubert (*Tod und das Mädchen*), D53, 1817, a setting for voice and piano of words by Claudius. Schubert used its theme for variations in the second movement of his String Quartet in D minor D810 (1824), which is known by the song's title.

Death and Transfiguration. *See* TOD UND VERKLÄRUNG.

Death in Venice. Opera in two acts by Britten to a libretto by Myfanwy Piper after Thomas Mann (1973, Aldeburgh).

Deborah. Oratorio by Handel to a biblical text compiled by S. Humphreys (1733, London).

Debussy, (Achille-)Claude (*b* St Germain-en-Laye, 22 Aug 1862; *d* Paris, 25 March 1918). French composer. He studied with Guiraud and others at the Paris Conservatoire (1872–84) and as prizewinner went to Rome (1885–7), though more important impressions came from his visits to Bayreuth (1888, 1889) and from hearing Javanese music in Paris (1889). Wagner's influence is evident in the cantata *La damoiselle élue* (1888) and the *Cinq poèmes de Baudelaire* (1889) but other songs of the period, notably the settings of Verlaine (*Ariettes oubliées, Trois mélodies, Fêtes galantes*, set 1) are in a more capricious style, as are parts of the still somewhat Franckian G minor String Quartet (1893); in that work he used not only the Phrygian mode but also less standard modes, notably the whole-tone mode, to create the floating harmony he discovered through the work of contemporary writers: Mallarmé in the orchestral *Prélude à 'L'après-midi d'un faune'* (1894) and Maeterlinck in the opera *Pelléas et Mélisande*, dating in large part from 1893–5 but not completed until 1902. These works also brought forward a fluidity of rhythm and colour quite new to Western music.

Pelléas, with its rule of understatement and deceptively simple declamation, also brought an entirely new tone to opera – but an unrepeatable one. Debussy worked on other opera projects and left substantial sketches for two pieces after tales by Poe (*Le diable dans le beffroi* and *La chûte de la maison Usher*), but nothing was completed. Instead the main works were orchestral pieces, piano sets and songs.

The orchestral works include the three *Nocturnes* (1899), characteristic studies of veiled harmony and texture ('Nuages'), exuberant cross-cutting ('Fêtes') and seductive whole-tone drift ('Sirènes'). *La mer* (1905) essays a more symphonic form, with a finale that works themes from the first movement, though the centrepiece ('Jeux de vagues') proceeds much less directly and with more variety of colour. The three *Images* (1912) are more loosely linked, and the biggest, 'Ibéria', is itself a triptych, a medley of Spanish allusions. Finally the ballet *Jeux* (1913) contains some of Debussy's strangest harmony and texture in a form that moves freely over its own field of motivic connection. Other late stage works, including the ballets *Khamma* (1912) and *La boîte à joujoux* (1913) and the mystery play *Le martyre de St Sébastien* (1911), were not completely orchestrated by Debussy, though *St Sébastien* is remarkable in sustaining an antique modal atmosphere that otherwise was touched only in relatively short piano pieces (e.g. 'La cathédrale engloutie').

The important piano music begins with works which, Verlaine fashion, look back at rococo decorousness with a modern cynicism and puzzlement (*Suite bergamasque*, 1890; *Pour le piano*, 1901). But then, as in the orchestral pieces, Debussy began to associate his music with visual impressions of the East, Spain, landscapes etc, in a sequence of sets of short pieces. His last volume of *Etudes* (1915) interprets similar varieties of style and texture purely as pianistic exercises and includes pieces that develop irregular form to an extreme as well as others influenced by the young Stravinsky (a presence too in the suite *En blanc et noir* for two pianos, 1915). The rarefaction of these works is a feature of the last set of songs, the *Trois poèmes de Mallarmé* (1913), and of the Sonata for flute, viola and harp (1915), though the sonata and its companions also recapture the inquisitive Verlainian classicism. The planned set of six sonatas was cut short by the composer's death from rectal cancer.

Operas Rodrigue et Chimène (1892); Pelléas et Mélisande (1902)
Cantatas Diane au bois (1886); L'enfant prodigue (1884); La damoiselle élue (1888)
Play with music Le martyre de St Sébastien (1911)
Orchestral music, ballets Printemps (1887); Fantaisie for piano and orchestra (1890); Prélude à 'L'après-midi d'un faune' (1894); Nocturnes (1899); La mer (1905); Danse sacrée et danse profane (1904); Khamma (1912); Images

(1912); La boîte à joujoux (1913); Jeux (1913)
Chamber music Str Qt (1893); Syrinx, fl (1913); Vc Sonata (1915); Sonata, fl, va, harp (1915); Vn Sonata (1917)
Piano music Suite bergamasque (1890); Pour le piano (1901); D'un cahier d'esquisses (1903); Estampes (1903); L'isle joyeuse (1904); Masques (1904); Images (1905, 1907); Préludes (1909–10, 1912–13); Six épigraphes antiques, 2/4 hands (1914); Études (1915); En blanc et noir, 2 pf (1915)
Songs Ariettes oubliées (1888); Cinq poèmes de Baudelaire (1889); Trois mélodies (1891); Fêtes galantes (1891, 1904); Proses lyriques (1893); Chansons de Bilitis (1898); Trois ballades de Villon (1910); Trois poèmes de Mallarmé (1913)

Decani, cantoris. The two halves of the choir in an English church: *decani* (the dean's side) is the south, *cantoris* (the cantor's side) the north. Traditionally, the *decani* singers took the leading part one week, the *cantoris* the next; or alternation might be daily during the festival seasons. Some items were sung in alternation between the two groups.

Deceptive cadence [false cadence; interrupted cadence]. A CADENCE in which the dominant chord resolves not on to the expected tonic but on to some other chord, usually the submediant (V–VI).

Decibel (dB). A unit used for expressing the difference in level between sounds of different intensities; as it is a logarithmic unit, it corresponds well to the listener's experience of volume.

Decius, Nikolaus (*b* Hof an der Saale, *c*1485; *d* after 1546). German Kantor and composer. His three evangelical hymns, settings of German versions of the Gloria, Sanctus and Agnus Dei based on Gregorian chants, are probably the earliest in existence.

Declamation. The relation between verbal stress and melodic accent in the setting and delivery of a text. It covers such matters as the relationship between speech rhythms and musical ones and was central to French ideas on singing.

Decoration Day. Orchestral work by Ives (1912) which became the second movement of *Holidays*.

Dedekind, Constantin Christian (*b* Reinsdorf, 2 April 1628; *d* Dresden, 2 Sept 1715). German composer and poet. He studied under Bernhard in Dresden, becoming a bass at the Dresden court chapel (1654) and director of the court orchestra (1666–75). His most important work is the *Aelbianische Musen-Lust* (1657), containing 146 sacred and secular solo songs with continuo. The sacred concertos for two voices and bass of his *Musicalischer Jahrgang* (1673–4) are examples of the German sacred cantata, with recitatives, ariosos and da capo arias. He was also a distinguished violinist.

Dedekind, Henning (*b* Neustadt am Rübenberge, 30 Dec 1562; *d* Gebesee, 28 July 1626). German theorist. A Kantor at Langensalza (1586–1615) and Gebesee (1615–26), he published two theoretical music primers (1589, 1590). A few three-part songs by him appeared in an anthology (1588). His brother Euricius (1554–1619), a composer, was a Kantor in Lüneburg.

Deering, Richard. *See* DERING, RICHARD.

De Fabritiis, Oliviero (Carlo) (*b* Rome, 13 June 1902; *d* there, 12 Aug 1982). Italian conductor and composer. After study in Rome he made his début there in 1920; from 1932 to 1943 he conducted at the Teatro dell'Opera and from 1938 often worked with

Beniamino Gigli. He visited Edinburgh with the Naples San Carlo company in 1963 and gave *Simon Boccanegra* at Covent Garden in 1965. He directed the premières of operas by Mascagni and Pizzetti.

De Fesch [Defesch], **Willem** (*b* Alkmaar, 1687; *d* London, 3 Jan 1761). Netherlands composer and violinist. He was a violinist in Amsterdam from 1710, and was *kapelmeester* at Antwerp Cathedral 1725–31. He later moved to London where he was a frequent soloist and directed the orchestra at Marylebone Gardens. An accomplished composer, he wrote 17 sets of sonatas and duets etc, 1716–*c*1750; they are Vivaldian in style and show a move from a virtuoso idiom to a simpler, more expressive one. His English vocal works include songs and oratorios.

DeGaetani, Jan (*b* Massillon, Ohio, 10 July 1933). American mezzo-soprano. She studied at the Juilliard School and from 1958 specialized in the avantgarde repertory; her impressive technique and powerfully expressive voice have been heard in many first performances, including Crumb's *Ancient Voices of Children* (1970). She also sings medieval music and Baroque cantatas.

Degen, Johann (*b* Weismain, *c*1585; *d* Bamberg, 29 Aug 1637). German composer. Organist of St Martin, Bamberg, from 1615, he published the first German Catholic hymnbook (1628), with 132 German and 26 Latin hymns with 96 tunes, most of which he harmonized. He also edited a collection (1631) of 53 Latin motets which are parodies of secular madrigals and concertos.

De Giosa, Nicola (*b* Bari, 3 May 1819; *d* there, 7 July 1885). Italian composer and conductor. He studied at the Naples Conservatory, where his teachers included Donizetti. He was a prolific song composer and in the 1860s and 1870s an admired conductor, but he is best remembered for his Neapolitan comic operas, especially *Don Checco* (1850).

De Grandis, Vincenzo (*b* Ostra, 6 April 1631; *d* there, 4 Aug 1708). Italian composer. He held various posts as *maestro di cappella*, notably at the ducal courts of Hanover (1674–80) and Modena (1682–3) and at Santa Casa, Loreto (1685–92). His three surviving oratorios (1682–9) contain stylistic features unusual for their period: all use accompanied and motto arias, and two include accompanied recitative – an early use of this form.

Degli Antoni, Pietro (*b* Bologna, 16 May 1639 ; *d* there, 1720). Italian composer. At first a cornettist at S Petronio, he became *maestro di cappella* of three Bolognese churches; he wrote sacred music, including an oratorio *L'innocenza depressa*, but was most important for his contribution to the development of the church and chamber sonatas, the most innovatory compositions being the sonatas for violin and continuo, opp.4 and 5 (1676, 1686). His brother Giovanni Battista (1636–after 1696), an organist in Bologna, wrote a set of *Ricercate* op.1 for solo cello, a forerunner of Bach's solo suites.

Degree. The position of a note in a diatonic scale. The first degree is the tonic, the second the supertonic, the third the mediant, the fourth the subdominant, the fifth the dominant, the sixth the submediant, and the seventh the leading note.

Degtyaryov, Stepan Anikiyevich (*b* Borisovka, 1766; *d* nr. Kursk, 5 May 1813). Russian composer and singer. He is remembered chiefly for his patriotic oratorio, *Minin i Pozharsky, ili Osvobozhdeniye Moskvii* (1811), the first written by a Russian.

Dehn, Siegfried (Wilhelm) (*b* Altona, 24 Feb 1799; *d* Berlin, 12 April 1858). German scholar and teacher. He was custodian of the royal music library in Berlin from 1842, the editor of *Cäcilia* (1842–8) and professor at the Royal Academy of the Arts from 1849, becoming widely respected as a theory teacher. He made a pioneering contribution to scholarship through his editions of Bach's instrumental music (notably the Brandenburg Concertos) and of Lassus's motets.

Deidamia. Opera in three acts by Handel to a libretto by Rolli (1741, London).

Deiters, Hermann (Clemens Otto) (*b* Bonn, 27 June 1833; *d* Koblenz, 11 May 1907). German writer on music. Besides his essays in the *Allgemeine musikalische Zeitung* (1865–82), he wrote on Brahms, whom he knew, including the first authoritative Brahms biography (1880). His most important work was the revision of Thayer's *Life of Beethoven* (1866–1908).

De Koven, (Henry Louis) Reginald (*b* Middletown, CT, 3 April 1859; *d* Chicago, 16 Jan 1920). American composer. He studied in Stuttgart, Oxford, Florence, Vienna and Paris, returning to the USA in 1882 and working as a music critic, notably in Chicago; he founded and conducted (1902–4) the Washington SO and composed, producing piano music, songs, two operas (at the end of his career) and 27 operettas (1887–1913), including *Robin Hood* (1890), in which he drew on 19th-century Italian opera and on folklike melody.

Delage, Maurice (Charles) (*b* Paris, 13 Nov 1879; *d* there, 21 Sept 1961). French composer. He came to music late and was helped by Ravel. His works are few and often of a refined exoticism; they include *Quatre poèmes hindous* for soprano and nonet (1913) and works based on Kipling.

Delalande, Michel Richard. *See* LALANDE, MICHEL RICHARD DE.

De Lamarter, Eric (*b* Lansing, MI, 18 Feb 1880; *d* Orlando, FL, 17 May 1953). American composer and organist. He studied in the Mid west and with Guilmant and Widor in Paris (1901–2); he later worked as a church musician, conductor and teacher in Chicago. His compositions, in a conservative style, include sacred choral and organ music and orchestral and chamber works.

Delannoy, Marcel (*b* La Ferté-Alain, 9 July 1898; *d* Nantes, 14 Sept 1962). French composer. He was encouraged by Honegger, and composed operas, notably *Le poirier de misère* (1927), ballets and two symphonies.

De Lara [Tilbury], (Lottie) Adelina (*b* Carlisle, 23 Jan 1872; *d* Woking, 25 Nov 1961). English pianist. She appeared as a child prodigy and studied with Clara Schumann, whose traditions of technique she maintained from her début in 1891.

De Latre, Petit Jean (*b c*1510; *d* Utrecht, 31 Aug 1569). Netherlands composer. A choirmaster in Liège and later Utrecht, he published a set of Lamentations (1554) and a volume of *chansons* (1555), and wrote other sacred and secular works (printed in anthologies). His motets are in a strict, imitative style expressing the atmosphere of the text rather than displaying technical skill; most of the *chansons* are restrained settings of classical love-songs.

Del Buono, Gioanpietro (*fl* Palermo, 1641). Italian composer. He worked in Sicily and published a book of *Canoni, oblighi et sonate* (1641), for three to eight voices, including 22 canons of different kinds, all on the *cantus firmus Ave maris stella*. His 14 harpsichord sonatas, the earliest examples of the genre, are interesting music; they are in effect self-contained partitas in Frescobaldi's style with a *cantus firmus* complete in long notes in every piece.

Delden, Lex van (*b* Amsterdam, 11 Sept 1919). Dutch composer. Self-taught, he has written symphonies, many concertos etc often in a tonal style, built from a concise idea imaginatively developed and varied. He is also active as administrator and critic.

Deldevez, Edouard [**Edme**] (**-Marie-Ernest**) (*b* Paris, 31 May 1817; *d* there, 6 Nov 1897). French conductor and composer. He studied with Reicha and Halévy at the Paris Conservatoire. He was associated with the Paris Opéra (principal conductor, 1873–7) and with the Société des Concerts du Conservatoire, also producing chamber and orchestral music. His writings include a treatise on conducting.

Delibes, (Clément Philibert) Léo (*b* St Germain du Val, 21 Feb 1836; *d* Paris, 16 Jan 1891). French composer. A church organist until 1871, he was drawn to the theatre, first writing light operettas in the style of his teacher Adolphe Adam (roughly one a year from 1856 to 1869), then becoming chorus master at the Théâtre-Lyrique and the Opéra. He is best known for his appealing classical ballets *Coppélia* (1870), with its charming character numbers, and the tuneful but more sophisticated *Sylvia* (1876), both admired by Tchaikovsky. Meyerbeer's influence is evident in his serious opera *Jean de Nivelle* (1880), and a gift for witty pastiche in his dances for Hugo's play *Le roi s'amuse* (1882). His masterpiece is *Lakmé* (1883), a highly successful opera indebted to Bizet and memorable for its oriental colour, strong characterization and fine melodies.

Delius, Frederick [**Fritz**] (**Theodore Albert**) (*b* Bradford, 29 Jan 1862; *d* Grez-sur-Loing, 10 June 1934). English composer. His father lent him money to set up as a citrus grower in Florida (1884–6), where he had lessons with Thomas Ward; he then studied at the Leipzig Conservatory (1886–8) and met Grieg. He settled in Paris as a man of bohemian habits, a friend of Gauguin, Strindberg, Munch and others, until in 1897 he moved to Grez with Jelka Rosen, later his wife. There he remained.

He had written operas, orchestral pieces and much else before the move to Grez, but nearly all his regularly performed output dates from afterwards while looking back to the musical and other experiences of earlier years: the seamless flow of Wagner, the airier chromaticism of Grieg, the rich colouring of Strauss

and Debussy, the existential independence of Nietzsche. His operas *A Village Romeo and Juliet* (1901) and *Fennimore and Gerda* (1910) are love stories cast in connected scenes and examining spiritual states within a natural world. Nature is important too in such orchestral pieces as *In a Summer Garden* (1908), *A Song of the High Hills* (with wordless chorus, 1911) or *A Song of Summer* (1930), though there are other works in which the characteristic rhapsodizing is made to serve symphonic forms, notably the Violin Concerto (1916) and three sonatas for violin and piano (1914, 1923, 1930). The choral works include two unaccompanied, wordless songs 'to be sung of a summer night on the water' (1917), the large-scale *A Mass of Life* with words from Nietzsche (1905) and a secular Requiem (1916). In the early 1920s he grew blind and paralysed as a result of syphilitic infection, and his last works were taken down by Eric Fenby.

Dramatic works Irmelin (1892, perf. 1953); The Magic Fountain (1895); Koanga (1904); A Village Romeo and Juliet (1901, perf. 1907); Margot la Rouge (1902); Fennimore and Gerda (1919); Hassan, incidental music (1923)
Orchestral music Pf Conc. (1897); Paris: the Song of a Great City (1899); Brigg Fair (1907); In a Summer Garden (1908); Summer Night on the River (1911); On Hearing the First Cuckoo in Spring (1912); North Country Sketches (1914); Vn and vc Conc. (1916); Vn Conc. (1916); Vc Conc. (1921)
Choral music Appalachia (1903); Sea Drift (1904); A Mass of Life (1905); A Song of the High Hills (1911); 2 Songs to be sung of a Summer Night on the Water (1917)
Chamber music 3 vn sonatas (1914, 1923, 1930); Str Qt (1916); Sonata, vc, pf (1916)
*Vocal music c*75 songs etc

Della Casa, Lisa (*b* Burgdorf, 2 Feb 1919). Swiss soprano. She sang at Zurich from 1943 and appeared at the Salzburg Festival from 1947; that year she joined the Vienna Staatsoper. Her smooth legato and attractive stage presence made her a favourite in Strauss: Arabella was the role of her Covent Garden début (1953) and she was well known as Ariadne, the Marschallin and Salome. She retired in 1974.

Della Ciaia, Azzolino Bernardino (*b* Siena, 21 May 1671; *d* Pisa, 15 Jan 1755). Italian composer. He is remembered chiefly for his six harpsichord sonatas (a rare designation at the time, *c*1727) and his novel design of a four-manual, 60-register organ (with a fifth keyboard controlling a harpsichord); it was first played in Pisa in 1737 and still exists.

Della Valle, Pietro (*b* Rome, 11 April 1586; *d* there, 21 April 1652). Italian theorist and composer. He was one of the most important and wide-ranging figures in early 17th-century Rome. Chiefly important for his discourse *Della musica dell'eta nostrà* (1640), a defence of modern 'decorated' music containing vivid information on contemporary Roman musical life, his interest in ancient music (stimulated by his friendship with G.B. Doni) is exemplified in his only surviving work, *Dialogo per la festa della santissima Purificazione* (1640). Oratorio-like in style, it is written in five different modes, for one to five voices, with special continuo instruments tuned to the required mode.

Deller, Alfred (George) (*b* Margate, 31 May 1912; *d* Bologna, 16 July 1979). English countertenor. His

London début was in 1943 and he made his first recording in 1949. The next year he began collaborating with the lutenist Desmond Dupré; together they were responsible for reviving the English lute-song in the 1950s. They founded the Deller Consort, a small group dedicated to the idiomatic performance of early music. At the Stour (Kent) Music Festival (which he founded in 1963) Deller was heard in the Baroque repertory. In 1960 he created Oberon in Britten's *A Midsummer Night's Dream*. His voice was a successful blend of the falsetto range with a light baritone and he was largely responsible for the postwar revival of interest in the high male voice. His son Mark (*b* 1938) is also a countertenor who sang in the Deller Consort.

Deller, Florian Johann (*b* Drosendorf, bap. 2 May 1729; *d* Munich, 19 April 1773). Austrian composer. A Stuttgart court violinist, he studied with Jommelli and in 1761–7 wrote music for six of J.G. Noverre's dramatic ballets, notably *Orfeo ed Euridice* (1763), gaining widespread fame. He also wrote comic operas, symphonies and sonatas.

Dello Joio, Norman (*b* New York, 24 Jan 1913). American composer. He studied with Wagenaar at the Juilliard School (1939–41) and with Hindemith (1941) and has taught at various institutions, in 1972 becoming professor of music at Boston University. His works, influenced by 19th-century Italian opera, Catholic church music and jazz, are in a bold style. Operas (including three on the story of St Joan), large-scale choral pieces and orchestral music predominate.

Del Mar, Norman (René) (*b* London, 31 July 1919). English conductor and writer on music. He studied at the RCM and played the horn in the RPO, under Beecham. He founded the Chelsea SO in 1944 and with it gave early British performances of Strauss, Busoni and Mahler. As guest conductor with leading orchestras he is heard to best advantage in complex, late Romantic scores. He is the author of a three-volume study of Richard Strauss (1962) and books on aspects of the orchestral repertory.

Del Monaco, Mario (*b* Florence, 27 July 1915; *d* Mestre, 16 Oct 1982). Italian tenor. He studied at the Pesaro Conservatory and in 1941 sang Puccini's Pinkerton in Milan. He visited Covent Garden with the San Carlo company in 1946 and sang regularly at the Met, 1951–9. In the Italian repertory he was widely admired more for the vigour of his interpretations than any subtlety.

Del Tredici, David (*b* Cloverdale, CA, 16 March 1937). American composer. He studied at Berkeley and Princeton, and taught at Harvard (1966–72), Boston University (1973–84) and the City University of New York (1984–). Since 1968 he has produced a large cycle of polystylistic works based on Lewis Carroll's Alice books; they include *An Alice Symphony* (1969–75) and the four-part *Child Alice* (1977–81).

De Luca, Giuseppe (*b* Rome, 25 Dec 1876; *d* New York, 26 Aug 1950). Italian baritone. He studied at the Accademia di S Cecilia and in 1897 sang Gounod's Valentine at Piacenza. He sang at La Scala from 1903 (including the première of *Madama But-*

terfly) and his stylish, well-schooled voice was heard at the Met, 1915–40 (début as Rossini's Figaro, farewell as Rigoletto). He created Puccini's Gianni Schicchi in 1918.

De Lucia, Fernando (*b* Naples, 11 Oct 1860; *d* there, 21 Feb 1925). Italian tenor. He studied in Naples and made his début there as Faust (1885). After early fame as Rossini's Almaviva he became identified with the *verismo* repertory; he was the first London Canio and Cavaradossi and created roles in four operas by Mascagni. Though admired for his technique and vocal control he was criticized for excessive vibrato.

Delvincourt, Claude (*b* Paris, 12 Jan 1888; *d* Orbetello, 5 April 1954). French composer. He studied with Widor and others at the Paris Conservatoire, of which he became director in 1941. He composed in many genres, often trying to recapture a medieval or Renaissance spirit.

Demantius, (Johannes) Christoph (*b* Liberec, 15 Dec 1567; *d* Freiberg, 20 April 1643). German composer. After matriculating at Wittenberg in 1593, he moved to Leipzig. He was Kantor at Zittau (1597–1604), then in Freiberg at the cathedral and municipal school. A prolific and versatile composer, he wrote many polyphonic Lutheran motets and a fine *St John Passion* (1631), showing Lassus's influence, as well as some 25 occasional pieces. His nine published secular volumes include songs based on Italian and Polish dance-song forms; some set his own poetry. His theoretical writings include the first German alphabetical musical dictionary (1632).

Dembiński, Bolesław (*b* Poznań, 9 May 1833; *d* there, 7 Aug 1914). Polish organist, conductor and composer. He was organist at Poznań Cathedral, conductor and music director of the Polish Theatre in Poznań and founder of many singing societies; he wrote two operas, church music and choral songs.

Demessieux, Jeanne (*b* Montpelier, 14 Feb 1921; *d* Paris, 11 Nov 1968). French organist and composer. She studied at the Paris Conservatoire and gave her first public recital in 1946. At her London début (1947) she showed her gifts for improvisation; tours of North America followed. Her prodigious technique was allied to considerable interpretative powers.

Demisemiquaver. The note in American usage called a 32nd-note, that is half the value of a semiquaver (or 16th-note) and double that of a hemidemisemiquaver (or 64th-note). It is first found in early 16th-century instrumental music. *See* NOTE VALUES.

Demus, Jörg (*b* St Polten, 2 Dec 1928). Austrian pianist. He studied in Vienna and made his début there in 1953. His flexible touch and expressive line have been most admired in the music of Mozart, Schubert and Debussy. He is often heard as accompanist to leading singers and instrumentalists and has recorded with his own collection of early instruments.

Demuth, Norman (*b* S. Croydon, 15 July 1898; *d* Chichester, 21 April 1968). English composer. He studied briefly at the RCM but was essentially self-taught, being sympathetic to French music (he wrote books on Franck, Dukas, Roussel, Gounod, Ravel and French opera). From 1930 he taught at the RAM.

Denisov, Edison (Vasil'yevich) (*b* Tomsk, 6 April 1929). Soviet composer. After training in mechanics and mathematics he studied with Shebalin and Peiko at the Moscow Conservatory (1951–6), where he later taught. He was one of the first Soviet composers to follow the advanced serialism of western Europe, and has produced a large output ranging from the cantata *Sun of the Incas* (1964) and opera (*L'écume des jours*, 1981) to diverse chamber pieces (Piano Trio, 1971).

Denner, Johann Christoph (*b* Leipzig, 13 Aug 1655; *d* Nuremberg, 20 April 1707). German woodwind instrument maker. He established a shop in Nuremberg (1680) and realizing the advantages of new-style imported French instruments, abandoned one-piece Renaissance construction in favour of three pieces with tuning-joints and a change in the bore. His surviving instruments include, besides recorders, members of the oboe, shawm and bassoon families; an early clarinet with a bell and three keys supports Doppelmayr's statement (1730) that Denner invented the instrument. He is also credited with the introduction of the Baroque racket. The surviving recorders, flutes, oboes and clarinets of Johann's son Jacob (1681–1735) show a move towards late Baroque elegance.

Density 21.5. Work for solo flute by Varèse (1936); 21.5 is the density of the metal of the flute.

Dent, Edward J(oseph) (*b* Ribston, 16 July 1876; *d* London, 22 Aug 1957). English musicologist. He was educated at Eton and Cambridge, where he taught from 1902. In 1918 he left for London, as a music critic; he returned to Cambridge as professor of music in 1926, instituting many reforms before he retired in 1941. As a scholar his main concerns were Italian music, especially of the Baroque period, and opera; his most influential books are those on A. Scarlatti (1905), Mozart's operas (1913) and English opera (1928). He was interested too in contemporary music and was first president of the ISCM. Dent did much to broaden the horizons of British musical life (not least through his many idiomatic opera translations) and had great influence on opera, scholarship and composition.

Dentice, Scipione (*b* Naples, 19 Jan 1560; *d* there, on or before 21 April 1635). Italian composer. After a period in Rome, he was a canon of Naples Cathedral by 1609 and joined the Oratorio Filippino there. His five madrigal books (1591–1607) include interesting chromatic pieces; he also published motets (1594) and spiritual madrigals (1629). He was related to Fabrigio Dentice (*c*1530–*c*1600), who worked in Naples, Barcelona and Parma, and published Lamentations (1593) and other sacred works and also wrote madrigals and lute music.

Denver Symphony Orchestra. American orchestra formed in 1934 from members of the Civic SO; both groups were conducted by Horace E. Tureman until 1944. Later conductors include Brian Priestman, Gaetano Delogu and Philippe Entremont (from 1986). Its home is Boettcher Concert Hall (opened

1978, cap. 2650). Summer activities include the Rocky Mountain Festival (in various places).

Déploration (Fr.). Term used for late medieval and early Renaissance compositions inspired by a composer's death. Many centre on Ockeghem and Josquin; they commonly use the Phrygian mode.

De Reszke. Polish family of singers. The most celebrated members were Jean (1850–1925), a tenor noted for his roles in Massenet's *Hérodiade* and *Le Cid*, Meyerbeer's *L'africaine* and *Le prophète* and Gounod's *Faust* and *Roméo et Juliette*, and his brother Edouard (1853–1917), a bass whose huge voice and stature made him a fine exponent of Wagner roles, including Hans Sachs in *Die Meistersinger* and King Mark in *Tristan und Isolde*.

Dering, Richard (*b* *c*1580; *d* London, bur. 22 March 1630). English composer. A Catholic, he spent his early working years abroad, but he entered Charles I's service in 1625. His English music includes works for the Anglican church, dances, and fantasias for viols (among his best works), two madrigals, and quodlibets for voices and viols (*City Cries, Country Cries*). The Italianate works include Catholic church music, canzonettas and madrigals and are strongly influenced by contemporary practice, though he never used solo instruments or recitative. The motets for two and three voices were especially popular in England after 1625.

Dernesch, Helga (*b* Vienna, 3 Feb 1939). Austrian soprano, later mezzo-soprano. She sang Musorgsky's Marina at Berne in 1957 and later appeared at Cologne and Bayreuth. Her lyric gifts, striking stage presence and intense acting were displayed as the Marschallin and Berlioz's Cassandra for Scottish Opera. She appeared with distinction, at Salzburg (under Karajan) and elsewhere, in many Wagner soprano roles, but in 1979 turned to the mezzo repertory.

De Sabata, Victor (*b* Trieste, 10 April 1892; *d* Santa Margherita Ligure, 11 Dec 1967). Italian conductor and composer. After early success as a composer he conducted at the Monte Carlo Opera from 1918, including the première of Ravel's *L'enfant et les sortilèges* (1925). He conducted at La Scala from 1930, repeating a fervently committed *Tristan und Isolde* at Bayreuth in 1939. He took the Scala company to Britain in 1950 (*Otello* and *Falstaff* at Covent Garden) and often appeared as guest in the USA.

Descant. DISCANT. The term is also used to signify a high instrument of a family, such as the descant recorder (in the USA, soprano recorder) or the descant (or treble) viol; it is also used to refer to a high, florid part added above the melody of a hymn.

Descartes, René (*b* La Haye, 31 March 1596; *d* Stockholm, 11 Feb 1650). French philosopher. His principal contribution to music theory was the *Compendium musicae* (1618), in which he attempted to define the dual relationship between the physical and psychological phenomena in music. The bulk of the work is devoted to the practical aspects of music as part of the process of sensory perception. He also contributed to music theory on period structure and harmonic inversion.

Deschamps, Emile (*b* Bourges, 20 Feb 1791; *d* Versailles, April 1871). French poet and librettist. He turned into verse Berlioz's prose for *Roméo et Juliette*, helped Meyerbeer with the librettos of *Robert le diable* and *Les Huguenots*, wrote texts for innumerable songs and cantatas and translated Schubert's lieder into French. He was partly responsible for introducing Romanticism, in the form of dramatic and picturesque poetry, into French opera.

Déserts. Work for wind, piano, percussion and tape by Varèse (1954).

Deshevov, Vladimir Mikhaylovich (*b* St Petersburg, 11 Feb 1889; *d* there, 27 Oct 1955). Soviet composer. He studied at the St Petersburg Conservatory (1908–14) and is remembered as one of those who wrote machine music (*Rails* for piano, 1926).

De Silva, Andreas (*b c*1475–80). ?Spanish singer and composer. Having trained probably in France and northern Italy, he was employed by Pope Leo X in Rome and, from 1522, by the Duke of Mantua. His output includes six masses, at least 31 motets and a *chanson*. An original composer who adapted many local stylistic influences, he was held in high regard both during his life and later. His style is characterized by simple, expressive melodies tending towards declamation, a dramatic sense of harmony and clearly defined structures. Some of the more adventurous pieces explore the new developments of such composers as Willaert and Gombert. He is not to be confused with Andreas Silvanus.

Desmarets, Henry (*b* Paris, Feb 1661; *d* Lunéville, 7 Sept 1741). French composer. As a boy chorister in the royal chapel he became a disciple of Lully. He maintained court links and his first opera was given at Versailles in 1682. Later he was *maître de chapelle* at a Jesuit college. An amorous imbroglio led to his exile in 1699, and in 1701 he took a court post in Madrid. From 1707 he was *surintendant de la musique* to the Duke of Lorraine at Lunéville, where he expanded musical activities. He wrote *c*20 stage works; the *tragédies lyriques*, such as *Iphigénie en Tauride* (1704), use more adventurous harmony and more flexible recitative than Lully's. His other works include impressive *grands motets*, cantatas, *airs* and sonatas.

Desormière, Roger (*b* Vichy, 13 Sept 1898; *d* Paris, 25 Oct 1963). French conductor and composer. After study at the Paris Conservatoire, he conducted at the Concerts Pleyels from 1921 and was later associated with Les Six. He toured widely with the Ballets Russes, 1925–9, and after Dyaghilev's death earned a reputation for sensitive performances of contemporary and pre-Classical music.

Desprez, Josquin. *See* JOSQUIN DESPREZ.

Dessau, Paul (*b* Hamburg, 19 Dec 1894; *d* E. Berlin, 28 June 1979). German composer. He was an opera coach and conductor from 1912 and began to make a name as a composer in the 1920s, but all his mature work dates from after a period in Paris (1933–9), when he became politically aware and studied serialism with Leibowitz. More important was his meeting with Brecht in the USA in 1942. In 1948 they returned to Germany, where their collaborations included the opera *Die Verurteilung des Lukullus*

(1951) and where Dessau became the leading composer of the Democratic Republic, producing a large quantity of choral music, incidental scores, chamber music and songs. His last major work was the opera *Einstein* (1973), which uses an array of styles from Bach quotations to electronic shrieks.

Dessauer, Josef (*b* Prague, 28 May 1798; *d* Mödling, 8 July 1876). Bohemian composer. He studied with Tomášek in Prague and settled in Vienna in 1835. He was successful as a songwriter and opera composer, the song *Lockung* being particularly popular, and well regarded by Berlioz and Chopin, whose Polonaises op.26 were dedicated to him.

Dessus (Fr.). The highest part in an ensemble or consort. In the 17th and 18th centuries, 'dessus' may mean violin. The word corresponds to the English 'treble'; 'dessus de viole' refers to the treble viol.

Destinn, Emmy (*b* Prague, 26 Feb 1878; *d* České Budějovice, 28 Jan 1930). Czech soprano. She appeared in Berlin, 1898–1908, as Santuzza, Carmen and Salome. At Bayreuth she was a successful Senta (1901) and at Covent Garden her gifts as an actress and singer were valued from 1904 as Donna Anna, Aida and Butterfly. At the Met, she was Minnie in the première of Puccini's *La fanciulla del West* (1910).

Destouches, André Cardinal (*b* Paris, bap. 6 April 1672; *d* there, 7 Feb 1749). French composer. He studied with André Campra. His *pastorale-héroïque Issé* (1697, Fontainebleau) was an immediate success; he later revised it, and up to 1726 presented ten more stage works (operas, ballets etc). He held posts from 1718 in the court *musique de la chambre* and at the Académie Royale de Musique, 1713–30.

Destouches' stage works show a fine dramatic sense and, like other French music of the day, use harmonies and scorings more adventurous than Lully's, helping to prepare the way for Rameau; the recitatives are notable for their flexibility and their arioso style. His other works include motets, cantatas and many *airs*.

Detroit Symphony Orchestra. American orchestra founded in 1914; it lapsed twice after 1940 and was re-formed in 1951 under Paul Paray. Concerts are usually at the Henry and Edsel Ford Auditorium (opened 1956, cap. 2900). Young people's concerts were soon given and summer concerts were started in 1922. It was the official orchestra at the Worcester Music Festival (MA) in 1958–74 and resident at Meadow Brook Festival, Rochester (MI), from 1964. In 1970 it instituted the Detroit Symphony Youth Orchestra as a training group. Ossip Gabrilowitsch was the first permanent conductor (1919–36). Under Antal Dorati (1977–81) it made its first European tour and gained worldwide recognition. Gunther Herbig became music director in 1984.

Dett, R(obert) Nathaniel (*b* Niagara Falls, 11 Oct 1882; *d* Battle Creek, MI, 2 Oct 1943). American composer. He studied at the Oberlin Conservatory and with Boulanger in France (1929). His music, which uses black folk music in a neo-Romantic style, includes oratorios, motets, partsongs, piano music and numerous arrangements of spirituals.

Dettingen Te Deum and Anthem. Choral works by

Handel composed to celebrate the British victory over the French at Dettingen, near Frankfurt, in 1743; the anthem is to the text *The king shall rejoice*.

Deuteromelia. 'Second honey': second collection of English rounds and catches published in 1609 by Thomas Ravenscroft; the first is *Pammelia*.

Deutsch, Max (*b* Vienna, 17 Nov 1892; *d* Paris, 22 Nov 1982). French composer, conductor and teacher. After study with Schoenberg in Vienna he worked as a theatre conductor in several countries and wrote music for Pabst's films, notably *Der Schatz* (1923). In 1924 he moved to Paris, where he introduced works by Berg and Schoenberg, worked as a pianist and cabaret composer and at the Ecole Normale de Musique.

Deutsch, Otto Erich (*b* Vienna, 5 Sept 1883; *d* there, 23 Nov 1967). Austrian musicologist. He was trained as an art historian and worked as a music librarian; he spent the years 1939–51 in Cambridge. A prolific scholar (he wrote nearly 150 articles on Schubert, 80 on Mozart), he invented the 'documentary biography' of composers (Schubert, 1914; Handel, 1955; Mozart, 1961), compiled a Schubert thematic catalogue (1951) and worked influentially and revealingly on Viennese composers, especially in bibliographical and iconographical fields.

Deutsche (Ger.). 'German': term for a GERMAN DANCE.

Deutsche Oper. Opera company and theatre in West Berlin. The company originally occupied the Deutsches Opernhaus (inaugurated 1912, destroyed 1942); in 1925 it was renamed the Städtische Oper. In 1961, after further changes, the company and its rebuilt theatre reopened as the Deutsche Oper. At first, repertory was mainly standard, but premières of Weill and Schreker were given (1932) and of Egk (1948) and Henze (1956). After 1961 forces were increased and the repertory (over 75 works) became the largest in the world.

Deutsches Requiem, Ein. *See* GERMAN REQUIEM, A.

Deutscher Verlag für Musik. German firm of music publishers. It was founded in Leipzig on 1 January 1954. The German Democratic Republic state music publishing house, it has produced complete critical editions, performing editions and numerous contemporary works, as well as specialized music literature, notably the series *Musikgeschichte in Bildern*.

Deutsche Staatsoper. Opera company established in East Berlin in 1945 from the Staatsoper, which in 1919 had replaced the former court opera. Dessau's *Die Verurteilung des Lukullus* (1951) was the first of a number of premières of works by East German composers.

Deux journées, Les [The Water Carrier]. Opera in three acts by Cherubini to a libretto by J.N. Bouilly (1800, Paris); its full title is *Les deux journées, ou Le porteur d'eau* and in England it is known as *The Water Carrier*, in Germany as *Der Wasserträger*.

Development. The procedure by which thematic material already stated is reshaped. In SONATA FORM the development section follows the exposition.

Devienne, François (*b* Joinville, 31 Jan 1759; *d* Paris, 5 Sept 1803). French composer. He was active in Paris as a flautist, bassoonist and composer, *c* 1780–85 and from 1788. He wrote successful operas in the

1790s, notably *Les visitandines* (1792) which brought him much fame. From 1790 he taught in the Paris National Guard school; when this became the Conservatoire in 1795, he was appointed an administrator and flute professor. Most of his *c* 300 instrumental works are for wind, among them seven *symphonies concertantes*, *c* 20 concertos and many chamber works, in an elegant melodic style; he also wrote *romances*, patriotic songs and an important flute method (1794). His works did much to raise the level of French wind music in the late 18th century.

Devils of Loudun, The [Diabły z Loudun]. Opera in three acts by Penderecki to his own libretto after John Whiting's play from Aldous Huxley's novel (1969, Hamburg).

Devil's Trill Sonata. Nickname of a violin sonata in G minor by Tartini (*c* 1714), published in J.B. Cartier's *L'art du violon* (1798), so called because of the long trill in the last of its four movements.

Devin du village, Le [The Village Soothsayer]. Opera in one act by Rousseau to his own libretto (1752, Fontainebleau); it provided the basis for Mozart's *Bastien und Bastienne*. Burney made an English version, *The Cunning Man* (1766).

Devisenarie (Ger.). Term for Baroque arias in which the opening vocal phrase is interrupted by an instrumental passage and then sung complete.

Devrient, Eduard (Philipp) (*b* Berlin, 11 Aug 1801; *d* Karlsruhe, 4 Oct 1877). German theatre historian, librettist and baritone. He sang the part of Christ in the famous Berlin revival of Bach's *St Matthew Passion* under Mendelssohn (1829), later turning to acting and writing. He supplied the libretto for Marschner's *Hans Heiling*.

De Waart, Edo (*b* Amsterdam, 1 June 1941). Dutch conductor. He began a career as an oboist and made his conducting début in 1964. In 1966 he became musical director of the Netherlands Wind Ensemble and assistant conductor of the Concertgebouw Orchestra. He conducted at Covent Garden in 1976 and Bayreuth in 1979. He was music director of the San Francisco SO, 1977–85, and was appointed to the Minnesota Orchestra from 1986.

Dezède, Nicolas (*b* ?1740–50; *d* Paris, 11 Sept 1792). Composer. Of obscure ancestry, he was in Paris from the 1770s. His successful first opera *Julie* (1772) was followed by *c* 20 more; several, notably his masterpiece *Blaise et Babet* (1783), were well known abroad. Most are comic, pastoral in tone, with a simple, elegant, expressive style. Mozart wrote piano variations on an air from *Julie*, 'Lison dormait'; the well-known air *Ah, vous dirais-je, Maman?* (also varied by Mozart, and famous in English as *Twinkle, twinkle little star*) is attributed to him.

D'Hooghe, Clement (Vital Ferdinand) (*b* Temse, 21 April 1899; *d* Wilrijk, 1 April 1951). Belgian organist and composer. He studied at the Antwerp Conservatory, where he later taught, and was organist at St Paul's, Antwerp (1926–51). A brilliant virtuoso, he toured as a recitalist. His works include masses and music for children.

Diabelli, Anton (*b* Mattsee, 6 Sept 1781; *d* Vienna, 7 April 1858). Austrian music publisher. With Pietro Cappi as business manager, he established the firm

Cappi & Diabelli in Vienna in December 1818, specializing in fashionable operatic and dance music. His shrewd idea in 1819 of sending a simple waltz theme to every notable Austrian composer, asking them to send him a variation apiece, gained notice: it resulted in the *Vaterländischer Künstlerverein* (1824), a set of some 50 variations, and also Beethoven's monumental Diabelli Variations op.120. Diabelli's reputation also rests on his championship of Schubert, whose first (1821) and principal publisher he became. The firm was highly productive as Anton Diabelli & Cie (1824–51) and as C.A. Spina (1852–72), when it published works by Johann Strauss the younger.

Diabelli Variations. Beethoven's 33 Variations on a Waltz by Diabelli for piano op.120 (1823).

Diabolus in musica (Lat.). 'Devil in music'. A medieval phrase for the tritone (e.g. F–B), an intractable interval harmonically or melodically in music of the period.

Diaghilev [Diaghileff], **Sergey Pavlovich**. *See* DYAGILEV, SERGEY PAVLOVICH.

Dialogue. A piece involving exchanges between two or more characters. Dialogue techniques are found in the 16th-century frottola and madrigal and in the Florentine *intermedi*. 'Dialogo' was used in the 17th century for short quasi-dramatic works with recitative but not intended for the stage; by 1700 the term gave way to 'cantata'. The sacred *laude* dialogues of the 16th century and the Latin recitative-dialogues of the early 17th were important in the formation of oratorio in Italy; sacred dialogues also played a part in the development of the church cantata in Germany before Bach.

Dialogues des Carmélites [The Carmelites]. Opera in three acts by Poulenc to a libretto by Bernanos (1957, Milan).

Diamond, David (Leo) (*b* Rochester, NY, 9 July 1915). American composer. He studied at the Eastman School with Rogers, in New York with Sessions and in France with Boulanger; he also made contacts in Paris with Gide, Roussel, Ravel and Stravinsky. His meticulously crafted works are in a brilliant neo-classical style with an individual vein of lyricism; they include ballets, eight symphonies (1941–61), concertos, ten string quartets (1940–66) and many songs. *Rounds* for strings (1944) was widely performed.

Dianda, Hilda (*b* Córdoba, 13 April 1925). Argentinian composer. She studied in Buenos Aires and with Malipiero in Venice (1949–50); she also worked with the Groupe de Recherches Musicales in Paris (1958–62) and attended the Darmstadt courses. Her works are mostly for orchestra or ensemble.

Diapason. In English, an organ stop (the fundamental sound of an organ); it may also denote the range of a voice or instrument. In French it may refer to the scaling of a string or organ pipe or to the distance between the finger-holes of a wind instrument.

Diary of One who Disappeared, The [Zápisník zmizelého]. Song cycle by Janáček (1919), settings for tenor, alto, three-part women's chorus and piano of 22 anonymous poems.

Diatonic. Based on an octave divided into five tones

(T) and two semitones (S), e.g. T–T–S–T–T–T–S. The major and natural minor scales are diatonic, as are the church modes. A diatonic interval is one that is found in the diatonic octave.

Dibdin, Charles (*b* Southampton, bap. 15 March 1745; *d* London, 25 July 1814). English composer and dramatist. His early works included a vocal collection (1763) and *The Shepherd's Artifice* (1764) an all-sung opera to his own libretto, in which he sang the leading role. But it was his flair for character parts and humorous accents that made his name, first as Ralph in Arnold's *The Maid of the Mill* (1765). In 1767–72 he collaborated with the librettist Isaac Bickerstaffe on comic works, the first English operas with 'action' finales: *Lionel and Clarissa* (1768), *The Padlock* (1768) and *The Ephesian Matron* (1769) were his finest. Also successful were his afterpiece *The Waterman* (1774) and opera *The Quaker* (1775), both with typically characterful vocal lines. After this, Dibdin's career and finances went into decline, owing to his truculent behaviour. He wrote short, all-sung dialogues for Sadler's Wells, children's operas, pantomimes and hundreds of strophic ballads and topical and comic songs, many for his one-man 'Table Entertainments' of 1789–1805; he was especially famous for his sea songs. The last of his *c*40 operas was given in 1811. He remained active as a writer (novels, periodicals, autobiography) and business speculator, but died destitute and friendless.

Dichterliebe [Poet's love]. Song cycle by Schumann (op.48, 1840), settings for voice and piano of 16 poems by Heine.

Dickinson, Peter (*b* Lytham St Annes, 15 Nov 1934). English composer. He studied at Cambridge and in New York, where he met and was influenced by Cage, Cowell and Varèse; he then held posts in England, notably as professor at Keele University (1974–84). His works, in diverse genres, show his interests in American music, Stravinsky and Satie; they include concertos for piano (1984) and violin (1986).

Diddley bow. Single-string instrument of the southern USA, usually a length of wire with the ends attached to a frame house wall.

Diderot, Denis (*b* Langres, 5 Oct 1713; *d* Paris, 31 July 1784). French critic. He was the chief architect of the *Encyclopédie* (for which he wrote articles on instruments) and had a strong impact on musical thought. In works such as *Le neveu de Rameau* (*c*1760) he judged the Italian style then popular to be too shallow (unlike Rameau's) and recommended a reform of French theatre, including the use of classical subjects in opera. Gluck and Traetta successfully took up these ideas. Unlike Rousseau, he defended 'pure' instrumental music as the highest form of art, unrestrained by concrete ideas and capable of rendering the deepest feelings.

Didjeridu. An end-blown, straight natural trumpet, without separate mouthpiece, used by the aborigines of northern Australia. It consists of a termite-hollowed eucalyptus branch, 1–1.5 m long, and is blown through the narrow end of the conical tube. It is played by male aborigines together with clapping sticks to accompany singing and dancing, usually in 'open' ceremonies and clan songs. It functions mainly as a drone of relatively constant pitch, over which voiced sounds are superimposed to form further rhythmic patterns and harmonize with the drone.

Dido and Aeneas. Opera in a prologue and three acts by Purcell to a libretto by Nahum Tate after Virgil (1689, London); Dido's Lament, 'When I am Laid in Earth', is in Act 3.

Didone abbandonata. Piano Sonata in G minor op.50 no.3 by Clementi (1821); Violin Sonata in G minor by Tartini (1734). It is the title of a well-known opera libretto by Metastasio (1724).

Diémer, Louis(-Joseph) (*b* Paris, 14 Feb 1843; *d* there, 31 Dec 1919). French pianist and composer of Alsatian origin. He studied at the Paris Conservatoire, gaining a reputation for the precision and purity of his playing, and in 1887 succeeded Marmontel as professor; he also played the harpsichord and helped found the Société des Instruments Anciens. His works are mainly for piano, including early music editions, transcriptions and a method.

Diepenbrock, Alphons (Johannes Maria) (*b* Amsterdam, 2 Sept 1862; *d* there, 5 April 1921). Dutch composer. Self-taught, he was influenced by Wagner, Netherlands polyphony, late Beethoven and, from 1910, Debussy. He occupied an important place in Dutch music at the turn of the century in that he was the first modern composer whose works could be judged by international standards. They include church music and an important sequence of symphonic poems with obbligato voice (e.g. *Zwei Hymnen an die Nacht*, 1899; *Die Nacht*, 1911).

Dieren, Bernard van (*b* Rotterdam, 27 Dec 1887; *d* London, 24 April 1936). British composer of Dutch birth. Largely self-taught, he settled in England in 1909 and formed friendships with Epstein (on whom he wrote a book) and Augustus John, besides leading musicians. He wrote in an intricate, broadly tonal and contrapuntal style, his works including six string quartets, *Diafonia* for baritone and chamber orchestra (1916) and the *Chinese Symphony* with soloists and chorus (1914).

Dies irae (Lat.: 'day of wrath'). The Sequence of the Mass for the Dead. It is normally included in choral and orchestral requiems (though not in Fauré's or Duruflé's) and has often been set independently. The plainchant has been used as a symbol in instrumental and orchestral pieces by Berlioz, Saint-Saëns, Rakhmaninov and others.

Dietrich, Albert (Hermann) (*b* Forsthaus Golk, 28 Aug 1829; *d* Berlin, 20 Nov 1908). German conductor and composer. A member of Schumann's circle at Düsseldorf, he worked in Bonn and in Oldenburg, championing the works of Bach, Schumann and Brahms. As a composer he had greatest success with his songs, also writing two operas and incidental music.

Dietrich, Sixt (*b* Augsburg, *c*1493; *d* St Gall, 21 Oct 1548). German composer. A teacher at Konstanz Cathedral (1517–19), he was ordained in 1522 and assisted with music at the cathedral. He was acquainted with several humanists, including Rudolfinger in Strasbourg and Amerbach in Basle, and with Luther. In 1527 he joined the Reformatory movement, giving lectures on music at universities, but withdrawing to St Gall after Konstanz was taken by Catholic imperial troops in 1548. As a student he composed mostly secular songs. The bulk of his later output is liturgical music for Konstanz Cathedral and the Catholic imperial choir, and commissioned works for the early Protestant service; most of it is based on pre-existing melodies and frequently uses canon and imitation techniques. His eight sacred songs in German are more chordal. He is one of the most important early Protestant composers.

Dietsch [Dietzch, Dietz], **(Pierre-)Louis(-Philippe)** (*b* Dijon, 17 March 1808; *d* Paris, 20 Feb 1865). French conductor and composer. He was a church musician and composition teacher at the Ecole Niedermeyer, Paris, producing mostly conservative works. He is remembered for controversies connected with his conductorship of the Opéra, especially those involving Wagner and Verdi.

Dieupart, Charles (*b* ?after 1667; *d c*1740). French composer. He wrote instrumental music for stage works in London, 1704–11, and later was a violinist and harpsichord teacher. His works include six dance suites (1701, for keyboard or ensemble), six flute sonatas (in a more conservative, Italian style), orchestral works and songs. Some of his music was copied out by Bach.

Diferencias (Sp.). Term for VARIATIONS in 16th-century Spanish music; it is also used (like the English DIVISION) for the subdivision of long notes into several shorter ones.

Difference tone. A particular case of COMBINATION TONE; it is produced when two tones are heard, and its frequency is the difference of the frequencies of the two tones. It is thus a lower note. The phenomenon was discovered by Giuseppi Tartini (he called it *terzo suono*, 'third sound') and they are therefore sometimes called 'Tartini tones'. In orchestral music they are often noticeable when two clarinets are playing in 3rds, for example in the recapitulation of the second subject of Mendelssohn's 'Hebrides' Overture.

Dilliger, Johann (*b* Eisfeld, 30 Nov 1593; *d* Coburg, 28 Aug 1647). German composer and editor. He was Kantor in Coburg 1625–33, during which time he published about 30 music collections. He composed only sacred music including over 100 contrapuntal, chorale-based motets, 200 homophonic songs and Italianate concertos for up to six voices with continuo. His interest in the modern style is reflected in the number of Italian compositions included in his publications.

Dillon, James (*b* Glasgow, 29 Oct 1950). Scottish composer. He studied music and linguistics at London University, but was self-taught as a composer. His music, influenced by Ferneyhough and Finnissy, is characterized by wild complexity and extreme instrumental demands. His early works are for solo instruments or small ensembles – ... *Once Upon a Time* for eight instruments (1980), *East 11th St NY 10003* for six percussionists (1982) – but in

Überschreiten for 16 instruments (1986) and his first orchestral score *Helle Nacht* (1987) he began to extend his techniques to larger forces.

Dilthey, Wilhelm (Christian Ludwig) (*b* Biebrich, 19 Nov 1833; *d* Seis, 3 Oct 1911). German philosopher. He had some impact on musicology in the early 20th century through his view that music history from Schütz to Beethoven was a continuous development.

Dima, Gheorghe (*b* Braşov, 10 Oct 1847; *d* Cluj, 4 June 1925). Romanian composer, conductor and teacher. He studied at the Leipzig Conservatory. He conducted Handel, Haydn and Mendelssohn oratorios in Sibiu, also founding a conservatory in Cluj. His vocal music is in a Romantic, folk-influenced idiom; he founded the tradition of modern Romanian songwriting.

Diminished interval. A perfect or minor interval from which a semitone has been subtracted.

Diminished seventh chord. A chord consisting of three superimposed minor 3rds (e.g. B–D–F–A♭).

Diminished triad. A chord built of two superimposed minor 3rds (e.g. B–D–F).

Diminuendo (It.). 'Diminishing': an instruction to become quieter, sometimes expressed with a 'hairpin' or abbreviated *dim.*

Diminution. Term denoting a kind of ornamentation involving the breaking down of a number of long notes into a larger number of short notes – that is, a diminution of note values through the increase in the number of notes to be played in the same time. It is one of the commonest methods in the Renaissance and Baroque periods of introducing melodic variation. The term is also used, particularly regarding fugue, for the playing of a melody in shorter notes (commonly at double speed).

D'Indy, Vincent. *See* INDY, VINCENT D'.

Dioclesian (The Prophetess, or The History of Dioclesian). Semi-opera by Purcell to a text by T. Betterton after J. Fletcher and P. Massinger (1690, London).

Direct [custos]. The symbol placed at the end of a staff, or a page, to indicate the first note of the next staff. It appears in musical sources from the 11th century onwards. It takes various forms, the commonest being akin to a sign for a mordent on the line or in the space of the note it stands for, with a tail extending upwards and forwards.

Dirge. A generic title for English burial poems and songs of mourning; the word comes from the antiphon 'Dirige, Dominus Deus meus' in the Roman Office for the Dead.

Diruta, Girolamo (*b* ?Deruta, nr. Perugia, *c*1554; *d* after 1610). Italian organist and theorist. In 1574 he entered the Franciscan monastery at Correggio and *c*1580 moved to Venice, where (he claimed) Zarlino, Merulo and Porta were his teachers. He was organist at the cathedrals of Chioggia (from 1593) and Gubbio (from 1609). His comprehensive treatise on organ playing (*Il transilvano*, 2 pts, 1593, 1609), in dialogue form, ranges widely from basic technique to the rules of counterpoint; it includes many compositions (toccatas, ricercares, hymns etc), some by Diruta himself, and is the first treatise

of its kind. He also published motets (1580).

His nephew Agostino (*c*1595–*c*1650) was organist at Venice, Asola and Rome and published over 20 books of sacred music.

Discant. A type of medieval polyphony based on a plainchant tenor, characterized by note-against-note contrary movement between the voices and the interchange of the consonances (octave, 5th and 4th). It originated as an improvisation technique, but in later written sources is found within organal plainchant settings, where it contrasts with a more melismatic style, and in clausulas and conductus. In English discant the *cantus firmus* was sometimes in the upper voice rather than the tenor; the added voice could be in a number of different ranges and a technical device known as the 'sight', involving mental transposition, was applied in improvisation.

Discography. Term referring to the description, listing and study of sound recordings, applicable alike to disc, tape, wire, cylinder, piano and organ roll and audio-visual media. Periodicals containing discographies appeared as early as 1923 but discography as a practice comparable to bibliography dates from 1936.

Discord. *See* DISSONANCE.

Disjunct. A term applied to a melodic line that moves by leap (i.e. in intervals of more than a 2nd) rather than in conjunct motion (by step).

Disposition. The arrangements of stops among the keyboards or divisions of a harpsichord or organ.

Dissonance. Two or more notes sounding together and forming a discord, or a sound which, in the prevailing harmonic system, is unstable and needs to be resolved to a consonance.

Dissonance Quartet. Nickname of Mozart's String Quartet in C K465 (1785), so called because of the striking dissonances in the introduction.

Di Stefano, Giuseppe (*b* Motta Santa Anastasia, 24 July 1921). Italian tenor. He sang at La Scala in 1947 and made the first of many appearances at the Met in the following season. His earlier singing was noted for beautiful tone and effective use of *pianissimo*; his natural elegance of delivery later became roughened with the assumption of heavier roles, such as Bizet's Don José and Verdi's Radamès. His British début was at Edinburgh in 1957, as Donizetti's Nemorino, and he sang Cavaradossi at Covent Garden in 1961. He was Callas's partner during her 1973–4 concert tour.

Distler, Hugo (*b* Nuremberg, 24 June 1908; *d* Berlin, 1 Nov 1942). German composer. He studied at the Leipzig Conservatory with Grabner, Ramin and Högner, who led him to an interest in Baroque and pre-Baroque organ music. He then worked as an organist, choral conductor and teacher in Lübeck, Stuttgart (1937–40) and Berlin. Harassment by the authorities led him to suicide. His works consist mostly of choral and organ music, characterized by harmonic boldness within a tonal milieu.

Distratto, Il. Haydn's Symphony no.60 in C (1774), so called because it uses incidental music Haydn wrote for the comedy *Der Zerstreute*, after J.F. Regnard's *Le distrait* (1774).

Dital. A lever for adjusting the pitch of such instruments as the harp, lute and guitar.

Ditfurth, Franz Wilhelm Freiherr von (*b* Rinteln an der Weser, 7 Oct 1801; *d* Nuremberg, 25 May 1880). German folksong collector. He collected folksongs from Franconia and historical songs from Germany and Austria, publishing nearly 20 volumes.

Dithyramb. Name for Dionysus and a song in his honour. Greek dithyrambs were written between about 700BC and AD200. The term was revived in the 19th century for pieces intended to evoke the wild and vehement qualities of Dionysus (Bacchus); there are examples this century by Medtner and Stravinsky.

Ditson, Oliver. American firm of music publishers. It was founded in Boston in 1857 but traces its history to the earliest music publishing firm in the USA (Ebenezer Batelle, 1783). By 1890 it was the largest in the nation, its catalogue listing over 100 000 titles (vocal, choral, instrumental, and music literature including books and journals); educational material was a speciality. In 1937 the firm was bought by Theodore Presser.

Dittersdorf, Carl Ditters von [Ditters, Carl] (*b* Vienna, 2 Nov 1739; *d* Neuhof, Bohemia, 24 Oct 1799). Austrian composer. He was a violinist in the Prince of Saxe-Hildburghausen's orchestra in Vienna, 1751–61, then served under Count Durazzo at the imperial court theatre. As Kapellmeister to the Bishop of Oradea, 1765–9, he wrote his first vocal works. In 1770–95 he was Kapellmeister to the Prince-Bishop of Breslau; he assembled an opera troupe and had several Italian comic operas staged. He was named Knight of the Golden Spur in 1770 and in 1773 ennobled. Beginning with the highly successful *Doctor und Apotheker* (1786), he wrote a series of Singspiels for Vienna; in the 1790s he wrote several for Oels.

Widely renowned in his day, Dittersdorf was a major figure of the Viennese Classical school. His instrumental output includes over 40 concertos, chamber music and (most important) *c*120 symphonies, including 12 based on Ovid's *Metamorphoses* (*c*1786). Witty effects, irregular phrases and folk elements appear, and some later works are tightly and subtly constructed. Most enduring were his Singspiels, which fuse folklike and *opera buffa* styles. He also composed other stage works, oratorios (notably *Esther*, 1773), cantatas and sacred music. His memoirs provide much fascinating information about musical life in his time.

Divertimento. A musical form prominent in the Classical period, much used by Haydn, Mozart and other Austrian composers. The title was commonly applied to a light piece for keyboard or, more often, an ensemble of soloists. There are usually between five and nine movements. Several 20th-century composers, including Bartók and Berkeley, have applied the title to easygoing pieces for string or chamber orchestra.

Divertissement. Term used in France since the 17th century for music, usually with spectacle and dance, intended for diversion. The major Baroque composers wrote *divertissements* in larger theatrical works. Others, such as the *grands divertissements* ordered by

Louis XIV in 1664 and 1674, were self-contained entertainments resembling Italian serenatas. *See also* DIVERTIMENTO.

Divine Office. A series of eight services performed each day and night in the Roman Catholic Church: Matins (originally Vigils), often at 3 a.m.; Lauds, at daybreak; Prime, at 6 a.m.; Terce, at 9 a.m.; Sext, at noon; None, at 3 p.m.; Vespers, at twilight; Compline, before retiring. Prime, Terce, Sext and None are often referred to as the Little Hours. Services are composed of psalms and canticles with antiphons, lessons followed by responsories, hymns, versicles with responsories and prayers; they are arranged in a fixed pattern throughout the day and year (the 'cursus'). Features of the Office existed in the early Jewish prayer hours: it was established in Christian communities by the 6th century.

Divine Poem, The [Bozhestvennaya poema]. Skryabin's Symphony no.3 in C minor, op.43 (1904).

Divisi (It.). 'Divided': an instruction for one section of the orchestra (particularly a string one) to divide into two or more, taking separate parts often notated on the same staff.

Division. 17th-century English term for a variation technique in which the notes of a *cantus firmus* or a ground bass are 'divided' into shorter ones. Divisions were extemporized, especially by viol players, and sometimes notated. Instructions are contained in Christopher Simpson's *The Division-Violist* (1659).

Division viol. An English form of bass viola da gamba (*see* VIOL), used in the 17th century for performing free ornamentation by varying given melodies (*see* DIVISION). It was the equivalent of the European viola bastarda, and was smaller than a consort bass viol but larger than a lyra viol.

Divitis, Antonius (*b* Louvain, *c*1470; *d* 1515–34). Flemish composer. Master of the choirboys at St Donatien, Bruges, from 1501 and of St Rombaut, Mechelen, from 1504, he became a singer in Philip the Handsome's chapel at Brussels in 1505 and travelled with the court to Spain. He later joined the court of Louis XII. His works include three parody masses, a requiem, two mass sections, three Magnificats, seven motets and a *chanson*. With his four-part parody masses, based on works by Mouton, Richafort and Agricola, he played an important role in shaping a technique that was to dominate mass composition in the 16th century. His *chanson* is a large-scale cantus firmus setting of the melody of Ockeghem's *Fors seulement*.

Dixieland jazz. A style of traditional jazz played by white musicians of the early New Orleans school; the term is often used for New Orleans jazz as a whole or for its post-1940 revival.

Dixon, (Charles) Dean (*b* New York, 10 Jan 1915; *d* Zug, 4 Nov 1976). American conductor. He studied in New York, founding a chamber orchestra there in 1938. He made frequent guest appearances with leading orchestras in the 1940s but held no permanent appointment. Wider scope came in Sweden (Göteborg SO, 1953–60), West Germany (Hesse RSO, Frankfurt, 1961–74) and Australia (Sydney SO, from 1964). His achievements did much to open doors to black musicians.

Dizi, François Joseph (*b* Namur, 14 Jan 1780; *d* Paris, Nov 1847). South Netherlands harpist and composer. The most renowned harpist in London during 1800–30, he was highly regarded as a teacher and composer, his most important work being 48 harp studies which are still used.

Djamileh. Opera in one act by Bizet to a libretto by Gallet (1872, Paris).

Dobbs, Mattiwilda (*b* Atlanta, 11 July 1925). American soprano. She studied with Lotte Lehmann and Bernac, and made her opera début as Stravinsky's Nightingale (Holland Festival, 1952). Her La Scala début followed in 1953, the year she sang Zerbinetta at Glyndebourne. In 1957 she joined the Met company, having made her début as Gilda the previous year; she sang coloratura roles, including Donizetti's Lucia.

Dobroven [Dobrowen], **Issay Alexandrovich** (*b* Nizhny-Novgorod, 27 Feb 1891; *d* Oslo, 9 Dec 1953). Norwegian conductor. He studied at the Moscow Conservatory under Taneyev and in Vienna with Godowsky, then embarked on a career in Russia but settled in Germany, holding posts in Berlin and Dresden (1924), in Frankfurt and San Francisco (from 1930) and Budapest (1936–9), specializing in Russian music. He went to Oslo in the 1930s and became a Norwegian citizen, escaping in 1940 to Sweden. In 1949 he conducted and produced a notable Russian season at La Scala.

Dobrowolski, Andrzej (*b* Lwów, 9 Sept 1921). Polish composer. He studied with Malawski (1945–51) and has taught at the conservatories of Kraków and Warsaw. His works, following a development parallel to Lutosławski's, include orchestral and instrumental pieces, electronic music and songs; later works are characterized by craftsmanship and animated wit.

Dobrzyński, Ignacy Feliks (*b* Romanów, 25 Feb 1807; *d* Warsaw, 9 Oct 1867). Polish composer. He studied at the Warsaw Conservatory, then travelled in Germany. He wrote three operas, vocal, chamber and orchestral music in the Viennese Classical tradition and piano music showing Chopin's influence.

Docteur Miracle, Le. Operetta in one act by Bizet to a libretto by Battu and Halévy (1857, Paris).

Dodd, John (Kew) (*b* ?London, 1752; *d* Richmond, Surrey, 1839). English bow maker. The finest before Tubbs, he probably began making bows in 1780–90, of the 'swan' head type and the more novel, squat 'hammer' head type; later he adopted continental innovations including the metal ferrule and the octagonally shaped stick. For their ideal length and weight his cello bows are sought after by modern players. His brother Thomas (*d* 1834) was a London instrument seller, and his nephew James a bow maker.

Dodecaphony (from Gk.). '12-sounding': a synonym for atonality or 12-note serial composition.

Dodge, Charles (Malcolm) (*b* Ames, IA, 5 June 1942). American composer. He studied at Columbia University, notably with Otto Luening, and at Princeton (computer music). He has composed computer music since the mid-1960s, seeking in such works as *Changes* (1970) to extend the medium's expressive range; *Speech Songs* (1972) uses computer techniques

to create a variety of vocal sounds. Since 1977 he has directed the Center for Computer Music at Brooklyn College.

Dodgson, Stephen (Cuthbert Vivian) (*b* London, 17 March 1924). English composer. He studied at the RCM, where he has taught since 1965. His music, generally on a modest scale, is tasteful and fluently written; it includes song cycles, reflecting his sensitivity to English poetry, and instrumental works (among them pieces for guitar, harpsichord and various wind instruments) which show his urbane style and grasp of idiomatic writing. He is married to the harpsichordist and scholar Jane Clark.

Dogleg jack. A form of jack on harpsichords without a manual coupler.

Döhl, Friedhelm (*b* Göttingen, 7 July 1936). German composer. He studied with Fortner at the Freiburg Musikhochschule (1956–64) and has taught in Berlin (1969–74) and Basle (director of the academy from 1974). His works include Webernian chamber music and collaborations with visual artists.

Dohnányi, Christoph von (*b* Berlin, 8 Sept 1929). German conductor, grandson of Ernő Dohnányi. His first major appointment was with the Frankfurt Opera, 1968–75, after which he joined the Hamburg Opera. His British début was with the LPO (1965) and in 1984 he became principal conductor of the Cleveland SO. Dohnányi's technical command is often placed at the disposal of modern music; premières he has given include Henze's *Der Junge Lord* (1965, Berlin) and *The Bassarids* (1966, Salzburg).

Dohnányi, Ernő [Ernst von] (*b* Bratislava, 27 July 1877; *d* New York, 9 Feb 1960). Hungarian composer and pianist. He studied with Thomán and Koessler at the Budapest Academy (1894–7) and came quickly to international eminence as both pianist and composer. After teaching at the Berlin Hochschule (1905–15) he returned to Budapest and worked there as pianist, teacher, conductor and composer. His influence reached generations in all spheres of musical life and he is considered one of the chief architects of 20th-century Hungarian musical culture; he championed the music of Bartók and Kodály. He also toured internationally as a pianist, ranking among the greatest of his time, and as a conductor (his pupils included Solti). He left Hungary in 1944 and in 1949 settled in the USA. His works are in a Brahmsian style, crossed with Lisztian virtuosity and thematic transformation; they include two symphonies (1901, 1944), two piano concertos (1898, 1947), two piano quintets (1895, 1914) and two violin concertos (1915, 1950), the popular Variations on a Nursery Song for piano and orchestra (1914) and three string quartets (1899, 1906, 1926).

Doktor Faust. Opera in eight scenes by Busoni to his own libretto after Marlowe; it was completed by Jarnach (1925, Dresden).

Dolce (It.). Sweet; *con dolcezza* means 'with sweetness'.

Doles, Johann Friedrich (*b* Steinbach, 23 April 1715; *d* Leipzig, 8 Feb 1797). German composer. He studied with Bach at Leipzig, conducting the Grosses Konzert there, then became Kantor at Freiberg and co-director of the Gymnasium, for which he wrote a school opera (1748). From 1756 he was Kantor at St Thomas's, Leipzig (Bach's former post), where Mozart visited him in 1789. A leading composer of Protestant church music, he wrote at least 160 cantatas, 35 motets and several Passions, oratorios and masses. Some cantatas and motets are of the 'figured chorale' type virtually invented by him, simple chorale settings with orchestral ritornellos. He also composed lieder, organ chorales and other keyboard music. Reflecting Bach's influence, his music is carefully crafted, but its style is more melodic. Some pieces are richly ornamented. Doles had a lasting influence as teacher and choir trainer.

Dollé, Charles (*fl*?1735–55). French composer. He was a viol player and teacher in Paris, possibly a pupil of Marais. He published six books of chamber music, some for viol, some for the pardessus and trio sonatas (1737–54), of which two are lost. The early viol works follow Marais's style, but the later works become progressively more Italianate while retaining French ornamentation.

Dolly. Suite (op.56) for piano duet by Fauré (1897).

Dolmetsch, (Eugène) Arnold (*b* Le Mans, 24 Feb 1858; *d* Haslemere, 28 Feb 1940). English musician of French, German, Swiss and Bohemian descent. He studied at the Brussels Conservatoire and the RCM. By 1889 he had begun to restore early instruments, giving concerts at his home in the 1890s. He made a lute in 1893, a clavichord in 1894; later he was noted for his reconstructions of recorders. He worked in the USA and France before World War I and in 1925 founded the early music festival at Haslemere. He studied, collected and edited MSS and published a pioneering book on the interpretation of 17th- and 18th-century music (1915), laying the foundations for later widespread interest in early music. His son Carl (*b* 1911), a virtuoso recorder player, became musical director of the Haslemere Festival in 1947 and is responsible for the Dolmetsch Foundation, established in 1929 to further the study and performance of early music. He is a frequent recitalist, for whom many works have been written.

Dolzaina. A reed instrument, similar to the medieval shawm, played primarily in France, the Netherlands and Spain (14th and 15th centuries) and Italy (16th century). Tinctoris described it as having seven finger-holes and a thumb-hole. It was made in several sizes of which the tenor (range *c–d'*) was the most common.

Domaine Musical. Organization founded in Paris by Boulez in 1954. It had its own ensemble and presented concerts of pre-Classical and 20th-century music and important new works. Boulez conducted (1957–67), then Amy; it disbanded in 1973, having served as a model for similar groups.

Domestic Symphony. *See* SYMPHONIA DOMESTICA.

Domgraf-Fassbänder, Willi (*b* Aachen, 19 Feb 1897; *d* Nuremberg, 13 Feb 1978). German baritone. Study in Berlin and Milan was followed by engagements at Dusseldorf and Stuttgart. He sang at the Berlin Staatsoper, 1928–45, taking part in the première of Egk's *Peer Gynt* admired by Hitler. At Glyndebourne his pleasing voice and lively personality were admired in Mozart.

Dominant. The fifth step or degree of the major or minor scale, important in tonal music as the highest note of the tonic triad; the key of the dominant is the natural complement to the tonic key.

Dominant seventh chord. Chord consisting of a major triad on the fifth scale degree (the dominant) with an added minor 7th from the root (e.g. G–B–D–F).

Domingo, Plácido (*b* Madrid, 21 Jan 1937). Spanish tenor. He was taken to Mexico in 1950 and sang baritone roles in zarzuelas from 1957. His first major tenor role was Donizetti's Arturo (1961, Dallas). After four years with the Israel National Opera he sang Pinkerton at the New York City Opera (1965). Engagements with the Met and at many European houses confirmed his position as the leading lyric-dramatic tenor of his time. In roles as diverse as Cavaradossi, Othello and Lohengrin he has performed with sensitive phrasing and dramatic conviction, his vocal gifts allied to a warm, outgoing stage personality. Since 1973 he has also conducted opera.

Dominicus Mass. Mass in C K66 by Mozart.

Donath, Helen (*b* Corpus Christi, TX, 10 July 1940). American soprano. She studied in New York and pursued a career in Germany, singing notably at Cologne (from 1962), Hanover and Munich. Her roles include Pamina (Salzburg, 1967), Sophie (San Francisco and with Vienna Staatsoper) as well as sacred music. She is noted for the flexibility and purity of her light lyric soprano.

Donati. German family of organ and clavichord builders. The most celebrated members were Christoph the elder (1625–1706), whose work included the organs at St Nicolai Cathedral, Luckau (1672–4), and the Schlosskirche, Eisenberg (1683–8); and his son Johannes Jacobus (*b* 1663), organ builder at the courts of Gotha and Altenburg and a prolific and talented craftsman. Members of the family were active in Zwickau, Glauchau and Altenburg until the end of the 18th century.

Donati, Ignazio (*b* Casalmaggiore, *c*1575; *d* Milan, 21 Jan 1638). Italian composer. He held many posts as *maestro di cappella*, notably at the cathedrals of Urbino (1596–8, 1612–15), Novara (1623–9) and Milan (from 1631). Composing almost exclusively church music, he was important as a pioneer of the small-scale concertato motet in which he contrasted varied vocal groupings with contrapuntal dexterity and melodic charm. The preface to the 1636 collection of solo motets, his most brilliant in style, contains interesting ideas on the teaching of singing, while the *Salmi boscarecci* (1623) are notable for their optional supporting parts and alternative methods of performance.

Donato, Baldassare (*b*?1525–30; *d* Venice, 1603, probably June). Italian composer. He spent his life in Venice, singing at St Mark's from 1550 and becoming vice-*maestro* (1588) and *maestro di cappella* (1590). He is an important figure in the history of Italian light secular music: his book of *napolitane* (1550) was very popular and influential and show him freeing the villanella from the restrictions of Neapolitan dialect song and giving it a more international flavour. Some serious madrigals (1553, 1568) and sacred music

(1599), less noteworthy, were also published.

Donato da Cascia (*fl* Florence, late 14th century). Italian composer. He was probably a Benedictine or Camaldolensian monk from Cascia, near Florence. 17 compositions ascribed to him – 14 madrigals, a caccia, a ballata and a virelai – have survived. All but the three-part caccia are for two voices and all but the virelai are in Tuscan sources. They vary widely in style: some use syllabic articulation throughout, others are based on rhythmic or melodic imitation.

Donatoni, Franco (*b* Verona, 9 June 1927). Italian composer. He studied with Pizzetti at the Accademia di S Cecilia (1952–3), Rome, and moved towards modernism as a result of meeting Maderna in 1953; he has taught at various Italian institutions. His works show remarkable powers of self-renewal, with the influence of Petrassi replaced successively by those of Webern, Boulez, Stockhausen and Cage, but leading, since the mid-1960s, to personal means of responding to the crisis in values through perfection of craftsmanship and the re-use of old materials. Nearly all his works are orchestral or instrumental; they include *Puppenspiel* nos.1 and 2 (1961–5) and *Per orchestra* (1962).

Donaueschingen Festival of Contemporary Music (West Germany). Annual (autumn) event revived in 1950 from a festival founded in 1921, which was the earliest devoted to contemporary music. Many internationally renowned composers had works first performed there, including Berio, Boulez, Henze, Hindemith, Ligeti, Messiaen, Nono, Penderecki, Stockhausen, Webern and Xenakis.

Don Carlos. Opera in five acts by Verdi to a French libretto by Méry and du Locle after Schiller (1867, Paris); Verdi revised it several times, notably in four acts in Italian (1884, Milan).

Don Giovanni. Opera in two acts by Mozart, to a libretto by Da Ponte (1787, Prague) based on one written by Casti for an opera by Gazzaniga (1787, Venice).

Doni, Giovanni Battista (*b* Florence, bap. 13 March 1595; *d* there, 1 Dec 1647). Italian classicist, philologist and music theorist. He served in diplomatic and administrative posts and was associated with Mersenne in Paris. From *c*1630 he dedicated himself to rediscovering ancient Greek music, believing that the application of its methods to modern composition would lead music to a new flowering. His revival of the Greek modes and the instruments he designed (notably the 'lyra Barberina') led to experiments by Frescobaldi, Luigi Rossi and others. He also wrote on the history and styles of modern dramatic music.

Donington, Robert (*b* Leeds, 4 May 1907). English musicologist. He studied the viol, the violin and interpretation with Arnold Dolmetsch. He has divided his career between performance and scholarship at universities in the USA. Among his writings on opera is a provocative Jungian interpretation of Wagner's *Ring* (1963). He has written *The Instruments of Music* (1949), but a major contribution is his *The Interpretation of Early Music* (1963), which has become an indispensable reference work with its many quotations from treatises, its valuable insights into problems of performing practice and its commonsense, musicianly attitude towards their solution.

Donnerstag aus Licht. Opera in three acts by Stockhausen to his own libretto (1981, Milan), the first completed work of the seven-opera cycle *Licht*.

Donizetti, (Domenico) Gaetano (Maria) (*b* Bergamo, 29 Nov 1797; *d* there, 8 April 1848). Italian composer. He was of humble origins but received help and a solid musical education (1806–14) from Mayr, producing apprentice operas and many sacred and instrumental works before establishing himself at Naples with *La zingara* (1822). Here regular conducting and a succession of new works (two to five operas a year) marked the real start of his career. With the international triumph of *Anna Bolena* (1830, Milan) he freed himself from Naples; the further successes of *L'elisir d'amore* and *Lucrezia Borgia* (1832, 1833, Milan), *Marino Faliero* (1835, Paris) and the archetype of Italian Romantic opera, *Lucia di Lammermoor* (1835, Naples), secured his pre-eminence. Some theatrical failures, however, as well as trouble with the censors and disappointment over losing the directorship of the Naples Conservatory to Mercadante, caused him to leave for Paris, where besides successful French versions of his earlier works he brought out in 1840 *La fille du régiment* and *La favorite*. His conducting of Rossini's *Stabat mater* (1842, Bologna) and enthusiasm in Vienna for *Linda di Chamounix* (1842) led to his appointment as Kapellmeister to the Austrian court. Declining health began to affect his work from this time, but in *Don Pasquale* (1843, Paris) he produced a comic masterpiece, and in the powerful *Maria di Rohan* (1843, Vienna), *Dom Sébastien, roi di Portugal* (1843, Paris) and *Caterina Cornaro* (1844, Naples) some of his finest serious music.

Donizetti's reputation rests on his operas: in comedy his position has never been challenged but in the tragic genre, though his work sums up a whole epoch, no single opera can be considered an unqualified masterpiece. His works survive through the grace and spontaneity of their melodies, their formal poise, their effortless dramatic pace, their fiery climaxes and above all the romantic vitality underlying their artifice. Like Bellini, Donizetti epitomized the Italian Romantic spirit of the 1830s. Having imitated Rossini's formal, florid style for ten years (1818–28) he gradually shed heavily embellished male-voice parts, conceiving melodies lyrically and allowing the drama to determine ensemble structures. From 1839 his style was further enriched by fuller orchestration and subtler, more varied harmony. If he contributed nothing so distinctive to the post-Rossinian tradition as Bellini's 'heavenly' melody, he still showed a more fluent technique and a wider-ranging invention, from the brilliant to the expressive and sentimental. He was particularly responsive to the individual qualities of his singers, including Persiani (*Lucia*), Pasta and Ronzi de Begnis (*Anna Bolena*, *Maria Stuarda*, *Roberto Devereux*), the baritone Giorgio Ronconi and the tenors Fraschini and Moriani (*L'elisir d'amore*, *Lucia*).

Although his practical facility and readiness to adapt scores themselves constructed of 'spare-part' set forms once brought criticism, since 1950 revivals and reassessment as well as a fuller understanding of the theatrical practices of his day have restored Donizetti to critical and popular favour.

Dramatic music Anna Bolena (1830); L'elisir d'amore (1832); Lucrezia Borgia (1833); Maria Stuarda (1835); Marino Faliero (1835); Lucia di Lammermoor (1835); Roberto Devereux (1837); La fille du régiment (1840); La favorite (1840); Linda di Chamounix (1842); Don Pasquale (1843); Maria di Rohan (1843); Dom Sébastien, roi di Portugal (1843); Caterina Cornaro (1844); Poliuto (1848; comp. 1838); *c*50 others; over 25 cantatas and occasional works
Vocal chamber music *c*250 songs and duets with pf acc.; choruses
Sacred music *c*100 works, incl. Requiem, d, for Bellini (1835); Miserere, g (1837); Ave Maria (1842)
Instrumental music 13 sinfonias; 5 concs., incl. Concertino, G, eng hn (1817); 19 str qts; chamber music; pf pieces

Don Juan. Tone poem by Richard Strauss (1889).
The legend of Don Juan has been the subject of many operas, the best known being Mozart's *Don Giovanni*. Other composers who have used the story include Melani, Gazzaniga, Fabrizi, Federici, Dibdin, Pacini, Dargomïzhsky, Delibes, Alfano and Goossens; Gluck wrote a ballet on it (1761).

Donohoe, Peter (*b* Manchester, 18 June 1953). English pianist. He studied at Chetham's School and the Royal Northern College in Manchester, and under Loriod in Paris. A silver medallist in the 1982 Moscow Tchaikovsky competition, he has shown a commanding technique and vitality in a broad repertory from Bach and Beethoven to Prokofiev and Bartók.

Donostia, José Antonio de (*b* San Sebastian, 10 Jan 1886; *d* Lecároz, 30 Aug 1956). Spanish composer. He studied in Barcelona, San Sebastian and Paris (with Roussel), and was an organist until he was appointed in 1943 to direct folk music studies at the Spanish Institute of Musicology (he was an authority on Basque music). His early works are Romantic-impressionist in style, his later (notably a Requiem, 1945, and choral music) show more refinement and concision.

Don Pasquale. Opera in three acts by Donizetti to a libretto by G. Ruffini and the composer after Anelli's *Ser Marc'Antonio* (1843, Paris).

Don Quichotte. Opera in five acts by Massenet to a libretto by Henri Cain after Le Lorrain's play based on Cervantes's novel (1910, Monte Carlo).

Don Quixote. Tone poem by Richard Strauss, with solo parts for cello and viola (1897). Cervantes's novel (1605, 1615) has inspired many musical works, including operas by Förtsch, Conti, Boismortier, Paisiello, Piccinni, Salieri, Mendelssohn, Mercadante, Donizetti, Massenet, Macfarren, Clay, Jaques-Dalcroze and Falla. Ballets include Petipa's (1869), with music by Minkus, and those by Petrassi, Ibert and Gerhard.

Doppio (It.). 'Double', e.g. *doppio movimento* ('double the tempo').

Doppioni. A woodwind instrument of the late 16th century and early 17th, known principally in Italy. Zacconi (1592) named three sizes, soprano (compass

c′–d′′′), tenor (*c–d′*) and bass (*C–a*).

Doppler, (Albert) Franz [Ferenc] (*b* Lwów, 16 Oct 1821; *d* Baden, 27 July 1883). Polish, later Hungarian, flautist and composer. From 1841 he was the first flautist at the Hungarian National Theatre, where five of his operas, notably *Benyovszky* (1847), were staged with success. He helped found the Hungarian PO, worked as flautist, later chief conductor, of the Vienna Court Opera ballet, writing some 15 ballets, and made well-known transcriptions of Liszt's Hungarian Rhapsodies. His brother Karl (1825–1900), also a flautist, wrote mainly songs and incidental music.

Dorati, Antal (*b* Budapest, 9 April 1906). American conductor of Hungarian birth. After study in Budapest he conducted at the Royal Opera there (1924). From 1933 to 1945 he was associated with ballet companies in Europe and the USA. His abilities as an orchestral trainer were recognized in appointments with the Dallas SO (1945–9), Minneapolis SO (1949–60), BBC SO (1962–6) and Detroit SO (1977–81). He has championed Bartók's music and given many first performances and with the Philharmonia Hungarica has recorded all Haydn's symphonies. His conducting is distinguished by vigorous direct rhythm and an ear for colour. His own compositions make no concessions to contemporary fashion.

Doret, Gustave (*b* Aigle, 20 Sept 1866; *d* Lausanne, 19 April 1943). Swiss composer. He studied with Dubois and Massenet in Paris, where he began his career as a conductor. Later he divided his time between Switzerland, where he was an important musical figure, and Paris, composing operas (often collaborating with Morax on Swiss subjects), songs and much choral music.

Dörffel, Alfred (*b* Waldenburg, 24 Jan 1821; *d* Leipzig, 22 Jan 1905). German music librarian and writer. He supervised music printing for Breitkopf & Härtel and C.F. Peters, opened his own music lending library, edited several volumes of the Bach Gesellschaft Gesamtausgabe and contributed to the *Neue Zeitschrift für Musik* and *Musikalisches Wochenblatt*.

Dorian. The second of the eight traditional church modes, the authentic MODE on D. The term 'Dorian sixth' means the raised sixth degree in the minor mode (e.g. F♯ in A minor).

Dorian Toccata and Fugue. Nickname of a toccata and fugue in D minor (BWV538) for organ by J.S. Bach (1717), so called because Bach omitted a B♭ from the key signature, giving the impression the work is in the Dorian mode.

Dorn, Heinrich Ludwig Egmont (*b* Königsberg, 14 Nov 1800; *d* Berlin, 10 Jan 1892). German conductor and composer. He was conductor to the Königsberg city theatre, subsequently working in Leipzig, Hamburg, Riga, Cologne (where he founded the Rheinische Musikschule, 1848) and Berlin. As a composer, his reputation was based on his humorous lieder, though he wrote many operas, including a setting of the Nibelung saga (1854).

Dornel, Louis-Antoine (*b c*1680; *d* Paris, soon after 1756). French composer. He was an organist in

Paris from 1706 and in 1725–42 *maître de musique* to the Académie Française, writing annual motets. His published works include trio and solo sonatas (influenced by Corelli), harpsichord pieces, solo cantatas and *airs*.

Dot. Above a note, a dot signifies that the note is to be played STACCATO (or, if beneath a slur, PORTATO). In 16th-century keyboard music, it may indicate chromatic alteration. To the right of a note, it indicates that the value of that note should be increased by half (in some earlier notations and systems of performing practice, the modification may be different). In early mensural notation, a dot may indicate a rhythmic division. Dots in vertical pairs or groups of four alongside a double bar or a bar-line indicate a passage to be repeated.

Dotted rhythms. Rhythms in which long notes alternate with one or more short ones, so called because the long notes are usually written with the aid of the dot of addition (*see* NOTE VALUES). In the 17th and 18th centuries, particularly, dotted rhythms were not always performed in exact accordance with their notation, so that short notes in different voices could be brought into synchronization (see ex.1, where the

Ex. 1 Bach: Goldberg Variations, variation 16

two dotted crotchets need to be performed as double dotted crotchets, and the following quavers as semiquavers, if the notes in the two hands are to sound together). Similarly, dotted figures are often found against triplets and in some cases the rhythms may be accommodated; however, there is evidence that in such a context as ex.2 the dotted rhythms should

Ex. 2 Bach: Sonata no. 4 for violin and harpsichord BWV*1017, 3rd movt*

rather be sharpened and the duplet quavers (left hand, bar 14; violin, bar 15) played as triplets. In French overtures and other pompous and arresting music, notated in dotted rhythm, contemporary writers suggested that the short note following the dot should be played rapidly and energetically, exaggerating the rhythm; whether it is correct practice automatically to 'double-dot' in such contexts – that is, play the rhythms in a ratio nearer to 7:1 than 3:1 – remains a matter of controversy. Another context where rhythms need to be sharpened is shown

Ex. 3

in ex.3, where the initial note may need to be played short to match the rhythms that follow. *See also* NOTES INÉGALES.

Dotzauer, (Justus Johann) Friedrich (*b* Häselrieth, 20 Jan 1783; *d* Dresden, 6 March 1860). German cellist, teacher and composer. He played in the court orchestras at Meiningen and Leipzig and in the Dresden royal orchestra (1811–50). His four influential cello tutors and his teaching ability resulted in the 'Dresden School' of playing.

Double. Term used to qualify particular instruments, either to mean of double size and pitched an octave lower (for example, the double bassoon) or to signify a double mechanism or a paired instrument (double horn, double flageolet). The French word *double* means variation, usually (as in Bach's keyboard music) of an elaborate melodic character.

Double bar. Two vertical lines (one of them normally heavy) drawn through the staff to mark off a section of a piece; *see* BAR.

Double bass [contrabass, string bass, bass]. The largest and lowest-pitched bowed string instrument (for illustration, *see* VIOLIN). The modern double bass has four or five strings and often plays an octave lower than the cello. In the orchestra it supplies power, weight and a rhythmic foundation. More rarely, it is heard as a soloist (its repertory includes over 200 concertos). There are two basic designs, one shaped like a viola da gamba, with sloped shoulders, the other like a violin. Small basses are little bigger than a cello, while full-size instruments can have a body of up to *c*140 cm; the standard (three-quarter) size is *c*115 cm. Normal four-string instruments are tuned E'–A'–D–G. Strings are tuned with brass machines with steel worm-screws; early basses had large wooden pegs. Music for the instrument is notated an octave higher than pitch.

The double bass, or its predecessor the violone, entered the orchestra in the late 17th century and early 18th. Court orchestras of the mid-18th century included basses, sometimes more numerous than the cellos. It was often used without a cello in Classical divertimento-style music. A modern symphony orchestra generally has at least eight. Chamber music with double bass includes Beethoven's Septet and Schubert's 'Trout' Quintet and Octet and Dvořák's String Quintet. 20th-century composers have exploited the bass in their search for less familiar tone colours, e.g. Prokofiev's Quintet and works by Henze, many of which use artificial harmonics. In jazz considerable virtuosity in pizzicato technique is required, particularly since the advent of amplification. In many countries the bass is used in military and concert bands.

Double bassoon [contrabassoon, contrafagotto]. A bassoon with a basic pitch one octave below the normal BASSOON (for illustration, *see* WOODWIND INSTRUMENTS).

Double counterpoint. Two-part INVERTIBLE COUNTERPOINT.

Double dot. Term referring to the use of two dots after a note, so prolonging it by three-quarters of its original length. It also refers to the rhythmic convention of the Baroque period by which (it is supposed) certain single-dotted rhythms should be played more sharply than notated, i.e. as if they were double dotted. Double-dotted rhythms, though found in French music as early as *c*1660, were little notated until the 19th century. *See* DOTTED RHYTHMS.

Double fugue. A fugue with two main subjects: they may appear initially as subject and counter-subject, or the second may have its own exposition.

Double harpsichord. A two-manual HARPSICHORD.

Double horn. A HORN with a fourth valve to change it from one key to another (usually *F* to *B*♭).

Double stop. The playing of two notes simultaneously on a bowed string instrument, by stopping two strings. *See* MULTIPLE STOPPING.

Double tonguing. *See* TONGUING.

Douglas, Clive Martin (*b* Rushworth, 27 July 1903; *d* Melbourne, 29 April 1977). Australian composer. He studied at the Melbourne University Conservatorium and worked as a conductor with ABC orchestras (1936–66). His richly orchestrated works show an interest in aboriginal culture; *Three Frescoes* (1971) approaches serialism.

Dowd, William (Richmond) (*b* Newark, NJ, 28 Feb 1922). American harpsichord maker. He was in partnership with Frank Hubbard at Boston, but later established his own workshop in Cambridge, Massachusetts (1958), building *c*20–22 harpsichords a year on historical models; a workshop in Paris (from 1971) produces 20–24 a year. Most are two-manual harpsichords based on those of the Blanchets, Hemsch and Taskin. Dowd's instruments are in wide use by leading players.

Dowland, John (*b* ?London, 1563; *d* there, bur. 20 Feb 1626). English composer. He became a Catholic while serving the English ambassador in Paris (1580–84) and in 1588 graduated BMus at Oxford. In 1592 he played the lute to the queen, then travelled in Europe, visiting the courts of Brunswick, Kassel, Nuremberg and cities in Italy, where he met Marenzio. He was back in London in 1597, then became a lutenist at the Danish court (1598–1603, 1605–6). On his return he served Lord Walden (1609–12) and eventually achieved his ambition, the post of court lutenist, in 1612. He had been awarded a doctorate by 1621 and played at James I's funeral in 1625. He was succeeded by his son Robert (*c*1591–1641), also known for the lute collections he edited.

Though known in his day as a virtuoso lutenist and singer, Dowland was also a prolific, gifted composer of great originality. His greatest works are inspired by a deeply felt, tragic concept of life and a preoccupation with tears, sin, darkness and death. In the best of his 84 ayres for voice and lute (published mainly in 4 vols., 1597, 1600, 1603, 1612), he markedly raised the level of English song, matching perfectly in music the mood and emotion of the verse; in his best songs, such as *In darknesse let mee dwell*, he freed himself of almost all conventions, accompanying the singer's strange, beautiful melody with biting discords to express emotional intensity to an extent unsurpassed at the time. His 70-odd pieces for solo lute include intricate polyphonic fantasias, expressive dances and elaborate variation sets; foremost among his other instrumental music is the variation set *Lachrimae*, which contains the famous 'Semper Dowland semper dolens', characterizing his air of melancholy. But he could also write in a lighter vein, as in the ballett-like *Fine Knacks for Ladies*. He also wrote psalm settings and spiritual songs.

Secular vocal music over 80 ayres, v, lute, incl. In darknesse let mee dwell, Flow my teares, Fine Knacks for Ladies
Instrumental music Lachrimae, viol consort, lute (1604); *c*70 lute fantasias, pavans, galliards, almains, jigs
Sacred vocal music 14 psalms and spiritual songs

Downbeat. The accented beat at the beginning of a bar, by analogy with the downward stroke in conducting; opposites are UPBEAT and OFF-BEAT.

Down by the Greenwood Side. 'Dramatic pastoral' by Birtwistle to a text by Michael Nyman (1969, Brighton).

Downes, Edward (Thomas) (*b* Birmingham, 17 June 1924). English conductor. He studied at the RCM and with Scherchen. In 1952 he joined Covent Garden and gave notable readings of Russian opera and the *Ring*. In 1972 he conducted the première of Maxwell Davies's *Taverner* and the following year gave Prokofiev's *War and Peace* at the Sydney Opera House, of which he was musical director (1972–6). In 1980 he became principal conductor of the BBC Northern SO (BBC Philharmonic from 1983).

Downes, (Edwin) Olin (*b* Evanston, IL., 27 Jan 1886; *d* New York, 22 Aug 1955). American music critic. He wrote for the *Boston Post* (1906–24) and the *New York Times* (1924–55) and lectured and broadcast widely. His reviews strongly influenced taste in the USA: he recognized the value of new works by Richard Strauss, Stravinsky, Prokofiev and Shostakovich and was a passionate advocate of Sibelius's music.

Downes, Ralph (William) (*b* Derby, 16 Aug 1904). English organist. After study at the RCM, in 1928 he became organist and musical director of the Princeton University chapel. From 1936 he was organist at Brompton Oratory, London, soon earning a reputation as a recitalist and broadcaster; his Bach recordings were widely praised. His pioneering design for the Festival Hall organ (1948–51) had much influence.

Doxology. Christian liturgical formula praising God. The greater doxology is the Gloria ('Gloria in excelsis deo') of the Latin Mass; the lesser is the text beginning 'Gloria Patri' ('Glory to God the Father and to the Son and to the Holy Spirit, now and always and to the ages of ages. Amen') adopted in the 4th century, which concludes most Office Psalms, introits and canticles. Its music is determined by the music of the psalm etc with which it is associated.

Doyagüe, Manuel José (*b* Salamanca, 17 Feb 1755; *d* there, 18 Dec 1842). Spanish composer. He was choirmaster at Salamanca Cathedral and professor at the University; one of the best-known Spanish composers of his time, he wrote sacred vocal music, notably dramatic *Miserere* settings.

Draeseke, Felix (August Bernhard) (*b* Coburg, 7 Oct 1835; *d* Dresden, 26 Feb 1913). German composer. He showed progressive tendencies at the Leipzig Conservatory and was influenced by Wagner and by Liszt at Weimar, but had little success with his early, programmatic works. Later, cultivating Classical instrumental forms, he gained contrapuntal mastery and produced much vocal music as well as the operas *Gudrun* (1884), *Herrat* (1892) and *Fischer und Kalif* (1905) and the oratorio trilogy *Christus* (1895–9).

Drag. A type of stroke in side-drum playing, involving a rapid double prefatory stroke before the main one.

Draghi, Antonio (*b* Rimini, ? 17 Jan 1634–16 Jan 1635; *d* Vienna, 16 Jan 1700). Austrian composer. He was probably trained in Venice, and entered the dowager Empress Eleonora's service in Vienna in 1658, becoming assistant Kapellmeister in 1668 and Kapellmeister in 1669. During this decade he was active as a librettist. He presented his first stage work in 1666; many of his later works were for the court of the Emperor, Leopold I, where he became director of dramatic music in 1673. From 1682 he was imperial court Kapellmeister. His son Carlo Domenico (1669–1711) became a court organist and a composer.

Draghi was one of the most prominent and prolific composers in Vienna in his day, especially in dramatic music. He frequently collaborated with the librettist Nicolò Minato and the stage designer L.O. Burnacini. Nearly half of his 124 secular stage works are three-act operas with classical subject matter. They make increasing use of da capo arias and like his other works are based on the mid-17th-century Venetian style. His *c*40 sacred dramatic works include *sepolcri* (for Maundy Thursday or Good Friday), notable for their subdued tone and low instrumental sonorities, and oratorios. Draghi also composed several other sacred works and 50 serenatas, chamber cantatas etc.

Draghi, Giovanni Battista (*b c*1640; *d* London, 1708). Italian composer, possibly a brother of Antonio Draghi. He went to England in connection with Charles II's abortive plans to establish opera there, and in 1673 was installed as organist of the queen's Catholic chapel in Somerset House, moving to James II's private chapel in 1687. For a time he was music master to the royal princesses. Important for his part in establishing the 'seriousness and gravity' of the Italian style at a time when French influence was still strong in England, he composed mainly songs (many for plays) and instrumental music, including six suites of harpsichord lessons (*c*1707).

Drăgoi, Sabin V(asile) (*b* Selişte, 18 June 1894; *d* Bucharest, 31 Dec 1968). Romanian composer. He studied at the conservatories of Cluj (1919–20) and Prague (1920–22, with Novák), and worked as a teacher, notably as director of the Timişoara Conservatory (1925–43). His works are based on Romanian folk music (of which he made many editions). His opera *The Plague* (1927) was a major contribution to the Romanian repertory.

Dragonetti, Domenico (Carlo Maria) (*b* Venice, 10 April 1763; *d* London, 16 April 1846). Italian double bass player and composer. He played in Venetian theatre orchestras before settling in London in 1794, appearing regularly in concerts and provincial festivals for the next half century; he was renowned for his expressive, virtuoso performances, on a large, three-string instrument, with the cellist Robert Lindley. His numerous works, mostly for double bass, include eight concertos and over 30 string quintets. His giant double bass is now in the Victoria and Albert Museum, London.

Drame lyrique. Term for a genre of late 19th- and early 20th-century French opera. Epitomized by many of Massenet's operas, it was more intimate than grand opera and richer in style than the serious sort of *opéra comique*.

Dramma giocoso. Term used by Goldoni and other late 18th-century librettists for operas in which elevated characters appear alongside the peasants and servants of *opera buffa*. An example is Mozart's *Don Giovanni*.

Dramma [drama] per musica. The usual term for a Baroque Italian opera libretto, especially of a serious or heroic kind.

Drdla, František Alois (*b* Žďár nad Sázavou, 28 Nov 1869; *d* Bad Gastein, 3 Sept 1944). Czech composer and violinist. He studied at the conservatories of Prague and Vienna, played in Viennese opera orchestras and toured widely as a violinist. He composed operettas and chamber music, but was known internationally for his salon pieces.

Dream of Gerontius, The. Choral work by Elgar (op.38), a setting of Cardinal Newman's poem for mezzo-soprano, tenor, bass, chorus and orchestra (1900, Birmingham).

Drechsler, Joseph (*b* Vlachovo Březí, 26 May 1782; *d* Vienna, 27 Feb 1852). Bohemian composer, conductor and organist. He wrote music for Singspiels and farces at the Theater in der Leopoldstadt, Vienna, and was Kapellmeister of St Stephen's Cathedral; once highly regarded for his pedagogical works, he is now known for his music for Ferdinand Raimund's plays.

Dreigroschenoper, Die *See* THREEPENNY OPERA, THE.

Drei Pintos, Die. Comic opera in three acts by Weber to a libretto by Theodor Hell after C. Seidel's *Der Brautkampf*; Weber left it unfinished and Mahler completed the score (1888, Leipzig).

Dresden, Sem (*b* Amsterdam, 20 April 1881; *d* The Hague, 30 July 1957). Dutch composer. He studied with Pfitzner in Berlin (1903–5), then returned to the Netherlands, where he was director of the conservatories of Amsterdam (1924–37) and The Hague (1937–49). His music up to *c*1935 consists of chamber and vocal works influenced by French and German contemporaries; thereafter he wrote concertos and large choral works.

Dresden Amen. A cadence to 'Amen', composed in

Dresden by J.G. Naumann. Wagner used it extensively in *Parsifal*.

Dresden Philharmonic Orchestra. East German orchestra founded in Dresden *c*1870; its home is the Palace of Culture (opened 1969). It soon made foreign tours; early guest conductors and soloists included Brahms, Dvořák, R. Strauss and Tchaikovsky. Popular symphony concerts were given from 1912. Festivals with the Staatsoper and of modern music were given under Paul van Kempen (1934–42), under whom the orchestra achieved world fame.

Dresden Staatsoper. Opera company in Dresden, originally the court opera. In the 18th century it had an Italian repertory and visited Russia and Poland. From 1817 German opera was conducted by Weber and later by Wagner, including premières of *Der fliegende Holländer* (1843) and *Tannhäuser* (1845). One of its greatest periods was under Ernst von Schuch (1882–1914), who gave 51 new works, including four by R. Strauss. Later conductors included Fritz Busch (1922–33) and Karl Böhm (1934–42). It continues to give contemporary as well as standard works.

Drese, Adam (*b* Thuringia, *c*1620; *d* Arnstadt, 1701). German composer and viola da gamba player. While music director to Duke Wilhelm IV at Weimar he compiled a catalogue (1662) of his music which shows that he played an important role in transmitting the Italian style from region to region (he had studied in Warsaw, Regensburg and Dresden, under Schütz). By 1663 he was Kapellmeister at the Jena court, also directing opera, but on Duke Bernhard's death (1678) he moved to the Schwarzburg court where he came into contact with the Bach family. His surviving music includes songs, funeral music and dances.

Dressler, Gallus (*b* Nebra, 16 Oct 1533; *d* Zerbst, 1580–89). German composer. After studies in the Netherlands and at Jena, he became Kantor at Magdeburg (1558). He took a degree at Wittenberg (1570) and later held posts at Zerbst and Anhalt. He published many polyphonic Latin sacred works, but is more important for his contribution to the German motet and his psalm settings. Three theoretical treatises by him survive.

Dretzel, Cornelius Heinrich (*b* Nuremberg, bap. 18 Sept 1697; *d* there, 7 May 1775). German composer. He was a grandson of Georg Dretzel (*c*1610–after 1676; organist of St Michael, Schwäbisch Hall) and nephew of Valentin, the most important member of the family. He was organist of St Lorenz (from 1743) and of St Sebald. His reputation as a virtuoso player and contrapuntist is supported by his solo harpsichord concerto, *Harmonische Ergötzung*, influenced by Bach's *Italian Concerto*. Of hymnological importance is his *Evangelisches Choralbuch* (1731) which contains over 900 melodies with continuo, most appearing in print for the first time in their local versions; the preface discusses the origin and development of the chorale.

Dretzel, Valentin (*b* Nuremberg, bap. 30 May 1578; *d* there, bur. 23 March 1658). German composer. He was from a Nuremberg family of musicians ac-

tive from the 16th century to the 18th. A virtuoso organist, he succeeded Johann Staden as organist of St Lorenz (1618) and St Sebald (1634), holding the latter post until his death. His principal publication, *Sertulum musicale* (1620), is a collection of motets for three to eight voices with instruments and continuo, and includes two ricercares and two canzonas.

Dreyfus, George (*b* Wuppertal, 22 July 1928). Australian composer. He went to Melbourne in 1939 and studied as a bassoonist at the university conservatorium. In 1960–65 he consolidated a serial technique and thereafter concentrated on composition, working in all genres and for films and television. He has promoted Australian music through his New Music Ensemble (founded 1958) and chamber orchestra (1970).

Drigo, Riccardo (*b* Padua, 30 June 1846; *d* there, 1 Oct 1930). Italian conductor and composer. He worked in Russia for over 40 years, as conductor of the Italian Opera in St Petersburg and later of the Imperial Ballet, conducting the premières of Tchaikovsky's *Sleeping Beauty* and *Nutcracker*. His own ballet *Arlekinada* (1900) enjoyed international renown.

Driving. 17th-century term for syncopation.

Drone. A sustained sound, or a musical instrument or part of one that produces such a sound and maintains it through a section of music. Bagpipes usually have one or more drones.

Drottningholm. Theatre at the royal palace, Stockholm, opened in 1766 (cap. 400; restored 1920s); it replaced a smaller theatre (1754, burnt 1762). It was not used after 1800 but its costumes, scenery and machinery survived and have provided information on 18th-century performing practice. A summer season of 18th-century operas (including Swedish) has been given since the 1940s; a festival (May–Sept) was established in 1953.

Drouet, Louis (*b* Amsterdam, 1792; *d* Berne, 8 Sept 1873). French flautist. He was immensely successful in Paris and London, touring throughout Europe as a virtuoso and producing an admirable tutor (1827) and many technical studies, notably the *Cent études*.

Druckman, Jacob (Raphael) (*b* Philadelphia, 26 June 1928). American composer. He studied with Persichetti and Mennin at the Juilliard School (1949–56), with Copland at Tanglewood (1949–50) and in Paris (1954). He has taught at the Juilliard School and, since 1972, at Brooklyn College. His works of the 1950s and 1960s are generally of vocal or instrumental chamber music, including tape in the important *Animus* series (1966–9). Since the early 1970s he has produced sophisticated, characterful orchestral scores; the first, *Windows* (1972), won a Pulitzer Prize; *Mirage* (1976), *Aureole* (1979) and *Prism* (1980) quote from other composers' works, creating a 'new Romanticism'.

Drum. A percussion instrument with a skin (or plastic) head stretched over a frame or body shell of wood, metal, earthenware or bone. It is known in almost every age and culture. Drums are sounded in three ways: percussion, where they are struck with the hands or with beaters, or shaken; friction, where the membrane, or a stick or cord in contact with it, is rubbed; and plucking, where a string knotted below the membrane is plucked so that its vibrations are transferred to the skin. Most drums are struck. These have various shapes: kettledrums, which are bowl-shaped; tubular drums, which may be cylindrical, barrel-shaped, double-conical, hourglass-shaped, conical or goblet-shaped; and frame drums.

Drums were among the earliest instruments. In many areas they are used as message drums or served sacred or ritual purposes. They are represented in the art of ancient Egypt, Assyria, India and Persia. They were known to the Greeks and Romans; small kettledrums and tabors of Arab or Saracen origin came to Europe during the 13th-century crusades. Larger kettledrums reached the West from the Ottoman Empire during the 15th century.

In the orchestra, membrane drums are either of definite pitch (timpani) or of indeterminate pitch (bass, side and tenor drums). The bass consists of a cylindrical shell of wood with two heads. The bass drum is normally played from a standing position, supported on a stand or suspended in a frame. For the normal single stroke it is struck with a large felt-headed stick. The bass drum was rare in Europe until the 18th century when the imitation of the Turkish janissary bands became fashionable: Gluck seems to have made the earliest use of it; he was followed by Mozart (*Die Entführung aus dem Serail*, 1782), Haydn ('Military' Symphony, 1794) and Beethoven (Ninth Symphony, 1823). Romantic composers such as Berlioz, Liszt (credited with introducing the roll), Wagner, Verdi and Sibelius used it extensively. Stravinsky's use of it in the finale of *The Rite of Spring* remains one of its finest moments.

The side (or snare) drum, so called because the original military instrument was slung from the shoulder and worn angled at the player's side, consists of a cylindrical shell of wood or metal covered at each end with a head of calfskin or plastic. They range from 10 to 30 cm in depth and are 35–40 cm in diameter. Across the lower head are stretched snares, eight or more strings of gut, wire, wire-covered silk or nylon, whose vibration gives the drum its characteristic crisp timbre. It is played with tapered wooden drumsticks with acorn-shaped ends. The foundation of side-drumming is the 'roll', with such patterns as the 'paradiddle' and embellishments as the 'flam', 'drag' and 'ruff'. The earliest known side drum is the medieval tabor, represented in early 13th- and 14th-century art as a rope-tensioned drum with snares. Such music as was written down is military, consisting mainly of instructions for signalling and pace-making. The association of drum and fife, first recorded in 1332, continued for many centuries, as important to the foot regiment as the trumpets and kettledrums to the cavalry. By the 19th century composers, notably Rossini (*La gazza ladra*), made increasing use of the side drum; it is prominent in works by Rimsky-Korsakov, Elgar, Ravel, Nielsen, Bartók, Shostakovich, Britten, Sessions and Carter, some of whom have exploited its rhythmic resources and numerous tone colours.

The tenor drum is cylindrical, larger in diameter (*c*45 cm) than depth (*c*36 cm). Tonally it is between the bass drum and the unsnared side drum; it is played with hard or soft sticks. In England, France and Germany it appeared in the military band during the 19th century. Berlioz used a tenor drum in his *Grande messe des morts*; Wagner wrote for it in *Rienzi, Lohengrin, Die Walküre* and *Parsifal*, and Strauss in *Ein Heldenleben*.

Drum machine. See ELECTRONIC PERCUSSION.

Drumroll Symphony. Nickname of Haydn's Symphony no.103 in Eb, which begins with a roll on the kettledrums.

Drum set [drum kit, trap set]. The basic equipment of jazz, dance band and rock drummers, including a bass drum, snare drum and suspended cymbal, with ancillary instruments according to the style of music.

Drury Lane Theatre. London theatre, properly the Theatre Royal. It is the fourth (opened 1812) on the site; the first opened in 1663. Many new English operas were given there in the late 18th and the 19th centuries as well as British premières of many German (including Wagner) and Russian operas up to 1919.

Druschetzky [Družecký], **Georg** (*b* Druzek, Bohemia, 7 April 1745; *d* Budapest, 6 Sept 1819). Bohemian composer. An oboist, he was a regimental musician in Austria until 1775, and then a conductor and drummer in the public service. He later served at Bratislava, and from 1807 at Budapest. His large output includes over 200 works for wind ensemble, symphonies, other instrumental works, and stage and sacred music.

Drysdale, (George John) Learmont (*b* Edinburgh, 3 Oct 1866; *d* there, 18 June 1909). Scottish composer. He studied at the RAM, winning high praise and returning to Scotland only in 1904. His best works, far more Scottish idiomatically than those of Mackenzie or MacCunn, include the prize-winning overture *Tam o'Shanter* (1890), the opera *The Red Spider* (1898), the tone poem *A Border Romance* (1904) and the cantata *Tamlane* (1905).

Düben, Gustaf (*b* Stockholm, *c*1628; *d* there, 19 Dec 1690). Swedish collector of music and composer. He was one of a large family of musicians of German descent, and the son of Andreas Düben (*c*1597–1662), conductor of the Swedish court orchestra (from 1640) and organist of two Stockholm churches. He inherited his father's positions as conductor of the court orchestra and organist of the German Church in 1663. Most of his works are continuo songs (with a few choral and instrumental pieces), but his chief significance is as a collector. The Düben Collection, given by his son to Uppsala University in 1732, consists of 1500 vocal and over 300 instrumental works, one of the richest late 17th-century sources, containing many unique compositions. Among the autographs by foreign composers is Buxtehude's cantata cycle, *Membra Jesu nostri*, with a dedication to Düben. His son Anders von Düben (1673-1738) was also a musician at the Swedish court.

Dubois, (François Clément) Théodore (*b* Rosnay, Marne, 24 Aug 1837; *d* Paris, 11 June 1924). French composer, teacher and organist. After a rigorous training, he devoted himself to composing church music, serving as *maître de chapelle* of Ste Clotilde, Paris, where he produced his oratorio *Les sept paroles du Christ* (1867), and later of the Madeleine, and to teaching at the Conservatoire. His treatises on harmony and on counterpoint and fugue are still widely used.

Dubrovnik Festival (Yugoslavia). Annual (summer) music and drama festival founded in 1950; events include concerts, opera and dance.

Du Buisson. There are several composers of this name in 17th-century France. One (*d* by 1688) wrote the earliest surviving French viol music. Another worked at Louis XIV's court and wrote motets. A third apparently lived in Paris and composed almost entirely drinking-songs (16 books, 1686–96, and in collections), which were popular in their day.

Du Caurroy, Eustache (*b* ?Gerberoy, bap. 4 Feb 1549; *d* Paris, 7 Aug 1609). French composer. A singer at court from *c*1570, he was vice-*maître* of the Chapelle Royale until 1595 and then *surintendant de la musique*. He wrote motets, psalms, *chansons* and instrumental fantasias (many published posthumously). His requiem remained the official mass for French kings' funerals.

Duckles, Vincent H(arris) (*b* Boston, 21 Sept 1913; *d* Berkeley, 1 July 1985). American musicologist and librarian. He studied at Berkeley and Columbia University. After teaching he became head of the music library at Berkeley in 1947 (which he built into one of the finest research libraries) and subsequently professor of music. He has worked on 17th-century English song but is known for his valuable *Music Reference and Research Materials* (1964).

Duct flute. A wind instrument with a windway or duct to lead the air to the instrument's lip, e.g. the penny whistle and the recorder.

Ductia. Medieval Latin term used by Johannes de Grocheo (*De musica*, *c*1300) to describe two forms: a type of light, rapid song sung by boys and girls for dances and an instrumental dance similar to the *estampie*.

Due corde (It.). 'Two strings': a direction in piano music to depress the 'una corda' pedal partway, so that the hammers strike two of the three strings for each note, producing an effect between 'una corda' and 'tre corde'.

Due Foscari, I. Opera in three acts by Verdi to a libretto by Piave after Byron (1844, Rome).

Duet. A vocal or instrumental piece (or section of one) for two performers, with or without accompaniment. The operatic love duet and the piano duet are widely disseminated types.

Dufaut (*d* before 1682–6). French composer. One of the most renowned lutenists of his time, he appears to have travelled in England and Germany. Many of his 80 known pieces for ten or 11-course lute were printed in Ballard's important collections of 1631 and 1638. His music is characterized by rhythmic flexibility expressed through notated rubato and by the anticipation and retardation of melody notes.

Dufay, Guillaume (*b c*1398; *d* Cambrai, 27 Nov 1474). French composer, acknowledged by his contemporaries as the leading composer of his day. Having been trained as a choirboy at Cambrai Cathedral, where he probably studied under Loqueville, he seems to have entered the service of the Malatesta family in Pesaro some time before 1420. Several of his works from this period were written for important local events. After returning briefly to Cambrai and establishing links with Laon, where he held two benefices, he was a singer in the papal choir in Rome from 1428 until 1433, when he became associated with the Este family in Ferrara and the Dukes of Savoy. He rejoined the papal choir (1435–7), and composed the famous motet *Nuper rosarum flores* for the dedication of Brunelleschi's dome of Florence Cathedral in 1436, but spent his later years (apart from 1451–8, when he was again in Savoy) at Cambrai, where he was visited as a celebrity by such musicians as Binchois, Tinctoris and Ockeghem. Although he composed up to his death, most of his late works are lost.

Working in a period of relative stability in musical style, Dufay achieved distinction rather by consummate artistry than bold innovation. More than half his compositions, including most of his antiphons, hymns, Magnificats, sequences and single items of the Mass, are harmonizations of chant, with the melody usually in the upper part. Most of his motets are imposing compositions written to celebrate a political, social or religious event; four- and five-part textures, often alternating with duos, are common, two or more texts may be set simultaneously, and isorhythm is sometimes used. Others, in a three-voice, treble-dominated style, are more direct and intimate expressions of religious sentiment. Moving from early paired mass movements to the developing form of the cyclic tenor mass, he was apparently the first to base a cycle on a secular melody. Outstanding among his masses is the *Missa 'Ave regina celorum'*, perhaps his last composition. He also composed secular songs, three-quarters of them rondeaux. As an artist of international fame, he is represented in some 70 MSS in many countries.

Sacred music Missa sine nomine; Missa 'Ave regina celorum'; Missa 'Ecce ancilla Domini'; Missa 'L'homme armé'; Missa 'S Jacobi'; Missa 'Se la face ay pale'; Missa 'St Antony'; Missa 'Caput' (authorship uncertain); 2 three-section masses; 5 mass pairs; *c*20 single mass movts; *c*30 motets; *c*60 other works
Secular music over 50 rondeaux; *c*10 ballades; 4 virelais; *c*15 other works

Duff. Generic term for a single-headed instrument akin to the Western tambourine, usually with a goatskin membrane and often with rattles or jingles. It is known in the Middle East, Central Asia, southern Europe and parts of Africa, South Asia and Latin America.

Dukas, Paul (Abraham) (*b* Paris, 1 Oct 1865; *d* there, 17 May 1935). French composer. He studied with Guiraud at the Paris Conservatoire (1881–9) and became a friend of Debussy, d'Indy and Bordes. His Franckian leanings are evident in his first published work, the overture *Polyeucte* (1891), though Beethoven is also suggested, as again in his Symphony in C (1896). But the symphonic scherzo *L'apprenti sorcier* (1897) is more individual, not least in its augmented-triad and diminished-7th harmonies, which influenced Stravinsky and Debussy. The next years were devoted to the opera *Ariane et Barbe-Bleue* (1907), though at the same time he produced two piano works of Beethovenian range and power: the Sonata in E♭ minor and the *Variations, interlude et final sur un thème de Rameau*. Dukas' self-criticism constricted his later output. Apart from the exotic ballet *La péri* (1912) he published only a few occasional works. He cultivated craftsmanship to an extreme degree and his orchestration has been widely admired and imitated. His voluminous criticism reveals an unusual breadth of sympathy and he was a conscientious editor of Beethoven, Couperin, Rameau and Scarlatti and an admired teacher at the Conservatoire.

Duke Bluebeard's Castle [A Kékszakállú herceg vára]. Opera in one act by Bartók to a libretto by B. Balázs (1918, Budapest).

Dulcimer. A string instrument of the box zither family, without keyboard. It often has a trapeziform box. Its strings, commonly two to six for each course, are unfretted; the courses are usually in intersecting horizontal planes. The player may hit the strings with hammers or pluck them with the fingers or a plectrum. The instrument has been used in Western popular, folk and art music; it is widespread in eastern Europe, North Africa, Central Asia, India, Korea and China and is eminent in the classical music of Iran.

The body is almost always a box, commonly $c1$ m along the bottom side. Small instruments $c60$ cm long were made in Flanders in the 17th century and England in the 19th, and larger ones $c130$ cm long are known in England, the USA and Alpine areas. The concert cimbalom is even larger, $c160$ cm long. Bridges are of wood, usually with a wire rod in the top. Hammers may have hard or soft heads; steel piano wire is used for the strings.

The instrument was introduced to western Europe in the 15th century, possibly from Byzantium. The medieval psaltery is usually held flat against the body, the player looking out and away from the instrument. More detail is known about the Baroque dulcimer; surviving instruments have 18 to 25 courses. Dulcimers were played in Bohemia, England (Pepys mentioned it in 1662 as accompanying puppet shows) and Spain and became more widespread in Italy. Mersenne (1663–7) illustrated a double-course instrument with notes on only one side of a single bridge. In 1704 Pantaleon Hebenstreit brought a large version to Louis XIV, who is said to have decreed that it should be called 'pantaleon'. 18th-century instruments could have as many as five bridges and seven or eight strings to a course. The repertory includes Scottish and Irish dances.

The concert cimbalom was accorded orchestral status by Liszt, in the revised version of his *Ungarischer Sturmmarsch* (1876) and his Sixth Hungarian Rhapsody. The instrument's association with Hungarian gypsy music was exploited by Kodály (*Háry János*, 1926) and Bartók (Violin Rhapsody no.1, 1928). Stravinsky used it in *Reynard* (1915–16) and

Ragtime (1918).

Dulcken. Flemish family of harpsichord makers, of German origin. The founder of the family workshop in Antwerp was Joannes Daniel Dulcken (*d* 1757), whose renown as a harpsichord maker was second only to that of the Ruckers family. He made single- and double-manual instruments, generally with a five-octave compass, three registers and a florally decorated soundboard; eight examples survive, dated 1745 to 1755. After his death his widow and youngest son Joannes (1742–75) moved the workshop to Brussels (1764–70); his eldest son Johan Lodewijk (1736–after 1793) became known in Amsterdam as an organ builder.

Dulichius, Philipp (*b* Karl-Marx-Stadt, 18 Dec 1562; *d* Szczecin, 24 March 1631). German composer. He taught at Szczecin (Stettin) from 1587 and supervised music at the court. His 12 published books of liturgical works (1589–1630) are mostly for large forces, notably motets which are highly expressive of their texts; he ignored continuo and concertato techniques in favour of a synthesis of Venetian and Netherlands styles. He was nicknamed 'the Pomeranian Lassus'.

Dumbarton Oaks Concerto. Popular name for Stravinsky's Concerto in E♭ for chamber orchestra because it was first performed at Dumbarton Oaks, Washington, DC (1938), at the home of R.W. Bliss, who commissioned it.

Dumka. A type of Ukrainian folk music. The name (pl. *dumky*) was adopted in Slavonic countries in the 19th century for a sung lament or an instrumental piece of a melancholy character. In the latter context it is associated particularly with Dvořák, whose dumky sometimes have quicker middle sections.

Dumky Trio. Piano Trio in E minor op.90 (1891) by Dvořák.

Dump. A name for doleful English pieces (possibly written *in memoriam*), mainly for lute or keyboard, of $c1540$–1640; most have an ostinato bass.

Dunayevksy, Isaak Iosifovich (*b* Lokhvitsa, 30 Jan 1900; *d* Moscow, 25 July 1955). Soviet composer. He studied with Bogatïryov at the Khar'kov Conservatory (1915–19) and in the 1920s worked in theatres. With his 12 operettas (notably *The Bridegrooms*, 1927) he renewed Russian musical comedy, freeing it from the Viennese stereotype. Later he adapted jazz in his popular songs and film scores.

Dunhill, Thomas (Frederick) (*b* London, 1 Feb 1877; *d* Scunthorpe, 13 March 1946). English composer. After study with Stanford at the RCM he founded a series of chamber concerts in London to promote music by young British composers. He was most succesful with his chamber music and educational piano pieces.

Duni, Egidio (Romualdo) (*b* Matera, bap. 11 Feb 1708; *d* Paris, 11 June 1775). Italian composer. He studied with Durante in Naples and wrote some ten serious operas (most to Metastasio texts) for Italian theatres, 1735–55, beginning with the highly successful *Nerone* in Rome; he also presented an opera in London (1737). He had works given in various Italian cities but $c1750$ became *maestro di cappella* at the Parma court. There he composed his last serious opera and an *opera buffa* (1756–7), and was drawn by the French orientation there to *opéra comique*. Moving to Paris, he wrote *c*20 works in the form up to 1770; the first, *Le peintre amoureux de son modèle* (1757), was especially successful and influential. As music director of the Comédie-Italienne, 1761–8, he won success with *Mazet* (1761). One of the chief *opéra comique* composers of his day, Duni assimilated the French idiom and added to it Italianate *ariettes* and recitatives, helping to create the *comédie mêlée d'ariettes*. His operas contain natural and expressive declamation and skilful characterization. His brother Antonio (*c*1700–*c*1766), also a composer, held posts at Madrid, Moscow and elsewhere.

Dunstable [Dunstaple], **John** (*b c*1390; *d* 24 Dec 1453 [or later, ?1459]). English composer, acknowledged as the most eminent of the Englishmen who strongly influenced the generation of Dufay and later continental composers. Little is certainly known about his career; he was probably not the John Dunstavylle who was at Hereford Cathedral, 1419–40, but may have been in the service of the Duke of Bedford before 1427. He was in the service of Queen Joan of Navarre, second wife of Henry IV, 1427–36, and was *serviteur et familier domestique* in the household of Henry, Duke of Gloucester, in 1438. In the late 1430s he held lands in northern France. There is evidence that he was also an astronomer. He was buried at St Stephen's, Walbrook, where his epitaph described him as 'prince of music'.

Most of his surviving music is in continental sources. 51 compositions are consistently stated in MS sources to be his, but many others, anonymous or with conflicting ascriptions, are probably by him. Stylistically, his music can be divided into four categories: isorhythmic works in which a plainchant tenor forms the lowest of three or four parts; non-isorhythmic works based on a plainchant that may be in any of the three parts; works in 'free treble' or 'ballade' style, consisting of a freely composed melodic line (which may however incorporate traces of elaborated plainchant) and two slower supporting parts; and declamatory works in a syllabic style with careful accentuation of the text. Two of the earliest mass cycles, *Rex seculorum* and *Da gaudiorum premia*, are ascribed to him in some sources and some of his mass movements may originally have belonged to complete cycles. Most of his works are in three parts, except for the isorhythmic motets which are mostly in four, and, while nearly all begin in triple time, there is often a change to duple near the middle and sometimes a shorter return to triple towards the end. His melodies are characterized by stepwise and triadic movement, and the harmony, reflecting the English predilection for 3rds and 6ths, is predominantly consonant.

Sacred music Four-movement mass 'Da gaudiorum premia'; 2 pairs of mass movts; 2 complete masses (authorship uncertain); single mass movts; *c*12 motets; *c*20 other sacred works
Secular music chansons, ?other pieces

Duo. *See* DUET.

Duodrama. MELODRAMA with two principal characters.

Duparc, Elisabeth ['Francesina'] (*d* ?1778). French soprano. She trained in Italy, and from 1736 sang in London, where she appeared in many performances of Handel's operas and oratorios. She specialized in agile singing; her natural warble was ideal for bird songs. Her most famous role was Semele.

Duparc [Fouques Duparc], **(Marie Eugène) Henri** (*b* Paris, 21 Jan 1848; *d* Mont-de-Marsan, 12 Feb 1933). French composer. He studied the piano and composition with Franck, writing works that he later destroyed; this loss, together with a crippling psychological condition that caused him to abandon composition at the age of 36, has resulted in a legacy of just 13 songs (composed 1868–84). An important influence is Wagner, seen in the ambitious harmonic structure of *Chanson triste* and the shifting chromaticism of *Soupir*. Yet Duparc's feeling for poetic atmosphere and the craftsmanship he used to communicate it, as in the sinister drama of *La manoir de Rosemonde*, were unique, giving the French *mélodie* a rare musical substance and emotional intensity. From 1885 he led a quiet life, remaining close to Ernest Chausson and cultivating his aesthetic sensibility through reading and drawing.

Duphly, Jacques (*b* Rouen, 12 Jan 1715; *d* Paris, 15 July 1789). French harpsichordist and composer. He was briefly organist at Evreux Cathedral and then at Rouen. In 1742 he settled in Paris, making his name as a harpsichordist, teacher and composer. His four harpsichord collections (1744–68) are modelled chiefly on Rameau's. Book 3 (1758) includes a long, brilliant chaconne and a savage tirade, *La Médée*.

Du Plessis, Hubert (Lawrence) (*b* Malmesbury district, 7 June 1922). South African composer. He studied in South Africa and at the RAM and has taught at the universities of Cape Town and Stellenbosch. His works use Afrikaans and Cape Malay folksongs. He is a well-known pianist, harpsichordist and writer.

Duplet. A group of two notes or chords to be performed in the time of three.

Duplum, duplex (Lat.). 'Double': terms used in medieval theory to denote (1) two-voiced polyphony (e.g. 'organum duplum'); (2) compound, or composite, of an interval; (3) the second voice of a polyphonic work, composed in duet with the tenor; and (4) the lengthening of duration ('longa duplex') or the halving of it ('proportio dupla') in mensural notation.

Duport, Jean-Pierre (*b* Paris, 27 Nov 1741; *d* Berlin, 31 Dec 1818). French cellist and composer. He performed in Paris in the 1760s and from 1773 was first cellist at the Berlin court. Mozart wrote piano variations on a minuet of his in 1789 and Beethoven may have written his op. 5 sonatas for him. He composed mostly virtuoso cello music, including sonatas and a concerto.

His brother Jean-Louis (1749–1819), also a cellist, appeared with him in Paris and then went to Berlin, returning to Paris in 1806 and later serving at Marseilles; he wrote virtuoso cello concertos and sonatas and a cello method (*c*1813), which still serves as the basis of modern technique.

Du Pré, Jacqueline (*b* Oxford, 26 Jan 1945; *d* London, 19 Oct 1987). English cellist. After study with William Pleeth at the GSM she made her recital début in London in 1961. The following year her technical proficiency and romantic warmth were revealed in Elgar's Concerto, a work with which she was always associated. Her American début was in 1965. In 1967 she married Daniel Barenboim, with whom she also formed a musical partnership. Multiple sclerosis halted her playing career in 1973 but she continued as an influential teacher.

Dupré, Marcel (*b* Rouen, 3 May 1886; *d* Meudon, 30 May 1971). French composer and organist. He studied with Guilmant, Vierne and Widor at the Paris Conservatoire (1902–14), returning as professor of organ (1926–54) while also serving as organist of St Sulpice (1934–71) and appearing internationally as a recitalist. His works introduced a Lisztian virtuosity and a contemplative modality into organ music; he also wrote religious symphonic poems. Alain and Messiaen were among his pupils.

Duprez, Gilbert(-Louis) (*b* Paris, 6 Dec 1806; *d* there, 23 Sept 1896). French tenor and composer. He created the role of Edgardo in *Lucia di Lammermoor* (1835, Naples), also singing leading roles, often for their Paris premières, in works by Halévy, Auber and Donizetti and in Berlioz's *Benvenuto Cellini* (1838). He was greatly admired for his declamation and the smoothness of his *canto spianato*. Among his works are six operas and three books, notably *Souvenirs d'un chanteur* (1880).

Dupuy, Jean Baptiste Edouard (*b* Corcelles, Neuchâtel, *c*1770; *d* Stockholm, 3 April 1822). Swiss violinist, singer and composer. He was a touring violinist, an orchestral musician in Stockholm, a singer in Copenhagen and, from 1811, court conductor in Stockholm, where he produced his own theatrical works, Mozart operas and contemporary French operas.

Dur (Ger.: 'hard'). Major, as in *G dur* (G major).

Durand. French firm of music publishers. It was founded in 1869 by Marie Auguste Durand (1830–1909) in partnership with Schoenewerk, was reorganized in 1891 as A. Durand & Fils, and in 1909 by Jacques Durand (1865–1928) as Durand & Cie; both Auguste and his son Jacques were composers. In 1869 the firm bought the Flaxland catalogue of *c*1200 publications; to this it added the collected works of Rameau (ed. Saint-Saëns), Schumann's piano works (ed. Fauré), Mendelssohn's piano works (ed. Ravel) and other music for its enormous 'Edition classique'. Meanwhile promoting contemporary French music, the Durands became the original publishers of almost all the works of Saint-Saëns, Debussy and Ravel, most of those of Fauré and Dukas and many by Franck, Falla, Milhaud and Poulenc.

Duranowski, August (Fryderyk) (*b* Warsaw, *c*1770; *d* Strasbourg, 1834). Polish violinist and composer. He studied the violin in Paris with Viotti, becoming leader of the Brussels opera orchestra in 1790. He toured Europe and settled in Strasbourg. One of the most eminent virtuosos of his time and an important influence on Paganini, he was known for his extraordinary technique, especially in trilling, bowing and

passage-work. Among his compositions, the Concerto in A major op.8 and *airs variés* for violin and orchestra are noteworthy.

Durante, Francesco (*b* Frattamaggiore, 31 March 1684; *d* Naples, 30 Sept 1755). Italian composer. A pupil of his uncle in Naples, he also spent time in Rome and probably abroad before working as *primo maestro* at the Naples conservatory Poveri di Gesù Cristo, 1728–39. From 1742 he was *primo maestro* at S Maria di Loreto, the largest Neapolitan conservatory, and from 1745 also at St Onofrio. He was venerated as the finest composition teacher in Naples; among his pupils were Pergolesi, Anfossi and Piccinni.

Unusually among Neapolitan composers, Durante wrote no operas, although he wrote sacred dramas and secular and sacred cantatas. He made his name chiefly through his sacred works, which include all the current liturgical and devotional genres. Among them are masses (e.g. the *Missa in Palestrina*, 1739) in the traditional Palestrina style, to which Durante added more modern touches than did his contemporary Leo, and *stile moderno* works with instruments, such as motets and psalms, using lighter textures and sometimes thematic and harmonic contrasts, strong dissonances, and expressive dynamics and scoring. Careful construction distinguishes his latest works. Also notable are his instrumental pieces, including six harpsichord sonatas (*c*1732) and eight *Concerti per quartetto* (?*c*1740), and his many didactic works.

Durastanti, Margherita (*fl* 1700–34). Italian soprano. She had a longer association with Handel than any other singer: he wrote cantatas and other music for her in Rome in 1707–8 and operatic roles for her in England in the 1720s and in 1733–4, including Agrippina and Sextus (*Giulio Cesare*). She also sang in Italian and German theatres.

Durazzo, Count Giacomo (*b* Genoa, 27 April 1717; *d* Venice, 15 Oct 1794). Italian impresario. He was Genoan ambassador to Vienna, 1749–64, and in 1754 became *directeur des spectacles* in Vienna, responsible for the two main theatres. With Gluck, he established French-style *opéra comique* in Vienna; he also fostered Gluck's 'reforms' of *opera seria* and promoted Italian *opera buffa*. Later, as Viennese ambassador to Venice, he received musicians including the Mozarts.

Durchführung. German term for the DEVELOPMENT section in sonata form and also for the EXPOSITION of a fugue.

Durchkomponiert (Ger.). THROUGH-COMPOSED.

Durey, Louis (Edmond) (*b* Paris, 27 May 1888; *d* St Tropez, 3 July 1979). French composer. He studied at the Schola Cantorum and was one of Les Six, though he soon took an independent, more serious-minded path on the basis of Satie and Stravinsky. He wrote mostly chamber music (notably three string quartets, 1917, 1922, 1928), choral pieces and songs, some in support of socialist ideals.

Durkó, Zsolt (*b* Szeged, 10 April 1934). Hungarian composer. He studied with Farkas at the Budapest Academy and with Petrassi in Rome (1961–3), returning to Hungary to take a leading part in the modernist advance. He became internationally known as the leading Hungarian composer of his generation. His music holds a balance between tradition and novelty, his emotional expression marked by noble reserve. His works range from opera (*Moses*, 1977) through orchestral, vocal and chamber music to piano pieces.

Durón, Sebastián (*b* Brihuega, bap. 19 April 1660; *d* Cambó, 3 Aug 1716). Spanish composer. He held organist's posts at cathedrals including Seville (1680–85) and Palencia (1686–91), then at the royal chapel in Madrid (*maestro de capilla*, 1702). After exile in 1706 he lived mostly in Bayonne. He was a prolific composer, notable for his use of Italian style in zarzuelas and other works; he was among the first in Spain to write cantatas with da capo arias and recitative. His sacred works and organ music are more conservative. He also wrote villancicos, songs etc. His half-brother Diego (*c*1658–1731), *maestro de capilla* at Las Palmas Cathedral, was also a composer.

Duruflé, Maurice (*b* Louviers, 11 Jan 1902; *d* Paris, 16 June 1986). French composer and organist. He studied with Tournemire, whose deputy at Ste Clotilde he became, and then at the Paris Conservatoire (1920–28) with Gigout and Dukas. In 1930 he was appointed organist of St Etienne-du-Mont and he toured internationally as a recitalist. His works are few, in a vivid modal style, and include a Requiem (1947).

Dušek, František Xaver (*b* Chotěborky, bap. 8 Dec 1731; *d* Prague, 12 Feb 1799). Czech composer. An influential music teacher and pianist in Prague, he was one of the foremost Bohemian composers of his day, writing *c*40 symphonies and *c*20 string quartets (most in the 1760s), wind parthias, other chamber music and keyboard sonatas and concertos. His wife and pupil Josefa (1754–1824), a soprano, sang in Vienna, Prague and elsewhere; Mozart wrote three arias for her.

Dushkin, Samuel (*b* Suwaki, 13 Dec 1891; *d* New York, 24 June 1976). American violinist of Polish birth. He studied at the Paris Conservatoire and with Auer and Kreisler in New York. After his début with the New York SO in 1924 he became identified with contemporary music; he toured extensively with Stravinsky, giving the premières of the Violin Concerto (1931) and the Duo concertante (1932).

Dussek, Jan Ladislav (*b* Čáslav, 12 Feb 1760; *d* St Germain-en-Laye or Paris, 20 March 1812). Bohemian pianist and composer. After studying in Prague he toured widely, gaining a brilliant reputation; he was Kapellmeister to Prince Radziwill for two years, then worked in Paris, 1786–9. In 1789–99 he lived in London, much in demand as teacher and performer; he became a partner in his father-in-law's music publishing firm (Corri, Dussek & Co.), but fled to the Continent when it ran into debt. In 1804–6 he was Kapellmeister to the Prince of Prussia, on whose death (1806) he wrote the piano sonata *Elégie harmonique*. He briefly served Prince Isenburg, then worked again in Paris.

Dussek's reputation as a composer faded rapidly and unjustly. Foremost in his output are over 40 piano sonatas, *c*12 piano concertos and many chamber works (most with piano). The early works are classical in style, but those after *c*1790 show Romantic traits anticipating Schubert, Chopin and others and piano writing of an especially virtuoso character. He also wrote lighter piano pieces, harp music and a keyboard method (1796).

Dussek was one of a family of musicians. His father Jan (1738–1818) was an organist and composer; his brother Franz Benedict (1766–after 1816) composed operas, an oratorio and chamber works in Italy; and his sister Katerina Veronika [Cianchettini] (1769–1833) was a singer, pianist, harpist and composer. His wife Sophia (1775–1847) worked in London as a singer, pianist and harpist.

Du Tertre, Estienne (*fl* Paris, mid-16th century). French composer. He spent his creative years in Paris, where he may have been an organist, and from 1557 was an editor for the publisher Attaingnant. Over 70 of his *chansons* were published (1543–68).

Dutilleux, Henri (*b* Angers, 22 Jan 1916). French composer. He studied with the Gallons, Büsser and Emmanuel at the Paris Conservatoire (1933–8), where he was appointed professor in 1970 after periods with French radio (1943–63) and at the Ecole Normale de Musique (from 1961). His first works suggest influences from Debussy, Ravel, Roussel and Honegger, but he developed as an isolated and independent figure, producing a relatively small output of great breadth and originality, predominantly of instrumental works; they include two symphonies (1950, 1959) and other orchestral pieces, piano music and the string quartet *Ainsi la nuit* (1976).

Dutoit, Charles (*b* Lausanne, 7 Oct 1936). Swiss conductor. He studied at the Lausanne Conservatory and with Charles Munch. In 1967 he became principal conductor of the Berne SO. With the Zurich Tonhalle Orchestra he has toured widely as a convincing advocate of the 20th-century repertory, in particular Stravinsky.

Duval, François (*b* Paris, 1672–3; *d* Versailles, 27 Jan 1728). French composer. He was in the service of the Duke of Orleans by 1704, and from 1714 played in the 24 Violons du Roi. His seven sets of violin sonatas (1704–20) include elements of Corelli's style; the 1704 sonatas were the first such works published in France.

Duvernoy [Duvernois], **Frédéric Nicolas** (*b* Montbéliard, 16 Oct 1765; *d* Paris, 19 July 1838). French horn player, teacher and composer. Considered by many to be the leading player of his day, he was the first major figure of the French school. He specialized in the middle register, the *cor mixte*, and taught at the Paris Conservatoire, publishing an important method (1802). He wrote concertos and chamber music.

Dux, Claire (*b* Witkowicz, 2 Aug 1885; *d* Chicago, 8 Oct 1967). Polish soprano. She studied in Berlin, made her début in Cologne in 1906 as Pamina and sang in the Berlin Royal Opera, 1911–18; she sang Sophie at Covent Garden (1911) and appeared in Chicago and elsewhere in the USA from 1921. She retired early from the stage; her voice was a lyric soprano of exceptional purity, controlled by a firm technique.

Dux, comes (Lat.). Terms for 'leader' and 'follower' in a canon.

Dvořák, Antonín (Leopold) (*b* Nelahozeves, 8 Sept 1841; *d* Prague, 1 May 1904). Czech composer. He studied with Antonín Liehmann and at the Prague Organ School (1857–9). A capable viola player, he joined the band that became the nucleus of the new Provisional Theatre orchestra, in 1862 conducted by Wagner and from 1866 Smetana. Private teaching and mainly composing occupied him from 1873. He won the Austrian State Stipendium three times (1874, 1876–7), gaining the attention of Brahms, who secured the publisher Simrock for some of his works in 1878. Foreign performances multiplied, notably of the Slavonic Dances, the Sixth Symphony and the *Stabat mater*, and with them further commissions. Particularly well received in England, Dvořák wrote *The Spectre's Bride* (1884) and the Requiem Mass (1890) for Birmingham, the Seventh Symphony for the Philharmonic Society (1885) and *St Ludmilla* for Leeds (1886), besides receiving an honorary doctorate from Cambridge. He visited Russia in 1890, continued to launch new works in Prague and London and began teaching at the Prague Conservatory in 1891 (where Joseph Suk was among his most gifted pupils). Before leaving for the USA he toured Bohemia playing the new *Dumky* Trio. As director of the National Conservatory in New York (1892–5) he taught composition, meanwhile producing the well-known Ninth Symphony ('From the New World'), the String Quartet in F, the String Quintet in E♭ and the Cello Concerto. Financial strain and family ties took him back to Prague, where he began to write symphonic poems and finally had his efforts at dramatic music rewarded with the success of the fairytale opera *Rusalka* (1901). The recipient of honours and awards from all sides, he remained a modest man of simple tastes, loyal to his Czech nationality.

In matters of style Dvořák was neither conservative nor radical. His works display the influences of folk music, mainly Czech (*furiant* and *dumky* dance traits, polka rhythms, immediate repetition of an initial bar) but also ones that might equally be seen as American (pentatonic themes, flattened 7ths); Classical composers whom he admired, including Mozart, Haydn, Beethoven and Schubert; Wagner, whose harmony and use of leitmotifs attracted him; and his close friend Brahms (notably his piano writing and mastery of symphonic form). Despite his fascination with opera, he lacked a natural instinct for drama; for all their admirable wit and lyricism, his last five stage works rank lower than his finest instrumental music. Here his predilection for classical procedures reached its highest level of achievement, notably in the epic Seventh Symphony, the most closely argued of his orchestral works, and the Cello Concerto, the crowning item in that instrument's repertory, with its characteristic richness and eloquence, as well as in the popular and appealing Ninth Symphony and the colourful Slavonic Dances and Slavonic Rhapsodies. Among his chamber works, landmarks are the String Sextet in A op.48, a work in his national style which attracted

particular attention abroad; the F minor Piano Trio op.65, one of the climaxes of the more serious, classically 'Brahmsian' side of his output – unlike the E minor op.90, a highly original series of *dumka* movements alternately brooding and spirited; the exuberant op.81 Piano Quintet; and several of the string quartets, notably the popular 'American' op.96, with its pentatonic leanings, and the two late works, the deeply felt op.106 in G and the warm and satisfying op.105 in A♭.

Orchestral music Sym. no.1, c, 'Bells of Zlonice' (1865); Sym. no.2, B♭ (1865); Sym. no.3, E♭ (1873); Sym. no.4, d (1874); Sym. no.5, F (1875); Sym. no.6, D (1880); Sym. no.7, d (1885); Sym. no.8, G (1889); Sym. no.9, e, 'From the New World' (1893); Pf Conc., g (1876); Vn Conc., a (1880), Vc Conc., b (1895); Sym. Variations (1877); Scherzo capriccioso (1883); 8 ovs.; 2 serenades (str, E, 1879; wind, d, 1878); 3 Slavonic Rhapsodies (1878); 2 sets of Slavonic Dances (orig. for pf duet, 1878, 1886); 5 sym. poems (1896–7)
Chamber music 3 str qnts (incl. op.97, E♭, 1893); 14 str qts (incl. op.51, E♭, 1879; op.61, C, 1881; op.96, F, 1893; op.105, A♭, 1896; op.106, G, 1895); Str Sextet, op.48 (1878); 2 pf trios (incl. op.65, F, 1883; op.90, e, 'Dumky', 1891); 2 pf qts (incl. op.87, E♭, 1889); 2 pf qnts (incl. op.81, A, 1887); sonatas; other chamber works; many pf pieces (dances, eclogues, character-pieces, duets); org preludes and fugues
Dramatic music Dimitrij (1882, 1894); The Jacobin (1889, 1898); Kate and the Devil (1899); Rusalka (1901); Armida (1904); 9 other operas; incidental music
Vocal music Stabat mater (1877); The Spectre's Bride, cantata (1884); St Ludmilla, oratorio (1886); Requiem (1890); 2 masses, cantatas and sacred choral works; partsongs, choral arrs. of Czech folksongs; over 100 songs and duets with pf acc.; other arrs.

Dwight, John Sullivan (*b* Boston, 13 May 1813; *d* there, 5 Sept 1893). American writer on music. He was the influential editor of *Dwight's Journal of Music* (Boston, 1852–81), a primary source for the history of music in New England from the earliest orchestral concerts to the founding of the Boston SO.

Dyagilev [Diaghilev], Sergey Pavlovich (*b* Gruzino, 31 March 1872; *d* Venice, 19 Aug 1929). Russian impresario. He performed *Boris Godunov* in Paris in 1908 and the following year presented his first Ballets Russes season. Ravel's *Daphnis et Chloé* was given in 1912 and Debussy's *Jeux* in 1913. An association with Stravinsky began with the commissioning of *The Firebird* for 1910 and continued until 1928 (*Apollo*). Dyagilev's success was founded on an inspired collaboration with leading composers (Satie, Falla and Prokofiev also wrote for him) and a close relationship with such artists as Picasso, Rouault and Bakst and the choreographers Fokin, Nizhinsky, Massin and Balanchin.

Dyce, William (*b* Aberdeen, 19 Sept 1806; *d* Streatham, 14 Feb 1864). Scottish painter. He was a pioneer in the revival of plainchant in the Anglican liturgy, notably through his sumptuous edition of the Common Prayer (1842–4).

Dykes, John Bacchus (*b* Hull, 10 March 1823; *d* Ticehurst, 22 Jan 1876). English composer. Precentor and minor canon at Durham Cathedral (1849–62), he composed some 60 hymn tunes in *Hymns Ancient and Modern* (1861), of which *Nicaea* ('Holy, holy, holy'), *Horbury* ('Nearer my God to thee') and *St Cross* ('O come and mourn'), among others, remain in use.

Dylan, Bob [Zimmerman, Robert Allen] (*b* Duluth, MN, 24 May 1941). American singer and songwriter. He led the urban folk-music revival of the 1960s and 1970s. He sang his early blues and folksongs, in a distinctive speech-song style, with a harsh, nasal voice, to his own guitar accompaniment; several were associated with protest (*Blowin' in the wind*, 1962; *The times they are a-changin'*, 1964) and many have elusive, abstract lyrics. From 1965 he performed and recorded with an amplified blues band; in 1979 he embraced fundamentalist Christianity and in the 1980s he experimented with reggae rhythms.

Dynamics. The aspect of musical expression resulting from variation in the volume of sound. Dynamic instructions appeared in lute music as early as the 16th century but were rare until the 17th, when markings *piano* and *forte* came into general currency, as did 'loud' and 'soft' in English consort music. 'Hairpin' marks opening at the right for crescendo (growing louder) and the left for diminuendo (growing softer) are found from the early 18th century; the effects were however known earlier and indicated by a succession of dynamic markings. In much Baroque music, as the structure of the instruments bears out, level planes of volume are often implied. Crescendo and diminuendo of a conspicuous character were known in Italian orchestral music during the first half of the 18th century but became a particular feature of the Mannheim composers of the mid-century, where they served a structural purpose in the music. The use of crescendo as a choral effect is much later, probably dating only from the mid-19th century. Standard dynamic marks used in music are *pp* (*pianissimo*, very quiet), *p* (*piano*, quiet), *mp* (*mezzo piano*, moderately quiet), *mf* (*mezzo forte*, moderately loud), *f* (*forte*, loud) and *ff* (*fortissimo*, very loud); late Romantic composers have used further aggregations of *p*s and *f*s for even more marked effect, notably Tchaikovsky, who probably holds a record with his *pppppp* at the end of the first movement of his Symphony no.6 (*Pathétique*).

Dyson, Sir George (*b* Halifax, 28 May 1883; *d* Winchester, 28 Sept 1964). English composer. He studied at the RCM (1900–04) and later taught there (director from 1938), and at several schools. His works include choral and orchestral pieces (notably *The Canterbury Pilgrims*, 1931) and books.

Dzerzhinsky, Ivan (Ivanovich) (*b* Tambov, 9 April 1909; *d* Leningrad, 18 Jan 1978). Soviet composer. He studied at the Gnesin School (1929–30) and with Popov, Ryazanov and Asaf'yev, though from the first his works were strongly traditional. His opera *Quiet flows the Don* (1934) was acclaimed by Stalin as a model of socialist realism. From 1936 he held important administrative posts while continuing to write operas and orchestral music.

E

E. The name of a note, or a PITCH CLASS; *see also* PITCH NAMES. E is the third degree (or mediant) of the scale of C major.

Eames, Emma (*b* Shanghai, 13 Aug 1865; *d* New York, 13 June 1952). American soprano. She studied in Boston and in Paris, where she made her Opéra début as Gounod's Juliet (1889). Her Covent Garden début was as Marguerite (1891). She sang regularly at the Met up to 1909, her roles including Donna Anna, Leonora (*Il trovatore*), Tosca and Sieglinde. She had a pure lyric soprano, cool in timbre, and complete technical command.

Early music. Term used, mainly since the 1960s, to stand not only for music of an earlier era but also for a particular attitude towards its performance. It is sometimes applied to music of the Middle Ages and the Renaissance (i.e. up to 1600), sometimes to the Baroque period too (up to 1750), but increasingly up to 1800, so including much of the Classical period. But the usage of the term for such concepts as 'authentic' or historically informed performance, extends up to more recent times and could (for example) comprehend playing Schumann's piano music on instruments of his day or Mahler's symphonies using the kinds of portamento favoured by string players of the early 20th century.

The 'early music movement' is particularly concerned with performing practice and the revival and use of period instruments as well as period techniques and understandings of such matters as notation, rhythm, tempo and articulation, along with the establishment of texts that conform with the composer's intentions. The movement may be seen as going back to the musical antiquarianism of the 18th century and the critical scholarship that arose from it during the 19th. Its true father figure is ARNOLD DOLMETSCH who did much in the early 20th century to revive interest in early techniques and instruments; his pupils and followers continued the tradition. In the 1960s and 1970s, groups such as Concentus Musicus (Vienna), the Early Music Consort (London), the Studio für Frühe Musik (Munich), the Schola Cantorum Basiliensis (Basle) and the New York Pro Musica cultivated performance in period styles; their work has since been followed up by groups and individuals, particularly in such centres as London, the Low Countries and Boston. Most of these groups concentrated on Baroque music or earlier; with the work of the Academy of Ancient Music, the Collegium Aureum and the London Classical Players, the Classical and early Romantic repertories have also been examined in the light of period performance. The early music movement has been much fostered not only by scholars but also by modern builders of period instruments, by journals (notably the British quarterly *Early Music*, founded in 1973), by publishers (particularly of facsimile editions) and by the record industry.

Early Music Consort of London. A group formed by DAVID MUNROW in London in 1967.

Easdale, Brian (*b* Manchester, 10 Aug 1909). English composer. He studied at the RCM and from 1936 wrote music for films, notably *The Red Shoes* (1948). His *Missa coventrensis* (1962) was written for the consecration of Coventry Cathedral. Easdale's chamber music and songs owe something to Britten and the Bax–Bridge generation.

East, Michael (*b c*1580; *d* Lichfield, 1648). English composer. He took the MusB degree at Cambridge (1606) and then probably worked in London. He was a lay clerk at Ely Cathedral (1609–14) before becoming Master of the Choristers at Lichfield Cathedral (by 1618). His seven publications (1604–38) include italianate madrigals, consort songs, anthems and fancies for viols; though mostly unremarkable, they are in an up-to-date style using italianate idioms. He also contributed to *The Triumphes of Oriana* (1601).

East [Este], Thomas (*d* London, 1608). English music printer and publisher. He was the father of English music printing. Despite an uncertain market and the vicissitudes of the monopoly system under which he had to work, he flourished from 1588, when his print of Byrd's *Psalmes, Sonets and Songs* had immediate success. He printed most of the music of Byrd and Morley, as well as *Musica transalpina* (1588 and 1597), *The Triumphes of Oriana* (1601) and Lassus's *Novae cantiones*, the first single-composer Italian collection issued in England; his Italian edition (1595) of Morley's five-part balletts suggests a plan to export English music to Italy. His version of the English metrical Psalter, *The Whole Booke of Psalmes* (1592), ran into six

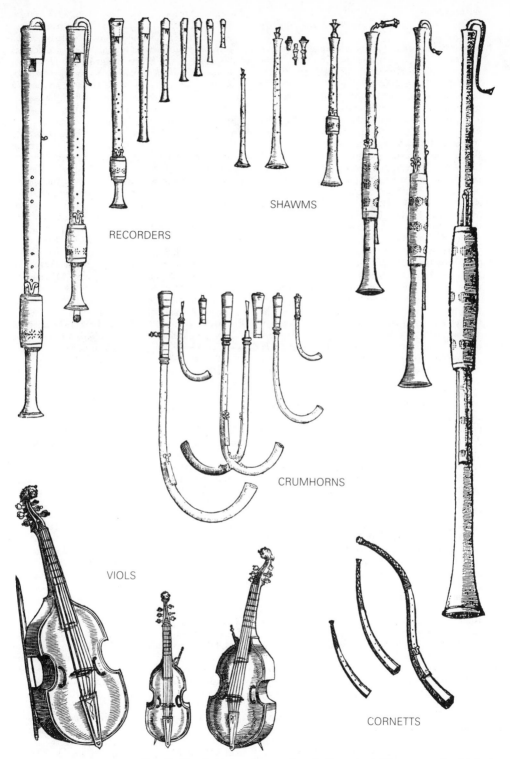

RECORDERS

SHAWMS

CRUMHORNS

VIOLS

CORNETTS

Some families of early instruments as shown by Praetorius in 'Syntagma musicum' (1620)

further editions.

East Asian music. *See* CHINESE MUSIC and JAPANESE MUSIC.

Eastman School of Music. American conservatory in Rochester, NY. It was founded in 1912 as the Dossenbach-Klingenberg School of Music (DKG Institute of Musical Art from 1914). In 1917 it was taken over by George Eastman and in 1921 became part of the University of Rochester.

Easton, Florence (*b* Middlesborough, 25 Oct 1882; *d* New York, 13 Aug 1955). English soprano. She studied in Paris and London; her career began in Berlin (1907–13) but was principally at the Met (1917–29) where she sang a great range of roles from Brünnhilde to Carmen with pure tone, sound technique and excellent musicianship.

Eastwood, Thomas (Hugh) (*b* Hawley, Hants., 12 March 1922). English composer. He studied in Berlin with Blacher and in London with Stein. His works include the chamber opera *Christopher Sly* (1960) and scores for the theatre and radio.

Eaton, John (Charles) (*b* Bryn Mawr, PA, 30 March 1935). American composer. He studied at Princeton (1953–9) with Babbitt, Cone and Sessions. In the late 1960s he wrote much for electronic synthesizers, with exceptional originality and virtuosity. In 1970 he began teaching at Indiana University, and turned to writing opera, notably *Heracles* (1968), *Myshkin* (1973), *The Cry of Clytaemnestra* (1980) and *The Tempest* (1985).

Ebeling, Johann Georg (*b* Lüneburg, 8 July 1637; *d* Stettin, 4 Dec 1676). German composer. He succeeded Crüger as Kantor of St Nicolai, Berlin (1662–7), where the poet Paul Gerhardt was deacon. Important as the first to collect Gerhardt's hymns, he published them in a volume (1666–7) for domestic devotions, providing melodies for 112 of the 120 pieces, which he harmonized in four parts with two optional parts for instruments; his setting of *Gib dich zufrieden* is outstanding. Ebeling wrote an early history of music, *Archaiologica Orphicae* (1675).

Eben, Petr (*b* Žamberk, 22 Jan 1929). Czech composer. He studied with Bořkovec at the Prague Academy (1948–54) and has taught at Prague University. His works, chiefly in vocal and chamber forms, show an involvement with Renaissance thought; they include *Apologia Sokrates* (1967), an oratorio reflecting his preoccupation with mortality, and *Faust* for organ (1982).

Eberl, Anton (Franz Josef) (*b* Vienna, 13 June 1765; *d* there, 11 March 1807). Austrian composer. Active as a pianist from the 1770s, he made two German concert tours, the first (1795–6) with Constanze Mozart. In 1796–1802 he stayed twice in St Petersburg as Kapellmeister. His output includes five symphonies, three piano concertos, chamber music, seven piano sonatas and other piano music; he also wrote stage works for Vienna (1787–1801), songs and cantatas. His early piano works show the influence of Mozart (possibly his teacher) and some, notably variations, appeared under Mozart's name; the later works show Romantic traits. Latterly Eberl's music, especially the E♭ Symphony and the Sonata op.39, was compared favourably with Beethoven's.

Eberlin, Daniel (*b* Nuremberg, bap. 4 Dec 1647; *d* ?Kassel, Dec 1713–5 July 1715). German composer. He studied in Rome. An unsettled career, probably the result of a volatile temper, included posts as Kapellmeister at Eisenach and Kassel. He was an accomplished contrapuntist and fine violinist and, according to his son-in-law Telemann, possessed a mind 'whose ability few have equalled'. His extant vocal works, mostly cantatas, show expressive word-setting and rather wilful harmonic writing.

Eberlin, Johann Ernst (*b* Jettingen, Bavaria, bap. 27 March 1702; *d* Salzburg, 19 June 1762). German composer. He was an organist at Salzburg Cathedral from 1726 and by 1749 court and cathedral Kapellmeister. Among his many vocal works, the operas, intermezzos, music for school plays and oratorios are mainly italianate. He also wrote organ pieces and, most influential, sacred works (including *c*70 masses); Leopold Mozart thought highly of these.

Ebers, John (*b* London, *c*1785; *d* there, *c*1830). English opera manager. As manager of the Italian Opera at the King's Theatre, Haymarket (1820–27), he introduced works by Rossini, Mercadante, Meyerbeer and Spontini to London. His account of his regime, *Seven Years of the King's Theatre* (1828/*R*1970), is vivid and entertaining.

Eberwein, (Franz) Carl (Adalbert) (*b* Weimar, 10 Nov 1786; *d* there, 2 March 1868). German violinist and composer. He was an influential court musician at Weimar, where he was closely associated with Goethe, writing songs and stage works, some to Goethe's texts. His brother Traugott Eberwein (1775–1831), also a violinist, was Kapellmeister at Rudolstadt, an early founder of music festivals in Germany and a composer, notably of songs.

Ebner, Wolfgang (*b* Augsburg, 1612; *d* Vienna, 11/12 Feb 1665). German composer. In 1637 he began a lifelong association with the imperial court in Vienna, first as organist of the Kapelle, then, from 1663, as Cathedral Kapellmeister; he was also official ballet composer. Highly esteemed by his contemporaries, little of Ebner's music survives. With his colleague Froberger he established the 17th-century Viennese keyboard school important for its fusion of French, German and English styles, his best-known composition being the 36 variations for harpsichord (1648) on a theme by Ferdinand III. He also wrote 15 rules of thoroughbass realization.

Ebony Concerto. Concerto by Stravinsky for clarinet and orchestra (1945), composed for the jazz musician Woody Herman.

Eccard, Johannes (*b* Mühlhausen, 1553; *d* Berlin, 1611). German composer. His teachers at Mühlhausen, the Weimar Kapelle (1567–71) and the Munich Hofkapelle (1571–3) included Joachim a Burck and Lassus. After serving Jacob Fugger in Augsburg (1577–8), he joined the Brandenburg Hofkapelle in Königsberg (1579), becoming Kapellmeister in Berlin in 1604. Among his dozen or so sacred publications, his German chorale motets (1642, 1644) were influential; he also published chorales, sacred odes and occasional pieces.

Eccles, John (*b* ?London, *c*1668; *d* Hampton Wick, 12 Jan 1735). English composer. The son of Henry Eccles (*c*1645–1711), a court musician, he was a composer for Drury Lane Theatre, where his dialogue in *The Richmond Heiress* (1693) was highly successful, and from 1695 he was music director at Lincoln's Inn Fields. In all, he wrote some 12 masques and operatic pieces, and incidental music for over 50 plays. He also was a court musician-in-ordinary, as Master of Musick writing court odes, 1700–1727. After Purcell's death (1695) he was the leading Restoration theatre composer. His masque *The Judgment of Paris* (1701) and dramatic opera *The British Enchanters* (1706, based on Lully's *Amadis*) were the last of their kinds as was his St Cecilia's Day Ode (1701). In his final stage work, *Semele* (1707), he created with Congreve a sensitive English recitative of the Italian *secco* type, but it remained unperformed.

Eccles came from a family of musicians, including Solomon (*c*1617–1682), a music teacher; Solomon (*c*1645–1710), a bass violin player at court and composer of music for several plays; and Henry (*c*1680–*c*1740), a violinist who worked in London and Paris and wrote violin sonatas.

Echappée (Fr.). 'Escaped [note]': in part-writing, an unaccented non-harmonic note in a melodic resolution, outside the interval circumscribing the resolution and approached in the direction opposite from that of the resolution.

Echo. Echo effects are caused by the reflection of sound waves from distant surfaces. The effect has been imitated in music, for example in 16th-century madrigals; it became popular in dramatic works in the 17th century and sometimes gave opportunities for punning effects (for example as in Cavalieri's *Rappresentazione di Anima, et di Corpo*, 1600, where the Soul asks 'Chi dalla morte al cor con dispiacere?' and is answered 'Piacere'). There are also examples, suggesting a 'deep-vaulted cell', in Purcell's *Dido and Aeneas*. Mozart uses echoes of diminishing length in his Serenade for four orchestras K286/269*a*; Wagner uses a sinister mis-echo in *The Flying Dutchman* to suggest a ghost ship.

An Echo Organ is an encased subsidiary chest within the main organ, usually with its own keyboard.

Eck, Friedrich Johann (Gerhard) (*b* Schwetzingen, 24 May 1767; *d* there, 22 Feb 1838). German violinist. He went with the Mannheim orchestra to Munich in 1778, and was Konzertmeister 1788–1800. He composed several violin concertos and may have had some hand in the concerto in E♭ ascribed to Mozart (K268). His brother Franz (1774–1804), also a Munich court violinist, later served at tne Russian court and taught Louis Spohr.

Eckard, Johann Gottfried (*b* Augsburg, 21 Jan 1735; *d* Paris, 24 July 1809). German pianist and composer. He lived in Paris from 1758, winning recognition as a pianist before the piano was well established there. His eight keyboard sonatas (1763–4) were the first in Paris to be conceived for the piano and include varied textures and advanced thematic development. Mozart was influenced by them and used one in an early piano concerto.

Eckhardt-Gramatté, S(ophie)-C(armen) (*b* Moscow, 6 Jan 1902; *d* Stuttgart, 2 Dec 1974). Canadian composer. She studied at the Paris Conservatoire and made a career as both violinist and pianist. In 1936 she studied composition with Trapp in Berlin, and in 1953 she settled in Canada. Her works include two symphonies (1939, 1970), concertos, three string quartets (1938, 1943, 1964) and much other chamber and piano music.

Eclats/Multiples. Orchestral work by Boulez, an expanded version of *Eclats* for 15 instruments (1965), regarded as a 'work in progress' by the composer.

Eclogue. Term applied to piano pieces in the 19th century by Tomášek, Liszt, Dvořák and others, to imply a pastoral character.

Ecole Niedermeyer. Conservatory in Paris. Founded in 1853 by L. Niedermeyer as a school of church music, it became a general music academy in 1895. Fauré was one of its first pupils.

Ecole Royale de Chant. The first French academy of music, it was founded in Paris in 1783, mainly to provide singers for the Opéra, and absorbed by the Conservatoire in 1795.

Ecossaise (Fr.: 'Scottish'). A lively kind of contredanse in 2/4 time, possibly of Scottish origin, popular in the early 19th century. Stylized *écossaises*, mostly for piano, were composed by Beethoven, Schubert, Weber and Chopin.

Ecuatorial. Work by Varèse for bass voice(s), brass, piano, organ, two ondes martenots and percussion, a setting of a Maya prayer in a Spanish translation by Jimines (1934).

Edel, Yitzhak (*b* Warsaw, 1 Jan 1896; *d* Tel-Aviv, 14 Dec 1973). Israeli composer of Polish birth. He studied with Rytel and Statkowsky in Warsaw, and moved to Palestine in 1929. There he worked as a teacher and choirmaster, producing much choral music deeply rooted in Jewish traditions.

Edelmann, Jean-Frédéric (*b* Strasbourg, 5 May 1749; *d* Paris, 17 July 1794). Alsatian composer. He lived in Paris from *c*1774, gaining widespread fame as a composer, keyboard player and teacher. He was an administrator in Strasbourg from 1789 but was guillotined after factional disputes. His keyboard works include sonatas (some with violin), quartets and concertos; their dramatic quality and dynamic markings suggest they were intended for the piano. He also wrote vocal music, notably the opera *Ariane dans l'isle de Naxos* (1782, Paris).

Eden–Tamir Duo. Israeli piano duo, formed in 1952 by Bracha Eden (*b* Jerusalem, 15 July 1928) and Alexander Tamir (*b* Vilnius, 2 April 1931). They first appeared in New York in 1955 and in London two years later and have often been heard in neglected works for two pianos, including music by Clementi, Dussek and Hummel. In 1968 they gave Stravinsky's piano-duet version of *The Rite of Spring*.

Edgar. Opera in four acts by Puccini to a libretto by F. Fontana after A. de Musset's verse-drama *La coupe et les lèvres* (1889, Milan); Puccini revised it, reducing it to three acts (1892, Ferrara), and made a final version (Buenos Aires, 1905).

Edinburgh International Festival (UK). Annual festival (Aug–Sept) established in 1947. Events include concerts, opera and dance, given by international performers. The Concerts Colonnes orchestra gave the inaugural concert and the Vienna PO appeared in the same year. Opera has always been included, first with the Glyndebourne company, then by visiting European and British groups and (from 1973) the ad hoc Festival Opera. Numerous fringe events are given independently during the festival.

Edmunds, John (*b* San Francisco, 10 June 1913; *d* Berkeley, 9 Dec 1986). American composer. He studied at Harvard and in England under Goldsbrough and Dart. He taught at Syracuse and Berkeley and worked at the New York Public Library, 1957–61, and was in England, 1968–76. His large output of songs is mostly inspired by English and Irish poetry (e.g. *The Faucon*, 1944), many showing an awareness of earlier music (e.g. *Psalms of David*, 1960); evocative accompaniments are matched by sensitive declamation. He has also written choral works and ballets.

Edward. Brahms's ballade in D minor op.10 no.1 for piano (1854).

Edwards, Richard (*b* Somerset, 1524; *d* London, 31 Oct 1566). English composer. By 1557 he had joined the Chapel Royal and became Master of the Children in 1561. Though well known as a poet, he composed a few secular partsongs, including the famous *In goinge to my naked bedde* (his own verse) and songs for his play *Damon and Pithias* (1564, only one extant).

Edwards, Ross (*b* Sydney, 23 Dec 1943). Australian composer. He studied in Sydney and Adelaide; Sculthorpe, Maxwell Davies and Veress were among his teachers. Chamber music is central to his output. An interest in medieval techniques is reflected in his nativity play *Quem quaeritis* (1967).

Egdon Heath. Orchestral work (op.47) by Holst, subtitled 'Homage to Hardy' (1927).

Egedacher. German family of organ builders. Their instruments include organs for Salzburg Cathedral (1704–5 and 1718), Salem Abbey (1714 and 1719) and Passau Cathedral (1733; the case survives). They built the first detached console in Austria and specified many more stops than was usual, including tierce-sounding ranks, the Cornet, the Italian Piffaro and the reeds Bombarde, Fagotto, Hautboy and Voix humaine.

Egge, Klaus (*b* Telemark, 19 July 1906; *d* Oslo, 7 March 1979). Norwegian composer. He studied with Valen in Oslo and at the Berlin Hochschule für Musik. His music uses folk material, later within the framework of an individual 12-note technique; it includes five symphonies (1942–69) and two piano concertos (1937, 1944).

Eggert, Joachim (Georg) Nicolas (*b* Gingst, 22 Feb 1779; *d* Thomestorp, 14 April 1813). Swedish composer and conductor of German birth. As conductor of the Swedish royal orchestra he introduced the Viennese Classics. In 1812 he conducted the first Swedish performance of a Mozart opera (*Die Zauberflöte*). His symphonies and chamber music are in the Classical tradition.

Egisto. Opera by Cavalli to a libretto by Faustini (1643, Venice).

Egk, Werner (*b* Auchsesheim, 17 May 1901; *d* Inning, 10 July 1983). German composer. He studied in Munich with Orff and worked there for the radio and theatre until in the late 1930s he moved to Berlin,

where he conducted at the Staatsoper. His most important works were operas (*Die Zaubergeige*, 1935; *Peer Gynt*, 1938; *Circle*, 1948; *Der Revisor*, 1957; *Die Verlobung in San Domingo*, 1963) and orchestral pieces in an often ironic, dissonant style, influenced by French music and Stravinsky.

Egmond, Max (Rudolf) van (*b* Semarang, 1 Feb 1936). Dutch baritone. He studied in the Netherlands and from the early 1960s became widely known in Baroque music. His warm tone and knowledge of performing practice have often been placed in the service of Bach's cantatas.

Egmont. Overture and incidental music, op.84, by Beethoven (1810) for Goethe's play.

Egressy, Béni [Galambos, Benjámin] (*b* Sajókazinc, 21 April 1814; *d* Pest, 17 July 1851). Hungarian composer, librettist and dramatist. Working at the National Theatre, Pest, from about 1840, he wrote librettos for some of Ferenc Erkel's operas, translated into Hungarian French and Italian works and wrote plays with music in a popular, national style. A self-taught composer, he wrote the prize-winning song *Szózat* (1843), recognized as a second Hungarian national anthem.

Egüés, Manuel de (*b* S Martin del Rio, 3 June 1657; *d* Burgos, 11 April 1729). Spanish composer. Choirmaster at Burgos Cathedral from 1685, and a leading Spanish composer of the Baroque, he composed *c*200 sacred works (mostly villancicos), contrapuntal in style but with some florid melodic writing.

Ehrlich, Abel (*b* Cranz, 3 Sept 1915). Israeli composer of German birth. He studied in Zagreb and with Rosovsky at the Jerusalem Academy (1939–44), remaining in the Holy Land as a teacher. His earlier works are Romantic with eastern Mediterranean influences, but after attending courses with Stockhausen and Pousseur in the late 1950s he has followed newer trends.

Ehrling, Sixten (*b* Malmö, 3 April 1918). Swedish conductor. He conducted at the Royal Opera, Stockholm, from 1940 and was music director there, 1953–70. He was music director of the Detroit SO, 1963–73, and gave a wide range of performances at the Met, including a complete *Ring* cycle. In 1979 he was appointed principal guest conductor of the Denver SO.

Eibenschütz, Ilona (*b* Budapest, 8 May 1873; *d* London, 21 May 1967). Hungarian pianist. She made her début in Vienna at the age of six and studied with Clara Schumann before her mature début at Cologne in 1890; her British début was in 1891. Until her retirement in 1902 she was a champion of Schumann and Brahms.

Eichendorff, Joseph (Karl Benedikt), Freiherr von (*b* Lubowitz Castle, 10 March 1788; *d* St Rochus, 26 Nov 1857). German poet. The melancholy beauty of his poetry attracted such composers as Brahms, Franz, Mendelssohn, Schumann and Wolf, among others.

Eichheim, Henry (*b* Chicago, 3 Jan 1870; *d* Montecito, CA, 22 Aug 1942). American violinist and composer. He studied at the Chicago Musical College and played in the Boston SO (1890–1912). As a composer he was a pioneer in the use of Asian material. He wrote large, atmospheric orchestral works; *Java* (1929) and *Bali* (1933), for example, juxtapose a small gamelan with an orchestra. He also composed songs.

Eichner, Ernst (Dieterich Adolph) (*b* Arolsen, bap. 15 Feb 1740; *d* Potsdam, early 1777). German bassoonist and composer. He was first a violinist, and from 1769 Konzertmeister, at the Zweibrücken court: he also toured as a virtuoso bassoonist, joining the Kapelle of the Prussian crown prince at Potsdam in 1773. He was a gifted composer of instrumental music. Of his 31 symphonies (1769–76), the later ones are mature and expressive; many use fully fledged sonata form. He also wrote 19 solo concertos (six for bassoon), chamber works and keyboard music. His daughter Adelheid (1760/62–1787), a soprano, also served at Potsdam; she sang in Berlin and composed songs.

1812 Concert overture, op.49, by Tchaikovsky (1880); commemorating Napoleon's retreat from Moscow in 1812, it incorporates *La Marseillaise* and the Tsarist national anthem and, intended for performance in a Moscow square, includes cathedral bells and cannon fire.

Eight foot. Term used of organ stops, and by extension other instruments, to indicate that they are pitched at unison or 'normal' pitch, as distinct from four foot (an octave higher) or 16 foot (an octave lower).

Eighth-note. American term for QUAVER; a note half the value of a quarter-note, or crotchet, and double the value of a 16th-note, or semiquaver. *See* NOTE VALUES.

Eight Songs for a Mad King. Music-theatre piece by Peter Maxwell Davies to a libretto by Randolph Stow (1969, London).

Eimert, Herbert (*b* Bad Kreuznach, 8 April 1897; *d* Cologne, 15 Dec 1972). German composer. He studied at the conservatory (1919–24) and university (1924–30) in Cologne, where from 1927 he worked for the radio, notably as director of the Studio for Electronic Music (1951–62). He was a pioneer of 12-note music in the 1920s and of tape music (e.g. Four Pieces, 1953) in the 1950s. His importance lies in his foundation-laying research: his *Atonale Musiklehre* (1923) gave the first systematic description of 12-note technique.

Eine kleine Nachtmusik. Serenade for four or five solo string instruments by Mozart, K525 (1787).

Einem, Gottfried von (*b* Berne, 24 Jan 1918). Austrian composer. In 1938 he started work as a répétiteur in Bayreuth and Berlin, where he studied composition with Blacher (1941–3). In 1944 the success of his ballet *Prinzessin Turandot* gained him a post at the Dresden Staatsoper, and in 1947 he came to international attention when his first opera, *Dantons Tod*, was staged at Salzburg. He moved to Vienna in 1953 and became a leading figure in Austrian musical life as teacher, administrator and composer. The most important of his later works are further operas: *Der Prozess* (1953), *Der Zerrissene* (1964), the admired Dürrenmatt opera *Der Besuch der alten Dame* (1971), *Kabale und Liebe* (1976) and *Jesu Hochzeit* (1980). Starting from a Bergian expressionist style, they draw on a wide range of influences including Stravinsky and Blacher.

Ein' feste Burg [A Safe Stronghold]. A Lutheran hymn, a setting of Psalm xlvi; it has been used by J.S. Bach in his cantata BWV80 and has been quoted in several other works, including Meyerbeer's *Les Huguenots*, Mendelssohn's 'Reformation' Symphony and Wagner's *Kaisermarsch*.

Eingang (Ger.). A brief improvisatory passage, usually over a dominant 7th chord, serving as a 'lead-in' to a new section in a work, especially the return of the main theme in a Classical rondo.

Einstein, Alfred (*b* Munich, 30 Dec 1880; *d* El Cerrito, CA, 13 Feb 1952). American musicologist of German origin. He studied at Munich University and became known both as scholar and critic (*Münchner Post* until 1927, then *Berliner Tageblatt*); in 1933 he left Germany and in 1939 went to the USA, where he taught at Smith College and elsewhere. A prolific and wide-ranging scholar, he wrote books on Schütz, Gluck, Schubert and Mozart (he revised the Köchel catalogue in 1937) as well as a *Short History of Music* (1936) and a study *Music in the Romantic Era* (1947).

Einstein on the Beach. Opera in four acts by Glass to his own libretto (1976, Avignon).

Eisler, Hanns (*b* Leipzig, 6 July 1898; *d* Berlin, 6 Sept 1962). German composer. He studied with Schoenberg (1919–23) and in 1925 began teaching in Berlin, where his left-wing political sympathies became more acute. He grew critical of his early works, which had sprung directly from Schoenberg, and wrote political songs. In 1930 he began a collaboration with Brecht (notably with *Die Massnahme*, 1930, and *Die Mutter*, 1931), which continued after both men went into exile in the USA; there he also produced many film scores. In 1950 he returned to Berlin and applied himself to the problems of creating music for a socialist state: his solution was to write functional music almost exclusively, including film scores, incidental music and songs, in a strenuous diatonic style still motivated by the Schoenbergian conscience of his youth.

Eisteddfod. A competitive festival, mainly of choral singing, originating from the medieval gatherings of Welsh bards. Many are held in Wales and by Welsh communities abroad. The annual National Eisteddfod was established in 1880 ('Royal' from 1966); proceedings are in Welsh and events include professional concerts. The annual (summer) International Eisteddfod at Llangollen (established 1947) consists mainly of folksongs and dances of the many nations represented.

Eitner, Robert (*b* Breslau, 22 Oct 1832; *d* Templin, 2 Feb 1905). German editor and bibliographer. A pioneer in musical scholarship, he founded the Gesellschaft für Musikforschung (1868) and its journal, the *Monatshefte für Musikgeschichte* (1869), also supervising the publication of much early music. His most important contribution was the systematic collection of information about printed and MS music in over 200 European libraries, published in ten volumes as the indispensable *Quellen-Lexikon* (1900–04).

Eklund, Hans (*b* Sandviken, 1 July 1927). Swedish composer. He studied at the Stockholm Musikhögskolan (1947–52), with Larsson and with Pepping in Berlin (1953–4). His works, mostly orchestral, are in a polyphonic style following Hindemith and Reger.

Ekphonetic notation. Notation system designed to facilitate the singing of a liturgical text. Such signs are found in medieval MSS, but their musical meaning is imperfectly understood; they may consist of letters, dots or shapes representing the motions of a conductor's hand. The system is used mainly in association with biblical texts, in the music of the Syrian, Armenian and other Eastern churches, as well as in the synagogue (where the present notational system derives from it).

Elder, Mark (*b* Hexham, 2 June 1947). English conductor. He studied at Cambridge and worked at Glyndebourne from 1970, making his professional début with the Royal Liverpool PO in 1971 and conducting with Australian Opera, 1972–4. He conducted from 1974 at the English National Opera, becoming principal conductor (1979), where he has shown himself vigorous and commanding over a large repertory of 19th- and 20th-century music. He conducted a new production of *Die Meistersinger* at Bayreuth in 1980, has conducted widely as a guest, and was appointed music director of the Rochester PO from 1989.

Electric bass. An electric guitar, usually with four heavy strings tuned $E'–A'–D–G$. The electric bass guitar was invented by Leo Fender and made available in 1951; it was designed to replace the double bass. It is extensively used in rock.

Electric guitar. An electronically amplified guitar. Vibrations in the metal strings are converted by means of one or more pickups mounted on the instrument into an electrical signal that is passed to an amplifier. There are two main types: the hollow-bodied (or semi-acoustic) and the solid-bodied; the former is generally favoured by jazz musicians, the latter by rock musicians. A standard electric guitar has the same tuning as an acoustic guitar ($E–A–d–g–b–e'$); an electric bass guitar is tuned like a double bass ($E'–A'–D–G$). The first electric guitars were manufactured in the 1930s. (For illustration, see LUTE.)

Electric piano. An electronically amplified keyboard instrument capable of producing piano-like sounds. Such instruments range from modified pianos or instruments closely resembling a normal piano to fully electronic keyboard instruments which may differ from electronic organs only in timbre. *See also* SOSTENENTE PIANO.

Electrification of the Soviet Union, The. Opera in two acts by Nigel Osborne to a libretto by Craig Raine after Pasternak's *The Last Summer* (Glyndebourne, 1987).

Electronic instruments. Instruments that incorporate electronic circuitry (i.e. circuits with thermionic valves or semiconductors) as an integral part of the sound-generating system. This article deals not only with electronic instruments proper (such as synthesizers) but also with electromechanical instruments (such as some types of electric organ) and electro-acoustic instruments (such as the electric guitar) which generate signals without using electronics but use electronic amplification to make the signals

audible. (Ordinary acoustic instruments that may be amplified electronically are not electronic instruments in the sense used here.)

Although experiments using electricity in musical instruments began as early as the mid-18th century, the first significant developments towards electronic instruments were made in the 1890s. The most important advance was the electromagnetic tone-wheel, which was employed in the TELHARMONIUM and Choralcelo, both made in the USA; restricted by the available technology, neither was a practical success.

The invention of the thermionic valve in 1904 opened up the new field of electronics. A number of experimental instruments employing the novel technology were soon made, but the first practical application was the THEREMIN (1920), devised in the USSR, an important centre of experiment in the 1920s. The theremin exploited the principle of heterodyning two radio-frequency oscillators, and was played by moving the hands in front of two antennae. It enjoyed considerable success and inspired several imitators.

Several innovations were made in Paris in the late 1920s, the most enduring of which was the ONDES MARTENOT (1928), the only early electronic instrument with an established place and an important literature. It operated on similar principles to the theremin and originally it too was space-controlled but it was soon adapted to a keyboard. Berlin in the 1930s produced several important developments, notably the trautonium (1930), which found some favour with composers, and two forms of electric piano: the Elektrochord (1932) and Neo-Bechstein-Flügel (1931).

From the 1920s, many different variations on the theme of the ELECTRONIC ORGAN were created. The principle of the electromagnetic tone-wheel was revived in a number of instruments, notably the HAMMOND ORGAN (1934), the first electronic instrument to achieve commercial success. The first fully electronic (as opposed to electromechanical) organ to be marketed was the Allen organ (1939). After experiments in the 1920s, the first electric guitars were commercially manufactured in the USA in 1931.

After World War II, the USA quickly established a lead in the development and manufacture of electronic instruments that was to last until Japan's rise to prominence in the 1970s. The postwar period is characterized largely by two types of instrument, the electronic organ and the SYNTHESIZER, both of which benefited from such advances in electronics as semiconductors, integrated circuits and microprocessors.

Electromechanical organs (such as the classic Hammond) were gradually replaced by all-electronic instruments. The challenge of producing a convincing imitation of a pipe organ led to new solutions using increasingly more sophisticated circuitry, including digital synthesis techniques.

The first analogue synthesizers, appearing in 1964, represented a return to the innovatory spirit of the 1920s: rather than attempting to imitate acoustic instruments, they opened out new possibilities. Since they were fully programmable, the player could control all aspects of the sound. Their subsequent development has seen an increase in technical sophistication and a move towards designs that are simpler to operate, even if at the cost of programming freedom. The availability of microprocessors led to the development of the digital synthesizer, which first appeared in the mid-1970s.

Electronic music. Music produced or modified by electronic means so that electronic equipment is required for it to be heard.

Experiments in constructing electronic instruments began as early as the 1890s, when Thaddeus Cahill constructed the TELHARMONIUM; it was first exhibited in 1906, and attempts to manufacture it continued sporadically until the venture failed shortly before World War I. During the 1920s and 1930s many electronic instruments were invented, among them the Theremin (1924) and the Ondes martenot (1928); although they were used by some composers of the time (among them Honegger, Milhaud and Messiaen), only the Ondes martenot remains in use. Experimental projects involving the manipulation of gramophone records to produce pieces of music began around the same time; a later, sophisticated example of this technique is Cage's *Imaginary Landscape no. 1* (1939), but the concept was not widely used. In the early days the technology of electronic music was evolving far more quickly than its aesthetics; many composers were reluctant to work in a field without traditions. It was not until after World War II that musicians began to formulate codes of practice: the electronic music tradition began at this time.

The first radical experiments were made by Pierre Schaeffer at the RTF studios in Paris in 1948. He worked with recordings of pre-existing sound which he manipulated and modified in playback, constructing pieces out of chains of noises. The use of natural, or concrete, sound sources caused this style to be named *musique concrète*. Schaeffer's first compositions, the *Etudes*, were realized in 1948; with others, including Pierre Henri, he developed a detailed syntax for the genre in the 1950s. At the same time, at the WDR studio in Cologne, Werner Meyer Eppler and Herbert Eimert were developing *Elektronische Musik*, using test equipment – oscillators as sound sources, modified by filters and modulators – rather than pre-recorded sound. Early compositions by Eimert, Goeyvaerts and others, were followed by Stockhausen's *Studie I* (1953) and *Studie II* (1954), the most sophisticated pieces of electronic music to that date. The aesthetics and techniques of such works were discussed in such journals as *Die Reihe*, and controversies arose between the supporters of the Paris and Cologne schools. These were effectively reconciled when Stockhausen's *Gesang der Junglinge* (1956) used both techniques, establishing them as twin facets of one genre.

During the 1950s and 1960s electronic music studios were founded in major cities in Europe, the USA and Japan, and such composers as Berio, Babbitt, Luening and Varèse used electronic techniques in their work. Although composers continued to create works in the studio for dissemination on tape

they also began to explore the use of electronics in performance. Works like Cage's *Atlas eclipticalis* (1961–2) and Stockhausen's *Mixtur* (1964), *Kurzwellen* (1968) and *Mantra* (1970), require conventional instruments and various electronic techniques. During the 1960s groups devoted to the concert presentation of 'live' electronic music were established; these included Musica Elettronica Viva and the Sonic Arts Union.

In the 1960s, when the voltage-controlled SYNTHESIZER became widely available (in systems manufactured first in the USA by Moog, Buchla and others), composers were able to work with portable machines for the first time. Around the same time programs for COMPUTERS were developed that facilitated the digital synthesis and manipulation of sound and the storage of information about sounds and structures. University departments at Princeton and Stanford, and such institutions as IRCAM in Paris established studios where computer synthesis could be explored. IRCAM's director, Pierre Boulez, produced one of the most effective works using electronic means, *Répons* (1980), in which the sounds of an orchestra are modified by computer analysis and synthesis. In the 1980s many works were produced suggesting that the medium, though still in places uncharted, continues to provide a stimulus to composers. By the mid-1980s digital synthesizers, smaller and more powerful than their analogue ancestors and offering the facility of linkage to home computer systems, have brought facilities previously only available in the most advanced studios into the composer's workroom.

Electronic organ. An electronically amplified keyboard instrument capable of imitating a pipe organ. There are numerous means of producing such sounds without pipes: the main systems are electromagnetic tone-wheels (as in the Hammond organ), electrostatic tone-wheels (Electrone), vibrating metal reeds (Wurlitzer organ), oscillators (Baldwin organ) and digital waveform synthesis (Allen computer organ).

Electronic percussion [drum machine, rhythm machine]. An electronic instrument, used in popular music, that synthesizes percussion sounds or stores and reproduces the sounds of conventional percussion instruments.

Electrophone [electronophone]. Generic term for musical instruments that produce vibrations that must be passed through a loudspeaker before they are heard as sound. Such instruments may be divided into three subcategories: electronic, which use no mechanical agency to generate sounds; electromechanical, which use mechanical tone-wheels that produce no acoustic sound but form part of an oscillator circuit; and electroacoustic, which convert the vibrations of strings, reeds, plates, rods or other components into voltage variations in an electrical circuit.

Elegy. A vocal or instrumental piece lamenting someone's death. The earliest type is the medieval PLANCTUS; later ones include the vocal DÉPLORATION and NENIA and the instrumental TOMBEAU, DUMP and APOTHÉOSE. Many Baroque laments (*see*

LAMENTO) are elegiac in tone; numerous other works, including some from Stravinsky's late years, are elegies in all but name.

Elegy for Young Lovers. Opera in three acts by Henze to a libretto by Auden and Kallman (1961, Schwetzingen).

Elektra. Opera in one act by Richard Strauss to a libretto by Hofmannsthal after Sophocles (Dresden, 1909). Other operas on the subject have been written by Haeffner (1787) and Gnecchi (*Cassandra*, 1905).

Eler, André-Frédéric (*b* Alsace, 1764; *d* Paris, 21 April 1821). French composer. He was librarian at the Paris Conservatoire from its foundation (1795) and later a counterpoint teacher; he wrote vocal and wind pieces for the students as well as operas, orchestral and chamber music and patriotic works. His collection of 16th- and 17th-century vocal works is still extant.

Eler, Franz (*b* Uelzen, *c*1500–05; *d* Hamburg, 22 Feb 1590). German composer. He taught at the Johannes Gymnasium, Hamburg, after 1529. His *Cantica sacra* (1588), containing Latin and German hymns, is a chief source for 16th-century Lutheran melody.

Elevation. Normally an organ piece played at Mass during the consecration. Five Frescobaldi toccatas were designed as elevation pieces.

Elgar, Sir Edward (William) (*b* Broadheath, nr. Worcester, 2 June 1857; *d* Worcester, 23 Feb 1934). English composer. He had violin lessons in Worcester and London but was essentially self-taught, learning much in his father's music shop. From the age of 16 he worked locally as a violinist, organist, bassoonist, conductor and teacher, also composing abundantly though not yet very individually: the accepted corpus of his works belongs almost entirely to the period after his 40th birthday.

His first attempt to establish himself in London was premature. He moved there with his wife Alice in 1889, but in 1891 they returned to Malvern, and he began to make a reputation more steadily with choral works: *The Black Knight, The Light of Life, King Olaf* and *Caractacus*. These were written within a specifically English tradition, but they were influenced also by German music from Weber, Schumann and Mendelssohn to Brahms and Wagner. The orchestral Enigma Variations (1899), in which each variation portrays a different friend of Elgar's, then proclaimed the belated arrival of a fully formed original style, taken further in the oratorio *The Dream of Gerontius* (1900), where the anxious chromaticism of a post-*Parsifal* manner is answered by the assurances of the Newman text: Elgar was himself a Roman Catholic, which may have been one cause of his personal insecurity.

Gerontius and the Variations made him internationally famous, but he remained in Worcestershire, composing mostly in the same two genres: *The Apostles* and *The Kingdom* were two parts of a never completed triptych of oratorios, and a sequence of short orchestral pieces was followed by a long awaited and much acclaimed First Symphony, swiftly joined by the Violin Concerto and Second Symphony. By 1912 the Elgars had at last settled again in London, but after the outbreak of war he achieved little besides the

deeply reflective Cello Concerto, and after his wife's death in 1920 almost nothing. In 1923 he went back to Worcester, and though he occasionally worked at new pieces – a completion of the oratorio trilogy, a Third Symphony, an opera after Jonson's *The Devil is an Ass* – his composing life was over. He did, however, work energetically at recording much of his music for the gramophone.

The celebrated nobility of his music has been seen as evocative of British imperial glory, but its deeper qualities are of aspiration and nostalgia: they are qualities of an intimately personal expression, but also of a style created at the end of a tradition. For though the Straussian tone poem *Falstaff* is one of his subtlest creations, most usually his symphonic forms looked back to Schumann and, in point of thematic transformation, Franck. But his highly characteristic and often extended melodic themes suggest a connection with Bruckner's in their tonal and rhythmic stability (there is often an underlying slow march metre) and their implication of unusual harmonic relationships.

Cantatas and oratorios The Black Knight (1892); The Light of Life (1896); Scenes from the Saga of King Olaf (1896); Caractacus (1898); Sea Pictures, mezzo, orch (1899); The Dream of Gerontius (1900); The Apostles (1902); The Kingdom (1906); The Music Makers (1912)

Orchestral music Froissart, ov. (1890); Serenade, str (1892); Enigma Variations (1899); Cockaigne, ov. (1901); Pomp and Circumstance, 5 marches (1901–30); In the South, ov. (1904); Introduction and Allegro, str (1905); Wand of Youth, Suites nos. 1 and 2 (1907–8); Sym. no.1 (1908); Vn Conc. (1910); Romance, bn, orch (1910); Sym. no.2 (1911); Falstaff, sym. poem (1913); Vc Conc. (1919); Severn Suite, brass band, (1930)

Chamber and instrumental music Salut d'amour, pf/vn, pf/etc (1889); Org sonata (1895); Chanson de nuit, Chanson de matin (*c*1897); Vn sonata (1918); Str Qt (1918); Pf Qnt (1919); pf music

Elijah. Oratorio, op.70, by Mendelssohn to a text by J. Schubring after *Kings* 1. xvii–xix (1846, Birmingham).

Elisabetta, regina d'Inghilterra. Opera in two acts by Rossini to a libretto by G. Schmidt after Federici (1815, Naples).

Elisir d'amore, L'. Comic opera in two acts by Donizetti to a libretto by Romani after Scribe's *Le philtre* (1832, Milan).

Elízaga, José Mariano (*b* Morelia, 27 Sept 1786; *d* there, 2 Oct 1842). Mexican composer. He worked in Mexico City and Guadalajara as a piano teacher and *maestro de capilla*, producing two notable didactic works (1823, 1835) and some church music. He co-founded Mexico City's Sociedad Filarmónica and was one of the first to promote Mozart and Beethoven in Mexico.

Elizalde, Fred [Federico] (*b* Manila, 12 Dec 1907; *d* there, 16 Jan 1979). Spanish conductor and composer. He studied in Madrid, in England and in California under Bloch. He then studied law at Cambridge, exercising in the 1920s much influence on jazz in Britain by importing high-level New York players. In 1930 he became conductor of the Manila SO, but was in Paris, 1931–3, then in Spain, where he was a friend of Falla and Lorca and fought in the Civil War, next in France and then in Manila as president of the broadcasting company from 1948. His works include an opera *Paul Gauguin* (1943) and concertos for piano and violin.

Elkus, Albert (Israel) (*b* Sacramento, 30 April 1884; *d* Oakland, 19 Feb 1962). American musician. He studied in California, Berlin, Paris and Vienna, and taught at Berkeley (1931–59) and elsewhere. His few works, mostly dating from his 20s and 30s, are well constructed and conservative. His son Jonathan (*b* 1931) has edited music by Ives, on whom he has written a book, and composed theatre, band and vocal music.

Ella, John (*b* Leicester, 19 Dec 1802; *d* London, 2 Oct 1888). English violinist, conductor and critic. He studied at the RAM and with Fétis in Paris. He promoted chamber music concerts in London through the Musical Union (1845–80) and was an outspoken critic for the *Morning Post, Musical World* and *The Athenaeum*.

Eller, Heino (*b* Tartu, 7 March 1887; *d* Tallinn, 16 June 1970). Estonian composer. He studied with Kalafati at the Petrograd Conservatory and taught composition in Tartu (1920–40) and then Tallinn. His works include three symphonies, five quartets and much music for violin and for piano (still played in Estonia), showing a northern colouring but also a nervous tension akin to Skryabin.

Ellerton, John Lodge (*b* Cheshire, 11 Jan 1801; *d* London, 3 Jan 1873). English composer. He studied at Oxford and in Rome. He is notable mainly for the quantity of his chamber music, in conventional style, including 50 string quartets.

Ellington, Duke [Edward Kennedy] (*b* Washington, DC, 29 April 1899; *d* New York, 24 May 1974). American jazz composer, bandleader and pianist. He played with the Washingtonians at the Kentucky Club, New York (1923–7), then moved to the Cotton Club (1927–32) with an enlarged band under his leadership. He pioneered the 'jungle' style of big-band jazz and made over 200 recordings. In 1931 he experimented with extended composition in *Creole Rhapsody* followed by *Reminiscin' in Tempo* and *Diminuendo and Crescendo in Blue*. The band developed further (it now had 14 pieces) and toured in the USA and Europe (1933, 1939). Ellington's writing was based on the styles of individual band members and suffered from its changes of personnel in the mid-1940s. His extended compositions continued, for the concert hall (*Black, Brown and Beige*, 1943) and later for LP records (a series of 'suites'). He wrote a film score and stage music and latterly mainly liturgical music. After he died his orchestra was taken over by his son, Mercer Ellington (*b* 1919).

Ellis, Osian (Gwynn) (*b* Ffynnongroew, 8 Feb 1928). Welsh harpist. He studied at the RAM, where he taught from 1959. He has played as a recitalist, in chamber music and in orchestras. Harp works written for him include Britten's Suite (1969) and concertos by Hoddinott and Mathias.

Ellis, Vivian (John Herman) (*b* Hampstead, 29 Oct 1903). English composer. He studied at the RAM and became a prolific composer of operettas in the 1930s; *Bless the Bride* (1947) is the best known.

Elman, Mischa (*b* Talnoye, 20 Jan 1891; *d* New York, 5 April 1967). American violinist. He studied in Odessa and with Auer at St Petersburg. His débuts in Berlin, London and New York (1904, 1905, 1908) established him as a great violinist, admired above all for his rich, sensuous, infinitely expressive tone and his passionate temperament.

Eloy, Jean-Claude (*b* Monte-St-Aignan, 15 June 1938). French composer. He studied with Milhaud at the Paris Conservatoire, with Scherchen and Pousseur at Darmstadt, and with Boulez at the Basle Academy (1961). Boulez and Varèse were the dominant influences on his early works (*Equivalences* for wind and percussion, 1963), but since the early 1970s he has looked more to oriental music and philosophy in a sequence of few but substantial works (e.g. *Kshara-akshara* for voices and orchestral groups, 1974).

Elsbeth, Thomas (*b* Neustadt, Franconia, ?mid-16th century; *d* ?Jawor, Silesia, after 1624). German composer. He seems to have worked in Franconia and Silesia, and is noteworthy as the composer of some 100 songs for three to five voices, and about 150 motets, the early ones in Latin, most of the rest in German, all without continuo. Of the motets, the two collections of *Evangelien* (1616, 1621) are interesting for their inclusion of explanatory paraphrases preceding the gospel texts.

Elsner, Józef Antoni Franciszek (*b* Grodków, 1 June 1769; *d* Warsaw, 18 April 1854). Polish composer and teacher of German origin. He was in charge of the Warsaw Opera (1799–1824), enriching its repertory with his own works. He also issued a collection of Polish songs, promoted concerts, contributed to the *Allgemeine musikalische Zeitung* and to the Polish press, organized music schools, wrote textbooks and became rector of the conservatory in 1821; Chopin was among his pupils. Through his use of native folk music elements, he was a precursor of the Polish national style.

Elssler, Johann (Florian) (*b* Eisenstadt, 3 May 1769; *d* Vienna, 12 Jan 1843). Austrian music copyist. He was Haydn's personal copyist from 1787 and later also his valet. His father Joseph (*d* 1782), copyist to Prince Esterházy, also copied works by Haydn, and was succeeded by his son Joseph jr (1767–1843). Johann's children included Therese (1808–78) and Fanny (1810–84), both eminent dancers.

Elston, Arnold (*b* New York, 30 Sept 1907; *d* Vienna, 6 June 1971). American composer. He studied with Goldmark (1928–30) and Webern (1932–5), and taught at the University of Oregon (1941–58) and at Berkeley (1958–71). His works include a chamber opera *Sweeney Agonistes* (1950), much choral music and chamber works, notably a String Quartet (1961) and a Piano Trio (1967).

Elvey, Sir George (Job) (*b* Canterbury, 27 March 1816; *d* Windlesham, 9 Dec 1893). English organist and composer. He was organist at St George's Chapel, Windsor (1835–82), and composer of notable hymn tunes, including *St George* ('Come, ye faithful people, come') and *Diademata* ('Crown him with many crowns').

Elwell, Herbert (*b* Minneapolis, 10 May 1898;

d Cleveland, 17 April 1974). American composer. He studied with Bloch in New York (1919–21) and Boulanger in Paris (1921–4), and taught at the Cleveland Institute (1928–45) and Oberlin. His works include many songs in a lyrical style related to Fauré.

Elwes, Gervase (Cary) (*b* Northampton, 15 Nov 1866; *d* Boston, 12 Jan 1921). English tenor. He went into the diplomatic service, then turned to singing and in 1903 became professional. He sang Gerontius in 1904 and the première of Vaughan Williams's *On Wenlock Edge* in 1909. He was much admired for his sensitive, refined singing, notably in lieder and Bach's Passions. The Musicians' Benevolent Fund was established in his memory.

Emanuel Moór pianoforte. A double-manual keyboard instrument invented by the Hungarian composer Emanuel Moór (1863–1931); the upper keyboard, which may be coupled to the lower, produces notes an octave higher.

Embellishment. The decoration of a musical line; *see* IMPROVISATION and ORNAMENTS.

Embouchure. The oral mechanism for playing a wind instrument, consisting of the lips, the lower facial muscles and the structure of jaws and teeth. The term is also the French for mouthpiece.

Emmanuel, (Marie François) Maurice (*b* Bar-sur-Aube, 2 May 1862; *d* Paris, 14 Dec 1938). French composer. In 1880 he entered the Paris Conservatoire (where he later taught, 1909–36) and had private lessons with Guiraud, which brought him into contact with Debussy. He was one of the few independents in French music. Concerned with modality (his Cello Sonata of 1887 is in the Phrygian mode), he studied folksong, plainchant and ancient Greek music, his works including two Aeschylean operas. He also wrote two symphonies, six piano sonatinas and songs and several books.

Emmett, Dan(iel Decatur) (*b* Mount Vernon, OH, 29 Oct 1815; *d* there, 28 June 1904). American composer and minstrel performer. In 1843–58 his four-man blackface troupe, the Virginia Minstrels, established the model for the black minstrel show – an evening of imitation black music, dancing, anecdotes and oratory. Later he performed with Dan Bryant's Minstrels, writing the tunes and words for the finales ('walk-arounds'); the most successful was *Dixie* (1860). Later he worked as a fiddler. The rough-hewn character of his *c*55 songs contrasts with the sentimental appeal of Foster's minstrel music.

Emperor Concerto. Nickname of Beethoven's Piano Concerto no.5 in E♭ (1809).

Emperor Quartet. Nickname of Haydn's String Quartet in C. op.76 no.3 (1797), so called because the slow movement is a set of variations on the tune he wrote for the Emperor, now the Austrian national anthem.

Empfindsamkeit (Ger.). Term associated with a particular aesthetic outlook prevalent in north Germany in the mid-18th century. The word comes from *Empfindung* ('expression') and refers to an intimate, sensitive, subjective kind of expression, designed to draw gentle tears of melancholy. It is the

equivalent of 'sensibility' in the 18th-century or Jane Austen sense or the kind of 'sentimentality' of Laurence Sterne. In music, the ideals of *Empfindsamkeit* (or the *Empfindsamer Stil*) are best represented in the music and writings of C.P.E. Bach.

Encina, Juan del (*b* Salamanca, 12 July 1468; *d* León, late 1529 or early 1530). Spanish poet, dramatist and composer. In 1484 he joined Salamanca Cathedral choir and in 1498 left for Rome, where he served at the Spanish pope's court. He also held posts at Málaga (1508–19) and León cathedrals (1519 until his death). He wrote most of his music and plays before he was 30. Many of his compositions are villancicos, featuring varied, flexible rhythms, a transparent polyphonic texture, expressive harmonies, syllabic word-setting and smooth melodies. His originality lies in his ability to combine rhythm and expression in an organic whole.

Encore. A French word meaning 'again', cried out by English audiences (not French ones, who use *bis*) to demand the repetition of a piece just heard or an extra item. An 'encore' now usually means an extra piece played at the end of a recital or by a soloist after a concerto.

Enescu, George [Enesco, Georges] (*b* Liveni Vîrnav [now George Enescu], 19 Aug 1881; *d* Paris, 3/4 May 1955). Romanian composer and violinist. He studied at the Vienna Conservatory (1888–94) and at the Paris Conservatoire (1895–9). Paris remained the centre of his professional life, though he spent much time in Romania as a teacher and conductor. He is regarded as the greatest and most versatile Romanian musician and was widely admired as a violinist. Apart from the two Lisztian *Rhapsodies roumains* for orchestra (1901) his music has been neglected, perhaps partly because of the complexity and diversity of his stylistic allegiances: Romanian folk music is a recurrent influence, but so too are Wagner and Reger and early Schoenberg. His output includes the opera *Oedipe* (1936), five symphonies (1905, 1914, 1921, 1934, 1941) and much chamber music.

Enfance du Christ, L' [The Childhood of Christ]. Oratorio, op.25, by Berlioz to his own text (1854, Paris).

Enfant et les sortilèges, L'. Opera in two parts by Ravel to a libretto by Colette (1925, Monte Carlo).

Enfant prodigue, L'. Cantata by Debussy, to a text by E. Guinard (1884, Paris) revised 1908.

Opera by Auber (1850, Paris). *See also* PRODIGAL SON, THE.

Engel, (A.) Lehman (*b* Jackson, MS, 14 Sept 1910; *d* New York, 29 Aug 1982). American composer and conductor. He studied in New York with Goldmark and Sessions. His reputation rests chiefly on his work in the theatre as a composer, conductor and music director. He wrote incidental music and conducted on Broadway.

Engelmann, Georg (*b* Mansfeld, *c*1575; *d* Leipzig, bur. 11 Nov 1632). German composer. He was musical director at St Pauli, Leipzig, and also from 1625 organist of the Thomaskirche. His music, widely known in central Germany, includes well-wrought motets and three noteworthy volumes of dances (1616–22). Consisting mostly of pavans and galliards paired in the English manner, they are characterized by idiomatic string writing and brilliant figuration in the two highest parts. His son Georg (c1603–63) succeeded him at the Thomaskirche.

Engelmann, Hans Ulrich (b Darmstadt, 8 Sept 1921). German composer. He studied with Fortner, Leibowitz and Krenek, and began teaching at the Frankfurt Musikhochschule in 1969. His works include dramatic, orchestral and instrumental pieces using a variety of techniques.

English Bach Festival (UK). Annual series (spring/summer) of events in London, established in 1963 by Lina Lalandi; it was at first in Oxford, then Oxford and London, but is now solely in London. Bach and the music of his time (played on Baroque instruments) are featured. British composers have been commissioned and British premières of continental works have been given. Operas have included rarely heard works by Handel, Rameau and Rossini.

English Baroque Soloists. Period instrument ensemble founded in 1978 by its conductor JOHN ELIOT GARDINER.

English Chamber Orchestra [ECO]. British orchestra. Originally the Goldsbrough Orchestra, formed in 1948 by Arnold Goldsbrough and Lawrence Leonard, it gave mainly 18th-century works until 1960, when it was renamed and adopted a wider repertory. It became the resident orchestra at the Aldeburgh Festival in 1961 and in 1969 made its first world tour. Its conductors have included Barenboim and Leppard.

English Concert. Group founded by Trevor Pinnock in 1972. Primarily for the performance of Baroque music on period instruments, it is led by Simon Standage. It is of variable size, from three or four players to a full chamber orchestra, with Pinnock as harpsichord (or organ) continuo player or soloist. The group has won acclaim for its lithe, spirited playing of Vivaldi, Bach and especially Handel, most of whose orchestral music it has recorded.

English flute. Term applied in the 18th century to the recorder to distinguish it from the transverse (or 'German') flute.

English Folk Dance and Song Society. Organization, with headquarters in London, formed in 1932 from the Folk-Song Society (founded in 1898 to collect and publish folk music) and the English Folk Dance Society (founded by Cecil Sharpe in 1911 to make known dances he had collected and published). Its international conference and festival in 1935 led to the formation of the International Folk Music Council (now the International Council for Traditional Music) in 1947. It publishes the *Folk Music Journal*.

English guitar. A type of cittern popular in England from c1750 to 1810. It has a flat or slightly convex back and six courses of strings tuned c–e–g–c′–e′–g′. The repertory consists principally of solo arrangements of theatre songs and dance-tunes.

English horn [cor anglais]. The tenor of the modern orchestra OBOE family, pitched in F, a 5th below the oboe; its lowest note is written b, sounding e. The bell is characteristically pear-shaped with a constricted opening. It is used in orchestras and wind ensembles; it sometimes plays parts written for the oboe da caccia (e.g. in Bach's *St Matthew Passion*). (For illustration, *see* WOODWIND INSTRUMENTS.)

English National Opera. Formerly Sadler's Wells Opera, which developed from the OLD VIC company and performed at Sadler's Wells Theatre, London, from 1931; it moved to the Coliseum in 1968 and was renamed in 1974. It performs in English and offers a broad repertory, including operetta, often in progressive production styles.

English Opera Group. Opera company established by Britten, Eric Crozier and John Piper in 1947; it was enlarged and renamed English Music Theatre Company in 1975; it was dissolved in 1980. Aiming to encourage the collaboration of writers and composers and to present their works and earlier chamber operas, it helped establish Aldeburgh Festival and formed a training school, the London Opera Centre. It toured abroad and gave annual seasons at Sadler's Wells Theatre. Premières included works by Berkeley, Birtwistle, Britten, Musgrave and Walton.

English violet. A bowed string instrument, described by L. Mozart (1756) as a kind of viola d'amore but with different tuning and with seven principal and 14 sympathetic strings. It was unknown under this name in England and might be identical with the violetta marina.

Englund, (Sven) Einar (b Ljugarn, 17 June 1916). Finnish composer. He studied with Palmgren and Carlsson at the Helsinki Academy (1933–41), with Copland at Tanglewood, and in Russia, where he was impressed by Prokofiev and Shostakovich. His works include five symphonies (1946–77), concertos and piano pieces.

Engramelle, Marie Dominique Joseph (b Nédonchel, 24 March 1727; d Paris, 9 Feb 1805). French builder of mechanical instruments. His *La tonotechnie ou L'art de noter des cylindres* (Paris, 1775), concerning the use of a numbered dial in 'notating' the studded barrels of mechanical instruments, contains much valuable information on French late Baroque performing practice, documenting minute shading and great freedom in tempo and articulation.

Enharmonic. Term used to denote different ways of 'spelling' the name of a note (e.g. B♯ = C = D♭♭). An 'enharmonic change' is the respelling of a note in accordance with its changing function (e.g. D♭ is renamed C♯ in a modulation from D♭ major to A major). An 'enharmonic modulation' involves the respelling of a key, usually when there is a change in mode (e.g. from C♯ minor to D♭ major).

Enharmonic keyboard. A keyboard with more than 12 keys and sounding more than 12 different pitches in the octave. Such keyboards may make available mean-tone temperament in tonalities with more than two flats or three sharps; make possible the playing of a number of chords in just intonation; and produce microtones. Enharmonic keyboards date back to the 15th century and are described by Zarlino and Praetorius.

Enigma Variations [Variations on an Original

Theme ('Enigma')]. Elgar's op.36 (1899), 14 variations for orchestra dedicated to his 'friends pictured within'; each variation portrays an individual, the last one the composer himself.

Enlightenment. A movement in 18th-century thought that aimed to combat superstition and prejudice and place human betterment above the supernatural. In music, it is reflected in the rise of a simpler, more accessible, *galant* style, in which graceful melody with a simple accompaniment predominated, replacing the elaborate counterpoint of the late Baroque era. The development of a light, Rococo style in French music after the death of Louis XIV, the reform of the Italian opera libretto towards simpler human dramas apt for treatment in a direct melodic style and the growth of a newly expressive instrumental style in north Germany (the *Empfindsamer Stil*) are all part of this movement.

Enna, August (Emil) (*b* Nakskov, 13 May 1859; *d* Copenhagen, 3 Aug 1939). Danish composer. Mostly self-taught, he composed many successful operas, notably *The Witch* (1892) and *Kleopatra* (1894).

Enríquez(-Salazar), Manuel (*b* Ocotlán, 17 June 1926). Mexican composer. He studied at the Juilliard School (1955–7) and became director of the Mexico City Conservatory. From 1960 he used serial and aleatory techniques, mostly in orchestral and instrumental pieces. In the 1960s he held a comparable position to Chávez's of the 1930s, but unlike Chávez he declared nationalism a dead end for Mexican musicians.

En saga. Symphonic poem, op.9, by Sibelius (1892, rev. 1902).

Ensalada (Sp.: 'salad'). A kind of QUODLIBET in 16th-century Spain. The best known are ten by Mateo Flecha (i). *Ensaladilla* is a Latin American villancico of a type popular in the 16th–18th centuries involving a quodlibet of other villancicos.

Ensemble. Term for a group of players and/or singers; it is also applied to the music they play and the degree of precision with which they play together.

Ensemble InterContemporain. French chamber orchestra founded in 1976 at the Institut de Recherche et de Coordination Acoustique/Musique, Paris. It is conducted by Boulez and Peter Eötvös, tours internationally and has given many premières.

Ensemble Modern. German ensemble. It was founded in 1980 from members of the National Youth Orchestra of West Germany for performing new music. It has appeared at festivals in Darmstadt, Donaueschingen, Warsaw and Huddersfield and several composers have written for it, notably Kagel, who also sometimes conducts it.

Entführung aus dem Serail, Die [The Abduction from the Seraglio]. Singspiel in three acts by Mozart to a libretto by J.G. Stephanie jr after C.F. Bretzner's *Belmonte und Constanze* (1782, Vienna).

Entr'acte (Fr.). A piece performed between the acts of a play or opera. Examples include Beethoven's entr'actes for Goethe's *Egmont* and Schubert's for Chézy's *Rosamunde*. *See also* COMÉDIE-BALLET, INTERMEDIO and INTERMEZZO.

Entrée. In the French 17th-century BALLET DE COUR, a group of dances unified by subject; in the *opéra-ballet* and *tragédie lyrique*, a march-like piece marking the beginning of the *divertissement* and the entry of the 'corps d'entrée'. *See also* INTRADA.

Entremés. A theatrical intermezzo, usually comic, in 17th-century Spain.

Eolides, Les. Symphonic poem by Franck (1876) after a poem by Lecomte de Lisle.

Eötvös, Peter [Péter] (*b* Székelyudvarhely, 2 Jan 1944). Hungarian conductor and composer. He studied at the Budapest Academy (1958–65) and in 1966 went to Cologne, where from 1968 he played in Stockhausen's live electronic ensemble. In the 1970s he turned to conducting (mostly 20th-century music), mainly with the Ensemble InterContemporain and the BBC SO.

Epinette de Vosges. A partly fretted zither called after the French mountain region where it survived. It consists of a shallow box tapered in width, with five metal strings stretched over 13–17 metal frets.

Episode. A subsidiary or intermediate section of a rondo or other musical form; in fugue, any passage in which the subject is not heard.

Epistle. In Eastern and Western Christian liturgies, a traditional biblical reading from the New Testament Epistles in the Liturgy of the Word or the first main division of the Eucharist. It is traditionally read or chanted by a sub-deacon (the 'epistoler') to a simple recitation tone which is occasionally elaborated; occasionally it was set to polyphony.

Epistle sonata. An instrumental piece, probably played between the reading of the Epistle and the Gospel at Mass. The usage was apparently peculiar to Salzburg Cathedral. Mozart wrote 17 examples, single movements for two violins, bass and organ, sometimes with other instruments.

Epithalamium. A marriage song or poem; an instrumental piece for a wedding or evoking one.

Epstein, David (Mayer) (*b* New York, 3 Oct 1930). American conductor and composer. He studied with Fine and Berger at Brandeis, Sessions and Babbitt at Princeton, and with Milhaud; in 1965 he was appointed professor at MIT. He made his conducting début in 1960, and as music director of the Harrisburg (Pennsylvania) SO (1974–8) improved its standards. With the MIT SO he has recorded 20th-century American music. His compositions are Webernian in their compression. He has written on music theory.

Equale. A piece for equal, i.e. similar, voices or instruments. The name was used especially for funeral pieces for trombones, of which Beethoven's three *equali* (1812) are the best-known examples.

Equal temperament. A tuning system based on the division of the octave into 12 equal semitones. This is the normal tuning of Western music today. The equality of semitones means that all other intervals are tempered, as compared with their frequency ratios. It is often supposed that Bach's *Well-Tempered Clavier* was intended for a system of equal temperament, but although many German theorists of Bach's time regarded equal temperament as a good tuning, many others preferred unequal temperaments and there is no firm evidence as to which system Bach favoured. Unequal temperaments continued in use well into the 19th century.

Equal voices. Term used when two or more voices of the same compass sing in two or more parts, for example music for a women's choir; it is usually laid out so that each of the voices is at some time singing the uppermost part.

Erard. French firm of piano and harp makers. It was founded in Paris c1780 by Sébastien Erard (1752–1831), assisted by his brother Jean-Baptiste (1745–1826). The success of Sébastien's *clavecin mécanique* (1779) and the patronage of Louis XVI led to the manufacture of pianos from 1785; experiments to improve the pedal harp were undertaken at J.B. Krumpholtz's suggestion. Sébastien opened a London shop in 1792. The firm introduced major improvements, notably the double escapement piano action (1821), which greatly improved key repetition and the player's control, and the harp's fork mechanism (now standard) which, by mechanically shortening the strings by a semitone, allowed the construction of a harp, tuned in Cb, that could be played in any key (1810). Jean-Baptiste's son Pierre (1794–1855) continued the firm's reputation for innovation, building chiefly harps in London and upright pianos in Paris.

Erb, Donald (James) (*b* Youngstown, OH, 17 Jan 1927). American composer. He studied in Cleveland, Bloomington and Paris and has taught at the Cleveland Institute and Case Western Reserve University. His works are mostly orchestral and instrumental, in traditional forms and exploiting unusual sounds, virtuosity and sometimes electronics. His style reached maturity with the concertos for trombone (1976), cello (1976), keyboards (1978) and trumpet (1980).

Erb, Karl (*b* Ravensburg, 13 July 1877; *d* there, 13 July 1958). German tenor. Self-taught, he made his début at Stuttgart (1907) and in 1913 joined Munich Opera. He created the title role in Pfitzner's *Palestrina* (1917); he left Munich in 1925 and retired from opera in 1930, concentrating on lieder and Bach's Passions. He was married to Maria Ivogün. He was noted for a strong but soft-grained voice and natural musicianship.

Erbach, Christian (*b* Gaualgesheim, 1568–73; *d* Augsburg, 1635). German composer. His early years were spent in Augsburg in the service of Marcus Fugger, for whose wedding in 1598 he composed a motet. In 1602 he was appointed organist of St Moritz and head of the Stadtpfeifer, before moving in 1614 to Augsburg Cathedral (principal organist 1625–35), where he enjoyed a wide reputation as a teacher. Italian influence is evident in much of Erbach's keyboard music (mostly toccatas, canzonas and ricercares) and vocal works, especially in the large, Venetian-style polychoral motets and smaller sacred canzonettas. The *Modi sacri tripertiti* (1604–6) contain *cantus firmus* settings of the introits, alleluia verses and communions for mass at most of the important liturgical feasts.

Erben, Balthasar (*b* Danzig, 1626; *d* there, bur. 3 Oct 1686). German composer. He travelled widely in Europe before becoming Kapellmeister at St Marien, Danzig, in 1658, where he was the central figure in local musical life. His surviving compositions consist mainly of sacred concertos showing rich scoring supported by expressive harmony, affective chromaticism and closely worked counterpoint.

Erede, Alberto (*b* Genoa, 8 Nov 1909). Italian conductor. After early study with Fritz Busch he conducted at Glyndebourne, 1938–9. He worked in the USA from 1937 and was engaged at the Met, 1950–55. At the Deutsche Oper am Rhein he was music director, 1958–61, becoming chief conductor of the Gothenburg SO in 1961. His rhythmically alert interpretations of Verdi and Puccini have been recorded.

Erismena. Opera by Cavalli to a libretto by Aureli (1655–6, Venice); it is unique among 17th-century Italian operas in that a contemporary English singing translation exists.

Erk, Ludwig (Christian) (*b* Wetzlar, 6 Jan 1807; *d* Berlin, 25 Nov 1883). German folksong editor, teacher and choral director. In Berlin he taught at the Royal Seminary and directed a choral union and the royal cathedral choir. He collected German folksongs, his most comprehensive publication being the *Deutscher Liederhort* (1856, enlarged 1893–4). Through his collections he established the character of the 19th-century German school song.

Erkel, Ferenc (*b* Gyula, 7 Nov 1810; *d* Budapest, 15 June 1893). Hungarian composer, conductor and pianist. He played and taught the piano in Kolozsvár, then settled in the capital c1835, conducting opera, appearing as a piano soloist and composing instrumental pieces with Hungarian themes (e.g. the *Duo brillant* for violin and piano, 1837). He decided not to compete with Liszt as a pianist but turned to writing for the stage: his well-received *Bátori Mária* (1840) led quickly to *Hunyadi László* (1844), the most successful of his operas in Hungary; it combines Italian and Viennese Classical influences with indigenous ones, notably the 'Hungarian scale', rhythms, heroic expression and tripartite form of the *verbunkos*, and the dramatic climaxes of the *csárdás*. He was conductor at the National Theatre, Pest (1838–74; succeeded by Hans Richter), and for the Philharmonic Concerts which he founded, composing mainly shorter works from this time onwards, including the well-known *népszínmű* (popular plays with interpolated songs) *Két pisztoly* and *A rab* and the Hungarian national anthem (1844). His strikingly successful *Bánk bán* (1861), written with his most talented sons Gyula (1842–1909) and Sándor (1846–1900), represents the culmination of his native operatic style. Neither his later comic works nor his experimental, nationalistic music dramas were as distinctive, though the Wagnerian *Brankovics György* (1868–72) was considered his masterpiece during his lifetime. He devoted his last years to choral music and the directorship of the Budapest Academy of Music.

Erlebach, Philipp Heinrich (*b* Esens, bap. 25 July 1657; *d* Rudolstadt, 17 April 1714). German composer, a leading figure in central Germany at the time. He was Kapellmeister at the Rudolstadt court from

1681. His six surviving trio sonatas and suites show his skill at uniting foreign and German stylistic features, while the dramatic works (only librettos and a few arias survive) demonstrate a preference for national, historical subjects with an emphasis on popular realism. He composed in a wide range of sacred genres among which the psalm settings are of interest for their colourful harmonies and contrasts of tempo and dynamics. But he is chiefly important as a cantata composer, developing a new expressive style which he called 'oratorio cantata'; his work represents the final stage in the form's evolution.

Erlkönig [The Erl-king]. Song by Schubert (D328, 1815), a setting for voice and piano of a ballad by Goethe. Several composers set it, including Loewe, Reichardt and Zelter.

Ernani. Opera in four acts by Verdi to a libretto by Piave after Hugo (1844, Venice).

Ernst, Heinrich Wilhelm (*b* Brno, 6 May 1814; *d* Nice, 8 Oct 1865). Moravian violinist and composer. He studied at the Vienna Conservatory. One of the outstanding violinists of his time, he reached (and occasionally surpassed) Paganini's wizardry, also impressing with his soulful, touching cantilena; he was highly regarded by Berlioz, Joachim and Mendelssohn. His compositions, notable for Romantic élan and technical ingenuity, include the *Concerto pathétique* op.23, the famous *Elégie* op.10 and the Six Polyphonic Studies.

Ernste Gesänge, Vier. *See* FOUR SERIOUS SONGS.

Eroica Symphony [Sinfonia eroica]. Beethoven's Symphony no.3 in E♭ (1804); it was originally called 'Bonaparte' but Beethoven removed the title when Napoleon proclaimed himself emperor and the work was published as 'Heroic Symphony', 'composed to celebrate the memory of a great man'.

Eroica Variations. Beethoven's op.35 (1802), 15 variations and a fugue for piano on an original theme in E♭; he also used the theme in his ballet *Die Geschöpfe des Prometheus*, the 'Eroica' Symphony and the seventh of his 12 *Contredanses*.

Erwartung [Expectation]. Opera in one act by Schoenberg to a libretto by Marie Pappenheim (1924, Prague), a monodrama for soprano and orchestra.

Eschenbach, Christoph (*b* Breslau, 20 Feb 1940). German pianist and conductor. After study in Cologne and Hamburg he was heard widely as a pianist, notably in Mozart, Beethoven and the early Romantic repertory; he also championed Henze's music. In 1969 he made his American début. He has conducted since 1973, in 1982 becoming chief conductor of the Zurich Tonhalle Orchestra.

Escher, Rudolf (George) (*b* Amsterdam, 8 Jan 1912; *d* De Koog, 17 March 1980). Dutch composer. He studied with Pijper at the Rotterdam Conservatory (1934–7) and taught at Utrecht University. His works, in a strongly polyphonic, expanded tonal style, using kernels that grow into motifs and melodies, cover all non-dramatic genres, including some fine *a cappella* choral works of the 1950s, a closely argued Wind Quintet (1967) and *Summer Rites at Noon* (1973) for spatially opposed orchestral groups.

Esclarmonde. Opera in four acts by Massenet to a libretto by Gallet and L. de Gramont (1889, Paris).

Escobar, Luis Antonio (*b* Villapinzón, 14 July 1925). Colombian composer. He studied with Nabokov in Baltimore and Blacher in Berlin. He founded the Colombia PO in 1966 and was later a diplomat in Germany. His music shows an awareness of Latin American dance rhythms and includes the ballet *Avirama* (1955) and the opera *Los hampones* (1961).

Escobar, Pedro de (*b* Oporto, *c*1465; *d* ?Évora, after 1535). Portuguese composer active in Spain. He was a singer in the chapel choir at the court of Isabella I (1489–99), *maestro de capilla* of Seville Cathedral (1507–14), and possibly *mestre da capela* to Cardinal Dom Affonso (1521). His works (in MSS), which include two masses and seven motets, show uncommon contrapuntal skill and sensitivity to text.

Escobedo, Bartolomé de (*b* diocese of Zamora, *c*1500; *d* 21 March/11 Aug 1563). Spanish composer. He spent most of his working life in the papal choir in Rome. His works include two masses and several motets (in MSS). In 1551 he was a judge in the debate between Vicentino and Lusitano on chromaticism.

Eshpay, Andrev Yakovlevich (*b* Koz'modem'yansk, 15 May 1925). Soviet composer. He studied with Myaskovsky, Golubev and Khachaturian at the Moscow Conservatory (1948–56) and has written orchestral, choral, chamber and light music; it draws on Mari folk music, of which his father Yakov Andreyevich (1890–1963) was a scholar (he, too, based compositions on it).

España. Orchestral rhapsody by Chabrier (1883).

Espansiva, Sinfonia. *See* SINFONIA ESPANSIVA.

Esplá (y Triay), Oscar (*b* Alicante, 5 Aug 1886; *d* Madrid, 6 Jan 1976). Spanish composer. He studied in Meiningen and Munich with Reger (1912) and in Paris with Saint-Saëns (1913); from 1930 he taught at the Madrid Conservatory. He was an accomplished musician, whose style, owing something to Debussy and Stravinsky as well as Spanish folk music, is simple, fresh and elegant. His works cover many genres and he wrote several books.

Esposito, Michele (*b* Castellammare di Stabia, 29 Sept 1855; *d* Florence, 23 Nov 1929). Italian pianist, composer and conductor. From 1882 to 1928 he was in Dublin, teaching at the Royal Irish Academy of Music, conducting the Dublin Orchestral Society and composing vocal and instrumental music using Irish melodies.

Espressivo (It.). Expressive.

Esquivel Barahona, Juan (de) (*b* Ciudad Rodrigo, *c*1563; *d* ?there, after 1613). Spanish composer. A pupil of Juan Navarro, he was *maestro de capilla* of Ciudad Rodrigo Cathedral from before 1608 until at least 1613. An important and prolific composer, he published masses (1608) and motets (1608, 1613), which were widely popular and stand comparison with Victoria's.

Estampes. Three piano pieces by Debussy (1903): *Pagodes*, *La soirée dans Grenade* and *Jardins sous la pluie*.

Estampie. Medieval term applied to certain textless melodies which may be instrumental dances and which consist of a number of versicles, each repeated. The last portion of the first versicle, varied at the repeat, is re-used at the end of each of the later ones. A few vocal works have forms resembling that of the *estampie* and a number of French poems called 'estampies' could have been sung to melodies of the same type.

Este. Italian family of patrons. Hereditary lords of Ferrara, they included conspicuous patrons of music, especially from the late 15th century when Duke Ercole I d'Este succeeded in making Ferrara a musical centre of European importance and began the tradition of importing first-rate musicians from northern Europe, notably Josquin Desprez and Obrecht. After 1598, when Ferrara was lost to the papacy, the Estensi continued to rule and to encourage music in neighbouring Modena. The tradition declined in the 18th century.

Esterházy. Hungarian noble family, noted as musical patrons. The earliest family member with an interest in music was Pál (1635–1713), a statesman and soldier and palatine of Hungary, who engaged a choir and orchestra at Eisenstadt in 1674 and composed 55 cantatas (published in 1711). Joseph Haydn served four of the princes: Paul Anton (reigned 1734–62), his brother Nikolaus 'the Magnificent' (1762–90), Nikolaus's son Anton (1790–94), and Anton's son Nikolaus (1794–1833). Their ancestral castle is in Eisenstadt (Kismarton); in the 1760s Prince Nikolaus built the family palace, Eszterháza, on the Neusiedler See. Prince Paul Anton and Prince Nikolaus 'the Magnificent' were both instrumentalists; Haydn wrote baryton works for the latter. Prince Anton disbanded the court orchestra in 1790, leaving Haydn free to go to London, but Prince Nikolaus revived it and commissioned six masses from Haydn and one from Beethoven. Subsequently music at the court declined. Other relatives of the family were active in Viennese musical life.

Esther. Oratorio by Handel, originally composed (perhaps as a masque, *Haman and Mordecai*) to a text probably by Pope and Arbuthnot, for performance at Cannons, c1718; it was adapted and given in London in 1732. It was the first English oratorio.

Estrada, Carlos (*b* Montevideo, 15 Sept 1909; *d* there, 7 May 1970). Uruguayan composer. He studied in Montevideo and with Roger-Ducasse and Büsser at the Paris Conservatoire. He was active in Uruguay as a conductor (he founded the Montevideo CO), teacher and composer of neo-classical, modal pieces, including two symphonies (1951, 1967).

Estrée, Jean d' (*b* early 16th century; *d* 1576). French composer. He was an oboist at the French court and edited four books of dances (1559–64); their over 120 branles and c60 other dances, for four to six instruments, provide a conspectus of dancing practices of the time.

Estro armonico, L' [Harmonic fancy]. Vivaldi's op.3, 12 concertos for different combinations of violin, two violins, four violins and cello, with orchestra and continuo (1712).

Eszterháza [Esterház]. Palace in Fertőd, Hungary. In 1766–90 it was the summer home of Prince Nikolaus Esterházy and it became an international centre for the arts. Haydn was employed there and wrote most of his operas for its theatre (opened 1768). 1038 opera

performances (67 premières, including Cimarosa and Paisiello) were given in 1780–90. After the prince's death (1790) the theatre was not used. In 1959 annual (summer) Haydn festival concerts were inaugurated.

Et exspecto resurrectionem mortuorum. Work by Messiaen for woodwind, brass and percussion (1964).

Ethnomusicology. A branch of MUSICOLOGY in which emphasis is given to the study of music in its cultural context; the anthropology of music. It had its origins during the late 19th century in Europe and the USA with the work of Carl Stumpf, Erich M. von Hornbostel, Curt Sachs, Alexander J. Ellis, Jesse Walter Fewkes, Franz Boas and others. Early studies dealt largely with the psychology of music, the reconstruction of world music history, the distribution of musical styles and instruments and, in the USA, with the analysis of American Indian music. Modern research combines anthropological techniques of fieldwork and ethnography with a variety of humanistic approaches, especially from musicology and aesthetics.

Etler, Alvin (Derald) (*b* Battle Creek, IA, 19 Feb 1913; *d* Northampton, MA, 13 June 1973). American composer. He studied with Hindemith at Yale (1942–4) and taught at Smith College (1949–73). His craftsmanlike works, mostly instrumental, are influenced by a Bartók and Copland style, serial after 1963.

Etoile du Nord, L'. Opera in three acts by Meyerbeer to a libretto by Scribe (1854, Paris).

Eton Choirbook. English MS, copied 1490–1502 for use at Eton College, where it is still held. It originally consisted of 224 folios, but now has 126; 29 of the 93 pieces originally indexed are missing. Most are motets; the composers include Browne, Davy and Cornysh.

Etude (Fr.). A STUDY.

Etudes d'exécution transcendante d'après Paganini. *See* TRANSCENDENTAL STUDIES AFTER PAGANINI.

Eugene Onegin. Opera in three acts by Tchaikovsky to a libretto by K. Shilovsky and the composer after Pushkin (1879, Moscow).

Eulenburg. German–British music publishers. The firm was established by Ernst Eulenburg (1847–1926) in Leipzig in 1874; at first it issued educational and choral material, but it became famous for its miniature scores (begun in 1891); over 1000 works have appeared in 'Eulenburgs kleine Partitur-Ausgabe'. Ernst's son Kurt (1879–1982) moved the firm to London in 1939, with a branch in Zurich; the London firm was taken over by Schott in 1957.

Eulenspiegel, Till. *See* TILL EULENSPIEGELS LUSTIGE STREICHE.

Euphonium. A brass instrument of widely conical profile, essentially a tenor tuba in 9′ B♭. It usually has four valves (occasionally three or five), its compass is F′ to b′♭ or higher. It was invented in 1843 and soon became the most important tenor brass instrument in bands. In English (and increasingly American) usage, the euphonium is a wider-bored instrument than the baritone. It is known in Germany as *Baryton* or *Tenorbasshorn*.

Euryanthe. Opera in three acts by Weber to a libretto by Helmina von Chézy after a 13th-century French romance (1823, Vienna).

Eustachio Romano (*fl* early 16th century). Italian composer. His *Musica duorum* (1521) is the earliest printed book of music for instrumental ensemble, containing 45 duets in the new imitative style of Josquin and his contemporaries; he also wrote frottolas.

Evangelisti, Franco (*b* Rome, 21 Jan 1926; *d* there, 28 Jan 1980). Italian composer. He studied with Daniele Paris in Rome (1948–53), Genzmer in Freiburg (1953–6) and at Darmstadt. In 1964 he founded the improvisation group Nuova Consonanza and he has taught electronic music in Rome. He exploited indeterminacy in *Proporzioni* (1958) for flute and *Aleatorio* (1959) for string quartet.

Evans, Sir Geraint (Llewellyn) (*b* Pontypridd, 16 Feb 1922). Welsh baritone. He studied at the GSM and made his Covent Garden début in 1948. Until his retirement from opera in 1984 he was highly valued for his keenly characterized portrayals of such comic roles as Beckmesser, Dulcamara and Papageno. At La Scala, the Met and Salzburg he was also successful as Falstaff and as Mozart's Figaro and Leporello.

Exaudet, André-Joseph (*b* Rouen, ?*c*1710; *d* Paris, 1762). French violinist and composer. He played in Paris from 1744. His 12 violin sonatas contain technical innovations, and op.3 (*c*1766) includes *intermèdes* for two violins. A minuet from his trio sonatas (1751) was highly popular.

Excursions of Mr Brouček, The [Výleti pana Broucka]. Opera in two parts by Janáček: *Mr Brouček's Excursion to the Moon*, in two acts with a libretto by the composer (with additions) after Čech; and *Mr Brouček's Excursion to the 15th Century*, in two acts with a libretto by F.S. Procházka after Čech (1920, Prague).

Eximeno (y Pujades), Antonio (*b* Valencia, 26 Sept 1729; *d* Rome, 9 June 1808). Spanish theorist. He was notorious for his bias against contrapuntal rules and scholastic pedantry, revealed in *Dell' origine e delle regole della musica* (1774) and in an attack on Padre Martini (1775).

Exposed fifths, exposed octaves. Hidden 5ths or octaves between the outer voices in a harmonic progression (*see* HIDDEN FIFTHS, HIDDEN OCTAVES).

Exposition. In fugue, the opening section in which the voices enter in turn with the subject; in sonata form, the first part of the movement in which the main material is stated, beginning in the tonic and closing in, usually, the dominant or relative major.

Expression. The idea that music can express emotion has many times been reiterated in the history of writing about music. In some areas, for example the Baroque, it was believed that certain types of phrase carry specific emotional connotations (i.e. a descending minor-key phrase connotes despair). Some writers have held that music could express specific emotions while others suggest it merely imitates them.

More commonly, 'expression' is applied to elements in musical performance that depend on personal response and vary between different interpretations, i.e. such nuances as can arise from articulation, tempo and dynamics. The term 'expression marks' is applied particularly to indications of dynamics, like *pp* (*pianissimo*, very quiet), *f* (*forte*, loud) or *cresc* (*crescendo*, growing louder); terms like *cantabile* (in a singing style) or *morendo* (dying away) are also expression marks.

Expressionism. Term, applied originally to painting and literature, used for the intensely emotional manner used in the arts from the second decade of the 20th century. It was first used in this sense in 1910, of the school of artists including Kandinsky, Marc and Nolde; Schoenberg, himself a painter, was associated with such artists. The term was probably first applied to music in 1918, especially to Schoenberg and (following Kandinsky's view) his avoidance of traditional forms of the beautiful in order to express his feelings in the most powerful, personal way. It is recognized that the strongest manifestation of expressionism in music is in Schoenberg's atonal, pre-12-note works (e.g. the Four Orchestral Songs op.22, 1915).

Expression marks. *See* TEMPO AND EXPRESSION MARKS.

Exsultate, jubilate. Motet by Mozart, K165 (1773).

Exultet. A lyrical prayer, chanted by a deacon once a year during the Easter Vigil, to bless the Paschal candle and celebrate its symbolism. It first appeared in the 8th-century Gallican liturgy and formed part of the Roman rite from the Middle Ages. It is also termed *Laus cerei*, *Benedictio cerei* or *Praeconium paschale* and is sung to a simple recitation or a more ornate melody.

Eybler, Joseph Leopold (*b* Schwechat, 8 Feb 1765; *d* Vienna, 24 July 1846). Austrian composer. He studied with Albrechtsberger, 1776–9, and later with his distant cousin Haydn; a friend of Mozart's, he began to complete the Requiem after his death (Süssmayr continued this task). He was choir director at the Carmelite Church in Vienna, 1792–4, and at the Schottenkloster, 1794–1824. He also held court posts, ultimately as court Kapellmeister (1824–33). His works include an opera, oratorios, cantatas, sacred works, instrumental music (notably string quintets) and songs. The early works reflect his respect for Haydn and Mozart.

Eyck, Jacob van (*b* *c*1589; *d* Utrecht, 26 March 1657). Dutch carillonist and composer. Working in Utrecht from 1625, he discovered that the purity of a bell's sound is directly related to its shape. As a composer he was known through three collections of pieces for solo recorder (1664–9), mostly variations on popular melodies.

Eye music. Music with a symbolic meaning apparent to the eye but not to the ear; Italian madrigalists, for example, sometimes used black notes to suggest darkness and white ones light, and Bach symbolized the Crucifixion with notes in the form of a cross.

F

F. Name for a note, or a PITCH CLASS; *see also* PITCH NAMES. F is the fourth degree (subdominant) of the scale of C. In a musical text (usually in lower case, bold italic type), *f* stands for *forte* (loud); *see* DYNAMICS. As the sign that fixes pitch on the bass staff is a stylized F, the bass clef is sometimes called the 'F clef'. Vivaldi's instrumental works may be listed by numbers prefixed with an F, indicating the thematic list by Fanna (1968).

Faber, Heinrich (*b* Lichtenfels, before 1500; *d* Oelsnitz, 26 Feb 1552). German music theorist, Kantor and composer. He was a singer at the court of Christian II at Copenhagen (1515–24) and studied in Wittenberg, where he later lectured (1551). His musical renown rests on three theoretical works; his *Compendiolum musicae* (1548), a textbook for beginners, was the most popular music treatise in Lutheran schools in the 16th and 17th centuries and an important source of two-voice compositions, including his own.

Faber, Johann Christoph (*fl* early 18th century). German composer. He was a court violinist and an indifferent composer, but is noted for his four instrumental pieces containing musically encoded messages.

Fabri, Annibale Pio (*b* Bologna, 1697; *d* Lisbon, 12 Aug 1760). Italian tenor. He sang in operas in Italy from 1711 and in Handel's operas in London, 1729–31. Several times president of the Accademia Filarmonica of Bologna, he later joined the royal chapel at Lisbon. One of the leading singers of his age, he did much to raise the status of the tenor voice.

Fabricius, Werner (*b* Itzehoe, 10 April 1633; *d* Leipzig, 9 Jan 1679). German composer. He was music director at St Pauli, Leipzig (from 1656), also serving as organist at the Nicolaikirche. A friend of Schütz, he was a composer of sacred vocal music (songs, dialogues, concertos), but also wrote a figured bass treatise (before 1675), a set of short preludes arranged by key and chorale settings.

Fabrizi, Vincenzo (*b* Naples, 1764; *d* ?after 1812). Italian composer. He worked first in Naples, then in northern Italy, and from 1786 in Rome, where he was a theatre musical director. His 14 comic operas (1783–8), notably *Il convitato di pietra* (*Don Giovanni Tenorio*, 1787), gained him international fame;

his last was written for Barcelona. He also composed chamber music.

Faburden. A style of improvised polyphony in English 15th-century music. From a plainchant in the middle voice, two other parts were derived: a treble, or the plainchant a 4th higher, and a 'faburden', in 3rds and 5ths below the middle. The result was a preponderance of 6-3 chords. By 1462 'faburden' was used for the three-voice texture. Continental FAUXBOURDON is a related style but in a mainly written tradition.

Façade. 'Entertainment' by Walton for reciter and ensemble, to poems by Edith Sitwell (1921); it has undergone several revisions and Walton made two orchestral suites from it.

Faccio, Franco [Francesco Antonio] (*b* Verona, 8 March 1840; *d* Monza, 21 July 1891). Italian conductor and composer. He studied at the Milan Conservatory with his (lifelong) friend Boito, producing the opera *I profughi fiamminghi* (1863) and the more successful *Amleto* (1865, text by Boito), as well as songs, cantatas and a popular scherzo for orchestra. But his true métier was as a conductor; he succeeded Terziani at La Scala, coming into close contact with Verdi and giving the premières of his *Otello* (1887), Puccini's *Le villi* (1885) and Ponchielli's *La gioconda* (1876). His final triumphs were *Lohengrin* and *Die Meistersinger*. He was an important historical link between Mariani and Toscanini.

Fado. Portuguese song and dance genre, the typical urban vocal music of cafés, cabarets and nightclubs. It may have a Moorish origin, or originally have been a maritime style. It is usually sung with guitar-like instruments, which play cross-rhythms against the vocal melody; the form is usually strophic and the songs may include improvised material.

F-A-E. A three-note motto, derived from the phrase 'Frei aber einsam' ('Free but lonely') and used as a unifying theme in the violin sonata composed in 1853 by Albert Dietrich (the first movement), Schumann (the second and fourth) and Brahms (the scherzo).

Faenza MS. Italian MS of the 15th century. It consists of 96 folios, some of which contain keyboard arrangements of vocal works and liturgical *cantus firmus* settings of the first two decades of the century, as well as 22 pieces in white mensural notation copies in 1473–4 (sections of the mass Ordinary, Magnificats, motets etc). It is now at the Biblioteca Comunale, Faenza.

Fagan, Gideon (*b* Somerset West, 3 Nov 1904; *d* Cape Town, 21 March 1980). South African composer. He studied at the RCM (1922–6) and held conducting posts in England. He returned to South Africa as a conductor, music director of SABC (1963–6) and lecturer at Cape Town University (1967–73).

Fago, (Francesco) Nicola (*b* Taranto, 26 Feb 1677; *d* Naples, 18 Feb 1745). Italian composer and teacher. He was *primo maestro* at the Turchini conservatory in Naples, 1705–40, and had a high reputation as a teacher; Leo and Jommelli were among his students. He was also *maestro di cappella* at the Tesoro S Gennaro of Naples Cathedral in 1709–31, and at S Giacomo degli Spagnuoli from 1736. After presenting stage works and oratorios, he turned to church music, writing over 50 works (psalms, masses etc). Some combine polychoral writing with a modern style, while others use the *stile antico*. His secular solo cantatas are modelled on Alessandro Scarlatti's.

His son Lorenzo (1704–93), like his father called 'Il Tarantino', succeeded him at the Tesoro di S Gennaro in 1731 and later at the Turchini conservatory (1744–93); he wrote sacred music and cantatas. Lorenzo's son Pasquale (*c*1740–before 1795), known as 'Pasquale Tarantino', held the former post, 1766–71, and composed several operas.

Fagotto. BASSOON; also an organ stop.

Fairground organ [band organ]. A mechanical organ, used from *c*1880 to 1930 to provide music for carousels and in amusement parks, circuses and skating rinks in Europe and the USA. They were usually housed in elaborate cases and included flue and reed pipes.

Fair Maid of Perth, The [La jolie fille de Perth]. Opera in four acts by Bizet to a libretto by St Georges and Adenis after Scott (1867, Paris).

Fairy Queen, The. Semi-opera in a prologue and five acts by Purcell to a libretto possibly by E. Settle after Shakespeare's *A Midsummer Night's Dream* (1692, London).

Fairy's Kiss, The. *See* BAISER DE LA FÉE, LE.

Falckenhagen, Adam (*b* Grossdalzig, 26 April 1697; *d* Bayreuth, 1761). German lutenist and composer. He served at German courts including Weissenfels (in the 1720s) and Bayreuth. One of the last significant lute composers, he wrote sonatas, partitas and concertos.

Falco, Michele (*b* Naples, ?1688; *d* after 1732). Italian composer. He was the only professional musician among the originators of Neapolitan *opera buffa*, setting several dialect librettos in 1709–23. The first two, *Lo Lollo pisciaportelle* (1709) and *Lo Masiello* (1712; Act 2 only), were given privately. Falco also wrote oratorios.

Falcone, Achille (*b* Cosenza, *c*1570–75; *d* there, 9 Nov 1600). Italian composer. *Maestro di capella* at Caltagirone, Sicily, he is noted for the musical dispute and competition he had in 1600 with the Spanish composer Sebastián Raval. His only publi-

cation, five-part madrigals (1603), describes the dispute and includes the competition pieces.

Falconieri, Andrea (*b* Naples, *c*1585; *d* there, 19/29 July 1656). Italian composer and lutenist. He worked in Parma, Modena and Genoa (also probably at Mantua and Florence) before becoming *maestro di cappella* at Naples in 1647. Most prolific as a songwriter, his surviving works are among the first to show a distinction between recitative or arioso and aria within the same song. His instrumental pieces, mostly for two violins, bass and continuo, display a spirited style midway between Monteverdi and Corelli; they underline the links between lute music, the dance suite and the *sonata da camera*.

Fall, Leo(pold) (*b* Olomouc, 2 Feb 1873; *d* Vienna, 16 Sept 1925). Austrian composer. He studied with the Fuchs brothers at the Vienna Conservatory and worked from 1895 as an operetta conductor. In 1906 he settled in Vienna, where his three operettas *Der Fidele Bauer* (1907), *Die Dollarprinzessin* (1907) and *Die geschiedene Frau* (1908) established him alongside Lehár and Strauss and brought him international renown.

Falla (y Matheu), Manuel de (*b* Cádiz, 23 Nov 1876; *d* Alta Gracia, 14 Nov 1946). Spanish composer. He studied in Cádiz and from the late 1890s in Madrid, where he was a pupil of Tragó for the piano and Pedrell for composition. In 1901–3 he composed five zarzuelas in the hope of making money; then in 1905 came his first important work, the one-act opera *La vida breve*, which he revised before its first performance, in Paris in 1913. He had moved to Paris in 1907 and become acquainted with Dukas, Debussy, Ravel, Stravinsky and Albéniz, all of whom influenced his development of a style using the primitive song of Andalusia, the *cante jondo*, and a modern richness of harmony and colour. This was not an immediate achievement: he wrote little before returning to Madrid in 1914, but then came the piano concerto *Noches en los jardines de España* (1915) and the ballets *El amor brujo* (1915) and *El sombrero de tres picos* (1919), the latter presented by Dyagilev and designed by Picasso.

Like Stravinsky a few years before, he turned to a much sparer style and to the format of touring theatre in *El retablo de maese Pedro* (1923). He also began to concern himself with the medieval, Renaissance and Baroque musical traditions of Spain, reflected in his Concerto for harpsichord and quintet (1926). Most of the rest of his life he devoted to a vast oratorio, *Atlántida*, on which he worked in Granada (where he had settled in 1919) and after 1939 in Argentina. With Albéniz and Granados he was one of the first Spanish composers to win international renown and the most gifted of the three.

False cadence, false close [deceptive cadence; interrupted cadence]. A CADENCE in which the dominent chord resolves not on to the expected tonic but on to some other chord, usually the submediant (V–VI).

False relation [cross-relation; non-harmonic relation]. A chromatic contradiction between two notes in a chord or in different parts in adjacent chords. False relations involve chromatic semitones and normally arise because of the melodic independence of the lines. Their potential for expressive text-setting attracted many 16th- and 17th-century composers, notably Gesualdo and Purcell.

Falsetto. The treble range produced by most adult male singers through a slightly artificial technique whereby the vocal cords vibrate in a length shorter than usual. Stroboscopic observations show that, in falsetto singing, the extreme membranous edges of the vocal cords appear to be the only parts in vibration; in ordinary singing, the cords vibrate as a whole. Falsetto singing has long been used in Western music and the term was known in Italy by the 16th century. In 17th-century Italian choirs, alto parts were often sung by falsettists but soprano parts were taken over by castratos; in northern Europe falsettists continued to be used (with boy sopranos) until the 19th century when women were admitted to Protestant church choirs – though in England there has been an uninterrupted tradition of falsetto singing, particularly in cathedral and collegiate choirs.

Falsobordone (It.). Term for a style of chordal recitation based on root-position triads, with the form and melody of a Gregorian psalm-tone. It was used for vesper psalms, and the style appears in many compositions from the 15th century to the 18th. The name relates (but the style does not) to the French FAUXBOURDON.

Falstaff. Opera in three acts by Verdi to a libretto by Boito after Shakespeare (1893, Milan).
Symphonic study (op.64) by Elgar (1913).

Famintsïn, Alexander Sergeyevich (*b* Kaluga, 5 Nov 1841; *d* Ligovo, 6 July 1896). Russian music historian and critic. A professor at the St Petersburg Conservatory, he is remembered chiefly for his critical writings attacking the music of the Balakirev–Stasov circle from the viewpoint of the German academicism in which he was steeped.

Fanciulla del West, La [The Girl of the Golden West]. Opera in three acts by Puccini to a libretto by G. Civinini and C. Zangarini after Belasco (1910, New York).

Fandango (Sp.). A courtship dance of Castille and Andalusia, in triple time and moderately fast tempo; the term is also used for a slow, plaintive sung melody of the flamenco type. Of popular origin, it became fashionable in the late 18th century and was used in dramatic music; one fandango melody was used by Gluck (*Don Juan*, 1761) and later by Mozart (*Le nozze di Figaro*, 1786). An outstanding example in art music is the 450-bar fandango for harpsichord by Antonio Soler; fandangos have also been composed by D. Scarlatti, Boccherini, Rimsky-Korsakov, Albeniz, Granados and Falla.

Fanfare. A flourish of trumpets or other brass instruments, often with percussion, for ceremonial purposes. Fanfares are distinct from military signals in usage and character. Their tradition goes back to the Middle Ages; in 18th-century France, 'fanfare' denotes a short bustling movement with many repeated notes. The modern meaning arose during the 19th century. Many British composers have composed fanfares for coronations; other notable examples are Copland's *Fanfare for the Common Man* (1942), Stravinsky's *Fanfare for a New Theatre* (1964) and Britten's *Fanfare for St Edmundsbury* (1959).

Fanfare for the Common Man. Work by Copland for brass and percussion (1942).

Fano, Michel (*b* Paris, 9 Dec 1929). French composer. He studied with Boulanger and Messiaen at the Paris Conservatoire (1948–53) and was influenced by Boulez in his Sonata for two pianos (1952). In 1954 he abandoned abstract composition films.

Fantasia (It.; Eng. fancy, fantasy; Fr. *fantasie*; Ger. *Fantasie, Phantasie*). An instrumental piece in which the imagination of the composer takes precedence over conventional styles and forms.

The lute fantasias of Francesco da Milano, widely imitated in the 16th century, integrate imitation techniques with brilliant idiomatic play. The lute (or vihuela) fantasia was also cultivated by Luis de Milán in Spain and composers elsewhere, notably Dowland in England. The keyboard fantasia, whose types included arrangements of vocal polyphony, variations on the hexachord, free ricercares and (in Germany) chorale-based pieces, came to the fore in the late 16th century and was popular in the 17th; composers include Frescobaldi, Sweelinck, Scheidt, Froberger, Byrd and Orlando Gibbons. Ensemble fantasias were written in many countries, too, but especially in England, where Purcell paid tribute to a long tradition to which Byrd, Gibbons, Jenkins, William Lawes and Locke had contributed.

While the ensemble type had largely died out by 1700, the keyboard fantasia remained important, especially in Germany. It soon severed its links with imitative counterpoint; J.S. Bach's best-known example, the Chromatic Fantasy and Fugue (BWV903), combines elements of toccata and recitative. C.P.E. Bach's fantasias are rhapsodic and improvisatory works for clavichord, many of them unbarred, but like Mozart's piano fantasias their sections are organized into a coherent structure. To the Romantics the fantasia offered the means of formal expansion without the constraints of rigid sonata form. Beethoven, in his two sonatas 'quasi una fantasia' (op.27), pointed the way for the piano fantasias of Schubert, Chopin and Schumann. The term 'fantasia' was also used, by Liszt and others, for virtuoso pieces based on themes from an opera or other work. 20th-century composers, too, have used the term for extended instrumental pieces (e.g. Schoenberg's op.47) and for free variations (e.g. Tippett's *Fantasia on a Theme by Corelli*).

Fantasia Concertante on a Theme of Corelli. Work for strings by Tippett (1953), on a theme from Corelli's Concerto grosso op.6 no.2, written for the tercentenary of Corelli's birth.

Fantasia contrappuntistica. Piano work by Busoni (1910) based on Bach's Contrapunctus XVIII from *The Art of Fugue*; Busoni created a fourth subject (Bach composed only three) and added a fifth.

Fantasia on a Theme by Thomas Tallis. Work by Vaughan Williams for double string orchestra and string quartet (1910), on the third of nine psalm tunes Tallis composed (1567) for Archbishop Parker's Psalter.

Fantasia on British Sea Songs. Henry Wood's orchestral arrangement of nine traditional and other songs (1905), celebrating the centenary of Nelson's victory at Trafalgar; it became the traditional finale to the last night of the Proms.

Fantasia on Greensleeves. Ralph Greaves's arrangement (1934) for one or two flutes, harp and strings of the interlude from Vaughan Williams's opera *Sir John in Love*.

Fantasia-suite. Modern term for a 17th-century English genre for strings and organ consisting of a fantasia followed by dances (usually almaine and galliard).

Fantasiestück (Ger.). A piece, usually for piano, related to the 19th-century FANTASIA but generally shorter and narrower in scope.

Fantasiestücke. *See* PHANTASIESTÜCKE.

Fantastic Symphony. Symphony, op.14, by Berlioz (1830).

Fantini, Girolamo (*b* in or nr. Spoleto, *c*1600; *fl* 1630–38). Italian trumpeter. Chief trumpeter at the Tuscan court from 1630, he wrote an early trumpet method (1638) important for its inclusion of the first known pieces for trumpet and continuo. He also extended the instrument's register to c''' (once to d''').

Farandole. A chain dance of southern France, usually in a moderate 6/8, played by flute and drum.

Farewell Symphony. Nickname of Haydn's Symphony no.45 in F♯ minor (1772), so called because in the final Adagio the number of players is gradually reduced to none.

Farina, Carlo (*b* Mantua, *c*1600; *d* *c*1640). Italian composer and violinist. He was at the Mantua court, among the early violin virtuosos who developed the instrument's techniques. He was Konzertmeister at the Dresden court, where Schütz worked, 1625–9, but after that is heard of only in Danzig in 1637; it is supposed that he returned to Italy. He published five books of music for two to four instruments and continuo, pavans, galliards and other dances, with sonatas and canzonas (1626–8). His sonatas for one or two violins and continuo are among the earliest for violin and show a highly developed virtuoso technique; some are stunt-like, using special effects, and in one (*Capriccio stravagante*, 1627) the violin has to imitate fighting cats, barking dogs and a variety of other instruments. But he is important for his extension of the violin's technique and for his influence, as the first virtuoso violinist in Germany, on German violinists and sonata composers.

Farinel, Michel (*b* Grenoble, bap. 23 May 1649; *d* there, ?early 18th century). French violinist and composer. A pupil of Carissimi in Rome, he was superintendent of music and ballets at the Spanish court in Madrid (1679–88) before returning to France as *maître de chapelle* at the convent of Montfleury, and at St Etienne, Toulouse. He is chiefly remembered for his variations on the folia, known in England as *Farinel's Ground* and published in Playford's *The Division Violin* (1685). His father François (*d* 1672) was a musician at the Savoy court and his son Jean-Baptiste (1665–*c*1720) Konzertmeister at Hanover and Osnabrück.

Farinelli [Broschi, Carlo] (*b* Andria, 24 Jan 1705; *d* Bologna, 15 July 1782). Italian soprano castrato. He sang from the 1720s in operas, including several by his teacher Porpora; in 1724–34 he travelled widely, appearing in operas by most of the principal composers of the day. At the height of his powers he sang in London (1734–7); he was highly praised for his agility, purity of tone and beauty of sound. Lastly he served at the Spanish royal court in Madrid, directing the chapel music and producing Italian operas and reputedly singing the same arias every day to cheer his melancholy monarch. He retired with enormous wealth to his estate near Bologna, *c*1760, where he received musicians including Padre Martini, Gluck and Mozart. He was influential in spreading the florid musical style in *opera seria*, and often introduced his own arias. His brother was the composer RICCARDO BROSCHI.

Farinelli, Giuseppe (*b* Este, 7 May 1769; *d* Trieste, 12 Dec 1836). Italian composer. He studied in Naples. With *c*60 stage works to his credit, most written during 1800–10 and showing a rich and facile invention, his success as an *opera buffa* composer rivalled Cimarosa's; among the most notable are *I riti d'Efeso* (1803) and *La contadina bizzarra* (1810).

Farkas, Ferenc (*b* Nagykanizsa, 15 Dec 1905). Hungarian composer. He studied with Weiner and Siklós at the Budapest Academy (1922–7) and with Respighi in Rome (1929–31), then worked mostly as a teacher, notably at the Budapest Academy (1949–75). Stravinsky was an influence on his orchestral virtuosity, displayed in theatre and concert works; his output also includes sacred and secular choral music and songs.

Farkas, Ödön (*b* Jászmonostor, 1851; *d* Cluj-Napoca, 11 Sept 1912). Hungarian composer, conductor and teacher. He studied in Budapest. As director of the Kolozsvár (now Cluj-Napoca) Conservatory from 1879, he fostered the study and composition of Hungarian music, his own works reflecting the metrical peculiarities of the Magyar language and its melodies, and the influence of Liszt and Erkel.

Farmer, Henry George (*b* Birr, Ireland, 17 Jan 1882; *d* Law, Scotland, 30 Dec 1965). British musicologist. He played the clarinet, horn and violin in the Royal Artillery Orchestra. He also worked as a conductor and taught in London schools. In 1914 he moved to Glasgow, where he continued conducting and studied Arabic. In 1929 he published *A History of Arabian Music to the XIIIth Century*, which established his reputation as a leading scholar of Middle Eastern music; he wrote prolifically on Arab, Persian, Turkish, Jewish and oriental music theory and instruments, as well as military music and Scottish music history.

Farmer, John (*b* *c*1570; *fl* 1591–1601). English composer. He was organist and Master of the Children (1595) and a vicar-choral (1596) of Christ Church Cathedral, Dublin, before moving to London in 1599. He contributed to East's psalter (1592) and published 40 two-part canons (1591). His four-part madrigals (1599) include the famous *Faire Phyllis I saw sitting all alone*.

Farmer, Thomas (*d* London, by 8 Dec 1688). English composer. During an apparently brief life he served as one of the king's violinists from 1671. He published *A Consort of Musick in Four Parts* (1686) and wrote over 40 songs (many for plays) that appeared in collections such as *Choice Ayres, Songs and Dialogues* (1676–84) and *The Theater of Music* (1685–7).

Farnaby, Giles (*b* c1563; *d* London, bur. 25 Nov 1640). English composer. A joiner by training, he graduated BMus at Oxford in 1592 and then lived mainly in London. In the early 1600s he taught music briefly at Aisthorpe, near Lincoln. An instinctive and original composer, he is noted for over 50 imaginative keyboard pieces – fantasias, variations, dances etc. He published a book of four-part canzonets (1598) and contributed to East's psalter (1592), as well as compiling his own. His son Richard (*b* London, *c*1594) was also a composer.

Farrant, Richard (*b* ?c1525–30; *d* London, 30 Nov 1580). English composer. A singer in the Chapel Royal from *c*1550, he became Master of the Choristers of St George's Chapel, Windsor, in 1564 and of the Chapel Royal in 1569. He wrote and staged plays (two stage songs survive) and was an early exponent of the verse anthem. Some liturgical pieces attributed to 'Farrant' may be his or may be by one of the John Farrants, father and son, who were organists at Salisbury in the late 16th century.

Farrar, Ernest Bristow (*b* Blackheath, 7 July 1885; *d* France, 18 Sept 1918). English composer. He studied with Stanford at the RCM, wrote much in a characteristically English style of pastoral lyricism, and was killed in action.

Farrar, Geraldine (*b* Melrose, MA, 28 Feb 1882; *d* Ridgefield, CT, 11 March 1967). American soprano. After her début at the Royal Opera, Berlin (as Gounod's Marguerite, 1901), she became a pupil of Lilli Lehmann. She sang at the Met, 1906–22. Her clear tone and shapely phrasing made her a favourite in such roles as Zerlina, Cherubino and Suor Angelica, which she created in 1918.

Farrenc, (Jeanne-) Louise [née Dumont] (*b* Paris, 31 May 1804; *d* there, 15 Sept 1875). French composer, pianist, teacher and scholar. A composition pupil of Reicha, she published piano works from 1825, notably the *Air russe varié* and the 30 Etudes op.26; her chamber music, including two piano quintets, two piano trios, violin sonatas, trios, a nonet and a sextet, was even more successful. She was piano professor at the Conservatoire (1842–73) and editor, initially with her husband Aristide Farrenc (1794–1865), of *Le trésor des pianistes*, an anthology of 17th- and 18th-century music (23 vols., 1861–74). A flautist, music publisher and scholar, he was an advocate of early music and contributed to French periodicals and to Fétis's *Biographie universelle* (1860–65).

Farsa (It.). 'Farce': term used in 18th-century Italian librettos for comic intermezzi or an afterpiece. 'Farsetta' is also found.

Farwell, Arthur (*b* St Paul, MN, 23 April 1872; *d* New York, 20 Jan 1952). American composer. He studied with Norris and Chadwick in Boston, and with Humperdinck and Pfitzner in Germany (1897–9). He looked more to France and Russia, however, in

his compositions, which are numerous (116 opus numbers) and diverse; they range from community choruses to tiny songs. He gradually abandoned a late Romantic harmonic style for a more idiosyncratic idiom. A turning-point was *Vale of Enitharmon* op.91 (1930) for piano; in 1940 he began a series of polytonal piano studies which culminated in the Piano Sonata op.113 (1949), probably his masterpiece. Among many activities, he founded the Wa-Wan Press for new American music (1901–12), collected and arranged American Indian music, wrote pageants for community performance and was a music critic (notably for *Musical America*).

Fasano, Renato (*b* Naples, 21 Aug 1902; *d* Rome, 3 Aug 1979). Italian conductor. After study at the Naples Conservatory he was director of the Cagliari Conservatory and in 1948 founded the Collegium Musicum Italicum. This split into I Virtuosi di Roma (1952) and the Teatro dell'Opera da Camera (1956), both devoted to performing the 18th-century Italian repertory in Italy and abroad. From 1972 he supervised the edition of Vivaldi's sacred works.

Fasch, Carl Friedrich Christian (*b* Zerbst, 18 Nov 1736; *d* Berlin, 3 Aug 1800). German harpsichordist, conductor and composer, son of J.F. Fasch. He was second harpsichordist at Frederick the Great's court, 1756–67, and a colleague of C.P.E. Bach; he next served as first accompanist, and in 1774–6 conductor, at the Berlin Opera. He was a famous teacher. Later he founded and conducted the influential Berlin Singakademie. He composed vocal works, sacred and secular, keyboard music and other instrumental pieces.

Fasch, Johann Friedrich (*b* Buttelstädt, 15 April 1688; *d* Zerbst, 5 Dec 1758). German composer. He worked first in Leipzig where he founded a collegium musicum. After travelling, he held court posts at Bayreuth, Greiz and Lukaveč. From 1722 he was Kapellmeister at Zerbst, writing 12 cycles of church cantatas, other sacred music and festival works for the court; he gained widespread fame, although none of his music was published in his lifetime. One of the most significant of Bach's German contemporaries, he wrote over 60 concertos (structured like Vivaldi's), *c*90 orchestral suites, and symphonies and trio sonatas. Unusual and progressive scorings feature in his orchestral music, and his output shows a transition from Baroque to early Classical style; some late works anticipate the idioms of Gluck, Haydn and Mozart. Most of his vocal works (including four early operas) are lost.

Faschingsschwank aus Wien [Carnival Jest in Vienna]. Schumann's op.26, for piano (1840).

Fasola. A traditional simplified method of solmization popular in England and North America; in effect an abbreviated form of the ancient gamut, it uses only four solmization syllables (*fa, sol, la, mi*) by repetition.

Fasolo, Giovanni Battista (*b* Asti, *c*1600; *d* ?Sicily, after 1659). Italian composer. He spent much of his life as an organ teacher in Sicily, becoming *maestro di cappella* to the Archbishop of Monreale in 1659. Two of his nine published collections survive: *An-*

nuale (1645) provides a parish organist with responses and independent organ pieces for the year, while *Arie spirituale* (1659) are concertato settings of his own texts.

Fassbaender, Brigitte (Berlin, 3 July 1939). German mezzo-soprano, daughter of Willy Domgraf-Fassbänder. She studied in Nuremberg and made her début at Munich (1961), joining the company there and singing in all the major European houses. Her roles have included Carmen, Eboli, Dorabella, Geschwitz (*Lulu*) and Octavian (at her Covent Garden and Met débuts, 1971, 1974); her firm, well-defined mezzo serves particularly well in travesty roles.

Fauré, Gabriel (Urbain) (*b* Pamiers, 12 May 1845; *d* Paris, 4 Nov 1924). French composer and teacher. He trained at the Ecole Niedermeyer (1854–65) as organist and choirmaster, coming under the influence of Saint-Saëns and his circle while working as a church musician (at Rennes, 1866–70; St Sulpice, 1871–3; the Madeleine, from 1874) and giving lessons. Though he met Liszt and was fascinated by Wagner, he sought a distinctive style in his piano pieces and numerous songs, which had to be composed during summer holidays. Recognition came slowly owing to the modernity of his music. In 1892 he became national inspector of the provincial conservatories, and in 1896 chief organist at the Madeleine and composition teacher at the Conservatoire, where his pupils included Ravel, Koechlin, Roger-Ducasse, Enescu and Nadia Boulanger; from 1905 to 1920 he was the Conservatoire's resolute and influential director, becoming celebrated for the vocal and chamber masterpieces he produced until his death.

Fauré's stylistic development can be traced from the sprightly or melancholy song settings of his youth to the bold, forceful late instrumental works, traits including a delicate combination of expanded tonality and modality, rapid modulations to remote keys and continuously unfolding melody. Widely regarded as the greatest master of French song, he produced six important cycles (notably the novel *La bonne chanson* op.61) and three collections each of 20 pieces (1879, 1897, 1908). In chamber music he enriched all the genres he attempted, while his works for piano (chiefly nocturnes, barcarolles and impromptus) embody the full scope of his stylistic evolution. Among his few large-scale works, the popular and delicately written Requiem op.48 and the 'song opera' *Pénélope* (1913) are noteworthy.

Dramatic music Prométhée, lyric tragedy (1900); Pénélope, lyric drama (1913); Masques et Bergamasques, lyrical comedy (1919); incidental music to 6 plays, incl. Pelléas et Mélisande (1898)
Vocal music Messe basse (1881); Requiem (1877); *c*15 other sacred pieces, incl. Cantique de Jean Racine (1865); secular choruses, duets; 6 song cycles, including La bonne chanson (1894); over 50 songs
Orchestral and chamber music pieces for solo inst and orch; orch suites from stage works; 2 pf qnts (op.89, d, 1895; op.115, c, 1921); str qt, e (1924); Pf Trio, d (1923); 2 pf qts (op.15, c, 1879; op.45, g, 1886); 2 vn sonatas; 2 vc sonatas; pieces for solo inst and pf; harp pieces
Piano music 13 nocturnes; 13 barcarolles; 9 preludes; 5 impromptus; 4 valse-caprices; Dolly, pf duet (1897)

Faure, Jean-Baptiste (*b* Moulins, 15 Jan 1830; *d* Paris, 9 Nov 1914). French baritone. His musicality, the stylishness of his singing and his gifts as an actor made him an unrivalled Don Giovanni; he was also particularly admired as Alphonse in Donizetti's *La favorite*, Tell in Rossini's *Guillaume Tell* and Mephistopheles in Gounod's *Faust*.

Faust. Opera in five acts by Gounod to a libretto by Barbié and Carré after Goethe (1859, Paris).

Faust, La damnation de. *See* DAMNATION DE FAUST, LA.

Faust, Scenes from Goethe's. Overture and six movements by Schumann (1853), for soloists, chorus and orchestra.

Faust, Two Episodes from Lenau's. Two orchestral works by Liszt (1860): *Der nächtliche Zug* and *Der Tanz in der Dorfschenke*, the latter being the Mephisto Waltz no.1, later transcribed for piano solo and piano duet.

Faust Overture, A. Concert overture by Wagner (1840), intended as the first movement of a Faust Symphony.

Faust Symphony, A. Symphony by Liszt for tenor, male voices and orchestra (1857) after Goethe.

Fauvel, Roman de. A medieval *roman* by Gervais du Bus that constitutes a satirical allegory upon the Roman Church. One of the 12 MSS in which it survives presents a much extended form of the poem with a great many musical interpolations, monophonic and polyphonic. These represent a rich and largely anonymous repertory of 13th- and 14th-century music which is of far-reaching significance in the history of music and stands at the beginning of the French Ars Nova. The first book was completed in 1310, the second in 1314 and enlarged in 1316. The 167 musical items are closely integrated into the purpose of the poem, at least some of them evidently having been written for it. They comprise 34 motets (the only polyphonic items), 30 prosae and lais, 25 rondeaux, ballades and other *chansons*, 52 alleluias, responses etc and 26 refrains.

Fauxbourdon. A technique of either improvised singing or shorthand notation particularly associated with 15th-century sacred music. The term was applied to certain apparently two-part works or sections of works, normally with an elaborated plainchant in the upper part. The two written parts are based on a framework of 6ths and octaves, to which a third part and even a fourth could be added by following strict formulaic procedures. The earliest method (from *c*1430) involved the exact duplication of the upper part at the 4th below, producing a chain of 6-3 chords punctuated by single 8-5 chords, with some decorative passing notes and suspensions. From *c*1450 an alternative method was to create a bass part by singing alternate 3rds and 5ths beneath the tenor, beginning and ending with a unison or octave; an alto part could then be added by singing alternate 3rds and 4ths above the tenor, beginning and ending with a 5th. As a method of improvisation, fauxbourdon acted as a simple means of harmonizing a plainchant.

Favart, Charles-Simon (*b* Paris, 13 Nov 1710; *d* Belleville, 12 March 1792). French librettist and impresario. Working in Paris theatres from the 1740s, he played a major part in the development of *opéra comique*. In the 1750s he presented *intermèdes* translated from Italian comic works, latterly including both traditional vaudevilles and parodies of Italian ariettas; from the 1760s he wrote librettos specifically for *opéras comiques* by Monsigny and others, notably *Les moissonneurs* (set by Duni, 1768).

Favola in musica (It.). 'Tale in music': a designation found on the title-pages of 17th-century opera scores and librettos. The phrase 'in musica', rather than 'per musica', may be intended to emphasize the composer's contribution.

Favorita. An Italian dance of the 16th and 17th centuries with the same harmonic structure as the ROMANESCA.

Favorite, La [La favorita]. Opera in four acts by Donizetti to a libretto by Royer and Vaëz after Baculard d'Arnaud's *Le comte de Comminges* (1840, Paris).

Fayolle, François (Joseph Marie) (*b* Paris, 15 April 1774; *d* there, 2 Dec 1852). French writer on music. He is best known for his compilation, with Choron, of the *Dictionnaire historique des musiciens* (1810–11), though he also wrote two books on 18th- and 19th-century violinists (1810, 1831), contributed significantly to *The Harmonicon* (he lived in London, 1815–29), to French periodicals and to Michaud's *Biographie universelle*.

Fayrfax, Robert (*b* Deeping Gate, 23 April 1464; *d* ?St Albans, ? 24 Oct 1521). English composer. He was a Gentleman of the Chapel Royal by 1497, graduated MusB (1501) and MusD (1504) at Cambridge and was incorporated DMus at Oxford (1511). From 1509 until his death he was senior lay clerk there, and received many payments from Henry VIII for music MSS. 29 compositions by him survive (more than by any other English composer of his generation), including two Magnificats, ten votive antiphons and secular pieces. He is important for his cultivation of the cyclic mass, of which six of his are known; all except one are based on a plainsong *cantus firmus* in the tenor of the full sections. His music is less elaborate than that of Cornysh and Taverner and uses restrained, carefully wrought melodic lines.

Fede, Johannes (*b* Douai, *c*1415; *d* ?Paris, ?1477). French composer. Vicar of St Amé, Douai (1439–40), he became a member of the papal chapel in 1443, entered the chapel of Leonello d'Este, Marquis of Ferrara (1445), and was chaplain of the Sainte-Chapelle, Paris, from 1449 and a member of the chapel of Louis XI (1473–4). Although he was included in lists of prominent musicians by three poets of the time, only six compositions attributed to him survive: two Magnificat antiphons and four *chansons* (one probably by Barbingant).

Fedeli, Ruggiero (*b* Venice, ?*c*1655; *d* Kassel, Jan 1722). Italian composer, singer and instrumentalist. He was active chiefly in Germany where he held a succession of court and theatre posts. Among his sacred and secular vocal works the cantatas and arias are notable for their virtuoso vocal writing, which may have influenced Handel and the Hamburg opera style through his surviving opera, *Almira* (1703, Brunswick). His father Carlo (*c*1622–1685) led the orchestra at St Mark's, Venice, from 1661 and wrote a

set of sonatas (1685) with lively fugal movements, echo effects and sometimes a solo cello part. His brother Giuseppe (*fl* 1680–1733) composed mainly chamber music, but also an English opera *The Temple of Love* (1706) and French songs.

Fedora. Opera in three acts by Giordano to a libretto by Colautti after Sardou (1898, Milan).

Feen, Die [The Fairies]. Opera in three acts by Wagner (his first) to his own libretto after C. Gozzi's poem *La donna serpente* (1888, Munich).

Feierlich (Ger.). Solemn, festive.

Feind, Barthold (*b* Hamburg, 1678; *d* there, 15 Oct 1721). German lawyer, poet and aesthetician. He was a leading librettist for the Hamburg Opera, writing texts for Keiser and Graupner. He insisted that opera must be a distinct and realistic genre, not simply spoken drama set to music.

Fel, Marie (*b* Bordeaux, 24 Oct 1713; *d* Chaillot, 2 Feb 1794). French singer. Trained in the Italian style, she sang in Paris from 1734 and became one of the most famous Opéra singers, performing major roles in many works (including most of Rameau's). Her brother Antoine (1694–1771) also sang at the Opéra.

Felciano, Richard (James) (*b* Santa Rosa, CA, 7 Dec 1930). American composer. He studied with Milhaud at Mills College and the Paris Conservatoire, and with Dallapiccola (1958–9). In 1967 he joined the faculty at Berkeley. His works are strongly theatrical, such pieces as *Background Music* (1969) blurring the distinction between music and theatre; many use electronics. *Contractions* for woodwind quintet (1965) and *In Celebration of Golden Rain* for organ and gamelan (1977) are typically dramatic.

Feld, Jindřich (*b* Prague, 19 Feb 1925). Czech composer. He studied with Řídký at the Prague Academy (1948–52) and has written much instrumental music influenced by Bartók and serialism, including several concertos and string quartets and a Chamber Suite for nonet.

Feldman, Morton (*b* New York, 12 Jan 1926; *d* Buffalo, 3 Sept 1987). American composer. He studied with Riegger and Wolpe and from 1950 was closely associated with Cage; he also gained much from contact with New York painters. In 1972 he joined the faculty of the State University of New York, Buffalo. His consistent concern has been with quiet, pure and open-textured music, sometimes elastically notated (as in the *Projection* series of 1950–51) but more often fully written out. The *Viola in my Life* series (1970–71) and *Rothko Chapel* (1971) are the best known of his works. Several later pieces are extremely long, for example the First String Quartet (1979) which lasts *c*100 minutes and the Second (1983), intended to last six hours.

Feldmusik (Ger.). 'Field music': term used for fanfares and other military compositions, or the ensembles that played such music (known in the 18th century as *Oboisten* because of the leading role played by the oboists). After *c*1750 the popularity of *Feldmusik* among amateurs led to the formation of many wind ensembles, and the tradition continued under the name of *Harmoniemusik*.

Feldparthie (Ger.). An 18th-century form of wind music related to FELDMUSIK and the Partie or

PARTITA.

Fellegara, Vittorio (*b* Milan, 4 Nov 1927). Italian composer. He studied with Chailly and at Darmstadt and has taught at the Donizetti Institute in Bergamo. His music synthesizes avant-garde elements with features of postwar Italian realism, connecting both with Nono and Petrassi.

Fellowes, Edmund H(orace) (*b* London, 11 Nov 1870; *d* Windsor, 21 Dec 1951). English scholar. From 1900 he was a minor canon of St George's Chapel, Windsor. His notable contribution was his extensive series of editions of English music of *c*1545–1640 and the critical and historical writings with which he surrounded them. His union of scholarship, completeness and practicality was in a small way revolutionary, and it was mainly through his work that knowledge of the music passed into the mainstream of English musical life.

Felsenstein, Walter (*b* Vienna, 30 May 1901; *d* Berlin, 8 Oct 1975). Austrian actor and producer. He studied in Vienna and held appointments at opera houses in Germany during the 1920s and 1930s, including those at Cologne and Frankfurt; he was later excluded from regular employment because of his progressive views. His productions from 1939 increasingly broke away from conventional 'singers' opera'. In 1947 he became director of the Komische Oper in East Berlin, where he developed his concept of opera: he believed that music should be subject to the laws of the theatre, serving the dramatic action and its 'historical reality', making the music and singing 'a credible, convincing, authentic and indispensable means of human expression', taking account of the 'associative ability of a contemporary audience'. He and his pupils (such as Götz Friedrich and Joachim Herz) have had great influence on opera production styles in the second half of the 20th century.

Felton, William (*b* Drayton, 1715; *d* Hereford, 6 Dec 1769). English composer. A clergyman at Hereford Cathedral from 1743, he was well known for his dexterous harpsichord and organ playing. His 16 harpsichord suites (1750–58) and 32 keyboard concertos (1744–60; Handel subscribed to one set) reflect his fluent playing.

Feminine ending. The melodic termination of a phrase or motif on a weak beat, or on an unstressed part of a bar.

Fenby, Eric (William) (*b* Scarborough, 22 April 1906). English writer on music and composer. He gained early experience as an organist. From 1928 to 1934 he was amanuensis to Delius, who dictated the *Songs of Farewell* and *A Song of Summer*; his experiences are related in *Delius as I knew him* (1936). He was a professor at the RAM from 1964.

Fenice, La. Theatre in Venice. It opened in 1792 (rebuilt 1837, cap. 1500) and became the most important opera house in the city. Its many premières included five Verdi operas. Its seasons now include concerts by the opera orchestra.

Fennelly, Brian (*b* Kingston, NY, 14 Aug 1937). American composer. He studied at Yale University with Perle and Schuller. He has been a music administrator and in 1981 became professor at New York University. His music includes 12-note works (Wind Quintet, 1967; String Quartet, 1971–3) and freely atonal works (*Tesserae I* and *III*).

Fennimore and Gerda. Opera in 11 scenes by Delius to his own libretto after J.P. Jacobsen's *Niels Lyhne* (1919, Frankfurt).

Feo, Francesco (*b* Naples, 1691; *d* there, 18/28 Jan 1761). Italian composer. A pupil of Nicola Fago, he was *maestro di cappella* at the Annunziata in Naples from 1726. One of the finest Neapolitan teachers of his day, he taught at the S Onofrio conservatory, 1723–39, and at the Poveri di Gesù Cristo, 1739–43.

His dramatic works include 16 operas (1713–40) for Naples, Rome (e.g. *Andromaca* 1730), Turin and Madrid, and 12 oratorios and sacred dramas (1714–43). His operas lie between Vinci's popular Neapolitan style and Leo's conservative one. In church music he was the most significant Neapolitan composer next to Leo and Durante, writing many masses, psalms, hymns, sacred cantatas etc. Unlike them he did not cultivate the Palestrina style, preferring instrumental accompaniments, sometimes with homophonic textures. His idiom combines *galant* and more traditional elements in an individual way, notably in the expressive *St John Passion* (1744).

Feragut, Beltrame (Bertrand di Avignone) (*b*?Avignon, *c*1385; *d c*1450). Priest and composer. Having worked in Vicenza, he was *maestro di cappella* of Milan Cathedral (1425–30) and may then have moved to Ferrara. By 1449 he was a chaplain at the court of René d'Anjou at Aix. Ten compositions by him survive: four mass sections (including a Gloria–Credo pair), a hymn, a Magnificat, three motets and a rondeau.

Ferdinand III (*b* Graz, 13 July 1608; *d* Vienna, 2 April 1657). Austrian emperor, patron and composer. He encouraged the Italian style at the Austrian court, employing the teacher Valentini and many Italian opera composers; some distinguished Germans, notably Froberger and Kerll, also worked at his court. He was the dedicatee of numerous publications, notably Monteverdi's eighth book of madrigals (1638); his own compositions, mainly sacred vocal music, show some skill and individuality.

Ferencsik, János (*b* Budapest, 18 Jan 1907; *d* there, 12 June 1984). Hungarian conductor. He conducted at the Budapest State Opera from 1930 and was musical director, 1953–74. In 1953 he became chief conductor of the Hungarian National PO and made his British and American débuts in 1957 and 1962. He appeared widely as a guest conductor, and was chiefly noted as a dynamic exponent of Hungarian music.

Ferguson, Howard (*b* Belfast, 21 Oct 1908). English composer and editor. He studied with Morris at the RCM, and made his reputation as a composer in the early 1930s, mostly for classically formed instrumental works in a style close to Walton, notably a fine Octet (1933). He was also a recital pianist. In 1959 he abandoned composition to concentrate on editing, producing many valuable editions of early keyboard music.

Ferlendis, Giuseppe (*b* Bergamo, 1755; *d* Lisbon,

1802). Italian oboist. He was a celebrated player in Salzburg, where he worked on improvements to the english horn and came to know Mozart, who probably wrote a concerto for him. He played in Italy and in London and Lisbon, publishing concertos for the oboe, the english horn and the flute.

Fermata (It.: 'pause'). The sign of the corona (a point surmounted by a semicircle) showing the end of a phrase or indicating the prolongation of a note or rest beyond its usual value. In some contexts it may indicate an improvisation. *See* PAUSE and ORGAN POINT.

Fernandes, Gaspar (*b* c1570; *d* Puebla, before 18 Sept 1629). Central American composer of Portuguese birth. He was a singer and organist at Évora Cathedral in 1590 and *maestro de capilla* at the cathedrals of Guatemala (1599–1606) and Puebla (1606–29). Between 1609 and 1620 he wrote over 250 festal chanzonetas and villancicos for Puebla (MS); his *Elegit eum Dominus* is the earliest known Latin secular work by a New World composer. A few liturgical works also survive.

Fernández Hidalgo, Gutierre (*b* Andalusia, 1553; *d* ?Cuzco, after 1620). South American composer. He was cathedral *maestro de capilla* and seminary instructor in Bogotá (1584), Quito (1588), Cuzco (1591) and, most notably, Sucre (1597–1620). His surviving output includes psalms and *Magnificat* and *Salve regina* settings, mostly for four voices.

Ferne Klang, Der [The Distant Sound]. Opera in three acts by Schreker to his own libretto (1912, Frankfurt).

Ferneyhough, Brian (*b* Coventry, 16 Jan 1943). English composer. He studied at the RAM (1966–7), in Amsterdam with de Leeuw (1968) and in Basle with Klaus Huber (1969–71). Since 1973 he has taught at the Freiburg Musikhochschule and at Darmstadt. His works, notated with fearsome complexity, extend from the avant-garde tradition of the 1950s; they incorporate philosophical and cultural ideas. Among the best known are *Transit* for amplified voices and orchestra (1975), *Time and Motion Study I–III* (1974–7) and the *Carceri d'invenzione* cycle (1981–6).

Ferrabosco, Alfonso (i) (*b* Bologna, bapt. 18 Jan 1543; *d* there, 12 Aug 1588). Italian composer. He was a member of a prominent Bolognese and later English family of musicians. His father Domenico Maria (*b* Bologna, 14 Feb 1513; *d* there, Feb 1574) had worked as *maestro di cappella* at S Petronio and in the papal chapel at Rome; he was composer of a book of madrigals (1542) and some miscellaneous pieces. Other composers in the family include two children of a cousin of Domenico's, Costantino (*fl* c1550–1600), who worked in Nuremberg and published a book of canzonettas, and Matthia (1550–1616), who worked at the court chapel in Graz (Kapellmeister, 1611) and composed canzonettas and villanellas.

Alfonso went to Rome as a child, but was in England in the early 1560s in the employment of Elizabeth I. He remained there up to the end of 1578, with visits to Italy in 1564 and 1568–c1571; he seems to have been involved in scandals or at least

misunderstandings. After he left Elizabeth tried to induce him to return; it has been suggested that he worked as a spy for her. He later worked in the service of the Duke of Savoy in Turin.

He wrote some 80 sacred works, mostly motets and Lamentations for five and six voices. Technically he was influenced by Lassus; in turn, he inspired Byrd and other English composers. Most of the texts he set are sad; his melodic lines reflect his preoccupation with plaintive and meditative subjects and emotions. Although his work as a madrigalist is not important in an Italian context, here too he had much influence on his English contemporaries as the only Italian madrigalist active in England in the period. He published two books of five-voice madrigals (1587) and wrote some 70 others, in five or six voices. His style is well-wrought but generally conservative; he was admired for his skill rather than his invention. His other works include a modest number of *chansons*, Latin songs, fantasias and dances for the lute, and some fantasias and In Nomines for viols.

Ferrabosco, Alfonso (ii) (*b* ?Greenwich, by 1578; *d* there, bur. 11 March 1628). English composer, son (probably illegitimate) of Alfonso (i). A lutenist, viol player and singer, he was employed at court from 1592, granted a pension and annuity by James I in 1605 and, under Charles I, also becoming Composer of Music in Ordinary and Composer of Music to the King. In 1605–11 he was concerned with the music for seven masques, with Ben Jonson and Inigo Jones; his songs are in a declamatory manner, with melismas on colourful words and some imitation in the accompaniments. Some of these appeared in his published book of *Ayres* (1609) along with more conventional lute songs. His other vocal music includes 23 fourpart 'madrigalette', short pieces for four high voices. His sacred music includes 13 motets and a set of Lamentations, all for five voices, similar to his father's music in the choice of sombre texts and in style though subtler in texture and harmonic treatment. He also wrote six anthems. Outstanding among his instrumental music, which includes dances for viols and pieces for lute and lyra viols, are his fantasias and In Nomines, in fluent, instrumental counterpoint and well-controlled textures.

He had three sons who were musicians. Alfonso (iii) (*c*1610–*c*1660), a viol and wind player, took over his father's appointments. Henry (*c*1615–1658), a singer, wind player and composer, was a musician until 1645 but was killed during a military expedition to Jamaica in 1658. John (*b* Greenwich, bapt. 9 Oct 1626; *d* ?Ely, bur. 15 Oct 1682) was an organist and composer at Ely Cathedral from 1662; his works include several services and anthems and some harpsichord dances.

Ferrandini, Giovanni Battista (*b* Venice, c1710; *d* Munich, 25 Sept 1791). Italian composer. He was an oboist at the Munich court, becoming chamber composer in 1732 and director of chamber music in 1737. In 1755–c1790 he lived in Padua. A successful opera composer, he wrote c14 operas for Munich, 1727–81, notably *Catone in Utica* (1753), as well as cantatas, arias, a *Fastenmeditation* (1738) and instrumental music.

Ferraresi del Bene, Adriana [Gabrielli, Adriana] (*b* Ferrara, *c*1755; *d* ?Venice, after 1799). Italian soprano. She sang in London in 1785–6, and, most successfully, Vienna in 1788–91. A mistress of Da Ponte, she created Fiordiligi in *Così fan tutte* (1790) and sang Susanna in the Vienna revival (1789) of *Le nozze di Figaro*, for which Mozart wrote her two new arias. She was noted for her remarkable range.

Ferrari, Benedetto (*b* Reggio Emilia, *c*1603; *d* Modena, 22 Oct 1681). Italian librettist and composer. He was employed at the Farnese court at Parma, and probably also at Modena before moving to Venice where his *Andromeda* (music by Manelli), staged at the Teatro S Cassiano in 1637, was the earliest Venetian opera to which the paying public were admitted. Further collaborations followed and a touring company was formed. He travelled to Vienna in 1651 and was appointed court choirmaster at Modena in 1653. Among Ferrari's later Venetian operas *Il pastor regio* (1640) is of particular interest: the final duet in the Bologna version of 1641, 'Pur ti miro, pur ti godo', was later re-used (perhaps with Ferrari's music) for the final duet in Monteverdi's *L'incoronazione di Poppea*. The three books of *Musiche varie* (1633–41; many are settings of Ferrari's own texts) show that although he could write attractive melodies, he was more at ease composing affective recitative.

Ferrari, Giacomo Gotifredo (*b* Rovereto, bap. 2 April 1763; *d* London, Dec 1842). Italian composer. He was a singing teacher and harpsichordist in Paris, moving to London in 1792. He presented operas in both cities and also wrote fashionable vocal and piano music. Later he worked in Italy and in Edinburgh. His writings include valuable memoirs (1830).

Ferrari, Luc (*b* Paris, 5 Feb 1929). French composer. He studied under Cortot, Honegger and Messiaen and was a founder-member of the Groupe de Recherches Musicales (1958). His music is characterized by virtuosity, violent contrasts and humour; he adopts an anti-intellectual approach to composition, calling into question the nature of art.

Ferretti, Giovanni (*b* c1540; *d* after 1609). Italian composer. He was *maestro di cappella* of Ancona Cathedral (1575–9), Gemona (1586–8), Cividale del Friuli (1589) and the Santa Casa, Loreto (1596–1603); he also had contact with Rome. Some of his seven published books of *napolitane* (1567–85) were immensely popular and influenced the growth of the English madrigal.

Ferrier, Kathleen (Mary) (*b* Higher Walton, 22 April 1912; *d* London, 8 Oct 1953). English contralto. She became established as a concert singer during World War II and in 1946 created Britten's Lucretia, at Glyndebourne. At Edinburgh and Salzburg she soon became known for her emotionally committed appearances in Mahler's *Das Lied von der Erde*. Her warm voice and noble phrasing were last heard in performances of Gluck's *Orfeo* at Covent Garden.

Fesca, Friedrich (Ernst) (*b* Magdeburg, 15 Feb 1789; *d* Karlsruhe, 24 May 1826). German composer and violinist. He studied in Leipzig and was court violinist in Kassel and Karlsruhe, also composing symphonies, Mozartian chamber music, two operas and sacred vocal music. His son Alexander (1820–49) was a pianist and a prolific song composer.

Festa, Costanzo (*b* c1490; *d* Rome, 10 April 1545). Italian composer and singer. After a period at the French court (*c*1514), he was in the employ of Costanza d'Avalos on the island of Ischia, off Naples (1510–17), then a singer in the papal choir. A consummate master of polyphony, he was probably the most important Italian composer between Josquin and Palestrina and marked a stage in Italy's rise to musical dominance. His music was widely admired and disseminated, its technique based on pervasive imitation, rich textures and vivacious rhythm. He wrote over 60 motets (in MSS), ranging from penitential works to settings of Marian antiphons. His four masses embrace parody, paraphrase and *cantus firmus* techniques and his Magnificats include one of the earliest polyphonic sets for all eight tones. Many of his (mainly four-part) madrigals were published in anthologies between 1530 and 1549. Sebastiano Festa (*c*1495–1524), composer of frottolas and other such works who lived in Emilia and Rome, may have been a relative of his.

Festa teatrale (It.). A Baroque operatic genre in which the subject was typically allegorical and the production usually part of a court celebration.

Feste romane. Orchestral work by Respighi (1828).

Festing, Michael Christian (*d* London, 24 July 1752). English violinist and composer. A pupil of Geminiani, he appeared in London from 1724 and directed the orchestras at the King's Theatre (from 1737), Ranelagh Gardens (from 1742) and elsewhere; he strongly influenced English string playing. Arne was among his pupils. In 1735 he became Master of the King's Musick. He was a co-founder of the (later Royal) Society of Musicians. His instrumental publications, including four sets of violin solos, three of trio sonatas and three of concertos, show Geminiani's influence, with virtuoso writing and elaborate ornamentation. His cantatas and songs for Ranelagh were highly popular.

Festival Casals of Puerto Rico (West Indies). Annual (summer) festival in San Juan, established in 1957; events concerts by the Puerto Rico SO and opera.

Festival d'Art Contemporain. See ROYAN FESTIVAL.

Festival of Two Worlds. See SPOLETO FESTIVAL.

Fêtes d'Hébé, Les. *Opéra-ballet* by Rameau in a prologue and three *entrées* to a libretto by Montdorge (1739, Paris).

Fêtes galantes. Two sets of songs by Debussy, settings for voice and piano of six poems by Verlaine (1891, 1904).

Fêtes Musicales en Touraine (France). Annual (summer) festival, established in 1964. Orchestral and chamber concerts are given by international groups and soloists.

Fétis, François-Joseph (*b* Mons, 25 March 1784; *d* Brussels, 26 March 1871). Belgian writer on music. One of the most influential musical figures of the 19th century, he produced a comprehensive biographical dictionary, showed a prescient intellectual interest in harmony, music history and non-

European music and yet his reactionary ideas adversely affected the public response to new music. He studied at the Paris Conservatoire and began his career as a harmony and singing teacher, organist and composer of comic operas in the Grétry tradition, soon teaching and serving as librarian at the Conservatoire (1826–30). In 1827 he founded the weekly *Revue* (later *et gazette*) *musicale*; in 1833 he became first director of the Brussels Conservatory. Tirelessly active in Belgian concert life, as royal *maître de chapelle* and organizer of historical concerts, he composed conservative orchestral, chamber and sacred vocal pieces in his late years; he also made historical anthologies of music. But it is for his writings, chiefly the rich if undependable *Biographie universelle des musiciens* (1835–44) and the unfinished *Histoire générale de la musique* (1869–76), and for his theory of art as non-progressive, that he is remembered. He believed that music of the past was capable of moving 19th-century listeners and thus became a pioneer in the revival of early music. His eldest son Edouard Fétis (1812–1909) edited his father's journal from 1833 and wrote books on Belgian artists and musicians.

Feuermann, Emanuel (*b* Kolomed, 22 Nov 1902; *d* New York, 25 May 1942). Austrian cellist, later naturalized American. After his Vienna début (1912) he studied with Klengel in Leipzig. He led the Gurzenich Orchestra cellos and taught at the Berlin Hochschule, 1929–33. From 1938 he lived in the USA (teaching at the Curtis Institute from 1941) and often played chamber music with Schnabel and Heifetz. He was admired for his warm tone and sure technique.

Feuersnot. Opera in one act by Richard Strauss to a libretto by E. von Wolzogen after a Flemish legend (1901, Dresden).

Feuillet, Raoul-Auger (*b* c1659; *d* 14 June 1710). French choreographer and dancing-master. He worked at the court of Louis XIV and is important for his *Chorégraphie* (1700) which describes a system of dance notation used in Europe throughout the 18th century, in which over 350 choreographies are extant. He published annual collections of choreographies from 1702 and in 1704 a superb volume of theatrical dances.

Févin, Antoine de (*b* ?Arras, c1470; *d* Blois, 1511–12). French composer. By 1507 he was associated with the French court. His music is characterized by the new style of the 1490s and by its clarity of texture and formal design. His sacred works include ten masses (most using parody technique), three Magnificats and over a dozen motets. Most of his numerous three-voice *chansons* incorporate a borrowed monophonic popular melody, usually in the tenor. He was esteemed by his contemporaries.

Fiala, Joseph (*b* Lochovice, ?3 Feb 1748 or 1754; *d* Donaueschingen, 31 July 1816). Czech composer and oboist. He held court posts at Wallerstein, Munich and Salzburg (1778–85), and from 1777 was a friend of the Mozart family. After periods in Vienna and in Russia (1786–90), he became Kapellmeister at Donaueschingen (1792). Also a cellist and viola da gamba player, he wrote chamber, orchestral and keyboard music, pieces for wind band and a mass.

Fibich, Zdeněk (Antonín Václav) (*b* Všebořice, 21 Dec 1850; *d* Prague, 15 Oct 1900). Czech composer. He studied in Prague and at the Leipzig Conservatory, then privately under Jadassohn. He had periods in Paris (1868–9) and Mannheim (1869–70). His first post was as a choir trainer in Vilnius, 1873–4; in 1875 he returned to Prague, working at the Provisional Theatre until he became, in 1878, choirmaster of the Russian Orthodox Church. From 1881 he worked only as a composer and private teacher.

Among 19th-century Czech composers, he cedes position only to Smetana and Dvořák; but his internationalist style and leanings (his music does not sound distinctively Czech) have led to his relative eclipse. His German training is evident in his solid technique, sturdy, direct rhythms and mellow orchestral palette. He wrote three complete, mature symphonies (1883–98), four-movement works which show his melodic gifts and his inventive craftsmanship, for example in the monothematic opening movement of no.2 (the first Czech cyclic symphony) and in the first of no.3, propelled by a powerful ostinato figure. But possibly Fibich's most successful sonata-form movements are in his ingenious concert overtures such as *A Night in Karlštejn* (1886) and *Komenský* (1892). He also wrote evocative tone-poems, some on Shakespearean themes, some concerned with Nature.

His chamber music is mostly early; the most distinguished work is the last, a Quintet (1893) for piano, violin, cello, clarinet and horn. Among his many piano works is a substantial theoretical collection, as well as sonatas and two late suites, one evocative of the Alps, the other of paintings. But his major piano work is the set of 376 *Moods, Impressions and Reminiscences*, inspired by and recording in great detail all aspects of his love affair with the young writer Anežka Schulzová, who was his pupil from 1886.

In his last years Fibich destroyed almost all his church music and more than half of his 200 songs (those that remain show the influence of Schubert and Schumann). Of his seven operas, the earliest show Smetana's influence; outstanding is *The Bride of Messina* (1884), arguably the finest Czech 19th-century tragic opera, which shows a severe declamatory style and a complex leitmotif system. Some of the later ones return to the 'number opera' pattern, including *Šárka* (1897), his most direct and most popular opera. His finest dramatic music, however, is found in his melodramas, notably the stage trilogy *Hippodamia* (1891), where he used a speaking voice against a dense web of leitmotifs, with the orchestral texture carefully controlled. He also composed concert melodramas, four with piano (including the popular *Queen Emma*, 1883, orchestrated 1889) and two with orchestra (*The Water Goblin*, 1883; *Hakon*, 1888), whose symphonically developed texture prepared the way for *Hippodamia*.

Fiddle. Generic term for any string instrument played with a bow. Colloquially, 'fiddle' is often used for a member of the violin family or for the kit ('dancing-master's fiddle'). During the Middle Ages and the early Renaissance the word was used not only for bowed instruments in general but also for the particular type now known as the medieval fiddle. The outline of the medieval fiddle varied, the most usual shapes being oval, elliptical or rectangular, while a spade-like fiddle was common in southern Europe. Strings were generally gut. The fiddle had no universal tuning; Tinctoris wrote that the 'viola' had three strings tuned in 5ths or five strings tuned in 5ths and unisons. The medieval fiddle was played in all strata of society; it was used to accompany song and in church on special occasions, particularly those of a non-liturgical nature.

Fiddle Fugue. Nickname of an organ fugue in D minor by J.S. Bach BWV539 (c1720), so called because it is adapted from a work for solo violin.

Fidelio. Opera in two acts by Beethoven (1805) to a libretto by Sonnleithner after Bouilly; a second version (1806) was made by Stephan von Breuning and a final one by Treitschke (1814, Vienna). Beethoven wrote four overtures: *Leonora* nos.1–3 were rejected but are now played as concert overtures.

Fiedler, Arthur (*b* Boston, 17 Dec 1894; *d* Brookline, MA 10 July 1979). American conductor and violinist. He studied in Berlin, making his début there at 17. Returning to the USA, he played the viola in the Boston SO and in 1924 formed the Boston Sinfonietta. From 1930 his lively personality and eclectic taste attracted a huge following for the Boston Pops Orchestra, which he conducted for over 40 years.

Field, John (*b* Dublin, July 1782, bap. 5 Sept; *d* Moscow, 23 Jan 1837). Irish composer and pianist. His early musical training came from his father and from Tommaso Giordani in Dublin, after which he was apprenticed to Muzio Clementi in London. He probably studied with Salomon. By 1801 he had established a reputation as a concert pianist and published his first important works, the piano sonatas op.1. As a result of a successful continental tour with Clementi (1802–3) he remained in St Petersburg, becoming an idol of fashionable society there and in Moscow, teaching, giving concerts and composing until 1823, when illness overwhelmed him; he died in Moscow, having made one return visit to London and to other European cities.

During his lifetime Field was known chiefly for the sensitivity of his playing, especially his expressive touch, singing phrases and extreme delicacy, a striking contrast to the fashion for virtuoso display. This legendary playing style was supported by the publication of his 17 nocturnes, each a self-sufficient piece evoking a dreamy mood of sadness consoled; songlike in manner and texture, they anticipated Chopin's pieces of the same type by nearly 20 years and influenced Liszt and Mendelssohn. Among Field's other, more numerous works, the most important are the rondos and fantaisies for piano, the *Kamarinskaya* variations (1809) and the *Air russe varié* for piano duet (1808), and the seven piano concertos. At his best, he was the equal of any of the Romantic pianist-composers.

Accompanied piano music 7 pf concs.; 2 other works with orch; Pf Qnt, A♭ (c1815); pieces for pf and str qt
Piano music 4 Sonatas; Fantaisie sur l'Andante de Martini (1811); 20 nocturnes; c50 other solo pieces, incl. rondos,

variations, romances; works for pf duet, incl. Air russe varié (1808)

Fiery Angel, The [Ognenniy angel]. Opera in five acts by Prokofiev to his own libretto after V. Bryusov (1955, Paris).

Fife. A small cylindrical transverse flute with a narrower bore and hence louder and shriller than the flute. Fifes were generally made from a single piece of wood, had six finger-holes and sometimes one or more keys. They have been associated with side drums in military use since at least the 14th century. In modern British 'drum and fife bands', fifes are short conical flutes with six keys, pitched in B♭ (a 6th above the concert flute).

Fifth. The INTERVAL between two notes four diatonic scale degrees apart (e.g. C–G). *See also* CIRCLE OF FIFTHS.

Fifths Quartet [Quintenquartett]. Nickname of Haydn's String Quartet in D minor op.76 no.2 (1797), derived from the leaps of a 5th of its opening theme.

Figner, Nikolay Nikolayevich (*b* Nikiforovka, 21 Feb 1857; *d* Kiev, 13 Dec 1918). Russian lyric-dramatic tenor. He studied at the St Petersburg Conservatory and made his début in Naples (1882); in 1887 he joined the Imperial Opera, St Petersburg, singing in the premières of operas by Tchaikovsky (including *The Queen of Spades*, 1890) and others. He was admired for his eloquence in such roles as Don José, Faust and Radamès. In 1897 he sang Verdi's Duke at Covent Garden. His second wife Medea (née Mei, 1859–1952) created Tchaikovsky's Lisa (*The Queen of Spades*) and Iolanta.

Figural, figurate, figured. Florid; the terms are used for a decorated line or to distinguish concerted music from plainchant or simple vocal polyphony. In figured bass, numerals indicate the harmonies to be used; *see* CONTINUO.

Figuration. A kind of continued, measured embellishment, accompaniment or passage-work. In principle, it is composed of 'figures' or small patterns of notes; often the term is used loosely for passage-work of other kinds.

Figure. A short melodic idea with a particular identity of rhythm and/or contour. *See* MOTIF.

For figured bass, *see* CONTINUO.

Figured bass. Term for a bass part in an ensemble work, usually of the 17th or 18th centuries, furnished with figures and other signs telling the player the harmonies required to be played above the bass part. *See* CONTINUO.

Figures, Doctrine of musical. The English equivalent of a German term, *Figurenlehre*, coined by scholars to describe the musical figures or motifs used, particularly during the Baroque period but also in the Renaissance, to illustrate ideas in the texts they set or the emotion they wish to convey (by analogy with the theory of rhetoric). *See* RHETORIC AND MUSIC.

Filar il suono [filar la voce] (It.). 'To spin the sound [the voice]': a direction in singing to sustain a long note without taking a fresh breath. It can also be used for a wind instrument and (meaning without a change of bow) for a string instrument. It implies that the note is to be 'spun out' quietly, without gradation in volume, though some writers expected a gradual *crescendo* and *diminuendo*.

Filippi, Filippo (*b* Vicenza, 13 Jan 1830; *d* Milan, 24 June 1887). Italian music critic. An ardent admirer of Verdi, he was connected with the *Gazzetta musicale di Milano* (1859–62), then with the Milan journal *La perseveranza*, attaining a commanding position among Italian music critics.

Fille aux cheveux de lin, La. Piano piece by Debussy, after Lecomte de Lisle, no.8 of his *Préludes* Book 1 (1910).

Fille du régiment, La [The Daughter of the Regiment]. Opera in two acts by Donizetti to a libretto by J.H.V. De Saint-Georges and J.F.A. Bayard (1840, Paris).

Fille mal gardée, La. Ballet in two acts planned by d'Auberval and Aumer to a medley of French songs (1789, Bordeaux). Hérold arranged a new score, composing some himself. Other versions include music by P.L. Hertel (1817–99).

Film music. For early silent films, music was needed to illustrate the action and to cover the sound of the projector. It was usually supplied by a pianist, but sometimes by an orchestra playing snippets from the classics or short 'mood' pieces. For some long films, special scores were played by musicians who travelled with the film.

With the introduction of 'talkies' in 1927 film music was recorded on the film itself, but it was some time before the potentialities of integrated film music were fully explored. Since about 1940 film music has been recognized as a highly specialized form of composition and several composers have devoted their talents to it almost exclusively, among them Miklós Rózsa, Dimitri Tiomkin and Bernard Herrmann (*Citizen Kane, Psycho*). At the same time a surprisingly large number of major composers in other fields, including Prokofiev (*Alexander Nevsky, Ivan the Terrible*), Shostakovich, Walton and Copland, have shown themselves ready to accept its discipline of precise synchronization and timing.

Fils, (Jan) Antonín [Filtz, (Johann) Anton] (*b* Eichstätt, bap. 22 Sept 1733; *d* Mannheim, bur. 14 March 1760). Bohemian composer and cellist. He played in the Mannheim court orchestra from 1754. A pupil of Johann Stamitz and a founder of the Mannheim school, he composed 70 symphonies, several concertos and various chamber works, using an original style with folk elements and irregular phrases. His works were widely popular.

Final. The concluding scale degree of any melody in a MODE.

Finale. The last movement of a multi-movement instrumental composition; the concluding section of an act of an opera or other stage work. The concluding movement in a set of variations (e.g. Schumann's *Etudes symphoniques* and Elgar's Enigma Variations) is often designated 'finale', indicating a freer and wider-ranging treatment of the theme than is found earlier in the work. The operatic ensemble finale, developed in Italian comic opera (especially *dramma giocoso*) during the 18th century, represents an essential step from the late Baroque number opera to the

continuous style of 19th-century music drama.

Finalmusik (Ger.). A composition of the divertimento or serenade type which could be used to conclude an outdoor concert. At the end-of-year celebrations at Salzburg University the students put on 'Finalmusik' performances to honour their professors; Mozart wrote several works for the purpose.

Finck, Heinrich (*b*?Bamberg, 1444 or 1445; *d* Vienna, 9 June 1527). German composer. After training as a choirboy in Poland he travelled widely in search of an appointment. Between 1498 and *c*1510 he served in the chapel of Prince Alexander of Lithuania, first in Vilnius, then (when Alexander became King of Poland in 1501) in Kraków. He was subsequently 'Singemeister' of the ducal Kapelle in Stuttgart (1510–14), a household musician to Cardinal M. Lang in Mühldorf (1516–19) and after 1519 composer to the Salzburg Cathedral chapter. Much of his music is lost but several masses, motets and motet cycles, hymns, songs and instrumental pieces survive. His creative life spans three generations: his early style, with its difficult melismatic lines, is rooted in the first flowering of German polyphony but his later works, with their full textures, show him to have assimilated the 'modern' styles of music written after 1500 by Isaac, Josquin and others.

His great-nephew, Hermann (1527–58), an organist in Wittenberg, wrote *Practica musica* (1556), a treatise on rudiments that gives examples from over 80 works by leading composers.

Fine (It.). 'End': an indication of where to finish a piece in forms in which the notation ends with the second section but the performance ends by repeating the first.

Fine, Irving (Gifford) (*b* Boston, 3 Dec 1914; *d* there, 23 Aug 1962). American composer. He studied with Hill and Piston at Harvard, and with Boulanger in Paris, then taught at Harvard (1939–50) and Brandeis (1950–62). His small output includes orchestral, choral and chamber pieces influenced by Stravinsky, using some serial elements from 1952 onwards.

Fine, Vivian (*b* Chicago, 28 Sept 1913). American composer and pianist. A pupil of Sessions, she worked as a teacher in New York and dance accompanist. Her early works are in a stern, dissonant contrapuntal style, but it became more relaxed with a wider expressive range, touched by humour (e.g. *A Guide to the Life Expectancy of a Rose*, 1956). Her best-known works are the ballet *Alcestis* (1960) and the *Paean* (1969) and *Missa brevis* (1972).

Fine Arts Quartet. American string quartet. Founded in Chicago in 1946, and led by Leonard Sorkin, it has given annual concerts at the University of Wisconsin and has toured widely in Europe and the Far East. Works by Babbitt, Wuorinen and Crawford are among its recorded repertory.

Fingal's Cave [The Hebrides]. Overture (op.26) by Mendelssohn (1830, rev. 1832).

Fingerboard. The part of a string instrument over which the strings are stretched and against which the fingers of the player's hand press them down.

Finger cymbals. Small cymbals in pairs, one on the

thumb and the other on the index or middle finger. Known since antiquity, they are still widely used in Asia.

Fingering. Principles of fingering keyboard instruments have varied greatly between the 15th century and the present day; it is widely felt among students of early keyboard music that, without a proper understanding of earlier fingering systems, it is impossible to articulate music in the manner the composer intended. Many early fingering systems use the thumb and the little finger sparingly, particularly in right-hand scale passages, where 'paired fingerings' (using the second and third, or third and fourth fingers repeatedly) were often recommended, demanding a style of finger-crossing manageable on instruments of light touch where the keys needed to be depressed only a short distance. By the time of Bach and Couperin more flexible forms of fingering were coming into use; by the late 18th century, in the time of Clementi, and with Czerny in the early 19th century, modern principles were established – that the long fingers should never be crossed, that the thumb should be used as the only pivot, that unnecessary hand position changes should be avoided and that the same finger should not be employed on two consecutive notes. The use of the thumb on black keys was long discouraged, but free and flexible use of all the digits is now accepted. Fingering is normally notated by numbering the thumb as 1, the forefinger 2 and the little finger 5; this system used to be known as 'continental fingering', while 'English fingering' (favoured in British publications from the late 18th century to the early 20th) showed a cross for the thumb, 1 for the forefinger and 4 for the little finger.

On string instruments, fingering involves the stopping of strings and is closely allied to notation, tone colour and expression. Here too systems have changed from one period to another depending on the instruments and their expressive requirements; they also depend on such factors as the presence or otherwise of frets and, because of the necessity of shifting the hand to different positions, on the way the instrument is held.

The fingering of wind instruments differs from that of keyboard and string instruments because the same figures are nearly always used to produce any given note. The basic principle with woodwind is that the fingers are lifted successively from a series of holes and the vibrating length of the air column is thus successively shortened. Normally the raising of fingers produces a diatonic scale, and intermediate notes are obtained by 'cross fingerings' (keeping lower holes covered while higher ones are raised) or by added keys, also normally operated by the fingers. With brass instruments, the fingers and sometimes the thumb are used to operate valves or pistons (*see* VALVE).

Fink, (Christian) Gottfried Wilhelm (*b* Sulza, 8 March 1783; *d* Leipzig, 27 Aug 1846). German theologian, critic and editor. He wrote for the *Allgemeine musikalische Zeitung* from 1808 and succeeded Rochlitz as editor (1828–41), initially welcoming the work of the younger Romantics but later refusing articles by Schumann, opposing Chopin and making a celebrated attack on A.B. Marx and representational music (1842).

Finke, Fidelio Friedrich (*b* Josefstal, 22 Oct 1891; *d* Dresden, 12 June 1968). German composer. He studied with Novák at the Prague Conservatory (1908–11), where he taught until moving to posts in Dresden (1946–51) and Leipzig (1951–9). His music is craftsmanlike, influenced by German composers and folk music. It includes eight orchestral suites, choral, piano and organ pieces and stage music; but he is best known for his chamber music.

Finlandia. Orchestral work, op.26, by Sibelius (1899); its affinity with Finnish folksong has led to its performance at important national events.

Finney, Ross Lee (*b* Wells, MN, 23 Dec 1906). American composer. He studied with Boulanger (1927–8), with Sessions at Harvard (1928–9) and with Berg in Vienna (1931–2), and has taught at Smith College (1929–48) and the University of Michigan (1949–). His music is strongly propelled and, from 1950, rooted in serialism: his large output includes four symphonies (1942, 1958, 1960, 1972), concertos, quartets and choral music.

Finnissy, Michael (Peter) (*b* London, 17 March 1946). English composer. He studied at the RCM. His large output includes much for ensembles of voices and instruments and for piano. It has a severe, uncompromising quality and is often violent or flamboyantly virtuoso.

Finscher, Ludwig (*b* Kassel, 14 March 1930). German musicologist. He studied at Göttingen and was professor of musicology at Frankfurt, then Heidelberg, and president of the IMS, 1977–82. His interests centre on the Josquin period and the Viennese Classics (especially the string quartet) repertory.

Finta giardiniera, La. [The Pretend Gardener]. Opera in three acts by Mozart to a libretto probably by Calzabigi and revised by Coltellini (1775, Munich). Anfossi set the same libretto (1774) and Piccinni wrote an opera on the subject (1770).

Finta semplice, La [The Pretend Simpleton]. Opera in three acts by Mozart to a libretto by M. Coltellini after Goldoni (1769, Salzburg).

Finzi, Gerald (Raphael) (*b* London, 14 July 1901; *d* Oxford, 27 Sept 1956). English composer. He studied privately with Farrar (1914–16) and Bairstow (1917–22) and lived most of his life in the country. Influenced by Elgar and Vaughan Williams as well as his teachers, he developed an intimate style and concentrated on songs, particularly settings of Hardy. Other works include a clarinet concerto (1949) and *Dies natalis* for high voice and strings (1939).

Fiocco. Italian family of musicians. Pietro Antonio (*c*1650–1714) settled in Brussels and became *maître de chapelle* at the court chapel; he also served at Notre Dame de Sablon and was an opera director, writing new prologues for Lully's operas and a pastorale (1699). His church music shows Venetian traits. His son Jean-Joseph (1686–1746), a keyboard player, was *maître de chapelle* at Notre Dame de Sablon and the court chapel and wrote motets, oratorios etc. Another son, Joseph-Hector (1703–41), also a keyboard player, was *sous-maître* at the court chapel, then *maître de chapelle* at Antwerp Cathedral, finally serving in Brussels again. His harpsichord pieces (1730) and *Leçons des ténèbres* show Couperin's influence, while his other sacred music is more italianate.

Fioravanti, Valentino (*b* Rome, 11 Sept 1764; *d* Capua, 16 June 1837). Italian composer. A formidable rival to Paisiello, Guglielmi and Cimarosa, he toured Italy writing comic and serious operas, (77; 1784–1824). His most important serious work was the Neapolitan trilogy *Adelaide e Comingio* (1817), but he is best remembered for his flexible, lively *opere buffe*, including *Le cantatrici villane* (1799) and *La capricciosa pentita* (1802). In 1816 he became *maestro di cappella* of the Sistine Chapel. His son Vincenzo (1799–1877) carried on the *opera buffa* tradition in a series of 35 works, of which *Il ritorno di Pulcinella da Padova* (1837) was the most popular.

Fiorè, Andrea Stefano (*b* Milan, 1686; *d* Turin, 6 Oct 1732). Italian composer. A child prodigy, he was in the service of the Turin court by 1699, when he published 12 trio sonatas; in 1707, after studying in Rome, he became *maestro di cappella* there. He presented over 20 operas (mostly *seria*) at Turin and elsewhere, starting with the successful *La casta Penelope* (1707, Milan). He also wrote solo cantatas and sacred music.

His father, Angelo Maria (*c* 1660–1723), was a cello virtuoso; he played at the courts of Parma and (from 1696) Turin, and composed cello music.

Fiorillo, Federigo (*b* Brunswick, 1 June 1755; *d* after 1823). Italian composer. He toured as a violinist and mandolin player and in 1782–4 was conductor at Riga. After a period in Paris he worked in London, from 1788 to the 1790s as viola player in Salomon's quartet. He was a popular composer, writing mostly instrumental and pedagogical works (notably 36 violin caprices). His father Ignazio (1715–87) was court conductor at Brunswick (1754–62), then at Kassel. He composed 20 or more stage works (some to Metastasio librettos) and sacred and instrumental music.

Fioritura (It.). 'Flourish': embellishment of a melodic line, whether improvised by a performer or written out by the composer.

Fioroni, Giovanni Andrea (*b* Pavia, ?1704; *d* Milan, 14/19 Dec 1778). Italian composer. After studying under Leo in Naples, he moved to Milan, becoming *maestro di cappella* at the cathedral in 1747 and later at other churches. An influential composer and teacher, he composed operas and oratorios and some 300 sacred vocal works, many for large forces and in a contrapuntal style.

Fipple. A word associated with part of the duct flute's sound mechanism. Its meaning varies from windway, lip and block, to the whole head.

Firebird, The [Zhar'-ptitsa]. Ballet in two scenes by Stravinsky based on Russian fairy-tales (1910, Paris).

Fires of London, The. British chamber ensemble, founded in 1967 as the Pierrot Players. Under Peter Maxwell Davies and (at first) Harrison Birtwistle, it was formed with the soprano Mary Thomas, the five players required for Schoenberg's *Pierrot lunaire*,

and a percussionist. The ensemble gave many first performances of works by Davies and other composers; it was extinguished in 1987.

Fire Symphony. Haydn's Symphony no.59 in A (by 1769).

Fireworks Music [Music for the Royal Fireworks]. Instrumental suite by Handel played at the fireworks display in London celebrating the Peace of Aix-la-Chapelle (1749).

Firkušný, Rudolf (*b* Napajedla, 11 Feb 1912). American pianist of Czech birth. Since his début at Prague in 1902 he has been closely identified with the music of Janáček, one of his teachers. He is admired in the standard repertory and has given premières of works by Barber, Ginastera and Martinů.

Firsova, Elena (*b* Leningrad, 21 March 1950). Soviet composer. She studied at the Moscow Conservatory until 1975, when a meeting with Edison Denisov proved decisive in shaping her subsequent music. Her output includes concertos, including two each for violin and cello, but it is in her smaller-scale works, particularly those including voices, that her most distinctive music is to be found – *Misterioso* (String Quartet no.3), written in memory of Stravinsky in 1980, and the cantata on texts by Mandelstam, *Earthly Life* for soprano and chamber ensemble (1984). In those her invention is seen to be predominantly melodic and intimate in effect.

First of May, The [Pervomayskaya]. Shostakovich's Symphony no.3 in E♭ (1929), with a choral setting of a text by S. Kirsanov in the finale.

Fischer, Annie (*b* Budapest, 5 July 1914). Hungarian pianist. She studied under Dohnányi and made her début in 1922. From her first concert abroad, in 1926, she has been widely admired for her powerful technique and interpretative insight, shown particularly in the concertos of Mozart and Beethoven and Schubert's sonatas.

Fischer, Carl. American music publishers. Founded in New York in 1872, the firm began with the dual objective of publishing music and selling instruments, music and methods, becoming the principal publisher of Sousa and Fillmore; its band catalogue, the oldest in the USA, is the world's largest. School music and, since 1946, contemporary choral and orchestral music by composers including Dello Joio, Foss and Thomson have been special interests. The firm acquired Boosey & Hawkes in 1986.

Fischer, Edwin (*b* Basle, 6 Oct 1886; *d* Zurich, 24 Jan 1960). Swiss pianist. After study at the Basle Conservatory he taught at the Stern Conservatory, Berlin, 1905–14. His interpretations of the German repertory were Romantic in spirit. With his chamber orchestra (founded in 1932) he revived the practice of conducting from the keyboard; he was also noted for his cadenzas for Mozart's concertos. He was an influential teacher in Lucerne and elsewhere.

Fischer, Irwin (*b* Iowa City, 5 July 1903; *d* Wilmette, IL, 7 May 1977). American composer. He studied at the American Conservatory in Chicago (where he was appointed to teach in 1928), with Boulanger in Paris (1931) and with Kodály in Budapest (1936). In the 1930s he developed a polytonal technique he called 'biplanal'; in the 1960s he began to use systematic serialism. His songs display an exceptional variety of styles and techniques.

Fischer, Johann (*b* Augsburg, 25 Sept 1646; *d* Schwedt, *c*1716). German composer and violinist. His restless career included brief spells as Lully's copyist in Paris, as Konzertmeister at the Schwerin ducal court (from 1704), and as Kapellmeister to the Margrave of Brandenburg-Schwedt. Chiefly a composer of chamber music, which is melodically fresh and engaging, he transplanted the French style into Germany and was a pioneer in the use of scordatura tunings.

Fischer, Johann Caspar Ferdinand (*b c*1662; *d* Rastatt, 27 Aug 1746). German composer of Bohemian origin. By 1695 he was Kapellmeister at the Baden court. Except for a Singspiel (1721) and sets of vespers (1701) and litanies (1711), he composed instrumental music, which was known to Bach and Handel. His orchestral suites in *Le journal du printems* (1695), among the finest influenced by French ballet music, include French overtures and dance movements in a Lullian style. In his *Pièces de clavessin* (1696) Fischer transferred this type of suite to the keyboard; the similar *Musicalischer Parnassus* (*c*1740) is more Italianate in style. His organ works are *Ariadne musica* (1702), containing a prelude and fugue in each of 20 keys (foreshadowing Bach's '48'), and *Blumen-Strauss* (1732), which has a group of pieces in each of the eight church tones.

Fischer, Johann Christian (*b* Freiburg, 1733; *d* London, bur. 3 May 1800). German oboist and composer. He worked mostly in London and was a leading player at the Bach–Abel concerts, 1768–82. He wrote concertos for oboe or flute, other instrumental works, and an oboe method. A minuet from his first oboe concerto became very popular; Mozart wrote keyboard variations on it.

Fischer, Kurt von (*b* Berne, 25 April 1913). Swiss musicologist. After studying at Berne (Conservatory and University) and teaching there, he was professor of musicology at Zurich and president of the IMS, 1967–72. His publications range widely, from 14th-century polyphony, Bach, Beethoven and Grieg to contemporary Swiss music, and he also worked on the Passion and variation form.

Fischer, (Johann Ignaz) Ludwig (*b* Mainz, 18 Aug 1745; *d* Berlin, 10 July 1825). German bass. Regarded as Germany's leading bass singer, he worked at Mannheim, Munich, Vienna (1780–83), Regensburg and Berlin; he created Osmin in Mozart's *Die Entführung aus dem Serail* (1782). His wife was the singer Barbara Strasser (1758–after 1825).

Fischer-Dieskau, Dietrich (*b* Berlin, 28 May 1925). German baritone. He made his concert début in 1947. The next year he sang Verdi's Posa in Berlin and was soon in demand throughout Europe in the operas of Strauss, Mozart and Wagner (Bayreuth from 1954). He made his British début in 1951 and sang in the USA from 1955. His commanding stage presence and full, resonant voice have been identified with such roles as Barak and Mandryka and Mozart's Count Almaviva and Don Alfonso. But his

greatest achievement has been in lieder: he has an unequalled repertory of over 1000 songs, many of which he has recorded. His command of rhythm, flawless technique and profound feeling for the relation of words to music have set a standard in the songs of Schubert, Schumann, Brahms and Wolf, making him one of the most highly valued singers of the century.

Fischietti, Domenico (*b* Naples, ?*c*1725; *d* ?Salzburg, ?after 1810). Italian composer. He studied under Leo and Durante in Naples, where he presented his first comic opera in 1749. Moving to Venice, he collaborated with Goldoni in four highly successful comic operas, 1754–8, including *Il mercato di Malmantile* (1757). He presented several operas in Prague and in Dresden, where he was Kapellmeister, 1765–72; he then lived mainly in Salzburg, initially as Kapellmeister. He wrote *c*20 operas (both serious and comic), an oratorio (1767), sacred music and solo cantatas.

Fisher, John Abraham (*b* Dunstable or London, 1744; *d* ?London, 1806). English violinist and composer. He played in London theatre orchestras and in *c*1769–1778 was leader at Covent Garden, contributing music for productions such as the burlesque *The Golden Pippin* (1773). He also wrote violin pieces, six symphonies (*c*1775), an oratorio, and many popular pleasure-garden songs. He then made a tour of the Continent, and while in Vienna married Nancy Storace but was expelled by the emperor for his behaviour towards her. Later he spent time in Ireland. His works have an energetic *galant* style; his three violin concertos (*c*1782) reflect his exceptional technical skill.

Fisher, Sylvia (Gwendoline Victoria) (*b* Melbourne, 18 April 1910). Australian soprano. She studied at the Melbourne Conservatory and moved to Europe in 1947, joining the Covent Garden company in 1948. Until 1958 she was successful as Sieglinde, the Marschallin and the Kostelnička in *Jenůfa*. From 1963 she sang Britten roles with the English Opera Group and in 1971 created the role of Mrs Wingrave (for television).

Fitelberg, Grzegorz (*b* Dynaburg, 18 Oct 1879; *d* Katowice, 10 June 1953). Polish conductor and composer. He studied at the Warsaw Conservatory as a violinist and was a member with Szymanowski of the Young Poland in Music movement, whose first concert (1906) he conducted. Most of his compositions date from this early period; thereafter he was active as a conductor of the Warsaw PO, for Dyagilev in Russia (1921–4) and elsewhere.

Fitelberg, Jerzy (*b* Warsaw, 20 May 1903; *d* New York, 25 April 1951). Polish composer, son of Grzegorz. He studied with Schreker in Berlin (1922–6) and lived there and in Paris (1933–9) and New York (1940–51). His works are mostly instrumental and neo-classical; among the best are the concertos, which display rich fantasy, expressive power and structural skill, and the chamber music, from which the cycle of five quartets excels.

Fitzenhagen, (Karl Friedrich) Wilhelm (*b* Seesen, 15 Sept 1848; *d* Moscow, 14 Feb 1890). German cellist. After playing in the Dresden Hofkapelle, from

1870 he was professor at the Imperial Conservatory, Moscow, gaining a reputation as the greatest teacher, soloist and chamber music performer in Russia; he gave the première of Tchaikovsky's Variations on a Rococo Theme op.33 (1877), which was dedicated to him.

Fitzgerald, Ella (*b* Newport News, VA, 25 April 1918). American jazz and popular singer. Her career began in 1935 with Chick Webb's band, with which she recorded. She took it over on Webb's death (1939) and embarked on a solo career in 1942. In 1946 she began an association with the impresario Norman Granz, through his 'Jazz at the Philharmonic' tours. During the 1950s she recorded a series of LP 'songbooks', arrangements by Nelson Riddle of American songs. She continued to perform and record jazz with a variety of musicians. Her agile, girlish voice has remarkable range.

Fitzwilliam Virginal Book. English MS of keyboard music. It consists of 220 folios, with nearly 300 pieces by English composers, notably Bull, Byrd and Farnaby. Copied by Francis Tregian, 1606–19, it is now in the Fitzwilliam Museum, Cambridge.

Five, The. A group of 19th-century Russian composers – Balakirev, Borodin, Cui, Musorgsky and Rimsky-Korsakov – united in their aim to create a distinctive nationalist school of Russian music; most were self-taught musicians based in St Petersburg. 'The Five' are called in Russia 'The Mighty Handful'.

Fjeldstad, Øivin (*b* Oslo, 2 May 1903). Norwegian conductor. He studied the violin and then conducting in Oslo and Leipzig and under Krauss in Berlin. He was first music director of the Norwegian Opera (1958) and also directed the Oslo Philharmonic Society. He toured widely and made many recordings of Scandinavian and other music, including, with Flagstad, an early one of *Götterdämmerung*.

Flackton, William (*b* Canterbury, bap. March 1709; *d* there, 5 Jan 1798). English composer. He was a Canterbury bookseller and a church organist. His output includes chamber works, notably four viola sonatas (sets of 1770 and 1776) in a conservative but expressive style, sacred music, a cantata and songs.

Flagellant songs. Songs sung during penitential rites in the 13th and 14th centuries; *see* GEISSLER-LIEDER.

Flagello, Nicolas (*b* New York, 15 March 1928). American composer, conductor and pianist. He studied composition with Giannini and in Rome; he conducted the Rome SO and CO and at Chicago Lyric Opera and New York City Opera. He has written operas, concertos and, choral works in a style marked by italianate lyricism but with a note of despair and agitation; his later music is intensely chromatic and dissonant.

Flageolet. End-blown flute of the late 16th century with four finger-holes and two thumb-holes, akin to a simplified recorder. It was popular in England in the 17th century. The compass was *d–a″* (or higher) and it was used for teaching birds to sing. Later versions had ivory mouthpieces and keys. Double flageolets, with two tubes, could be played in 3rds or 6ths.

Flagstad, Kirsten (Malfrid) (*b* Hamar, 12 July 1895; *d* Oslo, 7 Dec 1962). Norwegian soprano. She studied in Oslo and from 1913 to 1932 sang only in Scandinavia. Her first major roles abroad were Sieglinde and Gutrune at Bayreuth in 1934. The following year she was a great success at the Met, as Sieglinde, Isolde and Brünnhilde. She appeared at Covent Garden over many years, singing Wagner for the last time on stage in 1951. In 1950 she gave the première of Strauss's *Four Last Songs*. The nobility of her phrasing and the purity and beauty of her tone are well represented in the complete recording of *Tristan und Isolde* under Furtwängler.

Flam. A type of stroke in side-drum playing, involving a rapid prefatory stroke before the main one.

Flamenco (Sp.). Generic term for a particular body of song, dance and guitar music, mostly from Andalusia. There has been much speculation about its origins, which the name suggests may be related to the 16th-century Spanish-Flemish connection, to the flamingo bird, to Arab song or to several other possible sources. Flamenco song is based on a particular group of modes, several with Phrygian characteristics (especially the minor 2nd). Many different metres are used, sometimes in combination, and cross-rhythms are provided by heel-stamping and similar devices. Accompaniment is normally played on a guitar (or more than one guitar), which provides an introduction and has a dual role as both solo and accompanying instrument; the accompaniment takes three styles, *rasgueado* (strumming), *paseo* (lively melodic passage-work) and *falsetas* (improvised interludes).

Flanagan, William (*b* Detroit, 14 Aug 1923; *d* New York, 31 Aug/1 Sept 1969). American composer. He studied with Rogers and Phillips at the Eastman School and with Copland at Tanglewood (1947–8), the last a major influence. He wrote in a conservative style, excelling in songs and other smaller vocal forms. He was also a critic.

Flanders Festival (Belgium). Annual festival, founded in 1964, held in one or more towns (including Antwerp, Bruges, Brussels, Ghent) during spring and summer; events include orchestral concerts, recitals, opera, early music, dance and competitions.

Flat. A notational sign (♭), normally placed to the left of a note and indicating that the note is to be lowered in pitch by one semitone. A double flat, notated as two flats together, indicates that the note is to be lowered by two semitones. *See* ACCIDENTAL.

Flat trumpet. An early, English form of slide trumpet. Pitched in C, it had a double slide at the U-bend allowing several full positions. It could play in 'flat' (minor) keys and was used by Purcell in his funeral music for Queen Mary (1694).

Flautando [flautato] (It.). 'Flute-like': to a violinist, an instruction to bow lightly over the end of the fingerboard to produce a flute-like tone. To a harpist the term might suggest the use of harmonics.

Flauto. FLUTE. Until the mid-18th century, the term meant recorder and the flute was specified by 'flauto traverso' or 'traverso'. 'Flauto d'amore' refers to the flute in A, a minor 3rd below the concert instrument, and 'flauto piccolo' and 'flautino' signify a small recorder or flageolet. The term also refers to an organ stop.

Flaxland, Gustave-Alexandre (*b* Strasbourg, 26 Jan 1821; *d* Paris, 11 Nov 1895). French music publisher. As copyright owner of the French editions of three Wagner operas (and in spite of legal controversy surrounding some of the copyrights), he championed Wagner's music in Paris when feeling against the composer was strong.

Flebile (It.). Mournful, plaintive.

Flecha, Mateo (*b* Prades, 1481; *d* Poblet, 1553). Spanish composer. He worked in Lérida, Valencia and as *maestro de capilla* to Philip II's younger sisters in Arévalo. His eight *ensaladas* (1581) show vitality and variety of metre and texture; he also wrote villancicos. His nephew Mateo (*c*1530–1604) composed *ensaladas* and madrigals.

Flechtenmacher, Alexandru (Adolf) (*b* Iaşi, 23 Dec 1823; *d* Bucharest, 28 Jan 1898). Romanian composer, conductor and violinist of German descent. He studied in Vienna. His *The Witch Hîrca* (1848) is one of the earliest Romanian operettas, which, with his many patriotic choruses and solo songs, made him a pioneer of Romanian music; he founded the Craiova Philharmonic Society and the Bucharest Conservatory (1864).

Fleckno, Richard (*d* ?London, *c*1678). English composer and Roman Catholic priest. He travelled widely, supporting himself as a courtier. His importance lies in his two operas, both lost (and possibly never performed): *Ariadne Deserted by Theseus and Found and Courted by Bacchus* (1654) contained an important preface outlining Fleckno's ideas on opera, acquired in Italian visits; *The Mariage of Oceanus and Brittania* (1659) was a mixture of Italian recitative, French dance and English masque.

Fledermaus, Die. Operetta in three acts by Johann Strauss (ii) to a libretto by C. Haffner and Richard Genée after *Le réveillon* (1872) by Meilhac and Halévy (1871, Vienna).

Fleischmann, Aloys (Georg) (*b* Munich, 13 April 1910). Irish composer of German origin. He studied at Cork (where he was professor of music, 1934–80) and Munich (1932–4). He has contributed significantly to Irish music and written many dance scores for Cork Ballet.

Fleisher, Leon (*b* San Francisco, 23 July 1928). American pianist and conductor. He studied with Schnabel and made his début in 1942 with the San Francisco SO. His intellectual power and warmth of feeling are well displayed in Liszt, Brahms and Beethoven. He lost the use of his right hand in 1965 and after playing the left-hand repertory began a conducting career in 1968; he has worked with orchestras in Washington and Baltimore. In 1981 an operation restored the use of his right hand.

Flentrop, Dirk (Andries) (*b* Zaandam, 1 May 1910). Dutch organ builder. He learnt his craft in his father's workshop (founded 1903) and with Frobenius in Denmark. Both father (Hendrik Flentrop, 1866–1950) and son trained as church organists but devoted themselves to restoring early instruments and constructing new ones on traditional principles. His

first significant Baroque-style organ was for the Nederlands Hervormde Kerk, Loenen aan de Vecht (1950). Besides restoring organs in the Netherlands, Portugal and Mexico, he has built new ones at St Mark's Cathedral, Seattle (1965), and Duke University Chapel, Durham, North Carolina (1976).

Flesch, Carl (*b* Moson, 9 Oct 1873; *d* Lucerne, 14 Nov 1944). Hungarian violinist and teacher. He studied in Paris and Vienna. His concert career began in 1894 and after settling in Berlin (1908) he became internationally known also as a chamber music player and teacher. An impeccable technique and intellectual grasp of style were placed in the service of a wide repertory. His diagnostic ability as a performer made him a successful teacher; he published several methods, including *Die Kunst des Violin-Spiels* (1923).

Fletcher, (Horace) Grant (*b* Hartsburg, IL, 25 Oct 1913). American composer. He studied under Krenek at Michigan and under Hanson, Rogers and Ewell at the Eastman School and taught at various Mid west institutions from 1938. His compositions, including two symphonies and two piano concertos, are stylistically diverse; latterly he has been influenced by the legends and tribal cultures of the south-western USA.

Fleury, André (Edouard Antoine Marie) (*b* Neuilly-sur-Seine, 25 July 1903). French organist and composer. He studied at the Conservatoire and with Marchal and Vierne, became organist at St Augustin (1930) and taught at the Ecole Normale (1943). From 1949 he was organist at Dijon Cathedral, then he returned to Paris in 1971 as co-organist with Guillou of St Eustache. His playing was noted for its rhythmic verve; his works, mainly for organ, include two organ symphonies.

Flexatone. A percussion instrument invented in the 1920s, consisting of a small flexible metal sheet close to which wooden knobs are mounted on spring steel strips. When the player shakes the instrument a tremolo effect is produced; the pitch is adjusted by pressure on the sheet. It has been used by Schoenberg, Khachaturian, Henze and others.

Flicorno (It.). A valved bugle horn of widely conical profile; the Italian counterpart of the flugelhorn. They have been made in seven sizes, from a contrabasso in C or B♭ (compass E''–f) to the now obsolete *sopracuto* in B♭ or A, compass eb'–f'''. The standard model is the soprano in C, B♭ or A, compass $f\sharp'$–bb''.

Fliegende Holländer, Der. *See* FLYING DUTCHMMAN, THE.

Fliessend (Ger.). Flowing.

Flight of the Bumble Bee, The. Orchestral interlude in Rimsky-Korsakov's opera *The Legend of Tsar Saltan* (1900) of which many arrangements have been made.

Flonzaley Quartet. American string quartet. Led by Adolfo Betti, it was established in New York in 1902 by a private patron; it made its first European tour in 1904 and appeared regularly in the USA and Europe until it was disbanded in 1928. Admired for its finish, brilliance and beautiful tone, it was one of the earliest quartets to make records.

Flood, The. 'Musical play' by Stravinsky to a libretto arranged by Robert Craft from *Genesis* and the York and Chester mystery plays (televised 1962; 1963, Hamburg).

Floquet, Etienne Joseph (*b* Aix-en-Provence, 23 Nov 1748; *d* Paris, 10 May 1785). French composer. Active in Paris from the 1760s, he became Gluck's rival with the highly successful opera-ballet *L'union de l'Amour et des arts* (1773). He was briefly a viola player at the Opéra, then studied in Italy. Later he wrote several comic operas for Paris; *Le seigneur bienfaisant* (1780) was especially popular. His eight stage works include two *tragédies lyriques*; the second, *Alceste* (1783), an emulation of Gluck, was not performed.

Florid. Term used particularly in vocal music in the 18th century to refer either to passage-work (previously called 'divisions') or to the use of ornaments.

Florimo, Francesco (*b* S Giorgio Morgeto, 12 Oct 1800; *d* Naples, 18 Dec 1888). Italian librarian, writer on music and composer. He became archivist-librarian at the Naples Conservatory in 1826, also serving as a singing teacher and writing songs, many in a Neapolitan popular style, and a singing method. He was the devoted advocate and biographer of Bellini and author of the indispensable *Cenno storico sulla scuola musicale di Napoli* (1869–71).

Flos Campi [Flower of the Field]. Suite by Vaughan Williams for viola, (wordless) chorus and orchestra (1925).

Floss der 'Medusa', Das. 'Popular and military oratorio' by Henze to a text by Ernst Schnabel (1971, Vienna).

Flötenuhr (Ger.). A flute-playing musical clock, a mechanical instrument producing its sound from organ pipes activated by pinned cylinders. Mozart and Haydn wrote for it.

Flothuis, Marius (Hendrikus) (*b* Amsterdam, 30 Oct 1914). Dutch composer. He studied musicology at Amsterdam University but is self-taught as a composer. He wrote a large amount of generally lyrical, tonal and contrapuntal music, in many genres; as a scholar he has brought particular insights to Mozart.

Flotow, Friedrich (Adolf Ferdinand), Freiherr von (*b* Teutendorf, 27 April 1812; *d* Darmstadt, 24 Jan 1883). German composer. Of an aristocratic family, he attended the Paris Conservatoire and came under the influence of Auber, Rossini, Meyerbeer, Donizetti, Halévy and Adam, and later Gounod and Offenbach. By 1835 he had completed his first opera, *Pierre et Cathérine*, but he gained public notice only with *Le naufrage de la Médeuse* (1839). His most successful works were the tuneful if unsubstantial *Alessandro Stradella* (1844) and the delightful *Martha, oder Der Markt zu Richmond* (1847), both to texts by F.W. Riese. None of his 15 later operas rivalled the popularity of *Martha*, which in its concerted music shows dramatic flair and in its sentimental numbers (including 'The Last Rose of Summer') period charm and a delicate, romantic wistfulness. He also wrote instrumental music and songs.

Flourish. In Elizabethan plays, a fanfare, usually for trumpets. The term was used in England during the 17th and 18th centuries for short preludes, consisting largely of scales and arpeggios, to test the tuning and functioning of an instrument.

Floyd, Carlisle (Sessions) (*b* Latta, SC, 11 June 1926). American composer. He studied with Ernst Bacon at Syracuse University (1945–9). In 1947 he joined the faculty of Florida State University and in 1976 was appointed a professor at the University of Houston. His operas are an important part of American music-drama; they include *Susannah* (1955), *Wuthering Heights* (1958), *Of Mice and Men* (1970) and *Willie Stark* (1981), and are well crafted and stageworthy though eclectic and conservative.

Fludd, Robert (bap. Bearsted, 17 Jan 1574; *d* London, 8 Sept 1637). English writer and physician. In his many Latin treatises he touched on music, often in abstruse language and with fantastic diagrams; he criticized contemporary theorists, including Kepler and Mersenne. He composed some dances.

Flue-work. The flue stops of an organ, i.e. those in which wind is directed through a narrow windway to strike against a lip or edge above.

Flugelhorn. A valved brass instrument pitched in B♭ with the same compass as the cornet. It has the conical bore, wide bell and large format of the keyed bugle. It is a leading instrument in most continental bands but rare in British or American ones.

Flute [cross flute, German flute, transverse flute]. A broad term covering many instruments from the modern orchestral woodwind to folk instruments of most cultures. Generically a flute is any instrument with an air column confined in a hollow body and activated by a stream of air from the player's lips striking the sharp edge of an opening. The airstream may be shaped and directed by the player as on the orchestral flute or confined in a channel and directed against an edge as in the duct flute family of whistles and recorders.

The orchestral flute has a mainly cylindrical tube of wood or metal about 66 cm long and 2 cm in diameter, and is in three sections: a head joint with the mouth-hole or embouchure; the body or middle joint with the principal keywork; and the foot joint with keys for the right little finger (for illustration, *see* WOODWIND INSTRUMENTS). The instrument has a fully chromatic compass from *c'* (*b* on some flutes) for three octaves or more. It has 13 main tone holes, smaller holes to facilitate shakes and other fingerings, and elaborate keywork. The control of the sound is achieved by the player's lips; a proper embouchure is a crucial part of the instrument's technique.

The flute family includes the piccolo, half the size of the concert flute and pitched an octave higher; the alto flute (sometimes called bass flute), in G, a 4th lower than the concert flute, with a range *g–c'''*; and the true bass flute, an octave lower than the concert flute.

Flutes of various sorts were known in ancient civilizations. They disappear from Western art after the fall of Rome and reappear in the 10th and 11th centuries. After 1500, flutes appear in pictorial and literary sources throughout western Europe as members of whole and broken consorts and as solo instruments. In the early Baroque period the flute fell into a decline; the cylindrical Renaissance instrument with its inefficient cross-fingerings could not meet the music's demands. With the improvements of the Parisian makers the one-keyed conical Baroque flute became standard in the early 18th century, first in France and later in Germany and England. With the advent of public concerts the growth in amateur music-making and the rise of the expressive *galant* style well suited to it, the flute greatly gained in popularity. The fullest source on the 18th-century flute and its technique is Quantz's *Versuch einer Anweisung die Flöte traversiere zu spielen* (1752). Bach used the flute in his cantatas, Passions, and oratorios, and Handel and other composers of Italian opera also scored for the flute. Bach's chamber works include some eight sonatas and two trios for flute; Handel, Vivaldi and many others contributed to its large late Baroque repertory, Vivaldi writing concertos as well as sonatas. Other leading 18th-century composers of flute music include de la Barre, Hotteterre and Blavet from France, J.B. Loeillet from Belgium, Porpora and G.B. Sammartini from Italy, Telemann, Hasse, Quantz and Bach's sons from Germany, and Stanley and Hook from England. After the quartets and concertos of Mozart, the solo and chamber repertory declined, again because the flute could not compete expressively with other instruments or provide the louder or more brilliant sounds needed in ever-larger concert rooms. But there is a considerable repertory of trivial chamber music.

At the beginning of the 19th century flutes were made from boxwood, ebony, cocus wood or ivory, with one to eight keys. In the 1830s Theobald Boehm redesigned the instrument, to make the tone louder and more uniform, to improve its intonation and to make chromatic notes more accessible. Boehm's conical flute of 1832, with its powerful 'open' sound, improved intonation and ingenious mechanism, gradually gained acceptance, and with minor modifications it remains the standard model.

The flute entered the orchestra in the mid- to late 18th century; often flutes were an alternative to the standard oboes, but later one or two became standard. By the mid-19th century two flutes and sometimes a piccolo were used; later the alto flute too made an occasional appearance.

The 20th-century French school found the coolly expressive character of the flute specially appealing, as its use by Debussy, Honegger, Ibert and Milhaud testifies. Prokofiev, Piston, Schoenberg, Varèse and Vaughan Williams have also contributed to the repertory. Since 1945 composers to have written for flute include Henze, Berio and Boulez.

Flutter-tonguing. A type of tonguing in which the player rolls the letter 'r' on the tip of his tongue while playing; it is used especially on the flute.

Flying Dutchman, The [Der fliegende Holländer]. Opera in three acts by Wagner to his own libretto (1843, Dresden).

Fodor-Mainvielle, Joséphine (*b* Paris, 13 Oct 1789;

d St Genis-Laval, 14 Aug 1870). French soprano. She took part in the London or Paris premières of several Rossini operas, scoring her biggest success in the title role of *Semiramide* (1825). Her father Josephus Andreas Fodor (1751–1828) was a Dutch violin virtuoso.

Foerster, Josef Bohuslav (*b* Prague, 30 Dec 1859; *d* Vestec, 29 May 1951). Czech composer. He studied at the Prague Organ School (1879–82) and was acquainted with Dvořák and Smetana. His wife sang for Mahler, whom the couple followed to Vienna in 1903, returning in 1918 to Prague, where he taught. With his contemporaries Janáček, Novák, Suk and Ostrčil, Foerster led the development of Czech music from late 19th-century nationalism to the interwar avant garde. He produced a large output, much of it in sets or cycles; the bulk is vocal music, including six operas, over 300 choral works and 26 melodramas, but he also wrote chamber and instrumental music (including five symphonies). His language is restrained and conventional in harmony and structure, using free polyphony. His extensive literary work includes essays, memoirs, verse and criticism. He was also a gifted artist.

His father Josef (1833–1907) was a prominent organist and choirmaster in Prague and a leading figure in the church music reform movement in Bohemia and Moravia.

Foignet, Charles Gabriel [Jacques] (*b* Lyons, 1750; *d* Paris, 1823). French singer and composer. He wrote or collaborated in more than 25 *opéras comiques* and melodramas and created, with his son François (1782–1845), a highly regarded theatrical troupe at their Théâtre des Jeunes-Artistes. François, also a singer and composer, enjoyed his greatest success with his *La naissance d'Arlequin* (1803).

Foldes, Andor (*b* Budapest, 21 Dec 1913). American pianist. He made his début at eight, in a Mozart concerto with the Budapest PO; later he studied at the Academy, with Dohnányi and with Bartók. He has made particular impact as a Bartók interpreter, though his playing of the Viennese Classics and early Romantic music is also much admired.

Folia. A musical framework used during the Baroque period for songs, dances and variations. There were two versions: an early one with a history extending from 1577 to 1674 in Spain and Italy and a later type (ex.1) appearing from 1672 to 1750, mainly in

Ex.1

France and England. Corelli's is the best known of the numerous sets of variations on the folia.

Folk music. Term used, in areas (such as Europe, North America and India) where a tradition of cultivated music exists (ecclesiastical, courtly, urban), for musical traditions associated with rural, especially peasant, cultures. It is defined as music that is accepted in the community and passed through oral transmission; the existence of variants is a commonly cited feature, as is its ever-changing nature.

The term 'folk revival' has been used for a genre of popular music based on the revival of traditional folksongs and the new composition of music in a similar style.

Folquet de Marseille (b?Marseilles, c1150; d Toulouse, 25 Dec 1231). Provençal troubadour. At first a merchant, he was at the Aragon court and in cities in southern France; he entered the church c1195 and established Toulouse University in 1229. He left 29 poems, and melodies for 13 survive; these are notable for their use of characteristic melodic formulae.

Fomin, Evstigney Ipatovich (b St Petersburg, 16 Aug 1761; d there, May 1800). Russian composer. He studied with G.B. Martini in Bologna, 1782–6, then returned to St Petersburg, composing Russian stage works, notably the melodrama *Orfey i Evridika* (1792) and sacred pieces. After becoming répétiteur at the Imperial Theatres in 1797, he wrote three more operas, often to librettos on national subjects. He was one of the most significant Russian opera composers of his day; his style includes Russian folk elements, lyrical melodies and dramatic harmonies.

Fonseca, Julio (b San José, 22 May 1885; d there, 22 June 1950). Costa Rican composer. He studied at the Milan and Brussels conservatories, then returned to Costa Rica in 1906. He is the most prolific composer in Costa Rican history, his works including the *Gran fantasía sinfónica* (1937) which quotes the national anthem and his own waltz *Leda* (1914).

Fontaine, Pierre (b?1390–95; d c1450). French composer. Having been trained probably at Rouen Cathedral, he was a member of the chapel of Philip the Bold, Duke of Burgundy, by 1403 and served Philip's successor, John the Fearless, as a chaplain (1415–19). In 1420 he became a member of the papal chapel but between 1428 and 1430 returned to the court of Burgundy as a singer in Philip the Good's chapel. Seven *chansons* (six rondeaux and a ballade) by him survive.

Fontana, Giovanni Battista (b Brescia; d Padua, c1630). Italian composer and violinist. He was a leading figure in the early history of the sonata. Knowledge of his life and work is confined to one important posthumous collection of sonatas (1641), six for violin (or cornett) and bass, 12 for two violins and bass (often with concertante parts for bassoon or cello). Divisible into numerous contrasting sections, they are conservative in melodic and harmonic style but characterized by a complex, nervous rhythmic idiom with elaborate ornamentation, especially in the solo works.

Fontane di Roma. Orchestral work by Respighi (1916).

Fontanelli, Alfonso (b Reggio Emilia, 15 Feb 1557; d Rome, 11 Feb 1622). Italian composer and statesman. An influential nobleman, he served the Fer-rarese court, recruiting its virtuosos, from at least 1586 to 1597, its most brilliant period. He also worked in Modena, Florence and notably Rome and travelled widely in Italy, France and Spain. His two madrigal books (1595, 1604) are in an up-to-date style and include bold, experimental use of dissonance.

Fontei, Nicolò (b Orciano di Pesaro; d?Verona or Venice, 1647 or later). Italian composer. He probably settled in Venice before 1634 but moved to Verona in 1645 as cathedral choirmaster. He had become a master of the Venetian triple-time bel canto aria by the third volume (1639) of his *Bizarrie poetiche*, using the form with equal success in his sacred music. He was a pioneer of refrain structures in secular vocal music, notably in the pastoral dialogue *Lilla, se Amor non fugga* (in op.4). His only known opera (performed Venice, 1642) is lost.

Foote, Arthur (William) (b Salem, MA, 5 March 1853; d Boston, 8 April 1937). American composer. He studied with Paine at Harvard (1870–75), then became a highly regarded teacher and organist and leading figure in Boston musical life. His music, often reflective in tone, consists mostly of chamber and choral pieces, piano music and songs; his Suite in E for strings (1907) and *A Night Piece* for flute and strings (1922) were popular in his lifetime.

Forbes, Sebastian (b Amersham, 22 May 1941). Scottish composer. He studied at the RAM and Cambridge and was organist at Trinity College. His Piano Trio (1964) established him as a composer of intellectual toughness; later works include the *Essay* for orchestra (1970), Symphony (1972) and two string quartets.

Force of Destiny, The. See FORZA DEL DESTINO, LA.

Ford, Thomas (d London, bur. 17 Nov 1648). English composer. He was a court musician from 1611 to 1642, serving as a viol player. His only publication (1607) includes some famous ayres (e.g. *Faire sweet cruell, There is a ladie*), as well as dances etc for two lyra viols. He also wrote partsongs, anthems and viol fantasias.

Forefall. An ascending APPOGGIATURA.

Forelle, Die See TROUT, THE.

Forest (d?1446). English composer of the early 15th century. His first name is not known but he may have been the John Forest who was Archdeacon of Surrey from 1415 and Dean of Wells from 1425 until his death in 1446. A Credo setting, five Marian antiphons (one in the Old Hall MS) and an isorhythmic motet by him have survived. Two further Credo settings may be his. His style has much in common with that of Power's later motets.

Forkel, Johann Nikolaus (b Meeder, 22 Feb 1749; d Göttingen, 20 March 1818). German music historian. He held various musical posts in Göttingen, including university music director from c1780; he was an influential scholar and teacher, and a founder of modern musicology. His main works are an incomplete history of music (1788–1801), a bibliography of writings on music (1792) and a biography of J.S. Bach (1802); he also planned a complete edition of Bach's works. He composed keyboard and vocal music.

Forlana [forlane]. A lively north Italian dance in 6/4 or 6/8 with repeated motifs. It flourished from c1697 to 1750 as a French court dance, and during the 18th century it was popular in Venice with gondoliers and 'street people'. Stylized forlanas include those in Bach's Suite no.1 for orchestra and Ravel's *Le tombeau de Couperin*.

Form. The structure, shape or organizing principle of music. It has to do with the arrangement of the elements in a piece of music to make it coherent to the listener, who may be able to recognize, for example, a theme heard earlier in the piece or a key change that establishes links between one part of a composition and another. Themes and keys are only two of many elements that composers use to help articulate the structure of a piece to give it clarity and unity. There are numerous ways – subconscious as well as conscious – in which composers have done, or attempted to do, this, depending upon the style in which they are writing.

The word 'form' is mostly used, however, in reference to the structural plan of a single movement: such terms as binary, ternary, ritornello, sonata, rondo and variations stand for particular formal schemes. (For information on individual forms, see under the name of the form concerned.)

Formé, Nicolas (*b* Paris, 26 April 1567; *d* there, 27 May 1638). French composer. From 1609 he was *sous-maître* and composer at the royal chapel. Notorious for his arrogant and undisciplined nature, he was nevertheless a fine composer, now known only by his sacred music. In a double-choir mass dedicated to Louis XIII (1638) and the two motets from the same volume, he made explicit use of the concertante style, thus heralding the Versailles *grand motet*. He also wrote Magnificats based on the eight church tones, in a more traditional manner.

Formes fixes (Fr.). Poetic 'fixed forms', such as the 14th-century ballade and the 15th-century rondeau, which directly affected the musical forms of that period.

Forqueray, Antoine (*b* Paris, 1671–2; *d* Mantes, 28 June 1745). French composer and bass viol player. He was appointed *musicien ordinaire de la chambre* to Louis XIV in 1689, played at court and taught many eminent people. He was famous for his brilliant exploitation of the viol, in contrast to Marais' more graceful style. This is seen in the complex and demanding style of his *Pieces de viole*, published in 1747 by his son, Jean-Baptiste-Antoine (1699–1782), also a viol player of great skill, who edited them and may at least have recomposed parts of them; he also issued a keyboard version. Antoine's nephew Michel (1681–1757) and Michel's nephew Nicolas-Gilles (1703–61) were organists in Paris.

Forrester, Maureen (*b* Montreal, 25 July 1930). Canadian contralto. After a successful New York recital (1956) she soon appeared widely in the USA and Europe; her singing of Mahler was particularly memorable. Her first operatic role was Gluck's Orpheus (1962, Toronto) and she was later heard in New York in operas by Wagner, Handel and Menotti.

Förster, Christoph (Heinrich) (*b* Bibra, 30 Nov 1693; *d* Rudolstadt, ?5/6 Dec 1745). German composer. He worked at the courts at Merseburg (from 1717) and Rudolstadt (1743). He was respected for his church music, including over 25 cantatas. Among his many instrumental works are Frenchstyle orchestral suites, Italianate sinfonias, concertos and chamber works; he also composed stage works, occasional cantatas etc.

Förster, Emanuel Aloys (*b* Niederstein, 26 Jan 1748; *d* Vienna, 12 Nov 1823). Austrian composer. He settled in Vienna in the 1780s as a composer, theorist and teacher, his works including over 40 piano sonatas and various chamber pieces (string quartets and quintets, piano quartets etc); he was a pioneer in writing for large chamber ensembles with piano. He also wrote keyboard variations, secular vocal music and pedagogical works. His piano works of the 1780s show C.P.E. Bach's influence, but from the 1790s his models were mature works by Haydn and Mozart; his style lies between theirs and early Beethoven.

Forster, Georg (*b* Amberg, c1510; *d* Nuremberg, 12 Nov 1568). German editor and composer. A chorister at Elector Ludwig V's court in Heidelberg c1521, he became an eminent physician in Amberg. He collected songs, pursued an interest in literature and met Luther, who encouraged him to compose settings of biblical texts. Among his esteemed editions is an influential collection of 382 (mostly fourpart) German songs, *Frischer tentscher Liedlein* (Nuremberg, 1539–56), which covers the German Tenorlied from the late 15th century to the middle of the 16th and enjoyed great popularity.

Förster, Kaspar (*b* Danzig, bap. 28 Feb 1616; *d* Oliva, nr. there, 2 Feb 1673). German composer. A pupil of Scacchi and (in the 1660s) Carissimi, he was a bass singer and choral conductor at the Polish court in Warsaw (1638–c1643) and Kapellmeister to King Frederik III of Denmark at Copenhagen (1652–5, 1661–7), making periodic journeys to Venice. He is important for his role in transmitting the Italian style to the north. His surviving vocal works (mostly sacred concertos) are usually for three solo voices (with very low bass parts) with two violins and continuo. He wrote two oratorios modelled on Carissimi's; his surviving instrumental music includes six trio sonatas.

Forte (It.). 'Loud', 'strong', abbreviated *f*; hence *fortissimo* (*ff*, very loud). See DYNAMICS.

Forte, Allen (*b* Portland, OR, 23 Dec 1926). American music theorist. He studied at Columbia University and in 1959 began teaching at Yale. He is a leading figure in the study of music analysis by Schenkerian methods and his own extensions of them involve set theory and computer technology.

Fortepiano. Term sometimes used for the piano of the 18th century and early 19th to distinguish it from the 20th-century instrument.

Fortner, Wolfgang (*b* Leipzig, 12 Oct 1907). German composer. He grew up in the Protestant tradition of Leipzig, studying with Grabner at the conservatory. In 1931 he began teaching at the Heidelberg Institute for Church Music; he also taught at Darmstadt in the late 1940s and at the Freiburg Musikhoch-schule (1957–72). He holds an important position in West German music both as a composer and teacher, his standing being comparable with Mess-iaen's. His earlier music is neo-classical influenced by Hindemith and Stravinsky, but from 1945 he used serialism, in an individual way. His main works are operas (notably *Die Bluthochzeit*, 1957; *In seinem Garten liebt Don Perlimplin Belisa*, 1962; *Elisabeth Tudor*, 1972) and orchestral pieces.

Förtsch, Johann Philipp (*b* Wertheim am Main, bap. 14 May 1652; *d* Eutin, 14 Dec 1732). After travelling in Europe he settled in Hamburg, where he became the leading opera composer (1684–90). The few surviving arias from his 12 known lost operas suggest a strongly personal style, characteris-tically German in its use of strophic, song-like arias and affective word setting. He was also a prolific composer of cantatas, probably written for the Gottorf Hofkapelle (1686–88).

Fortspinnung (Ger.). Term devised in 1915 to stand for the process of continuation or development of musical material in which a short idea or motif is 'spun out' into an entire phrase or period, for exam-ple by sequence or intervallic change. It was much used in the Baroque period, rather less in the Classical.

48. Familiar title of the two collections of 24 preludes and fugues in all the keys by J.S. Bach. The first book, entitled *Das wohltemperirte Clavier*, was com-posed in 1722; the second, untitled, dates mainly from 1738–42. *See* WELL-TEMPERED CLAVIER.

Forza del destino, La. Opera in four acts by Verdi to a libretto by Piave after A.P. de Saavedra (Duke of Rivas) (1862, St Petersburg); Verdi revised it (1869, Milan), to a libretto revised by Ghislanzoni.

Foss [Fuchs], Lukas (*b* Berlin, 15 Aug 1922). Ameri-can composer, conductor and pianist of German parentage. He studied in Berlin, Paris (1933–7) and with Scalero and Thompson at the Curtis Institute, as well as with Hindemith at Yale (1939–40). In 1953 he was appointed professor of music at UCLA. He was music director of the Buffalo PO (1963–70) and in 1971 became conductor of the Brooklyn PO, introducing much new music. From 1981 to 1986 he was also music director of the Milwaukee SO. As a programme planner and conductor he has been un-orthodox. His early music, with neo-classical and American folk elements, made his reputation as a composer, but in the late 1950s he began working with improvisation, and his subsequent works draw on diverse modernisms, including electronics.

Foster, Lawrence (Thomas) (*b* Los Angeles, 23 Oct 1941). American conductor. After study in Los Angeles and at Tanglewood he held appointments in California. His London début was in 1967 and he was chief guest conductor with the RPO, 1969–74; he has given well-prepared first performances (in-cluding music by Birtwistle) and was musical direc-tor of the Houston SO, 1970–78.

Foster, Stephen C(ollins) (*b* Pittsburgh, 4 July 1826; *d* New York, 13 Jan 1864). American composer of popular 'household' and minstrel songs. A self-taught musician, he produced *c*200 songs, 1844–64.

Most are simple, sentimental solo songs 'of the hearth and home', such as *My old Kentucky home* (1853), *Jeanie with the light brown hair* (1854) and *Beautiful dreamer* (1864). But his *c*30 minstrel songs are often strongly rhythmic, in black dialect and with a choral refrain and instrumental interlude; they include *Oh! Susanna* (1848), *Camptown Races* (1850) and *Old Folks at Home* (1851). He also wrote hymns and Sunday school songs.

Foucquet, Pierre-Claude (*b* Paris, 1694–5; *d* there, 13 Feb 1772). French composer. He was one of a line of Parisian organists, including his grandfather An-toine (*d* 1708), his father Pierre (*d* 1734–5; one of the first Frenchmen to write Italian-style sonatas) and his uncle Antoine (*d* by 1740). He played at St Eus-tache, the royal chapel (from 1758) and also at Notre Dame (from 1761), and composed three harpsi-chord books (1749–51), which include many charac-ter pieces, some with extended forms and keyboard devices. Both his sons were also organists.

Foulds, John (Herbert) (*b* Manchester, 2 Nov 1880; *d* Calcutta, 24 April 1939). English composer. Influ-enced by Indian music, he was concerned with un-usual modalities and quarter-tones in his large, diverse output of orchestral and chamber music. His best-known work is *A World Requiem* for the World War I dead.

Fountains of Rome. *See* FONTANE DI ROMA.

Four foot. Term used of organ stops, and by exten-sion other instruments, to indicate that they are pitched an octave above 'normal' (eight foot) pitch.

Four Last Songs [Vier letzte lieden]. Songs by Ri-chard Strauss, settings for soprano (or tenor) and orchestra of poems by Hesse and Eichendorff (1948).

Fournier, Pierre (Léon Marie) (*b* Paris, 24 June 1906; *d* Geneva, 8 Jan 1986). French cellist. After study at the Paris Conservatoire he soon became known in a wide repertory, cultivating a smooth tone, graceful phrasing and firm intellectual control. His first tour of the USA was in 1948. As a chamber musician he was heard with Primrose and Schnabel and, latterly, Szeryng and Kempff. He gave the premières of concertos by Roussel, Martin and Martinů.

Four Saints in Three Acts. Opera in four acts by Virgil Thomson to a libretto by Gertrude Stein (1934, Hartford, Conn.).

Four Seasons, The [Le quattro stagioni]. Four con-certos by Vivaldi, from his *Il cimento dell'armonia e dell'inventione* op.8 (*c*1725). No.1 in E RV269 is 'La primavera' (Spring), no.2 in G minor RV315 is 'L'es-tate' (Summer), no.3 in F RV293 'L'autunno' (Autumn) and no.4 in F minor RV297 'L'inverno' (Winter); seasonal events are pictured in sonnets preceding each concerto.

Four Serious Songs [Vier Ernste Gesänge]. Song cycle by Brahms (op.121, 1896), settings for bari-tone and piano of biblical texts.

Four Temperaments, The. Sub-title of Nielsen's Symphony no.2 in C minor (1902), inspired by a painting of that name.

Fourth. The INTERVAL between two notes three dia-tonic scale degrees apart (e.g. C–F).

Fou Ts'ong (*b* Shanghai, 10 March 1934). British pianist of Chinese birth. He studied in Shanghai and Warsaw, made his Chinese début in 1953 and in 1959 his début in Britain, where he settled. His delicate touch and keen sensibility make him a notable interpreter of Mozart, Chopin and Debussy.

Fox, Virgil (Keel) (*b* Princeton, IL, 3 May 1912; *d* West Palm Beach, 25 Oct 1980). American organist. He studied in Baltimore and with Marcel Dupré in Paris. In 1931 he played at Carnegie Hall and from 1946 to 1965 was organist at Riverside Church, New York. His dazzling technique and flamboyant performing style, often at an electronic organ, earned him a wide following.

Foxtrot. A social dance dating from *c*1910; like other 'animal' dances, it had its origins in the one-step, two-step and syncopated ragtime dances in the USA.

Fra Diavolo. Comic opera in three acts by Auber to a libretto by Scribe (1830, Paris).

Frame drum. A drum with one or two heads stretched over a frame or hoop. The many types, used in most parts of the world, vary in shape, size and method of attaching the skins. The tambourine is a frame drum.

Framery, Nicolas Etienne (*b* Rouen, 25 March 1745; *d* Paris, 26 Nov 1810). French writer and composer. He composed an *opéra comique* (1768) but was mainly active as a writer and translator: he wrote *c*12 librettos (most based on Italian works) as well as reviews, notices on musicians and a theoretical work.

Françaix, Jean (*b* Le Mans, 23 May 1912). French composer. He studied at the Paris Conservatoire and with Boulanger and quickly made a reputation for elegant chamber music, especially for wind instruments, following in the direction of Poulenc; notable is the Quintet (1934) for flute, harp and string trio. His large output also includes operas, ballets, orchestral and choral pieces and songs. A brilliant piano virtuoso, he has toured internationally.

Francesca da Rimini. Symphonic fantasia by Tchaikovsky (op.32) after a picture by Doré (1876).

Opera in a prologue, two scenes and an epilogue by Rakhmaninov to a libretto by Modest Tchaikovsky (1906, Moscow).

Francescatti, Zino (*b* Marseilles, 9 Aug 1902). French violinist. He studied in Marseilles, where he made his début in 1918; later he played duos with Ravel and R. Casadesus. A champion of 20th-century music, he was also noted for the relaxed lyricism and eloquence of his playing in the Romantic repertory.

Franceschini, Petronio (*b* Bologna, *c*1650; *d* Venice, *c*18 Dec 1680). Italian composer. He worked in Bologna where he was a cellist at the cathedral (1675–80) and an early member of the Accademia Filarmonica. He wrote four operas for performance there and died while writing one for Venice. His surviving operatic music has great rhythmic energy and makes much use of the trumpet in dialogue with the voice. He also wrote sacred music and sonatas.

Francesco Canova da Milano (*b* Monza, 18 Aug 1497; *d* Milan, 15 April 1543). Italian composer and lutenist. He was lutenist and viol player to the papacy (1516–39), to Ippolito de' Medici and Cardinal Alessandro Farnese. He was the first Italian Renaissance musician to achieve an international reputation and more music by him survives than by any other lutenist of the time, in more than 40 publications (1536–1603) and 25 MSS. He wrote ricercares, fantasias and arrangements of vocal works, by Sermisy, Janequin and Josquin, among others.

Francés de Iribarren, Juan (*b* Sangüesa, 1698; *d* Málaga, 2 Sept 1767). Spanish composer. He worked at Salamanca Cathedral from 1717. One of the most prolific Spanish composers of the century, he wrote *c*500 villancicos and many other sacred works, in a highly polished style.

Franchetti, Baron Alberto (*b* Turin, 18 Sept 1860; *d* Viareggio, 4 Aug 1942). Italian composer. He studied in Turin, Venice and Germany (with Rheinberger), and was influenced by Meyerbeer and Wagner in his operas (e.g. *Asrael*, 1888).

Franchois (de Gemblaco), Johannes (*fl* 1378–1415). Franco-Flemish composer. By 1378 he was in Avignon as a member of the Archbishop of Rouen's chapel. In 1384 he was a cantor at St Denis, Liège, but by 1393 he had returned to Avignon as a member of Pope Clement VII's chapel. He later became a chaplain at the court of Philip the Bold, Duke of Burgundy, and retired after 1404 to Evreux, where he held a prebend at the cathedral. Two Glorias, two Credos, an isorhythmic motet and three rondeaux by him survive.

Franchomme, Auguste (Joseph) (*b* Lille, 10 April 1808; *d* Paris, 21 Jan 1884). French cellist and composer. He studied at the Paris Conservatoire. The most distinguished French cellist of his day, he was renowned for his expressive, singing tone. He was close to Chopin, with whom he collaborated on a Grand Duo Concertante (1833) and whose Cello Sonata op.65 was dedicated to him. His own works include studies, a concerto and numerous accompanied solos for cello.

Franck, César (- Auguste - Jean - Guillaume - Hubert) (*b* Liège, 10 Dec 1822; *d* Paris, 8 Nov 1890). French composer, teacher and organist of Belgian birth. Intended by his ambitious father for a career as a piano virtuoso, he studied at the Liège (1830–35) and Paris (1837–42) conservatories but found his true vocation only later through organist's appointments in Paris, chiefly that of Ste Clotilde (from 1858), and part-time teaching. His improvisatory skill attracted notice and led to his first major work, the remarkable *Six pièces* (1862), though another decade passed before he was appointed organ professor at the Conservatoire. From the mid-1870s until his death his creative powers lasted unabated. He wrote large-scale sacred works, notably the oratorio *Les béatitudes* (1879), and several symphonic poems such as *Le chasseur maudit* (1882) and *Psyché* (1888). But his achievements are evident especially in the symphonic, chamber and keyboard works in which he made one of the most distinguished contributions to the field by any French musician. Here, in the Piano Quintet (1879), the *Prélude, choral et fugue* for piano (1884), the Violin Sonata (1886), the Symphony in D minor (1888) and the String Quartet (1889), his inherent emotionalism and a preoccupation with counterpoint and traditional forms found a balance, in turn decisively impressing his band of disciples, from Duparc, d'Indy and Chausson to Lekeu, Vierne, Dukas and Guilmant. Features of his mature style, indebted alike to Beethoven, Liszt and Wagner, are his complex, mosaic-like phrase structures, variants of one or two motifs; his rich chromaticism, often put to structural use in the 'chord pair'; and his fondness for cyclic, tripartite forms.

Sacred music Ruth (1846); Rédemption (1874); Les béatitudes (1879); Rébecca (1881); 3 cantatas; 2 masses; c25 sacred pieces, incl. Panis angelicus (1872)
Secular vocal music Hulda (1885, perf. 1894); Ghiselle, unfinished (1890, perf. 1896); patriotic odes and hymns; songs
Orchestral music Sym., d (1888); Les Éolides, sym. poem (1876); Le chasseur maudit, sym. poem (1882); Psyché, sym. poem (1888); Sym. Variations, with pf (1885); Pf Conc. (1835)
Chamber and keyboard music Str Qnt (1878); Pf Qnt (1879); Str Qt, D (1889); 5 pf trios (1834–42); Vn Sonata, A (1886); other vn pieces; Six pièces, org (1862); over 100 org and harmonium pieces; Prélude, choral et fugue, pf (1884); Prélude, aria et final, pf (1887); pf fantaisies

Franck, Johann Wolfgang (*b* Unterschwaningen, bap. 17 June 1644; *d* ?*c*1710). German composer. After studying in Italy he settled in Ansbach as 'Director der Comoedie' in 1672. His importance lies in his synthesis of French, German and Italian stylistic elements in the operas (*c*20) he wrote for Ansbach and Hamburg (where he was musical director of the Theater am Gänsemarkt, 1679–86). His last years were spent in London. Equally important are his sacred songs, notable for their attractive melodies and balanced formal structures. Franck also wrote numerous cantatas.

Franck, Melchior (*b* Zittau, *c*1579; *d* Coburg, 1 June 1639). German composer. He was in a church choir in Augsburg, *c*1600, and moved to Nuremberg in 1601, working at St Egidien's Church. Soon after he became Kapellmeister at the Coburg court. He remained there for the rest of his life, though the depredations of the Thirty Years War reduced the Kapelle and Franck's situation. He was however one of the leading German Protestant composers of his time, publishing more than 40 collections of motets in the period 1601–36, with over 600 works. Nearly all are for choir, performable with or without instruments; only four collections require continuo. Franck typically used simple chorale tunes as the basis of his motets, which follow a straightforward style, with some fugal writing and carefully worked-out counterpoint, but also much homophonic writing; he occasionally used word-painting. He also published many books of secular music, including quodlibets and several sets of convivial songs and dances.

Franco, Hernando (*b* Galizuela, 1532; *d* Mexico City, 28 Nov 1585). Spanish composer. He was *maestro de capilla* at Guatemala (1573) and Mexico City (1575) cathedrals and one of the most notable Renaissance composers of the New World. His surviving *Magnificat* and *Salve regina* settings, psalms and *Lamentations* are characterized by a fluent but rather austere polyphonic style.

Francoeur, François (*b* Paris, 21 Sept 1698; *d* there, 5 Aug 1787). French composer and violinist. His father Joseph (*c*1662–*c*1741) was a double bass player in the 24 Violons du Roi and the Opéra. François served the court as *compositeur de la chambre* (1727) and a member of the 24 Violons (1730), and worked at the Opéra, becoming *maître de musique* (1739) and *inspecteur adjoint* (1743). He collaborated with François Rebel in 20 successful stage works, starting with the opera *Pyrame et Thisbé* (1726); the two were directors of the Opéra, 1757–67. Francoeur's other works include violin sonatas and orchestral pieces.

François's brother Louis (1692–1745) was also a violinist at the Opéra and in the 24 Violins and composed violin sonatas. Louis' son Louis-Joseph (1738–1804) was a violinist at the Opéra, *maître de musique* (1767–79), intermittently director of the orchestra and later an administrator; he wrote stage and other vocal works.

Franco of Cologne (*fl* mid-13th century). German theorist. Nothing is known of his life except that he was a papal chaplain and preceptor of an order of knights, and that he had some connection with Paris University. He wrote, probably *c*1280, the treatise *Ars cantus mensurabilis*, which deals in a practical way with all the main issues and genres of 13th-century music, with apt and up-to-date illustrations. Its special importance lies in its treatment of notation, for it contains the first major statement of an idea that has been fundamental to Western notation ever since: that different durations should be represented by different note shapes (not merely by different contexts, as previously). The system he advocated held good, with some modifications, for the next two centuries. Franco is thus seen as the principal figure in the establishment of the standard system of musical notation.

Francs-juges, Les. Overture (op.3) by Berlioz (1826).

Frank, Ernst (*b* Munich, 7 Feb 1847; *d* Oberdöbling, 17 Aug 1889). German conductor and composer. He studied in Munich and was one of the most gifted German conductors of his time, holding appointments in Würzburg, Vienna and Mannheim, eventually succeeding Bülow as court Kapellmeister in Hanover (1879). He was a friend of Brahms and collaborated with Clara Schumann on the complete edition of Robert Schumann's works. His compositions include over 200 songs and the opera *Hero* (1884).

Frankel, Benjamin (*b* London, 31 Jan 1906; *d* there, 12 Feb 1973). English composer. He studied at the GSM while working as a jazz violinist and worked as an orchestrator and film music composer. He produced over 100 outstanding film scores while also writing orchestral and chamber music in an individual style influenced by Shostakovich, Bartók and Sibelius. In the 1950s he began using serialism, notably in his eight symphonies (1958–71).

Franklin, Benjamin (*b* Boston, 17 Jan 1706; *d* Philadelphia, 17 April 1790). American statesman, scientist and amateur musician. At his shop in Philadelphia he printed three hymnbooks (1730–36) for the Ephrata Community. He played the harp, guitar and glass dulcimer, and invented an improved form of MUSICAL GLASSES or 'armonica'. He also wrote a treatise on music aesthetics.

Franz [Knauth], Robert (*b* Halle, 28 June 1815; *d* there, 24 Oct 1892). German composer. He studied theory with J.C.F. Schneider and, on his own, the works of Bach, Handel, Schubert and Schumann, working chiefly as conductor of the Halle Singakademie and as a teacher at Halle University. As a composer he enjoyed the admiration of Schumann (who secured a publisher for his first songs), Liszt (who wrote a book about him) and the public, though he suffered irreparably from the loss of his hearing. Nearly all his many works are songs; Romantic miniatures, they show a fondness for motivic construction and strophic form, a lyricism, simplicity and restricted emotional range typical of the *Volkslied*, conservative homophonic accompaniments and an emphasis on poetic mood rather than individual words. Their characteristic feeling is of delicacy, often tinged with melancholy, as in *Mutter, o sing' mich zur Ruh'* (op.10 no.3) and the *Schilflieder* op.2. About a quarter are settings of Heine.

Fränzl. German family of musicians. The most celebrated members were Ignaz (1736–1811), a violinist who was the first musical director of the Nationaltheater, Mannheim, and his son Ferdinand (1767–1833), the most important German violinist of Spohr's generation, who became Kapellmeister at the Munich court and wrote popular overtures and violin concertos.

Frauenliebe und -leben [Woman's Love and Life]. Song cycle (op.42) by Schumann, settings for female voice and piano of eight poems by Adalbert von Chamisso (1840).

Frauenlob [Heinrich von Meissen] (*b* ?Meissen, *c*1255; *d* Mainz, 29 Nov 1318). German Minnesanger, the most important representative of late courtly and *Spruch* poetry. He travelled mainly in northern and eastern Germany and was much esteemed for his skills and his temperament. He combined traditional chivalrous themes with a profound veneration of God and nature, showing virtuosity and erudition, and was one of the Meistersingers' 12 *alte Meister*. His name probably refers to his songs in praise of the Virgin.

Frau ohne Schatten, Die [The Woman without a Shadow]. Opera in three acts by Richard Strauss to a libretto by Hofmannsthal (1919, Vienna).

Frederick II, King of Prussia [Friedrich II; Frederick the Great] (*b* Berlin, 24 Jan 1712; *d* Potsdam, 17 Aug 1786). German monarch, patron of the arts, flautist and composer. As crown prince he maintained a musical ensemble; after his accession (1740) he expanded it, running musical affairs with quasi-military discipline, and established the Berlin Opera. Among his finest musicians were C.H. Graun (Kapellmeister), Quantz (who wrote hundreds of flute concertos and sonatas for him) and C.P.E. Bach (his accompanist). J.S. Bach visited in 1747, later basing his *Musical Offering* on a theme by Frederick. During and after the Seven Years War (1756–63) the court music declined. Frederick's compositions include many flute sonatas and concertos (modelled on Quantz's) and several arias for Graun's operas; he also wrote librettos including *Montezuma* (set by Graun, 1755).

Free counterpoint. The free application of the principles of consonance and dissonance and of part-writing in the working out of contrapuntal ideas, as opposed to STRICT COUNTERPOINT.

Freedman, Harry (*b* Lódź, 5 April 1922). Canadian composer of Polish origin. He moved to Canada when he was three and studied with Weinzweig at the Toronto Conservatory, after gaining experience as a painter and in jazz. He played the english horn in the Toronto SO, 1946–69. His music, showing the influence of jazz, of Bartók and latterly serialism, includes ballets, orchestral pieces and songs. Among the best-known works are *Tableau* (1952), *Images* (1957–8) and *Klee Wyck* (1970), which translate the essence of several Canadian paintings into musical counterparts.

Freemasonry. *See* MASONIC MUSIC.

Free reed. A reed not under the direct control of the player. They are found in certain organ pipes, the accordion and concertina, the mouth organ or harmonica, and wind-cap instruments.

Free Trade Hall. Hall in Manchester, opened in 1856 and rebuilt in 1951; it has a capacity of 2500 and is the home of the Hallé Orchestra.

Freischütz, Der. Opera in three acts by Weber to a libretto by F. Kind and J.A. Apel and F. Laun's *Gespensterbuch* (1821, Berlin).

Freisslich, Johann Balthasar Christian (*b* Immelborn, bap. 30 March 1687; *d* Danzig, 1764). German composer. After directing the Sondershausen Hofkapelle he became Kapellmeister of St Mary's, Danzig, succeeding his half-brother Maximilian Dietrich (1673–1731, also a composer). A prolific composer, he wrote Passions and both church and occasional cantatas in a warm lyrical style.

Freitas (Branco), Frederico (Guedes) de (*b* Lisbon, 15 Nov 1902). Portuguese composer. He studied at the National Conservatory. In 1940 he founded the Lisbon Choral Society, later conducting the Oporto SO (1949–53). His works are diverse in style and genre and include fine ballet scores.

Freitas Branco, Luís de (*b* Lisbon, 12 Oct 1890; *d* there, 27 Nov 1955). Portuguese composer. He studied in Lisbon, with Humperdinck in Berlin and with Grovlez in Paris, then taught at the National Conservatory in Lisbon from 1916. As composer, musicologist and critic he was a leading figure in Portuguese musical life. He introduced European developments (impressionism and expressionism) into Portuguese music and left much orchestral and choral works and songs.

Freithoff, Johann Henrik (*b* Christiansand, 1713; *d* Copenhagen, 24 June 1767). Norwegian composer. A virtuoso violinist, he travelled to Italy and elsewhere before being appointed at the Copenhagen court in 1744. He wrote attractive violin sonatas and trios.

Fremstad, Olive (*b* Stockholm, 14 March 1871; *d* Irvington-on-Hudson, 21 April 1951). Swedish-American mezzo-soprano and soprano. She studied in Berlin with Lilli Lehmann and made her début at Cologne in 1895. She was successful in Vienna and London and sang at the Met, 1903–14. Her portrayals of Carmen, Tosca, Salome and Brünnhilde won her an affectionate following. She sang her first Isolde (1908) at Mahler's début at the Met.

French horn. *See* HORN.

French overture. An instrumental introduction to an opera, ballet or suite, combining a slow opening, marked by stately dotted rhythms and suspensions, with a lively fugal second section. There is often a return to the style of the opening at the end of the fast section. The form originated with Lully's ballet overtures of the 1650s and flourished for over 60 years in France and even longer elsewhere. Handel used it for his London operas and oratorios and Bach in his orchestral suites and other works.

French sixth chord. An AUGMENTED SIXTH CHORD with both a major 3rd and an augmented 4th in addition to an augmented 6th above the flattened submediant (e.g. A♭–C–D–F♯).

Freni, Mirella (*b* Modena, 27 Feb 1935). Italian soprano. She made her début at Modena in 1955 as Micaela, sang with the Netherlands Opera, then in 1960–62 appeared at Glyndebourne as Zerlina, Susanna and Adina. She has appeared at Covent Garden since 1961, La Scala since 1962 (both débuts as Nannetta), and the Met since 1965, at first in light lyric roles including Violetta and Mimì, but has successfully moved on to heavier ones such as Butterfly, Amelia (*Simon Boccanegra*) and Aida, adding weight and dramatic force to her appealing charm.

Frequency. The number of vibrations per second of a tone. It is normally measured in Hertz (Hz).

Freschi, Domenico (*b* Bassano del Grappa, *c*1630; *d* Vicenza, 2 July 1710). Italian composer. He worked at Vicenza Cathedral (*maestro di cappella* from 1656), and was active as an opera composer, particularly in Venice, and for the private Contarini theatre near Padua (for which he also wrote dramatic cantatas). His church music includes simple four-part hymn settings.

Frescobaldi, Girolamo (*b* Ferrara, mid-Sept 1583; *d* Rome, 1 March 1643). Italian composer and organist. He studied with Luzzaschi at Ferrara, where he also came under Gesualdo's influence. Soon after 1600 he went to Rome where in 1607 he became organist of S Maria in Trastevere. The same year he travelled with his patron, Guido Bentivoglio, to Brussels, but his experience of this centre of keyboard music left little imprint on him, except perhaps in the fantasias of 1608. In July 1608 Frescobaldi was elected organist of St Peter's, Rome; during the following years he was employed also by Cardinal Pietro Aldobrandini and other patrons.

In 1615 Frescobaldi secured a position with Duke Ferdinando Gonzaga at Mantua, but after three months he returned to Rome, remaining there until 1628 when he became organist at the Medici court in Florence. By the time he returned once more to Rome, in 1634, his fame was international and he was moving in the highest circles of patronage. In 1637 Froberger came from Vienna to study with him. Little is known of his other pupils, but his influence on keyboard playing and composition remained important for a century or more.

Frescobaldi is remembered chiefly for his keyboard music, much of which was published in 12 volumes (1608–14) with toccatas, canzonas, ricercares, dances and variations. The most famous is *Fiori musicali* (1635), with pieces for use in the Mass: the Kyrie-Christe unit from the Ordinary, toccatas to be played during the Elevation and other pieces corresponding to items of the Proper (introit, gradual, offertory, communion). Bach owned a copy and learnt from it.

Frescobaldi's vocal music is of relatively small importance. His sacred works, including *c*40 motets, mostly for one to three voices and continuo, show none of the complexity and expressive intensity of the keyboard works. Perhaps his most characteristic vocal music is in an early volume of madrigals (1608), but two volumes of *Arie musicali* published during Frescobaldi's years in Florence (1630) are also of interest.

Instrumental music over 130 keyboard works incl. toccatas, capriccios, fantasias, ricercares, variations, dances, some (incl. 3 organ masses) in Fiori musicali (1635); over 50 ensemble canzonas
Vocal music 2 masses; over 30 sacred pieces; 65 secular pieces (madrigals, songs)

Fresneau, Jehan (*b* Cambrai; *fl c*1470–1505). French composer. He held posts in the royal chapel (1470–75), the Duke of Milan's chapel choir (1476) and at Chartres Cathedral (1495–1505). A mass and five *chansons* by him survive, the latter in conventional style. He was considered a musician of some stature by his contemporaries.

Fret. A strip of gut, bone, ivory, wood or metal across the fingerboard of certain string instruments. The hard ridge of the fret, against which the finger presses the string, affects the tuning and restores something of the 'open string' quality to the sound. The lute, viol and guitar and the Indian sitar have frets.

Freyer, August (*b* Mulda, 15 Dec 1803; *d* Pilica, 28 May 1883). Polish organist, composer and teacher of German birth. As organist at the Evangelical Church in Warsaw for over 40 years, director of a free school of organ playing and a distinguished performer, he reawakened Polish interest in the declining art of the organ. Of his compositions the virtuoso organ works are still in the repertory.

Fricassée (Fr.). A kind of QUODLIBET popular in 16th-century France, usually nonsensical and sometimes obscene.

Frick, Gottlob (*b* Ölbronn, 28 July 1906). German bass. He sang at Coburg from 1934 and joined Karl Böhm at the Dresden Staatsoper in 1941. He sang at Covent Garden, 1951–71, and was heard at Bayreuth, Salzburg and the Met. His large, dark voice suited him to the Wagnerian repertory, Hagen and Gurnemanz being his best roles.

Fricker, Peter Racine (*b* London, 5 Sept 1920). English composer. He studied with Morris at the RCM (1937–41) and after the war with Seiber; he then taught in London before moving to Santa Barbara in 1964. He was the most prominent British composer to emerge after World War II, his free atonal style having much impact after a period when British music had been dominated by the pastoral folksong tradition. His early works were influenced by Bartók, Hindemith and Schoenberg and consisted mostly of orchestral and chamber pieces, notably the first three symphonies (1949, 1951, 1960) and concertos. Later works, in a fluent contrapuntal style, are more economical and concentrated; they include choral music and songs.

Fricsay, Ferenc (*b* Budapest, 9 Aug 1914; *d* Basle, 20 Feb 1963). Hungarian conductor. He was a pupil of Bartók and Kodály, with whom he became identified after his career began at Szeged (1936–44). He became musical director of the Budapest Opera in 1945. He was heard in Britain from 1950 and the USA from 1953 but his major work was with the Berlin Radio SO, (1948–52, 1956–63).

Friction drum. A drum sounded by friction. The membrane may be rubbed by the hand or by a stick which passes through a hole in the membrane. Played in Africa, Asia, Europe and South America, they are often associated with religion.

Frid, Géza (*b* Máramarossziget, 25 Jan 1904). Dutch composer and pianist of Hungarian origin. He studied with Bartók and Kodály at the Budapest Academy (1912–24) and settled in Amsterdam in 1929. He became internationally renowned for his Bartók performances and as an accompanist. His works (mostly instrumental) use novel techniques within a conventional style based on Hungarian folk music.

Friderici, Daniel (*b* Klein Eichstedt, 1584; *d* Rostock, 23 Sept 1638). German composer and writer. After a restless period of study he was appointed Kantor of St Marien, Rostock (1618), where he became a leading musical figure. He composed much music, both sacred and secular, preferring for the former texts from the Psalms and prophets which he set in predominantly homophonic style, occasionally varied to illustrate the text. His secular pieces are generally simple choral songs designed to drive out melancholy and encourage virtue. The influential treatise *Musica figuralis* (1618, eight edns) is notable for its rules on singing and the treatment of modes; it states that the beats should be regulated according to the words of the text, not by the regular stroke of a clock.

Friebert [Frieberth], (Johann) Joseph (*b* Gnadendorf, bap. 5 Dec 1724; *d* Passau, 6 Aug 1799). Austrian tenor and composer. After singing in Vienna, he was Kapellmeister at the Passau court from 1763, composing mostly stage works. His brother Karl Frieberth (1736–1816), also a tenor, served Prince Esterházy (under Haydn) until 1776, then became a Kapellmeister in Vienna; he wrote lieder and other vocal music.

Fried, Oskar (*b* Berlin, 1/10 Aug 1871; *d* Moscow, 5 July 1941). German conductor and composer. He studied briefly with Humperdinck and in Munich and made his reputation as both composer and conductor (notably of Mahler). He wrote many lieder and three successful large vocal-orchestral pieces, but after 1913 he gave up composing.

Friedenstag. Opera in one act by Richard Strauss to a libretto by Gregor after Calderón (1938, Munich).

Friml, (Charles) Rudolf (*b* Prague, 2 Dec 1879; *d* Los Angeles, 12 Nov 1972). American composer and pianist of Czech birth. He settled in the USA in 1906.

He wrote 30 operettas and revue scores, including *The Firefly* (1912), *Rose Marie* (1924), *The Vagabond King* (1925) and *The Three Musketeers* (1928). From 1925 he lived in Hollywood, writing new works and adapting his popular operettas for the screen.

Fritz, Gaspard (*b* Geneva, 18 Feb 1716; *d* there, 23 March 1783). Swiss composer and violinist. A virtuoso player in the Italian style, he was active in Geneva and performed in Paris. His compositions, including ornate violin sonatas, other chamber works and six symphonies (?1770–71), show Italian traits; some were highly successful.

Fritzsche, Gottfried (*b* Meissen, 1578; *d* Ottensen, 1638). German organ builder. An intimate of Praetorius, Schütz and Scheidt, he was one of the foremost German masters of his day. He was probably a pupil of Johann Lange, but he provided a wider range of stops. In 1626 he broke new ground by giving each of three manuals and the pedal-board (at St Ulrich, Brunswick) a separate Principal chorus. With this technique and many ingeniously differentiated new stops, he reformed organ building in Hamburg, notably with the instruments of St Katharinen and the Jakobikirche, helping to create the prototype of the Hanseatic Baroque organ, which remained standard for almost a century.

Frobenius. Danish firm of organ builders. Founded in 1909 at Copenhagen by Theodor Frobenius (1885–1972), it began building organs with mechanical action in 1944. The firm specializes in carefully designed modern casework and specifications following north German, early Baroque lines. Its important organs include those at St Jakobs, Copenhagen (1953) and Ribe Cathedral (1974).

Froberger, Johann Jacob (*b* Stuttgart, bap. 19 May 1616; *d* Héricourt, 6/7 May 1667). German composer and keyboard player. Trained at the Stuttgart court, he went in the 1630s to Vienna, where he became a court organist. He studied in Rome with Frescobaldi and made further travels, performing in the Low Countries, England, France and Germany. In 1653 he was made Vienna court organist, but he was released in 1658; lastly he worked as tutor to Princess Sibylla of Württemberg-Montbéliard at Héricourt.

Froberger was the foremost German keyboard composer of his day. By combining features of different national styles, he created a German keyboard style which became very influential after his death. Italian elements are prominent in his *c*70 toccatas, ricercares, fantasias, canzonas and capriccios for organ or harpsichord. His counterpoint is more conservative than Frescobaldi's, but his toccata structures point towards the later north German form of the toccata and fugue, and his thematic invention looks towards Bach. His best works are his 30 harpsichord suites, in which he combined French forms with a more expressive idiom and livelier textures. Among the earliest examples of their genre, they contain dance movements in various orderings; there are also laments, other character pieces and a variation suite, *Partita auff die Mayerin*. Froberger's only other surviving works are two sacred vocal pieces.

Frog. In a bow for string instruments, the device that secures the hair and holds it away from the bow stick at the lower end.

Frog Quartet. Nickname of Haydn's String Quartet in D op.50 no.6 (1787); it comes from the 'croaking' theme in the finale.

Fröhlich. Austrian family of singers. The most celebrated members were the sopranos Anna (1793–1880) and Josefine (1803–78). Their house was a well-known centre of musical activity, at which Schubert often played; at Anna's instigation he wrote works for her, for her pupils and for Josefine.

Fröhlich, Friedrich Theodor (*b* Brugg, 20 Feb 1803; *d* Aarau, 16 Oct 1836). Swiss composer. Influenced by his studies and friends in Berlin, he was a prolific composer of choral works and songs in Romantic style. Suffering from artistic isolation, he committed suicide, only later being recognized as a gifted composer.

Frøhlich, Johannes Frederik (*b* Copenhagen, 21 Aug 1806; *d* there, 21 May 1860). Danish composer, violinist and conductor of German descent. He was connected with the Royal Theatre, Copenhagen, from 1821, also becoming known as a composer of string quartets, overtures and ballets, one of which contains the popular Danish march *Riberhusmarch* (1843). His Symphony in E♭ op.33 (1830) marked a revival of Danish interest in the genre.

Froissart. Concert overture, op.19, by Elgar (1890).

From Bohemia's Woods and Fields [Z Českých luhů a hajů]. Symphonic poem by Smetana (1875), the fourth of his cycle *Má vlást*.

Fromm, Andreas (*b* Pänitz, 1621; *d* Prague, 16 Oct 1683). German composer. Kantor at the Marienkirche in Stettin, he is chiefly known for his innovatory oratorio *Actus musicus* (1649): he used instrumental sinfonias to represent affections and Protestant chorales in ornamented solos or as chorale fantasias. Influenced by Italian monody, the work demands a staged performance in church and was published together with a *Dialogus Pentecostalis* which provides further evidence of his dramatic leanings.

Fromm Music Foundation. Institution, based at Harvard University, founded in 1952 by Paul Fromm; it promotes contemporary music by commissioning works and sponsoring concerts, including the annual Tanglewood Festival of Contemporary Music.

From my Life [Z mého života; Aus meinem Leben]. Smetana's autobiographical String Quartet no.1 in E minor (1876); he gave the same title to the Quartet no.2 in D minor (1883) but the title is now used only for no.1.

From the House of the Dead [Z mrtvého domu]. Opera in three acts by Janáček to his own libretto after Dostoyevsky (1930, Brno).

From the New World. *See* NEW WORLD, FROM THE.

Frottola. A type of north Italian polyphonic song of the period *c*1470–1530, sometimes known as *barzelletta*. It embraces a variety of poetic forms, including the ode, sonnet, *strambotto*, *capitolo* and *canzone*. Most early frottolas are for three voices, the later ones for four, with the main tune in the soprano.

Rhythms are simple and straightforward and the texture basically homophonic. Some were adapted for voice and lute and lower parts were probably often played on viols, winds or even a keyboard instrument. 11 books of frottolas were printed by Petrucci in 1504–14. The chief centre of frottola writing was Mantua, where the leading composers, Tromboncino and Cara, worked.

Frühbeck de Burgos, Rafael (*b* Burgos, 15 Sept 1933). Spanish conductor. He studied at Bilbao and Madrid and later at Munich. In 1962 he became chief conductor of the Madrid National Orchestra, and later held posts at Düsseldorf, Montreal and Washington, DC. He is noted for the vigour and discipline of his performances.

Frumerie, (Per) Gunnar (Fredrik) de (*b* Nacka, 20 July 1908). Swedish composer. He studied at the Stockholm Conservatory (1923–8) and began teaching there in 1945. Of impulsive and florid temperament, he has composed much in many genres, especially concertos, chamber and piano music; he has few Swedish equals in the field of song and wrote an opera, *Singoalla* (1940).

Fry, William Henry (*b* Philadelphia, 19 Aug 1813; *d* Santa Cruz, Virgin Islands, 21 Dec 1864). American composer and critic. He wrote three operas, notably *Leonora* (1845, Philadelphia; possibly the first public performance of a grand opera by a native American), and numerous orchestral works, besides campaigning in the New York press for a native American musical art. His admonitions encouraged Bristow and others; but his own music remained rooted in the French and Italian operatic and German symphonic traditions of the early 19th century.

Frye, Walter (*fl c*1450–75). English composer. He may have been in charge of the lay choir at Ely Cathedral from 1443–4 or earlier and was probably the Walter Frye who joined the London Gild of Parish Clerks in 1456–7. The will of a man with the same name was proved at Canterbury in 1475. His works are characteristically English in style but seem to have enjoyed a remarkable vogue on the Continent. His three mass cycles are based on tenor *cantus firmi* (*Flos regalis*, *Nobilis et pulchra* and *Summe Trinitati*) and are unified by motto themes. Of his other works only *Sospitati dedit* is based on chant. *Salve virgo* may be a version of the missing Kyrie from the *Summe Trinitati* Mass, but the remaining compositions may all have originated as songs, though most also exist with sacred texts.

Fuchs, Aloys (*b* Rázová, 22 June 1799; *d* Vienna, 20 March 1853). Austrian librarian and writer on music. His important music library (now dispersed) was rich in early printed editions and in autographs of works by Bach, Handel, Haydn, Gluck, Mozart and Beethoven; his epoch-making catalogues and published articles relate chiefly to Gluck and Mozart.

Fuchs, Robert (*b* Frauenthal, 15 Feb 1847; *d* Vienna, 19 Feb 1927). Austrian composer, teacher, organist and conductor. From 1875 he was conductor of the orchestral society of the Gesellschaft der Musikfreunde and professor at the Vienna Conservatory, where his pupils included Mahler, Sibelius,

Schrecker, Wolf and Zemlinsky. Brahms thought highly of his compositions, especially the prize-winning First Symphony (1885). His brother Johann Nepomuk (1842–99), an opera conductor and editor, became director of the conservatory in 1893.

Fučík, Julius (Arnošt Vilém) (*b* Prague, 18 July 1872; *d* Berlin, 25 Sept 1916). Czech composer. He studied with Dvořák at the Prague Conservatory (1885–91) and worked as an orchestral player and bandmaster, producing almost 300 dances, marches and overtures.

Fuenllana, Miguel de (*b* Navalcarnero, early 16th century; *d* after 1568). Spanish composer and vihuelist. He was *músico de cámara* to Elisabeth de Valois (1562–8). His only known work is *Orphénica lyra* (1554), which contains 52 fantasias by him for vihuela, in the polyphonic, full-textured style typical of Morales' generation; more than half the book consists of arrangements of vocal works by other composers, among them Josquin, Morales and Verdelot.

Fugato (It.). Term used for a fugal passage in an otherwise non-contrapuntal movement.

Fugger. German family of merchants and bankers. Under their patronage Augsburg flourished throughout the Renaissance as a centre of art, literature and music. Over 40 printed music volumes were dedicated to members of the family by such composers as Aichinger, Eccard, A. and G. Gabrieli, Hassler, Lassus and Monte.

Fughetta. A short or 'light' FUGUE.

Fuging-tune [fuguing-tune, fugue-tune]. An Anglo-American psalm tune or hymn tune which contains one or more groups of contrapuntal voice entries involving textual overlap. It originated in Britain and was taken up in the late 18th century by American composers, notably William Billings.

Fugue (Ger. *Fuge*; It. *fuga*). A composition, or compositional technique, in which a theme (or themes) is extended and developed mainly by imitative counterpoint.

In the opening section, the 'exposition', the main theme or 'subject' is announced in the tonic, after which the second 'voice' enters with the ANSWER, i.e. the same theme at the dominant (or subdominant) pitch (but *see also* DOUBLE FUGUE) while the first may proceed to a COUNTER-SUBJECT. This procedure is repeated at different octaves until all the voices have entered and the exposition is complete. An extra statement of the subject or answer following on the exposition is called a 'redundant entry'; a set of such entries is a 'counter-exposition'.

The exposition is the only essential for the definition of a piece as a fugue, but most fugues proceed to further entries of the subject, which may be separated by 'episodes', often based on material from the exposition. The 'middle entries', normally in keys other than the tonic or dominant, may treat the theme in stretto (with overlapping entries) or vary it in some way. In 'augmentation' the note values are lengthened; in 'diminution' they are shortened; in 'inversion' the subject is upside down. A 'false entry' begins the subject but does not complete it. The final entry of the subject is usually in the tonic key.

The term *fuga* was used from the late Middle Ages to the early Baroque for strict imitation or canon, but fugal writing in the modern sense first appears in 16th-century vocal polyphony and in instrumental forms, including the ricercare, fantasia and canzone, derived from it. *Fuga*, in its present sense, appears alongside 'fantasia' in the *Tabulature nova* (1624) of Scheidt. Another kind of fugue emerged from the keyboard toccatas of Froberger and Buxtehude, and the idea of including fugal passages in the toccata led to the 'prelude and fugue' combination. J.C.F. Fischer's *Ariadne musica* (1702) is a collection of preludes and fugues in various keys which served as an example for Bach's '48'. Bach's two volumes contain some of his greatest fugues but did not exhaust his command of fugal technique. His suites, concertos and cantatas frequently combine fugue and ritornello form, and he introduced the combination of the subject and a number of counter-subjects in various vertical permutations. In the *Art of Fugue* he explored the potentialities of a single main theme in a cycle of 14 fugues, including pairs of invertible or mirror fugues, a species unique to this work. Handel's oratorio fugues, by contrast, aim at broader, more dramatic effects and tend to become homophonic at climaxes, as do his instrumental fugues.

The use of fugal material in Classical sonata-style movements was common – it has a special significance in the late piano sonatas and string quartets of Beethoven – and fugues were considered almost *de rigueur* in liturgical music throughout the 19th century. At the same time it ceased to be a normal mode of expression and became increasingly associated with academicism. Mendelssohn's E minor fugue op.35 no.1 is a good example of the Baroque fugue seen through the eyes of a Romantic composer, and both Schumann and Brahms, with their academic leanings, made significant use of fugue in a number of works. Less predictable is Verdi's mastery of fugal technique in the Requiem and the final scene of *Falstaff*.

In the 20th century a return to an essentially contrapuntal outlook and to Baroque ideals brought a temporary revival of interest in fugue. Hindemith's *Ludus tonalis* and Shostakovich's 24 Preludes and Fugues, both for piano, are modern equivalents of Bach's '48', and the first movement of Bartók's Music for Strings, Percussion and Celesta is a notable example of the use of traditional fugal procedures in a harmonic idiom based on the tritone.

Führer, Robert (Jan Nepomuk) (*b* Prague, 2 June 1807; *d* Vienna, 28 Nov 1861). Czech composer and organist. He studied with Vitásek and was an organist at Prague Cathedral. A prolific, popular composer, he wrote over 400 works, mostly sacred, in an appealing lyrical style; the finest include his Mass in A♭ (1843) and the oratorio *Christus im Leiden und im Tode*.

Fukushima, Kazuo (*b* Tokyo, 11 April 1930). Japanese composer. Self-taught, he associated with Takemitsu, Yuasa and others in the 1950s. His works, usually for small ensembles, are often meditative and have connections with gagaku and noh music.

Fuleihan, Anis (*b* Kyrenia, 2 April 1900; *d* Stanford, 11 Oct 1970). American composer of Cypriot origin. He arrived in the USA in 1915 and was mostly self-taught in composition. He taught at Indiana University (1947–53), then lived mostly in Beirut and Tunis. His first works have an oriental colouring, but he became less inclined towards that style after visiting the Near East in 1924–8; his music also became less dissonant. He is best known for his orchestral music, which includes three piano concertos (1936, 1937, 1963) and two symphonies (1936, 1962).

Full cadence, full close [authentic cadence; perfect cadence]. A CADENCE consisting of a dominant chord followed by a tonic chord (V–I), both normally in root position.

Fuller Maitland, J(ohn) A(lexander) (*b* London, 7 April 1856; *d* Carnforth, 30 March 1936). English critic and scholar. He studied at Cambridge and with W.S. Rockstro; in 1889 he became music critic of *The Times*, holding that post for 22 years, during which period he edited *Grove 2*, contributed to *The Oxford History of Music* and worked on an edition of the Fitzwilliam Virginal Book. He was also involved in editing folksong collections and music by Purcell and published several monographs on Bach and 19th-century composers.

Fumagalli. Italian family of musicians. The most celebrated members were Adolfo (1828–56), a renowned pianist and composer of over 100 salon pieces for piano, and his brother Luca (1837–1908), also a pianist and composer.

Funcke, Friedrich (*b* Nossen, 1642; *d* Römstedt, 20 Oct 1699). German composer and writer. As Kantor of St Johannis, Lüneburg (1664–94), he composed much music for civic occasions including a large-scale concerto (1666) with descriptive music in commemoration of a damaging storm. An original and dramatic *St Matthew Passion* (*c*1668–74), important in the history of the Passion oratorio, is attributed to him.

Functional analysis. A form of musical analysis put forward by Hans Keller in the 1950s and 1960s, based on the postulation that 'contrasts are but different aspects of a single basic idea, a background unity'. In his analyses, which latterly were wordless (i.e. conducted purely in music itself), Keller aimed to elucidate the way in which an entire musical structure proceeded from a single, cell-like 'basic idea'. His method was applied chiefly to music from the Classical era to the Second Viennese School. *See* ANALYSIS.

Fundamental. In acoustics, the lowest note in a harmonic series of frequencies that are multiples of its frequency.

Fundamental bass. *See* BASSE FONDAMENTALE.

Funeral march. A slow, ceremonial MARCH. Marches have often been used within larger works for their specific meaning or emotional suggestiveness. Well-known examples include the Dead March from Handel's *Saul* (1739), Beethoven's 'Marcia funebre sulla morte d'un eroe' from his Piano Sonata in A♭ op.26 (1800–01) and the slow movement of his Symphony no.3 in E♭ ('Eroica', 1803), the 'Marche

funèbre' (1837) in Chopin's Piano Sonata in B♭ minor op.35 (he also wrote another, in C minor, 1827) and Siegfried's Funeral March in Wagner's *Götterdämmerung* (1876); Mahler's Symphony no.1 in D (1888) includes a parody funeral march based on a minor-key version of *Frère Jacques*.

Für Elise. Bagatelle in A minor for piano by Beethoven (1810), of which the autograph is inscribed 'Für Elise'.

Furiant (Cz.). An exuberant Bohemian folkdance in which 2/4 and 3/4 metre alternate. Stylized examples are in 3/4 though with accents to make clear its rhythmic character. Dvořák wrote several, for piano, and in his orchestral music (Symphony no.6 in D) and his chamber music (Piano Quintet in A op.81).

Furlanetto, Bonaventura (*b* Venice, 27 May 1738; *d* there, 6 April 1817). Italian composer. From 1768 he was *maestro* at S Maria della Visitazione (the Pietà), Venice. Later he had duties at St Mark's and *c*1808 became *maestro di cappella* there; by then he ranked as Venice's foremost sacred composer. His large output includes *c*25 oratorios, sacred cantatas, solo motets and other sacred works, many of them for the Pietà. Such early works as the highly successful oratorio *Giubilo celeste al giungervi della sant' anima* (1765) use a simple theatrical style; later works include parts for highly skilled singers and unusual instruments. He also wrote a few secular and instrumental pieces and at least one counterpoint treatise.

Furno, Giovanni (*b* Capua, 1 Jan 1748; *d* Naples, 20 June 1837). Italian teacher. He taught in Naples from 1772 and was later considered the Conservatory's best teacher; Bellini was among his most famous pupils. He composed several vocal and keyboard works.

Fürstenau. German family of musicians. The most celebrated members were Anton Bernhard (1792–1852), a flautist and flute composer who worked under Weber in Dresden and was praised for the expressiveness of his playing, and his son Moritz (1824–89), a flautist and composer who wrote on musical life in Dresden.

Furtwängler, (Gustav Heinrich Ernst Martin) Wilhelm (*b* Berlin, 25 Jan 1886; *d* Baden-Baden, 30 Nov 1954). German conductor and composer. His ambition was to be a composer but by 1907 he had conducted his first concert, at Munich. After appointments at Breslau, Zurich, Munich and Strasbourg he became director of the Lübeck Opera (1911–15). There and at the Mannheim Opera (1915–20) he became established as the leading young German conductor. He conducted orchestras in Frankfurt and Berlin from 1920; from 1928 he was in charge of the Leipzig Gewandhaus Orchestra and the Berlin PO. He was a regular visitor to London from 1924 (he gave *Tristan* and the *Ring* in the 1930s) and was heard in the USA from 1925. Although he often conducted the Vienna PO he was most closely associated with the Berlin PO, touring with it throughout Europe. An ambivalent relationship with the Nazi regime led him in 1934 to resign his posts (earlier in the year he had given the first performance of Hindemith's *Mathis der Maler* symphony, which was denounced by Goebbels).

Furtwängler resumed his career in 1935 and after leaving Germany in 1945 enjoyed a successful career in Milan, Salzburg, Berlin and London, though he was not able to conduct in the USA.

His art lay in his ability to approach each performance as a spontaneous re-creation of the composer's thought. He cultivated an imprecise beat to achieve a large, unforced sonority and allowed fluctuations of tempo that conveyed through a mastery of transition a unique spiritual insight. The German Classics were at the centre of his repertory, but he also conducted Tchaikovsky, Berlioz and Debussy and gave the first performances of Bartók's First Piano Concerto and, less successfully, Schoenberg's Orchestral Variations. His compositions include three symphonies, settings of Goethe for chorus, and chamber and piano music.

Fusz, János (*b* Tolna, 16 Dec 1777; *d* Budapest, 9 March 1819). Hungarian composer. He worked mainly in Vienna, where he studied with Albrechtsberger, writing stage works, chamber music and lieder; his most important composition is a prelude to Schiller's *Die Braut von Messina* (1811).

Futurism. A movement initiated by the writer F.T. Marinetti (1876–1942) in 1909, primarily in the visual arts, concerned with establishing an art appropriate to an industrial society. It was adapted to music by the composer F.B. Pratella (1880–1955) and Luigi Russolo (1885–1947), a painter who turned to music in 1913 and created works made up of noises from 'intonarumori' ('noise-intoners'). A few other composers briefly took up futurist ideals, but interest soon faded; however, the movement may have had some influence on Varèse and possibly Mosolov (*The Foundry*, 1928). Some aspects of musical futurism anticipated the methods of *musique concrète* and electronic music.

Fux, Johann Joseph (*b* Hirtenfeld, 1660; *d* Vienna, 13 Feb 1741). Austrian composer and theorist. He settled in Vienna in the 1690s and worked as organist at the Schottenkirche until 1702. Gaining favour at the imperial court, he became court composer (1698), vice-Kapellmeister (1713) and principal Kapellmeister (1715). He was also vice-Kapellmeister at St Stephen's Cathedral, 1705–12, and Kapellmeister, 1712–15. Among his occasional works was the coronation opera *Constanza e Fortezza* (1723), lavishly produced in Prague). He continued composing into old age, and was also a famous teacher.

Foremost in Fux's output are over 400 church works, including *c*80 masses. He is most noted for his unaccompanied polyphony, modelled on Palestrina's and found in such works as the *Messa di San Carlo* (1718). Counterpoint is also a feature of his accompanied church music and other works, among them 20 operas, 13 oratorios and over 100 instrumental works (mostly church sonatas, partitas and overtures). His operas and oratorios are both monumental and expressive, and include ornamentation and dance-like melodies. His *Gradus ad Parnassum* (1725), the most important modern textbook on counterpoint, influenced many later composers. Fux's works form the culmination of Baroque music in Austria.

Fuzelier, Louis (*b* Paris, 24 Oct 1674; *d* there, 19 Sept 1752). French librettist and dramatist. He wrote many successful plays with music (later known as *opéras comiques*) for Paris, many of them parodies of other works. Among his librettos are the first examples of *ballet héroïque*, notably Rameau's *Les Indes galantes* (1735). He favoured unusual subjects and novel stage effects.

G

G. Name of a note, or a PITCH CLASS; *see also* PITCH NAMES. G is the fifth degree (or dominant) of the scale of C major. Followed by a numeral, it identifies a work by Boccherini by its number in Yves Gérard's thematic catalogue (1969), or a work by Beethoven by its number in the list published in the second edition of *Grove's Dictionary* (1904–10), which supplements the existing opus numbers by assigning new ones (beyond 138) to works that lack them.

Gabrieli, Andrea (*b* Venice, 1533; *d* there, 30 Aug 1585). Italian composer. Possibly a pupil of Willaert, in 1557–8 he was organist of S Geremia, Cannaregio, and in 1562 was working in Munich, where he met Lassus. In 1566 he became organist of St Mark's, Venice, where he remained all his life. A prolific and exceptionally versatile composer, he was a leading figure in Venice, respected as a performer and teacher, and one of the most important figures of his generation. He composed masses (1572), motets (1565, 1576) and psalms (1583), as well as secular and instrumental works (1566–80); many pieces were published posthumously by his nephew Giovanni. He is chiefly famous for his sacred ceremonial music (notably *Concerti*, 1587), in which he brilliantly exploited the architecture of St Mark's, separating voices and instruments into *cori spezzati* to create imposing stereophonic effects, a style that greatly influenced other Venetian and German composers. His madrigals are more lightweight and homophonic than others of the time, some showing Lassus's influence.

Sacred music c130 motets, many in Concerti (1587); 7 masses (1 inc.); psalms
Secular vocal music c190 madrigals; choruses for the tragedy Edippo Tiranno (1588); 3 mascheratas (1601)
Instrumental music over 50 canzonas, ricercares, preludes, toccatas, kbd; 3 org masses; ensemble ricercares; battaglia for wind

Gabrieli, Giovanni (*b* Venice, c1553–6; *d* there, Aug 1612). Italian composer, nephew of Andrea Gabrieli. Like his uncle, with whom he studied, he worked briefly at the Munich court (c1575–8) and in 1585 he became organist of St Mark's, Venice, and of the confraternity of S Rocco, posts he held for the rest of his life. After Andrea's death, he edited many of his works for publication. His own fame and influence were widespread and crucial, notably in northern Europe – Schütz was among his many pupils – and he represents the highest point of the High Renaissance Venetian school. He composed motets and mass movements (*Symphoniae sacrae*, 1597, 1615, MSS), instrumental ensemble music (1597, 1615, MSS) and organ works (1593, MSS), as well as a few madrigals (1587 and anthologies). Much of his sacred ceremonial music exploits the architecture of St Mark's, using contrasting groups of singers and players to create *cori spezzati* effects, but often in a more intense and dissonant style than his uncle's. His music for wind ensemble is lively and colourful and includes up-to-date concertato writing; the organ ricercares are in a well-developed and specific keyboard style.

Sacred vocal music 94 motets, incl. In ecclesiis, Timor et tremor, many in Symphoniae sacrae (1597, 1615); 7 mass movts; 7 Magnificats
Secular vocal music c30 madrigals
Instrumental music c50 ensemble canzonas, sonatas, incl. Sonata pian e forte (1597), Sonata for 3 vns (1615); over 60 kbd ricercares, canzonas, toccatas

Gabrieli Quartet. British string quartet, led by Kenneth Sillito. Founded in 1966, it has toured widely abroad and is noted for its well-balanced performances of the standard repertory and its championship of 20th-century music.

Gabrielli, Caterina (*b* Rome, 12 Nov 1730; *d* there, 16 Feb/April 1796). Italian soprano. Already famous in Italy, she sang in Vienna, 1755–8, becoming a protégée of Metastasio and a favourite of Gluck and Traetta. Later she sang at centres including St Petersburg (1772–5) and London (1775–6), retiring in 1782. She was known as one of the most intelligent and perfect singers of her time.

Gabrielli, Domenico (*b* Bologna, 15 April 1651; *d* there, 10 July 1690). Italian composer. A pupil of Legrenzi, he was a cellist at S Petronio, Bologna, from 1680. Although he composed operas (12, 1682–94), oratorios and cantatas that show a flair for the dramatic, his significance lies primarily in his virtuosity as a cellist and as composer of some of the earliest music for the instrument. His canons, ricercares and sonatas show an advanced technique and acute awareness of sonority. Besides further chamber music he wrote two sonatas (with orchestra) for his other favoured instrument, the trumpet, and often used this and the cello in a concertante manner, or as obbligato instruments, in his vocal music.

Gabrilowitsch, Ossip (Salomonovich) (*b* St Petersburg, 7 Feb 1878; *d* Detroit, 14 Sept 1936). American pianist and conductor. He studied the piano with A. Rubinstein and later with Leschetizky in Vienna, making his début in Berlin (1896). He first went to America in 1900. He conducted in Munich, 1910–14, then the Detroit SO, 1918–35, but continued playing the piano and accompanying his wife, the contralto Clara Clemens. He was admired for his delicate yet expressively penetrating style.

Gaburo, Kenneth (Louis) (*b* Somerville, NJ, 5 July 1926). American composer. He studied with Rogers at the Eastman School and Petrassi in Rome (1954–5), and has taught at the University of Illinois (1955–68) and San Diego. Much of his music is connected with experiments with verbal language and vocal performance, for example *Antiphonies II* and *III* (1962) and the *Lingua* series (1965–70). He founded and conducted several groups called 'New Music Choral Ensemble' (NMCE).

Gace Brulé (*b* ?Champagne, *c*1160; *d* after 1213). French trouvère. He probably lived in the Meaux area and spent some time at the Breton court and the court of the Countess of Brie and Champagne. Possibly he took part in the third or fourth crusade, or both. He was the most prolific and one of the best known of the early trouvères; his popularity derives more from the fact that he satisfied the conventions of his time than from any particular originality. He left more than 60 songs, and some 20 more have been attributed to him.

Gade, Niels (Wilhelm) (*b* Copenhagen, 22 Feb 1817; *d* there, 21 Dec 1890). Danish composer, the most important figure in 19th-century Danish music. He trained as a violinist and played in the Royal Orchestra, Copenhagen, producing his official op.1, the prize-winning concert overture *Efterklange af Ossian* in 1840. Encouraged by Mendelssohn, who was enthusiastic about his First Symphony (1841–2), he went to Leipzig as an assistant conductor of the Gewandhaus Orchestra, also meeting Schumann and composing the Mendelssohnian Third Symphony (1847) and String Octet (1848). In Copenhagen he reorganized the Musical Society, establishing a permanent orchestra and choir which gave the premières of his Symphonies nos.4–8 and his large choral works ('Koncertstykke'), notably *Comala* (1846), and serving as co-director of the Copenhagen Academy of Music. Although the personal, Scandinavian colouring of his early works gave way to the German Romantic influence in his music after *c*1850, he had an immense influence on the next generation of Danish composers.

Gadski, Johanna (*b* Anklam, 15 June 1872; *d* Berlin, 22 Feb 1932). German soprano. She sang in Berlin from 1889 and in 1895 appeared as Elsa in New York, with the Damrosch Company. She sang Aida at Covent Garden (1898–1901) and appeared at the Met (1900–17). Until her retirement she often sang Verdi, and brought to Wagnerian roles an unfailing beauty of voice and purity of style.

Gaffi, Tommaso Bernardo (*b* Rome, 1665–70; *d* there, 11 Feb 1744). Italian composer. He was organist at various Roman churches before succeeding his teacher Pasquini at S Maria in Aracoeli (1710). He wrote at least seven oratorios, and 12 chamber cantatas (1700) unusual for their arias with obbligato instruments, including the harpsichord.

Gaffurius [Gafurius, Gafori], **Franchinus** (*b* Lodi, 14 Jan 1451; *d* Milan, 25 June 1522). Italian theorist and composer. He entered the priesthood in 1474 and, after periods in Lodi, Mantua and Verona (1474–7) and Genoa (1477–8), he went to Naples, where he met Tinctoris, who became a close friend. After a year as director of music at Bergamo Cathedral, in 1484 he became *maestro di cappella* of Milan Cathedral, establishing himself as one of the leading and renowned musical figures of his time. He enjoyed the friendship of many *litterati*, composers and artists, among them Leonardo da Vinci. His three most important treatises, *Theorica musicae* (1492), *Practica musicae* (1496) and *De harmonia musicorum instrumentorum opus* (1518), offer a course of study in theoretical and practical music and show conservative and progressive tendencies. Most of his extant music, which includes masses, motets, Magnificats, hymns and madrigals, was composed for Milan Cathedral. His influence in the history of music theory is considerable and his erudition, research and humanistic views stamp him a true Renaissance man.

Gafori, Franchino. *See* GAFFURIUS, FRANCINUS.

Gagaku. The traditional court music of medieval Japan, originally derived from China. There are various genres of gagaku, including *bugaku* ('dance music'), *komagaku* ('Korean music') and *tōgaku* ('Tang music'), performed on combinations, normally including two plucked instruments, three wind, a gong and drums. The style is smooth and precise; the tempo is initially slow but later fast.

Gagliano. Italian family of violin makers. They were active in Naples from *c*1700 to the mid-19th century. The instruments of Nicola and his brother Gennaro (both *fl c*1740–*c*1780), sons of the first maker in the family and the first known Neapolitan maker Alessandro (*fl c*1700–*c*1735), are the most sought after of the Gaglianos' work. They show the influence of Stradivari, the cellos in particular being good; tonally they tend towards brightness. Gennaro often made Amati copies, but he and Nicola also introduced the very narrow cello design used by most later Neapolitans.

Gagliano, Marco da (*b* Florence, 1 May 1582; *d* there, 25 Feb 1643). Italian composer. He first worked at S Lorenzo, Florence (from 1602), and took part in performances by the Compagnia dell' Arcangelo Raffaello, becoming its *maestro di cappella* in 1609. In 1607 he founded the Accademia degli Elevati, a society of leading Florentine musicians. In this period he had contact with the Mantuan court, where his opera *Dafne* was successfully staged in 1608. He was *maestro di cappella* of Florence Cathedral from 1608 and of the Medici court from 1608–9, composing for both establishments. Later he also held ecclesiastical posts.

Gagliano's *Dafne*, to a text by Rinuccini, is a milestone in the early history of opera. It is much less austere in style than similar works by other Florentines, and like Monteverdi's *Orfeo* it includes traditional genres – airs, duets, trios and choruses – as well as recitative passages. His other opera, *La Flora* (1628, Florence), is similar in style; this and others of his stage works were composed with Jacopo Peri. His secular vocal music, much acclaimed in his time, includes some 90 madrigals and several monodies (notably *Valli profonde*, 1615). The madrigals (mostly in five parts) are often homophonic, and the later ones are especially direct in expression. He also composed well over 100 sacred works, among them Latin masses, motets etc and some spiritual madrigals; they range from monodies to double-choir settings. His Holy Week responsories (1630–31) remained in use long after his death.

His brother Giovanni Battista (1594–1651) succeeded him as *maestro di cappella* of Florence Cathedral and the Medici court in 1643, and wrote occasional and sacred music, including two oratorios (lost) and *Varie musiche* (1623, unusual in grouping madrigalian and strophic pieces with sacred works).

Gagliarda (It.). GALLIARD.

Gagnebin, Henri (*b* Liège, 13 March 1886; *d* Geneva, 2 June 1977). Swiss composer. He studied in Lausanne, Berlin, Geneva and Paris (with d'Indy) and was director of the Geneva Conservatory (1925–57). His large output extends from Franckism towards Stravinsky and includes three symphonies (1911, 1921, 1955).

Gai (Fr.). Merry, cheerful.

Gaita. A double-reed instrument of southern Europe, the Middle East and Latin America. The term, variously spelt (*gaida, gajde, gajdy, ghayta* etc), comes from the Gothic *gait* or *ghaid* ('goat') and originally denoted a bagpipe with a goatskin bag; in southeastern Europe it still signifies a bagpipe.

Gál, Hans (*b* Brunn, 5 Aug 1890; *d* 3 Oct 1987). Austrian musicologist and composer. He studied with Mandyczewski at Vienna University (1908–13) and taught there (1919–29). In 1945 he was appointed lecturer at Edinburgh University and he played a leading role in the city's musical life as a conductor and pianist. His works include early operas, symphonies, string quartets and much choral music etc, in a traditional Austro-German style. Among his writings are studies of Brahms and Schubert.

Galamian, Ivan (Alexander) (*b* Tabriz, 23 Jan 1903; *d* New York, 14 April 1981). American violinist and teacher of Iranian birth. He studied in Moscow and Paris (début 1924). After moving to the USA in 1937 he was appointed to the Curtis Institute in 1944 and the Juilliard School in 1946. His rational, analytical approach benefited such pupils as Perlman, Zukerman, Laredo and Zukovsky.

Galán, Cristóbal (*b c*1630; *d* Madrid, 24 Sept 1684). Spanish composer. He directed the choir at Segovia Cathedral (1664–7), moving to Madrid, where in 1680 he became music director of the royal chapel. Composing in most of the current vocal forms, he wrote many secular and devotional villancicos for one to 13 voices.

Galant. Term, from the French word for 'gallant' (also implying 'elegant', 'courtly'), used in the 18th century for music in a graceful style, with lightly accompanied, periodic melodies. It implies, in tune with Enlightenment ideals, music that is clear, pleasing and 'natural' as opposed to the elaborate counterpoint of the previous generation. Typical composers are Vinci, Hasse, G.B. Sammartini, J.C. Bach and the young Mozart. Although a term of praise when the style prevailed, *galant* later became identified with lightness and even triviality.

Galanterie. In the early 18th century, a German term for an up-to-date work, in the GALANT style, especially a keyboard piece. The term has sometimes been supposed, without good reason, to refer to the light pieces placed between the sarabande and gigue in the classical suite.

Galeazzi, Francesco (*b* Turin, 1758; *d* Rome, Jan 1819). Italian theorist. He worked in Rome as a violin teacher, composer and theatre music director, and later lived in Ascoli. His *Elementi teorico-pratici di musica* (1791–6), the most comprehensive 18th-century Italian treatise, is a key to the understanding of the Classical style. It contains the earliest known description of sonata form in thematic terms.

Galilei, Vincenzo (*b* S Maria a Monte, probably late 1520s; *d* Florence, bur. 2 July 1591). Italian theorist and composer. A pupil of Zarlino in Venice, he lived in Padua and from 1572 in Florence. With Giovanni de' Bardi among his patrons, he became a leading member of the Camerata; through his published writings (notably *Dialogo*, 1581) he advocated the revival through monody of the ancient Greek union of poetry and music. His output includes madrigals, lute pieces and an important treatise on lute playing (*Fronimo*, 1568).

Galimberti, Ferdinando (*fl c*1730–50). Italian composer. Active in Milan, he composed sacred music and instrumental works; his *c*12 symphonies are among the earliest written. His style resembles that of G.B. Sammartini.

Galindo Dimas, Blas (*b* Venustiano Carranza, 3 Feb 1910). Mexican composer. He studied with Chávez at the Mexico City Conservatory, of which he became director (1947–61). His works have embraced all the current vogues from peppery folklore through dissonant, contrapuntal abstracts to light shows; they include seven ballets performed in Mexico City (1940–52).

Galin-Paris-Chevé method. A French system of teaching sight-singing, based on a system proposed by Rousseau in 1742 but modified by the three people whose name it bears. It uses a numeral system of notation, numbering the notes from 1 to 7, with dots above or below to signify a change of octave. Coupled with a series of syllables to define rhythm, it was widely used in France and then elsewhere in the second half of the 19th century.

Galli, Amintore (*b* Rimini, 12 Oct 1845; *d* there, 8/13 Dec 1919). Italian critic, teacher and composer. He was in charge of Sonzogno's music publishing and taught at the Milan Conservatory, also writing historical and pedagogical works, editing periodicals and composing.

Galli, Filippo (*b* Rome, 1783; *d* Paris, 3 June 1853). Italian bass. He appeared in over 60 different operas at La Scala, Milan, including 26 first performances, but he is remembered mainly for the roles Rossini wrote for him, especially Maometto (1820) and Assur in *Semiramide* (1823).

Galliard. A lively, triple-metre court dance of the 16th–17th centuries, often associated with the PAVAN. A feature was the use of hemiola. It probably originated in northern Italy, but the earliest surviving music was published in Paris by Attaingnant in 1529–30. Most 16th-century galliards are in a simple homophonic style with the tune in the upper part; some are thematically related to a preceding pavan. The galliard survived into the 17th century but in its later style became quite a slow piece.

Galliard, John Ernest (*b*?Celle, *c*1687; *d* London, 1749). German composer. He settled in London in 1706 as an oboist to Prince George of Denmark and from 1710 was also organist at Somerset House. As a composer he concentrated on stage music. His early attempts at all-sung English opera, *Calypso and Telemachus* (1712) and *Circe* (1719), were unsuccessful, but he achieved popularity with his eight pantomimes of 1723–36, such as *The Rape of Proserpine* (1727), which include much operatic music. He also wrote a third all-sung opera (1741), masques, sacred music, cantatas and sonatas for recorder and bassoon. His dramatic works contain evocative writing and fluent English word-setting. He translated Tosi's singing treatise as *Observations on the Florid Song* (1742).

Gallican rite, Music of the. The tradition of monophonic liturgical music used in the Christian churches of Gaul before Gregorian (Roman) chant was imposed under Pepin (*d* 768) and Charlemagne (*d* 814). Remnants of this tradition survive in the Gregorian repertory and elsewhere. Differences include the preference for two recitation notes in psalmody, the importance of melismatic chants and the use of expressive effects; certain liturgical peculiarities are paralleled in Ambrosian and Mozarabic chant. In a more general sense, 'Gallican' is sometimes used to mean 'non-Roman', and 'Gallican chant' the chant of the churches of the Iberian peninsula, Septimania, Merovingian and Belgic Gaul, the Celtic areas and (in part) Milan.

Galliculus [Alectorius, Hähnel], **Johannes** (*fl* early 16th century). German theorist and composer. He was in Leipzig in 1520, when his successful counterpoint treatise, the *Isagoge*, was published there. His music, all sacred, includes a *St Mark Passion*, three Magnificats and nine motets; he became closely allied to the Wittenberg Church through his friend Georg Rhau, who included many works by Galliculus in the collections he published for the new church.

Galli-Curci, Amelita (*b* Milan, 18 Nov 1882; *d* La Jolia, CA, 26 Nov 1963). Italian soprano of Italian-Spanish parentage. She was largely self-taught and made her début in 1906. In Europe and in South and Central America she became successful as a coloratura. At Chicago (1916–36) and the Met (1921–30) she was admired for her beauty of timbre in such roles as Rosina, Lucia, Linda and Violetta.

Galliera, Alceo (*b* Milan, 3 May 1910). Italian conductor and composer. After study at the Milan Conservatory he made his début in Rome in 1941. Though he has conducted opera in Milan and Genoa his career as an orchestral conductor has been largely outside Italy. In 1964 he became artistic director of the Strasbourg Municipal Orchestra. He has recorded with London orchestras, notably the LSO, his repertory reflecting a cosmopolitan taste.

Gallignani, Giuseppe (*b* Faenza, 9 Jan 1851; *d* Milan, 14 Dec 1923). Italian teacher and composer. With Verdi's support he became director of the Parma, later of the Milan, conservatories, also serving as *maestro di cappella* at Milan Cathedral from 1884 and composing church music.

Gallo, Domenico (*fl* mid-18th century). Italian composer. He was a violinist, and wrote instrumental and sacred music. 12 of his trio sonatas appeared in England under Pergolesi's name; some were used, as Pergolesi's, by Stravinsky in *Pulcinella* (1920).

Galop. A lively ballroom dance of German origin, popular throughout Europe in the 19th century. The music, in 2/4 time, was played at *c*126 bars per minute and was usually quite short.

Galoubet. A three-holed pipe, of Provençal origin, of a PIPE AND TABOR ensemble; it was used to accompany dancing in the Middle Ages.

Galpin, Francis W(illiam) (*b* Dorchester, 25 Dec 1858; *d* Richmond, Surrey, 30 Dec 1945). English writer. A clergyman by profession, he had a large collection of instruments; he wrote a study, *Old English Instruments of Music* (1910), a pioneering work, and a *Textbook of European Musical Instruments* (1937) as well as a study of Sumerian music. The Galpin Society, founded in 1946 for the study of instruments, was named after him.

Galuppi, Baldassare ['Il Buranello'] (*b* Burano, 18 Oct 1706; *d* Venice, 3 Jan 1785). Italian composer. He studied with Lotti and worked briefly in Florence, then returned to Venice, where his successful *opera seria Dorinda* (1729) launched his theatrical career: many others followed. In 1740–51 he taught at the Mendicanti orphanage. He worked in London, 1741–3, presenting four operas. Subsequently he enjoyed growing fame both in Italy and abroad. He was a *vice-maestro* at St Mark's, 1748–62, then *maestro di cappella* (Venice's highest musical post). An extended collaboration followed with the librettist Carlo Goldoni. With *L'Arcadia in Brenta* (1749, Venice) he was successful in comic opera; *Il filosofo di campagna* (1754, Venice) was especially popular. As music director of Catherine the Great's chapel, 1765–8, he staged operas at St Petersburg and Moscow and composed Russian sacred music. Returning to Venice, he became *maestro di coro* at the Ospedale degli Incurabili; latterly his operatic output decreased.

Galuppi was a crucial figure in the development of *opera buffa*, and his *c*30 works in the genre were the first to gain widespread fame. Most of them are cast in the new *dramma giocoso* genre, with partly serious elements, that he created with Goldoni. They use an early Classical style, with simple but inventive melodies carefully matched to the text. Often the orchestra carries the musical continuity. Many aria forms appear, and his use of the sectional 'chain finale' was influential. His c70 serious operas show a growing use of 'reform' elements. Among his other works are cantatas, 27 oratorios, church music and instrumental works (including over 100 harpsichord pieces).

Galway, James (b Belfast, 8 Dec 1939). British flautist. He studied in London and at the Paris Conservatoire and after playing in London orchestras (1961–9) joined the Berlin PO. From 1975 he has pursued a career as soloist, dazzling audiences with his technique and sensitive articulation. His 14-carat gold flute has also been heard in contemporary music and many recordings.

Gamba. The Italian for leg, sometimes used as an abbreviation for VIOLA DA GAMBA ('leg viol', a viol played between the legs). It is also the term for an organ stop with a string-like sound quality.

Gambler, The [Igrok]. Opera in four acts by Prokofiev to his own libretto after Dostoyevsky (1929, Brussels).

Gamelan. A type of orchestra or ensemble of southeast Asia. It includes various combinations of gongs, metallophones, xylophones, drums, bowed and plucked strings, a flute or oboe, small cymbals and singers. Its main function is to accompany religious or ceremonial rituals and dances in temple, village or court. Because there are two basic tuning systems – a five-note scale (slendro) and a seven-note one (pelog) – complete gamelan may consist of two sets of instruments, one tuned to each.

Interest in gamelan has flourished in the West since Debussy was captivated by the Javanese gamelan at the Paris World Exhibition of 1889. Many universities, museums and other institutions own gamelan.

Gamut. Term commonly used for musical range; strictly, derived from solmization, it means the notes shown on the Guidonian hand. Historically, the word (which could take the form gamma ut, gamma or gamme) stood for the system of scales based on the hexachord; or it could mean the note G, the note one below the acknowledged lowest note of that system. See NOTATION; SOLMIZATION.

Gänsbacher, Johann (Baptist) (b Sterzing, 8 May 1778; d Vienna, 13 July 1844). Austrian composer and conductor. A lifelong friend of Weber, he was Kapellmeister at St Stephen's Cathedral, Vienna, from 1824 and a composer of conventional vocal works. His son Josef (1829–1911), an esteemed singing teacher in Vienna, received the dedication of Brahms's cello sonata op.38.

Ganz, Rudolf (b Zurich, 24 Feb 1877; d Chicago, 2 Aug 1972). American pianist and conductor. He studied the cello and the piano, with Busoni and others, and made his début in 1899 with the Berlin PO in Beethoven's Piano Concerto no.5 and Chopin's no.1. He conducted the orchestra in his own Symphony no.1 the next year. He taught at Chicago Musical College, 1901–5, and was director there, 1929–54; he also conducted in St Louis and New York. His compositions include piano music, songs and orchestral music.

Gapped scale. A scale with at least one interval greater than a whole tone (e.g. the pentatonic scale).

Garant, (Albert Antonio) Serge (b Quebec, 22 Sept 1929). Canadian composer. He studied with Champagne (1949–50) and in Paris with Messiaen (1951–2). In 1967 he was appointed professor at the University of Montreal. His music has been influenced by Boulez and Webern and much of it has aleatory elements; it includes a series of pieces based on Bach's Musical Offering.

Garaudé, Alexis (-Adélaide-Gabriel) de (b Nancy, 21 March 1779; d Paris, 23 March 1852). French composer and singing teacher. A renowned teacher at the Paris Conservatoire (1816–41), he published many didactic vocal works and composed c200 songs.

Garcia, José Maurício Nunes (b Rio de Janeiro, 20/22 Sept 1767; d there, 18 April 1830). Brazilian composer (in Brazil referred to as José Maurício). He was mestre de capela of Rio de Janeiro Cathedral from 1798 and of the royal chapel from 1808; he remained active as organist, conductor, composer and teacher until c1816. Over 230 of his works survive, mostly sacred pieces for four-part chorus with orchestra, including c20 masses. The early works are typically simple, clear and devotional, while those of after c1810 show the influence of Italian opera. The noble and grandiose Requiem of 1816, his best work, is one of the finest written in the Americas and confirms Garcia's position as the most distinguished Brazilian composer up to his time.

García, Manuel (del Popolo Vicente Rodríguez) (b Seville, 21 Jan 1775; d Paris, 9 June 1832). Spanish tenor and composer. He was already well known in Spain before his successful Paris début (1808) and stay in Italy (1811–16), where he created roles in several Rossini operas (including Almaviva in Il barbiere di Siviglia); an excellent singer, actor and teacher, he became the principal exponent of Rossini's music in Paris, London and New York, and led the first Italian opera company to visit America (1825). Among his compositions (tonadillas, songs and over 40 operas and operettas), the opera El poeta calculista (1805) was particularly successful in Spain and abroad. García had four children who all became singers; the most celebrated were Pauline Viardot, Maria Malibran and his son Manuel García (1805–1906), a baritone whose investigations into the voice's physiology, invention of the laryngoscope (1855) and singing method brought him world fame.

Gardane [Gardano]. Family of music printers, active in Venice. Using Attaingnant's single-impression printing method, Antonio (1509–69) began his career in 1538, issuing chansons, masses, motets and chiefly madrigals, notably by Arcadelt, Willaert, Rore and Lassus. With Girolamo Scotto, his only serious rival, he printed almost every important music book in Italy during his time, including lute tablatures (from 1546) and keyboard scores (from 1551). Alessandro (c1539–c1591), his first son, issued music in Venice (1579–81) and later in Rome (1583–91), especially religious works by Marenzio, Palestrina and Victoria; Angelo, his second (1540–

1611), increased the firm's output and was the first to print vocal music in score with bar-lines for performance on keyboard instruments (1577).

Gardel, Pierre Gabriel (*b* Nancy, 4 Feb 1758; *d* Paris, 18 Oct 1840). French dancer and ballet-master. He assisted his brother Maximilien Léopold Philippe Joseph (1741–87) as a ballet-master at the Paris Opéra from 1783, succeeding to the post in 1787. He choreographed many ballets until the 1790s, also appearing as dancer. Both brothers were also musicians. Their father Claude (*d* 1774) was a ballet-master and from 1760 court choreographer in Paris.

Gardelli, Lamberto (*b* Venice, 8 Nov 1915). Italo-Swedish conductor. He studied in Pesaro and Rome, working with Serafin and making his début in *La traviata* (1944). He was at the Stockholm Opera, 1946–55, and with the Danish Radio SO, 1955–61, also conducting elsewhere, notably in New York (1964) and at Covent Garden, London (1969); in 1983 he became principal conductor of Munich RSO. He is noted as an outstanding Verdi conductor, in command of both structure and expression.

Gardellino [Cardellino], Il (It.: 'goldfinch'). Title of Vivaldi's Flute Concerto in D RV428 and of his chamber concerto RV90, because of flute passages supposedly akin to the goldfinch's song.

Garden, Mary (*b* Aberdeen, 20 Feb 1874; *d* Inverurie, 3 Jan 1967). American soprano of Scottish birth. She studied in Chicago and Paris; her début was as Charpentier's Louise at the Opéra-Comique (1900). She created Debussy's Mélisande (1902) and was successful as Manon and Thaïs. At Chicago she was the leading soprano, 1910–31.

Gardiner, Henry Balfour (*b* London, 7 Nov 1877; *d* Salisbury, 28 June 1950). English composer. He studied with Knorr at the Hoch Conservatory in Frankfurt (1894–6), where he was influenced by Wagner and Tchaikovsky. In London he helped considerably to establish the music of his English contemporaries. He composed abundantly before World War I, but in 1925 abandoned composition.

Gardiner, John Eliot (*b* Fontmell Magna, 20 April 1943). English conductor. He studied at Cambridge and with Nadia Boulanger. In 1964 he founded the Monteverdi Choir, with which he commemorated Monteverdi's quatercentenary in a performance of the Vespers in Ely Cathedral (1967). His authority in Baroque style has been notable in performances of Rameau; he gave a pioneering concert performance of *Les boréades* in London (1975) and at the 1982 Aix Festival conducted the opera's stage première. He made his USA début in 1979, became artistic director of Göttingen Festival in 1981 and was musical director of Lyons Opéra, 1982–7. His vigorous, shapely performances of Handel, Gluck and Mozart with period-instrument ensembles (notably his own English Baroque Soloists) have attracted much attention.

Gardner, John (Linton) (*b* Manchester, 2 March 1917). English composer. He studied at Oxford and has worked mostly as a teacher, writing operas (notably *The Moon and Sixpence*, 1957) and much cho-

ral music in a diatonic style.

Gardner, Samuel (*b* Kirovograd, 25 Aug 1891; *d* New York, 23 June 1984). American composer and violinist. Taken to the USA in 1892, he toured as a violinist and conductor, teaching at the Juilliard School (1924–41) and elsewhere. He was pre-eminently a composer for the violin; his String Quartet in D Minor (1918) won a Pulitzer Prize.

Garsi, Santino (*b* Parma, 22 Feb 1542; *d* there, ?17 Jan 1604). Italian composer. After studying in Rome he was a lutenist at the Farnese court in Parma from 1594 until his death. Some 45 dances for lute, mainly galliards, survive in MS. His son Ascanio and son or grandson Donino (*d* 1630) were also musicians; Donino compiled a famous lute MS.

Garth, John (*b* ?Durham, *c*1722; *d*, ?London, *c*1810). English composer. He was an organist in Co. Durham, and composed 30 accompanied keyboard sonatas, solo keyboard music and six cello concertos. With Charles Avison, he edited music by Benedetto Marcello.

Gascongne, Mathieu [?Johannes]. French composer. A *magister* and priest in Cambrai diocese (1518), he may have served the French royal court. Willaert ranked him with Josquin and Ockeghem as one of the 'buoni antichi' and based a parody mass on one of his motets. His sacred music includes eight masses, two four-part Magnificats and 19 motets. His *chansons*, mostly for three voices, are forward-looking.

Gaspard de la nuit. Three piano pieces by Ravel (1908): *Ondine*, *Le gibet* and *Scarbo*.

Gaspari, Gaetano (*b* Bologna, 15 March 1807/8; *d* there, 31 March 1881). Italian bibliographer and music historian. From 1839 he was associated with the Liceo Musicale, Bologna, classifying material in the superb music library and teaching and writing on the history of music in Bologna.

Gasparini, Francesco (*b* Camaiore, 5 March 1668; *d* Rome, 22 March 1727). Italian composer and teacher. He presented his first opera in Rome in 1694. In 1701–13 he was *maestro di coro* at the Ospedale della Pietà in Venice, composing several operas each year. He then returned to Rome, becoming *maestro di cappella* at S Lorenzo in Lucina in 1717. Among the finest composers of his generation, he wrote *c*50 operas, as well as solo cantatas, oratorios and church music (in both strict and concerted styles). Much of his music is contrapuntal, but the arias in his later operas have pre-Classical features. Highly esteemed as a teacher (D. Scarlatti was one of his pupils), he wrote theoretical works including a treatise on figured bass (1708).

Gasparini, Quirino (*b* Gandino, 1721; *d* Turin, 30 Sept 1778). Italian composer. He worked in various Italian centres before becoming *maestro di cappella* of Turin Cathedral (1760). Greatly respected, he wrote much sacred music, two operas (including *Mitridate*, 1767, Turin; the model for Mozart's setting) and several instrumental works. His motet *Adoramus te* was once attributed to Mozart.

Gasparo de Salò [Bertolotti] (*b* Salò, bap. 20 May 1540; *d* 14 April 1609). Italian string instrument maker. Active in Brescia from 1568, he made mostly tenor violas; now often reduced in size, they are highly regarded for their full, reedy tone quality.

Gassenhauer. A German street song or urban folksong. The term was used in the 16th century for a popular song but later acquired a pejorative connotation. In Act 1 of Wagner's *Die Meistersinger von Nürnberg* it is used by Beckmesser to belittle Sachs's art.

Gassmann, Florian Leopold (*b* Most, 3 May 1729; *d* Vienna, 20 Jan 1774). Bohemian composer. He studied in Italy and worked in Venice, where he presented six operas (including *Issipile*, 1758). In 1763 he succeeded Gluck as Viennese court ballet composer. Most of his 15 operas, 1764–73, were comic; the most popular was *La contessina* (1770). In 1772 he became court Kapellmeister. He founded the oldest Viennese musical society, the Tonkünstler-Sozietät, for which he wrote the oratorio *La Betulia liberata* (1772). Although best known for his operas, he also wrote church music, secular cantatas and many instrumental works. Of his 33 symphonies, the more italianate, earlier ones have three movements, the later ones four; some use experimental forms and unusual keys. His chamber works (string quartets, trios etc) tend to be more conservative and include many fugues.

Gast, Peter [Köselitz, Johann Heinrich] (*b* Annaberg, 10 Jan 1854; *d* there, 15 Aug 1918). German composer. He studied at the Leipzig Conservatory and became friend and secretary of Nietzsche, who greatly admired his music, including the comic opera *Die heimliche Ehe* (1891).

Gastein Symphony. Symphony on which Schubert worked in Gastein during 1825; it was long thought lost but is now taken to be the work we know as the Great C major Symphony, no.9, D944.

Gastoldi, Giovanni Giacomo (*b* Caravaggio, ? 1550s; *d* Mantua, 1609). Italian composer. He served in the Gonzaga chapel in Mantua from 1572 and was in charge of the music there from 1592 to 1608, when he went to Milan. He published at least 16 books of sacred music in a wide variety of styles and 11 of secular, but is chiefly famous for his ballettos, of which he published two sets, for five voices (1591) and for three (1594); their homophonic textures and simple harmonies made them immensely popular. The 1591 volume was ten times reprinted in Venice alone and they greatly influenced the English ballett composers (notably Morley). In his madrigals his style was like Marenzio's in his bright sonorities, crisp, rhythmic melodies and diatonic harmonies. He was a skilful composer of dance music.

Gates, Bernard (*b* Westminster, *c*1685; *d* North Aston, 15 Nov 1773). English bass and teacher. In his main post as Master of the Children of the Chapel Royal he trained a number of future leading musicians. He sang solos in several Handel premières in 1713. His revival in 1732 of *Esther* was important in provoking Handel to take up seriously the composition of English oratorio.

Gatti, Guido M(aggiorino) (*b* Chieti, 30 May 1892; *d* Grottaferrata, 10 May 1973). Italian musicologist. He was editor of several journals, book series and reference works as well as a prolific writer, particu-

larly on contemporary music. He was also an energetic administrator. He should not be confused with Carlo Gatti (1876–1965), the composer and scholar who was a leading figure in Verdi studies.

Gatti, Luigi (Maria Baldassare) (*b* Castro Lacizzi, 11 June 1740; *d* Salzburg, 1 March 1817). Italian composer. He worked at Mantua, becoming *vicemaestro* at S Barbara in 1779. From 1783 he was Kapellmeister of the Salzburg court and cathedral (the last Italian to hold the post). His works include six serious operas, five oratorios, many cantatas and much sacred music (including a mass based on Haydn's *Creation*); he also wrote instrumental music.

Gatti-Casazza, Giulio (*b* Udine, 3 Feb 1869; *d* Ferrara, 2 Sept 1940). Italian opera impresario. He held posts at La Scala, Milan (1898–1908), where he worked with the conductor Arturo Toscanini to revitalize the opera house, and at the Metropolitan Opera, New York, until 1935. His early years, with Toscanini, were artistically outstanding, but during his long tenure at the Metropolitan he introduced a new level of professionalism.

Gaudeamus Foundation. Organization founded in 1945 at Bilthoven, the Netherlands. It promotes new, especially Dutch, music. From 1959 it has held an annual international music week and in 1962 established the Competition for Interpreters of Contemporary Music.

Gaultier, Denis (*b* 1603; *d* Paris, 1672). French composer and lutenist. He is often referred to as 'le jeune' to distinguish him from his cousin Ennemond. *La rhétorique des dieux* (*c*1652) was the most important of his publications which include *Pièces de luth* (*c*1670) and *Livre de tablature* (*c*1672; completed by his pupil Montarcis). His output comprises principally dances, and he developed with his cousin Ennemond the portrait in music and the *tombeau*. Their use of tonality is often more adventurous than their predecessors'.

Gaultier, Ennemond (*b* Villette, 1575; *d* Nèves, 11 Dec 1651). French composer and lutenist. He is often referred to as 'le vieux' to distinguish him from his cousin Denis. He was a lutenist at the French court until *c*1630. Although his dances are scattered in various anthologies, lack of publication has made it more difficult to distinguish between his music and his cousin's; their works are the most significant French contribution to the lute music of the time.

Gauntlett, Henry John (*b* Wellington, Salop, 9 July 1805; *d* London, 21 Feb 1876). English organist, composer and critic. He was a church organist in London, introducing the C organ compass, compiling hymn books and composing hymn tunes, notably *Irby* ('Once in royal David's city'). He also contributed to several music journals on topics including Bach, Beethoven and Gregorian plainsong.

Gautier, Jacques (*b* late 16th century; *d* before 1660). French lutenist and composer. He is sometimes known as 'Gautier d'Angleterre'. Attached to the English court (1625–*c*1641), he taught Queen Henrietta Maria and was praised for his brilliant playing. A few of his compositions exist in MS.

Gautier, Pierre (*b* Le Ciotat, ?1642; *d* at sea nr. Sète, 1696). French composer and opera director. In 1684 he founded an academy of music in Marseilles, inaugurated the following year with one of his two lost operas, *Le triomphe de la paix*. In subsequent seasons operas by Lully were successfully performed and taken to other musical centres in southern France. As an opera director he was concerned with the quality of performance and repertory. His surviving instrumental works and songs, though influenced by Lully, are lively and individual.

He should not be confused with the lutenist-composer Pierre Gautier of Orleans (*d* after 1638), who worked in Rome.

Gautier, Théophile (*b* Tarbes, 30 Aug 1811; *d* Paris, 23 Oct 1872). French poet and critic. He created several ballets, among them the well-known *Giselle* (music by Adam, 1841), and contributed to the *Moniteur universel*. His daughter Judith Gautier (1845–1917), a writer on music, was an ardent partisan of Wagner.

Gautier de Coincy (*b* Coincy-l'Abbaye, 1177–8; *d* Soissons, 25 Sept 1236). French trouvère. He may have studied at Paris University; in 1214 he became prior at Vic-sur-Aisne and in 1233 abbot at Soissons. He wrote a massive verse narrative, *Miracles de Nostre-Dame*, in 1214–33, including songs, and composed religious *chansons*. His work represents the earliest substantial collection of sacred, Marian songs in the vernacular, and drew on secular melodies, which are set to sacred or devotional words.

Gautier de Dargiès (*b* ?Dargies, nr. Beauvais; *d* after 1236). French trouvère. He came from a well-known family and took part in the third crusade. More than 20 songs by him are known, notable for their individuality of form, richness of rhythmic design and melodic vitality.

Gavazzeni, Gianandrea (*b* Bergamo, 27 July 1909). Italian conductor, composer and writer. After study at the Milan Conservatory he conducted operas in the *verismo* and contemporary Italian repertory. He was a successful composer during the 1930s but concentrated on conducting from 1949. In 1957 he took the La Piccola Scala company to the Edinburgh Festival. He has written books on Donizetti and Beethoven.

Gaveaux, Pierre (*b* Béziers, 9 Oct 1760; *d* Charenton, 5 Feb 1825). French singer and composer. He sang in Béziers, then in Bordeaux, where he studied with Beck. In Paris from 1789, he took major operatic roles, and up to 1818 composed over 30 stage works, mostly *opéras comiques*. Especially successful was his *fait historique*, *Léonore* (1798); Beethoven's *Fidelio* was based on the same Bouilly libretto. He also composed songs, Revolutionary works and overtures, publishing many of them himself.

Gaviniès, Pierre (*b* Bordeaux, 11 May 1728; *d* Paris, 8 Sept 1800). French violinist and composer. He appeared in Paris in 1741 and soon became the leading virtuoso there. In 1760 he presented a stage work and began publishing instrumental music. As leader of the Concert Spirituel orchestra he performed his own works; he was joint director,

1773–7. From 1795 he was violin professor at the Paris Conservatoire. Especially praised for his pure, expressive tone, Gaviniès succeeded Leclair as leader of the French violin school and taught many famous pupils. His concertos, sonatas, duos and other violin works reflect his virtuosity; his *24 matinées* (1800) were the most difficult violin studies before Paganini. He also wrote vocal pieces.

Gavotte. A French folkdance; also a court dance and instrumental form popular from the late 16th century to the late 18th. The early court gavotte was related to the branle; a later type, introduced *c*1660, was characterized by two crotchet upbeats. The stylized gavotte, which often appeared in the Baroque suite after the sarabande, had a time signature of 2 or ¢, a moderate tempo and four-bar phrases. It was considered a pastoral dance, and several gavottes by Bach and others have drone basses suggesting a bagpipe or musette.

Gawroński [Rola-Gawroński], **Wojciech** (*b* Sejmany, 28 March 1868; *d* Kowanówko, 5 Aug 1910). Polish pianist and composer. He studied in Warsaw and Berlin (under Moszkowski). He was admired for his interpretations of Chopin and Bach. His compositions include works for piano and violin, two prize-winning string quartets and the opera *Maria* (1899).

Gay, John (*b* Barnstaple, bap. 16 Sept 1685; *d* London, 4 Dec 1732). English poet and dramatist. His *The Beggar's Opera* (1729, London), put together from popular tunes, was the first important ballad opera; its music and subject matter made it an instant theatrical success. Bass parts for the tunes and an overture were added by Pepusch. Gay's second ballad opera, *Polly*, was banned; his third, *Achilles* (1733, London), was unsuccessful. He wrote at least part of the libretto for Handel's *Acis and Galatea* (1718).

Gayane. Ballet in three acts by Khachaturian to a libretto by Derzhavin (1942, Leningrad); it includes the famous 'Sabre Dance'.

Gaztambide (y Garbayo), Joaquín (Romualdo) (*b* Tudela, 7 Feb 1822; *d* Madrid, 18 March 1870). Spanish composer and conductor. He was a successful conductor of opera and zarzuela companies in Madrid and of the Madrid Concert Society. Of his 44 zarzuelas *Catalina* (1854) was the best.

Gazza ladra, La. *See* THIEVING MAGPIE, THE.

Gazzaniga, Giuseppe (*b* Verona, 5 Oct 1743; *d* Crema, 1 Feb 1818). Italian composer. He studied with Porpora and Piccinni in Naples, where he presented his first stage work (1768). Returning to Venice in 1770, he wrote over 40 operas (mostly comic) for Italian theatres, and one for Dresden (1778). Most famous was his *Don Giovanni Tenorio* (1787, Venice); Mozart's *Don Giovanni* was based on the same Bertati libretto. From 1791 he was *maestro di cappella* at Crema Cathedral. He was one of the last Italian *opera buffa* composers; his works are less Neapolitan in style than those of Piccinni or Cimarosa. He composed several sacred works.

Gazzelloni, Severino (*b* Roccasecca, 5 Jan 1919). Italian flautist. He studied in Rome and became first flute of the Italian RSO. He is noted for his performance of Baroque music and particularly of avant-garde works where his full tone and brilliant articulation serve well. Maderna and Haubenstock-Ramati are among those to have written music for him.

Geary, Thomas Augustine [Timothy] (*b* Dublin, 1775; *d* there, Nov 1801). Irish composer. A keyboard player, he composed fine canzonets (*c*1795) and other vocal works. He was the first Irish composer to exploit systematically the form of sets of keyboard variations and rondos based on popular airs.

Gebauer. French family of musicians, apparently of Saxon origin. The most celebrated members were Michel Joseph (1763–1812), an oboist and bandmaster who composed marches and chamber music, and his brother François René (1773–1845), a noted bassoonist who composed concertos and much bassoon chamber music.

Gebrauchsmusik (Ger.). 'Utility music': term coined in the 1920s to refer to music that is socially useful and relevant, including music for films and radio, mechanical instruments, for amateurs and to stimulate political debate. A product of Germany during the Weimar republic, it is characteristic of the period in its avoidance of subjectivity of expression. Composers associated with the concept included Hindemith and Weill.

Gédalge, André (*b* Paris, 27 Dec 1856; *d* Chessy, 5 Feb 1926). French composer. He studied with Guiraud at the Paris Conservatoire, where he remained as a notable teacher of counterpoint; he published the monumental *Traité de la fugue* (1901). His works include three symphonies, theatre pieces, chamber and piano music and songs.

Gedda, Nicolai (Harry Gustaf) (*b* Stockholm, 11 July 1925). Swedish tenor. He made his début at the Stockholm Opera in 1952 and appeared at La Scala from the 1952–3 season. He sang the Duke of Mantua at Covent Garden in 1955, returning in later seasons as Benvenuto Cellini. At the Met in 1958 he created Anatol in Barber's *Vanessa*. A refined artist and fine linguist, he has a large song repertory and is one of the most versatile and gifted singers of his generation.

Gehot, Joseph (*b* Brussels, 8 April 1756; *d c*1820). South Netherlands composer. He toured in Europe and from *c*1780 played the violin in London, where he published chamber music and theoretical works and played in Haydn's orchestra, 1791–2. He then went to the USA, where his first concert (1792, New York) included his *Overture in Twelve Movements, Expressive of a Voyage from England to America*. He later played in orchestras in Philadelphia.

Geige. German term for violin or 'fiddle', used in the Middle Ages for any bowed string instrument.

Geigenwerk. Bowed keyboard instrument invented *c*1575. It had five parchment-covered wheels against which individual strings were drawn by operating the keyboard.

Geiringer, Karl (Johannes) (*b* Vienna, 26 April 1899). American musicologist. He studied in Vienna and Berlin, became involved in music publishing and became librarian of the Gesellschaft der Musikfreunde. In 1938 he moved to London, then to the

USA, teaching at Boston for 21 years and later at Santa Barbara. His writings include studies of Brahms, Haydn and the Bach family.

Geisslerlieder. Religious folksongs sung by German flagellants of the 13th and 14th centuries during pilgrimages and acts of penance.

Geister Trio. *See* GHOST TRIO.

Geistliches Konzert. 'Sacred concerto': term used in 17th-century Germany for a sacred vocal work.

Gelinek, Josef (*b* Sedlec, 3 Dec 1758; *d* Vienna, 13 April 1825). Czech composer and pianist. After working as an organist in Prague, he went to Vienna (probably in 1789) as chaplain and tutor to the Kinsky family. He studied with Albrechtsberger and had contact with Haydn, Mozart and Beethoven. He wrote over 100 sets of piano variations (many on operatic melodies), arrangements of works by Beethoven and others, piano pieces, chamber music and songs.

Geminiani, Francesco (Xaverio) (*b* Lucca, bap. 5 Dec 1687; *d* Dublin, 17 Sept 1762). Italian violinist, composer and theorist. He studied in Rome with Corelli and A. Scarlatti, and in 1711 became leader of the opera orchestra in Naples. Settling in London in 1714, he earned instant success as a violin virtuoso and became one of the most influential teachers (of the violin and composition). He published a series of instrumental works, starting with the highly acclaimed violin sonatas op.1 (1716). In the 1730s he made two lengthy visits to Ireland, and later spent time in the Netherlands and Paris. He settled in Dublin in 1759, giving his last known concert in 1760.

Geminiani's principal works are solo sonatas and concerti grossi. His model was Corelli, but he composed with originality, writing for a wider range of solo instruments and using a more sonorous and chromatic idiom; his music is more expressive and dramatic than Corelli's (though still contrapuntal). Most works have the traditional four-movement plan still popular in England. The violin sonatas op.1 and op.4 (1739) are especially difficult to play, and include cadenzas. Geminiani revised the former set as trio sonatas (*c*1757), and also made arrangements of others of his works. His 45 concerti grossi have a concertino of two violins, viola and cello; they include arrangements of sonatas by Corelli.

Geminiani also composed harpsichord pieces (mostly arranged from his sonatas) and *The Inchanted Forrest*, an instrumental piece for a stage work (1754, Paris). His most influential treatise was *The Art of Playing on the Violin* (1751), the first such work for advanced players; he also wrote on musical taste, harmony, accompaniment and guitar playing.

Chamber music 12 violin sonatas, op.1 (1716, rev. 1739), later arr. as trio sonatas; 12 vn sonatas, op.4 (1739); 6 vc sonatas, op.5, also as vn sonatas (1746); sonatas and arrs.
Orchestral music conc. grossi – 6, op.2 (1732); 6, op.3 (1732); 6, op.7 (1746); 9 others; The Inchanted Forrest, in conc. grosso style (1754); 18 Corelli sonatas arr. as conc. grossi
Other works hpd pieces and arrs.; minuets

Gemshorn. A medieval folk instrument of the recorder type, made originally from an animal horn. It was made at different pitches and had a soft, husky tone; it is suitable for medieval or early Renaissance dance music or secular polyphony. The name is also used for an organ stop with a gentle, ocarina-like quality.

Gendang [kendang]. Generic south-east Asian term for a double-headed laced drum, cylindrical or conical. It is also used in Sumatra and Malaysia for instrumental pieces in which it is prominent and hence for the ensembles that play them.

Gendron, Maurice (*b* Nice, 26 Dec 1920). French cellist. He studied at Nice and the Paris Conservatoire, making his début in London in 1945 with the Western première of Prokofiev's Cello Concerto. He has played widely in Europe and also conducted; his cello playing is noted for its elegance, style and resonant tone.

Generalbass (Ger.: 'thoroughbass'). Term for figured or unfigured bass parts (*see* CONTINUO), first used by theorists in the 17th century; the term came to stand for the science of tonal harmony in general.

Generali, Pietro (*b* Masserano, 23 Oct 1773; *d* Novara, 3 Nov 1832). Italian composer. He studied in Naples and Rome and wrote sacred works and *c*54 operas, the most successful including *Pamela nubile* (1804) and *I baccanali di Roma* (1816). Although his use of dramatic orchestral effects anticipated Rossini's, his works show triviality.

Generalpause (Ger.). A rest for the whole orchestra, usually unexpected and sometimes marked with the letters 'GP'.

Genlis [née Ducrest de Saint-Aubin], **Stéphanie-Félicité**, Countess of (*b* Champcéry, 25 Jan 1746; *d* Paris, 31 Dec 1830). French writer, educationist and harpist. Her musical importance lies in her pedagogical works, including a harp manual (1802, 1811), and in her theory of harmonics.

Genoveva. Opera in four acts by Schumann to a libretto by R. Reineck after L. Tieck and C.F. Hebbel (1850, Leipzig).

Gentilucci, Armando (*b* Lecce, 8 Oct 1939). Italian composer. He studied with Donatoni at the Milan Conservatory and in 1969 became director of the Reggio Emilia Liceo Musicale. His works show a left-wing political commitment and musical style comparable with Nono's; *Studi per un Dies irae* (1971) incorporates a partisan song, and in *Come qualcosa palpita nel fondo* (1973) electronic and live instrumental performance are combined.

Genuino, Francesco (*b* ?Naples, *c*1580–85; *d* ? there, before 1633). Italian composer. From a prominent Neapolitan family, he published five madrigal books, only three of which survive (1605, 1612, 1614); they contain mainly serious pieces in a dense contrapuntal style.

Genzmer, Harald (*b* Blumenthal, 9 Feb 1909). German composer. He studied with Hindemith at the Berlin Musikhochschule (1928–34) and taught in Berlin, Freiburg (1946–57) and Munich. During the war he also worked with Sala and Trautwein on electronic instruments and wrote two trautonium concertos (1939, 1952). His other works are in most genres except opera and reveal a craftsmanlike, Hindemithian approach.

Geoffroy, Jean-Nicolas (*d* Perpignan, 11 March

1694). French composer, author of the largest collection of harpsichord music of 17th-century France. He held posts as organist in Paris (to 1690) and at Perpignan Cathedral (from 1692). The only music clearly ascribed to him is a posthumous MS copy of 217 pieces, mostly grouped into 19 harpsichord suites. Although an extraordinarily inventive composer, particularly in his harmony, he had limited control of his ideas and his effects can seem arbitrary.

Gerarde, Derick (*fl* 1540–80). Flemish composer. He probably spent time in Italy, and perhaps in Munich, before moving to England, where he served the Earl of Arundel at Nonesuch, Surrey. His surviving works (*c*90 motets, over 120 secular and *c*45 instrumental pieces) form one of the largest MS collections of polyphony by a single composer of the period in England and show a resourceful musical technique with mastery of declamation and text illustration.

Gerber, Ernst Ludwig (*b* Sondershausen, 29 Sept 1746; *d* there, 30 June 1819). German music scholar. He worked first as a lawyer and in 1775 succeeded his father Heinrich Nikolaus (1702–75), a former J.S. Bach pupil, as Sondershausen court organist. The owner of a large music library, he became famous as a lexicographer, writing a highly influential dictionary of musicians (1790–92, amplified 1812–14) and other works on music. Both he and his father composed keyboard music.

Gerbert, Martin, Freiherr von Hornau (*b* Horb am Neckar, 11–12 Aug 1720; *d* St Blasien, 13 May 1793). German music historian. A priest, he became Prince-Abbot at St Blasien in 1764. He was a founder of modern historical musicology through his works on the history of chant and church music and his three-volume edition of over 40 medieval music treatises (1784).

Gerbič, Fran (*b* Cerknica, 5 Oct 1840; *d* Ljubljana, 29 March 1917). Slovenian composer and singer. He was a choral director and teacher in Ljubljana (from 1886); his most important compositions are piano mazurkas, the orchestral *Jugoslovanska balada* (1910) and *Hunting Symphony*, and solo songs.

Gerhard, Roberto (*b* Valls, 25 Sept 1896; *d* Cambridge, 5 Jan 1970). Spanish composer, later naturalized British. He studied in Barcelona with Granados and Pedrell and in Vienna and Berlin with Schoenberg (1923–8), returning to Barcelona to take an active part in musical life. His compositions from this period are few: they include the Schoenbergian Wind Quintet (1928), the cantata *L'alta naixença del rei en jaume* (1932) and the ballet *Ariel* (1934). In 1939 he left Spain and eventually settled in England, where he became much more productive, in a distinctly Spanish style. There were three more ballets (*Don Quixote*, 1941; *Alegrias*, 1942; *Pandora*, 1944), an opera (*The Duenna*, 1947), the symphony *Homenaje a Pedrell* (1941) and songs, besides the Violin Concerto (1943), which looks back to the early atonal works and forward to the dynamic, boldly colourful, serial compositions of his last two decades.

This late development was rapid, from the Schoenbergian style of the First Quartet (1955) to the athematic, block-form, effect-filled Second (1962). It can be seen too in the cycle of four symphonies (1953,

1959, 1960, 1967) and the Concerto for Orchestra (1965), which move towards a Varèsian sound-drama (the Third Symphony has the sub-title 'Collages' and includes tape). Other late works include electronic pieces, much incidental music and pieces for ensemble (Concert for Eight, 1962; *Hymnody*, 1963; *Libra*, 1968; *Leo*, 1969).

Gerhardt, Elena (*b* Leipzig, 11 Nov 1883; *d* London, 11 Jan 1961). German mezzo-soprano (originally soprano), later naturalized British. She gave her first recital in 1903, accompanied by Nikisch, and sang in England from 1906, the USA from 1912. She settled in England in 1934 and after successful wartime concerts taught in London. The sensuous beauty of her voice, with strong chest notes, made her a distinguished interpreter of Wolf, Schubert and Brahms.

Gericke, Wilhelm (*b* Schwanberg, 18 April 1845; *d* Vienna, 27 Oct 1925). Austrian conductor. Although he was known in Vienna for his performances of French, Italian and Wagnerian opera, his most important contribution was as conductor of the Boston Symphony Concerts (1884–9, 1898–1906).

Gerl, Franz Xaver (*b* Andorf, 30 Nov 1764; *d* Mannheim, 9 March 1827). Austrian bass and composer. In 1789–93 he sang in Schikaneder's company in Vienna, creating Sarastro in *Die Zauberflöte* (1791). He composed and contributed to over a dozen stage works, mostly Singspiels, notably *Der dumme Gärtner aus dem Gebirge* (*Der dumme Anton*, 1789). He was a friend of Mozart's. His wife Barbara (1770–1806), also a singer, created Papagena in *Die Zauberflöte*.

Gerle, Conrad (*d* Nuremberg, 4 Dec 1521). German lute maker. He worked in Nuremberg and became well known for his lutes in France and Germany. One of his sons was probably the instrumentalist and lute maker Hans Gerle (*c*1500–1570), who published three volumes of instrumental music including the valuable *Musica teusch* (1532); he may have been related to Georg Gerle (*d c*1589), an instrument maker in Innsbruck.

German, Sir Edward [Jones, German Edward] (*b* Whitchurch, Salop, 17 Feb 1862; *d* London, 11 Nov 1936). English composer. He studied the violin at the RAM (where he became known as J.E. German), also composing songs and instrumental works, teaching and playing in theatre orchestras. He soon became popular for his incidental music in an old English country-dance style (*Richard III*, 1889; *Henry VIII*, 1892; *English Nell*, 1900); the comic operas *Merrie England* (1902) and *Tom Jones* (1907) confirmed his standing as Sullivan's heir. Of his works in other genres, the refined orchestral piece *Welsh Rhapsody* (1904), the song *Glorious Devon* (1904), and the settings of Kipling's *Just So Stories* (1903) were the most successful, full of charm and showing his gift for melody.

German dance (Ger. *Deutsche*). Term used from *c*1760 for triple-metre couple-dances until replaced *c*1815 by the names of the two most common types, the LÄNDLER and the WALTZ. Haydn, Mozart, Beethoven and Schubert wrote sets of *Deutsche*.

German flute. Name for the transverse flute, used to distinguish it from the recorder or 'English flute'.

Germani, Fernando (*b* Rome, 5 April 1906). Italian organist. He studied in Rome and in 1921 began a career as organist. He has taught in Siena and Rome and played widely in the USA. He gave Bach's complete organ works for the first time in Italy in 1945, repeating them several times, and was first organist at St Peter's, Rome, 1948–59.

German Reed, Thomas (*b* Bristol, 27 June 1817; *d* London, 21 March 1888). English musician and entertainer. Besides directing the music for plays at the Haymarket Theatre (1838–51) and English operas at London and provincial theatres, he gave (with his wife, the actress Priscilla Horton) a well-known series of light entertainments in non-theatrical venues.

German Requiem, A [Ein deutsches Requiem]. Choral work by Brahms, with soprano and baritone soloists (op.45, 1868), so called because the text, treating death, is from Luther's translation of the Bible.

German sixth chord. An AUGMENTED SIXTH CHORD with both a major 3rd and a doubly augmented 4th or perfect 5th in addition to an augmented 6th above the flattened submediant (e.g. A♭–C–E♭–F♯).

Gernsheim, Friedrich (*b* Worms, 17 July 1839; *d* Berlin, ?10 Sept 1916). German composer, conductor and pianist. He studied in Mainz (with Pauer), in Frankfurt, at the Leipzig Conservatory (with Moscheles, Hauptmann and David) and in Paris. As a conductor, in Cologne, Rotterdam and (from 1890) Berlin, he favoured the works of Brahms, whose harmony and orchestration influenced his own compositions. He was at his best in chamber music, notably the Piano Quintet in B minor.

Gershwin, George (*b* Brooklyn, 26 Sept 1898; *d* Hollywood, 11 July 1937). American composer. Essentially self-taught, he was first a song plugger in Tin Pan Alley and an accompanist. In his teens he began to compose popular songs and produced a succession of musicals from 1919 to 1933 (*Lady, be Good!*, 1924; *Oh, Kay!*, 1926; *Strike up the Band*, 1927; *Funny Face*, 1927; *Girl Crazy*, 1930); the lyrics were generally by his brother Ira (1896–1983). In 1924 he became famous: he wrote *Rhapsody in Blue* as a concerto for piano and Paul Whiteman's jazz band. Its success led him to devote increasing energy to 'serious' composition. His more ambitious works include the Piano Concerto in F (1925) and the tone poem *An American in Paris* (1928). But he continued composing for the musical theatre, and some of his most successful musicals (*Strike up the Band, Girl Crazy, Of Thee I Sing*) date from this period. In 1934–5 he wrote his 'American folk opera' *Porgy and Bess*, which draws on Afro-American idioms; given on Broadway, it was only a limited success. Gershwin went to Hollywood in 1936 and wrote songs for films. He was a sensitive songwriter of great melodic gifts and did much to create syntheses between jazz and classical traditions in his concert music and black folk music and opera in *Porgy and Bess*.

Operas Blue Monday Blues (1922); Porgy and Bess (1935), incl. Summertime, It ain't necessarily so, I got plenty o' nuttin'

Musicals La La Lucille (1919); Broadway Brevities of 1920, incl. Swanee; Lady, be Good! (1924), incl. Fascinating Rhythm; Oh, Kay! (1926), incl. Do, do, do, Someone to watch over me; Strike up the Band (1927); Funny Face (1927), incl. 'S wonderful; Girl Crazy (1930), incl. Embraceable you, I got rhythm; Of Thee I Sing (1931); 6 film scores
Songs 40 incl. The man I love (1924), How long has this been going on? (1927)
Instrumental music Rialto Ripples, pf (1917); [3] Preludes, pf (1926); Rhapsody in Blue, jazz band, pf, orch (1924); Conc., F, pf, orch (1925); An American in Paris, tone poem, orch (1928); Cuban Ov., orch (1932)

Gervais, Charles-Hubert (*b* Paris, 19 Feb 1671; *d* there, 15 Jan 1744). French composer. He served the Duke of Chartres and after the duke became Regent of France he became a *sous-maître* to the royal chapel (1723). His three operas, especially *Hypermnèstre* (1716, Paris), move away from the Lullian style towards Rameau. He also wrote a ballet, cantatas, *airs* and motets.

Gervaise, Claude (*fl* Paris, 1540–60). French editor, composer and arranger. Employed as an editor by Attaingnant in Paris until 1558, he is known principally for his instrumental music. As well as editing three books of *Danceries*, he composed the music of the sixth (1555) – *pavanes, gaillardes* and branles, mostly for four-part ensemble. He also wrote 46 polyphonic *chansons* (published in anthologies).

Gesamtkunstwerk (Ger). 'Total art work': term used by Wagner to signify his music dramas in which all the arts (music, poetry, movement, design) should combine to the same artistic end. The concept was not original to Wagner, but the term was.

Gesang der Jünglinge. Electronic work by Stockhausen (1956) in which a boy's voice, singing the *Benedicite*, is transformed etc.

Geschöpfe des Prometheus, Die. Ballet (overture, introduction and 16 numbers) by Beethoven, op.43 (1801, Vienna).

Geschwind (Ger.). Quick.

Gesellschaft der Musikfreunde. Austrian society founded in 1812 in Vienna to promote music; it is also known by the name of its home, the Musikverein (opened 1870). Its conservatory (founded 1817) became the city's chief music school (Hochschule für Musik und Darstellende Kunst); among its teachers have been Mahler and Wolf. The Singverein (1858) is one of Vienna's principal choirs. Its concert series, with Viennese and visiting orchestras, are also broadcast; conductors have included Brahms, Hans Richter and Furtwängler.

Gesellschaftslied. German polyphonic song cultivated among the middle classes in the 15th–17th centuries (in contrast with *Hoflied*, courtsong, and *Volkslied*, folksong). The term has been extended in Germany to cover songs of predominantly popular character that reflect the interests and tastes of clearly defined social groups. The term has also been applied to choral songs of the 18th–20th centuries and sometimes serves as a synonym for 'Geselliges Lied' ('sociable song').

Gesius, Bartholomäus (*b* Müncheberg, ?1555–62; *d* Frankfurt an der Oder, 1613). German composer. After studying at the University of Frankfurt an der Oder (1575–80) he lived at Müncheberg (1582), Muskau and Wittenberg. From 1593 until his death he was Kantor at the Marienkirche, Frankfurt. His many sacred publications include Latin pre-Reformation songs, Protestant hymns, two important Passions and occasional pieces.

Gestopft (Ger.). 'Stopped': term applied to hand-stopping on a horn, affecting pitch and tone quality.

Gesualdo, Carlo, Prince of Venosa (*b* ?Naples, *c*1561; *d* Gesualdo, 8 Sept 1613). Italian composer. A nobleman and amateur musician, he is notorious for having his first wife and her lover murdered in 1590; he married Leonora d'Este of Ferrara three years later. While at the Ferrarese court (1594–6) he played the lute and showed a passion for music and came to be accepted as a serious composer. He eventually retired to his castle at Gesualdo, sunk into a deep melancholy from which music alone could provide relief. His music was strongly influenced by Luzzaschi and Nenna, particularly the former in his use of serious, expressive, richly worked music even for quite light texts. He took great pains over word setting, allowing texts to be clearly heard and strongly expressed. Much of the music in his six madrigal books (1594–1611) and three sacred books (1603–11) uses unexpected harmonies and changes of key, dissonances and striking chromaticism in a highly original way, usually prompted by the emotions of the texts. Stravinsky made arrangements of some of his madrigals.

*Sacred music c*40 motets; *c*30 responsories
*Secular music c*120 madrigals; inst pieces

Gevaert, François-Auguste (*b* Huysse, 31 July 1828; *d* Brussels, 24 Dec 1908). Belgian musicologist, teacher and composer. He was an energetic and influential director of the Brussels Conservatory (succeeding Fétis) and author of much-praised pedagogical works on orchestration (1885), the organ (1871) and harmony (1905–7). He wrote extensively on ancient and medieval music.

Gewandhaus Orchestra. German orchestra formed in 1781 and named after the hall in Leipzig which opened that year (rebuilt 1884, destroyed 1943). Mendelssohn was its conductor in 1835–47 and gave many premières, including symphonies of Schumann and Schubert. It has toured since 1916.

Ghedini, Giorgio Federico (*b* Cuneo, 11 July 1892; *d* Nervi, 25 March 1965). Italian composer. He studied at the Turin Liceo Musicale and taught in Turin, Parma and Milan (1941–62). Most of his published works date from after the late 1920s; they show the emergence of a personal style out of neoclassicism and more radical elements. His output includes operas (*Maria d'Alessandria*, 1937; *Le baccanti*, 1948), orchestral pieces (Partita, 1926; *Marinaresca e baccanale*, 1933; *Architetture*, 1940; *Concerto dell'albatro* with spoken text, 1945), choral and chamber music and songs.

Gheerkin de Hondt (*fl* 1539–47). Flemish composer. He was choirmaster to the Marian Brotherhood in 's-Hertogenbosch (1539–47). His extant works include six masses, four motets and numerous four-part *chansons*. But the attribution of works to him is complicated by the assignment in contemporary sources of all but one to composers identified simply as 'Gheerkin'.

Gherardello da Firenze (*b* 1320–25; *d* Florence, 1362–3). Florentine composer. A clerk at Florence Cathedral in 1343, and later a chaplain there, he became a prior at S Remigio, Florence. He was known for his liturgical compositions but only two mass movements have survived. His secular works include monophonic ballate and two-part madrigals as well as a three-part caccia.

Gherardeschi, Filippo Maria (*b* Pistoia, 1738; *d* Pisa, 1808). Italian composer. A pupil of Padre Martini, he worked in Livorno, Volterra, Pisa and Pistoia before becoming *maestro di cappella* of a church in Pisa (*c*1766) and soon after concert director for the Grand Duke of Tuscany. He wrote much church music and seven operas (1763–9). His family long played a leading role in the musical life of Pistoia.

Ghersem, Géry (de) (*b* Tournai, *c*1574; *d* there, 25 May 1630). Franco-Flemish composer. After an early career at the Spanish court in Madrid, where a seven-part mass of his was published (1598), he returned home in 1604, becoming director of the chapel of Archduke Albert in Brussels. Highly esteemed by his patrons, he composed much sacred music and 170 villancicos, but only the mass and an eight-part motet, *Benedicam Dominum*, survive.

Ghiaurov, Nicolai (*b* Velingrad, 13 Sept 1929). Bulgarian bass. After study in Russia he made his début at Sofia in 1955. He has sung at La Scala from 1959 and at Covent Garden from 1962. His Met début was in 1965, as Gounod's Mephistopheles. To such roles as Philip II and Boris Godunov he brings a secure technique and vivid characterization.

Ghiselin [Verbonnet], Johannes (*fl* early 16th century). Flemish composer. He was a singer in Florence, then was associated with the Ferrarese court. In 1503 he accompanied Josquin from Paris to Ferrara and in 1504 they were joined by Obrecht to serve the court chapel. Josquin and Ghiselin returned to the Netherlands in 1505 to avoid the plague. He was one of the most famous composers of his day. Nine of his masses survive and several motets and *chansons*. Many of his works display great technical skill (e.g. his hexachord mass *De les armes*).

Ghisi, Federico (*b* Shanghai, 25 Feb 1901; *d* Luzerna San Giovanni, 18 July 1975). Italian musicologist. He studied in Milan, Turin and Florence, where he taught music history at the university (1937–40), later teaching at Perugia and Pisa. His research centred on Renaissance Florence, instruments, the music of Carissimi and Valdesi folk music; he also composed operas, ballets and chamber, choral and orchestral music.

Ghislanzoni, Antonio (*b* Lecco, 25 Nov 1824; *d* Caprino Bergamasco, 16 July 1893). Italian writer and librettist. Though best known for his collaboration on the librettos for Verdi's *La forza del destino* and *Aida*, he also wrote *c*85 librettos for other composers and over 2000 articles; among the important reviews he edited were the *Italia musicale* and the *Gazzetta musicale di Milano*.

Ghost Trio. Nickname of Beethoven's Piano Trio in D op.70 no.1 (1808), so called because of the slow movement's ghostly atmosphere.

Giacobbi, Girolamo (*b* Bologna, bap. 10 Aug 1567; *d* there, by 13 Feb 1629). Italian composer. He served at S Petronio, Bologna, from 1581 (*maestro di cappella*, 1604–8) and was a member of the Accademia de' Floridi. One of the first outside Florence to use the new monodic style, he wrote *intermedi* (1608) and other stage music as well as sacred works (1601–18).

Giacosa, Giuseppe (*b* Colleretto Parella, 21 Oct 1847; *d* there, 2 Sept 1906). Italian writer and librettist. He collaborated with Luigi Illica on the librettos for Puccini's *La bohème*, *Tosca* and *Madama Butterfly*.

Giannettini, Antonio (*b* Fano, 1648; *d* Munich, bur. 14 July 1721). Italian composer. He held posts as a singer and organist in Venice (notably at St Mark's) and was appointed *maestro di cappella* to the Duke of Modena in 1686. More often required to write occasional pieces (serenatas etc) and oratorios than operas, he moved to Venice *c*1702, returning to Modena in 1707. Of his *c*10 operas, mostly written for Venice, *Medea in Atene* (1675) was most widely performed; it has a large range of gesture and a lively rhythmic style, making use of the *stile concitato*.

Gianni Schicchi. Opera in one act by Puccini to a libretto by Forzano after Dante's *Inferno*; it is the third of *Il Trittico*, the other operas being *Il tabarro* and *Suor Angelica* (1918, New York).

Giant Fugue. Nickname of J.S. Bach's organ chorale prelude *Wir gläuben all an einen Gott*, BWV680, so called because of the pedal part's giant strides.

Giardini, Felice (de) (*b* Turin, 12 April 1716; *d* Moscow, 8 June 1796). Italian violinist and composer. He played in opera orchestras in Rome and Naples, and in 1748 began a concert tour, but settled in England in 1750. There he was successful as soloist, teacher and orchestral leader (notably at the King's Theatre, where his style of playing was influential). He wrote three operas (1757–65) and contributed to others, and in 1763 collaborated with Avison in the oratorio *Ruth*; a more popular version of 1768 was by Giardini alone. After living in Naples, 1784–90, he returned to England, but later left for Russia. His many chamber works include sonatas, trios, quartets etc. His accompanied harpsichord sonatas of 1751 and his harpsichord quintets (1767) were among the first of their types.

Gibbons, Christopher (*b* Westminster, bap. 22 Aug 1615; *d* there, 20 Oct 1676). English composer, son of Orlando Gibbons. Brought up in London and Exeter, he was organist of Winchester Cathedral (1638–42), of the Chapel Royal (1660–76) and organist (1660–66) and Master of the Choristers (1664–6) of Westminster Abbey. He took the DMus at Oxford in 1663. An outstanding keyboard player, he composed anthems, masque music, viol fantasias and keyboard pieces. Blow was among his pupils.

Gibbons, Orlando (*b* Oxford, 1583; *d* Canterbury, 5 June 1625). English composer. He came from a musical family and was a chorister (1596–8) and student (1599–1603) at King's College, Cambridge. He joined the Chapel Royal in *c*1603 and was one of its organists by 1615 (senior organist, 1625). In 1619 he became a virginal player at court and in 1623 organist at Westminster Abbey. He took the MusB at Cambridge (1606) and the DMus at Oxford (1622). One of the most important English composers of sacred music in the early 17th century, he wrote several Anglican services, popular in their day, and over 30 anthems, some imposing and dramatic (e.g. *O clap your hands*), others colourful and most expressive (*See, the word is incarnate*; *This is the record of John*). His instrumental music, also important, includes over 30 elaborate contrapuntal viol fantasias and over 40 masterly keyboard pieces. His madrigals (1612) are generally serious in tone (e.g. *The Silver Swanne*).

Sacred vocal music over 30 anthems; 2 services; psalms; Te Deum; hymn tunes
Secular vocal music 14 madrigals, incl. The Silver Swanne; consort songs
Instrumental music over 30 fantasias, viol; pavans and galliards; In Nomines; kbd almans, pavans, fantasias, galliards

Gibbs, Cecil Armstrong (*b* Great Baddow, 10 Aug 1889; *d* Chelmsford, 12 May 1960). English composer. He studied at Cambridge and with Vaughan Williams at the RCM, where he taught (1921–39). His best works are his songs, especially to poems by de la Mare, but he also wrote much for choirs and chamber orchestras and achieved immense success with his slow waltz *Dusk*.

Gibbs, Joseph (*b* 23 Dec 1699; *d* Ipswich, 12 Dec 1788). English composer. He was organist at Dedham and (from 1748) at Ipswich, and gave many concerts in the region. He composed eight violin sonatas (*c*1746) in an intense, chromatic style, quartets and organ music.

Gibson, Sir Alexander (Drummond) (*b* Motherwell, 11 Feb 1926). Scottish conductor. He studied in Glasgow and London. In 1957 he became musical director of Sadler's Wells Opera and in 1959 was appointed principal conductor of the Scottish National Orchestra, remaining until 1984 and often giving new music. In 1962 he co-founded Scottish Opera, conducting a notable *Ring* cycle in 1971. His American début was in 1970, with the Detroit SO.

Gielen, Michael (Andreas) (*b* Dresden, 20 July 1927). Austrian conductor. After a career as a pianist in Buenos Aires he worked at the Vienna Staatsoper (1951–60). He has held posts at the Royal Opera, Stockholm, the Netherlands Opera, the Belgian National Orchestra, the Cologne Opera, Frankfurt Opera, South German Radio, the BBC SO and the Cincinnati SO. He is noted for the force and vitality he brings to complex modern scores and has given many premières and performances of works of the Second Viennese School.

Gieseking, Walter (*b* Lyons, 5 Nov 1895; *d* London, 26 Oct 1956). German pianist. His early career was in Hanover. After World War I he was often heard in modern music, performing Schoenberg, Busoni and Pfitzner. He was admired for his delicacy of tone and refinement of nuance, especially in Ravel, Debussy, and Mozart.

Gifford, Helen (Margaret) (*b* Melbourne, 5 Sept 1935). Australian composer. Her works are indebted to Polish and Asian music. She has written several scores (with electronics) for the theatre.

Gigault, Nicolas (*b* ?Paris, *c*1627; *d* there, 20 Aug 1707). French composer. A leading keyboard player of his time, he was organist at four Parisian churches, and may have been a teacher of Lully. He published two collections, *Livre de musique* (1683, 1685), the second specifically for organ. The 1683 volume contains 20 popular noëls with variations, the earliest example of this genre; that of 1685 contains 183 versets, many showing the influence of contemporary secular music.

Gigli, Beniamino (*b* Recanati, 20 March 1890; *d* Rome, 30 Nov 1957). Italian tenor. He made his début at Rovigo in 1914, as Ponchielli's Enzo. At La Scala he had great success as Boito's Faust (1918) and in 1920 made his Met début, returning to New York until 1932. He appeared at Covent Garden between 1930 and 1946. He was admired for the fluency of his singing but sometimes criticized for his taste.

Gigout, Eugène (*b* Nancy, 23 March 1844; *d* Paris, 9 Dec 1925). French composer. He studied with Saint-Saëns at the Ecole Niedermeyer and associated with Fauré and Franck. In 1863 he became organist of St Augustin, Paris, and in 1911 began teaching at the Conservatoire. Most of his music is for organ.

Gigue. (1) (Fr.: 'jig'; It. *giga*) A popular Baroque dance and a standard movement of the suite. It apparently originated in the British Isles. By the end of the 17th century two distinct styles had emerged: the French gigue, in a moderate or fast tempo (6/4, 3/8 or 6/8) with irregular phrases and imitative texture; and the Italian *giga*, a faster dance in 12/8 metre with regular four-bar phrases and homophonic texture. Bach wrote examples of both types, as well as other gigues which are difficult to classify; Handel's are mostly of the Italian type.

(2) Medieval French name for a bowed string instrument, related to the German *Geige*.

Gilbert, Anthony (*b* London, 26 July 1934). English composer. He came to music late, and from 1959 studied with Seiber, Milner and Goehr. Messiaen and Birtwistle were notable influences on his earlier scores, though in the 1970s his music became calmer and more lyrical, sometimes influenced by Indian music and mythology (e.g. in *The Lakravaka Bird*, 1977). In 1973 he began teaching at the Royal Northern College.

Gilbert, Henry F(ranklin Belknap) (*b* Somerville, MA, 26 Sept 1868; *d* Cambridge, MA, 19 May 1928). American composer. He studied at the New England Conservatory (1886–7) and with MacDowell (1889–92), but devoted himself to composition only after hearing *Louise* in Paris in 1901. He wrote operas, orchestral pieces (including *The Dance in Place Congo*, *c*1908) and songs and was the first to use black spirituals and ragtime in concert orchestral works.

Gilbert, Kenneth (*b* Montreal, 16 Dec 1931). Canadian harpsichordist. He studied in Montreal and Paris, as organist and harpsichordist, and held a post as organist in Montreal, 1955–67; he has taught in Canada and the Low Countries. He is chiefly admired as a harpsichordist, for his elegance and precision in Couperin and his brilliance and vitality in D. Scarlatti. He has edited the harpsichord music of both composers.

Gilels, Emil (Grigor'yevich) (*b* Odessa, 19 Oct 1916; *d* Moscow, 14 Oct 1985). Soviet pianist. He studied in Odessa and performed in public from 1933. He first appeared outside the USSR in 1947, making his New York début in 1955 and his British début in 1959. A flawless technique, powerful discipline and physical strength were heard in a repertory ranging from Bach to Bartók.

Giles, Nathaniel (*b* in or nr. Worcester, *c* 1558; *d* Windsor, 24 Jan 1634). English composer. He was Master of the Choristers at Worcester Cathedral (1851–5), Master of the Children and an organist at St George's Chapel, Windsor, from 1585 and Master of the Children of the Chapel Royal from 1597. His surviving works include three services and some two dozen anthems.

Gillebert de Berneville (*fl* c1250–80). French trouvère. He was active in the Arras region. He left *c*30 songs, notable less for originality than for their facility, grace and mastery of form, with simple melodies having a strong insistence on the final.

Gilles, Jean (*b* Tarascon, 8 Jan 1668; *d* Toulouse, 5 Feb 1705). French composer. He was *maître de musique* at Aix-en-Provence Cathedral from 1693, at Agde from 1695 and at Toulouse from 1697. He mainly composed in the form of the Versailles *grand motet*, showing an unusual expressiveness, bordering on pathos, in his text setting. Two of these works remained popular for most of the 18th century; still more so was his *Messe des morts*, which was widely praised and sung at Rameau's funeral (1764) and Louis XV's (1774).

Gillespie, Dizzy [John Birks] (*b* Cheraw, SC, 21 Oct 1917). American jazz trumpeter. After playing in various bands he joined Cab Calloway's orchestra in 1939, making *c*60 recordings. A founder of bop, he was largely responsible for introducing into jazz whole-tone scales, altered chords, substitute harmonies and 9th, 11th and 13th chords. His 1945 recordings with Charlie Parker were much praised and in the late 1940s he experimented with big-band bop. His *Manteca* (with Gil Fuller, 1947) established Afro-Cuban jazz. His late career was largely with small groups. Gillespie's technique and versatility make him the leading jazz trumpeter after Armstrong.

Gillier, Jean-Claude (*b* Paris, 1667; *d* there, 31 May 1737). French composer. He was a double bass player at the Paris Comédie Française from 1693, and in 1694–1717 composed music for plays there. From 1713 he composed mostly for the *opéras comiques* at the Paris fair theatres. He wrote music for over 70 works in all; he was important for introducing a growing proportion of new music, as divertissements, vaudeville finales and prologues. For dramatic purposes he sometimes called for unusual scorings.

Gillier's brother Pierre ['Gillier l'aîné'] (*b* 1665) was a singing teacher and a song composer; his son 'Gillier le fils' also wrote music for plays.

Gillis, Don (*b* Cameron, MN, 17 June 1912; *d* Columbia, SC, 10 Jan 1978). American composer. After study in Texas he worked for NBC in New York; in 1955 he formed the Symphony of the Air from former members of the NBC SO. His music was often based on American subject matter and popular and traditional material, his whimsical bent being revealed in such works as Symphony no.5$\frac{1}{2}$ (1947). His band works have been widely performed.

Gilly, Dinh (*b* Algiers, 19 July 1877; *d* London, 19 May 1940). French baritone. He studied in Toulouse, Rome and at the Paris Conservatoire, and sang at the Opéra, 1902–8; he was at the Met, 1909–14, in such roles as Rigoletto, Albert (*Werther*) and Sonora in the première of *La fanciulla del West*. He retired in 1924. He was a musical, expressive singer and a fine actor.

Gilman, Lawrence (*b* Flushing, NY, 5 July 1878; *d* Franconia, NH, 8 Sept 1939). American critic. He was music critic of *Harper's Weekly* from 1901 and from 1923 of the *New York Tribune*; noted as a sympathetic writer, he supported Wagner and the impressionists and was early to recognize Ives's importance.

Gilmore, Patrick S(arsfield) (*b* Ballygar, 25 Dec 1829; *d* St Louis, 24 Sept 1892). Irish-American bandmaster and impresario. He had his own band in Boston by 1859 but gained more notice for his gigantic concert-festivals: his World Peace Jubilee in 1872 boasted over 20 000 performers. Of his Civil War songs the most popular was *When Johnny comes marching home* (1863). The Gilmore Band toured until the early 1890s.

Gilson, Paul (*b* Brussels, 15 June 1865; *d* there, 3 April 1942). Belgian composer. Mostly self-taught, he was impressed by Wagner and the Russian Five. He wrote his most important works around the turn of the century, including the orchestral *La mer* (1892) and the opera *Prinses Zonneschijn* (1901); he found the subsequent development of music uncongenial and devoted more attention to teaching and writing textbooks.

Giménez [Jiménez] **(y Bellido), Jerónimo** (*b* Seville, 10 Oct 1854; *d* Madrid, 19 Feb 1923). Spanish composer and conductor. A theatre and concert director in Madrid, he wrote one-act zarzuelas showing a flair for orchestral effects and the influence of folk music. His most popular works include *De vuelta del vivero* (1895) and *La tempranica* (1900).

Ginastera, Alberto (Evaristo) (*b* Buenos Aires, 11 April 1916; *d* Geneva, 25 June 1983). Argentinian composer. He studied at the National Conservatory (1936–8) and made an early reputation with his ballet *Panambí* (1940). Another nationalist ballet, *Estancia*, followed in 1941, when he was also appointed to the staff of the National Conservatory. During an extended visit to the USA (1945–7) he attended Copland's courses at Tanglewood; thereafter his life was divided between Argentina and abroad, his travels sometimes necessitated by changes of government. In 1971 he settled in Geneva.

Until the mid-1950s his music was essentially nationalist in a manner comparable with Bartók, Falla and Stravinsky, but he moved towards an atonal expressionism that has links with Berg and Penderecki: this made possible his late emergence as a composer of highly charged opera in which magic and fantastic elements are prominent (*Don Rodrigo*, 1964; *Bomarzo*, 1967; *Beatrix Cenci*, 1971). Other works include two piano concertos (1961, 1972), the *Cantata para América mágica* for soprano and percussion (1960) and three string quartets (1948, 1958, 1973).

Gioconda, La. Opera in four acts by Ponchielli to a libretto by 'Tobia Gorrio' (Arrigo Boito) after Hugo's *Angelo, tyran de Padoue* (1876, Milan); the well-known *Dance of the Hours* is in Act 3.

Giocoso (It.). Jocular, playful.

Gioielli della Madonna, I. *See* JEWELS OF THE MADONNA, THE.

Giordani, Tommaso (*b* Naples, *c*1733; *d* Dublin, late Feb 1806). Italian composer. He toured with his father's opera company, which in 1756 gave its first opera in London. In 1765–7 he presented five English comic operas and an *opera seria* in Dublin. In 1768–83 he lived in London where he composed three operas and made contributions to, and adaptations of, others' works. The overture to his pantomime *The Elopement* (1767) was particularly successful. Returning to Dublin, he opened an English Opera House and presented seven new works there, but soon became bankrupt. Later he achieved some success, notably with the pantomime *The Island of Saints* (1785). He became music director at the Theatre Royal, Crow Street, in 1788. Among his other works are odes, sacred music, cantatas, canzonets and *c*40 instrumental works including many chamber works with keyboard; his keyboard concertos were very popular in his time. His style is generally *galant*, resembling J.C. Bach's.

He is sometimes confused with Giuseppe Giordani (*c*1753–1798), an opera composer active in Italy and *maestro di cappella* at Fermo Cathedral from 1791.

Giordano, Umberto (*b* Foggia, 28 Aug 1867; *d* Milan, 12 Nov 1948). Italian composer. He studied with Serrao at the Naples Conservatory between 1880 and 1890 and was commissioned, after showing promise in a competition, to write an opera: this was *Mala vita*, a *verismo* opera of some violence and crudity, given at Rome in 1892. After another failure (an old-fashioned romantic melodrama), he moved to Milan, where his *Andrea Chénier* was given, at La Scala, in 1896; with its French Revolutionary subject and its fervent, assertive style, it was an immediate success and has remained popular in Italy and beyond. Comparable success, at least in Italy, was met by *Fedora* (1898, Milan), but of his seven later operas only the comic *Il re* (1929, Milan), which was taken up by coloratura sopranos, enjoyed any real success although he remained a master of the intense, vehement, Massenet-influenced, theatrically effective style that gives *Andrea Chénier* its appeal.

Giorgetti, Ferdinando (*b* Florence, 25 June 1796; *d* there, 22 March 1867). Italian composer and violinist. An early advocate of German instrumental music in Italy, he composed chamber works in the Viennese Classical style and co-founded the first Italian music magazine, the *Revista musicale fiorentina* (1840).

Giorno di regno, Un. Comic opera in two acts by Verdi to a libretto by Romani after A.V. Pineu-Duval's play *Le faux Stanislas* (1840, Milan).

Giornovichi [Jarnowick etc], **Giovanni Mane** (*b* ?Palermo, ?1735–45; *d* St Petersburg, 23 Nov 1804). Italian violinist and composer. He lived in Paris, 1770–79, becoming the city's favourite violinist. He next became leader of the Prussian crown prince's orchestra. Later he served at the Russian court (1782–6, 1803–4); he was in London, 1791–6, then in Hamburg. He was admired for his charming and unaffected playing though was a difficult, arrogant man. His 17 violin concertos, his most popular works, are mostly in a simple *galant* style; they began a fashion for *romance* slow movements. He also wrote violin sonatas, duos and other pieces.

Giovannelli, Ruggiero (*b* Velletri, *c*1560; *d* Rome, 7 Jan 1625). Italian composer. Possibly a pupil of Palestrina, he was *maestro di cappella* at many Roman institutions, including S Luigi dei Francesi (1583–91), the Cappella Giulia (1599) and the Sistine Chapel (1614–24). His output includes six published books of madrigals (1585–1606) and two of motets, some polychoral (1593, 1604), as well as four masses.

Giovanni da Cascia (*fl* northern Italy, 1340–50). Italian composer. Probably from Cascia, near Florence, he may have been associated with the Visconti court at Milan in the 1340s and later with that of Mastino II della Scala in Verona, 16 madrigals and three caccias by him survive, and there is evidence that some were still being performed as late as 1420. He played a decisive part in consolidating the style of the Italian madrigal.

Giovanni d'Arco. Opera in four acts by Verdi to a libretto by Solera partly after Schiller (1845, Milan).

Gipps, Ruth (*b* Bexhill-on-Sea, 20 Feb 1921). English composer and conductor. She was a pupil of Vaughan Williams at the RCM, where she returned to teach. Her works include five symphonies (1942–80), concertos and chamber and choral music.

Gipsy Baron, The. *See* ZIGEUNERBARON, DER.

Giraffe piano. A type of upright PIANOFORTE, popular in the early 19th century.

Girl of the Golden West, The. *See* FANCIULLA DEL WEST, LA.

Giroust, François (*b* Paris, 10 April 1737; *d* Versailles, 28 April 1799). French composer. He held posts at Orléans Cathedral (1756–69) and S Innocents, Paris (1769–75). Already popular for his motets, he composed others as *sous-maître* at the royal chapel (from 1775); from 1785 he was also *surintendant de la musique de chambre*. He wrote *c*70 motets, which combine archaic and modern traits and include notable descriptive passages, besides oratorios, other sacred music, stage works and patriotic and masonic pieces.

Giselle, ou Les Wilis. 'Fantastic ballet' in two acts by Adam to a scenario based on a legend recounted by Heine (1841, Paris); modern productions are based on a St Petersburg production (1884).

Gittern [gyterne]. A short-necked medieval lute, similar to the 16th-century MANDORE. It had a rounded back like the Renaissance lute but was smaller and had no clear division between body and neck; it usually had an angled pegbox. Its three or four (later five) strings or pairs of strings were probably tuned like those of a four-course lute, with the intervals 4th–3rd–4th, and were plucked with a quill.

The gittern probably entered Europe from Arab countries in the late 13th century; in the 14th it was played by minstrels and amateur musicians. In the 15th it was eclipsed by the lute.

Giuditta. Opera in five acts by Lehár to a libretto by Knepler and Löhner (1934, Vienna).

Giuliani, Mauro (Giuseppe Sergio Pantaleo) (*b* Bisceglie, 27 July 1781; *d* Naples, 8 May 1829). Italian guitarist and composer. In Vienna from 1806, he became famous as the greatest living guitarist, teaching, performing and composing a rich repertory for the guitar. He was also a cellist, playing in the première of Beethoven's Symphony no.7 (1813). In 1814 he became honorary chamber musician to Napoleon's second wife. He returned to Italy in 1819 and was patronized by the nobility. His works include three guitar concertos, sonatas, studies and variations for solo guitar, quartets and many duos (with flute or violin) for guitar and songs.

Giulini, Carlo Maria (*b* Burletta, 9 May 1914). Italian conductor. He conducted in Rome from 1944 and made his theatre début in 1950 with *La traviata*. Experience with the Milan RO led to his appointment as principal conductor at La Scala (1953). He conducted a memorable *Don Carlos* at Covent Garden in 1958, returning until 1967 when he decided to concentrate on orchestral engagements. With the Philharmonia Orchestra and the Chicago SO he became known for lyrical yet dynamic performances of a limited repertory. He returned to opera in 1982, with *Falstaff* in Los Angeles and London. He was conductor of the Los Angeles PO, 1978–84.

Giulio Cesare. Opera in three acts by Handel to a libretto by Haym after Bussani (1724, London).

Giuseppino (*fl* 1600). Italian singer and composer. He was probably Giuseppe del Biabo, an entertainer from Bologna who sang his own songs and played the jew's harp and theorbo. Ten of his pieces survive; one, *Fuggi, fuggi, fuggi da questo cielo*, became popular throughout Europe and was later used by Smetana as the main theme of *Vltava*.

Giustini, Lodovico (Maria) (*b* Pistoia, 12 Dec 1685; *d* there, 7 Feb 1743). Italian composer. An organist in Pistoia, he wrote a set of 12 *Sonate da cimbalo di piano e forte* (1732), the earliest known music written specifically for the piano. It includes dynamic markings and other pre-Classical features.

Giustiniana. Term used in the 15th and early 16th centuries for a setting for voice and instruments of verses by LEONARDO GIUSTINIANI; later, from *c*1560 to *c*1600, it signified a type of VILLANELLA in which the text ridicules aged, stuttering Venetians.

Giustiniani, Vincenzo (*b* Chios, 1564; *d* Rome, 1637). Italian theorist and patron. From a noble family, he moved in the highest social circles in Rome. His *Discorso sopra la musica* (MS, 1628) is a valuable source of information on performers and musical practices in the early 17th century.

Giusto (It.). 'Just', 'exact', as in TEMPO GIUSTO.

Glachant, Antoine-Charles (*b* Paris, 19 May 1770; *d* Versailles, 9 April 1851). French composer. A military commander, he founded a conservatory in Arras and wrote stage works for Paris before moving there, *c*1823, as first violinist at the Théâtre Français. He was most popular for his chamber music (flute duos, string quartets and trios), more ambitious than many French works of the time.

Gladwin, Thomas (*b c*1710; *d* ?London, ?1799). English composer. Organist at Vauxhall Pleasure Gardens, London, he played concertos there probably from *c*1740 and was popular for his songs and his eight *Lessons* for keyboard (*c*1755); the three with violin were probably the first of this type by an English composer.

Glagolitic Mass. Cantata by Janáček to a Slavonic church text adapted by Miloš Weingart (1926).

Glanville-Hicks, Peggy (*b* Melbourne, 29 Dec 1912). Australian composer. She studied at the Melbourne Conservatorium, at the RCM with Vaughan Williams (1931–5), in Vienna with Wellesz and in Paris with Boulanger. She then lived in the USA (1942–59) before returning to Australia. Her works include operas (notably *The Transposed Heads*, 1953), orchestral, chamber and vocal pieces.

Glarean, Heinrich [Glareanus, Henricus; Loriti] (*b* Mollis, June 1488; *d* Freiburg, 28 March 1563). Swiss theorist, scholar, poet and humanist. A pupil of Michael Rubellus (*c*1501–6), he studied at Cologne University (music with Cochlaeus) from 1506 to 1510. In 1514 he went to Basle, where he met Erasmus, who became a dominant influence, and taught. Opposed to the Reformation movement, of which Basle was now a centre, he moved to Freiburg, where he was a professor and influential in school music teaching. He knew many musicians of his day, including Mouton and Senfl. His first treatise, *Isagoge in musicen* (1516), deals with the elements of music, solmization and the eight modes; but his fame rests on the vast *Dodecachordon* (1547), which made great impact on Renaissance musical thought. Apart from its extraordinary breadth and diversity, its outstanding contribution lay in Glarean's exposition of his new modal system, in which four modes (the Ionian, Hypoionian, Aeolian and Hypoaeolian) were added to the medieval eight. It is also a valuable musical anthology containing over 120 works by Josquin, Obrecht, Ockeghem and others. Many composers, such as Merulo and the Gabrielis, applied his modal principles to their instrumental compositions.

Glasenapp, Carl Friedrich (*b* Riga, 3 Oct 1847; *d* there, 14 April 1915). German writer. A trusted member of the Wagner circle, he used valuable documentary material in his writings on the composer, which are unreliable because of his blind loyalty.

Gläser, Franz (Joseph) (*b* Horní Jiřetín, 19 April 1798; *d* Copenhagen 29 Aug 1861). Bohemian composer. He studied at the Prague Conservatory, then went to Vienna (1817–30), where he supplied popular theatres with scores for farces and pantomimes. He wrote his best-known works including the popular *Des Adlers Horst* (1832), in Berlin, and later was court conductor in Copenhagen.

Glass, Louis (Christian August) (*b* Copenhagen, 23/4 March 1864; *d* there, 22 Jan 1936). Danish composer. He studied at the Brussels Conservatory. A contemporary of Nielsen, he cultivated a distinctive style; his best works include the Fourth String Quartet op.35 (1901–6) and the programmatic symphonies, especially the Brucknerian 'Skovsymfoni' (no.3, 1901) and the 'Svastica' (no.5, 1919).

Glass, Philip (*b* Baltimore, 31 Jan 1937). American composer. He studied at the Juilliard School and with Boulanger in Paris (1964–6) and worked with the Indian musicians Ravi Shankar and Alla Rakha. His minimalist works of 1965–8 (e.g. *Two Pages*) are 'experimental and exploratory' but later ones, for his own amplified ensemble, are more complicated (e.g. *Music in Fifths*). Since 1975 his works have nearly all been for the theatre. With the Met staging of *Einstein on the Beach* (1976) he became famous; two further operas, *Satyagraha* (1980) and *Akhnaten* (1984), followed. He has become the most popular serious composer in the USA and has performed in rock and jazz.

Glasser, Stanley (*b* Johannesburg, 28 Feb 1926). South African composer. He studied with Seiber and at Cambridge, and became head of music at Goldsmiths' College in 1969. His works include serious and popular pieces, some of his later music reflecting his study of South African folk music.

Glass harmonica. *See* MUSICAL GLASSES.

Glass harp. A type of MUSICAL GLASSES devised in 1929 by Bruno Hoffmann.

Glazunov, Alexander Konstantinovich (*b* St Petersburg, 10 Aug 1865; *d* Paris, 21 March 1936). Russian composer. He studied privately with Rimsky-Korsakov (1879–81) and had his First Symphony performed when he was 16. He became a member of the circle around the patron Belyayev, who took him to meet Liszt in Weimar, and in 1899 was appointed to the St Petersburg Conservatory, which he directed from 1905 until leaving the Soviet Union in 1928. During these later years he composed relatively little: the bulk of his output, which includes nine symphonies, much else for orchestra, the ballet *Raymonda* (1897) and seven quartets, dates from before World War I. He has a significant place in Russian music in that he reconciled Russianism and Europeanism. He absorbed Balakirev's nationalism, Rimsky-Korsakov's orchestral virtuosity, Tchaikovsky's lyricism, Borodin's epic grandeur and Taneyev's contrapuntal skill.

Gleason, Frederick G(rant) (*b* Middletown, CT, 17/18 Dec 1848; *d* Chicago, 6 Dec 1903). American composer. He worked as an organist in Connecticut, then as a teacher, editor and music critic in Chicago from *c*1877. His output includes two operas and four large-scale cantatas, sacred choral pieces and orchestral and chamber works.

Glee. A simply harmonized, unaccompanied English song. Early glees, from the 17th century, were for three or more male voices (alto, tenor, bass was a popular combination); texts were often about eating and drinking, but also love, patriotic themes and the hunt. The genre gradually became more refined and by the late 18th century glees were also written for mixed voices. Societies such as the Glee Club and the Anacreontic Society were formed, but glee singing remained essentially an amateur activity, in taverns and the home, which lasted well into the 19th century. Leading glee composers included Thomas Arne and Samuel Webbe.

Glier, Reyngol'd Moritsevich (*b* Kiev, 11 Jan 1875; *d* Moscow, 23 June 1956). Soviet composer. He studied at the Moscow Conservatory, where he became professor of composition (1920–41). His works, in the Russian epic tradition of Borodin and Glazunov, include three symphonies (the third subtitled 'Il'ya Muromets', 1911), concertos (one for coloratura soprano, 1943) and ballets (notably *The Red Flower*), as well as operas on central Asian themes using indigenous musical traditions, and chamber and piano music.

Glinka, Mikhail Ivanovich (*b* Novospasskoye [now Glinka], 1 June 1804; *d* Berlin, 15 Feb 1857). Russian composer. Having come to know rural folk music in its purer forms, and receiving an unsystematic musical education in St Petersburg and on his sojourn in Italy (1830–33), he neither inherited a tradition of sophisticated composition nor developed a distinctive and consistent personal style. But he exerted a profound and freely acknowledged influence on Balakirev, Rimsky-Korsakov, Musorgsky, Borodin and Tchaikovsky, as well as on Prokofiev and Stravinsky. His first important compositions, written in Berlin (1834), where he studied briefly with Siegfried Dehn, were a Capriccio for piano duet and an unfinished symphony, both applying variation technique to Russian themes. It was his opera *A Life for the Tsar* (1836; originally *Ivan Susanin*) that established him overnight as Russia's leading composer. Though its national character derives from melodic content alone (mostly merely quasi-Russian), it is nevertheless significant for its novel, expressive Russian recitative and for its use of the leitmotif. His next opera, *Ruslan and Lyudmila* (1842), based on Pushkin's fantastic, ironic fairy-tale, was less well received, being structurally unsuited to the stage and musically haphazard, yet it contains elements of striking originality, including Chernomor's grotesque little march, pungent touches of chromatic colour, exuberant rhythms, the use of the whole-tone scale and the 'changing background' technique for folktune presentation. Inspiring the oriental and 'magic' idioms of later Russian composers, this opera proved to be seminal in the history of Russian music. At Paris (1844–5) Glinka enjoyed Berlioz's music and in Spain (1845–7) folk music and fresh visual impressions; two Spanish Overtures resulted, exceeded in inventiveness however by the kaleidoscopic orchestral variations *Kamarinskaya* (1848). Among the rich legacy of his songs, the Pushkin settings *Where is our rose?*, *I recall a wonderful moment*, *Adèle* and *The toasting cup* are particularly fine.

Dramatic music Ivan Susanin [A Life for the Tsar], opera (1836); Ruslan and Lyudmila, opera (1842); incidental music

Instrumental music Kamarinskaya, orch (1848); ovs., other orch pieces; Str Qt, F (1830); Sextet, E♭ (1832); variations, mazurkas for pf; pf duets, incl. Capriccio on Russian Themes, A (1834)

Vocal music songs, partsongs, choruses, hymns

Glissando. A sliding effect; the word, pseudo-Italian, comes from the French *glisser*, 'to slide'. Applied to the piano and harp, it refers to the effect obtained by sliding rapidly over the keys or strings (so that every individual note is articulated, no matter how rapid the 'sliding'). On the voice, violin or trombone, the effect can be of a smooth rise or fall of pitch (as in PORTAMENTO), but a true glissando in which each note is distinguishable is also possible.

Globokar, Vinko (*b* Anderny, 7 July 1934). Yugoslav composer and trombonist. He studied at the Ljubljana Conservatory, at the Paris Conservatoire, with Leibowitz (1959–63) and with Berio (1965), who wrote *Sequenza V* for him. In 1972 he was a founder-member of the quartet New Phonic Art. His works depend on his experience as a performer of jazz, avant-garde and improvised music: many require a creative contribution from the performers (e.g. *Correspondences*, 1969).

Globular flute. A spherical VESSEL FLUTE; an example is the ocarina. African examples are often made from seed shells or small spherical gourds.

Glock, Sir William (*b* London, 3 May 1908). English music administrator, pianist and critic. He studied at Cambridge and with Artur Schnabel in Berlin (1930–33). Though a fine pianist, he at first became a music critic and joined *The Observer* as chief critic (1934–45). In 1948 he founded an influential Summer School of Music at Dartington, remaining its director until 1979; he was also an active promoter of contemporary music. In 1959 he became Controller of Music at the BBC, where he invigorated British musical life by breathing new vitality into what had become a stagnant scene, particularly by bringing together old and new music and introducing artists and composers. He retired in 1973.

Glockenspiel. A percussion instrument with tuned metal (usually steel) bars, arranged like the piano keyboard. Most orchestral glockenspiels are of the open type, played with beaters; the keyboard type, inferior in tone, is now rare. The open type has two standard patterns with a range of *g″* to *c′′′′* and *c″* to *c′′′′*. The keyboard type has a compass of two and a quarter to two and a half octaves, and the bars are struck from below by small metal hammers. (For illustration, *see* PERCUSSION INSTRUMENTS.)

The glockenspiel's earliest use is in Handel's *Saul* (1739): Handel's instrument (called 'carillon') had a keyboard. Glockenspiels played with beaters entered the orchestra in the mid-19th century. Modern models (often called simply 'glock' or 'bells') may have a foot-operated damping mechanism or movable suspension to affect the resonance. Its music is notated in the treble clef, usually two octaves lower than sounding.

Gloria in excelsis deo. The second item of the Ordinary of the Latin Mass, a hymn of praise sung after the Kyrie on festal occasions. The text is considered one of the great prose hymns of Christian literature and the chant melodies are among the most important of medieval chant. Omitted during Advent and Lent, it is also known as the Great Doxology and the Angelic Hymn, and its text begins with *Luke* ii.14. Greek versions were known at an early date in the East and by the 6th century in the West; the received version is first found in Frankish sources of the 9th century. The celebrant intones the first phrase, 'Gloria in excelsis deo' and the choir continues with 'Et in terra pax', which is where most polyphonic settings begin. In later settings the Gloria is often divided into several movements. The Lutheran Mass consists of Kyrie and Gloria alone.

Gloriana. Opera in three acts by Britten to a libretto by William Plomer after Strachey (1953, Covent Garden), written to celebrate the coronation of Elizabeth II.

Glosa (Sp.). 'Gloss': term used in the 16th century, as a musical equivalent of poetic glossing, for variations, usually on a religious theme; it could also mean ornamentation (as in Ortiz's *Trattado de glosas*, 1553).

Gloucester Festival (UK). *See* THREE CHOIRS FESTIVAL.

Glover, Jane (*b* Helmsley, 13 May 1949). English conductor. She studied at Oxford, doing research on Cavalli, and became known as a TV presenter. Her conducting début was at Wexford in 1975, and she worked at Glyndebourne; in 1984 she became artistic director of the London Mozart Players.

Glover, Sarah Anna (*b* Norwich, 13 Nov 1786; *d* Malvern, 20 Oct 1867). English teacher. Her 'Norwich Sol-fa Ladder' provided the basis for John Curwen's tonic sol-fa system of teaching singing.

Gluck, Christoph Willibald Ritter von (*b* Erasbach, 2 July 1714; *d* Vienna, 15 Nov 1787). Bohemian-German composer. His father was a forester in the Upper Palatinate (now the western extreme of Czechoslovakia); Czech was his native tongue. At about 14 he left home to study in Prague, where he worked as an organist. He soon moved to Vienna and then to Milan, where his first opera was given in 1741. Others followed, elsewhere in Italy and during 1745–6 in London, where he met Handel's music. After further travel (Dresden, Copenhagen, Naples, Prague) he settled in Vienna in 1752 as Konzertmeister of the Prince of Saxe-Hildburghausen's orchestra, then as Kapellmeister. He also became involved in performances at the court theatre of French *opéras comiques*, as arranger and composer, and he wrote Italian dramatic works for court entertainments. His friends tried, at first unsuccessfully, to procure a court post for him; but by 1759 he had a salaried position at the court theatre and soon after was granted a royal pension.

He met the poet Calzabigi and the choreographer Angiolini, and with them wrote a ballet-pantomime *Don Juan* (1761) embodying a new degree of artistic unity. The next year they wrote the opera *Orfeo ed Euridice*, the first of Gluck's so-called 'reform operas'. In 1764 he composed an *opéra comique*, *La rencontre imprévue*, and the next year two ballets; he followed up the artistic success of *Orfeo* with a further collaboration with Calzabigi, *Alceste* (1767), this time choreographed by Noverre; a third, *Paride ed Elena* (1770), was less well received.

Gluck now decided to apply his new ideals to French opera, and in 1774 gave *Iphigénie en Aulide* (as well as *Orphée*, a French revision of *Orfeo*) in

Paris; it was a triumph, but also set the ground for a controversy between Gluck and Italian music (as represented by Piccinni) which flared up in 1777 when his *Armide* was given, following a French version of *Alceste* (1776). *Iphigénie en Tauride* followed in 1779 – his greatest success, along with his greatest failure, *Echo et Narcisse*. He now acknowledged that his career was over; he revised *Iphigénie en Tauride* for German performance, and composed some songs, but abandoned plans for a journey to London to give his operas and died in autumn 1787, widely recognized as the doyen of Viennese composers and the man who had carried through important reforms to the art of opera.

Gluck's opera reforms – they are not exclusively his own, for several other composers (notably Jommelli and Traetta, both like Gluck French-influenced) had been working along similar lines – are outlined in the preface he wrote, probably with Calzabigi's help, to the published score of *Alceste*. He aimed to make the music serve the poetry through its expression of the situations of the story, without interrupting it for conventional orchestral ritornellos or, particularly, florid and ornamental singing; to make the overture relevant to the drama and the orchestration apt to the words; to break down the sharp contrast between recitative and aria: 'in short ... to abolish all the abuses against which good sense and reason have long cried out in vain'. *Orfeo* exemplifies most of these principles, with its abandonment of simple recitative in favour of a more continuous texture (with orchestral recitative, arioso and aria running into one another) and its broad musical-dramatic spans in which different types of solo singing, dance and choral music are fully integrated. It also has a simple, direct plot, based on straightforward human emotions, which could appeal to an audience as the complicated stories used in contemporary *opera seria*, with their intrigues, disguises and subplots, could not. He had a limited compositional technique, but one that was sufficient for the aims he set himself. His music can have driving energy, but also a serenity reaching to the sublime. His historical importance rests on his establishment of a new equilibrium between music and drama, and his greatness on the power and clarity with which he projected that vision; he dissolved the drama in music instead of merely illustrating it.

Dramatic music Artaserse (1741); La caduta dei giganti (1746); Le nozze d'Ercole e d'Ebe (1747); La Semiramide riconoscuita (1748); La clemenza di Tito (1752); Le cinesi (1754); L'innocenza giustificata (1755); L'île de Merlin (1758); L'ivrogne corrigé (1760); Le cadi dupé (1761); Orfeo ed Euridice (1762, Fr. version, Orphée, 1774); La rencontre imprévue (1764); Telemaco (1765); Alceste (1767, Fr. version 1776); Paride ed Elena (1770); Iphigénie en Aulide (1774); Armide (1777); Iphigénie en Tauride (1779, Ger. version 1781); Echo et Narcisse (1779); *c*20 others; 4 ballets incl. Don Juan (1761), Semiramis (1765)
Vocal music 7 Klopstock songs (1786); other songs; sacred works incl. De profundis (1787)
Instrumental music 8 trio sonatas; syms.

Glückliche Hand, Die. Drama with music in one act by Schoenberg to his own libretto (1924, Vienna).

Glyndebourne Festival Opera. Company founded in 1934 by John Christie at his estate in Glyndebourne, Sussex. It gives annual summer seasons in the opera house he built there (1934, cap. 311; enlarged to 800). Directors have included Fritz Busch (1934–9, 1950–51), Vittorio Gui, John Pritchard and Bernard Haitink (from 1977). Orchestras have been the RPO (1948–63) and the LPO (since 1964). Its first productions were of Mozart, whose works are still presented each year as part of a wider repertory including Cavalli, Debussy, Rossini, Verdi, Stravinsky and especially R. Strauss. Glyndebourne Touring Opera (founded 1968) takes the productions on tour in Britain.

Gmunden-Gastein Symphony. *See* GASTEIN SYMPHONY.

Gnattali, Radamés (*b* Pôrto Alegre, 27 Jan 1906). Brazilian composer. He studied in Rio de Janeiro and was first a pianist, later a string quartet violist and conductor of the radio orchestra. He has written music of a nationalist flavour, including a *Brasiliana* series for various instrumental combinations, drawing on dance rhythms and jazz, and concertos, symphonies, chamber music and songs.

Gnecco, Francesco (*b* Genoa, *c*1769; *d* Milan, 1810/11). Italian composer. He was *maestro di cappella* of Savona Cathedral for a time and wrote sacred and chamber music, but was most famous for his 25 operas, notably *La prova d'un opera seria* (1805, Milan), a comedy with a backstage plot.

Gnesin, Mikhail Fabianovich (*b* Rostov-na-Donu, 2 Feb 1883; *d* Moscow, 5 May 1957). Russian composer and teacher. He studied with Lyadov and Rimsky-Korsakov at the St Petersburg Conservatory. After teaching in Leningrad and Moscow he became principal of the Gnesin State Institute, Moscow; Khachaturian was among his pupils. From 1941 his music was largely devoted to Jewish subjects.

Gnocchi, Pietro (*b* Alfianello, 1677; *d* Brescia, 4 Sept 1771). Italian composer. He lived as a scholar, priest and ascetic in Brescia, and became *maestro di cappella* at the cathedral in 1762. He composed mostly sacred works, often using alternating choirs in the Venetian style.

Gobbi, Tito (*b* Bassano del Grappa, 24 Oct 1915; *d* Rome, 5 March 1984). Italian baritone. He sang in Italy from 1935 (La Scala début 1942, as Donizetti's Belcore) and appeared at Covent Garden in 1951, where his best London roles were Puccini's Scarpia and Verdi's Posa and Boccanegra. He sang in Chicago from 1954, producing several operas there, and at the Met from 1956. His musicianship and acting ability, allied to a fine though not very large voice, made him one of the finest singing actors of his generation.

Goblet drum. Single-headed drum shaped like a goblet, usually made of pottery, wood or metal; it is used in the Islamic world.

Godard, Benjamin (Louis Paul) (*b* Paris, 18 Aug 1849; *d* Cannes, 10 Jan 1895). French composer. He studied at the Paris Conservatoire. Though most of his works are sentimental salon pieces for piano, his serious music (e.g. the piano studies opp.42 and 107 and the symphonies, chamber music and violin pieces) shows a more classical orientation.

Godefroid, (Dieudonné Joseph Guillaume) Félix (*b* Namur, 24 July 1818; *d* Villers-sur-Mer, 12 July 1897). Belgian harpist and composer. Well known as a harp virtuoso, he wrote an opera, *La harpe d'or* (1858), a useful method and solo pieces that are still in the repertory.

Godowsky, Leopold (*b* Soshly, 13 Feb 1870; *d* New York, 21 Nov 1938). American pianist and composer of Polish birth. He toured widely from the age of nine, making his American début in Boston in 1884. Tours of the USA and Canada followed and until 1900 he taught in Philadelphia and Chicago. Until World War II he continued to appear in Europe; his reputation as a Chopin interpreter was not enhanced by a series of elaborate Studies on the Etudes. His concert career ended in 1930.

Goehr, (Peter) Alexander (*b* Berlin, 10 Aug 1932). British composer. His father, the conductor Walter Goehr (1903–60), brought the family to England in 1933, and he studied with Hall at the Royal Manchester College (1952–5), where fellow students included Birtwistle and Davies. He then followed Messiaen's classes at the Paris Conservatoire (1955–6). Family and education thus fitted him to marry Schoenbergian with post-Webernian influences, which he did in two cantatas, *The Deluge* (1958) and *Sutter's Gold* (1960), and in instrumental pieces of this period. With the Violin Concerto (1962) and Little Symphony (1963) he moved into a broader style made possible by greater understanding of serialism. His first opera, *Arden Must Die* (1967), is a morality on the borders of Weill, and a triptych of music-theatre pieces (1968–70) also shows a concern with social behaviour. Orchestral and chamber works of this period move still closer to the ethos of the two Viennese schools, but in doing so display a more confident individuality (String Quartet no.3, 1976). His second opera, *Behold the Sun* (1985), is about the clash between revolutionary and established thought in 16th-century Germany. In 1976 he became professor of music at Cambridge.

Goethe, Johann Wolfgang von (*b* Frankfurt, 28 Aug 1749; *d* Weimar, 22 March 1832). German writer and poet. He served at the Weimar court from 1775. One of the seminal figures of world literature, he intended many of his writings for music. His greatest work, *Faust*, envisages musical sections, and though never set complete, inspired compositions by Mendelssohn, Schumann, Berlioz, Liszt, Gounod, Mahler and others. Beethoven wrote music for the tragedy *Egmont*. Goethe wrote several Singspiel texts, such as *Claudine von Villa Bella* (later set by Schubert), and his poetry dominated German song from Schubert (e.g. *Erlkönig*) to Wolf – though he himself preferred simple settings, like Zelter's or Reichardt's, to ones as elaborate as Schubert's.

Goetz, Hermann (Gustav) (*b* Königsberg, 7 Dec 1840; *d* Hottingen, 3 Dec 1876). German composer. He studied at the Stern Conservatory, Berlin, soon distinguishing himself as organist and choirmaster in Winterthur, also conducting oratorio and opera performances there. Though he produced some sensitive choral settings (*Nenie*, 1874) and notable orchestral and chamber works (the Mendelssohnian Piano Concerto in B♭, 1867, and Piano Quintet in C minor, 1874), his best-known work is the lively and refined *Der Widerspenstigen Zähmung* (1868–72), considered one of the finest 19th-century German comic operas.

Goeyvaerts, Karel (August) (*b* Antwerp, 8 June 1923). Belgian composer. He studied with Messiaen at the Paris Conservatoire (1947–56) and wrote highly systematic serial music (Sonata for two pianos, 1951) that led to a close creative relationship with Stockhausen. After a spell of writing electronic music, in the 1960s he sought to combine electronic and live sound (e.g. in *Pièce pour piano*, 1964).

Goffriller, Matteo (*b* Bressanone, *c*1659; *d* Venice, 23 Feb 1742). Italian string instrument maker. He was the first important maker of the Venetian school and is best known for his cellos, mostly large instruments (now reduced) based on those of the Amati family.

Göhler, (Karl) Georg (*b* Zwickau, 29 June 1874; *d* Lübeck, 4 March 1954). German composer. He studied in Leipzig with Kretzschmar, had a conducting career, and wrote over 200 songs in a traditional style.

Goldberg, Johann Gottlieb (*b* Danzig, bap. 14 March 1727; *d* Dresden, bur. 15 April 1756). German keyboard virtuoso and composer. Perhaps a pupil of Bach, he was harpsichordist (at Dresden) to Count Keyserlingk, who reportedly commissioned Bach's Goldberg Variations (*c*1741) for him to play to cure or alleviate his insomnia. From 1751 he was in the service of Count von Brühl. Among his works are church cantatas and trio sonatas in a Bachian style, and keyboard music (including concertos) in a more modern idiom.

Goldberg, Szymon (*b* Włoclawek, 1 June 1909). American violinist and conductor of Polish birth. He studied with Flesch in Berlin and made his début in Warsaw (1921). He was leader of the Dresden PO from 1925 and of the Berlin PO under Furtwängler, 1929–34. After World War II, he toured widely becoming an American citizen in 1953; from 1955 he was soloist and conductor with the Netherlands CO.

Goldberg Variations. 30 variations on an original theme for harpsichord by J.S. Bach, BWV988 (*c*1741), written for J.G. Goldberg. Every variation whose number is a multiple of three is some form of canon, at progressively larger intervals (e.g. variation 12 is a canon at the 4th).

Golden Cockerel, The [Zolotoy petushok]. Opera in three acts by Rimsky-Korsakov to a libretto by Bel'sky after Pushkin (1909, Moscow).

Golden Sonata. Nickname of Purcell's Trio Sonata in F, z810, for two violins and continuo.

Goldman, Richard Franko (*b* New York, 7 Dec 1910; *d* Baltimore, 19 Jan 1980). American conductor and critic. He studied at Columbia and from 1937 conducted the Goldman Band, founded by his father, Edwin (1878–1956). He also taught at the Juilliard School (1947–60) and the Peabody Conservatory (1968–77) and wrote criticism, chiefly for the *Musical Quarterly*.

Goldmann, Friedrich (*b* Karl-Marx-Stadt, 27 April 1941). German composer. He studied at the Dresden Musikhochschule (1959–62) and with Wagner-Régeny (1962–4), and has used serial and aleatory procedures. His best-known work is the Sonata for wind quintet and piano (1970).

Goldmark, Carl [Karl; Károly] (*b* Keszthely, 18 May 1830; *d* Vienna, 2 Jan 1915). Hungarian composer. Experienced as a theatre violinist but largely self-taught as a composer, he settled in Vienna in the 1860s, gaining recognition for his String Quartet op.8 (1860) and tirelessly supporting Wagner's works. His fame derived mainly from his colourful first opera, *Die Königin von Saba* (1875), with its Wagnerian harmony and rich melodic style. His other works show him the heir of Schumann, Mendelssohn or Spohr (Violin Concerto op.28), but his late piano pieces are impressionistic.

Goldmark, Rubin (*b* New York, 15 Aug 1872; *d* there, 6 March 1936). American composer and teacher, nephew of Carl Goldmark. He studied with Robert Fuchs at the Vienna Conservatory and with Dvořák at the National Conservatory in New York. He is remembered as a distinguished teacher, privately and at the Juilliard School, 1924–36; his pupils included Copland and Gershwin.

Goldoni, Carlo (*b* Venice, 25 Feb 1707; *d* Paris, 6–7 Feb 1793). Italian playwright and librettist. He was active in opera throughout his career. From the 1740s he wrote only comic works, his librettos dominating the Venetian comic opera stage. They were widely influential: among the most successful were *Il filosofo di campagna* (Galuppi) and *La buona figliuola* (Piccinni). Several were set by Haydn and a version of one, *La finta semplice*, by Mozart (1768). Goldoni reformed *opera buffa* by speeding up the action, simplifying the plot, incorporating a partly serious element (in the new *dramma giocoso* genre, developed with Galuppi) and calling both for more elaborate scenery and more music in a greater variety of forms; he developed especially the full-scale ensemble finale.

Goldsbrough Orchestra. *See* ENGLISH CHAMBER ORCHESTRA.

Goldschmidt, Berthold (*b* Hamburg, 18 Jan 1903). British conductor and composer of German origin. He studied with Schreker in Berlin (1922–5) and moved to England in 1935; he has conducted at Glyndebourne and the Edinburgh Festival. His works, in many genres, have connections with Busoni, Weill and Shostakovich.

Goldschmidt, Otto (Moritz David) (*b* Hamburg, 21 Aug 1829; *d* London, 24 Feb 1907). German pianist, conductor and composer. He was Jenny Lind's accompanist (from 1852 her husband) and the founder and conductor of the London Bach Choir (1875–85); his best-known composition is the oratorio *Ruth* (1867).

Golestan, Stan (*b* Vaslui, 7 June 1875; *d* Paris, 21 April 1956). Romanian composer. He studied with d'Indy, Dukas and Roussel at the Schola Cantorum (1895–1903) and composed orchestral and chamber music and songs in a lyrical, nationalist style.

Golinelli, Stefano (*b* Bologna, 26 Oct 1818; *d* there, 3 July 1891). Italian composer and pianist. Acclaimed throughout Europe in the 1840s and 1850s, he made successful concert tours, taught at the Liceo Musicale in Bologna and wrote over 200 piano pieces in a lyrical yet classically influenced style.

Golishev, Efim [Jef] (*b* Kherson, 20 Sept 1897; *d* Paris, 25 Sept 1970). Russian composer. He studied the violin with Auer and in 1909 went to Berlin, where he wrote a pioneering 12-note composition, the String Trio (1914). He was then, as visual artist and musician, a member of the Berlin dada group; in his *Antisymphonie* and *Kenchmanenver* he invented instruments and equipped the musicians with kitchen utensils. In 1933 he left for peregrinations through western Europe and South America.

Golitsïn [Galitsin], Prince **Nikolay Borisovich** (*b* 19 Dec 1794; *d* Bogorodskoye, 3 Nov 1866). Russian music patron and cellist. He commissioned from Beethoven the quartets op.127, op.132 and op.130, all dedicated to him. His son Yury Nikolayevich Golitsïn (1823–72) was a conductor and composer.

Gombert, Nicolas (*b* c1495; *d* c1560). Flemish composer. Probably a native of Flanders and possibly a pupil of Josquin (he composed a *déploration* on Josquin's death, 1545), he was a singer (from 1526) and *maître des enfants* (from 1529) in Emperor Charles V's court chapel, with which he travelled in Europe and for which he also served unofficially as composer. He was canon of Notre Dame, Tournai, by 1534. By 1540 he had been dismissed from the imperial chapel but was probably pardoned (and granted a benefice) c1552. Highly regarded by his contemporaries as a great innovator, he favoured dense textures and often used dark, rich timbres. He used pervading imitation more consistently than anyone of his own or an earlier generation, creating textures in which the voices tend to be equally important. All but two of his ten extant masses elaborate existing motets or *chansons*. His motets (over 160 survive) (from books, 1539, 1541, many in collections), are his most representative works, each phrase of text having its own expressive motif worked through the texture. Other sacred works include eight fine Magnificats and multi-voice works. His *chansons* (over 70) are like the Netherlands motet only more animated and often conceived on a broad scale. His music continued to be printed until long after his death.

Gomes, (Antônio) Carlos (*b* Campinas, 11 July 1836; *d* Belém, 16 Sept 1896). Brazilian composer. He studied under his father, a bandmaster, began composing at an early age and entered the conservatory at Rio de Janeiro. He was naturally drawn to opera and his first, *A noite do castelo*, was given in Rio in 1861; this and *Joana de Flandres* (1863) were successful and in 1864 he went to study in Milan. Two comic works showed evidence of his ability in a popular style. But it was *Il Guarany*, given at La Scala in 1870 and in Rio on the emperor's birthday later in the year, that brought him international fame; Verdi called it a work of genius and it was performed in most European musical centres. Three further Italian operas followed, with mixed success. Gomes visited Brazil in 1880 and wrote *Lo* *schiavo*, inspired by the abolition of slavery; it was successfully given in Rio in 1889. His last opera, *Condor* (1891, Milan) moves towards *verismo*. An oratorio, *Colombo*, was given in Rio in 1892. Because of political change Gomes had lost official support, and in 1896 he was appointed director of Belém conservatory. A master of late 19th-century Italian opera, he had a high dramatic sense and his melodic invention is richly lyrical. He followed Italian conventions of the time but moved towards leitmotif in certain works; some of his operas show Brazilian feeling, with reminiscence of folk polyphony. He also wrote songs and piano music.

Gomółka, Mikołaj (*b* Sandomierz, *c*1535; *d* ?Jazłowiec, ?5 March 1609). Polish composer. He was educated at the Polish court, where he was a wind player (1555–63), before moving to Sandomierz (1566–78) and Kraków. His 150 four-part psalms (1580) comprise the earliest known published musical setting of the Polish psalter.

Gondoliers, The. Operetta by Sullivan to a libretto by Gilbert (1889, London).

Gong. A circular metal percussion instrument, of definite or indefinite pitch. Gongs may be flat, with the rim turned over ('kettle gong'), or with turned-down rim and central boss (like the gongs of Java and Burma). Most are cast and hammered from an alloy of copper and tin. The gong's primary importance is in south-east Asia but several types are used in the Western orchestra. The most common orchestral gong is large and flat (76 cm or more in diameter), of indefinite pitch, with a shallow lip, and is suspended in a frame to be struck by a heavy beater covered with felt or wool; originally Chinese, it is known as the 'tam-tam'. Other types may be tuned and played in sets. (For illustration, *see* PERCUSSION INSTRUMENTS.)

Gong-chime. A set of small bossed gongs placed upright, usually in a row in pitch order, in a wooden frame, and played by one to four musicians; they are common in south-east Asian ensembles.

Gönnenwein, Wolfgang (*b* Schwäbisch-Hall, 29 Jan 1933). German conductor. He studied in Stuttgart and in 1959 became director of the South German Madrigal Choir, appearing in London in 1964 and South America in 1971. He also conducted the Cologne Bach Choir and taught in Stuttgart. He has conducted some opera but is chiefly known for his clear, well-balanced performances of the standard choral repertory.

Gonzaga. Italian family of music patrons who ruled Mantua, 1328–1627. The most brilliant years at the Gonzaga court began with Isabella d'Este's arrival in 1490 as wife of Francesco II (*d* 1519). Many leading frottolists flourished there. In 1510 Francesco II established a court chapel, while Cardinal Ercole (ruled 1540–63) founded a rival ecclesiastical chapel. Guglielmo (*d* 1587) composed madrigals, motets and masses in a conservative style and founded the palatine basilica of S Barbara; during his reign, and in particular that of his son Vincenzo I (*d* 1612), such composers as Striggio, Gastoldi, Wert, Pallavicino and Monteverdi were employed. Musical productions under Vincenzo I included Monteverdi's early operas and Marco da Gagliano's *Dafne* (1608). Francesco Gonzaga (1590–1628), of the family's cadet branch, wrote sacred music, canzonettas and arias.

Goodall, Sir Reginald (*b* Lincoln, 13 July 1901). English conductor. He studied at the RCM and joined Sadler's Wells Opera in 1944, conducting the première of Britten's *Peter Grimes* in 1945. He joined Covent Garden the following year but opportunities were limited; full recognition came in 1968, with his spacious, refulgent, grandly unified performances of *The Mastersingers* at Sadler's Wells. At the London Coliseum he has conducted the *Ring* (1973) and *Parsifal* (1986) and with the Welsh National Opera *Tristan und Isolde* (1979).

Good Friday Music [Karfreitagszauber]. Music by Wagner from Act 3 scene i of *Parsifal*, sometimes performed as a concert item.

Goodman, Benny [Benjamin] **(David)** (*b* Chicago, 30 May 1909; *d* New York, 13 June 1986). American jazz clarinettist and bandleader. In the early 1920s he played in Chicago, with the 'Austin High School Gang', before joining Ben Pollack's band (1925). From 1929 he was a leading freelance clarinettist. In 1934 he formed his first big band, which used arrangements by Benny Carter, Fletcher Henderson and Dean Kincaide, becoming the leading one of the swing era (1936–9). He also used a jazz trio, quartet and (later) sextet in his programmes. A peerless improviser, Goodman was also a concert performer; he commissioned works from Bartók (*Contrasts*, 1939), Copland and Hindemith (clarinet concertos, both 1947). His big band broke up in 1940, was re-formed later that year, and again (to play bop-style arrangements) in 1948–9. Thereafter he formed bands only for engagements, including tours of South America (1961) and the USSR (1962).

Goossens, Sir (Aynsley) Eugene (*b* London, 26 May 1893; *d* Hillingdon, 13 June 1962). English conductor and composer. He studied in Bruges, Liverpool and London (RCM, with Stanford). He played the violin in the Queen's Hall Orchestra, 1912–15, but after conducting Stanford's opera *The Critic* (1916) established a reputation as a conductor of great technical resource in unfamiliar music. He gave the first British concert performance of *The Rite of Spring* in 1921. After experience with the Handel Society and the Carl Rosa Opera Company his career was largely in the USA: he conducted the Rochester PO from 1923 and the Cincinnati SO, 1931–46. From 1947 to 1956 he did pioneering work in Australia, as director of the New South Wales Conservatorium and conductor of the Sydney SO. Among his many compositions, which are accomplished if eclectic in style, are two operas produced at Covent Garden, *Judith* (1929) and *Don Juan de Mañara* (1937), as well as much orchestral and choral music.

Goossens, Leon (*b* Liverpool, 12 June 1897; *d* Tunbridge Wells, 12 Feb 1988). English oboist, brother of Eugene. He studied at the RCM and at 17 was principal oboist of the Queen's Hall Orchestra; he later played at Covent Garden and in the LPO. He was chiefly known however as a soloist, where his technical mastery, his expressive refinement and his beauty of tone were long recognized as beyond comparison. Many composers, including Vaughan Williams and Britten, wrote works for him.

Goovaerts, Alphonse (Jean Marie André) (*b* Antwerp, 25 May 1847; *d* Brussels, 25 Dec 1922). Belgian musicologist. He is known principally for his valuable *Histoire et bibliographie de la typographie musicale dans les Pays-Bas* (1880).

Gopak. See HOPAK.

Gora. MOUTH BOW sounded by the breath. Found chiefly in southern Africa, it was formerly played mainly by the Khoikhoi (Hottentots) though Bushmen and, later, Bantu peoples also adopted it. It resembles a simple mouth-resonated musical bow, but is sounded by blowing on a piece of quill attached to the string; this gives it a distinctive tone quality, similar to the free reed of the harmonica.

Gorczycki, Grzegorz Gerwazy (*b* Bytom, *c*1667; *d* Kraków, 30 April 1734). Polish composer. He studied in Vienna and Prague and worked in Kraków and Chelmno. A notable figure in Polish Baroque music, he wrote not only *a cappella* polyphony but also in the new concertato style.

Górecki, Henryk (Mikołaj) (*b* Czernica, 6 Dec 1933). Polish composer. He studied with Szabelski at the Katowice Conservatory (1955–60) and with Messiaen in Paris. His music has connections with Penderecki, but its deepest affinities are with ancient Polish religious music, and it often shows a saintly simplicity. Most of his works are for orchestra or chamber ensemble; they include the chamber trilogy *Genesis* (1963) and three symphonies.

Gorgia (It.). Term for improvised ornamentation of the kind described by Caccini (*Le nuove musiche*, 1601/2).

Görner, Johann Valentin (*b* Penig, 27 Feb 1702; *d* Hamburg, end of July 1762). German composer. He was director of music at Hamburg Cathedral from 1756. He composed a collection of odes and songs (1742–52) and other vocal music. His brother Johann Gottlieb (1697–1778) worked with Bach as organist of several Leipzig churches; his appointment as musical director to the University Church (1723) caused a dispute with Bach. He composed cantatas, keyboard music etc.

Gorr, Rita (*b* Zelzaete, 18 Feb 1926). Belgian mezzosoprano. She studied in Ghent and Brussels, made her début in Antwerp (Fricka, *Die Walküre*, 1949) and sang in Strasbourg and from 1952 in Paris. She sang at Bayreuth from 1958, Covent Garden from 1959, La Scala from 1960 and the Met from 1962. She was noted for her large, rich, metallic voice and dramatic temperament, heard to outstanding effect in Wagner and Verdi (Eboli, Amneris) and Gluck's Tauris Iphigeneia.

Gorzanis, Giacomo (*b* Puglia, *c*1520; *d* ?Trieste, 1575–9). Italian composer. A virtuoso lutenist, he was blind. He may have been at the Spanish court in Bari before settling in Trieste (by 1567). His four lutebooks (1561–*c*1575) contain dances arranged in short suites; two books of *napolitane* (1570, 1571) also survive.

Gospel. In Eastern and Western Christian liturgies, the final biblical lesson in the Liturgy of the Word,

or first main division of the Eucharist. It is traditionally chanted by a deacon ('the gospeller') to a simple recitation tone which is occasionally elaborated, but was occasionally set to polyphony.

'Gospel hymnody' is the term for American revivalist religious song from the late 19th century. 'Gospel music' stands for the type of religious popular song that succeeded the SPIRITUAL; *see also* SOUL MUSIC and COUNTRY MUSIC.

Goss, Sir John (*b* Fareham, 27 Dec 1800; *d* London, 10 May 1880). English organist and composer. He succeeded Attwood as organist of St Paul's Cathedral (1838) and composed mainly glees and anthems, long popular for their grace and careful word-setting.

Gossec, François-Joseph (*b* Vergnies, 17 Jan 1734; *d* Passy, 16 Feb 1829). South Netherlands composer. At Paris he was a violinist in La Pouplinière's orchestra, *c*1751–1762, as well as a composer. In 1762–70 he directed the Prince of Condé's theatre at Chantilly, from *c*1766 also serving the Prince of Conti; meanwhile he composed *opéras comiques*, notably *Les pêcheurs* (1766, Paris). He founded the Concert des Amateurs in 1769 and directed it until 1773; the orchestra was one of Europe's finest. In 1773–7 he was a director of the Concert Spirituel. From 1775 he held posts at the Opéra and presented various stage works there; the ballets were the most successful. From 1784 he directed the new Ecole Royale de Chant. At the Revolution he directed the band of the Garde Nationale and wrote numerous Revolutionary works for large forces. After 1799 his output declined, and he concentrated on teaching at the Conservatoire.

Gossec's *c*50 symphonies, showing many Mannheim traits, are his most important works and contributed significantly to the development of the genre in France. One of them (1761) was among the first French orchestral works to use clarinets. Novel effects of scoring also appear in his *Messe des morts* (1760) and oratorio *La nativité* (1774). He also wrote other sacred works, songs, *symphonies concertantes*, chamber music and treatises.

Gosswin, Antonius (*b* ?Liège, *c*1546; *d* 1597–8). Flemish composer. Possibly a pupil of Lassus, he served the Bavarian court chapel from 1558 for many years, twice attending the Diet of Regensburg (1576, 1594). He became organist of St Peter's, Munich, in 1576 and moved to Freising in 1580. His masses, motets and German secular songs (1581) show Lassus's influence.

Gostling, John (*b* East Malling, *c*1650; *d* ?Canterbury, 17 July 1733). English singer. He held clerical posts and was a Gentleman of the Chapel Royal from 1679. A favourite of Charles II, he was a notable deep bass singer for whom Purcell probably wrote *They that go down to the sea in ships*, and copyist of important collections of cathedral music.

Gothic Symphony. Havergal Brian's Symphony no.1 (1927).

Gotovac, Jakov (*b* Split, 11 Nov 1895; *d* Zagreb, 16 Oct 1982). Yugoslav composer. He studied with Marx in Vienna and worked in Zagreb as a conductor and composer of Croatian nationalist music. His works include operas and orchestral pieces; the *Symphonic Reel* (1926) is the most popular Croatian orchestral piece and the opera *Ero the Joker* (1935) was performed in over 80 European opera houses.

Götterdämmerung [Twilight of the Gods]. Music drama in a prologue and three acts by Wagner to his own libretto (1876, Bayreuth), the last of the cycle DER RING DES NIBELUNGEN.

Göttingen Handel Festival (West Germany). Annual (summer) event established in 1920 and organized since 1931 by the Göttinger Händel-Gesellschaft. Operas and other works are given.

Gottlieb, (Maria) Anna (*b* Vienna, 29 April 1774; *d* there, 4 Feb 1856). Austrian singer and actress. She created Barbarina in Mozart's *Le nozze di Figaro* (1786) and Pamina in *Die Zauberflöte* (1791). Thereafter she had a long and popular career in Singspiel.

Gottlieb, Jack S. (*b* New Rochelle, NY, 12 Oct 1930). American composer and writer. He was Bernstein's assistant at the New York PO (1958–66) and has remained associated with Bernstein. His works consist mostly of operas, choral music and songs, many setting Jewish religious texts.

Gottschalk, Louis Moreau (*b* New Orleans, 8 May 1829; *d* Tijuca, Brazil, 18 Dec 1869). American composer and pianist. At 13 he went to Paris for piano and composition lessons, and by 19, through the success of his 'Creole' piano pieces *Bamboula, La savane* and *La bananier* (the so-called Louisiana trilogy), his name was a household word throughout Europe. He was hailed as the New World's first authentic musical spokesman and his keyboard virtuosity was compared with Chopin's. After another charming genre piece, *Le mancenillier* (1851), and tours of Switzerland, France and Spain, 1850–52, he made his New York début. In touring the USA to increase his income, 1853–6, he catered ever more to the public taste for sensational effects (e.g. in *Tournament Galop* and *The Last Hope*). His most fruitful period, 1857–61, was spent in the Caribbean, where in relative seclusion he wrote some of his finest works, including *Souvenir de Porto Rico, Ojos criollos* (four hands), the Symphony no.1 ('La nuit des tropiques') and the one-act opera *Escenas campestres*. A second extended tour of the USA, 1862–5, produced little but the well-known *Dying Poet* and the duet *La gallina*. From his last years in South America, feverishly devoted to concert-giving, the most notable works are *Pasquinade*, the *Grand scherzo* and the *Grande tarantelle* for piano and orchestra. Although not an 'advanced' composer, Gottschalk was sensitive to local colour and often used quotation as both a musical and psychological device, as well as syncopated rhythms and jagged melodic lines – all traits associated with later music.

Gottsched, Johann Christoph (*b* Juditten, 2 Feb 1700; *d* Leipzig, 12 Dec 1766). German writer and critic, a leading figure in the literary reform movement of the German Enlightenment. Though he rejected opera, his ideas for the theatre foreshadowed Gluck. He was one of the first to urge the use of incidental music between the acts of plays. He wrote texts for several secular works by Bach.

Goudimel, Claude (*b* Besançon, 1514–20; *d* Lyons, 28–31 Aug 1572). French composer. After studies in Paris (1549), he was an employee (1551) and partner (1552–5) of the publisher Du Chemin. In 1557 he moved to Metz and by 1567 was in Lyons. His many psalm publications include two complete settings of the Genevan psalter. He also wrote Latin sacred works, humanist odes and nearly 70 *chansons*. Some of the psalms are set in a free motet style; in others the traditional melody is in the top voice with imitative counterpoint or in the tenor with note-against-note harmonization (these last were for domestic use).

Gould, Glenn (Herbert) (*b* Toronto, 25 Sept 1932; *d* there, 4 Oct 1982). Canadian pianist. He appeared with the Toronto SO at the age of 14 and throughout Canada in recitals and broadcasts. From 1957 he performed in the USA and in Europe; his rhythmic dynamism and clarity of part-playing were widely admired in Bach. He was known as an interpreter of Schoenberg. His appearances were unorthodox for their programming and repertory as well as for his mannerisms. In 1964 he abandoned the concert platform for the recording studio, but continued to compose and write articles.

Gould, Morton (*b* New York, 10 Dec 1913). American composer and conductor. He studied in New York and gave piano recitals in his teens including improvisations on submitted themes; he then worked for radio stations. A versatile composer, he has written in many genres, including Broadway musicals (*Billion Dollar Baby*, 1945), but is best known for his orchestral music, in a light style drawing on elements of jazz and folk music, with ingenious rhythms and skilful orchestration. His works include four symphonies (1943–76), two 'symphonettes' (1938–41) and five concertos (1938–84, including one for tap dance, 1952).

Gounod, Charles (François) (*b* Paris, 17 June 1818; *d* St Cloud, 18 Oct 1893). French composer. He studied privately with Reicha and at the Paris Conservatoire with Halévy (counterpoint) and Le Sueur (composition), winning the Prix de Rome in 1839. At Rome (1840–42) he was deeply impressed by the 16th-century polyphonic music (particularly Palestrina's) he heard in the Sistine Chapel and wrote some rather austere masses; for a time a church organist in Paris, he considered joining the priesthood. The climax of his liturgical work came in 1855 with the florid *Messe solennelle de Ste Cécile*, a favourite setting scarcely superseded by his 12 later ones (1870–92). Meanwhile he wrote a Gluckian, then a Meyerbeerian opera, both failures; the succeeding five, all first performed at the Théâtre-Lyrique, are the works by which he is remembered, namely the small-scale *Le médecin malgré lui* (1858) and *Philémon et Baucis* (1860), the triumphant *Faust* (1859), in which sensitive musical characterization and a refreshing naturalness set new standards on the French operatic stage, and the major successes *Mireille* (1864) and *Roméo et Juliette* (1867).

In 1870 Gounod took refuge in England from the Franco-Prussian War, staying some four years to exploit the English demand for choral music. The first conductor of the Royal Albert Hall Choral

Society (1871), he produced dozens of choruses and songs. But he experienced considerable intrigue in his private life, effectively marking the end of his fruitfulness as a composer. His oratorios for Birmingham, *La rédemption* and *Mors et vita*, if banal and facilely emotional, were nonetheless successful. Gounod's influence on the next generation of French composers, including Bizet, Fauré and especially Massenet, was enormous. Tchaikovsky and later Poulenc, Auric and Ravel admired his clean workmanship, delicate sentiment, gift for orchestral colour and, in his best songs, unpretentious lyrical charm.

Dramatic music Le médecin malgré lui (1858); Faust (1859); Philémon et Baucis (1860); Mireille (1864); Roméo et Juliette (1867); Polyeucte (1878); 6 other operas; incidental music to Jeanne d'Arc (1873) and 4 other plays
Vocal music Messe solennelle de Ste Cécile (1855); 16 other masses; 4 oratorios, incl. La rédemption (1882), Mors et vita (?1885); sacred pieces; partsongs, solo songs, duets
Instrumental music 2 syms.; Petite symphonie, wind (1885); Str Qt; chamber and orch pieces; pf, org music

Gouvy, Louis Théodore (*b* Goffontaine, 3/5 July 1819; *d* Leipzig, 21 April 1898). French composer. Dividing his time between Paris and Germany, he wrote over 90 works, including much traditional instrumental music and several large choral works; his music is commonly compared with Mendelssohn's.

Gow. Scottish family of folk fiddlers. The most celebrated members were Niel (1727–1807), whose distinctive playing style and published collections of strathspey reels (1784, 1788, 1792) gained him widespread recognition, and his son Nathaniel (1766–1831), a dance-band leader, music publisher and composer of airs, reels and strathspeys in the Scottish folk style.

Goyescas. Suite of seven piano pieces by Granados (1911) inspired by Goya's paintings. Granados incorporated some of their music in his opera of the same title, in three scenes to a libretto by F. Periquet (1916, New York).

G.P. Abbreviation for *Generalpause* (Ger.), a rest for the entire orchestra or ensemble.

Grabner, Hermann (*b* Graz, 12 May 1886; *d* Bolzano, 3 July 1969). German teacher and composer. In 1910 he began studies in Leipzig with Reger, whose assistant he became in 1912, teaching later in Leipzig and Berlin. His importance lies in his work as a theorist and teacher.

Grabu, Louis (*fl* 1665–94). French composer working in England. He succeeded Nicholas Lanier as Master of the King's Musick (1666–74), taking charge of the bands of violins. He composed songs and incidental music for plays and was chosen by Dryden to set his opera *Albion and Albanius* (1685), the music of which is Lullian in style.

Grace notes. Ornamental notes written or printed smaller than the main text, not reckoned within the written bar length. Some are ornaments, with a conventional realization (the term is sometimes taken to imply ornaments sounded before the main note); others, as in the piano music of Chopin, Liszt etc, may be lengthy passages of figuration that defy precise notation in rhythmic terms or invite freedom in performance.

Gradual. Chant of the Proper of the Roman Mass which follows the reading of the Epistle. It evolved in the 5th century and is an example of responsorial psalmody (in which soloists alternate with a choir), consisting of a choral respond intoned by a soloist, a solo verse and a repetition of the last part of the choral respond. Texts are usually from the psalms. The melodies, which are melismatic, are arranged in groups by mode.

Gradus ad Parnassum (Lat.: 'Steps to Parnassus'). Title of a textbook in counterpoint by J.J. Fux, first published in 1725; its method of teaching strict counterpoint was not only used by the Viennese Classical composers but became the foundation of contrapuntal study for more than two centuries. Debussy used the title for the first piece in his piano suite *Children's Corner*.

Graener, Paul (*b* Berlin, 11 Jan 1872; *d* Salzburg, 13 Nov 1944). German composer. He studied at the Veit Conservatory, Berlin, then lived in London (1896–1908) before returning to teach and compose in Austria and Germany. His music has connections with Strauss, Reger and Pfitzner. On the basis of his 130 lieder and nine operas he was among the most frequently performed of living German composers in the 1920s; the operas include *Hanneles Himmelfahrt* (1927), *Friedemann Bach* (1931) and *Der Prinz von Homburg* (1935).

Graf. German family of musicians. Johann (1684–1750), a violinist, served at Mainz, Bamberg and Rudolstadt (Konzertmeister, 1722–39, Kapellmeister from 1739); he composed mostly violin sonatas. His son Christian Ernst (1723–1804), also a violinist, succeeded him and in 1765 became Kapellmeister to Prince William of Orange at The Hague; his output includes symphonies, chamber and keyboard music and songs. A second son, Friedrich Hartmann (1727–95), toured as a flautist and held posts in Hamburg, Steinfurt, The Hague and Augsburg (as a music director from 1772); Mozart visited him in 1777. A director of the London Professional Concerts, 1783–4, he composed instrumental works (many with flute), oratorios, cantatas etc.

Graf, Conrad (*b* Riedlingen, 17 Nov 1782; *d* Vienna, 18 March 1851). Austrian piano maker of German birth. Active in Vienna from 1804, he is recognized as a maker of fine instruments rather than an innovator, a typical Graf piano having virtually all-wood construction, a range of six octaves and a 4th or 5th and three to five pedals. Beethoven, Chopin, the Schumanns and Liszt were among his admirers.

Graf, Max (*b* Vienna, 1 Oct 1873; *d* there, 24 June 1958). Austrian music critic. He studied with Hanslick and Bruckner and wrote a dissertation on the music of women in the Renaissance; he taught in Vienna but was chiefly occupied as a critic for the *Wiener Allgemeine Zeitung* and other newspapers. During World War II he taught and wrote in the USA, returning to Vienna in 1947. Well known as a progressive critic, a supporter of the Second Viennese School, he wrote several books, notably a history of music criticism, *Composer and Critic* (1946). His son Herbert (1904–73) was a noted opera prodducer, appearing at the Met (1936–60), Salzburg, Covent Garden and elsewhere.

Gräfe, Johann Friedrich (*b* Brunswick, 1711; *d* there, 8 Feb 1787). German poet and composer. In 1737–43 he published four volumes of lieder set by himself, C.F. Hurlebusch, C.H. Graun and C.P.E. Bach, which helped establish the lied as a significant form.

Grainger, (George) Percy (Aldridge) (*b* Brighton, Melbourne, 8 July 1882; *d* White Plains, NY, 20 Feb 1961). American composer of Australian origin. He studied with Knorr and Kwast at the Hoch Conservatory in Frankfurt (1895–9), where he became linked with Balfour Gardiner, Quilter and C. Scott, and settled in London in 1901. Another close friend was Grieg. During the next decade he appeared widely as a concert pianist; he also took part in the folksong movement, collecting and arranging numerous songs. He was an unconventional man, in his attitudes, his lifestyle and his music where he experimented with a variety of techniques, including rhythm freed from regular metre, polytonality, improvisation and highly unusual instrumentation. In 1914 he moved to the USA, where he taught in Chicago and New York; he visited Australia several times, helping the establishment of the Grainger Museum at Melbourne. His large output, complicated by the fact that he often made several versions of a piece, includes both original works and folksong arrangements. He has suffered the fate of being remembered more for what he called his 'fripperies' (*Country Gardens, Handel in the Strand, Molly on the Shore*) than his larger works, but even in them his originality of spirit comes through.

Gram, Peder (*b* Copenhagen, 25 Nov 1881; *d* there, 4 Feb 1956). Danish composer. He studied with Krehl in Leipzig (1904–7) and worked in Denmark as a leading teacher, conductor and administrator. His few works include three symphonies and three string quartets.

Granada International Festival (Spain). Annual (summer) festival established in 1952; events include concerts by visiting orchestras, soloists and chamber groups in the Alhambra, the Generalife and other venues.

Granados (y Campiña), Enrique (*b* Lerida, 27 July 1867; *d* English Channel, 24 March 1916). Spanish composer. He studied in Barcelona with Pedrell and in Paris (1887–9), then returned to Barcelona to work as a teacher, pianist and composer. His greatest success came with the piano suite *Goyescas* (1911), a sequence of highly virtuoso studies after paintings by Goya; he expanded them to form an opera of the same title, produced in New York in 1916. His other works include songs, orchestral pieces and more piano music.

Granata, Giovanni Battista (*b* Turin; *d* after 1684). Italian composer, focal point of a guitar school centred on Bologna. He published seven books of music for the instrument, some with strings and continuo, the last four of which are among the most important in the Italian Baroque guitar repertory; dominated by lute-like plucked textures, as opposed to strummed, they display a virtuoso exploitation of the in-

strument's resources and extend its range.

Gran cassa (It.). Bass drum; *see* DRUM.

Grancini, Michel'Angelo (*b* Milan, 1605; *d* there, 1669). Italian composer. *Maestro di cappella* at Milan Cathedral from 1650, he was a prolific church music composer. At his best in settings of motet texts with expressive potential, he wrote in most of the current liturgical forms; the largest published works are the *Varii concerti* (1652) and *Giardino spirituale* (1655).

Grancino, Giovanni (*fl c*1685–*c*1726). Italian violin maker. He was the most important Milanese violin maker, at least until the time of Guadagnini, showing good workmanship if serving a less wealthy clientèle than that of his Cremonese competitors. He made an unusually large number of cellos.

Grand choeur. The Great chorus of a French organ.

Grand Duo. Sub-title given by the publisher to Schubert's Sonata in C for piano duet, D812 (1824). It was once thought to be a piano version of a 'lost' symphony but this theory has been discredited by scholars. There are orchestral versions of the work by Joachim and Anthony Collins.

Grande-Duchesse de Gérolstein, La. Opera in three acts by Offenbach to a libretto by Meilhac and Halévy (1867, Paris).

Grande Ecurie et la Chambre du Roy, La. French early music ensemble, founded in 1966 by the oboist Jean-Claude Malgoire (*b* 1940). They have given many performances in France and elsewhere, mostly on period instruments, and have made recordings of Baroque works, chiefly French (Lully, Rameau) but also operas by Handel.

Grande messe des morts. Berlioz's Requiem, op.5 (1837).

Grande symphonie funèbre et triomphale. Work by Berlioz for chorus, military band and orchestra to a text by A. Deschamps (1840).

Grandi, Alessandro (*b* ?1575–80; *d* Bergamo, 1630, after June). Italian composer. He may have studied with Giovanni Gabrieli in Venice. His first posts were in Ferrara: he became *maestro di cappella* of the Accademia della Morte in 1597, of the Accademia dello Spirito Santo in 1610 and of the cathedral in 1615. In 1617 he moved to Venice as a singer at St Mark's, where Monteverdi was *maestro di cappella*; he was made his deputy in 1620. From 1627 he was *maestro di cappella* of S Maria Maggiore, Bergamo.

Grandi was one of the most talented and popular composers of his day in northern Italy. He contributed importantly to church music in the new concertato style, particularly in his *c*200 motets (including 11 published collections). The earlier of these, mostly for two to five voices, are distinctive for their emotional intensity and interesting textures. Many of his motets of after *c*1620 are for solo voice with instruments; this new genre was to lead to the 'sacred concertos' of Schütz and later German composers. Grandi also composed three books of large-scale psalms and masses (1629–30). His secular works include strophic solo cantatas and arias, written in a progressive, tuneful style, and two books of concertato madrigals.

He should not be confused with the Alessandro

Grandi (1638–97) who worked at Rimini Cathedral and composed sacred music.

Grand jeu. Term in French organ music denoting either the early Diapason chorus, without Flute mutations or reeds, or a combination of Bourdons, mutations, Cornet and reeds.

Grand macabre, Le. Opera in two acts by Ligeti to a libretto by M. Meschke after Ghelderode (1978, Stockholm).

Grand opera. A serious, all-sung opera. The term also means, in French (*grand opéra*), the Paris Opéra and the operas performed there. It is applied more narrowly to the monumental works given at the Opéra during its period of greatest magnificence, including Rossini's *Guillaume Tell* (1829) and works by Meyerbeer and others of the 1830s to librettos by Scribe. Normally they were in four or five acts, dealt with passionate human relationships against a conflict of peoples, classes or religions, and involved spectacular staging. The term may also be applied to operas by Donizetti and Verdi (whose French *Don Carlos*, 1867, is arguably the supreme example of the genre, and to his Italian *Aida*), and to Wagner's German opera *Rienzi* (1842).

Grand orgue (Fr.). Full organ; it may also refer to the Great organ (*see* ORGAN) and can be used to distinguish a true pipe organ from other types.

Grand pianoforte. A piano in a horizontal wing-shaped case of a form directly derived from the harpsichord's. The earliest recorded use of the term is a 1777 patent to Robert Stodart for a HARPSI-CHORD-PIANO. *See* PIANOFORTE; for illustration, *see* KEYBOARD INSTRUMENTS.

Granier, Louis (*b* Toulouse, 1740; *d* there, 1800). French composer. He directed the opera at Bordeaux, went to Paris (1766), to Toulouse (music director of the theatre, 1770–73), then back to Paris, playing in the royal chapel, the Concert Spirituel and at the Opéra (assistant to the director, 1777–86). He contributed to several operas, notably *Théonis* (1767, Paris: with P.-M. Berton and J.C. Trial). He was related to François Granier (1717–79), a composer, cellist and violinist active in Lyons and in Paris, 1760–66, where he wrote ballets for Noverre.

Graphic notation. Type of notation used by some composers of the second half of the 20th century, which gives no precise indication of what notes are to be played, or when, but uses graphic means (sometimes but not always incorporating material akin to musical notation) to suggest what the performer might play. Some graphic scores are accompanied by verbal instructions. The technique was used by Morton Feldman (in *Projections*) as early as 1951; other composers to have used it include Ligeti, Stockhausen and Cardew. *See* NOTATION and ALEATORY.

Graun, Carl Heinrich (*b* Wahrenbrück, 1703–4; *d* Berlin, 8 Aug 1759). German composer, brother of J.G. Graun. After singing in the opera chorus at Dresden he joined the Brunswick Opera (1725), becoming vice-Kapellmeister *c*1727 and writing six operas for the court. From 1735 he was Kapellmeister to the Prussian crown prince, after whose accession (as Frederick the Great) in 1740 he became Kapellmeister. He recruited singers in Italy for the new Berlin Opera, which opened with his *Cesare e Cleopatra* (1742), and remained its chief composer, writing 26 works; some (e.g. *Montezuma*, 1755) have librettos by the king, who also controlled musical content. They are strongly influenced by Hasse, and with his are the foremost Italian operas of mid-18th-century Germany, but they also bear signs of the reform tendencies of the Gluck epoch. Graun's sacred works, notably the long-popular and intensely felt Passion *Der Tod Jesu* (1755, Berlin), tend to be more adventurous, as do his expressive Italian solo cantatas. He also wrote concertos, trio sonatas and other instrumental music.

Graun, Johann Gottlieb (*b* Wahrenbrück, 1702–3; *d* Berlin, 27 Oct 1771). German composer. He studied the violin and composition with J.G. Pisendel and later with Tartini in Prague (*c*1723–4). After serving briefly at Merseburg and Arolsen he joined the musical establishment of the Prussian crown prince in 1732; when the prince became king (Frederick the Great) in 1740, Graun became Konzertmeister at the new Berlin Opera. One of the foremost German instrumental composers of the pre-Classical era, he wrote *c*400 works, including symphonies, concertos (most for violin), trio sonatas etc. The symphonies have a fresh, individual style, and use clear sonata forms. He also composed sacred music, solo cantatas and songs.

His brother August Friedrich (1698/9–1765), a musician at Merseburg, was also a composer.

Graupner, (Johann) Christoph (*b* Kirchberg, 13 Jan 1683; *d* Darmstadt, 10 May 1760). German composer. He was a friend of Telemann and an opera harpsichordist in Hamburg, 1707–9; there he presented five operas, notable for their independent and dramatic instrumental writing. *Bellerophon* (1708) was especially successful. He then became vice-Kapellmeister to the Darmstadt court and in 1712 Kapellmeister; in 1723 he declined the post of Kantor at the Leipzig Thomaskirche before it was offered to Bach. After several more operas (up to 1719), he turned to other genres, and was unusually prolific. His *c*1400 church cantatas contain a variety of solo and choral numbers, many with chorales; he also wrote 24 secular cantatas. Foremost in his instrumental output are 113 symphonies, some thoroughly italianate. Among his other works are orchestral overture-suites, over 40 concertos (many with wind solos) in a Vivaldian style, chamber music and keyboard works; his Partien (keyboard suites) combine French and Italian features.

Graupner, (Johann Christian) Gottlieb (*b* Verden, 6 Oct 1767; *d* Boston, 16 April 1836). German-American musician. He was oboist in a Hanover regiment until 1788, when he went to London, playing in Haydn's orchestra in 1791–2, and then went to America where he is recorded as playing an oboe concerto in Charleston in 1796. He published and sold music there and became a leading musical figure in Boston, organizing orchestras and helping in the foundation of the Handel and Haydn Society.

Grave (Fr., It.). Serious, grave.

Gravicembalo. Italian 17th-century name for the

HARPSICHORD.

Graz Festival. *See* STEIRISCHE HERBSTFESTIVAL.

Graziani. Italian family of singers. The most celebrated members were Francesco (1828–1901), a baritone noted for his Verdi roles, and his brother Lodovico (1820–85), a tenor, who sang in the première of *La traviata*.

Graziani, Bonifazio (*b*?Marino, *c*1604; *d* Rome, 15 June 1664). Italian composer. *Maestro di cappella* at the Gesù and the Roman Seminary from 1648, he ranks with Carissimi as an outstanding member of the Roman school. In addition to two oratorios his 25 published collections contain polyphonic masses, psalms and motets (his most important works). In those for solo voice (six collections, 1652–72) Graziani demonstrates his mastery of declamation and free arioso.

Grazioli, Giovanni Battista (Ignazio) (*b* Bogliaco, 6 July 1746; *d* Venice, *c*1820). Italian composer. He worked at St Mark's, Venice (second organist, 1782–5, first 1785–9). Among his works are 12 attractive harpsichord sonatas (*c*1780) and much sacred music. His son Alessandro was also a composer.

Grazioso (It.). Graceful, agreeable, dainty.

Great C major Symphony. Nickname of Schubert's Symphony no.9 (1828).

Great octave. Term used by organ builders to refer to the (pipes of the) octave *C–c*.

Greatorex, Thomas (*b* N. Wingfield, 5 Oct 1758; *d* Hampton, 18 July 1831). English conductor, teacher and organist. He is remembered chiefly as conductor of ·the aristocratic Ancient Concerts (1793–1831) and as a private music teacher; he became organist of Westminster Abbey in 1819.

Great organ. Term denoting either a large organ (as distinct from a smaller chamber organ) or the larger, main manual of a two-manual or double organ.

Greber, Jakob (*d* Mannheim, bur. 5 July 1731). German composer. In 1703–5 he composed stage music in London, including the pastoral *Gli amori d'Ergasto* (1705), the first Italian opera staged there. He then became Kapellmeister to Duke Karl Philipp at Innsbruck and (when the duke became Elector Palatine in 1717) Neuburg, Heidelberg and Mannheim. He composed several more stage works, and solo cantatas.

Grechaninov, Alexander Tikhonovich (*b* Moscow, 25 Oct 1864; *d* New York, 4 Jan 1956). Russian composer. He studied at the Moscow Conservatory (1881–90) and with Rimsky-Korsakov at the St Petersburg Conservatory (1890–93) and worked as a piano teacher and folksong arranger; in 1910 he received a pension for his liturgical music. But that ceased with the Revolution, and in 1925 he settled in Paris, moving to the USA in 1929. His large output (nearly 200 opus numbers) includes operas, five symphonies, masses, songs and piano music.

Green, Ray (Burns) (*b* Cavendish, MO, 13 Sept 1908). American composer. He studied with Bloch at the San Francisco Conservatory (1927–33) and with Milhaud in Paris (1935–7), then returned to the USA to work as a composer, teacher and publisher: in 1951 he founded American Music Editions. His works incorporate American elements and cover all genres; the best known are *Festival Fugues* (1936), *Holiday for Four* (1936) and *Sunday Sing Symphony* (1940).

Greenberg, Noah (*b* New York, 9 April 1919; *d* there, 9 Jan 1966). American conductor and musicologist. He was largely self-taught. In 1952 he founded the New York Pro Musica, a group of singers and instrumentalists devoted to medieval and Renaissance music. His revival of the medieval *Play of Daniel* in 1958 had particular impact. Greenberg and the Pro Musica's vital, exciting presentation of early music changed current attitudes and influenced the formation of similar ensembles.

Greene, Maurice (*b* London, 12 Aug 1696; *d* there, 1 Dec 1755). English composer and organist. After working as a church organist in London, he succeeded to every major musical post in England, becoming organist at St Paul's Cathedral (1718), organist and composer of the Chapel Royal (1727) and Master of the King's Musick (1735). He was also professor of music at Cambridge, and active in groups including the Academy of Ancient Music; later he set up the Apollo Academy as a rival. With Festing he founded the Royal Society of Musicians in 1738. His project to issue a collection of church music, ancient and modern, was unfinished at his death (Boyce carried it through).

Greene is remembered chiefly for his church music, including *c*100 anthems (mostly of the verse and solo types) and several services and canticles. He also wrote three oratorios (notably *The Song of Deborah and Barak*, 1732), an Ode for St Cecilia's Day (1730), 35 court odes, two dramatic pastorals, various cantatas, songs etc and attractive keyboard suites. His large-scale works include dramatic touches and simple but monumental effects; his style is generally Baroque and italianate, with both contrapuntal material and fluent melodic writing.

Greene, (Harry) Plunket (*b* Old Connaught House, Co. Wicklow, 24 June 1865; *d* London, 19 Aug 1936). Irish bass-baritone. After study in Florence and London he sang in *Messiah* in 1888. He was soon in demand as a lieder singer but was best known in the large choral works of Parry and Elgar. He first toured the USA in 1893.

Greeting, Thomas (*d* London, 1682). English instrumentalist and teacher. In the service of Charles II (from 1662) and the Duke of York (from 1677), he is now known chiefly for his *Pleasant Companion* (*c*1667–8) containing instructions and 54 pages of tunes for the flageolet, printed in dot notation.

Grefinger, Wolfgang (*b*?1470–80; *d* after 1515). German or Austrian composer. He studied under Hofhaimer, probably in Innsbruck, and became organist at St Stephen's Cathedral, Vienna. In 1515 he published his *Cathemerinon*, containing four-voice settings of hymns. His music was greatly esteemed in his lifetime and long remained popular. His numerous Tenorlieder were his most important works, though he also composed Latin motets.

Greghesca. A light 16th-century song, related to the VILLANELLA, to words by ANTONIO MOLINO which mixed Venetian and Greek dialects.

Gregoir, Edouard (Georges Jacques) (*b* Turnhout, 7 Nov 1822; *d* Wijneghem, 28 June 1890). Belgian writer on music. He is known chiefly for his historical writings on music in Belgium and on Belgian composers. His brother Jacques (1817–76) was a pianist and composer.

Gregora, František (*b* Netolice, 9 Jan 1819; *d* Písek, 27 Jan 1887). Czech composer and teacher. He studied in Vienna. A choirmaster, he wrote songs, partsongs and much church music, as well as 17 double bass concertos and an important harmony manual (1876).

Gregorian and Old Roman chant. Old Roman chant is a liturgical repertory of melodies which survives in MSS of the 11th–13th centuries but can be traced to at least the 8th. It is no longer thought that 'Gregorian' chant represents Roman chant in the time of Gregory (590–604) but that it originated in the Frankish Empire *c*800, with the introduction of the Roman liturgy there; Old Roman chant was the Roman version of this Gregorian chant. The Roman tradition continued to develop until the 11th century, absorbing certain Frankish elements; it was finally ousted by Gregorian chant in Rome in the high Middle Ages. Standard melodic formulae and melismas are less clearly outlined and less stable in some parts of the Old Roman repertory, and the melodic lines have less flexibility than in Gregorian chant.

Gregory, William (*fl* 1651–87). English composer and viol player. He served at court throughout Charles II's reign in both the King's Musick and the Chapel Royal. Noted for two keyboard suites in Locke's *Melothesia* (1673), he also composed ten suites for other instruments and songs printed in anthologies (1667–93). He is often confused with another William Gregory (*c*1605–63), also a court musician.

Greig, Gavin (*b* Parkhill, 10 Feb 1856; *d* Whitehill, 31 Aug 1914). Scottish folk music scholar. He collected and studied some 100 000 lines of text and over 3000 tunes of Scottish folksongs and balladry.

Greiss, Yusef (*b* Cairo, 13 Dec 1899; *d* Venice, 7 April 1961). Egyptian composer. He was a pioneer of Egyptian nationalism. His symphonic poem *Egypt* (1932) was the first orchestral work composed by an Egyptian; he composed three more symphonic poems and two symphonies.

Grell, (August) Eduard (*b* Berlin, 6 Nov 1800; *d* there, 10 Aug 1886). German conductor and composer. Principal conductor of the Singakademie (1853–76) and an advocate of the *a cappella* movement, he was one of the greatest exponents of early church music, particularly of works in the Palestrina style; his best-known composition is a 16-part *a cappella* mass (1861).

Grenon, Nicolas (*b c*1380; *d* 1456). French composer and pedagogue. A clerk at Notre Dame, Paris, he became a canon (later sub-deacon, then deacon) of the church of the Holy Sepulchre there. By 1403 he was master of the choirboys at Laon Cathedral. In 1408–9 he was a teacher and singer in Cambrai and by 1412 he had joined the service of John the Fearless, Duke of Burgundy. Having returned briefly to Cambrai Cathedral, he was master of the choirboys of the papal chapel in Rome (1425–7), but spent the rest of his life in Cambrai. Five *chansons* (three rondeaux, a ballade and a virelai), four isorhythmic motets and an incomplete Gloria by him survive.

Gresnick, Antoine-Frédéric (*b* Liège, bap. 2 March 1755; *d* Paris, 16 Oct 1799). South Netherlands composer. He studied in Naples, and in 1779–80 presented two *opere buffe* in Italy. He then moved to Lyons, visiting London in 1786 to give his opera *Alceste*, and directing the theatre orchestra, 1787–9. Settling in Paris in 1794, he composed many *opéras comiques* in a fluent melodic style akin to Grétry's; he was well regarded internationally. Among his other compositions are vocal music (including 'dialogued' *romances* with a violin or flute) and concertos.

Gretchen am Spinnrade. Song by Schubert (D118), a setting for voice and piano of a passage from Goethe's *Faust* (1814).

Grétry, André-Ernest-Modeste (*b* Liège, 8 Feb 1741; *d* Paris, 24 Sept 1813). French composer. Of Walloon descent, he was a distinguished boy soprano. In 1761–5 he studied in Rome, composing sacred music and two intermezzos (1765). He settled in Paris in 1767 and began writing in the new *opéra comique* genre; his second work, *Le Huron* (1768), was an instant success. As his output continued he rose in esteem, and many works were given abroad (especially in Liège). Some (e.g. *Zémire et Azor*, 1771) used oriental subjects. His serious opera *Andromaque* (1780) was a failure, but with *Colinette à la cour* (1782) and *Panurge dans l'île des lanternes* (1785) he successfully introduced comic subject matter to the Opéra, helping to remove the barriers between tragedy and comedy. In the rivalry between supporters of Gluck and Piccinni, Grétry favoured the Gluckists, whose applause made his *La caravane du Caire* (1783) a particular triumph. After *Richard Coeur-de-lion* (1784) his inspiration declined. Several works were banned after the Revolution, and his later operas were obliged to support the new regime. Latterly he concentrated on literature, notably his *Mémoires* (1789), which comment on his works and his ideas about composition, and his *Reflexions d'un solitaire* (1801–13).

Grétry dominated *opéra comique* in his day and contributed significantly to the development of French opera as a whole. He skilfully combined Italian features and clear French declamation; with his simple, delicately expressive style and natural characterization he implemented Rousseau's ideas for opera. His operas include both Italian and French aria and song forms. Clear characterization is a particular feature of his ensembles, and the instrumental pieces (overtures and dances) are colourfully but economically scored. Among his other compositions are *romances*, Revolutionary songs and early instrumental and sacred works.

Dramatic music Zémire et Azor (1771); L'amant jaloux (1778); La caravane du Caire (1783); Richard Coeur-de-lion (1784); Panurge dans l'île des lanternes (1785); *c*35 other operas; prologues, divertissements

*Vocal music c*20 romances; 4 Revolutionary songs; sacred works

Instrumental music 6 str qts, op.3 (1773)

Grieg, Edvard (Hagerup) (*b* Bergen, 15 June 1843; *d* there, 4 Sept 1907). Norwegian composer. He studied with E.F. Wenzel at the Leipzig Conservatory (1858–62), where he became intimately familiar with early Romantic music (especially Schumann's), gaining further encouragement in Copenhagen and encouragement from Niels Gade. Not until 1864–5 and his meeting with the Norwegian nationalist Rikard Nordraak did his stylistic breakthrough occur, notably in the folk-inspired *Humoresker* for piano op.6. Apart from promoting Norwegian music through concerts of his own works, he obtained pupils, became conductor of the Harmoniske Selskab, projected a Norwegian Academy of Music and helped found the Christiania Musikforening (1871), meanwhile composing his Piano Concerto (1868) and the important piano arrangements of 25 of Lindeman's folksongs (op.17, 1869). An operatic collaboration with Bjørnson came to nothing, but his incidental music to Ibsen's *Peer Gynt* (1875), the most extensive and best known of his large compositions, produced some of his finest work. Despite chronic ill-health he continued to tour as a conductor and pianist and to execute commissions from his base at Troldhaugen (from 1885); he received numerous international honours. Among his later works, *The Mountain Thrall* op.32 for baritone, two horns and strings, the String Quartet in G minor op.27, the popular neo-Baroque *Holberg Suite* (1884) and the *Haugtussa* song cycle op.67 (1895) are the most distinguished.

Grieg was first and foremost a lyrical composer; his op.33 Vinje settings, for example, encompass a wide range of emotional expression and atmospheric colour, and the ten opus numbers of *Lyric Pieces* for piano hold a wealth of characteristic mood-sketches. But he also was a pioneer, in the impressionistic uses of harmony and piano sonority in his late songs and in the dissonance treatment in the *Slåtter* op.72, peasant fiddle-tunes arranged for piano.

Dramatic music Peer Gynt, incidental music (1875); music for 2 other plays
Orchestral music Sym., c (1864); Pf Conc., a (1868); Holberg Suite (1884); *c*15 other pieces
Chamber music 3 vn sonatas (1865, 1867, 1887); Str Qt, g (1878); Vc Sonata, a (1883)
Piano music Humoresker, op.6 (1865); Sonata, e (1866); Lyric Pieces, 10 sets; dances
Vocal music Folksong arrs., psalms, cantatas; *The Mountain Thrall*, Bar, 2 hn, strs (1878); *Haugtussa*, song cycle (1895); over 150 other songs

Griepenkerl, Friedrich (Conrad) (*b* Peine, 10 Dec 1782; *d* Brunswick, 6 April 1849). German music scholar. He promoted J.S. Bach's music, including the performance of choral works in Brunswick and the publication of keyboard and organ works.

Griffes, Charles T(omlinson) (*b* Elmira, NY, 17 Sept 1884; *d* New York, 8 April 1920). American composer. He studied with Mary Selena Broughton in Elmira and with Humperdinck in Berlin, where he lived, 1903–7. He returned to teach in Tarrytown, NY. Up to *c*1911 his music was within the German Romantic tradition but he then developed a more Debussian style in piano pieces (*The Pleasure-Dome of Kubla Khan*, 1912; *Roman Sketches*, 1915–

16) and songs (*Tone-Images*, 1912–14; *Four Impressions*, 1912–16). He became closely concerned with oriental culture (*Five Poems of Ancient China and Japan*, 1916–17; ballet *Sho-jo*, 1917), while his last works, including the Piano Sonata (1918), show a free handling of dissonance paralleling Skryabin.

Grigny, Nicolas de (*b* Rheims, bap. 8 Sept 1672; *d* there, 30 Nov 1703). French composer. Organist of St Denis, Paris, and of Rheims Cathedral from *c*1697, he published a volume of organ music (1699) consisting of nine groups of pieces, based on the Mass and hymns: each begins with a *cantus firmus* movement followed by a fugue and then duos, récits, dialogues etc. Characterized by greater contrapuntal complexity and contrast of colour than most contemporary French organ music, as well as rich texture and expressive embellishment, the volume was copied by Bach.

Griller Quartet. British string quartet. It was founded in 1928 with Sidney Griller as leader. It toured widely from 1930 and was in residence at the University of California at Berkeley from 1949 to 1961. It was heard in a wide repertory, including works written for it by Bloch, Milhaud and Bax.

Grimani, Maria Margherita (*fl* early 18th century). ?Italian composer. The last of a line of female oratorio composers at the Viennese court, she had two oratorios performed there (1713, 1718). Her *Pallade e marte* (1713) was the first operatic work by a woman composer to be given at the imperial court.

Grimm, Friedrich Melchior, Baron von (*b* Regensburg, 25 Dec 1723; *d* Gotha, 19 Dec 1807). German critic. He worked as a diplomat in Paris from 1749. Influenced by the Encyclopedists, he favoured the use of the Italian style in French operas (especially those of Rameau); in the Querelle des Bouffons of the 1750s he rejected all French music in favour of Rousseau, writing the satirical tract *Le petit prophète de Boehmischbroda* (1753) and other works. He was a friend to the visiting Mozart family, 1763–4 and 1778.

Grisi, Giulia (*b* Milan, 22 May 1811; *d* Berlin, 29 Nov 1869). Italian soprano. She sang throughout Europe (1828–61), and with a voice perfectly placed and even over two octaves, she easily made the transition from the florid writing of Rossini and Donizetti to the heavier style of Verdi and Meyerbeer; a forceful and convincing actress, she was admired particularly as Donna Anna, Semiramis and Norma. Her sister Giuditta Grisi (1805–40), a mezzo-soprano, excelled in Bellini's music.

Grofé, Ferde (Rudolf von) (*b* New York, 27 March 1892; *d* Santa Monica, 3 April 1972). American composer, arranger and pianist. He was a viola player in the Los Angeles SO (1909–19) and from 1917 worked as an arranger for the Paul Whiteman band, for which in 1924 he arranged Gershwin's *Rhapsody in Blue*, making his reputation. Much of his own music was based on American motifs; the best known is *Grand Canyon Suite* (1931).

Groh, Johann (*b* Dresden, ?*c*1575; *d* ?Weesenstein, Saxony, ?1627). German composer. He was organist at Meissen from 1604, then in service at Weesenstein from 1621. His output of vocal music, almost all sacred, is small but varied. Particularly interesting is his instrumental music which includes 36 fresh, attractive intradas (1603) and 30 pavans and galliards (1604) characterized by homophonic textures and piquant rhythmic answering phrases.

Grøndahl [née Backer], **Agathe (Ursula)** (*b* Holmestrand, 1 Dec 1847; *d* Oslo, 4 June 1907). Norwegian composer and pianist. She studied with Bülow in Florence and Liszt in Weimar. She was influential as performer and teacher but is remembered chiefly as a composer of shapely, lyrical songs (*c*190), among which the cycles *The Child's Spring Day* (1899) and *Ahasverus* (1902) are the best.

Groppo (It.). Term for a group of ornaments involving a note of anticipation or a changing note; *see* SPRINGER and CADENT.

Grosse Fuge. Beethoven's op.133, a fugue in B♭ for string quartet (1826), intended as the finale of his String Quartet op.130 (he substituted another).

Grosse Orgelmesse. Haydn's Mass no.4 in E♭ (1768–9), in which the organ plays an important part.

Grossi, Giovanni Francesco ['Siface'] (*b* Chiesina Uzzanese, 12 Feb 1653; *d* nr. Ferrara, 29 May 1697). Italian singer. A soprano castrato, he sang Siface in Cavalli's *Scipio affricano* (1671, Rome) and was thereafter always known by that name. He worked for the Duke of Modena from 1679 but also appeared in opera, notably in Venice and Naples, and visited London in 1687. He was murdered after boasting about an affair with someone of high family.

He should not be confused with the singer Carlo Grossi (*c*1634–1688), who worked in Modena and Venice and composed madrigals and sacred music; or with Giovanni Antonio Grossi (*d* Milan, 1684), who wrote sacred music.

Grossin, Estienne (*fl c*1420). French composer. A priest from Sens, he held church posts in Paris and wrote mass settings, motets and *chansons*.

Ground. A melody, usually in the bass (and often called 'ground bass', in Italian *basso ostinato*), recurring many times, with continuous variation in the upper parts. 'Ground' may refer to the bass melody itself, to the musical scheme including the harmonies and upper voices, to the process of repetition, or to the composition. It was first used in England in the late 16th century and frequently in the Baroque period, sometimes associated with improvisation. The term has been applied more broadly, including to the recurrence of an essentially harmonic progression even without a recurring bass-line. Byrd was among the first to use the term as a title. Christopher Simpson gave instructions in *The Division-Viol, or the Art of Playing Extempore upon a Ground* (1659); the English master of the ground was Purcell, who used the form freely and extensively in vocal as well as instrumental music, varying the harmony with great skill and breaking down the uniformity of phrase structure by devising melodic lines that overlapped the breaks.

Ground bass patterns are found in many of the standard Italian and Spanish dance patterns of the Renaissance and Baroque eras: traditional grounds such as the Ruggiero, the romanesca and the folia

were used for variations and for songs. The passacaglia and chaconne were based on grounds but with the formulae conceived rather as bass melodies than as harmonic progressions; sometimes the ground bass was treated strictly (especially in vocal music of the period 1625–50), but later composers tended to transpose the ground (often into the dominant or the minor mode) to facilitate variety. In the chaconnes of Lully and Rameau the ground is very freely treated, and in late chaconnes (for example those by Gluck and Mozart) any ground-bass element is at best vestigial. Later composers to use ground basses include Beethoven (32 Variations in C minor for piano), Brahms (Symphony no.4, finale), Stravinsky (*Symphony of Psalms*, finale: here the ground is of four minims, in 3/2 rhythm, so that it constantly shifts its position in the bar), Britten (in Act 2 of *Peter Grimes*) and Riegger (Symphony no.3, fourth movement).

Grout, Donald J(ay) (*b* Rock Rapids, IA, 28 Sept 1902; *d* Skaneateles, NY, 9 March 1987). American musicologist. He studied at Harvard University, then in France, Germany and Austria. He taught at Harvard (1936–42), the University of Texas (1942–5) and Cornell. Grout had a special interest in A. Scarlatti and his operas, but was best known for his *Short History of Opera* (1947) and his *History of Western Music* (1960).

Grove, Sir George (*b* London, 13 Aug 1820; *d* Sydenham, 28 May 1900). English engineer, writer on music, educationist and editor of the first edition of the *Dictionary of Music and Musicians*. Trained as a civil engineer, he worked on projects in Glasgow, Jamaica, Chester and Bangor, succeeding J.S. Russell, another engineer, as secretary of the Society of Arts (1850) and becoming secretary of the Crystal Palace (1852). Through various introductions he became interested in biblical research and while contributing to the *Dictionary of the Bible* developed the idea of a music dictionary. Meanwhile he helped organize the Crystal Palace concerts, writing analytical programme notes (from 1856) on the works of Beethoven, Mendelssohn, Schubert and Schumann, and he began long friendships with Arthur Sullivan (1862), Clara Schumann (1863) and, in Vienna, C.F. Pohl (1867), in addition becoming a frequent contributor to *The Times* and the editor of *Macmillan's Magazine* (1868). His work for Macmillan on the *Dictionary of Music and Musicians* (four vols., 1879–89; later edns. 1904–10, 1927, 1940, 1954, 1980) began in 1873 and incorporated his own research and writing in many articles, notably those on Beethoven, Mendelssohn and Schubert. He took an energetic part in establishing the RCM and became its first director (1882), continuing to write about music in articles and in the valuable *Beethoven and his Nine Symphonies* (1896). Though pre-eminently a self-taught amateur, he received numerous awards for his services to literature and music; he was knighted in 1883.

Grové, Stefans (*b* Bethlehem, Orange Free State, 23 July 1922). South African composer. He studied in the USA with Piston and Copland and taught at the Peabody Conservatory (1957–72) before returning to South Africa (teaching at Pretoria University from 1973). His works include orchestral and chamber pieces in a linear contrapuntal style.

Groven, Eivind (*b* Lårdal, 8 Oct 1901; *d* Oslo, 8 Feb 1977). Norwegian composer and ethnomusicologist. He grew up in a strong folk music tradition, and studied in Oslo and Berlin. He collected *c*2000 melodies, most of them Hardanger fiddle tunes, and constructed several organs tuned in just intonation.

Groves, Sir Charles (Barnard) (*b* London, 10 March 1915). English conductor. After study at the RCM he joined the BBC as chorus master in 1938. With the BBC Northern Orchestra (1944–51), Bournemouth SO (1951–61) and Royal Liverpool PO (1963–77) he was convincing in a wide standard repertory, notably in early 20th-century choral music.

Grovlez, Gabriel (Marie) (*b* Lille, 4 April 1879; *d* Paris, 20 Oct 1944). French composer. He studied at the Paris Conservatoire and was active as an opera conductor (Opéra-Comique, 1905–8; Opéra, 1914–34). He wrote finely coloured operas, ballets, symphonic poems, songs and piano music in a style close to Fauré.

Grua. Family of Italian and German musicians. Gasparo Pietragrua (late 16th century–after 1651) was an Italian composer of vocal music and an organist, active at Pallanza, Canobio and Milan; his relationship to the rest of the family is unclear.

Carlo Luigi Pietro Grua (*c*1665–*c*1726) was vice-Kapellmeister at Dresden (1693–4) and Düsseldorf (1694–1713 or later) and composed four operas, the last two (1721–2) for Venice. He also wrote duets and sacred music. Carlo Pietro Grua (*c*1700–1773), probably his son, was Kapellmeister at the Mannheim court from 1734, writing two operas, five oratorios and church music. His son Franz Paul Grua (1753–1833) was a Mannheim court violinist and went with the orchestra to Munich (1778), becoming vice-Kapellmeister in 1779 and court Kapellmeister in 1784; he composed an opera (1780) and many sacred works.

Gruber, Franz Xaver (*b* Unterweizburg, 25 Nov 1787; *d* Hallein, 7 June 1863). Austrian composer. He was Kantor and organist at St Nicholas's, Oberndorf, where, at the request of Josef Mohr, the assistant priest and author of the text, he wrote the famous Christmas song *Stille Nacht* (24 Dec 1818).

Gruber, H(einz) K(arl) (*b* Vienna, 3 Jan 1943). Austrian composer. He studied at the Vienna Hochschule with Katz, Jehiek and von Einem and began a career as a double bass player. His *Frankenstein!!* for vocalist and orchestra (1977) is an ironically tonal piece of musical surrealism. He has also written a Violin Concerto (1978).

Gruberová, Edita (*b* Bratislava, 23 Dec 1946). Czechoslovak soprano. She studied in Prague and Vienna, making her début in Bratislava as Rosina (1968) and going on to sing widely in Austria (including the Vienna Staatsoper) and Germany, and later in Britain (notably at Glyndebourne) and the USA (Met début, as Queen of Night, 1977). Her roles include the three heroines of *Contes d'Hoffmann*, Verdi's Gilda and Violetta and Strauss's Zer-

binetta; she is admired as a fine coloratura singer and a stylish Mozartian.

Gruenberg, Louis (*b* nr. Brest-Litovsk, 3 Aug 1884; *d* Beverly Hills, 10 June 1964). American composer of Russian origin. He studied in New York and with Busoni in Berlin and in 1923 was one of the founders of the League of Composers. He essayed a distinctively American style through using jazz and black spirituals; his works include symphonies, chamber music, songs and operas, of which *The Emperor Jones* (1933, Met) is rated the best.

Grumiaux, Baron Arthur (*b* Villers-Perwin, 21 March 1921; *d* Brussels, 16 Oct 1986). Belgian violinist. He studied at the Brussels Conservatory and with Enescu in Paris. His career was interrupted by World War II and he made his British début in 1945, rapidly winning international acclaim. As a concerto soloist and in chamber music he was known for the purity and classical elegance of his playing.

Gruppen. Work by Stockhausen for three small orchestras in different parts of an auditorium (1957).

Gruppetto (It.). *See* TURN.

Grützmacher, Friedrich (Wilhelm Ludwig) (*b* Dessau, 1 March 1832; *d* Dresden, 23 Feb 1903). German cellist and composer. A pupil of Drechsler, he was solo cellist of the Dresden Hofkapelle for over 40 years, also touring, teaching and writing useful technical studies, workmanlike concertos and other music for the cello. He is remembered especially for his arrangement of a cello concerto in B♭ by Boccherini.

Guaccero, Domenico (*b* Palo del Colle, 11 April 1927). Italian composer and writer. He studied in Rome with Petrassi and from 1973 has taught at the Frosinone Conservatory. He has written stage and instrumental music, drawing on many techniques, and 'action music'.

Guadagni, Gaetano (*b* Lodi or Vicenza, *c*1725; *d* Padua, Nov 1792). Italian alto (later soprano) castrato. He sang in many Italian and other European cities, especially London (1748–53, when Handel wrote for him, and later, when J.C. Bach did); the title role of Gluck's *Orfeo* was written for him (1762, Vienna). He was praised as both actor and singer.

Guadagnini. Italian family of violin makers. They were active from before 1740 until the early 20th century. The most important member was Giovanni Battista [J.B.] (*c*1711–1786), a prolific maker who worked in Piacenza (from 1740), Milan (1750), Cremona (1758), Parma (1759) and Turin (1771) and whose violins are the most highly prized mid- to late 18th-century Italian instruments. Their appearance was gradually modified, but their outline remained Stradivarian, with slightly more sloping shoulders and scrolls cut with great character. His varnish was usually orange-brown, sometimes with a rich red tint. They give a direct, powerful sound which, if lacking the warmth of some other makes, is equalled by few instruments.

Guami, Francesco (*b* Lucca, *c*1554; *d* there, 30 Jan 1602). Italian composer, brother of Gioseffo Guami. A trombonist in the Bavarian court chapel (1568–80), he became *maestro di cappella* at several Italian churches, including the Cappella Palatina, Lucca (1598). He composed madrigals (3 bks, 1588–98), showing Venetian influence, instrumental ricercares (1598) and masses (1591, lost).

Guami, Gioseffo (*b* Lucca, *c*1540; *d* there, 1611). Italian composer. A pupil of Willaert and a singer at St Mark's, Venice (1561–8), he was organist at the Munich court (1568–79), where he met Lassus, at St Mark's, Venice (1588–91), and Lucca Cathedral (1591–1611). His many motets, madrigals and instrumental works show the influence of Venetian composers and of Lassus. Three of his sons (Domenico, Valerio and Vincenzo) were also musicians.

Guardasoni, Domenico (*b*?Modena, *c*1731; *d* Vienna, 13/14 June 1806). Italian impresario, tenor and opera producer. He sang in Bustelli's touring opera company, later becoming its director. He presented operas by Mozart (including the première of *Don Giovanni*, 1787), and in 1791 commissioned his *La clemenza di Tito* for Prague.

Guarini, (Giovanni) Battista (*b* Ferrara, late 1538; *d* Venice, Oct 1612). Italian poet. From a learned Veronese family, he served several Italian courts, including Ferrara (1579–88). His play *Il pastor fido* (1589) brought the pastoral vogue to its height; together with his other verses (e.g. *Tirsi morir volea*) it attracted musical settings by hundreds of composers in the 17th century, among them Wert, Marenzio and Monteverdi.

Guarneri. Italian family of violin makers. The first member, Andrea (*c*1626–1698), learnt his craft under Nicolo Amati, establishing his own workshop in 1654; though his work lacks Amati's elegance, he made fine violins and smaller violas. His son Pietro Giovanni (1655-1720), called 'da Mantova' as he settled in Mantua by 1683, was a court musician and meticulous workman, producing distinctive but relatively few violins. Pietro's brother Giuseppe Giovanni Battista (1666–1739/40), known as 'filius Andreae', inherited Andrea's business in 1698 and made first-rate instruments, particularly cellos, until *c*1720. Among third-generation members, G.G.B.'s elder son Pietro (1695–1762), known as 'da Venezia', worked in Venice from *c*1718, blending Cremonese and Venetian traits in his instruments. The younger son Giuseppe ('del Gesù') became one of the greatest violin makers of all time. He set up on his own in 1722 or 1723, soon using labels with the IHS cipher (perhaps indicating that he was a Jesuit); he reached his peak *c*1735, in instruments renowned for their strength, tonal beauty and ease of response. He is sometimes rated higher than Stradivari.

Guarneri Quartet. American string quartet. It was formed at the 1964 Marlboro Festival, and led by Arnold Steinhardt; it appeared at Spoleto in 1965 and played Beethoven's quartets in London in 1970. It has recorded quintets with Artur Rubinstein and is noted for its tonal sweetness and command of dynamics.

Guarnieri, (Mozart) Camargo (*b* Tietê, São Paulo, 1 Feb 1907). Brazilian composer and conductor. He studied with Baldi and in Paris with Koechlin and Boulanger (1938–9); he was conductor of the São Paolo SO and in 1960 became director of the conservatory. The leading Brazilian nationalist of his time, he has written orchestral and instrumental music, songs and a comic opera. His three symphonies (1944–52) typify his nationalist, technically refined style.

Gubaydulina, Sofiya Asgatovna (*b* Chistopol', 24 Oct 1931). Soviet composer. She studied with Peyko and Shebalin at the Moscow Conservatory (1954–62) and since the late 1960s has used avant-garde techniques. After a period of iconoclasm, she has returned to traditional forms, writing three string quartets and a symphony *Stimmen ... verstummen...* (1986).

Gudmundsen-Holmgreen, Pelle (*b* Copenhagen, 21 Nov 1932). Danish composer. He studied at the Copenhagen Conservatory, and in the late 1950s was, with Nørholm and Nørgård, one of the leaders of Danish modernism, working with serialism. From the mid-1960s he has been involved with a minimalist movement: *Tricolore IV* (1969) for orchestra, a static piece of simple rhythmic pattern and slow chord change, is perhaps the most remarkable achievement of 'absurd' simplicity.

Gueden, Hilde (*b* Vienna, 15 Sept 1917). Austrian soprano. She studied in Vienna and made her début in operetta there (1939); she sang in Zurich and Munich, then in Italy (1942–6), at Salzburg (Zerlina, 1946) and then regularly at the Vienna Staatsoper as well as at the Met, 1951–60. Her assured technique and dramatic ability, and her Viennese style, served well in Strauss and Mozart.

Guédron, Pierre (*b* Beauce, ?1570–75; *d* ?Paris, *c*1619). French composer. He held appointments at the French court from *c*1588 until his death, was a notable singing teacher and an important composer of *airs de cour* and *ballets de cour*. The dramatic quality of his music and sensitivity to texts can best be seen in his contributions to at least nine ballets (1602–19), especially in the *récits*, virtually the only early 17th-century French songs to show up-to-date Italian influence. He published numerous *airs de cour*, polyphonic as well as solo (1602–20), notable for their sensitive word-setting.

Guénin, Marie-Alexandre (*b* Maubeuge, 20 Feb 1744; *d* Etampes, 22 Jan 1835). French violinist and composer. He made his solo début in Paris in 1773, became assistant director of the Concert Spirituel, the Prince of Condé's music director (1777) and principal violinist at the Opéra (1783). By 1808 he was in the King of Spain's service; in 1814–16 he served Louis XVIII. He composed symphonies, concertos and chamber music.

Guerau, Francisco (*b* mid-17th century; *d* early 18th century). Spanish guitarist and composer. In the service of the Spanish royal family from 1659, he published *Poema harmónico* (1694) containing instructions and 27 compositions of the variation type for five-course Baroque guitar which place him among the leading Spanish guitar composers of his day.

Guéroult, Guillaume (*b* Rouen, early 16th century; *d c*1565). French poet and music publisher. He lived mainly in Geneva and Lyons. His poem *Susanne ung* *jour* (1548) was perhaps the most popular 16th-century *chanson spirituelle* text. As a publisher he issued many music volumes in partnership with Simon Du Bosc in Geneva (1554–5).

Guerrero, Antonio (*b* Seville, *c*1700; *d* Madrid, 1776). Spanish composer. Initially a guitarist and musician in Madrid theatrical companies, he wrote one of the earliest pieces (1752) with all the characteristics of a *tonadilla*. His output comprises over 100 stage works.

Guerrero, Francisco (*b* Seville, ?4 Oct 1528; *d* there, 8 Nov 1599). Spanish composer. A pupil of Morales, he also taught himself the vihuela, harp, cornett and organ. He was *maestro de capilla* of Jaén Cathedral (1546–9) and then vice-*maestro* (1551) and *maestro* (1574–99) of Seville Cathedral. He visited Rome (1581–2), Venice and the Holy Land (1588–9). The most important 16th-century Spanish composer of sacred music after Victoria, he published 18 masses and *c*150 motets; because of their singable, diatonic lines, they remained in use in Spanish and Spanish-American cathedrals for more than two centuries after his death. He also published secular songs; many other works survive in anthologies and MSS. His brother Pedro (*b* Seville, *c*1520), his first teacher, was also a composer.

Guerrini, Guido (*b* Faenza, 12 Sept 1890; *d* Rome, 14 June 1965). Italian composer. He studied with Torchi and Busoni at the Bologna Liceo Musicale and directed the conservatories of Florence (1928–47), Bologna and S Cecilia, Rome (1950–60). His earlier works include luxuriant symphonic poems; later he wrote religious music, notably a gravely expressive *Missa pro defunctis* (1939).

Guest [Miles], **Jane Mary** (*b* Bath, *c*1765; *d* after 1814). English pianist and composer. She appeared publicly in Bath before she was six and in London from 1779. Possibly she was a pupil of J.C. Bach. She was known in court circles and became a prominent teacher, with a royal pupil. She composed a graceful set of accompanied keyboard sonatas (1783) and other works.

Guézec, Jean-Pierre (*b* Dijon, 29 Aug 1934; *d* Paris, 9 March 1971). French composer. He studied with Messiaen at the Paris Conservatoire (1953–63) and wrote highly colourful, dynamic pieces suggestive of Xenakis, Varèse and Webern (*Textures enchaînées* for wind and percussion, 1967; *Onze pour cinq* for percussion, 1970). He was one of the first to seek to express in music certain aspects of 20th-century pictorial technique.

Guglielmi, Pietro Alessandro (*b* Massa, 9 Dec 1728; *d* Rome, 19 Nov 1804). Italian composer, son of the *maestro di cappella* Jacopo (*d c*1731). He studied with Durante in Naples and presented his first operas (mostly comic) there and in Rome, 1757–63; later he composed for north Italian centres. In 1767–72 he was joint composer and music director of the King's Theatre, London, where his *I viaggiatori ridicoli* (1768) was particularly successful. Returning to Naples in 1776, he was judged the equal of Paisiello and Cimarosa and had operas performed abroad. He was *maestro di cappella* at St Peter's, Rome, from 1793, and from 1797 also at S Lorenzo Lucina; he continued composing operas up to 1802.

In his *c*50 comic operas, intermezzos and *farsette* Guglielmi used more ensembles than normal (latterly with more action and characterization) and a wider range of aria forms. His *c*30 serious operas and his later sacred works were equally progressive. Among his other compositions are oratorios (notably *Debora e Sisara*, 1789, Naples), cantatas, keyboard quartets and sonatas, and other instrumental pieces.

His son Pietro Carlo (*b* ?Rome, or Naples, ?*c*1763; *d* ?Naples, 28 Feb 1817), also a composer, presented 40 or more operas, mostly comic, in Naples and other cities (including Lisbon and London). By 1813 he was *maestro di cappella* to the Archduchess Beatrice in Massa. His operas were popular but show less originality than his father's. Notable among his other works is the oratorio *La distruzione di Gerusalemme* (1803, Naples). His brother Giacomo (1782–after 1820) was a comic opera singer.

Guglielmo Ebreo da Pesaro (*b* ?Pesaro, *c*1425; *d* ?after 1480). Italian Jewish dance-theorist and choreographer. He served many courts, including those of Naples, Urbino and Ferrara. His treatise, *De pratica seu arte tripudii vulgare opusculum*, written by 1510, contains both theoretical instructions and choreographies of *balli* and *basses danses*.

Guhr, Karl (Wilhelm Ferdinand) (*b* Militsch, 30 Oct 1787; *d* Frankfurt, 22 July 1848). German conductor and composer. Praised by Spontini, Wagner and Berlioz, he held conducting appointments in Nuremberg, Wiesbaden, Kassel and Frankfurt (1821–48). He composed operas, concertos, quartets and violin pieces.

Gui, Vittorio (*b* Rome, 14 Sept 1885; *d* Florence, 17 Oct 1975). Italian conductor. After study in Rome he made his début there in 1907 with *La Gioconda*. He conducted at La Scala from 1923 and in 1928 formed the Orchestra Stabile of Florence, later to develop as the Maggio Musicale Fiorentino. He conducted at Salzburg from 1933 and Covent Garden from 1938. In Florence and at Glyndebourne (1952–64) he conducted operas by Mozart and Verdi, but he was distinguished above all as an interpreter of Rossini. Among his compositions are two operas.

Guido of Arezzo (*b c*991; *d* after 1033). Music theorist. Educated at the Benedictine Abbey of Pomposa, he later moved to Arezzo where Bishop Theodaldus invited him to train singers for the cathedral. In *c*1028 he was called to Rome by Pope John XIX to expound his new methods of notation and teaching, and shortly afterwards entered a monastery (probably at Avellana, near Arezzo). His fame as a pedagogue was legendary. His famous treatise *Micrologus* is the earliest comprehensive treatise on musical practice that includes a discussion of polyphonic music and plainchant; in it he developed both a system of precise pitch notation relying (like the modern staff) on lines and spaces representing pitches defined by letters (clefs) and a technique of sight-singing based on the syllables *ut, re, mi, fa, sol, la* and on the so-called 'Guidonian hand'. Next to Boethius's treatise it was the most copied and read instruction book in the Middle Ages.

Guignon, Jean-Pierre (*b* Turin, 10 Feb 1702; *d* Versailles, 30 Jan 1774). Italian violinist and composer. Among the most brilliant virtuosos of his era, he often appeared in Paris from 1725. He served at the French court, 1733–62; his appointment as 'Roy des violons' in 1741 led to controversy. His compositions, mostly for violin, include sonatas and duos.

Guilbert, Yvette (*b* Paris, 20 Jan 1865; *d* Aix-en-Provence, 2 Feb 1944). French diseuse and folksinger. She made her acting début in 1877, then sang in *cafés-concerts*, in songs of her own or adapted by her; by 1891 she was a leading figure in Paris entertainment. She appeared in England and the USA in the 1890s. Later she sang songs from the Middle Ages onwards, her performances being notable for subtle colouring, clear diction and her strong personality.

Guildhall School of Music and Drama [GSM]. London conservatory founded in 1880 as the Guildhall School of Music. It was mainly for amateurs until 1892, then became a school for professional training, including opera and drama; it was renamed in 1935 and in 1977 moved to the Barbican.

Guilds. Musicians have formed guilds first to promote their interests and rights, secondly to regulate the profession and establish welfare provision. The earliest known guilds were formed in Vienna (1288) and Paris (by 1321) by freelance musicians emulating the trade guilds and religious fraternities: this helped them gain professional acceptance and legal protection. A guild of parish clerks was formed in London in 1240; in Germany there were guilds of court trumpeters and drummers. Civic musicians are reported in the 13th and 14th centuries; they played at weddings and other festive occasions. *See also* MINSTRELS; STADTPFEIFER; and WAITS.

Guillaume li Vinier (*b* Arras, *c*1190; *d* 1245). French trouvère. He was among the more imaginative and prolific of the Arras trouvère poets of his time; he left 26 songs and eight jeux-partis, often unusual in metric structure, and influenced by Gace Brulé. His brother Gille li Vinier (*c*1190–1252) was also a trouvère.

Guillaume Tell. *See* WILLIAM TELL.

Guillelmus Monachus (*fl* late 15th century). ?Italian theorist. He wrote a treatise, *De preceptis artis musicae*; its haphazard organization suggests a compilation, but it is important for the information it provides not only on plainchant, modes, solmization and mensuration but particularly on fauxbourdon and gymel. He uses 'fauxbourdon' to mean improvised polyphony and includes descriptions of parallel discant and gymel, distinguishing this English practice from the continental usage with the cantus in the top voice.

Guillemain, Louis-Gabriel (*b* 15 Nov 1705; *d* Chaville, 1 Oct 1770). French composer and violinist. After studying in Italy, he worked in Lyons and Dijon. From 1737 he served at the French court, becoming one of the most esteemed musicians there; his most successful work was his ballet-pantomime *L'opérateur chinois* (1748). He published 18 sets of instrumental works, 1734–62, light, graceful music including virtuoso violin sonatas, *sonates en quatuor*

and 12 *symphonies … en trio* (1740–48) in a more italianate manner with clear sonata forms.

Guilmant, (Félix) Alexandre (*b* Boulogne-sur-Mer, 12 March 1837; *d* Meudon, 29 March 1911). French organist, composer and editor. Largely self-taught, he became well known throughout Europe and North America as a recitalist, also holding the post of organist at the Trinité, Paris, and teaching at the Schola Cantorum and the Conservatoire. The quality and range of the new Cavaillé-Coll organs that he played enabled him, with Widor, to establish the French 'organ symphony'. Besides composing much organ and sacred vocal music, he made numerous editions of 16th- to 18th-century organ works.

Guiraud, Ernest (*b* New Orleans, 23 June 1837; *d* Paris, 6 May 1892). French composer. He studied with Marmontel and Halévy and won a Prix de Rome in 1859. Though his fame rests on his contact with Bizet, Offenbach, Debussy (one of his pupils) and Dukas, especially his supplying of recitatives for *Carmen* and his orchestration of *Les contes d'Hoffmann*, he was himself a composer; besides light stage works, he wrote a serious opera (*Frédégonde*, 1895; completed by Saint-Saëns and Dukas) and distinctive orchestral music, especially the *Ouverture d'Arteveld* (1882). He was professor at the Paris Conservatoire from 1876.

Güiro. A scraped percussion instrument, originally from the Caribbean, Panama and South America, now used in the orchestra and in folk and popular bands. It consists of an elongated gourd, with notches cut into it, along which a switch is rubbed to produce a rasping sound.

Guitar. A string instrument of the lute family. The modern classical guitar has a fretted fingerboard (usually with 19 frets), six strings, a wooden resonator with a waisted figure-of-eight shape, a circular soundhole and a flat back (for illustration, *see* LUTE). A rosewood bridge acts as a stringholder. The strings are nylon (the three lower overspun with fine metal), tuned by rear pegs activating a geared mechanism. The standard tuning is $E–A–d–g–b–e'$; guitar music is notated an octave higher than it sounds.

It is not known whether the guitar was introduced to medieval Europe by the Arabs or was an indigenous European instrument. Names related to 'guitar' occur in medieval literature from the 13th century but may refer to such instruments as the gittern. Its history in Europe can be traced back to the Renaissance; during the 15th century a four-course guitar appeared, having much in common with the lute and vihuela.

16th-century guitars were much smaller than modern ones; their gut strings (the three lower ones doubled) were tuned to a pattern of 4th–major 3rd–4th (e.g. $g/g'–c'/c'–e'/e'–a'$). In polyphonic music, technique was similar to that of the lute and vihuela, with the right-hand little finger resting on the bridge or soundtable, while the thumb and first two fingers plucked the strings. Music, notated in TABLATURE, included simple dances, *chansons* and fantasias. The four-course guitar continued in use in the 17th and 18th centuries, mainly in popular music, and survives in Spanish and Portuguese cultures as a small treble guitar.

Five-course guitars, often called 'viola' or 'viola da mano', were played from the late 15th century, especially in Italy. They were typically tuned $a/a–d'/d'–g/g–b/b–e'$ (with the third course at the lowest pitch), though some had a lower octave (bourdon) on some courses (e.g. $A/a–d/d'–g/g–b/b–e'$). Guitar music called for strumming, plucking individual strings and other techniques.

In the mid-18th century a special type of guitar, the *chitarra battente*, developed, probably for accompanying popular music. It had a deeply vaulted back and metal strings and frets; the strings, passing over a movable bridge, were fixed at the bottom of the body and probably played with a plectrum.

Baroque guitars are richly decorated. During the 17th century many tutors were published, often containing solos and dance suites and many in an alphabetical system of notating left-hand chords. A huge repertory of Italian arias with guitar accompaniment was published.

In the late 18th century, first in France, guitar tablature was replaced by staff notation, single strings were used in place of double courses and a sixth string was added. In the early 19th other changes established the form that developed into the modern guitar. Machine heads replaced wooden pegs, fixed frets (of ivory or ebony, then metal) were used instead of gut, and a flat back became standard. Some players rested the right hand on the table, some used fingernails. The instrument was held in various ways.

Fernando Sor, a Spaniard who moved to Paris (a centre of interest in the guitar), and the Italian Mauro Giuliani were among the most influential guitarist-composers, establishing a repertory of large-scale works (including concertos and chamber music) as well as easy pieces and studies, characterized by their elegance and vivacity. With the Spanish maker Antonio de Torres Jurado (1817–92), the guitar achieved a standard size and form. He made it larger and established the vibrating length of the strings at 65 cm; he developed fan-strutting of the soundboard and introduced the modern bridge. The instrument is now rested on the left thigh but right-hand position and technique varies.

In the early 20th century the guitar lacked a repertory to give it a status comparable with other instruments. Works were transcribed from other media (e.g. music for lute and vihuela, other string instruments and keyboard). The Spanish guitarist Andrés Segovia was influential in making it a respected concert instrument; he made many transcriptions and inspired composers to write for him. Falla (*Homenaje pour le tombeau de Claude Debussy*), Rodrigo (*Concierto de Aranjuez*), Castelnuovo-Tedesco, Manuel Ponce, Villa-Lobos (*Douze études, Cinq préludes*), Britten and Gerhard are among those who have written for the guitar. The 20th-century repertory has introduced new techniques and sonorities, sometimes derived from folk music, flamenco and jazz.

Variants include the LYRE GUITAR, guitars with extra strings and instruments that varied in size and hence in pitch. Of 20th-century variants, the flamenco guitar is closest to the classical, but lighter. Guitarists playing in jazz, blues, folk etc have required instruments with greater volume and penetration such as the 'Dreadnought' (larger and broader than the normal guitar), acoustic guitars and, most recently, the ELECTRIC GUITAR.

Guitar violoncello. *See* ARPEGGIONE.

Gulda, Friedrich (*b* Vienna, 16 May 1930). Austrian pianist and composer. He made his début in 1944 and appeared at Carnegie Hall, New York, in 1950. Until 1962 he was most successful in Viennese classical music, then developed an interest in jazz; he appeared at the Newport Festival and founded the Eurojazz Orchestra. His technically skilled performances, with improvised cadenzas, seek to reconcile distinctions between musical idioms.

Gumpelzhaimer, Adam (*b* Trostberg, 1559; *d* Augsburg, 3 Nov 1625). German composer and writer on music. Kantor and *Präzeptor* at the school and church of St Anna, Augsburg, from 1581 until his death, he is best known for his *Compendium musicae* (1591, 13 edns. to 1681), a comprehensive textbook in Latin and German on music rudiments. Its *c*150 music examples include many of his own ricercares, canons, motets etc. His other works (motets, lieder) were published in 13 volumes (1591–1620).

Guntram. Opera in three acts by Richard Strauss to his own libretto (1894, Weimar; revised 1940, Weimar).

Guridi (Bidaola), Jesús (*b* Vitoria, 25 Sept 1886; *d* Madrid, 7 April 1961). Spanish composer. He studied with d'Indy and Sérieyx at the Schola Cantorum, with Jongen in Liège (1906) and with Neitzel in Cologne (1908), then returned to Bilbao to work as an organist, choirmaster (notably of the Bilbao Choral Society), teacher and composer. He studied Basque folk music and used it in some of his output of operas and orchestral pieces. His opera *Amaya* (1920) was widely acclaimed, and his Basque zarzuela *El caserío* (1926) is considered a jewel of the Spanish lyric theatre.

Gurilyov, Alexander L'vovich (*b* Moscow, 3 Sept 1803; *d* there, 11 Sept 1858). Russian composer. He had piano lessons with John Field. He is remembered chiefly as a composer of songs, many of which appeared in the journal *Nouvelliste* in the 1840s and 1850s, and of piano transcriptions and folksong settings.

Gurlitt, Manfred (*b* Berlin, 6 Sept 1890; *d* Tokyo, 29 April 1973). German composer and conductor. He studied with Muck and Humperdinck in Berlin. From 1911 he conducted at German opera houses, returning to Berlin (Staatsoper) in 1924. His *Wozzeck* (1926, Bremen) was written at almost the same time as Berg's opera. From 1939 he worked in Japan, doing much to make German opera known there. His cousin Wilibald Gurlitt (1889–1963) was an eminent music historian and lexicographer, active in Freiburg.

Gurney, Ivor (Bertie) (*b* Gloucester, 28 Aug 1890; *d* Dartford, 26 Dec 1937). English composer and poet. He studied with Stanford and Vaughan Williams at the RCM, before and after war service during which he was wounded, gassed and shell-shocked. Between 1919 and 1922 he composed intensively, especially songs in a flowing, sensuous style more influenced by Parry and German lieder than by the folksong movement. His later years were spent in mental hospitals.

Gurrelieder. Work by Schoenberg for solo voices, choruses and huge orchestra to a German translation of J.P. Jacobsen's poems (1911); it includes the *Lied der Waldtaube* ('Song of the Wood Dove').

Gusle. Single-string fiddle of Yugoslavia, in which the hollow resonator (covered with stretched skin) and the neck are carved together from one piece of wood, usually maple. It resembles a large spoon and can be oval, round, leaf-shaped or pear-shaped. The player, who sings to his own accompaniment, holds the instrument upright between his knees.

Gusli. A Russian folk psaltery, originally in the form of a rounded-off trapezoid with concave sides, and with 11 to 36 strings, covering a range of two to three octaves.

Gutheil-Schoder, Marie (*b* Weimar, 10 Feb 1874; *d* Ilmenau, 4 Oct 1935). German soprano. After coaching at Weimar from Richard Strauss she joined Mahler at the Vienna Hofoper (1900), where she was the first Viennese Electra. In 1913 she sang Octavian at Covent Garden. She was admired for her vivid dramatic characterizations. Throughout her career she was associated with Schoenberg; she was often heard in *Pierrot lunaire* and created the Woman in *Erwartung* (1924, Prague).

Guy, Barry (John) (*b* London, 22 April 1947). English double bass player and composer. He studied with Orr at the GSM and played in jazz and avant-garde groups, founding the London Jazz Composers' Orchestra (1971). He has evolved a new vocabulary of timbres for the double bass (eloquently demonstrated in *D* for 15 strings, 1972) which, with his vigorous performing style, has been a stimulus to other composers.

Guyot (de Châtelet) [Castileti], **Jean** (*b* Châtelet, 1512; *d* Liège, 11 March 1588). South Netherlands composer. He worked in Liège (1557/8–63) and

briefly at the imperial court at Vienna (1563). His works, which include a mass, two settings of the Te Deum, 20 motets and ten *chansons*, feature dense polyphonic textures and skilful use of counterpoint.

Gymel. 15th- and 16th-century English term (probably from the Latin *gemellus*, 'twin'), denoting the splitting of one voice part in a polyphonic composition into two voices of equal range. It was used in an English treatise of *c*1450 to describe a method of improvisation in which the two parts begin and end on unisons, but although the technique is found in at least two earlier English compositions, the earliest practical sources that use the term are continental and date from the mid-15th century. Its earliest English source is the Eton Choirbook, written in the last years of the 15th century. The practice seems to have died out by the late 1560s.

Gymnopédies. Three piano pieces by Satie (1888).

Gypsy Baron, The. *See* ZIGEUNERBARON, DER.

Gypsy Rondo. The last movement of Haydn's Piano Trio in G HXV:25, so called because of its lively rhythms drawing on gypsy music.

Gypsy scale. Name for the scale type $c–d–eb–f\sharp–g–ab–b–c'$, so called because of its use in much Hungarian music (it is sometimes referred to as the 'Hungarian' mode or scale).

Gyrowetz, Adalbert [Jírovec, Vojtěch Matyáš] (*b* Česke Budějovice, 20 Feb 1763; *d* Vienna, 19 March 1850). Bohemian composer and conductor. He studied in Prague and in 1785 went to Vienna, but soon left for Italy, Paris and then London, where he assisted Haydn and had some of his own works published. He returned to Bohemia and then Vienna, and from 1804 was conductor of the Court Theatre, writing German operas and ballets until he retired in 1831. He knew Beethoven and was a pall-bearer at his funeral. His music, which includes *c*40 symphonies and much chamber music (nearly 50 each of string quartets and piano trios), is in a style chiefly modelled on Haydn's though he also assimilated that of early Beethoven; some of his songs show Czech national features. His music is polished, but generally light; by the 1820s it was stylistically outmoded.

H

H. In German, the note, or the PITCH CLASS, B♮; *see* PITCH NAMES. H is sometimes used (as is 'Hob.') to identify works by Haydn by their numbers in Anthony van Hoboken's thematic catalogue (2 vols., 1957, 1971).

Haas, Joseph (*b* Maihingen, 19 March 1879; *d* Munich, 30 March 1960). German composer. He was a pupil of Reger from 1904 and teacher in Stuttgart and Munich, where he strove, as president, to rebuild the Musikhochschule (1945–50). His works, including 'folk oratorios', Catholic masses and instrumental pieces, are popular music on the highest level.

Haas, Pavel (*b* Brno, 21 June 1899; *d* Auschwitz, 17 Oct 1944). Czech composer. He studied with Janáček at the Brno Conservatory (1920–22) but made an individual departure from Janáček's style in his opera *The Charlatan* (1938) and other works. His set of four Chinese songs (1944) is among the most forceful Czech pieces of the period.

Hába, Alois (*b* Vizovice, 21 June 1893; *d* Prague, 18 Nov 1973). Czech composer. He played in his father's folk band and studied with Novák at the Prague Conservatory (1914–15) and with Schreker in Vienna and Berlin (1918–22), though he was influenced more by Schoenberg in developing an athematic, highly chromatic style. A suite for strings (1917) was his first work to use quarter-tones, which became a sphere of interest and which he used in his opera *The Mother* (1931). He taught microtonal composition at the Prague Conservatory (1924–51) and wrote choral music, 16 string quartets and much else using quarter-tones and sixth-tones.

Hába, Karel (*b* Vizovice, 21 May 1898; *d* Prague, 21 Nov 1972). Czech composer, brother of Alois. He studied at the Prague Conservatory with Novák (1921) and his brother (1925–7) and performed quarter-tone music throughout Europe on the violin and viola. His compositions, in many genres, draw on eastern Moravian folksong and include educational music.

Habanera. A Cuban dance and song, named after the capital, Havana. The music is in a moderate to slow duple metre. The habanera (*not* habañera) became popular in the early 19th century and was much used by French and Spanish composers; an outstanding example appears in Bizet's *Carmen*.

Habeneck, François-Antoine (*b* Mézières, 22 Jan 1781; *d* Paris, 8 Feb 1849). French violinist, conductor and composer. He was Baillot's pupil at the Paris Conservatoire and principal violinist of the Opéra orchestra. He became director, then conductor, of the Paris Opéra (1821–46), conducting many premières, including Rossini's *Guillaume Tell*, Meyerbeer's *Robert le diable* and Berlioz's *Benvenuto Cellini*. Founder of the Société des Concerts du Conservatoire (1828), he also introduced Beethoven's music to France and attained an unrivalled orchestral standard and position of influence in Paris music. His compositions are mainly for the violin.

Haberl, Franz Xaver (*b* Oberellenbach, 12 April 1840; *d* Regensburg, 5 Sept 1910). German musicologist. He completed the first Palestrina edition (1894), issued plainchant editions, began a Lassus edition and contributed to scholarly journals, also founding a school of ecclesiastical music.

Habermann, Franz (Johann or **Wenzel)** (*b* Kynžvart, 20 Sept 1706; *d* Cheb, 8 April 1783). Bohemian composer. He was music director to the Prince of Condé and then to the Duke of Tuscany in Florence. Returning to Prague (by 1743), he became a choirmaster and from 1773 was Kantor at Cheb. Famous for his contrapuntal writing, he composed an *opéra comique*, oratorios, church music and instrumental works; the later music has early Classical elements. Handel used material from five of his masses (in *Philomela pia*, 1747) in *Jephtha* and an organ concerto.

Hacker, Alan (*b* Dorking, 30 Sept 1938). English clarinettist. He studied at the RAM and in Paris, Vienna and Bayreuth, and taught at the RAM from 1959. He played in the LPO and in various specialist contemporary music groups, including his own, Matrix (1971). From 1976 to 1988 he taught at York University. He is noted for his playing of contemporary music (he has given premières of works by Birtwistle, Maxwell Davies etc) and for his performances of Mozart and early 19th-century music on period instruments, including the basset clarinet.

Hacquart, Carolus (*b* Bruges, *c*1640; *d*?1701). Netherlands composer and instrumentalist. He worked in Amsterdam and The Hague and possibly (from 1689) in England. His most important work is

Harmonia parnassia (1686), ten varied and original sonatas in which features of the *sonata da chiesa* and *sonata da camera* are fused; he also wrote sacred music, 12 suites (*Chelys*, 1686) for viola da gamba, and a Dutch pastoral *De triomfeerende min* (1680).

Hadden, J(ames) Cuthbert (*b* Banchory-Ternan, 9 Sept 1861; *d* Edinburgh, 2 May 1914). Scottish organist and writer on music. He wrote biographies of Handel, Mendelssohn, Haydn and Chopin, also contributing to periodicals; his outstanding work is *George Thomson, the Friend of Burns* (1898).

Hadjidakis, Manos (*b* Xanthi, 23 Oct 1925). Greek composer. Self-taught, he has drawn on Greek urban folk music in a large output of stage music and popular songs. He has also promoted and conducted music by other Greek composers and has written scores for Greek cinema and theatre (including *Never on Sunday*).

Hadley, Henry (Kimball) (*b* Somerville, MA, 20 Dec 1871; *d* New York, 6 Sept 1937). American composer and conductor. He studied with Chadwick, an important influence, as was R. Strauss, whom he met in London (1905). His late Romantic compositions were successful in his lifetime (the opera *Cleopatra's Night* was produced at the Met, 1918) but he is remembered most as an effective advocate of American music, conducting on both sides of the Atlantic.

Hadley, Patrick (Arthur Sheldon) (*b* Cambridge, 5 March 1899; *d* King's Lynn, 17 Dec 1973). English composer. He studied at Cambridge and with Vaughan Williams at the RCM. In 1938 he returned to Cambridge as lecturer, and became professor (1946–62). His music, much of it for choral-orchestral forces, is essentially Delian; in his finest work, *The Trees so High* (1931), for baritone and orchestra, he reconciled folksong with symphonic form.

Haebler, Ingrid (*b* Vienna, 20 June 1929). Austrian pianist. She studied in Salzburg, Vienna, Geneva and Paris and has toured widely; her repertory includes Romantic music, but she is chiefly admired for her playing of Schubert and above all Mozart, where her natural feeling for a shapely line and her gentle warmth and intimate expression find an ideal outlet. She has recorded all Mozart's concertos and sonatas, Schubert's sonatas and (on a fortepiano) J.C. Bach's concertos.

Haeffner, Johann Christian Friedrich (*b* Oberschönau, 2 March 1759; *d* Uppsala, 28 May 1833). Swedish conductor, singing teacher and composer of German birth. He held posts with the Swedish Royal Opera and the Royal Orchestra in Stockholm, then from 1808 worked as music director at Uppsala University, also playing the organ at the cathedral. As a composer he is remembered for his sacred choral works and hymns.

Haffner Serenade. Nickname of Mozart's Serenade in D K250/248*b* for orchestra (1776), so called because it was composed for a Haffner family wedding.

Haffner Symphony. Nickname of Mozart's Symphony no.35 in D (1782), written for a Haffner family ennoblement celebration.

Hageman, Richard (*b* Leeuwarden, 9 July 1882; *d* Beverly Hills, 6 March 1966). American composer and conductor. After study in Amsterdam he conducted opera in the USA, notably at the Met (1908–22), where his own work *Caponsacchi* was staged in 1937. He also wrote film music and was head of the opera department at the Curtis Institute.

Hahn, Reynaldo (*b* Caracas, 9 Aug 1874; *d* Paris, 28 Jan 1947). French composer of Venezuelan origin. He studied with Massenet at the Paris Conservatoire. While in his teens he gained a reputation as a composer of songs, which he sang to his own accompaniment in fashionable salons, gaining admittance to Proust's circle. But after 1900 he concentrated on the theatre, as conductor (at the Opéra from 1945) and as a composer of ballets, operas and operettas (*Ciboulette*, 1923; *Mozart*, 1925).

Haibel, (Johann Petrus) Jakob (*b* Graz, 20 July 1762; *d* Đakovo, *c*27 March 1826). Austrian composer, singer and choirmaster. He sang in Schikaneder's company at the Freihaus-Theater auf der Wieden, from the mid-1790s writing incidental music and Singspiels, among which *Der Tiroler Wastel* (1796) was his greatest success. From 1807 he was a provincial choirmaster in Slavonia and the posthumous brother-in-law of Mozart.

Haiden [Heyden]. German family of musicians working in Nuremberg. Sebald (1499–1561), theorist and Kantor at the Spitalkirche from 1521, is notable for his treatises, *Musicae stoicheiōsis* (1532), on polyphony and mensural notation, and *Musicae* (1537; enlarged as *De arte canendi*, 1540), a more comprehensive work with many music examples by, among others, Josquin and Obrecht. His son Hans (1536–1613) was an instrument maker and writer. He is chiefly remembered as the inventor of the *Geigenwerk*, a keyboard instrument shaped like a harpsichord but sounded by parchment-covered wheels which could sustain notes indefinitely and produce dynamic shadings and vibrato; the first (1575) was built for the Elector of Saxony. Hans's son Hans Christoph (1572–1617) was a composer and poet and organist of St Sebald (1596–1616). Despite an irregular life he made an important contribution to German song: his two collections (1601, 1614) of homophonic songs for singing and dancing have a carefree freshness and the 1614 set can be seen as an early attempt at a unified song cycle. His brother David (1580–1660) was an instrumentalist and probably a composer.

Haigh, Thomas (*b* London, 1769; *d* ? there, April 1808). English composer. He studied with Haydn in London, 1791–2, and returned there in 1801 after a time in Manchester. A pianist, he arranged music by Haydn for the piano and composed many sonatas, solo and accompanied.

Hainl, François [Georges] (*b* Issoire, 16 Nov 1807; *d* Paris, 2 June 1873). French conductor and cellist. He studied at the Paris Conservatoire. From 1863 he was conductor at the Paris Opéra, where he directed the premières of *L'africaine*, *Don Carlos* and *Hamlet*; Berlioz praised his clarity and expressiveness.

Hainlein, Paul (*b* Nuremberg, bap. 12 April 1626; *d* there, 6 Aug 1686). German composer and instrument maker. He was organist at the Egidienkirche (from 1655) and St Sebald, Nuremberg (from 1658), and co-directed the Nuremberg company of musicians (from 1656). His music includes strophic songs and instrumental pieces. His grandfather Sebastian (*d* 1631) and his father, also Sebastian (1594–1655), his uncle Hans (1598–1671) and his son Michael (1659–before 1725) were instrument makers, particularly of trombones.

Haitink, Bernard (Johann Herman) (*b* Amsterdam, 4 March 1929). Dutch conductor. He studied with Leitner and in 1957 became principal conductor of the Netherlands Radio PO. In 1961 he became principal conductor of the Concertgebouw (at first jointly with Eugen Jochum), retaining the post until 1988. His American début was in 1958 with the Los Angeles SO. With the LPO (principal conductor, 1967–79) he has been admired for his well-thought-out performances of the standard repertory, notably of Mahler and Bruckner (whose complete symphonies he has recorded). At Glyndebourne he conducted operas by Mozart and Stravinsky, and in 1987 he became musical director at Covent Garden.

Hajibeyov [Gadzhibekov], Uzeir (Abdul Huseyn) (*b* Agjabedï, 17 Sept 1885; *d* Baku, 23 Nov 1948). Azerbaijani composer. Trained as a teacher, he wrote the first opera of eastern Islam, *Leylï i Mejnun* (1907), based on Azerbaijani music and with improvised solo parts. He then studied in Moscow and St Petersburg (1911–14), returning to Baku to take a leading part in musical life as teacher, critic, folksong collector and composer. The main work of his later years was the opera *Kyor-oglï* (1936), a more sophisticated example of Azerbaijani–Western synthesis.

Hakim, Talib Rasul [Chambers, Stephen Alexander] (*b* Asheville, NC, 8 Feb 1940). American composer. Robert Starer and Morton Feldman were among his teachers. He has taught at Adelphi University (1972–9) and Nassau Community College (1971–81). From the 1970s he became strongly influenced by Sufism, his music cultivating a dissonant language characterized by original timbral combinations.

Halévy, (Jacques-François-) Fromental [Fromentin] (-Elie) [-Elias] (*b* Paris, 27 May 1799; *d* Nice, 17 March 1862). French composer, teacher and writer. He was a pupil of Cherubini, Berton and Méhul at the Paris Conservatoire, winning the Prix de Rome in 1819. Back in Paris he became an opera composer and a professor at the Conservatoire (where his pupils included Gounod, Bizet and Saint-Saëns), also acting as *chef du chant* at the Théâtre-Italien and later at the Opéra. His first true success was *Le dilettante d'Avignon* (1829). By 1835 he had composed his first serious grand opera, *La juive* (libretto by Scribe), which became his greatest and the work on which his fame chiefly rests. *L'éclair* (1835) consolidated his position, followed by the grand operas *La reine de Chypre* (1841) and *Charles VI* (1843), among other, less successful, works. Fluent and professional, though owing much to Italian music and to Boieldieu and Auber, his writing is particularly imaginative in its orchestration and its ability to evoke period and place. His literary output includes *Souvenirs et portraits* (1861) and the posthumous *Derniers souvenirs et portraits* (1863).

Half cadence, half close [imperfect cadence; semi-cadence]. A CADENCE that comes to rest on the dominant.

Halffter, Cristobal (Jiménez) (*b* Madrid, 24 March 1930). Spanish composer and conductor, nephew of Ernesto and Rodolfo. He studied with del Campo at the Madrid Conservatory (1947–51) and conducted the Falla Orchestra (1953–63). In the mid-1960s he became the leading Spanish exponent of avant-garde music. His main works are orchestral or vocal-orchestral, some with electronics.

Halffter (Escriche), Ernesto (*b* Madrid, 16 Jan 1905). Spanish composer and conductor. He was a precocious composer and came to the attention of Falla, who gave him lessons from 1922; Ravel was another influence, though his style has more in common with Poulenc's. He wrote ballets, orchestral pieces, songs and chamber music, and also completed Falla's *Atlántida*.

His brother Rodolfo (*b* 1900) also had lessons with Falla. In 1939 he settled in Mexico City, becoming a leading figure in musical life in a post-Falla style.

Half-note. American term for minim; a note half the value of a whole-note, or semibreve, and double the length of a quarter-note, or crotchet. *See* NOTE VALUES.

Halka. Opera in two acts by Moniuszko to a libretto by Wolski (concert performance, 1848, Vilnius), revised in four acts (1858, Warsaw); it was the first widely successful Polish opera.

Hall, Henry (*b c*1656; *d* Hereford, 30 March 1707). English composer. One of the Children of the Chapel Royal, he became organist of Exeter (1674) and Hereford (1688) cathedrals, and composed church music and secular songs, dialogues and catches, some of which appeared in anthologies (1685–1707). His son, also Henry (*d* 1714), succeeded him at Hereford.

Hall, Richard (*b* York, 16 Sept 1903; *d* Horsham, 24 May 1982). English composer. He studied at Cambridge and taught at the Royal Manchester College (1938–56), where his pupils included Birtwistle, Davies and Goehr. His works, including five symphonies (1941–64) and two string quartets, blend Hindemith and Schoenberg into a lyrical English style.

Hallé, Sir Charles (*b* Hagen, 11 April 1819; *d* Manchester, 25 Oct 1895). English pianist and conductor of German birth. He studied in Darmstadt and Paris, where he introduced the complete Beethoven sonata series, appeared as a chamber music player and came to know Chopin, Liszt, Berlioz and Wagner. Leaving for London in 1848, he settled in Manchester and reorganized the old Gentlemen's Concerts orchestra, establishing the adventurous Hallé Concerts in 1858, which he conducted for the rest of his life; he was also instrumental in the founding of the Royal Manchester College of Music (1893). He was knighted in 1888.

Halle Handel Festival (East Germany). Annual (summer) festival established in 1952 at Handel's birthplace. It has played an important part in the revival of Handel's operas.

Hallelujah Chorus. Popular name for the chorus at

the end of Part II of Handel's *Messiah*.

Hallelujah Concerto. Nickname of Handel's Organ Concerto in Bb op.7 no.3 (1751), so called because it resembles the Hallelujah Chorus in *Messiah*.

Hallén, (Johannes) Andreas (*b* Göteborg, 22 Dec 1846; *d* Stockholm, 11 March 1925). Swedish conductor and composer. He studied with Reinecke in Leipzig, with Rheinberger in Munich and with Rietz in Dresden. He worked in Göteborg, Berlin and Stockholm, where he conducted the Filharmoniska Sällskapet (1885–95), the Royal Opera (1892–7) and the Sydsvenska Filharmoniska Sällskapet (1902–7), later teaching at the Stockholm Conservatory. His works, though accomplished, are often derivative, particularly his three Wagnerian operas.

Hallé Orchestra. British orchestra. It was founded by Charles Hallé in 1858, when he inaugurated the annual Hallé Concerts in the Free Trade Hall, Manchester (opened 1856; rebuilt 1951, cap. 2500), and was conducted by him until his death (1895); later conductors included Hans Richter, Hamilton Harty and John Barbirolli.

Halling. A Norwegian dance, from the town of Hallingdal, in a fairly fast duple (sometimes triple) metre.

Hallnäs, (John) Hilding (*b* Halmstad, 24 May 1903). Swedish composer. He studied with Grabner in Leipzig and from 1933 lived in Göteborg as an organist, teacher, composer and vigorous proponent of new music. His works include symphonies, songs and chamber music.

Hallström, Ivar Christian (*b* Stockholm, 5 June 1828; *d* there, 11 April 1901). Swedish composer. He wrote primarily vocal music in an eclectic style reflecting Swedish classical and folk traditions (the opera *The Bewitched One*, 1874) and the influences of Gounod and Wagner.

Hamal, Jean-Noël (*b* Liège, 23 Dec 1709; *d* there, 26 Nov 1778). South Netherlands composer, son of Henri Guillaume (1685–1752), cantor of Liège Cathedral. After studying in Rome, he sang at Liège Cathedral, becoming director of music in 1738. French and Italian features appear in his output, which includes stage works, oratorios, sacred and instrumental pieces; his six overtures (1743) foreshadow the early Classical symphony. His nephew Henri (1744–1820), who also studied in Italy, succeeded him at the cathedral from 1778 until the Revolution; he composed a similar range of works, some of them in collaboration with Jean-Noël.

Hambourg, Mark (*b* Boguchar, 31 May 1879; *d* Cambridge, 26 Aug 1960). British pianist and composer. He studied in his native Russia with his father, Michael (1855–1916), and made his London début in 1889, giving 1000 concerts by 1906. In 1896 he became a British subject. As a soloist he was in the Romantic tradition; he also formed a successful piano trio with his brothers Jan (1882–1947) and Boris (1884–1954).

Hambraeus, Bengt (*b* Stockholm, 29 Jan 1928). Swedish composer. He studied with Moberg at Uppsala University (1947–56) and at Darmstadt and in 1957 joined the staff of Swedish radio; in 1972

he was appointed professor at McGill University, Montreal. He was one of the first to use the organ as an avant-garde instrument (*Konstellationer I*, 1958). Other works, in many genres including tape pieces, are influenced by medieval and non-European (especially Japanese) music.

Hamburg Opera [Hamburger Staatsoper]. The first German-language opera company was established in 1678 at the Theater am Gänsemarkt in Hamburg; it flourished for 60 years. Reinhard Keiser directed in 1703–6 and wrote *c*50 works for it; operas by Handel, Mattheson and Telemann (director, 1722–38) were also given. In 1827 interest revived with the opening of a new theatre (known as the Staatsoper from 1934; rebuilt 1955, cap. 1674) and again after 1874 under the impresario Bernhard Pollini; Mahler conducted in 1891–7. Later conductors included Klemperer and Böhm. Under Rolf Liebermann (1959–73) it became a leading international company.

Hamerik [Hammerich]. Danish family of musicians. Asger Hamerik (1843–1923) was a composer who studied with Berlioz (1864–9) and who, as director of the Peabody Conservatory in Baltimore (1871–98), became an exponent of Scandinavian Romanticism in the USA. His brother Angul (1848–1931) was a music historian who published important studies based on Danish sources and his son Ebbe (1898–1951) was a leading conductor in Copenhagen in the 1920s and a composer of operas and symphonies.

Hamerik, Ebbe (*b* Copenhagen, 5 Sept 1898; *d* the Kattegat, 11 Aug 1951). Danish composer and conductor, son of Asger Hamerik. After study with his father he was a conductor from 1919, notably in modern music. His opera *Marie Grubbe* was successfully performed in 1940; his five symphonies are short, monothematic *cantus firmus* works.

Hamilton, Iain (Ellis) (*b* Glasgow, 6 June 1922). Scottish composer. He studied with Alwyn at the RAM (1947–51) and took an active part in London musical life as a university teacher while making a reputation as a modernist. His music of the early 1950s was influenced by Bartók, Berg and Hindemith; then in 1958 he began to use serialism with Webernian strictness. This style continued after his appointment to Duke University, North Carolina, in 1961, but he developed a broader style, which he has used in operas to his own librettos (*The Royal Hunt of the Sun*, 1977; *The Catiline Conspiracy*, 1974; *Anna Karenina*, 1980; *Lancelot*, 1985). He has also written instrumental and vocal music.

Hamlet. Fantasy-overture by Tchaikovsky (1888).

Symphonic poem by Liszt (1858).

Shakespeare's play has been the subject of several operas, including those by Ambroise Thomas (1868), Gasparini, D. Scarlatti, Mercadante, Grandi and Searle, and of ballets (Tchaikovsky, Blacher, Shostakovich etc).

Hammer. The part of a piano action that strikes the strings. The term is also applied to the beater used for such instruments as the xylophone or tubular bells.

Hammerklavier. Term for the piano popular in

Germany in the early part of the 19th century.

Hammerklavier Sonata. Beethoven's Piano Sonata no.29 in B♭ op.106 (1818).

Hammerschmidt, Andreas (*b* Brüx, 1611–12; *d* Zittau, 29 Oct 1675). German composer and organist. His first post was as organist at the castle at Weesenstein, Saxony (1633–4); he returned to Freiberg, his home town, as organist of St Petri in 1635–9. From 1639 he was organist of St Johannis, Zittau. Here he produced most of his output and became well known; he was also esteemed as a teacher and an organ expert.

Hammerschmidt is the most representative composer of mid-17th-century German church music. His 14 sacred collections, 1639–71 (including the five-volume *Musicalische Andachten*), contain over 400 motets, concertos, arias, masses etc. The most traditional are his motets, some using madrigalian style. His sacred concertos for many parts anticipate the form of the later German church cantata in their use of distinct sections (including chorales); notable among his small sacred concertos are the sacred dialogues of 1645, scored for two, three or four voices and continuo. His arias are in an up-to-date song style. He also wrote hymn tunes, several occasional works, three volumes each of secular songs (1642–9) and instrumental dances (1636–50).

Hammerstein, Oscar (Greeley Clendenning) II (*b* New York, 12 July 1895; *d* Doylestown, PA, 23 Aug 1960). American librettist, lyricist, producer and publisher. He wrote the books, lyrics or both for over 30 shows, by composers including Youmans, Friml and Romberg. He is best known for his collaborations with Jerome Kern (*Showboat*, 1927) and Richard Rodgers (*Oklahoma!*, 1943; *South Pacific*, 1949; *The King and I*, 1951; *Flower Drum Song*, 1958; *The Sound of Music*, 1959). Oscar Hammerstein I, his grandfather (1846–1919), was an important opera impresario in New York.

Hammond, Dame Joan (Hood) (*b* Christchurch, NZ, 24 May 1912). New Zealand soprano. She studied in Sydney and played the violin in the Sydney SO; her operatic début was there in 1929, her London and Vienna (Staatsoper) débuts in 1938. She sang at Covent Garden, 1948–51, as Leonora (*Il trovatore*), Leonore (*Fidelio*) and Aida. She also appeared in New York, Russia (singing Tatyana in *Eugene Onegin*) and Australia. Her strong, vibrant voice and warm personality served particularly well in Puccini; she sang Tosca 149 times and Butterfly 147, and more than a million copies were sold of her recording of Lauretta's aria from *Gianni Schicchi*.

Hammond organ. An electronic organ developed in 1933–4 by the American engineers Laurens Hammond and John M. Hanert. The instrument was manufactured from 1935 by Hammond Clock (later Hammond Organ) of Chicago and was an immediate success: over 2 million Hammond organs of various models have been sold. Hammond organs built before the mid-1960s made use of the electromagnetic tone-wheel principle to generate sounds. Timbre could be precisely controlled by a system of drawbars which regulated the combination and volume of the overtones of notes. Later models imitated the characteristic sound of the tone-wheel instrument.

Hampel, Anton Joseph (*b* Prague, *c*1710; *d* Dresden, 30 March 1771). Bohemian horn player. A member of the Dresden royal orchestra, he was the first to master the horn's low register and to develop the hand-stopping technique. He also devised the *Inventionshorn*, allowing crooks to be inserted into the horn's body rather than at the mouthpiece. Punto was among his pupils.

Hampel, Hans [Jean, Giovanni, Jan] (*b* Prague, 5 Oct 1822; *d* there, 30 March 1884). Czech composer. A distinguished piano pupil of Tomášek, he is remembered for his deeply felt Romantic character-pieces in the style of Schumann and Chopin.

Hampton, Lionel ['Hamp'] (*b* Louisville, KY, 12 April 1909). American jazz vibraphonist, drummer and bandleader. He played as a drummer in Chicago, and (from 1927) in California, where he took up the vibraphone in the early 1930s. He joined Benny Goodman's big band and trio in 1936, leaving in 1940 to form his own big band. The first notable jazz musician to play the vibraphone, he was largely responsible for establishing its use in jazz.

Handbell. A bell with a handle (a shaft or loop) enabling it to be held in the hand for ringing. Usually it has a clapper and is swung, although it may be held stationary and struck. It is the only type of bell that ·can be damped. Handbells are mostly used in sets, from about six to over 60 covering a range from a short melodic scale to five chromatic octaves. Large sets include bells, 40 cm to 5 cm in diameter, sounding *c* to *c′′′′′*. A 'team' or 'choir' of four to 15 perform either by holding one or two bells in each hand or by lifting them from a table as required.

The oldest extant handbells are from China, from about 1600BC; handbells were also known in India, from the 5th or 6th century BC. They are used in Africa for religious rites, signalling and musical performance.

Handel, George Frideric (*b* Halle, 23 Feb 1685; *d* London, 14 April 1759). English composer of German birth. He was born Georg Friederich Händel, son of a barber-surgeon who intended him for the law. At first he practised music clandestinely, but his father was encouraged to allow him to study and he became a pupil of Zachow, the principal organist in Halle. When he was 17 he was appointed organist of the Calvinist Cathedral, but a year later he left for Hamburg. There he played the violin and harpsichord in the opera house, where his *Almira* was given at the beginning of 1705, soon followed by his *Nero*. The next year he accepted an invitation to Italy, where he spent more than three years, in Florence, Rome, Naples and Venice. He had operas or other dramatic works given in all these cities (oratorios in Rome, including *La resurrezione*) and, writing many Italian cantatas, perfected his technique in setting Italian words for the human voice. In Rome he also composed some Latin church music.

He left Italy early in 1710 and went to Hanover, where he was appointed Kapellmeister to the elector. But he at once took leave to take up an invitation to London, where his opera *Rinaldo* was produced early in 1711. Back in Hanover, he applied for a second leave and returned to London in autumn 1712. Four more operas followed in 1712–15, with mixed success; he also wrote music for the church and for court and was awarded a royal pension. In 1716 he may have visited Germany (where possibly he set Brockes's Passion text); it was probably the next year that he wrote the Water Music to serenade George I at a river-party on the Thames. In 1717 he entered the service of the Earl of Carnarvon (soon to be Duke of Chandos) at Edgware, near London, where he wrote 11 anthems and two dramatic works, the evergreen *Acis and Galatea* and *Esther*, for the modest band of singers and players retained there.

In 1718–19 a group of noblemen tried to put Italian opera in London on a firmer footing, and launched a company with royal patronage, the Royal Academy of Music; Handel, appointed musical director, went to Germany, visiting Dresden and poaching several singers for the Academy, which opened in April 1720. Handel's *Radamisto* was the second opera and it inaugurated a noble series over the ensuing years including *Ottone, Giulio Cesare, Rodelinda, Tamerlano* and *Admeto*. Works by Bononcini (seen by some as a rival to Handel) and others were given too, with success at least equal to Handel's, by a company with some of the finest singers in Europe, notably the castrato Senesino and the soprano Cuzzoni. But public support was variable and the financial basis insecure, and in 1728 the venture collapsed. The previous year Handel, who had been appointed a composer to the Chapel Royal in 1723, had composed four anthems for the coronation of George II and had taken British naturalization.

Opera remained his central interest, and with the Academy impresario, Heidegger, he hired the King's Theatre and (after a journey to Italy and Germany to engage fresh singers) embarked on a five-year series of seasons starting in late 1729. Success was mixed. In 1732 *Esther* was given at a London musical society by friends of Handel's, then by a rival group in public; Handel prepared to put it on at the King's Theatre, but the Bishop of London banned a stage version of a biblical work. He then put on *Acis*, also in response to a rival venture. The next summer he was invited to Oxford and wrote an oratorio, *Athalia*, for performance at the Sheldonian Theatre. Meanwhile, a second opera company ('Opera of the Nobility', including Senesino) had been set up in competition with Handel's and the two competed for audiences over the next four seasons before both failed. This period drew from Handel, however, such operas as *Orlando* and two with ballet, *Ariodante* and *Alcina*, among his finest scores.

During the rest of the 1730s Handel moved between Italian opera and the English forms, oratorio, ode and the like, unsure of his future commercially and artistically. After a journey to Dublin in 1741–2, where *Messiah* had its première (in aid of charities), he put opera behind him and for most of the remainder of his life gave oratorio performances, mostly at the new Covent Garden theatre, usually at or close to the Lent season. The Old Testament provided the basis for most of them (*Samson, Belshazzar, Joseph, Joshua, Solomon*, for example), but he sometimes experimented, turning to classical mythology (*Semele, Hercules*) or Christian history (*Theodora*), with little public success. All these works, along with such earlier ones as *Acis* and his two Cecilian odes (to Dryden words), were performed in concert form in English. At these performances he usually played in the interval a concerto on the organ (a newly invented musical genre) or directed a concerto grosso (his op.6, a set of 12, published in 1740, represents his finest achievement in the form).

During his last decade he gave regular performances of *Messiah*, usually with about 16 singers and an orchestra of about 40, in aid of the Foundling Hospital. In 1749 he wrote a suite for wind instruments (with optional strings) for performance in Green Park to accompany the Royal Fireworks celebrating the Peace of Aix-la-Chapelle. His last oratorio, composed as he grew blind, was *Jephtha* (1752); *The Triumph of Time and Truth* (1757) is largely composed of earlier material. Handel was very economical in the re-use of his ideas; at many times in his life he also drew heavily on the music of others (though generally avoiding detection) – such 'borrowings' may be of anything from a brief motif to entire movements, sometimes as they stood but more often accommodated to his own style.

Handel died in 1759 and was buried in Westminster Abbey, recognized in England and by many in Germany as the greatest composer of his day. The wide range of expression at his command is shown not only in the operas, with their rich and varied arias, but also in the form he created, the English oratorio, where it is applied to the fates of nations as well as individuals. He had a vivid sense of drama. But above all he had a resource and originality of invention, to be seen in the extraordinary variety of music in the op.6 concertos, for example, in which melodic beauty, boldness and humour all play a part, that place him and J.S. Bach as the supreme masters of the Baroque era in music.

Dramatic music operas – Almira (1705); Rodrigo (1707); Agrippina (1710); Rinaldo (1711, rev. 1731); Il pastor fido (1712); Teseo (1713); Silla (1713); Amadigi di Gaula (1715); Radamisto (1720); Act 3 of Muzio Scevola (1721); Floridante (1721); Ottone (1723); Flavio (1723); Giulio Cesare (1724); Tamerlano (1724); Rodelinda (1725); Scipione (1726); Alessandro (1726); Admeto (1727); Riccardo Primo (1727); Siroe (1728); Tolomeo (1728); Lotario (1729); Partenope (1730); Poro (1731); Ezio (1732); Sosarme (1732); Orlando (1733); Arianna (1734); Ariodante (1735); Alcina (1735); Atalanta (1736); Arminio (1737); Giustino (1737); Berenice (1737); Faramondo (1738); Serse (1738); Imeneo (1740); Deidamia (1741); 3 pasticcios; arrs.; music for The Alchemist (1710), Comus (1745), Alceste (comp. 1750)

Oratorios, odes etc Il trionfo del Tempo e del Disinganno (1707); La resurrezione (1708); Ode for the Birthday of Queen Anne (?1713); Brockes Passion (?1716); Acis and Galatea, masque (1718); Esther (1718, rev. 1732); Deborah (1733); Athalia (1733); Parnasso in festa (1734); Alexander's Feast (1736); Il trionfo del Tempo e della Verità (1737); Saul (1739); Israel in Egypt (1739); Ode for St Cecilia's Day (1739); L'Allegro, il Penseroso ed il Moderato (1740); Messiah (1742); Samson (1743); Semele (1744); Joseph and his Brethren (1744); Hercules (1745); Belshazzar (1745); Occasional Oratorio (1746); Judas Maccabaeus (1747); Joshua (1748); Alexander Balus (1748); Susanna (1749); Solomon (1749); Theodora (1750); The Choice of Hercules (1751); Jephtha (1752); The Triumph of Time and Truth (1757)

Sacred music Latin works incl. Dixit Dominus (1707), Laudate pueri Dominum (1707), Nisi Dominus (1707); English works – 11 'Chandos' anthems; 4 Coronation anthems, incl. Zadok the Priest (1727); Chapel Royal anthems; 'Foundling Hospital Anthem' (1749); 'Anthem on the Peace' (1749); 'Funeral Anthem' (1737); 'Utrecht' Te Deum and Jubilate (1713); 'Dettingen' Te Deum (1743); other pieces; hymns

Secular vocal music 7 dramatic cantatas; *c*25 solo and duo cantatas with insts; *c*70 solo cantatas with bc; *c*20 duets and trios with bc; songs (most to English texts)

Orchestral music 6 concerti grossi op.3, B♭, B♭, G, F, d, D/d; 12 Grand Concertos, op.6, G, F, e, a, D, g, B♭, c, F, d, A, b (1739); 3 concerti a due cori, B♭, F, F (*c*1747); conc. for Alexander's Feast, C (1736); 3 ob concs.; 6 concs. op.4, nos.1–5, g/G, B♭, g, F, F, org, no.6, B♭, for harp (1738); 2 org concs., F, A, in 'A Second Set' (1740); 6 org concs. op.7, B♭, A, B♭, d, g, B♭; other org concs.; Water Music (1717); Music for the Royal Fireworks (1749); other pieces; dances

Chamber music 6 trio sonatas op.2; 7 trio sonatas op.5; solo sonatas with bc (12 pubd as op.1) – 6 for rec, 5 for fl, 3 for ob, 5 for vn, 1 for va da gamba

Keyboard music 2 bks suites (1720, 1733); 6 fugues (1735); preludes, sonatinas, airs

Handel and Haydn Society. American oratorio society founded in Boston, MA, in 1815, 'for cultivating and improving a correct taste in the performance of sacred music'. It was the first organization of its kind in the USA. C.E. Horn was its first conductor; others have included Emil Mollenhauer and Christopher Hogwood. It ran triennial festivals, for choirs of 300–600, and toured internationally.

Handel Opera Society. English company founded in 1955 by Charles Farncombe (renamed Handel Opera, 1977); it was discontinued in 1985. It aimed to revive interest in staged performances of Handel's dramatic works; it opened with *Deidamia*, and gave annual seasons from 1959 at Sadler's Wells Theatre, of oratorios as well as operas, and later took productions abroad.

Handl, Jacob [Gallus, Jacobus] (*b* probably Ribniča 15 April–31 July 1550; *d* Prague, 18 July 1591). Slovenian composer. He lived in Austria from *c*1565 and in 1574–5 sang in the Vienna Hofkapelle under Monte. After extensive travels, he was choirmaster to the Bishop of Olomouc (*c*1579–85) and Kantor of St Jan na Brzehu, Prague (*c*1586–91). In his published music (20 masses, 445 motets, three Passions and many secular songs) he successfully used Italian and Netherlands techniques with skilful use of counterpoint; many of his polychoral pieces show the influences of Willaert and Lassus.

Handschin, Jacques (Samuel) (*b* Moscow, 5 April 1886; *d* Basle, 25 Nov 1955). Swiss musicologist. He studied theory and the organ with Reger in Munich and Leipzig and taught the organ at St Petersburg (1909–20), inspiring leading Russian composers to write for the instrument. Later he taught at Basle University, 1924–55. Handschin's studies were wide-ranging but his chief achievements were in medieval music, where he developed an approach through style criticism; he published many articles on the schools of St Martial and Notre Dame and on early English polyphony.

Handy, W(illiam) C(hristopher) (*b* Florence, AL, 16 Nov 1873; *d* New York, 28 March 1958). American composer. He played the trumpet, organized his own bands and became co-owner of a music publishing firm in Memphis; there he published his *Memphis Blues* (1912) and *St Louis Blues* (1914), which paved the way for public acceptance of black folk blues. In New York in the 1920s and 1930s he continued to promote the welfare of black composers and performers.

Hannikainen, (Toivo) Ilmari (*b* Jyväskylä, 19 Oct 1892; *d* Kuhmoinen, 25 July 1955). Finnish pianist, composer and teacher. His teachers included Schreker, Žiloti, Steinberg and Cortot. He made his Helsinki début in 1914 and appeared in London from 1921, being best known for his interpretations of Sibelius and Rakhmaninov. With his brothers Tauno (1896–1968), a conductor and cellist who worked in the USA from 1940, and Arvo (1897–1942), a violinist, he formed a trio.

Hänsel und Gretel. Opera in three acts by Humperdinck to a libretto by Adelheid Wette after the brothers Grimm (1893, Weimar).

Hansen. Danish firm of music publishers. It was founded in Copenhagen (1853) by Jens Wilhelm Hansen. At first issuing mainly educational and salon music, it soon began to publish new works by Danish composers including Gade and Hartmann; in 1879 it acquired a virtual monopoly of the music trade in Denmark. Branches in Leipzig (1887), Oslo (1909), Stockholm (1915) and Frankfurt (1951) have secured its promotion of northern European composers, notably Nielsen, Svendsen, Stenhammar and Sibelius; Wilhelm Hansen is now the leading Scandinavian publisher.

Hans Heiling. Opera in a prelude and three acts by Marschner to a libretto by E. Devrient (1833, Berlin).

Hanslick, Eduard (*b* Prague, 11 Sept 1825; *d* Baden, 6 Aug 1904). German music critic, aesthetician and pioneer of musical appreciation. He studied music with Tomášek and read law at Prague University, writing his earliest essays for the Prague journal *Ost und West* and for the *Wiener Musikzeitung*, the *Sonntagsblätter* and the *Wiener Zeitung*. From 1849 to 1861 he was a civil servant, chiefly for the ministry of culture, meanwhile writing for the *Presse*, publishing his important book *Vom Musikalisch-Schönen* (1854) and lecturing on music appreciation at Vienna University, becoming full professor in 1870. He was also active as a musical emissary and helped promote the standardization of musical pitch. Among his longstanding friends were Brahms and the philosopher Robert Zimmermann. Though his aesthetic enshrined the classical ideals of orderliness and formal perfection, his interests were limited to the music of his own time. He is perhaps most widely known for his anti-Wagnerian stance and the controversy it nurtured; his basic contention was that music's value lies in its autonomous formal relations and not in its expressiveness. A shrewd grasp of technical details, a systematic approach and clear, lively prose gave added authority to his writings.

Hanson, Howard (Harold) (*b* Wahoo, NE, 28 Oct 1896; *d* Rochester, NY, 26 Feb 1981). American composer and conductor. He studied with Goetschius in New York and became director of the Eastman

School (1924–64), where he was an influential teacher and founded the Institute of American music; he also promoted modern American music through his work as a conductor. His own music shows the influence of Sibelius, Grieg and Respighi (his teacher in Rome in the early 1920s). Among his works are seven symphonies, symphonic poems, choral pieces, chamber and piano music and songs.

Harawi, chant d'amour et de mort. Song cycle by Messiaen (1945), settings for soprano and piano of 12 of his own texts.

Harbison, John (b Orange, NJ, 20 Dec 1938). American composer. He studied with Piston at Harvard, with Blacher in Berlin (1961) and with Sessions and Kim at Princeton; in 1969 he took a post at MIT. Operas and larger vocal works predominate in his output, including *Winter's Tale* (1979, San Francisco) and *Full Moon in March* (1979, New York); in a lucid, lyrical style, they also include concertos for piano and violin (1978, 1980), chamber and vocal pieces. He has appeared as guest conductor of several leading ensembles in the USA, including the San Francisco SO and the Boston SO.

Hardanger fiddle [Harding fiddle]. A folk violin of western Norway, with four melody strings, four or five wire sympathetic strings below the fingerboard, and characteristic national decoration.

Hardel. French family of instrument makers and musicians active from 1611. Gilles Hardel, his son Guillaume (d c1676), and his sons François (b 1642) and Jacques (in 1676 an officer of the Duchess of Orleans) were makers of lutes and harpsichords. One of the Hardels (possibly Jacques) was a composer whose surviving nine pieces include a Gavotte in A minor (to which Louis Couperin composed a *double*) found in many MS collections; six other dances in D minor constitute the only fully 'classical' French harpsichord suite from the 17th century.

Hardingfele (Nor.). *See* HARDANGER FIDDLE.

Harington, Henry (b Kelston, 29 Sept 1727; d Bath, 15 Jan 1816). English composer. Principally a physician and author, he became one of the leading glee writers of his day. He also wrote songs, duets etc.

Harmonica [mouth organ]. An instrument consisting of a small casing containing a series of free reeds in channels leading to holes on the instrument's side. It is placed between the lips and played by inhalation and exhalation, unwanted holes being masked by the tongue. By moving the instrument to and fro, the different notes are brought into play.

There are two main types of harmonica, the diatonic and the chromatic. The invention of the instrument in 1821 is credited to C.F.L. Buschmann (1805–64); it soon gained wide popularity in light entertainment and folk music. The chromatic harmonica evolved in the early 1920s; it was brought into prominence by Larry Adler, for whom Milhaud and Vaughan Williams among others have composed. The instrument has played an essential role in the American blues tradition and is used in modern jazz and educational music.

Harmonic analysis. The analysis of harmony, in the modern sense, goes back to Gottfried Weber (1817–21). It is based on the description of chords by the scale position of their root (I, the tonic; II, supertonic etc) with the addition of b, c etc for inversions (thus VIb means first inversion on the submediant); or figures, as in figured bass, can be used.

Harmonic minor. *See* MINOR.

Harmonic rhythm. The rhythm of harmonic progression in a piece of music (i.e. the rhythm articulated by the chords in a progression). The term is often used, however, simply for the rate of change of chords, in which case the term 'harmonic tempo' would be more precise.

Harmonics. The individual pure sounds normally present as part of an ordinary musical tone. They are present because a string or an air column can vibrate not only as a whole but also as two halves, three thirds etc simultaneously. The relative strength of each harmonic gives the tone quality to the note as heard. The first 16 harmonics of the note C are shown in ex.1. The richer the upper harmonics, the brighter the tone of an instrument; the oboe and the violin are instruments with many higher harmonics, whereas the flute and the recorder have a stronger fundamental and fewer and weaker harmonics. The 'hollow' sound of the clarinet is created by the predominance of odd-numbered harmonics. In some vibrating bodies, particularly bells, their irregular form will cause sounds that are not harmonic partials; this may give a confused or dubious perception of pitch.

Harmonics are used in a variety of ways in musical instruments. Woodwind players can 'overblow' their instruments in the octave (oboe) or 12th (clarinet) and thus extend their compass; this may be done by lip pressure and/or by opening a nodal hole in the tube. On brass instruments, which have longer and narrower tubes, the player can choose the harmonic to be sounded by means of lip pressure; before valves were invented (c1815), only notes of the harmonic series (and in some circumstances their near neighbours) could be played. On string instruments, players can cause a string to vibrate only in sections by touching it lightly at the appropriate point; this can produce a note of a cool, silvery quality (sometimes called 'flageolet notes'). These are 'natural harmonics', based on the open string; 'artificial harmonics' can be produced by fingering a note and touching lightly a 4th higher, thereby producing a note two octaves higher (these can be used

Ex. 1

(black notes are imperfectly tuned)

to produce an effect of great virtuosity, for example in the finale of Sibelius's Violin Concerto). Ex.2

Ex. 2

natural harmonic (open string)   artificial harmonic (stopped string)

shows how harmonics may be notated. On the harp, the use of the second harmonic (ex.3) can produce an effect of particular delicacy.

Ex. 3

'Harmonic', applied to an organ stop, means one where the sounding note is a harmonic of the pipe's natural sounding length.

Harmonic series. *See* HARMONICS, especially, ex.1.

Harmonie. Besides being the French or German for 'harmony', 'Harmonie' was used from *c*1750 to the 1830s for a wind band, ranging from a pair of instruments (normally horns or clarinets) to the 13 required in Mozart's Serenade K361/370*a*. Its principal function was to provide music, known as Harmoniemusik, for dinners and social events.

Harmonie der Welt, Die. Opera in five acts by Hindemith to his own libretto (1957, Munich); he wrote a symphony with the same title (1951).

Harmoniemesse. Haydn's Mass in B♭ (1802), so called because of its extensive use of wind instruments.

Harmoniemusik. *See* **Harmonie.**

Harmonious Blacksmith. Name for the Air from Handel's Harpsichord Suite no.5 in E (1720), so called because it was supposedly derived from the singing of a harmonious blacksmith of Edgware (whose grave can be seen at Whitchurch, Stanmore, Middx); the story is however a 19th-century fabrication.

Harmonium. A small reed organ. The original instrument, patented in 1842, had a three-octave keyboard, one set of reeds (later four sets) and a single blowing pedal; more advanced models had a five-octave keyboard, stops and couplers. The name has been used in England and on the Continent to refer to reed organs in general (larger instruments in Germany were sometimes called 'Kunstharmonium').

The first standard model was manufactured by A.F. Debain (1809–77) in Paris. Until the first half of the 20th century it was regarded as a substitute for the orchestra in domestic music and light music arrangements; it was also popular for church music and in the cinema. Original compositions have been written by virtuoso players, above all Karg-Elert, and adaptations for it were made by Schoenberg. *See* REED ORGAN.

Harmony. The combining of notes simultaneously, to produce chords, and their successive use to produce chord progressions.

Different eras of Western music (harmony is much more highly developed in Western music than in any other) have held different ideas as to what kinds of harmony are acceptable or good. In the Middle Ages, the concept of harmony concerns combinations of two notes. In the Renaissance, three-note harmony became the norm and the triad had become the main unit of harmony (a three-note chord built up in 3rds). This remained the basic element in Western harmony until the 20th century, even when harmony was composed in four parts or more. From the beginning of the Baroque era (*c*1600), harmony was widely understood as the chords with which a melody was accompanied (as the practice of basso continuo, or figured bass, implies). The study of harmony also dictates acceptable relationships between successive chords. For example, if one chord is a dissonance, that dissonance needs to be resolved in the next chord (even though that next chord may itself incorporate another dissonance). In triadic harmony, the root of each chord – not necessarily the same as its bass – is the note in that chord from which the other notes can be derived in a series of rising 3rds. Thus the triad C–E–G has C as its root; but it may be heard with E as the lowest note.

In medieval and early Renaissance music, even a full major triad was felt inappropriate for the last chord of a piece, which normally would embody the final note (in more than one octave) and the 5th above it. In the period 1600–1900, full triads are usual for concluding chords; but in the 20th century, composers have treated dissonance more freely and have not felt it necessary to resolve chords that in earlier eras would be considered dissonant. During the 19th century, much more chromatic alteration of notes was being used, particularly by Wagner, and in the early 20th the principles of triadic harmony were under attack: from such composers as Bartók, who (inspired by the folk music of the area from which he came) was constructing chords based on the interval of a 4th; by Schoenberg, using first atonal and then 12-note methods of composition; and Stravinsky, who, though his music was predominantly tonal, left dissonances unresolved to tease the ear.

Harmony cannot be dissociated from the rhythmic aspects of music. In particular, the use of dissonance and consonance can generate, by the tensions it creates, a powerful forward momentum. Harmony can also provide punctuation marks in the form of cadences – simple, readily recognizable chord progressions that mark a natural end to a phrase in a stereotyped way. Harmony is sometimes seen as the 'opposite' to counterpoint, because it primarily operates vertically whereas counterpoint seems to operate horizontally. The two are not opposed: most contrapuntal writing, particularly of the 1600–1900 period, is governed by harmonic progression while, equally, harmony is concerned with the movement of individual voices.

Harmony of the Spheres. *See* MUSIC OF THE SPHERES.

Harnisch, Otto Siegfried (*b* Reckershausen, *c*1568; *d* Göttingen, bur. 18 Aug 1623). German composer. He was a Kantor in Brunswick, Helmstedt, Wolfenbüttel and Göttingen (1603–23). His works include three-part German secular songs in the Italian villanella style (3 bks, 1587, 1588, 1591), motets (1592, 1621), a Passion (1621) and a theoretical treatise (1608).

Harnoncourt, Nikolaus (*b* Berlin, 6 Dec 1929). Austrian conductor and cellist. After study at the Vienna Academy he played in the Vienna SO (1952–69). In 1953 he formed the Vienna Concentus Musicus, an influential early music group using period instruments, notable for their performances of Monteverdi's operas, Bach's choral and orchestral music and the Viennese Classics. Insights gained from period performance have informed his conducting with modern instruments. His wife Alice (*b* 1930) leads the Concentus Musicus.

Harold en Italie. Symphony (op.16) by Berlioz for viola and orchestra after Byron (1834).

Harp. Generic name for plucked string instruments in which the plane of the strings is perpendicular to the soundboard. The Western concert harp, or double-action pedal harp, patented by Erard in 1810, has 47 strings, seven per octave, C' to g''''. A pedal-activated system enables each string to be shortened, raising its pitch by two semitones.

Normally triangular in shape, all harps have three basic structural elements: resonator, neck and strings. Frame harps have a forepillar or column which connects the lower end of the resonator to the neck, adding structural support and helping bear the string tension. European harps are the frame type: most others are 'open harps', which may be 'arched' or 'angular'.

Resonators are topped with a wood soundboard or a skin soundtable and a string holder to which one end of a string is usually attached; the other end is attached to the neck directly, or indirectly to plugs or tuning-pegs. Buzzing mechanisms (brays), attached near one end of the string, on either the neck or soundboard, and activated by the plucked string, were used on Renaissance European harps and on most African harps today. Harps may have from one to over 90 strings; mechanisms for their chromatic alteration range from manually operated hooks to complex pedal-activated systems. Harps are played in six basic positions. Tunings may be pentatonic, tetratonic, heptatonic (including diatonic) and chromatic. The strings may be plucked, struck or strummed with the fingers or a plectrum, and the resonators may be percussively struck with the fingers, hand or hooked rattles.

The earliest representations, from *c*2200BC, depict Sumerian harps with boat-shaped resonators and up to six strings. The instrument was used in Egypt and Mesopotamia and had spread to Greece and Rome by the 4th century BC. By the 8th century AD it appears in European illuminated MSS and carvings and resembles the ancient Egyptian arched type. After the 12th century, frame harps are almost the only kind shown, mostly in psalm illustrations in the hands of David. Their features include a neck curved inwards towards a trapezoidal box resonator and joined to its narrower end by a narrow shank, and a forepillar curved outwards from the longest string. By the late 14th century the instrument usually had 24 gut strings, a range of almost three octaves and

probably chromatic tuning in at least one octave. The bass registers were extended downwards during the 15th century; by the 16th the compass was F–c'''.

The oldest extant Irish or Celtic harp dates from the 14th century. The instrument today is small and single-rank with 24–34 strings, a flat soundboard on a round-backed resonator and levers for shortening the strings; it is used for educational purposes.

In the 16th century harps were built with two rows of strings to make the instrument chromatic. One type had parallel ranks; in the other, the ranks crossed ('cross-strung'). The latter, which usually had a compass of four octaves, is the Italian Renaissance *arpa doppia*. By 1897, when the Pleyel cross-strung harp was patented, the compass was over five octaves; Debussy and others wrote for it despite its thin sonority and awkward technique. A three-rank harp, with parallel outer ranks identically tuned and an inner rank of chromatic notes, was developed in 16th-century Italy at the time of monody and early opera; it was used in England by William Lawes and Handel. Its vigorous attack and bright sound was kept alive during the 18th and 19th centuries by Welsh makers and performers, later by Welsh gypsy players.

In late 17th-century Germany and Austria the hook harp was developed, with metal hooks in the neck below the tuning pegs to shorten each string, operated by pedals from the early 18th century; later this was popular in Paris. The instrument had 36–43 strings tuned to E♭, and seven pedals, enabling wide modulation. Erard's improved model of 1792 formed the basis for the modern double-action harp.

The late 18th-century establishment of the single-action pedal harp was paralleled by developments in technique and repertory. C.P.E. Bach and Mozart composed for the instrument, while Krumpholtz, Dussek and Spohr contributed to the solo and ensemble literature. Writing was mostly in scale and arpeggio figurations and spread chords, with harmonics and damped notes for special effects. The harp entered the orchestra through the opera house, where it was used by Gluck and Haydn and later by Meyerbeer and Donizetti. The virtuoso Parish-Alvars pioneered the numerous effects possible on the double-harp, including the chordal glissando. Much 19th-century harp repertory was scarcely more than salon music for talented amateurs. Berlioz was the first to use the harp in the symphony orchestra (*Symphonie fantastique*, 1830) and later in the century it was idiomatically used by Liszt, Richard Strauss, Sibelius and Debussy among others. The French school of playing dominated in the early 20th century, with a repertory including works by Fauré and Saint-Saëns. Many new percussive effects were introduced by Carlos Salzedo and extended by Berio, Boulez and others.

Harps have a place in many cultures outside Europe. The instrument was introduced into the New World by the early conquistadors; at first it was mainly used for continuo parts in sacred music, but by the 19th century it was primarily a folk and salon instrument. Today it is particularly used, in various forms, in Mexico, Paraguay, Argentina, Venezuela and Peru. African forms of harp compare with those of ancient Egypt; the instrument is widely used in the traditions of some 50 African peoples. Harps have rich symbolic meanings and harpists are often central figures in rituals. Angular harps of the ancient world were carried eastwards: the arched to south and south-east Asia, where it is still played, and the angular to the Far East, where it was last depicted in 17th-century miniature paintings.

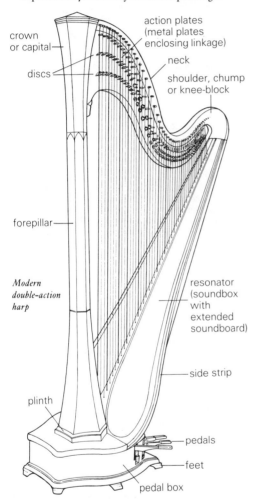

crown or capital

discs

action plates (metal plates enclosing linkage)

neck

shoulder, chump or knee-block

forepillar

Modern double-action harp

resonator (soundbox with extended soundboard)

side strip

plinth

pedals

feet

pedal box

Harpégé (Fr.). 'Arpeggiated': term found in French Baroque music to indicate that a chord or passage is to be played in an arpeggiated manner.

Harper, Edward (James) (*b* Taunton, 17 March 1941). English composer. He studied at Oxford and the RCM, and later in Milan. In 1964 he became a lecturer in music at Edinburgh University. His works include a series of three fantasias (1976–7, for chamber orchestra, 11 strings and brass quintet respectively), a symphony (1979), a Clarinet Concerto (1982) and two operas, *Fanny Robin* (after Thomas Hardy, 1975) and *Hedda Gabler* (after Ibsen, 1985).

Harper, Heather (*b* Belfast, 8 May 1930). British soprano. She studied in London and made her professional début at Glyndebourne in 1957, singing Anne Trulove (*Rake's Progress*) there in 1963. Her Covent Garden début was in 1962, in Britten's *Midsummer Night's Dream*; she has also sung at Bayreuth (from 1967) and Buenos Aires (1969). She is a noted interpreter of Britten and of soprano parts in the choral repertory. She retired from the stage in 1984.

Harp-lute. Generic term for two different types of instrument. One is an instrument of the guitar type, used in England and France in the early 19th century; called variously harp-guitar, harp-lute, harp-lyre, harp-lute-guitar or lute-harp (or 'harp ventura' in the form developed by A.B. Ventura), it had eight to 20 strings with stops, 'ditals' or other devices for raising their pitch by a semitone. An instrument on which ladies accompanied their songs, its life was brief, from *c*1798 to 1828.

'Harp-lute' also describes a West African instrument with a long neck piercing a wood or calabash body with sets of strings attached along the neck, across a bridge on the soundtable and anchored on the neck's lower protrusion; the bridge is designed so that the strings are in two planes. The best-known example is the 21-string *kora*.

Harp Quartet. Nickname of Beethoven's String Quartet in E♭ op.74 (1809), so called because of its harp-like pizzicato arpeggios in the first movement.

Harpsichord. A stringed keyboard instrument, distinguished from the clavichord and the piano by the fact that its strings are plucked, not struck. The earliest known reference to a harpsichord is from 1397, in Padua ('clavicembalum'); a Minden altarpiece of 1425 is the earliest known representation. The harpsichord remained in use to the late 18th century for solo keyboard music, and primarily as a continuo instrument in chamber and orchestral music and opera. It fell into disuse by *c*1810; its modern revival dates from the 1880s. (For illustration, *see* KEY-BOARD INSTRUMENTS.)

The heart of its mechanism is the jack, a slender slip of wood which stands on the back of each key. The top of the jack carries a plectrum of quill, leather or plastic in a pivoted tongue; when the key is depressed, the jack rises and the plectrum is forced past the string, plucking it (a releasing mechanism permits the jack to return without plucking the string again). A piece of cloth in a slot next to the tongue damps the string's vibrations and silences it. A padded bar (the jackrail) prevents the jack from flying out of the instrument when the key is struck.

Although this mechanism is capable of producing a sensitive legato or staccato, changes in dynamics are possible only if the harpsichord has special devices or if each key has additional jacks and strings which may be engaged at will. Many harpsichords have at least two sets of strings, one at normal pitch (8′) and one an octave above (4′).

A typical 18th-century northern European harpsichord has two manuals, three sets of strings (2 × 8′, 1 × 4′), three registers and a manual coupler. Foot- or knee-operated devices for dynamic and register changes appeared in the late 1750s; most instruments had a 'lute stop', plucking close to the nut and producing a nasal timbre, and a 'buff stop', dampening the overtones of the 8′ string. Compasses increased from three octaves in the 15th century (some chromatic notes were omitted in the lower octave), to four in the 16th ($C–c'''$), and five by the 18th ($F–f'''$).

No 15th-century harpsichords apparently survive, but representations show short instruments with thick cases. Most surviving 16th-century instruments are from Italy, where the main centre was Venice. Most instruments had an 8′ register (or $1 × 8′, 1 × 4′$) and thin, slender cases of cypress, with a separate, decorated outer case. Their sound had a marked 'attack' and shorter resonance than later Flemish instruments.

The most important centre in northern Europe was Antwerp, where the Ruckers family worked for a century from 1579. Their instruments had long stringing, thicker cases (usually painted) and by the 1590s two manuals. Harpsichords falling between the Italian and Flemish types were made in France, Germany and England in the 17th century; several French two-manual instruments with unpainted walnut cases survive. This type was succeeded in the 1690s by a national variant of the Ruckers type with French keyboard and action. The soundboards and cases were painted or lacquered in fashionable styles. Blanchet founded the most important dynasty of Paris harpsichord makers: his workshop was inherited by Taskin in 1766.

English harpsichord-building in the 18th century was dominated by Shudi and Kirckman whose instruments, in veneered oak cases, had a rich, powerful tone. In 18th century Germany, the centre was Hamburg; some instruments have complex dispositions, including 2′ and 16′ registers and, in one case, three manuals. An unusually long model was evolved by J.D. Dulcken of Antwerp, the leading 18th-century maker in the Low Countries.

With the invention of the pianoforte and its propagation in the later 18th century, the harpsichord seemed to be superseded. After the last Kirckman was produced in c1809, it was not revived until the late 1880s when Arnold Dolmetsch presented Renaissance and Baroque music on original instruments in London. He built his first harpsichord in 1896, and soon workshops were established in Boston, Paris and Haslemere. Pleyel and Erard in Paris also produced instruments; after 1923 a new Pleyel model incorporated an iron frame holding thick strings at high tension on which Wanda Landowska in Berlin trained a generation of harpsichordists. Hubbard and Dowd in Boston were the first to construct harpsichords to historical principles; they were soon widely followed although modern concert instruments continued in use in Germany. Instruments in kit form, pioneered by W.J. Zuckermann in 1960, have assisted the growth of interest.

Harpsichord-piano. An instrument combining the hammer action of the piano with the plucking jacks of the harpsichord. Combination instruments were produced in the later 18th century by such piano makers as Stein and Erard.

Harp way. A tuning name which, together with such others as 'viol way', 'lute way', 'plain way', 'lyra way' is found in 17th-century tablatures for the LYRA VIOL.

Harrer, (Johann) Gottlob (b Görlitz, 8 May 1703; d Carlsbad, 9 July 1755). German composer. After studying in Italy, he served Count von Brühl in Dresden and in 1750 succeeded Bach as Kantor at St Thomas's, Leipzig. He composed oratorios, Passions, church music and many instrumental works (symphonies, sontatas etc), often using an italianate style akin to Hasse's.

Harris, Renatus (b ?Quimper, c1652; d ?Bristol, 1724). English organ builder. Son of Thomas Harris (d c1684), who built cathedral organs for Gloucester (1666), Salisbury (1668–9) and Chichester (1675–7), he was the most flamboyant English organ builder of his time, with a flair for publicity and not above sharp practice to gain advantage over his hated rival 'Father' Smith. A Roman Catholic, he enjoyed the support of Catherine of Braganza and built an organ for the Popish Chapel at Whitehall (1686–8); over half his new organs after 1684 were for London churches. His specifications often include mutation work and reed voicing in the French manner; his action work was considered superior to Smith's. Among his most notable surviving organs are those for Bristol Cathedral (1685), St Bride, Fleet Street (1694), All Hallows, Twickenham (1700), and St Peter Mancroft, Norwich (1707). He was succeeded by his son John Harris (d 1743) in partnership with John Byfield (i) (c1694–1751).

Harris, Roy (b Lincoln County, OK, 12 Feb 1898; d Santa Monica, 1 Oct 1979). American composer. He studied with Farwell in Los Angeles and, after successful performances of his orchestral Andante (1926), with Boulanger in Paris. From the first his music was identified as distinctively American in its ruggedness, its expansiveness and its hymn-like modal melody: his early symphonies, particularly the Third (1937), were widely acclaimed and imitated, and he came to write much on patriotic themes. His large output consists mostly of orchestral and choral music, two of his 14 symphonies being choral; among the best are *Kentucky Spring* (1949) and *Memories of a Child's Sunday* (1945). He taught at various institutions in the USA, notably UCLA (1961–71) and California State University, Los Angeles (1971–6).

Harris, Sir William H(enry) (b London, 28 March 1883; d Petersfield, 6 Sept 1973). English composer. He studied at the RCM and taught there (1923–53) while also working as a church musician in Oxford and at St George's, Windsor, 1933–61. His works include choral music (notably the double-choir motet *Faire is the Heaven*, 1925) and organ pieces.

Harrison, Beatrice (b Roorkee, India, 9 Dec 1892; d Smallfield, 10 March 1965). English cellist. She studied at the RCM and in Berlin, where she won a Mendelssohn Prize. She toured much in Europe and became an admired performer of contemporary works, notably by Delius, Goossens and Elgar (whose Cello Concerto she recorded under the composer). She and her sister, the violinist May (1891–1959), a pupil of Auer, were noted exponents of Brahms's Double Concerto, and of Delius's, dedicated to them. Beatrice was famous for a radio performance in which she played her cello in a wood to induce the nightingales to sing.

Harrison, Frank [Francis] **Ll(ewellyn)** (*b* Dublin, 29 Sept 1905; *d* Canterbury, 29 Dec 1987). Irish musicologist. He studied in Dublin and taught in Kingston, Canada, and at St Louis, until 1952 when he was appointed lecturer at Oxford University. In 1970 he became professor of ethnomusicology at Amsterdam University. He was founder-editor of the series Early English Church Music and author of *Music in Medieval Britain* (1958); he also worked on folk and non-European music in the British Isles and Latin America.

Harrison, Lou (*b* Portland, OR, 14 May 1917). American composer. He studied with Cowell in San Francisco (1934–5) and Schoenberg in Los Angeles and has spent most of his life in California. During World War II he worked with Cage on percussion music. He also studied Korean and Chinese traditions: Western symphonism is much more remote from his music of melismatic melody, often for unusual forces (including folk instruments and everyday objects), over ostinatos and drones. He has constructed a wide range of instruments, often tuned in just intonation, including a 'tack piano', jade flutes and gamelan.

Harrison & Harrison. English firm of organ builders. Founded in Rochdale in 1861 by Thomas Hugh Harrison (1839–1912), it moved to Durham in 1870, becoming Harrison & Harrison when Thomas' brother James joined him in 1872. Like Willis, they and their successors (notably Thomas's son Arthur) built or rebuilt many cathedral organs, including those at York (1915), Manchester (1916), Gloucester (1920) and Exeter (1933), as well as instruments in college chapels and parish churches, including King's, Trinity and St John's colleges, Cambridge, and St Mary Redcliffe, Bristol. The firm's most ambitious work was the reconstruction and enlargement of the Willis instrument in the Royal Albert Hall, London (1924, 1934). Its most important contribution was the revival of chorus and mixture work. More recent Harrison organs include those in the Royal Festival Hall (1954; designed by Ralph Downes) and the cathedrals of Wells, Ely, Coventry and St Albans.

Harrogate Festival (UK). Festival in North Yorkshire, inaugurated in 1927, annual (summer) from 1966. Events include concerts in Ripon Cathedral. Works are commissioned and performers include young artists.

Harsányi, Tibor (*b* Magyarkanisza, 27 June 1898; *d* Paris, 19 Sept 1954). French composer. He studied with Kodály at the Budapest Academy and settled in Paris in 1924, associating with Honegger. His works, in most genres, were latterly neo-classical.

Hart, Fritz (Bennicke) (*b* London, 11 Feb 1874; *d* Honolulu, 9 July 1949). English composer. He studied at the RCM (1893–6) and became a friend of Holst and Vaughan Williams. In 1908 he moved to Australia, where he directed the Melbourne Conservatory and the SO; from 1932 he conducted the Honolulu SO, and in 1936 became professor at Hawaii

University. He wrote 20 operas and many songs.

Hart, Philip (*b* ?London, ?c1674; *d* London, 17 July 1749). English composer. He had a high reputation as an organist and worked at several London churches. An accomplished composer, he wrote an ode (1702), solo cantatas, other vocal music and keyboard pieces.

Harteveld, (Julius Napoleon) Wilhelm (*b* Stockholm, 5 April 1859; *d* there, 1 Oct 1927). Swedish composer. He studied in Stockholm and Leipzig and worked in Russia (1882–1918) as a teacher, conductor and folksong collector. His works include marches (probably including the *Marcia Carolus rex*) and choral music.

Hart House Quartet. Canadian string quartet. Led first by Geza de Kresz (from 1935, by James Levey), it was founded in 1924, and linked with Toronto University; it also played in the USA and Europe. It was noted for its performances of 20th-century works as well as the standard repertory. It disbanded in 1946.

Hartmann, Emil [Wilhelm Emilius Zinn] (*b* Copenhagen, 21 Feb 1836; *d* there, 18 July 1898). Danish composer and organist, son of J.P.E. Hartmann. A church musician, he wrote successful stage works and orchestral music inspired by Scandinavian subjects, notably the overture to Ibsen's *Haermaendene paa Helgeland* op.25 and the symphonic poem *Hakon Jarl* op.40.

Hartmann, Johan Peter Emilius (*b* Copenhagen, 14 May 1805; *d* there, 10 March 1900). Danish composer and organist. He was a grandson of Johann Ernst Hartmann (1726–93), a German composer and violinist who, settling in Denmark in 1766, wrote Singspiels that laid the foundation for Danish national Romantic opera. J.P.E. Hartmann followed both a government career and that of cathedral organist, conservatory teacher and director and conductor in Copenhagen, becoming a leading figure in Denmark though attracting little attention elsewhere (unlike his son-in-law Niels Gade). His 'Norse' aspect was evident from the 1830s, particularly in the melodramas he wrote to Oehlenschlaeger's texts, from *Guldhornene* (1832) to *Yrsa* (1883), and in his operatic masterpiece evoking a medieval atmosphere, *Liden Kirsten* (1846); through numerous hymns and songs he further satisfied rising national feelings in 19th-century Denmark.

Hartmann, Karl Amadeus (*b* Munich, 2 Aug 1905; *d* there, 5 Dec 1963). German composer. He studied with Haas at the Munich Academy (1924–7), with Scherchen and with Webern (1941–2). After the war he started the Musica Viva festival in Munich to present music that had been banned during the Nazi years, and most of his published works date from after this period. They include most importantly a cycle of eight symphonies (1936, 1946, 1947, 1949, 1950, 1953, 1958, 1962), which have a Brucknerian breadth while suggesting the influences of Reger, Berg, Stravinsky, Bartók and Blacher. He also wrote several concertos and vocal music including a chamber opera *Simplicius Simplicissimus* (1949), a strongly expressive work combining popular song, chorale and psalm-like recitation with symphonic method.

Harty, Sir (Herbert) Hamilton (*b* Hillsborough, 4 Dec 1879; *d* Brighton, 19 Feb 1941). Irish composer and conductor. He held organist's posts in Ireland and in 1900 moved to London. After early success as a composer and accompanist he turned to conducting, working with the LSO and becoming conductor of the Hallé Orchestra, 1920–33; he gave new British music and British premières of Strauss, Mahler (including the Ninth Symphony) and Shostakovich. He then worked with London orchestras. He was a noted Berlioz interpreter and made arrangements of popular Handel works; his own compositions include an attractive *Irish Symphony*, a Violin Concerto, chamber and vocal works, some written for his wife, the soprano Agnes Nicholls.

Harvey, Jonathan (Dean) (*b* Sutton Coldfield, 3 May 1939). English composer. He studied at Cambridge, privately with Erwin Stein and Hans Keller, and with Babbitt at Princeton (1969–70). He has taught at the universities of Southampton (1964–77) and Sussex. His early music shows enthusiasms ranging from Britten and Messiaen to Stockhausen and Davies, but since the early 1970s he has developed a more integrated style and has emerged as an outstanding composer of electronic music (*Mortuos plango, vivos voco*, 1980). Later pieces include *Madonna of Winter and Spring* (1986).

Harwood, Elizabeth (Jean) (*b* Barton Seagrave, 27 May 1938). English soprano. She studied in Manchester and joined Sadler's Wells in 1961; her Covent Garden début was in 1967 as the Fiakermilli (*Arabella*). She is noted for the elegance and refinement of her high, silvery soprano.

Háry János. Opera in a prologue, five scenes and an epilogue by Kodály to a libretto by Paulini and Harsányi after Garay (1926, Budapest).

Haskil, Clara (*b* Budapest, 7 Jan 1895; *d* Brussels, 7 Dec 1960). Romanian pianist. She studied in Vienna and with Cortot in Paris. After her début in 1910 she often appeared with Ysaÿe, Casals and latterly Grumiaux. She was a brilliant pianist of restricted scale but remarkable power, a sensitive interpreter of Mozart, Schubert and early Beethoven.

Haslemere Festival (UK). Annual (summer) festival in Surrey, founded in 1925 by Arnold Dolmetsch. Concerts of early music, on original instruments, are given by the Dolmetsch family and others.

Haslinger. Austrian firm of music publishers. Founded as the Chemische Druckery in Vienna (1803) by Alois Senefelder, it was soon transferred to S.A. Steiner (1773–1838), who went into partnership with his employee Tobias Haslinger (1787–1842) between 1815 and 1826. In 1826 Haslinger took over, followed by his son Carl in 1842; the firm was sold to Schlesinger in 1875. The firm acquired a worldwide reputation during the period 1815–26; Haslinger replaced lithographic printing with clear engraving and brought out a handsome edition of Beethoven's works. Publications included the first editions of Beethoven's opp.90–101, 112–18 and 121*a*, a 38-volume edition of Mozart's keyboard works and pieces by Czerny, Hummel, Moscheles, Spohr and Weber. From 1828 the firm began a complete Beethoven edition (73 vols. by 1845), adding

Schubert first editions and works of Chopin, Schumann and above all Johann Strauss (i) and (ii); light music sustained the firm, by 1850 dominating its output.

Hasse, Johann Adolf (*b* Bergedorf, bap. 25 March 1699; *d* Venice, 16 Dec 1783). German composer. From a family of musicians, he began his career as a tenor in Hamburg; he then studied in Italy, under A. Scarlatti and others, and wrote several works for performance in Naples, where he held a position. With his wife, the soprano Faustina Bordoni, he went to Dresden in 1731 as Kapellmeister to the Saxon court. His reputation, however, was such that he was in demand in Italy (especially Venice, where he worked particularly for the Incurabili hospital) and Vienna as well as in Dresden. Besides his operas, he composed oratorios and large quantities of church music, chiefly for the Dresden court; he also wrote concertos and chamber works.

It was as an opera composer, however, that Hasse was above all esteemed. He wrote *c*70 stage works, mostly serious operas to texts by Metastasio, many of which were widely given, not only in Dresden but in Naples, in Venice during his later years at the important Viennese court, and wherever Italian opera was admired. Metastasio himself favoured Hasse above all others who set his librettos, for his polished style, his feeling for the words and his sensitivity to the human voice. Burney called him 'the most natural, elegant, and judicious composer of vocal music, as well as the most voluminous'. In his last years, when he preferred to compose church music, he came to be regarded as old-fashioned.

Dramatic music Artaserse (1730); Cleofide (1731); Siroe rè di Persia (1733); Tito Vespasiano (1735); Didone abbandonata (1742); Piramo e Tisbe (1768); Il Ruggiero (1771); *c*45 others; 11 intermezzos; 10 stage works

Other vocal music 11 oratorios, incl. I pellegrini al sepolcro di Nostro Signore (1745 or 1751), La conversione di S Agostino (1750); over 80 secular cantatas; songs, arias, solfeggi; Mass, d (1751); 11 other masses; 3 Requiems; *c*40 mass movts; over 80 psalms, antiphons, hymns; *c*40 solo motets; sacred arias

Instrumental music *c*25 fl concs.; *c*30 trio sonatas; over 30 fl sonatas and vn sonatas; kbd sonatas, toccatas

Hassell, Jon (*b* Memphis, 22 March 1937). American composer and trumpeter. He studied with Stockhausen and Pousseur in Cologne (1965–7) and in the late 1960s began performing with Terry Riley and La Monte Young. His works, some with Brian Eno, synthesize ethnic and electronic music. He developed a new technique for trumpet playing.

Hasselmans, Alphonse (Jean) (*b* Liège, 5 March 1845; *d* Paris, 19 May 1912). French harpist and composer of Belgian birth. As solo harpist with the orchestras of the Paris Conservatoire, Opéra and Opéra-Comique, and as professor at the Conservatoire, he played a significant part in the harp revival at the turn of the century; he wrote *c*50 pieces.

Hassler, Hans Leo (*b* Nuremberg, bap. 26 Oct 1564; *d* Frankfurt, 8 June 1612). German composer. He was first taught by his father, the organist Isaak Hassler (*c*1530–1591), then by A. Gabrieli in Venice (1585–6). From 1586 to 1600 he was chamber musician to the Fuggers in Augsburg and was chamber organist and (later) Kapellmeister at the Saxon court chapel in Dresden from 1608. Influenced by Lassus and the Venetians, he was a prolific composer of Latin and German sacred music, as well as secular and instrumental music. Though no innovator, he coordinated and developed current styles and earned a high reputation for his practical approach and craftsmanship. His brother Kaspar (1562–1618) was a music editor and a leading organist in Nuremberg; his brother Jakob (1569–1622) was an organist and composer of madrigals, sacred and keyboard music.

Hässler, Johann Wilhelm (*b* Erfurt, 29 March 1747; *d* Moscow, 29 March 1822). German organist and pianist. At first an organist in Erfurt, he performed in cities including Dresden (1789), where he met Mozart. After working as a pianist in London (1790–92) and St Petersburg he settled in Moscow (1794), becoming an influential piano teacher. He composed much piano music (sonatas, fantasias etc) and various chamber and vocal pieces.

Hatton, John Liptrot (*b* Liverpool, 12 Oct 1809; *d* Margate, 20 Sept 1886). English composer, pianist, conductor and singer. He composed numerous songs, edited song collections and worked as a theatre conductor and arranger. Among his most successful works, the *Songs by Herrick, Ben Jonson and Sedley* (1850) and the popular ballad *The Wreck of the Hesperus* show his catholic taste and gift for simple, fresh invention.

Haubenstock-Ramati, Roman (*b* Kraków, 27 Feb 1919). Austrian composer of Polish origin. He studied with Malawski in Kraków (1934–8) and Koffler in Lwów (1939–41), then in 1950 moved to Tel-Aviv. In 1957 he settled in Vienna. His earlier works were serial; most of the later ones incorporate aleatory elements and use graphic notation. The opera *Amerika* (1964) is typical.

Haubiel, Charles Trowbridge (*b* Delta, OH, 30 Jan 1892; *d* Los Angeles, 26 Aug 1978). American pianist and composer. After study in Europe he taught in Oklahoma City, then at New York University (1923–47). He founded the Composer's Press in 1935. A prolific composer in a traditional idiom, he achieved success with the orchestral pieces *Karma* (1928) and *Portraits* (1935).

Hauer, Josef Matthias (*b* Wiener Neustadt, 19 March 1883; *d* Vienna, 22 Sept 1959). Austrian composer. Self-taught as a composer, he began in 1912–19 by writing strongly chromatic miniatures, mostly songs and piano pieces. In 1919 he discovered the serial method he used exclusively thereafter: he understood the 12-note set as a hexachordal trope (i.e. a sequence of two unordered groups of six notes each). Schoenberg had his music performed by his concert society, but both men insisted on priority in the discovery of serialism, and their relationship did not continue. Hauer remained an isolated figure. He produced a large output, including operas, choral works, orchestral suites and string quartets, but had few performances. In 1938 he retired, thereafter concentrating on gamelike *Zwölftonspiele*, of which he left *c*1000.

Hauk, Minnie (*b* New York, 16 Nov 1851; *d* Trib-schen, 6 Feb 1929). American mezzo-soprano. She sang the female lead in the American première of Gounod's *Roméo et Juliette* (1867, New York), then after many successful appearances in Europe, notably in Vienna, Berlin and London, sang the title roles in the American premières of *Carmen* (1878) and *Manon* (1885). Her repertory was vast; her voice had great force and richness.

Haunted Manor, The [Straszny dwór]. Opera in four acts by Moniuszko to a libretto by Chęciński (1865, Warsaw).

Hauptmann, Moritz (*b* Dresden, 13 Oct 1792; *d* Leipzig, 3 Jan 1868). German composer, theorist and teacher. At Kassel he was a violinist under Spohr for 20 years, then Kantor of the Thomasschule, Leipzig, and theory teacher in the newly founded conservatory there. He edited the *Allgemeine musikalische Zeitung* (1843) and, with Otto Jahn and Schumann, founded the Bach Gesellschaft (1850). His output consists chiefly of sacred vocal music; his theoretical system stresses the dualism of major and minor.

Hauptstimme (Ger.: 'chief voice'). The name given by Schoenberg and Berg to the most important polyphonic voice in a passage of 12-note or other rigorously non-tonal music, as opposed to the *Nebenstimme* ('under-voice') and accompanying voices.

Hauptwerk (Ger.). Like GREAT ORGAN, *Grand orgue* and *Organo primo, Hauptwerk* denotes the main manual of an organ, as distinct from the CHAIR ORGAN or the POSITIVE.

Hausmann, Robert (*b* Rottleberode, 13 Aug 1852; *d* Vienna, 18 Jan 1909). German cellist. He studied with Joachim and Piatti. A member of the Joachim Quartet (1879–1907), he was associated with Brahms, whose Cello Sonata op.99 was written for him; with Joachim he also gave the première of Brahms's Double Concerto (1887).

Hausmusik. German term for music intended for performance in the home, particularly among the middle classes.

Haussermann, John (William jr) (*b* Manila, 21 Aug 1909). American composer. He studied in Cincinnati and in Paris with Dupré (many of his works include the organ). He wrote in all non-dramatic forms; whole-tone harmonies reflect his French experience. A sufferer from cerebral palsy, he wrote much of his music with an assistant.

Haussmann, Valentin (*b* Gerbstedt, 1565–70; *d* *c*1614). German composer, music editor and poet. He travelled in Germany finding employment from princely courts, city councils and bourgeois patrons, without apparently seeking a permanent post. As well as occasional music his output (mostly published in Nuremberg) includes sacred vocal works, numerous collections of dance-songs and instrumental dances (1592–1608), anthologies of Italian music in his own translation and instrumental music. His two collections of intradas, pavans and galliards (1604) are a landmark in the development of independent instrumental music and include some of the earliest parts specifically for the violin in Germany. The monothematic 'Fuga prima' (*Neue*

Paduane und Galliarde) is a significant step in the early history of the fugue.

Hautbois (Fr.). 'Loud woodwind': term for the smaller members of the shawm family, used in France and England after 1500; in the 17th century the name was taken into English as 'oboe'.

Haut-dessus (Fr.). 'High treble': term used in French music of the 17th and 18th centuries for the uppermost part in an ensemble; if there are two high parts, the one immediately below the *haut-dessus* is called *bas-dessus*.

Haute-contre (Fr.). A high tenor voice, cultivated in France until *c*1800, and again in the late 20th century; it is also used for the corresponding member of an instrumental family. The voice is in some respects equivalent to the English countertenor, using a natural voice but possibly with some falsetto at the top of the range. The important male roles in the operas of Lully and Rameau are normally assigned to *haute-contres*.

Havergal, William Henry (*b* High Wycombe, 18 Jan 1793; *d* Leamington, 19 April 1870). English composer. A clergyman, he wrote cathedral music, hymn tunes and chants, also bringing a number of German chorales into English use.

Havingha, Gerhardus (*b* Groningen, 15 Nov 1696; *d* Alkmaar, 6 March 1753). Netherlands composer. He was organist at Appingedam and (from 1722) in Alkmaar; he was also a carillonist. He composed harpsichord suites (1724) and ensemble pieces.

Hawaiian guitar [steel guitar]. A type of GUITAR held flat across the player's knees; it was developed in the late 19th century from the classical guitar, taken to Hawaii by American settlers *c*1830. It has a raised steel nut to hold the strings; the player slides a steel bar along the strings, producing glissando or vibrato effects. Leg-mounted electric steel guitars were introduced in the 1930s; later models incorporated several necks or knee-levers and pedals for tuning-changes.

Hawes, William (*b* London, 21 June 1785; *d* there, 18 Feb 1846). English teacher, composer and conductor. Master of the Choristers at St Paul's Cathedral (1812–17) and Master of the Children of the Chapel Royal (1817–46), he was conductor of the Madrigal Society and from 1824 director of the English Opera House, composing theatrical music, glees and church music.

Hawkins, Coleman ['Hawk', 'Bean'] (*b* St Joseph, MO, 21 Nov 1904; *d* New York, 19 May 1969). American jazz tenor saxophonist. As a member of Fletcher Henderson's orchestra (1924–34) he became the leading jazz saxophonist of his generation, establishing a deep-toned, melodic and arpeggio-based style that freed the instrument from the earlier slap-tongued vaudeville style of solo playing. He worked in Britain and Europe (1936–9) before returning to the USA, where he led bands and was a member of 'Jazz at the Philharmonic' tours. He kept abreast of developments in jazz, successfully embracing bop and subsequent modern styles.

Hawkins, Sir John (*b* London, 29 March 1719; *d* there, 21 May 1789). English music historian. He worked as an attorney in London and was active in musical and literary circles; Handel and John Stanley were among his friends. He owned a fine collection of treatises and music. His *A General History of the Science and Practice of Music* (1776) appeared soon after Charles Burney's history and led to rivalry between the two writers. It contains valuable information about London musical society of the period and emphasizes the achievement of 16th- and early 17th-century composers. He also wrote a life of Samuel Johnson.

Haydn, (Franz) Joseph (*b* Rohrau, 31 March 1732; *d* Vienna, 31 May 1809). Austrian composer. The son of a wheelwright, he was trained as a choirboy and taken into the choir at St Stephen's Cathedral, Vienna, where he sang from *c*1740 to *c*1750. He then worked as a freelance musician, playing the violin and keyboard instruments, accompanying for singing lessons given by the composer Porpora, who helped and encouraged him. At this time he wrote some sacred works, music for theatre comedies and chamber music. In *c*1759 he was appointed music director to Count Morzin; but he soon moved, into service as Vice-Kapellmeister with one of the leading Hungarian families, the Esterházys, becoming full Kapellmeister on Werner's death in 1766. He was director of an ensemble of generally some 15–20 musicians, with responsibility for the music and the instruments – and was required to compose as his employer – from 1762, Prince Nikolaus Esterházy – might command. At first he lived at Eisenstadt, *c*30 miles south-east of Vienna; by 1767 the family's chief residence, and Haydn's chief place of work, was at the new palace at Eszterháza. In his early years Haydn chiefly wrote instrumental music, including symphonies and other pieces for the twice-weekly concerts and the prince's *Tafelmusik*, and works for the instrument played by the prince, the baryton (a kind of viol), for which he composed *c*125 trios in ten years. There were also cantatas and a little church music. After Werner's death church music became more central, and so, after the opening of a new opera house at Eszterháza in 1768, did opera. Some of the symphonies from *c*1770 show Haydn expanding his musical horizons from occasional, entertainment music towards larger and more original pieces, for example nos.26, 39, 49, 44 and 52 (many of them in minor keys, and serious in mood, in line with trends in the contemporary symphony in Germany and Austria). Also from 1768–72 come three sets of string quartets, probably not written for the Esterházy establishment but for another patron or perhaps for publication (Haydn was allowed to write other than for the Esterházys only with permission); op.20 clearly shows the beginnings of a more adventurous and integrated quartet style.

Among the operas from this period are *Lo speziale* (for the opening of the new house), *L'infedeltà delusa* (1773) and *Il mondo della luna* (1777). Operatic activity became increasingly central from the mid-1770s as regular performances came to be given at the new house. It was part of Haydn's job to prepare the music, adapting or arranging it for the voices of the resident singers. In 1779 the opera house burnt down; Haydn composed *La fedeltà premiata* for its reopening in 1781. Until then his operas had largely been in a comic genre; his last two for Eszterháza, *Orlando paladino* (1782) and *Armida* (1783), are in mixed or serious genres. Although his operas never attained wider exposure, Haydn's reputation had now grown and was international. Much of his music had been published in all the main European centres; under a revised contract with the Esterháza his employers no longer had exclusive rights to his music.

His works of the 1780s that carried his name further afield include piano sonatas, piano trios, symphonies (nos.76–81 were published in 1784–5, and nos.82–7 were written on commission for a concert organization in Paris in 1785–6) and string quartets. His influential op.33 quartets, issued in 1782, were said to be 'in a quite new, special manner': this is sometimes thought to refer to the use of instruments or the style of thematic development, but could refer to the introduction of scherzos or might simply be an advertising device. More quartets appeared at the end of the decade, op.50 (dedicated to the King of Prussia and often said to be influenced by the quartets Mozart had dedicated to Haydn) and two sets (opp.54–5 and 64) written for a former Esterházy violinist who became a Viennese businessman. All these show an increasing enterprise, originality and freedom of style as well as melodic fluency, command of form, and humour. Other works that carried Haydn's reputation beyond central Europe include concertos and notturnos for a type of hurdy-gurdy, written on commission for the King of Naples, and *The Seven Last Words*, commissioned for Holy Week from Cadíz Cathedral and existing not only in its original orchestral form but also for string quartet, for piano and (later) for chorus and orchestra.

In 1790, Nikolaus Esterházy died; Haydn (unlike most of his musicians) was retained by his son but was free to live in Vienna (which he had many times visited) and to travel. He was invited by the impresario and violinist J.P. Salomon to go to London to write an opera, symphonies and other works. In the event he went to London twice, in 1791–2 and 1794–5. He composed his last 12 symphonies for performance there, where they enjoyed great success; he also wrote a symphonie concertante, choral pieces, piano trios, piano sonatas and songs (some to English words) as well as arranging British folksongs for publishers in London and Edinburgh. But because of intrigues his opera, *L'anima del filosofo*, on the Orpheus story, remained unperformed. He was honoured (with an Oxford DMus) and fêted generously, and played, sang and conducted before the royal family. He also heard performances of Handel's music by large choirs in Westminster Abbey.

Back in Vienna, he resumed work for Nikolaus Esterházy's grandson (whose father had now died); his main duty was to produce masses for the princess's nameday. He wrote six works, firmly in the Austrian mass tradition but strengthened and invigorated by his command of symphonic technique. Other works

of these late years include further string quartets (opp.71 and 74 between the London visits, op.76 and the op.77 pair after them), showing great diversity of style and seriousness of content yet retaining his vitality and fluency of utterance; some have a more public manner, acknowledging the new use of string quartets at concerts as well as in the home. The most important work, however, is his oratorio *The Creation* in which his essentially simple-hearted joy in Man, Beast and Nature, and his gratitude to God for his creation of these things to our benefit, are made a part of universal experience by his treatment of them in an oratorio modelled on Handel's, with massive choral writing of a kind he had not essayed before. He followed this with *The Seasons*, in a similar vein but more a series of attractive episodes than a whole.

Haydn died in 1809, after twice dictating his recollections and preparing a catalogue of his works. He was widely revered, even though by then his music was old-fashioned compared with Beethoven's. He was immensely prolific: some of his music remains unpublished and little known. His operas have never succeeded in holding the stage. But he is regarded, with some justice, as father of the symphony and the string quartet: he saw both genres from their beginnings to a high level of sophistication and artistic expression, even if he did not originate them. He brought to them new intellectual weight, and his closely argued style of development laid the foundations for the larger structures of Beethoven and later composers.

Sacred vocal music masses – Missa brevis, F (?1749); Missa Cellensis, C, 'Cecilia Mass' (1766); Missa Sancti Nicolai, G (1772); Missa in honorem BVM, Eb, 'Great Organ Mass' (by 1774); Missa brevis Sancti Joannis de Deo, Bb, 'Little Organ Mass' (by 1778); Missa Cellensis, C, 'Mariazell Mass' (1782); Missa Sancti Bernardi von Offida, Bb, 'Heiligmesse' (1796); Missa in tempore belli, C, 'Paukenmesse' (1796); 'Nelson Mass', d, 'Coronation Mass', 'Missa in angustiis' (1798); Theresienmesse, Bb (1799); Creation Mass, Bb (1801); Harmoniemesse, Bb (1802); other church music, incl. Te Deum, C (by 1800)

Oratorios Stabat mater (1767); Applausus, allegorical oratorio/cantata (by 1768); Il ritorno di Tobia (1775); Die sieben letzten Worte ('The Seven Last Words') [based on orch work] (by 1796); The Creation (1798); The Seasons (1801)

Dramatic music operas – Acide (frag.) (1762); La canterina (1766); Lo speziale (1768); Le pescatrici (1769); L'infedeltà delusa (1773); Philemon und Baucis (1773); L'incontro improvviso (1775); Il mondo della luna (1777); La vera costanza (by 1779, rev. 1785); L'isola disabitata (1779); La fedeltà premiata (1781); Orlando paladino (1782); Armida (1783); L'anima del filosofo (comp. 1791); music for plays

Miscellaneous vocal music Arianna a Naxos, cantata (by 1790); arias, scenas, partsongs; songs to English and German texts; folksong arrs.; canons

Symphonies 1, D (by 1759); 2, C (by 1764); 3, G (by 1762); 4, D (by 1762); 5, A (by 1762); 6, D, 'Le matin' (?1761); 7, C, 'Le midi' (?1761); 8, G, 'Le soir' (?1761); 9, C (?1762); 10, D (by 1766); 11, Eb (by 1769); 12, E (1763); 13, D (1763); 14, A (by 1764); 15, D (by 1764); 16, Bb (by 1766); 17, F (by 1765); 18, G (by 1766); 19, D (by 1766); 20, C (by 1766); 21, A (1764); 22, Eb, 'The Philosopher' (1764); 23, G (1764); 24, D (1764); 25, C (by 1766); 26, d, 'Lamentatione' (1770); 27, G (by 1766); 28, A (1765); 29, E (1765); 30, C, 'Alleluja' (1765); 31, D, 'Hornsignal' (1765); 32, C (by 1766); 33, C (by 1767); 34, d/D (by 1767); 35, Bb (1767); 36, Eb (by 1769); 37, C (?by 1758); 38, C (by 1769); 39, g (by 1770); 40, F (1763); 41, C (by 1770); 42, D (1771); 43, Eb, 'Mercury' (by 1772); 44, e,

'Trauersinfonie' (by 1772); 45, f♯, 'Farewell' (1772); 46, B (1772); 47, G (1772); 48, C, 'Maria Theresia' (?by 1769); 49, f, 'La passione' (1768); 50, C (1773); 51, B♭ (by 1774); 52, c (by 1774); 53, D, 'Imperial', 'Festino' (?1778/9); 54, G (1774); 55, E♭, 'The Schoolmaster' (1774); 56, C (1774); 57, D (1774); 58, F (by 1775); 59, A, 'Fire' (by 1769); 60, C, 'Il distratto' (by 1774); 61, D (1776); 62, D (by 1781); 63, C, 'La Roxelane' (by 1781); 64, A, 'Tempora mutantur' (by 1778); 65, A (by 1778); 66, B♭ (by 1779); 67, F (by 1779); 68, B♭ (by 1779); 69, C, 'Laudon', 'Loudon' (by 1779); 70, D (by 1779); 71, B♭ (by 1780); 72, D (by 1781); 73, D, 'La chasse' (by 1782); 74, E♭ (by 1781); 75, D (by 1781); 76, E♭ (?1782); 77, B♭ (?1782); 78, C (?1782); 79, F (?by 1784); 80, d (by 1784); 81, G (by 1784); 6 Paris syms.: 82, C, 'L'ours', 'The Bear' (1786); 82, g, 'La poule', 'The Hen' (1785); 84, E♭ (1786); 85, B♭, 'La reine', 'The Queen' (?1785); 86, D, (1786); 87, A (1785); 88, G (?1787); 89, F (1787); 90, C (1788); 91, E♭ (1788); 92, G, 'Oxford' (1789); 12 London syms.: 93, D (1791); 94, G, 'The Surprise' (1791); 95, c (1791); 96, D, 'The Miracle' (1791); 97, C (1792); 98, B♭ (1792); 99, E♭ (1793); 100, G, 'Military' (1793/4); 101, D, 'The Clock' (1793/4); 102, B♭ (1794); 103, E♭ 'Drumroll' (1795); 104, D, 'London' (1795); 106, D (?1769); 107, B♭ (by 1762); 108, B♭ (by 1765)
Other orchestral music 3 vn concs. – C (by 1769), A (by 1771), G (by 1769); 2 vc concs. – C (?c1765), D (1783); Hn Conc., D (1762); Tpt Conc., E♭ (1796); Concertante, vn, vc, ob, bn, orch, B♭ (1792); 3 hpd concs. – F (by 1771), G (by 1781), D (by 1784); other concs.; concertinos and divertimentos for hpd and orch; dances, marches etc; Die sieben letzten Worte ('The Seven Last Words') (by 1787)
String quartets op.1 nos.1, B♭ 'La chasse', 2, E♭, 3, D, 4, G, 'O', E♭, 6, C (?c1757–1764) [op.1 no.5 = arr. of Sym. no.107]; op.2 nos.1, A, 2, E, 4, F, 6, B♭ (?c1760–1765) [op.2 nos.3, 5 = arrs. of divertimentos]; [op.3 probably not by Haydn] op.9 nos.1–6, C, E♭, G, d, B♭, A (by 1771); op.17 nos.1–6, E, F, E♭, c, G, D (1771); op.20 nos.1–6, E♭, C, g, D, f, A (1772); op.33, 'Russian', nos.1–6, b, E♭ 'The Joke', C 'The Bird', B♭, G 'How do you do', D; op.42, d (1785); op.50, 'Prussian', nos. 1–6, B♭, C E♭, f♯, F, D 'The Frog' (1787); op.54 nos.1–3, G, C, E (by 1788); op.55 nos.1–3, A, f 'The Razor', B♭ (by 1788); op.64 nos.1–6, C, b, B♭, G, D 'The Lark', E♭ (1790); op.71 nos.1–3, B♭, D, E♭ (1793); op.74 nos.1–3, C, F, g, 'The Rider' (1793); op.76 nos.1–6, G, d 'Fifths', C 'Emperor', B♭ 'Sunrise', D, E♭ (by 1797); op.77 nos.1–2, G, F (1799); op.103, d (unfinished, by 1803)
Other chamber music over 120 trios for baryton, va and bass; 29 kbd trios; other trios, trio sonatas, duos; pieces for flute-clock; 8 notturnos for 2 lire organizzate (c1790); numerous divertimentos
Keyboard music c40 sonatas; Variations, f (1793); other variations, capriccios

Haydn, (Johann) Michael (*b* Rohrau, bap. 14 Sept 1737; *d* Salzburg, 10 Aug 1806). Austrian composer, younger brother of Joseph Haydn. He sang with his brother at St Stephen's Cathedral, Vienna, and in 1757–63 was Kapellmeister to the Bishop of Gross-wardein. From 1763 he was court musician and Konzertmeister to the Prince-Archbishop of Salz-burg, also writing music for the court. He had much contact with the Mozart family, and he, Mozart and Adlgasser wrote an act each of the oratorio *Die Schuldigkeit des ersten Gebots* (1767). He became organist at the Holy Trinity Church in 1777, and cathedral organist (succeeding Mozart) in 1781. Under the church reforms of the 1780s he wrote simpler sacred music; meanwhile his reputation grew, and he later composed several works for the Empress Maria Theresia. Among his pupils was the young Carl Maria von Weber.

Haydn contributed most in the field of sacred music, writing 38 masses and over 300 other church works; most are for four solo voices, four-part choir and orchestra (sometimes with wind instruments). Fugues often appear, and some masses are in a strict contrapuntal style; there is less florid solo writing than in many sacred works of the day. His Requiem in C minor (1771) probably influenced Mozart's later setting. His instrumental works include c40 symphonies, many of them vigorous and inventive and some having fugal finales, concertos, minuets etc, and chamber music including many divert-imentos, 12 string quartets and four duets for violin and viola (which Mozart made into a set of six). He also composed Singspiels, incidental music to Vol-taire's *Zaire* (1777), an *opera seria* (1787), oratorios, cantatas and other secular vocal works. His part-songs for unaccompanied male voices were among the earliest written.

Sacred vocal music over 30 Latin masses; 3 Requiems; 6 Te Deum; c200 motets; over 100 other works
Dramatic music Zaire, incidental music (1777); 1 opera seria; Singspiels and other stage works; oratorios
Secular vocal music 10 cantatas; 1 serenata; c50 songs; c80 partsongs; c80 canons
Orchestral music c40 syms.; 11 concs.; cassations, serenatas, divertimentos, dances, marches
Chamber music Str qnt (1784); 12 str qts; 2 fl qts; 4 sonatas, vn, va (1784)

Haydn Quartets. Six string quartets by Mozart: in G K387 (1782), in D minor K421/417*b* (1783), in E♭ K428/421*b* (1783), in B♭ K458 ('Hunt', 1784), in A K464 (1785), in C K465 (1785), so called because they are dedicated to Haydn.

Haydn Variations. *See* ST ANTONY VARIATIONS.

Hayes, William (*b* Gloucester, bap. 26 Jan 1708; *d* Oxford, 27 July 1777). English composer. After working in Shrewsbury, he was organist at Worces-ter Cathedral (1731–4) and then at Magdalen Col-lege, Oxford. In 1742 he became professor of music at Oxford. His works include two oratorios, church music, a masque, cantatas, glees, instrumental pieces and several writings on music.

His son Philip (1738–97), a Gentleman of the Chapel Royal, succeeded him in 1777 at Magdalen College and as professor of music. His output in-cludes a similar range of works but shows signs of the new continental style. He edited works by his father and by Boyce. A second son, William (1741–90), was a clergyman and composed psalm tunes.

Haym, Nicola Francesco (*b* Rome, 6 July 1678; *d* London, 11 Aug 1729). Italian cellist, composer and librettist. He played under Corelli in Rome, 1694–1700, and was then a composer and cellist to the Duke of Bedford in London; later he served the Duke of Chandos. He took a leading part in the establishment of Italian opera in London and wrote arias for works by A. Scarlatti and others. Among his other works are oratorios, church music and sonatas. As a librettist he collaborated especially with Handel, writing or adapting texts for operas including *Teseo* (1713) and *Giulio Cesare* (1724). He was also an antiquarian.

Hayne [Ayne, Scoen Hayne] **van Ghizeghem** (*b* c1445; *d* 1472–97). Franco-Burgundian compo-ser. He was employed by Charles, Count of Charolais, and in July 1472 was with him at the siege of Beauvais. 20 *chansons* are attributed to him in late 15th- and early 16th-century sources. All have a treble-dominated texture, a contrapuntal structure built on a duet to which a countertenor is added, and a break roughly halfway through (following the poetic form). His best works (e.g. *Allez regrets* and *De tous biens plaine*) are among the finest of their genre, distinguished by melodic elegance and expressive intensity.

Hays, Doris (Ernestine) (*b* Memphis, 6 Aug 1941). American composer and pianist. She studied in Munich and at several American universities and is a noted exponent of Ives, Cowell and Cage. Her works, within that experimental tradition, sometimes draw on her Southern background; *Sens-Events* (1970–77) is typical of several multi-media works.

Head, Michael (Dewar) (*b* Eastbourne, 28 Jan 1900; *d* Cape Town, 24 Aug 1976). English composer. He was a pupil of Corder at the RAM (1919–25), where he taught from 1927. He is best known for his 85 songs, which fall between the popular ballad and the art song, which he performed widely in one-man recitals.

Headington, Christopher (John Magenis) (*b* London, 28 April 1930). English composer, teacher and writer. He studied at the RAM and with Berkeley. From 1965 he has been associated with the BBC and Oxford University. His fluent, fastidious compositions include string quartets and song cycles.

Head-motif. A musical idea or 'motto' which, by appearing at the beginning of each of a series of pieces or movements, establishes a relationship between them.

Heartz, Daniel (*b* Exeter, NH, 5 October 1928). American musicologist. He studied at Harvard and taught at Chicago (1957–60), then at Berkeley. He has worked on French Renaissance music, especially dance and music printing, and on 18th-century opera, especially Mozart, towards a new history of the Classical era.

Heavy metal. An Anglo-American style of rock, characterized by loud, sustained 'power chords' played on the electric guitar and a persistent beat that may be aggressively fast or intentionally ponderous. Lyrics (concerning sex, rebellion and violence) are delivered in an extreme, screeching and barking style between guitar chords. Exponents include Jimi Hendrix, The Who and Led Zeppelin.

Hebenstreit, Pantaleon (*b* Eisleben, 1667; *d* Dresden, 15 Nov 1750). German pantaleonist. He developed the cimbalom, or pantaleon (as it was called by Louis XIV in 1705), from the rustic form of the dulcimer and performed on it with much success in Germany, Paris and Vienna. It was especially popular for its dynamic variation, but was later overshadowed by the piano. Hebenstreit served at the Eisenach court, 1706–9 (he left after Telemann became Kapellmeister), and at Dresden from 1714, later becoming vice-Kapellmeister and (in 1734) court director of Protestant church music. He was also a violinist and composed orchestral suites and overtures.

Hebrides, The. *See* FINGAL'S CAVE.

Heckel. German family of woodwind instrument makers. It was through them that the German bassoon, based on the work of Carl Almenraeder, reached its present degree of refinement. Having worked for Schott of Mainz, Johann Adam Heckel (1812–77) started his own business at Biebrich in 1831; it has remained there, directed by successive members of the family. Besides the bassoon and double bassoon, it produces all kinds of woodwind instruments; among several new ones, the heckelphone and heckel-clarina (1890) are the most important. In Dresden a collateral branch has long been established as brass instrument makers.

Heckel, Wolff (*b* Munich, *c*1515; *d* in or after 1562). German lutenist and composer. He apparently lived in Strasbourg. His lutebook (1556), containing over 100 wide-ranging dances and vocal arrangements, is important for its 40 pieces for two lutes, written in German tablature.

Heckelclarina. An instrument akin to a saxophone invented in 1890 by the Heckel family.

Heckelphone. A baritone double-reed woodwind instrument, invented by the Heckel family in response to a suggestion from Wagner and first produced in 1904. It is similar to the oboe but has a wider bore, a bulbous bell and a bassoon-type reed on a curved crook. Its range is A–g''; Strauss gave it an important part in *Salome* (1905). Smaller varieties, a minor 3rd and a 4th higher, have been built.

Hegar, Friedrich (*b* Basle, 11 Oct 1841; *d* Zurich, 2 June 1927). Swiss conductor and composer. He studied at the Leipzig Conservatory under Hauptmann, Rietz and David and was a violinist at the Gewandhaus. He was a conductor in Zurich for more than 50 years, also helping to found the Zurich Music School and composing choral works, many for the male choirs he transformed into serious musical institutions; his best-known work is the oratorio *Manasse* (1888).

Heidenröslein. Song by Schubert (D257, 1815), a setting for voice and piano of words by Goethe.

Heider, Werner (*b* Fürth, 1 Jan 1930). German composer. He studied with Höller at the Munich Musikhochschule and has written much using avant-garde techniques; many of his pieces explore the sound possibilities of a single instrument (e.g. clarinet).

Heifetz, Jascha (*b* Vilna, 2 Feb 1901; *d* Los Angeles, 10 Dec 1987). American violinist of Russian birth. He studied at the St Petersburg Conservatory with Auer and appeared in the West from 1912, making his début in Berlin. He left Russia in 1917 and settled in the USA after his Carnegie Hall début the same year, becoming an American citizen in 1925. His first London appearance was in 1920. Heifetz was noted for his immaculate technique, coupled with an intense vibrato and a preference for fast tempos. He was heard in chamber music with Piatigorsky, Feuermann and Rubinstein.

Heiliger Dankgesang (Ger.). 'Song of thanks to heaven': Beethoven's title for the slow movement of his String Quartet in A minor op.132 (1825), written on his recovery from illness; music in a style recalling the old ecclesiastical modes and chorale-prelude techniques is contrasted with more vigorous music, marked 'Feeling new strength'.

Heiligmesse. Nickname of Haydn's Mass no.10 in B♭ (1796), so called because of the treatment of the words 'Holy, Holy' in the Sanctus.

Heiller, Anton (*b* Vienna, 15 Sept 1923; *d* there, 25 March 1979). Austrian composer and organist. He studied at the Vienna Academy and was internationally esteemed as a Bach performer. His works include masses and cantatas in the polyphonic tradition of Hindemith and organ music.

Heinichen, Johann David (*b* Krössuln, 17 April 1683; *d* Dresden, 16 July 1729). German composer and theorist. Initially an advocate, he composed music for the Weissenfels court, then moved to Leipzig (1709), where he presented operas and directed a collegium musicum. He also worked at Zeitz and Naumburg. In 1710–16 he lived in Italy and had two operas staged in Venice in 1713. From 1717 he was Kapellmeister (with J.C. Schmidt) at the Dresden court. He wrote serenatas, cantatas, sacred works, and instrumental music for the court, combining German, French and Italian features; his concertos and sonatas are italianate, with unusual instrumental combinations and sonorities. He wrote two versions of a thoroughbass treatise, the second (1728) among the major musical writings of the period.

Heininen, Paavo (Johannes) (*b* Helsinki, 13 Jan 1938). Finnish composer. He studied with Englund and Kokkonen at the Helsinki Academy (1956–60), with Zimmermann in Cologne (1960–61) and with Persichetti in New York (1961–2), then returned to teach at the academies in Helsinki and Turku. His powerful works include symphonies, concertos, much chamber music, and the opera *The Silken Drum* (1983); his style developed from one influenced by Hindemith and Bartók to a more delicate one.

Heinrich, Anthony Philip (*b* Krásný Búk, 11 March 1781; *d* New York, 3 May 1861). American composer of German-Bohemian birth. Considered America's first 'professional' composer, he worked in Philadelphia, Pittsburgh, Kentucky, Boston and New York, where he settled in 1837. As a violinist he led the first known performance of a Beethoven symphony in the USA (Lexington, KY, 1817) and in 1842 he helped organize the New York Philharmonic Society. His large output of orchestral, vocal, instrumental and keyboard works, 1818–58, includes many expressive or descriptive pieces (e.g. *The Dawning of Music in Kentucky, or The Pleasures of Harmony in the Solitudes of Nature*, 1820; *Pushmataha, a Venerable Chief of a Western Tribe of Indians*, 1831); some are eccentric and unusually complex.

Heinze, Sir Bernard (Thomas) (*b* Shepparton, 1 July 1894; *d* Sydney, 9 June 1982). Australian conductor and music administrator. He studied at the RCM in London, then under d'Indy in Paris and Willy Hess in Berlin. In 1924 he joined the staff of the Melbourne University Conservatorium, where he did much to develop musical life, conducting the

Victorian SO. In 1929 he became director-general of music to the Australian Broadcasting Company and in 1922 music adviser to its successor; in this role he exercised much influence on musical standards. He was director of the New South Wales Conservatorium, 1956–66, and continued after retirement to work for the advancement of music in Australia.

Heise, Peter (Arnold) (*b* Copenhagen, 11 Feb 1830; *d* Tårbaek, 12 Sept 1879). Danish composer. He studied with Hauptmann in Leipzig. His chief importance is as a composer of *c*300 songs showing a great lyrical gift. The tragic opera *King and Marshal* (1878), the most significant Danish opera of the century, stands at the crossroads of the older national Singspiel and new, freer expression in music drama.

Heldenleben, Ein. Tone poem by Richard Strauss (1898).

Heldentenor (Ger.). 'Heroic tenor': term for a robust and enduring tenor voice, particularly of the kind suited to Wagner's heroic roles (Tristan, Siegfried).

Hèle, George de la (*b* Antwerp, 1547; *d* Madrid, 27 Aug 1586). Flemish composer. He sang in the royal chapel in Madrid (1560–70) and was a choirmaster at Malines (1572–4) and Tournai Cathedral (1574–80). He became *maître* of the French royal chapel in 1580. His book of eight masses, printed by Christopher Plantin in Antwerp (1578), is reckoned a model of printing artistry.

Helffer, Claude (*b* Paris, 18 June 1922). French pianist. He studied under Casadesus and Leibowitz, making his début in 1948. He has been active in presenting 20th-century music in Paris, combining creative dexterity and definition with traditional skills. He has given premières of works by Amy, Boucourechliev and others, as well as championing French music generally. His wife Mireille, head of ethnomusicology at the Musée de l'Homme, is an authority on the music of Burma and Indo-China.

Helicon. A valved bass brass instrument, first produced in Vienna in 1845, in circular form, usually with a narrow bell: it rests on the player's left shoulder, passing under his right arm, and like the sousaphone can be carried for long periods. It is pitched in F, E♭ or B♭.

Hellendaal, Pieter (*b* Rotterdam, bap. 1 April 1721; *d* Cambridge, 19 April 1799). Dutch composer. He studied with Tartini in Italy, then gave concerts in the Netherlands (1749–51) before moving to London, where he was a successful violin soloist and composer. From 1762 he worked in Cambridge, latterly as a teacher; he was also an organist. His output includes virtuoso violin sonatas in the Italian late Baroque style, six concerti grossi (*c*1758), other instrumental music, glees, a cantata and other vocal works.

Heller, Stephen [István] (*b* Budapest, 15 May 1813; *d* Paris, 14 Jan 1888). French pianist and composer of Hungarian birth. He studied in Vienna with Anton Halm, making an extended concert tour in 1828 which resulted in a long stay in Augsburg, where he began to write lieder and the first of his 160 published piano pieces. From 1839 he was in Paris, teaching the piano and contributing to the *Gazette* *musicale*. Encouraged by Schumann in print and by Liszt in performance (playing his study *La chasse* op.29), he became so well known as a composer of studies that he had difficulty attracting attention for his other music. Yet his importance as a transitional figure between German Romanticism and French Impressionism is clear both from his evocative character-pieces and imaginative 'nature' music of the 1850s and from his later, exploratory works using unusual pedal effects, registration changes and parallelism (the barcarolles op.141 and preludes op.150).

Hellermann, William (David) (*b* Milwaukee, 15 July 1939). American composer and guitarist. He studied at Columbia, where he later taught (1965–72). He has composed prolifically, especially for small ensembles, and has had several gallery exhibitions of his 'Eyescores'. He is internationally known as a guitarist.

Hellinck, Lupus [Wulfaert] (*b* c1496; *d* Bruges, c14 Jan 1541). Flemish composer. A singer at St Donatian, Bruges, he also served briefly as *maître de chapelle* of Notre Dame, Bruges. He was a master craftsman, particularly interested in thematic unity. He did not use *cantus firmus* or canon, preferring evenly flowing polyphony achieved through pervading imitation. His 13 parody masses are his most important works; he also wrote motets, *chansons* and German chorales. His music was disseminated throughout Europe.

Hellmesberger. Austrian family of musicians. The most celebrated members were Georg (1800–73), a popular violinist who helped establish the Viennese school of playing and counted Joachim and Ernst among his pupils; his son Joseph (i) (1828–93), also a violinist, who besides conducting the Gesellschaft der Musikfreunde concerts and directing the Vienna Conservatory founded and led (1849–91) the famous string quartet that bore his name; and his grandson Joseph (ii) (1855–1907), a violinist and composer of operettas and ballets who became Mahler's rival as conductor of the Vienna PO (1900–03).

Helm, Theodor Otto (*b* Vienna, 9 April 1843; *d* there, 23 Dec 1920). Austrian writer on music. An admirer particularly of Bruckner, and contributor to periodicals including the *Musikalisches Wochenblatt* (1870–1905) and the *Deutsche Zeitung* (1884–1901), he was a leading figure in Viennese musical life.

Helmholtz, Hermann (Ludwig Ferdinand) von (*b* Potsdam, 31 Aug 1821; *d* Berlin, 8 Sept 1894). German scientist. After studying in Berlin he taught in Berlin, Königsberg, Bonn and Heidelberg. He contributed more to the musical aspect of acoustics than has any other individual. He analysed and explained the significance of overtones, explained combination tones and discovered summation tones; through his work on the ear he founded the present theory of hearing. He also worked on phase, wave patterns, beats and their role in consonance and dissonance, and temperament systems. Helmholtz devised a type of resonator for his experiments, built harmoniums and improved previous acoustical instruments. His classical work on acoustics (1863) was translated by A.J. Ellis as *On the Sensations of Tone* (1875).

Helmont, Charles-Joseph van (*b* Brussels, 19 March 1715; *d* there, 8 June 1790). South Netherlands composer. He was titular organist at Ste Gudule, Brussels, and became choirmaster there in 1741, after four years at Notre Dame de la Chapelle. He composed mostly sacred music, including masses and numerous motets, in an italianate style. Among his other works are keyboard pieces reflecting French influence, an opera and a divertissement. His son Adrien-Joseph (1747–1830), his successor at Ste Gudule, composed sacred music and an *opéra comique*.

Helmore, Thomas (*b* Kidderminster, 7 May 1811; *d* London, 6 July 1890). English teacher and choir trainer. As precentor of St Mark's College, Chelsea (1842–77), he set a new standard for unaccompanied services through the use of plainsong. His *Primer of Plainsong* (1877) became a standard text and he played a large part in establishing a choral tradition in parish churches.

Helsinki Festival (Finland). Annual (Aug–Sept) arts festival inaugurated in 1957; events include concerts, especially of Sibelius's music.

Hemel, Oscar van (*b* Antwerp, 3 Aug 1892; *d* Hilversum, 9 July 1981). Dutch composer. He moved to Holland in 1914 and studied with Pijper (1931–3). His works include symphonies, concertos, choral pieces and chamber music in a traditional but lively, lyrical style.

Hemidemisemiquaver. The note, in American usage called a 64th-note, that is half the value of a demisemiquaver. It is first found in late 17th-century music. Although the semihemidemisemiquaver (128th-note) is known, and even shorter notes appear very occasionally in some repertories, the hemidemisemiquaver is the shortest note in normal use. *See* NOTE VALUES.

Hemiola. In early music theory, the ratio 3:2. In the modern metrical system it denotes the articulation of two bars in triple metre as if they were three bars in duple. It is often used in Baroque dances such as the courante and the sarabande, generally just before a cadence; it also appears in the Viennese waltz.

Hemony. Netherlands family of bronze casters. The brothers François (c1609–1667) and Pieter (1619–80) originated in Lorraine and were outstanding makers of carillons, working first in Zutphen (until 1657), then Ghent and Amsterdam (from 1664). They produced probably 300–400 church bells and 53 carillons; among their most beautiful carillons are those in Nieuwe Kerk, Delft (1659–60), Onze-Lieve-Vrouw, Amersfoort (1659–63), and Utrecht Cathedral (1663–4). The unparalleled beauty and purity of their bells was due to the high proportion of tin they used and to the accuracy of their tuning method after the bell was cast. As the first to make chromatic carillons and to extend the compass to three or more octaves, the Hemonys developed it into a musically viable instrument.

Hempel, Frieda (*b* Leipzig, 26 Jun 1885; *d* Berlin, 7 Oct 1955). German soprano, later naturalized American. She studied in Berlin and sang there from 1905 to 1912. Her pure tone, with great facility in decorative passages, ensured her success in Verdi and Mozart; in 1914 she sang the Queen of Night at Drury

Lane. Her major success was at the Met (1912–19) as the Marschallin and Violetta, and in operas by Donizetti, Weber and Rossini. During the 1920s she gave concert impersonations of Jenny Lind.

Hemsi (Chicurel), Alberto (*b* Kasaba, 23 Dec 1896; *d* Aubervilliers, 7 Oct 1975). Italian composer. He studied in Izmir (1911–13) and Milan (1914–19) and from 1920 was absorbed in the study of the music of Sephardic Jewry. He lived in Alexandria (1927–57), where he taught (founding a conservatory), conducted (the Alexandria PO, 1928–40), composed and founded the Edition Orientale de Musique.

Hen, The. Nickname of Haydn's Symphony no.83 in G minor (1785), because of the first movement's 'clucking' second subject.

Henderson, (James) Fletcher ['Smack'] (*b* Cuthbert, GA, 18 Dec 1898; *d* New York, 29 Dec 1952). American jazz bandleader, arranger and pianist. He began leading bands while he was house pianist for the Black Swan record company (1922) and in 1923 formed a group which, the following year, moved to the Roseland Ballroom, New York; it became the most important pioneering big band, setting the pattern for most later ones. He employed such musicians as Louis Armstrong, Coleman Hawkins and Benny Carter as soloists and his arranger, Don Redman, established what was to become the accepted use of brass and reed sections in jazz arranging. Henderson made most of his own arrangements from 1927, and in 1934 arranged for Benny Goodman, joining him in 1939 as staff arranger. He continued to work with his own bands until 1950.

Henkemans, Hans (*b* The Hague, 23 Dec 1913). Dutch composer and pianist. He studied with Pijper in Utrecht, where he also trained in medicine (1933–8), later practising as a psychiatrist. Up to 1969 he was a concert pianist, specializing in Mozart and Debussy; his earliest works include two piano concertos (1932, 1936) and the Passacaglia and Gigue for piano and orchestra (1940), showing his conscientious, timbrally diversified adaptation of Pijper's motivic technique. His small output also includes concertos for flute, violin, viola and harp, vocal orchestral pieces, chamber music and orchestrations of Debussy's Preludes.

Henle. German firm of music publishers. Founded in Munich in 1948 by Günter Henle (1899–1979), it is noted for its clear 'Urtext' editions of the Classical and Romantic piano and chamber repertory and for its collaborations in academic music books.

Henrici, Christian Friedrich [Picander] (*b* Stolpen, 14 Jan 1700; *d* Leipzig, 10 May 1764). German cantata librettist. He held administrative posts in Leipzig and collaborated with Bach there for nearly 20 years, writing (under the pseudonym 'Picander') texts for his *St Matthew Passion*, *St Mark Passion*, many of his secular and occasional cantatas and church cantatas.

Henry VIII (*b* Greenwich, 28 June 1491; *d* Windsor, 28 Jan 1547). King of England, 1509–47. He was trained in music from an early age and music occupied a prominent place at his court. 34 compositions by him survive. Of the 20 vocal items, some are arrangements of existing music. *Helas madam* and *Pastyme with*

good companye, two of his most famous works, are based on continental models. The same MS contains 13 instrumental pieces by him, in three or four parts. He also wrote a three-part motet, *Quam pulchra es*.

Henry, Pierre (*b* Paris, 9 Dec 1927). French composer. He studied with Messiaen at the Paris Conservatoire (1938–48) and in 1949 joined Schaeffer's studio for *musique concrète*; he left in 1958 and founded his own studio. All his works are composed on tape; they include ballets for Béjardt (*Orphée*, 1958; *Nijinsky, clown de Dieu*, 1971) and religious works (*La messe de Liverpool*, 1968). His music has become known for its diverse and striking expressive force and immediate communicative power.

Henry Wood Promenade Concerts (UK). Annual (July–Sept) series of concerts in London. They were held from 1895 at the Queen's Hall (destroyed 1941), then at the Royal Albert Hall. Henry J. Wood was conductor until his death in 1944, when they were named after him. Since 1927 (except 1940–41) they have been organized by the BBC, whose chief orchestra, the BBC SO, takes part in many of the concerts. Under the direction of William Glock (1959–72) concert versions of national opera productions and experimental and chamber works were introduced and several works commissioned each season. Additional concerts are now given in other London venues.

Henselt [Hänselt], **(Georg Martin) Adolf** [Adolphe] **(von)** (*b* Schwabach, 9 May 1814; *d* Cieplice, 10 Oct 1889). German pianist and composer. He was a pupil of Hummel and Sechter and became court pianist in St Petersburg. Though he performed publicly less than any other celebrated pianist (he ceased touring in 1838), he was hailed by Schumann, Liszt and others as one of the greatest players, and in technique represents a link between Hummel and Liszt. He used arpeggio figuration in an individual way. His works include two sets of 12 studies, opp.2 and 5, and the Concerto in F minor op.16.

Henze, Hans Werner (*b* Gütersloh, 1 July 1926). German composer. He studied at a music school in Brunswick and then, after war service, with Fortner at the Institute for Church Music in Heidelberg (1946–8). At first he composed in a Stravinskian neo-classical style (First Symphony, 1947), but lessons with Leibowitz in 1947 and 1948 encouraged his adoption of 12-note serialism. Unlike such contemporaries as Stockhausen, however, he held his music open to a wide range of materials. Occasionally he made his obeisance to Darmstadt (Second Quartet, 1952), but his large, varied output of this period also shows the continuing importance to him of neo-classicism, Schoenbergian or Bergian expressionism and jazz. Nor was he dismissive of old forms or, in particular, the theatre: he conducted the Wiesbaden ballet (1950–53) and composed ballets (*Jack Pudding*, 1951; *Labyrinth*, 1951) and operas (*Boulevard Solitude*, 1952).

In 1953 he moved to Italy, where his music became more expansive, sensuous and lyrical and he concentrated on a sequence of operas (*König Hirsch*, 1956; *Elegy for Young Lovers*, 1961) and cantatas (*Kammermusik*, 1958; *Cantata della fiaba estrema* 1963). The climax to this period came with a rich and elaborate but also dynamic treatment of *The Bacchae* in the opera *The Bassarids* (1966), followed by a period of self-searching; that was externalized in the Second Piano Concerto (1967) and eventually gave rise to an outspoken commitment to revolutionary socialism. Henze visited Cuba (1969–70), where he conducted the first performance of his Sixth Symphony, incorporating the tunes of revolutionary songs. He also developed a bold, poster style in music-theatre works (*El Cimarrón*, 1970), leading to his dramatization of class conflict in the opera *We Come to the River* (1976).

But he was also continuing his exploration of an expressionist orchestral sumptuousness in such works as *Heliogabalus imperator* (1972) and *Tristan* (1974), and an enjoyment in reinterpreting old musical models (*Aria de la folía española* for chamber orchestra, 1977). Later works, including the opera *The English Cat* (1983) and the Seventh Symphony (1984), continue his highly personal synthesis of past and present, lyricism and rigour.

Dramatic music Boulevard Solitude (1952); König Hirsch (1956); Der Prinz von Homburg (1960); Elegy for Young Lovers (1961); Der junge Lord (1965); The Bassarids (1966); Moralities (1968); Der langwierige Weg in die Wohnung der Natascha Ungeheuer (1971); La cubana (1974); We Come to the River (1976); Pollicino (1979); The English Cat (1983); Tre opere di burattini (1984)
Ballets Jack Pudding (1951); Labyrinth (1951); Der Idiot (1952); Maratona (1957); Ondine (1958); L'usignolo dell' imperatore (1959); Tancredi (1966); Orpheus (1979)
Orchestral music 7 syms. (1947, 1949, 1950, 1955, 1962, 1969, 1984); 2 vn concs. (1947, 1971); 2 pf concs. (1950, 1967); Sym. Variations (1950); Ode to the Westwind (1953); Quattro poemi (1955); Sonata per archi (1958); Antifone (1960); Los caprichos (1963); In memoriam: Die weisse Rose (1965); Double Conc., ob, harp, str (1966); Db Conc. (1966); Telemanniana (1967); Compases para preguntas ensimismadas (1970); Heliogabalus imperator (1972); Tristan (1974); Aria de la folía española (1977); Il Vitalino raddoppiato (1977)
Choral music Novae de infinito laudes (1962); Cantata della fiaba estrema (1963); Das Floss der 'Medusa' (1968)
Solo vocal music Kammermusik (1958); Being Beauteous (1963); Versuch über Schweine (1968); El Cimarrón (1970); Voices (1973); The King of Harlem (1979)
Chamber music 5 str qts (1947, 1952, 1976, 1976, 1977); Pf Sonata (1959); Vn Sonata (1976); Va Sonata (1979)
Incidental music, film scores

Heptachord. A seven-note SCALE, e.g. the major or minor scale.

Herbain [first name unknown], Chevalier d' (*b* Paris, *c*1730–34; *d* there, 1769). French composer. He composed three operas for Italian theatres, then three at the Opéra and Comédie-Italienne, Paris. He wrote other vocal music and several instrumental works; some of his airs became very popular.

Herbeck, Johann Ritter von (*b* Vienna, 25 Dec 1831; *d* there, 28 Oct 1877). Austrian conductor and composer. He was choirmaster of the Männergesangverein, Vienna (1856–66), soon becoming choral and concert director of the Gesellschaft der Musikfreunde (1859–70, 1875–7), court Kapellmeister (from 1866) and director of the Vienna Court Opera (1870–75). In 1865 he conducted the première of Schubert's Unfinished Symphony. Of his music, owing something to Schumann, the choral works are the most important.

Herbert, Edward, Lord of Cherbury (*b* Eyton-on-Severn, 3 March 1583; *d* London, 1 Aug 1648). English amateur musician. He was the brother of the poet George Herbert. Between *c*1600 and *c*1648 he compiled a well-known MS of lute music, much of it French (Fitzwilliam Museum, Cambridge).

Herbert, Victor (August) (*b* Dublin, 1 Feb 1859; *d* New York, 26 May 1924). American composer of Irish birth. Brought up in Stuttgart, he studied at the conservatory and began his career as a cellist, teacher and composer. In 1886 he moved to New York, where he taught at the National Conservatory; he also conducted the Pittsburgh SO (1898–1904) and wrote orchestral works, including two cello concertos. He found most success, though, as an operetta composer (he wrote over 40) in the first two decades of the century (*Babes in Toyland*, 1903; *Naughty Marietta*, 1910); they are skilfully orchestrated and include songs that became staples of the recital repertory.

Herbst, Johann Andreas (*b* Nuremberg, bap. 9 June 1588; *d* Frankfurt, 24 Jan 1666). German theorist and composer. He held posts as Kapellmeister, notably at Frankfurt (from 1623) and Nuremberg (1636–44). Of his theoretical works, *Musica practica* (1642; based on Praetorius) presents the art of singing, especially ornamentation, emphasizing practical exercises for use in schools; *Musica poetica* (1643) is the first German instruction book on composition. In his predominantly sacred music Herbst was a pioneer in introducing the basso continuo and concertato style to Germany.

Herbst, Johannes (*b* Kempten, 23 July 1735; *d* Salem, NC, 15 Jan 1812). German composer. He was educated in Germany and England and ordained in 1774. In 1786 he went to the USA, taking an important collection of Moravian choral music and serving in Pennsylvania and (from 1811) Salem. He wrote *c*180 choral anthems with accompaniment and *c*145 songs; a gifted melodist and effective writer for the voice, he used an unusually chromatic harmonic style.

Hercules. Musical drama by Handel to a text by T. Broughton after Sophocles (1745, London); it is distinct from his *The Choice of Hercules* (1751).

Herder, Johann Gottfried (*b* Mohrungen, 25 Aug 1744; *d* Weimar, 18 Dec 1803). German man of letters. He served at the Bückeburg court, 1771–6, and then at Weimar, where he came into contact with Goethe. A central figure in the development of several disciplines (history, language, theology, philosophy, sociology), he considered music fundamental to culture and education. He wrote essays on music and texts for stage and other works (some set by J.C.F. Bach) besides publishing folksong collections. His poems, some dealing with music, were set by Beethoven, Brahms, Schubert and others.

Hereford Festival (UK). *See* THREE CHOIRS FESTIVAL.

Her Majesty's Theatre. London theatre (opened 1897) on the site of earlier theatres known under various names. Many new works, including Handel operas and oratorios, were given at its predecessor, the King's Theatre (opened 1705 as Queen's, renamed 1714 and on other royal changes of sex). It was the main London site for Italian opera for most of the 18th and 19th centuries; Verdi's *I masnadieri* had its première there (1847).

Herman, Woody [Woodrow] (**Charles**) (*b* Milwaukee, 16 May 1913; *d* Los Angeles, 28 Oct 1987). American jazz bandleader, clarinettist, alto saxophonist and vocalist. In 1934–6 he worked with Isham Jones's band, and when it broke up used its leading players as a nucleus for his own orchestra. In the mid-1940s it became internationally famous for its force and originality. The many bands he subsequently led were noted for their brilliant improvisation and incisive ensemble playing; Stravinsky composed his *Ebony Concerto* (1945) for Herman's musicians. Compositions like *Caldonia* and *Apple Honey* confirmed his reputation. In the 1950s he was influenced by the harmonic procedures of bop and in the 1960s he added elements of rock to his scoring. Herman was an admired soloist: his clarinet playing was hard-edged, his saxophone tone smooth and mellifluous.

Hernando (y Palomar), Rafael (José María) (*b* Madrid, 31 May 1822; *d* there, 10 July 1888). Spanish composer and teacher. He studied at the Madrid Conservatory. He wrote mainly small theatrical works, among which the zarzuelas *Colegiales y soldados* (1849) and *El duende* (1849) were his greatest triumphs. From the late 1850s he supported various musical causes, including a national music academy and a national opera.

Hérodiade. Opera in four acts by Massenet to a libretto by P. Milliet, H. Grémont (G. Hartmann) and Zamadini after Flaubert (1881, Brussels).

Hindemith wrote a ballet (with recitation after Mallarmé) on the same story (1944).

Hérold, (Louis Joseph) Ferdinand (*b* Paris, 28 Jan 1791; *d* there, 19 Jan 1833). French composer of Alsatian descent. He studied at the Paris Conservatoire with Louis Adam, Kreutzer, Catel and Méhul (who became the dominant influence on his style), composing his first opera in Italy in 1814. For several years he had difficulty finding adequate texts and his works frequently failed. Not until the delightful *Marie* (1826) did he score a triumphant success, meanwhile working as an accompanist at the Théâtre-Italien in Paris and later as singing coach at the Opéra, where he composed music for five ballets, including *La somnambule* and *La fille mal gardée*. The two operas for which he is remembered – *Zampa, ou La fiancée de marbre* (1831; originally *Le corsaire*) and the finer *Le pré aux clercs* (1832) – were both popular successes, the first full of effective theatrical situations and showing the brilliant tenor Chollet to advantage, the second treating thoughtfully a controversial subject. Such accomplished scores suggest that had Hérold lived longer, he might have fulfilled his ambitions to compose grand opera.

Herpol, Homer (*b* St Omer, *c*1520; *d* Konstanz, 12 Dec 1573–8 Jan 1574). South Netherlands composer. Kantor at the collegiate church of St Nikolaus, Fribourg (1554–67), and a pupil of Glarean (1555–7), he became *Informator choralium* at Kon-

stanz Cathedral in 1569. His main work is a collection of 54 motets (1565) on the Gospel texts of the ecclesiastical year, the first known complete cycle; he also wrote motets, Magnificats and several four-voice works, notably a *Salve regina* and *Regina coeli*. His style is influenced by Josquin and he is one of the most important representatives of the Franco-Flemish school in Switzerland and south-west Germany.

Herrmann, Bernard (*b* New York, 29 June 1911; *d* Los Angeles, 24 Dec 1975). American composer and conductor. He studied at the Juilliard School and worked with CBS from 1934, notably as chief conductor of the CBS SO (1942–59), but also in London. He wrote vivid and finely integrated film scores (*Citizen Kane*, 1940; *Psycho*, 1959; *Fahrenheit 451*, 1966). Among his other works are the cantata *Moby Dick* (1938) and the opera *Wuthering Heights* (1952).

Herrmann, Gottfried (*b* Sondershausen, 15 May 1808; *d* Lübeck, 6 June 1878). German instrumentalist, composer and conductor. In Kassel he had violin lessons with Spohr and studied theory and composition with Hauptmann. As city music director in Lübeck (1833–43, from 1852) and royal Kapellmeister at Sondershausen (1842–59), he organized and conducted chamber and orchestral concerts and directed opera performances, occasionally appearing as violinist. He wrote operas, symphonies, concertos and chamber music, some showing Spohr's influence.

Herschel, Sir William (*b* Hanover, 15 Nov 1738; *d* Slough, 25 Aug 1822). English musician and astronomer. Initially a regimental oboist and violinist, he settled in England in the 1750s and was active in Durham, Newcastle, Leeds, Halifax and (from 1766) Bath; he was a prominent concert director and teacher and played the violin and organ. From the 1770s he concentrated increasingly on astronomy (he discovered Uranus in 1781). He composed 24 symphonies, concertos and chamber works, organ music, many anthems etc and other vocal works. Much of his instrumental music shows north German influences, but his later concertos and accompanied keyboard sonatas (written in the 1760s) use the italianate *galant* style popularized by J.C. Bach. Several members of his family were musicians.

Hertel, Johann Wilhelm (*b* Eisenach, 9 Oct 1727; *d* Schwerin, 14 June 1789). German violinist, keyboard player and composer. As a boy he accompanied his father as harpsichordist on concert tours; later he was a violin pupil of Franz Benda. He worked at the Strelitz court, 1744–53, and was court composer in Schwerin, 1754–67, remaining active there. His output includes masses, Passions and cantatas etc for the court, numerous keyboard concertos (which rank beside C.P.E. Bach's) and over 40 symphonies. He also wrote lieder, incidental music, chamber and solo keyboard works, a thoroughbass treatise and two autobiographies.

Hertel's father Johann Christian (1699–1754) was one of the best viol players of his time and a violinist. He served at the Eisenach court (from 1733 as Konzertmeister and director of music) and then at Strelitz, composing many instrumental works. His father, Jakob Christian (*fl c*1667–*c*1726), was Kapellmeister in Oettingen and later Merseburg.

Hertz (Hz). The unit of frequency, equal to one cycle per second.

Hervé [Ronger, Florimond] (*b* Houdain, 30 June 1825; *d* Paris, 3 Nov 1892). French composer, singer and conductor. In Paris he studied with Auber and became organist at St Eustache (1845–53). He produced or conducted many short musical farces of his own as well as works by Offenbach, Delibes and others; among his more substantial works are the operettas *Chilpéric* (1868), *Le petit Faust* (1869) and, most important, *Mam'zelle Nitouche* (1883).

Hervortretend (Ger.). 'Coming forward': a direction to bring out a part that might otherwise be buried in the texture.

Herz, Henri [Heinrich] (*b* Vienna, 6 Jan 1803; *d* Paris, 5 Jan 1888). German pianist and composer. He studied at the Paris Conservatoire. One of the most celebrated pianists of the 1830s and 1840s, he toured extensively in Europe and the Americas. In Paris he founded his own piano factory, built a famous concert hall and taught at the Conservatoire (1842–74). He composed popular salon pieces and variations in the style of Czerny and Moscheles, which were criticized for their empty virtuosity, as well as valuable finger exercises.

Herzogenberg, (Leopold) Heinrich (Picot de Peccaduc), Freiherr von (*b* Graz, 10 June 1843; *d* Wiesbaden, 9 Oct 1900). Austrian composer. A lifelong friend of Brahms and a colleague of Philipp Spitta (with whom he founded the Bach Society, 1874), he was professor of composition at the Hochschule für Musik, Berlin. His strongly derivative music includes Wagnerian orchestral works, Schumannesque piano works and songs, Brahmsian chamber music, and church music in the spirit of Bach and Schütz.

Hesdin, Nicolle des Celliers de (*d* Beauvais, 21 Aug 1538). French composer. He was a master of the choirboys at Beauvais Cathedral from at least 1536 until his death. His music began to circulate in the late 1520s and by 1533 had earned him a reputation alongside that of Festa, Jacquet of Mantua and Willaert as one of the eminent 'moderni'. His works, which include three masses, two Magnificats, over a dozen motets and numerous *chansons*, are of high quality, revealing a sensitivity to sonority and a feeling for structural articulation.

Hess, Ernst (*b* Schaffhausen, 13 May 1912; *d* Egg, 2 Nov 1968). Swiss composer. He studied at the Zurich Conservatory and with Boulanger and Dukas in Paris. From 1938 he taught at the Winterthur Conservatory; he was also a conductor, especially of Mozart, some of whose music he edited and whom he emulated in his compositions.

Hess, Dame Myra (*b* London, 25 Feb 1890; *d* there, 25 Feb 1965). English pianist. She studied at the GSM and the RAM, under Tobias Matthay, and made her London début in 1907; her USA début was in 1922. She had a wide following for her warm, thoughtful interpretations, above all of Mozart,

Beethoven and Schumann. Her arrangement of Bach's *Jesu, joy* was a universal favourite. She organized lunchtime recitals at the National Gallery, London, during the war years, for which she was made a DBE.

Hesse, Ernst Christian (*b* Grossgottern, 14 April 1676; *d* Darmstadt, 16 May 1762). German composer and viola da gamba player. He served at Giessen until 1694, and then at the Darmstadt court, where he became Kapelldirektor in 1707. As a player he studied in Paris and made concert tours; he also studied operatic style in Italy under Vivaldi. He composed an Italian opera (*c*1712), a divertimento and instrumental pieces.

Heterophony. Term used to describe simultaneous variation of a single melody. Its meaning can range from reference to minute discrepancies in unison performance to complex contrapuntal writing. It applies to much accompanied vocal music of the Near and Far East where an instrument provides an embellished version of a vocal part.

Heuberger, Richard (Franz Joseph) (*b* Graz, 18 June 1850; *d* Vienna, 28 Oct 1914). Austrian composer and critic. He was director of choirs in Vienna from the 1870s and active as a music critic, succeeding Hanslick on the *Neue freie Presse* in 1896. He wrote several stage works which enjoyed success, above all *Der Opernball* (1898, Vienna), which remains a mainstay of the Viennese operetta repertory.

Heugel. French firm of music publishers, active in Paris from 1839. Though built at first on the weekly journal *Le ménestrel* and illustrated song albums, the catalogue expanded to include didactic works and theatre music; stage works by Offenbach, Thomas and Delibes were successful. The firm took over others in the late 19th century and by the early 20th composers included Fauré, Ibert, d'Indy, Milhaud, Poulenc and Widor. The firm publishes early music in the series 'Le Pupitre' (ed. F. Lesure) and works of the Société Française de Musicologie.

Heugel, Johannes (*b* ?1500–10; *d* Kassel, by 31 Jan 1585). German composer. He was a musician, and from 1547 probably Kapellmeister, at the Hesse court in Kassel. About 500 compositions by him survive, including motets for church festivals, Te Deums and Magnificats, Latin psalms and occasional motets, a complete German psalter, German songs and instrumental pieces. His early polyphonic works are sonorously scored for voices and instruments and influenced by the old Flemish school; his eight-voice *Consolamini, popule meus* (1539) is probably the earliest German piece for double choir. The later works are more homophonic and the four-voice psalm motets show the influence of a simpler Flemish style.

Heure espagnole, L'. Opera in one act by Ravel to a libretto by Franc-Nohain (1911, Paris).

Heutling Quartet. German string quartet, led by Werner Heutling. It made its début in 1958 and has played widely throughout Europe and Asia. Its recordings include the complete quartets of Mozart and Schubert.

Hewitt, James (*b* ?Dartmoor, 4 June 1770; *d* Boston, 2 Aug 1827). American conductor, composer and publisher of English birth. In New York, 1792–1811, he was conductor at the Park Street Theatre and operated a 'musical repository'; he pursued similar activities in Boston, 1811–16, then travelled between Boston, New York and several southern cities. Besides music by Handel, Haydn, Mozart, Shield and Hook, he published c160 of his own works, from ballad operas to hymn tunes. His son John Hill Hewitt (1801–90) was a travelling music teacher and newspaper journalist, mainly in the south-eastern USA; he is remembered as a composer of sentimental songs, including *The Minstrel's Return'd from the War* (c1828) and *All Quiet along the Potomac Tonight* (1863). Three other children of James's were musicians, the pianist Sophia Henrietta Emma (1799–1845), the publisher James Lang (1803–53) and the composer George Washington (1811–93).

Hexachord. An ascending series of six notes that proceeds by whole tones except between the third and fourth notes, which are a semitone apart. It was first described by Guido of Arezzo in the early 11th century and became the foundation of the earliest standard notational system for polyphonic music, being used as an aid to singing as well as a basis for composition. Hexachords were named according to whether they had B♮ or B♭ or neither. The G hexachord was called *hexachordum durum* because it contained the 'hard' square B (B♮) on its third step; the F hexachord was called the *hexachordum molle* because its fourth step was the soft or rounded B (B♭); the C hexachord was called the *hexachordum naturale* because it included neither B♭ nor B♮.

Hexaméron. Six variations for piano by different composers on a theme from Bellini's *I puritani*; they are by Liszt (who also wrote introductory and transitional material), Thalberg, Pixis, Herz, Czerny and Chopin (1837, Paris).

Hexenmenuett. *See* WITCHES' MINUET.

Hey, Julius (*b* Irmelshausen, 29 April 1832; *d* Munich, 22 April 1909). German singing teacher. He taught at the Royal Music School, Munich, and coached singers for the first complete *Ring* cycle at Bayreuth (1876). His chief publication, the four-volume manual *Deutscher Gesangunterricht* (1885), condensed as *Der kleine Hey* (1912), is still the standard textbook for German vocal training.

Heyther, William (*b* Harmondsworth, c1563; *d* July 1627). English musician. A singer at Westminster Abbey (1586–1616) and Gentleman of the Chapel Royal from 1615, he founded a music lectureship at Oxford (1627) and gave the university instruments and music; the Oxford chair of music is named after him.

Hiawatha. Cantata by Coleridge-Taylor to a text from Longfellow: its three parts are *Hiawatha's Wedding Feast* (1898), *The Death of Minnehaha* (1899) and *Hiawatha's Departure* (1900).

Hibernian Catch Club. Male-voice choir founded c1680 in Dublin by the vicars-choral; it claims to be the oldest surviving musical society in Europe.

Hibernicon. A contrabass wind instrument of the BASS-HORN class, invented in Ireland and patented in 1823; it is a keyed brass instrument, 5 m long, of conical bore, to stand upright, and has *D'* as its fundamental note.

Hichiriki. A Japanese double-reed instrument, with reverse conical bore, used in *gagaku* (court music). It has a narrow range (*g'–a''*), but the large reed, about 4 cm long, allows for great flexibility of pitch.

Hickson, William Edward (*b* London, 7 Jan 1803; *d* Fairseat, Kent, 22 March 1870). English social reformer. Through articles, lectures and books, beginning with *The Singing Master* (1836) and *Vocal Music as a Branch of National Education* (1838), he campaigned vigorously for music teaching in schools.

Hidalgo, Juan (*b* Madrid, c1614; *d* there, 30 March 1685). Spanish composer. In c1631 he became a harpist and harpsichordist at the Madrid royal chapel, remaining there until his death. The most famous and most gifted composer of his time, he composed many villancicos and *tonos humanos* and some Latin church music, but is chiefly important for popularizing Italian operatic styles at the Spanish court, in particular through his stage works, written mainly in collaboration with Calderón. *La púrpura de la rosa*, their first, is lost, but their next, *Celos aun del aire matan* (1660), is the earliest surviving Spanish opera. His style represents a synthesis of Italian and Spanish characteristics.

Hidden fifths, hidden octaves. In part-writing, the approach to a 5th or an octave by similar motion between two voices. The rules of strict counterpoint permit the occurrence of hidden 5ths anywhere except between the outer voices ('exposed 5ths'); the type called 'HORN' FIFTHS is permitted anywhere.

Highlife. A dance style that appeared on the West African coast in the early 20th century; it has developed into one of the most popular modern dance styles in the area. The name comes from an association with 'high living'. Musically, the style arose from the impact of Western military and popular music on African populations; the idiom is bold and spirited, with most music in quick duple metre, and sonorities mixing African, Caribbean and Western traditions.

Hi-hat. A pair of cymbals horizontally mounted and operated by a pedal; it is a component of the jazz DRUM SET.

Hilaire [Hylaire] **Daleo** [Turleron] (*b* diocese of Clermont; *fl* early 16th century). Composer. After court service at Ferrara and Mantua, in 1513 he joined the chapel of Pope Leo X and remained there until at least 1522. His music, which follows the styles of Févin and Mouton, is not particularly distinguished, but his mass and *chansons* use the French idiom with skill.

Hildebrandt, Zacharias (*b* Münsterberg, 1688; *d* Dresden, 11 Oct 1757). German organ builder and instrument maker. He worked under Gottfried Silbermann (1713–22), becoming court organ builder to the Prince of Saxe-Weissenfels in 1730 and moving in 1734 to Leipzig, where he built a 'lute-harpsichord' for Bach and worked as overseer of the town's organs. Among his own, which normally have elements of the Hamburg Baroque organ with more string-tone stops and richer mixtures than Silbermann's, that at St Wenzel, Naumburg (1743–6; extant) is considered outstanding. His son Johann Gottfried (1724/5–75) assisted him, also building the organ of St Michaelis, Hamburg (1762–7 and 1769).

Hildegard of Bingen (*b* Bemersheim, Rheinhessen, 1098; *d* Rupertsberg, 17 Sept 1179). German composer, abbess and mystic. Her writings include much lyrical and dramatic poetry which has survived with monophonic music. The *Symphonia armonie celestium revelationum* contains musical settings of 77 poems arranged according to the liturgical calendar. The poetry is laden with imagery and the music, based on a few formulaic melodic patterns, is in some respects highly individual. Her morality play *Ordo virtutum* contains 82 melodies in a more syllabic style. She also wrote medical and scientific treatises, hagiography and letters and recorded her many visions.

Hill (1). English family of organ builders. The firm started as Elliot & Hill in 1825 but from 1832 was managed alone by William Hill (1789–1870), whose early work included huge organs for York Minster (1829–33) and Birmingham Town Hall (1832–4). The work of his middle period (1838–*c*1858), associated with a radical redesign of the English organ, shows an awareness of historic European methods as well as a desire to provide an instrument for performing Bach and choral and orchestral transcriptions. Manual and pedal choruses were extended to include 16′ tone, with a pedal compass of *C* to *d*′ or *e*′; manual compasses (including the Swell) were standardized as *C* to *f*‴; and a variety of novelty registers was provided. Among the resulting 'German system' organs were those at Christ Church, Newgate Street (1838), Worcester Cathedral (1842) and the Royal Panopticon, Leicester Square (1854; the first to substitute steam power for manual blowing). Hill's later organs, using equal temperament and retaining a bright, rich tonal character, included those for St Albans Abbey (1860) and Melbourne Town Hall (1870).

William's son Thomas (1822/3–93) built instruments on the same lines, notably the vast Sydney Town Hall organ (1886–90); his son Arthur George (1857–1923), a skilled draughtsman, presided over a less vigorous, 'Edwardian' phase of organ building, opulent but slightly old-fashioned.

In 1916 the firm amalgamated with Norman & Beard of Norwich. Since 1945 it has been a chief supporter of the organ reform movement in England, restoring or building important instruments at Norwich Cathedral, Bath Abbey and the Royal College of Organists, London.

(2). English firm of violin and bow makers, restorers and valuers. It was active in London from the mid-18th century. Its most important work has been in restoration, unprecedented at the time. With William Ebsworth Hill (1817–95), and especially under the supervision of his four sons, notably Alfred Ebsworth (1862–1940), thousands of fine string instruments were saved by ingenuity and meticulous workmanship. The firm's bow workshop, established in the 1890s, set a new, unsurpassed standard in England.

Hill, Alfred (Francis) (*b* Melbourne, 16 Nov 1870; *d* Sydney, 30 Oct 1960). Australian composer. He studied at the Leipzig Conservatory (1887–91), then worked in Australia and New Zealand as a conductor, teacher and composer. He became the most widely recognized of pre-World War I Australian composers. His works include operas, string quartets and 13 symphonies (most from his last two decades and 12 of them transcriptions of chamber works), using Maori and aborigine elements within a conventional Romantic style.

Hill, Edward Burlingame (*b* Cambridge, MA, 9 Sept 1872; *d* Francestown, NH 9 July 1960). American composer. He studied with Paine at Harvard (where he taught, 1908–40) and Widor in Paris. His music (all instrumental) shows the influence of MacDowell, French impressionism and latterly jazz.

Hill, Uri K(eeler) (*b* ?Richmond, MA, 1780; *d* Philadelphia, 9 Nov 1844). American composer. He grew up in Vermont and published a collection of sacred pieces as *The Vermont Harmony* (1801). He set up in Boston in 1806 as a teacher and piano tuner and in 1810 moved to New York, founding a Handelian Academy (1814) and compiling *The Handelian Repository* (1814) and *Solfeggio Americano ... with a Wide Variety of Psalmody* (1820), which used Italian solmization; he taught in Philadelphia, 1822–44. He is remembered as a composer and arranger of tunebooks, both sacred and secular. His son Ureli Corelli Hill (1802–75) was a violinist and conductor.

Hillbilly music. Term used to describe American country music of the type current between 1920 and 1941; it is characterized by traditional songs, non-electric instruments and rural imagery.

Hillemacher, Paul Joseph Guillaume (*b* Paris, 29 Nov 1852; *d* Versailles, 13 Aug 1933). French composer. He studied with Bazin at the Paris Conservatoire, winning a Prix de Rome (1876). He often worked with his brother Lucien Joseph Edouard (1860–1909). Their collaboration began in 1879 and flourished from 1881, when they adopted the pen name of Paul-Lucien Hillemacher. They were noted for songs and dramatic works, in particular the delightful *Vingt mélodies* and the symphonic legend *Loreley* (1882).

Hiller, Ferdinand (von) (*b* Frankfurt, 24 Oct 1811; *d* Cologne, 11 May 1885). German conductor and composer. After studying the piano with Alois Schmitt and with Hummel (1825–7) he made sojourns in Paris and Italy, eventually replacing his friend Mendelssohn as conductor of the Leipzig Gewandhaus Orchestra (1843–4). From 1844 he was in Dresden, from 1847 Düsseldorf and from 1850 Cologne, where he reorganized the music school, conducted concerts and assisted at the Rhenish festivals. Though at first in sympathy with progressive composers, he drifted towards conservative circles and was esteemed as a Mozart interpreter. A productive composer of operas, oratorios, chamber, orchestral and choral works, he was at his best in his songs and in the piano pieces that are still in the teaching repertory.

Hiller, Johann Adam (*b* Wendlich-Ossig, 25 Dec 1728; *d* Leipzig, 16 June 1804). German composer. Active in Leipzig's musical life from 1751, he served Count Brühl in Dresden, 1754–8, then returned to Leipzig, becoming the most prominent and respected musical figure there. He was influential as director of the Grosses Concert, 1763–71. From 1766 he wrote music for middle-class comedies by C.F. Weisse and others, thus creating the north German Singspiel. He also founded a singing school and a musical society in Leipzig and became musical director of two churches and conductor (1781) of the Gewandhaus concerts. He left in 1785 to become Kapellmeister to the Duke of Courland but returned in 1786. He was director of music in Breslau, 1787–9, and afterwards Kantor of St Thomas's, Leipzig.

Hiller's 14 Singspiels, his most important works, promoted the revival of German song, which he combined with styles from Italian and French opera to give a wide range of characterization and expression. He also composed single songs, italianate secular cantatas, sacred music (including choral settings) and instrumental works. He wrote on many aspects of music, notably in his *Wöchentliche Nachrichten* (1766–70), the first specialized musical periodical in the modern sense. His didactic works include several treatises on singing.

Hiller's son Friedrich Adam (*c*1767–1812) was a theatre musical director at Altona and later Königsberg; he composed stage works, songs and string quartets.

Hiller, Lejaren (*b* New York, 23 Feb 1924). American composer. He took lessons from Sessions and Babbitt. In 1968 he became professor of composition at the State University of New York at Buffalo. Much of his music is electronic and much composed with computers (his *Illiac Suite* (1956) was the first work written with one); his other music includes the *Computer Cantata* (1963).

Hilliard Ensemble. English vocal ensemble, founded in 1974 by the baritone Paul Hillier and named after the miniaturist painter Nicholas Hilliard. It specializes in the precise performance of small-scale works and has acquired a particular reputation for its vigorous, accurate and well-informed readings of late medieval and Renaissance music. It normally consists of a male ensemble of four voices, headed by the countertenor David James, a founder-member, but can expand to eight voices and makes occasional use of female singers.

Hilton, John (*b* ?Cambridge, 1599; *d* Westminster, bur. 21 March 1657). English composer. A Cambridge MusB (1626), he became organist of St Margaret's, Westminster, in 1628. His *Catch that Catch Can* (1652), a collection of catches, rounds and canons including 42 of his own, was very popular. He also wrote ayres (1627), songs and dialogues (1669) and instrumental pieces (MS). Several services and anthems in MS may be by him or his father, John Hilton (*d* by 20 March 1608).

Hilverding van Wewen, Franz (Anton Christoph) (bap. Vienna, 17 Nov 1710; *d* there, 30 May 1768). Austrian choreographer. A dancer at the Viennese court, he arranged and directed dances, pantomimes and ballet interludes for Viennese theatres, and in 1752–8 was court ballet-master; he returned in 1764 after a period at the Russian court. He created ballets and dances in operas by Starzer, Gassmann and others, and was the first to fashion fully developed pantomime-ballets instead of the usual decorative divertissements. His successor and pupil Angiolini continued this development.

Himmel, Friedrich Heinrich (*b* Treuenbrietzen, 20 Nov 1765; *d* Berlin, 8 June 1814). German composer. A talented pianist, he became chamber composer to the Prussian court in 1792. In 1793–5 he was in Italy, where he had two operas staged. Returning to Berlin, he became Kapellmeister (1795), but continued to make concert tours, and presented an *opera seria* at St Petersburg in 1799. His tuneful Singspiel *Fanchon das Leyermädchen* (1804, Berlin) enjoyed lasting success; he wrote his final stage work (1813) for Vienna. His other works include lieder, oratorios, sacred music, cantatas and instrumental pieces. He remained in favour at the Prussian court despite frequent drunkenness.

Hindemith, Paul (*b* Hanau, nr. Frankfurt, 16 Nov 1895; *d* Frankfurt, 28 Dec 1963). German composer. He studied as a violinist and composer (with Mendelssohn and Sekles) at the Hoch Conservatory in Frankfurt (1908–17) and made an early reputation through his chamber music and expressionist operas. But then he turned to neo-classicism in his *Kammermusik* no.1, the first of seven such works imitating the Baroque concerto while using an expanded tonal harmony and distinctively modern elements, notably jazz. Each uses a different mixed chamber orchestra, suited to music of linear counterpoint and, in the fast movements, strongly pulsed rhythm.

During this early period Hindemith lived as a performer: he was leader of the Frankfurt Opera orchestra (1915–23, with a break for army service), and he played the viola in the Amar-Hindemith Quartet (1921–9) as well as in the first performance of Walton's Viola Concerto (1929). Much of his chamber music was written in 1917–24, including four of his six quartets and numerous sonatas, and he was also involved in promoting chamber music through his administrative work for the Donaueschingen Festival (1923–30). However, he also found time to compose abundantly in other genres; including lieder (*Das Marienleben*, to Rilke poems), music for newly invented mechanical instruments, music for schoolchildren and amateurs, and opera (*Cardillac*, a fantasy melodrama in neo-classical forms). In addition, from 1927 he taught at the Berlin Musikhochschule.

His concern with so many branches of music sprang from a sense of ethical responsibility that inevitably became more acute with the rise of the Nazis. With the beginning of the 1930s he moved from chamber ensembles to the more public domain of the symphony orchestra, and at the same time his music became harmonically smoother and less intensively contrapuntal. Then in the opera *Mathis der Maler* (preceded by a symphony of orchestral excerpts) he dramatized the dilemma of the artist in society, eventually opposing Brechtian engagement and insisting on a greater responsibility to art. Nevertheless, his music fell under official disapproval, and in 1938 he left for Switzerland, where *Mathis* had its first performance. He moved on to the USA and taught at Yale (1940–53), but spent his last decade back in Switzerland.

His later music is in the style that he had established in the early 1930s and that he had theoretically expounded in his *Craft of Musical Composition* (1937–9), where he ranks scale degrees and harmonic intervals in order from most consonant (tonic, octave) to most dissonant (augmented 4th, tritone), providing a justification for the primacy of the triad. His large output of the later 1930s and 1940s includes concertos (for violin, cello, piano, clarinet and horn) and other orchestral works, as well as sonatas for most of the standard instruments. His search for an all-encompassing, all-explaining harmony also found expression in his Kepler opera *Die Harmonie der Welt*.

Operas Mörder, Hoffnung der Frauen (1919); Sancta Susanna (1921); Cardillac (1926, rev. 1952); Hin und zurück (1927); Neues vom Tage (1929); Mathis der Maler (1935); Die Harmonie der Welt (1957); The Long Christmas Dinner (1960)
Ballets Der Dämon (1922); Nobilissima visione (1938); Hérodiade (1944)
Orchestral music Conc. for Orch (1925); Philharmonisches Konzert (1932); Mathis der Maler, sym. (1934); Sym., E♭, (1940); The Four Temperaments, pf, str (1940); Symphonic Metamorphosis on Themes of Carl Maria von Weber (1943); Die Harmonie der Welt, sym. (1951)
Chamber orchestral music Kammermusik no.1 (1922); no.2 with solo pf (1924); no.3 with solo vc (1925); no.4 with solo vn (1925); no.5 with solo va (1927); no.6 with solo va d'amore (1927); no.7 with solo org (1927)
Chamber music 6 str qts (1919, 1921, 1922, 1923, 1943, 1945); 2 str trios (1924, 1933); numerous sonatas etc
Choral music Das Unaufhörliche, oratorio (1931); When Lilacs Last in the Door-yard Bloom'd (1946); Mass (1963)
Songs Das Marienleben (1923, rev. 1936–48); many others

Hines, Earl (Kenneth) ['Fatha'] (*b* Duquesne, PA, 28 Dec 1905; *d* Oakland, 22 April 1983). American jazz pianist and bandleader. He moved to Chicago in 1923, joining several bands, in 1927 becoming director of Carroll Dickerson's under Louis Armstrong's leadership. In 1929 he founded his own, which he led until 1948, when he joined Armstrong's All Stars, working as a soloist and in small groups after 1951. He devised a 'trumpet style' of linear right-hand solo and ensemble playing, and dissolved the conventional left-hand patterns into a less regular pulse, allowing greater freedom in improvisation.

Hingeston [Hingston], **John** (*b* York, ?1599–1606; *d* London, 17 Dec 1683). English composer. He was in the choir of York Minster and later in private service to the 4th Earl of Cumberland and Lord Henry Clifford, his son, 1621–45. In 1654–8 he was organist and Master of the Music to Oliver Cromwell, and at the Restoration became a royal viol player and Keeper of His Majesty's Wind Instruments; Purcell was his apprentice. Besides two anthems, his surviving works consist of fantasy-suites for viols and for violins.

Hin und Zurück [There and back]. Opera in one act by Hindemith to a libretto by M. Schiffer after an English revue sketch (1927).

Hippolyte et Aricie. *Tragédie en musique* in a prologue and five acts by Rameau to a libretto by Pellegrin after Racine (1733, Paris).

Hirt auf dem Felsen, Der. *See* SHEPHERD ON THE ROCK, THE.

Histoire du soldat, L'. *See* SOLDIER'S TALE, THE.

Histoires naturelles. Song cycle by Ravel (1906), settings for voice and piano of five poems by Jules Renard.

Historia. Term used by Schütz and other German Baroque composers for the musical setting of a biblical story. In the late Middle Ages the term designated a day's antiphons and responsories of the Divine Office.

Hitchcock, H(ugh) Wiley (*b* Detroit, 28 Sept 1923). American musicologist. He studied in Michigan and Paris, and since 1961 has taught in New York, at Hunter College and Brooklyn College. He is particularly known for his work on the history of American music.

Hlobil, Emil (*b* Veselí nad Lužnicí, 11 Oct 1901). Czech composer. He studied with Suk at the Prague Conservatory (1924–30) and taught there (1941–58) before moving to the Academy. His works include operas, symphonies, concertos and string quartets in the Czech impressionist tradition of Suk and Novák.

H.M.S. Pinafore. Operetta by Sullivan to a libretto by Gilbert (1878, London).

Hoboken, Anthony van (*b* Rotterdam, 23 March 1887; *d* Zurich, 1 Nov 1983). Dutch collector and bibliographer. He studied at Frankfurt and with Schenker in Vienna. From 1919 he built up a collection of first and early editions amounting to some 5000 items, over 1000 of Haydn, of whose music he published a thematic catalogue (1957, 1971), with works identified by H or Hob. numbers.

Hochbrucker. German family of instrument makers and musicians. The most celebrated members were Jakob (*b c*1673), a lute and viola maker who invented the pedal harp; his son Simon (1699–*c*1750), a harpist who popularized the innovation; and his great nephew Christian (1733–after 1792), a harp teacher, virtuoso and composer of harp sonatas and duos, who won great renown in Paris and London.

Hoch Conservatory. Frankfurt conservatory established in 1878, endowed by a bequest by J. Hoch. Its staff, which included Clara Schumann, Julius Stockhausen and Humperdinck, quickly gained it an international reputation. In 1937 it divided into a Staatliche Hochschule and a conservatory for amateurs.

Hochschule für Musik. Music school founded in Berlin in 1869. It incorporates the Akademie für Kirchen- und Schulmusik (founded 1820, renamed 1822, 1875, 1922, amalgamated 1944) and the Städtisches Konservatorium (founded 1850, renamed 1857, 1935, 1945, amalgamated 1966). Under Joachim (1869–1907) it became one of Germany's finest schools; public concerts were given from 1872.

Hocket. Medieval term, probably related to onomatopoeic words such as the French *hoquet* and the English hiccup, for a contrapuntal technique of the 13th and 14th centuries in which sounds and silences are dovetailed through a staggered arrangement of rests in two or more voices. The technique was used in the caudas of some conductus and (often with exclamatory or pictorial significance) in short passages in motets and secular songs. It also forms the basis of a number of textless compositions; the best known is Machaut's *Hoquetus David*.

Höckh, Carl (*b* Ebersdorf, 22 Jan 1707; *d* Zerbst, 25 Nov 1773). German violinist and composer. After serving as a regimental oboist he toured with F. Benda and others. From 1734 director of music at the Zerbst court, he was famous as a violinist and teacher and a founder of the German violin school. His violin works (concertos, sonatas etc) are unusually demanding for their date.

Hoddinott, Alun (*b* Bargoed, 11 Aug 1929). Welsh composer. He studied at University College, Cardiff, and privately with Benjamin, returning to Cardiff as lecturer in 1959; in 1967 he became professor, and founded the Cardiff Festival of 20th-century Music. His music is essentially tonal though not diatonic, in a vigorous style that has roots in Bartók, Rawsthorne and Hindemith. His large output consists mostly of orchestral and chamber music (symphonies, concertos, sonatas), but he has also written operas and choral music.

Hodges, Edward (*b* Bristol, 20 July 1796; *d* there, 1 Sept 1867). English organist and composer. A church organist in Bristol, 1819–38, he was a Bach enthusiast and an early English advocate of a full pedal-board. He emigrated in 1838, becoming music director at Trinity Church, New York, 1839–59; he wrote services, psalms and essays on church and organ music. His daughter Faustina (1823–95), an organist in Brooklyn and later Philadelphia, edited his works. Three sons were also organists, notably Sebastian (1830–1915), rector of St Paul's Church, Baltimore, 1870–1905.

Hoérée, Arthur (Charles Ernest) (*b* St Gilles, 16 April 1897; *d* Paris, 3 June 1986). Belgian composer. He studied at the Paris Conservatoire (1919–26) and remained in the city as a teacher and composer, closely associated with Honegger; his works include many film and radio scores.

Hofer, Andreas (*b* [Bad] Reichenhall, 1629; *d* Salzburg, 25 Feb 1684). Austrian composer. Kapellmeister at Salzburg Cathedral (from 1666) and at the court of the Prince-Archbishop (from 1679), his compositions range from large-scale sacred works to pieces for solo voice showing the influence of Italian monody. The 53-part *Missa salisburgensis*, formerly attributed to Benevoli, has been tentatively ascribed to him.

Høffding, (Niels) Finn (*b* Copenhagen, 10 March 1899). Danish composer. He studied with Jeppesen in Copenhagen and Marx in Vienna (1921–2) and in the 1920s composed three symphonies and other works in a post-Nielsen style. During the 1930s he turned to educational music and from 1931 he also taught at the Copenhagen Conservatory. His later works include 'symphonic fantasias', some with vocal parts.

Höffer, Paul (*b* Barmen, 21 Dec 1895; *d* Berlin, 31 Aug 1949). German composer. He was a pupil of Schreker at the Berlin Musikhochschule, where he taught from 1923. His large output covers many genres and includes much *Gebrauchsmusik*.

Hoffmann, Bruno (*b* Stuttgart, 15 Sept 1913). German player and maker of the musical glasses, or 'glass harp' (as he calls it). He studied keyboard and singing but specialized in musical glasses from 1929; he constructed a chromatic, four-octave instrument, becoming known in the 1930s as a soloist. The tone he draws is sweet and powerful and of extraordinary resonance.

Hoffmann, E(rnst) T(heodor) A(madeus) (*b* Königsberg, 24 Jan 1776; *d* Berlin, 25 June 1822). German writer and composer. He was educated as a lawyer; his earliest compositions date from 1798–9 at Berlin, where he studied briefly with Reichardt. He moved to Warsaw in 1804, getting some of his works performed and conducting concerts. Periods as a theatre director, composer and producer in Bamberg (1808, 1810–12) raised his hopes, but he was more successful as a writer of stories, essays and reviews for the *Allgemeine musikalische Zeitung* (1809–15) and other journals. In 1813 he became conductor to a Dresden–Leipzig opera company and began work on *Undine*, to be his greatest success (1816); but he was obliged to return to law and wrote only a few more works. Praised by Weber for its pace, drama and melody, the magic opera *Undine* remains the most important of his six extant stage works; along with the heroic *Aurora* (1812), it enlarges German Singspiel by giving greater scope to the ensembles and a more prominent role to the chorus. He also wrote sacred works, piano sonatas and orchestral and chamber pieces. He is chiefly remembered as a writer on music; apart from his imaginative stories (e.g. 'Kreisleriana') which influenced Schumann, Offenbach and Wagner, his finest achievements were his perceptive reviews of Beethoven's works, which did much for contemporary understanding of the composer's music.

Hoffmann, Melchior (*b* Birnstein, *c*1685; *d* Leipzig, 6 Oct 1715). German composer. He succeeded Telemann in 1704 as director of music at the Leipzig Neukirche, opera house and collegium musicum, and wrote operas and sacred music. Two of Bach's cantatas have been ascribed to him.

Hoffmann von Fallersleben, August Heinrich (*b* Fallersleben 2 April 1798; *d* Schloss Corvey, 29 Jan 1874). German philologist and poet. He was a pioneering folksong editor and a popular children's poet but is most widely known as the author of *Das Lied der Deutschen* ('Deutschland, Deutschland über Alles', 1841).

Hoffmeister, Franz Anton (*b* Rothenburg am Neckar, 12 May 1754; *d* Vienna, 9 Feb 1812). Austrian music publisher and composer. By 1785 he had established a firm in Vienna, publishing his own works and orchestral and chamber music by Haydn and Mozart; it was apparently successful until 1791. From 1788 he began selling off works to Artaria, meanwhile negotiating with Beethoven (whose op.10 sonatas and a set of variations appeared in 1799); in 1801 he joined A. Kühnel (proprietor of the Bureau de Musique) in a new business at Leipzig. Despite a certain professional dilettantism, Hoffmeister's firm was shrewd in its choice of composers: the catalogue includes Albrechtsberger, Clementi, Pleyel and Süssmayr; Mozart (a personal friend) is represented by several first editions between K478 and 577, including the 'Hoffmeister' Quartet K499. The firm was eventually taken over by C.F. Peters. Hoffmeister was a prolific composer: he wrote several German operas, *c*66 symphonies and much chamber music.

He should not be confused with Friedrich Hofmeister (1782–1864), the Leipzig publisher and bibliographer.

Hoffmeister Quartet. Name given to Mozart's String Quartet in D K499, written (supposedly to repay a debt) for the publisher F.A. Hoffmeister.

Hoffnung, Gerard (*b* Berlin, 22 March 1925; *d* London, 28 Sept 1959). British musician and illustrator. A refugee from Germany, he studied art, teaching in schools and working as a freelance. He is remembered for his musical cartoons, featuring imaginatively grotesque portrayals of musicians and instruments, rich in allusive humour. He was also a tuba player and from 1956 organized 'Hoffnung Music Festivals', for which many composers wrote humorous works.

Hoffstetter, Roman (*b* Laudenbach, 24 April 1742; *d* Miltenburg, 21 May 1815). German composer. He was *regens chori* at the Benedictine monastery of Amorbach until 1803 and wrote string quartets (modelled on Haydn's) and orchestral and sacred music. He probably composed at least two of the six quartets op.3 formerly attributed to Haydn. His brother Johann Urban Alois (1742–1808 or later) was also a composer.

Hofhaimer, Paul (*b* Radstadt, 25 Jan 1459; *d* Salzburg, 1537). Austrian organist and composer. In 1480 he was given a life appointment as an organist at the court of Duke Sigmund of Tyrol in Innsbruck, and from 1489 also served Maximilian I. He travelled widely and settled in Augsburg in 1507. In 1519 he became organist at Salzburg Cathedral and organist to the archbishop. The most important organist of his time and a master of improvisation, he was also a gifted and influential teacher whose pupils held posts throughout Europe. He was also an expert on organ construction. Few of his compositions survive, though his music was popular in his day; his German songs, many in *Harmoniae poeticae* (Nuremberg, 1539), are noteworthy.

Hofmann, Heinrich (Karl Johann) (*b* Berlin, 13 Jan 1842; *d* Gross-Tabarz, 16 July 1902). German composer. He studied in Berlin and was well known in the 1870s and 1880s for his orchestral and choral works, such as the *Ungarische Suite* op.16 and *Das Märchen von der schönen Melusine* op.30, and his operas *Cartouche, Armin* and *Ännchen von Tharau*, but his amiable traditionalism, seen also in the piano duets and chamber music, did not ensure lasting success.

Hofmann, Josef (Casimir) (*b* Kraków, 20 Jan 1876; *d* Los Angeles, 16 Feb 1957). American pianist of Polish birth. His precocious gifts were displayed from the age of seven and his American début in 1887 caused a sensation. After study with Anton Rubinstein he made his mature début in 1894, quickly establishing a reputation unequalled among Romantic pianists. He was renowned for his fault-

less pedalling, even passage-work and wide dynamic range, but a limited repertory and a tendency to improvisatory excess limited his success. As director of the Curtis Institute, Philadelphia (1926–38), he did much to shape piano teaching methods.

Hofmann, Leopold (*b* Vienna, 14 Aug 1738; *d* there, 17 March 1793). Austrian composer. After a period as Kapellmeister at St Peter's, Vienna, he became court keyboard teacher (1769); from 1772 he was second court organist and also Kapellmeister at St Stephen's Cathedral. He enjoyed wide fame as both player and composer. His many sacred works (including over 30 masses) combine Austrian Baroque and Neapolitan traits, while his *c*55 symphonies are in a *galant* style. Among his other works are lieder, concertos and chamber music.

Hofmannsthal, Hugo von (*b* Vienna, 1 Feb 1874; *d* there, 15 July 1929). Austrian poet and dramatist. He wrote librettos for Strauss's *Elektra, Der Rosenkavalier, Ariadne auf Naxos, Die Frau ohne Schatten, Die ägyptische Helena* and *Arabella*.

Hoftanz. German 16th-century parallel of the BASSE DANSE.

Hofweise (Ger.) Term for a medieval monophonic song type, dealing with courtly love. It was used by the Meistersinger. In some modern literature it is used for polyphonic song around 1500.

Hogarth, George (*b* Carfrae Mill, 1783; *d* London, 12 Feb 1870). Scottish writer on music. He contributed to numerous journals including *The Harmonicon*, the *Morning Chronicle* and the *Daily News* (1846–66; edited briefly by his son-in-law Dickens), also writing valuable books on opera and on Victorian musical life.

Hogwood, Christopher (Jarvis Haley) (*b* Nottingham, 10 Sept 1941). English harpsichordist and conductor. He studied at Cambridge University and with Gustav Leonhardt. With David Munrow he founded the Early Music Consort (1967) and from 1973 has directed the ACADEMY OF ANCIENT MUSIC. He has appeared as a conductor in Sydney and widely in the USA, especially in Los Angeles and New York, and in 1986 was appointed conductor of the Handel and Haydn Society of Boston. His harpsichord recordings include brilliant accounts of French music and works by J.S. and C.P.E. Bach. He has written books on the trio sonata (1979) and Handel (1985).

Hoiby, Lee (*b* Madison, 17 Feb 1926). American composer and pianist. He studied with Menotti at the Curtis Institute, and has written operas, ballets, choral and instrumental music and songs, in a modern Romantic, lyrical style. He has played as a recitalist throughout the USA.

Holberg Suite [Fra Holbergs tid; From Holberg's Time]. Suite by Grieg (1884) for orchestra (originally for piano), written for the bicentenary of Holberg's birth.

Holborne, Antony (*fl* ?1584; *d* ?29 Nov–1 Dec 1602). English composer. 150 instrumental pieces, mostly dances, by him survive in *The cittharn Schoole* (1597) and other collective volumes (1596–1612) and in MS; they include music for consort, lute, bandora and cittern. His brother William (*fl* 1597) also composed.

Holbrooke, Joseph (*b* Croydon, 5 July 1878; *d* London, 5 Aug 1958). English composer. A pupil of Corder at the RAM, he was influenced by Wagner and early Strauss. His large output, dating mostly from the beginning of the century, includes operas (among them the huge trilogy *The Cauldron of Anwyn*), symphonies, symphonic poems, chamber music and much for piano.

Holęwa, Hans (*b* Vienna, 26 May 1905). Swedish composer of Austrian origin. He studied as a conductor at the Vienna Conservatory; in 1937 he moved to Sweden and in 1939 began to write in a strict, 12-note serial style, making his mark with the String Trio (1959).

Holiday, Billie [Lady Day; Fagan, Eleanora] (*b* Baltimore, 7 April 1915; *d* New York, 17 July 1959). American jazz singer. She first recorded in 1933 with Benny Goodman and in 1935 began recording with the pianist Teddy Wilson (under her own name from 1936). She sang with the big bands of Count Basie and Artie Shaw (1937–8) but subsequently usually appeared on her own. She was in the film *New Orleans* (1946) and toured Europe (1954, 1958). She was the leading jazz singer of her time, creating an innovatory and widely imitated style, using blues devices and a languid, relaxed approach to rhythmic attack, and a distinctive timbre.

Holidays. Orchestral work by Ives assembled from *Washington's Birthday* (1909), *Decoration Day* (1912), *The Fourth of July* (1913) and *Thanksgiving and/or Forefathers' Day* (1904).

Holländer, Alexis (*b* Ratibor, 25 Feb 1840; *d* Bonn, 5 Feb 1924). German conductor and composer. As choral director of the Cäcilienverein for 32 years (1870–1902), he gave the Berlin premières of Brahms's *German Requiem*, Handel's *Semele* and Liszt's *Christus*. His compositions, mainly piano pieces and chamber music, show Schumann's influence.

Holland Festival. Annual arts festival (June), established in 1947 to revive culture in the Netherlands after World War II. It is held in several centres concurrently. Many premières, including opera, by Netherlands and other composers have been given (including Britten and Stockhausen). Haydn's operas, Michael Haydn's choral works and experimental theatre productions have been prominent.

Höller, Karl (*b* Bamberg, 25 July 1907). German composer. He was a pupil of Haas in Munich, where he became a leading teacher, administrator and composer. His compositions, mostly orchestral, chamber and keyboard works, are characterized by a love of polyphony and colourful harmony arising from impressionism.

Höller, York (George) (*b* Leverkusen, 11 Jan 1944). German composer. He studied with Zimmermann at the Cologne Musikhochschule (1963–8) and has been influenced also by Stockhausen and Boulez, especially in pieces for instruments and tape. His works include *Arcus* (1978) and a Piano Concerto (1985).

Holliger, Heinz (*b* Langenthal, 21 May 1939). Swiss oboist and composer. He studied with Veress, in Paris, and with Boulez in Basle. Since the mid-1960s he has appeared internationally in a repertory ranging from Baroque oboe concertos to works written for him by Berio, Henze and Lutosławski. He has a bright tone and extraordinary phrasing technique and has introduced new effects (e.g. harmonics, double trills, chords). His compositions were initially Boulezian but have drawn nearer to Berio and Kagel in making the actual performance the main point (String Quartet, 1973).

Holloway, Robin (Greville) (*b* Leamington Spa, 19 Oct 1943). English composer. He studied with Goehr (from 1960) and at Cambridge, where in 1974 he was appointed lecturer. His large output covers many genres (including numerous songs) and shows a remarkable command of diverse styles: some pieces lovingly reinterpret Romanticism (*Scenes from Schumann* for orchestra, 1970); others are strikingly positive in their modernism (*The Rivers of Hell* for chamber ensemble, 1977).

Hollywood Bowl. A 60-acre canyon in California which forms a natural amphitheatre; it seats *c*25 000. An annual summer festival, mainly of art music, was established there in 1922. It is the summer home of the Los Angeles PO.

Holmboe, Vagn (*b* Horsens, 20 Dec 1909). Danish composer. He studied with Høffding and Jeppesen in Copenhagen, and with Toch in Berlin, then returned to Copenhagen to work as a teacher (at the conservatory), critic and composer. He is the leading Danish symphonist after Nielsen (he has composed 11, 1935–82) and composer of a series of 14 string quartets (1949–75), regarded as the most important Scandinavian contributions to the genre since World War II. He has also written operas, vocal and chamber music. His style is unproblematic if not immediately accessible, influenced by Nielsen, Hindemith and Stravinsky.

Holmès [Holmes], Augusta (Mary Anne) (*b* Paris, 16 Dec 1847; *d* there, 28 Jan 1903). French composer of Irish parentage. A pupil of Franck and a devotee of Wagner, she wrote music of great breadth and virility, including operas, dramatic symphonies and symphonic poems, successful choral works, notably *Les Argonautes* (1881), and many songs. But she is remembered chiefly for her striking personality, which dominated musical and literary salons.

Holmes, Edward (*b* Hoxton, 10 Nov 1799; *d* London, 28 Aug 1859). English music critic. A pupil of Vincent Novello, he came to know Shelley, Hazlitt, Leigh Hunt and Charles Lamb as well as Attwood, Cramer and Mendelssohn and later Berlioz. These influences, together with his enthusiasm for Mozart and Bach (whose music he knew as an organist) formed the basis of his critical stance. Besides writing the vivid *A Ramble among the Musicians of Germany* (1828) and the pioneering *Life of Mozart* (1845), he contributed significantly to journals including *The Atlas*, *The Spectator*, *Fraser's Magazine* and *Musical Times*, giving English music criticism technical authority and intellectual respectability.

Holst, Gustav(us Theodore von) (*b* Cheltenham, 21 Sept 1874; *d* London, 25 May 1934). English composer. He studied at the RCM with Stanford, and in

1895 met Vaughan Williams, to whom he was close for the rest of his life. From 1905 he taught at St Paul's Girls' School in Hammersmith.

Like Vaughan Williams, he was impressed by English folksong, but also important was his reading in Sanskrit literature (chamber opera *Sāvitri*, composed 1908; *Choral Hymns from the Rig Veda*, 1912) and his experience of the orchestral music of Stravinsky and Strauss (he had played the trombone professionally). In *The Planets* (1916) he produced a suite of seven highly characterful movements to represent human dispositions associated with the planets in astrology, and his interest in esoteric wisdom is expressed too in his cantata *The Hymn of Jesus* (1917). But his very varied output also includes essays in a fluent neo-classicism (*A Fugal Concerto* for flute, oboe and strings, 1923; Double Violin Concerto, 1929), a bare Hardy impression (*Egdon Heath*, 1927) and operas.

Operas Sāvitri (1916); The Perfect Fool (1923); At the Boar's Head (1925); The Wandering Scholar (1934)
Choral-orchestral music Choral Hymns from the Rig Veda (1912); The Hymn of Jesus (1917); Ode to Death (1919); First Choral Symphony (1924); A Choral Fantasia (1930)
Other choral music The Evening-Watch (1924); 8 Canons (1932); partsongs; folksong arrs.
Orchestral music St Paul's Suite (1913); The Planets (1916); Egdon Heath (1927); Brook Green Suite (1933); Hammersmith (1930); Lyric Movement, va, chamber orch (1933)
Songs 4 Songs (anon., 15th century), S/T, vn (1917); 12 Songs (H. Wolfe) (1929)

Holst, Imogen (*b* Richmond, Surrey, 12 April 1907; *d* Aldeburgh, 9 March 1984). English writer, conductor and administrator, daughter of Gustav. She studied at the RCM and worked as organizer for the Council for the Encouragement of Music and the Arts in World War II and later at Dartington Hall. She went to Aldeburgh as amanuensis to Britten in 1952, engaging also in conducting (with the Purcell Singers), editing, composing and writing (the standard study of her father and works on Renaissance and Baroque composers).

Holstein, Franz von (*b* Brunswick, 16 Feb 1826; *d* Leipzig, 22 May 1878). German composer. He studied at the Leipzig Conservatory with Moscheles, Richter and Hauptmann. A follower of Weber and Marschner, later of Mendelssohn, he wrote operas, most notably *Der Haideschacht* (1868), orchestral works, many songs, chamber music and piano pieces.

Holywell Music Room. Concert room in Oxford. It opened in 1748 (cap. *c*300) for public concerts and is the oldest of its kind in Europe still in use. It was for many years part of the university Faculty of Music.

Holzbauer, Ignaz (Jakob) (*b* Vienna, 17 Sept 1711; *d* Mannheim, 7 April 1783). Austrian composer. He was Kapellmeister to Count Rottal of Holešov in Moravia, then musical director at the Vienna court theatre; he also visited Italy. After a period as Oberkapellmeister at the Stuttgart court, he was Kapellmeister at Mannheim, 1753–78, remaining there when the court moved to Munich. He presented 19 stage works, most of them at Mannheim; the most successful, the Singspiel *Günther von Schwarzburg* (1777, Mannheim), helped revive interest in German opera. Holzbauer was notable for his many sacred works (Mozart adapted a *Miserere* for Paris) and also composed symphonies, chamber music and concertos.

Holzmann, Rudolf (*b* Breslau, 27 Nov 1910). Peruvian composer and ethnomusicologist of German origin. Trained in Berlin, Strasbourg and Paris, he moved in 1938 to Lima, where he worked as a teacher, ethnomusicologist and composer; from 1972 he taught at Huánuco University. He published a collection of Peruvian folksong (1966) and catalogues of the works of contemporary Peruvian composers. His early music exploits folk melodies; later works (*Dodedicata*, 1966) use serial techniques.

Holztrompete (Ger.). 'Wooden trumpet': an ALPHORN or a wooden instrument with the bell of an english horn, one valve and a cup mouthpiece, invented to play the shepherd's melody in the third act of Wagner's *Tristan und Isolde*.

Homilius, Gottfried August (*b* Rosenthal, 2 Feb 1714; *d* Dresden, 2 June 1785). German composer, organist and Kantor. A pupil of Bach, he was organist at the Frauenkirche, Dresden, from 1742; from 1755 he also worked at the Kreuzkirche and the Sophienkirche. With J.F. Doles, he was the leading German Protestant composer of his day, writing *c*60 motets, over 200 sacred cantatas and Magnificats, Passion music and oratorios. Though rooted in Baroque style, they increasingly show pre-Classical traits such as homophony, simple melodies and expressive devices. Also significant are his chorale preludes and other organ pieces, which combine the contrapuntal styles of Bach and Pachelbel with more modern features.

Homme armé, L'. A 15th-century melody which was used as the basis for mass settings of *c*1450–*c*1600 by such composers as Dufay, Ockeghem, Obrecht, Josquin, Morales and Palestrina.

Hommel [hummel, humle]. A folk dulcimer used in the Low Countries, adjacent parts of Germany, and in Scandinavia. It may have up to 12 strings in double or triple courses; the fretted strings are stopped and all the strings sounded by a plectrum. Its onomatopoeic name is derived from *hommelen* (Dutch), 'to hum' or 'to buzz'.

Homophony (Gk.: 'same-sounding'). Literally, voices or instruments sounding together. The term, originally applied to unison singing (for which MONOPHONY is now preferred) signifies partwriting in which there is a clear distinction between melody and accompanying harmony or in which all the parts move in the same rhythm ('chordal style'), as opposed to polyphonic treatment in which parts may move independently.

Homorhythmic. Term for music with the same rhythmic structure in all parts, as in a hymn harmonization. *See* HOMOPHONY.

Honauer, Leontzi (*b* ?Strasbourg, *c*1730; *d c*1790). Alsatian harpsichordist and composer. He served the Prince of Rohan in Paris and wrote keyboard sonatas and chamber works with keyboard which were very popular. Mozart adapted four movements from his solo sonatas (1761–3) in his early keyboard concertos.

Honegger, Arthur (*b* Le Havre, 10 March 1892; *d* Paris, 27 Nov 1955). Swiss composer. He studied from 1911 at the Paris Conservatoire, then returned to Switzerland for military service (1914–15), though Paris remained his home. He was a member of Les Six, and set Cocteau's libretto in his stylized opera *Antigone* (1927), but he had no time for Satie or for the group's flippancy: he was acutely aware of artistic responsibility and took his guidelines from Bach and Beethoven. His harmony, though fundamentally tonal, is often dense and wide-ranging, set in motion by a vigorous rhythmic propulsion that suggests Baroque formality wielding modern means: that is the manner of his oratorio-style stage works, including *Le roi David* (1921) and *Jeanne d'Arc au bûcher* (1938). His other works include five symphonies (1930, 1941, 1946, 1946, 1951), three 'symphonic movements' (*Pacific 231*, 1923; *Rugby*, 1928; no.3, 1933), chamber pieces, songs and much incidental music.

Dramatic music Le roi David, dramatic psalm (1921); Antigone, opera (1927); Judith, biblical opera (1926); Jeanne d'Arc au bûcher, stage oratorio (1938); Nicolas de Flue, dramatic legend (1941); 14 ballets; incidental music for 26 plays; 8 radio scores; over 40 film scores
Orchestral music Pastorale d'été (1920); Chant de joie (1923); Pacific 231 (1923); Pf Concertino (1925); Rugby (1928); Mouvement symphonique no.3 (1933); Vc Conc. (1934); 5 syms. (1930, 1941, 1946, 1946, 1951); 10 vocal orchestral works, incl. La danse des morts (1938), Une cantate de Noël (1953)
Chamber and instrumental music 3 str qts (1917, 1936, 1936); sonatas, suites, sonatinas, preludes, dance movts
Songs over 60

Hong Kong Festival. Annual (spring) festival established in 1973; events include concerts, recitals, dance and Chinese opera.

Hook, James (*b* Norwich, ? 3 June 1746; *d* Boulogne, 1827). English organist and composer. He gave concerts and composed from a very young age and *c*1763–4 settled in London as an organist. He became organist and composer at Marylebone Gardens, *c*1768–9, and at Vauxhall Gardens in 1774; also a fine piano teacher, he wrote a successful keyboard manual. He retired in 1820. His large output includes some 30 stage works (comic operas, pantomimes etc), odes, cantatas, over 2000 songs and much instrumental music (overtures, keyboard concertos and chamber and keyboard works). He was the most successful English exponent of the *galant* style and wrote mainly in a light-hearted vein, often using the popular pseudo-Scottish idiom; latterly he was much influenced by Haydn.

Hook harp. A diatonic frame harp, fitted with hooks in the neck to permit the player to raise the pitch of each string by a semitone. The device was developed in Germany and Austria in the late 17th century.

Hooper, Edmund (*b* North Halberton, *c*1553; *d* London, 14 July 1621). English composer. After singing at Exeter Cathedral, he joined the Westminster Abbey choir (1582), becoming Master of the Choristers (1588) and organist (1606). A Gentleman of the Chapel Royal from 1604, he became its joint organist (with Gibbons) in 1615. He was a popular

and respected composer of service music, anthems and keyboard works (mostly MS).

Hopak [gopak]. A Ukrainian and Belorussian folkdance and folksong, in strongly marked duple metre with a robust character. It was used by Musorgsky in *Sorochintsy Fair* and by Tchaikovsky in *Nutcracker*.

Hopkins, Antony (*b* London, 21 March 1921). English musician. He studied at the RCM (1939–42) and has written much occasional music, chiefly vocal, though his fame is as a broadcaster, lecturer and writer.

Hopkins, Bill [G(eorge) W(illiam)] (*b* Prestbury, Cheshire, 5 June 1943; *d* Chopwell, 10 March 1981). English composer. He studied at Oxford and with Messiaen and Barraqué in Paris (1964–5), sharing with the latter a deep self-criticism that may become the subject for a paradoxically rapturous lyricism. His few works are for piano or chamber forces.

Hopkins, Edward (John) (*b* London, 30 June 1818; *d* there, 14 Feb 1901). English organist and composer. Well known as organist and choirmaster at the Temple Church (1843–98), London, he composed numerous anthems and services and wrote an important treatise on the organ (1855).

Hopkinson, Francis (*b* Philadelphia, 21 Sept 1737; *d* there, 9 May 1791). American statesman and musician. An amateur, he played the harpsichord in public concerts in the 1760s and 70s and composed songs, including *My days have been so wondrous free* (1759), the earliest surviving American secular composition (unpublished), and *Seven Songs* (1788). He also played the organ and compiled tune books for congregational singing.

Hopp, Julius (*b* Graz, 18 May 1819; *d* Vienna, 28 Aug 1885). Austrian composer and dramatist. A prolific composer of stage works for suburban theatres in Vienna, he is best known for the 16 Offenbach adaptations he made, mostly for the Theater an der Wien, during the 1860s and 1870s.

Hora lunga [doina]. A Romanian vocal or instrumental folk-music genre of lyrical character; it consists of variations on a single, richly ornamented melody, which the performer constructs on a traditional skeletal theme.

Horenstein, Jascha (*b* Kiev, 6 May 1898; *d* London, 2 April 1973). Russian-Austrian conductor, naturalized American. He studied in Vienna with Marx and Schreker. In the 1920s he conducted the Vienna SO and the Berlin PO. He moved to the USA in 1940. After World War II he gave performances of modern opera in the USA and Europe. He was best known for his intense interpretations of Bruckner and Mahler at a time when those composers were not fashionable.

Horizon chimérique, L'. Song cycle (op.118, 1921) by Fauré, settings for voice and piano of four poems by J. de la Ville Mirmont.

Horký, Karel (*b* Štěměchy u Třebíče, 4 Sept 1909). Czech composer. A pupil of Haas in Brno (1937–9), he taught at the Brno Conservatory from 1961 (director from 1964) and wrote operas, concertos, chamber and vocal music. His oratorio-opera *Jan-Hus* (1950) created a new form of music drama.

Horn. A wind instrument usually of the lip-reed class. Horns for signalling have been made from conch shells, wood, animal horns etc as well as metal. Horns capable of many notes usually consist of a conical brass tube in a curved, coiled or folded shape. This article is concerned with the European orchestral horn, or french horn.

In its simplest form the horn is a slender, gradually tapered tube between 2 and 5.5 m long, coiled in one, two or three circles and expanding into a widely flared bell (for illustration, see BRASS INSTRUMENTS). The natural horn as used in 18th- and 19th-century orchestras had crooks, lengths of tubing fitted next to the mouthpipe which added to its basic length, enabling it to play different harmonic series. Modern horns have four or three (sometimes five) valves, which act to extend or shorten the basic length of tubing. 'Single' horns are pitched in Bb or F; in 'double' horns the fourth valve transforms the instrument from one pitch to another (that in F/Bb is the commonest). The range of the horn is from the 2nd partial to the 16th.

The two types of 16th-century horn influenced the hoop-like horn of the 17th. One was a slender, one-note hunting horn, crescent-shaped with a small coil in the middle; the other was longer and close-coiled in helical form, and represents the first stage in the development of the modern horn. It was used in works by Cavalli and Lully in the late 17th century. The more elegant and slender circular *trompe*, with two and a half coils, probably first used in France c1660 for hunting, was introduced to Bohemia by Count Sporck in the 1680s. Bohemian horn players were famous in the later 18th century. The french horn was familiar in England by 1680; Handel included it in his *Water Music* (c1717). In France it remained simply the hunting horn until c1748 when it was imported in its orchestral form from Germany. Its earliest players were probably trumpeters who took over the horn when required.

Crooks were apparently first used on German horns in the early 18th century. Despite the instrument's limitations, Bach, Handel and others wrote high, florid parts for it similar to those for trumpet. At the same time, Bohemian players cultivated the lower and middle registers and discovered the use of 'stopped' notes by partial occlusion of the bell with the hand, allowing notes adjacent to those in the harmonic series to be played. This technique also induced a refinement of tone quality. Mozart used stopped notes in his concertos, as did he and Beethoven in their chamber music. During the latter part of the 18th century it became standard for orchestras to include a pair of horns, with crooks that allowed them to play notes in the key of the piece.

Valve horns, designed to play chromatically, were developed by Stölzel and Blühmel in Silesia and patented in 1818. In the mid-1820s, they reached Paris, where the model was improved. The valve horn made its orchestral début in 1835. Weber was the first to explore the Romantic potential of the natural instrument. Wagner used natural and valve horns together in his early works. Schumann's Adagio and Allegro for horn and piano (1849) broke away from the hand-horn tradition; Brahms's op.40 (1865) is still conceived for the older instrument. 20th-century composers such as Hindemith and Britten have exploited the qualities of the valve horn in their compositions. Horn players can produce stopped notes by pushing a hand into the bell, or with a mute; a loud stopped note produces a fierce, brassy sound. Strauss used muted horns in *Don Quixote* to imitate the bleating of a flock of sheep.

Horn, Charles Edward (*b* London, 21 June 1786; *d* Boston, 21 Oct 1849). English composer and singer, son of Karl Friedrich Horn. He sang in London theatres, soon having success as a composer of light operas in Mozartian style; *The Devil's Bridge* (1812) was widely popular, as were individual songs from longer dramatic works, above all 'Cherry ripe' in *Paul Pry* (1826). From 1827 he had three spells in the USA, making stage appearances, conducting, adapting Mozart operas and introducing English works, also becoming a music publisher in New York, winning prizes for his glees and composing an oratorio, *The Remission of Sin* (1835). In 1847 he was elected conductor of the Handel and Haydn Society in Boston, where he spent the last two years of his life. His *Dirce* (1821) is thought to have been the first all-sung English opera since 1762.

Horn, Johann Caspar (*b* Valtice, *c*1630; *d* Dresden, *c*1685). Austrian composer. A physician by profession, he spent most of his adult life in Leipzig and composed several collections of French-style ballets and character pieces, for amateur performance; he also wrote a cantata cycle, *Geistliche Harmonien* (1680–81), one of the first to require instruments in addition to the continuo.

Horn, Karl Friedrich (*b* Nordhausen, 13 April 1762; *d* Windsor, 5 Aug 1830). German organist and composer. He went to London in 1782, became a royal music master and organist of St George's Chapel, Windsor (1823), and with Samuel Wesley was a pioneer of the Bach revival in England.

Horn band. A band of hunting horns, each able to play only a single note. It originated in Russia: the first was formed at the court of Empress Elizabeth in 1751 or 1754, with 37 wide-bore horns. Such bands became popular among the Russian nobility, while smaller ensembles (of about 13 horns) were used in Bohemia and Saxony. Horn bands are common in Africa, the horns being made of ivory, antelope horn, wood or gourd.

Hornbostel, Erich M(oritz) von (*b* Vienna, 25 Feb 1877; *d* Cambridge, 28 Nov 1935). Austrian scholar. He studied under Mandyczewski, then turned to the sciences (Heidelberg and Vienna, 1895–1900). Moving to Berlin he took up experimental psychology and musicology and directed the Berlin Phonogramm-Archiv (1906–33). He was dismissed in 1933 and went to New York, then London. He was a pioneer in the application of concepts of acoustics, psychology and physiology to non-European musical cultures and thus in the establishment of 'comparative musicology'. His many publications include the standard classification of instruments (with Sachs, 1914).

Horne, Marilyn (Bernice) (*b* Bradford, PA, 16 Jan 1934). American mezzo-soprano. After performing in California she sang in Europe from 1956, making her Covent Garden début in 1964. A long association with Joan Sutherland has included appearances in operas by Rossini and Bellini. A versatile artist, she has been heard as Rinaldo, Zerlina and Carmen. She made her Met début in 1970.

Horneman, Christian Frederik Emil (*b* Copenhagen, 17 Dec 1840; *d* there, 8 June 1906). Danish composer. He was son of the composer Johan Ole Emil Horneman (1809–70), with whom he established a music publishing firm in 1860. He studied with Moscheles, Richter and Hauptmann in Leipzig, where he met Grieg, who became a lifelong friend. Besides popular arrangements, he composed the opera *Aladdin* (1865–87), the overture to which was his best-known work, and instrumental music. He helped found a musical society (1865), concert society (1874) and conservatory (1880).

'Horn' fifths. In part-writing, a type of hidden 5ths occurring when each voice approaches its note from an adjacent note of an overtone series containing that 5th, akin to two-voice writing for natural horns. *See* HIDDEN FIFTHS, HIDDEN OCTAVES.

Hornpipe. (1) A single-reed wind instrument incorporating animal horn either around the reed, as a bell at the lower end, or both. A pipe of elder, cane or bone is sounded by a beating reed; most hornpipes have two pipes in parallel, ending in single or double bells. Many folk instruments are played with an inflated skin bag, like the bagpipe. The melodic range may reach a 9th.

The earliest hornpipe was probably the Phrygian *aulos*, with two pipes. Hornpipes are depicted in art from the 10th century; the Welsh pibgorn or pibcorn and the Scottish stock-and-horn were in use in the 18th century. Folk hornpipes are still known in Russia, the Greek islands and North Africa.

(2) A British dance, resembling the JIG, popular from the 16th century to the 19th: there were various solo or group types, in 3/2, 2/4 or 4/4 time. The dance was not associated particularly with sailors as is often supposed.

Horn Signal. Nickname of Haydn's Symphony no.31 in D (1765), so called because four horns are used in the slow movement.

Hornwerk. Term for certain 16th- and 17th-century tower organs of Central Germany and Austria. Originally they could play only a few chords, and were used in the manner of bells. Later they were supplied with playing mechanisms of the pinned barrel type enabling them to play melodies. Examples still exist in Salzburg and Heilbrunn.

Horovitz, Joseph (*b* Vienna, 26 May 1926). British composer. He studied at Oxford, at the RCM and with Boulanger in Paris. A versatile and witty composer, he has written much in both light and serious styles, including the parody *Horrortorio* (1959).

Horowitz, Vladimir (*b* Kiev, 1 Oct 1904). American pianist of Ukrainian birth. He appeared in Russia from 1922 and made his London and New York débuts in 1928. In 1940 he settled in the USA, becoming a citizen in 1944. He continued to perform until the early 1970s, with several breaks through ill-health, and played again in the USSR in 1986. He is admired for his legendary technique, with immaculate control of articulation and dynamics, uncanny speed and force, individual tone and a curious combination of urbanity and power; he is at his best in Schumann, Liszt and the late Romantics.

Horsley, William (*b* London, 15 Nov 1774; *d* there, 12 June 1858). English composer and organist. Under the influence of John Wall Callcott (from 1813 his father-in-law), he concentrated on vocal composition, also becoming a founder of the Concentores Sodales and the Philharmonic Society. Among his most justly renowned works are the glees *By Celia's arbour* and *See the chariot at hand* (he wrote 124), the song *Gentle lyre* and the ballad *The sailor's adieu*. He also wrote influential if conservative didactic works. His son Charles Edward Horsley (1822–76) studied in Germany and came under Mendelssohn's influence, writing competent instrumental music and, later, oratorios and anthems.

Horst, Anthon van der (*b* Amsterdam, 20 June 1899; *d* Hilversum, 9 March 1965). Dutch composer. He studied at the Amsterdam Conservatory (1914–17) and worked as a church organist. His main works, often using a particular mode, include a symphony (1939) and eight large-scale choral pieces with the title *Choros*.

Horwood, William (*d*?1484). English composer. A vicar-choral and *Informator* at Lincoln Cathedral, he composed (*c*1460–84) some of the earliest examples of the full choral style of English music associated with the Eton Choirbook.

Hostinský, Otakar (*b* Martinèves, 2 Jan 1847; *d* Prague, 19 Jan 1910). Czech aesthetician and music critic. He founded the first Czech school of musicology, initiated studies in the science of harmony and made advances in ethnomusicological method (rejecting folksong as the source of Czech stylistic individuality). He was the first writer to defend Smetana. Besides music he wrote librettos.

Hothby, John (*b c*1410; *d* 1487). English theorist and composer. An Oxford graduate and Carmelite monk, he travelled extensively on the Continent before studying at Pavia in the 1450s. Later he spent time in Florence and by 1467 was a teacher, choirmaster and chaplain at the Cathedral of St Martin, Lucca. His surviving compositions are two Magnificats, a Kyrie, three motets and three secular works, all showing Dunstable's influence. Many of his treatises are elementary pedagogical texts, others are more speculative or polemical. He sought, particularly in *Calliopea legale*, to reconcile new musical practices with past theory, but elsewhere objected to the more radical reforms proposed by some contemporary theorists.

Hotter, Hans (*b* Offenbach am Main, 19 Jan 1909). Austrian bass-baritone of German birth. His early career was in Prague and Hamburg; he sang at Munich from 1937, taking part in the premières there of Strauss's *Friedenstag* and *Capriccio*. At Covent Garden (from 1947) and Bayreuth (début 1952) he became known as the leading Wagnerian bass-baritone of his time, bringing an intense declamation and commanding stage presence to his roles, above all Wotan. He sang character roles at Munich more than ten years after his offical retirement. In the 1960s he produced the *Ring* at Covent Garden.

Hotteterre, Jacques (-Martin) ['Le Romain'] (*b* Paris, 29 Sept 1674; *d* there, 16 July 1763). French composer and instrumentalist. A bassoonist and flautist at the French court, he also played the musette and was a successful teacher and instrument maker. Among his works are suites for flute and bass, pieces for one and two unaccompanied flutes (the first such music in France) and trio sonatas; the latter contain Italian as well as French traits. His *Principes de la flûte traversière* (1707) was the first treatise on flute playing; he also wrote a treatise on improvising (1719) and a musette method (1737).

Hotteterre was one of a large family of woodwind instrument makers. His grandfather Jean (*c*1605–?1690–92) and father Martin (*c*1640–1712) specialized in musette making. Martin and his cousins Jean (*c*1648–1732), Nicolas (*c*1637–1694), Louis (? *c*1645/50–1716) and Nicolas (1653–1727), also instrument makers, all played at the French court, as did Jacques's brother Jean (*d* 1720), like his father Martin, a composer. The family was related to the Chédeville family.

Hourglass drum. Drum with a constricted waist and open cup-shaped ends, usually of wood, metal, earthenware or even bone, known from Africa to Japan and Oceania. In some types the player can vary the tension of the skin, and thus the pitch, by pressing on a thong (as in the West African talking drum).

House of the Dead, From the. *See* FROM THE HOUSE OF THE DEAD.

Houston Grand Opera. American company founded in 1955; it was directed by Walter Herbert until 1972. Its home is the Wortham Theater Center (1987; two halls, cap. 2300 and 1100). Its repertory includes modern works and light opera and its activities include a free spring festival, international tours and the Houston Opera Studio for young American singers. It has a touring group, Texas Opera Theater.

Houston Symphony Orchestra. American orchestra founded in 1913; it was conducted by Paul Blitz until 1916. Its home is Jesse H. Jones Hall (cap. 3001). It became fully professional under Ernst Hoffmann (1935–47). Under Stokowski (1955–61) contemporary works were given; John Barbirolli (1961–7) instituted tours. Sergiu Comissiona became music director in 1983. Activities include free park concerts, young people's concerts and a summer festival. Houston Symphony Chorale was established in 1947.

Hove, Joachim van den (*b* Antwerp, 1567; *d* The Hague, 1620). South Netherlands composer. Highly esteemed as a lutenist in Leiden, he travelled widely before dying destitute. His collections show him as a sensitive composer and arranger: *Praeludia testudinis* (1616) contains his own music, while Italian composers are represented in *Florida* (1601) and *Delitiae musicae* (1612).

Hovhaness, Alan [Chakmakjian, Alan Hovhaness] (*b* Somerville, MA, 8 March 1911). American composer. He studied with Converse at the New England Conservatory. His earliest music, though Romantic in harmony, reflects his interest in Renaissance style; from 1943 he began to incorporate elements of his Armenian heritage, and in the 1950s, when he travelled widely, he embraced non-Western and experimental procedures. From *c*1960 he took a keen interest in Japanese and Korean music, which affected his style; only in the 1970s did he return to a more Western style, richer and more spacious. An individual feature is his way of treating elements (harmony, tone colour etc) as either predominant or else neutral; any note may be exclusively linear, vertical, textural or rhythmic. Most of his work is broadly religious in inspiration; he is enormously prolific, having reached his first 60 symphonies in the mid-1980s, with corresponding production in other orchestral music, choral and solo vocal works, piano and chamber music.

Howells, Herbert (Norman) (*b* Lydney, 17 Oct 1892; *d* Oxford, 23 Feb 1983). English composer. He studied with Stanford and Wood at the RCM, where he taught from 1920 almost to his death. He also succeeded Holst at St Paul's Girls' School (1932–62) and was professor of music at London University. His music is within an English diatonic tradition embracing Elgar, Walton and Vaughan Williams. The earlier works include two piano concertos and chamber pieces, but most of his music is choral, including *c*15 anthems, a concert Requiem (*Hymnus Paradisi*, 1938, first performed 1950), masses, anthems and motets and some fine songs. Deeply tinged by the English choral tradition, Howells's music reflects a subtle and fastidious craftsman capable of a restrained, individual eloquence.

Howes, Frank (Stewart) (*b* Oxford, 2 April 1891; *d* Standlake, 28 Sept 1974). English critic. He studied at Oxford and, after a period at the RCM, joined the staff of *The Times* in 1925, succeeding H.C. Colles as chief critic (1943–60). He also lectured at the RCM, 1938–70. One of his interests found expression in his book *The Borderland of Music and Psychology* (1926); another is reflected in *Folk Music of Britain – and Beyond* (1970). A champion of contemporary English music, he did much to further the music of Vaughan Williams and Walton; his *The English Musical Renaissance* (1966) declared natural affinities which made him out of sympathy with the more cosmopolitan tastes after 1945. He was an untiring figure in musical administration and organization.

Hoyland, Vic(tor) (*b* Wombwell, 11 Dec 1945). English composer. He studied fine art and drama at Hull University, but subsequently took the doctorate in composition at York University, where he worked with Sherlaw Johnson and Rands. Since 1980 he has taught at Birmingham University. His music has continued to be informed by the visual arts, and by theatre in particular. *Xingu* for orchestra and three children's groups (1979) first crystallized these preoccupations, while his intricate, somewhat italianate instrumental writing was refined in *Andacht zum Kleinen* for nine instruments (1980) and its companion work *Fox* (1983), and his String Quartet (1985).

Hoyoul, Balduin (*b* Liège, 1547–8; *d* Stuttgart, 26 Nov 1594). South Netherlands composer. A choirboy at the Stuttgart Hofkapelle, he was sent to study with Lassus in Munich (1564–5) and returned as a composer and singer; he was court Kapellmeister from 1589. He published Latin and German motets (1587, 1589); eight parody Magnificats (based on works by Lassus) survive in MS.

Hřímalý. Czech family of musicians of Polish origin. The most celebrated members were Vojtech (1842–1908), a violinist and conductor in Prague, then Chernovtsy, whose best-known works include the operas *The Enchanted Prince* (1872) and *Švanda the Bagpiper* (1896); and Jan (1844–1915), a violinist who taught at the Imperial Conservatory, Moscow, and played in premières of Tchaikovsky's chamber works.

Hsu, Tsang-houei (*b* Changhua, 6 Sept 1929). Chinese composer. He studied in Taiwan and with Jolivet and Messiaen in Paris (1954–9), then returned to introduce avant-garde techniques to Taiwan. He has worked extensively on Taiwanese folk music, on which he has written, and used elements of traditional Chinese music in an output embracing many genres.

Hubay, Jenő (*b* Budapest, 15 Sept 1858; *d* there, 12 March 1937). Hungarian composer and violinist. He studied with Joachim in Berlin, then worked in Paris and Brussels before returning to Budapest in 1886 to teach at the conservatory; from 1919 he directed the academy. His pupils included Szigeti and d'Aranyi. He played throughout Europe. His works include operas, four symphonies and four violin concertos.

Huber, Hans (*b* Eppenburg, 28 June 1852; *d* Locarno, 25 Dec 1921). Swiss composer, pianist and teacher. He studied at the Leipzig Conservatory. From 1877 he was mainly in Basle, where his works were performed and highly praised, especially the 'Tell' Symphony (no.1) and the choral work *Pandora*. For his Romantic style (modelled on Schumann and later on Liszt, Brahms and Richard Strauss) and wide-ranging output he may be regarded as the most important 19th-century Swiss composer.

Huber, Klaus (*b* Berne, 30 Nov 1924). Swiss composer. He studied with Burkhard, and with Blacher in Berlin (1955–6), and has taught at conservatories in Basle and Freiburg. His music uses avant-garde techniques in the exploration of spiritual truth with a Renaissance seriousness and precision. Among his works are an opera (*Jot*, 1973), vocal orchestral works, some with tape (e.g. *Erniedrigt–Geknechtet–Verlassen-Verachtet*, 1983), and orchestral and chamber pieces.

Huberman, Bronisław (*b* Częstochowa, 19 Dec 1882; *d* Corsier-sur-Vevey, 15 June 1947). Polish violinist. After study in Berlin he toured widely from 1893, visiting the USA in 1896–7. With the rise of the Nazis he moved to Palestine, co-founding the Palestine SO (later Israel PO) in 1936; he settled in the USA in 1940. He was admired for his sensitivity and intense expression but his individualism and fallible technique attracted criticism.

Hucbald (*b* at or nr. Tournai, *c*840; *d* St Amand, 20 June 930). Theorist and composer. A monk of the abbey of St Amand (called Elnon) at Tournai, he wrote the first known systematic exposition of Western music theory, *De harmonica institutione* (*c*880). His chief purpose was to instruct the monastic choir in singing chant and to develop systematic, rational ways of understanding music; his method was to illustrate every point of theory with a specific example of chant. The treatise considers intervals, consonances, tones and semitones, scales, tetrachords and modes. He also composed several Offices for saints' days.

Huddersfield Choral Society. British amateur choir (*c*230 members) founded in 1836. It performed regularly in Huddersfield from 1881 and first visited London in 1887; its first foreign visit was to the Netherlands in 1928. Malcolm Sargent was guest conductor for *c*30 years. John Pritchard was principal conductor, 1973–80, and was succeeded by Owain Arwel Hughes.

Huddersfield Contemporary Music Festival (UK). Annual (autumn) festival founded at Huddersfield Polytechnic, Yorkshire, by Richard Steinitz in 1978. Among the composers on whose works it has concentrated are Xenakis, Carter, Henze, Davies, Berio and Ferneyhough.

Hudson, George (*b*?1615–20; *d* Greenwich, Dec 1672). English composer. He contributed music (lost) to Davenant's opera *The Siege of Rhodes* (1656) and was a member of the King's Private Music from 1660. His surviving music includes pieces for lyra viol and suites for one or two violins and bass.

Hüe, Georges (Adolphe) (*b* Versailles, 6 May 1858; *d* Paris, 7 June 1948). French composer. He was a pupil of Franck and Reber at the Paris Conservatoire. His works include operas and songs, many reflecting his travels to the orient, Africa and America.

Hueffer, Francis [Hüffer, Franz] (*b* Münster, 22 May 1843; *d* London, 19 Jan 1889). English music critic of German birth. He wrote for leading journals, was music critic of *The Times* (1878–89), author of several books (including *The Troubadours*, 1878), and one of the first to draw English attention to Wagner, Liszt and Berlioz.

Hughes, Arwel (*b* Rhosllanerchrugog, 25 Aug 1909). Welsh composer. He studied at the RCM and worked for the BBC in Wales (1935–71). His most important works are choral-orchestral, notably the oratorio *Pantycelyn* (1963).

His son Owain Arwel (*b* 1942) is a conductor often heard in the popular repertory.

Hugh the Drover, or Love in the Stocks. Romantic ballad opera in two acts by Vaughan Williams to a libretto by Harold Child (1924, London).

Huguenots, Les. Opera in five acts by Meyerbeer to a libretto by Scribe and Deschamps (1836, Paris).

Hullah, John (Pyke) (*b* Worcester, 27 June 1812; *d* London, 21 Feb 1884). English teacher and composer. With government support he introduced from continental models a fixed *doh* system of teaching singing to school teachers and the public in 1840, eventually securing a permanent place for music in the school curriculum. Though his system was replaced by Curwen's, he had a great influence on amateur music in England, publishing textbooks, essays and choral and vocal collections and writing songs including the popular *The Three Fishers*.

Hüllmandel, Nicolas-Joseph (*b* Strasbourg, 23 May 1756; *d* London, 19 Dec 1823). Alsatian composer. Settling in Paris *c*1776, he won instant success as player, on the harpsichord, piano and glass harmonica, and composer. In 1789 he moved to London, where he concentrated on playing and teaching and published arrangements and a didactic work. He composed 26 keyboard sonatas (some with violin) and shorter pieces. The sonatas, gracefully written, include polyphony as well as melodic writing, and have dynamics and sonorities idiomatic to the piano as well as some brilliant passage-work; most of the violin parts are optional and simple.

Humble, (Leslie) Keith (*b* Geelong, 6 Sept 1927). Australian composer. He studied at the RAM (1950–51) and with Leibowitz in Paris (1953–5), where he remained, writing music for experimental theatre works. In 1966 he returned to Australia as lecturer at Melbourne University, becoming a vigorous champion and performer of new music. His later works have included dramatic, electronic and instrumental pieces, notably the *Nunique* and *Arcade* series.

Hume, Tobias (*b* ?*c*1569; *d* London, 16 April 1645). English composer. An officer in the Swedish and Russian armies, he played the viol and entered Charterhouse almshouse in London in 1629. His two published lyra viol tablatures (1605, 1607) contain all his known works – dances, descriptive and programmatic pieces and songs.

Humfrey, Pelham (*b* 1647; *d* Windsor, 14 July 1674). English composer. He was a chorister in the Chapel Royal until 1664, and then travelled in France and Italy, where he probably had contact with Lully and Carissimi. He became a Gentleman of the Chapel Royal in 1667; in 1672 he was made composer for the royal band of violins and soon afterwards succeeded Henry Cooke as Master of the Children and composer in the Private Musick. He was also a leading figure in the Corporation of Music. He probably taught Purcell composition. Though not a prolific composer, Humfrey played a central role in consolidating an English Baroque style. His 19 verse anthems combine modern influences from Lully's music (especially in their string writing) and from Italian music (in their vocal writing), and are distinctive for their powerful expressive language. French influence is also obvious in one of his two masques for *The Tempest* (1674), while the other shows Italianate features. His other works include a service, three court odes and nearly 30 songs (most to secular texts).

Hummel. *See* HOMMEL.

Hummel, Johann Nepomuk (*b* Bratislava, 14 Nov 1778; *d* Weimar, 17 Oct 1837). Austrian pianist and composer. A child prodigy and a pupil of Mozart (Vienna, 1786–8), he undertook an extended tour (1789–92) throughout northern Europe with his father, arousing particular interest in England, where he met Haydn. Back in Vienna he studied with Albrechtsberger, Salieri and Haydn, giving lessons to support himself. He held a position as Konzertmeister to Prince Nikolaus Esterházy (1804–11) and, after a period of writing piano and chamber music for Vienna, returned to the concert platform. He was Kapellmeister in Stuttgart (1816–18) and Weimar (from 1819), where he conducted the court theatre and many concerts, knew Goethe and other luminaries and still had time to teach and compose; he toured regularly as a pianist and worked tirelessly on his important piano method (1828). The climax of his career came in 1830 with a trip to Paris and London. Despite his public and financial success – he had an excellent business sense and systematized multi-national music publishing – he remained a warm and simple person. His playing was praised for its clarity, neatness, evenness, superb tone and delicacy, products of his preference for the lighttoned Viennese piano; he excelled at improvisation. Ferdinand Hiller was among his pupils. Hummel wrote some of the finest music of the last years of Classicism, with ornate Italianate melodies and virtuoso embroidery; his later music shows more expression and variety, including imaginative harmony and long flights of lyricism.

Piano music 6 solo sonatas; over 50 other solo works, incl. variations, rondos, fantasies; pf duets

Chamber music Septet, d (*c*1816); Septett militaire, C (1829); Pf Qnt, eb/Eb (1802); 3 str qts (before 1804); 2 str trios; 8 pf trios; 7 acc. kbd sonatas; *c*20 other works

Orchestral music 8 pf concs.; Tpt Conc., Eb (1803); other works for solo inst(s) and orch; dances, marches

*Dramatic music c*12 operas; contributions to other composers' operas; incidental and ballet music

Vocal music 5 masses; oratorio; other sacred works; secular cantatas, partsongs, solo songs

Humoreske [humoresque]. Term used by Schumann as the title for an extended piano piece (op.20) and by later composers for pieces of a relaxed and genial kind.

Humperdinck, Engelbert (*b* Siegburg, 1 Sept 1854; *d* Neustrelitz, 27 Sept 1921). German composer and teacher. He studied at the Cologne Conservatory (1872–6) and at the Royal Music School in Munich (1877–9), meeting Wagner in Naples and assisting him with *Parsifal* at Bayreuth (1881–2). After interludes in Paris, Spain, Cologne and Mainz (working for B. Schotts Sohne), he moved to Frankfurt as a teacher and opera critic, also writing his most famous work, *Hänsel und Gretel* (1890–93; given its première at Weimar under Richard Strauss); by 1900 he was in Berlin, teaching, composing operas and writing Shakespearean incidental music (among his most successful work). The operatic version of *Königskinder*, another characteristic piece in his naive, folklike style, was first performed in New York in 1910; like *Hänsel und Gretel* it started from simple song settings and went through an intermediate stage to a full opera, showing Wagnerian harmonic and textural influences.

Humpert, Hans Ulrich (*b* Paderborn, 9 Oct 1940). German composer. A pupil of Petzold and Eimert at the Cologne Musikhochschule (1961–7), he succeeded Eimert in 1972 as director of the electronic music studio.

Humphries, John [?J.S.] (*b c*1707; *d* before *c*1740). English composer. A violinist, he published violin solos and 24 concertos (*c*1740–1741), among the first in England to use wind instruments. A set of 12 trio sonatas (1734) by 'J.S. Humphries' is probably also his.

Humstrum. An English folk fiddle, now extinct, that resembled a REBEC, made of a tin canister and four wire strings.

Hungarian Dances. 21 piano duets by Brahms, published in four volumes (1852–69); three were orchestrated and some arranged for piano solo.

Hungarian Quartet. String quartet, founded in Budapest in 1935, led first by Sándor Végh, then by Zoltán Székely. It was resident in the Netherlands before moving to the USA in 1950, and it disbanded in 1970. Although it played a wide repertory, it was specially noted for its authority in Beethoven and Bartók.

Hungarian Rhapsodies. 20 piano pieces by Liszt (1840s–1885). The Hungarian Fantasy for piano and orchestra is based on no.14.

Hunnenschlacht. Symphonic poem by Liszt (1857) after a mural by W. von Kaulbach.

Hunold, Christian Friedrich ['Menantes'] (*b* Wandersleben, 29 Sept 1681; *d* Halle, 6 Aug 1721). German librettist. He wrote several librettos for Keiser in Hamburg and some of his cantata texts (written later in Halle) were set by Bach at Cöthen. He also wrote on poetic theories governing music.

Hunt. Title given to several works incorporating hunt-like rhythms or themes, notably Mozart's String Quartet in Bb K458 (1784), two works by Haydn, his String Quartet in Bb op.1 no.1 (*c*1758) and Symphony no.73 in D (*c*1781, also known as 'LA CHASSE'), and Bach's Cantata no.208 (1713).

Hunter, Rita (Nellie) (*b* Wallasey, 15 Aug 1933). English soprano. She studied with Eva Turner and in 1960 became a principal at Sadler's Wells. Her début was as Marcellina (*Figaro*), but she moved on to larger roles, including Senta and Leonora (*Il trovatore*). Her main triumph, however, was as Brünnhilde in the ENO *Ring*, a grandly-scaled performance with sweetness as well as power. She sang Brünnhilde at the Met (1972) as well as Norma, and has sung widely in Europe, the USA and in Australia, where she settled.

Hunyady László. Opera in four acts by Erkel, to a libretto by Egressy after Tóth (1844, Budapest); it was the first widely successful opera in Hungarian.

Hurd, Michael (*b* Gloucester, 19 Dec 1928). English composer. He studied at Oxford and with Berkeley (1953–9) and has composed much choral and educational music, notably *Jonah-man Jazz* (1966), and written several books on English music.

Hurdy-gurdy [organistrum]. A string instrument bowed mechanically, with three main elements: a set of melody and drone strings, a resin-coated wooden wheel which acts as a bow, and a keyboard with tangents that bear on the strings when depressed.

In the Middle Ages the hurdy-gurdy (*organistrum*) was used in the teaching and performance of religious music. 12th-century pictures show it as fiddle-shaped with three strings, up to 2 m long, resting on the laps of two players (one operated the tangents, the other turned the wheel. Eight tangents provided a diatonic octave (with Bb as well as B) from C. The drone strings were an octave apart with the centre melody string a 4th or 5th below the higher. In the 13th century the instrument was smaller and played by one musician, often to accompany songs. It became established as a popular minstrel instrument. Its social standing has varied; in the 17th century it was a beggar's instrument. During the 18th, when 'rusticity' was in vogue, it saw an upsurge of popularity among the French aristocracy (as the *vielle à voue*), and pieces were written specially for it (e.g. Mozart's four German dances, K602). Haydn wrote for a related instrument, the *lira organizzata*.

The hurdy-gurdy is usually viol-shaped, with two melody strings passing through the box housing the tangents. One of the drones causes its bridge to rattle. The instrument is slung around the neck and held so that the keys fall back into place after being released. The player can articulate rhythm with minute interruptions of the wheel's rotation while pressing the keys with the left-hand fingers.

The hurdy-gurdy is still played in parts of Europe as a folk instrument; variant forms include the Swedish *nyckelharpa*, played with a bow in place of the wheel.

Hurford, Peter (John) (*b* Minehead, 22 Nov 1930). English organist. He studied under Darke, at Cambridge and with Marchal in Paris. He emerged as an authoritative performer of 18th-century French music and particularly Bach, whose complete works he has recorded. He was master of the music at St Albans Abbey, 1958–79, and has travelled widely in the USA and elsewhere as recitalist and teacher. He has written church and organ music.

Hurlebusch, Conrad Friedrich (*b* Brunswick, *c*1696; *d* Amsterdam, 17 Dec 1765). German composer. He travelled in Germany and Italy as a harpsichord virtuoso and was briefly Kapellmeister at the Swedish court (from 1722). He presented operas in Brunswick and elsewhere and in 1743 became organist at the Oude Kerk, Amsterdam. He wrote cantatas, psalms, odes, concertos and keyboard sonatas, in a generally direct style.

Hurlstone, William (Yeates) (*b* London, 7 Jan 1876; *d* there, 30 May 1906). English composer. He studied under Stanford at the RCM and was a brilliant pianist, but ill-health prevented a concert career. A composer of great promise, he died young, leaving orchestral works (including a Piano Concerto, 1896, and Fantasie-Variations on a Swedish Air, 1904), chamber works (Phantasie String Quartet, 1906) and instrumental sonatas, as well as piano music, part-songs and songs.

Hurník, Ilja (*b* Poruba, 25 Nov 1922). Czech composer and pianist. He studied with Řídký and Novák (1941–4) and has written in most genres, moving from a post-Janáček to a more wide-ranging style.

Hurwitz, Emanuel (Henry) (*b* London, 7 May 1919). English violinist. He studied at the RAM and with Huberman. He was leader of the ECO, 1948–68, then of the New Philharmonia, and was active as a chamber music player in his own string quartet, the Melos

Ensemble and the Aeolian Quartet, with which he recorded Haydn's complete quartets. In 1968 he formed his own orchestra. He is also known as a capable and sympathetic teacher.

Husa, Karel (*b* Prague, 7 Aug 1921). American composer of Czech origin. He studied in Prague with Řidký and in Paris with Boulanger and Honegger (1946–51). Since 1954 he has lived in the USA, teaching at Cornell University and conducting major orchestras. His music is clear in style, often with powerful rhythms and dramatic ostinatos, and sometimes including quarter-tones and serialism; he is a brilliant orchestrator. Most of his works are instrumental; *Music for Prague 1968* (1968) and *Apotheosis of this Earth* (1970) are among the first concert band works to use aleatory procedures and are classics of their kind.

Husla [husle]. A bowed instrument played by the Wends or Sorbs of eastern Germany and Slavonic countries. It resembles a medieval fiddle and is held across the chest and supported by a strap; its traditional tuning is $d'-a'-e''$.

Huston, Scott (*b* Tacoma, WA, 10 Oct 1916). American composer. He studied with Phillips, Rogers and Hanson at the Eastman School (1938–42, 1950–52), and began teaching at the Cincinnati Conservatory in 1952. His works include orchestral, choral and instrumental pieces, and the opera *Blind Girl* (1984, New York).

Hutchinson. American 'singing family', active from 1840 to the 1880s. The most popular of such groups in the 19th century, it was drawn from the 13 children of Jesse and Mary Hutchinson of Milford, New Hampshire. They wrote many of their own songs and were known particularly for their espousal of progressive social causes (anti-slavery, temperance, universal suffrage).

Hüttel, Josef (*b* Mělník, central Bohemia, 18 July 1893; *d* Plzeň, 6 July 1951). Czech conductor and composer. He studied with Novák at the Prague Conservatory (1908–12) and with Taneyev in Moscow (1912–13), then worked in Russia and Egypt (1921–46) as a conductor. His works (all instrumental) were at first influenced by Skryabin, but later tended towards Stravinsky.

Hüttenbrenner, Anselm (*b* Graz, 13 Oct 1794; *d* Ober-Andritz, 5 June 1868). Austrian composer. A pupil of Salieri and friend of Beethoven and Schubert, he wrote operas, vocal, orchestral and chamber music, and songs (some modelled on Beethoven's). He was Kapellmeister of the Steiermärkischer Musikverein (1825–39).

Huygens, Christiaan (*b* The Hague, 14 April 1629; *d* there, 8 June 1695). Dutch scientist and theorist, second son of Constantijn Huygens. His importance to music theory lies in the *Novus cyclus harmonicus* (1661) in which he demonstrated the mathematical basis of the old theory of division of the octave into 31 equal parts. He also worked on the comma fault of mean-tone temperament.

Huygens, Sir Constantijn (*b* The Hague, 4 Sept 1596; *d* there, 28 March 1687). Dutch poet, diplomat, musician and scientist. During 60 years' service for the House of Orange he travelled widely, notably to London, Paris, and Venice, corresponding with many eminent musicians and theorists. The psalms and songs of his *Pathodia* (1647) show an accomplished technique with strong Italian influence and are virtually all that survive of his 900 reputed compositions. He wrote a treatise (1641) in support of organ accompaniment for psalm singing in the Dutch Reformed Church and proposed improvements to the Genevan Psalter (1658).

HWV. Abbreviation for 'Händel Werke Verzeichnis', referring to *Händel-Handbuch* (vols. i–iii, 1978, 1984, 1986), by Bernd Baselt, a thematic catalogue in which each work by Handel is assigned a number.

Hydraulis. An ancient pneumatic organ in which water was used to control the wind pressure; an important instrument of later classical antiquity, it is the direct ancestor of the modern pipe organ.

Hymbert de Salinis (*fl c*1400). Franco-Flemish composer. His surviving works, a ballade and eight sacred pieces (mass movements, motets and a *Salve regina*), range in style from the complex Ars Subtilior practice of the late 14th century to the more restrained manner of the young Dufay.

Hymn. Term applied in ancient times to songs in honour of gods, heroes or notable men, and in Christian worship to strophic songs in praise of God.

The first Latin hymnals with melodies date from the 11th or 12th century, and polyphonic settings have been a regular feature of Vespers since the 15th. A group of three-part settings, probably composed for the papal court at Avignon in the late 14th century, place an ornamented form of the traditional plainchant in one voice (usually the top); this was a feature of the polyphonic hymn for the next 200 years. The style is predominantly note against note. Most of the hymns in a complete annual cycle by Dufay use chant and polyphony for alternate stanzas, as was usual in the Renaissance.

By 1500 four-part settings were normal. In Germany, a style was established which was used throughout Europe in the 16th century, with the plainchant as a *cantus firmus* in equal notes and the other voices weaving a contrapuntal background to it. Some hymn cycles use this style in alternation with chant. There are examples by Festa, Lassus, Victoria, Guerrero and Palestrina. Important cycles came also from Germany and France, and in England Byrd and Tallis wrote settings in the main 16th-century tradition. In the 17th century the vocal bass was doubled by the organ, and various combinations of voices (including solo) and instruments were used. Hymn cycles continued to be written but the tendency was to compose isolated settings independent of chant. 18th-century hymn composers include Padre Martini in Italy, and Fux and Wagenseil in Vienna, but most 18th- and 19th-century settings were occasional works for local use.

The vernacular hymn began with the Reformation and has been a constant part of Lutheran worship (*see* CHORALE). The English Reformation however moved towards Calvinism, leading to opposition to the hymn in the liturgy, and for two centuries English parish church music was essentially the metrical psalm. In the 18th century non-conformists such as

John Wesley promoted hymns to a central place in their worship, thereby attracting numerous converts. The established church responded in the 19th century, commissioning new hymns and requiring parishes to provide congregational hymnbooks; this reached a climax with *Hymns Ancient and Modern* (1861), which popularized a new, Victorian type of hymn tune which is still the norm, despite the varied contents of *The English Hymnal* (1906) and the more interdenominational *Songs of Praise* (1928).

The main American contributions to hymnody have been the gospel hymn of the 19th century revivalist movement, culminating in the works of Moody and Sankey, and the SPIRITUAL.

Hymnen. Work by Stockhausen for four-track tape based on national anthems (1967).

Hymn of Jesus, The. Choral work, op.37, by Holst to his own text translated from the apocryphal Acts of St John (1917).

Hymn Society of America. Organization founded in 1922 to promote the writing and the wider use of hymns. Its headquarters are at Wittenberg University, Springfield, Ohio. Publications include a quarterly, hymnology studies and a microfilm index (*Dictionary of American Hymnology*) to hymn texts.

Hymn to St Cecilia. Britten's op.27 (1942), a setting for unaccompanied chorus of a text by Auden.

Hymnus paradisi. Requiem by Howells to liturgical and biblical texts (1938, performed 1950).

Hyperaeolian. A term used by Glarean (*Dodecachordon*, 1547) for the octave species *B–b* divided at F, the basis of what is now referred to as the LOCRIAN mode.

Hyperprism. Work for wind and percussion by Varèse (1923).

Hypo-. Prefix used with the names of the church modes to signify their plagal forms, as follows: *Hypoaeolian*, on A, using a range *e–e'*; *Hypodorian*, on D, range *A–a*; *Hypoionian*, on C, *g–g'*; *Hypolydian*, on F, *c–c'* or *c–d'*; *Hypomixolydian*, on G, *d–d'* or *c–e'*; and *Hypophrygian*, on E, *B–b* or *A–c'*. See MODE; PLAGAL MODE.

I

Ibach. German firm of piano and organ makers. Founded in 1794 at Beyenburg by Johannes Adolph Ibach (1766–1848), it developed a reputation for building both fine and good medium-class instruments, including many modern uprights from 1885. Tributes to the Ibach piano have come from Wagner, Bartók, Schoenberg, Webern and Richard Strauss.

Iberia. 12 piano pieces by Albéniz in four volumes (1906–9).

Ibéria is also the title of the second of Debussy's orchestral IMAGES.

Ibert, Jacques (François Antoine) (*b* Paris, 15 Aug 1890; *d* there, 5 Feb 1962). French composer. He studied with Vidal at the Paris Conservatoire and won the Prix de Rome in 1919; later he returned to Rome as director of the French Academy (1937–60). Writing in an urbane style that suggests Debussy, Poulenc or Stravinsky (or Chabrier in his lighter music), he produced a large output of comic operas, ballets, songs, chamber music (notably the String Quartet, 1942) and orchestral pieces (including the evocative triptych *Escales*, 1922, and the witty Divertimento, 1930).

Ice Break, The. Opera in three acts by Tippett to his own libretto (1977, London).

Ichiyanagi, Toshi (*b* Kobe, 4 Feb 1933). Japanese composer. He was a pupil of Ikenouchi. While in the USA (1952–61) he was impressed by Cage, whose ideas he put into practice on his return to Japan. He performed with Cage, Tudor and others in the USA, 1966–7, writing *Appearance* and *Music for Living Space*, among other works, for their concerts.

Iconography of music. The analysis and interpretation of musical subject-matter in works of art. Iconography is used by musical historians for the study of obsolete instruments, historical performing techniques, the numbers, disposition and relative positioning of players in ensembles, the role of music in a society and aspects of stage settings, operatic costumes and concert rooms etc. Many of these apply equally to Western and non-Western musical traditions. The student of musical iconography needs, for the interpretation of what he sees, the equipment of an art historian, a social historian and an intellectual historian in understanding the degree of realism of any representation, not only because of the licence an artist may exercise in producing an attractive, well-balanced picture or sculpture, but also because of the symbolic or associative factors that may be incorporated and the degree of stylization or idealization. Many individual composer iconographies, or pictorial biographies, have been published, showing representations of the composer himself, the people whom he knew and the places in which he worked.

Idée fixe. Term coined by Berlioz for a theme which recurs, perhaps obsessively, in different movements of a work (e.g. his *Symphonie fantastique*).

Idiophone. Term for an instrument that produces sound from the substance of the instrument itself, being solid or elastic enough not to require stretched membranes or strings. An idiophone may be struck, plucked, blown or made to vibrate by friction; examples include cymbals, rattles (struck), jew's harps (plucked), sets of wind-chimes (blown) or the glass harmonica (friction).

Idomeneo, rè di Creta. Opera in three acts by Mozart to a libretto by G.B. Varesco after Danchet's for Campra (1781, Munich).

Ifukube, Akira (*b* Kushiro, 7 March 1914). Japanese composer. He was briefly a pupil of Tcherepnin. His music, mostly orchestral and including several ballets, uses Ainu and other folk traditions and is rhythmically violent (his style has been described as 'ethnic exoticism'). He published a treatise on orchestration (1953).

Ikenouchi, Tomojirō (*b* Tokyo, 21 Oct 1906). Japanese composer. He studied with Büsser at the Paris Conservatoire (1927–36), then returned to Tokyo to teach and compose, becoming one of the most influential composition teachers. A perfectionist, he wrote few and compact works, showing his admiration for Mozart, Saint-Saëns and Ravel.

Ileborgh, Adam (*fl c*1448). German composer. He taught and possibly played the organ in Stendal, Brandenburg, and is remembered as composer and/or compiler of one of the earliest organ books, the 'Ileborgh Tablature', consisting of five free preludes and three *cantus firmus* settings of modest quality.

Iliev, Konstantin (*b* Sofia, 9 March 1924). Bulgarian composer. He studied in Sofia and with Řídký and Hába in Prague, then returned to Sofia to work as a conductor (Sofia State PO, 1956–72), teacher and composer. His works make virtuoso use of 12-note and aleatory means, sometimes with Bulgarian folk elements.

Illica, Luigi (*b* Castell'Arquato, 9 May 1857; *d* Colombarone, 16 Dec 1919). Italian librettist. With Giuseppe Giacosa he produced the librettos of Puccini's *La bohème, Tosca* and *Madama Butterfly*, independently writing for other *verismo* composers including Giordano and Mascagni (*Isabeau*, 1911).

Illuminations, Les. Song cycle (op.18, 1939) by Britten, settings for soprano or tenor solo and strings of nine prose-poems by Rimbaud.

Il Verso, Antonio (*b* Piazza Armerina, ?*c*1560; *d* Palermo, *c*23 Aug 1621). Italian composer. A pupil of Pietro Vinci (1582–4), he worked mainly as a freelance teacher and composer in Palermo, visiting northern Italy (probably Venice) in *c*1600–03. Ten books of madrigals, three of motets and one of instrumental works by him survive.

Images. Orchestral work by Debussy, its three pieces being *Gigues* (1912), *Ibéria* (1908) and *Rondes de printemps* (1909).

He also wrote two sets of three piano pieces with the same title (1905, 1907).

Imaginary Landscape. Five percussion works by Cage (1939–52); no.4 uses 12 radios and no.5 is electronic.

Imbrie, Andrew (Welsh) (*b* New York, 6 April 1921). American composer. He studied with Sessions at Princeton and in 1947 began teaching at Berkeley. His works include symphonies, concertos and quartets in a Sessions-influenced style of sharply profiled melody, brilliant orchestration, rhythmic animation and conscientious development. In his opera *Angle of Repose* (1976, San Francisco) American folk idioms are integrated with atonal harmony.

Imbroglio (It.). Term for a scene of confusion in an Italian 18th-century *opera buffa*, typically an act finale where everyone is singing in some degree of agitation, matched by complexity in the music.

Imeneo. Opera in three acts by Handel to a libretto after Stampiglia (1740, London).

Imitation. Immediate or overlapping repetition of the melodic contour of one part by another, often at a different pitch. The technique was intrinsic to certain medieval forms, such as the ROTA and CACCIA, and became increasingly important after the middle of the 15th century. A more-or-less consistent use of imitation ('through imitation') was the main structural principle of late Renaissance vocal polyphony, for example that of Josquin and Palestrina. CANON employs the device in a strict and thorough manner; it is also fundamental to FUGUE.

The term is also used for imitations of nature (e.g. birdsong) or non-musical sounds in a musical work.

Immortal Hour, The. Music drama in two acts by Boughton to his own libretto after 'Fiona Macleod' (William Sharp) (1914, Glastonbury).

Imperfect. Term applied in early mensural NOTATION to a relationship of 2:1 (as opposed to perfect, 3:1) in time (the relation between semibreve and breve) or prolation (the relation between minim and semibreve).

Imperfect cadence [half cadence; half close]. A CADENCE that comes to rest on the dominant.

Imperfect consonance. The interval of a major or minor 3rd or 6th, or compounds of these, as opposed to a perfect consonance.

Impériale, L'. Title given to Haydn's Symphony no.53 in D (1778–9) in a 19th-century Paris catalogue of Haydn's symphonies.

Haydn's Mass in D minor, the Nelson Mass, is nicknamed the Imperial Mass.

Impresario, The [Der Schauspieldirektor]. Singspiel in one act by Mozart to a libretto by G. Stephanie (1786, Vienna).

Impressionism. Term, first used in the 1870s of Monet, Pissarro and their circle of painters, and later applied to music. In 1882, Renoir mentioned 'musical impressionists' in discussion with Wagner. It was applied, as a criticism, to Debussy's *Printemps* in 1887, to signify that the writer thought the work lacking in structural precision and exaggeratedly occupied with colour. Although Debussy is still generally regarded as the prototype impressionist composer, it has been argued that analogies between him and the Monet school are misleading. But many critics regard it as a useful critical concept, particularly for music that blurs the outlines of traditional tonal progression with modal or chromatic features and conveys moods and emotions around a subject rather than presenting a detailed musical picture.

Impromptu. A title used for single-movement piano pieces; it implies a free, casual nature to the composer's inspiration. Among the earliest examples are Schubert's; later composers include Chopin, Schumann, Skryabin and Fauré.

Improperia (Lat.: 'reproaches'). A series of chants sung on Good Friday during the Veneration of the Cross.

Improvisation. The creation of a musical work, or the final form of one, as it is being performed. It may involve the work's immediate composition by its performers, the elaboration or adjustment of detail in an existing work, or anything in between.

A number of forms of improvisation are familiar in Western art music. In early ecclesiastical music, singers were taught how to add another line to a liturgical chant while it was being performed; such techniques probably had a place in the development of ORGANUM, and early examples of written-out organum, discant or motets show signs of improvisational origins. Improvisatory techniques were similarly used in the FAUXBOURDON style of the early 15th century. Such techniques continued to be used in the 16th, when singers improvised over a *cantus firmus* in long notes and even improvised in imitative counterpoint.

Other kinds of improvisation in the Renaissance and Baroque periods include DIMINUTION, where the notes of a melody are broken down into a larger number of shorter ones, and DIVISION, where a player (usually on the viol) improvises in accordance with a given harmonic pattern. Particularly important during the Baroque period was the tradition of improvisation of the CONTINUO player, whose task was to provide, usually on a keyboard instrument or a plucked one, the required harmonic background (to which clues might be provided by figures in the bass part). Another form of improvisation in the Baroque period was the filling out of a given chord-sequence by figuration, as in the French harpsichord tradition of the PRÉLUDE NON MESURÉ or in passages left not fully realized in works such as Corelli's violin solos.

Ornamentation also represents a form of improvisation; here the player or singer embellishes a given line, often quite freely, to enhance its expression and to show his or her inventiveness and brilliance. The tradition of added ornamentation, important in repeat sections of operatic arias, in Italian *adagio* movements and in passages intentionally left in a skeletal state by the composer, persisted throughout the 18th century and well into the 19th, when it retained an important place in Italian opera in particular. It had a more important position in music for a soloist than in chamber music (from the Classical period onwards) or orchestral music, although it was practised extensively in these too.

A special case of improvisation is the CADENZA: a point, usually close to the end of the first movement of a solo concerto, or near the end of a vocal aria, where the composer indicated with a fermata sign that something was to be added – either a simple flourish or, from Mozart's time onwards, a more elaborate passage which might involve the working-out of themes already heard.

The idea of executing an improvisation in a fixed musical form has always held attractions. Bach and Handel were famous for their improvised fugues, Mozart and Beethoven for their improvised variations. The tradition of organ improvisation, usually fugal in character, flourished particularly in the French organ school of the late 19th century and the early 20th.

The idea of improvisation as a return to a more spontaneous form of music-making, in which different members of an ensemble react to what other members are playing, has been encouraged by some composers in the 20th century, particularly in the field of ALEATORY composition.

Outside Western art music, improvisation has an important place in jazz (mainly where individual performers improvise within fixed harmonic patterns) and in many non-Western musical systems. It is particularly central to Indian classical music, in which a sitar player, for example, may improvise within particular rhythmic constraints on a RAGA. The term 'extemporisation' is used more or less interchangeably with improvisation.

In a Summer Garden. Rhapsody for orchestra by Delius (1908). The garden was Delius's own at Grez.

Inbal, Eliahu (*b* Jerusalem, 16 Feb 1936). Israeli conductor. He studied the violin in Jerusalem, then conducting under Celibidache and at the Paris Conservatoire (1960–63). He first appeared mainly in Italy (La Scala, 1965), later in Britain and the USA; he was appointed conductor of Frankfurt RSO, 1974. He is noted as a lively conductor of the standard repertory, and especially powerful in late Romantic music, notably Mahler.

Incalzando (It.). 'Chasing': a direction to increase speed.

Incidental music. Music composed for, or used in, a dramatic production, film or radio or television programme. In ancient Greek drama, music intervened at significant points, and in medieval miracle and mystery plays it accompanied entrances and exits, imitated real-life effects and enhanced symbolism. The earliest surviving secular play with significant music is Adam de la Halle's *Le jeu de Robin et Marion* (*c*1283), but it was the Renaissance that saw the first play with incidental music in the modern sense. In the 16th century and the early 17th, music was considered more appropriate for comedies and pastorals than for tragedies. Shakespeare's example led to an increased use of music in plays in England, and the tradition increased at the Restoration, when composers included John Eccles and Henry Purcell, in whose works a distinction is not always possible between plays with music and 'semi-operas'. The same is true of the *comédies-ballets* of Molière and Lully.

In the 18th century, Goethe and Schiller wrote plays with provision for incidental music, Beethoven and Weber being among the composers who provided it. Schubert's score for Chézy's *Rosamunde von Cypern* and Mendelssohn's for *A Midsummer Night's Dream* are among the most notable examples of 19th-century incidental music, the latter belonging to a tradition of supplying music for Shakespeare's plays to which Spohr, Humperdinck, Tchaikovsky, Balakirev and others also contributed.

The composition of substantial orchestral scores for dramatic productions continued to the end of the 19th century and beyond; outstanding are those by Fauré and Sibelius for Maeterlinck's *Pelléas et Mélisande*. After World War I Stravinsky's music for Ramuz's *Soldier's Tale* set a precedent for more modest forces, and also for a close collaboration between writer and composer, both features of Brecht's work with Weill, Eisler and Dessau. Since the 1930s composers have found a demand for incidental music in the cinema (*see* FILM MUSIC) and to some extent in broadcasting, although radio and television programmes often draw on recorded music originally written for the concert hall.

Incipit (Lat.: 'it begins'). The opening words or music in a text or composition, used for identification in a THEMATIC CATALOGUE.

Incledon, Charles [Benjamin] (*b* St Keverne, bap. 5 Feb 1763; *d* London, 18 Feb 1826). English tenor. He was well known for his performances at Covent Garden Theatre (where he sang in the première of Haydn's *Creation*, 1800) and at Vauxhall, the Lenten Oratorios and provincial festivals; from 1804 he was associated with nautical and patriotic ballads.

Incoronazione di Poppea, L' [The Coronation of Poppaea]. Opera in a prologue and three acts by Monteverdi to a libretto by G.F. Busenello (1642, Venice).

Incredible Flutist, The. Ballet by Walter Piston (1938, Boston).

Indes galantes, Les. *Opéra-ballet* in a prologue and two to four *entrées* by Rameau to a libretto by Fuzelier (1735, Paris).

India, Sigismondo d' (*b* Palermo, *c*1582? *d* ?Modena, by 19 April 1629). Italian composer. As a young man he travelled in Italy, notably to Florence, and in 1611 he became chamber music director at the Turin court; he left in 1623, working in Modena and Rome. His five books *Le musiche* (1609–23) contain chamber monodies, varied in style but often of great emotional intensity, and duets; he also published eight volumes of madrigals (1606–24), some highly chromatic and expressive, as well as villanellas and motets.

Indianapolis Symphony Orchestra. American orchestra founded in 1930 and first conducted by Ferdinand Schaeffer. Its home (since 1984) is the Circle Theater (cap. 1847). Under Fabien Sevitzky (1937–55) programmes included contemporary American music, young musicians were engaged and concert series were instituted. Izler Solomon (1956–76) increased its international reputation. John Nelson was music director, 1976–87.

Indian music. One of the world's most ancient and distinguished musical cultures is that of the Indian subcontinent, including the modern nations of India, Pakistan, Bangladesh, Nepal and Sri Lanka. Indian music is divided into two main traditions, Hindustani, of north India, Pakistan and Bangladesh, and Karnatic or south Indian, of the Indian peninsula, south of Hyderabad.

It is thought that the purest and most ancient music of India is preserved in the south, where the aboriginal Dravidian Hindu population was driven over millennia by waves of invasions, first by the Aryans (2nd millennium BC) and later by the Muslims (13th century onwards). North Indian music has been heavily influenced by central Asian and Persian forms introduced to the Moghul courts, and many of the famous hereditary performers are Muslims. Despite the many differences between these two great traditions, the fundamental concepts of composition and performance are shared and have been enshrined over the centuries in theoretical treatises, beginning with the much-studied *Nātya-śāstra* (probably 4th and 5th centuries AD), a treatise on ancient dramaturgy.

Most Indian classical music has three main components, a solo melody line, usually highly embellished, a rhythmic accompaniment and a drone. Vocal music is predominant; instrumental styles and genres, though better known in the West through famous performers such as Ravi Shankar and Ali Akbar Khan, are based on vocal models. Indian melodies are based on scalar-modal structures called 'ragas'. Each raga has an ascending and descending form (which may differ), prescribed ornaments, characteristic melodic phrases, a specified time of day for performance, a predominant mood (*rasa*) and two primary notes, a main melodic note and a secondary one usually a 4th or 5th higher. Thousands of ragas are described in theoretical writings, but in practice only *c*50 are played in the Hindustani tradition and 50 in the Karnatic. Indian

rhythm is conceived of in time cycles called 'talas', usually with six to 16 beats. Talas are subdivided into groups of beats: for example, the Hindustani *jhap-tāl* tala with ten beats is subdivided 2 + 3 + 2 + 3 and the Karnatic *jhampā* tala, also with ten, is subdivided 7 + 1 + 2. Each tala has characteristic patterns and phrases which are memorized by Indian drummers.

Improvisation, another important feature of Indian music, is based on the elaborate rules that govern the performance of raga and tala. Most Indian genres, such as the Hindustani *dhrupad* and *khayāl* vocal forms, begin with a slow unmeasured improvisatory section in which the characteristics of the raga are introduced. Performances are often something of a contest between soloist and drummer, with each introducing increasingly complex permutations of the tala, often spanning several cycles.

Indian instruments reflect the main requirements of the musical system – flexibility of pitch to perform the many ragas and their microtonal ornaments, rhythmic complexity and an ever-present drone. There are very few instruments of fixed pitch, such as the metallophones and xylophones that predominate in South-east Asia, although the harmonium has become popular in the 20th century. Most melody instruments have drone strings which the player strums while performing the raga. The sitar, the best known of north Indian string instruments, is a long-necked plucked lute with four melody strings, three drone strings and 13 sympathetic strings, which vibrate independently when the instrument is played, enriching the timbre. The *sarod*, another Hindustani plucked lute, has a shorter neck than the sitar, six melody, two drone and several sympathetic strings. The *vīṇā*, the principal string instrument of Karnatic music and one of India's oldest instruments, is a long-necked plucked lute with four melody and three drone strings. The European violin is also played in Indian classical music; the performer sits crosslegged on the floor and holds it against his chest with the scroll braced against the instep of his right foot. The drums of classical Indian music, all played with the hands and fingers, are tuned to the main pitch of the raga. In the south the main drum of the classical tradition is the *mṛdaṅgam*, a double-headed barrel drum. In the north, the tabla, a pair of small single-headed drums, accompanies vocal and instrumental music, often with great virtuosity and amazing speed. The basic drone is supplied by the *tamburā*, a long-necked lute with four strings that are never stopped but strummed slowly and evenly throughout the raga, often by a pupil of the soloist.

Over 70% of the population of India lives in villages where urban art music is seldom heard. Village music includes songs of the life cycle, seasons and Hindu festivals. In recent decades the most popular music in India has been Indian film music disseminated by the large Bombay film industry.

Indian Queen, The. Semi-opera in five acts by Purcell to a text by Dryden and R. Howard (1695, London); the final masque is by Daniel Purcell.

Indonesian music. The rich musical diversity of the Indonesian archipelago – *c*3000 islands populated by

300 ethnic groups speaking 250 distinct languages – results from Mongul, Arab, Indian and Chinese influences on ancient indigenous styles, still preserved in the outlying islands and in the interiors of Sumatra and Java. Bronze technology, which achieved a high level by the 3rd and 2nd centuries BC, encouraged the spread of gong-chime ensembles from mainland South-east Asia to Indonesia.

Java is the most densely populated of the Indonesian islands and its musical traditions the best known and most thoroughly studied. Javanese music is dominated by the gamelan (musical ensemble), found in settings ranging from the great courts to towns and remote villages. Gamelan music is performed at religious and state functions, ritual gatherings and temple festivals (especially in Bali); it accompanies theatrical and social dance, classical dance-dramas and all-night puppet plays (*wayang kulit*), and is played as concert music as well as on daily radio programmes and in music schools. The ensembles vary in size from a few members to large court ensembles of up to 75 instruments. The music is characterized by homogeneous percussive sounds of large and small hanging bronze gongs (*gong ageng, kempul*), bronze kettle gongs (*kenong, keṭuk*), gong-chimes (*bonang*), single and multi-octave metallophones (*saron, gender*) and xylophones (*gambang*), and various sizes of drums (*kendang gending, kendang ketipung, kendang batangan*), which together may accompany one or more vocalists, flute (*suling*) or *rebab* (bowed spike fiddle of Middle Eastern origin). A typical Javanese gamelan consists of *c*25 instruments and about six singers.

The structure of gamelan music is extremely complex and has been much studied. It is based on two principal scales, the five-note *slendro* and the seven-note *pelog*. Each has several modes (*paṭet*), characterized by a hierarchy of pitches, cadential formulae and a specified time of day for performance. A full gamelan orchestra consists of two sets of instruments, one tuned in *pelog*, the other in *slendro*. Javanese compositions (*gending*) are characterized by complex polyphony and are divided into small units, each marked by the stroke of the largest gong. Within these units, instruments play interlocking parts, the notes combining to form the melody. This technique, with each player adding his notes to the total melody, yields fast complex pieces without making excessive demands on any one musician. Individual parts are based on a nuclear melody; several thousand of these are in court MSS and *c*1000 are commonly performed. In a typical Javanese composition, some instruments play expanded versions of the melody, others play it in long note values, others abstractions (for example every 4th note), while others double, paraphrase and ornament it. Cipher notation is used for instruction, supplementing the traditional pedagogical techniques of imitation and rote. The seemingly mathematical style of gamelan music, with its highly patterned repetitions, stratified structure and homogeneous percussive sound, results in a music of unusual beauty, with a distinctively rich timbre and sedate character.

The ensemble music of Bali shares many features with that of Java, including instrument types and the complex polyphonic structure of the compositions, based on permutations of a nuclear melody. Balinese gamelan are distinguished by their unusual resonance, resulting from the tuning of paired metallophones – two identical instruments, one tuned slightly higher than the other. The resulting acoustical beats lend to Balinese music its uniquely transparent shimmering texture.

Indy, (Paul Marie Théodore) Vincent d' (*b* Paris, 27 March 1851; *d* there, 2 Dec 1931). French composer. He studied with Lavignac from 1865 and with Franck at the Paris Conservatoire from 1872, becoming Franck's staunchest adherent. From here he gained his devotion to what he saw as the standards of German symphonism and in 1894 he was the leading founder of the Schola Cantorum, set up as a Franckist conservatory. In his own music he insisted on logical construction, preferring sonata and variation forms, though his scoring could be brilliant and his contrapuntal skill is often at the service of airiness rather than density. He also contrasted Wagnerism (three *Wallenstein* overtures, 1873–81) with use of folksongs from the Ardèche (*Symphonie sur un chant montagnard français* for piano and orchestra, 1886). Other works include two more symphonies (1903, 1916–18), the symphonic variations *Istar* (1896), operas (*Le chant de la cloche*, 1883, perf. 1912; *Fervaal*, 1897; *L'étranger*, 1903), motets, songs, chamber and piano music.

Inégales. *See* NOTES INÉGALES.

Inextinguishable, The [Det Undslukkelige]. Nielsen's Symphony no.4 (1916).

Inflection. A deviation from pitch. It is used in plainchant for deviations from a monotone reciting note, for reasons of punctuation, at least partly to aid intelligibility. In other music, deviations of pitch are used for expressive purposes as a form of ornamentation, as in the 'blue' notes of jazz.

Ingegneri, Marc'Antonio (*b* Verona, *c*1547; *d* Cremona, 1 July 1592). Italian composer. A pupil of Ruffo and a choirboy at Verona Cathedral, he later moved to Cremona, becoming *maestro di cappella* at the cathedral in 1581. His nine surviving volumes of sacred music and nine of madrigals, in the north Italian tradition, show him to have been a highly competent polyphonist. He taught Monteverdi, whose early music shows his influence.

Inghelbrecht, D(ésiré)-E(mile) (*b* Paris, 17 Sept 1880; *d* there, 14 Feb 1965). French conductor and composer. After experience as an orchestral violinist, he conducted in Paris from 1908 including at the Opéra, 1945–50, championing the music of Debussy, Ravel and Roussel. His own works, which include ballets and piano music, are highly polished and subtly orchestrated.

Inharmonicity. The quality of timbre present when the partial tones that constitute a musical note do not match the harmonic series (i.e. are not multiples of the fundamental frequency). Inharmonicity appears mildly in wind and string instruments, and in pianos, but is strong in such instruments as gongs and bells.

In Nature's Realm [V přírodě]. Concert overture, op.91, by Dvořák (1891), the first of his *Nature, Life and Love* cycle.

In Nomine (Lat.). Title of over 150 English instrumental pieces of the 16th and 17th centuries which use as a *cantus firmus* the Sarum antiphon *Gloria tibi Trinitas*. Composers include Tye, Tallis, Byrd, Orlando Gibbons and Purcell. They draw on an extract, beginning with the words 'In nomine Domini', from a mass by Taverner.

Inori. Work by Stockhausen for orchestra with one or two mimes (1974).

Insanguine [Monopoli], **Giacomo (Antonio Francesco Paolo Michele)** (*b* Monopoli, 22 March 1728; *d* Naples, 1 Feb 1795). Italian composer and teacher. He taught at the S Onofrio conservatory, Naples, becoming *primo maestro* in 1785. He was also an organist at the Tesoro di S Gennaro, *maestro di cappella* from 1781. Of his *c*20 stage works, 1756–82, the earlier ones are mostly comic, the later serious; he also revised and contributed to other composers' operas and wrote sacred music and didactic works. His music is carefully worked and progressive in style.

Institut de Recherche et de Coordination Acoustique/Musique [IRCAM]. Organization founded in 1969 in Paris, attached to the Centre Pompidou. It opened in 1977 with Boulez as director, offering facilities for computer composition and presenting concerts (many with the Ensemble Inter-Contemporain).

Instruments, Classification of. The most comprehensive scholarly system for classifying instruments on a worldwide basis is that devised in 1914 by Hornbostel and Sachs. Using the physical characteristics of sound-production as the basic principle of division, they distinguished four categories: self-sounders (idiophones), membrane instruments (membranophones), string instruments (chordophones) and wind instruments (aerophones), as opposed to the traditional threefold division into percussion, string and wind instruments. Their use of the Dewey decimal system heralded the important role of non-verbal symbols in years to come. Drägner (1948) extended the Hornbostel and Sachs system, taking account of instruments' musical and physiological functions. Hood (1971) devised 'organograms' using symbolic language and diagrams incorporating performance techniques, musical function and social and cultural considerations; he also added the electrophone to the Hornbostel and Sachs divisions. Reinecke (1974) correlated classes of instruments with emotional stereotypes, in line with current thinking about the instrument as aspect as opposed to object.

Intabulation. An arrangement of a vocal composition for keyboard, lute or other plucked string instrument. The term is especially applied to music of the 14th, 15th and 16th centuries, and written in TABLATURE (the system of notation using letters, figures or other symbols instead of notes on a staff). In later intabulations, the arranger often embellished the original, with scale passages, figurative writing etc, and sometimes omitted details of the inner part-writing.

The Italian equivalent term, *intavolatura*, could signify a collection of music intabulated for lute or keyboard, but in later Italian and German music it might also be applied to keyboard scores and sometimes also to repertory written specifically for the instrument as opposed to arrangements.

Intavolatura (It.). INTABULATION; the word or one of its variants was often used as a title for music published in tablature, usually for lute or keyboard.

Intégrales. Work for wind and percussion by Varèse (1925).

Interlude. Something played or sung between the main parts of a larger work, such as an opera. In instrumental music, modulating interludes may provide a transition from the key of one movement or section to that of the next.

Intermède (Fr.). Music and dance inserted between the acts of a larger entertainment; the French counterpart of the Italian *intermedio* or *intermezzo*. Its history goes back to the mid-16th century. By the late 17th, *intermèdes* could be extended compositions in their own right, comparable to an entire opera. An *intermède* was not necessarily related to the work into which it was inserted. Those by Lully and Charpentier for Molière's comedies represent a climax of the genre.

Intermedio (It.; Fr. *intermède*). A form of musico-dramatic entertainment performed between the acts of plays in the Renaissance. Staged *intermedi* were inserted in classical comedies at Ferrara in the late 15th century, with a *moresca* (mimed dance) interspersed with songs or recitations explaining the action. Subjects included pastoral and hunting scenes, classical mythology and love stories. In the early 16th century this *moresca* type was supplanted by others with humanistic literary themes glorifying the ruling house and the absolutist regime.

At Florence spectacular *intermedi* were given on state occasions. The music for only two sets, for Medici weddings, has survived. In 1539 a play was given with six *intermedi*, set by Francesco Corteccia. The most lavish *intermedi* were those for Ferdinando de' Medici's wedding to Christine of Lorraine in 1589: the music, mainly by Malvezzi and Marenzio, ranged from solo songs to ballets and polychoral madrigals for 60 singers and at least 24 instruments.

Monteverdi's *Orfeo* (1607) and other early operas owe much to the *intermedio* tradition. The principal environment of the *intermedio* itself in the early 17th century was in plays put on by literary academies, but after about 1650 *intermedi* were composed as entr'-actes for public opera and may be seen as precursors of the 18th-century Neapolitan INTERMEZZO.

The French equivalent of the *intermedio* was the *intermède*, in which ballet played a major role. The *intermèdes* to Mazarin's Italian opera importations in mid-17th-century Paris proved more popular than the operas themselves. The full range of possibilities in *intermèdes* may be seen in those by Lully and Charpentier for Molière's comedies.

Intermezzo. (1) Term used in the 18th century (generally in the plural, 'intermezzi') for comic interludes performed between the acts or scenes of an *opera seria*. The practice of emphasizing the division of acts with interludes in the manner of the Renaissance INTERMEDIO (for which the word 'intermezzo' is sometimes used) was common in early 17th-century operas. As the century progressed these sections became more grotesque and began to involve stock comic characters, whose *scene buffe* gravitated towards the ends of acts. With the reforms of *c*1700, comic scenes were banished from serious opera in Venice and the intermezzo was given its own plot, usually built round a cunning servant girl who tricks her male partner or ensnares him in matrimony. There were usually two or three short parts, each with recitative, one or two da capo arias and a duet. Popular librettos were repeated in different *opera serie* with either original or new music. Pariati's *Pimpinone* was set at least three times, by Albinoni, Conti and Telemann. In Naples *scene buffe* were preferred to intermezzos until about 1720, when the intermezzo entered a golden age with such composers as Sarri, Hasse and Pergolesi, whose *La serva padrona* (1733) is the most famous example of the genre. By 1750, however, the intermezzo had been largely supplanted by ballets as the principal entr'acte diversion in *opera seria*.

In the 19th century the term 'intermezzo' was used for lyrical pieces or movements, often for piano solo. Mendelssohn called the third movement of his Piano Quartet no.2 'Intermezzo' and Schumann made frequent use of this title in his early piano music. Brahms composed numerous independent intermezzos for piano, and the term has been used for operatic entr'actes, as in Mascagni's *Cavalleria rusticana*.

(2) Opera in two acts by Richard Strauss to his own libretto (1924, Dresden).

International Council for Traditional Music. Organization founded in London in 1947, as the International Folk Music Council, to study and promote folk music and dance. Its headquarters are in Kingston, Ontario. It has national committees and study groups, and publishes a yearbook. It was renamed in 1981.

Internationale Stiftung Mozarteum. Austrian institution established in Salzburg in 1880, when the Internationale Mozart-Stiftung (founded 1870) and the Mozarteum (founded 1841 with the Dommusikverein) were combined. A centre of Mozart scholarship and of music in the city, it includes a conservatory and a museum.

International Folk Music Council. *See* INTERNATIONAL COUNCIL FOR TRADITIONAL MUSIC.

International Institute for Comparative Music Studies and Documentation. Organization founded in West Berlin in 1963, with Alain Daniélou as director. Its aim is to study and promote nonEuropean music. Its publications include the series Les Traditions Musicales and (with the International Music Council) the quarterly *World of Music*.

International League of Women Composers. Organization which promotes serious music by women composers; its headquarters are in Three Mile Bay, New York. Originally the League of Women Composers, founded in Knoxville in 1975 by Nancy Van de Vate, it expanded and was renamed in 1978. It

publishes the catalogue *Contemporary Concert Music by Women* (1981–).

International Music Centre. Organization founded in Vienna in 1961 to investigate and present music through television, radio, films and recordings. It holds meetings and publishes information on technical and ethical aspects of music in these media.

International Music Council. Organization based in Paris, formed in 1949 by UNESCO to serve music through international exchange of music and musicians, the use of audio-visual media, cooperation with other groups and support of musicians' rights. It holds annual meetings and publishes (with the International Institute for Comparative Music Studies) the quarterly *World of Music*. It formed the Musicians International Mutual Aid Fund in 1974.

International Musicological Society. Society, with headquarters in Basle, founded in 1927 to replace the International Musical Society (1899–1914). Congresses are held every five years and it publishes the series *Documenta musicologica*, the periodical *Acta musicologica* and (with the International Association of Music Libraries) the International Inventory of Musical Sources (*RISM*), International Repertory of Musical Iconography (*RIdIM*), International Repertory of Music Literature (*RILM*) and International Repertory of the Musical Press (*RIPM*).

International Society for Contemporary Music. Society founded in 1922 (with headquarters in London) to promote contemporary music through annual festivals. Berg's Violin Concerto (Barcelona, 1936) and Boulez's *Le marteau sans maître* (Baden-Baden, 1955) are among works to have been given premières at such events. Autonomous national sections (30 in the 1980s) organize activities.

International Society for Music Education. Society founded in Brussels in 1953 by the International Music Council; it is based in Birkerød, Denmark. Its aims are to promote music education at all levels throughout the world by arranging meetings, cooperating with other organizations and through research. It publishes the *ISME Yearbook*.

Interpretation. The aspect of music arising from the difference between notation, which preserves a written record of the music, and performance, which brings the musical experience into renewed existence. While traditionally, since the Romantic era, interpretation has been seen as dependent on a performer's view of the work and his capacity for presenting a plausible view of it to an audience, more recently it has also been taken to embrace an understanding of the composer's own aural vision of the work as affected by the conventions of notation and performance of his time (as embraced by the concept of PERFORMING PRACTICE). While there is no substitute for a knowledge of performing practice, the insights brought by intuitive musicianship and trained imagination to the expression of a work are central to its interpretation.

Interrupted cadence [deceptive cadence; false cadence]. A CADENCE in which the dominant chord resolves not on to the expected tonic but on to some other chord, usually the submediant (V–VI).

Ex. 1

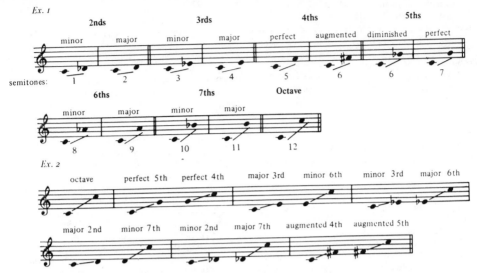

Ex. 2

Interval. The distance between two pitches. Intervals are described according to the number of steps they embrace in a diatonic scale, counted inclusively: from C up to D or down to B is a 2nd, C up to E or down to A a 3rd etc. Ex.1 shows the basic diatonic intervals above and below middle C. Other intervals are used in non-Western music.

Intervals may be identified by their frequency ratios. An octave is 2:1, a perfect 5th 3:2 (in just intonation). Two intervals that add up to an octave are said to be inversions of each other (for example, the minor 3rd is the inversion of the major 6th; see ex.2). Intervals an octave larger than those in ex.1 are considered their compounds.

In the South [Alassio]. Concert overture, op.50, by Elgar (1904), an impression of Italy sketched at Alassio.

In the Steppes of Central Asia [V sredney Azii]. 'Musical picture' for orchestra by Borodin (1880).

Intimate Letters [Listy duvěrné]. Sub-title of Janáček's autobiographical String Quartet no.2 (1928).

Intolleranza 1960. Opera in two parts by Nono to his own libretto after A.M. Ripellino (1961, Venice).

Intonarumori (It.). 'Noise intoners': a family of ten types of instrument, mostly based on the principle of the hurdy-gurdy, invented by LUIGI RUSSOLO and constructed in Milan, 1913–21. They were used in works by Russolo himself and other futurist composers.

Intonation. In plainchant, the initial melodic phrase usually sung by the priest or cantor before the other voices enter. The term is particularly used for the phrase intoned at the beginning of the Gloria and the Credo of the Mass. In performance, 'intonation' is used to describe the accuracy of pitch of a singer's or instrumentalist's individual notes.

Intonazione. A short toccata-like piece designed to introduce in its correct key some kind of vocal music in the church service. The term was used by the Gabrielis (*Intonationi d'organo*, 1593) but rarely by later composers.

Intrada. An instrumental piece used to accompany an entrance, to inaugurate a festive event or to begin a suite, mainly in the Baroque period. A collection of intradas was published by Alessandro Orologio in 1597, and intradas in duple or triple metre occur in 17th-century German orchestral suites.

Introduction. A preparatory section, often in a slow tempo, prefixed to an extended movement. The concept is an old one but the term is chiefly associated with music of the Classical and Romantic periods. The introductions in Haydn's quartets and symphonies range from a few chords to a fully structured section, and this development is carried further in the long introductions to Beethoven's Symphonies nos.2, 4 and 7. Some introductions contain thematic material for the movement that follows, as in Brahms's Symphony no.1, or motto themes for the whole work, as in Tchaikovsky's Fourth and Fifth Symphonies. In some cases the introduction is so important that the term is included in the title, e.g. in pieces called 'Introduction and Allegro' by Schumann, Elgar and Ravel.

Introduction and Allegro. Elgar's op.47 for string quartet and string orchestra (1905).

Introit. In Gregorian chant, the first item in the Proper of the Mass, sung during the procession of the celebrant to the altar. It consists of an antiphon, verse, antiphon, verse, antiphon, Gloria Patri and antiphon, the verse and Gloria Patri being sung to the same simple formula, or tone. There are eight tones, one in each ecclesiastical mode. Texts are usually from the psalms. Sundays are often identified by the introit's first word. It originated by the 6th century as a psalm sung antiphonally by the congregation and gradually became shortened.

The term is also used for an instrumental piece replacing all or part of the sung introit of the Mass. There are organ settings of introit plainchants in collections up to *c*1600; later they are rare, but Liszt and others included short

'Introit' movements in their organ accompaniments to Low Mass.

Invention. (1) Term used since the 16th century as a title for short vocal or instrumental works; it often bears the connotation of 'original idea'. Bach made copies of Bonporti's *Invenzioni* for violin and continuo (1712), and his own 15 inventions for keyboard in two-part counterpoint are the best-known examples.

(2) As applied to valveless brass instruments, a curved sliding CROOK to be inserted into the body of the horn or trumpet without disturbing the mouthpiece. The player could keep the instrument close to the body, making hand-stopping possible. The *Inventionshorn* was first used in Dresden in the early 1750s.

Inversion. (1) The rearrangement of the notes of a chord built in 3rds so that the lowest note is not the root of the chord. If the lowest note is the 3rd of the triad it is said to be a 'first inversion', if the 5th, a 'second inversion'.

(2) The complement of an interval within some fixed interval. Within an octave a 2nd inverts to a 7th, a 3rd to a 6th, a 4th to a 5th and vice versa.

(3) The mirroring of a succession of notes about a fixed note, usually the first note or interval in the succession. Composers of the Renaissance and Baroque often wrote imitative counterpoint in inversion; Bach composed several inverted fugues and canons. 12-note rows, in Schoenberg's system of composition with 12 notes, may be used in inversion, and retrograde inversion.

Inverted cadence. *See* MEDIAL CADENCE.

Inverted mordent. *See* MORDENT; SCHNELLER; and ORNAMENTS.

Invertible counterpoint. The contrapuntal design of two or more voices in a polyphonic texture so that any of them may serve as an upper voice or as the bass. Invertible counterpoint involving two (three, four) voices is called double (triple, quadruple) counterpoint.

Invisible City of Kitezh, The [Skazaniye o nevedimomm grade Kitezhe i deve Frevronii: 'Legend of the Invisible City of Kitezh and the Maiden Fevroniya']. Opera in four acts by Rimsky-Korsakov to a libretto by Bel'sky (1907, St Petersburg).

Invitation to the Dance [Aufforderung zum Tanze]. Weber's *Rondo brillant* in D♭ op.65 for piano; it was orchestrated by Berlioz (1841) and, much altered, by Weingartner.

Ioannidis, Yannis (*b* Athens, 8 June 1930). Greek composer. He studied at the Athens Conservatory and the Vienna Academy, then worked in Caracas, 1968–76, as a conductor and teacher (he founded the Caracas CO). His works, mostly instrumental, are elegantly structured with rich textures.

Iolanta. Opera in one act by Tchaikovsky to a libretto by Modest Tchaikovsky after Hertz (1892, St Petersburg).

Iolanthe. Operetta in two acts by Sullivan to a libretto by Gilbert (1882, London).

Ionian. The name coined by Glarean (*Dodecachordon*, 1547) for one of his additions to the eight traditional church modes, the authentic mode on C, range *c–c'*. It is identical with the modern major scale. *See*

Mode.

Ionisation. Work for percussion by Varèse (1931).

Ipavec, Benjamin (*b* Šveti Jurij, 24 Dec 1829; *d* Graz, 20 Dec 1909). Slovene composer. His songs (1862–1909) are the finest examples of Slovene Romantic lieder, and his *The Noblemen of Teharje* (1802) a valuable contribution to Slovene opera.

Iphigénie en Aulide. Opera in three acts by Gluck to a libretto by Du Roullet after Racine (after Euripides) (1774, Paris).

Iphigénie en Tauride. Opera in four acts by Gluck to a libretto by N.F. Guillard and Du Roullet after Euripides (1779, Paris).

Ippolitov-Ivanov, Mikhayl (Mikhaylovich) (*b* Gatchina, 19 Nov 1859; *d* Moscow, 28 Jan 1935). Russian composer. He studied at the St Petersburg Conservatory (1875–82) and taught from 1893 at the Moscow Conservatory (as director, 1905–22), while also being active as an opera conductor (including at the Bol'shoy from 1925) and composer. His works include operas and orchestral pieces in a style close to Rimsky-Korsakov's; latterly he wrote mass songs and marches.

IRCAM. *See* INSTITUT DE RECHERCHE ET DE COORDINATION ACOUSTIQUE/MUSIQUE.

Ireland, John (Nicholson) (*b* Bowdon, 13 Aug 1879; *d* Rock Mill, 12 June 1962). English composer. He studied at the RCM, first as a pianist, then as a composer under Stanford (1897–1901), under whom he gained command of a solid Brahmsian style radically altered during the next two decades by the impressions of Debussy, Ravel and Stravinsky. The result was a sequence of lyrical piano pieces, but also substantial chamber works, including two piano trios (1906, 1917) and two violin sonatas (1909, 1917). Meanwhile he served as organist and choirmaster at St Luke's, Chelsea (1904–26), later returning to the RCM to teach (1923–39). His postwar works include the symphonic rhapsody *Mai-Dun* (1921, one of many works suggestive of English landscape), the Piano Concerto (1930), a classic of 20th-century English music, and *Legend* for piano and orchestra (1933).

Irino, Yoshirō (*b* Vladivostok, 13 Nov 1921; *d* Tokyo, 28 June 1980). Japanese composer. A pupil of Moroi and prominent in Japanese music as a teacher and festival director, he was also the first Japanese composer to adopt serialism (1950). His works are mostly for orchestral and chamber forces, some using traditional Japanese instruments (e.g. *Wandlungen* for two *shakuhachi* and orchestra, 1973).

Irish harp (Ir. *cláirseach*). A type of harp used in Ireland up to the late 18th century. It had a resonator carved out of a block of willow, a curved forepillar, and 30–36 diatonically tuned heavy brass strings, set in the left side of the neck. It was held on the left shoulder, the left hand playing in the upper register and the right the lower.

Irish Symphony. Sullivan's Symphony in E (1864). It is also the sub-title of Stanford's Symphony no.3 in F minor (1887) and of a symphony by Harty (1904).

Irmelin. Opera in three acts by Delius to his own

libretto, composed in 1892 (1953, Oxford).

Isaac, Heinrich (*b* Flanders, *c*1450; *d* Florence, 26 March 1517). Flemish composer. Though he was born in Flanders, no references to him there are known; the earliest (1484) concerns an apparent journey south, through Innsbruck, to Italy. Serving the Medici in Florence, 1485–93, he sang at the cathedral and probably taught Lorenzo the Magnificent's children. From 1496 he worked intermittently in Vienna, Torgau, Konstanz and Florence, notably as court composer to the Habsburg Emperor Maximilian I. From 1514 he remained in Florence, holding both a Medici pension and a diplomatic post under Maximilian.

Isaac's works reflect his knowledge of the distinctions among Netherlands, Italian and German musical practices; he adapted well to local tradition wherever he found himself. Half his nearly 40 settings of the Mass Ordinary, for example, use 'foreign' borrowed material (e.g. secular songs) and imaginative cyclic structures in accordance with Netherlands-Italian practice, while the other half (dating from after 1496) use plainchant and more conservative, self-contained structures, often with unison sections. The German style is found above all in his nearly 100 settings of the Proper, especially in the posthumous three-volume collection *Choralis constantinus*, written for the Habsburg court chapel and for Konstanz. His secular works include imitative *chansons* and homophonic frottolas as well as German Tenorlieder (*Isbruck, ich muss dich lassen* is famous for the lyricism of its polyphony). In quality and scope Isaac's works stand beside those of Obrecht, Compère, Agricola and La Rue as some of the finest of the Josquin period; his influence, through his music and his pupil Senfl, was particularly important in Germany.

Sacred music 36 masses; 15 mass movts; 99 cycles of mass Propers; over 30 other mass Propers; over 40 free motets
Secular music c80 songs: German lieder, incl. Isbruck, ich muss dich lassen; French chansons; Italian frottolas

Isaack, Bartholomew (*b* Windsor, bap. 22 Sept 1661; *d* 1703). English music copyist and composer. A clerk at Eton College from 1673, he compiled (1675–95) a huge collection of English Restoration church music (including an anthem of his own), now a primary source of works by Blow and Humfrey. Other MSS copied by him contain scores of important works by Blow and Purcell.

Isabella Leonarda (*b* Novara, 1620; *d* there, *c*1700). Italian composer. A nun – her civil name was Isabella Calegari – at S Ursula at Novara, she published over 200 works (mainly solo motets showing Carissimi's influence) in 20 collections (1665–1700).

Isamitt, Carlos (*b* Rengo, 13 March 1887; *d* Santiago, 6 July 1974). Chilean composer. He studied in Chile and Europe and became professor at the National Conservatory in Chile. A pioneer in his country of 12-note music (from 1939), he was also influenced by his studies of American Indian music. He wrote vocal and orchestral works and ballets.

Ishii, Maki (*b* Tokyo, 28 May 1936). Japanese composer. He studied with Ifukube and Ikenouchi (1952–8), and with Blacher and Rufer in Berlin (1958–61). His works use avant-garde techniques, sometimes in combination with Japanese traditions and instruments.

Islamey. 'Oriental fantasy' for piano by Balakirev (1869, rev. 1902).

Isle of the Dead, The [Ostrov myortvïkh]. Symphonic poem, op.29, by Rakhmaninov (1909) after Böcklin's painting.

Isola disabitata, L'. Opera in two acts by Haydn to a libretto by Metastasio (1779, Eszterháza).

Isorhythm. Term coined to refer to the periodic repetition or recurrence of rhythmic patterns in 14th- and early 15th-century motets. The tenors even of early 13th-century clausulais and motets were characterized by reiterated rhythmic figures, but the larger proportions of the 14th-century motet, typified by the works of Vitry and Machaut, demanded at least some degree of similar organization in the upper voices too, to emphasize the structure. Repetitions of the pitch content (*color*) of the tenors of such works do not necessarily coincide with those of the rhythmic unit (*talea*). Some English Gloria and Credo settings from the later 14th and early 15th centuries also use isorhythm.

Isouard, Nicolas [Nicolò de Malte] (*b* Malta, 6 Dec 1775; *d* Paris, 23 March 1818). French composer of Maltese birth. From 1794 he was an opera composer, having success in Florence, Livorno and Malta before establishing himself (1800) in Paris, where he collaborated with Rodolphe Kreutzer and formed the publishing concern Le Magasin de Musique (1802–11; with Cherubini, Méhul, Rode, Kreutzer and Boieldieu). From 1802 he produced numerous successful works, many with the librettist C.J. Etienne, becoming the most influential figure at the Opéra-Comique. Among his important operas are *Cendrillon* (1810; a fairy-tale opera), the expressive *Jeannot et Colin* (1814) and his masterpiece, *Joconde* (1814). His melodic gift went hand in hand with craftsmanship and a sure instinct for matching words and music.

Israel Festival. Annual (summer) festival established in 1961; concerts are given in Jerusalem, Tel-Aviv and Haifa. Israeli composers and biblical subjects have been prominent.

Israel in Egypt. Oratorio by Handel to a biblical text (1739, London).

Israel Philharmonic Orchestra. Orchestra (later the Palestine SO, the Palestine PO from 1946 and the Israel PO again from 1948) founded in 1936 by Huberman in Tel-Aviv. It gave its first concert under Toscanini; in 1968 Zubin Mehta became musical director. It has performed with many renowned conductors and soloists and has toured abroad since 1951.

Istampita (It.). ESTAMPIE.

Istesso tempo, L' (It.). 'The same pace': a direction to maintain the tempo in spite of a change of time signature, note value etc.

Ištvan, Miloslav (*b* Olomouc, 2 Sept 1928). Czech composer. He studied with Kvapil at the Brno Academy (1948–52), where he has lectured. His works grow out of the Janáček tradition into serial and electronic regions.

Italiana in Algeri, L' [The Italian Girl in Algiers]. Opera in two acts by Rossini to a libretto by Anelli (1813, Venice).

Italian Caprice [Capriccio italien]. Orchestral work, op.45, by Tchaikovsky (1880).

Italian Concerto. Work for harpsichord (BWV971) by J.S. Bach, published in *Clavier-Übung*, ii (1735).

Italian overture. Term for the introduction to an 18th-century opera, oratorio or similar work, consisting of three movements (fast–slow–fast/dance); it was established in the late 17th century, in the time of Alessandro Scarlatti, and is an important precursor of the symphony.

Italian Quartet [Quartetto Italiano]. Italian string quartet, led by Paolo Borciani. It was founded in 1945 and has toured widely in a wide repertory ranging from Mozart, Beethoven and Schubert to Webern and new Italian music. The quartet usually play from memory; they are noted for their scrupulous technical preparation and their intensity of style.

Italian Serenade. Work for string quartet by Wolf (1887); there are arrangements for orchestra and for piano by Reger.

Italian sixth chord. An AUGMENTED SIXTH CHORD that has a major 3rd in addition to an augmented 6th above the flattened submediant (e.g. A♭–C–F♯).

Italian Symphony. Mendelssohn's Symphony no.4 in A op.90 (1933), begun in Italy.

Italienisches Liederbuch. Collection of songs by Wolf, settings for voice and piano of 46 poems translated from the Italian by Paul von Heyse; they were published in two volumes (1892, 1896).

Iturbi, José (*b* Valencia, 28 Nov 1895; *d* Hollywood, 28 June 1980). Spanish pianist. He studied at Valencia Conservatory and first played in the USA in 1928. He was admired for his idiomatic performances of Spanish music. He conducted the Rochester PO (1936–44) and appeared in several Hollywood films.

Iturriaga, Enrique (*b* Lima, 3 April 1918). Peruvian composer. He studied with Holzmann in Lima and Honegger in Paris; in 1973 he became director of the Escuela Nacional de Música. His works integrate Arequipan folk music with modern styles, from Hindemith to Webern; *Vivencias* (1965) was his first step towards 12-note serialism.

Ivan IV. Opera in four acts by Bizet to a libretto by F.H. Leroy and H. Trianon, completed in 1865.

Ivanhoe. Opera in three acts by Sullivan to a libretto by J.R. Sturgis after Scott (1891, London).

Ivanov, Mikhail Mikhaylovich (*b* Moscow, 23 Sept 1849; *d* Rome, 20 Oct 1927). Russian critic and composer. As music critic of the St Petersburg journal *Novoye vremya* (1880–1918) he held conservative views, showing hostility towards the 'National School'; his compositions include four operas, choral pieces, songs and orchestral works in the style of Tchaikovsky.

Ivanovs, Jānis (*b* Preili, 9 Oct 1906). Latvian composer. He was a pupil of Vītols at the Riga Conservatory, where he taught from 1944. His works include a cycle of symphonies drawing on Latvian folk music, especially the early ones, which are tinged by

impressionism; the middle ones reflect wartime experience, while later ones move into philosophical realms and more complex harmony and textures, and ultimately social themes, with a simpler more chamber-like style.

Ivan Susanin. *See* LIFE FOR THE TSAR, A. *Ivan Susanin* was the original title of Glinka's opera (1836) and is now normally used, especially in the USSR.

Ives, Charles (Edward) (*b* Danbury, CT, 20 Oct 1874; *d* New York, 19 May 1954). American composer. He was influenced first by his father, a bandmaster who had libertarian ideas about what music might be. When he was perhaps 19 (the dating of his music is nearly always problematic) he produced psalm settings that exploit polytonality and other unusual procedures. He then studied with Parker at Yale (1894–8) and showed some sign of becoming a relatively conventional composer in his First Symphony (1898) and songs of this period. He worked, however, not in music but in the insurance business, and composition became a weekend activity – but one practised assiduously: during the two decades after his graduation he produced three more symphonies and numerous other orchestral works, four violin sonatas, two monumental piano sonatas and numerous songs.

The only consistent characteristic of this music is liberation from rule. There are entirely atonal pieces, while others are in the simple harmonic style of a hymn or folksong. Some are highly systematic and abstract in construction; others are filled with quotations from the music of Ives's youth: hymns, popular songs, ragtime dances, marches etc. Some, like the *Three Places in New England*, are explicitly nostalgic; others, like the Fourth Symphony, are fuelled by the vision of an idealist democracy. He published his 'Concord' Sonata in 1920 and a volume of 114 songs in 1922, but composed little thereafter. Most of his music had been written without prospect of performance, and it was only towards the end of his life that it began to be played frequently and appreciated.

Orchestral music 4 syms. (1898, 1900–02, 1904, 1909–16); Three Places in New England (1908–?14); Decoration Day (1912); The Fourth of July (1913); Second Orchestral Set (1915)
Chamber orchestral music The Unanswered Question (1906); Central Park in the Dark (1906); Tone Roads no.1 (1911), no.3 (1915)
Chamber music 2 str qts (1896, 1913); 4 vn sonatas (1908, 1910, 1913–?14, 1906–?16)
Piano music Three-Page Sonata (1905); Sonata no.1 (1909); Sonata no.2 'Concord' (1915)
Vocal music c185 songs; psalms, unison songs

Ives, Simon (bap. Ware, 20 July 1600; *d* London, 1 July 1662). English composer and instrumentalist. He became organist of Christ Church, Newgate, and a vicar-choral at St Paul's Cathedral in c1630 and a London wait in 1637. He was among the most prominent musicians of his day, as composer and performer. His surviving works (over 100) include music for Shirley's masque *The Triumph of Peace* (1633–4), much consort music and pieces for solo lyra viol. Another composer of the same name (c1626–by 1662) also wrote lyra viol pieces.

Ivogün, Maria (*b* Budapest, 18 Nov 1891; *d* Beatenberg, 2 Oct 1987). Hungarian soprano. She was engaged by Bruno Walter for Munich in 1913 and sang there until 1925, notably as Mimì and Mozart's Constanze and Queen of Night; she then joined the Städtische Oper, Berlin. She was particularly successful (and admired by the composer) as Strauss's Zerbinetta, the role she sang at her Covent Garden début (1924). Her appearances in the USA were confined largely to the concert platform.

Ivrea MS. French MS of the period *c*1365–80, probably from Avignon or from the court of Gaston Fébus. It consists of 64 folios containing 81 compositions, mostly motets and masses but with a few *chansons* and other secular pieces, composed 1320–75; composers include Vitry and Machaut. It was largely written by two scribes in black and red notation. It is in the Biblioteca Capitolare, Ivrea, where it has probably been kept since the 14th century.

J

Jacchini, Giuseppe Maria (*b* Bologna, *c*1663; *d* there, 2 May 1727). Italian cellist and composer. A renowned performer and accompanist, he played at S Petronio, Bologna, 1689–96 and 1701–27, and also became *maestro di cappella* in the Collegio dei Nobili and at S Luigi. He composed trumpet and string sonatas and concertos in the Bolognese tradition of Cazzati and Torelli; some include solo cello passages.

Jachino, Carlo (*b* San Remo, 3 Feb 1887; *d* Naples, 23 Dec 1971). Italian composer. A pupil of Riemann in Leipzig (1910–11), he taught in Italy and Colombia and from 1961 was director of the S Carlo opera house, Naples. His works include two piano concertos, chamber music (three string quartets, 1925–30) and an opera *Giocondo e il suore*, successfully performed at La Scala (1924) and elsewhere.

Jack. The part of a harpsichord action that carries the plectrum past the string. The word is also used for the pivoted vertical lever in a piano action that forces the hammer upward when a key is depressed.

Jackson, Francis (Alan) (*b* Malton, 2 Oct 1917). English organist and composer. He studied with Bairstow whom he succeeded as master of the music at York Minster (1946–82). He is a noted recitalist and an esteemed composer of church and organ music (sonatas, anthems etc) as well as a symphony.

Jackson, William (*b* Exeter, 29 May 1730; *d* there, 5 July 1803). English composer. After working as a teacher and organist in Exeter, he became organist at the cathedral there in 1777. He composed three dramatic works for London, notably the comic opera *The Lord of the Manor* (1780), and was popular for some of his many songs and canzonets, in which he sought to revive a true English melodic tradition. His other works include sacred music and instrumental pieces; his sonatas for harpsichord and violin (*c*1757) were among the first and most adventurous English examples of the genre. He wrote articles and critical essays on music and an autobiography (published 1882), and was also a painter and a friend of Gainsborough and Reynolds.

He is sometimes called 'Jackson of Exeter' to distinguish him from 'Jackson of Masham' (1815–66), a Yorkshire musician who wrote and conducted oratorios and cantatas for the Bradford Festival.

Jacob, Gordon (Percival Septimus) (*b* London, 5 July 1895; *d* Saffron Walden, 8 June 1984). English composer. He studied with Stanford and Howells at the RCM and taught there (1926–66). He composed mostly orchestral and chamber music in a traditional style, and was drawn to wind instruments, for which he wrote concertos. He also wrote several textbooks on instrumentation.

Jacob, Gunther (Wenceslaus) (*b* Kačerov, bap. 30 Sept 1685; *d* 21 March 1734). Bohemian composer. He was a Benedictine monk at St Nicolas, Prague. Renowned for his sacred music, he wrote over 30 masses, four oratorios and *c*100 other sacred works. Most use the late Baroque concerto style, with pre-Classical elements. His music is notable for its expressive treatment of words.

Jacob, Maxime (*b* Bordeaux, 13 Jan 1906; *d* Tarn, 26 Feb 1977). French composer. A pupil of Koechlin and Gédalge and a member of Satie's circle, he took holy orders in 1929 and wrote liturgical music as well as eight string quartets, 15 piano sonatas and songs.

Jacob de Senleches (*fl* 1378–95). French composer. He was presumably from St Luc, near Evreux. Having studied at Bruges, he entered the court of John I of Castile in 1379 and was harpist to Cardinal Pedro de Luna, the future Pope Benedict XIII, in Navarre in 1383. By the early 1390s he had moved to the court of Aragon. His six surviving *chansons* include some of the most difficult and notationally complex examples of the Ars Subtilior.

Jacobi, Frederick (*b* San Francisco, 4 May 1891; *d* New York, 24 Oct 1952). American composer. He studied with Goldmark, Bloch and (in Berlin) Juon. His works cover all genres, sometimes influenced by American Indian music (e.g. *Indian Dances*, 1928) but more by the central Western tradition (e.g. Concertino for piano and strings, 1946).

Jacobin, The [Jakobin]. Opera in three acts by Dvořák to a libretto by M. Červinková-Riegrová (1889, Prague).

Jacobs, René (*b* Ghent, 30 Oct 1946). Belgian countertenor. He was a choirboy at Ghent Cathedral, and later studied in Brussels and The Hague. He has performed with many madrigal ensembles and early music groups, including the Leonhardt Consort, La Petite Bande, Il Complesso Barocco and his own

Collegium Vocale. Principally a singer of Baroque music, he has sung in (and sometimes conducted) performances of operas by Monteverdi, Cavalli and Cesti, and he is also a stylish exponent of the French repertory (notably *airs de cour* and sacred works by Charpentier and Couperin); his rich, full and flexible countertenor has been heard to advantage in Handel and in Gluck's *Orfeo*, which he has recorded with period instruments while singing the title role.

Jacopo da Bologna (*fl* northern Italy, 1340–?1360). Italian composer and theorist. A native of Bologna, he apparently worked at the courts of the Visconti in Milan and della Scala in Verona and may later have been connected with the Aragonese court. The texts of some of his works suggest that he was acquainted with other leading Italian composers, particularly Giovanni de Cascia and Piero, and with the poet Petrarch; and his treatise *L'arte del biscanto misurato* indicates that he may have been a university teacher. At least 34 works (25 two-voice madrigals, seven three-voice madrigals and caccias, a *lauda*-ballata and a motet) can be attributed to him, and their popularity continued into the 15th century. His early madrigals frequently use parallel 5ths and octaves and their tenors often have passages of long-held notes; the shape of the later works is increasingly governed by the texts, by more rational tonal structures and by a closer relationship between the voices, achieved through imitation.

Jacotin (*fl* 1st half of the 16th century). Composer(s) of *chansons* and sacred works (published 1519–56). Although all the pieces attributed to Jacotin (which include over 30 *chansons*, eight motets and four Magnificats) may be the work of a single composer, his identity is still a subject of speculation. The likeliest contender for his identity is Jacotin Le Bel who sang in the papal chapel choir (1516–21) and was a singer and canon in the French royal chapel (1532–55).

Jacovacci [Jacobacci], **Vincenzo** (*b* Rome, 14 Nov 1811; *d* there, 30 March 1881). Italian impresario. Celebrated for his shrewd management of the Apollo Theatre, Rome, he gave the premières of Verdi's *Il trovatore* (1853) and *Un ballo in maschera* (1859).

Jacques, (Thomas) Reginald (*b* Ashby de la Zouch, 13 Jan 1894; *d* Stowmarket, 2 June 1969). English organist and conductor. He studied at Oxford and in 1931 he began conducting the Bach Choir, London. He founded in 1936 the Jacques Orchestra for performances on a chamber orchestral scale. He was best known in the choral repertory, particularly for his deeply felt readings of Bach's Passions.

Jacques de Liège (*b* Liège, *c*1260; *d* there, after 1330). French theorist. He wrote *Speculum musice*, the largest surviving medieval music treatise; it has 521 chapters in seven books. The first five deal with speculative music (following Boethius and others), the sixth with plainchant and the seventh with discant and other mensural music. In this last he attacks 'modern errors' and argues in favour of traditional authority. His book is without parallel as a statement of the theory and practice of the Ars Antiqua.

Jacquet de la Guerre, Elisabeth-Claude (*b c*1666; *d* Paris, 27 June 1729). French composer. She was the daughter of Claude Jacquet (*d* 1702), member of a well-known family of harpsichord makers and organists. An accomplished harpsichordist with a talent for improvisation, she became a protégée of Louis XIV and Mme de Montespan. She wrote music for the Théâtres de la Foire. Her surviving music includes a ballet, an opera *Cephale et Procris* (1694), three collections of cantatas (1708–*c*1715), solo and trio sonatas with violin and bass viol, and two sets of *Pièces de clavecin* (1687, 1707). She was among the first in France to use the sonata and cantata genres, was the only woman to write a *tragédie lyrique* and among the earliest to publish harpsichord collections.

Jacquet of Mantua [Colebault, Jacques] (*b* Vitré, 1483; *d* Mantua, 2 Oct 1559). French composer active in Italy. He was a singer to the Modenese house of Rangoni and in 1525, with Willaert, served at the Este court at Ferrara. The following year he settled in Mantua, where for 30 years he dominated musical life. He was also titular *maestro di cappella* of the Cathedral of SS Peter and Paul there (1534–59). Jacquet was the leading master of sacred polyphony between Josquin and Palestrina and a prolific composer. In his sacred music (which includes over 20 masses and numerous motets) he appears a skilled craftsman alert to new ideas: smoothly arched lines, symmetry of phrase and fluency. His later motets show clearly his stylistic change to pervading imitation as the generating principle.

Jadin, Louis Emmanuel (*b* Versailles, 21 Sept 1768; *d* Montfort-l'Amaury, 11 April 1853). French pianist, teacher and composer. He was a keyboard accompanist at the Théâtre de Monsieur, also composing Italianate musical comedies from the early 1790s and teaching solfège at the Paris Conservatoire (1796–8, 1802–16). His prolific output includes, besides some 35 stage works (notably *Le siège de Thionville*, 1793, an *opéra-vérité*), numerous instrumental sonatas, solo songs and chamber music. His father Jean (*d c*1789) was a Netherlands violinist and composer active in Brussels and Versailles and his brother Hyacinthe (1769–1802) was a pianist.

Jaëll [née Trautmann], **Marie** (*b* Steinseltz, 17 Aug 1846; *d* Paris, 4 Feb 1925). French pianist and teacher. She studied in Stuttgart and Paris. She developed a famous piano method based on economy of hand movement, set out in several books (1895–1927). With her husband, the Austrian pianist Alfred Jaëll (1832–82), she made European concert tours supporting the cause of contemporary music (she was a friend of Liszt and stayed regularly at Weimar).

Jahn, Otto (*b* Kiel, 16 June 1813; *d* Göttingen, 9 Sept 1869). German philologist, archaeologist and musicographer. A leading classical scholar, he is best known for his important biographical study *W.A. Mozart* (Leipzig, 4 vols., 1856–9; rev. 2/1867), remarkable for its scale, lucidity and above all critical method.

Jähns, Friedrich Wilhelm (*b* Berlin, 2 Jan 1809; *d* there, 8 Aug 1888). German scholar and singing teacher. He is best known for his collection and classification of Weber's works and the resulting thematic catalogue with critical comment, *Carl Maria von Weber in seinen Werken* (1871).

Jahreszeiten, Die. *See* SEASONS, THE.

Jakobsleiter, Die [Jacob's Ladder]. Unfinished oratorio by Schoenberg to his own text (1922), completed posthumously by Winfried Zillig.

Jamaican Rumba. Piece for two pianos by Arthur Benjamin (1938), arranged for other instruments, including orchestra.

Jambe de Fer, Philibert (*b* Champlitte, *c*1515; *d* ?Lyons, *c*1566). French composer and writer on music. A Protestant, he moved to Lyons while young and later supervised the music for Charles IX's visit (1564). He is known for his many polyphonic settings of French psalm translations and for his treatise (*Epitome musical*, 1556), the earliest to include lengthy discussion of the violin and the only one that provides insight into the national difference between Italian and French practices.

James, John (*d* London, *c*1745). English composer. Renowned as an organist, he played at St Olave, Southwark, 1730–36, and from 1738 at St George-in-the-East. His organ voluntaries, among the finest of their day, were very popular; he also wrote songs and a funeral anthem.

Jam session. An informal gathering of jazz musicians, playing (normally improvising) for their own pleasure as a spontaneous diversion.

Janáček, Leoš [Leo Eugen] (*b* Hukvaldy, 3 July 1854; *d* Moravská Ostrava, 12 Aug 1928). Czech composer. He was a chorister at the Augustinian 'Queen's' Monastery in Old Brno, where the choirmaster Pavel Křižkovský took a keen interest in his musical education. After completing his basic schooling he trained as a teacher and, except for a period at the Prague Organ School, he spent 1872–9 largely as a schoolteacher and choral conductor in Brno. In 1879 he enrolled at the Leipzig Conservatory, where he developed his interest in composition under the strict and systematic supervision of Leo Grill. After a month in Vienna he returned to Brno in May 1880; there he became engaged to one of his pupils, Zdenka Schulzová, whom he married in July 1881.

In Brno, Janáček took up his former activities, and he also founded and directed an organ school and edited a new musical journal, *Hudební listy*. After composing his first opera, *Šárka*, he immersed himself in collecting and studying Moravian folk music, which bore fruit in a series of orchestral suites and dances and in a one-act opera, *The Beginning of a Romance*. This was favourably received in 1894, but Janáček withdrew it after six performances and set to work on *Jenůfa*.

During the long period of composition of *Jenůfa* (1894–1903), Janáček rethought his approach to opera and to composition in general. He largely abandoned the number opera, integrated folksong firmly into his music and formulated a theory of 'speechmelody', based on the natural rhythms and the rise and fall of the Czech language, which was to influence all his ensuing works and give them a particular colour through their jagged rhythms and lines. *Jenůfa* was soon followed by other operatic ventures, but his

reputation in Brno was as a composer of instrumental and choral music and as director of the Organ School. Outside Moravia he was almost unknown until the Prague première of *Jenůfa* in 1916. The creative upsurge of a man well into his 60s is explained partly by the success of *Jenůfa* in Prague and abroad, partly by his patriotic pride in the newly acquired independence of his country, and perhaps most of all by his passionate, though generally distant, attachment to Kamila Stösslová, the young wife of an antique dealer in Pisek, Bohemia.

Between 1919 and 1925 Janáček composed three of his finest operas, all on subjects with special resonances for him: *Katya Kabanova* with its neglected wife who takes a lover, *The Cunning Little Vixen* with its sympathetic portrayal of animals (and particularly the female fox), and *The Makropoulos Affair* with the 'ageless' woman who fascinates all men. Each was given first in Brno and soon after in Prague. His 70th birthday was marked by a doctorate from the Masaryk University in Brno. Early in 1926 he wrote the Sinfonietta for orchestra, characteristic in its blocks of sound and its forceful repetitions, and later that year his most important choral work, the *Glagolitic Mass*. While performance of his music carried his fame abroad, he started work on his last opera, *From the House of the Dead*, which he did not live to see performed. It received its première in April 1930 in a version prepared by his pupils Břetislav Bakala and Osvald Chlubna.

Janáček's reputation outside Czechoslovakia and German-speaking countries was first made as an instrumental composer. He has since come to be regarded not only as a Czech composer worthy to be ranked with Smetana and Dvořák, but also as one of the most substantial and original opera composers of the 20th century.

Operas Šárka (early, perf. 1925); The Beginning of a Romance (1894); Jenůfa (1904); Osud (1903–7, perf. 1958); The Excursions of Mr Brouček (1920); Katya Kabanova (1921); The Cunning Little Vixen (1924); The Makropoulos Affair (1926); From the House of the Dead (1930)
Vocal music Glagolitic Mass (1926); Diary of One who Disappeared, cycle (1919); cantatas, choruses, sacred pieces
Orchestral music Taras Bulba (1918); Sinfonietta (1926)
Piano music Sonata 1.x.1905 (1905); On the Overgrown Path (1908); In the mists (by 1912)
Instrumental music Str Qt no.1, 'Kreutzer Sonata' (1923); Str Qt no.2, 'Intimate Letters' (1928); Mládí [Youth], fl/pic, ob, cl, b cl, hn, bn (1924)

Janáček Quartet. Czech string quartet, led first by Jiří Trávníček and from 1973 by Bohumil Smejkal. Formed in 1947, it toured widely from 1955, performing from memory with an expressive intensity and technical virtuosity. Since 1969 the players have taught at the Brno Academy.

Janequin [Jannequin], **Clément** (*b* Châtellerault, *c*1485; *d* Paris, 1558). French composer. A 'clerc' in Bordeaux (1505–23) and holder of minor prebends there (1525–30), he served briefly (1531) as master of the choirboys at Auch Cathedral. From 1534 to 1537 he was *maître de chapelle* at Angers Cathedral, where he probably lived until *c*1549, when he settled in Paris. In the 1550s he was *chantre ordinaire du roi* and, during the last years of his life, *compositeur ordinaire* *du roi.* Janequin was much more a specialist than most Renaissance composers: over 250 *chansons* and 150 settings of psalms and *chansons spirituelles* overshadow his two masses and one motet. He and Claudin de Sermisy were the best and most prolific of the many composers who cultivated the Parisian *chanson*. His genius lay in creating witty narrative and programmatic pieces, such as *Le chant des oiseaux, L'alouette, La chasse, Les cris de Paris* and *La bataille*; they are filled with onomatopoeic effects, such as fanfares, birdsong and street cries. His *chansons* are mostly based on short, simple musical formulae creating a mosaic of superimposed fragments. Often the music is harmonically static, depending for effect on rhythmic invention and witty superimposition. In addition to programmatic *chansons* (many written early) he composed shorter, pithier ones.

Janiewicz, Feliks (*b* Vilnius, 1762; *d* Edinburgh, 21 May 1848). Polish violinist and composer. He first played in the Polish royal chapel. In 1785 he went to Vienna, where he met Haydn and Mozart, and then appeared in Italy and later Paris (he played in the Duke of Orleans's chapel). From 1792 he lived in Britain; still a successful virtuoso, he also ran a music publishing and instrument firm (from 1803) and organized musical events. He composed violin concertos and sonatas, piano music and songs.

Janissary music [Turkish music]. An ensemble of Turkish percussion instruments introduced into European military music in the 18th century and later adopted by the orchestra; it also refers to the kind of music composed for such a group, such as certain choruses in Mozart's *Die Entführung aus dem Serail* (1782).

Janitsch, Johann Gottlieb (*b* Swidnica, 19 June 1708; *d* Berlin, *c*1763). Silesian composer. After studying law, he joined the Prussian crown prince's orchestra as a bass viol player in 1736, following him to Berlin after his accession (as Frederick the Great) in 1740. He also directed performances and from the 1730s ran an influential concert series. A much-respected composer, he wrote vocal music for Berlin and elsewhere, and many *galant*-style instrumental works including sinfonias, quartets for wind and strings, trio sonatas and keyboard sonatas.

Janko, Paul von (*b* Tata, 2 June 1856; *d* Constantinople, 17 March 1919). Hungarian musician and engineer. In 1882 he patented a radical design for the piano keyboard, comprising two interlocking 'manuals' with three touch-points for each key lever, so that the keyboard appears to have six tiers of short, narrow keys. This effort to systematize scale fingerings, reduce the octave span and compensate for unequal finger lengths met with enthusiasm in Austria, Germany and the USA, but failed because few were prepared to relearn their repertory with new fingering.

Jannequin, Clément. *See* JANEQUIN, CLÉMENT.

Janotha, (Maria Cecylia) Natalia (*b* Warsaw, 8 June 1856; *d* The Hague, 9 June 1932). Polish pianist and composer. Her teachers included Brahms and Clara Schumann. One of the finest pianists of her time, she was admired as a Chopin interpreter. She wrote *c*400 piano works influenced by Chopin and translated Polish books on him.

Janovka, Tomáš Baltazar (*b* Kutná Hora, bap. 6 Jan 1669; *d* Prague, bur. 13 June 1741). Czech lexicographer and organist of the Týn Church, Prague, for 50 years. His only completed work, *Clavis ad thesaurum magnae artis musicae* (1701), was the first musical dictionary of the Baroque period. Placing special emphasis on the organ and church music, he was primarily concerned with definitions of Latin and Italian terms but also included a few German and French words.

Janowitz, Gundula (*b* Berlin, 2 Aug 1937). German soprano. She appeared under Karajan at the Vienna Staatsoper from 1960 and sang Mozart roles at Salzburg from 1968; she was Ilia at Glyndebourne in 1964 and Donna Anna at Covent Garden in 1976, and also sings Strauss and Wagner. Possessor of a warm, clear voice, she is one of the finest lyric sopranos of her generation.

Jansa, Leopold (*b* Ústí nad Orlicí, 23 March 1795; *d* Vienna, 25 Jan 1875). Bohemian violinist and composer. He was renowned as a concert violinist, teacher and chamber music player, becoming musical director and professor at Vienna University and from 1845 first violinist of Schuppanzigh's quartet. His compositions include chamber and violin works.

Janson, Jean-Baptiste-Aimé Joseph ['l'aîné'] (*b* Valenciennes, *c*1742; *d* Paris, 2 Sept 1803). French cellist and composer. He served the Prince of Conti and later the Duke of Brunswick and was a successful soloist. He became *surintendant de la musique* to Louis XVIII's brother in 1788, and later professor at the new Paris Conservatoire. He wrote mostly cello music, making several technical innovations. His brother Louis-Auguste-Joseph Janson ['le jeune'] (1749–*c*1815) was also a cellist and composer.

Janssen, Werner (*b* New York, 1 June 1899). American conductor and composer. He studied at the New England Conservatory, and with Weingartner, Scherchen and Respighi in Europe. His international reputation was established with performances of Sibelius in Helsinki (1934). His compositions incorporate jazz idioms.

Janue, Antonius (*fl c*1460). Italian composer. He was employed at the ducal palace, Genoa, in 1456, and his 13 extant sacred works form the only substantial collection of mid-15th-century polyphony by an Italian composer.

Japanese music. The traditional music of Japan has been much influenced by foreign cultures, initially of China, Manchuria and Korea, latterly the West. These styles have blended with indigenous repertories and with one another, lending Japanese music a richness and idiosyncratic nature unequalled in Asia. The philosophies of Shintō and Buddhism, especially Zen Buddhism, provide the aesthetic bases of the Japanese approach to the arts.

Japanese music emphasizes monophonic or nonharmonic texture. This has produced other characteristics: the delicate use of microtones, the importance of timbre and the refinement of free rhythm. Musical aesthetics have varied from period to period: in early antiquity purity was of prime importance, in late antiquity refined and courtly taste, in the early Middle Ages symbolism and sobriety, and in the later Middle Ages precision and elegance. Traditional Japanese music falls into three main classes: *gagaku* theatre music, *nō* theatre music, and the repertories for the koto (13-string long zither), shamisen (three-string plucked lute) and shakuhachi (end-blown bamboo flute).

Gagaku ('elegant music') refers to all the traditional court music of Japan, which flourished during the Nara and Heian periods (710–1185). Its tonal systems, scales and modes are derived in theory from ancient Chinese practice but have developed independently in Japan. The main genres are *tōgaku*, based on Chinese and Indian practices, and *komagaku*, based on Korean and Manchurian models. *Gagaku* style is steady, unhurried and graceful. Instrumental techniques require ease and control, without virtuoso display; singing is regarded as similar to natural speech, but intoned. In neither vocal nor instrumental technique is vibrato used and there is little ornament or artifice. The spare style clearly displays the music's outlines. Instruments of the *gagaku* ensembles include the hichiriki (oboe), ryūteki (transverse flute), shō (mouth organ), kakko (barrel drum), shōko (small gong), biwa (lute), sō (long zither) and tsuridaiko (barrel drum).

Nō theatre was established in the late 14th century and early 15th; it is acknowledged to have achieved the highest synthesis of literature, theatre, dance and music among Japanese performing arts and its aesthetic theory is considered the most profound. The principal feature of the music is its rhythm which, measured or free, is built on an eight-beat unit (four-beat units often appear, six- and two-beat occasionally). The sung text is based on phrases of 12 syllables $(7 + 5)$. The ensemble includes nōkan (transverse bamboo flutes), kotsuzumi and ōtsuzumi (hourglass drums) and shimedaiko (shallow barrel drum).

Kabuki, a Japanese theatrical form popular since the Edo period (1603–1868), includes dance numbers and purely dramatic plays. In contrast to *nō*, there is no singing by the actors. *Kabuki* instrumental music is played by onstage or offstage groups. Both use percussion and flutes and perform different genres of shamisen music, including *gidayū* and *nagauta*. Offstage music may give sound effects, set the mood, support stage action or imply unspoken thoughts; onstage music is generally narrative commentary or dance accompaniment.

By the mid-20th century, music in Japan reflected mixtures of three basic types: Japanese traditional music, Western traditional music and international modern trends. In Tokyo, audiences enjoy concerts of music ranging from Bach to Webern, played by Japanese orchestras, while on television young Japanese singers nightly perform Western or Japanese popular songs. On the surface, traditional music seems neglected. But although the number of professional performers and lovers of such music has

decreased, the surviving traditions have been maintained at a high level, partly through the strong musicians' guilds. Such continuing traditions are sustained not only in art music but also in the rich variety of folk traditions in the country.

Japanese Philharmonic Orchestra of Los Angeles. Orchestra formed in 1961, the only Japanese symphony orchestra outside Japan.

Jaques-Dalcroze, Emile (*b* Vienna, 6 July 1865; *d* Geneva, 1 July 1950). Swiss educationist and composer. His early musical studies were under Fauré, Delibes and Bruckner. He is remembered for his influential system of coordinating music and bodily movement ('eurhythmics'), which he developed at the Institut Jaques-Dalcroze at Geneva; it involved the translation of whole compositions into movement.

Járdányi, Pál (*b* Budapest, 30 Jan 1920; *d* there, 29 July 1966). Hungarian composer. He studied with Kodály and Siklós at the Budapest Academy (1938–42), where he later taught (1946–59). His works, in the tradition of Bartók and Kodály, include the 'Vörösmarty' Symphony (1952), two string quartets (1947, 1954) and piano music. He has worked extensively on Hungarian folksong, developing a new system of classification, and written many articles.

Jardin clos, Le. Song cycle (op.106, 1914) by Fauré, settings for voice and piano of eight poems by Charles van Lerberghe.

Jarecki, Henryk (*b* Warsaw, 6 Dec 1846; *d* Lwów, 18 Dec 1918). Polish composer and conductor. He had composition lessons with Moniuszko in Warsaw. Through his efforts the Lwów Opera became the leading opera theatre in Poland (1874–1900). He composed mainly vocal works, including nine operas strongly influenced by Moniuszko.

Jarnach, Philipp (*b* Noisy, 26 July 1892; *d* Bernsen, 17 Dec 1982). German composer of Spanish-French parentage. He studied with Lavignac in Paris and gained help from Debussy and Ravel. In 1914 he began teaching at the Zurich Conservatory, and in 1915 he met Busoni there, becoming a close colleague. He followed Busoni to Berlin in 1921, and completed *Doktor Faust* for its posthumous première (1925). He then taught in Cologne (from 1927) and Hamburg (1949–59). His works, in Busonian neo-classical style, include orchestral pieces (*Musik mit Mozart*, 1935), chamber music (String Quintet, 1920; String Quartet, 1924) and two piano sonatas (1925, 1952).

Jarzębski, Adam (*b* Warka; *d* Warsaw, *c*1648). Polish composer. A musician at the Warsaw royal chapel for most of his career, he is best known for his *Canzoni e concerti* (1627) for two to four instruments with continuo. Important in the development of central European chamber music, they feature Italianate trio-sonata textures with richly ornamented, harmonically based melodies. Jarzębski was a master of variation technique and handled chromaticism and dissonance to lively effect.

Jazz. A music created mainly by black Americans in the early 20th century through an amalgamation of elements drawn from European-American and tribal African musics. Among its distinctive characteristics are the use of improvisation, bent pitches or 'blue notes', swing and polyrhythms.

The earliest form, New Orleans jazz, evolved from the fusion of black folk forms such as ragtime and blues with various popular musics. It emerged in the 1910s and spread to other parts of the USA. The first jazz recordings were made in 1917 by the Original Dixieland Jazz Band. By the end of the decade jazz had attracted a large, mainly white audience throughout the USA.

In the 1920s, Paul Whiteman's jazz-influenced dance music enjoyed enormous success. Chicago became a centre for New Orleans jazz: King Oliver, Jimmie Noone, Earl Hines, Jelly Roll Morton and Louis Armstrong were leading figures. Armstrong's extraordinary talent was quickly recognized and his playing was much imitated. When the illegal cabarets and dance halls in Chicago were swept away by a reformist government in 1928 the New Orleans musicians lost their base; the style declined and was of little importance until the Dixieland Revival movement of the 1940s.

New York became the new focus for jazz, swing became the dominant style and there was an emphasis on big bands and commercial dance music. Fletcher Henderson's band was a model for many others, including those of Duke Ellington and Benny Goodman. The Count Basie Orchestra represented the Kansas City style.

A more serious-minded interpretation of swing was developed by small, informal groups, often put together for a brief club engagement or single recording session. Musicians particularly associated with this style of work were Billie Holiday, Art Tatum, Roy Eldridge, Coleman Hawkins and Lester Young.

The early 1940s saw the creation of the bop style, representing a considerable advance in complexity: the best bop soloists were adept at improvising rapid melodies full of asymmetrical phrases and accent patterns. Leading exponents were Dizzy Gillespie and Charlie Parker.

Beginning in the mid-1940s there was a movement, mainly among white musicians, to adopt more advanced harmonies suggested by European art music, especially that of Stravinsky and Debussy, and to play in lighter, understated fashion. This produced the styles of cool jazz (notably represented by Miles Davis and the Modern Jazz Quartet) and West Coast jazz (the groups of Dave Brubeck and Gerry Mulligan). Hard bop, a vigorous offshoot of bop, was sometimes called East Coast jazz by contrast.

Bop, cool, Dixieland and Mainstream jazz (a modified form of swing) co-existed through the 1950s. But by the early 1960s the decline of bop as an active force and the effects of a contraction of audiences brought about changes. A new era of experiment was begun. The movements of modal jazz, in which Miles Davis was particularly influential, and the avant-garde free jazz sprang up; John Coltrane was an important exponent of both. Later in the decade, Davis again acted as a catalyst for jazz-rock or 'fu-

sion music', which united jazz improvisation with the amplified instruments and rhythmic character of rock.

Jeanne d'Arc au bûcher [Joan of Arc at the Stake]. Dramatic oratorio by Honegger to a text by Claudel (1938, Basle).

Jebe, Halfdan (*b* Trondheim, ?1868; *d* Mexico City, 17 Dec 1937). Norwegian violinist and composer. He studied with Joachim in Berlin and Massenet in Paris, where he was part of a circle to which Strindberg, Munch and Delius were attached; he became a close friend of Delius, with whom he travelled to Norway, Florida and England. In 1901–3 he travelled through Europe and the Far East, then in 1906 left for the Americas, eventually settling in Mexico. There he wrote chamber and orchestral pieces, and an opera and ballets on Mayan subjects.

Jeep, Johannes (*b* Dransfeld, *c*1581; *d* Hanau, 19 Nov 1644). German composer. He held Kapellmeister posts at Weikersheim (1613) and Frankfurt (1637) before moving to Hanau (1640). Four-part hymn and psalm settings form the bulk of his surviving output, but he was best known for the 34 secular songs of his *Studentengärtlein* (1605–14); homophonic strophic songs on the threshold of monody, they are notable for their folklike character and matching of words and music.

Jeffreys, George (*b c*1610; *d* Weldon, 1 July 1685). English composer. He was a member of the Chapel Royal by 1643, when he became organist at Charles I's Oxford court. From *c*1646 he served the Hatton family at Kirby, Northants. An important forerunner of Purcell, he wrote service music, anthems, devotional songs and Latin motets, as well as secular songs and string fantasias (mostly MS), in an unusually intense style, successfully combining English and Italian idioms.

Jehan des Murs. *See* JOHANNES DE MURIS.

Jehannot de l'Escurel (*d* Paris, 23 May 1304). French composer. A young cleric of Notre Dame, Paris, he was hanged for debauchery. His 34 surviving songs, apparently only half of the original collection, appear in a source of the *Roman de Fauvel*. All but one are monophonic. They exploit a variety of forms, show a lyrical spirit and charm and occasionally use word-painting.

Jelić, Vincenz (*b* Rijeka, 1596; *d* Saverne, ?1636). Croatian composer. After an early career in Graz, in 1618 he joined the Saverne court in Alsace as an instrumentalist. His sets of church concertos (1622–8) show influence of the expressive north Italian style and are unusual for their frequent use of tempo indications.

Jelinek, Hanns (*b* Vienna, 5 Dec 1901; *d* there, 27 Jan 1969). Austrian composer. He had lessons with Schoenberg (1918–19) and with Schmidt at the Vienna Academy (1920–22), but largely taught himself by studying the early serial scores of Schoenberg, Berg and Webern. Until he was appointed to the Vienna Musikhochschule in 1958, he earned his living in light music; he used jazz in his Second Symphony for big band and orchestra (1929, rev. 1949) and other works. The last two of his six symphonies, however, are serial compositions, as are his didactic collections *Zwölftonwerk* (pieces for piano and chamber ensembles, 1947–52) and *Zwölftonfibel* (12 vols. for piano, 1953–4).

Jélyotte, Pierre de (*b* Lasseube, 13 April 1713; *d* 12 Oct 1797). French singer and composer. He created many of Rameau's leading *haute-contre* roles at the Paris Opéra (often appearing with Marie Fel), and was guitar teacher to the king and a cellist to Madame de Pompadour. He composed a *comédie-ballet* (1746) and other vocal music.

Jemnitz, Sándor (*b* Budapest, 9 Aug 1890; *d* Balaton-földvár, 8 Aug 1963). Hungarian composer. He studied with Koessler at the Budapest Academy (1906–8), with Reger in Leipzig and with Schoenberg in Berlin. After further study he returned to Budapest, becoming a widely respected critic and promoter of modern music. His works, mostly in the smaller forms, are rooted in Regerian counterpoint, though he was influenced too by the expressionist Schoenberg. His music was well known in western Europe.

Jena Codex. German MS, prepared in the second quarter of the 14th century. It consists of 133 folios (originally 154) written by three scribes, containing 91 Minnesang melodies and many poems. The earliest Minnesang source, from the northern area of Minnesinger activities, it is now in Jena University library.

Jena Symphony. Name given to a symphony by Witt found in 1909 at Jena, long attributed to Beethoven.

Jeney, Zoltán (*b* Szolnok, 4 March 1943). Hungarian composer. He was a pupil of Farkas at the Budapest Academy (1961–6) and Petrassi in Rome (1969). His early works were influenced by Bartók and Webern; later ones reflect Cage's thought.

Jenkins, David (*b* Trecastell, 30 Dec 1848; *d* Aberystwyth, 10 Dec 1915). Welsh composer and conductor. Besides composing hymn tunes and large choral works (*Job, The Storm, The Psalm of Life*), he taught at Aberystwyth, edited *Y Cerddor* (from 1889) and was a choral conductor in Wales and the USA.

Jenkins, John (*b* Maidstone, 1592; *d* Kimberley, 27 Oct 1678). English composer. A lutenist and lyra viol player, he was in London in 1634 and was appointed a court theorbo player in 1660. He lived with several East Anglian families, including Roger North's at Kirtling, Cambs. (1660–66), but was never officially attached to any. He was important for his consort music, notably for viols, which were widely popular among amateur players; his *c*800 surviving pieces are pre-eminent in lyrical invention, structural organization and sonority. He had a command of the English virtuoso 'division' style. He composed both in the traditional many-voice consort style and in the new Italian three-part manner, often writing for treble, two basses and organ or two trebles and bass, moving towards a new violin-influenced phrase structure.

Jenko, Davorin (*b* Dvorje, 9 Nov 1835; *d* Ljubljana, 25 Nov 1914). Slovene composer. Composer and conductor at the National Theatre, Belgrade (1871–1902), he wrote the first Serbian operetta, *The Sorceress* (1882), and the first Serbian orchestral works.

Jenůfa [Jeji pastorkyna: 'Her foster-daughter']. Opera in three acts by Janáček to his own libretto after Pressová (1904, Brno).

Jephtha. Oratorio by Carissimi to a Latin text (*Jephte*) after the Bible (by 1650).

Oratorio by Handel to a biblical text compiled by Morell (1751, London).

Jeppesen, Knud (Christian) (*b* Copenhagen, 15 Aug 1892; *d* Risskov, 14 June 1974). Danish musicologist and composer. He began as an opera conductor, then studied under Carl Nielsen and Thomas Laub. From 1920 he taught at the Royal Danish Conservatory, Copenhagen; later he was professor of musicology at Århus University (1946–57). He was the leading authority on Palestrina and in his many writings influenced the appreciation of Italian Renaissance music. He also worked on Danish music from the Renaissance to Nielsen.

Jeremiah. Leonard Bernstein's Symphony no.1 (1943), setting words from the *Book of Jeremiah* for mezzo-soprano in the last movement.

Jeremiáš, Otakar (*b* Písek, 17 Oct 1892; *d* Prague, 5 March 1962). Czech composer. He studied with Novák (1909–10) and worked in Prague as a conductor, notably of the New Prague SO, which he brought to a high standard. His works include operas (*The Brothers Karamazov*, 1928), much choral music and songs in a post-Smetana style. He wrote books on conducting and instrumentation.

His father Bohuslav (1859–1918) and brother Jaroslav (1889–1919) were also composers; the former conducted, taught and wrote choral music; the latter was an accompanist and critic whose most important work was his oratorio *Mistr Jan Hus* (1915).

Jeritza, Maria (*b* Brno, 6 Oct 1887; *d* Orange, NJ, 10 July 1982). Czech soprano. She sang at the Vienna Staatsoper for two decades from 1912, becoming a celebrated Tosca and Turandot; she introduced Janáček's Jenůfa to Vienna and was Strauss's Ariadne and Empress in *Die Frau ohne Schatten*. At the Met her radiant, secure voice was heard from 1921 and she became the company's most glamorous star. She sang at Covent Garden, 1925–6.

Jerome of Moravia (*fl* 1272–1304). Theorist. A Dominican monk, he wrote an encyclopedic treatise on music in his time, considering it as liberal art and a mathematical science, and discussing chant and polyphony. Much is derivative, from Boethius and others, but two original chapters treat the composition of chants and styles of singing.

Jersild, Jørgen (*b* Copenhagen, 17 Sept 1913). Danish composer. A pupil of Roussel, he taught at the Copenhagen Conservatory (1943–75) and worked as a music critic, while composing in a neo-classical style that developed into a characteristic Danish elegance. His works include choral songs, piano pieces (*Trois pièces en concert*, 1945) and harp music (including a concerto, 1972). He has written pedagogical books.

Jessonda. Opera in three acts by Spohr to a libretto by Gehe after Lemierre (1823, Kassel).

Jeté. In string playing, a bowstroke that bounces or ricochets off the string.

Jeu de cartes. Ballet 'in three deals' by Stravinsky to a scenario by the composer and M. Melaïeff (1937, New York).

Jeunehomme. Title sometimes given to Mozart's Piano Concerto in E♭ K271 after the French pianist who first performed it; nothing is known of her beyond the one name.

Jeunesses Musicales. Movement established in 1940 in Belgium to promote music and related arts among young people. The Fédération Internationale des Jeunesses Musicales (founded 1945) set up an international centre in Yugoslavia in 1969; 39 countries were members by 1987. Music camps, orchestras, concert tours, courses and competitions are arranged.

Jeu-parti (Fr.). A type of debate in poetry and music, used in the 12th and 13th centuries by the troubadours and trouvères. They are usually concerned with courtly love. Some 200 survive, about half with music.

Jeux. Ballet ('poème dansée') by Debussy to a scenario by Nizhinsky (1913, Paris).

Jeux d'eau. Piano piece by Ravel (1901).

Jeux d'enfants. Suite of 12 pieces for piano duet by Bizet (1871), five of which he orchestrated as the *Petite suite*.

Jewels of the Madonna, The [I gioielli della Madonna]. Opera in three acts by Wolf-Ferrari to a libretto by Golisciani and Zangarini (1911, Berlin).

Jewish music. The earliest evidence of Jewish musical culture is found in the Old Testament. Hebrew music was established by King David between 1002 and 970 BC in the Temple of Jerusalem, where Levite musicians were in charge of instrumental and vocal performance. Biblical instruments include the 'asor (a string instrument, presumed to have had ten strings), ḥalil (wind instrument, probably including flutes and reed instruments), ḥatzotzerah (trumpet, probably used to produce rhythmic blasts on a single pitch), kaithros (probably a lyre), kinnor (probably a lyre, played by David for Saul: the most important melodic instrument of ancient Israel), metziltayim (probably pair of cymbals), minnim (probably string instrument), nevel (probably a lyre or a harp), qarna (animal horn played at Nebuchadnezzar's court), tof (probably a round frame drum like the tambourine but without jingles), 'ugav (probably a wind instrument) and the shofar (ram or ibex horn, used for signalling), the only instrument played in modern times. After the destruction of the Temple by the Romans in AD70, instrumental music was banned; vocal forms, particularly psalm singing, survive to the present, however, apparently with little change, and are the oldest living forms of Jewish music. Other vocal forms are cantillation of the prose books of the Bible (including the Pentateuch, Prophets and Ruth) and virtuoso, improvisatory prayers and hymns, orally transmitted by cantor-composers.

Since the Middle Ages, music has been linked with Jewish mysticism, as in the eastern European Hasidic movement, with its distinctive *niggunim*, strongly rhythmical men's songs sung to non-lexical syllables. The Hasidic style influenced east European synagogue music. Precentors developed virtuoso styles, often drawing on local classical idioms (e.g. the *maqām* system in the East diaspora and Baroque variation techniques in the West).

German synagogues began to incorporate choirs, organ and other instrumental music from c1700, drawing on a contemporary non-Jewish repertory of secular pieces, dance and even operatic tunes. The 19th century saw the increasing assimilation of Western styles in synagogue music, as well as the formation of cantoral schools. The first Reform temple, of Israel Jacobson, used German chorales with Hebrew texts. American synagogue music was originally based on European models, though more recently such composers as Ernest Bloch, Frederick Jacobi, Lazare Saminsky and Isadore Freed have contributed pieces in Hebraic idiom.

There is no unified body of Jewish folksong, rather a multitude of folk traditions that reflect conditions in the many scattered communities formed after the destruction of the Second Temple and the dispersion of Jewry around the world. These diverse traditions blend Jewish trends with local forms; for example, Yiddish folksongs of eastern Europe retain something of their medieval German character while drawing on the style of the host culture – Russian, Polish or Romanian. In North Africa and the eastern Mediterranean, songs of the Sephardim, driven from Spain in 1492, retain Spanish elements.

Unlike Islam, which has steadily expanded, influencing musical cultures from Spain to Indonesia, the creation of Israel in 1948 resulted in a sudden compression of Jews from widely dispersed regions. Because of this unusual concentration of cultures, Israel has been the focus of intensive ethnomusicological investigation: of Yeminite traditions (believed to be the oldest), of the Sephardim (with their Spanish *romanzas*, surviving from the 15th century), of the Ethiopian Falasha, of Jewish congregations from India and of the Ashkenazim from German, Slavonic and Baltic states (with their complex history of cultural exchange).

Jew's harp [jaw's harp, trump]. A mouth-resonated instrument consisting of a flexible metal tongue fixed at one end to a surrounding stirrup-shaped frame. The player places the free end of the tongue in front of his mouth cavity and plucks it; the resulting vibration produces a sound of constant pitch, rich in overtones. By regulating the frequency of the air in his mouth cavity the player can amplify selected overtones to produce a wide variety of effects and melodies.

The jew's harp has many vernacular names, including 'trump' and 'tromp'; there is no evidence that it was ever associated with the Jewish people. Most jew's harps made and played in Europe and North America are metal (brass, iron or steel), but in Asia, Indonesia and Oceania they may be made of bamboo, palm wood, bone or ivory.

Ježek, Jaroslav (b Prague, 25 Sept 1906; d New York, 1 Jan 1942). Czech composer. He studied with Jirák (1924–7) and Suk (1927–9) at the Prague Conservatory and worked with the Prague Free Theatre (1928–39), providing songs and dances, growing out of jazz and dance music, for left-wing satirical plays.

When the company disbanded he moved to New York. His concert works include neo-classical orchestral and chamber music, songs and piano pieces.

Jig. A vigorous dance of the British Isles documented since the 15th century. It has many historical and regional variants and in some versions is akin to the hornpipe and the reel. The Baroque GIGUE may derive from it.

Jigg [jig, jygge]. A short burlesque comedy for two to five characters, sung in verse to well-known tunes, with lively dancing; it was popular in England and on the Continent from c1550. In the London theatre it was given with more serious entertainments but in the early 17th century it became increasingly rowdy and was transformed into a more formal song-and-dance act or a prose farce or 'droll', the form in which it persisted until the late 18th century.

Jingles. A cluster of small bells, such as sleigh bells, arranged on a strap or a loop of wire or a wooden handle; it is also applied to the small metal discs in the frame of a tambourine.

Jingling johnny. *See* TURKISH CRESCENT.

Jirák, K(arel) B(oleslav) (*b* Prague, 28 Jan 1891; *d* Chicago, 30 Jan 1972). Czech composer. He studied with Novák (1909–11) and Foerster (1911–12) and took a prominent part in Czech music as critic, conductor and head of radio music (1930–45). In 1947 he left to teach at Roosevelt College, Chicago. His earlier music suggested Mahler and showed an awareness of innovation, but while working on his Third Symphony (1929–38) he developed a closer identification with Czech Romanticism. He wrote six symphonies, nine string quartets, instrumental sonatas, choral music and many songs, as well as several books.

Jitterbug. An informal, unconventional and some-times violent style of dance, generally performed to syncopated music. Originating in New York dance halls (e.g. the Savoy) as an acrobatic, improvised style, it came to be performed in the 1940s and 1950s throughout North America and Europe.

Jive. American urban folk music of the 1940s. The term is also applied to a style of jitterbugging or athletic dancing, and to marijuana. Jive music is a form of blues (later rhythm-and-blues) character-ized by the extrovert style of its principal exponent, the saxophonist and singer Louis Jordan.

Joachim, Joseph (*b* Köpcsény, 28 June 1831; *d* Berlin, 15 Aug 1907). Austro-Hungarian violinist and composer. He studied in Budapest and Vienna, and was influenced by Mendelssohn in Leipzig where he studied composition. He briefly led Liszt's orchestra at Weimar but soon associated himself rather with the Schumanns and Brahms. In spite of personal disputes he was a powerful advocate of Brahms's music, as conductor as well as violinist. From 1868 he taught in Berlin. He founded and led an influential string quartet in 1869. His playing was in the French classical tradition, marked by seriousness and nobil-ity of style. His own music, which includes pieces for violin and orchestra and chamber music, besides cadenzas for other composers' works and arrange-ments, shows no strong creative personality.

Joachim, Otto (*b* Düsseldorf, 13 Oct 1910). Canadian composer of German origin. Trained as a violinist, he fled the Nazis to the Far East (1934–49), then settled in Montreal as a viola player, teacher, instrument builder and composer. His compositions, mostly dat-ing from his Canadian period, include 12-note, alea-tory and electronic pieces.

Joan of Arc. Subject of several works, including operas by Verdi (GIOVANNI D'ARCO) and Tchaikovsky (THE MAID OF ORLEANS) and a dramatic oratorio by Honeg-ger (JEANNE D'ARC AU BÛCHER).

Job. Masque for dancing in nine scenes and an epilogue by Vaughan Williams to a scenario by G. Keynes and G. Raverat after Blake (1931, London).
  Oratorio by Parry (1892, Gloucester).
  Sacred opera in one act by Dallapiccola to his own text (1950, Rome).

Jochum, Eugen (*b* Babnenhausen, 1 Nov 1902; *d* Munich, 26 March 1987). German conductor. He studied in Augsburg and Munich, where he worked at the State Opera. In 1932 he became music director of Berlin Radio and conducted the Berlin PO. At Hamburg Opera (from 1934) he presented music by Hindemith, Stravinsky and Bartók banned else-where by the Nazis. During the war he conducted the Amsterdam Concertgebouw Orchestra, returning in 1949 to Munich as music director of Bavarian Radio and forming its SO. He was admired for his perform-ances of the German symphonic repertory, especially Bruckner. His brothers Otto (1898–1969) and Georg (1909–70) were also conductors.

Johann Ernst, Prince of Weimar (*b* Weimar, 1696; *d* Frankfurt, 1 Aug 1715). German composer. Recog-nized for his musical talent, he studied composition with J.G. Walther and was a violinist. He wrote instrumental music, including violin concertos; Bach, Weimar court organist in 1708–17, based key-board concerto arrangements on four of his works.

Johannes Afflighemensis (*fl* 1100). Theorist. His identity is uncertain; he may come from Lorraine or Flanders, but some scholars think he was an English-man (John Cotton), others south German, and others from Brabant (Afflighem). His *De musica* is a practical didactic treatise of unusual clarity and originality, which avoids speculative discussion; it covers solmi-zation, the modes, intervals, notation and organum, and was the most copied and cited of all medieval treatises.

Johannes de Garlandia (*fl* c1240). Theorist. He taught at Paris University; he may be identifiable with an Englishman of the same name (c1190–c1272) who also taught there. He wrote two treatises: *De plana musica*, on plainchant, deals with classification of music, proportions and the description of inter-vals; *De mensurabili musica* is the first work to give full treatment to rhythm and notation, and it further covers intervals, organum and discant. His systema-tization of the theory of rhythmic modes and Notre Dame polyphony made possible the development of the mensural system and late medieval polyphony.

Johannes de Grocheo (*fl* c1300). French theorist. He worked in Paris in the late 13th century. In his treatise *De musica* he was contemporary and independent in his account of practical music and was the first to discuss secular monophonic forms in any detail.

Johannes de Lymburgia (*fl* 1400–40). Composer, probably from Limbourg (Belgium). After being attached to the collegiate church of St Jean l'Evangéliste, Liège, he moved in 1431 to Vicenza as an instructor of young clerics and in 1436 was appointed canon of Notre Dame, Huy. His compositions, mainly for three voices, include mass movements and pairs and a cycle (probably assembled from these), Magnificats, hymns and *laude*. His style and notation is skilful, emphasizing variety of texture – solo and choral, polyphonic, fauxbourdon and monophonic.

Johannes de Muris (*b* nr. Lisieux, *c*1300; *d c*1350). French theorist. He studied at Paris University and lived mainly in Paris with periods at Evreux, Fontevroult and Mezières-en-Brenne. A mathematician and astronomer, he wrote between three and five works on music theory which had an exceptional distribution and influence. *Ars nove musice* (*c*1321) deals with definitions and acoustical matters, *Musica pratica* (*c*1322) with time and notation; *Musica speculativa* (1323) follows Boethius and considers consonance and proportion mathematically. Other books ascribed to him deal with mensural practice and counterpoint.

Johannes de Quadris (*fl* mid-15th century). Composer. He probably worked in the Veneto, *c*1430–40. His surviving music, which includes Magnificats and Lamentations, reveals such a stylistic diversity that until recently it was thought to have been composed by two people of the same name. But, as a whole, his output developed in a way typical of the 15th century, from a northern late Gothic idiom to the expressive, tuneful simplicity of Italian music.

Johannes de Sarto (*fl* 1390–1440). Composer and priest. Having been associated with St Jean l'Evangéliste, Liège, he was probably a singer in the court chapel of Albert II, King of Germany, at the time of the latter's death in 1439. Three introits and three antiphons are ascribed to him. Two of the introits use fauxbourdon technique and the antiphons use imitation extensively.

Johansen, David Monrad (*b* Vefsn, 8 Nov 1888; *d* Sandvika, 20 Feb 1974). Norwegian composer. He studied at the Oslo Conservatory, with Humperdinck and Kahn in Berlin (1915–16) and with Grabner in Leipzig (1933–5), and was a music critic. He is perhaps the most outstanding of those Norwegian composers who have continued the nationalist tradition. His style is marked by broad lines and vigorous harmony that often uses archaisms. His modest output includes choral and vocal music, orchestral pieces (*Pan*, 1939; Symphonic Variations, 1946; Piano Concerto, 1954), a string quartet (1969) and piano pieces.

Johanson, Sven-Eric (Emanuel) (*b* Västervik, 10 Dec 1919). Swedish composer. He was a pupil of Rosenberg. Working as a church musician, he has composed much choral music but also operas, symphonies, chamber pieces and songs in a serial, contrapuntal style.

John [João] IV, King of Portugal (*b* Vila Vicosa, 19 March 1604; *d* Lisbon, 6 Nov 1656). Collector, writer and composer. He reigned from 1640 and was heir to the music-loving dukes of Bragança whose music library he expanded into one of the most sumptuous collections in history. It was lost in the 1755 earthquake but its recorded contents reveal a devotion to the *stile antico*, as do the king's two surviving four-part motets.

As a writer, he produced two brief works: a defence of modern music and a response to criticisms of a Palestrina mass.

John F. Kennedy Center. *See* KENNEDY CENTER FOR THE PERFORMING ARTS.

Johnny Strikes Up. *See* JONNY SPIELT AUF.

Johnson, Edward (*fl* 1572–1601). English composer. He served the Kitson family of Hengrave Hall, Suffolk (1572–5), and took the Cambridge MusB in 1594. A contributor to *The Triumphes of Oriana* (1601), he was highly rated in his day though only a few vocal and instrumental pieces by him survive.

Johnson, John (*fl* 1579–94). English composer, father of Robert Johnson (ii). He served as a court lutenist (1579–94). His lute music (all MS) includes pavans, galliards and popular tunes in contrapuntal style; he also developed the lute duet to a high technical standard.

Johnson, Robert (i) (*b* Duns, *c*1500; *d c*1560). Scottish composer. According to the St Andrews Psalter he was a priest who, accused of heresy, fled to England. He was in York *c*1530, returned to Scotland and then left finally for England *c*1535. He wrote Latin sacred music, characterized by imitation, chordal music to English texts, service music, secular English songs and instrumental consorts.

Johnson, Robert (ii) (*b* ?London, *c*1583; *d* there, by 26 Nov 1633). English composer, son of John Johnson. He served the Lord Chamberlain (1596–1603) and was a court lutenist from 1604 until his death. An able and respected composer, he wrote songs for plays (including some by Shakespeare) in an up-to-date, often declamatory style, masque music, well-developed dances for lute and a few sacred vocal and other instrumental works.

Johnson, Robert Sherlaw (*b* Sunderland, 21 May 1932). English composer and pianist. He studied at Durham University (1950–53), at the RAM (1953–7) and with Boulanger and Messiaen in Paris (1957–8); he has taught at the universities of York (1965–70) and Oxford. His works, reflecting his admiration for Messiaen, Varèse and Boulez, include Catholic liturgical music, three piano sonatas (1963, 1967, 1976) and the opera *The Lambton Worm* (1977).

Johnson, Tom (*b* Greeley, CO, 18 Nov 1939). American composer. He studied at Yale and with Feldman, and was an influential critic on the *Village Voice* (1971–83). His works include *The Four-note Opera* (1972) and *Nine Bells* (1979).

Johnston, Ben(jamin Burwell jr) (*b* Macon, GA, 15 March 1926). American composer. He studied with Milhaud (1951–2) and Cage (1959–60), but most importantly with Partch (1950–51), whose interest in just intonation and microtones he shares. He is regarded as a foremost microtonal composer; his works cover all genres and include a series of string quartets and much music for dance.

Johnstone, Maurice (*b* Manchester, 28 July 1900;

d Harpenden, 3 April 1976). English composer. He studied in Manchester and at the RCM and worked as a freelance journalist before becoming Beecham's secretary (1933–5). He then joined the BBC, where he was head of music, 1953–60. His works, conservative in style and folksong-influenced, include *A Welsh Rhapsody* (1932) and *Tarn Hows: a Cumbrian Rhapsody* (1949), both for orchestra.

Joke. Name sometimes given to Haydn's String Quartet in E♭ op.33 no.2 (1781), on account of the ending of the finale, where Haydn's teases the listener's expectation with rests and recurring phrases. Mozart wrote a parodistic *Musical Joke* (*Ein musikalischer Spass* K522, 1787) for strings and horns.

Jolas, Betsy (*b* Paris, 5 Aug 1926). French composer. Brought up in a literary family, she studied at Bennington College, New York (1945–6), and at the Paris Conservatoire with Messiaen and Milhaud (1948–55); since 1971 she has been Messiaen's deputy at the Conservatoire. She commands a lyrical style close to Boulez and has written mostly for small ensembles of voices and/or instruments. In her *Quatuor II* (1964) she replaced the leader of a string quartet with a coloratura soprano.

Jolie fille de Perth, La. *See* FAIR MAID OF PERTH, THE.

Jolivet, André (*b* Paris, 8 Aug 1905; *d* there, 20 Dec 1974). French composer. He studied with Le Flem (1928–33) and Varèse (1930–33), who influenced his development of a style of fluid, incantatory melody supported by rich harmony and powerful rhythmic impulse; this style seemed to restore the primitive magical attributes of music (*Mana* for piano, 1935; *Cinq incantations* for flute, 1936; *Danse incantatoire* for orchestra, 1936; *Cinq danses rituelles* for orchestra or piano, 1939). Messiaen was impressed by *Mana* and joined him in forming the Jeune France group (1936); they shared a taste for the exotic and for sumptuous instrumentation. During World War II his music became less esoteric, nearer to Bartók. He was musical director of the Comédie Française (1943–59), for which he wrote and conducted numerous incidental scores. His other works include ballets, three symphonies, highly virtuoso concertos (for piano, violin, cello, harp, trumpet, percussion and ondes martenot), choral works, songs and instrumental pieces.

Jommelli, Nicolò (*b* Aversa, 10 Sept 1714; *d* Naples, 25 Aug 1774). Italian composer. A pupil of Feo and others in Naples (he was also influenced by Hasse), he presented his first comic opera there in 1737 and his first serious opera in Rome in 1740. Moving to Bologna in 1741, he became a pupil and friend of Padre Martini. In 1743–7 he was musical director of the Ospedale degli Incurabili, Venice, and in 1749 he became *maestro coadiutore* to the papal chapel in Rome; he wrote sacred music for both institutions, but still concentrated on opera, achieving international fame. After writing two operas for the Stuttgart court, he became its Ober-Kapellmeister in 1754. His serious operas there used the court's fine musicians, dancers and designers, often following the favoured French taste; his last one for Stuttgart was *Fetonte* (1768). He also composed serenatas, pastorales and comic operas. After he left in

1769, he composed for the Lisbon court and had revisions of his works staged there. Among his later works for Italy was *Armida abbandonata* (1770, Naples).

Jommelli wrote *c*100 stage works. In his *c*60 serious operas (many to Metastasio texts) he was a pioneer in modifying the singer-dominated Italian style. Increasingly, he omitted items superfluous to the drama and added ensembles and more choruses and accompanied recitatives. He gave the orchestra (notably the wind) a greater role and used more text-painting. With the Stuttgart resources he could develop these principles further, writing prologues, orchestral pieces and ballets. He also adopted more flexible forms, especially in arias and finales. Among his other works are Italian cantatas (secular and sacred), oratorios, many Latin sacred works and several instrumental pieces.

Dramatic music Demofoonte (3 settings: 1743, 1753, 1764); Didone abbandonata (3 settings: 1747, 1749, 1763); Enea nel Lazio (1766); Fetonte (2 settings: 1753, 1768); Armida abbandonata (1770); *c*55 other serious operas; *c*21 comic operas, intermezzi, pastorales; *c*2 serenatas; contributions to pasticcios
Secular vocal music solo cantatas, duet cantatas
Sacred music *c*15 oratorios and sacred cantatas; 1 Passion; 18 masses; many graduals, psalms, motets
Instrumental music 4 concs.; sonatas and other chamber works; kbd pieces

Jones, Daniel (Jenkyn) (*b* Pembroke, 7 Dec 1912). Welsh composer. He studied at the RAM (1935–8) and has written ten symphonies in an essentially tonal but vigorously chromatic style. Other works include operas, music for Dylan Thomas's *Under Milk Wood* (1954; poet and composer were friends from boyhood), choral and chamber music.

Jones, Edward (*b* Llandderfel, bap. 29 March 1752; *d* London, 18 April 1824). Welsh harper and composer. He was a successful player and teacher in London from the 1770s and *c*1788 became harper to the Prince of Wales. He published Welsh and other national melodies and encouraged competitive eisteddfods. His compositions include sonatas and other works for harp or keyboard, and songs.

Jones, Dame Gwyneth (*b* Pontewynydd, 7 Nov 1936). She studied at the RCM and in Zurich and sang Sieglinde at Covent Garden in 1965 and for her Bayreuth (1966) and Met (1972) débuts. Other Wagner roles have included Isolde, Eva and Brünhilde, which she sang in the Bayreuth centenary *Ring* of 1976. Her powerfully emotional, vibrant singing is also well suited to Strauss and Puccini (notably as Turandot).

Jones, John (*b* ?London, 1728; *d* there, 17 Feb 1796). English composer. He was organist in London at the Middle Temple, the Charterhouse and St Paul's Cathedral. His works include a book of psalm chants, songs and three vigorous, dramatic collections of harpsichord music (1754–61).

Jones, Philip (*b* Bath, 12 March 1928). English trumpeter. He studied under Hall at the RCM and has played with many London orchestras as well as freelance. He is noted for the Philip Jones Brass Ensemble, active 1951–87, a group of flexible size which won a high reputation for its playing of early music and new works, some specially written.

Jones, Richard (*b* late 17th century; *d* London, 20 Jan 1744). English violinist and composer. He was leader of the Drury Lane Theatre orchestra in London from *c*1730. He composed keyboard suites (1744) and two sets of violin sonatas, using an italianate but original style.

Jones, Robert (*fl* 1597–1615). English composer. He graduated BMus at Oxford in 1597 and in 1615 was living at Blackfriars, London. He published five books of ayres for voice and lute (1600–10) and one of madrigals (1607) and contributed to *The Triumphes of Oriana* (1601). Of another Robert Jones (early 16th century), a singer in the royal household, two sacred pieces and a song survive.

Jones, (James) Sidney (*b* London, 17 June 1861; *d* there, 29 Jan 1946). English composer. A theatre musician and conductor, he wrote musical comedies and operettas (notably *A Gaiety Girl*, 1893, and *The Geisha*, 1896, the most popular of all British operettas). He retired after writing the musical play *The Happy Day* (1916).

Jong, Marinus de (*b* Oosterhout, 14 Aug 1891). Belgian pianist and composer. He studied at the Antwerp Conservatory, returning there to teach in 1931. His early career was as a piano virtuoso and he then turned to composition, using Gregorian melodies harmonized in modern style. His works include three operas, ballets, three symphonies, many concertos and much chamber music.

Jongen, Joseph (Marie Alphonse Nicolas) (*b* Liège, 14 Dec 1873; *d* Sart-lez-Spa, 12 July 1953). Belgian composer. He studied at the Liège Conservatory, then spent 1898–1902 acquainting himself with music in Germany, Italy and France. Back in Belgium he taught at the conservatories of Liège (from 1902) and Brussels (1920–39) and composed in a Franckian style, though influenced by Debussy and Ravel from the early 1920s. One of the best-known Belgian composers of the early 20th century, he wrote mostly for orchestral or chamber forces.

His brother Léon (1884–1969) succeeded him as director of the Brussels Conservatory (1939–49) and wrote operas, orchestral, choral and piano music.

Jongleur (Fr.). A medieval entertainer, sometimes a minstrel. The term (also *joglëor, janglëor, juggler*) covers a range of instrumentalists and story-tellers. *See* MINSTREL; GUILDS.

Jongleur de Notre Dame, Le. Opera in three acts by Massenet to a libretto by M. Léna after Anatole France (after a medieval miracle play) (1902, Monte Carlo).

Masque in one act by Peter Maxwell Davies to his own libretto (1978, Kirkwall).

Jonny spielt auf [Johnny strikes up]. Opera in two parts (11 scenes) by Krenek to his own libretto (1927, Leipzig).

Joplin, Scott (*b* nr Marshall, TX, or Shreveport, LA, 24 Nov 1868; *d* New York, 1 April 1917). American composer and pianist. Known in the late 19th century as the 'King of Ragtime', Joplin became famous after the publication in 1899 of his *Maple Leaf Rag*. He published many rags (some collaborative), 1900–06, including *The Entertainer* (1902), and later produced more extended compositions, *The Ragtime Dance* (1902) and the operas *A Guest of Honor* (1903) and *Treemonisha* (1911). The latter was not successfully performed in Joplin's lifetime, but was revived in 1972 (Joplin was awarded a posthumous Pulitzer Prize in 1976).

Jordan, Sverre (*b* Oslo, 25 May 1889; *d* Bergen, 10 Jan 1972). Norwegian composer. He took a leading musical role in Bergen as a critic and conductor and composed diatonic orchestral and chamber works in standard forms, and songs.

Joseph. Oratorio by Handel to a biblical text compiled by J. Miller (1744, London); its full title is *Joseph and his Brethren*.

Opera in three acts by Méhul to a libretto by A. Duval (1807, Paris).

Josephs, Wilfred (*b* Newcastle upon Tyne, 24 July 1927). English composer. He studied with Nieman at the Guildhall School (1954–6) and Deutsch in Paris (1958–9). His large, varied output is fundamentally tonal, strongly willed and often in standard forms (nine symphonies, concertos, much chamber music). His largest works include the Jewish Requiem (1963), the oratorio *Mortales* (1969) and the opera *Rebecca* (1983).

Josephslegende. Ballet in one act by Richard Strauss to a scenario by H. Kesler and Hofmannsthal (1914, Paris).

Joshua. Oratorio by Handel to a text probably by Morell (1748, London).

Josquin Desprez [Près, Josquin des] (*b* c1440; *d* Condé-sur-l'Escaut, 27 Aug 1521). Northern French composer. Perhaps a native of the Vermandois region of Picardy, he was a singer at Milan Cathedral in 1459, remaining there until December 1472. By July 1474 he was one of the 'cantori di capella' in the chapel of Galeazzo Maria Sforza. Between 1476 and 1504 he passed into the service of Cardinal Ascanio Sforza, whom he probably accompanied in Rome in 1484. His name first appears among the papal chapel choir in 1486 and recurs sporadically; he had left the choir by 1501. In this Italian period Josquin reached artistic maturity.

He then went to France (he may also have done so while at the papal chapel) and probably served Louis XII's court. Although he may have had connections with the Ferrara court (through the Sforzas) in the 1480s and 1490s, no formal relationship with the court is known before 1503 when, for a year, he was *maestro di cappella* there and the highest-paid singer in the chapel's history. There he probably wrote primarily masses and motets. An outbreak of plague in 1503 forced the court to leave Ferrara (Josquin's place was taken by Obrecht, who fell victim in 1505). He was in the north again, at Notre Dame at Condé, in 1504; he may have been connected with Margaret of Austria's court, 1508–11. He died in 1521. Several portraits survive, one attributed to Leonardo da Vinci.

Josquin's works gradually became known throughout western Europe and were regarded as models by many composers and theorists. Petrucci's three books of his masses (1502–14) reflect contemporary esteem, as does Attaingnant's collection of his *chan-*

sons (1550). Several laments were written on his death (including Gombert's elegy *Musae Jovis*), and as late as 1554 Jacquet of Mantua paid him tribute in a motet. He was praised by 16th-century literary figures (including Castiglione and Rabelais) and was Luther's favourite composer.

Josquin was the greatest composer of the high Renaissance, the most varied in invention and the most profound in expression. Much of his music cannot be dated. Generally, however, his first period (up to *c*1485) is characterized by abstract, melismatic counterpoint in the manner of Ockeghem and by tenuous relationships between words and music. The middle period (to *c*1505) saw the development and perfection of the technique of pervasive imitation based on word-generated motifs. This style has been seen as a synthesis of two traditions: the northern polyphony of Dufay, Busnois and Ockeghem, in which he presumably had his earliest training, and the more chordal, harmonically orientated practice of Italy. In the final period the relationship between word and note becomes even closer and there is increasing emphasis on declamation and rhetorical expression within a style of the utmost economy.

His many motets span all three periods. One of the earliest, the four-part *Victimae paschali laudes* (1502), exemplifies his early style, with its dense texture, lack of imitation, patches of stagnant rhythm and rudimentary treatment of dissonance. Greater maturity is shown in *Planxit autem David*, in which homophonic and freely imitative passages alternate, and in *Absalon, fili mi*, with its flexible combination of textures. His later motets, such as *In principio erat verbum*, combine motivic intensity and melodic succinctness with formal clarity; they are either freely composed, four-part settings of biblical texts, or large-scale *cantus firmus* pieces. Transparent textures and duet writing are common.

Josquin's 18 complete masses combine elements of *cantus firmus*, parody and paraphrase techniques. One of the earliest, *L'ami Baudichon*, is a *cantus firmus* mass on a simple dance formula; the simplicity of melody and rhythm and the clarity of harmony and texture recall the Burgundian style of the 1450s and 1460s. *Fortuna desperata*, on the other hand, is an early example of parody. Canonic writing and ostinato figures are features. His last great masses, notably the *Missa de beata virgine* and the *Missa 'Pange lingua'*, were preceded by works in which every resource is deployed with bravura.

Josquin's secular music comprises three settings of Italian texts and numerous *chansons*. One of the earliest, *Cela sans plus*, typifies his observance of the *formes fixes* and the influences of the Burgundian styles of Busnois and Ockeghem. Later works, such as *Mille regretz*, are less canonic, the clear articulation of lines and points of imitation achieved by a carefully balanced hierarchy of cadences. Some, like *Si j'ay perdu mon ami*, look forward to the popular 'Parisian' *chanson* of Janequin.

Sacred vocal music 18 masses; 6 mass sections; 112 motets
Secular vocal music *c*70 chansons; settings of Spanish, German and Italian texts; many doubtful works

Josten, Werner (Erich) (*b* Elberfeld, 12 June 1885;

d New York, 6 Feb 1963). American composer of German origin. He studied with Siegel in Munich and Jaques-Dalcroze in Geneva, then moved to the USA in 1920 and worked as a teacher at Smith College (1923–49), conductor and composer. His works, mostly from the 1920s and 1930s, have connections with the medieval and exotic (*Jungle* for orchestra, 1928).

Jota. A Spanish song and dance, originating from Aragon but common in many parts of Spain. It is in rapid triple time with a short upbeat and four-bar phrases (they cadence alternately on dominant and tonic). It is known as early as the 17th century, and was used in art music by Glinka and Liszt as well as by Spanish composers.

Joteyko, Tadeusz (*b* Poczujki, 1 April 1872; *d* Cieszyn, 20 Aug 1932). Polish composer. A pupil of Gaevert in Brussels and Noskowski in Warsaw, he wrote operas and orchestral pieces in a lyrical, simple style showing elements of folk music, and craftsmanlike choral works. He taught and conducted in Warsaw.

Joubert, John (Pierre Herman) (*b* Cape Town, 20 March 1927). British composer of South African origin. He studied at the RAM (1946–50) and has taught at the universities of Hull (1950–62) and Birmingham (1962–87). His works, of traditional integrity in a style growing out of Britten and Walton, include operas (*Under Western Eyes*, 1969), orchestral and chamber works, and much sacred and secular choral music.

Jovernardi, Bartolomé (*b* Rome, *c*1600; *d* Madrid, 22 July 1668). Italian harpist and theorist. He was employed at the Spanish royal chapel from 1633. He invented a cross-strung chromatic harp and a harpsichord allegedly capable of *crescendo*, but is principally known for his bilingual *Tratado de la mussica* (1634) on the classification of instruments.

Joyce, Eileen (*b* Zeehan, 21 Nov 1912). Australian pianist. She studied in Leipzig, attending Schnabel's master classes. She later settled in London and made a reputation for her spirited playing of the Romantic repertory, later moving on to 20th-century music and playing the harpsichord.

Jozzi, Giuseppe (*b* ?Rome, *c*1710; *d* ?Amsterdam, *c*1770 or earlier). Italian singer, harpsichordist and composer. A castrato soprano, he sang in Italy until 1745, then in London and later Stuttgart. He composed harpsichord sonatas in a *galant* style like Domenico Alberti's, and is chiefly remembered for trying to pass off some of Alberti's sonatas as his own.

Juanas, Antonio (*b* ?Spain; *d* there, after 1819). Composer. He was *maestro de capilla* of Mexico City Cathedral, *c*1790–1816, and later moved to Spain. Among the most prolific of colonial composers, he wrote over 200 Latin sacred works.

Jubilate. Psalm xcix in the Latin psalter, Psalm c in the Authorized Version and Prayer Book. In the Anglican church it is used as an alternative to the *Benedictus* in the service of Matins. Festal settings include one by Purcell.

Judas Maccabaeus. Oratorio by Handel to a text by Morell (1747, London).

Judenkünig, Hans (*b* Schwäbisch Gmünd, *c*1450; *d* Vienna, March 1526). German lutenist. He was a member of a Viennese fraternal order from 1518 to 1526, becoming the leading Viennese lute composer of his day. His two lutebooks (*c*1515–19, 1523), with music in German tablature, were important manuals of self-instruction.

Judith. Oratorio by Parry (1888, Birmingham).

Oratorio by Arne to a text by Bickerstaffe (1761, London).

Biblical opera in three acts by Honegger to a libretto by R. Morax (1926, Monte Carlo).

Juditha triumphans. Oratorio by Vivaldi to a libretto by Cassetti (1716, Venice).

Jug band. An instrumental ensemble developed among black Americans in the 1920s and 1930s. The jug player purses his lips over the narrow opening of the jug, usually an earthenware demijohn, and blows short bursts that are amplified by the jug. The band includes strings and a melody instrument such as a harmonica or kazoo.

Juilliard Quartet. American string quartet. It was established in 1946 by William Schuman, then president of the Juilliard School of Music, and in 1962 was appointed quartet-in-residence at the Library of Congress, Washington, DC. Led by Robert Mann, it has given several Beethoven cycles and is also known for its performances of modern American music and that of the Second Viennese School.

Juilliard School. Conservatory in New York. It was formed in 1946 as the Juilliard School of Music from the Institute of Musical Art (founded 1905) and the Juilliard Graduate School (opened 1924). In 1968 it moved to the Lincoln Center and was renamed. Its departments include the Dance Division (1951), Theater Center (1968) and American Opera Center (1970).

Juive, La [The Jewess]. Opera in five acts by Halévy to a libretto by Scribe (1835, Paris).

Jukebox. A coin-operated gramophone that originated in American amusement arcades at the turn of the century; they became widespread in Europe and the USA in the 1930s and were an important medium for disseminating popular music.

Julien. Opera in a prologue and four acts by Charpentier to his own libretto (1913, Paris), a sequel to *Louise*.

Julietta, or The Key of Dreams. Opera in three acts by Martinů to his own libretto after Georges Neveux (1938, Prague).

Julius Caesar. *See* GIULIO CESARE.

Jullien, Gilles (*b c*1651; *d* Chartres, 14 Sept 1703). French composer. He was organist of Chartres Cathedral from 1667. His surviving music is in the *Premier livre d'orgue* (1690), a collection of 80 pieces grouped into eight sets, in each church mode. The preludes are solidly contrapuntal; some pieces carry directions suggesting mood and tempo, while others, notably those in five parts, have registration schemes.

Jullien, Louis (George Maurice Adolphe Roch Albert Abel Antonio Alexandre Noé Jean Lucien Daniel Eugène Joseph-le-brun Joseph-Barême Thomas Thomas Thomas-Thomas Pierre Arbon Pierre-Maurel Barthélemi Artus Alphonse Bertrand Dieudonné Emanuel Josué Vincent Luc Michel Jules-de-la-plane Jules-Bazin Julio César) (*b* Sisteron, 23 April 1812; *d* Paris, 14 March 1860). French conductor and composer. He served in the army and attended the Paris Conservatoire but found his metier giving lively entertainments of dance music, first in Paris (1836–8), then in London (1840–58), where he conducted some 24 promenade concert seasons; he also toured the provinces, the USA and the Netherlands, his showmanship ensuring popular success. Though his programmes offered a mixed fare of quadrilles (notably the celebrated *British Army Quadrilles* for orchestra and four military bands, 1846), instrumental solos, galops, waltzes, overtures and favourite symphonic movements, they sometimes included a complete Beethoven or Mendelssohn symphony. His role in presenting classical music to the public was considerable.

Jumping Frog of Calaveras County, The. Opera in one act by Lukas Foss to a libretto by J. Karsavina after Twain (1950, Bloomington, Indiana).

Junge Lord, Der. Opera in two acts by Henze to a libretto by I. Bachmann after Hauff (1965, Berlin).

Juon, Paul (*b* Moscow, 6 March 1872; *d* Vevey, 21 Aug 1940). German composer of Russian origin. He studied with Arensky and Taneyev at the Moscow Conservatory and with Bargiel at the Musikhochschule in Berlin (1894–5), where he settled in 1897, teaching at the Hochschule (1906–34). His creative allegiances were to Tchaikovsky, Dvořák and Brahms: his output includes three violin concertos, other orchestral works, three string quartets, much chamber music, sonatas and piano pieces.

Jupiter Symphony. Nickname of Mozart's Symphony no.41 in C K551 (1788); the nickname is believed to have been coined by Salomon in the early 19th century.

Jürgens, Jürgen (*b* Frankfurt, 5 Oct 1925). German conductor. He studied in Frankfurt and Freiburg and in 1955 became director of the Hamburg Monteverdi Choir and in 1966 Hamburg University. He has given many concerts in the USA and Europe, with a repertory ranging from Ockeghem to Henze. Monteverdi's Vespers and *Orfeo* are among the choir's recordings.

Jürgenson, Pyotr Ivanovich (*b* Tallinn, 17 July 1836; *d* Moscow, 2 Jan 1904). Russian music publisher. He established his business in Moscow in 1861, soon the largest in Russia; besides Tchaikovsky the catalogue included other Russian composers and Beethoven, Chopin and Wagner.

Jurinac, Sena (*b* Travnik, 24 Oct 1921). Austrian soprano of Yugoslav birth. After study at Zagreb she sang Cherubino at the Vienna Staatsoper in 1945. She appeared at Salzburg and Covent Garden from 1947 and at Glyndebourne from 1949. Her rich, even voice was heard to best advantage in Mozart, notably Ilia and Fiordiligi, and she was also distinguished as Beethoven's Leonore, the Marschallin and Desdemona.

Jurjāns, Andrejs (*b* Ērgļi, 30 Sept 1856; *d* Riga, 28 Sept 1922). Latvian composer. He was a pupil of

Rimsky-Korsakov in St Petersburg. One of the founders of Latvian classical music, he particularly developed the choral song, cantata and orchestral piece using folk music. He undertook pioneering research into Latvian folksong.

Just, Johann August (*b* Gröningen, *c*1750; *d* ?The Hague, Dec 1791). German keyboard player and composer. A music master at the Prince of Orange's court, he wrote pedagogical keyboard sonatas and divertimentos etc (some with violin), specifying the harpsichord rather than the piano. His other works include Singspiels, songs and chamber and orchestral music.

Just intonation. Term used for a manner of tuning in performance so that intervals are tuned so pure that they do not beat. String players normally try to play in this manner (when they are not accompanied by a keyboard). The term is sometimes used for a keyboard tuning in which some 5ths are tuned very small in order that the others and most of the 3rds should be pure. One consequence of just intonation is that there are two different sizes of major 2nd, represented by the frequency ratios 9:8 and 10:9. Various elaborate keyboard instruments have been constructed, with alternative pitches for certain notes, to enable music to be played in just intonation; more recently, computer systems have been devised to produce just intonation from a normal keyboard.

Juzeliūnas, Julius (*b* Čepolė Žeimelis region, 20 Feb 1916). Lithuanian composer. He studied in Kaunas and Leningrad and in 1952 began teaching at the Vilnius Conservatory. His earlier music is Romantic, but later works fuse national and newer elements; his output includes orchestral, vocal and chamber works and music for the stage.

K

K [KV]. Abbreviation for Köchel (Köchel-Verzeichnis), the chronological thematic catalogue of Mozart's works prepared by Ludwig von Köchel (1862, 6/1964). Köchel's original numberings have often been changed in the light of discoveries about the chronology of different works; where the more recent number differs from the better-known original one, both are commonly given, usually in the form 191/186*e* (as in this dictionary) or 191(186*e*). Sometimes K is printed with a superscript number (K^3) to distinguish the edition cited. The letter K is also sometimes used for numbers in R. Kirkpatrick's catalogue of D. Scarlatti's harpsichord sonatas, though Kk is often preferred to avoid confusion with Köchel numbers.

Kabalevsky, Dmitry Borisovich (*b* St Petersburg, 30 Dec 1904; *d* Moscow, 27 Feb 1987). Russian composer. He had a liberal education, wrote poetry and painted and showed promise as a pianist. The family moved to Moscow in 1918, where he studied the piano with Selyanov and from 1925 at the Moscow Conservatory with Catoire and Myaskovsky, the latter a formative influence; in 1932 he returned to teach at the conservatory (full professor from 1939). He was also involved in organizational and union activities, and worked in the music publishing house. The period 1932–41 was prolific, with much dramatic music (including the first version of his opera *Colas Breugnon*) and the first three symphonies. In the war years he turned to topical works on heroic patriotism. After the party decree of 1948 he worked towards a more lyrical idiom, as seen in his concertos of the ensuing years; later he worked in operetta and topical cantatas. Kabalevsky occupied an important role in Soviet music, as writer, spokesman on cultural policy, teacher and administrator as well as composer.

Operas Colas Breugnon (1938); The Taras Family (1947); Nikita Vershinin (1955); Spring Sings, operetta (1957); The Sisters, operetta (1967)
Orchestral music 3 pf concs. (1928, 1935, 1952); 4 syms. (1932, 1934, 1933, 1954); The Comedians (1940); Vn Conc. (1948); 2 vc concs. (1949, 1964); Spring, sym. poem (1960); Rhapsody, pf, orch (1963)
Choral music The Mighty Homeland (1942); Song of Morning, Spring and Peace (1958); Leninists (1959); Requiem (1962); Of the Homeland (1965); Letter to the 30th Century (1972)

Chamber music 2 str qts (1928, 1945); Sonata, vc, pf (1962)
Piano music 3 sonatas (1927, 1945, 1946); 2 sonatinas (1930, 1933); 24 Preludes (1944); 6 Preludes and Fugues (1959)

Kabeláč, Miloslav (*b* Prague, 1 Aug 1908; *d* there, 17 Sept 1979). Czech composer. He was a pupil of Jirák at the Prague Conservatory (1928–34). In 1932 he joined Czech radio and for some years concentrated on conducting. His works, drawing on ancient, exotic and modern music, include eight symphonies (three of them vocal) and the spatially conceived *Euphemias mysterion* (1965).

Kabuki. Traditional form of Japanese theatre, including dance numbers and purely dramatic plays. It is accompanied by offstage music (wood blocks, gongs, xylophone, bells etc, for sound effects), as well as on-stage musicians (singers and *shamisen*, or lute, players).

Kade, Otto (*b* Dresden, 6 May 1819; *d* Bad Doberan, 19 July 1900). German writer on music and editor. He promoted 16th-century Lutheran church music, both as court music director in Schwerin (from 1860) and as a scholar, contributing to the *Monatshefte für Musikgeschichte*, editing church music collections and publishing a supplementary volume to Ambros's *Geschichte der Musik*.

Kadosa, Pál (*b* Levice, 6 Sept 1903; *d* Budapest, 30 March 1983). Hungarian composer. He studied with Kodály at the Budapest Academy (1921–7), where he taught from 1945. His music grows out of the sphere of Bartók, Stravinsky and Hindemith, though with 12-note elements in pieces from the late 1950s onwards. Among his works are eight symphonies (1941–68), four piano concertos (1931–66), vocal music and much piano music (he was a noted exponent of Bartók's piano works).

Kagel, Mauricio (Raúl) (*b* Buenos Aires, 24 Dec 1931). Argentinian composer. Self-taught as a composer, he worked in Buenos Aires as a conductor and in films before moving to Cologne in 1957; he has taught at the Musikhochschule there since 1974. The first work he completed in Europe was *Anagrama* for voices and instruments (1958), using all sorts of improper vocal sounds in textures of Boulezian fastidiousness; this absurd combination of strict form and unconventional, subversive ingredients has remained characteristic. Many of his works are explicitly theatrical: at one extreme they include pieces for the opera house (*Staatstheater*, 1971; *Die Erschöpfung der Welt*, 1985) and radio dramas, though in other works the instrumentalists' actions are the drama (*Match* for two cellists and percussionist, 1964). The intention is often satirical, to examine ways in which music is used as psychological therapy, marketable commodity, religious devotion, subject of learned expertise etc. Several works have also been filmed by the composer (e.g. *Ludwig van*, 1970).

Kahn, Robert (*b* Mannheim, 21 July 1865; *d* Biddenden, 29 May 1951) German composer. He studied in Berlin and Munich and was acquainted with Brahms, the greatest influence on his music, though he also admired Reger. He taught at the Berlin Musikhochschule (1894–1930) and moved to England in 1937. His works include chamber music in standard forms, 180 lieder and distinguished choral works.

Kaisermarsch. Work by Wagner for unison male voices and orchestra (1871), celebrating the German victory in the Franco-Prussian War and the election of Wilhelm I as emperor.

Kaiser-Walzer. Waltz, op.437, by Johann Strauss (ii) (1888), written in honour of Emperor Franz Josef.

Kajanus, Robert (*b* Helsinki, 2 Dec 1856; *d* there, 6 July 1933). Finnish conductor and composer. He studied in Leizpig and Paris. In 1882 he founded the Helsinki Orchestral Society, which he conducted for the rest of his life. After a successful period as a composer in the 1880s he became an early champion of Sibelius's music, performing it widely and making authoritative recordings. His own works, several with a Finnish nationalist flavour, include orchestral and choral music.

Kakadu Variations. Beethoven's Variations for piano trio, op.121*a* (1803) on Wenzel Müller's song *Ich bin der Schneider Kakadu.*

Kalabis, Viktor (*b* Červený Kostelec, 27 Feb 1923). Czech composer. A pupil of Hlobil (1945–8) and Řídký (1952), in 1953 he joined Czech radio; his works include four symphonies, concertos and string quartets in a forceful, economical diatonic style (e.g. *Chamber Music* for strings, 1963).

Kalaš, Julius (*b* Prague, 18 Aug 1902; *d* there, 12 May 1967). Czech composer. He was a pupil of Foerster, Křička and Suk at the Prague Conservatory (1921–8). He wrote satirical ballads and songs for a popular male-voice sextet of which he was pianist and director, orchestral and chamber works, operettas and film scores.

Kalbeck, Max (*b* Breslau, 4 Jan 1850; *d* Vienna, 4 May 1921). German writer, music critic and editor. He was an influential critic in Vienna from 1880, contributing to the *Wiener allgemeine Zeitung*, the *Neue freie Presse*, the *Neues Wiener Tageblatt* and the *Wiener Montags-Revue*. A friend and partisan of Brahms, he produced an important biography of him (4 vols., 1904–14) and edited his correspondence. He was also a librettist and poet.

Kalinnikov, Vasily Sergeyevich (*b* Voina, 13 Jan 1866; *d* Yalta, 11 Jan 1901). Russian composer. He studied in Moscow, living in poverty playing in theatre orchestras. Tchaikovsky thought highly of him. His reputation rests mainly on his successful First Symphony (1894–5; dedicated to his teacher S.N. Kruglikov), which shows Borodin's influence in its folksong-like themes and unexpected modulations but also an individual handling of material, particularly polyphonically. Among his other works, the symphonic picture *The Cedar and the Palm* (1897–8) and the incidental music to *Tsar Boris* (1899) are notable.

Kalkbrenner, Frédéric [Friedrich Wilhelm Michael] (*b* early Nov 1785; *d* Enghien-les Bains, 10 June 1849). French pianist, teacher and composer of German extraction. He studied at the Paris Conservatoire and visited Vienna, where he received guidance from Haydn and heard Clementi. From 1815 to 1824 he lived in England, winning the reputation that placed him in the front rank of European pianists, for the clarity and beauty of his playing. He toured, played in London and taught, in 1824 settling in Paris, where he joined the Pleyel firm (in a largely financial capacity) and continued to give concerts of his own music until 1839. A prolific composer, especially of piano works, he made concessions to virtuosity even in his sonatas and chamber music, showing a propensity for dramatic effects. Among his didactic works, the *Méthode pour apprendre le piano-forte à l'aide du guide-mains* op.108 (1831) had a lasting influence.

Kalliwoda, Johann Wenzel [Kalivoda, Jan Křtitel Václav] (*b* Prague, 21 Feb 1801; *d* Karlsruhe, 3 Dec 1866). Bohemian composer and violinist. He studied at the Prague Conservatory and in 1822 became conductor of the royal orchestra in Donaueschingen, where he staged operas (including his own *Prinzessin Christine von Wolfenburg*, 1828), performed as a soloist and invited leading international virtuosos to play. Of his large output (mainly orchestral, chamber and piano music) only the chorus *Das deutsche Lied* remained in the repertory after 1850.

Kallstenius, Edvin (*b* Filipstad, 29 Aug 1881; *d* Danderyd, 22 Nov 1967). Swedish composer. He studied at the Leipzig Conservatory (1904–7) and pioneered advanced techniques in Sweden (including an adapted 12-note method) in his five symphonies, eight string quartets and other works.

Kálmán, Imre (*b* Siofok, 24 Oct 1882; *d* Paris, 30 Oct 1953). Hungarian composer. He studied with Koessler at the Budapest Academy. The success of his first operetta, *The Gay Hussars* (1908), led him to settle in Vienna, where he produced more such works in Viennese–Hungarian style (*Die Csárdásfürstin*, 1915; *Gräfin Mariza*, 1924). In 1939 he moved to Paris, and from there in 1940 to the USA.

Kalmus, Alfred (August Uhlrich) (*b* Vienna, 16 May 1889; *d* London, 25 Sept 1972). English music publisher of Austrian birth. He studied under Adler and in 1909 joined the enterprising Viennese firm, Universal Edition, where he fostered such composers as Schoenberg, Berg, Webern, Bartók and Janáček. He went to London in 1936 and inaugurated the London branch of Universal Edition, where he was eventually able to carry on the enterprise shown earlier by the parent company with young radical composers.

Kalomiris, Manolis (*b* Smyrna, 26 Dec 1883; *d* Athens, 3 April 1962). Greek composer. He studied with Grädener in Vienna (1901–6) and settled in Athens in 1910, working as a teacher, administrator, composer and writer; he founded the National Conservatory, directing it from 1926 to 1948. Largely responsible for the revival of Greek composition, he based his art on folk music and the German and Russian late Romantics, producing a flamboyant, epic style. His large output includes operas, large-scale vocal works, songs and piano music, as well as a few orchestral pieces.

Kamānche. Spike fiddle of Iran and the Caucasus, also known in other Middle Eastern and Central Asian countries (sometimes under different names, such as *rabāb*). It normally has a spherical body of wood, a long neck, and nowadays four metal strings (originally three silk ones). It is the only bowed string instrument in Iranian classical music.

Kamarinskaya. Orchestral work by Glinka (1848).

Kamieński, Maciej (*b* Sopron or Magyar-Ovar, 13 Oct 1734; *d* Warsaw, 25 Jan 1821). Polish composer. After a period in Vienna he was a teacher and concert organizer in Warsaw and presented several Polish stage works; the first (1778) was the earliest Polish opera given in public. He also wrote songs, sacred music and piano pieces.

Kaminski, Heinrich (*b* Tiengen, 4 July 1886; *d* Ried, 21 June 1946). German composer. Largely self-taught, he spent most of his life in the village of Ried, apart from a period teaching in Berlin (1930–33). His concern was with music as a spiritual art (not a 'craft'), and his works are austere, introspective and intricately contrapuntal; there are connections with Brahms, Bach and late Beethoven in the earlier music, but by the beginning of the 1920s his style was coherently his own. His small output includes sacred choral music and songs, chamber, organ and piano pieces, and a few orchestral works, of which the Concerto grosso for double orchestra (1922) was the most successful.

Kaminski, Joseph (*b* Odessa, 17 Nov 1903; *d* Tel-Aviv, 14 Oct 1972). Israeli composer. He studied in Berlin and Vienna (with Gál) and settled in Tel-Aviv as leader of the Palestine Orchestra (1937–69: it became the Israel PO). His works include a Violin Concerto (1948) and a witty Trumpet Concertino (1941).

Kammel, Antonín (*b* Běleč, bap. 21 April 1730; *d* ?London, by 1787). Bohemian composer. He was a violin pupil of Tartini in Padua. By 1764 he was in London, where he became a concert soloist and probably a royal chamber musician and had contact with J.C. Bach and Abel. A fluent and successful composer, he published *c*40 sets of instrumental works, mostly for amateurs. Among them are violin concertos, string quartets and duos, sonatas, sinfonias and divertimentos; in style they resemble J.C. Bach.

Kammerton. *See* CAMMER-TON and PITCH.

Kamu, Okko (Tapani) (*b* Helsinki, 7 March 1946). Finnish conductor. His early career was as a violinist in Helsinki; he had conducting experience with the Finnish National Opera when he won the Karajan Competition of 1969, which led to engagements in Europe and the USA which brought him a reputation for spontaneity tempered by sensitivity and disciplined feeling. He held posts with the Finnish Radio SO (1971), the Oslo PO (1975), the Helsinki PO (1979), the Dutch Radio SO (1983), as guest conductor of the CBSO (1985) and the Sjaelland SO, Copenhagen (1988).

Kancheli, Giya Alexandrovich (*b* Tbilisi, 10 Aug 1935). Soviet composer. He studied at the Tbilisi Conservatory (1958–63), where he has taught since 1972. He is recognized as one of the most radical thinkers in Georgian music. His works, using folk music, include six symphonies (1967–81), jazz pieces and musicals.

Kandler, Franz Sales (*b* Klosterneuburg, 23 Aug 1792; *d* ?Baden, 26 Sept 1831). Austrian writer on music. As a military official in Venice and later Naples (1817–25) he pursued research privately, producing the first biography of Hasse (1820), editing an early Palestrina study and writing on Italian music for periodicals.

Kantele. Folk psaltery of Finland and the Baltic. It is made from a narrow, smooth piece of wood in a trapezoidal shape, hollowed out at the side, bottom or top. The player rests the instrument in his lap. There are usually five wire strings; 20th-century instruments have several wooden strips and cross bridges with 12 to 46 strings.

Kantionale (Ger.). *See* CANTIONAL.

Kantor (Ger.). Term for a post as director of music in a Lutheran church and usually the musical head of an educational establishment attached to the church. From the Reformation until the mid-18th century the post of Kantor in a large city such as Hamburg or Leipzig (where Bach was Kantor of St Thomas's Church and School from 1723 until his death) was one of the most highly esteemed. Besides composing and directing sacred music, the duties often included training a choir, teaching practical and theoretical music and sometimes other subjects, and playing a part in civic music, sacred and secular. *See also* CANTOR.

Kantorei (Ger.). Term sometimes used for the musicians at a Protestant German court (as opposed to Kapelle, the normal Catholic term); it could also signify a group of voluntary musicians who performed in a Protestant church under a Kantor.

Kapelle (Ger.). CHAPEL; term for a court music establishment, secular as well as sacred.

Kapellmeister (Ger.). 'Chapel-master': the musician in charge of a Kapelle or chapel, meaning a musical establishment, which may be sacred, secular or both. It can be used for the conductor of an orchestra or a band.

Kapr, Jan (*b* Prague, 12 March 1914). Czech composer, pupil of Řídký and Křička. He worked as a critic and as a teacher at the Brno Academy (1961–70), while writing most importantly a cycle of eight symphonies (1943–70) showing an increasing refinement of style and moving from lyricism towards more astringency.

Kapsberger, Johann Hieronymus (*b* Venice, *c*1580; *d* Rome, 1651). German composer. Having spent his first 20–25 years in Venice, he moved to Rome *c*1604 where he quickly achieved fame as a lute virtuoso, gaining access to noble and artistic circles and securing the patronage of the papal family. He played an important role in developing for plucked instruments a virtuoso style characterized mainly by lively ornamentation, as can be seen in his published toccatas, partitas and dances for lute and chitarrone. His *Sinfonie a quattro* (1615) have richer textures, including parts for violin and cornett. His vocal music, which includes villanellas, madrigals, arias and motets, is uneven; the *Cantiones sacrae* (1628) are the most successful.

Karajan, Herbert von (*b* Salzburg, 5 April 1908). Austrian conductor. After study at the Salzburg Mozarteum and the Vienna Academy he conducted opera at Ulm, 1929–34, gaining a reputation for seeking technical perfection. He became music director at Aachen in 1934. A performance of *Tristan und Isolde* at the Berlin Staatsoper in 1937 launched an international career. Former Nazi associations caused an interruption in his career but from 1947 his progress as 'Generalmusikdirektor of Europe' was unimpeded: he recorded with the Philharmonia, London, and the Vienna PO from 1950, succeeded Furtwängler in 1955 as principal conductor of the Berlin PO and was director of the Vienna Staatsoper, 1957–64 (not without tensions). He was artistic director of the Salzburg Festival, 1956–60, and from 1967 was responsible for productions at the Easter festival there of operas by Wagner, Verdi, Musorgsky and Strauss. He had links with Paris and Milan, but Berlin and Vienna were his chief bases. His Met début was in 1968 with his Salzburg production of *Die Walküre*. He conducts an orchestral repertory ranging from Bach to Henze, in which Mozart, Beethoven and Bruckner are central; his interpretations are noted for their smoothness of line and luxuriance of sound.

Karayev, Kara (Abul'faz-oglï) (*b* Baku, 5 Feb 1918; *d* Moscow, 13 May 1982). Azerbaijani composer. He studied at the Azerbaijan State and Moscow conservatories, and with Shostakovich (1942–6). Active in both Azerbaijani and Soviet musical organizations, notably as secretary of the Composers' Union (since 1962), he wrote ballets, symphonies, choral works etc in an expressive style blending Azerbaijani folk music with the tradition of Prokofiev. His ballet *In the Path of Thunder* (1958) was a new achievement in Soviet musical theatre.

Karelia. Overture and suite for orchestra, opp.10 and 11, by Sibelius (1893).

Karg(-Elert), Sigfrid (*b* Oberndorf am Neckar, 21 Nov 1877; *d* Leipzig, 9 April 1933). German composer and organist. He studied at the Leipzig Conservatory and in 1902 was appointed to the Magdeburg Conservatory, though he soon abandoned teaching to concentrate on composing, supported and encouraged by Grieg. In 1919 he succeeded Reger (also an admirer) at the Leipzig Conservatory, while continuing his career as a touring organist and harmonium player, becoming internationally known (he visited the USA, 1931–2). His large output includes much for both instruments, besides chamber, piano and sacred choral music. Many of his works are tone poems indicating his closeness to Grieg, Skryabin, Schoenberg and Debussy; others, including the monumental 66 Chorale Improvisations (1910) and 20 Pre- and Postludes (1912) for organ, are polyphonic, influenced by Bach. With Reger he is one of the major organ composers of the 19th and early 20th centuries.

Kargel, Sixt (*b c*1540; *d* ?Zabern, after 1594). German lutenist. He was an editor for the printer Jobin in Strasbourg. He was lutenist to the Landgrave of Alsace from 1574 and to the Prince-Bishop of Zabern from 1593; he edited two collections for lute (1574, 1586) and two for cittern (1575, 1578) and composed a few lute fantasias.

Karkoff, Maurice (Ingvar) (*b* Stockholm, 17 March 1927). Swedish composer. He studied at the Stockholm Academy (1945, 1948–53) and in the 1950s broke away from Swedish orthodoxy in his experiments with new techniques, though his personality is essentially Romantic. His large output includes eight symphonies, choral and chamber music and much-valued educational pieces for piano and for chorus.

Karłowicz, Mieczysław (*b* Wiszniewe, 11 Dec 1876; *d* Tatra Mountains, 8 Feb 1909). Polish composer. Trained as a violinist, he was active in the Warsaw Music Society and a strong supporter of the 'Young Poland' artistic movement, advocating the newest techniques in Polish orchestral music. Among his works are symphonic poems using thematic transformation and reflecting pantheism, sorrow and Wagnerian ideas of love and death, including *Eternal Songs* (1908) and *Stanisław i Anna Oswiecimowie* (1912).

Karol Szymanowski Philharmonic. Polish society inaugurated in 1945 as the Kraków Philharmonic; it was renamed in 1962. Its ensembles include the Kraków PO (which has given many Penderecki premières), mixed and boys' choirs, a string quartet and the Capella Cracoviensis. It presents *c*700 concerts each season and organizes festivals.

Károlyi, Pál (*b* Budapest, 9 June 1934). Hungarian composer. He was a pupil of Viski and Farkas at the Budapest Academy (1956–62). His works are latterly mostly chamber and instrumental and influenced by avant-garde techniques. He has made important contributions to educational music.

Karr, Gary (Michael) (*b* Los Angeles, 20 Nov 1941). American double bass player. He appeared as a soloist in New York from 1962 and toured Europe in 1964. In 1967 he founded the International Institute for the String Bass and that year gave the première of a concerto by Henze which he had commissioned. He is noted for his rich and powerful tone.

Karrer, Paul [Karrerēs, Paulos] (*b* Zante, 12 May 1829; *d* there, April 1896). Greek composer. For his two operas on Greek subjects, *Marcos Botsaris* (1857) and *Kyra Frosyni* (1869), he may be regarded (with Xyandas) as the initiator of authentic Greek opera.

Kasemets, Udo (*b* Tallinn, 16 Nov 1919). Canadian composer of Estonian origin. He studied in Tallinn, Stuttgart and Darmstadt, moving in 1951 to Canada where he undertook a wide range of musical activities. In the 1950s he combined 12-note serialism with folk elements, but since the early 1960s he has been involved with post-Cageian experimental music; some works involve audience participation in their realization, others have indeterminate numbers of performers or tape elements.

Kashin, Daniil Nikitich (*b* Moscow, 1769; *d* there, Dec 1841). Russian folksong collector and composer. He wrote three operas, one successful (*Natal'ya, the Boyar's Daughter*, 1800 or 1805), but is now remembered for his three-volume collection of Russian folksongs (1833–4).

Kashkin, Nikolay Dmitriyevich (*b* Voronezh, 9 Dec 1839; *d* Kazan, 15 March 1920). Russian teacher and critic. A professor of theory, music history and the piano at the Moscow Conservatory (1866–96), he produced an influential theory textbook (1875) and contributed significantly to the press (1862–1918). His recollections of Borodin, Balakirev, Rimsky-Korsakov and, above all, Tchaikovsky are still valuable.

Kashperov, Vladimir Nikitich (*b* Chufarovo, 6 Sept 1826; *d* Romantsevo, 8 July 1894). Russian composer. He studied in St Petersburg, having success as an opera composer there and in Italy, though his style remained close to Donizetti's, and he was sought after as a singing teacher in Moscow. His (published) correspondence with leading literary and musical figures gives valuable insight into Russian cultural life.

Kašlík, Václav (*b* Poličná, 28 Sept 1917). Czech composer and opera producer. He studied with Karel and Hába, and was influenced by Burian. His daring stagings of Janáček in Prague have been widely acclaimed; he has worked internationally, often using television, film and projections. Of his own operas and ballets, *Krakatit* (1961) is notable.

Kassern, Tadeusz Zygfryd (*b* Lwów, 19 March 1904; *d* New York, 2 May 1957). Polish composer. He studied at the conservatories of Lwów and Poznań and in 1931 went to Paris, where he was a member of Boulanger's circle; in 1948 he moved to New York as a diplomat. Among his works are operas, concertos (including one for soprano, 1928) and piano music, some based on Polish folk music.

Kastner, Alfred (*b* Vienna, 10 March 1870; *d* Hollywood, 24 May 1948). American harpist of Austrian origin. He studied with Zamara at the Vienna Conservatory and played in Poland, Hungary, Switzerland and London before becoming principal harpist with the newly founded Los Angeles PO (1919–36). He was a highly regarded teacher.

Kastner, Jean-Georges (*b* Strasbourg, 9 March 1810; *d* Paris, 19 Dec 1867). French theorist and composer. He studied at the Paris Conservatoire. He won acclaim for his writings, especially his pioneering *Traité général d'instrumentation* (1837), which influenced his friend Berlioz, and his nine *livres-partitions*, lengthy essays followed by music, in which he synthesized art and knowledge of a phenomenological or mystical cast (e.g. *Les danses des morts*, 1852). His compositions include operas, songs and wind music, notably pieces for the saxhorn and the alto saxophone.

Katchen, Julius (*b* Long Branch, NJ, 15 Aug 1926; *d* Paris, 29 April 1969). American pianist. He studied in New York and made his début in 1937 with the Philadelphia Orchestra. His adult career was centred on Europe, where he became known for his formidable technique and intellectually challenging performances of Mozart, Beethoven and particularly Brahms.

Katerina Izmaylova. Title of the revised version of Shostakovich's LADY MACBETH OF THE MTSENSK DISTRICT.

Katin, Peter (Roy) (*b* London, 14 Nov 1930). British pianist. He studied at the RAM with Craxton and made his début in 1948. He toured widely and is admired for his solid technique and his sensitive playing of a large repertory, in which he excels in Chopin, Schubert and the impressionists.

Katya Kabanova [Kát'a Kabanová]. Opera in three acts by Janáček to his own libretto after A.N. Ostrovsky's translation of Červinka's *The Storm* (1921, Brno).

Kauer, Ferdinand (bap. Dyákovice, 18 Jan 1751; *d* Vienna, 13 April 1831). Austrian composer. He was a keyboard teacher, organist and violinist in Vienna from *c*1777. In the 1790s he became second Kapellmeister at the Leopoldstadt Theatre, where he presented stage works; the most successful was *Das Donauweibchen* (1798), a romantic-heroic folktale with songs. In 1814–18 he was Kapellmeister at the Josefstadt Theatre. His *c*200 stage works include Singspiels, parodies, local plays, pantomimes etc, and contain simple strophic songs and airs, with frequent echoes of Mozart and Wenzel Müller. He also wrote oratorios, church music, symphonies, chamber and keyboard music and instrumental tutors.

Kauffmann, Georg Friedrich (*b* Ostermondra, 14 Feb 1679; *d* Merseburg, 24 Feb 1735). German composer. He became court and cathedral organist at Merseburg in 1710; later he was director of church music at the court. In 1722 he competed unsuccessfully with Bach for the Thomaskantorate at Leipzig. As a composer he had a high reputation; he was one of the finest of Bach's German contemporaries. His works include church cantatas, an Ascension Oratorio and organ music. The *Harmonische Seelenlust* (1733–6), a collection of chorale preludes and figured bass settings, was a landmark in German organ music; it has preludes of various types, with inventive motivic and harmonic treatment.

Kaun, Hugo (*b* Berlin, 21 March 1863; *d* there, 2 April 1932). German composer. He lived in the USA, 1886–1902; later he taught in Berlin. His works, Wagnerian in style, include operas, three symphonies and four quartets. His male choruses were popular with German singing societies.

Kay, Ulysses (Simpson) (*b* Tucson, 7 Jan 1917). American composer, nephew of the jazzman King Oliver. He studied at the Eastman School and with Hindemith at Yale. In 1968 he began teaching at Lehman College, New York. His works include orchestral and choral compositions in a warmly melodic, vibrant diatonic style.

Kayn, Roland (*b* Reutlingen, 3 Sept 1933). German

composer. He was a pupil of Blacher (1955–8) in Berlin, and worked in electronic studios throughout Europe. His works, often motivated by information theory, include electronic and orchestral compositions.

Kayser, Isfrid (*b* Türkheim, 13 March 1712; *d* Marchtal, 1 March 1771). German composer. He was music director at the Premonstratensian monastery of Marchtal in the 1740s. A leading Bavarian composer of sacred music, he published several collections of masses, psalms etc on an ambitious scale, with a progressive idiom and varied textures; he also composed keyboard suites.

Kayser, Leif (*b* Copenhagen, 13 June 1919). Danish composer. He studied at the Copenhagen Conservatory (1936–40), abandoned music and took holy orders, but then studied with Boulanger and returned to composition in a post-Nielsen style. His works include ingenious symphonies and instrumental music; he has contributed substantially to modern Danish church music with organ and choral works in a retrospective style influenced by Gregorian chant.

Kayser, Philipp Christoph (*b* Frankfurt, 13 March 1755; *d* Oberstrass, 24 Dec 1823). German composer. A music teacher in Zurich, he met Goethe there and later visited him twice. He composed a Singspiel (1785–6) and several songs to Goethe texts, music for *Egmont* (*c*1785–6) and over 100 other songs, a cantata and chamber works; he ceased composing in 1789.

Kazoo. An instrument which amplifies the voice, imparting a buzzing, rasping quality to it (a 'singing membrane'). Manufactured in the USA since *c*1850, it was used in early jazz ensembles but is now often regarded as a toy. It consists of a cigar-shaped metal or plastic tube with a flattened opening at one end, a smaller, circular opening at the other, and a circular disc of membrane over a hole on top: as the performer sings or hums into it the membrane vibrates.

Keats, Donald (Howard) (*b* New York, 27 May 1929). American composer. He studied at Yale, Columbia and Minnesota universities. He was professor of music at Antioch College, 1967–75, and Denver University from 1975. His music is dissonant but based on clearly articulated tonal centres; the *Elegiac Symphony* (1960) is his most successful work.

Kee, Piet (Willem) (*b* Zaandam, 30 Aug 1927). Dutch organist and composer, son of the organist and composer Cor Kee (*b* 1900). He studied at the Amsterdam Conservatory. His repertory on extensive tours of Europe and the USA has consisted largely of Dutch and German music; he is also known as a skilful improviser and has composed for the organ as well as choral and chamber music.

Kegelstatt (Ger.: 'skittle alley'). Title sometimes given to Mozart's Trio in E♭ K498 for clarinet, viola and piano (1786), supposedly composed at a skittle game.

Keil, Alfredo (*b* Lisbon, 3 July 1850; *d* Hamburg, 4 Oct 1907). Portuguese composer and painter of German descent. His importance to music rests on his three operas, notably *Serrana* (1899), the first successful, full-scale Portuguese opera, and his hymn *A Portugueza* (1894), which became the national anthem in 1911.

Keiser, Reinhard (*b* Teuchern, bap. 12 Jan 1674; *d* Hamburg, 12 Sept 1739). German composer. He wrote operas for Brunswick from *c*1693 and in 1694 became court chamber composer. From 1696–7 he was Kapellmeister at Hamburg, and from 1700–01 also Kapellmeister to the Schwerin court. As joint director of the Hamburg Theater-am-Gänsemarkt, 1702–7, he presented 17 of his own operas. *Der Carneval von Venedig* (1707), which included local dialect, was especially successful. He remained active in Hamburg until 1718. After a period as a guest Kapellmeister at Stuttgart he served intermittently at Copenhagen. He was back in Hamburg by 1723 and in 1728 became Kantor of the cathedral. The Singspiel *Der hochmüthige, gestürtzte und wieder erhabene Croesus* (1730), a version of a 1710 opera, was among his last stage works.

Keiser was the central and most original figure in German Baroque opera, and wrote over 80 stage works. Most have serious German texts, which cover a wide range of subjects and often include allegorical or comic elements. They are notable for their dramatic flavour and skilful characterization. Italian and French musical elements appear (including Italian arias from 1703), with dramatic recitatives and ariosos, varied aria forms and inventive instrumentation. His several Passions, oratorios and cantatas show similar features. Among his other works are sacred music and trio sonatas. Handel drew heavily on his works in his own.

Kelemen, Milko (*b* Podravska Slatina, 30 March 1924). Yugoslav composer. He studied at the Zagreb Academy, at the Paris Conservatoire with Messiaen and Aubin (1954–5) and at the Freiburg Musikhochschule with Fortner. These latter studies led him from a neo-classical style influenced by folk music to a highly personal 12-note style, used chiefly in operas and orchestral pieces. He has taught in Yugoslavia and Germany and in 1961 founded the Zagreb Biennale.

Keller, Gottfried (*d* London, 1704, before 25 Nov). German composer resident in England. Well known in London as a teacher of the harpsichord, he wrote a *Compleat Method* (published 1705) for thoroughbass, and many sonatas primarily for combinations of wind instruments, of which three for trumpet (1700) are especially interesting.

Keller, Hans (*b* Vienna, 11 March 1919; *d* London, 6 March 1985). British critic of Austrian birth. He studied the violin in Vienna and fled to England in 1938, working as a violinist and writing criticism. In 1959 he joined the BBC Music Division. From the mid-1950s he put forward a method of 'functional analysis', designed to identify a single unifying idea from which a whole composition, in his view, was derived. His many articles, often controversial, cover a wide range of subjects.

Kellner, David (*b* Leipzig, *c*1670; *d* Stockholm, 6 April 1748). German composer. Church organist in Stockholm and one of the last lutenist virtuoso-composers, he wrote a collection of lute pieces (1747) and a popular thoroughbass manual (1732).

Kellner, Johann Peter (*b* Gräfenroda, 28 Sept 1705; *d* there, 19 April 1772). German organist and composer. He was assistant Kantor at Gräfenroda, 1728–32, and Kantor from 1732. A famous organist, he met Bach (some of whose works he copied) and Handel. He wrote mostly keyboard music, including suites, variations and organ preludes and fugues, in a modern *galant* style.

His son Johann Christoph (1736–1803) was court organist and Kantor in the Lutheran church at Kassel; his works include concertos, preludes, fugues etc for keyboard, chamber music and cantatas.

Kelly, Michael (*b* Dublin, 26 Dec 1762; *d* Margate, 9 Oct 1826). Irish tenor and composer. From 1779 he studied singing and appeared in operas in Italy. In 1783–7 he sang in Vienna, creating the roles of Don Curzio and Don Basilio in Mozart's *Le nozze di Figaro* (1786). He then worked as a singer, music publisher and theatre manager in London, and composed over 60 dramatic works (notably the opera *Blue Beard*, 1798). His autobiographical *Reminiscences* appeared in 1826.

Kelly, Thomas Alexander Erskine, 6th Earl of (*b* Kellie Castle, Fife, 1 Sept 1732; *d* Brussels, 9 Oct 1781). Scottish composer. A pupil of Stamitz in Mannheim (1753–6), he became a successful composer in Edinburgh, writing many overtures and symphonies. At first he used the Mannheim style; his later works, including six trio sonatas (1769), show a wider range of techniques. He was the most important Scottish composer between the late 16th century and the late 19th.

Kelterborn, Rudolf (*b* Basle, 3 Sept 1931). Swiss composer. He studied at the Basle Academy, privately with Burkhard, with Blacher (1953), and with Fortner and Bialas at Detmold, where he taught (1960–68) before returning to a post at the Zurich Musikhochschule. He made an international name, bringing avant-garde techniques into a Swiss neo-Baroque style in orchestral, chamber and choral works; he has written a sequence of successful operas (*Ein Engel kommt nach Babylon*, 1977; *Der kirschgarten*, 1984).

Kempe, Rudolf (*b* Niederpoyritz, 14 June 1910; *d* Zurich, 12 May 1976). German conductor. After a career as an oboist he conducted at the Leipzig Opera from 1935. He was musical director at the Dresden Opera (1949–52) and the Bavarian Staatsoper, Munich (1952–4). He was associated with the RPO, 1961–75, and the Zurich Tonhalle Orchestra, 1965–72. The complete orchestral works of Strauss are among his recordings, but he was admired above all for his spacious, finely textured performances of Wagner's operas.

Kempff, Wilhelm (*b* Jüterbog, 25 Nov 1895). German pianist. He studied in Berlin and Potsdam and began his concert career in 1916. He toured widely after World War I but did not appear in London until 1951 or in New York until 1964. He was a lyrical and lucid exponent of Beethoven, Schumann and Brahms.

Kenessey, Jenő (*b* Budapest, 23 Sept 1906; *d* there, 19 Aug 1976). Hungarian composer, pupil of Lajtha and Siklós. He worked at the Budapest Opera as coach and conductor (1929–65) and wrote ballets and orchestral music in a style influenced by Lajtha, Kodály and the *verbunkos*. His opera *Gold and the Woman* (1943) is his masterpiece.

Kenins, Talivaldis (*b* Liepāja, 23 April 1919). Canadian composer of Latvian origin. He studied at the Riga Conservatory (1940–44) and with Aubin and Messiaen at the Paris Conservatoire (1945) and moved to Canada in 1951; the next year he joined the staff at Toronto University. His works include symphonies and chamber music, mostly in a style with concertante and contrapuntal elements.

Kennedy, David (*b* Perth, 15 April 1825; *d* Stratford, Ontario, 12 Oct 1886). Scottish tenor. From the 1860s he was internationally known for his singing of traditional Scottish folksongs. His daughter Marjorie Kennedy-Fraser (1857–1930) promoted interest in Hebridean song through her publications and lecture-recitals.

Kennedy, (George) Michael (Sinclair) (*b* Manchester, 19 Feb 1926). English writer on music. He joined the *Daily Telegraph* in Manchester in 1941 and became its northern music critic (1950) and editor (1960). A prolific and sensitive writer, he has written valuable studies of several English composers (Elgar, Vaughan Williams, Britten), books on Mahler and Strauss and music dictionaries.

Kennedy Center for the Performing Arts. Arts complex in Washington, DC, opened in 1971. Its music facilities include the Opera House (cap. 2334), Concert Hall (cap. 2759), Terrace Theater (cap. 513) and a performing arts library; musicals are given in the Eisenhower Theater.

Kent bugle. *See* KEYED BUGLE.

Kentner, Louis (Philip) (*b* Karviná, 19 July 1905; *d* London, 21 Sept 1987). British pianist and composer of Hungarian birth. After study at the Budapest Academy he made his début in 1920; he settled in England in 1935. He was a fine interpreter of Mozart and Beethoven but was mainly noted for his delicacy and grandeur in Chopin and especially Liszt. He made a speciality of Bartók, giving the Hungarian première of Piano Concerto no.2, the European of no.3, and taking part in the world première of the concerto version of the Sonata for Two Pianos and Percussion (1942, London). He was also an admired chamber musician.

Kenton, Stan(ley Newcomb) (*b* Wichita, KS, 15 Dec 1911; *d* Los Angeles, 25 Aug 1979). American jazz-band leader. He formed his 14-piece band in 1941 and in 1949 founded a new 20-piece orchestra, called Progressive Jazz after the movement it represented. He also briefly had a 43-piece band. He established his first university 'jazz clinic' in 1959; thereafter his career centred on university campuses. Many leading big-band jazzmen and soloists began their careers with him.

Kent Opera. English company founded in 1969 by Norman Platt (artistic director) and Roger Norrington (music director) to give professional performances of opera outside London. It appears in southern England and abroad (including festivals).

Its repertory is wide ranging and it sometimes uses period instruments for works of the 17th and 18th centuries.

Kentucky dulcimer. *See* APPALACHIAN DULCIMER.

Kepler, Johannes (*b* Weil der Stadt, 27 Dec 1571; *d* Regensburg, 15 Nov 1630). German scientist and philosopher who wrote on music. Mathematician at the Prague court of Emperor Rudolf II (1601–12), he later settled in Linz where his major contribution to music theory, *Harmonices mundi*, was completed and published in 1619. In the first two books he traced the origin of the seven 'harmonies' of a string back to archetypes inherent in geometry and God. Book 3 contains a treatise on consonance and dissonance, intervals, modes, melody and notation; book 4 is on astrology. In book 5 Kepler described his harmony of the spheres.

Kerckhoven, Abraham van den (*b* ?Malines, *c*1618; *d* Brussels, Dec 1701). Flemish composer. He was from a family active in Brussels from the late 16th century to the mid-18th. In 1648 he replaced Kerll as organist to Archduke Leopold Wilhelm of Austria, Governor of the Low Countries. Many of his works (all are for organ) use early 17th-century ricercare techniques, but in the longer fantasies and fugues his harmonic and formal developments are more forward-looking. Some have registration indications.

Kerle, Jacobus de (*b* Ieper, 1531–2; *d* Prague, 7 Jan 1591). South Netherlands composer. Among the many posts he held in the Netherlands, Italy and Germany was that of organist at Augsburg Cathedral (1568–74); he also served the emperor in Vienna (1582) and Prague (1583). One of the last important composers of the Netherlands school, he wrote masses, other liturgical music and motets (15 vols., 1557–85), combining traditional Flemish polyphonic techniques with a more modern italianate clarity.

Kerll, Johann Kaspar (*b* Adorf, 9 April 1627; *d* Munich, 13 Feb 1693). German composer and organist. His precocious talent was quickly recognized by Archduke Leopold Wilhelm of Austria, who sent him to Rome to study with Carissimi. By 1656 he was Kapellmeister at the Munich court, where his opera *L'Oronte* was produced for the inauguration of the opera house (1657); this and ten further operas (1658–72) are lost. In 1673 he returned to Vienna, becoming organist at St Stephen's Cathedral (1674–7), assisted by his pupil Pachelbel, and imperial court organist (1677). He was in Vienna during the Turkish siege of 1683, composing a mass.

Kerll was an imaginative enough composer to imbue a new spirit into contemporary forms. Among his keyboard works the eight sets of versets of *Modulatio organica* (1686) are outstanding, with masterly fugal writing. He also wrote toccatas, canzonas, suites and other pieces. Venetian influence is detectable in his surviving dramatic work, the school drama *Pia et fortis mulier S Natalia* (1677), while his 18 extant masses range in style from traditional polyphony to a highly developed concertante idiom, including occasional symphonies and

sonatas. The works in *Delectus sacrarum cantionum* (1669), for two to five voices with continuo (some with obbligato violins), recall Schütz's *Kleine geistliche Concerte*.

Kerman, Joseph (Wilfred) (*b* London, 3 April 1924). American scholar and critic. He studied at New York University and Princeton and in 1951 began teaching at the University of California at Berkeley. His main areas of work have been opera, Elizabethan music (especially Byrd), Beethoven and Verdi. He has vigorously expressed (and his writings exemplify) the controversial view that musicology should partake of criticism.

Kern, Jerome (David) (*b* New York, 27 Jan 1885; *d* there, 11 Nov 1945). American composer. He wrote songs to be interpolated into shows, and by the outbreak of World War I had contributed over 100 to 30 shows. His own first scores were failures, but in 1915–18 he composed four shows for the Princess Theatre, New York, which were seen as a new type of sophisticated musical show with much more fully integrated songs and story than was usual; the best (written with Guy Bolton) was *Very Good, Eddie* (1915). He wrote many musical comedies, of which the most successful and influential was *Show Boat* (1927), with words by Oscar Hammerstein II. From 1939 he lived in Hollywood, contributing to films some of his best-known songs, notably *The last time I saw Paris* and *The way you look tonight*. He bridged the stylistic gap between the European operetta tradition and the American musical, developing the technique of using lyrical song to advance plot and character.

Kertész, István (*b* Budapest, 28 Aug 1929; *d* Kfar Saba, Israel, 16 April 1973). German conductor of Hungarian birth. After study at the Liszt Academy, Budapest, he worked in Hungary until the 1956 uprising. He was music director at Augsburg, 1958–63, and at the Cologne Opera from 1964. His London début was in 1960, with the LSO, of which he was principal conductor, 1965–8. He gave direct interpretations across a wide repertory including 20th-century classics.

Kes, Willem (*b* Dordrecht, 16 Feb 1856; *d* Munich, 21 Feb 1934). Dutch conductor and violinist. His teachers included Wieniawski and Joachim. He created and conducted the Amsterdam Concertgebouw Orchestra (1888–95), helping to establish its outstanding reputation; he held conducting appointments in Glasgow, Moscow and Koblenz.

Ketèlbey, Albert (William) (*b* Birmingham, 9 Aug 1875; *d* Cowes, 26 Nov 1959). English composer. He appeared as a solo pianist and conducted internationally. He was a popular composer of light orchestral pieces (*In a Monastery Garden*, 1915; *In a Persian Market*, 1920).

Kettledrum. A drum with a hemispherical body as resonator; the most familiar are the orchestral TIMPANI. Kettledrums may be made from materials ranging from tortoise shells and hollowed-out tree trunks to clay or metal bowls; the head is attached over the open body by lacing, thong-tensioning, pegs etc. The shape strengthens certain overtones in the harmonic series so that the kettledrum produces a definite pitch and can be tuned.

Such drums were known in Mesopotamia in the 2nd millennium BC and were used by the Huns in the 3rd and 2nd centuries BC. They are often paired; common in the Middle East, they were adopted in Europe during the Crusades (13th century). The Arabic term *naqqāra* became the French *nacaires* and the English NAKERS. In India a small thong-tensioned kettledrum constitutes the lower drum of the TABLĀ.

Keussler, Gerhard von (*b* Gulbene, 5 July 1874; *d* Niederwartha bei Dresden, 21 Aug 1949). German conductor and composer. He studied in St Petersburg and Leipzig, and conducted the Hamburg PO (from 1918), and in Australia (1932–6). A philosopher, critic and poet, he set his own verse in songs and oratorios.

Key. (1) The quality of a musical passage or composition that causes it to be sensed as gravitating towards a particular note, called the key note or the tonic. One therefore speaks of a piece as being in C major or minor etc. *See* TONALITY.

Key is also taken to mean pitch; the expression to sing 'off key' signifies out of tune; 'on key' can mean at concert (i.e. standard) pitch.

(2) In keyboard instruments, a balanced lever which when depressed either operates a valve to admit air to a pipe or reed or mechanically strikes or plucks a string. In mouth-blown instruments, the key is a device controlling a tone hole out of the reach of, or too large for, the fingers: it consists of a touchpiece for the finger, a pivoted lever and a padded plate or cup to close the hole.

Keyboard. A set of levers (keys) actuating the mechanism of a musical instrument such as the organ, harpsichord, clavichord, piano etc. It probably originated in the Greek hydraulis. Its influence on Western musical systems was great: the primacy of the C major scale is partly due to its being played on the white keys, and the 12-semitone chromatic scale could also be derived from the keyboard's design.

Up to the 13th century, keyboards were diatonic with a C as first key, except for the inclusion of B♭ which permitted transpositions compressing the compass of plainchant to less than two octaves. By the early 14th century, the development of polyphony had caused a widening of compass and the addition of chromatic notes. The arrangement of the keys in two rows, with the sharps and flats grouped by two and three in the upper, existed by the early 15th century. A compass *F–a″* was frequent by the 16th, and in Italy upper limits of *c‴* or even *f‴* were common. The compass increased further in the 17th century, and reached five octaves by 1700. Pianos now usually cover seven octaves and a 3rd, *A″–c″″*: organ keyboards rarely cover more than five octaves.

In the 18th and 19th centuries, keyboard instruments gained a leading position in European musical practice, which led to attempts to provide many types of instrument with a keyboard mechanism (e.g. the harmonium and celesta). Electronic technology has led to many adaptations of the conventional keyboard, including split and staggered manuals and touch-sensitive keyboard. Experimental keyboards include the 'sequential keyboard' (1834), the reversed keyboard (1876) and the ENHARMONIC KEYBOARD.

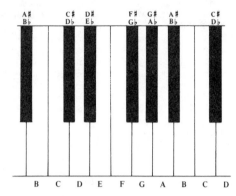

Keyboard instruments. Generic term for instruments whose playing mechanisms are operated from a keyboard. The oldest is the organ; other early types include such plucked instruments as the harpsichord, the virginal and the spinet, as well as the clavichord (a struck instrument); more recent examples include the pianoforte, the harmonium, the celesta, the glockenspiel and the synthesizer. The term 'keyboard music' is often used for music before 1750, much of which is intended for any available keyboard instrument rather than a specific type. See illustration, pp. 394–5.

Keyed bugle [key bugle, Kent bugle]. A conical, wide-bore, soprano brass instrument, with side-holes controlled by keys similar to those on woodwind instruments; it was invented in 1810. It may have only five keys but bugles with up to 12 are found. Most early keyed bugles were in C with a crook to B♭; others later appeared in high E♭. The wide conical bore and the deep conical mouthpiece produce a mellow, woolly sound similar to that of the modern flugelhorn.

Keyed bugles were common in British bands by 1815, the year of the earliest known use of the instrument in the USA. It continued in use up to the mid-1860s.

Keyed trumpet. The first trumpet with keys was made in Dresden, *c*1770. Early instruments were pitched in D and E♭, later (*c*1820) also in G, A or A♭ with crooks for lower pitches. Five is the most common number of keys but some trumpets have four or six. The keyed trumpet was successful as a solo instrument in the 1790s and early 19th century (Haydn's concerto, for Anton Weidinger, dates from 1796); it was also used in military music from about 1820, especially in Austria and Italy, but towards 1840 it was superseded by the valve trumpet.

Key note. The note by which the key of a composition, or a section of it, is named and on which its scale starts (i.e. the FINAL of a church mode or the TONIC of the major or minor mode).

Key signature. The sharp or flat signs placed at the beginning of a composition, immediately after the clef, or in the course of a composition generally after a double bar. The signs affect all notes of the same names as those on which they stand and so define the key of the composition. The earliest use of accidentals in this context is found in the 11th and 12th centuries; the association of a signature with a definite key is an 18th-century development. Key signatures have increasingly been abandoned in highly chromatic music since the late 19th century.

The chart below shows the number of sharps or flats in the signature of each major and minor key.

mid-century, such makers as the Triéberts, Buffet, Heckel and Boehm had established the principles of keywork which today is completely reliable. Tone holes on wind instruments can now be placed exactly according to theoretical principles, disregarding the limitations of the unaided human hand; but most players dislike the resulting departure from traditional tone quality.

Khachaturian, Aram Il'yich (*b* Tbilisi, 6 June 1903; *d* Moscow, 1 May 1978). Soviet composer. A bookbinder's son, he at first studied medicine and received his musical education comparatively late, studying the cello and composition under

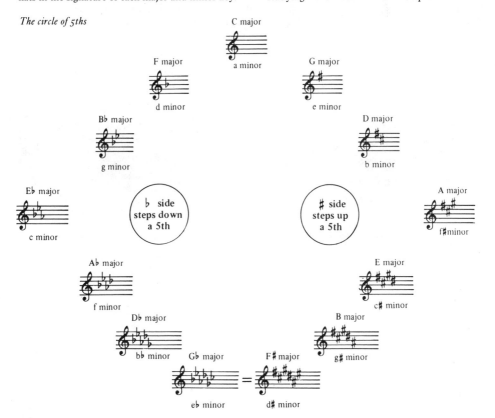

The circle of 5ths

Keywork. Term denoting the various mechanical devices to aid the fingers in controlling the tone holes of wind instruments. The simplest wind instruments (recorders, shepherds' flutes) can be played by fingering the soundholes, but when instruments began to be made in various sizes paralleling the different ranges of the human voice (by the early 16th century), the wider spacing needed between the holes on larger, deeper instruments began to exceed the stretch of the normal hand. The first keys were probably designed to assist the little finger, followed by thumb-keys on large shawms and bassoon types. The use of keys to make a chromatic scale possible probably began in the late 18th century, on the transverse flute. The first half of the 19th, however, saw the greatest changes. By the

Myaskovsky at the Moscow Conservatory (1929–37). He came to wider notice in 1936 with his Piano Concerto and his Violin Concerto (1940), and was active from 1937 in the Union of Soviet Composers. Most of his best-known works, including the ballet *Gayane*, date from the 1940s. In common with other Soviet composers, he was subject to official criticism in 1948; but his colourful, nationally tinged idiom was far removed from modernistic excess. He concentrated on film music in the ensuing years, and took up conducting and teaching (at the Gnesin Institute and the Conservatory). His later works include 'concert rhapsodies' which re-interpret concerto form. His career represents the Soviet model of the linking of regional folklorism with the central Russian tradition; his Armenian heritage is

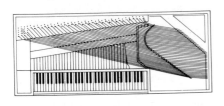

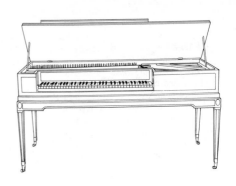

square piano

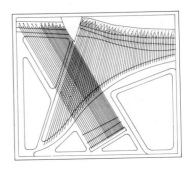

upright piano

grand piano

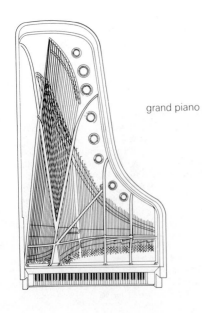

virginals

clavichord

spinet

harpsichord

Keyboard instruments: external and internal views

clear in his melodies and his vitality, but in disciplined form. His greatest strengths lie in colourful orchestration and effective pictorialism.

Ballets Gayane (1942); Spartak (1954)
Orchestral music Dance Suite (1933); 3 syms. (1935, 1943, 1947); Pf Conc. (1936); Vn Conc. (1940); Masquerade (1944); Vc Conc. (1946); Funeral Ode in Memory of Lenin (1949); The Battle for Stalingrad (1952); The Widow of Valencia (1953); Concert Waltz (1955); Concert-rhapsodies, vn, orch (1962), vc, orch (1963), pf, orch (1965)
Choral music Song of Stalin (1937); Ode of Joy (1956)
Chamber music Sonata, vn, pf (1932); Trio, cl, vn, pf (1932); Recitative and Fugue, str qt (1967)
Piano music Poem (1927); Album of Children's Pieces, 2 vols. (1946, 1964); Sonatina (1959); Sonata (1961)

Khan, Ali Akbar (*b* Shibpur, 14 April 1922). Indian *sarod* player and composer. He first performed in public at the age of 14 and was court musician to the Maharaja of Jodhpur in his early 20s. Since 1955 he has performed extensively in the West. He founded colleges in Calcutta (1956) and California (1967).

Khandoshkin, Ivan Yevstafyevich (*b* 1747; *d* St Petersburg, 29/30 March 1804). Russian composer. He was a violinist at the Russian court, teaching at the Academy of Fine Arts; later he was court Kapellmeister and played in a theatre. He wrote three unaccompanied violin sonatas and variations on Russian folktunes, which display the level of his virtuosity.

Khovanshchina. Opera in five acts by Musorgsky to his own libretto (1880), completed and orchestrated by Rimsky-Korsakov (1886, St Petersburg).

Khrennikov, Tikhon (Nikolayevich) (*b* Elets, 10 June 1913). Soviet composer. He studied with Shebalin at the Moscow Conservatory (1932–6) and in 1948 became head of the Soviet Composers' Union, in which position he has attacked modernism and stood out for socialist realism. His works include operas (notably the melodious *Into the Storm*, 1939), operettas, ballets, symphonies and concertos.

Kidson, Frank (*b* Leeds, 15 Nov 1855; *d* there, 7 Nov 1926). English folksong collector and bibliographer. Among his most important publications are *Old English Country Dances* (1890), *Songs of Britain* (1913), *A Garland of English Folk-songs* (1926) and the valuable *British Music Publishers and Engravers* (1900).

Kienzl, Wilhelm (*b* Waizenkirchen, 17 Jan 1857; *d* Vienna, 3 Oct 1941). Austrian composer. He studied in Graz, Prague and Leipzig and attended the first complete *Ring*, becoming a member of Wagner's circle. His works include operas continuing from early Wagner, as well as choral music and songs, and he was a prolific writer.

Kiesewetter, Raphael Georg (*b* Holešov, 29 Aug 1773; *d* Baden, 1 Jan 1850). Austrian scholar. In government service, he also pursued music research and took part in Viennese concert life. He collected scores and produced books and articles on the Netherlands style, the history of song and Arabic and ancient Greek music; his major work was the *Geschichte der europäisch-abendländischen oder unsrer heutigen Musik* (1834).

Kilar, Wojciech (*b* Lwów, 17 July 1932). Polish composer. He studied in Katowice and Kraków and with Boulanger in Paris. He began as a neo-

classicist, though since 1962 he has used new techniques and is most successful in orchestral pieces.

Kilpinen, Yrjö (Henrik) (*b* Helsinki, 4 Feb 1892; *d* there, 2 May 1959). Finnish composer. He studied in Helsinki, Vienna and Berlin, and made his name as a composer of lyrical songs, of which he produced over 750. His other works include male choruses and piano music.

Kimball. American firm of reed organ, piano and organ makers. It was founded in Chicago in 1857 by William Wallace Kimball (1828–1904). Stressing volume, reasonable price and quality of construction, it manufactured reed organs (1880–1922), pianos (from 1887) and pipe organs (1890–1942), including many notable instruments for Chicago churches. After 1945 the firm concentrated on pianos; besides building a new factory in 1955, it took over Bösendorfer in 1966. Now in Indiana, it also makes electronic organs for home use.

Kindermann, Johann Erasmus (*b* Nuremberg, 29 March 1616; *d* there, 14 April 1655). German composer. He studied under Staden and in Italy and worked as organist of the Egidienkirche, Nuremberg. An influential composer, he wrote contrapuntal organ music (published in tablature), collections of sonatas and dances for strings and much sacred vocal music, including motets, concertato-style works and sacred songs; he also wrote some humorous pieces.

Kinderszenen. Schumann's op.15, 13 piano pieces (1838).

Kindertotenlieder. Song cycle by Mahler (1904), settings for baritone or contralto and orchestra of five poems by Rückert.

King, Alec [Alexander] Hyatt (*b* Beckenham, 18 July 1911). English musicologist. He studied at Cambridge and in 1944–77 was superintendent of the Music Room of the British Museum. A leading music bibliographer, he has written much on music collection and early printing; he is also a leading Mozart scholar of his generation.

King, Matthew Peter (*b* London, *c*1773; *d* there, Jan 1823). English composer and theorist. He published a series of piano sonatas (some with violin) before 1800 and later presented many comic operas and other stage works. He also wrote an oratorio (1816), songs, glees etc and theoretical treatises.

King, Robert (*fl* London, 1676–1728). English composer. Appointed to the Private Musick of Charles II in 1680, he retained this position under five monarchs, becoming composer-in-ordinary under William and Mary with a licence to give public concerts. His compositions, though uneven, show Italian influence; the vocal music (mainly songs) is more successful than the instrumental airs and other pieces. King was also involved in selling music from Rome and Amsterdam publishers.

King Arthur, or The British Worthy. Semi-opera in a prologue, five acts and an epilogue by Purcell to a libretto by Dryden (1691, London).

Kingdom, The. Oratorio (op.51) by Elgar to his own biblical text (1906, Birmingham), a sequel to *The Apostles*.

King Goes Forth to France, The. Opera in three

acts by Sallinen to a libretto by Paavo Haavikko (1984, Savonlinna).

King Lear. Overture by Berlioz (1831).

Overture and incidental music by Balakirev (1861).

Opera by Aribert Reimann to a libretto by Henneberg (1978, Munich).

Operas on the subject were contemplated by Verdi and Britten.

King of Prussia Quartets. Mozart's last three string quartets: in D K575 (1789), in B♭ K589 (1790) and in F K590 (1790), so called because they were commissioned by Friedrich Wilhelm II of Prussia.

King Priam. Opera in three acts by Tippett to his own libretto (1962, Coventry).

King Roger. Opera in three acts by Szymanowski to a libretto by J. Iwaszkiewicz and the composer (1926, Warsaw).

King's Band of Music. Group formally established at the English court in the 1620s, though royal minstrels go back to the 11th century. Its formal role under a MASTER OF THE QUEEN'S MUSIC terminated in the 20th century; it played for royal entertainment and on ceremonial occasions during the 17th to 19th centuries.

King's Singers. British ensemble. It originally consisted of two countertenors, a tenor, two baritones and a bass, five of them former choral scholars of King's College, Cambridge. It made its début in 1968. The combination of the traditional King's sound with intense professionalism and a faintly camp humour has led to their success in a wide repertory, ranging from Renaissance polyphony through 18th-century glees and American barbershop harmony to new works (written for them by Penderecki, Berio and others) and arrangements of popular songs.

King Stephen [König Stephan]. Overture and incidental music, op.117, by Beethoven (1811), written for A. von Kotzebue's prologue given at the first night of the German theatre in Budapest (1812).

King's Theatre. *See* HER MAJESTY'S THEATRE.

Kinkeldey, Otto (*b* New York, 27 Nov 1878; *d* Orange, NJ, 19 Sept 1966). American musicologist. He studied music with Edward MacDowell and in Berlin (1902–9), taking the doctorate (then rare for an American in a German university). He taught at Breslau University but returned to New York, where he became head of the public library's music division (1915–23). He later settled at Cornell University with the first American chair of musicology, created for him. Kinkeldey was the founder of American musicology: it was primarily owing to him that it became an accepted subject and it was chiefly to him that subsequent American music scholars owed their livelihood. His own research was mainly on early keyboard music and Renaissance dance.

Kinnor. Biblical string instrument, usually assumed to have been a plucked lyre, and the most important melodic instrument in ancient Israel. The term is also the modern Hebrew name for the violin.

Kipnis, Alexander (*b* Zhitomir, *c*13 Feb 1891; *d* Westport, CT, 14 May 1978). American bass. He studied in Berlin, made his début in Hamburg (1915) and sang in Berlin, Salzburg, Bayreuth and London (début 1927). After his American début (1923, Boston, as Pogner) his career was centred in the USA. At the Met (1940–46) he sang Gurnemanz and Boris Godunov with a skilful variety of colour. His son Igor (*b* 1930) is a harpsichordist.

Kirbye, George (*d* Bury St Edmunds, bur. 6 Oct 1634). English composer. He served the Jermyn family at Rushbrooke Hall and later moved to nearby Bury St Edmunds. He published a madrigal volume and contributed 19 settings to East's psalter (1592) and a piece to *The Triumphes of Oriana* (1601).

Kircher, Athanasius (*b* Geisa, 2 May 1601; *d* Rome, 27 Nov 1680). German polyhistorian, theologian and music theorist. He lived mainly in Italy, where he became a professor at the Collegio Romano in 1633. His chief work on music is *Musurgia universalis* (1650), one of the most influential of all music treatises. It covers many aspects of the music of the time, and contains original ideas on topics including musical expression and the classification of styles.

Kirchner, Leon (*b* Brooklyn, 24 Jan 1919). American composer, pianist and conductor. He studied with Schoenberg in Los Angeles, with Bloch at Berkeley and with Sessions in New York. From 1949 he taught in California, moving to Harvard in 1961. His works, in a powerful Schoenbergian style, include the opera *Lily* (1977), two piano concertos (1953, 1963) and three string quartets. He has an international reputation as a pianist and conductor.

Kirckman. English family of harpsichord and piano makers, of Alsatian origin. In *c*1770 Jacob Kirckman (1710–92), who had been in England since the early 1730s, went into partnership with his nephew Abraham Kirckman (1737–94); successive family members managed the firm, building their last harpsichord in 1809 and continuing as piano makers until 1896. With Shudi, Jacob Kirckman had a near monopoly of the English harpsichord at its apogee (the latter apparently making over twice as many instruments as his rival). Although Kirckman was experienced in related keyboard instruments and repertory and open to experimentation, his harpsichord types were fundamentally the same as Shudi's, including their machine stop activated by a pedal (from *c*1766) to alter the registration and another mechanism to operate the lid or Venetian swell. It has been suggested that Kirckman's instruments probably had a more incisive, nasal tone, especially the lute registers.

Kiriac-Georgescu, Dumitru (*b* Bucharest, 18 March 1866; *d* there, 8 Jan 1928). Romanian composer, conductor and teacher. A professor at the Bucharest Conservatory (where he had studied) and founder of an important choir (the 'Carmen' society, 1901), he used folk music and modes to create a new style of Romanian music.

Kirkby, Emma (*b* Camberley, 26 Feb 1949). English soprano. After study at Oxford she made her London début in 1974. She has sung with the Academy of Ancient Music, London Baroque and the Taverner Players and has appeared widely with the lutenist Anthony Rooley. Her pure, almost vibrato-free, coolly expressive voice has been heard most in Renaissance and Baroque music; she is a distinguished interpreter of Dowland and Handel. She made her American début in 1978.

Kirkpatrick, Ralph (Leonard) (*b* Leominster, MA, 10 June 1911; *d* Guilford, CT, 13 April 1984). American harpsichordist. He studied at Harvard and with Landowska in Paris, making his début as a harpsichordist in 1930. He first performed on the clavichord in 1946, making his British début the following year. His repertory ranged from Bach to Elliott Carter, performed with rhythmic vitality and stylistic authority. His important study of Domenico Scarlatti (1953) includes a valuable catalogue of the sonatas on which the standard numbering system (Kk) is based.

Kirnberger, Johann Philipp (*b* Sealfeld, bap. 24 April 1721; *d* Berlin, 26–7 July 1783). German theorist and composer. He was a pupil of J.S. Bach. In 1741–51 he served in Poland and was a convent music director. After studying the violin at Dresden, he held court posts in Berlin; from 1758 he was in Princess Anna Amalia's service. Among the most significant theorists centred in Berlin, he wrote several treatises – notably *Die Kunst des reinen Satzes* (1771) – in which he tried to propagate Bach's methods. His own compositions, including sacred, chamber and keyboard music and songs, are correct but uninspired; some are modelled on Bach's music, and others have a *galant* style akin to C.P.E. Bach.

Kirov Theatre (Leningrad). Formerly the Mariinsky Theatre (built 1860), it was renamed in 1935 and renovated in 1963–70 (cap. 1621). Premières of operas by Musorgsky, Rimsky-Korsakov and Tchaikovsky were given there; from the 1920s repertory included new works by Soviet and foreign composers. The Kirov Opera and Ballet are among the leading companies in the USSR.

Kiss, The [Hubička]. Opera in two acts by Smetana to a libretto by Krásnohorská after Světlá (1876, Prague).

Kistler, Cyrill (*b* Grossaitingen, 12 March 1848; *d* Bad Kissingen, 1 Jan 1907). German composer. Apart from writing stage works, among which the folk opera *Röslein im Hag* (1903) was the most successful, he made noteworthy arrangements of Wagner, whose friend he was, and edited the neo-German *Musikalischen Tagesfragen*.

Kit [kytte]. A small unfretted fiddle, generally with four strings, used from the 16th century to the 19th. There were two main types: pear- or boat-shaped, with a vaulted back, and viol- or violin-shaped, with a slightly arched back and a long neck. The kit was probably derived from the rebec; early examples are often elaborately carved or decorated.

The tuning was generally in 5ths, sometimes at violin pitch but more often a 4th or 5th higher or even an octave if there were only three strings. The French names (*poche, pochette*) imply that it could be carried in the pocket, and the German term *Tanzmeistergeige* indicates its use by dancing-masters. The kit was played at all social levels; performers played violin pieces or popular tunes, as little music was composed specifically.

Kithara [cithara]. The most important string instrument of Greco-Roman antiquity, larger and heavier than the LYRE, which it resembles. It had two wooden arms rising vertically from the soundchest (also of wood), crossed by a yoke. Strings were stretched between yoke and the soundchest: three to five in early examples, seven or more from the 7th century BC. The soundbox could be rectangular or smaller and rounded (the 'cradle kithara'). The left hand plucked, strummed or damped the strings from behind while the right plucked them with a plectrum.

The kithara probably originated in Asia Minor; in Greece it was indispensable in singing the praises of Hellenic heroes and in choral performances, while in Rome it appeared in virtually every area of musical life including the theatre, the *convivium* and cult music.

Harry Partch used the name 'kithara' for instruments he built resembling the Greek ones.

Kittel, Caspar (*b* Lauenstein, 1603; *d* Dresden, 9 Oct 1639). German composer. A pupil and colleague of Schütz, he served at the Dresden Hofkapelle from *c*1616. He studied in Italy and introduced the term 'cantata' into Germany with his *Arien und Cantaten* (1638), his only known music; the term is used to denote pieces – five arias and four duets – of the strophic variation type. His son Christoph (*fl* 1641–80) and grandson Johann Heinrich (1652–82), composer of a set of 12 preludes in successive keys, were also musicians at the Dresden Hofkapelle.

Kittel, Johann Christian (*b* Erfurt, 18 Feb 1732; *d* there, 17 April 1809). German organist, composer and teacher. A favourite pupil of Bach, he was an organist at Langensalza and then Erfurt (from 1762 at the Predigerkirche), famous as virtuoso and teacher. He wrote an influential organ textbook (1801–8), various organ pieces and piano sonatas; though aiming to uphold Bach's principles, he often used a *galant*, melodic style.

Kittl, Jan Bedřich (*b* Orlík nad Vltavou, 8 May 1806; *d* Leszno, 20 July 1868). Czech composer. He studied with Tomášek. He achieved European success with his refreshing second symphony (*Jagdsymphonie*, 1837), becoming director of the Prague Conservatory (1843) and a progressive influence on the city's musical life until 1865: he introduced the music of Berlioz and Wagner and encouraged the use of Czech in the conservatory, also composing Czech songs and choruses. His *Bianca und Giuseppe* (1848; libretto by Wagner) was one of the most successful operas written in Bohemia before Smetana.

Kjerulf, Halfdan (*b* Oslo, 17 Sept 1815; *d* there, 11 Aug 1868). Norwegian composer and piano teacher. He studied in Copenhagen (with Gade) and at the Leipzig Conservatory, settling in Oslo (1851) as a piano teacher and writing songs (*c*130), male choruses (*c*40 original works, 50 arrangements) and piano pieces (Romantic character-pieces; two volumes of folk arrangements, 1861, 1867). In their fusion of German Romanticism and Norwegian folk music, the songs represent his outstanding achievement, virtually creating the Norwegian art song.

Kk. *See* K.

Klagend (Ger.). Plaintive, lamenting.

Klagende Lied, Das. Cantata by Mahler to his own text (1880).

Klami, Uuno (Kalervo) (*b* Virolahti, 20 Sept 1900; *d* there, 29 May 1961). Finnish composer. He studied with Melartin at the Helsinki College of Music (1915–24), with Ravel in Paris (1924–5) and Willner in Vienna (1928–9). His most important works are orchestral, bringing the influences of French music and early Stravinsky into the post-Sibelian tradition: they include the *Kalevala Suite* (1933), two symphonies (1937, 1945), two piano concertos (1925, 1950) and a violin concerto (1943).

Klangfarbenmelodie (Ger.: 'sound, colour, melody'). A term coined by Schoenberg (*Harmonielehre*, 1911) to denote a succession of tone colours related in a way analogous to the relationship between the pitches in a melody.

Klavier (Ger.). Term for 'manual', 'keyboard' or 'keyboard instrument'. From *c*1800 it referred to the piano or Hammerklavier, especially in southern Germany and Austria, and was occasionally used for clavichord. As a modern term, 'Klavier' usually denotes stringed keyboard instruments only; in popular usage, it normally stands for piano (*Klavierkonzert*, *Klavierspiel* etc). *See also* CLAVIER.

Klavierbüchlein. *See* CLAVIER-BÜCHLEIN.

Klavierstücke I–XI. 11 piano pieces in two sets by Stockhausen (*I–IV*, 1953; *V–XI*, 1956).

Klebe, Giselher (*b* Mannheim, 28 June 1925). German composer. He studied with Rufer and Blacher in Berlin (1946–51) and has taught at Detmold since 1957. Rather like Henze, he has used a 12-note style to vigorously expressive ends in a sequence of operas, to his own librettos: *Die Räuber* (1957), *Die tödliche Wünsche* (1959), *Die Ermordung Cäsars* (1959), *Alkmene* (1961), *Jacobowsky und der Oberst* (1965), *Ein wahrer Held* (1975), *Das Mädchen aus Domrémy* (1976) etc.

Kleber, Leonhard (*b* Göppingen, *c*1495; *d* Pforzheim, 4 March 1556). German organist. He studied at Heidelberg; the holder of several organist's posts, he is known chiefly for the 332-page organ tablature which he compiled in Pforzheim, 1521–4.

Kleczyński, Jan (*b* Janiewicze, 8 June 1837; *d* Warsaw, 15 Sept 1895). Polish writer, pianist, teacher and composer. His more than 1700 reviews and articles, on composers, music history, Polish folk music and Chopin's music, helped to popularize music in Poland. Besides contributing to journals, he edited *Echo muzyczne* (1880–95) and published folksongs and a Chopin edition.

Kleiber, Carlos (*b* Berlin, 3 July 1930). Argentinian conductor, son of Erich Kleiber. He studied in Buenos Aires and held posts at several European opera houses, notably Zurich and Stuttgart, appearing too at Munich, Vienna and London. In his favoured repertory – Strauss, Wagner, late Verdi, Berg – he is an interpreter of great passion and dramatic tension, with a powerful intellectual grasp, and is noted for the intense discipline and high precision he demands.

Kleiber, Erich (*b* Vienna, 5 Aug 1890; *d* Zurich, 27

Jan 1956). Austrian conductor. After study in Vienna and Prague he conducted opera at Darmstadt, Düsseldorf and Mannheim. From 1923 he was music director at the Berlin Staatsoper, conducting many new works, notably (after 137 rehearsals) the première of Berg's *Wozzeck* in 1924. His USA début was with the New York PO in 1930. Political pressure forced his resignation at Berlin in 1934 and from 1937 he directed the German opera seasons at Buenos Aires, also appearing elsewhere in Latin America. He was heard again in London (Covent Garden, 1950–53) and elsewhere in Europe after World War II. He was admired for his minutely rehearsed, and finely balanced performances especially of Berg, Strauss, Beethoven and Mozart.

Klein, Bernhard (Joseph) (*b* Cologne, 6 March 1793; *d* Berlin, 9 Sept 1832). German composer. Influenced by his friend Thibaut, he became known in Germany primarily as a sacred choral composer, drawing on Handel's style. In Berlin he was known for his lieder (over 100) in a simple, syllabic style.

Kleine Orgelmesse. Haydn's Mass no.7 in B♭ (*c*1775); its full title is *Missa brevis Sancti Joannis de Deo*.

Kleinknecht. German family of musicians. The main members were Johann Wolfgang (1715–86), a violinist who served at Stuttgart, Eisenach and Bayreuth (director of music, 1738–69), and composer of sonatas and other works; and his brother Jakob Friedrich (1722–94), a flautist and violinist at Bayreuth, Kapellmeister from 1761 (from 1769 at Ansbach), composer of trio sonatas, concertos etc.

Klemm, Johann (*b* Oederan, *c*1595; *d* ?Dresden, after 1651). German composer and music publisher. Court organist at Dresden from 1625, he was also active as a publisher producing music of his own as well as collections by his teacher Schütz. In 1631 he published his *Partitura seu Tabulatura italica*, 36 fugues for two to four voices, in each of the 12 modes, for organ or other instruments. It is a pedagogical model of instrumental *prima prattica* stressing strict counterpoint as the basis of compositional technique.

Klemperer, Otto (*b* Breslau, 14 May 1885; *d* Zurich, 6 July 1973). German conductor. He studied in Frankfurt and Berlin, receiving early encouragement from Mahler. After opera appointments at Prague, Barmen and Strasbourg he worked at Cologne, 1917–24, giving premières of operas by Zemlinsky and Schreker. He made his American début in 1927 and in that year became director of the Kroll Opera, Berlin. Until its closure in 1931 performances were given there of operas by Schoenberg, Stravinsky and Janáček as well as the standard repertory. He further enhanced his reputation as a champion of modern music with orchestral concerts in Berlin, the USSR and elsewhere. After emigrating to the USA in 1933 he conducted the Los Angeles PO (1933–9), the New York PO, the Philadelphia Orchestra and the Pittsburgh SO. He was engaged at the Budapest Opera, 1947–50 and conducted the Philharmonia Orchestra, London, from 1951, becoming principal conductor in 1959. Until his retirement in 1972 he was regarded as the most authoritative interpreter of the Austro-German tradition. Within a context of generally steady tempos his interpretations were notable for their heroic dimensions and architectural grasp. His performances of Beethoven and Bruckner were marked by tragic grandeur and Mahler's symphonies were given without Viennese sentiment. At Covent Garden in the early 1960s Klemperer conducted performances of *Fidelio*, *Die Zauberflöte* and *Lohengrin*. Among his compositions are an opera, and string quartets.

Klenau, Paul (August) von (*b* Copenhagen, 11 Feb 1883; *d* there, 31 Aug 1946). Danish composer. He studied in Berlin and Munich, and spent most of his life in Germany and Vienna as a composer and conductor. His works, looking to Bruckner and Strauss, include operas, seven symphonies (1908–41) and piano music.

Klien, Walter (*b* Graz, 27 Nov 1928). Austrian pianist. He studied in Frankfurt, Graz and Vienna, and was a pupil of Michelangeli and Hindemith. He won many prizes and toured widely, making his USA début in 1969. He has played much 20th-century music but is chiefly known for his cool, precise and stylish playing of the Viennese Classics, especially Mozart and Schubert.

Klindworth, Karl (*b* Hanover, 25 Sept 1830; *d* Stolpe, 27 July 1916). German pianist, conductor and teacher. A pupil of Liszt and an admirer of Wagner, he was active in London (1854–68), Moscow (as professor at the conservatory, 1868–82), Berlin and Potsdam, where he conducted new music and founded a piano conservatory (1884). He prepared the vocal scores of the *Ring* and made arrangements or editions of Schubert, Chopin and Bach.

Kling, Henri (Adrien Louis) (*b* Paris, 14 Feb 1842; *d* Geneva, 2 May 1918). Swiss horn player, teacher, conductor and composer of Franco-German birth. He played and taught chiefly in Geneva, also producing many textbooks and articles, arrangements for wind ensemble and four operas.

Klingenstein, Bernhard (*b* probably Peiting, 2 March 1545–1 March 1546; *d* Augsburg, 1 March 1614). German composer. He was a choirboy, subdeacon and Kapellmeister (from 1574) at Augsburg Cathedral. His motet volume (1607) includes the first solo vocal concerto published in Germany as well as pieces showing Venetian influence; ten other sacred works by him are in two volumes he edited (1604–5).

Klöffler, Johann Friedrich (*b* Kassel, 20 April 1725; *d* Burgsteinfurt, 21 Feb 1790). German composer. He served at the Steinfurt court, becoming music director in 1754; later he directed public concerts and made extensive concert tours. He composed numerous orchestral and chamber works, notably a battle symphony for two opposing orchestras (1777).

Klose, Friedrich (*b* Karlsruhe, 29 Nov 1862; *d* Ruvigliana, 24 Dec 1942). German-Swiss composer. He studied with Bruckner in Vienna (1886–9) and wrote a fairy opera (*Ilsebill*, 1903), choral works and symphonic poems. His memoirs (1927) provide insight into Bruckner's personality and Viennese musical life.

Klotz. German family of violin makers. The most celebrated members were Mathias (1653–1743), the originator of violin making in Mittenwald; his son Sebastian (1696–1775), a prolific maker whose instruments show delicacy and good taste; and his grandsons Aegidius (1733–1805) and Joseph (1743–late 18th century). The term 'Klotz school' is often used to describe late 18th-century Mittenwald instruments by lesser-known craftsmen.

Klughardt, August (Friedrich Martin) (*b* Cöthen, 30 Nov 1847; *d* Rosslau, 3 Aug 1902). German conductor and composer. He was court music director at Weimar (1869), and conductor at theatres in Neustrelitz (1873) and Dessau (1882). Of his compositions, the oratorios (notably *Die Zerstörung Jerusalems*) and concertos for cello (1894) and violin (1895) had some success.

Knaben Wunderhorn, Des. Collection of German folk poetry edited by Ludwig Achim von Arnim and Clemens Brentano (3 vols., 1805–8). Its magical evocation of Romanticism and its German national spirit attracted composers. Mahler wrote over 20 *Wunderhorn* songs for voice and piano or orchestra and incorporated texts from it in his Second, Third and Fourth symphonies. Other composers who set its poems include Weber, Mendelssohn, Schumann, Brahms, Strauss, Schoenberg and Webern.

Knappertsbusch, Hans (*b* Elberfeld, 12 March 1888; *d* Munich, 25 Oct 1965). German conductor. He studied at the Cologne Conservatory and was assistant to Richter and Siegfried Wagner at Bayreuth. He conducted at the Munich Opera from 1922, moving to Vienna in 1936 to work at the Staatsoper and with the Vienna PO. He often conducted Bruckner and at Bayreuth (from 1951) was noted for broadly conceived performances of *Parsifal* and the *Ring*.

Knecht, Justin Heinrich (*b* Biberach, 30 Sept 1752; *d* there, 1 Dec 1817). German composer. He was music director at Biberach except for a time at the Stuttgart court (1806–8). He wrote theoretical treatises, Singspiels (in Hiller's style), other vocal music and various instrumental pieces, notably a programmatic symphony (*c*1784) anticipating the subject of Beethoven's Pastoral Symphony.

Kneller Hall. *See* ROYAL MILITARY SCHOOL OF MUSIC.

Knipper, Lev (Konstantinovich) (*b* Tbilisi, 3 Dec 1898; *d* Moscow, 30 July 1974). Soviet composer. He served in the army (1917–22) before studying at the Gnesin School and in Berlin and Freiburg. In the late 1920s he belonged to the modernist stream in Soviet music: his opera *The North Wind* (1930) is comparable with Shostakovich's *The Nose*. But in later works, particularly his cycle of 14 symphonies (1929–54), he turned to the ideals of socialist realism and wrote blander music. He also wrote works on central Asian themes.

Knorr, Iwan (Otto Armand) (*b* Mewe, 3 Jan 1853; *d* Frankfurt, 22 Jan 1916). German composer and teacher. He studied with Moscheles, Richter and Reinecke at the Leipzig Conservatory. An admired teacher at the Hoch Conservatory, Frankfurt (from 1883), he wrote several pedagogical works. His compositions, influenced by Ukrainian folk music, reveal his contrapuntal mastery.

Knot Garden, The. Opera in three acts by Tippett to his own libretto (1970, London).

Knüpfer, Sebastian (*b* Aš, 6 Sept 1633; *d* Leipzig, 10 Oct 1676). German composer. Kantor of the Thomaskirche, Leipzig (from 1657), and director of the city's music, he initiated a final period of musical excellence there that culminated in the careers of Schelle, Kuhnau and Bach. His output consisted almost entirely of sacred works to Latin or German texts. Most are in the 17th-century vocal concerto style, with a substantial orchestra used to brilliant and colourful effect. He often based his German works on the text and melody of a chorale and was a master at deriving contrapuntal ideas from motivic fragmentation of the chorale. He also published a collection of secular madrigals and canzonettas (1663) for the collegium musicum students.

Knussen, (Stuart) Oliver (*b* Glasgow, 12 June 1952). English composer. He studied in London and with Schuller at Tanglewood. His works display a fine ear for complex textural blendings; they include three symphonies (1967, 1971, 1979) and the operas *Where the Wild Things Are* (1983) and *Higglety Pigglety Pop!* (1985).

Knyvett, William (*b* London, 21 April 1779; *d* Ryde, IOW, 17 Nov 1856). English composer. An alto, he sang at the Chapel Royal and Westminster Abbey and was later a concert and festival director. He specialized in singing and composing glees, and also wrote songs and anthems. His father Charles (1752–1822), a famous glee and catch singer, directed concerts of Handel's music.

Koanga. Opera in three acts by Delius to a libretto by C.F. Keary after G.W. Cable (1904, Elberfeld).

Kobelius, Johann Augustin (*b* Waehlitz, 21 Feb 1674; *d* Weissenfels, 17 Aug 1731). German composer. He was an organist at Sangerhausen. The last important composer to write operas for the Weissenfels court, he presented over 20 German works there, 1715–29.

Koch, (Sigurd Christian) Erland von (*b* Stockholm, 26 April 1910). Swedish composer. He studied in Stockholm, France and Germany, and has used Dalecarlian folk music in a large output of mostly instrumental works, including symphonies, concertos and string quartets. His fresh, well-scored pieces have made him one of the most popular Swedish composers abroad.

Koch, Heinrich Christoph (*b* Rudolstadt, 10 Oct 1749; *d* there, 19 March 1816). German theorist. After serving as a violinist (and later Konzertmeister) at the Rudolstadt court, he devoted himself to writing. His principal work, *Versuch einer Anleitung zur Composition* (1782–93), the most comprehensive composition treatise of the Classical era, was influential especially for its detailed treatment of musical form. He also wrote an important dictionary of musical terms, *Musikalisches Lexikon* (1802).

Köchel, Ludwig (Alois Ferdinand) Ritter von (*b* Stein, 14 Jan 1800; *d* Vienna, 3 June 1877). Austrian botanist, mineralogist and music bibliographer. An amateur of private means, he compiled the monumental chronological thematic catalogue of Mozart's works (Leipzig, 1862) which provided the basis for scholarly publication. Though subsequent editions alter his numbering of some of the pre-1784 works, his framework and 'K' numbers have largely endured.

Koczwara, František (*b* ?Prague, *c*1750; *d* London, 2 Sept 1791). Bohemian composer. A performer on various instruments, he settled in England in the 1770s and was in Dublin in the late 1780s. He published mostly chamber and keyboard music for amateurs; his programmatic sonata *The Battle of Prague* (*c*1788), for piano and optional accompaniment, had a wide success.

Kodály, Zoltán (*b* Kecskemét, 16 Dec 1882; *d* Budapest, 6 March 1967). Hungarian composer. Brought up in the country, he knew folk music from childhood and also learnt to play the piano and string instruments, and to compose, all with little tuition. In 1900 he went to Budapest to study with Koessler at the Academy of Music, and in 1905 he began his collaboration with Bartók, collecting and transcribing folksongs. They also worked side by side as composers, and Kodály's visit in 1907 to Paris, bringing back Debussy's music, was important to them both: their first quartets were played in companion concerts in 1910, marking the emergence of 20th-century Hungarian music.

Kodály, however, preferred to accept rather than analyse folk material in his music, and his style is much less contrapuntal and smoother harmonically. His major works, notably the comic opera *Háry János*, the *Psalmus hungaricus*, the 'Peacock' Variations for orchestra and the Dances of Marosszék and Galánta draw on Magyar folk music (unlike Bartók, he confined himself to Hungarian material). His collecting activity also stimulated his work on musical education, convincing him of the value of choral singing as a way to musical literacy. He taught at the Budapest Academy from 1907, and after World War II his ideas became the basis of state policy, backed in part by his own large output of choral music, much of it for children, as well as other exercise pieces, and was widely used as a model abroad.

Operas Háry János (1926); The Transylvanian Spinning-Room (1932); Czinka Panna (1948)

Orchestral music Summer Evening (1906); Háry János suite (1927); Dances of Marosszék (1930); Dances of Galánta (1933); Peacock Variations (1939); Conc. for Orch. (1940); Sym. in C (1961)

Choral music Psalmus hungaricus (1923); Budavári Te Deum (1936); Missa brevis (1944); At the Martyr's Grave (1945); The Music Makers (1964); sacred pieces, chorus and pf/org; many choruses, folksong settings etc for mixed, high, male and children's chorus

Chamber and instrumental music 2 str qts (1909, 1918); Sonata, vc, pf (1910); Duo, vn, vc (1914); Sonata, vc (1915); Capriccio, vc (1915); Magyar rondo, vc, pf (1917); Serenade, 2 vn, va (1920); Sonatina, vc, pf (1922); Wind qt (*c*1960); pf pieces, org pieces

Kodály method. A way of training children in music, devised by Zoltán Kodály, which is based on giving them a thorough grounding in solfeggio (using a 'movable doh' system), aimed at developing aural ability with emphasis on sight-singing, dictation and the reading and writing of music; a progressive repertory of songs and exercises, based on Hungarian folk music, is used.

Koechlin, Charles (Louis Eugène) (*b* Paris, 27 Nov 1867; *d* Le Canadel, 31 Dec 1950). French composer. He studied with Massenet, Gédalge and Fauré at the Paris Conservatoire from 1890 and was associated with such contemporaries as Ravel, Schmitt and Debussy (whose *Khamma* he largely orchestrated in 1913). As a public figure he soon became noted more for his writings on music and for his teaching (Milhaud and Poulenc were pupils) than for his composing, which at all periods was prolific. His output is enormous: there are over 200 works with opus numbers, many of them big symphonic, choral or chamber pieces. His symphonic poem *Les bandar-log* (1939), one of seven works based on the *Jungle Book* stories, shows his knowledgeable and sometimes satirical view of a wide range of contemporary musical languages, as does his *Seven Stars' Symphony* (1933), a portrait gallery of the contemporary cinema. Other works include symphonic poems, choral works, songs and instrumental sonatas, as well as numerous small pieces for diverse combinations. Some reflect his communist sympathies, some are polytonal, some influenced by his love of Bach. His uncompromising and unworldly nature contributed to his unjust neglect.

Koeckert, Rudolf (Josef) (*b* Ústí nad Labem, 27 June 1913). German violinist. He studied in Prague and held appointments there, in Bamberg and with the Bavarian RSO in Munich. He is known chiefly for the Koeckert Quartet, formed in 1939, which has given many premières and sound performances of the Classical and Romantic repertory.

Koenig, Gottfried Michael (*b* Magdeburg, 5 Oct 1926). German composer. He studied with Bialas at Detmold (1947–50) and at the Cologne Musikhochschule (1953–4), then worked at the electronic music studio in Cologne (1954–64), where he assisted Stockhausen and others. In 1964 he moved to Utrecht University, where he has developed computer systems in the generation of live and taped music.

Koessler, Hans (*b* Waldeck, 1 Jan 1853; *d* Ansbach, 23 May 1926). German composer, cousin of Reger. He studied in Munich and became a distinguished teacher at the Budapest Academy (1882–1908), where his pupils included Bartók, Kodály and Dohnányi. His output, notable for accomplished technique, includes fine choral works, two symphonies, an opera, chamber music and lieder.

Koffler, Józef (*b* Stryj, 28 Nov 1896; *d* Wieliczka, 1943). Polish composer. He studied with Schoenberg in Vienna (1920–24) and taught at the Lwów Conservatory (1929–41). His works include three symphonies, chamber and piano pieces in a lucid serial but distinctively Polish style (he was the first Pole to use 12-note serialism).

Kogan, Leonid (Borisovich) (*b* Dnepropetrovsk, 14 Nov 1924; *d* Mytishcha, 17 Dec 1982). Soviet violinist. He studied in Moscow, making his début at the age of 17. His London and Paris débuts were in 1955, his American one (at Boston) in 1958. He performed with technical mastery and a cool temperament in a repertory ranging from Bach to Berg; he was also heard in much contemporary Soviet music.

Kogoj, Marij (*b* Trieste, 27 May 1895; *d* Ljubljana, 25 Feb 1956). Yugoslav composer. He studied in Vienna with Schreker and Schoenberg (1914–18), then worked as a coach and conductor at the Ljubljana Opera. He was a pioneer of expressionism in Slovene music, his works including the opera *Black Masks* (1929).

Kohaut, Karl (*b* Vienna, bap. 26 Aug 1726; *d* there, 6 Aug 1784). Austrian lute virtuoso and composer. He was a civil servant in Vienna and a famous performer; his lute concertos are outstanding in the repertory.

Kohs, Ellis (Bonoff) (*b* Chicago, 12 May 1916). American composer. He studied at the Juilliard School and Harvard and in 1950 began teaching at the University of Southern California. His compositions, which include much chamber music, show imaginative use of variation technique, the later ones including serialism. His textbooks, notably *Music Theory* (1961), are widely used.

Kokkonen, Joonas (*b* Iisalmi, 13 Nov 1921). Finnish composer. He studied at the Helsinki Academy, where he remained as a teacher (1950–63). Influenced by Bartók and Hindemith as much as Sibelius, his works include symphonies, string quartets and the opera *The Last Temptations* (1975).

Kolb, Barbara (*b* Hartford, CT, 10 Feb 1939). American composer. She studied at Hartt College as a composer and clarinettist, and with Foss and Schuller. She has developed a vigorous eclectic style in instrumental and solo vocal works, *Appello* for piano (1976) being representative.

Kolberg, (Henryk) Oskar (*b* Przysucha, 22 Feb 1814; *d* Kraków, 3 June 1890). Polish folklorist and composer. He is best known for his systematic collection (from 1838) of Polish folktunes and for his ethnographic and historical studies of Polish music.

Kolęda [colenda]. Polish Christmas song; the term is associated with an anonymous folk-influenced repertory of the 17th and 18th centuries.

Kolisch, Rudolf (*b* Klamm am Semmering, 20 July 1896; *d* Watertown, MA, 1 Aug 1978). American violinist of Austrian birth. He studied with Schreker and Schoenberg (later his brother-in-law) and in 1922 formed the Kolisch Quartet; he settled in the USA in 1935 and gave performances of modern works, notably music of the Second Viennese School and of Bartók. Kolisch became leader of the Pro Arte Quartet in 1942 and taught at the University of Wisconsin, 1944–67.

Kollmann, Augustus Frederic Christopher (*b* Engelbostel, 21 March 1756; *d* London, 19 April 1829). German theorist and composer. He was organist and schoolmaster of the Royal German Chapel in St James's Palace, London, from 1782. To provide a simple system of music theory, he wrote several composition treatises (including *An Essay on Practical Musical Composition*, 1799) and theoretico-practical works (music with theoretical explanations). He also wrote articles, his own musical journal, piano music and vocal pieces. He was active in the Bach revival. His daughter Joanna (1786–1849) was a singer and organist; his son George Augustus (1789–1845), a pianist, organist and composer, designed a new piano action and railway carriages.

Kollo, René (b Berlin, 20 Nov 1937). German tenor, grandson of the operetta composer Walter Kollo (1878–1940). His early career was in lighter music; he made his serious début at Brunswick (1965, a Stravinsky triple bill), mainly singing lyrical roles, and sang the Steersman on his Bayreuth début (1969). He went on to sing in Vienna and Italy, with a heavier repertory, including Parsifal and Walther. His Met début was as Lohengrin and his Covent Garden début as Siegmund (both 1976), and he sang Siegfried in the Bayreuth centenary *Ring*. Basically a lyrical singer, he can nevertheless bring due force to *Heldentenor* roles.

Kol nidrei [Kol nidre]. Work for cello and orchestra by Bruch (1881).
Schoenberg's op.39, a setting for speaker, chorus and orchestra of the *Kol Nidre*.

Komische Oper. The name of two separate opera companies in Berlin. The first, 1905–11, founded by Hans Gregor, presented comic opera, operetta and works from Mozart to Puccini. Another, in East Berlin, was established at the Metropoltheater in 1947. Under Walter Felsenstein it became internationally recognized for its progressive productions. In 1966, after it moved to a new theatre, the company expanded and had a wider repertory, including new works. Notable performances have been directed by Joachim Herz and Götz Friedrich.

Komitas [Gomidas] (b Kyotaya, 8 Oct 1869; d Paris, 22 Oct 1935). Armenian composer. Trained in a seminary from 1881, he attracted notice as a singer, folksong collector and self-taught composer: he adopted 'Komitas', the name of a 7th-century hymn writer, as his religious pseudonym on becoming an archimandrite. He was one of the first Armenians to have a classical Western musical education. After studies in Berlin (1896–9) he returned to Edjmiadsin, but his activities became increasingly international and secular and in 1910 he settled in Constantinople, founding a choir. Deported to the interior during the Armenian persecution, he suffered a breakdown, and from 1919 lived in a hospital outside Paris. His works consist mostly of folksong arrangements, remarkable for their exactness and variety, for the Armenian choirs he directed. Most of his own vocal works are based on folk or sacred melodies.

Komorous, Rudolf (b Prague, 8 Dec 1931). Czech composer. He was a pupil of Bořkovec in Prague. He played the bassoon in ensembles, and taught it at the Peking Conservatory (1959–61); in 1971 he was appointed professor at the University of British Columbia. His works use avant-garde means, notably graphic notation.

Kondrashin, Kirill (Petrovich) (b Moscow, 6 March 1914; d Amsterdam, 7 March 1981). Soviet conductor. After study at the Moscow Conservatory he conducted at the Malïy Theatre, Leningrad,

1936–43. From 1943 he was at the Bol'shoy Theatre, Moscow, and in 1956 began a career in the orchestral repertory. He made his American and British débuts in 1958. As artistic director of the Moscow PO, 1960–75, he conducted (without a baton) memorable performances of Mahler and Shostakovich. In 1979 he was appointed conductor of the Concertgebouw Orchestra.

Kongelige Kapel. *See* DANISH ROYAL ORCHESTRA.

König, Johann Balthasar (b Waltershausen, bap. 28 Jan 1691; d Frankfurt, bur. 2 April 1758). German composer. He was music director at the Katharinenkirche, Frankfurt, from 1721, and at the city Kapelle from 1727. His *Harmonischer Lieder-Schatz* (1738) was the most comprehensive chorale book of the century and includes tunes of his own. He also composed sacred and occasional cantatas.

König Hirsch. Opera in three acts by Henze to a libretto by H. von Cramer (1956, Berlin); it was revised as *Il re cervo, or The Errantries of Truth* (1963, Kassel).

Königskinder. Opera in three acts by Humperdinck to a libretto by 'Ernst Rosmer' (Elsa Bernstein-Porges) (1897, Munich).

Königsperger, Marianus [Johann Erhard] (b Roding, 4 Dec 1708; d Prüfening, 9 Oct 1769). German composer. He was organist and choirmaster at the Benedictine Abbey of Prüfening from 1734, and one of the most popular and prolific composers of his generation in south Germany. His 29 Latin sacred collections include masses, offertories, psalms etc, intended for parish choirs (with instruments). He also wrote chamber and keyboard music and Singspiels.

Konink, Servaas de (d Amsterdam, 9 Dec 1717–28 Feb 1718). Netherlands composer. A teacher and member of the Amsterdam theatre orchestra, he wrote two of the earliest Dutch operas (1688, 1699), music for Racine's *Athalie* (1697) and other vocal music. These use the French style; his instrumental works (trio sonatas etc) are italianate.

Konjović, Petar (b Čurug, 5 May 1883; d Belgrade, 1 Oct 1970). Yugoslav composer. He studied at the Prague Conservatory and worked in Zagreb as a conductor (1917–39) and in Belgrade as a teacher (1939–50). Influenced by Smetana, Novák and Janáček, he used folk music in his operas (*Koštana*, 1931), instrumental music and songs (including 100 folksong arrangements).

Konrad of Würzburg (b Würzburg, c1225; d Basle, 31 Aug 1287). German Minnesinger. He was an itinerant musician, then settled in Basle and Strasbourg; probably he was the first Minnesinger to make a living from writing. He had a virtuoso talent and a vast output and influenced many later poets (he was one of the Meistersingers' 12 *alte Meister*). Much music survives in his name but it is uncertain how much he actually composed.

Kont, Paul (b Vienna, 19 Aug 1920). Austrian composer. He studied with Lechthaler at the Vienna Academy (1945–8) and with Messiaen, Honegger and Milhaud in Paris (1952). His works include operas (*Traumleben*, 1963), orchestral pieces and chamber music in a 12-note, serial style.

Kontakte. Work for four-track tape by Stockhausen (1960); he also made a version with piano and percussion.

Kontarsky. German pianists. The brothers Aloys (*b* Iserlohn, 14 May 1931) and Alfons (*b* Iserlohn, 9 Oct 1932) formed a duo in 1955, which has won an international reputation for performing modern music. They have given first performances of works by Berio, Bussotti, Kagel and Stockhausen.

Kontra-Punkte. Work for ten instruments by Stockhausen (1952), a revision of his orchestral piece *Punkte*.

Konwitschny, Franz (*b* Fulnek, 14 Aug 1901; *d* Belgrade, 28 July 1962). German conductor. He played the viola in Leipzig and Vienna before turning to conducting in 1927. Appointments in Stuttgart, Freiburg and Frankfurt were followed in 1949 by the conductorship of the Leipzig Gewandhaus Orchestra. In East Germany, and widely as guest conductor elsewhere in Europe, he was heard most often in Wagner, Strauss and Bruckner.

Konyus, Georgy Eduardovich (*b* Moscow, 30 Sept 1862; *d* there, 29 Aug 1933). Russian musicologist and composer of French-Italian descent. He studied with Taneyev and Arensky at the Moscow Conservatory, where he himself taught Skryabin, Khachaturian and others. His chief work was the creation and exposition of an original theory of musical form; his music includes orchestral and choral pieces.

Konzertmeister (Ger.). 'Concertmaster': term for the principal violin (leader) of an orchestra or ensemble.

Konzertstück (Ger.). A 'concert-piece' for solo instrument(s) and orchestra, frequently in one movement (e.g. Weber's *Konzertstück* for piano and orchestra).

Kool Jazz Festival (USA). Annual (summer) festival, formerly Newport Jazz Festival (founded 1954); it moved to New York in 1972 and was renamed in 1981.

Kopelent, Marek (*b* Prague, 28 April 1932). Czech composer. He studied with Řídký at the Prague Academy (1951–5), and since around 1960 has been influenced by Webern and the Western avant garde.

Koppel, Herman (David) (*b* Copenhagen, 1 Oct 1908). Danish composer of Polish parentage. He studied at the Copenhagen Conservatory (1926–9), where he came to know Nielsen, and in 1949 began teaching there. His works include a *Macbeth* opera (1970), symphonies, concertos, string quartets and vocal music, adapting influences from Bartók, Stravinsky, jazz and serialism to a post-Nielsen style.

Kora. A 21-string plucked harp-lute. It is used by professional male musicians of the Manding linguistic and cultural family, in West Africa. It has a long neck which passes through a large hemispherical gourd resonator covered with a leather soundtable, and has two parallel ranks of strings at right angles to the soundtable. It is used to accompany narrations, recitations and songs in honour of a patron. The term is occasionally applied to the gora of southern Africa and to the fiddle of Flores, Indonesia.

Kornauth, Egon (*b* Olmütz, 14 May 1891; *d* Vienna, 28 Oct 1959). Austrian composer. He studied with Fuchs, Schreker and Schmidt in Vienna, where he remained, though with periods touring as a trio pianist throughout Europe, in the Far East (1928–9) and Brazil (1933–5). His works, in a tonal Romantic style, include orchestral suites, chamber and piano pieces and lieder.

Korngold, Erich Wolfgang (*b* Brno, 29 May 1897; *d* Hollywood, 29 Nov 1957). American composer of Austro-Hungarian origin. Son of the music critic Julius Korngold (1860–1945), he studied with Zemlinsky and had spectacular early successes with his ballet *Der Schneemann* (1910, Vienna) and operas *Violanta* (1916) and *Die tote Stadt* (1920). In 1934 he went to Hollywood and wrote some fine film scores. After World War II he wrote orchestral and chamber pieces, including a Violin Concerto and Symphony in F♯, in a lush, Romantic style.

Kortholt. Term for double-reed instruments of the 16th and 17th centuries with bores that double back on themselves (as in the bassoon). The pitch of such instruments is thus deeper than their length suggests. 'Kortholt' was applied to the dulzian or early bassoon ('curtal' in England), the racket, the sordun or 'courtaut' and the wind-cap sordun.

Kósa, György (*b* Budapest, 24 April 1897; *d* there, 16 Aug 1984). Hungarian composer and pianist. He studied with Bartók and Kodály, played the piano in the première of Bartók's *Wooden Prince*, and taught at the Budapest Academy (1927–60). His large output covers most genres and is coloured by his concern with fate, existence and beliefs.

Koto. Japanese zither. Introduced from China in the 8th century, it has a long, slender rectangular wooden body. 13 strings of equal length and thickness are stretched over movable wooden or ivory bridges, one per bridge, tuned to various types of pentatonic scale. The strings are plucked with plectra worn on the thumb, index and middle finger of the right hand; the left hand is used to press on the string to the left of the bridge.

There are several schools of koto playing; the koto is used in *gagaku* (court music), solo music, songs with accompaniment and ensemble music with *shamisen* (lute) and *shakuhachi* (end-blown flute). In the 20th century Japanese composers (notably Miyagi Michio) have used the koto in Western-style works and introduced new types, including a 17-string bass koto.

Kotoński, Włodzimierz (*b* Warsaw, 23 Aug 1925). Polish composer. He studied with Rytel in Warsaw (1945–51), with Szeligowski in Poznań (1950–51), and at Darmstadt (1957–60). In 1967 he began teaching at the Warsaw Conservatory. His music has moved from a neo-Baroque to an avant-garde style, many works making a point of percussion or electronics.

Kotter, Hans (*b* Strasbourg, *c*1485; *d* Berne, 1541). German organist and composer. An organ pupil of Hofhaimer (1498–*c*1500), he held court and church posts in Torgau, Fribourg and Berne. He helped plan and copy three organ books, which include some of his compositions; he was a skilful, inventive composer, whose freely composed pieces are good early examples of an individual instrumental style.

Kotzwara, Francis. *See* KOCŻWARA, FRANTIŠEK.

Koussevitsky, Sergey (Alexandrovich) (*b* Kalinin,

26 July 1874; *d* Boston, MA, 4 June 1951). American conductor and composer of Russian birth. He began his career in 1896 as a double bass soloist. In 1908 he conducted the Berlin PO and gave concerts with the LSO. The following year he founded a publishing house, promoting contemporary Russian music, and formed an orchestra which toured in Russia. After the Revolution he worked in the West and in 1924 became conductor of the Boston SO. He gave many persuasive performances of music by American composers, including Barber, Copland and Harris, as well as commissioning works from Ravel, Stravinsky and Hindemith. An influential teacher, he established the Berkshire Music Center at Tanglewood in 1940; Bernstein was among his pupils. In 1942, in his wife's memory, he established the Koussevitzky Music Foundation to commission new works; among them were Britten's *Peter Grimes* and Bartók's Concerto for Orchestra. He was a colourful, flamboyant figure whose performances were marked by emotional intensity, vivid phrasing and dramatic character.

Kovařovic, Karel (*b* Prague, 9 Dec 1862; *d* there, 6 Dec 1920). Czech conductor and composer. He was a pupil of Fibich (1878–80) and in 1900 became opera director of the Prague National Theatre, making an important contribution to Czech musical life; he conducted *Jenůfa* in his own edition (1916), leading to performances that established Janáček's reputation abroad. His compositions consist mostly of operas and ballets.

Kox, Hans (*b* Arnhem, 19 May 1930). Dutch composer. He was a pupil of Badings in Utrecht. His earlier works are in traditional forms; later pieces use mobile form and spatially separated ensembles (e.g. in *Requiem for Europe*, 1971).

Kozeluch [Koželuh], **Johann Antonín** (*b* Velvary, 14 Dec 1738; *d* Prague, 3 Feb 1814). Bohemian composer, cousin of Leopold Kozeluch. He studied in Vienna (*c*1763–6) with Gluck, Gassmann and Hasse. Settling in Prague, he became Kapellmeister at the church of St Francis at the Crusaders' monastery, and from 1784 was choirmaster at St Vitus's Cathedral; he was also a famous teacher. One of the major Bohemian composers of his day, he wrote two operas (in Jommelli's style), *c*400 sacred works and several orchestral pieces.

Kozeluch [Koželuh], **Leopold** [Jan Antonín] (*b* Velvary, 26 June 1747; *d* Vienna, 7 May 1818). Bohemian composer. He studied in Prague with his cousin J.A. Kozeluch and with F.X. Dušek. Moving to Vienna in 1778, he became a successful pianist, teacher and composer, and in 1785 founded a music publishing house. From 1792 he held posts at the imperial court. One of the foremost Czech composers in 18th-century Vienna, he wrote chiefly piano music, including 49 solo sonatas, other piano pieces and piano trios and concertos. He also composed symphonies, violin sonatas and other chamber music, 12 stage works, cantatas, songs and many folksong arrangements. His vocal music is mostly *galant* in style. His instrumental works are in the Viennese Classical style; later ones have Romantic traits foreshadowing Schubert and Beethoven.

Kozlovsky, Alexey (*b* Kiev, 15 Oct 1905; *d* Tashkent, 9 Jan 1977). Soviet composer. He studied at the Kiev and Moscow conservatories, and in 1936 moved to Tashkent; there he taught at the conservatory, collected Uzbek folksongs, conducted the Uzbek Philharmonic SO and composed in most genres, bringing Uzbek elements into a colourful, Romantic style.

Kozłowski, Józef (*b* Warsaw, 1757; *d* St Petersburg, 27 Feb 1831). Polish composer and conductor. A prolific composer, he wrote songs, choral works, incidental music and several hundred polonaises, which he introduced to Russia and popularized as a dance form.

Krafft. South Netherlands family of composers and musicians. Jean-Laurent (1694–1768) was a Brussels engraver, music publisher and composer. His son François-Joseph (1721–95), music director of St Baaf Cathedral, Ghent, composed sacred music. François (1733–after 1783), son of Jean-Laurent, was a conductor at Brussels *c*1760 and a famous harpsichord teacher; he composed sacred and instrumental works.

Kraft. Austrian family of composers and cellists. The most celebrated members were Anton (1749–1820), first cellist in Prince Esterházy's orchestra and a composition pupil of Haydn (who wrote his Cello Concerto in D for him); and his son Nikolaus (1778–1853), a leading cellist of his day, who toured, performed with Mozart in Dresden, played in the Schuppanzigh Quartet in Vienna from the 1790s, and served at the Stuttgart court, 1814–34. Both father and son composed cello music.

Kraft, Anton (*b* Rokycany, 30 Dec 1749; *d* Vienna, 28 Aug 1820). Austrian composer and cellist. He held posts in Prince Nikolaus Esterházy's orchestra from 1778 (when he studied composition with Haydn), later in Bratislava and from 1796 in Prince Lobkowitz's orchestra in Vienna. Haydn's Cello Concerto in D (long attributed to Kraft) was written for him, as was the cello part of Beethoven's Triple Concerto. His own works include cello sonatas, duets for violin and cello, cello duos, a concerto and some miscellaneous pieces. His son Nikolaus (*b* Eszterháza, 14 Dec 1778; *d* Cheb, 18 May 1853) was also a distinguished cellist who played in the Lobkowitz orchestra and the Schuppanzigh Quartet; he composed cello concertos and numerous salon pieces.

Kraft, Leo (Abraham) (*b* Brooklyn, 24 July 1922). American composer. He studied at Queens College (where he joined the faculty in 1947), at Princeton and with Boulanger in Paris (1954–5). His music, mostly instrumental, was at first neo-classical but later works are atonal. An admired teacher, he is author of several theory and ear-training texts.

Krakowiak. Polish folkdance from the Kraków region, in fast duple time with syncopated rhythms. Chopin and Paderewski have used it in art music.

Kraków Philharmonic Orchestra. *See* KAROL SZYMANOWSKI PHILHARMONIC.

Kramer, Jonathan D. (*b* Hartford, CT, 7 Dec 1942). American composer. He studied at Harvard and Berkeley, and has taught at several American institutions, from 1978 at the Cincinnati College-Conservatory. His works, mostly instrumental and electronic, range from the experimental to the highly structured; *Music for Piano V* (1980) is one of the most admired.

Kraus, Alfredo (*b* Las Palmas, 24 Sept 1927). Spanish tenor. He made his début in Cairo in 1956 as the Duke (*Rigoletto*) and his Covent Garden début was in 1959 (opposite Sutherland in *Lucia di Lammermoor*). The next year he sang at La Scala, and his Met début was in 1966 (in *Rigoletto*). A smooth lyric tenor of fine taste, he is much admired for the elegance and stylishness of his singing.

Kraus, Joseph Martin (*b* Miltenberg am Main, 20 June 1756; *d* Stockholm, 15 Dec 1792). German composer. After studying at Mannheim and elsewhere in Germany, he moved to the Swedish royal court, becoming deputy orchestral conductor in 1781 and, after a long study tour of Europe, *Kapellmästare* in 1788. Gustavus III's finest composer, he wrote operas (notably *Proserpina*, 1781, and *Aeneas i Carthago*, perf. 1799), other stage music, cantatas, songs, sacred music, symphonies (including a fine one in C minor) and string quartets; many of his works use rich harmonies and show a Mannheim influence.

Kraus, Lili (*b* Budapest, 4 March 1903; *d* Asheville, NC, 6 Nov 1986). American pianist. She studied in Budapest, working with Kodály and Bartók, and in Vienna under Schnabel. She became known for her clear and musicianly interpretations of the Viennese Classics, especially Mozart; she toured widely and later taught in the USA.

Kraus, Otakar (*b* Prague, 10 Dec 1909; *d* London, 28 July 1980). British baritone. He studied in Prague and Milan, and made his début in Brno as Amonasro (1935), then sang in Bratislava but settled in London in 1940. A member of the Covent Garden company, 1951–68, he created several roles and was an outstanding Alberich. He also created Nick in Stravinsky's *The Rake's Progress* (1951, Venice). He later taught in London.

Krause, Christian Gottfried (*b* Wińsko, bap. 17 April 1719; *d* Berlin, 4 May 1770). German composer. A prominent lawyer, he established a musical and artistic salon in Potsdam and wrote a treatise (1752) which, proposing a simple song style, laid the foundation for the first Berlin Lied School. He published collections of songs by C.P.E. Bach, himself and others; he also wrote cantatas, stage and instrumental music and essays.

Krauss, Clemens (*b* Vienna, 31 March 1893; *d* Mexico City, 16 May 1954). Austrian conductor. His opera début was at Brno in 1913; after other appointments, he worked in Frankfurt, 1924–9. He was director of the Vienna Staatsoper, 1929–35, then at the Berlin Staatsoper for two years before going to the Munich Opera. Later he was associated with the Vienna PO. A friend of Strauss, he conducted the premières of four of his operas, some when other conductors withdrew for political reasons. He was a notable interpreter of light Viennese music. His wife was the soprano Viorica Ursuleac (1894–1985).

Krauze, Zygmunt (*b* Warsaw, 19 Sept 1938). Polish composer. He studied with Sikorski in Warsaw and Boulanger in Paris, and in the mid-1960s became a leading Polish modernist. His most successful piece is the orchestral *Folk Music* (1972).

Krebs, Johann Ludwig (*b* Buttelstedt, bap. 12 Oct 1713; *d* Altenburg, 1 Jan 1780). German composer and organist. His father, Johann Tobias (1690–1762), was a pupil of J.G. Walther and Bach, and became an organist and composer at Buttelstedt and later Buttstädt. Johann Ludwig also studied with Bach (who regarded him highly) before becoming organist at the Marienkirche, Zwickau, in 1737. He was organist of the castle in Zeitz, 1744–55, and court organist at Gotha from 1755. He competed unsuccessfully for Bach's Leipzig post in 1750. He composed over 100 organ works (chorales, fantasias, preludes and fugues etc), other keyboard music, chamber and orchestral works and sacred choral works. Much of his music is contrapuntal, and some (notably an organ fugue on B–A–C–H) reflects Bach's influence. Italian and French idioms appear in the keyboard suites and sonatas, and some works have *galant* elements.

His three sons were all musicians; the most important, Johann Gottfried (1741–1814), organist and later Kantor at Altenburg, wrote sacred and keyboard music.

Krebs [Miedke], Karl August (*b* Nuremberg, 16 Jan 1804; *d* Dresden, 16 May 1880). German conductor and composer. He studied in Vienna. He was Kapellmeister at Hamburg (1827–50), then at the Dresden Court Opera in succession to Wagner. His works include church music and operas but he is best known for his many songs.

Krehbiel, Henry Edward (*b* Ann Arbor, 10 March 1854; *d* New York, 20 March 1923). American music critic. He studied law and became a music critic, first in Cincinnati (1874–80) and then for the *New York Tribune* (until 1923). He was an influential advocate of Wagner's late works in the USA and of the music of Brahms, Tchaikovsky and Dvořák. His writings include a study of black folksong (1914) and a revision of Thayer's *Life of Beethoven* (1921).

Kreisler, Fritz (*b* Vienna, 2 Feb 1875; *d* New York, 29 Jan 1962). American violinist and composer of Austrian birth. After study at the Vienna Conservatory and the Paris Conservatoire he toured the USA (1888–9). Real recognition came in 1899, after a concert with the Berlin PO under Nikisch. His London début was in 1902 and in 1910 he gave the première of Elgar's Concerto. He lived in Berlin, 1924–34, and in 1939 settled in the USA, becoming an American citizen in 1943. His last concert was in 1947. Kreisler played with grace, elegance and a sweet, golden tone with a pronounced vibrato. His repertory included brief pieces of his own, some of them semi-pastiche pieces which he initially ascribed to composers such as Tartini and Pugnani, some of them sugary Viennese morsels, all beautifully written to display brilliant, subtle and expressive violin playing.

Kreisleriana. Schumann's op.16, eight fantasies for piano (1838), named after E.T.A. Hoffmann's fictional Kapellmeister.

Krejčí, Iša (František) (*b* Prague, 10 July 1904; *d* there, 6 March 1968). Czech composer and conductor. He studied composition at the Prague Conservatory with Jirák and Novák and conducting with Talich and worked for Bratislava Opera (1928), Czech radio (1934), Olomouc Opera (1945) and from 1958 Prague National Theatre. He wrote an opera *Antigona* (after Sophocles, 1934) and *Revolt in Ephesus* (after Shakespeare, 1943); he also wrote four symphonies, but his best work is in his chamber music, which demonstrates his neo-classical lyricism and wit.

Krejčí, Miroslav (*b* Rychnov nad Kněžnou, 4 Nov 1891; *d* Prague, 29 Dec 1964). Czech composer. He was a pupil of Novák and later taught in schools and at the Prague Conservatory (1943–53). He was a prolific composer in many genres in a style related to Novák and Foerster. His works include three symphonies (1944–57), two operas (*Summer*, 1940; *The Last Hetman*, 1948) as well as chamber music, piano and organ pieces and vocal music.

Kremenliev, Boris (*b* Razlog, 23 May 1911). American composer and ethnomusicologist of Bulgarian origin. He went to the USA in 1929 and studied with Hanson at the Eastman School and later taught at UCLA. His music has similarities to Bartók's. His research is on Slavonic music.

Krenek [Křenek], Ernst (*b* Vienna, 23 Aug 1900). American composer of Austrian origin. He studied in Vienna and Berlin with Schreker, who was an influence on his early works (Symphonies nos.1–3, 1921–2). After a visit to Paris, he began to emulate Stravinsky's neo-classicism, producing an eclectic style out of which, with the addition of mild jazz elements, he wrote his opera *Jonny spielt auf* (1926), a spectacular success in its day. He followed it up with more jazz operas, including *Leben des Orest* (1930), and then assimilated 12-note serialism in his most ambitious opera, *Karl V* (1938). In 1938 he moved to the USA, where he taught and continued to compose prolifically, his later works including further operas: *Pallas Athene weint* (1955), *Der goldene Bock* (1964), *Sardakai* (1970). Nearly all his music since *Karl V* is serial, several works of the 1950s and 1960s being abstract speculations in the technique. In scope and style his music embraces almost all the major trends, displayed in a highly accomplished technique.

Dramatic music Jonny spielt auf (1926); Leben des Orest (1930); Karl V (1938); Pallas Athene weint (1955); Der goldene Bock (1964); Sardakai (1970); *c*14 other operas; ballets; incidental music
Choral music Lamentatio Jeremiae prophetae (1942); other Catholic church music
Orchestral music 5 syms. (1921, 1922, 1922, 1947, 1949); 4 pf concs. (1923, 1937, 1946, 1950); Quaestio temporis (1959); Horizon Circled (1967)
Vocal music *c*20 songs, 1V, pf; *c*17 others, incl. Sestina (1957)
Chamber music 8 str qts (1921, 1921, 1923, 1924, 1930, 1937, 1944, 1981); other pieces
Piano music *c*25 pieces incl. 6 sonatas (1919, 1928, 1943, 1948, 1950, 1951)
Ballets, incidental music, tape music

Kretzschmar, (August Ferdinand) Hermann (*b* Olbernhau, 19 Jan 1848; *d* Berlin, 10 May 1924).

German music historian and conductor. He studied in Leipzig. A teacher and choral conductor in Leipzig (1871–6, 1887–1903), Rostock (1877–86) and Berlin (from 1904), he was regarded as second only to Riemann among German music historians, notably for his work on Venetian opera, performing practice and Baroque *Affektenlehre* and as an editor of early music. He did much to popularize Bach's works.

Kreutzer [Kreuzer], Conradin (*b* Messkirch, 22 Nov 1780; *d* Riga, 14 Dec 1849). German composer and conductor. He was Kapellmeister intermittently in Stuttgart, Donaueschingen, Vienna and Cologne, having his greatest success at the Viennese Theater in der Josefstadt with the pleasing and expressive operas *Das Nachtlager in Granada* and *Der Verschwender* (both 1834); the latter is still performed in Austria. He also produced atmospheric choral settings of Uhland and effective chamber music.

Kreutzer, Rodolphe (*b* Versailles, 16 Nov 1766; *d* Geneva, 6 Jan 1831). French violinist, composer and teacher. He studied with his father and with Anton Stamitz and played the first of his 19 violin concertos at the Concert Spirituel in 1784, establishing himself as a leading virtuoso. From 1790 he produced a series of stage works, of which the colourful *opéra comique Lodoiska* (1791), the ballet *Paul et Virginie* (1806) and the comedy *Aristippe* (1808) were the most popular; but the less successful biblical opera *Abel* (1810) contains some of his best music. His concert career, in Paris and on tour (Beethoven heard him in Vienna and dedicated his Violin Sonata op.47 to him), continued until 1810, complemented by teaching at the Paris Conservatoire (1793–1826); from 1817 he was chief conductor of the Opéra. Kreutzer's playing was praised by Spohr, Beethoven and Fétis. His skill as a teacher is shown by the remarkable *42 études ou caprices* (1796); he, Baillot and Rode form the founding trinity of the French violin school. His brother Jean Nicolas Auguste (1778–1832) was also a violinist and composer, and his nephew Léon Charles François (1817–68) a writer on music.

Kreutzer Sonata. Nickname of Beethoven's Violin Sonata in A op.47 (1803), dedicated to Rodolphe Kreutzer.

Sub-title of Janáček's String Quartet no.1 (1924), on the score of which he wrote 'Inspired by L.N. Tolstoy's *Kreutzer-sonata*'.

Kreuzchor. Choir of Dresden Kreuzkirche (founded 1216). The choir school was known as the Kreuzschule by the 14th century. In 1559 adults were added to the choir, which in the 18th century also served as an opera chorus. Under Rudolf Mauersberger (1930–71) it toured and gained an international reputation.

Kreyn, Yulian (Grigor'yevich) (*b* Moscow, 5 March 1913). Soviet composer. The son and nephew of composers, he studied with Dukas in Paris and settled in Moscow in 1934, writing orchestral and chamber music in a complex, lyrical style. His musicological interests centre on Debussy and Ravel.

Krieger, Adam (*b* Driesen, 7 Jan 1634; *d* Dresden, 30 June 1666). German composer. He was organist of the Nicolaikirche, Leipzig (from 1655), and of the

Dresden court (from 1658). His importance lies chiefly in his two song collections (1657, 1667), for one to five voices with instrumental ritornellos, which brought German song to a new peak of development, firmly establishing Italian expressiveness within the existing tradition of simple strophic songs. He also wrote sacred cantatas and funeral songs.

Krieger, Armando (*b* Buenos Aires, 7 May 1940). Argentinian composer, pianist and conductor. A pupil of Ginastera, he has appeared as a pianist throughout the Americas, is a conductor at the Teatro Colón and founded his own contemporary music orchestra. His works have been widely performed.

Krieger, Edino (*b* Brusque, 17 March 1928). Brazilian composer. He studied with Koellreutter (1944–8) and at the Juilliard School (1948–9), where his teachers included Copland, and has worked in Brazil as broadcaster, critic, teacher and administrator. His early works are serial, but *c*1952 he turned to slightly nationalist neo–classicism, later synthesizing both styles.

Krieger, Johann (*b* Nuremberg, bap. 1 Jan 1652; *d* Zittau, 18 July 1735). German composer, brother of J.P. Krieger. He was briefly Kapellmeister at Greiz and Eisenberg, and was organist of St Johannis, Zittau, from 1682 until his death. Admired (by Handel and Bach among others) as a contrapuntist, especially for his double fugues, he wrote two volumes of keyboard music, *Sechs musicalische Partien* (1697) and *Anmuthige Clavier-Übung* (1699, written *c*1680), which reveal him as an outstanding German keyboard composer of the generation before Bach. His only other published work is a collection of sacred and secular strophic songs (1684) for one to four voices. Of his 235 known sacred vocal works only 33 survive; and apart from a few arias, his ten operas are lost.

Krieger, Johann Philipp (*b* Nuremberg, bap. 27 Feb 1649; *d* Weissenfels, 6 Feb 1725). German composer. A child prodigy, he was playing in public at nine and at about 15 went to study in Copenhagen. He then held posts in Nuremberg, Zeitz and Bayreuth before further study in Italy; later he worked in Halle and at the Weissenfels court.

Krieger was a prolific and influential composer. He wrote 18 operas, from which only a few arias survive; he also produced over 2000 cantatas, of which 74 survive, notable for forthright melody and direct harmony and rhythm, apt to the new style of verse he favoured. His instrumental works include two sets each of 12 trio sonatas (1688, 1693) and a set of Lullian suites for wind; he also wrote early examples of the German concerto (now lost) and some keyboard music.

Krips, Josef (*b* Vienna, 8 April 1902; *d* Geneva, 13 Oct 1974). Austrian conductor. He studied at the Vienna Academy and made his début in 1921. After appointments at Dortmund and Karlsruhe he became conductor at the Vienna Staatsoper in 1935. From 1945 he helped to re-establish Viennese musical life. He toured with the Vienna PO and was principal conductor of the LSO, 1950–54. Later positions were with the Buffalo PO (1954–63) and the San

Francisco SO (1963–70). He was an accomplished conductor, particularly at home with Mozart and Schubert. His brother Henry (1912–87) was also a conductor, admired for his performances of Viennese operetta; he spent most of his life in Australia.

Křížkovský, (Karel) Pavel (*b* Holasovice, 9 Jan 1820; *d* Brno, 8 May 1885). Czech composer and choirmaster. Belonging to the founding generation of Czech national music, he excelled in writing secular choruses to Czech words, using authentic folktunes. Typical of these largely homophonic 'folksong echoes' are his choruses *Enchantment* and *The Drowned Maiden* (1848), *Turn Round* (1851) and *The Recruit's Prayer* (1857–61).

Kroepfl, Francisco (*b* Szeged, 26 Feb 1931). Argentinian composer of Hungarian origin. Taken to Buenos Aires in 1932, he studied with Paz and taught. A pioneer of electronic music, he is one of the most prominent composers of the Argentinian avant garde.

Kroll Opera. Company established in Berlin in 1927 as a branch of the Deutsche Staatsoper to perform new and standard works in a non-traditional manner at the theatre opened by Josef Kroll in 1844; among the conductors was Klemperer. It was forced to close after four seasons but its designers (including Ewald Dülberg, Oskar Schlemmer and László Moholy-Nagy) influenced the development of opera production after 1945.

Krombholc, Jaroslav (*b* Prague, 30 Jan 1918; *d* there, 16 July 1983). Czech conductor. He studied in Prague and made his début at the National Theatre there in 1940, later becoming chief conductor (1968–75) and giving operas by Smetana, Cikker and Janáček. From 1959 he was guest conductor at the Vienna Staatsoper and he was heard at the Holland and Edinburgh festivals. From 1973 to 1978 he was chief conductor of the Czechoslovak Radio SO.

Krommer, Franz (Vinzenz) [Kramář, František Vincenc] (*b* Kamenice u Třebíče, 27 Nov 1759; *d* Vienna, 8 Jan 1831). Czech composer. A violinist and organist, he settled in Vienna in 1795; in 1798 he became Kapellmeister to Duke Ignaz Fuchs. He was Ballett-Kapellmeister of the imperial court theatre from 1810 and director of chamber music and court composer from 1818. Writing mainly in the style of Haydn and Mozart, he was one of the most successful Czech composers in Vienna. His output includes symphonies, concertos (notably for wind instruments), wind partitas, many string quartets, violin duets and other chamber works and a few sacred pieces.

Kropfreiter, Augustinus Franz (*b* Hargelsberg, 9 Sept 1936). Austrian composer and organist. He was a choirman at St Florian, then studied in Linz (1954–5) and Vienna (1956–60) before returning as organist of St Florian; he has travelled throughout Europe as an organist. His works, sacred and secular, are in a traditional style drawing on Hindemithian counterpoint and sequences of triadic chords.

Krumpholtz, Jean-Baptiste (*b* Budenice, 3 May 1742; *d* Paris, 19 Feb 1790). Bohemian harpist and composer. He was the most gifted and acclaimed harp virtuoso of his day. He studied with Haydn and joined Prince Esterházy's retinue in 1773; later he made concert tours and improved the pedal harp's mechanism. He wrote harp sonatas, concertos, variations etc and a harp method (1800). His wife, Anne-Marie (*c*1755–after 1824), was also a famous harpist. His brother Wenzel (*c*1750–1817) was a violinist to Prince Esterházy and later a close friend of Beethoven.

Kruyf, Ton de (*b* Leerdam, 3 Oct 1937). Dutch composer. He was self-taught before he had lessons with Fortner in 1966. His works, in many genres, are in a lyrical, serial style (e.g. *Sinfonia II*, 1968).

Kubelík, Jan (*b* Michle, 5 July 1880; *d* Prague, 5 Dec 1940). Czech violinist and composer. After study at the Prague Conservatory he began his career as a soloist in 1898. He toured the USA from 1902 and until his retirement in 1940 was widely known in a broad repertory for his technical mastery and depth of musical perception. Six violin concertos are among his compositions.

Kubelík, Rafael (Jeronym) (*b* Býchory, 29 June 1914). Swiss conductor and composer of Czech birth, son of Jan Kubelík. He studied at the Prague Conservatory and made his conducting début with the Czech PO in 1934. He conducted Glyndebourne Opera at the 1948 Edinburgh Festival and was musical director of the Chicago SO, 1950–53. At Covent Garden (1955–8) he gave operas by Janáček and Berlioz. He was principal conductor of the Bavarian SO, 1961–79. His works include two operas and two symphonies.

Kubik, Gail (Thompson) (*b* South Coffreyville, OK, 5 Sept 1914; *d* Claremont, CA, 20 July 1984). American composer. He studied under Sowerby in Chicago (1935–6) and under Piston at Harvard (1937–8), later having contacts with Boulanger. He worked for the NBC, 1940–41, and for the US Army Air Force Picture Unit (1943–6); he later lectured and was composer-in-residence at Scripps College (1970–80). His work for radio, television and films influenced his other music, which includes orchestral, chamber and vocal compositions and uses jazz rhythms in a neo-classical style. His Second and Third Symphonies (1955–6) and the *Symphony concertante* (1952) are notable.

Kučera, Václav (*b* Prague, 29 April 1929). Czech composer. He studied with Shebalin at the Moscow Conservatory (1951–6), then worked in Prague for the radio and the composers' union. Contact with Western music in the mid-1960s took him from socialist realism to an avant-garde style, often using electronics (e.g. *Invariant*, 1969).

Kufferath. German (later Belgian) family of musicians. The most celebrated members were Hubert-Ferdinand (1818–96), a violinist who settled in Brussels as a teacher and composer, and his son Maurice (1852–1919), director of the Théâtre de la Monnaie, Brussels (1900–14), editor (later proprietor) of *Le guide musical* (1875–1914) and author of several books, notably on Wagner.

Kuhlau, (Daniel) Friedrich (Rudolph) (*b* Uelzen, 11 Sept 1786; *d* Copenhagen, 12 March 1832). Danish composer and pianist of German birth. After studying in Hamburg he established himself in Copenhagen as a pianist and composer, gaining success with his Piano Concerto op.7 and his Singspiel *Røverborgen* (1814). He was well received in Stockholm and in Vienna he met Beethoven, whose works he championed. Though best known for his Classical piano works and fashionable flute music, he also wrote fine chamber music including the Quintet op.51 and the Flute Sonata op.69, the opera *Lulu* (1824) and the popular incidental music (incorporating folktunes and the national hymn) to Heiberg's frequently performed play *Elverhøj* (1828). His piano sonatas are popular teaching pieces and his sonatinas for piano duet have become classics. With C.E.F. Weyse Kuhlau was the foremost composer of the late Classical and early Romantic periods in Denmark.

Kühmstedt, Friedrich Karl (*b* Oldisleben, 20 Dec 1809; *d* Eisenach, 8 Jan 1858). German composer. A pupil of Hummel, he was prominent in Eisenach as a teacher, director of church music and Kapellmeister; with Liszt he drew up a plan for improving musical life in Weimar. His works are contrapuntal, many modelled on Bach, and include organ pieces, an oratorio and pedagogical and theoretical writings.

Kuhnau, Johann (*b* Geising, 6 April 1660; *d* Leipzig, 5 June 1722). German composer and theorist. He studied in Dresden and Zittau, where he briefly served as Kantor and organist, and then at Leipzig, where in 1684 he became organist at the Thomaskirche and, in 1701, Kantor. His secular vocal music is all lost, but many sacred works survive, mostly cantatas, anticipating the style of Bach, his successor: they show lyrical vocal writing, powerful fugues and dramatic contrasts of texure which stress the rhetorical sense. He published four sets of keyboard pieces, including two sets called *Clavier-Übung* (each with seven suites, one set in the major keys and one in the minor) and, his best-known work, the *Biblical Sonatas*, which describe in music, sometimes naively but with enterprising use of the harpsichord's resources, the emotional states aroused by particular stories from the Bible.

Kühnel, August (*b* Delmenhorst, 3 Aug 1645; *d c*1700). German composer. A leading performer on the viola da gamba, he held posts at Zeitz and Darmstadt and as Kapellmeister at Darmstadt and Weimar. He also studied in Paris and visited London. He published a set of 14 attractive *Sonate ô partite* (1698) for one and two violas da gamba with continuo.

Kuijken. Belgian family of musicians. Wieland (*b* Dilbeek, 31 Aug 1938), viol player and cellist, studied at the Bruges and Brussels conservatories, played in the new music group Musiques Nouvelles, the Alarius Ensemble (1959–72) and a family trio; he is widely regarded as the leading exponent of the bass viol, especially in French music. Sigiswald (*b* Dilbeek, 16 Feb 1944), violinist and conductor, followed the same training and played in the same groups as Wieland; he is noted as a Bach interpreter and conducts LA PETITE BANDE, a period-instrument orchestra which he founded in 1972, with which he has given notable performances of Handel and

Rameau operas. Barthold (b Dilbeek, 8 March 1949), flautist and recorder player, studied at the same institutions and at The Hague under Brüggen; he has played in several early music groups and as soloist has played 18th-century flute music with stylish musicianship.

Kujawiak. Polish folkdance from the Kujawy region, in moderately fast triple time with misplaced accents, in effect a slightly slower form of the MAZURKA.

Kulintang. Gong-chime of the Philippines, Indonesia and other parts of south-east Asia. The term is also used for a percussion ensemble in which the *kulintang* gong-chime is the main constituent. It consists of bossed bronzed gongs laid horizontally, the largest on the left, in a row in front of the performer on two parallel strings stretched in a wooden frame, and played with two soft wooden mallets. *Kulintang* ensembles are used for feasts, weddings and entertainments; the gong-chime provides the melody and the punctuating instruments provide drones.

Kullak. German family of musicians. The most celebrated members were Theodor (1818–82), a pianist and teacher who founded the Neue Akademie der Tonkunst for pianists in Berlin and wrote the indispensable *Schule des Oktavenspiels* (1848), and his son Franz (1844–1913), a piano teacher regarded as highly as his father.

Kullervo. Symphonic poem, op.7, by Sibelius for soprano, baritone, male chorus and orchestra (1892) after the *Kalevala*.

Kummer, Friedrich August (b Meiningen, 5 Aug 1797; d Dresden, 22 Aug 1879). German cellist and composer. He was principal cellist with the Dresden court orchestra (1852–64) as well as a soloist and chamber music player, also teaching at the conservatory and composing c400 works, notably the *Concertino en forme d'une scène chantante* op.73.

Künneke, Eduard (b Emmerich, 27 Jan 1885; d Berlin, 27 Oct 1953). German composer. A pupil of Bruch, he worked in Berlin theatres. He wrote more than 30 light operas, enjoying particular success with *Das Dorf ohne Glocke* (1919) and *Der Vetter aus Dingsda* (1921). He drew on jazz in his later works.

Kunst, Jaap [Jakob] (b Groningen, 12 Aug 1891; d Amsterdam, 7 Dec 1960). Dutch ethnomusicologist. He studied the violin and became interested in Netherlands folk culture. In 1919 he went with a string trio to Indonesia, remaining until the mid-1930s; in 1930 he was given a government appointment as musicologist. He established an archive of instruments, recordings, books and photographs for the museum at Djakarta. In 1936 he became curator of the Royal Tropical Institute in Amsterdam and began to amass the collections there. From 1953 he taught at Amsterdam University. Kunst was a founder of modern ethnomusicology (a word he himself coined): he showed deep concern for humanity and the need to comprehend music in the widest possible frame of reference.

Kunst der Fuge, Die. *See* ART OF FUGUE, THE.

Kunzen. German family of musicians. Johann Paul (1696–1757), an organist and Kapellmeister, directed the Hamburg Opera briefly (1723–5) and visited London before settling in 1732 at Lübeck, where he was organist of the Marienkirche and a prominent composer of oratorio-like *Abendmusiken*. His son Adolf Carl (1720–81), also an organist, worked at the Schwerin court and (in 1754–7) in London; he then succeeded his father at Lübeck, composing notably vivid oratorios, besides occasional works, lieder and instrumental pieces. Adolf's son Friedrich Ludwig Aemilius (1761–1817) worked at Copenhagen, Berlin, Frankfurt and Prague before becoming royal Kapellmeister at Copenhagen (1795). A protégé of J.A.P. Schulz, he wrote c20 stage works, 1789–1817, mostly to Danish texts, including operas and Singspiels that recall Mozart and sometimes (in *Holger Danske*, 1789) Gluck. He also composed large-scale oratorios and folklike lieder akin to Schulz's songs.

Kuri-Aldana, Mario (b Tampico, 15 Aug 1931). Mexican composer. He studied in Mexico and at the Di Tella Institute, and has worked in Mexico as a conductor, teacher and musical ethnologist. The roots of his style are in a folkloristic neo-classicism, but he has drawn on the styles of his other teachers, notably Messiaen.

Kurka, Robert (Frank) (b Cicero, IL, 22 Dec 1921; d New York, 12 Dec 1957). American composer. Mostly self-taught, he wrote in a neo-classical style influenced by the folk music of Czechoslovakia, his parents' homeland. He is best known for the orchestral suite *The Good Soldier Schweik* (1956).

Kurpiński, Karol Kazimierz (b Włoszakowice, 6 March 1785; d Warsaw, 18 Sept 1857). Polish composer and conductor. A central figure in Warsaw musical life, he was Kapellmeister of the royal chapel (1819), founder and editor of the first Polish music periodical, *Tygodnik muzyczny* (1820–21), conductor of the Warsaw Opera (1824–40) and a music and singing teacher. Operas (notably *The Castle of Czorsztyn*, 1819) and polonaises for piano or orchestra are his most important works, which helped to lay the foundations of a national style in Polish music.

Kurtág, György (b Lugoj, 19 Feb 1926). Hungarian composer. He studied with Veress and Farkas at the Budapest Academy (1946–55) and with Milhaud and Messiaen in Paris (1957); in 1967 he began teaching at the Budapest Academy. His works are few and mostly short, suggesting a combination of the most abstract Bartók and late Webern, though with a strong lyrical, expressive force (and sometimes ingenious wit). Most of his compositions are for chamber forces, sometimes with solo voice. Among the best known are *The Sayings of Péter Bornemisza* (1968), a 'concerto' for soprano and piano in 24 short movements, and *Messages of the Late R.V. Troussova* (1980) for soprano and orchestra. Some of his pieces (e.g. 15 songs, 1982) use the cimbalom.

Kurz, Selma (b Biala, 15 Oct 1874; d Vienna, 10 May 1933). Austrian soprano. After an early career in Hamburg and Frankfurt she sang in Vienna from 1899. Until her retirement in 1927 she was admired in the coloratura repertory, as Gilda, Violetta and

Zerbinetta. At Covent Garden (1904–7, 1924) she was heard as Mimì and Wagner's Elisabeth.

Kürzinger, Paul Ignaz (*b* Mergentheim, 28 April 1750; *d* Vienna, after 1820). Bavarian composer. He was a court violinist at Munich and (from 1777) Regensburg, where he directed the court opera theatre, 1780–83. He composed operas and ballets. His father Ignaz Franz Xaver (1724–97) served at Mergentheim and later Würzburg; he wrote vocal music and a singing and violin manual.

Kusser, Johann Sigismund (*b* Bratislava, bap. 13 Feb 1660; *d* Dublin, Nov 1727). Composer of Hungarian parentage active in Germany, England and Ireland. After six years in Paris studying with Lully, his first significant post was as opera Kapellmeister at the Brunswick-Wolfenbüttel court (1690–94). A brief association with the Hamburg opera led him to form his own travelling opera company, but by 1700 he was Oberkapellmeister at the Stuttgart court. After disagreements he moved in 1705 to London, and spent much of his remaining career in Dublin, where he composed for royal celebrations. Often basing his music on French dance forms, he excelled in arias of more dramatic appeal; of his 23 known stage works only two collections of arias survive. He developed a more cosmopolitan repertory at Hamburg, raising standards of performance there by his excellence as an orchestral director.

Kuula, Toivo (Timoteus) (*b* Vaasa, 7 July 1883; *d* Viipuri, 18 May 1918). Finnish composer. He studied in Helsinki, Bologna, Paris and Germany and was a conductor in Finland. His best works are vocal, with a vein of dark pathos and folk influence, suggesting he was the most talented Finnish composer of his generation.

Kwela. Zulu term for a popular urban musical style of southern Africa. In the 1950s it was used for whistle-playing boys; the standard *kwela* ensemble today consists of one or two each of guitars and end-blown flutes with a one-string bass, the flutes played far into the mouth to produce a loud, rounded tone. The idiom draws on American popular music.

Kyrie eleison. The first acclamation in the Ordinary of the Latin Mass, sung directly after the introit. The basic text, which is Greek, consists of 'Kyrie eleison' (three times), 'Christe eleison' (three times), 'Kyrie eleison' (three times): 'Lord, have mercy... Christ, have mercy... Lord, have mercy'. The phrase 'Kyrie eleison' was used in Eastern and Western litanies from at least the 4th and 5th centuries, and St Gregory the Great (pope 590–604) is credited with establishing its use together with 'Christe eleison' in the Roman Mass. By the 10th century the ninefold shape was established.

In Renaissance and later polyphonic settings of the Mass the Kyrie may be in three movements. The Lutheran Mass consists of the Kyrie and Gloria only.

The term 'Kyriale' is used for a collection or a book of chants not only for the Kyrie of the Mass but for the entire Ordinary.

Kyung-Wha Chung. *See* CHUNG, KYUNG-WHA.

L

L. Abbreviation for Longo, used for identifying D. Scarlatti's harpsichord sonatas by their numbers in the edition by Alessandro Longo (1906–10); this numbering, however, is now superseded by others, especially Kirkpatrick's.

L.H. Left hand.

La Barbara, Joan (*b* Philadelphia, 8 June 1947). American composer and singer. She has been an influential figure in experimental music as a performer since the early 1970s, when she developed a repertory of extended vocal techniques, including multiphonics and circular breathing. Most of her compositions are for her own performance.

La Barre, de [Chabanceau de la Barre]. French family of musicians active mainly at the French court from the late 16th century to the early 18th. The foremost member was Pierre (i) (1592–1656), who played the organ and harpsichord at court and wrote instrumental and vocal music. His children included Anne (1628–1688 or earlier), a leading court singer, Joseph (1633–1678 or earlier), an organist and composer, and Pierre (ii) (1634–1710 or earlier), an instrumentalist and singer and a composer of keyboard pieces and *airs*. Some of the music attributed to the last-named may be by his father.

La Barre, Michel de (*b* c1675; *d* 1743/4). French composer and flautist. A highly renowned performer, he played in the Académie Royale de Musique, the Musettes and Hautbois de Poitou and the court chamber music. His suites for two unaccompanied flutes (1709 onwards, the first of their kind in France) and flute solos and trio sonatas established a French flute style and contributed to the instrument's popularity; Italian influence shows especially in the later works. He also wrote songs and two *opéra-ballets*.

L'abbé 'le fils' [Joseph-Barnabé Saint-Sévin] (*b* Agen, 11 June 1727; *d* Paris, 25 July 1803). French composer and violinist. A child prodigy, he studied with Leclair, 1740–42, then joined the Paris Opéra orchestra. He gave many concerts and wrote an important violin treatise, *Principes du violon* (1761). His compositions include violin sonatas (similar to Leclair's), symphonies (in a modern style) and *airs* for violin. His father, L'abbé 'l'aîné' [Pierre-Philippe Saint-Sévin] (?c1700–1768), was a prominent orchestral cellist in Paris, as was his uncle, L'abbé 'le cadet' [Pierre Saint-Sévin] (?c1710–1777).

Lablache, Luigi (*b* Naples, 6 Dec 1794; *d* there, 23 Jan 1858). Italian bass. The most famous bass of his generation, he began his career as a *buffo napoletano*, appearing throughout Italy and in Vienna before making brilliant débuts in London and Paris (1830); he continued to appear regularly in both capitals until the early 1850s. Among his most celebrated roles were Sir George Walton in Bellini's *I puritani* and the title roles in Donizetti's *Marino Faliero* and *Don Pasquale*, all of which he created.

La Borde, Jean-Benjamin(-François) de (*b* Paris, 5 Sept 1734; *d* there, 22 July 1794). French composer and writer on music. He had a political and financial career at the French court and was a pupil of Rameau. A violinist and pioneer in the study of old music, he composed c40 stage works (mostly *opéras comiques*) and many songs, arias etc. His writings include the important *Essai sur la musique ancienne et moderne* (1780). He designed a *clavecin chromatique* with 21 notes to the octave – which encourages his confusion with Jean-Baptiste de La Borde (1730–77), a scientist who designed a *clavecin électrique*.

Labroca, Mario (*b* Rome, 22 Nov 1896; *d* there, 1 July 1973). Italian composer. He studied with Respighi and Malipiero, but was closer to Casella as a propagandist on behalf of contemporary music in Florence, Milan and Venice, and while working for Italian radio. His works include vocal orchestral (*Stabat mater*, 1933) and instrumental pieces.

Labunski, Felix (*b* Ksawerynów, 27 Dec 1892; *d* Cincinnati, 28 April 1979). American composer of Polish origin. He studied with Dukas and Boulanger in Paris (1924–34) and moved to the USA in 1936. There he taught, and composed in a Romantic, partly neo-classical style.

His brother Wiktor (1895–1974) was a pianist and composer who also emigrated to the USA.

Lacépède, Bernard Germain Etienne Médard de la Ville-sur-Illon, Count of (*b* Agen, 26 Dec 1756; *d* Epinay-sur-Seine, 6 Oct 1825). French theorist and composer. An eminent naturalist, he studied composition with Gossec and wrote dramatic and instrumental works; he destroyed his *Armide* on learning of Gluck's. His *Poétique de la musique* (1785) offered an unusually serious discussion of instrumental music.

Lacerda, Osvaldo (Costa de) (*b* São Paulo, 23

March 1927). Brazilian composer. He studied with Guarnieri (1952–62) and in the USA; in 1969 he began teaching in São Paulo. His works, in all non-dramatic genres, bring Brazilian folk music into a modern idiom. His best-known orchestral piece is the nationalist suite *Piratininga* (1962).

Lachenmann, Helmut (Friedrich) (*b* Stuttgart, 27 Nov 1935). German composer. He studied with David at the Stuttgart Musikhochschule (1955–8) and with Nono in Venice (1958–60). In 1966 he began teaching. In later works he simplified his forms and lessened the extent of aesthetic intervention in his material.

Lachner, Franz Paul (*b* Rain am Lech, 2 April 1803; *d* Munich, 20 Jan 1890). German composer and conductor. Having been conductor of the Kärntnertor Theater, Vienna (1829), he became prominent in musical life in Munich (1836), conducting the court opera, concerts of the Musikalische Akademie and Königliche Vokalkapelle and festivals; personal confrontation with Wagner brought his career to an abrupt end in 1864. A prolific and craftsmanlike composer, he was influenced mainly by Beethoven and Schubert; the opera *Catarina Cornaro* (1841), the seventh orchestral suite (1881) and the Requiem op.146 had particular success. His brothers Theodor (1788–1877), Ignaz (1807–95) and Vinzenz (1811–93) were all musicians.

Lachnith, Ludwig Wenzel (*b* Prague, 7 July 1746; *d* Paris, 3 Oct 1820). Bohemian composer and horn player. After serving the Duke of Zweibrücken (from 1768) he settled in Paris and became *instructeur* at the Opéra. He composed stage works and was later notorious for his pasticcios, including a mutilated version (1801) of *Die Zauberflöte*. He made keyboard arrangements of music by Haydn and others, and composed symphonies and chamber works.

Lachrimae, or Seaven Teares. Collection of 21 pieces by Dowland for five viols and lute (1604), the 'seaven teares' being seven pavans called *Lachrimae*, each a set of variations on his song *Flow my Teares* (the 14 other pieces are dances).

Britten wrote *Lachrymae* (op.48) for viola and piano after Dowland (1950).

Lacombe [Trouillon-Lacombe], Louis (*b* Bourges, 26 Nov 1818; *d* St Vaast-la-Hougue, 30 Sept 1884). French composer and writer. He studied at the Paris Conservatoire and had piano lessons with Czerny in Vienna. Among his hundreds of works in many genres, the songs, piano pieces and small-scale, folk-orientated operas show his unpretentious, sensitive style at its most effective, though his best-known work is the dramatic symphony *Sapho* (1878). He contributed to *La chronique musicale*.

Laderman, Ezra (*b* Brooklyn, 29 June 1924). American composer. He studied with Wolpe (1946–9) and with Luening at Columbia (1950–52), and in 1971 was appointed professor at Binghamton. His works are vigorous and Romantic and include several on Jewish subjects; he has a melodic gift and an ability to combine tonal with atonal or aleatory material, often in unusual structures. Some of his most interesting experiments are in his eight string quartets (1953–85).

Lady Macbeth of the Mtsensk District [Ledi Makbet Mtsenskovo uyezda]. Opera in four acts by Shostakovich to a libretto by Preys after Leskov (1934, Leningrad); Shostakovich revised it as *Katerina Izmaylova* (1963, Moscow).

L'Affilard, Michel (*b* c1656; *d*?Versailles, 1708). French composer, theorist and singer. He was a member of the Versailles royal chapel from 1683. The first composer to supply metronome indications, he is best known for his sight-singing treatise *Principes très-faciles pour bien apprendre la musique* (five edns., 1694–1705); the dance-songs it contains provide valuable insights on the performance and quality of movement of early 18th-century dance music.

Lafont, Charles Philippe (*b* Paris, 1 Dec 1781; *d* nr. Tarbes, 10 Jan or 14 Aug 1839). French violinist and composer. He inherited the classical technique of the Viotti school through his teachers Kreutzer and Rode, making it more brilliant and idiomatic, notably in a 'contest' with Paganini (1816). Besides fashionable virtuoso music he composed *duos concertants* for violin and piano and over 200 romances.

La Garde, Pierre de (*b* nr. Crécy-en-Brie, 10 Feb 1717; *d* c1792). French composer and baritone. He worked at the French court, was an assistant conductor at the Paris Opéra, 1750–55, and in 1756 became *compositeur de la chambre du roi*. He composed a successful *pastorale heroïque*, *Aeglé* (1748), three other stage works, *airs* (including brunettes with harp or guitar), cantatas and *cantatilles* in an attractive lyrical style.

La Guerre, Michel de (*b* Paris, c1605; *d* there, bur. 13 Nov 1679). French composer. The most important member of a family of musicians who flourished in Paris for about 100 years from 1630. He was organist of the Sainte-Chapelle from 1633. His pastorale *Le triomphe de l'Amour sur des bergers et bergères* (1655, staged 1657; music lost) has claims to be reckoned the earliest French opera.

Lai (Ger. *Leich*). The lai proper or lyric lai, as distinct from the narrative lai cultivated by Marie de France in the second half of the 12th century, is an extended song form of the 13th and 14th centuries. Each stanza (if it is in stanzas) has a different form and consequently different music. Starting from extreme freedom of structure in the 13th century, the lai developed in the 14th into a more regular form, typically of 12 stanzas of which the first and last may be related. Its principal 14th-century exponent was Machaut, in whose hands it developed a variety of metre and a control of polyphonic accompaniment which anticipated the later larger forms. Its demise is attributable both to the declining status of monophonic song in the 15th century and to the emergence of the cyclic mass as primary focus for the aspiration to extend musical structures.

Laissez vibrer (Fr.). 'Let vibrate': term used in music for certain percussion instruments, particularly cymbals.

Lajtha, László (*b* Budapest, 30 June 1892; *d* there, 16 Feb 1963). Hungarian composer. He studied with Herzfeld at the Budapest Academy and from 1910 was associated with Bartók and Kodály in their folksong collecting. He then taught at the National Conservatory (1919–49). He travelled widely in Europe and was internationally renowned for his folk music research. In 1952 he was appointed professor at the Budapest Academy. Though influenced by Bartók, he was closer to French and Italian music than were any of his Hungarian contemporaries, and his music shows a progression from chromatic harmony through a strongly contrapuntal period (from the end of World War I to the mid-1930s) to an assertion of melody, his many fugal movements giving way to aria forms. His works include nine symphonies (1936–61), ten string quartets (1922–53), choral and vocal music.

Lakmé. Opera in three acts by Delibes to a libretto by Gondinet and Gille (1883, Paris).

Lakner, Yehoshua (b Bratislava, 24 April 1924). Israeli composer. He settled in Palestine in 1941 and studied with Partos and Boskovich; in 1959–60 he studied in Germany with Stockhausen and Zimmermann. He moved to Zurich in 1963, and has written much electronic music for plays.

Lalande [Delalande], Michel-Richard de (b Paris, 15 Dec 1657; d Versailles, 18 June 1726). French composer. An organist at four Paris churches, and a harpsichordist, he became *sous-maître* at the royal chapel in 1683 and *compositeur de la musique de la chambre* in 1685, gaining total control of these posts in 1714 and 1709 respectively. He was also *surintendant de la musique de la chambre* (from 1689), then *maître* (from 1695). After Louis XIV's death in 1715 he gradually gave up all these responsibilities.

Lalande was the leading composer of the late Baroque *grand motet*, writing over 70 such works for the royal chapel. They bring together disparate elements (Gregorian melodies, counterpoint, *galant* style) with a new depth of feeling and are notable for their adventurous harmonies. Later he adapted certain works, creating larger, autonomous movements and adding elaborate arias or duets and more counterpoint. He also composed other sacred pieces, various stage works (from which he compiled instrumental *Symphonies*), *Sinfonies pour les soupers du Roi, Symphonies des Noëls* and airs. His *Ballet de la jeunesse* (1686) was a precursor of the *opéra-ballet*.

La Laurencie, Comte (Marie-Berband-) Lionel (-Jules) de (b Nantes, 24 July 1861; d Paris, 21 Nov 1933). French musicologist. In 1898 he abandoned a career in government for music. He gave lecture courses, founded the Société Française de Musicologie in 1917 and became editor of the *Encyclopédie de la musique et dictionnaire du Conservatoire* in 1919. His main interest was French music from Lully to Gluck, of which he provided both general and detailed studies; his greatest contribution was his three-volume study (1922–4) of French violin music.

Lalo, Edouard(-Victoire-Antoine) (b Lille, 27 Jan 1823; d Paris, 22 April 1892). French composer. He studied at the Lille Conservatory and in Habeneck's class at the Paris Conservatoire. As a violinist and teacher in Paris in the 1850s he showed an unfashionable inclination towards chamber music, playing Classical string quartets and composing string trios and a noteworthy quartet. During the 1870s he attracted attention for his instrumental works, especially for the *Symphonie espagnole* (1874), a five-movement violin concerto, and the powerful Cello Concerto (1877). After disappointment at the poor reception of his opera *Fiesque* (1866–7), he took up stage music again in 1875, winning success with *Le roi d'Ys* (1888), on which his operatic fame has rested; his ballet score *Namouna* (1881–2) became popular as a series of orchestral suites. Among the hallmarks of Lalo's music, the vigour of which stands in contrast to the style of Franck's pupils and the impressionists, are his strongly diatonic melody, piquant harmony and ingenious orchestration.

Lambardi, Camillo (b Naples, c1560; d there, Nov 1634). Italian composer. A pupil of Nola at the Annunziata church, Naples, he sang there from 1569, becoming *maestro di cappella* in 1592. He published responsories for double chorus (1592), motets (1613, 1628) and madrigals (1600, 1609). His son Francesco (c1587–1642), a singer and *maestro di cappella* in Naples, published secular works (1607, 1614, 1616) that include some of the earliest Neapolitan arias with continuo.

Lambe, Walter (b ?1450–51; d after Michaelmas 1499). English composer. He may have been the Lambe born in Salisbury, elected scholar of Eton College in 1467 and admitted a lay clerk at St George's Chapel, Windsor, in 1479. An esteemed and popular composer, he contributed many sacred pieces to the Eton Choirbook.

Lambert, (Leonard) Constant (b London, 23 Aug 1905; d there, 21 Aug 1951). English composer. He entered the RCM when he was 17, and was becoming well known by the time he was 20. He was the first English composer commissioned by Dyagilev (*Romeo and Juliet*, 1926), initiating a lifelong association with ballet as a conductor and composer: he wrote *Pomona* (1927) for Nizhinska and *Horoscope* (1938) for the Vic-Wells Ballet, of which he was founder musical director (from 1931). But he also wrote concert pieces, preferring unconventional genres and anti-traditional tastes for jazz and Stravinsky: such works include *The Rio Grande* for piano, chorus and orchestra (1927), the Concerto for piano and nonet (1930–31) and the choral orchestral 'masque' *Summer's Last Will and Testament* (1932–5). He stood in sharp relief against the background of English musical life and had wide-ranging interests. A lively critic, he wrote the stimulating *Music Ho! a Study of Music in Decline* (1934).

Lambert, John (Arthur Neill) (b Maidenhead, 15 July 1926). English composer. He studied at the RCM (1943–50) and with Boulanger in Paris (1950–53), and in 1963 returned to the RCM as a teacher. His music may be compared with Lutosławski's in its wary modernism (e.g. *Formations and Transformations*, 1969).

Lambert, Michel (b Champigny-sur-Veude, 1610; d Paris, 29 June 1696). French composer and singer. One of the most important French composers of *airs* in the second half of the 17th century, he succeeded Cambefort as *maître de musique de la chambre du roi* in 1661, having been granted a 20-year-old royal privilege for printing his music in 1659. His surviving 300 *airs* are models of elegance in which careful attention is paid to correct declamation; most are short binary structures followed by a *double*, while some use chaconne basses or are organized as dialogues. French opera composers were influenced by his dialogues and more dramatic *récits* and he was in demand as a singing teacher.

Lamellaphone. Term for an instrument whose sound is produced by the vibration of thin lamellae or tongues of metal, wood or other material. It is found throughout Africa and in parts of Latin America. Examples are the *mbira* and the *likembe*, of Zimbabwe and Zaïre. It consists of a set of tuned tongues fitted to a board or resonator so that one end of each tongue can vibrate freely; the free ends are plucked (depressed and released) by the player. The instrument is commonly used to accompany song.

Lament. Term for a variety of musical and poetic forms related to mourning rites for the dead or ritual leave-taking. The domestic funeral lament, which goes back to antiquity, is still widely practised in some rural areas as an outlet of emotion and as part of the rites of transition. Most domestic laments take the form of alternating cries of grief (the 'planctus') and the framing of a message (the 'discourse'). Laments are normally performed by women, either relatives of the dead person or women of prestige with a talent for keening. Their song usually has a narrow compass, often within five notes.

For particular kinds of lament, *see* APOTHÉOSE; CAOINE; DÉPLORATION; DIRGE; DUMP; ELEGY; LAMENTO; PLAINTE; PLANCTUS; TOMBEAU; *and* THRENODY.

Lamentations. Verses of the prophet Jeremiah sung as lessons in the Holy Week Tenebrae services in the Roman Catholic church. A distinguishing feature is the inclusion of Hebrew letter-names (Aleph, Beth etc) at the beginning of the text of each verse. The Lamentations were sung to a simple recitation tone, also found in many polyphonic settings, including those in an early printed collection (1506) by Arcadelt, Isaac, La Rue and their contemporaries. Carpentras's Lamentations were sung in the papal chapel until replaced in 1587 by Palestrina's. In his and Lassus's settings the recitation tone was not always used; the Lamentations of Byrd and Tallis dispense with it. 17th-century Lamentations include a famous setting by Allegri; many solo settings with continuo were also composed in Italy. Interest waned in the 18th century, although at Naples Alessandro Scarlatti, Porpora and Jommelli contributed to the tradition.

Lamentations settings were also made in France after 1600 under the title *leçons de ténèbres*; those of Charpentier, Lalande and Couperin exemplify the florid French style.

Lamentation Symphony. Nickname of Haydn's Symphony no.26 in D minor (late 1760s), so called because some of its themes resemble plainsong melodies sung in the week before Easter.

Lamento. A setting of a mournful text common in baroque operas and cantatas. The most influential early 17th-century example was Monteverdi's *Lamento d'Arianna* (1608), an expressive operatic recitative. His *Lamento della ninfa* (1638) established

a type 'in stile recitativo' over a repeated descending four-note figure which was widely imitated, notably by Cavalli. Pathetic lament arias, many of them with some form of descending four-note bass, are found in Purcell's operas and early 18th-century works. 'Lamento' is occasionally used as a title of instrumental works.

Lamoureux, Charles (*b* Bordeaux, 28 Sept 1834; *d* Paris, 21 Dec 1899). French conductor and violinist. He studied at the Paris Conservatoire, joining the Société des Concerts du Conservatoire and forming his own concert-giving chamber groups (1860, 1872); by 1873–4 he was mounting large-scale choral performances (*Messiah, St Matthew Passion, Judas Maccabaeus*, Gounod's *Gallia* and Massenet's *Eve*). His chief importance lies in his direction of the Société des Nouveaux-Concerts (the Concerts Lamoureux), which from 1881 gave weekly orchestral performances noted for their precision and expressiveness; he travelled to Russia and regularly to London with his orchestra. A committed Wagnerian, he introduced selections from Wagner's operas and eventually produced *Lohengrin* (1887, 1891) and *Tristan und Isolde* (1899).

Lampe, John Frederick [Johann Friedrich] (*b* Saxony, *c*1703; *d* Edinburgh, 25 July 1751). German composer. He worked in London as a bassoonist from *c*1724 and a dramatic composer from 1732. His several attempts at serious English opera in the Italian manner failed, but he had success with lighter works, notably the burlesque *The Dragon of Wantley* (1737) and the satirical all-sung mock opera, after Shakespeare, *Pyramus and Thisbe* (1745). His other works include songs, hymn tunes (to words by Charles Wesley) and two harmony manuals.

Lampugnani, Giovanni Battista (*b* Milan, 1706; *d* there, 12 June 1788). Italian composer, possibly a son of the Italian writer Giovanni Battista Lampugnani (*fl* 1690–98). Presenting his first serious operas in Milan in the 1730s, he established a wide reputation. In 1743–4 he was resident composer at the King's Theatre, London, where he presented two operas and contributed to pasticcios. After returning to Italy he composed several more operas, including his five comic ones (1758–69, Milan). Later he worked in Milan as a singing teacher and harpsichordist. His *c*23 serious operas are unusual for combining light, tuneful writing (like that in his comic works) with elaborate melodic ornamentation. He also composed two serenatas, sacred pieces, many songs and arias, and several trio sonatas and sinfonias similar to G.B. Sammartini's.

Lancers. A 19th-century variant of the quadrille, danced to music from popular songs and stage works. The name derives from the *Quadrille des lanciers*.

Land des Lächelns, Das [The Land of Smiles]. Operetta in three acts by Lehár to a libretto by L. Herzer and F. Löhner (1929, Berlin).

Landi, Stefano (*b* Rome, 1586/7; *d* there, 28 Oct 1639). Italian composer. He studied at the Collegio Germanico and the Seminario Romano, under Agazzari. By 1618 he was *maestro di cappella* to the Bishop of Padua, where his first opera, *La morte d'Orfeo*, was given in 1619; the next year he was back in Rome, where he remained, working for a number of churches, the papal choir and the Borghese and Barberini families. It was for the Barberini that his most important work, the sacred opera *Sant' Alessio*, was written in 1631 or 1632: this was the first opera on a historical topic, the first about a human's inner life and one of the first about a saint. It is notable for its instrumental sinfonias, its use of comic characters, its choral writing, its dances and the expressive use of recitative and also of ensemble. Landi's other works include madrigals, several books of arias, psalms, masses and motets, some in a conservative Roman style.

Landini, Francesco (*c*1325–97). Italian composer, poet and performer. Blinded by smallpox in childhood, he mastered the organ and other instruments, working at home in Florence and probably also in Venice, as well as writing on philosophical, religious and political topics of the day. He is buried at S Lorenzo, Florence. Most of his surviving works are ballate, of which roughly two-thirds are for two voices and one-third for three. His style ranges from simple dance-song to intricate canonic or isorhythmic forms, synthesizing the Italian style of his predecessors with French influences and displaying a distinctive gift for melody. The so-called Landini (under-3rd) cadence is frequent in upper parts. Hardly any poetry can be securely attributed to him, although the texts of the autobiographical songs, in the Italian *dolce stil novo* associated with Dante, Boccaccio and Petrarch, are presumably his.

*Works c*140 ballate; 1 virelai; 1 canonic madrigal; 9 other madrigals; 1 caccia

Landini cadence [Landino 6th]. A name often used for a cadential formula in which the sixth degree of the scale is interposed between the leading note and its resolution on the tonic or final degree. Examples appear in the music of Francesco Landini but it is common in 15th- and early 16th-century polyphony.

Ländler. A folkdance in slow 3/4 time, popular in Austria, south Germany and German Switzerland. In the 17th and 18th centuries it was an outdoor round dance with hopping and stamping; later, it became a quicker, more elegant ballroom dance, and initiated the waltz which superseded it. The *ländler* was used by such Austrian symphonists as Haydn, Mozart and Mahler. A genuine Carinthian *ländler* is quoted in Berg's Violin Concerto.

Landon, H(oward) C(handler) Robbins (*b* Boston, 6 March 1926). American musicologist. After studying music in Philadelphia and Boston, he worked as a music critic in Europe. He began to establish his reputation as a Haydn scholar in the late 1940s, culminating in his book on the symphonies (1955) and his five-volume *Haydn: Chronicle and Works* (1976–80), both landmarks. He has edited many other Haydn works, notably the operas, stimulating performances and provoking a reappraisal of Haydn as a dramatic composer. He has also worked on other 18th-century music, written articles and reviews and broadcast and lectured widely.

Landowska, Wanda (*b* Warsaw, 5 July 1897; *d* Lakeville, CT, 16 Aug 1959). Polish harpsichordist. She studied in Warsaw and Berlin and in 1900 moved to Paris. Her early career was as a pianist but from 1903 she played the harpsichord. In 1923 she made her début in the USA and settled there in 1940. Both in her writings and as a vigorous and vital performer with a powerful yet flexible rhythmic sense she did much to develop modern harpsichord playing and became the leading figure in the instrument's revival. Many eminent players were her pupils and several works were written for her (including concertos by Falla and Poulenc).

Landowski, Marcel (*b* Pont L'Abbé, 18 Feb 1915). French composer. He studied at the Paris Conservatoire and after military service (1939–40) had advice from Honegger. In 1966 he was appointed director of music for the ministry of culture. His works include operas, symphonies and vocal music, in which he sought a middle path between conservatism and the avant garde.

Landré, Guillaume (*b* The Hague, 24 Feb 1905; *d* Amsterdam, 6 Nov 1968). Dutch composer. A pupil of Pijper, he was an administrator in Dutch new music, and moved in his own works from a motivic style to one of longer, often elegiac melodies. His works include operas, four symphonies and four string quartets.

Láng, István (*b* Budapest, 1 March 1933). Hungarian composer. He studied at the Budapest Academy, where he began teaching in 1973. His works, in a refined modernist style and favouring cyclic form, are in many genres, including opera.

Lang, Johann Georg (*b* Svojšín, 1722; *d* Ehrenbreitstein, 17 July 1798). German composer of Bohemian descent. He played the keyboard and violin, and in 1746 joined the Prince-Bishop of Augsburg's orchestra; he was Konzertmeister by 1758. His output includes 29 concertos for keyboard (one was falsely attributed to Haydn), 38 symphonies, chamber music with keyboard, keyboard sonatas and vocal works (mostly sacred).

Lang, Josephine (Caroline) (*b* Munich, 14 March 1815; *d* Tübingen, 2 Dec 1880). German composer. A pupil of Mendelssohn, she published several books of songs highly praised for their lyricism and literary sensibility.

Lang, Paul Henry (*b* Budapest, 28 Aug 1901). American musicologist of Hungarian birth. He studied in Budapest and became a conductor and bassoonist. In 1924 he turned to musicology, studying at Heidelberg and Paris, then went to the USA, teaching at Columbia University (1933–69). He was editor of *The Musical Quarterly* (1945–73), a critic for the *New York Herald Tribune* (1954–63) and president of the IMS (1955–8). He wrote many articles and a book on Handel (1966), his monumental *Music in Western Civilization* (1941) being an outstanding contribution to cultural history.

Lange, de. Dutch family of organists and composers. The most celebrated members were Samuel (1840–1911), a teacher and conductor who played an influential part in the Dutch Bach renaissance, and his brother Daniël (1841–1918), an acclaimed choral conductor and champion of early Netherlands polyphony and author of several books and articles.

Lange, Francisco Curt (*b* Eilenburg, 12 Dec 1903). Uruguayan musicologist of German origin. He studied at Leipzig, Berlin, Munich and Bonn universities. In 1930 the Uruguayan government invited him to help organize the country's musical life and he settled in Montevideo. He played a central role not only in Uruguay but also in other South American countries, editing music, writing books and articles, organizing concerts and building cultural links.

Langeleik. Norwegian ZITHER in box form. It has one melody string, three to seven drone strings and a fretted fingerboard; it is played with a plectrum. It was established *c*1600 and remained common in domestic music until the mid-19th century.

Lange-Müller, Peter Erasmus (*b* Frederiksberg, 1 Dec 1850; *d* Copenhagen, 26 Feb 1926). Danish composer. Largely self-taught, Romantic by inclination and isolated by choice, he evolved an individual vocal style, the subtlety of which was unprecedented in Danish music; it is seen at its best in his songs and in the choral *Madonnasange* op.65. His many operas were unsuccessful but the incidental music for *Der var engang* op.25 and the Piano Trio op.53 secured him recognition.

Langer, Susanne K(atherina) (*b* New York, 20 Dec 1895; *d* Old Lyme, CT, 17 July 1985). American philosopher. After studying at Radcliffe College and in Vienna, she taught at various institutions, notably Connecticut College. Her publications of 1940–60 centred on a philosophy of art derived from a theory of musical meaning, involving the use of music as paradigm of a symbol system; she regards the principles of musical form as structurally the same as those of the patterns of human feeling.

Langgaard, Rued (Immanuel) (*b* Copenhagen, 28 July 1893; *d* Ribe, 10 July 1952). Danish composer. The son of a Liszt pupil, he had works performed from boyhood. After World War I he reacted violently against neo-classicism and adopted a Romantic style based on Gade and Wagner; this, and his attacks on Danish musical life, made him an isolated figure. His works include the opera *Antikrist* (1916–36), 16 symphonies (1911–51) and six string quartets (1914–31).

Langhans, (Friedrich) Wilhelm (*b* Hamburg, 21 Sept 1832; *d* Berlin, 9 June 1892). German writer, composer and violinist. An admirer of Wagner and an advocate of reforms in music education, he contributed to music periodicals including the *Neue Berliner Musikzeitung*, the *Neue Zeitschrift für Musik* and *Echo*.

Langlais, Jean (*b* La Fontenelle, 15 Feb 1907). French composer and organist. He studied at blind school, with Dupré and Dukas at the Paris Conservatoire, and with Tournemire, whom he succeeded in 1945 as organist at Ste Clotilde. He has visited the USA several times. His works are mostly masses and organ music, some based on Gregorian themes, enhanced by rich polymodal harmonies.

Langridge, Philip (Gordon) (*b* Hawkhurst, 16 Dec 1939). English tenor. He studied the violin at the RAM but in 1962 turned to singing, studying under

Bruce Boyce. Apart from Mozart roles, notably Idomeneus (at La Scala and Glyndebourne) and Ferrando (at the Met), he has chiefly sung in Baroque music (Monteverdi, Rameau, Handel's Scipio) and a wide range of 20th-century roles – including Tom in Stravinsky's *Rake's Progress*, Janáček's Laca (at Covent Garden), Schoenberg's Aaron, Britten's Quint and Vere (1988, ENO) and the title role in Birtwistle's *Mask of Orpheus* (1986, ENO) – where his careful musicianship, clear diction and attractively astringent timbre serve well.

Langsam (Ger.). Slow.

Langspil. Icelandic ZITHER in box form. It has one to six strings and a fretted fingerboard and is played with a horsehair bow. It became obsolete in the late 19th century but has been reintroduced in music education.

Lanier, Nicholas (*b* London, bap. 10 Sept 1588; *d* there, bur. 24 Feb 1666). English composer, singer and artist. He was a member of a family of musicians of French descent. Master of the King's Musick from 1625 (lutenist from 1616), he was important as a songwriter, and particularly as an early exponent of the Italian declamatory style. He wrote music for four masques by Jonson, in the first of which, *Lovers Made Men* (1617), he is described as introducing 'stylo recitativo' into England. Between 1625 and 1628 he travelled to Italy buying pictures for Charles I, and on his return composed the long recitative *Hero and Leander*; remarkable for its expressive force, the music shows the influence of Italian laments. Another Italian form that he may have imported was the strophically varied aria over a repeated bass.

Lanner, Joseph (Franz Karl) (*b* Vienna, 12 April 1801; *d* Oberdöbling, 14 April 1843). Austrian composer and violinist. From a quintet in which he played the violin and the elder Johann Strauss the viola (1820), he built a full orchestra that performed popular dance music in taverns in Vienna and in the Prater; it split, forming the rival Lanner and Strauss dance bands which laid the foundations of the classical Viennese waltz. Lanner's gift for a coaxing, Schubertian lyricism was matched by his sense of Romantic harmonic colour, notably in his dances *Die Pesther* op.93, *Die Werber* op.103, *Die Romantiker* op.167 and *Die Schönbrunner* op.200.

Lantins, de. Family of early 15th-century composers and musicians from Liège. Of Berthold, Ray and Johannes little is known, but numerous works survive by Arnold and Hugo (both *fl* 1420–30). Arnold's brief career in the papal choir overlapped with Dufay's and his works include items for the mass, a mass cycle on 'Verbum incarnatum', and several *chansons*. Hugo, also closely connected with Dufay, is represented in the same MSS as Arnold. Hugo's works, comprising principally Glorias, motets and rondeaux, are distinguished by the exceptionally lavish use of imitation.

Lanza. Italian family of musicians. The most celebrated members were Gesualdo (1779–1859), a singing teacher in London, and his brother Francesco (1783–1862), a pupil of Field, who taught and composed for the piano, becoming the founder of the Neapolitan piano school.

Lanzetti, Salvatore (*b* Naples, *c*1710; *d* Turin, *c*1780). Italian cellist and composer. He served at Turin and also made concert tours, spending much time in London. His cello sonatas (1736 onwards), unusually demanding for their date, helped to establish a taste for the cello in England.

Lapicida, Erasmus (*b* ?1440–45; *d* Vienna, 19 Nov 1547). Composer. He was a singer in the Elector Ludwig V's court chapel in Heidelberg (1510–21) and was later connected with the Habsburgs and with the Archduke Ferdinand of Austria, settling in Vienna *c*1520. His works, in numerous styles, include seven Latin motets and some excellent polyphonic adaptations of German folksongs and *Hofweisen*, whose frottola-like traits suggest Italian influence.

Lara, Isidore de [Cohen] (*b* London, 9 Aug 1858; *d* Paris, 2 Sept 1935). English composer and pianist. He studied in Milan and with Lalo in Paris and was a successful composer of songs and small-scale piano pieces; he also promoted new music. Private patronage enabled him to write operas, staged at Covent Garden (*Amy Robsart*, 1893), Monte Carlo (*Messalina*, 1899) and in Paris (*Naïl*, 1912).

Lardenois, Antoine (*b* Paris; *d* ?Dax, *c*1672). French composer. He worked in Nîmes and Paris, becoming choirmaster of Dax Cathedral in the late 1660s. He was a Protestant, 1652–60, and devised a simplified solmization system for the Protestant psalter, using it in his editions of *Les psaumes de David* after Marot and de Bèze (1651) and *Paraphrase des pseaumes* by Godeau (1655), which were widely used by French Protestants.

Largamente (It.). 'Broadly': a term denoting a stately manner, or an instruction to slow the tempo.

Larghetto (It.). Less slow and dignified than Largo.

Largo (It.). Broad, slow.

Larigot. A French organ mutation stop of $1\frac{1}{3}'$ pitch, i.e. two octaves and a 5th above the fundamental.

Lark Ascending, The. Romance by Vaughan Williams for violin and orchestra (1914) after Meredith's poem.

Lark Quartet. Nickname of Haydn's String Quartet in D op.64 no.5, so called because of its soaring melody at the beginning.

La Rochelle. Site of the RENCONTRES INTERNATIONALES D'ART CONTEMPORAIN.

Larrocha (y de la Calle), Alicia de (*b* Barcelona, 23 May 1923). Spanish pianist. She made her concerto début at the age of 12 with the Madrid SO. After her British and American débuts (1953, 1955) she formed a duo with the cellist Gaspar Cassadó. In 1959 she became director of the Marshall Academy, Barcelona. Her performances of Mozart and Romantic music are marked by a lively attack and subtle, poetic shading; her recordings of Granados and Albéniz have won prizes.

Larsen, Jens Peter (*b* Copenhagen, 14 June 1902). Danish musicologist. He studied at Copenhagen University and taught there, 1939–70. He has worked on Danish music and Handel, but his central interest is Haydn, on whom he has published many articles and done much to provide a sound base for future study.

Larsson, Lars-Erik (Vilner) (*b* Åkarp, 15 May 1908; *d* Helsingborg, 26 Dec 1986). Swedish composer. He studied with Ellberg at the Stockholm Conservatory (1925–9) and with Berg and Reuter in Vienna and Leipzig (1929–30), then worked for Swedish radio and taught at the Stockholm Conservatory (1947–59) and Uppsala University (1961–6). He was the first Swede to write serial music (1932), but other works of the period are post-Sibelian or neoclassical, and his output generally is characterized by variety of style. His works include concertos, a series of 12 concertinos, chamber and vocal music.

LaRue, (Adrian) Jan (Pieters) (*b* Kisaran, Sumatra, 31 July 1918). American musicologist. He studied at Harvard and Princeton, and in 1957 began teaching at New York University. He has studied the music of Okinawa, but his central interests are late 18th-century music (especially the symphony), style analysis and music-bibliographical research, including computer applications.

La Rue, Pierre de (*b* ?Tournai, *c*1460; *d* Courtrai, 20 Nov 1518). Flemish composer. He was a tenor at Siena Cathedral (1482/3–5) and at 's-Hertogenbosch Cathedral (1489–92). He served the Burgundian court chapel and went with Philip the Fair to Spain (1501–3, 1506); on his journeys he met leading composers in France and Germany. Later he worked at Marguerite of Austria's court in Mechelen and in Archduke Karl's private Kapelle (1514–16). La Rue stands alongside Josquin, Obrecht, Isaac, Compère and Brumel as one of the leading Flemish composers of the period, and is significant for the extent and diversity of his work, as well as for its quality and individuality. Central to his output are his masses (which include 31 cycles, two Kyries and five Credos); they feature *cantus firmus* treatments (La Rue preferred plainchant to secular models), canon and simple two-voice sections used to contrast with the fuller four- and five-voice texture. Most of his motets are for four voices; his *chansons* are usually for four voices and range in style from the late-Burgundian type with textless lower parts to the 16th-century type with vocal parts of equal design. He also composed seven Magnificats and a set of Lamentations. His music, which is probably closest to Josquin's in style, influenced the succeeding generation.

Sacred music 31 masses; 7 mass movts; 7 Magnificats; 1 Lamentations; 26 motets
Secular music *c*30 chansons

Laruette, Jean-Louis (*b* Paris, 7 March 1731; *d* there, 10 Jan 1792). French composer. A highly successful singer at the Opéra-Comique, he popularized comic tenor roles (fathers, bankers etc) which became known as 'laruettes'. He composed *c*12 stage works, 1753–72; like Duni's, these developed the *opéra comique* into the form later used by Philidor and others, introducing more new music but retaining spoken text.

LaSalle Quartet. American string quartet, led by Walter Levin. It was formed in 1949 by students from the Juilliard School, making its European début in 1954 and touring extensively. Though it performs works of all periods, it is best known for its performances of the Second Viennese School and other 20th-century music.

Laschi [Mombelli], Luisa (*b* Florence, 1760s; *d c*1790). Italian soprano. Working in Vienna from 1784, she created the role of the Countess in Mozart's *Le nozze di Figaro* (1786) and sang Zerlina in the première there (1788) of *Don Giovanni*.

Laserna, Blas de (*b* Corella, bap. 4 Feb 1751; *d* Madrid, 8 Aug 1816). Spanish composer. He was conductor at the Teatro de la Cruz, Madrid, from 1790, and wrote at least 700 *tonadillas*; the later ones show Italian traits. His other works include *sainetes, melólogos*, instrumental pieces and prologues.

Laskovksy, Ivan Fyodorovich (*b* St Petersburg, 1799; *d* there, 1855). Russian composer. A pupil of John Field, he produced valuable piano works, including a set of variations on the folk melody *Kamarinskaya*, elaborate nocturnes and ballades and some Chopinesque mazurkas and waltzes.

Lassen, Eduard (*b* Copenhagen, 13 April 1830; *d* Weimar, 15 Jan 1904). Belgian composer of Danish origin. He studied at the Brussels Conservatory, winning the Belgian Prix de Rome (1851). He succeeded Liszt as court music director at Weimar (1858), writing operas, notably *Le roi Edgard* (1855), incidental music and songs.

Lassù. Slow introductory section of the Hungarian *verbunkos* dance form.

Lassus, Orlande [Roland] de [Lasso, Orlando di] (*b* Mons, ?1530 or 1532; *d* Munich, 14 June 1594). Franco-Flemish composer. He served Ferrante Gonzaga of Mantua from *c*1544, accompanying him to Sicily and Milan (1546–9). He worked for Constantino Castrioto in Naples, where he probably began to compose, then moved to Rome to join the Archbishop of Florence's household, becoming *maestro di cappella* at St John Lateran in 1553. After returning north, to Mons and Antwerp, where early works were published (1555–6), he joined the court chapel of Duke Albrecht V of Bavaria in Munich as a singer (1556). He married in 1558. Although a Catholic, he took over the court chapel in 1563 and served the duke and his heir, Wilhelm V, for over 30 years, until his death. In this post he consolidated his position by having many works published and travelling frequently (notably to Vienna and Italy, 1574–9), establishing an international reputation. The pope made him a Knight of the Golden Spur in 1574.

One of the most prolific and versatile of 16th-century composers, Lassus wrote over 2000 works in almost every current genre, including masses, motets, psalms, hymns, responsorial Passions and secular pieces in Italian, French and German. Most of his masses are parody masses based on motets, *chansons* or madrigals by himself or others; the large number of Magnificats is unusual. His motets include didactic pieces, ceremonial works for special occasions, settings of classical texts (some secular, e.g. *Prophetiae Sibyllarum*, 1600), liturgical items (offertories, antiphons, psalms, e.g. *Psalmi...poenitentiales*, 1584) and private devotional pieces. He issued five large volumes of sacred music as *Patro-*

cinium musices (1573–6), and after his death his sons assembled another (*Magnum opus musicum*, 1604).

Admired in their day for their beauty, technical perfection and rhetorical power, the motets combine the features of several national styles – expressive Italian melody, elegant French text-setting and solid northern polyphony – enhanced by Lassus's imaginative responses to the texts. His secular works reveal a cosmopolitan with varied tastes. The madrigals range from lightweight villanellas (*Matona mia cara*) to intensely expressive sonnets (*Occhi, piangete*); the *chansons* include 'patter' songs and reflective, motet-like works; and among the German lieder are sacred hymns and psalms, delicate love-songs and raucous drinking-songs. This versatility and wide expressive range place him among the most significant figures of the Renaissance.

Lassus's sons Ferdinand (*c*1560–1609) and Rudolph (*c*1563–1625) also served the Bavarian court chapel and assembled many of their father's works for publication. Ferdinand succeeded to his father's post at court; Rudolph composed much sacred music.

*Sacred vocal music c*70 masses, 4–8vv; 4 Passions, 4, 5vv; *c*100 Magnificats, 4–10vv; *c*30 hymns, 4, 5vv; over 500 motets, 2–12vv; many other liturgical works (Offices, lessons, Lamentations, litanies, falsibordoni etc)
*Secular vocal music c*200 madrigals and villanellas, 3–10vv; *c*150 chansons, 3–8vv; *c*90 lieder, 3–8vv

Lates, James (*b* ?*c*1740; *d* Oxford, 21 Nov 1777). English composer. He was active as a violinist in Oxford and the vicinity, working for the Duke of Marlborough at Blenheim. He published five sets of gracefully written chamber works (mostly in a *galant* style), including six trio sonatas for violin, cello and continuo (*c*1775).

Latilla, Gaetano (*b* Bari, 10 Jan 1711; *d* Naples, 15 Jan 1788). Italian composer. Trained in Naples, he presented operas (mostly comic) there from 1732, and from 1738 in other cities including Madrid (1747) and Barcelona (1754); he wrote over 40 operas, most of them before 1756. He was assistant *maestro* at S Maria Maggiore, Rome (1738–41), and in Venice, *maestro di coro* at the Pietà conservatory (1753–66) and assistant *maestro* at St Mark's (from 1762), composing oratorios and other sacred music. By 1774 he was back in Naples. His other works include arias, ensembles and instrumental pieces.

Latin American music. The many cultures of South and Central America and the Caribbean islands blend American Indian, African and European (particularly Spanish and Portuguese) traditions. In folk music, the particular combination of elements varies from region to region, from the purely Indian forms of highland Bolivia and Amazon rain forests peoples to the *mestizo* ('mixed') music of Bolivia, Peru and Ecuador, the largely Hispanic music of Argentina, and the distinctive style of Brazil, which blends African and Portuguese forms. Minorities such as the East Indians of Trinidad and Guyana, the Javanese of Surinam and the Japanese of Brazil complete this rich musical scenario.

Less Iberian heritage has in general been preserved in Latin America than British in North America;

many areas are devoid of Latin influence. But some Hispanic poetic forms dating from the Middle Ages and Renaissance (for example the *romance*) are performed in a variety of forms throughout the continent, such as the *copla* of Colombia, the Andean countries and Argentina. Other folksongs, such as the Argentinian and Chilean *tonadas* and *tonos*, also preserve old Spanish literary forms. In contrast to the thriving Anglo-American tune repertory of the USA, however, few extant Iberian melodies are current in Latin America except the Hispanic children's repertory, which is similar in its Old and New World settings. In the Andean region of Bolivia, Peru and Ecuador, indigenous Indian music has absorbed Spanish elements, a process that began under the influence of 16th-century Christian missionaries. Andean tunes are essentially European, but often have much repetition and use tetratonic and pentatonic scales. This blend stands in contrast with the marked lack of acculturation between Anglo and Indian styles in North America.

Afro-Hispanic folk music is especially important in Brazil, Venezuela and Colombia. Black communities in Brazil preserve styles close to their African counterparts, with driving rhythms using syncopations, responsorial forms and the dominance of percussion instruments. The combination of Portuguese with African traits is particularly apparent in Brazilian folk dances, including the samba, *batuque, jongo, luindu* and more recent urban forms such as the bossa-nova. The best-preserved African music of the New World is found in the cult repertories, notably the Lucumi of Cuba, Rada and Vodoun of Haiti, Shango of Trinidad, and Ketu and Candomble of Brazil. Cult ritual combines Christian belief with traditional West African practices; the music of these groups retains African call-and-response form, complex rhythms and drum and bell accompaniment based on African models. In some cases African-derived peoples of Latin America have invented entirely novel musical forms, the most notable example being the Trinidadian steel band. During the 20th century, they have contributed many local styles to the international pop repertory, including Latin jazz, Afro-Cuban jazz, calypso, reggae, salsa and soca.

The indigenous music of Latin America is that of the American Indians who, during the pre-Conquest era, ranged from small nomadic bands to the highly developed cultures of the Maya, Aztec and Inca. Modern Indian music includes songs for hunting, fishing and other work songs, entertainment songs, epics, laments and ritual songs, the texts of which preserve the tribe's heritage of myth. The style is primarily vocal, with melodies based on two, three or sometimes five pitches; melodies based on a major triad are also widespread. A simple rhythmic accompaniment is typical but polyphony is found among Indians of Brazil, Peru, Ecuador and Venezuela.

Instrumental music is more important among South American Indians than those of the North. Indigenous instruments include flutes, whistles, rattles, maracas, trumpets of simple clay, bark or bamboo, conch-shell trumpets and various drum types including the double-headed frame drum. Instruments often have ritual significance, particularly bullroarers, maracas, stamping tubes, pellet-bells, bark trumpets and certain flutes. Complex instrumental styles include the interlocking panpipe pieces of Panamanian Cuna Indians, the panpipe ensembles of the Aymara of Argentina, Bolivia and Peru and the flute duets of Camayura of Brazil. Some groups have adopted Western instruments which they play in local styles, for example the Tzotzil of Mexico who play violins, harps and guitars. Some of the most complex music of Latin America is practised in the Andean region, where harps, guitars, violins, lutes and other European instruments are played as well as indigenous flutes and panpipes.

Latrobe [La Trobe], **Christian Ignatius** (*b* Leeds, 12 Feb 1758; *d* Fairfield, 6 May 1836). English composer. A Moravian minister, he composed and edited much church music for Moravian and more general use, notably the influential *Selection of Sacred Music* (6 vols., 1806–26), which introduced to Britain the church music of Graun, Pergolesi, Haydn and Mozart.

Laub, Ferdinand (*b* Prague, 19 Jan 1832; *d* Gries, 18 March 1875). Czech violinist. He studied at the Prague Conservatory. Renowned for his beautiful tone, virtuosity and stylishness, he succeeded Joachim as Konzertmeister in Weimar (1853) and became professor in Berlin (1855–7) and Moscow (from 1866), performing with his most eminent contemporaries. He was also an acclaimed chamber player; Tchaikovsky dedicated his Third String Quartet op.30 to Laub's memory.

Laub, Thomas (Linnemann) (*b* Langaa, 5 Dec 1852; *d* Gentofte, 4 Feb 1927). Danish church musician and composer. He studied with Gebauer at the Copenhagen Conservatory (1873–6) and became interested in the Cecilian movement: as writer, editor and composer he devoted himself to restoring the traditions of Danish church music based on plainsong and the chorale. The most important collection of his compositions is *Dansk kirkesang* (1918). As organist he followed Gebauer at Helligåndskirken in Copenhagen (1884–91) and Gade at Holmens Kirke (1891–1925).

Lauda [laude] **spirituale**. The principal form of nonliturgical religious song in Italy in the Middle Ages and Renaissance. It developed in the 13th-century wave of religious hysteria in north Italy, Provence and Germany. *Lauda* texts alternate a two-line refrain with stanzas of four or more lines, and this structure is mirrored in the music. Many monophonic *laude* are in a simple syllabic style, with a small range; others resemble the more florid troubadour and trouvère songs. In the 15th century the polyphonic *lauda* replaced the monophonic among the élite. Most early examples were for two or three voices in a simple style akin to that of the frottola. With the advent of the Counter-Reformation the singing of *laude* was given new impetus and influenced the beginnings of Roman oratorio.

Laudon [Loudon] **Symphony**. Haydn's Symphony no.69 in C (mid-1770s), dedicated to the Austrian field-marshal Ernst Gideon Freiherr von Loudon.

Launeddas. A triple single-reed wind instrument of Sardinia, consisting of three cane pipes, two with finger-holes and one serving as a drone. All three are inserted into the mouth.

Laurenti. Italian family of musicians, active mainly in Bologna. Bartolomeo Girolamo (1644–1726), a violin virtuoso, composed instrumental music. Two of his sons were composers. Girolamo Nicolò (1678–1751), also a violinist, replaced him in the orchestra of S Petronio, Bologna, and later directed it; he composed instrumental works. Pietro Paolo (1675–1719) was a string player at S Petronio, *maestro di cappella* at the Collegio dei Nobili from 1703, and an opera singer; he wrote mostly oratorios and operas. Other members of the family included Antonia Maria Novelli ['La Coralli'] (*fl* 1715–35), one of the most celebrated singers of her day; Angelo Maria (*fl* early 18th century), a composer, string player and organist; and Lodovico Filippo (*fl* early 18th century), a composer and string player.

Laurenzi, Filiberto (*b* Bertinoro, *c*1620; *d* after 1651). Italian composer. A singer in Rome, he probably later worked in Venice; he wrote a book of florid *Concerti ed arie* (1641) and contributed to two operas, notably *La finta savia* (1643, Venice), which uses a refined mixture of Roman and Venetian styles.

Lauri-Volpi, Giacomo (*b* Rome, 11 Dec 1892; *d* Valencia, 17 March 1979). Italian tenor. He made his début in 1919 and sang at La Scala and the Met from 1923. His bright tone and beautiful legato made him a favourite in such roles as Calaf, Othello, the Duke of Mantua and Manrico. His last public appearance was in 1959.

Lausanne Chamber Orchestra. Swiss orchestra founded in 1940 for Lausanne Radio by Victor Desarzens, conductor until 1953. It takes part in European festivals and gives subscription concerts.

Lausanne International Festival (Switzerland). Annual (summer) festival founded in 1956; events include opera, concerts, ballet and jazz given by visiting performers.

Lavallée, Calixa (*b* Ste Théodosie de Verchères [now Calixa-Lavallée], Quebec, 28 Dec 1842; *d* Boston, 21 Jan 1891). Canadian composer. He worked as a travelling theatre musician, bandsman and choirmaster before writing the song *O Canada* (*c*1880), which has become the national anthem of Canada. He settled in Boston, had several works performed and published and became active in the Music Teachers' National Association. He was the first native-born Canadian composer.

Lavignac, (Alexandre Jean) Albert (*b* Paris, 21 Jan 1846; *d* there, 28 May 1916). French teacher and writer. From 1871 he taught solfège and harmony at the Paris Conservatoire (where he had studied), writing important pedagogical works on musical dictation (1882) and on piano pedalling (1889), also founding the *Encyclopédie de la musique et Dictionnaire du Conservatoire* (published 1920–31).

Lavotta, János (*b* Pusztafödémes, 5 July 1764; *d* Tállya, 11 Aug 1820). Hungarian composer and violinist. He studied in Vienna. With Bihari and Csermák he helped to create the *verbunkos*, a new Hungarian national style. Besides Hungarian and German instrumental dances he composed extended programmatic works, including the suite *Nobilium hungariae insurgentium nota insurrectionalis hungarica* (1797).

Lavrangas, Dionyssios (*b* Argostolion, 17 Oct 1860/1864; *d* Razata, 18 July 1941). Greek composer. He studied in Naples (1882–5) and in Paris with Delibes, Massenet and Franck. In 1894 he settled in Athens, where he was co-founder of the Greek Opera (in 1900), for which he wrote operas and operettas in a style indebted to Bizet, Delibes and Massenet and to Italian models. He was also a conservatory teacher, publisher and critic, besides composing orchestral and choral music and songs.

Lavry, Marc (*b* Riga, 22 Dec 1903; *d* Haifa, 24 March 1967). Israeli composer of Latvian origin. He studied at the Riga and Leipzig conservatories and with Glazunov, then emigrated to Palestine in 1935. His works, including opera, oratorio, and symphonic poems, were influenced by oriental folk music and Jewish cantillation.

Lawes, Henry (*b* Dinton, 5 Jan 1596; *d* London, 21 Oct 1662). English composer. He was a Gentleman of the Chapel Royal from 1626 and a musician to Charles I from 1631; he was involved in masques and other court music. After working as a teacher of singing and the viol during the Commonwealth, he regained his former posts in 1660. As a composer he was best known for his songs, some of which he wrote for dramatic works; over 400 survive (more than 200 were published in three books, 1653–8), ranging from simple strophic pieces to dramatic, declamatory settings. Lawes contributed, with Henry Cooke and Matthew Locke, to the opera *The Siege of Rhodes* (1656), and also composed anthems and some instrumental works.

Lawes, William (Salisbury, bap. 1 May 1602; *d* Chester, 24 Sept 1645). English composer, younger brother of Henry Lawes. He was probably a chorister at Salisbury Cathedral until the Earl of Hertford placed him under the tutelage of his own music master, John Coprario. In 1635 Lawes was appointed 'musician in ordinary for the lute and voices' to Charles I, though he was probably in Charles's service before then. In 1642 he enlisted in the royalist army and accompanied the king on campaigns; he was killed during the battle to relieve the garrison at Chester.

Lawes was a gifted, versatile and prolific composer. The stylized dance suite is the basic vehicle for his chamber music, often with a preceding fantasia or pavan. In his viol consorts he exhibited late Renaissance traits, but the larger part of his chamber music uses violins in the concertante style of early Baroque violin music with continuo. It includes the 'Harpe' consorts, a unique collection of variation suites for violin, bass viol, theorbo and harp. Of Lawes's vocal music, over 200 songs are extant, many of them composed for court masques and other theatrical entertainments. He is considered the leading English dramatic composer before Purcell. Much of his church music – *c*50 anthems and ten sacred canons or rounds – is also of high quality, *The Lord is my Light* being one of the finest verse anthems of its period.

Instrumental music 30 consort suites, incl. 18 with vn(s); 8 vn sonatas; 8 trio sonatas; ensemble suites; over 100 ensemble dances; keyboard suites and dances
Vocal music c50 anthems, incl. The Lord is my Light; 10 sacred canons; over 200 songs, duets, trios, some orig. for dramatic works (incl. The Triumph of Peace, masque, 1634)

Layolle, Francesco de (*b* Florence, 4 March 1492; *d* Lyons, *c*1540). Italian composer and organist. He was a singer in the Florentine church of the Ss Annunziata, where he became acquainted with the organist Bartolomeo degli Organi, who taught him. In 1521 he settled at Lyons where he was organist at the Florentine church of Notre Dame de Confort. A leading figure in Lyons intellectual life, he also composed, collected and edited music for printers there; in the 1530s he worked closely with Jacques Moderne, contributing to and editing volumes of sacred music. He cultivated all the principal forms of vocal polyphony, and his extant works include three masses, seven penitential psalms, 35 motets and a few *chansons* and madrigals. His music combines beauty of melody and harmony with contrapuntal skill, placing him among the leading composers of his generation.

Lazăr, Filip (*b* Craiova, 18 May 1894; *d* Paris, 3 Nov 1936). Romanian composer. He studied with Kiriac and Castaldi at the Bucharest Conservatory (1907–12) and with Krehl at the Leipzig Conservatory (1913–14), then toured as a pianist, playing much new music. From 1928 he was based in France and Switzerland, and his music moved from Romanian nationalism to serialism and neo-classicism. His works include four piano concertos, vocal and chamber music.

Leader. English term for the principal first violinist in an orchestra; in American usage the word is 'concertmaster' (Ger. *Konzertmeister*). He normally sits on the outside chair of the first desk of the first-violin section and is responsible for executing the conductor's wishes in technical matters, such as the marking and bowing of parts. He normally plays solo violin passages, serves as a deputy conductor, organizes sectional rehearsals and acts as liaison between the orchestra and its management. In earlier periods, before the advent of the conductor, the leader or concertmaster played a part in directing performances. *See* CONDUCTING.

Leading motif. *See* LEITMOTIF.

Leading note. The seventh degree of the major or harmonic minor scale, so called because it lies a semitone below the tonic and has a strong tendency to lead up to it.

Lear, Evelyn (*b* Brooklyn, 8 Jan 1928). American soprano. She studied at the Juilliard School, made her New York recital début in 1955, then after further study in Berlin made her operatic début there as the Composer (*Ariadne auf Naxos*). She has sung in several new works (including Levy's *Mourning becomes Electra* on her Met début, 1967) and is especially associated with Berg's Lulu. She has also sung such roles as Handel's Cleopatra, most of the Mozart soprano roles, Verdi's Desdemona and Strauss's

Octavian and the Marschallin. She is noted for her warm voice and intelligent, appealing stage manner.

Leardini, Alessandro (*b* Urbino; *fl* 1643–62). Italian composer. He wrote stage works, including two intermezzos for the opera *La finta savia* (1643) and an opera *Argiope* (*c*1649), both performed in Venice. While *maestro di cappella* at the Mantuan court (*c*1649–52) his *Psiche* was produced for a ducal marriage. A motet and four solo cantatas (1662) also survive.

Lebègue, Nicolas-Antoine (*b* Laon, *c*1631; *d* Paris, 6 July 1702). French composer. He was organist at St Merry, Paris, from 1664 and an *organiste du Roi* from 1678. Of his five extant volumes for keyboard (1676–*c*1687) those for harpsichord contain his most elegantly turned music; though more formal in style and organization, they owe much to Chambonnières and Louis Couperin. In his organ music, especially the suites of the first of his three volumes (1676), he appears as an innovator: rejecting more severe counterpoint, he evolved the *récit en taille* and pioneered genres requiring an independent pedal part. He was an influential teacher and an adviser on organ design.

Lebewohl, Das. Beethoven's title for his Piano Sonata no.26 in E♭ op.81*a*, usually known as *Les Adieux*.

Lebhaft (Ger.). Lively, sprightly, brisk.

Lebič, Lojze (*b* Prevalje, 23 Aug 1934). Yugoslav composer. He was a pupil of Kozina in Ljubljana, where he has conducted and taught. Influenced by the Polish avant garde, his works include orchestral, vocal and chamber pieces.

Lebrun, Louis-Sébastien (*b* Paris, 10 Dec 1764; *d* there, 27 June 1829). French tenor and composer. A singing tutor at the Paris Opéra and singing director in the imperial chapel, he composed chiefly stage works, mostly *opéras comiques*; among these, *Marcelin* (1800) and *Le rossignol* (1816) were quite successful.

Lebrun, Ludwig August (*b* Mannheim, bap. 2 May 1752; *d* Berlin, 16 Dec 1790). German oboist and composer. He played in the Mannheim court orchestra and travelled widely. He was one of the finest oboists of his day. His compositions include oboe concertos, ballet music (for London) and chamber works. His wife Franziska Lebrun [née Danzi] (1756–91), the leading soprano at the Mannheim court opera (later at Munich), toured with him; she composed violin sonatas. Of their children, Sophie [Dülken] (1781–after 1815) became a well-known pianist, and Rosine (1783–1855) a singer and actress. The horn player and composer Jean Lebrun (1759–*c*1809), a Frenchman, is unrelated to them.

Le Cerf de la Viéville, Jean Laurent (*b* Rouen, 1674; *d* there, 10 Nov 1707). French author and amateur musician. His defence of French music in his major work, the *Comparaison de la musique italienne et de la musique française* (1704–6), forms an important contribution to the development of musical criticism and aesthetics in the early 18th century.

Lechner, Leonhard (*b* valley of R. Adige, *c*1553; *d* Stuttgart, 9 Sept 1606). German composer. He was a singer in the Munich Hofkapelle under Lassus (probably 1564–8) and in the Landshut Hofkapelle before 1570. After ten years as a schoolmaster in

Nuremberg he became Kapellmeister at Hechingen, a Catholic court, in 1584. His Lutheranism soon caused problems, and in 1585 he fled to Tübingen and then to Stuttgart, where he sang in the Hofkapelle. He became Hofkapellmeister in 1594; during his tenure standards greatly improved. The leading German composer of choral music in the later 16th century, he issued masses (1584), Magnificats (1578), psalms (1587) and motets (1575, 1581), as well as eight books of lieder (1576–c1606) and occasional works. His four-part Passion (1593) brought the German motet Passion to its peak; his other sacred works were influenced by Lassus and Italian composers. His lieder (German villanellas, Gesellschaftslieder, song motets etc) are more individual; and he was the first to set a complete cycle of German poems.

Leclair, Jean-Marie (*b* Lyons, 10 May 1697; *d* Paris, 22 Oct 1764). French composer and violinist. Initially a dancer, he lived from 1723 in Paris, where he became a prominent soloist and began producing violin sonatas (from 1723). He also appeared abroad, and in 1733 became *ordinaire de la musique du roi* at the French court. In 1738–43 he served the court of Orange in the Netherlands and (in 1740–43) François du Liz at The Hague. He then lived mainly in Paris, where he was murdered (probably by his nephew).

Foremost in Leclair's output are over 60 solo, duet and trio sonatas for violin. In these he imbued the Italian style with French elements more successfully than most of his contemporaries, using short ornamented phrases and colourful harmonies; the idiom reflects his own virtuoso technique. He also composed concertos, minuets, suites etc, ballet music, an opera (*Scylla et Glaucus*, 1746) with many striking features and other vocal music. He was an influential teacher and is considered the founder of the French violin school.

Leclair was one of several musical brothers. The most important were Jean-Marie (1703–77), a violinist, who directed the Académie des Beaux-Arts in Lyons and composed sonatas and other works, Pierre (1709–84) and Jean-Benoît (1714–after 1759), both violinists and composers in Lyons.

Le Clerc, Charles-Nicolas (*b* Sézanne en Brie, 20 Oct 1697; *d* Paris, 20 Oct 1774). French violinist and music publisher. A violinist at the Opéra from 1729 and later in the royal band, he began publishing in 1736, issuing mainly instrumental works by well-known Italian, German and Flemish composers, in which he had sole rights; later he published vocal music. His brother Jean-Pantaléon (before 1697–after 1760), also a violinist in the royal band, from 1720, was a music publisher on commission from 1728; he dealt mainly in French chamber music, dances and songs, engraved at the composers' expense.

Lecocq, (Alexandre) Charles (*b* Paris, 3 June 1832; *d* there, 24 Oct 1918). French composer. At the Paris Conservatoire he studied with Bazin and Halévy and became a friend of Bizet and Saint-Saëns. The acclaim accorded his operettas *Les cent vierges* (1872), *La fille de Madame Angot* (1872) and *Giroflé-Girofla* (1874), all first produced in Brussels, established him as a natural successor to Offenbach. In Paris he confirmed his international reputation with *La petite mariée* (1875) and *Le petit duc* (1878), both still in the repertory; they demonstrate his light touch, pleasing melodies, deft use of rhythm and lively theatrical effects.

Leçons de ténèbres. A name for French settings of the LAMENTATIONS of Jeremiah.

Ledger line. *See* LEGER LINE.

Leduc, Simon (*b* Paris, ? before 1748; *d* there, bur. 22/5 Jan 1777). French violinist, composer and publisher. He was a successful soloist and an orchestral player at the Concert Spirituel, in 1773 becoming a director. His works include violin concertos, symphonies and chamber music. He published some of his own music; this business was expanded by his brother and pupil Pierre Leduc ['le jeune'] (1755–1816), also a violinist. Pierre's son Auguste (1779–1823) took over the publishing firm and in c1807 became one of the first publishers to use lithography.

Lee, Dai-Keong (*b* Honolulu, 2 Sept 1915). American composer. He studied with Sessions at the Juilliard School, with Copland, and with Luening at Columbia. Writing in all genres, he has used Polynesian instruments and scales. He has maintained an interest in stage music, writing short operas in the Weill tradition.

Leeds Musical Festival (UK). Biennial (from 1970) autumn festival, established in 1858 to mark the opening of Leeds Town Hall. Large choral works have been commissioned since 1880, when it became a triennial event with Sullivan as conductor. It gained international status through the quality of its chorus and the works presented, including Dvořák's *St Ludmilla* (1886) and Elgar's *Caractacus* (1898). Orchestral and chamber music are part of its programme.

Lees, Benjamin (*b* Harbin, China, 8 Jan 1924). American composer of Russian parentage. In the USA from childhood, he studied at the University of Southern California (1945–8) and with Antheil, then went to Europe in 1954 to develop an individual style; in 1961 he returned to the USA to work as a composer and teacher. His works, in a vigorous style of extended tonality, include large-scale choral works (e.g. *Visions of Poets*, 1961), four symphonies (1953–85), concertos, chamber and piano music.

Leeuw, Ton de (*b* Rotterdam, 16 Nov 1926). Dutch composer. He was a pupil of Badings and Messiaen and from 1960 has taught at the Amsterdam Conservatory. Until the mid-1950s he was influenced by Bartók, Hindemith and Pijper, but later works move towards Boulez and Berio; Asian thought has also been important. His works cover many genres and include a *Spatial Music* series (1966–71) for separated or moving players.

LeFanu, Nicola (Frances) (*b* Wickham Bishops, 28 April 1947). English composer, daughter of Elizabeth Maconchy. She studied at Oxford and the RCM, and in 1977 was appointed lecturer at King's College, London. Her works, ranging from music-theatre (*Dawnpath*, 1977) to chamber music, are distinguished by their linear qualities.

Lefèvre. French organ builders. They were active from the 16th century to the 19th. The name belonged to at least 23 builders, mostly members of the same family, but the most celebrated was Jean-Baptiste Nicolas (1705–84), of comparable importance to F.-H. Cliquot. Characteristic of his style were an extension of the manual compass up to *e′′′*, the addition of extra trumpets, up to five cornets, the use of a Bombarde 16′ and the addition on the *Pédale* of a Nazard and a 16′ Trompette. Chief among his organs were those at St Martin, Tours (1761; the largest French classical organ), Evreux Cathedral (1744) and St Pierre, Caen (1753, 1778).

Lefèvre, (Jean) Xavier (*b* Lausanne, 6 March 1763; *d* Paris, 9 Nov 1829). French clarinettist and composer. A soloist and orchestral player in Paris, and teacher at the Conservatoire, he wrote orchestral and chamber works (most with clarinet), vocal pieces and a clarinet method (1802).

Le Flem, Paul (*b* Lezardrieux, 18 March 1881; *d* Trégastel, 31 July 1984). French composer. He studied at the Paris Conservatoire and with d'Indy and Roussel at the Schola Cantorum, where he returned to teach. He was also a choral conductor. His works, in most genres, are in the d'Indy tradition and have a gracious melancholy. His criticism was open-minded.

Le Gallienne, Dorian (Leon Marlois) (*b* Melbourne, 19 April 1915; *d* there, 29 July 1963). Australian composer. He studied in Melbourne and at the RCM (1938–9) and was influenced by English lyricism, French wit and Stravinsky–Bartók bitonality. His works include a symphony (1953) and chamber music.

Legato (It.: 'bound'). Term meaning connected smoothly, with neither a perceptible break in the sound nor special emphasis; the opposite of STACCATO.

Légende. A title used by Liszt, Tchaikovsky and other 19th-century composers for pieces of a legendary character or which depict a legend.

Legende von der Heiligen Elisabeth, Die. Oratorio by Liszt to a text by O. Roquett (1865, Budapest).

Legend of Tsar Saltan, The. *See* TALE OF TSAR SALTAN, THE.

Leger [ledger] **line.** A short horizontal line drawn above or below the staff to accommodate a note that is too high or too low to be printed on the staff itself.

Legge, Walter (*b* London, 1 June 1906; *d* St Jean, Cap Ferrat, 22 March 1979). English music administrator. In 1927 he joined the HMV record company, for which he eventually became manager for artists and repertory. He was responsible for greatly enlarging the repertory of recorded music, for forming the Philharmonia Orchestra and for supervising many of the most distinguished recordings of the early LP era.

Leggero [leggiero] (It.). Light.

Leggiadro (It.). Pretty, graceful.

Legley, Vic(tor) (*b* Hazebrouck, 18 June 1915). Belgian composer. A pupil of Absil, he has worked as a viola player, radio producer and teacher at the Brussels Conservatory (from 1949). His works include symphonies, concertos, string quartets and vocal music; among the best known is *La cathédrale d'acier* (1958).

Legnani, (Rinaldo) Luigi (*b* Ferrara, 7 Nov 1790; *d* Ravenna, 5 Aug 1877). Italian guitarist, instrument maker and composer. After touring successfully both as a soloist and with Paganini, he retired to Ravenna (*c*1840), where he built fine guitars and violins; most of his 250 compositions are light guitar pieces.

Legrant, Guillaume (*fl* 1418–56). French composer. A singer in the chapel of Pope Martin V from 1418 until at least 1421, he held several benefices in the diocese of Rouen and may have sung in the chapel of Duke Charles of Orleans in 1455–6. His three mass movements are among the earliest to distinguish between solo and choral polyphony. Three virelais also survive.

Legrenzi, Giovanni (*b* Clusone, bap. 12 Aug 1626; *d* Venice, 27 May 1690). Italian composer. An organist, he served at S Maria Maggiore, Bergamo, from 1645, later becoming a chaplain there and in 1653 first organist. In 1656–65 he was *maestro di cappella* of the Accademia dello Santo Spirito at Ferrara. Later he unsuccessfully sought various posts and refused others (one of them at the French court). Moving to Venice, he worked at the Conservatorio dei Mendicanti, probably from 1671, and was its *maestro di coro* by 1683. Finally he gained distinction at St Mark's, as *vice-maestro di cappella* from 1681 and *maestro* from 1685; the musical forces there attained their largest recorded size in these years.

One of the most gifted and influential composers of his time, Legrenzi was a major force in the development of the late Baroque style. His music owes much to Cazzati, Merula and others, but is dominated by a stronger tonal sense. His fugal writing is especially notable. His most forward-looking works are his *c*100 ensemble sonatas (for strings and continuo), which influenced the sonatas and concertos of Torelli, Vivaldi and Bach; he also composed instrumental dances. In his operas (six of his 19 survive complete), arias have a growing importance and display a variety of forms. Among his other vocal works are solo cantatas, seven oratorios and much sacred music, ranging from small motets to massive polychoral settings. His aria style strongly influenced Alessandro Scarlatti and Handel.

Legros, Joseph (*b* Monampteuil, 7/8 Sept 1739; *d* La Rochelle, 28 Dec 1793). French singer and composer. He was a choirboy at Laon and developed into a powerful, sweet-toned *haute-contre*, making his début at the Paris Opéra in 1764. He sang in operas by Rameau, and created several Gluck roles, including Pylades (*Iphigénie en Tauride*); later he directed the Concert Spirituel, 1777–90, where he promoted Haydn's music and commissioned works from Mozart, but put commercial interests ahead of artistic ones. He composed two works for the stage.

Leguerney, Jacques (Alfred Georges Emile) (*b* Le Havre, 19 Nov 1906). French composer. He studied with Boulanger at the Ecole Normale de Musique from 1927, but began composing seriously only in the 1940s. He produced a body of songs distinguished by elegant lines and supple, sophisticated harmony, at the time reckoned second only to Poulenc's.

Lehár, Franz [Ferencz] (*b* Komarón, 30 April 1870; *d* Bad Ischl, 24 Oct 1948). Austrian composer of Hungarian origin. The son of a military bandmaster and composer, he studied in Prague with Foerster and Fibich and followed his father in an army career.

In 1902 he resigned to work in Vienna as a conductor and composer, notably of operettas, achieving spectacular international success with *Die lustige Witwe* (1905), *Der Graf von Luxemburg* (1909) and *Zigeunerliebe* (1910). These and others restored the fortunes of the Viennese operetta and opened the genre to a greater musical and dramatic sophistication. After World War I his time seemed to have passed, but then came new successes, many written for Richard Tauber: *Paganini* (1925), *Der Zarewitsch* (1927), *Friederike* (1928), *Das Land des Lächelns* (1929) and *Giuditta* (1934). His other works include waltzes, marches and songs.

Le Heurteur, Guillaume (*fl* 1530–45). French composer. In 1545 he was a canon and preceptor of the choirboys at St Martin, Tours. Virtually all his surviving works, which include four masses, two Magnificats, 21 motets and 23 *chansons*, were published in Paris or Lyons (1530–45). His masses are based on pre-existent material; his sacred music is in varied contrapuntal style and reflects the French predilection for harmony. The four-part *chansons* are freely composed and, in their short phrases, concise structure, frequent cadences and melodic stereotypes, follow Parisian *chanson* style.

Lehmann, Hans Ulrich (*b* Biel, 4 May 1937). Swiss composer. He studied with Boulez and Stockhausen at the Basle Academy (1960–63) and taught there and (from 1972) in Zurich. His works are indebted to Boulez in their measured sonorities and serial organization.

Lehmann, Lilli (*b* Würzburg, 24 Nov 1848; *d* Berlin, 17 May 1929). German soprano. She sang principally in Berlin, Bayreuth (taking part in the first complete *Ring* cycle, 1876) and New York (début, 1885), and later at the Salzburg Festival (1901–10), her enormous repertory ranging from the light, coloratura parts of Mozart (Donna Anna) and Bellini to the more dramatic roles of Wagner (Isolde, Brünnhilde) and Verdi. Among her famous pupils were Olive Fremstadt and Geraldine Farrar.

Lehmann, Liza [Elizabeth] (**Nina Mary Frederica**) (*b* London, 11 July 1862; *d* Pinner, 19 Sept 1918). English soprano and composer. Her teachers included Jenny Lind. She is remembered for her song cycles, notably *In a Persian Garden* (1896), and as a recitalist and witty diarist.

Lehmann, Lotte (*b* Perleberg, 27 Feb 1888; *d* Santa Barbara, 26 Aug 1976). German soprano, later naturalized American. She sang in Hamburg from 1910, after study in Berlin, and in 1914 moved to Vienna where, until forced to leave in 1938, she was a favourite in such roles as Strauss's Composer and Marschallin and Wagner's Eva and Elsa. At Covent Garden she sang every season from 1924 to 1938 (Mozart's Countess, Beethoven's Leonore). Her Chicago and Met débuts (1930, 1934) were both as Sieglinde. One of the leading lyric-dramatic sopranos of the time, her lovely voice was matched by a vivid personality and theatrical gift. She retired to Santa Barbara in 1951 and taught there and in London.

Lehrstück (Ger.). 'Teaching piece': term used, and probably invented, by Brecht for a theatrical genre, usually with political content, designed to teach the participants rather than to divert an audience. Music for *Lehrstücke* was composed by Weill, Hindemith, Eisler and others.

Leibowitz, René (*b* Warsaw, 17 Feb 1913; *d* Paris, 29 Aug 1972). French composer of Polish origin. He studied with Schoenberg and Webern in Berlin and Vienna (1930–33) and in 1945 settled in Paris to work as a conductor, teacher (of Boulez and others) and composer; in 1947 he founded the International Festival of Chamber Music. His two books on 12-note music, published in the late 1940s, were influential; later theoretical writings reflect his interest in existentialism. His works are close to Schoenberg and Berg, and include operas, concertos, cantatas and four string quartets.

Leich. German term for medieval type of song, equivalent to the French LAI.

Leider, Frida (*b* Berlin, 18 April 1888; *d* there, 4 June 1975). German soprano. From 1915 she sang at Halle, Hamburg and elsewhere. At the Berlin Staatsoper she excelled from 1923 in operas by Mozart, Verdi and Strauss. At Covent Garden (début 1924) and in the USA (Chicago from 1928) she was a distinguished Wagnerian, singing Isolde, Brünnhilde and Kundry.

Leifs, Jón (*b* Sólheimer Farm, 1 May 1899; *d* Reykjavík, 30 July 1968). Icelandic composer. He studied in Leipzig (1916–22) and conducted various German orchestras. He wrote orchestral, vocal and piano music based on Icelandic folk music, of which he was an ardent champion.

Leigh, Walter (*b* London, 22 June 1905; *d* nr. Tobruk, 12 June 1942). English composer. A pupil of Hindemith in Berlin (1927–9), he wrote light and functional music but also some more ambitious pieces, notably a Harpsichord Concertino (1936).

Leighton, Kenneth (*b* Wakefield, 2 Oct 1929). English composer. He studied at Oxford and with Petrassi in Rome, and in 1970 was appointed professor at Edinburgh University. His music is in a 12-note but fundamentally diatonic style; its romanticism is expressed in lyrical melody, instrumental colour and virtuoso solo writing. It includes Catholic church music, concertos, chamber and instrumental pieces.

Leighton, Sir William (*b* ?Plash, *c* 1565; bur. London, 31 July 1622). English poet and composer. A member of the landed gentry, he is known for his *Teares and Lamentations of a Sorrowfull Soule* (1614), a collection of 55 consort songs and unaccompanied partsongs by 21 English composers setting his own verse; it includes eight of his own works.

Leinsdorf, Erich (*b* Vienna, 4 Feb 1912). American conductor of Austrian birth. After early experience as assistant to Webern, Toscanini and Walter he conducted at the Met from 1938, notably in Wagner and Strauss. He was conductor of the Rochester PO (1947–55) and musical director of the Boston SO (1962–9). In London he was guest conductor with the LSO and in Berlin he was principal conductor of the RSO, 1977–80.

Leipzig Conservatory. German music school, established in 1843 by Mendelssohn, its first principal; it was renamed the Mendelssohn Akademie in 1946.

Schumann and Reger taught there. It attracted many students from abroad, including Grieg, Sullivan and Delius.

Leise. A devotional Germanic song stanza of the later Middle Ages; the term is supposedly derived from the refrain 'Kyrie eleison'.

Leisentrit, Johannes (*b* Olomouc, May 1527; *d* Bautzen, 24 Nov 1586). German hymnologist. One of the great church reformers of the early Counter-Reformation, he is known for his *Geistliche Lieder und Psalmen* (1567), the most important Counter-Reformation hymnbook; its 250 texts and 180 melodies include several of his own.

Leitmotif (Ger.). 'Leading motif': a clearly defined theme or musical idea, representing or symbolizing a person, object, idea etc, which returns in its original or an altered form at appropriate points in a dramatic (mainly operatic) work. The term was coined by F.W. Jähns in 1871, but the device itself has a long ancestry. Its significance for Romantic opera was first appreciated by Weber, and Wagner elevated it to a position of paramount importance as a means of both symphonic development and dramatic allusion. Leitmotif was taken up by Wagner's disciples, including Cornelius and Humperdinck, and by other composers. Strauss's use derives both from Wagner and from Liszt's technique of thematic metamorphosis.

Leitner, Ferdinand (*b* Berlin, 4 March 1912). German conductor. He studied in Berlin and conducted there from 1943. At the Stuttgart Opera he was musical director, 1950–69, giving notable performances of operas by Berg and Orff. He was principal conductor of the Zurich Opera, 1969–84, and often heard as guest conductor in the Netherlands, Germany and South America. Bruckner, Strauss and Mozart were prominent in his repertory.

Le Jeune, Claude (*b* Valenciennes, 1528–30; *d* Paris, bur. 26 Sept 1600). French composer. Educated at or near Valenciennes, he was a Protestant, and by 1564 he had settled in Paris. After serving the Duke of Anjou (*c*1580–84), he fled in 1589 to La Rochelle because of his Protestant sympathies, but he was back in Paris in Henri IV's service by 1596. One of the most prolific and original French composers of the late 16th century, he composed nearly 350 psalms, nearly 150 *airs*, over 100 *chansons*, over 40 Italian madrigals, a mass, motets and instrumental fantasias (most published posthumously). He was a chief exponent of *musique mesurée*; his application of this and other theories of musical and textual relationships had a lasting influence. His *airs* supplied a model for the later *air de cour* and his psalms were popular throughout the 17th century.

Lekeu, Guillaume (Jean Joseph Nicolas) (*b* Heusy, 20 Jan 1870; *d* Angers, 21 Jan 1894). Belgian composer. He studied with Franck and d'Indy, absorbing the influences of late Beethoven and Wagner and composing prolifically, often with feverish intensity. His most important works include the Violin Sonata (1892; commissioned by Ysaÿe) and the orchestral *Fantaisie sur deux airs populaires angevins* (1892).

Lélio, ou Le retour à la vie. Monodrama by Berlioz to his own text (one number is by A. Duboys after Goethe), for soloists, chorus and orchestra (1832), a sequel to the *Symphonie fantastique*.

Lemacher, Heinrich (*b* Solingen, 26 June 1891; *d* Cologne, 16 March 1966). German composer. He studied at the Cologne Conservatory (1911–16) and was a critic, teacher and composer. Influenced by Bruckner, he composed much Catholic church music, a subject on which he wrote books.

Lemaire, Louis (*b* 1693–4; *d* Tours, *c*1750). French composer. He is notable as the most prolific composer of *cantatilles*, publishing 66 of them in Paris, 1728–50; most are for high voice with instruments. He also wrote *airs*, cantatas, motets and instrumental pieces.

Le Maistre, Matthaeus (*b* ?Roclenge-sur-Geer, *c*1505; *d* Dresden, by April 1577). Netherlands composer. He was Kapellmeister of the Dresden Kantorei from 1554 but retired in 1568. He was a conservative musician who followed the Protestant tradition of J. Walter and G. Rhau. His masses were influenced by the post-1500 Netherlands style and most use *cantus firmus* and parody techniques. Most of his numerous motets, too, show characteristics of an earlier style. His most important works are his German sacred and secular songs, a late echo of a vernacular partsong tradition that had reached its peak in the music of Senfl. The sacred pieces range from simple homophonic songs to great motets using *cantus firmus* and imitation.

Lemmens, Jaak Nikolaas [Jacques Nicolas] (*b* Antwerp, 3 Jan 1823; *d* Zemst, 30 Jan 1881). Belgian organist and teacher. He studied with Girschner and Fétis at the Brussels Conservatory, where he became an organ professor (1849–69). An early advocate of Bach's organ works in Belgium and France, he was renowned for his pedal technique and skilful registration. His wife Helen Lemmens-Sherrington (1834–1906) was a celebrated English soprano.

Lemnitz, Tiana (Luise) (*b* Metz, 26 Oct 1897). German soprano. She studied in Metz and Frankfurt, later singing in Hanover and Berlin in a wide range of lighter soprano roles. She made her Covent Garden début as Eva (1936) and was especially admired for her sensitive, polished singing as Octavian and Pamina.

Lemoyne, Jean-Baptiste (*b* Eymet, 3 April 1751; *d* Paris, 30 Dec 1796). French composer. He studied at the Prussian court, then worked at Warsaw. By 1780 he was in Paris, where he presented 12 stage works. His Gluckian first serious opera, *Electre* (1782), was poorly received, but *Nephté* (1789) was long popular. Of his *opéras comiques* (written after a visit to Italy, 1787), *Les prétendus* (1789) was especially successful. He also composed Revolutionary music and other pieces.

Lendvay, Kamilló (*b* Budapest, 28 Dec 1928). Hungarian composer. He studied with Viski at the Budapest Academy, where he was appointed professor in 1973. His music has moved from the Bartók–Kodály tradition to embrace serial and Polish avant-garde elements.

Léner Quartet. Hungarian string quartet, led by Jenő Léner. It was founded in 1919, made its début in Vienna the next year, and was at once invited to Paris;

from 1922 to 1939 it appeared regularly in London, where it gave complete Beethoven cycles, and in 1929 a New York début followed. The group was admired for its immaculate ensemble and beautifully finished playing.

Leningrad Philharmonic Orchestra. Russian orchestra formed in 1921 to replace the court orchestra (founded 1882). Under Yevgeny Mravinsky (chief conductor from 1938) it won international acclaim and toured many countries. It gave the first performances of eight Shostakovich symphonies.

Leningrad Symphony. Sub-title of Shostakovich's Symphony no.7 in C (1941), composed during the siege of Leningrad.

Lento (It.; Fr. *lent, lentement*). Slow.

Lenton, John (*b* mid-17th century; *d* London ?1718). English composer. A violinist in the King's Private Musick and a Gentleman of the Chapel Royal, he served under successive monarchs from 1681. He composed incidental and instrumental music, songs and catches, but is notable for *The Gentleman's Diversion* (MS, 1693); containing some 30 solos and duets composed for Lenton by his English contemporaries, it is probably the earliest English violin tutor.

Lenya, Lotte (*b* Vienna, 18 Oct 1898; *d* New York, 27 Nov 1981). American singing actress of Austrian birth. Her early career was in Zurich and in 1920 she moved to Berlin. Her marriage to Kurt Weill in 1926 led to a close association with his stage works. She created Jenny in *Die Dreigroschenoper* (1928) and later appeared on stage in Paris and New York, establishing herself as one of the outstanding *diseuses* of the time. After Weill's death in 1950 she revived many works from his German years.

Lenz, Wilhelm von (*b* Riga, 1 June 1809; *d* St Petersburg, 19 Jan 1883). Russian official and writer of German descent. He wrote extensively on Beethoven and was the first to elaborate the idea, suggested by Fétis, that Beethoven's works may be divided into three periods.

Leo, Leonardo (Ortensio Salvatore de) (*b* S Vito de Normanni, 5 Aug 1694; *d* Naples, 31 Oct 1744). Italian composer. Trained in Naples, he became supernumerary organist in the viceroy's chapel in 1713; he was later promoted, eventually reaching *maestro di cappella* (1744). He taught at the Turchini Conservatory from 1734, becoming *primo maestro* in 1741.

Leo composed over 60 stage works, 1714–44, mostly for Naples. He contributed significantly to Neapolitan musical comedy, and in his *opera seria* revivals, 1742–3, introduced the chorus into Neapolitan opera. After Hasse's departure and Vinci's death in 1730 he was the city's dominant composer. He was especially famous for his oratorios and also wrote church music, latterly using *a cappella* textures and scholarly counterpoint. Among his other works are chamber cantatas, concertos, sinfonias, keyboard music and didactic writings.

León, Argeliers (*b* Pinar del Rio, 7 May 1918). Cuban composer and ethnomusicologist. He studied with Ardévol in Havana, where he has worked as a teacher, librarian, composer and ethnologist. Some of his works combine serialism with Afro-Cuban rhythms, the piquant combination of the austere and the popu-

lar earning him a niche in Cuban composition.

Leon, Felipe Padilla de (*b* Peneranda, 1 May 1912). Filipino composer. He studied in Manila and the USA and has taught at Manila institutions. His works include operas and symphonic poems in a nationalist style.

Leoncavallo, Ruggero (*b* Naples, 23 April 1857; *d* Montecatini, 9 Aug 1919). Italian composer and librettist. He studied literature at Bologna University. The failure of an early opera, *I Medici* (1893), conceived as the first of a Renaissance trilogy (unrealized) and written for Giulio Ricordi who rejected it, prompted him, in a defiant quest for fame, to write the poem and music of *Pagliacci* (Milan, 1892), the single work for which he is widely known. In its economy and consistent impetus, notably with the *commedia dell'arte* playlet and the Zola-inspired prologue invoking naturalism, the opera represents a skilful exploitation of the 1890s *verismo* trend; it made Leoncavallo a celebrity overnight. That success was never repeated. However, he set *La bohème* (1897) in opposition to Puccini and the sentimental *Zazà* (1900) was favourably received. One of the first composers to become involved with gramophone records, he wrote the popular song *Mattinata* (recorded by Caruso, 1904) and conducted *Pagliacci* (1907), both for the G&T Company.

Leonhardt, Gustav (Maria) (*b* 's Graveland, 30 May 1928). Dutch harpsichordist, organist and conductor. After study in Basle he made his début in Vienna in 1950, playing Bach's *Art of Fugue* on the harpsichord. Widely regarded as the leading harpsichordist of his day, he has taught at Amsterdam Conservatory since 1954 and has toured widely in Europe and North America, performing Frescobaldi, Bach and Froberger with tasteful ornamentation and an alert sense of rhythm.

Leoni, Franco (*b* Milan, 24 Oct 1864; *d* London, 8 Feb 1949). Italian composer. He studied with Dominiceti and Ponchielli at the Milan Conservatory and worked in Italy and England as a composer of Puccinian operas (including *L'oracolo*, 1905), oratorios and songs.

Leoni, Leone (*b* Verona, *c*1560; *d* Vicenza, 24 June 1627). Italian composer. He was *maestro di cappella* of Vicenza Cathedral from 1588 until his death. Six books of madrigals (1588–1602) and six of motets (1606–22) survive; many items reappeared in anthologies. He emphasized contrasts of texture and expressive setting.

Léonin (*fl* Paris, *c*1163–1201). Composer, possibly the 'Magister Leoninus' mentioned in 1193 who died in or soon after 1201. According to the 13th-century theorist Anonymous IV, he was the 'best composer [or singer] of organum' and compiled a *Magnus liber* containing two-part settings of the solo portions of graduals, alleluias and responsories for all the principal feasts of the year. The *Liber* no longer exists in its original form, and although Anonymous IV states that the books of polyphony initiated by Léonin and modified by Pérotin were still being used at Notre Dame Cathedral in Paris in the early 13th century, it is no longer believed that Léonin was choirmaster there. The music of the *Liber* is an extension of a primary improvisatory tradition, and Léonin should probably be seen not as its composer in the modern sense but as one who encapsulated the increasing inventiveness of singers. It is difficult to determine whether Léonin consistently employed the principles of modal rhythm or whether these were fully developed only by the compilers of the later sources.

Leonore. Beethoven's original title for his opera known as *Fidelio*. It was based on a libretto *Léonore ou L'amour conjugal* by J.N. Bouilly, but was staged as *Fidelio* first in 1805 and then, in its first revision, in 1806; at its second revision, in 1814, Beethoven accepted the title *Fidelio*. The overtures he wrote for it – no.2 for the original production, no.3 for the 1806 version, no.1 probably for a planned Prague production of 1807 – are known as *Leonore* to distinguish them from the 1814 *Fidelio* overture.

Leontovych, Mykola Dmytrovich (*b* Monastïryok, 13 Dec 1877; *d* Markovka, 25 Jan 1921). Ukrainian composer. He studied in seminaries and had consultations with Yavorsky (1909–14). The most brilliant of Lisenko's successors, he collected and arranged Ukrainian folk music; his *Shchedryk* (1916) established him as the most popular Ukrainian composer.

Leopold I (*b* Vienna, 9 June 1640; *d* there, 5 May 1705). Holy Roman Emperor (from 1658), composer and patron of music, a member of the house of Habsburg. He expanded the imperial Hofkapelle and, by the judicious hiring of librettists, composers and stage designers (notably Draghi, Schmelzer and L.O. Burnacini), fostered a court theatrical life unequalled in Europe and epitomized by the sumptuous production of Cesti's *Il pomo d'oro* in 1668. As a composer he was most successful in his concertato liturgical works (notably the *Missa angelis custodis*, 1673), but he also wrote sacred and secular Italian dramatic compositions, including *sepolcri* marked by skilful handling of recitative and arioso sections, and preference for a simple melodic style. He also wrote songs for German-language comedies in a simple, light idiom.

L'Epine, (Francesca) Margherita de (*b* c1683; *d* London, 8 Aug 1746). Italian soprano. In London from 1702, she was the first Italian singer to establish a lasting reputation there, appearing in English operas and masques (notably by Pepusch, whom she later married) and some of the first Italian operas produced in London. She was sister to the singer Maria Gallia and mistress of the composer Jakob Greber.

Leppard, Raymond (John) (*b* London, 11 Aug 1927). English conductor. He studied at Cambridge and made his London début in 1952, gaining an early reputation for his lively, crisply articulated interpretations of 17th- and 18th-century harpsichord music. He has often been heard with the ECO, was principal conductor of the BBC Northern SO (1973–80) and became principal guest conductor of the St Louis SO in 1984. In 1962 he conducted his version of Monteverdi's *L'incoronazione di Poppea* at Glyndebourne, inaugurating an influential series of revivals there and elsewhere of 17th-century Italian operas.

Lerdahl, Fred [Alfred] (Whitford) (*b* Madison, 10 March 1943). American composer and theorist. He studied at Princeton with Babbitt, Cone and Kim, and at Freiburg with Fortner (1968–9), and has taught at Berkeley, Harvard, Columbia and the University of Michigan. His early works suggest Berio, but in the mid-1970s he began to incorporate tonal elements in a highly original way: the First and Second String Quartets (1978, 1982), though written independently, are linked. He has been productive as a theorist.

Le Roux, Gaspard (*b*?c1660; *d*?Paris, c1706). French composer. Listed in his day among the foremost harpsichordists, he is important for his one collection *Pièces de clavessin* (1705). Grouped by tonality into suites (though he did not use the term), a unique feature is that most pieces are also given in trio form (for strings, wind or a single melody instrument with keyboard). The allemandes and courantes are sophisticated examples of a developed, lute-based French keyboard style, while the sarabandes show an unusual diversity.

Le Roux, Maurice (*b* Paris, 6 Feb 1923). French composer. He studied with Messiaen at the Paris Conservatoire (1946–52) and followed Boulez in his works. Subsequently he made a reputation as a cinema composer and conductor, of the Orchestre National de l'ORTF (1960–68) and at the Opéra.

Le Roy, Adrian (*b* Montreuil-sur-Mer, c1520; *d* Paris, 1598). French music printer and lutenist. He was in partnership with his cousin Robert BALLARD.

Lésbio, António Marques (*b* Lisbon, 1639; *d* there, 21 Nov 1709). Portuguese writer and composer. He became master of the royal chamber musicians in 1668 and thereafter held a succession of royal appointments. Of the Spanish villancicos and Portuguese villancicos for which he is remembered, only 16 survive with music; they show him as a composer of grace and polish. His larger church works were lost in the Lisbon earthquake of 1755.

Leschetizky, Theodor [Leszetycki, Teodor] (*b* Łańcut, 22 June 1830; *d* Dresden, 14 Nov 1915). Polish pianist, teacher and composer. A pupil of Czerny and a friend of Anton Rubinstein, he was in great demand as a piano teacher, first in St Petersburg (1852–77), then in Vienna (from 1878); his vigorous, practical methods earned him the respect of hundreds of pupils, among them Paderewski, Artur Schnabel and Ossip Gabrilovich. Most of his 49 compositions are piano miniatures.

Lesson. Term originally used in England to denote an exercise in performance or composition but later applied to many types of domestic keyboard music and some of chamber music. It appears in 16th-century titles such as Morley's *First Booke of Consort Lessons* (1599) and was later used for individual movements of the keyboard suite and for pieces that Italian composers might have called 'sonatas'.

L'Estocart, Paschal de (*b* Noyon, ?1539; *d* after 1584). French composer. He visited Italy several times and was variously at Basle, Nancy and Evreux. An austere, essentially Huguenot composer, yet thoroughly italianate, he published five books of motets, psalms and other religious pieces in Geneva

(1582–3). A hallmark of his style is his daring harmony.

Le Sueur [Lesueur], **Jean-François** (*b* Drucat-Plessiel, 15 Feb 1760; *d* Paris, 6 Oct 1837). French composer and writer. Originally a choirmaster (including a spell at Notre Dame, Paris, 1786–7), he turned to the theatre during the Revolution, making his début as an opera composer with *La caverne* (1793), followed by *Paul et Virginie* (1794) and *Télémaque* (1796). While musical director (co-director with Cherubini from 1816) of the Tuileries Chapel he had his greatest triumph with *Ossian ou Les bardes* (1804) and began teaching at the Conservatoire (1818), where his pupils included Berlioz, Ambroise Thomas and Gounod. From 1830 he devoted himself to writing. His major contribution was the *Exposé d'une musique* (1787), which treats the aim of music as imitation, along the lines of Rousseau. Among his compositions, *La caverne* is noteworthy for its strong dramatic character, effective choral writing and fusion of elements from *opera seria*, *opera buffa* and *opéra comique*; his sacred music includes 29 large works notable for their simplicity.

Lesure, François (-Marie) (*b* Paris, 23 May 1923). French musicologist. He studied at the Sorbonne, the Conservatoire, the Ecole des Chartes and at the Ecole Pratique des Hautes-Etudes. He was a librarian in the music department of the Bibliothèque Nationale in Paris for 20 years before becoming head keeper in 1970. In 1965 he became professor of musicology at the Free University, Brussels. His research has been concerned principally with the sociology of music, 16th-century French music, Debussy and bibliography.

Let's Make an Opera. 'Entertainment for young people', op.45, by Britten to a libretto by Eric Crozier (1949, Aldeburgh); the second part is *The Little Sweep*, the opera itself.

Letter V. Title sometimes attached to Haydn's Symphony no.88 in G; it is a relic of a system for cataloguing Haydn's symphonies with letters of the alphabet, before the standard numbering was done.

Leutgeb, Joseph [Ignaz] (*b* ?Salzburg, *c*1745; *d* Vienna, 27 Feb 1811). Austrian horn player. He served at the Salzburg court and gave many concerts elsewhere. He was a friend of Mozart, who wrote music including three horn concertos for him.

Leveridge, Richard (*b* 1670–71; *d* London, 22 March 1758). English bass and composer. He was a leading London singer from the 1680s until 1751, and performed both in English works (by Purcell and others) and Italian operas (including Handel's; he was Polyphemus in the 1731 public première of *Acis and Galatea*. He composed several stage works, 1698–1723, and numerous popular songs, notably 'Roast Beef'.

Levi, Hermann (*b* Giessen, 7 Nov 1839; *d* Munich, 13 May 1900). German conductor. He studied with Hauptmann and Rietz at the Leipzig Conservatory. As Hofkapellmeister in Karlsruhe (1864–72) and Munich (1872–90), he became an esteemed interpreter of Brahms and of Mozart's operas, but he made his strongest mark at Bayreuth, notably with *Parsifal* (1882, 1889–94). For his economy of gesture, quality of interpretation and influence, he ranks with Richter as one of the greatest early Bayreuth conductors.

Levidis, Dimitrios (*b* Athens, 8 April 1885/1886; *d* Palaeon Phaleron, 29 May 1951). Greek composer, later naturalized French. He studied in Athens, Lausanne and Munich (with Klose, Mottl and Strauss, 1907–8), then settled in France (1910–32) before returning to Athens to work as a teacher and composer. He wrote abundantly, in many genres, with a refined technique combining Straussian harmony and Ravelian impressionism. His *Poème symphonique*, using an ondes martenot, was given at the first demonstration of the instrument (1928, Paris).

Levine, James (*b* Cincinnati, 23 June 1943). American conductor and pianist. He was a piano soloist with the Cincinnati SO at the age of ten. After study at the Juilliard School he joined the Cleveland Orchestra as assistant to Szell. He made his Met début in 1971 and became music director there in 1975. He made his Salzburg début in 1975, Bayreuth in 1982, and has also appeared at the Vienna Staatsoper. As an orchestral conductor his repertory ranges from the 18th century to Xenakis and Cage; he is an outstanding Mahler interpreter. He has conducted Mozart from the keyboard and plays chamber music.

Levy, Marvin David (*b* Passaic, NJ, 2 Aug 1932). American composer. He studied at New York University and under Luening at Columbia University. His music is atonal, theatrical in character and flexible in its treatment of rhythm. His best known work is the opera *Mourning Becomes Elektra* (1967), commissioned by the Met.

Lewis, Sir Anthony (Carey) (*b* Bermuda, 2 March 1915; *d* Haslemere, 5 June 1983). English musicologist and conductor. He studied at Cambridge and joined the BBC music department, in 1945 planning the music for the new Third Programme. In 1947 he became Professor of Music at Birmingham University, where he conducted many revivals of Handel operas, and in 1968 he became principal of the Royal Academy of Music. He was largely responsible for the inception of the Musica Britannica edition and worked too for the Purcell Society and the Royal Musical Association. He did much for the revival of Baroque music.

Lewis, Richard (*b* Manchester, 10 May 1914). English tenor. From 1947 he sang at Glyndebourne in operas by Britten, Stravinsky, Mozart and Monteverdi. At Covent Garden he created roles in operas by Walton (Troilus) and Tippett (Mark, Achilles) and was Aaron in the British premières of Schoenberg's *Moses und Aron*. With a mellifluous voice of great flexibility, he was also distinguished in concert and oratorio (particularly as Gerontius) and toured much abroad.

Lewkovitch, Bernhard (*b* Copenhagen, 28 May 1927). Danish composer. He studied with Schierbeck and Jersild at the Copenhagen Conservatory, and worked as a church musician and choral conductor: his works include much Catholic church music. In the mid-1950s he moved from modality to serialism; some works of the 1960s use avant-garde effects and brought him international renown.

Lhéritier, Jean [Johannes] (*b* c1480; *d* after 1552). French composer. A disciple of Josquin, he worked in Ferrara (1506–8), Rome (1521–2) and may have had connections with Florence in the late 1520s. His compositions survive in many MSS and printed collections. Central to his output is the motet, of which he composed many. They are characterized by imitation relieved by homophonic writing for formal reasons. His melodies are nicely balanced arches, predominantly in stepwise motion. His single extant mass is of a type cultivated by Févin and Mouton c1500 and borrows melodic material from one of the former's *chansons*.

Lhévinne, Josef (*b* Orel, 13 Dec 1874; *d* New York, 2 Dec 1944). Russian pianist. He graduated from the Moscow Conservatory in 1891 and after living in Berlin (1907–19) moved to New York and taught at the Juilliard School from 1922. His wife Rosina (1880–1976) also taught there; Browning, Van Cliburn and Levine were among her pupils. Lhévinne was known for his prodigious technique, notably in Chopin and Tchaikovsky.

Lhotka, Fran (*b* Mlada Vožice, 25 Dec 1883; *d* Zagreb, 26 Jan 1962). Yugoslav composer of Czech origin. A pupil of Dvořák, he taught at the Zagreb Academy (1920–61) and wrote ballets and instrumental music using Croatian elements.

His son Ivo Lhotka-Kalinski (*b* 1913), who studied with him and with Pizzetti, is also a composer, notably of radio and television operas in a neo-classical style incorporating atonal elements.

Liber usualis (Lat.). 'Book of common practice': short title of a book, first issued by the monks of Solesmes in 1896, of prayers, lessons and chants for the more important services of both Mass and Office in the Roman Catholic Church. It combines elements of the missal, gradual, breviary and antiphoner.

Libretto. A printed 'small book' containing the words of an opera, oratorio etc; by extension, the text itself (*see* OPERA). Librettos, designed to be read during a performance of the work, list casts and include stage directions, and where the opera was performed in a language other than that of the audience a translation was normally given. The printing of librettos for theatre use declined in the 19th century when gas lighting made it possible to dim auditorium lights and the publication of vocal scores became more widespread.

Libuše. Opera in three acts by Smetana to a libretto by Wenzig translated by Špindler (1881, Prague).

Licenza (It.). 'Licence': in the 17th and 18th centuries a passage or cadenza inserted into a piece by a performer. The term was also used for an epilogue added to an opera or play, in honour of a patron's birthday or wedding or some other festive occasion. The directions 'Con alcuna licenza' or 'con alcune licenze' indicate some degree of freedom in either performance or composition.

Lichnowsky, Prince Karl (Alois Johann Nepomuk Vinzenz Leonhard) von (*b* Vienna, 21 June 1761; *d* there, 15 March 1814). Austrian nobleman and patron of the arts. He was a pupil and patron of Mozart and later of Beethoven in Vienna, supporting an ensemble for the performance of Beethoven's early chamber works. His sister Henriette (1769–after 1829) had contact with Chopin in Paris, and his brother Moritz (1771–1837), also a patron of both Mozart and Beethoven, was a fine amateur composer.

Lichtenstein, Karl August, Freiherr von (*b* Lahm, 8 Sept 1767; *d* Berlin, 10 Sept 1845). German composer and theatre manager. He worked in Bamberg, Dessau, Vienna, Strasbourg and Berlin, writing c17 stage works and, for other composers, four librettos (including *Die Hochzeit des Gamacho*, 1825, for Mendelssohn); he translated or arranged many operas by leading composers.

Lidholm, Ingvar (Natanael) (*b* Jönköping, 24 Feb 1921). Swedish composer. A pupil of Rosenberg, he has worked as a conductor, radio producer and teacher at the Stockholm Musikhögskolan (from 1965). His early works are in a Nielsen–Hindemith style, but in 1949 he took up serialism, followed in the 1960s by more avant-garde practices, though certain features of his music (sensitive choral writing, colourful orchestration and an essential lyricism) have remained constant. His most important works are choral, but his output includes dramatic, orchestral and instrumental pieces. His vocal techniques are integrated in ... *a riveder le stelle* (1973).

Lidl, Andreas (*b* ? Vienna; *d* London, ?by 1789). Austrian baryton and viola da gamba player. He played in the Esterházy Kapelle (under Haydn) in the early 1770s, and later worked in London. He composed instrumental duets, trios, quartets and quintets, mostly adapted from baryton originals.

Lie, Sigurd (*b* Drammen, 23 May 1871; *d* Vestre Aker, 30 Sept 1904). Norwegian composer. He studied in Oslo and at the Leipzig Conservatory. Among his sizeable output of chamber music, orchestral pieces and songs, the two Norwegian dances for violin and piano and the famous song *Sne* ('Snow') are still in the repertory.

Liebe der Danae, Die. Opera in three acts by Richard Strauss to a libretto by Gregor after Hofmannsthal (1952, Salzburg).

Liebermann, Rolf (*b* Zurich, 14 Sept 1910). Swiss composer and opera director. He studied with Scherchen and Vogel and managed the Hamburg Staatsoper (1959–73) and Paris Opéra (1973–80). His compositions, mostly predating these appointments, include operas and orchestral pieces (Concerto for jazz band and orchestra, 1954).

Lieberson, Peter (*b* New York, 25 Oct 1946). American composer. He was a pupil of Babbitt and Wuorinen and studied Tibetan Buddhism, 1976–81. His works include a large, romantic Piano Concerto (1983) conceived to reflect Buddhist concepts.

Liebesliederwalzer. 18 waltzes, op.52, by Brahms for two pianos with soprano, alto, tenor and bass soloists to texts from G.F. Daumer's *Polydora* (1869); they were also published without vocal parts. Brahms composed 15 *Neue Liebesliederwalzer* (op.65).

Liebestod (Ger.: 'love-death'). Isolde's final aria at

the end of Act 3 of *Tristan und Isolde* (often played in an orchestral arrangement as a concert item with the Prelude). Wagner used the title to refer to the Prelude itself.

Liebesträume. Three piano nocturnes by Liszt (*c*1850), transcriptions of three of his songs.

Liebesverbot, Das. Opera in two acts by Wagner to his own libretto after Shakespeare's *Measure for Measure* (1836, Magdeburg).

Lied (Ger.: 'song'). Term generally used in English for the Romantic art song from Schubert to Wolf and Strauss.

The earliest forms of lied, however, come from the 15th century, including 36 by Oswald von Wolkenstein; they are in two or three parts. A specifically German type, the *Tenorlied*, first appearing in the *Lochamer Liederbuch* (*c*1460), is based on a pre-existing vocal line used as a *cantus firmus* (or Tenor). In the songs of Isaac and other early 16th-century composers four-part writing was the norm, with the Tenor virtually always in the highest male part. The 260 songs of his pupil Senfl explore many stylistic possibilities, including imitation, and often have a soprano *cantus firmus*. The heyday of the *Tenorlied* ended *c*1550. Later the form received decisive impetus from Lassus; the highpoint of this period was reached in the *c*60 lieder of Hans Leo Hassler, whose synthesis of Italian style with German lyricism was influential. The polyphonic lied figures slightly in the works of Schein and thereafter hardly at all.

In the 17th century a new kind of lied arose, the Generalbass or continuo lied, mainly for literati, students and the cultivated middle class; they were simpler and often cruder than the courtly solo songs of other countries. Adam Krieger was the greatest continuo lied composer; his *Arien* (1667), mostly solos with continuo and instrumental ritornellos, vary from pastoral love-songs to lascivious drinking-songs. After 1670 the continuo lied declined, but it had a resurgence towards the mid-18th century with such composers as Telemann and J.V. Görner.

After 1750, a new aesthetic led to strophic lieder set to simple folklike melody with uncomplicated harmony and independent accompaniment. Berlin (where lied composers included C.P.E. Bach) was the principal centre. The Second Berlin Lied School of *c*1770, including Reichardt and Zelter, used a more complex style and sought out better poetry, including Goethe's and Schiller's. Of Viennese composers only Mozart contributed significantly to the lied development.

Beethoven can be claimed as creator of the Romantic lied, but it was Schubert's setting of Goethe's *Gretchen am Spinnrade* (1814) and *Erlkönig* (1815) that first embodied the close identification with poet, character, scene and singer, as well as the concentration of lyric, dramatic and graphic ideas into an integrated whole, which characterize the finest 19th-century lieder. In addition to onomatopoeic devices (of which the cycles *Die schöne Müllerin* and *Winterreise* provide numerous examples) there are in Schubert's 610 songs hundreds of more deeply

personal and less readily explicable verbo-musical ideas, corresponding to sunlight, evening, sleep, love, grief and so on, which occur in infinitely variable permutation.

Schubert's perfect compound of text and music was rarely matched by his successors. In Loewe's 375 songs music is subordinate to words; his best settings are of narrative ballads such as *Edward* and *Erlkönig*. Mendelssohn aimed at formal perfection, in strophic songs with a varied last verse or coda. Schumann's 260 lieder recombine the basic elements of verbal equivalence and musical independence, revealing him as Schubert's true heir; his personal innovation was to elevate the role of the piano. The rich flowering of German Romantic song with piano, to which Franz, Wagner, Liszt, Cornelius and others contributed, was maintained to the end of the century by two composers who represent opposite ends of the spectrum of lied composition. Brahms was the supreme traditionalist: most of his 200 songs are carefully unified strophic or ternary structures, with often complex but rarely independent accompaniments. They reach heights of nostalgia and longing scaled by no other songwriter. Wolf's procedures, in contrast, were poetry-orientated; he published songbooks devoted to particular poets (Mörike, Goethe, Eichendorff). His basic style is keyboard writing enriched by vocal and instrumental counterpoint, employing an extended harmonic language; his 300 songs encompass a wider emotional range than any other composer's since Schubert.

Although cultivated with distinction by Strauss and others, the lied with piano lost its central position after 1900, and in the orchestral cycles of Mahler it was taken from drawing room to concert hall. Schoenberg and Berg followed Mahler, but neither paid much attention to the lied after World War I.

Liederbuch (Ger.: 'songbook'). Term for certain 15th- and 16th-century German collections of polyphonic songs or short lyric poems that were usually sung. Among MSS commonly associated with it are the Glogauer Liederbuch and the Lochamer Liederbuch.

Lieder eines fahrenden Gesellen. Song cycle by Mahler (1885), settings for baritone or mezzosoprano and orchestra (or piano) of four of his own poems after *Des knaben Wunderhorn*.

Liederkreis (Ger.). 'Song circle': either a SONG CYCLE or a circle or club of people dedicated to the cultivation of popular song. The term was first used by Beethoven to describe his *An die ferne Geliebte*. Schumann used it as a title for two cycles for voice and piano: op.24, settings of nine poems by Heine, and op.39, settings of 12 poems by Eichendorff (both 1840).

Lieder ohne Worte. Eight books of piano pieces by Mendelssohn (1830–*c*1845); they are characterized by a songlike melody in the right hand. He also wrote a *Lied ohne Worte* op.109 for cello and piano (*c*1845).

Liederspiel (Ger.). A type of dramatic entertainment of early 19th-century Germany in which existing lyric verses were set to music. The first was *Lieb und Treue* (1800) by J.F. Reichardt, the form's leading figure.

Liedertafel. Term for a male society of 19th-century Germany which met to perform vocal music and take refreshments; the first was founded by Zelter in Berlin in 1808.

Lied von der Erde, Das. *See* SONG OF THE EARTH, THE.

Lienas, Juan de (*fl* Mexico, *?c*1620–50). Mexican composer, possibly of Spanish birth. His surviving music, 16 works for women's voices, was apparently written for use in the Convento del Carmen and in the élite Encarnación convent in Mexico City; it ranks among the finest, technically most fluent music in the large colonial repertory.

Lieto (It.). 'Happy'; *lieto fine* is the term for the happy ending obligatory in serious opera of the 18th century. *See* OPERA.

Lieutenant Kijé [Poruchik Kizhe]. Suite for orchestra, op.60, by Prokofiev (1934), derived from music he wrote for a film.

Life for the Tsar, A [Zhizn'za tsarya; Ivan Susanin]. Opera in four acts and an epilogue by Glinka to a libretto by Baron Georgy Rosen (1836, St Petersburg); the original title was *Ivan Susanin*.

Ligature. A notational symbol of the kind used between the 12th century and the 16th that combines within itself two or more pitches and by its shape defines their rhythm. The earliest ligatures derived from the rising and falling two-note neume of chant notation. Ligatures were codified and systematized in the mid-13th century by Franco of Cologne; his rhythmic schemes for them were largely unchanged as long as ligatures remained in use. Ligatures became increasingly rare in the 15th century and virtually went out of use in the 16th, particularly as note values became shorter and the note-lengths signified by ligatures, mainly longs, breves and semibreves, were used less than minims and semiminims. Ligatures still appear, however, in printed editions of the 16th century and even occasionally later.

The term 'ligature' is sometimes applied to a slur indicating that two or more notes are to be sung to the same syllable (although the earlier ligature, described above, did not necessarily carry that implication); it is sometimes applied to the tie. The term also signifies the metal band with screws by which the single reed of the clarinet or saxophone is attached to the mouthpiece.

Ligeti, György (Sándor) (*b* Tirnăveni, 28 May 1923). Austrian composer of Hungarian origin. He studied with Farkas, Veress and Járdányi at the Budapest Academy, where he began teaching in 1950. During this period he followed the prevailing Bartók–Kodály style in his works while also writing more adventurous pieces (First Quartet, 1954) that had to remain unpublished. In 1956 he left Hungary for Vienna. He worked at the electronic music studio in Cologne (1957–8) and came to international prominence with his *Atmosphères* (1961), which works with slowly changing orchestral clusters. This led to teaching appointments in Stockholm (from 1961), Stanford (1972) and Hamburg (from 1973). Meanwhile he developed the 'cloud' style in his Requiem (1965) and *Lontano* for orchestra (1967), while writing an absurdist diptych for vocal soloists and ensemble: *Aventures* (1966) and *Nouvelles aventures*

(1966). His interests in immobile drifts and mechanical processes are seen together in his Second Quartet (1968) and Chamber Concerto (1970), while the orchestral *Melodien* (1971) introduced a tangle of melody. The combination of these elements, in music of highly controlled fantasy and excess, came in his surreal opera *Le grand macabre* (1978). His subsequent output has been diminished by ill-health, though it includes a Horn Trio (1982) in which perverse calculation is carried into Romanticism. Other later works include *Monument, Selbstporträt, Bewegung*, for two pianos (1976), two pieces for harpsichord (1978), two Hungarian studies for chorus (1983) and a book of piano studies (1985).

Dramatic music Aventures (1966); Nouvelles aventures (1966); Le grand macabre (1978)
Orchestral music Apparitions (1959); Atmosphères (1961); Fragment (1961); Poème symphonique, 100 metronomes (1962); Vc Conc. (1966); Lontano (1967); Ramifications, str (1969); Chamber Conc. (1970); Melodien (1971); Double Conc., fl, ob, orch (1972); San Francisco Polyphony (1974); Pf Conc. (1983)
Choral music Requiem (1965); Lux aeterna (1966); Clocks and Clouds (1973); Drei Phantasien (1983); Magyar Etüdök [Hungarian studies] (1983)
Chamber music 2 str qts (1954, 1968); Continuum, hpd (1968); Ten pieces, wind qnt (1968); Horizont, rec (1971); Monument, Selbstporträt, Bewegung, 2 pf (1976); 3 Objekte, 2 pf (1976); Passacaglia ungherese, hpd (1978); Trio, vn, hn, pf (1982); Studies, pf (1985)
Organ music Volumina (1962); 2 studies (1967, 1969)

Light Cavalry [Die leichte Kavallerie]. Operetta in two acts by Suppé to a libretto by C. Costa (1866, Vienna).

Lighthouse, The. Opera in a prologue and one act by Peter Maxwell Davies to his own libretto (1980, Edinburgh).

Lilburn, Douglas (Gordon) (*b* Wanganui, 2 Nov 1915). New Zealand composer. He studied at the RCM (1937–40), where Vaughan Williams was a decisive influence, and in 1947 began teaching at Victoria University, Wellington; in the early 1960s he established the first electronic music studio in Australasia and he has trained a generation of young composers. His earlier works, including the overture *Aotearoa* (1940) and his first two symphonies (1948, 1951), are in a diatonic style sensitive to the New Zealand landscape. He then drew on Bartók, Stravinsky, contemporary Americans and the Second Viennese School in developing his style towards the Third Symphony (1961), after which he began to compose electronic music (*Three Inscapes*, 1972).

Liliencron, Rochus, Freiherr (Traugott Ferdinand) von (*b* Plön, 8 Dec 1820; *d* Koblenz, 5 March 1912). German scholar. With his expertise in philology, literature and theology, he contributed much as editor (with F.X. von Wegele) of the *Allgemeine deutsche Biographie* (1875–1907), also supervising the publication of *c*45 volumes of the Denkmäler deutscher Tonkunst.

Lill, John (Richard) (*b* London, 17 March 1944). English pianist. He studied at the RCM and with Kempff. He made his London début in 1963 (Beethoven's Piano Concerto no.5) and won the 1970

Tchaikovsky Competition in Moscow. He is noted for his broad, vigorous Beethoven playing and his commanding technique in the Romantic concerto repertory.

Lima, Candido (*b* nr. Viana do Castelo, 22 Aug 1939). Portuguese composer. He trained in Portugal and at Darmstadt and has done important educational work, as a teacher at the Oporto Conservatory and as a writer. His large, diverse output embraces avantgarde techniques.

Lima, Jeronymo Francisco de (*b* Lisbon, 30 Sept 1743; *d* there, 19 Feb 1822). Portuguese composer. He studied in Naples and worked in Lisbon, becoming cathedral *mestre de capela* in 1798 and organist of the royal chamber in 1802. He composed stage works and much sacred music. His brother Braz Francisco de Lima (1752–1813) was also a composer.

Lincoln Center for the Performing Arts. Arts complex in New York, established in the 1960s. Music facilities include Avery Fisher Hall (formerly Philharmonic Hall, opened 1962, renamed 1973; rebuilt 1976, cap. 2742); New York State Theater (1964; renovated 1981–2, cap. 2737); METROPOLITAN OPERA HOUSE (1966, cap. 3788); JUILLIARD SCHOOL; Alice Tully Hall (1969, cap. 1096). Free outdoor concerts are given in the Plaza and Damrosch Park.

Lincoln Portrait. Work for speaker and orchestra by Copland (1942).

Lind [Lind-Goldschmidt], **Jenny** [Johanna Maria] (*b* Stockholm, 6 Oct 1820; *d* Wynds Point, 2 Nov 1887). Swedish soprano. She was nicknamed 'the Swedish nightingale'. Her operatic career in Stockholm (1838–43) launched her on a series of triumphant appearances in Germany, Austria and Britain (1844–9), where her Alice (in Meyerbeer's *Robert le diable*; her London début, 1847), Amina (Bellini's *La sonnambula*) and Marie (Donizetti's *La fille du régiment*) were favourites, confirming her acting ability and the extraordinary power, flexibility and purity of her voice. From 1850, beginning with an extended tour of the USA, she sang only in concert and oratorio, settling in England (1858) with her husband and accompanist, Otto Goldschmidt. Her last public performance was in 1883.

Lindberg, Oskar (Fredrik) (*b* Gagnef, 23 Feb 1887; *d* Stockholm, 10 April 1955). Swedish composer and church musician. He studied with Ellberg and Hallén at the Stockholm Conservatory (where from 1919 he taught), and worked as an organist. He wrote late Romantic orchestral pieces as well as a Requiem, cantatas and hymns, and helped compile the 1939 Swedish hymbook.

Lindblad, Adolf Fredrik (*b* Skenninge, 1 Feb 1801; *d* Löfvingsborg, 23 Aug 1878). Swedish composer. While studying with Zelter in Berlin he became a close friend of Mendelssohn's. He directed a music and piano school (1827–61), and composed a successful symphony (1831), an opera (*Frondörerna*, 1835) and 215 lieder, some modelled on Swedish folk melodies. Among his finest works are the colourful nature songs *En sommardag* and *Aftonen*.

Lindeman. Norwegian family of musicians. The most important members were Ludvig Mathias (1812–87), an organist and folksong collector who published a chorale book (1878) and folksong collections, particularly *Aeldre og nyere norske fjeldmelodier* (1853–67); and his son Peter Brynie (1858–1930), with whom he founded the Christiania (Oslo) Conservatory (1883).

Lindgren, (Karl) Adolf (*b* Trosa, 14 March 1846; *d* Stockholm, 8 Feb 1905). Swedish critic and historian. Apart from contributing to numerous Scandinavian and German journals, he co-founded the important Swedish journal *Svensk musiktidning* (1881–1913) and wrote discerningly on music for the encyclopedia *Nordisk familjebok* (1875–99).

Lindley, Robert (*b* Rotherham, 4 March 1776; *d* London, 13 June 1855). English cellist. From 1794 to 1846 he was principal cellist at the Italian Opera in London and at all the major concerts, sharing a desk with his friend Dragonetti. He was noted for his outstanding technique and elaborate accompaniment of recitative.

Lindpaintner, Peter Josef von (*b* Koblenz, 9 Dec 1791; *d* Nonnenhorn, 21 Aug 1856). German conductor and composer. Kapellmeister of the royal orchestra at Stuttgart (1819–56), he was one of the most highly regarded conductors of his time. He composed Weberian operas, notably *Der Bergkönig* (1825) and *Der Vampyr* (1828), much chamber music and many songs, including the popular *Roland*.

Lindsay Quartet. English string quartet, led by Peter Cropper. It was founded in 1965, when its players were students at the RAM; it was taught by Griller and Kolisch. The quartet was in residence at Keele University from 1968, later at Sheffield and (from 1978) Manchester. It is notable for its high standard of ensemble and the insight it brings to the standard repertory; it has made complete recordings of the Bartók and Beethoven quartets and has devised ingenious quartet festivals based on particular repertories. The quartet has appeared widely in the USA and Europe.

Lindy [lindy hop]. A lively, often acrobatic social dance that originated in Harlem, New York, in the 1920s; it became increasingly athletic and increasingly popular in the next two decades and was also called 'jitterbug'. It included a section in which the dancers improvised. In the 1950s it served as a basis for some rock-and-roll dances.

Linike [Linigke], **Johann Georg** (*b* c1680; *d* Hamburg, after 1737). German composer. After serving at Berlin he was music director at the Weissenfels court; later he went to London (1721–5) and then became first violinist at the Hamburg Opera. He composed mainly instrumental music and cantatas. Other musicians in the family included Ephraim (1665–1726), a violinist who served mostly at Berlin, and Christian Bernhard (1673–1751), a cellist and composer at Berlin and later Cöthen.

Lining-out. A method of performing a psalm or hymn in which a leader gives out the words and/or the melody one line at a time, followed by the congregation. It began in 17th-century England and is still used in parts of the USA.

Linke, Norbert (*b* Steinau, 5 March 1933). German composer. He studied with Klussmann at the Hamburg Musikhochschule (1952–7) and has worked as a critic, teacher and composer. In his compositions he has tried to abolish the barriers between 'serious' and 'light' music.

Linley, Thomas (*b* Bath, 5 May 1756; *d* Grimsthorpe, 5 Aug 1778). English composer and violinist. One of England's most precocious musicians, he studied with Boyce, then became Nardini's violin pupil in Florence (1768–71), where he met Mozart (1770). Returning to England, he performed in Bath and London and from 1773 was leader at Drury Lane theatre. He composed prolifically, writing stage works (the first, 1775, with his father), sacred music, an *Ode on the Spirits of Shakespeare* (1776), songs etc, violin sonatas and 20 or more violin concertos. His works are fluent and imaginative; his death (in a boating accident) was a great loss to English music.

His father Thomas (1733–95) was a composer, harpsichordist, concert director and singing teacher in Bath; he also worked at Drury Lane theatre, becoming joint manager in 1776. He presented several stage works and composed and arranged music for plays and pantomimes.

The other Linley children included Elizabeth Ann (1754–92), a distinguished soprano; Mary (1758–87), also a soprano; Ozias Thurston (1765–1831), an organist and clergyman; and William (1771–1835), a pupil of C.F. Abel and later a civil servant, composer of operas and other vocal works.

Linz Symphony. Nickname of Mozart's Symphony no.36 in C (1783), composed and first performed in Linz.

Lioncourt, Guy de (*b* Caen, 1 Dec 1885; *d* Paris, 24 Dec 1961). French composer. He studied with Roussel and d'Indy at the Schola Cantorum, Paris, and remained there as a teacher, leaving in 1935 to become founder-director of the Ecole César Franck. His music, including masses and liturgical dramas, places a high value on plainchant.

Lion's roar. *See* STRING DRUM.

Lipatti, Dinu (*b* Bucharest, 19 March 1917; *d* Geneva, 2 Dec 1950). Romanian pianist. He studied in Bucharest and Paris. His career was interrupted by the war and later concert appearances were curtailed by illness. Largely through recordings he became known for his poetic sensibility and delicacy of touch: he was most often heard in Chopin, Schumann and Mozart.

Lipiński, Karol Józef (*b* Radzyń, 30 Oct 1790; *d* Urłów, 16 Dec 1861). Polish violinist. From 1839 he worked in Dresden as a conductor, composer and teacher, his pupils including Wieniawski and Joachim. He represented the classical school of Viotti and Spohr. His tone was renowned throughout Europe for its strength and depth, and his technique compared to that of Paganini (with whom he played).

Lipkin, Malcolm (Leyland) (*b* Liverpool, 2 May 1932). English composer. He studied at the RCM and with Seiber (1954–7). His music displays economy of means and includes a Piano Concerto (1957), *Sinfonia da Roma* (1965) and a choral setting of Psalm xcvi. Since 1975 he has taught at Kent University.

Lippius, Johannes (*b* Strasbourg, 24 June 1585; *d* Speyer, 24 Sept 1612). Alsatian music theorist. A pupil of Calvisius at the Leipzig Thomasschule, he died before taking up a theological professorship at Strasbourg. His importance as a music theorist rests on *Synopsis musicae novae* (1612) in which Renaissance theory is replaced with four-part composition over a bass, the most significant component being the triad (symbolic equivalent to the Trinity). He was thus early to recognize in theory the practice of the early 17th century, primarily in Italian music, in which the bass is the most important functional part in a texture of several voices.

Lipsius, Marie ['La Mara'] (*b* Leipzig, 30 Dec 1837; *d* Schmölen, 2 March 1927). German writer on music. A member of Liszt's circle, she edited several volumes of his letters and wrote prolifically on a wide range of subjects, including many leading composers, whom she knew personally.

Lira. Term used for various string instruments: *see* LIRA DA BRACCIO; LIRA ORGANIZZATA; LIRONE (or lira da gamba); and LYRA. It also applied to the hurdy-gurdy and is still used for a hurdy-gurdy with three or four strings and four to 13 keys used in the Ukraine, Belorussia and Poland.

Lira da braccio. An important bowed string instrument of the Renaissance, used especially by courtly Italian poet-musicians of the 15th and 16th centuries to provide a chordal accompaniment to improvised recitations. It was also used in *intermedio* orchestras. It had a body like a violin's, but a wide fingerboard, a relatively flat bridge and a leaf-shaped pegbox with frontal pegs. There were normally seven strings, five on the fingerboard tuned in 5ths and two off-board drones tuned in octaves. Often called simply 'lira' or even 'viola', it was the principal instrument of Francesco di Viola, Alfonso dalla Viola and the other Italian composer-performers similarly named. It was often associated with mythological or allegorical characters such as Orpheus and Apollo. Like the *lirone*, it disappeared from use in the early 17th century.

Lira organizzata. A HURDY-GURDY with one or two ranks of organ pipes and bellows housed in its body. A crank operates the wheel that activates the strings and the bellows that make the pipes sound. It reached a peak of popularity *c*1780; Pleyel and Haydn are among those who wrote for it.

Lirone. A bass counterpart to the LIRA DA BRACCIO, of which it is a larger version, played between the knees rather than under the chin. It was usually fretted, with shallow ribs. It could accommodate as many as nine to 14 strings on the fingerboard and two to four drone strings. Its ingenious tuning system involved a series of ascending 5ths and descending 4ths, with the drones adapted to the tonality of the piece being played. Its remarkable sound provided a dynamic nuance like that of the viol or even a consort of viols.

The *lirone* was designed for sustained chordal playing, its chief use being to accompany the voice. The earliest known reference is from 1536, in a Venetian religious confraternity. Its impressive repertory extended from the mid-16th century to the 17th; Venice, Florence and Rome were the main centres of its cultivation.

Lisinski, Vatroslav [Fuchs, Ignacije] (*b* Zagreb, bap.

8 July 1819; *d* there, 31 May 1854). Croatian composer. He studied at the Prague Conservatory. The leading early Romantic composer in Croatia and founder of modern Croatian music, he wrote 142 works between 1841 and 1852; some draw on Czech and Croatian folk melody (the opera *Porin*, 1848–51), while others show his advanced harmonic and orchestral sense (the overture *Bellona*, 1849).

Lissa, Zofia (*b* Lwów, 19 Sept 1908; *d* Warsaw, 26 March, 1980). Polish musicologist. She studied at Lwów and Poznań and from 1948 taught at Warsaw University. She was active in many Polish and foreign institutions; her scholarly work, founded on Marxist method, was focussed on aesthetics, the methodology of the history of music and recent Polish music.

Liszt, Franz [Ferenc] (*b* Raiding, 22 Oct 1811; *d* Bayreuth, 31 July 1886). Hungarian composer and pianist. He was taught the piano by his father and then Czerny (Vienna, 1822–3), establishing himself as a remarkable concert artist by the age of 12. In Paris he studied theory and composition with Reicha and Paer; he wrote an opera and bravura piano pieces and undertook tours in France, Switzerland and England before ill-health and religious doubt made him reassess his career. Intellectual growth came through literature, and the urge to create through hearing opera and especially Paganini, whose spectacular effects Liszt eagerly transferred to the piano in original works and operatic fantasias. Meanwhile he gave lessons and began his stormy relationship (1833–44) with the (married) Countess Marie d'Agoult. They lived in Switzerland and Italy and had three children.

He gave concerts in Paris, maintaining his legendary reputation, and published some essays, but was active chiefly as a composer (*Années de pèlerinage*). To help raise funds for the Bonn Beethoven monument, he resumed the life of a travelling virtuoso (1839–47); he was adulated everywhere, from Ireland to Turkey, Portugal to Russia. In 1848 he took up a full-time conducting post at the Weimar court, where, living with the Princess Carolyne Sayn-Wittgenstein, he wrote or revised most of the major works for which he is known, conducted new operas by Wagner, Berlioz and Verdi and, as the teacher of Hans von Bülow and others in the German avant-garde, became the figurehead of the 'New German school'. In 1861–9 he lived mainly in Rome, writing religious works (he took minor orders in 1865); from 1870 he journeyed regularly between Rome, Weimar and Budapest. He remained active as a teacher and performer to the end of his life.

Liszt's personality appears contradictory in its combination of romantic abstraction and otherworldliness with a cynical diabolism and elegant, worldly manners. But though he had a restless intellect, he also was ceaselessly creative, seeking the new in music. He helped others generously, as conductor, arranger, pianist or writer, and took artistic and personal risks in doing so. The greatest pianist of his time, he composed some of the most difficult piano music ever written (e.g. the *Transcendental Studies*) and had an extraordinarily broad repertory, from Scarlatti onwards; he invented the modern piano recital.

Two formal traits give Liszt's compositions a personal stamp: experiment with large-scale structures (extending traditional sonata form, unifying multi-movement works), and thematic transformation, or subjecting a single short idea to changes of mode, rhythm, metre, tempo or accompaniment to form the thematic basis of an entire work (as in *Les préludes*, the *Faust-Symphonie*). His 'transcendental' piano technique was similarly imaginative, springing from a desire to make the piano sound like an orchestra or as rich in scope as one. In harmony he ventured well beyond the use of augmented and diminished chords and the whole-tone scale; the late piano and choral works especially contain tonal clashes arising from independent contrapuntal strands, chords built from 4ths or 5ths, and a strikingly advanced chromaticism.

Piano works naturally make up the greater part of Liszt's output; they range from the brilliant early studies and lyric nature pieces of the first set of *Années de pèlerinage* to the finely dramatic and logical B minor Sonata, a masterpiece of 19th-century piano literature. The piano works from the 1870s onwards are more austere and withdrawn, some of them impressionistic, even gloomy (*Années*, third set). Not all the piano music is free of bombast but among the arrangements, the symphonic transcriptions (notably of Berlioz, Beethoven and Schubert) are often faithful and ingenious, the operatic fantasias (on *Norma* and *Ernani*, for example) more than mere salon pieces.

Liszt invented the term 'sinfonische Dichtung' ('symphonic poem') for orchestral works that did not obey traditional forms strictly and were based generally on a literary or pictorial idea. Whether first conceived as overtures (*Les préludes*) or as works for other media (*Mazeppa*), these pieces all emphasize musical construction much more than scene-painting or story-telling. The three-movement *Faust-Symphonie* too, with its vivid character studies of Faust, Gretchen and Mephistopheles, relies on technical artifice (especially thematic transformation) more than musical narrative to convey its message; it is often considered Liszt's supreme masterpiece. Although he failed in his aim to revolutionize liturgical music, Liszt did create in his psalm settings, *Missa solemnis* and the oratorio *Christus* some intensely dramatic and moving choral music, successful in his lifetime and well suited to concert performance.

Dramatic and vocal music Don Sanche, opera (1825); *c*70 songs; recitations
Choral music Die Legende von der heiligen Elisabeth, oratorio (1857–62); Christus, oratorio (1853–66); Missa solemnis (1855); Missa choralis (1865); Hungarian Coronation Mass (1867); Requiem (1867–8); Psalm xiii (1855); Psalm xviii (1860); Via crucis (1878–9); *c*50 others; 2 Beethoven cantatas (1845; 1869–70); An die Künstler (1853); Hungaria 1848, cantata (1848); *c*26 others.
Orchestral and chamber music Les préludes, sym. poem (1848); Ce qu'on entend sur la montagne, sym. poem (1849); Tasso, sym. poem (1849); Héroïde funèbre, sym. poem (1850); Prometheus, sym. poem (1850); Mazeppa, sym. poem (1851); Festklänge, sym. poem (1853); Orpheus, sym. poem (1854); Hungaria, sym. poem (1854); Hunnenschlacht, sym. poem (1857); Die Ideale, sym.

poem (1857); Faust-Symphonie (1857); Dante Symphony (1857); Hamlet, sym. poem (1858); First Mephisto Waltz (1861); Trois odes funèbres (1866); Second Mephisto Waltz (1881); Pf Conc. no.1, E♭ (1855); Pf Conc. no.2, A (1857); Totentanz, pf/orch (1865); other orch works; 9 chamber works

Keyboard music Grand galop chromatique (1838); Grosses Konzertsolo (1849); [12] Transcendental Studies (1851); [6] Paganini Studies (1851); Années de pèlerinage, i, Suisse (1854), ii, Italie (1849), iii (1877); Sonata, b (1853); [19] Hungarian Rhapsodies (1853, 1885); Third Mephisto Waltz (1883); ballades, nocturnes, bagatelles, marches, polonaises, variations, legends, fantasias, mood pictures; Fantasy and Fugue on Ad nos, ad salutarem undam, org (1850); Prelude and Fugue on B–A–C–H, org (1855)

Arrangements, transcriptions c250 paraphrases, mostly for pf, of works by other composers, incl. fantasias on opera themes by Rossini, Bellini, Donizetti, Auber, Mozart, Meyerbeer, Gounod, Verdi; transcrs. of orch works, songs and opera themes by Beethoven, Berlioz, Mendelssohn, Schubert, Weber, Wagner, Saint-Saëns; c90 arrs. of his own works

Litaize, Gaston (Gilbert) (*b* Ménil-sur-Belvitte, 11 Aug 1909). French organist and composer. He studied at the Paris Conservatoire and became organist of St François-Xavier, Paris, in 1946. Blind from birth, he taught at the National Institute for the Blind. He has toured as a recitalist in Europe and North America. 24 liturgical preludes (1954) are among his compositions.

Litany. A liturgical prayer, or the procession during which it may be recited, in the form of invocations or supplications usually pronounced by a deacon with brief responses from the congregation (e.g. 'Kyrie eleison', 'Domine miserere', 'Ora pro nobis', 'Te rogamus audi nos'). Its melodies are syllabic. Litanies originated in antiquity and are still used in the Byzantine rite and the synagogue. In 592 a litany of the saints was instituted at Rome on 25 April of each year, called the 'Major Litanies'; the (originally Gallican) 'Minor Litanies' were sung immediately preceding the Ascension. The litany has three sections: an invocation of Christ or the Trinity; invocations of the saints; and a series of supplications. The Anglican litany, using plainchant adapted by Archbishop Cranmer, dates from 1544 and is sung throughout the year with no procession. Litanies were set polyphonically from the 16th century; Mozart and Michael Haydn are among the composers who contributed to the genre.

Líteres (Carrión), Antonio (*b* Artá, Majorca, ?18 June 1673; *d* Madrid, 18 Jan 1747). Spanish composer. He was a bass viol player to the royal choir in Madrid and from 1693 bassist of the royal chapel. He became known as the leading court composer, writing zarzuelas (notably *Accis y Galatea*, 1708), secular cantatas, an oratorio and much sacred music.

Lithophone. A series of resonant stone slabs or plaques which produce musical sounds when struck. It is found throughout Asia and in parts of Africa, South America and Europe. Carl Orff used it (as *Steinspiel*) in several works.

Litolff. German firm of music publishers. It was founded by Gottfried Martin Meyer at Brunswick in 1828; after his death his widow in 1851 married the composer HENRY LITOLFF, who became active in the firm. Known for its careful editions, teaching material and light music for domestic use, the firm has – since 1940, when it was taken over by Peters of Leipzig – stressed contemporary music and musicology.

Litolff, Henry (Charles) (*b* London, 7 Aug 1818; *d* Bois-Colombes, 5 Aug 1891). French composer and pianist. He was a concert artist, conductor, music publisher, festival organizer, piano teacher and salon composer but is remembered chiefly for his four piano concertos entitled *concertos symphoniques* (c1844–67); their conception as symphonies with piano obbligato greatly impressed Liszt (who dedicated his Concerto no.1 to Litolff), and their scherzos contain some of his most brilliant writing.

Little Organ Mass. *See* KLEINE ORGELMESSE.

Little Russian Symphony. Nickname of Tchaikovsky's Symphony no.2 in C minor (1872); it uses folksongs from the Ukraine ('Little Russia').

Little Sweep, The. The second part of Britten's LET'S MAKE AN OPERA.

Liturgical books. Books used for the performance of the liturgies or services of the Christian rites. In the Roman Catholic rite, there are seven books: the *missale* (missal) contains texts for the Mass without musical notation; the *graduale* (gradual, *Antiphonale missarum* for early graduals) chants of the Proper and Ordinary of the Mass; the *breviarium* (breviary) texts for the Divine Office; the *antiphonale* or *antiphonarium* (antiphoner) chants for the Office, except Matins; the *martirologium* (martyrology) the lives of the saints; the *pontificale* (pontifical) the ceremonies performed by a bishop; and the *rituale* ceremonies performed by a priest in the administration of sacraments. Other modern books include the *Kyriale*, containing the chants of the Ordinary; the *Vesperale*, with Vespers and sometimes Compline; and the LIBER USUALIS. The *Liber responsorialis* includes chants, particularly responsories, for Matins, and the *Processionale monasticum* chants for processions before Mass. Both are used in monastic communities.

Books used in the Middle Ages include the sacramentary, with prayers for Mass; the lectionary, with lessons for Mass; the evangeliarium, with the Gospel readings for Mass; the ordinal, describing the order and procedures of the liturgy; and the cantarium, with the gradual alleluia chants and tract of the Mass.

Liturgical drama. *See* MEDIEVAL DRAMA.

Lituus. A Roman brass instrument consisting of a long tube turning in upon itself at the end, in the shape of a 'J'. It was used for military and ceremonial, especially funereal, occasions. Bach used the term for a type of horn in Cantata no.118, a funeral motet.

Litvinne, Félia (Vasil'yevna) (*b* St Petersburg, ?11 Oct 1861; *d* Paris, 12 Oct 1936). Russian soprano of German and Canadian descent. She studied in Paris and sang with Mapleson's company, New York, in 1885. Best known in Wagner, she sang Brünnhilde at the Paris Opéra and in several Russian *Ring* cycles, and Isolde at Covent Garden in 1899. She appeared at the Met from 1896, in operas by Verdi, Mozart and Meyerbeer.

Liuto attorbiato. Term for an archlute or a theorbo.

Liverati, Giovanni (*b* Bologna, 27 March 1772; *d* Florence, 18 Feb 1846). Italian composer. Initially an opera singer, he became Kapellmeister of the Italian Opera at Potsdam in 1796 and of the Prague National Theatre in 1799. In 1805–14 he taught singing in Vienna; later he was composer and music director at the King's Theatre, London. He composed 12 operas and other vocal music.

Liverpool Philharmonic Orchestra. *See* ROYAL LIVERPOOL PHILHARMONIC ORCHESTRA.

Llangollen. *See* EISTEDDFOD.

Lloyd, A(lbert) L(ancaster) (*b* London, 29 Feb 1908; *d* Greenwich, 29 Sept 1982). English ethnomusicologist. He learnt folksongs on an Australian sheep farm (1926–35) and whaling-songs as an Antarctic whaling fisherman (1937–8); later he travelled in South America and the Middle East. As an ethnomusicologist his interests centred on south-east Europe. He lectured in the USA and Australia and made numerous folksong recordings. His studies of folk music emphasize social context and economic conditions.

Lloyd, George (*b* St Ives, 28 June 1913). English composer. He studied at the RAM and has written operas, ten symphonies (1932–82) and concertos, in a diatonic, colouristic style.

Lloyd [Floyd, Flude], **John** (*b c*1475; *d* London, 3 April 1523). English (or Welsh) composer. A Gentleman of the Chapel Royal from *c*1510, he wrote a fine mass, *O quam suavis*, a highly florid and melismatic work with soaring melodic lines and euphonious counterpoint.

Lloyd, Robert (*b* Southend, 2 March 1940). English bass. He studied at London Opera Centre and under O. Kraus. He became a member of Covent Garden Opera in 1972 and has appeared in a wide range of bass roles, notably as Donizetti's Raimondo, Mozart's Sarastro and Boris Godunov; he has also appeared at the Paris Opéra, La Scala, many German houses and San Francisco. His firm, controlled, imposing voice serves well in such roles as Gurnemanz (*Parsifal*) and Verdi's Fiesco (*Simon Boccanegra*).

Lloyd Webber, Andrew (*b* London, 22 March 1948). English composer. He has written musicals in a highly eclectic style (*Jesus Christ Superstar*, 1970; *Evita*, 1978; *Cats*, 1981; *Starlight Express*, 1984; *The Phantom of the Opera*, 1986) and a requiem (1984). His brother Julian (*b* 1951), a cellist, is a pupil of Fournier and has given premières of works by Bliss and Rodrigo.

Lobe, Johann Christian (*b* Weimar, 30 May 1797; *d* Leipzig, 27 July 1881). German writer on music, composer and flautist. He wrote five operas, produced at Weimar (he was a friend of Goethe's), then edited the *Allgemeine musikalische Zeitung* (1846–8); he was author of the series *Fliegende Blätter für Musik* (1855–7) and several didactic works.

Lobgesang. Symphony-cantata, op.52, by Mendelssohn, his Symphony no.2 (1840).

Lobkowitz, Prince Joseph Franz Maximilian (*b* Roudnice nad Labem, 7 Dec 1772; *d* Třeboň, 15 Dec 1816). Bohemian nobleman and patron of the arts. A bass singer, violinist and cellist, he maintained a private orchestra and was a leading figure in Vienna's musical life. He supported Haydn and especially Beethoven, whose 'Eroica' was first heard at one of his concerts in 1804.

Many other members of his family were musical patrons. Notable were his grandfather Philipp Hyacinth (1680–1734), a lutenist, and his father, Ferdinand Philipp Joseph (1724–84), both composers and patrons of the young Gluck; and his son Ferdinand Joseph Johann (1797–1868), who had an orchestra in Vienna. The family's valuable music collections are now in Prague.

Lobo, Alonso (*b* Osuna, *c*1555; *d* Seville, 5 April 1617). Spanish composer. A choirboy at Seville Cathedral, he studied at Osuna University and was a canon there by 1591. He assisted Guerrero at Seville Cathedral from 1591, becoming *maestro de capilla* of Toledo Cathedral in 1593 and of Seville in 1604. He published masses and motets, some for double choir (1602); many other sacred works are in MSS. Victoria esteemed him as an equal and he was long regarded as one of the finest Spanish composers.

Lobo, Duarte (*b* Alcáçovas, ?1565; *d* Lisbon, 24 Sept 1646). Portuguese composer. He studied at Évora and was *maestro de capilla* at the cathedral there, and in Lisbon at the Hospital Real and the cathedral (by 1594). The most famous Portuguese composer of his day, he published six books of polyphonic liturgical music (1602–39); several of his pupils were notable composers.

Locatelli, Pietro Antonio (*b* Bergamo, 3 Sept 1695; *d* Amsterdam, 30 March 1764). Italian composer and violinist. He studied the violin in Rome and in 1717–23 played in the basilica of S Lorenzo in Damaso. He was appointed to the Mantuan court in 1725 but gave concerts elsewhere (especially Germany), gaining a high reputation; his playing was noted for its virtuosity and sweetness. From 1729 he worked mostly as a teacher and orchestral director in Amsterdam.

Locatelli wrote almost exclusively sonatas and concertos. The first of his four concerto grosso sets (1721) is the most Corellian (particularly its Christmas Concerto); his later music is more progressive. His influential *L'arte del violino* (1733) contains 12 solo violin concertos in a Venetian idiom like Vivaldi's and 24 caprices for solo violin. Among his other works are solo and trio sonatas.

Lochamer [Locheimer] **Liederbuch.** German MS, assembled in the 1450s. It consists of 92 folios containing 41 German secular pieces (mostly monophonic) and three other pieces, with C. Paumann's *Fundamentum organisandi*, including 32 keyboard pieces. It is now in the Staatsbibliothek, West Berlin.

Locke, Matthew (*b* ?Devon, 1621–2; *d* London, Aug 1677). English composer. He was a chorister and secondary at Exeter Cathedral, where he became friendly with Christopher Gibbons. He probably also became acquainted with Prince Charles (later Charles II) at Exeter, and may have spent some time with the royalist forces in the Netherlands. He returned to England by 1651, and two years later he and Gibbons wrote the music for James Shirley's masque *Cupid and Death*. Locke probably married in the mid-1650s, and in 1656 he joined with others in writing the music (all lost) for Davenant's opera *The Siege of Rhodes*, in which he also sang.

After the Restoration in 1660 Locke was awarded three posts at court, to which in 1662 he added that of organist to the queen (facilitated by his conversion to Roman Catholicism). He continued to write for the theatre and also (perhaps while in Oxford) engaged in a polemical exchange with Thomas Salmon over the latter's proposals for a new form of musical notation. Locke was of a vain, contentious and vindictive temperament, but his vitriolic attack on Salmon may have sprung also from his frustration at not being awarded high honours at Oxford (Salmon, an MA at Trinity College, was supported by the Oxford faculty).

Locke's importance lies in his chamber music and dramatic music, which influenced Purcell's. His consort music and other ensemble works, mainly suites and separate dances, display robust and daring melody, harmony and form, as well as a conscious preoccupation with contrasting rhythms, tempos and dynamics. Although sometimes experimental, it is the work of a gifted and inspired craftsman. His extant sacred music, while not as maturely conceived, is often of high quality. His dramatic music, best represented by *Cupid and Death*, the masque in *The Empress of Morocco* (1673) and the vocal music for *Psyche* (1675), shows a sure dramatic instinct, especially in the recitatives and in several of the curtain tunes.

Locke's other music includes the well-known pieces 'ffor His Majesty's Sagbutts & Cornetts', probably performed on the eve of Charles II's coronation, and *Melothesia* (1673), a collection of keyboard works with an important preface giving the first extant English rules for realizing a figured bass.

Dramatic music Cupid and Death, masque, composed with Christopher Gibbons (1st version, 1653, lost; rev. 1659); music for over 10 stage works, incl. *The Empress of Morocco* (1673), *Psyche* (1675)
Vocal music 2 services; over 30 English anthems; 15 Latin motets; sacred songs and canons; secular songs
Instrumental music Consort of Fower Parts, 6 suites for strings; over 40 suites and many separate pieces for strs; hpd pieces, some in Melothesia (1673); org pieces; music for wind, incl. 'ffor His Majesty's Sagbutts and Cornetts'; canons

Lockwood, Annea [Anna] (*b* Christchurch, 29 July 1939). New Zealand composer and instrument maker. She studied at Christchurch, the RCM in London, the Hochschule für Musik in Cologne and the Electronic Music Centre, Bilthoven. She has been involved in experimental music of several kinds, some involving environmental sound, others involving the burning or submersion in water of old pianos and documenting their decay; but her best-known interest lies in experimentation with glass, as in her *Glass Concert* (1967–9), which involved different types of glass object. Other works include *Humm* (for a large number of hummers, 1971) and *World Rhythms* (using a variety of recorded sounds involving transcendental meditation, 1975). She has lived in New York since 1973.

Lockwood, Normand (*b* New York, 19 March 1906). American composer. He studied with Respighi in Rome and with Boulanger (1927–9), and taught at various American universities, notably at Denver (1961–75). His large output is tonal or polytonal and includes expressive vocal works, especially settings of American poetry.

Loco (Lat.). 'In its place': a term used to countermand a previous instruction such as *8va bassa* or *sul ponticello*.

Locrian. Term used for a MODE of the form *B–b*. Glarean (*Dodecachordon*, 1547) called this division of the octave 'hyperaeolian'.

Loder, Edward (James) (*b* Bath, 1813; *d* London, 5 April 1865). English composer, son of the violinist and publisher John David (1788–1846). He studied with his father and under Ries in Frankfurt; in 1834 he wrote an opera, *Nourjahad*, which was well received, but he spent the ensuing years earning a living with hackwork (songs and partsongs) for a publisher and writing operatic potboilers. However, he also wrote a successful string quartet and an opera, *The Night Dancers* (1846), for the Princess's Theatre, of which he was musical director. In 1851 he moved to the Manchester Theatre Royal, in charge of music. There in 1855 his *Raymond and Agnes* was given; it shows a remarkable mastery of orchestration and dramatic tension. For most of his remaining years he was ill.

His cousin George (1816–68) was a double bass player and conductor who directed the American première of Beethoven's Ninth Symphony and died in Australia. George's sister Kate (1825–1904) had a notable career as a pianist, teacher and composer, of chamber music and an opera, *L'elisir d'amore*.

Lodoïska. Opera in three acts by Cherubini to a libretto by Fillette-Loreaux (1791, Paris). Kreutzer (1791), Storace (1794) and Mayr (1796) wrote operas on the same subject.

Loeffler, Charles Martin (*b* Schöneberg or Mulhouse, 30 Jan 1861; *d* Medfield, MA, 19 May 1935). American composer. He studied in Berlin and Paris and emigrated to the USA in 1881. He was assistant leader of the Boston SO (1882–1903) and a proponent of contemporary music; in 1910 he retired to the country. He was a skilled, self-critical composer. His works, in all genres, are in a Romantic impressionist style that drew on medieval and later jazz elements: they include *A Pagan Poem* for orchestra with piano obbligato (1906) and Music for Four Stringed Instruments (1919).

Loeillet. Flemish family of composers. Jean Baptiste (*b* Ghent, bap. 18 Nov 1680; *d* London, 19 July 1730) was active in London from *c*1705, well known as a player and teacher of the harpsichord and an oboist and flautist; he helped popularize the transverse flute in England. Besides nine suites of English-type keyboard lessons, he wrote 12 solo and 18 trio sonatas, distinguishing between a conservative, contrapuntal style for recorder and oboe and a more *galant* expressive one for flute; these contain more adventurous, italianate writing. He was known as 'John Loeillet of London' to distinguish him from other family members.

His uncle Pieter (1651–1735) was a violinist at Ghent and later Bordeaux, and his stepbrother Pierre (1674–1743) was a Ghent violinist. His brother Jacques (b Ghent, bap. 7 July 1685; d there, 28 Nov 1748), an oboist, held court posts at Munich and Versailles and composed instrumental works including six each of solo and trio sonatas. His cousin Jean Baptiste (b Ghent, bap. 6 July 1688; d Lyons, c1720), known as 'Loeillet de Gant', son of Pieter, served the archbishop at Lyons and published five sets of solo sonatas for recorder and continuo and one of trio sonatas in the style of Corelli, mainly *da chiesa* but with some dance movements and incorporating French-style ornamental writing in the slow movements.

Loesser, Frank (Henry) (b New York, 29 June 1910; d there, 28 July 1969). American composer and librettist. Largely self-taught in music, he worked in Hollywood from 1936. Best known for his Broadway shows, notably *Guys and Dolls* (1950) and *How to Succeed in Business without Really Trying* (1961), he is particularly successful in catching the flavour of colloquial speech, in his rhymes and his witty melodies, and was inventive in his use of form and harmony.

Loewe, (Johann) Carl (Gottfried) (b Loebjuen, 30 Nov 1796; d Kiel, 20 April 1869). German composer. A pupil of Türk at Halle, he began composing songs and instrumental pieces at an early age, also singing his own ballads to great acclaim. Among his finest early solo vocal works are settings of Goethe's *Erlkönig* (1818) and Byron's *Hebrew Melodies* (opp.4, 5, 13 and 14). He was a prolific composer in many media, but his other works, including the operas (notably *Emmy*, 1842) and oratorios, string quartets and piano works (in particular some programmatic sonatas and the tone poem *Mazeppa* op.27), were not as acclaimed as his narrative songs. Their accompaniments and modified strophic style, incorporating dramatic and lyrical passages, make a vivid impression (e.g. *Archibald Douglas* op.128); the fairy element in many of his folklore settings (e.g. *Herr Oluf* and *Tom der Reimer*) creates colour and melodic interest. From 1820 to 1865 Loewe worked in Stettin as a conductor, organist and teacher, yet it was through his recital tours that he won international fame; the Viennese called him 'the north German Schubert'.

Loewe, Frederick (Fritz) (b Berlin, 10 June 1901; d Palm Springs, 14 Feb 1988). American composer. He studied with Busoni, d'Albert and Reznicek, then went to the USA in 1924 and from the 1930s worked on Broadway (from *Life of the Party*, 1942, with Alan Jay Lerner). Their particular successes include *Brigadoon* (1947), which retains aspects of European operetta style, and *My Fair Lady* (1956), where the music is sensitively accommodated to character. He also wrote music for the film *Gigi* (1958).

Loewenguth Quartet. French string quartet, led by Aldred Loewenguth. It was formed in 1929 but became well known outside France only after 1945 – notably for its Beethoven cycles, its playing of Bartók and particularly French music.

Logier, Johann Bernhard (b Kassel, 9 Feb 1777; d Dublin, 27 July 1846). German pianist, teacher, author and composer. A piano teacher and music seller in Dublin from 1810, he developed and patented the chiroplast or 'hand-director' mechanism, a laterally sliding frame for the hands fitted above the keyboard, which though controversial had success in Britain and Germany (it was adopted by Kalkbrenner and defended by Spohr). His method, described in his writings (1814–27), also involved group piano teaching and his *System der Musik-Wissenschaft* (1827) marks the earliest known use of the now standard German word for 'musicology'.

Logothetis, Anestis (b Pyrgos, 27 Oct 1921). Austrian composer of Greek origin. Resident in Vienna from 1942, he studied at the Academy and has produced numerous graphic scores which, generally offering a degree of freedom in instrumentation as well as other dimensions, are often captivating works of visual art.

Logroscino, Nicola Bonifacio (b Bitonto, bap. 22 Oct 1698; d ?Palermo, 1765–7). Italian composer. He was organist to the Bishop of Conza (Avellino), 1729–31, then worked mostly in Naples, where he had studied. He presented numerous comic operas and between Leo's death (1744) and Piccinni's first successes (in the 1750s) was easily the most popular *buffo* composer there. He also composed a few serious operas (mostly for Rome), oratorios and church music. He spent his last years teaching at the Ospedale dei Figliuoli Dispersi, Palermo; his last opera was given in Venice in 1765.

Lohengrin. Opera in three acts by Wagner to his own libretto (1850, Weimar).

Löhlein, Georg Simon (b Neustadt an der Heide, 16 July 1725; d Danzig, 16 Dec 1781). German composer and theorist. After working in Jena, 1761–3, he became a music teacher (influenced by J.A. Hiller) in Leipzig. He wrote theoretical works (including a famous keyboard method, 1765), keyboard concertos, sonatas etc and vocal music.

Löhner, Johann (b Nuremberg, bap. 21 Nov 1645; d there, 2 April 1705). German composer. He was an organist in Nuremberg, notably at the Spitalkirche (from 1682) and St Lorenz (from 1694), and composed for home use over 300 devotional songs for voice and continuo in a folklike melodic style. His most significant work is the *Auserlesene Kirch- und Tafel-Music* (1682), with 12 through-composed works for solo voice, two violins and continuo. Of his three known operas only two collections of arias survive.

Lolli, Antonio (b Bergamo, c1725; d Palermo, 10 Aug 1802). Italian violinist and composer. He was solo violinist at the Württemberg court, 1758–74, and made lengthy concert tours to Vienna, Paris and elsewhere. He continued touring as chamber virtuoso to the Russian court, 1774–83 (his former pupil G.M. Giornovichi succeeded him), and later appeared in London, Paris and Italy. Noted for his technical precision, he was a highly influential performer and a popular composer of violin sonatas and concertos.

Lombardi alla prima crociata, Il. Opera in four

acts by Verdi to a libretto by Solera after T. Grossi (1843, Milan).

Lombardic rhythm. Reversed dotting. *See* SCOTCH SNAP.

Lonati, Carlo Ambrogio (*b*?Milan, *c*1645; *d*? there, *c*1712). Italian composer. A singer and one of the most brilliant violinists of his time, he worked in Rome (1668–77), where he played in many oratorios and enjoyed the patronage of Queen Christina of Sweden (he led her string orchestra from 1673) and the friendship of Stradella, his companion in notoriety. During the 1680s he worked at the Mantuan court, then spent his last years in Milan where five of his ten known operas were performed. Lonati's few extant violin works reveal a bold, fluent style with (in his 1701 sonatas) prominent double stopping and use of *scordatura*, as well as the idiosyncratic melodic writing that runs through all his music. His cantatas – long, varied and of unusual expressive force – rank with those of Stradella and A. Scarlatti, while his surviving operas, in Venetian style, are characterized by mature da capo arias and a penchant for the *stile concitato* with brilliant writing for obbligato instruments.

London, George (*b* Montreal, 5 May 1919; *d* Armonk, 24 March 1985). American bass-baritone. He sang in California from 1941 and from 1949 appeared in Europe (1950, Glyndebourne, as Mozart's Figaro; 1951, Bayreuth, as Amfortas). In 1960 he sang Boris Godunov at the Bol'shoy. After retiring in 1967 he produced opera, including the *Ring* at Seattle (1975).

London Bach Society. British choir founded in 1946 by Paul Steinitz to perform Renaissance and modern works as well as Bach. Its main home was St Bartholomew the Great, where it gave annual performances of the *St Matthew Passion* in German. Activities included tours abroad. The Steinitz Bach Players (founded 1969) performed with it.

London Classical Players. Orchestra founded by ROGER NORRINGTON in 1979 to perform music of the Classical era on period instruments.

London Festival, City of. *See* CITY OF LONDON FESTIVAL.

London Mozart Players. British orchestra founded in 1949 by Harry Blech, the first chamber orchestra to specialize in the Viennese Classics. From 1969 music of other periods was also given, with guest conductors. Jane Glover was appointed music director in 1983.

London Overture, A. Orchestral work by Ireland (1936).

London Philharmonic Orchestra [LPO]. British orchestra formed in 1932 by Thomas Beecham. Under his direction (1932–9) it became London's chief orchestra. Other conductors have included Boult, Pritchard, Haitink, Solti and Tennstedt. It has made many foreign tours and in 1964 became resident orchestra for Glyndebourne Festival Opera. The London Philharmonic Choir, an amateur choir, was founded in 1947, succeeding the Philharmonic Choir (founded 1919); its activities include performing with the LPO.

London Sinfonietta. British orchestra founded in 1968, with David Atherton as conductor, to present 20th-century works, including commissions; among conductors who work regularly with it are Elgar Howarth and Simon Rattle. It gives annual series in London, tours abroad and has given premières of works by Berio, Stockhausen, Henze, Birtwistle and Carter. The London Sinfonietta Voices was formed to sing with it. With Opera Factory (as Opera Factory London Sinfonietta), under its director, the producer and baritone David Freeman, it presents opera and music theatre, notably avant-garde works.

London Symphonies [Salomon Symphonies]. Haydn's last 12 symphonies, nos.93–104, composed for Salomon and first performed in London during Haydn's visits (1791–2, 1794–5). No.104 is known as the 'London' Symphony.

London Symphony, A. Vaughan Williams's Second Symphony (1913).

London Symphony Orchestra [LSO]. The oldest surviving London orchestra, formed in 1904 from members of the Queen's Hall Orchestra. Richter was its first principal conductor; others include Harty, Monteux and Abbado. It was the first British orchestra to tour North America (1912, under Nikisch) and to make a world tour (1964). Recordings were made from 1920. Activities include London seasons and appearances at international festivals. Its home since 1982 has been the Barbican Arts Centre. The London Symphony Chorus, an amateur choir, was founded in 1966 (as the London Symphony Orchestra Chorus); it became independent of the orchestra in 1976.

Long. The note that is twice the value of a breve; the longer of the two notes of early mensural music. First found in early 13th-century music, it has a value of two or three breves. *See* NOTE VALUES.

Longman & Broderip. English firm of music publishers and instrument makers, active in London under various names from 1767 to 1798. It was one of the most enterprising firms of its type, not only issuing music by Arne, Avison, Shield and other English composers and works by foreign composers including J.C. Bach, Haydn (notably the symphonies commissioned by Salomon) and Pleyel, but also supplying through its agents continental music and producing a wide range of harpsichords and pianos alongside more unusual instruments. From the 1780s it had a circulating music library and two provincial branches. The firm went bankrupt in 1798; it was succeeded by Broderip & Wilkinson.

Longo, Alessandro (*b* Amantea, 30 Dec 1864; *d* Naples, 3 Nov 1945). Italian pianist and composer. He studied and later taught in Naples. He is remembered for his publication of 11 volumes containing 544 sonatas and a fragment of Domenico Scarlatti's keyboard music, which did much to awaken interest in the composer. Scarlatti's sonatas are often referred to by their 'L' numbers although Longo's classification of them (by key) has been superseded.

Longueval, Antoine de (*b*?Longueville-sur-Somme; *fl* 1507–22). French composer. A singer in the royal chapel, he is best known for his Passion, perhaps the oldest extant four-voice motet setting.

Lonquich, Heinz Martin (*b* Trier, 23 March 1937). German composer. He studied at the Saarbrücken Musikhochschule (1954–7) and with Zimmermann and Eimert at the Cologne Musikhochschule (1966–9); in 1973 he became organist of St Nikolaus Cologne-Sülz. The experience of writing Catholic church music has given his freely serial music a distinct, pithy style.

Lontano. British ensemble. It was founded in 1976 by Odaline de la Martinez, its director, for performing contemporary music. A group of up to 20 players, it has commissioned new works, notably from British composers, and has toured widely and made recordings.

Loosemore, Henry (*b* ?Devon; *d* 1670). English composer, brother of George Loosemore. He was organist of King's College, Cambridge, from 1627 until his death and took the MusB in 1640. With John Jenkins, he was a central figure at the musical gatherings of the North family at Kirtling, Cambs. He composed service music and at least 30 anthems (all MS, many incomplete). His brother George (*d* 1682) was an organist in Cambridge, MusD (1665), and wrote sacred works (all MS, many incomplete) including 22 anthems.

Loosemore, John (*b* ?Bishops Nympton, 1613/14; *d* Exeter, 18 April 1681). English organ builder and virginal maker. His father, Samuel Loosemore, was also an organ builder. Among his surviving instruments is a positive-regal at Blair Atholl Castle (1650) and the Exeter Cathedral organ (1665; part of the case remains). He may be related to George and Henry Loosemore, both organists and composers.

Lopatnikoff, Nikolai (Lvovich) (*b* Tallinn, 16 March 1903; *d* Pittsburgh, 7 Oct 1976). American composer and pianist of Russian origin. He studied at the St Petersburg and Helsinki conservatories and privately with Toch. His music attracted attention in the 1930s and he was often heard as a solo pianist. In 1939 he moved to the USA and taught at Carnegie-Mellon University, Pittsburgh (1945–69). His works, in a Russian Romantic style, include four symphonies, two piano concertos, chamber and piano music.

Lopes-Graça, Fernando (*b* Tomar, 17 Dec 1906). Portuguese composer. He studied with Borba at the Lisbon Conservatory (1924–31) and with Koechlin in Paris (1937–9), where he came under Bartók's influence. Back in Lisbon he was a teacher, conductor and critic. His music in the 1960s moved away from folk traditions to embrace wider tonal and rhythmic possibilities. His large output includes much vocal and piano music.

López Capillas, Francisco (*b* ?Andalusia, *c*1615; *d* Mexico City, 18 Jan–7 Feb 1673). Mexican composer and organist, probably of Spanish birth. He was organist and *maestro de capilla* at Mexico City Cathedral, 1654–68, and wrote over 30 works, among the finest produced in New Spain. Their smooth polyphony masks a learned and greatly varied technique.

Loqueville, Richard (*d* Cambrai, 1418). French composer. In 1410 he was harp tutor to the son of the Duke of Bar and taught plainchant to the duke's choirboys. From 1413 to his death he taught music at Cambrai Cathedral. Four rondeaux, a ballade, an isorhythmic motet in honour of the Breton saint Yvo, a Marian motet, and several mass movements can be attributed to him.

Loreley, Die. Unfinished opera in three acts by Mendelssohn (1847) to a libretto by E. Von Giebel. Lachner, Wallace, Bruch, and Catalani are among those who wrote operas on the same subject.

Lorentzen, Bent (*b* Stenvad, 11 Feb 1935). Danish composer. A pupil of Jersild, he has taught in Århus and Copenhagen and has composed electronic and political-theatrical music.

Lorenz, Max (*b* Düsseldorf, 17 May 1901; *d* Salzburg, 11 Jan 1975). German tenor. After study in Berlin he sang at Dresden from 1928. He was best known in Wagner, singing Walther at the Met in 1931 and Siegfried at Bayreuth in 1933. At the Vienna Staatsoper he was admired as Othello and Strauss's Bacchus.

Lorenzani, Paolo (*b* Rome, 1640; *d* there, 28 Nov 1713). Italian composer. He was a chorister in the Cappella Giulia in the Vatican and a pupil of Benevoli; after an early career as *maestro di cappella* in Rome and Messina, he fled during the wars of 1678 to Paris and became an important figure in the struggle to gain recognition for Italian music and thus to break Lully's monopoly. He gained the support of Louis XIV (who helped him become director of the queen's music) and leading aristocrats (who arranged performances of his dramatic music, notably the pastorale *Nicandro e Fileno* in 1681), but after Queen Marie-Thérèse's death in 1683 his influence waned, despite successful Roman-style oratory performances he arranged as *maître de chapelle* to the Theatine order (from 1685) and an opera, *Orontée*, given at Chantilly. In 1694 he returned to Italy as director of the Cappella Giulia. Though rooted in the Roman tradition, his style was readily adaptable to French taste, and the instrumental writing particularly shows Lully's influence. Among his surviving works are airs, cantatas, motets (a set of 25 was published) and a mass and Magnificat, both for two choirs.

Lorenzini (*fl* 1570–71). Italian composer. There is confusion about his identity. He was lutenist to Ippolito d'Este at Tivoli (1570–71) and later at Ferrara. He probably wrote *c*70 preludes, fantasias and dances for solo lute (in printed collections, 1603–17, and MSS; some attributed under sobriquets).

Lorenzo da Firenze (*d* Florence, Dec 1372–Jan 1373). Florentine composer. He may have been a canon, from 1348, at S Lorenzo, Florence, where he was possibly a pupil of Landini's. That he moved in Florentine circles is borne out by the fact that the Squarcialupi MS contains all his monophonic ballate, which set texts by Boccaccio among others. Ten madrigals, a caccia and two mass movements are also attributed to him. His style is complex and experimental, with extended melismas, imitation and part-crossing, and accidentals used to striking effect. French elements can be detected in some of his works and their notation.

Lorenzo Fernândez, Oscar (*b* Rio de Janeiro, 4 Nov

1897; *d* there, 27 Aug 1948). Brazilian composer. He studied at the National Music Institute, where he taught from 1924; in 1936 he founded the Brazilian Conservatory. He wrote in a nationalist style and essayed all genres, though his songs are most valued. His *Malazarte* (1933) may be considered the first successful Brazilian nationalist opera.

Loriod, Yvonne (*b* Houilles, 20 Jan 1924). French pianist. She studied at the Paris Conservatoire. In 1943 she took part with Messiaen in the first performance of *Visions de l'Amen* for two pianos and has since been heard in all the premières of his works with piano. She became Messiaen's second wife. Her sonorous, rhythmically acute playing has also been heard in new music by Barraqué and Boulez. Her pupils at the Conservatoire and Darmstadt include many pianists who became prominent in the 1960s and 70s.

Lortzing, (Gustav) Albert (*b* Berlin, 23 Oct 1801; *d* there, 21 Jan 1851). German composer. In his youth he gained experience as an actor, singer and conductor, which he put to effective use in the 20 operas (1824–51) forming the main part of his output. The comic operas, from *Die beiden Schützen* (1835) to *Die Opernprobe* (1851), are his most characteristic, showing a vivid personal vein of sentimental humour which though limited in range was popular in appeal and made him the most inventive composer of opera with spoken dialogue in mid-19th-century Germany. If his own theatre career was insecure, his best works nevertheless hold their place in German repertory. He began as an imitator, even borrower, of other composers' works. With *Zar und Zimmermann* (1837) – followed up in such popular works as *Der Wildschütz* (1842) and *Der Waffenschmied* (1846) – he hit upon the formula, from Singspiel and *opéra comique*, of number opera with dialogue in a theatrically sound pattern. The numbers, usually solo songs, were often to a formula he could diversify by his melodic fluency to suit accepted singer-types (e.g. the comic bass); duets and choruses, less often ensembles, lead up to the finale. By also absorbing the example of the reminiscence-motif and the idiom of Spohr and Weber, seen for example in the advanced chromatic harmony of the magic operas *Undine* (1845) and *Rolands Knappen* (1849), he showed a sensitivity and craft well beyond the rigid pattern of number opera. Yet he remained essentially outside the development of Romantic opera and is remembered as an effective composer of theatrical entertainment.

Dramatic music Die beiden Schützen (1835); Zar und Zimmermann (1837); Hans Sachs (1840); Casanova (1841); Der Wildschütz (1842); Undine (1845); Der Waffenschmied (1846); Zum Grossadmiral (1847); Regina (1848, perf. 1899); Rolands Knappen (1849); Die Opernprobe (1851); 7 other Singspiels and operas; incidental music for 6 plays
Other works choral music; ovs., variations, dances for orch; songs

Los Angeles, Victoria de (*b* Barcelona, 1 Nov 1923). Spanish soprano. She sang at the Teatro Liceo, Barcelona, from 1945 and soon became internationally known as a concert singer. At Covent Garden (1950–61) she attracted attention particularly for Butterfly and Massenet's Manon. She also became a favourite, notably as Gounod's Marguerite and as Desdemona. Her voice is warm, vibrant and flexible, heard at its best in Spanish music.

Los Angeles Philharmonic Orchestra. American orchestra founded in 1919. Its first conductor was Walter Henry Rothwell; later conductors included Klemperer, Van Beinum, Mehta, Giulini and Previn (from 1985). Its home is the Dorothy Chandler Pavilion (cap. 3200) at Los Angeles County Music Center. Summer seasons are at Hollywood Bowl, where the orchestra gave the opening concert of the first festival in 1922. The Roger Wagner Chorale, founded in 1946 by Roger Wagner, was renamed the Los Angeles Master Chorale in 1965 and has become the resident choir of the Los Angeles PO.

Lothar, Mark (*b* Berlin, 23 May 1902; *d* Munich, 7 April 1985). German composer. He was a pupil of Schreker and Wolf-Ferrari and became music director of the Bavarian State Theatre, Munich (1945–55). His works include operas, instrumental music and songs.

Lott, Felicity (*b* Cheltenham, 8 April 1947). English soprano. She studied at the RAM and made her ENO début in 1975 as Pamina, also singing such roles as Fiordiligi and Natasha (*War and Peace*), while at Glyndebourne she appeared as Anne Trulove (*The Rake's Progress*), Octavian and Arabella. She has appeared at the Paris Opéra and the Hamburg Opera, and made her Covent Garden début in Henze's *We Come to the River* (1976), also singing Helena (*Midsummer Night's Dream*) and the Marschallin there (1987). She is admired for her naturally beautiful and flexible voice and her warm personality.

Lotti, Antonio (*b* Venice or Hanover, *c*1667; *d* Venice, 5 Jan 1740). Italian composer. A pupil of Legrenzi in Venice, he became an organist at St Mark's in 1690, eventually becoming *maestro di cappella* (1736). He also taught at the Ospedale degli Incurabili (Galuppi was one of his pupils); he wrote sacred music for both institutions. From 1692 he composed operas, mostly serious: he presented *c*30, the last four (1717–19) in Dresden. His large output includes oratorios, secular cantatas, duets, madrigals, instrumental pieces and numerous masses, motets and psalms. Most of his sacred choral works have no orchestral accompaniment; many, such as a *Miserere* of 1733, remained in use long after his death. His output bridges the late Baroque and early Classical styles and his late works are notable for their elegance and skilful counterpoint.

Loughran, James (*b* Glasgow, 30 June 1931). Scottish conductor. He worked first in Bonn and Amsterdam but became known only with a competition success in 1961; he then became conductor of the Bournemouth SO (1962–5), the BBC Scottish SO (1965–71), the Hallé Orchestra (1971–83) and the Bamberg SO (1979–83). He made his USA début with the New York PO in 1972.

Louis XIV (*b* St Germain-en-Laye, 5 Sept 1638; *d* Versailles, 1 Sept 1715). King of France, and patron of music, he assumed the throne in 1661. Obsessively preoccupied with music and dance –

partly as political instruments – from an early age he surrounded himself with distinguished composer-performers, above all Lully, to whom he granted privileges that enabled him to dominate the French musical world, but also d'Anglebert, Chambonnières, F. Couperin, Lalande and Marais. He founded the Académie de Danse (1661) and the Académie de Musique (1669). His own excellence as a dancer contributed to the popularity of the *ballet de cour*, and his wide tastes led to the development of many sacred and secular genres (cantatas, motets, *symphonies*, ballets and *tragédies lyriques*), notably by Lully, Lalande and Charpentier. Crucial to the development of the orchestra in the 18th century were the two ensembles Louis created as part of his vast musical establishment: the 24 Violons du Roi and the wind, brass and drums of the *écurie*.

Louise. Opera in four acts by Gustave Charpentier to his own libretto (1900, Paris).

Louis Ferdinand, Prince of Prussia (*b* Friedrichsfelde, 18 Nov 1772; *d* Saalfeld, 13 Oct 1806). German composer and pianist. A nephew of Frederick the Great, he served in the Prussian army and became an outstanding pianist, often performing in Berlin salons. He composed mostly chamber works with piano in an early Romantic style akin to that of his teacher, J.L. Dussek.

Louisville Orchestra. American orchestra founded in 1937 (known as the Louisville Philharmonic Society, 1942–77). It had a programme for commissioning works for ensembles of *c*50 players from renowned composers; in 1948–60 *c*120 works by over 100 composers were given at subscription concerts and most were recorded on the orchestra's own label, First Edition. Since 1983 it has played in the Robert S. Whitney Hall (cap. 2400) at the Kentucky Center for the Arts.

Loulié, Etienne (*b* ?Paris, *c*1655; *d* there, *c*1707). French theorist. A *maître de musique* in Paris, he published three treatises important for their discussions of tempo, metre, key, transposition, ornamentation and temperament, and is also notable for his inventions – the *chronomètre* (a metronomic pendulum device) and the *sonomètre* (a tuning aid).

Loure. A French theatre dance of the 17th and 18th centuries, frequently used as an *entrée*. Sometimes described as a slow gigue, it is usually in 3/4 or 6/4; characteristic rhythms include dotted figures, syncopations, hemiolas and a quaver–crotchet or crotchet–minim upbeat. There are stylized loures in Bach's French Suite no.5 for keyboard and Partita in E for violin. (It should not be confused with the bowstroke *louré*, an articulated slur.)

Lourié, Arthur Vincent (*b* St Petersburg, 14 May 1892; *d* Princeton, 12 Oct 1966). Russian composer. He abandoned studies at the St Petersburg Conservatory to experiment with 12-note procedures (*Formes en l'air* and other piano pieces of 1915). In 1918 he was appointed music commissar but in 1921 he left for Berlin, where he met Busoni; in 1924 he moved to Paris and became a close friend of Stravinsky, whom he followed to the USA in 1941. He was, however, antipathetic to neo-classicism, preferring a modal, chant-like style in his *Sonata liturgica*

(1928) and *Concerto spirituale* (1929), both for chorus and orchestra. He also wrote two symphonies (1930, 1939) and two operas (*The Feast During the Plague*, 1935; *The Blackamoor of Peter the Great*, 1961).

Love for Three Oranges, The [Lyubov k tryom apelsinam]. Opera in a prologue and four acts by Prokofiev to his own libretto after Gozzi (1921, Chicago). Prokofiev arranged an orchestral suite from the score (1919, revised 1924).

Love in a Village. Ballad opera ('pasticcio') in three acts to a libretto by Bickerstaffe (1762, London); Arne composed 19 songs and arranged the other music (by 16 composers).

Love the Magician. *See* AMOR BRUJO, EL.

Lowe, Edward (*b* Salisbury, *c*1610; *d* Oxford, 11 July 1682). English composer and writer. Organist of Christ Church Cathedral at Oxford (1631–2, 1660–82), and professor of music there from 1662, he was also a co-organist at the Chapel Royal. His compositions include lessons for harpsichord, partsongs and anthems influenced by the declamatory style of the Lawes brothers. In 1661 he published *A Short Direction for the Performance of Cathedrall Service*, and was important for his compilation of two large anthologies of vocal music by his contemporaries.

Lowe, Thomas (*d* London, 1 March 1783). English tenor. He sang successfully in London theatres and pleasure gardens from 1740, particularly in works by Arne and Handel.

Löwe von Eisenach, Johann Jakob (*b* Vienna, bap. 31 July 1629; *d* Lüneburg, early Sept 1703). German composer. A pupil of Schütz in Dresden, he became Kapellmeister at the courts of Wolfenbüttel (1655) and Zeitz (1663–5); thereafter his career declined, and his last known post was as an organist in Lüneburg. His output includes collections of Italian-influenced secular songs, sacred concertos and suites for instrumental ensemble (1658, 1664) in a canzona-like style with innovatory free introductory movements.

Lowinsky, Edward E(lias) (*b* Stuttgart, 12 Jan 1908; *d* Chicago, 10 Oct 1985). American musicologist of German birth. He studied in Stuttgart and Heidelberg, then lived in the Netherlands and from 1940 in the USA. He taught in North Carolina (1942–7), New York (1947–56), Berkeley (1956–61) and Chicago. A major figure of postwar musicology, he did much to stimulate investigation of Renaissance sources and to formulate criteria for modern editions; he produced many provocative and challenging articles on the relationship between music and the history of ideas.

Lualdi, Adriano (*b* Larino, 22 March 1885; *d* Milan, 8 Jan 1971). Italian composer. A pupil of Wolf-Ferrari and an ardent fascist, he directed the conservatories of Naples (1936–44) and, after a period of enforced retirement, Florence (1947–56). He wrote several operas, widely performed in Italy.

Lübeck, Vincent (*b* Paddingbütel, *c*Sept 1654; *d* Hamburg, 9 Feb 1740). German composer and organist. He was organist at St Nicolai, Hamburg, where he achieved a brilliant reputation and was much in demand as a teacher. Only nine organ works by him are known, mostly preludes and fugues, yet they amply demonstrate his eminence in north German organ music: brilliant passage-work and pedal solos attest to the inspiration of his Schnitger organ. He also wrote three sacred cantatas, and a keyboard suite (1728) stylistically similar to the organ works.

Lubin, Germaine (Léontine Angélique) (*b* Paris, 1 Feb 1890; *d* there, 27 Oct 1979). French soprano. After study at the Paris Conservatoire she appeared at the Opéra, 1914–44, notably in Wagner, Strauss and Gluck. She was an imposing Kundry and Isolde at Covent Garden and Bayreuth; her career was clouded by Nazi associations.

Lucas, Clarence (*b* Smithville, Ont., 19 Oct 1866; *d* Paris, 1 July 1947). Canadian composer. He studied at the Paris Conservatoire and worked as a theatre conductor, journalist and editor on both sides of the Atlantic. He was at his best in small forms, particularly songs, and his music was much admired in its day.

Lucas, Leighton (*b* London, 5 Jan 1903; *d* there, 1 Nov 1982). English composer. He was a member of the Ballets Russes (1918–21) and later active as a conductor, lecturer and composer, chiefly of instrumental music (including many film scores).

Lucca, Francesco (*b* Cremona, 1802; *d* Milan, 20 Feb 1872). Italian music publisher. An engraver, he published from *c*1841, issuing operas, including three by Verdi. In 1888 Ricordi absorbed the Lucca concern.

Lucchesi, Andrea (*b* Motta di Livenza, 23 May 1741; *d* Bonn, 21 March 1801). Italian composer. He presented his first operas in Venice, where he met the Mozarts in 1771, then went to Bonn as director of a travelling opera company, succeeding Beethoven's grandfather as court Kapellmeister in 1774. He later became music director of the new National Theatre; in 1783–4 he presented two more operas in Italy. Besides 13 stage works, he wrote much sacred music, symphonies and other instrumental works.

Lucerne International Music Festival (Switzerland). Annual (summer) festival founded in 1938. Events include concerts by visiting orchestras and conductors, recitals, master classes and exhibitions. Lucerne Festival Strings (formed 1956) take part.

Lucia di Lammermoor. Opera in three acts by Donizetti to a libretto by Cammarano after Scott (1835, Naples).

Lucier, Alvin (Augustus jr) (*b* Nashua, NH, 14 May 1931). American composer. He studied at Yale and Brandeis, and privately with Quincy Porter, then taught at Brandeis (1963–9) and Wesleyan University (from 1969). He has also toured as a performer of live electronic music, co-founding the Sonic Arts Union. Several of his works explore the acoustic properties of rooms and other chambers or exploit unusual sound sources (e.g. brain waves in *Music for Solo Performer*, 1965).

Lucio Silla. Opera in three acts by Mozart to a libretto by G. da Gamerra (1772, Milan). Anfossi (1774) and J.C. Bach (1774) wrote operas on the same subject.

Łuciuk, Juliusz (*b* Brzeźnica, 1 Jan 1927). Polish composer. He studied with Wiechowicz at the Kraków Conservatory and with Deutsch and Boulanger in

Paris (1959–60). He has used a free 12-note technique, graphic notation and the prepared piano.

Lucrezia Borgia. Opera in a prologue and two acts by Donizetti to a libretto by Romani after Hugo (1833, Milan).

Ludecus, Matthäus (*b* Wilsnack, 21 Sept 1527; *d* Havelberg, 12 Nov 1606). German composer. He served as a civic official and ecclesiastic in various towns, including Havelberg. He published four important volumes of Lutheran music (1589), containing four unharmonized Latin Passions, and Latin hymns.

Ludford, Nicholas (*b c*1485; *d* ?Westminster, *c*1557). English composer. He was a member of the Royal Free Chapel of St Stephen's, Westminster. His music, probably written before *c*1530, includes 11 masses and other sacred works, all with Latin texts. The masses, large-scale five- and six-part works in the English tradition of full, sonorous, often florid writing, bridge the gap between Fayrfax and Taverner.

Ludus tonalis. Piano studies by Hindemith (1942), exercises in counterpoint as well as piano technique.

Ludwig, Christa (*b* Berlin, 21 March 1928). German mezzo-soprano. She sang at Frankfurt, 1946–52, and appeared at Salzburg from 1954, notably in Mozart's operas. At the Vienna Staatsoper her rich and expressive voice has been heard since 1955 in the major mezzo roles of Wagner, Strauss and Verdi. She has been a frequent visitor to the Met since 1959.

Luening, Otto (Clarence) (*b* Milwaukee, 15 June 1900). American composer. In 1912 the family moved to Munich, where he studied at the Musikhochschule (1915–17); he also had private lessons with Jarnach and Busoni in Zurich, where he was flautist at the opera and a member of Joyce's theatre company. In 1920 he moved to Chicago, where he undertook a wide variety of musical jobs. He taught at various institutions, notably Columbia University (1944–68), where with Ussachevsky he set up an electronic music studio. His diverse output includes an opera (*Evangeline*, 1948), orchestral pieces, tape compositions and much chamber music.

Luftpause (Ger.). 'Air-break': a momentary silence, often indicated by a comma or 'V' above the staff.

Lugge, John (*b* Exeter, *c*1587; *d* there, after 1647). English composer. He was organist (from 1603) and a lay vicar-choral (from 1605) of Exeter Cathedral until 1647. His works include notable organ pieces and a few services and anthems (all MS).

Luisa Miller. Opera in three acts by Verdi to a libretto by Cammarano after Schiller (1849, Naples).

Lulier, Giovanni Lorenzo (*b c*1650; *d* Rome, early 18th century). Italian composer of Spanish birth. He spent his career in Rome, where he was a leading cellist. In the employ of cardinals Ottoboni and Pamphili (whose orchestra he directed), he composed eight oratorios and many cantatas and arias as well as two operas; much of his music is lost.

Lullaby (Fr. *berceuse*; Ger. *Wiegenlied*). A quiet composition of a lulling character, usually in triple metre; a cradle song. As a vocal piece the lullaby is found in the folk music of all countries and in the art music of all periods, and the same vein was often exploited in piano pieces of the 19th and 20th centuries, e.g. in the berceuses of Chopin, Dvořák, Balakirev, Casella and Moeran. *See also* BERCEUSE.

Lully, Jean-Baptiste [Lulli, Giovanni Battista] (*b* Florence, 28 Nov 1632; *d* Paris, 22 March 1687). French composer of Italian birth. He was taken from Florence to Paris in 1646 by Roger de Lorraine, Chevalier de Guise, who placed him in the service of his niece, Mlle de Montpensier. At her court in the Tuileries Lully got to know the best in French music and, despite his patroness's dislike of Mazarin and her involvement in the Fronde, he was no stranger to Italian music either. After the defeat of the Frondists, Mlle de Montpensier was exiled to St Fargeau. Lully obtained release from her service and on the death of his friend Lazzarini, in 1653, was appointed Louis XIV's *compositeur de la musique instrumentale*. From 1655 his fame as dancer, comedian and composer grew rapidly, and his disciplined training of the king's 'petite bande' earned him further recognition. In 1661 he was made *surintendant de la musique et compositeur de la musique de la chambre* and in 1662 *maître de la musique de la famille royale*. By then he was a naturalized Frenchman, and in July 1662 he married Madeleine, daughter of the composer Michel Lambert.

Lully then collaborated with Molière on a series of *comédies-ballets* which culminated in *Le bourgeois gentilhomme* (1670). After that he turned to opera, securing the privilege previously granted to Perrin and forestalling potential rivals with oppressive patents granted by the king. He chose as librettist Philippe Quinault, with whom he succeeded in establishing a new and essentially French type of opera known as *tragédie lyrique*. Between 1673 and 1686 Lully composed 13 such works, 11 of them with Quinault.

During this time Lully continued to enjoy the king's support, despite Louis' displeasure at his overt homosexual behaviour and the resentment his highhandedness provoked in other musicians. His greatest personal triumph came in 1681 when in an impressive ceremony he was received as *secrétaire du Roi*. After the king's marriage to Mme de Maintenon in 1683 life at court took on a new sobriety; it was perhaps in response to this that Lully composed much of his religious music. During a performance of his *Te Deum* in January 1687 he injured his foot with the point of a cane he was using to beat time. Gangrene set in, and within three months he died, leaving a *tragédie lyrique*, *Achille et Polyxène*, unfinished.

At his death Lully was widely regarded as the most representative of French composers. Practically all his music was designed to satisfy the tastes and interests of Louis XIV. The *ballets de cour* (1653–63) and the *comédies-ballets* (1663–72) were performed as royal entertainments, the king himself often taking part in the dancing. The *tragédies lyriques* (1673–86) were kingly operas *par excellence*, expressing a classical conflict between *la gloire* and *l'amour*; Louis himself supplied the subject matter for at least four of them and certainly approved the political sentiments of the prologues. Lully's music was correspondingly elevated, in the stately overtures, the carefully moul-

ded 'récitatif simple' and the statuesque choruses; many of the *airs*, too, draw as much attention to the *galant* mores of the court as to the stage action. Finally, the Versailles *grand motet*, of which the *Miserere* is an outstanding example, was designed to glorify the King of France as much as the King of Heaven.

Lully's three sons, Louis (1664–1734), Jean-Baptiste (1665–1743) and Jean-Louis (1667–88), were all musicians in the king's service.

Dramatic music Cadmus et Hermione (1673); Thésée (1675); Alceste (1674); Isis (1677); Persée (1682); Amadis (1684); Roland (1685); Armide (1686); 5 other tragédies lyriques; 36 ballets (some with other composers); 14 comédies-ballets, incl. L'amour médecin (1665), Les amants magnifiques (1670), Le bourgeois gentilhomme (1670)
Sacred music 13 grands motets, incl. Miserere (1664), Te Deum (1677), De profundis (1683); 14 petits motets
Instrumental music dances, symphonies, airs

Lulu. Opera in three acts by Berg to his own libretto after Wedekind (1937, Zurich). Act 3 was unfinished; it was completed by Cerha and the first performance of the whole work was in Paris in 1979.

Lumbye, Hans Christian (*b* Copenhagen, 2 May 1810; *d* there, 20 March 1874). Danish conductor and composer. He was extremely popular as a dance band conductor and composer of light music (waltzes, polkas, galops, marches, ballet music), and was the first music director of the Tivoli Gardens (1843–72). His sons Carl (1841–1911) and Georg (1843–1922) were also conductors and composers of light music.

Lumsdaine, David (*b* Sydney, 31 Oct 1931). British composer. He studied in Sydney, at the RAM and with Seiber, then worked in London as a composition teacher until appointed to Durham University (1970). His music is founded on imaginative extensions of serial theory which convey a sturdy sense of growth. His works include the orchestral *Hagoromo* (1975) and pieces for smaller ensembles. He first used electronic distortion in *Looking-glass Music* (1970) for brass quintet and tape.

Lunga (It.). 'Long': a word often placed above a note or fermata to indicate a longer wait than might be expected.

Luonnotar. Tone poem, op.70, by Sibelius for soprano and orchestra (*c*1910).

Lupi [Leleu], **Johannes** (*b c*1506; *d* Cambrai, 20 Dec 1539). Franco-Flemish composer. After training as a choirboy at Notre Dame, Cambrai, he became master of the choirboys there (1527). He was among the foremost composers of his generation, his style featuring faultless imitative counterpoint, melismatic melodies, fine harmonic planning and sensitive declamation. Like Gombert, he preferred full textures and continuous counterpoint, but did not use *cantus firmus* or canon. His works include two masses and many *chansons* in the Parisian tradition, but his finest music is in his numerous motets.

Lupi Second, Didier (*fl* mid-16th century). French composer. He lived mainly in Lyons. His *chansons spirituelles* (1548, with the poet Guéroult), the first such important publication of its kind by a Protestant, includes *Susanne un jour*, which was arranged by many later composers. He also published psalms (1549), secular *chansons* (1548) and many pieces in collections.

Lupo, Thomas (*d* London, Jan 1628). English composer of Italian origin. From a musical family, he served the court as a viol player or violinist (from 1591) and composer to the violins (from 1621). As well as vocal music, he composed many instrumental fantasias, some with 'trio-sonata' scoring, and was a pioneer of the broken consort.

Lupu, Radu (*b* Galaţi, 30 Nov 1945). Romanian pianist. He studied at the Moscow Conservatory. In 1969 he won the Leeds Piano Competition and made his London début. He plays Schubert, Schumann and Brahms in a lyrical style with a smooth, rounded tone, and is often heard in Mozart and Beethoven.

Lupus (*fl* 1518–30). Composer. The earliest source for his music, the Medici Codex (1518), and his style suggest that he may have been a northerner. He probably worked mainly in Italy and may have been Pietro Lupato, singer and acting *maestro di cappella* at St Mark's, Venice, in the early 1520s. His music includes three masses and numerous motets, some of which enjoyed considerable success, judging from its appearance in numerous MSS and publications.

Lur. A large trumpet dating from the late Nordic Bronze Age. It consists of a conical tube in the shape of a contorted 'S'. At the speaking end in place of a bell is a bronze disc ornamented with geometric figures. Many pairs have been excavated from Danish peat bogs. The term is also used in Scandinavia for bark and wooden trumpets of a kind played by herdsmen until the late 19th century.

Lurano, Filippo de (*b* ?Cremona, *c*1475; *d* after 1520). Italian composer. He was apparently in Rome in the early 16th century and was composing by 1508. In 1512 he was listed as *maestro di cappella* of Cividale Cathedral, where he remained until 1515, moving to Aquileia Cathedral in 1519. He was one of the most productive and able frottola composers of the early 16th century; his 35 frottolas are characterized by carefully constructed melodic lines and skilful alternation of homorhythmic passages with imitative sections.

Lusingando (It.). Coaxing, caressing.

Lusitano, Vicente (*b* Olivença; *d* ?Rome). Portuguese composer and theorist active in the 16th century. A member of the papal choir in Rome in 1550, he wrote an important treatise (1553) about the three genera of music: diatonic, chromatic and enharmonic. In a debate before the papal choir he put forward a traditional view in opposition to that of Nicola Vicentino.

Lusse, (Charles) de (*b* ?1720–25; *d* after 1774). French composer. He was a flautist and flute teacher in Paris from the 1750s and composed several flute works, including solo sonatas (1751) with brilliant and complex effects. He also produced a flute treatise (1761), other writings and various vocal works.

Lustigen Weiber von Windsor, Die. *See* MERRY WIVES OF WINDSOR, THE.

Lustige Witwe, Die. *See* MERRY WIDOW, THE.

Lute. Plucked string instrument, central to Western music from the late Middle Ages to the 18th century. Features are a vaulted body constructed from separate ribs shaped, bent and glued together; a flat soundboard with an ornate soundhole or 'rose'; a neck and fingerboard with tied gut frets; a pegbox, usually at nearly a right angle to the neck, with tuning pegs inserted laterally; a bridge, to which the strings are attached, at the lower end of the soundboard, and courses or paired strings of gut (often the treble string is single).

The European lute descends from the Arab instrument, the '*ūd*, introduced into the West through the Moorish conquest and occupation of Spain (711–1492); it is also from the Arabic *al-'ūd* that the word 'lute' derives.

The lutenist holds the instrument vertically, often on his lap, with the soundboard perpendicular to the floor, pressing the strings along the fingerboard with his left hand and plucking with the right. The strings are thin compared with a guitar's and produce many more high harmonics; the instrument's acoustical system is designed to give a characteristically clear, almost nasal sound. The volume is modest but because of its distinctive edginess the lute is readily audible in appropriate circumstances. Lutes vary in the number of courses, tuning and size. Fewer courses than four would be exceptional. As more were introduced, they were added on to the bass end; by the mid-18th century many lutes had 13 or 14. When the number increased beyond seven it became awkward to finger the lowest ones, which accordingly were tuned downwards in a scale from the sixth course so that a useful selection of notes was available by plucking without fingering (these diatonic bass courses are called 'diapasons').

Of the many tunings, two types are most important. The one known as 'Renaissance tuning' was typically $G-c-f-a-d'-g'$ or $A-d-g-b-e'-a'$ (the pitch was not absolute). This sequence of intervals continued to apply on certain types of lute throughout the 17th century and early 18th. The other, which arose from experimentation with the Renaissance tuning among French lutenists in the early 17th century, was typically $A-a-f-a-d'-f'$, now known as 'Baroque tuning'; many variants existed.

The earliest surviving music specifically for the lute dates from the late 15th century. Most of the early repertory, apart from song accompaniments, was intabulated (transcribed into tablature, the notation used for the lute) from *chansons* and other vocal originals. In Italy, Petrucci published six volumes of lute tablature, 1507–11; an important manuscript is the Capirola lute book, containing works and instructions for playing by the outstanding lutenist of the time. The leading figure of the next generation was Francesco Canova da Milano, a virtuoso player who wrote ricercares and fantasias. These forms and dance settings formed the basis of the repertory in the later 16th century. In Germany, the publications of Hans Neusidler (from 1536) are important. Lute playing flourished in Germany throughout the 17th century and well into the 18th; the leading virtuoso and lute composer of his day was S.L. Weiss (1686–1750). Bach used the lute in solo music and the *St John Passion*. In England, the leading lute virtuoso of the period around 1600 was

cittern

lute

sitar

shamisen

mandolin

electric guitar

chitarrone

guitar

banjo

Important instruments in the lute family

John Dowland, who wrote many contrapuntal fantasias, dances and other pieces as well as using the lute for accompanying his ayres and in consort music. In France, too, the lute was used for song accompaniment, in the *air de cour*. There was a prominent school of lutenists in the 17th century (notably Ennemond Gaultier in the middle of the century and Robert de Visée into the 18th); French players developed a specific style involving arpeggiation (the *style brisé*). In Spain, the local variant of the lute, the vihuela, was favoured. The lute was prominent as a continuo instrument during the Baroque period and remained in use up to the Classical era (Haydn wrote for it), but its place as the leading domestic instrument was firmly lost to the piano.

Lute-harpsichord. A variety of harpsichord strung with gut and intended to imitate the sound of a lute.

Luther, Martin (*b* Eisleben, 10 Nov 1483; *d* there, 18 Feb 1546). German reformer. He became a monk in 1505 and two years later was ordained priest. From 1512 he lectured, preached and encouraged the progress of the Reformation, first in the University of Wittenberg, then throughout Germany. A musical boy, he possessed a fine singing voice which he retained as an adult; he played the flute and lute. His practical involvement was matched by an understanding of music theory; and a visit to Rome (*c*1510) brought him into contact with the music of many composers, including that of Senfl and Josquin.

Music occupied an important place in his concept of the Reformation, and in 1566 he collaborated with Walter in creating plainchant appropriate to the German language. The close association between words and music was extremely important to his belief that music was 'the excellent gift of God'. Although he composed two four-part polyphonic sacred pieces (one to a Latin text), his most important works are the numerous hymn melodies which he either composed or arranged.

Luthier (Fr.; It. *liutaio*). Literally, 'lute maker', it has become a general term for a maker of violins or other string instruments. Similarly, the derivative 'lutherie' (lute making) has acquired the meaning of instrument making in general.

Lutosławski, Witold (*b* Warsaw, 25 Jan 1913). Polish composer. He studied with Maliszewski at the Warsaw Conservatory (1932–7) and soon made his mark as a pianist and composer, though few works from before 1945 have been published: those that have include the Paganini Variations for two pianos (1941). He then developed a clear, fresh tonality related to late Bartók, displayed in the Little Suite for orchestra (1951), the Concerto for Orchestra (1954) and the Dance Preludes for clarinet and piano (1954). But that style was short-lived: in the late 1950s he was able to essay a kind of serialism (*Funeral Music* for strings, 1958) and to learn from Cage the possibility of aleatory textures, where synchronization between instrumental lines is not exact (*Venetian Games* for chamber orchestra, 1961). Most of his subsequent works have been orchestral, fully chromatic, finely orchestrated in a manner suggesting Debussy and Ravel, and developed from an opposition between aleatory and metrical textures. These include his Second (1967) and Third (1983) symphonies, concertos for cello (1970) and for oboe and harp (1980), and settings of French verse with chorus (*Three Poems of Henri Michaux*, 1963), tenor (*Paroles tissées*, 1965) and baritone (*Les espaces du sommeil*, 1975). During this period he has also been internationally active as a teacher and conductor of his own music.

Orchestral music Symphonic variations (1938); 3 syms. (1947, 1967, 1983); Little suite (1951); Concerto for Orchestra (1954); Dance preludes (1955); Funeral Music (1958); 3 Postludes (1960); Venetian Games (1961); Livre pour orchestre (1968); Cello Concerto (1970); Preludes and Fugue, str (1972); Mi-parti (1976); Novelette (1979); Chain I (1983); Chain II, vn, orch (1985)
Voice with orchestra Silesian Triptych (1951); 5 Songs (1958); 3 Poèmes of Henri Michaux (1963); Paroles tissées (1965); Les espaces du sommeil (1975)
Chamber music Trio, ob, cl, bn (1945); Dance Preludes, cl, pf (1954); String Quartet (1964); Sacher Variation, vc (1975); Epitaph, ob, pf (1979); Partita, vn, pf (1984)
Piano music Variations on a Theme of Paganini, 2 pf (1941); Melodie ludowe [Folk melodies] (1945); Bukoliki (1952)
Songs with piano

Lutyens, (Agnes) Elisabeth (*b* London, 9 July 1906; *d* there, 14 April 1983). English composer. A daughter of the architect Sir Edwin Lutyens, she studied in Paris and at the RCM and at the end of the 1930s began to produce serial compositions (Chamber Concerto no.1 for nonet, 1939) referable more to Webern and Stravinsky than Schoenberg; she was one of the first English composers to use 12-note methods. Her large subsequent output includes operas, orchestral and diverse chamber pieces (13 string quartets, 1938–82), and numerous varied settings of English verse; she also wrote film scores. She was an esteemed teacher and published her autobiography, *A Goldfish Bowl* (1972).

Luxon, Benjamin (*b* Redruth, 24 March 1937). English baritone. He studied at the GSM and worked with the English Opera Group, creating Britten's Owen Wingrave in 1971. Later he sang at Glyndebourne (the Count in *Figaro*, 1973), at Covent Garden and with the English National Opera; he is admired for his warm, sympathetic baritone and his attention to words, which make him a notable singer of lieder.

Luython, Carl (*b* Antwerp, ?1557; *d* Prague, Aug 1620). South Netherlands composer. He was educated in Antwerp, at the imperial court chapel in Vienna and in Italy. He served the court in Vienna for over 35 years, until 1612, as an organist (from 1576) and court composer (1596), achieving great fame. His works include four books of sacred music (1587–1609), mostly in a conservative, late Netherlands style, one of madrigals (1582) and keyboard pieces.

Luzzaschi, Luzzasco (*b* Ferrara, ?1545; *d* there, 10 Sept 1607). Italian composer. He spent his whole life at Ferrara, probably studying under Rore among others. He served the Este court as a singer (1561) and first organist (1564), and was the duke's private composer by 1570; he was also organist at Ferrara Cathedral and the Accademia della Morte. After 1597 he probably served Cardinal Pietro Aldobrandini. The leading musician at Ferrara in the later 16th century, he was best known in his lifetime as a keyboard player (Frescobaldi was among his pupils). His works include a book of madrigals for one to three sopranos with keyboard (1601), containing elaborate virtuoso pieces given at the duke's private concerts by the 'singing ladies' of Ferrara, a repertory long kept secret. Of his many influential five-part madrigals (7 bks, 1571–1604), some early ones recall Rore while later ones use rich colours and sonorous contrasts. A motet volume (1598) and a few keyboard works also survive.

L'vov, Alexey Fyodorovich (*b* Tallinn, 5 June 1798; *d* nr. Kaunas, 28 Dec 1870). Russian composer and violinist. In 1837 he succeeded his father as director of the imperial court chapel choir in St Petersburg, for which he composed communion hymns, a Lord's Prayer setting and a *Stabat mater* (1851). As a violinist he was praised by Schumann and by Mendelssohn, whose violin concerto he played in Leipzig. His violin works include a concerto and 24 caprices. He is best known for the famous national hymn *God Save the Tsar*, commissioned by Nicholas I (1833).

Lyadov [Liadov], Anatol [Anatoly] Konstantinovich (*b* St Petersburg, 11 May 1855; *d* Polïnovka, 28 Aug 1914). Russian composer and teacher. A pupil of Rimsky-Korsakov at the St Petersburg Conservatory, he showed promise and developed a lasting interest in counterpoint; from 1878 he taught at the conservatory (Prokofiev and Myaskovsky were among his pupils), also making appearances as a conductor. In the 1870s he was associated with 'The Five', and in the 1880s with the Belyayev circle. Many of his pieces are based on pre-existing motifs (folksongs, other composers' themes, a cantus firmus) or rely on a programme, revealing his sense of orchestral colour and gift for musical characterization (notably in the orchestral works *Baba-Yaga*,

?1891–1904, and *Kikimora*, 1909); later works, including the symphonic poem *Skorbnaya pesn* (1914), experiment with extended tonality. A series of charming piano miniatures is still in the repertory. Procrastination, indolence and self-doubt prevented him from completing a work of any size or scope.

Lyapunov [Liapunov], **Sergey Mikhaylovich** (*b* Yaroslavl, 30 Nov 1859; *d* Paris, 8 Nov 1924). Russian composer, pianist and conductor. He studied at the Moscow Conservatory but, attracted by the nationalism of the new Russian school, became a pupil of Balakirev, a dominating influence. He taught and conducted in St Petersburg, also appearing as a pianist and composing prolifically, often in the style of other composers (Schumann, Chopin, Mendelssohn, Balakirev and above all Liszt); his brilliant technical studies op.12 recall Liszt's *Transcendental Studies*. Besides piano showpieces (still in the repertory), he wrote distinctive, lyrical piano miniatures, orchestral works, notably the Solemn Overture on Russian Themes (1896), and many songs.

Lyatoshyns'ky, Boris Mykolayovich (*b* Zhitomir, 3 Jan 1895; *d* Kiev, 15 April 1968). Ukrainian composer. He studied with Glier at the Kiev Conservatory, where he remained as a teacher (1918–68). His attempt to create a distinctively Ukrainian style, on the basis of folksong and Russian Romanticism, was profoundly important to his successors. His works include operas (*The Golden Ring*, 1930; *Shchors*, 1938), five symphonies (1919, 1936, 1951, 1963, 1966), four string quartets (1915–43) and vocal and piano music.

Lydian. The fifth of the eight traditional church modes, the authentic MODE on F.

Lympany, Moura (*b* Saltash, 18 Aug 1916). English pianist. She studied at Liège and the RCM and with Matthay. She made her début at the age of 12, later becoming well known internationally, especially for her commanding performances of 20th-century English music and works of the Russian Romantics.

Lyon & Healy. American instrument manufacturers and music dealers. It was founded in 1864 in Chicago by George Washburn Lyon and Patrick Joseph Healy. Apart from its broad range of merchandise and advanced selling methods (its retail music stores closed in 1979), the firm is best known for its harps, from 1889 specially built for strength, pitch reliability and freedom from unwanted vibration.

Lyra [lira]. A term used for various instruments, most often string instruments. In army bands a lyra is a portable glockenspiel consisting of a lyre-shaped metal frame to which are attached tuned metal bars in the conventional two rows for diatonic and chromatic notes (*see* BELL-LYRA). The terms 'lyra' and 'lira' in medieval and Renaissance writings designated various string instruments of the time (LIRA DA BRACCIO, LIRONE and LYRA VIOL) as well as the ancient Greek lyre, but seldom members of the zither family. The term is also used for a short-necked Greek fiddle.

Lyra-glockenspiel. *See* BELL-LYRA.

Lyra viol. A small bass viol popular in England during the 17th century. It differed little from the standard bass viol. Its repertory, notated in tablature, is predominantly polyphonic and played mainly with the bow. The sources include pieces for one lyra viol or more, and lyra viol accompaniment for songs, by composers such as Coprario, Jenkins, William Lawes and Tobias Hume. At least 60 different tunings have been noted.

Lyre. A string instrument whose strings are attached to a yoke in the same plane as the soundchest, with two arms and a crossbar. The earliest known examples, from the 3rd millennium BC, are from sites in Mesopotamia. Lyres appeared in several Mediterranean lands in antiquity and spread throughout medieval Europe; in modern times they are played in Ethiopia and neighbouring countries. The resonator may be in the shape of a bowl or a box; the arms may be symmetrical or otherwise; the strings may run parallel or may fan out.

The lyre and the KITHARA were the most important string instruments of ancient Greece and Rome. The lyre had a soundchest of tortoise-shell (as set out in the myth of its invention by Hermes); the kithara was larger, with a wooden soundchest. The lyre first appears in late 7th-century illustrations and becomes increasingly common; the number of strings increases from three or four to seven. It is normally depicted with the player sitting, his left hand against the strings and his right with a plectrum; the left hand may have played an accompaniment to a singer, and the right perhaps preludes and postludes.

The lyre was traditionally regarded as the instrument of Apollonian restraint; in the Middle Ages it was associated with King David, patron of music and Christ figure.

Lyre guitar. A lyre with a fingerboard. Pictorial evidence shows the existence of such an instrument as early as the 9th century; a six-string lyre guitar was popular as an accompanying instrument in Paris and London, *c*1780–1817.

Lyric. Term used (usually in the plural) for the words of a song; also to describe a voice, usually soprano or tenor, of a light and unforced quality. It is also used simply to mean 'to do with music': the 'lyric theatre', 'lyric stage'.

Lyric Opera of Chicago. Established as the Lyric Theatre of Chicago in 1954, renamed 1956. Early seasons were mainly Italian, with European principals. Later, a wider repertory included more American artists; Lyric Opera Center for American Artists (founded 1973) provides young singers. The company commissioned Penderecki's *Paradise Lost* (première 1978).

Lyric Suite. Work for string quartet by Berg (1926).

Orchestral work by Grieg (1904), orchestrations of four of his *Lyric Pieces* for piano.

Lysarden. English term, related to 'lizard', thought to serve for the bass of the CORNETT family before the SERPENT came into use in the 17th century.

Lysenko, Mykola Vytal'yevych (*b* Hrynky, 22 March 1842; *d* Kiev, 6 Nov 1912). Ukrainian composer, pianist and folksong collector. His nationalist sympathies, study of folk music and Shevchenko's poetry stimulated him to become the leading figure in Ukrainian music in Kiev, where he settled in 1876. A prolific composer and a fine pianist, he produced folksong arrangements, choral settings of Ukrainian poetry, small-scale piano pieces showing Chopin's influence and several Ukrainian operas, notably *Natalka-Poltavka* (1889) and the epic *Taras Bul'ba* (1880–90). He also wrote essays on folk music and founded a Ukrainian School of Music.

Lyudkevych, Stanislav Pylypovych (*b* Jarosław, 24 Jan 1879; *d* L'vov, 10 Sept 1979). Ukrainian composer. He studied with Zemlinsky in Vienna (1907–8), then taught in L'vov, notably at the conservatory (1945–72). He played a leading role in establishing musical culture in western Ukraine. In his music he used Ukrainian folk music in a late Romantic style, his works including operas, patriotic cantatas and orchestral pieces; he also made editions and arrangements of folk music.

M

M.D. [mano destra] (It.). Right hand.

M.M. Abbreviation for Maelzel's metronome; see MAELZEL, JOHANN NEPOMUK, and METRONOME.

M.S. [mano sinistra] (It.). Left hand.

Maag, (Ernst) Peter (Johannes) (*b* St Gall, 10 May 1919). Swiss conductor. Among his early appointments were as assistant to Ansermet with the Suisse Romande Orchestra, then at Düsseldorf and Bonn (1954–9) where he introduced unfamiliar repertory. He made his British début at Covent Garden in 1959, his American with the Cincinnati SO the same year and at the Met in 1972. He was principal conductor at the Vienna Volksoper (1964–8) and has also worked in Parma and Turin. He is admired especially for his direction of Mozart but is also a sensitive conductor of 19th-century music.

Maayani, Ami (*b* Ramat-Gan, 13 Jan 1936). Israeli composer. He studied with Ben-Haim (1956–60) and at the Columbia-Princeton Electronic Music Center. His works, using Near Eastern elements, include choral and orchestral pieces. He is best known for his harp music, notably Harp Concerto no.1 (1960) and the Toccata (1961).

Maazel, Lorin (Varencove) (*b* Neuilly, 6 March 1930). American conductor and violinist. After study at Pittsburg he conducted the New York PO in 1939. His début as a violinist was in 1945 and his adult début as a conductor at Catania in 1953. Wider attention came in 1960 with performances in London and Bayreuth. He was director of the Deutsche Oper, Berlin (1965–71), and of the Vienna Staatsoper, 1982–4. He was music director of the Cleveland Orchestra, 1972–82, and from 1986 of the Pittsburgh SO. His performances are notable for their vitality and attention to detail.

Macbeth. Opera in four acts by Verdi to a libretto by Piave after Shakespeare (1847, Florence; revised, 1865, Paris).

Tone poem by Richard Strauss (1888).

McCabe, John (*b* Huyton, 21 April 1939). English composer and pianist. He studied at the Royal Manchester College and with Genzmer in Munich, then returned to England to work as a pianist, critic and composer; in 1983 he became director of the London College of Music. His works, in an extended tonal style relating to Hartmann and Nielsen, include three symphonies (1965, 1971, 1978), much other orches-

tral music, chamber and keyboard pieces.

McCormack, John (*b* Athlone, 14 June 1884; *d* Dublin, 16 Sept 1945). Irish tenor, later American. After study in Milan he sang Mascagni's Turiddù at Covent Garden in 1907, returning until 1917 in operas by Gounod, Bellini and Puccini. His fine technique and sweet tone made him a favourite at the Met where he sang up to 1918. In the 1920s he appeared as a concert singer, earning some disfavour for his singing of inferior music but giving pleasure with his sweet tone and polished individual style.

McCracken, James (Eugene) (*b* Gary, IN, 16 Dec 1926; *d* New York, 29 April 1988). American tenor. He sang small roles at the Met from 1953 and in 1960 appeared with the Washington, DC, Opera as Othello, a role well suited to his robust style and which he repeated at his Covent Garden début in 1964 and at the Met. He was a noted Florestan and Don José.

McCredie, Andrew D(algarno) (*b* Sydney, 3 Sept 1930). Australian musicologist. He studied in Europe, taking the PhD in Hamburg and composition with Berkeley in London. He returned to teach at Adelaide. His research has been in early German opera and instrumental music; he has also contributed to research on Australian music and the development of musicology there.

MacCunn, Hamish (*b* Greenock, 22 March 1868; *d* London, 2 Aug 1916). Scottish composer, conductor and teacher. He studied at the RCM (with Parry and Stanford), becoming professor at the RAM (1888–94) and the Guildhall School of Music (from 1912) but from the late 1890s turning increasingly to conducting light opera. As a composer he had most success with his superficially 'Scottish' works, particularly the tuneful overture *Land of the Mountain and the Flood* (1887); he also wrote operas (including *Jeanie Deans*, 1894), choral works and songs.

MacDowell, Edward (Alexander) (*b* New York, 18 Dec 1860; *d* there, 23 Jan 1908). American composer. He studied the piano in Paris (with Marmontel), Wiesbaden and Frankfurt (Carl Heymann), as well as composition (with Raff, at the Hoch Conservatory in Frankfurt), taking his first post at the Darmstadt Conservatory. Liszt heard his *First Modern Suite* and First Piano Concerto and strongly encouraged him; by 1884 German firms had published ten of his works. After several years in Wiesbaden he moved to

Boston in 1888 to pursue a performing career. His Second Piano Concerto and First and Second Orchestral Suites won success there and in New York, and he was increasingly accepted as a leading figure in American musical life. Compositions of the Boston years included his popular *Woodland Sketches*, *Sonata tragica* and *Sonata eroica* and the *Six Love Songs*. In 1896 he became the first professor of music at Columbia University; besides organizing the new department, he conducted a New York men's glee club and composed some of his best piano music – *Sea Pieces*, the Third and Fourth Sonatas, *New England Idyls* – and many male choruses. He left Columbia in 1904 but continued to teach privately; after his death his summer home at Peterborough, New Hampshire, was converted into an artists' colony (still active).

MacDowell was a Romantic by temperament, with a musical imagination shaped by nature and literature (notably poetry and Celtic and Nordic legends). His style derives largely from Schumann, Liszt, Wagner, Raff and especially Grieg and, though not innovatory, influential or distinctively American, retains a certain melodic freshness and attractive orchestral colouring.

Orchestral music Pf Conc. no.1, a (1882); Pf Conc. no.2, d (1884–6); sym. poems – Hamlet, Ophelia (1884–5), Lancelot und Elaine (1886), Lamia (1888); Romanze, vc, orch (1887); Orch Suite no.1 (1891); Orch Suite no.2, 'Indian' (1895); other works
Piano music First Modern Suite (1881); Second Modern Suite (1882); Sonata tragica (1891–2); Sonata eroica (1895); Woodland Sketches (1896); Sea Pieces (1898); Sonata no.3, 'Norse' (1899); Sonata no.4, 'Keltic' (1900); Fireside Tales (1902); New England Idyls (1902); 25 others; edns. of pieces by other composers
Vocal music 11 song sets, incl. Six Love Songs (1890), Eight Songs (1893), Four Songs (1899), Three Songs (1899), Three Songs (1901); 28 partsongs, incl. College Songs, male vv (1901); edns. of choruses by other composers

Mace, Thomas (*b* ?Cambridge/York, 1612–13; *d* ?Cambridge, *c*1706). English writer and composer. He was appointed a singing-man at Trinity College, Cambridge, in 1635, and probably spent most of his life there. He is remembered for his *Musick's Monument* (1676), an important source of information about English musical life and practices in the mid-17th century, including discussion of church music, the use of instruments, acoustics, tempo and notation. The book includes eight lute suites; he also wrote 15 pieces for viol.

Maceda, José (*b* Manila, 31 Jan 1917). Filipino composer. He studied in Manila and with Boulanger in Paris (1937–41), then toured internationally as a pianist. In 1958 he worked briefly in the Paris *musique concrète* studio and met Xenakis and Boulez, and in 1960 he began teaching Asian music at the University of the Philippines. His music draws on ethnic and avant-garde models; primitive ritual informs his *Pagsamba* for 241 performers (1968).

McEwan, Sir John (Blackwood) (*b* Hawick, 13 April 1868; *d* London, 14 June 1948). Scottish composer. He studied at Glasgow University and the RAM (1893–5), where he was appointed professor in 1898

and became principal (1924–36). His works include orchestral compositions (including *Grey Galloway*, 1908), 17 string quartets, seven violin sonatas and choral music. He introduced Schoenbergian Sprechgesang into British music with the 14 Poems for 'inflected' voice and piano (1943).

Macfarren, Sir George (Alexander) (*b* London, 2 March 1813; *d* there, 31 Oct 1887). English composer. He studied at the RAM, becoming professor (from 1875 principal) there and at Cambridge. In spite of being blind (from 1860) he remained active as an author and lecturer, editor and composer, receiving a knighthood in 1883. One of the most prolific 19th-century composers, he won modest success with his operas, notably *King Charles II* (1849) and *Robin Hood* (1860), but wrote mainly choral, orchestral and chamber music (including nine symphonies and five string quartets) and songs; his best-known piece was the overture *Chevy Chace* (1837). His brother Walter (1826–1905) was a pianist and esteemed teacher at the RAM; he composed songs, partsongs and accomplished piano pieces.

McGibbon, William (*b* Edinburgh, *c*1690; *d* there, 3 Oct 1756). Scottish composer. The leading Scottish composer of the late Baroque period, he wrote sonatas, concertos and folktune arrangements and variations. He was also a violinist.

Machaut, Guillaume de (*b* ?Reims, *c*1300; *d* there, ?13 April 1377). French composer and poet. Probably educated in Reims, he entered the service of John of Luxembourg, King of Bohemia, as a royal secretary, *c*1323. The king helped him to procure a canonry in Reims, which was confirmed in 1335; Machaut settled there *c*1340, although he continued in royal service until the king's death (1346). He then served various members of the French high nobility, including John, Duke of Berry, his later years being dedicated to the MS compilation of his works.

With his prolific output of motets and songs, Machaut was the single most important figure of the French Ars Nova. He followed and developed the guidelines of Philippe de Vitry's treatise *Ars nova* and, in particular, observed Vitry's unprecedented advocation of duple time in many of his works, even in his setting of the Ordinary of the Mass. Only in some of his lais and virelais and the *Hoquetus David* did he consistently adhere to 13th-century rhythmic patterns and genres. His own rhythmic style is novel in its use of variety and motivic interest, particularly through syncopation, and in his development of isorhythmic techniques (which he often extended to all voices): all but three of his 23 motets, and four of the movements of the *Messe de Nostre Dame*, are isorhythmic. The mass is one of the earliest polyphonic settings of the Mass Ordinary; the four isorhythmic movements are based on Gregorian tenors, while the Gloria and Credo are freely constructed. In secular music, Machaut set a wide range of poetic forms, all of which are illustrated in his long narrative poem, the *Remede de Fortune* (probably an early work). While the relationship between text and music is most closely observed in the monophonic lais and virelais, a highly flexible approach is adopted in the three-voice motets so that the subtle treatment of the text avoids the symmetricality of complete isorhythm. His inventive approach to isorhythm resulted in freely-constructed introductions to five of his Latin motets. More progressive features of Machaut's style – an increased awareness of tonality, the use of unifying rhythmic motifs – are found in his polyphonic settings of rondeaux and ballades, while melodic considerations are to the fore in his virelais. Typical of Machaut's compositional flair and imagination is the rondeau *Ma fin est mon commencement* in which the text provides the key to an ingenious canon.

Sacred music Messe de Nostre Dame; 23 motets; Hoquetus David, double hocket
Secular music 42 ballades; 22 rondeaux, incl. Ma fin est mon commencement; 33 virelais; 19 lais; 1 complainte; 1 chanson royal

Machavariani, Alexey Davidovich (*b* Gori, 23 Sept 1913). Soviet composer. He studied at the Tbilisi Conservatory, where he began teaching in 1940. Influenced by Georgian national art and contemporary musical trends, his works include operas, ballets (notably *Otello*, 1957, performed throughout Europe), large-scale choral works and symphonies.

Machicotage (Fr.). The practice of embellishing certain sections of plainchant to add solemnity; widespread in France and Italy since the Middle Ages, it consisted chiefly in the addition of passing notes.

Machine head. A tuning device that uses mechanical advantage to tune or maintain the pitch of a string. It dates back to the 16th century; the most efficient form is the worm-gear device used on the double bass and some plucked instruments.

Machine stop. A device applied to English harpsichords in the second half of the 18th century to enable a single pedal to control two or more separate registers, overriding their individual handstops. A similar device on chamber organs allowed an extra slider to cancel the higher-pitched stops when a pedal was depressed, even though their knobs remained drawn.

Mackenzie, Sir Alexander (Campbell) (*b* Edinburgh, 22 Aug 1847; *d* London, 28 April 1935). Scottish composer and conductor. He studied in Germany and at the RAM, by 1865 becoming known in Edinburgh as a violinist and conductor. In the 1880s he won a reputation as one of England's leading composers, chiefly with the oratorio *The Rose of Sharon* (1884). From 1885 he lived in London, conducting the Novello Oratorio Concerts and, from 1888, serving as an influential principal of the RAM; he also conducted for the Philharmonic Society (1892–9) and occasionally for the Royal Choral Society, making a tour of Canada in 1903. He was knighted (1895) and created KCVO (1922). A workmanlike composer, he produced successful choral works, vocal settings (many of Scottish poets) and descriptive orchestral pieces, often imaginative and satisfying if also derivative.

Mackerras, Sir (Alan) Charles (MacLaurin) (*b* Schenectady, NY, 17 Nov 1925). Australian conductor. After playing the oboe in the Sydney SO he

studied in Prague; he was later closely associated with Janáček's operas, conducting *Katya Kabanova* at Sadler's Wells in 1951 and recording it and other operas with the Vienna PO. He was musical director of Sadler's Wells/English National Opera (1970–79). His conducting is marked by exuberance of rhythm and keen sense of colour; to these he added a scholarly concern for textural accuracy and interpretative style: his *Le nozze di Figaro* (1965) adopted 18th-century practices. He has been guest conductor with many leading orchestras and in 1986 became musical director of Welsh National Opera.

McLeod, Jennifer (Helen) (*b* Wellington, 12 Nov 1941). New Zealand composer. She studied with Lilburn and in Europe with Messiaen, Stockhausen and Boulez, and in 1967 was appointed to Victoria University. Her works include music-theatre and ensemble pieces, some for children and amateurs. In 1967 she abandoned music.

MacMillan, Sir Ernest (Alexander Campbell) (*b* Mimico, 18 Aug 1893; *d* Toronto, 6 May 1973). Canadian conductor, composer and organist. He played the organ in Toronto from 1903 and obtained the Oxford BMus in 1911, DMus 1918. He was principal at the Toronto Conservatory (1926–42) and conductor of the Toronto SO (1931–56), giving many premières of works by Canadian composers and becoming widely known for his annual *Messiah* and *St Matthew Passion*. Choral music and song are central among his compositions. A gifted musician of broad interests, he played an important part in the expansion of Canadian musical life after 1945, serving on several national committees and editing *Music in Canada* (1955).

Macnaghten, Anne (Catherine) (*b* Whitwick, 9 Aug 1908). English violinist. She studied in Leipzig, made her solo début in Dublin in 1930 and with her string quartet (originally entirely of women) in London in 1932. In 1931 she founded an important concert series in London, to perform music by young or little-known British composers; the Macnaghten Concerts have done much to bring new music and budding composers to wider notice.

Maconchy, Elizabeth (*b* Broxbourne, 19 March 1907). English composer. She studied at the RCM (1923–9) and with Jirák in Prague, which gave her music a central European tone: she shares Bartók's intensive motivic working, vigorous counterpoint and feeling for the string quartet (her works include 14, 1933–84, besides much other chamber music). Her Englishness is perhaps more apparent in her occasional operas, songs and choral works; among the most successful is *Ariadne* (1970), a cantata for soprano and chamber orchestra.

McPhee, Colin (Carhart) (*b* Montreal, 15 March 1900; *d* Los Angeles, 7 Jan 1964). American composer and ethnomusicologist of Canadian origin. He studied at the Peabody Conservatory, in Paris with Le Flem and in New York with Varèse. In 1934–6 he was in Bali, studying the music that became the subject of his *Balinese Ceremonial Music* for two pianos (1940) and of pioneering research, culminating in *Music in Bali* (1966). After the war he taught in Los Angeles, from 1960 at UCLA. The hallmark of his style is sensitivity to timbres with a predilection for textures of multi-layered rhythms. His best-known work is *Tabuh-tabuhan* (1936) which uses a symphony orchestra, a 'nuclear gamelan' of Western instruments and Balinese gongs.

Macque, Giovanni de (*b* Valenciennes, ?1548–50; *d* Naples, Sept 1614). Flemish composer. As a boy he sang in the imperial court chapel in Vienna. He studied under Monte, moved to Rome by 1574 and to Naples in 1585, serving as organist (1594) and *maestro di cappella* (1599) of the Spanish viceroy's chapel. Trabaci and Mayone were among his many pupils. A leading composer of the Neapolitan school, he published 13 books of madrigals (1576–1613) and other pieces in anthologies, as well as composing many keyboard and instrumental works.

Madama Butterfly. Opera in two acts by Puccini to a libretto by Giacosa and Illica after Belasco (1904, Milan).

Maderna, Bruno (*b* Venice, 21 April 1920; *d* Darmstadt, 13 Nov 1973). Italian composer. As a boy he appeared in Italy and abroad as a violinist and conductor; he then studied at the conservatories of Rome and Venice, and with Scherchen, who in 1948 guided him towards 12-note serialism. In 1951 he visited Darmstadt, where he taught and conducted from 1954, and where he settled. He was internationally admired as an orchestral conductor, notably in contemporary music. He played an unequalled part in the early postwar development of Italian music. His earlier works are Schoenbergian, but in the mid-1950s, like Berio with whom he was closely associated, he developed a relaxed Italian accent within the avant-garde language: in 1954 the two founded an electronic music studio in Milan, and there he produced several tape compositions (*Continuo*, 1958). His other works include the theatrical project *Hyperion* (1964), the opera *Satyricon* (1973), solo instrumental pieces and much for orchestra (three oboe concertos, 1962, 1967, 1973; *Quadrivium* with percussion quartet, 1969).

Madetoja, Leevi (Antti) (*b* Oulu, 17 Feb 1887; *d* Helsinki, 6 Oct 1947). Finnish composer. He studied with Sibelius in Helsinki (1906–10), with d'Indy in Paris (1910–11), and in Vienna and Berlin (1911–12), then worked in Helsinki as a teacher, critic and composer. His works, often using Ostrobothnian folk music and French techniques, are skilfully orchestrated; they include the operas *The Ostrobothnians* (1923) and *Juha* (1934), three symphonies (1916, 1918, 1926) and much choral music.

Madonis, Luigi (*b* Venice, *c*1690; *d* St Petersburg, *c*1770). Italian violinist and composer. Known as an excellent player, he was leader of an Italian touring opera troupe and later to the Russian court orchestra, which he joined in 1733. His output (mostly chamber music) includes some of the few Baroque works written in Russia.

Madrigal. The term 'madrigal' has two distinct, unconnected meanings: a poetic and musical form of 14th-century Italy, and a 16th- or 17th-century setting of secular verse.

The earliest madrigals of the 14th-century type probably date from the 1320s; the genre was fully developed in the 1340s, with two- or three-line verses (usually with identical music) and a one- or two-line terminating ritornello. All but a few of the 190 surviving examples are for two voices, the rest for three. The style, as seen in the madrigals of Giovanni da Cascia and Jacopo da Bologna, is basically syllabic, with a fairly florid upper part supported by a plainer lower one. After *c*1360 the genre declined and by 1450 it was virtually extinct.

From *c*1530 the term 'madrigal' came to be used for verse owing its style, imagery and even vocabulary to Petrarch. Its seriousness and refinement demanded a kind of musical setting that the contemporary frottola could not provide but which was now developed by Verdelot and others from the French *chanson* and the motet. Festa's three-voice madrigals were popular but Verdelot's for four to six voices were considered the leading examples until Arcadelt's appeared in 1539. Venice was the main centre for the madrigal; there Willaert's madrigals were widely imitated by Rore and others.

They however brought many changes to the genre, in declamation and harmony. Four to six (usually five) parts became the norm in the 1550s and 1560s, when Palestrina and Lassus contributed to the genre and such great madrigalists as Andrea Gabrieli and Wert began their careers. Late in the century, Rome and the duchies of Ferrara and Mantua became centres of progressive influence; stylistic changes included the absorption of elements of the popular villanella and bold experimentation in chromaticism, word-painting and harmonic and rhythmic contrast which, in the madrigals of Marenzio, Luzzaschi, Gesualdo and Monteverdi, threatened the balanced style of Renaissance polyphony.

The move towards a concerted style is seen in Monteverdi's madrigal output. In his fifth book (1605) he provided a continuo part for the last six pieces, and his seventh book (1619), called *Concerto*, consists of concerted pieces. He favoured the duet for high voices and continuo; other instrumental parts do not figure consistently. Solo madrigals were also composed in the first quarter of the 17th century by Caccini, d'India and others, after which the genre became virtually indistinguishable from the new DIALOGUE and CANTATA. However, the polyphonic madrigal survived as an archaic genre in occasional works by A. Scarlatti and others.

The rise of the English madrigal in the last decades of the 16th century coincided with the heyday of the English sonnet sequence. In musical style, its terminus was set by the translated Italian madrigals in Yonge's *Musica transalpina* (1588) and in particular by examples from Marenzio's early period. English composers did not adopt the extravagant styles then in favour in Italy. Morley was the guiding force of the English school. His light, Italianate madrigels and canzonets, some of them transcriptions of Gastoldi and Anerio, inspired Farnaby, Farmer and Bennet in the late 1590s; but it was left to Kirbye, Weelkes and Wilbye to emulate the more serious Italian madrigal for five or six voices in an imaginative and individual style. In 1601, 21 Englishmen contributed to Morley's *The Triumphes of Oriana*, a collection in praise of Queen Elizabeth I. Thereafter the English madrigal declined; although some charming light pieces and striking serious ones were written, the lute ayre and 'recitative musicke' marked the madrigal as a thing of the past.

Ties between Italy and other European countries encouraged the composition of madrigals in Spain, Germany, the Netherlands, Denmark and Poland, but nowhere to the same extent as in England.

Madrigal comedy. Term for a late Renaissance work consisting of secular vocal pieces held together by a plot or story. Vecchi's *L'Amfiparnaso* (1597) and Banchieri's *La pazzia senile* (1598) are among the best-known examples. They were not intended to be staged and their importance as forerunners of opera has been overestimated.

Madrigale spirituale. A general term for the settings of Italian devotional texts, not for liturgical use, which became fashionable in the Counter-Reformation. Many are versions of secular madrigals or new settings of *laude*, but the repertory includes also original works by Palestrina, Gesualdo and others.

Madrigali guerrieri ed amorosi. Monteverdi's eighth book of madrigals (1638).

Madrigalism. Term to denote the illustrative devices used in madrigals, particularly those of the late 16th century and the early 17th (*see* WORD-PAINTING).

Maegaard, Jan (Carl Christian) (*b* Copenhagen, 14 April 1926). Danish composer and musicologist. He studied with Jeppesen, Schierbeck and Jersild at the Copenhagen Conservatory, and with Larsen at the university, where he was appointed professor in 1971. His academic work has centred on Schoenberg, who has deeply influenced his own music (much of it vocal).

Maelzel, Johann Nepomuk (*b* Regensburg, 15 Aug 1772; *d* at sea, 21 July 1838). German inventor. Settling in Vienna in 1792, he built mechanical musical instruments, including the 'Panharmonicon' and the 'Trumpeter'; *c*1808 he made ear trumpets (one of which Beethoven used) and brought out a musical chronometer (*c*1813), an improved version of a machine by Stöckel. A shrewd and energetic businessman, for a time friendly with Beethoven, he is chiefly remembered for his 'metronome' (so named in his 1815 patent), a further improved chronometer. Although there is dispute over his contribution, the familiar wooden-boxed metronome remains almost exactly like Maelzel's last models of *c*1830.

Maessens, Pieter [Massenus Moderatus, Petrus] (*b* Ghent, *c*1505; *d* Vienna, Oct 1563). Flemish composer. He was a choirboy in the Archduchess Margaret of Austria's chapel, then a soldier of fortune for Charles V and the King of Spain. In 1540 he was appointed Kapellmeister of Notre Dame, Courtrai, and from 1546 Kapellmeister in the Viennese court chapel. He wrote numerous sacred and secular choral pieces and several literary works.

Maestoso (It.). Majestic.

Maestro (It.). 'Master': a title applied in musical parlance in several senses. It may refer to a composer, a virtuoso, a teacher, an instrument maker, a conductor or leader of an ensemble. *Maestro al cembalo* means leader at the harpsichord (it was commonly used in 18th-century operatic contexts); *maestro di cappella* and its equivalents *maestro de capilla* (Sp.), *maître de chapelle* (Fr.) and *Kapellmeister* (Ger.) mean master of a chapel, the musician in charge of a musical establishment, sacred, secular or both. For the role of the *maestro*, *see* CHAPEL.

Magadis. A term for the Greco-Roman angular HARP. The word 'magadize', to sing or play in octaves, suggests that the instrument had pairs of strings an octave apart.

Magaloff, Nikita (*b* St Petersburg, 8 Feb 1912). Swiss pianist. His family left Russia in 1918 and he studied at the Paris Conservatoire, where he met Ravel and Prokofiev. He has played widely and is seen as a leading interpreter of the Franco-Russian school of music by Chopin and Russian composers of the 19th and 20th centuries.

Magelone, Die Schöne. 15 songs by Brahms (op.33, 1868), settings for voice and piano of extracts from Ludwig Tieck's novel.

Maggio Musicale Fiorentino (Italy). Annual (summer) festival of opera, concerts and ballet in Florence, inaugurated in 1933 by the Orchestrale Fiorentino under Vittorio Gui. The originality of its opera productions (including many premières) and the presence of such conductors as Furtwängler and Bruno Walter soon led to its international renown.

Magic Flute, The [Die Zauberflöte]. Singspiel in two acts by Mozart to a libretto by Schikaneder after Liebeskind's story *Lulu* in Wieland's *Dschinnistan* and other sources (1791, Vienna).

Magnard, (Lucien Denis Gabriel) Albéric (*b* Paris, 9 June 1865; *d* Baron, 3 Sept 1914). French composer. Of a serious disposition, he produced severe, formalistic works – mainly orchestral and chamber music and operas – taking Wagner, Beethoven, Gluck and his teacher d'Indy as models. Canon and fugue pervade much of his output, though the Third Symphony (1896) and the opera *Bérénice* (1909), his masterpiece, show a refreshing clarity of scoring and a lyric simplicity.

Magnificat. A canticle (text from *Luke* i. 46–55), sung with an antiphon near the end of Vespers. Polyphonic settings began in the 14th century and many were composed in the 15th and 16th for both Catholic and Protestant services. Dufay wrote five settings, Victoria 18, Palestrina over 30, Lassus *c*100. Complete Magnificat cycles (eight settings) were composed by Sixt Dietrich (1535), Senfl (1537) and several later composers.

Most Renaissance settings alternate polyphony with verses sung monophonically to plainchant or instrumental music; except among English composers, the polyphonic sections are normally based on the canticle chant. This is the case in the two settings in Monteverdi's Vespers of 1610. The sectional style of his and of Schütz's great Magnificat evolved into a series of free arias, choruses etc. This type of Magnificat reached its most developed form in Bach's E♭ setting, performed in 1723 with Christmas pieces interpolated between some verses (Bach later rearranged the work in D, without the interpolations).

C.P.E. Bach's Magnificat of 1749 uses a similar 'number' technique, but the methods are those of the Classical period, the words being subordinated to the musical design. This style is carried to its logical conclusion in the Magnificat from Mozart's K339 Vespers (1780), a sonata-form Allegro with an Adagio introduction. After a dearth of Magnificats in the Romantic period, the Latin text has inspired several modern composers, including Berkeley and Penderecki.

Magnus Liber. Term used, following the late 13th-century theorist known as Anonymous IV, for the most important and widely-influential collection of two-voice polyphony from the early Notre Dame period. Originally compiled *c*1170, from the period Notre Dame Cathedral was under construction (1163–82), the *Magnus Liber* is said to have been the work of Léonin with subsequent revisions by Pérotin. The three main extant versions reveal that the original corpus comprised settings of the solo sections of responsories for Vespers and Mass for certain major feasts of the liturgical year, as celebrated at Notre Dame, in the earlier, sustained-note style of organum. Before 1200 these were reworked in the new styles brought about by the adoption of rhythmic modes, formulated in Paris *c*1180, and compositions selected from other churches of the city or diocese were introduced. The repertory underwent several stages of development before the discant style, in which both voices are governed by rhythmic modes, was reached. While Pérotin was undoubtedly responsible for much of the reworking of the *Magnus Liber*, he cannot be credited as sole creator of the modal system, the new discant style or the resulting items for three or four voices, composed for the most important festal occasions; it is more likely that such far-reaching developments were evolved by a school of composers based at Notre Dame and consolidated by him.

Mahagonny. *See* AUFSTIEG UND FALL DER STADT MAHAGONNY.

Mahaut, Antoine (*b ?c*1720; *d ?c*1785). Netherlands flautist and composer. He lived in Amsterdam, but visited Paris and Dresden. Foremost in his output are flute sonatas, duets etc among the finest of their day, and symphonies; he also edited song collections and wrote a flute method (1759) which marked a major advance in flute teaching.

Mahillon. Belgian family of wind instrument makers. The most celebrated members were Charles (1813–87), who founded the family business in Brussels in 1836 (ceased 1935, with a London branch 1844–1922) and became famous for his clarinets, and his eldest son Victor-Charles (1841–1924), remembered as an acoustician, writer and curator of the Brussels Conservatory Instrumental Museum.

Mahler, Gustav (*b* Kalište, Bohemia, 7 July 1860; *d* Vienna, 18 May 1911). Bohemian-Austrian composer. In 1860 his family moved to Jihlava, where Gustav took piano and theory lessons. From 1875 to 1878 he was at Vienna Conservatory, where he studied the piano, harmony and composition. After that he attended university lectures, worked as a music teacher and composed *Das klagende Lied*, a cantata indebted to the operas of Weber and Wagner but also showing many conspicuously Mahlerian features.

In 1880 Mahler accepted a conducting post at a summer theatre at Bad Hall, and he was engaged in a similar capacity in 1881 and 1883 at the theatres in Ljubljana and Olomouc. Between these appointments he engaged in composition and other conducting until, in autumn 1883, he became music director at Kassel. He found conditions uncongenial, and the repertory consisted solely of light opera; but an unhappy love affair with one of the singers led to the composition of his first masterpiece, the song cycle *Lieder eines fahrenden Gesellen*, and the inception of the closely related First Symphony.

Early in 1885 Mahler secured the post of second conductor at the Neues Stadttheater in Leipzig, to begin in July 1886, and a few months later he resigned his post at Kassel. The intervening year he spent at the Landestheater in Prague, where he had the opportunity of conducting operas by Gluck, Mozart, Beethoven and Wagner. There were at first fewer such opportunities at Leipzig, but in January 1887 he took over the *Ring* cycle from Arthur Nikisch, who fell ill, and convincingly established among critics and public his genius as an interpretative artist. The following year he completed Weber's unfinished comic opera *Die drei Pintos* (its successful performances in 1888 made Mahler famous and provided a useful source of income) and fell in love with the wife of Weber's grandson. Another consequence of his friendship with the Webers was the discovery in 1887 of the musical potential of *Des Knaben Wunderhorn*, a collection of folklike texts by Arnim and Brentano which provided Mahler with words for all but one of his songs for the next 14 years.

Disagreements with colleagues led to Mahler's resignation at Leipzig in May 1888 and to his dismissal a few months later from Prague, where he had been engaged to prepare *Die drei Pintos* and a production of Cornelius's *Der Barbier von Bagdad*; but within a few weeks he secured a far more important appointment at the Royal Opera in Budapest. His first year there was overshadowed by the illness and deaths of his parents and his sister. Though he was successful in bringing the opera house into profit and improving standards and repertory, the imminent appointment of an Intendant with artistic control made his situation untenable; he resigned and became first conductor at the Stadttheater, Hamburg. Despite a stifling artistic atmosphere and a heavy workload, Mahler returned to composition and at his summer retreat in the Salzkammergut completed the Second and Third Symphonies. 1895 brought both tragedy, when his youngest brother committed suicide, and success, with the première of the Second Symphony in Berlin in December. Now a conductor of international stature and a composer of growing reputation, he turned his attention to the Vienna Hofoper. The main obstacle was his Jewish origins; so he accepted Catholic baptism in February 1897 and was appointed Kapellmeister at Vienna two months later.

At Vienna Mahler brought a stagnating opera house to a position of unrivalled brilliance, especially during 1903–7, when he collaborated with the designer Alfred Roller on a series of memorable productions. In 1901 he had a villa built at Maiernigg on the Wörthersee in Carinthia, where he spent the summers composing. In 1902 he married Alma, daughter of the artist Anton Schindler, and though their life together was not untroubled (its strains caused him to consult Freud for psychoanalysis in 1910) the security benefited his creative life. At Maiernigg he completed symphonies nos.5–8 and in 1904 the *Kindertotenlieder*, settings of five poems by Rückert on the death of children. The death of Mahler's own elder daughter, Maria, from scarlet fever three years later left him distraught.

In Vienna Mahler was surrounded by radical young composers, including Schoenberg, Berg, Webern and Zemlinsky, whose work he supported and encouraged. His propagation of his own music, however, aroused opposition from a section of the Viennese musical establishment, and when the campaign against him, led by an anti-semitic press, gained momentum he was again forced to look elsewhere. This time he turned to New York, where he spent his last winters as conductor, first of the Metropolitan Opera and, from 1910, of the New York PO. He continued to spend the summers in Europe, where he undertook further conducting and completed the valedictory Ninth Symphony and *Das Lied von der Erde*. This last, a setting of six Chinese poems in German translation, took the shape of a large-scale symphony for two voices and orchestra; but Mahler, whose fear of death and sense of fate had been intensified by the diagnosis of a heart condition in 1907, refused to number the work 10, citing Beethoven, Schubert and Bruckner. He did, however, start work on a tenth symphony, but died before he could complete it.

Although as a conductor Mahler achieved fame primarily in opera, his creative energies were directed almost wholly towards symphony and song. Even in the early *Das klagende Lied*, there are stylistic features to be found in his mature music, for example the combining of onstage and offstage orchestras, the association of high tragedy and the mundane, the drawing on folksong ideas and the dramatic-symbolic use of tonality. This last reappeared in his early masterpiece, the *Lieder eines fahrenden Gesellen*, which has an evolutionary tonal scheme paralleling the changing fortunes of the travelling hero. In the 1890s Mahler was much influenced by the *Wunderhorn* poems, in his symphonies as well as his songs, for he often used song to clarify an important moment in the structure of a symphony, for example 'Urlicht' in no.2, which he found himself unable to continue after writing the imposing first movement. No.3 is more idiosyncratic; again, its dramatic scheme evolved with recourse to song and chorus. No.4 returns to tradition, in a first movement of rare wit and subtlety; here the poetic idea is the progress from experience to innocence (with a *Wunderhorn* song finale). While no.2, 'The Resurrection', moves from C minor to E♭,

no.4 goes from G major to the 'heavenly' E major. Parody, irony and satire are important in Mahler's thinking during these years, with popular invention (like the children's round in no.1 and the march tunes of no.3) and elements of distortion.

Nos.5, 6 and 7 are sometimes regarded as a trilogy, although no.5 is a heroic work, with a narrative running from its opening funeral march through the agitated Allegro to a Scherzo and a triumphant conclusion. The symphony moves from C♯ minor to D major. No.6, a tragic work – and in many musicians' view, his greatest symphony for its equilibrium between form and drama – begins and ends in A minor; the finale makes it clear that there is no escape for the implied hero and indeed his death is symbolically enacted in the movement's shattering climax. The shape of no.7, which moves from E minor to C major, is less satisfying; possibly, with its dark, nocturnal middle movement, it is consciously built round the poetic concept of darkness moving towards the light of the finale. The largest-scale of Mahler's symphonies is no.8, the so-called 'Symphony of a Thousand', in which the second part is a vast synthesis of forms and media embodying the setting of the final scene of Goethe's *Faust* as an amalgam of dramatic cantata, oratorio, song cycle, Lisztian choral symphony and instrumental symphony. This public pronouncement was followed by one of his most personal, *Das Lied von der Erde*, influenced in its vocal writing and woodwind obbligatos by Mahler's new interest in Bach. His last two symphonies return to the four-movement scheme of the middle-period ones, incorporating extensions of the character movements of his earlier works with the new type of slow first movement (followed up in the unfinished Tenth) and ending with an Adagio in a mood of profound resignation. Mahler's extension of symphonic form, of the symphony's expressive scope and the use of the orchestra (especially the agonized timbres he obtained by using instruments, particularly wind, at the top of their compass) represent a pained farewell to Romanticism; they were followed up only in the music of the Second Viennese School.

Symphonies no.1, D (1888); no.2, c–E♭, with S, A, mixed vv (1894); no.3, d, with A, women's vv, boys' vv (1896); no.4, G–E, with S (1900); no.5, c♯–D (1902); no.6, a (1904); no.7, e–C (1905); no.8, E♭, with 3S, 2A, T, Bar, B, boys' vv, mixed vv (1907); no.9, D–D♭ (1909); no.10, f♯/F♯, inc. (1910)
Songs (3) Lieder, T, pf (1880); Das klagende Lied, S, A, T, mixed vv, orch (1880); 15 Lieder und Gesänge, v, pf (1880–90); (4) Lieder eines fahrenden Gesellen, v, orch/pf (1885); Des Knaben Wunderhorn, v, pf/orch (1892–8); (5) Kindertotenlieder, v, orch (1904); (5) Rückert-Lieder, v, orch/pf (1901–2); Das Lied von der Erde, T, A/Bar, orch (1909)
Other works Pf Qt, a, inc. (?1876–8); Rübezahl, opera (?1879–83, lost)

Mahon. English family of musicians of Irish origin. John (c1749–1834), a famous clarinettist, did much to popularize the instrument in England; he also played the basset-horn, violin and viola and composed various pieces, mostly for clarinet. His brother William (c1751–1816) was similarly a pioneer on the clarinet and also played the oboe, violin and viola. Especially notable among their brothers and sisters was Sarah Second (c1767–1805), a soprano, who sang at Covent Garden and many festivals.

Maid of Orleans, The [Orleanskaya deva]. Opera in four acts by Tchaikovsky to his own libretto after Schiller (1881, St Petersburg).

Maid of Pskov, The [Pskovityanka]. Opera in four acts by Rimsky-Korsakov to his own libretto after L.A. Mey (1873, St Petersburg).

Maid of the Mill, The. *See* SCHÖNE MÜLLERIN, DIE.

Mainstream. Term coined in the 1950s to refer to music in the swing idiom; it is now used of any jazz based on the chord sequences of the style developed by Louis Armstrong and others in the late 1920s and has been extended to apply to jazz-rock and other fusion styles.

Mainzer, Joseph (*b* Trier, 21 Oct 1801; *d* Manchester, 10 Nov 1851). German teacher. He is best known for the free classes he opened in Paris (1835), London and Edinburgh (1841), in which hundreds of adults learnt to sing. His journal *Mainzer's Musical Times* (founded 1842) was taken over by Novello and in 1844 became *The Musical Times*.

Maistre Jhan [Jan, Jehan] (*b* c1485; *d* c1545). French composer. He was on the payroll of the Ferrarese court as early as 1512 and remained until 1543, serving as *maestro di cappella*. His madrigals, of which over 20 survive, are awkward in style when compared with those of Verdelot or Arcadelt, but he was nevertheless one of the 'founders' of this genre. His numerous motets show him a skilful emulator of Josquin; they reveal a preference for four-voice writing, imitative duets and occasional chordal writing. He also composed a large-scale *cantus firmus* mass for five voices.

Majo, Gian Francesco (de) (*b* Naples, 24 March 1732; *d* there, 17 Nov 1770). Italian composer. As a young man he worked in the Naples royal chapel. His first opera (1758, Parma) was a great success; others followed, including several in northern Italy (1761–2), where he studied with Padre Martini. Later he presented operas in Vienna, Madrid and elsewhere. He wrote 20 or more stage works, mostly *opere serie*. Like Jommelli and Traetta he (independently) approached Gluck's reforms of this genre, using more dramatic music, modifying aria form and giving the orchestra more importance. *Ifigenia in Tauride* (1764, Mannheim) has an overture related to the drama (anticipating Gluck) and many ensembles and choruses. But some works are more conventional. Majo also composed oratorios, cantatas and church music.

His father Giuseppe (1697–1771) served in the Naples royal chapel (*maestro di cappella* 1745); he composed mostly operas and sacred music.

Major. (1) The name given to a scale whose octave species is built of the following ascending sequence of intervals: T–T–S–T–T–T–S (T = tone, S = semitone). The note chosen to begin the sequence, the key note, becomes part of the name of the scale, i.e. the scale beginning on C is the scale of C major. A piece or passage whose melodic basis is a major scale (say, that on C) and whose harmonic basis is the major triad on the key note of that scale is said to be 'in C major'.

(2) A major INTERVAL is any one that can be reckoned between the key note of a major scale and a higher note in that scale, other than those called 'perfect' (the 4th, 5th and octave). A major TRIAD is a three-note chord which, reckoned from the lowest note, is built of a major 3rd and a perfect 5th.

Major [Mayer], **(Jakab) Gyula** [Julius] (*b* Košice, 13 Dec 1858; *d* Budapest, 30 Jan 1925). Hungarian composer and pianist. He studied the piano with Erkel and Liszt. His music combines a nationalistic melodic flavour and Germanic formalism, resolved most successfully in the prize-winning 'Hungarian' Symphony op.17 and the 'Hungarian' Piano Sonata op.35. Notable among his other works are the symphonic poem *Balaton* (1906) and the folk opera *Mila* (1913).

Maklakiewicz, Jan Adam (*b* Chojnata, 24 Nov 1889; *d* Warsaw, 7 Feb 1954). Polish composer. He studied with Statkowski at the Warsaw Conservatory (1922–5) and with Dukas in Paris, then was a conservatory teacher, church musician and critic in Warsaw. His works of 1928–32 make adventurous use of new techniques (Cello Concerto, 1930; Symphony no.2 with baritone and chorus, 1928). The later music is radically simpler (he wrote much church music in the 1930s).

Makropulos Affair, The [Věc Makropulos]. Opera in three acts by Janáček to his own libretto after Čapek (1926, Brno).

Maksymiuk, Jerzy (*b* Grodno, 9 April 1936). Polish conductor. He studied at Warsaw and had early sucess as a pianist. When conducting at the theatre, he was invited to form a chamber orchestra to play for the opera; this soon became independent as the Polish CO. He was also principal conductor of the Polish National RO, 1975–7. The Polish CO has toured widely in Europe, the USA, Japan and Australia and has appeared at many festivals and made recordings. In 1984 Maksymiuk was appointed chief conductor of the BBC Scottish SO.

Malagueña. Term, either for a fandango-type dance from Málaga and Murcia, or for an emotional, sensuous gypsy song on a repeated descending bass pattern. Stylized *malagueñas* were composed by Chabrier (*España*, 1883), Ravel (*Rapsodie espagnole*, 1908) and Albéniz (*Iberia*, 1909).

Malawski, Artur (*b* Przemysl, 4 July 1904; *d* Kraków, 26 Dec 1957). Polish composer. He studied with Sikorksi at the Warsaw Conservatory and taught at the Kraków Conservatory (1945–57). His earlier music was influenced by Szymanowski, but his works of 1945–50 are unusualy audacious for that time in Polish music (Overture, 1949; Toccata and Fugue in Variation Form for piano and orchestra, 1949). In his late works he adopted a dramatic, romantic expressiveness (e.g. Symphony no.2, 1956).

Malbecque, Guillaume (*b* c1400; *d* Soignies, 29 Aug 1465). Netherlands composer, evidently from the area of Maalbeck, north of Brussels. By November 1431 he had joined the chapel of Pope Eugene IV where he remained until 1438. From 1440 he was canon of St Vincent in Soignies. He apparently knew both Dufay and Binchois. The five songs ascribed to him display a great variety of compositional techniques and are equal to the best *chansons* of his contemporaries.

Malcolm, George (John) (*b* London, 28 Feb 1917). English harpsichordist. He studied at the RCM and Oxford and was Master of the Music at Westminster Cathedral, 1947–59, where he did much to develop a lively, forthright style. He has conducted orchestras but is best known as a harpsichordist, with a brilliant style that freely exploits the resources of the modern instrument.

Maldere, Pierre van (*b* Brussels, 16 Oct 1729; *d* there, 1 Nov 1768). South Netherlands composer. He played in the royal chapel at Brussels from 1746, later advancing to director. He travelled widely and presented operas in Vienna and Paris. In 1762–7 he was director of the Brussels Grand Theatre, for which he composed two comic operas (one in collaboration). His principal works are over 40 symphonies, which have a Classical three-movement form and orchestral style. His violin solo and trio sonatas show some Italian Baroque features.

Malec, Ivo (*b* Zagreb, 30 March 1925). Yugoslav composer. He studied at the Zagreb Academy and with Messiaen at the Paris Conservatoire, where he was appointed professor (1972). He has worked in the *musique concrète* studios, besides composing ballets, orchestral pieces etc, and was one of the first Yugoslav composers to make an international reputation.

Maler, Wilhelm (*b* Heidelberg, 21 June 1902; *d* Hamburg, 29 April 1976). German composer. A pupil of Grabner, Haas and Jarnach, he taught at the Musikhochschule in Cologne (from 1928) and Hamburg (1959–69), and wrote concertos, piano sonatas and choral works influenced by Reger and Busoni, but also by impressionist and folk elements. Under his leadership the Detmold Academy became a leading European music school.

Malgoire, Jean-Claude (*b* Avignon, 25 Nov 1940). French conductor and oboist. He is known chiefly for his work with the early music ensemble, LA GRANDE ECURIE ET LA CHAMBRE DU ROY, which he founded in 1966.

Malherbe, Charles (Théodore) (*b* Paris, 21 April 1853; *d* Cormeilles, 5 Oct 1911). French musicologist and composer. He was archivist-librarian of the Paris Opéra (from 1899) and a noteworthy collector of musical autographs (including Bach cantatas, Beethoven sketches and the *Symphonie fantastique*). Among his writings, the *Histoire de l'Opéra-Comique: la seconde salle Favart* (1892–3; with A. Soubies) and his historical notes for 16 volumes of Rameau's works are particularly useful.

Malibran [née Garcia], Maria(-Felicia) (*b* Paris, 24 March 1808; *d* Manchester, 23 Sept 1836). Spanish mezzo-soprano, sister of Pauline Viardot. She studied with her father, the tenor Manuel Garcia, whose harsh treatment prompted her to marry in order to escape. From 1828 to 1832 she sang alternately in Paris and London, then from 1833 in Italy and London, making her greatest impression in Bellini's *La sonnambula* and *Norma*. Renowned for the range and flexibility of her voice and unpredict-

able stage performances, she died at the height of her career, after a riding accident.

Malinconico (It.). Sad, melancholy.

Malipiero, Gian Francesco (*b* Venice, 18 March 1882; *d* Treviso, 1 Aug 1973). Italian composer. He studied with Bossi at the Licei Musicali in Venice (1899–1902) and Bologna (1904–5), and began transcribing the music of Monteverdi and other early Italians in 1902; he also learnt much from serving as amanuensis to Smareglia. In 1913 he visited Paris, where he formed a lasting friendship with Casella and heard *The Rite of Spring*: he then suppressed everything he had previously written. The influences of Stravinsky and particularly Debussy were to remain fundamental, and they gave rise to his first masterpieces: the orchestral *Pause del silenzio I* (1917), the ballet *Pantea* (1919, perf. 1932) and the seven miniature operas *Sette canzoni* (1919).

In 1924 he retired to Asolo in the Veneto and in 1926 embarked on his complete Monteverdi edition, while continuing to compose copiously. Archaic and contemporary elements were combined in the operas, his main works of the 1920s, including *San Francesco d'Assisi* (1922) and *Torneo notturno* (1931). His enormous later output includes more operas, orchestral music, eight string quartets and vocal pieces. He was the most original and inventive Italian composer of his generation.

His nephew Riccardo (*b* 1914) is a composer who has taught in Italy and abroad, and written 12-note works in many genres.

Operas L'orfeide (1925); Tre commedie goldoniane (1926); Torneo notturno (1931); Giulio Cesare (1936); Antonio e Cleopatra (1938); I capricci di Callot (1942); Vergilii Aeneis (1958); Venere prigioniera (1957); *c*32 others
Ballets Pantea (1932); 5 others
Choral music La cena (1927); La Passione (1935); *c*11 others
Vocal music 8 works with orch; 4 with ens; 13 with pf
Orchestral music 11 syms. (1933–69); 6 pf concs. (1934–64); 2 vn concs. (1932, 1963); Impressioni dal vero (1911–22); Pause del silenzio (1917–26); Concerti (1931); others
Chamber music 8 str qts (1920–64); *c*22 other pieces
Piano music *c*30 pieces

Maliszewski, Witold (*b* Mohylew on the Dniestr, 20 July 1873; *d* Zlesie, 18 July 1939). Polish composer. He studied with Rimsky-Korsakov at the St Petersburg Conservatory (1898–1902) and taught at the conservatories of Odessa (1908–21) and Warsaw (1931–9). His greatest achievements were in sacred and orchestral music (four symphonies, 1902, 1903, 1907, 1925).

Malko, Nikolay (Andreyevich) (*b* Brailov, 4 May 1883; *d* Sydney, 23 June 1961). American conductor of Russian birth. He studied with Rimsky-Korsakov at St Petersburg, where he conducted stage works from 1908. He taught and conducted in Moscow and was chief conductor of the Leningrad PO, 1926–9. From 1929 he appeared widely in Europe, notably with the Danish State RO. In 1940 he settled in Chicago, appearing as guest conductor with American orchestras; later he conducted the Yorkshire SO (1954) and the Sydney SO (1957).

Mallarmé, Stéphane (*b* Paris, 18 March 1842; *d* Valvins, 9 Sept 1898). French poet. His poem *L'après-midi d'un faune* inspired Debussy's orchestral piece, and Boulez's *Pli selon pli* (1957–62) uses both his words and the elusive atmosphere of his poetry.

Malling, Otto (Valdemar) (*b* Copenhagen, 1 June 1848; *d* there, 5 Oct 1915). Danish composer. Organist in several Copenhagen churches, he wrote a long series of Romantic character-pieces for organ (1892–1910) as well as orchestral and chamber works, also teaching at the Copenhagen Conservatory (from 1885; director from 1899).

Malvezzi, Cristofano (*b* Lucca, bap. 28 June 1547; *d* Florence, 22 Jan 1599). Italian composer. He lived in Florence from 1551, serving the Medici family at S Lorenzo as a canon from 1562. He became organist of S Trinità in 1565, *maestro di cappella* jointly of the cathedral and S Giovanni Battista in 1573 and organist of S Lorenzo in 1574. Peri was his pupil. He wrote music for Florentine *intermedi* (1583–9), editing for publication the famous one of 1589, as well as instrumental ricercares (1577) and madrigals (3 bks, 1583–90). His brother Alberigo (*c*1550–1615) was also an organist and composer.

Mamangakis, Nicos (*b* Rethymnon, Crete, 3 March 1929). Greek composer. He studied with Orff and Genzmer at the Munich Musikhochschule (1957–64), and has used both avant-garde techniques and a popular style; the social and political criticism found in his lighter music has made his reputation in Greece.

Mambo. A dance of the 1940s, of Cuban origins. It is in a fairly quick 4/4 time, to music characterized by ostinato and riff passages for wind instruments.

Mamelles de Tirésias, Les. Opera in two acts by Poulenc to a libretto by Apollinaire (1947, Paris).

Ma mère l'oye. *See* MOTHER GOOSE.

Mamiya, Michio (*b* Asahikawa, 29 June 1929). Japanese composer. A pupil of Ikenouchi (1947–52), he has collected and arranged folk music. His compositions draw on it and since 1963 also on African music and jazz. His works include dramatic, choral and orchestral pieces, some for Japanese instruments.

Mancando (It.). Growing quieter, dying away.

Manchicourt, Pierre de (*b* Béthune, *c*1510; *d* Madrid, 5 Oct 1564). Franco-Flemish composer. A choirboy at Arras Cathedral (1525) he was choirmaster at Tours (1539) and Tournai (1545) cathedrals, and, from 1559, master of Philip II's Flemish chapel in Madrid. Of his many motets, the earliest have the attenuated lines and full textures of Ockeghem and the shorter phrases and voice-pairings of Josquin, while the later ones are closer to Gombert in combining elegant melody with constant imitation. He also composed many masses and Parisian *chansons*.

Mancinelli, Luigi (*b* Orvieto, 5 Feb 1848; *d* Rome, 2 Feb 1921). Italian conductor and composer. The leading Italian conductor of the generation between Faccio and Toscanini, he was an immediate success from his début in *Aida* (Perugia, 1874), soon working at the Teatro Apollo, Rome (1874–80), and in Bologna (1881–6); chief conductorships at the Madrid opera (1887–93), Covent Garden (1888–1905) and the new Metropolitan in New York (1893–1903) followed, though in later years, as the Wagner repertory began to be sung in German, he confined his activities to Italy, South America, Spain and Portugal. He was an authoritarian, charismatic figure who put great emphasis on fidelity to the score and championed the German classics. As a composer he never fulfilled the promise of his early incidental music for *Cleopatra* (1877) and the opera *Isora di Provenza* (1884).

Mancini, Francesco (*b* Naples, 16 Jan 1672; *d* there, 22 Sept 1737). Italian composer. He was organist at the Turchini Conservatory in Naples, then in 1704 first organist at the court; he served as music director, 1707–8 and 1725–37 (succeeding A. Scarlatti). In 1720–35 he directed the Conservatorio di S Maria di Loreto. Most active as a composer *c*1702–23, he wrote *c*20 operas, over 200 secular cantatas, liturgical music, oratorios and serenatas. His style combines Baroque counterpoint with more progressive melodic ideas.

Mancini Codex. Italian MS of the early 15th century. It consists of 42 folios and contains 76 secular pieces (50 of them ballatas) of the period 1365–1430, by Ciconia and others. It is in the hand of one main scribe and comes from the Lucca and Padua areas; called after A. Mancini, who discovered it in 1938, it is in two parts, of which 33 folios are at the Archivo di Stato, Lucca, and six at the Biblioteca Comunale, Perugia.

Mancinus, Thomas (*b* Schwerin, 1550; *d* there, 1611/12). German composer. He was a Kantor at Schwerin and Kapellmeister at Gröningen before founding the Hofkantorei (court music college) at Wolfenbüttel in 1589. He retired in 1604. Though best known for his two simple, dramatic Passions (before 1602), he also published motets (1608), secular songs (1588) and bicinia (1597).

Mander, Noel (Percy) (*b* Crouch, 19 May 1912). English organ builder and restorer. His new and rebuilt organs, chiefly mechanical-action instruments, combine traditional English methods with neoclassical elements. Among his most important are those in St Paul's Cathedral (1972–7), Canterbury Cathedral (1978–9), Corpus Christi College, Cambridge (1969), and St Giles, Cripplegate, London (1968–9).

Mandini, Stefano (*b* 1750; *d* ?*c*1810). Italian baritone. He was a leading member of Joseph II's Italian opera company in Vienna, 1783–6, and created Count Almaviva in Mozart's *Le nozze di Figaro* (1786). Later he sang in Paris and St Petersburg. His wife was the soprano Maria Mandini (*fl* 1780s), the first Marcellina in *Le nozze di Figaro*. His brother Paolo (1757–1842), a tenor, sang in Haydn's company at Eszterháza, 1783–4, and later in Vienna.

Mandolin. A plucked string instrument with a fingerboard and a rounded body. The body is either carved from solid wood or (since the 17th century) built up like a lute. The pegbox is usually curved. (For illustration, *see* LUTE.)

'Mandore' and 'mandola', terms found from 1570, were used for larger instruments with six to eight courses in Germany and Italy; small mandores had four or five strings, single or partly paired, typically tuned $c'-g'-c''-g''$ or $c-f-c'-f'-c''$. This instrument, which persisted in Italy, was usually called 'mandola' or (standard by the 18th century) 'mandolino'; it was tuned in 4ths, $b-e'-a'-d''-g''$, strung with gut and plucked with the fingers or a quill plectrum. The modern four-course mandolin or 'Neapolitan mandolin' goes back to the mid-18th century; it has a deep body and an angled soundboard with florid decoration, and is tuned like a violin, $g-d'-a'-e''$, and played with a plectrum.

Repertory for the mandore goes back to the late 16th century. Parts for the five- or six-course instrument began to appear in concerted music and opera in the late 17th century. Vivaldi wrote concertos for one and two mandolins, probably the six-course instrument, and Telemann and Albrechtsberger composed for the large German mandore. It is probably the 'Neapolitan' four-course instrument that Mozart called for in the *Don Giovanni* serenade and that Beethoven and Hummel used. Verdi used the mandolin for atmosphere in *Otello* and *Falstaff*, as did Mahler in three works and Schoenberg in two. It has become popular as a 'folk' instrument in the USA, Latin America (*bandolín, bandolim*) and Japan.

Mandore (It. *mandola, pandora*; Sp. *bandurria*). A name used from the 16th century for a family of small plucked string instruments with a rounded body. Larger instruments that developed in Germany and Italy from the later 17th century were termed 'mandore' or 'mandola' and the smaller ones 'mandolin' or 'mandolino'. *See also* MANDOLIN.

Mandurria. *See* BANDURRIA.

Mandyczewski, Eusebius (*b* Chernovtsy, 17 Aug 1857; *d* Vienna, 13 July 1929). Romanian musicologist. At Vienna University he studied with Hanslick and Notebohm. In 1879 he met Brahms, who became a lifelong friend and to whom he became amanuensis. As director of the Gesellschaft der Musikfreunde archives, he was concerned with the Schubert Gesamtausgabe (editing the songs, 10 vols., 1887–97) and with a second volume of Nottebohm's pioneering *Beethoveniana* (1887).

Manén, Juan (*b* Barcelona, 14 March 1883; *d* there, 26 June 1971). Spanish violinist and composer. He began touring internationally in 1892. He was a self-taught composer of operas, violin music etc and author of several books.

Manfred. Incidental music by Schumann, op.115, for Byron's verse drama (1849).

Symphony (unnumbered) by Tchaikovsky, after Byron (1885).

Manfredini, Francesco Onofrio (*b* Pistoia, bap. 22 June 1684; *d* there, 6 Oct 1762). Italian composer. A violin pupil of Torelli in Bologna, he joined the S Petronio orchestra there in 1704 after a period in Ferrara. Later he probably served at the Monaco court; by 1727 he was *maestro di cappella* at St Philip's Cathedral, Pistoia. He composed oratorios and instrumental works, mainly in the Bolognese idiom of Torelli.

Manfredini, Vincenzo (*b* Pistoia, 22 Oct 1737; *d* St Petersburg, 16 Aug 1799). Italian theorist and composer, son of F.O. Manfredini. He served at St Petersburg, and in 1762–5 directed the court opera

company, composing several operas, ballets, cantatas and other works. He returned to Bologna in 1769, where he was engaged in theoretical controversies on singing (with Mancini) and opera reform (with Arteaga). When his former pupil became tsar, he returned to St Petersburg, in 1798. His output includes harpsichord sonatas, string quartets and symphonies.

Mangolt, Burk (*fl* early 15th century). Squire and minstrel. A citizen of Bregenz, he was employed by the poet Hugo von Montfort to set his verse to music. The ten extant melodies ascribed to him are preserved in a beautifully-worked MS of Montfort's poetry, which may have been worked by Mangolt himself. His melodic style has been compared with that of Oswald von Wolkenstein.

Manhattan School of Music. Conservatory in New York, founded in 1917 as the Neighborhood Music School. Its facilities include the Martinson Electronic Music Laboratory.

Manieren (Ger.: 'manners'). Embellishment, including free ornamentation and specific ornaments, especially the latter.

Mann, Arthur Henry (*b* Norwich, 16 May 1850; *d* Cambridge, 19 Nov 1929). English organist and choir trainer. As organist and choirmaster of King's College, Cambridge (1876–1929), he transformed the chapel choir from one of the worst into the most famous Anglican choir in the world.

Mann, William S(omervell) (*b* Madras, 14 Feb 1924). English music critic. He studied in London and Cambridge, and in 1948 joined *The Times*, becoming chief music critic (1960–82). He is a fluent and direct writer whose work ranges widely and includes studies of the operas of Richard Strauss (1964) and Mozart (1977).

Manna, Gennaro (*b* Naples, 12 Dec 1715; *d* there, 28 Dec 1779). Italian composer. A nephew of Feo, he was *maestro di cappella* of Naples Cathedral from 1744 and later also of Ss Annunziata. He composed 13 stage works (mostly *opere serie*) for Italian theatres, 1742–61, oratorios and over 150 other sacred works. Independent instrumental parts are a feature of his output. Other composers in Manna's family include his cousin Cristoforo (*b* 1704) and his nephew Gaetano (1751–1804), his successor at Ss Annunziata and *secondo maestro* of the cathedral, who wrote sacred music.

Mannelli, Carlo (*b* Rome, 4 Nov 1640; *d* there, 6 Jan 1697). Italian composer. A soprano (castrato) singer and violinist, he was Corelli's predecessor at S Luigi dei Francesi in Rome and a member of the Congregazione di S Cecilia. As a violinist he forms a stylistic link between Caproli and Corelli. Mannelli's surviving music includes a piece for violin and continuo which makes extensive use of double stopping, and some technically demanding trio sonatas (1682–92) notable for their cantabile slow movements and fugal allegros. His violin tutor is lost.

Mannerism. Term borrowed from art criticism to stand for aspects of the style of the later 16th century and the early 17th in which striking effects (in particular, harmonic ones) to illustrate particular textual points, usually in a madrigal, take precedence over broader treatment of musical form. Composers considered mannerist include Willaert, Rore and above all Gesualdo; some of the works of Marenzio and Monteverdi may also be seen as in this category.

Mannes College of Music. Conservatory in New York. Founded in 1916 as the David Mannes School by Mannes and his wife (formerly Clara Damrosch), it was the first music school in the USA to offer a degree course in the performance of early music.

Mannheim School. A group of composers who worked at Mannheim, in the employ of the Elector of the Palatinate Carl Theodor (reigned at Mannheim 1742–78). They were assembled by the musical director, Johann Stamitz, and included many outstanding figures, such as Cannabich, Fils, the Toeschis, Stamitz's sons, Fränzl, Wendling and the Lebruns; Holzbauer was Kapellmeister, 1753–78. Burney called them 'an army of generals equally fit to plan a battle as to fight it'; Schubart wrote that 'no orchestra in the world has ever excelled the Mannheim'. The orchestra developed a new range of effects which the Mannheim composers exploited, especially in their symphonies. Their crescendo was particularly famous; so were the 'Mannheim sigh' (an appoggiatura figure) and the 'Mannheim rocket' (a leaping triad). Mozart and other composers were influenced by the Mannheim School, who made important contributions to the development of the orchestra and the history of the symphony.

Manns, Sir August (*b* Stolzenberg, 12 March 1825; *d* London; 1 March 1907). German, later British conductor. As conductor at the Crystal Palace, with George Grove, he made the adventurous Saturday Concerts (1855–1901) the principal source of classical music at popular prices.

Manon. Opera in five acts by Massenet to a libretto by Meilhac and P. Gille after Prévost (1884, Paris).

Manon Lescaut. Opera in four acts by Puccini to a libretto by Leoncavallo, Praga, Oliva, Illica and Giacosa after Prévost (1893, Turin).

Mantra. Work by Stockhausen for two amplified, ring-modulated pianos with woodblock and crotales (played by the pianists) (1970).

Mantzaros [Halikiopoulos], **Nicolaos** (*b* Corfu, 26 Oct 1795; *d* there, 30 March 1872). Greek composer and teacher. The first important modern Greek composer, he is considered father of the Ionian School. He taught in Corfu and founded the Corfu Società Filarmonica (his role in organizing musical life affected the whole of Greece). He collected folksongs, wrote treatises and composed numerous conservative works. Part of one of his 'Hymn to liberty' settings became the Greek national anthem.

Manual. A KEYBOARD played by the hands (in contrast to one played by the feet; *see* PEDAL). *Manualiter*, a quasi-Latin term derived from *manualis* ('hand keyboard'), indicates that a piece of organ music so labelled is played on manuals only, as distinct from *pedaliter*.

Manualiter. Term used to indicate that a piece of organ music should be played on manuals only, not with pedals; it was chiefly used in Germany in the Baroque period.

Manuel, Roland. *See* ROLAND-MANUEL.

Manziarly, Marcelle de (*b* Kharkov, 13 Oct 1899). French composer. She was a pupil of Boulanger. Her works, in many genres, use modal extensions to diatonic harmony. She has appeared internationally as a pianist.

Manzoni, Giacomo (*b* Milan, 26 Sept 1932). Italian composer. He studied in Messina, Milan and at Darmstadt (1956–7) and, like Nono, has been directed in his musical radicalism by left-wing sympathies. His works include operas on political subjects and instrumental music, using many techniques including electronics. He has translated several books by Adorno and Schoenberg and edited and contributed to musical journals.

Manzoni Requiem. Title sometimes used for Verdi's Requiem (1874), written in memory of Alessandro Manzoni.

Mapleson, James Henry (*b* London, 4 May 1830; *d* there, 14 Nov 1901). English impresario. From 1861 to 1889 he managed opera seasons intermittently at the Lyceum, Her Majesty's Theatre, Drury Lane and Covent Garden, giving many English premières, including those of *Faust, Carmen* and *La forza del destino*.

Maqām. Arabic term for a melodic mode: each *maqām* consists of a selection of notes (sometimes involving quarter-tone intervals) from which melodies may be drawn, observing the particular sequences, cadences and motifs appropriate to it.

Mara [née Schmeling], **Gertrud Elisabeth** (*b* Kassel, 23 Feb 1749; *d* Tallinn, 20 Jan 1833). German soprano. After singing in Hiller's Leipzig concerts, she served in the Berlin opera, 1771–9, marrying the cellist Mara. Later she appeared in Germany, Italy and elsewhere, but was most successful in London (1784–1802), especially in concerts and oratorios: she was a bravura singer, noted for her sound technique, beautiful tone and professional high-handedness.

Maracas. A pair of gourd rattles, usually oval; the gourds contain the dried seeds of the fruit. Imitations are made in modern materials containing rattling objects. Maracas, probably of South American Indian origin, are part of the rhythm section of Latin American bands and have been adopted by Western rhythm bands and orchestral percussion. Composers writing for maracas include Varèse (*Ionisation*, 1934) and Prokofiev (*Romeo and Juliet*, 1935). Maracas have been used as 'drumsticks', for example in Leonard Bernstein's *Jeremiah Symphony* (1942).

Marais, Marin (*b* Paris, 31 May 1656; *d* there, 15 Aug 1728). French composer. The central figure in the French bass viol school, he spent his life in Paris, much of it in royal service. A pupil of Sainte-Colombe and protégé of Lully, he composed four operas (1693–1709 – notably *Alcione*, 1706, famous for its storm scene) that form an important link between Lully and Campra. But his greatest significance lies in his five collections of music for one to three bass viols (1686–1725), comprising over 550 pieces. As well as the usual dances, they include character pieces that are among his finest works, and they possess an eloquence and refinement of line and richness of ornamental detail that perfectly display the qualities of his instrument. The *Pieces en trio* (1692) are recognized as the first appearance of the trio sonata in France.

Marazzoli, Marco (*b* ?Parma, *c*1602–8; *d* Rome, 26 Jan 1662). Italian composer. After a period as a priest and singer at Parma Cathedral, he served in Rome as a tenor in the papal chapel from 1637; he was also associated with the Barberini family. Several of his operas were successfully staged in Rome, notably the comic *Chi soffre speri* (1639), a revision with Virgilio Mazzocchi of the latter's *Il falcone* (1637). He also presented operas in Ferrara, Venice and Paris (1643). The comic opera *Dal male il bene* (1653, Rome), which he composed with Antonio Maria Abbatini, was staged after the Barberinis returned from exile in France.

Marazzoli was one of the most versatile and gifted composers of vocal music in the Italy of his day. Of the eight or more operas wholly or partly by him, *Chi soffre speri* and *Dal male il bene* are remembered as the earliest comic operas; he also played a part in the development of *secco* recitative and the ensemble finale. He wrote over 350 cantatas (mostly for one or two solo voices and continuo), lyrical works in a wide variety of styles and forms. His sacred output includes some ten oratorios (Latin and Italian), four Italian oratorio-dialogues and a few church compositions.

Marcabru (*b* Gascony, ?1100–10; *fl* 1128–50). Provençal troubadour. He is one of the earliest troubadours for whom music survives and he clearly enjoyed a considerable reputation with his successors. Biographical details found in his works point to service at the court of Guillaume X of Aquitaine (who ruled 1127–37), a period seeking work in Portugal and Barcelona, leading to employment with Alfonso VII of Castile, and in 1144 a return to Provence where he composed the song *Cortazamen voill comensar* (inspired by the preparations for the second crusade), the last work to contain biographical information. The 43 *chansons* attributed to Marcabru are remarkable for the complexity of their texts, most of which discuss the niceties of courtly love, in comparison with the simple melodies to which they are set.

Marcato (It.). Marked, stressed, accented.

Marcello, Alessandro [Stinfalico, Eterio] (*b* Venice, 1684; *d* there, 1750). Italian composer. He was a dilettante musician and held concerts at his home in Venice. His compositions include solo cantatas, arias, canzonets, violin sonatas and concertos. His six concertos *La cetra* (*c*1740) are unusual for their wind solo parts, concision and use of counterpoint within a broadly Vivaldian style, placing them as a last outpost of the classic Venetian Baroque concerto. Bach transcribed the Oboe Concerto in D minor (*c*1717) for harpsichord.

Marcello, Benedetto (*b* Venice, 1/2 Aug 1686; *d* Brescia, 24/25 July 1739). Italian composer and writer, brother of Alessandro Marcello. He held important posts in the public service and was also an advocate, magistrate and teacher. He achieved international fame with his 50 psalm settings in can-

tata style, *Estro poetico-armonico* (1724–6), and composed other church music, oratorios and stage works, over 400 solo cantatas, duets etc, and several sets of sonatas, concertos and sinfonias (influenced by Vivaldi). His output is characterized by imagination and a fine technique and includes both counterpoint and progressive, *galant* features. Notable among his writings is the celebrated satire on contemporary opera, *Il teatro alla moda* (*c*1720).

March. Music for marching is essentially an ornamentation of a regular and repeated drum rhythm. The earliest extant military marches are those by Lully and André Philidor *l'aîné* for the bands of Louis XIV. Many early military marches were adapted from popular tunes. The French Revolution and Napoleonic wars lent a new impetus to the genre; marches for particular regiments and armies were composed by Cherubini, Hummel, Beethoven and others. Most of the marches now in the military band repertory were written between 1880 and 1914, among the most original and lasting being those of J.P. Sousa and K.J. Alford.

The march seems to have entered art music through Lully's operas and ballets, and processional marches appear in operas by Handel, Mozart, Verdi, Wagner and others. March music for keyboard can be traced back at least to Byrd's *Battell*; the piano literature of the 19th century includes many marches, e.g. those of Schubert, Schumann and Chopin. Marches introduce and conclude many 18th-century serenade-type works, representing the players' entry and departure. Haydn wrote a march as the slow movement of his 'Military' Symphony, no.100, the fourth movement of Berlioz's *Symphonie fantastique* is a 'Marche au supplice', and funeral marches are included in Beethoven's Third Symphony and Mahler's First. Examples of orchestral marches intended as separate concert pieces include Liszt's Rakoczy march and the five *Pomp and Circumstance* marches of Elgar.

Marchal, André(-Louis) (*b* Paris, 6 Feb 1894; *d* St Jean-de-Luz, 27 Aug 1980). French organist. Blind from birth, he studied at Paris Conservatoire and was organist at St Germain-des-Prés (1915–45) and St Eustache (1945–63). He gave his first recital in 1923 and toured widely in Europe and North America, gaining fame as a colourist and for his skill in improvisation. He took a leading part in the revival of French classical organ building.

Marchand, Heinrich (Wilhelm Philipp) (*b* Mainz, 4 May 1769; *d* after 1812). German keyboard player and composer. A pupil and protégé of Leopold Mozart, he played the keyboard and violin at the Salzburg court (1786–8) and later at Regensburg. He also made concert tours and composed keyboard music. His sister Margarethe (1768–1800), a singer, married Franz Danzi; his father Theobald Hilarius (1741–1800), a singer and actor, directed the German National Theatre at Mannheim (later at Munich) from 1775.

Marchand, Louis (*b* Lyons, 2 Feb 1669; *d* Paris, 17 Feb 1732). French harpsichordist, organist and composer. He settled in Paris by 1689, becoming organist at several churches (including the Cordeliers) and a much admired virtuoso. From 1708 he was an *organiste du roi*. He toured Germany, 1713–17, but failed to appear in a planned contest with J.S. Bach in Dresden (1717). Afterwards he returned to the Cordeliers and became famous as a teacher. Foremost in his output are organ pieces and harpsichord suites, all early works. He also wrote an opera, cantatas, *airs* and a composition treatise.

Marchand, (Simon-)Luc (*b* 31 May 1709; *d* 27 April 1799). French composer. He was an organist and lutenist at the French court until 1761, and also a violinist. He was among the first (1748) to write accompanied keyboard music. His grandfather Jean (1636–91) was a violinist at the French court, and his father Jean-Baptiste (1670–1751) a lutenist. Jean-Noël (1666–1710), Jean-Baptiste's brother, was a player in the royal chapel, organist of Notre Dame de Versailles, and a composer; his sons included Jean-Noël (1689–1740/57), a musician, and his half-brother Guillaume (1694–1738), an organist in the royal chapel.

Marchesi. Italian family of singers. The most celebrated members were Salvatore (1822–1908), a baritone, and his wife Mathilde (de Castrone) Marchesi [née Graumann] (1821–1913), a German mezzo-soprano and singing teacher. She taught in Vienna, Cologne and Paris (where she opened her own school), working with, among others, Emma Calvé, Mary Garden, Nellie Melba and her own daughter Blanche Marchesi (1863–1940).

Marchesi [Marchesini], Luigi (*b* Milan, ?8 Aug 1755; *d* there, 14–18 Dec 1829). Italian castrato. One of Italy's foremost singers, he appeared in operas from 1773 and travelled widely, notably to St Petersburg (1785–6) and London (1788–90); he was especially associated with the composers Bianchi and Sarti. He composed songs, arias and duets.

Marchetti, Filippo (*b* Bolognola, Macerata, 26 Feb 1831; *d* Rome, 18 Jan 1902). Italian composer. He studied at the Naples Conservatory. Of the seven operas he composed in 1856–80 only *Ruy Blas* (1869) won real fame, with its Spanish colouring, melodic delicacy and effective orchestration. But his work represents a point of transition on the line towards the *verismo* of Puccini.

Marchetto da Padova (*b* Padua, ?1274; *fl* 1305–26). Italian theorist and composer. He was *maestro di canto* at Padua Cathedral, 1305–7, and left his home town the following year. He composed motets but was best known for his three treatises: *Lucidarium* (1309–18), *Pomerium* (1318–26) and *Brevis compilacio* (essentially a summary of *Pomerium*). The first two were written with the help of a Dominican friar, suggesting that Marchetto was not a scholar, but a musician who wanted to codify his practical experience. The *Lucidarium* is largely concerned with oral teaching. It presents traditional ideas on the definition and origins of music and explains the Gregorian tones. This material is largely based on other authors; more original is the section on intervals and consonances where he rejects the accepted Pythagorean system to propose a division of the tone into five equal parts – a theory that aroused much controversy, initiating a polemic which lasted until the late 15th century. The *Pomerium* provides a detailed discussion of mensural music and concludes with a definition of discant, the rules for ligatures and an exposition of the rhythmic modes, based on Franco but going beyond him. His system was never widely adopted, but his authority was long respected.

Marcuse, Sibyl (*b* Frankfurt, 13 Feb 1911). American musicologist. Of Swiss and English parentage, she emigrated to the USA. She studied in New York and in 1950 established herself as a harpsichord and piano technician, soon gaining a reputation as an organologist. She published two reference books, *Musical Instruments: a Comprehensive Dictionary* (1964), which defines and describes individual instruments, and *A Survey of Musical Instruments* (1975), a historical survey by groups.

Marcussen. Danish firm of organ builders. It was founded in 1806 by Jürgen Marcussen (1781–1860). Among its organs are those in St Nicholas, Copenhagen (1930), St Oscar, Stockholm (1949), Lübeck Cathedral (1970) and the Nieuwe Kerk, Amsterdam (restoration, 1981). The firm was one of the first to return to the sonic, structural and technical principles of the Baroque organ.

Marenzio, Luca (*b* Coccaglio, 1553–4; *d* Rome, 22 Aug 1599). Italian composer. Possibly a pupil of Contino in Brescia, he moved to Rome in *c*1574 and served cardinals and other wealthy patrons (including Luigi d'Este) until 1586. During these years he published copiously and gained an international reputation. He travelled in 1587, visiting Verona, and briefly served Ferdinando de' Medici in Florence, where in 1589 he composed *intermedi* for the ducal wedding festivities. He returned to Rome later that year, residing with the Duke of Bracciano until *c*1593, when he entered Cardinal Cinzio Aldobrandini's service; he held a Vatican apartment in 1594. In 1595–6 he visited the Polish court, returning to Rome in 1598.

One of the most prolific madrigalists of the period, Marenzio published over 400 madrigals and villanellas in at least 23 books (1580–99). They range widely, from light pastorals to serious sonnets (these mostly from later years), and are notable for their striking mood- and word-painting. They long remained popular in Italy and elsewhere, especially England. His motets, though less well known, also feature much verbal imagery and religious symbolism.

Secular vocal music over 400 madrigals; *c*80 villanellas
Sacred vocal music *c*75 motets

Mareš, Jan Antonín (*b* Chotěboř, 1719; *d* St Petersburg, 30 May 1794). Czech horn player and music director. He worked at the St Petersburg court from 1748 and established a band of 36 single-note horns, for which he wrote and arranged music; it was the model for later Russian horn bands.

Marescalchi, Luigi (*b* Bologna, 1 Feb 1745; *d* after 1805). Italian music publisher and composer. In the early 1770s he issued *c*60 vocal and instrumental publications in Venice, then concentrated on composition, writing operas and many ballets, before establishing a music-printing concern in Naples (1786–99) protected by royal privilege.

Maria Antonia Walpurgis, Electress of Saxony (*b* Munich, 18 July 1724; *d* Dresden, 23 April 1780). German princess and amateur musician. The wife of Elector Friedrich Christian of Saxony, she was an important artistic patron (notably of Hasse) at Dresden, and a fine singer and keyboard player. She composed two operas and other works, and was also a poet and painter.

Maria di Rohan. Opera in three acts by Donizetti to a libretto by Cammarano (1843, Vienna).

Maria Golovin. Opera in three acts by Menotti to his own libretto (1958, Brussels).

Mariani, Angelo (Maurizio Gaspare) (*b* Ravenna, 11 Oct 1821; *d* Genoa, 13 June 1873). Italian conductor and composer. After his début as an instrumental composer in 1843 he turned to conducting opera, having his first great success with Verdi's *I due Foscari* (Milan, 1846) and *Nabucco* (1847). From 1852 he worked mainly in Genoa at the Teatro Carlo Felice, and in Bologna at the Teatro Comunale, where he gave many successful Wagner and Verdi performances, notably the *Don Carlo* of 1867. Though his skill and dedication to each opera as 'theatre' drew praise from Verdi, Meyerbeer, Rossini and Wagner, he became estranged from Verdi after 1869.

Maria Stuarda. Opera in three acts by Donizetti to a libretto by G. Bardari after Schiller (1835, Milan).

Maria Theresa. Haydn's Symphony no.48 in C, probably composed in the late 1760s.

Mariazell. Haydn's Mass in C, HXXII:8 (1782), also sometimes known as Missa Cellensis.

Marić, Ljubica (*b* Kragujevac, 18 March 1909). Yugoslav composer. She studied at the Prague Conservatory with Suk and Hába and taught at the Belgrade Academy (1945–67). Her works include a cycle in Orthodox church modes (1958) and a much-praised cantata, *The Songs of Space* (1956).

Marie, Jean-Etienne (*b* Pont-l'Evêque, 22 Nov 1917). French composer. He studied with Messiaen at the Paris Conservatoire (1947–50) and has worked with electronics and new instruments, exploring microtones: one of his pieces uses thirdtones, *Ecce ancilla Domini* for 32 strings (1973) uses a quarter-tone note row.

Marienleben, Das. Songs by Hindemith, settings for voice and piano of 15 texts by Rilke (1923); Hindemith orchestrated six of them.

Mariés de la tour Eiffel, Les. Ballet in one act by five of Les Six (not Durey) to a libretto by Cocteau (1921, Paris).

Mariétan, Pierre (*b* Monthey, 23 Sept 1935). Swiss composer. He studied with Zimmermann and Koenig in Cologne (1960–62), at Darmstadt and with Stockhausen and Boulez in Basle (1961–3). In the mid-1960s he turned from a Boulezian style towards guided improvisation. He has conducted contemporary music throughout Europe.

Mariinsky Theatre. *See* KIROV THEATRE.

Marimba. Term for a group of idiophones, some of which are plucked (lamellaphones) and some struck (xylophones), found in Africa (mainly Central and Southern) and Latin America; it is also a modern orchestral instrument. With calabash-resonated instruments, the calabashes are individually tuned to the pitch of each key. Manufacture of the modern orchestral marimba began in the USA in 1910; its compass is normally about $c-c'''$ or higher (bass instruments may have a compass $C-c'$). The xylorimba (or marimba-xylophone) has an extended compass, $C-c''''$. Composers such as Grainger, Milhaud, Orff and Messiaen have written for a marimba; Berg, Dallapiccola, Messiaen and Gerhard have used the xylorimba. In the mid-20th century Harry Partch constructed five tuned idiophones, four of which form a family based on the traditional marimba principle of rectangular blocks mounted over resonators and struck with mallets.

In Africa the terms *mbila* and *mbira* represent instruments of the marimba type; *sanza* represents the lamellaphone sub-type.

Marimbaphone. A steel marimba introduced *c*1920, now obsolete. Percy Grainger was one of the few composers to call for it.

Marine-shell trumpet. *See* CONCH-SHELL TRUMPET.

Marine trumpet. *See* TRUMPET MARINE.

Marini, Biagio (*b* Brescia, *c*1587; *d* Venice, 1663). Italian composer. He was a nephew of Giacinto Bondioli. He first worked at St Mark's, Venice, as a violinist under Monteverdi (from 1615), and was an instrumentalist at the Parma court in 1621–3. He then served, part of the time as Kapellmeister, at the court at Neuburg an die Donau, but travelled to other countries. From 1649 he worked in Italy; latterly he lived in Brescia and Venice. Marini is an important figure in the early development of the violin and the sonata. Instrumental music is foremost in his output. In his op.8 collection (1629) there is a clear distinction between sonatas and sinfonias, and some of the sonatas in his last book, op.22 (1655), are progressive in being divided into separate sections. His works also show advances in idiomatic string writing. Among his vocal works are both sacred and secular pieces.

Marino, Carlo Antonio (*b* ?Albino, *c*1670; *d* ?there, *c*1717). Italian violinist, cellist and composer. Employed as a violinist at S Maria Maggiore, Bergamo, and much in demand among north Italian opera orchestras, he composed amorous, often humorous solo cantatas but was better known for his instrumental chamber music: a set of solo violin sonatas (1705) and three of church sonatas remarkable for their fresh and lively melodic invention and their elaborate cello parts.

Marinuzzi, Gino (*b* Palermo, 24 March 1882; *d* Milan, 17 Aug 1945). Italian conductor and composer. After study in Palermo he gained a wide reputation as a fervent conductor of Wagner and Strauss, giving *Parsifal* at Buenos Aires in 1913. In Monte Carlo, Rome and London he was admired in Puccini. He wrote three operas and a symphony. His son Gino (*b* 1920) has conducted opera and ballet in Rome and written film and orchestral music.

Mario, Giovanni Matteo, Cavaliere de Candia (*b* Cagliari, 17 Oct 1810; *d* Rome, 11 Dec 1883). Italian tenor. Succeeding Rubini as the outstanding lyric tenor of his day, he made his début at the Paris

Opéra in the title role of Meyerbeer's *Robert le diable*
(1838), becoming closely associated with the
Théâtre-Italien from 1841 and with the Royal Italian Opera, Covent Garden, from 1847 to his retirement in 1871. Rossini's Almaviva (*Il barbiere di
Siviglia*), Donizetti's Nemorino (*L'elisir d'amore*)
and Ernesto (*Don Pasquale*), Verdi's Duke of Mantua (*Rigoletto*) and Gounod's Faust were among his
most admired roles.

Markevich, Igor (*b* Kiev, 27 July 1912; *d* Antibes, 7
March 1983). Italian conductor and composer of
Russian birth. He began his career as a composer,
notably in association with Dyagilev. After spending World War II in Italy he travelled widely as a
guest conductor, appearing with the Boston SO in
1955. From 1967 he conducted the Monte Carlo
Orchestra, giving lively performances of modern
music as well as the standard repertory. An oratorio,
Le paradis perdu (1935), is among his compositions.

Markig (Ger.). Vigorous.

Marlboro Music Festival (USA). Annual (summer)
festival of chamber music, founded in 1950. Concerts are given in Persons Auditorium (cap. 650) at
Marlboro College, Vermont. Many recordings of
concerts are later broadcast and groups tour for the
rest of the year as 'Music from Marlboro'.

Marmontel, Jean François (*b* Bort, 11 July 1723;
d Abloville, 31 Dec 1799). French man of letters. A
prominent literary figure in Paris, he wrote opera
librettos for Rameau, Grétry, Piccinni and others.
He supported Italian music; some of his texts for
Piccinni are italianate adaptations of Quinault's.

Maros, Rudolf (*b* Stachy, 19 Jan 1917). Hungarian
composer. He studied with Kodály at the Budapest
Academy (1939–42), where he began teaching in
1949. His music developed from a diatonic, folk-
influenced style to 12-note serialism in 1959, many
works using Bartókian arch form.

Marpurg, Friedrich Wilhelm (*b* Seehof, 21 Nov
1718; *d* Berlin, 22 May 1795). German writer on
music and composer. He wrote books, periodicals
and music in Berlin from 1749. Among his major
works on music are three journals (which he edited
and largely wrote), discussing practical, theoretical
and aesthetic matters. He also wrote manuals on
keyboard performance, thoroughbass and composition, and an authoritative treatise on fugue (1753–4)
reflecting his admiration of Bach. His compositions
include songs and keyboard pieces.

Marriage of Figaro, The [Le nozze di Figaro].
Opera in four acts by Mozart to a libretto by Da
Ponte after Beaumarchais (1786).

Marriner, Sir Neville (*b* Lincoln, 15 April 1924). English conductor and violinist. He studied at the
RCM, where he later taught, 1949–59. He played in
the Philharmonia Orchestra, 1952–68, then in the
LSO. He founded the Academy of St Martin-in-
the-Fields and directed it 1959–78; it became widely
known particularly through recordings, which show
a graceful, warm, polished style. He was music
director of the Minnesota Orchestra, 1978–86.

Marschner, Heinrich August (*b* Zittau, 16 Aug
1795; *d* Hanover, 14 Dec 1861). German composer.
Originally intended for a legal career, he devoted

himself to music from 1815–16, when he met Beethoven and became a private music teacher in Bratislava. From 1821 he worked as a stage composer and
conductor in Dresden, then at the Leipzig
Stadttheater (swiftly winning fame with *Der Vampyr*, 1827, and *Der Templer und die Jüdin*, 1829) and,
from 1830, at the Hanover Hoftheater, where his
Hans Heiling (1831–2) made his name as a leading
German opera composer. Outspoken in his advocacy of a true German opera, he was held in high
esteem by Mendelssohn and Schumann, and later
by Bülow, Hanslick, Spitta and Pfitzner, for his 13
operas, which in content and form represent a link
between Weber and Wagner, making him one of the
central figures of the Romantic era. They are characterized by a consistent integration of all theatrical
means. From creating a protagonist psychologically
divided within himself (*Der Vampyr*), he evolved a
drama less dependent on local setting or comic and
folk elements than Weber's operas but more
melodramatic, stressing explicit musical characterization, motivic development, leitmotif technique and ultimately, in *Hiarne* (1857–8), through-
composition. Since he often sacrificed music for
dramatic ends, most of his work is forgotten, but his
masterpiece, *Hans Heiling*, is the definitive expression of the spirit of his age. He also wrote Singspiels,
pageants, incidental music, a ballet, over 400 songs
and 120 male-voice choruses, and chamber music.

Marsh, John (*b* Dorking, 1752; *d* Chichester, 1828).
English composer and writer on music. A lawyer by
profession, he led orchestras in Salisbury, Canterbury and Chichester, and was the most prolific
orchestral composer in England in his time, writing
at least 28 symphonies and overtures and 12 concerti
grossi. He also wrote chamber music, organ voluntaries (many arranged from music by other composers), anthems and psalm tunes. He cultivated
both the late Baroque and the Classical styles, discussing the two in *A Comparison between the Ancient
and Modern Styles of Music* (1796), one of his principal writings.

Marshall-Hall, George W(illiam) L(ouis) (*b* London, 26 March 1862; *d* Melbourne, 18 July 1915).
English conductor and composer. He studied in
Berlin and at the RCM and in 1890 was appointed
professor at Melbourne University, becoming a
leading controversial figure in the city's musical life
and founding a conservatory. He wrote five operas,
orchestral and chamber music.

Marteau sans maître, Le. Work by Boulez for alto
and ensemble, a setting of three poems by René
Char (1954, revised 1957).

Martenot, Maurice. Inventor of the ONDES
MARTENOT (1928).

Martha, oder Der Markt zu Richmond. Opera in
four acts by Flotow to a libretto by F.W. Riese after
V. de Saint-Georges (1847, Vienna); it includes the
song ''Tis the Last Rose of Summer'.

Martín, Edgardo (*b* Cienfuegos, 6 Oct 1915). Cuban
composer. He studied with Ardévol at the Havana
Conservatory (1939–46) and taught there (1945–
68), leaving to found the National Composers' Collective.

Martin, François (*b* 1727; *d* Paris, 1757). French composer and cellist. He played in the Paris Opéra orchestra and appeared as a soloist from the 1740s; his patron was the Duke of Gramont. His principal works are instrumental, including six symphonies and overtures of the pre-Classical type (1751), trios for two violins and cello (1746), sonatas and dances. He also composed *cantatilles* and motets.

Martin, Frank (*b* Geneva, 15 Sept 1890; *d* Naarden, 21 Nov 1974). Swiss composer. The son of a Calvinist minister, he was deeply impressed by a performance of the *St Matthew Passion* he heard at the age of ten. He studied with Joseph Lauber and worked from 1926 with Jaques-Dalcroze, then in his Piano Concerto no.1 (1934) and Symphony (1937) adopted Schoenbergian serialism while retaining an extended tonal harmony that looked to Debussy: the mature fusion of these elements into a style marked by dissonant chords, smooth part-writing and 'gliding tonality' did not come until the dramatic chamber oratorio *Le vin herbé* (1941), soon followed by two larger oratorios, *In terra pax* (1944) and *Golgotha* (1948), as well as by the *Petite symphonie concertante* for harp, harpsichord, piano and strings (1945) and the *Sechs Monologe aus 'Jedermann'* (1943, orchestrated 1949). In 1946 he moved to the Netherlands; he also taught at the Cologne Musikhochschule (1950–57). His later works include the operas *Der Sturm* (1956, Vienna Staatsoper) and *Monsieur de Pourceaugnac* (1963, Geneva), a large-scale Requiem (1972) and many concertante pieces, among them concertos for violin and harpsichord (both 1952) and a second for piano (1969).

Martinelli, Caterina (*b* Rome, *c* 1589; *d* Mantua, bur. 7 March 1608). Italian singer in the service of the Gonzagas at Mantua. Monteverdi composed the title role of his *L'Arianna* with her in mind, though she died before the first performance. In her memory he wrote the madrigal cycle *Lagrime d'amante al sepolcro dell'amata*, published in his sixth collection (1614).

Martinelli, Giovanni (*b* Montagnana, 22 Oct 1885; *d* New York, 2 Feb 1969). Italian tenor. After early appearances in Milan and Rome he sang Cavaradossi at Covent Garden in 1912 and Rodolfo at the Met the following year. Until 1945 his singing there was distinguished by pure, strong declamation and immaculate breath control. He was without equal as Othello, Don Carlos and Radamès.

Martinet, Jean-Louis (*b* Ste Bazeille, 8 Nov 1912). French composer. He studied with Koechlin at the Schola Cantorum and with Roger-Ducasse and Messiaen at the Paris Conservatoire, also having lessons with Leibowitz. In 1971 he was appointed professor at the Montreal Conservatory. His music is indebted to Messiaen and Bartók.

Martini, Padre Giovanni Battista (*b* Bologna, 24 April 1706; *d* there, 3 Aug 1784). Italian writer on music, teacher and composer. A monk and later priest, he served at S Francesco, Bologna, as organist (1722–5), then *maestro di cappella*. Widely and deeply respected as a teacher (mainly of counterpoint), he taught Mozart, J.C. Bach, Jommelli and *c* 100 others; he also corresponded with many emi-

nent figures, and built up a magnificent library including portraits of musicians (preserved in Bologna). He composed prolifically, mostly in an early Classical idiom; his output includes oratorios, church music (some in the *stile antico*), stage works, other secular vocal works (including *c* 1000 canons), sinfonias, concertos, 96 keyboard sonatas and numerous organ pieces. Foremost among his writings are a history of ancient music (1761–81) and a counterpoint treatise (1774–5). He is one of the most famous figures in 18th-century music.

Martini, Johannes (*b* Brabant, *c* 1440; *d* Ferrara, late Dec 1497–early 1498). Flemish composer. His long, distinguished association with the chapel of Duke Ercole I d'Este at Ferrara began in 1473 and lasted until his death, though he also sang for a short time in the Sforza chapel in Milan (1474). He composed sacred and secular music. The preponderance of masses over motets is more characteristic of Ockeghem's generation than of Josquin's, and his musical style is more conservative than Josquin's. His ten masses and motets are in an elaborate contrapuntal style, with skilful imitative devices; his vesper psalms (written with Brebis) are simple and homophonic. His secular music consists of three-voice settings of French and Italian texts.

Martini [Martini il Tedesco, Schwarzendorf], Johann Paul Aegidius (*b* Freystadt, 31 Aug 1741; *d* Paris, 10 Feb 1816). German composer. After serving the Duke of Lorraine, he moved to Paris (1764) where he worked for private patrons and at the Théâtre de Monsieur; in 1800–02 he taught at the Conservatoire, and from 1814 he directed the court orchestra. His works include 13 operas, other vocal music (notably the popular song *Plaisir d'amour*), chamber, orchestral and band music and several treatises.

Martino, Donald (James) (*b* Plainfield, NJ, 16 May 1931). American composer. He studied with Sessions and Babbitt at Princeton and with Dallapiccola in Florence (1954–6), then taught at Yale (1959–69) and the New England Conservatory (1969–81) and Harvard (from 1983). His imaginative and craftsmanlike music shows a strong feeling for instrumental gesture within a lucid dramatic continuity. An accomplished clarinettist, he has written a Triple Concerto for clarinet, bass clarinet and contrabass clarinet (1977) and other wind works.

Martinon, Jean (*b* Lyons, 10 Jan 1910; *d* Paris, 1 March 1976). French conductor and composer. He studied with Münch and Roussel. After World War II he became conductor of the Concerts du Conservatoire in Paris and the Bordeaux SO. He appeared as guest conductor with the Boston SO (1957) and was principal conductor of the Chicago SO (1963–9). His works include two violin concertos and four symphonies.

Martinů, Bohuslav (Jan) (*b* Polička, 8 Dec 1890; *d* Liestal, 28 Aug 1959). Czech composer. He studied at the Prague Conservatory (1906–10), then worked as a teacher and orchestral violinist before going to Paris in 1923. There he studied with Roussel and developed a neo-classical style, sometimes using jazz (*La bagarre*, 1926; *Le jazz*, 1928, both for orchestra). He began to apply himself to Czech subjects (ballet *Špalíček*, 1933; opera *The Miracles of Mary*, 1935; *Field Mass* for male voices, wind and percussion, 1939), but not exclusively: this was also the period of his fantasy opera *Julietta* (1938) and of numerous concertos. In 1940 he left Paris, and the next year arrived in New York, where he concentrated on orchestral and chamber works, including his first five symphonies. From 1948 his life was divided between Europe and the USA: this was the period of his Sixth Symphony (1953), *Frescos of Piero della Francesca* for orchestra (1953) and opera *The Greek Passion* (1961). He was one of the most prolific composers of the 20th century, imaginative in style, with energetic rhythms and powerful, often dissonant harmony, but uneven in quality.

Martín y Soler, (Atanasio Martín Ignacio) Vicente (Tadeo Francisco Pellegrín) (*b* Valencia, 2 May 1754; *d* St Petersburg, 11 Feb 1806). Spanish composer. He was in the service of the Spanish Infante by 1780 and composed operas and ballets for Italian cities in 1779–85; he also wrote zarzuelas. He then began a famous collaboration with the librettist Da Ponte in Vienna, presenting three Italian *opere buffe* (notably *Una cosa rara*, 1786). In 1788–94 he was at the Russian court as a composer and teacher, returning there in 1796 after a period in London, and becoming inspector of the Italian court theatre. He composed some 20 stage works in all; his ten *opere buffe*, among the finest of the period, contain expressive and dance-like melodies.

Martirano, Salvatore (*b* Yonkers, NY, 12 Jan 1927). American composer. He studied with Rogers at the Eastman School and Dallapiccola in Florence (1952–4), and in 1963 began teaching at Urbana. His works have included essays in 'pop-art' synthesis, leading to *L.'s G.A.* (Lincoln's Gettysburg Address), his most popular mixed-media work in the 1960s. Subsequently he has written tape pieces.

Martucci, Giuseppe (*b* Capua, 6 Jan 1856; *d* Naples, 1 June 1909). Italian composer, pianist and conductor. He studied at the Naples Conservatory. As a touring piano virtuoso, he won praise from Liszt and Anton Rubinstein in 1874, but from 1880–81 was professor of the piano (in 1902, director) at the Naples Conservatory. He was an enthusiastic conductor of the German (sometimes English and French) repertory in Naples and Bologna, where he was director of the Liceo Musicale (1886–1902). Besides piano music, he composed distinctive chamber works, often Schumannesque or Elgarian in their gentle lyricism and caprice (e.g. the popular *Notturno* op.70 no.1 and *Novelletta* op.82 no.2); his attractive Second Symphony has been called 'the starting point of the renaissance of non-operatic Italian music'.

Martyrdom of St Magnus, The. Chamber opera in one act by Peter Maxwell Davies to his own libretto after George Mackay Brown (1977, Kirkwall).

Martyre de Saint Sébastien, Le. Incidental music by Debussy for voices, chorus and orchestra for a mystery play by D'Annunzio (1911).

Marx, Adolf Bernhard (*b* Halle, 28 Nov 1795; *d* Berlin, 17 May 1866). German music theorist, author and composer. A pupil of Türk and Zelter and a friend of Mendelssohn, he edited the *Berliner allgemeine musikalische Zeitung* (1824–30), becoming professor at Berlin University in 1830 and co-founding in 1850 the Berliner Musikschule (later the Stern Conservatory). Of his compositions, mainly vocal and choral works, only the oratorio *Moses* (1841) aroused interest. His writings, especially the textbooks (*Die Lehre von der musikalischen Komposition*, 1837–47) and aesthetic works (*Die alte Musiklehre im Streit mit unserer Zeit*, 1841), brought more lasting fame. He is noted for his sectional and schematic treatment of form emphasizing thematic material, including a pioneering discussion of sonata form.

Marx, Joseph (*b* Graz, 11 May 1882; *d* there, 3 Sept 1964). Austrian composer. He composed *c*120 songs in 1908–12 which are comparable with Wolf's in their spontaneity and brought him international fame. He then taught at the Vienna Academy (1914–27) and worked as a critic. His later instrumental works were influenced by Bruckner, Brahms and Reger but were of purely local importance.

Marx, Karl (*b* Munich, 12 Nov 1897; *d* Stuttgart, 8 May 1985). German composer. He studied with Orff and at the Munich Academy (1920–24), where he remained as a teacher; later he taught in Graz and Stuttgart. His works include much choral music, especially for youth choir.

Marxsen, Eduard (*b* Nienstädten, 23 July 1806; *d* Altona, 18 Nov 1887). German pianist, teacher and composer. He was a much sought-after teacher in Hamburg; he taught Brahms, who dedicated his B♭ Piano Concerto to him.

Mary, Queen of Scots. Opera in three acts by Thea Musgrave to her own libretto after Amalia Elguera (1977, Edinburgh).

Masaniello. *See* MUETTE DE PORTICI, LA.

Mascagni, Pietro (*b* Livorno, 7 Dec 1863; *d* Rome, 2 Aug 1945). Italian composer. He studied with Ponchielli and Saladino at the Milan Conservatory (1882–4), then worked as a touring conductor and wrote *Guglielmo Ratcliff* (*c*1885). His next opera was the one-act *Cavalleria rusticana*, which was staged in Rome in 1890 and won him immediate international acclaim: it effectively established the vogue for *verismo*. None of his later operas was anything like so successful, though some numbers from *L'amico Fritz* (1891) and the oriental *Iris* (1898) have survived in the repertory. Later works include the comedy *Le maschere* (1901), the unexpectedly powerful *Il piccolo Marat* (1921) and *Nerone* (1935), this last testifying to his identification with fascism.

Maschera, Florentio (*b* ?Brescia, *c*1540; *d* there, *c*1584). Italian composer. An organ pupil of Merulo, he was organist at Santo Spirito, Venice, and Brescia Cathedral (1557–84) and played the viola da braccio and violin. His popular four-part canzonas (1584), suitable for viol ensembles or lute, are among the earliest pieces specifically for instrumental ensemble.

Mascherata (It.). 'Masked', 'masquerade': a type of

VILLANELLA, probably intended for performance during Carnival.

Mascitti, Michele (*b* S Maria, 1663–4; *d* Paris, 24 April 1760). Italian composer. After travelling through Europe as a violinist, he won great popularity in Paris. A figurehead of Italian instrumental music there, he published 100 violin sonatas and 16 other works, 1704–38, in a Corellian style modified with French features.

Maskarade. Opera in three acts by Nielsen to a libretto by V. Anderson after Holberg (1906, Copenhagen).

Masked Ball, A. *See* BALLO IN MASCHERA, UN.

Mask of Orpheus, The. Opera in three acts by Birtwistle to a libretto by Peter Zinovieff (1986, London).

Mask of Time, The. Work by Tippett for soprano, alto, tenor and bass soloists, chorus and orchestra (1984), to a text compiled by the composer.

Masnadieri, I. Opera in four acts by Verdi to a libretto by Maffei after Schiller (1847, London).

Mason, Daniel Gregory (*b* Brookline, MA, 20 Nov 1873; *d* Greenwich, CT, 4 Dec 1953). American composer, grandson of Lowell Mason. He studied at Harvard (1891–5) and with Chadwick and Goetschius and taught at Columbia (1905–42). At first he concentrated on writing about music but from 1907 he gave more attention to composing, and in 1913 he had further lessons in Paris with d'Indy, who influenced him strongly without turning him from Brahms. He was a conservative composer and meticulous technician. His works include three symphonies (1914, 1929, 1936), chamber music (String Quartet on Negro Themes, 1919) and songs.

Mason, Lowell (*b* Medfield, MA, 8 Jan 1792; *d* Orange, NJ, 11 Aug 1872). American music educator, composer and conductor. He was the chief pioneer in introducing music instruction to American schools and a leading reformer of American church music. In Savannah, 1812–27, then in Boston to 1851, he was highly successful as a church choirmaster, and he directed the Boston Handel and Haydn Society, 1827–32. Through his singing classes for children, his hymn tunebooks and music instruction books (based on European models), and especially through the teacher training offered at his Boston Academy of Music (1833), he succeeded in giving music a regular place in Boston schools. He continued to teach until 1851. In later years he produced further books, church music collections and compositions, mostly sacred vocal works. Among the best known are the hymn arrangements *Azmon* ('O for a thousand tongues to sing') and *Hamburg* ('When I survey the wondrous cross') and the original tunes *Olivet* ('My faith looks up to thee') and *Bethany* ('Nearer, my God, to thee').

His son Daniel Gregory (1820–69) founded the religious music publishing firm Mason Brothers in 1853 with his brother Lowell (1823–85). A third son William (1829–1908) was a concert pianist, teacher and composer, and a fourth, Henry (1831–90), was an instrument builder and father of DANIEL GREGORY MASON.

Mason & Hamlin. American firm of piano and reed organ makers. Founded in Boston in 1854 by Henry Mason (1831–90) and Emmons Hamlin (1821–85), it made reed organs, from the traditional melodeon type to the larger, two-manual-and-pedal 'Church' organ; by 1867 it was manufacturing about a quarter of the USA's reed organs. From 1883 it made pianos, introducing the 'tension resonator' and the 'duplex scale' to improve sound quality. High-quality grands and uprights were built from *c*1900 to 1920. Both sides of the business passed to other companies, but the firm continues to make pianos under its own name.

Masonic music. Music used in connection with the ritual and social functions of freemasons. Hymn singing, while never an integral part of masonic rites, was frequently included at meetings, and masonic hymnals and cantatas were published in considerable numbers from the 1730s onwards. Haydn, Mozart, Loewe, Spohr, Liszt and Puccini are among composers who became freemasons; Wagner planned to join.

Mozart's masonic music is of particular importance. He became a mason in 1784, but as early as 1773 wrote music for Baron von Gebler's masonic play *Thamos, König in Ägypten*. He took part in musical performances at his lodge, and composed for various Viennese lodges, notably cantatas, wind works and a piece of funeral music. Musical reflections of masonic imagery are present in *Die Zauberflöte*.

Masque. A genre of entertainment developed in England during the 16th and 17th centuries. It involved poetry, music and elaborate sets, and reached its highest development in the court masques of *c*1600–30 and in the stage masques of the Restoration. It had its origins in the English disguising of the 15th century and its Italian counterparts, introduced to the English court by Henry VIII. The 16th-century court masque combined speech, songs and formal dances with 'revels', during which the masquers engaged in dancing, gallantry and intrigue with members of the audience.

In the early 17th century, court masques were given either in the Great Hall at Whitehall or in the Banqueting House; similar entertainments were put on at the Inns of Court. The high quality of the Jacobean masques is due largely to the poetry of Ben Jonson and the stage designs of Inigo Jones, who together produced about 30 works, 1605–31. They usually included four songs, with dances in between, and introductory and concluding numbers. No complete score is extant but many items by the main composers, Alfonso Ferrabosco (ii), Robert Johnson, Thomas Campion and Nicholas Lanier, survive. The songs are influenced by Italian recitative.

As dramatic presentations, Caroline masques were superior to Jacobean. Shirley's *Triumph of Peace* (1634) was probably the most elaborate, with music by William Lawes, the main dramatic composer of the time. Among masques performed for the lesser nobility, the most famous is Milton's *Comus* (Ludlow Castle, 1634), with music by Henry Lawes. Shirley's *Cupid and Death* (1653) is the only surviving masque from the Commonwealth, with music by Locke and Christopher Gibbons. After the Restoration the masque survived in the theatre, as diversions resembling court masque entries at the ends of acts. They included dances, a song and/or recitative and a dialogue or chorus. Masque tradition influenced Purcell's *Dido and Aeneas* (1689) and his semi-operas. After 1700 the term 'masque' was applied to short semi-operas.

Masques et bergamasques. *Comédie musicale* by Fauré to a libretto by Fauchois (1919, Monte Carlo).

Mass. The ritual of the Eucharist, celebrated primarily in the Catholic church, has given rise to a large musical repertory. The Mass is known to music historians in the form in Table 1. The Proper – the sections that vary from day to day – attracted a large repertory of plainchant; the Ordinary texts and chants evolved between the 7th and 11th centuries.

The chants of the Proper served as melodic material for early organum in the 10th century; in the 12th century the new polyphonic art was enriched by organum settings of Mass items. In the 14th cen-

TABLE 1: *Structure of the Mass*

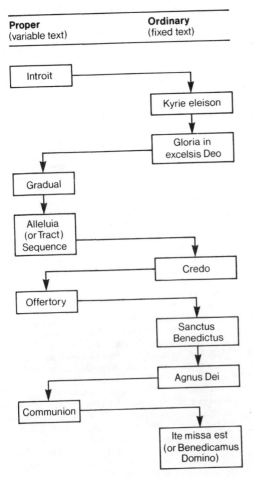

tury, polyphonic settings concentrated on the Ordinary, which was used at all times of the liturgical year. Early settings were compiled in Tournai and in Italy; the *Messe de Nostre Dame* by Machaut (*c*1350) stands out as the earliest by a single composer. English composers continued to set mass sections throughout the 15th century; Dunstable is credited with an early cyclic mass unified by a tenor *cantus firmus*.

By 1450, when the Mass Ordinary was regarded as central in composition, the 'cantus firmus' or 'tenor' mass predominated. Dufay used both sacred and secular melodies as the basis for his masses, and in the period of Ockeghem and his contemporaries (*c*1460–90) the *chanson* was increasingly used as a source of tenor melodies around which an often very intricate contrapuntal web was woven. Josquin's 20-odd masses form a culmination of traditions while opening the way to further developments in the use of free *cantus firmi* and in drawing on the entire polyphonic substance of a model. This 'parody' technique was much used in 16th-century mass composition. The principal movements normally begin with varied treatment of the model's opening subject and close with its final cadence; the borrowed material is interlaced with new. Masses based on motets, *chansons* or madrigals were written by most late Renaissance composers, including Palestrina, Victoria, Lassus and Morales; freely invented masses were also composed. Other types include the canonic mass and the paraphrase mass with free use of plainchant; the old tenor mass is also found.

Parody techniques and even *cantus firmi* survived into the Baroque period, and the *stile antico* was used as late as Domenico Scarlatti. But the development of a style with choruses in *stile antico* (with instruments doubling) or independent instrumental support and music for solo voices led to a type in which the various sections (especially the Gloria and Credo) were divided into several movements. This 'cantata mass' was associated with early 18th-century Neapolitan composers, but the greatest work of this kind is Bach's B minor Mass.

The early Classical Viennese composers introduced a more integrated structure, often on symphonic lines. The masses of Haydn and Mozart served a liturgical function, and even Beethoven's *Missa solemnis* was intended for a church service. But thereafter most musically significant masses were written either for the concert hall or for some splendid occasion. Liszt's for the coronation of Emperor Franz Joseph as King of Hungary (1867) and Bruckner's F minor Mass (1867–8), commissioned by the Viennese chapel royal, are outstanding examples of large-scale settings; and it is significant that the greatest 20th-century mass, that by Stravinsky (1948), has been most often performed in the concert hall.

Massaino, Tiburtio (*b* Cremona, by 1550; *d* Piacenza or Lodi, *c*1610). Italian composer. An Augustinian, he worked in Cremona before becoming *maestro di cappella* of Salò Cathedral (by 1587). He was briefly at Innsbruck (*c*1589), Salzburg and Prague (1591), returning in 1594. His music – he published at least

20 volumes of sacred music (1576–1609) and nine of madrigals (1569–1604) – was much admired in his time.

Massarani, Renzo (*b* Mantua, 26 March 1898; *d* Rio de Janeiro, 28 March 1975). Italian composer. He was a pupil of Respighi. In the early 1920s he was one of I Tre, a group formed in imitation of Les Six, and he wrote in most genres. His works were banned by Mussolini and many were destroyed. After World War II he emigrated to Brazil, and abandoned composition to work as a music critic.

Massart, (Joseph) Lambert (*b* Liège, 19 July 1811; *d* Paris, 13 Feb 1892). Belgian violinist. Noted as a chamber music player, he was violin professor at the Paris Conservatoire (1843–90), where Wieniawski and Kreisler were among his pupils.

Massé, Victor [Félix Marie] (*b* Lorient, 7 March 1822; *d* Paris, 5 July 1884). French composer. He studied at the Paris Conservatoire, winning the Prix de Rome (1844). He was chorus master at the Opéra from 1860 and composition professor at the Conservatoire from 1866. He wrote over 20 operas, but his talents are best represented by three collections of romances, some drawing-room operettas and by the delightful *opéra comique Les noces de Jeannette* (1853).

Massenet, Jules (Emile Frédéric) (*b* Montand, St Etienne, 12 May 1842; *d* Paris, 13 Aug 1912). French composer. His family moved to Paris in 1847 and he entered the Conservatoire at the age of 11 as a piano pupil of Adolphe Laurent. He later studied harmony with Reber and composition with Ambroise Thomas, winning the Prix de Rome in 1863. In Rome he got to know Liszt and, through him, Constance de Sainte-Marie, who became his pupil and, in 1866 after his return to Paris, his wife. The following year his opera *La grand'tante* was given at the Opéra-Comique, and in 1873 *Marie-Magdeleine* at the Théâtre de l'Odéon initiated a series of *drames sacrés* based on the lives of female biblical characters. Many of his secular operas, too, are in effect portraits of women.

In 1878 Massenet was made a teacher of composition at the Conservatoire, where he remained all his life, influencing many younger French composers, including Charpentier, Koechlin, Pierné and Hahn. In his own music he began to move away from the suave, sentimental melodic style derived from Gounod and to adopt a more Wagnerian type of lyrical declamation. The change is apparent in *Manon* (1884), which placed Massenet in the forefront of French opera composers, and still more in *Werther* (1892).

But as early as 1877, in *Hérodiade*, Massenet had begun to modify the symmetry and loosen the syntax of his melodies to give them a more speaking, intimate, conversational character. Repetitions are usually masked or transferred to the orchestra while the voice takes a lyrical recitative line in the Wagnerian manner; literal repetitions are carefully calculated to provide an insistent, emotional quality. Often his melodies have a swaying, hesitant character (9/8 or 6/8) – first and most effectively used in

Act 1 of *Manon* to express a girl's hesitant yet delighted awareness of her own charms. By *Werther*, the relationship of voice and orchestra is more sophisticated, and that opera contains clear examples of Massenet's dissolution of formal melody into rhapsodic recitative-like writing as evolved by Wagner. Massenet's music is harmonically conservative, rarely venturing beyond modest chromaticisms; rhythmically, it is original in the variations he uses to give the melody a more caressing, intimate character. He had a characteristically French ear for orchestral nuance. Though primarily a lyrical composer, he was also a master of scenes of action, as for example at the opening of *Manon*.

After *Sapho* (1897) Massenet scored few major successes. His conception of opera became outdated long before his death and his position as France's leading opera composer was finally challenged when Debussy's *Pelléas et Mélisande* was given at the Opéra-Comique in 1902. The unpretentiousness of his best works recommends their melodic charm and gracefulness, and they remain firmly in the standard opera-house repertory.

Dramatic music Hérodiade (1877); Manon (1884); Le Cid (1885); Esclarmonde (1889); Werther (1892); Thaïs (1894); Sapho (1897); Cendrillon (1899); Le jongleur de Notre-Dame (1902); Thérèse (1907); Don Quichotte (1910); *c*20 others; incidental music for 13 plays, incl. Notre-Dame de Paris (1879); Phèdre (1900); 3 ballets
Choral music Requiem (*c*1863); motets, cantatas, partsongs
Vocal music over 200 songs, incl. cycles
Instrumental music Scènes alsaciennes, suite (1881); other suites; 3 ovs.; Pf Conc. (1903); chamber music; pf music

Mässig (Ger.). Moderate.

Mass of Life, A. [Eine Messe des Lebens]. Choral work by Delius to a German text from Nietzsche's *Also sprach Zarathustra* (1905).

Massonneau, Louis (*b* Kassel, 10 Jan 1766; *d* Ludwigslust, 4 Oct 1848). German violinist, composer and conductor of French descent. After working in Göttingen, Frankfurt, Altona and Dessau, he settled at Ludwigslust in 1803, becoming Kapellmeister in 1812. Of his instrumental works (dating from before 1800) the three symphonies are noteworthy; the Third Symphony op.5 (*La tempête et le calme*, 1794) uses harmonic and dynamic effects to suggest a tempest, thus anticipating Beethoven's Pastoral Symphony.

Master of the Queen's [King's] **Music** [Musick]. The title of the one remaining officer of the musicians (King's Band of Music) who from the 17th century provided secular music at the English court. Nicholas Lanier was the first holder of the title, which is now honorary and held by a distinguished British composer from whom occasional works are commissioned. Holders of the title include Boyce (1755–79), Elgar (1924–34), Bax (1942–52), Bliss (1953–75) and Malcolm Williamson (1975–).

Master Peter's Puppet Show [El retablo de maese Pedro]. Opera in one act by Falla to his own libretto after Cervantes (1923, Seville).

Mastersingers of Nuremberg, The [Die Meistersinger von Nürnberg]. Opera in three acts by Wagner to his own libretto (1868).

Masterson, (Margaret) Valerie (*b* Birkenhead, 3 June 1937). English soprano. She studied in Liverpool, at the RCM and in Milan and made her début in Salzburg in 1964. She sang in Gilbert and Sullivan, 1966–70, then joined the Coliseum company, playing such roles as Violetta and Massenet's Manon. After successes in Mozart at Aix-en-Provence, she made her Paris Opéra debut as Marguerite (1978); her American début was in *La traviata* (1980, San Francisco). Her ENO roles included Handel's Cleopatra, to which she added his Semele at Covent Garden (1982). Her lustrous, agile soprano is supported by clear diction and an attractive stage presence.

Masur, Kurt (*b* Brieg, 18 July 1928). German conductor. After appointments at Halle and Leipzig he was conductor of the Dresden PO (1955–8, 1967–72). He worked at the Komische Oper, Berlin (1960–64) and in 1970 became conductor of the Leipzig Gewandhaus Orchestra. He made his London début in 1973, with the New Philharmonia, and is particularly admired in Bruckner, Schumann and Beethoven.

Mata, Eduardo (*b* Mexico City, 5 Sept 1942). Mexican conductor and composer. His teachers include Halffter, Chávez, Rudolf, Leinsdorf and Schuller. Among his posts have been music directorships of the Phoenix SO (1974–7), the Mexico National SO (1976–7) and the Dallas SO (from 1977); he has appeared widely as a guest conductor in Europe and the USA. As a composer he was chiefly active up to 1967; he has written three symphonies (1962–6) and three *Improvisations* for different combinations (1961–5).

Matachin. A battle dance popular from the 16th century to the 18th and later in Mexico and Spanish-speaking America; in one form it was grotesque, in another a skilful sword dance.

Matačić, Lovro von (*b* Susak, 14 Feb 1899; *d* Zagreb, 4 Jan 1985). Yugoslav conductor. After an early career in Vienna and Cologne (début 1919) he returned to Yugoslavia in 1938, becoming music director of the Belgrade Opera and conductor of the Belgrade PO. He conducted opera at Dresden, Frankfurt (1961–6) and Monte Carlo (from 1974) and was often heard in the symphonies of Bruckner and Tchaikovsky.

Matasin. *See* MATACHIN.

Materna(-Friedrich), Amalie (*b* St Georgen, 10 July 1844; *d* Vienna, 18 Jan 1918). Austrian soprano. Her bright, powerful voice was ideal for the role of Brünnhilde, which she sang in the first complete *Ring* cycle at Bayreuth (1876); she sang Kundry in the première of *Parsifal* (Bayreuth, 1882).

Mather, Bruce (*b* Toronto, 9 May 1939). Canadian composer. He studied at Toronto University (1953–9), with Milhaud and Messiaen in Paris (1959–62) and with Leland Smith at Stanford (1962–4); in 1966 he began teaching at McGill. His works, in a Boulezian style, include many for small forces.

Matheus de Sancto Johanne (*fl* 1365–?1389). French composer. In 1378 he was a member of the chapel of Louis I of Anjou, and from 1382 until at least 1386 he was a chaplain at the papal chapel in Avignon. He may subsequently have served at the court of the Duke of Orleans. His surviving compositions – three or four ballades, two rondeaux and a motet – reveal him as one of Machaut's successors in developing the Ars Subtilior. The rhythm and notational technique is most complex in the three-voice works; his motet, in an English source, is unusual for its five-voice scoring.

Mathews, Max (Vernon) (*b* Columbus, NE, 13 Nov 1926). American computer scientist and composer. He was a pioneer of computer sound synthesis at Bell Telephone Laboratories in Murray Hill, New Jersey, in the late 1950s and 1960s, and has also worked at Stanford University and IRCAM in Paris.

Mathias, William (James) (*b* Whitland, 1 Nov 1934). Welsh composer. He studied with Berkeley at the RAM and in 1959 began teaching at University College, Bangor. His music draws on Bartók, Hindemith, Stravinsky and Tippett: the style is essentially tonal and his preference for standard multi-movement forms allows for lyrical and dynamic expression. He has written much choral music, besides concertos (three for piano), chamber music (two string quartets, 1968, 1982), and the opera *The Servants* (1980).

Mathieson, Muir (*b* Stirling, 24 Jan 1911; *d* Oxford, 2 Aug 1975). British conductor. He studied at the RCM and in 1934 became musical director of London Films; he later worked for Alexander Korda and Rank. He directed the music for 500 films and commissioned scores from Bliss, Vaughan Williams and Walton. Britten wrote the *Young Person's Guide to the Orchestra* (1946) for a film directed by him.

Mathieu. French family of musicians. Michel (1689–1768), a violinist, served at the French court and composed instrumental and vocal music. His son Julien-Amable (1734–1811), at first a court violinist, was music master of the royal chapel, 1765–92, and composed mostly violin music and motets. A second son, Michel-Julien Mathieu [Lépidor] (1740–after 1777) was a composer, violinist and writer.

Mathis, Edith (*b* Lucerne, 11 Feb 1938). Swiss soprano. She studied at Lucerne and sang in Cologne and Berlin; her English début was at Glyndebourne (Cherubino, 1962) and she sang at Covent Garden in 1970 (Susanna, Sophie). She has sung at many leading festivals and appeared with distinction as Strauss's Zdenka (*Arabella*) and in music by Bach, but is especially admired for her fresh, characterful singing in Mozart.

Mathis der Maler. Opera in seven scenes by Hindemith to his own libretto on Matthias Grünewald (1938, Zurich); Hindemith wrote a symphony with the same title (1934).

Matho, Jean-Baptiste (*b* Brittany, *c*1660; *d* Versailles, 16 March 1746). French composer. The only important Breton musician of the 17th and 18th centuries, he sang at the French court from 1684 and became *maître de musique du Roi* in 1722. He composed ballets, divertissements and other stage works in the Lullian tradition.

Matin, Le. Haydn's Symphony no.6 in D (?1761), the

first of a group of three: no.7 is 'Le midi' and no.8 'Le soir'.

Mátray, Gábor (*b* Nagykáta, 23 Nov 1797; *d* Budapest, 17 July 1875). Hungarian musicologist. He was the first music director of the Hungarian National Theatre (Pest, 1837) and his music for the play *Csernyi György* (1812) is the earliest document in Hungarian opera history. As director of the National Conservatory (from 1840) he introduced concerts of early Hungarian music. His historical writings, folk music editions and informed criticism earned him the title 'father of Hungarian musicology'.

Matrimonio segreto, Il. Opera in two acts by Cimarosa to a libretto by G. Bertati after Colman and Garrick (1792, Vienna).

Matsudaira, Yoritsune (*b* Tokyo, 5 May 1907). Japanese composer. A pupil of Komatsu, he was influenced by French music from Debussy to Les Six, but in the mid-1930s began to take a creative interest in gagaku, which after the war he combined with 12-note methods (Theme and Variations for piano and orchestra, 1951). His output consists mostly of instrumental music.

Mattei, Stanislao (*b* Bologna, 10 Feb 1750; *d* there, 12 May 1825). Italian teacher and composer. Padre Martini's closest friend, he was *maestro di cappella* at leading Bologna churches. He taught Donizetti, Rossini and others at the Liceo Musicale, and wrote a theoretical work and many compositions, mostly sacred.

Matteis, Nicola (i) (*b* Naples; *d* ?London, ?1707 or later). Italian violinist and composer. Active in England from the 1670s, he was a renowned performer and a popular composer of music for violin and bass and of songs. Many of his pieces (preludes, dances etc) are grouped into suites; they include idiomatic violin writing more advanced than that in contemporary Italian music.

Matteis, Nicola (ii) (*b* ? late 1670s; *d* Shrewsbury, 26 Oct 1760). English violinist and composer, son of Nicola Matteis (i). He was a violinist at the Viennese imperial court from 1700, and in 1712–30 director of instrumental music. He wrote ballet music for many court operas, and a few instrumental works.

Matteo da Perugia (*d* by 13 Jan 1418). Italian composer. He was the first *magister capellae* at Milan Cathedral, 1402–7 and 1414–16. He spent many years serving the Archbishop of Milan, Petros Filargo di Candia, who in 1409 became the Antipope Alexander V. After his patron was poisoned the following year, Matteo may have served Pope John XXIII before returning to Milan Cathedral, where he remained. He was a prolific composer, though his works are confined to a few sources and he was less influential than his contemporary Ciconia. He was, however, master of the compositional techniques of the period, writing Italian ballate as well as in the French secular forms, isorhythmic motets and mass movements. His later rondeaux introduce several stylistic innovations of the 15th century, including instrumental openings, a simpler rhythmic style, and a vertically conceived texture. Imitative entries are a feature of his mass movements. Both Matteo

and his patron Filargo (who had studied theology at the Sorbonne) were responsible for encouraging the growth of French culture in northern Italy.

Matthay, Tobias (Augustus) (*b* London, 19 Feb 1858; *d* High Marley, 15 Dec 1945). English teacher and pianist. He studied at the RAM and taught there (1876–1925). In 1900 he founded a school to propagate his theories of piano technique (based on muscular relaxation) and teaching, as expounded in *The Act of Touch* (1903). His theories were questioned, but the success of many of his pupils (Hess, Craxton, Bowen, Lympany) speaks for itself.

Mattheson, Johann (*b* Hamburg, 28 Sept 1681; *d* there, 17 April 1764). German composer, critic and theorist. From a young age he sang in the Hamburg Opera and performed on various instruments; later he took solo tenor roles, and up to 1705 he appeared in works by Handel (who became a personal friend), Reinhard Keiser and others. He was also a virtuoso organist. As secretary to the English ambassador to Hamburg (from 1706) he travelled widely; in 1715–28 he was music director at Hamburg Cathedral, for which he composed many works.

Mattheson's output (now mostly lost) comprises operas, cantatas and other vocal music, chamber works and keyboard suites, fugues etc. His religious commitment was best expressed in his 26 oratorios and Passions (including *Das Lied des Lammes*, 1723, Hamburg), which contain dramatic writing and homophonic choruses. His vocal melodies are notable for their expressive simplicity. His many writings cover almost every aspect of the music of his day and reflect his practical experience and expertise. The most important, *Der vollkommene Capellmeister* (1739), is an encyclopedia of knowledge for music directors. Among the rest, *Das neu-eröffnete Orchestre* (1713), presenting a progressive approach to musical instruction, and *Critica musica* (1722–5), the first German music periodical, are especially valuable.

Matthews, Colin (*b* London, 13 Feb 1946). English composer, brother of David. After study at Nottingham University he worked with Deryck Cooke on the performing version of Mahler's Tenth Symphony. He was later an assistant to Britten. His music, in an intense, sometimes atonal style, includes a series of sonatas for orchestra, a Cello Concerto (1984) and two string quartets (1979, 1982).

Matthews, David (*b* London, 9 March 1943). English composer, brother of Colin. After study at Nottingham University he worked as an assistant to Britten (1966–9). Other influences have been Tippett (he published a study in 1980) and the expressionist music of Schoenberg. His works include three symphonies, five string quartets (1970–85) and Variations for Strings (1986).

Matthews, Denis (James) (*b* Coventry, 2 Feb 1919). English pianist and writer. He studied at the RAM and made his London début in 1939. From 1946 he toured widely, appearing with major orchestras and the Griller and Amadeus quartets. His taste inclines towards the Viennese Classics, which he plays with an awareness of the performing practice of the period. He was professor of music at Newcastle University (1971–84). Among his books is *Beethoven* (1985).

Mauduit, Jacques (*b* Paris, 16 Sept 1557; *d* there, 21 Aug 1627). French composer. Of aristocratic origins and widely educated, he was a leading member of Baïf's Académie and organized its musical functions. His published works include *chansonnettes* (1586) and psalms (1623), setting Baïf's *vers mesurés*, and a requiem for Ronsard's funeral (1585). Many of his works are lost.

Mauersberger, Rudolf (*b* Mauersberg, 29 Jan 1889; *d* Dresden, 22 Feb 1971). German conductor and composer. After study at the Leipzig Conservatory he was choirmaster at Aachen and Eisenach, where he established a flourishing Bach tradition. From 1930 until his death he was choirmaster at the Kreuz-kirche, Dresden. He toured widely with the boys' choir (the Dresden Kreuzchor), notably in music by Schütz, but was also an advocate of contemporary music.

Maugars, André (*b* c1580; *d* c1645). French bass viol player and writer. Praised by Mersenne and Rousseau as one of the first great French viol virtuosos, he held a church appointment near Puy. The open letter he published after his visit to Rome (c1637) is an invaluable account of Italian music of the period and provides early comparisons between French and Italian styles.

Maurel, Victor (*b* Marseilles, 17 June 1848; *d* New York, 22 Oct 1923). French baritone. He sang at the Paris Opéra (1879–94), also appearing frequently at La Scala, Milan, Covent Garden and the Metropolitan Opera, New York. Among the roles he created were Verdi's Iago (*Otello*, 1887) and Falstaff (1893) and Leoncavallo's Tonio (*Pagliacci*, 1892). Outstanding for his breath control and acting skill, he also appeared on the dramatic stage, co-directed the Théâtre-Italien (1883–5) and wrote books on singing and opera staging.

Má vlast [My Country]. Cycle of six symphonic poems by Smetana, including *Vltava* and *From Bohemia's Woods and Fields*.

Mavra. Opera in one act by Stravinsky to a libretto by Kochno after Pushkin's *The Little House at Kolomna* (1922, Paris).

Maw, (John) Nicholas (*b* Grantham, 5 Nov 1935). English composer. He studied with Berkeley at the RAM (1955–8) and Boulanger and Deutsch in Paris (1958–9). He has taught in England and the USA. His music represents the extension of a solid tonal tradition, traceable back through Britten, Tippett, Bartók and Strauss, all influences on a style of fresh vigour. Among his works are two comic operas, *One Man Show* (1964) and *The Rising of the Moon* (1970), orchestral pieces and chamber music. His monumental orchestral work *Odyssey* was given in 1987.

Maxixe. Brazilian urban popular dance that appeared in Rio de Janeiro c1870. The term first referred to a free manner of dancing but soon became synonymous with the Brazilian popularized polka and tango. The maxixe is akin to a polka, with much syncopation; it has a buoyant melodic line and eight-bar sections, in an *ABACA* form.

Maxwell Davies, Peter. *See* DAVIES, PETER MAXWELL.

May, Frederick (*b* Dublin, 1911; *d* there, 8 Sept 1985). Irish composer. He studied with Vaughan Williams at the RCM and Wellesz in Vienna, then was music director of the Abbey Theatre, Dublin. His works include a quartet, songs and *Songs from Prison* (1958) for baritone and orchestra.

Maynard, John (*b* St Albans, bap. 5 Jan 1577; *d* after 1614). English lutenist and composer. He was engaged as a bass singer by King Christian of Denmark in 1599 but absconded in suspicious circumstances in 1601. He is best remembered for his *The XII Wonders of the World* (1611), 12 satires on stock characters for voice, lute and bass viol, followed by six 'Lute-Lessons', and seven pavans for lyra viol with optional bass viol.

May Night [Mayskaya noch']. Opera in three acts by Rimsky-Korsakov to his own libretto after Gogol (1880, Moscow).

Mayone, Ascanio (*b* Naples, c1565; *d* there, 9 March 1627). Italian composer. He studied with Nola and was organist (1593) and joint *maestro di cappella* (1595) of the Annunziata, Naples. In 1602 he joined the Spanish viceroy's chapel as organist. He also played the harp. His keyboard pieces (3 vols., 1603, 1606, 1609) helped pioneer a new 'Baroque' keyboard style. A book of five-part madrigals also survives (1604).

Mayr, Richard (*b* Henndorf, 18 Nov 1877; *d* Vienna, 1 Dec 1935). Austrian bass-baritone. After study in Vienna he made his début at Bayreuth as Hagen (1902). He was engaged by Mahler for the Vienna Hofoper, where he was successful for 30 years in Mozart, Wagner and Strauss; his Covent Garden début (1924) was as Baron Ochs, his most admired role.

Mayr [Mayer], (Johannes) Simon [Giovanni Simone] (*b* Mendorf, 14 June 1763; *d* Bergamo, 2 Dec 1845). German composer. From 1789 he studied with Bertoni in Venice, soon establishing himself as one of the foremost opera composers in Italy. Among his most successful works, *Che originali* (1798), *Ginevra di Scozia* (1801), *La rosa bianca e la rosa rossa* (1813) and *Medea in Corinto* (1813) were staged repeatedly throughout Italy and performed abroad up to 1850, long after his reputation had been eclipsed by Rossini, Mercadante and Donizetti, his devoted pupil. From 1802 he was *maestro di cappella* in Bergamo, teaching, composing sacred music (over 600 items) and organizing performances of works by Haydn, Mozart and Beethoven. His works show diverse influences from Gluck to the late Neapolitan opera composers, but they also reveal a colourful orchestration new to Italy and a skilful construction of long dramatic segments bridging several scenes.

Mayseder, Joseph (*b* Vienna, 26 Oct 1789; *d* there, 21 Nov 1863). Austrian violinist and composer. He had lessons from Wranitzky. From 1800 to 1837 in Vienna he was an eminent soloist, quartet player (in such private circles as those of Beethoven's patrons) and orchestral leader, composing conservative works mainly for his own performance.

Mayuzumi, Toshirō (*b* Yokohama, 20 Feb 1929). Japanese composer. A pupil of Ikenouchi and Ifukube, and of Aubin at the Paris Conservatoire

(1951–2), he has introduced avant-garde techniques to Japan and produced a large output covering most genres, including tape music. From 1958 his music has embraced Japanese and Buddhist tradition.

Mazarin, Jules (*b* Pescina, 14 July 1602; *d* Vincennes, 9 March 1661). French politician of Italian birth. He is important in music for his advocacy of Italian opera in France. A cardinal (from 1641) and first minister from 1643, he saw Italian opera in France as a smoke-screen for political manoeuvres, and brought to Paris the composers Marazzoli and Rossi and the designer Torelli. Rossi's *Orfeo* (1647) and Caproli's *Le nozze di Peleo e di Theti* (1654) were successfully performed under his patronage.

Mazeppa. Opera in three acts by Tchaikovsky to a libretto by Burenin and the composer after Pushkin (1844, Moscow).

Two piano pieces by Liszt (1840, 1851); he also used the title for a symphonic poem (1851) after Hugo.

Mazurka. A Polish dance from Mazovia, around Warsaw. Its three regional types, *masur, obertas* and *kujawiak*, are in fast triple time with strong accents on the second or third beat. Usually performed by four, eight or 12 couples, it was originally accompanied on a kind of bagpipe. During the 18th and 19th centuries it became fashionable in many European capitals, and its scope is demonstrated in Chopin's piano mazurkas.

Mazurok, Yury (Antonovich) (*b* Krasnik, 8 July 1931). Polish baritone, working in the USSR. He studied in Moscow and joined the Bol'shoy Theatre in 1963, later becoming a soloist there. His firm tone and vivid temperament have served particularly well as Eugene Onegin and Andrey (*War and Peace*); his other roles include Renato (Covent Garden début, 1975) and Escamillo (Vienna Staatsoper, 1979). He is also a noted interpreter of songs, especially the Russian repertory.

Mazzaferrata, Giovanni Battista (*b* Como or Pavia; *d* ?Ferrara, 26 Feb 1691). Italian composer. He held posts as *maestro di cappella* at Vercelli Cathedral, at the Accademia della Morte and cathedral in Ferrara, and may have worked in Tuscany. One of the most individual composers of his day, he wrote sacred cantatas and madrigals as well as a notable set of sonatas (1674) whose light, fluent style foreshadows that of the early Classical period.

Mazzinghi, Joseph (*b* London, 25 Dec 1765; *d* Downside, 15 Jan 1844). English composer of Corsican origin. A child prodigy, he studied with J.C. Bach in London and at 19 became music director and harpsichordist at the King's Theatre. Before leaving there in 1798 he presented over 20 ballets (most including pieces by other composers), two English and two Italian operas. Later he taught the piano (notably to the Princess of Wales) and composed other English stage works and numerous instrumental works for amateurs, especially piano sonatas with violin accompaniment and (from 1810) variations and arrangements for piano, harp and flute. He also wrote many songs, glees etc.

Mazzocchi, Domenico (*b* Civita Castellana, bap. 8 Nov 1592; *d* Rome, 21 Jan 1665). Italian composer. By 1621 he was living in Rome, where he served Cardinal Ippolito Aldobrandini as a musician until 1638. His other patrons included Pope Urban VIII (Maffeo Barberini), who secured a lifelong benefice for him in 1637. The most elegant and expressive of his music appears in his vocal chamber works, among them motets, dialogues, sonnets (notably the lament *Lagrime amare all' anima*, 1638) and a book of madrigals (1638); the latter combine old and new techniques. All the published works, unusually, contain dynamic and tempo markings. Mazzocchi also composed two operas and one Italian and several Latin oratorios.

Mazzocchi, Virgilio (*b* Civita Castellana, bap. 22 July 1597; *d* there, 3 Oct 1646). Italian composer, brother of Domenico Mazzocchi. A pupil of his brother in Rome, he later held a series of posts there as a *maestro di cappella*, first at the Chiesa del Gesù and later at St John Lateran (1628–9) and the Cappella Giulia of St Peter's (from 1629). He wrote various sacred works, some secular vocal pieces and a sacred opera, and collaborated with Marco Marazzoli in the comic opera *Chi soffre speri* (1639, Rome).

Mazzucato, Alberto (*b* Udine, 28 July 1813; *d* Milan, 31 Dec 1877). Italian composer, teacher and writer. He studied at the Padua Conservatory and wrote for the stage (notably *Esmeralda*, 1838) until the 1840s, when he abandoned composition for a teaching career at the Milan Conservatory (director from 1872). He contributed to the *Gazzetta musicale di Milano* (1845–58) and was *maestro direttore e concertatore* at La Scala (1859–68).

Mbira [mbila]. Term used in southern and south-eastern Africa for various types of MARIMBA, LAMELLAPHONE or XYLOPHONE. One of the most powerful African melodic instruments, it is made in several pitch ranges and accompanies singer-dancers in orchestras which often represent political power.

Meale, Richard (Graham) (*b* Sydney, 24 Aug 1932). Australian composer. Essentially self-taught, he was influenced by Messiaen and Boulez and by Lorca's poetry, then from 1965 by Japanese art (*Clouds now and then* for orchestra, 1969); his works since the early 1970s are less related to literary or metaphysical sources and include *Viridian* for strings (1978).

Meane. English term originally referring to the middle part of a three-voice polyphonic texture. In the late 16th century and the 17th it was sometimes used synonymously with altus or countertenor.

Mean-tone. A system of temperament or a tuning of the scale, used particularly for earlier music on instruments lacking any capacity for flexibility of intonation during performance. The system is based on pure major 3rds (frequency ratio 5:4) divided into two equal whole tones; to achieve this, the 5th has to be made smaller than pure by a quarter of the syntonic comma. This system is sometimes called 'quarter-comma mean-tone'. The term is, however, also applied to other Renaissance and Baroque keyboard tunings in which major 3rds are slightly modified; these include, for example, $\frac{2}{7}$-comma mean-tone and $\frac{1}{5}$-comma mean-tone temperaments. In mean-tone temperaments, E♭ is higher in pitch than D♯ (etc), and triads mostly sound more resonant than in equal temperament. *See* TEMPERAMENT; JUST INTONATION.

Measure. (1) English term of *c*1550–1650 for a sequence of dance steps in slow or moderate duple time roughly corresponding to one strain of music. Measures were usually set to pavans and almans.

(2) American term, equivalent to the English 'bar', for the metrical units marked off along the staff by vertical lines (bars or bar-lines). *See* BAR.

Mechanical instrument. A musical instrument in which the sound is produced automatically or mechanically, usually without a performer (some instruments involve a degree of human participation). The most important part of a mechanical instrument or automatophone is the device for regulating the musical sounds, that is, a cylinder, punched cardboard strip, metal disc or similar mechanism; of these, the cylinder is by far the oldest.

With the development of clockwork mechanism, clock towers were often equipped with carillons that played a melody by means of a cylinder with pins; carillon production continued in the Low Countries throughout the 16th and 17th centuries. In the late Renaissance, artistic cabinets contained organ automatophones, or mechanical organs, and smaller organs were incorporated in flute-playing clocks, popular in the second half of the 18th century (*see* MUSICAL CLOCK). The first barrel organs appeared in the 18th century (*see* BARREL ORGAN and BIRD INSTRUMENTS) and often replaced the organ in smaller churches. Modifications of this instrument were used in amusement enterprises, in circuses and with merry-go-rounds (*see* FAIRGROUND ORGAN). Attempts to imitate the sound of the orchestra resulted in the invention of the ORCHESTRION or a mechanical organ; these were often combined with percussion instruments or a piano.

Good tone, small size and reasonable price contributed to the development and wide distribution of the MUSICAL BOX in the 19th century; it was based on a metal comb with teeth of different lengths. Intensive mechanization of string instruments did not take place until the 19th century, when 'crank-handle pianos' or 'piano organs' appeared in Italy and England (*see* BARREL PIANO). Their sound is rather like a xylophone; there are no dampers and the pins on the cylinder are not adapted to achieve dynamic effects. The PIANOLA, patented in 1897, incorporated a pneumatic mechanism operated by pedals; it was equipped with 88 mechanical 'fingers', which could be used freely with a perforated strip, enabling rhythmical extravagance and harmonizations never previously attempted by composers (*see* PLAYER PIANO).

In 1908 the first mechanical violin, the 'virtuosa', was constructed in the USA. This was an ordinary violin placed in an instrument containing a number of levers and mechanical 'fingers'; a disc replaced the bow. It was followed by the 'violina' in 1911 and the 'violinista' in 1920. With the advance of electronic and cybernetic musical machines, automatophones had virtually ceased to exist by the 1930s. Their cylinders and perforated strips, however, fulfil the same function as modern sound recordings,

and they can provide valuable information about historical tuning, performing practice and tempo.

Médée. Opera in three acts by Cherubini to a libretto by F.B. Hoffmann after Euripides (1797, Paris). Operas on the same subject have been written by M.-A. Charpentier (1693), Benda (1775), Mayr (1813) and Milhaud (1938) among others; Barber wrote a Medea ballet (1946).

Meder, Johann Valentin (*b* Wasungen, bap. 3 May 1649; *d* Riga, end July 1719). German composer. He worked as a court singer, then (1674–80) as Kantor at Tallinn, where he presented the opera *Die beständige Argenia* (1680), the first of his four stage works. After a period at Riga, he was Kapellmeister at St Marien, Danzig (1687–98) then at Königsberg Cathedral and from 1700 at Riga Cathedral. He was an excellent organist. Besides stage works he composed some 150 motets, cantatas, masses etc which show Buxtehude's influence; those surviving include an oratorio Passion (1700).

Mederitsch(-Gallus), Johann (Georg Anton) (*b* Vienna, bap. 27 Dec 1752; *d* L'vov, 18 Dec 1835). Austrian composer. After a period as theatre Kapellmeister at Olomouc, 1781–2, he worked in Vienna as a composer, teacher and double bass player. In the 1790s he was Kapellmeister at Buda. A popular and prolific composer, he wrote Singspiels and music for plays (mostly for Vienna), and instrumental and sacred works.

Medial cadence [inverted cadence]. A CADENCE whose penultimate chord is in inversion, as opposed to a 'radical' cadence, whose chords are in root position. (Some writers regard the medial cadence as a type of imperfect cadence.)

Mediant. The third step or degree of the major or minor scale, so called because of its intermediate position between the key note (tonic) and the 5th degree (dominant).

Medici. Italian family of music patrons. The rulers of Florence for most of the period 1434–1737, they were renowned for their patronage of learning, literature, the arts and science. Musical chapels were maintained at the city's cathedral and baptistry from 1438; especially influential were Lorenzo the Magnificent (ruled 1449–92) and his son Giovanni, who ruled as Pope Leo X from 1513 and patronized many famous musicians. Duke Cosimo I (ruled 1537–74) reorganized and enlarged the chapels and began the practice of retaining musicians and dancers at court. He was also the first to commission musical festivities for family and state occasions. *Intermedi* were staged between the acts of plays, and in 1600 the first operas were given: Caccini's *Il rapimento di Cefalo* and Peri's *Euridice* (the earliest complete extant opera). A later Medici heir apparent, Prince Ferdinando (1663–1713), patronized Alessandro and Domenico Scarlatti, Handel and others.

Medieval drama. The vast corpus of medieval drama comprises essentially two types of religious drama: liturgical drama, in which a Latin text is sung monophonically, and the vernacular play, in which various kinds of music are introduced into spoken dialogue. Some secular plays with incidental music also exist from the Middle Ages, but the liturgy was the main source of medieval drama although various types of lyric song (notably dance-song), the *lauda spirituale*, the *planctus* and the *Marienklage* were also important.

The development of liturgical drama (mostly not strictly part of the liturgy) was not chronological, nor was medieval drama cultivated equally all over Europe. Different traditions emanate from the various centres. Important early ones were St Martial, St Gall, Winchester and Fleury, but others flourished in northern France, England, northern Italy and eastern Spain. The dialogue tropes of the Introit of the Mass, particularly the *Quem queritis* dialogues of Christmas and Easter, provide the most important source for dramatic ceremony in church. From the 10th century to the 16th an enlarged version of the Easter dialogue, known as the *Visitatio sepulchri*, accounts for about two-thirds of the extant repertory. In addition to the Introit trope, it included antiphons, hymns, laments and often the Easter sequence *Victimae paschali*. Its function was to celebrate the joy of the Resurrection; the Christmas plays centred on the adoration of the shepherds (*Officium pastorum*) and of the Magi (*Officium Stelle*). Plays with biblical subjects (notably the celebrated *Play of Daniel*), saints' plays (Miracles) and Passion plays have also been preserved, though the latter, with its human approach to the suffering of Christ, border on the province of vernacular drama.

In contrast to liturgical drama, plays in the vernacular were almost always performed outdoors, dependent on a number of sites, or 'houses', in the streets and squares of a town, whether use was made of pageant-wagons or not. Musically, the most important types of vernacular plays are: (*a*) the *planctus* of the Virgin Mary (*Marienklagen*), which took place as an extra-liturgical event on Good Friday; (*b*) a variety of non-liturgical religious plays, like the *Play of Adam*, which follow no particular pattern; and (*c*) early secular drama, such as Adam de la Halle's *Robin et Marion* of *c*1283. The richest surviving repertory of vernacular plays is to be found in Germany but, as in the case of liturgical drama, traditions and developments varied greatly throughout Europe.

Mediņš, Jānis (*b* Riga, 9 Oct 1890; *d* Stockholm, 4 March 1966). Latvian composer. He studied in Riga, where he worked as a conductor and teacher; in 1948 he settled in Stockholm. He wrote operas, orchestral works and songs in a nationalist Romantic style; his *Love's Victory* (1935) was the first Latvian ballet.

His brothers Jāzeps (1877–1947) and Jēkabs (1885–1971) were also composers.

Medium, The. Opera in two acts by Menotti to his own libretto (1946, New York).

Medley. A selection (or potpourri) of well-known tunes. The 18th-century 'medley overture' was revived in Victorian times, when it usually consisted of a string of tunes from the work it precedes (as in Sullivan's operas).

Medtner [Metner], Nikolay (Karlovich) (*b* Moscow, 5 Jan 1880; *d* London, 13 Nov 1951). Russian composer. He studied the piano under Safonov at the Moscow Conservatory (1897–1900) and had

composition lessons with Arensky and Taneyev, though was mostly self-taught. In 1921 he left Russia. He settled in Paris (1925–35), but was out of sympathy with musical developments there and found a more receptive audience in London, where he spent his last 16 years. He belonged in the line of Russian composer-pianists, though his music is close too to the Schumann-Brahms tradition. His works include three piano concertos (1918, 1927, 1943), much solo piano music, three violin sonatas and songs.

Meester, Louis de (*b* Roeselare, 28 Oct 1904). Belgian composer. In 1945 he began working for Belgian radio; he has undertaken much electronic research. Many of his compositions are incidental music.

Méfano, Paul (*b* Bassorah, 6 March 1937). French composer. He studied with Messiaen and Milhaud at the Paris Conservatoire (1960–64) and has developed a vigorous, post-Boulezian style while also working as a conductor. *La messe des voleurs* (1972) successfully combines live and electronic resources.

Mefistofele. Opera in a prologue and five acts by Boito to his own libretto after Goethe (1868, Milan).

Mehta, Zubin (*b* Bombay, 29 April 1936). Indian conductor. After study in Vienna he won the 1958 Liverpool International Conductors' Competition. He was appointed to the Montreal SO (1960–67) and was musical director of the Los Angeles PO (1962–77). From 1977 he was musical director of the Israel PO and from 1978 of the New York PO. His performances are noted for warm expression and rhythmic vigour, not without some flamboyance.

Méhul, Etienne-Nicolas (*b* Givet, 22 June 1763; *d* Paris, 18 Oct 1817). French composer. Trained as an organist, he was taken to Paris in 1778 or 1779, where he became a pupil of J.-F. Edelmann; he published keyboard sonatas in 1783 but worked mainly on setting opera librettos, developing the *opéra comique* tradition of Grétry and Dalayrac. *Euphrosine* (1790) and *Stratonice* (1792) made him famous throughout France. In 1793 he joined the staff of the Institut National de Musique and began producing civic pieces in the republican vein, notably the *Chant du départ*; from 1795 he was an inspector of the new Conservatoire. Although the failure rate of his operas after 1800 increased, their overtures were successful (*La chasse du jeune Henri* incorporates hunting-calls) and many numbers became popular. He turned to symphonic writing: the two published symphonies (1808–9) are, with the tuneful *Joseph* (1807; his most famous *opéra comique* and last important stage work), the climax of his achievement. In structure they resemble Haydn's, but in rhythmic drive and unity the G minor symphony is comparable to Beethoven's Fifth. As an opera composer Méhul is important for his exploitation of the orchestra – he expanded the cello's role and made extensive use of stopped horn notes and subdivided strings (his opera without violins, *Uthal*, 1806, is well known) – and for his use of the reminiscence-motif and chromaticism to convey psychological or atmospheric description. Beethoven's trumpet-calls in *Fidelio* and Weber's scoring and use of reminiscence-motifs are alike indebted to Méhul.

Dramatic music Euphrosine (1790); *Stratonice* (1792); Le jeune Henri (1797); Ariodant (1799); Uthal (1806); Joseph (1807); Les amazones (1811); La journée aux aventures (1816); *c*25 others; ballet music
Vocal music Mass, A♭ (?1804); cantatas, incl. Chant national du 14 juillet 1800 (1800); patriotic hymns, songs
Instrumental music 4 syms.; music for wind ensemble; chamber pieces; 6 keyboard sonatas

Mei, Girolamo (*b* Florence, 27 May 1519; *d* Rome, July 1594). Italian music historian. His pioneering *De modis musicis antiquorum* (MS, 1566–73), a comprehensive four-volume study of ancient Greek music, was a decisive influence on the development of monody and music drama in the late 16th and early 17th centuries.

Mei, Orazio (*b* Pisa, 26 May 1731; *d* Livorno, 1 March 1788). Italian composer. He became organist at Pisa Cathedral in 1759 and *maestro di cappella* at Livorno Cathedral in 1763; he wrote chiefly sacred music, including a *Stabat mater* of much expressive intensity generated by skilful use of chromaticism.

Meier, Waltraud (*b* Würzburg, 9 Jan 1956). German mezzo-soprano. She made her début in Würzburg and sang in other German houses (Mannheim, Dortmund, Hanover and Stuttgart), making her Bayreuth début in 1983 as Kundry, a role she has sung at the Vienna Staatsoper (1987) and Covent Garden (1988: her début there was as Eboli, 1985). She has also sung in Buenos Aires, Paris and at La Scala, chiefly in the dramatic Wagner roles, where her powerful singing and intense dramatic involvement make her a compelling performer.

Meifred, Pierre-Joseph Emile (*b* Colmar, 13 Nov 1791; *d* Paris, 28 Aug 1867). French horn player and designer. He studied with Dauprat at the Paris Conservatoire, where he later taught. He gave the first French performance on the valve horn (recently introduced from Germany), and designed great improvements to it, making it possible to use crooks in different pitches.

Meistergesang. A German tradition of song-writing and performance among the rising bourgeois classes that flourished from the 14th century to the 17th, reaching its apogee in the 16th. The Meistersinger were usually members of the professional classes who formed themselves into guilds (*Gesellschaften*), under the strict control of the city authorities; they enforced the *Schulordnung*, or rules for the composition and performance of *Meisterlieder* laid down in the 16th century. About 16 000 Meistersinger Lieder survive in 120 MSS, the earliest of which dates from the 15th century, but melodies (or *Töne*) are found in few sources. The exact origins of the Meistergesang are unknown, but it was clearly related to the *Sangspruchdichter*, or wandering troubadour tradition of the 13th and 14th centuries, in that its founders imitated their poetry. Of the many guilds, details are extant only for that in Nuremburg, which received great impetus from the activities of the shoemaker Hans Sachs (1494–1576), a romanticized version of whose career is presented in Wagner's opera *Die Meistersinger von Nürnberg*. Some of the guilds continued to thrive into the 19th and 20th centuries; the last Meistersinger died in 1922. Many of the songs are about the Meistergesang itself, but are otherwise largely religious in inspiration and moralizing in tone, and thus provided a means for broadening the education of the lower and middle classes. The Meistersinger always showed awareness of their art and its significance.

Meistersinger von Nürnberg, Die. *See* MASTERSINGERS OF NUREMBERG, THE.

Mel, Rinaldo del (*b* Mechlin, *c*1554; *d c*1598). Flemish composer. His family was connected with the duchy of Lorraine and he was well educated. He was at the Lisbon court (*c*1572–80), then lived mainly in Italy, visiting Liège (1587–8) and Antwerp (1588–9). He published four books of motets (1581–95), showing Netherlands and Palestrinian influence, and at least 13 of madrigals (1583–96), where melodic interest tends to be in the top voice.

Melani, Alessandro (*b* Pistoia, 4 Feb 1639; *d* Rome, Oct 1703). Italian composer, brother of Jacopo Melani. After serving as *maestro di cappella* in Orvieto and Ferrara and then at Pistoia Cathedral (1667), he moved to Rome, where he became *maestro di cappella* of S Maria Maggiore and (by 1672) of S Luigi dei Francesi. He was the leading composer of sacred music there and an important precursor of Alessandro Scarlatti, writing ten oratorios and over 100 motets and other liturgical works, many of them polychoral. He also composed several operas and a number of cantatas, arias etc.

Melani, Jacopo (*b* Pistoia, 6 July 1623; *d* there, 19 Aug 1676). Italian composer. He served at Pistoia Cathedral as organist and then *maestro di cappella*; in 1667 he moved to Rome. He was the leading 17th-century composer of comic operas. Of his *c*10 stage works, the most successful was the satirical opera *Il Girello* (1668, Rome), which began a revival of Roman opera. Most of the others were written for Florence.

All six of Melani's brothers were musicians. The most notable, apart from Alessandro, was Atto Melani (1626–1714), an alto, who sang in operas in Paris and Rome and was a composer, a diplomat and a politician.

Melba, Dame Nellie [Mitchell, Helen Porter] (*b* Richmond, Melbourne, 19 May 1861; *d* Sydney, 23 Feb 1931). Australian soprano. After study in Paris her career began at the Théâtre de la Monnaie, Brussels (1887). From 1888 until World War I she was heard in London, notably as Lucia, Gilda and Gounod's Juliette; she also appeared with the Chicago Opera and sang at the Met, 1883–1910. She retired in 1926. She was valued for her beautiful tone and perfect technique, though these qualities were not always matched by taste and musicianship.

Melcer-Szczawiński, Henryk (*b* Kalisz, 21 Sept 1869; *d* Warsaw, 18 April 1928). Polish pianist, composer, conductor and teacher. His teachers included Leschetizky in Vienna. As a pianist he won acclaim throughout Europe, particularly playing his own piano concertos (1895, 1898). He was conductor of the Warsaw PO (1910–12) and Warsaw Opera (1915–16), a teacher and influential concert organizer and a valued director of the conservatory (1922). His works include operas, piano music and songs.

Melchior, Lauritz (*b* Copenhagen, 20 March 1890; *d* Santa Monica, 18 March 1973). Danish tenor, later American. He sang at the Royal Opera, Copenhagen, from 1913, first as a baritone. His international career dates from 1924, when he sang Siegmund at Covent Garden. In London until 1939 and at the Met, 1926–50, he was the outstanding Heldentenor of his generation, and sang Parsifal, Siegfried and Tristan at Bayreuth (1924–31).

Melik-Pashayev, Alexander Shamil'yevich (*b* Tbilisi, 23 Oct 1905; *d* Moscow, 18 June 1964). Georgian conductor. He studied with Tcherepnin and at Leningrad with Gauk and held appointments as conductor at Tbilisi and at the Bol'shoy in Moscow (1953–62). His British début was at Covent Garden (*Queen of Spades*, 1961). He was admired for his control and shaping of large-scale Romantic works, seen in operas of Verdi and Russian composers of the 19th and 20th centuries.

Meliš [Zminský], Emanuel (Antonín) (*b* Zminný, 15 Oct 1831; *d* Prague, 27 June 1916). Czech writer on music. He founded and edited the first regular Czech music journal, *Dalibor* (1858–64; 1869), to which he contributed the first biography of Smetana (1863).

Melisma (Gk.:'song'). A group of more than five or six notes sung to a single syllable, especially in liturgical chant. They are characteristic of graduals, tracts, responsories and alleluias in the Gregorian repertory. In early medieval chant they could be inserted into or removed from a chant, and so acquired stereotyped melodic characteristics. Chant melismas served as tenors for polyphony from the 12th century to the 15th; melismatic style has been used regularly in polyphonic vocal music since the 14th century.

Melkus, Eduard (*b* Baden, 1 Sept 1928). Austrian violinist. He studied in Vienna and in 1958 was appointed professor at the Hochschule für Musik there; he has also taught widely abroad. He specializes in Baroque and Classical music and in 1965 founded the Vienna Capella Academica; his recordings show his sweet tone, fluent phrasing and effervescent ornamentation.

Mell, Davis (*b* Wilton, 15 Nov 1604; *d* London, 4 April 1662). English violinist and composer. He served as a violinist under Charles I and during the Commonwealth and in 1660 became Master of the King's Band. His instrumental works include masque music and many dances for violin and bass, grouped in suites.

Mellers, Wilfrid (Howard) (*b* Leamington, 26 April 1914). English composer and writer on music. He studied at Cambridge (1933–8) and had composition lessons from Wellesz and Rubbra in Oxford; he taught at Cambridge (1945–8), Birmingham (1948–59), Pittsburgh (1960–63) and York (1964–82). His large, varied output belongs within an English visionary tradition going back through Britten and Tippett, Blake and the high Baroque, to medieval esoterism, though he has also been influenced by the openness of American music, on which he has written with wide-ranging enthusiasm. His books include a pioneering study of Couperin, many stimulating works on the Beatles and other popular topics, and volumes on Bach and Beethoven.

Melli [Megli], Domenico Maria (*b* Reggio Emilia; *fl* early 17th century). Italian composer. He was a lawyer, for a time at Padua. He published three volumes of monodies, two of them as early as 1602 (the year of Caccini's *Le nuove musiche*); they also include some duets and dialogues. His monodies are mostly madrigals in a less ornamented style than Caccini's. His relative Pietro Paolo (*fl* 1612–20) was a lutenist at the imperial court in Vienna and composed for his instrument.

Mellnäs, Arne (*b* Stockholm, 30 Aug 1933). Swedish composer. He studied with Larsson and Blomdahl at the Stockholm Musikhögskolan (1953–63), where he remained as a teacher. His works have involved Ligetian and aleatory features. He became internationally known for the orchestral *Collage* (1962).

Mellophone. A valved brass instrument of circular form in E♭ or F (alto); common in the USA, it corresponds with the English TENOR COR and is intended to replace the horn in marching bands.

Mel'nikov, Ivan Alexandrovich (*b* St Petersburg, 4 March 1832; *d* there, 8 July 1906). Russian baritone. He was a favourite with St Petersburg audiences from 1867 to 1890, his best-known roles including Borodin's Prince Igor, Ruslan in Glinka's *Ruslan and Lyudmila* and Boris Godunov in Musorgsky's opera (a part he created).

Melodeon. (1) Term extensively used in the USA in the early 19th century for a small reed organ with one keyboard and one or two sets of reeds.

(2) A button accordion: a rectangular, bellows-operated, free-reed instrument with buttons on the right-hand end of the bellows and buttons or keys on the left; different notes are produced by the press and draw of the bellows. Such an instrument was first patented in 1829. Melodeons have been widely used in non-Western societies.

Melodic minor. *See* MINOR.

Mélodie. French song of the 19th and 20th centuries, usually for solo voice and piano. The first major composer associated with the *mélodie* was Berlioz; others who contributed to the genre included Gounod, Massenet, Saint-Saëns, Duparc and Fauré. In their *mélodies*, the term implied a type of serious lyric song distinct from the German lied, and a distinctively French style marks the Verlaine settings of Debussy and the songs of Poulenc and others of Les Six.

Melodrama. A kind of drama, or a section of one, in which spoken lines are accompanied or punctuated by music. The music of French *mélodrames*, of which Rousseau's *Pygmalion* (score by Coignet) is an early and influential example, was divided into short, independent numbers to be played between the spoken passages. The German form (*Melodram*), perfected by Georg Benda in such works as *Ariadne auf Naxos*, aimed for greater musical continuity. Mozart's enthusiasm for Benda's work bore fruit in the Singspiel *Zaide* (1779–80), and Beethoven's interest in the genre is evident in the dungeon scene in *Fidelio* and in the incidental music to *Die Ruinen von Athen*, *König Stephan* and *Egmont*. Weber, Schubert, Schumann, Liszt and many 19th-century opera composers tried their hand, and the melodrama thrived in the lands that are now Czechoslovakia. 20th-century examples are no less numerous, and include some which make use of SPRECHGESANG.

The term is also used for a kind of play, popular in the 19th century, in which romantic and frequently sensational happenings are carried through until Good triumphs and Evil is frustrated.

Melodramma. An Italian term used during the Baroque era, and often in later periods, for the libretto of a serious opera.

Melody. A series of musical notes arranged in succession, in a particular rhythmic pattern, to form a recognizable unit. Melody is a universal human phenomenon, traceable to pre-historic times. The origins of melodic thinking have been sought in language, in birdsong and other animal sounds, and in the crying and playing of young children. The early development of melody may have proceeded from one-step voice inflections through combinations of such small intervals as minor 3rds and major 2nds to pentatonic patterns (i.e. based on a five-note scale) such as are found in many parts of the world (including some quite highly developed forms of Western art music where they often serve as a basis).

The concept of melody differs widely across cultures. One might compare the intensity of detail in an Indian raga with the austere lines of Western ecclesiastical chant, or the static, repetitive melodies of Japanese noh plays with the expansively lyrical lines of a Schubert song or the motivically generated melodies of Beethoven. In some cultures, specific melodies are associated with particular texts, as in Japanese noh plays and Western plainchant. Most melodies display patterns of rise or fall, of motivic patterning and of final cadencing that are specific to their cultures. Often such matters are related to the key or mode in which they are cast, which is likely to dictate their final note.

Melody is traditionally considered, along with rhythm and harmony, as one of the three fundamental elements in music. It is an oversimplification to regard them as independent, however. Rhythm is an important element within melody itself, not only because each note of the melody has a duration but also because larger-scale rhythmic articulation gives shape and vitality to a melody; while, at least in Western music, harmony often plays a fundamental role in determining the contour and direction of a melodic line, and the harmonic implications of a line of melody may accordingly give it life. Ideas of what constitutes a melody, and in particular a beautiful melody, are constantly changing in Western music; almost every generation has criticized the next for producing music lacking in melody when it is simply that ideas of good melody are changing – a point strongly made by Wagner in *Die Meistersinger* (1868) where, incorporating melodic ideas from the mastersingers of the 16th century, Wagner opposed the conservative Beckmesser, who believes in a set of rules for the composition of melody, with the young knight Walther from Stolzing, who has a new, imaginative idea (as Wagner felt he did himself) of what melody can be. In vocal music, from the time of the medieval troubadours through the

song composers of the late Renaissance and the composers of bel canto opera, melody has always been of primary importance, and it remained so particularly in the Classical and Romantic eras, in instrumental music as well as vocal. The breakdown of the tonal system in the 20th century, and the freer use of chromaticism and large leaps, has made melody less easy to apprehend.

Melograph. An electronic instrument invented in the 1950s that converts a melody into a continuous graphic representation; it is important in the study of elements of non-Western music that cannot conveniently be expressed in traditional notation.

Mélophone. A portable free-reed instrument, invented in Paris in 1837, shaped like a guitar, harp or cello with a keyboard and bellows. It is 80–130 cm high by 32–65 cm and is rested on the right thigh; the right hand works the bellows and the left the 40 to 84 keys, some with octave couplings, controlling a range of three to five octaves.

Melos Quartet. German string quartet, based at Stuttgart and led by Wilhelm Melcher. It was formed in 1965, has toured widely (after winning competitions in Geneva and Rio de Janiero in 1966) and has recorded all Beethoven's and Schubert's quartets. (It should not be confused with the Melos Ensemble of London, formed in 1950 as a variable group of up to 12 players.)

Melusina, The Fair. *See* SCHÖNE MELUSINE, DIE.

Membranophone. Generic term for instruments that produce their sound from tightly stretched membranes. They are subdivided according to whether they are struck drums, plucked drums, friction drums (*see* DRUM) or singing membranes (which are made to vibrate by speaking or singing into them).

Mendel, Arthur (*b* Boston, 6 June 1905; *d* Newark, NJ, 14 Oct 1979). American musicologist. He studied at Harvard and in Paris with Nadia Boulanger (1925–7), then worked as a critic, in music publishing and as a conductor of Baroque music. He taught in New York and from 1952 at Princeton. He worked on the history of pitch, on Josquin and on the application of computer technology to musicological problems; but above all he produced studies of Bach's life and editions of his works (notably the documentary biography *The Bach Reader* (1945), with Hans T. David). He was the foremost American Bach scholar of his generation.

Mendelssohn, Arnold (Ludwig) (*b* Racibórz, 26 Dec 1855; *d* Darmstadt, 19 Feb 1933). German teacher, composer and organist, son of a second cousin of Felix Mendelssohn. He studied in Berlin. An advocate of Bach and Schütz, he contributed to the renewal of interest in Lutheran church music, teaching at Bonn, Cologne, Darmstadt and Frankfurt, where Hindemith was among his pupils. His compositions include polyphonic sacred music, folklike stage works and songs.

Mendelssohn (-Bartholdy) [Hensel], **Fanny (Cäcilie)** (*b* Hamburg, 14 Nov 1805; *d* Berlin, 14 May 1847). German pianist and composer, sister of Felix Mendelssohn. She was a gifted pianist and composer of songs (some published under her brother's

ser of songs (some published under her brother's name) and piano music. Her diary and correspondence provide vivid and essential material on Felix and the musical life of her time.

Mendelssohn (-Bartholdy), (Jakob Ludwig) Felix (*b* Hamburg, 3 Feb 1809; *d* Leipzig, 4 Nov 1847). German composer. Of a distinguished intellectual, artistic and banking family in Berlin, he grew up in a privileged environment (the family converted from Judaism to Christianity in 1816, taking the additional 'Bartholdy'). He studied the piano with Ludwig Berger and theory and composition with Zelter, producing his first piece in 1820; thereafter, a profusion of sonatas, concertos, string symphonies, piano quartets and Singspiels revealed his increasing mastery of counterpoint and form. Besides family travels and eminent visitors to his parents' salon (Humboldt, Hegel, Klingemann, A.B. Marx, Devrient), early influences included the poetry of Goethe (whom he knew from 1821) and the Schlegel translations of Shakespeare; these are traceable in his best music of the period, including the exuberant String Octet op.20 and the vivid, poetic overture to *A Midsummer Night's Dream* op.21. His gifts as a conductor also showed themselves early: in 1829 he directed a pioneering performance of Bach's *St Matthew Passion* at the Berlin Singakademie, promoting the modern cultivation of Bach's music.

A period of travel and concert-giving introduced Mendelssohn to England, Scotland (1829) and Italy (1830–31); after return visits to Paris (1831) and London (1832, 1833) he took up a conducting post at Düsseldorf (1833–5), concentrating on Handel's oratorios. Among the chief products of this time were *The Hebrides* (first performed in London, 1832), the G minor Piano Concerto, *Die erste Walpurgisnacht*, the Italian Symphony (1833, London) and *St Paul* (1836, Düsseldorf). But as a conductor and music organizer his most significant achievement was in Leipzig (1835–45), where to great acclaim he conducted the Gewandhaus Orchestra, championing both historical and modern works (Bach, Beethoven, Weber, Schumann, Berlioz), and founded and directed the Leipzig Conservatory (1843). Composing mostly in the summer holidays, he produced *Ruy Blas* overture, a revised version of the *Hymn of Praise*, the Scottish Symphony, the now famous Violin Concerto op.64 and the fine Piano Trio in C minor (1845). Meanwhile, he was intermittently (and less happily) employed by the king as a composer and choirmaster in Berlin, where he wrote highly successful incidental music, notably for *A Midsummer Night's Dream* (1843). Much sought after as a festival organizer, he was associated especially with the Lower Rhine and Birmingham music festivals; he paid ten visits to England, the last two (1846–7) to conduct *Elijah* in Birmingham and London. Always a warm friend and valued colleague, he was devoted to his family; his death at the age of 38, after a series of strokes, was mourned internationally.

With its emphasis on clarity and adherence to classical ideals, Mendelssohn's music shows alike the influences of Bach (fugal technique), Handel (rhythms, harmonic progressions), Mozart (dramatic characterization, forms, textures) and Beethoven (instrumental technique), though from 1825 he developed a characteristic style of his own, often underpinned by a literary, artistic, historical, geographical or emotional connection; indeed it was chiefly in his skilful use of extra-musical stimuli that he was a Romantic. His early and prodigious operatic gifts, clearly reliant on Mozart, failed to develop (despite his long search for suitable subjects), but his penchant for the dramatic found expression in the oratorios as well as in *Ruy Blas* overture, his *Antigone* incidental music and above all the enduring *Midsummer Night's Dream* music, in which themes from the overture are cleverly adapted as motifs in the incidental music. The oratorios, among the most popular works of their kind, draw inspiration from Bach and Handel and content from the composer's personal experience, *St Paul* being an allegory of Mendelssohn's own family history and *Elijah* of his years of dissension in Berlin. Among his other vocal works, the highly dramatic *Die erste Walpurgisnacht* op.60 (on Goethe's poem greeting springtime) and the Leipzig psalm settings deserve special mention; the choral songs and lieder are uneven, reflecting their wide variety of social functions.

After an apprenticeship of string symphony writing in a classical mould, Mendelssohn found inspiration in art, nature and history for his orchestral music. The energy, clarity and tunefulness of the Italian have made it his most popular symphony, although the elegiac Scottish represents a newer, more purposeful achievement. In his best overtures, essentially one-movement symphonic poems, the sea appears as a recurring image, from *Calm Sea and Prosperous Voyage* and *The Hebrides* to *The Lovely Melusine*. Less dependent on programmatic elements and at the same time formally innovatory, the concertos, notably that for violin, and the chamber music, especially some of the string quartets, the Octet and the two late piano trios, beautifully reconcile classical principles with personal feeling; these are among his most striking compositions. Of the solo instrumental works, the partly lyric, partly virtuoso *Lieder ohne Worte* for piano (from 1829) are elegantly written and often touching.

Dramatic music incidental music for 6 plays, including Antigone (1841), A Midsummer Night's Dream (1843), Athalie (1845); opera; 5 Singspiels
Choral music St Paul, oratorio (1836); Elijah, oratorio (1846); c30 psalms, sacred cantatas, larger sacred works; over 30 motets, anthems, shorter sacred works; 6 secular cantatas, incl. Die erste Walpurgisnacht (1832); over 60 choral songs
Vocal music 6 concert arias; over 70 songs; 12 duets
Orchestral music 13 str sinfonias; Sym. no.1, c (1824); Sym. no.2, 'Hymn of Praise', B♭ (1840); Sym. no.3, 'Scottish', a (1842); Sym. no.4, 'Italian', A (1833); Sym. no.5, 'Reformation', D (1830); A Midsummer Night's Dream, ov. (1826); Calm Sea and Prosperous Voyage, ov. (1828); The Hebrides, ov. (1830); The Lovely Melusine, ov. (1833); Ruy Blas, ov. (1839); Pf Conc. no.1, g (1831); Pf Conc. no.2, d (1837); Vn Conc., e (1844); other orch movements
Chamber music Octet, strs, op.20, E♭ (1825); 2 str qnts (op.18, A, 1826; op.87, B♭, 1845); 6 str qts (op.12, E♭, 1829; op.13, a, 1827; op.44 nos.1–3, D, e, E♭, 1837–8; op.80, f, 1847); 3 pf qts; 2 pf trios (op.49, d, 1839; op.66, c, 1845); 2

vn sonatas; 2 vc sonatas; Va Sonata
Piano music Lieder ohne Worte (8 sets) (1829–45); Variations
sérieuses op.54 (1841); sonatas, fugues, fantasias
Other works org preludes and fugues, sonatas; *c*60 canons;
transcrs. and arrs. of Bach, Handel, Mozart, Beethoven

Mendelssohn Akademie. *See* LEIPZIG CONSERVA-
TORY.

Mendès, Catulle (*b* Bordeaux, 20 May 1841; *d* St
Germain-en-Laye, 8 Feb 1909). French writer. He
published the first full-length biography of Wagner
(1886), also championing native French composers
including the young Debussy, with whom he collaborated on an abandoned opera (1889–91). Chabrier
and Messager are among the composers who used
his opera librettos.

Mengelberg, Willem (Josef) (*b* Utrecht, 28 March
1871; *d* Zuort, 22 March 1951). Dutch composer.
He studied in Utrecht and Cologne and in 1891 took
up a post in Lucerne, but in 1895 returned to the
Netherlands as conductor of the Amsterdam Concertgebouw, a post he held for the rest of his working life. He brought the orchestra into the front rank
of European ensembles. He was noted as an outstanding interpreter of Mahler and Strauss, but
brought much vigour to the entire Romantic repertory, also conducting admired Palm Sunday performances of Bach's *St Matthew Passion*. He was a
meticulous disciplinarian but often treated composers' markings freely. Having conducted in Germany during World War II, he was thereafter
banned in the Netherlands and spent his last years
in retirement. Two of his nephews were musicians:
Rudolf (1892–1959), a musicologist and composer,
and Karel (*b* 1902), a conductor in Germany and
elsewhere, a critic and composer in a wide range of
genres. Misha (*b* 1935), son of Karel, is an avant-
garde composer, involved in the use of improvisatory and jazz techniques.

Mennin, Peter (*b* Erie, PA, 17 May 1923; *d* New York,
17 June 1983). American composer. He studied with
Hanson and Rogers at the Eastman School and in
the 1940s established himself as a composer of diatonic symphonies; he composed nine (1941–81),
which have been widely performed. He was director
of the Peabody Conservatory (1958–62) and the
Juilliard School (1962–83).

Meno (It.). Less; 'meno mosso' means less fast.

Menotti, Gian Carlo (*b* Cadegliano, 7 July 1911).
American composer of Italian origin. He studied at
the Milan Conservatory and the Curtis Institute
(with Scalero, 1928–33), where a co-student was
Samuel Barber, his close friend for whom he later
wrote librettos. He won success with his comic one-
act opera *Amelia Goes to the Ball* (1937), which was
taken up by the Met in 1938 and led to an NBC
commission for a radio opera, *The Old Maid and the
Thief* (1939). A grand opera, *The Island God* (1942,
Met), was a failure; but it was followed after the war
by the chamber opera *The Medium* (1946), a supernatural tragedy notable for its sinister atmosphere; it
was paired with his short comedy *The Telephone*
(1947) for a Broadway run of 211 performances,
1947–8. The full-scale political melodrama *The
Consul* (1950), in a post-Puccini *verismo* style, and

The Saint of Bleecker Street (1954), an effective
drama in the same serious style, enjoyed much success, as had the television Christmas opera *Amahl
and the Night Visitors* (1951). His later works include more operas and orchestral pieces, including
several works for children written in a direct and
appealing style. More ambitious works (such as
Goya, 1986), have been criticized as musically thin
and too derivative. In 1958 he founded the Spoleto
Festival of Two Worlds, which he directed until
1967.

Operas Amelia al ballo (1937); The Old Maid and the Thief
(1939); The Island God (1942); The Medium (1946); The
Telephone (1947); The Consul (1950); Amahl and the
Night Visitors (1951); The Saint of Bleecker Street (1954);
Maria Golovin (1958); Labyrinth (1963); Le dernier sau-
vage (1963); Help, Help, the Globolinks! (1968); The Most
Important Man (1971); Tamu-Tamu (1973); The Hero
(1976); La loca (1979); Goya (1986)
Children's operas Martin's Lie (1964); The Egg (1976); The
Trial of the Gypsy (1978); Chip and his Dog (1979); A
Bride from Pluto (1982); The Boy who Grew too Fast
(1982)
Cantatas The Death of the Bishop of Brindisi (1963); Land-
scapes and Remembrances (1976); Muero porque no
muero (1982)
Choral music Missa O pulchritudo (1979)
Ballets Sebastian (1944); Errand into the Maze (1947); The
Unicorn, the Gorgon and the Manticore (1956)
Orchestral music Pf Conc. (1945); Apocalypse (1951); Vn
Conc. (1952); Triple Conc. (1970); Fantasia, vc, orch
(1976); Sym. no.1 (1976); Db Conc. (1983)
Chamber music; songs

Mensuration. The system devised in the late Middle
Ages governing rhythmic relationships between
long, breve and semibreve. The system was established *c*1250 by Franco of Cologne and continued in
use until the end of the 16th century. Under the
mensural system, the relationship between the long
and the breve (*modus*, 'mode'), the breve and the
semibreve (*tempus*, 'time') and the semibreve and the
minim (*prolatio*, 'prolation') may be either 3:1 (or
perfect) or, as in modern notation, 2:1 (or imperfect). *Modus* is normally imperfect. Imperfect time
and imperfect (or minor) prolation produce a metre
the equivalent of modern 2/4; imperfect time and
perfect (or major) prolation produce 6/8; perfect
time and imperfect prolation produce 3/4; and both
perfect produce 9/8. Other devices, such as the placing of a dot and the substitution of black notes for
white ones ('coloration'), are used to define particular aspects of rhythmic notation.

Menuet. A French dance in triple time of the 17th and
18th centuries. *See* MINUET.

Menuetto [tempo di menuetto]. Title for non-Italian
MINUET style movements of the later 18th century.

Menuhin, Sir Yehudi (*b* New York, 22 April 1916).
American-born violinist of Russian parentage. His
professional début was in San Francisco in 1924,
after study with Persinger, and he made his European début in Paris in 1927. After further study with
Enescu he played in New York and became an overnight celebrity, at the age of 11. His technical assurance and depth of understanding ensured lasting
success in the USA and Europe. In 1932 he made a
famous recording of Elgar's Concerto with the composer. After the war his playing was clouded by

technical problems but he continued to be a favourite, for his personal qualities as well as his interpretative ability. In 1959 he settled in London. In 1985 he became a British subject. His sisters Hephzibah (1920–81) and Yaltah (b 1922), and his son Jeremy (b 1951) are noted pianists. He has directed several festivals (Bath, Gstaad), played with and conducted his own chamber orchestra (founded 1958), throughout the world, and established a music school for talented children. He has achieved a remarkable position as a world citizen with diverse interests outside music and has collaborated in performing Indian music in Western culture.

Mephisto Waltzes. Four works by Liszt, their title referring to Mephistopheles. The first two were originally for orchestra (one as the second of *Two Episodes from Lenau's Faust*) and transcribed for piano solo and piano duet; the third and the fourth were for piano (1885).

Mer, La. Three symphonic sketches by Debussy (1905).

Merbecke [Marbeck], **John** (b ?Windsor, c1505–c1510; d c1585). English composer. A lay clerk at St George's Chapel, Windsor, in 1531 and subsequently an organist there, in 1543 he was arrested for his heretical adherence to Calvinism and narrowly escaped execution. He returned to St George's after his release from prison and devoted the rest of his life to the study of Protestantism. Although he composed Latin church music before c1550, he is best known for his *The Booke of Common Praier Noted* (1550), the first musical setting of services in the 1549 Prayer Book. It was probably designed for use in parish churches rather than cathedrals and consists of simple monodic music in the style of plainchant written in a special form of rhythmic notation.

Mercadante, (Giuseppe) Saverio (Raffaele) (b Altamura, bap. 17 Sept 1795; d Naples, 17 Dec 1870). Italian composer and teacher. He studied in Naples and was Zingarelli's favourite pupil (1816–20); from instrumental music he turned to opera in 1820, establishing a European reputation with the Rossinian *opera buffa Elisa e Claudio* (1821). After a time in Spain and Portugal (1826–30), while serving as *maestro di cappella* at Novara Cathedral (1833–40), he reconsidered his operatic style. *Il giuramento* (1837), considered his masterpiece, inaugurates the reforms for which he is remembered: seriousness of purpose and the strengthening of musico-dramatic integrity. By 1840 he was the most respected figure on the purely Italian operatic scene and director of the Naples Conservatory. Increasingly occupied with instrumental works, church music and teaching, but jealous of Verdi's success, he slowed down his operatic output. Among Mercadante's 60 operas, the most important are the 'reform' group from *Il giuramento* to *Il reggente* (1843), in which he deliberately varied the forms and accompaniments, eliminated brash and trivial orchestral effects, simplified vocal lines, reduced repetition and emphasized the drama. Verdian melodrama was influenced by these works (*Aida* has literal echoes of *La vestale*, 1840), though beside the powerful genius of Verdi they inevitably appeared old-fashioned and lacking in human appeal.

Mercure, Pierre (b Montreal, 21 Feb 1927; d Avallon, 29 Jan 1966). Canadian composer. He studied at the Quebec Conservatory and in Paris with Boulanger. In Montreal he was a bassoonist, administrator and the first Canadian producer of music on television. His early works looked towards Stravinsky, Milhaud, Honegger and jazz, but from 1959 he aligned himself with the avant garde, using tapes in many works. He died after a car accident.

Mercury. Haydn's Symphony no.43 in E♭ (by 1772).

Mercy, Lewis (b c1695; d ?London, c1750). English composer and recorder player. He served the Earl of Caernarvon in London and was a celebrated performer on the recorder (then becoming less popular than the transverse flute). He composed italianate solos for flute and for bassoon, with continuo.

Méreaux, Jean-Amédée Le Froid de (b Paris, 17 Sept 1802; d Rouen, 25 April 1874). French musicologist, pianist and composer. His main achievement is *Les clavecinistes de 1637 à 1790* (1864–7), an edition with essays on the composers represented. His grandfather Nicolas-Jean Le Froid de Méreaux (1745–97) was an organist and composer of operas and oratorios.

Merelli, Bartolomeo (b Bergamo, 19 May 1794; d Milan, 3/4 April 1879). Italian impresario. Though disliked as a manager, he is remembered for launching Verdi on his operatic career (1839). He also wrote librettos for Mayr, Vaccai and Donizetti (1818–24).

Merikanto, Aarre (b Helsinki, 29 June 1893; d there, 29 Sept 1958). Finnish composer. He was son of the composer Oskar Merikanto (1868–1924). He studied with Reger in Leipzig (1912–14) and Vasilenko in Moscow (1915–16), and taught at the Helsinki Academy (1936–58). His opera *Juha* (1922) invites comparison with Janáček; other works, in a highly coloured, chromatic style, include three symphonies (1916, 1918, 1953), three piano concertos (1913, 1937, 1955) and chamber music.

Meriläinen, Usko (b Tampere, 27 Jan 1930). Finnish composer. He studied at the Helsinki Academy (1951–6) and with Vogel in Ascona (1958), then worked in Tampere as a conductor and teacher. His works include symphonies, piano concertos, piano sonatas and ballets (notably *Arius*, 1960) in a highly structured style.

Merkù, Pavle (b Trieste, 12 July 1929). Yugoslav composer. He studied privately, and has worked in Trieste as a teacher and for the radio. His music makes discriminating use of new procedures; it includes the expressionist cantata *Von der Kindermörderin Maria Farrar* (1958).

Merques, Nicolas (fl 1433–6). French composer. A singer and cleric from Arras who entered the chapel of the Council of Basle in November 1433 is assumed to be the composer of a number of works attributed to N. (or C.) Merques. These include liturgical pieces and secular songs, all in the style of the mid-1430s – though his one extant motet is archaic in its use of separate texts in the three voices.

Merrick, Frank (b Bristol, 30 April 1886; d London, 19 Feb 1981). English pianist. He studied with Leschetizky and taught at conservatories in Manchester and

London. In 1928 he won a prize for finishing Schubert's 'Unfinished'; he also composed piano concertos and other works. He was a noted champion of the piano music of John Field, several of whose concertos and other works he recorded.

Merrie England. Light opera in two acts by German to a libretto by Basil Hood (1902, London).

Merrill, Robert (*b* Brooklyn, 4 June 1917). American baritone. He made his Met début in 1945 and over the next 30 years appeared in all the major French and Italian baritone roles. He recorded Germont and Renato with Toscanini and made his Covent Garden début in 1967. He was admired most for the natural beauty of his voice.

Merry Widow, The [Die lustige Witwe]. Operetta in three acts by Lehár to a libretto by V. Léon and L. Stein after Meilhac (1905, Vienna).

Merry Wives of Windsor, The [Die lustigen Weiber von Windsor]. Opera in three acts by Nicolai to a libretto by S.H.Mosenthal after Shakespeare (1849, Berlin).

Mersenne, Marin (*b* La Soultière, 8 Sept 1588; *d* Paris, 1 Sept 1648). French mathematician, philosopher and theorist. One of the leading French thinkers of the 17th century, he lived in Paris from 1619 as a Jesuit priest. His work is central to the academic and scientific movements of his time, and a major part of it is devoted to music. On the basis of practical experiment and observations, he made important discoveries concerning the nature and behaviour of sound, which are the foundation of the science of acoustics in later times. He also wrote on the theory and practice of music. His principal musical treatise is the *Harmonie universelle* (1636–7).

Merula, Tarquinio (*b* Cremona, 1594/5; *d* there, 10 Dec 1665). Italian composer and organist. His first posts as an organist were at Cremona, Lodi (1616–21) and the Polish court. From 1626 he held posts at Cremona Cathedral, with periods at Bergamo (1631–2, 1638–46). One of the finest and most progressive composers of his generation, he published several volumes of church music (1624–52); his sacred concertos for few voices resemble Monteverdi's, while those for more voices are in the style of Giovanni Gabrieli. His secular music comprises monodies, dialogues and accompanied madrigals; also important are his instrumental works, among them four books of ensemble canzonas (1615–51) and some keyboard pieces.

Merulo, Claudio (*b* Correggio, 8 April 1533; *d* Parma, 5 May 1604). Italian composer. He was organist of Brescia Cathedral (1556–7) and of St Mark's, Venice (1557–84), where he was also an organ consultant, publisher and teacher. From 1586 he was in Parma as organist to the duke, the cathedral (1587) and the Steccata company (1591). Famed for his organ playing, he developed a distinctive idiom (toccatas, ricercares etc; 10 bks, 1567–1611); nine books of sacred vocal music and four of madrigals also survive.

Mesangeau, René (*b* late 16th century; *d* Paris, 1638). French lutenist and composer. One of the greatest lutenists of the 17th century, he served at the French court from *c*1620 and wrote pieces for his instrument.

Messa di voce (It.: 'placing of the voice'). The singing or playing of a long note so that it begins quietly, swells to full volume and then diminishes. It was originally (in the early 17th century) regarded as an ornament; some later writers call for it on all long notes. Though primarily a vocal effect, it was also used (and has been much over-used) by instrumentalists. It should not be confused with the term *mezza voce*, an instruction (meaning 'half-voice') to use a subdued tone.

Messager, André (Charles Prosper) (*b* Montluçon, 30 Dec 1853; *d* Paris, 24 Feb 1929). French composer, conductor, pianist, opera administrator and writer. At the Ecole Niedermeyer, Paris, his teachers included Fauré and Saint-Saëns, who were to remain close friends. On leaving (1874) he was appointed organist at St Sulpice under Widor. Though best known as a skilled composer of light music – he achieved particular success with the operetta *Véronique* (1898) and the ballet *Les deux pigeons* (1886) – he won respect for his conducting, notably of Wagner and Mozart, for his versatility as a pianist (performing with Fauré) and orchestrator and for his administration of the Opéra-Comique (1898–1903; 1919–20), the Opéra (1907–14) and Covent Garden (1901–7). Encouraging Debussy with *Pelléas et Mélisande*, he conducted its première (1902), also introducing Charpentier's *Louise* and Massenet's *Grisélidis*. He was music critic of several newspapers, including *Le Figaro*.

Messiaen, Olivier (Eugène Prosper Charles) (*b* Avignon, 10 Dec 1908). French composer. He studied at the Paris Conservatoire (1919–30) with Dukas, Emmanuel and Dupré, and taught there (1941–78) while also serving as organist of La Trinité in Paris. Right from his first published work, the eight Preludes for piano (1929), he was using his own modal system, with its strong flavouring of tritones, diminished 7ths and augmented triads. During the 1930s he added a taste for rhythmic irregularity and for the rapid changing of intense colours, in both orchestral and organ works. Most of his compositions were explicitly religious and divided between characteristic styles of extremely slow meditation, bounding dance and the objective unfolding of arithmetical systems. They include the orchestral *L'ascension* (1933), the organ cycles *La nativité du Seigneur* (1935) and *Les corps glorieux* (1939), the song cycles *Poèmes pour Mi* (1936) and *Chants de terre et de ciel* (1938), and the culminating work of this period, the *Quatuor pour la fin du temps* for clarinet, violin, cello and piano (1941).

During the war he found himself surrounded by an eager group of students, including Boulez and Yvonne Loriod, who eventually became his second wife. For her pianistic brilliance he conceived the *Visions de l'amen* (1943, with a second piano part for himself) and the *Vingt regards sur l'enfant Jésus* (1944), followed by an exuberant triptych on the theme of erotic love: the song cycle *Harawi* (1945), the *Turangalîla-symphonie* with solo piano and ondes martenot (1948) and the *Cinq rechants* for small chorus (1949). Meanwhile the serial adventures of Boulez and others were also making a mark, and Messiaen produced his most abstract, atonal and irregular music in the *Quatre études de rythme* for piano (1949) and the *Livre d'orgue* (1951).

His next works were based largely on his own adaptations of birdsongs: they include *Réveil des oiseaux* for piano and orchestra (1953), *Oiseaux exotiques* for piano, wind and percussion (1956), the immense *Catalogue d'oiseaux* for solo piano (1958) and the orchestral *Chronochromie* (1960). In these, and in his Japanese postcards *Sept haïkaï* for piano and small orchestra (1962), he continued to follow his junior contemporaries, but then returned to religious subjects in works that bring together all aspects of his music. These include another small-scale piano concerto, *Couleurs de la cité céleste* (1963), and the monumental *Et exspecto resurrectionem mortuorum* for wind and percussion (1964). Thereafter he devoted himself to a sequence of works on the largest scale: the choral-orchestral *La Transfiguration* (1969), the organ volumes *Méditations sur le mystère de la Sainte Trinité* (1969), the 12-movement piano concerto *Des canyons aux étoiles...* (1974) and the opera *Saint François d'Assise* (1983).

Opera Saint François d'Assise (1983)
Orchestral music Les offrandes oubliés (1930); Le tombeau resplendissant (1931); Hymne au Saint Sacrement (1932); L'ascension (1933); Turangalîla-symphonie (1948); Réveil des oiseaux (1953); Oiseaux exotiques (1956); Chronochromie (1960); Sept haïkaï (1962); Couleurs de la cité céleste (1963); Et exspecto resurrectionem mortuorum (1964); Des canyons aux étoiles... (1974)
Choral music Trois petites liturgies de la Présence Divine (1944); Cinq rechants (1949); La Transfiguration de Notre Seigneur Jésus-Christ (1969)
Solo vocal music Poèmes pour Mi (1936); Chants de terre et de ciel (1938); Harawi (1945)
Piano music Visions de l'amen, 2 pf (1943); Vingt regards sur l'enfant Jésus (1944); Cantéyodjayâ (1948); Quatre études de rythme (1949); Catalogue d'oiseaux (1958); La fauvette des jardins (1972)
Organ music Le banquet céleste (1928); Diptyque (1930); Apparition de l'église éternelle (1932); L'ascension (1934); La nativité du Seigneur (1935); Les corps glorieux (1939); Messe de la Pentecôte (1950); Livre d'orgue (1951); Méditations sur le mystère de la Sainte Trinité (1969); Le livre du Saint Sacrament (1986)
Chamber music Quatuor pour la fin du temps, cl, vn, vc, pf (1941); Le merle noir, fl, pf (1951)

Messiah. Oratorio by Handel to a text compiled by Jennens from the Bible and the Prayer Book Psalter (1742, Dublin).

Messner, Joseph (*b* Schwaz, 27 Feb 1893; *d* Salzburg, 23 Feb 1969). Austrian composer and church musician. He worked at Salzburg Cathedral from 1922 and was a distinguished improviser. His works include Brucknerian church music, three symphonies and organ music.

Mesto (It.). Sad, sorrowful, dejected.

Metallophone. Generic term for percussion instruments that consist of a series of tuned metal bars arranged in a single or double row. Instruments made of metal slabs were known in China by AD700, and bronze slabs appeared in Japan in the 9th century. Such instruments have distinctive roles in the GAMELAN ensemble. Far Eastern metallophones have influenced certain Western orchestral percussion instruments such as the glockenspiel and vibraphone.

In modern compositions 'metallophone' is applied to a row of alloy bars suspended over a resonance box. Carl Orff scored for them; in a simple form metallophones are included in school percussion groups.

Metamorphosen. Work by Richard Strauss for 23 solo strings (1945).

Metastasio, Pietro [Trapassi, Antonio Domenico Bonaventura] (*b* Rome, 3 Jan 1698; *d* Vienna, 12 April 1782). Italian poet. He worked first in Rome and Venice; from 1730 he was imperial court poet in Vienna, writing texts for stage works and oratorios given there. He was especially productive in the 1730s. His *c*70 librettos were set over 800 times by composers throughout Europe during the 18th and early 19th centuries (including Handel, Gluck and Mozart as well as Hasse, Jommelli, Caldara and numerous others). He acquired an unmatched reputation. Best known were his 27 texts for three-act heroic operas, featuring noble behaviour and inner conflict but usually happy endings, to show the triumph of reason and virtue and the benevolence of gods (or God) and kings. He took a deep interest in the way his librettos were set and corresponded voluminously with composers; he had a great influence on serious opera and its musical forms for close on a century.

Metre. The organization of notes in a composition or passage, with respect to time, in such a way that a regular pulse made up of beats can be perceived and the duration of each note can be measured in terms of these beats. The beats are grouped regularly into larger units called bars or measures. Metre is identified at the beginning of a composition, or at any point where it changes, by a TIME SIGNATURE.

Metronome. An apparatus for establishing musical tempo: more specifically the clockwork-driven double-pendulum device perhaps invented about 1812 by D.N. Winkel but refined and patented by J.N. Maelzel in 1815. Its distinct main purposes are to establish an appropriate tempo for a piece and to establish consistency of tempo through a work or an exercise. In the 20th century, synchronization in commercial music has brought the need for more sophisticated mechanisms. The metronome appears as a musical instrument in its own right in works by Ravel, Villa-Lobos and Ligeti.

Etienne Loulié's *chronomètre* (1696) was the first device for defining tempo. Its calibrated pendulum mechanism was further refined throughout the 18th century and by the 1780s clockwork machines were being developed. Maelzel's metronome, which aroused the interest of Beethoven and Salieri, calculated tempo in beats per minute, ranging from 48 to 160. Within a few years several major composers had issued Maelzel metronome (M.M.) numbers for their works. Attempted refinements have been few and short-lived; modern metronomes differ little from his final model. Electronic devices have however been developed during the 20th century for teaching purposes and to cope with the rhythmic complexities of avant-garde scores.

Metropolitan Opera House. The chief opera house in New York. It opened in 1883, on Broadway and 39th Street (cap. 3625); the resident company was soon successful, with German opera under Leopold Damrosch. In 1891 the emphasis shifted to fine singing. Caruso first sang there in 1903; Mahler conducted *Tristan* in 1908. That year, Gatti-Casazza (from La Scala) became director, bringing Toscanini with him; during his directorship (up to 1935) operas were given in their original language and several new American works were performed. Rudolf Bing (general manager, 1950–72) modernized the house, broadened casts and repertory and supervised the move to the new house (cap. 3788) in Lincoln Center (1966). James Levine became artistic director in 1986.

Metz. Site of the RENCONTRES INTERNATIONALES DE MUSIQUE CONTEMPORAIN.

Meulemans, Arthur (*b* Aarschot, 19 May 1884; *d* Etterbeek, 29 June 1966). Belgian composer, pupil of Tinel at the Lemmens Institute in Mechelen (1900–06). He was conductor for Belgian radio and wrote brilliantly scored impressionist tone poems, concertos etc.

Meyer, Ernst Hermann (*b* Berlin, 8 Dec 1905). German composer and musicologist. He studied in Berlin and Heidelberg, his teachers including Eisler, Butting and Hindemith. After working against Nazism he went into exile in England (1933–48), where he was active politically, as a composer of film music, and as a musicologist (*English Chamber Music*, 1946). He returned to Berlin to teach at the Humboldt University (1948–70). He soon became a leading figure in East German music. His works include choral, orchestral and chamber music in a style of passionate commitment to Marxist–Leninist ideals.

Meyer, Kerstin (Margareta) (*b* Stockholm, 3 April 1928). Swedish mezzo-soprano. She studied in Stockholm, Salzburg, Rome and Vienna and made her début in Stockholm as Azucena (1952), later singing Carmen at Hamburg (1959) and Dido in *Les troyens* at Covent Garden (1960). She has sung at the Met (1960–63) and Bayreuth (1962–5), and created many new roles, notably in operas by Henze.

Meyer, Philippe-Jacques (*b* Strasbourg, 1737; *d* London, 1819). Alsatian harpist and composer. A pupil of Christian Hochbrucker, he worked in London, Paris and Strasbourg before settling in London in 1784. He wrote many harp works and an early harp tutor (1763).

Meyerbeer [Meyer Beer], **Giacomo** [Jakob Liebmann] (*b* Vogelsdorf, 5 Sept 1791; *d* Paris, 2 May 1864). German composer. Of a wealthy Jewish merchant family in Berlin, he studied composition with Zelter (1805), B.A. Weber (1808) and Abbé Vogler in Darmstadt (1810–11), winning success more as a pianist than a composer. After a study tour in Italy (1816–25), where he met artists, librettists and impresarios and wrote six notable operas (especially the impressive *Il crociato in Egitto*, 1824), he gained a reputation equal to Rossini's. From 1825 he worked chiefly in Paris but was always on the move,

taking cures, producing his operas in major European cities and auditioning new singers; in 1842, indisputably the world's leading active opera composer, he became Prussian Generalmusikdirektor – he was dismissed in 1848 but directed the Berlin royal court music until his death. Having first conquered the Paris Opéra with the five-act *Robert le diable* (1831), he and his most important collaborator Eugène Scribe created the famous *Les Huguenots* (1836), then began work on *Le prophète* and *L'africaine*, both of which suffered long delays from casting difficulties; *Le prophète* was eventually received enthusiastically with Pauline Viardot as Fidès (1849), while the première of *L'africaine* (1865) became a brilliant posthumous tribute to its composer.

Cultivating a consistently realistic style, 'expressive monumentalism', Meyerbeer conceived of grand opera as a whole, blending social content, historical material and local colour; exploitation of the horrific was an essential ingredient, along with massive crowd scenes building up a grandiose volume of sound and long passages of demanding solo singing. But these were allied to innovations, notably in the orchestra and in the deliberate creation of 'unbeautiful' sound. He was widely admired for his care over historical details, his melodic invention in ballet scenes and his grasp of the capabilities of individual singers.

Operas Il crociato in Egitto (1824); Robert le diable (1831); Les Huguenots (1836); Le prophète (1849); L'étoile du nord (1854); Le pardon de Ploërmel (1859); L'africaine (1865); 9 others
Vocal music secular cantatas, hymns; sacred works; over 60 songs
Instrumental music Sym., E♭ (1811); 2 concs.; ov., variations, marches for orch; marches for military band

Meyerowitz, Jan (*b* Wrocław, 23 April 1913). American composer of German origin. He studied in Berlin with Gmeindl and Zemlinsky, and in Rome with Respighi, Casella and Molinari. He has worked in the USA as a teacher (at the City University of New York, 1962–80), and also composed operas (notably *The Barrier*, 1950), choral and instrumental music in a style drawing on Schoenberg, Berg and the Italian 19th century.

Mezzo, mezza (It.). 'Half', 'medium', e.g. MEZZO-SOPRANO, *mezzo-forte* (*mf*, less loud than *forte*), *mezzo-piano* (*mp*, less quiet than *piano*), *mezza voce* ('half-voice', i.e. a restrained tone).

Mezzo-contralto (It.). A voice of contralto timbre but mezzo-soprano compass.

Mezzo-soprano (It.). A female voice normally with a range of approximately a–$f\sharp''$. The distinction between soprano and mezzo-soprano dates from the mid-18th century but was particularly taken up by composers of the 19th, who often assigned important roles to mezzo-sopranos, particularly from Rossini's time onwards, when the castrato voice (usually of roughly the same pitch) fell out of favour. In the early 19th century there are heroic roles for mezzo but later it was used more for dramatic secondary ones (like Eboli in Verdi's *Don Carlos*); it was also commonly used for such roles as nurse or confidante. The voice is effectively exploited by Saint-Saëns for the seductive Dalila.

mf. Abbreviation for *mezzo-forte*; *see* DYNAMICS.

Míča, František Adam (*b* Jaroměřice nad Rokytnou, 11 Jan 1746; *d* Lwów, 19 March 1811). Czech composer. A government official in Vienna (until 1785) and later abroad, he was a fluent successful composer, especially of symphonies and string quartets. His uncle František Antonín (1694–1744), Kapellmeister to Count Questenberg at Jaroměřice, composed stage works, cantatas and oratorios.

Michael, Tobias (*b* Dresden, 13 June 1592; *d* Leipzig, 26 June 1657). German composer. He first served as Kapellmeister of the Neue Kirche at Sondershausen. From 1631 he was Kantor of the Leipzig Thomaskirche, succeeding Schein. His principal works are the two volumes *Musicalische Seelenlust* (1634–7), which are Italianate in style. The first contains 30 German motets for five voices and continuo, the second 50 sacred concertos. Michael also composed sacred songs and occasional works.

Michael's father, Rogier (*b* Mons or Bergen op Zoom, *c*1552; *d* Dresden, 1619 or later), was court Kapellmeister at Dresden from 1587 (where Schütz was his assistant and Schein his pupil) and composer of sacred histories, chorale settings, motets etc. His brothers Christian (*c*1593–1637) and Samuel (*c*1597–1632) were also composers. Samuel was organist of the Nicolaikirche, Leipzig (1628–32); Christian succeeded him in 1633.

Michaelides, Solon (*b* Nicosia, 12 Nov 1905; *d* Athens, 9 Sept 1979). Greek composer. He studied in London (1927–30) and in Paris with Boulanger (1930–34), then taught in Limassol (1934–56) and Salonica (1957–70), taking a leading part in musical life. His works, in many genres, use folk and Byzantine elements.

Michelangeli, Arturo Benedetti (*b* Brescia, 5 Jan 1920). Italian pianist. He studied at the Milan Conservatory and in 1939 won the Geneva International Piano Competition. He made his London début in 1946 and appeared in the USA two years later. He is renowned as a superlative technician for his control of colour and counterpoint, and a characteristic blend of romantic fervour and classical poise. A highly temperamental artist, he has cancelled nearly as many concerts as he has given.

Micheli, Romano (*b* Rome, *c*1575; *d* there, after 1659). Italian composer. He spent time in various Italian cities, and in 1625 became *maestro di cappella* at S Luigi dei Francesi, Rome; later he lived in Naples. A controversial figure, he challenged other composers to compositional tests and published polemical writings. As a composer he devoted himself to complex canons, for which he gained a high reputation.

Michna, Adam Václav (*b*?Jindřichův Hradec, *c*1600; *d* there, 2 Nov 1676). Czech composer. He was the town organist of Jindřichův Hradec from *c*1633, and the dominant composer of the Czech lands in the 17th century. All his surviving works are sacred. His two hymnals (1647, 1661) contain simple settings of folklike melodies, while *The Czech lute* (1653) consists of hymns in aria style. He also

composed Italianate concertato works to Latin texts; the collection *Sacra et litaniae* (1654) is notable for using folk elements in an elaborate idiom.

Mico, Richard (*b* Taunton, *c*1590; *d* London, bur. 10 April 1661). English composer. From 1608 he was resident musician at Thorndon Hall, Essex, with the Petre family, Byrd's patrons. In 1631 he moved to London. He was a leading composer of consort music; some 40 pieces, including 30 fantasias, survive.

Microtone. A musical interval distinctly smaller than a semitone. Microtones occur in the melodic intervals of ancient Greece, in the various theoretical divisions of the octave into more parts than 12, and in the discrepancies among 'pure intervals' or between such notes as G♯ and A♭ in certain temperaments.

Microtones have been used in Western music since the end of the 19th century, when Julian Carillo experimented with quarter tones in the 1890s. Ives wrote for pianos a quarter tone apart; Hába and Vïshnegradsky used quarter-tone music in the 1920s (Hába also used smaller divisions). Several composers have used octaves with more than 12 divisions, 53 and particularly 31 being favoured (organs have been built in 31-interval octave systems). The difficulty of devising instruments to play in microtones has been overcome in recent years by electronic means.

Middle C. A colloquial name for the note of which the pitch is 256 Hz; it is probably so called because it is written on a leger line midway between two staves bearing a treble and bass clef. The note is also near the middle of the keyboard and near the top of the male vocal range and the bottom of the female.

Middle Eastern music. *See* ARAB MUSIC.

Midi, Le. Haydn's Symphony no.7 in C (?1761), the second of a group of three: no.6 is 'Le matin' and no.8 'Le soir'.

Midsummer Marriage, The. Opera in three acts by Tippett to his own libretto (1955, London); the *Ritual Dances* from Acts 2 and 3 are often performed as a concert item.

Midsummer Night's Dream, A. Overture and incidental music, op.61, by Mendelssohn (1862).

Opera in three acts by Britten to a libretto by the composer and Peter Pears (1960, Aldeburgh).

Shakespeare's play has attracted several composers, among them Purcell (*The Fairy Queen*, 1691).

Mielczewski, Marcin (*d* Warsaw, Sept 1651). Polish composer. A musician of the royal chapel in Warsaw, in 1645 he became director of music to the king's brother, the Bishop of Płock. A leading Polish composer of his day, he wrote a wide variety of sacred concertos for both few and many voices; others of his sacred works are polyphonic in style. He also composed instrumental canzonas and probably secular vocal music. A number of his works include popular Polish melodies.

Mignon. Opera in three acts by Ambroise Thomas to a libretto by J. Barbier and M. Carré after Goethe (1866, Paris).

Mignone, Francisco (Paulo) (*b* São Paulo, 3 Sept 1897; *d* Rio de Janeiro, 20 Feb 1986). Brazilian composer. He studied at the conservatories of São Paulo and Milan and from 1933 was a teacher, conductor and composer in Rio de Janeiro. His early works are Italianate, but from *c*1929 to the late 1950s he wrote in a nationalist style influenced by Andrade, his later compositions drawing on modernist techniques. His large output covers all genres but he had most success in Brazil with solo songs and piano pieces.

Migot, Georges (*b* Paris, 27 Feb 1891; *d* Levallois, 5 Jan 1976). French composer. He studied with Widor, d'Indy and Emmanuel at the Paris Conservatoire (1909–20), and between the wars struggled against neo-classicism in his writings and compositions: he continued rather in the tradition of Debussy and late Fauré, using the term 'permodality' for his harmonic technique. His works include ballets, sacred cantatas, six oratorios on the life of Christ, 13 symphonies (1920–67), songs, chamber and instrumental music.

Mihalovich, Ödön Péter József de (*b* Feričance, 13 Sept 1842; *d* Budapest, 22 April 1929). Hungarian composer and educationist. He studied with Hauptmann in Leipzig and Cornelius in Munich. He greatly contributed to Hungarian musical life in his role as the influential principal of the Budapest Music Academy (from 1887), supporting, among others, the young Bartók and Kodály. Most of his output, including operas, orchestral works and lieder, was influenced by Wagner and the New German School.

Mihalovici, Marcel (*b* Bucharest, 22 Oct 1898; *d* Paris, 12 Aug 1985). French composer. He studied in Bucharest and with d'Indy and Gastoué in Paris. His music, in most genres, draws on a wide range of current trends; member of a Parisian émigré group, Ecole de Paris, from eastern Europe, he was also indebted to his compatriot Enescu. His works include five symphonies, five operas and much chamber and piano music; the pianist Monique Haas (1909–87) was his wife.

Mihály, András (*b* Budapest, 7 Nov 1917). Hungarian composer. He studied at Budapest Academy as a cellist, but had private composition lessons with Kadosa and Strasser, and in the early 1940s was influenced by Bartók and the Second Viennese School. In 1950 he began teaching at the Budapest Academy and in 1968 he founded the Budapest Chamber Ensemble for performing new music. From 1965 he was more influenced by the Western avant garde: *Monodia* (1970) for orchestra uses clusters and aleatory writing.

Mikado, The. Operetta by Sullivan to a libretto by Gilbert (1885, London).

Miki, Minoru (*b* Tokushima, 16 March 1930). Japanese composer. He was a pupil of Ikenouchi and Ifukube. His works essay a synthesis of Western and Japanese elements, in operas, choral music and pieces for Japanese instruments.

Mikrokosmos. Six volumes of 'progressive pieces' for piano by Bartók (1926–39).

Milán, Luis de (*b c*1500; *d c*1561 or later). Spanish musician. He apparently spent most of his life in Valencia, associated with its ducal court at least until 1538. His *Libro de música de vihuela de mano intitulado El maestro* (1536) is distinguished not only as the first collection of vihuela (and therefore guitar) music, but also as the earliest source employing verbal indications of tempo. It contains 40 fantasias, formally free with a blend of homophony and polyph-

ony, and six pavans. The fantasias feature virtuoso passage-work and occasional experiments in chromaticism. It also contains a rich repertory of vocal music – villancicos in Castilian and Portuguese.

Milan Conservatory (Conservatorio di Musica 'G. Verdi']. Music school founded in 1807, the most important in Italy. Early students trained mainly for La Scala. It was named after Verdi in 1901.

Milanov, Zinka (*b* Zagreb, 17 May 1906). Yugoslav soprano. She studied at Zagreb and sang there, 1928–35. At the Met she gave more than 400 performances between 1937 and 1966, notably as Leonora in *Il trovatore*, Bellini's Norma and Mozart's Donna Anna. Her voice was of great beauty and power if occasionally unsteady in tone.

Milanuzzi, Carlo (*b* Sanatoglia; *d c*1647). Italian composer. He first worked in Venice, Perugia, Verona, Finale di Modena and Camerino, and became *maestro* and organist at S Mauro, Noventa di Piave, in 1643. He was also a poet and a priest. He composed in a progressive style, particularly in his nine volumes of secular monody (1622–43), which consist mostly of tuneful arias. Some of his sacred works are unified by the use of repeated material.

Mildenburg, Anna von. *See* BAHR-MILDENBURG, ANNA.

Milder-Hauptmann, (Pauline) Anna (*b* Constantinople, 13 Dec 1785; *d* Berlin, 29 May 1838). German singer. Beethoven wrote the part of Leonore for her (1805), and Schubert *Der Hirt auf dem Felsen* and the second *Suleika* song. Her greatest triumph was in Gluck's *Iphigénie en Tauride* (1812).

Milhaud, Darius (*b* Aix-en-Provence, 4 Sept 1892; *d* Geneva, 22 June 1974). French composer. He studied with Widor, Gédalge and Dukas at the Paris Conservatoire and became associated with Claudel, who took him to Rio de Janeiro as his secretary (1916–18): he wrote incidental music for Claudel's translation of the *Oresteia* (1922), making innovatory use of chanting chorus and percussion, he also drew on Brazilian music in his ballet *L'homme et son désir* (1918). But Claudel's influence was briefly succeeded by Cocteau's, and he became a member of Les Six; works of this period include the ballet *Le boeuf sur le toit* (1919). In 1922 he sought out jazz in Harlem and used the experience in another ballet, *Le création du monde* (1923). Thereafter he travelled widely, taught on both sides of the Atlantic and produced a colossal output in all genres, normally in a style of fluent bitonality. His operas include *Les malheurs d'Orphée* (composed 1925), *Le pauvre matelot* (1926), *Christophe Colomb* (1928), *Maximilien* (1930), *Bolivar* (1943), *David* (1952) and *Saint Louis* (1970). There are also 12 symphonies and much other orchestral music, sacred and secular choral music, 18 quartets and songs.

Dramatic music 15 operas, incl. Les malheurs d'Orphée (1925); Le pauvre matelot (1927); Christophe Colomb (1930); Maximilien (1932); Bolivar (1950); David (1954); Saint Louis (1972); 17 ballets, incl. L'homme et son désir (1918); Le boeuf sur le toit (1919); La création du monde (1923); Moïse (1940); incidental music for 40 plays, incl. Protée (1919); Les choëphores (1915); Les euménides (1917–22); 26 film scores, incl. Madame Bovary (1933); 11 radio scores and miscellanea

Orchestral music 2 sym. suites; 6 chamber syms.; 12 syms. (no.3 with chorus); 5 pf concs.; 3 vn concs.; 2 va concs.; 2 vc concs.; Le carnaval d'Aix, pf, orch (1926); Concertino de printemps, vn, chamber orch (1934); Suite provençale (1936); Kentuckiana (1948); Suite cisalpine, vc, orch (1954); other ovs., concs., concertinos, fanfares; 5 works for brass band, incl. Suite française (1944)

Vocal music 39 choral works, incl. Service sacré (1947); 34 solo vocal works, incl. Alissa, cycle, S, pf (1913, rev. 1931), Catalogue de fleurs, 1v, pf/7 insts (1920); c30 sets of songs, incl. Poèmes juifs (1916); many single songs

Chamber and instrumental music 18 str qts, 20 other chamber works, incl. trios, 4 qnts; c25 sonatas, sonatinas; 20 pf works, incl. Saudades do Brasil (1921); 5 works for 2 pf, incl. Scaramouche (1937), Carnaval à la Nouvelle-Orléans (1947); 5 org works

Other 9 children's works; arrs. of Auric, Poulenc, Satie; 3 bks, incl. Notes sans musique (1949) [autobiography]

Military. Nickname of Haydn's Symphony no.100 in G (1793–4), so called because it uses 'military' instruments and has a trumpet call in the second movement.

Military band. Term from the late 18th century to denote a regimental band of woodwind, brass and percussion instruments. It is also applied to any ensemble that plays military music, including signals and military calls. In British usage it may (misleadingly) refer to any type of mixed wind band. *See* BAND.

Milkina, Nina (*b* Moscow, 27 Jan 1919). British pianist. She studied in Paris and with Craxton in London, making her début at 11. She has been admired for her freshness in Chopin and, above all, for her neat, clear-textured playing of Mozart's sonatas and concertos.

Miller, (Alton) Glenn (*b* Clarinda, IA, 1 March 1904; *d* between London and Paris, c15 Dec 1944). American bandleader, trombonist, arranger and composer. He joined the Dorsey Brothers' Orchestra (1934) and while with Ray Noble's group (1935) conceived his characteristic reed-section sound of a clarinet over four saxophones. The orchestra he formed in 1938, noted for its precision, rapidly became the most popular 'sweet' swing band through its recordings *Moonlight Serenade, Little Brown Jug* and *In the Mood*. In 1942 Miller assembled a service band, later posted to England. Mystery surrounding his death (he was declared missing after an aeroplane flight) helped translate his international fame into near legend.

Milleville. French family of musicians, largely active in Ferrara. Alessandro (?1521–1589) was a composer who sang in the papal chapel (1553–8) and from 1560 was second organist (under Luzzaschi) at the Ferrarese court; a fine player, he wrote madrigals (four bks, 1573–84) and motets (1584). His son Francesco (?1565–after 1639), also a composer, went from Ferrara to Rome (1614) and held many posts as organist (e.g. Gubbio, Chioggia, Siena) between 1616 and 1628, probably returning to Ferrara by 1639; his extant publications (11 bks, 1616–39) include sacred works and continuo madrigals.

Millico, (Vito) Giuseppe (*b* Terlizzi, 19 Jan 1737; *d* Naples, 2 Oct 1802). Italian soprano castrato and composer. He sang in operas throughout Europe, becoming associated especially with Gluck, and composed operas, arias and other works. He was also a famous teacher.

Millöcker, Carl (*b* Vienna, 29 April 1842; *d* Baden, 31 Dec 1899). Austrian composer. His successes of the 1880s, notably *Der Bettelstudent* (1882) and *Gasparone* (1884), established him with Johann Strauss and Suppé as one of the three leading exponents of Viennese operetta of the time.

Mills College Center for Contemporary Music. Electronic studio at Mills College, Oakland, California. Originally San Francisco Tape Music Center (founded 1961 at San Francisco Conservatory), in 1966 it moved to Mills College and later merged with Mills Performing Group.

Milner, Anthony (Francis Dominic) (*b* Bristol, 13 May 1925). English composer. He studied with R.O. Morris at the RCM and with Seiber, and has taught at London institutions since 1947. He has been influenced by 12-note and medieval music, but has stood out for traditional harmony. His output consists mostly of choral, orchestral and chamber pieces, often reflecting his Roman Catholic adherence.

Milnes, Sherrill (Eustace) (*b* Downers Grove, IL, 10 Jan 1935). American baritone. He made his début in 1960 and in 1965 sang Valentin in Gounod's *Faust* at the Met. His forthright, vigorous performances of Escamillo, Don Giovanni and the leading Verdi baritone roles have made him much in demand in USA and Europe. His Covent Garden début was in 1971, as Renato.

Milojević, Miloje (*b* Belgrade, 28 Oct 1884; *d* there, 16 June 1946). Yugoslav composer. He studied in Belgrade, Munich and Prague, and worked in Belgrade as a critic and choirmaster; he composed piano music, songs and partsongs in a folksong-influenced style.

Milstein, Nathan (Mironovich) (*b* Odessa, 31 Dec 1904). American violinist of Russian birth. He made his début at Odessa in 1920 and toured Russia for five years, often appearing with Horowitz. After leaving Russia in 1925 he studied further with Ysaÿe and in 1929 played with the New York PO, settling in the USA and becoming an American citizen in 1942. He is noted for his consistency and musicianship and his silvery tone, performing largely in the standard repertory.

Milton, John (*b* Stanton St John, c1563; *d* London, bur. 15 March 1647). English composer, father of the poet. After a period at Christ Church, Oxford, he moved to London and joined the Scriveners' Company (1600). He retired to Horton, Bucks., in 1632 but later returned to London. He composed anthems and other sacred music, madrigals and consort music.

Milwaukee Symphony Orchestra. American orchestra founded in 1958; its home is the Uihlein Hall (built 1969, cap. 2331) at Milwaukee County Performing Arts Center. Its first conductor was Henry John Brown. Activities include a summer series at Milwaukee County Zoo and free parks concerts.

Minato, Count Nicolò (*b* Bergamo, c1630; *d* Vienna, 1698). Italian librettist. A lawyer by profession, he became prominent as a librettist and impresario in Venice, where his chief musical collaborator was Cavalli. From 1669 he was imperial court poet in Vienna; there he wrote over 170 secular librettos and *c*40 sacred texts, many of them for Antonio Draghi. Later composers to set them include G. Bononcini and Telemann. Most of his secular librettos are based on events of ancient history.

Mines of Sulphur, The. Opera in three acts by Richard Rodney Bennett to a libretto by Beverley Cross (1965, London).

Mingus, Charles (*b* Nogales, AZ, 22 April 1922; *d* Cuernavaca, Mexico, 5 Jan 1979). American jazz double bass player, pianist and composer. He first became known as a bass player with Louis Armstrong (*c*1943) and Lionel Hampton (1947–8), achieving national fame with Red Norvo's trio (1950–51); he settled in New York, where he worked with many leading players, becoming famous as a virtuoso. He turned to composition in the mid-1950s. In 1955 he founded a workshop to specialize in playing his compositions, dictated to the players as a basis for improvisation. Notable players in his four- to 11-piece group were the saxophonists Eric Dolphy and Roland Kirk and the drummer Dannie Richmond. His *Pithecanthropus erectus* (1956) broke away from conventional structure and displayed a range of unusual instrumental sonorities. A remarkable blend of sustained composition and improvisation was achieved in *The Black Saint and the Sinner Lady* (1963).

Minim. The note, in American usage called a half-note, that is half the value of a semibreve and double the value of a crotchet. The shortest of the five note values of early medieval music (hence its name), it is first found in early 14th-century music. *See* NOTE VALUES.

Minimalism. Term applied from the early 1970s to various compositional practices, current from the early 1960s (when they were generally known as 'systematic music'), the features of which – static harmony, patterned rhythms and repetition – aim radically to reduce the range of compositional materials. Leading composers of minimalist music include La Monte Young, Terry Riley, Steve Reich, Philip Glass, Cornelius Cardew and Michael Nyman. The origins of minimalism may be traced back to music by Satie and the early works of Cage, and also to the music of Bali, black Africa and India. Young's Trio for Strings (1958) with its even, extended notes and its absence of rhythm, prepared the way. Riley's *In C* (1964) introduced the elements of pulse and the repetition of tiny motivic cells in a single harmony; it lasts more than 90 minutes. Reich pursued not only the possibilities of pulse but also the gradually shifting relationships that occur when material gradually moves out of phase with itself; his first experiments with phasing (*Come Out*, 1966) were achieved with tape loops, but he also worked with live performers, notably in *Drumming* (1971), which he called 'music as a gradual process'. Glass's distinctive, equally stringent approach creates rhythmic change by the addition and subtraction of sub-cells of a musical phrase; characteristically, a loud, fast, intense motif is established by repetition and fragments of it then begin to be repeated or omitted, as in *1 + 1* (1968). Other composers have developed individual minimalist

approaches, including paring down compositional means to a handful of notes. Ceaseless repetition of material with an unchanging pulse, the prolongation of single notes, the phasing of rhythms, additive treatment of small motivic cells, the use of simple tonal or modal harmonies, and the exploitation of single timbres are all among minimalist techniques. Composers have applied these to opera (for example Glass's *Einstein on the Beach*, 1976, and *Akhnaten*, 1984; John Adams's *Nixon in China*, 1987). Minimalism, with its abduration of the increasing complexity that has marked most Western music since 1600, represents a departure from avant-garde development in the usual sense, and its trance-like, hypnotic qualities have put it close to other types of development in intellectual circles of the 1980s (for example, the interest in meditation and non-Western thought processes); it has also brought one wing of the serious music establishment closer to popular and rock music.

Minkus, Léon (Fyodorovich) [Alois; Aloysius Ludwig] (*b* Vienna, 23 March 1826; *d* there, 7 Dec 1917). Composer and violinist of Czech or Polish origin. From the 1850s he was a violinist and teacher in St Petersburg and from 1862 to 1872 conductor at the Bol'shoy Theatre, Moscow. His ballet *Don Quixote* (1869; scenario by Petipa) was well received and remained in the repertory. In 1872 he was appointed ballet composer to the imperial theatres in St Petersburg, producing with Petipa several ballets popular in their day but now forgotten.

Minneapolis Symphony Orchestra. *See* MINNESOTA ORCHESTRA.

Minnesang. The German tradition of courtly lyric and secular monophony that flourished in the 12th to the 14th centuries. It can be considered the German branch of the Provençal troubadour tradition, though it has independent features. It was cultivated particularly by the nobility, and diffused by travelling musicians. The word 'Minne' can be taken to represent love with both its spiritual and sensual overtones, and its essentially aristocratic poetry was based on the concept of *Minnedienst* – servitude to love – itself inextricably linked to the feudal system. A recurrent theme is that of the knight's love for an unattainable lady, of undying service without reward. During the peak period of Minnesang (*c*1165–1200), the *hôhiu minne* ('high *Minne*') represented the ideal spiritual love between man and woman, the *nideriu minne* (low *Minne*) the more physical demands of the man for possession of a woman. There are three main forms – *Lied*, *Spruch* and *Leich* – of which the first two are in stanzas while the last is a complex, through-composed structure. The extant melodies are preserved in MSS from the 14th and 15th centuries, and cannot necessarily be applied to earlier verses. The Minnesang is generally categorized according to content, the basic types being the *Minnelied* (the man's expression of love), the *Frauenlied* (the woman's song), the *Wechsel* (in which the lovers 'exchange' their views), the *Tagelied* (like the Provençal *Alba*, the parting of the lovers at dawn), the *Tanzlied* (dance-song) and the *Kreuzlied* (crusading song). As the tradition developed, verse structures and content become more intricate, notably in the Minnesang of Walter von der Vogelweide and the witty, ironic style cultivated by Neidhart von Reuental (*d c*1250). In the 14th century, the rising importance of the towns and the bourgeoisie shifted the emphasis from the courtly idealism to songs in a more spiritual and didactic tone, but the influence of the Minnesang is still discernible in the works of the Monk of Salzburg (*c*1400) and Oswald von Wolkenstein (*d* 1445).

Minnesota Orchestra. American orchestra, originally the Minneapolis SO, founded in 1903; Emil Oberhoffer was its first director. Its homes are Orchestra Hall (Minneapolis; built 1974, cap. 2543) and Ordway Music Theatre (St Paul); it was renamed in 1968. Tours began in 1906 and under Eugene Ormandy (1931–6) it gained an international reputation; Dimitri Mitropoulos (1937–49) added contemporary works to the repertory; Neville Marriner (1979–86) initiated a plan to enlarge the orchestra from 1987.

Minor. (1) The name given to a scale whose octave species, in its natural form, is built of the following ascending sequence of intervals: T–S–T–T–S–T–T (T = tone, S = semitone). The note chosen to begin the sequence, the key note, becomes part of the name of the scale, i.e. the scale beginning on A is the scale of A minor. A piece or passage whose melodic basis is a minor scale (say, that on A) and whose harmonic basis is the minor triad on the key note of that scale is said to be 'in A minor' (lower-case letters, 'a minor' or simply 'a' are sometimes used to distinguish minor from major).

In the minor scale, some notes are altered chromatically to increase the harmonic or melodic sense of direction: the 'harmonic minor' scale has a raised 7th, in accordance with the major triad on the fifth step (the dominant); the melodic minor scale has a raised 6th and a raised 7th when it is ascending, borrowing the leading-note function of the seventh step from the major scale; when descending it is the same as the natural minor scale. See ex.1.

Ex. 1

(2) A minor INTERVAL is one a semitone smaller than a major interval of the same name but contains the same number of diatonic scale steps. A minor TRIAD is a three-note chord which, reckoned from the lowest note, is built of a minor 3rd and a perfect 5th.

Minstrel. A professional entertainer of any kind from the 12th century to the 17th, with particular reference to a professional secular musician, usually an instrumentalist (the term also covered jugglers, acrobats, story tellers etc). The Middle Ages witnessed the heyday of minstrelsy, but it is often difficult to establish the exact nature of their music-making, not least because of the varied use of terminology in sources from the period. The term

'minstrel' seems to have disappeared from common usage by the end of the 16th century. In the early part of the period it was applied to the poet-composer, and clearly embraced the singer as well as the instrumentalist. Most documentary evidence gathered so far relates to court minstrels, a necessary adjunct to court life throughout the Middle Ages, whether salaried (common later in the period) or itinerant. Hardly any minstrel music has survived – most was transmitted orally – but dance music undoubtedly formed a large part of the repertory. In the 14th century the distinction between *haut* and *bas* groups emerged, and the *alta capella* (a trio or quartet of shawms and sackbuts) appeared in the 15th. During this time there were annual assemblies of minstrels in the Low Countries, at which instrumentalists gathered from all over Europe; the last recorded was in 1447. The disappearance of the minstrel would seem to have coincided with the shift to written instrumental styles from the later 15th century. The tradition was however continued in some measure by the town musicians, waits and *Stadtpfeifer* of the 16th–18th centuries.

Minuet (Fr. *menuet*; Ger. *Menuett*; It. *minuetto*). A dance, of French origin, in a moderate triple metre. It was known at Louis XIV's court as an elegant social dance performed by one couple at a time, and remained the most popular dance among the European aristocracy until the late 18th century. Lully introduced numerous minuets into his operas and ballets and the dance was frequently included in Baroque keyboard and ensemble suites. Italian minuets, often in 3/8 or 6/8 time, used a faster tempo.

The minuet was the only important dance to survive into the Classical period. Italian opera overtures of the early 18th century often close with a minuet, as do many symphonies by G.B. Sammartini, Abel, J.W. Stamitz and Monn and some early piano sonatas by Haydn. After about 1770 the ternary minuet–trio–minuet (*da capo*), derived from the Baroque practice of playing two minuets 'alternativement', became the standard third (occasionally second) of four movements in symphonies and string quartets. Haydn was the first to substitute movements called 'scherzo' for minuets (in his string quartets op.33) and Beethoven preferred vigorous and robust scherzos in the standard minuet and trio layout, sometimes extended to include a repeat of the trio and a second repeat of the scherzo.

19th-century composers were less interested in the minuet, but some 20th-century composers, including Françaix, Bartók, Schoenberg and Ravel, have revived it for its associations with the past.

Minute Waltz. Nickname of Chopin's Waltz in D♭, op.64 no.1 for piano (1847), so called because it can be played (too fast) in one minute.

Miracle. Nickname of Haydn's Symphony no.96 in D

(1791), so called because it was said (incorrectly) that at its first performance the audience miraculously escaped being injured by a falling chandelier (the incident actually occurred in 1795 after a performance of his Symphony no.102).

Miraculous Mandarin, The [A csodálatos mandarin]. Pantomime (ballet) in one act by Bartók to a scenario by Menyhért Lengyel (1926, Cologne).

Mireille. Opera in three acts by Gounod to a libretto by Carré after Mistral (1864, Paris).

Mirliton. A group of acoustic devices that modify the tonal characteristics of sounds fed into them. The French term 'mirliton' is used generically for musical auxiliaries depending on the forced vibration of a thin membrane. This membrane may be free, as in the 'comb-and-paper', or may form part of the wall of a tube or vessel containing an air column; its effect is to add a buzzing or nasal quality.

Miroglio, Francis (*b* Marseilles, 12 Dec 1924). French composer. A pupil of Milhaud at the Paris Conservatoire (1951–2), he has written much in a Boulezian style and in 1965 founded a festival at St Paul de Vence.

Miroirs. Five piano pieces by Ravel (1905).

Mirror canon. A canon in which the following voice is an inversion or (less often) a retrograde of the leading one.

Mirror fugue. A fugue in which all the parts may be inverted simultaneously to form a second fugue (e.g. Bach's *Art of Fugue*, Contrapunctus 12 and 13).

Mirror on which to Dwell, A. Song cycle by Carter (1975), settings for soprano and ensemble of six poems by Elizabeth Bishop.

Miry, Karel (*b* Ghent, 14 Aug 1823; *d* there, 3 Oct 1889). Belgian composer. A prolific composer, noted for his children's songs, he is remembered for *De vlaamse leeuw* (1845), the Flemish national hymn.

Miserere (Lat.: 'have mercy'). The first word of Psalm l, sung in the Roman Office for the Dead and at Tenebrae. Polyphonic settings, often in nine parts, are mostly in simple chordal style alternating with plainchant. A celebrated example is Allegri's; other noteworthy settings are those by Palestrina, Victoria and Gesualdo, while more elaborate ones were composed by Josquin, Lassus and G. Gabrieli. Tye's *Miserere* is a setting of Psalm lv, and several other texts from the Roman psalter begin with the same word.

Missa. The Latin term for the Roman Catholic MASS.

Missa brevis. A short mass. The term was in use by *c*1500, and more widely after 1560, for a brief setting of the Ordinary. It is also used for 17th- and 18th-century settings of the first two sections only (Kyrie and Gloria) of the Mass Ordinary.

Missa in tempore belli. *See* PAUKENMESSE.

Missal. A liturgical book of the Western church, containing all the material for the celebration of Mass. The oldest complete missals including musical notation originated in Italy in the 10th century; by the 11th a missal was formed in each church.

Missa solemnis. Solemn mass; it has become the name by which Beethoven's Mass in D op.123 (1823) is known.

Misura (It.). 'Measure', 'time', 'bar', e.g. *senza misura* ('without barring', i.e. freely).

Mitridate, rè di Ponto. Opera in three acts by Mozart to a libretto by V.A. Cigna-Santi after G. Parini and Racine (1770, Milan).

Mitropoulos, Dimitri (*b* Athens, 1 March 1896; *d* Milan, 2 Nov 1960). American conductor and composer. He studied in Athens, Brussels and Berlin and in 1930 was engaged to conduct the Berlin PO; at this time he started his practice of conducting from the keyboard. After his American début, with the Boston SO (1936), he settled in the USA. He was conductor of the Minneapolis SO (1937–49), raising the orchestra's standards and giving works by Berg, Krenek and Schoenberg. He conducted the New York PO (1949–58) and worked at the Met from 1954, notably in operas by Strauss and Barber. An unorthodox conductor, he obtained performances of impassioned intensity, particularly in Mahler.

Mixolydian. The seventh of the eight traditional church modes, the authentic MODE on G.

Mixture stop. An organ stop composed of several ranks of pipes at various pitches (most often octaves and 5ths). The term is generic, referring to compound stops in general, and specific, in that Mixture is the name used in some areas and periods for the chief mixture of the Diapason chorus or *pleno*. The contents and planning of mixture stops distinguish national organ schools and test the skill of builders.

Miyagi, Michio (*b* Kobe, 7 April 1894; *d* Kariya, 25 June 1956). Japanese composer. Blind from the age of seven, he was trained as a koto player and became a famous master. He wrote much music for the koto with Japanese or Western instruments, the most celebrated work being *The Sea in Spring* (1929) for koto and *shakuhachi*.

Mizler von Kolof, Lorenz Christoph (*b* Heidenheim, 25 July 1711; *d* Warsaw, March 1778). German writer on music. From 1737 he lectured on music at Leipzig University. He served a Polish count in the 1740s and became court physician at Warsaw in 1752. He advocated a musical science based on mathematics and philosophy. His main work was the monthly *Neu-eröffnete musikalische Bibliothek* (1736–54), including essays and reviews of books on music; it became the official periodical of his corresponding society of musical scholars (Bach, Handel and Telemann were among the 20 members).

Mizmār. Generic term from the Arab world for various kinds of wind instrument with single or double reed; in the past it applied to all wind instruments. It refers primarily to a double clarinet with pipes of equal length and made from wood, reed, ivory or bone.

Mizuno, Shūkō (*b* Tokushima, 24 Feb 1934). Japanese composer. He studied with Shibata and Hasegawa at the Tokyo Geijutsu Daigaku (1958–63), where he began teaching in 1971. His works have used improvisation, graphics (*Orchestra 1966*) and jazz (*Jazz Orchestra '73*).

Mlada. Opera-ballet in four acts by Rimsky-Korsakov to his own libretto after Krílov (1892, S

Petersburg); it is based on an unfinished project in collaboration with Borodin, Cui, Musorgsky and Minkus.

Mládí [Youth]. Suite for wind sextet by Janáček (1924).

Młynarski, Emil (*b* Kibarty, 18 July 1870; *d* Warsaw, 5 April 1935). Polish composer. He studied with Auer and Lyadov at the St Petersburg Conservatory, and returned to Warsaw in 1898, working there as director of the conservatory; he was also a conductor (Scottish SO, 1910–16; Warsaw Opera; Philadelphia). He promoted new Polish music, but his own works combine 19th-century traditions with folksong elements.

Mock trumpet. Term apparently used *c*1700 for an undeveloped CHALUMEAU. It has been confused with the trumpet marine, with which it has no connection. It had three finger-holes for each hand, a thumb-hole and no keys. Its length is said to be *c*23 cm and its range g′–g″; its tone was probably strident.

Modal. Term for music based on a mode rather than a major or minor scale. In the Western tradition it applies particularly to music using the church modes of the Middle Ages and the Renaissance (and music imitating them, such as the movement of Beethoven's String Quartet in A minor op.132 in the Lydian mode) and to works that draw on folk music elements, for example Mozart's 'Moorish Song' for Pedrillo in *Die Entführung aus dem Serail*, Brahms's *Fünf Stücke im Volkston* for cello and piano, much music by Russian nationalist composers (e.g. in Glinka's *Ivan Susanin* or Musorgsky's *Boris Godunov*) and by such composers as Vaughan Williams and Bartók. An effect of modality may also be provided by unorthodox scales, such as the one used in Verdi's *Ave Maria* and the whole-tone scale of Debussy, though in fact neither of these is in a real sense modal. *See* MODE.

Mode. Term in Western music theory with three main applications, all connected with meanings of the Latin word *modus* ('measure', 'standard', 'manner'). The first is concerned with the relationship between note values in early notation, the second with intervals in early medieval theory, and the third with scale type and melody type. In its commonest sense, 'mode' stands for the scale or the selection of notes used as the basis for a composition; this selection has implications about where melodies will end, the shapes they may take and (according to early theory) the expressive character of a piece.

'Mode' is also used as an acoustical term, referring to ways in which a string or an air column can be made to vibrate (for example in segments; *see* HARMONICS). *See also* RHYTHMIC MODES.

Moderato (It.). 'Moderate', 'restrained', e.g. *allegro moderato* ('a little slower than *allegro*').

Moderator pedal. A pedal or knee lever that causes a strip of cloth to be introduced between the hammers and strings of a piano to produce a muted effect.

Moderne, Jacques (*b* Pinguente, *c*1495–1500; *d* Lyons, *c*1562). French music printer of Italian birth. One of the first to adapt Attaingnant's single-impression method, he began issuing music books in

Lyons in 1532 and was Attaingnant's only rival in France for 15 years; he issued *c*50 music books (over 800 pieces including masses, motets, *chansons* and instrumental music), with works by local and Parisian composers, Gombert, Willaert, Arcadelt and a variety of Italians, Spanish and Germans.

Modern Jazz Quartet. American jazz ensemble. Its members for its first recording in 1952 were Milt Jackson (vibraphone), John Lewis (piano and director), Kenny Clarke (drums) and Percy Heath (double bass). In 1955 Clarke was replaced by Connie Kay. The quartet, a leading exponent of cool jazz in the 1950s and 1960s, disbanded in 1974 but was re-formed in the early 1980s.

Modinha. A Portuguese and Brazilian sentimental art song of the 18th and 19th centuries, generally with guitar accompaniment; it came to be influenced by Italian opera in the late 18th century and later popularized. The Brazilian *modinha* survives as a lyrical folk genre.

Mödl, Martha (*b* Nuremberg, 22 March 1912). German soprano. She studied at Nuremberg and appeared with the Düsseldorf Opera, 1945–9, when she sang mezzo roles. She was at the Hamburg Staatsoper from 1949, sang Leonora (*Fidelio*) at the 1955 reopening of the Vienna Staatsoper and at Bayreuth (1951–67) was admired for her vivid characterizations of Kundry, Isolde and Brünnhilde. She appeared in London between 1950 and 1972.

Modulation. (1) In tonal music, the movement out of one key into another as a continuous musical process. The most common and simplest modulations are to keys most closely related to the main key: the relative minor or major, the dominant and its related keys and the subdominant and its related keys. Modulations are often effected by using a PIVOT. They play an important part in a work's formal organization.

(2) The term is also used in ELECTRONIC MUSIC for certain processes of change, for example of frequency or amplitude, or the more complex changes that can be made with a RING MODULATOR.

Moeck. German firm of music publishers and instrument makers. Founded by Hermann Moeck (1896–1982), in 1925 at Celle, it originally promoted recorders and their music, but it now makes high-quality early instruments of almost every kind, including viols.

Moeran, E(rnest) J(ohn) (*b* Heston, 31 Dec 1894; *d* Kenmare, 1 Dec 1950). English composer. He studied at the RCM (1913–14) then, after war service, with Ireland (until 1923) who, with Delius, was a dominant influence on his early music. In the early 1930s he retired to the Cotswolds, where he wrote his Symphony in G minor (1937), a work of Nature lyricism drawing on Sibelian thematic methods. His other works, all marked by meticulous craftsmanship, include the Sinfonietta (1944) and orchestral Serenade (1948), concertos for violin (1942) and cello (1945), chamber music and songs.

Moeschinger, Albert (*b* Basle, 10 Jan 1897; *d* Thun, 25 Sept 1985). Swiss composer. A pupil of Courvoisier in Munich, he taught at the Berne Conservatory (1937–43). Influenced by Reger, Debussy,

Stravinsky and Bartók, his large output includes choral music, five symphonies, six string quartets and piano and organ music.

Moffo, Anna (*b* Wayne, PA, 27 June 1932). American soprano. She studied in Philadelphia and Rome, making her début in Spoleto as Donizetti's Norina in 1955. Her American début was as Mimì in Chicago, 1957; she joined the Met in 1959, singing light, lyric soprano roles. Her Covent Garden début was as Gilda (1964). She was admired for her warm, radiant tone and her coloratura singing.

Mohaupt, Richard (*b* Wrocław, 14 Sept 1904; *d* Reichenau, 3 July 1957). German composer. He studied with Prüwer and Bilke at Breslau University and worked in New York from 1939, returning to Austria in 1955. His works include operas and ballets, mostly comic, as well as children's songs, and music for films and broadcasting.

Moiseiwitsch, Benno (*b* Odessa, 22 Feb 1890; *d* London, 9 April 1963). British pianist of Russian birth. After study in Odessa and Vienna he made his London début in 1909, later settling in England and taking British nationality in 1937. He made regular tours of Europe and the USA after World War I, notably as a powerful and poetic exponent of Beethoven and Rakhmaninov.

Mokranjac, Stevan (Stojanović) (*b* Negotin, 9 Jan 1856; *d* Skopje, 28 Sept 1914). Serbian composer. He studied in Munich, Rome and Leipzig. He established the Belgrade String Quartet (he played second violin), co-founded (1899) and directed the Serbian School of Music and conducted the Serbian Choral Society (from 1887). His methodical collection and study of Slav folk melodies influenced his own (predominantly choral) compositions, as in the 15 *Rukoveti* or choral rhapsodies (1884–1909).

Molchanov, Kirill Vladimirovich (*b* Moscow, 7 Sept 1922). Soviet composer, pupil of Alexandrov at the Moscow Conservatory. His works include vividly theatrical operas – notably *The Stone Flower* (1950) on tales from the Urals and the revolutionary *Daybreak* (1956) – and songs. He has also written film and incidental music.

Molière [Poquelin, Jean-Baptiste] (*b* Paris, bap. 15 Jan 1622; *d* there, 17 Feb 1673). French playwright and actor. Musically he is important for his works in the new genre of *comédie-ballet*, for which Lully composed ballet music and other pieces; the last was *Le malade imaginaire* (1673). He also wrote with Lully the *tragédie-ballet Psyché* (1671).

Molinaro, Simone (*b c*1565; *d* Genoa, 1615). Italian composer, nephew of Della Gostena, whom he succeeded as *maestro di cappella* of S Lorenzo, Genoa, by 1602. He published nine books of sacred works (1597–1616, two lost) and four of secular (1595–1615), as well as a lutebook (1599) containing dances, arrangements of vocal works and some adventurous fantasias.

Molino, Antonio [Blessi, Manoli] (*b c*1495–7; *d* ?Venice, in or after 1571). Italian poet and musician. He was widely educated and lived in Venice, where he founded a music academy. As a poet he was important in the early history of the *commedia dell'arte*; his verses were set by many leading Venetians, notably

A. Gabrieli. He also composed madrigals (2 bks, 1568, 1569).

Molique, (Wilhelm) Bernhard (*b* Nuremberg, 7 Oct 1802; *d* Cannstadt, 10 May 1869). German violinist and composer. He had lessons from Spohr and Rovelli. From 1826 to 1849 he was orchestra leader and royal music director in Stuttgart, training the orchestra to excellence and making extensive tours in Europe. In 1849 he settled in London as a performer, teacher and composer. Among his many, mainly conservative, works, the Violin Concerto no.5 (1841) and Cello Concerto (1853) enjoyed great popularity.

Moll (Ger.: 'soft'). Minor, as in *A moll* (A minor).

Moll, Kurt (*b* Buir, 11 April 1938). German bass. He studied in Cologne and sang widely in Germany before joining Hamburg Staatsoper in 1970. He has appeared at the main European opera houses and festivals and made his Covent Garden début as Kaspar in *Der Freischütz* (1977); other notable roles include Ochs (*Rosenkavalier*) and Osmin (*Die Entführung*), which show his deep voice and dramatic command.

Molter, Johann Melchior (*b* Tiefenort, 10 Feb 1696; *d* Karlsruhe, 12 Jan 1765). German composer. He worked at the Baden-Durlach court at Karlsruhe, studied in Italy (1719–21) and became Kapellmeister (1722). After a period as Kapellmeister at Eisenach, 1734–41, he returned to Karlsruhe, where he later reorganized the Kapelle. Prominent in his output are 170 sinfonias, over 40 solo concertos (some are among the earliest for clarinet), 21 orchestral sonatas (a genre unique to Molter), other orchestral music and over 100 chamber works. His music reflects many influences and shows a move from late Baroque to *galant* style; imaginative instrumentation is often a feature. He also composed oratorios, cantatas and keyboard music.

Molto (It.). Much, very.

Molza, Tarquinia (*b* Modena, 1542; *d* Rome, 8 Aug 1617). Italian singer. She was a member of the famous virtuoso 'singing ladies' at the Ferrarese court (1583–9) when her liaison with Wert, then *maestro di cappella*, caused her dismissal.

Momente. Work by Stockhausen for soprano, setting a varied collection of texts for chorus and instruments (1964).

Moment musical. A term used by Schubert's publisher for that composer's six lyrical piano pieces op.94 (D780) and occasionally by later composers, including Paderewski and Rakhmaninov, for pieces of a similar kind.

Momigny, Jérôme-Joseph de (*b* Philippeville, 20 Jan 1762; *d* Charenton, 25 Aug 1842). Belgian theorist and composer. His writings on rhythm and harmony (1803–34) in some ways ingeniously anticipate modern music theory; he proposed, for example, that the real rhythmic unit straddles the barline and that a single tonality embraces 17 notes. His compositions are mainly salon music.

Mompou, Federico (*b* Barcelona, 16 April 1893; *d* there, 3 June 1987). Spanish composer. He studied in Barcelona and with Motte-Lacroix and Samuel-Rousseau in Paris, where he remained until

1941 except for a return to Barcelona in 1914–21; he then settled in his native city. His output consists almost entirely of small-scale piano pieces and songs in a fresh, naive style indebted to Satie and Debussy; he aimed for maximum expressiveness through minimum means, often achieving a melancholy elegance.

Monari, Bartolomeo ['Monarino'] (*fl* Bologna, ?1670–1707). Italian composer. He became *maestro di cappella* of S Giovanni in Monte, Bologna, in ?1679, and later assistant organist of S Petronio. He wrote vocal and organ music. Clemente Monari (*c*1660–*c*1729), probably his brother, cathedral *maestro di cappella* at Reggio Emilia and Forlì, composed operas and oratorios.

Monckton, (John) Lionel (Alexander) (*b* London, 18 Dec 1861; *d* there, 15 Feb 1924). English composer. He studied at Oxford and was called to the Bar; later he wrote music criticism and applied his skill as a melodist to the writing of musical comedies, notably *The Arcadians* (1909) and *The Quaker Girl* (1910).

Mondo della luna, Il [The World on the Moon]. Opera in three acts by Haydn to a libretto by Goldoni (1777, Eszterháza). The libretto was previously set by Galuppi, Paisiello, Piccinni and others.

Mondonville, Jean-Joseph Cassanéa de (*b* Narbonne, bap. 25 Dec 1711; *d* Belleville, 8 Oct 1772). French violinist and composer. In the 1730s he was in Lille; then he settled in Paris, where he won fame as soloist and composer. He became *sous-maître* to the royal chapel in 1740 and *intendant* in 1744. His music is notable for its imaginative textures. Best known were his sonatas for harpsichord and violin (1734), among the earliest accompanied keyboard music, and those for harpsichord, violin and voice (1748); his 17 *grands motets* (among the finest since Lalande's and like his, much performed at the Concert Spirituel) and ten stage works (1742–71) were also popular.

Monferrato, Natale (*b* Venice, *c*1603; *d* there, by 23 April 1685). Italian composer. A singer at St Mark's, Venice, from 1639, he was made *vicemaestro di cappella* there in 1647 and *maestro di cappella* (succeeding Cavalli) in 1676. He was also an organist and a teacher. His output, mostly sacred, includes masses in the *stile antico* and motets and psalms in a more modern style.

Monferrina. A country dance in 6/8 metre of Piedmontese origin, popular in early 19th-century England: Clementi composed two sets for piano.

Mongini, Pietro (*b* Rome, 1830; *d* Milan, 27 April 1874). Italian tenor. Noted for his brilliance of sound in such Verdi roles as Manrico (*Il trovatore*) and Don Alvaro (*La forza del destino*), he created Radamès in the first performance of *Aida*, in Cairo (24 December 1871).

Monica. A song, popular in 17th-century Italy, used by Frescobaldi and others for instrumental variations.

Moniot d'Arras (*fl* 1213–39). French trouvère, probably associated with the Abbey of St Vaast in Arras. Poems by him are addressed to various members of the nobility, and his extant songs are in a variety of genres and forms. Most are the usual *chansons courtoises* but two set religious texts. His quotation of existing motets in some of his songs gives clues to their rhythmic interpretation. He should not be confused with Moniot de Paris, active in the mid-13th century, who is known by nine songs in a simple, even rustic style.

Moniuszko, Stanisław (*b* Ubiel, 5 May 1819; *d* Warsaw, 4 June 1872). Polish composer. After studying with Rungenhagen in Berlin he returned to Poland and became organist at St John's, Vilnius, also giving piano lessons and conducting the theatre orchestra. Contacts with literary figures stimulated his interest in dramatic music, which he began to compose prolifically. His opera *Halka*, performed first in Vilnius (1848) then in Warsaw (1857), established him as the foremost Polish nationalist opera composer. He became conductor of the Grand Theatre, Warsaw (1859), and from 1864 taught at the Music Institute. A national element is apparent chiefly in the librettos of his operas, the plots representing the Polish world of nobility (*The Haunted Manor*, 1861–4; *The Countess*, 1859) and often introducing common people as victims (*Halka*); in a country deprived of statehood they fostered patriotic feeling. Stylistically close to Rossini and Auber's *opéras comiques*, they make greater use of the chorus and rely on Polish dance rhythms (the mazurka and polonaise). The significance of his popular *Songbooks for Home Use* (267 songs with piano accompaniment in 12 books; 1843–59, 1877–1910) lies in their freer dissemination, testimony to the 'Polishness' of society when large-scale public performances were impossible. The songs are simple, usually strophic, displaying a rich melodic inventiveness and folkdance rhythms; they became a model for later Polish composers.

Monk, Thelonious (Sphere) (*b* Rocky Mount, NC, 10 Oct 1917; *d* Weehawken, NJ, 17 Feb 1982). American jazz pianist and composer. In the early 1940s, as pianist at Minton's Playhouse, New York, he contributed to the harmonic idiom of bop. He led several small groups, but was little known until *c*1957 when he first met critical acclaim. In the 1960s he achieved popular success but after 1971 went into virtual retirement. His piano style was unorthodox, using a distinctive 'clanging' timbre, crushed notes, clusters and unconventional harmonies. His economical use of material emphasized his often humorous sense of rhythmic anticipation and delay, tempo suspension and silence, allowing him to explore themes with unusual rigour.

Monk, William Henry (*b* London, 16 March 1823; *d* there, 18 March 1889). English organist and editor. He was a leader in the Anglican choral revival, holding London posts as organist and choirmaster and editing *Hymns Ancient and Modern* (1861), for which he wrote the well-known tune 'Eventide' (*Abide with me*).

Monk of Salzburg (*fl* late 14th century). German poet and composer. Although there is confusion as to his name and monastic order, 49 sacred and 57 secular songs are attributed to him in MSS from the heyday of the Meistergesang. His songs were composed at the court of his patron, the Archbishop of Salzburg, Pilgrim II von Puchheim (1365–96). Almost half his religious songs, written in a style close to that of Latin hymns and sequences, are in praise of the Virgin; his secular songs embrace all the genres of late medieval poetry. His works include the earliest known examples of polyphonic (and so rhythmically notated) songs in German.

Monn, Matthias Georg (*b* Vienna, 9 April 1717; *d* there, 3 Oct 1750). Austrian composer. He became organist at St Charles's Church, Vienna, in 1738 or later, and was also a teacher. Though little known abroad, he was, like Wagenseil, a leading Viennese composer. In his *c*20 symphonies he approached Classical sonata form; most have three movements, but one (1740) is the first known four-movement symphony with a third-movement minuet. His several concertos (most for harpsichord) also have progressive elements; his various chamber, vocal and keyboard works are more conservative.

Monn's works have been confused with those of his brother Johann Christoph (1726–82), who also worked in Vienna and composed keyboard and other instrumental music.

Monnikendam, Marius (*b* Haarlem, 28 May 1896; *d* Heerlen, 22 May 1977). Dutch composer. He studied with Dresden at the Amsterdam Conservatory, and with d'Indy and Aubert in Paris, then worked in the Netherlands as a critic and teacher. His works, in a broadly traditional style, include much church music and orchestral pieces.

Monochord [canon harmonicus]. An ancient single-string instrument first mentioned in Greece in the 5th century BC, said to have been an invention of Pythagoras. It remained a viable musical device, for teaching, tuning and experimentation, until the advent of more accurate instruments in the late 19th century. In its earliest form its single string was stretched across two fixed bridges erected on a plank or table; a movable bridge was then placed under the string, dividing it into two sections. The marks indicating the position of the fixed bridge were inscribed on the table beneath the string. The length of the instrument was about 90–122 cm. Monochord-based diagrams and directions for determining the consonances abound in medieval treatises.

The monochord is cited in Greek and medieval writings as an ensemble instrument; in the late Middle Ages and the Renaissance, it is often mentioned as a tool in the design or measurement of bells and organ pipes.

Monodrama. A MELODRAMA for one character. The term was also used by Schoenberg for his *Erwartung* (1909).

Monody. Accompanied Italian solo song, especially secular, of *c*1600–40. The term stands equally for an individual song or the entire repertory. It covers songs for solo voice and continuo (usually lute, chittarone, theorbo, harpsichord or occasionally guitar). Monodies fall into two groups, the madrigal type (with a polarized bass and vocal line, the latter often quite elaborately embellished), and the aria type, more varied in form and style but often strophic, in

triple time and little ornamented. This distinction was already established by Caccini in his epoch-making *Le nuove musiche* (1601/2). The form was largely Florentine up to *c*1620, then primarily Venetian; but monodies were written elsewhere in Italy, particularly Rome. Composers included Caccini, Peri, Grandi, da Gagliano and d'India. Monodies were usually dramatic in style, closely illustrating the sense of the words with ornamentation, abrupt leaps, changes in rhythmic texture and unexpected harmonies.

Monophony. Music for a single voice or part, e.g. plainchant and unaccompanied solo song. The term is contrasted with 'polyphony' (music in two or more independent voices), 'homopohony' (which implies rhythmic similarity in a number of voices) and 'heterophony' (simultaneous variations of a single melody).

Monothematic. Term used to describe a piece or movement constructed on a single theme. Sonata-form movements (including many by Haydn) in which second-group material is derived from the opening theme are often described as monothematic, even though contrasting themes may appear elsewhere.

Monotone. A single unvaried tone, or a succession of sounds at the same pitch. Liturgical texts are often recited 'in monotone'; the device is also used for special effects in opera.

Monpou, (François Louis) Hippolyte (*b* Paris, 12 Jan 1804; *d* Orleans, 10 Aug 1841). French composer. A pupil of Choron and Fétis, he won recognition principally as an innovatory composer of piquant little songs, often to texts by Alfred de Musset (*L'Andalouse*, 1830) or Victor Hugo (*Les deux archers*, 1834). Among his comic operas *Le Piquillo* (1837) and *Le planteur* (1839) show his natural talent.

Monsigny, Pierre-Alexandre (*b* Fauquembergues, 17 Oct 1729; *d* Paris, 14 Jan 1817). French composer. He presented *opéras comiques* in Paris from 1759, from 1761 collaborating with the librettist Sedaine, notably in *Le roy et le fermier* (1762) and *Le déserteur* (1769). *Félix et l'enfant trouvé* (1777), a particular success, was his last work. Later he was Inspector of Musical Education (1800–02). He composed 18 stage works in all; his *opéras comiques*, often unusually serious for the genre, show a melodic gift and dramatic instinct and are strikingly forward-looking in their instrumental writing.

Montbuisson, Victor de (*b* Avignon, *c*1575; *d* after 1638). French music editor. He was a lutenist at the Kassel court (1598–1627), then taught in The Hague until 1638. In 1611 he began to compile an important MS lutebook, containing *c*80 dances and over 50 arrangements of vocal pieces by many composers.

Monte, Philippe de (*b* Mechlin, 1521; *d* Prague, 4 July 1603). Flemish composer. He was a choirboy at Mechlin and then served the Pinelli family in Naples (1542–51). In 1554 he was in Antwerp and then England (where he met Byrd), serving in the private chapel of Philip II of Spain (Mary Tudor's husband). He was next in Rome, probably with Cardinal Orsini, and from 1568 until his death he was Kapellmeister at the Habsburg court in Vienna (later Prague). Prolific, successful and progressive in outlook, he composed over 1100 madrigals in 34 books (1554–1600, often reprinted), spiritual madrigals (5 bks, 1581–93) and *chansons* (1585), as well as some 40 masses (mostly MS) and over 250 motets (10 bks, 1572–1600).

Montéclair, Michel Pignolet de (*b* Andelot, bap. 4 Dec 1667; *d* Aumont, 22 Sept 1737). French composer and theorist. He arrived in Paris in 1687 and soon played the *basse de violon* and double bass in the Paris Opéra orchestras; he was also eminent as a teacher. One of the most versatile composers of his time, his output includes several stage works, which influenced Rameau (especially their dramatic scoring), and 20 French and four Italian cantatas with many operatic features. He also wrote collections of *airs*, sacred music, instrumental pieces (though none for keyboard) and treatises; his *Principes de musique* (1736) is a major source on French vocal ornamentation.

Montella, Giovanni Domenico (*b* Naples, *c*1570; *d* there, by 2 July 1607). Italian composer. A pupil of Macque, he was a lutenist in Fabrizio Gesualdo's academy in Naples in the late 1580s and in the Spanish viceroy's chapel (1591, organist from 1599). A prolific composer, he published 14 books of secular music (1595–1607) and five of sacred (1600–05), with much contrapuntal device and extravagant harmonies.

Montemezzi, Italo (*b* Vigasio, 31 May 1875; *d* there, 15 May 1952). Italian composer. He studied at the Milan Conservatory and won success with his introduction of Wagnerian elements into an Italian operatic style, notably in *L'amore dei tre re* (1913).

Montesardo, Girolamo (*b* ?Naples; *fl* 1606–*c*1620). Italian composer. A singer, he served first at Bologna, was *maestro di cappella* at Fano in 1608 and later lived in Naples. He wrote vocal music and a volume of guitar pieces (1606), which popularized a system of chord notation for use in *rasgueado* playing of the five-course guitar.

Monteux, Pierre (*b* Paris, 4 April 1875; *d* Hancock, ME, 1 July 1964). American conductor of French birth. After study at the Paris Conservatoire his early experience was as a viola player. He was conductor of Dyagilev's Ballets Russes, 1911–14, and gave the premières of Stravinsky's *Rite of Spring* and *Petrushka*, Ravel's *Daphnis et Chloé* and Debussy's *Jeux*. He conducted the Boston SO, 1920–24, then went to Amsterdam and to Paris where he founded and conducted the Orchestre Symphonique (1929–38). He directed the San Francisco SO, 1936–52. In 1961, aged 86, he signed a 25-year contract as chief conductor of the LSO. His conducting was noted for its sure grasp of musical structure and its feeling for sound over a wide repertory.

Monteverdi [Monteverde], Claudio (Giovanni Antonio) (*b* Cremona, 15 May 1567; *d* Venice, 29 Nov 1643). Italian composer. He studied with Ingegneri, *maestro di cappella* at Cremona Cathedral, and published several books of motets and madrigals before going to Mantua in about 1591 to serve as a string player at the court of Duke Vincenzo Gonzaga. There he came under the influence of Giaches de Wert, whom he failed to succeed as *maestro di cappella* in 1596. In 1599 he married Claudia de Cattaneis, a court singer, who bore him three children, and two years later he was appointed *maestro di cappella* on Pallavicino's death. Largely as the result of a prolonged controversy with the theorist G.M. Artusi, Monteverdi became known as a leading exponent of the modern approach to harmony and text expression. In 1607 his first opera, *Orfeo*, was produced in Mantua, followed in 1608 by *Arianna*. Disenchanted with Mantua, he then returned to Cremona, but failed to secure his release from the Gonzaga family until 1612, when Duke Vincenzo died. The dedication to Pope Paul V of a grand collection of church music known as the Vespers (1610) had already indicated an outward-looking ambition, and in 1613 Monteverdi was appointed *maestro di cappella* at St Mark's, Venice.

There Monteverdi was active in reorganizing and improving the *cappella* as well as writing music for it, but he was also able to accept commissions from elsewhere, including some from Mantua, for example the ballet *Tirsi e Clori* (1616) and an opera, *La finta pazza Licori* (1627, not performed, now lost). He seems to have been less active after *c*1629, but he was again in demand as an opera composer on the opening of public opera houses in Venice from 1637. In 1640 *Arianna* was revived, and in the following two years *Il ritorno d'Ulisse in patria*, *Le nozze d'Enea con Lavinia* (lost) and *L'incoronazione di Poppea* were given first performances. In 1643 he visited Cremona and died shortly after his return to Venice.

Monteverdi can be justly considered one of the most powerful figures in the history of music. Much of his development as a composer may be observed in the eight books of secular madrigals published between 1587 and 1638. The early books show his indebtedness to Marenzio in particular; the final one, *Madrigali guerrieri et amorosi*, includes some pieces 'in genere rappresentativo' – *Il ballo delle ingrate*, the *Combattimento di Tancredi e Clorinda* and the *Lamento della ninfa* – which draw on Monteverdi's experience as an opera composer. A ninth book was issued posthumously in 1651.

Orfeo was the first opera to reveal the potential of this then novel genre; *Arianna* (of which only the famous lament survives) may well have been responsible for its survival. Monteverdi's last opera, *L'incoronazione di Poppea*, though transmitted in not wholly reliable sources and including music by other men, is his greatest masterpiece and arguably the finest opera of the century. In the 1610 collection of sacred music Monteverdi displayed the multiplicity of styles that characterize this part of his output. The mass, written on themes from Gombert's motet *In illo tempore*, is a monument of the *prima prattica* or old style. At the other extreme the motets, written for virtuoso singers, are the most thorough-going exhibition of the modern style and the *seconda prattica*.

Dramatic music L'Orfeo (1607); Il ritorno d'Ulisse in patria (1640); L'incoronazione di Poppea (1642); ballets: Il ballo delle ingrate (1608); Tirsi e Clori (1616); Volgendo il ciel (?1636); Combattimento di Tancredi e Clorinda, dramatic dialogue (1624)

Secular vocal music c220 works incl. 9 madrigal bks: Bk 1 (1587), Bk 2 (1590), Bk 3 (1592), Bk 4 (1603), Bk 5 (1605), Bk 6 (1614), Bk 7, incl. Chiome d'oro (1619), Bk 8, Madrigali guerrieri et amorosi (1638), Bk 9 (1651); Lamento d'Arianna, from lost opera (1608); canzonettas (1584); Scherzi musicali, 2 bks (1607, 1632)

Sacred vocal music Vespers (1610); 3 masses; 2 Magnificats; Madrigali spirituali (1583); c140 works, incl. motets, psalms etc, some in Selva morale e spirituale (1640)

Monteverdi, Giulio Cesare (*b* Cremona, bap. 31 Jan 1573; *d* Salò, ?1630/31). Italian composer and writer on music, brother of Claudio. Until 1612 he served the Duke of Mantua; he was later an organist at Castelleone and then *maestro di cappella* at Salò Cathedral. A composer of vocal music, he edited his brother's *Scherzi musicali* (1607), adding an explanation of his ideas.

Monteverdi Choir. English semi-professional chamber choir founded in 1964 by its conductor JOHN ELIOT GARDINER.

Montezuma. Opera by C.H. Graun to a libretto by Frederick the Great, translated into Italian (1755, Berlin).

Monti, Marianna (*b* Naples, 1730; *d* there, 1814). Italian soprano. She appeared in comic operas in Naples from 1746, becoming perhaps the most popular *prima buffa* there, 1760–80, and helping promote the more complex type of comic opera already current in Venice. Among the composers who created roles for her was her brother Gaetano (*c*1750–?1816), an organist who wrote, besides comic operas, intermezzos, a serious opera and other pieces.

The sisters Anna Maria (1704–after 1727), Grazia (*fl* 1728) and Laura Monti (after 1704–1760), cousins of Marianna, were also Neapolitan *opera buffa* singers; Laura was the first Serpina in Pergolesi's *La serva padrona* (1733).

Montpellier MS. French MS, possibly from Paris, of the period *c*1270–1310. It consists of 400 folios containing 336 compositions, almost all of them motets, from the 13th century; it is the largest surviving collection of medieval motets. It is now at the Faculté de Médecine, Montpellier University.

Montreal Symphony Orchestra. Canadian orchestra founded in 1930 as the Montreal Orchestra; in 1934 some of its members formed Les Concerts Symphoniques, which in 1954 became the Orchestre Symphonique de Montréal–Montreal SO. Concerts are given in the Salle Wilfrid Pelletier (1967; cap. 3000). Activities include subscription series and popular, choral and educational concerts.

Montreux(-Vevey) Music Festival (Switzerland). Annual (Aug–Oct) festival established in 1946 as the Septembre Musical; among its events are orchestral and chamber concerts (which include contemporary works), and oratorios and church music in Vevey.

Montsalvatge, Xavier (*b* Gerona, 11 March 1912). Spanish composer. He studied at the Barcelona Conservatory (1923–36), then wrote *c*20 ballets for the Goubé-Alexander company, drawing on Stra-

vinsky and Les Six and on Caribbean music. His later works, in most genres, have been more eclectic. He has also been active as a teacher and critic.

Monza, Carlo (*b* Milan, *c*1735; *d* there, 19 Dec 1801). Italian composer. He succeeded Sammartini as organist at the Milan court in 1768 and *maestro di cappella* in 1775; he was also *maestro* of three churches and from 1787 of Milan Cathedral. He presented *c*20 operas at Italian theatres, 1758–85; later he wrote sacred music, in both contrapuntal and operatic styles, and came to be regarded as one of the leading Italian sacred composers of the time.

He was probably not related to Carlo Antonio Monza (late 17th century–1736), who may also have been Milanese and who had operas given at Venice, Messina and elsewhere and was *maestro di cappella* in Vercelli from 1735.

Moog, Robert A(rthur) (*b* Flushing, NY, 23 May 1934). American designer of electronic instruments. He formed his own company, built theremins (1954–62) and marketed the first commercial modular synthesizer in 1964. After 14 years (his role as designer of the synthesizers bearing his name ended *c*1973), he formed a new company, manufacturing devices for precision control of analogue and digital synthesizers. He has developed several electronic devices and designed electronic music systems.

Moonlight Sonata. Nickname of Beethoven's Piano Sonata no.14 in C♯ minor op.27 no.2 (1801), so called because in a review of it Heinrich Rellstab wrote that the first movement reminded him of moonlight on Lake Lucerne.

Moór, Emanuel. *See* EMANUEL MOÓR PIANOFORTE.

Moore, Carman (Leroy) (*b* Lorain, OH, 8 Oct 1936). American composer. He studied with Persichetti and Berio at the Juilliard School, and with Wolpe. He co-founded the Society of Black Composers (1968). His works blend jazz, gospel, rock and avant-garde idioms. *Gospel Fuse* (1974) and *Wildfires and Field Songs* (1974), both for orchestra, established his reputation.

Moore, Douglas (Stuart) (*b* Cutchogue, NY, 10 Aug 1893; *d* Greenport, NY, 25 July 1969). American composer. He studied at Yale, in Paris with d'Indy and Boulanger (1919–21), and in Cleveland with Bloch, then taught at Barnard College, Columbia (1926–62). His most important works are operas, generally dealing with rural or pioneer life and drawing on folk music; they include *The Devil and Daniel Webster* (1938) and *The Ballad of Baby Doe* (1956).

Moore, Gerald (*b* Watford, 30 July 1899; *d* Penn, Bucks., 13 March 1987). English pianist. He studied in Canada and with Mark Hambourg in England. From 1921 he was associated with HMV as a recording artist, providing discreet and sympathetic accompaniments for many leading instrumental and vocal soloists. Early partnerships were with Casals, Schumann and Teyte. He later recorded most of the lieder of Schubert, Wolf and Strauss, notably with Schwarzkopf and Fischer-Dieskau, and raised the art of accompanying to the highest level. His writings include *The Unashamed Accompanist* (1943) and his memoirs *Am I too Loud?* (1962).

Moore, Thomas (*b* Dublin, 28 May 1779; *d* nr. Devizes, 25 Feb 1852). Irish poet and musician. In London from 1799, he won a vast following for his verses, personal charm and singing and above all for his *Selection of Irish Melodies* (1808–34; accompaniments by John Stevenson), kindling interest in little-known Irish folk music. Similar collections of *Sacred Songs* (1816) and *Popular National Airs* (1818–28) followed. But it was with the exotic story-poem *Lalla Rookh* (1817) that his colourful imagery made an impact on Romantic composers; portions of it were set by Spontini, Félicien David, Sterndale Bennett, Schumann and C.V. Stanford among others.

Morago, Estêvão Lopes (*b* Madrid, *c*1575; *d* ?Orgens, after 1630). Portuguese composer of Spanish birth. He was *mestre de capela* of the cathedral at Veseu, 1599–1630, and also a priest. He left *c*100 liturgical works, some of them for double choir; their style, though mainly conservative and contrapuntal, includes expressive harmonic writing. Some of his hymns remained popular into the 18th century.

Morales, Cristóbal de (*b* Seville, *c*1500; *d* ?Marchena, 4 Sept–7 Oct 1553). Spanish composer. He is recognized as the most important figure in early 16th-century Spanish sacred music. He received his early musical education in Seville and in 1526 was appointed *maestro de capilla* of Avila Cathedral. In 1531 he resigned and by September 1535 was a singer in the papal chapel in Rome. He left in 1545 and was appointed *maestro de capilla* at Toledo Cathedral. He then fell ill and in 1547 renounced the position. On returning to Andalusia he became *maestro de capilla* to the Duke of Arcos at Marchena (1548–51). In 1551 he became *maestro de capilla* at Málaga Cathedral.

His works, almost all liturgical, include over 20 masses, 16 Magnificats, two Lamentations and over 100 motets. The Magnificats, perhaps the best known of his works, are permeated by Gregorian *cantus firmi*; his Lamentations are characterized by a sober homophonic style. In his motets he often used chant associated with the text, as a melodic point of departure (e.g. *Puer natus est*) or as an ostinato figure (e.g. the five-voice *Tu es Petrus*), but he seldom borrowed entire melodies. Their texture is characterized by free imitation with exceptional use of homophonic sections to stress important words or portions of text. The two masses for the dead and the *Officium defunctorum* are the most extreme examples of Morales's sober style. He had thorough command of early 16th-century continental techniques and his style is better compared to Josquin, Gombert and Clemens than to his Spanish contemporaries. He favoured cross-rhythms, conflicting rhythms, melodic (but not harmonic) sequence and repetition, harmonic cross-relations, systematic use of consecutives and occasional daring use of harmony.

Sacred music over 20 masses; 16 Magnificats; 2 Lamentations settings; over 100 motets
Secular music Spanish songs; intabulations

Morales, Olallo (Juan Magnus) (*b* Almeria, 15 Oct 1874; *d* Tällberg, 29 April 1957). Swedish composer of Spanish birth. He studied in Stockholm and Berlin, and was a conductor, critic and teacher (at the conservatory, 1917–39). His works colourfully blend Spanish impressionism with Nordic romanticism.

Moravians, American. A religious sect whose communities, established in the mid-18th century, produced a highly developed musical culture for over 100 years. The Moravian Church, organized as the Bohemian Brethren in 1457, renewed itself at Herrnhut, Saxony, in 1722 and sent missionaries to North America from 1735. They established Bethlehem (1741), Nazareth (1748) and Lititz (1756) in Pennsylvania and Salem in North Carolina (1766, now Winston-Salem), where they carried on strong musical traditions, congregational and concerted. Choirs divided by age, sex and marital status had their own devotionals and festivals; the principal musical service, the love feast (a simple congregational meal), required anthems with instrumental accompaniment, hymns, duets and solo songs; song hours (several a week) introduced new hymns, to be sung at Sunday services, German and English. Most of this music was provided by composers within the Church. Notable German Moravian musicians in the communities were J.F. Peter (1746–1813), Johannes Herbst (1735–1812), D.M. Michael (1751–1827) and J.C. Bechler (1784–1857); among American-born Moravians, Peter Wolle (1792–1871) edited the first Moravian tunebook published in the USA (1836) and wrote anthems and songs, and E.W. Leinbach (1823–1901) wrote a remarkable *Hosanna*. By *c*1850 musical life in the communities began to decline, owing to changes in taste, secularizing influences and a decreasing need for new music.

Morawetz, Oskar (*b* Světlá nad Sázavou, 17 Jan 1917). Canadian composer of Czech origin. He studied at Toronto University, where in 1958 he was appointed professor. Most of his works are serious, often tragic; they include orchestral pieces, songs and chamber music. Some of his earlier orchestral pieces such as the *Carnival Overture* (1946), the Divertimento for Strings (1948) and the *Overture to a Fairy Tale* (1956) are popular for their colourful orchestration and rhythmic vitality; the Scherzo for piano (1947) is a minor classic for Canadian pianists.

Morceaux en forme de poire, Trois. Work for piano duet by Satie (1903), a group of six (not three) pieces.

Mordent. An ornament, consisting in its normal form of the rapid alternation of the main note with the note a step below. This is also known as a lower mordent; a variant is the inverted or upper mordent, when the main note alternates with the note above. It is known in German as the *Schneller* (from *schnellen*, 'to jerk'), and in French as the *pincé*, *battement* or *martellement*. A double mordent has two (occasionally more) iterations, and is considered suitable in a slower tempo; in ex.1 (from Gottlieb Muffat, *c*1739), the outer mordents show a normal realization, the central one a double. Ex.2 shows both with the French mordent sign (from Couperin,

Ex. 1

1713). The upper mordent is notated with the same sign as in the first example but without the vertical

Ex. 2

Pincé simple   Pincé double

line through it (identical with that for the PRALL-TRILLER). Sometimes the sign is prolonged to indicate extra iterations.

Moreau, Jean-Baptiste (*b* Angers, 1656; *d* Paris, 24 Aug 1733). French composer and teacher. He was *maître de musique* at Langres and Dijon; in the late 1680s he was *musicien ordinaire* at the royal school at St Cyr. He was famous for his dramatic music, especially that for Racine's plays *Esther* (1689) and *Athalie* (1691), and also composed sacred pieces. In 1694 he became superintendent of Languedoc but soon returned to Paris. Montéclair was his pupil.

Moreira, António Leal (*b* Abrantes, 1758; *d* Lisbon, 21 Nov 1819). Portuguese composer. An organist in Lisbon, he became *mestre de capela* of the royal chapel in 1787, composing numerous sacred works. He was also a theatre music director. One of the most gifted and successful stage composers of his day, much influenced by Paisiello and Cimarosa, he wrote 16 operas, serenatas etc (both Italian and Portuguese), notably *A vingança da cigana* (1794).

Morel, François (d'Assise) (*b* Montreal, 14 March 1926). Canadian composer. He studied with Champagne at the Montreal Conservatory (1944–53) and had decisive contact with Varèse in New York in 1958. He has written functional music for radio and orchestral and chamber pieces using serial methods.

Morendo (It.). Dying.

Morera, Enrique (*b* Barcelona, 22 May 1865; *d* there, 12 March 1942). Spanish composer. A pupil of Pedrell, he wrote operas, zarzuelas and orchestral music, strongly influenced by folk music, and became one of the most popular Catalan composers.

Moresca [morisca]. (1) A Renaissance dance of exotic character, often simulating a battle between Moors and Christians. Blackening of the face, bells attached to costumes and the participation of a fool are common features, as in the English derivation, the morris dance. In the 17th century the term 'moresca' was used for ballet or pantomimic dance in opera (e.g. at the end of Monteverdi's *Orfeo*).

(2) A type of VILLANELLA parodying the dialect of Africans living in Venice and Naples. The music was lively and uncomplicated, characterized by rhythmic freedom, chordal texture and occasional passages in parallel 5ths.

Mori. English family of musicians. Nicolas (1796/7–1839), a pupil of Viotti, led the Philharmonic

Society and King's Theatre orchestras, composed violin music, and married into music publishing (Mori & Lavenu). Of his sons, Frank (1820–73), a conductor and vocal composer, tried to found a permanent London orchestra in 1854; Nicholas (1822–*c*1890) wrote theatre music and opera fantasias.

Mörike-Lieder. Collection of songs by Wolf, settings for voice and piano of 53 poems by Mörike (most written in 1888).

Morin, Jean-Baptiste (*b* Orléans, 1677; *d* Paris, 1754). French composer. He was *ordinaire de la musique* to the Duke of Orléans (the Regent) in Paris, and *maître de chapelle* to his daughter. His 18 published cantatas (1706–12), which unite French and Italian styles, influenced many composers; he also wrote divertissements and motets.

Morlacchi, Francesco (Giuseppe Baldassare) (*b* Perugia, 14 June 1784; *d* Innsbruck, 28 Oct 1841). Italian composer and conductor. He studied in Loreto and Bologna. His career as an opera composer began in Italy in 1807; by 1811 he was Kapellmeister of the Italian Opera in Dresden where, despite a heated rivalry with Weber (Kapellmeister of the Dresden German Opera, 1817–26), he was esteemed for his musical leadership. His effective if superficial style approaches Donizetti and Rossini and is seen to best advantage in comic scenes; among his considerable successes were *Il nuovo barbiere di Siviglia* (1816), *La simplicetta di Pirna* (1817), *La gioventù di Enrico V* (1823), *Il Colombo* (1828) and *Il rinnegato* (1832). He also composed sacred works.

Morley, Thomas (*b* Norwich, 1557–8; *d* London, early Oct 1602). English composer. A pupil of Byrd, he was master of the choristers at Norwich Cathedral (1583–7) before becoming organist of St Paul's Cathedral, London (by 1589), and a Gentleman of the Chapel Royal (1592). From 1598 he held the patent for music printing that had once been Byrd's. At some period he was also employed as a government spy. A most influential figure, as composer, music editor and theorist, he wrote service music, anthems, psalms and Latin motets as well as over 100 madrigals and lighter secular works (1593–7), accompanied solo songs (1600) and keyboard and other instrumental music. His editions and anthologies of Italian music, some with new English texts, were chiefly responsible for the Elizabethan vogue for Italian madrigals; and he edited the famous English madrigal anthology *The Triumphes of Oriana* (1601). His renowned *Plaine and Easie Introduction* (1597), a practical and lively treatise in dialogue form, was long popular.

Sacred music 3 services; service music; English anthems, psalms, Latin motets
*Secular vocal music c*100 madrigals and canzonets, incl. Aprill is in my mistris face, Now is the month of maying; songs
Instrumental music dances, variations, kbd; ensemble pieces

Mornington, Garret Wesley, 1st Earl of (*b* Dublin, 19 July 1735; *d* Kensington, 22 May 1781). Irish composer. He showed remarkable precocity as a violinist, keyboard player and composer. Later he founded a music society in Dublin and was the first professor of music at the university there (1764–74).

He is best known for his prizewinning glees.

Moroi, Makoto (*b* Tokyo, 17 Dec 1930). Japanese composer. A pupil of Ikenouchi, he worked at the electronic music studio in Cologne (1955–6) and returned to take a leading part in the Japanese avant garde, as composer and as teacher (from 1968 at the Osaka Geijutsu Daigaku). Many of his works, in most genres, use Japanese instruments (e.g. Five Pieces for shakuhachi, 1964).

His father Saburō Moroi (1903–77) was the principal representative in Japan of the German tradition, his works including five symphonies, concertos and chamber music.

Moross, Jerome (*b* Brooklyn, 1 Aug 1913; *d* Miami, 25 July 1983). American composer. He worked in Hollywood as an arranger (1940–48) and wrote film scores, stage pieces (many in hybrid on experimental forms), orchestral and chamber music; they combine spontaneous, popular appeal with strength of musical purpose.

Morris, R(eginald) O(wen) (*b* York, 3 March 1886; *d* London, 14 Dec 1948). English teacher. He studied at Oxford and the RCM, where he taught. A leading figure in the institution of contrapuntal study on the basis of actual music rather than arbitrary theory, with his sharp intellect he influenced a generation of composers in England. He was himself a fastidious composer.

Morris dance. An English genre of folkdance, covering processional and sword dances; in the central tradition, it is danced by two groups of three men holding handkerchiefs or sticks, with small bells attached to their legs. It has sometimes been called the 'morisco', supporting the theory that it derives from the *moresca*.

Mortari, Virgilio (*b* Passirana di Lainate, 6 Dec 1902). Italian composer, pupil of Bossi in Milan and Pizzetti in Parma. His works, covering all genres including opera, are in a neo-classical, often humorous style.

Mortaro, Antonio (*fl* 1587–1610). Italian composer. A Franciscan friar, he was organist at the monastery in Milan by 1598 and of Novara Cathedral in 1602; he returned to Brescia after 1606. Most of his sacred music (10 bks, 1595–1610) is for multiple choirs in the Venetian style and includes forward-looking concertato-like pieces. He also wrote pleasing canzonets (*Fiammelle amorose*). His music was popular and widely disseminated.

Mortensen, Finn (Einar) (*b* Oslo, 6 Jan 1922). Norwegian composer. A pupil of Egge in Oslo and Bentzon in Copenhagen, both important influences, he has written largely instrumental music, at first in a polyphonic, neo-classical style, but from *c*1960 using serialism. He has also taught in Oslo.

Mortensen, Otto (Jacob Hübertz) (*b* Copenhagen, 18 Aug 1907). Danish composer. He studied with Jeppesen at the Copenhagen Conservatory (1925–9), in Berlin, and in Paris with Milhaud (1939). He has worked as a conductor, pianist and teacher and has written songs in the Nielsen tradition.

Morthenson, Jan W(ilhelm) (*b* Örnsköldsvik, 7 April 1940). Swedish composer. He studied at Uppsala University and Darmstadt, and has been motivated, like Kagel, by a view of music as decadent and disintegrating. He has been a prolific writer on theory.

Morton, Jelly Roll (*b* New Orleans, 20 Oct 1890; *d* Los Angeles, 10 July 1941). American jazz composer and pianist. From *c*1904 he worked in southern cities; by 1911 he was in New York, by 1917 Los Angeles. In 1922 he settled in Chicago, where he made his first recordings, post-ragtime in style. He was recording with the Red Hot Peppers in 1927, and in 1928 went to New York where he worked with larger groups, using elaborate harmony and solo improvisation. The first important jazz composer, he developed the New Orleans style to its finest expression.

Morton, Robert (*b c*1430; *d* 1476 or later). English composer. He was a member of the Burgundian chapel choir, 1457–76, in the reigns of Philip the Good and Charles the Bold. A reference to him as 'chappellain angloix' is the only evidence of his provenance; further biographical details are found in his songs, which suggest that he knew the influential Bouton family and was acquainted with Flemish composers such as Hayne van Ghizeghem. Only secular works survive; they have traces of an English style. Some of his pieces were exceptionally widely distributed and represent the height of musical achievement at the Burgundian court.

Mosca, Giuseppe (*b* Naples, 1772; *d* Messina, 14 Sept 1839). Italian composer. He was a composer and later music director at various Italian theatres, and in 1803–5 *maestro al cembalo* at the Théâtre-Italien, Paris. His 42 operas resemble Rossini's in style.

His brother Luigi (1775–1824), also a composer, was *maestro al cembalo* at the S Carlo opera house, Naples, and later *vice-maestro* of the royal chamber and chapel and a singing teacher. He wrote 16 operas and much sacred music.

Moscheles, Ignaz (*b* Prague, 23 May 1794; *d* Leipzig, 10 March 1870). German pianist, conductor and composer of Czech birth. A pupil of B.D. Weber in Prague and of Albrechtsberger and Salieri in Vienna, he became a piano recitalist, travelling throughout Europe (1815–25). Settling in London (1825–46), he taught at the RAM, established a series of 'historical soirées' (in which he performed Bach and Scarlatti on the harpsichord), wrote fashionable salon music and conducted the Philharmonic Society; he was a friend of Mendelssohn, conducted the London première of Beethoven's *Missa solemnis* (1832) and translated Schindler's biography as *The Life of Beethoven* (1841). From 1846 he was professor at the Leipzig Conservatory. His best compositions are his piano sonatas (some for duet), in which a classical balance is tempered with an early Romantic dynamism, and his studies (still used).

Moscow Conservatory. One of the music schools founded by the RUSSIAN MUSICAL SOCIETY. It opened in 1866 and Nikolay Rubinstein was its first principal. After 1918 its scope was enlarged to include music schools for children and an opera studio.

Mosè in Egitto. Opera (azione tragico-sacra) in three acts by Rossini to a libretto by A.L. Tottola after F. Ringhieri's *L'Osiride* (1818, Naples); Rossini revised it in four acts as *Moïse et Pharaon, ou Le passage de la Mer Rouge* with a new libretto by Balocchi and E. de Jouy (1827, Paris).

Moses und Aron. Opera in three acts by Schoenberg to his own libretto, composed 1932 (1957, Zurich). Schoenberg wrote only a libretto (to be spoken) for the third act, which is not generally given.

Mosolov, Alexandr Vasil'yevich (*b* Kiev, 11 Aug 1900; *d* Moscow, 11 July 1973). Soviet composer. He studied with Glier, Myaskovsky and Prokofiev at the Moscow Conservatory (1922–5) and was active during the mid-1920s as a modernist: works of this period include the ballet *Steel* (1928), song cycles and piano sonatas. Later he turned to a more conventional style, often using central Asian folk music.

Mosonyi, Mihály [Brand, Michael] (*b* Frauenkirchen, bap. 4 Sept 1815; *d* Pest, 31 Oct 1870). Hungarian composer, teacher and writer on music. In Pest from 1842, he taught the piano and composition; among his most famous pupils were Kornél Ábrányi and Ödön Mihalovich. He made his début as a composer in 1843–4 with the Overture and First Symphony, then the more innovatory, one-movement Piano Concerto (1844). In his Second Symphony (1846–56) he first used Hungarian idioms, becoming acquainted with Liszt, who encouraged him to write in the national style; he took the Hungarian name of Mosonyi in 1859 and produced piano works using native dance and song elements. Of his larger Hungarian compositions, the orchestral rhapsody *Homage to Kazinczy* (1860) uses the cimbalom and a characteristic ostinato, and the cantata *Festival of Purification at the River Ung* (1859) recounts 9th-century Hungarian conquests. As a contributor to the music journal *Zenészeti lapok* he campaigned vigorously for the new national style.

Mosso (It.). 'Moved', 'agitated', e.g. *più mosso* ('more moved', i.e. faster).

Mostly Mozart Festival (USA). Annual (summer) festival founded in 1966 at Lincoln Center, New York; it became the model for other festivals in the USA. Events include orchestral, choral and chamber concerts.

Motet. One of the most important forms of polyphonic music from *c*1250 to 1750. It originated in the 13th century in the practice of Pérotin and his contemporaries at Notre Dame, Paris, of adding words to the upper voice or voices of a CLAUSULA, with a plainchant tenor ('motet' derives from the French *mot*, 'word'). Sometimes two upper voices had different words. At first Latin texts, mainly concerning the Virgin, were used, but French secular texts became common as the motet shed its connection with church and liturgy. With the notational reforms of the late 13th century, motets with tenors rhythmically similar to the upper voices, or which quote secular songs and dances, became possible. Several motet types flourished in France, but these reduced to one definitive type capable of much variety in the reforms of Philippe de Vitry. Machaut's works show a preference for French texts and use ISORHYTHM in the tenor and occasionally the upper parts as well; this became increasingly common in the late 14th century, as did rhythmic refinements. Many large-scale and complex 'mensuration motets' are found in English and French sources of the late 14th century and early 15th; Dufay, in his 14 isorhythmic and mensuration motets, achieved a magnificent synthesis of numerically constructed *cantus firmus* polyphony with new techniques that hastened its decline.

With the gradual abandonment of isorhythm after *c*1420, composers began to return to the liturgical and devotional contexts in which the motet had originated. They used a variety of structural principles and contrapuntal techniques, setting mostly Marian texts and juxtaposing vocal and instrumental pairs of voices. For three-part song motets Dufay adopted a treble-dominated texture derived from the *chanson*. With the next generation, including Ockeghem and Busnois, the motet built on a tenor *cantus firmus* became once more important. Four to six parts is the norm. The key figure in the late 15th and early 16th centuries was Josquin, in whose motets all the traditional styles found a place but in whose later works *cantus firmus* technique and canon gave way to imitative counterpoint, with homophonic writing to provide variety and text illustration.

By Josquin's death in 1521, the musical language of the 16th-century motet was essentially formed. The Franco-Netherlands style, exemplified by Mouton, Gombert and Clemens non Papa, took firm root in Italy and saw a synthesis in the motets of Lassus, which draw on rhetorical gestures borrowed from the madrigal, and in those of the more conservative Palestrina. A distinctive Italian contribution to the development of the motet was the use of divided choirs (*cori spezzati*), associated particularly with St Mark's, Venice. It was there that G. Gabrieli, in such works as *In ecclesiis*, sowed the seeds of a new manner in motet writing.

Motet composition in the Baroque period follows two independent lines. The Palestrina tradition, maintained by the Vatican, predominated in Italy, Austria, south Germany and Iberia, where the motet showed studious craftsmanship, schematic sequences and monotonous harmony; later a more harmonic conception developed, with a periodic style of vocal melody, *da capo* form (Caldara, Lotti), and normally instrumental doubling and continuo accompaniment. The other line of development lay in the vocal concerto. Viadana's *Cento concerti ecclesiastici* (1602) showed the feasibility of a small-scale medium, using a handful of modest voices with continuo. There was a vogue in Venice in the 1620s for such works, which often included violins and increasingly reflected the influence of opera and cantata. Important mid-Baroque composers include Cazzati and Bassani. At Rome the old and new styles co-existed, while with Neapolitans such as A. Scarlatti, Durante and Leo the orchestral motet came nearest to current operatic forms.

The motets of G. Gabrieli and Viadana served as starting-points for German composers such as Praetorius, Schütz and Scheidt. The sectional structures of their sacred concertos led to the introduction of such elements as arias and chorales and finally to the church cantata of the 18th century. At the same time the choral motet was cultivated locally, for weddings, funerals and other special occasions. Bach's six motets represent its culmination.

In England the anthem superseded the motet in

church music. In France the *grands motets* of Du Mont, Lully, Charpentier, Lalande, Campra and others formed an impressive repertory for the king's chapel and were heard at the Concert Spirituel. Most were psalm settings for soloists, ensembles, chorus and orchestra. The *petit motet* for one, two or three voices and continuo was more appropriate to convents, though some by F. Couperin and others also had concert performances.

After 1750 the history of the motet is largely an account of individual and mostly isolated works. Mozart, Liszt and Bruckner are important as composers of Latin motets, while the German Protestant tradition is best represented by the seven motets of Brahms.

Motetus. Medieval term (first used by Franco of Cologne, *c*1280) for the voice immediately above the tenor in motets; it was also used to designate the entire composition, whether it consisted of two voices or more. In the earliest stages of the motet, when only Latin texts appear, the compositions were called 'tropi' or 'prose'. Theorists also used 'discantus' or 'motellus' for the voice above the tenor.

Mother, The [Matka]. Opera in ten scenes by Alois Hába to his own libretto, the first opera to use quarter-tones (1931, Munich).

Mother Goose. [Ma mère l'oye]. Suite by Ravel after fairy-tales by Péricault (1910); originally for two pianos, it was orchestrated in 1911.

Mother of Us All, The. Opera by Virgil Thomson to a libretto by Gertrude Stein (1947, New York).

Motif [motive]. A short musical idea, melodic, harmonic or rhythmic, or all three. It may be of any size but is generally regarded as the shortest subdivision of a theme or phrase that maintains its identity. *See also* LEITMOTIF.

Moto (It.). 'Movement', 'motion', e.g. *con moto* ('with motion', i.e. quickly).

Moto perpetuo [perpetuum mobile] (It.). 'Perpetual motion': term used for rapid, persistently maintained figuration, of such pieces as the finale of Chopin's Piano Sonata op.35. It is used as a title for the last movement of Weber's Piano Sonata no.1, Mendelssohn's op.119 and Paganini's *Allegro de concert* op.11.

Motown. A style of recorded soul music originated by the Motown Corporation of Detroit in the early 1960s. It made black popular music acceptable to white audiences for the first time through sophisticated arrangements and a muting of the more vigorous characteristics of Afro-American music and performing practices.

Motte, Diether de la (*b* Bonn, 20 March 1928). German composer. He studied with Maler at Detmold and at Darmstadt; in 1962 he began teaching at the Hamburg Musikhochschule. His works are influenced by a view of 'singing' music informed as much by the gamelan and plainsong as by Schubert and Berg.

Mottl, Felix (Josef) (*b* Vienna, 24 Aug 1856; *d* Munich, 2 July 1911). Austrian conductor, composer and editor. He studied at the Vienna Conservatory, where he was in Bruckner's theory class. As

conductor of the court opera in Karlsruhe (1881–1903) he made standards virtually second to none in Germany. From 1886, when he first worked at Bayreuth, he became internationally known for his Wagner performances (noted for their clarity). He moved to the Munich opera house in 1903. Besides editing vocal scores of Wagner's operas he made orchestral arrangements of German songs and French ballet music, also composing stage works and songs.

Motto. A motif which recurs at various points in a work. 'Motto aria' is sometimes used for a Baroque aria which opens with a motto phrase, followed by an instrumental passage, before the voice resumes. *See also* HEAD-MOTIF, IDÉE FIXE and LEITMOTIF.

Moulinié, Etienne (*b* Languedoc, *c*1600; *d* there, after 1669). French composer. Director of music to Gaston of Orleans, the king's younger brother, 1628–60, he later became director of music to the Languedoc estates. He was most popular for his *airs de cour*, which are unusual for their rhythmic freedom; some were used with new texts for sacred songs. He also composed Italian and Spanish songs, ballet music, dance pieces and sacred music.

Moulu, Pierre (*b c*1480–90; *d c*1550). French or Flemish composer. He may have been employed at the French royal chapel in the early 16th century. He was influenced by Josquin, whose pupil he may have been. His *c*20 motets use *cantus firmus* and canon and often consist of a chain of imitative points. His four masses use paraphrase technique and one is based on a motet by Josquin. Most of his eight *chansons* also use borrowed material, chiefly popular melodies, which he treated with considerable contrapuntal sophistication.

Mountain dulcimer. *See* APPALACHIAN DULCIMER.

Mouret, Jean-Joseph (*b* Avignon, 11 April 1682; *d* Charenton, 22 Dec 1738). French composer. A fine singer, he was in Paris by 1707 and soon *maître de musique* for the Marshall of Noailles. In *c*1708–1736 he was court *surintendant de la musique*, at Sceaux; as a theatre composer his main post was at the New Italian Theatre, 1717–37. From 1720 he also sang in the king's chamber; and he was artistic director of the Concert Spirituel, 1728–34. Highly popular in his day, he wrote nine operas and ballets and over 400 divertissements for plays. His controversial *opéra-ballet*, *Les fêtes ou Le triomphe de Thalie* (1714), was among the first to use comedy. His other works include motets, cantatas, *cantatilles*, *airs* and instrumental works, notably the *Suites de symphonies* (1729).

Mouth bow. A type of MUSICAL BOW held against the player's mouth. It is widely distributed in Africa, Central and South America and Oceania. As with the jew's harp, harmonic partials are selectively resonated with the mouth cavity. Most have a single string.

Mouth organ [mouth harp]. Term applied to several types of free-reed wind instrument; in the West it is generally applied to the HARMONICA and to mouth-blown instruments of south-east Asia and the Far East.

Mouthpiece. The part of a wind instrument that is

placed in or against a player's mouth, and which, with the lips or a reed, forms the tone generator. In brass instruments, the bell-shaped mouthpiece has three important internal elements, the cup, the throat and the backbore, which have much influence on the instrument.

Mouton, Jean (*b* Haut-Wignes, by 1459; *d* St Quentin, 30 Oct 1522). French composer. He was appointed a singer and teacher in the collegiate church of Notre Dame, Nesle, in 1477 and *maître de chapelle* there in 1483. By 1500 he was *maistre des enfans* at Amiens Cathedral, and in 1502 had taken charge of the music in the collegiate church of St André, Grenoble. In 1502 he became associated with Louis XII's court, to which he remained attached for the rest of his life.

He is one of the most important motet composers of the early 16th century. Over 100 motets, *c*15 masses and over 20 *chansons* by him survive, many published in his lifetime. Though he shared many of Josquin's techniques – paired imitation, canonic *cantus firmi* etc – it seems unlikely he was Josquin's pupil. His music is characterized by smooth, flowing melody and clear, sharply profiled motifs. He favoured full sonorities but kept textures clear by keeping the voice ranges separate. His motets are often built on a canon and show his dazzling contrapuntal skill, especially in those in which all the voices are canonic (e.g. *Nesciens mater virgo virum*). His masses span the transition from *cantus firmus* to the newer procedures of paraphrase and parody; his *chansons* (like his motets) display a variety of styles.

Movement. Term applied to any portion of a musical work sufficiently complete in itself to be regarded as an entity.

Moyse, Marcel (Joseph) (*b* St Amour, 17 May 1889; *d* Brattleboro, VT, 1 Nov 1984). French flautist. He studied at the Paris Conservatoire and played in several Paris orchestras. He was a frequent soloist under leading conductors and was eminent as a teacher; his sweet tone and clear articulation were much admired. Ibert is among those who wrote concertos for him.

Moyzes, Alexander (*b* Kláštor pod Znievom, 4 Sept 1906). Slovak composer. He studied with Novák at the Prague Conservatory (1925–30) and taught in Bratislava. His works, including nine symphonies (1929–71) and concertos, contributed importantly to the revival of Slovak Music.

His father Mikuláš (1872–1944) was also a Slovak nationalist composer.

Mozarabic rite, Music of the. The repertory of chant belonging to the church of Spain until its suppression in favour of the Roman rite in 1085; 'Mozarabic' refers to Christians under Muslim domination (though the rite antedates the Muslim invasion in 711). Music survives in more than 20 MSS and fragments from the 9th–14th centuries; most has no precise indication of pitch. Melodies are classified by a scheme analogous to the modal system of Gregorian chant, and the structures of Mass and Office are similar to those of other rites, especially the Roman, Ambrosian and Gallican. There have been attempts to revive the rite since the late 15th century and it is still in occasional use.

Mozart, Franz Xaver Wolfgang ['Wolfgang Amadeus'] (*b* Vienna, 26 July 1791; *d* Karlovy Vary, 29 July 1844). Austrian composer and pianist, the sixth child and younger surviving son of Wolfgang Amadeus and Constanze Mozart. He was trained by Hummel, Salieri and others, and had his first works published in 1802. After teaching in L'vov, he lived there as a freelance musician, 1813–38, making a long concert tour, 1819–21. Later he lived in Vienna. He composed a wide range of piano music (concertos, sonatas, etc), some of which looks forward to the piano style of Chopin and Liszt. His output also includes songs and other vocal music. His brother was Carl Thomas (1784–1858), the Mozarts' other surviving son.

Mozart, (Johann Georg) Leopold (*b* Augsburg, 14 Nov 1719; *d* Salzburg, 28 May 1787). German composer, violinist and theorist, father of Wolfgang Amadeus Mozart. He became a musician to the Count of Thurn and Taxis in Salzburg in 1739. In 1743, already active as a composer, he joined the prince-archbishop's court orchestra, advancing in 1757 to composer of the court and chamber and in 1763 to deputy Kapellmeister. A prominent violin teacher, he gained international fame with his *Versuch einer gründlichen Violinschule* (1756). After *c*1760 his own career took second place to the education of his children, Maria Anna ('Nannerl') and (especially) Wolfgang, whom he took on numerous musical tours.

Leopold Mozart's output includes numerous symphonies, other orchestral pieces (concertos, divertimentos etc), chamber and keyboard music, oratorios, masses and other sacred works. 'Popular' and programmatic elements appear in some of his instrumental music. Of his writings, the *Versuch* (1756), which deals with violin technique and music theory, is one of the foremost musical didactic works of the 18th century.

Mozart, (Johann Chrysostom) Wolfgang Amadeus (*b* Salzburg, 27 Jan 1756; *d* Vienna, 5 Dec 1791). Austrian composer, son of Leopold Mozart. He showed musical gifts at a very early age, composing when he was five and when he was six playing before the Bavarian elector and the Austrian empress. Leopold felt that it was proper, and might also be profitable, to exhibit his children's God-given genius (Maria Anna, 'Nannerl', 1751–1829, was a gifted keyboard player): so in mid-1763 the family set out on a tour that took them to Paris and London, visiting numerous courts en route. Mozart astonished his audiences with his precocious skills; he played to the French and English royal families, had his first music published and wrote his earliest symphonies. The family arrived home late in 1766; nine months later they were off again, to Vienna, where hopes of having an opera by Mozart performed were frustrated by intrigues.

They spent 1769 in Salzburg; 1770–73 saw three visits to Italy, where Mozart wrote two operas (*Mitridate, Lucio Silla*) and a serenata for performance in Milan, and acquainted himself with Italian styles. Summer 1773 saw a further visit to Vienna, probably in the hope of securing a post; there Mozart wrote a set of string quartets and, on his return, wrote a group of symphonies including his two earliest, nos.25 in G minor and 29 in A, in the regular repertory. Apart from a journey to Munich for the première of his opera *La finta giardiniera* early in 1775, the period from 1774 to mid-1777 was spent in Salzburg, where Mozart worked as Konzertmeister at the Prince-Archbishop's court; his works of these years include masses, symphonies, all his violin concertos, six piano sonatas, several serenades and divertimentos and his first great piano concerto, K271.

In 1777 the Mozarts, seeing limited opportunity in Salzburg for a composer so hugely gifted, resolved to seek a post elsewhere for Wolfgang. He was sent, with his mother, to Munich and to Mannheim, but was offered no position (though he stayed over four months at Mannheim, composing for piano and flute and falling in love with Aloysia Weber). His father then dispatched him to Paris: there he had minor successes, notably with his Paris Symphony, no.31, deftly designed for the local taste. But prospects there were poor and Leopold ordered him home, where a superior post had been arranged at the court. He returned slowly and alone; his mother had died in Paris. The years 1779–80 were spent in Salzburg, playing in the cathedral and at court, composing sacred works, symphonies, concertos, serenades and dramatic music. But opera remained at the centre of his ambitions, and an opportunity came with a commission for a serious opera for Munich. He went there to compose it late in 1780; his correspondence with Leopold (through whom he communicated with the librettist, in Salzburg) is richly informative about his approach to musical drama. The work, *Idomeneo*, was a success. In it Mozart depicted serious, heroic emotion with a richness unparalleled elsewhere in his works, with vivid orchestral writing and an abundance of profoundly expressive orchestral recitative.

Mozart was then summoned from Munich to Vienna, where the Salzburg court was in residence on the accession of a new emperor. Fresh from his success, he found himself placed between the valets and the cooks; his resentment towards his employer, exacerbated by the Prince-Archbishop's refusal to let him perform at events the emperor was attending, soon led to conflict, and in May 1781 he resigned, or was kicked out of, his job. He wanted a post at the imperial court in Vienna, but was content to do free-lance work in a city that apparently offered golden opportunities. He made his living over the ensuing years by teaching, by publishing his music, by playing at patrons' houses or in public, by composing to commission (particularly operas); in 1787 he obtained a minor court post as *Kammermusicus*, which gave him a reasonable salary and required nothing beyond the writing of dance music for court balls. He always earned, by musicians' standards, a good income, and had a carriage and servants; through lavish spending and poor management he suffered times of financial difficulty and had to borrow. In 1782 he married Constanze Weber, Aloysia's sister.

In his early years in Vienna, Mozart built up his reputation by publishing (sonatas for piano, some with violin), by playing the piano and, in 1782, by having an opera performed: *Die Entführung aus dem Serail*, a German Singspiel which went far beyond the usual limits of the tradition with its long, elaborately written songs (hence Emperor Joseph II's famous observation, 'Too many notes, my dear Mozart'). The work was successful and was taken into the repertories of many provincial companies (for which Mozart was not however paid). In these years, too, he wrote six string quartets which he dedicated to the master of the form, Haydn: they are marked not only by their variety of expression but by their complex textures, conceived as four-part discourse, with the musical ideas linked to this freshly integrated treatment of the medium. Haydn told Mozart's father that Mozart was 'the greatest composer known to me in person or by name; he has taste and, what is more, the greatest knowledge of composition'.

In 1782 Mozart embarked on the composition of piano concertos, so that he could appear both as composer and soloist. He wrote 15 before the end of 1786, with early 1784 as the peak of activity. They represent one of his greatest achievements, with their formal mastery, their subtle relationships between piano and orchestra (the wind instruments especially) and their combination of brilliance, lyricism and symphonic growth. In 1786 he wrote the first of his three comic operas with Lorenzo da Ponte as librettist, *Le nozze di Figaro*: here and in *Don Giovanni* (given in Prague, 1787) Mozart treats the interplay of social and sexual tensions with keen insight into human character that – as again in the more artificial sexual comedy of *Così fan tutte* (1790) – transcends the comic framework, just as *Die Zauberflöte* (1791) transcends, with its elements of ritual and allegory about human harmony and enlightenment, the world of the Viennese popular theatre from which it springs.

Mozart lived in Vienna for the rest of his life. He undertook a number of journeys: to Salzburg in 1783, to introduce his wife to his family; to Prague three times, for concerts and operas; to Berlin in 1789, where he had hopes of a post; to Frankfurt in 1790, to play at coronation celebrations. The last Prague journey was for the première of *La clemenza di Tito* (1791), a traditional serious opera written for coronation celebrations, but composed with a finesse and economy characteristic of Mozart's late music. Instrumental works of these years include some piano sonatas, three string quartets written for the King of Prussia, some string quintets, which include one of his most deeply felt works (K516 in G minor) and one of his most nobly spacious (K515 in C), and his last four symphonies – one (no.38 in D) composed for Prague in 1786, the others written in 1788 and forming, with the lyricism of no.39 in Eb, the tragic suggestiveness of no.40 in G minor and the grandeur of no.41 in C, a climax to his orchestral music. His final works include the Clarinet Concerto and some pieces for masonic lodges (he had been a freemason since 1784; masonic teachings no doubt affected his thinking, and his compositions, in his last years). At his death from a feverish illness whose precise nature has given rise to much speculation (he was not poisoned), he left unfinished the Requiem, his first large-scale work for the church since the C minor Mass of 1783, also unfinished; a completion by his pupil Süssmayr was long accepted as the standard one but there have been recent attempts to improve on it. Mozart was buried in a Vienna suburb, with little ceremony and in an unmarked grave, in accordance with prevailing custom.

Masses, mass movements Missa solemnis K139/47a, c, 'Waisenhausmesse' (1768); Missa brevis K49/47d, G (1768); Missa brevis K65/61a, d (1769); Missa K66, C, 'Dominicus' (1769); Missa K167, C, 'In honorem Ssmae Trinitatis' (1773); Missa brevis K192/186f, F (1774); Missa brevis K194/186h, D (1774); Missa brevis K220/196b, C, 'Spatzenmesse' (1776); Missa [longa] K262/246a, C (1775); Missa K257, C, 'Credo' (1776); Missa brevis K258, C, 'Spaur' (1776); Missa brevis K259, C, 'Organ solo' (1776); Missa brevis K275/272b, Bb (1777); Missa K317, C, 'Coronation' (1779); Missa solemnis K337, C (1780); Missa K427/417a, c (inc., 1783); Requiem K626, d (inc., 1791); 2 Kyrie settings
Other sacred music 4 litanies K109/74e, 125, 195/186d, 243 (1771–6); Dixit Dominus, Magnificat K193/186g, C (1774); Vesperae de Dominica K321, C (1779); Vesperae solennes de confessore K339, C (1780); c20 motets etc, incl. Exsultate, jubilate K165/158a (1773), Ave verum corpus K618 (1791); 17 church sonatas, org, orch
Oratorios, sacred dramas etc Pt I of Die Schuldigkeit des ersten Gebots, sacred drama, K35 (1767); La Betulia liberata, oratorio, K118/74c (1771); Davidde penitente, oratorio, K469 (1785); 2 sacred cantatas; 3 masonic cantatas
Dramatic music operas – La finta semplice K51/46a (1769); Bastien und Bastienne K50/46b (1768); Mitridate, rè di Ponto K87/74a (1770); Lucio Silla K135 (1772); La finta giardiniera K196 (1775); Il rè pastore K208 (1775); Zaide K344/336a (inc., 1780); Idomeneo K366 (1781); Die Entführung aus dem Serail K384 (1782); Der Schauspieldirektor K486 (1785); Le nozze di Figaro K492 (1786); Don Giovanni K527 (1787); Così fan tutte K588 (1790); Die Zauberflöte K620 (1791); La clemenza di Tito K621 (1791); other works – Apollo et Hyacinthus, Latin intermezzo, K38 (1767); Ascanio in Alba, festa teatrale, K111 (1771); Il sogno di Scipione, serenata, K126 (1772); Les petits riens, ballet, KA10/299b (1778)
Secular vocal music several duets and ensembles; c50 arias and scenas; c30 songs, incl. Das Veilchen K476 (1785), Als Luise die Briefe K520 (1787), Abendempfindung K523 (1787); canons
Symphonies no.1, K16, Eb (1765); no.4, K19, D (1765); KA223/19a, F (1765); no.5, K22, Bb (1765); KA221/45a, G, 'Lambach' (1766); no.6, K43, F (1767); no.7, K45, D (1768); KA214/45b, Bb (1768); no.8, K48, D (1768); K81/73l, D (1770); K97/73m, D (1770); K95/73n, D (1770); no.11, K84/73q, D (1770); no.10, K74, G (1770); KA216/74g, Bb (1770–71); K75, F (1771); no.12, K110/75b, G (1771); K96/111b, C (1771); no.13, K112, F (1771); no.14, K114, A (1771); no.9, K73, C (1772); no.15, K124, G (1772); no.16, K128, C (1772); no.17, K129, G (1772); no.18, K130, F (1772); no.19, K132, Eb (1772); no.20, K133, D (1772); no.21, K134, A (1772); no.26, K184/161a, Eb (1773); no.27, K199/161b, G (1773); no.22, K162, C (1773); no.23, K181/162b, D (1773); no.24, K182/173dA, Bb (1773); no.25, K183/173dB, g (1773); no.29, K201/186a (1774); no.30, K202/186b, D (1774); no.28, K200/189k, C (1774); no.31, K297/300a, D, 'Paris' (1778); no.33, K319, Bb (1779); no.34, K338, C (1780); no.35, K385, D, 'Haffner' (1782); no.36, K425, C, 'Linz' (1783); no.38, K504, D, 'Prague' (1786); no.39, K543, Eb (1788); no.40, K550, g (1788); no.41, K551, C, 'Jupiter' (1788); symphony movements [no.37: slow introduction to sym. by M. Haydn]
Concertos piano – 7 arrangements (1767, 1772); K175, D (1773); K238, Bb (1776); K246, C (1776); K271, Eb (1777); K414/385p, A (1782); K413/387a, F (1783); K415/387b, C

(1783); K449, Eb (1784); K450, Bb (1784); K451, D (1784); K453, G (1784); K456, Bb (1784); K459, F (1784); K466, d (1785); K467, C (1785); K482, Eb (1785); K488, A (1786); K491, c (1786); K503, C (1786); K537, D, 'Coronation' (1788); K595, Bb (1791); Conc., 2 pf, K365/316a, Eb (1779); Conc., 3 pf, K242, F (1776); violin – K207, Bb (?1773); K211, D (1775); K216, G (1775); K218, D (1775); K219, A (1775); Concertone, 2 vn, K190/186E, C (1774); Sinfonia concertante, vn, va, K364/320d, Eb (1779); Bn Conc. K191/186e (1774); 2 fl concs. K313–4/285c–d, G, D (1778); Ob Conc. K314/285d, C (1778); Conc., fl, harp, K299/297c, C (1778); 3 hn concs. K417, 447, 495, all Eb (1783–7); Cl Conc. K622, A (1791); various conc. movements
Miscellaneous orchestral music 3 cassations (1769); 7 divertimentos (1771–80); 6 serenades, incl. K250/248b, D, 'Haffner' (1776), K320, D, 'Posthorn' (1779); 1 notturno; Masonic Funeral Music K477/479a, c (1785); A Musical Joke K522, F (1787); Eine kleine Nachtmusik K525, G (1787); marches, minuets, German dances, ländler, contredanses
Music for wind ensemble Serenade for 13 insts. K361/370a, Bb (?1783–4); Serenade K375, Eb (1781); Serenade K388/384a, c (1782–3); various divertimentos; horn duos; miscellaneous movements
Chamber music without keyboard str qnts – K174, Bb (1773); K515, C (1787); K516, g (1787); K406/516b, c (1788); K593, D (1790); K614, Eb (1791); str qts – K80/73f, G (1770); 3 divertimentos K136–8/125a–c, D, Bb, F (1772); K155–60/134a–b, 157–9, 159a, D, G, C, Bb, Eb (1772–3); K168–73, F, A, C, Eb, Bb, d (1773); 6 'Haydn' qts: K387, G (1782), K421/417b, d (1783), K428/421b, Eb (1783), K458, Bb, 'Hunt' (1784), K464, A (1785), K465, C, 'Dissonance' (1785); K499, D, 'Hoffmeister' (1786); Adagio and Fugue K546, c (1788); 3 'Prussian' qts: K575, D (1789), K589, Bb (1790), K590, F (1790); 4 fl qts; Ob qt; Qnt, hn and str; Cl qnt K581, A (1789); 2 duos, vn and va (1783); Str trio K563, Eb (1788); other pieces
Chamber music with keyboard Qnt, pf and wind K452, Eb (1784); Pf qt K478, g (1785); Pf qt K493, Eb (1786); 7 pf trios; Trio, pf, cl, va, K498, Eb (1786); vn sonatas – 16 youthful works (1762–6); K301/293a, G (1778); K302/293b, Eb (1778); K303/293c, C (1778); K305/293d, A (1778); K296, C (1778); K304/300c, e (1778); K306/300l, D (1778); K378/317d, Bb (1779–81); K379/373a, G (1781); K376/374d, F (1781); K377/374e, F (1781); K380/374f, Eb (1781); K454, Bb (1784); K481, Eb (1785); K526, A (1787); K547, F (1788); 2 sets of variations for pf, vn
Keyboard music sonatas – K279–83/189d–h, C, F, Bb, Eb, G (1775); K284/205b, D (1775); K309/284b, C (1777); K311/284c, D (1777); K310/300d, a (1778); K330/300h, C (1783); K331/300i, A (1783); K332/315k, F (1783); K333/315c, Bb (1784); K457, c (1784); K533, F (1788); K545, C (1788); K570, Bb (1789); K576, D (1789); 5 sonatas for kbd duet; sonata for 2 kbds; 16 sets of variations; many miscellaneous pieces, incl. Fantasia K397/385g, d (1782–?); Fantasia K475, c (1785); Rondo K485, D (1786); Rondo K511, c (1787); Fugue for 2 kbds, K426, c (1788); pieces for mechanical organ and armonica

Mozart and Salieri. Opera in one act by Rimsky-Korsakov to his own libretto after Pushkin (1898, Moscow).

Mozarteum. *See* INTERNATIONALE STIFTUNG MOZARTEUM.

Mravinsky, Evgeny (Alexandrovich) (*b* St Petersburg, 4 June 1903; *d* Leningrad, 21 Jan 1988). Soviet conductor. After study at Leningrad Conservatory he was conductor of the Kirov Theatre Ballet, 1932–8. From 1938 he was chief conductor of the Leningrad PO, touring widely in a broad repertory and giving the premières of Shostakovich's Symphonies nos.5, 6, 8, 9 and 10. He is an outstanding representative of the Soviet school, his finely detailed performances being marked by an atmosphere of spontaneous emotion.

Mṛdaṅga. An Indian term, in use for over two millennia, for tuned, finger-played, double-headed drums, primarily elongated barrel drums, which give the principal accompaniment to indigenous art music styles of the Indian high tradition. Earlier they were used in theatre music, later in concert forms and more elaborate temple and devotional music.

Mshvelidze, Shalva (Mikhaylovich) (*b* Tbilisi, 28 May 1904). Soviet composer. He studied at the Tbilisi Conservatory (where he taught from 1929) and with Shcherbachov. His operas and symphonies have contributed to the foundation of a Georgian music school. His ethnomusicological studies have been of Indian music.

Muck, Carl (*b* Darmstadt, 22 Oct 1859; *d* Stuttgart, 3 March 1940). German conductor. He made his début at Leipzig in 1880 and after opera engagements at Zurich, Salzburg and Prague became Kapellmeister of the Berlin Opera (1892, music director 1908). He gave the first Russian performance of the *Ring* and conducted *Parsifal* at Bayreuth, 1901–30. His meticulous standards of preparation were heard to advantage in Bruckner's symphonies.

Mudarra, Alonso (*b* Palencia diocese, *c*1510; *d* Seville, 1 April 1580). Spanish vihuelist and composer. After associations with the dukes of Infantado and Charles V, he became a canon of Seville Cathedral in 1546. That year his *Tres libros de musica* was published. It contains over 70 compositions for six-course vihuela, four-course guitar and voice and vihuela; the instrumental pieces include 27 fantasias and other dances for vihuela.

Mudd, Thomas (*b* ?Peterborough; *d* ?Durham, bur. 2 Aug 1667). English composer. From a musical family, he was a chorister at Peterborough Cathedral (1619) and organist there (1631–2) and at Lincoln (1662) and Exeter (1664) cathedrals. He briefly worked at York Minster (1666). Services and anthems in MSS ascribed to 'Mudd' may be by him or members of his family.

Mudge, Richard (*b* Bideford, 1718; *d* Great Packington, 3 April 1763). English composer. He was a cleric in the Midlands and composed a fine set of concertos (1749, one with solo trumpet) in the late Baroque style.

Muette de Portici, La [Masaniello]. Opera in five acts by Auber to a libretto by Scribe and Delavigne (1828, Paris).

Muffat, Georg (*b* Mégève, bap. 1 June 1653; *d* Passau, 23 Feb 1704). German composer of French (Savoy) birth, father of Gottlieb. He studied with Lully and others in Paris in 1663–9. After a period as an organist at Molsheim he travelled widely and in 1678 became organist and chamber musician to the Archbishop of Salzburg. In the 1680s he went to Rome, where he studied with Pasquini and had contact with Corelli. From 1690 he was Kapellmeister to the Bishop of Passau.

A prominent composer of instrumental music, Muffat was a pioneer in bringing French and Italian styles into Germany, and in the prefaces to his works he also gave details of Lully's and Corelli's performing practices. The first of his five publi-

cations, *Armonico tributo* (1682), contains five ensemble sonatas which owe much to Corelli's concerti grossi op.6 and also show French features. Muffat drew on them for his 12 concerti grossi, *Ausserlesene Instrumental-Music* (1701). Lully's influence predominates in the 15 orchestral suites of his two *Florilegium* volumes (1695, 1698); each suite begins with a French overture. Muffat also wrote a book of organ music, including 12 Italianate toccatas (1690), three stage works (now lost) and a major treatise on continuo practice.

Muffat, Gottlieb [Theophil] (*b* Passau, bap. 25 April 1690; *d* Vienna, 9 Dec 1770). German composer and organist, son of Georg. Trained under Fux's supervision at the Viennese court, he became a court organist there in 1717, later acquiring teaching duties. He was promoted to second organist in 1729 and to first organist in 1741 and retired in 1763.

Muffat was Vienna's leading keyboard composer in the 18th century, and wrote little other than keyboard music. In general he used the Italianate styles and forms traditionally favoured in Vienna. Particularly conservative are his 72 fugal versets (1726) and his 32 strictly contrapuntal ricercars (1733 at latest); the latter, like Bach's *Art of Fugue*, are notated in open score. He also composed over 30 toccatas (some of which resemble his father's) and some capriccios, preludes etc. His most progressive works are the six keyboard suites of his *Componimenti musicali* (1639). These combine *galant* features and contrapuntal writing, and show the influence of French composers (notably Couperin) and also of Handel and Fux. Handel in turn borrowed heavily from Muffat's suites in some of his own works.

Mühlfeld, Richard (Bernhard Herrmann) (*b* Salzungen, 28 Feb 1856; *d* Meiningen, 1 June 1907). German clarinettist. Principal clarinet at the court of Saxe-Meiningen (1879–1907), but known internationally, he was admired particularly by Brahms, who composed the Trio op.114, Quintet op.115 and the two Sonatas op.120 for him.

Muldowney, Dominic (*b* Southampton, 19 July 1952). English composer. He studied at York University with Rands and Blake. In 1976 he was appointed music director at the National Theatre (*The Beggar's Opera*, 1982). His works include Brecht settings, orchestral and chamber pieces, characterized by a searching attitude to formal conventions.

Mulè, Giuseppe (*b* Termini Imerese, 28 June 1885; *d* Rome, 10 Sept 1951). Italian composer. He studied at the Palermo Conservatory, which he directed before moving to a similar post at the Conservatorio di S Cecilia, Rome (1925–43). He worked with Sicilian folk music and wrote incidental music for the Greek theatre at Syracuse and operas.

Mulet, Henri (*b* Paris, 17 Oct 1878; *d* Draguignan, 20 Sept 1967). French composer. He studied at the Paris Conservatoire and held appointments as an organist but in 1937 withdrew to Provence. He burnt most of his MSS, and is remembered only by two fine organ pieces, *Esquisse byzantines* (*c*1919) and *Carillon sortie*.

Müller [Schmid], **Adolf** (*b* Tolna, 7 Oct 1801; *d* Vienna, 29 July 1886). Austrian composer. Kapellmeister at Viennese theatres from 1826, principally the Theater an der Wien (1847–78), he was extremely prolific, producing *c*580 theatre scores by 1868; though most proved ephemeral, many of his 41 scores to Nestroy's plays are still performed in Vienna. He also wrote church music and *c*400 songs.

Müller, August Eberhard (*b* Northeim, 13 Dec 1767; *d* Weimar, 3 Dec 1817). German composer. He worked as a flautist, conductor and organist in northern Germany, moving in 1794 to Leipzig, where in 1800 he became assistant Kapellmeister at St Thomas's and Kapellmeister in 1804. From 1810 he was musical director at the Weimar court. He composed concertos, keyboard and chamber music and various vocal works. His early output is Mozartian; his later piano music is more virtuoso in style. He wrote influential piano and flute tutors and a guide to Mozart's keyboard concertos.

Müller(-Zürich), Paul (*b* Zurich, 19 June 1898). Swiss composer. He studied with Jarnach and Andreae at the Zurich Conservatory (1917–19), where he later taught from 1927 to 1969, and in Paris and Berlin. Influenced by Reger, he developed a neo-Baroque style characterized by advanced but tonal harmony and wrote choral and organ music, concertos, chamber music etc.

Müller, Wenzel (*b* Trnava, 26 Sept 1767; *d* Baden, 3 Aug 1835). Austrian composer. He was Kapellmeister to the Leopoldstädter-Theater (1786–1807; 1813–30), where he won his earliest success with *Das Sonnenfest der Braminen* (1790). Among later theatre scores *Die Schwestern von Prag* (1794), *Der verwunschene Prinz* (1818) and *Die Alpenkönig* (1828) are noteworthy, though many of his simple but effective individual songs achieved more lasting popularity as street songs and *Volkslieder*.

Mulliner Book. English MS of keyboard music, copied by T. Mulliner, *c*1550–75. It contains pieces by Redford, Tallis and others, liturgical organ pieces, dances and arrangements. It is now in the British Library, London.

Multiphonics. Term for the sounding of two or more pitches simultaneously on an instrument that normally sounds only single notes, or with the voice. Bruno Bartolozzi described multiphonic techniques for wind instruments in 1967; vocal multiphonics are traditional in South-east and East Asia.

Multiple stopping. In string playing, the pressing of two, three or four strings simultaneously to produce double, triple or quadruple (i.e. multiple) stops.

Mumma, Gordon (*b* Framingham, MA, 30 March 1935). American composer. He studied at the University of Michigan and was active with Ashley from 1957 as an experimental composer; from 1966 he was associated with the Merce Cunningham Dance Company. Collaboration has been central to his career. A wide-ranging innovator, he is best known for his contributions to electroacoustic music, particularly his pioneering of 'cybersonic music' (e.g. in *Medium Size Mograph*, 1963).

Münch [Munch], Charles (*b* Strasbourg, 26 Sept 1891; *d* Richmond, VA, 6 Nov 1968). Alsatian conductor and violinist. After study in Paris and Berlin he led the Leipzig Gewandhaus Orchestra, 1926–33, under Furtwängler. From 1932 he conducted orchestras in Paris, presenting much new music. As chief conductor of the Boston SO (1948–62) he gave spontaneous, dynamic performances especially of French and American music.

Münchinger, Karl (*b* Stuttgart, 29 May 1915). German conductor. After study in Stuttgart and Leipzig he conducted the Hanover SO during World War II. In 1945 he founded the Stuttgart CO, touring widely with it and making many highly praised recordings, particularly of music by Bach. His performances are characterized by clear textures and rich tone.

Mundy, John (*b c*1555; *d* Windsor, 29 June 1630). English composer. He was organist of St George's Chapel, Windsor, for over 40 years, taking the BMus (1586) and DMus (1624) at Oxford. A versatile and effective composer, he published sacred and secular songs and metrical psalms (1594) and wrote anthems, motets and keyboard works. His father, William (*c*1529–*c*1591), was a composer who sang in various London churches, the cathedrals and the Chapel Royal and wrote services, anthems and large-scale complex Latin antiphons.

Munich Festival (West Germany). An opera festival established in summer 1875 has been held annually since 1901. Other events include concerts, ballet and a Bach festival.

Munich Philharmonic Orchestra. West German orchestra established in 1924 from the Kaim Orchestra. Its conductors have included Pfitzner, Rosbaud and Kempe.

Munrow, David (John) (*b* Birmingham, 12 Aug 1942; *d* Chesham Bois, 15 May 1976). English player of early wind instruments. He studied at Cambridge and gained experience of folk music in South America. In 1967 he formed the Early Music Consort of London (its members included Bowman and Hogwood); it gave many exciting and revealing performances of medieval and Renaissance pieces in an authentic, polished and lively style, introducing an important repertory of music to the public. It also gave several first performances of contemporary music.

Muradeli, Vano Il'ich (*b* Gori, 6 April 1908; *d* Tomsk, 14 Aug 1970). Soviet composer. He studied in Tbilisi and with Shekhter and Myaskovsky in Moscow, and later directed the Soviet navy songs ensemble. He wrote numerous propaganda songs, operas, two symphonies etc.

Murky. A keyboard style, originating in the 1730s, in which the bass consists of an extended pattern of alternating octaves. A famous example is the main theme (Allegro) of the first movement of Beethoven's Piano Sonata in C minor op.13 ('Pathétique').

Murray, Ann (*b* Dublin, 27 Aug 1949). Irish mezzo-soprano. She studied in Manchester and at the London Opera Centre, making her début with Scottish Opera as Gluck's *Alceste* (1974). In 1976 she first appeared at Covent Garden (Mozart's Cherubino) and at the Met (in *La clemenza di Tito*, where she has sung both Annius and Sextus; she has also appeared at the Vienna Staatsoper, La Scala and at Salzburg Festival (notably as Rossini's Cinderella). Her firm, ringing, high mezzo has been heard to advantage in a wide range of roles and in the concert repertory.

Murrill, Herbert (Henry John) (*b* London, 11 May 1909; *d* there, 25 July 1952). English composer. He studied at the RAM and Oxford, and worked for the BBC from 1936. His compositional tastes were Francophile and mildly Stravinskyan, and he wrote mostly in smaller forms.

Muscadin. A dance similar to the allemande. The melody associated with it was used for settings and variations by the English virginalists.

Muselar. Term of the late 17th century, revived by modern writers, for Flemish virginals with keyboards off-centre to the right and so having strings centrally plucked for most of the instrument's range. This produces a distinctive flute-like tone of great beauty.

Muset, Colin (*fl c*1200–50). French trouvère poet and composer, active in the Champagne region. Only half the works attributed to him survive with melodies, but they represent a wide variety of types. They also contain interesting references to instruments and the playing of them, and reveal him to have been a jongleur by profession; this may account for the folksong-like simplicity of his melodies.

Musette. *Term used for several instruments.* The 'musette de Poitou' of the 17th century was a simple bagpipe, accompanied by an 'hautbois de Poitou' (a bagless chanter) or by a consort of such instruments. It was used by musicians of the Grande Ecurie du Roi at Versailles. In 17th- and early 18th-century France, the musette was a small bagpipe, of aristocratic design; many works for it as a solo, ensemble or accompanying instrument were written in the 1720s and 1730s by Boismortier, Rameau and others. In the 1830s, the name was given to a small oboe, without reed-cap, pitched a 5th above the normal instrument, used for rural colour and domestic amusement (it was sometimes called 'hautbois pastorale'). The *basse du musette* is a basset oboe, probably of Swiss 18th-century origin.

The term is also used for a gavotte-like piece of pastoral character whose style suggests the sound of the musette or bagpipe, generally with a drone bass. Musettes appeared in 18th-century French ballets and as keyboard pieces.

Musgrave, Thea (*b* Barnton, 27 May 1928). Scottish composer. She studied with Gál in Edinburgh and with Boulanger in Paris (1950–54), then gradually came towards a 12-note style, which around the time of her first opera *The Decision* (1965) became galvanized into a dramatic vigour. Her later works include orchestral and chamber pieces in which the instruments are viewed as characters, as well as further operas: *The Voice of Ariadne* (1973), *Mary, Queen of Scots* (1977), *A Christmas Carol* (1979) and *Harriet, the Woman Called Moses* (1985).

Musica Antiqua Köln. German early music ensemble. It was founded in 1973, initially to perform Italian 17th-century and French early 18th-century music; it has also come to specialize in the music of J.S. Bach and his predecessors. The group, usually of about six players (led by Reinhard Goebel, violin), can expand to a chamber orchestra of up to 30. It has toured extensively and made many recordings.

Musica enchiriadis. A Latin treatise on music, one of the best-known medieval writings, written *c*900 in the north of the West Frankish empire. Its authorship is uncertain, but it could be by Otgerus, Count Laon and Abbot of St Amand (924–52). Its primary concern is the tetrachord as an organizing principle for song and individual pitches; it thus provides a link between Hellenistic music theory and Western liturgical music. It is best known for its instructions for parallel organum.

Musica ficta (Lat.: 'false music'). Term used to describe accidentals that need to be added, in performance or editing, to the texts as written in early music. The basic principle underlying *musica ficta* is that, because of certain theoretical rules of medieval and Renaissance music, accidentals were understood to be implied in particular contexts so were not written. Modern performers need to have them added, but it is not always clear where they may be presumed and authorities differ substantially over their addition.

Musical bow. An ancient bow-shaped string instrument consisting of a flexible stave, curved by the tension of a string (or strings) stretched between its ends; where there is a resonator, it is unattached or detachable. Widely distributed in Africa, America, Oceania, part of Asia and formerly in Europe, it is often played recreationally as a solo instrument or (with a resonator) for song accompaniment; more pitches can be obtained by stopping the string or by changing the size of the resonator. In some areas it is important in magic or religion.

Musical box. A mechanical instrument in which tuned steel prongs are made to vibrate by contact with moving parts driven by a clockwork mechanism. In 1796, Antoine Favre produced the first known music from steel prongs sounded by pins set in a disc or drum. Originally adjuncts to watches, these evolved into brass cylinders with steel pins playing a line of tuned teeth, which gave rise to the one-piece tuned steel comb with the essential refinement of steel dampers.

By *c*1825, the musical box was well established, with combs having as many as 250 teeth covering a range of about six octaves. Manufacture grew up mainly in Switzerland, and such makers as Henriot and Paillard became renowned. There were several varieties, and refinements such as tuned bells, drum and castanet were occasionally added. Besides sacred and popular music, arias and overtures from most favourite operas of 1830–90 were reproduced.

Musical clock. A clock combined with a mechanical instrument which played music at regular time intervals (every quarter of an hour, half-hour or hour) or at will. In the Middle Ages astronomical clocks were equipped with carillons; when spring mechanisms were invented, small carillons were built in portable clocks, in which eight to 16 glass bells played short folksongs by means of a cylinder. Watches with miniature carillons were produced as early as the 16th century. In the early 19th the metal bells were replaced either by chromatically tuned metal rods or with comb mechanisms.

While the manufacture of musical clocks with carillons was concentrated in London in the 18th century, flute-playing clocks were produced in Berlin, and Haydn, Mozart and Beethoven composed for them. Harp-playing clocks were also made, equipped with a stringed automatophone.

Musical comedy. The musical comedy – sometimes called simply 'musical' – is the chief form of popular musical theatre in the 20th-century English-speaking world. It developed from comic opera and burlesque in London at the end of the 19th century and reached its most durable form in the work of such American composers as Jerome Kern, George Gershwin, Cole Porter and Irving Berlin in the 1920s and 1930s. Most musical comedies have a loosely constructed plot combining comic and romantic interest; the musical score usually consists of catchy or sentimental songs, ensembles and dances. The tradition continues in the work of such composers as Stephen Sondheim and Andrew Lloyd Webber. Closely related to the musical comedy is the musical play, a work with a more substantial plot and score (e.g. Bernstein's *West Side Story*), and the musical film, of which Harry Warren's *42nd Street* (1933) is a notable example (though most musical films of this era were simply film versions of stage musicals, e.g. Rodgers's *The Sound of Music*).

The distinction between musical comedy and operetta is not precise; generally 'operetta' is taken to denote an older-style work, with a romantic story and a score using 19th-century European styles.

Musical Fund Society. Charitable organization founded in 1820 in Philadelphia, probably the oldest musical society in the USA; it presents free concerts, grants scholarships and sponsors competitions.

Musical glasses [armonica, glass harmonica]. Bell-type instruments of glass or other brittle material which if rubbed in a certain fashion respond like the strings of a bowed instrument. They may also be struck, with moderate force, for effects as on a xylophone (a method that prevails in Asia).

Musical glasses in the West were derived from Asian antecedents from the 11th century onwards and came into serious musical use during the early 18th. In England the technique of stroking the rims with the fingertips, as opposed to striking the glasses with a stick, was first used in 1744 by Richard Pockrich, whose glasses were graded by size and tuned by the addition of water. Gluck played a concerto in London on 26 glasses in 1746. In 1761 Benjamin Franklin improved the instrument by fitting the glasses concentrically on a horizontal rod, actuated by a crank attached to a pedal; his instrument, known as the armonica or glass-chord, became popular, with its distinctive tone of vibrant, piercing sweetness. Mozart composed a Quintet with flute, oboe, viola and cello in 1791. Playing the instrument, however, had a damaging effect on the player's nerves. Its popularity lasted until *c*1830. The musical glasses have been revived in the 20th century by Bruno Hoffmann under the name 'glass harp'.

Musical Joke, A [Ein musikalischer Spass]. *See* JOKE.

Musical Offering, The [Das musikalische Opfer]. 13 works by J.S. Bach, ricercars and canons on a theme by Frederick the Great as well as a trio sonata; some are for keyboard, others for up to four instruments (flute, violin and continuo).

Musical saw. *See* SAW, MUSICAL.

Musica Nova (UK). *See* SCOTTISH NATIONAL ORCHESTRA.

Musica reservata. Term applied to an aspect of the style or performance of music in the late 16th century. It is found with various definitions and implications in writings from 1552 to 1625 and has been interpreted in contradictory ways, remaining a subject of debate among scholars. However, it is generally agreed that *musica reservata* is music with heightened expressiveness, that presents a text with intensity and in a style 'reserved' for connoisseurs. Thus it is not characterized by a single technique but by such factors as chromaticism or striking modulations.

The name 'Musica Reservata' was used by a British early music group from the 1950s, founded by Michael Morrow, to perform medieval and Renaissance music in a vigorous and direct style.

Musica Sacra. American choir formed in 1970 by Richard Westenburg. It became the most notable professional choir in New York, especially for its annual (summer) Basically Bach Festival (from 1978).

Musica transalpina. Anthology of Italian madrigals translated into English, compiled by Nicolas Yonge and published in 1588 by Thomas East; it contains 57 madrigals, by Alfonso Ferrabosco (i), Marenzio, Palestrina, de Monte and others. A second book, of 24, followed in 1597. The collections much influenced the development of the madrigal in England.

Musica Viva (West Germany). Annual festival of contemporary music founded in Munich in 1946 by K.A. Hartmann. It played a leading part in postwar German musical life (reintroducing much important 20th-century music) and was the prototype for many other festivals.

Musica Viva Australia. Organization formed in 1945 as Sydney Musica Viva, a professional chamber group led by Robert Pikler. It promotes chamber music tours by Australian and other groups in Australia and abroad, and its programmes include commissioned Australian works.

Music drama. A term applied to Wagner's operas and to others in which the musical, verbal and scenic elements are intended to cohere to serve one dramatic end.

Musicescu, Gavriil (*b* Ismail, 1 April 1847; *d* Iaşi, 21 Dec 1903). Romanian composer, teacher and choirmaster. He studied in St Petersburg, then became professor, later director, of the Iaşi Conservatory. As conductor of the Metropolitan Choir he developed a new repertory and a Romanian choral tradition. His own works (liturgies, hymns and secular choruses) draw on folksong and modal harmony.

Music hall. A place for a type of entertainment (and accordingly the entertainment itself) which flourished in Britain in the late 19th century and early

20th. The entertainment consisted of musical acts and popular songs; it was taken up in the USA and to some extent on the European mainland, though in France and Germany cabaret, aimed at a narrower public, was the natural counterpart.

The first use of the term 'music hall' was probably in 1848 and several such institutions opened in London soon afterwards. They presented ballads and other popular songs, 'nigger minstrel' acts, selections from popular operas and comic turns and monologues to audiences seated at tables where they were served with drinks. Music halls declined during the second decade of the 20th century, but not before they had created many reputations, of such artists as George Robey (1869–1954), Marie Lloyd (1870–1922) and Harry Lauder (1870–1950), and a large repertory of popular songs.

Musici, I. Italian chamber ensemble. It was formed in 1952 by 11 string players and a harpsichordist at the Accademia di S Cecilia, Rome. Felix Ayo led it until 1968, then Salvatore Accardo and Pina Carmirelli and it has toured widely. Its reputation is founded on Italian Baroque music but it also plays 20th-century works. Brilliance, firm attack and discipline mark its playing.

Music Makers, The. Ode, op.69, by Elgar (1912), a setting for alto, chorus and orchestra of a poem by A. Shaughnessy.

Musico (It.). 'Musician': term used in the 17th and 18th centuries for a professional musician, mainly one associated with secular music or opera, and in particular a castrato singer (in which context it had a derogatory implication).

Music of the Spheres. An ancient Greek (Pythagorean) doctrine postulating harmonious relationships among the planets governed by their proportionate speeds of revolution and their fixed distance from the earth. The concept can be traced back to Jewish beliefs about an orderly cosmos hymning the praises of its creator. The idea continued to appeal to thinkers about music until the end of the Renaissance, influencing scholars of many kinds, including humanists; the last creative statement of the idea was made by Kepler in 1619, but for some later thinkers cosmic imagery of a Pythagorean cast has persisted and for 20th-century musicians such as Hindemith the music of the spheres has remained a vital if metaphorical concept.

Musicology. The scholarly study of music. Traditionally, the term has implied the study of music history, but it has been broadened during the 20th century to embrace all aspects of the study of music, including comparative musicology (i.e. the study of non-Western music and folk music, or ethnomusicology) and systematic musicology (embracing such topics as theory, music education, music as a socio-cultural phenomenon, psychology and acoustics). The study of musical history began in Europe during the Enlightenment, with the work of such men as the encyclopedists in France, Burney and Hawkins in England, Padre Martini in Italy and in Germany Martin Gerbert and J.N. Forkel. Ethnomusicological studies began later and made real progress only at the beginning of the 20th century. The field of musicology as a whole was first methodically defined by the Viennese scholar Guido Adler in 1885.

Music theatre. Term current since the 1960s for musical works that involve a dramatic element in their presentation. They may be small-scale operas, song cycles with instrumental accompaniment that are 'staged' on a concert platform (e.g. Davies's *Eight Songs for a Mad King*) or pieces that resist classification (e.g. Cardew's school operas and numerous works by Kagel). Earlier examples include Stravinsky's *Soldier's Tale* and *Reynard*.

Music therapy. The use of music to cure, alleviate or stimulate. It is familiar from ancient mythology and has been used increasingly in the treatment of physical as well as mental handicaps and emotional disturbance, although there is little theoretical work to explain its effectiveness. Of the elements of music, it is rhythm that is acknowledged to be the vital therapeutic factor by virtue of its power to focus energy and to bring structure into the perception of temporal order; music has stimulated the passive or withdrawn patient into more alert response. It has served to make an emotionally ill patient more accessible, while for physical disabilities it can be used to organize the scale and sequence of small goals in acquiring muscular skill and control, and for mental retardation it can assist in the acquisition of elementary concepts. Mentally retarded and autistic children often respond to music where all else has failed. Music is an expressive vehicle for relief of emotional tension, bypassing difficulties of speech and language. Music therapy has been used to improve motor coordination in cerebral palsy and muscular dystrophy; it is also used to teach breath and diction control when there is speech impairment.

Musikverein. The home of the GESELLSCHAFT DER MUSIKFREUNDE in Vienna; it opened in 1870. It contains the city's chief concert hall, the Grosser Musikvereinssaal (cap. c1950) and the Brahmssaal (cap. c750).

Musique concrète (Fr.). Term coined by a group of experimenters in electronic music working in Paris in the late 1940s. It was intended to denote their use of natural or 'concrete' sound sources in their manner of composing 'concretely' on tape rather than abstractly through notation and performance. Pierre Schaffer and Pierre Henry were leading members of the group.

Musique mesurée. *See* VERS MESURÉS.

Musorgsky [Moussorgsky], **Modest Petrovich** (*b* Karevo, 21 March 1839; *d* St Petersburg, 28 March 1881). Russian composer. His mother gave him piano lessons, and at nine he played a Field concerto before an audience in his parents' house. In 1852 he entered the Guards' cadet school in St Petersburg. Although he had not studied harmony or composition, in 1856 he tried to write an opera; the same year he entered the Guards. In 1857 he met Dargomïzhsky and Cui, and through them Balakirev and Stasov. He persuaded Balakirev to give him lessons and composed songs and piano sonatas.

In 1858 Musorgsky passed through a nervous or spiritual crisis and resigned his army commission. A visit to Moscow in 1859 fired his patriotic imagination and his compositional energies, but although his music began to enjoy public performances his nervous irritability was not entirely calmed. The emancipation of the serfs in March 1861 obliged him to spend most of the next two years helping manage the family estate; a symphony came to nothing and Stasov and Balakirev agreed that 'Musorgsky is almost an idiot'. But he continued to compose and in 1863–6 worked on the libretto and music of an opera, *Salammbô*, which he never completed. At this time he served at the Ministry of Communications and lived in a commune with five other young men who ardently cultivated and exchanged advanced ideas about art, religion, philosophy and politics. Musorgsky's private and public lives eventually came into conflict. In 1865 he underwent his first serious bout of dipsomania (probably as a reaction to his mother's death that year) and in 1867 he was dismissed from his post.

Musorgsky spent summer 1867 at his brother's country house at Minkino, where he wrote, among other things, his first important orchestral work, *St John's Night on the Bare Mountain*. On his return to St Petersburg in the autumn Musorgsky, like the other members of the Balakirev–Stasov circle (ironically dubbed the 'Mighty Handful'), became interested in Dargomïzhsky's experiments in operatic naturalism. Early in 1869 Musorgsky re-entered government service and, in more settled conditions, was able to complete the original version of the opera *Boris Godunov*. This was rejected by the Mariinsky Theatre and Musorgsky set about revising it. In 1872 the opera was again rejected, but excerpts were performed elsewhere and a vocal score published. The opera committee finally accepted the work and a successful production was mounted in February 1874.

Meanwhile Musorgsky had begun work on another historical opera, *Khovanshchina*, at the same time gaining promotion at the ministry. Progress on the new opera was interrupted partly because of unsettled domestic circumstances, but mainly because heavy drinking left Musorgsky incapable of sustained creative effort. But several other compositions belong to this period, including the song cycles *Sunless* and *Songs and Dances of Death* and the *Pictures at an Exhibition*, for piano, a brilliant and bold series inspired by a memorial exhibition of drawings by his friend Victor Hartmann. Ideas for a comic opera based on Gogol's *Sorochintsy Fair* also began to compete with work on *Khovanshchina*; both operas remained unfinished at Musorgsky's death. During the earlier part of 1878 he seems to have led a more respectable life and his director at the ministry even allowed him leave for a three-month concert tour with the contralto Darya Leonova. After he was obliged to leave the government service in January 1880, Leonova helped provide him with employment and a home. It was to her that he turned on 23 February 1881 in a state of nervous excitement, saying that there was nothing left for

him but to beg in the streets; he was suffering from alcoholic epilepsy. He was removed to hospital, where he died a month later.

Many of Musorgsky's works were unfinished, and their editing and posthumous publication were mainly carried out by Rimsky-Korsakov, who to a greater or lesser degree 'corrected' what Musorgsky had composed. *Boris Godunov*, in particular, was reshaped and repolished, with drastic cuts, wholesale rewriting and rescoring, insertion of new music and transposition of scenes. It was only many years later that, with a return to the composer's original drafts, the true nature of his rough art could be properly understood, for Musorgsky shared with some of the painters of his day a disdain for formal beauty, technical polish and other manifestations of 'art for art's sake'. His desire was to relate his art as closely as possible to life, especially that of the Russian masses, to nourish it on events and to employ it as a means for communicating human experience.

Operas Salammbô (1863–6), inc.; Boris Godunov (1st version 1868–9; 2nd version 1871–3; staged 1874); Khovanshchina (1872–80), inc.; Sorochintsy Fair (1874–80), inc.

Songs incl. cycles The Nursery (1870), Sunless (1874), Songs and Dances of Death (1875–7)

Other works St John's Night on the Bare Mountain, orch (1867); Pictures at an Exhibition, pf (1874)

Muta (It.). 'Change': a performing instruction; 'Muta in La' would mean change to an instrument in A, or change the tuning crook of a wind instrument to put it in A.

Mutation stop. Single-rank stops, usually of wide or fairly wide-scale pipes with a high lead content, pitched at the 5th, 3rd, 7th, 9th etc of an upper octave; hence their other names, 'overtone stops', *Aliquotstimmen* etc. Examples are the Nasard, Larigot and Tierce.

Mute. A mechanical device used on musical instruments to muffle the tone. In instruments of the violin family the typical mute is a three-pronged clamp of metal, ivory, bakelite or wood; attached to the bridge, it absorbs some of the vibration and makes the sound relatively veiled and slightly nasal. Muting of woodwinds has been accomplished by stuffing a cloth into the bell, although this is unevenly effective since the proportion of sound issuing from the bell varies. Mutes applied to brass instruments modify tone colour and reduce the volume, and some alter the pitch. With the influence of jazz, a large range of mutes has been developed, including the straight mute, cup mute, wah-wah mute and bucket mute. The hand over or in the bell is also used.

A buff stop on the harpsichord presses felts or leathers against a set of strings, muting the tone. The 'soft' or *una corda* pedal is the modern version of a mute on the piano and reduces the volume by shifting the hammers to the right so that they hit only two (or one) of the strings for each note.

Müthel, Johann Gottfried (*b* Mölln, Lauenburg, 17 Jan 1728; *d* Bienenhof, 14 July 1788). German composer. He became chamber musician and organist at the Schwerin court in 1747 and in 1750 visited J.S. Bach at Leipzig. From 1753 he directed a private musical establishment at Riga. An individual composer, he wrote chiefly harpsichord music (sonatas, concertos etc) in an expressive and virtuoso style influenced by C.P.E. Bach. His other works include organ pieces and songs.

Muti, Riccardo (*b* Naples, 28 July 1941). Italian conductor. He studied at the Naples and Milan conservatories and made his début in 1968, with the Italian RSO. He has conducted at Florence from 1969, giving operas by Rossini, Spontini and Meyerbeer. He was chief conductor of the (New) Philharmonia, 1973–82, and principal conductor of the Philadelphia Orchestra from 1981; in 1986 he became musical director of La Scala, Milan. His performances are distinguished for their vitality, warmth and expressiveness.

Muzïka. The Soviet state-controlled publisher of music and music literature. It was established in 1964 through an amalgamation of Muzgiz and Sovetskiy Kompozitor. Besides orchestral and instrumental works by Soviet and foreign composers, vocal music and folk and educational material, it has been responsible for important scholarly works including editions of the complete works of Glinka, Rimsky-Korsakov, Tchaikovsky, Balakirev and Prokofiev.

Muzio, Claudia (*b* Pavia, 7 Feb 1889; *d* Rome, 24 May 1936). Italian soprano. She made her début at Arezzo in 1910. Wider attention came in 1914, with Desdemona at La Scala and Covent Garden. She sang at the Met from 1916, notably as Tosca and in the première of *Il tabarro* (1918), and was also successful in South America. She brought drama and pathos to all her roles.

Muzio [Mussio], (Donnino) Emanuele (*b* Zibello, 24 Aug 1821; *d* Paris, 27 Nov 1890). Italian conductor and composer. A friend and assistant to Verdi, with whom he studied in Milan, he gave the first performances in the USA of *Un ballo in maschera*, *Aida* and the Requiem, also conducting in Cuba, Egypt and throughout Europe. He composed four operas and numerous songs.

Myaskovsky, Nikolay Yakovlevich (*b* Novogeor-giyevsk, 20 April 1881; *d* Moscow, 8 Aug 1950). Soviet composer. He studied for a military career but entered the St Petersburg Conservatory (1906–11), where his teachers included Lyadov and Rimsky-Korsakov. He served in the war, and from 1921 taught at the Moscow Conservatory. He was not an innovator but was an influential, individual figure working within the Russian tradition. His large output is dominated by the cycle of 27 symphonies (1908–50, highly regarded in and outside Russia in his lifetime. He also wrote 13 string quartets (1913–49), choral and chamber music.

My Ladye Nevells Booke. English MS of keyboard music, completed in 1591 by John Baldwin, thought to have been written for the wife of Sir Edward Nevill. It consists of 192 folios containing 42 pieces by Byrd and is privately owned.

Mylius, Wolfgang Michael (*b* Mannstedt, 1636; *d* Gotha, 1712–13). German composer and writer on music. He was a court musician at Altenburg and later at Gotha, becoming Kapellmeister there in 1676, and wrote Singspiels, many sacred works, and a practical musical manual (1686). He came of the same family as Johann Daniel Mylius (*c*1585–*c*1628), scientist, lutenist and composer.

Mysliveček, Josef (*b* Horní Šárka, 9 March 1737; *d* Rome, 4 Feb 1781). Czech composer. Active as a composer from 1760, he settled in Italy and presented his first opera in Parma in 1764. The success of *Bellerofonte* (1767, Naples) led to commissions from all the major Italian cities. His fame spread abroad and in 1773 he presented an opera in Munich; on a second visit (1777) he met and advised Mozart. His last three operas (1779–80) were failures.

Mysliveček wrote 27 *opere serie*; their arias show grateful vocal writing and appealing melodic invention. Stronger dramatic expression appears in his oratorios, notably *Isacco figura del Redentore* (1776, Florence; also called *Abramo ed Isacco*, 1777, Munich). His instrumental music, including symphonies, concertos and chamber music, was also highly popular. His style is often similar to Mozart's.

N

Nabokov, Nicolas [Nikolay] (*b* Lyubcha, 17 April 1903; *d* New York, 6 April 1978). American composer. He studied in Russia, Stuttgart and Berlin (with Juon and Busoni, 1922–3), then lived in France (1926–34) and the USA, returning to Paris in the 1950s. As a composer he is identified with music for dance (e.g. *Ode*, 1927; *Union Pacific*, 1934); he also wrote operas, three symphonies, vocal orchestral pieces and books and articles.

Nabucco. Opera in four acts by Verdi to a libretto by Solera after A. Cortesi's ballet after Anicet-Bourgeois and F. Cornue (1842, Milan).

Nachschlag (Ger.). 'After-beat': term for a group of ornaments involving 'after-notes'. It may signify a passing appoggiatura, taking its value from the preceding rather than the following note; it may be an anticipation (cadent) or changing-note (springer); or it may be the turned ending of a trill.

Nachtanz (Ger.). Term for the second of a pair of dances, usually a fast triple-metre reworking of the music of the first. Examples include the saltarello, galliard and *tripla*.

Nacht in Venedig, Eine. Operetta in three acts by Johann Strauss (ii) to a libretto by 'F. Zell' (Camillo Walzel) and Genée (1883, Berlin).

Nachtmusik. German equivalent of the Italian Notturno or the Nocturne.

Naderman. French family of musicians, publishers and instrument makers. The most celebrated members were Jean-Henri (1735–99), a prominent builder of single-action pedal harps and publisher of much chamber music, especially for harp; and his son François-Joseph (1781–1835), a leading harpist and composer who became the first harp professor at the Paris Conservatoire (1825) and wrote studies that are still used.

Nagārā. *See* Naqqāra.

Nägeli, Hans Georg (*b* Wetzikon, 26 May 1773; *d* Zurich, 26 Dec 1836). Swiss composer, music publisher and educationist. He founded the first music lending library in Switzerland and as a publisher issued first editions of piano works by Beethoven, Clementi and Cramer as well as music by Bach and Handel. He also lectured and wrote essays (many on aesthetics) and compiled a singing tutor. His compositions are chiefly choral music and songs.

Nail violin. A friction idiophone (not a violin) consisting of metal, glass or wooden rods fastened at one end to a soundboard. It was invented *c*1740. The flat wooden soundboard is usually half-moon in shape and the nails are fastened perpendicularly around the curved edge. Chromatic nails are slightly bent; the shorter the nail, the higher the pitch. The instrument was held in the left hand by a hole and sound produced by rubbing a strong, well-rosined, black-haired bow across the nails. A keyboard model, with a treadle-operated band replacing the bow, was introduced in 1791. The principle of the nail violin has been revived in the 20th century in several instruments, often sound sculptures.

Naïs. *Pastorale héroïque* in a prologue and three acts by Rameau to a libretto by Cahusac (1749, Paris).

Nakers. Small kettledrums of medieval Europe, of Arab origin (*see* Naqqāra). They are recorded as early as the 13th century in France and Italy (*nacaires, naccheroni*) and as late as the 16th. They were more or less hemispherical, 15–25 cm in diameter, frequently with snares and usually played in pairs, suspended in front of the player. They were usually played with drumsticks, mainly for martial purposes but also in chamber music, dance and processional music and probably for accompanying songs.

Nameday [Namensfeier]. Overture (op.115) by Beethoven, composed for the name-day festivities of Emperor Francis II of Austria (1815).

Nancarrow, Conlon (*b* Texarkana, AR, 27 Oct 1912). Mexican composer of American origin. He studied with Slonimsky, Piston and Sessions in Boston (1933–6) and has lived in Mexico since 1940. From the late 1940s he has composed exclusively for player piano. His studies exploit the instrument's potential for rhythmic complexity and textural variety, creating showpieces of virtuosity far beyond a human performer's capabilities, with arpeggios, trills, glissandos, leaps, widely spaced chords and complex counterpoint. He is concerned with tempo, especially the 'temporal dissonance' of several rates occurring simultaneously, and with formal structure. His music first received serious attention only in the 1970s.

Nanino, Giovanni Bernardino (*b* Vallerano, *c*1560; *d* Rome, 1623). Italian composer, brother of G.M. Nanino. He was *maestro di cappella* of S Maria de' Monti, Rome (after 1588), S Luigi dei Francesi, where he excelled as a teacher (1591–1608), and Cardinal Montalto's church, S Lorenzo in Damaso (from 1608). He published three books of madrigals (1588–1612), four of motets (1610–18) and psalms (1620).

Nanino, Giovanni Maria (*b* Tivoli, 1543–4; *d* Rome, 11 March 1607). Italian composer. Possibly a pupil of Palestrina, he was *maestro di cappella* of S Maria Maggiore, Rome (*c*1567–75), and of S Luigi dei Francesi (1575–7). From 1577 until his death he was a tenor in the papal choir. Chiefly famous as a teacher, he influenced many Roman musicians and was a versatile and imaginative composer of secular music (4 bks, *c*1571–93) and sacred (1586).

Naples Conservatory. Italian music school. In the 17th century music schools were established at four orphanages in Naples (S Onofrio, Poveri di Gesù Cristo, S Maria di Loreto, Pietà dei Turchini). The boys were taught counterpoint and singing and to play instruments; they took part in church services and concerts. In 1806 the remaining schools merged as the Real Collegio di Musica, which moved to the monastery S Pietro a Majella in 1826 and was later named after it.

Nápravník, Eduard (Francevič (*b* Býšť, 24 Aug 1839; *d* Petrograd, 23 Nov 1916). Czech conductor and composer. He studied in Prague and in 1861 became director of Prince Yusupov's private orchestra in St Petersburg. In 1869 he succeeded Lyadov as principal conductor of the Mariinsky Theatre, also conducting concerts of the Russian Musical Society and the Philharmonic Society; he was noted for his industry and attention to detail. Acclaimed by Stasov and Bülow, he conducted important foreign works and the premières of over 80 Russian operas, including Musorgsky's *Boris Godunov* (1874) and Cui's *William Ratcliff* (1869). He was competent but less distinctive as a composer, being influenced by Glinka and Tchaikovsky.

Naqqāra. Type of kettledrum of the Islamic world, the Caucasus and Central and South Asia, used in military, religious and ceremonial music. *Naqqāra* are usually played in pairs, tuned to different pitches; larger instruments can be carried on horseback or on camels. European kettledrums and nakers developed from them. In South Asia, as *nagārā*, they have been used (generally in pairs) for military, court and temple functions and are also known as folk and tribal instruments, often for dancing.

Nardini, Pietro (*b* Livorno, 12 April 1722; *d* Florence, 7 May 1793). Italian violinist and composer. A pupil of Tartini, he became his most eminent disciple and was especially noted for his fine tone in Adagios. He was solo violinist and orchestral leader at the Stuttgart court in 1762–5, music director at the ducal court in Florence from 1770, and a famous teacher (Thomas Linley was among his pupils). He wrote many violin sonatas and several concertos, duets etc in a pre-Classical style.

Nares, James (*b* Stanwell, bap. 19 April 1715; *d* London, 10 Feb 1783). English composer and organist. He was organist of York Minster in 1735–56, then

served at the Chapel Royal as organist, composer and later Master of the Choristers (1757–80). He composed chiefly church music, including services and over 40 anthems (with much solo writing). Among his other works are a set of lively keyboard lessons, fugues, a trio sonata, a dramatic ode (*c*1742), catches, canons and glees. Also a teacher, he wrote treatises on singing and keyboard playing.

Narváez, Luys de (*b* Granada; *fl* 1530–50). Spanish composer and vihuelist. He may have been in the service of Charles V's secretary and, in the 1540s, as music teacher to the children of Prince Philip's chapel, he travelled to Italy and northern Europe. Apart from two motets, his music is for solo vihuela. A collection published in 1538 contains fantasias, variation sets, arrangements of vocal pieces and songs and a setting of a basse danse tenor. His fantasias are of the highest quality.

Nasard [nazard]. An organ stop, a mutation sounding one octave (or two) and a 5th above the main note; it was particularly used in France in the 16th and 17th centuries.

Nasco, Jan (*b c*1510; *d* Treviso, 1561). Flemish composer active in northern Italy. He is not to be confused with Maistre Jahn of Ferrara. In 1547 he became musical director of the Accademia Filarmonica of Verona and, though he was appointed *maestro di cappella* of Treviso Cathedral in 1551, he maintained a close association with the academy. With Ruffo, he belonged to the group of musicians working near Venice, greatly influenced by Willaert. He composed in all sacred forms (including a Passion). His secular works (madrigals and canzone) are characterized by careful text-setting. In general he inclined towards homophonic writing.

Nash, Heddle (*b* London, 14 June 1896; *d* there, 14 Aug 1961). English tenor. He sang in Italy until 1926, then in London with the Old Vic and the British National Opera Company and from 1929 at Covent Garden. With a charming, sweet voice, he was admired as Mozart's Ottavio and Wagner's David and sang leading roles at the early Glyndebourne seasons. He was an outstanding oratorio singer, excelling in Handel and as Elgar's Gerontius.

Nasidze, Sulkhan Ivanovich (*b* Tbilisi, 17 March 1927). Soviet composer. He studied with Tuskiya at the Tbilisi Conservatory, where he began teaching in 1963. His works, in most genres, have attracted interest for their organic synthesis of new expressive means with traditional Georgian music; they include five symphonies (1957, 1964, 1969, 1972, 1975).

Nasolini, Sebastiano (*b* Piacenza, *c*1768; *d* ?Naples, 1816). Italian composer. He was *maestro al cembalo* at the S Pietro theatre, Trieste, 1787–90; in 1788 he presented his first opera there and became *maestro di cappella* of the Cathedral of S Giusto. Subsequently he presented over 20 operas (comic and serious), in Venice and other Italian cities, enjoying almost unbroken success. Among his other works are oratorios and many arias and duets. His style is graceful, light and fluent, akin to Paisiello's.

Nathan, Isaac (*b* Canterbury, 1790; *d* Sydney, 15 Jan 1864). Australian composer of English birth. He was educated at Cambridge. A writer, teacher, music publisher and opera composer in London, he won early success as Byron's collaborator in *Hebrew Melodies* (1815–19); court intrigues led to his emigration to Australia in 1841. In Sydney he opened a singing academy, became a choral director, gave concerts and produced patriotic odes as well as the first operas written in Australia (1843, 1846); noteworthy were his experiments in transcribing aboriginal music, including *Koorinda Braia* (1842).

National anthems. Hymns, marches, anthems or fanfares used as official patriotic symbols. The term for these became current in the early 19th century (in most countries it is the equivalent of 'national hymn'). Such pieces are performed on ceremonial occasions and at some types of theatrical or sporting event. The earliest is the British one, *God Save the King/Queen*, which came to be used in the 1740s; several other countries adopted national anthems later in the 18th century, including France (*La marseillaise*) and Austria (Emperor's Hymn, by Haydn). Many more were adopted during the 19th century, but only since the mid-20th century have Eastern countries followed. The texts of national anthems usually embody patriotic fervour; the music is sometimes hymn-like, often martial, occasionally operatic and sometimes based on local folk-music traditions.

National Conservatory of Music of America. Music school founded in 1885 in New York by Jeannette Thurber to encourage a national musical culture. Dvořák was director in 1892–5. Its standards were high but it ceased to exist *c*1928 for lack of funds.

Nationalism. Term applied to the movement in music, about the middle of the 19th century, in which composers became eager for their music to embody elements that proclaimed its nationality. The expression of nationality in music is much older than this; 17th- and 18th-century theorists and composers, for example, were keenly aware of aspects of their music that reflected nationality, and by the late 18th century, composers in Britain in particular were incorporating folk melodies (or supposed ones) in their music. However, the purpose of the nationalist movement of the mid-19th century was more self-consciously assertive of national tradition. It manifested itself in the music of Chopin, who was not the first but was the best composer to embody Polish dance rhythms in his music. Glinka's opera *A Life for the Tsar* (1856) (now known as *Ivan Susanin*), with its nationalist topic as well as its use of folk music, is considered an important landmark in the nationalist movement, as are the operas of Musorgsky and Borodin and many orchestral works of the Five. In Bohemia, there were manifestations of nationalism as early as the 1820s, in the operas of Škroup, but it was only with the work of Šebor, Smetana and Dvořák that Czech nationalism made a strong impact; its growth was connected with the Czechs' desire to free themselves from Austrian domination. Other east European countries were similarly motivated and created such nationalist works as Moniuszko's Polish opera *Halka* (1848) and Erkel's *Hunyadi László* (1844), though Hungarian nationalism took fire only with Kodály and Bartók. Nationalism, though less motivated by political events, is also found in Spain

(Albéniz, Granados), northern Europe (Grieg, Sibelius) and England (Vaughan Williams, Holst). It would be misleading, however, not to note the nationalism of the central countries in the European musical tradition: in Germany, from Schumann and Brahms (who used German folksong) and Wagner; in Italy, from Verdi (whose operas are assertively Italian, whatever their topic) and even France, where Debussy was anxious to create a national music. Nationalism takes somewhat different forms in the Americas: in South America the emphasis has been on the use of dance rhythms of local significance, while in the USA the national spirit has been most strongly expressed in such characteristically American forms as jazz and the musical (though distinctively American idioms have also been used within European-based musical forms).

National Philharmonic Orchestra (Poland). Orchestra founded in Warsaw in 1946 (renamed in 1947 and 1955); it replaced the Warsaw PO (1901–39). Concerts are given in the National Philharmonic Hall (rebuilt 1955). Activities include youth concerts and international tours.

National Symphony Orchestra. American orchestra founded in 1931 in Washington, DC. Hans Kindler was its first conductor; its home is the Concert Hall, Kennedy Center. Activities include concerts in parks and at Wolf Trap Farm Park. Recent conductors have included Dorati and Rostropovich.

Nativité du Seigneur, La. Nine organ works (meditations) by Messiaen (1935).

Natra, Sergiu (*b* Bucharest, 12 April 1924). Israeli composer of Romanian origin. He studied with Klepper at the Bucharest Academy, and in 1961 settled in Tel-Aviv, where he became professor at the University (1976). The works he has composed in Israel are atonal, influenced by the landscape, religion and language of Israel; his music is characterized by working short motifs in variation form.

Natural. A notational sign (♮), normally placed to the left of a note and thereby cancelling a flat or sharp that would otherwise affect it. The adjective 'natural' indicates a note neither sharpened nor flattened.

Natural notes. The notes of the harmonic series of a brass instrument, particularly of one without valves, slides or keys, and so confined to one series of HARMONICS.

Naudot, Jacques-Christophe (*b c*1690; *d* Paris, 26 Nov 1762). French composer and flautist. He was a well-known player and teacher in Paris. A popular composer, he produced over 20 sets of instrumental works, 1726–52, including solo, duet and trio sonatas for flute, flute concertos (by 1737) and pieces for vielle (hurdy-gurdy) or musette. His flute music was influential for its virtuosity, italianate features and 'Aria' movements.

Naumann, Johann Gottlieb (*b* Blasewitz, 17 April 1741; *d* Dresden, 23 Oct 1801). German composer. He studied in Italy and presented his first operas there and at the Dresden court, where he became second church composer in 1764 and chamber composer in 1765; in 1776 he became Kapellmeister. He next served at the Stockholm court, 1777–86, where he wrote three stage works, notably the Swedish operas *Cora och Alonzo* (1782) and *Gustaf Wasa* (1786), long regarded as the Swedish national opera; he also wrote a Danish opera, *Orpheus og Eurydike* (1786), for Copenhagen. From 1786 he was Oberkapellmeister at Dresden.

Naumann was the foremost Dresden musician of his day and a prolific composer, writing *c*25 stage works, 12 oratorios, church music, cantatas and instrumental music. His early output is italianate; later he was influenced by Gluck and French opera, and in other vocal music by early Romantic style.

His grandson Emil (1827–88) wrote books and pamphlets on music and composed stage works, sacred music, lieder etc. Emil's cousin Ernst (1832–1910) was an editor of Bach's music, composer and arranger.

Naumann, Siegfried (*b* Malmö, 27 Nov 1919). Swedish composer. His teachers included Pizzetti in Rome (1949–53). He has worked as a conductor, especially of new music, and in 1962 founded the ensemble Musica Nova; his own acknowledged works, from 1959 and later, are in an avant-garde style, showing a strong feeling for sonority and pregnant rhythm. *Il cantico del sole* for solo voices, chorus and orchestra (1963) won him international renown.

Navarra, André(-Nicolas) (*b* Biarritz, 13 Oct 1911). French cellist. After study at Toulouse and Paris he made his solo début in 1931 at the Colonne Concerts, Paris. His thoughtful, refined playing was heard in Elgar's Concerto and he gave first performances of concertos by Jolivet and Tomasi. He has taught in Paris, Siena and Vienna.

Navarraise, La. Opera in two acts by Massenet to a libretto by J. Claretie and H. Cain (1894, London).

Navarro, Juan (*b* Seville or Marchena, *c*1530; *d* Palencia, 25 Sept 1580). Spanish composer. After singing in the cathedral choirs of Jaén and Málaga (1553–5, briefly under Morales), he was *maestro de capilla* of the cathedrals of Avila (1563–6), Salamanca (1566–74), Ciudad Rodrigo (1574–8) and Palencia (from 1578). His psalms, hymns and Magnificats long remained among the most popular vesper collections in Spain, Portugal and Mexico.

Another composer of the same name (*c*1550–*c*1610), born in Cádiz, published in 1604 the earliest music composed and printed in Mexico, a collection of Passion settings and Lamentations.

Nāy [nai, nay, ney]. Obliquely held rim-blown flute of the Middle East, Iran and Central Asia. It is the only wind instrument used in Arab and Persian art music; many folk forms are known.

Naylor, Bernard (*b* Cambridge, 22 Nov 1907; *d* Victoria, BC, 19 May 1986). Canadian composer of English origin, son of the composer and organist Edward (1867–1934). He studied at the RCM (1924–7) and Oxford (1927–31), and in 1932 went to Canada; in 1942 he founded the Little SO in Montreal. He spent periods in England as an organist and teacher (Oxford, 1950–52; Reading, 1953–9). His music is deeply rooted in the English choral tradition and includes much Anglican church music marked by acute sensitivity to words (e.g. Nine Motets, 1952).

Nazareth, Ernesto (Júlio de) (*b* Rio de Janeiro, 20 March 1863; *d* there, *c*2 Feb 1934). Brazilian composer. He wrote *c*100 tangos, establishing him as the most influential Brazilian popular composer of the 20th century.

NBC Symphony Orchestra. American orchestra formed in New York in 1937 specifically for Toscanini, who conducted it until 1954 when he retired; it was disbanded by the NBC but continued independently for several years as 'Symphony of the Air'.

Neander, Valentin (*b* ?Treuenbrietzen, ?1575–80; *d* in or after 1619). German composer. A pupil of Gesius in Frankfurt an der Oder, he published an important collection of 89 four-part sacred pieces (1619), showing the influence of French psalm setting on Lutheran music. His father Valentin (*c*1540–*c*1584) was also a composer of sacred pieces and a writer on music.

Neapolitan school. A term used to denote the operatic style favoured by composers born or trained in Naples from the end of the 17th century until the 1770s. It is now held that no 'Neapolitan school' existed, but the term remains useful and not irrelevant since most of the leading opera composers of this period studied in Neapolitan conservatories. These composers include A. Scarlatti, traditionally regarded as founder of the group, Porpora, Vinci, Hasse (although a German), Pergolesi, Jommelli, Traetta, Piccinni, Paisiello and Cimarosa.

Neapolitan sixth. A chord, the first inversion of the major triad built on the flattened second degree of the scale; in C major or minor, F–A♭–D♭. It may precede a V–I CADENCE and function like a subdominant. It is associated with the so-called 'Neapolitan' school of 18th-century Italian opera composers.

Neate, Charles (*b* London, 28 March 1784; *d* Brighton, 30 March 1877). English pianist. An esteemed performer and teacher in London, he is remembered for his friendship with Beethoven, whom he met in Vienna in 1815 and on whose behalf he acted in Beethoven's dealings with the Philharmonic Society.

Nebenstimme (Ger.: 'under-part'). *See* HAUPTSTIMME.

Nebra (Blasco), José (Melchior de) (*b* Calatayud, bap. 6 Jan 1702; *d* Madrid, 11 July 1768). Spanish composer. He was principal organist of the Spanish royal chapel and the Descalzas Reales convent at Madrid from 1724; in 1751 he became deputy director of the chapel and head of the choir school. A highly successful theatre composer, he had 57 stage works performed in Madrid and Lisbon in 1723–30 and 1737–51 (none in 1731–6). Whether secular or sacred, they combine comic, folklike and tragic elements, and all include spoken dialogue. He also wrote (especially from the 1740s) music for the royal chapel.

Neck. As applied to such string instruments as the violin, viol, lute and guitar families, the neck is the projecting handle to which part of the fingerboard is fastened. The player holds the instrument by the neck and fingers the strings with the same hand. The neck can be separate (as on the violin) or an integral part of the body (as in a rebec). Its size and shape depend on its function and the number, tension and length of strings involved.

Nedbal, Oskar (*b* Tábor, 26 March 1874; *d* Zagreb, 24 Dec 1930). Czech composer. He studied with Dvořák at the Prague Conservatory (1885–92) and became internationally known as viola player in the Czech Quartet (1891–1906) and conductor of the Czech PO (1896–1906) and Vienna Tonkünstlerorchester (1906–18); his later years were spent in Bratislava. He was renowned for his tasteful operettas, to Viennese librettos and enlivened with fresh, folkdance rhythms; he also wrote successful ballets.

Neefe, Christian Gottlob (*b* Chemnitz, 5 Feb 1748; *d* Dessau, 26 Jan 1798). German composer. He moved to Bonn in 1779 as music director of a theatre troupe, and from *c*1780 taught the young Beethoven the piano, organ, thoroughbass and composition. He became court organist but from 1784 concentrated increasingly on teaching. His output includes nine German stage works (for Leipzig and elsewhere) and many lieder, their dramatic effects and novel forms at times anticipating Schubert. He also wrote instrumental pieces, an autobiography and essays.

Neel, (Louis) Boyd (*b* Blackheath, 19 July 1905; *d* Toronto, 30 Sept 1981). English conductor. After study at the GSM he founded his own string orchestra in 1932, taking it to Salzburg in 1937 for the première of Britten's Variations on a theme of Frank Bridge, written for it. He was a pioneer of chamber orchestra performances of Baroque music; his 18 players gave Bach, Handel and little-known Italian music in a lively, chamber style, and toured widely. Neel was later dean of the Royal Conservatory of Music, Toronto, 1953–70, and founded the Hart House Orchestra.

Negrea, Marţian (*b* Vorumloc, 10 Feb 1893; *d* Bucharest, 13 July 1973). Romanian composer. A pupil of Mandyczewski and Schmidt at the Vienna Academy (1918–21), he taught at the conservatories of Cluj (1921–41) and Bucharest (1941–63). He wrote in a lyrical, pastoral style using folk material, evoking the Romanian landscape (e.g. in the chorus *Shepherdess* and the orchestral *Grui Tales*, 1940).

Negri, Cesare (de') (*b* Milan, *c*1535; *d* ?there, after 1604). Italian dancing-master. His comprehensive treatise *Le gratie d'amore* (1602) is an important source for social and theatrical dance, containing choreographies and music for 43 dances (including, unusually, some for two and four couples).

Negrilla (Sp.). A villancico (more specifically a *canario*), mimicking the music, song and dance of black African slaves.

Neidhart von Reuental (?*c*1180; *d* after 1237). Influential German Minnesinger who served members of the Bavarian and Austrian aristocracy. The amount of surviving music for his poetry is exceptionally large for so early a Minnesinger: 17 melodies survive for 68 poems. These are all written as dance pieces, in two categories, for summer (outdoor, in simple rhyming couplets) and winter (indoor, in more elaborate, three-section forms). He broke with the conventions of the country ambience with a new realism

and vigour, in music as well as poetry, and was much imitated.

Neidlinger, Gustav (*b* Mainz, 21 March 1912). German bass-baritone. He sang at the Hamburg Staatsoper, 1936–50, then joined the Stuttgart Opera. He appeared at Bayreith, 1952–75, and made his Met début in 1972. As guest in London, Vienna and elsewhere he was noted for his powerful portrayals of Alberich, Klingsor and Telramund.

Nelson, Judith (Anne) (*b* Chicago, 10 Sept 1939). American soprano. She sang in early music groups at universities in Chicago and Berkeley, showing distinction in 15th-century music; in Europe she sang widely in Paris, London and the Low Countries, making her operatic début in Brussels as Monteverdi's Drusilla (1979). She has made many recordings of Charpentier, Couperin and Handel, with René Jacobs and Emma Kirkby, and has recorded Schubert songs with fortepiano. She is noted for her pure-toned, spirited and stylish singing.

Nelson Mass. Haydn's Mass no.11 in D minor (1798); Haydn inscribed it 'Missa in angustiis' but its connection with Nelson is unclear.

Nelsova, Zara (*b* Winnipeg, 23 Dec 1918). American cellist of Canadian birth and Russian parentage. She studied in London and made her début there in 1932. With her two older sisters she toured extensively in a piano trio and made her solo New York début in 1942. She excels in Romantic works but her repertory includes 20th-century music; Bloch dedicated three suites to her.

Nenna, Pomponio (*b* Bari, *c*1550–55; *d* ?Rome, by 22 Oct 1613). Italian composer. Probably a pupil of Felis, he was governor of Andria, near Bari. He served in Gesualdo's household in Naples (*c*1594–9), moving to Rome in 1608. Seven books of his madrigals (1582–1618) – probably influenced by Gesualdo – and two of responsories (1607, 1622) survive.

Neo-classical. Term used to describe the style of certain 20th-century composers who, notably in the period between the two world wars, revived the balanced forms and perceptible thematic processes of earlier styles. The term is particularly applied to Stravinsky, from *Pulcinella* (1920), which draws on music purportedly by Pergolesi, to *The Rake's Progress* (1951), which uses Mozartian techniques of recitative and aria. It is also applied to Prokofiev (the 'Classical Symphony', with its 18th-century dance forms), Hindemith and (though he abhorred the idea of neo-classicism) Schoenberg. *See also* CLASSICAL.

Neo-Gallican chant. Chant composed for the neo-Gallican liturgical movement in France from the late 17th century to the early 19th. It consisted either of a pseudo-plainchant style or newly-composed, tonal melodies.

Nepomuceno, Alberto (*b* Fortaleza, 6 July 1864; *d* Rio de Janeiro, 16 Oct 1920). Brazilian composer. From 1888 to 1895 he studied in Rome, Berlin and Paris. He then worked in support of Brazilian music as a teacher, conductor and composer in Rio de Janeiro, playing a major role in Brazilian musical nationalism and being one of the first to use Brazilian elements in his works (e.g. *Série brasileira*, 1892). These include operas, orchestral and chamber pieces, church music and over 80 songs.

Neri [Negri], Massimiliano (*b* ?Brescia, ?1615; *d* Bonn, 1666). Italian organist and composer. He was first organist of St Mark's, Venice, in 1644–64, also working at SS Giovanni e Paolo, and later served at Cologne. His principal works are his sonatas and canzonas (1644, 1651).

Neri, Filippo (*b* Florence, 21 July 1515; *d* Rome, 26 May 1595). Italian religious leader. With the 'spiritual exercises' he conducted in Roman churches, he influenced the use of the LAUDA SPIRITUALE and the rise of the ORATORIO.

Nerone. Opera in four acts by Boito to his own libretto; it was completed by Toscanini, Tommasini and Smareglia (1924, Milan).

Opera in three acts by Mascagni to a libretto by Targioni-Tozzetti after Cossa (1935, Milan).

Monteverdi (*L'incoronazione di Poppea*) and Handel (*Agrippina*) also wrote Nero operas.

Neruda. Moravian family of musicians. The most celebrated members were Wilma (Lady Hallé, ?1838–1911), a violinist acclaimed throughout Europe, and her brother Franz (1843–1915), a cellist, conductor and instrumental composer who worked mainly in Copenhagen.

Nesterenko, Evgeny (Evgenyevich) (*b* Moscow, 8 Jan 1938). Russian bass. He studied in Leningrad and made his début there as Gremin (*Eugene Onegin*). In 1971 he became a principal at the Bol'shoy where his roles included Boris Godunov, the role of his débuts at La Scala, the Vienna Staatsoper and the Met (1973–5). His full, resonant, typically Russian bass serves well in these roles and as Philip II in *Don Carlos*, as well as in Russian song.

Nestroy, Johann Nepomuk (Eduard Ambrosius) (*b* Vienna, 7 Dec 1801; *d* Graz, 25 May 1862). Austrian playwright, actor and singer. The last and greatest figure in a long line of Viennese actor-dramatists, he played *c*880 different parts during his career. Among his most successful stage works are witty parodies of Rossini's *Cenerentola* (*Nagerl und Handschuh*, 1832; music by Adolf Müller), Meyerbeer's *Robert le diable* (*Robert der Teufel*, 1833; music by Müller) and *Tannhäuser* (1857; music by Carl Binder).

Nešvera, Josef (*b* Praskolesy, 24 Oct 1842; *d* Olomouc, 12 April 1914). Czech composer. In Prague his teachers included J.B. Foerster. In 1884 he became music director at Olomouc Cathedral, playing a leading role in the city's musical life. He was a prolific composer: among his best-known works were the *Czech Passion* op.17, *De profundis* op.49 and the male-voice chorus *To Moravia*.

Nettl, Bruno (*b* Prague, 14 March 1930). American ethnomusicologist. He studied at Indiana University, taught at Detroit and, from 1964, at the University of Illinois. He has written extensively on North American Indian music, music of the Middle East and European and American folk music; his general interests include acculturation and modernization in traditional music. In his writings on ethnomusicology Nettl has shown himself one of the

leading thinkers of his time. His father, Paul Nettl (1889–1972), was also a musicologist; he taught in Prague and at Indiana Univeristy (1946–59) and published many books and articles, mainly on 17th- and 18th-century music.

Neubauer, Franz Christoph (*b* Hořin, 21 March 1750; *d* Bückeburg, 11 Oct 1795). Bohemian violinist and composer. After touring as a violinist, he served at Weilburg (1790), Minden and Bückeburg, where he later became Kapellmeister (1795). An imaginative and prolific composer, he wrote symphonies, string quartets, concertos etc and sacred and secular vocal music, with interesting modulations and textures.

Neuhaus, Max (*b* Beaumont, TX, 9 Aug 1939). American composer. He studied at the Manhattan School and was an avant-garde percussionist before devoting himself, in 1968, to composing electronic music, often for public installations, for example in parks, or swimming pools (*Water Whistle I–XVII*, 1970–75).

Neukomm, Sigismund Ritter von (*b* Salzburg, 10 July 1778; *d* Paris, 3 April 1858). Austrian composer and pianist. He was a pupil of Michael Haydn in Salzburg and in 1797–1804 Joseph Haydn in Vienna, where he taught the piano and singing. He was Kapellmeister at the German Theatre in St Petersburg, 1804–8, and in 1809 settled in Paris, where he enjoyed growing success. In 1816–21 he was in Rio de Janeiro as teacher to the court of John VI of Portugal; later journeys took him to Italy, the British Isles, Algiers and elsewhere. He championed the music of Mozart and Haydn and composed some 1300 works; he was especially prolific in sacred music and song.

Neumann, Angelo (*b* Vienna, 18 Oct 1838; *d* Prague, 20 Dec 1910). Austrian tenor and opera impresario. He made his début in Berlin in 1859 and sang in Vienna, 1862–76. He then became manager of the Leipzig opera, moving to Bremen (1882) and Prague (1885). In 1882 he formed a touring company that gave Wagner's operas (including the *Ring*) in London, Paris, St Petersburg and elsewhere. He left a book of Wagnerian memoirs.

Neumann, František (*b* Přerov, 16 June 1874; *d* Brno, 25 Feb 1929). Czech conductor and composer. After study at the Leipzig Conservatory he worked at opera houses in Karlsruhe, Hamburg and Frankfurt. He became chief conductor of the Brno National Theatre in 1919 and collaborated closely with Janáček in the premières of *Katya Kabanova*, *The Cunning Little Vixen*, *Šárka* and *The Makropoulos Affair*; he also conducted the première of *Taras Bulba* (1921). Several of his operas were produced during his early years in Germany.

Neumann, Václav (*b* Prague, 29 Oct 1920). Czech conductor. He studied at the Prague Conservatory and after engagements in Karlsbad and Brno conducted at the Komische Oper, Berlin (1956–64). He worked in Leipzig, 1964–8, and then became chief conductor of the Czech PO. His repertory includes Janáček's operas and strongly structured performances of Czech classical and contemporary works.

Neumark, Georg (*b* Langensalza, 7 March 1621; *d* Weimar, 8 July 1681). German writer and composer. Chief poet at the Weimar court, he wrote sacred and secular poetry and set much of it to music; he was one of the most imaginative German composers of continuo songs. He was also a viol player.

Neumatic style [group style]. In plainchant, the setting of text mainly with one neume (a group of usually two or four notes written together) per syllable (e.g. in introits and communion chants). It is contrasted with syllabic style (mainly one note per syllable) and melismatic style (florid groups of notes sung to one syllable).

Neumeister, Erdmann (*b* Uichteritz, 12 May 1671; *d* Hamburg, 18 Aug 1756). German poet and theologian. A pastor (from 1715 in Hamburg), he was a leading opponent of Pietism. In his nine cycles of church cantata texts, he reformed the genre by including opera-like poetry. Telemann set the 1711 and 1714 cycles, and J.S. Bach five texts from them.

Neumes. Notational signs used in the Middle Ages that represented specific kinds of melodic motion and manners of performance. They are mainly associated with vocal music, especially the plainchant of the Western, Byzantine and Orthodox churches and the Buddhist chant of India. Each neume may represent anything from a single note to a group of four notes. Even within western Europe, there exist many different neumatic systems, used at different periods, for example those in the MSS from St Gall, Switzerland, in the 10th century, the Beneventan neumes used in Italy in the 12th century, and the Aquitanian neumes of southern France a little later (this notation eventually became dominant). *See also* CHEIRONOMY; EKPHONETIC NOTATION.

Neupert. German firm of piano and harpsichord makers. Founded in 1868 by Johann Christoph Neupert (1848–1921) as piano builders, it added harpsichords, clavichords and fortepianos to its production in 1907–8. The harpsichords are typical of the pre-1939 modern German school (heavily constructed, open at the bottom), though from 1970 the firm also followed 18th-century prototypes.

Neusidler, Hans (*b* Bratislava, *c*1508–9; *d* Nuremberg, 2 Feb 1563). German composer and lutenist, a principal figure in early German lute music. From 1530 he lived in Nuremberg as a lute teacher and maker. His eight lutebooks (1536–49) contain arrangements of German and Italian vocal music, dances and preludes; the first includes his own lute method, the earliest to give left-hand fingering.

Neusidler, Melchior (*b* Nuremberg, 1531; *d* Augsburg, 1590). German lutenist and composer, son of Hans Neusidler. From *c*1552 he worked in Augsburg, visiting Italy (1565–6) and Innsbruck (1580–81), where he was briefly employed. His two lutebooks of 1566, in Italian tablature, contain arrangements of vocal works, dances and imitative ricercares; another (1574) includes comments on tuning. His brother Conrad (1541–*c*1604) was also a lutenist and composer.

Neveu, Ginette (*b* Paris, 11 Aug 1919; *d* San Miguel, Azores, 28 Oct 1949). French violinist. She appeared with the Colonne Orchestra in Paris at the age of seven. After study with Enescu and Flesch she toured widely from 1935; her London début was in 1945. Her playing was distinguished by a strong emotional involvement and a sure sense of style.

Nevin, Ethelbert (Woodbridge) (*b* Edgeworth, PA, 25 Nov 1862; *d* New Haven, 17 Feb 1901). American composer. He wrote mainly songs and short piano pieces, which are graceful and daintily chromatic but often predictable and over-sentimental; his song *The Rosary* (1898) was particularly popular. His brother Arthur (1871–1943) was also a composer.

Newark, William (*b*?*c*1450; *d* Greenwich, 11 Nov 1509). English composer. In 1477 he was a Gentleman of the Chapel Royal and at Christmas 1492 was rewarded by Henry VII for composing a song (unnamed). The following year he became Master of the Children of the Chapel Royal, and from 1503 until his death he was responsible for devising the annual Christmas entertainment at court. His seven known works are secular songs, competent and often charming.

New England Conservatory. Boston conservatory. It was established in 1867 and had nearly 1500 students by 1881. Directors have included George Chadwick and Gunther Schuller (1967–77), under whom its programmes expanded to include courses in early and Afro-American music.

New German school. Term for the group of musicians associated with Liszt in the mid-19th century, including Cornelius, von Bülow and Raff; they championed such 'progressive' composers as Berlioz and Wagner for their advanced harmonic language and their interest in music as expressing literary or pictorial ideas, as opposed to the more conservative 'absolute' music favoured by their sturdiest opponent, Brahms.

Newman, Alfred (*b* New Haven, 17 March 1900; *d* Los Angeles, 17 Feb 1970). American composer. A pupil of Goldmark in New York and Schoenberg in California, he went to Hollywood in 1930 and worked as a composer and conductor of film music. He was a key figure in American film music, among the first to establish the Hollywood romantic, symphonic style (e.g. in *The Prisoner of Zenda*, 1937; *The Hunchback of Notre Dame*, 1939).

Newman, Ernest [Roberts, William] (*b* Everton, 30 Nov 1868; *d* Tadworth, 7 July 1959). English music critic. He was the most celebrated British music critic in the early 20th century. He studied at Liverpool University and became a bank clerk, then studied music (among other subjects) and wrote his first book (on Gluck) in 1895. In 1905 he joined the *Manchester Guardian* as music critic; he soon moved to the *Birmingham Daily Post*, *The Observer* and in 1920 to *The Sunday Times*, where he remained until 1958. Newman wrote books on Beethoven, Liszt, Strauss and Elgar, but it is chiefly for his four-volume *Life of Richard Wagner* (1933–47), a monumental biography that has still not been surpassed, that he is remembered. He also wrote a valuable series of books, *Opera Nights*, *More Opera Nights* and *Wagner Nights*, with detailed analyses and historical commentary. As a critic, he aimed for scientific precision in evaluation; his writing is closely argued yet marked by its lively humanity.

Newman, William S(tein) (*b* Cleveland, 6 April

1912). American musicologist. He studied at Western Reserve University and Columbia, and taught at the University of North Carolina from 1945. He has written valuably on performing practice but is noted for his three-volume *History of the Sonata Idea* (1959), a study of the term and its applications from the Baroque to the early 20th century.

New Music America (USA). Annual (summer or autumn) festival inaugurated in New York in 1979; it is held in various places and is the largest contemporary music festival in the USA.

New Opera Company. British company founded in Cambridge in 1957 to promote contemporary British opera and other 20th-century works in English. It became associated with Sadler's Wells Opera and gave the London première of Stravinsky's *The Rake's Progress* at Sadler's Wells Theatre in its first season.

New Orleans jazz. A style of small-ensemble JAZZ that originated before World War I and became widely known through recordings in the 1920s; it involves a degree of improvisation, using formulae and conventional figurations.

New Orleans Opera. American company founded in 1943 by Walter Loubart. Seasons (Nov–May) are at New Orleans Theater of the Performing Arts (opened 1973). Its repertory emphasizes 19th-century French works.

New Orleans Philharmonic Symphony Orchestra. American orchestra founded in 1936; its home is the Orpheum Theater. Arthur Zack was its first conductor; his successors included Philippe Entremont (1979–86) and Maxim Shostakovich (from 1986).

New Philharmonia Orchestra. *See* PHILHARMONIA ORCHESTRA.

Newport Jazz Festival. *See* KOOL JAZZ FESTIVAL.

New South Wales State Conservatorium of Music. Australian conservatory founded in Sydney in 1915. Directors have included Alfred Hill, Sir Eugene Goossens and Sir Bernard Heintze.

New Wave. A type of ROCK music developed in the late 1970s. The term was at first a milder synonym for PUNK ROCK, but came to refer to a clearcut, lean style of pop-rock.

New World, From the [Z nového světa]. Sub-title of Dvořák's Symphony no.9 in E minor (1893), in which some melodies are akin to American folktunes.

New York City Opera. Company founded in 1943 as the City Center Opera Company. Its home (since 1966) has been the New York State Theater at Lincoln Center (cap. 2737). Young musicians and audiences have always been encouraged. Julius Rudel (director 1957–79) presented a broad repertory, stressing ensemble production rather than the star system. Under Beverly Sills (director from 1979) musical comedy was introduced, with an annual (spring) season from 1986.

New York Philharmonic Orchestra. American orchestra founded in 1842; it was first conducted by Ureli Corelli Hill (with D.-G. Etienne and H.C. Timm). Its home is Avery Fisher Hall at Lincoln Center. In the 1920s it absorbed other orchestras, including the New York SO, and became the Philharmonic–Symphony Society Orchestra. It has had many renowned conductors (including Mengelberg, Furtwängler and Walter) and a changing repertory: Bernstein (1958–69) gave new American works, Boulez (1971–8) introduced unfamiliar works from the 18th century to the 20th, Mehta (from 1978) returned to mainly standard repertory. Broadcasts began in 1922, children's concerts in 1924, tours abroad in 1930 (with Toscanini). Seasons include free park concerts and festivals.

New York Pro Musica. American ensemble and school founded in 1952 as Pro Musica Antiqua by Noah Greenberg, who aimed to revive early music through study and performance. Its medieval drama productions were televised, recorded and taken abroad. Many members of performing groups in the USA trained there. It ceased in 1974.

New York Symphony Orchestra. American orchestra founded in 1878 by Leopold Damrosch. It was the first American orchestra to tour Europe (1920). In 1928 it merged with the Philharmonic Society orchestra (*see* NEW YORK PHILHARMONIC ORCHESTRA).

Nibelung's Ring, The. *See* RING DES NIBELUNGEN, DER.

Niccolò da Perugia (*fl* Florence, late 14th century). Italian composer. His works include settings of the Florentine poet Sacchetti and point to musical activities in Florence. His two-voice madrigals and caccias reveal Jacopo da Bologna's influence. He also cultivated the ballate with a one-line *ripresa* and with the moralizing content favoured in Florentine circles.

Nichelmann, Christoph (*b* Treuenbrietzen, 13 Aug 1717; *d* Berlin, 1761/2). German composer. He was a pupil of Keiser, Telemann and Mattheson in Hamburg and served noble families. Moving to Berlin in 1739, he studied with Quantz and C.H. Graun, and in 1745–56 was (with C.P.E. Bach) a harpsichordist to Frederick the Great. Like other Berlin composers, he wrote keyboard concertos (at least 16) with early Classical features; his other works include sinfonias, keyboard sonatas, vocal pieces and two treatises.

Nicholson, Richard (*fl* 1595; *d* Oxford, 1639). English composer. From 1595 he was *Informator choristarum* (and probably organist) at Magdalen College, Oxford (BMus, 1596), and from 1626 taught music in the university. He wrote a few anthems, consort songs and madrigals and contributed to *The Triumphes of Oriana* (1601).

Nicolai, (Carl) Otto (Ehrenfried) (*b* Kaliningrad, 9 June 1810; *d* Berlin, 11 May 1849). German composer and conductor. He studied in Berlin (with Zelter) and in Rome (with Baini), where he was organist at the Prussian Embassy chapel (1833–6). Contact with the theatre led him to drop contrapuntal studies and turn to composing opera. He made a reputation in Trieste and Turin before becoming principal conductor at the Vienna Hofoper (1841–7), where his uncompromising standards, and energy in founding the Vienna Philharmonic Concerts, made a great impact. In 1848 he returned to Berlin as opera Kapellmeister and cathedral choir director. His new German opera *Die lustigen Weiber von Windsor* (1849), which brought to a peak the bourgeois Romantic comic opera and his own creativity, was his masterpiece, reconciling his conflicting imaginative and intellectual impulses. His church and orchestral music is conventional, while his partsongs and choruses show his penchant for felicitous melodies.

Nicolai, Philipp (*b* Mengeringhausen, 10 Aug 1556; *d* Hamburg, 26 Oct 1608). German theologian, poet and composer. He is known for two songs (using traditional melodies), *Wie schön leuchtet der Morgenstern* and *Wachet auf* (1599), both important in Protestant church music history.

Nicolet, Aurèle (*b* Neuchâtel, 22 Jan 1926). Swiss flautist. He studied in Zurich and with Moyse in Paris, and was solo flautist in the Berlin PO, under Furtwängler, 1950–59. He taught in Berlin and Freiburg, and later in Basle. His playing of Bach and Mozart show his stylistic assurance, fine phrasing and French tonal quality; he has played and recorded much new music.

Nicolini [Grimaldi, Nicolo] (*b* Naples, bap. 5 April 1673; *d* there, 1 Jan 1732). Italian alto castrato. He sang first in Naples, notably in operas by A. Scarlatti. In 1708–12 and 1715–17 he sang in London and was largely responsible for the growing popularity of Italian opera there, appearing in many performances. The leading male singer of his day and a fine actor, he created the title roles in Handel's *Rinaldo* and *Amadigi*.

Nicolini [Niccolini], **Giuseppe** (*b* Piacenza, 29 Jan 1762; *d* there, 18 Dec 1842). Italian composer. He studied in Naples. Though he was one of the last representatives of the old Neapolitan school, between 1793 and 1820 producing *c*51 operas (largely using stereotyped formulae), his works were performed by the best virtuosos and attracted an enormous public; *Traiano in Dacia* (1807) enjoyed particular favour. From 1819 he was *maestro di cappella* in Piacenza, devoting himself increasingly to sacred composition.

Niedermeyer, (Abraham) Louis (*b* Nyon, 27 April 1802; *d* Paris, 14 March 1861). Swiss composer and educationist. He studied with Moscheles and E.A. Förster in Vienna, then in Rome and Naples, where he formed a lasting friendship with Rossini. Failure as a stage composer led him to cultivate sacred music in Paris, where he dedicated himself to reviving traditional methods of performing the Catholic liturgy. He reopened Choron's school of church music as the Ecole Niedermeyer and collaborated with Joseph d'Ortigue in plainsong publications. His gift for attractive melody is best seen in his songs, a genre to which he gave new life.

Niehaus, Manfred (*b* Cologne, 18 Sept 1933). German composer. He was a pupil of Zimmermann in Cologne (1954–61). He has become known for small-scale, absurd or surrealist pieces, latterly for amateur music.

Nielsen, Carl (August) (*b* Sortelung, 9 June 1865; *d* Copenhagen, 3 Oct 1931). Danish composer. He had a poor, rural upbringing, though his father was a musician and he learnt to play the violin, brass instruments and the piano. He studied at the Copenhagen Conservatory (1884–6), then continued having lessons with Orla Rosenhoff. In 1890–91 he travelled to Germany, France and Italy, and began his Brahmsian First Symphony (1892); from 1889 to 1905 he played the violin in the Danish court orchestra.

During the decade from the First Symphony to the Second ('The Four Temperaments', 1902) he developed an extended tonal style, but compacted and classical in its logic: the relatively few works of this period include the string quartets in G minor and Eb, the cantata *Hymnus amoris* and the opera *Saul and David*. Here he showed a gift for sharp musical characterization, pursued in his second opera, the comedy *Maskarade* (1906) and other works, while his parallel command of large-scale, dynamic forms was affirmed by the Third Symphony (*Sinfonia espansiva*, 1911) and the Violin Concerto (1911).

From this period he was an international figure and went abroad often to conduct his own music, while working in Copenhagen as a conductor and teacher. At the same time his music became still more individual in its progressive tonality (movements or works ending in a key different from the initial one), 'group polyphony' (the orchestra being treated as an assembly of ensembles in counterpoint), vigorous rhythmic drive and dependence on a harmony not so much of chords as of focal pitches. His chief works were still symphonies (no.4 'The Inextinguishable', 1916; no.5, 1922) and chamber pieces (F major quartet, 1919; *Serenata in vano* for quintet, 1914), but he also produced numerous songs and hymn tunes, besides incidental scores.

The range of his output remained broad during his last decade, but his textures became still more polyphonic and his ideas still more vividly characterized, bringing a conversational style, intimate or dramatic, to such works as the Sixth Symphony (*Sinfonia semplice*, 1925), the Wind Quintet (1922) and the concertos for flute (1926) and clarinet (1928). His last works, going still deeper into the great contrapuntal tradition, include the Three Motets (1929) and *Commotio* for organ (1931).

Operas Saul og David (1902); Maskarade (1906)

Orchestral music Little Suite (1888); Sym. no.1, g (1892); Sym. no.2, 'The Four Temperaments' (1902); Sym. no.3, 'Sinfonia espansiva' (1911); Sym. no.4, 'The Inextinguishable' (1916); Sym. no.5 (1922); Sym. no.6, 'Sinfonia semplice' (1925); Helios (1903); Saga-drøm (1908); Vn Conc. (1911); Pan and Syrinx (1918); Fl Conc. (1926); En fantasirejse til Faerøerne (1927); Cl Conc. (1928); Bøhmiskdansk folketone (1928)

Choral music Hymnus amoris (1897); Fynsk foraar (1921); 3 motets (1929); *c*11 occasional cantatas

Solo vocal music Melodramas, songs, incl. 40 Danish songs (1914, 1917), collab. T. Laub; 20 Popular Melodies (1921); 10 Little Danish Songs (1924)

Chamber music Str qts, g, G, f, Eb, F (1888, 1888, 1890, 1898, 1919); 2 vn sonatas (1895, 1912); Serenata in vano, cl, bn, hn, vc, db (1914); Wind Qnt (1922)

Piano music Chaconne (1916); Theme and Variations (1917); Suite (1920); 3 Pieces (1928)

Organ music 29 Little Preludes (1929); Commotio (1931)

Nielsen, Ludvig (*b* Borge in Østfold, 3 Feb 1906).

Norwegian composer and organist. He studied in Oslo and Leipzig, and in 1935 became organist and choirmaster at Trondheim Cathedral. He is considered one of the finest Scandinavian organists and is among the leading Norwegian church music composers.

Nielsen, Riccardo (b Bologna, 3 March 1908). Italian composer. He was a pupil of Gatti and later director of the Ferrara Conservatory. His works were at first in a style akin to Casella's and Stravinsky's but in the 1940s he adopted 12-note procedures (e.g. in the monodrama *L'incubo*, 1948).

Niemann, Walter (b Hamburg, 10 Oct 1876; d Leipzig, 17 June 1953). German composer and writer on music. He studied at the Leipzig Conservatory, becoming a teacher abd critic in Leipzig; he also composed prolifically for the piano and wrote numerous books, notably on the history of piano music.

Nietzsche, Friedrich (Wilhelm) (b Röcken, 15 Oct 1844; d Weimar, 25 Aug 1900). German philosopher. His significance for musical aesthetics is the distinction he drew between the 'Romantic' and the 'Dionysian', which led to the repudiation of Romanticism as a product of sickness. He applied it to Wagner's music, which he had originally championed; his volte-face anticipated the 20th-century reaction against all that is over-burdened, over-decorated and heavy in 19th-century art. Many musical works have been inspired by his writings, particularly *Also sprach Zarathustra*.

Niewiadomski, Stanislaw (b Saposzyn, 4 Nov 1859; d Lwów, 15 Aug 1936). Polish composer. A pupil of Paderewski and Jadassohn, he taught at the conservatories of Lwów (1887–1914) and Warsaw (from 1919). He was one of the greatest Polish song composers; his songs, many extremely popular, are characterized by melodic richness, simple rhythm and colourful harmony and they often incorporate folk elements.

Nigg, Serge (b Paris, 6 June 1924). French composer. He studied with Messiaen at the Paris Conservatoire and with Leibowitz, and like his fellow student Boulez adopted 12-note serialism. His communist sympathies led him to adopt a more immediate style in the 1950s; later works have tended to be exuberantly eclectic. A characteristic of his music is a mixture of tenderness and aggressiveness reminiscent of Ravel, with whom he has a deep affinity. His most important pieces are orchestral, with or without voices; *Visages d'Axel* (1967) is an accomplished example.

Nightingale, The [Solovey]. Opera in three acts by Stravinsky to a libretto by the composer and S. Mitusov after Hans Andersen (1914, Paris).

Night on the Bare Mountain [St John's Night on the Bare Mountain; Ivanova noch' na Lïsoy gore]. Orchestral work by Musorgsky (1867) after Gogol's story *St John's Eve*; it is well known in a revision by Rimsky-Korsakov.

Night Ride and Sunrise [Öinen ratsastus ja auringonnousu]. Tone poem, op.55, by Sibelius (1907).

Nights in the Gardens of Spain. *See* NOCHES EN LOS JARDINES DE ESPAÑA.

Nikisch, Arthur (b Lébényi Szent Miklós, 12 Oct 1855; d Leipzig, 23 Jan 1922). Austro-Hungarian conductor. He studied at the Vienna Conservatory and played the violin in the Vienna Court Orchestra under Brahms, Liszt, Verdi and Wagner. In 1879 he became principal conductor of the opera at Leipzig, soon winning international renown; he held posts with the Gewandhaus Orchestra, the Boston SO, the Budapest Opera and the Berlin PO, and was guest conductor of the Amsterdam Concertgebouw Orchestra, the Vienna PO and the LSO. Famous for the passionate yet controlled string tone he elicited and for his flexible sense of tempo, he excelled in the music of Beethoven, Schumann, Brahms, Bruckner, Tchaikovsky and Wagner, becoming the most influential conductor of his day.

Nilsson, (Märta) Birgit (b West Karup, 17 May 1918). Swedish soprano. After study in Stockholm she sang at the Royal Opera there from 1946. Her international career developed in 1954–5, with Wagner's Elsa at Bayreuth and Brünnhilde in Munich. She sang at Covent Garden from 1957 and at the Met from 1959. She was a distinguished Electra and Turandot but it was as a Wagner interpreter that she was most valued; her bright and powerful voice, perfect in intonation, made her a worthy successor to Flagstad. She retired from the stage in 1982.

Nilsson, Bo (b Skelleftehamn, 1 May 1937). Swedish composer. In the late 1950s he was a notable follower of Boulez and Stockhausen; in the 1960s he turned to late Romanticism (*Entrée*, 1962), writing film scores of simple, Swedish lyricism. He is one of the most enigmatic and gifted postwar Swedish composers. Characteristic of his music is the use of silvery percussion sounds as a backcloth for finely wrought vocal or flute (often alto flute) lines and a feeling for miniature, calculated forms (*Szene I–II* for chamber orchestra, 1961). The fourth *Szene* (1975) includes a jazz saxophone and chorus.

Nilsson, Christine (b Sjöabol, 20 Aug 1843; d Stockholm, 22 Nov 1921). Swedish soprano. With a pure and brilliant voice, immensely flexible and perfectly even, she was outstanding as Thomas's Ophelia and Mignon and Gounod's Marguerite. Berwald wrote *The Queen of Golconda* for her but she never sang in it.

Nilsson, Torsten (b Höör, 21 Jan 1920). Swedish composer and church musician. He studied in Stockholm (1938–43) and with Heiller in Vienna (1961–3) and has worked as an organist and choirmaster in Köping, Helsingborg and Stockholm. His compositions, often forceful and dramatically intense, attempt to break barriers between sacred and secular styles; they include pioneering church operas, oratorios and instrumental music.

Nimsgern, Siegmund (b St Wendel, 14 Jan 1940). German baritone. He first appeared at Saarbrücken Opera, but later his career became international, with appearances in London (Amfortas, *Parsifal*, 1973), La Scala (Jokanaan, *Salome*, 1974) and the Met (Pizarro, *Fidelio*, 1978). His repertory is wide but his well-focussed voice and approach to interpretation suit him particularly well to Wagner and Strauss.

Nin (y Castellanos), Joaquín (*b* Havana, 29 Sept 1879; *d* there, 24 Oct 1949). Cuban composer. He studied in Barcelona and the piano with Moszkowski in Paris, becoming internationally known as an exponent of Bach and early Spanish music. His works include songs and piano pieces influenced by Spanish Baroque music and French impressionism.

Nin-Culmell, Joaquín (María) (*b* Berlin, 5 Sept 1908). American composer and pianist of Cuban origin. He studied in Paris and Spain (with Falla), settling in the USA in 1938. He wrote a Mass for the consecration of St Mary's Cathedral, San Francisco (1970), and the opera *La celestina* (1965–80), as well as instrumental and chamber pieces and songs with strong Spanish elements.

Ninna (It.). A lullaby or Christmas pastorale.

Ninot le Petit [Johannes Baltazar] (*b* Rome, Dec 1501–16 June 1502). Franco-Netherlands composer. Under his real name (Baltazar) he was a singer in the Sistine Chapel from 1488 until his death. Highly regarded by his contemporaries, he was principally a composer of *chansons*, in which he paraphrased popular melodies. Four lengthy motets, in the most advanced style of the day, fusing Italian harmonic clarity and Netherlands skill, and a mass by him also survive.

Ninth chord. A chord which, when arranged in close position with its fundamental (root) in the bass, encompasses the interval of a 9th.

Nissen, Georg Nikolaus (*b* Haderslev, 22 Jan 1761; *d* Salzburg, 24 March 1826). Danish music historian and diplomat. He married Mozart's widow Constanze in 1809, and wrote a biography of Mozart (1828; completed by J.H. Feuerstein) which remains a basic source on the composer.

Nivers, Guillaume Gabriel (*b* ?Paris, *c*1632; *d* Paris, 30 Nov 1714). French organist, composer and theorist. He was organist of St Sulpice, Paris, and also became an organist of the royal chapel (1678), master of music to the queen (1681) and music director at the Maison Royale de St Louis (1686). His three *Livres d'orgue* (1665–75) contain organ versets for alternation with the choir in the divine service. Their use of both traditional church forms (*cantus firmus* movements, preludes and fugues) and secular forms, and their idiomatic organ style, greatly influenced later French organ works. Nivers also wrote sacred vocal music, edited Gregorian chant and wrote four theoretical works, notably *Traité de la composition* (1667).

Nixon in China. Opera in two acts by John Adams to a libretto by Alice Goodman (1987, Houston).

Nō [noh]. A genre of Japanese musical dance-drama. Nō plays are accompanied by the *nōkan* (transverse flute), *kotsuzumi* and *ōtsuzumi* (hourglass drums) and the *shimedaiko* (barrel drum), termed collectively the *hayashi*.

Nobilissima visione. Dance legend in six scenes by Hindemith on the life of St Francis of Assisi (1938, London).

Nobilmente (It.). Nobly, majestically.

Noble, Dennis (William) (*b* Bristol, 25 Sept 1899; *d* Javea, 14 March 1966). English baritone. He was singing at Bristol Cathedral and in a cinema when he was invited to audition for Covent Garden, where he

was particularly successful in Verdi and Puccini and in new music. He sang in the première of Walton's *Belshazzar's Feast* (1931) and was always associated with the work, to which his firm, vigorous voice was ideally suited.

Noblemen and Gentlemen's Catch Club. *See* CATCH CLUB.

Nobre, Marlos (*b* Recife, 18 Feb 1939). Brazilian composer. He was a pupil of Koellreutter and Guarnieri in São Paulo (1960–62) and of Ginastera at the Di Tella Institute (1963–4). His music uses avant-garde and Brazilian elements.

Noces, Les [Svadebka: 'The wedding']. Choreographic scenes (four) by Stravinsky for soprano, mezzo-soprano, tenor and bass soloists, chorus, four pianos and percussion to texts compiled by the composer from traditional Russian sources (1923, Paris).

Noches en los jardines de España. Symphonic impressions by Falla for piano and orchestra (1916).

Nocturne. A title used by Field, Chopin, Fauré and others for piano pieces suggesting night and usually quiet and meditative in character. Orchestral nocturnes include one in Mendelssohn's incidental music for *A Midsummer Night's Dream* and Debussy's *Trois nocturnes*.

Nocturnes. Orchestral work by Debussy in three parts: *Nuages*, *Fêtes* and *Sirènes* (with women's chorus) (1899).

Noël. Term used since the 15th century for French non-liturgical Christmas verses sung to the tunes of chant, popular songs or dances. Collections appeared in the 16th century and arrangements for instruments were made in the 17th and 18th. With the French Revolution the genre fell from favour, but it was revived in the late 19th century with more symphonically conceived examples for organ by Franck, Guilmant and (in the 20th) Tournemire.

Nola, Giovanni Domenico del Giovane da (*b* Nola, 1510–20; *d* Naples, May 1592). Italian composer. He was appointed *maestro di cappella* at the Ss Annunziata, Naples, in 1563; under his leadership the choir made an outstanding contribution to the city's musical life. He published two volumes of *Canzoni villanesche* (1541), containing 31 villanesche and 11 mascheratas for three voices, and several books of madrigals; they use expressive dissonances, mainly imitative textures and, sometimes, advanced harmonic language. He also published a book of motets for five voices.

Nonet. A piece for nine solo instruments. An outstanding example is the Nonet of Spohr (op.31), for five wind instruments and four strings.

Non-harmonic note. In part-writing, a note that is not consonant with the other notes of the chord to which it belongs and must therefore be 'resolved', usually by step, to a note that is consonant in the next chord. Among common types are the passing note, anticipation, auxiliary note, 'échappée', cambiata and appoggiatura.

Nono, Luigi (*b* Venice, 29 Jan 1924). Italian composer. He studied with Malipiero at the Venice Conservatory (1941–5) and with Maderna and Scherchen, both of whom orientated him towards 12-note serialism (he married Schoenberg's daughter Nuria in

1955). His avant-garde partisanship has been inseparable from a commitment to socialism, twin aspects of a revolt against bourgeois culture: hence his avoidance of normal concert genres in favour of opera and electronic music, his frequent recourse to political texts and his work in bringing music to factories. His works include the operas *Intolleranza 1960* (1961) and *Al gran sole carico d'amore* (1975), the cantata *Il canto sospeso* (1956), orchestral works and tape pieces. Much of his music of the 1950s and 1960s has a fervent lyricism; later works have tended to be more pessimistic (*Ein Gespenst geht um in der Welt*, 1971).

Dramatic music Intolleranza 1960 (1961); Al gran sole carico d'amore (1975)
Ballet Il mantello rosso (1954)
Orchestral music Variazioni canoniche (1950); Composizione no.1 (1951), no.2 (1959); Due espressioni (1953); Incontri (1955); Varianti (1957); Per Bastiana Tai-Yang Cheng (1967)
Chamber music Polifonica – monodia – ritmica (1951); Canti per 13 (1955); Sofferrte onde sereee (1976); Con Luigi Dallapiccola (1979); Fragmente-Stille (1980)
Choral music Epitaffio per Federico Garcia Lorca (1953); Liebeslied (1954); La victoire de Guernica (1954); Il canto sospeso (1956); La terra e la compagna (1958); Cori di Didone (1958); Y entonces comprendió (1970); Ein Gespenst geht um in der Welt (1971); Das atmende Klarsein (1981)
Other vocal music Ha venido (1960); Sarà dolce tacere (1960); Canti di vita e d'amore (1962); Canciones a Guiomar (1963); La fabbrica illuminata (1964); A floresta è jovem e cheja de vida (1967); Un volto e del mare (1960); Como una ola de fuerza y luz (1972); Siamo la gioventù del Vietnam (1973); Quando stanno morendo (1982); Guai ai gelidi mostri (1983); Prometeo (1984)
Tape Omaggio a Emilio Vedova (1960); Ricorda cose ti hanno fatto in Auschwitz (1966); Contrappunto dialettico alla mente (1968); Non consumiamo Marx (1969); Musiche per Manzu (1969); Für Paul Dessau (1974)

Noordt, Anthoni van (*b* Amsterdam, bur. 23 March 1675). Netherlands composer. He worked in Amsterdam, latterly at the Nieuwe Kerk, and published a book of organ pieces (1659) in the style of Sweelinck. Among the other musicians in his family were the composer, flautist and organist Jacob van Noordt (1619–after 1679) and the organist and composer Sybrand van Noordt (bur. 1705), probably his brother and son respectively.

Nordheim, Arne (*b* Larvik, 20 June 1931). Norwegian composer. He studied at the Oslo Conservatory (1948–52) and in the late 1960s began touring internationally as a performer of live electronic music. His early works are traditional, but since the late 1950s he has used avant-garde methods. He has written orchestral pieces, some with tape or voices (e.g. the ballet *Katharsis*, 1962; *Epitaffio*, 1963), but also for small combinations as well as live electronic music.

Nordica [Norton], Lillian (*b* Farmington, ME, 12 Dec 1857; *d* Batavia, 10 May 1914). American soprano. She studied in Boston and made her New York début in 1876 before further training in Milan, where she made her opera début in 1879 as Mozart's Donna Elvira. Her Paris début was as Gounod's Marguerite (1882) and she appeared at Covent Garden as Violetta (1887). She made her Met début in 1891 and was especially known for her Wagner roles

there (1893–1909); her success was more the result of hard work than natural gifts.

Nordoff, Paul (*b* Philadelphia, 4 June 1909; *d* Herdecke, 18 Jan 1977). American composer. He studied with Goldmark at the Juilliard School and was a conventional composer before in 1959 devoting his energies to music therapy, on which he wrote several books (with C. Robbins).

Nordraak, Rikard (*b* Oslo, 12 June 1842; *d* Berlin, 20 March 1866). Norwegian composer. He studied in Berlin and Oslo and became a member of the New Norwegian Society. Apart from his music for the Norwegian national anthem *Ja, vi elsker dette landet* (1864), his importance lies in the musical nationalism he generated in his contemporaries, especially in his friend Grieg.

Norfolk and Norwich Triennial Festival of Music and the Arts (UK). Autumn festival established in 1824. It has commissioned works and presented many premières, mainly of choral music; events include orchestral and choral concerts and exhibitions.

Norfolk Rhapsody. Orchestral work by Vaughan Williams (1906).

Nørgård, Per (*b* Gentofte, 13 July 1932). Danish composer. He studied with Holmboe (from 1949) at the Copenhagen Conservatory (1952–5) and in Paris with Boulanger (1956–7), and has taught at the conservatories of Odense (1958–61), Copenhagen (1960–65) and Århus (from 1965). He has occupied a central position among younger Danish composers as a leader and originator of ideas. His earliest works were post-Sibelian and a feeling for slow harmonic growth survived his contact with the avant garde in the late 1950s: but from that time, while composing the instrumental series *Fragmenter*, he adopted a system for establishing intervallic hierarchies in textures that are often repetitive, sometimes suggesting (though independent of) American minimalism. He used this in the ballet *The Young Man Shall Marry* (1965). His works include operas, four symphonies (1954–81) and much vocal and chamber music.

Nørholm, Ib (*b* Copenhagen, 24 Jan 1931). Danish composer. He studied with Holmboe at the Copenhagen Conservatory (1950–56), where he began teaching in 1961. His large output, in most genres, shows a development from works in a post-Nielsen, tonal, lyrical tradition to a moderate use of avant-garde techniques. He has been part of a Danish movement in which simplicity of conception (reacting against avant-garde complexity) and accessibility for the listener are main concerns. His use of collage reflects this aim (e.g. in the third and fourth of his five string quartets). He has also written operas, symphonies, chamber and piano music.

Norma. Opera in two acts by Bellini to a libretto by Romani after Soumet (1831, Milan).

Norman, Barak (*b c*1670; *d* London, *c*1740). English string instrument maker. He was the most important early English maker, noted for his viols and lutes; he also made violins and was one of the earliest English cello makers. His work is characterized by beautiful modelling, good wood and very dark brown varnish; the tone is strong and rich. Early specimens are highly arched but later ones have medium arching and elaborate double purfling. The earliest recorded label (on a viol) is dated 1690.

Norman, Jessye (*b* Augusta, GA, 15 Sept 1945). American soprano, After study in the USA she made her début in Berlin in 1969 as Wagner's Elisabeth. She made her La Scala and Covent Garden débuts in 1972, as Aida and Berlioz's Cassandra. In the 1970s she turned increasingly to concert work, but in 1985 returned to Covent Garden as Strauss's Ariadne. Her large, resplendent voice is capable of uncommon refinement of nuance.

Norman, (Fredrik Vilhelm) Ludvig (*b* Stockholm, 28 Aug 1831; *d* there, 28 March 1885). Swedish composer and conductor. After training in Leipzig, he settled in Stockholm, teaching at the conservatory, conducting the royal orchestra and founding the Nya Harmoniska Sällskapet. As a pianist he accompanied the violinist Wilma Neruda (his wife, 1864–9). His well-crafted works, including three symphonies and chamber music, show the influence of Mendelssohn, Gade and Schumann.

Norrington, Roger (Arthur Carver) (*b* Oxford, 16 March 1934). English conductor. He studied at Cambridge and the RCM, sang as a professional tenor, 1962–70, and founded choirs specializing in the music of Schütz and Monteverdi. He was musical director of Kent Opera, 1969–84, conducting many performances of operas, from Monteverdi to Verdi, in period performances. With his groups the London Baroque and London Classical Players, giving performances of many repertory works of the 18th and early 19th centuries (including arresting ones of Haydn's *Creation* and Beethoven's symphonies), he has done much to make a wider public aware of the significance of period-style performance.

North, Alex (*b* Chester, PA, 4 Dec 1910). American composer. He studied at the Juilliard School and in Moscow and was a pupil of Copland and Toch. In the 1950s he became a leading Hollywood composer after the success of *A Streetcar Named Desire* (1951); he has also written music for dance.

North, the Hon. Roger (*b* ?Tostock, *c*1651; *d* Rougham, March 1734). English author. He was an amateur musician, and after working as a lawyer wrote on music and many other subjects. His musical writings (including *The Musicall Grammarian*, 1728) show an exceptional breadth and shrewdness, dealing with aesthetics, theory, performing practice etc; he may be called the first English music critic. His brother Francis (1637–85), 1st Baron Guilford, was also a lawyer, musician and author.

North Country Sketches. Orchestral work by Delius (1914).

Northern Sinfonia. British orchestra established in 1961 in Newcastle upon Tyne by Michael Hall. The first permanent British chamber orchestra, it performs throughout Britain and abroad. The Sinfonia Chorus was formed in 1973.

Nose, The [Nos]. Opera in three acts by Shostakovich to a libretto by E. Zamyatin, G. Ionin and A. Preys after Gogol (1930, Leningrad).

Nose flute. A flute sounded by nasal breath. Such flutes are common in the Pacific Islands and Southeast Asia. Their origin may lie in the association of nasal breath with magic and religious rites.

Noske, Frits (Rudolf) (*b* The Hague, 13 Dec 1920). Dutch musicologist. He studied at Amsterdam, The Hague and in Paris and has taught at Leiden, Amsterdam and elsewhere. His work ranges widely, from French 19th-century song to Dutch Baroque music, Italian opera and musical sociology. His brother, Willem Noske (*b* 1918), is a leading violinist, specializing in early Dutch and Italian music.

Noskowski, Zygmunt (*b* Warsaw, 2 May 1846; *d* there, 23 July 1909). Polish composer and conductor. His teachers in Warsaw included Moniuszko; later he studied in Berlin. He contributed much to Warsaw musical life, directing the Music Society, the Philharmonic Orchestra and the Opera and teaching a generation of Polish composers. Though most of his numerous works are conservative, he composed the first Polish symphonic poem (*The Steppe*, 1896–7) and made the first attempts at a musical drama.

Nota cambiata (It.: 'changed note'). A term introduced in the 17th century for an accented passing note but which has come to mean an unaccented non-harmonic note that is quitted by a leap of a 3rd downwards (or by extension upwards). See ex.1.

Ex. 1

Notari, Angelo (*b* Padua, 14 Jan 1566; *d* London, Dec 1663). Italian composer. He was in England from 1610–11, serving Prince Henry and (by 1618) Prince Charles (later Charles II). His book of monodies, chamber duets and canzonettas (*c*1613) helped introduce modern Italian styles in England.

Notation. A visual analogue of musical sound, intended either as a record of sound heard or imagined, or as a set of visual instructions for performers.

The earliest known forms of notation seem to have been through hand signs (*see* CHEIRONOMY). The first alphabetical system is Greek and probably existed by 500BC. The Chinese had a system by the 3rd century BC. A system of EKPHONETIC NOTATION existed for Hebrew biblical texts by the 6th century AD. But the first substantial neume system in the West dates from the 9th century, from St Gall, Switzerland. Two centuries later, neumes were in use in the Eastern church; in the West, the staff, the Guidonian hand (a type of cheironomy) and SOLMIZATION syllables had been invented by Guido of Arezzo. His system of staff notation was widely copied in western Europe, existing for a time alongside neumatic notations.

In the 13th century, Franco of Cologne codified a rhythmic system (*see* MENSURATION). Franco also codified the LIGATURE system. Rhythmic notation was further modified by Philip de Vitry early in the 14th century; other modifications involving varied subdivisions of the breve, introduced by Petrus de Cruce, were used in Italy, leading to a complex system ('mannered notation'). During the 15th, the system of notation with black note-heads gradually gave way to one where white note-heads were used, basically as they are today. The rhythmic notation of the mensuration system used a system of circles and broken circles (like the letters O and C), sometimes with a dot in the middle, to indicate to the performer the triple or duple relationship between successive note values. A system of proportional signs, in the form of vertical strokes through the circles, or using figures, could indicate a change in note values. For example, a diminution of note values in the ratio 2:3 would be shown as the fraction 3/2; for the particular case of halving, a vertical stroke through the mensuration sign was used. The modern system of time signatures could arise only when music came to be regularly barred; here the rhythmic structure is shown by two figures, the lower signifying the unit of measurement (4 is a crotchet or a quarter-note, 8 a quaver or eighth-note), the upper the number of such units in the bar. Thus 3/2 represents a bar with three minims or half-notes; 4/4 represents one with four crotchets or quarter-notes. Where the upper numeral is a multiple of three, the time is 'compound' and the notes of the unit defined by the lower number are grouped in threes; thus 6/8 represents a bar of six quavers or eighth-notes, divided into two dotted-crotchet (dotted quarter-note) beats.

Void or white notation, with duple relationships for the most part between successive note values, and dots (when used for rhythmic purposes) serving only to augment by half the value of the notes they follow, was widely adopted by the early 16th century for both vocal and instrumental music, apart from tablatures. Printers also adopted it, as it was suitable for printing from movable type. Black note-heads, besides being used for the lesser note values, occasionally signified particular kinds of rhythmic change (such as HEMIOLA rhythms in 3/2 time). In certain special contexts, void notation for shorter notes remained in use. In 15th-century music, note-heads were generally lozenge-shaped; later, rounded note shapes replaced them.

Void notation was developed mainly for singing; for instruments, particularly plucked string instruments like the lute, and to some extent keyboard instruments, systems of TABLATURE were preferred, showing how the performer obtained a particular note rather than the note itself. Tablatures for the lute and guitar have remained in use; those for the keyboard fell out of use in the ensuing centuries. Instrumental features adopted during the 16th and 17th centuries included the bar-line, the beam (linking a group of notes of like length) and the slur, and clefs became standardized, facilitating reading. The demisemiquaver (32nd-note) and the hemidemisemiquaver (64th-note) were added to note values between the 16th and the 18th centuries, and keyboard notation used a score layout (sometimes with more than two staves to the system). In the 19th century, the vocabulary of signs for dynamics, accents and articulation was greatly extended.

There are many other aspects of notation that are imprecise: the system of ornaments, where small signs (akin to neumes) indicate how particular groups of notes are to be performed; tempo (though time signatures have a certain if ill-defined significance); volume, where dynamic marks cannot indicate precise levels; and rhythmic alteration, where music was not intended to be played exactly as notated (e.g. in the 18th-century French overture). Nor can articulation be precisely conveyed by notation. In some experimental 20th-century music, music is not notated in conventional terms and the player may be left to improvise on the basis of musical patterns, verbal instructions or even the impressions he receives from a picture or a few lines of prose.

Notched flute. An end-blown flute (open or stopped) with a U- or V-shaped notch cut or burnt into the upper rim to facilitate tone production. Notched flutes, used solo and in ensembles, are distributed across Africa, the Far East, the Pacific Islands and Central and South America.

Notes inégales (Fr.). 'Unequal notes': a rhythmic convention of French music mainly of the Baroque period according to which certain divisions of the beat move in alternately long and short values even if they are written equal. Evidence of this practice comes from several theoretical works (notably Couperin's *L'art de toucher le clavecin*, 1716) and can sometimes be inferred from the music itself. The convention applies chiefly to even quavers (when the unit of time is a crotchet) moving conjunctly (stepwise), where it specifies that the first note should be played distinctly longer than the second (vice-versa if the notes are slurred with a dot above the second). Sometimes composers indicated whether notes were to be played equal by adding an appropriate performing direction (conventional signs may be used to indicate the absence of *notes inégales*). The extent to which notes written equal should be 'unequalized' in music other than French (e.g. by Handel and Bach) remains in question; it is clear that non-French composers (e.g. Handel and Bach) occasionally expected rhythms to be adjusted, but equally clear that this was not to be done constantly or indiscriminately. Conventions akin to *notes inégales* also occur in jazz.

Note values. The relationships between note-shapes and the rhythmic values they represent were first codified in the 13th century by Franco of Cologne and others; in the ensuing period, however, a note could represent either two or three times the value of the next lower in value. The present 'orthochronic' system, in which a fixed duple relationship obtains between any note value and the next smaller, has been in use since the 16th century. The placing of a dot after a note, since that time, has indicated that the value of the note be increased by half.

Over the last 700 years, note values have slowed down, and smaller note values have come to serve as the basic unit of movement. a semibreve (or whole note) is a not eof short or moderate lenth in 15th-century music but a long note today. Normally the crotchet (or quarter-note) is now regarded as the standard pulse; in the transcription of early music, it is thereore customary to reduce note values by a factor of anything from 16 (for early medieval music)

TABLE 1

Latin	British	American	French	German	Italian	Spanish
maxima	large	–	maxime	–	massima	maxima
longa	long	–	carrée à queue	–	longa	longo
brevis	breve	double whole note, double note	carrée, brève, double-ronde	Doppelganze (-Note), Doppeltaktnote	breve	breve
semibrevis	semibreve	whole note	ronde	Ganze (-Note)	semibreve	redonda
minima	minim	half-note	blanche	Halbe (-Note)	bianca	blanca
semiminima	crotchet	quarter-note	noire	Viertel (-Note)	nera	negra
fusa	quaver	eighth-note	croche	Achtel (-Note)	croma	corchea
semifusa	semiquaver	16th-note	double croche	Sechzehntel (-Note)	semicroma	semicorchea
fusella	demisemiquaver	32nd-note	triple croche	Zweiunddreissigstel (-Note)	biscroma	fusa
fusellala	hemidemi-semiquaver	64th-note	quadruple croche	Vierundsechzigstel (-Note)	semibiscroma	semifusa

TABLE 2

British		American	Rests
semibreve		whole-note	(also used for a one-bar rest whatever the metre)
minim		half-note	
crotchet		quarter-note	
quaver		eighth-note	
semiquaver		sixteenth-note	
demisemiquaver		thirty-second-note	

ties are used to join notes together; *dots* increase a note by half its value

eval music) down to two (for 16th-century music).

The accompanying tables show the nomenclature of notes in seven languages, along with the standard forms of notes and rests, and the note shapes.

Notker (*b* nr. St Gall, *c*840; *d* there, 912). Monk of the Benedictine Abbey of St Gall, sometimes known as 'Notker Balbulus' ('the stammerer'). He was the most famous author of SEQUENCE texts in the Middle Ages, in his *Liber hymnorum* of 884, which includes an explanatory and autobiographical preface. He should not be confused with Notker Labeo (*c*950–1022), also a monk at St Gall, who wrote five short essays on musical topics.

Notre Dame School. Name for the group of musicians associated with Notre Dame Cathedral, Paris, or the previous church on the site, 1190–1210, who were credited with the development of ORGANUM.

Nottara, Constantin C. (*b* Bucharest, 1 Oct 1890; *d* there, 19 Jan 1951). Romanian composer. He studied in Bucharest, Paris (1907–9) and Berlin (1909–13), and was an orchestral violinist, quartet leader (1914–33), conductor and critic. His works include *verismo* operas, nationalist orchestral pieces and popular violin miniatures.

Notte, La [The Night]. Title of three concertos by Vivaldi: for bassoon (in B♭, RV501), for flute (in G minor, RV439), and a chamber concerto for flute, two violins, bassoon and continuo (in G minor, RV104).

Nottebohm, (Martin) Gustav (*b* Lüdenscheid, 12 Nov 1817; *d* Graz, 29 Oct 1882). German musicologist. After studying in Berlin and Leipzig (where he knew and was taught by Mendelssohn and Schumann), he settled in Vienna (1846), where he became a member of Brahms's circle. One of the first acknowledged experts in textual criticism, he studied Beethoven's MSS, above all the sketches and exercises, publishing his findings in important articles and monographs (1865–80). His work not only led to substantial revisions of the chronology of Beethoven's works and to an improved understanding of his creative processes but also provided procedural models and source materials for a century of Beethoven scholarship.

Notturno (It.). Term used in the 18th century for a SERENADE to be performed late at night. Mozart used it as a title for his *Serenata notturna* K239 and his Notturno K286/269a and Haydn for his eight notturnos of 1790. Several chamber works in two movements were published as notturnos, for example J.C. Bach's op.2 string trios.

Nourrit, Adolphe (*b* Montpellier, 3 March 1802; *d* Naples, 8 March 1839). French tenor. He was principal tenor at the Paris Opéra (1826–37), creating such roles as Masaniello in *La muette de Portici* (1828), Count Ory (1828), Arnold in *Guillaume Tell* (1829), Robert in *Robert le diable* (1831), Eléazar in *La juive* (1835) and Raoul in *Les Huguenots* (1836), and was noted for his intelligence and subtlety. He was appointed professor at the Conservatoire in 1827. His career declined quickly when he left Paris for Italy and he committed suicide. His father Louis (1780–1831) and his brother Auguste (1808–53) were both well-known tenors.

Nouvelles aventures. Work by Ligeti for three singers and seven instrumentalists (1965; staged 1966), a sequel to *Aventures* (1962).

Novák, Jan (*b* Nová Říše na Moravě, 8 April 1921; *d* Ulm, 17 Nov 1984). Czech composer. He studied with Petrželka at the Brno Conservatory (1940–46), with Bořkovec at the Prague Academy and with Copland and Martinů in the USA (1947–8). Under Martinů's influence he began by exploring a specifically Czech neo-classicism, as in the Oboe Concerto (1952) and the two-piano Concerto (1955); but in the late 1950s he began using 12-note methods, for example in the jazz-influenced Capriccio for cello and orchestra (1958). His dramatic gifts are seen in the oratorio *Dido* (1967). In 1970 he settled in Italy. His works include orchestral, vocal and keyboard music.

Novák, Vítězslav [Viktor] **(Augustín Rudolf)** (*b* Kamenice nad Lipou, 5 Dec 1870; *d* Skuteč, 18 July 1949). Czech composer. He studied with Jiránek and Dvořák at the Prague Conservatory (1889–92) and was powerfully influenced by the folk

music of Moravia and Slovakia, which he began to collect and study in 1896. The result was an outpouring of symphonic poems and songs, culminating in the dramatic cantata *The Storm* (1910) and the large-scale tone poem *Pan* for piano (1910). In 1909 he began teaching at the Prague Conservatory, and this occupied him more than composition in his later years, though he wrote several operas, much choral music and a few late instrumental scores, of which the *Autumn Symphony* (1934) and the *South Bohemian Suite* are representative. A skilled melodist and contrapuntist, he retained an essentially late Romantic style, supported by a meticulous technique.

Novello. London firm of music publishers. It was established in 1829 by Alfred Novello (1810–96). By concentrating mainly on cheap editions of choral works (Handel, Mendelssohn) it fostered the huge growth of interest in choral singing from the 1840s; its monthly journal, the *Musical Times* (founded 1844), began the tradition of 'octavo editions' for choral music. In the later 19th century, concert promotion and the publication of opera scores, orchestral music and school music became strong interests. Notable composers associated with the firm include Dvořák, Elgar, Bliss and Musgrave. The firm became part of the Granada group in 1970.

Novello, Ivor [Davies, David Ivor] (*b* Cardiff, 15 Jan 1893; *d* London, 6 March 1951). Welsh composer. He began his career as a composer of popular songs when he was 17 and in 1914 composed the song *Till the Boys Come Home* ('Keep the home fires burning'), which was immensely popular during World War I. He starred in his own musicals, including *Glamorous Night* (1935), *The Dancing Years* (1939) and *Jing's Rhapsody* (1949).

Novello, Vincent (*b* London, 6 Sept 1781; *d* Nice, 9 Aug 1861), English organist, choirmaster, editor and publisher of Italian origin. As organist and choirmaster at the Portuguese Embassy chapel in London, he introduced Haydn's and Mozart's masses to England, meanwhile (from 1811) editing and publishing, at his own expense, these and other collections of sacred works notably by Purcell, Boyce and Handel). His adoption of a vocal score format with keyboard accompaniment, making the music more readily accessible to amateurs, laid the foundation for the success of Novello & Co., opened commercially in 1829 by his eldest son Alfred (1810–96), whose business sense – he founded two journals, the *Musical World* (1836) and the *Musical Times* (1844), acquired the copyrights to Mendelssohn's choral works and set up as his own printer – gave tremendous impetus to the amateur choral movement in Britain. Vincent was also active in England on behalf of Mozart's family and took part in the early stages of the Bach revival. His fourth daughter, the soprano Clara Novello (1818–1908), won great acclaim as an oratorio singer.

Noverre, Jean-Georges (*b* Paris, 29 April 1727; *d* St Germain-en-Laye, 19 Oct 1810). French-Swiss choreographer. He was a dancer and ballet-master from the 1740s. After working in Lyons, Strasbourg, London and elsewhere, he served at the Stuttgart court, 1760–67; he then became ballet-master to the imperial family and the two theatres in Vienna, 1767–74. At the peak of his career, he staged c40 new ballets (music by Starzer and others) and choreographed operas including Gluck's *Alceste* (1767). Though he was less successful at Milan and Paris, his late productions in London were well received.

Like his pupil Gaspero Angiolini, Noverre helped establish the *ballet en action*, creating unified dramatic and realistic works without irrelevant spectacle and decoration. His writings, especially *Lettres sur la danse* (1760), had much influence.

Novotný, Václav Juda (*b* Vesce, 17 Sept 1849; *d* Prague, 1 Aug 1922). Czech writer on music and composer. He contributed to *Dalibor, Hudební revue* and other journals (notably on Smetana and Dvořák) and translated into Czech numerous opera librettos. A friend of Smetana's, he also accompanied Dvořák to England (1884). As a composer his reputation rests on his songs and c300 folksong arrangements.

Nowak, Leopold (*b* Vienna, 17 Aug 1904). Austrian musicologist. He studied at the Vienna Academy and Vienna University, where he took the doctorate in 1927 with a dissertation on the Gesellschaftslied of Heinrich Finck, Paul Hofhaimer and Heinrich Isaac; in 1932 he completed his *Habilitation* with a work on the history of the basso ostinato, and subsequently taught until 1973. In 1946 he became director of the Österreichische Nationalbibliothek music collection. His main scholarly work has been in preparing a critical edition of Bruckner's output, and he was personally responsible for new, revised editions of nearly all the symphonies and masses. His interests extend to Haydn, Liszt, Rezniček, Catholic church music and Austrian folk music.

Nowowiejski, Feliks (*b* Barczewo, 7 Feb 1877; *d* Poznań, 18 Jan 1946). Polish composer. A pupil of Bruch and Dvořák, he was an organist, conductor and teacher in Kraków and Poznań. He composed prolifically in most genres in a late Romantic style, his oratorio *Quo vadis* (1903) becoming popular through performances in 150 cities in Europe and the USA.

Noye's Fludde. Children's opera in one act by Britten, a setting of the Chester miracle play (1958, Aldeburgh).

Nozze di Figaro, Le. *See* MARRIAGE OF FIGARO, THE.

Nucius, Johannes (*b* Görlitz, *c*1556; *d* Himmelwitz, 25 March 1620). German theorist and composer. He was a Cistercian monk and from 1591 abbot at Himmelwitz. His counterpoint treatise, *Musices poeticae* (1613), describing 17th-century compositional practices, includes an important chapter on music-rhetorical figures. He also published over 100 motets (1591, 1609).

Nuits d'été, Les [Summer Nights]. Song cycle, op.7, by Berlioz, settings for voice and orchestra of six poems by Gautier (1841).

Nuitter [Truinet], **Charles-Louis-Etienne** (*b* Paris, 24 April 1828; *d* there, 23/24 Feb 1899). French librettist and music librarian. With collaborators he produced over 60 librettos, including some for Offenbach, Delibes and Lalo, also writing books on the Paris Opéra, of which he was archivist from 1866.

Number opera. Term for an opera consisting of individual, easily detachable sections or 'numbers', as distinct from those (e.g. Wagner's) in which the music is continuous.

Nunc dimittis. The canticle of Simeon, *Luke* ii.29–32, sung at Compline in the Latin rite and as the second canticle at the Anglican Evensong.

Nuove musiche, Le. Collection by Giulio Caccini of madrigals and songs, including a manifesto on the new style of MONODY; it was published in Florence in 1602 (dated 1601, in old style).

Nursery, The [Detskaya]. Song cycle by Musorgsky (1870), seven settings for voice and piano of his own words.

Nursery Suite. Orchestral suite by Elgar (1931).

Nut. In string instruments, the thin ridge between pegbox and fingerboard, at a right angle to them; it is usually made of hardwood, sometimes of ivory. The term 'nut' may also be applied to the heel or frog of a bow.

Nutcracker [Shchelkunchik]. Ballet in two acts and three scenes by Tchaikovsky to a libretto by M. Petipa after Alexandre Dumas *père*'s version of E.T.A. Hoffmann's story (1892, St Petersburg).

Nyckelharpa. A keyed fiddle, known since the 15th century. It was used in Scandinavia and north Germany for popular dance and festive music; it is still used in Sweden. There are generally two gut melody strings, up to three gut or wound drones and several sympathetic strings, with up to 24 wooden keys giving a nearly complete chromatic sequence. It is slung from the player's neck, held horizontally with keys downwards and bowed from below.

Nystedt, Knut (*b* Oslo, 3 Sept 1915). Norwegian composer. A pupil of Brustad at the Oslo Conservatory, he has worked as a church organist and written choral, orchestral and chamber works in a lyrically classical style, introducing 12-note elements in the mid-1950s; later works are preoccupied with timbre.

Nystroem, Gösta (*b* Silvberg, 13 Oct 1890; *d* Särö, 9 Aug 1966). Swedish composer. He studied with Lundberg, Bergenson and Hallén in Stockholm, then went to Paris (1920–32), where he had lessons from d'Indy. Back in Sweden he was a pugnacious music critic. His early works were influenced by Debussy and Ravel; in the 1930s his study of Baroque polyphony led him to a more intense dissonant style (e.g. *Sinfonia breve*, 1931). Then later his music became more harmonic: nature, especially the sea, became a stimulus as did the work of Piero della Francesca and Braque (he was himself a painter). His last works saw a return to a tauter style. As well as symphonies, symphonic poems, concertos and two late string quartets, he wrote many songs.

O

Oakeley, Sir Herbert (Stanley) (*b* London, 22 July 1830; *d* Eastbourne, 26 Oct 1903). English composer and organist. He studied at Oxford and in Leipzig and Dresden. As Reid Professor of Music at Edinburgh University (1865–91) he instituted academic reforms and founded the University Musical Society. He was music critic of *The Guardian* (1858–66) and composed much church music.

O Antiphons [Great Antiphons]. A set of seven antiphons to the Magnificat, each text beginning with 'O' ('O sapienta', 'O adonai' etc); they are sung (to the same melody of the second mode) on the seven days preceding Christmas Eve. They had entered the liturgy by the 9th century; their number increased during the Middle Ages.

Obbligato (It.). 'Necessary': term used for an independent and essential part in concerted music, secondary to the principal melody. If referring to a keyboard part, it designates a part fully written out instead of notated as a figured bass. A song with instrumental obbligato (like Schubert's *Shepherd on the Rock*, with clarinet) means one in which the obbligato instrument has an important, semi-solo role. A sonata for keyboard with violin obbligato means one in which the violin part cannot be omitted (as opposed to one with violin *ad libitum*, where it can).

Obbligo [obligo]. A 17th-century term indicating a problem which the composer chooses to set himself in a piece. The solmization symbols in Frescobaldi's *Ricercar quarto, obligo mi re fa mi*, for example, form the structural basis for the composition.

Oberek [obertas]. A Polish dance related to the MAZURKA.

Oberlin, Russell (Keys) (*b* Akron, OH, 11 Oct 1928). American countertenor. He studied at the Juilliard School and in 1952 was a founder with Noah Greenberg of the New York Pro Musica. His sweet tone and subtle phrasing made him a leading exponent of early music. He turned to teaching in the mid-1960s, from 1971 at Hunter College, New York.

Oberlin College Conservatory of Music. American music school founded near Cleveland, Ohio, in 1865 and affiliated with Oberlin College (founded 1833) from 1866. Under Fenelon B. Rice (director 1871–1901) it attained national status.

Oberon. Opera in three acts by Weber to a libretto in English by J.R. Planché after Wieland's (1826, London).

Oberthür, Charles [Karl] (*b* Munich, 4 March 1819; *d* London, 8 Nov 1895). German harpist and composer. He worked in Brussels, Mannheim and London, becoming unrivalled as a virtuoso and teacher, producing over 450 compositions and a useful harp method (op.36).

Oberto, Conte di San Bonifacio. Opera in two acts by Verdi to a libretto by A. Piazza revised by Solera (1839, Milan).

Oberwerk (Ger.). The upper chest and manual of an organ, often (since *c*1840) provided with Swell shutters. In many sources *Oberwerk* denotes *Hauptwerk*, i.e. the main chest above the player, as opposed to the Chair organ.

Oboe. The principal soprano double-reed woodwind instrument. It consists of a slender bore of hardwood, *c*59 cm long and in three sections, which open out to form a moderate bell (for illustration, *see* WOODWIND INSTRUMENTS). The reed is formed of two hollowed-out blades of thin 'cane' bound face to face to a narrow tapered metal tube (a 'staple'). At their free ends, the blades are scraped down to a feather edge: placed between the lips and blown through, they vibrate together, transmitting bursts of energy to the air column in the body. The compass of the modern oboe is $bb'-a'''$; the first 16 notes are fundamental tones, the remainder harmonics. In addition to the soprano in C, the oboe family includes the oboe d'amore in A, the english horn (cor anglais) in F and the baritone oboe in C, all distinguished by the bulb bell, of ancient origin.

The French word 'hautbois' (high-, strong-, loud- or principal-wood) was applied in its various spellings to the smaller members of the shawm family, in France and England, and these instruments had an important place in the 'loud' music of the Middle Ages. The true oboe originated *c*1660 at the French court; its creator is said to be the elder Jean Hotteterre. The new instrument reached England in 1674; *The Sprightly Companion*, an instruction book of 1695, describes it as 'not much inferior to the Trumpet' and that 'with a good reed and skilful hand it sounds as easy and soft as the flute'. Its distinguishing features included a two-octave compass and two or three keys.

The years before 1750 saw technical improvements

531

and the emergence of national characteristics. The 19th century was the period of mechanization and between 1800 and 1825 eight keys appeared, at first as alternatives to accepted fingerings or to improve intonation, but later as primary facilities. The instrument became fully chromatic from *b* upwards and the range extended to *f'''* or *a'''*. In the early 19th century, French instruments tended to sensitivity and refinement, Viennese ones favouring warmth and robustness. By 1825, Josef Sellner of the Vienna court orchestra had created an advanced '13-key oboe', which gained ascendancy in the 1830s; the French-style instrument, however, with its 'Boehm style' improvement to the key mechanism, remains predominant.

While J.M. Hotteterre wrote much to popularize the oboe in the early 18th century, works by Couperin, C.P.E. Bach and J.-B. Loeillet fully established the instrument, enabling it to become reliable in the hands of skilled players; as an alternative to the flute or violin it often appeared as a solo instrument with continuo or in the trio sonata. Handel, Albinoni and Vivaldi used it in solo concertos and concerti grossi, and Bach exploited it extensively in an obbligato role. In the Classical period pairs of oboes became a standard part of the orchestra, and developments at Mannheim helped encourage the composition of numerous solo concertos, of which there are examples by Mozart, J.C. Bach and Lebrun. The requirements of the oboe as an orchestral instrument were considerably increased in the 19th century; the symphonies of Beethoven, Schubert, Brahms and Mahler use it in highly effective but often demanding ways. As a solo instrument it was less appreciated until 20th-century concertos by Richard Strauss and Vaughan Williams among others revived it. The chamber music repertory, particularly that of the wind quintet, has expanded considerably since 1900, and in recent decades players have been required to produce a wide range of multiple sonorities, microtones and other special effects.

The origin of the oboe d'amore is obscure. It may at first have been used simply as an alternative a minor 3rd lower than the C instrument. After the 18th century it passed into oblivion until its revival in the 1880s. She tenor oboe (english horn) was built a 4th or 5th below the treble, and used mainly in a military context during the 18th century. The baritone oboe, probably developed before 1750, is today replaced by the HECKLEPHONE.

Oboe da caccia (It.). Tenor OBOE (english horn) or, specifically, a mid-18th-century tenor oboe with a large open bell, used in formal music associated with the hunt; it is usually pitched a 5th below the soprano instrument.

Oboe d'amore (It.). The alto of the OBOE family, a transposing instrument pitched a minor 3rd below the oboe. Bach used it extensively in his *St Matthew Passion* and other sacred works.

Oborin, Lev (Nikolayevich) (*b* Moscow, 11 Sept 1907; *d* there, 5 Jan 1974). Russian pianist. He studied in Moscow, where he later taught at the conservatory. He was noted for his simple, clear, expressive playing over a wide range of styles from Mozart to Shostakovich; he gave the première of Khachaturian's Piano Concerto and was an advocate of new Soviet music. He played much with D. Oistrakh and composed piano music.

Obradović, Aleksandar (*b* Bled, 22 Aug 1927). Yugoslav composer. He studied with Logar at the Belgrade Academy, where he began teaching in 1969; he also studied with Berkeley in London (1959–60) and at the Columbia-Princeton Electronic Music Center (1966–7). His music, which includes five symphonies, choral and chamber pieces, shows a bold harmonic quality and a concentration on tightly knit formal structures.

Obraztsova, Elena (Vasil'yevna) (*b* Leningrad, 7 July 1937). Soviet mezzo-soprano. After graduation from the Leningrad Conservatory she sang at the Bol'shoy from 1964, notably as Musorgsky's Marina and Marfa. She first appeared in the USA in 1975 and at La Scala in 1976. Her voice has been noted for its flexibility and full timbre.

Obrecht, Jacob (*b* Bergen op Zoom, 22 Nov *c*1450; *d* Ferrara, 1505). Netherlands composer. He was *zangmeester* at Utrecht, *c*1476–1478, then choirmaster for the Corporation of Notre Dame at St Gertrude, Bergen op Zoom, 1479–84. He then became singing master at Cambrai, and on 13 October 1486 was installed as succentor at St Donatien, Bruges. After a visit to Italy he was appointed *maître de chapelle* at Bruges in 1490. In 1494 his name appears in the records of Notre Dame, Antwerp, and from then until his retirement in 1500 he alternated between Antwerp and Bergen op Zoom. He died of the plague while on a visit to Ferrara. As early as 1475 Tinctoris had mentioned him with the best and most renowned musicians, and other evidence suggests that he commanded the greatest respect. He wrote mainly sacred music. In his masses, and to a lesser extent in his motets, he brought to a culmination certain aspects of style that appeared in Dufay's last works and were developed by his successors, notably Busnois. One of his earliest masses, *Missa 'Forseulement'*, combines the earlier practice of quoting the *cantus firmus* literally with newer, more varied techniques, such as the combination of the *cantus firmus* with the traditional chant in the Credo. Such variety of treatment continued to be a feature of his later masses. He normally changed the type of statement from movement to movement and exploited part-quotation, a *cantus firmus* moving from part to part and the simultaneous statement of material in two or more voices. His ingenuity in the quoting of borrowed material was inexhaustible. His counterpoint ranges from the serene (e.g. the Kyrie of the *Missa Graecorum*) to the hyperactive (e.g. the *Missa 'Caput'*) but, unlike Josquin, he rarely maintained a single motivic pattern throughout a section and his counterpoint thus lacks long-range function. His style also features full and sonorous writing, parallel 10ths between outer voices, skilful use of canon and emphasis on root-position chords.

Sacred music 28 masses; 28 motets
Secular music over 30 songs, inst. pieces, intabulations

Obukhov, Nikolay (*b* Kursk, 22 April 1892; *d* Paris, 13 June 1954). Russian composer. He studied with Shteynberg and Tcherepnin at the St Petersburg Conservatory and in 1914, influenced by Skryabin, began writing 12-note pieces. In 1918 he moved to Paris and began a Christian mystical testament *Le livre de vie* for voices, piano duet and an electronic instrument of his own invention, the 'croix sonore'; he worked on the piece almost throughout his creative life, drawing arrangements from it as independent compositions.

Ocarina. A vessel flute in the shape of a large, elongated egg, hollow and usually made of terracotta. In its side is a flattened tube with a hole at its base; the player blows down the tube, and so across the hole, setting the mass of air in the instrument in vibration. The standard Western ocarina was probably invented by Giuseppe Donati of Budrino, Italy, *c*1860, with eight finger-holes in front and two thumb-holes at the back; pitch is affected solely by the number of holes opened. It is popular as a child's instrument in the USA and in Europe and varieties are used in folk music.

Oceanic music. The diverse cultures of Australia and the 7000 to 10 000 islands of the Pacific have been shaped by isolation, migration and contact within their vast ocean setting, forces that have in turn influenced local styles of music and dance. The region may be divided into four principal areas: Melanesia, Polynesia, Micronesia and Australia.

Our knowledge of the music of Oceania dates from accounts of early explorers and missionaries, including Captain James Cook, who provided excellent descriptions of native art in journals from his three voyages (1768–80); early accounts portray a relatively homogeneous musical style which still persists. Music and dance are important throughout the area and are inextricably linked with poetry, particularly in Polynesia and Melanesia. Vocal music predominates; many remote atolls lack indigenous instruments. Since the second half of the 18th century there has been much musical change throughout the Pacific, with the introduction of Western church music, whalers' chanties and modern genres of popular music. Indigenous forms are preserved, either as an aspect of deliberate traditionalism as in New Zealand and Hawaii or as a result of slower acculturative processes on more remote islands. In modern times, inter-island festivals have encouraged the mixing of local indigenous styles, supplying a complex mosaic of cultural processes: acculturation, especially Westernization as in Christian hymns and 'pan-Pacific pop', modernization, revitalization of traditional forms and the marginal survival of archaic music and dance.

The region of Melanesia includes Fiji, the Solomon Islands and Papua New Guinea as well as many smaller atolls. Melanesian music is less dominated by text than is that of Polynesia or Micronesia. Songs are often in archaic languages unintelligible to performers and listeners alike. The dominant style is monophonic singing in unison or octaves, with call-and-response forms. Melodies may be triadic or pentatonic, though some have a limited range, often a 3rd. Music and dance accompany long ceremonial cycles, often lasting ten years or more. The Solomon Islands are distinguished by complex polyphonic panpipe music. Bamboo panpipes are made in various sizes and may be played solo, to accompany song, or in orchestras which rehearse regularly; panpipe pieces have composers, and highly developed local theories exist for this music.

The islands of Polynesia cover a wide area, from New Zealand to Hawaii, with a surprisingly unified musical style, partly due to extensive migration prompted by overpopulation. Music and dance are usually associated with poetry and the rhythm of songs is generally bound to that of the text. Among the Maori of New Zealand, the importance of text encourages strict rhythms and firm unison singing. Traditional Maori chants include lullabies, laments, incantations, love songs, historical and genealogical recitations and dance songs. Some Maori chant is based on a reciting tone and has a style between speech and song; other genres have three- or four-note melodies (the pitches do not generally correspond to those of the Western diatonic scale). Chants may be accompanied by body percussion – stamping, clapping and slapping. The music most often heard in Polynesia, however, reflects Western influence, for example the *himene* of Tahiti, which use Western-style counterpoint with a local-style drone.

Micronesian music is little researched. Song predominates, often with simple drone polyphony or parallel intervals, especially 4ths. As in Polynesia, music and dance are an extension of poetry. Line dances and sitting dances, with arm and hand movements, are common throughout the Micronesian islands.

Australian music includes the genres of the Anglo-European settlers who arrived in Australia from the 18th century onwards, as well as songs of the various European-derived ethnic minorities, such as Greeks and Italians, and some Asian groups, particularly Indians. The oldest culture of Australia is preserved by the Aborigines. Music and dance form an integral part of their daily life, accompanying rites of passage, embodying their mythology and genealogy and providing entertainment, especially in the gossip-song repertory. Aboriginals have had little contact with other Oceanic peoples and their musical style is distinct. Unison group performance is the norm, although polyphony is practised in Arnhem Land. The most common Aboriginal instrument is the didjeridoo, a long, hollow eucalyptus branch, blown like a trumpet; through the technique of circular breathing the player can achieve a sustained note and it is possible to produce two pitches a 10th apart. Rhythmic accompaniment to song is provided by clapping and concussion rhythm sticks. As elsewhere throughout the Pacific region the bullroarer, a small wooden plaque whirled on a string, is used in religious ceremonies.

Most instruments of the Pacific islands have extra-musical functions, in rituals, for signalling, as lures, to imitate the voices of supernatural beings and as toys. They are generally of simple construction, for example, bamboo flutes without finger-holes, sounded by mouth in Melanesia and Micronesia, or by nasal breath in Polynesia and Micronesia ('nose flutes'). Drums usually lack tuning devices. Open-ended, single-headed hourglass drums are common in New Guinea and Melanesia; the open end is often elaborately carved, in imitation of the mouth of a crocodile or bird. Cylindrical drums are more common in Polynesia. Slit-drums, found throughout the region, are not true membrane drums but hollowed-out tree trunks beaten with sticks. Some indigenous instruments are unique to the Pacific such as the friction blocks of New Ireland, three to four wooden plaques rubbed with the hands. String instruments include simple musical bows and bamboo tube zithers. The conch-shell trumpet is used in most areas for signalling. Instruments introduced from overseas include the Hawaiian ukulele, a native form of the Portuguese mandolin, brought to the islands *c*1879.

Ochs, Siegfried (*b* Frankfurt, 19 April 1858; *d* Berlin, 5 Feb 1929). German chorus master. He founded and conducted the Berlin Philharmonic Choir (1882–1920), concentrating on the works of Schütz, Bach, Handel, Beethoven, Schubert and Brahms; he was celebrated for his performances of the *St Matthew Passion*.

Ockeghem [Okeghem], **Johannes** [Jean] (*b c*1410; *d* ?Tours, 6 Feb 1497). Franco-Flemish composer. The earliest reference to him as a singer shows that he was a *vicaire-chanteur* at Notre Dame, Antwerp, for a year from 24 June 1443. His *déploration* on Binchois' death (1460) suggests a connection with the Burgundian ducal chapel where Busnois and Dufay worked. He entered the service of Charles I, Duke of Bourbon, in Moulins in the mid-1440s and was a member of the chapel in 1446–8. In the year ending 30 September 1453 he is cited in the French court archives 'nouveau en 1451'. This service continued during Louis XI's reign, though he held other offices, including a canonry at Notre Dame, Paris (1463–70). In 1470 he visited Spain, in 1484 Bruges and Dammes. After Louis' death he remained *premier chapelain* and was still on the payroll in 1488. He enjoyed an enviable personal and professional reputation.

His most imposing works are his mass settings. Several are based on pre-existing material, sacred or secular. One of the earliest is probably the *Missa 'Caput'* which states the *cantus firmus* in the lowest voice, but in other (probably later) works, such as the *Missa 'De plus en plus'*, he varied the treatment of the *cantus firmus*, assimilating it increasingly to the rhythmic and melodic character of the other voices; his two incomplete mass cycles are based on late *chansons* of his own, and his polyphonic *Requiem* is the earliest known setting. Others of his masses, including the *Missa prolationum* and the *Missa 'Mi-mi'*, are freely composed. The former is perhaps the most extraordinary contrapuntal achievement of the 15th century, with its simultaneous use of all four prolations in complex canonic combinations, while the other clearly shows his own characteristic

style, with its variations in mensuration, texture and sonority. His motets display even greater inventiveness, combining homophonic textures, skilful *cantus firmus* treatments, sweeping melodic lines, energetic rhythmic figures and frequent imitation. Most of his *chansons* use traditional *formes fixes* and feature treble-dominated textures, though some are canonic and occasionally anticipate early 16th-century *chanson* style. The level of contrapuntal skill and artistic excellence of his music laid a foundation for the achievements of Josquin's generation.

*Sacred vocal music c*14 masses; Requiem; *c*9 motets;
*Secular vocal music c*20 chansons; many doubtful works

Octandre. Work for wind septet and double bass by Varèse (1923).

Octave. The INTERVAL between two notes seven diatonic scale degrees apart (e.g. *c–c'*), giving a frequency ratio 1:2. The term usually implies 'perfect octave', the sum of five whole tones and two diatonic semitones; but a diminished or augmented octave (*c– c'♭* or *c–c'♯*) is equally possible.

Octet. A piece for eight solo instruments. Mendelssohn's Octet is an outstanding example for strings only. The wind octet, typically two each of oboes, clarinets, horns and bassoons, has a rich repertory, including some of Mozart's finest serenades. Schubert's D803 is one of several octets for mixed ensembles of wind and strings.

October. *See* TO OCTOBER.

Ode. In classical antiquity, a poem intended to be sung, usually in honour of some special occasion or as part of a play. Some Horatian odes were set to music in medieval court circles and monastery schoolrooms, and in the 1490s Conradus Celtes at Ingolstadt commissioned Petrus Tritonius to compose four-voice illustrations of the 19 poetic metres in Horace's odes. Tritonius's work enjoyed great success and similar German collections were published in the 16th century.

In England between 1660 and 1820 odes were regularly composed for royal occasions, and from 1715 the preparation of odes on the monarch's birthday and the New Year was part of the duties of the poet laureate and the Master of the King's Musick. Blow, Purcell, Handel and Boyce were important composers of court odes. Like the Cecilian odes composed annually (with few exceptions) between 1683 and 1720, and sporadically since then, these works are indistinguishable in structure from the contemporaneous cantata.

Ode for St Cecilia's Day. Four choral works by Purcell (1683, 1683, 1685, 1692).
    Choral work by Handel (1739), a setting of Dryden's poem.
    Cantata by Parry (1889).

Odense. Title given to a symphony in A minor discovered in the Danish city of Odense in 1983 and identified (probably wrongly) as by Mozart (as K16*a*).

Ode to Napoleon. Work by Schoenberg, op.41, a setting of Byron's poem for reciter, piano and string quartet (later arranged for string orchestra) (1942).

Odhecaton. Short title of the first series of publications of polyphonic music, issued by the printer OTTAVIANO PETRUCCI in 1501 as *Harmonice Musices Odhecaton A* (further books, *B* and *C*, followed). It is printed in movable type and contains mainly French *chansons*.

Odington, Walter (*fl* 1298–1316). English music theorist and scientist. His treatise on music (*Summa de speculatione musice*) is the most systematic and comprehensive work of its period. The first four sections serve the *musicus* or theorist, the last two the performer; it covers chant, the ecclesiastical modes and discant.

Odo [Oddo]. Name of several medieval musicians whose identities have been confused. A tonary and treatise of the late 10th century attributed to 'Abbot Odo' may be by an Abbot Odo of Arezzo rather than Abbot Odo of Cluny (*b* 878/9), composer of hymns and antiphons. A *Dialogus* on music attributed to Odo of Cluny is probably from north Italy, of unknown authorship. Another tonary, probably Franciscan, has also been wrongly attributed to 'Abbot Odo'; a simple Cluny monk named Odo has been confused with the Abbot.

Oedipus rex. Opera-oratorio in two acts by Stravinsky to a libretto by Cocteau after Sophocles translated by J. Daniélou (first staged 1928, Vienna).

Off-beat. Any impulse in a measured rhythmic pattern except the first (the DOWNBEAT); the term is usually applied to rhythms that emphasize the weak beats of the bar. The impulse that precedes and anticipates the downbeat of a bar is the UP BEAT.

Offenbach, Jacques (*b* Cologne, 20 June 1819; *d* Paris, 5 Oct 1880). French composer of German origin. His career began with a year's study at the Paris Conservatoire and several years' experience as a solo and orchestral cellist; he became a theatre conductor in 1850, finally getting his own stage works performed in 1855. Writing mainly for the Bouffes Parisiens, he reached the peak of his international success in the 1860s; revivals and tours, as well as the score of his serious opera *Les contes d'Hoffmann* (unfinished, completed by Guiraud), dominated the 1870s.

With Johann Strauss (ii), Offenbach was one of the two outstanding composers in popular music of the 19th century and writer of some of the most exhilaratingly gay, tuneful music ever written. *Les contes d'Hoffmann* has retained a place in the international repertory for its fantasy and its strongly appealing music; but his most significant achievements lie in operetta: *Orphée aux enfers* (1858), *La belle Hélène* (1864), *La vie parisienne* (1866), *La Grande-Duchesse de Gérolstein* (1867) and *La Périchole* (1868) are striking examples. Moreover, it was through the success of Offenbach's works abroad that operetta became an established international genre, producing major national exponents in Strauss, Sullivan and Léhar and evolving into the 20th-century musical.

Offenbach was well served both by his skilful chief librettist Ludovic Halévy and by his talented leading ladies Hortense Schneider and Zulma Bouffer. His comic subjects, usually satirical treatments of familiar stories with a sharp glance at contemporary

society and politics, are enhanced by none-too-subtle musical devices, including the quotation of well-known operatic music in incongruous settings: his tunes are often built upon a rising phrase in a major key and his finales are made exciting by gradual tempo acceleration and the use of brass at climaxes. He had a rare gift for catchy tunes, usually in dance rhythms, and telling harmonic touches. Through its famous overture (in fact composed by Carl Binder) and can-can, *Orphée aux enfers* has remained his best-known operetta.

Dramatic music Orphée aux enfers (1858); La belle Hélène (1864); Barbe-bleue (1866); La vie parisienne (1866); La Grande-Duchesse de Gérolstein (1867); La Périchole (1868); Les contes d'Hoffmann, completed by Guiraud (1881); *c*80 others; vaudevilles, incidental music; 5 ballets
Vocal music songs, duets, partsongs
Instrumental music works for vc, orch; vc, pf; chamber works with vc; pieces for vc solo, cello duo, etc; dance music

Offertory. In the Western church, a chant of the Proper of the Mass; sung as the offerings (in the early church, usually bread and wine) were being received, it marks the beginning of Mass of the Faithful. It was introduced by St Augustine (*d* 430). Gregorian offertories begin with an antiphon, followed by two or three verses with freely composed, ornate and wide-ranging melodies and a refrain (usually from the end of the antiphon). From the Renaissance era there are many polyphonic offertory settings in the style of short motets, notably by Lassus and Palestrina (a set of 68 settings for the entire year, published in 1593); Mozart and Haydn are among later composers who have written offertories.

Office de Radiodiffusion-Télévision Française [ORTF]. French broadcasting body. It was established in 1964, replacing RTF (1945; regular broadcasts began in 1923). Its musical forces include the Orchestre Nationale (founded 1934), Orchestre Philharmonique, the Nouvel Orchestre Philharmonique de Radio France, Groupe de Recherches Musicales (for electronic music), Ars Nova (modern music), choirs and regional orchestras. All give public concerts.

Office, Divine. *See* DIVINE OFFICE.

Offrandes. Work for soprano and small orchestra by Varèse, a setting for soprano and small orchestra of texts by V. Huidobro and J.J. Tablada (1921).

Offrandes oubliées, Les. Orchestral work ('méditation symphonique') by Messiaen (1930).

Ogdon, John (Andrew Howard) (*b* Mansfield Woodhouse, 27 Jan 1937). English pianist. He studied at the RMCM and while a student gave first performances of works by Goehr, Maxwell Davies and himself. He made his London début with Busoni's Piano Concerto at the 1958 Proms and in 1962 won joint first prize at the Tchaikovsky Competition, Moscow. A powerful player, he has a large repertory of Romantic and 20th-century music, notably Liszt and Messiaen.

Ohana, Maurice (*b* Casablanca, 12 June 1914). French composer of Andalusian origin. He studied with Daniel-Lesur at the Schola Cantorum, Paris (from 1937), and after the war with Casella at the

Accademia di S Cecilia, Rome. In 1946 he returned to Paris, where he has taught and composed. His first major work, the oratorio *Llanto por Ignacio Sanchez Mejias* (1950), brought his name to a wide audience. His music is cosmopolitan and independent, related to French composers from Debussy to Boulez but also to the music of Spain and north Africa. He has written for diverse vocal and instrumental groupings, often including zither, guitar and percussion in his ensembles, and has exploited micro-intervals.

Oiseaux exotiques. Work by Messiaen for piano, wind and percussion (1956).

Oistrakh, David (Fyodorovich) (*b* Odessa, 30 Sept 1908; *d* Amsterdam, 24 Oct 1974). Soviet violinist. After study at the Odessa Conservatory he made his début in Leningrad in 1928. His international career began in 1927 but the war years were spent performing in Russia. His technical mastery and powerful tone were often heard in Soviet music; he was the dedicatee of both Shostakovich's violin concertos. He was among the greatest violinists of his day, a fine interpreter of the great Romantic concertos, and the most characteristic representative of the Russian school.

Oistrakh, Igor (Davidovich) (*b* Odessa, 27 April 1931). Soviet violinist. He studied under his father and at Moscow Conservatory, where he has taught since 1958. A player of high refinement and technical command, he is cooler in tone and approach than his father and more detached in interpretation.

Ojai Music Festival (USA). Annual (spring) festival inaugurated in 1947 at Ojai, CA. Music of the 13th to 20th centuries is given, with emphasis on rare and new works.

Oktōēchos. A Byzantine term for liturgical books arranged according to the system of eight ecclesiastical modes; the term is now used for the eight-mode system itself. In the Greek and other Eastern Christian churches, the *oktōēchos* contains Proper chants for the Offices of Saturday evening and Sunday in eight-weekly cycles, with one mode for each week. The systems in Byzantine and Gregorian chant date back at least to the 8th and 9th centuries.

Olah, Tiberiu (*b* Arpăşel, 2 Jan 1928). Romanian composer. He studied at the conservatories of Cluj (1946–9) and Moscow (1949–54), then began teaching at the Bucharest Conservatory. As a composer for films he has achieved a leading position in Romania. He has also written vocal, orchestral and chamber music.

Old Hall MS. An important MS collection of 14th–early 15th-century English sacred music which, for the first time, attaches an English repertory to named composers such as Leonel Power, Pycard, Queldryk, Roy Henry etc. It was possibly compiled for the chapel of Thomas, Duke of Clarence (*d* 1421), by a single scribe *c*1410–15; additions were made up to *c*1420 of works by Dunstable, Sturgeon and others. Questions remain as to its early history and the identity of Roy Henry. The MS, now in the British Library, is organized according to liturgical category based on settings of the movements of the Mass Ordinary (a gathering of Kyries may have been lost). Music notated in score in English discant

style begins each section, followed by more complex polyphonic works drawing on techniques such as canon and isorhythm notated in parts. It provides an instructive compendium of the stages through which such techniques passed, from the use of short rhythmic patterns through flexible structures to the strict isorhythm of Dunstable. Only the second-layer pieces reflect the pan-consonant, melodically fluent style of the so-called *contenance angloise*.

Oldham, Arthur (William) (*b* London, 6 Sept 1926). English composer. He studied with Howells at the RCM (1943–5) and with Britten, who was an influence on his early ballets (including *Mr Punch*, 1946) and choral pieces. He has worked as a choirmaster in Edinburgh, London (LSO Chorus, 1969–76) and Paris. Much of his music is for children.

Old Hundredth. A name used from *c*1696 for the hymn tune by Loys Bourgeois set to Psalm cxxxiv in the Genevan Psalter (1551). In 1561 it was appropriated by the Anglo-Genevan Psalter for a version of Psalm c, *All people that on earth do dwell*.

Old Vic. London theatre, built 1817–18; opera given there from 1900. From 1931 its company performed also at Sadler's Wells Theatre; it was known as the Vic-Wells Opera and became Sadler's Wells Opera (later ENGLISH NATIONAL OPERA).

Oliphant. Medieval end-blown ivory horn, finely carved and prized by the wealthy classes as a token of land tenure, or by churches as a reliquary, rather than as a musical instrument. It was made largely by Muslim craftsmen in south Italy and Sicily, particularly in the 11th century.

Oliphant, Thomas (*b* Condie, 25 Dec 1799; *d* London, 9 March 1873). Scottish writer and editor. An influential member of the Madrigal Society, he published popular editions of English and Italian madrigals, completed the first catalogue of MS music in the British Museum (1842) and laid the foundation for that of printed music.

Oliver, King [Joe] (*b* in or nr. New Orleans, 11 May 1885; *d* Savannah, 8 April 1938). American jazz cornettist and bandleader. He moved in 1918 to Chicago, where in 1920 he formed what was to be King Oliver's Creole Jazz Band. The band was reorganized in 1924 as the Dixie Syncopators. After 1927 Oliver led bands but seldom performed. One of the most important musicians in the New Orleans style, he was renowned for 'wa-wa' effects.

Oliver, Stephen (*b* Liverpool, 10 March 1950). English composer. He studied at Oxford University (electronic music with Sherlaw Johnson). His music is largely associated with the theatre, and includes numerous operas (*Tom Jones*, 1976; *Beauty and the Beast*, 1984), music for the Royal Shakespeare Company (*Nicholas Nickleby*, 1980) and the musical *Blondel* (1983).

Olivero, Magda (*b* Saluzzo, 25 March ?1910–14). Italian soprano. She studied in Turin where she made her début in *Gianni Schicchi* (1933). She sang widely in Italy in the central repertory including such roles as Violetta, Butterfly and Mimì. But from 1940 she was especially associated with Cilea's

Adriana Lecouvreur, of which the composer regarded her as the ideal interpreter. She retired on marriage in 1940, but returned to the stage in 1950 at Cilea's request, and became a soprano of outstanding appeal, in the USA and Europe, in Tosca and other dramatic roles.

Oliveros, Pauline (*b* Houston, 30 May 1932). American composer. She studied with Robert Erickson (1954–60) and worked at the San Francisco Tape Music Center (1961–7), then in 1967 began teaching electronic music at San Diego. Her large output includes much electronic music and pieces for mixed media and she is concerned with improvisation guided by meditation.

Olsen, Poul Rovsing (*b* Copenhagen, 4 Nov 1922; *d* there, 2 July 1982). Danish composer. He studied with Jeppesen at the Copenhagen Conservatory (1943–6) and with Boulanger and Messiaen in Paris (1948–9), then worked in Copenhagen as a music critic. His early works showed the influences of Bartók, Stravinsky and Nielsen, joined in the 1950s by 12-note serialism, but from the 1960s his music began to reflect his work as a musical ethnologist (*A L'inconnu* for voice and 13 instruments, 1962): he did fieldwork in Greenland and the Persian Gulf and taught at the univerrities of Lund (1967–9) and Copenhagen (from 1969). His output includes an opera, orchestral and chamber music, piano pieces and songs.

Olsson, Otto (Emanuel) (*b* Stockholm, 19 Dec 1879; *d* there, 1 Sept 1964). Swedish organist and composer. He studied at the Stockholm Conservatory, where he taught (1908–45) while also serving as organist of the Gustav Vasa church: one of the great virtuosos of his time, he also worked as teacher, committee member and composer to strengthen church music in Sweden. His largest, best-known work is the *Te Deum* (1906) for chorus, strings, harp and organ; he also wrote organ music.

Olympians, The. Opera in three acts by Bliss to a libretto by J.B. Priestley (1949, London).

Ondeggiando (It.; Fr. *ondulé*). In string playing, a wavy motion involving moving the bow back and forth across two or more strings.

Ondes martenot. A monophonic electronic instrument invented in 1928 by Maurice Martenot (1898–1980). A keyboard controls the frequency of a variable oscillator; the signal is amplifed and radiated as sound from a loudspeaker. The right hand plays the keyboard, of which each key is capable of slight lateral movement, creating a vibrato; the left controls potentiometers governing filters which change timbre and dynamics. The instrument has been used by Varèse, Messiaen and Boulez, among others, and is still used by young French composers.

Ondine. Ballet in three acts and five scenes by Henze (1958, Covent Garden).

Piano piece by Ravel, the first of *Gaspard de la nuit*.

Ondříček, František (*b* Prague, 29 April 1857; *d* Milan, 12 April 1922). Czech violinist and composer. He studied at the Prague Conservatory and with Massart at the Paris Conservatoire. Internationally known as a violinist, he gave the première of Dvořák's Violin Concerto (1883), also playing solo

and chamber works. He composed fantasias on Slavonic themes and taught in Vienna and Prague. His father Jan (1832–1900) was a bandmaster, and his brother Emanuel (1880–1958) a violinist who settled in Boston.

Ondulé (Fr.; It. *ondeggiando*). In string playing, a wavy motion executed by moving the bow with an up-and-down wrist action across two or more adjacent strings.

Onegin, (Elisabeth Elfriede Emilie) Sigrid [Hoffmann, Lilly] (*b* Stockholm, 1 June 1889; *d* Magliaso, 16 June 1943). German mezzo-soprano. After study in Munich and Milan she sang at the Stuttgart Opera from 1912. Later engagements took her to Munich (1919–22), Berlin (1926–31) and Zurich (1931–5), and she also sang at Salzburg and the Met. A fine Wagner singer, she was also distinguished in roles ranging from Gluck's Orpheus to Verdi's Amneris.

O'Neill, Norman (Houstoun) (*b* London, 14 March 1875; *d* there, 3 March 1934). English composer. A pupil of Somervell (1890–93) and of Knorr in Frankfurt (1893–7), he taught at the RAM (from 1924). He was the most skilful conductor and composer of incidental music (over 50 scores) for London theatres of his time.

One-step. A fast ballroom dance first made popular *c*1910; it was danced to music in 2/4 or 6/8 time, at *c*60 bars per minute.

On Hearing the First Cuckoo in Spring. Orchestral work by Delius (1912), the first of his Two Pieces for Small Orchestra (the other is *Summer Night on the River*).

Onslow, (André) George (Louis) (*b* Clermont-Ferrand, 27 July 1784; *d* there, 3 Oct 1853). French composer of English descent. An amateur cellist of independent means, he pursued his interest in chamber music through composition, studying briefly with Reicha but also trying out new works with musical friends. His substantial output of chamber music, unusual for the time, includes over 70 string quartets and string quintets and ten piano trios, the best showing fresh, idiomatic ideas and good craftsmanship. Of his larger works, only the overture to *Le colporteur* (1827) achieved success.

On this Island. Song cycle (op.11, 1937) by Britten, settings for soprano or tenor and piano of five poems by Auden.

On Wenlock Edge. Song cycle by Vaughan Williams (1909), settings for tenor, string quartet and piano of six poems from A.E. Housman's *A Shropshire Lad* (1896), the first is *On Wenlock Edge*.

Open notes. On valved brass instruments, the notes of the harmonic series produced without lowering any valve; in brass parts 'open' countermands 'muted' or 'stopped'.

Open position [open harmony]. The spacing of a chord in such a way that the interval between the highest and lowest parts is relatively large (e.g. greater than a 12th in four-part harmony) and the upper parts do not lie close together.

Open string. In string instruments, a string played at its full sounding-length without 'stopping' (i.e. without being touched or pressed down with the finger); in unfretted string instruments there is a difference in sound between an open string and a stopped one at the same pitch.

Opera. A musical dramatic work in which the actors sing some or all of their parts; a union of music, drama and spectacle, with music normally playing a dominant role.

Antecedents of opera include the intermedio, but the earliest operas staged by the group of 'camerata' around patrons in Florence were courtly entertainments in the form of the pastorale. The spread of the new *stile rappresentativo* to other Italian courts began with Monteverdi's *Orfeo* (Mantua, 1607). As opera became a public entertainment, from 1637 at Venice, its content and structure changed to meet the demands of new audiences. A more accessible type of opera can be seen in the romantic dramas of Faustini which Cavalli set in 1642–52 with expressive recitative and fluid arias.

By the 1660s the aria structure in opera had become standardized as either *ABA* or *ABB*; the proportion of arias increased as arioso became less promiment and recitative less melodic. Plots and action became more varied and violent and spectacular stage effects were featured. The Venetian repertory and the operatic style of Cavalli, Sartorio, Pallavicino, Legrenzi and others spread elsewhere, partly through the activities of travelling troupes. In 1650 one of these, the Febiarmonici, took opera to Naples, a city soon to rival Venice as a centre for and disseminator of opera. By 1700 opera in Italy had been more or less standardized in a form familiar from the middle-period works of Alessandro Scarlatti: a three-movement overture followed by three acts, each consisting of a succession of sharply differentiated recitatives and arias (almost invariably ternary, *ABA*, in structure), with the occasional duet or ensemble and a final *coro* for the entire cast.

The situation in France was somewhat different. French opera, as seen in the *tragédies lyriques* of Lully, was essentially a court spectacle, predominantly on legendary or mythological themes, and in five acts, with big choral and ceremonial scenes reflecting the magnificence and social order of the age of Louis XIV. France and Germany both imported Italian opera in the later 17th century, and there were attempts at German-language opera, especially at Hamburg, where an opera house had opened in 1678, Keiser was the leading figure and Handel wrote his first operas. In England, French influence was at first dominant in the 'semi-opera' with spoken dialogue; all-sung English operas, of which Purcell's *Dido and Aeneas* is the outstanding 17th-century example, were to be a rarity until well after 1900.

In the early 18th century there was a reaction in Italy against the alleged extravagance, over-elaboration and confusions of the 17th-century libretto; this was initiated by Zeno and completed after 1720 by Metastasio, whose *opera seria* librettos were set by numerous composers throughout the 18th century, including Vinci, Leo, Porpora, Hasse, Jommelli, Paisiello and Cimarosa. (Handel, whose mature operas were written for London and lie off the mainstream of the Italian tradition, set only three of them, adjusted to his requirements.) Metastasio's librettos serve as a model of the prevailing rationalist philosophy, the action moving through conflicts and misunderstandings to an inevitable *lieto fine* (happy ending), in which merit receives its due reward, often brought about through an act of renunciation by a benevolent despot. The music is equally orderly, largely an alternation of recitatives (in which the action takes place) and arias (in which the characters give vent to their emotional states). It is, however, important to realize that in 18th-century opera, particularly as given in public opera houses, the composer was not the dominant figure he was to become: operas were usually put together by house composers and poets, often drawing on several composers' music, old and new, to suit the available singers, who (then as now) were the chief draw – above all the castratos and the sopranos.

As the century went on, the structure of *opera seria* was again challenged, this time from below. Lighter forms of opera, such as *opera buffa* in Italy, *opéra comique* or *comédie mêlée d'ariettes* in France, ballad opera or comic opera in England and Singspiel in Germany, came from humble beginnings to flourish alongside *opera seria* and even to penetrate its substance. Serious opera began to change in the direction of freer choice and more imaginative treatment of subject matter, reflected in the music by modifications of the strict *da capo* and the rise of new aria forms, greater use of accompanied recitatives and of the chorus, and in the end a virtual fusion of the formerly distinct French and Italian characteristics. The 'reforms' of Traetta, Jommelli and especially Gluck (*Orfeo ed Euridice*, 1762) were stages in this process; the final stage is best represented by the operas of Mozart from *Idomeneo* (1781), including his three with Da Ponte with their many ensembles (including extended act finales, following the Venetian reforms of the poet Goldoni and the composer Galuppi) which bring a new emotional weight to comic opera. Two-act form came to be preferred, especially in comic opera, at this period.

By the early 19th century, even 'serious' opera had moved from its earlier aristocratic milieu into the great public theatres with their mass audiences. One manifestation of this was the popularity of 'rescue' operas, of which Beethoven's *Fidelio* (1805) is the best known. Popular audiences were undoubtedly an influential factor in the growth of French grand opera, with its emotion-charged plots, colourful orchestration and massive choral numbers; this is seen at its most successful in the collaboration between the librettist Scribe and the composer Meyerbeer. Nature and the supernatural entered into the substance of the drama, particularly in Germany with Weber, Marschner and others.

While Italian serious opera as cultivated by Rossini, Donizetti and Verdi remained relatively conservative, there was a move towards greater musical continuity during the 19th century. The rigid separation of recitative and aria was gradually broken down, and virtually eliminated in the Wagnerian music drama, with its 'endless melody' and elaborate system of leitmotifs, and (in a different way) in the final works of Verdi and the *verismo* operas of his Italian successors, above all Puccini.

Characteristic for the age was the rise of new types of opera based on national history, legends and folklore and drawing on national idioms in the music. Russia took the lead with works such as Musorgsky's *Boris Godunov*; similar examples in the 20th century were the operas of Janáček and, on an epic scale, Prokofiev's *War and Peace*. The underlying note of 20th-century opera is tragedy, whether conveyed in terms of symbolism (as in Debussy's *Pelléas et Mélisande*), expressionism (Strauss's *Salome* and *Elektra*, Schoenberg's *Erwartung*) or naturalism (*Peter Grimes* and other operas by Britten). At the same time composers have engaged in fantasy (e.g. Prokofiev's *The Love for Three Oranges*, Ravel's *L'enfant et les sortilèges*), allegory (Tippett's *The Midsummer Marriage*), grotesque comedy (Shostakovich's *The Nose*), patriotism (Prokofiev's *War and Peace*), irony (Stravinsky's *The Rake's Progress*, the last and greatest neo-classical opera), political or philosophical tract (Henze's *Der junge Lord* and *The Bassarids*) and personal epic (Stockhausen's cycle on the days of the week). New operas continue to be composed; but the expense of staging them and the difficulty of reconciling advanced forms of musical utterance with the requirements of the traditional opera house and its audience have induced many composers to prefer chamber opera or other kinds of music theatre susceptible to concert, 'workshop' or experimental production.

See also AZIONE TEATRALE, BALLAD OPERA, FARSA, FESTA TEATRALE, INTERMEDIO, INTERMEZZO, MELODRAMA, MUSIC DRAMA, NUMBER OPERA, OPÉRA COMIQUE, OPERA SEMISERIA, OPERETTA, PASTICCIO, PUPPET OPERA, SEMI-OPERA, SINGSPIEL, TRAGÉDIE LYRIQUE and ZARZUELA.

Opéra. The principal opera company in Paris and its theatre. Originally the Académie de Musique, founded in 1669, the name and theatre changed many times; it is now Théâtre National de l'Opéra. The company was established in 1672 as the Académie Royale de Musique by Lully, who presented many of his own works. In the 19th century it was noted for performances of grand opera, a term that became associated with the company as well as the works performed. Works by Rameau, Gluck, Berlioz, Verdi and Messiaen have had their premières there.

Opéra-ballet. A French genre of lyric theatre cultivated in the period between Lully and Rameau (1687–1733). It normally consisted of a prologue and three or four independent acts or *entrées*. Leading exponents were Campra, Mouret and Montéclair.

Opéra bouffe. A form of OPERETTA derived from the *opéra comique*; the first example is Offenbach's *Orphée aux enfers* (1858).

Opera buffa. A full-length Italian comic opera with recitative rather than spoken dialogue.

Opéra comique. Term for a French stage work with spoken dialogue interspersed with songs etc. Originally comic, farcical or parodistical, it broadened its scope in the late 18th century with subjects from the *drame bourgeois*, and by the late 19th century the music was usually continuous. The leading early exponent of the form was Grétry; the best-known example of it is Bizet's *Carmen* (1875).

Opéra-Comique. Parisian institution, founded in 1715 after the Théâtres de la Foire. It was in competition with the Opéra and the Comédie-Française, and because of this and its often satirical bent it had a much interrupted existence, flourishing 1724–44, 1752–8 and merging with the Comédie-Italienne in 1762. There were rival companies bearing the name in the 1790s, but in 1801 the Théâtre de l'Opéra-Comique was established, first at the Salle Feydeau (until 1829), then at the Salle Favart (1840–87, 1898 onwards). The company primarily performed opera with spoken dialogue (not necessarily comic opera); among its premières have been works by Méhul, Boieldieu, Auber, Thomas, Bizet (*Carmen*), Offenbach (*Les contes d'Hoffmann*), Chabrier, Debussy (*Pelléas et Mélisande*) and Ravel (*L'heure espagnole*, *L'enfant et les sortilèges*).

Opera Factory. *See* LONDON SINFONIETTA.

Opera North. British opera company based in Leeds. It was founded in 1977, as English National Opera North, with David Lloyd-Jones as musical director.

Opera semiseria. A type of Italian opera, derived from the 18th-century French *comédie larmoyante*, of a serious, melodramatic character, with subsidiary comic material often provided by servants. Stimulus to the new genre was given by Paisiello's *Nina, o sia La pazza per amore* (1789). It introduced spoken prose dialogue into Italian opera, where it continued to be used occasionally well into the 19th century.

Opera seria. A term used for heroic or tragic Italian opera of the 18th and early 19th centuries, and particularly the period when Metastasio's librettos dominated the stage.

Opera Theatre of St Louis. American opera company founded in 1976. Its premières include commissions and the first stage performances of Prokofiev's *Maddalena* (1982) and Delius's *Margot la rouge* (1983). It was the first American company to appear at the Edinburgh Festival (1983).

Operetta. Term used in the 17th and 18th centuries for a variety of stage works shorter or less ambitious than opera, and in the late 19th and early 20th centuries for a light opera with spoken dialogue and dances. This type evolved in the 1850s from the French *opéra comique*, the style being set by Offenbach in works such as *Orphée aux enfers* (1858) and *La belle Hélène* (1864). Offenbach was followed in France by Lecocq, Planquette, Messager and others, and his success abroad brought into being other national schools of operetta. In Vienna, where Suppé's one-act operettas were popular, Offenbach's monopoly of large-scale productions was unchallenged until 1871, when Johann Strauss's *Indigo und die vierzig Räuber* established the individual style of Viennese operetta, with more exotic settings and scores built around dance forms, particularly the waltz. His *Die Fledermaus* (1874) and Lehár's *Die lustige Witwe* (1905) are the most celebrated examples of the rich Viennese operetta tradition.

In England the influence of French and Viennese operetta eventually bore fruit in the comic operas of Sullivan, and towards the end of the 19th century American examples by Sousa and others began to appear, to be superseded in the 1920s by the MUSICAL COMEDY.

Ophicleide. An obsolete lip-energized brass wind instrument belonging to the keyed bugle family, to which it forms the bass. It was patented by the French maker Halary in 1821. The word 'ophicleide' (French 'ophicléide') was compounded from the Greek 'ophis' (a serpent) and 'kleis' (a cover or stopper) so can be translated as keyed serpent', although it has little in common with the serpent. 'Ophicleide', though intended as the name for the largest of the set covered by Halary's patent, soon became generic for all sizes.

The ophicleide's bore, except for a moderate bell flare, is conical, and the main tube is bent in the form of a narrow U. The crook, usually either circular or elliptical, completes the bore and carries at its narrow end the mouthpiece, usually similar to a bass trombone's. Ophicleides have been built with nine to 12 keys. The tone is full and resonant and such composers as Mendelssohn, Schumann, Verdi and Wagner wrote important parts for it which are not always well replaced by the blander-toned tuba.

Opitz, Martin (*b* Bunzlau, 23 Dec 1597; *d* Danzig, 20 Aug 1639). German poet, librettist and literary theorist. Active both in Silesia and abroad, he wrote a highly influential treatise (1624) introducing modern High German. His reform verses (sacred and secular) were set by many German composers in the 17th century, following his emphasis on proper diction. He also wrote other sacred texts and adapted the libretto for the first German opera, Schütz's *Dafne* (1627, Torgau).

Opus [op.] (Lat.). 'Work': a term used with a number to identify a work or group of works in a composer's output. Opus numbers are not always a reliable guide to chronology.

Oratorio. An extended musical setting of a sacred, usually non-liturgical, text. Except for a greater emphasis on the chorus throughout much of its history, the forms and styles of oratorio tend to approximate to those of opera in any given period, but the normal manner of performance is without scenery, costumes or action.

Oratorio originated in the informal meetings, or 'spiritual exercises', of the Congregazione dell' Oratorio in Rome, founded in the 1550s by St Filippo Neri. The name comes from the oratory or prayer hall in which the meetings were held. Music, particularly *laude*, helped attract people and membership spread to other cities. Important in introducing the new monodic style was the performance at the Chiesa Nuova in Rome of Cavalieri's sacred opera, *Rappresentatione di Anima, et di Corpo* (1600). But the most important type of oratory music during the next 50 years was sacred dialogue of the kind in Anerio's *Teatro armonico* (1619).

By the mid-17th century two types had developed. The *oratorio volgare*, in Italian, is represented by Carissimi's *Daniele*, Marazzoli's *S Tomaso* and similar works attributed to Foggia and Luigi Rossi. Lasting some 30–60 minutes, they were performed in two sections, separated by a sermon; their music resembles that of contemporary operas and chamber cantatas. The *oratorio latino*, in Latin, was first developed at the Oratorio del Ss Crocifisso, related to the church of S Marcello in Rome; the most significant composer is Carissimi, whose *Jephte* may be considered the first masterpiece of the genre. Like most other Latin oratorios of the period, it is in one section only.

By the 1660s oratorio was established, and until *c*1720 it flourished in oratories and secular surroundings. Handel's *La resurrezione* (1708) was given at the Ruspoli residence in Rome, and oratorios by A. Scarlatti, Caldara and many others were given in similar locations. Other centres were Bologna, Modena, Florence and Venice; composers include F. Gasparini, Vivaldi and many leading opera composers. Their oratorios are mostly in two sections, lasting *c*90–120 minutes, with librettos based mainly on the Bible, hagiography and moral allegory. Musical style is akin to that of the opera, with few choruses and many *da capo* arias.

Outside Italy, the Italian oratorio was primarily a Lenten substitute for opera at the Roman Catholic courts of central Europe, notably Vienna, where oratorios were performed in a chapel during services. A related genre was the one-section *sepolcro*, in which the Passion story was narrated in a chapel, at Easter, with scenery, costumes and action. The leading composer of oratorios and *sepolcri* at Vienna was Antonio Draghi; another was Caldara, who set oratorio texts by the court poets, Zeno and Metastasio.

Only in the early 18th century was a clearly defined genre of 'Oratorium', with German text, accepted in German concert life and Lutheran services. One root was the *historia*, exemplified by Schütz's settings of the Christmas, Passion and Easter narrations. From the mid-17th century composers began including music with non-biblical texts; this resulted in the 'oratorio Passion', a genre that culminated in the Passions of Bach. Other antecedents of German oratorio were the sacred dramatic dialogue, which sometimes served as a Lutheran motet, and the oratorio-like works performed as ABENDMUSIK in Lübeck under Buxtehude.

Hamburg was the chief centre for the early 18th-century German oratorio in spite of opposition to Keiser's setting of Hunold's *Der blutige und sterbende Jesus* (1704). A direct successor was Brockes's Passion oratorio, set by Handel, Keiser, Telemann, Mattheson and others. Such composers made more prominent a use of the chorus than did Italian composers and also introduced chorales. The works Bach called 'Oratorium' stand outside the true oratorio tradition.

Although it had an antecedent in the sacred dialogue, English oratorio was essentially Handel's creation – a synthesis of elements from the English masque and anthem, French classical drama, Italian *opera seria* and *oratorio volgare*, and the German Protestant oratorio. For Handel 'oratorio' normally meant a three-act dramatic work on a biblical subject, with prominent use of the chorus, performed as a concert in a theatre. It originated, almost by accident, when in 1732 Handel's intention of presenting a revised stage version of his earlier *Esther* was thwarted by the Bishop of London's ban. Its success in a concert version prompted Handel to compose two more in 1733, and his other English oratorios followed in 1738–52. Of these, *Messiah* (1742) is the best known, though as a setting of a purely biblical, non-dramatic text it is not representative of Handelian oratorio. Few Englishmen attempted to emulate Handel's mastery of oratorio, though there are examples by Greene, Arne and Stanley.

Charpentier, who studied with Carissimi in Rome, appears to have been the first French composer of oratorios; he preferred the terms 'historia', 'canticum', 'dialogue' or 'motet' for oratorio-like works apparently performed as extended motets during festive masses, at church concerts and at private Lenten gatherings. The chorus is of special importance as narrator, crowd and commentator. Few oratorios were composed in France during the 50 years following Charpentier's death in 1704.

In Italy and Vienna, *oratorio volgare* predominated in the late 18th century, with the emphasis on solo singing. The Dresden court played an important role in cultivating the pre-Blassical and Classical oratorio. The Lutheran oratorio continued to function liturgically, as a substitute for the cantata, and in public concerts at Hamburg (under Telemann and C.P.E. Bach), Berlin (where Graun's *Der Tod Jesu* was performed almost annually) and Lübeck. The music of Haydn's late oratorios, *The Creation* and *The Seasons*, reflects his experience of Handelian oratorio in London.

After 1800 fewer major composers devoted their main energies to oratorio, but the genre continued to occupy a central place, especially in England and Germany, with the emphasis on massive performances at music festivals. The oratorios of Spohr and Mendelssohn took their place beside Handel's and Haydn's in the repertory of large choral societies, but after Mendelssohn the musical history of oratorio becomes more and more an account of individual masterpieces, among which Berlioz's *L'enfance du Christ* (1854), Liszt's *Christus* (1862–7), Elgar's *The Dream of Gerontius* (1900), Schoenberg's *Die Jakobsleiter* (1917–22), Honegger's *Le roi David* (1923) and Walton's *Belshazzar's Feast* (1931) are particularly significant. Stravinsky's 'opera-oratorio' *Oedipus rex* (1926–7) is the most successful of modern attempts to apply certain characteristics of the oratorio to secular ends.

Orb and Sceptre. March by Walton, composed for the coronation of Elizabeth II (1953).

Orbón (de Soto), Julián (*b* Avilés, 7 Aug 1925). Cuban composer of Spanish birth. He was a pupil of Ardévol. He directed the conservatory founded by his father in Havana (1946–60), then worked in Mexico City (1960–63) and New York (from 1964). His works are in a Spanish-Cuban style influenced by Falla, the Halffters, Chávez and Villa-Lobos.

Orchestra (from Gk. 'dancing place'). An organized body of bowed strings, with more than one player to a part, to which may be added wind and percussion instruments. An ensemble wholly of wind instruments, whether woodwind and brass or brass alone, is normally described as a BAND.

In the Greek theatre the term denoted the semicircular space in front of the stage where the chorus sang and danced; in the Roman theatre, it was reserved for the senators' seats. The term was revived in late 17th-century France and defined as the place in front of the stage where the instruments and their director sat. By the early 18th century, the word was applied to the players themselves.

The origins of the orchestra can be seen in the 16th century in the separate consorts of instruments in the major courts, and the special assemblies of instruments for important ceremonies. In the 17th century the composition of the ensemble varied from place to place both in number and type of instrument. The string ensemble was fostered in Italy, particularly in Rome, and brass ensembles were used in Germany to perform suites. The French and English court ensembles grew out of Italian viol consorts; by 1626 the 24 Violons du Roi (6 violins, 12 violas, 6 cellos) was established in France, to be imitated by the English during the Restoration.

By the 18th century a number of German and Austrian courts maintained ensembles closely modelled on the court orchestras of Versailles. The basic ensemble consisted of four-part strings, two oboes, bassoon and continuo. Recorders and sometimes transverse flutes were used in French and Venetian opera, and trumpets and timpani were introduced for music of a festal or military character. Trombones were reserved for church music. By the second half of the century a standard orchestra would include strings, two oboes (the players could often 'double' flutes, later clarinets), one or two bassoons and two horns (with trumpets and drums for festive occasions or in the opera house). Later, a pair of clarinets was added. The harpsichord was the standard continuo instrument for most of the century. The orchestra was directed by the first violinist or the keyboard player. A standard orchestra of 1790 consisted of 23 violins, seven violas, five cellos, seven double basses, five flutes and oboes, two clarinets, three bassoons, four horns, two trumpets, timpani and two harpsichords.

In the mid-19th century string instruments were rebuilt to allow for higher string tension which permitted a more brilliant timbre, greater volume and higher standard pitch. The wind instruments were redesigned to facilitate legato playing and chromatic notes, and they had a more powerful tone. The orchestras of Bruckner, Mahler and Wagner came to be known for their huge size as composers searched for new tone colours, and some string sections numbered 70. The number and variety of wind instruments in use became highly variable: the piccolo, double bassoon and trombones were introduced by 1810 and the bass clarinet, tuba and cornet invented in the mid-century. The english horn (cor anglais) reappeared, having been used during the 18th century. Harps also came into regular use.

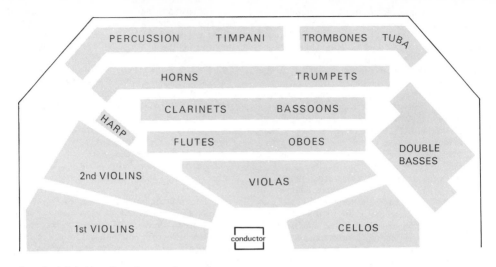

A standard disposition of a modern symphony orchestra

The 20th-century orchestra saw a large increase in the number of percussion instruments, including many of Eastern or exotic origin, used by Stravinsky and Bartók among others. The symphony orchestra of today is constituted according to the formulae of the late 19th century, with typically 32 violins, 12 each of violas and cellos, eight double basses, four of each woodwind (flute, oboe, clarinet, bassoon), eight horns, four trumpets, three trombones, tuba and several percussion. Further lines of development include the chamber orchestra, founded out of a reaction against the overblown post-Romantic orchestra; the modified orchestra of avant-garde works, which exploits timbre through the medium of synthesizers; and the orchestra of period instruments, featuring ensembles for the performance of Baroque, Classical and early Romantic music.

Orchestre de la Suisse Romande. Swiss orchestra based in Geneva, founded by Ernest Ansermet in 1918. Conducted by him until 1966, it was noted for performances of Debussy, Ravel and Stravinsky.

Orchestrion. (1) Name given by G.J. Vogler to a large, revolutionary organ with which he toured Europe in 1789 and 1790. It had four manuals, pedals and 63 stops, all fitted into a case *c*3 m square.

(2) Term widely used in the 19th and 20th centuries to denote a complex MECHANICAL INSTRUMENT played by pinned barrels or perforated cards or paper rolls. It was popular as a domestic entertainment for the wealthy, and its indoor use mainly for the performance of classical music etc, differentiated it from the related street and fairground organ. In the early 20th century it gave way to the player piano and electronic organ. Cherubini and Beethoven composed for J.N. Maelzel's PANHARMONICON; D.N. Winkel's componium (1821) played variations on a given composition of 80 bars.

Ordinary chants. Chants from the Mass and Office whose texts remain constant from day to day in the services of the Western church, as distinct from those whose texts vary (PROPER CHANTS). It chiefly refers to the Mass chants KYRIE, GLORIA, CREDO, SANCTUS and AGNUS DEI, which were usually set polyphonically from the 14th century onwards.

Ordonez, Carlo d' (*b* Vienna, 19 April 1734; *d* there, 6 Sept 1786). Austrian composer. An administrator in Vienna, he was active as a composer (from the 1750s) and violinist. By the 1770s his works were known throughout Europe: his marionette parody *Alceste* (1775, Eszterháza), after Gluck, was especially popular. Important in the development of the new instrumental style, he wrote over 70 symphonies and over 30 string quartets, which feature driving rhythms, imitation and sometimes fugue. His other works include trios and a Singspiel (1778, Vienna).

Ordre. Term used by F. Couperin for a group of harpsichord pieces in the same key. Couperin's imitators used it as a synonym for suite.

Orefice, Antonio (*fl* 1708–34). Italian composer. Beginning with the highly successful *Patrò Calienno de la Costa* (1709, Naples), he was the first to have operas in Neapolitan dialect performed publicly (one by Tommaso de Mauro followed within weeks) and helped establish the genre, later taken up by Vinci and Leo. He also composed heroic operas and other pieces.

Orefice, Giacomo (*b* Vicenza, 27 Aug 1865; *d* Milan, 22 Dec 1922). Italian composer and critic. A pupil of Mancinelli, he composed *verismo* operas and impressionistic piano works. Through his lectures, editions and criticism he aided the development of Italian musicology.

Oregon Symphony Orchestra. American orchestra founded in 1896 as the Portland SO (renamed 1967); it was the first major orchestra in the western USA. Its first permanent conductor was Carl Denton (1918–25). Its home is the Arlene Schnitzer Concert Hall (formerly Paramount Theater; cap. 2800) at Portland Center for the Performing Arts.

Orejón y Aparicio, José de (*b* Huacho, 1706; *d* Lima,

7–21 May 1765). Peruvian composer and organist. As chief organist at Lima Cathedral from 1742 (and *maestro de capilla*, 1764–5), he enjoyed unprecedented acclaim for the poignant beauty of his music. Some 19 works survive, mostly elegiac minor-key settings, which were in the repertory long after his death.

Orfeo, L'. Opera in a prologue and five acts by Monteverdi to a libretto by A. Striggio the younger (1607, Mantua). *See also* ORPHEUS.

Orfeo ed euridice. Opera in three acts by Gluck to a libretto by Calzabigi (1762, Vienna); Gluck made a French version *Orphée* (1774, Paris).

Orff, Carl (*b* Munich, 10 July 1895; *d* there, 29 March 1982). German composer. He studied at the Munich Academy and later, in 1920, with Kaminski. In 1924, with Dorothee Günther, he founded a school for gymnastics, music and dance, and out of this came his later activity in providing materials for young children to make music, using their voices and simple percussion instruments. His adult works also seek to make contact with primitive kinds of musical behaviour, as represented by ostinato, pulsation and direct vocal expression of emotion; in this he was influenced by Stravinsky (*Oedipus rex*, *The Wedding*), though the models are coarsened to produce music of a powerful pagan sensual appeal and physical excitement. All his major works, including the phenomenally successful *Carmina burana* (1937), were designed as pageants for the stage; they include several versions of Greek tragedies and Bavarian comedies.

Dramatic music Klage der Ariadne (1925); Orpheus (1925); Tanz der Spröden (1925); Carmina burana (1937); Der Mond (1939); Catulli carmina (1943); Die Kluge (1943); Die Bernauerin (1947); Antigonae (1949); Astutuli (1953); Trionfo di Afrodite (1953); Comoedia de Christi resurrectione (1957); Oedipus de Tyrann (1959); Ludus de nato infante mirificus (1960); Ein Sommernachtstraum (1964); Prometheus (1966); De temporum fine comoedia (1973)

Orff-Schulwerk. System of music education devised by Carl Orff. It involves training children to play and sing together, to improvise, usually with the special set of percussion instruments for which Orff composed.

Orford Quartet. Canadian string quartet, led by Andrew Dawes. It was founded at Mount Orford in 1965 and has served as resident quartet at Toronto University and toured extensively in Europe and North America. It plays the standard repertory and many contemporary works.

Orgad, Ben-Zion (*b* Gelsenkirchen, 21 Aug 1926). Israeli composer of German birth. Taken to Palestine in 1933, he studied with Ben-Haim (1942–7) and at Brandeis (1960–62). Much of his music uses words or ideas from the Bible. His later choral compositions (e.g. *Story of a Pipe*, 1972) exploit the simultaneous enunciation of different texts by solo voices or groups, recalling the antiphonal singing of cantor and congregation. He has worked in music education and has lectured widely.

Organ. A wind instrument consisting of one or more scale-like rows of individual pipes which are made to sound by air under pressure admitted to the pipes by valves operated from one keyboard or more. Most organs have several stops which, when drawn, enable one or more ranks of pipes to be used. The wind-chest is fed by bellows. When a key is depressed, mechanical (or tracker) action causes wind to accumulate in the corresponding pallet valve; the wind is admitted to each stop by means of a perforated slip of wood ('slider'), which can be aligned either to allow wind to pass to each pipe or to prevent it from doing so by means of rods, trundles and levers operated by a 'stop-knob' near the player. With tubular-pneumatic action, air under pressure in the touch-box above the depressed key flows along tubing to the pneumatic motor operating the pipe-chest pallet. In a 'direct electric action', a magnet pulls the pallet open.

Flue pipes are the most common type, made of a tin-lead alloy or pure tin. Air from the chest passes through the foot-hole (bore) at the base of the pipe-foot and through the flue or windway to strike the edge of the upper lip. Reed pipes have a thin, flexible brass reed-tongue which sets the air column in the pipe into vibration. In a flue pipe, the pitch of the note is primarily affected by the pipe's length; the size of flue and bore, and position of the lips, affect the tone quality. In reed pipes, the frequency is determined by the length of the air column and by the length, mass and stiffness of the reed-tongue (the longer it is, the lower the pitch). The regulation of tone quality and loudness is termed 'VOICING'. A 'stopped' pipe will sound an octave lower than of it were open. A unison open flue stop at *C* is eight feet long (8'); a 4' stop sounds an octave above, a 16' an octave below. Measurements in feet are used to describe the pitch of a rank of pipes: see Table 1.

TABLE 1

32'	C''	$3\frac{1}{5}'$	e	$\frac{4}{5}'$	e''
16'	C'	$2\frac{2}{3}'$	g	$\frac{2}{3}'$	g''
$10\frac{2}{3}'$	G'	2'	c'	$\frac{1}{2}'$	c'''
8'	C	$1\frac{3}{5}'$	e''	$\frac{1}{3}'$	g'''
$5\frac{1}{3}'$	G	$1\frac{1}{3}'$	g'	$\frac{2}{5}'$	e'''
4'	c	1'	c''	$\frac{1}{4}'$	c''''

Tone families, controlled by the 'stop-knob' mechanism, are determined by the diameters of pipes in relation to their length (*see* SCALING). A narrow scaling in flue pipes produces a bright quality known as Principal tone. Principals are open pipes and include the narrow *Geigen* and the fuller Open Diapason. Flutes are produced from wider scaling and are usually stopped (*Bourdon*, *Gedackt*); they can be made of wood or metal (Principals are usually of metal). Some stop names describe only the tone family (Principal 8', Flute 4') or the construction of the pipe (*Hohlflöte*); others take their name from the instrument imitated (Trumpet, Horn). By the late 16th century, names had become regular and reliable as indication of a stop's purpose. Mixture stops are composed of several ranks of pipes at various pitches, most often octaves, and 5ths, to add brilliance. Mutation (overtone) stops, similarly, are pitched at the 5th, 3rd, 7th, 9th etc of an upper octave. The selection and combination of stops is known as REGISTRATION.

Manual keyboards (usually two or three) are operated by the hands and a pedalboard by the feet; a coupling device enables the pipes of one manual to be sounded from another. The pipes for each division are placed on separate cases, the most usual being the Great or *Hauptwerk*, Chair or Choir or *Rückposotov, Oberwerk, Brustwerk* and Pedal. Many organs have a Swell manual, controlled by shutters so that the player can decrease the volume.

The invention of the pipe organ is credited to Ctesibius, an Alexandrian engineer in the 3rd century BC, whose HYDRAULIS was more a demonstration of the principles of hydraulics than a musical instrument as such. By the 2nd century AD the Roman organ was heard in theatres and games; a surviving model dated 228 from Aquincum is very small, with four rows of 13 bronze flue pipes, one open and three stopped. Organ construction was abandoned until the 9th and 10th centuries when the instrument was reintroduced from Byzantium, with bellows often replacing the cylinder-pump water organ. Instruments were used as diplomatic gifts or signs of royal power. The 10th-century monastic revival contributed to the introduction of organs in the Western church.

By the 15th century the large organ, usually located near the *cantores*, could be distinguished from the smaller portative and positive organs. Portatives were portable, with a compass of up to two octaves, and were blown by bellows operated by one of the player's hands. Positives were blown by larger bellows operated by a second person. By 1500 the average church organ in northern Italy or southern France had about ten stops and one manual. Those of the upper Rhineland were the most advanced in Europe, with two or three manuals. In England, organs remained single-manual until the 17th century; pipes were wooden and the key compass slightly larger than northern European models. A number of new stops were invented (above all Flutes and Reeds, often for specific colour imitations) and instruments were able to produce a variety of tonal effects.

In the 16th century regional schools began to emerge. By the mid-17th, the French organ had achieved its classic form; its reeds had a bass depth and brilliance, and the flute mutation rank (Tierce) was very popular; builders included Thierry, Joyeuse and the Clicquot family. The instrument demonstrated extravagant contrasts, big choruses (plein jeu and grand jeu), echoes and clearly marked colours. Its development was set back by the French Revolution, but revived in the 1840s by Cavaillé-Coll who introduced many tonal innovations.

Organ building in England, hindered during the Reformation, had increased considerably by the late 17th century with the instruments of Bernard ('Father') Smith and Renatus Harris, in which French influence was strong. The pedalboard was probably not used until c1720 and the Swell developed at the same time, ousting the Choir organ as the chief second manual. Mid-18th century instruments by the émigré Snetzler introduced continental features such as colourful stops, manual

coupler and Tremulant. These techniques were incorporated on concert-hall organs on the 19th century.

16th-century Spanish organs were influenced by the Flemish school. By the 18th, reed pipes were placed horizontally, projecting from the organ case, and were used for 'battle-pieces' and ceremonial occasions; half-stops providing separate registrations for each hand were also developed. The standard Italian instrument by 1575 was modelled on the one-manual Brescian classical organ; second manuals, reed stops and swell boxes were not widely used until the 18th century.

In central Germany extravagant court chapel organs were built with rich mechanical layouts, allowing an immense array of stop combinations, and were geared towards subtle colour and musical variety. A flourishing school of builders grew up, including the Fritzsche and Compenius families, Silbermann and Casparini; such composers as Froberger, Pachelbel and J.S. Bach were inspired by the instrument. As it became increasingly associated with congregational hymn singing in the 18th century it developed a powerful 16' pedal tone and extremes of loud and soft. 17th-century Dutch organs were used for secular purposes, and demonstrate a magnificent array of mutations and flute and reed colours. German builders dominated the instrument during the 18th century and produced large, powerful instruments which lacked the older German brilliance or French distinction. Organs were used in Central America by 1530 and in Canada by 1657. English instruments were imported in North America throughout the 18th century and a vigorous native school was established in Boston and New York, its work rooted in the English tradition.

The 19th-century Bach revival resulted in the alteration of countless old English and French organs and some Italian and Spanish: pedals and second choruses were added and short manuals completed, but the national identity was usually retained. Technical developments on Germany c1825 had an influence throughout Europe: octave couplers became popular and double pedalboards and solo manuals were used on larger instruments. In England, swell boxes were improved, higher pressure was applied to reed pipes and the mechanical-pneumatic action ('Barker lever') was in use by 1833. Fully pneumatic and electric actions, which helped establish the organ as an imitator of the orchestra, were developed in France and England in the mid-century; the latter became the norm in the USA in the early 20th century.

An organ revival (*Orgelbewegung*) was instigated in Germany during the 1920s, concerned with reviving some of the instrument's historic principles. Attempts were made to reconstruct the tonal character of a Baroque instrument and old models were restored. The movement spread throughout Europe and the USA, awareness for historical accuracy increasing in the years after World War II. The tendency towards strict and specific stylistic imitation has become increasingly marked, particularly in the field of authentic temperaments.

Organ by Flentrop (1967) at the Queen Elizabeth Hall, London

Organ chorale. *See* CHORALE and CHORALE PRELUDE.

Organ hymn. A liturgical form in which verses of a hymn were taken alternately by the choir and the organ. The earliest source of liturgical organ music is the Faenza MS (*c*1400); there are also early German examples. In the 16th century, English organists (notably John Redford, *d* 1547) produced outstanding organ hymns, on a *cantus firmus*. Organ hymns were published in the early 17th century by Frescobaldi and Titelouze, but the genre did not develop further and in Protestant countries it gave way to the organ chorale.

Organostrum. *See* HURDY-GURDY.

Organ mass. A collection of pieces (versets) for the organ replacing parts of the Mass and played in alternation with the sung portions. Until the mid-17th century the planchant replaced by the organ was generally used structurally in the verset. The earliest source, the Faenza MS (*c*1400), contains examples, two-part settings with tenor *cantus firmo* in long notes. More advanced settings are in the Buxheom Organbook (*c*1470), in 16th-century English sources and in Attaingnant's *Tabulature pour le jeu d'orgues* (1531). Cavazzoni (*ontabulatura d'organo*, ii, 1543) broke away from the *cantus firmus* style in favour of a more unified, motet-like texture; he was followed in Italy by A. Gabrieli, Merulo and Frescobaldi.

The 17th century is the most important period for the organ mass. French settings include those of Nivers, Lebègue, Gogault, Raison, de Grigny and F. Couperon, in which polyphonic structures were discarded for the new concertato style, with less structural use of plainchant. French publications continued to dominate the scene in the 18th and 19th centuries. In 1903 the *Motu proprio* of Pope Pius X banned *alternatim* organ music from the liturgy.

Organology. The descriptive and analytical study of muscal instruments. The term was introduced by Bessaraboff in 1941 to distinguish the 'scientific and engineering aspects' of instruments from the broader study of music. An essential part of organology is the analytical classfication of instruments from different epochs and cultures (*see* INSTRUMENTS, CLASSIFICATION OF); their historical development and musical uses can also fall under this heading, though not necessarily the development of associated genres or details of their repertory.

Organo pleno [pieno] (It.: 'full organ'). Term for an organ REGISTRATION using the major choruses of the instrument. It has rarely if ever denoted that the composer has required the organist to draw every stop; since *c*1850 most composers other than the French have left it to the organist's discretion and the organ-bellows' capacity. *See* FULL ORGAN and GRAND CHOEUR.

Organ point. Ambiguous term in English, equivalent to the French *point d'orgue* and the German *Orgelpunkt*. Any of these may imply either a harmonic pedal (also called 'pedal point' or simply 'pedal' in English), where a note in the bass is sustained while the other parts continue in motion (it can also apply to an ornamental cadenza above a sustained note); they can also be used simply for a pause or fermata, which may also imply a sustained note in the bass with improvised music above. In present-day usage, *Orgelpunkt* and the French *pédale*, and the English 'pedal point' or 'pedal', carry the first meaning, *point d'orgue*, the German *Fermate* and the English 'pause' or 'fermata' the second. 'Organ point' is better avoided.

Organ Solo Mass. Mozart's *Missa brevis* in C K259 (1776), so called because there is an important solo in the Benedictus.

Organ Symphony. Saint-Saëns's Symphony no.3 in C minor (1886).

Organum. Term, originally connected with the organ but later with 'consonant music', used for medieval polyphony; from the 12th century specifically referred to music with a sustained-note tenor (usually based on a pre-existing melody) and faster-moving upper part(s). From the late 13th century it was used for plainchant in general, as distinct from the motet and conductus.

The concept of consonance and the idea of a voice (*vox organalis*) added to a pre-existing chant melody (*vox principalis*) were fundamental to the development of organum. In the early Middle Ages the *vox organalis* generally lay below the *vox principalis* and the concept of consonance was based on parallel 4ths and 5ths. Influenced by the theoretical need to avoid the tritone and the demands of the tetrachord system, other intervals became acceptable; by the 11th century parallel movement in 3rds and contrary motion were important and the *vox organalis* enjoyed greater freedom of movement, eventually becoming established as the upper voice.

As the century progressed, a distinction was made between organum, in which the *vox organalis* forms melismas over the sustained notes of the *vox principalis*, and discant, where it forms more or less strict note-for-note counterpoint. In the melismatic type the *vox organalis* became the 'main voice' in effect, and drew on a number of melodic formulae (*see* CENTONIZATION) in relatively short melismas. The extension of these melismas marks the achievement of the Notre Dame school (notably Léonin and Pérotin) as represented in the *Magnus liber* (*c*1170). This collection also reveals that, towards the end of the 12th century, melismatic organum was gradually superseded by the more fashionable discant counterpoint introducing modal rhythm. Nonmodal melismatic organum (*organum purum*) disappeared, but a third type emerged in which modal rhythm was cultivated in the melismatic upper voice over the sustained notes of the tenor (as the *vox principalis* became known in the 13th century). Modal rhythm opened up new possibilities for three- and four-voice music, and was eventually responsible for the transformation to mensural, or rhythmically measured, polyphony.

Organ verset. A short organ piece, often improvised, which replaces a verse of a liturgical item sung by the choir. *See also* ALTERNATIM, ORGAN HYMN and ORGAN MASS.

Orgelbüchlein. Collection of short chorale-preludes for organ by J.S. Bach.

Orgelpunkt (Ger.). *See* ORGAN POINT.

Ó Riada, Seán [Reidy, John] (*b* Cork, 1 Aug 1931; *d* London, 3 Oct 1971). Irish composer. He studied with Fleischmann at Cork (1948–52), where he taught (1963–71) after periods at Irish radio and the Abbey Theatre, Dublin. He made arrangements of Irish folk music but wrote more speculative compositions, notably the *Nomos* series, of which no.2 (1963) for baritone, chorus and orchestra is the most important.

Orlandini, Giuseppe Maria (*b* Florence, 19 March 1675; *d* there, 24 Oct 1760). Italian composer. He was *maestro di cappella* to the Prince of Tuscany in Florence and of Florence Cathedral from 1732). He composed *c*50 stage works for theatres in Florence, Naples, Venice and elsewhere, using a progressive, simple melodic idiom. Best known were his 12 comic intermezzos; *Il marito giocatore* (1719, Venice; also given as *Serpilla e Bacocco*, 1721, Munich) was apparently the most frequently performed piece of musical drama in the 18th century. His other works include oratorios and cantatas.

Orlando. Opera in three acts by Handel to a libretto by Capece after Ariosto (1733, London). Vivaldi wrote two operas on Orlando (1714, 1727).

Ormandy, Eugene (*b* Budapest, 18 Nov 1899; *d* Philadelphia, 12 March 1985). American conductor of Hungarian birth. After study at the Budapest Conservatory he began touring as a solo violinist during World War I. He moved to the USA in 1921 and was conductor of the Minneapolis SO, 1931–6. From 1936 to 1980 he worked with the Philadelphia Orchestra which he shaped into a fine instrument, full in tone and immaculate in technique, especially in the late Romantic and early 20th-century music.

Ormindo. Opera by Cavalli to a libretto by Faustini (1644, Venice).

Ornaments. The brief, conventional formulae of embellishment to music, which may be added extemporaneously by performers working within traditions of free ornamentation or may be notated by means of conventional signs or small notes. They have been used in all periods of Western music but proliferated particularly in the late Renaissance, the Baroque and the Classical periods. They divide into two main classes: graces, melodic ornaments applied to individual notes; and divisions or *passaggi*, where figuration patterns are applied to an existing melody. The use of ornaments was encouraged in particular musical contexts, for example, in Italian monodic singing and (later) Italian opera arias, slow movements in sonatas, in French lute (and later harpsichord and viol) music and in the music of the English virginalists. In some contexts ornaments were often left unnotated or notated only vaguely. In others, more or less precise systems of signs were devised; many composers and theorists, especially towards the end of the Baroque period, presented tables of these signs and their execution (for example Couperin and Bach). But ornament signs were often used in a casual, inconsistent and uncertain manner, partly because performers were anyway often expected to add ornamentation of their own (*see* IMPROVISATION).

For discussion of individual ornaments and their realization, see under the name of the ornament itself; the following are entered in this dictionary: ANSCHLAG, ACCIACCATURA, APPOGGIATURA, BEAT, BEBUNG, CADENT, CHUTE, GRACE NOTES, GROPPO, MESSA DI VOCE, MORDENT, NACHSCHLAG, PRALLTRILLER, PORTAMENTO, RELISH, SLIDE, SPRINGER, TIRADE, TRILL, TRILLO, TURN and VIBRATO.

Ornithoparchus, Andreas (*b* Meiningen, *c*1490). German theorist. A graduate of Rostock and Tübingen universities and a disciple of Erasmus, he published his first treatise on music, *Musicae activae micrologus*, at Leipzig in 1517. In four books, it dealt with practical music and composition and showed his wide experience. It was clearly popular, for it went through several editions; it was translated into English by Dowland in 1609.

Ornstein, Leo (*b* Kremenchug, 2 Dec 1892). American composer and pianist of Russian birth. He studied in Petrograd and New York, where he arrived in 1907. From 1911 to 1920 he appeared widely as a composer-pianist, playing pieces that made extravagant use of dissonance, polyrhythm and unusual colour effects (e.g. *Wild Men's Dance*, *c*1915); his later works seem more conservative.

Orologio, Alessandro (*b c*1550; *d* Vienna, ?1633). Italian composer. He served the imperial court in Prague as a trumpeter (from 1580) and as vice-Kapellmeister (1603–13) and travelled extensively. Widely known as an ensemble instrumentalist and composer, he published six books of secular vocal music (1586–96) and one of instrumental pieces, short, sonorous intradas for five or six instruments (1597).

Orozco, Rafael (*b* Córdoba, 24 Jan 1946). Spanish pianist. He studied at the Cordoba and Madrid conservatories, graduating in 1964, and in 1966 won the Leeds Piano Bompetition. An exuberant virtuoso, he is at his best in the central Romantic repertory.

Orpharion. A wire-strung, plucked instrument of the BANDORA family, of similar scalloped shape but smaller and tuned like the lute. From the end of the 16th century it was largely regarded as interchangeable with the lute, but had fallen into disuse by the end of the 17th. It had seven, eight or nine double courses, a 'viol' type pegbox with lateral pegs, and a sloping bridge and frets enabling a larger range than the lute's.

Orphée aux enfers. *See* ORPHEUS IN THE UNDERWORLD.

Orphéon. French popular male-voice choral movement; it began to develop *c*1815 and the original Orphéon choral society was established in Paris in 1833. By the turn of the century there were more than 2000 Orphéon societies in France.

Orpheus. Symphonic poem by Liszt, an introduction to his Weimar production of Gluck's *Orphée et Euridice* (1854).

Ballet in three scenes by Stravinsky (1948, New York).

The Orpheus legend has been the subject of many operas, by Peri and Caccini (both *Euridice*), Monteverdi (L'ORFEO), Gluck (ORFEO ED EURIDICE), Benda, Paer, Offenbach, Milhaud, Malipiero,

Casella, Krenek and Birtwistle (THE MASK OF ORPHEUS), among others, and of ballets (including Henze's).

Orpheus in the Underworld [Orphée aux enfers]. Opera in two acts by Offenbach to a libretto by Crémieux and Halévy (1858, Paris); Offenbach expanded it into four acts (1874, Paris).

Orphica. A portable piano, invented c1795 and designed for outdoor use; it could be carried or supported on a strap round the neck. It had a compass of two or four octaves.

Orr, C(harles) W(ilfred) (b Cheltenham, 31 July 1893; d Painswick, 24 Feb 1976). English composer. One of the finest British songwriters of the century, he wrote 35 songs (24 of them settings of Housman) in a modal-diatonic, elegiac style.

Orr, Robin [Robert] **(Kemsley)** (b Brechin, 2 June 1909). Scottish composer. He studied at the RCM, at Cambridge, with Casella in Siena and with Boulanger in Paris. In 1938 he returned to Cambridge, where he became professor (1965–76). His works, drawing on mid-century masters, include two symphonies (1963, 1970), chamber music, the opera *Hermiston* (1975) and much Anglican church music.

Orrego-Salas, Juan (Antonio) (b Santiago, 18 Jan 1919). Chilean composer and musicologist. He studied in Chile and the USA (with Thompson and Copland), then was active in Santiago as a teacher, critic and composer. In 1961 he founded the Latin American Music Center at Indiana University. His works, in all genres, show a neo-classical craftsmanship.

ORTF. *See* OFFICE DE RADIODIFFUSION-TÉLÉVISION FRANÇAISE.

Ortigue, Joseph (Louis) d' (b Cavaillon, 22 May 1802; d Paris, 20 Nov 1866). French writer on music. He contributed articles and reviews to over 20 journals, notably *Le ménestrel* (chief editor, 1863) and the *Journal des débats* (succeeding his friend Berlioz, 1864), but his major work was his study of religious music, especially in the *Dictionnaire liturgique, historique et théorique de plain-chant* (1853). He collaborated with Louis Niedermeyer.

Ortiz, Diego (b Toledo, c1510; d ?Naples, c1570). Spanish theorist and composer. He was in Naples by 1553 and *maestro de capilla* of the Spanish viceroy's chapel from 1558 until at least 1565. His *Trattado de glosas* (1553), the first printed ornamentation manual for bowed string instruments, includes c24 viol pieces. A book of sacred music also survives (1565).

Orto [Dujardin], Marbrianus de (b ?diocese of Tournai, c1460; d Nivelles, by Feb 1529). Franco-Flemish composer. A singer in the papal chapel choir, 1483–96, he became dean at St gertrude, Nivelles; subsequently he sang in Philip the Fair's chapel, with which he went to Spain, then worked in Antwerp and Brussels. His seven masses and six motets show a preference for varied *cantus firmus* techniques. He also wrote *chansons*. His *Dulces exuviae*, a setting for four voices of Dido's lament from the *Aeneid*, is an outstanding example of musical humanism in the Renaissance.

Osborne, George Alexander (b Limerick, 24 Sept 1806; d London, 16 Nov 1893). Irish pianist and composer. He studied in Paris with Pixis and Fétis, then with Kalkbrenner, of whose style he became one of the finest exponents. He was a fashionable pianist, well-known teacher and salon composer in London and Paris, where his friends included the most eminent musicians, Berlioz and Chopin among them.

Osborne, Nigel (b Manchester, 23 June 1948). English composer. He studied at Oxford and with Rudziński in Warsaw (1970–71) and is a prolific composer of operas, diverse vocal works and ensemble pieces. His interest in 20th-century literature is reflected in his opera after Pasternak, *The Electrification of the Soviet Union* (1987, Glyndebourne).

Oslo Philharmonic Orchestra. Norwegian orchestra formed in 1919 to replace the Musikforening and the National Theatre Orchestra; it is now the foremost orchestra in Norway, conducted by Mariss Jansons (1979–).

Ospedale della Pietà. One of the Venetian charitable institutions for girls that became famous in Europe as conservatories in the 17th and 18th centuries. The virtuoso music composed by Vivaldi and others who taught there influenced the style of instrumental music in northern Italy.

Ossia (It.). 'Alternatively': an indication used in scores for an alternative to a passage (e.g. simplified, embellished, another reading).

Ostinato. A term used to refer to the repetition of a musical pattern many times in succession. A melodic ostinato may occur in the bass (*see* GROUND), as an upper melody (e.g. the 'Dargason' from Holst's *St Paul's Suite*) or simply as a succession of pitches (e.g. the 'Carillon' from Bizet's *L'Arlésienne* Suite no.1). A constantly repeated chord progression produces a harmonic ostinato, as in Chopin's *Berceuse*, while rhythmic ostinato occurs in Ravel's *Bolero*.

Ostrčil, Otakar (b Prague, 25 Feb 1879; d there, 20 Aug 1935). Czech composer. A pupil of Fibich, he worked in Prague as a conductor, notably as director of the National Theatre (1920–35), whose standards he raised, and where he gave important new Czech operas (including Janáček's) and foreign works. His own works include operas and orchestral pieces in an expanded tonal style.

Osud. Opera in three acts by Janáček to a libretto by F. Bartošová and the composer (composed 1905, broadcast 1934).

O'Sullivan, Denis (b San Francisco, 25 April 1868; d Columbus, OH, 1 Feb 1908). Irish-American baritone. He studied in San Francisco and later in Florence, London and Paris. He made his London début in 1895 and later worked with the Carl Rosa company, singing the title role in *The Flying Dutchman* in Dublin at five hours' notice. He later divided his time between England and the USA. He was admired for his phrasing and enunciation.

Oswald, James (b Scotland, 1711; d Knebworth, 1769). Scottish composer and music publisher. After a period in Edinburgh, 1736–41, he settled in London, where he published collections of folktunes and other popular music. In 1761 he became chamber composer to George III. He wrote variations, trio sonatas, pieces depicting flowers etc, with a Scottish flavour which helped popularize a Scottish idiom in London.

Oswald von Wolkenstein (*b* Schöneck in Pustertal, *c*1377; *d* Merano, 2 Aug 1445). South German poet-musician, one of the last knightly ones of the region. Second son of a Tyrolean family, he was important as an emissary and in local politics; events from his active life are recorded in his songs. His poetry covers a variety of themes, from a battle-cry to satirical and para-liturgical texts, as well as much love poetry inspired by his wife Margarete (whom he married in 1417) and other ladies. His individual, often innovatory approach to composition (notably his through-composed stanzas, his approach to word-setting and his use of large melodic steps and instrumental interludes) sets him apart from Meistergesang, although he is sometimes classified as a Meistersinger. While his polyphonic songs reveal Italian trecento influence, his individual treatment can best be seen in his songs recognizable as contrafacta, especially in the division of the melodic lines and syllabic treatment of melismas. His texting of the tenor foreshadows the TENORLIED. His polyphonic compositions also include canons, songs in the style of organum and conductus and several lieder with short passages of hocket. Towards the end of his life he seems to have rejected these more complex compositional devices and concentrated on setting songs with a greater emphasis on the need to instruct others to 'do right' (*rechttun*) in this world.

Otaño (y Eugenio), Nemesio (*b* Azcoitia, 19 Dec 1880; *d* S Sebastian, 29 April 1956). Spanish composer. He studied in Valladolid with Vicente Goicoechea, with whom he began his work reforming sacred music. In 1911 he founded the Schola Cantorum at Comillas: his performances with them of plainsong and polyphony were highly influential. From 1939 he was director of the Madrid Conservatory. His works range from popular sacred songs (e.g. *Estrella hermosa*) to large-scale choral pieces.

Otello. Opera in four acts by Verdi to a libretto by Boito after Shakespeare (1887, Milan).

Opera in three acts by Rossini to a libretto by F. Berio di Salsa after Shakespeare (1816, Naples).

Otescu, Ion Nonna (*b* Bucharest, 15 Dec 1888; *d* there, 25 March 1940). Romanian composer. A pupil of Kiriac and Castaldi in Bucharest and of d'Indy and Widor in Paris (1908–11), he taught at the Bucharest Conservatory from 1913 (director, 1918–40) and conducted the Bucharest PO. He wrote operas and orchestral pieces in a nationalist French-influenced style.

Othello. Concert overture, op.93, by Dvořák, the third of his *Nature, Life and Love* cycle.

Othmayr, Caspar [Othmarus, Gasparus] (*b* Amberg, 12 March 1515; *d* Nuremberg, 4 Feb 1553). German composer. While a student at Heidelberg University (1533–6) he belonged to the Hofkantorei; he may have been a composer at the Palatine court during the next decade, though he held posts in Heilsbronn and Ansbach. He was an important and versatile composer whose output, covering the main genres of vocal music except the mass, amounts to *c*230 compositions. Most of his sacred pieces are clearly Luth-

eran, with their references to hymn tunes and settings of Lutheran biblical texts. His secular songs, which include 50 four- or five-part German songs and 16 four-part ones (published 1549 and *c*1550), occupy a central position in his output. He used both *cantus firmus* tenor parts (frequently folktunes) and duo sections in the manner of Josquin and Senfl.

Ottani, Bernardo (*b* Bologna, 8 Sept 1736; *d* Turin, 26 April 1827). Italian composer. A pupil and friend of Padre Martini, he had an early success with a comic opera for Venice (1767–8) and later composed two operas for Dresden (1769) and ten (mostly serious) for Italian cities. He was *maestro di cappella* in Bologna from 1769; in 1770 Mozart heard an oratorio of his. He became *maestro di cappella* of Turin Cathedral in 1779 and thereafter wrote mostly sacred music. His brother Gaetano (before 1736–1808) was a tenor.

Otto, Georg (*b* Torgau, 1550; *d* Kassel, bur. 30 Nov 1618). German composer. From 1569 he was Kantor at Langensalza and from 1586 Hofkapellmeister to the Landgrave of Hessen-Kassel, where he taught his heir, Moritz; Schütz was also among his pupils, and music flourished there under his supervision. He composed mainly sacred works (3 vols., 1574–1604, and many MSS).

Ottone. Opera in three acts by Handel to a libretto by Haym after Pallavicino (1723, London).

Our Hunting Fathers. Symphonic song cycle, op.8, by Britten (1936), a setting of a text by W.H. Auden for soprano or tenor and orchestra.

Our Man in Havana. Opera in three acts by Williamson to a libretto by Sidney Gilliat after Graham Greene (1963, London).

Ours, L'. *See* BEAR, THE.

Ouseley, Sir Frederick Arthur Gore (*b* London, 12 Aug 1825; *d* Hereford, 6 April 1889). English church musician, scholar and composer. A high churchman (ordained 1849), deeply influenced by the Oxford movement, he dedicated his wealth to the musical profession, founding St Michael's College, Tenbury (1854), and the Musical Association (1874) and becoming professor at Oxford (1855). He thus established musical scholarship as a respected field of learning. At St Michael's he developed his ideal of the English cathedral service, meanwhile collecting a library rich in early English church music and Spanish theory, his chief interests. As a composer he showed early precocity and a vivid imagination but moderated his style, especially in sacred vocal works, towards classical models.

Ouvert, clos (Fr.). Terms that signify, respectively, the first-time and second-time endings in a piece with a repeat. The words appear particularly in 14th-century music.

Overblowing. The process by which a wind player produces higher modes of vibration in his air column, and thus sounds not the fundamental but the octave, 12th etc of its lowest note.

Over-dotting. A convention in the performance of Baroque music according to which, it is supposed, dotted rhythms should be exaggerated. *See* DOTTED RHYTHMS.

Overspun string. String with a core of gut or metal wound round along its length with a coil or coils of a (relatively thin) ductile wire to increase its mass without increasing stiffness.

Overstrung. Term applied to a piano in which the strings are arranged in two nearly parallel planes, with the bass strings passing diagonally over those in the middle range. Both groups may thus fan out over the soundboard and make more effective use of its entire area (*see* PIANOFORTE). The term should not be confused with CROSS-STRUNG.

Overton, Hall (*b* Bangor, MI, 23 Feb 1920; *d* New York, 24 Nov 1972). American composer. He studied with Persichetti at the Juilliard School (1947–51), where he later taught (1960–71), and privately with Riegger and Milhaud. Deeply influenced by jazz, he wrote operas including *Huckleberry Finn* (1971), two symphonies, and chamber music.

Overtone. A mode of vibration of a body other than that of its fundamental frequency. An overtone need not be harmonic. *See* HARMONICS and ACOUSTICS.

Overture (Fr. *ouverture*; Ger. *Ouvertüre*; It. *sinfonia*). An orchestral piece introducing an opera or other longer work, or one written for concert performance. Overtures to mid-17th-century Venetian operas typically consisted of a slow section in duple metre followed by a faster one in triple; this served as a model for the FRENCH OVERTURE developed by Lully, Purcell, Handel and others. In Germany, 'Ouvertüre' was often used for an orchestral suite beginning with an overture of this type. The Italian overture (*see* SINFONIA), developed at Naples in the late 17th century, was in three short sections (fast–slow–fast), often with a prominent trumpet part. This type, or rather its first section extended on sonata lines, survived into the Classical period, but it was not until Gluck and Mozart that composers began to connect the overture thematically or in other ways to the opera that followed. The standard operatic overture between 1790 and 1820 consisted of a slow introduction and a fast movement in common time and in sonata form but without repeats and with little or no melodic development.

After Wagner's *Tannhäuser* (1845) independent overtures to serious operas were largely replaced by shorter preludes, but the overture survived in comic operas and operettas and as a concert piece. Many concert overtures, such as Mendelssohn's *The Hebrides*, are descriptive pieces; others, like Berlioz's *King Lear* and *The Corsair*, are based on literary subjects or, like Brahms's *Academic Festival Overture*, celebrate a particular event.

Owen Wingrave. Opera in two acts by Britten to a libretto by Myfanwy Piper after Henry James; it was written for television (1971) but later staged (1973, Covent Garden).

Oxford Elegy, An. Work by Vaughan Williams for speaker, chorus and small orchestra, to a text adapted from Matthew Arnold (1949).

Oxford Symphony. Nickname of Haydn's Symphony no.92 in G (1789), so called because it was performed when Haydn received an honorary doctorate at Oxford University.

Oxford University Press. English publishing concern, a division of Oxford University since 1478. Its musical activities have been almost entirely a 20th-century development, the printed music programme in particular flourishing under the management (1921–41) of Hubert J. Foss. The emphasis has been on contemporary British music, notably by Vaughan Williams, Lambert, Rawsthorne and Walton; standard collections include *The Oxford Book of Carols* and *The Church Anthem Book*.

Ozawa, Seiji (*b* Hoten, 1 Sept 1935). Japanese conductor. After early conducting experience in Tokyo he studied at the Berkshire Music Center, Tanglewood; Münch, Bernstein and Karajan were early mentors. He was music director of the Toronto SO, 1965–70, and after a period with the San Francisco SO became music director of the Boston SO in 1973. His London début was in 1965, with the LSO, and he has conducted at Salzburg since 1969. He is at his best in large-scale, late Romantic music.

Ozi, Etienne (*b* Nîmes, 9 Dec 1754; *d* Paris, 5 Oct 1813). French bassoonist and composer. He was a highly successful soloist and orchestral player in Paris and served at the French court (1786–8) and elsewhere. After the Revolution he taught at the Conservatoire and played widely; he was regarded as the best bassoonist of his time. He wrote concertos, *symphonies concertantes* and chamber music for his instrument as well as wind-band music and three bassoon methods.

P

P. Abbreviation for *piano* (It.: 'quiet'); in musical text, it is usually in lower case, bold italic type. *See* DYNAMICS. Followed by a numeral, it identifies a concerto or symphony by Vivaldi by its number in Pincherle's thematic catalogue (1948).

Pablo, Luis de (*b* Bilbao, 28 Jan 1930). Spanish composer. Self-taught as a composer, he began working on behalf of new music in Madrid in the mid-1950s and attended the Darmstadt courses in 1958. Through his large, varied output and his teaching at the Madrid Conservatory he has influenced younger Spanish composers. Since the mid-1960s his works have used aleatory forms; later they embraced electronics.

Paccagnini, Angelo (*b* Castano Primo, 17 Oct 1930). Italian composer. He studied at the Milan Conservatory, where he teaches, and worked from 1956 at the Milan electronic music studio; he also leads Ars Antiqua, an early music ensemble. His works, in many genres, are concerned with the condition of men in the contemporary world and are often violent and dramatic.

Pacchiarotti, Gasparo (*b* Fabriano, bap. 21 May 1740; *d* Padua, 28 Oct 1821). Italian soprano castrato. He achieved much success in operas throughout Italy, and in 1778–84 sang in England, where William Beckford was one of his patrons. In 1791 he revisited London and in 1793 he retired to Padua. He was the last great soprano castrato; his rendition of pathetic airs was especially moving.

Pacchioni, Antonio Maria (*b* Modena, bap. 5 July 1654; *d* there, 15 July 1738). Italian composer. A priest, he became *maestro di cappella* of Modena Cathedral in 1694; he was also *vice-maestro* (1699–1722) and then *maestro di cappella* at the ducal court. His three oratorios (1677–82), among the first given in the Modena area, have many strophic arias and two make unusually extensive use of the chorus. He also wrote church music and a few secular pieces.

Pace, Pietro (*b* Loreto, 1559; *d* there, 15 April 1622). Italian composer. He was organist of the Santa Casa, Loreto (1591–2, 1611–22), and of Pesaro Cathedral (1597) and had connections with the Urbino court. A prolific composer of motets etc (11 bks, 1613–19) and madrigals (5 bks, 1597–1617), he often used continuo and affective ornamentation.

Pacelli [Pecelli], **Asprilio** (*b* Vasciano, 1570; *d* Warsaw, 4 May 1623). Italian composer. He served at two Rome churches before becoming *maestro di cappella* of the Collegio Germanico there by 1595. He held a similar post at St Peter's in 1602, but in 1603 went to Warsaw as director of the Polish royal chapel, where he was a champion of Italian music. His own works, which became widely known, are mainly motets, psalms etc in the learned Roman style deriving from Palestrina; some are polychoral. He also composed two books of madrigals.

Pachelbel [Bachelbel], **Johann** (*b* Nuremberg, bap. 1 Sept 1653; *d* Nuremberg, bur. 9 March 1706). German composer and organist. He was taught by two local musicians, Heinrich Schwemmer and G.C. Wecker. In 1669 he entered the university at Altdorf and was organist of the Lorenzkirche there, but left after less than a year for lack of money and in 1670 enrolled in the Gymnasium Poeticum at Regensburg, where he continued musical studies with Kaspar Prentz.

After about five years as deputy organist at St Stephen's Cathedral, Vienna (1637–7), and a year as court organist at Eisenach, Pachelbel was appointed organist of the Predigerkirche at Erfurt in June 1678, where he remained for 12 years. During this time he was outstandingly successful as organist, composer and teacher (his pupils included J.S. Bach's elder brother, Johann Christoph) and was twice married. He left Erfurt in 1690 and, after short periods as organist in Stuttgart and Gotha, returned to his native Nuremberg, where he was organist at St Sebald until his death.

Pachelbel was a prolific composer. His organ music includes *c*70 chorales (mostly written at Erfurt), 95 Magnificat fugues (for Vespers at St Sebald) and non-liturgical works such as toccatas, preludes, fugues and fantasias. His preference for a lucid, uncomplicated style found fullest expression in his vocal music, which includes two masses and some important Vespers music as well as arias and sacred concertos. His modest contributions to chamber music include the canon that has become his best-known work.

*Organ music c*70 chorales; 95 Magnificat fugues; over 60 toccatas, preludes, fugues, ciacconas, fantasias, ricercares
Other keyboard music 21 suites; 7 sets of chorale variations; 10 arias with variations, incl. 6 in Hexachordum Apollinis (1699)

Chamber music Musicalische Ergötzung, 6 suites (1695); Partita, G; Canon and Gigue, D
Sacred music 11 concs.; vespers music, incl. 13 Magnificats; 2 masses; 11 motets; arias

Pachelbel, Wilhelm Hieronymus (*b* Erfurt, bap. 29 Aug 1686; *d* Nuremberg, 1764). German composer and organist, eldest son of Johann. He held posts at Fürth, Erfurt and (from 1706) Nuremberg. He left several organ works and other keyboard pieces; some resemble his father's, while others, including *Musicalisches Vergnügen* (?1725), are more progressive.

Pachman, Vladimir de (*b* Odessa, 27 July 1848; *d* Rome, 6 Jan 1933). Ukrainian pianist. He studied at the Vienna Conservatory and made his début in Odessa in 1869. After further study he did not reappear until 1879, when he toured widely in Europe and the USA. He was renowned for his sensitive touch, notably in Chopin, and eccentric platform manner.

Pacific Island music. *See* OCEANIC MUSIC.

Pacific Northwest Wagner Festival (USA). Annual (summer) festival established in 1975; Seattle Opera presents Wagner's *Ring* in German and English (German with supratitles from 1986).

Pacific 231. Orchestral work by Honegger (*Mouvement symphonique no.1*, 1923), named after a locomotive.

Pacini, Antonio Francesco Gaetano Saverio (*b* Naples, 7 July 1778; *d* Paris, 10 March 1866). Italian composer and music publisher. He studied in Naples, went to Nîmes and, in 1804, to Paris, where he wrote *opéras comiques* and songs. In 1806 he began a career as a music publisher. In 1820–35 he issued operas by Mercadante, Bellini, Donizetti and Rossini; he also published monthly periodical collections of light music, piano concertos by Field and Paganini's caprices.

Pacini, Giovanni (*b* Catania, 17 Feb 1796; *d* Pescia, 6 Dec 1867). Italian composer. He studied singing with Marchesi in Bologna, then turned to composition. Between 1813 and 1867 he wrote nearly 90 operas, first modelling them on Rossini and later, after contact with Bellini's works, giving more attention to harmonic and instrumental colour. He was gifted with melodic invention, used to effect in a variety of cabaletta types; his accompaniments and ensemble writing are weak by comparison. Among the earlier works, *Alessandro nelle Indie* (1824), *L'ultimo giorno di Pompei* (1825), *Gli arabi nelle Gallie* (1827) and *Ivanhoe* (1832) were notable successes. In 1833 increased competition from Bellini and Donizetti caused his five-year withdrawal from the stage and he established a music school at his home in Viareggio and composed sacred works for the ducal chapel in Lucca, of which he was director from 1837. But with the immensely successful *Saffo* (1840), considered his masterpiece, he entered a period of more mature opera composition, producing *La fidanzata corsa* (1842), *Maria, regina d'Inghilterra* and *Medea* (1843). Though his success and reputation outside Italy were limited, his musical weaknesses can be attributed chiefly to the circumstances in which he worked. In the face of for-midable competition within Italy, he satisfied a sophisticated public for half a century.

Pacius, Frederik (*b* Hamburg, 19 March 1809; *d* Helsinki, 8 Jan 1891). Finnish composer. A pupil of Spohr, he was a violinist in Stockholm and in 1835 settled in Helsinki, where he did much for musical life. He taught at the university and wrote two operas, orchestral works and the Finnish national anthem, and is regarded as the father of Finnish music.

Packe, Thomas (*fl* c1480–c1520). English composer. He may have been a chapel clerk at Eton College. His compositions include a five-voice *Nunc dimittis*, a motet and two masses, among the few English polyphonic Ordinary settings of the time.

Padbrué, Cornelis Thymanszoon (*b* Haarlem, c1592; *d* there, bur. 18 Jan 1670). Netherlands composer. A schalmei player, he was a city musician at Haarlem in 1610–35. His seven volumes of music (1631–46) include sacred and secular vocal pieces and instrumental works; the last is the only surviving example of *stile rappresentativo* from the northern Low Countries. Among the other musicians in his family was his uncle David Janszoon Padbrué (c1553–1635), a composer, singer and lute player.

Paderewski, Ignacy Jan (*b* Kuryłówka, 18 Nov 1860; *d* New York, 29 June 1941). Polish pianist, composer and statesman. He studied at the Warsaw Music Institute, in Berlin and with Leschetizky in Vienna, his career as a pianist beginning in 1888 with an exhausting concert schedule (Europe, North and South America, Australia, New Zealand, South Africa); he was noted for his individual treatment of rubato. Meanwhile he composed during the summers, producing the opera *Manru* (1892–1901), the Symphony op.24 and the *Fantaisie polonaise* op.19 for piano and orchestra, typical products of the late Romantic Polish national school; perhaps better known are his programmatic piano miniatures and the Piano Concerto (1888). Between 1910 and 1921 he was active on behalf of Poland, making speeches, assisting victims of oppression and eventually becoming prime minister (1919). He also supported young Polish composers and worked on a new Chopin edition.

Padilla, Juan Gutiérrez de (*b* Málaga, c1590; *d* Puebla, by 22 April 1664). Mexican composer. He was *maestro de capilla* at Puebla Cathedral from 1629 and one of the most important Spanish-born composers of his time. Most of his music survives, including c35 sacred vocal works, chiefly for double choir, and over 80 villancicos.

Padoana [paduana, padovana]. Term used in the 16th and 17th centuries for at least two kinds of dance. It is sometimes equivalent to the duple-metre PAVAN, or it may denote the first triple-metre after-dance of a PASSAMEZZO.

Padovano, Annibale (*b* Padua, 1527; *d* Graz, 15 March 1575). Italian composer. He was organist at St Mark's, Venice (1552–65), then at the Graz court (from 1566, director of music 1567). Though important chiefly for his distinctive ricercares and improvisatory toccatas for organ (1556, 1604), he also published sacred works (1567, 1573) and madrigals (1561, 1564).

Paer, Ferdinando (*b* Parma, 1 June 1771; *d* Paris, 3 May 1839). Italian composer. He studied in Parma. He made his mark as an opera composer principally in the *semiserio* style, first in Parma and then in Vienna (at the Kärntnertor-Theater from 1797), Dresden (as court Kapellmeister from 1801) and Paris (as Napoleon's *maître de chapelle* from 1807), where he also directed the Théâtre Italien until 1827. Gifted with a fund of sweet, Italianate melody and a fluent technique, he was a prolific if conservative composer who, with Mayr, dominated Italian opera in the first decade of the 19th century. In his best works, including *Griselda* (1798), *Camilla* (1799), *I fuorusciti di Firenze* (1802), *Sargino* (1803), *Leonora* (1804) and *Agnese* (1809), tragic and comic elements appear side by side, fully developed *airs* alternate with homely *romances* and an important role is given to the chorus. The lighter numbers show his wit, lyric charm, rhythmic thrust and skill at instrumentation and the intertwining of voices – the qualities that have made his popular comedy *Le maître de chapelle* (1821) enduring.

Paganelli, Giuseppe Antonio (*b* Padua, 6 March 1710; *d* ?Madrid, *c*1763). Italian composer. He had several operas staged in Venice (1732–3, 1742–3) and also presented operas in Prague (1735), Brunswick (1737–8) and elsewhere. He was director of chamber music to the Margravine of Bayreuth, 1737–8, and later perhaps to the King of Spain. He also wrote trio sonatas and other instrumental vocal works.

Paganini, Nicolò. (*b* Genoa, 27 Oct 1782; *d* Nice, 27 May 1840). Italian violinist and composer. By his technique and his extreme personal magnetism he was not only the most famous violin virtuoso but drew attention to the significance of virtuosity as an element in art. He studied with his father, Antonio Cervetto and Giacomo Costa and composition with Ghiretti and Paer in Parma. From 1810 to 1828 he developed a career as a 'free artist' throughout Italy, mesmerizing audiences and critics with his showmanship; notable compositions were the bravura variations *Le streghe* (1813), the imaginative 24 Caprices op.1 and the second and third violin concertos, surpassing in brilliance any that had been written before. After conquering Vienna in 1828 he was equally successful in Germany (Goethe, Heine and Schumann admired him), Paris and London (1831–4). His hectic international career finally shattered his health in 1834, when he returned to Parma. Apart from his unparalleled technical wizardry on the instrument, including the use of left-hand pizzicato, double-stop harmonics, 'ricochet' bowings and a generally daredevil approach to performance – all of which influenced successive violinists (Ernst, Bériot, Vieuxtemps) – he is most important for his artistic impact on Liszt, Chopin, Schumann and Berlioz, who took up his technical challenge in the search for greater expression in their own works.

Violin and orchestra 6 concertos; *c*12 sets of variations, including Le streghe (1813); sonatas; miscellaneous pieces
Chamber music 32 sonatas, 4 sonatinas and 2 sets of variations for vn, gui; qts and other works with gui; 3 str qts; Vn

Sonata (1830); other vn pieces with pf; 24 Caprices, vn (*c*1805); variations for vn; gui pieces
Vocal music songs, duet

Pagliacci [Clowns]. Opera in two acts by Leoncavallo to his own libretto (1892, Milan). It is usually performed in a double bill with Mascagni's *Cavalleria rusticana*, hence the colloquial abbreviation 'Cav' and 'Pag'.

Pagliughi, Lina (*b* New York, 27 May 1911 *d* Rubicone, 1 Oct 1980). Italian soprano. She studied in San Francisco and Milan, where she made her début in 1927 as Gilda (the role of her Covent Garden début, 1938). Donizetti's Lucia and the Queen of Night were also among her roles. Her sweet tone, polished technique and expressive delicacy made her one of the leading Italian light sopranos. She retired in 1957.

Paine, John Knowles (*b* Portland, ME, 9 Jan 1839; *d* Cambridge, MA, 25 April 1906). American composer. He was the first American to win acceptance as a composer of large-scale concert music and one of the first to be named professor of music in an American university (Harvard). German-trained, he returned to Boston in 1861 and gave organ recitals and public lectures in musical style and history before turning to composition and teaching. He organized the music department at Harvard and made Cambridge a centre of musical America; his students included J.A. Carpenter, Arthur Foote, D.G. Mason, Richard Aldrich and A.T. Davison. Besides over 100 works for the university, notably incidental music to *Oedipus tyrannus* (1881), he produced important large works that were frequently performed, including the Mass in D (1867), the oratorio *St Peter* (1872) and the classically inspired First Symphony (1875). He was idolized by the critic J.S. Dwight and highly regarded by the American public.

Paisible, James (*b* France; *d* London, ?Aug 1721). Composer and recorder and oboe player. Resident in England by 1674, he served at court and in the band at Drury Lane Theatre. He had a high reputation as a player, and wrote mainly instrumental music, much of it for the theatre. His wife was the singer Mary Davis.

Paisiello, Giovanni (*b* Roccaforzata, 9 May 1740; *d* Naples, 5 June 1816). Italian composer. He was trained in Naples; after presenting several operas in northern Italy, 1764–5, he returned there and established himself as a leading comic opera composer. In 1776–84 he served in St Petersburg as *maestro di cappella* to Catherine II, composing operas including *Il barbiere di Siviglia* (1782). He then became successively dramatic and chamber composer to the King of Naples. Especially successful was his sentimental comedy *Nina* (1789, Caserta). From 1790 most of his operas were serious. After a period in Paris directing the music in Napoleon's chapel, he returned to Naples and remained at the court under French control (1806–15).

Paisiello was one of the most successful and influential opera composers of his time. Most of his over 80 operas are comic and use a simple, direct and spirited style, latterly with sharper characterization, more colourful scoring and warmer melodies (features that influenced Mozart). His serious operas have less than the conventional amount of virtuoso vocal writing; those for Russia are the closest to Gluck's 'reform' approach. He also composed sacred, chamber and keyboard works.

Dramatic music Il barbiere di Siviglia (1782); Il re Teodoro in Venezia (1784); Le gare generose (1786); La molinara (1789); Nina (1789); Proserpine (1803); over 75 others
Secular vocal music cantatas, occasional works, duets
Sacred music oratorios; cantatas; over 20 masses; motets, other liturgical works
Instrumental music kbd concs.; divertimentos, minuets; str qts; fl qts; hpd sonatas, other pieces

Paiva, Heliodoro de (*b* Lisbon, 1502; *d* Coimbra, 21 Dec 1552). Portuguese composer and organist. He must have been trained at the royal court, where his parents served. He spent most of his life in S Cruz monastery, Coimbra. Besides being an excellent scribe, he was an able singer, instrumentalist and contrapuntist. His compositions, in an idiomatic Iberian keyboard style, show a fine harmonic sense. Other composers borrowed from his work, notably Palestrina and Scheidt.

Paix, Jakob (*b* Augsburg, 1556; *d* ?Hiltpolstein, after 1623). German composer. He was an organist and schoolteacher at Lauingen an der Donau from 1576, then organist at the ducal court of Neuburg (1609–17). His important organ tablatures (1583, 1589) contain arrangements of motets, popular songs and dances and advice on how to perform them. A few sacred vocal works also survive (1581–9).

Palazzotto e Tagliavia, Giuseppe (*b* Castelvetrano, Sicily, ?*c*1587; *d* after 1633). Italian composer. He was a priest at Palermo and lived in Naples in 1617–20. In 1633 he became archdeacon at Cefalù Cathedral. With d'India he was one of the foremost Sicilian composers of his time, notable especially for his three books of madrigals; he also wrote motets and masses. His music shows the influence of Gesualdo and Monteverdi, and features florid melody, flawless counterpoint and bold harmonies.

Palester, Roman (*b* Śniatyn, 28 Dec 1907). Polish composer. He studied with Sikorski at the Warsaw Conservatory (1925–31), then divided his time between Poland and Paris, where he settled in 1948. His works up to 1945 are in a vital, Hindemithian style with elements of folk music: they established his international reputation. In the 1950s he acquired 12-note techniques, but since 1956 he has pursued a dynamic style more concerned with expression than technical sophistication. His versatility, technical accomplishment and receptivity to new ideas make him an interesting figure of his generation in Poland. His works, mostly in conventional genres, include four symphonies (1936–51).

Palestrina. Opera by Pfitzner to his own libretto (1917, Munich).

Palestrina, Giovanni Pierluigi da (*b* ?Palestrina, ?3 Feb 1525–2 Feb 1526; *d* Rome, 2 Feb 1594). Italian composer. He was a pupil of Mallapert and Firmin Lebel at S Maria Maggiore, Rome, where he was a choirboy from at least 1537. He became organist of S Agapito, Palestrina, in 1544 and in 1547 married Lucrezia Gori there; they had three chil-

dren. After the Bishop of Palestrina's election as pope (Julius III) he was appointed *maestro di cappella* of the Cappella Giulia in Rome (1551), where he issued his first works (masses, 1554); during 1555 he also sang in the Cappella Sistina. Two of Rome's greatest churches then procured him as *maestro di cappella*, St John Lateran (1555–60) and S Maria Maggiore (1561–6), and in 1564 Cardinal Ippolito d'Este engaged him to oversee the music at his Tivoli estate. From 1566 he also taught music at the Seminario Romano, before returning to the Cappella Giulia as *maestro* in 1571.

During the 1560s and 1570s Palestrina's fame and influence rapidly increased through the wide diffusion of his published works. So great was his reputation that in 1577 he was asked to rewrite the church's main plainchant books, following the Council of Trent's guidelines. His most famous mass, *Missa Papae Marcelli*, may have been composed to satisfy the council's requirements for musical cogency and textual intelligibility. He was always in tune with the Counter-Reformation spirit; after his wife's death in 1580 he considered taking holy orders, but instead he remarried (1581). His wife, Virginia Dormoli, was a wealthy fur merchant's widow; his investments in her business eased his financial strains, and his last years at St Peter's were among his most productive.

Palestrina ranks with Lassus and Byrd as one of the greatest Renaissance masters. A prolific composer of masses, motets and other sacred works, as well as madrigals, he was (unlike Lassus) basically conservative. In his sacred music he assimilated and refined his predecessors' polyphonic techniques to produce a 'seamless' texture, with all voices perfectly balanced. The nobility and restraint of his most expressive works established the almost legendary reverence that has long surrounded his name and helped set him up as the classic model of Renaissance polyphony.

Sacred vocal music over 100 masses, 4–8vv; *c*375 motets, 4–8vv; 35 Magnificats, 4–8vv; 68 offertories, 5vv; Lamentations, 4–8vv; 11 litanies, 3–8vv; *c*80 hymns, 3–6, 12vv; 49 sacred madrigals, 5vv
Secular vocal music over 90 madrigals, 3–6vv

Paliashvili, Zakhary Petrovich (*b* Kutaisi, 16 Aug 1871; *d* Tbilisi, 6 Oct 1933). Georgian composer. He learnt music in the Catholic church, in a folk choir and at the Moscow Conservatory under Taneyev (1900–03). Back in Georgia he worked as a teacher, folksong collector and composer. He is most renowned for his operas Abesalom da Eteri (1919) and Twilight (1923).

Palindrome. Title given to Haydn's Symphony no.47 in G (1772) because of its perfectly palindromic minuet.

Palisca, Claude V(ictor) (*b* Rijeka, 24 Nov 1921). American musicologist of Yugoslav birth. He studied in New York and at Harvard and in 1959 began teaching at Yale. His main interests lie in late Renaissance and Baroque music, and the history of music theory; his writings include a short study *Baroque Music* (1968) and a comprehensive revision of Grout's history (1988).

Pallandios, Menelaos G. (*b* Piraeus, 11 Feb 1914). Greek composer. He was a pupil of Mitropoulos in Athens and Casella in Rome (1939–40), and has taught at the Athens Conservatory since 1936 (director from 1962). His works, including ballets and orchestral pieces, are in the national school, some of the best suggested by ancient Greek subjects.

Pallavicino, Benedetto (*b* Cremona, 1551; *d* Mantua, 26 Nov 1601). Italian composer. He was an organist in the Cremona area before 1579, when he moved to Vespasiano Gonzaga's service at Sabbioneta. By 1584 he was at the Mantuan court, succeeding Wert as *maestro di cappella* in 1596 and remaining there until he died. A prolific and popular madrigalist (10 bks, 1579–1612), he also published masses (1603) and motets (1605).

Pallavicino, Carlo (*b* Salò, Lake Garda; *d* Dresden, 29 Jan 1688). Italian composer. He was an organist at S Antonio, Padua, in 1665–6, and had his first operas staged in Venice in 1666. In 1667 he went to the Dresden court as a vice-Kapellmeister; he was Kapellmeister in 1672–3, but then returned to S Antonio. After a period as musical director of the Ospedale degli Incurabili, Venice, he resumed his Dresden post in 1685, becoming director of chamber and theatre music in 1687. He had two operas staged there (1687, 1689), but continued to compose mainly for Venice. He wrote 24 operas, among which *Vespasiano* (1678, Venice) was especially popular. Their melodic writing is notably inventive, and they make increasing use of da capo arias (instead of simple songs) and of the orchestra. He also composed several oratorios and church works. His son Stefano Benedetto (1672–1742) was a librettist and poet.

Palm, Siegfried (*b* Wuppertal, 25 April 1927). German cellist. He was principal cellist with orchestras in Lübeck, Hamburg and Cologne (1945–67), then pursued a solo career. He has played a leading part in the development of cello technique, specializing in avant-garde music. He has taught in Germany and the USA from 1962 and was Intendant of the Deutsche Oper, Berlin, 1977–81.

Palmgren, Selim (*b* Pori, 16 Feb 1878; *d* Helsinki, 13 Dec 1951). Finnish composer. A pupil of Wegelius and Busoni, he worked in Helsinki as a conductor, teacher (at the Sibelius Academy, 1936–51), pianist and composer and toured widely, from 1923 teaching at the Eastman School. His output, mostly songs, partsongs and lyric piano pieces, is distinguished by its pianistic writing. He also wrote five piano concertos (1904–40).

Paminger, Leonhard (*b* Aschach an der Donau, 25 March 1495; *d* Passau, 3 May 1567). Austrian composer. While a student at Vienna University (1513–16) he sang in St Stephen's *Stadtkantorei* and taught himself composition. In 1516 he settled in Passau. His music combines the style of Josquin's successors with the native German style. He won international recognition early in his career and his works were included in French and Italian anthologies. They include settings of Latin antiphons, responsories, psalms, hymns, and German Protestant hymns.

Pammelia. Collection of anonymous vocal rounds, catches and canons (1609), the first published in England; the second part is *Deuteromelia* (also 1609).

Pampani, Antonio Gaetano (*b* Modena, *c*1705; *d* Urbino, Dec 1775). Italian composer. After working at the opera in Urbino, he was *maestro di cappella* of Fano Cathedral, 1726–34, then conducted in Pesaro. Later, as director of the chorus and orchestra of the Ospedaletto orphanage in Venice, he wrote oratorios, solo motets, other sacred music and concertos, 1749–64. In 1767 he became *maestro di cappella* of Urbino Cathedral. He was most active as a stage composer after 1746, presenting *opere serie* and other works at Venice and elsewhere; he also wrote sonatas and other instrumental pieces.

Pandiatonicism. A term coined by N. Slonimsky for the free use of dissonant diatonic degrees in a single chord (as for example by Stravinsky).

Pandora. *See* BANDORA.

Pandoura. A Greco-Roman lute with a long, thick neck and a small soundbox.

Panerai, Rolando (*b* Campi Bisenzio, 17 Oct 1924). Italian baritone. He studied in France and Milan and made his début in Naples in 1947. He sang regularly at La Scala from 1951; among his best roles are Verdi's Luna and Germont and Rossini's Figaro. He is noted for his dark, vibrant tone and incisive diction, and for the panache of his acting.

Panharmonicon. A mechanical instrument capable of imitating a large variety of orchestral sounds. It was invented and exhibited in Vienna in 1804 by Johann Nepomuk Maelzel. Beethoven's 'Battle Symphony' was originally written for it.

Panizza, Ettore (*b* Buenos Aires, 12 Aug 1875; *d* Milan, 27 Nov 1967). Argentine conductor and composer of Italian descent. After study in Milan he conducted in Europe from 1899, giving operas by Zandonai, Massenet and Wolf-Ferrari at Covent Garden, 1907–14. He was assistant to Toscanini at La Scala in the 1920s and conducted widely in the Americas from 1921, at the Met, 1934–42. His compositions include four operas.

Panpipes. Instrument consisting of pipes of graduated lengths, joined together in the form of a bundle or a raft. They have no mouthpiece and are blown across their tops, while the lower ends are stopped. The earliest extant European depictions appear on bronze urns from north-east Italy and date from the 5th and 6th centuries BC. Panpipes were popular among the Etruscans and the ancient Greeks who considered them an instrument of low, merely rustic status. They appeared early in China where they are still popular. Today the panpipes are an important part of the folk music of Romania, Burma, Oceania (they are highly developed in the Solomon Islands) and all parts of South America, particularly in the Andean chain. The instrument's pastoral sound has attracted such composers as Telemann and Mozart, who used it in *The Magic Flute*; its tones have recently been used as a basis for electronic music.

Pantaleon. A large, versatile dulcimer named (allegedly at Louis XIV's command) after Pantaleon Hebenstreit (1667–1750), who invented it in 1697.

Pantalon stop. A device found in a few unfretted late 18th-century clavichords. A series of tangent-like brass blades cause the strings to continue to sound rather than have their vibrations damped out. It is named after the PANTALEON.

Pantomime. Pantomime or dumb show is of great antiquity, but the traditional British musical type had its origins in the modified form of the *commedia dell-'arte* established north of the Alps, above all in Paris. Pantomimes appeared on the London stage in the early 18th century. It was a popular mixed-medium entertainment staged as an adjunct to more serious fare, with songs and instrumental pieces during which the action was mimed. Dialogue was introduced in the late 18th century. Extravagant stage effects and a harlequinade were important. John Rich established the London tradition, which was continued by Garrick; Galliard and Pepusch supplied much of the music, and later the Arnes, Dibdin, Linley, Boyce and Shield.

During the 19th century the nature of pantomime changed, and in the 20th the traditional harlequinade has been replaced by topical songs and allusions for which a children's tale is hardly more than a pretext, with vestiges of its old character in the acrobatic antics of comedians.

Pantonality. Term, coined by Rudolf Réti in the 1950s, to explain the continued extension of tonal language in the late 19th century beyond the point at which it could be said to be in a key, or in two or more keys simultaneously, or shifting in and out of several keys.

Panufnik, Andrzej (*b* Warsaw, 24 Sept 1914). Polish composer, naturalized British. He studied with Sikorski at the Warsaw Conservatory (1932–6) and worked in Poland and abroad as a conductor. In 1954 he moved to England, where he concentrated on composition, combining a constructivist, cellular approach with a command of large forms and Romantic rhetoric. His works include symphonies, other orchestral pieces, choral music (including the choral *Universal Prayer*, 1969) and a few chamber and piano compositions.

Paolo da Firenze (*d* Arezzo, Sept 1419). Italian composer and theorist. A member of the Camaldolese order, he died in the monastery of S Viti but had Florentine connections; he moved in the same circles as Landini and may have been involved with the Squarcialupi MS. In his authenticated songs – 11 madrigals and 22 ballate – his style displays both traditional and progressive features, with French influence becoming more marked during his development. In his two liturgical works he combines an Italianate melodic line with a *cantus firmus*. He wrote a treatise, *Ars ad adiscendum contrapunctum*.

Papaioannou, Yannis Andreou (*b* Cavala, 6 Jan 1911). Greek composer. He studied at the Hellenic Conservatory (1922–34), where he began teaching in 1953. His music has progressed from neo-classicism and Byzantine modality to serial and avant-garde practices.

Papandopulo, Boris (*b* Honnef, 25 Feb 1906). Yugoslav composer and conductor. A pupil of Bersa in Zagreb and Foch in Vienna, he became a prominent conductor in Yugoslavia. His large, varied output synthesizes neo-classical and folk elements; he has written cantatas and concertos, including one for four timpani (1969).

Papavoine [1st name unknown] (*b* ?Normandy, *c*1720; *d* ?Marseilles, 1793). French composer. An orchestral violinist in Paris, he wrote four operas and music for many plays and pantomimes. His instrumental output includes *c*20 symphonies (1752–*c*1765), among the first in France in the Classical style, and various chamber works.

Papillons. Schumann's op.2 (1831), 12 short piano pieces.

Papineau-Couture, Jean (*b* Montreal, 12 Nov 1916). Canadian composer. He studied in Montreal, with Porter at the New England Conservatory and with Boulanger at the Longy School (1941–3); in 1951 he began teaching at the University of Montreal and he has been deeply involved in Canadian cultural life. His works, in all genres except opera, are in a highly structured neo-classical style, some using serialism. Counterpoint is prominent in his music.

Papp, Lajos (*b* Debrecen, 18 Aug 1935). Hungarian composer. He was a pupil of Szabó at the Budapest Academy (1954–60). He has concentrated on chamber music, but made an international name with his *Dialogo* for piano and orchestra (1967).

Parabosco, Girolamo (*b* Piacenza, *c*1524; *d* Venice, 21 April 1557). Italian composer. He was a pupil of Willaert's and, after travelling throughout Italy, was elected first organist at St Mark's, Venice, in 1551, becoming active in musical and literary academies in the city. His 'motet-like', five-voice madrigals, of which 25 survive, use dense imitative polyphony and show Willaert's influence. He also wrote three instrumental pieces.

Parade. 'Ballet réaliste' in one act by Satie to a scenario by Cocteau (1917, Paris).

Paradiddle. A pattern of strokes on the side-drum consisting (onomatopoeically) of four semiquavers.

Paradies [Paradisi], **(Pietro) Domenico** (*b* Naples, 1707; *d* Venice, 25 Aug 1791). Italian composer and teacher. After presenting two stage works in Italy, he settled in London. There he had two operas staged (1747, 1751) and later wrote arias for pasticcios but was most successful as a singing teacher and harpsichord master. Notable among his instrumental works are 12 harpsichord sonatas (1754).

Paradies und die Peri, Das. Cantata, op.50, by Schumann (1843) to a text after Moore's poem *Lalla Rookh*.

Paradis, Maria Theresia von (*b* Vienna, 15 May 1759; *d* there, 1 Feb 1824). Austrian composer and pianist. Blind from childhood, she was a prominent pianist in Vienna and also appeared as an organist and singer. On a concert tour, 1783–6, she played in Paris, London, Berlin and elsewhere; Mozart wrote a piano concerto for her in 1784 (K456). Her compositions include three stage works, cantatas, songs and piano concertos and sonatas and show the influence of her teachers Salieri and Kozeluch.

Paradise Lost. Opera in two acts by Penderecki to a libretto by Christopher Fry after Milton (1978,

Chicago).

Parallel fifths, parallel octaves. *See* CONSECUTIVE FIFTHS, CONSECUTIVE OCTAVES.

Parallel key. A minor key having the same tonic as a given major key, or vice versa, e.g. C major and C minor.

Parallel motion. In part-writing, the simultaneous melodic movement of two or more voices in the same direction at a distance of the same interval or intervals.

Paraphrase. In Renaissance polyphony, a compositional process involving the quotation in one or more voices of a plainchant melody in altered form. In the 19th century, the term was applied to an elaboration of pre-existing material, usually as a vehicle for expressive virtuosity, as in Liszt's paraphrases on Italian opera themes.

Paray, Paul (M.A. Charles) (*b* Le Treport, 24 May 1886; *d* Monte Carlo, 10 Oct 1979). French conductor and composer. He studied at the Paris Conservatoire and in 1923 became conductor of the Concerts Lamoureux. As principal conductor of the Concerts Colonne (1933–52) and the Detroit SO (1952–63) he earned a reputation for reliability in a wide repertory, especially French music. His works include two symphonies, a symphonic poem, piano and chamber music.

Pardessus. French term for an instrument that plays an upper descant part, especially the 'pardessus de viole', a descant viol of the 18th century, tuned *g–c′–e′–a′–d″* or sometimes *c′–e′–a′–d″–g″* and also known as the 'quinton'. Louis de Caix d'Hervelois (*d* c1760) wrote for it.

Pari, Claudio (*b* Burgundy; *fl* Sicily, 1611–19). Italian composer. He was director of music at the Jesuit house at Salemi, Sicily, in 1615–18. Among the best Sicilian madrigalists of the day, he published four books of five-part madrigals and one of six-part madrigals. The pieces are mostly grouped in cycles, one of them (in book 4, 1619) called *Il lamento d'Arianna*. They show mannerist features such as careful interpretation of the text, complex counterpoint and experiments in harmony and structure.

Paride ed Elena. Opera in five acts by Gluck to a libretto by Calzabigi (1770, Vienna).

Parikian, Manoug (*b* Mersin, Turkey, 15 Sept 1920; *d* London, 24 Dec 1987). English violinist of Armenian descent. He studied in London, made his solo début in 1947 and led several orchestras (Philharmonia, 1949–57) and ensembles. He was an admired teacher and a champion of young composers, many of whom wrote concertos for him.

Paris, Orchestre de. French orchestra formed in 1967 under the direction of Munch; he was succeeded by Karajan (1969), Solti (1971) and Barenboim (1976).

Paris Conservatoire. The principal music school in France. Founded by BERNARD SARRETTE in 1795 as a teaching academy and to provide music for public occasions, it was intended to be the first of many such schools throughout France. It became the model for conservatories in other countries.

Parish Alvars, Elias [Eli] (*b* Teignmouth, 28 Feb 1808; *d* Vienna, 25 Jan 1849). English harpist. Based

mainly in Vienna from 1834, he developed new techniques on the double-action harp. Many of his harp works, including solo pieces and concertos, are of phenomenal difficulty.

Paris Opéra. *See* OPÉRA.

Paris Symphonies. Haydn's six symphonies nos.82–7, composed for the Concert de la Loge Olympique (1787).

Paris Symphony. Mozart's Symphony no.31 in D (1778), written in Paris and first performed at the Concert Spirituel.

Paris: the Song of a Great City. Orchestral work by Delius (1899).

Parke. English family of musicians. John (1745–1829) and his brother William Thomas (1762–1847) were both oboists in London. William Thomas, the more eminent, extended the oboe's upper range and composed concertos, overtures and songs; he was also a flautist. He left a valuable set of memoirs (1830). John's daughter Maria Hester Park(e) (1775–1822) was a singer, pianist and composer (of keyboard music and glees) and a friend of Haydn during his years in London.

Parker, Charlie ['Bird', 'Yardbird'] (*b* Kansas City, 29 Aug 1920; *d* New York, 12 March 1955). American jazz alto saxophonist. In 1942 he joined Earl Hines's band and in 1944 Billy Eckstine's. In New York he first led his own group, with Dizzy Gillespie. In Los Angeles, he had a nervous breakdown, exacerbated by addictions. Back in New York from 1947, he formed a quintet which recorded many of his most famous pieces. He toured Europe and had a large following, but drugs forced him into a more peripatetic life and sporadic employment. A virtuoso with distinctive tone and thorough control, he was a brilliant improviser. His line combined drive and a complex organization of pitch and rhythm; he used pitches outside the harmony, with a variety of melodic devices, but his best work retained a clear, coherent line.

Parker, Horatio (William) (*b* Auburndale, MA, 15 Sept 1863; *d* Cedarhurst, 18 Dec 1919). American composer. He studied with Chadwick, and with Rheinberger in Munich (1882–5), then worked as a teacher and organist and choirmaster in New York. In 1894 he was appointed professor at Yale, though he continued to work as a church musician in New York and Boston and to produce much choral music, in a conservative style looking to Brahms, Dvořák and Gounod. He also wrote for the theatre, notably the opera *Mona*, given at the Met in 1912; this, the oratorio *The Legend of St Christopher* (1898) and the lyric rhapsody *A Star Song* (1902) typify his period of increasing concern for dramatic expression, with a style more integrated and more chromatic. His final period returns to more traditional melody and diatonic harmony, in tune with his wish to communicate with a wide public. His output also includes many songs and a few keyboard, chamber and orchestral works.

Parlando (It.). 'Speaking': a direction that the music should be performed in a speech-like manner.

Parody. Term for a technique of Renaissance polyphony, primarily associated with the mass, involving the use of earlier composed material. The essential feature is that the substance of the source, not merely a single line, is absorbed into the new piece, creating a fusion of old and new elements. An example of a parody mass is Palestrina's *Missa 'Assumpta est Maria'*, based on his own motet. The term is also used for such works as the short masses of Bach, which re-use earlier material but are better described as reworkings or arrangements. The term has further been used for a humorous or satirical composition in which features (sometimes actual melodies) of another composer or of a period or style are employed and made to appear ridiculous.

Parody mass. A setting of the Mass Ordinary that is unified by the use of substantial elements from a pre-existing polyphonic work in each movement.

Paroles tissées. Work for tenor and chamber orchestra by Lutosławski (1965) to a text by Jean-François Chabrun.

Parratt, Sir Walter (*b* Huddersfield, 10 Feb 1841; *d* Windsor, 27 March 1924). English organist, teacher and composer. He was organist at Magdalen College, Oxford, from 1872, and in 1882 appointed to St George's Chapel, Windsor, soon becoming chief organ professor at the RCM and Master of the Queen's Musick (1893). The foremost organ exponent of his time, he is best remembered for his role (with Parry and Stanford) in the renaissance of English music. He had impeccable taste and skill, founded on his love of Bach's works; he advocated Baroque registration principles and adherence to original texts, setting a similarly high standard in his choice of choral works from Tallis to Wesley.

Parrenin Quartet. French string quartet, led by Jacques Parrenin. It was formed in 1942 and began its international career in 1949; it has appeared in the USA and eastern Europe. It plays not only the standard repertory but also music of the Second Viennese School – its playing of Webern came to be seen as definitive – and more recent music.

Parrott, Andrew (*b* Walsall, 10 March 1947). English conductor. He studied at Oxford, where he was engaged in research in the performing practice of early music. In 1973 he founded the Taverner Choir; he has directed performances of large-scale choral works (Monteverdi's Vespers, Bach's B minor Mass and Passions) with period instruments and has made several recordings, of these and the English choral repertory.

Parrott, (Horace) Ian (*b* London, 5 March 1916). English composer. He studied at the RCM and Oxford, and in 1950 was appointed professor at Aberystwyth. His works, many (like the opera *The Black Room*, 1966) coloured by his interest in Welsh culture, include three symphonies (1946, 1960, 1966) and four string quartets.

Parry, Sir (Charles) Hubert (Hastings) (*b* Bournemouth, 27 Feb 1848; *d* Rustington, 7 Oct 1918). English composer and teacher. He studied at Oxford and with Pierson and Dannreuther, publishing songs, church music and piano works from the 1860s. He taught at the RCM from 1883 (succeeding Grove as director in 1894), also becoming professor at Oxford (1900–08) and president of the Musical Association (1901–8). Among his scholarly interests were Bach and the history of musical style, on which he wrote perceptively. His cantatas *Scenes from Prometheus Unbound* (1880), *Blest Pair of Sirens* (1887) and *L'allegro ed il penseroso* (1890) made a decisive impact for their poetic merit and advanced (Wagnerian) idiom. The anthem *I was glad* (1902), the choral *Songs of Farewell* (1916) and many of the unison songs including *The Lover's Garland* and *Jerusalem* show a similar regard for text and a fresh lyricism. His forceful personality and social position, together with his ethical views and intellectual vigour, enabled him to exercise a revitalizing influence on English musical life in the late 19th century.

Parry, John (*b* Bryn Cynan, *c*1710; *d* Ruabon, 7 Oct 1782). Welsh harper. The finest harper of his generation in Great Britain, he served a Welsh baronet and later the Prince of Wales. His instrumental collections of Welsh and other melodies, 1742–81, began a vogue for the harp air.

Parry, Joseph (*b* Merthyr Tydfil, 21 May 1841; *d* Penarth, 17 Feb 1903). Welsh composer. He studied with Sterndale Bennett at the RAM and taught in Aberystwyth, at his own music school in Swansea, and in Bardiff. His standing among Welsh musicians was almost legendary. His compositions include *Blodwen* (1878), believed to be the first Welsh opera, the oratorio *Saul of Tarsus* (1892) and the hymn tune *Aberystwyth*, for which he is best remembered.

Parsifal. Sacred festival drama (*Bühnenweihfestspiel*) in three acts by Wagner to his own libretto (1882, Bayreuth).

Parsley, Osbert (*b* 1511; *d* Norwich, 1585). English composer. He spent most of his life in Norwich where he sang in the cathedral choir. He wrote music for both the Latin and English rites and seems to have found the former more congenial. The psalm *Conserva me, Domine*, in which flowing lines weave expressive webs of polyphony, is noteworthy. His English church music includes two four-part Morning Services and an anthem. Five In Nomines for five viols show him as a varied and ingenious instrumental composer.

Parsons, Geoffrey (Penwill) (*b* Sydney, 15 June 1929). Australian accompanist. He studied in Sydney and Munich. In 1950 he went to London as accompanist to Peter Dawson and remained there, appearing with Schwarzkopf and others; he is admired as a player of subtlety and taste.

Parsons, Robert (*b c*1530; *d* Newark-upon-Trent, 25 Jan 1570). English composer. In 1563 he became a Gentleman of the Chapel Royal in London, and he may have had connections with Lincoln. He was a respected, prolific composer of Latin and Anglican church music, consort songs and music for viols. He is not apparently related to the Robert Parsons (1596–1676) of Exeter Cathedral, composer of anthems and services, nor to the other contemporary composers of the name.

Parsons, William (*fl* 1545–63). English composer. In 1555 he was a vicar-choral at Wells Cathedral and may have been chief composer and copyist there,

1552–60. He was the major contributor (81 settings) to Day's psalter (1563) and may have helped compile it. Most of his services, anthems and motets are lost or incomplete in MSS.

Part. (1) The line or lines of music read by an individual performer or performing section in the realization of a musical work; that music itself, hence 'the piano part', 'the soprano part'.

(2) In polyphonic music, one of the individual musical lines that contribute to one or more elements of the music, e.g. two-part counterpoint, four-part harmony. (The word 'voice' is sometimes preferred in this context.)

(3) The primary division of certain large-scale works (especially oratorios), equivalent to the act in theatrical works. In musical form, one of the sections of a work by which its form is defined, e.g. three-part song form.

Pärt, Arvo (b Paide, 11 Sept 1935). Estonian composer. He was a pupil of Eller at the Tallinn Conservatory until 1963 while working as a sound producer for Estonian radio (1957–67); in 1962 he won a prize for a children's cantata (*Our Garden*) and an oratorio (*Stride of the World*). Early works followed standard Soviet models, but later he turned to strict serial writing, in rhythm as well as pitch (*Perpetuum mobile*, 1963) and then collage techniques (Symphony no.2, 1966; *Pro et contra* for cello and orchestra, 1966). In the 1970s he came into contact with plainchant and the music of the Orthodox Church, which affected his music both technically and spiritually. This is seen in, for example, Symphony no.3 (1971) and the cantata *Song for the Beloved* (1973) as well as *Tabula rasa* for three violins, strings and prepared piano (1977). The music of other composers is evoked, drawing on minimalist techniques of repetition, in such works as *Arbos* for chamber ensemble (1977, Janáček), *Summa* for tenor, baritone and ensemble (1980, Stravinsky), *Cantus in Memory of Benjamin Britten* for bell and strings (1980, Britten). Of more recent works, *Pari intervalli* echoes Bach chorale preludes, *An den Wassern zu Babylon* calls on 13th-century music and the *St John Passion* (1981) uses choral and instrumental heterophony recalling ancient incantation, always intense yet pure and ritualistic in effect. Pärt went to live in Berlin in the early 1980s.

Partbooks. Manuscript or printed books that contain music for only a single vocal or instrumental part of a composition, as opposed to ones that supply the complete music. They were probably devised in the late 15th century and were the standard medium for ensemble music in the next two centuries. For vocal music their use declined from the 17th century, but the practice of performing from separate partbooks remains normal in, for example, chamber and orchestral music.

Partch, Harry (b Oakland, CA, 24 June 1901; d San Diego, 3 Sept 1974). American composer and instrument maker. Largely self-taught, he worked from the early 1930s with his own and adapted instruments, playing music in just intonation. He was skilled at realizing the musical potential of wood; many of his instruments were visually spectacular,

forming the stage set of his theatrical works. All his instruments are featured in *And on the Seventh Day Petals Fell in Petaluma* (1966). His other works include *Oedipus* (1951) and *Delusion of the Fury* (1969).

Part-crossing. In part-writing, the rising of the lower of two voices above the higher or the falling of the higher below the lower. In polyphonic music, the term also signifies the use of a voice or instrument higher (lower) than another which by nature lies above (below) it, usually for special effect.

Partenope. Opera in three acts by Handel to a libretto after Stampiglia (1730, London).

Parthenia. Title of the first book of keyboard music published in England, in full *Parthenia or the Maydenhead of the First Musicke that ever was Printed for the Virginals*; it appeared in 1613 (many later reprints) and contains pieces by Byrd, Bull and O. Gibbons. It was followed the next year by a volume with the punning title *Parthenia In-Violata*, with music for virginals and bass viol.

Parthia [parthie, partie]. Term for a SUITE or other multi-movement genre of the 17th and 18th centuries; *see also* PARTITA.

Partial. A component vibration at a particular frequency in a compound tone. It need not be harmonic. Fundamentals or overtones are sometimes described as partials but the term is generally used in referring to components in the tone of such a body as a bell. *See* HARMONICS.

Partimento (It.). Term used in the Classical period for an exercise in figured bass playing.

Partita. Term used in the 16th and 17th centuries for a single instrumental piece or variation, and by Kuhnau (1689) and later German composers (including Bach) as a synonym for suite.

Partos, Oedoen (b Budapest, 1 Oct 1907; d Tel-Aviv, 6 July 1977). Israeli composer of Hungarian origin. A pupil of Hubay and Kodály at the Budapest Academy, he moved in 1938 to Palestine, where he worked as a violist (with the Israel PO and the Israel Quartet), teacher and composer. His works use eastern Jewish folksongs and, from 1960, 12-note technique; his writing for strings, prominent in most of his works, includes Eastern practices (e.g. long notes, varied embellishments and microtones), all found in *Maqamat*, *Psalms* and *Shiluvim* for viola and chamber orchestra (1970).

Partsong. A song for more than one voice. It usually implies an unaccompanied choral song. It has been particularly cultivated in the last 200 years, especially in England and Germany.

Part-writing. An aspect of counterpoint and polyphony that recognizes each part or voice as an individual strand, not merely an element in the resultant harmony; thus each must have a melodic shape and rhythmic life of its own. (The term 'voice-leading' from the German *Stimmführung*, is preferred in American usage.)

Pasatieri, Thomas (b New York, 20 Oct 1945). American composer. He was a pupil of Giannini and Persichetti at the Juilliard School. Most of his works are operas in a conservative, neo-romantic style; they include *The Seagull* (1974) and *Washington Square* (1976).

Pasdeloup, Jules Etienne (*b* Paris, 15 Sept 1819; *d* Fontainebleau, 13 Aug 1887). French conductor. He studied at the Paris Conservatoire where from 1841 he taught (solfège, piano and choral music). With his former pupils he launched the Société des Jeunes Artistes (1852–61), giving premières of symphonies by Gounod, Saint-Saëns and others. Financial crisis led him to initiate the Concerts Populaires de Musique Classique, which offered a wider, culturally deprived public good performances of Classical, German Romantic and French symphonic music. Though from 1871 his popularity waned in the rivalry with Colonne and Lamoureux, he was a great stimulus to French musical life and his orchestra inspired the writing of symphonic music by composers who might otherwise have ignored this form.

Pashchenko, Andrey Filippovich (*b* Rostov-na-Donu, 15 Aug 1885; *d* Moscow, 16 Nov 1972). Soviet composer. A pupil of Witohl and Shteynberg at the St Petersburg Conservatory (1914–17), he was an orchestral librarian (1911–31). His large output includes much choral music, where his epic style is most evident, operas, 15 symphonies (1915–70), nine string quartets and over 60 songs.

Pashkevich, Vasiliy Alexeyevich (*b c*1742; *d* St Petersburg, 9 March 1797). Russian composer. He was a violinist at the St Petersburg court from 1763 and later court composer. He wrote several Russian operas, some comic, some on folk or historical themes; they use both Russian melodies and Italian musical features.

Paso doble (Sp.: 'double step'). Hispanic social dance, in a moderately quick duple metre (often 6/8), of a march-like character.

Pasquali, Niccolo (*b c*1718; *d* Edinburgh, 13 Oct 1757). Italian composer. He was active in London from *c*1743, then Dublin (1748–9) and Edinburgh, where he wrote stage works and led orchestras. His other works include an oratorio, overtures, violin sonatas and songs; he also left a useful and popular figured bass manual (1757).

Pasquini, Bernardo (*b* Massa e Cozzili, Lucca, 7 Dec 1637; *d* Rome, 21 Nov 1710). Italian composer and keyboard player. By 1650 he was living in Rome, where he was reputedly taught by Cesti. After a year as organist of S Maria Maggiore, he became organist of S Maria in Aracoeli in 1664; he served there for the rest of his life. He was also harpsichordist and musical director to Prince Giambattista Borghese and served other eminent patrons. Renowned for his keyboard virtuosity, he performed with Corelli in Rome and also appeared abroad. Domenico Scarlatti was among his pupils.

Pasquini was the foremost Italian composer of keyboard music between Frescobaldi and D. Scarlatti. His 17 keyboard suites and 14 variation sets, clearly conceived for harpsichord, show great melodic inventiveness, and his 11 contrapuntal pieces and 34 toccatas are very varied in style and form, some of them recalling Frescobaldi's influence. He also left 28 keyboard sonatas written only in figured bass. His large vocal output includes operas, oratorios, cantatas, arias and motets, and stands between Cesti

and Alessandro Scarlatti in style. He also wrote two musical treatises.

Pasquini, Ercole (*b* Ferrara, mid-16th century; *d* Rome, 1608–19). Italian composer. A pupil of Alessandro Milleville, he was an organist at the Ferrarese court, then organist of the Cappella Giulia in Rome (1597–1608). An important precursor of Frescobaldi, he composed distinctive toccatas, dances and variations for keyboard (30 extant in MS).

Passacaglia (It.; Fr. *passacaille*, *passecaille*). Originally, a standard type of ritornello for a category of 17th-century Spanish, French or Italian song. Most 'ritornello-passacaglias' used the harmonic progression I–IV–V–(I) in either major or minor, duple or triple, to match the song. In the second quarter of the century the passacaglia began to be used as a basis for variations for guitar, voice and continuo, keyboard instruments and chamber groups. The basic harmonic formula (ex.1a) was transformed into a number of melodic bass lines (ex.1b–f) which, influenced by the *ciaconna*, were nearly always in triple metre but (unlike the *ciaconna*) favoured the minor mode. When the formula was used for every phrase the result was a ground bass, but most Italian passacaglia variations have a plural title (*passacagli*), indicating that the singular term referred not to the whole composition but to a single phrase.

Ex. 1 The principal passacaglia formulae (usually minor)

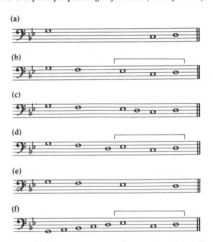

In France the distinction between the *passacaille* and the CHACONNE was not always clear, and in Germany their relationship became even more confused. The chaconne in Bach's D minor Partita for solo violin is in a minor key; the same composer's passacaglia for organ extends a ground melody used by Raison in his *Christe, Trio en passacaille*. German theorists tried in vain to distinguish between the forms whose earlier history was by then forgotten.

The Classical and Romantic periods produced very few passacaglias (the finale of Brahms's Fourth Symphony is often cited as one); but as a set of variations on a ground bass, and often with Bach's organ passacaglia as a model, the title has been used by 20th-century composers.

Passage. Term used, much as in a literary reference, to refer to part of a composition generally characterized by some particular treatment (e.g. 'an arpeggio passage'). The term 'passage-work' is often used to describe sections, especially of keyboard works, consisting of brilliant figuration but of modest thematic substance (like the Italian *passaggio*).

Passaggio (It.). A florid piece or section of a piece, designed to display the performer's skill; it may be notated or improvised as a DIVISION. The term may also apply to a linking section or 'bridge passage', usually incorporating a modulation.

Passamezzo. An Italian dance in duple metre, popular *c*1550–1650. It is somewhat faster than the pavan, to which it is related. The *passamezzo antico*, in the minor mode, used the chordal framework i–VII–i–V–III–VII–i–(V)–i; the *passamezzo moderno*, in the major, used I–IV–I–V–I–IV–I–(V)–I. The basic scheme was repeated a number of times and was often followed by a triple dance on the same scheme. Numerous passamezzos were written for lute, keyboard or ensemble, mostly variations on one of the above harmonic schemes.

Passepied. A French court dance and instrumental form of the 17th and 18th centuries. A faster version of the minuet, in 3/8 or 6/8, usually danced by one couple at a time, it had fairly constant movement in quavers and semiquavers. It was used in many French operas and ballets, often in pastoral scenes, and in Baroque keyboard and orchestral suites.

Passereau, Pierre (*fl* 1509–47). French composer. He was a tenor in the Duke of Angoulême's chapel (1509) and may have sung at Cambrai Cathedral (1525–30). Apart from a single motet, his output consists entirely of *chansons*, of which Attaingnant published nearly 30 during the 1530s; they were popular during his lifetime. He set a few doleful texts, but most are narrative or descriptive songs of a cheerful nature, with graceful melodies, syllabic settings in freely imitative polyphony alternating with chordal passages, and with lively rhythms and repeated notes. His *chansons* were very popular during his lifetime.

Passing note. In part-writing, a non-harmonic note that leads from one note to another in a single direction, by conjunct motion.

Passion. A musical setting of the Crucifixion story as recorded in the Gospels.

At an early date special lesson tones were developed for reciting the Passion. From the 13th century it became usual to divide them among three singers and in the 15th the practice began of setting polyphonically some or all of the *turba* sections (passages of speech by groups or individuals, except Christ), resulting in the responsorial Passion (also known as the 'choral' or 'dramatic' Passion). The earliest extant examples, of English origin, date from *c*1440; the most famous 15th-century example is by Richard Davy (*c*1490). The responsorial Passion is widespread in 16th-century Italy, often with the words of Christ in the polyphonic sections (e.g. in the settings of Asola and Soriano); outside Italy the responsorial type is represented by the Passions of Lassus, Victoria and Guerrero. In the through-composed (or 'motet') Passion the complete text, including the narration (Evangelist), was set polyphonically. Examples include the *St Matthew Passion* of Nasco and the *St John Passions* of Rore and Ruffo; settings based on all four Gospels were composed by Longueval, Handl and Regnart.

In Lutheran Germany both types are found. There are responsorial Passions by Luther's friend Johannes Walter (i), with simple homophony in the polyphonic sections. Scandello's *St John Passion* (before 1561) was the first in German to include Christ's words: only the narrative was monophonic. There are settings based on all four Gospels and also through-composed works based on single Gospels with shortened Latin text, such as the Passions of Resinarius (1543) and Daser (1578). Lechner's *St John Passion* (1594) is representative of the German 16th-century Passion. Others are based on the German Passion by Joachim a Burck, an abridged version of St John's Gospel, which abandons the old Passion tone; among these, Machold's *St Matthew Passion* begins the tradition of inserting hymn verses into the Passion.

The most vital development of the Passion in the 17th and 18th centuries was in Lutheran Germany, where both types were followed though the strongest tradition in the early 17th century was based on Walter. The composer remained responsible only for the polyphonic sections, the traditional recitation tone being used for the narrative; but Schütz in his three Dresden Passions (*c*1665) created his own highly expressive recitations.

About 1650, north German composers began to insert sinfonias, new madrigalian verse and hymns into their settings. The earliest of these 'oratorio Passions' were those by Selle, which included continuo and other instruments. Other composers of this type include Theile, who replaced the recitation tone with recitative.

In the 18th century there were basically four types. The old type without instruments was largely ignored. The oratorio Passion, closer to Lutheran devotional requirements, is the commonest in the first third of the century; the genre reached its height in Bach's *St John Passion* (1724) and the *St Matthew Passion* (1727 or 1729). The Passion oratorio, usually without narrator and with a poetic text, belongs to the ORATORIO. Fourthly, the lyrical Passion meditation is represented in Italy and elsewhere by Metastasio's *La Passione di Gesù Cristo* (set by Caldara, Jommelli, Paisiello and others) and in Germany by C.H. Graun's *Der Tod Jesu*. Classification of the 18th-century Passion is, however, made difficult by hybrid works (such as Telemann's *St Luke Passion*, 1728) and 18th-century parody and pasticcio practices.

Works of the 19th and 20th centuries dealing with the Passion belong mainly to the oratorio and to the concert hall rather than the church. Exceptions include Hugo Distler's *Choralpassion* (1933) and Eberhard Wenzel's liturgical Passion of 1968.

Passione, La. Nickname of Haydn's Symphony no.49 in F minor (1768), so called because the opening Adagio is akin to Passion music.

Passy, Ludvig Anton Edmund (*b* Stockholm, 3 Sept 1789; *d* Drottningholm, 16 Aug 1870). Swedish pianist and composer of French parentage. He studied with John Field in St Petersburg. The most famous Swedish pianist of his time, he was attached to the royal court. His compositions display a restrained virtuoso style in the manner of Hummel and Clementi.

Pasta [née Negri], Giuditta (Maria Costanza) (*b* Saronno, 28 Oct 1797; *d* Blevio, Como, 1 April 1865). Italian soprano. She studied in Milan and made her first appearance in Paris in 1816. She first excelled in Rossini's roles, especially Desdemona, Tancredi and Semiramis, but it was her creation of Donizetti's Anna Bolena (1830) – an essential factor in that opera's immense success – and of Bellini's Amina in *La sonnambula* (1831) and the title roles in his *Norma* (1831) and *Beatrice di Tenda* (1833) that marked the highpoint of her career. For more than a decade the greatest soprano in Europe, she was unrivalled in her combination of lyric genius and dramatic power.

Pasticcio (It.: 'mess', 'hotch-potch'). A dramatic or sacred work whose parts are wholly or partly taken from existing works by various composers (it should not be confused with collaborative works; an essential feature is the borrowing of individual parts). Operatic pasticcio arose in the early 18th century primarily because impresarios wanted to gain public approval by offering favourite pieces, while itinerant singers found it convenient to appear before new audiences with proven successes. The practice reached a highpoint *c*1750. Important composers (e.g. Handel, Keiser and Vivaldi) arranged pasticcios only when they were acting as impresarios.

Pastorale. A work that depicts the characters and scenes of rural life or expresses its atmosphere.

The earliest musical settings of pastoral poetry were made by the troubadours and trouvères. Adam de la Halle's *Jeu de Robin et Marion* (13th century) is a pastoral play set to music. Pastoral themes are found in *chansons* and frottolas *c*1500 and are common in the Italian and English madrigal; Tasso's *Aminta* (1573) and Guarini's *Il pastor fido* (1590) provide many of the texts. The pastoral language of the madrigal was carried to the 17th-century cantata, and most early operas were based on pastoral material. Towards mid-century interest shifted to historical themes in serious opera, but with the Arcadian Academy's influence pastoral elements again became common after 1690. The initial interest in Italy was followed by an equally large wave in France, as in operas by Lully, Destouches and Rameau.

A special category is the Christmas pastorale, vocal or instrumental. It perhaps drew on features of the music-making of Italian shepherds (*pifferari*) who played at Christmas in the towns: lilting melodies usually in 6/8 or 12/8, parallel 3rds, drone basses and symmetrical phrases. Such movements appear in Baroque vocal works and concertos for performance at the Vatican on Christmas Eve, but the style was widely disseminated. The sinfonia of the second section of Bach's *Christmas Oratorio* and the 'Pifa' ('pastoral symphony') of Handel's *Messiah* are familiar examples.

Beethoven adapted conventions of 18th-century pastoral music in his Pastoral Symphony op.68, and motifs suggesting the sounds and sights of nature permeate much music of Schubert and Weber. In the 'Scène aux champs' from the *Symphonie fantastique* Berlioz intended to evoke a mood of unsatisfied passion in a romantic pastoral setting, and similar imaginative re-creations of archaic pastoral melodies occur in later works, including Wagner's *Tristan und Isolde*, Debussy's *L'après-midi d'un faune* and Vaughan Williams's *Pastoral Symphony*.

Pastoral Sonata. Publisher's name for Beethoven's Piano Sonata no.15 in D op.28 (1801), presumably so called because of the finale's country-dance-like character.

Three harpsichord sonatas by Scarlatti (in D K415, in F K446, in C K513) are also known by this title because of their particular use of 6/8 time.

Pastoral Symphony. Symphony no.6 in F by Beethoven (1808).

Symphony by Vaughan Williams, his third (1921).

Pastorella. A church composition for Christmas, usually telling of the birth of Christ. Found from the late 17th century to the 19th in German and Slavonic Roman Catholic areas, it is normally for choir or soloists and small orchestra.

Pastor fido, Il. Opera in three acts by Handel to a libretto by Rossi after Guarini (1712, London).

Opera in four acts by Salieri to a libretto by Da Ponte (1789, Vienna).

Pastourelle [pastorella]. A French (or Provençal) medieval lyric characterized by its pastoral theme, usually the attempted seduction of a shepherdess by a gallant knight. Many examples survive from the troubadour and trouvère repertory of the 12th and 13th centuries.

Pastrana, Pedro de (*b c*1480; *d* after 1559). Spanish composer. He was a singer in the Aragonese chapel of Ferdinand the Catholic (1500), served Charles V, and was *maestro de capilla* to Ferdinand of Aragon and to Prince Philip (1547). His associates were illustrious musicians. His extant works include a six-part mass, four four-part Magnificats, motets, villancicos and short, homophonic psalm settings.

Patachich, Iván (*b* Budapest, 3 June 1922). Hungarian composer. A pupil of Siklós, Viski and Farkas at the Budapest Academy (1941–7), he began composing in the Bartók–Kodály tradition, but studied at Darmstadt and pioneered electronic music in Hungary, establishing the first studio.

Paṭaha. Elongated barrel drum of ancient and medieval India; it was capable of considerable volume and thus associated with warfare, public announcements and religious and theatrical presentations.

Patanè, Giuseppe (*b* Naples, 1 Jan 1932). Italian conductor, son of the conductor Franco Patanè (1908–68). He studied at the Naples Conservatory and worked at the Teatro San Carlo there; in the 1960s he conducted mainly in Austria and Germany (Deutsche Oper, Berlin, 1962–8); he made his La Scala début in 1969 and has also been heard in the

USA and at Covent Garden. He is noted for his dynamic direction of both the operatic and the symphonic repertories.

Paṭet. Term for 'mode' or 'melody type' in INDONESIAN MUSIC; it carries implications about tonality, cadences and compass.

Pathétique. Beethoven's Piano Sonata no.8 in C minor op.13 (1797–8), which Beethoven called 'Grande sonate pathétique'.

Sub-title of Tchaikovsky's Symphony no.6 in B minor (1893).

Patience. Operetta by Sullivan to a libretto by Gilbert (1881, London).

Patterson, Paul (*b* Chesterfield, 15 June 1947). English composer. He studied with Stoker at the RAM and returned there in 1975 as director of electronic studies. His works use aleatory methods and include *Cracovian Counterpoints* for 14 instruments (1977) and *Mass of the Sea* for vocal soloists, chorus and orchestra (1984).

Patter song. A comic song in which the humour derives from having the greatest number of words uttered in the shortest possible time. The tradition begins as early as A. Scarlatti, was extensively cultivated by the *opera buffa* composers of the late 18th century, then by Rossini (especially in his ensembles of confusion) and Sullivan.

Patti, Adelina [Adela] **(Juana Maria)** (*b* Madrid, 19 Feb 1843; *d* Craig-y-Nos Castle, 27 Sept 1919). Italian soprano. She came from a family of singers, touring the USA (with Ole Bull and later Gottschalk) before making her European début at Covent Garden (1861), where she reigned for 25 years. With her perfectly placed voice and remarkable acting skills she excelled in the roles of Amina, Lucia, Violetta, Norina and Rosina. Later she was noted for the slightly heavier roles of Semiramis, Marguerite, Leonora (*Il trovatore*) and Aida – as well as her legendary temperament, fees and jewels.

Patzak, Julius (*b* Vienna, 9 April 1898; *d* Rottach-Egern, 26 Jan 1974). Austrian tenor. Self-taught, he sang at the Munich Opera from 1928 and joined the Vienna Staatsoper in 1945. His voice was not large, but well projected and with a slightly nasal timbre; he was successful in Mozart, as Beethoven's Florestan, in the lighter Wagner roles and as the Evangelist in Bach's Passions, as well as in Viennese operetta.

Pauer, Ernst (*b* Vienna, 21 Dec 1826; *d* Jugenheim, 9 May 1905). Austrian pianist, teacher and editor. He studied in Munich. As professor at the RAM (1859–64) and the RCM (1876–96) in London, he lectured on the history of keyboard music and produced numerous historical editions and several books. He gave concerts abroad and in 1866 was appointed Austrian court pianist. His son Max von Pauer (1866–1945) was a pianist and notable teacher in Germany.

Pauer, Jiří (*b* Kladno-Lisbušín, 22 Feb 1919). Czech composer. He studied with Hába at the Prague Conservatory (1943–6) and Bořkovec at the Academy (1946–50) and in 1958 was appointed artistic director of the Czech PO. His works include operas, orchestral music and mass songs.

Paukenmesse. Haydn's Mass no.9 in C (1796); Haydn called it *Missa in tempore belli* and it is sometimes known as 'Mass in Time of War'.

Paukenwirbel Symphonie. *See* DRUMROLL SYMPHONY.

Paul Bunyan. Opera in two acts with a prologue by Britten to a libretto by W.H. Auden (1941, New York); Britten revised it (1976, Aldeburgh).

Paulus, Stephen (Harrison) (*b* Summit, NJ, 24 Aug 1949). American composer. He studied at Minnesota University and in 1983 became a composer-in-residence of the Minnesota Orchestra. He came to notice with his one-act opera *The Village Singer* (1979, St Louis), which was followed by *The Postman Always Rings Twice* (1982, St Louis), a powerful music drama if conservative in style.

Paumann, Conrad (*b* Nuremberg, *c*1410; *d* Munich, 24 Jan 1473). German composer and organist. Born blind, he held a number of organist's posts in Nuremberg before travelling secretly to Munich in 1450 to become organist at the Bavarian court. In this capacity he travelled widely in Germany, Italy and Burgundy, attracting tributes to his skill. His son and pupil Paul succeeded him in Munich, and he had many other pupils; his influence is clearly seen in the works of the Buxheim Organ Book. Few of his own works, however, survive; because of his blindness many of his performances were improvised. Virdung's attribution to him of the invention of German lute tablature seems plausible, as it would have been particularly suitable for the dictation of music. His settings of secular *cantus firmi* for organ and his one surviving polyphonic vocal work, reveal that he was aware of the latest developments in the Burgundian *chanson*. His organ works balance an ornamented discant and a solid tenor-countertenor basis; he was the leading German instrumental composer of his type.

Paur, Emil (*b* Czernowitz, 29 Aug 1855; *d* Mistek, 7 June 1932). Austrian violinist, conductor and composer. He studied at the Vienna Conservatory and held court appointments. In 1893 he succeeded Nikisch as conductor of the Boston SO; he was conductor of the New York Philharmonic Concerts (1898) and the Pittsburgh SO (1904–10) and director of the National Conservatory, New York.

Pause. The sign of the corona, a point surmounted by a semicircle, showing the end of a passage or indicating the prolongation of a note or rest beyond its usual value; it is often called 'fermata'. Sometimes it indicates that a cadenza or flourish should be performed.

Pavan. A court dance of the 16th and 17th centuries, probably Italian in origin. It was similar choreographically to the 15th-century *bassadanza*, sedate and normally in duple metre. In 16th-century sources it is frequently the first dance in a group, followed by one or more after-dances in fast triple metre, often based on the same melodic or harmonic material. In Italy such after-dances are usually labelled SALTARELLO, but the most usual pairing in the late 16th century, particularly in northern Europe, was pavan and galliard. By that time the pavan was giving way to the PASSAMEZZO in Italy, but it remained popular until c1625 in England where examples for lute, keyboard and ensemble abound.

Pavane pour une infante défunte [Pavan for a dead princess]. Piano piece by Ravel (1899), later orchestrated.

Pavaniglia. An instrumental dance popular in Italy during the first half of the 17th century.

Pavarotti, Luciano (*b* Modena, 12 Oct 1935). Italian tenor. He made his début in Reggio Emilia in 1961 and from 1963 sang outside Italy, appearing at Covent Garden in *La bohème* and in 1965 sang Edgardo in *Lucia di Lammermoor* in Australia with Sutherland. He made his La Scala début that year as Verdi's Duke and his USA début as Edgardo in Miami; at the Met, he sang Rodolfo in 1968. In the central Italian repertory (Bellini, Verdi, Puccini) and Mozart, his rich, even, vibrant voice, with splendid high notes, produced with great fluency and idiomatic musicianship, establishes him as one of the finest and most appealing Italian tenors of the century.

Pavesi, Stefano (*b* Casaletto Vaprio, 22 Jan 1779; *d* Crema, 28 July 1850). Italian composer. During the late 1820s he served as music director of the Vienna Court Opera, succeeding Salieri. *Maestro di cappella* at Crema, he wrote nearly 70 operas, *seria* and *buffa*, among which *Ser Marcantonio* (1810) enjoyed great success.

Pavillon (Fr.). The bell of a wind instrument, particularly a brass one. The direction 'pavillon en l'air' tells the player to raise the bell of his instrument so that the sound rings out more strongly.

Paxton, Stephen (*b* London, 1735; *d* there, 18 Aug 1787). English composer. He was an important composer of cello solos and lessons, in a fluent and graceful melodic style; he wrote Latin church music and was also a notably successful composer of glees. His brother William (1737–81), a cellist, also composed glees.

Payen, Nicolas [Colin] (*b* Soignies, c1512; *d* Madrid, after 24 April 1559). South Netherlands composer. Most of his career was in the service of Charles V's chapel in Spain. Five *chansons* and 11 motets by him survive, some of the latter showing his concern for expressing the emotional content of his texts.

Payne, Anthony (Edward) (*b* London, 2 Aug 1936). English composer. He studied at Durham and became a critic for the *Daily Telegraph*; later he wrote for *The Independent*. Most of his compositions date from after his mid-30s and show an atonal development of English rhapsodism, reflecting his interest in Bridge and Bax, on whom he has written. He has also published a study of Schoenberg (1968). In 1966 he married the soprano Jane Manning.

Pazdírek. Czech family of publishers and musicians. The most celebrated members were Bohumil [Johann Peter Gotthard] (1839–1919), who brought out the 34-volume *Universal-Handbuch der Musikliteratur* (Vienna, 1904–10), and his nephew Oldřich (1887–1944), who raised the family firm in Brno to its leading position, concentrating on Moravian works.

Peabody Conservatory. Part of the Peabody Institute, Baltimore (affiliated with the Johns Hopkins University since 1977). Founded in 1857 by George Peabody as the Academy of Music, it opened in 1868.

Its activities have been imaginative and wide ranging. Reginald Stewart, director 1941–58 and conductor of the Baltimore SO, instituted the appointing of the orchestra's principals as teachers.

Peacham, Henry (*b* North Mimms, 1578; *d* ?London, 1642–3). English writer. He is of interest to musicians primarily for the much-quoted chapter on music in his *Compleat Gentleman* (1622), which defends music in the church and home and stresses its practical value.

Peacock Variations. Orchestral work by Kodály (1939), variations on the Hungarian folksong *The Peacock*.

Pearl Fishers, The [Les pêcheurs de perles]. Opera in three acts by Bizet to a libretto by M. Carré and E. Cormon (1863, Paris).

Pears, Sir Peter (Neville Luard) (*b* Farnham, 22 June 1910; *d* Aldeburgh, 3 April 1986). English tenor. After study at the RCM he sang in the BBC Chorus, 1934–8. He sang at Sadler's Wells from 1943, creating Britten's Peter Grimes there in 1945. Britten wrote all his major tenor roles, including Albert Herring (1947), Vere in *Billy Budd* (1951) and Aschenbach in *Death in Venice* (1971), and many of his solo vocal works with Pears's voice in mind. It had a clear, reedy almost instrumental quality, capable of a wide range of expression; its timbre was inward and reflective. His repertory ranged from the 16th century to the 20th. With Britten as accompanist he gave intelligent, eloquent performances of Schubert lieder and other songs, many of them recorded.

Pearsall, Robert Lucas (*b* Clifton, 14 March 1795; *d* Wartensee, 5 Aug 1856). English composer and antiquarian. He trained as a barrister but from 1825 devoted himself to studying early music and to composition, living at Mainz, Karlsruhe and Wartensee; he made occasional return visits to Bristol, where his music was performed by the Bristol Madrigal Society. His works range from Latin motets and Anglican cathedral music to orchestral overtures, but he is best remembered for his Romantic partsongs, notably *O who will o'er the downs so free* and *When Allen-a-dale*, and 'madrigals' in Elizabethan style; these, including the six-part *O ye roses*, the eight-part *Lay a garland* and the four-part ballett *No, No, Nigella*, revive and extend the Renaissance style with striking success. He was a respected contrapuntist and devoted time to the reform of English Church Music.

Peasant Cantata. Nickname of J.S. Bach's Cantata no.212, *Mer hahn en neue Oberkeet*, to a libretto by Picander (1742); it includes folk melodies.

Pêcheurs de perles, Les. *See* PEARL FISHERS, THE.

Pedal. A lever operated by the foot; pedals are variously used on musical instruments. A pedal can alter pitch, as in the harp or timpani; or it can facilitate the playing of an instrument, as in the drum-kit where it controls the bass drum and the high-hat cymbal. Its most frequent uses fall into two categories. First it may produce expressive effects, change the tone colour or the length of decay of a note (as in the left and right pedals on a piano) or its volume (as in the swell pedal on an organ); some electric instruments such as the vibraphone, guitar and synthesizer have 'effects pedals' of this sort. Second, it is widely used for a series of pedals arranged like a piano keyboard but played with the feet and thus termed a 'pedalboard'; this device is most often found on the organ, where it commonly provides bass notes but has long been used for a wide range of musical purposes. Various other pedal instruments have been developed; the pedal clavichord and pedal harpsichord were mostly used as practice instruments for organists, but the pedal pianoforte was for a while taken seriously in its own right. Mozart owned one; Gounod, Alkan and Schumann all composed music for one.

Pedal clarinet. Name for the contrabass CLARINET.

Pedaliter. Term to indicate that a piece of organ music is to be played both by hand and feet.

Pedal notes. The fundamental sounds of a brass instrument, obtained when the air column is set in vibration as a whole instead of in parts. They are not often used in orchestral writing, except in the case of the trombone, whose pedal notes (sounding from $B'\flat$ downwards) have been called for quite frequently since Berlioz's time.

Pedal organ. The chest, towers, chamber etc given to the pipes of the pedal department, as distinct from the pedal-keys or pedalboard which play them or which, in instruments without a Pedal organ, play the stops of the manual(s). Since the late 14th century the largest organs have had some kind of Pedal organ; by 1600, in central Germany, the Pedal organ often contained three distinct chests.

Pedal point. A sustained or repeated note, usually in the bass, above or around which other parts move.

Pedersøn, Mogens (*b c*1583; *d* ?Copenhagen, ?Jan–Feb 1623). Danish composer. He studied with Giovanni Gabrieli in Venice in 1599–1600 and 1605–9, and from 1603 was an instrumentalist in the Danish royal chapel. After serving Queen Anne at the English court, 1611–14, he became assistant director of the Danish chapel in 1618. The most important Danish composer of the era, he wrote two books of madrigals (1608, 1611) in the modern Italian style and a volume of church music (1620), which contains settings of post-Reformation Danish liturgical melodies and some fine Latin polyphonic pieces. He also left two pavans for viols.

Pederzuoli, Giovanni Battista (*d* in or after 1692). Italian composer. He was *maestro di cappella* of S Maria Maggiore, Bergamo, in 1664–5; in 1677–82 he was organist at the court of the Dowager Empress in Vienna; he then succeeded Antonio Draghi as Kapellmeister (until 1686). He composed 14 dramatic works and seven *sepolcri* and oratorios, which like Draghi's are in a rather conservative middle Baroque style; they contain some imaginative scorings. His output also includes philosophical cantatas and other vocal pieces.

Pedrell, Felipe (*b* Tortosa, 19 Feb 1841; *d* Barcelona, 19 Aug 1922). Spanish composer and musicologist. Though devoted originally to composition – he regarded his masterpiece as the Wagnerian trilogy *Los Pirineos* (1890–91) – he worked increasingly as a writer and editor. His publications include the complete works of Victoria, a biographical series on Catalan musicians, a dictionary of Spanish, Portuguese

and Latin American musicians and a critical reassessment of Spanish popular song. The creator of modern Spanish musicology, he contributed greatly to the revival of interest in church music in Spain.

Pedrotti, Carlo (*b* Verona, 12 Nov 1817; *d* there, 16 Oct 1893). Italian conductor and composer. He established his reputation first as a composer of operas in the *buffa* or *semiseria* style, notably with the tuneful *Tutti in maschera* (1856), given at Verona, where he taught and conducted. As director and conductor of the Teatro Regio, Turin (1868–82), he not only improved the quality of opera performance, conducting a highly successful *Lohengrin* and premières of works by Rossi, Bottesini and Catalani, but also founded a series of Concerti Populari, stimulating interest in German instrumental music. He helped place Turin beside Milan as a leading Italian musical centre.

Peebles, David (*fl* 1530–76; *d* before 1592). Scottish composer. A canon of the Augustinian Priory of St Andrews, he composed a motet, *Si quis diligit me* (*c*1530), using structural imitation and showing his striking melodic gift. His works include 106 Protestant psalm tunes for four voices.

Peerce, Jan (*b* New York, 3 June 1904; *d* there, 15 Dec 1984). American tenor. His broadcasts in the 1930s attracted the attention of Toscanini, with whom he sang in several recordings. He sang at the Met, 1941–68, specializing in the French and Italian repertories; his strong technique and secure upper register also made him a favourite in Europe and Russia.

Peer Gynt. Incidental music by Grieg for Ibsen's play (1876, Oslo), from which he arranged two orchestral suites.

Saeverud also wrote incidental music for the play (1947) and Egk wrote an opera on the subject (1938).

Peerson, Martin (*b* ?March, 1571–3; *d* London, bur. 15 Jan 1651). English composer. A virginalist and organist active in London, he was probably sacrist at Vestminster Abbey, 1623–30. He was also almoner and master of the choristers at St Paul's Cathedral from 1624–5 until services ceased in 1642, and remained later as almoner. Experiments with form and unusual harmonic procedures are characteristic of his works. His two books of secular vocal music (1620, 1630) include settings for up to six voices with instruments and combine elements from the ayre, madrigal, consort song and verse anthem; the second – the earliest English published collection with figured bass – is strikingly sombre in mood. A more modern idiom appears in his 20 (mostly verse) anthems. He also composed motets, keyboard pieces and consort music.

Peeters, Flor (*b* Tielen, 4 July 1903; *d* Antwerp, 4 July 1986). Belgian composer. He studied at the Lemmens Institute, Mechelen, where he was appointed professor in 1923; later he taught at the conservatories of Ghent (1931–8), Tilburg (1935–48) and Antwerp (1948–68), while also pursuing an international career as an organist. His works, characterized by a preference for classical forms, consist mostly of sacred choral and organ music, in a style looking to Dupré and Tournemire; his fluent melodies are influenced by Gregorian chant, Flemish Renaissance polyphony and folk themes. He published many editions and teaching works.

Peirol (*b* Peirol, ?1160; *d* after 1221). Provençal troubadour poet and composer. He may have served the Dauphin of Auvergne at Clermont until *c*1202. His songs reveal that he was involved in the crusades. Half of the 34 poems attributed to him survive with music.

Peixinho, Jorge (Manuel Rosado Marques) (*b* Montijo, 20 Jan 1940). Portuguese composer. He studied at the Lisbon Conservatory (1951–8) and abroad with Petrassi, Boulez, Nono and others. From the early 1960s he was an acknowledged leader of the Portuguese avant garde and in 1970 he founded the Lisbon Contemporary Music Group. He has taught at the Oporto Conservatory and in Brazil.

Pękiel, Bartłomiej (*d* ?Kraków, *c*1670). Polish composer. He became an organist at the Polish royal court in Warsaw in the 1630s, and was deputy director of music under Scacchi. After Scacchi left (1649) he acted as director, gaining the title in 1653. From 1656 he lived in Kraków, becoming director of music in the cathedral chapel in 1658; he also composed for the male Rorantist chapel. He was the leading Polish composer of the middle Baroque period. Of his 30 surviving sacred works, those from Warsaw are dramatic concertato works and polychoral masses with instruments; later arones include traditional polyphonic masses and motets (such as the *Missa pulcherrima ad instar Praenestini*, 1669). Some of his works use themes from plainchant or Polish sacred songs. He also wrote instrumental pieces.

Peking [Beijing] opera. A Chinese opera style dating from the late 18th century, combining singing, speech, mime and acrobatics, with instrumental support; it uses a set melodic repertory. *See* CHINESE MUSIC.

Pelissier, Victor (*b* ?Paris, *c*1755; *d* ?NJ, *c*1820). French composer. He appeared in Philadelphia as a horn player in 1792, and also played in New York; he was again in Philadelphia, 1811–14. He was a prolific composer of theatre music, for pantomimes, melodramas and operas; most of the music is lost but items appeared in a 12-volume collection (1811–12).

Pelléas et Mélisande. Opera in five acts by Debussy, a setting of Maeterlinck's play abridged by the composer (1902, Paris).

Symphonic poem, op.5, by Schoenberg after Maeterlinck (1903: *Pelleas und Melisande*).

Incidental music for Maeterlinck's play was written by Fauré (1898) and Sibelius (1905).

Pellegrin, Claude Mathieu (*b* Aix-en-Provence, 25 Oct 1682; *d* there, 10 Oct 1763). French composer. Organist at Aix Cathedral, he became *maître de chapelle* in 1706; after a period at the Sainte-Chapelle, Paris, he returned there 1731–48. His motets and other sacred works are notable for their rhythmic variety and descriptive writing.

Pelletier, Wilfrid (*b* Montreal, 20 June 1896; *d* New York, 9 April 1982). American conductor and music educationist of Canadian birth. He studied in Paris. From 1918 to 1950 he was assistant conductor at the Met, and in 1935 he founded the Société des Concerts Symphoniques de Montréal. Until his retirement in 1970 he worked for educational institutions, notably establishing children's concerts in Montreal.

Pelog. One of the two tuning systems (the other is *slendro*) used by GAMELAN ensembles in Java; normally it is heptatonic. *See* INDONESIAN MUSIC.

Peñalosa, Francisco de (*b* Talavera de la Reina, *c*1470; *d* Seville, 1 April 1528). Spanish composer. He was appointed a singer in Ferdinand V's chapel choir in 1498 and in 1511 *maestro de capilla* to Ferdinand's grandson. After a period at Burgos (1512–16) he served at Seville Cathedral and in 1517 became a singer in the papal chapel in Rome. He was the most skilful Spanish polyphonist before Morales and admired by his contemporaries. His extant works (almost all sacred) include seven complete masses and motets; his secular music includes eight trios, a duo and a six-voice quodlibet in the Cancionero de Palacio.

Penberthy, James (*b* Melbourne, 3 May 1917). Australian composer. He studied at the Melbourne University Conservatorium and in Europe and began composing in a relatively conservative style, though since the late 1960s he has used new techniques. His works include operas (notably *Dalgerie*, 1958) ballets and symphonies.

Penderecki, Krzysztof (*b* Dębica, 23 Nov 1933). Polish composer. He was a pupil of Malawski at the Kraków Conservatory (1955–8), where he has also taught. He gained international fame with such works as *Threnody for the Victims of Hiroshima* for 52 strings (1960), exploiting the fierce expressive effects of new sonorities, but in the mid-1970s there came a change to large symphonic forms based on rudimentary chromatic motifs. Central to his work is the *St Luke Passion* (1965), with its combination of intense expressive force with a severe style with archaic elements alluding to Bach, and its sequel *Utrenia*, in which Orthodox chant provides musical material and at the same time a sense of mystery. His operas have been admired for their dynamic expression even if their discrete vignettes offer more opportunity for characterization than development.

Operas The Devils of Loudon (1969); Paradise Lost (1978); Die schwarze Maske (1986)
Choral music From the Psalms of David, perc (1958); Strophes, S, reciter, 10 insts (1959); Dimensions of Time and Silence, 40vv, insts (1959); Stabat mater (1962); Cantata on the 600th anniversary of the Jagellonian University, orch (1964); Funeral Song for Rutkowski (1964); St Luke Passion, narrator, orch (1965); Dies irae, orch (1967); Kosmogonia, orch (1970); Utrenia, orch (1971); Canticum canticorum Salomonis, orch (1972); Ecloga VIII, 6 male vv (1972); Magnificat, B, orch (1974); Te Deum, orch (1979)
Orchestral music Emanations, 2 str orch (1958); Anaklasis, 42 str, perc (1960); Threnody for the Victims of Hiroshima, 52 str (1960); Fluorescences (1961); Fonogrammi (1961); Polymorphia, 48 str (1961); Kanon, str, tapes (1962); Vn Conc. (1963); Sonata, vc, orch (1963); Capriccio, ob, 11 str (1965); De natura sonoris I (1966), II (1971); Capriccio, vn (1967); Pittsburgh Ov. (1967); Actions, 14 jazz insts (1971); Partita, hpd (1971); Praeludium, woodwind, dbs (1971); Vc Conc. no.1 (1972); Vn Conc. no.2 (1982); Sym. no.1 (1973); Sym. no.2 (1980); The Dream of Jacob (1974); Va Conc. (1938)
Chamber music 2 str qts (1960, 1968)

Pénélope. Opera in three acts by Fauré to a libretto by René Fauchois (1913, Monte Carlo).

Composers to write operas on the Penelope legend include Monteverdi (IL RITORNO D'ULISSE IN PATRIA), Cimarosa, Galuppi, Piccinni and Jommelli.

Penet, Hilaire (*b* diocese of Poitiers, ?1501). French composer. A choirboy at the papal court (1514–16), he became a regular member in 1516 and entered Leo X's private chapel in 1519. Magnificats, motets and *chansons* by him survive. His motet *Descendit angelus Domini* served as a model for masses by Palestrina and Porta. Clarity and smooth craftsmanship mark his *chansons*.

Penillon. A Welsh form of improvised bardic song, with harp accompaniment.

Pentatonic. A term applied to music, a mode or a scale based on a system of five different pitches to the octave.

Pentland, Barbara (Lally) (*b* Winnipeg, 2 Jan 1912). Canadian composer. She studied with Gauthiez in Paris (1929–30) and with Jacobi and Wagenaar at the Juilliard School (1936–9), then began to make her name with vigorous music in a style drawing on Copland and Schoenberg. She taught at the University of British Columbia (1949–63) and came under Webern's influence in the mid-1950s; latterly her music has been aleatory and used quarter-tones. Most of her works are instrumental.

Pépin, (Jean-Josephat) Clermont (*b* St Georges-de-Beauce, 15 May 1926). Canadian composer and educationist. He studied with Scalero at the Curtis Institute (1941–5) and with Honegger, Jolivet and Messiaen at the Paris Conservatoire (1949–55), then taught at the Montreal Conservatory (1955–64, 1967–72). His works, allied with the French avant garde, cover all genres and include five symphonies (1948–83) and five string quartets (1948–76).

Pepping, Ernst (*b* Duisburg, 12 Sept 1901; *d* Berlin, 1 Feb 1981). German composer. He studied with Gmeindl at the Berlin Musikhochschule and taught in Berlin from 1934, at the Spandau Church Music School and at the Musikhochschule. His works consist mostly of Protestant sacred choral and organ music in neo-Baroque style. They include the *Spandauer Chorbuch* (1938), 20 volumes of austere, unaccompanied choral pieces.

Pepusch, Johann Christoph (*b* Berlin, 1667; *d* London, 20 July 1752). German composer and theorist. After serving at the Prussian court he settled in London (by 1704) as a viola player and later harpsichordist at Drury Lane theatre, where in 1707–16 he presented five masques, notably *Venus and Adonis* (1715) and *Apollo and Daphne* (1716). By 1721 he was music director to James Brydges (later Duke of Chandos), writing verse anthems and other sacred works. Having composed the basses and an overture for John Gay's *The Beggar's Opera* (1728), he wrote a sequel, *Polly* (not staged until 1777). He also composed odes, secular solo cantatas (most to English texts), over 100 instrumental sonatas and other instrumental pieces. In 1737 he became organist to the Charterhouse; he was in constant demand as a teacher. Latterly his main interest was the performance and study of ancient music, in which he was the leading expert of his day. He edited music by Corelli and published (anonymously) *A Treatise on Harmony* (1730). His wife was the singer Marguerite de l'Epine.

Perahia, Murray (*b* New York, 19 April 1947). American pianist and conductor. He studied at Mannes College and with Horszowski. After appearances as soloist throughout the USA he won the 1972 Leeds International Competition. He is noted for his delicacy and sensitivity, notably in Chopin and Schumann, and has recorded all Mozart's concertos, directing from the keyboard.

Peranda, Marco Gioseppe (*b* Rome/Macerata, *c*1625; *d* Dresden, 12 Jan 1675). Italian composer. An alto singer in the Dresden court chapel from the 1650s, he worked with Schütz as vice-Kapellmeister in 1661–3 and as Kapellmeister in 1663–72, finally becoming first court Kapellmeister. He is important chiefly for his many sacred concertos and motets (mostly to Latin texts). Like works by his Italian contemporaries, they tend to be more theatrical than Schütz's, with contrasts of time and texture; they strongly influenced other German composers. His other works include masses, Magnificats etc, three oratorios, madrigals, instrumental pieces and parts of two operas.

Peraza. Spanish family of organists. Jerónimo de Peraza (de Sotomayor) (*c*1550–1617), son of a famous shawm player, was organist of the cathedrals of Seville (1573–9) and Toledo (1580–1617); his nephew Jerónimo (1574–1604) was organist of Palencia Cathedral for nearly ten years. The elder Jerónimo's brother, Francisco (1564–98), was an esteemed organist of Seville Cathedral from 1584; his son Francisco (*c*1597–after 1636) was organist at the cathedrals of Toledo (1618–21), Cuenca (1626) and Segovia (1628–9).

Percussion instruments. Term for instruments played by shaking, or by striking a membrane or a plate or a bar of metal, wood or other hard material. One using a membrane is a MEMBRANOPHONE; one where the sound is produced by the vibration of the material struck is an IDIOPHONE. Percussion instruments may be divided into those that produce a sound of definite pitch and those that do not.

Perdendosi (It.). Losing itself, dying away.

Perez, David (*b* Naples, 1711; *d* Lisbon, 30 Oct 1778). Italian composer. Trained in Naples, he presented his first opera there in 1735. He held posts in the royal chapel in Palermo, becoming *maestro di cappella*. In 1740–51 he composed operas for Palermo, Genoa and elsewhere, gaining an international reputation. Finally he served the Portuguese court as *maestro di cappella* and music master to the royal princesses (from 1752). One of the finest *opera seria* composers of his day, he wrote over 35 such works, many to texts by Metastasio. Those for Lisbon, including *Solimano* (1757), are more *galant* in style and flexible in structure, and achieve an impressive dramatic effect. Perez also wrote an *opera buffa* (1740, Naples), serenatas and much sacred music.

Perfall, Karl, Freiherr von (*b* Munich, 29 Jan 1824; *d* there, 14 Jan 1907). German administrator and composer. While he was intendant of the National

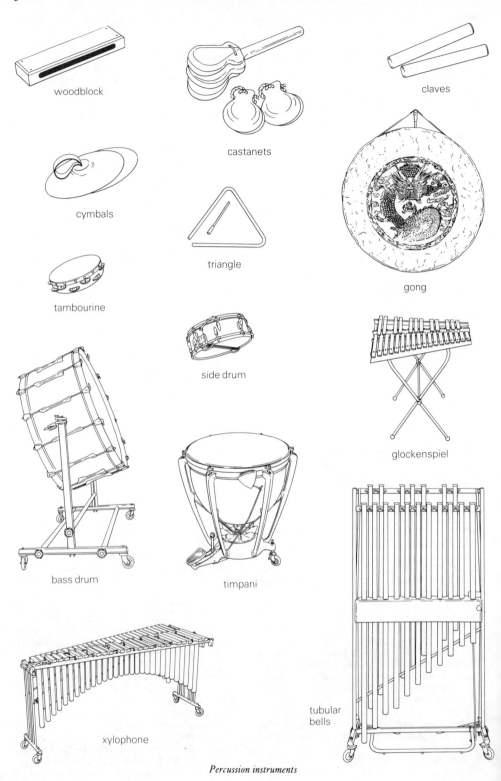

woodblock

castanets

claves

cymbals

triangle

gong

tambourine

side drum

glockenspiel

bass drum

timpani

tubular bells

xylophone

Percussion instruments

Theatre, Munich (1867–93), over 700 Wagner performances were given; his energy and practicality contributed to saving Bayreuth. His operas were performed in Munich.

Perfect. Term used in early mensural NOTATION to denote a relationship of 3:1 (as opposed to imperfect, 2:1) in time (the relation between semibreve and breve) or prolation (the relation between minim and semibreve).

Perfect cadence [authentic cadence; final cadence; full cadence; full close]. A CADENCE consisting of a dominant chord followed by a tonic chord (V–I), both normally in root position. Some theorists specify that a cadence is 'perfect' only if the uppermost voice sounds the tonic note in the final chord.

Perfect Fool, The. Opera in one act by Holst to his own libretto (1923, London).

Perfect interval [perfect consonance]. The interval of an octave, 5th, 4th or unison, or any compound of one of these (11th, 12th etc); an 'imperfect consonance' refers to major and minor 3rds and their compounds.

Perfect pitch. *See* ABSOLUTE PITCH.

Performing practice [performance practice]. Term adapted from the German *Aufführungspraxis*. As applied to Western music, it involves all aspects of the way in which music is and has been performed; its study is of importance to the modern performer concerned with 'authentic' style. Aspects of performing practice include notational ones (i.e. the relationship between written notes and the sounds they symbolize, especially in such matters as rhythm, tempo and articulation); improvisation and ornaments; instruments, their history and physical structure and the ways in which they are played; voice production; matters of tuning, pitch and temperament; and ensembles, their size, disposition and the modes in which they are directed. Performing practice is generally approached through the study of treatises and instruction books, critical writings and iconographical material, as well as actual instruments and music. It is also an inseparable part of the central concerns of ethnomusicologists who work with orally transmitted repertories and of those scholars who work with the music of ancient civilizations, such as those of Egypt, Greece and Rome.

Pergament, Moses (*b* Helsinki, 21 Sept 1893; *d* Gustavsberg, 5 March 1977). Swedish composer of Finnish birth. He trained in St Petersburg and Berlin and spent much of the interwar period in Berlin and Paris, settling in Stockholm, where he composed and was an influential and trenchant music critic. His works, in many genres, testify to his cosmopolitan background though equally important was his Jewish heritage; central to his output is the choral symphony *Der Judiska sången* (1944).

Pergament, Ruvim (*b* Petrozavodsk, 12 Sept 1906; *d* there, 6 March 1965). Soviet composer. He studied as a violinist at the Leningrad Conservatory but was self-taught as a composer. He was vital in establishing Karelo-Finnish art music, writing operas, oratorios etc and arranging folksongs. The vocal-symphonic poem *Ayno* (1954), based on the Kalevala, is his major work.

Pergolesi, Giovanni Battista (*b* Iesi, 4 Jan 1710; *d* Pozzuoli, 16 March 1736). Italian composer. While studying with Durante in Naples he worked as a violinist, and in 1731 he presented his first stage work, a *dramma sacro*. He became *maestro di cappella* to the Prince of Stigliano in 1732 and to the Duke of Maddaloni in 1734. Several more stage works followed for Naples and an *opera seria*, *L'Olimpiade* (1735), for Rome.

Though only moderately popular in his lifetime, Pergolesi posthumously attained international fame as a leading figure in the rise of Italian comic opera. He wrote two *commedie musicali*, with both *buffo* and *seria* elements, and three comic intermezzos, each staged with an *opera seria* by him. The intermezzo *La serva padrona* (1733, Naples) is a miniature masterpiece of *buffo* style, spirited, with touches of sentiment and with clear, lively characterization; it was widely performed and in 1752 initiated the Parisian Querelle des Bouffons. *Livietta e Tracollo*, also known as *La contadina astuta* (1734, Naples), became popular too. His other works include sacred music (notably a *Stabat mater* of 1736), chamber cantatas and duets, and a few instrumental pieces. Numerous works have been wrongly attributed to him.

Dramatic music Salustia (1732); Lo frate 'nnamorato (1732); Il prigionier superbo (1733); La serva padrona, intermezzo (1733); Livietta e Tracollo, intermezzo (1734); Adriano in Siria (1734); L'Olimpiade (1734); Flaminio (1735); 2 sacred dramas

Sacred vocal music 2 masses; Vespers; Stabat mater, f (1736); 2 Salve regina; 2 motets

Secular music 5 arias and cantatas; 4 sonatas

Peri, Jacopo (*b* Rome, 20 Aug 1561; *d* Florence, 12 Aug 1633). Italian composer and singer. Trained in Florence, he was organist at the Badia in 1579–1605, and by 1586 was a singer at S Giovanni Battista. From 1588 he served the Medici court as composer and singer; he also played keyboard instruments and the chitarrone. In the 1590s he met with musicians, poets and philosophers at the home of Jacopo Corsi and began to compose in the new recitative style, intended to match the expressive power of ancient Greek music. His first two operas, both to texts by Rinuccini, were *Dafne* (1598, Florence), composed with Corsi, and *Euridice* (1600, Florence), partly rewritten by Giulio Caccini for the first performance. *Euridice*, based on the Orpheus legend, is the earliest opera for which complete music survives. Peri's setting emphasizes both the structure of the libretto (a prologue and five scenes) and its varied emotions, and includes choral numbers, strophic songs and continuous expressive recitatives. His later dramatic works, mostly written with other Florentine composers such as Marco da Gagliano, include several operas, three oratorios (1622–4) and some shorter pieces; one work was staged in Mantua (1620), where he held a court position from 1618. He also wrote a book of songs, *Le varie musiche* (1609), with some recitative settings, and an instrumental ricercare.

Péri, La. Ballet ('poème dansée') by Dukas (1912, Paris).

Périchole, La. Operetta in three acts by Offenbach to

a libretto by Meilhac and Halévy after Mérimée (1868, Paris).

Perigourdine. A French folkdance from Périgord, usually in 3/8 or 6/8, similar to the PASSEPIED.

Period. A musical statement terminated by a cadence or built of complementary members, each generally two to eight bars long ('antecedent' and 'consequent').

Perissone [Pierreson, Pyrison], **Cambio** (*b* ?*c*1520; *fl* 1540–50). Singer and composer of French or Flemish origin active in Venice. He belonged to a circle of well-known Venetian musicians, including Rore and Willaert, and published four volumes of secular music, 1545–50. Apart from a surviving motet, all his works are secular, his four-voice madrigals being modelled on Rore's and his villanellas and five-voice madrigals on Willaert's.

Perle, George (*b* Bayonne, NJ, 6 May 1915). American composer and theorist. He studied with Wesley LaViolette (1934–8) and Krenek, and in 1961 began teaching at Queens College, New York. During the 1930s he was one of the first Americans to take an interest in 12-note music; from that grew his '12-tone modality', which makes possible a relatively concordant atonality having connections with Berg and Bartók. His works are almost all instrumental and include string quartets and wind quintets. It eschews the veneer of the avant garde and unfolds in a relatively uncomplicated way. He has also written many influential essays and books, particularly on Berg.

Perlemuter, Vlado (*b* Kaunas, 26 May 1904). French pianist of Polish birth. He studied with Moszkowski and Cortot. His early experience was with the music of Ravel, to whom he played, using a wide range of 'orchestral' sonorities. Later he became known as a distinguished interpreter of Chopin. In 1950 he became a professor at the Paris Conservatoire.

Perlman, Itzhak (*b* Tel-Aviv, 31 Aug 1945). Israeli violinist. Though a victim of poliomyelitis, he had given numerous recitals by the age of ten. After study at the Juilliard School with Galamian, from 1958, he made his Carnegie Hall début in 1963. His British début was in 1968 with the LSO. His instinctive musicianship, allied to a brilliant technique, has been admired in the concerto repertory and in recitals with Barenboim, Zukerman and others.

Perne, François-Louis (*b* Paris, 4 Oct 1772; *d* Laon, 26 May 1832). French music historian, composer, singer and double bass player. He played in the Paris Opéra orchestra and was administrator of the Conservatoire (librarian from 1819). His scholarly interests were chiefly in Greek and medieval music; he studied original documents but published little. Fétis acquired his important library.

Perosi, Lorenzo (*b* Tortona, 20 Dec 1872; *d* Rome, 12 Dec 1956). Italian composer and church musician. A pupil of Haberl at Regensburg, he was appointed choirmaster at St Mark's, Venice (1894), and the Sistine Chapel (1898). At the turn of the century his oratorios had extraordinary international success; he also wrote 33 masses and smaller sacred pieces and concertos. Though naive and eclectic, his best pieces have an appealing freshness and gentle spirituality.

Pérotin (*fl* Paris, *c*1200). French composer, the most celebrated musician involved in the revision and renotation of the *Magnus liber* (attributed to Léonin). Two decrees by the Bishop of Paris concerning the 'feast of the fools' and the performance of quadruple (four-voice) organum, from 1198 and 1199, have been associated with Pérotin since the theorist known as Anonymous IV stated that he composed four-voice settings of both the relevant texts. Attempts to identify him at Notre Dame have proved inconclusive. He may have been born *c*1155–60, revised the *Magnus liber* 1180–90 subsequently composed his three- and four-voice works and died in the first years of the 13th century; or he wrote the four-voice works early in his career, revised the *Magnus liber* in the first decade of the 13th century and died *c*1225. He was not necessarily attached to Notre Dame. As regards his *Magnus liber* revisions, Anonymous IV refers to his abbreviations and improvement of the work by substituting succinct passages in discant style for the more florid organum; this would seem to be confirmed by one source of the *Magnus liber*, although the substitute sections are not attributed there to a specific composer. The creation of three- and four-voice organum *c*1200 is an important step in the development of polyphony which until then had been conceived in terms of two voices, and Pérotin's compositions show great awareness of the implications for structure and tonality. The confusion over dating derives from unresolved problems of notation.

Sacred music 2 four-voice organa; *c*10 three-voice organa; 3 conductus; 5 clausulas and probably 156 for *Magnus liber*

Perpetuum mobile. *See* MOTO PERPETUO.

Perrachio, Luigi (*b* Turin, 28 May 1883; *d* there, 6 Sept 1966). Italian composer and pianist. He taught at the Turin Liceo Musicale (1925–55) and, as a writer, pianist and conductor, was a propagandist for contemporary music and educational reformer. Of his modest output, in the Debussy–Ravel tradition, the 25 Preludes (1927) for piano are best known.

Perrault, Charles (*b* Paris, 12 Jan 1628; *d* there, 16 May 1703). French author. He first worked as a lawyer, and was a supporter of Lully's style of opera, writing two librettos. His well-known *Contes*, such as *La belle au bois dormant* and *Cendrillon*, have inspired music by Rossini, Tchaikovsky and others. His brother Claude (1613–88) was a polymath whose interests included music and acoustics.

Perrin, Pierre (*b* Lyons, *c*1620; *d* Paris, bur. 26 April 1675). French poet and librettist. He founded the first opera academy in Paris and wrote the libretto for its successful first production, Cambert's *Pomone* (1671); however, financial troubles led him to surrender his privilege to Lully in 1672. His other works include texts for two pastorals by Cambert and verses for songs and cantatas.

Perrin d'Angicourt (*fl* 1245–70). French trouvère. His jeux-partis with others centred in Arras suggest connections with that area. Several of his songs are dedicated to members of the Franco-Flemish nobility. He was one of the more prolific trouvères, his 35 extant songs favouring strophes employing different line lengths, though he preferred shorter verses. Musically he favoured songs in bar form (*AAB*).

Perséphone. Melodrama in three scenes by Stravinsky to a libretto by André Gide for narrator, tenor, chorus, children's chorus and orchestra (1934, Paris).

Persichetti, Vincent (*b* Philadelphia, 6 June 1915; *d* there, 14 Aug 1987). American composer and educationist. A pupil of Nordoff and Harris at the Philadelphia Conservatory, where he taught (1941–7), he began teaching at the Juilliard School in 1947. He produced a large, eclectic output in all concert genres, from which the piano works and music for wind band are important. His mastery of compositional technique was prodigious but he has been criticized for a cool detachment in his style.

Persimfans [Perviy Simfonicheskiy Ansambl' bez Dirizhora; First Conductorless Symphony Ensemble]. Russian orchestra, 1922–32, formed from leading players in Moscow, which achieved a high standard using chamber-music rehearsal methods. Its success led to the formation of similar groups in other towns and to a higher standard of orchestral playing in the USSR.

Persinger, Louis (*b* Rochester, IL, 11 Feb 1887; *d* New York, 31 Dec 1966). American violinist, pianist and teacher. He studied at Leipzig Conservatory and with Ysaÿe. His solo début was in 1912 and in 1915 he became leader of the San Francisco Orchestra; he moved to New York in 1925. He was also a highly influential teacher (Menuhin was a pupil); at the Juilliard School from 1930, he did much to establish an American school of violin playing.

Perti, Giacomo Antonio (*b* Bologna, 6 June 1661; *d* there, 10 April 1756). Italian composer. He was trained in Bologna and also studied with Giuseppe Corso ('Celano') in Parma. After serving as *maestro di cappella* at Bologna Cathedral in 1690–96, he was *maestro di cappella* at S Petronio and simultaneously held similar posts at S Domenico (1704–55) and S Maria in Galliera (1706–50). He was five times chosen as *principe* of the Accademia Filarmonica, and also achieved fame as a teacher; Giuseppe Torelli and G.B. Martini were among his pupils.

Perti was a skilful, highly esteemed composer; he wrote over 300 sacred works, over 20 operas (for Bologna, Venice, Pratolino and elsewhere) and *c*20 oratorios. His sacred works are mostly concerted masses, psalms, motets etc; typically, they show melodic inventiveness, variety of form and colourful scoring. Among his other works are secular cantatas, arias and liturgical instrumental pieces.

Perugia Festival. *See* SAGRA MUSICALE UMBRA.

Pes. Term found in some English sources of polyphony the later 13th century for the untexted, non-Gregorian tenor (often borrowed from a song or dance-tune) of certain motets. It usually denotes a strict or varied melodic (as opposed to rhythmic) ostinato.

Pesante (It.). Heavy, weighty.

Pescetti, Giovanni Battista (*b* Venice, *c*1704; *d* there, 20 March 1766). Italian composer. He studied with Lotti in Venice and up to 1732 composed and revised

operas for theatres there (some in collaboration with Galuppi). In 1737–44 he composed and contributed to stage works in London; he then returned to Italy, presenting his last opera in Padua, 1761. From 1762 he was second organist at St Mark's, Venice. His other works include sacred pieces and keyboard sonatas.

Pešek, Libor (*b* Prague, 22 June 1933). Czech conductor. He studied under Ancerl, Neumann and Smetáček in Prague and worked as repetiteur at first Polzen and then Prague Opera. He became conductor of the Czech State CO (1970–77), then of the Slovak PO (1980–81); in 1982 he was appointed conductor-in-residence of the Czech PO and in 1987 he became principal conductor of the Royal Liverpool PO. He has appeared widely as a guest conductor and on tour and has made many records, of the Czech repertory and also works by Bruckner, Stravinsky and Skryabin.

Pesenti, Martino (*b* Venice, *c*1600; *d* there, *c*1648). Italian harpsichordist and composer. Blind from birth, he devoted himself mainly to chamber music. He published five volumes of dances, seven of madrigals and canzonettas, three of arias and one of church music. The dances, composed for harpsichord with optional string parts, are mostly correntes and galliards in a simple style typical of his output.

Pesenti [Vicentino], **Michele** (*b* in or near Verona, *c*1470; *d* after 1524). Italian singer, composer and lutenist. He served the d'Este family at Ferrara and may then have worked for the Gonzagas at Mantua. He was one of the most important frottola composers: he wrote 36, published 1504–21. Two motets also survive.

Pessard, Emile (Louis Fortuné) (*b* Paris, 29 May 1843; *d* there, 10 Feb 1917). French composer. He studied at the Paris Conservatoire, where from 1881 he was a professor of harmony, and composed operas, notably *Les folies amoureuses* (1891), light instrumental music and highly regarded songs.

Peter, Johann Friedrich (*b* Heerendijk, 19 May 1746; *d* Bethlehem, PA, 13 July 1813). American composer. He trained at a Moravian seminary in Saxony, then went to America (1770), taking several MSS of J.C.F. Bach's music. He served in Pennsylvania, Salem and the North, composing over 100 anthems and solo songs that display fine vocal and orchestral writing and depth of musical expression. His six string quintets (1789), in the early Classical style, are the earliest known chamber music composed in America.

Peter and the Wolf [Petya i volk]. Symphonic fairy-tale, op.67, by Prokofiev to his own libretto, for narrator and orchestra (1936).

Peter Grimes. Opera in a prologue and three acts by Britten to a libretto by Montagu Slater after Crabbe (1945, London).

Peters. German firm of music publishers. Its origins go back to the 'Bureau de Musique' opened in Leipzig in 1800 by F.A. Hoffmeister and A. Kühnel (which issued Forkel's monograph on Bach and Beethoven's opp.19–22 and 39–42); under Kühnel alone (1895–13) Spohr's first works were published. The business was purchased by Carl Friedrich Peters (1779–1827) in 1814, then successively taken over by C.G.S.

Böhme (1828), J. Friedländer (1860) and Max Abraham (1880), under whom it achieved a worldwide reputation for efficiency and quality, with Grieg, Wagner, Brahms, Bruch and Sinding in the catalogue. Abraham's nephew Henri Hinrichsen (1868–1942) directed the firm from 1900, acquiring works by Wolf, Mahler, Reger, Pfitzner, Schoenberg and Richard Strauss; his son Max founded the London branch in 1938 (as Hinrichsen Edition) and his son Walter the New York branch in 1948, while Johannes Petschull established a firm at Frankfurt in 1950. The original Leipzig firm, state-owned since 1949, now promotes the work of contemporary composers in eastern Europe (Eisler, Khachaturian, Shostakovich); the American one publishes Babbitt, Cage and many avant-garde composers.

Peterson, Oscar (Emmanuel) (*b* Montreal, 15 Aug 1925). Canadian jazz pianist. His international reputation was established in the 1950s when he worked mainly with a trio. His solo performances in the 1970s showed him to be one of the greatest of solo jazz pianists, with an extraordinary technique and comprehensive grasp of jazz piano history.

Peterson-Berger, Wilhelm (*b* Ullånger, 27 Feb 1867; *d* Östersund, 3 Dec 1942). Swedish composer. He studied at the Stockholm Conservatory (1886–9) and with Kretzschmar in Dresden (1889–90), then worked as an influential music critic in Stockholm (1896–1930) before retiring to northern Sweden. He became well known as the composer of the *Frösöblomster* (1896) for piano and the song collection *Svensk lyrik*. He also wrote music dramas in the Wagnerian spirit (e.g. *Arnljot*, 1910, often viewed as the Swedish national opera), five symphonies (1903–33) and choral music in a nationalist Romantic style.

Petite Bande, La. Early music ensemble. It was founded in 1971 by Sigiswald Kuijken and is normally directed by him from the violin. The original objective was to record operatic music by Lully but it has also recorded many other French works (notably by Rameau), Handel operas and orchestral music from Muffat to Mozart. It is notable for its precision and its light, vivacious style.

Petite messe solennelle. Choral work by Rossini, a setting of the Mass for soprano, mezzo-soprano, tenor and baritone soloists, chorus, two pianos and harmonium (1863), later arranged with orchestra (1867).

Petite Suite. Work by Debussy for piano duet (1889).

Petrarch (*b* Arezzo, 20 July 1304; *d* Arquà, 18 July 1374). Italian poet. Though he was fond of music, little of his verse belongs to the category of *poesia per musica* (ballate and madrigals) and only one contemporary polyphonic setting (by Jacopo da Bologna) survives, although others may have been performed in improvised settings. The important 16th-century Petrarch revival begins with the work of Benedetto Gareth and Pietro Bembo's edition of the *Canzoniere* (1501). His work inspired at least two generations of Italian poets, including Sannazaro and Tasso, all of whom provided texts for madrigalists. Willaert and other composers in Venice set his verse, but settings became less frequent later in the 16th century,

though they never disappeared, and the influence of the Petrarchan revival was felt throughout Europe. Schubert, Liszt and Schoenberg are among the later composers to draw inspiration from him.

Petrassi, Goffredo (*b* Zagarolo, 16 July 1904). Italian composer. A pupil of Bustini at the Conservatorio di S Cecilia, Rome (1928–33), he began teaching there in 1939. During the 1930s he was influenced by Hindemith, Stravinsky and the later Casella, but in the 1950s his music became atonal and in the 1960s athematic, while its bold colouring and rhythmic energy were intensified. His major works include a cycle of eight concertos for orchestra (1934–72), large-scale choral pieces (*Magnificat*, 1940; *Coro di morti*, 1941; *Noche oscura*, 1951), much chamber and instrumental music. After Dallapiccola he was the most important and influential Italian musician of his generation.

Petrella, Errico (*b* Palermo, 10 Dec 1813; *d* Genoa, 7 April 1877). Italian composer. He studied at the Naples Conservatory and wrote operas in the old *buffo* style, winning special recognition for the spirited *Le precauzioni* (Naples, 1851). Of his later, serious works, *Marco Visconti* (1854), *Jone* (1858) and *I promessi sposi* (1869) are the best.

Petri, Egon (*b* Hanover, 23 March 1881; *d* Berkeley, CA, 27 May 1962). German pianist of Dutch descent. He received early encouragment from Busoni and became his most important pupil and interpreter. In Berlin, London (from 1921) and New York (début 1932) he was admired for his profound and masculine style in Bach, Beethoven and Liszt. He moved to the USA in 1938 and taught at Cornell University (1940–46) and Mills College, Oakland.

Petri, Georg Gottfried (*b* Žary, 9 Dec 1715; *d* Görlitz, 6 July 1795). German composer. After working in law, he became music director in Guben and then Kantor in Görlitz (1764). He was a prolific composer, of songs, keyboard and violin pieces and sacred works including at least three cycles of church cantatas. A son of Balthasar Adam (1704–93), he had two musician nephews: Johann Samuel (1738–1808), writer of sacred music and a popular treatise *Anleitung zur practischen Musik* (1767, enlarged 1782), and Christopher (1758–?), Kantor and composer.

Petrić, Ivo (*b* Ljubljana, 16 June 1931). Yugoslav composer. He studied with Škerjanc at the Ljubljana Academy (1950–58) and developed a refined style influenced by Škerjanc and Osterc and, since the early 1960s, by avant-garde techniques. His works, mostly for orchestra or ensemble, include *Croquis sonores* (1963) for five instruments and percussion.

Petridis, Petros (John) (*b* Nigde, 23 July 1892; *d* Athens, 17 Aug 1977). Greek composer. He was educated in Istanbul and Paris and was a critic for over 50 years. He was a self-taught composer, influenced by Greek folk music and Byzantine modality; his works include five symphonies (1929–51), concertos, music for the stage and vocal pieces.

Petrini, Francesco (*b* Berlin, 1744; *d* Paris, 1819). French harpist and composer. He studied the harp under his father (*d* 1750), a harpist at Frederick the Great's court. After serving at the Mecklenburg-Schwerin court, 1765–9, he performed and taught in

Paris and published harp concertos, sonatas, duets etc, a harp method and books on harmony. His sister Therese (1736–after 1800) was a singer and harpist in Berlin.

Petrov, Andrey Pavlovich (*b* Leningrad, 2 Sept 1930). Soviet composer. A pupil of Evlakhov at the Leningrad Conservatory (1949–54), he is a versatile composer who has produced stage works, symphonic poems, light music and song cycles, generally based on literary or pictorial subjects. He is an eminent figure in Leningrad.

Petrov, Osip (Afanas'yevich) (*b* Kirovograd, 15 Nov 1806; *d* St Petersburg, 12 March 1878). Russian bass. He won outstanding acclaim during his 50 years on the stage for, among other roles, Glinka's Ivan Susanin and Ruslan, Dargomïzhsky's Miller (*Rusalka*) and Leporello (*The Stone Guest*) and Varlaam in *Boris Godunov*, all of which he created. His voice was of peculiarly Russian character. He married Anna Yakovlevna Vorob'yova (1816–1901), an internationally admired contralto for whom Glinka wrote Vanya (*A Life for the Tsar*).

Petrovics, Emil (*b* Zrenjanin, 9 Feb 1930). Hungarian composer. He was a pupil of Farkas at the Budapest Academy (1952–7), where he began teaching in 1969. His works include operas, cantatas and much incidental music drawing on a wide range of influences. The opera *C'est la guerre* (1961) established his reputation.

Petrucci, Ottaviano (dei) (*b* Fossombrone, 18 June 1466; *d* Venice, 7 May 1539). Italian music printer. He was the first to print polyphonic music from movable type. He went to Venice *c*1490 and in 1501 issued *Harmonice musices odhecaton A* ('100 songs in harmonic music'), an oblong quarto of 103 folios with 96 pieces, predominantly three- and four-voice French *chansons* by Agricola, Busnois, Compère, Isaac and Josquin; the series was completed by *Canti B* (1501/2) and *Canti C* (1503/4). Though his new printing process required three (later two) impressions – one for staves, another for notes, a third for texts – most of his surviving books show good alignment and graceful type. In 1507 he published the first lute tablature to be printed. At Fossombrone from 1511 until 1520 or 1521 he continued to print frottolas, masses and motets. Petrucci's editions constitute the most representative body of music issued by any printer of his time; his successful method initiated the dissemination of polyphonic music.

Petrus de Cruce (*fl c*1290). Composer and author. He may have lived in Amiens. He wrote a *Tractatus de tonis* and a treatise on mensural polyphony, now lost. His main achievement in the development of mensural music was to progress beyond Franco's subdivision of the breve into two or three semibreves into anything up to seven, and to establish that any two successive groups of semibreves should be separated by a dot. He aroused both opposition and support. In his motets the Petronian semibreves are restricted to the tripla or upper part; the motetus generally falls into a rhythmic mode and the tenor moves in unpatterned longs. The motets seem orientated towards the declamation of often highly irregular French verses. His ideas influenced Italian trecento notation.

Petrushka. Ballet (burlesque) in four scenes by Stravinsky to a story by Benois (1911, Paris).

Pettersson, (Gustaf) Allan (*b* Västra Ryd, 19 Sept 1911; *d* Stockholm, 20 June 1980). Swedish composer. A pupil of Olsson and Blomdahl at the Stockholm Conservatory (1930–39), he played the viola in the Stockholm PO (1939–51), then went to Paris for further study with Honegger and Leibowitz. Back in Sweden he concentrated on composition, in particular on large-scale, single-movement symphonies in an impassioned diatonic style (there were eventually 15, *c*1950–1978); he also wrote concertos, songs and chamber pieces.

Petyrek, Felix (*b* Brno, 14 May 1892; *d* Vienna, 1 Dec 1951). Austrian composer. A pupil of Schreker and Adler in Vienna, he taught in Berlin (1921–5), Stuttgart (1930–39), Leipzig (1939–49) and Vienna, and wrote stage works, songs, piano music (including duos and duets) etc, in a Romantic style suggesting comparison with Mahler.

Petzold, Rudolf (*b* Liverpool, 17 July 1908). German composer. He was a pupil of Jarnach at the Cologne Musikhochschule (1930–33), where he taught (1946–70). His works include chamber, sacred choral and orchestral scores, those up to *c*1949 being tonal, the later ones atonal; the 'imaginary ballet' *Incarnatus est homo* (1966) for orchestra and chorus is important.

Peuerl, Paul (*b* ?Stuttgart, bap. 13 June 1570; *d* after 1625). German composer, organist and organ builder. He was an organist at Horn, Lower Austria, but by 1609 had moved to a church at Steyr. His three instrumental collections (1611–25) contain early examples of the variation suite; he also composed a volume of songs (1613).

Peverara, Laura (*b* Mantua, *c*1545; *d* Ferrara, 4 Jan 1601). Italian singer. She was the leading member of the group of virtuoso 'singing ladies' at the Ferrarese court (1580–98). Three important anthologies were dedicated to her.

Pevernage, Andreas (*b* Harelbeke, 1543; *d* Antwerp, 30 July 1591). Flemish composer. He was choirmaster of St Salvator, Bruges (1563), and of Notre Dame, Courtrai (1563–79), before religious troubles drove him to Antwerp. He returned to Courtrai in 1584 and became choirmaster of Notre Dame, Antwerp. His works include over 100 *chansons* (5 bks, 1589–1607) and over 50 motets (1578 and collections).

Peyote drum. A WATER-DRUM used in meetings of the Native American Church of the Indians in North America. It consists of well-soaked buckskin stretched over an iron kettle *c*25 cm high; the kettle is half-filled with water and beaten, producing a loud, resonant sound. During a ceremony the Peyote rattle (a gourd filled with small stones, with a wooden handle) is also used.

Pez, Johann Christoph (*b* Munich, 9 Sept 1664; *d* Stuttgart, 25 Sept 1716). German composer. An instrumentalist and singer, he first served in Munich as chamber musician at the court, 1688–94 (but he spent part of that period in Rome). He then served at the Bonn court, as Kapellmeister from 1696; after returning to Munich (1701–6) he was court Kapellmeister at Stuttgart. Strong Italian influences appear in his output, which includes sacred music, dramatic works, cantatas and instrumental pieces.

Pezel, Johann Christoph (*b* Glatz, 1639; *d* Bautzen, 13 Oct 1694). German town bandsman and composer. Until 1681 he served as a string player in Leipzig, becoming Stadtpfeifer in 1670. He then moved to Bautzen, near Glatz in Silesia. He was a prolific composer, chiefly writing instrumental and sacred music. His principal works are his two collections of tower music, scored for two cornetts and three trombones. The first book (1670) contains 40 one-movement sonatas (most of them apparently grouped in pairs); the second (1685) contains 76 intradas and dance movements. The pieces alternate between imitative and homophonic sections and make imaginative use of the simple style traditional to tower music.

Pfeiffer, (Johann) Michael Traugott (*b* Wilfershauzen, 5 Nov 1771; *d* Wettingen, 20 May 1849). German teacher. He was the first to apply Pestalozzian principles to school music teaching, publishing the results (1809–21) in collaboration with H.G. Nägeli.

Pfitzner, Hans (Erich) (*b* Moscow, 5 May 1869; *d* Salzburg, 22 May 1949). German composer. A pupil of Knorr and Kwast at the Hoch Conservatory, Frankfurt, he was a teacher in Berlin, Strasbourg and Munich until 1934, when he was relieved of his post. His earlier works, including the operas *Der arme Heinrich* (1895) and *Die Rose vom Liebesgarten* (1901), are Wagnerian, but in *Palestrina* (1917) he produced a remarkable piece of operatic spiritual autobiography, contrasting the pressures of the everyday world with the inner certainties of artistic genius. One of his certainties was of the supremacy of the German Romantic tradition – he was a patriot but not a nationalist – which he supported in polemical exchanges with Berg and implicitly in the cantatas (*Von deutscher Seele*, 1921; *Das dunkle Reich*, 1929) which were his main works after *Palestrina*. He also wrote three symphonies, (1932, 1939, 1940), concertos for the piano (1922), the violin (1923) and two for the cello (1935, 1944), chamber music (including three string quartets) and *c*100 songs.

Pfleger, Augustin (*b* Schlackenwerth, *c*1635; *d* ?there, after 23 July 1686). German composer. He was Kapellmeister at the court at Schlackenwerth, Bohemia, until 1662. By 1686 he returned to this post, having served as court vice-Kapellmeister at Güstrow (1662–5) and as court Kapellmeister at Gottorf (1665–73). He composed over 200 sacred works (both German and Latin) and several secular odes. His German works, such as the cycle of 72 dramatic dialogues, whose texts combine poetry and biblical passages, show him as a forerunner of the composers who developed the German sacred cantata.

Phaëton. *Tragédie lyrique* in a prologue and five acts by Lully to a libretto by P. Quinault (1683, Versailles).

Phagotus. A type of bagpipe invented in the early 16th century by Afranio degli Albonesi of Pavia. Its name is from 'fagotto', ('a bundle of sticks') but it has little in common with the bassoon. A more sophisticated version of the Yugoslavian bagpipe, it consists of twin ornamental pillars joined by crosspieces; the upper part was bored with parallel cylindrical tubes joined at the top, forming a continuous tube with holes for fingers and keys, and the lower parts contained single beating reeds. One pillar could produce ten diatonic notes from *c*, the other ten from *G*. Cross-fingering could produce chromatic notes and either pillar could be silenced or sounded at will. Air was provided by a small underarm bellows, as in the Irish bagpipes. The instrument would not stay in tune.

Phalèse. Family of music publishers. They were active in Louvain and Antwerp, 1545–1647. Pierre (i) of Louvain (*c*1510–1573/6) issued *chanson* and motet books by composers of the Low Countries, especially Clemens non Papa, books of lute tablature and books using large choirbook type. His son Pierre (ii) (*c*1550–1629), who took over *c*1576 and moved to Antwerp in 1581, added volumes of Italian madrigals. The firm continued under his daughters Madeleine (1586–1652) and Marie (1589–*c*1674).

Phantasiestücke. Schumann's op.12 (1837), eight piano pieces with descriptive titles.

Phantasy. The name for English single-movement chamber works written for competitions established in 1905 by W.W. Cobbett; prizewinners include Bridge, Vaughan Williams, Howells and Britten.

Phasing. A technique used by minimalist composers, particularly Reich, in which the same rhythm is heard from two performers, with one of them accelerating so that they move in and out of phase.

Philadelphia Orchestra. American orchestra founded in 1900; it was first conducted by Fritz Scheel. Under Leopold Stokowski (1912–41) it became one of the world's leading orchestras and was widely known through broadcasts and recordings; tours and outdoor summer seasons began in the 1930s. Subsequent conductors include Ormandy (1938–80) and Muti. Its homes are the Academy of Music (opened 1857, cap. 2900) and the summer festivals at Mann Music Center and Saratoga (NY).

Philharmonia Orchestra. London orchestra founded in 1945 by Walter Legge; it was known as the New Philharmonia in 1964–77. It soon gained an international reputation, especially for the quality of its recordings. From 1952 it made many tours. Principal conductors have included Klemperer (from 1959, president until 1973) and Giuseppe Sinopoli (from 1983). The Philharmonia Chorus, an amateur choir, was founded in 1957 by Legge to work with the Philharmonia Orchestra; it was known as the New Philharmonia Chorus, 1964–77, but became independent of the orchestra in 1964. It makes broadcasts and recordings and gives concerts outside Britain.

Philharmonic. A name used by many musical organizations, meaning 'music-loving' (from Gk. *phil-*: 'loving'; *harmonic*: 'concerning music').

Philidor, François-André Danican (*b* Dreux, 7 Sept 1726; *d* London, 31 Aug 1795). French composer. After training with Campra at Versailles, he worked in Paris as a copyist, teacher and (most famously) chess player; he also spent much time in England.

Gaining fame as a composer, he presented over 20 *opéras comiques* in Paris, notably *Tom Jones* (1765), and several serious operas, such as *Ernelinde* (1767). His major choral work, the oratorio *Carmen saeculare*, was given in London in 1779.

Philidor was among the most gifted of the early *opéra comique* composers and contributed to its increasing sophistication. His works have an italianate style, with expressive melody, skilful ensembles and sensitive scoring; *Tom Jones* also contains accompanied recitative. His serious operas, though less well received, anticipated the styles of French operas by Gluck and Piccinni; *Ernelinde* was the first French serious opera with italianate arias throughout instead of the traditional *airs*. He also composed church music and other vocal works.

Philidor was one of a large family of musicians. His father, André Danican (*c*1647–1730), was an instrumentalist at the French court and (from 1684) the king's music librarian, organizing a large collection of works (now partly in the Paris Conservatoire); he composed stage, sacred and instrumental works. His sons Jacques Danican (1657–1708) and Anne Danican (1681–1728) were also court instrumentalists. Anne Danican, composer of sacred and instrumental works, founded the Paris Concert Spirituel in 1725. Jacques's son Pierre Danican (1681–1731) was a composer and wind player at the French court.

Philippe the Chancellor (*b* Paris, *c*1160–80; *d* there, 1236). French poet. His duties as Chancellor of Paris (1218–36) included responsibility for the University. His Latin poems and at least one French song survive with music, though it is not clear whether he was the composer. The high proportion of contrafacta reveals an extensive knowledge of the repertory. His primary importance lies in his substantial contribution to the repertory of Notre Dame conductus and his role in the early motet.

Philippot, Michel (Paul) (*b* Verzy, 2 Feb 1925). French composer. He was a pupil of Dandelot at the Paris Conservatoire (1946–8) and of Leibowitz (1948–50). In 1949 he began working for French radio, and much of his music has been electronic, though he has composed instrumental scores, influenced by Xenakis. He has written on aesthetics, acoustics, the evolution of music and *Stravinsky* (1965); his use of principles drawn from scientific knowledge is exemplified in *Commentariolus Copernicae* for nine instruments (1973).

Philippus de Caserta (*fl* Avignon, *c*1370). French theorist and composer. The treatise *Tractatus de diversis figuris*, sometimes attributed to Egidius de Murino, may be by Philippus: in it notational systems (using tails, flags, dots, red and hollow notes) are put forward to allow new rhythmic combinations. Philippus used some of these in his works, which comprise six ballades, one Credo and one (doubtful) rondeau. Ciconia drew on three of his ballades in a virelai.

Philips, Peter (*b*?London, 1560–61; *d* Brussels, 1628). English composer. He was a choirboy at St Paul's Cathedral, London, in 1574 and in 1582 fled to the Continent because of his Catholic faith. He was organist of the English College, Rome, until 1585, when he travelled in Europe, settling in Antwerp in 1590. In 1593 he was imprisoned for treason but was released. He moved to Brussels in 1597, serving as an organist in the vice-regal chapel of the Spanish Netherlands until he died. Famous in northern Europe as a fine organist and versatile composer, Philips was second only to Byrd as the most published English composer of his day. His music for keyboard and instrumental ensemble is mainly in the traditional English style, while his Italian madrigals (3 bks, 1596–1603) and his wide-ranging motets (5 bks, 1612–28), including some for double choir, show continental (notably Roman) influence.

Phillips, Burrill (*b* Omaha, NE, 9 Nov 1907). American composer. He was a pupil of Rogers and Hanson at the Eastman School, where he remained to teach (1933–49), later moving to other American institutions. His first important orchestral work, *Selections from McGuffey's Reader* (1933), established his reputation as a composer with a consciously American style. His works also include choral and chamber music.

Philomel. Work by Babbitt for soprano and tape (1964), a setting of a text by Hollander.

Philosoph, Der [The Philosopher]. Haydn's Symphony no.22 in E♭ (1764), a reference to the opening Adagio.

Phinot [Finot, Finotto], **Dominique** [Dominico] (*b c*1510; *d c*1555). Franco-Flemish composer. He spent most of his career in Italy, where he was associated with the court of Urbino (*c*1545–*c*1555) and with Pesaro. The four volumes of his motets and *chansons* published in Lyons (1547–8) suggest that he had moved there. He was a prolific composer, whose output also includes masses, Magnificats, psalms and *chansons*, and was held in high esteem by his contemporaries. His most important contribution lies in his development of the eight-voice double-choir technique.

Phoebus and Pan [Der Streit zwischen Phoebus und Pan]. Cantata by J.S. Bach, BWV201 (1731) to a text by Picander after Ovid.

Phorminx. An early Greek string instrument, frequently mentioned by Homer; it was probably a 'cradle KITHARA', with three to five strings.

Phrase. A term used for short musical units of various lengths, generally regarded as longer than a motif but shorter than a period. It carries a melodic connotation: 'phrasing' is applied to the subdivision of a melodic line.

Phrygian. The third of the eight church modes, the authentic MODE on E. The expression 'Phrygian mode' is often used as a covering term for Renaissance and Baroque polyphonic compositions whose final sonority is an E major triad established by a Phrygian cadence and within the Phrygian or Hypophrygian range.

A Phrygian CADENCE is one in which the lowest part descends to the final or tonic by a semitone step (from a so-called 'upper leading note') while the highest part normally rises to the final or tonic by a whole-tone step; the minor-key imperfect cadence, common in the Baroque period at the ends of slow movements, is of this kind.

Piacere, a. *See* A PIACERE.

Piacevole (It.). Agreeable, pleasant.

Piani, Giovanni Antonio (*b* Naples, 1678; *d*?Vienna, after 1757). Italian violinist and composer. He worked first in Paris, then from 1721 at the imperial court in Vienna, latterly as director of instrumental music. His main works are 12 sonatas (1712), which include detailed expression markings.

Pianissimo (It.). Very quiet, the superlative of *piano*; abbreviated *pp*. *See* DYNAMICS.

Piano (It.). 'Flat', 'low', i.e. quiet, abbreviated *p*; hence *pianissimo* (*pp*, very quiet). Also the normal abbreviation for PIANOFORTE.

Piano accordion. An ACCORDION with a piano keyboard.

Piano duet. A piece for two players at one piano; less commonly, a piece for two pianos. Some English duets date from the early 17th century, but the first masterpieces are the sonatas of Mozart. Schubert and Brahms enriched the repertory in the 19th century and notable works have since been written by Debussy, Hindemith, Milhaud and others. Arrangements for piano duet of orchestral works are numerous, since they provided the principal means for amateur musicians to acquaint themselves with the concert repertory before the arrival of the gramophone record. All the above-mentioned composers made significant contributions to the two-piano repertory, as did Saint-Saëns, Rakhmaninov, Bartók and Messiaen.

Pianoforte. A keyboard instrument distinguished by the fact that its strings are struck by rebounding hammers rather than plucked (as in the harpsichord) or struck by tangents (as in the clavichord). It has been central in professional and domestic musical life from the third quarter of the 18th century not only because it can sound ten or more notes at once, and thus give an approximate rendering of any piece of Western music, but also because it can be played both soft and loud (whence its name) according to touch, which produces its vast expressive range.

The modern grand piano consists of six main elements: the strings – three for each note down to *B* or *B*♭, then two for each, except for the extreme bass with just one; the massive metal frame which supports the strings' considerable tension (*c*16,400 kg); the wooden soundboard beneath the strings, without which the tone would be faint and thin; the wooden case enclosing all the foregoing; the action, comprising the keys (normally 88), the hammers and the mechanism that operates them; and the pedals. The one on the right (the sustaining pedal) removes the dampers from the strings, giving added duration and resonance to the sound, even though the hands have been removed from the keys; the one on the left (the 'una corda' or 'soft' pedal) reduces the volume either by shifting all the hammers sideways so that they strike one less string, or, in upright pianos, by moving the hammers nearer to the strings so that their impact is diminished, or even by the simple interposition of a piece of felt. Some pianos have a middle pedal, usually a 'sostenuto' pedal which allows the player to sustain a selected group

of notes while still dampening the remaining strings; more rarely the third pedal is a muffling device used for practicing purposes.

The first pianofortes were made by Bartolomeo Cristofori, who began work on them in 1698. He was keeper of instruments at the Medici court in Florence and his invention, which he called 'harpsichord with loud and soft', has a remarkable number of features in common with later, highly developed versions of the instrument, notably the sophisticated 'escapement mechanism' which stopped the hammer rebounding against the string it had just struck. Cristofori's idea was taken up in Germany by Silbermann whose improvements met with J.S. Bach's approbation in 1747. The main thrust of German and Austrian piano building, however, concentrated on developing the piano along the lines of the clavichord. This led to the invention of the 'Prellmechanik' (a simple action in which the hammer is facing the player and attached to the key) or 'Viennese action' which, as developed particularly by the Stein family, formed the characteristic Viennese pianoforte whose lightness of touch and subtlety of nuance ensured its popularity well into the 19th century. The English school began with Johann Zumpe, an associate of Silbermann who started making square pianos (shaped like a clavichord) in London in 1760; they were enthusiastically endorsed by J.C. Bach, and improved by John Broadwood, Robert Stodart and Americus Backers, all important in the development of the English piano. The English action was first developed by Backers in the early 1770s; Stodart patented it in 1777 and the Broadwood firm adopted and improved it. Further improvements in the action were made in France by Sébastien Erard who, while mainly following English models, made modifications to the action to improve note repetition.

At the end of the 18th century, the idea of using metal bracing to bear the tension of the strings was developed in England and in the USA. Many firms were involved, including John Isaac Hawkins, an English maker working in the USA, who invented the upright piano and devised a new system of metal bracing; Broadwood and Erard also used metal, but the first maker to use a single-cast metal frame including hitchpin plate was Alpheus Babcock, who worked in Boston and Philadelphia and patented his invention in 1825. The use of iron frames, which allowed for greater tension and thus thicker strings and a fuller, more ringing tone, was the last fundamental development in the piano's history. String tension was later distributed across the frame by the practice of 'overstringing', whereby one set of strings is laid diagonally over another.

In the 19th century, the greater volume and flexibility of the English action led to its prevailing over the Viennese type, although the Viennese instrument (by such makers as Walter, Schantz, Streicher, the Steins and Graf, and ultimately Bösendorfer) was preferred by many composers and players for its greater sensitivity (a notable exception was Chopin, who preferred the English and French types). The upright (developed by Robert Wornum in London

Action of a modern grand piano. When the key is pressed the movement is transmitted via the pilot to the intermediate lever; the jack then acts on the roller of the hammer which rises towards the string. The backward projection of the jack contacts the set-off button and the jack moves back permitting the hammer to escape and to continue in free flight to strike the string and begin its descent; it is then caught and retained by the check and repetition lever as long as the key remains depressed. If the key is partly released the hammer is freed, and the roller is acted on directly by the repetition lever; it is thus possible to strike the string again by depressing the key a second time (the jack will re-engage with the roller only when the key has been fully released so that a full hammer stroke may be made).

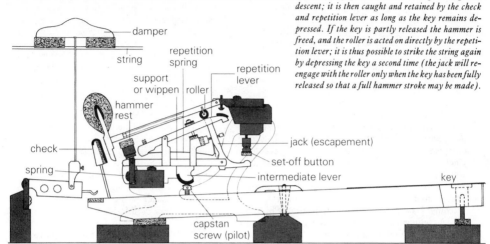

and others) came during the 19th century to replace the square – although that was extensively developed in the USA – as the standard domestic instrument. The Steinway firm in New York developed both the square and the upright, but also became the leading manufacturers of the large grand piano; they, with the German firms Bechstein and Blüthner – all three were founded in 1853 – and to a lesser extent Bösendorfer of Vienna, came to be regarded as the leading makers.

20th-century developments include the 'baby grand', appropriate to domestic use, and many smaller types of upright. The piano as a symbol of domestic social prestige was at its height in the years before World War I; in 1910 about 600,000 pianos were built worldwide (more than half in the USA). This figure dipped in the inter-war years, but by 1980 the figure was over 800,000, of which well over a third were made in Japan (mostly by Yamaha). Miscellaneous developments to the piano during the present century include attempts at a sustaining instrument (*see* SOSTENENTE PIANO), developments of various other electric attachments and ultimately of an ELECTRIC PIANO. There have also been experiments in microtonal pianos. The automatic PLAYER PIANO was popular in the early part of the 20th century. (For further illustration, *see* KEYBOARD INSTRUMENTS.)

Pianola. An early make of automatic PLAYER PIANO. The trademark 'Pianola', property of the Aeolian Corporation, has become widely known and is frequently misapplied to other makes.

Piano quartet. A piece for piano and three instruments, usually violin, viola and cello. The piano quartets of Mozart (K478 and 493), Beethoven (op.16), Schumann, Dvořák, Brahams and Fauré are among the finest in the rather slender and uneven Classical–Romantic repertory. Among outstanding 20th-century works for piano and mixed ensemble are those of Webern, Hindemith and Messiaen.

Piano quintet. A piece for piano and four other

instruments. The outstanding Classical works are those for piano and wind instruments by Mozart (K452) and Beethoven (op.16), but the combination of piano and string quartet is more usual. Among the finest works for this medium are the quintets of Schumann, Brahms, Dvořák, Franck, Fauré, Elgar, Bloch and Shostakovich. Perhaps the most familiar piano quintet is Schubert's 'Trout' Quintet D667, for piano, violin, viola, cello and double bass.

Piano score [piano-vocal score]. A score of a work including orchestra or other instruments in which the instrumental part is arranged on two staves to facilitate playing on the piano.

Piano trio. A piece for piano and two other instruments, usually violin and cello. The genre originated in the mid-18th century from the accompanied sonata in which the string parts were often merely optional. In Haydn's piano trios the cello is rarely independent of the piano's bass line, but in those of Mozart, Beethoven and Schubert its emancipation is gradually made complete; Beethoven and Schubert adopted a four-movement scheme, lending their works a scale and importance previously associated with the quartet and the symphony. Later composers wrote for all three instruments in an increasingly brilliant style. Mendelssohn, Schumann, Brahms, Dvořák, Franck, Tchaikovsky and Arensky, and in the 20th century Fauré, Ravel and Shostakovich, made important contributions to the genre. Among other trio combinations with piano are those with clarinet and viola (Mozart's K498), clarinet and cello (Beethoven and Brahms) and violin and horn (Brahms and Berkeley).

Piantanida, Giovanni (*b* Florence, 1705; *d* Bologna, 1782). Italian violinist and composer. He toured widely as a virtuoso, notably to St Petersburg (1735–7), and performed with Handel in London (1739–42) and at the Paris Concert Spirituel. Later he settled in Bologna. His playing was compared to Tartini's. He composed violin sonatas, concertos etc. His son Gaetano (1768–1835) was a pianist and composer.

Piatigorsky, Gregor (*b* Ekaterinoslav, 17 April 1903; *d* Los Angeles, 6 Aug 1976). American cellist. He studied at the Moscow Conservatory and left Russia in 1921. From 1924 he was principal of the Berlin PO, under Furtwängler, and pursued a solo career from 1928. After his New York début (1929) he came to be regarded as the leading cellist of his generation, combining an innate flair for virtuosity with exquisite taste in style and phrasing; he was at his best in Romantic music. At Los Angeles in 1961 he established a chamber music series with Heifetz.

Piatti, Alfredo (Carlo) (*b* Bergamo, 8 Jan 1822; *d* Crocetto di Mozzo, 18 July 1901). Italian cellist and composer. He studied at the Milan Conservatory. Encouraged by Liszt and Mendelssohn, he pursued a solo career that won him praise throughout Europe. In London he played with the Italian Opera, in Joachim's quartet and at the Popular Concerts, also teaching; Hausmann and Stern were among his pupils. A connoisseur of instruments, he was noted for his superb technique and unsentimental interpretations and he played in the old style without an end-pin. Among his compositions are six cello sonatas, two concertos and the valuable *12 caprices* for solo cello; he also made editions of 18th-century works.

Piave, Francesco Mario (*b* Murano, 18 May 1810; *d* Milan, 5 March 1876). Italian librettist. Verdi's life-long friend and collaborator, he wrote the texts for *Ernani* (1844), *Macbeth* (1847), *Rigoletto* (1851), *La traviata* (1853) and *La forza del destino* (1862), among other operas.

Pibgorn [pibcorn]. Folk instrument of the single HORNPIPE type from Wales. A mouth horn was fixed to the top of the pipe and it was played with a single reed.

Pibroch. Term used since the early 19th century for the more serious repertory of Scottish highland bagpipe music (as opposed to dances, military music etc). It apparently evolved as courtly ceremonial music. Pibrochs are in theme and variation form.

Picard. *See* PYCARD.

Picardy third. TIERCE DE PICARDIE.

Piccaver, Alfred (*b* Long Sutton, 25 Feb 1884; *d* Vienna, 23 Sept 1958). English tenor. After study in New York he made his début in Prague (1907) as Gounod's Romeo. In Vienna he was a favourite from 1910 to 1937, singing roles by Verdi, Wagner, Beethoven and Puccini in a robust style sometimes compared with Caruso's. He taught in Vienna from 1955.

Piccinini, Alessandro (*b* Bologna, 30 Dec 1566; *d* ?there, *c*1638). Italian composer and lutenist. With his father and brothers, also lutenists, he served the Ferrarese court (1582–97), then Cardinal Aldobrandini in Bologna (to 1621). His two publications (1623, 1639) contain toccatas and dances for lute and chitarrone and advice on how to play them. He developed a new bass lute and modified the chitarrone.

Piccinni, (Vito) Niccolò (Marcello Antonio Giacomo) (*b* Bari, 16 Jan 1728; *d* Passy, 7 May 1800). Italian composer. He studied with Leo and Durante in Naples and had operas staged there from the 1750s. His reputation grew fast; *La Cecchina*, better known under its alternative title *La buona figliuola* (1760, Rome), was an international success. Besides composing prolifically, he taught singing and was second *maestro di cappella* at Naples Cathedral and from 1771 second organist of the Naples royal chapel. In 1776, after a decline in his popularity, he went to Paris and composed French operas (serious and comic). His *tragédies lyriques Roland* (1778), *Iphigénie en Tauride* (1781) and *Didon* (1783) were notable successes, despite challenges from Gluckists and others. After his return to Italy (1791) his output declined; finally he went back to France.

Piccinni was a central figure in both Italian and French opera. His Italian operas number over 100 and are notable for their varied expression (their elegance of style was especially admired) and progressive textures and orchestration; in comic opera he was a pioneer of the multi-sectional finale. His serious operas, both Italian and French, also reflect his flexible approach to form. The French works established a synthesis of the modern italianate style and the traditional French forms, which was less radical but more influential than Gluck's. He also composed oratorios and other sacred works, cantatas and instrumental pieces.

Piccinni's son Luigi (1764–1827) composed mostly French and Italian comic operas. His grandson Louis Alexandre (1779–1850) was a conductor and accompanist in Paris, and composed melodramas and ballets.

Operas La Cecchina, also as La buona figliuola (1760); Roland (1778); Iphigénie en Tauride (1781); Didon (1783); over 90 others
Sacred music 3 oratorios; 2 masses; other pieces
Secular and instrumental music cantatas, songs; ov.; hpd music

Piccioni, Giovanni (*b* Rimini, *c*1550; *d* Orvieto, after 17 June 1619). Italian composer. From 1577 he was *maestro di musica* of an academy in Conegliano, Veneto, and from 1590 organist of Orvieto Cathedral. He published polyphonic madrigals (9 bks, 1577–after 1602) and sacred works (at least 5 bks, 1589–1619), some with a continuo part and advice on how to play it.

Piccolo (It.: 'small'). A small flute sounding an octave higher than the concert instrument; its range is $c''–c''''$, written an octave below sounding pitch (for illustration, *see* WOODWIND INSTRUMENTS). The word is applied to other miniature instruments, such as the violino piccolo.

Piccolo trumpet. A TRUMPET in B♭, pitched an octave above the normal valved trumpet.

Pichl, Václav (*b* Bechyně, 25 Sept 1741; *d* Vienna, 23 Jan 1805). Czech composer. He held several posts, notably at the Vienna court theatre (*c*1770–1777), and was finally music director for the Austrian governor at Milan, returning to Vienna in 1796. His music, much admired in his day, stands between the early and high Classical styles, his many symphonies resembling those of Haydn's middle period. A founder of the Viennese violin school, he composed violin concertos and much solo violin music, besides chamber works, several operas (and opera librettos) and over 100 sacred works.

Pick-Mangiagalli, Riccardo (*b* Strakonice, 10 July 1882; *d* Milan, 8 July 1949). Italian composer of Czech birth. He studied at the Milan Conservatory (1896–1903) and wrote ballets, orchestral pieces etc, in a style drawing on Strauss and Ravel; the most successful was *Il carillon magico* (1918). He was also a pianist and teacher and directed the Milan Conservatory (1936–49).

Pictures at an Exhibition [Kartinki s vïstavki]. Piano suite by Musorgsky (1874), a description of ten pictures by Victor Hartmann, linked by a 'promenade'; it has been orchestrated by several composers, including Ravel, Henry Wood and Stokowski.

Piece. Term for a composition or a self-contained section of one, usually but not necessarily instrumental. The word was first for the numerous *pièces de clavecin* and *pièces de viole* published in France in the 17th and 18th centuries. The Italian (*pezzo*) and German forms (*Stück*) are much used, the German often in compound forms.

Pieltain, Dieudonné-Pascal (*b* Liège, bap. 4 March 1754; *d* there, 10 Dec 1833). South Netherlands violinist and composer. He played at the Paris Concert Spirituel before working in London (1782–*c*1792), and composed violin concertos and many string quartets. His brother Pierre-Joseph (*b* 1751) was a well-known horn player.

Pieno (It.). 'Full', as in *organo pieno* (full organ), *coro pieno* (full choir) and *a voce piena* (with full voice).

Pierné, (Henri Constant) Gabriel (*b* Metz, 16 Aug 1863; *d* Ploujean, 17 July 1937). French composer. He studied with Franck and Massenet at the Paris Conservatoire and succeeded the former as organist of Ste Clotilde (1890–98), thereafter concentrating on composition and conducting (principal conductor of the Concerts Colonne, 1910–34), enjoying a high reputation. His works range from operettas of sensuous charm (e.g. *Sophie Arnould*, 1927) to sacred oratorios, all marked by his clear technique and pleasing synthesis of Franckian and Debussian traits.

Piero (*fl* northern Italy, 1340–50). Italian composer of the earliest generation of trecento musicians. Possibly from Assisi, his works were known among the nobility of Milan and Verona, and he may have served there alongside Jacopo da Bologna and Giovanni de Cascia. His two- and three-voice madrigals and caccias are striking in their use of canonic techniques.

Pierre, Constant(-Victor-Désiré) (*b* Passy, 24 Aug 1855; *d* Paris, 12 Feb 1918). French musicologist. His searching and accurate studies of the music of the French Revolution and the history of the Paris Conservatoire are still invaluable.

Pierrot lunaire. Song cycle, op.21, by Schoenberg, settings for female voice (in *Sprechgesang*), flute, piccolo, clarinet, bass clarinet, violin, viola, cello and piano of poems by Albert Giraud translated into German by Otto Erich Hartleben (1912); it is in three parts, each containing seven songs.

Pierson [Pearson], **Henry Hugo** [Hugh] (*b* Oxford, 12 April 1815; *d* Leipzig, 28 Jan 1873). German composer of English origin. He studied with Attwood and Corfe in London, with Rinck and Reissiger in Ger-

many (1839–44) and under Tomašek at Prague. He first worked mainly in Dresden but made trips to Britain (Edinburgh, where he was briefly Reid Professor, 1844–5; Norwich, 1852), settling in Stuttgart in 1863. He established his reputation in Germany with the opera *Leila* (1848), the incidental music to Goethe's *Faust* (1854) and the symphonic poem *Macbeth* (1859); these use colourful instrumentation and short motifs in an episodic framework. But his most remarkable works are the songs (*c*100), often with English texts, in which his complex melodies and gift for surprise result in a freely original style avoiding sentimentality; striking examples include *All my Heart's Thine Own* and *Heimweh, Ruhe*. He also mastered the German male-voice chorus idiom.

Pietkin, Lambert (*b* Liège, bap. 22 June 1613); *d* there, 16 Sept 1696). Walloon composer. He was an organist at Liège Cathedral and was made *maître de chapelle* in 1644. Motets and several sonatas by him survive.

Piéton, Loyset [Aloysis] (*fl c*1530–45). Composer. His works were widely disseminated in MS and printed sources, 1532–74, suggesting that he was in Italy and Lyons. His works were also known in Germany and the Netherlands. His output includes a mass, a Magnificat and many motets, demonstrating his affinity with the Flemish school.

Pietoso (It.). Pitiful, piteous.

Pietrobono [Pietrobono del Chitarino; Petrus Bonus Ferrariensis] (*b* ?Ferrara, *c*1417; *d* there, 20 Sept 1497). Italian lutenist and singer. He spent most of his career at the Estense court, Ferrara, and in the 1480s spent time at the Hungarian court. He was considered one of the most remarkable lutenists of the period.

Piffaro [piffero]. An Italian shawm. The term goes back at least to the 15th century and is still used in the Abruzzi region of Italy during the Christmas festivities. (It should not be confused with *fiffaro*, a flute or fife.)

Piguet, Michel (*b* Geneva, 30 April 1932). Swiss oboist. He studied in Geneva and Paris, becoming solo oboe of the Zurich Tonhalle Orchestra in 1961. He left in 1964, devoting himself to the Baroque oboe and teaching at the Schola Cantorum Basiliensis; he also plays the Baroque recorder. His refinement of tone and polished technique make him an outstanding exponent of period instruments.

Pijper, Willem (*b* Zeist, 8 Sept 1894; *d* Leidschendam, 18 March 1947). Dutch composer. He studied with Wagenaar in Utrecht (1911–16) and taught at the conservatories of Amsterdam (1918–30) and Rotterdam (1930–47); he had a great influence on succeeding Dutch composers, especially in his way of building movements from 'germ cells' (melodic motifs or chords). His works include the opera *Halewijn* (1933), three symphonies (1917, 1921, 1926), concertos for piano, cello and violin, four string quartets (1914–28) and piano music. He was the leading Dutch composer in the first half of the 20th century.

Pilarczyk, Helga (Käthe) (*b* Schöningen, 12 March 1925). German soprano. She studied singing in Hamburg from 1948, made her début at Brunswick in 1951 and joined the Hamburg Opera in 1953, specializing in 20th-century opera: she has sung such roles as Berg's Marie and Lulu, the Woman (Schoenberg's *Erwartung*) and Jocasta (Stravinsky's *Oedipus rex*). She sang Salome at Covent Garden in 1959 and Marie at the Met in 1965. She is a singer of much intelligence and dramatic power.

Pilgrim's Progress, The. Opera (morality) in four acts by Vaughan Williams to his own libretto after Bunyan (1951, London).

Pilkington, Francis (*b c*1565; *d* Chester, 1638). English composer. He took the Oxford BMus in 1595. By 1602 he was a lay clerk at Chester Cathedral, where he served all his life, becoming precentor in 1623. He composed lute-songs (1605), two books of madrigals (1613–14, 1624) and a few lute pieces.

Pincé (Fr.). Plucked, as in plucked instruments, hence PIZZICATO; also an ornament of the MORDENT type.

Pineapple Poll. Ballet in one act and three scenes to music by Sullivan (arranged by Mackerras) to a scenario by John Cranko after Gilbert (1951, London).

Pinello di Ghirardi, Giovanni Battista (*b* Genoa, *c*1544; *d* Prague, 15 June 1587). Italian composer. He held posts at Landshut, Vicenza, Innsbruck and Dresden (court Kapellmeister, 1580–84), then sang in the Prague Hofkapelle. He was much involved in the quarrels between German and Italian musicians at the Dresden court. His secular works (4 bks, 1571–84) helped spread the Italian vocal style in Germany; some sacred works also survive (3 bks, 1583–8).

Pingoud, Ernest (*b* St Petersburg, 14 Oct 1888; *d* Helsinki, 1 June 1942). Finnish composer of Russian origin. A pupil of Siloti in St Petersburg and Reger in Leipzig, he worked in Helsinki from 1924 and wrote mostly orchestral music, influenced by impressionism and Skryabin; his works have held a place in the Finnish repertory.

Pini-Corsi, Antonio (*b* Zadar, June 1858; *d* Milan, 22 April 1918). Italian baritone. He excelled in character roles including Ford in Verdi's *Falstaff* and Schaunard in Puccini's *La bohème*, both of which he created, singing throughout Italy and at the Metropolitan Opera, New York.

Pini di Roma. Symphonic poem by Respighi (1924).

Pinkham, Daniel (Rogers) (*b* Lynn, MA, 5 June 1923). American composer. He studied at Harvard and with Boulanger and in 1959 joined the staff at the New England Conservatory. He is a prolific composer whose early music is neo-classical, but in the 1950s he began to use serial techniques.

Pinto, George Frederick (*b* Lambeth, 25 Sept 1785; *d* Chelsea, 23 March 1806). English composer. He studied the violin with J.P. Salomon, who soon presented him as a prodigy, and also learnt the piano. He played in London and provincial concerts from 1796 to 1804, when he became ill; his early death from an unknown cause provoked regret especially for the promise held by his compositions, some showing astonishing anticipations of Beethoven and Schubert. He produced several remarkable piano works (notably the two sonatas op.3, a Fantasia and Sonata in C minor and three variation sets), violin duets and sonatas and charming songs. He was an early advocate of Bach's music in England.

Pinza, Ezio (Fortunato) (*b* Rome, 18 May 1892; *d* Stamford, CT, 9 May 1957). Italian bass. He made his début in 1914 and sang at La Scala from 1922. At the Met (1926–48) he was a favourite for his cultivated voice, handsome presence and engaging personality, singing all the major Italian bass roles and becoming the pre-eminent Italian bass of his day. There and at Covent Garden and Salzburg he shone especially in Mozart. Latterly he had a second career in musical comedy, operetta and musical films.

Piozzi, Gabriele Mario (*b* Quinzano, Venice, 8 June 1740; *d* Tremerchion, Wales, 26 March 1809). Italian tenor, composer and keyboard player. After travels on the Continent he worked in England from *c*1776 as a singer, teacher and pianist. He composed accompanied keyboard sonatas and quartets and several vocal works. He was a member of the Burney–Johnson circle and married the wealthy literary lady Mrs Thrale.

Pipa [pip'a]. A pear-shaped, fretted lute played in China and Korea, corresponding with the Japanese *biwa*; it has four strings (sometimes five in Korea).

Pipe and tabor. A pair of instruments played together by one person chiefly to provide music for dancing. The pipe is an end-blown flute, usually with three holes, and is held in the left hand while the tabor, a small drum with snares, is worn over the player's shoulder and struck with a stick held in the right hand. Although popular throughout Europe since the 13th century, the pipe and tabor were used particularly in England in the 16th and 17th centuries, especially to accompany Morris and other dancing. The combination survives in the folk music of southern France, Spain and parts of Latin America.

Pipelare, Matthaeus (*b c*1450; *d c*1515). Flemish composer. He worked in Antwerp and was Master of the Choristers for the Marian Brotherhood at 's-Hertogenbosch (1498–1500). In Ornithoparchus's words he was a composer whose works 'flow from the very fountaine of Art'. His style is diverse, ranging from dense polyphony to homophonic writing; he was a master of large complex structures, *cantus firmus* technique and expressive vocal writing. 11 masses, motets and French and Flemish four-voice *chansons* by him survive.

Piquer [picquer] (Fr.). Term used in French Baroque music, sometimes to mean that an even series of notes so indicated should be played as if in dotted rhythm (*see* NOTES INÉGALES) or that they should be played staccato.

Pirata, Il. Opera in two acts by Bellini to a libretto by Romani (1827, Milan).

Pirates of Penzance, The. Operetta by Sullivan to a libretto by Gilbert (1879, Paignton).

Pirouette. The turned wooden component, cylindrical or funnel-shaped, within which the reed is mounted in the shawm and certain other instruments; it protected the reed and supported the player's lip muscles.

Pirro, André (Gabriel Edme) (*b* St-Dizier, 12 Feb 1869; *d* Paris, 11 Nov 1943). French musicologist. He studied the organ and at the Sorbonne and taught at the Schola Cantorum (from 1896) and at the Sorbonne (1912–37), where he established the first practical music university course in France and had many distinguished pupils. He worked at first on Bach and his precursors, but moved to earlier music; a study of Renaissance music (1948) crowns his work.

Pirrotta, Nino (b Palermo, 13 June 1908). Italian musicologist. He studied at Palermo and Florence. He taught at the Palermo Conservatory, was librarian of the S Cecilia Conservatory, Rome (1948–56), then professor at Harvard, returning to Italy in 1972 as professor at Rome University. His work, chiefly on Italian music from the 14th century to the 17th, is informed by a rare logic and clarity of thought and an unusually wide cultural knowledge, seen at their best in his *Li due Orfei: da Poliziano a Monteverdi* (1969).

Pisador, Diego (b Salamanca, 1509/10; d there, after 1557). Spanish vihuelist and composer. His *Libro de música de vihuela* (1552) contains arrangements of music by Josquin and others, as well as fantasias and variations of his own.

Pisano [Pagoli], Bernardo (b Florence, 12 Oct 1490; d Rome, 23 Jan 1548). Italian composer, singer and classical scholar. Trained at the cathedral school in Florence, he became master of the choristers there, then master of the cathedral chapel. From 1514 he was a singer in the papal chapel. His wide interests brought him into contact with leading intellectual and artistic figures: Michelangelo was among his friends. Of his numerous responsories, those for Good Friday and Holy Saturday are in a simple, solemn chordal style. His secular pieces are in two styles: the strophic ballatas and canzonettas (composed before 1515) are lightly homophonic with sprightly rhythms; the later ones are madrigalian, four voices. 17 of the latter were published by Petrucci (1520), the first printed collection of secular music containing the works of a single composer. They helped establish him as a leading figure in the history of the early 16th-century madrigal.

Pisendel, Johann Georg (b Cadolzburg, 26 Dec 1687; d Dresden, 25 Nov 1755). German violinist and composer. The foremost German violinist of his day, he studied with Torelli while at the Ansbach court and with Vivaldi in Venice, 1716–17. He was a member of the Dresden court orchestra in 1712, becoming Konzertmeister in 1730, and continued to tour widely. He composed several fine instrumental works, including seven violin concertos in an italianate style and a solo violin sonata.

Pistocchi, Francesco Antonio Mamiliano (b Palermo, 1659; d Bologna, 13 May 1726). Italian composer and singer. He was a child prodigy, and later had a brilliant operatic career as a contralto. He served at the Parma court in 1686–95, and in 1696 became court Kapellmeister at Ansbach. After travels with Giuseppe Torelli, he returned to Bologna. In 1702 he was named *virtuoso di camera e di cappella* to Prince Ferdinando of Tuscany. Latterly he was famous as a singing teacher and was a priest. His music includes operas, oratorios, cantatas etc, notable for their melodic elegance and colourful harmony.

Piston. On brass instruments, the moving component of a piston (as opposed to a rotary valves). The cornet, or *cornet à pistons*, has sometimes been called simply 'piston'. On an organ a piston is a button that controls a pre-set combination of stops.

Piston, Walter (Hamor) (b Rockland, ME, 20 Jan 1894; d Belmont, MA, 12 Nov 1976). American composer and teacher. He trained as a draughtsman before studying composition at Harvard (1919–24) and with Dukas and Boulanger in Paris; he then returned to Harvard (1926–60), becoming a renowned theory teacher. His textbook *Harmony* (1941) has been widely used. His music is in a clear, tonal style suggesting the neo-classical Stravinsky, Fauré and Roussel: the main works include eight symphonies (1937–65), five string quartets (1933–62) and the ballet *The Incredible Flutist* (1938); little of his output is vocal.

Pitch. The quality of a sound that fixes its position in the scale. Sounds produced by such instruments as a cymbal or a bass drum are said to be of indefinite pitch. Pitch is determined by what the ear perceives as the most fundamental wave-frequency of a sound.

In normal concert usage today, a standard pitch is used, defined as $a' = 440$ cycles per second (or Hz). There has not always been a standard pitch. The oldest extant instructions for tuning a harpsichord suggest that one fixes the initial note as one wishes; and as recently as the early 19th century, woodwind instruments were commonly equipped with interchangeable joints to accommodate different pitch levels. Evidence from between $c1500$ and $c1800$, usually in the form of surviving organs, pitch pipes or tuning forks, or from written sources, shows a variation in pitch for a' between modern $f'\sharp$ and c''. The pitch for opera performances in Paris in Lully's time ($c1675$) was $a' = c410$; this was also the low chamber pitch ('Cammer-Ton') of J.S. Bach. Bach's organ pitch ('Chor-Ton') at Leipzig and Weimar, however, was $a' = c480$. Pitch levels between $c415$ and $c430$ were much used: a tuning fork associated with Handel gives $a' = 422.5$, and this is the approximate pitch of French orchestras $c1700$ and the 'high chamber pitch' of J.S. Bach. This is the pitch, too, used by the Philharmonic Society of London in 1813. In Vienna, pitch was then $a' = 435$. It rose during the 19th century as the pressures during increasing public performance, in larger halls, led to a striving for more brilliant effect. In the 1850s, it stood at 449 at the Paris Opéra and 451 at La Scala, Milan. The rise gave particular concern to singers as the higher pitch increasingly strained their voices. A standard of $a' = 435$ was established in France in 1859.

The present standard of $a' = 440$ was laid down by the International Organization for Standardisation in 1955. Most performers on period instruments use a lower pitch, generally $c430$ for music of the Classical period and 415 for Baroque music.

Pitch class. Term used in modern music theory for all notes bearing the same name: all Cs, for example, form a pitch class C.

Pitch names. Names given to the seven pitches A–G. In English usage only letter names are given; French, Italian and Spanish use names derived from the Guidonian hexachord. In German, suffixes added to let-

TABLE 1

		A	B	C	D	E	F	G
♭♭	Eng.	A double flat	B double flat	C double flat	D double flat	E double flat	F double flat	G double flat
	Fr.	La double bémol	Si double bémol	Ut double bémol	Re double bémol	Mi double bémol	Fa double bémol	Sol double bémol
	Ger.	Asas	Bes (Heses)	Ceses	Deses	Eses	Feses	Geses
	It.	La doppio bemolle	Si doppio bemolle	Do doppio bemolle	Re doppio bemolle	Mi doppio bemolle	Fa doppio bemolle	Sol doppio bemolle
	Sp.	La doble bemol	Si doble bemol	Do doble bemol	Re doble bemol	Mi doble bemol	Fa doble bemol	Sol doble bemol
♭	Eng.	A flat	B flat	C flat	D flat	E flat	F flat	G flat
	Fr.	La bémol	Si bémol	Ut bémol	Re bémol	Mi bémol	Fa bémol	Sol bémol
	Ger.	As	B	Ces	Des	Es	Fes	Ges
	It.	La bemolle	Si bemolle	Do bemolle	Re bemolle	Mi bemolle	Fa bemolle	Sol bemolle
	Sp.	La bemol	Si bemol	Do bemol	Re bemol	Mi bemol	Fa bemol	Sol bemol
♮	Eng.	A	B	C	D	E	F	G
	Fr.	La	Si	Ut	Re	Mi	Fa	Sol
	Ger.	A	H	C	D	E	F	G
	It.	La	Si	Do	Re	Mi	Fa	Sol
	Sp.	La	Si	Do	Re	Mi	Fa	Sol
♯	Eng.	A sharp	B sharp	C sharp	D sharp	E sharp	F sharp	G sharp
	Fr.	La dièse	Si dièse	Ut dièse	Re dièse	Mi dièse	Fa dièse	Sol dièse
	Ger.	Ais	His	Cis	Dis	Eis	Fis	Gis
	It.	La diesis	Si diesis	Do diesis	Re diesis	Mi diesis	Fa diesis	Sol diesis
	Sp.	La sostenido	Si sostenido	Do sostenido	Re sostenido	Mi sostenido	Fa sostenido	Sol sostenido
✕	Eng.	A double sharp	B double sharp	C double sharp	D double sharp	E double sharp	F double sharp	G double sharp
	Fr.	La double dièse	Si double dièse	Ut double dièse	Re double dièse	Mi double dièse	Fa double dièse	Sol double dièse
	Ger.	Aisis	Hisis	Cisis	Disis	Eisis	Fisis	Gisis
	It.	La doppio diesis	Si doppio diesis	Do doppio diesis	Re doppio diesis	Mi doppio diesis	Fa doppio diesis	Sol doppio diesis
	Sp.	La doble sostenido	Si doble sostenido	Do doble sostenido	Re doble sostenido	Mi doble sostenido	Fa doble sostenido	Sol doble sostenido

ters denote modification, but English, French, Italian and Spanish add words for sharp, flat etc to the basic name. See Table 1.

Pitch notation. The earliest pitch notation of the type used now (to distinguish by their octave notes of the same pitch class) is based on the scale or gamut of Guido of Arezzo (*see* HEXACHORD; SOLMIZATION). Most standard pitch systems nowadays follow, or are based on, the system devised by Helmholtz in 1862. Here the notes are named in octave groups extending from C to the B above. The octave below middle C is notated *c*, middle C is *c'*, then *c''* etc. The octave below the C below middle C is *C*, the octave below that *C,* (in the Helmholtz system) or *C'* in the system used in this dictionary etc. Another traditional system shows middle C as c, an octave above c', an octave below C, two octaves below CC, etc. Several systems have been devised using inferior numerals, with middle C as c_4, with the octave below c_3 and the octave above c_5 etc. Other systems have been used based on numerals, with 12 to each octave in ascending order (such systems are favoured for the notes of keyboard instruments).

Pitchpipe. A wooden pipe with a variable and graduated stopper, which when blown gives any desired note of the scale as marked on the stopper. They were used principally in Britain in churches that had neither organs nor gallery bands for giving the starting-notes of metrical psalms. Surviving specimens date from *c*1750 to 1850; a typical pitchpipe might be of mahogany, with a scale *c'–c''* or *e'–e''*. There are two types: in one, the fipple is shaped like a recorder's and the plunger is of soft wood with an inlaid, stamped pewter scale; the other has a central turned fipple and a mahogany plunger with an inlaid boxwood scale.

Pitoni, Giuseppe Ottavio (*b* Rieti, 18 March 1657; *d* Rome, 1 Feb 1743). Italian composer and writer on music. He was *maestro di cappella* at Rieti Cathedral in 1676–7 and thereafter at S Marco, Palazzo Veneziana, Rome; he also held similar posts at St John Lateran (1708–19) and then at the Cappella Giulia. He was a prolific composer of church music, leaving over 3000 masses, psalms, hymns etc. They are basically in the contrapuntal Palestrina tradition, but contain elements of the concertato and polychoral styles; some of his later works are largely chordal. His writings deal with music history and theory.

Pitt, Percy (*b* London, 4 Jan 1869; *d* there, 23 Nov 1932). English conductor, composer and manager. He studied in Leipzig and Munich and conducted at Covent Garden from 1907, at first as Richter's assistant. He gave operas by Musorgsky and Debussy in Beecham's 1919–20 season and was musical director of the BBC, 1922–30, conducting its first public concert and opera relay.

Pittsburgh Symphony Orchestra. American orchestra founded in 1926. Its first conductor was Antonio Modarelli (1927–37); subsequently conductors have included Reiner, William Steinberg, Previn and Maazel. Its home is Heinz Hall for the Performing Arts (formerly Penn Theater;

cap. 2847). Activities include a summer festival and free park concerts. The Mendelssohn Choir (formed 1909) performs with it. The Pittsburgh Orchestra, founded in 1895, gave *c*1000 concerts before it disbanded in 1910.

Più (It.). 'More', e.g. *più animato*.

Piva. An Italian dance of the 15th and 16th centuries, a faster variety of the courtly *bassadanza*. It went out of fashion by *c*1450, but the term was used in the 16th century for a quick triple-time dance often preceded by a pavan and saltarello.

Pivot. A chord (or a note) which has different harmonic (or melodic) functions in two different keys, this property being used to effect a smooth transition from one key to another.

Pixis, Johann Peter (*b* Mannheim, 10 Feb 1788; *d* Baden-Baden, 22 Dec 1874). German pianist and composer. From 1806 he lived in Vienna, where he studied with Albrechtsberger and met Beethoven, Meyerbeer and Schubert. He became famous in Paris as a piano virtuoso and teacher (1823–40), composing chiefly keyboard pieces in a brilliant, often derivative style; one of his most frequently performed compositions was the concert rondo op.120, *Les trois clochettes*. His brother Friedrich Wilhelm Pixis (1785–1842), a violinist and composer, was an admired teacher at the Prague Conservatory.

Pizzetti, Ildebrando (*b* Parma, 20 Sept 1880; *d* Rome, 13 Feb 1968). Italian composer. He studied at the Parma Conservatory (1895–1901), then taught at Florence (1908–24), Milan (1924–36) and the Accademia di S Cecilia, Rome (1936–58). He was also active as a music critic. A serious-minded conservative, he looked for a renewal of Italian opera on the basis of a flexible arioso developed from Wagner, Debussy and Musorgksy and in some ways looking back to Florentine monody, as well as using imaginative choral writing: his main works in this genre include his first two operas, *Fedra* and *Debora e Jaele*, and especially *Assassinio nella cattedrale*. He also wrote an unaccompanied Requiem, one of his several unaccompanied choral works to demonstrate his sympathy for the expressive power of vocal polyphony.

Operas Fedra (1915); Debora e Jaele (1922); Lo straniero (1930); Fra Gherardo (1928); Orséolo (1935); L'oro (1947); Vanna Lupa (1949); Ifigenia (1950); Cagliostro (1952); La figlia di Iorio (1954); Assassinio nella cattedrale (1958); Il calzare d'argento (1961); Clitennestra (1965); incidental music

Orchestral music Per l'Edipo re di Sofocle, 3 preludes (1903); Conc. dell'estate (1928); Canti della stagione alta, pf, orch (1930); Vc Conc., C (1934); Sym., A (1940); Vn Conc., A (1944); Preludio a un altro giorno (1952); Harp Conc., B♭ (1960)

Choral music 2 canzoni corali (1913); Canto d'amore, male vv (1914); Messa di requiem (1922); De profundis (1937); Epithalamium, orch (1939); 3 composizioni corali (1943); Cantico di gloria, 3 choruses, wind, 2 pf, perc (1948); Vanitas vanitatum, solo vv, male chorus, orch (1958); 2 composizioni corali (1961); Filiae Jerusalem, S, female chorus, orch (1966)

Solo vocal music 3 liriche (1904); 5 liriche (incl. I pastori, 1908–15); Erotica (1911); 2 liriche drammatiche napoletane (1918); 3 sonetti di Petrarca (1922); Altre 5 liriche (1933); 3 liriche (1944); 3 canti d'amore (1960)

Chamber and instrumental music 2 str qts, A (1906), D (1933); Vn Sonata, A (1919); Vc Sonata, F (1921); Pf Trio, A (1925); pf music (incl. Sonata, 1942).

Pizzicato (It.). A direction to pluck the string or strings of a (generally bowed) instrument with the fingers.

Plagal cadence [Amen cadence]. A CADENCE consisting of a subdominant chord followed by a tonic chord (IV–I), both normally in root position.

Plagal mode. A church mode whose *ambitus* (range) includes the octave lying between the 4th below and the 5th above the final of the MODE (as opposed to the 'authentic mode', whose *ambitus* is from the final to its octave). The term is thus applied to the even-numbered modes of Gregorian chant, each of which takes its name from the corresponding odd-numbered one, with the addition of the prefix HYPO-.

Plainchant [plainsong]. The official monophonic unison chant, originally unaccompanied, of the Christian liturgies. The term refers particularly to the chant repertories with Latin texts, i.e. those of the major Western Christian liturgies (AMBROSIAN, GALLICAN, MOZARABIC and GREGORIAN AND OLD ROMAN); and in a more restricted sense to the repertory of Gregorian chant, the official chant of the Roman Catholic Church.

The origins of Christian liturgical chant lie in Jewish synagogue practice and in pagan music at early church centres (Jerusalem, Antioch, Rome and Constantinople). By the 4th century there were distinct families of Eastern and Western (Latin) rites, each with its own liturgy and music. As political and liturgical unification began under Carolingian rule in the mid-8th century, all the local Latin musical rites except the Ambrosian were suppressed in favour of the Gregorian. Notation appears nowhere before the 9th century, precise pitch representation being found only a century or two later. Of the Latin rites, only the Gregorian, Old Roman and Ambrosian survive complete.

Each plainchant family has its distinctive modal idioms; in some repertories (Gregorian-Old Roman, Byzantine, Slavonic, Coptic) the modes are assigned numbers or names. The Byzantine modal theory OKTŌĒCHOS developed with a symmetrical arrangement of eight modes and was adopted by the Gregorian repertory in the late 8th century. These use four final pitches (D, E, F and G), with sub-forms in a higher range (authentic) and lower range (plagal) for each final. Certain modes are preferred for certain liturgical categories, liturgical seasons or particular feasts. In the Gregorian tradition tonaries from the 9th century onwards listed melodies by mode, imposing the modal system only after the repertory had been fixed.

The forms of the chant repertory can be divided into psalmodic and non-psalmodic. There are three main forms of psalmody: antiphonal, in which two halves of a choir sing psalm verses in alternation with a refrain (antiphon); responsorial, in which one or more soloists alternate with the choir in singing psalm verses and a refrain (respond); and direct, in which the cantors sing verses without a refrain.

Non-psalmodic forms include the strophic form of the hymn, in which a single melody is repeated for all strophes; the sequence, in which there is repetition within each couplet; the repetitive forms of the Kyrie and Agnus Dei; and the non-repetitive forms of the Sanctus, Gloria and Credo. In the Mass, the chants of the Ordinary are all non-psalmodic and those of the Proper are psalmodic. Recitation formulae are used for both psalmodic and non-psalmodic texts. The syllabic psalm tones are the musical patterns based on mode that accommodate the recitation of psalm verses. The beginning, middle and end of each verse are punctuated with small intonation, flex, mediant and cadential formulae.

There are three melodic styles of chant: syllabic, in which each syllable of text is set to a single note; neumatic, in which two to a dozen notes accompany a syllable; and melismatic, in which single syllables may be sung to dozens of notes. The Christian liturgies are divided into the Eucharistic Mass and the DIVINE OFFICE, and it is the liturgy that determines the musical style of plainchant. In general, the more solemn the occasion, the more florid the music, although the most solemn chants are intoned by the celebrant. Each family of chant is characterized by a specific melodic type: antiphons and psalms are normally set syllabically, introits, Sanctus and Agnus Dei melodies are neumatic, and graduals, alleluias and offertories contain extensive melismas.

Chant composition involves the contrived selection of traditional modal materials, which may be divided into cells, formulae and patterns. Cells are miniature melodic gestures, which either stand alone or contribute to the larger stylized formulae; formulae are longer, more individual melismatic elements; and patterns are flexible frameworks or pitches that accommodate whole phrases of text. These melodic idioms are chosen and ordered according to established modal procedures (*see* CENTONIZATION).

Plainchant musical (Fr.). Term for a reformed or newly composed kind of chant used in France from the 17th century to the 19th. It was designed in the 1630s because of the desire of the Oratorians of the rue St Honoré, Paris, to attract Louis XIII's courtiers. Existing chants were revised, altered in rhythm and accidentals, with rules for ornamentation and tempo; new melodies were invented in the same vein by Bourgoing, Du Mont and Nivers. It remained in use until the Benedictines of Solesmes instituted their reforms.

Plainte (Fr.). Term used mainly in the 17th and 18th centuries for a slow, expressive piece of lamenting character.

Plançon, Pol (Henri) (*b* Fumay, 12 June 1851; *d* Paris, 11 Aug 1914). French bass. He made his début at Lyons in 1877 and sang in Paris from 1880. His Opéra (1883) and Covent Garden (1891) débuts were as Gounod's Mephistopheles. At the Met, 1893–1908, his polished voice and elegant style were admired, notably in Flotow, Thomas and Verdi.

Planctus. A song of lamentation and a literary and musical genre widespread in the Middle Ages, in

Latin and the vernaculars. Various types of planctus are known from the 9th century, both sacred and secular; in the 12th, laments of the Virgin Mary and *complaintes d'amour* were particularly common. Formally, the 12th-century planctus (like those of Abelard) can be related to the sequence or to the north French lai. The Provençal *planh* is a variant of the sirventes, with a topical subject – such as the death of Richard Coeur-de-lion (*d* 1199) – and often with borrowed form and melody. The Marian planctus is non-liturgical but according to local custom may on occasion have been performed in church. The planctus – whether of the three Marys or other biblical figures – was important in the development of liturgical drama.

Planets, The. Orchestral suite, op.32, by Holst (1916).

Planquette, (Jean) Robert (*b* Paris, 31 July 1848; *d* there, 28 Jan 1903). French composer. He studied at the Paris Conservatoire. A conscientious craftsman, he had his greatest success with the immensely popular operettas *Les cloches de Corneville* (Paris, 1877) and *Rip van Winkle* (London, 1882).

Planson, Jean (*b* ?Paris, *c*1559; *d* after 1612). French composer. He was organist of St Germain l'Auxerrois, Paris (1575), and St Sauveur, Paris (1586–8). Two of his pieces won prizes at Evreux in 1578. He published motets and sonnets (1583) and *airs*, sometimes folklike, for four voices (1587), which were popular and often reprinted.

Plantade, Charles-Henri (*b* Pontoise, 14/19 Oct 1764; *d* Paris, 18/19 Dec 1839). French composer and teacher. Active first in Paris, he was *maître de chapelle* at the Dutch court, 1806–10, singing master and stage director at the Paris Opéra, 1812–15, and music master to the royal chapel from 1816. He composed operas, sacred works, songs etc.

Plantin, Christopher (*b* ?Tours, *c*1520; *d* Antwerp, 1 July 1589). Flemish printer of French birth. The most prolific and important Antwerp publisher in the 16th century, and official printer to Philip II of Spain, he issued learned books including missals and breviaries; between 1578 and 1589 he published ten books of music by Monte, Le Jeune and others. His successors brought out sacred music by Lobo and Palestrina, while a branch in Leiden issued works by Sweelinck. Plantin's extant business records and his collection of music type increase the firm's historical importance.

Plaqué (Fr.). 'Laid down': an instruction to perform the notes of a chord simultaneously rather than successively.

Platania, Pietro (*b* Catania, 5 April 1828; *d* Naples, 26 April 1907). Italian composer and teacher. He was *maestro di cappella* at Milan Cathedral (from 1882) and director of the Naples Conservatory (1885–1902). The greatest Italian contrapuntist of his day, admired by Rossini and Verdi, he composed much church music and, unusually, orchestral music.

Platée. *Comédie-lyrique* in a prologue and three acts by Rameau to a libretto after Autreau (1745, Paris).

Platti, Giovanni Benedetto (*b* Padua, 9 July 1697; *d* Würzburg, 11 Jan 1763). Italian composer. He served at the Würzburg episcopal court from 1722 as teacher and composer, playing the oboe, violin, cello,

harpsichord and flute. He composed an opera (1729), other vocal music (mostly sacred) and *c*120 instrumental works, including harpsichord sonatas, violin sonatas and concertos. These show a transition from Baroque to *galant* style and reflect German influences, with rhythmic vitality and polyphonic devices among their notable features.

Player piano. A piano that automatically plays music recorded, usually by means of perforations in a paper roll. It had three phases of development. Early models, from the 1890s, consisted of a cabinet, pushed in front of an ordinary piano, with a row of wooden 'fingers' poised over the keyboard; perforations in a moving roll caused suction (generated by pedals, as in a harmonium) to force the fingers on to the keys. Dynamics, balance of bass and treble, and pedalling were controlled by levers at the front of the cabinet. By 1900 these features were built into the piano itself; expression knobs and tempo regulators were set into the front with the pumping pedals at the base. Finally, piano rolls capable of reproducing nuances were introduced; thus changes of tempo and dynamics were no longer at the whim of performers and the original artist's style could be re-created. Stravinsky and Hindemith composed for the instrument; Gershwin, Rakhmaninov and Paderewski were among those who made player-piano recordings. Its popularity began to decline *c*1923 with the increased use of the radio and gramophone.

Playford. English family of music publishers and booksellers. In 1651–84 John Playford (i) (1623–86) dominated London music publishing, operating from a shop by Temple Church, where he was clerk. He printed Royalist political tracts but is more important for his music, comprising lesson books and theory, song and instrumental collections, and psalms and hymns (including *The Whole Book of Psalmes*). Among his best-known publications are *The English Dancing Master* (1651; many enlarged editions until 1728) and *A Musicall Banquet* (1651); composers represented in his works include Purcell, Locke, William and Henry Lawes and Simpson. His son Henry (1657–*c*1707), who joined the business *c*1680, updated and amended much of what his father had begun, particularly in light music and 'favourite songs'. Henry's publications include Tom D'Urfey's songs in *Wit and Mirth* and Purcell's *Orpheus Britannicus*.

Plectrum. A piece of material (usually plastic, wood, bone or quill) with which the strings of an instrument are plucked. Plectra are particularly effective on such lute-type instruments as the mandolin and guitar, where they facilitate vigorous strumming and tremolando effects.

Plein jeu (Fr.: 'full registration'). In the 16th century the term described the combination of stops that gave the same Principal chorus as the old undivided, stop-less *Blockwerk*, i.e. Principals 16', 8', 4' etc. It also denotes one of two distinct choruses in French Classical organ music of 1670–1770, i.e. the Diapason chorus or *plein jeu* as distinct from the Flute, Cornet, mutation and reed combination of *grand jeu*.

Pleyel. French firm of instrument makers. It was

founded in 1807 in Paris by the composer and publisher Ignace Pleyel. Adopting the best features of
English piano making, it first built cottage pianos
('pianinos') then grands; Kalkbrenner and Chopin
became closely associated with the firm, which in the
mid-1830s had an annual production of 1000 instruments (2500 by the 1870s). Among family members
in charge of the business, Gustave Lyon (1857–1936)
is remembered for developing the chromatic harp in
the 1890s. The firm also made chromatic timpani,
chimes, two-manual pianos, a player piano ('Pleyela')
and, from 1912, two-manual harpsichords designed
and promoted by Wanda Landowska.

Pleyel, Ignace Joseph [Ignaz Josef] (*b* Ruppersthal,
18 June 1757; *d* Paris, 14 Nov 1831). Austrian
composer, publisher and piano maker. He became
Haydn's pupil and lodger in Eisenstadt *c*1772 and
was probably Kapellmeister to Count Erdődy later in
the decade. After travels in Italy, he became assistant
and in 1789 full Kapellmeister of Strasbourg Cathedral. In 1791–2 he conducted the Professional Concerts in London; though less popular there than
Haydn, he had much success, especially with his
symphonies concertantes and quartets. He returned to
Strasbourg but in 1795 settled in Paris, where he
opened a music shop, founded a major publishing
house (active until 1834) and reduced his composing
activities; in 1802 he issued the first miniature scores
(of music by Haydn). He visited Haydn in Vienna in
1805, and in 1807 founded a piano factory in Paris.

Pleyel's music enjoyed enormous popularity in his
lifetime. He composed several hundred works,
among them symphonies and other orchestral pieces,
chamber music, keyboard solos, stage works and
other vocal items. His earlier works are the most
original, notable for their thematic treatment.

His son Camille (1788–1855) became his business
associate and a successful pianist, appearing in
France and England; he composed many piano pieces
and was a friend of Chopin. Camille's wife, Marie
Moke Pleyel (1811–75), toured widely as a pianist,
taught in Belgium and composed for the piano; Chopin and Liszt dedicated works to her.

Pli selon pli. Work by Boulez for soprano and orchestra, sub-titled 'Portrait de Mallarmé' (1962, but continually revised).

Plowright, Rosalind (*b* Worksop, 21 May 1949).
English soprano. She studied in Manchester and at
the London Opera Centre and made her London
stage début with the ENO in *The Turn of the Screw*
(1979), appearing at Covent Garden the next year.
She has sung Aida and Donna Anna at Covent Garden, and has appeared at the Vienna Staatsoper, the
Paris Opéra, La Scala and widely in the USA. Her
powerful, gleaming, tautly-focussed voice and dramatic vitality serve particularly well in such roles as
Verdi's Desdemona.

Plüddemann, Martin (*b* Kolobrzeg, 29 Sept 1854;
d Berlin, 8 Oct 1897). German composer, singer and
critic. He rekindled interest in the German ballad by
establishing 'ballad schools' in Berlin and Graz and
composing over 50, notable for their narrative style,
characterization and unity; examples are *Siegfrieds
Schwert* and *Der alte Barbarossa*.

Plummer, John (*b* c1410; *d* c1484). English composer.
He was a member of the Chapel Royal by 1441 and
Master of the Chapel Children by 1444. Although as
late as 1467 he was still nominally a Gentleman of the
Chapel Royal, he had settled in Windsor *c*1458 and
from 1460 was verger of St George's Chapel. He was a
progressive composer who experimented with invertible counterpoint and imitation. In addition to three
votive antiphons and a motet, some mass movements
have also been attributed to him.

Pluriarc. A plucked string instrument of west, south-
west and central Africa, consisting of several musical
bows attached to a single resonator.

Poco (It.). 'Little', 'somewhat', e.g. *poco a poco* ('little
by little').

Poème. Chausson's op.25 (1896) for violin and
orchestra.

Poème électronique. Work for three-track tape by
Varèse (1958).

Poèmes pour Mi. Song cycle by Messiaen (1936),
settings for soprano and piano of his own poems.

Poem of Ecstasy [Poema ekstasa]. Orchestral work,
op.54, by Skryabin (1908).

Poet and Peasant [Dichter und Bauer]. Comedy with
songs by Suppé, in three acts, to words by Elmar
(1846, Vienna); the overture has long been especially
popular.

Poglietti, Alessandro (*b* ?Tuscany, early 17th century; *d* Vienna, July 1683). Austrian composer.
From 1661 he was court and chamber organist in the
Kapelle of the Emperor Leopold I in Vienna, where
he enjoyed great favour and was highly regarded as a
teacher of keyboard playing and composition. As a
keyboard composer he represents one of the most
vital links between Frescobaldi and the composers
of the late Baroque. His works include 12 ricercares
and many programmatic pieces, notably *Rossignolo*
(1677), a cycle of movements imitating musical instruments and folk music, as well as battle music
and imitations of bird calls. He also wrote an opera
(*Endimiome festiggiante*, 1677) and various sacred
works.

Pohjola's Daughter [Pohjolan tytär]. Symphonic
fantasia op.49 by Sibelius (1906) after the *Kalevala*.

Pohl, Carl Ferdinand (*b* Darmstadt, 6 Sept 1819;
d Vienna, 28 April 1887). German music historian.
From 1866 he was archivist and librarian to the
Gesellschaft der Musikfreunde in Vienna; besides
monographs on the society's collections, he wrote
Mozart und Haydn in London (1867), the result of
three years' research in London, and the invaluable
Joseph Haydn (1875–82).

Pohl, Richard (*b* Leipzig, 12 Sept 1826; *d* Baden-
Baden, 17 Dec 1896). German critic. A friend of
Wagner, Liszt and Berlioz, especially when he lived
in Weimar (1854–64), he became their champion in
opposition to Hanslick. He wrote under the
pseudonym 'Hoplit' in the *Neue Zeitschrift für
Musik*.

Pohle, David (*b* Marienberg, 1624; *d* Merseburg, 20
Dec 1695). German composer. An instrumentalist,
he was trained by Schütz at Dresden and held court
posts before settling at Halle, where he was Konzertmeister by 1660 and Kapellmeister by 1661. He

was also Kapellmeister at Zeitz (1678–82) and later at Merseburg (from 1682). He composed sacred concertos (mainly to Latin texts), a cycle of cantatas for the church year (of which one aria survives), secular arias, chamber sonatas and suites.

Point. English term in use since the 16th century for a motif or theme suitable for imitation (hence 'counterpoint'). It has also been used as a title for a piece in imitative style.

Point d'orgue (Fr.). *See* ORGAN POINT.

Pointer (Fr.). Term used in French Baroque music to indicate that notes written as equal be played in a dotted rhythm (*see* NOTES INÉGALES); it could also simply mean staccato.

Pointillism. Term borrowed from painting for a musical texture in which notes of different tone-colours are presented in isolation rather than in linear sequence, as in post-Webern music of the 1950s and 1960s. *See* KLANGFARBENMELODIE.

Poisoned Kiss, The. Opera (romantic extravaganza) in three acts by Vaughan Williams to a libretto by Evelyn Sharp after Garnett and Hawthorne (1936, Cambridge).

Poissl, Johann Nepomuk, Freiherr von (*b* Hauken-zell, 15 Feb 1783; *d* Munich, 17 Aug 1865). German composer. Early association with Danzi and with Weber (1811) was decisive in his career as an opera composer in Munich, where he was briefly director of the court theatre. Though his works lack original-ity, his greatest successes, the grand operas *Athalia* (1814) and *Der Wettkampf zu Olympia* (1815), were praised by Weber for their melodic construction, rich harmony and apt scoring.

Pokorny, Franz Xaver (Thomas) (*b* Střibro, 20 Dec 1729; *d* Regensburg, 2 July 1794). Bohemian com-poser. He studied at Mannheim and from 1766 served at the Regensburg court. He composed many orchestral works, mostly symphonies and concertos. Two of his sons became musicians; some of the other Bohemian musicians named Pokorny may have been related to him.

Polacca (It.). Term indicating a Polish style ('alla pol-acca'); usually taken as implying a dance rhythm equivalent to that of a POLONAISE.

Poldini, Ede (*b* Budapest, 13 June 1869; *d* Corseaux, 28 June 1957). Hungarian composer. A pupil of Tomka in Budapest and Mandyczewski in Vienna, he settled in Switzerland in 1908 and wrote suc-cessful operettas and operas, notably *Vagabund und Prinzessin* (1903) and *Hochzeit im Fasching* (1924), and popular piano music.

Poliphant [polyphon(e)]. An early 17th-century English plucked instrument. It was an attempt at a diatonically tuned hybrid of all the wire-strung instruments, with short treble strings played across a lute- or bandora-shaped body, and long bass diapasons like a theorbo's.

Polish Chamber Orchestra. Orchestra formed by JERZY MAKSYMIUK.

Polish Symphony. Nickname of Tchaikovsky's Symphony no.3 in D (1875), so called because of the finale's polonaise rhythm.

Poliziano, Angelo (*b* Montepulciano, 1454; *d* Flor-ence, 1494). Italian humanist and poet. He spent most of his life in the service of the Medici family. His poetry was set by contemporary composers and his celebrated *Fabula di Orfeo* (*c*1480), an entertain-ment in various verse forms for a half-spoken, half-sung performance, looks forward to the rise of the *intermedio*.

Polka. A lively couple-dance in 2/4 time. Of Bo-hemian origin, it became one of the most popular 19th-century ballroom dances. The music, usually in ternary form, employed characteristic rhythms emphasizing the third quaver of the bar (ex.1). Pol-

Ex. 1

kas were written by the Strausses and other leading dance composers, and several are found in Smeta-na's music. 20th-century examples include those in Weinberger's *Schvanda the Bagpiper*, Walton's *Façade* and Stravinsky's *Circus Polka*.

Pollarolo, (Giovanni) Antonio (*b* Brescia, bap. 12 Nov 1676; *d* Venice, 30 May 1746). Italian compo-ser, son of Carlo Francesco. He was a pupil of his father and substituted for him as *vicemaestro di cap-pella* at St Mark's, Venice, from 1702 before suc-ceeding to the post in 1723. In 1740 he became *primo maestro*; he was also *maestro di cappella* at the Ospe-daletto conservatory from 1716. Apart from several oratorios and other sacred works he wrote mainly operas (1700–29), which – now mostly lost – are notable for their extended da capo arias.

Pollarolo, Carlo Francesco (*b c*1653; *d* Venice, 7 Feb 1723). Italian composer. After serving as a church organist in Brescia, he succeeded his father as organist at the cathedral there in 1767 and became head of the music in 1680. In 1689 he moved to Venice, where he became second organist at St Mark's in 1690 and *vicemaestro di cappella* in 1692; his son Antonio took over his duties in 1702. At least from 1696 he was also musical director of the Ospe-dale degl'Incurabili, for which he wrote several oratorios. Pollarolo was a leading opera composer, composing over 80 operas in all between 1680 and 1722 (only *c*20 survive); they were popular both in Italy and abroad. They are typical of the transition from the late Venetian to the Neapolitan style of opera: whereas the earlier works alternate flexibly between recitative and arioso, the later ones are increasingly standardized, with long passages of *secco* recitative and large-scale da capo arias, using a virtuoso vocal style. His other works include secular solo cantatas, arias and duets and church music.

Polledro, Giovanni Battista (*b* Piovà, 10 June 1781; *d* there, 15 Aug 1853). Italian violinist and compo-ser. He studied in Turin with Pugnani and held appointments in Bergamo and Moscow. He led the Dresden court orchestra under Weber and was later court *maestro di cappella* in Turin (1824–44). Ac-claimed as the best violinist since Viotti, he played with Beethoven in 1812. Among his compositions are six études.

Pollini, Maurizio (*b* Milan, 5 Jan 1942). Italian pianist. He studied at the Milan Conservatory and in 1960 won the Warsaw Chopin competition, soon gaining a wide reputation for his brilliance and his clarity of exposition in a repertory ranging from Bach and Schubert to Boulez and Schoenberg. He has conducted from the keyboard and in 1981 conducted Rossini's *La donna del lago* at the Pesaro Festival.

Polly. Ballad opera in three acts by Gay with music arranged by Pepusch and Arnold (1779, London), a sequel to *The Beggar's Opera*.

Pololáník, Zdeněk (*b* Brno, 25 Oct 1935). Czech composer. A pupil of Petrželka and Schaefer at the Brno Academy (1957–61), he has written symphonies, choral and chamber works using Moravian modality and avant-garde techniques. Elements of pop music are used in *Rhythmic Mass* (1973).

Polonaise (Fr.). A stately Polish processional dance or an instrumental piece. The dance, accompanied by singing, has long been used at weddings and public ceremonies. The melodies are in triple metre and have a simple structure, consisting of short phrases usually without upbeat. As a court dance, accompanied by instruments rather than by singing, it became the most highbred expression of the Polish national spirit and the most representative of Polish dances throughout Europe.

The 18th century saw the stylization of the polonaise. Those of Bach (French Suite no.1, Orchestral Suite no.2) show the characteristic features of triple metre, phrases without upbeat and a closing rhythm which throws the accent on to the second beat. German composers propagated the dance as a musical form and many polonaises were written by Telemann, J.G. Goldberg, Mozart, Beethoven, Schubert, Weber and others. Chopin's famous examples established ex.1 as the typical polonaise

Ex. 1

rhythm. Among other notable piano polonaises are those of Schumann and Liszt, and the form was used by several Russian composers, including Musorgsky (*Boris Godunov*), Tchaikovsky (*Sleeping Beauty, Eugene Onegin*) and Glinka.

Polovinkin, Leonid Alexeyevich (*b* Kurgan, 13 Aug 1894; *d* Moscow, 8 Feb 1949). Soviet composer. He studied with Myaskovsky and Vasilenko at the Moscow Conservatory (1914–24) and was a leader of Russian modernism in the mid-1920s; his later works are simpler, many connected with his work for the Moscow Central Children's Theatre from 1927–8.

Polovtsian Dances. Dances for chorus and orchestra by Borodin from Act 2 of *Prince Igor*.

Polska. A dance type of central and northern Europe: it has both duple- and triple-time versions and was parent to such local dances as the mazurka and polonaise. Dating from the Renaissance it has its roots in Polish folk choruses and dance pairs, and was also popular in Scandinavia. Dvořák and Grieg are among composers who have written stylized polskas.

Polychoral. Term for music written for two or more

choirs. The technique developed in the 16th century, in Venice and Rome. *See* CORI SPEZZATI.

Polyphony. Term, derived from the Greek for 'many-sounding', used for music in which two or more strands sound simultaneously. It is used in distinction to monophony ('one-sounding', for music consisting of a single line) and homophony ('like-sounding', implying music in which the melody is accompanied by voices in the same rhythm). In fact, polyphony strictly comprehends homophony, though in common usage there is a distinction between them.

The term 'polyphonic era' is generally applied to the late Middle Ages and the Renaissance; the late Renaissance (the time of Palestrina and Lassus) is regarded as the 'golden age of polyphony'. The kind of polyphony used in the Baroque era, by Bach and Handel, is usually described by the term 'counterpoint'.

Polyrhythm. The superposition of different rhythms or metres; it is characteristic of some medieval polyphony and common in 20th-century music.

Polytextuality. Many-texted: the use of two or more texts in a vocal work. The technique was much used in the motet and certain other forms of the 13th and 14th centuries. The texts may be in different languages and may or may not be related in sense.

Polytonality. The simultaneous use of more than two different keys.

Pommer. German name for the alto, tenor and bass SHAWM.

Pomo d'oro, Il. Opera by Cesti in a prologue and five acts, to a libretto by Sbarra; it was performed with vast splendour, following the marriage of Leopold I, at the Viennese court, with a large orchestra and 24 sets by Burnacini, in 1668.

Pomp and Circumstance. Five orchestral marches, op.39, by Elgar; no.1 includes the melody later used for 'Land of Hope and Glory'.

Pomposo (It.). Pompous, ceremonious.

Ponc, Miroslav (*b* Vysoké Mýto, 2 Dec 1902; *d* Prague, 1 April 1976). Czech composer. A pupil of Suk and Hába at the Prague Conservatory and of Schoenberg privately, he wrote avant-garde pieces in the 1920s, but subsequently devoted himself to the theatre: he conducted at the National Theatre in Prague from 1945 and wrote over 100 incidental scores.

Ponce, Manuel (María) (*b* Fresnillo, 8 Dec 1882; *d* Mexico City, 24 April 1948). Mexican composer. From boyhood he was active as a pianist, church organist and composer; he completed his studies in Bologna and Berlin before being appointed to the Mexico City Conservatory in 1909. There followed periods in Havana (1915–17) and Paris (1925–33), during which time he had consultations with Dukas), but otherwise he worked in Mexico City as a teacher and composer. His works are mostly sentimental songs and piano salon pieces, but he also wrote large orchestral music. His guitar music, including many solo pieces and a *Concierto del sur* (1941), was taken up by Segovia and his followers and has become part of the standard repertory.

Ponchielli, Amilcare (*b* Paderno Fasolaro [now

Paderno Ponchielli], 31 Aug 1834; *d* Milan, 16 Jan 1886). Italian composer. After studying at the Milan Conservatory he settled in the provinces as an organist and municipal band conductor, repeatedly attempting to establish himself as an opera composer. He finally won success in 1872 with the much-revised *I promessi sposi*, in 1874 with the Ricordi commission *I lituani* and above all in 1876 with *La Gioconda*. As professor of composition at the Milan Conservatory (from 1880) he taught Puccini and, briefly, Mascagni. He also composed much sacred music for S Maria Maggiore, Bergamo. Of his works, only *La Gioconda*, on a text drawn by Boito from Hugo, is in the modern repertory. An inspired stylization of grand opera, it contains music that is alive, varied and sensitive, notably the tenor romanza 'Cielo e mar' and the famous 'Suicidio', and that foreshadows aspects of late Verdi and of *verismo* opera. Elsewhere Ponchielli's atmospheric colouring and symphonic treatment (*I lituani, Il figliuol prodigo*) show remarkable imagination and workmanship, despite his lack of a strong personality.

Pons, Lily (Alice Joséphine) (*b* Draguignan, 12 April 1898; *d* Dallas, 13 Feb 1976). American soprano. She studied at the Paris Conservatoire and made her opera début in 1928 as Delibes's Lakmé. Her Met début was in 1931 as Donizetti's Lucia; she was a sensational success and remained there for 25 years, singing such roles as Verdi's Gilda and Bellini's Amina. She sang widely in other countries and made films; in 1938 she married André Kostelanetz. Her voice was frail, agile and extremely high-pitched.

Pons de Capdoil (*b* c1165; *d* c1215). Provençal troubadour. A member of the nobility of the Haute-Loire region, he was considered by his contemporaries the epitome of the courtly knight. He was active in Marseilles and closely associated with the Count of Auvergne, whose beautiful wife inspired some of his finest love poetry. His crusading songs date from the time of the third crusade, in which he may have participated. Of his 27 known poems, four survive with music; his melodies are among the finest in the repertory and were often used as contrafacta.

Ponselle, Rosa (*b* Meriden, CT, 22 Jan 1897; *d* Green Spring Valley, MD, 25 May 1981). American soprano. Her opera début was at the Met in 1918, opposite Caruso, as Leonora in *La forza del destino*. Her warmth, perfect technique and opulent tone made her a success in operas by Bellini, Verdi, Mozart and Meyerbeer; she never sang Puccini or Wagner. At Covent Garden (début 1929) she sang Violetta and Norma.

Ponte, Lorenzo da. *See* DA PONTE, LORENZO.

Ponticello. The bridge of a string instrument. *See* SUL PONTICELLO.

Pontio, Pietro (*b* Parma, 25 March 1532; *d* there, 27 Dec 1595). Italian composer. He was *maestro di cappella* at S Maria Maggiore, Bergamo (1565–7), Madonna della Steccata, Parma (1567–9, from 1582), and Milan Cathedral (1577–82). His treatises, *Ragionamento* (1588) and *Dialogo* (1595), show his concern with good counterpoint and textual clarity. He also published 11 books of sacred music (1580–95).

Poot, Marcel (*b* Vilvoorde, 7 May 1901). Belgian composer. He studied at the Brussels and Antwerp conservatories, privately with Gilson (1916) and with Dukas in Paris. He taught at the Brussels Conservatory, latterly as director (1949–66), and was a critic; with Gilson he founded the *Revue musicale belge*. His output includes stage works, five symphonies (1929–74), concertos and chamber music, in an essentially tonal, rhythmic style influenced by jazz and middle-period Stravinsky and Prokofiev. The *Vrolijke ouverture* (1935) is one of the most played Belgian orchestral pieces.

Pop music. Term applied since the late 1950s to the central, most widely circulated and commercially successful kinds of popular music.

Popov, Gavriil Nikolayevich (*b* Novocherkassk, 12 Sept 1904; *d* Repino, 17 Feb 1972). Soviet composer. A pupil of Shcherbachov at the Leningrad Conservatory, he wrote a modernist Sextet (1927) and five symphonies in the epic tradition of Borodin and Glazunov.

Popp, Lucia (*b* Uhorská Ves, 12 Nov 1939). Austrian soprano of Czechoslovak birth. She sang at Salzburg and the Vienna Staatsoper from 1963. She made her Covent Garden début in 1966 and sang the Queen of Night at the Met in 1967. Her bright, well-focussed voice and charming stage presence have made her much in demand in Strauss, Mozart and Verdi. She is also a noted recitalist.

Popper, David (*b* Prague, 9 Dec 1843; *d* Baden, 7 Aug 1913). Austrian cellist. He studied at Prague Conservatory and undertook the first of many virtuoso tours in 1863. He was principal cellist of the Vienna Court Opera, 1868–73, then resumed touring, but settled in Budapest in 1896 as professor at the conservatory. He has periods with the Hellmesberger and Hubay quartets. He was a prolific composer of cello music; his works include four concertos but the most famed is his *Requiem* for three cellos and orchestra (1891). His brother Wilhelm (1846–1905) also had a distinguished career as a cellist, in London, New York and Vienna, and composed for the cello.

Popular music. Music of the populace. The term embraces all kinds of traditional or 'folk' music which, originally made by illiterate people, was not written down. Forms of popular music designed to entertain large numbers of people arose particularly with the growth of urban communities as a result of industrialization. The term 'popular music' is most commonly applied to music of, and since, the 'Tin Pan Alley' era, i.e. from the 1880s in the USA and the early 20th century in Europe. It has however been developing distinctive characteristics since the early 19th century, for example in the sentimental ballads of the mid-19th century, the music of the dance halls and pleasure gardens (including military marches), the music hall and the operetta repertory, and (under American influence) the development of styles more or less based on black music, as heard in American minstrel shows. American popular music gained further ground in Europe with the coming of ragtime in the years immediately preceding World War I.

For popular music since World War I *see* MUSICAL COMEDY, BLUES, JAZZ, SWING, COUNTRY MUSIC, SOUL MUSIC, RHYTHM-AND-BLUES and ROCK.

Porena, Boris (*b* Rome, 27 Sept 1927). Italian composer. He was a pupil of Petrassi in Rome and in 1972 was appointed to teach at the Rome Conservatory. His individual musical style has responded to influences from the neo-classical Stravinsky and the Darmstadt avant garde: cantatas and smaller vocal pieces, often setting German poetry, figure among his works. He has written an educational collection *Kinder-Musik* (1972) and published articles.

Porgy and Bess. Opera in three acts by Gershwin to a libretto by Du Bose Heyward and Ira Gershwin (1935, Boston).

Poro. Opera in three acts by Handel to a libretto after Metastasio's *Alessandro nell'Indie* (1731, London).

Porpora, Nicola (Antonio) (*b* Naples, 17 Aug 1686; *d* there, 3 March 1768). Italian composer and singing teacher. He was *maestro di cappella* to the Prince of Hessen-Darmstadt and the Portuguese ambassador in Naples. In 1708 he presented his first opera there; later he wrote operas for Rome, Vienna (1714, 1718) and elsewhere. He moved to Venice in 1726 as *maestro* of the Incurabili orphanage but spent 1733–6 in London composing for the Opera of the Nobility (which rivalled Handel's company). He then held conservatory posts in Naples (*maestro di cappella* at S Maria di Loreto, 1739–42) and Venice. In 1747–51 he taught singing at the Dresden court, where from 1748 he was also Kapellmeister. In 1752–3 he became a music teacher at the imperial court in Vienna; he taught the young Haydn, who became his valet and accompanist. He returned to Naples in 1760.

Reflecting his understanding of the art of singing, Porpora's music often features intricate, embellished vocal writing. His main works are his *c*50 operas, of which the five for London are the most dramatic. Among his other works are serenatas, cantatas, oratorios and sacred operas and over 100 other sacred works. He also wrote didactic pieces (solfèges etc) and several instrumental works.

Porro, Giovanni Giacomo (*b* Lugano [then in Italy], *c*1590; *d* Munich, Sept 1656). Italian composer. An organist, he moved in 1635 to Munich, where he became court vice-Kapellmeister and then Kapellmeister. He introduced opera to Munich, composed over 900 sacred works and *c*200 madrigals: only four small pieces survive.

Porsile, Giuseppe (*b* Naples, 5 May 1680; *d* Vienna, 29 May 1750). Italian composer and singing-master. He served in the Spanish chapel in Naples and then (from 1695) in Barcelona, where he organized the music chapel and taught singing. Moving to Vienna in 1713–14, he became singing-master to the empress and in 1720 court composer. He produced over 20 secular dramatic works and 13 oratorios, 1717–37, also writing chamber cantatas, duets etc and instrumental pieces. His music combines north Italian elements (familiar in Vienna) with Neapolitan features and is frequently contrapuntal.

Port. Old Scottish term for an instrumental piece, usually played on the harp.

Porta, Costanzo (*b* Cremona, 1528–9; *d* Padua, 19 May 1601). Italian composer. A minorite friar, he went in *c*1549 to the Frari church in Venice, where he became a pupil of Willaert at St Mark's and formed a lifelong friendship with Merulo. He was *maestro di cappella* at the cathedrals of Osimo (1552–65), Padua (1565–7) and Ravenna (1567–74) and of the Santa Casa, Loreto (1574–80), and was an influential teacher. He visited Florence, Ferrara and Mantua, gaining important patrons and meeting other leading musicians. He returned to Padua Cathedral in 1589. A highly disciplined composer renowned for his contrapuntal skill, he wrote mainly sacred music (12 bks, 1555–1605), including over 200 polyphonic motets, 15 masses, introits and a large vesper hymn cycle. His secular works include five madrigal books (1555–86).

Porta, Giovanni (*b* Venice, ?*c*1690; *d* Munich, 21 June 1755). Italian composer. After serving (latterly as *maestro*) in Cardinal Ottoboni's *cappella* in Rome, he began presenting operas in Venice (1716); in 1720 he had one staged in London (*Numitore*, opening the new Royal Academy of Music: Handel later drew on it in the 'Arrival of the Queen of Sheba' in *Solomon*). Later he also composed for Milan and elsewhere. In 1726 he became *maestro di coro* at the Incurabili orphanage in Venice and from 1737 was court Kapellmeister in Munich. He wrote over 25 *opere serie*, cantatas, arias etc and sacred works.

Portamento (It.). A smooth and rapid 'sliding' between two pitches, executed continuously. It is characteristic of the voice, trombone and strings; it has long been regarded as an expressive device, though in string playing changes in technique and taste have led it to be used much less often than in the past. The term is also used in the sense of *port de voix* as a synonym for an ascending appoggiatura.

Portative. A small ORGAN of treble flue pipes common in the 14th and 15th centuries. It was strapped to the player's shoulder and played with the right hand while the bellows was operated by the left.

Portato (It.). A bowstroke, an articulated slur, represented by a slur over notes with dots.

Port de voix Fr.). *See* APPOGGIATURA.

Porter, Andrew (*b* Cape Town, 26 Aug 1928). British writer on music. He studied at Oxford and embarked on a career in music criticism in London, joining the *Financial Times* in 1952; he was also editor of the *Musical Times* (1960–67). From 1972 he wrote for the *New Yorker*, settling in New York in 1974. An elegant and well-informed writer, sympathetic to new music and particularly authoritative on opera, he has made singing translations of many operas and published much on Verdi as well as collections of reviews.

Porter, Cole (Albert) (*b* Peru, IN, 9 June 1891; *d* Santa Monica, 15 Oct 1964). American composer. His talent showed young, but he had few formal studies in music until 1919 (after a period at law school and another in the French Foreign Legion), when he took lessons from d'Indy. He had meanwhile composed a number of musicals, often to his own lyrics; his first success was with *Wake Up and Dream* (1929, London). Among those that followed were *Gay Divorce* (1932) and *Anything Goes* (1934); he also wrote music for films. His finest musical, *Kiss Me, Kate*, followed in 1948. Besides being an inventive and witty lyricist, he was an ingenious melodist who produced some of the most sophisticated and musically complex songs of American popular music.

Porter, (William) Quincy (*b* New Haven, 7 Feb 1897; *d* Bethany, CT, 12 Nov 1966). American composer. He was a pupil of Parker at Yale, d'Indy in Paris (1920) and Bloch in New York. After a further stay in Paris (1928–31), during which he developed his personal style, he taught at Vassar (1932–8), the New England Conservatory (1938–46) and Yale (1946–65). His style is marked by smooth melodic movement in a highly chromatic polyphony, at its best in chamber music. He wrote nine string quartets (1923–58), two symphonies (1934, 1962), keyboard and incidental music and songs.

Porter, Walter (*b* ?c1587 or c1595; *d* London, bur. 30 Nov 1659). English composer. He was a tenor at the Chapel Royal (from 1617) and later Master of the Choristers of Westminster Abbey (1639–44); he also played the lute. He published madrigals and motets; the former (1632), virtually the only English madrigals in concertato style, support his claim that he was a pupil of Monteverdi.

Portland Symphony Orchestra. *See* OREGON SYMPHONY ORCHESTRA.

Portsmouth Point. Concert overture by Walton (1925), after an etching by Rowlandson.

Portugal [Portogallo], Marcos Antônio (da Fonseca) (*b* Lisbon, 24 March 1762; *d* Rio de Janeiro, 7 Feb 1830). Portuguese composer. He was singer and organist of the Seminário Patriarchal in Lisbon and from 1785 conductor at the Teatro do Salitre, where he presented Portuguese comic operas. Already widely popular, he spent 1792–1800 in Italy, producing 21 Italian operas (*seria* and *buffa*) in Naples and elsewhere. Returning to Libson, he became *mestre de capela* of the royal chapel and director of the S Carlos Opera. The court left for Rio de Janeiro in 1807; he joined it there in 1811, and remained successful as a composer. Besides over 50 operas in a Neapolitan style, he composed cantatas, occasional pieces and numerous sacred works.

His brother Simão (1744–?1842) also went to Rio de Janeiro, where he became organist of the royal chapel; he composed sacred music.

Porumbescu, Ciprian (*b* Şipotele-Sucevei, 14 Oct 1853; *d* Stupca, 6 June 1883). Romanian composer, choirmaster and teacher. He studied at the Vienna Conservatory with Bruckner. A founder of the Romanian school of instrumental and vocal music, he wrote folkdances, salon pieces for piano, songs and choruses and the popular Romanian operetta *New Moon* (1882). The Bucharest Conservatory now bears his name.

Posaune (Ger.). TROMBONE; in German, it also means the last trumpet.

Posch, Isaac (*d* ?Klagenfurt, 1622–3). Austrian composer, organist and organ builder. He worked in Carinthia from 1614 and Carniola from 1617–18, and was probably a Protestant. His instrumental en-

semble works (2 bks, 1618, 1621) made a distinctive contribution to the early Baroque variation suite. His 42 sacred vocal concertos (1623) are also notable and some have obbligato parts.

Position. Term applied to playing positions on string instruments and on the trombone. On a string instrument it indicates the placing of the left hand on the fingerboard so that the fingers can play from 1 on the lowest string to 4 on the highest without a SHIFT. On the trombone it refers to the degree of extension of the slide.

Positive. A small, movable ORGAN such as the English 'chamber organ'; the term also refers to a manual of a larger organ derived from such an organ.

Poss, Georg (*b* Franconia, c1570; *d* Czerwienczyce, after 1633). German composer. A trumpet and cornett player, he served the Habsburgs at Graz (1597–1618) and then at Neisse, Silesia (1618–22). He composed a number of polychoral sacred works, which helped introduce the Venetian style of G. Gabrieli into Austria.

Posse (Ger.). A farce or broad comedy. In the 19th century the term *Posse mit Gesang* was used in Vienna for a comic play with solo songs, rudimentary ensembles, incidental music and sometimes short choruses. Composers of music for *Possen* included Wenzel Müller, Ferdinand Kauer, Adolf Müller and Franz von Suppé.

Posse, Wilhelm (*b* Bromberg, 15 Oct 1852; *d* Berlin, 20 June 1925). German harpist and composer. Solo harpist of the Berlin PO and Opera (1872–1903), he taught at the Berlin Hochschule für Musik; besides transcribing Liszt's piano pieces, he wrote important pedagogical works.

Possenti, Pellegrino (*fl* 1623–8). Italian composer. Possibly an amateur composer, he published two volumes of secular music which reflect his admiration for Monteverdi; the first (1623) contains two laments, the second (1625) a strophic-bass cantata. He also wrote a book of 18 one-movement sonatas (1628) with early use of tremolo and the direction 'da capo'.

Post horn. A small brass instrument, originally with a fundamental about *bb'*, used in the past by postillions and guards on mail coaches. In Germany it reached its standard form, circular and with three turns, in the late 18th century. As it graduated to use in concert music it acquired crooks, keys and finally valves. Telemann and Bach imitated it. Mozart, Beethoven and Mahler actually wrote for it. The English instrument, long and straight, in A or Ab, is still made; it is used in performances of Koenig's famous *Post Horn Galop* (1844).

Posthorn. Nickname of Mozart's Serenade in D K320 (1779), in which a posthorn is used in the second trio of the second minuet.

Postlude. The concluding movement or section of a composition; a piece played during the congregation's exit at the end of a church service.

Postnikova, Victora (Valentinovna) (*b* Moscow, 12 Jan 1944). Soviet pianist. She studied at the Moscow Conservatory and won several prizes; her international career began in 1967, when she showed unusual freshness, spontaneity and delicacy in her playing of the central Romantic repertory. In 1969 she married the conductor Rozhdestvensky.

Poston, Elizabeth (*b* nr. Walkern, Herts., 24 Oct 1905; *d* there, 18 March 1987). English composer. She studied at the RAM and worked for the BBC. Her output is modest (songs, chamber music etc) but she evolved a personal style based on neo-classicism and emphasizing craftsmanship and melodic fluency. She was a respected editor of folk-songs, carols and hymns.

Potpourri. An instrumental medley of popular and previously unconnected tunes from operas or other works. The term was first used in the 18th century for collections of dances or other pieces and such compilations as Josef Gelinek's *Potpourri tiré des airs de 'Zauberflöte', 'Domjuan' et 'Figaro' pour le piano-forte*. The repertory of 19th-century military bands and café orchestras was composed largely of potpourris.

Potter, A(rchibald) J(ames) (*b* Belfast, 22 Sept 1918; *d* Greystones, 5 July 1980). Irish composer. A pupil of Vaughan Williams at the RCM (1936–8), he taught at the Royal Irish Academy of Music from 1955 and was a journalist and broadcaster. His large output includes orchestral and choral works, ballets and folksong arrangements in a broadly Romantic style, his *Sinfonia de profundis* (1968) for orchestra achieving popularity.

Potter, (Philip) Cipriani (Hambly) (*b* London, 3 Oct 1792; *d* there, 26 Sept 1871). English composer, pianist and teacher. He was son of the flautist Richard Huddleston Potter (1755–1821) and grandson of the flute maker Richard Potter (1726–1806). He studied with Attwood, Crotch and Joseph Woelfl, and later with Aloys Förster in Vienna, where he met Beethoven. From 1819 he appeared often as a soloist, giving the English premières of several Mozart and Beethoven concertos, and as conductor of the Philharmonic Concerts (until 1844). Admired for the brilliance of his playing, he taught the piano at the newly founded RAM, serving as principal from 1832 to 1859. Although his composing was limited to 1816–37, he produced remarkable works, chiefly instrumental, including nine symphonies (notably one in G minor), chamber works (Three Grand Trios op.12, two sextets, a string quartet, three overtures and three piano concertos, in which he displayed contrapuntal skill, harmonic ingenuity and a telling use of instrumental colour.

Pougin [Paroisse-Pougin], **(François-Auguste-) Arthur** (*b* Châteauroux, 6 Aug 1834; *d* Paris, 8 Aug 1921). French writer on music. He was a theatre violinist and conductor in Paris until 1863, then turned to writing. He was a frequent contributor to *Le ménestrel* (from 1885 chief editor), *La France musicale*, *L'art musical*, *Le soir*, *La tribune* and the *Journal officiel* (from 1878) and edited the supplement to Fétis's *Biographie universelle*. His most important single work was on Verdi's life (1881).

Poule, La. See HEN, THE.

Poulenc, Francis (Jean Marcel) (*b* Paris, 7 Jan 1899; *d* there, 30 Jan 1963). French composer. His background gave him a musical and literary sophistication from boyhood, and he was already a publicly

noted composer by the time he took lessons with Koechlin (1921–4): such works as his Apollinaire song cycle *Le bestiaire* (1919) and Sonata for two clarinets (1918) had shown the Stravinsky–Satie inclinations that assure him a place among Les Six. His ballet *Les biches* (1924), written for Dyagilev, established his mastery of the emotions and musical tastes of the smart set, opening a world of suavity and irony that he went on to explore in a sequence of concertante pieces: the *Concert champêtre* for harpsichord, the *Aubade* with solo piano and the Concerto for two pianos,.

Around 1935 there came a change in his personal and spiritual life, reflected in a sizable output of religious music, a much greater productivity and an important contribution to French song (from this time he gave recitals with the baritone Pierre Bernac). Yet the basis of his style was unchanged: Stravinsky, Fauré and contemporary popular music continued to be his sources, even in the devotional music (*Litanies à la vierge noire* for female voices and organ) and the larger sacred works (*Stabat mater*, *Gloria*). The songs include four cycles. But his output of instrumental music, apart from the many piano pieces of a private character, continued to be modest: his most important later orchestral piece is the G minor organ concerto with strings and timpani (1938), which journeys between Bach and the fairground, while his main chamber works were the sonatas for flute, oboe and clarinet.

Music for the stage also continued to occupy him. There was another ballet, *Les animaux modèles* (1942), scores for plays and films, and a new departure into opera, begun with the absurd Apollinaire piece *Les mamelles de Tirésias* and pursued with more seriousness in his deeply-felt tragedy of martyrdom, *Dialogues des Carmélites* (1957), as well as a setting of Cocteau's telephone monologue *La voix humaine* (1959).

Operas Les mamelles de Tirésias (1947); Dialogues des Carmélites (1957); La voix humaine (1959)
Other dramatic music Les biches, ballet (1924); Aubade, pf, 18 insts (1929); Les animaux modèles (1942); incidental music for 11 plays; 5 film scores
Orchestral music Concert champêtre, hpd, orch (1928); Conc. d, 2 pf, orch (1932); Conc., g, org, str, timp (1938); 8 others
Choral music Litanies à la vierge noire 1936); Mass, G (1937); Figure humaine (1943); Stabat mater (1950); Quatre motets pour le temps de Moël (1952); Gloria (1959); Sept répons des ténèbres (1961)
Solo vocal music 7 works with ens, incl. Le bestiaire (1919), Cocardes (1919), Le bal masqué (1932), La dame de Monte Carlo (1961); *c*50 works with pf, incl. Trois poèmes de Louise Lalanne (1931), Cinq poèmes (1935), Tel jour, telle nuit (1936–7), Fiançailles pour Rire (1939), La fraicheur et le feu (1950), La courte paille (1960); Colloque (1940), 2vv
Chamber and instrumental music Sextet, wind qnt, pf (1939); Vn Sonata (1943); Vc Sonata (1948); Fl Sonata (1956); Cl Sonata (1962); Ob Sonata (1962)
Piano music over 30 works, incl. Trois mouvements perpétuels (1918), Promenades (1921), [6] nocturnes (1938), [15] improvisations (1959), Les soirées de Nazelles (1936)

Pound, Ezra (Loomis) (*b* Hailey, ID, 30 Oct 1885; *d* Venice, 1 Nov 1972). American poet. He was concerned with music as a critic, an admirer of troubadour song and Antheil, a harmony theorist and as the composer of two operas: *The Testament of François Villon* and *Cavalcanti* (both 1923).

Pousseur, Henri (Léon Marie Thérèse) (*b* Malmedy, 23 June 1929). Belgian composer. He studied at the conservatories of Liège (1947–52) and Brussels (1952–3) and had contact with Froidebise and Souris, though more decisive was his meeting in 1951 with Boulez: from that time he was a leading figure in the European avant garde, teaching at Darmstadt (1957–67), Cologne (1963–8), in the USA and in Belgium. His early works owe much to the initiatives of Boulez and Stockhausen, but they already showed a feeling for harmonic consistency that was to become crucial (and to gain political overtones). Also important was the concept of mobile form, often allied with stylistic heterogeneity, as in the opera *Votre Faust* (1969), which in his own output has seemed less a 'work' than a source of derivatives (*Miroir de Votre Faust, Jeu de Miroirs de Votre Faust*), implying a view of the art work as endlessly mutable, even corrigible. His later works have tended to be for the most diverse media, ranging from symphony orchestra to electronic means, from solo cello in unusual tuning to improvising ensemble. He is a prolific writer, chiefly on 20th-century music and theory.

Powell, Mel (*b* New York, 12 Feb 1923). American composer. He was a pupil of Hindemith at Yale, where he taught (1958–69) before moving to the California Institute of the Arts. His works, in many genres, have used serial and electronic means, and several of them reflect his own experience as a jazz pianist.

Power, Leonel (*b* ?1370–85; *d* Canterbury, 5 June 1445). English composer. He shared with his younger contemporary Dunstable the leadership of English style in the early 15th century. He served in the household chapel of Thomas Duke of Clarence (*d* 1421) and in 1423 was admitted to the fraternity of Christ Church, Canterbury, where he was master of the choir that sang in the nave or Lady Chapel outside the monastic liturgy. 40 works are undisputedly attributed to him, and more mass movements and Marian compositions have conflicting ascriptions; he is not known to have written secular works, isorhythmic motets or canonic compositions. An elementary discant treatise by Power survives, supporting the idea that he may have been a teacher. His influence is notable in the Old Hall MS, which includes 23 works by him in the original layer. With Dunstable, he was a pioneer of the unified mass cycle. Power seems to have taken the initiative in pairing movements of the Ordinary, and at least one Ordinary cycle, *Alma Redemptoris mater*, can be ascribed to him. Power's Old Hall music covers most of the genres of his age, including simple descant settings, freely-composed pieces for four and five voices, isorhythmic mass movements and works in which a complex upper part is supported by slower-moving lower parts. The English love of full sonorities, the syncopated rhythms of the French Ars Nova and the proportional ingenuity of the Ars Subtilior are fused in Power's earlier works; his later motets lean towards the more equal-voiced, homogeneous texture of the succeeding generation of composers.

Sacred music Four-movement mass 'Alma redemptoris mater'; 2 other masses (authorship uncertain); 2 Gloria-Credo pairs; 2 Sanctus-Agnus pairs; *c*20 single mass movements; *c*15 other works

Pozzi Escot, (Olga) (*b* Lima, 1 Oct 1931). Peruvian composer. She studied at the Juilliard School and the Hamburg Musikhochschule, and has spent most of her life teaching in the USA. She composes generally for small forces, in a clear, meticulous, timbrally striking style, mathematically planned.

pp. Abbreviation for *pianissimo*, very quiet; *ppp* implies still quieter. *See* DYNAMICS.

Prades Festival (France). Annual (summer) festival. It was established in 1950, when eminent musicians were invited to Prades to play with Casals for the Bach bicentenary. Concerts are mainly of Classical and earlier works.

Praetorius, Christoph (*b* Bunzlau; *d* Lüneburg, 1609). German composer. He studied at Wittenberg (1551) and was Kantor at the Johanneum, Lüneburg, 1563–81, when deafness forced him to retire. A well-known musical figure, he published chorale motets and occasional pieces (1560–87) and a music textbook (1574).

Praetorius, Hieronymus (*b* Hamburg, 10 Aug 1560; *d* there, 27 Jan 1629). German composer. He was an organ pupil of his father Jacob (*c*1530–86), a copyist and organist of St Jacobi, Hamburg. After serving at Erfurt (1580–82) he assisted his father, succeeding him in 1586; he remained there until he died. A leading composer of sacred music, he wrote *c*100 motets (4 bks, 1599–1618), among the earliest Venetian-inspired polychoral works published in north Germany. Six masses (1616), nine Magnificats (1602) and some organ works also survive. His music editions include chorales (1604), the first to specify organ accompaniment.

Praetorius, Jacob (*b* Hamburg, 8 Feb 1586; *d* there, 21/22 Oct 1651). German composer, son of Hieronymus Praetorius. An organ pupil of Sweelinck, he was organist of St Petri, Hamburg, from 1603 until his death; Weckmann was among his pupils. He wrote large-scale organ works, chorale settings (1604, 1651) and wedding motets. His brother Johannes (*c*1595–1660) was also a Hamburg organist and a composer.

Praetorius, Michael (*b* Creuzburg an der Werra, 15 Feb ?1571; *d* Wolfenbüttel, 15 Feb 1621). German composer and theorist, nephew of Christoph Praetorius. The son of a strict Lutheran, he was educated at Torgau, Frankfurt an der Oder (1582) and Zerbst (1584). He was organist of St Marien, Frankfurt (1587–90), before moving to Wolfenbüttel, where he was court organist from 1595 and Kapellmeister from 1604. He temporarily served the Saxon court (1613–16), chiefly at Dresden, where he met Schütz and got to know the latest Italian music, and he worked in many other German cities. The most versatile German composer of his day, he was also one of the most prolific. His 21 extant sacred vocal publications include over 1000 Protestant hymn-based works (e.g. *Musae Sioniae*, 9 vols., 1605–10), many for multiple choirs, as well as Latin music for the Lutheran service, motets, psalms and instrumental dances (*Terpsichore*, 1612). His encyclopedic treatise *Syntagma musicum* (3 vols. pubd 1614–20), with detailed information on instruments and performing practice, is of immense documentary value. (For an illustration from this book, *see* EARLY MUSIC.)

Prague Quartet. Czech string quartet, led by Bretislav Novotný. Founded in 1955, it has toured widely, playing the standard classical repertory and a broad range of Czech music.

Prague Spring Festival (Czechoslovakia). Annual festival established in 1946 to attract musicians to the city after World War II. Events include opera, concerts and ballet.

Prague Symphony. Mozart's Symphony no.38 in D (1786), first performed during Mozart's visit to Prague in 1787.

Prague Symphony Orchestra. Czech orchestra founded in 1934 under Rudolf Pekárek; its conductors have included Smetáček and Neumann.

Pralltriller (Ger.). 'Compact trill': term for a trill of only four notes (or 'half-trill'). Ex.1 shows its nota-

Ex. 1

Ex. 2

tion (*a*); a common but strictly incorrect reading, appropriate only in fast passages, is shown in (*b*) and the correct reading in (*c*). Ex.2 shows another common context of the *Pralltriller*.

Pratella, Francesco Balilla (*b* Lugo di Romagna, 1 Feb 1880; *d* Ravenna, 17 May 1955). Italian composer. A pupil briefly of Mascagni at the Pesaro Liceo Musicale, in 1910 he became associated with the futurist movement as a prolific polemicist as well as a composer (e.g. the opera *L'aviatore Dro*, 1920). His later music, however, has more to do with Pizzetti and Romagnan folktunes. He directed the Licei Musicali at Lugo (1910–29) and Ravenna (1927–45).

Pratt, Silas G(amaliel) (*b* Addison, VT, 4 Aug 1846; *d* Pittsburgh, 30 Oct 1916). American composer. He worked in Chicago, partly as an organist, and studied under Bendel and Kullak in Berlin (1868–71) and later (1875–7) took lessons from Liszt. In 1888 he went to New York and in 1906 he founded the Pratt Institute of Music and Art in Pittsburgh. Two of his three operas, *Lucille* and *Zenobia, Queen of Palmyra* were produced in Chicago in the 1880s; he also wrote much orchestral and piano music.

Prausnitz, Frederik (William) (*b* Cologne, 26 Aug 1920). American conductor of German birth. After study at the Juilliard School he conducted the New England Conservatory SO, 1961–9, and was music director of the Syracuse SO, 1971–4. He became chief conductor of the Peabody Institute, Baltimore, from 1976. In the USA and Europe he is noted as a champion of contemporary music.

Precentor. One who leads the singing in church. In cathedrals the precentor is an important musical office among the clergy.

Pre-Classical. Term applied to the music immediately before the Classical era, i.e. the *galant* or Rococo period, represented by such composers as Vinci, Pergolesi, Hasse and J.C. Bach. More loosely it is sometimes used to signify any music before the late 18th century.

Predieri, Luca Antonio (*b* Bologna, 13 Sept 1688; *d* there, 3 Jan 1767). Italian composer. A violinist, he was *maestro di cappella* in several Bolognese churches including the cathedral (1728–31). After moving to Vienna he became *vicemaestro* of the court chapel in 1739 and succeeded Fux as its director in 1741. He composed oratorios, other sacred music and *c*30 operas, mainly given in Florence and Vienna.

Several other members of Predieri's family were musicians, but some of the relationships are unclear. Giacomo (Maria) (1611–95) was organist at the cathedral in Bologna, 1679–93, a cornettist and founder of the Accademia Filarmonica. His nephew Antonio (*c*1650–1710) was a tenor singer taking character parts in operas. Angelo (1655–1731) was a singer, composer and *maestro di cappella*, and teacher of G.B. Martini. Giacomo Cesare (1671–1753), another nephew of Giacomo and an uncle of Luca Antonio, was a composer (notably of oratorios), singer and *maestro di cappella* at six Bologna institutions. Giovanni Battista (*fl* 1730–55) was a composer and *maestro di cappella*.

Preghiera (It.). 'Prayer': term for the number in many 19th-century operas in which a character prays for divine help; Desdemona's 'Ave Maria' in Verdi's *Otello* is an example.

Preindl, Josef (*b* Marbach, 30 Jan 1756; *d* Vienna, 26 Oct 1823). Austrian composer. He held a series of organists' posts in Vienna before becoming vice-Kapellmeister of St Stephen's Cathedral in 1795 and Kapellmeister (succeeding his teacher Albrechtsberger) in 1809. He was also a popular piano teacher. He wrote sacred music, songs, piano pieces and a music theory manual (1827).

Prelleur, Peter (*b c*1705; *d* London, 1741). English organist and composer. He was organist at Christ Church, Spitalfields (from 1735), and theatre harpsichordist and composer in London. He wrote three stage works, songs, hymns and concertos, but is chiefly remembered for his introduction to singing and instructions for playing various instruments in *The Modern Musick-Master* (1731), which also includes a history of music and a dictionary.

Prelude (Fr. *prélude*; Ger. *Vorspiel*; It. *preludio*; Lat. *praeludium, praeambulum*). An instrumental movement intended to precede a larger work or group of pieces. Preludes evolved from improvisations made by players to test the tuning, touch or tone of their instruments and by church organists to establish the pitch and mode of the music to be sung during the liturgy. The oldest to survive are in Adam

Ileborgh's tablature of 1448, Paumann's *Funda-mentum organisandi* (1452) and the Buxheim Orgelbuch (1460–70); 16th-century sources contain many more. Unattached preludes in an improvis-atory style continued to be written after 1600, but during the 17th century and the first half of the 18th the prelude followed by a fugue or a suite of dances became the predominant type. The prelude and fugue is a mainly German form which reached its highest point of development in Bach's organ works and his '48'. The improvisatory element is absent from many of Bach's preludes but is to the fore in the PRÉLUDE NON MESURÉ with which French composers often prefaced their suites.

Few preludes date from the Classical period, but the attached prelude reappeared in 19th-century Bach-influenced works such as Mendelssohn's Six Preludes and Fugues op.35, Liszt's Prelude and Fugue on B–A–C–H and Brahms's two preludes and fugues for organ. More typical of the Romantic period was the set of independent preludes for piano. Hummel's set of 24 'in the major and minor keys' op.67 (*c*1814–15) was followed by Chopin's op.28 (1836–9), which in turn served as a model for those of Heller (op.81), Alkan (op.31), Cui (op.64) and Busoni (op.37). Rakhmaninov's, although issued under three different opus numbers (3, 23 and 32), also embrace all 24 keys. The idea of a prelude as a non-programmatic characteristic piece for piano was taken up by such composers as Skrya-bin, Szymanowski, Shostakovich and Martinů. Debussy's two sets have descriptive titles, which are otherwise rare. His *Prélude à l'après-midi d'un faune* is an orchestral tone poem.

For chorale preludes, *see* CHORALE.

Prélude non mesuré (Fr.). Term for 17th-century French harpsichord preludes written without orthodox indications of rhythm and metre. The notation as devised by Louis Couperin consists of a succession of unbarred semibreves, with slurs indicating sustained notes (as in ex.1) or notes with ornamental significance or melodic importance (ex.1, at asterisk), or isolating notes from what pre-cedes and follows. Lebègue preferred a more precise indication of note values but Marchand, Cléram-bault and Rameau followed D'Anglebert's system, which uses bar-lines to mark off significant musical sentences, quavers to indicate a melodic (rather than a rapid) arpeggio and semiquavers for ornamental notes (ex.2). Most unmeasured preludes are either

toccatas, relating to those of Frescobaldi and Froberger, or elegiac *tombeaux*.

Ex. 2 D'Anglebert: Prelude no.2

Préludes. 24 piano pieces by Debussy, in two books (1910, 1913), each piece having a descriptive title.

Préludes, Les. Symphonic poem by Liszt (1848, re-vised 1854) after Lamartine.

Preparation. In part-writing, the 'softening' of the dissonant effect of an accented non-harmonic note (i.e. an appoggiatura) by presenting it as a consonant note in the previous chord (a 'prepared appog-giatura').

Prepared piano. A piano in which the pitches, tim-bres and dynamic responses of individual notes have been altered with screws, rubber erasers and other objects placed between the strings. The technique was developed by John Cage for his *Bacchanale* (1940).

Prés, Josquin des. *See* JOSQUIN DESPREZ.

Pressenda, Joannes Franciscus (*b* ?1777; *d* Turin, 1854). Italian violin maker, who with his pupil Joseph Rocca is regarded as the finest Italian violin maker of the 19th century. He worked in Turin and produced instruments with rich orange or red varnish.

Presser, Theodore (*b* Pittsburgh, 3 July 1848; *d* Phil-adelphia, 27 Oct 1925). American publisher and musical philanthropist. In 1883 he founded the monthly magazine *The Etude* and established a music publishing business at Philadelphia (moving to Bryn Mawr in 1949), which through acquisitions and agencies maintains a huge stock of classical, educational and light music. Among the American composers represented are Babbitt, Carter, Cowell, Ives, Piston and Riegger.

Preston, Jørgen (*d* Copenhagen, by 28 Nov 1553). Composer, presumably of Netherlands origin, active

Ex. 1 Louis Couperin: Prelude no. 6

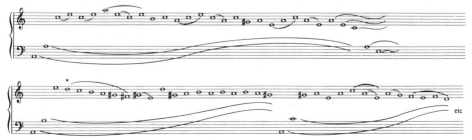

in Denmark. He led Christian III's chapel choir (1551–3), and may previously have been in Duke Albrecht's service. The most productive foreign composer at the Danish court, he composed six Latin motets, ten German hymns and three instrumental canons. Much of his music uses *cantus firmi*, but the instrumental pieces are more interesting.

Presto (It.). Quick, fast; hence *prestissimo*, very fast.

Preston, Simon (John) (*b* Bournemouth, 4 Aug 1938). English organist. He studied at the RAM and Cambridge and was sub-organist at Westminster Abbey, 1962–7. He was organist and lecturer in music at Christ Church, Oxford, 1970–81, conducting notable recordings of choral music by Walton and Haydn. From 1981 to 1987 he was organist and master of the choristers at Westminster Abbey. A perfectionist with an instinct for colour in registration, he is a leading interpreter of Liszt's organ music and Handel's concertos.

Preston, Thomas (*d* ?Windsor, after 1559). English composer. He may have been organist and choirmaster at Magdalen College, Oxford, in 1543. A Preston was organist and choirmaster at Trinity College, Cambridge (1548–52, 1554–9), and also organist at St George's Chapel, Windsor (1558–9). His surviving music is for organ, all for the Latin liturgy, and features virtuoso keyboard technique.

Prêtre, Georges (*b* Waziers, 14 Aug 1924). French conductor. He studied at the Paris Conservatoire and under Cluytens and conducted in provincial French opera houses from 1946. His Paris début was at the Opéra-Comique in *Capriccio*; he appeared at the Opéra in 1960, in London the next year and at the Met in 1964. He worked much with Callas, with whom he recorded *Tosca* and *Carmen*, and is a noted interpreter of Poulenc's music.

Previn, André (George) (*b* Berlin, 6 April 1929). American conductor, pianist and composer of German birth. He studied in Berlin and at the Paris Conservatoire and moved to Los Angeles in 1939. His early career was in the film industry and as a jazz pianist. He made his conducting début in 1963 and was conductor-in-chief of the Houston SO, 1967–70. From 1965 he has been heard with the LSO (principal conductor, 1969–79), notably in strongly coloured late Romantic or early 20th-century music. He conducted the Pittsburg SO, 1976–86, and became music director of the Los Angeles PO in 1986. He has composed musicals and orchestral and chamber works.

Previtali, Fernando (*b* Adria, 16 Feb 1907; *d* Rome, 1 Aug 1985). Italian conductor and composer. After study at the Turin Conservatory he became associated with Gui, assisting him in establishing the Maggio Musicale Fiorentino. He conducted modern music with the Rome Radio SO and took the S Cecilia Orchestra on many foreign tours. He also appeared with the Cleveland Orchestra and has held appointments in opera houses in Turin, Genoa and Naples.

Prévost, André (*b* St Jérôme, 30 July 1934). Canadian composer. He was a pupil of Pépin at the Montreal Conservatory and of Messiaen and Dutilleux in Paris (1960–63). In 1964 he was appointed professor at the Montreal Conservatory. He quickly established himself as an important, lively force in Canadian music, notably with *Fantasmes* (1963) and *Pyknon* (1966) for orchestra.

Prey, Hermann (*b* Berlin, 11 July 1929). German baritone. He sang at the Hamburg Staatsoper from 1953 and in Vienna from 1957. At the Met he sang Wagner's Wolfram in 1960, repeating the role at his Bayreuth début in 1965. From 1959 he has been heard at the Salzburg Festival, notably as Mozart's Figaro, Guglielmo and Papageno. His genial manner and mellifluous tone make him a popular lieder singer.

Pribaoutki. Work by Stravinsky, a setting of four Russian rhymes for male voice and ensemble (1914).

Přibyl, Vilém (*b* Náchod, 10 April 1925). Czech tenor. He made his début in 1952 and joined the Brno Opera in 1961, singing heroic tenor parts. He sang at many international festivals and at Covent Garden; his roles include Othello, Don José and Florestan but he has had outstanding success in the Czech repertory.

Price, (Mary Violet) Leontyne (*b* Laurel, MS, 10 Feb 1927). American soprano. She studied at the Juilliard School and made an early success as Gershwin's Bess, the role of her London début in 1952. She was best known as an interpreter of Verdi, singing Aida in Europe from 1958. In 1966 she sang Barber's Cleopatra in the production that opened the new Met at Lincoln Center.

Price, Margaret (Berenice) (*b* Blackwood, 13 April 1941). Welsh soprano. She made her début with the Welsh National Opera as Cherubino in 1962, the role of her Covent Garden début the next year. Other successful Mozart roles have been Constanze and Fiordiligi (notably at Glyndebourne), Pamina (1969, San Francisco début) and Donna Anna (1971, Cologne). Her full, creamy lyric soprano has also been heard in many Verdi roles, and she has recorded Isolde. She is equally at home as a recitalist, often accompanied by the conductor James Lockhart.

Prick-song. Term of the 15th and 16th centuries to signify the notation of mensural music; hence the music itself.

Prigioniero, Il. Opera in a prologue and one act by Dallapiccola to his own libretto after Villiers de l'Isle Adam and Charles de Coster (broadcast 1949; 1950, Florence).

Prima donna (It.). 'First lady': term for the principal female singer in an opera cast or an opera company. The term has been used for the leading singer since the mid-17th century. Normally the *prima donna* is a soprano, singing the role of the heroine; but in a few operas (notable examples are Rossini's *Il barbiere di Siviglia* and Saint-Saëns's *Samson et Dalila*) she is a mezzo-soprano. Sometimes such expressions as 'prima donna assoluta' ('absolute first lady') are used to distinguish the *prima donna* from any other possible claimant to the role. The term has entered the non-musical vocabulary as an expression for anyone who behaves in an outrageously egotistical manner.

Prima prattica (It.). 'First practice': term first used in the early 17th century to distinguish the Renaissance polyphonic style from the new style (*seconda prattica*) of Caccini, Monteverdi and others.

Prima volta (It.: 'first time'). Term for the first-time bar, or first ending, in a repeated passage; *seconda volta* denotes the second-time bar. They are usually numbered 1 and 2.

Primo musico (It.). 'First musician': term used in the 17th and 18th centuries for the leading singer in an opera cast or an opera company, normally a castrato.

Primo uomo (It.). 'First man': the principal male singer in the cast of an opera or in an opera company; when first used, in the late 17th century, the term normally denoted the leading castrato, but later it was applied to leading tenors.

Primrose, William (*b* Glasgow, 23 Aug 1904; *d* Provo, UT, 1 May 1982). Scottish viola player. He studied the violin in Glasgow, at the GSM and under Ysaÿe, who advised him to change to the viola. He played in a quartet and was chosen by Toscanini as principal viola for the NBC SO (1937–42). Later he taught at the universities of Southern California, Indiana, Tokyo and at Brigham Young University. He produced a tone of rare sweetness and beauty and induced several composers to write for him, notably Bartók (his Viola Concerto), Britten, Milhaud and Rochberg.

Prin, Jean-Baptiste (*b* England, *c*1669; *d* Strasbourg, after 1742). French performer and composer. Active mostly in Lyons, he was a prominent performer on the trumpet marine, for which he composed many works in a simple style, and wrote a method (1742). He was also a teacher and dancing-master.

Prince Igor. Opera in four acts and a prologue by Borodin to his own libretto after Vladimir Stasov. Borodin worked on it 1869–70, 1874–87, but left it unfinished; Rimsky-Korsakov and Glazunov completed and orchestrated much of it (1890, St Petersburg).

Prince of the Pagodas, The. Ballet in three acts by Britten (1957, London).

Princesse de Navarre, La. *Comédie-ballet* in three acts by Rameau to a libretto by Voltaire (1745, Paris).

Princess Ida. Operetta in two acts by Sullivan to a libretto by Gilbert (1884, London).

Principal. Term for an organ stop; originally (*c*1500–1700) it denoted the diapason chorus but from the 18th century it usually signified a 4′ stop. In 20th-century Germany, *Prinzipal* stands for basic 8′ tone.

Principale. Term for the lower register of the natural trumpet, from its lowest note (*C*) to *c″* (as opposed to the clarino register, from *c″* upwards). The term also stood for a style of playing, with a strong tone and a rapid tongue technique. In the field the *principale* trumpet was used for signals.

Prinner, Johann Jacob (*b* ?Münzbach, 1624; *d* Vienna, 18 March 1694). Austrian composer. An organist, he first held posts at Kremsmünster and Graz and in 1680–85 was chamberlain to Archduchess Maria Antonia in Vienna. He was also a poet. He wrote songs in a popular style, suites, and a treatise which includes instructions on violin playing.

Printemps. Symphonic suite by Debussy for orchestra and female chorus (1887).

Printing. The printing of music, because it involves a variety of symbols, some of which need to be presented as if superimposed, developed more slowly than the printing of literary material. The earliest printed music came in liturgical books, in the 1470s; most early examples show staff lines in red with notes printed in black. These were produced by two impressions from blocks of wood (or occasionally metal) cut in relief. The use of wood or metal blocks continued in the early 16th century, and was occasionally used much later, even into the 19th century. The first music to be printed in America, the *Bay Psalm Book* (Boston, 1698) was printed from woodblocks.

In 1501 Ottaviano Petrucci, working in Venice, printed the first mensural music. His *Harmonice musices odhecaton A*, 96 pieces for three or four voices, was printed from movable type. His printing method involved three (later two) impressions, for the staves, for the notes and for the text. The first music printed by single impression was a short item produced by John Rastell in London, *c*1526, but it was Pierre Attaingnant of Paris, publisher of many books of *chansons* from 1527–8 onwards, who set the example in single-impression printing. The single-impression process involved casting each note, its stem and a fragment from the staff-lines on the same unit of type. Notes at this period were lozenge-shaped or square, with centred stems; during the 16th century engravers designed round notes (corresponding with contemporary calligraphy) but these were not universally used until the late 17th century. Music printing from movable type remained in use during much of the 17th century and the 18th, and persisted in some kinds of publication into the 19th and even the 20th, by which time the fragmentary staff-lines and uneven beaming of much of the early and inferior work had given way to music of a clear and smooth appearance.

Movable type, however, was inadequate for some kinds of music, particularly keyboard music with rapid notes and chords and florid instrumental or vocal lines. The closest analogy to the hand of the copyist was the hand of the engraver, wielding a steel point on a copper plate. Engraving ('intaglio') had been used for printing in the 15th century and was adapted to music in the 1530s, though only for lute tablature; for mensural music it was used late in the 16th century, notably by Simone Verovio of Rome, in music for voices or keyboard or lute. The technique was quickly taken up in England and the Low Countries and, in the late 17th century, in France and Germany. The process involves taking a metal plate (copper or, later, pewter), planning the layout in detail, then marking the staff-lines, the note-heads, the stems and various symbols (clefs, accidentals etc), either by scoring with a steel point (sometimes acid was used for deeper etching) or by using a series of punches; traditions differed between periods, countries and individual workshops. The music could then be printed direct from the plate on a press. At the beginning of the 18th century, Paris, London and Amsterdam were the largest centres of music publishing; later in the century and in the 19th, Vienna and particularly Leipzig became increasingly important.

In 1796 a process called lithography was invented

by Alois Senefelder. This is based on the principle that a surface (originally of stone, but many other substances were used) could be prepared in such a way that some parts of it would accept a greasy ink and others would not; the image of music could be inscribed on such a surface and it could then be used for the printing of further copies. This offset process has remained the basis for music printing, though today the 'stone' is normally prepared photographically. The process of origination of the image, however, is still needed, and engraving remains one of the principal methods; others in use today include transfers ('Notaset'), stencils, music typewriters and various computer-based systems.

Printz, Wolfgang Caspar (*b* Waldthurn, 10 Oct 1641; *d* Žary, 13 Oct 1717). German music theorist. In the early 1660s he travelled in Italy; his main post was as Kantor at Žary, from 1665. His work greatly influenced later German writers; his *Phrynis Mitilenaeus* (1676–9) was one of the most extensive summaries of music theory of its time, and his *Historische Beschreibung* (1690) was the major history of German music. Several novels are attributed to Printz, but none of his music is known to survive.

Prinz von Homburg, Der. Opera in three acts by Henze to a libretto by Bachmann after Kleist (1960, Hamburg).

Prioris, Johannes (*b* ?Brabant, *c*1460; *d c*1514). Franco-Netherlands composer. He was *maître de chapelle* to Louis XII. A follower of Ockeghem, he was named among the best-known contemporary musicians. His works, which include one of the earliest-known polyphonic settings of the Mass for the Dead, five other masses, six Magnificats, motets and *chansons*, show him to have been a polished musician capable of using the wide variety of current compositional techniques.

Pritchard, Sir John (Michael) (*b* London, 5 Feb 1921). English conductor. He worked at Glyndebourne from 1947 and conducted three Mozart operas there in 1951; he was musical director, 1969–78. He first conducted at Covent Garden in 1952, giving there the premières of Britten's *Gloriana* (1953) and Tippett's *The Midsummer Marriage* (1955). He has been associated with the Royal Liverpool PO and the LPO and in 1978 became principal conductor of Cologne Opera.

Priuli, Giovanni (*b* Venice, *c*1575; *d* 1629). Italian composer. A pupil of G. Gabrieli, he moved to Graz in 1614–15 as Hofkapellmeister to Archduke Ferdinand and continued to serve him in 1619–22 after he became emperor. His teacher's influence is apparent in his five volumes of sacred music, which include instrumental works for church use. He also composed five volumes of secular music. The composer Marieta Morosina Priuli (*fl*1665) was probably related to him by marriage.

Prix de Rome. Composition prize established in 1803 by the Institut de France, awarded annually up to 1968. It involved a period of study in Rome; winners have included Berlioz, Gounod, Bizet, Massenet and Debussy.

Pro Arte Quartet. Belgian string quartet, originally led by Alphonse Onnou. Founded in 1912, it gave lucid performances of works by Bartók, Martinů and Milhaud as well as the classical repertory, and appeared in Britain and the USA from 1925. In the 1930s it made many pioneer recordings of Haydn's quartets. It moved to the USA in 1940; Rudolf Kolisch was leader from 1944 until its disbandment in 1947.

Prodigal Son, The. Britten's third church parable (op.81) to a text by William Plomer (1968, Aldeburgh).

Ballet (*Bludnïy sin*) in three acts by Prokofiev to a scenario by Kochno (1929, Paris).

Oratorio by Sullivan to his own text (1869, Worcester).

Programme music. Music of a narrative or descriptive kind. The term was introduced by Liszt, who defined a programme as 'a preface added to a piece of instrumental music . . . to direct [the listener's] attention to the poetical idea of the whole or to a particular part of it'. Programme music, which has been contrasted with ABSOLUTE MUSIC, is distinguished by its attempt to depict objects and events. The concept is much older than Liszt. Kuhnau's six Bible sonatas (1700) are each preceded by a summary of what the music is meant to convey, and the 'programmes' of Vivaldi's 'Four Seasons' concertos are contained in sonnets appended to the music.

By Beethoven's time even the most abstract and classical of musical forms had become capable of bearing a programmatic meaning. The Pastoral Symphony and the 'Lebewohl' Sonata op.81*a* both have precedents, in the 18th-century depictions of Nature and in Bach's capriccio for his departing brother. The decisive step towards programme music of a subjective, Romantic kind was taken by Berlioz. By his use of the solo viola in *Harold en Italie* and of the IDÉE FIXE there and in the *Symphonie fantastique*, he was able to distinguish between the individual protagonist and the external circumstances of his experience. The *idée fixe* was a substantial step towards the Wagnerian LEITMOTIF by means of which Liszt and Strauss, in the SYMPHONIC POEM, were able to associate specific themes with a fixed representational meaning.

The 'programme' as a basic determining idea in symphonic music gave rise to many of the great works of Czech and Russian nationalism, to Mahler's symphonies and to the French school of orchestral writing, and survived into the 20th century, receiving no serious intellectual setback until the reaction led by Schoenberg, Bartók and Stravinsky. Composers then tended to turn their backs on programme music and find their way to expression through more abstract musical means; but in the 1960s and 1970s some revival of programmatic devices could be noted in works by younger composers.

Progression. A succession of chords or chord-like constructions having a coherence as an expression of harmony ('chord progression', 'harmonic progression'), especially one based on a familiar pattern ('blues progression').

Progressive jazz. Term applied to attempts, chiefly in the 1940s and 1950s, to continue and extend the jazz orchestral tradition; it is generally associated with the work of Stan Kenton.

Prokofiev, Sergey (Sergeyevich) (*b* Sontsovka, 27 April 1891; *d* Moscow, 5 March 1953). Russian composer. He showed precocious talent as a pianist and composer and had lessons from Glier from 1902. In 1904 he entered the St Petersburg Conservatory, where Rimsky-Korsakov, Lyadov and Tcherepnin were among his teachers; Tcherepnin and Myaskovsky, who gave him valuable support, encouraged his interest in Skryabin, Debussy and Strauss. He had made his début as a pianist in 1908, quickly creating something of a sensation as an *enfant terrible*, unintelligible and ultra-modern – an image he was happy to cultivate. His intemperateness in his early piano pieces, and later in such works as the extravagantly Romantic Piano Concerto no.1 and the ominous no.2, attracted attention. Then in 1914 he left the conservatory and travelled to London, where he heard Stravinsky's works and gained a commission from Dyagilev: the resulting score was, however, rejected (the music was used to make the *Scythian Suite*); a second attempt, *Chout*, was not staged until 1921.

Meanwhile his gifts had exploded in several different directions. In 1917 he finished an opera on Dostoyevsky's *Gambler*, a violently involved study of obsession far removed from the fantasy of his nearly contemporary Chicago opera *The Love for Three Oranges*, written in 1919 and performed in 1921. Nor does either of these scores have much to do with his 'Classical' Symphony, selfconsciously 18th-century in manner, and again quite distinct from his lyrical Violin Concerto no.1, written at the same period and in the same key. There were also piano sonatas based on old notebooks alongside the more adventurous *Visions fugitives*, all dating from 1915–19.

Towards the end of this rich period, in 1918, he left for the USA; then from 1920 France became his base. His productivity slowed while he worked at his opera *The Fiery Angel*, an intense, symbolist fable of good and evil (it had no complete performance until after his death, and he used much of its music in Symphony no.3). After this he brought the harsh, heavy and mechanistic elements in his music to a climax in Symphony no.2 and in the ballet *Le pas d'acier*, while his next ballet, *L'enfant prodigue*, is in a much gentler style: the barbaric and the lyrical were still alternatives in his music and not fused until the 1930s, when he began a process of reconciliation with the Soviet Union.

The renewed relationship was at first tentative on both sides. *Romeo and Juliet*, the full-length ballet commissioned for the Bol'shoy, had its première at Brno in 1938, and only later became a staple of the Soviet repertory: its themes of aggression and romantic love provided, as also did the Eisenstein film *Alexander Nevsky*, a receptacle for Prokofiev's divergent impulses. Meanwhile his own impulse to remain a Westerner was gradually eroded and in 1936 he settled in Moscow, where initially his concern was with the relatively modest genres of song, incidental music, patriotic cantata and children's

entertainment (*Peter and the Wolf*, 1936). He had, indeed, arrived at a peculiarly unfortunate time, when the drive towards socialist realism was at its most intense; and his first work of a more ambitious sort, the opera *Semyon Kotko*, was not liked.

With the outbreak of war, however, he perhaps found the motivation to respond to the required patriotism: implicitly in a cycle of three piano sonatas (nos.6–8) and Symphony no.5, more openly in his operatic setting of scenes from Tolstoy's *War and Peace*, which again offered opportunities for the two extremes of his musical genius to be expressed. He also worked at a new full-length ballet, *Cinderella*. In 1946 he retired to the country and though he went on composing, the works of his last years have been regarded as a quiet coda to his output. Even his death was outshone by that of Stalin on the same day.

Operas The Gambler (1917, perf. 1929); The Love for Three Oranges (1921); The Fiery Angel (1923, perf. 1954); Semyon Kotko (1940); War and Peace (1943, perf. 1957); The Story of a Real Man (1948, perf. 1960)

Ballets Chout (1921); Le pas d'acier (1927); L'enfant prodigue (1929); Sur le Borysthène (1932); Romeo and Juliet (1938); Cinderella (1945); The Tale of the Stone Flower (1954)

Film scores Lieutenant Kijé (1933); Alexander Nevsky, Mez, chorus, orch (1938); Ivan the Terrible 1945)

Orchestral music Sym. no.1, 'Classical', D (1917); Sym. no.2, d (1925); Sym. no.3, c (1928); Sym. no.4, C (1930); Sym. no.5, B♭ (1944); Sym. no.6, E♭ (1947); Sym. no.7, c♯ (1952); Pf Conc. no.1, D♭ (1912); Pf Conc. no.2, g (1913); Pf Conc. no.3, C (1921); Pf Conc. no.4, B♭ (1931); Pf Conc. no.5, G (1932); Vn Conc. no.1, D (1917); Vn Conc. no.2, g (1935); Scythian Suite (1915); Vc Conc., e (1938), rev. as Sym. Conc. (1952); Peter and the Wolf, narrator, orch (1936); Vc Concertino, g (1952)

Chamber music Qnt, g, ob, cl, vn, va, db (1924); 2 str qts, b, F (1930, 1941); Vn Sonata, f (1946); Fl/Vn Sonata, D (1943); Vc Sonata, C (1949)

Piano music Sonata no.1, f (1909); Sonata no.2, d (1912); Sonata no.3, a (1917); Sonata no.4, c (1917); Sonata no.5, C (1923); Sonata no.6, A (1940); Sonata no.7, B♭ (1942); Sonata no.8, B♭ (1944); Sonata no.9, C (1947); Sarcasms (1914); Visions fugitives (1917)

Vocal music cantatas, songs, partsongs, folksong arrs.

Proksch, Joseph (*b* Liberec, 4 Aug 1794; *d* Prague, 20 Dec 1864). Czech-Austrian teacher. In 1830 he opened his *Musikbildungsanstalt* in Prague, a progressive institution contributing much to the city's musical life; Smetana was among his pupils.

Prolation (Lat. *prolatio*). In early mensural notation, the relationship between semibreve and minim.

Prologue. The introductory scene to a dramatic work, usually explaining the context and meaning of what follows. Prologues were a usual feature of Baroque opera, the earliest being for only one character, usually Tragedia (Rinuccini, Peri's *Euridice*) or Musica (Monteverdi's *L'Orfeo*). By the mid-17th century it was customary for several allegorical characters to appear. Topical prologues, such as Quinault's for Lully's *Alceste* (1674), were usually political allegories designed to show the ruler (in this case, Louis XIV) in a favourable light.

Prologues became less common in the 18th century, but Naples had an important tradition of operatic prologues during the monarchy (1734–82) and later composers and librettists have occasionally provided them. Leoncavallo's *Pagliacci* opens with a prologue explicitly modelled on those of ancient drama, and 20th-century examples range from the brief spoken prologue of Stravinsky's *Oedipus rex* to the lion-taming scene that sets the tone for Berg's *Lulu*.

Promenade concerts. Informal concerts at which cheap tickets are sold for standing room for a large part of the audience; the most famous are the HENRY WOOD PROMENADE CONCERTS.

Prometheus. Symphonic poem by Liszt (revised 1855).

Prometheus, the Poem of Fire [Prometei, Poema Ogyma]. Symphonic poem, op.60, by Skryabin (1910), for orchestra with piano, optional chorus, and colour organ (projecting colours).

Pro Musica Antiqua. Belgian ensemble of singers and instrumentalists. Formed in 1933 by the conductor Safford Cape, it specialized in 13th- to 16th-century music, making many influential recordings and touring throughout Europe and the Americas. It disbanded in 1974.

See also NEW YORK PRO MUSICA.

Proper chants. Chants from the Mass and Office whose texts vary from day to day, as distinct from those whose texts remain constant (ORDINARY CHANTS). It chiefly refers to the Mass chants INTROIT, GRADUAL, ALLELUIA, TRACT, OFFERTORY and COMMUNION, which are usually sung as plainchant.

Prophète, Le. Opera in five acts by Meyerbeer to a libretto by Scribe (1849, Paris).

Proportion. The relationship between numbers for pitches and time-units; for pitches, *see* INTERVAL. In time-units, the word refers to the system of time signatures which indicate proportional alteration of note values in 15th- and 16th-century music. It might affect one voice, or several, or all voices, for a short passage or an entire piece.

Proportz (Ger.). 16th- and 17th-century term for an after-dance derived from a duple-metre dance by the application of *proportio sesquialtera*, three notes in the after-dance taking the time of two in the model.

Prosa. A text for a sequence, usually in Latin and constructed largely in 'couplets' (two lines of text set to the same music). The term is first applied regularly to sequence texts in 10th-century MSS although it was also used for texts of other kinds of chant or as underlay for melismas. In the early repertory (*c*850–1000) *prosae* neither scanned nor rhymed, but later they did both, becoming almost indistinguishable from verse. They were regularly sung rather than recited, and were composed in a wide variety of styles, from works of little literary value to the exquisite 12th-century meditations on sacred subjects, in rhyme and scansion, by Adam of St Victor's.

Prosdocimus de Beldemandis (*b* ?Padua; *d* there, 1428). Italian theorist. He studied at Bologna and Padua universities where he subsequently taught. His first musical treatise (1404) is a commentary on the work of the French theorist Johannes de Muris. Subsequent works cover aspects of late medieval music theory, from proportions of intervals and ratios between rhythmic values, the rules of counterpoint and matters of 14th-century Italian notation (by then submerged in the French system). In 1425 he attacked Marchetto da Padova's division of the tone into five equal parts. Though inclined to favour older theorists and practice, his writings offer much valuable information about early 15th-century Italian music.

Proses lyriques. Songs by Debussy, four settings for voice and piano of his own texts (1893).

Prosula. Term used for a text created to fit a melisma in Gregorian chant (other medieval terms include 'prosa', 'tropus' and 'verba'). There are prosulas for chants in the Ordinary and Proper of the Mass and the Office. Always strictly syllabic (one syllable to each note of the melisma), they seem to have served two purposes: to enrich the liturgy with new devotional texts and to make it easier to memorize the melodies. The best known are for the Kyrie, but those for offertory verses and alleluias proliferated in the 10th and 11th centuries. Prosulas for the Office are confined to the responsories of Vespers and Matins.

Prota. Italian family of musicians, active in Naples. Ignazio (1690–1748) taught at the Neapolitan conservatory S Onofrio a Capuana, where Jommelli was among his pupils. He composed four operas for Naples. Of his sons, Tommaso (*d* after 1768) composed stage and other vocal works and sonatas, sinfonie etc, and Giuseppe (1737–1807) was oboist in the Naples royal chapel. Ignazio's grandson Gabriele (1755–1843) was a *maestro di cappella* and a composer of operas and sacred works; his son Giovanni (*c*1786–?1843) wrote church music, operas and instrumental pieces.

Provenzale, Francesco (*b* Naples, *c*1626; *d* there, 6 Sept 1704). Italian composer. Active in Naples, he had operas staged between 1654 and 1674 and became city *maestro di cappella* in 1665; he was later *maestro di cappella* to the treasury of S Gennaro (1686–99) and served for two periods at the viceregal court. An important teacher, he worked as chief *maestro* at the conservatories S Maria di Loreto (1663–75) and the Turchini (1675–1701). He was the first prominent Neapolitan musician to compose opera and forerunner of the Neapolitan school of the 18th century. *Il schiavo di sua moglie* (1671) and *La Stellidaura vendicata* (1674), which survive complete, are largely modelled on the style of Venetians such as Cesti, but also include melodies of a dance-like, popular character. Provenzale wrote at least six other operas (two may have been adaptations of Cavalli's), secular cantatas and sacred music.

Prowo, Pierre (*b* Altona, 8 April 1697; *d* there, 8 Nov 1757). German organist and composer. He was organist in Altona and composed mostly instrumental music, including chamber concertos for wind and mixed ensembles, and sonatas.

Prozession. Work by Stockhausen for live electronic ensemble (1967), the score containing instructions for performing and adapting passages from the composer's earlier works.

Prunières, Henry (*b* Paris, 24 May 1886; *d* Nanterre, 11 April 1942). French musicologist. He studied in Paris, where he taught (1909–14). He founded and directed (to 1939) the *Revue musicale* and from 1921 its series of concerts (largely of contemporary music). His writings centre on 17th-century French music, above all Lully, whose importance he diagnosed and of whose music he began a collected edition.

Prussian. Title given to C.P.E. Bach's Six Sonatas for keyboard w48 (1742) and Haydn's six string quartets op.50 (1787), because of their dedications to Prussian royalty. Mozart's string quartets in D K575, B♭ K589 and F K590 are similarly named.

Psalm. Ancient Greek term for 'striking' or 'plucking', given to the verses of the Hebrew 'Book of Praises' (i.e. the biblical *Psalms*) by the translators of the Septuagint. The numbering of the Hebrew text, followed in the Authorized Version and most other Protestant versions, differs from that of the Septuagint and the Vulgate, as shown in Table 1.

TABLE 1

Masoretic, Protestant	Septuagint, Vulgate, Roman Catholic
1 8	1 8
9 10	9
11 113	10 112
114 15	113
116 vv. 1 9	114
116 vv. 10–19	115
117 46	116–45
147 vv. 1 11	146
147 vv. 12 29	147
148 50	148 50

In the Temple, the psalms were chanted daily by professional singers (Levites), with instruments. In the Eastern churches they are seldom sung entire; in Western churches they are sung complete or a few verses of a psalm are sung in an antiphonal or responsorial chant.

The history of Western psalmody has three stages. Up to the Edict of Milan (AD313), the psalms were interspersed with lessons. By the time of Gregory I (*c*600), the Mass and Office had assumed a fixed shape and antiphonal psalmody (the chanting of a psalm alternately by two choirs) and responsorial psalmody (when the congregation responded to a psalm sung by a cantor) were institutionalized. The distinction between these types later faded.

The stabilization of psalmody between Gregory I and the 11th century is known from the service book for Mass and Office, theoretical writings and the tonaries, which categorized chants by mode and specified the ending of the psalm tone for each antiphon. In Gregorian chant there are eight such tones, one for each church mode.

In the 16th century, Protestant churches encouraged congregational psalm singing by adopting metrical versions in the vernacular. An important early translation was Clément Marot's, the basis of the Calvinist psalter. A repertory of tunes came into being; these were set in a simple chordal style in collections which included Loys Bourgeois's complete psalter (1563), widely recognized as a standard version. Some later settings were more contrapuntal; Le Jeune and others dropped the tunes and composed what amounted to free motets.

In England, after the Catholic Mary Tudor's reign (1553–8), metrical psalms became popular, the standard psalter being that of Sternhold and Hopkins. Other metrical psalters included that of Archbishop Parker (1567), for which Tallis provided several harmonized tunes.

In the Roman church only Italy, and to a lesser extent Spain, had any strong tradition in the 16th century of written psalm polyphony. Settings using two alternating choirs ('salmi spezzati'), by Jacquet of Mantua, Willaert and others, were in principle through-composed, permitting a more varied texture.

Psalms were used as texts for the new motet repertory evolved by Josquin and his contemporaries *c*1500. Many settings treat them freely and cannot have been used as liturgical psalms; if sung in church, they must have served a function outside the liturgy. Collections such as Lassus's penitential psalms were probably used domestically as sacred madrigals.

After 1600 the singing of metrical psalms continued in the reformed churches of northern Europe. More ambitious psalm composition in this period is largely confined to the motet and anthem, but some composers continued issuing psalm collections, notably Sweelinck who set all 150 psalms in French metrical versions for three to eight voices, using melodies from the Genevan psalter as *cantus firmi*. Schütz also set the complete psalter in German metrical versions, as well as composing some more elaborate settings. Among later psalm collections those of G.B. Bassani and Benedetto Marcello are noteworthy. Most subsequent psalm settings are for concert use, for chorus and orchestra, often with soloists; Bruckner's large-scale settings and Kodály's *Psalmus Hungaricus* are representative. Stravinsky's *Symphony of Psalms* and Pendericki's *Psalmy Dawida* are multi-movement works using psalm texts.

See also ANGLICAN CHANT.

Psalmodikon. A bowed zither popular in the mid-19th century in Scandinavia, where it was used to regulate choral singing, particularly in schools. It consisted of a long, flat soundbox with one bowed and several resonating drone strings.

Psalms, Metrical. Paraphrases of the biblical psalms in verse, often designed for singing to tunes of a simple, popular type (known today as hymn tunes). *See* PSALM.

Psalmus hungaricus. Choral work by Kodály, a setting of Mihály Kecskeméti Vég's paraphrase of Psalm lv (1923).

Psalterer. A bowed instrument used in the early 18th century in English churches where no other accompanying instrument was available. It was shaped like a large viol with a fretted fingerboard and two strings tuned an octave apart.

Psaltery. An instrument of the zither family consisting of a wooden soundbox on which rows of strings are stretched between metal pins or wooden pegs. The word has its origins in the Latin *psalterium* which, historically, denoted any of the plucked instruments associated with David and the psalms. Psaltery and *psalterium* seem to have become synonymous around the 12th century when the Middle Eastern psaltery (or *qānūn*) entered Europe via Spain and influenced the shape of the psaltery, which was widely used throughout the Middle Ages. It could not cope with Renaissance chromaticism and from the late 15th century it was decreasingly used. It is the ancestor of the dulcimer (and thus, arguably, of the harpsichord and the pianoforte).

Psyché. *Tragédie lyrique* in five acts by Lully to a libretto by Corneille and Fontenelle (1679, Paris).

Opera by Locke to a libretto by Shadwell (1675, London).

Puccini, Giacomo (i) (*b* Celle di val di Roggio, Lucca, bap. 26 Jan 1712; *d* Lucca, 16 May 1781). Italian composer. Organist of S Martino in Lucca, 1739–72, and, from 1739 to his death, director of the republic's Cappella Palatina, he was prominent in the organization of music in Lucca. He wrote much sacred music, marked by its good vocal writing, its skilful counterpoint and its varied treatment of the text; he also wrote dramatic music for the local election festivities, the *tasche*, consisting of orchestral pieces, recitatives and arias, and also an oratorio.

His son, Antonio Puccini (1747–1832), succeeded him at S Martino and the Cappella Palatina; he too was a prolific church composer and wrote music for several *tasche*. Antonio's son Domenico Puccini (1772–1815) held appointments in Lucca; he composed much sacred music, two works for the *tasche*, cantatas and songs, two symphonies and a concerto.

Puccini, Giacomo (Antonio Domenico Michele Secondo Maria) (ii) (*b* Lucca, 22 or 23 Dec 1858; *d* Brussels, 29 Nov 1924). Italian composer, son of Michele Puccini and fifth in a line of composers from Lucca. After studying music with his uncle, Fortunato Magi, and with the director of the Istituto Musicale Pacini, Carlo Angeloni, he started his career at the age of 14 as an organist at S Martino and S Michele, Lucca, and at other local churches. However, a performance of Verdi's *Aida* at Pisa in 1876 made such an impact on him that he decided to follow his instinct for operatic composition. With a scholarship and financial support from an uncle, he was able to enter the Milan Conservatory in 1880. During his three years there his chief teachers were Bazzini and Ponchielli.

While still a student, Puccini entered a competition for a one-act opera announced in 1882 by the publishing firm of Sonzogno. He and his librettist, Ferdinando Fontana, failed to win, but their opera *Le villi* came to the attention of the publisher Giulio Ricordi, who arranged a successful production at the Teatro del Verme in Milan and commissioned a second opera. Fontana's libretto, *Edgar*, was unsuited to Puccini's dramatic talent and the opera was coolly received at La Scala in April 1889. It did, however, set the seal on what was to be Puccini's lifelong association with the house of Ricordi.

The first opera for which Puccini himself chose the subject was *Manon Lescaut*. Produced at Turin in 1893, it achieved a success such as Puccini was never

to repeat and made him known outside Italy. Among the writers who worked on its libretto were Luigi Illica and Giuseppe Giacosa, who provided the librettos for Puccini's next three operas. The first of these, *La bohème*, widely considered Puccini's masterpiece, but with its mixture of lighthearted and sentimental scenes and its largely conversational style was not a success when produced at Turin in 1896. *Tosca*, Puccini's first excursion into *verismo*, was more enthusiastically received by the Roman audience at the Teatro Costanzi in 1900.

Later that year Puccini visited London and saw David Belasco's one-act play *Madam Butterfly*. This he took as the basis for his next collaboration with Illica and Giacosa; he considered it the best and technically most advanced opera he had written. He was unprepared for the fiasco attending its first performance in February 1904, when the La Scala audience was urged into hostility, even pandemonium, by the composer's jealous rivals; in a revised version it was given to great acclaim at Brescia the following May. By then Puccini had married Elvira Gemignani, the widow of a Lucca merchant, who had borne him a son as long ago as 1896. The family lived until 1921 in the house at Torre del Lago which Puccini had acquired in 1891. Scandal was unleashed in 1909 when a servant girl of the Puccinis, whom Elvira had accused of an intimate relationship with her husband, committed suicide. A court case established the girl's innocence, but the publicity affected Puccini deeply and was the main reason for the long period before his next opera.

This was *La fanciulla del West*, based on another Belasco drama; it was given its première at the Metropolitan Opera, New York, in December 1910. In all technical respects, notably its Debussian harmony and Straussian orchestration, it was a masterly reply to the criticism that Puccini repeated himself in every new opera. What it lacks is the incandescent phrase, and this is probably why it has not entered the normal repertory outside Italy.

Differences with Tito Ricordi, head of the firm since 1912, led Puccini to accept a commission for an operetta from the directors of the Vienna Karltheater. The result, *La rondine*, though warmly received at Monte Carlo in 1917, is among Puccini's weakest works, hovering between opera and operetta and devoid of striking lyrical melody. While working on it Puccini began the composition of *Il tabarro*, the first of three one-act operas (*Il trittico*) which follow the scheme of the Parisian Grand Guignol – a horrific episode, a sentimental tragedy (*Suor Angelica*) and a comedy or farce (*Gianni Schicchi*). This last has proved to be the most enduring part of the triptych and is often done without the others, usually in a double bill.

In his early 60s Puccini was determined to 'strike out on new paths' and started work on *Turandot*, based on a Gozzi play which satisfied his desire for a subject with a fantastic, fairy-tale atmosphere, but flesh-and-blood characters. During its composition he moved to Viareggio and in 1923 developed cancer of the throat. Treatment at a Brussels clinic seemed successful, but his heart could not stand the strain and he died, leaving *Turandot* unfinished. (It is usually played today with Franco Alfano's ending.) All Italy went into mourning and two years later his remains were interred at his house at Torre del Lago which, after his wife's death in 1930, was turned into a museum.

Puccini's choral, orchestral and instrumental works, dating mainly from his early years, are unimportant, though the Mass in A♭ (1880) is still performed occasionally. His operas may not engage us on as many different levels as do those of Mozart, Wagner, Verdi or Strauss, but on his own most characteristic level, where erotic passion, sensuality, tenderness, pathos and despair meet and fuse, he was an unrivalled master. His melodic gift and harmonic sensibility, his consummate skill in orchestration and unerring sense of theatre combined to create a style that was wholly original, homogeneous and compelling. He was fully aware of his limitations and rarely ventured beyond them. He represents Verdi's only true successor, and his greatest masterpiece and swansong, *Turandot*, belongs among the last 20th-century stage works to remain in the regular repertory of the world's opera houses.

Operas Le villi (1884); Edgar (1889); Manon Lescaut (1893); La bohème (1896); Tosca (1900); Madama Butterfly (1904); La fanciulla del West (1910); La rondine (1917); Il trittico [Il tabarro, Suor Angelica, Gianni Schicchi] (1918); Turandot (1926), inc.
Vocal music Mass, A♭ (1880); motets, cantatas, songs
Instrumental music orch pieces, chamber music, pf pieces

Puccini, Michele (*b* Lucca, 27 Nov 1813; *d* there, 23 Jan 1864). Italian composer, son of Domenico Puccini and father of Giacomo Puccini (ii). He studied under his grandfather and others and in Naples under Donizetti and Mercadante and taught in Lucca at the Istituto Musicale Pacini, where he became director in 1862. He was organist at S Martino. He wrote a large quantity of sacred music, which shows little imagination, and two operas. He had two sons who were musicians, Giacomo and Michele (1864–91).

Puerto Rico Festival. *See* FESTIVAL CASALS OF PUERTO RICO.

Pugnani, (Giulio) Gaetano (Gerolamo) (*b* Turin, 27 Nov 1731; *d* there, 15 July 1798). Italian violinist and composer. A pupil of G.B. Somis, he played in the Teatro Regio orchestra, Turin, from the age of ten and had an international reputation by the 1760s. After conducting at the King's Theatre, London, 1767–9, he became first violinist of the King's Music in Turin in 1770 and director of music in 1776. Meanwhile he had several operas staged in Italy and abroad, and in 1780–82 made a concert tour with his pupil Viotti. He was one of the foremost violinists of the 18th century, especially famous for his powerful playing, and probably contributed to the development of the modern bow. Besides stage works, he composed 20 sonatas for violin and continuo, *c*40 trio sonatas, other chamber music and symphonies, often in four movements, influenced by Mannheim and Vienna models. The Praeludium and Allegro ascribed to him are by Kreisler.

Pugni, Cesare (*b* Genoa, 31 May 1802; *d* St Petersburg, 26 Jan 1870). Italian composer. He studied in Milan. He contributed all or part of the music to over 300 ballets staged principally in London or in St Petersburg, where he was ballet composer to the imperial theatres from 1851. His choreographers included Cerrito, Paul Taglioni, Petipa and notably Jules Perrot, with whom he produced the well-known *Ondine* (1843), *La Esmeralda* (1844), *Pas de quatre* (1845) and *Le jugement de Paris* (1846).

Pugno, (Stéphane) Raoul (*b* Montrouge, 23 June 1852; *d* Moscow, 3 Jan 1914). French pianist, teacher and composer. He studied at the Paris Conservatoire. Perhaps the leading French pianist of his time, he excelled in the music of Mozart, Chopin and Franck, performing as a soloist and with Ysaÿe and with Debussy. He was professor at the Conservatoire (1892–1901) and composed light stage works.

Pulcinella. 'Ballet with song' in one act by Stravinsky to a libretto by Massin (1920, Paris); for soprano, tenor, bass and chamber orchestra, it adapts works attributed to Pergolesi.

Puliaschi, Giovanni Domenico (*b* Rome; *fl* early 17th century). Italian composer and singer. He was a tenor in the papal chapel from 1612 but also sang bass and played the chitarrone. One of the most remarkable singers of his time, his virtuoso technique is reflected in his collection *Musiche varie* (1618), which also includes an essay on singing.

Pullois, Johannes (*d* 23 Aug 1478). Netherlands composer. He sang in Antwerp Cathedral, 1442–7, and in the papal chapel from at least 1453 to 1459. Until 1463 he sang in the Burgundian court chapel, returning then to Antwerp where he remained, apart from a couple of visits to Rome, until his death. His extant works includes a cyclic mass, a number of other liturgical compositions and secular songs, two to Dutch texts. Well known in the 15th century, they are generally of a conservative nature.

Punch and Judy. Opera in one act by Birtwistle to a libretto by Stephen Pruslin (1968, Aldeburgh).

Punk rock. A genre that evolved in the USA and later in London in the mid-1970s, when a number of outrageous and eccentric musicians played in a deliberately raw, amateurish style and espoused nihilistic political sentiments; it later changed into a brutal, monochromatic 'hardcore' style, played fast and at high volume.

Puntato (It.). An indication that notes are to be played staccato when indicated by 'points' (dots) above or below the notes in question; the term may also be used for 'dotted' notes.

Punteado (Sp.). The plucking of individual strings of the guitar with the right-hand fingertips, as opposed to RASGUEADO.

Punto, Giovanni [Stich, Johann Wenzel] (*b* Žehušice, 28 Sept 1746; *d* Prague, 16 Feb 1803). Bohemian hornist and composer. He first served Count Thun; from 1768 he travelled widely as a virtuoso, holding posts at Mainz, Würzburg and Paris (for a time as violinist-conductor). He had an exceptional reputation, and Mozart and Beethoven both composed for him. He wrote 11 horn concertos and many chamber works for his instrument.

Puppet opera. The earliest known operas for puppets were Venetian burlesques staged at the Teatro S Moisè from 1679. There were puppet theatres in Paris and London during the 18th century, and Haydn wrote puppet operas for performance at the summer palace of Prince Nikolaus Esterházy. Interest in puppet theatre then declined, but the late 19th century brought a regeneration in several countries. Falla's *El retablo de Maese Pedro* is perhaps the best-known 20th-century puppet opera.

Purcell, Henry (*b* Westminster, 21 Nov 1659; *d* Westminster, 21 Nov 1695). English composer. He was a chorister in the Chapel Royal until his voice broke in 1673, and he was then made assistant to John Hingeston, whom he succeeded as organ maker and keeper of the king's instruments in 1683. In 1677 he was appointed composer-in-ordinary for the king's violins and in 1679 succeeded his teacher, Blow, as organist of Westminster Abbey. It was probably in 1680 or 1681 that he married. From that time he began writing music for the theatre. In 1682 he was appointed an organist of the Chapel Royal. His court appointments were renewed by James II in 1685 and by William III in 1689, and on each occasion he had the duty of providing a second organ for the coronation. The last royal occasion for which he provided music was Queen Mary's funeral in 1695. Before the year ended Purcell himself was dead; he was buried in Westminster Abbey on 26 November 1695.

Purcell was one of the greatest composers of the Baroque period and one of the greatest of all English composers. His earliest surviving works date from 1680 but already show a complete command of the craft of composition. They include the fantasias for viols, masterpieces of contrapuntal writing in the old style, and some at least of the more modern sonatas for violins, which reveal some acquaintance with Italian models. In time Purcell became increasingly in demand as a composer, and his theatre music in particular made his name familiar to many who knew nothing of his church music or the odes and welcome songs he wrote for the court. Much of the theatre music consists of songs and instrumental pieces for spoken plays, but during the last five years of his life Purcell collaborated on five 'semi-operas' in which the music has a large share, with 'divertissements', songs, choral numbers and dances. His only true opera (i.e. with music throughout) was *Dido and Aeneas*, written for a girls' school at Chelsea; despite the limitations of Nahum Tate's libretto it is among the finest of 17th-century operas.

Several other members of the Purcell family were musicians, notably Henry's brother Daniel (*d* London, bur. 26 Nov 1717), who was organist of Magdalen College, Oxford (1688–95), and of St Andrew's, Holborn, London (1713–17), and in the years between these two appointments was active as a theatre composer in London.

Dramatic music Dido and Aeneas (1689); semi-operas: Dioclesian (1690); King Arthur (1691); The Fairy Queen (1692); The Indian Queen (1695); The Tempest (*c*1695); songs and incidental music for over 40 plays
*Sacred music c*65 anthems, including My heart is inditing (1685), Rejoice in the Lord alway (*c*1683); Morning and Evening Service, B♭; Magnificat and Nunc Dimittis, g; Te Deum and Jubilate, D (1694); Jehovah quam multi sunt, psalm (*c*1680)
Other vocal music 24 odes and welcome songs, incl. Welcome to all the pleasures (St Cecilia's Day, 1683), Hail, bright Cecilia (St Cecilia's Day, 1692), Come, ye sons of art away (1694); over 100 songs, v, bc; over 50 songs, 2/3 vv, bc; *c*60 catches, 3/4 vv
Instrumental music 13 fantasias, 3–5 viols (*c*1680); 2 In nomines, viols (*c*1680); Chacony, g, 4 str; 22 sonatas, 2 vn, b viol, bc (*c*1680, pubd 1683, 1697); 8 suites (pubd 1696), other works, hpd/spinet; 5 org voluntaries

Purcell Room. *See* SOUTH BANK CENTRE.

Purfling. A narrow inlay of wood inset in a trough cut inside the border edge of the belly and back of certain instruments, notably violins and viols. The inlay, of three narrow strips (occasionally made of mother-of-pearl), helps protect the edges of the instrument as well as ornamenting it.

Puritani di Scozia, I. Opera in three acts by Bellini to a libretto by C. Pepoli after F. Ancelot and X.B. Saintine, after Scott (1935, Paris).

Puschman, Adam (Zacharias) (*b* Görlitz, 1532; *d* Breslau, 4 April 1600). German poet and Meistersinger. He was taught by Hans Sachs in Nuremberg, 1556–60; from 1578 he lived in Breslau. He composed some 200 Meisterlieder, sacred and secular, and more than 30 *Meistertöne* for which he also composed melodies. His importance in Meistergesang rests primarily on his recodification of the artistic and organizational rules for Meistersinger and the collections he made of *Meistertöne* melodies (which previously had been transmitted only orally).

Pushkin, Alexander Sergeyevich (*b* Moscow, 26 May 1799; *d* St Petersburg, 29 Jan 1837). Russian poet. For the extraordinary breadth and variety of their character and the musical appeal of their language, his writings have had enormous attraction for Russian composers, including Glinka (*Ruslan and Lyudmila*), Dargomïzhsky (*The Stone Guest*), Rimsky-Korsakov (*The Golden Cockerel*), Tchaikovsky (*Eugene Onegin, Mazeppa*) and Stravinsky (*Mavra*).

Puy. Name for literary and musical societies founded mainly in northern France from the 12th century to the early 17th and the contests they held. It probably derives from the Latin *podium*, referring to the raised place from which competitors delivered their *chansons*. Early *puys* were in honour of the Virgin Mary; contests were held for the best *chanson royale* or *serventois*. There were *puys* in many major French towns, and in London; from the 16th century they were exclusively literary.

Puyana, Rafael (*b* Bogotà, 14 Oct 1931). Colombian harpsichordist. He studied at the New England Conservatory, Boston, as a pianist, then in 1951 became a harpsichord pupil of Landowska. He made his New York début in 1957, his London début in 1966. His rhythmic drive, decisive characterization and virtuosity recall Landowska herself, particularly in Scarlatti. Several new works have been written for him.

Puzzi, Giovanni (*b* Parma, 1792; *d* London, 1 March 1876). Italian horn player. The leading horn virtuoso in London from 1817 to 1840, he was a dazzling exponent of the chromatic late hand-horn technique. Two of his horns survive, one in the Horniman Museum, the other in the Victoria and Albert Museum.

Pycard (*fl* c1410). French composer working in England; a man of his name was a clerk of John of Gaunt's chapel, 1391–7. After Power he was the most fully represented in the original layer of the Old Hall MS. His extant works are all mass movements in four or five voices, and include four canons; other anonymous canonic compositions may be attributable to him. One of his non-canonic mass movements is isorhythmic, the other imitative in all four voices.

Pygmalion. *Acte de ballet* in one act by Rameau to a libretto by Sovot after La Motte (1748, Paris).

Pygott, Richard (*fl* early 16th century). English composer. He was a Gentleman of the Chapel Royal from 1524. His few surviving compositions, mostly sacred pieces, are of high quality, combining complex textures and beauty of melodic line.

Pylkkänen, Tauno (*b* Helsinki, 22 March 1918; *d* there, 13 March 1980). Finnish composer. He was a pupil of Madetoja, Palmgren and Ranta at the Helsinki Academy (1937–40), where he began teaching in 1967, having also worked in radio, as a critic, and as artistic director of the Finnish National Opera

(1960–70). He has written operas described as a kind of Finnish *verismo*, (e.g. *The Shadow*, 1952), song cycles and orchestral music.

Pyne, Louisa (Fanny) (*b* ?27 Aug 1832; *d* London, 20 March 1904). English soprano. Noted for her leading roles in English opera (Macfarren's *King Charles II*, Balfe's *The Bohemian Girl*, Benedict's *Lily of Killarney*), she formed the Pyne–Harrison Opera Company (1857–64) with the tenor William Harrison.

Pythagoras. Greek philosopher and religious teacher. He emigrated from Samos to Croton in southern Italy *c*531 BC. Doctrines of his school include the harmony of the spheres and a belief in the importance of numbers as a guide to the interpretation of the world. The discovery of the numerical ratios corresponding to the principal intervals of the musical scale is attributed to him. He became an almost legendary figure, and from the 5th century onwards his followers constituted one of the principal schools of Greek musical theory.

The term 'Pythagorean intonation' is applied to temperament systems based on pure perfect 4ths and 5ths; such systems were much used in the early Renaissance.

Pythagorean intonation. A tuning of the scale in which all the 5ths are pure (in the frequency ratio 3:2). Pythagorean intonation has large major 2nds and 3rds and small minor 2nds and 3rds; it is appropriate for use in certain types of medieval music.

Q

Qanbūs. A short-necked, fretless lute once common in southern Arabia; it has seven strings and a skin soundbox and was used to accompany vocal music.

Qānūn. A plucked zither of the Middle East, North Africa and parts of Asia. An ancient version of it was widespread in Egypt and Syria. The modern *qānūn* is popular in the folk and art music of Turkey (*kanūn*) and many Arab countries. It has *c*75 strings with a compass of three to four octaves and is played resting on a table or the player's knees. The strings are plucked with ring-shaped plectra on the index fingers; there are levers on the left of the instrument for tuning the strings.

Qin [ch'in]. An ancient Chinese plucked zither consisting of a narrow box strung with seven silk strings. It has no bridge or frets but a lacquered, inlaid body. It originated as early as the 14th or 15th century BC and has been used as a court instrument (particularly in ritual and ceremonial music), for accompanying and, in its highest form of development, during the Ming dynasty (1368–1644), as an expressive solo instrument.

Quadran pavan. 16th-century term for the *passamezzo moderno*, (see PASSAMEZZO). The term derives from 'B quadro' (the sign for B♮), which distinguished the major-mode *passamezzo moderno* from the minor-mode *antico* type.

Quadrille. An early 19th-century ballroom dance, based on the contredanse. Performed by sets of four, six or eight couples, it was popular in Paris during the First Empire and later elsewhere. The music, usually adapted from popular tunes, was in eight- or 16-bar sections and in duple time.

Examples were written by the Strausses and other major dance composers; there are also quadrilles based on such unlikely works as *Tristan und Isolde* and Rossini's *Stabat mater*.

Quadruplet. A group of four equal notes to be performed in the time of three in a time signature where the regular units are divisible by three.

Quadruplum, quadruplex (Lat.). 'Quadruple': terms used in medieval theory to denote (1) four-voiced polyphony (e.g. *organum quadruplum*); (2) the fourth voice of a polyphonic work, an independent voice composed against a tenor, duplum and triplum; or (3) diminution or augmentation by a factor of four in mensural notation.

Quagliati, Paolo (*b* Chioggia, *c*1555; *d* Rome, 16 Nov 1628). Italian composer. From *c*1574 for over 50 years he worked in Rome for wealthy families and was organist of S Maria Maggiore from at least 1608. His secular works include canzonettas (2 bks, 1588), madrigals (1608), a composite festive work (1611) and a volume of concertato solos, duets and madrigals (1623). Five sacred publications also survive.

Quantz, Johann Joachim (*b* Oberscheden, Hanover, 30 Jan 1697; *d* Potsdam, 12 July 1773). German flautist, composer and writer on music. He joined the Polish chapel of Augustus III as an oboist in 1718, working mainly in Dresden, and later turned to the transverse flute. He became a member of the Dresden court Kapelle after a European tour, 1724–7. From 1728 he visited Berlin to teach the flute to the young Prince Frederick, whom (as Frederick the Great) he served from 1740, supervising his concerts, composing and making flutes. His main works are over 200 sonatas for flute and continuo, *c*60 trio sonatas and over 300 flute concertos; these contain French and Italian elements and reflect the transition from late Baroque to early Classical style. He also wrote solo flute pieces, duets, songs etc, and the comprehensive *Versuch einer Answeisung die Flöte traversiere zu spielen* (1752), a flute treatise influential for its detailed discussion of performance.

Quartal harmony. Term for a harmonic system based on the interval of a 4th (as in early two-part organum), as opposed to the TERTIARY HARMONY of the major–minor tonal system. In 'non-quartal harmony' of the 15th century the 4th is used only as a discord.

Quarter-note. American term for crotchet: a note half the value of a half-note, or minim, and double the value of an eighth-note, or quaver. *See* NOTE VALUES.

Quarter-tone. An interval half the size of a semitone. Some 20th-century composers (including Alois Hába and Bartók) have used quarter-tones.

Quartet. A piece for four voices or instruments, or a group that performs such a piece. The STRING QUARTET and PIANO QUARTET are among the most important forms of chamber music.

Quartetto Italiano. *See* ITALIAN QUARTET.

Quartetto serioso. Beethoven's String Quartet in F minor op.95 (1810).

Quartettsatz. Title given to an unfinished movement for string quartet in C minor, D703, by Schubert (1820).

Quartfagott. A bassoon pitched a 4th above (or, if prefixed 'hoch', below) the normal one.

Quartposaune. A TROMBONE pitched a 4th below the ordinary trombone; the term is mentioned from the mid-16th century. (The *Quintposaune* is pitched a 5th below.) By the 19th century, the word came to be equivalent to 'Bassposaune'.

Quasi (It.). Almost, approximately, like.

Quatreble. Term in medieval and Renaissance music for the voice or part pitched a 5th higher than the treble.

Quattro rusteghi, I [School for Fathers]. Opera in four acts by Wolf-Ferrari to a libretto by Sugana and Pizzolato after Goldoni (1906, Munich).

Quattro stagioni, Le. *See* FOUR SEASONS, THE.

Quatuor concertant (Fr.). A title used in the late 18th century for a quartet in which four instruments (usually two violins, viola and cello) are essential to the musical discourse, as opposed to one in which the first violin is dominant.

Quatuor pour la fin du temps. Work by Messiaen for clarinet, piano, violin and cello (1940) after the Apocalypse.

Quaver. The note, in American usage called an eighth-note, that is half the value of a crotchet and double that of a semiquaver. The equivalent of the old *fusa*, it is first found in 15th-century music. In early sources it is shown as a void note with two flags. The French term for it, *croche*, should not be confused with the English crotchet. *See* NOTE VALUES

Queen Elizabeth Hall. *See* SOUTH BANK CENTRE.

Queen Mary's Funeral Music. Music by Purcell for the funeral of Queen Mary (1695), a setting of two sentences from the burial service, the anthem *Thou know'st, Lord, the secrets of our hearts*, two canzonas for slide trumpets and trombones and a march.

Queen of Spades, The [Pikovaya dama]. Opera in three acts by Tchaikovsky to a libretto by the composer and Modest Tchaikovsky (1890, St Petersburg).

Queen's Hall. London concert hall built in 1893 (cap. 2492). Many musicians from Britain and abroad appeared there and as the home of the Henry Wood Promenade Concerts (from 1895) it became a national centre of music; it was destroyed in 1941.

Quentin, Jean-Baptiste (*fl* Paris, 1718–*c*1750). French composer. A violinist of high reputation, he played at the Opéra and composed much chamber music for violin and continuo, trio sonatas and quartet sonatas. His brother Bertin (*d* ?1767) was also a violinist and composer.

Querelle des Bouffons. *See* BOUFFONS, QUERELLE DES.

Querflöte (Ger.). Transverse FLUTE.

Quickstep. A duple-time dance of the 1920s, a fast version of the FOXTROT, taken at 50 or more bars per minute. The term is also sometimes used for a fast march.

Quiet City. Work for english horn, trumpet and strings by Copland (1939), an arrangement of incidental music he wrote for a play.

Quilter, Roger (*b* Brighton, 1 Nov 1877; *d* London, 21 Sept 1953). English composer. He studied at the Hoch Conservatory, Frankfurt. He is best known for his songs, most written 1900–30, in a style of seeming effortlessness and extreme sensitivity. He also wrote successful light orchestral pieces (e.g. *A Children's Overture*, 1919).

Quinault, Philippe (*b* Paris, bap. 5 June 1635; *d* there, 26 Nov 1688). French dramatist, librettist and poet. The prime literary creator of the *tragédie lyrique*, he was active at the French court, where he wrote the librettos for 14 of Lully's stage works between 1672 and 1686 – including *Alceste* (1674) and *Armide* (1686) – many of which were also set by later composers, notably Gluck.

Quinet, Marcel (*b* Binche, 6 July 1915; *d* Woluwé-St Lambert, 16 Dec 1986). Belgian composer. Son of the conductor and teacher Fernand Quinet (1898–1971), he studied at the Brussels Conservatory, where he began teaching in 1943; he was also a pupil of Absil. His large output, especially of orchestral, chamber and piano music, has links with Hindemith, Absil and Bartók and is distinguished by formal clarity and objectivism.

Quinible. Medieval term for a voice or part pitched an octave above the treble.

Quintanar, Héctor (*b* Mexico City, 15 April 1936). Mexican composer. He was a pupil of Chávez (1960–64) and studied at Columbia University. His works use electronic, improvisatory and other avant-garde techniques (he was the first Mexican to compose an electronic film score, for *Una vez un hombre*) and he is a promoter of new music.

Quintet. A piece for five voices or instruments, or a group that performs such a piece. The STRING QUINTET, the PIANO QUINTET and the WIND QUINTET are among the most important forms of chamber music.

Quinton. A five-string instrument, used during the 18th century, with the body of a violin and the fretted neck and sloping shoulders of a viol, and tuned *g–d'–a'–d''–g''*. The term is also applied to the *pardessus de viole* (*see* PARDESSUS).

Quintuplet. A group of five equal notes occurring irregularly and occupying the space of a note or notes (usually four or five) of regular metric duration.

Quintuple time. A metre of five beats to the bar. Its irregularity has made it an oddity in Western music; the common division into alternative groups of two and three beats is often found disturbing. It has been used for special effect by several composers, notably Tchaikovsky in the waltz-like second movement of his Symphony no.6 (1893) and by Handel and Wagner to convey unease or excitement. There are however earlier examples, among them some songs in the *Canciero musical de Palacio* (1516–20). It occurs more commonly in folk music, particularly east European; composers who drew on elements of folk music style early in the 20th century have used it.

Quintus (Lat.). 'Fifth': the fifth part in a piece of vocal polyphony. The term was particularly used for printed partbooks in five-voice music, where the *quintus* part might be for different voices (e.g. 'discantus 2' or 'contratenor 2') in addition to the standard four.

Quodlibet (Lat.: 'What you please'). A composition, usually of a light or humorous kind, in which snatches of well-known melodies and texts appear in successive or simultaneous combination. The term was first used in this sense in Germany in 1544.

There are three main types. The catalogue quodlibet consists of a free setting of catalogue poetry (ridiculous lists of items loosely combined). In the successive quodlibet, one voice has short musical and textual quotations while the others form a homophonic accompaniment. In the simultaneous quodlibet, two or more pre-existing melodies are combined.

Parallel types of quodlibet in the Renaissance were the *fricassée* (France), *misticanza* or *messanza* (Italy), *ensalada* (Spain) and medley (England).

R

R. Abbreviation used for works by Vivaldi according to the catalogue by Mario Rinaldi (1945), and for works by Liszt according to the catalogue by Peter Raabe (1931, 2/1968). *See also* Rv.

R.H. Right hand.

Raaff, Anton (*b* Gelsdorf, bap. 6 May 1714; *d* Munich, 28 May 1797). German tenor. A pupil of Bernacchi in Bologna, after appearing in Germany and abroad, he was the principal operatic tenor in Naples and Florence in the 1760s. He later served at the Mannheim and Munich courts and sang in the première of Mozart's *Idomeneo* (1781, Munich).

Rabāb. Term for string instruments, both bowed and plucked, found mainly in Arab and Islamic countries as a fiddle or spike fiddle, and in Central Asia and India as a kind of lute, long-necked or double-chested. The name appears variously in different regions (e.g. *rebab*, *ribāb*, *rubāb* etc) and may be related to the European REBEC. The two-string *rebab* is used in gamelan music in Java and Bali. The Ethiopian *rababa* is a bowl-shaped lyre.

Rabaud, Henri (*b* Paris, 10 Nov 1873; *d* there, 11 Sept 1949). French composer and conductor. A pupil of Massenet and Gédalge at the Paris Conservatoire, he made his name with his colourful oriental opera *Mârouf, savetier du Caire* (1914) and was director of the Paris Opéra (1914–18) and of the Conservatoire (1922–41). His output includes five other operas, two symphonies and film scores.

Rachmaninoff [Rachmaninov], **Sergey.** *See* RAKHMANINOV, SERGEY.

Racket. A double-reed Renaissance woodwind instrument. It was squat and cylindrical, had a bassoon-type reed and was characterized by a throaty tone and deep compass. It was made in four sizes, of ranges from *C'–G* to *G–d'*. But it lacked the strength and expression of the contemporary shawm and dulcian and was obsolete by the mid-17th century. The Baroque racket or racket-bassoon, a modified version with an increased range, appeared later, but died out in the 18th century.

Radamisto. Opera in three acts by Handel to a libretto by Haym after Lalli (1720, London): his first opera for the Royal Academy of Music.

Radesca di Foggia, Enrico (*b* Foggia, late 16th century; *d* Turin, early 1625). Italian composer. He worked at Turin Cathedral as organist (until *c*1615)

and then as choirmaster, and from 1610 also served at the ducal court, becoming choirmaster by 1615. He was one of the earliest composers of sacred music for small vocal ensemble and continuo, but in his seven secular collections concentrated on duets, using a lively style derived from the canzonetta.

Radetzky March. March, op.228, by Johann Strauss (i) (1848).

Radical bass. In Rameau's theory of harmony (1722), an imaginary bass line produced by linking the roots of the chords in a progression. *See* BASSE FONDAMENTALE.

Radical cadence. A CADENCE whose penultimate and final chords are in root position, as opposed to a 'medial' or 'inverted' cadence, whose penultimate chord is in inversion.

Radicati, Felice Alessandro (*b* Turin, 1775; *d* Bologna, 19 March 1820). Italian violinist and composer. He studied with Pugnani, then worked in Vienna, London and Lisbon before settling in Bologna as orchestra director, *maestro di cappella* at S Petronio and professor at the conservatory. He composed chiefly operas and chamber music, earning the epithet 'Restorer of the Italian quartet'.

Radino, Giovanni Maria (*b* mid-16th century; *d* after 1607). Italian composer. He served the Count of Frankenburg's family in Carinthia, becoming organist of S Giovanni in Verdare, Padua, by 1592. His collection of dances (1592) is the first such Italian volume specifically for the harpsichord. He edited a madrigal book in 1598. His son Giulio (*d* before 1607) also composed.

Raff, (Joseph) Joachim (*b* Lachen, 27 May 1822; *d* Frankfurt, ?24/25 June 1882). German composer and teacher. Through the influence and encouragement of Liszt, whom he met in 1845 and for whom he worked at Weimar (1850–55), he joined the New German School, becoming a lifelong friend of Bülow and composing prolifically in nearly every form and genre. His attempt at fusing past and present methods (contrapuntal techniques with programmes) often led to an unattractive mixture of styles, while his penchant for salon-like music made him susceptible to triviality. His skilled instrumentation was praised and his programme symphonies on rustic subjects (e.g. no.7, 'In den Alpen', 1875; no.10, 'Zur Herbstzeit', 1879) had a progressive influence. During his lifetime he enjoyed great fame as a modern master and won esteem as teacher and administrator at the Hoch Conservatory, Frankfurt (from 1877), where his pupils included Edward MacDowell and Alexander Ritter.

Raga. Indian term, often translated as 'mode', 'scale' or 'melody type'; a raga represents a series of notes, presented in ascending and descending forms. Each raga is associated with a particular mood and a particular time of the day or the year; a raga is used as a basis for improvisation in Indian classical music (*see* INDIAN MUSIC).

Rage over a lost penny. Title given to Beethoven's *Rondo a capriccio* in G op.129 for piano (in fact an early work, written in 1795); completed by an unknown editor from Beethoven's unfinished autograph, it is a stormy piece.

Ragtime. American popular music style that flourished *c*1896–1918. Its main trait is its ragged (i.e. syncopated) rhythm. Although now thought of as a piano style, it also referred to other instrumental music, vocal music and dance. Most instrumental rags follow the forms of earlier duple-and quadruple-metre dances – the march, two-step, polka and schottische – with three or more independent 16-bar phrases, each consisting of four-bar phrases in patterns of repeats and reprises. There might also be an introduction or interpolations. A school of 'classic' ragtime whose principal exponent was Scott Joplin achieved considerable sophistication, though simpler, more accessible rags were more popular. Ragtime gave way to jazz after World War I. The change was at first more in terminology than in the music; and many ragtime musicians such as Morton began to call themselves jazz musicians.

Ragué, Louis-Charles (*b* by 1760; *d* Moulins, after 1793). French composer and harp teacher. He was active in Paris, 1783–93, and wrote two harp concertos, many harp sonatas, duos etc and two harp methods. His other works include three symphonies, two *opéras comiques*, a ballet and an oratorio.

Raimbaut de Vaqueiras (*b* Vaqueiras, ?1150–60; *d* ?Greece, ?4 Sept 1207). Provençal troubadour and composer. Of humble origins, he spent most of his life in Italy as companion-at-arms to Boniface, Marquis of Monferrat (1152–1207). He earned a knighthood saving his patron's life in Sicily in 1194, and was again at his side in the fourth crusade. Of the 35 poems attributed to him, seven survive with music; the best known is *Calenda maya*, called an *estampida* in its last line and thus a very early example of the *estampie*.

Raimon de Miraval (*fl* 1180–1215). Provençal troubadour. A member of the lesser nobility, he was associated with aristocratic patrons in southern France. 48 *chansons* can be attributed to him and 22 survive with melodies, the largest extant troubadour musical output after Guiraut Riquier's. They display great variety in poetic and musical construction, with courtly and political songs, debates and a *dompnejaire* (*salut d'amour*).

Raimondi, Pietro (*b* Rome, 20 Dec 1786; *d* there, 30 Oct 1853). Italian composer. He studied at the Naples Conservatory, later teaching there and in Palermo. He wrote *c*50 operas, but it is as a remarkable contrapuntist that he is remembered. He composed (as 'experiments') combinations of up to six independent fugues that could be performed simultaneously, two eight-part masses, each with its own orchestra, which could be performed together (1836), and similarly three oratorios (1847–8) juxtaposing disparate tempos, metres, performing bodies and types of expression. His direction of a performance of these oratorios in Rome made him a celebrity, and he was made *maestro di cappella* at St Peter's in 1852.

Raindrop Prelude. Nickname of Chopin's Prelude in D♭ op.28 no.15 (1839) for piano, so called because of its 'pattering' repeated A♭s.

Rainier, Priaulx (*b* Howick, 3 Feb 1903; *d* Besse-en-Chandesse, 10 Oct 1986). South African composer. She lived in England from 1920, when she began studying as a violinist at the RAM. In 1937 she had composition lessons with Boulanger, then came to notice for her lucid, rhythmically powerful music in a style indebted to Bartók and Stravinsky (Clarinet Suite, 1943; *Barbaric Dance Suite* for piano, 1949; *Requiem*, 1956); in the 1960s her work became more compressed and less tonal. Her small output consists mostly of orchestral, chamber and vocal music.

Raison, André (*b* before 1650; *d* Paris, 1719). French composer. He was organist at the royal abbey of Ste Geneviève, Paris, from *c*1666, and later at the convent and college of the Jacobins of St Jacques. Clérambault was one of his pupils. He published two organ collections, the first of which (1688) contains five organ masses and a preface on performance. His pieces are notable for their colourful registrations and changes of tempo and metre.

Raitio, Väinö (Eerikki) (*b* Sortavala, 15 April 1891; *d* Helsinki, 10 Sept 1945). Finnish composer. He studied in Helsinki, Moscow (1916–17), Berlin (1921) and Paris (1925–6), coming into contact with foreign trends (Skryabin, expressionism, Debussy) which influenced his tone poems of the 1920s and operas of the next decade.

Rake's Progress, The. Opera in three acts and an epilogue by Stravinsky to a libretto by W.H. Auden and Chester Kallman after Hogarth (1951, Venice).

Rakhmaninov [Rachmaninoff], Sergey (Vasil'yevich) (*b* Semyonovo, 1 April 1873; *d* Beverley Hills, 28 March 1943). Russian composer and pianist. He studied at the Moscow Conservatory (1885–92) under Zverev (where Skryabin was a fellow pupil) and his cousin Ziloti for piano and Taneyev and Arensky for composition, graduating with distinction as both pianist and composer (the opera *Aleko*, given at the Bol'shoy in 1893, was his diploma piece). During the ensuing years he composed piano pieces (including his famous C♯ minor Prelude), songs and orchestral works, but the disastrous première in 1897 of his Symphony no.1, poorly conducted by Glazunov, brought about a creative despair that was not dispelled until he sought medical help in 1900: then he quickly composed his Second Piano Concerto. Meanwhile he had set out on a new career as a conductor, appearing in Moscow and London; he later was conductor at the Bol'shoy, 1904–6.

By this stage, and most particularly in the Piano Concerto no.2, the essentials of his art had been assembled: the command of the emotional gesture conceived as lyrical melody extended from small motifs, the concealment behind this of subtleties in orchestration and structure, the broad sweep of his lines and forms, the predominant melancholy and nostalgia, the loyalty to the finer Russian Romanticism inherited from Tchaikovsky and his teachers. These things were not to change, and during the remaining years to the Revolution they provided him with the materials for a sizable output of operas, liturgical music, orchestral works, piano pieces and songs, even though composition was generally restricted to periods of seclusion between concert engagements. In 1909 he made his first American tour as a pianist, for which he wrote the Piano Concerto no.3.

Soon after the October Revolution he left Russia with his family for Scandinavia; in 1918 they arrived in New York, where he mainly lived thereafter, though he spent periods in Paris (where he founded a publishing firm), Dresden and Switzerland. There was a period of creative silence until 1926 when he wrote the Piano Concerto no.4, followed by only a handful of works over the next 15 years, even though all are on a large scale. During this period, however, he was active as a pianist on both sides of the Atlantic (though never again in Russia). As a pianist he was famous for his precision, rhythmic drive, legato and clarity of texture and for the broad design of his performances.

Operas Aleko (1893); The Miserly Knight (1906); Francesca da Rimini (1906)
Choral music 6 choruses, women's or children's vv (1896); Spring, Bar, chorus, orch (1902); Liturgy of St John Chrysostom (1910); The Bells, S, T, Bar, chorus, orch (1913); All-Night Vigil (1915); 3 Russian songs (1926)
Piano and orchestra Pf Conc. no.1, f♯ (1891); Pf Conc. no.2, c (1901); Pf Conc. no.3, d (1909); Pf Conc. no.4, g (1926, rev. 1941); Rhapsody on a Theme of Paganini (1934)
Orchestral music Prince Rostislav, sym. poem (1891); The Rock, sym. poem (1893); Capriccio on Gypsy Themes (1894); Sym. no.1, d (1895); Sym. no.2, e (1907); The Isle of the Dead, sym. poem (1909); Sym. no.3, a (1936); Sym. Dances (1940)
Piano music Morceaux de salon, (1894); 6 Duets, 4 hands (1894); Moments musicaux (1896); Suite, 2 pf (1901); Chopin Variations (1903); 10 Preludes op.23 (1903); Sonata no.1, d (1907); 13 Preludes op.32 (1910); 6 Etudes-tableaux op.33 (1911); Sonata no.2, b♭ (1913); 9 Etudes-tableaux op.39 (1917); Corelli Variations (1931)
Chamber music Trio élégiaque, g, pf, vn, vc (1892); Trio élégiaque, d, pf, vn, vc (1893); Sonata, vc, pf (1901)
Songs 6 op.4 (1893); 6 op.8 (1893); 12 op.14 (1896); 12 op.21 (1902); 15 op.26 (1906); 14 op.34 (1912); 6 op.38 (1916)

Raking. A technique of playing broken chords on the lute.

Rákóczi March. Hungarian march (c1810), possibly by János Bihari, named after Prince Rákóczi, leader of the Hungarian revolt against Austria; it has been quoted by several composers, including Berlioz, Strauss and Liszt.

Rallentando (It.). Becoming slower.

Ramann, Lina (*b* Mainstockheim, 24 July 1833; *d* Munich, 30 March 1912). German writer and teacher. She is remembered chiefly for her books on Liszt (with whom she studied), including the 'official' though inaccurate biography *Franz Liszt als Künstler und Mensch* (1880–94).

Rameau, Jean-Philippe (*b* Dijon, bap. 25 Sept 1683; *d* Paris, 12 Sept 1764). French composer and theorist. His early training came from his father, a professional organist; he went to a Jesuit school, then had a short period of music study in Italy. He may have played the violin for a time in a theatre orchestra. In 1702 he was appointed *maître de musique* at Avignon Cathedral, but later in the same year he moved to Clermont Cathedral; by 1706 he was in Paris as organist of the Jesuit college. He returned to Dijon in 1709 as organist at Notre Dame (a shared position); but by 1713 he was in Lyons and in 1715 he was back in Clermont with a 29-year contract as organist.

By 1722, however, he was in Paris, where he was to remain; he had left Clermont to supervise the publication of his *Traité de l'harmonie*, a substantial and controversial work, particularly as regards his new theory, based on his understanding of the physical properties of sound, about the relationship of bass to harmony. The *Traité* brought him to wide attention. As a composer, he was known only for his keyboard music (a second collection appeared in 1729–30) and his cantatas, though he had also written some church music.

His ambitions, however, lay in opera; and at the age of 50, in 1733, he had his first opera, *Hippolyte et Aricie*, given at the Opéra. It aroused great excitement, admiration, bewilderment and (among the conservative part of the audience who saw no good in anything since Lully) disgust. It was fairly successful, as were the other operas that followed in the ensuing years; his *opéra-ballet Les Indes galantes* had 64 performances over two years, and the least successful, *Castor et Pollux*, had an initial run of 21 performances.

Rameau had various patrons, notably the financier La Pouplinière; he moved in intellectual circles and counted Voltaire among his friends. He continued his theoretical work in the 1740s and was embroiled in several controversies. In 1745 he was appointed a royal chamber music composer; thereafter several of his works had their premières at court theatres. Nine new theatre works followed in the mid-late 1740s, beginning with *La princesse de Navarre* and the comedy *Platée*; but from 1750 onwards only two major works were written, for Rameau was increasingly involved with theory and with a number of disputes, with Rousseau, Grimm and even former friends, pupils and collaborators such as Diderot and D'Alembert. When Rameau died, in 1764, he was widely respected and admired, though he was seen too as unsociable and avaricious.

Rameau's harpsichord music is notable for its variety of texture, its originality of line and its boldness of harmony. But his chief contribution lies in his operas, especially those in the *tragédie lyrique* genre. He anticipated Gluckian reform by relating the overture to the ensuing drama. He brought to the numerous dances a remarkably wide range of moods, even within the constraints of the standard dance forms, using a richly varied orchestral palette and bold melodic lines. Diderot praised his ability to distinguish the tender, the voluptuous, the impassioned and the lascivious. He wrote many fine pathetic monologues, usually at the beginnings of acts, with intense, slow-moving vocal lines and rich, sombre accompaniments. His recitative, while following the Lullian model, is more flexible in rhythms and more expressive in its declamation. Such *tragédies* as *Hippolyte et Aricie* and *Castor et Pollux*, with their noble characters and their eloquent lines, harmonies and orchestration, supported by skilfully placed divertissements that strengthen rather than dilute the force of the action, stand among the great creations of French musical drama.

Dramatic music Hippolyte et Aricie (1733); Les Indes galantes (1735); Castor et Pollux (1737); Les fêtes d'Hébé (1739); Dardanus (1739); La princesse de Navarre (1745); Platée (1745); Les fêtes de Polymnie (1745); Le temple de la gloire (1745); Les fêtes de l'Hymen et de l'Amour (1747); Zaïs (1748); Pygmalion (1748); Les surprises de l'Amour (1748); Naïs (1749); Zoroastre (1749); La guirlande (1751); Acante et Céphise (1751); Daphnis et Eglé (1753); Les Sybarites (1753); La naissance d'Osiris (1754); Anacréon (1754); Les Paladins (1760); Les boréades (1764)
Other vocal music c9 chamber cantatas; 4 canons; other secular pieces; c4 motets
Keyboard music 4 hpd bks – 10 pieces (1706), 22 pieces (1724), 16 pieces incl. La poule (c1728), 7 pieces (1741)
Chamber music 4 concerts, hpd, vn/fl, viol/vn

Ramifications. Work by Ligeti for string orchestra or 12 solo strings (1969).

Ramin, Günther (*b* Karlsruhe, 15 Oct 1898; *d* Leipzig, 27 Feb 1956). German organist and conductor. He studied at the Leipzig Conservatory and became organist of the Thomaskirche in 1918; in 1940 he was appointed Kantor (12th in line from Bach). He toured Europe and the USA (1933–4) as an organist and was active as a choral conductor in Leipzig, Berlin and the USSR.

Ramos de Pareia, Bartolomeo (*b* Baeza, c1440; *d* c1491). Spanish theorist and composer. He taught at Salamanca University, at Bologna (from c1472) and at Rome (c1484–91). His treatise, *Musica practica* (1482), marks him as one of the most original music theorists. He claimed that the tetrachord system of Boethius and the hexachord of Guido were too complicated for performers and proposed a new solmization method. He also attacked Boethius's ideas on tuning and pleaded for clarity and practicality in other areas. Many of his ideas were taken up by later theorists, including Glarean, Aaron and Zarlino.

Rampal, Jean-Pierre (Louis) (*b* Marseilles, 7 Jan 1922). French flautist. He studied at Marseilles and the Paris Conservatoire (where he later taught); his concert career began with international tours in 1947, and he was solo flautist at the Paris Opéra, 1956–62. He is admired particularly for his performances of 18th-century music, where his clear, mellow tone, attractive shading and delicate articulation, is heard to particular advantage in music by Bach and Mozart.

Rampini, (Giovanni) Giacomo (*b* Padua, 1680; *d* there, 27 May 1760). Italian composer. He was

maestro di cappella of Padua Cathedral from 1704 and composed sacred music, operas and oratorios. Among his pupils was his nephew Giacomo (*d* 1811), who became organist and later *maestro di cappella* at Udine Cathedral; he too composed sacred music.

Ramsey, Robert (*fl* Cambridge, c1612–44). English composer. He graduated at Cambridge (1616) and was organist of Trinity College (1628–44). Some two dozen Latin and English sacred works by him, including a service, are known, as well as consort songs, continuo songs and dialogues, and madrigals; some show Italian influence, others that of the early English Baroque style.

Randall, J(ames) K(irtland) (*b* Cleveland, 16 June 1929). American composer. He studied at Columbia, Harvard and Princeton, with Sessions and Babbitt, and in 1958 joined the Princeton faculty. He has been particularly concerned with computer sound synthesis and from 1980 with improvised group performances (with painters and dancers) in which he participates.

Randegger, Alberto (*b* Trieste, 13 April 1832; *d* London, 18 Dec 1911). English conductor, teacher and composer of German and Italian descent. He settled in London in 1854, becoming an influential singing teacher (at the RAM and RCM) and opera conductor; he was particularly admired for his Verdi interpretations. His textbook (1893) remains useful.

Rands, Bernard (*b* Sheffield, 2 March 1935). English composer. He studied at Bangor and in Italy and Germany with Dallapiccola, Maderna, Boulez and Berio, of whom the last has been a particular influence (e.g. in *Actions for Six*, 1963). In 1969 he was appointed lecturer at York University, moving to San Diego in the mid-1970s. Like Berio, he has written works in which the potential of a single instrument is explored (*Memos I–V*).

Range. The compass of an instrument or voice, or of a piece of music, from the lowest note to the highest; the interval between those notes.

Rangström, (Anders Johan) Ture (*b* Stockholm, 30 Nov 1884; *d* there, 11 May 1947). Swedish composer. A pupil of Lindegren (1903–4) and of Pfitzner in Berlin (1905–6), he was a critic and singing teacher in Stockholm. He conducted throughout Sweden. He wrote four symphonies and other works in a clearcut homophonic style, though is best remembered for his many songs.

Rank. In an organ, a complete set or row of pipes, controlled by one stop-knob (some compound stops have more than one rank).

Ránki, György (*b* Budapest, 30 Nov 1907). Hungarian composer. A pupil of Kodály at the Budapest Academy (1926–30), he later worked on oriental folk music. His works are in several genres, the most successful being for the theatre (e.g. the opera *King Pomádé's New Clothes*, 1953).

Rankl, Karl (*b* Gaaden, 1 Oct 1898; *d* Salzburg, 6 Sept 1968). British conductor and composer of Austrian birth. He studied with Schoenberg and Webern in Vienna and held conducting posts at opera houses in the 1920s, notably with Klemperer at the Kroll, Berlin (1928–31). He helped re-establish opera at Covent Garden from 1946 but was obliged to resign in 1951. He was conductor of the Scottish Orchestra, 1952–7.

Rant. A country dance of the jig variety in binary form and duple metre, from the Scottish lowlands and northern England. Surviving examples date from the 17th and 18th centuries.

Ranz des vaches (Fr.). A melody sung or played on an alphorn by Swiss herdsmen in the Alps to summon their cows. About 50 melodies survive, an early printed example being the one used by Meyerbeer in his opera *Dinorah* and by Grétry and Rossini in the overtures to their William Tell operas. Other, more stylized, imitations occur in Berlioz's *Symphonie fantastique* and Wagner's *Tristan und Isolde*.

Raoul de Ferrières (*fl* 1200–10). French trouvère, a member of the Norman nobility. 11 *chansons* are ascribed to him, including *Quant li rossignols*, probably the song referred to by Johannes de Grocheo as a *cantus coronatus*. All his melodies are in bar form (*AAB*) and some show signs of regular rhythmic organization.

Two other trouvères are known as Raoul: Raoul de Beauvais, probably of the mid-13th century, and Raoul de Soissons, who took part in crusades in the period 1239–70.

Rap. A style of black American popular music consisting of improvised rhymes performed to a rhythmic accompaniment; it originated in New York in the mid-1970s.

Rape of Lucretia, The. Chamber opera in two acts by Britten to a libretto by Ronald Duncan after André Obey (1946, Glyndebourne).

Raphael, Günter (Albert Rudolf) (*b* Berlin, 30 April 1903; *d* Herford, 19 Oct 1960). German composer. He was a pupil of Kahn at the Berlin Musikhochschule (1922–5). From 1926 he taught in Leipzig, but his music was banned by the Nazis, and in 1934 he resigned; he returned to teaching in Duisburg, Mainz and Cologne after the war. His earlier music is Regerian, but during his retirement he developed a sparer style reaching back to Bach and Schütz, and later used 12-note technique. His large output includes much church music, five symphonies, chamber, organ and piano works.

Rappresentativo. *See* STILE RAPPRESENTATIVO.

Rappresentazione di Anima, et di Corpo, La. Oratorio by Cavalieri to a text by Manni (1600, Rome).

Rappresentazione sacra. Term used in the 15th and 16th centuries for a kind of religious play in Italian with music, a significant forerunner of both opera and oratorio. In the late 17th century the term was often applied to the Viennese *sepolcro*.

Rapsodie espagnole. Orchestral work by Ravel (1908).
  Piano work by Liszt (*c*1863).

Raselius, Andreas (*b* Hahnbach, *c*1563; *d* Heidelberg, 6 Jan 1602). German composer. After studies at Heidelberg, he was a Kantor in Regensburg, 1584–1600, then returned to Heidelberg as court Kapellmeister. He wrote the first published German motet cycle for the church year (1594–5), chorales for congregational singing and two treatises.

Rasgueado (Sp.). The downward strumming of the strings of the guitar with the right-hand thumb or the back (flat side) of the right-hand fingernails, or an upward sweep over the strings with the fingertips or the thumb.

Rasi, Francesco (*b* Arezzo, ?4 May 1574; *d* after 1620). Italian composer and tenor. Reputedly a pupil of Caccini, he had great success as a singer and a chitarrone player, and was also a poet. After a period in Gesualdo's service he worked from 1598 at the Mantuan court, where in 1607 he probably created the title role in Monteverdi's *Orfeo*. He published two volumes of monodies (1608, 1610), which use an expressive style similar to Caccini's; among his other works are songs and Latin motets.

Rasse, François (Adolphe Jean Jules) (*b* Helchin, 17 Jan 1873; *d* Brussels, 4 Jan 1955). Belgian composer. He was a pupil of Huberti at the Brussels Conservatory, where he taught from 1920, and directed the Liège Conservatory (1925–38). He also conducted at the Théâtre de la Monnaie. His large output, in a late Romantic style, includes several song cycles.

Rastell, John (*b* London, *c*1475; *d* there, 1536). English MP, dramatist, historian and printer. A small but important quantity of surviving music – a three-part song from his play *A New Interlude* and a broadside ballad – printed from type in a single impression, probably by 1525, gives him priority over Attaingnant as the pioneer of this far-reaching innovation in music printing.

Rastrum. A pen with a number of nibs or styli, used for drawing staves. The study of the layout of stafflines on MS paper, which can yield information about such matters as dates of composition, is called 'rastrology'.

Ratchet. A handle-operated rattle consisting of a cogwheel scraped against wooden or metal tongues. A large ratchet appears in Beethoven's 'Battle' Symphony, smaller ones in Leopold Mozart's 'Toy' Symphony, Strauss's *Till Eulenspiegel* and Respighi's *Pini di Roma*; they are also a familiar feature of football matches.

Rathaus, Karol (*b* Tarnopol, Poland, 16 Sept 1895; *d* New York, 21 Nov 1954). American composer. He studied in Vienna and Berlin and lived in Paris and London (1932–8) before moving to the USA. He taught at Queen's College, New York (1939–54), and in 1952 re-orchestrated parts of *Boris Godunov* for the Met. His music, which includes chamber music and songs, is characterized by its rhythmic vitality, angular melodies and bold dissonances; his predilection for the piano and vivid orchestration are noteworthy.

Rathgeber, Johann Valentin (*b* Oberelsbach, 3 April 1682; *d* Banz, 2 June 1750). German composer. He was a chamber musician at the Benedictine abbey of Banz in 1707 and from 1711 choirmaster; later he made a tour of Germany. He was well known and influential for his church music, including 19 large collections of Latin mass settings, Vesper psalms, offertories etc (most for SATB solo and chorus and instruments). He also wrote 24 concertos (1728), keyboard pieces (1743) and the *Tafel-Confect* (1733, 1737, 1746), a three-volume collection of popular song settings. Simple textures and attractive melodies are features of his style.

Rattle. A shaken vessel, often with a handle, filled or strung with small hard objects such as seeds or pebbles, found worldwide and in all periods. Gourd rattles (MARACAS) are common in Latin American dance.

Rattle, Simon (Denis) (*b* Liverpool, 19 Jan 1955). English conductor. After study at the RAM he became conductor of the Bournemouth SO and Sinfonietta in 1974. In 1975 he became associate conductor of the Royal Liverpool PO and in 1979 principal conductor of the CBSO. He is noted for his fluent style and lucid direction, notably in 20th-century music; he has conducted at Glyndebourne and worked with period-instrument orchestras.

Raupach, Hermann Friedrich (*b* Stralsund, 21 Dec 1728; *d* St Petersburg, Dec 1778). German harpsichordist and composer. He served mostly at the St Petersburg court, where he presented several stage works. While in Paris, 1762–8, he published some sonatas, from which Mozart arranged four movements in his early keyboard concertos.

His father Christoph (1686–1744) was an organist in Stralsund, a composer and a writer on music. Another relative, Ernst Benjamin Salomo Raupach (1784–1848), was a dramatist and librettist.

Rauschpfeife. Term used in late-medieval Germany and the Low Countries for woodwind instruments, particularly the shawm.

Rautavaara, Einojuhani (*b* Helsinki, 9 Oct 1928). Finnish composer. He studied with Merikanto at the Helsinki Academy (1948–52), where from 1966 he taught, and with Persichetti at the Juilliard School (1955–6). His large output shows a variety of stylistic resource (Russian nationalists, Hindemith and advanced serialism) and he has written in many genres; notable is *The True and False Unicorn* (1971) for chorus, orchestra and tape.

Rauzzini, Venanzio (*b* Camerino, bap. 19 Dec 1746; *d* Bath, 8 April 1810). Italian soprano castrato and composer. He served at Munich, 1766–72, and presented two operas there; he also played the harpsichord. Mozart composed the title role of *Lucio Silla* and solo motet *Exsultate, jubilate* for him in 1772–3. In 1774 he settled in England. Besides singing at the King's Theatre, London (1774–7), he composed new operas, revised his earlier ones and contributed to pasticcios, 1774–87. From 1777 he lived mostly in Bath, where he became a concert manager. A composer of some popularity, he also wrote incidental music, cantatas, duets, arias, songs, vocal exercises etc and instrumental pieces. His brother Matteo (1754–91), active in Munich, Vienna and finally Dublin, was a composer and singing teacher.

Raval, Sebastián (*b* Cartagena, *c*1550; *d* Palermo, before 27 Oct 1604). Spanish composer. A soldier, then a friar, he served at the Urbino court and in 1592 went to Rome. In 1595 he became *maestro* of the royal chapel in Palermo, where he took part in a competition with Falcone. He composed motets (1593, 1600), Lamentations (1594) and secular music (4 bks, 1593–6), conservative works aiming at contrapuntal complexity.

Ravel, (Joseph) Maurice (*b* Ciboure, 7 March 1875; *d* Paris, 28 Dec 1937). French composer. His father's background was Swiss and his mother's Basque, but he was brought up in Paris, where he studied at the Conservatoire, 1889–95, returning in 1897 for further study with Fauré and Gédalge. In 1893 he met Chabrier and Satie, both of whom were influential. A decade later he was an established composer, at least of songs and piano pieces, working with luminous precision in a style that could imitate Lisztian bravura (*Jeux d'eau*) or Renaissance calm (*Pavane pour une infante défunte*); there was also the String Quartet, somewhat in the modal style of Debussy's but more ornately instrumented. However, he five times failed to win the Prix de Rome (1900–05) and left the Conservatoire to continue his life as a freelance musician.

During the next decade, that of his 30s, he was at his most productive. There was a rivalry with Debussy and some dispute about priority in musical discoveries, but Ravel's taste for sharply defined ideas and closed formal units was entirely his own, as was the grand virtuosity of much of his piano music from this period, notably the cycles *Miroirs* and *Gaspard de la nuit*. Many works also show his fascination with things temporally or geographically distant, with moods sufficiently alien to be objectively drawn: these might be historical musical styles, as in the post-Schubertian *Valses nobles et sentimentales*, or the imagination of childhood, as in *Ma mère l'oye*. Or the composer's inspection might be turned on the East (*Shéhérazade*) or, as happened repeatedly, on Spain (*Rapsodie espagnole*, the comic opera *L'heure espagnole*). Or there might be a double focus, as in the vision of ancient Greece through the modification of 18th-century French classicism in the languorous ballet *Daphnis et Chloé*, written for Dyagilev.

The Ballets Russes were also important in introducing him to Stravinsky, with whom he collaborated on a version of Musorgsky's *Khovanshchina*, and whose musical development he somewhat paralleled during the decade or so after *The Rite of Spring*. The set of three Mallarmé songs with nonet accompaniment were written partly under the influence of Stravinsky's *Japanese Lyrics* and Schoenberg's *Pierrot lunaire*, and the two sonatas of the 1920s can be compared with Stravinsky's abstract works of the period in their harmonic astringency and selfconscious use of established forms. However, Ravel's *Le tombeau de Couperin*, just as selfconscious, predates Stravinsky's neoclassicism, and the pressure of musical history is perhaps felt most intensely in the ballet *La valse*, where 3/4 rhythm develops into a *dance macabre*: both these works, like many others, exist in both orchestral and piano versions, testifying to Ravel's superb technique in both media (in 1922 he applied his orchestral skills tellingly to Musorgsky's *Pictures at an Exhibition*). Other postwar works return to some of the composer's obsessions: with the delights and dangers of the child's world in the sophisticated fantasy opera *L'enfant et les sortilèges*, with musical Spanishness in *Boléro* and the songs for a projected

Don Quixote film, and with the exotic in the *Chansons madécasses*. His last major effort was a pair of piano concertos, one exuberant and cosmopolitan (in G major), the other (for left hand only) more darkly and sturdily single-minded. He died after a long illness.

Operas L'heure espagnole (1911); L'enfant et les sortilèges (1925)
Ballets Ma mère l'oye (1911); Daphnis et Chloé (1912); La valse (1920, perf. 1928); Boléro (1928)
Orchestral music Rapsodie espagnole (1908); Pavane pour une infante défunte (1910); Valses nobles et sentimentales (1912); Pf Conc., left hand (1930); Pf Conc., G (1931)
Chamber music, Str Qt (1903); Introduction and Allegro, harp, 6 insts (1905); Pf Trio (1914); Sonata, vn, vc (1922); Tzigane, vn, pf (1924); Sonata, vn, pf (1927)
Piano music Menuet antique (1895); Pavane pour une infante défunte (1899); Jeux d'eau (1901); Sonatine (1905); Miroirs (1905); Gaspard de la nuit (1908); Ma mère l'oye, 4 hands (1910); Valses nobles et sentimentales (1911); Le tombeau de Couperin (1917)
Songs with instruments Shéhérazade (1903); Trois poèmes de Mallarmé (1913); Don Quichotte à Dulcinée (1933); Chansons madécasses (1926)
Songs with piano 5 mélodies populaires grecques (1906); Histoires naturelles (1906); Chants populaires (1910); 2 mélodies hébraïques (1914); Ronsard à son âme (1924)

Ravenscroft, John (*d* by 1708). English composer. An amateur violinist, he lived in Italy, where he took lessons with Corelli and published 12 trio sonatas, modelled closely on Corelli's but less virtuoso, in 1695; a second book appeared in London in 1708. A different John Ravenscroft played the violin in London, *c*1720–50, and composed dance music.

Ravenscroft, Thomas (*b* ?*c*1582; *d c*1635). English editor, composer and theorist. A singer at St Paul's Cathedral until at least 1600 and a student at Gresham College, he took the Cambridge MusB (?1605) and taught at Christ's Hospital (1618–22). His editions include *Pammelia* (1609), the first English printed collection of rounds and catches, and one of the most important psalters of the period (1621); 55 of its 105 settings are by him. He also wrote anthems, instrumental works and a treatise, the *Briefe Discourse* (1614).

Ravinia Festival (USA). Annual (summer) festival established in 1936 from an earlier concert series at Ravinia Park, Chicago. Events include concerts by the Chicago SO and visiting orchestras, chamber music, concert performances of operas, jazz, popular music and master classes.

Ravvivando (It.). 'Reviving': term used to instruct the performer to return to an earlier faster tempo or livelier mood.

Rawsthorne, Alan (*b* Haslingden, 2 May 1905; *d* Cambridge, 24 July 1971). English composer. He studied as a pianist at the RCM and abroad with Petri; only at the end of the 1930s did he begin to make a name as a composer. Influenced by Hindemith, he developed a highly crafted and abstract style, chiefly in concertos and other orchestral works. His inclination towards motivic thinking and variation structures brought some approximation to 12-note techniques, but tonal centres remained important. He wrote three symphonies (1950, 1959, 1964), two piano concertos (1939, 1951), two violin

concertos (1948, 1956), three string quartets (1939, 1954, 1964) and sonatas for viola, cello and violin.

Raymond. Opera in three acts by Ambroise Thomas to a libretto by Rosier and de Leuven (1851, Paris).

Raymonda. Ballet in three acts by Glazunov (1898, St Petersburg).

Razor Quartet [Rasiermesserquartett]. Nickname of Haydn's String Quartet in F minor op.55 no.2 (late 1780s), which he is said to have given to the London publisher John Bland in exchange for an English razor.

Razumovsky, Count Andrey Kyrillovich (*b* St Petersburg, 2 Nov 1772; *d* Vienna, 23 Sept 1836). Russian music patron. From 1792, he was Russian ambassador in Vienna, where he knew Haydn, Mozart and Beethoven. He is specially associated with Beethoven's three string quartets op.59, in two of which Beethoven introduced Russian folk themes in his honour. He established a string quartet in 1808 which Beethoven was allowed to use; it was disbanded in 1814 when his palace was ravaged by fire.

Razumovsky, Dmitry Vasil'yevich (*b* Tula province, 7 Nov 1818; *d* Moscow, 14 Jan 1889). Russian scholar. He studied Russian chant, becoming the first lecturer in the history of Russian church music at the Moscow Conservatory (1866).

Razumovsky Quartets. Beethoven's String Quartets op.59 nos.1–3 (1805–6), dedicated to Count Andrey Razumovsky.

Read, Daniel (*b* Attleboro, MA, 16 Nov 1757; *d* New Haven, CT, 4 Dec 1836). American composer and tunebook compiler. He may have attended singing schools from *c*1772; by 1774 he was composing and in 1782 he moved to New Haven. His first published music appeared in *The Chorister's Companion* (1782); *The American Singing Book* (1785) was devoted entirely to his pieces. Read's style was based on the English *a cappella* tradition but with more harmonic flexibility and less regard for conventions; after 1795 he chiefly revised his earlier music. By the early 1800s a number of his tunes (including 'Calvary', 'Greenwich' and 'Windham') had become part of the American psalmody repertory. Read was also joint compiler/publisher of the *American Musical Magazine* (1786–7), the first American periodical music publication.

Reading, John (*b c*1685; *d* London, 2 Sept 1764). English composer and organist, probably a son of the Lincoln, Chichester and Winchester organist John Reading (*d* 1692). He was organist at Dulwich College and at London churches including St John's, Hackney (1708–27). A skilled and versatile composer, he wrote songs, anthems and organ and harpsichord pieces, some showing an Italian influence. He also collected, transcribed and arranged a large amount of music.

Real, tonal. Terms used in fugue, referring to the ANSWER, which is described as 'real' if an exact transposition of the subject and 'tonal' if not.

Realize. Term used for the working-out for performance of some element left uncertain, or indefinitely notated, in the original. Thus a CONTINUO player 'realizes' a figured bass, by playing his or her version of the chords implied; a singer will 'realize' ORNAMENTS notated in a conventional form. A fully written-out continuo part is often described as a 'realization'. The term may also be applied to the preparation of an edition that goes beyond writing out what is implicit and includes elements freshly written in what is supposed to be the style of the original.

Rebab. A spiked fiddle with two or three strings, found in Indonesia and Malaysia, used in gamelan music in Java and Bali. *See* RABĀB.

Rebec. A bowed stringed instrument of 10th-century origin, used in European art music chiefly during the Middle Ages and Renaissance. There were two basic forms, pear-shaped or straight and narrow. The pegbox was sometimes right-angled and later became sickle-shaped. The strings varied from one to five or more, three being typical; it was usually tuned in 5ths (a 1545 authority gives different sizes, tuned *g–d'–a'*, *c–g–d'* and *F–G–d–a*). It could be played on the lap, as in southern Europe, or on the shoulder, as in the north. It was commonly played in processions, dances and at court, notably that of Henry VIII; later it was used in consorts.

Rebel, François (*b* Paris, 19 June 1701; *d* there, 7 Nov 1775). French composer, son of Jean-Féry Rebel. A violinist and theorbist, at 13 he joined the orchestra of the Académie Royale. With his colleague François Francoeur, he played at the Concert Spirituel in 1726 and put on an opera *Pirame et Thisbé*, the first of their several collaborative operas or ballets. They were concerned too in performance and administration at the Concert Spirituel and at the Opéra, 1743–67. In their joint works, Rebel was said to provide the forceful element, Francoeur the expressive.

Rebel, Jean-Féry (*b* Paris, bap. 18 April 1666; *d* there, 2 Jan 1747). French violinist and composer, father of François Rebel. After serving the Count of Ayen in Spain, 1700–05, he became a leading member of the French king's 24 Violons and the Académie Royale de Musique orchestra. He later held court posts including that of chamber composer (from 1726) and was active as a harpsichordist and conductor. An innovatory and esteemed composer, he wrote various vocal works, string sonatas, 'symphonies' for the Académie Royale dancers including *Les caractères de la danse* (1715), *Terpsichore* (1720) and the much admired *Les élémens* (1737), which begins with a famously alarming dissonance to represent chaos.

His father Jean (early 17th century–*c*1691) and sister Anne-Renée (1663–1722) were both singers at the French court.

Rebelo, João Soares or **João Lourenço** (*b* Caminha, 1610; *d* Apelação, 16 Nov 1661). Portuguese composer, brother of Marcos Soares Pereira. He was made a nobleman of the royal house by King John IV in 1646. He wrote a large amount of sacred music, much of it in a grandiose polychoral idiom (including a 39-voice mass for John IV's 39th birthday). He should not be confused with Manuel Rebello (*c*1575–1647), a leading Portuguese composer of sacred music and *mestre de capela* at Évora Cathedral.

Rebikov, Vladimir Ivanovich (*b* Krasnoyarsk, 31 May 1866; *d* Yalta, 4 Aug 1920). Russian composer. He studied with Klenovsky at the Moscow Conservatory and in Berlin. His early music was Tchaikovskian, but *c*1900 he began to write expressionist dramatic and vocal pieces using whole-tone harmony and other modernisms; his most adventurous works are 'musico-psycholographic dramas' and the 'mélomimiques' for voice and piano.

Recapitulation. The third main division of a movement in SONATA FORM, in which the thematic material of the first section is restated, normally all in the tonic key.

Rechants, Cinq. Works by Messiaen, five settings of his own texts for 12 voices (1949).

Récit (Fr.). Term, distinct from 'recitative', for a piece sung by a solo voice, in French 17th-century usage; it was later extended to embrace solo instrumental sections in larger works. In the 17th-century *ballet de cour*, a *récit* was usually placed at the beginning of each act, to serve as commentary. In organ music the term denotes a manual on the French classical organ, used for solo stops.

Recital. Term for a concert given by one performer or a small group. It was used in the 16th century for a speech or narrative and transferred to music in the 19th century. The first to popularize the term was Liszt, who used it in 1840 for his solo piano performances in London.

Recitative. A type of vocal writing, normally for a single voice, which follows the natural rhythms and accentuation of speech and its pitch contours. The 'stile recitativo' was linked with the Florentine Camerata's development, in the late 16th century, of a style with a precise rhythmic notation, harmonic support, a wide melodic range and affective (emotionally charged) treatment of the words.

During the 17th century, the aria became the dominant element in opera, and recitative a vehicle for dialogue and a connecting link between arias. The carefully notated declamation of early recitative was replaced by a more rapid, even delivery notated mainly in quavers (a trend taken further in late 18th-century *opera buffa*). Among several conventions applied to recitative by 1700 was that of ending a passage with a falling 4th, or with a 4–3–(2)–1 descent, in advance of the cadence. Later the continuo cadence was often delayed until the singer had finished (though not usually in opera). This kind of recitative is now called *recitativo semplice* or *recitativo secco*, to distinguish it from accompanied recitative (*recitativo accompagnato*, *recitativo stromentato*, i.e. with instruments other than continuo), which was rare until *c*1680. In the 18th century a more elaborate kind of accompanied recitative (*recitativo obbligato*), in which the orchestra has independent passages of a violent or pathetic character, became important at dramatic junctures in *opera seria* and in the oratorio and cantata. In Gluck's *Orfeo ed Euridice* (1762) and his Paris operas (1774–9) the orchestra accompanies throughout. While Italian-style recitative was adopted in Germany and England, in France there was greater resistance: the French language favoured a type more melodic and rhythmically flexible.

With the continuous texture of opera and oratorio in the 19th century, recitative disappeared as an independent form while remaining an essential means of expression for passages in a libretto for which lyrical treatment was inappropriate. Recitative with keyboard accompaniment did not long survive the 18th century, except where it was artificially revived, as in Britten's *The Rape of Lucretia* (1946) and Stravinsky's *The Rake's Progress* (1951). Many composers have introduced recitative-like passages into instrumental works. Examples include Haydn's Symphony no.7 ('Le midi') and Beethoven's piano sonatas op.31 no.2 and op.110. The passage for cellos and basses in the finale of Beethoven's Choral Symphony is marked 'selon le caractère d'un Récitatif mais *in tempo*'.

Recorder (Fr. *flûte à bec*; Ger. *Blockflöte*; It. *flauto dolce*). A woodwind instrument with seven finger-holes and a thumb-hole; it is end-blown through a whistle mouthpiece. The modern recorder is usually made in three jointed sections: the head with its characteristic beak-shaped mouthpiece, the middle joint, and the foot joint which contains the seventh finger-hole (for illustration, *see* EARLY MUSIC). The main instruments in use today (with the lowest note of their two-octave range) are the descant, or in the USA soprano (*c″*); the treble, USA alto (*f′*); the tenor (*c′*) and the bass (*f*); rarer are the sopranino (*f″*), the great bass (*c*) and double bass (*F*). (There have also been recorders of intermediate pitches.)

The recorder, at different periods, has been called 'fipple flute', 'English flute' and 'common flute'. It probably had its origins as an art instrument in Italy in the 14th century. The first tutor was published in Venice in 1535. During the Renaissance it was primarily a consort instrument; Praetorius described eight different sizes (from *Exilent* to *Grossbass*) and Henry VIII's inventory mentions 76 recorders in cases of four to nine instruments, which were doubtless made and tuned together for consort music. The Baroque period saw an increased use of the recorder as a solo instrument or as a member of ensembles. Purcell's 'flute' parts in his dramatic works are for recorder and Bach used it extensively in his cantatas as well as in two of the Brandenburg Concertos. Handel, the Loeillets and especially Telemann composed for recorder in smaller combinations. It was replaced in popularity by the more expressive transverse flute during the 18th century but has been widely revived in the 20th as a school instrument, particularly in England and Germany. Many modern composers have written for recorder, notably Britten and Henze.

Recoupe. A French 16th-century dance, often used as an after-dance to the basse danse.

Reda, Siegfried (*b* Bochum, 27 July 1916; *d* Mülheim, 13 Dec 1968). German composer and organist. A pupil of Pepping and Distler at the Spandau Church Music School, he taught at Essen from 1946 and from 1953 directed church music in Mülheim (Altstadt), becoming a strong influence on new currents in Protestant church music. He developed Distler's style in his choral music (Requiem, 1963) and moved from neo-classicism to serialism in his organ works.

Redford, John (*d* London, ?Nov 1547). English composer and organist. He was a vicar-choral at St Paul's Cathedral in 1534 but by 1547 was Master of the Choristers and organist. He is one of the earliest English composers of any importance whose organ music has survived. Apart from three four-voice Latin motets, all his extant music is for organ and was designed to alternate with, and partly replace, the sung plainchant of the Latin services. His music is instrumental in idiom and almost completely independent of vocal technique; he raised the organ antiphon to the status of written, rather than improvisatory, composition. He was a poet and dramatist too.

Redoutensaal. Hall in Vienna, built in 1740; it was the city's main concert hall until the Musikverein opened (1870).

Reduction. Term used for the arrangement (usually for piano) of music for orchestra or other ensemble.

Reed. A thin layer of metal, plastic or most frequently natural reed (or 'cane'), set into vibration by air from bellows or a player's lungs. There are two types used in Western art music: 'beating' and 'free'. The former may be single (as in the clarinet, saxophone and the reed stop of an organ), where the reed beats against a fixed surface, or double (as in the oboe and bassoon), where two reed surfaces beat together. The free reed, which vibrates freely under air pressure, is found in certain organ pipes and reed organs such as the harmonium, accordion and concertina (all bellows-blown). The mouth organ is one of the few mouth-blown free reeds.

Reed organ. Generic term for keyboard instruments whose sound is produced by freely vibrating reed tongues (usually without individual resonators) and activated by air under pressure or suction. Common names for such instruments include HARMONIUM, melodeon, vocalion, seraphine, *orgue expressif*, cabinet organ or American organ (this last is generally used in Europe to distinguish suction from pressure instruments). In the 19th century many patents were taken out for types of reed organ under such names as Aeolina, Euphonion, Mélodiflute, Organochordium and Physharmonika. Other reed organs include such portable instruments as the ACCORDION and CONCERTINA.

Reed organs range from compact single-manual instruments with one set of reeds, powered by one or two foot treadles, to large two-manual (rarely three) and pedal instruments having several sets, of differing colours and pitches, and powered by a separate blowing lever or an electric motor, as in pipe organs. The commonest types had two to five sets of reeds, one manual and such accessories as octave couplers and tremulant. Such instruments vied with the piano as domestic instruments in the 19th century and were used extensively in small churches as substitutes for the pipe organ.

During the late 19th century in Europe the reed organ was regarded as a serious instrument for serious musicians; composers such as Franck, Karg-Elert, Louis and René Vierne and Reger wrote works for it. Many transcriptions were made, and it was extensively used to accompany voices. In the USA the literature tended to be simpler and aimed at the amateur. In the early 20th century interest began to wane, and by the mid-century, electronic instruments had taken over the domestic market. But more lately interest in the reed organ and its music has been renewed: it occasionally appears in concerts and has been restored for church use.

Reel. A Scottish dance, common also in Ireland and North America. The earliest reference to it dates from 1590, but the dance is of much greater antiquity. The music is in a rapid, smooth-flowing quaver movement in *alla breve* time, minim = 120. The reel has existed in various forms with qualifying names such as 'threesome' and 'foursome', indicating the number of dancers; those most often danced today are the eightsome and the Reel of Tulloch, devised c1880.

Reese, Gustave (*b* New York, 29 Nov 1899; *d* Berkeley, 7 Sept 1977). American musicologist. He attended New York University and taught there from 1927. His two most important books, *Music in the Middle Ages* (1940) and *Music in the Renaissance* (1954), gave tremendous impetus to the study of early music and to musicology in general in English-speaking countries. His work set new standards in the documentation, orderly marshalling and clear exposition of fact.

Reeve, William (*b* London, 1757; *d* there, 22 June 1815). English composer. Initially an organist in Totnes, Devon, he moved to London in the 1780s and composed music for stage works. Several in the 1790s were pantomime ballets, with songs but no spoken dialogue; he also composed operas (mostly short) and 'aqua dramas'.

Refice, Licinio (*b* Patrica, 12 Feb 1883; *d* Rio de Janeiro, 11 Sept 1954). Italian composer and church musician. He studied and taught in Rome, where he was *maestro di cappella* at S Maria Maggiore (1911–47), and toured as a conductor in Europe and North and South America. He composed oratorios and masses and two religious operas, notably *Cecilia* (1934), staged in many countries.

Reformation Symphony. Mendelssohn's Symphony no.5 in D op.107 (1832), written for (but not played at) the tercentenary in Augsburg of the foundation of the Lutheran Reformed Church.

Refrain. In poetry, a phrase or verse which recurs at intervals, especially at the end of a stanza. The term has been used analogously for recurring passages in musical forms, with or without text repetition.

The French *refrain*, applied to medieval song, means a segment of melody with words which is interpolated in other works where it may be repeated as part of a strophic song; they are in the nature of courtly aphorisms or amorous proverbs and were introduced into polyphonic motets and monophonic songs.

The French late medieval *formes fixes* (rondeau, virelai and ballade) involve refrains in the more usual sense. The refrain of the ballata and frottola is known as *ripresa*, that of the villancico as *estribillo* and that of the carol as burden.

Regal. A kind of small portable organ in which the sound is produced by reeds. It flourished in the 16th and 17th centuries, mainly in Germany, but also in England and in Italy, where it featured in early operas such as Monteverdi's *Orfeo*.

Regent's bugle. A rare kind of trumpet introduced by J.G. Schmidt into the Prince Regent's band, c1815. Probably it had a cylindrical tube, with a telescopic mouthpiece, a U-shaped slide for adjusting its fundamental and five keys.

Reger, (Johann Baptist Joseph) Max(imilian) (*b* Brand, Upper Palatinate, 19 March 1873; *d* Leipzig, 11 May 1916). German composer. He studied with Riemann (1890–95) in Munich and Wiesbaden (where his drinking habits began); in 1901 he settled in Munich, and in 1907 he moved to Leipzig to take a post as professor of composition at the university, though he was also active internationally as a conductor and pianist. He was appointed conductor of the court orchestra at Meiningen in 1911 and in 1915 moved to Jena.

During a composing life of little more than 20 years, he produced a large output in all genres, nearly always in abstract forms. He was a firm supporter of 'absolute' music and saw himself in a tradition going back to Bach, through Beethoven, Schumann and Brahms; his organ music, though also affected by Liszt, was provoked by that tradition. Of his orchestral pieces, his symphonic and richly elaborate Hiller Variations and Mozart Variations are justly remembered; of his chamber music the lighter-textured trios have retained a place in the repertory, along with some of the works for solo string instruments. His late piano and two-piano music places him as a successor to Brahms in the central German tradition. He pursued intensively, and to its limits, Brahms's continuous development and free modulation, often also invoking, like Brahms, the aid of Bachian counterpoint. Many of his works are in variation and fugue forms; equally characteristic is a great energy and complexity of thematic growth.

Orchestral music Sinfonietta, A (1905); Serenade, G (1906); Variations and Fugue on a Theme of Hiller (1907); Vn Conc., A (1908); Sym. Prologue to a Tragedy, a (1908); Pf Conc., f (1910); Overture to a Comedy (1911); Romantic Suite (1912); 4 Portraits after Arnold Böcklin (1913); Ballet Suite, D (1913); Variations and Fugue on a Theme of Mozart (1914)
Choral music Psalm c (1909); Die Nonnen (1909); 8 geistliche Gesänge (1914); Requiem, inc. (1914); 2 Gesänge (Der Einsiedler; Requiem) 1915; male- and mixed-voice choruses, sacred works
Chamber music 9 sonatas, vn, pf (1890, 1891, 1899, 1903, 1905, 1909, 1911, 1915); 4 sonatas, vc, pf (1892, 1898, 1904, 1910); 2 pf qnts (1898, 1902); 11 sonatas, vn (1900, 1905); 2 sonatas, cl, pf (1900); 5 str qts (1900, 1904, 1909, 1911); Serenade, fl, vn, va (1904); 2 str trios (1904, 1915); Pf Trio (1908); Suite, vn, pf (1908); Sonata, cl/va, pf (1909); 2 pf qts (1910, 1914); Str sextet (1910); Preludes and Fugues, vn (1912, 1914); 3 Duos im alten Stil, 2 vn (1914); 3 suites, vc (1915); 3 suites, va (1915); Serenade, fl/vn, vn, va (1915); Cl Qnt (1915); 12 Kleine Stücke eigenen Liedern, vn, pf (1916)
Solo vocal music An die Hoffnung, A/Mez, orch/pf (1912); Hymnus der Liebe, Bar/A, orch (1914); over 250 lieder
Piano music Variations and Fugue on a Theme of Bach (1904); Variations and Fugue on a Theme of Beethoven, 2 pf (1904); 4 sonatinas (1905, 1908); 6 pieces, pf duet (1906); Introduction, Passacaglia and Fugue, 2 pf (1906); 6 prel-

udes and fugues (1907); Episoden (1910); Aus meinem Tagebuch (1912); Variations and Fugue on a Theme of Telemann (1914); Träume am Kamin, 12 pieces (1915)
Organ music 7 chorale fantasias (1898–1900); 4 fantasias and fugues (1 on B–A–C–H) (1898–1916); 2 sonatas (1899, 1901); 6 trios (1900); 62 pieces (1901–16); 95 chorale preludes (1902–14); Variations and Fugue on an Original Theme (1903); 9 preludes and fugues (1904); Introduction, Passacaglia and Fugue (1913)

Reggae. An urban popular music and dance style, originating in Jamaica in the mid-1960s. It fuses elements of North American popular music and traditional Afro-Jamaican music. The characteristic rhythmic texture is an amalgam of short ostinatos on electric guitars, organ, electric bass and drums emphasizing the off-beats of quadruple metre.

Regina caeli laetare (Lat.: 'Queen of Heaven, rejoice'). One of the four Marian antiphons sung at the end of Compline from Easter Sunday to the Friday after Pentecost. Polyphonic settings were made by Dunstable, Busnois, Victoria and others.

Regis, Johannes [Leroy, Jehan] (*b* c1430; *d* ?Soignies, c1485). Netherlands composer. A 'Jehan Leroy' was at St Vincent, Soignies, in 1458. In 1463 he was appointed *magister puerorum* of Notre Dame, Antwerp. He also became Dufay's secretary in Cambrai. His works, which were widely known and include two masses and eight motets, use *cantus firmi* and imitative procedures. His motets are more advanced stylistically, with strong cadences, greater rhythmic activity and full scoring.

Register. A part of the range or compass of an instrument, singing voice or composition.

Registration. In organ and harpsichord playing, the selection of different available pitches and tone colours. The musical forces of the organ are available selectively by means of separate stops or registers which together provide the entire tonal capacity of the instrument. Each of the registers controls the 'on' or 'off' position for a series of pipes, grouped so that one or more pipes will respond to each key on a manual or pedal keyboard.

Large harpsichords from the late 16th century to c1800 rarely had fewer than three colours (two stops which could be used separately or together), and any late 17th-century instrument with two manuals and three choirs was capable of at least ten distinct registrations. Although no conventions of harpsichord registration developed, indications by French composers imply that most pieces were to begin with full registration, and manuals were uncoupled and registers retired for special effects. After the Baroque period, large harpsichords were fitted with 'machine' stops which shifted registration from full to a single 8' on each manual and enabled graduated dynamic effects.

Regnart, Jacob (*b* Douai, ?1540–45; *d* Prague, 16 Oct 1599). South Netherlands composer. From 1557 he served the Habsburg courts, first as a singer in Prague, then in Vienna. In 1568–70 he studied in Italy. After 1576 he was back in Prague (vice-Kapellmeister from 1579 then from 1596), with a spell in Innsbruck (from 1585). A respected and successful composer, he is known for his immensely popular German secular songs for three voices in

villanella style (1576–9). He also published four- and five-part lieder (1591, 1580), madrigals (1574, 1581) and at least ten books of sacred music contributing to the Catholic reform movement.

Regola dell'ottava (It.). 'Rule of the octave': term used in the theory of figured bass for a simplified harmony system in which each note of a scale (ascending and descending an octave) was assumed to indicate a particular pattern of chordal harmony.

Regondi, Giulio (*b* Genoa, c1822; *d* London, 6 May 1872). Italian guitar and concertina player. He won fame as a guitarist in Paris and London, later becoming a distinguished player and popularizer of the concertina (invented by Wheatstone, 1829), for which he wrote concertos and chamber and solo works.

Reich, Steve [Stephen] **(Michael)** (*b* New York, 3 Oct 1936). American composer. He studied drumming when he was 14 with the New York PO timpanist; later he took a degree in philosophy at Cornell (1953–7) and studied composition at the Juilliard School (1958–61) and at Mills College (1962–3) with Milhaud and Berio, also becoming interested in Balinese and African music. In 1966 he began performing with his own ensemble, chiefly of percussionists, developing a music of gradually changing ostinato patterns that move out of phase, creating an effect of shimmering surfaces; this culminated in *Drumming* (1971), a 90-minute elaboration of a single rhythmic cell. From c1972 he added harmonic change to his music, and later (*Tehillim*, 1981) melody. He has also worked with larger orchestral and choral forces (*The Desert Music*, 1983).

Reicha [Rejcha], **Antoine(-Joseph)** [Antonín] (*b* Prague, 26 Feb 1770; *d* Paris, 28 May 1836). Czech, later French, composer, theorist and teacher. He studied with his uncle Josef Reicha (1752–95), a cellist and conductor, learning the violin and the flute; at Bonn and Hamburg he developed an interest in harmony and composition, soon fertilized at Vienna (1801) by his friendship with Haydn and lessons with Albrechtsberger. In Paris from 1808, he hoped for operatic success but had only three operas performed, one of which, *Sapho* (1822), he considered his masterpiece. Meanwhile his fame as a wind quintet composer, theorist and teacher increased, assisted by his *Traité de mélodie* (1814), the fugal Etudes op.97 and the success of his students, including Baillot, Habeneck and Rode. Professor of counterpoint and fugue at the Conservatoire from 1818 – Berlioz and Liszt were among his pupils in 1826, Franck in 1835 – he wrote one of the first modern classroom harmony texts, *Cours de composition musicale* (?1816–18). His most important treatise however was the *Traité de haute composition musicale* (1824–6), dealing with invertible counterpoint, fugue, rhythm and form.

Reichardt, Johann Friedrich (*b* Königsberg, 25 Nov 1752; *d* Giebichenstein, 27 June 1814). German composer and writer on music. A virtuoso violinist and fine keyboard player, he toured north Germany and Bohemia in 1771–4. After a year as a government official, he became Kapellmeister to the royal Berlin opera in 1775. While traditional Italian opera predominated there, his own works were mostly staged elsewhere; later he had successes at Berlin with German works, notably his Singspiel *Claudine von Villa Bella* (1789, libretto by Goethe). Meanwhile he continued to travel and to meet leading artists and intellectuals. He founded the Berlin Concert Spirituel in 1783. Latterly he grew unpopular at court and in 1794 he was dismissed. He worked briefly at Kassel and visited Vienna, but died largely forgotten.

Reichardt composed chiefly vocal music. His *c*1500 songs are early Romantic in spirit, and depart from the plain style of the Berlin school, ranging from folklike settings to near-operatic scenes. In his *c*30 dramatic works he abandoned the older styles of *opera seria* for forward-looking Italian opera and German forms. He also wrote incidental music (e.g. for *Macbeth*, 1787), ballets, oratorios, cantatas, sacred music and many instrumental works (most for keyboard). Also important are his many writings, notably the *Briefe eines aufmerksamen Reisenden* (1774–6), based on his travel notes and letters. As editor of the *Musikalisches Kunstmagazin* (1782–91) he was a pioneer of modern music journalism.

Reichardt's daughter Louise (1779–1826) was a singing teacher and chorus director in Hamburg, and a popular composer of songs and choruses.

Reiche, Gottfried (*b* Weissenfels, 5 Feb 1667; *d* Leipzig, 6 Oct 1734). German trumpeter. He worked in Leipzig (from 1719 as senior city piper) and in 1723–34 played all Bach's first trumpet parts. He composed many sonatas and other pieces.

Reicher-Kindermann, Hedwig (*b* Munich, 15 July 1853; *d* Trieste, 2 June 1883). German soprano. One of the Valkyries in the first complete *Ring* cycle at Bayreuth (1876), she later sang to great acclaim the roles of Erda, Fricka, Isolde, Ortrud and Brünnhilde for Angelo Neumann's touring company. She was the outstanding opera singer of her generation.

Reichmann, Theodor (*b* Rostock, 15 March 1849; *d* Marbach, 22 May 1903). German baritone. During his 30-year career he excelled in the Wagner roles of Amfortas, Hans Sachs, the Dutchman and Wotan. He sang at Munich, Bayreuth and the Vienna Court Opera.

Reid, John (*b* Straloch, 13 Feb 1721; *d* London, 6 Feb 1807). Scottish flautist, composer and musical benefactor. Besides pursuing an army career, he was famous as a flautist and wrote sonatas, marches etc for the instrument. He endowed the chair of music at Edinburgh University.

Reigenlied. Medieval round-dance song. It was a conceptual mould for performance rather than a form; it is characterized by triple metre, repeated notes and phrase repetition. Cries, stamping and clapping were features of its presentation, reflecting its basic function of expressing *joie de vivre* in springtime. It played an important role in the summer songs of Neidhart von Reuental and was used by others in the 13th century and in Meisterlieder.

Reimann, Aribert (*b* Berlin, 4 March 1936). German composer and pianist. He studied with Blacher and Pepping at the Berlin Musikhochschule (1955–9)

and established himself as a pianist, notably as accompanist to Fischer-Dieskau, with whom he has recorded 20th-century German songs. He has written ten operas in an expressionist style (*Lear*, 1978; *Die Gespenstersonate*, 1984), orchestral, vocal and chamber music.

Reimann, Heinrich (*b* Kłodzko, 14 March 1850; *d* Berlin, 24 May 1906). German organist and writer. From 1887 he was an organist, theory teacher, choral conductor and librarian in Berlin, also writing music criticism, programme notes for the Berlin PO and books on Bach and Brahms and editing an international folksong collection. He supported the music of Wagner, Brahms and Reger.

Reina Codex. Italian MS of the early 15th century. It consists of 122 folios with 220 secular pieces, Italian and French, of the period *c*1400–40, madrigals, ballatas, ballades, rondeaux, virelais etc, by Bartolino da Padova, Jacopo da Bologna, Landini, Machaut, Dufay and others. Copied by several scribes, it comes from the Padua-Venice area, was owned by a Signor Reina in the early 19th century and now belongs to the Bibliothèque Nationale, Paris.

Reinagle, Alexander (*b* Portsmouth, bap. 23 April 1756; *d* Baltimore, 21 Sept 1809). English composer and pianist of Austrian descent. After working in Glasgow and meeting C.P.E. Bach in Hamburg, he settled in Philadelphia (1786), becoming an eminent teacher, concert organizer and theatre musician. For 15 years he worked with the New Company, a theatrical company in Philadelphia and Baltimore, which he conducted and for which he composed the music for hundreds of light stage productions. His four piano sonatas are perhaps the first sonatas written in the USA (*c*1790). Reinagle's brother Joseph (1762–1825) was a string player and composer and his nephew Alexander Robert (1799–1877) an organist in Oxford who wrote the well-known hymn tune *St Peter* ('In Christ there is no east or west').

Reincken [Reinken, Reinike], Johann Adam (*b* 27 April 1623; *d* Hamburg, 24 Nov 1722). Dutch or German composer and organist. He may have been born in the Netherlands or Alsace. In 1654–7 he studied with Sweelinck's former pupil Heinrich Scheidemann in Hamburg. After a year as organist in Deventer he became Scheidemann's assistant at St Catherine's, Hamburg, in 1658 and succeeded him in 1663; he was not assisted in his duties until his 80th year. He was famous as a concert performer, organ expert and teacher. The nine of his keyboard works known to survive, which include a fugue, a toccata, a fantasia (*An den Wasserflüssen Babylon*), variations and three suites, reflect both the style of the north German organ school and his own virtuoso technique. A set of six instrumental suites, *Hortus musicus* (1687), is foremost among his other surviving works.

Reine, La. Nickname of Haydn's Symphony no.85 in Bb (1785), so called because it was admired by Marie Antoinette, Queen of France.

Reinecke, Carl (Heinrich Carsten) (*b* Altona, 23 June 1824; *d* Leipzig, 10 March 1910). German composer, teacher, administrator, pianist and conductor. He was court pianist in Copenhagen then taught in Cologne, giving concerts with Hiller. He is remembered primarily as a stern but sympathetic teacher (from 1860) at the Leipzig Conservatory, where as director (from 1897) he perpetuated tradition and upheld the example of the Classical composers; among his pupils were Grieg, Riemann, Sullivan and Weingartner. He conducted the Gewandhaus Orchestra (until 1895) and composed, chiefly numerous piano works in the style of Schumann, Brahmsian chamber music and the simpler forms of popular 'Hausmusik'.

Reiner, Fritz (*b* Budapest, 19 Dec 1888; *d* New York, 15 Nov 1963). American conductor of Hungarian birth. His career began in Budapest. He was principal conductor of the Dresden Staatsoper, 1914–22, then settled in the USA, becoming principal conductor of the Cincinnati SO, 1922–31. Later he had charge of the Pittsburg SO (1938–48) and Chicago SO (1953–63). He demanded rhythmic precision and clear textures, resulting in elegant and unsentimental performances, often with great dramatic impact.

Reiner [Rainer], Jacob (*b* Altdorf, Württemberg, before 1650; *d* Weingarten, 12 Aug 1606). German composer. After studying with Lassus in Munich, he worked at the abbey of Weingarten, where he became Kapellmeister. His numerous sacred works show the influence of Lassus and of Venetian composers. His son Ambrosius Reiner (1604–72) was also a composer.

Reinhardt, Johann Georg (*b* 1676/7; *d* Vienna, 6 Jan 1742). Austrian composer. He played in the imperial chapel in Vienna, becoming first organist in 1728; from 1727 he was also Kapellmeister at St Stephen's Cathedral. He was one of Vienna's most significant and prolific composers of church music and also wrote operas and oratorios. His style resembles Fux's. Several other members of his family were musicians.

Reining, Maria (*b* Vienna, 7 Aug 1903). Austrian soprano. She made her début at the Vienna Staatsoper in 1931, returning after a period in Munich in 1937, the year she first appeared at Salzburg. She sang at Covent Garden (Elsa, *Lohengrin*) and Chicago (Eva, *The Mastersingers*, and Butterfly) in 1938; her beautiful voice and elegant manner were particularly admired as the Marschallin, a role she sang in Paris and New York.

Reinitz, Béla (*b* Budapest, 15 Nov 1878; *d* there, 27 Oct 1943). Hungarian composer. A pupil of Siklos in Budapest, he wrote over 500 songs, notably settings of Ady as well as cabaret repertory. He was politically active and forced into exile (1920–31), but returned to Budapest.

Reinken, Johann Adam. *See* REINCKEN, JOHANN ADAM.

Reinmar (der Alte) von Hagenau (*fl* 1185–1205; *d c*1205). German Minnesinger, a leading representative of high Minnesang. Presumably a member of the family of imperial ministerial rank from Hagenau in Alsace, he was court poet to the Babenbergs. His highly original poetry was very influential on contemporary poets such as Neidhart von Reuental; four poems survive with music and three more can be reconstructed. Characteristic features of his style are sensitivity, veiled circumlocutions and affected turns of phrase.

Reinmar von Zweter (*b c*1200; *d c*1260). German Minnesinger. From a noble family of Rhenish Franconia, he was an itinerant musician who visited several south German and Austrian courts. He is generally considered the most important *Spruch* poet of the generation after Walther von der Vogelweide and his *Sprüche*, on a variety of themes from religious to political, show the influence of that master. Well over 200 *Spruch* stanzas have been preserved, as well as several love poems and one *Leich* with music; but the musical evidence regarding his songs is confusing.

Reissiger, Karl Gottlieb (*b* Belzig, 31 Jan 1798; *d* Dresden, 7 Nov 1859). German composer, conductor and teacher. He took theory lessons from Salieri in Vienna, then studied in Munich. Succeeding Weber as director of the Dresden Court Opera in 1826, also becoming Hofkapellmeister in 1828, he gained a reputation as a gifted conductor and gave the première of Wagner's *Rienzi* (1842). Under his direction the Dresden Opera was acknowledged as the best in Europe. He also taught theory (Clara Schumann was one of his pupils), directed music festivals and composed prolifically without distinction.

Reizenstein, Franz (Theodor) (*b* Nuremberg, 7 June 1911; *d* London, 15 Oct 1968). British composer and pianist of German birth. He studied with Hindemith in Berlin (1930–34) and Vaughan Williams at the RCM, then remained in England, at first as an internee, later as a teacher (at the RAM, 1958–68) and pianist (as a soloist and in a trio he formed). His early music shows Hindemith's influence, but later his style became smoother and more relaxed. He wrote much chamber and piano music, two piano concertos and choral music (*Voices of Night*, 1951).

Réjouissance. A lively, 'rejoicing' movement included in some 18th-century orchestral suites, including Bach's Ouverture no.4 in D and Handel's Music for the Royal Fireworks.

Relâche. 'Ballet instantanéiste' in two acts by Satie to a scenario by Picabia (1924, Paris).

Relative key. A key with the same key signature as another given key: C major is the relative major of A minor, E minor is the relative minor of G major.

Relative pitch. The ability to identify intervals by ear without being able to identify individual pitches, as with ABSOLUTE PITCH.

Relish. Term for an ornament; a single relish is a trill with a turned ending, or simply a turn; a double relish is a compound ornament, differently understood by writers, but it normally included a trill and often a turn and/or an appoggiatura.

Rellstab, Johann Carl Friedrich (*b* Berlin, 27 Feb 1759; *d* there, 19 Aug 1813). German publisher and composer. He took over his father's Berlin printing firm in 1779, later adding a publishing house and music shop. He also established a music lending library (1783) and a concert series (1787). Later he worked as a teacher and critic. Among his works are a Singspiel, cantatas, songs, orchestral and keyboard pieces and writings on music.

Rellstab, (Heinrich Fredrich) Ludwig (*b* Berlin, 13 April 1799; *d* there, 27 Nov 1860). German music critic and poet, son of J.C.F. Rellstab. Besides independently published works, he wrote articles for many periodicals and in 1830 founded the important Berlin weekly, *Iris im Gebiete der Tonkunst* (1830–41). He was the first to refer to Beethoven's Piano Sonata op.27 no.2 in terms of moonlight. Schubert and Liszt set some of his poems, Mendelssohn and Meyerbeer his librettos.

Reményi [Hoffmann], Ede [Eduard] (*b* Miskolc, 17 Jan 1828; *d* San Francisco, 15 May 1898). Hungarian violinist. At the Vienna Conservatory he studied with Joseph Böhm. His career as a virtuoso took him to the USA (1848, 1855, 1878) and throughout Europe, where he played with Brahms, became Liszt's friend and held court posts in London and Pest. His soulful and fiery playing combined technical mastery with a national flavour.

Rémy, W.A. [Mayer, (Benjamin) Wilhelm] (*b* Prague, 10 June 1831; *d* Graz, 23 Jan 1898). Austrian composer. Among his many Schumannesque orchestral works, the overture *Sardanapal*, the symphonic poem *Helena* and a Symphony in F were successful. A strict but inspiring teacher, he counted Busoni and Weingartner among his pupils.

Renaissance. Term applied, in Western music history, to the era lasting from *c*1430 to the end of the 16th century. The word means 'rebirth', referring to the objective of intellectuals and artists of the time to repudiate the previous era (the Middle Ages) and to restore the philosophical and artistic ideals of classical antiquity.

The relationship between this movement and music is complex and it is not easy to cite musical features that reflect Renaissance ideals, at least until rather later. However, the Renaissance spirit is often felt to be reflected in such music as the *chansons* of Dufay and Binchois, with their smoother, more flowing lines, and particularly in Josquin's music, from the end of the 15th century, in which imitative counterpoint in four or more parts (replacing the predominant three-part writing of the previous generation) came to be the norm, with all parts alike in texture and frequent imitative writing. Josquin's music, in particular, is often paralleled with the beginnings of humanism, at much the same time. This was also the period when, with the European invention of printing, knowledge began to spread more readily and music came to be published instead of circulating only in manuscript.

The characteristic musical style of the Renaissance period is the smooth, homogeneous, imitative polyphonic style, used by Palestrina, Lassus and Byrd. It was used not only in sacred music (predominantly masses and motets) but also in secular madrigals and instrumental consort music. The favoured instrument was the lute, which during the 16th century became established as the standard instrument for domestic music-making.

The Renaissance period was succeeded by the Baroque. Elements of Baroque style are found early in the second half of the 16th century but Renaissance imitative polyphony remained in use, particu-larly in sacred music, during the 17th century and beyond, widely recognized as a fitting manner for church music.

Renard. 'Burlesque in song and dance' in one act by Stravinsky to his own libretto after Russian rhymes (1922, Paris).

Rencontres Internationales d'Art Contemporain (France). Annual (summer) festival established in 1973; it took over from the Royan Festival. Stockhausen, Boulez and Ferneyhough are among the composers whose works have been prominent.

Rencontres Internationales de Musique Contemporain (France). Annual (autumn) festival established in Metz in 1972; Stockhausen, Boulez, Kagel and Xenakis are among those whose works have been performed.

Rendall, David (*b* London, 11 Oct 1948). English tenor. He studied at the RAM and in Salzburg. He appeared as Alfredo and Pinkerton at the ENO and in Paris in the title role of *Idomeneo*. He has sung at La Scala and in Vienna and made his New York début at the City Opera in 1978 and the Met in 1980 (as Donizetti's Ernesto). At Covent Garden (début 1975) he has sung Don Ottavio and Rossini's Almaviva, to which his fluent, lyrical high tenor is happily suited.

Rener, Adam (*b* Liège, *c*1485; *d* Altenburg, *c*1520). South Netherlands composer and singer. He was a choirboy at Maximilian's court, studied in Burgundy and from 1507 was a musician in the Saxon Elector's Court at Torgau; under his direction the Saxon Chapel became an important musical centre. Like Isaac, he took the spirit of Netherlands music into Germany soon after 1500. His compositions include nine masses, eight Magnificats and motets.

Renvoisy, Richard de (*b* Nancy, *c*1520; *d* Dijon, 6 March 1586). French composer. He was at Besançon Cathedral from 1545 to 1554, when he became *maître des enfans* at the Sainte-Chapelle, Dijon; in 1586 he was arrested for sodomy and burnt at the stake. A highly reputed lutenist, he published musical settings, of 13 Greek lyric odes in French translation (1559).

Rè pastore, Il. *Dramma per musica* in two acts by Mozart to a libretto after Metastasio (1775, Salzburg). The Metastasio text was also set by Bonno, Gluck and others.

Repeat. The restatement of a passage of music, usually indicated by enclosing the material to be repeated between double bars with vertical pairs of dots.

Repiano. A corruption of RIPIENO, used in band music for players other than those at the leading desk.

Reports. 17th-century English term for points of imitation or imitative entries.

Reprise. A repetition. In sonata form the term has been used both for the repeat of the exposition and for the recapitulation. In French Baroque harpsichord music the word often appears to indicate, especially in a rondeau, the point to which the player should return.

Requiem Mass. The Mass for the Dead of the Roman Catholic Church, taking its name from the first word of its introit, *Requiem aeternam dona eis, Domine* ('Give them eternal rest, O Lord'). Its sections are:

Introit; Kyrie; Gradual (*Requiem aeternam*) and Tract (*Absolve, Domine*); Sequence (*Dies irae, dies illa*); Offertory (*Domine Jesu Christe*); Sanctus and Benedictus; Agnus Dei; and Communion (*Lux aeterna*); the responsory *Libera me, Domine* follows the communion on solemn occasions.

The oldest extant polyphonic requiem is that of Ockeghem (*c*1470), who set only four sections. Some 41 settings survive from the period between Ockeghem's and the end of the 16th century, including those of La Rue, Morales, Lassus and Palestrina; they are generally conservative in style. Most Renaissance requiems do not include the sequence.

Hundreds of requiems were composed in the 17th century, by G.B. Bassani, Cazzati, J.K. Kerll, Johann Stadlmayr, Viadana and others. Many were for special occasions. In the 18th century Jommelli, Paisiello and others wrote requiems. Mozart's unfinished Requiem (1791) is the first large-scale setting with instruments in the concert repertory, to which 19th-century composers, starting with Cherubini, added notable works. The requiems of Berlioz (1837) and Verdi (1874) are large-scale works employing huge forces. Those of Liszt, Saint-Saëns, Bruckner and Dvořák are more expressive, in the expressive tradition of Cherubini, and Fauré's is notable for its songlike character and its restraint. These qualities are present also in Duruflé's Requiem of 1947, probably the most frequently performed 20th-century setting before the *War Requiem* (1961) of Britten, which combines the Latin texts with war poems by Wilfred Owen.

Brahms's *German Requiem* (1857–68) is a setting of biblical texts on the theme of death and mourning; it is not a Requiem Mass.

Rescue opera. A type of opera, popular especially in France during the years after the Revolution, in which the hero or heroine is rescued at the last moment from death at the hands of an oppressor or from some natural catastrophe by an act of heroism. The most famous example is Beethoven's *Fidelio*.

Residentie-Orkest. Dutch orchestra established in The Hague in 1904 by Henri Viotta, who conducted until 1917. It has an international reputation (foreign visits were made from 1910) and attracts many guest conductors.

Resnik, Regina (*b* New York, 30 Aug 1922). American soprano and mezzo-soprano. She was engaged by Fritz Busch to sing Lady Macbeth in New York in 1942; she also sang under Kleiber in Mexico City. She made her Met début as Leonora (*Il trovatore*) in 1944; her roles there included Leonore (*Fidelio*), Donna Anna and Sieglinde, which she sang at Bayreuth in 1953. Her voice changed to mezzo-soprano in 1955; thereafter she made a successful Covent Garden début as Carmen (1957), also singing Clytemnestra there, and she appeared in Vienna and at other continental opera houses. She was noted for her warm and vibrant voice and her fine, intelligent musicianship. She produced operas in Hamburg and Venice in 1971.

Resolution. The conclusive ending of a musical idea, be it a melodic line on the key note or a chord progression on tonic harmony. In counterpoint a resolution converts a dissonant configuration (e.g. a suspension) into a consonance.

Reson, Johannes (*fl c*1425–35). Composer, probably of French origin, though possibly identifiable with a member of the London Gild of Parish Clerks (*c*1448–*c*1458) of the same name. His two compositions with French texts hint that he had travelled and had not served at court. His most important work is an early cyclic mass, clearly conceived as a whole with melodic and tonal recurrences between movements.

Resonator. Term referring to the element of an instrument showing the properties of resonance, including the air columns of wind instruments and organ pipes, the bodies of string instruments and the soundboards of pianos and harpsichords. The term also refers to air vessels or electronic devices designed to respond to specific vibration frequencies.

Respighi, Ottorino (*b* Bologna, 9 July 1879; *d* Rome, 18 April 1936). Italian composer. He studied with Torchi and Martucci at the Liceo Musicale in Bologna (1891–1901), then had lessons with Rimsky-Korsakov during visits to Russia (1900–03). In 1913 he settled in Rome, teaching and composing. He is best known as the composer of highly coloured orchestral pieces, capitalizing on the most brilliant aspects of Rimsky-Korsakov, Ravel and Strauss: *Fontane di Roma* (1916), *Pini di Roma* (1924), *Vetrate di chiesa* (1925), *Trittico botticelliano* (1927), *Gli uccelli* (arrangements of pieces by earlier composers, 1927) and *Feste romane* (1928). His interest in the past is to be heard not only in his arrangements of *Arie antiche* for orchestra but in the use of plainchant and the church modes in such pieces as the *Concerto gregoriano* (for violin, 1921) and the *Quartetto dorico* (1924). He also wrote operas (*La bella dormente nel bosco*, 1921) and vocal works.

Respond. Term sometimes used synonymously with RESPONSORY, but better reserved for the first part of a chant in responsorial form as distinct from the verse that follows. 'Respond' and 'verse' are often abbreviated to 'R' and 'V', each crossed with a diagonal slash.

Response. In Christian liturgies, the short text sung or spoken by the choir or congregation in response to the versicle.

Responsory. A category of Western chant serving as musical postludes to the reading of lessons. Great responsories are prominent in Matins and monastic Vespers. Their earliest source is from the 11th century. They involve the chanting of a psalm in alternation between a soloist, who sings a verse, and a chorus, who sing a refrain or 'respond'. The solo sections are set polyphonically in the Notre Dame repertory; by the 16th century, texts were often set as elaborate motets. Sets of responsories continued to be composed during the 18th century. Short responsories are sung after the short readings or chapters of the lesser hours and Compline in the secular Office, and at Lauds and Vespers in the monastic Office.

Rest. A notational sign that indicates the absence of a sounding note; in traditional notation, each note value has an equivalent rest (*see* NOTE VALUES). The semibreve rest is normally used, in modern notation, to signify a whole bar's rest irrespective of the actual time value of the bar.

Resurrection Symphony. Sub-title of Mahler's Symphony no.2 in C minor (1894), so called because the finale is a setting for soprano, chorus and orchestra of the Klopstock's (*Aufersteh'n*) 'Resurrection' chorale.

Resurrezione, La. Oratorio by Handel to a text by C.S. Capece (1708, Rome).

Retablo de maese Pedro, El. *See* MASTER PETER'S PUPPET SHOW.

Rethberg, Elisabeth (*b* Schwarzenberg, 22 Sept 1894; *d* Yorktown Heights, NY, 6 June 1976). German soprano. She studied in Dresden and made her début there in 1915. At the Met she was leading soprano for 20 seasons (1922–42) and took 35 roles, including Aida, Desdemona, Eva, Sieglinde and Donna Anna. She regularly returned to Dresden where in 1928 she created the title role in Strauss's *Die aegyptische Helena*. Her pure style and beautiful tone were much admired.

Réti, Rudolph (*b* Uzice, 27 Nov 1885; *d* Montclair, NJ, 7 Feb 1957). American writer on music. He studied in Vienna and as a pianist gave the première of Schoenberg's op.11 (1911), later becoming music critic of the Vienna *Das Echo* (1930–38). He emigrated to the USA in the 1930s. He is remembered for *The Thematic Process in Music* (1951), which arose from intensive analyses of Beethoven piano sonatas; in it he saw the process of composition as linear, based on a motif that has arisen in the composer's mind and that he allows to grow by constant transformation. This is argued in his *Thematic Patterns in Sonatas of Beethoven* (1965). Réti also wrote books on aspects of tonality.

Retirada (It.). Term sometimes used for the final movement of a Baroque suite, particularly in eastern Europe.

Retransition. In a sonata-form movement, the last part of the development section that prepares for the recapitulation, often with a passage which leads to, and emphasizes, the dominant of the main key.

Retrograde (Lat. *cancrizans*: 'crab-like'). A succession of notes played backwards. It has always been regarded as an esoteric way of handling a musical structure and one that does not invite the listener's appreciation. In the Middle Ages and Renaissance it was applied to *cantus firmi*; it is important in Schoenberg's system of composition with 12 notes, in which 12-note rows may be used in retrograde and retrograde inversion.

Reubke, Adolf (*b* Halberstadt, 6 Dec 1805; *d* Hausneindorf, 3 March 1875). German organ builder, father of Julius Reubke. His business was based in Hausneindorf and his son Emil (1836–85) was in partnership with him from 1860. One of the most important 19th-century German organ builders, he built the instruments at the Jakobikirche, Magdeburg (1858), Magdeburg Cathedral (1861) and the Gewandhaus, Leipzig (1860), among others. Ernst Röver took over the firm in 1885.

Reubke, Julius (*b* Hausneindorf, 23 March 1834; *d* Pillnitz, 3 June 1858). German composer, pianist

and organist. He studied the piano with Kullak at the Berlin Conservatory, then in 1856 went to Weimar where he became one of Liszt's favourite pupils. His strikingly advanced Piano Sonata in B♭ minor and programmatic Organ Sonata in C minor (1857) are masterpieces of the German Romantic style and show him to have been a promising composer. His brother Otto (1842–1913) was an admired organist, pianist, conductor and composer in Halle.

Reusch, Johannes (*b* Rodach, *c*1525; *d* Wurzen, 27 Feb 1582). German composer. After studies at Wittenberg, he was a Kantor in Meissen from 1543 to 1555, when he moved to Wurzen. He is known for his psalms (1551), among the earliest of German-language settings and the first to be separately published; he also published odes (1554), occasional pieces and an elementary treatise (1553).

Reusner [Reussner], **Esaias** (*b* Lwówek Śląski, 29 April 1636; *d* Cölln, Berlin, 1 May 1679). German composer. After working in Silesia, he became a lutenist at the electoral court in Berlin in 1674. He wrote mainly instrumental music; his volumes of lute suites, *Delitiae testudinis* (1667) and *Neue Lauten-Früchte* (1676), were the first by a German composer to use the French lute style. His father, Esaias Reusner (*d* 1660–80), was also a composer and lutenist.

Reutter, (Johann Adam Joseph Karl) Georg (von) (*b* Vienna, bap. 6 April 1708; *d* there, 11 March 1772). Austrian composer. An organist and a pupil of Caldara, he became imperial court composer in Vienna in 1731, after a visit to Italy. He held a collection of Kapellmeisterships at court and St Stephen's Cathedral from *c*1736. Music however declined at both places during these years, partly because of Maria Theresa's economies; and Haydn, Gluck and others were unable to obtain posts because of him. One of the most prolific composers of his time, he wrote over 30 stage works, several oratorios, over 500 sacred works and various instrumental pieces. Baroque features (particularly sequences) predominate in his style.

Reutter's father Georg (1656–1738) was organist at court (from 1700) and St Stephen's (1686–1720), where he was Kapellmeister (1715–28); he composed sacred and organ works.

Reutter, Hermann (*b* Stuttgart, 17 June 1900; *d* Heidenheim an der Brenz, 1 Jan 1985). German composer and pianist. A pupil of Courvoisier at the Munich Academy, he became a teacher (from 1936 director of the Hoch Conservatory, Berlin) accompanist to leading German singers and composer. At first he adopted a Hindemithian style, though later works are more traditional. His large output covers most genres, but he is admired for his stage works and songs.

Revolutionary hymn. A general term for music sung to embody the idea of revolution. A substantial repertory of such music was sung at festivals and on other occasions in France *c*1790–1800. It includes *La marseillaise*, numerous songs by Gossec and more ambitious pieces by Méhul, Cherubini and others.

Revolutionary Study. Nickname of Chopin's Study in C minor op.10 no.12 (1830) for piano, so called because it was said to express Chopin's patriotic reaction to the news that Warsaw had been captured by the Russians.

Revue. A topical, satirical theatrical entertainment consisting of a series of scenes having a central theme but no plot; it included singing and dancing. It originated in France early in the 19th century, grew in sophistication later in the century and in the 20th provided a vehicle for such artists as Mistinguett, Maurice Chevalier and Josephine Baker. The music, partly compiled from existing material, included songs by such composers as Maurice Yvain and José Padilla. English revue also goes back to the early 19th century, but only c1900 were revues regularly given theatrically; they flourished in the 1920s with such composers as Noel Coward and Ivor Novello as well as interchange with New York. There the revue was a more recent development; it had become established in 1907 with the inauguration of what was to be the *Ziegfeld Follies*, an increasingly spectacular series. This and its many imitators generally had collaborative music and were sentimental rather than satirical in tone. Composers included Irving Berlin and Harold Arlen. The genre declined after the 1940s, particularly under the impact of television, though in the USA intimate revue continued locally and in Britain waves of satirical shows (such as *Beyond the Fringe*, 1961) used revue techniques. Rock and electronic music were increasingly used to reflect the flavour of social protest.

Revueltas, Silvestre (*b* Santiago Papasquiaro, 31 Dec 1899; *d* Mexico City, 5 Oct 1940). Mexican composer. He studied in Mexico City, Austin and Chicago, his teachers including Tella and Borowski. From 1929 to 1935 he was assistant conductor of the Mexico SO, for which he composed rhythmically vigorous, boldly coloured pieces, most famously *Sensemayá* (1938).

Rey. French family of musicians. Jean-Baptiste Rey (i) (1734–1810) was a prominent opera conductor. He served at several provincial theatres and from 1776 at the Paris Opéra where he directed works by Gluck; in 1779 he became master of the *musique de chambre* at the French court, and he sometimes conducted at the Concert Spirituel. His works include an opera and arrangements of other composers' operas. His brother Louis-Charles-Joseph (1738–1811), a cellist at the Opéra, composed stage and instrumental works. Jean-Baptiste (ii) (c1760–c1822), possibly a son of Louis-Charles-Joseph, was an organist and theorist.

Reyer [Rey], (Louis-Etienne-)Ernest (*b* Marseilles, 1 Dec 1823; *d* Le Lavandou, 15 Jan 1909). French composer and critic. An admirer (but not imitator) of Berlioz and Wagner, he composed orchestral and stage works with a fashionably exotic flavour and two highly successful operas, *Sigurd* (1884) and *Salammbô* (1890). His music shows discipline and delicate orchestral colouring yet lacks melodic distinction and individuality. As a writer contributing to several journals including *Journal des débats* (1866–98), he preferred the music of Gluck, Weber,

Schumann and Berlioz, distrusting progressive ideas, especially uncritical Wagnerism.

Reymann, Matthias (*b* Torún, c1565; *d* after 1625). German lutenist and composer. He was a law student in Leipzig by 1582. His lutebook of 1598 contains 74 idiomatic preludes, fantasias and dances, many with rich figuration; a second book (lost) included 152 settings of psalm melodies.

Reynolds, Roger (Lee) (*b* Detroit, 13 July 1934). American composer. He was a pupil of Finney and Gerhard (1957–60) and since the early 1960s has been active in mixed-media and electronic music, working at Ann Arbor, IRCAM and elsewhere. In 1969 he joined the faculty at San Diego. His work has been informed by a concern for the ways in which human consciousness interacts with musical experience.

Reys, Jakub (*b* Poland, c1540; *d* Paris, c1605). Polish composer and lutenist. He served Henri III of France from 1574 until his death. Highly praised by contemporaries as a lutenist, he composed over 60 preludes, fantasias and dances for lute, notable for their technical difficulty.

Reyzen [Reisen], Mark (Osipovich) (*b* Zaytsevo, 3 July 1895). Soviet bass. He made his début at Kharkov in 1921, sang in Leningrad (1925–30) then at the Bol'shoy, Moscow (1930–54). He had a warm, powerful and beautiful bass, capable of fine dramatic inflection, which served well in such Musorgsky roles as Boris Godunov and Dosifey; he was also outstanding as Ivan Susanin and Verdi's King Philip II.

Reznicek, E(mil) N(ikolaus) von (*b* Vienna, 4 May 1860; *d* Berlin, 2 Aug 1945). Austrian composer. A pupil of Reinecke and Jadassohn at the Leipzig Conservatory, he worked widely as a conductor and wrote light operas (*Donna Diana*, 1894), four symphonies and three string quartets.

Rhapsody. Term borrowed from ancient Greek epic poetry, first used as a musical title by Tomášek for a set of six pieces for piano (c1803). These and other early examples are restrained in character, but free fantasias of an epic, heroic or national character were later often given the title. Examples include the 19 Hungarian Rhapsodies of Liszt and the rhapsodies by Brahms and Dohnányi (for piano), Dvořák, Enescu, Chabrier and Vaughan Williams (for orchestra) and Bartók (for solo instruments and orchestra).

Rhapsody in Blue. Work by Gershwin for piano and orchestra (1924).

Rhapsody on a Theme of Paganini. Rakhmaninov's op.43 (1934), 24 variations for piano and orchestra on Paganini's violin Caprice no.2 in A minor.

Rheinberger, Joseph (Gabriel) (*b* Vaduz, 17 March 1839; *d* Munich, 25 Nov 1901). German composer and teacher. After studying at the Munich Conservatory he was a church organist, piano teacher and conductor of the Munich Choral Society, becoming professor at the conservatory in 1867 and Hofkapellmeister in 1877. He composed indefatigably and with mastery of traditional polyphonic and formal concepts, but remained aloof from modern ideas; his best music is in the 20 organ sonatas and his sacred works after 1877. There are also symphonies, two organ concertos and much chamber music. His lasting influence was as a revered composition teacher; among his pupils were Humperdinck, Thuille, Horatio Parker and Furtwängler.

Rheineck, Christoph (*b* Memmingen, 1 Nov 1748; *d* there, 29 July 1797). German composer. In 1769–75 he worked in Lyons, where he had two operas staged. Later he presented concerts in Memmingen and appeared as a singer, pianist and clarinettist. He was a successful lied composer, adept at setting humorous and folklike poetry, and also wrote a Singspiel and choral and keyboard pieces.

Rheingold, Das [The Rhine Gold]. Music drama in four scenes by Wagner to his own libretto (1869, Munich), the first of the cycle DER RING DES NIBELUNGEN.

Rhenish Symphony. Schumann's Symphony no.3 in E♭ (1850), composed after a journey down the Rhine.

Rhetoric and music. The idea of music as a rhetorical art has its origins in classical times. At the end of the Middle Ages and during the Renaissance, music theorists, noting the new kind of expressiveness in music, began to draw parallels between the art of the orator and that of the musician. From soon after 1600, writers on music often drew analogies between the procedures of rhetoric and those of music, culminating in the 17th century and the early 18th with attempts to transform specific rhetorical concepts into musical equivalents. This was first attempted by Burmeister (1606), in analysing the rhetorical structure and use of musical figures in a motet by Lassus; the idea was followed up by later theorists, most of them in Germany. This in turn linked with Baroque ideas on the affections and the concept of conveying a rationalized emotional state or passion in music; to this end musical-rhetorical figures could be used to add force to the expression.

Rhine Gold, The. *See* RHEINGOLD, DAS.

Rhumba. *See* RUMBA.

Rhymed office. The rhymed office or *historia* refers to a liturgical text drawn from the historical books of the Bible. Historical narrative, usually based on the life of a local saint, characterizes most later offices, the musical items of which (mostly antiphons and responsories) are provided with rhymed and metrical texts. One of the earliest not dedicated to a saint, that of Trinity Sunday, also gained general and lasting use. Rhymed offices, like sequences, were widely used and composed until the 16th century; they possibly influenced the rhymed and metrical sacred paraphrases of the Renaissance.

Rhythm. The subdivision of a span of time into perceptible sections; the grouping of musical sounds, principally by means of duration and stress. With melody and harmony, rhythm is one of the three basic elements of music.

In Western music, time is usually organized to establish a regular pulse, and by the subdivision of that pulse into regular groups. Such groups are commonly of two or three units (or their com-pounds, such as four or six); the arrangement of the pulse into groups is the metre of a composition, and the rate of pulses is its tempo. Most Western music, from the late Middle Ages to the 20th century, possesses a regular rhythmic pulse and metre; these may be absent, however, from some types of earlier music, for example ecclesiastical plainchant, which apparently lacked a metric structure, leaving its rhythm to be realized according to conventions and as dictated by the verbal text. In some 20th-century music, composers have sought to avoid regular rhythmic structures in order to achieve a more flexible rhythm; in some cases their methods have been influenced by folk music lacking a regular metric structure. But even in periods when composers accepted 'the tyranny of the bar-line', they have used various devices to prevent dull or sterile rhythmic structures: syncopation (displacement of accent); shorter notes at stressed parts of the bar (as opposed to the more natural longer notes at accented points); phrases that avoid regular four-bar or eight-bar patterns; eliding phrases into one another or extending phrases; short-term displacement of accent (common in cadences in the Baroque era: *see* HEMIOLA); in vocal music, following a natural speech rhythm (either one that contradicts metric regularity, as in much recitative, or one that follows a broad metric structure created by a verbal text).

Rhythm, as a fundamental element – no music can exist other than in time – has a part to play in many other aspects of music: it is an important element in melody, it affects the progression of harmony, and has a role in such matters as texture, timbre and ornamentation. It is fundamental to the dance; dance patterns, derived from natural rhythms of bodily motion, have dictated many of the rhythmic patterns that pervade Western music.

While in Western music rhythm is multiplicative (i.e. rhythmic patterns are derived by multiplying or dividing, normally by two or three), in many non-Western cultures they are additive; an eight-unit rhythm in Western music is invariably constructed on the basis $2 \times 2 \times 2$, in Middle Eastern music it may well be $3 + 2 + 3$.

Rhythm-and-blues [R & B]. A style of popular music performed principally by American blacks from the late 1940s to the early 1960s. The term replaced 'race music' and was supplanted by 'soul'. Rhythm-and-blues grew out of the blues and related styles but is played by an ensemble, typically of a lead singer or instrumentalist, a rhythm section (bass, drums and some combination of piano, electric organ and electric guitar) and a group consisting of voices, wind instruments, guitar or organ. Most rhythm-and-blues music is in the major mode (with 'blue notes'), uses forms based on the blues and Tin Pan Alley songs and is in quadruple metre with off-beats emphasized. Much is vocal; the lyrics range from those akin to mainstream popular music to the blues vision of the human condition.

Rhythmic modes. The medieval concept by which rhythmic patterns, all in triple metre, were defined and systematized. Applying chiefly to music of the 12th and 13th centuries, they were defined by Johannes de Garlandia (*c*1240): he listed six modes, each of a particular rhythmic pattern (or *ordo*). These patterns served as the basis of much early polyphony.

Rhythm machine. *See* ELECTRONIC PERCUSSION.

Rhythm section. The part of a jazz band that principally articulates the rhythm: usually a combination of (or selection from) piano, drums, double bass (played pizzicato), guitar and electric bass guitar.

Riadis, Emilios (*b* Salonica, 1 May 1885; *d* there, 17 July 1935). Greek composer. He studied in Salonica, in Munich (1908–10) and with Charpentier and Ravel in Paris (1910–15), then returned to teach at the Salonica State Conservatory. His works are in most genres, but his songs are particularly valued for their sensitivity, folk echoes and oriental sensuality.

Ribattuta (It.). A trill in jerky (dotted) rhythm; it starts on the main note and normally accelerates.

Ricci, Federico (*b* Naples, 22 Oct 1809; *d* Conegliano, 10 Dec 1877). Italian composer, brother of Luigi Ricci. He studied at the Naples Conservatory with Raimondi, his own brother and Bellini. Though less original than his brother, he was the more accomplished and versatile composer, showing a lighter, more graceful touch in comedy, notably in *Il marito e l'amante* (1852) and *Une folie à Rome* (1869), and creating serious works worthy of Mercadante, particularly *Corrado d'Altamura* (1841), his masterpiece. His most sensational success was the *opera semiseria* drawn from Scott, *La prigione di Edimburgo* (1838). Apart from four comedies composed with Luigi, he wrote vocal chamber works for his pupils at the St Petersburg Conservatory.

Ricci, Francesco Pasquale (*b* Como, 17 May 1732; *d* Loveno di Menaggio, 7 Nov 1817). Italian composer. He was *maestro di cappella* of Como Cathedral from 1759 but also travelled widely; in 1766–80 he appeared in concerts at The Hague. He composed symphonies, chamber music, sacred works etc and contributed (perhaps with J.C. Bach) to a keyboard method (*c*1788).

Ricci, Luigi (*b* ?Naples, 8 June/8 July 1805; *d* Prague, 31 Dec 1859). Italian composer, brother of Federico Ricci. He studied at the Naples Conservatory. One of the more individual voices in Italian opera of the period, he brought a mastery of traditional *buffo* devices and a new, robust melodic manner to his natural gift for comedy, scoring successes with his *opera semiseria Chiara di Rosembergh* (1831), the witty farce *Un avventura di Scaramuccia* (1834) and the fantastic comedy *Crispino e la comare* (1850), the last in collaboration with his brother.

Ricci, Ruggiero (*b* San Francisco, 24 July 1918). American violinist. His San Francisco and New York débuts (1928, 1929) were followed by a tour of Europe in 1932. He has specialized in the bravura repertory, playing Paganini with accuracy and elegance. From 1975 he has taught at the Juilliard School.

Ricciarelli, Katia (*b* Rovigo, 18 Jan 1946). Italian soprano. She studied in Venice and made her début in Mantua as Mimì (1969); but it is as a Verdi singer that she is chiefly known. She sang Leonora (*Il trovatore*) at Parma in 1970 and has sung Elisabeth (*Don Carlos*) in Paris and Munich, Desdemona in Brussels and in 1987 at Covent Garden as well as in the Zeffirelli film). Her American début was at Chicago in *I due Foscari* (1972); she has also sung at the Met and San Francisco. Her warmly attractive *spinto*-style voice and her spacious phrasing have been much admired.

Riccio, Teodore (*b* Brescia, *c*1540; *d* Ansbach, *c*1600). Italian composer. He was *maestro di cappella* of S Nazaro, Brescia (1567). In 1575 he moved to the Ansbach court and in 1578 to Königsberg, where he became a Protestant and, in 1585, court Kapellmeister for life. His seven sacred publications (1576–90) are in the traditional Lutheran style and contain much polychoral writing; secular works also survive (3 bks, 1567–77).

Ricciotti, Carlo [Bacciccia] (*b c*1681; *d* The Hague, 13 July 1756). Italian violinist and impresario. Until 1725 he worked (ultimately as director) in a French opera company at The Hague, and he was violin teacher to Count Willem Bentinck. Six *Concerti armonici* formerly ascribed to Pergolesi have been attributed to him; they are now known to be by Count Unico van Wassenaer.

Ricercare [ricercar] (It.: 'to search out'). Term originally used for a lute or keyboard piece of preludial character, later for an imitative piece similar in scope to the fantasia or the fugue. The title (the French equivalent is *recherché*) implies a piece of a complex or esoteric nature.

The term first occurs in Spinacino's *Intabulatura de lauto, libro primo* (1507), for pieces designed to try out the tuning of an instrument. The style was transferred to the keyboard in M.A. Cavazzoni's *Recerchari, motetti, canzoni* (1523). Examples of the non-imitative ricercare for solo viol are found in the works of Ganassi and Ortiz, where the term bears a didactic connotation.

The origin of the imitative ricercare is uncertain. The ensemble ricercares in *Musica nova* (1540) are in an imitative motet style. But the type may have arisen not from vocal music but from the occasional use of imitation in preludial ricercares such as Cavazzoni's. The early imitative organ ricercare is represented by four examples in G. Cavazzoni's *Intavolatura cioe recercari canzoni himni magnificati* (1543). Many early collections, including Willaert's, have title-pages indicating their suitability for voice, organ or other instruments. The monothematic ricercare (akin to the early FANTASIA) appears first in 1547 and was developed by A. Gabrieli, whose organ ricercares use contrapuntal devices that foreshadow the fugue. The highpoint was reached in the work of Frescobaldi, whose later examples (in *Fiori musicali*, 1635) were among those designed to replace the liturgical offertory.

In Austria and Germany Frescobaldi's severe manner was continued in the ricercares of Froberger. Other German composers include Krieger and Pachelbel, but the form underwent no rejuvenation until Bach, who revived the term for two fugal pieces in the *Musical Offering*. Modern composers who have used the term have mostly implied by it a severe fugue with archaic mannerisms.

Richafort, Jean (*b* ?Hainaut, *c*1480; *d* ?Bruges, *c*1547). Franco-Flemish composer. He was *maître de chapelle* at St Rombaud, Mechelen (1507–9), then served the French chapel, and finally was *maître de chapelle* at St Gilles, Bruges (1542–7). One of the most gifted of Josquin's younger disciples, he was a master contrapuntist who attempted to enhance the relationship between words and music. His two surviving masses are among the earliest to use fully-fledged parody technique and his many *chansons* are motet-like in style. But his preeminence is revealed most clearly in his motets, in which he used *cantus firmi*, ostinatos, canons, paraphrase technique and imitation; the best known is *Quem dicunt homines*, a model of formal clarity. He also composed a Requiem for six voices and two secular motets.

Richard Coeur-de-Lion. Opera in three acts by Grétry to a libretto by Sedaine after La Curne de Sainte-Palaye (1784, Paris).

Richard I, Coeur-de-lion (*b* Oxford, Sept 1157; *d* Limoges, 11 April 1199). King of England (1189–99), Duke of Aquitaine from 1171, and Count of Poitou from 1169, poet and composer. Son of Henry II of England and Eleanor of Aquitaine, he spent most of his life in France. His reputation as poet and composer has been exaggerated by the fictitious story of his rescue from prison by Blondel de Nesle in 1194. But two of his poems, one with music, survive, both 'topical' in theme. Though his contribution as a member of the earliest generation of trouvères is slight, he did leave one of the earliest examples of the rotrouenge.

Richard de Fournival (*d* 1260). French trouvère poet and composer. Son of a doctor to King Philippe Auguste of France, and himself a doctor, he became a canon of Notre Dame and in 1246 chancellor. His 18 monophonic songs are remarkable for their variety of structure and subtle musical treatment. He is also of importance for his involvement in the early motet.

Richart de Semilli (*fl* late 12th or early 13th century). French trouvère, probably a native of Paris. His musical structures stand apart from the mainstream of trouvère music in their heavy reliance on repetition.

Richter, Ferdinand Tobias (*b* Würzburg, 22 July 1651; *d* Vienna, 3 Nov 1711). Austrian composer. After serving as organist at the monastery of Heiligenkreuz, Lower Austria, in 1675–9, he became court and chamber organist at the imperial court in Vienna in 1683, and first organist in the court chapel from 1690. His keyboard works, which were his best-known music, include five suites and other pieces; a talented dramatic composer, he also wrote music for 11 Latin school plays and several operas and oratorios.

Richter, Franz Xaver (*b* ?Holešov, 1 Dec 1709; *d* Strasbourg, 12 Sept 1789). German composer. He served from 1740 as vice-Kapellmeister to the Prince-Abbot in Kempten, Allgäu. By 1747 he had joined the Mannheim court as a bass singer; after a

period as court chamber composer, he became Kapellmeister at Strasbourg Cathedral (1769). One of the foremost Mannheim composers, he wrote many symphonies, concertos, chamber works (including string quartets) and vocal pieces (mostly sacred). But he stood apart from the Mannheim style, and his music is often contrapuntal, reflecting Viennese influence. He was a respected teacher and wrote a composition treatise.

Richter, Hans (*b* Györ, 4 April 1843; *d* Bayreuth, 5 Dec 1916). Austro–Hungarian conductor. He studied the violin, the horn and theory at the Vienna Conservatory. He was closely associated with Wagner and Bülow from 1866–7, becoming conductor at the National Theatre, Pest, the Vienna Hofoper (and Philharmonic concerts) and Gesellschaft der Musikfreunde. In 1876 he conducted the first *Ring* cycle at Bayreuth. From 1877 he appeared regularly in England, directing the Birmingham Festival and conducting the LSO (1904–11) and the Hallé Orchestra (1897–1911); he introduced London audiences to *Die Meistersinger, Tristan* and the *Ring* in English (1908). Known for his enthusiasm and precision not only in Wagner but in Beethoven, Brahms, Bruckner and Dvořák, he was a great admirer of Elgar, whose First Symphony is dedicated to him.

Richter, Karl (*b* Plauen, 15 Oct 1926; *d* Munich, 15 Feb 1981). German organist and conductor. He studied in Leipzig and became organist of the Thomaskirche there in 1947. Later he taught and played in Munich, directing the Munich Bach Choir and Orchestra. He performed a wide repertory but, although he avoided any concessions to historical style, was chiefly known for his performances and recordings of Bach and Handel.

Richter, Sviatoslav (Teofilovich) (*b* Zhitomir, 20 March 1915). Soviet pianist. He was largely self-taught, making his recital début in 1934. After study at the Moscow Conservatory he gave many early performances of Prokofiev's music. From his first appearances in the West, in 1960, he won fame for his supreme virtuosity, poetic phrasing and ability to use a wide range of tone colour. He is at his best in 19th-century Romantic music, notably Schubert and Schumann.

Ricieri, Giovanni Antonio (*b* Venice, 12 May 1679; *d* Bologna, 15 May 1746). Italian composer and singer. A soprano, he joined the *cappella* of S Petronio, Bologna, in 1701 and in 1722–6 served Count Rzewuski in Poland. Thereafter he lived mostly in Bologna, where his pupils included G.B. Martini. He composed three operas (for Poland), oratorios, church music etc, showing skill in both concertato and contrapuntal styles.

Ricordi. Italian firm of music publishers, founded in Milan in 1808 by Giovanni Ricordi (1785–1853). Its dominant position in 19th-century Italy and continued power in the 20th, achieved through astuteness, initiative and the rights on Verdi's and Puccini's operas, are unsurpassed in music publishing. Giovanni was a violinist and copyist who in 1811 became publisher to the Milan Conservatory and won exclusive contracts with La Scala and other theatres in Milan, Venice and Naples. By 1825 the catalogue had over 2300 items, including opera arrangements, method books, works by Paganini and guitar pieces; in the next 15 years they added vocal scores and performing material (for hire) by Rossini, Bellini, Donizetti, Mercadante, Pacini, Meyerbeer and, in 1839, Verdi (Ricordi published all but three of Verdi's operas). Giovanni's son Tito (i) (1811–88) directed the firm during its greatest expansion, but it was the founder's highly cultured grandson Giulio (1840–1912) who dealt with Verdi and was central in Puccini's development. He maintained the company's operatic tradition, also publishing Boito, Ponchielli and Catalani. After 1919 the management passed out of the family. More emphasis was given to editions of earlier music (Vivaldi, D. Scarlatti), and modern Italian composers were added to the catalogue. A new Verdi critical edition is among the firm's most recent developments.

Rider Quartet. Title given to Haydn's String Quartet in G minor op.74 no.3 (1793), because of the galloping motion of its opening phrase.

Riders to the Sea. Opera in one act by Vaughan Williams, a setting of Synge's play (1937, London).

Ridout, Godfrey (*b* Toronto, 6 May 1918; *d* there, 24 Nov 1984). Canadian composer. He studied at the Toronto Conservatory, where in 1940 he began teaching, moving in 1948 to Toronto University. His works consist mostly of orchestral and choral pieces in an eclectic, affirmative and tuneful diatonic style.

Riedl, Josef Anton (*b* Munich, 11 June 1927). German composer. He was a pupil of Orff and Schaeffer and has worked in several electronic studios. He is noted for environmental events and mixed-media works.

Riedt, Friedrich Wilhelm (*b* Berlin, 5 Jan 1710; *d* there, 5 Jan 1783). German flautist, writer on music and composer. He played in Frederick the Great's Kapelle from 1741, and in 1749 became director of the Berlin Musikübende Gesellschaft. He wrote a study of intervals (1753); in an essay (1756) he criticizes excessive improvisation in performance. He wrote much chamber music.

Riegel, Henri-Joseph. *See* RIGEL, HENRI-JOSEPH.

Riegger, Wallingford (Constantin) (*b* Albany, GA, 29 April 1885; *d* New York, 2 April 1961). American composer. He studied with Goetschius at the Institute of Musical Art in New York, and with Bruch and Stillman-Kelley in Germany (1907), where he returned as a conductor (1914–17). He returned to the USA, settling in 1928 in New York, where he taught. In 1919–20 he turned seriously to composition, but only in 1926 began to develop the freely atonal, strongly contrapuntal and often rhythmically vigorous style of his major works: *Study in Sonority* for massed violins (1927), *Dichotomy* for chamber orchestra (1932). He gained a reputation as one of the most articulate exponents of avant-garde modernism and was involved with new music organizations. His output includes much dance music, vocal works and numerous arrangements of folksongs and carols.

Orchestral music Study in Sonority (1927); Dichotomy (1932); Scherzo (1932); Canon and Fugue (1941); Sym. no.3 (1947); Music for Brass Choir (1949); Music for Brass

(1951); Music for Orch (1951); Variations, pf, orch (1953); Suite for Younger Orch (1954); Dance Rhythms (1954); Sym. no.4 (1957); Variations, vn, orch (1959); Quintuple Jazz (1959); Sinfonietta (1959); Duo, pf, orch (1960)
Chamber music 2 str qts (1939, 1948); Pf Qnt (1951); Woodwind Qnt (1952); Conc., pf, wind qnt (1952)
Dance music c18 works incl. New Dance (1935); With my Red Fire (1936)
Vocal works c16

Riemann, (Karl Wilhelm Julius) Hugo (*b* Gross-Mehlra, 18 July 1849; *d* Leipzig, 10 July 1919). German music theorist and writer. He studied harmony with Jadassohn and the piano and composition with Reinecke in Leipzig and taught at the Hamburg and Wiesbaden conservatories and at Leipzig University (he was appointed director of the new Collegium Musicum in 1908). One of the most original and creative scholars of his time, he set out systematically a theory of functional harmony, counterpoint and phrasing in the monumental *Grosse Kompositionslehre* (3 vols., 1902–13) and initiated the analysis of music on principles of historical style and genre. This led him to discover forgotten composers and sources whose music he transcribed, edited or analysed, including Byzantine MSS of the 10th to the 15th centuries, John Dunstable, the Mannheim symphonists and Johann Schobert. His contribution is reflected in the *c*60 books, among them the celebrated *Musik-Lexikon* (1882, 8/1916), 70 compositions and over 200 other publications he produced.

Rienzi [Cola Rienzi, der letzte der Tribunen]. Opera in five acts by Wagner to his own libretto after E. Bulwer Lytton and Mary Russell Mitford (1842, Dresden).

Riepel, Joseph (*b* Hörschlag, 22 Jan 1709; *d* Regensburg, 23 Oct 1782). Austrian theorist and composer. After working in Dresden and Poland, he served from the 1750s at the Regensburg court as violinist, composer and music director. His most important work is *Anfangsgründe zur musikalischen Setzkunst* (1752–68), a five-volume composition treatise based on the principle of arranging combinations and permutations of musical elements; it had a strong influence on H.C. Koch's theories. His compositions include orchestral and chamber music.

Ries, Ferdinand (*b* Bonn, bap. 28 Nov 1784; *d* Frankfurt, 13 Jan 1838). German pianist and composer. He was the eldest son of the violinist Franz (Anton) Ries (1755–1846), Beethoven's teacher. He studied the piano with Beethoven in Vienna (1802–4), often acting as his secretary and copyist, and after a time in Paris and on tour moved to London (1813–24), where he or his works were often heard at Philharmonic Society concerts and where he acted for Beethoven in dealings with London publishers. In his native Rhineland from 1825 he composed and conducted, also collaborating on an early biography of Beethoven (with F.G. Wegeler, 1838). His prolific output consists chiefly of salon pieces and songs. His brother Hubert (1802–86) was a distinguished violinist in Berlin.

Rieti, Vittorio (*b* Alexandria, 28 Jan 1898). American composer of Italian descent. He was a pupil of Frugatta in Milan (1912–17) and Respighi in Rome (until 1920). In the 1920s and 1930s he was influenced by Les Six and spent much time in Paris; in 1940 he moved to the USA, where he taught at various institutions. His large output, in an idiom akin to neo-classicism, includes many ballets (among them *Barabau* (1925, for Dyagilev), symphonies, concertos, chamber and piano pieces.

Rietz, (August Wilhelm) Julius (*b* Berlin, 28 Dec 1812; *d* Dresden, 12 Sept 1877). German cellist, conductor, composer and editor. He held conducting posts in Düsseldorf, Leipzig and Dresden, also teaching at the Leipzig Conservatory and preparing scores for collected editions of Bach, Handel, Mozart and Mendelssohn. His brother Eduard (1802–32), a violinist, founded the Berlin Philharmonic Society in 1826 and was the teacher and friend of Mendelssohn.

Riff. In popular music, particularly jazz, a short melodic ostinato, usually two or four bars long. Probably deriving from the repetitive call-and-response patterns of West African music, it has appeared prominently in jazz from earliest times.

Rifkin, Joshua (*b* New York, 22 April 1944). American musicologist, pianist and conductor. He studied at the Juilliard School, at New York University, at Göttingen and at Princeton, and worked with Stockhausen at Darmstadt. He worked with Nonesuch Records and taught at Brandeis University. He is well known for his playing of Scott Joplin's piano rags. As a scholar he has worked particularly on Renaissance* sources, Schütz and Bach. He has proposed that Bach's choral music is authentically performed with one voice to a part and has directed recordings in support of that theory.

Rigatti, Giovanni Antonio (*b* Venice, 1615; *d* there, 25 Oct 1649). Italian composer. After serving as *maestro di cappella* at Udine Cathedral (1635–7) he sang at St Mark's, Venice, and taught singing. By 1646 he was *maestro di cappella* to the Patriarch of Venice. An outstanding composer of church music, he published two books of solo motets, three of small-scale concertato motets and four of psalms; most have parts for obbligato instruments. He also left two volumes of secular vocal works.

Rigaudon [rigadon, rigadoon]. A French folkdance, court dance and instrumental form popular in France and England in the 17th and 18th centuries. It was a gay duple-metre dance in two or more strains characterized by four-bar phrases, usually with an upbeat. It appears in the ballets and operas of Campra, Rameau and their French contemporaries and in keyboard and ensemble works by French and German composers. Among later works to include a rigaudon are Grieg's *Holberg Suite* and Ravel's *Le tombeau de Couperin*.

Rigel, Henri-Jean (*b* Paris, 11 May 1772; *d* Abbeville, 16 Dec 1852). French pianist, teacher and composer, son of Henri-Joseph Rigel. He taught at the Ecole Royale de Chant (later the Conservatoire) in Paris from 1785 and became known as one of the best piano professors of his time; later he taught César Franck. He was also an eminent accompanist. He wrote two operas, other vocal works (*scènes*,

romances etc), several piano concertos, overtures etc, chamber music (most with piano) and solo piano works.

Rigel [Riegel], Henri-Joseph (*b* Wertheim, 9 Feb 1741; *d* Paris, 2 May 1799). German composer and teacher. After studying with Jommelli he settled in France, moving to Paris in 1768 and becoming one of the city's most respected musicians, active as a composer and a teacher of *solfège* and the piano. He was piano professor at the new Conservatoire from 1795. He had greatest success with his instrumental works, mostly from the 1770s, which exploit the piano's dynamic range. His orchestral music, notable for its lyricism, includes *c*15 symphonies and several concertos. He also wrote oratorios, motets, 14 operas (1778–99), Revolutionary hymns and other vocal works.

His brother Anton (*c*1745–after 1807) travelled throughout Europe as a teacher and composer, writing mostly chamber music. He had two musician sons, Henri-Jean (above) and Louis (1769–1811), a pianist, composer and teacher.

Righini, Vincenzo (*b* Bologna, 22 Jan 1756; *d* there, 19 Aug 1812). Italian composer, singing teacher and conductor. In 1776 he joined an opera troupe in Prague, for which he wrote his first three operas. He next served in Vienna where he directed the Italian Opera (1780–87) and in Mainz as court Kapellmeister (1787–93). In 1793 he became Kapellmeister and director of the Italian Opera in Berlin. He stayed there after the Opera was disbanded (1806), becoming Kapellmeister of the royal theatre in 1811, but returned to Bologna in 1812. Of his 16 stage works the finest are his Berlin operas, which feature dramatic ballets and expressive vocal writing and instrumentation. His output also includes cantatas, sacred music, songs and piano pieces.

Rigoletto. Opera in three acts by Verdi to a libretto by Piave after Hugo's *Le roi s'amuse* (1851, Venice).

Rihm, Wolfgang (*b* Karlsruhe, 13 March 1952). German composer. He studied first at Karlsruhe (1968–72), where Fortner was among his teachers, and later at Darmstadt, in Cologne under Stockhausen, and with Huber and Nono. An atonal, post-expressionist composer who favours pungent, hard-edged sonorities, and uses tonality in moments of repose (for example in the opera *Jakob Lenz*, 1980), he has written a ballet (*Tutuguri*, 1982) and orchestral works including symphonies, a series of pieces (some with voices) under the title *Abgesangsszene*, *Segmente* for 18 strings (1974) and *Cuts and Dissolves*, a concerto for 29 players (1977), as well as chamber music, lieder and organ music.

Riisager, Knudåge (*b* Port Kunda, 6 March 1897; *d* Copenhagen, 26 Dec 1974). Danish composer. He studied in Copenhagen with Malling and Gram, in Paris with Roussel and Le Flem (1921–3) and in Leipzig with Grabner (1932), developing a cosmopolitan neo-classicism quite distinct from the post-Nielsen tradition (Trumpet Concertino, 1933). While working in the civil service he wrote ballets, five symphonies (1925–50), six string quartets (1918–43) and vocal music.

Riley, Terry (Mitchell) (*b* Colfax, CA, 24 June 1935).

American composer and saxophonist. He studied at Berkeley and began working with tape loops at the studios of French radio in 1962–3. Out of this activity came minimalist pieces for instrumental ensemble, including Keyboard Studies (1963) and *In C* (1964). Since then he has toured internationally as a performer of his own and Indian music (which he studied). He taught at Mills College, 1971–80.

Rilling, Helmuth (*b* Stuttgart, 29 May 1933). German conductor, chorus master and organist. He studied at Stuttgart and with Fernando Germani and Bernstein. In 1954 he founded the Gächinger Kantorei, touring widely with this and other choruses; the instrumental ensemble the Bach-Collegium of Stuttgart was added in 1965. He conducts regularly in the USA and has been internationally known as an organist since the 1960s.

Rimbault, Edward (Francis) (*b* London, 13 June 1816; *d* there, 26 Sept 1876). English scholar. Trained as an organist (he was a pupil of Samuel Wesley), he lectured and collected, edited and wrote about early music, particularly English. His discoveries and revivals, including published editions for the Musical Antiquarian, Percy, Motett and Handel societies, enriched the Victorian choral repertory; he also wrote books on the organ and piano.

Rimksy-Korsakov, Georgy Mikhaylovich (*b* St Petersburg, 26 Dec 1901; *d* there, 10 Oct 1965). Soviet composer, nephew of Nikolay Rimsky-Korsakov. He graduated from the Leningrad Conservatory in 1927 and began teaching there the same year. In the 1920s he wrote quarter-tone pieces, some for electronic instruments.

Rimsky-Korsakov, Nikolay Andreyevich (*b* Tikhvin, 18 March 1844; *d* Lyubensk, 21 June 1908). Russian composer. Apart from piano lessons, a love for the music of Glinka and a fascination with opera orchestras, he had little preparation for a musical career – he trained as a naval officer – until he met Balakirev (1861), who captivated him, encouraging his attempts at composition, performing his works and introducing him to Borodin, Dargomïzhsky, Cui and Musorgsky. He wrote songs, orchestral works and an opera (*The Maid of Pskov*, 1873) before becoming professor at the St Petersburg Conservatory (1871) and inspector of naval bands (1873–84), teaching himself harmony and counterpoint, conducting at Balakirev's Free School and collecting folksongs. His next opera, *May Night* (1880), engaged his full creative powers with its blend of the fantastic and the comic (the realm in which he was to score most of his greatest successes), while *Snow Maiden* (1882) evoked a deeper world of nature-mysticism. Official duties at the imperial chapel (1883–91), work on the deceased Musorgsky's and Borodin's MSS and advising for the publisher Belyayev interrupted composition, but he did produce the three colourful orchestral works by which he is best known, *Sheherazade*, the *Spanish Capriccio* and the *Russian Easter Festival* overture, during 1887–8, after which he devoted himself to opera; of the 12 dramatic works from *Mlada* (1892) to *The Golden Cockerel* (1909), *Kitezh*

(1907) stands out for its mystical and psychological depths. Rimsky-Korsakov's operas far outweigh in importance his other compositions, for both their brilliant scoring and fine vocal writing. If they lack dramatic power and strong characterization, they nevertheless set delightful fantastic puppets in the context of musico-scenic fairy tales, using a dual musical language to delineate 'real' from 'unreal'. He transmitted his pellucid style to two generations of Russian composers, from Lyadov and Glazunov to Stravinsky and Prokofiev, all of whom were his pupils.

Operas The Maid of Pskov (1873); May Night (1880); Snow Maiden (1882); Mlada, opera-ballet (1892); Christmas Eve (1895); Sadko (1898); Mozart and Salieri (1898); The Tsar's Bride (1899); Tsar Saltan (1900); Legend of the Invisible City of Kitezh (1907); The Golden Cockerel (1909)
Choral works folksong settings, traditional chants, cantatas
Orchestral and chamber works Sym. no.1 (1884); Sym. no.2 'Antar' (1897); Sym. no.3, C (1886); Overture on Russian Themes (1880); Fantasia on Two Russian Themes, vn/orch (1887); Spanish Capriccio (1887); Sheherazade, suite (1888); Russian Easter Festival, ov. (1888); Sadko (1892); 5 str qts; Str Sextet (1876); Trio (1897); wind pieces
Other *c*20 pf works, incl. variations, fugues, character-pieces, dance movts; 23 sets of songs; 2 folksong collections; orchestrations, revisions, completions of works by Dargomïzhsky, Musorgsky, Borodin, Glinka

Rinaldo. Opera in three acts by Handel to a text by Rossi and Hill after Tasso (1711, London) – his first opera for London. He revised it extensively in 1731.

Rinaldo di Capua (*b* Capua or Naples, *c*1705; *d* ?Rome, *c*1780). Italian composer. He lived and worked mainly in Rome, where he presented over 20 operas, 1737–78. He also composed operas for other Italian cities and, as his fame grew, for Lisbon (1741) and Paris (1752–3). His greatest successes included the *opera seria Vologeso re de' Parti* (1739) and the intermezzo *La zingara* (1753, Paris), later adapted as an *opéra comique* (1755). His later operas are mostly farces and intermezzos; few date from after 1770. Based on the Neapolitan style, they use expansive forms and a wide expressive range; *La zingara* contains *seria* arias as well as *buffo* numbers. Among his other works are oratorios, arias, overtures, cantatas and symphonies.

Rinforzando (It.). 'Reinforcing': a more sudden increase in volume than *crescendo*; it is abbreviated *rf* or *rinf*.

Ringbom, Nils-Eric (*b* Turku, 27 Dec 1907). Finnish composer and critic. He has played a leading role in the administration of musical life in Finland, and has written several books. His distinctive music includes symphonies, choral and instrumental music.

Ring des Nibelungen, Der [The Nibelung's Ring]. Four music dramas by Wagner to his own librettos: *Das Rheingold* (1869), *Die Walküre* (1870), *Siegfried* (1876) and *Götterdämmerung* (1876).

Ring modulator. A device much used in live and recorded electronic music. A given sound is fed in and mixed with a second sound: it then re-emerges in modified form, at its simplest as the sum and difference of the frequency. Stockhausen used it in several works, e.g. *Mixtur, Mantra* and *Hymnen*.

Rinuccini, Ottavio (*b* Florence, 20 Jan 1562; *d* there, 28 March 1621). Italian librettist and poet. From a noble family, he wrote verses for Florentine academies and for court entertainments from 1579. In his librettos, which include those for Peri's *Dafne* (1598), the first fully sung opera, and Monteverdi's *Arianna* (1608), he successfully adapted lyric conventions to the new recitative style of early dramatic composers. His madrigal verses were widely popular (e.g. *Zefiro torna*).

Riotte, Philipp Jakob (*b* St Wendel, 16 Aug 1776; *d* Vienna, 20 Aug 1856). German composer. In Vienna he worked at the court opera and as music director of the Theater an der Wien. He was best known for his Singspiels and stage works (*c*50) at Viennese popular theatres.

Ripa (da Mantova), Alberto da (*b* Mantua, *c*1500; *d* Paris, 1551). Italian lutenist and composer. He served Ercole Gonzaga in Mantua, then spent most of his life at the French court, first as lutenist then (after 1533) as *valet de chambre du roi*. His excellence is often mentioned in literature of the time. Of his many lute pieces, the arrangements of *chansons* and motets are little more than transcriptions with ornamentation and his dance pieces are simple and undistinguished; several of the fantasias, however, are excellent examples of the full-textured, polyphonic lute style of the 1530s and 1540s. He was probably not related to Jacquet de Ripa.

Ripa (y Blanque), Antonio (*b* Tarazona, *c*1720; *d* Seville, 3 Nov 1795). Spanish composer. He held a series of *maestro de capilla* posts, the first when he was 17, the last at Seville Cathedral in 1768; he won a wide reputation as one of the finest composers of his day. His *c*500 works include Latin sacred music and villancicos.

Ripieno (It.). The tutti (or 'concerto grosso'), as distinct from the solo group (or 'concertino'), in an orchestra performing music, especially concertos, of the Baroque period.

Riposo, Il. Vivaldi's Violin Concerto in E rv270.

Ripresa (It.). Term for a repeat or refrain in 16th- and 17th-century songs and dances; it may signify a small instrumental unit which appears before, after or between repetitions of the main music. *Riprese* use standard chord progressions, mostly in triple metre.

Riquier, Guiraut (*b* Narbonne, *c*1230; *d c*1300). Provençal troubadour poet and composer, usually considered the last of the troubadours. His 89 extant poems are, in some sources, assigned an exact date, ranging from 1254 to 1292, and reveal facts about his life. He served Amalrich IV, Viscount of Narbonne (1239–70), and then Alfonso X the Wise of Castile until 1279, when he left, probably to serve Henry II, Count of Rodez (1275–1302). Remarkably, no fewer than 48 of his poems have survived with their melodies. 29 are in bar form, but even with this type there is great formal variety. In addition to being dated, Riquier's songs are labelled as to type: 25 of those with music are called *cansos* (through-composed or part strophic) and 20 *vers* (in bar form).

Rise and Fall of the City of Mahagonny. *See* AUF-STIEG UND FALL DER STADT MAHAGONNY.

Rising of the Moon, The. Opera in three acts by Maw to a libretto by Beverley Cross (1970, Glyndebourne).

Risoluto (It.). Resolved, decisive.

Risset, Jean-Claude (*b* Le Puy, 13 March 1938). French composer. A pupil of Jolivet, he worked with Mathews at the Bell Telephone Laboratories from 1964, and has developed computer music in the USA and Paris (at IRCAM from 1971).

Ristori, Giovanni Alberto (*b* ?Bologna, 1692; *d* Dresden, 7 Feb 1753). Italian composer. After presenting his first operas in Italy he went to Dresden, and in 1717–33 was a composer to the Italian comic theatre; he was also director of the *cappella polacca* at Warsaw. In 1731–2 he visited St Petersburg, where a revival (1731) of one of his works was probably the first performance of an Italian opera in Russia. He was demoted to chamber organist at Dresden in 1733 but became court *Kirchenkomponist* in 1746 and vice-Kapellmeister (under Hasse) in 1750. He composed *c*20 operas and other stage works, mostly for Dresden, as well as oratorios, cantatas, sacred works (masses, psalms, motets etc) and a few instrumental pieces. His music is skilfully composed and at times matches Hasse's in breadth and melodic beauty.

Ritardando (It.). Holding back, becoming slower.

Ritenuto (It.). 'Held back': an indication of a more sudden, extreme slowing down than is implied by *rallentando* and *ritardando*.

Rite of Spring, The [Vesna svyashchennaya]. Ballet (scenes of pagan Russia) in two parts by Stravinsky to a scenario by N. Roerich (1913, Paris).

Ritornello. A short recurring passage, particularly the tutti section of a Baroque aria or concerto movement. Most of the recurring instrumental sections in Monteverdi's operas are entitled 'ritornello' and the term was similarly used in England, Germany and France, where the *ritournelle*, usually in triple time, came to signify a section to be danced after a song.

By the 18th century a typical form of the ritornello aria was: ritornello in the tonic key; first solo, moving to the dominant or relative major; shortened ritornello in the new key; second solo, modulating and cadencing in the tonic; full ritornello in the tonic (sometimes with solo interruptions). In a *da capo* aria this pattern was repeated after a central section. The same basic design, extended to cover more key centres, was used for fast movements in Baroque concertos (Vivaldi, Bach etc); and combined with sonata-form elements it reached a new level of complexity in Mozart's piano concertos.

Ritorno d'Ulisse in patria, Il. Opera in a prologue and five acts by Monteverdi to a libretto by G. Badoaro (1640, Venice).

Ritschel, Johannes (Michael Ignaz) (*b* Mannheim, bap. 29 July 1739; *d* there, 25 March 1766). German violinist and composer. After studying in Bologna (with Padre Martini) and Naples, he became *Protector Electoralis chori musici* at the Mannheim court (1763). One of the most gifted of the second-generation Mannheim composers, he wrote many sacred works, showing Italian influence.

His father Franz Joseph (*d* 1763) was first organist at the Mannheim court and a brother of Georg Wenzel Ritschel (*c*1680–1757), a double bass player there. His son Georg (1744–1805), a violinist, went with the court to Munich in 1778 and composed chamber works.

Ritter, Alexander [Sascha] (*b* Narva, 7 June 1833; *d* Munich, 12 April 1896). German composer and violinist. Wagner's nephew by marriage, he studied with Ferdinand David at the Leipzig Conservatory. He was second Konzertmeister under Liszt at Weimar (1854–6) and Bülow at Meiningen, where he met the young Richard Strauss whom he strongly influenced. He also worked in Stettin, Schwerin and Würzburg. His compositions include two operas, tone poems, choral works and lieder.

Ritter, Christian (*b*?1645–50; *d* after 1717). German composer. After serving at Halle, he became court organist (1681) and then vice-Kapellmeister at Stockholm. He held equivalent posts at Dresden in 1683–8, then returned to Stockholm for at least 11 years. His surviving output includes sacred works, notable for their expressive power, and keyboard pieces.

Ritter, Hermann (*b* Wismar, 16 Sept 1849; *d* Würzburg, 25 Jan 1926). German viola player. He constructed and exhibited the *viola alta* (1876), an exact enlargement of a violin more brilliant in tone than the viola; it was used by Wagner at Bayreuth.

Ritter, Peter (*b* Mannheim, 2 July 1763; *d* there, 1 Aug 1846). German cellist and composer. He played in the Mannheim theatre orchestra, becoming Konzertmeister in 1801, and was also a soloist. In 1803–23 he was Kapellmeister to the orchestra of the Grand Duchy of Baden. He composed over 20 German stage works (mostly for Mannheim), sacred music and various instrumental pieces.

His uncle Georg Wenzel (1748–1808), a bassoonist and composer, served at Mannheim, Munich and Berlin; for him Mozart wrote the bassoon part of his lost *sinfonia concertante* for wind. Among the other musicians of the family was the Mannheim violinist Heinrich (*fl* 1779–93), Peter's brother.

Ritual Dances. Four orchestral dances by Tippett from his opera *The Midsummer Marriage* (1955).

Ritual Fire Dance. Dance from Falla's ballet *El amor brujo* (1915).

Rivier, Jean (*b* Villemomble, 21 July 1896). French composer. He studied with Caussade at the Paris Conservatoire (1922–6) and taught there after World War II. He became one of the most progressive younger composers of the interwar period, his works including symphonies, concertos, chamber music and songs in a strongly purposeful, tonal style.

Roberday, François (*b* Paris, bap. 21 March 1624; *d* Auffargis, 13 Oct 1680). French composer. He was a valet at the French court and an organist. His keyboard fugues and capriccios (1660) show a strong Italian influence.

Robert, Pierre (*b* Louvres, *c*1618; *d* Paris, bur. 30 Dec 1699). French composer. A priest, he was *maître de chapelle* at Notre Dame (1653–63) before becoming a *sous-maître* at the royal chapel and *compositeur de la musique de la chapelle et de la chambre du roi* (1672–83). His principal works are 24 *grands motets* (1684), which resemble Lully's.

Robert de Handlo (*fl* early 14th century). English music theorist, possibly from a distinguished Kent family. His treatise (*Regule cum maximis Magistri Francoris cum additionibus aliorum musicorum*, 1326), which remained influential for several centuries, is a practical handbook using a clear didactic method of maxims and rules by Franco of Cologne, Handlo himself and other theorists such as Petrus de Cruce and Johannes de Garlandia. Not much is original, but Handlo gave a useful synoptic history of notation, with an English emphasis. He was among the last to embrace the theory of the rhythmic modes while they were still a basis for polyphony.

Robert de Reins [La Chievre] (*fl* 13th century). French trouvère poet and composer. He came from the Ile de France. Of nine works attributed to him, three are motets; he is one of an exclusive group of trouvères, including Richart de Fournival, associated with the early motet.

Robert le diable. Opera in five acts by Meyerbeer to a libretto by Scribe and Delavigne (1831, Paris).

Roberto Devereux. Opera in three acts by Donizetti to a libretto by Cammarano after F. Ancelot's *Elisabeth d' Angleterre* (1837, Naples).

Robertsbridge Codex. English MS dating from the second quarter of the 14th century. It is famous for the very early examples of keyboard music on two of its folios, consisting of three *estampies* and three motet arrangements. It is now in the British Library, London.

Robertus de Anglia (*fl* 1469–75). English composer. In September 1460 he went to Ferrara Cathedral to instruct the vicars in singing, and from 1467 to October 1474 was *magister cantus* at S Petronio, Bologna; he then returned to England. Two Italian songs are attributed to him; a third is lost.

Robeson, Paul (*b* Princeton, NJ, 9 April 1898; *d* Philadelphia, 23 Jan 1976). American bass-baritone. Known at first as an actor, he gave his first concert in 1925, singing negro spirituals. He quickly became internationally known, and in the 1930s made films. His voice had great richness and earthy resonance.

Robin et Marion. A play in courtly-popular style by ADAM DE LA HALLE, written *c*1283; the music consists largely of traditional *refrains*.

Robinson, Anastasia (*b* Italy, *c*1692; *d* Southampton, April 1755). English soprano, later contralto. She was a popular opera singer in London, 1714–24, and created several Handel roles, including Oriana in *Amadigi* (1715) and Cornelia in *Giulio Cesare* (1724). Her voice was notable for its expressiveness. She was married to the Earl of Peterborough. She is often confused with her contemporary, the soprano Ann Turner Robinson (*d* 1741), who sang in some of the same operas, such as *Radamisto*, and Ann's daughter, 'Miss Robinson', who sang in Handel oratorios in the 1740s.

Robinson, Earl (Hawley) (*b* Seattle, 2 July 1910). American composer. He went to New York in 1934, studied with Copland and Eisler, and began writing musicals and topical cantatas (e.g. *Ballad for Ameri-*

cans, 1938) and songs based on folk music. Later works include concertos for banjo and piano.

Robinson, Thomas (*fl* 1589–1609). English lutenist and composer. The Cecil family were among his patrons. He probably taught the lute to the future Queen Anne in Denmark before 1589, when she married James I. His lute method *The Schoole of Musicke* (1603) helped advance lute technique in England and his music is charming and of outstanding quality. He also published lessons for the cittern (1609).

Rocca, Lodovico (*b* Turin, 29 Nov 1895 *d* there, 25 June 1986). Italian composer. A pupil of Orefice in Milan, he is best known for his eclectic but powerful opera *Il Dibuk* (1934); he also directed the Turin Conservatory (1940–66).

Rochberg, George (*b* Paterson, NJ, 5 July 1918). American composer. He studied at the Mannes School (1939–42) and with Scalero and Menotti at the Curtis Institute (1945–7). In 1950 he went to Rome and met Dallapiccola, becoming strongly impressed by Schoenbergian serialism, followed *c*1957 by a turn towards Webern. During this period he worked as an editor for Presser, then in 1960 joined the faculty at the University of Pennsylvania. During the mid-1960s he began to work with quotations, drawing on music from Bach to the present, which seems to have led him to an overtly Romantic style in most of his music since the early 1970s. His works cover most genres and include five symphonies (1957–85), a Violin Concerto (1974), seven string quartets (1952–79) and other chamber and vocal music.

Rochester Philharmonic Orchestra. American orchestra. It was founded in 1921 as the Eastman Theatre Orchestra to accompany silent films. In 1923 it began annual concert seasons, with Eugene Goossens as conductor; its home is the Eastman Theatre (opened 1921, cap. 3100). It takes part each summer in the Finger Lakes Music Festival, Canandaigua.

Rochlitz, (Johann) Friedrich (*b* Leipzig, 12 Feb 1769; *d* there, 16 Dec 1842). German critic and editor. He studied in Leipzig, where he met Mozart in 1789. A writer trained in music and theology, he became the first editor (1798–1818) of Breitkopf & Härtel's *Allgemeine musikalische Zeitung*, remaining a well-respected contributor until 1835. His viewpoint was conservative and his first appraisals of Beethoven were severely critical, but from 1800 he came to regard him as the most important exponent of the new German music. Weber and Spohr set texts by Rochlitz and Goethe held him in high esteem.

Rock. The term, strictly defined, refers to a musical style that emerged in the mid-1960s; more broadly, it encompasses this and rock and roll, which prevailed in the late 1950s and early 1960s. The two styles have similarities: both use amplified singing and electric instruments (usually a lead electric guitar, a prominent rhythm section of bass guitar and drums and often a rhythm guitar and keyboard instrument), have a strong rhythmic drive intended to encourage listeners to dance, and appeal principally to young people.

Rock and roll emerged in the USA in the mid-1950s as a development of rhythm-and-blues, but whereas rhythm-and-blues had an almost exclusively black audience, rock and roll appealed to a mass audience mainly of young whites. Black rhythm-and-blues performers like Chuck Berry, Little Richard and Bo Diddley soon found success with this larger audience. But the greater popularity was for such white performers as Bill Haley and the Comets, Elvis Presley, Buddy Holly, Gene Vincent and the Everly Brothers, most from southern country-music backgrounds. Rock and roll quickly gained an international following and in the early 1960s British groups such as the Beatles, the Rolling Stones and the Who helped broaden its stylistic boundaries and ushered in rock – a more diverse musical category.

Key themes for the early rock movement were youth protest, the counterculture and hallucinogenic drugs. San Francisco became its leading centre. Californian groups of the late 1960s such as the Grateful Dead, Jefferson Airplane and the Doors broke away from the established format of the three-minute song and played loose, extended, improvisatory numbers. Eclecticism and experiment abounded.

By the mid-1970s, much of the experiment was felt to be self-indulgent and the political stances unrealistic. There were attempts to recapture the vigour of 1950s rock and roll and to work within the discipline of the short song, and the distinction between rock and pop music became blurred. Rock now became divided into several sub-categories such as heavy metal, punk and new wave, each with its own audience.

Rock and roll. *See* ROCK.

Röckel. German family of musicians. The most celebrated members were Joseph (1783–1870), a tenor and producer of German opera in Paris and London, and his son August (1814–76), a conductor remembered mainly for his correspondence with Wagner.

Rockstro [Rackstraw], William S(mith) (*b* North Cheam, 5 Jan 1823; *d* London, 2 July 1895). English writer on music, pianist and composer. He studied in Leipzig (1845), where his teachers included Mendelssohn. He wrote successful pedagogical works, biographies of Handel, Mendelssohn and Jenny Lind and editions of early English vocal music.

Rococo. Term from art that has been applied by analogy to music, especially French music, of the 18th century. It stands for a style of architectural decoration that began in France at the end of the 17th century and is light, graceful and ornamental, involving the breaking-up of the severe lines of the previous era; it was widely imitated, especially in south Germany and Austria. In music, the term has been applied to the lighter works of the French Regency period, especially the *opera-ballet*; it has also been applied to François Couperin's keyboard music, with its decorative style and its emphasis on character-pieces, to the music of the French flute and violin composers of the time and even to Rameau's operas. By extension, it has been applied to non-French music, for example the chamber music of Telemann.

Rode, (Jacques) Pierre (Joseph) (*b* Bordeaux, 16 Feb 1774; *d* Château de Bourbon, 25 Nov 1830). French violinist and composer. He was a favourite pupil of Viotti's in Paris and made his début in 1790. Professor at the newly founded Paris Conservatoire (1795) and solo violinist to Buonoparte (1800), he also won success in Spain, Germany and in Russia, where he was solo violinist to the tsar in St Petersburg (1804–8). In 1812 he gave the first performance of Beethoven's Violin Sonata op.96 with the Archduke Rudolph at the piano. He was the most finished representative of the French violin school, imbuing the classicism of his teacher Viotti with typically French verve, piquancy and a kind of nervous bravura. His best music is in his 13 concertos, but he also wrote popular *airs variés*, 12 string quartets, 24 duos for two violins and the famous 24 Caprices.

Rodelinda. Opera in three acts by Handel to a libretto by Haym after Salvi (1725, London).

Rodeo. Ballet in one act by Copland to a scenario by Agnes de Mille (1942, New York).

Röder. Leipzig music engraving and printing firm, founded in 1846 by C.G. Röder (1812–83). The largest and most progressive music printers of the time, it worked with many publishers and was nationalized after World War II.

Rodgers, Richard (Charles) (*b* Hammels Station, 28 June 1902; *d* New York, 30 Dec 1979). American composer. He studied at Columbia University (1919–21) and the Institute of Musical Art (1921–3). With Lorenz Hart, he aimed to use good poetry in place of the banal lyrics of current popular songs. Their association produced 30 stage musicals as well as films. On Hart's death in 1943 Rodgers formed a partnership with Oscar Hammerstein II which led to a series of musicals that enjoyed unprecedented success, from *Oklahoma!* (1943, which integrated song, dance and drama) to *South Pacific* (1949) and *The Sound of Music* (1959).

Rodio, Rocco (*b* Bari, *c*1535; *d* Naples, after 1615). Italian composer. He worked mainly in Naples and is known for his advanced *Regole di musica* (1600) and the counterpoint and progressive features of his madrigals and canzonas.

Rodolphe, Jean Joseph (*b* Strasbourg, 14 Oct 1730; *d* Paris, 12/18 Aug 1812). Alsatian horn player, violinist and composer. A pupil of Leclair, he played in the court orchestra at Stuttgart, where he studied with Jommelli and wrote several ballets for Noverre (notably *Médée et Jason*, 1763). By 1767 he was in Paris, where he composed stage works and horn music and was a teacher; he wrote two theory methods (1784, *c*1785). He popularized the horn as a solo instrument and was probably the first in Paris to use a hand-stopping technique.

Rodrigo, Joaquín (*b* Sagunto, 22 Nov 1901). Spanish composer. Blind from the age of three, he studied with Antich in Valencia and Dukas in Paris (from 1927), also receiving encouragement from Falla. His *Concierto de Aranjuez* for guitar and orchestra (1939) made his name and established his style of

tuneful and smoothly colourful Hispanicism: later works include similar concertos for violin, piano, cello, harp and flute as well as songs and small instrumental pieces, several for guitar.

Rodrigues Coelho, Manuel (*b* Elvas, *c*1555; *d* probably at Lisbon, *c*1635). Portuguese composer. He was organist at Elvas Cathedral (until 1602) and then at the court in Lisbon. His collection *Flores de musica pera o instrumento de tecla & harpa* (1620) is the earliest surviving keyboard music printed in Portugal.

Rodríguez de Hita, Antonio (*b c*1724; *d* Madrid, 21 Feb 1787). Spanish composer. He was *maestro de capilla* at Palencia Cathedral (*c*1740–*c*1757) and at the Madrid Convento Real de la Encarnación. His works include four zarzuelas (1768–70), which helped establish a native Spanish opera, much church music and some instrumental pieces. His treatise (1757) reflects his progressive approach.

Rodwell, George (Herbert Bonaparte) (*b* London, 15 Nov 1800; *d* there, 22 Jan 1852). English composer and playwright. He was a pupil of Vincent Novello and Henry Bishop. Between 1824 and 1846 he wrote the music for *c*23 stage pieces (and the words to another 20 or more), of which *Teddy the Tiler* (1830) was most successful. He also composed popular songs and glees, taught at the RAM and was music director at Covent Garden Theatre (from 1836), advocating a national opera.

Rodzinski, Artur (*b* Split, 1 Jan 1892; *d* Boston, MA, 27 Nov 1958). American conductor of Polish descent. After study in Vienna, with Marx, Schreker and Schalk, he conducted in Poland from 1920. He was assistant to Stokowski in Philadelphia from 1926 and in 1929 became conductor of the Los Angeles PO. His periods with the Cleveland Orchestra (1933–43) and the New York PO (1943–7) were notable for his raising of standards. He gave energetic performances of a wide repertory, including concert performances of operas.

Roeser, Valentin (*b* Germany, *c*1735; *d* Paris, probably 1782). German composer and clarinettist. By 1762 he was in Paris, where he served the Prince of Monaco and later the Duke of Orléans. He composed much instrumental music: his early orchestral trios and symphonies show a Mannheim influence, but the later works are in the French taste. More important were his didactic works, among them an instrumentation treatise of 1764 (the first of its kind) and a translation (1770) of L. Mozart's *Violinschule*.

Rogalski, Theodor (*b* Bucharest, 11 April 1901; *d* Zurich, 2 Feb 1954). Romanian composer. He studied at the Bucharest Conservatory (1919–20), with Karg-Elert at the Leipzig Conservatory (1920–23) and with d'Indy and Ravel in Paris (1924). He was conductor of the Radio Bucharest SO (1930–51) and taught at the conservatory. He wrote a handful of polished orchestral works, notable for their lavish colouring.

Roger, Estienne (*b* Caen, 1665/6; *d* Amsterdam, 7 July 1722). French music publisher. Active in Amsterdam, he issued music 1696–1722, after which his son-in-law Michel-Charles Le Cène acquired the firm, running it until 1743. His practice was to copy music of publishers in other countries, and he built up an impressive international list, enhancing his business by distribution throughout Europe. His catalogue was strong in Italian works, including the first editions of most of Vivaldi's printed works and all of Corelli's; also in the catalogue are Albinoni, Caldara, A. Scarlatti, Torelli, Veracini and (from Paris) Lully, Marais and Mouton. During Le Cène's time Geminiani, Locatelli, Quantz, Tartini and Telemann were added. Roger was the first music printer to use publisher's plate numbers. His music was beautifully printed using the new process of copperplate engraving.

Roger, Gustave-Hippolyte (b Paris, 17 Dec 1815; d there, 12 Sept 1879). French tenor. With his intelligence, fine bearing and pure tone he won great success, creating (among other roles) Berlioz's Faust (1846) and John of Leiden in Le prophète (1849).

Roger, Victor (b Montpellier, 22 July 1853; d Paris, 2 Dec 1903). French composer and critic. He studied at the Ecole Niedermeyer. Among the vaudeville-operettas that were his speciality, Les vingt-huit jours de Clairette (1892) and L'auberge du Tohu-Bohu (1897) were particularly successful, showing melodic grace and effective use of rhythm.

Roger-Ducasse, Jean (Jules Aimable) (b Bordeaux, 18 April 1873; d Taillan-Médoc, 19 July 1954). French composer. He was a pupil of Fauré at the Paris Conservatoire, where he later taught. His works, in an elaborate, personal style, include the ingenious ballet Orphée (1913, perf. 1926) and the opera Cantegril (1931), choral and orchestral music, songs and piano pieces.

Rogers, Benjamin (b Windsor, bap. 2 June 1614; d Oxford, June 1698). English organist and composer. After serving in Dublin, he held a series of posts as a singer and organist at St George's Chapel, Windsor, and Eton College (from 1641). He was organist and informator choristarum at Magdalen College, Oxford, 1665–86. He composed consort and keyboard music and several services and anthems.

Rogers, Bernard (b New York, 4 Feb 1893; d Rochester, NY, 24 May 1968). American composer. He studied with Goetschius at the Institute of Musical Art in New York (1921–2) and in Europe with Bridge and Boulanger (1927–9); until 1967 he taught at the Eastman School. His works include oratorios and psalm settings, five symphonies (1926–59) and other orchestral music in a finely coloured tonal style. His The Art of Orchestration (1951) is a standard work.

Rogers, Nigel (David) (b Wellington, 21 March 1935). English tenor. He studied at King's College, Cambridge, in Rome, Milan and in Munich where he was concerned in the foundation of the Studio der frühen Musik. A Baroque specialist, he has sung in several early music groups and is admired as an interpreter of Monteverdi, with his natural feeling for the music's expressive character, his command of florid writing and his clear, incisive tone.

Roger Wagner Chorale. See LOS ANGELES PHILHARMONIC ORCHESTRA.

Rogier, Philippe (b Arras, c1561; d Madrid, 29 Feb 1596). Flemish composer. A chorister at Philip II of Spain's chapel from 1572, he was ordained, becoming vicemaestro (1584) and maestro de capilla (1586). Of his large output (at least 250 works), only 16 motets (1595), five masses (1598) and a few chansons and other sacred works survive.

Rogowski, Ludomir Michal (b Lublin, 3 Oct 1881; d Dubrovnik, 14 March 1954). Polish composer. A pupil of Noskowski at the Warsaw Conservatory and of Nikisch and Riemann in Leipzig (1906–9), he directed the Vilnius Organ School and founded the Vilnius SO (1910). In 1926 he settled in Dubrovnik. His works include operas, seven symphonies, chamber and choral music using folksong and oriental modes.

Roi Arthus, Le. Opera in three acts by Chausson to his own libretto (1903, Brussels).

Roi David, Le. Dramatic psalm in five parts by Honegger, a setting for narrator, soloists, chorus and orchestra of a text by Morax (1921, Mézières).

Roi d'Ys, Le. Opera in three acts by Lalo to a libretto by Blau (1888, Paris).

Roi malgré lui, Le. Opera in three acts by Chabrier to a libretto by E. de Najac and P. Burani after A. and M. Ancelot (1887, Paris).

Roland. Tragédie lyrique in a prologue and five acts by Lully to a libretto by P. Quinault (1685, Versailles).

Roland-Manuel [Lévy, Roland Alexis Manuel] (b Paris, 22 March 1891; d there, 2 Nov 1966). French composer. He was a pupil of Roussel and Ravel, and devoted follower of the latter. His works include operas, oratorios, orchestral pieces and songs in a fastidious, refined, anti-Romantic style. He wrote books on Ravel and Falla, ghosted Stravinsky's Poetics of Music and popularized music as a broadcaster.

Roldán, Amadeo (b Paris, 12 July 1900; d Havana, 7 March 1939). Cuban composer. A pupil of del Campo in Madrid, he settled in Havana in 1921, and was an invigorating influence as conductor of the Havana PO, founder of the Havana String Quartet, composer and conservatory teacher. A mulatto, he drew on Afro-Cuban music and myth and wrote ballets, orchestral pieces and a set of Rítmicas (1930: I–IV for wind quintet and piano, V–VI for percussion ensemble).

Rolfe Johnson, Anthony (b Tackley, Oxon, 1940). English tenor. He took up singing only in 1967, studied at the GSM and appeared first at Glyndebourne. Later he sang for the English National Opera, chiefly in Mozart roles and as Monteverdi's Orpheus; he has also sung Lensky (Netherlands Opera) and Aschenbach (Scottish Opera). Noted for his elegant and lyrical singing, he has enjoyed particular success in oratorios by Handel.

Roll. On a drum, a tremolo effect (sometimes notated tr) obtained by the rapid alternation of strokes with two sticks.

Rolla, Alessandro (b Pavia, 6 April 1757; d Milan, 15 Sept 1841). Italian violinist and composer. He joined the ducal court in Parma as first viola player in 1782, later becoming first violinist (1792) and concert director. In 1803–33 he was first violinist and orchestral director at La Scala, Milan; he also taught at the new Milan Conservatory. An influential and respected musician, he composed virtuoso concertos and solos, chamber music and pedagogical pieces.

Rolland, Romain (*b* Clamecy, 29 Jan 1886; *d* Vézelay, 30 Dec 1944). French man of letters and writer on music. He studied in Paris and Rome, became director of the music school of the Ecole des Hautes Etudes Sociales (1902–11) and in 1903 was appointed to the first chair of music history at the Sorbonne, retiring in 1913 because of ill-health. As historian, critic, biographer, novelist, playwright and polemicist, Rolland ranged wide. He took a personal view of history of a rigorously moral tone; this gave a distinctive flavour to his biographies of Beethoven (of whom he wrote a single-volume life and a seven-volume study) and Handel and to his numerous articles. He saw history primarily in terms of the noble, superior soul; because of music's universality, profundity and spontaneity, he believed it was often the first to give expression to fundamental changes in society. In this spirit he composed his vast 'roman fleuve' *Jean-Christophe* (1904–12), using the life of a fictional composer as a symbol around which to synthesize his convictions about the nature, history and moral significance of music, its racial characteristics and its function.

Rolle, Johann Heinrich (*b* Quedlinburg, 23 Dec 1716; *d* Magdeburg, 29 Dec 1785). German composer. After serving as organist in Magdeburg, 1732–6, he went to Leipzig and then to Berlin, where he played in Frederick the Great's court orchestra (1741–7). Returning to Magdeburg, he became organist at the Johanniskirche, and in 1751 succeeded his father, Christian Friedrich Rolle (1681–1751) as city music director. In 1764 he founded a series of public concerts (the second of its kind in Germany), at which he presented his own biblical-historical oratorios with great success. These *c*20 works (1766–85), more dramatic and emotional than most contemporary oratorios, have sacrificial subjects (e.g. *Der Tod Abels*, 1769). Influenced by Berlin composers such as C.H. Graun, they are unusually flexible in structure. Rolle also wrote other oratorios, two stage works, many motets, cantatas and songs, and orchestral, chamber and keyboard music.

Rolli, Paolo Antonio (*b* Rome, 13 June 1687; *d* Todi, 20 March 1765). Italian librettist. He worked in London, 1715–44, and wrote librettos for Italian operas there; Handel set several, notably *Deidamia* (1741). His writings also include poetry, cantata texts, satires and translations.

Röllig, Karl Leopold (*b* Hamburg; *d* Vienna, 4 March 1804). German glass harmonica player and composer. He was music director of a theatre company in Hamburg and had an opera staged in 1771. He toured in the 1780s, then settled in Vienna. Besides improving the glass harmonica, he invented the orphica, a small, portable piano (*c*1795). He wrote pieces for both instruments and essays on instrument building.

He should not be confused with Johann Georg Röllig (1710–90), a court musician at Zerbst and composer of cantatas, motets, orchestral and chamber music.

Roman, Johan Helmich (*b* Stockholm, 26 Oct 1694; *d* Haraldsmåla, 20 Nov 1758). Swedish composer. He joined the Swedish royal chapel as a violinist and oboist in 1711, and *c*1715–21 studied in England, where he had contact with Handel. Returning to Stockholm, he became deputy master of the chapel (1721), later chief master (1727). Besides improving the chapel standards, he founded Stockholm's first public concerts (1731) and toured Europe (1735–7). He retired in 1745.

Roman, the first Swedish composer of real significance, is a leading figure in the country's musical history. His output includes occasional vocal works, sacred music, songs etc, orchestral suites and concertos, symphonies and chamber works; best known is the orchestral suite *Drottningholmsmusiquen*, written for a royal wedding in 1744. Some of his music shows Handel's influence, but his style also has *galant* features. He arranged works by other composers and translated theoretical works into Swedish.

Roman Carnival. *See* CARNAVAL ROMAIN, LE.

Romance. From the 15th century, *romance* in Spain and *romanza* in Italy have nearly always signified a ballad. The narrative *romance* was, next to the villancico, the most popular song-type in Spanish-speaking countries. Over 50 settings of *romance* tunes of 1450–1550 survive. Up to the mid-16th century they were probably sung mostly at court as three- or four-part choruses or as solo songs with lute. After *c*1550 a new type of *romance* with a refrain was taken up and by 1630 the *romance* was virtually indistinguishable from the villancico.

From the early 18th century 'romance' in France and 'Romanze' in Germany were used for extravagant, sentimental or 'romantic' tales. The *romance* was ideally suited to the sentimental vein of *opéra comique* and to drawing-room performance. Such German poets as Herder, Goethe and Schiller provided texts and the *Romanze*, with its folksong elements, became a feature in the Singspiel.

The vocal romance was often imitated in instrumental slow movements of a simple, lyrical character. The *romance* of Mozart's Piano Concerto K466 and Beethoven's two *Romanzen* for violin and orchestra opp.40 and 50 exemplify the genre's lyric capabilities. In the 19th century the term was used for small character-pieces, for example Schumann's *Drei Romanzen* op.28.

Roman de Fauvel. *See* FAUVEL, ROMAN DE.

Romanesca. A sequence of chords, used in Italy from *c*1550 to 1650, for songs and instrumental variations. The harmonic pattern, used both in duple or triple metre, was varied with extra chords or notes. In the 17th century the bass was increasingly treated as a melody. The romanesca was occasionally used for dancing. The chordal scheme also occurred in such forms as the *favorita* and the *fantinella*.

Romani, Felice (*b* Genoa, 31 Jan 1788; *d* Moneglia, 28 Jan 1865). Italian librettist. His classically elegant verses and dramatic sense made Italian composers eager to work with him (over 100 19th-century composers set his texts). His most important collaborations were with Rossini, Donizetti (notably *L'elisir d'amore, Anna Bolena, Lucrezia Borgia*) and above all Bellini (*Il pirata* to *Beatrice di Tenda*). He was also a literary critic.

Romanov. Russian imperial family. As patrons of the

arts they exercised a decisive influence on Russian music, which until the 18th century had remained isolated from Western developments. During the reigns of Empress Anna (1730–40) and Empress Elizabeth (1741–62) foreign musicians were invited to the Russian court and Italian opera became popular; in 1755 Francesco Araia composed the first opera to a Russian text. Catherine II (1762–96), herself a librettist, gave particular encouragement to opera.

Romantic. Term applied to the era in music history, from c1790 to 1910, that succeeded the Classical period. The word 'romantic' has to do with romance, imagination, the strange and the fantastic; in music it is applied (as to literature and painting) to works in which fantasy and imagination are in their own right more important than classical features such as balance, restraint and good taste.

Romanticism has early manifestations in English 18th-century literature, but its chief development was in Paris and Germany. In post-Revolution Paris, it is seen in the new types of opera that began to emerge and in the massive scale of patriotic music-making. In Germany, it appeared in the work of E.T.A. Hoffmann, the operas of Weber and the songs of Schubert, for example. The influence of Goethe, and particularly his *Faust*, was widely felt: Faust's search for immortality and transcendental sensual experience, leading him to meddle with the forces of darkness, typifies some of the attitudes of early Romanticism, seen in music in such works as Schubert's song *Der Erlkönig*, Weber's *Der Freischütz* and Berlioz's *Symphonie fantastique*. The position of the creative artist began to change: the artist could lead the way into a transcendental world and thus came to be regarded as a spiritual hero.

In music, Romanticism led to looser and more extended musical forms, including the symphonic poem (an orchestral work that related a story, or at least had a literary or artistic background), the expressive miniature for piano (especially the nocturne, cultivated by Field, Chopin and others, in which clear outlines were blurred to provide a dreamy, nocturnal effect), the art song (in which great emphasis was placed on the music's detailed expression of the verbal text and the symbolic meanings it carried) and opera, with plots that dealt with the escape of individuals from political repression ('rescue operas') or the fates of national or religious groups (especially in French grand opera) or events in exotic, far-off settings, usually in medieval times (Italian composers especially favoured plots set in Scotland based on the writings of Walter Scott).

Another manifestation of Romanticism is found in the exaltation not only of the composer but of the virtuoso performer; pianists such as Chopin and Liszt, and the violinist Paganini, acquired European reputations for their unique insights or heroic brilliance. A further aspect of Romanticism is found in the search for national identity, often through their history and folk-music repertory, by many of the European countries just attaining political maturity or independence.

The early period of Romanticism is generally seen as ending about the middle of the century, and the middle period as ending in c1890; the final period can be reckoned as ending in c1910 or at the time of World War I.

Romantic Symphony. Sub-title of Bruckner's Symphony no.4 in E (1874).

Romanza, Romanze (It., Ger.) *See* ROMANCE.

Romberg. German family of musicians. The most celebrated members were Andreas Jakob (1767–1821), a violinist and composer who settled in Hamburg, winning recognition for his songs and choral works, especially the setting of Schiller's *Lied von der Glocke* op.25 (1809); and his cousin Bernhard Heinrich (1767–1841), an internationally known cellist.

Rome Conservatory. *See* ACCADEMIA DI S CECILIA.

Romeo and Juliet. Dramatic symphony, op.17, by Berlioz for soprano, tenor and bass soloists, chorus and orchestra to a text by E. Deschamps (1839).

Opera in five acts by Gounod to a libretto by Barbier and Carré (1867, Paris).

Fantasy overture by Tchaikovsky (1869).

Ballet in a prologue, three acts and an epilogue by Prokofiev to a libretto by Lavrovsky, the composer and Radlov (1938, Brno).

Other composers have written works on the subject, among them Bellini (*I Capuleti ed I Montecchi*).

Romero, Mateo [Rosmarin, Mathiea] (*b* Liège, 1575–6; *d* Madrid, 10 May 1647). Spanish composer. He was *maestro de capilla* of the Flemish chapel in Madrid, 1598–1634, and served as a chaplain. Highly regarded in his time, he was a master of polychoral writing; in his secular music he used both madrigalian and villancico-like styles. He was influential in introducing the new style into Spain.

Ronald, Sir Landon (*b* London, 7 June 1873; *d* there, 14 Aug 1938). English conductor and composer, son of the opera impresario Henry Russell. He studied at the RCM, worked with touring opera companies, accompanied Melba on a tour in the USA, and made his Covent Garden début in 1896. He worked with the new LSO, 1904–7, then conducted with distinction in Berlin and Rome and widely in Britain, notably with the Royal Albert Hall Orchestra (1909–14). He was principal of the GSM, 1910–38, wrote criticism, and composed operettas, orchestral music and many songs.

Ronconi, Giorgio (*b* Milan, 6 Aug 1810; *d* Madrid, 8 Jan 1890). Italian baritone. One of the finest singing actors of the mid-19th century, he was equally gifted in tragedy and comedy; he appeared in several Donizetti premières and created the title role of Verdi's *Nabucco* (1842).

Rondeau. (1) One of the three fixed forms, together with the ballade and the virelai, that dominated French song and poetry in the 14th and 15th centuries. It had taken on its definitive structure by the early 13th century, when it was already a dance-song of importance. Its derivation from the Latin forms *rotundettum* or *rotundellum* implies circular motion in the dances for which such pieces were originally sung. The earliest dated rondeau is in a collection of courtly and popular songs of 1228, the essential features being the presence of a final refrain and the anticipation of the first part of this refrain in line two. Later the refrain was also introduced at the beginning of the poem, giving the form which was to remain the basis of the rondeau: I–II–I–I–I–II–I–II. This eight-line type is the most common in the late 13th and 14th centuries. Adam de la Halle's 14 three-voice settings in conductus style are the first polyphonic examples. It is distinguished from the virelai in that the rondeau refrain requires the whole melody, not simply part of it. This may explain why these refrains enjoyed an independent life and were inserted into other songs and motets. The *motet enté* ('grafted motet') uses a rondeau refrain in one voice but with new textual and musical material interpolated between the original opening and closing lines. The rhyme and metre may vary, particularly in the early period; from Machaut onwards the eight- and 16-line type dominates, the 21-line type becoming popular in the 15th century when it outshone the other lyric forms. Like the virelai and ballade, the rondeau is generally concerned with courtly love, usually in a rather lighter vein. It was also used in religious drama, although few examples are preserved with music and most were probably contrafacta of existing secular rondeaux.

(2) French term of the Baroque period for a composition based on the alternation of a main section (refrain, reprise, *grand couplet* or 'rondeau'), with subsidiary sections (*couplets*, episodes); *see* RONDO. Rondeaux are common in harpsichord music, for example Couperin's; they also appear in dance music, as in Rameau's opera *Hippolyte et Aricie* where there is a 'Menuet en rondeau'. In England the corruption 'Round O' was common.

Rondellus. A technique of three-voice composition cultivated in 13th-century England, or a piece composed in this manner. It uses the device known as voice-exchange. The exchange could be restricted to the two upper voices supported by a repetitive tenor (or *pes*), or it could be applied to all three. The only medieval writer to describe it was an Englishman, Walter Odington (*c*1300), although a Welsh account of 1198 clearly refers to the practice and early examples seem to come near the Welsh border. On the Continent it was known as an English practice from at least *c*1225; in continental treatises the term is generally found as the Latin for rondeau. Apart from the famous Summer Canon (which can be regarded as a potential multipart rondellus), no examples for more than three voices are known. The form died out, along with voice-exchange, after *c*1300.

Rondine, La. Opera in three acts by Puccini to a libretto by Adami (1917, Monte Carlo).

Rondo. A musical form in which the first or main section recurs, normally in the home key, between subsidiary sections (*couplets*, episodes) and to conclude the composition. The familiar Classical rondo had an important precursor in the French rondeau of Lully, François Couperin and Rameau. Englishmen such as Purcell and Germans such as Georg

Muffat and Bach adopted French forms and techniques, and by the mid-18th century the rondeau of French stamp was widely established. In the 1770s there began a vogue for rondos of a simple, tuneful kind for which *opera buffa* provided much of the impetus. C.P.E. Bach's rondos in the series for 'Connoisseurs and Amateurs' are extended leisurely compositions which stand outside the mainstream of the genre's evolution. The independent rondo for piano was cultivated with yet greater distinction by Mozart (K494 and 511), Beethoven (opp.51 no.1 and 129) and Mendelssohn (*Rondo capriccioso* op.14).

More often the Classical rondo (*ABAC...A*) functioned as a movement within a large composition, especially as the finale in a sonata, serenade or concerto. Haydn began composing rondos in the early 1770s; examples are found in his symphonies, string quartets and piano trios. Mozart used the form in a variety of media throughout his career. Beethoven used it in his early chamber works, sonatas and concertos, but later largely abandoned it. A significant innovation of the Classical period is the sonata-rondo, a fusion of rondo design with a sonata-allegro tonal plan. This entails the recapitulation in the tonic of the first episode and, possibly, the replacement of the contrasting central episode (*C*) with development of earlier material.

The sonata-rondo survived after Beethoven mainly in the finales of concertos (by Mendelssohn, Tchaikovsky, Grieg, Brahms and others). A famous later rondo is Strauss's *Till Eulenspiegel*. Mahler's Fifth Symphony has a Rondo-Finale and the third movement of his Ninth Symphony, Rondo-Burleske, is a free, expansive treatment of the Classical rondo.

Rondò [rondo]. A type of aria popular in the late 18th century, consisting of two sections, one slow and one fast, each of which may be repeated. One or both may be in gavotte rhythm. The best-known examples are by Mozart; they include 'Non mi dir' (*Don Giovanni*) and 'Per pietà' (*Così fan tutte*). The rondò is an important precursor of the 19th-century cantabile–cabaletta scheme.

Ronnefeld, Peter (*b* Dresden, 26 Jan 1935; *d* Kiel, 6 Aug 1965). German composer and conductor. A pupil of Blacher at the Berlin Musikhochschule (1950–54) and of Messiaen at the Paris Conservatoire (1954–5), he was Karajan's assistant at the Vienna Staatsoper, then conducted opera in Bonn and Kiel. He wrote operas and ballets in an advanced style, making brilliant use of parody.

Rontani, Raffaello (*b* ?Florence; *d* Rome, 1622). Italian composer. After serving in Florence he became *maestro di cappella* of S Giovanni dei Fiorentini, Rome, in 1616. He was one of the most popular composers of secular vocal chamber music. He published six volumes of *Varie musiche* (1614–22), mainly of solo songs, and one of madrigals (1610).

Röntgen, Julius (*b* Leipzig, 9 May 1855; *d* Bilthoven, 13 Sept 1932). Dutch composer, conductor and pianist. He studied composition in Leipzig with Lachner, Hauptmann and Richter and the piano with Plaidy and Reinecke. In Amsterdam from 1877 to 1925, he was a piano teacher and director of the conservatory, a recitalist and conductor of the Toonkunstkoor (1886–98); he became friendly with Brahms and Grieg. With his sons Julius (1881–1951), a violinist, and Engelbert (1886–1958), a cellist, he formed a trio (his sons Johannes and Joachim were also leading musicians). As a composer, chiefly of orchestral and chamber works, he was influenced by Schumann, Brahms and later, Reger.

Root. The lowest note of a chord when the notes are rearranged as a sequence of 3rds. If no rearrangement is necessary the chord is said to be in root position; if the root is not the lowest note, it is in INVERSION.

Rootham, Cyril (Bradley) (*b* Bristol, 5 Oct 1875; *d* Cambridge, 18 March 1938). English composer. He studied at St John's, Cambridge, and with Stanford at the RCM, and from 1902 was organist and musical director at his Cambridge college. His works include two symphonies and much choral music, notably the *Ode on the Morning of Christ's Nativity* (1928).

Ropartz, (Joseph) Guy (Marie) (*b* Guingamp, 15 June 1864; *d* Lanloup, 22 Nov 1955). French composer. He was a pupil of Dubois and Massenet at the Paris Conservatoire (1885–6) and of Franck, whose faithful disciple he was, though his music has a personal, often Breton flavour. He directed the conservatories of Nancy (1894–1919) and Strasbourg (1919–29), then retired to Brittany, the landscape and Celtic folklore of which he drew on in his works. They include the opera *Le pays* (1910), five symphonies (1894–1944), six string quartets (1893–1951), sacred choral pieces, songs, and verse and other writings.

Rore, Cipriano de (*b* Machelen, 1515–16, *d* Parma, Sept 1565). Flemish composer. He was in Italy by the 1540s; he was associated with Willaert and others in Venice. He was established as a composer by 1547, when he was *maestro di cappella* at the Ferrarese court. In 1559 he moved to Brussels to serve Margaret of Parma, governor of the Netherlands, in 1561 to Parma, to enter Ottavio Farnese's service, and in 1563 to Venice, where he was briefly *maestro di cappella* at St Mark's. He returned to Parma in 1564. The most influential of the earlier madrigalists, he produced over 120 Italian madrigals (mainly in 10 bks, 1542–66), as well as *c*80 sacred motets (5 bks, 1544–63, 1595, and MSS), masses, a Passion, secular motets and *chansons*. His early madrigals, mainly serious in tone, show a masterly fusion of sophisticated Franco-Flemish polyphony and Italian lyricism, with controlled use of imagery, while his later ones include marked progressive elements; these were much admired by Monteverdi.

Rorem, Ned (*b* Richmond, IN, 23 Oct 1923). American composer. He studied with Sowerby in Chicago (1938–9) and with Thomson (1944) and Diamond in New York, also attending the Curtis Institute (1943) and the Juilliard School. From 1949 to 1958 he was based in Paris, though spent two of those years in Morocco: his published diaries of this and later periods are flamboyantly candid. His large output includes symphonies, instrumental pieces and choral music, though he has been most productive

and successful as a composer of songs, latterly almost entirely in extended cyclic structures.

Rosa [Rose], Carl (August Nikolaus) (*b* Hamburg, 22 March 1842; *d* Paris, 30 April 1889). German impresario, violinist and conductor. He studied in Leipzig and Paris. With his wife, the soprano Euphrosyne Parepa, he formed and managed the Carl Rosa Opera Company, famous for its performances in English (1876–87) of foreign works (notably Wagner and Verdi) and new British operas.

Rosalia. A pejorative name, taken from an old Italian popular song *Rosalia, mia cara*, for the identical repetition of a melody a step higher.

Rosamunde. Play (*Rosamunde, Fürstin von Zypern*) by Helmina von Chézy (1823) for which Schubert wrote incidental music (entr'actes, ballets and vocal numbers). The overture used was one he had written in 1822 for the opera *Alfonso und Estrella*; the one now known as *Rosamunde* overture was composed for *Die Zauberharfe* (1820).

Rosbaud, Hans (*b* Graz, 22 July 1895; *d* Lugano, 29 Dec 1962). Austrian conductor. He studied in Frankfurt and conducted the radio orchestra there, 1928–37, becoming associated with music by Bartók, Stravinsky and the Second Viennese School. After periods in Münster, Strasbourg and Munich he conducted the South-West German RO at Baden-Baden from 1948 until his death and was also conductor of the Zurich Tonhalle Orchestra from 1957. His objectivity and intellectual strength were well suited to Schoenberg's music and he gave the first concert and stage performances of *Moses und Aron* (1954, 1957).

Rosé, Arnold (Josef) (*b* Iaşi, 24 Oct 1863; *d* London, 25 Aug 1946). Austrian violinist. He studied at the Vienna Conservatory and in 1881 became leader of the Vienna Court Opera orchestra and the Vienna PO. The following year he founded the Rosé Quartet, touring widely with it until 1938 and giving the first performances of works by Brahms, Reger and Schoenberg; he was regarded as a great chamber player. He married Mahler's sister Justine and collaborated closely with the composer during his years as director of the Vienna Court Opera.

Rose, Leonard (Joseph) (*b* Washington, DC, 27 July 1918; *d* White Plains, NY, 16 Nov 1984). American cellist. After study in Miami, Philadelphia and New York he became principal cellist of the Cleveland Orchestra in 1939, leaving for the New York PO in 1943. His concerto début was in 1944 and he toured as a soloist from 1951, making his London début in 1958. He was at his best in the Romantic repertory and was much admired as a chamber player and teacher (at the Juilliard School and the Curtis Institute).

Roseingrave, Thomas (*b* Winchester, 1688; *d* Dun Laoghaire, 23 June 1766). English organist and composer. In 1709 he studied in Italy, where he became a friend of Domenico Scarlatti. After settling in London (by 1718), he popularized Scarlatti's music in England and later made a famous edition (1739) of 42 of his sonatas. He was organist of St George's, Hanover Square, from 1725 and had an outstanding reputation as player and teacher, especially until the late 1730s. Later, after an unhappy love affair that depressed him and 'render'd [him] incapable of playing the organ', he retired to Dublin. His most original works are his harpsichord suites (1725), organ fugues and other keyboard pieces, which feature chromaticism and irregular phrases. He also composed Italian cantatas, anthems and songs.

His father, Daniel (d 1727), held cathedral organist's posts in England before becoming organist of Christ Church Cathedral and St Patrick's Cathedral, Dublin, in 1698; he composed sacred works. Daniel's son Ralph (c1695–1747), who succeeded him at Christ Church in 1719 and at St Patrick's in 1727, was also a church composer.

Rosen, Charles (Welles) (b New York, 5 May 1927). American pianist and writer on music. He studied at the Juilliard School and Princeton and with Moriz Rosenthal; his interests embrace mathematics, philosophy and literature. From 1951 he has been prominent as a pianist; he is severe and intellectual, at his best in Bach and Beethoven. His chief contribution to music literature is *The Classical Style* (1971); he has also written a monograph on Schoenberg (1975) and a book on sonata form (1980).

Rosenberg, Hilding (Constantin) (b Bosjökloster, 21 June 1892; d Stockholm, 19 May 1985). Swedish composer. He studied with Ellberg at the Royal Academy of Music in Stockholm (1915–16), and with Stenhammar. In 1920 he journeyed abroad, encountering the music of Hindemith and Schoenberg, which influenced his own: particularly important were Hindemith's neo-Baroque textures, though in harmony he continued to belong to a Scandinavian world of Sibelius, Nielsen and folk music. His music became more diatonic in the 1930s, when he also began writing operas (*Marinetter*, 1938). His large output includes eight symphonies (1917–74) and many other orchestral scores, incidental music, seven operas, ballets, oratorios and 12 string quartets. He was also active as a conductor (including at the Stockholm Royal Opera) and exerted an important influence on Swedish musical life as a teacher.

Rosenkavalier, Der. Opera in three acts by Richard Strauss to a libretto by Hofmannsthal (1911, Dresden).

Rosenman, Leonard (b Brooklyn, 7 Sept 1924). American composer. A pupil of Schoenberg, Sessions and Dallapiccola, he is an important figure in American film music, notably for *East of Eden* (1954) and *Rebel Without a Cause* (1955).

Rosenmüller, Johann (b Oelsnitz, c1619; d Wolfenbüttel, bur. 12 Sept 1684). German composer. He first worked as an organist and teacher in Leipzig, but was imprisoned (on suspicion of homosexuality) in 1655. From 1658 he was a trombonist at St Mark's, Venice, and in 1678–82 also composer at the Ospedale della Pietà. Finally he returned to Germany as court Kapellmeister at Wolfenbüttel. A prolific composer, he was important in transmitting Italian styles to Germany, where his music was especially popular. He published four instrumental collections (1645–82), which move from simple

dance suites to Italianate ensemble sonatas; the 12 sonatas of 1682 include much fugal writing. His sacred works number c200. The earliest are mainly small German concertos (many were published in two books, *Kern-Sprüche*, 1648 and 1652–3), but the later are mostly Latin, including psalms, solo cantatas and music for the Mass; these too show strong Italian features, and are notable for their expressiveness, clarity of form and idiomatic vocal writing.

Rosenthal, Manuel (b Paris, 18 June 1904). French conductor and composer. A pupil of Ravel at the Paris Conservatoire, he had an international conducting career (including at the Seattle SO, 1948–51), specializing in the 20th-century French repertory. His works, in many genres, are in a noble, neo-classical style.

Rosenthal, Moriz (b L'vov, 18 Dec 1862; d New York, 3 Sept 1946). Ukrainian pianist. After study in L'vov he moved to Vienna in 1875 and made his début there in 1876. From 1877 he was supervised by Liszt, after whose death he made his first tour of the USA. His playing of Chopin was noted for its virtuosity and tonal variety. He taught in New York from 1938.

Roser [von Reiter], Franz de Paula (b Naarn, 17 Aug 1779; d Budapest, 12 Aug 1830). Austrian composer. He studied with his father, the composer Johann Georg Roser (1740–97), and reputedly with Mozart. From 1800 he worked mainly as a theatre Kapellmeister and tenor in Vienna, composing over 60 works for the Vienna stage. He also wrote sacred and instrumental music.

Rosetti, Antonio [Rösler, Franz Anton] (b Litoměřice, c1750; d Ludwigslust, 30 June 1792). Bohemian composer. He joined the Wallerstein court as a double bass player in 1773, later becoming deputy (by 1780) and then full Kapellmeister (1785). From 1789 he was Kapellmeister to the Ludwigslust court. He also visited centres including Paris (1781) and Prague (where he conducted his Requiem for Mozart, 1791). Widely respected as a composer, he was especially influenced by Haydn. His large instrumental output, written mainly in the 1780s, includes over 30 symphonies, over 50 concertos (many for one or two horns), music for the Wallerstein wind ensemble and chamber and keyboard music. He also wrote oratorios, sacred works and many songs, arias etc.

Rosin [resin; colophony]. A substance, refined from distilled oil of turpentine, that is rubbed on the hair of the bow of a string instrument to give the bow-hair the roughness needed to enable it to set the strings in vibration. It can be used in powdered form. Strictly, 'resin' is the natural gummy exudation from tree trunks, as distinct from rosin.

Roslavets, Nikolay (Andreyevich) (b Dushatino, 5 Jan 1881; d Moscow, 23 Aug 1944). Soviet composer. He was a pupil of Vasilenko at the Moscow Conservatory (1902–12). At first influenced by French impressionism and Skryabin, he had by 1915 developed a technique of 12-note organization. In the 1920s he became prominent in Russian musical life, on the modernist wing, but later he and his music fell into obscurity. His works include piano and chamber pieces, choral music, songs and a violin concerto (1925); he wrote many articles.

Rospigliosi, Giulio (*b* Pistoia, 28 Jan 1600; *d* Rome, 9 Dec 1669). Italian librettist. He was the foremost librettist of his day for Roman opera; his works include the text to the earliest comic opera, Virgilio Mazzocchi's *Chi soffre speri* (1639). He was made pope (Clement IX) in 1667.

Rosseter, Philip (*b* 1567–8; *d* London, 5 May 1623). English composer. He became a court lutenist in London in 1603. From 1609 to 1617 he managed theatre companies, presenting plays at court and in public theatres. An associate of Campion, he published lute-songs with him (1621) and wrote many lute pieces in a traditional, contrapuntal style as well as consort music (1609).

Rossi, Francesco (*fl* Milan, *c*1670–1692). Italian composer. He worked in Milan as a church organist and later as a *maestro di cappella*, and composed a number of operas, some of them comic. Several musicians of this name were active in Italy, *c*1650–*c*1725.

Rossi, Lauro (*b* Macerata, 19 Feb 1812; *d* Cremona, 5 May 1885). Italian composer and teacher. He studied at the Naples Conservatory and achieved individuality as an opera composer in the post-Rossinian tradition, showing invention and a flair for comedy in, for example, *I falsi monetari* (1834, rev. 1844) and *Il domino nero* (1849). He was famous chiefly as an academic, as director of the Milan (1850–70) and Naples (1870–80) conservatories. He encouraged institutional reforms, revived old music (notably by Frescobaldi and Janequin) and wrote a lucid harmony textbook (1858).

Rossi, Luigi (*b* Torremaggiore, *c*1597; *d* Rome, 20 Feb 1653). Italian composer. Trained by Giovanni de Macque in Naples, he entered the service of the Borghese family in Rome in the early 1620s and became organist of S Luigi dei Francesi in 1633; he was also a singing teacher and lutenist. In 1641 he went to serve Cardinal Antonio Barberini, who commissioned his opera *Il palazzo incanto* (1642). Rossi presented his second opera, *Orfeo* (1647), at the French court; both were highly successful. After a second visit to Paris he moved to Lyons and later returned to Italy.

Rossi was recognized as one of the leading musicians of his time. His operas, both grand, spectacular works, represent the culmination of Roman opera in the period. During his lifetime, however, he was best known for his chamber cantatas, of which *c*300 survive; these use an expressive *bel canto* style and are mostly in short, clearly-defined forms. He also composed several oratorios, other sacred music, and instrumental pieces.

His brother Giovan Carlo (*c*1617–1692) was a harpist, organist and composer.

Rossi, Michelangelo (*b* Genoa, 1601–2; *d* Rome, bur. 7 July 1656). Italian composer and violinist. He first worked as an organist in Genoa, and by 1621 was in the service of Cardinal Maurizio of Savoy in Rome, where he also became a pupil and friend of Frescobaldi. He was next patronized by the Barber-

ini family (1630–38) and then by the Este family in Modena; he later returned to Rome. In his lifetime he was known as a virtuoso violinist, but his only surviving instrumental pieces are for keyboard: these include a collection of ten toccatas and correntes (?1640), similar to Frescobaldi's music though the toccatas are less dramatic. He also composed two operas, of which the earlier, *Erminia sul Giordano* (1637), is extant.

Rossi, Salamone (*b* ?Mantua, 19 Aug 1570; *d* ?Mantua, *c*1630). Italian composer. An instrumentalist, he had close links with the Gonzaga court at Mantua, though as a Jew he held a salaried position only intermittently. The majority of his vocal music, including five books of madrigals (1600–22) and some Hebrew settings (1622–3), is conservative in style, but his three-part canzonettas (1589) and especially his chamber duets (entitled *Madrigaletti*, 1628) are notably progressive. In his four instrumental collections (1607–22) he contributed to the development of the Baroque trio-sonata texture.

Rossini, Gioachino (Antonio) (*b* Pesaro, 29 Feb 1792; *d* Passy, 13 Nov 1868). Italian composer. Both his parents were musicians, his father a horn player, his mother a singer; he learnt the horn and singing and as a boy sang in at least one opera in Bologna, where the family lived. He studied there and began his operatic career when, at 18, he wrote a one-act comedy for Venice. Further commissions followed, from Bologna, Ferrara, Venice again and Milan, where *La pietra del paragone* was a success at La Scala in 1812. This was one of seven operas written in 16 months, all but one of them comic.

This level of activity continued in the ensuing years. His first operas to win international acclaim come from 1813, written for different Venetian theatres: the serious *Tancredi* and the farcically comic *L'italiana in Algeri*, the one showing a fusion of lyrical expression and dramatic needs, with its crystalline melodies, arresting harmonic inflections and colourful orchestral writing, the other moving easily between the sentimental, the patriotic, the absurd and the sheer lunatic. Two operas for Milan were less successful. But in 1815 Rossini went to Naples as musical and artistic director of the Teatro S Carlo, which led to a concentration on serious opera. But he was allowed to compose for other theatres, and from this time date two of his supreme comedies, written for Rome, *Il barbiere di Siviglia* and *La Cenerentola*. The former, with its elegant melodies, its exhilarating rhythms and its superb ensemble writing, has claims to be considered the greatest of all Italian comic operas, eternally fresh in its wit and its inventiveness. It dates from 1816; initially it was a failure, but it quickly became the most loved of his comic works, admired alike by Beethoven and Verdi. The next year saw *La Cenerentola*, a charmingly sentimental tale in which the heroine moves from a touching folksy ditty as the scullery maid to brilliant coloratura apt to a royal maiden.

Rossini's most important operas in the period that followed were for Naples. The third act of his *Otello* (1816), with its strong unitary structure, marks his maturity as a musical dramatist. The Neapolitan operas, even though much dependant on solo singing of a highly florid kind (to the extent that numbers could be, and have been, interchanged), show an enormous expansion of musical means, with more and longer ensembles and the chorus an active participant; the accompanied recitative is more dramatic and the orchestra is given greater prominence. Rossini also abandoned traditional overtures, probably in order to involve his audiences in the drama from the outset. In Naples the leading soprano was Isabella Colbran, mistress of the impresario, Barbaia. She transferred her allegiance to Rossini, who in 1822 married her; they were not long happy together.

Among the masterpieces from this period are *Maometto II* (1820) and, written for Venice at the end of his time in Naples, *Semiramide* (1823). Barbaia gave a Viennese season in 1822; Rossini and his wife returned to Bologna, then in 1823 left for London and Paris where he took on the directorship of the Théâtre-Italien, composing for that theatre and the Opéra. Some of his Paris works are adaptations (*Le siège de Corinthe* and *Moïse et Pharaon*); the *opéra comique Le Comte Ory* is part-new, *Guillaume Tell* wholly. This last, widely regarded as his *chef d'oeuvre*, and very long, is a rich tapestry of his most inspired music, with elaborate orchestration, many ensembles, spectacular ballets and processions in the French tradition, opulent orchestral writing and showing a new harmonic boldness.

And then, silence. At 37, he retired from opera composition. He left Paris in 1837 to live in Italy, but suffered prolonged and painful illness there (mainly in Bologna, where he advised at the Liceo Musicale, and in Florence). Isabella died in 1845 and the next year he married Olympe Pélissier, with whom he had lived for 15 years and who tended him through his ill-health. He composed hardly at all during this period (the *Stabat mater* belongs to his Paris years); but he went back to Paris in 1855, and his health and humour returned, with his urge to compose, and he wrote a quantity of pieces for piano and voices, with wit and refinement, that he called *Péchés de vieillesse* ('Sins of Old Age'), including the graceful and economical *Petite messe solennelle* (1863). He died, universally honoured, in 1868.

Operas L'inganno felice (1812); La scala di seta (1812); La pietra del paragone (1812); Tancredi (1813); L'italiana in Algeri (1813); Il turco in Italia (1814); Elisabetta, regina d'Inghilterra (1815); Il barbiere di Siviglia (1816); Otello (1816); La Cenerentola (1817); La gazza ladra (1817); Armida (1817); Mosè in Egitto (1818); Ermione (1819); La donna del lago (1819); Maometto II (1820); Zelmira (1822); Semiramide (1823); Il viaggio a Reims (1825); Le siège de Corinthe (1826); Moïse et Pharaon (1827); Le Comte Ory (1828); Guillaume Tell (1829); 16 others

Vocal music Stabat mater (1841); Petite messe solennelle (1863); over 20 other sacred works; *c*16 cantatas; hymns, choruses; songs, arias, duets, trios; studies, exercises, cadenzas

Instrumental music 6 sonatas, strs (*c*1804); 3 sinfonias; other orch pieces; chamber works; pieces for military band; over 60 pf pieces

Rössler [Rösler], **Franz Anton.** *See* ROSETTI, ANTONIO.

Rostal, Max (*b* Teschen, 7 Aug 1905). British violinist of Austrian birth. He studied with Flesch and Rosé and gave recitals from 1911. He was a professor at the Berlin Hochschule, 1930–33, and taught at the GSM, 1944–58; Yfrah Neaman and members of the Amadeus Quartet were among his pupils. As a soloist in Britain he won acclaim for his sweet, transparent tone underlaid by rhythmic drive and incisive attack; he was distinguished in Bartók's Second Concerto and gave many first performances. In 1958 he became a professor at the Berne Conservatory.

Rostropovich, Mstislav (Leopoldovich) (*b* Baku, 27 March 1927). Russian cellist, pianist and conductor. He studied at Moscow Conservatory and became cello professor there in 1956, the year of his London and New York débuts. He introduced Shostakovich's First Concerto to London in 1960 and began an association with Britten, who wrote the Cello Sonata, suites and the Cello Symphony for him. He is often heard as piano accompanist to his wife, Galina Vishnevskaya; they left the USSR in 1974 and lost their citizenship in 1978. In 1977 he became music director of the National SO, Washington, DC. As a cellist Rostropovich is noted for his commanding technique and intense, visionary playing; as a conductor his style is free and flexible.

Rosvaenge, Helge (*b* Copenhagen, 29 Aug 1897; *d* Munich, 19 June 1972). Danish tenor. He made his début in 1921 as Don José; he later sang at Cologne and was leading tenor at the Berlin Staatsoper, 1930–44, appearing also in Vienna, Munich and Salzburg. He sang Parsifal at Bayreuth in the 1930s but was chiefly admired in Italian roles, with his warm, sonorous tone and his brilliant top register.

Rota (Lat.: 'wheel'). Term for a ROUND in the 13th century and possibly the 14th. The only differences between rota and rondellus are the successive rather than simultaneous entries of the voices; the rota has therefore to end arbitrarily. The singing of rotas in medieval England was probably practised to a greater extent than the sources reveal; rounds are easily improvised and were probably not regarded as art music requiring notation unless they were particularly complex. The only known piece specifically labelled 'rota' in the MS is the famous *Sumer is icumen in*, and the term is not discussed in medieval treatises.

Rota, Nino (*b* Milan, 3 Dec 1911; *d* Rome, 10 April 1979). Italian composer. He studied at the Milan Conservatory, privately with Pizzetti (1925–6), with Casella in Rome, and at the Curtis Institute (1931–2). In 1939 he joined the staff at the Bari Conservatory (director from 1950). He wrote fluently in a cool, direct style: his output includes operas (notably *The Italian Straw Hat*, 1955), three symphonies, concertos and instrumental pieces, besides numerous film scores (many for Fellini, Visconti and Zeffirelli).

Rothenberger, Anneliese (*b* Mannheim, 19 June 1924). German soprano. She made her début at Koblenz (1943) and sang in the Hamburg Opera, 1946–56, singing light soprano roles; she sang Sophie (*Rosenkavalier*) at Glyndebourne (1959) and in the film of 1960, the year of her Met début

(Zdenka, *Arabella*). She was a regular singer at Munich and Vienna, her roles including Berg's Lulu, Mozart's Susanna and J. Strauss's Adele.

Roto-toms. Set (usually seven) of small, tunable drums, each with a compass of an octave. Maxwell Davies has used them frequently in his works.

Rotrouenge. Medieval term applied to certain troubadour and trouvère poems, apparently denoting the presence of a refrain and distinguishing features of rhyme scheme. It is rarely found; only four troubadour and six trouvère songs are so designated. By the late 12th and 13th centuries it had lost its identity, if it ever had one.

Rotta, Antonio (*b* ?Padua, *c*1495; *d* there, 1549). Italian lutenist. He was virtually unrivalled in Italy as a lutenist and was an excellent teacher. His surviving compositions (all for lute) include arrangements of vocal music, dances and ricercares, many in his *Intabolatura* (Venice, 1546).

Rotte. Name for various string instruments of many periods. In the 11th and 12th centuries it referred to the triangular psaltery. However, it also designated a six-string, plucked lyre ('Germanic lyre'), a descendant of the ancient Greek kithara, which was widely used in north-west Europe from pre-Christian times to the 13th century. Thereafter bowed versions became popular, and by the 15th century 'rotte' seems to have been synonymous with 'fiddle'. The name, a German one, is cognate with the Celtic 'crwth', English 'crowd' and French and English 'rote'.

Rotterdam Philharmonic Orchestra. Dutch orchestra founded in 1918; its home is De Doelen (opened 1966, cap. 2230).

Rouge, Guillaume (*b* *c*1385; *d* *c*1456). French composer. He was named in an early 16th-century poem as one of the 'grans musiciens' with Binchois and Dufay. He was trained at Rouen Cathedral and played the organ there in 1399. In 1415 he joined the Burgundian court chapel and in the 1420s served in the Sainte-Chapelle, Dijon. By 1431 he had returned to Burgundy where he served for 20 years, leaving in 1451 to enter Duke Charles of Orleans's chapel. His three-voice mass cycle is one of the earliest to incorporate a secular *chanson*.

Rouget de Lisle, Claude-Joseph (*b* Lons-le-Saumier, 10 May 1760; *d* Choisy-le-Roi, 26/27 June 1836). French poet and composer. Posted as a lieutenant to Strasbourg in 1791, he became popular as a poet, violinist and singer. His *Chant de guerre pour l'armée du Rhin* (1792), later known as the *Marseillaise*, became an official national song in 1795 and the French national anthem in 1879. It has been quoted by composers including Tchaikovsky (*1812 Overture*) and Schumann. Rouget de Lisle also wrote other Revolutionary works, songs and opera librettos.

Roulade. A decorative passage, usually in vocal music.

Roullet, Johannes (*fl* *c*1435–45). ?French composer. Most of his compositions are functional settings of liturgical texts with chant paraphrase in the upper voice and fauxbourdon-like accompaniment, but his four sequence settings are of great interest for the

variety of formal solutions he offers to accommodate the lengthy texts. His songs survive in sacred versions.

Round. (1) A perpetual canon at the unison (or octave) for three or more voices. The medieval Latin term was *rota* ('wheel'), used in the rubric of the 13th-century *Sumer is icumen in*, a round sung over a two-part vocal ostinato (strictly a RONDELLUS). A particular form of round, distinguished by its frivolous text, was the CATCH, popular in the 16th–18th centuries. On the Continent the round is known by the generic term 'canon'.

(2) A country dance, particularly one in which the dancers are grouped in a circle.

Round O. English corruption of the French 'rondeau'.

Rousseau, Jean (*b* Moulins, 1 Oct 1644; *d* ?*c*1700). French bass violist, composer, theorist and teacher. He is best known for his comprehensive *Traité de la viole* (1687).

Rousseau, Jean-Jacques (*b* Geneva, 28 June 1712; *d* Ermenonville, 2 July 1778). Swiss philosopher, author and composer. He lacked formal training as a composer and his first attempts at French opera, in the 1740s, were unsuccessful; but his *intermède Le devin du village* (1752, Fontainebleau), modelled on Italian intermezzos, was an instant success and affected the growth of French *opéra comique*. It has a folklike simplicity of tone and includes some italianate music but no spoken dialogue. Also influential was *Pygmalion* (1770, Lyons), a spoken monodrama with music (composed mostly by Horace Coignet); this led to the genre known as melodrama. He also wrote motets, songs and instrumental pieces.

Rousseau's views on music had a strong impact, though not all are borne out by his compositions; his belief that music should express feelings rather than ideas influenced Romantic thought. He claimed that this was possible only through language, and in his *Lettre sur la musique française* (1753; his main contribution to the Querelle des Bouffons) he attacked French opera, praising Italian music. Among his other writings is a *Dictionnaire de musique* (1768).

Roussel, Albert (Charles Paul Marie) (*b* Tourcoing, 5 April 1869; *d* Royan, 23 Aug 1937). French composer. After embarking on a naval career, in 1894 he began studies with Gigout, moving on to train with d'Indy and others at the Schola Cantorum (1898–1908) where in 1902 he began teaching. In 1909 he made a tour of India and Indo-China, and he drew on that experience in writing his Hindu opera-ballet *Padmâvatî* (1923), though other works, like the vocal-orchestral *Evocations* (1911) and ballet *Le festin de l'araignée* (1913), had already shown his ability to leaven d'Indyism with exotic material and Ravellian brilliance. In the Symphony no.2 (1921), he moved on to an almost polytonal density, but in the 1920s his music (like Ravel's) became more spare and astringent, though still with a rhythmic vigour and motivic intensity that can be seen as a highly personal extension of Schola thinking. His later, neo-classical works, marked by wide-ranging regular themes and motoric rhythms, include the Symphonies nos.3 and 4, the orchestral Suite in F, the Piano Concerto, the String Quartet and two ballets, *Bacchus et Ariane* and *Aenéas*.

Ballets Le festin de l'araignée (1913); Bacchus et Ariane (1931); Aenéas (1935)
Opera-ballet Padmâvatî (1923)
Orchestral music Résurrection (1903); 4 syms. (1906, 1921, 1930, 1934); Evocations (1911); Pour un fête de printemps (1920); Suite, F (1926); Conc., small orch (1927); Pf Conc. (1927); Little Suite (1929); Sinfonietta (1934); Rapsodie flamande (1936); Concertino, vc, orch (1936)
Chamber music Pf Trio (1902); Divertissement, wind qnt, pf (1906); 2 vn sonatas (1908, 1924); Sérénade, ens (1925); Trio, fl, va, vc (1929); Str Qt (1932); Str Trio (1937)
Piano music Rustiques (1906); Suite, f♯ (1910); Sonatine (1912); 3 pièces (1933); Prélude et fugue (1934)
Songs c20

Rovescio, Al. *See* AL ROVESCIO.

Rovetta, Giovanni (*b* Venice, *c*1595; *d* there, 23 Oct 1668). Italian composer. He spent his life at St Mark's, Venice: after serving as a bass singer (1623–7), he became assistant *maestro di cappella* to Monteverdi, succeeding him as full *maestro* in 1644. A leading composer in the concertato style, he concentrated on sacred music, of which he published nine collections (1626–62). His motets are mostly for two to four voices and organ, while some of his masses and psalms are scored for larger forces. Like Monteverdi's music they reflect an interest in musical form. He also composed two operas (now lost) and four books of madrigals.

Rovigo, Francesco (*b* 1541–2; *d* Mantua, 7 Oct 1597). Italian composer. A pupil of Merulo in Venice (1570), he held court appointments in Mantua (from 1577) and Graz (from 1582) and became organist at S Barbara, Mantua (1590). He published madrigals (1581), a mass (1592) and instrumental ensemble music (*c*1583).

Rovsing Olsen, Poul. *See* OLSEN, POUL ROVSING.

Roxburgh, Edwin (*b* Liverpool, 6 Nov 1937). English composer. He studied at the RCM (with Howells) and at Cambridge, and later under Dallapiccola and Boulanger. He was a professional oboist but in 1967 became director of the 20th-century department at the RCM. His earliest work is serial; since 1961 he has used a less formal, more experimental style. His compositions include Variations (1963) and *Montage* (1977) for orchestra as well as much vocal music and chamber works including series called *Dithyramb* (I for clarinet and percussion, II for three percussion and piano, 1972) and *Nebula* (I for clarinet, II for wind quintet, 1974).

Roxelane, La. Nickname of Haydn's Symphony no.63 in C (?1779), so called because material from the incidental music for the play *Soliman II*, in which the heroine was Roxolane, occurs in the second movement.

Royal Academy of Music [RAM]. Conservatory founded in London in 1822. William Crotch was its first principal. The first professional music school in England, it provides full-time courses for composers, performers and teachers, and degree courses.

The same name was used by the organization that put on opera in London, 1720–28, with Handel as musical director.

Royal Albert Hall. Large rotunda in London. It was built as a memorial to Queen Victoria's consort, Prince Albert, and opened in 1871; it seats *c*6500. It is used for music, exhibitions, sport and meetings and has been the home of the Henry Wood Promenade Concerts since the Queen's Hall was destroyed in 1941.

Royal Choral Society. British choral society, the oldest surviving in London. It was founded in 1871 as the Royal Albert Hall Choral Society (renamed 1888). Gounod conducted the first concert (1872), in which *c*1000 took part; membership is now *c*250. Activities include annual seasons, tours abroad and recordings (from 1926); its carol concerts (from 1912) served as a model. Under Malcolm Sargent (1928–67) repertory was broadened and from 1973 works were commissioned.

Royal College of Music [RCM]. Conservatory founded in London in 1883. George Grove was its first director. It provides full-time courses for composers, performers and teachers, and degree courses.

Royal College of Organists. Institution in London, founded in 1864; mainly an examining body, it also arranges lectures and recitals.

Royal Festival Hall. *See* SOUTH BANK CENTRE.

Royal Hunt of the Sun, The. Opera in two acts by Iain Hamilton to his own libretto after Peter Shaffer (1977, London).

Royal Italian Opera. Name given in the 19th century to London theatres and their companies which presented seasons of opera in Italian; they included Covent Garden, Drury Lane, Her Majesty's and Lyceum.

Royal Liverpool Philharmonic Orchestra. British orchestra. Formerly the Liverpool PO, founded in 1840 as the mainly amateur orchestra of the Liverpool Philharmonic Society, it was renamed in 1957; its home is Philharmonic Hall (opened 1939), redesigned after the original hall (1849) burnt down (1933). Under Malcolm Sargent (1942–8) it became one of the best-known orchestras in Britain. Later conductors have included John Pritchard (1957), Charles Groves (1963), Walter Weller (1977), David Atherton (1980), Marek Janowski (1983) and Libor Pešek (1987).

Royal Military School of Music [Kneller Hall]. Conservatory founded in 1857 in Twickenham as the Military School of Music (renamed 1865). Students are trained as performers or bandmasters for British Army bands and may also prepare for diplomas or external degrees.

Royal Musical Association. Society founded in 1874 in London as the Musical Association (renamed 1944). Activities include regular meetings to hear research papers and an annual conference. Publications include a biennial *Journal* (which replaced the annual *Proceedings* in 1987) and the association inaugurated the series *Musica Britannica*.

Royal Northern College of Music [RNCM]. Conservatory formed from the Royal Manchester College of Music (opened 1893) and the Northern

School of Music (1942, formerly Matthay School of Music, 1920). It opened in a new building in 1972 as the Northern College of Music and was renamed in 1973.

Royal Opera. Formerly COVENT GARDEN Opera, established in London in 1945 as the British national company, it was renamed in 1968. Works are performed, usually in their original language, with international soloists. Music directors have included Karl Rankl (1945–51), Kubelik, Solti, Colin Davis and Haitink (from 1987).

Royal Philharmonic Orchestra [RPO]. British orchestra formed in London in 1946 by Thomas Beecham and conducted by him until 1960. It gave Royal Philharmonic Society subscription concerts and became resident orchestra at Glyndebourne and the Edinburgh Festival. Its activities include tours abroad and concerts with pop groups.

Royal Philharmonic Society. Organization formed in London in 1813 (as the Philharmonic Society, 'Royal' since 1912) to give seasons of orchestral concerts, mainly of music new to London; Beethoven was commissioned in 1815 and 1822 (Ninth Symphony). Its first permanent orchestra, the London Philharmonic (1932–46), was succeeded by the Royal Philharmonic (founded 1946); both became independent. Outside orchestras have played in RPS concerts since 1945. The Society's Gold Medal is awarded to an eminent musician; there are annual competitions for young composers.

Royal School of Church Music. British institution founded in 1927 as the School of English Church Music (renamed 1945), with headquarters at Addington Palace, Croydon, since 1954.

Royal Scottish Academy of Music and Drama. The chief conservatory in Scotland, it was founded in Glasgow in 1890 as the Athenaeum School of Music. The Drama School was opened in 1950 and the opera department in 1968.

Royan Festival [Festival d'Art Contemporain] (France). Annual (spring) festival, held from 1964 to 1973, one of the leading contemporary music festivals; the many premières given there included works by Barraqué and Xenakis. Its activities were taken over by the Rencontres Internationales d'Art Contemporain at La Rochelle.

Royer, Joseph-Nicolas-Pancrace (*b* Turin, *c*1705; *d* Paris, 11 Jan 1755). French composer. He settled in Paris in 1725 as a teacher of singing and the harpsichord and took administrative posts at the Opéra (1730–33) and the Concert Spirituel (from 1748) where he widened the repertory; from 1749 he was also composer and director of the Opéra orchestra. He was also teacher of the royal children. His output includes stage works, other vocal music and many harpsichord pieces; his style is fiery, with brilliant vocal writing and an assured command of harmony.

Roy Henry (*fl c*1410). English composer. He wrote a Gloria and a Sonatus in the Old Hall MS. Identity with an English monarch has not been ascertained, though Henry IV (ruled 1399–1413) and Henry V (1413–22) have been suggested; the former could be consistent with the style of the pieces, though Henry V is definitely credited with a composition (com-

pletely different in style) elsewhere. Possibly he was not a king.

Rozhdestvensky, Gennady (Nikolayevich) (*b* Moscow, 4 May 1931). Soviet conductor. He made his début at the Bol'shoy in 1941, while still a student at the Moscow Conservatory. He conducted further at the Bol'shoy, 1951–70 (principal conductor from 1964), and with Soviet Radio from 1961. He made his London début in 1956, and became chief conductor of the Stockholm PO in 1974 and the BBC SO in 1978. In 1981 he left for the Vienna SO. He is noted as a brilliant executant of late Romantic and contemporary music.

Rozkošný, Josef Richard (*b* Prague, 21 Sept 1833; *d* there, 3 June 1913). Czech composer. He became a leading figure in the cultural and social life of Prague. He is remembered for his successful opera *The Rapids of St John* (1871), with its fairytale motifs, nature scenes and descriptive tone-painting, indebted to Smetana; his one-act *Stoja* (1894) was the first Czech *verismo* opera.

Rózsa, Miklós (*b* Budapest, 18 April 1907). American composer. He studied in Leipzig and moved to Paris (1931) and later London (1935), where he began to write film music. In 1940 he went to the USA and continued his career as a film composer, later also teaching at the University of Southern California, conducting and lecturing. His music, which includes four concertos and other orchestral and chamber music, achieves a synthesis of Hungarian folksong and symphonic form, though does not directly quote folk material; his film scores in particular have benefitted from the use of folk idioms, e.g. *The Thief of Bagdad* (1940), *Quo Vadis?* (1951) and *Ben-Hur* (1959).

Rózsavölgyi [Rosenthal], **Márk** (*b* Balassagyarmat, 1789; *d* Pest, 23 Jan 1848). Hungarian composer and violinist. A theatre musician and the leader of his own gypsy band, he was celebrated as the last important master of the *verbunkos* and the first of the more modern *csárdás*. Over 40 volumes of his music, chiefly Hungarian dances, appeared in Pest during his lifetime; Liszt used some of his tunes in the Hungarian Rhapsodies nos.8, 12 and 13.

Rubato (It.). 'Stolen': of tempo, extended beyond the time mathematically available; thus slowed down, stretched or broadened.

Rubbra, (Charles) Edmund (*b* Northampton, 23 May 1901; *d* Gerrards Cross, 13 Feb 1986). English composer. A pupil of Scott and of Holst and Morris at the RCM (1921–5), he worked as a pianist, teacher and critic before his appointment as lecturer at Oxford (1947–68). His music took some while to develop independence from Ireland, Bax and Holst, but his First Symphony (1937) begins to show a characteristic style of rhapsodic growth tautened by thematic working and almost incessant polyphonic activity. His later works include ten more symphonies, of which no.9 is an oratorio-like work (*Sinfonia sacra*, 1972), besides concertos for viola, piano and violin, four string quartets (1933–77), masses and motets (he became a Roman Catholic in 1948).

Rubini, Giovanni Battista (*b* Romano, 7 April 1794; *d* there, 3 March 1854). Italian tenor. He was first renowned as a Rossini tenor but made his mark in the newer Romantic style, creating the tenor leads in, among other works, Bellini's *Il pirata* (1827), *La sonnambula* (1831) and *I puritani* (1835) and Donizetti's *Anna Bolena* (1830). From 1831 he performed chiefly with London or Paris casts that included Grisi (from 1836 Pasta), Tamburini and Lablache, also singing at concerts and festivals until his retirement in 1845. Though not noted for his looks or acting, he was celebrated for his supreme vocal artistry, including his phenomenally high range, natural phrasing and forceful expression.

Rubinstein, Anton (Grigor'yevich) (*b* Vikhvatinets, 28 Nov 1829; *d* Peterhof, 20 Nov 1894). Russian pianist, composer and teacher, brother of Nikolay Rubinstein. After a cosmopolitan childhood as a virtuoso, he enjoyed enormous international success, becoming one of the greatest 19th-century pianists, his playing being compared with Liszt's. From 1859, when he founded the Russian Musical Society with his patron the Grand Duchess Elena Pavlovna, he was an influential if controversial figure in Russian musical life; in 1862 he founded and directed (1862–7, from 1887) the St Petersburg Conservatory to combat what he perceived to be the amateurishness of the new nationalist movement in music. But his dogmatism relaxed by the 1870s and his work in education made its mark on musical standards throughout the country. Exceptionally prolific as a composer, he worked in haste, unable to rise above the commonplace; only the Melody in F op.3 no.1 for piano and the opera *Demon* (1871) achieved success. Tchaikovsky was among his pupils.

Rubinstein, Artur [Arthur] (*b* Łódź, 28 Jan 1887; *d* Geneva, 20 Dec 1982). Polish pianist, later American. He studied in Berlin, notably with Heinrich Barth, and played in public there from 1900. By the time of his first American tour, in 1906, his playing was noted for its flair and vivacity. During World War I he was largely in London. In the 1930s he withdrew for further study and by the time he settled in the USA, during World War II, his standing as one of the century's great players was recognized. He was often heard in concertos by Brahms and Beethoven and in chamber music. In his later years he was noted for his Chopin interpretations, marked by impeccable style, warm lyricism and passionate eloquence.

Rubinstein, Nikolay (Grigor'yevich) (*b* Moscow, 14 June 1835; *d* Paris, 23 March 1881). Russian pianist and teacher, brother of Anton Rubinstein. A child virtuoso who became a charming *bon vivant*, he was a vigorous organizer and uninhibited teacher, founding the Moscow branch of the Russian Musical Society (1859) and what became the Moscow Conservatory (1864). His playing was more detached and analytical than his brother's but he was more generous in support of Tchaikovsky and Balakirev and the new Russian school. Among his best-known pupils were Taneyev and Emil Sauer.

Rubio, David (Joseph) (*b* London, 17 Dec 1934). English maker of violins, lutes, guitars and harpsichords. In his workshops at New York (1964), Duns Tew, near Oxford (1968), and Cambridge (1979) he has produced instruments along historical lines, admired for their finish and exceptional tonal qualities.

Ruckers. Flemish family of harpsichord and virginal makers, probably of German origin. Hans (*c*1545–1598) established himself at Antwerp in 1584, building virginals and single-manual harpsichords. He was succeeded by his sons Joannes (1578–1642) and Andreas (i) (1579–after 1645) in partnership. In 1608 Joannes became sole owner of the business, which at his death was continued by his nephew Joannes Couchet. Meanwhile Andreas (i) and his son Andreas (ii) (1607–*c*1655) maintained a separate workshop, the father making *c*35–40 instruments a year; surviving ones made or signed by one of them are dated between 1608 and the early 1650s.

Ruckers virginals, rectangular and with only one set of strings, were made in six sizes up to six Flemish feet long; the larger ones were subdivided into spinetten (keyboard to the left, bright in sound) and muselars (keyboard to the right, rounder sound). The most elaborate stored on one side a small instrument at octave pitch (the 'child'), which could be slid on top of the main instrument at unison pitch (the 'mother'). The harpsichords had two sets of strings, an octave apart; the two-manual ones, with keyboards non-aligned and uncoupled, served as two instruments in one, playable at either of two pitches a 4th apart. Extended-compass instruments were made for export to England and France. All were elaborately decorated and marked with the maker's soundboard rose. Ruckers instruments had a rich, resonant sound, balanced throughout the register. They were more highly valued than those of any other maker and were often altered, redecorated, restored or counterfeited throughout Europe in the 17th and 18th centuries.

Rückpositiv (Ger.). The little organ placed at the organist's back, in front of the gallery (an English counterpart is 'Chair organ'); it is the second main manual of all major organs until about 1700, when it was replaced by the *Brustwerk*, Choir organ or Swell.

Rudall, Carte. English firm of wind instrument makers and flute specialists. Makers and dealers since 1747, it has made esteemed models of its own design, built flutes to commission and held the British manufacturing rights in Boehm's flutes. The firm became Rudall, Carte & Co. in 1871 and was absorbed by Boosey & Hawkes in 1955.

Ruddigore. Operetta by Sullivan to a libretto by Gilbert (1887, London).

Rudel, Jaufre (*fl* mid-12th century). Troubadour poet and composer, possibly from Bordeaux. He is known for his poems addressed to his 'distant love'. He took part in the second crusade in 1147. His distant love may have been the Countess of Tripoli, although neither she nor anyone else is named in any of his poems, and the mystery has given rise to wide-ranging speculation.

Rudel, Julius (*b* Vienna, 6 March 1921). American conductor. He emigrated to the USA in 1938 and studied in New York. His début was at New York

City Opera in 1944; he was the company's director, 1957–79, giving skilful performances and developing a strong ensemble company in a wide repertory. He has appeared as guest conductor with most major American orchestras and was music director of the Buffalo PO, 1979–85.

Rudhyar, Dane [Chennevière, Daniel] (*b* Paris, 23 March 1895; *d* San Francisco, 13 Sept 1985). American composer of French origin. He studied at the Paris Conservatoire (1912–13), then moved to the USA in 1916 and settled in southern California in 1919; in 1926 he took American nationality under a Hindu name and he became a pioneer in advocating Asian musical concepts. During the 1920s he wrote piano and orchestral pieces in a post-Skryabin style, but by the mid-1970s was best known as an astrologer. After 1970 he composed prolifically in a poignant, stop-and-go style.

Rudolf, Max (*b* Frankfurt, 15 June 1902). American conductor. After posts at Freiburg, Darmstadt and Prague, he worked in Göteborg during World War II. He moved to New York in 1945, conducting at the Met until 1958 when he became musical director of the Cincinnati SO. He then worked at the Curtis Institute, 1970–73, and later returned to the Met, continuing to give meticulous performances of Mozart.

Rudolf von Fenis-Neuenberg (*b* c1150; *d* by 30 Aug 1196). German Minnesinger. From the aristocratic Neuenberg family, with ties to the royal house of Burgundy, he belonged to an important group of Minnesinger who provided a link with trouvère song, absorbing and adapting form and subject matter from Romance verse and laying the foundation for the period of high Minnesang in Germany. His kinship with French culture is seen in the intellectual tone of his songs, particularly his thinking in antitheses. Seven or eight poems survive; melodies are provided by the Old French and Provençal models on which he based his songs.

Rudolph (Johann Joseph Rainer), Archduke of Austria (*b* Florence, 8 Jan 1788; *d* Baden, 24 July 1831). Austrian patron of music and amateur composer. He was Beethoven's pupil for 20 years, as well as his friend and greatest patron; among the works dedicated to him are the 'Archduke' Trio op.97 and the Mass in D op.123.

Rudorff, Ernst (Friedrich Karl) (*b* Berlin, 18 Jan 1840; *d* there, 31 Dec 1916). German composer. At the Leipzig Conservatory he studied with Moscheles, Reinecke and Richter, then taught and conducted at Cologne (1865–9) and Berlin (1869–1910). He composed in a style reminiscent of Mendelssohn, Schumann and Weber; among his best works are the orchestral Variations op.24 and the three symphonies opp.31, 40 and 50.

Rudziński, Witold (*b* Siebież, 14 March 1913). Polish composer. He studied at the Vilnius Conservatory (1928–36) and with Boulanger and Koechlin in Paris (1938–9), and taught at the conservatories of Vilnius (1939–42), Łódź (1945–7) and Warsaw (from 1957). He has written in many genres in an expansive, Romantic style.

Ruff. A type of stroke in side-drum playing, involving a rapid triplet of prefatory strokes before the main one.

Ruffino d'Assisi (*b* Assisi, ?c1490; *d* c1532). Italian composer. He was *maestro di cappella* at Padua Cathedral (1510–20), at the Basilico del Santo until 1525, then at Vicenza Cathedral. His extant works include a mass, two motets, two complete psalm-settings and three secular pieces. His sacred works reveal an adventurous if sometimes clumsy composer.

Ruffo, Titta (*b* Pisa, 9 June 1877; *d* Florence, 5 July 1953). Italian baritone. He made his début at Rome in 1898 and sang in South America from 1900, notably at the Colón, Buenos Aires (1908–31). He made his USA début at Philadelphia in 1912; in Chicago and at the Met (1922–9) he was popular for his forthright, darkly coloured portrayals of Rigoletto, Di Luna and Renato.

Ruffo, Vincenzo (*b* Verona, c1508; *d* Sacile, 9 Feb 1587). Italian composer. He was trained at Verona Cathedral, where he became *maestro di cappella* (1544). From 1563 to 1572 he was *maestro di cappella* at Milan Cathedral. There he was influenced by Cardinal Borromeo, who commissioned him to write a mass in which the text was as intelligible as possible (Borromeo's efforts on behalf of the Counter-Reformation included a famous trial of sacred compositions by several composers). After 1572 he held less important posts, at Pistoia Cathedral and in Verona. A prolific composer of sacred and secular vocal music, he was also one of the most adaptable of the period 1540–80. By 1563, when he abandoned secular music, he had written at least 260 madrigals; in the new *note nere* notation, they are rhythmically lively and flexible. They occupy an important place in the genre's development between the generation of Festa and Willaert and that of A. Gabrieli. His sacred music shows a long and complex development, from the traditional imitative style of his motets of 1542 to the experimental style of his post-1563 works, heavily influenced by Counter-Reformation ideals. Much of his music was published during his lifetime.

Ruge, Filippo (*b* Rome, c1725; *d* ?Paris, after 1767). Italian composer and flautist. He was active in Paris in the 1750s and 1760s. His works are mostly instrumental, including flute concertos, symphonies, solo flute sonatas and trio sonatas. Both these and other Italian works he played helped to popularize the Italian style in France.

Rugeri, Francesco ['Il Per'] (*b* 1620; *d* c1695). Italian violin maker. Although he worked in Cremona in the shadow of his teacher, Nicolo Amati, he is also regarded as a great maker, his best instruments almost equal in value to the Amatis'. He copied their style with care, normally signing his instruments after c1670 with his name, 'detto Il Per'. His son Vincenzo (active c1675–c1730) was also an excellent craftsman. The Rugeris made many cellos; Francesco experimented with their form and seems to have been the first Cremonese to produce the smaller, more manageable instrument.

Ruggiero. A musical scheme for songs, dances and instrumental variations, popular particularly in Italy in the early 17th century. It involves a bass melody in four phrases, in the major mode and usually in duple metre. Composers of variation sets on this bass include Frescobaldi, who wrote five. The scheme also appeared, sometimes as 'aria di Ruggiero', in vocal music, and it was occasionally used for dances. The name may have originated in a stanza from Ariosto's *Orlando furioso* beginning 'Ruggier, qual sempre fui'.

Ruggles, Carl [Charles] **(Sprague)** (*b* East Marion, MA, 11 March 1876; *d* Bennington, VT, 24 Oct 1971). American composer. He had lessons with Paine and others and took musical jobs in Boston and Minnesota, writing, teaching and conducting, before moving to New York in 1917. There he was in contact with Varèse, Cowell and especially Ives, a close friend, and developed a style of dissonant counterpoint held in suspense or else moving with vigour. His music, intensely chromatic, is notable for its sense of declamatory striving, heard at its finest in *Sun-Treader* (1931) – performed in Paris and Berlin in 1932 but not in the USA until 1966. From the 1920s he spent most summers in Vermont, where he settled; he taught in Miami, 1938–43. He composed little after the late 1940s but continued to paint.

Principal works Angels, 6 tpt (1921), rev. 4 tpt, 3 trbn (1938); Vox clamans in deserto, S, small orch (1923); Men and Mountains, small orch (1924), rev. orch (1936); Portals, 13 str (1925); Sun-Treader, orch (1931); Evocations, 4 chants, pf (1943); Organum, orch (1947)

Ruins of Athens, The [Ruinen von Anthen, Die]. Overture and incidental music, op.113, by Beethoven (1811), for A. von Kotzebue's epilogue given at the first night of the German theatre in Budapest (1812).

Rumba [rhumba]. Popular dance of Afro-Cuban origin, in duple time with syncopated rhythms. It was known in the USA by 1914 but became popular there and in Europe only in the 1930s (when it absorbed jazz elements). It is characterized by repetitive melody and ostinato rhythmic figures on the maracas, claves and other percussion. It served as a model for other Latin American types of ballroom dance.

Ruppe, Christian Friedrich (*b* Salzungen, Saxe-Meiningen, 22 Aug 1753; *d* Leiden, 25 May 1826). Netherlands composer and theorist. By the 1780s he had moved to Leiden, where he became an organist, university music director and professor, and founded a choral society. His large output includes cantatas, songs, chamber music, piano pieces and a theoretical treatise (1809–10). His brother Friedrich Christian (1771–1834) was a violinist, keyboard player and composer at the court in Meiningen; his works include oratorios and a keyboard concerto with choir.

Rusalka. Opera in three acts by Dvořák to a libretto by J. Kvapil (1901, Prague).

Opera in four acts by Dargomïzhsky to his own libretto after Pushkin (1856, St Petersburg).

Rush, George (*fl* London, *c*1760–80). English composer. After studying in Italy he presented in London two successful English operas (1764) and an afterpiece (1768). His instrumental output, in a progressive, pre-Classical style, includes four harpsichord concertos (*c*1770–*c*1777), overtures, guitar pieces and chamber works. He was a harpsichordist and guitarist.

Ruslan and Lyudmila. Opera in five acts by Glinka to a libretto by V.F. Shirkov and V.A. Bakhturin after Pushkin (1842, St Petersburg).

Russell, William (*b* London, 6 Oct 1777; *d* there, 21 Nov 1813). English composer. Much admired as a keyboard player, he worked in London as an organist and (in 1800–04) as pianist and composer at Sadler's Wells Theatre. He wrote *c*20 stage works, mainly pantomimes, as well as oratorios, anthems and odes.

Russian and Slavonic church music. The plainchant of the Eastern Orthodox Slavs: those who accepted the Christian religion and ritual from the Greeks but translated the services into Old Slavonic. Their chant is entirely vocal, monodic and unaccompanied. The earliest surviving music MSS, from the 11th and 12th centuries, transmit Byzantine chant, notation and mode systems, but there are some original hymns. New religious centres appeared; by 1500 notation had developed and chant was influenced by Russian melodies (primarily folksongs). The melismatic 'demestvenniy chant', for trained singers, appeared in the 16th century, and some aspects of the service were staged like liturgical drama.

Western polyphonic styles and notation entered Russian church music from Poland, probably in the 16th century. Early scores were settings of *demestvenniy* chant, but by the late 17th century, works had much in common with German choral music. Syllabic chant settings for three voices in block chords ('kant') appeared at this time; those with secular texts became popular. In the 18th century Italian composers brought their style into the Russian church. Following Glinka's suggestions in the 1830s, church music was harmonized modally rather than in the major and minor keys. A new awareness of a Russian idiom emerged in the 1860s.

The Serbian church gained independence from the Greek in 1219. In the late 15th century, composers were following Byzantine models; with the Ottoman invasion delaying cultural growth, late 18th-century documents still show Byzantine features and not until the mid-19th century do polyphonic settings of Serbian church music appear.

Russian bassoon. A variety of upright serpent of the early 19th century, shaped like a bassoon but played with a cup mouthpiece. It was often capped with a brass flared bell or a painted dragon's head.

Russian Easter Festival Overture. Overture by Rimsky-Korsakov (1888), based on Russian Orthodox melodies.

Russian Musical Society. Organization instituted in 1859 in St Petersburg by Anton Rubinstein. It soon had many branches; Anton's brother Nikolay was director in Moscow (1860). It arranged concert series, at which new Russian works were given, and founded conservatories; Tchaikovsky was among the first graduates at St Petersburg and was an influential teacher at Moscow. The society was disbanded in 1917.

Russian Quartets. Haydn's six string quartets op.33

(1781), dedicated to Grand Duke Paul of Russia.

Russo, William (*b* Chicago, 25 June 1928). American composer. A pupil of Becker (1953–5) and Jirák (1955–7), he has worked since his teens as a jazz musician in the USA and Europe, using jazz and rock elements (particularly improvisation) in his large output of dramatic and orchestral works. He composed much of Kenton's experimental material in the 1950s and several rock cantatas in the 1960s.

Russolo, Luigi (*b* Portogruaro, 30 April 1885; *d* Cerro di Laveno, 6 Feb 1947). Italian composer. Not fully trained in music, he began his association with futurism as a painter, but in 1913–14 gave concerts with 'intonarumori', noise machines of his own invention. In the 1920s he made more machines, but all were destroyed during World War II; they are regarded as forerunners of machines used in *musique concrète*.

Rust, Friedrich Wilhelm (*b* Wörlitz, 6 July 1739; *d* Dessau, 28 Feb 1796). German composer and violinist. He served at the Dessau court from 1762; after studying with C.P.E. Bach and F. Benda, he returned there, becoming court music director in 1775 and establishing Dessau as a vital musical centre. His large output includes chamber and keyboard music, dramatic works and sacred and secular vocal pieces.

His son Wilhelm Karl (1787–1855) became a pianist, organist and teacher.

Rust, Giacomo (*b* Rome, 1741; *d* Barcelona, 1786). Italian composer. He studied in Naples and Rome and made his reputation as an opera composer in Venice. After a few months (1777–8) as court Kapellmeister in Salzburg, he resumed his Italian operatic career; in 1783 he became *maestro di cappella* at Barcelona Cathedral. He composed over 20 operas.

Rust, Wilhelm (*b* Dessau, 15 Aug 1822; *d* Leipzig, 2 May 1892). German organist and scholar, grandson of F.W. Rust. He studied under his uncle W.K. Rust and settled in Berlin, where he was organist of St Luke's (1881), teacher, and director of the Bach Society (1862–75). In 1878 he went to Leipzig as organist, and 1880 Kantor, of St Thomas's. From 1858 he was chief editor of the works of J.S. Bach; he edited 26 volumes of the Bach-Gesellschaft edition (1855–81). He composed some songs and keyboard music.

Rustica, Alla. Title of Vivaldi's Violin Concerto in G RV151, because of its bucolic rhythms.

Rustic Wedding. Symphonic poem, op.26, by Karl Goldmark (1877): originally *Ländliche Hochzeit* (literally 'Country Wedding').

Rustle of Spring. Piano piece by Sinding (op.32 no.3, 1896); it exists in many arrangements.

Rutini, Giovanni Marco (*b* Florence, 25 April 1723; *d* there, 22 Dec 1797). Italian composer. After training in Naples he went to Prague, where he composed his first harpsichord sonatas (1748) and opera (1753). Later he taught the harpsichord to the future Catherine II in St Petersburg. Returning to Florence (1761), he won wide success as a comic opera and sonata composer; he became *maestro di cappella* to the Duke of Modena, but remained in Florence.

Rutini's *c*80 harpsichord sonatas were important in the development of the Classical style and influenced Haydn and Mozart. They have incisive themes, and (especially to *c*1760) improvisatory passages and expressive chromaticism. The later sonatas are more pianistic; some have violin accompaniment. Besides 17 operas, he wrote oratorios, cantatas and sacred music.

His son Ferdinando (*c*1764–1827) composed comic operas, sonatas etc and held *maestro di cappella* positions in Ancona and elsewhere.

Ruy Blas. Overture, op.95, by Mendelssohn (1839) written for a performance of Hugo's play.

Ruyneman, Daniel (*b* Amsterdam, 8 Aug 1886; *d* there, 25 July 1963). Dutch composer. A pupil of Zweers at the Amsterdam Conservatory, he worked on behalf of new music as an administrator and concert promoter. His works use neo-classical and later developments.

Rv. Abbreviation used for works by Vivaldi according to the thematic catalogue of his works (Ryom *Verzeichnis*) by Peter Ryom (1974).

Rychlík, Jan (*b* Prague, 27 April 1916; *d* there, 20 Jan 1964). Czech composer. He was a pupil of Řídký at the Prague Conservatory (1939–46). His music took account of postwar developments; he also wrote film scores and jazz pieces and was one of the earliest jazz scholars.

Rysanek, Leonie (*b* Vienna, 12 Nov 1926). Austrian soprano. After study at the Vienna Conservatory her early career was at Innsbruck and Saarbrucken. Wider notice came with her Sieglinde at the 1951 Bayreuth Festival, and she joined the Bavarian Staatsoper, Munich, singing Strauss, Verdi and Puccini. Her rich voice and fiery temperament served well in Salome and other major Strauss roles, as Lady Macbeth (at her Met début, 1959) and in the dramatic Puccini roles.

Rzewski, Frederic (Anthony) (*b* Westfield, MA, 13 April 1938). American composer, pianist and conductor. He was a pupil of Thompson and Spies at Harvard (1954–8) and of Wagner and Strunk at Princeton (1958–60). In 1962–4 he was associated with Stockhausen and in 1966–71 he was a member of Musica Elettronica Viva, based in Rome. During this period his music gained a socialist message (e.g. *Coming Together*, 1972) and he has explored folk and popular melodies; his works are characterized by drive and intensity.

S

Sabadini, Bernardo (*b* ?Venice; *d* Parma, 26 Nov 1718). Italian composer. He held posts as organist and *maestro di cappella* at the Parma court and the ducal church in the 1680s and 90s. As court composer he wrote or part-wrote more than 30 operas and other dramatic works for performance in Parma, Piacenza and elsewhere; many were sumptuously staged with designs by the Bibienas.

Sabbatini, Luigi Antonio (*b* Albano Laziale, ?1732; *d* Padua, 29 Jan 1809). Italian theorist and composer. A pupil of Padre Martini in Bologna, he was *maestro di cappella* at Marino and from 1786 at S Antonio, Padua. Like Vallotti and Tartini, he was a leading theorist of the Paduan school and wrote several treatises on counterpoint. He composed much sacred music.

Şabrá, Wadí' (*b* Beirut, 23 Feb 1876; *d* there, 11 April 1952). Lebanese composer. He studied at the Paris Conservatoire (from 1893), then divided his time between France and the Lebanon; much of his theoretical work was concerned with scales. In his compositions he united Western and Arab traditions; they include the operas *The Shepherds of Canaan* (the first in Turkish) and *The Two Kings* (the first in Arabic), choral music and the Lebanese national anthem.

Sabino, Ippolito (*b* Lanciano, *c*1550; *d* there, 25 Aug 1593). Italian composer. He probably worked at Lanciano. He is remembered for his madrigals, seven books for six and two for five voices, notable for their traditional polyphonic writing.

Saccadé (Fr.). 'Jerked': a kind of sharply accented bowing.

Sacchetti, Franco (*b* Ragusa, 1332–4; *d* San Miniato, 1400). Italian poet. His love lyrics, after Dante and Boccaccio, were set by many composers of the day, including Landini and Niccolò da Perugia. He himself set some of his 14 madrigals, 18 ballatas and two caccias.

Sacchini, Antonio (Maria Gasparo Gioacchino) (*b* Florence, 14 June 1730; *d* Paris, 6 Oct 1786). Italian composer. He was a favourite pupil of Durante's at the S Maria di Loreto conservatory in Naples, where he presented his first two stage works (1756–7) and became *secondo maestro* (1761). From the 1760s he composed operas, comic and serious, for Naples, Rome and elsewhere; in 1768 he became director of the Ospedaletto conservatory in Venice, writing oratorios and sacred pieces. He presented three operas in Germany in 1770; in 1772–81 he worked in London, where he won great popularity. Finally he settled in Paris; he was welcomed by Piccinni's supporters, but Gluck's faction intrigued against him. Of his three French operas, *Oedipe* (1786, Versailles) was hailed as his masterpiece.

More than half Sacchini's 45 operas are *opere serie*. Among the most admired of the period, they are notable for their expressive melodies and wide range of harmony. His French operas, especially *Oedipe*, successfully combine these features with impressive choral scenes (influenced by Gluck) and point towards Spontini's grand opera.

Sacconi, (Simone) Fernando (*b* Rome, 30 May 1895; *d* Point Lookout, Long Island, 26 June 1973). Italian maker and restorer of violins. At 16 he was an experienced maker and an able copyist; he became familiar with the moulds, patterns and tools of Stradivari, copying the 'Piatti' cello of 1720 and the 'Paganini' Stradivari viola, among others. In New York from 1931, he continued to be the most renowned restorer.

Sacher, Paul (*b* Basle, 28 April 1906). Swiss conductor. In 1926 he founded the Basle CO; with it and the Collegium Musicum of Zurich (from 1941) he gave the first performances of works by Bartók, Hindemith, Honegger, Strauss and Stravinsky and many works were commissioned by him. In 1933 he founded the Schola cantorum basiliensis for research into early music and its performance.

Sachs, Curt (*b* Berlin, 29 June 1881; *d* New York, 5 Feb 1959). American musicologist. He studied music history and art history in Berlin and only from 1909 devoted himself to music. In 1919 he became director of the Staatliche Instrumentensammlung, a distinguished collection of musical instruments, and taught at the university and elsewhere. Deprived of all his academic positions in 1933, he went to Paris and in 1937 to the USA, where he taught at New York and Columbia universities. Sachs was a giant among musicologists, as much for his astounding mastery of several subjects as for his ability to present a comprehensive view of a vast panorama. He was a founder of modern organology and he wrote a comprehensive dictionary and the best history of instruments. He became interested in non-Western music and hence a pioneer ethnomusicologist and also wrote on music of the ancient world, on rhythm and tempo and on the relationship between music and the other arts.

Sachs, Hans (*b* Nuremberg, 5 Nov 1594; *d* there, 19 Jan 1576). German poet and Meistersinger. He went to school in Nuremberg and then learnt shoemaking, travelling throughout Germany during his apprenticeship (1511–16). He became a master shoemaker in 1520 and prospered in his home town, then at the height of its cultural and economic development. In 1509–11 he had joined the Meistersinger guild, and through him Meistergesang was brought into the service of the Reformation. His guild was a model throughout Germany. His massive output (over 6000 works) includes Meisterlieder, satirical and didactic poems (*Spruchgedichte*), prose dialogues and plays, as well as 13 *Meistertöne* for which he composed melodies. His posthumous fame was assured above all by Wagner's *Die Meistersinger von Nürnberg* (1868).

Sackbut. Early English name for the TROMBONE.

Sacra rappresentazione. *See* RAPPRESENTAZIONE SACRA.

Sacrati, Francesco (*b* Parma, bap. 17 Sept 1605; *d* ?Modena, 20 May 1650). Italian composer. He was active in Venice as an opera composer in the early 1640s and in 1649 became *maestro di cappella* of Modena Cathedral. In 1645 his first opera, *La finta pazza* (1641), became one of the earliest Italian operas staged in France. He may have written some of the music of *L'incoronazione di Poppea*.

Sacred and Profane. Eight songs, op.91, by Britten, settings of medieval lyrics for five unaccompanied voices (1975).

Sacred Harmonic Society. Amateur choral society founded in 1832 in London. In 1847 it gave the first performances of the revised version of Mendelssohn's *Elijah*, with the composer conducting. It disbanded in 1888.

Sacre du printemps, Le. *See* RITE OF SPRING, THE.

Sadai, Yizhak (*b* Sofia, 13 May 1935). Israeli composer of Bulgarian birth. He went to Israel in 1949 and studied with Boskovich at the Tel-Aviv Academy, then with Haubenstock-Ramati (1957). While teaching at the music academies in Jerusalem and Tel-Aviv, he has essayed post-Bergian and post-Webernian styles, using oriental melodic shapes.

Sadko. Opera in seven scenes by Rimsky-Korsakov to a libretto by V.I. Bel'sky (1898, Moscow).

Sadler's Wells. London theatre on the site of a 17th-century pleasure garden. A Music House of the 1680s was replaced by a theatre (1765) which was rebuilt in 1930 (cap. 1548); it became the home of Sadler's Wells Opera (1934–68; now English National Opera). Other opera, ballet and drama groups gave seasons from 1954 and since 1968 it has been the London home of companies from Britain and abroad.

Saeverud, Harald (Sigurd Johan) (*b* Bergen, 17 April 1897). Norwegian composer. He was a pupil of Holmsen at the Bergen Conservatory (1915–20) and of Koch at the Berlin Musikhochschule

(1920–21). His works show a development from late Romanticism through atonal expressionism to a freely tonal and (since 1940) increasingly nationalist style. Primarily a composer of symphonies and concertos, he has also written fine piano pieces and a score for *Peer Gynt* (1947).

Safonov, Vasily Il'ich (*b* Cossack settlement, nr. Itsyursk, 6 Feb 1852; *d* Kislovodsk, 27 Feb 1918). Russian conductor, pianist and teacher. He studied with Leschetizky and at the St Petersburg Conservatory, where he later taught. In Moscow (1889–1905) he was professor and director of the conservatory and the 'batonless' conductor of the Russian Musical Society; he made guest appearances in New York (1906–9) and England. An outstanding pianist, he counted Skryabin and Medtner among his pupils.

Sagra Musicale Umbra (Italy). Annual (autumn) festival in Perugia, established in 1946. Concerts are mainly of sacred music.

Sahl, Michael (*b* Boston, 2 Sept 1934). American composer. He was a pupil of Sessions and Babbitt at Princeton and studied with Foss, Copland and Dallapiccola. His works include stage, electronic and orchestral pieces, combining avant-garde and popular features.

Śahnāī [shahnāī]. Conical oboe of North India *c*50 cm long, cylindrical with seven fingerholes, related to the *suona* of China, *sarunai* of Indonesia, *zūrnā* of the Arab world, *zurla* of Macedonia and south Serbia and many other similar shrill-sounding double-reed instruments of Europe and Asia.

Sainete (Sp.). 'Farce': a comic one-act dramatic vignette, with music, which from the mid-18th century was often played at the end of Spanish theatrical entertainments. Among its composers were Ramón de la Cruz and Antonio Soler.

St Anne Fugue. The fugue of Bach's Prelude and Fugue in E♭ for organ (BWV552), so called because of the resemblance of the subject to the hymn tune 'St Anne'.

St Antony Variations. Orchestral work, op.56a, by Brahms (1873), a set of variations on a theme ascribed to Haydn.

Sainte-Colombe (*d* ?Paris, 1691–1701). French bass violist and composer. He lived in Paris and was an outstanding bass viol virtuoso; he was Marais' teacher. His most noted compositions are 67 *Concerts* for two viols.

St François d'Assise. Opera in eight tableaux by Messiaen to his own libretto (1983, Paris).

St Gall [St Gallen]. A collection of 9th–11th-century MSS at the Benedictine monastery of St Gall, Switzerland, reflects its importance as a musical and literary centre; they transmit a distinct tradition of chant in a notation rich in rhythmic signs.

Saint-Georges, Joseph Boulogne, Chevalier de (*b* nr. Basse Terre, Guadeloupe, *c*1739; *d* Paris, 9/10 June 1799). French composer and violinist. After moving to Paris *c*1749, he became an expert fencer and athlete as well as a virtuoso violinist. From 1769 he played in the Concert des Amateurs under Gossec and in 1773–81 was its musical director and leader; it was soon one of France's best orchestras.

In this period he wrote violin concertos, *symphonies concertantes*, symphonies, chamber music and the first of his seven stage works (which had mixed success). In 1781 he founded another orchestra, the Concert de la Loge Olympique, for which Haydn's Paris symphonies were composed. Later he twice visited London; in 1791 he joined the National Guard. He briefly directed a new musical organization in Paris before his death.

St John Passion. Choral work by J.S. Bach, a setting for soloists, chorus and orchestra of the Passion narrated in St John's Gospel, with interpolations partly based on B.H. Brockes's poem (1724, Leipzig).

There are *St John Passion* settings by Selle (1623), Schütz (1665), Telemann (eight extant) and many other composers.

St John's, Smith Square. London concert hall (opened 1969, cap. 600), originally a church (built 1713–28, damaged in World War II). Concerts are given by young performers as well as by established British musicians and visitors from abroad. Weekly lunchtime concerts are broadcast live by the BBC.

St John's Night on the Bare Mountain. *See* NIGHT ON THE BARE MOUNTAIN.

St Louis, Opera Theatre of. *See* OPERA THEATRE OF ST LOUIS.

St Louis Symphony Orchestra. American orchestra formed in 1907 from an orchestra founded in 1880; Max Zach was its conductor, 1907–21. Its home is Powell Symphony Hall (from 1968; cap. 2689). Its first European tour was in 1968.

St Ludmilla [Svatá Ludmila]. Oratorio by Dvořák to a text by Vrchlický (1886, Leeds).

St Luke Passion. Oratorio by Penderecki for soloists, choruses and orchestra (1966, Münster). There are settings by Schütz (1666), Telemann (five extant) and other composers.

St Mark Passion. Bach set the *St Mark Passion* in 1731 but the music is largely lost. Of Telemann's several settings, four survive.

St Mark's, Venice. Italian cathedral. In the 16th century it became a major musical centre through the compositions of its *maestro di cappella* Willaert and his school, especially the Gabrielis; their style, using several groups in different choir galleries, influenced church music elsewhere in Italy and abroad.

St Martial. Former monastery at Limoges (Aquitaine), in south-west France, with which an important repertory of medieval music is associated. It was founded in 848, flourished especially in the period 930–1130, was secularized in 1535 and demolished in 1792. The MSS assembled there during its prosperous periods found their way to Paris in the 18th century. The collection numbers some 30 MSS, all but two now in the Bibliothèque Nationale, covering many kinds of liturgical music, mostly plainchant but three of them polyphonic, many originating from St Martial itself or elsewhere in Limoges, some from slightly further afield. The notation is mostly in the local 'Aquitanian neumes', varying from a primitive 9th-century style to the more developed 'square notation' of the late 12th century. Their rhythmic interpretation is uncertain.

St Matthew Passion. Choral work by J.S. Bach, a setting for soloists, chorus and orchestra of the Passion narrated in St Matthew's Gospel, with interpolations by Picander (Good Friday 1727 and/or 1729, Leipzig). There are *St Matthew Passion* settings by Davy, Schütz (1666), Telemann (six surviving) and other composers.

Saint of Bleeker Street. Opera in three acts by Menotti to his own libretto (1954, New York).

Sainton, Prosper (Philippe Catherine) (*b* Toulouse, 5 June 1813; *d* London, 17 Oct 1890). French violinist. At the Paris Conservatoire he studied the violin with Habeneck. After touring Europe, in 1845 he settled in London, teaching at the RAM, playing in chamber music concerts and leading major London orchestras (Philharmonic Society, 1846–54; Royal Italian Opera, 1847–71; Her Majesty's Theatre, 1871–80; Sacred Harmonic Society, from 1848). His wife Charlotte Sainton-Dolby (1821–85) was well known as a contralto and teacher.

St Paul. Oratorio, op.36, by Mendelssohn, to a text by Julius Schubring after the *Acts of the Apostles* (1836, Düsseldorf).

St Paul Chamber Orchestra. American orchestra founded in 1959; its home is the I.A. O'Shaughnessy Auditorium (opened 1970, cap. 1800). Its first conductor was Leopold Sipe. It has performed many contemporary works, including commissions, and under Pinchas Zukerman (director from 1980) Romantic and earlier works.

St Paul's Suite. Suite for strings, op.29 no.2 by Holst (1913), written for St Paul's Girls' School, Hammersmith.

St Petersburg Philharmonic Society. Russian institution, founded in 1802; it existed for 100 years and presented over 200 concerts, including the première of Beethoven's *Missa solemnis* (1824), sung by the court chapel choir.

Saint-Saëns, (Charles) Camille (*b* Paris, 9 Oct 1835; *d* Algiers, 16 Dec 1921). French composer, pianist and organist. Showing Mozartian precocity as both a pianist and composer, he had childhood lessons with Stamaty and Boëly before entering the Conservatoire (1848), where Halévy was his teacher; his dazzling gifts early won him the admiration of Gounod, Rossini, Berlioz and especially Liszt, who hailed him as the world's greatest organist. He was organist at the Madeleine, 1857–75, and a teacher at the Ecole Niedermeyer, 1861–5, where Fauré was among his devoted pupils. With only these professional appointments, he pursued a range of other activities, organizing concerts of Liszt's symphonic poems (then a novelty), reviving interest in older music (notably of Bach, Handel and Rameau), writing on musical, scientific and historical topics, travelling often and widely (in Europe, North Africa and South America) and composing prolifically; on behalf of new French music he co-founded the Société Nationale de Musique (1871). A virtuoso pianist, he excelled in Mozart and was praised for the purity and grace of his playing. Similarly French characteristics of his conservative musical style – neat proportions, clarity, polished expression, elegant line – reside in his best compositions, the classically orientated sonatas (especially the first each for violin and cello), chamber music (Piano Quartet op.41), symphonies (no.3, the 'Organ' Symphony, 1886) and concertos (no.4 for piano, no.3 for violin). He also wrote 'exotic', descriptive or dramatic works, including four symphonic poems, in a style influenced by Liszt, using thematic transformation, and 13 operas, of which only *Samson et Dalila* (1877), with its sound structures, clear declamation and strongly appealing scenes, has held the stage. *Le carnaval des animaux* (1886) is a witty frolic; he forbade performances in his lifetime, 'Le cygne' apart. From the mid-1890s he adopted a more austere style, emphasizing the classical aspect of his aesthetic which, perhaps more than the music itself, influenced Fauré and Ravel.

Dramatic music Samson et Dalila (1877); Etienne Marcel (1879); Henry VIII (1883); Ascanio (1890); 9 others; incidental music for 6 plays; 1 ballet; 1 film score (1908)
Vocal music over 40 sacred works, incl. Le déluge, oratorio (1875); c40 secular choral works; c140 songs; 7 duets
Orchestral music Sym., A (c1850); Sym. no.1, E♭ (1853); Sym. 'Urbs Roma', F (1856); Sym. no.2, a (1859); Sym. no.3 'Organ', c (1886); 4 sym. poems, incl. Danse macabre (1874); 4 ovs.; Suite algérienne (1880); Pf Conc. no.1, D (1858); Pf Conc. no.2, g (1868); Pf Conc. no.3, E♭ (1869); Pf Conc. no.4, c (1875); Pf Conc. no.5 'Egyptian', F (1896); 3 vn concs.; 2 vc concs.; 16 other works with solo inst, incl. Africa, pf/orch (1891), Caprice andalous, vn/orch (1904), Odalette, fl/orch (1920)
Chamber music 2 vn sonatas; 2 vc sonatas; 3 solo wind sonatas; 2 str qts; 2 pf trios; Pf Qnt (1855); Pf Qt (1875); Le carnaval des animaux (1886)
Keyboard music c45 pf works, incl. mazurkas, waltzes, souvenirs; 3 sets of Etudes; Variations on a Theme of Beethoven, pf duo (1874); works for harmonium, org
Other transcrs., arrs. of works by other composers; books, essays; Ecole buissonnière, memoirs (1913)

Saint-Simonians. Followers of a French social and philosophical movement, among whom several, notably Félicien David, were musicians. Stressing fraternal cooperation and the reorientation of society towards the poorest class, the movement used music, chiefly choruses, to propagate its ideas. Berlioz and Liszt attended the soirées of 1830–31, later becoming alienated by the group's increasing mysticism.

Salazar, Antonio de (*b* c1650; *d* Mexico City, 27 May 1715). Mexican composer of Spanish birth. Originally a prebendary in Seville, he went to Mexico and became cathedral *maestro de capilla* in Puebla (1679) and then in Mexico City (1688); a skilled organizer and teacher, he supervised the installation of a new organ there in 1695. His music, all sacred, is conservative in style, with little chromaticism; some works (e.g. *Salve regina*) are for double choir. He had a reputation for writing extended villancicos for feast days and composed 20 such pieces, 1680–1704.

Sales, Franz (*b* Namur, ?c1550; *d* Prague, 15 July 1599). Netherlands composer. He sang in the Innsbruck court chapel (1580–87), was a Kapellmeister at Hall, Tyrol (1587–91), then sang at the imperial court in Prague, under Monte. He is important for his conservative, richly polyphonic Mass Propers (3 vols., 1594–6).

Salicional. An organ stop, made of narrow, open cylindrical pipes, giving a delicate, string-like tone

at 4' or 8' pitch; it was popular from the late 16th century.

Salieri, Antonio (*b* Legnano, 18 Aug 1750; *d* Vienna, 7 May 1825). Italian composer. He studied with Gassmann and others in Vienna, and also knew Gluck (who became his patron) and Metastasio. In 1774 he succeeded Gassmann as court composer and conductor of the Italian opera; from 1788 he was also court Kapellmeister. He made his reputation as a stage composer, writing operas for Vienna from 1768 and presenting several in Italy, 1778–80. Later he dominated Parisian opera with three works of 1784–7; *Tarare* (1787), his greatest success, established him as Gluck's heir. In 1790 he gave up his duties at the Italian opera. As his style became old-fashioned his works lost favour, and he composed relatively little after 1804, but he remained a central and influential figure in Viennese musical life. His many pupils included Beethoven, Schubert and Liszt. There is little evidence of any intrigues against Mozart, still less of the charge of poisoning.

Salieri's c40 Italian operas are traditional in their emphasis on melodic expression, but they also show Gluck's influence, with dramatic choral writing, much accompanied recitative and careful declamation: some combine *seria* and *buffa* elements. In *Tarare* he came close to Gluck's dramatic ideals. Among his many other compositions are oratorios, church music, cantatas, arias, vocal ensembles, songs and orchestral and chamber works.

Salinas, Francisco de (*b* Burgos, 1 March 1513; *d* Salamanca, 13 Jan 1590). Spanish theorist and organist. He served the Archbishop of Santiago de Compostela, with whom he went to Rome. He was organist at the vice-regal chapel at Naples (1553–8) and at Sigüenza and León cathedrals. In 1567 he took the chair of music at Salamanca University. His treatise, *De musica libri septem* (1577), discusses proportions, intervals and chromatic and enharmonic genera and surveys the major theorists from antiquity to Zarlino. Among the music examples are 57 Spanish and Italian folk melodies.

Salisbury Festival (UK). *See* SOUTHERN CATHEDRALS FESTIVAL.

Sallé, Marie (*b* Paris, 1707; *d* there, 27 July 1756). French dancer. She danced in ballets and other stage works in Paris and London until 1740, appearing in operas by Rameau and Handel. An important figure in 18th-century dance, she adopted a new expressive style and simpler dress – major steps towards the ideal union of elements in the *ballet en action*, and anticipating many of Noverre's ideas.

Sallinen, Aulis (*b* Salmi, 9 April 1935). Finnish composer. He was a pupil of Merikanto and Kokkonen at the Helsinki Academy (1955–60), where he returned to teach in 1970. In the late 1960s he began melding triads with avant-garde techniques; then in the 1970s he turned to opera, drawing on sources as diverse as Shostakovich, Janáček and Orff in *The Horsemen* (1976), *The Red Line* (1978) and *The King Goes Forth to France* (1984). His concert works include four symphonies, five string quartets and concertos for violin and for cello.

Salmenhaara, Erkki (Olavi) (*b* Helsinki, 12 March

1941). Finnish composer. A pupil of Kokkonen at the Helsinki Academy and of Ligeti in Vienna (1963) he has taught at Helsinki University since 1963. His works, in most genres (including symphonies, an opera and a requiem), are influenced by Sibelius and Ligeti; latterly he has established an individual, expressive language with simple means.

Salmhofer, Franz (*b* Vienna, 22 Jan 1900; *d* there, 22 Sept 1975). Austrian composer and conductor. Schreker, Franz Schmidt and Adler were among his teachers. He was conductor at the Burgtheater (1929–39), for which he wrote *c*300 incidental scores, and after the war was director of the Staatsoper and the Volksoper. His operas, ballets and six string quartets are rooted in the Viennese tradition.

Salmon, Jacques (*b* Picardy, *c*1545; *fl* 1571–86). French composer. He served the Duke of Anjou (1571) and Henri III (at least 1575–83) as a singer and is known for the music he wrote (possibly with Beaulieu) for Beaujoyeux's *Balet comique de la Royne* (staged 1581).

Salmon, Karel (*b* Heidelberg, 13 Nov 1897; *d* Beit Zayit, 15 Jan 1974). Israeli composer of German birth. A pupil of Strauss in Berlin, he moved to Palestine in 1933 and was first musical director of Jerusalem radio (1936). He played a part in the Handel revival. His works, mostly in conventional forms, are influenced by Mediterranean and oriental folklore.

Salmon, Thomas (*b* Hackney, 24 June 1648; *d* Mepsal, Beds., bur. 16 Aug 1706). English musical theorist. He was a clergyman and an amateur musician. In the first of his writings on music, *An Essay to the Advancement of Musick* (1672), he proposed certain simplifications in notation, provoking a virulent and celebrated musical pamphlet war. Some of his ideas were later adopted.

Salome. Opera in one act by Richard Strauss, a setting of Hedwig Lachmann's translation of Wilde's play (1905, Dresden).

Other composers have written dramatic works on the same subject, among them Mariotte and Schmitt.

Salomon, Johann Peter (*b* Bonn, bap. 20 Feb 1745; *d* London, 28 Nov 1815). German violinist, impresario and composer. He first served at the Bonn court, and by 1764 was music director to Prince Heinrich of Prussia. In 1780–81 he settled in England, where he made his name as a brilliant violinist; then he turned to promoting concerts. He secured Haydn's visits to London in 1790–91 and 1794–5, led the orchestra in his London symphonies and played in performances of his quartets. He was also active as a conductor. His compositions include stage works, vocal pieces and various instrumental items; he arranged some of Haydn's symphonies for chamber ensemble. He is thought to have given Mozart's 'Jupiter' Symphony its nickname.

Salomon Quartet. English string quartet. It was established in 1981 by its leader Simon Standage for performances of the Classical and early Romantic repertory on period instruments.

Salomon Symphonies. *See* LONDON SYMPHONIES.

Salón Mexico, El. Orchestral work by Copland (1936) based on Mexican themes, also arranged for piano.

Salpinx. A trumpet-like instrument of the ancient Greeks, probably Etruscan in origin. It consisted of a thin, straight bronze tube with a bone mouthpiece and ending in a bell; it is traditionally associated with war.

Salsa. A popular music style of the 1940s, Cuban in origin. Salsa musicians who moved to New York introduced the style to the USA where it absorbed jazz influences. Traditionally each piece has three sections: a head (melodic) section, a *montuno* in which the lead singer improvises against a repeated vocal refrain, and a *mambo* section of contrasting riffs.

Saltarello. A generic term for moderately rapid Italian dances, usually in triple metre and involving jumping movements. The earliest known examples date from the late 14th or early 15th century. By the early 16th, the saltarello usually appeared as an after-dance to the *paduana* or passamezzo and derived its material from its duple-metre partner. An important characteristic was its ambiguity of metre, which in modern terms often seems to alternate between 6/8 and 3/4. In the 17th century the saltarello waned in popularity.

Towards the end of the 18th century a popular folkdance called the saltarello began to gain favour, first in Rome and then more widely. In 3/4 or 6/8, it was accompanied by guitars, tambourines and often by singing. The saltarello finale of Mendelssohn's Italian Symphony probably uses tunes for the 19th-century folkdance.

Saltbox. A wooden box, struck with a piece of wood to provide a makeshift percussion instrument in 17th- and 18th-century England.

Salt Lake Mormon Tabernacle Choir. American choir formed in 1847 in Salt Lake City; it has been internationally known since weekly broadcasts began in 1929.

Salvatore, Giovanni (*b* Castelvenere, early 17th century; *d* ?Naples, ?1688). Italian composer. He worked in Naples as a church organist, *maestro di cappella* and teacher, serving latterly at the conservatory Poveri di Gesù Cristo. A skilful composer of organ and vocal music, he is noted for his *Ricercari* (1641), a collection of ricercares, canzonas etc similar in style to Frescobaldi's.

Salve regina (Lat.: 'Hail, queen'). One of the four Marian antiphons, sung at the end of Compline from Trinity Sunday to the Saturday before the first Sunday in Advent. Among numerous polyphonic settings are those of La Rue, Josquin, Obrecht and Ockeghem.

Salzburg Festivals (Austria). Mozart festivals were held occasionally from 1842. The annual summer festival was established in 1920; it includes opera and concerts (especially Mozart), ballet and contemporary music. The Easter festival (founded 1966) features Wagner. A Mozart Week is held in the winter.

Salzedo, Carlos (Léon) (*b* Arcachon, 6 April 1885; *d* Waterville, ME, 17 Aug 1961). American harpist and composer. He studied in Bordeaux and Paris and moved in 1909 to New York, where he played in the Met orchestra (1909–13). His early harp compositions have a Ravellian harmonic vocabulary; in the USA his music became increasingly astringent. He made a large contribution to the harp repertory, bringing it abreast at least of Hindemith.

Salzman, Eric (*b* New York, 8 Sept 1933). American composer and writer on music. He studied at Columbia, with Sessions and Babbitt at Princeton and with Petrassi in Rome. Since 1958 he has worked in New York as a critic (for the *New York Times* and *Herald Tribune*), teacher and composer, notably of music-theatre (e.g. *Foxes and Hedgehogs*, 1967) and mixed-media pieces (*Toward a new American Opera*, 1985). His writings include *Twentieth-century Music: an Introduction* (1967); he was editor of the *Musical Quarterly*, 1984–7.

Samaras, Spyridon (Filiskos) (*b* Corfu, 29 Nov ?1863; *d* Athens, 7 April 1917). Greek composer. He studied in Athens and with Delibes at the Paris Conservatoire and was the first Greek composer to achieve international recognition, notably with his *verismo* operas from *Flora mirabilis* (1886) to *Rhea* (1908).

Samazeuilh, Gustave (Marie Victor Fernand) (*b* Bordeaux, 2 June 1877; *d* Paris, 4 Aug 1967). French writer and composer. He studied at the Schola Cantorum (1900–06) and with Dukas. His works include orchestral, chamber and piano pieces and songs, influenced by early Ravel and Debussy. He was also a critic and musical translator.

Samba. An Afro-Brazilian couple-dance and popular musical form. Mostly in binary metre, samba melodies and accompaniments are highly syncopated: a semiquaver–quaver–semiquaver figure is characteristic.

Sambuca. A name for the Greco-Roman angular harp.

Saminsky, Lazare (*b* Vale-Hotzulovo, 8 Nov 1882; *d* Port Chester, NY, 30 June 1959). American composer of Russian origin. He was a pupil of Lyadov and Rimsky-Korsakov at the St Petersburg and Moscow conservatories (1906–10); he moved in 1920 to New York, where in 1923 he was a founder of the League of Composers. He was musical director of Temple Emanu-El (1924–56) and author of several books; he wrote Jewish liturgical music and drew on Jewish sources in his five symphonies, choral music and songs.

Samisen. *See* SHAMISEN.

Sammartini, Giovanni Battista (*b* ?Milan, 1700/01; *d* there, 15 Jan 1775). Italian composer, brother of Giuseppe Sammartini. He held posts as *maestro di cappella* of Milan churches from 1728, and (from 1768) the ducal chapel; he was an excellent organist and teacher (his pupils probably included Gluck). By the 1740s he was the city's most famous composer and his music was gaining popularity abroad. Later he had contact in Milan with J.C. Bach, Boccherini, Mozart and others.

Sammartini was a leading figure in the development of the Classical style. His music is notable for its strong continuity, rhythmic drive and variety of structure and texture. The first master of the sym-

phony, he wrote over 60 such works; while the earliest combine Baroque and Classical traits, the middle-period ones (*c*1740–58) have an early Classical idiom, many using wind instruments (usually two horns or trumpets) as well as strings. The last symphonies point towards later styles (e.g. Mozart's). He also wrote concertos, other orchestral pieces and over 200 chamber works, including many trio sonatas. His late chamber works (notably six string quintets, 1773) are the most complex. Serious moods and expressive writing often appear in his three operas (1732–43) and his religious music, which includes oratorios, cantatas and psalms.

Orchestral music over 60 syms.; 8 solo concs. (most for vn); 2 ensemble concs.; 7 orch concertinos
Chamber music 6 str qnts (1773); 21 qts (some for strs only); over 100 trios; fl duets; *c*30 solo sonatas; *c*30 kbd sonatas
Vocal music 3 operas; secular cantatas, arias; miscellaneous sacred music, incl. 8 Lenten cantatas

Sammartini, Giuseppe [Gioseffo] **(Francesco Gaspare Melchiorre Baldassare)** (*b* Milan, 6 Jan 1695; *d* London, ?17/23 Nov 1750). Italian oboist and composer. He settled in London *c*1728 and soon won recognition as a brilliant performer, playing in concerts and operas (including Handel's). From 1736 he was music master to the Princess of Wales and her children. Noted for his fine tone, he transformed oboe playing in England. He was also a leading composer of solo flute and oboe sonatas, trio sonatas, concerti grossi, solo concertos etc; these are mainly conservative in style but have *galant* features of form and idiom. His other works include cantatas, arias and an English pastoral (*c*1740).

Sammons, Albert (Edward) (*b* London, 23 Feb 1886; *d* Southdean, 24 Aug 1957). English violinist. Largely self-taught, he led the Beecham Orchestra from 1908 and was later leader of the orchestra of Dyagilev's Ballets Russes. As leader of the London String Quartet (1907–16) and as soloist and in recital he was closely associated with English music, notably Elgar, Ireland and Delius. He was also a distinguished teacher.

Samosud, Samuil Abramovich (*b* Tbilisi, 14 May 1884; *d* Moscow, 6 Nov 1964). Soviet conductor. He conducted at theatres in Leningrad, 1917–36, and Moscow, 1936–50; later he was principal conductor of the Moscow Philharmonia SO and the All-Union Radio SO. He championed many operas by Soviet composers, including Shostakovich's *The Nose* and Prokofiev's *War and Peace*.

Samson. Oratorio by Handel to a text adapted by Hamilton from Milton (1743, London).

Samson et Dalila. Opera in three acts by Saint-Saëns to a libretto by Lemaire after the Bible (1877, Weimar).

Samstag aus Licht. Opera by Stockhausen to his own libretto (1984, Milan), the second completed work of the seven-opera cycle *Licht*.

Samuel, Harold (*b* London, 23 May 1879; *d* there, 15 Jan 1937). English pianist. He studied at the RCM, where he later taught and was at first known as an accompanist. But a series of Bach recitals he gave in 1921 aroused a keen interest in Bach's keyboard music and he became widely known in England and the USA for his clear and shapely playing of it. He was also admired for his playing of Brahms and as a chamber musician.

San Antonio Symphony Orchestra. American orchestra founded in 1939; Max Reiter was its first conductor. Its homes are the Lila Cockrell Theatre for the Performing Arts (completed 1968) and the Laurie Auditorium at Trinity University. In 1945–83 it sponsored the annual Grand Opera Festival. Various quartets of orchestra members give a summer concert series.

San Carlo. Theatre in Naples. It was built in 1737 and at once replaced the old Teatro di S Bartolomeo as the principal Neapolitan house for *opera seria*. Operas by leading Neapolitan composers (Pergolesi, Jommelli, Paisiello, Cimarosa) were given there in the 18th century. The present theatre (cap. 3500) was opened in 1816; its manager was Domenico Barbaia, who put on several important serious Rossini operas (*Mosè, Otello, La donna del lago*); Donizetti's *Lucia di Lammermoor* and Verdi's *Attila* and *Luisa Miller* were first given there. It remains the leading house in Naples.

San Cassiano. Theatre in Venice, the first public opera house, opened in 1637.

Sances, Giovanni Felice (*b* Rome, *c*1600; *d* Vienna, bur. 12 Nov 1679). Italian composer. A singer, he first worked in Rome, Bologna and Venice, and presented his first opera in Padua in 1636. Later that year he entered the imperial chapel in Vienna; he became assistant court Kapellmeister in 1649 and court Kapellmeister in 1669. He helped establish Italian dramatic music there and presented four operas and six *sepolcri* of his own. In addition to *c*600 sacred works, he composed secular vocal chamber music, of which four published volumes (1633–57) survive: these include both strophic songs and through-composed pieces and are notable for their suave, sometimes florid melodic writing.

Sánchez Málaga, Carlos (*b* Arequipa, 8 Sept 1904). Peruvian composer and teacher. He was director of the Lima National Conservatory, 1943–69, and a leader of Peruvian musical life. His works look to the mestizo folk traditions of his native city.

Sancho Marraco, José (*b* La Garriga, 27 Feb 1879; *d* there, 17 Sept 1960). Spanish composer and church musician. He was a boy chorister at Barcelona Cathedral, where he was appointed choirmaster in 1923. One of the greatest 20th-century composers of liturgical music in Spain, he wrote craftsmanlike masses and motets.

Sanctus. The fourth and oldest acclamation of the Ordinary of the Latin Mass, sung at the close of the Preface, just before the Canon, as the item most closely associated with the eucharistic phase of the Mass. It was added to the liturgy between the 1st and 5th centuries. Its melodic repertory was established by the 10th–11th centuries. The text, from *Isaiah* vi.3, usually has five main phrases: 'Sanctus', 'Pleni', 'Hosanna', 'Benedictus', 'Hosanna'; elaborate settings use melodic repetition or parallelism among these.

Sanderling, Kurt (*b* Arys, 19 Sept 1912). German conductor. After early experience with the Berlin Städtische Oper he left Germany in 1936 and was conductor of the Moscow Radio SO until 1941. He then became joint conductor of the Leningrad PO, returning to Germany in 1960 as conductor of the East Berlin SO. With it and the Dresden Staatskapelle he has toured widely in Europe. His blend of intellectual clarity and expressive shading has been admired in Mahler, Sibelius and Russian symphonic music.

Sanders, Robert L(evine) (*b* Chicago, 2 July 1906; *d* Delray Beach, FL, 26 Dec 1974). American composer. He was a pupil of Respighi, Bustini and Dobici in Rome, and of de Lioncourt and Braud in Paris. He worked in the USA as a conductor and teacher (notably at Brooklyn College, 1947–72), and wrote notably for brass in a neo-classical, dissonant style.

San Diego Opera Company. American company formed in 1964. Under Tito Capobianco (1975–83) its seasons and annual Verdi festivals (from 1978) emphasized lesser-known works. Premières include Menotti's *La loca* (1979) and a 20th-anniversary commission from Leonardo Balada.

San Diego Symphony Orchestra. American orchestra founded in 1902; R.E. Tragwitz was its first conductor. Its home is Symphony Hall (formerly Fox Theatre, cap. 2400; renamed 1985).

Sandoni, Pietro Giuseppe (*b* Bologna, 1 Aug 1685; *d* there, 16 Aug 1748). Italian composer and harpsichordist. As an organist in Bologna, he presented several oratorios, 1701–6. Later he travelled as a harpsichordist and had his third opera (1735) staged in London. He also composed a few instrumental works; his three keyboard sonatas (*c*1727) were the first published in England. He was married to the soprano Francesca Cuzzoni.

Sandrin [Regnault], Pierre (*b* ?St Marcel, ?*c*1490; *d* ?Italy, after 1561). French composer. While serving the French royal chapel he also spent time in Italy as *maestro di cappella* at Ippolito d'Este's court in Ferrara. His elegant *chansons* were highly esteemed by his contemporaries and range in style from the predominantly homophonic textures favoured by Claudin de Sermisy to the more flexible, sophisticated and chromatic music written after 1543; many were used as models for parody masses and arranged by lutenists and keyboard players for their instruments.

San Francisco Opera. American company formed in 1923; its home is the War Memorial Opera House (opened 1934, cap. 3252). Early seasons were of standard Italian and French works. Under Kurt Herbert Adler (director 1953–82) a broader repertory included premières of 20th-century works, many singers made their operatic or American débuts and the company supported groups for young performers (now San Francisco Opera Center) and gave the Summer Opera Festival (from 1980), with international casts.

San Francisco Symphony Orchestra. American orchestra established in 1911. Henry Hadley was its first conductor. It was brought to international level under Pierre Monteux (1936–52). Foreign tours began in 1968 under Josef Krips. From 1977, under Edo de Waart, works were commissioned and annual festivals given. With the opening of the

Louise M. Davies Symphony Hall (1980, cap. 3063) it became independent of San Francisco Opera and increased its activities.

Santa Croce, Francesco (*b* Padua, *c*1487; *d* Loreto, ?1556). Italian composer. He was *maestro di cappella* of Treviso Cathedral. One of the earliest composers to use *cori spezzati*, his extant music includes four five-part motets and psalm settings for double choir.

Santa Cruz (Wilson), Domingo (*b* La Cruz, Valparaiso, 5 July 1899; *d* Santiago, 7 Jan 1987). Chilean composer. He was a pupil of Soro in Santiago (1917–21) and del Campo in Madrid (1922–4), and became highly influential in Chilean musical life as a choral conductor, teacher at the National Conservatory (1928–53), administrator and composer. His works, in a Hispanic variety of Hindemithian counterpoint, include four symphonies, three string quartets, choral and piano music.

Santa Fe Chamber Music Festival (USA). Annual (summer) season established in 1973; concerts by renowned groups include new music by an American resident composer.

Santa Fe Opera. American company founded in 1956 as the Opera Association of New Mexico; it performs in the open-air Santa Fe Opera Theater. It has a wide repertory and uses mainly American singers. Activities include a summer festival of five productions, including premières, with players from major American orchestras.

Santa María, Tomás de (*b* Madrid; *d* Ribadavia, 1570). Spanish theorist and composer. A Dominican friar, he was organist in various monasteries in Castilla, principally S Pablo in Valladolid; there he may have met A. and J. de Cabezón, with whom he conferred in preparing *Arte de tañer fantasia* (1565). It aimed to teach the playing of fantasias (improvised pieces in fugal style) on the clavichord and is remarkable for its clarity and systematic organization.

Santiago, Francisco (*b* Santa Maria, 29 Jan 1889; *d* Manila, 28 Sept 1947). Filipino composer. He was trained at the University of the Philippines Conservatory and in Chicago and became the first Filipino director of the conservatory, 1931–45. He used standard European forms as well as folk-style songs.

Santiago, Francisco de (*b* Lisbon, *c*1578; *d* Seville, 5 Oct 1644). Portuguese composer. He was a *maestro de capilla* in Madrid (1601–17) and then at Seville Cathedral, where he was the first to bring castrato singers to the city. He wrote church music and over 500 villancicos.

Santini, Fortunato (*b* Rome, 5 Jan 1778; *d* there, 14 Sept 1861). Italian composer and collector. An enthusiast for Italian polyphony, he is remembered for his collection of *c*4500 MSS and *c*1100 printed items, many unique (now in Münster).

Santley, Sir Charles (*b* Liverpool, 28 Feb 1834; *d* London, 22 Sept 1922). English baritone. Apart from creating several roles in English operas by Wallace, Balfe and Benedict (1859–63), he sang Valentine to great acclaim in the English première of Gounod's *Faust* and the Dutchman (in Italian) in the first Wagner production in England. Admired for his expressiveness, he performed only in concert

and oratorio from 1877; he was knighted in 1907.

Santoliquido, Francesco (*b* S Giorgio a Cremano, 6 Aug 1883; *d* Anacapri, 26 Aug 1971). Italian composer. Trained at the Liceo di S Cecilia, Rome, he lived in Tunisia (1912–21), where he founded a music school, and from 1933 in Anacapri. He wrote in many genres, in a style influenced by Wagner and Debussy, and contributed to the fascist press, decrying 'modern music'.

Santoro, Cláudio (*b* Manaus, 23 Nov 1919). Brazilian composer and violinist. A pupil of Koellreutter and, in Paris, of Boulanger, he co-founded and played in the Brazilian SO (1941–7). His early music, influenced by Koellreutter, was inclined towards atonality, but in the late 1940s and 1950s his political and musical allegiances were with Prokofiev and Shostakovich. In the mid-1960s, however, he returned to a qualified serialism and began to use other avant-garde techniques. His large output is mostly instrumental and includes eight symphonies, three piano concertos and seven string quartets.

Santórsola, Guido (*b* Canosa, 18 Nov 1904). Uruguayan composer of Italian birth. Trained in São Paulo, Naples and London as a violinist, he settled in Montevideo as a string player, teacher and composer. His works, which include guitar music and several concertos, use Brazilian folk music and modernist techniques.

Santo Sepolcro, Al. Title given to two works by Vivaldi of a solemn, contrapuntal character, and presumably intended for Easter use: Sinfonia in B minor RV169 and Sonata in Eb RV130.

Santūr. A dulcimer-type instrument of great antiquity known throughout the Middle East, the Caucasus, south-eastern Europe and South Asia. The Iranian instrument, part of the traditional orchestra, has nine or 11 groups of strings fixed to a trapeziform case, played by striking with hammers; the Iraqi version has 23–5 strings, the Caucasian 13–26.

Sanza [sansa]. Term used generically for an African LAMELLAPHONE.

Sanzogno, Nino (*b* Venice, 13 April 1911). Italian conductor. He studied in Venice and under Scherchen in Brussels. His career was mainly at Venice and Milan, where he first appeared at La Scala in 1939, inaugurated La Piccola Scala in 1955 and introduced several important 20th-century works at La Scala and Venice festivals. He has appeared widely as a guest conductor. His compositions include symphonic poems and concertos, written in the 1930s.

Sarabande. One of the most popular of Baroque instrumental dances. It originated in the 16th century as a sung dance in Latin America and Spain and came to Italy early in the 17th century in the repertory of the Spanish guitar. The harmonic progression I–IV–I–V, often in alternating 6/8 and 3/4 metre, was a feature up to *c*1640. Around 1620 a new type called the *zarabanda francese* began to appear,

Ex. 1   (a) 𝄴 ♩ ♩. ♪|♩

(b) 𝄴 ♩ ♩ ♩ |♩. ♪♩ |

associated particularly with the rhythms of ex.1. That of ex.1a was preferred in France, along with an increasingly slow tempo and deliberate articulation. This type, in binary form and often in 3/2, was taken up by German composers as the third standard movement in the suite.

Saracini, Claudio (b Siena, 1 July 1586; d ?there, after 1649). Italian composer. A singer and lutenist of noble birth, he travelled widely and knew many eminent figures in Italy. With Sigismondo d'India he was one of Italy's two finest composers of monody in the early 17th century. His six published volumes (1614–24) consist almost entirely of secular songs, ranging from long recitatives and arias to simple strophic settings. The more declamatory and expressive pieces may owe something to Monteverdi.

Sárai, Tibor (b Budapest, 10 May 1919). Hungarian composer. A pupil of Kadosa, he has taught in Budapest at the conservatory (1953–9) and academy (from 1959) and became a leader of Hungarian musical life. His music developed from folklorism to humanism (*Variations on the Theme of Peace*, 1964); of professional finish, his works cover many non-dramatic genres and include *Musica per 45 corde* (1971).

Sāraṅgī. Short-necked fiddle of South Asia, found in classical raga music in north India and Pakistan and in folk music particularly of Rajasthan. It is played like a Western cello with the performer seated and the instrument against the left shoulder. The bow is held in the right hand and the strings are stopped with the fingernails of the left. There are three or four playing strings and steel sympathetic strings.

Sarasate (y Navascuéz), Pablo (Martín Melitón) de (b Pamplona, 10 March 1844; d Biarritz, 20 Sept 1908). Spanish violinist and composer. He studied at the Paris Conservatoire. From 1859 concert tours made him famous throughout Europe and in North and South America, his playing being distinguished by beautiful tone and a superb, apparently effortless technique. Among the many composers who dedicated works to him were Bruch, Saint-Saëns, Joachim and Dvořák. Best known of his own 54 opus numbers, chiefly virtuoso violin works, are the *Zigeunerweisen* op.20 (1878) and the four books of *Spanische Tänze* (opp.21, 22, 23, 26).

Sardou, Victorien (b Paris, 5 Sept 1831; d there, 8 Nov 1908). French dramatist. With his popular *comédies-vaudevilles* and later his 'well-made' comedies he can be seen as Scribe's natural successor. But it was his historical melodramas – *Patrie!* (1869), *La haine* (1874), *Théodora* (1884) and *La Tosca* (1887) – that attracted opera composers including Verdi, Giordano and Puccini.

Sargent, Sir (Harold) Malcolm (Watts) (b Ashford, Kent, 29 April 1895; d London, 3 Oct 1967). English conductor. After an early career as an organist he made his conducting début in 1921 at a London Promenade Concert. He was an outstanding choral conductor, directing the Royal Choral Society and the Huddersfield Choral Society for many years. An energetic popularizer, he conducted many children's concerts and was chief conductor of

the Proms, 1948–67, and of the BBC SO, 1950–57. He travelled widely and gave assured performances across a wide repertory.

Sarod. A plucked, fretless, double-chested, long-necked lute of the north Indian subcontinent, one of the most important instruments of Hindustani classical music. It is similar in appearance and in repertory to the SITAR. Its strings, six to eight with several added punctuating and sympathetic ones, are plucked with a wooden plectrum; many examples have a second small resonator of wood or gourd behind the pegbox.

Sarrette, Bernard (b Bordeaux, 27 Dec 1765; d Paris, 11 April 1858). French musical administrator. He organized the school of military music which became the Institut National de Musique (1793) and later the Paris Conservatoire (1795).

Sarro [Sarri], Domenico Natale (b Trani, Apulia, 24 Dec 1679; d Naples, 25 Jan 1744). Italian composer. He studied in Naples and had court posts as *vice-maestro di cappella* (1704–7, 1725–35) and acting *maestro di cappella* (from 1735). He had his first operas staged in 1706–7 and from 1718 he emerged as a prominent and prolific writer of operas, oratorios, serenatas etc; most were given in Naples. His earliest works use a Baroque style akin to Scarlatti's, but he contributed to the evolution of the simpler, more melodic Neapolitan style later popularized by Vinci and Leo. Around 1720 he was an innovatory composer; by 1740 his style was out of fashion.

Sarrusophone. A brass instrument designed in 1856 by Sarrus, a bandmaster in the French army; his intention was to design a family of double-reed instruments to replace oboes and bassoons in military bands. The family (ranging from the sopranino in E♭ to the contrabass in E♭ or B♭) closely resembles the saxophone family in range and fingering. They enjoyed brief popularity in wind and military bands; only the contrabass achieved lasting success in orchestras, where it was used by French composers, notably Saint-Saëns and Massenet, as a substitute for the double bassoon.

Sarti, Giuseppe (b Faenza, bap. 1 Dec 1729; d Berlin, 28 July 1802). Italian composer. After studying with Padre Martini he was organist of Faenza Cathedral, 1748–52, and presented his first opera in 1752. In 1753–75 he worked mainly in Copenhagen, as court Kapellmeister. Back in Italy in 1766–8, he served at the Pietà conservatory in Venice; in 1768–75 he was working at the Copenhagen royal chapel and court theatre. He was *maestro di cappella* of Milan Cathedral, 1779–84, also reaching the height of his fame as a composer, notably with *Giulio Sabino* and the comic opera *Fra i due litiganti* (1782). He then went (via Vienna) to St Petersburg as director of the imperial chapel; here he had several more operas staged and contributed to the Russian opera *The Early Reign of Oleg* (1790). He died on his way back to Italy.

Sarti's c70 stage works, which won him high popularity, are most inventive in their accompanied recitatives, varied aria forms, orchestration and (in comic operas) ensembles. In *The Early Reign of Oleg* he tried to imitate ancient Greek music; this was an isolated experiment, but the Russian subject matter and folk music foreshadow the later Russian national opera. He also wrote cantatas, sacred works (some in Russian), instrumental pieces and essays on music.

Sartori, Claudio (*b* Brescia, 1 April 1913). Italian musicologist. He studied at Pavia and Strasbourg and taught at Bologna and Milan. An outstanding bibliographer, he has done much to lay a firm foundation for studies in early Italian music, Italian music publishing and librettos. He has also worked on Josquin and edited *L'enciclopedia della musica* (1963–4).

Sartorio, Antonio (*b* Venice, 1630; *d* there, 30 Dec 1680). Italian composer. After writing two operas in Venice, he served as court Kapellmeister in Hanover (1666–75) but returned frequently to present further operas, among them *L'Adelaide* (1672). He later settled there, becoming *vice-maestro di cappella* of St Mark's in 1676. His 15th opera was unfinished when he died.

For Sartorio, opera was primarily a brilliant spectacle. Arias were the chief means of expression; several of his operas have more than 70. Especially notable are his laments, often written over a chromatic ostinato bass, and his trumpet arias. Among his other works are cantatas, separate arias and sacred pieces. His brother Gasparo Sartorio (1625/6 –1680) was also active in Venice as a composer and organist.

Sartorius, Paul (*b* Nuremberg, bap. 16 Nov 1569; *d* Innsbruck, 28 Feb 1609). German composer. He studied under Lechner and then in Rome and by 1594 was organist to Archduke Maximilian II in Mergentheim and later at Innsbruck. His sacred music (3 bks, 1599–1602, and MSS) is up-to-date and shows Italian influence; he also published Italian madrigals (1600) and lieder (1601).

Sarum rite, Music of the. A local medieval modification of the Roman rite used by the secular (non-monastic) chapter of Salisbury Cathedral. It was used there between the 13th century and the Reformation, became increasingly popular throughout England and spread to Scotland, Ireland and even Portugal. It was also adopted by religious houses, and underwent revisions before it was abolished in 1559.

Sarum melodies are essentially the same as their counterparts in the Roman rite but differ in points of detail. The rite provided the liturgical setting, the ritual texts and many of the plainsong themes for much English polyphony, including votive antiphons, hymn settings, responsories, festival masses, Magnificats and Lamentations.

Sáry, László (*b* Györ, 1 Jan 1940). Hungarian composer. He studied at the Budapest Academy (1961–6) and went to Darmstadt. Since *c*1970 he has been influenced by Stockhausen, Cage and minimalism. He wrote *Pentagram* (1974) for solo voices and ensemble for the centenary of Budapest.

Sas (Orchassal), Andrés (*b* Paris, 6 April 1900; *d* Lima, 26 Aug 1967). Peruvian composer of Belgian-French origin. He studied at the Brussels Conservatory (1920–23) and in 1924 was appointed to the Lima Academy; in 1930 he founded the Sas–Rosay Academy with his wife. His works treat Peruvian materials in a Debussian manner and his articles established him as the leading historian of Peruvian music in Lima.

SATB. Abbreviation for soprano, alto, tenor, bass, the make-up of a standard mixed choir.

Satie, Erik (Alfred Leslie) (*b* Honfleur, 17 May 1866; *d* Paris, 1 July 1925). French composer. In 1879 he entered the Paris Conservatoire, but his record was undistinguished. After leaving he wrote the triptychs of *Sarabandes* (1887), *Gymnopédies* (1888) and *Gnossiennes* (1890), of which the latter two sets are modal and almost eventless: all three sets see no need to resolve dissonances in a traditional manner. In the 1890s he began to frequent Montmartre, to play at the café Chat Noir and to involve himself with fringe Christian sects, notably the Rosicrucian movement. He also made the acquaintance of Debussy.

In 1898 he moved to the southern suburb of Arcueil-Cachan while continuing to work in Montmartre as a café pianist. He wrote little, though he completed the *Trois morceaux en forme de poire* for piano duet (1903). Then he became a student again, at the Schola Cantorum (1905–8). At last in 1911 his music began to be noticed, and this seems to have stimulated a large output of small pieces, mostly for solo piano and mostly perpetuating his earlier simplicity in pieces with ironic titles. *Sports et divertissements* (1914), published with illustrations by Charles Martin, contains 20 miniatures eccentrically and beautifully annotated by Satie. In 1915 he came to the attention of Cocteau, who seized on him as the ideal of the anti-Romantic composer and who facilitated the more ambitious works of his last years: the ballets *Parade* (1917), *Mercure* (1924) and *Relâche* (1924), and the cantata *Socrate* (1918). These have the same flatness as the smaller pieces and songs, achieved by means of directionless modal harmony, simple rhythm and structures made up through repetition or inconsequential dissimilarity. In different ways the style had an effect on French composers from Debussy and Ravel to Poulenc and Sauguet, as later on Cage.

Dramatic music Le piège de Méduse (1913)
Ballets Parade (1917); La belle excentrique (*c*1920); Mercure (1924); Relâche (1924); Jack-in-the-box (1926)
Choral music Messe des pauvres (1895); Socrate (1918)
Piano music 3 sarabandes (1887); 3 gymnopédies (1888); 3 gnossiennes (1890); Vexations (*c*1893); Pièces froides (1897); Nouvelles pièces froides (1910); Embryons desséchés (1913); Croquis et agaceries d'un gros bonhomme en bois (1913); Vieux sequins et vieilles cuirasses (1913); Sports et divertissements (1914); Avant-dernières pensées (1915); Sonatine bureaucratique (1917)
Piano duets 3 morceaux en forme de poire (1903); En habit de cheval (1911); Aperçus désagréables (1912)
Songs 3 mélodies (1887); Salut drapeau! (1891); 3 poèmes d'amour (1914); café-concert songs, incl. Tendrement, Je te veux, La diva de l'empire

Satz (Ger.). A word with several meanings in music: the commonest is a movement, but it may also signify a theme (*Hauptsatz* means 'head theme', 'main theme'), a section or group of themes, or a 'setting' (the way of composing a piece, or its structure or style).

Sauguet, Henri(-Pierre) (*b* Bordeaux, 18 May 1901). French composer. A pupil of Canteloube in Bordeaux, he moved in 1923 to Paris, where he joined the circle round Satie and developed a style of equable detachment and charm. His large output includes an opera on *La chartreuse de Parme* (1936), a Dyagilev ballet (*La chatte*, 1927), four symphonies (1945, 1949, 1955, 1971), concertos, chamber and choral music and numerous songs. Although he experimented with *musique concrète* and expanded tonality, he remained opposed to particular systems and his music has evolved little: he develops tonal or modal ideas in smooth curves, producing an art of clarity, simplicity and restraint.

Saul and David [Saul og David]. Opera in four acts by Nielsen to a libretto by E. Christiansen (1902, Copenhagen).

Saùng-gauk. Horizontal arched harp of Burma. There are two types: one, from Lower Burma, has five to seven strings tuned by pegs; the other, long associated with Buddhist royal dynasties and dating back at least to the 7th century, is the highly decorated *saùng-gauk* tuned by cords encircling the arm or arch. They were used in medieval ceremonial ensembles; a virtuoso style of playing developed in the late 18th century and is still maintained. The instrument is placed horizontally across the lap, the arch forward and to the harpist's left; there are usually 16 strings.

Sauret, Emile (*b* Dun-le-Roi, 22 May 1852; *d* London, 12 Feb 1920). French violinist and composer. An international virtuoso and a fine representative of the Franco-Belgian school of violin playing, he was particularly well received in the USA, Scandinavia, Berlin and London, where he was professor at the RAM and at Trinity College of Music. His compositions include two Rhapsodies for violin and orchestra and a Concerto in D minor; he also wrote a valuable method.

Sautillé (Fr.). A bowstroke played rapidly in the middle of the bow, one bowstroke per note, so that the bow bounces very slightly off the string of its own accord. *See* SPICCATO.

Savage, William (*b* ?London, 1720; *d* there, 27 July 1789). English composer, organist and singer. He was a pupil of Pepusch and Geminiani and a friend of Handel, in whose operas he sang as a boy from 1735. Later he sang as a bass in the Chapel Royal and at St Paul's, where he became Master of the Choristers (1747–8). He wrote mainly church music, including 40 anthems. His daughter Jane (*fl c*1780–90), a virtuoso keyboard player, was also a composer.

Savart. Term used for the logarithmic (base 10) measurement of intervals, named after the French scientist Félix Savart (1791–1841). There are 301.03 savarts to the octave.

Savioni, Mario (*b* Rome, 1608; *d* there, 22 April 1685). Italian composer. He joined the papal choir in 1642 and was its director, 1659–68; he also won a reputation as a teacher. He was one of the more important Italian cantata composers. His numerous cantatas range from single arias to large works with several arias and recitatives. He also wrote solo motets and madrigals.

Sāvitri. Chamber opera in one act by Holst to his own libretto from the *Mahābharata* (1916, London).

Savonlinna Festival (Finland). Opera festival founded in 1907 by the soprano Aino Ackté and reconstituted in its present form in 1967; performances are given by members of the Finnish State Opera and take place in Olavinlinna Castle. Festival commissions include Sallinen's *The Horseman* (1974) and *The King goes forth to France* (1984).

Savoy operas. Name given to the operettas of Gilbert and Sullivan: from *Iolanthe* (1882) onwards they were produced at the Savoy Theatre, London, built for them.

Savoy Theatre. London theatre built by Richard D'Oyly Carte as the home for Gilbert and Sullivan operettas; it opened in 1881 with a revival of *Patience* and was rebuilt in 1930 (cap. 1122).

Saw, Musical. A novelty instrument of mid-19th-century origin which gained popularity on the music-hall and vaudeville stages. A long hand-saw is bent into an S-shape on the player's knee; it is bowed with the right hand while the left changes the pitch. The vibrato, usually lavish, is caused by a quivering of the leg.

Sawallisch, Wolfgang (*b* Munich, 26 Aug 1923). German conductor and pianist. His career began at Augsburg and he was music director at Aachen, 1953–8. In 1957 he conducted *Tristan und Isolde* at Bayreuth and made his London début. He was principal conductor from 1961 of the Vienna SO, with which he made his American début in 1964. From 1971 to 1986 he was music director of the Bavarian Staatsoper, Munich. He has been a sympathetic accompanist in song recitals by many singers including Schwarzkopf and Fischer-Dieskau.

Sax, Adolphe [Antoine-Joseph] (*b* Dinant, 6 Nov 1814; *d* Paris, 4 Feb 1894). Belgian wind instrument maker. Son of a skilled wind instrument maker, Charles-Joseph Sax (1791–1865), and himself a player, he made flutes and clarinets from the early 1830s, moving to Paris in 1842 to set up his own workshop (with Berlioz's help). His range was extraordinarily wide, encompassing improvements and inventions, notably the families of saxhorns (1843) and saxotrombas (1845), the saxophones (1846), an adjustable rotary valve for the clairon (1849), a bassoon on 'rational' lines (1840, 1851), an improved trombone (1852) and an original system of six independent valves for brass instruments (1852). Only the SAXHORN and SAXOPHONE are still used, appreciated from the first by civil and military musicians; Sax taught the saxophone at the Paris Conservatoire (1858–71). Despite the virtual monopoly he enjoyed in French military music from 1845, attacks from rival Paris makers and many damaging lawsuits, perhaps exacerbated by his quarrelsome temperament, troubled his later years.

Saxhorn. A family of brass instruments with a fairly wide, tapered bore, using a cup mouthpiece and played with valves. They were evolved by the Belgian maker Adolphe Sax in Paris in the period

1842–5. There are many varieties, from a sopranino in E♭ to a B♭ contrabass, and although the larger members have a wider bore there is a strong homogeneity in the group's appearance. The tubing is usually folded in the manner of a large trumpet set on end and the mouthpiece projects at a right angle. The most distinctive members are the alto and tenor saxhorns (in E♭ and B♭ respectively) which appear in British and American brass bands as the tenor and baritone horns. The lower instruments, the bass in E♭ and the contrabass in B♭, are rather narrower in bore than the equivalent tubas. At the other end of the range, the sopranino saxhorn in E♭ and the soprano in B♭ are similar in basic design to the cornets in those keys, though most of Sax's instruments were built to be played upright rather than in the manner of a trumpet. It is understandable that Sax's claims to have produced an entirely new and therefore patentable instrument were hotly contested in his day.

Saxophone. A family of orchestral and military band instruments invented by Adolphe Sax, c1840. They are played with a single beating reed, like a clarinet, but are conical in bore like an oboe. The body, which is of metal, commonly brass, expands at the open end into a small flare. There are 18–21 holes along its length, all controlled by keys which, in the original design, were arranged according to a fingering system that combined simple oboe fingering with the Boehm system. The larger instruments contain a U-bend and, from the baritone downwards, a double folding at the upper end of the instrument. The family members (and their compasses) are: sopranino (or 'soprano') in E♭ (d♭'–a♭'''), soprano in B♭ (a♭–e'''), alto in E♭ (d♭–b♭''), tenor in B♭ (A♭–f''), baritone in E♭ (C–b♭'), bass in B♭ (A♭'–e♭') and contrabass in E♭ (D♭'–b♭). (These are the original 'military' group; an orchestral group a whole tone higher, alternately in F and C, was also built.) A sub-contrabass in B♭ has also been constructed though it falls outside Sax's original conception. The saxophone was rapidly assimilated into military bands where it formed, as its originator intended, a good tonal link between the clarinets and the tenor brasses, but it was soon taken up by French orchestral composers, notably Bizet, Meyerbeer and Massenet. Strauss asked for a quartet for his *Sinfonia domestica* and thanks to its use by, among others, Ravel, Debussy and Prokofiev, the saxophone has become an increasingly familiar colour in orchestral and chamber music. Sousa's wind bands introduced the instrument to the USA in the 1890s, and its power and expressive range, coupled with a technique comparatively easy to master, made it one of the instruments of the earliest days of jazz and blues. In the 1930s jazz bands normally included a four-piece saxophone section; though capable of cloying sweetness they could also play, as in Ellington's arrangements, with great refinement. The alto and tenor have been the most important saxophones used in jazz, though the soprano and baritone have also been heard. The instrument long retained an important place in popular music, as a soloist in jazz and as an essential

member of every dance band, but its role diminished sharply with the rock era.

Saxton, Robert (*b* London, 8 Oct 1953). English composer. He studied with Lutyens, then with Holloway at Cambridge; Berio has also been an influence. He is best known for his orchestral music, which includes *Ring of Eternity* (1983), *Circles of Light* (1985) and a Viola Concerto (1986).

Saygun, Ahmet Adnan (*b* Izmir, 7 Sept 1907). Turkish composer. He was a pupil of Borrel and d'Indy in Paris (1928–31); thereafter he worked in Turkey as a teacher (at the Ankara State Conservatory from 1946), folk-music scholar and composer. The work that brought him fame was the oratorio *Yunus Emre* (1946) and his opera *Köroğlu* (1973) is often heard. He also wrote symphonies and string quartets.

Sayve, Lambert de (*b*? nr. Liège, 1548–9; *d* Linz, 16–28 Feb 1614). Flemish composer. He was in Habsburg service all his life, as a choirboy and pupil of Monte in Vienna (from 1562), later at Melk, Graz and Vienna again; he became Hofkapellmeister in 1612. His collected motets (1612) range widely and include Venetian-influenced polychoral works; others are in anthologies and MSS. He also published Italian secular works (1582) and lieder (1602). His brother Mathias (*c*1545–?1619) and nephews Erasme (*c*1563–*c*1631) and Arnold (*c*1574–1618) also served the Habsburgs.

Scacchi, Marco (*b* Gallese, *c*1600; *d* there, 1681–7). Italian composer and writer on music. A disciple of G.F. Anerio, he served at the Polish court in Warsaw from 1626 and was choirmaster, 1628–49. He was a versatile composer, writing *stile antico* masses, madrigals with continuo, sacred concertos and operas (now lost). He believed that each genre demanded a distinct style and his classification of styles influenced later writers. In *Cribrum musicum* (1643) he accused the conservative composer Paul Siefert of incorrect technique; the resulting dispute continued for several years.

Scala, La [Teatro alla Scala]. Theatre in Milan, on the site of the church of S Maria della Scala; it opened in 1778 (destroyed 1943; reopened 1948, cap. 3000). It has always been the main centre for Italian opera and a leading international opera house. A. Sanquirico's sets (1817–32) had a long-lasting influence on stage design. Several Verdi operas, including his first four and his last two, had their first performances there. Its company has given many premières and since the 1920s has toured abroad. Its orchestra gives concert seasons in Milan.

Scala di seta, La. *See* SILKEN LADDER, THE.

Scale. A sequence of notes in ascending or descending order of pitch. It is long enough to define unambiguously a mode or tonality and begins or ends on the fundamental note of that mode or tonality. A scale is DIATONIC if the sequence of notes is based on an octave species consisting of five tones and two semitones; the MAJOR and natural MINOR scales are diatonic, as are the church modes (*see* MODE). A CHROMATIC scale is based on an octave of 12 semitones. The WHOLE-TONE SCALE proceeds entirely by whole tones. A PENTATONIC scale has five pitches within the octave.

Scaletta, Orazio (*b* Crema, *c*1550; *d* Padua, 1630). Italian composer. He was *maestro di cappella* at Lodi (1590), Crema (1601–9), Salò (1609–11), Bergamo (1615–20) and possibly Padua. His *Scala di musica* (1585) is a straightforward, practical didactic manual; madrigals (6 bks, 1585–1604) and sacred works by him (3 bks, 1610–15) also survive.

Scaling. In organ pipes, the relationship between the width of a pipe and its length. Narrow-scaled pipes produce a sound richer in overtones and more penetrating than that of wide-scaled ones. In string keyboard instruments, the term refers to the sounding length of the strings in relation to their intended pitch. Given constant tension and diameter, a string sounding an octave below another will be twice its length; for practicality the scaling is normally shortened in the bass.

Scandello, Antonio (*b* Bergamo, 17 Jan 1517; *d* Dresden, 18 Jan 1580). Italian composer. He worked in Trent and in 1549 entered the service of the Elector of Saxony at Dresden. He became a Protestant and in 1568 was appointed Kapellmeister. He made several journeys to Italy, and with the chapel went to other German cities. His reputation as a cornettist and sackbut player led musicians to travel great distances for tuition and his chapel was second only to Lassus's in Munich. His masses and motets use parody and *cantus firmus* techniques. His *St John Passion* (1561), influenced by the Lutheran-inspired tradition of Dresden, combines chorale and motet styles in Germany for the first time. He also composed many German and Italian secular songs, some synthesizing madrigal and villanella styles with German *cantus firmus* technique.

Scaramouche. Suite for two pianos by Milhaud (1937) based on music for a production at the Théâtre Scaramouche, Paris.

Ballet in three scenes by Sibelius (1922, Copenhagen).

Scarlatti, Alessandro (Gaspare) (*b* Palermo, 2 May 1660; *d* Naples, 22 Oct 1725). Italian composer. When he was 12 he was sent to Rome, where he may have studied with Carissimi. He married in 1678 and later that year was appointed *maestro di cappella* of S Giacomo degli Incurabili (now 'in Augusta'). By then he had already composed at least one opera (the title is unknown and it was not performed) and a second, *Gli equivoci nel sembiante*, was a resounding success in 1679. It confirmed Scarlatti in his chosen career as an opera composer and attracted the attention of Queen Christina of Sweden, who made him her *maestro di cappella*.

In 1684 Scarlatti was appointed *maestro di cappella* at the vice-regal court of Naples, at the same time as his brother Francesco was made first violinist. It was alleged that they owed their appointments to the intrigues of one of their sisters (apparently Melchiorra) with two court officials, who were dismissed. For the next two decades over half the new operas given at Naples were by Scarlatti. Two of them, *Il Pirro e Demetrio* (1694) and *La caduta dei Decemviri* (1697), were especially successful, but by 1700 the War of the Spanish Succession was beginning to undermine the privileged status of the Neapolitan nobility, rendering Scarlatti's position insecure. In 1702 he left with his family for Florence, where he hoped to find employment for himself and his son Domenico with Prince Ferdinando de' Medici.

When these hopes failed, Scarlatti accepted the inferior position in Rome of assistant music director at S Maria Maggiore. With a papal ban on public opera, he found an outlet for his talents in oratorio and in writing cantatas for his Roman patrons, notably Prince Ruspoli and the cardinals Ottoboni and Pamphili. In 1706 he was elected to the Arcadian Academy, with Pasquini and Corelli. The following year he attempted to conquer Venice, the citadel of Italian opera, with *Mitridate Eupatore* and *Il trionfo della libertà*, but they both failed and Scarlatti was forced to return to Rome, where he was promoted to the senior post at S Maria Maggiore.

Scarlatti found little satisfaction in the life of a church musician, and towards the end of 1708 he accepted an invitation from the new Austrian viceroy to resume his position at Naples. He remained there for the rest of his life, but maintained close contacts with his Roman patrons and made several visits there, some of them of long duration. It was probably in 1715 that he received a patent of nobility from Pope Clement XI. His final opera, *La Griselda*, was written for Rome in 1721, and he seems to have spent his last years in Naples in semi-retirement. Quantz visited him in 1724 and Hasse was his pupil for a time.

Scarlatti's reputation as the founder of the Neapolitan school of 18th-century opera has been exaggerated. He was not influential or even very active as a teacher, nor was he the sole originator of the musical structures (*da capo* aria, Italian overture, accompanied recitative) with which his name is associated, though he did bring to these a level of skill and originality which surpassed those of his contemporaries. Some of his best music is in the chamber cantatas, too few of which are known today.

Alessandro's sisters, Anna Maria (1661–1703) and Melchiorra Brigida (1663–1736), were both singers who worked in Rome and Naples; their relations with church authorities may have assisted Alessandro in his career. His brother Francesco (1666–*c*1745) was a court violinist in Naples and had works performed there and in Rome. His brother Tommaso (*c*1670–1760) was a tenor who sang in Naples. Alessandro's son Pietro Filippo (1679–1750) was *maestro di cappella* at Urbino and later organist at the Naples royal chapel; his works include an opera and cantatas. For his son Domenico, see below.

Operas Gli equivoci nel sembiante (1679); La Statira (1690); Il Pirro e Demetrio (1694); *La caduta dei Decemviri* (1697); L'Eraclea (1700); Il Mitridate Eupatore (1707); Il Tigrane (1715); Telemaco (1718); Il trionfo dell'onore (1718); Marco Attilio Regolo (1719); La Griselda (1721); over 30 others; contributions to other composers' operas

Secular vocal music over 700 cantatas; *c*33 serenatas; 8 madrigals

Sacred vocal music at least 35 oratorios (some lost); St John Passion; 10 masses; responsories for Holy Week; Lamentations for Holy Week; Stabat mater; 2 Magnificats; Te Deum; over 70 motets

Instrumental music 12 sinfonie di concerto grosso (1715); 4

sonatas, str; 7 sonatas, fl, str, bc (1725); kbd toccatas, variations

Scarlatti, (Giuseppe) Domenico (*b* Naples, 26 Oct 1685; *d* Madrid, 23 July 1757). Italian composer and keyboard player, son of Alessandro Scarlatti. In 1701 he was appointed organist and composer of the vice-regal court at Naples, where his father was *maestro di cappella*. The following year he took leave of absence and travelled with the family to Florence where Alessandro hoped for employment from Prince Ferdinando de' Medici. When this was not forthcoming Domenico returned to Naples, where he tried his hand at opera before his father removed him in 1705 and sent him to Venice to try his luck there. It may have been in Venice that he first met Handel, with whom he formed a strong attachment. (Another friendship made in Italy was with Thomas Roseingrave, who later championed Scarlatti's music in England and Ireland.) By 1707, however, Scarlatti was in Rome, assisting his father at S Maria Maggiore, and he remained in Rome for over 12 years, occupying posts as *maestro* to the dowager Queen of Poland from 1711, to the Marquis de Fontes from 1714, and at St Peter's (assistant *maestro* of the Cappella Giulia from November 1713, *maestro* from December 1714). He thus provided music for both sacred and secular employers, but he was unable to free himself from a domineering father until he obtained legal independence in January 1717.

In 1719 Scarlatti resigned his positions in Rome and apparently spent some years in Palermo before taking up his next post, as *mestre* of the Portuguese court in Lisbon. The Lisbon earthquake of 1755 destroyed documents about his career there, but his duties included giving keyboard lessons to John V's daughter, Maria Barbara, and his younger brother, Don Antonio. When Maria Barbara married the Spanish crown prince in 1729 Scarlatti followed her to Seville and then, in 1733, to Madrid, where he spent the rest of his life. Although he continued to write vocal music, sacred and secular, the main works of his Iberian years are the remarkable series of keyboard sonatas, copied out in his last years and taken to Italy by his colleague, the castrato Farinelli.

Scarlatti married twice: in 1728 a Roman, Maria Catarina Gentili, and in 1739 a Spaniard, Anastasia Maxarti Ximenes. None of his nine children became a musician. In 1738 he was honoured with a knighthood from King John V of Portugal, to which he responded by dedicating to the king a volume of *Essercizi per gravicembalo*, the only music published during his lifetime under his supervision.

The seven operas Scarlatti wrote in Rome for Queen Maria Casimira were by no means failures, and his church music and secular cantatas contain much admirable music. But his fame rightly rests on the hundreds of keyboard sonatas, nearly all in the same binary form, in which he gave free rein to his imagination, stimulated by the new sounds, sights and customs of Iberia and by the astonishing gifts of his royal pupil and patron. In these he explored new worlds of virtuoso technique, putting to new musical ends such devices as hand-crossing, rapidly repeated notes, wide leaps in both hands and countless other means of achieving a devastating brilliance of effect.

Instrumental music over 550 kbd sonatas, incl. 30 in Essercizi per gravicembalo (1738); 17 sinfonias, fl, ob, str, bc
Secular vocal music 12 operas, incl. *La Dirindina* (1715); 2 oratorios; serenatas; *c*70 cantatas (some doubtful)
Sacred vocal music 3 masses; Stabat mater; Te Deum; 2 Salve regina; 2 Miserere; motets

Scarlatti, Giuseppe (*b* Naples, *c*1718 or 18 June 1723; *d* Vienna, 17 Aug 1777). Italian composer, believed to be either a nephew or (if he was a son of Tommaso, Alessandro's youngest brother) a cousin of Domenico. He probably lived in Rome from 1739, then in Florence and by 1744 Lucca. He and his wife Barbara, a singer, were in Vienna in 1748, but were soon back in Italy (two of his operas were heard in Venice in 1752), then briefly in Spain and Naples, but thereafter mainly in Venice and Vienna where he was a ballet composer for the Kärntnertortheater. Further travels may have taken him to Italy and Spain in the mid-1760s, but later he worked for the Schwarzenberg family in Vienna. He composed more than 30 operas, which were performed in many Italian cities and in Vienna; he was noted for his natural melodic gift, his ingenious handling of *opera buffa* aria form and his generally charming if simple style.

Scat singing. A technique of jazz singing in which onomatopoeic or nonsense syllables are sung to improvised melodies.

Scelsi, Giacinto (*b* La Spezia, 8 Jan 1905). Italian composer. Of aristocratic birth, he had no formal training and ranged over many styles in his earlier works while remaining constant to an ideal of music as a link with the transcendental. That has remained his conviction in works since the 1950s, in which he has often used microtones, thin textures and extremely slow movement.

Scena. A term used in opera to mean either the stage, or the scene represented on the stage, or a division of an act. In Italian opera it has also the specific meaning of an episode made up of diverse elements (recitative, arioso, aria, orchestral passages etc) with no set formal construction, and it was also used for a concert setting of a scene from an opera libretto, e.g. Mozart's *Misera, dove son* K369.

Scenes from Childhood. *See* KINDERSZENEN.

Scenes from Goethe's Faust. *See* FAUST, SCENES FROM GOETHE'S.

Schack, Benedikt (Emanuel) (*b* Mirotice, 7 Feb 1758; *d* Munich, 10 Dec 1826). Austrian tenor and composer. A member of Schikaneder's theatre company, he was its principal tenor when it settled in Vienna in 1789, and Mozart (a close friend) wrote the part of Tamino in *Die Zauberflöte* (1791) for him. He also played the flute. Later he worked in Graz and Munich. His *c*25 stage works (1784–95) include a series of 'Anton' Singspiels for Vienna (most composed with F.X. Gerl).

Schaefer, Theodor (*b* Telč, 23 Jan 1904; *d* Brno, 19 March 1969). Czech composer. A pupil of Kvapil at the Brno Conservatory (1922–6) and Novák in Prague (1926–9), he was a leading figure in Brno as a teacher (at the academy), conductor and composer. He extended Novák's harmony towards modality and later serialism. His small output covers many genres, his Symphony (1962) being his principal work.

Schaeffer, Pierre (*b* Nancy, 14 Aug 1910). French composer. Trained as a technician, he worked for French radio from 1936 and in 1948 created the first works of *musique concrète* by manipulating and re-recording sounds from gramophone records. Most of his later pieces were made in collaboration, and in 1960 he abandoned composition, though he continued to teach at the Paris Conservatoire and to publish treatises on aesthetics, novels and essays.

Schafer, R(aymond) Murray (*b* Sarnia, 18 July 1933). Canadian composer. He was a pupil of Weinzweig at the Toronto Conservatory and a teacher at Simon Fraser University, British Columbia (from 1965). His output is large and diverse, using mixed media, electronics and quotations and he has a predilection for texts in dead languages. He has also written much against noise pollution and in favour of creative music education in schools.

Schäffer, Bogusław (*b* Lwów, 6 June 1929). Polish composer. He was a pupil of Malawski at the Kraków Conservatory, where he began teaching in 1963. He is an unusual figure in Polish music: his enormous output covers many genres and diverse musical styles and he is involved in numerous activities as a theorist and teacher. He has also published studies of new music. In his *TIS MW2* (1963), his first work of instrumental theatre, there are allusions to the past and 'absurd' confrontations of music, poetry, dance and visual arts.

Schaffrath, Christoph (*b* Hohenstein, 1709; *d* Berlin, 17 Feb 1763). German composer. He served Crown Prince Frederick (later Frederick the Great) from 1733–4, and was harpsichordist to the Berlin court Kapelle after his accession (1740); he may have left this post on becoming musician to Princess Amalia in 1741. He composed much instrumental music (especially keyboard sonatas, concertos and chamber works) in a *galant* style.

Schalk, Franz (*b* Vienna, 27 May 1863; *d* Edlach, 3 Sept 1931). Austrian conductor. He studied under Bruckner at the Vienna Conservatory and conducted at the Vienna Opera from 1900 under Mahler, becoming joint director with Strauss in 1918 and sole director, 1924–9. He appeared at the Met and Covent Garden from 1898. He and his brother Josef (1857–1900) were early champions of Bruckner's symphonies, but presented them in would-be improved versions, with cuts and other emendations.

Schall, Claus Nielsen (*b* Copenhagen, 28 April 1757; *d* there, 9 Aug 1835). Danish composer and dancer. He became ballet director at the Royal Theatre, Copenhagen, in 1776, and composer in 1795. Also a violinist, he was Konzertmeister at the Opera from 1792 and music director, 1818–34. Much influenced by Gluck and Mozart, he wrote ballet music as well as Singspiels, songs, instrumental pieces and pedagogical works.

Schalmei (Ger.). SHAWM; *see also* TRISTAN SCHALMEI.

The term was also used for a reed stop on the organ, *c*1550–*c*1750.

Scharwenka, (Franz) Xaver (*b* Szamotuły, 6 Jan 1850; *d* Berlin, 8 Dec 1924). Polish-German pianist, composer and educationist. He studied with Kullak in Berlin. A touring artist from 1874, he became increasingly active as a concert organizer and teacher in Berlin, founding his own conservatory in 1881 (the Klindworth-Scharwenka, with a New York branch in 1891). He was renowned as a Chopin interpreter. Among his best compositions are the Polish Dance op.3 no.1 and the Piano Concerto in Ab minor (1877). His brother Philipp (1847–1917) was a composer and teacher at the Scharwenka Conservatory.

Schat, Peter (*b* Utrecht, 5 June 1935). Dutch composer. He was a pupil of Van Baaren at the Utrecht Conservatory (1952–8), of Seiber in London and of Boulez in Basle (1960–62). In the 1960s he became a prominent modernist, requiring instrumentalists to move while playing (*Improvisations and Symphonies* for wind quintet, 1960), and referring to music of the past (*Clockwise and Anticlockwise* for 16 wind, 1967). In 1967 he visited Cuba and gained a political awareness that affected most of his later music, though the influence of American minimalism has also been important: later works include the opera *Houdini* (1976).

Schauspieldirektor, Der. *See* IMPRESARIO, THE.

Schede, Paul Melissus (*b* Mellrichstadt, 20 Dec 1539; *d* Heidelberg, 3 Feb 1602). German composer. A Kantor at Jönigsberg, Franconia, he was crowned poet in Vienna (1561) and ennobled (1564). He became a Calvinist in Geneva and travelled widely, visiting England in 1585–6. His psalms for the Reformed Church (1572), motets (1566) and other sacred works set his own verses, scrupulously following their metrical structure.

Scheibe, Johann Adolph (*b* Leipzig, 5 May 1708; *d* Copenhagen, 22 April 1776). German composer and theorist. He was the son of Johann Scheibe (*c*1680–1748), a well-known organ builder. Largely self-taught as a musician and scholar, he began his career in Hamburg. In 1740–47 he was Kapellmeister to the Danish court; he stayed in Denmark, returning to the court as a composer after 1766.

Scheibe was a major music theorist of the Enlightenment and an influential critic. In his main work, the periodical *Der critische Musikus* (1737–40), he advocated a simple and natural German national style and in 1737 made a controversial attack on Bach's music. He composed many cantatas, oratorios, church works, songs and instrumental pieces including sinfonias and concertos; most are now lost.

Scheibler, Johann Heinrich (*b* Monschau, 11 Nov 1777; *d* Krefeld, 20 Nov 1837). German theorist. Apart from his experiments in tuning and equal temperament, he is remembered for proposing the pitch $a' = 440$ as a standard at Stuttgart (1834).

Scheidemann, Heinrich (*b* Wöhrden, *c*1595; *d* Hamburg, early 1663). German composer. He studied with Sweelinck in Amsterdam, 1611–14, and in 1629 took up his father's former post as organist of the Catharinenkirche, Hamburg. He was highly esteemed as organist, organ expert, composer and teacher; his pupil J.A. Reincken became his assistant and later succeeded him.

A founder of the north German organ school, Scheidemann concentrated almost exclusively on organ music, where he extended Sweelinck's keyboard style into a specifically organ idiom. At least 50 of his organ works survive (he also left harpsichord pieces and sacred songs). His chorale and Magnificat settings were influential for their use of new forms (notably the chorale fantasia) as well as Sweelinck's techniques, while his praeambula approach the structure of the prelude and fugue.

Scheidemantel, Karl (*b* Weimar, 21 Jan 1859; *d* there, 26 June 1923). German baritone. He was acclaimed in Wagner, notably as Wolfram, Hans Sachs, Kurwenal, Klingsor and Amfortas, and created two Richard Strauss roles, Kunrad in *Feuersnot* (1901) and Faninal in *Der Rosenkavalier* (1911).

Scheidt, Samuel (*b* Halle, bap. 3 Nov 1587; *d* there, 24 March 1654). German composer and organist. He was organist of the Moritzkirche, Halle, for several years, and studied with Sweelinck in Amsterdam before becoming Halle court organist in 1609. From 1619–20 he was also court Kapellmeister, but the musical establishment almost disbanded (because of the Thirty Years War) in 1625. In 1627–30 he was director of music in Halle, also composing for the Marktkirche. His duties as court Kapellmeister resumed in 1638. Scheidt was active as an organ expert and a teacher (notably of Adam Krieger), and knew both Schütz and Schein.

Scheidt distinguished himself in both keyboard and sacred vocal music, in which he combined traditional counterpoint with the new Italian concerto style. Contrapuntal chorale settings are important among his *c*150 keyboard pieces. Some appear in his three-volume *Tabulatura nova* (1624), the first German publication of keyboard music to be in open score rather than in German organ tablature or in two-staff format; the collection also contains variations and liturgical pieces. Scheidt left some 160 sacred vocal works. His first book, *Cantiones sacrae* (1620), consists of polychoral motets, some of them based on chorales, and his second (1620) of large concertos with obbligato instrumental parts. Small concertos for few voices make up the four volumes of *Geistliche Concerte* (1631–40). Scheidt also composed dances, canzonas, sinfonias etc and canons.

His brother Gottfried (1593–1661) was organist at Altenburg and composer of sacred music.

Schein, Johann Hermann (*b* Grünhain, 20 Jan 1586; *d* Leipzig, 19 Nov 1630). German composer and poet. Trained as a soprano in the Dresden court chapel, he studied at Schulpforta and Leipzig and later worked as music director and tutor to the children of Gottfried von Wolffersdorff, 1613–15. After a year as Kapellmeister at the Weimar court, he became Kantor of St Thomas's, Leipzig – a post later held by Bach – in 1616. His pupils included Heinrich Albert; he knew both Schütz, a close friend, and Scheidt.

Primarily a composer for the voice, Schein was significant as one of the first composers to graft the modern Italian style on to the traditional elements of Lutheran church music. Much of his large sacred vocal output (nearly 400 works) is in five published volumes. The first part of *Opella nova* (1618) contains sacred concertos with continuo, clearly influenced by Viadana's but based (in most cases) on chorale melodies; the second part (1626), which uses fewer chorales, includes obbligato instrumental parts. His other sacred publications are a motet collection (1615), a book of sacred madrigals (1623) and the *Cantional* (1627), a hymnbook. Schein left some 90 secular vocal pieces, all of them to his own texts. Especially Italianate are the three-part settings in *Musica boscareccia* (1621–8) and his German continuo madrigals (1624–the first such works to be published). He also composed songs and many occasional works. His main instrumental work is the *Banchetto musicale* (1617), containing 20 variation suites.

Scheitholt (Ger.). A strummed ZITHER of Germany and the Alpine areas.

Schelle, Johann (*b* Geising, bap. 6 Sept 1648; *d* Leipzig, 10 March 1701). German composer. After serving as Kantor at Eilenburg, near Leipzig, he became Kantor of the Leipzig Thomaskirche in 1677. Composing sacred music to German texts almost exclusively, he was important for establishing the Gospel cantata as an independent form and for consolidating the various types of chorale cantata in use. Of his *c*50 surviving works, the 26-part setting *Lobe den Herrn* is one of the most elaborate.

Schenck [Schenk], Johannes (*b* Amsterdam, bap. 3 June 1660; *d c*1712). German–Dutch composer and viola da gamba player. The leading viol virtuoso in northern Europe, he served at the Düsseldorf court; the style of his music for viola da gamba shows the influence of English players. He published some seven books of sonatas or suites and three of vocal music.

Schenk, Johann Baptist (*b* Wiener Neustadt, 30 Nov 1753; *d* Vienna, 29 Dec 1836). Austrian composer. He studied with Wagenseil in Vienna and began composing for the theatre in 1780. Between 1785 and 1802 he had some 12 Singspiels and other stage works given in Vienna, and was Kapellmeister to Prince Auersperg for a time. His masterpiece, *Der Dorfbarbier* (1796), enjoyed international success into the 19th century; it exemplifies Viennese Singspiel at its best, with charming melodies, a variety of solos, duets and larger ensembles, and a well-constructed, witty yet affecting libretto. Among his other works are cantatas, sacred works, canons, symphonies, concertos and chamber music. Beethoven was one of his counterpoint and composition pupils in 1793.

Schenker, Heinrich (*b* Wisniowczyki, 19 June 1868; *d* Vienna, 13 Jan 1935). Austrian theorist. He studied under Bruckner in Vienna and became a lied accompanist, chamber music performer, critic, editor and private teacher. His interest in masterpieces and in the creative processes of great composers motivated his theoretical and editorial work.

Among his most significant editions are those of Beethoven's last five sonatas (1913–21). His first theoretical work was *Harmonielehre* (1906); it culminated in *Der freie Satz* (1935). He also issued two periodicals. Schenker's theory of tonal music can be described in terms of *Urlinie* (fundamental melodic line), the *Ursatz* (fundamental composition) and – the most general concept – *Schichten* (structural layers: background, middleground and foreground). The *Urlinie* spans, in effect, the upper voice of an entire composition and is coordinated with large-scale structural *Bassbrechung* ('bass arpeggiation'), ascending from tonic to dominant and returning to tonic; the resulting contrapuntal structure is the *Ursatz*. Thus harmony and counterpoint are combined at the deepest level of structure where the *Ursatz* represents the large-scale *Auskomponierung* ('composing out') of the fundamental harmony, the tonic triad. The concept of structural levels provides for a hierarchical differentiation of musical components, which establishes a basis for describing and interpreting relations among the elements of any composition. In Schenker's view the total work at all levels, not only at the background level, is the object of study and aesthetic perception. His theories have been highly influential, especially in the USA.

Scherchen, Hermann (*b* Berlin, 21 June 1891; *d* Florence, 12 June 1966). German conductor. His début was on tour with Schoenberg's *Pierrot lunaire*, in 1912. He was director of the Frankfurt Museumskonzerte from 1922 and the next year began a close involvement with the ISCM. He settled in Switzerland in 1933, conducting the Zurich RO and in 1954 opening a studio for electroacoustical research. He continued to champion contemporary music, giving first performances of works by Dallapiccola, Henze and Schoenberg in the 1950s and promoting experiment.

Scherer. German family of organ builders. Jakob (*d* 1754 or later) was active 1538–70. His son Hans the elder (*d* 1611), the most important member of the family, assisted him from 1541, and his grandson Hans the younger (*fl* c1600–1631) was responsible for the most mature examples of the famous 'Hamburg organ front' (introduced at St Jakobi, Hamburg, in 1576). They successfully combined features of the early Hamburg organ, the Brabant organ and the central German instrument. Examples survive in Tangermünde and Lübeck.

Scherzando (It.). Jokingly, playfully; also *scherzevole*.

Scherzetto, scherzino. A short or very slight piece in the character of a SCHERZO.

Scherzi, Gli. Title sometimes given to Haydn's six string quartets op.33 (1781) because of the *scherzando* (jocular) character of their minuets.

Scherzi musicali. Two sets of madrigalian songs by Monteverdi: 15 for three voices (1607) and ten for one or two voices with continuo (1632).

Scherzo (It.: 'joke'). Term, first used in early 17th-century Italian music, for light madrigals of the balletto type, e.g. Monteverdi's *Scherzi musicali* (1607). The rare examples of 'scherzi' from the period 1650–1750 are all instrumental works. Bach's use of the term for the penultimate movement of his Partita no.3 in A minor may derive from its use in Bonporti's *Invenzioni* (c1713). The scherzo's admission to the canon of movements in regular Classical usage dates from Haydn's quartets op.33 (1781), but it was Beethoven who established the scherzo and trio as a regular alternative to the minuet in sonatas, symphonies and chamber works. As an independent movement the scherzo came vigorously to life in Chopin's four examples for the piano. Brahms's Scherzo op.4 is of a similar kind, with two trios. With models like Stravinsky's *Scherzo fantastique* and *Scherzo à la Russe*, scherzos for orchestra or other instruments have been common in the 20th century.

Schetky, Johann Georg Christoph (*b* Darmstadt, 19 Aug 1737; *d* Edinburgh, 30 Nov 1824). German cellist and composer, father of the Philadelphia cellist and composer J. George Schetky (1776–1831). A pupil of Fils, he served in the Darmstadt court orchestra until 1768, also playing his own works in Hamburg and elsewhere. He went to London in 1772, then to Scotland, becoming principal cellist to the Edinburgh Musical Society. With the Earl of Kelly he was Scotland's foremost serious composer in the 18th century, and his cello sonatas and duets were especially popular. He also wrote other chamber music (notably six string quartets, 1777), keyboard sonatas, songs, orchestral music and two cello methods.

Schiassi, Gaetano Maria (*b* Bologna, 10 March 1698; *d* Lisbon, 1754). Italian composer. He worked as a violinist at a court in Italy and then Darmstadt; he had ten operas and two oratorios given in Italy including a Bolognese dialect comedy. From c1734 he was in Lisbon, where he served in the royal chapel; he wrote an opera and four oratorios for Lisbon as well as virtuoso sonatas and concertos for violin.

Schibler, Armin (*b* Kreuzlingen, 20 Nov 1920; *d* Zurich, 7 Sept 1986). Swiss composer. He studied in Zurich, in England with Rubbra and Tippett (1946) and at Darmstadt (1949–53). As a young man he was one of the best-known string composers. His works include melodramas, music-theatre pieces, choral, vocal, orchestral and chamber music.

Schicht, Johann Gottfried (*b* Reichenau, 29 Sept 1753; *d* Leipzig, 16 Feb 1823). German conductor and composer. He was musical director of the Leipzig Gewandhaus concerts (1785), founder of the Singakademie (1802) and Kantor of the Thomasschule (1810). As a composer he is remembered for his *Allgemeine Choralbuch* (1819).

Schickhardt, Johann Christian (*b* Brunswick, c1682; *d* Leiden, by 26 March 1762). German composer. Trained as a woodwind player and composer, he first served patrons in the Netherlands. By 1712 he was a publisher's agent in Hamburg; later he was active in central Germany and (in the 1720s) probably Scandinavia. By 1745 he was in Leiden. A popular and accomplished composer, he wrote mostly chamber music for recorder and oboe (notably a set of solo sonatas in all the keys, 1735), besides two instrumental tutors.

Schicksalslied. *See* SONG OF DESTINY.

Schieferdecker, Johann Christian (*b* Teuchern, 10 Nov 1679; *d* Lübeck, 5 April 1732). German organist and composer. He was first in Leipzig and Hamburg and had several operas staged, 1700–02. In 1706 he became deputy organist at the Marienkirche, Lübeck, succeeding Buxtehude as organist in 1707. There he wrote sacred music (some for the *Abendmusiken*), concertos and organ pieces.

Schierbeck, Poul (Julius Ouscher) (*b* Copenhagen, 8 June 1888; *d* there, 9 Feb 1949). Danish composer. A pupil of Nielsen and Laub, he was organist at Skovshoved Church (1916–49) and taught at the Copenhagen Conservatory from 1931. He made an important contribution to Danish song. His works also include much choral and organ music, a symphony and piano pieces.

Schiff, András (*b* Budapest, 21 Dec 1953). Hungarian pianist. He studied in Budapest and with George Malcolm in London. His Budapest début in 1972 was followed by tours abroad. He has acquired a reputation not only in the standard Classical and Romantic repertory but in contemporary music and in Bach, where his recordings of the '48' and other works have won praise for their stylistic grasp. He is active as a chamber musician.

Schikaneder, Emanuel (Johann Joseph) (*b* Straubing, 1 Sept 1751; *d* Vienna, 21 Sept 1812). Austrian dramatist, singer and composer. He was initially a dancer and actor, and enjoyed particular success as Hamlet. In 1778–85 he directed a travelling theatre troupe, for which he wrote plays and librettos; the troupe visited Salzburg in 1780. After directing other companies, he settled at the Freihaus-Theater auf der Wieden, Vienna, in 1789; here he produced his own plays and commissioned settings of his opera and Singspiel librettos – notably *Die Zauberflöte* (Mozart, 1791), in which he played Papageno. In 1801–6 he wrote for the Theater an der Wien; he later worked in Brno. He was one of the most talented and influential theatre men of his age; in all he wrote *c*50 librettos (two of which he himself set).

Schikaneder's brother Urban (1746–1818) was in his company for some years, as was Urban's son Karl, who became a dramatist, composer and producer. Urban's daughter Anna (1767–1862) was also a singer.

Schildt, Melchior (*b* Hanover, 1592–3; *d* there, 18 May 1667). German composer. A pupil of Sweelinck, he served at Wolfenbüttel and then at the Danish court (1626–9) before becoming organist at the Marktkirche, Hanover. Except for a masterly chorale concerto, *Ach mein herzliebes Jesulein* (1657), his surviving music is all for keyboard, comprising several chorale settings (notably a *Magnificat I. modi*), variations and praeambula.

Schiller, (Johann Christoph) Friedrich von (*b* Marbach, 10 Nov 1759; *d* Weimar, 9 May 1805). German dramatist, poet, aesthetician and historian. Though he was not a musician, his dramas and poetry had a great impact on composers – notably Beethoven, who set verses from his *Ode to Joy* in his Ninth Symphony. Other works based on Schiller

include Rossini's *Guillaume Tell*, Verdi's *Don Carlos* and songs by Schubert and others.

Schilling, Hans Ludwig (*b* Mayen, 9 March 1927). German composer. A pupil of Genzmer and Hindemith, he has taught in Freiburg since 1954 and developed from the Brahms–Reger tradition to serialism and the use of jazz. His works include orchestral, chamber and choral music.

Schillinger, Joseph (Moiseyevich) (*b* Khar'kov, 31 Aug 1895; *d* New York, 23 March 1943). American theorist of Ukrainian origin. He studied at the Petrograd Conservatory (1914–18) and worked in Russia as a teacher and composer. In 1928 he moved to the USA, where he taught theory according to his own quasi-mathematical system; Gershwin, Dorsey, Benny Goodman and Glenn Miller were among his pupils.

Schillings, Max von (*b* Düren, 19 April 1868; *d* Berlin, 24 July 1933). German composer and conductor. He was a pupil of von Königslow and Brambach in Bonn and associate of Strauss in Munich. In 1892 he took an appointment at Bayreuth, where in 1902 he was appointed choirmaster. His first three operas, *Ingwelde* (1894), *Der Pfeifertag* (1899) and *Moloch* (1906), were Wagnerian; he had more success in the horrific *Mona Lisa* (1915), dating from his period as conductor at the Stuttgart Opera (1908–18). He was then Intendant at the Berlin Opera (1918–25), after which he toured widely as a conductor, also making recordings.

Schindelmeisser, Louis (Alexander Balthasar) (*b* Königsberg, 8 Dec 1811; *d* Darmstadt, 30 March 1864). German conductor and composer. He studied in Berlin and Leipzig. He was an early and enthusiastic partisan of Wagner, arranging for first performances in Wiesbaden and Darmstadt of *Tannhäuser, Rienzi* and *Lohengrin*. His own operas were in the tradition of Weber and Spohr.

Schindler, Anton Felix (*b* Meedl, 13 June 1795; *d* Bockenheim, 16 Jan 1864). Moravian violinist, conductor and writer. A theatre violinist in Vienna and conductor at Aachen, he was Beethoven's tireless secretary and errand boy (1820–24, 1826–7) who, as a self-appointed guardian of the composer's legacy, tampered with documents and wrote a notoriously biased *Biographie* (1840, 2/1845 with supplements).

Schiøtz, Askel (Hauch) (*b* Roskilde, 1 Sept 1906; *d* Copenhagen, 19 April 1975). Danish tenor. He made his concert début in 1938 and sang Ferrando at the Royal Opera, Stockholm, the following year. He sang in England from 1946 and in the USA from 1948. He was a stylish interpreter of Schubert and Schumann songs. He taught in North America until 1968.

Schipa, Tito (*b* Lecce, 2 Jan 1888; *d* New York, 16 Dec 1965). Italian tenor. He sang in Italy from 1910, specializing in lyrical roles. At the Chicago Opera (1919–32) and the Met the natural grace and elegance of his singing was admired in such roles as Don Ottavio, the Duke of Mantua, and Massenet's Des Grieux and Werther. He retired in 1957, after a concert tour of Russia.

Schippers, Thomas (*b* Kalamazoo, MI, 9 March

1930; *d* New York, 16 Dec 1977). American conductor. He studied in Philadelphia and made his début in New York in 1948. He became conductor of Menotti's Spoleto Festival in 1950 and joined New York City Opera in 1951; in 1955 he made his débuts with the New York PO, at the Met and at La Scala. He conducted a new production of *The Mastersingers* at Bayreuth in 1963 and Barber's *Anthony and Cleopatra* at the new Met opening in 1966. He was music director of the Cincinnati SO from 1970.

Schirmer, G. American firm of music publishers. It was established in New York in 1866 by Gustav Schirmer (1829–93). From 1891 it had its own engraving and printing plant (used up to 1984) and a number of affiliated companies, making it one of the largest firms of its type in the USA. Composers in the catalogue have included Victor Herbert, Granados, Ives, Barber, Schuman, Bernstein, Menotti and Carter; it also published *Baker's Biographical Dictionary of Musicians* and *Musical Quarterly*. It became a part of Macmillan in 1968; in 1986 the music-publishing section became a part of Music Sales.

G. Schirmer is distinct from the Boston firm E.C. Schirmer, founded by a member of the same family in 1921.

Schleppend (Ger.). Dragging; more commonly *nicht schleppen* ('do not drag').

Schlesinger. German family of music publishers. A Berlin firm was established in 1810 by A.M. Schlesinger (1769–1838) and carried on by his son Heinrich (1810–79) until 1864, when he sold the firm to Robert Lienau. It was among the most important Prussian firms, becoming Weber's original publishers (1814), issuing Beethoven's opp.108–12, 132 and 135, sponsoring the *Berliner allgemeine musikalische Zeitung* and bringing out the first edition of Bach's *St Matthew Passion*. Works by Berlioz, Liszt and Chopin were later added to the catalogue. A.M. Schlesinger's son Maurice (1798–1871), who was responsible for the contact with Beethoven, founded a firm in Paris, active *c*1821–46, specializing in opera, including first editions of works by Meyerbeer and Donizetti, and piano music, notably by Moscheles, Weber and Hummel as well as Beethoven. Works by Mendelssohn, Liszt, Berlioz (Requiem, *Symphonie fantastique*) and Chopin followed in the late 1820s and early 1830s. His most enduring publication was the weekly *Gazette musicale de Paris* (1834; later *Revue et gazette musicale*).

Schlick, Arnolt (*b* ?Heidelberg, *c*1460; *d* ?there, after 1521). German organist and composer. He travelled widely in Germany and the Low Countries as an organist and organ consultant. His *Spiegel der Orgelmacher und Organisten* (1511) is the first German treatise on organ building and organ playing. Some of his organ pieces were published in his *Tabulaturen etlicher lobgesang* (1512), the first printed German organ tablatures. He was a skilful contrapuntist.

Schlusnus, Heinrich (*b* Braubach, 6 Aug 1988; *d* Frankfurt, 18 June 1952). German baritone. He made his début at Hamburg in 1915 and was leading baritone of Berlin Staatsoper, 1917–45, also touring extensively. His smooth, steady singing made him much admired as a lieder singer.

Schmelzer [Schmeltzer], **Johann Heinrich** (*b* Scheibbs, *c*1620–23; *d* Prague, 29 Feb–20 March 1680). Austrian composer and violinist. He was trained in Vienna and served in the court chapel from the mid-1630s, becoming a member of the orchestra in 1649 and vice-Kapellmeister in 1671. In 1679 he was made Kapellmeister, the first of a series of native Austrians. The leading Austrian composer of instrumental music before Biber, he wrote 150 ballet suites for court dramatic productions and over 100 sonatas. The former each have between two and nine separate dances, sometimes thematically related; some include elements of folk music. Notable among the sonatas are the six *Sonatae unarum fidium* (1664), the earliest published set for solo violin and continuo. Schmelzer's prolific output also includes *sepolcri* and other dramatic pieces, nearly 200 sacred works and some secular vocal music. His son Andreas Anton (1653–1701) was a composer and violinist at the same court.

Schmid, Balthasar (*b* Nuremberg, bap. 20 April 1705; *d* there, bur. 27 Nov 1749). German music printer and composer. Active in Nuremberg, he became one of the best-known and most accurate music engravers in 18th-century Germany, and printed music by Telemann, J.S. and C.P.E. Bach and others as well as his own. He was also an organist. His compositions are mostly keyboard works (some with flute or violin) for amateur players.

Schmidt, Franz (*b* Bratislava, 22 Dec 1874; *d* Perchtoldsdorf, 11 Feb 1939). Austrian composer. A pupil of Bruckner and Fuchs at the Vienna Conservatory, he was cellist in the Vienna Hofoper orchestra (1896–1911, for much of the time under Mahler), then taught at the Staatsakademie (1914–27) and the Musikhochschule (1927–31). In his music he continued the grand tradition, with peripheral influence from Schoenberg, Debussy and Hindemith: his works include four symphonies (1899, 1913, 1928, 1933), by which he made his name, the orchestral *Variationen über ein Husarenlied* (1931), chamber music (two string quartets, a piano quintet and two quintets for clarinet, piano and strings), organ pieces, the oratorio *Das Buch mit sieben Siegeln* (1937) and two operas (*Notre Dame*, 1904; *Fredigundis*, 1921).

Schmidt, Johann Christoph (*b* Hohnstein, 6 Aug 1664; *d* Dresden, 13 April 1728). German composer. A singer and instrumentalist at the Dresden court, he advanced to positions there including Kapellmeister (1698) and Oberkapellmeister (1717). Under him the Dresden orchestra became one of the most famous in Europe. He composed a number of sacred works (masses, cantatas, motets), a French festival divertissement (1719) and orchestral pieces.

Schmidt-Isserstedt, Hans (*b* Berlin, 5 May 1900; *d* Holm-Holstein, 28 May 1973). German conductor. He first worked at the Hamburg Staatsoper and from 1943 at the Deutsche Oper, Berlin. From 1945 to 1971 he conducted the North German Radio SO, and the Stockholm PO, 1955–64. He appeared widely as a guest conductor, valued for his transparent textures and rhythmic precision.

Schmieder, Wolfgang (*b* Bromberg, 29 May 1901). German music bibliographer. He studied at Heidelberg, worked in Dresden, at Breitkopf & Härtel in Leipzig (1933–42) and at Frankfurt. He is best known for his catalogue of Bach, the *Bach-Werke-Verzeichnis*, of which the numbers (BWV) are used to identify Bach's works.

Schmitt, Florent (*b* Blamont, 28 Sept 1870; *d* Neuilly-sur-Seine, 17 Aug 1958). French composer. A pupil of Massenet and Fauré at the Paris Conservatoire, he made his mark with three early works boldly uniting German (Strauss) and French (Debussy, Fauré) traditions: the choral-orchestral Psalm xlvii (1904), the ballet *La tragédie de Salomé* (1907) and the Piano Quintet (1908). His later works, developing little in style, cover most genres except opera. He was director of the Lyons Conservatory (1922–4) and critic.

Schmitt, Joseph (*b* Gernsheim am Rhein, bap. 18 March 1734; *d* Amsterdam, 28 May 1791). German composer and music publisher. A pupil of C.F. Abel, he was a priest and (by 1763) choirmaster at a monastery at Eberbach. By 1774 he was in Amsterdam, where he became eminent as a composer, concert director, publisher and teacher. His compositions include symphonies and chamber music (quartets, trios etc); many show a Mannheim influence, but Viennese features appear in his later works. Several of his works have been wrongly attributed to Haydn.

Schmittbaur, Joseph Aloys (*b* Bamberg, 8 Nov 1718; *d* Karlsruhe, 24 Oct 1809). German composer, conductor and glass harmonica maker. He served first at the Rastatt court (Kapellmeister 1765); after three years as court Konzertmeister at Karlsruhe, he was cathedral Kapellmeister and director of public concerts at Cologne, 1775–7. He then returned to Karlsruhe as Kapellmeister, also making glass harmonicas, enlarging that instrument's compass. His output, pre-Classical in style, covers all the standard genres of his time.

Schnabel, Artur (*b* Lipnik, 17 April 1882; *d* Axenstein, 15 Aug 1951). Austrian pianist and composer, later naturalized American. He studied with Leschetizky. From his début in 1890 he eschewed the usual virtuouso's repertory and concentrated on intellectually more worthy music: he played Schubert with lyrical expression and late Beethoven with intensity and great visionary force. He emigrated to the USA in 1939. Among his compositions are symphonies and string quartets. His son Karl Ulrich (*b* 1909), a pianist, made his début in Berlin in 1926 and moved to the USA in 1939.

Schnebel, Dieter (*b* Lahr, 14 March 1930). German composer, writer and theologian. He studied in Freiburg and taught in Frankfurt and from 1970 in Munich. His works have drawn on Stockhausen, Cage and Kagel in critical extensions of vocal possibility (*Maulwerke*, 1968), concert giving, music for reading (*mo-no*, 1969) etc; he has arranged music by Bach, Beethoven, Webern and Wagner.

Schnéevoigt, Georg (Lennart) (*b* Vyborg, 8 Nov 1872; *d* Malmö, 28 Nov 1947). Finnish conductor. He studied the cello in Helsinki and Germany and played in the Helsinki PO. He made his conducting début in 1901, held posts in Munich and Kiev and founded orchestras in Riga and in Helsinki, where his career thereafter centred, though he also held posts in other Scandinavian cities, Düsseldorf and Los Angeles. He was known for his forceful and intense performances of Romantic music.

Schneider. German family of musicians. The most celebrated members were Friedrich (1786–1853), a conductor and teacher at Dessau who composed prolifically, especially oratorios, cantatas and partsongs, and a pianist (he is believed to have given the première of Beethoven's 'Emperor' Concerto in 1811); and his brother Johann (1789–1864), a leading organist who influenced Schumann and Liszt.

Schneider, (Abraham) Alexander (*b* Vilna, 21 Oct 1908). American violinist and conductor of Russian birth. After study at Frankfurt he worked for German orchestras before joining the Budapest Quartet in 1932; he left in 1944 and rejoined in 1955. He continued to play chamber music and was associated with Casals in festivals at Prades (from 1950), Perpignan and Marlboro. In 1972 he founded and directed the Brandenburg Players and he has appeared as a guest conductor with other American orchestras.

Schneider, Hortense (Catherine-Jeanne) (*b* Bordeaux, 30 April 1833; *d* Paris, 6 May 1920 or 1922). French soprano. One of Offenbach's most successful leading ladies, she was triumphant in *La belle Hélène* (1864), *La Grande-duchesse de Gérolstein* (1867) and *La Périchole* (1868).

Schneiderhan, Wolfgang (Eduard) (*b* Vienna, 28 May 1915). Austrian violinist. After study in Vienna he made his adult solo début in Copenhagen in 1926. He was leader of the Vienna PO from 1937, leaving in 1951 to pursue a solo career. He has been heard largely in the Viennese repertory, giving direct, well balanced performances, often with his wife Irmgard Seefried. He has taught in Salzburg, Vienna and Lucerne.

Schnell (Ger.). Fast.

Schneller (Ger.). A type of MORDENT; it may also mean 'faster'.

Schnitger, Arp (*b* Schmalenfleth, 2 July 1648; *d* 24 July 1719). German organ builder. With his sons Georg (1690–after 1733) and Franz Caspar (1693–1729), and the benefit of official privileges, he built *c*150 organs of all sizes, achieving fame while young and establishing his own type of instrument in north Germany and the Netherlands. His organs have well-developed chorus work with mixtures on all manuals and pedals, flutes and reeds at many pitches, almost all metal pipework, a short octave on the manuals and slider-chests. The best was that at St Nicolai, Hamburg (1682–7).

Schnittke [Schnitke], Alfred. *See* SHNITKE, ALFRED.

Schnitzer. Two German families of instrument makers, both of Munich origin and active in Nuremberg; it is not known whether they were related. The members of one were Stadtpfeifers and woodwind instrument makers; Sigmund the elder (*d* 1557) was perhaps the most important woodwind maker before Denner: he expanded the family of shawms to include seven sizes and invented the first 16' bass instrument, the *Doppelquint-Basspommer*.

The other family made brass instruments, Anton the elder (*d* 1608) being the founder and greatest master. Most of their surviving trumpets and trombones are elaborate, ceremonial instruments of the highest quality; among them are the oldest signed and dated trombone (1551, by Erasmus Schnitzer), two trumpets by Anton the elder (1581, in modern E♭; 1585, in modern E) and the earliest trombone with a double slide (1612, by Jobst Schnitzer).

Schnorr von Carolsfeld, Ludwig (*b* Munich, 2 July 1836; *d* Dresden, 21 July 1865). German tenor. Principal tenor of the Karlsruhe opera (1858), he became famous in Dresden for his Tannhäuser and Lohengrin, eventually creating the role of Tristan in Wagner's *Tristan und Isolde* (10 June 1865) with his wife Malvina, née Garrigues (1825–1904), as Isolde. He died from the strains of the performance. Wagner praised his voice as 'full, soft and gleaming', admiring his dramatic power and intelligence.

Schnyder von Wartensee, (Franz) Xaver (*b* Lucerne, 18 April 1786; *d* Frankfurt, 27 Aug 1868). Swiss composer. He studied in Vienna. In Frankfurt he gave recitals on the glass harmonica. One of Switzerland's leading late Classical and early Romantic composers, he wrote chiefly choral music, including the oratorio *Zeit und Ewigkeit* (1838), in a delicately contrapuntal style.

Schobert, Johann (*b* ?Silesia, *c*1735; *d* Paris, 28 Aug 1767). Harpsichordist and composer. From *c*1760 he served the Prince of Conti in Paris: by his death (from eating poisonous mushrooms) he had earned much admiration as performer and composer. He wrote *c*30 harpsichord sonatas, mostly accompanied by one or more instruments; he also wrote harpsichord concertos, symphonies and an (unsuccessful) *opéra comique* (1766). A skilled and original composer, he evolved new formal and stylistic features; he influenced Mozart, who arranged movements from his sonatas in his earliest piano concertos and drew on Schobert's ideas in his own early sonatas.

Schoeck, Othmar (*b* Brunnen, 1 Sept 1886; *d* Zurich, 8 March 1957). Swiss composer. He studied at the Zurich Conservatory and with Reger in Leipzig (1907–8), then worked in Zurich and St Gall as a conductor. He was one of the leading Swiss composers of his generation. His numerous songs, usually setting German Romantic poetry, establish him among the foremost lieder composers, but he also wrote important operas: the dense and richly scored *Penthesilea* (1927) and *Vom Fischer und syner Fru* (1930), which like other works is more folklike. The rest of his output includes choral and orchestral scores and a few chamber pieces.

Schoelcher, Victor (*b* Paris, 21 July 1804; *d* Houilles, 24 Dec 1893). French writer on music. His interest in Handel, Italian opera and English 18th-century musical life resulted in *The Life of Handel* (1857), one of the earliest scholarly works on the composer.

Schoenberg [Schönberg], **Arnold (Franz Walter)** (*b* Vienna, 13 Sept 1874; *d* Los Angeles, 13 July 1951). Austro-Hungarian composer, an American citizen from 1941. He began violin lessons when he

was eight and almost immediately started composing, though he had no formal training until he was in his late teens, when Zemlinsky became his teacher and friend (in 1910 he married Zemlinsky's sister). His first acknowledged works date from the turn of the century and include the string sextet *Verklärte Nacht* as well as some songs, all showing influences from Brahms, Wagner and Wolf. In 1901–3 he was in Berlin as a cabaret musician and teacher, and there he wrote the symphonic poem *Pelleas und Melisande*, pressing the Straussian model towards denser thematic argument and contrapuntal richness.

He then returned to Vienna and began taking private pupils, Berg and Webern being among the first. He also moved rapidly forwards in his musical style. The large orchestra of *Pelleas* and the *Gurrelieder* was replaced by an ensemble of 15 in Chamber Symphony no.1, but with an intensification of harmonic strangeness, formal complexity and contrapuntal density: like the String Quartet no.1, the work is cast as a single movement encompassing the characters of the traditional four and using every effort to join unconventional ideas (a sequence of 4ths in the Chamber Symphony, for instance) into a conventional discourse. When atonality arrived, therefore, as it did in 1908, it came as the inevitable outcome of a doomed attempt to accommodate ever more disruptive material. However, Schoenberg found it possible a quarter-century later to return to something like his tonal style in such works as the Suite in G for strings, the completion of the Chamber Symphony no.2 and the Theme and Variations for band.

That, however, was not possible immediately. The sense of key was left behind as Schoenberg set poems by George in the last two movements of String Quartet no.2 and in the cycle *Das Buch der hängenden Gärten*, and for the next few years he lived in the new, rarefied musical air. With tonality had gone thematicism and rhythmic constraint; works tended to be short statements of a single extreme musical state, justifying the term 'expressionist' (Five Orchestral Pieces; Three Pieces and Six Little Pieces for piano). The larger pieces of this period have some appropriate dramatic content: the rage and despair of a woman seaching for her lover (*Erwartung*), the bizarre stories, melancholia and jokes of a distintegrating personality (*Pierrot lunaire*, for reciter in SPRECHGESANG with mixed quintet), or the progress of the soul towards union with God (*Die Jakobsleiter*).

Gradually Schoenberg came to find the means for writing longer instrumental structures, in the 12-note serial method, and in the 1920s he returned to standard forms and genres, notably in the Suite for piano, String Quartet no.3, Orchestral Variations and several choral pieces. He also founded the Society for Private Musical Performances (1919–21), involving his pupils in the presentation of new music under favourable conditions. In 1923 his wife died (he remarried the next year), and in 1925 he moved to Berlin to take a master class at the Prussian Academy of Arts. While there he wrote much of his unfinished opera *Moses und Aron* which is concerned with the impossibility of communicating truth without some distortion in the telling: it was a vehement confrontation with despair on the part of a composer who insisted on the highest standards of artistic honesty.

In 1933 he was obliged as a Jew to leave Berlin: he went to Paris, and formally returned to the faith which he had deserted for Lutheranism in 1898. Later the same year he arrived in the USA, and he settled in Los Angeles in 1934. It was there that he returned to tonal composition, while developing serialism to make possible the more complex structures of the Violin Concerto and the String Quartet no.4. In 1936 he began teaching at UCLA and his compositional output dwindled. After a heart attack in 1945, however, he gave up teaching and made some return to expressionism (*A Survivor from Warsaw*, String Trio), as well as writing religious choruses.

Operas Erwartung (1909, perf. 1924); Die glückliche Hand (1913, perf. 1924); Von heute auf morgen (1930); Moses und Aron (inc., 1932, perf. 1954)
Choral-orchestral music Gurrelieder (1911); Die Jakobsleiter (1922); Kol nidre (1938); Prelude 'Genesis' (1945); A Survivor from Warsaw (1947); Modern Psalm (1950)
Smaller choral music Friede auf Erden (1907); 4 Pieces (1925); 3 Satires (1925); 6 Pieces (1930); Dreimal tausend Jahre (1949); De profundis (1950); folksong arrs.
Orchestral music Pelleas und Melisande (1903); Chamber Sym no.1 (1906); 5 Pieces (1909); Variations (1928); Music to Accompany a Film Scene (1930); Vc Conc, after Monn (1932–3); Str Qt Conc., after Handel (1933); Suite in G (1934); Vn Conc. (1936); Chamber Sym. no.2 (1939); Pf Conc. (1942); Theme and Variations (1943)
Chamber music Verklärte Nacht, 2 vn, 2 va, 2 vc (1899); 4 str qts (1905, 1908 [with S], 1927, 1936); Serenade (1923); Wind Qnt (1924); Suite, septet (1926); Str Trio (1946); Phantasy, vn, pf (1949)
Piano music 3 Pieces (1909); 6 Little Pieces (1911); 5 Pieces (1923); Suite (1923); 2 Pieces (1931)
Organ music Variations on a Recitative (1941)
Songs 6 Orchestral Songs (1905); Das Buch der hängenden Gärten (1909); Herzgewächse, S, cl, celesta, harp, harmonium (1911); Pierrot lunaire, reciter, qnt (1912); 4 Orchestral Songs (1916); Ode to Napoleon, reciter, qnt (1942); many others with pf

Schöffler, Paul (*b* Dresden, 15 Sept 1897; *d* Amersham, 21 Nov 1977). Austrian bass-baritone. He studied in Dresden and Milan and was at the Dresden Staatsoper from 1925 to 1937, when he joined the Vienna Staatsoper. He sang in London (mainly Wagner and Mozart) from 1934 and at the Met from 1950. His roles included Sachs, Don Giovanni, Pizarro and Hindemith's Mathis. His warm, expressive voice was also admired in lieder.

Schola Cantorum Basiliensis. Institution founded in Basle, Switzerland, in 1933 by Paul Sacher for research into early music; in 1954 it was amalgamated with the Basle Musikschule and the conservatory to form the Musikakademie der Stadt Basel.

Scholes, Percy A(lfred) (*b* Headingley, 24 July 1877; *d* Vevey, 31 July 1958). English writer on music. He taught in Canterbury, South Africa and Manchester, then took up music criticism and wrote for *The Observer* (1920–25). He also gave fortnightly impromptu radio reviews of musical broadcasts. In 1928 he moved to Switzerland, where he took the doctorate with *The Puritans in Music* (1934). He is best known for his *Oxford Companion to Music* (1938), 'the most extraordinary range of musical knowledge, ingeniously "self-indexed", ever written and

assembled between two covers by one man' (*Grove 5*); he also wrote studies of Burney and Hawkins.

Schollum, Robert (*b* Vienna, 22 Aug 1913). Austrian composer. He studied with Marx and Lustgarten and in 1959 began teaching at the Vienna Music Academy. His works, in a neo-classical, serial style, include symphonies, chamber and choral music.

Scholz, Bernhard (*b* Mainz, 30 March 1835; *d* Munich, 26 Dec 1916). German conductor and composer. Holding posts in Hanover, Florence, Berlin, Breslau and Frankfurt, he assiduously promoted the works of Brahms, whose influence is evident in his own compositions (mainly chamber and piano music).

Schönbach, Dieter (*b* Stolp, 18 Feb 1931). German composer. A pupil of Bialas and Fortner in Detmold and Freiburg (1949–59), he is one of the foremost German exponents of mixed-media composition; in his works for conventional media he often uses graphics, electronics etc.

Schonberg, Harold C(harles) *b* New York, 29 Nov 1915). American music critic. He studied at Brooklyn College and at New York University and served as music critic and record reviewer for the *American Music Lover* (1939–42), the *Musical Courier* (1948–52) and the *New York Sun* (1946–50). He became associated with the *New York Times* in 1950 and was its senior music critic (1960–80). He was the first music critic to be awarded a Pulitzer Prize for criticism (1971). His special interests are piano literature and performance and lesser 19th-century composers.

Schönbrunn. The Habsburg royal and imperial palace in Vienna. In the 18th century French comic opera, including premières of works by Gluck, was given in its theatre (opened 1747), which is still used for chamber operas.

Schöne Melusine, Die. Overture, op.32, by Mendelssohn (1833) after Kreutzer's opera *Melusine*.

Schöne Müllerin, Die. Song cycle by Schubert (D795, 1823), settings for voice and piano of 20 poems by Wilhelm Müller.

Schönherr, Max (*b* Maribor, 23 Nov 1903; *d* Vienna, 13 Dec 1984). Austrian conductor and composer. He studied in Graz and worked in Vienna as a conductor, mostly of light music. As a composer he was known internationally for his Austrian dances. In the 1970s he took up musicology: he combined practical experience and critical judgment in preparing editions of Viennese music that are unique in studies of popular forms.

School for Fathers, The. See QUATTRO RUSTEGHI, I.

Schoolmaster, The. Nickname of Haydn's Symphony no.55 in E♭ (1774).

Schop, Johann (*d* Hamburg, 1667). German composer. A versatile instrumentalist, he worked from 1621 as the leading municipal viol player in Hamburg, and was also an exponent of early German violin music. He composed many dance pieces and vocal works. His sons Johann (1626–after 1670) and Albert (1632–?after 1667) were both composers.

Schopenhauer, Arthur (*b* Danzig, 22 Feb 1788; *d* Frankfurt, 21 Sept 1860). German philosopher. His view, expressed in *Die Welt als Wille und Vor-*

stellung (1818), that music directly articulates ultimate reality had a profound influence on Wagner, notably in the drama, verbal imagery and role of the music in *Tristan und Isolde*.

Schöpfung, Die. *See* CREATION, THE.

Schöpfungsmesse. *See* CREATION MASS.

Schorr, Friedrich (*b* Nagyvarad, 2 Sept 1888; *d* Farmington, CT, 14 Aug 1953). Hungarian bass-baritone, later naturalized American. He sang at Graz, 1912–16, and appeared with Klemperer at the Cologne Opera, 1918–23. At the Berlin Staatsoper (1923–30) he was heard in operas by Wagner, Strauss and Busoni. At Bayreuth (1925–31) and the Met (1924–43) he won fame as the outstanding Wagnerian bass-baritone of the day, with a voice of majesty and unfailing beauty.

Schott. German firm of music publishers. It was founded by Bernhard Schott (1748–1809) in Mainz in 1780 and began by issuing salon music but achieved eminence in the 1820s by its first publication of Beethoven's *Missa solemnis*, Ninth Symphony and the string quartets opp.127 and 131; the periodical *Cäcilia* (1823–48), Fétis's *Biographie universelle* and, from 1859, publication of the works of Wagner (*Der Ring*, *Die Meistersinger*) and his circle consolidated the firm's reputation. The encouragement of modern music has continued, with 20th-century composers from Stravinsky and Hindemith to Ligeti, Penderecki and Tippett in the catalogue; educational and school music, including many recorder works, also find a place. Scholarly activities include critical editions of the complete works of Wagner, Hindemith and Schoenberg.

Schott, Johann Georg (*b* Niederkleen, *c*1548; *d* Butzbach, 9 Jan 1614). German composer. He held civic posts in Butzbach and directed the collegium musicum there from 1610. His Lutheran chorale book, with nearly 200 settings, is among the largest known.

Schottische (Ger.). A round dance, like a polka but slower. It was introduced into England in 1848 as the 'German Polka'. A connection with the faster *écossaise* (also meaning 'Scottish') has been suggested.

Schramm, Melchior (*b* Münsterberg, *c*1553; *d* Offenburg, 6 Sept 1619). German composer. He was an organist in Halle (1571–2), Sigmaringen (1574–after 1594) and Offenburg (1605–19). An important forerunner of Hassler, he composed German madrigals (1579), motets (3 bks, 1576–1612) and other sacred works.

Schrammel. Term for a type and ensemble of popular Austrian music, named after the brothers Johann (1850–93) and Joseph Schrammel (1852–95). They were violinists who in 1878 founded a trio with a bass guitarist to play popular dances, marches and songs in wine-houses, inns and private gatherings around Vienna; a high-pitched clarinet (in G) was later added, regularly from 1886, but when the clarinettist died in 1893 the clarinet was replaced by an accordion. 'Schrammel quartets' have continued to flourish in this form.

Schreier, Peter (*b* Meissen, 29 July 1935). German tenor and conductor. He studied in Dresden,

making his solo début there in 1961. He soon joined the Berlin Staatsoper and has sung at most leading centres from the mid-1960s. His best roles are Ottavio, Ferrando, Rossini's Almaviva and Wagner's David, to all of which he brings distinctive tone and fastidious phrasing. He is also a distinguished singer of lieder and music by Bach. He has conducted since 1970, in opera and sacred music.

Schreker, Franz (*b* Monaco, 23 March 1878; *d* Berlin, 21 March 1934). Austrian composer. He studied with Fuchs at the Vienna Conservatory (1892–1900) and won success with his ballet *Der Geburtstag der Infantin* (1908) and still more with his opera *Der ferne Klang* (1912), which established his mastery of a harmonically rich, luxuriantly eventful orchestral style, used to suggest the surreal power of music over the characters. In 1908 he established the Philharmonic Choir, which performed many new works, and in 1912 he was invited to teach at the Music Academy in Vienna, from where he moved in 1920 to the directorship of the Berlin Musikhochschule: for the next ten years his fame was at its peak. Meanwhile the operas *Die Gezeichneten* (1918) and *Der Schatzgräber* (1920) had shown a more Wagnerian manner, though he returned to his earlier style, influenced by the more expressionist Strauss, in *Irrelohe* (1924). *Der singende Teufel* (1928) and *Der Schmied von Gent* (1932) are more neo-classical, but continue his abiding concern with the metaphysics of artistic creation (he wrote all his own librettos). *Christophorus* (1927), unperformed in his lifetime and dedicated to Schoenberg, is the most extraordinary expression of his existential anguish and vision of voluptuousness. His few non-operatic works include a Chamber Symphony (1916) and songs.

Schreyerpfeife [Schreierpfeife]. A loud wind-cap SHAWM (*see* WIND-CAP INSTRUMENTS) of the 16th and 17th centuries, with expanding conical bore (pl. *Schryari*). There are four sizes, pitched a 4th or 5th apart.

Schröder-Devrient, Wilhelmine (*b* Hamburg, 6 Dec 1804; *d* Coburg, 26 Jan 1860). German soprano. A singing actress who brought new dramatic powers to opera, she impressed audiences everywhere as Beethoven's Leonore, a role she created (1822) and which laid the foundations of her fame. Until the late 1830s she also excelled as Donna Anna, Euryanthe, Reiza, Norma, Romeo, Valentine and Rossini's Desdemona, receiving praise from Goethe, Weber, Moscheles, Chorley, Schumann and the young Wagner. Despite her vocal deficiencies and her increasingly heavy execution, she influenced the course of German Romantic opera.

Schroeder, Hermann (*b* Bernkastel, 26 March 1904). German composer. He studied at the Cologne Musikhochschule (1926–30) and taught at various German institutions. He did much to reform Roman Catholic church music, his works combining medieval techniques and 20th-century polyphony in a Hindemithian style.

Schröter, Christoph Gottlieb (*b* Hohnstein, 10 Aug 1699; *d* Nordhausen, 20 May 1782). German composer. After travelling in Germany and abroad and then teaching in Jena, he was a church organist in Minden (1726–32) then Nordhausen. His works include an important thoroughbass treatise (1772), many other writings, and both vocal and instrumental music (now mostly lost). Also an inventor, he devised the hammer action of the piano independently of (though later than) Cristofori.

Schröter, Johann Samuel (*b* ?Guben, *c*1752; *d* London, 2 Nov 1788). German pianist and composer. After studying with Hiller in Leipzig he settled in London, where Count Brühl was his patron. He was helped by J.C. Bach, whom he surpassed in popularity as player and fashionable teacher; on Bach's death in 1782 he became music master to Queen Charlotte, and later he held an appointment to the Prince of Wales. His wife, Rebecca, was later a pupil and admirer of Haydn. He wrote mostly accompanied keyboard sonatas and keyboard concertos, which helped to popularize a 'singing-allegro' style in England; his concertos (*c*1774–7) were among the earliest there specifically for the piano. Mozart wrote cadenzas for some of his concertos.

Schröter was one of a family of musicians. His sister Corona Elisabeth Wilhelmine (1751–1802), also a Hiller pupil, was a favourite singer in Leipzig and later Weimar, where she served Duchess Anna Amalia from 1776; she acted in Goethe's dramas and composed lieder and music for stage works. His brother Heinrich (*c*1760–after 1782) was a violinist and composer, and his sister Marie Henriette (1766–after 1804) was a singer. In the early 1770s all four children toured with their father, Johann Friedrich (1724–1811), who was later an oboist and teacher at Hanau.

Schubart, Christian Friedrich Daniel (*b* Obersontheim, 24 March 1739; *d* Stuttgart, 10 Oct 1791). German poet, writer on music and composer. A distinguished keyboard player, he served at the Württemberg court, 1769–73, then worked in Augsburg and Ulm. After imprisonment, 1777–87 (for insulting a duke's mistress), he became court and theatre poet at Stuttgart. As a composer he was best known for his lieder. His writings, including an important work on musical aesthetics (1806) and essays in his own periodical, stress expression in music. His poetry was often set; Schubert's four settings include *Die Forelle* and *An meine Klavier*.

Schubert, Franz (Peter) (*b* Vienna, 31 Jan 1797; *d* there, 19 Nov 1828). Austrian composer. The son of a schoolmaster, he showed an extraordinary childhood aptitude for music, studying the piano, violin, organ, singing and harmony and, while a chorister in the imperial court chapel, composition with Salieri (1808–13). By 1814 he had produced piano pieces, settings of Schiller and Metastasio, string quartets, his first symphony and a three-act opera. Although family pressure dictated that he teach in his father's school, he continued to compose prolifically; his huge output of 1814–15 includes *Gretchen am Spinnrade* and *Erlkönig* (both famous for their text-painting) among numerous songs, besides two more symphonies, three masses and four stage works. From this time he enjoyed the

companionship of several friends, especially Josef von Spaun, the poet Johann Mayrhofer and the law student Franz von Schober. Frequently gathering for domestic evenings of Schubert's music (later called 'Schubertiads'), this group more than represented the new phenomenon of an educated, musically aware middle class: it gave him an appreciative audience and influential contacts (notably the Sonnleithners and the baritone J.M. Vogl), as well as the confidence, in 1818, to break with schoolteaching. More songs poured out, including *Der Wanderer* and *Die Forelle*, and instrumental pieces – inventive piano sonatas, some tuneful, Rossinian overtures, the Fifth and Sixth Symphonies – began to show increased harmonic subtlety. He worked briefly as music master to the Esterházy family, finding greater satisfaction writing songs, chamber music (especially the 'Trout' Quintet) and dramatic music. *Die Zwillingsbrüder* (for Vogl) was only a small success, but brought some recognition and led to the greater challenge of *Die Zauberharfe*.

In 1820–21 aristocratic patronage, further introductions and new friendships augured well. Schubert's admirers issued 20 of his songs by private subscription, and he and Schober collaborated on *Alfonso und Estrella* (later said to be his favourite opera). Though full of outstanding music, it was rejected. Strained friendships, pressing financial need and serious illness – Schubert almost certainly contracted syphilis in late 1822 – made this a dark period, which however encompassed some remarkable creative work: the epic 'Wanderer' Fantasy for piano, the passionate, two-movement Eighth Symphony ('Unfinished'), the exquisite *Schöne Müllerin* song cycle, *Die Verschworenen* and the opera *Fierabras* (full of haunting music if dramatically ineffective). In 1824 he turned to instrumental forms, producing the A minor and D minor ('Death and the Maiden') string quartets and the lyrically expansive Octet for wind and strings; around this time he at least sketched, probably at Gmunden in summer 1825, the 'Great' C major Symphony. With his reputation in Vienna steadily growing (his concerts with Vogl were renowned, and by 1825 he was negotiating with four publishers), Schubert now entered a more assured phase. He wrote mature piano sonatas, notably the one in A minor, some magnificent songs and his last, highly characteristic String Quartet, in G. 1827–8 saw not only the production of *Winterreise* and two piano trios but a marked increase in press coverage of his music; and he was elected to the Vienna Gesellschaft der Musikfreunde. But though he gave a full-scale public concert in March 1828 and worked diligently to satisfy publishers – composing some of his greatest music in his last year, despite failing health – appreciation remained limited. At his death, aged 31, he was mourned not only for his achievement but for 'still fairer hopes'.

Schubert's fame was long limited to that of a songwriter, since the bulk of his large output was not even published, and some not even performed, until the late 19th century. Yet, beginning with the Fifth Symphony and the 'Trout' Quintet, he produced major instrumental masterpieces. These are marked by an intense lyricism (often suggesting a mood of near-pathos), a spontaneous chromatic modulation that is surprising to the ear yet clearly purposeful and often beguilingly expressive, and, not least, an imagination that creates its own formal structures. His way with sonata form, whether in an unorthodox choice of key for secondary material (Symphony in B minor, 'Trout' Quintet) or of subsidiary ideas for the development, makes clear his maturity and individuality. The virtuoso 'Wanderer' Fantasy is equally impressive in its structure and use of cyclic form, while the String Quartet in G explores striking new sonorities and by extension an emotional range of a violence new to the medium. The greatest of his chamber works however is acknowledged to be the String Quintet in C, with its rich sonorities, its intensity and its lyricism, and in the slow movement depth of feeling engendered by the sustained outer sections (with their insistent yet varied and suggestive accompanying figures) embracing a central impassioned section in F minor. Among the piano sonatas, the last three, particularly the noble and spacious one in B♭, represent another summit of achievement. His greatest orchestral masterpiece is the 'Great' C major Symphony, with its remarkable formal synthesis, striking rhythmic vitality, felicitous orchestration and sheer lyric beauty.

Schubert never abandoned his ambition to write a successful opera. Much of the music is of high quality (especially in *Alfonso und Estrella, Fierabras* and the attractive Easter oratorio *Lazarus*, closely related to the operas), showing individuality of style in both accompanied recitative and orchestral colour if little sense of dramatic progress. Among the choral works, the partsongs and the masses rely on homophonic texture and bold harmonic shifts for their effect; the masses in A♭ and E♭ are particularly successful.

Schubert effectively established the German lied as a new art form in the 19th century. He was helped by the late 18th-century outburst of lyric poetry and the new possibilities for picturesque accompaniment offered by the piano, but his own genius is by far the most important factor. The songs fall into four main structural groups – simple strophic, modified strophic, through-composed (e.g. *Die junge Nonne*) and the 'scena' type (*Der Wanderer*); the poets range from Goethe, Schiller and Heine to Schubert's own versifying friends. Reasons for their abiding popularity rest not only in the direct appeal of Schubert's melody and the general attractiveness of his idiom but also in his unfailing ability to capture musically both the spirit of a poem and much of its external detail. He uses harmony to represent emotional change (passing from minor to major, magically shifting to a 3rd-related key, tenuously resolving a diminished 7th, inflecting a final strophe to press home its climax) and accompaniment figuration to illustrate poetic images (moving water, shimmering stars, a church bell). With such resources he found innumerable ways to illuminate a text, from the opening depiction of morning in *Ganymed* to the leaps of anguish in *Der Doppelgänger*.

Schubert's discovery of Wilhelm Müller's narrative lyrics gave rise to his further development of the lied by means of the song cycle. Again, his two masterpieces were practically without precedent and have never been surpassed. Both identify nature with human suffering, *Die schöne Müllerin* evoking a pastoral sound-language of walking, flowing and flowering, and *Winterreise* a more intensely Romantic, universal, profoundly tragic quality.

Dramatic music Des Teufels Lustschloss (1814, perf. 1879); Die Zauberharfe (1820); Alfonso und Estrella (1822, perf. 1854); Fierabras (1823, perf. 1897); 5 Singspiels, incl. Die Zwillingsbrüder (1820), Die Verschworenen (1823, perf. 1861); incidental music to Rosamunde (1823)

Choral music 6 masses, incl. no.5, A♭ (1822), no.6, E♭ (1828); Stabat mater (1816); Deutsche Messe (1827); other liturgical pieces; Lazarus, oratorio (1820) inc.; Ständchen (1827); Mirjams Siebesgesang (1828); *c*60 secular and occasional pieces for female, mixed or unspecified vv; *c*100 male-voice trios, qts and qnts

Orchestral music Sym. no.1, D (1813); Sym. no.2, B♭ (1815); Sym. no.3, D (1815); Sym. no.4, c, 'Tragic' (1816); Sym. no.5, B♭ (1816); Sym. no.6, C (1818); Sym. no.8 [no.7], b, 'Unfinished' (1822); Sym. no.9 [no.8], C, 'Great' (?1825–8); 11 ovs., sym. movts

Chamber music Pf Qnt, A, 'The Trout' (1819); Quartettsatz, c (1820); Octet, F (1824); Str Qt, a (1824); Str Qt, d, 'Death and the Maiden' (1824); Str Qt, G (1826); 2 pf trios, B♭ and E♭ (1827–8); Str Qnt, C (1828); other works, incl. str qts, sonatas, vn, pf

Piano music Fantasy, C, 'Wanderer' (1822); Sonatas incl. A, D664 (1819/25), a, D845 (1825), D, D850, (1825), G, D894, (1826), c, D958, (1828), A, D959, (1828), B♭, D960, (1828); *c*33 others; fantasies, *c*50 dances, dance sets (waltzes, Ländler, ecossaises); over 30 works for pf duet, incl. Sonata, C, 'Grand Duo' (1824), Divertissement à l'hongroise (1824), Fantasie, f (1828)

Songs over 600, incl. Gretchen am Spinnrade (1814), Heidenröslein (1815), Erlkönig (1815), Der Wanderer (1816), Der Tod und das Mädchen (1817), Ganymed (1817), An die Musik (1817), Gruppe aus dem Tartarus (1817), Die Forelle (*c*1817), Prometheus (1819), Frühlingsglaube (1820), Sei mir gegrüsst (1821/2), Du bist die Ruh (1823), Die junge Nonne (1825), [4] Gesänge aus Wilhelm Meister (1826), An Sylvia (1826), Schwanengesang (14 songs, incl. Der Doppelgänger; 1828); cycles – Die schöne Müllerin, 20 songs (1823), Winterreise, 24 songs (1827)

Schubert, Franz Anton (*b* Dresden, 20 July 1768; *d* there, 5 March 1827). German composer and double bass player. He played in the orchestra at Dresden, directed the Italian Opera there from 1808 and was royal church composer from 1814. He is remembered solely for his remarks when a publisher mistakenly returned to him an MS of the other Schubert's *Erlkönig*, about the composer who 'impertinently sent you that sort of rubbish . . . and misused my name'. He had a brother Franz (1808–78), a Dresden violinist and composer, whose daughter Georgine (1840–78) was an international soprano. Joseph Schubert (1757–1837), violinist and opera composer, and Louis Schubert (1828–84), violinist, composer and singing teacher, both active in Dresden, were not related to him; nor were the Szczecin and Cologne composer and violinist Johann Friedrich Schubert (1770–1811) or FRANZ SCHUBERT.

Schuch, Ernst Edler **von** (*b* Graz, 23 Nov 1846; *d* Kotzschenbroda, 10 May 1914). Austrian conductor. From 1873 he was Kapellmeister (from 1889

music director) of the Dresden Hofoper, making it one of the most brilliant in the world. He conducted the premières of Strauss's *Salome* (1905), *Elektra* (1909) and *Der Rosenkavalier* (1911), brought Wagner's *Ring*, *Tristan und Isolde* and *Die Meistersinger* to the Dresden stage and introduced Puccini's operas to German audiences.

Schuëcker, Edmund (*b* Vienna, 16 Nov 1860; *d* Bad Kreuznach, 9 Nov 1911). Austrian harpist and composer. He studied with Zamara at the Vienna Conservatory, played in German orchestras and taught at the Leipzig Conservatory. He also worked in the USA (Chicago SO, 1891–1900; Pittsburgh SO, 1903–4; Philadelphia, 1904–9), publishing numerous harp studies and salon pieces including the popular Mazurka op.12.

Schulhoff, Ervín (*b* Prague, 8 June 1894; *d* Wülzbourg, 18 Aug 1942). Czech composer and pianist. He was a pupil of Reger in Leipzig (1908–10) and later in Germany (1919–23) he associated with Klee and the dadaists; back in Prague he was active as a pianist, in jazz and as an exponent of Hába's quarter-tone music. His works include stage pieces, six symphonies and two piano sonatas, displaying diverse styles. He died in a concentration camp.

Schuller, Gunther (*b* New York, 22 Nov 1925). American composer, conductor and teacher. He studied at the St Thomas Choir School (1938–42) and had a career as a horn player, notably at the Met (1945–59). He has taught at Tanglewood (from 1963) and was an innovatory, energetic president of the New England Conservatory, 1967–77. He has conducted internationally (notably new music), studied jazz and produced a large output, mostly of orchestral and chamber music, but also opera (including *The Visitation*, 1966). His works draw on Schoenberg, Babbitt, Stravinsky and jazz.

Schuloper (Ger.). 'School opera': the term usually refers to 20th-century operas written for didactic use in schools (although there is a long tradition of school music drama promoted by Jesuits and other religious orders). Suitability for performance by children is secondary to the teaching of music, drama and communal spirit. Important examples are Weill's *Der Jasager* and Hindemith's *Wir bauen eine Stadt*.

Schultheiss, Benedict (*b* Nuremberg, 20 Sept 1653; *d* there, 1 March 1693). German composer. He was an organist in Nuremberg, serving at the Frauenkirche in 1686–7 and then at St Egidien. His output comprises sacred music and two volumes of keyboard suites (1679–80), in which he was the first German to use the order allemande–courante–sarabande–gigue.

Schulz, Johann Abraham Peter (*b* Lüneburg, 31 March 1747; *d* Schwedt an der Oder, 10 June 1800). German composer and conductor. After studying with Kirnberger in Berlin, he travelled widely from 1768 as accompanist and music teacher to a Polish princess. Returning to Berlin in 1773, he helped Kirnberger with theoretical works. He became music director at the French theatre there in 1776. His productions of new operas brought him into

disfavour, and in 1787 he went to Copenhagen as court Kapellmeister and director of the royal theatre. By his retirement in 1795, Copenhagen was one of Europe's foremost musical centres.

Schulz's most important works were his four lied collections (1779–86); he set texts by leading poets and aimed to reflect the meaning in a simple musical style. His other vocal music (some in Danish) includes 12 stage works and oratorios, cantatas and sacred pieces; he also wrote keyboard and chamber music. He should not be confused with the Leipzig composer and conductor J.P.C. Schulz (1773–1827).

Schulze [Praetorius], Christian Andreas (*b* Dresden, *c*1660; *d* Meissen, 11 Sept 1699). German composer. He was Kantor of the municipal church at Meissen from 1678, and also became Kantor at the cathedral there. His *c*40 surviving works, all sacred, are carefully structured and expressive; they include a *Historia resurrectionis* to a German text (1686), sacred concertos and various kinds of early Protestant church cantata.

Schuman, William (Howard) (*b* New York, 4 Aug 1910). American composer. He studied at Columbia University and under Harris at the Juilliard School. He came firmly to public notice with his Symphony no.3 (1941). He taught at Sarah Lawrence College, 1935–45, then became president of the Juilliard School, which he extensively reorganized. He was president of the Lincoln Center, 1962–9. He has received many honours and awards. His symphonies (ten up to 1975) are central to his work; they embody vigorous drive, febrile rhythms and expansive musical and orchestral gestures, with a broad melodic line and a generally tonal idiom. Sometimes his music is layered, using different instrumental groups at different speeds. His chamber music includes four string quartets; he has also composed, especially since the mid-1970s, large-scale vocal pieces.

Schumann [née Wieck], Clara (Josephine) (*b* Leipzig, 13 Sept 1819; *d* Frankfurt, 20 May 1896). German pianist and composer. Developed by her father, Friedrich, into a musician of consummate artistry, she won dazzling success as a touring piano virtuoso both before and after she married Robert Schumann (1840), being praised not only for her mastery of a progressive repertory (Chopin, Schumann and Brahms) but also for her thoughtful interpretations and singing tone. She taught privately in Dresden and Düsseldorf and at the conservatories in Leipzig and Frankfurt. As a composer she showed imagination and control, notably in the Piano Trio op.17 and the songs op.23, but her ambitions were not serious; she ceased composing in 1854, the year of Robert's collapse. She prepared a complete edition of his music, attended to family duties and maintained a close relationship with Brahms to the end of her life.

Schumann, Elisabeth (*b* Merseburg, 13 June 1888; *d* New York, 23 April 1952). German soprano. She made her début in Hamburg in 1909, remaining until 1919, when she joined Strauss at the Vienna Staatsoper. She remained there until 1937, gaining admiration for her charming stage presence and beautifully controlled high soprano in such roles as Sophie, Eva and Mozart's Susanna, Despina and Zerlina. At Covent Garden she was successful from 1924. She was also a distinguished recitalist, notably in the songs of Schubert and Schumann.

Schumann, Frederic Theodor (*fl* London, 1760–80). German guitarist, composer and player of the musical glasses. One of many German musicians in London, he composed mainly accompanied harpsichord sonatas and guitar pieces.

Schumann, George (Alfred) (*b* Königstein 25 Oct 1866; *d* Berlin, 23 May 1952). German composer and conductor. A pupil of Reinecke and Jadassohn at the Leipzig Conservatory (1882–8), he directed the Berlin Singakademie from 1900 for 50 years, touring with it and developing an individual performing style. He taught at the Prussian Academy of Arts from 1907. His works include oratorios and orchestral music.

Schumann, Robert (Alexander) (*b* Zwickau, 8 June 1810; *d* Endenich, 29 July 1856). German composer. The son of a bookseller, he early showed ability as a pianist and an interest in composing as well as literary leanings. He was also enthusiastic over the writings of 'Jean Paul' (J.P.F. Richter), girl friends and drinking champagne, tastes he retained. In 1821 he went to Leipzig to study law but instead spent his time in musical, social and literary activities. He wrote some piano music and took lessons from Friedrich Wieck. After a spell in Heidelberg, ostensibly studying law but actually music, he persuaded his family that he should give up law in favour of a pianist's career, and in 1830 he went to live with Wieck at Leipzig. But he soon had trouble with his hands (allegedly due to a machine to strengthen his fingers, but more likely through remedies for a syphilitic sore). Composition, however, continued; several piano works date from this period.

In 1834 Schumann founded a music journal, the *Neue Zeitschrift für Musik*; he was its editor and leading writer for ten years. He was a brilliant and perceptive critic: his writings embody the most progressive aspects of musical thinking in his time, and he drew attention to many promising young composers. Sometimes he wrote under pseudonyms, Eusebius (representing his lyrical, contemplative side) and Florestan (his fiery, impetuous one); he used these in his music, too. His compositions at this time were mainly for piano: they include variations on the name of one on his lady friends, Abegg (the musical notes A–B–E–G–G), the character-pieces *Davidsbündlertänze* ('Dances of the league of David', an imaginary association of those fighting the Philistines), *Carnaval* (pieces with literary or other allusive meanings, including one on the notes A–S–C–H after the place another girl friend came from), *Phantasiestücke* (a collection of poetic pieces depicting moods), *Kreisleriana* (fantasy pieces around the character of a mad Kapellmeister) and *Kinderszenen* ('Scenes from Childhood'). Affairs of the heart played a large part in his life. By 1835 he was in love with Wieck's young daughter Clara, but Wieck did his best to separate them. They pledged

themselves in 1837 but were much apart and Schumann went through deep depressions. In 1839 they took legal steps to make Wieck's consent unnecessary, and after many further trials they were able to marry in 1840.

Schumann, understandably, turned in that year to song; he wrote *c*150 songs, including most of his finest, at this time, among them several groups and cycles, the latter including *Frauenliebe und -leben* ('A Woman's Love and Life') and *Dichterliebe* ('A Poet's Love'), which tells (to verse by Heine) a tragic Romantic story of the flowering of love, its failure and poet's exclusion from joy and his longing for death. Schumann, as a pianist composer, made the piano partake fully in the expression of emotion in such songs, often giving it the most telling music when the voice had finished.

In 1841, however, Schumann turned to orchestral music: he wrote symphonies and a beautiful, poetic piece for piano and orchestra for Clara that he later reworked as the first movement of his Piano Concerto. Then in 1842, when Clara was away on a concert tour (he disliked being in her shadow and remained at home), he turned to chamber music, and wrote his three string quartets and three works with piano, of which the Piano Quintet has always been a favourite for the freshness and Romantic warmth of its ideas. After that, in 1843, he turned to choral music, working at a secular oratorio and at setting part of Goethe's *Faust*. He also took up a teaching post at the new conservatory in Leipzig of which Mendelssohn was director. But he was an ineffectual teacher; and he had limited success as a conductor too. He and Clara moved to Dresden in 1844, but his deep depressions continued, hampering his creativity. Not until 1847–8 was he again productive, writing his opera *Genoveva* (given in Leipzig in 1850 with moderate success), chamber music and songs. In 1850 he took up a post in Düsseldorf as town musical director. He was at first happy and prolific, writing the eloquent Cello Concerto and the Rhenish Symphony (no.3: one movement depicts his impressions in Cologne Cathedral). But the post worked out badly because of his indifferent conducting. In 1852–3 his health and spirits deteriorated and he realized that he could not continue in his post. In 1854 he began to suffer hallucinations; he attempted suicide (he had always dreaded the possibility of madness) and entered an asylum, where he died in 1856, almost certainly of the effects of syphilis, cared for at the end by Clara and the young Brahms.

Dramatic music Genoveva, opera (1850); Manfred, incidental music (1852)

Orchestral music Sym. no.1, B♭, 'Spring' (1841); Sym. no.2, C (1846); Sym. no.3, E♭, 'Rhenish' (1850); Sym. no.4, d (1841, rev. 1851); 2 ovs.; Pf Conc., a (1845); Conzertstück, 4 horns, F (1849); Vc Conc., a (1850); other pieces

Instrumental music 3 str qts op.41, a, F, A (1842); Pf Qnt, op.44, E♭ (1842); Pf Qt, op.47, E♭ (1842); 3 pf trios; 3 vn sonatas; Adagio and Allegro (hn/vc, pf); fantasy pieces (cl, pf), romances (ob, pf) etc; org pieces incl. fugues

Piano music Sonata no.1, f♯ (1835); Sonata no.2, g (1838); Papillons (1831); Carnaval (1835); Concert sans orchestre, f (1836); Davidsbündlertänze (1837); Phantasiestücke (1837); Kinderszenen (1838); Kreisleriana (1838); Phantasie, C (1838); Faschingsschwank aus Wien (1840); Album

für die Jugend (1848); character-pieces, variations, impromptus, fantasias; duets
Songs over 300, incl. song cycles Frauenliebe und -leben (1840), Dichterliebe (1840); over 70 partsongs; *c*30 duets, trios
Choral music Das Paradies und die Peri, oratorio (1843); Szenen aus Goethes Faust (1853, perf. 1862); 17 others

Schumann-Heink, Ernestine (*b* Lieben, 15 June 1861; *d* Hollywood, 17 Nov 1936). Austrian mezzo-soprano, later naturalized American. After an early career at Dresden (début 1878) she sang at Hamburg from 1883, notably as Carmen and in Wagner. Chiefly a Wagner singer, she appeared at Bayreuth, 1896–1914, and sang Wagner roles at the Met from 1899, returning to Dresden in 1909 to create Strauss's Clytemnestra. Her dramatic temperament and vivid enunciation made her much in demand as a concert singer throughout the USA.

Schuppanzigh, Ignaz (*b* Vienna, 20 Nov 1776; *d* there, 2 March 1830). Austrian violinist and conductor. The greatest figure among the original Beethoven quartet players, notably leader of Count Razumovsky's quartet (1808–14), he played in first performances of Beethoven's works from the 1790s to 1828, including opp.16, 20, 59, 95, 97, 125, 127, 130, 132 and 135. He also led orchestral concerts at the Augarten and, after a time in St Petersburg (1816–23), became director of the Viennese court opera. His obesity was a source of amusement to Beethoven, who called him 'Milord Falstaff'.

Schürer, Johann Georg (*b* ?Roudnice, Bohemia, *c*1720; *d* Dresden, 16 Feb 1786). German composer. He worked as composer and music director to an opera troupe in Dresden and presented several of his own operas there, 1746–8. In 1748 he became church composer at the Dresden court. Before retiring in 1780, he composed several hundred sacred works (masses, psalms etc, oratorios) besides operas and cantatas. His style, showing contrapuntal mastery and a serious, expressive vein, differs from the neo-Neapolitan idiom then favoured in Dresden.

Schuricht, Carl (*b* Gdańsk, 3 July 1880; *d* Corseaux-sur-Vevey, 7 Jan 1967). German conductor. He studied in Berlin and Leipzig and was musical director at Wiesbaden, 1911–44, when he was active in promoting 20th-century music. Later he worked as a guest conductor. He was admired for his well-disciplined, often deliberate and usually very free performances of the classical repertory.

Schürmann, Georg Caspar (*b* Idensen, 1672/3; *d* Wolfenbüttel, 25 Feb 1751). German composer. In the 1790s he sang at the Hamburg Opera before becoming solo alto to the Brunswick-Wolfenbüttel court, where he established himself as a gifted composer; his first stage works were given in 1700–01. After a study visit to Venice, he became Kapellmeister and composer at the court of Meiningen, writing operas and church cantatas. After his return to Brunswick-Wolfenbüttel (*c*1707), he composed over 30 more German operas and was also active as a conductor, opera producer, translator and arranger of Italian operas.

Schürmann was a leading composer of the German Baroque. His works combine the north German idiom of Keiser and others with Italian traits and feature lyrical melodies and colourful textures and scorings; they point strongly towards the Classical style.

Schuster, Joseph (*b* Dresden, 11 Aug 1748; *d* there, 24 July 1812). German composer and conductor. Trained in Venice, he became a church composer at the Dresden court in 1772 and presented his first Italian opera there in 1773. Returning to Italy in 1774–7 and 1778–81, he studied with Padre Martini and wrote operas for Naples and elsewhere. Notable among his German successes was the singspiel *Der Alchymist* (1778). From 1781 he conducted in the Dresden court church and theatre, and in 1787 he became joint Kapellmeister with Seydelmann. A popular composer, he wrote *c*20 operas (mostly comic) up to 1802, as well as oratorios, sacred music, cantatas and instrumental works; Mozart was influenced, in matters of texture and form, by his divertimento of *c*1777 for keyboard and violin. Some of his output, including *Der Alchymist*, shows a Viennese influence.

Schütz, Heinrich [Sagittarius, Henricus] (*b* Bad Löstriz, bap. 9 Oct 1585; *d* Dresden, 6 Nov 1672). German composer. In 1590 he moved with his family to Weissenfels. In 1598 Landgrave Moritz, impressed by his musical accomplishments, took him to Kassel, where he served as a choirboy and studied music with the court Kapellmeister, Georg Otto. In 1609 Schütz proceeded to the University of Marburg to study law, but Landgrave Moritz advised him to abandon his university studies and to go to Venice as a pupil of G. Gabrieli; moreover, the landgrave provided the financial means to do this. Schütz remained in Venice for over three years, returning to Moritz's court at Kassel in 1613. The following year he was seconded to serve for two months at the electoral court in Dresden, and in 1615 the Elector Johann Georg I requested his services for a further two years. Moritz reluctantly agreed, and was obliged, for political reasons, to comply when the elector insisted on retaining Schütz in his permanent employ.

As Kapellmeister at Dresden, Schütz was responsible for providing music for major court ceremonies, whether religious or political. He also had to keep the Kapelle adequately staffed and supervise the musical education of the choirboys. His pupils during the following decades included the composers Bernhard, Theile and Weckmann. In 1619 Schütz published his first collection of sacred music, the *Psalmen Davids*, dedicated to the elector, and later that year he married Magdalena Wildeck. She died in 1625, leaving Schütz with two daughters whom he placed in the care of their maternal grandmother; he never remarried.

Schütz was often absent from Dresden on his own or the elector's business, and in 1627 he was at Torgau, where his *Dafne* (the first German opera) was performed for the wedding of the elector's daughter Sophia Eleonora. Visits to Mühlhausen and possibly Gera were undertaken later in the year. Towards the end of the 1620s economic pressures of the Thirty Years War began to affect the electoral court. Musicians' wages fell into arrears, and in 1628 Schütz decided on a second visit to Venice, where he was able to study developments in dramatic music under Monteverdi's guidance. He returned to Dresden in 1629, but two years later Saxony entered the war and musical activities at court soon came to a virtual halt. Schütz then accepted an invitation to direct the music at the wedding of Crown Prince Christian of Denmark. He arrived in Copenhagen in December 1633 and was paid a salary as Kapellmeister by King Christian IV until his return to Dresden in May 1635.

From Michaelmas 1639 Schütz was again absent from Dresden, this time for about 15 months in the service of Georg of Calenberg. On his return he found the Kapelle further depleted and its members living in penury, and for most of 1642–4 he was again employed at the Danish court. After a year in and around Brunswick he went into semi-retirement, spending much of his time in Weissenfels, though he retained the title and responsibilities of Kapellmeister at Dresden. The end of the Thirty Years War had little immediate effect on musical conditions and in 1651 Schütz renewed an earlier plea for release from his duties and the granting of a pension. This and later petitions were ignored and Schütz obtained his release only on the elector's death in 1656. He was far from inactive during his remaining 15 years. He continued to supply music for occasions at Dresden, frequently travelled and worked on the masterpieces of his last years – the Christmas History, the three Passions and the settings of Psalms cxix and c.

Schütz was the greatest German composer of the 17th century and the first of international stature. His output was almost exclusively sacred; he set mainly biblical texts and wrote little chorale-based music. His early works explore a variety of styles and genres: the polychoral *Psalmen Davids* (1619) are notable for their contrasting textures and sonorities, while the *Cantiones sacrae* (1625) present a wide range of motet settings, from the polyphonic to the concertato. Later, he exploited the Italian concertato idiom to the full, notably in the three books of *Symphoniae sacrae* (1629, 1647, 1650), which give equal weight to voices and instruments. His two sets of *Kleine geistliche Concerte* (1636, 1639), written after the Thirty Years War and for limited forces, emphasize the meaning of the text, combining principles of monody and counterpoint to create powerful and expressive declamation. Schütz's late works are dominated by the oratorical pieces and by the three unaccompanied 'dramatic' Passions, said to be the last great examples of the genre. His music, largely to German texts, constitutes the ultimate realization of Luther's endeavours to establish the vernacular as a literary and liturgical language, and embodies the Protestant and humanistic concept of *musica poetica* in perhaps its most perfect form.

Sacred vocal music Psalmen Davids, 26 psalms (1619); Resurrection History (1623); Cantiones sacrae, 41 motets (1625); Becker Psalter (1628, rev. 1661); Symphoniae sacrae, i, 20 motets (1629), ii, 27 motets (1647), iii, 21 motets (1650); Musicalische Exequien (1636); Kleine geistliche Concerte, i, 24 motets (1636), ii, 32 motets (1639); Geistliche Chor-Musik (29 motets, 1648); 12 geistliche Gesänge (1657); Die sieben Worte (?c1660); Christmas History (1664); St Matthew, St Luke and St John Passions (1666)
Secular vocal music 19 madrigals (1611); Dafne, opera (1627), lost; occasional works

Schütz Choir of London. British choir formed in 1973 by Roger Norrington to replace the Schütz Chorale and the amateur Heinrich Schütz Choir, both founded by him in 1962. Its repertory is centred on Schütz and early music, but since the mid-1970s 19th-century and contemporary British works have been given.

Schützendorf, Gustav (*b* Cologne, 1883; *d* Berlin, 27 April 1937). German baritone. After engagements in Berlin, Wiesbaden and Basle he sang in Munich, 1914–20. At the Met (1922–35) he appeared in Strauss, Wagner and Janáček. His brother Leo (1886–1931), a bass-baritone, sang widely in Germany before joining the Berlin Staatsoper (1920–29); in 1925 he created Berg's Wozzeck, under Kleiber.

Schuyt, Cornelis (Floriszoon) (*b* Leiden, 1557; *d* there, 9 June 1616). Netherlands composer. From 1593 he was assistant town organist to his father in Leiden and from 1601 first organist. A leading writer of Dutch madrigals (1603), he also composed Italian ones (1600, 1611) and instrumental music (1611) in a marked northern style.

Schwanda the Bagpiper [Švanda Dudák]. Opera in two acts by Weinberger to a libretto by M. Brod and M. Kareš (1927, Prague).

Schwanendreher, Der. Concerto for viola and small orchestra by Hindemith (1935) based on German folksongs.

Schwanengesang [Swansong]. Collection of songs by Schubert, D957 (1828), issued in two books after his death as a 'cycle', settings for voice and piano of 14 poems by Heine, Rellstab and Seidl.

Schwantner, Joseph (*b* Chicago, 22 March 1943). American composer. Trained in Chicago, he began teaching at the Eastman School in 1970. His works have moved from serialism to a freer style characterized by lyricism, impressionist colours and clear tonal centres.

Schwartz, Elliott (Shelling) (*b* Brooklyn, 19 Jan 1936). American composer. He was a pupil of Luening and Beeson at Columbia and of Creston. While working as a teacher he has produced a large output showing knowledge of a wide range of contemporary techniques.

Schwarz, Rudolf (*b* Vienna, 29 April 1905). British conductor. He studied in Vienna and made his début in Dusseldorf in 1924, then working in Karlsruhe and later Berlin. He went to England after World War II, working with the Bournemouth orchestra, 1947–51, then the CBSO, BBC SO (1957–62) and the Northern Sinfonia (1964–73); he also conducted in Bergen.

Schwarzkopf, (Olga Maria) Elisabeth (Friederike) (*b* Jarotschin, 9 Dec 1915). German soprano. After study at the Berlin Hochschule she made her stage début at the Städtische Oper in

1938, then studied further with Ivogün. She joined the Vienna Staatsoper in 1942, made her Salzburg début in 1947 and that year joined the Covent Garden company, remaining for four seasons. She made her La Scala début as Mozart's Countess in 1948, created Stravinsky's Anne Trulove in 1951 and made her Met début as the Marschallin in 1964. Her lustrous lyric soprano and her fine musicianship (supported by her husband, Walter Legge) made her the leading Mozart and Strauss opera singer of her day; whe was also the foremost female singer of lieder, performing Schubert and Wolf with beauty of tone and line and great musical intelligence.

Schweigsame Frau, Die. Opera in three acts by Richard Strauss to a libretto by Stefan Zweig after Ben Jonson's *Epicoene* (1935, Dresden).

Schweitzer, Albert (*b* Kayserberg, 14 Jan 1875; *d* Lambaréné, Gabon, 4 Sept 1965). Alsatian philosopher, organist, scholar, physician and humanist. He studied music as a child and after taking theology and philosophy at Strasbourg University, he studied the organ under Widor in Paris, also studying the psychology of sound in Berlin. His most important musical publications appeared in 1905–13 when he was a practising minister, a theology lecturer at Strasbourg and studying medicine in preparation for his first journey to Africa. His epoch-making study of Bach appeared when he was 30, in French; in 1908 he brought out the German version of it, almost twice the original length (all translations are based on this). Schweitzer was also much concerned with the organ reform movement.

Schweitzer, Anton (*b* Coburg, bap. 6 June 1735; *d* Gotha, 23 Nov 1787). German composer. He served the Duke of Hildburghausen and from 1769 was Kapellmeister to the Seyler theatre company, working at Weimar, 1771–4, and at Gotha, where he directed the ducal chapel from 1778. He composed over 50 dramatic works, including Singspiels, operas and incidental music. Several works have librettos by C.M. Wieland, who aimed to create a German national opera; of these *Alkeste* (1773) was the first grand, through-composed German opera, and shows Jommelli's influence. His *Pygmalion* (1772) was the first German melodrama (predating G. Benda's *Ariadne*). His last opera was *Rosamunde* (1780, Mannheim); he also wrote cantatas, songs and instrumental pieces.

Schwencke. German family of musicians. The most celebrated members were Christian Friedrich Gottlieb (1767–1822), a pianist and composer who made one of the first editions of the '48' (1801), and his son Johann Friedrich (1792–1852), an organist whose most important work is the *Choralbuch zum Hamburgischen Gesangbuch* (1832).

Schwertsik, Kurt (*b* Vienna, 25 June 1935). Austrian composer. A pupil of Marx and Schiske at the Vienna Academy (1949–57), he also studied at the Cologne electronic studio and at Darmstadt. In 1958 he and Cerha founded the ensemble Die Reihe. While working as a horn player in Vienna he produced a large output inclined towards a Viennese aesthetic of 'fantastic realism', using well-worn extracts of tonal music in collages.

Schwindl, Friedrich (*b* 3 May 1737; *d* Karlsruhe, 7 Aug 1786). Composer and violinist. In the 1760s he served private patrons and in the 1770s Prince William V of Orange at The Hague. After spending time in Switzerland he became Konzertmeister at the Karlsruhe court (1780). He was also a soloist and a concert orgaaniser. Widely popular as a composer, he wrote over 30 symphonies (some he later revised and extended), much chamber music and several vocal works.

Sciarrino, Salvatore (*b* Palermo, 4 April 1947). Italian composer. A pupil of Evangelisti, he came to prominence early as an avant-garde composer and has written in most genres, often exploiting marginal instrumental effects. His orchestral music (e.g. *Rondò*, 1972) depends on the elaboration of tiny elements.

Scimone, Claudio (*b* Padua, 23 Dec 1934). Italian conductor. He founded I Solisti Veneti in 1959, specializing in 18th-century and 20th-century Italian music. He is known for his lively direction of music by Vivaldi, Tartini and their contemporaries; he has also taught at conservatories in Venice, Verona and Padua.

Sciolto (It.). A direction asking for an easy, somewhat loose and flexible delivery of a passage or for a detached articulation.

Sciroli, Gregorio (*b* Naples, 5 Oct 1722; *d* after 1781). Italian composer. He studied with Fago and Leo in Naples and in 1747–57 composed comic operas, intermezzos etc for theatres there and in Rome and Palermo. As a teacher, his most famous singing pupil was Giuseppe Aprile. From the late 1750s he worked chiefly in north Italy, writing operas for Venice and elsewhere. He also wrote much sacred music (he may have held a church post in Genoa) and several instrumental works.

Sciutti, Graziella (*b* Turin, 17 April 1927). Italian soprano. She made her début at Aix-en-Provence in 1951, later singing there such roles as Mozart's Susanna and Zerlina. In 1954 she made her British début (Rosina, *Barber of Seville*) but she appeared at Covent Garden (as Verdi's Oscar) only in 1976. Her American début (1961) was in San Francisco as Susanna; she sang too in Salzburg and Vienna. She is admired for her vivacious personality, her pointed phrasing and her clear diction, and has also produced several operas.

Scolari, Giuseppe (*b* Vicenza, ? 1720; *d* ? Lisbon, after 1774). Italian composer. He presented *c*30 operas in Venice, other Italian cities, Barcelona and Lisbon. His comic works (notably *La cascina*, 1755) were among the earliest by a north Italian to use the new style developed in Naples and Rome. He also composed instrumental music.

Scordatura [descordato, discordato] (It., from *scordare*). A 'mistuning' of string instruments, notably lutes and violins. It was first used in the 16th century and enjoyed a vogue 1600–1750 but is now rare. Scordatura was used to extend an instrument's range downwards by tuning the lowest string a tone lower, to make certain passages easier to play, to produce special effects, to increase brilliance and to produce mixed sonorities. It was generally applied to single instruments but occasionally several of the same ensemble are in scordatura.

Score. A form of written or printed music in which the staves, normally linked by bar-lines, are vertically aligned so as to represent visually the musical coordination. The use of the word derives from the 'scoring' or vertical lines through the staves to form bars. The verb 'to score' means to compose or arrange for ensemble performance; 'to score up' implies writing out a score from a set of parts.

The term 'full score' signifies a score for orchestra containing full details of a work as it is intended to be performed; a 'miniature score' is a printed score of pocket size for individual use. An 'open score' is one that shows each voice of a composition (normally a polyphonic one) on a separate staff. A 'piano score' is an arrangement of an ensemble composition for piano; the term is sometimes used synonymously with 'vocal score', in which the voices are fully shown but the instrumental accompaniment is reduced for piano (or organ). A 'short score' is a condensed score in which some of the instrumental or vocal lines share a staff. The term 'study score' may be synonymous with 'miniature score' or may stand for a medium-sized version of a full score.

In modern orchestral scores, the orchestra is ordered in groups from the top down: woodwind, brass, percussion and strings. Each group is subdivided in roughly descending order of pitch range. The solo part of a concerto is written above the first violins; voice parts may be shown above the first violins or, traditionally, between the viola and the cellos. For clarity, bar-lines normally connect only those staves belonging to each group.

Scotch snap. A melodic figuration consisting of a stressed semiquaver followed by an unstressed dotted quaver, usually applied to melodies that fall or rise by steps. It was current in European art music, 1680–1800, and Scottish strathspeys, and in France and Italy was regarded as a Lombard characteristic ('Lombardic rhythm').

Scott, Cyril (Meir) (*b* Oxton, 27 Sept 1879; *d* Eastbourne, 31 Dec 1970). English composer and pianist. He studied at the Hoch Conservatory, Frankfurt (1892–3, 1895–8), with Humperdinck and Knorr and made his reputation during the first quarter of the century as a composer of rhapsodic languour in a style bearing comparison with Skryabin and Debussy; the Piano Concerto (1915) is the outstanding work of this period. He was also a notable writer on occultism, a poet and an internationally known pianist. His output includes operas and ballets, three symphonies, two piano concertos, chamber music, and numerous small piano pieces.

Scott, Sir Walter (*b* Edinburgh, 15 Aug 1771; *d* Abbotsford, 21 Sept 1832). Scottish poet and novelist. His writings inspired much music. Among his novels, *The Bride of Lammermoor* (1819), *Ivanhoe* (1820) and *Kenilworth* (1821) were especially popular as models for librettos, attracting such composers as Carafa, Donizetti, Marschner, Pacini, Auber and Sullivan. But the best Scott music was composed to his own words, notably by Schubert in seven song settings (1825) from *The Lady of the Lake* (1810).

Scottish Fantasy. Fantasia by Bruch on Scottish folktunes, for violin and orchestra (1880).

Scottish National Orchestra. The leading orchestra in Scotland, based in Glasgow. It was established in 1894 as the Scottish Orchestra and was attached to Glasgow Choral Union (founded 1874); it was renamed in 1951. Its conductors have included Barbirolli, Rankl, Szell, Susskind, Alexander Gibson (1959–84) and Neeme Järvi (from 1984). With the University of Glasgow it has organized Musica Nova, a festival of contemporary music held every two or three years since 1971; programmes concentrate on the works of two or three composers, who have included Berio, Davies, Birtwistle and Takemitsu.

Scottish Opera. Company based in Glasgow, founded in 1962 by Alexander Gibson. Its home is the Theatre Royal (1867, reopened 1975). Scottish operas have been commissioned since 1972. The company tours in Britain and abroad.

Scottish Symphony. Mendelssohn's Symphony no.3 in A minor (1842), inspired by a visit to Scotland.

Scotto. Italian family of booksellers, music printers and composers. Ottaviano (i) (*d* 1498) issued some missals, those of 1482 making him the first Italian to use movable type. His heirs were his nephews, including Ottaviano (ii) (*fl* 1498–1552), who produced (1533–9) music editions with Andrea Antico; and Girolamo (*c* 1505–1572), a madrigal composer and bookseller whose principal interest was music printing, using movable type and a single impression. Girolamo's nephew Melchiorre (*fl* 1566–1613) printed a great quantity of music, notably editions of Palestrina and Lassus, anthologies and lute tablatures.

Scotto, Renata (*b* Savona, 24 Feb 1934). Italian soprano. She sang at La Scala from 1953, notably in Bellini and Puccini; she appeared as Amina in *La sonnambula* at Edinburgh in 1957 and as Butterfly at Covent Garden in 1962, the role of her Met début in 1965. From 1973 she sang such heavier roles as Bellini's Norma and Donizetti's Anne Boleyn, to which she brought agility and dramatic power. She has also been active as a producer.

Scraper. Any instrument whose sound is produced by friction with a corrugated surface, such as the GÜIRO, the RATCHET or even the WASHBOARD.

Scriabin, Alexander Nikolayevich. *See* SKRYABIN, ALEXANDER NIKOLAYEVICH.

Scribe, (Augustin) Eugène (*b* Paris, 24 Dec 1791; *d* there, 20 Feb 1861). French dramatist and librettist. A highly skilled theatrical craftsman, he produced 'well-made' comedies and dramas concentrating attention on the plot, forward-moving action, contrasting characters and artful engagement of the audience; his librettos use similar principles, blended with the Romantic elements of passionate love, religious or social conflict and a period setting, to create a sequence of stirring scenes that builds to a huge finale. He is remembered for his distinctive contribution to French grand opera, especially with Meyerbeer, but also for his work with Auber, Bellini, Donizetti, Gounod, Halévy,

Offenbach and Verdi.

Sculthorpe, Peter (Joshua) (*b* Launceston, Tasmania, 29 April 1929). Australian composer. He studied at Melbourne University and with Rubbra and Wellesz at Oxford (1958–61) and in 1963 he began teaching at Sydney University. His music features an expressive brilliance of colour and vigorous use of ostinato, sometimes reflecting his interest in Balinese music. Among his works are the opera *Rites of Passage* (1974), orchestral and vocal pieces (including the series *Sun Music*) and a sequence of nine string quartets.

Sea Drift. Work by Delius for baritone, chorus and orchestra (1904), a setting of part of Whitman's *Out of the Cradle Endlessly Rocking*.

Sea Interludes. Four pieces making up Britten's op.33*a*, the descriptive orchestral music from *Peter Grimes* (1945), often performed with the passacaglia from Act 2 (op.33*b*).

Sea Pictures. Song cycle, op.37, by Elgar, settings for alto and orchestra of five poems by Noel, C.A. Elgar, E.B. Browning, R. Garnett and A. Lindsay Gordon (1899).

Searle, Humphrey (*b* Oxford, 26 Aug 1915; *d* London, 12 May 1982). English composer. He was a pupil of Webern in Vienna (1937–8), though he did not adopt 12-note serialism fully until 1946 and his Romantic mode of expression suggests comparison more with Schoenberg and Berg (and with Liszt, on whom he was an authority). He worked for the BBC, with the Sadler's Wells Ballet (1951–7) and as a teacher (at the RCM from 1965). His output includes operas (*Hamlet*, 1968), five symphonies (1953–64) and other orchestral works, cantatas (notably *Gold Coast Customs, The Riverrun* and *The Shadow of Cain*, setting Edith Sitwell and Joyce, 1949–51) and instrumental pieces. He also taught and wrote several books.

Seasons, The [Die Jahreszeiten]. Oratorio by Haydn to a libretto by van Swieten after Thomson (1801, Vienna). Tchaikovsky and Glazunov are among the composers who wrote works based on the seasons; for Vivaldi, *see* FOUR SEASONS, THE.

Sea Symphony, A. Vaughan Williams's First Symphony (1909), a setting for soprano and baritone soloists, chorus and orchestra of poems by Walt Whitman.

Seattle Opera. American company established in 1962. Its first director, Glynn Ross, initiated the Pacific Northwest Wagner Festival (1975), at which the *Ring* was given in English and German each summer (German from 1985, with English sur-titles).

Seattle Symphony Orchestra. American orchestra founded in 1903 with Harry F. West as conductor; it was reorganized in 1926. Its home is Seattle Center Opera House (formerly Civic Auditorium; converted 1962, cap. 3100).

Sebastiani, Claudius (*b* Metz; *fl* 1557–65). German music theorist. His *Bellum musicale* (Strasbourg, 1563) depicts the theories of plainchant and polyphony in the form of a war.

Sebastiani, Johann (*b* nr. Weimar, 30 Sept 1622; *d* Königsberg, spr 1683). German composer. He reputedly studied in Italy. In *c*1650 he settled in Königsberg, becoming Kantor at the cathedral in 1661. He was court Kapellmeister, 1663–79. His works include sacred and occasional pieces and songs; the most famous is his *St Matthew Passion* (written by 1663). Mainly conservative in style, it includes recitatives and arias but avoids a dramatic operatic idiom though it uses scorings symbolically: the two violins accompany Christ's words, while the four viols accompany the other soloists. Several of the chorales are repeated; later composers took up this device.

Sebastian z Felsztyna (*b* Felsztyn, ?1480–90; *d* after 1543). Polish composer and theorist. A student at Kraków University (1507–9), he was appointed priest at Felsztyn *c*1528. Three four-part Latin motets by him have survived; they are among the earliest examples of Polish four-voice music and are based on Gregorian melodies. He wrote five music treatises (only three have survived).

Sebenico, Giovanni [Šibenčanin, Ivan] (*b* ?Šibenik, *c*1640; *d* Cividale del Friuli or Corbola, Nov 1705). Croation composer, organist and tenor. After a period in Italy, he served at the English court in 1666–73; he was *maestro di cappella* at the Turin court in 1683–90 and then at Cividale del Friuli. He wrote three operas and sacred music.

Sec (Fr.). 'Dry': an indication that a note or chord should be struck and released abruptly.

Secco (It.). Short for *recitativo secco* ('dry recitative'), a 19th-century term for RECITATIVE accompanied only by continuo.

Sechter, Simon (*b* Friedberg, 11 Oct 1788; *d* Vienna, 10 Sept 1867). Austrian theorist, composer and teacher. The foremost master of music theory in Vienna, he counted Schubert, Vieuxtemps, Nottebohm, Thalberg and Bruckner (who succeeded him as professor at the conservatory) among his pupils, meanwhile composing. Of his over 8000 pieces (mostly fugues), the few published works include an opera (1844), the chorus from Schiller's *Die Braut von Messina*, folksong arrangements and organ and piano pieces. His most important theoretical work is *Die Grundsätze der musikalischen Komposition* (3 vols., 1853–4).

Seckendorff, Karl Siegmund, Freiherr von (*b* Erlangen, 26 Nov 1744; *d* Ansbach, 26 April 1785). German composer. He was chamberlain and steward at the Weimar court, 1775–84, also directing the Kapelle. He composed music for several of Goethe's stage works and set his poems; he also wrote chamber music and articles on music and aesthetics.

Second. The INTERVAL between any adjacent diatonic scale degrees (e.g. C–D, E♭–F). If the interval is a whole tone it is a major 2nd, if a semitone, a minor 2nd.

Seconda prattica. Term, used in opposition to 'prima prattica', to stand for the new styles of music developing at the beginning of the 17th century. The term may have originated in Monteverdi's circles or in Ferrara, apropos the new, freer, less strictly contrapuntal style favoured there, in which the music follows the sense of the words.

Second Viennese School. Term for the group of

composers who worked in Vienna in the early 20th century around Schoenberg, especially his pupils and those who adopted 12-note composition; in particular, it is used in reference to the three leading figures, Schoenberg, Berg and Webern.

Secret, The [Tajemstvi]. Opera in three acts by Smetana to a libretto by Krásnohorská (1878, Prague).

Secret Marriage, The. *See* MATRIMONIO SEGRETO, IL.

Seedo [Sidow] (*b c*1700; *d* ?Prussia, *c*1754). German musician. In the 1730s he contributed to several ballad operas at Drury Lane Theatre, London, notably *The Devil to Pay* (1731), which as a shortened afterpiece was the most popular ballad opera of the century after *The Beggar's Opera*. He also directed the band and composed an all-sung masque (1733). About 1736 he left to serve at the Prussian court.

Seefried, Irmgard (*b* Köngetried, 9 Oct 1919). Austrian soprano of German birth. She sang at the Aachen Opera from 1939, and in 1943 joined the Vienna Staatsoper after making her début as Eva; in 1947 she sang Fiordiligi and Susanna with the company at Covent Garden. She has appeared widely in concert, often with her husband, the violinist Wolfgang Schneiderhan, and with her light voice and charming manner is an admired singer of lieder.

Seeger, Charles (Louis) (*b* Mexico City, 14 Dec 1886; *d* Bridgewater, CT, 7 Feb 1979). American musicologist. His initial interest was in composition and conducting, and after graduating at Harvard he studied in Europe. He taught at Berkeley (1912–19), where he gave the first American courses in musicology in 1916, at the Institute of Musical Art, New York (1921–33), and at the New School for Social Research (1931–5), where, with Henry Cowell, he taught the first courses in ethnomusicology in the USA (1932). He was active in the organization and development of the Composers Collectives and worked as a music critic for several newspapers and journals, including the *Daily Worker*. He moved to Washington, DC, as music technical adviser in Roosevelt's Resettlement Administration (1935–8), deputy director of the Federal Music Project of the Works Progress Administration (1938–41) and chief of the music division of the Pan-American Union (1941–53). He returned to teaching in 1950 and was at the Institute of Ethnomusicology at the University of California, Los Angeles (1960–70), and lecturer at Harvard (from 1972). Seeger concentrated on general ethnomusicology and its theory and had influence as a largely prescriptive and philosophical writer. His lifelong interest in American folk music has been continued in the work of his children, the folksingers, songwriters and authors, Pete(r) R. Seeger (*b* 1919), Michael Seeger (*b* 1933) and Peggy Seeger (*b* 1935); his second wife was the composer RUTH CRAWFORD.

Seelewig. Opera (Singspiel) by Sigmund Theophil Staden; published in 1644 as *Das geistliche Waldgedicht oder Freudenspiel genant Seelewig*, it is the earliest surviving German music drama, with recitative in imitation of the Italian style.

Seger, Josef (Ferdinand Norbert) (*b* Řepín, bap. 21 March 1716; *d* Prague, 22 April 1782). Czech composer, organist and educationist. He was organist at Týn

(from *c*1741) and at the Crusaders' Church in Prague (from 1745). The most prolific Czech organ composer of the 18th century, he wrote many preludes, fugues, toccatas etc in a rich harmonic idiom, as well as sacred works. He was an influential teacher and wrote a popular volume of thoroughbass lessons.

Segerstam, Leif (Selim) (*b* Vasa, 2 March 1944). Finnish composer and conductor. He studied at the Helsinki Academy (1952–63) and the Juilliard School (1963–5) and has conducted the Finnish National Opera, Stockholm Royal Opera the Deutsche Oper, Berlin and the Austrian Radio SO, (1975–82). His works include orchestral and vocal pieces and string quartets using contemporary techniques in a colourful idiom; comprehensibility is a prime concern.

Segni, Julio [Julio da Modena; Biondin] (*b* Modena, 1498; *d* Rome, 23 July 1561). Italian keyboard player and composer. A singer at Modena Cathedral (1513) he sang in Rome and by 1530 was in Venice as first organist at St Mark's. He left Venice, probably for Rome, in 1533. He was the best organist of his day. Of his surviving ricercares, only one is for keyboard; it is unique for its thick, free-voiced writing.

Segno. *See* DAL SEGNO.

Segovia, Andrés (*b* Linares, 21 Feb 1893; *d* Madrid, 2 June 1987). Spanish guitarist. Self-taught, he made his début at 15 and in 1916 successfully toured Latin America. After his Paris début in 1924 he made several world tours, doing much to establish the guitar as an instrument for serious attention. His subtlety and virtuosity, his transcriptions of Bach, Handel, the lutenists and the Spanish vihuelists, and his encouragement of young players have further contributed to the instrument's renaissance. Falla, Ponce, Rodrigo and Turina are among those to have written for him.

Segreto di Susanna, Il. *See* SUSANNA'S SECRET.

Segue (It.). 'Follows': an indication that the next section or movement must follow without a break or that an established pattern must continue.

Seguidilla. A Spanish dance and song in moderately fast triple time, usually in a major key, with off-beat initial notes and cadential melismas. It is set to strophes (*coplas*) of alternate long and short lines separated by instrumental refrains for guitar, castanets and tambourine. As music, the *seguidilla* seems to have originated in the 1590s. The Castilian type is probably the earliest, but among notable variants are the *murcianas* (from Murcia) and the quicker *sevillanas* (from Seville). *Seguidillas* were sung and danced in the 18th-century *tonadilla* and in the *sainete* and zarzuela of the 19th and 20th centuries. The most famous operatic example is 'Près des ramparts de Seville' from Bizet's *Carmen* (1875).

Seiber, Mátyás (György) (*b* Budapest, 4 May 1905; *d* Kruger National Park, 24 Sept 1960). British composer of Hungarian origin. A pupil of Kodály at the Budapest Academy (1919–24), he taught jazz at the Hoch Conservatory, Frankfurt (1928–33), and settled in England in 1935; he taught at Morley College (1942–57), becoming the most widely known and respected composition teacher in Britain. His music shows the range of his enthusiasms, from Bach and Haydn to jazz and folk music, though his later works often achieve a fine balance between Bartók and Schoenberg: they include the cantata *Ulysses* (setting Joyce, 1947), his most widely admired work, his Third Quartet (1951) and his Violin Sonata (1960).

Seidl, Anton (*b* Pest, 7 May 1850; *d* New York, 28 March 1898). Austro-Hungarian conductor. He studied in Leipzig and went to Bayreuth, where he assisted Wagner with the first performance of the *Ring* (1876). Conducting the Metropolitan Opera (from 1885) and the New York Philharmonic Society (from 1891), he paved the way for the recognition of Wagner's music in the USA.

Seixas, (José António) Carlos de (*b* Coimbra, 11 June 1704; *d* Lisbon, 25 Aug 1742). Portuguese composer. After working as organist of Coimbra Cathedral, 1718–20, he was organist at the Lisbon royal chapel and (until 1728) a colleague of D. Scarlatti; he was a famous virtuoso on both organ and harpsichord and the leading composer in 18th-century Portuguese music. Most important are his keyboard sonatas (88 of a possible 700 survive), which unlike Scarlatti's are mostly in several movements; they feature idiomatic writing and experiments with motivic development. He also wrote sacred and orchestral pieces.

Séjan, Nicolas (*b* Paris, 19 March 1745; *d* there, 16 March 1819). French organist and composer. A famous virtuoso, he played at Notre Dame Cathedral (1772–89), the royal chapel (1790–91, from 1814) and elsewhere in Paris, and was organ professor at the Conservatoire (1795–1802). He composed several keyboard works; those of the 1780s were among the first in France specifically for the piano.

Sekles, Bernhard (*b* Frankfurt, 20 March 1872; *d* there, 8 Dec 1934). German composer. A pupil of Knorr at the Hoch Conservatory, Frankfurt, and of Humperdinck, he became a widely admired teacher at the Hoch Conservatory and was its director (1923–33). His music is essentially conservative but includes jazz, Slavonic and oriental elements.

Selle, Thomas (*b* Zörbig, 23 March 1599; *d* Hamburg, 2 July 1663). German composer. He studied in Leipzig, probably with Calvisius, and was influenced by Schein. He worked in north-west Germany, successively as at Heide, Wesselburen and Itzehoe and from 1641 as Kantor at the Johanneum, Hamburg and as civic director of music in the city. A prolific composer, he wrote sacred and secular vocal music in a wide range of current forms and styles. His sacred concertos and Passion music feature flexible scorings, varied sonorities and clearcut forms; his *St John Passion* (1641) was the first Passion with instrumental interludes.

Selmer. French, American and British firms of instrument manufacturers. Founded in 1885 in Paris by the clarinettist Henri Selmer, the company made mouthpieces, reeds and, by 1904, clarinets. Henri's brother Alexandre opened an import shop in New York (sold to George M. Bundy in 1918) and the French firm expanded; it offers a full range of high-quality woodwind and brass instruments. The American distributorship moved to Elkhart, Indiana, in 1927 and from World War II began making its own clarinets and flutes; it specializes in wind and brass and educational material for school bands. Selmer London is known chiefly for its manufacture (until 1975) of electronic instruments.

Selmer, Johan Peter (*b* Oslo, 20 Jan 1844; *d* Venice, 21 July 1910). Norwegian composer. His travels abroad, especially in France (he studied in Paris), gave him what were considered advanced musical ideas; his main works are for large orchestra, sometimes with vocal parts, showing the influence of Berlioz, Liszt and Wagner. He also produced songs and choruses whose simple lyricism has contributed to their popularity in Norway.

Sembrich, Marcella (*b* Wiśniewczyk, 15 Feb 1858; *d* New York, 11 Jan 1935). Polish soprano, later naturalized American. After study in Vienna and Milan she made her début in 1877, as Bellini's Elvira. She sang Donizetti's Lucia at Covent Garden in 1880 and was successful at the Met, 1883–1909. Among the foremost coloratura singers of her time, she was admired for her pure tone and elegant style.

Semele. Musical drama by Handel to a text by Congreve (1743, London), also set by John Eccles (1707).

Semibreve. The note, in American usage called a whole-note, that is half the value of a breve and double that of a minim. It is first found in late 13th-century music. Before *c*1600 its value was half or a third of a breve. *See* NOTE VALUES.

Semi-opera. A type of English Restoration drama with extensive musical scenes, often masque-like in character, performed by subsidiary characters, the main action being carried out in speech. The best-known examples are Purcell's *Dioclesian* (1690), *King Arthur* (1691), *The Fairy Queen* (1692) and *The Indian Queen* (1695).

Semiquaver. The note, in American usage called a 16th-note, that is half the value of a quaver and double the value of a demisemiquaver. It is normally a black note with two flags; in some forms of early notation it is found as a void note with three. *See* NOTE VALUES.

Semiramide. Opera in two acts by Rossini to a libretto by Rossi after Voltaire (1823, Venice).

Many composers wrote operas on the same subject, including Porpora, Vivaldi, Hasse, Gluck, Galuppi, Paisiello, Salieri, Cimarosa, Meyerbeer and Respighi.

Semitone. Half a tone; the smallest interval of the modern Western tone system. A chromatic scale proceeds by semitones.

Semplice (It.). 'Simple': an indication that a passage should be performed in a simple style, without ornament or deviation. 'Recitativo semplice' means recitative with only continuo accompaniment.

Sempre (It.). Always.

Senaillé, Jean Baptiste (*b* Paris, *c*1688; *d* there, 15 Oct 1730). French violinist and composer. He joined the 24 Violons du Roi in 1713, rejoining in 1720 after a break which included a visit to Italy. He was also renowned as a soloist. His 50 violin sonatas (1710–27) were among the first in France to combine French and Italian elements.

Sendrey, Alfred (*b* Budapest, 29 Feb 1884; *d* Los Angeles, 3 March 1976). Hungarian-American conductor and composer. A pupil of Koessler at the

Budapest Academy (1901–5), he worked in Germany, the USA and Austria as an opera conductor, (also of the Leipzig SO, 1924–32), then moved to Paris (1933–40) and finally to the USA, where he completed his studies of Jewish music.

Senefelder, Alois (*b* Prague, Nov 1771; *d* Munich, 26 Feb 1834). Bavarian actor and playwright, the inventor of lithography. Seeking a cheap method of printing his plays, he experimented first with etched stone and later (1797) with 'chemical printing' from stone, which immediately found an important commercial application in music printing. He began developing lithography all over Europe, with the music publisher J.A. André of Offenbach, in London and from his Chemische Druckery in Vienna.

Senesino [Bernardi, Francesco] (*b* Siena; *d* ?there, by 27 Jan 1759). Italian alto castrato. He served at the Dresden court, 1717–20, then sang in Handel's opera company in London, creating many of Handel's finest heroic roles (including Julius Caesar and Admetus); he was renowned for his power and his skill in both coloratura and expressive singing. On increasingly bad terms with Handel, he joined the rival Opera of the Nobility in 1733 and in 1736 he returned to Italy.

Senfl, Ludwig (*b* ?Basle, *c*1486; *d* Munich, 2 Dec 1542/10 Aug 1543). Swiss composer active in Germany. A choirboy in Emperor Maximilian I's Hofkapelle (1496), he probably studied with Isaac, 1507–*c*1510. In 1513 he succeeded Isaac as court composer at the Kapelle in Vienna. After a brief stay at Augsburg (1519–20) he travelled widely; by 1523 he was in Munich, in the service of Duke Wilhelm of Bavaria's Hofkapelle, where he spent the rest of his life. After *c*1530 he corresponded with Luther and, though he did not support Luther's reformation openly, he seems to have sympathized with it. Within his lifetime he won the praise of musicians throughout German-speaking Europe; examples of his work appeared in numerous treatises.

Senfl was the most significant representative of Netherlands-German motet and lied composition in German-speaking regions during the Reformation. His music, which includes seven masses, eight Magnificats, numerous Latin motets and German lieder, four-voice Latin odes and a few instrumental pieces, forms both the climax to the old German music and a highpoint of the new styles at the beginning of the Reformation. His motet style is based on that of Isaac and Josquin. He developed a wide range of techniques, above all in his polyphonic settings of the Proper, using as structural bases archaic patterns (such as isorhythm), ostinatos, canon and *cantus firmus* techniques. His textures are rich in sonority, with much movement in parallel 3rds and 6ths. His lieder, which range from courtly love-songs, through the folksong to the comic or satirical song, use techniques that originated in the German Tenorlied of the early 16th century. His Latin odes, with the tune in the descant set in a simple homophonic manner, were later taken up in German Protestant hymn settings.

Sennet. Term used in stage directions of plays in the Elizabethan and Jacobean period for a signal on the ceremonial entrance or exit of a group of players. The term may be cognate with 'signet' (signal) and/or sonata.

Sentence. Term for a complete musical idea (e.g. a self-contained theme); a sentence generally consists of two or four phrases arranged in a complementary manner and ending with a perfect cadence. It serves as an intermediary term between PHRASE and PERIOD.

Senza (It.). Without.

Sepolcro. A sacred dramatic genre in Italian, based on the Passion story and cultivated at the Viennese court in the late 17th century. It was like an oratorio, but in only one section and performed with scenery, costumes and action on Maundy Thursday and Good Friday. Composers of *sepolcri* include Draghi and Caldara.

Septembre Musical. *See* MONTREUX(-VEVEY) MUSIC FESTIVAL.

Septet. A composition for seven instruments or voices (or a group that performs such a composition). The best known is Beethoven's op.20; there are others by Hummel, Spohr, Saint-Saëns, Ravel and Stravinsky.

Sequence. (1) A category of medieval Latin chant (also called *prosa* or 'prose') which flourished *c*850–1150, during which time its musical and literary importance was great. It can be defined as an extensive, wide-ranging piece of sacred chant with a Latin text which is set syllabically; but the genre underwent structural modifications during the period. The text consisted mostly of couplets each having two isosyllabic lines sung to the same melody, each couplet being different from the preceding one in melody and length. In earlier sequences the text was not governed by regular accent patterns or end-rhyme (so was indeed 'prose'). After 1000, the texts scanned and rhymed increasingly, finally becoming verse. The texts were often associated with a particular season, feast or saint's day, and were probably sung at Mass, immediately after the alleluia, as a medieval addition to the Proper. Its relationship with the alleluia and its own genesis remain subjects of controversy, largely because of notation problems.

The main source for the early repertory is the work of NOTKER of St Gall (*c*840–912) whose *Liber hymnorum* is presumed to have been completed by 880 (it is only preserved in MSS from after 950). His works present a wide variety of styles and structures. Nine 'partially texted' early sequences have provoked various interpretations. The regularization of accent and influx of rhyme after 1000 became dominant features in the 12th century. The five sequences remaining in standard chant books – *Victimae Paschali laudes, Lauda Sion, Veni sancte spiritus, Stabat mater dolorosa* and *Dies irae* – date from this second phase.

The sequence was considered suitable for polyphonic setting from its earliest stages, from the parallel organum of the 10th-century *Musica enchiriadis* to the two-voice discant style of the 13th and 14th centuries, although at this time it was a choral chant and not commonly associated with polyphony for solo voices. However, there was a revival of it as a major polyphonic form in the early 15th century in the works of Dufay and Brumel and subsequently in those of Josquin and Willaert. Isaac included sequences in his *Choralis constantinus*. In the Renaissance, polyphonic settings of sequences for ritual purposes were rare and, particularly in England, were more commonly set as votive antiphons. After the Council of Trent and the reduction in the number of accepted sequences, it was only an intermittent genre, the last example of which is Byrd's setting of *Victimae paschali* in his *Gradualia*.

(2) A melodic or polyphonic idea consisting of a figure or motif stated successively at different pitches. Sequences may be used in the construction of a melody or theme, and usually function in the spinning out of material by developing a motif. *See also* ROSALIA.

Sequentia. Medieval term for a wordless melody associated with the alleluia of the Mass (as opposed to *prosa*, used for melodies with texts).

Sequenzae. Series of nine works by Berio (1958–75) for different solo instruments (one for solo female voice).

Serafin, Tullio (*b* Rottanova di Cavarzere, 1 Sept 1878; *d* Rome, 2 Feb 1968). Italian conductor. He studied at Milan Conservatory and made his début at Ferrara in 1898. He was principal conductor at La Scala, 1909–14, notably in Strauss and Montemezzi. At the Met (1924–34) he conducted premières of several new American works. He was artistic director of the Teatro ˙Reale, Rome (1934–43), giving well-balanced performances of the *Ring* and *Wozzeck*. Latterly he was often associated with Callas. An outstanding conductor of Italian Romantic opera, he did much to foster the revival of interest in Bellini and Donizetti.

Serebrier, José (*b* Montevideo, 3 Dec 1938). Uruguayan conductor and composer. He was a pupil of Santórsola and Estrada in Montevideo and of Giannini, Copland, Monteux and Dorati in the USA, where he has held appointments with the American SO (1962–7) and the Cleveland PO (1968–71). His works include orchestral and mixed-media pieces (e.g. *Colores mágicos*, 1971).

Serenade. A musical form, closely related to the DIVERTIMENTO. The word, from the Latin *serenus*, was used in its Italian form, SERENATA, for vocal works of various kinds, and serenade arias (love songs performed out of doors in the evening) occur in Mozart's *Die Entführung aus dem Serail* and *Don Giovanni*. In the Classical period the serenata's function was increasingly taken over by the instrumental serenade, of which Mozart's are the finest examples. Such works were often performed in the evenings or on social occasions; in the Salzburg tradition they might include as many as ten movements, often with three in concerto style set within four or more for orchestra. In the 19th century the orchestral serenade began to predominate, whether for strings (e.g. Dvořák's op.22, Tchaikovsky's op.48 and Elgar's op.22), wind instruments (Dvořák's op.44 and Strauss's op.7) or full orchestra

(Brahms's opp.11 and 16, the latter without violins). Smaller-scale serenades include Wolf's *Italienische Serenade* for string quartet. Britten's *Serenade* op.31 for tenor, horn and string orchestra is a cycle of songs about evening.

Serenade for Tenor, Horn and Strings. Song cycle, op.31, by Britten, settings of six poems about evening by English poets (1943).

Serenade Quartet. Title given to a string quartet long attributed to Haydn (as his op.3 no.5), on account of its serenade-like slow movement; the work is now no longer accepted as Haydn's and has been ascribed to Roman Hoffstetter.

Serenade to Music. Work by Vaughan Williams (1938), a setting of a passage from *The Merchant of Venice* for 16 solo voices and orchestra.

Serenata. In its general sense, a musical performance in someone's honour. The term is used as the Italian equivalent of SERENADE for a song sung in the evening with instrumental accompaniment by a lover beneath the beloved's window. More specifically it is used for large-scale Baroque cantatas usually performed out of doors in the evenings to celebrate a particular occasion such as a royal anniversary. Serenatas were often given in elaborate scenic settings and with rich costumes, but (like the oratorio) without stage action or change of scene. There were at least two (usually more) solo singers, typically representing pastoral, allegorical or mythological figures; on particularly important occasions a chorus might be introduced. One feature was the progressive orchestration, frequently for larger forces than are found in contemporary operas. A. Scarlatti is prominent among composers who wrote serenatas for performance in Rome and Naples. The genre was particularly cultivated in Venice, and outside Italy in Vienna, Munich and Dresden and by aristocratic families in Spain and Portugal.

Serenata notturna. Mozart's Serenade no.6 in D, K239 (1776).

Serialism. A method of composition in which one or more musical elements is subject to ordering in a fixed series. Most commonly the elements so arranged are the 12 pitch classes of the equal-tempered scale. This was a technique introduced by Schoenberg in the early 1920s and used by him in most of his subsequent compositions. Serialism was quickly taken up by his pupils, including Berg and Webern, and by their pupils, but not at first by many outside the circle, the most important exceptions being Dallapiccola and Krenek. The method spread more widely and rapidly after World War II, when Babbitt, Boulez, Nono and Stockhausen produced their first acknowledged works. Some of these composers, influenced by Messiaen's piano piece *Mode de valeurs et d'intensités* (1949), developed a method for controlling different musical parameters through permutations of a single series of 12 numbers, and they accordingly extended serialism to elements other than pitch, notably duration, dynamics and attack. At the same time, serial techniques began to be used by established composers, notably Stravinsky. Serialism cannot be described as constituting in itself a system of composition, still less a style; nor is it necessarily incompatible with tonality, as certain works of Berg and Stravinsky show, though it has usually been used as a means of erecting pitch structures in atonal music.

The term 'serialism' is now reserved, in some theoretical writings, only for music that goes beyond the pitch serialism of Schoenberg and applies serial methods to other elements.

For a fuller account of Schoenbergian 12-note methods, *see* TWELVE-NOTE MUSIC.

Series. An ordered succession of elements to be used as basic material in a composition. The term is most frequently applied to an ordering of the 12 pitch classes (in which case it is identical in meaning with note-row or tone-row), but it may also be used for a succession of fewer or more than 12 of any element (pitch classes, pitches, durations, dynamics, time points, timbres etc). *See also* SERIALISM.

Sérieyx, Auguste (Jean Maria Charles) (*b* Amiens, 14 June 1865; *d* Montreux, 19 Feb 1949). French composer. At the Schola Cantorum (1897–1907), he was a pupil of d'Indy, to whom he remained close. He wrote sacred choral music.

Serkin, Rudolf (*b* Eger, 28 March 1903). American pianist of Austrian birth. He studied in Vienna and made his début there in 1915. In 1920 a concert with the Busch CO led to a duo-sonata partnership with the violinist Adolf Busch. In 1939 he settled in the USA, becoming head of the piano department at the Curtis Institute. As a soloist he is known as a profound, precise interpreter of the Viennese Classics. His son Peter (*b* 1947) is also a pianist with interests ranging from Bach to Messiaen.

Serly, Tibor (*b* Losonc, 25 Nov 1901; *d* London, 8 Oct 1978). American composer of Hungarian origin. He was a pupil of Kodály at the Budapest Academy (1922–4); after settling in the USA he played the violin in several orchestras and conducted. In 1929 he began an enduring friendship with Ezra Pound. After Bartók and his wife arrived in New York he supported them and completed Bartók's Third Piano Concerto and Viola Concerto. In his compositions he used the 'modus lascivus' music, and allowed for 'multi-dimensional' music, and wordless singing.

Sermisy, Claudin de (*b c*1490; *d* Paris, 13 Oct 1562). French composer. He was a cleric at the Sainte-Chapelle in 1508 and later a singer in the king's personal chapel. In 1524 he went to Cambron (diocese of Amiens), but in 1532 was back in Paris as *sous-maître* of the royal chapel. He remained in the service of the kings of France until at least 1554, and probably until his death. The popularity of much of his music attests to the high reputation he enjoyed in his lifetime: he was ranked alongside Josquin, Févin and Certon by one of his contemporaries and in a *déploration* on his death by Certon (1570) was called 'grand maistre, expert et magnifique compositeur'.

His sacred works, which include 12 masses, many motets and Magnificats, exhibit some of the traits found in the music of Josquin and Févin's generation: voice-pairing, imitation and occasional canonic writing, though he avoided close-knit continuous counterpoint which obscured the text. His Passion is one of only two surviving French polyphonic Passions of the 16th century. His French *chansons*, of which *c*175 survive, show a logical development from those of Févin and Mouton in abandoning melismatic settings in favour of a simpler, more syllabic, more homophonic and faster-moving style. From *c*1528 he led the development of the lyrical, four-voice Parisian *chanson*. Some (e.g. *Je n'ay point plus d'affection*) are homorhythmic, others predominantly polyphonic; a few (e.g. *Ton feu s'estaint*) have two voices in canon. Perfect cadences tend to emphasize tonality in such works as *Tant que vivray* and *Maulgré moy vis*, which sound unequivocally tonal.

Serocki, Kazimierz (*b* Toruń, 3 March 1922; *d* Warsaw, 9 Jan 1981). Polish composer. He studied with Sikorski at the Łódź Conservatory and with Boulanger in Paris (1947–8). He was one of the leaders of the opening of Polish music in the 1950s to avant-garde techniques, his own works showing a dynamic treatment of percussion sonorities and, in his vocal music, a high expressive intensity. Notable among his later works are *Continuum* (1966), for six percussionists on 123 instruments, *Dramatic Story* (1971) for orchestra and the *Fantasia elegiaca* (1972) for organ and orchestra.

Serov, Alexander Nikolayevich (*b* St Petersburg, 23 Jan 1820; *d* there, 1 Feb 1871). Russian composer and critic. He took up music seriously from 1851, writing operas and narrow musical criticism showing him at odds with both factions in Russian musical life, the Slavophiles and the Westerners. His importance rests mainly in his astonishingly successful, Meyerbeerian operas *Judith* (1861–3) and *Rogneda* (1863–5), not only for their contemporary appeal but also for the great influence they had on later, more subtly skilled Russian composers: Musorgsky's crowd scenes, Tchaikovsky's dances and Borodin's folklike choruses owe something to them. Though not influenced by Wagner, Serov was the first Russian critic to champion Wagner's music.

Serpent. An obsolete wind instrument, originally a bass member of the CORNETT family. It derives its name from its shape, a long, sinuous tube, roughly S-shaped with an extra twist and often supported with vertical struts. The tube, markedly conical, is just over 2 metres long. The smaller end holds a metal crook with a cup mouthpiece similar to that of a bass trombone but usually of ivory or horn. The body was made of wood and covered with leather or canvas and contained two sets of three holes, although 19th-century models sometimes had extra holes and keys to govern them. The serpent was invented *c*1590 by a French churchman, Edmé Guillaume, for use in church music, particularly to double male voices in plainsong. It continued to be played in church bands in France and in England until the mid-19th century (Thomas Hardy mentioned it in this connection) but received a new lease of life in the mid-18th century by its adoption into military bands in Germany and England.

Serpette, (Henri Charles Antoine) Gaston (*b* Nantes, 4 Nov 1846; *d* Paris, 3 Nov 1904). French composer. He studied at the Paris Conservatoire, winning the Prix de Rome in 1871. A miniaturist with a gift for parody, he succeeded chiefly in salon pieces and theatrical scores for vaudeville operettas.

Serse. Opera in three acts by Handel to a libretto after Stampiglia and Minato (1738, London); on the story of Xerxes, it opens with his aria 'Ombra mai fù', 'Handel's Largo'.

Servais, Adrien François (*b* Hal, 6 June 1807; *d* there, 26 Nov 1866). Belgian cellist. A pupil of Platel at the Brussels Conservatory, he was described by Berlioz as 'Paganinian'. He was probably the finest cellist of his day. His son Joseph (1850–85), also an admired cellist, taught at the Brussels Conservatory.

Serva padrona, La [The Maid as Mistress]. Intermezzo (to *Il prigionier superbo*) in two parts by Pergolesi to a libretto by Federico (1733, Naples).

Serventois. *See* SIRVENTES.

Service. Term in the Anglican liturgy for musical settings of the canticles for Matins and Evensong and of parts of the Ordinary of Holy Communion. A service may comprise any or all of the following: for Matins: *Venite, Te Deum, Benedicite, Benedictus, Jubilate*; for Evensong: *Magnificat, Cantate Domino, Nunc dimittis, Deus misereatur*; and for Communion: Kyrie, Gloria, Creed, Sanctus, Benedictus, Agnus Dei. The term is also applied to settings of sentences from the Burial Service.

By 1549, Latin services had been almost entirely replaced in the Anglican liturgy by the English of *The Booke of the Common Prayer*. There are partbooks from that date devoted to Communion settings, from simple note-against-note compositions to adaptations of Taverner's complex Masses. The 1552 Prayer Book referred to music only in connection with the Gloria, now at the end of the service. The shift of emphasis from the Communion continued during the later 16th century. Composers usually set only the Kyrie and Creed; in the early 17th some also supplied settings of the Sanctus and occasionally the Gloria. After the Restoration the Sanctus was frequently sung as an introit to the ante-Communion, but late 17th- and 18th-century settings of both Sanctus and Gloria are few. A result of the 19th-century Oxford Movement was the restoration of Holy Communion to a more central position in sung worship, and in the 20th English composers found new inspiration in both the Communion Service and the Latin Mass; there are settings by Vaughan Williams, Rubbra and Britten.

Early partbooks contain comparatively little music for Matins and Evensong. In Day's *Certaine Notes* (1565) the various service elements are consistently grouped, with music for the Communion between that for Matins and Evensong (a 'full service'). Pre-Commonwealth settings fall into three basic categories: the 'short' service (e.g. Tallis's), essentially chordal in structure and for four voices without independent organ accompaniment; the 'long' or 'great' service, a festal composition, for large choir in up to eight parts (Byrd's Great Service is a fine example); and the service 'for verses', short with interpolated solos (the earliest substantial example is Morley's, and the type became increasingly popular in the early 17th century). Until the 19th cen-

tury, the service was less important than the anthem. S.S. Wesley broke new ground with his big E major Service (1845), blending an important organ part with the voice and striving for a new and more expressive idiom. Stanford's services represent the culmination of Wesley's work, and Charles Wood continued in a similar vein. The most successful 20th-century contributions are those of Howells and the composers mentioned above.

Sesquialtera. The ratio 3:2. The term is used in music for a reduction of note values, in mensural notation, in that ratio. In Hispanic music, it may refer to the mixture of duple and triple time within groups of six quavers.

Sessions, Roger (Huntington) (*b* Brooklyn, 28 Dec 1896; *d* Princeton, 16 March 1985). American composer. He studied with Parker at Yale and with Bloch in New York, becoming Bloch's assistant at the Cleveland Conservatory. Then he lived in Europe (1925–33) before returning to teach at Princeton (1935–44, 1953–65) and other institutions. He was the principal exponent of the internationalist approach to composition in the 1920s and the leading composition teacher, 1935–80. His pupils include Babbitt, Cone, Nancarrow and Weisgall. His writings address many difficult issues, from the practical to the philosophical.

Operas The Trial of Lucullus (1947); Montezuma (1964)
Incidental music The Black Maskers (1923)
Orchestral music 9 syms. (1927, 1946, 1957, 1958, 1964, 1966, 1967, 1968, 1978); Vn Conc. (1935); Pf Conc. (1956); Divertimento (1960); Rhapsody (1970); Conc., vn, vc (1971); Concertino, chamber orch (1972); Conc. for Orch (1981)
Vocal music Idyll of Theocritus (1954); When Lilacs Last in the Dooryard Bloom'd (1970)
Chamber music 2 str qts (1936, 1951); Duo, vn, pf (1943); Vn Sonata (1953); Str Qnt (1958)
Piano music 3 sonatas (1930, 1946, 1965); Pages from a Diary (1939); Five Pieces (1975)

Set. Term borrowed from a branch of mathematics known as set theory, where it refers to a collection of objects classified according to a given rule.

In music, it is generally used in connection with the 12-note system, where a 12-note set consists of all 12 pitch classes. The various operations of the 12-note system can, when pitch classes are expressed as numbers, be defined through arithmetic operations.

Seter, Mordecai (*b* Novorossiysk, 26 Feb 1916). Israeli composer of Russian origin. He studied in Paris with Dukas and Boulanger, then worked in Palestine as a composer and folksong collector; since 1972 he has been a professor at Tel-Aviv University. His early music is nationalist but later scores use 12-note serialism; his style is marked by a sense of drama and by the principle of variation. His output includes ballets, piano and orchestral music, string quartets and choral pieces, including the oratorio *Midnight Vigil* (1961).

Set piece. Term used, in Anglo-American sacred music of the 18th and 19th centuries, for a through-composed setting of a metrical text. In a dramatic work, it implies a self-contained number, such as an aria or a trio.

Settimana Musicale Senese (Italy). Annual (autumn) festival in Siena established in 1939; events include concerts of early Italian music and lectures.

Ševčík, Otakar (*b* Horaždovice, 22 March 1852; *d* Písek, 18 Jan 1934). Czech violinist. He studied in Prague, led orchestras in Salzburg and Vienna, and taught in Kiev, Prague and Vienna. He was greatly in demand and highly influential as a teacher (he had nearly 5000 pupils), using methods that stress perfection of detail.

Seven Deadly Sins, The. Ballet in a prologue, seven scenes and an epilogue by Weill to a libretto by Brecht, for soprano, male chorus and orchestra (1933, Paris).

Seven Last Words of Christ on the Cross, The. Composition by Haydn, written in 1785 or 1786 as a series of Easter meditations on commission from Cádiz Cathedral for performance in 1786 or 1787. It was originally for orchestra; Haydn later made arrangements for string quartet (op.51, 1787) and with voices as an oratorio (*c*1795); a piano version was also published with his approval. The work consists of seven Adagios with an introduction and epilogue.

Seventh. The INTERVAL between two notes of the diatonic scale six degrees apart (e.g. C–B, G–F); it is the interval produced when the 2nd is inverted at the octave. An octave less a diatonic semitone is a major 7th; an octave less a whole tone is a minor 7th.

Seventh chord. A chord consisting of a note with a 3rd, a 5th (usually) and a 7th above it; it may be inverted. *See also* DIMINISHED SEVENTH CHORD; DOMINANT SEVENTH CHORD.

Séverac, (Marie Joseph Alexandre) Déodat de (*b* St Félix de Caraman en Lauragais, 20 July 1872; *d* Céret, 24 March 1921). French composer. A pupil of d'Indy, Magnard and Albéniz at the Schola Cantorum, Paris (1896–1907), he spent most of his life in southern France, whose landscape and music were important to him, as was Debussy. His relatively small output includes operas (*Le coeur du moulin*, 1909; *Héliogabale*, 1910), sacred choral music and a few symphonic poems, but consists mostly of piano pieces and songs.

Severi, Francesco (*b* Perugia, late 16th century; *d* Rome, 25 Dec 1630). Italian composer. He was a soprano castrato in the papal choir, Rome, and wrote sacred and secular vocal pieces. In his *Salmi passaggiati* (1615) the solo voice's ornamentation is (unusually) written out in full, giving insight into the current style of improvisation.

Sextet. A composition for six instruments or voices (or a group that performs such a composition). The string sextet of Classical and post-Classical chamber music is commonly for two violins, two violas and two cellos. Brahms's opp.18 and 36 are the masterpieces of this repertory; others were composed by Boccherini, Spohr, Raff, Dvořák, Rimsky-Korsakov, Borodin, Reger, Martinů and Schoenberg (*Verklärte Nacht*). Wind sextets include those of Mozart, Beethoven (op.71) and Janáček (*Mladí*), and there are sextets for piano with various instruments by Mendelssohn, Glinka, Dohnányi,

Poulenc and others.

Sextolet [sextuplet]. A group of six notes of equal length taking the place of several (normally four) notes of the same kind. Properly, a sextolet is formed by the division into two of each note of a triplet, not by the division into three of a pair of notes (which is a double triplet).

Sextus (Lat.). 'Sixth': term for the sixth part in vocal polyphony, particularly in the 16th and 17th centuries.

Seydelmann, Franz (*b* Dresden, 8 Oct 1748; *d* there, 23 Oct 1806). German composer. After a study tour of Italy (1765–8) he became a church composer to the Dresden court in 1772, and joint Kapellmeister with Schuster in 1787. His 12 stage works, 1773–95, include Italian comic operas and German Singspiels, and share features with those by his teacher J.G. Naumann. He also wrote oratorios, other sacred works, cantatas and some chamber and keyboard pieces. His later works reflect the influences of C.P.E. Bach and Haydn.

Seyfried, Ignaz (Xaver), Ritter von (*b* Vienna, 15 Aug 1776; *d* there, 27 Aug 1841). Austrian composer, conductor and writer on music. Between 1797 and 1827 he was associated with the Freihaus-Theater and the Theater an der Wien, providing innumerable scores for plays, operas, Singspiels, biblical dramas and parodies, as well as conducting (notably the première of Beethoven's *Fidelio* in 1805). His versatility – he also wrote church music, pedagogical works and journal articles – if not his creative ingenuity, won him a unique place in Viennese musical life.

Sf [sfz]. *See* SFORZANDO, SFORZATO. The abbreviation *sfp* stands for *sforzando-piano*, i.e. play quietly immediately after an accented note.

Sfogato (It.). 'Let loose': in a light, easy style.

Sforza. Italian family of music patrons. During their rule of the Duchy of Milan, 1450–1535, Milan was one of the most active centres of Renaissance culture. Galeazzo Maria (ruled 1466–76) employed *c*40 singers, among them Josquin, Alexander Agricola and Compère. Musical development reached a high level under Ludovico il Moro, who ruled in the period from 1480, and his wife Beatrice d'Este; there were sumptuous musical festivities, some with sets and stage machines designed by Leonardo da Vinci.

Sforzando, sforzato (It.). 'Forcing', 'compelling': a strong accent, abbreviated *sf* or *sfz*.

Sgambati, Giovanni (*b* Rome, 28 May 1841; *d* there, 14 Dec 1914). Italian composer and pianist. A pupil and protégé of Liszt, an internationally successful pianist and co-founder of the Liceo Musicale (later Conservatorio) di S Cecilia, Rome, he was a leading figure in the late 19th-century resurgence of non-operatic music in Italy. His orchestral, chamber and keyboard works, reminiscent of Mendelssohn, Chopin, Schumann and Liszt, show a fluent talent but have endured less well than his Requiem (1895–6), used at Italian royal funerals. He conducted the première of Liszt's *Christus* (Part I, 1866–7).

Shake. *See* TRILL.

Shakespeare, William (*b* Stratford-on-Avon, bap. 26 April 1564; *d* London, 23 April 1616). English playwright. Music had an important part in his plays: *c*100 songs and many instrumental cues, ranging from sophisticated character-songs to functional battle-calls, are fully integrated into the dramas. Most of the original tunes are lost, but they included well-known ballads and popular instrumental music as well as art songs. His verses have inspired countless composers, notably of songs (Arne, *Where the bee sucks*; Schubert, *Who is Sylvia?*). Among many others who have written incidental or dramatic orchestral music are Mendelssohn (*A Midsummer Night's Dream*), Berlioz (*Romeo and Juliet, King Lear*), Liszt (*Hamlet*), Tchaikovsky (*Romeo and Juliet*), Elgar (*Falstaff*), Prokofiev (*Romeo and Juliet*, ballet) and Walton (*Henry V*, film). Operas and other dramatic works composed to librettos based on the plays include Purcell *The Fairy Queen* (*A Midsummer Night's Dream*), Rossini *Otello*, Berlioz *Béatrice et Bénédict* (*Much Ado*), Verdi *Macbeth*, *Otello* and *Falstaff*, Wagner *Das Liebesverbot* (*Measure for Measure*) and Britten *A Midsummer Night's Dream*.

Shakuhachi. Small end-blown Japanese bamboo Notched flute. It was imported from China by the 8th century but reached its modern form in the 15th. The standard instrument is 54.5 cm long and has four finger-holes and a thumb-hole, producing the approximate notes $d'-f'-g'-a'-c''$; it is widely used in all forms of Japanese folk and art music.

Shalyapin [Chaliapin], Fyodor Ivanovich (*b* nr. Kazan, 13 Feb 1873; *d* Paris, 12 April 1938). Russian bass. Largely self-taught, he first sang at Tbilisi and the Imperial Opera, St Petersburg. His career developed at Mamontov's private opera in Moscow and he sang at the Bol'shoy, 1899–1914. From 1901 he sang in the West, appearing at La Scala, the Met (1907–8) and with the Dyagilev seasons in Paris. He left Russia in 1921 and sang in opera and concerts throughout the world. Regarded as the greatest singing actor of his day, his voice was sufficiently flexible for him to undertake baritone as well as bass roles. He inspired, particularly as Boris Godunov, a series of imitators.

Shamisen. A three-string plucked lute from Japan, since the 17th century a popular contributor to all forms of folk and art music. Standard tunings are $b-e'-b''$, $b-f\sharp'-b'$ and $b-e'-a'$. The shamisen is played with an ivory plectrum; its distinctive sound is caused by a cavity in its long neck which allows the lowest strings to vibrate against the wood. (For illustration, *see* Lute.)

Shankar, Ravi (*b* Varanasi, Uttar Pradesh, 7 April 1920). Indian sitar player and composer. By the mid-1940s he had embarked on a performing career in India. He toured Europe and the USA (1956–7) and laid the foundations of an international reputation that has greatly furthered the popularity of Indian music in the West.

Shanty. A song with chorus sung by sailors as an aid to work on a ship. The earliest references to sailors' songs date from the 16th century, but most shanties known today (such as *Blow the Man Down*, *Rio*

Grande and *A-rovin'*) are of 19th-century origin, while the term itself is even more recent.

Shape notes. A tradition of rural American sacred music, marked by the use of unorthodox notational systems, in which differently shaped notes used for different pitches enabled a beginner to recognize pitches from the note-head shapes without having to learn the names of keys or lines and spaces. The first shape-notation (sometimes known as 'character', 'patent' or 'buckwheat' notation) to gain acceptance, at the beginning of the 19th century, was based on four-syllable solmization; this was superseded by a seven-syllable system. The four-syllable system was sometimes called 'fasola' because it was based on the syllables *fa, sol, la* and *mi*. Shape-note hymnody was published in many singing-school tune books and other collections of sacred music. The best known was *The Sacred Harp* (1844, using the four-shape system); shape-note gospel hymnody was propagated from the 1870s, notably through the monthly periodical, *Musical Million* (1870–1914).

Shapero, Harold (Samuel) (*b* Lynn, MA, 29 April 1920). American composer. He was a pupil of Piston and Krenek at Harvard (1938–41) and of Hindemith and Boulanger. In 1951 he joined the faculty at Brandeis. His works combine Stravinskyan neo-classicism with serialism. During the 1940s he was closely associated with Bernstein, Berger and Fine with whom he shared an interest in popular music and jazz.

Shapey, Ralph (*b* Philadelphia, 12 March 1921). American composer and conductor. He was a pupil of Wolpe. He has conducted and taught widely in the USA (at the University of Chicago, 1964–85, then at Queens College), and composed mostly instrumental music in a style described as 'abstract expressionist'. He withdrew his works, 1969–76, as a protest against world conditions.

Shaporin, Yury (Alexandrovich) (*b* Glukhov, 8 Nov 1887; *d* Moscow, 9 Dec 1966). Soviet composer. A pupil of Sokolov, Shteynberg and Tcherepnin at the St Petersburg Conservatory (1913–18), he allied himself with revolutionary trends in the theatre and music in the 1920s, but thereafter wrote comparatively little, much of his creative energy going into the opera *The Decembrists* (1920–53), which is comparable with *Prince Igor* in its epic sweep and lyricism. His other works include songs, piano music, film scores and oratorios, of which *The Story of the Battle for the Russian Land* (1944) was acclaimed.

Sharp. A notational sign (♯), normally placed to the left of a note, indicating that the note is to be raised in pitch by a semitone. The word is used as an adjective to denote intonation above notated pitch. Double sharps (notated **×**) indicate that the note they precede is to be raised in pitch by two semitones.

Sharp, Cecil (James) (*b* London, 22 Nov 1859; *d* London, 28 June 1924). English folk music collector and editor. He studied at Cambridge, then taught in Australia and England. He turned his attention to folk music *c*1900 and soon became the most important English folksong collector. He published numerous collections of songs and dances from 1904 onwards; he also visited the USA to collect songs of English origin and 'square dances' in Appalachia, thus giving impetus to American efforts. His aim of 'restoring their songs and dances to the English people' was realized by his collecting 4977 tunes, of which he published 1118 and provided accompaniments for 501. Composers such as Vaughan Williams, Holst and Butterworth used material he had collected.

Shaw, (George) Bernard (*b* Dublin, 26 July 1856; *d* Ayot St Lawrence, 2 Nov 1950). Irish dramatist and critic. Born into a musical household, he was early initiated into Italian opera and Mozart. In 1876 he moved to London and wrote his first music criticisms for *The Hornet*. From the start his views were trenchant and articulate, couched in a lithe and vivid prose that would venture with assurance on to any subject that might serve the cause of truth as he saw it. He became music critic of *The Star* in 1888–9 as 'Corno di Bassetto'; in 1890 he transferred to *The World* and continued to write weekly criticism until August 1894. Shaw's collected writings on music stand alone in their mastery of English and compulsive readability. Determined to interest stockbrokers in the art, he eschewed academic jargon. He was fortunate in having in Wagner a musical giant whose cause still needed pleading in London, but his admiration for Wagner never ousted Verdi from his affection, even if it blinded him to the merits of Brahms. After abandoning professional criticism, he continued to follow musical developments, supporting Strauss, recognizing Elgar's genius and approving Arnold Dolmetsch's work and sitting out the latest Schoenberg or Skryabin.

Shaw, Martin (Fallas) (*b* London, 9 March 1875; *d* Southwold, 24 Oct 1958). English composer. He was a pupil of Stanford at the RCM and organist in London churches. As composer and performer he worked to improve the standards of public sung music, in opera, church music and solo song; his numerous editions were influential. His brother Geoffrey Shaw (1879–1943) also wrote church music and worked in music education.

Shaw, Robert (Lawson) (*b* Red Bluff, CA, 30 April 1916). American conductor. His early career was as director of the Fred Waring Glee Club (1938–48). He was founder of the Collegiate Chorale in New York (1941), conducting it until 1954. From 1948 to 1966 he was conductor of the Robert Shaw Chorale, touring internationally with it, and in 1967 he became music director of the Atlanta SO.

Shawm. A double-reed woodwind instrument, used extensively in European music from the late 13th century to the 17th. It was made in seven sizes, high treble (*a′–e‴*), treble (*d′–b″*), alto (*g–d″*), tenor (*c–g′* or *a′*), basset (*G–g′*), bass (*C–c′*) and great bass (variable). Usually made in one piece, it had a conical bore that widened more than that of its successor the oboe, was played with a pirouette (lip rest) and had a loud, shrill tone. Shawms were much used in court ceremonial music and in town bands. Various names were given to the instrument in France, Germany and England, the larger sizes being 'bombarde' or 'pommer' in the 15th century; the term 'hautbois' appeared after 1500 and was eventually transferred to the newly developed oboe by the late 17th century. The term 'Schalmei' was also common. Shawm-type instruments are known by cognate names outside Europe, such as *śahnāī* (India) and *zūrnā* (Arab countries). (For illustration, *see* EARLY MUSIC.)

Shchedrin, Rodion (Konstantinovich) (*b* Moscow, 16 Dec 1932). Soviet composer. He was a pupil of Shaporin at the Moscow Conservatory (1951–5). His early music is close to Soviet-period Prokofiev in its colourful orchestration and fluency and gained him official approval which continued when he began to use serial and aleatory techniques in the mid-1960s. His works include an opera, ballets (*The Little Humpbacked Horse*, 1956; *Anna Karenina*, 1972), symphonies and other orchestral scores, string quartets and piano music.

Shcherbachov, Vladimir Vladimirovich (*b* Warsaw, 25 Jan 1889; *d* Leningrad, 5 March 1952). Russian composer. He was a pupil of Lyadov and Shteynberg at the St Petersburg Conservatory (1908–14). His early works are highly Romantic, showing influences from Skryabin, Grieg, Debussy and Rakhmaninov, but during the 1920s he moved to a style of gloom and impassioned drama in his many Blok settings, or else of light, dry grotesqueness in his instrumental music; during this period he taught at the Leningrad Conservatory (1923–31). His output includes five symphonies (1913–48, two of them choral), piano music and songs.

Shebalin, Vissarion (Yakovlevich) (*b* Omsk, 11 June 1902; *d* Moscow, 28 May 1963). Soviet composer. He was a pupil of Myaskovsky at the Moscow Conservatory (1923–8), where he immediately joined the staff, becoming an outstanding teacher and rising to become director in 1941: in 1948 he was dismissed in the anti-progressive purge but he returned in 1951. The dismissal was ironic, since he had already moved away from the modernist tendencies he had shown in the 1920s, becoming concerned with folksong arrangements, mass songs and patriotic cantatas. His works include five symphonies and other orchestral scores, an opera on *The Taming of the Shrew* (1946–56, his greatest success), nine string quartets and many songs, marked by his exquisite feeling for poetry.

Shedlock, J(ohn) S(outh) (*b* Reading, 29 Sept 1843; *d* London, 9 Jan 1919). English writer on music. A piano teacher and music critic (*The Athenaeum*, 1898–1916), he made pioneering studies of Beethoven's sketchbooks and letters and wrote on the history of the piano sonata.

Sheherazade. Symphonic suite, op.35, by Rimsky-Korsakov (1888).

Overture for orchestra by Ravel (1898).

Song cycle by Ravel, settings for voice and orchestra of three poems by Tristan Klingsor (1903).

Sheldonian Theatre. Auditorium in Oxford, built in 1669 as part of the university. Music has been performed there since its opening; Handel conducted the première of his *Athalia* there (1733).

Sheng. Chinese mouth organ, consisting of a bowl-shaped wind chamber surmounted by 17 bamboo pipes arranged in a circular bunch. The *sheng* is an important part of the modern Chinese orchestra.

Shepherd, Arthur (*b* Paris, ID, 19 Feb 1880; *d* Cleveland, 12 Jan 1958). American composer. He studied at the New England Conservatory (1892–7), later teaching there (1909–19) and at Western Reserve University (1926–50). An inspiring teacher, he was a traditional, craftsmanlike composer; he wrote two symphonies, four string quartets, choral works and songs in a tonal style with folksong elements.

Shepherd on the Rock, The [Der Hirt auf dem Felsen]. Song for soprano and piano, with clarinet obbligato, by Schubert (D965), a setting of words by Müller and possibly I. von Chézy (1828).

Sheppard, John (*b c*1515; *d* ?1559/60). English composer. He was at Magdalen College, Oxford, 1543–8, and by 1552 was a Gentleman of the Chapel Royal. Most of his extant music for the Latin rite probably dates from Mary's reign. The six-voice Magnificat, for example, with its florid counterpoint and lack of imitation, belongs to the tradition of the Eton Choirbook composers. Among his more modern works are the four-voice Magnificat, the *Missa 'Cantate'* and the Mass *'The Western Wynde'*. He was at his best when writing vigorous counterpoint around a plainchant. The English works, which include 15 anthems and service music, seem to date from Edward's reign.

Sherard, James (*b* Bushby, 1 Nov 1666; *d* Evington, 12 Feb 1738). English composer. He was a successful London apothecary and an amateur violinist. His 24 trio sonatas (1701, *c*1711), all of the *da chiesa* type, combine Italian and English features.

Sheriff, Noam (*b* Tel-Aviv, 7 Jan 1935). Israeli composer. He was a pupil of Ben Haim and of Blacher in Berlin. His works seek a fusion of Near Eastern and European elements, and are mostly instrumental; they include the *Chaconne* (1968) written for the Philadelphia Orchestra.

Sherlaw Johnson, Robert. *See* JOHNSON, ROBERT SHERLAW.

Shibata, Minao (*b* Tokyo, 29 Sept 1916). Japanese composer. He was a pupil of Moroi. His works show a development from Germanic Romanticism to serialism and electronics in the 1950s and then to more avant-garde techniques, including graphic notation and aleatory writing. His output covers most concert genres. He has also taught, notably at the Tokyo Geijutsu Daigaku (1959–69), and is one of the foremost Japanese writers on European music history.

Shield, William (*b* Swalwell, 5 March 1748; *d* London, 25 Jan 1829). English composer. A pupil of Avison, he began his career as a violinist in the north-east. In the 1770s and 1780s he played the viola in the orchestra of the King's Theatre, London. Beginning in 1778, he presented over 30 operas (full-length works and afterpieces) and several pantomimes and ballets in London, winning especial success with the opera *Rosina* (1782). He also wrote song collections and chamber works. In his operas he often collaborated with the librettist John O'Keeffe (notably in *The Poor Soldier*, 1783) and tended to use pastoral topics; most contain borrowed material, including folktunes (*Rosina* popularized the tune now known as 'Auld lang syne'). Exotic colouring features in his pantomime music. In old age he published two anthologies of music (1800, 1815) and was Master of the King's Music. In his chamber music, which includes some attractive string quartets and trios, he wrote occasional movements in quintuple metre.

Shifrin, Seymour (*b* New York, 28 Feb 1926; *d* Boston, 26 Sept 1979). American composer. He was a pupil of Schuman at the Juilliard School and of Luening at Columbia. He taught at Berkeley (1952–66) and Brandeis. In the 1950s he was associated with a group of composers in New York who were deeply involved with the Second Viennese School. But he developed a style of formal clarity and fleeting, ambiguous tonality. A turning-point came with *Satires of Circumstance* for mezzo-soprano and ensemble (1964). His works are mostly for small forces.

Shift. In string playing, the movement of the left hand from one position to another on the fingerboard.

Shilkret, Nat(haniel) (*b* New York, 1 Jan 1895; *d* Franklin Square, NY, 18 Feb 1982). American conductor and composer. He worked in orchestras from his teens and was musical director for Victor records (1916–35), then a Hollywood arranger. He commissioned Schoenberg, Stravinsky and others to contribute to the biblical cantata *Genesis*, for which he also wrote a movement.

Shimizu, Osamu (*b* Osaka, 4 Nov 1911). Japanese composer. Son of a gagaku musician and pupil of Hashimoto at the Tokyo Music School (1936–9), he has had most success as a composer of operas (*Tale of Shuzerji*, 1954), choral music (*The Prayer to the Mountains*, 1960) and songs, sometimes of Buddhist inspiration. Latterly he has written for Japanese instruments.

Shimmy. A dance popular in the USA in the 1910s and particularly the 1920s. It originated among American blacks but became a national craze when introduced in the revue *Ziegfeld Follies* (1922).

Shinohara, Makoto (*b* Osaka, 10 Feb 1931). Japanese composer. He studied in Tokyo and under Messiaen, later working with Stockhausen and settling in Berlin. His music is noted for his use of novel technqiues, timbres and space effects.

Shirinsky, Vasily Petrovich (*b* Krasnodar, 17 Jan 1901; *d* Mamontovka, 16 Aug 1965). Russian composer, violinist and conductor. He was a pupil of Myaskovsky, played in the Beethoven Quartet and worked with the Radio Orchestra and in theatres. His own style moved from Skryabin lyricism to a Prokofievan linearity.

Shirley, George (Irving) (*b* Indianapolis, 18 April 1934). American tenor. He made his début in New York as Eisenstein (*Die Fledermaus*) in 1959, then sang in Milan and Spoleto and made his Met début as Ferrando (*Così fan tutte*) in 1961. His roles at Covent Garden included Pelléas (1969) and Loge in *Das Rheingold* (1974), and at Santa Fe he sang Alwa in *Lulu* (1963). He later taught in Baltimore.

Shirley-Quirk, John (Stanton) (*b* Liverpool, 28 Aug 1931). English bass-baritone. He studied with Roy Henderson, sang at Glyndebourne in the early 1960s, then joined the English Opera Group in 1964, creating leading baritone roles in Britten's church parables and *Owen Wingrave* (1971) and the seven baritone roles in *Death in Venice* (Covent Garden, 1973; Met, 1974). He also sang Eugene Onegin at Glyndebourne and several Mozart roles. His concert repertory encompasses Bach, Berlioz, Brahms, Elgar and Tippett and his sensitivity, expressive intensity and characterful tone make him an admired lieder singer.

Shivaree. The American term for CHARIVARI.

Shnitke, Al'fred Garriyevich (*b* Engel's, 24 Nov 1934). Soviet composer. He was a pupil of Rakov and Golubev at the Moscow Conservatory (1953–61), where he taught until 1972. His works often use quotations, parodies and stylistic imitations in a highly charged manner, though some are more unified in expression. Textures are rich and complexly varied and string instruments feature prominently in his output, which, apart from four symphonies and various stage works, includes four violin concertos, two violin sonatas and chamber music. He is a prolific writer on Russian music.

Shofar. The ram's horn of the Bible; it is the only ancient Jewish instrument to survive the destruction of the Second Temple by the Romans (AD 70) and is still in use during services on high holy days and symbolically on certain other occasions, with a series of four calls using the 2nd and 3rd harmonics.

Shore, John (*b c*1662; *d* London, 1752). English trumpeter. He played at the English court and became Sergeant-trumpeter in 1707; he performed many of Purcell's difficult trumpet parts. He was also a lutenist and probably a violinist. He has been credited with the invention of the tuning-fork. His father, Matthias Shore (*d* 1700), had served as Sergeant-trumpeter from 1687; another member of the family, William Shore (*d* 1707), held the post from 1700. Matthias's daughter Catherine Shore (*c*1668–1730) was a soprano.

Short octave. Term to denote the tuning of some of the lowest notes of a keyboard instrument to pitches below their apparent ones, a practice used from the 16th century to the early 19th to allow the commonest bass notes to be available while making it unnecessary to extend the full keyboard to their depth. The system was probably first used in the early 16th century and persisted until the 19th.

Shostakovich, Dmitry (Dmitriyevich) (*b* St Petersburg, 25 Sept 1906; *d* Moscow, 9 Aug 1975). Soviet composer. He studied with his mother, a professional pianist, and then with Shteynberg at the Petrograd Conservatory (1919–25): his graduation piece was his Symphony no.1, which brought him early international attention. His creative development, however, was determined more by events at home. Like many Soviet composers of his generation, he tried to reconcile the musical revolutions of his time with the urge to give a voice to revolutionary socialism, most conspicuously in his next two symphonies, no.2 ('To October') and no.3 ('The

First of May'), both with choral finales. At the same time he used what he knew of contemporary Western music (perhaps Prokofiev and Krenek mostly) to give a sharp grotesqueness and mechanical movement to his operatic satire *The Nose*, while expressing a similar keen irony in major works for the ballet (*The Golden Age, The Bolt*) and the cinema (*New Babylon*). But the culminating achievement of these quick-witted, nervy years was his second opera *The Lady Macbeth of the Mtsensk District*, where high emotion and acid parody are brought together in a score of immense brilliance.

Lady Macbeth was received with acclaim in Russia, western Europe and the USA, and might have seemed to confirm Shostakovich as essentially a dramatic composer: by the time he was 30, in 1936, he was known for two operas and three full-length ballets, besides numerous scores for the theatre and films, whereas only one purely orchestral symphony had been performed, and one string quartet. However, in that same year *Lady Macbeth* was fiercely attacked in *Pravda*, and he set aside his completed Symphony no.4 (it was not performed until 1961), no doubt fearing that its Mahlerian intensity and complexity would spur further criticism. Instead he began a new symphony, no.5, much more conventional in its form and tunefulness – though there is a case for hearing the finale as an internal send-up of the heroic style. This was received favourably, by the state and indeed by Shostakovich's international public, and seems to have turned him from the theatre to the concert hall. There were to be no more operas or ballets, excepting a comedy and a revision of *Lady Macbeth*; instead he devoted himself to symphonies, concertos, quartets and songs (as well as heroic, exhortatory cantatas during the war years).

Of the next four symphonies, no.7 is an epic with an uplifting war-victory programme (it was begun in besieged Leningrad), while the others display more openly a dichotomy between optimism and introspective doubt, expressed with varying shades of irony. It has been easy to explain this in terms of Shostakovich's position as a public artist in the USSR during the age of socialist realism, but the divisions and ironies in his music go back to his earliest works and seem inseparable from the very nature of his harmony, characterized by a severely weakened sense of key. Even so, his position in official Soviet music certainly was difficult. In 1948 he was condemned again, and for five years he wrote little besides patriotic cantatas and private music (quartets, the 24 Preludes and Fugues which constitute his outstanding piano work).

Stalin's death in 1953 opened the way to a less rigid aesthetic, and Shostakovich returned to the symphony triumphantly with no.10. Nos.11 and 12 are both programme works on crucial years in revolutionary history (1905 and 1917), but then no.13 was his most outspokenly critical work, incorporating a setting of words that attack anti-semitism. The last two symphonies and the last four quartets, as well as other chamber pieces and songs, belong to a late period of spare texture, slowness and gravity, often used explicitly in images of death: Symphony no.14 is a song cycle on mortality, though no.15 remains more enigmatic in its open quotations from Rossini and Wagner.

Operas The Nose (1930); The Lady Macbeth of the Mtsensk District (1934, rev. as Katerina Izmaylova, 1963)
Ballets The Golden Age (1930); The Bolt (1931); The Limpid Stream (1935)
Orchestral music Sym. no.1, f (1925); Sym. no.2, 'To October', B, with chorus (1927); Sym. no.3, 'The First of May', Eb, with chorus (1929); Sym. no.4, c (1936); Sym. no.5, d (1937); Sym. no.6, b (1939); Sym. no.7, 'Leningrad', C (1941); Sym. no.8, c (1943); Sym. no.9, Eb (1945); Sym. no.10, e (1953); Vn Conc. no.1, a (1948, rev. 1955); Festive Ov. (1954); Pf. Conc. no.1, c, pf, tpt, str (1933); Pf Conc. no.2, F (1957); Sym. no.11, 'The Year 1905', g (1957); Sym. no.12, 'The Year 1917', d (1961); Sym. no.13, 'Babiy Yar', bb, B, chorus (1962); Sym. no.14, S, B, str, perc (1969); Sym. no.15, A (1971); Vc Conc. no.1, Eb (1959); Ov. on Russian and Kirghiz Folk Themes (1963); Vc Conc. no.2, G (1966); Vn Conc. no.2, c# (1967); October, sym. poem (1967); many suites after theatre and film scores
Chamber music Pf Trio no.1, c (1923); 2 Pieces, str octet (1925); Vc Sonata, d (1934); Str Qt no.1, C (1938); Pf Qnt, g (1940); Pf Trio, e (1944); Str Qt no.2, A (1944); Str Qt no.3, F (1946); Str Qt no.4, D (1949); Str Qt no.5, Bb (1952); Str Qt no.6, G (1960); Str Qt no.7, f# (1960); Str Qt no.8, c (1960); Str Qt no.9, Eb (1964); Str Qt no.10, Ab (1964); Str Qt no.11, f (1966); Str Qt no.12, Db (1968); Vn Sonata (1968); Str Qt no.13, bb (1970); Str Qt no.14, F# (1973); Str Qt no.15, eb (1974); Va Sonata (1975)
Vocal music cantatas, oratorios, incl. Song of the Forests, 1949; The Sun Shines on our Motherland, 1952; The Execution of Stepan Razin, 1964; folksong arrs.; many solo songs with pf/ens/orch
Piano music 8 Preludes, (1920); 3 Fantastic Dances (1922); Suite, f# (1922); Pf Sonata no.1 (1926); 10 Aphorisms (1927); 24 Preludes (1933); Pf Sonata no.2, b (1943); Children's Notebook, 7 pieces (1945); 24 Preludes and Fugues (1951); Concertino, 2 pf (1953)

Shostakovich, Maxim (*b* Leningrad, 10 May 1938). Soviet conductor and pianist, son of Dmitry Shostakovich. He studied at Moscow under Fliyer and took conducting under Gauk, Rozhdestvensky and Markevich. He was assistant conductor of the Moscow PO from 1963 and the USSR State SO from 1966, later principal conductor of the State RSO. He has conducted the premières of several of his father's works, including Symphony no.15, and was soloist in Piano Concerto no.2 (written for him). In 1981 he settled in the West. He is a conductor of considerable dynamism and intensity.

Shropshire Lad, A. A book of poems (1896) by A.E. Housman which hit off the mood of a generation of English composers and drew settings from them – among others, Butterworth, Gurney, Ireland, Orr, Somervell and Vaughan Williams (*On Wenlock Edge* and *Along the Field*); Butterworth also wrote an orchestral rhapsody (1913).

Shteynberg, Maximilian Oseyevich (*b* Vilna, 4 July 1883; *d* Leningrad, 6 Dec 1946). Soviet composer. He was a pupil of Rimsky-Korsakov, Lyadov and Glazunov at the St Petersburg Conservatory, where he taught from 1908. He gained the reputation of being the creative heir of Rimsky-Korsakov, his father-in-law: he edited several of his works for posthumous publication and his own music aims to assimilate folk music and extend the possibilities of

timbre. He wrote five symphonies, ballets (including *Metamorphosis*, 1913) and songs.

Shtogarenko, Andriy Yakovlevich (*b* Noviye Kaydaki, 15 Oct 1902). Ukrainian composer. He was a pupil of Bogatïrev at the Khar'kov Conservatory, a board member of the USSR composers' union from 1948 and taught at the Kiev Conservatory from 1960. His work is clear, optimistic and distinctively national, including mostly orchestral and vocal orchestral scores (e.g. *My Ukraine*, 1943).

Shuard, Amy (*b* London, 19 July 1924; *d* there, 18 April 1975). English soprano. She studied in London, made her operatic début in Johannesburg and sang with Sadler's Wells Opera, 1949–55, singing Katya Kabanova, Carmen, Eboli, Tatyana and Tosca. She joined Covent Garden in 1954, first in the Italian repertory, later in Wagner, as a striking Brünnhilde and Kundry. She sang Isolde in Geneva (1972) and appeared widely in Europe and the Americas.

Shudi [Schudi, Tschudi, Tshudi], **Burkat** [Burkhardt] (*b* Schwanden, 1702; *d* London, 19 Aug 1773). English harpsichord maker of Swiss birth. He arrived in England in 1718, settling in Soho in 1739; after his son's death in 1803, ownership of the firm passed to his son-in-law and partner John Broadwood (an employee since 1761). With Kirckman he was a leading English maker of the period, his clients including Frederick the Great, Maria Theresa, Haydn, the Prince of Wales, and his friends Gainsborough, Reynolds and Handel. He made three basic models, two single harpsichords (8', 8'; 8', 8,' 4') and a double (8', 8', 4' and lute). Normally there was a buff stop, with modifications ranging from the music desk, the machine stop (allowing variety of tone and dynamics) and a long compass down to C' (all from c1765), to the Venetian swell (from c1769) and a change in scaling to longer bass strings (from c1770).

Shumsky, Oscar (*b* Philadelphia, 23 March 1917). American violinist. He made his début with the Philadelphia Orchestra when he was eight and studied with Auer and Zimbalist. He has appeared widely as a soloist and has taught at several conservatories, including the Juilliard School. His playing combines virtuoso technique with purity of style.

Sibelius, Jean [Johan] (Julius Christian) (*b* Hämeenlinna (Tavastehus), 8 Dec 1865; *d* Järvenpää, 20 Sept 1957). Finnish composer. He studied in Helsinki from 1886 with Wegelius, also gaining stimulus there from Busoni, though at the same time he fostered ambitions as a violinist. In 1889 he went to Berlin to continue his composition studies with Becker, then after a year to Vienna under Goldmark and Fuchs. He returned to Helsinki in 1891 and immediately made a mark with his choral symphony *Kullervo*, though it took him another decade to establish a wholly consistent style and to emerge from the powerful influence of Tchaikovsky: important stages on the journey were marked by the *Karelia* suite, the set of four tone poems on the legendary hero Lemminkäinen (including *The Swan of Tuonela*), the grandiose *Finlandia* and the first two symphonies.

As these titles suggest, he was encouraged by the Finnish nationalist movement (until 1917 Finland was a grand duchy in the Russian empire), by his readings of Finnish mythology (Kullervo and Lemminkäinen are both characters from the *Kalevala*, which was to be the source also for subjects of later symphonic poems) and in some degree by the folk music of Karelia. But the most important stimulus would seem to have been purely musical: a drive towards continuous growth achieved by means of steady thematic transformation, and facilitated by supporting the main line very often with highly diversified ostinato textures instead of counterpoints. The singleness of purpose also has to do with the frequently modal character of Sibelius's harmony.

The Violin Concerto of 1903 was effectively a farewell to 19th-century Romanticism, followed by a pure, classical expression of the new style in the Symphony no.3. This was also a period of change in his personal life. In 1904 he bought a plot of land outside Helsinki and built a house where he spent the rest of his life with his wife and daughters, removed from the city where he had been prone to bouts of heavy drinking. Also, his music gained a large international following, and he visited England (four times in 1905–12) and the USA (1914). Symphony no.4, with its conspicuous use of the tritone and its austere textures, took his music into its darkest areas; no.5 brought a return to the heroic mould, developing the process of continuous change to the extent that the first movement evolves into the scherzo.

But that work took him some time to get right (written in 1915, it was revised in 1916 and again in 1919), and after World War I he produced only four major works: the brilliant and elusive Symphony no.6; no.7, which takes continuity to the ultimate in its unbroken unfolding of symphonic development; the incidental music for *The Tempest*; and the bleak symphonic poem *Tapiola*. He lived for another three decades, but published only a few minor pieces; an eighth symphony may possibly have been completed and destroyed. His reputation, however, continued to grow, and his influence has been profound, especially on Scandinavian, English and American composers, reflecting both the traditionalism and the radical elements in his symphonic thinking.

Orchestral music Sym. no.1, e (1899); Sym. no.2, D (1902); Sym. no.3, C (1907); Sym. no.4, a (1911); Sym. no.5, E♭ (1915); Sym. no.6, d (1923); Sym. no.7, C (1924); En saga (1892); Karelia, suite (1893); Lemminkäinen, suite (1895); Finlandia (1900); Vn Conc. (1903); Pelléas et Mélisande, suite (1905); Pohjola's Daughter (1906); Pan and Echo (1906); Nightride and Sunrise (1907); The Dryad (1910); The Bard (1913, rev. 1914); The Oceanides (1914); The Tempest (1925); Tapiola (1926); many lighter works
Choral orchestral music Kullervo (1892); The Origin of Fire (1902); cantatas
Chamber music Str Qt, 'Voces intimae', d (1909); early qts, vn pieces
Other incidental theatre music *c*90 songs; small choral pieces; pf pieces

Sibyl, Song of the. The song of the Erythrean Sibyl. One of the most popular prophecies of the coming of

Christ, it was incorporated in the 8th century into the Christmas Office was sung widely in the Middle Ages (the tradition is preserved in Majorca). Originally a clandestine early Christian 'pamphlet' in Greek verse, it appears in Latin in Augustine's *Civitas Dei*. The earliest surviving musical texts are from the 10th century and, despite melodic variants, the chant has remained remarkably stable. Two uses must be distinguished: a purely liturgical one, where it is inserted as a chant, usually into a lesson read in the Christmas season; and as part of a liturgical drama, where it may have formed an important part in the development of the *Ordo Prophetarum*.

Sicard, Jean (*fl* 1660–1700). French composer and singer. His most productive years were spent in Paris; later he was active in Marseilles. His 17 song collections (1666–83) include over 300 *airs à boire* and *airs sérieux* which show great inventiveness and variety.

Sicher, Fridolin (*b* Bischofszell, 6 March 1490; *d* there, 13 June 1546). Swiss organist. A pupil of Buchner, he was later organist of the collegiate church at St Gall. He wrote an organ tablature (1503–31) containing 176 pieces. (He did not write the *Liber Fridolini Sichery*, which came into his possession in 1545.)

Siciliana [siciliano]. Term for an aria type and instrumental movement of the late 17th and 18th centuries, probably related to an earlier dance, 'La Siciliana', akin to a slow gigue. It was normally in a slow 6/8 or 12/8, characterized by clear one- or two-bar phrases, lilting rhythms, simple melodies and direct harmonies, and was associated particularly with pastoral scenes and melancholy emotion. The siciliana was much used as an aria type in the operas and cantatas of A. Scarlatti and Handel (often featuring the chord of the Neapolitan 6th), and the style is frequently present in the vocal and instrumental music of the late Baroque (*see* PASTORALE).

From the 14th century to the early 17th, the term denoted the singing or accompanied recitation of a poetic form, the *strambotto siciliano* (*see* STRAMBOTTO).

Sicilian Vespers, The [Les vêpres siciliennes; I vespri siciliani]. Opera in five acts by Verdi to a French libretto by Scribe and Duveyrier from the libretto for Donizetti's *Le duc d'Albe* (1855, Paris).

Side drum. A DRUM slung from the shoulder and worn at the player's side; it is also called a snare drum. (For illustration, *see* PERCUSSION INSTRUMENTS.)

Sieben letzten Worte des Erlösers am Kreuz, Die. *See* SEVEN LAST WORDS OF CHRIST ON THE CROSS, THE.

Sieben Todsünden der Kleinbürger, Die. *See* SEVEN DEADLY SINS, THE.

Siefert, Paul (*b* Danzig, 28 June 1586; *d* there, 6 May 1666). German composer and organist. A pupil of Sweelinck, he worked first in Danzig and in 1611–16 in Königsberg. After a period as court organist in Warsaw, he was principal organist at the Danzig Marienkirche from 1623. He had a famous theoretical dispute with the Polish court choirmaster Marco Scacchi. He wrote both sacred and keyboard music;

his psalm settings (1640, 1651) show a move away from Sweelinck's style towards the techniques of the concertato chorale motet and the chorale cantata.

Siège de Corinthe, Le. Opera in three acts by Rossini to a French libretto (1826, Paris), a revision of an earlier opera, *Il Maometto II*, to an Italian libretto by C. della Valle (1820, Naples).

Siege of Rhodes, The. The first English opera, with music by Matthew Locke, Henry Lawes, Henry Cooke, Charles Coleman and George Hudson to a libretto by Davenant (1656, London); it is now lost.

Siegfried. Music drama in three acts by Wagner to his own libretto (1876, Bayreuth), the third in the cycle DER RING DES NIBELUNGEN.

Siegfried Idyll. Orchestral work by Wagner (1870).

Siegmeister, Elie (*b* New York, 15 Jan 1909). American composer. He was a pupil of Bingham at Columbia, Riegger, and Boulanger in Paris (1927–31), and has taught, notably at Hofstra University (1949–76). He has sought distinctively American modes of expression, influenced by Copland, Ives and jazz. His output includes a musical, operas, six symphonies (1947–83), string quartets, choral music and songs.

Siena Festival. *See* SETTIMANA MUSICALE SENESE.

Siface. *See* GROSSI, GIOVANNI FRANCESCO.

Sight, sighting. Terms used in Middle English discant treatises (*c*1390–*c*1450) for a method of improvising a discant or faburden by 'sighting' (or 'imagining') the notes to be sung as consonances above or below the notes of the chant on the four-line staff.

Sight-reading, sight-singing. The performing of a piece of music at first sight.

Signature. A sign or signs placed at the beginning of a composition. A key signature indicates which notes in the piece are to be sharpened or flattened; a time signature indicates its metre.

Signor Bruschino, Il. Opera in one act by Rossini to a libretto by Foppa after A. de Chazet and E.-T. Maurice Ourry (1813, Venice).

Sigtenhorst Meyer, Bernhard van den (*b* Amsterdam, 17 June 1888; *d* The Hague, 17 July 1953). Dutch musicologist and composer. He studied at the Amsterdam Conservatory and became known as a pianist and teacher in The Hague. His earliest works were in a Debussian style but his pioneering studies of Sweelinck led to a more lucid, controlled manner. He wrote songs and much chamber music.

Sigurbjörnsson, Thorkell (*b* Reykjavík, 16 July 1938). Icelandic composer. He studied in Reykjavík and the USA (under R.G. Harris, Gaburo and Hiller) and has worked in Reykjavík as a teacher, critic and broadcaster. He is internationally known as a pianist and composer: his works are in diverse styles and genres, tending to assimilate seemingly unrelated elements.

Siklós, Albert (*b* Budapest, 26 June 1878; *d* there, 3 April 1942). Hungarian educationist and composer. A pupil of Koessler at the Budapest Academy, where he began teaching in 1910, he wrote important textbooks providing a complete course in professional music education. He also wrote much criticism and essays. His large output of music is in a traditional Germanic style, influenced by Hungarian Baroque music and latterly Debussy.

Sikorski, Kazimierz (*b* Zurich, 28 June 1895). Polish composer. He studied with Szopski in Warsaw, and in Paris (1925–7, 1930), then taught at various institutions. His reputation rests largely on his educational work. His works include symphonies, wind concertos, chamber music and songs, expanding steadily from a late Romantic style and distinguished by their clear construction and expressive individuality.

Silbermann. German family of organ builders and instrument makers. Andreas (1678–1734), who worked in Paris (1704–6) under François Thierry, built 34 organs, including four in Strasbourg (1702–16) and two in Basle (1710–12). His brother Gottfried (1683–1753) settled in Freiberg in 1711, becoming acquainted with J.S. Bach and J.L. Krebs. Among his most important organs are those at Freiberg Cathedral (1710–14; extant) and, his masterpiece, the Katholische Hofkirche, Dresden (1750–54; pipework extant). Gottfried was also renowned for his clavichords, one of them prized by C.P.E. Bach; he even developed an improved grand piano said to have been approved by J.S. Bach. Johann Andreas (1712–83), son of Andreas, built 54 organs, in Alsace, Lorraine, Baden and Switzerland; they include those at St Thomas (1741) and the Neue Kirche (1749), Strasbourg and Arlesheim Cathedral (1761). Most of the stops on Silbermann organs are of a type common to the French and German schools, the instruments having a tonal wealth and craftsmanship among the finest of their time.

Silcher, (Philipp) Friedrich (*b* Schnait, 27 June 1789; *d* Tübingen, 26 Aug 1860). German folksong collector. With Pestalozzi and Nägeli he became a leading promoter of popular music education through folksong; he collected and edited songs from Germany and composed in a folklike style.

Silja, Anja (*b* Berlin, 17 April 1940). German soprano. Her début was as Rosina (*Barber of Seville*) in Berlin; later she worked at Brunswick, Stuttgart and Frankfurt, making her Bayreuth début as Senta in 1960 and working closely under Wieland Wagner in other Wagner roles such as Elsa and Eva. She sang Fidelio on her débuts in London (1963) and at the Met (1972); her other roles include Lulu and Marie, Isolde and Brünnhilde. Her voice is bright and vivid if unsteady; her intense stage presence, however, is always compelling. She married the conductor Christoph von Dohnányi.

Silken Ladder, The [La scala di seta]. Opera in one act by Rossini to a libretto by Rossi after Planard (1812, Venice).

Sills, Beverly (*b* Brooklyn, 25 May 1929). American soprano. Her early opera roles included Boito's Elena in San Francisco, 1953. She sang with touring companies and in 1955 joined the New York City Opera. In 1966 she gained prominence as Cleopatra in Handel's *Giulio Cesare*, and was successful in the lighter *bel canto* repertory, singing Donizetti at the City Opera and Covent Garden and Rossini at the Met and La Scala. She became general director of the City Opera in 1979 and retired from the stage in 1980.

Silva, Francisco Manuel da (*b* Rio de Janiero, 21 Feb 1795; *d* there, 18 Dec 1865). Brazilian composer. He studied counterpoint under Neukomm, 1816–21. He became a dynamic organizer of Rio's musical life from 1831, holding important posts as conductor and composer, and in 1847 founding the conservatory. Much of his music is sacred; his *Hino ao 7 de Abril*, written in 1831 on the abdication of Dom Pedro I, became the Brazilian national anthem.

Silverstein, Joseph (*b* Detroit, 21 March 1932). American violinist. He studied at Philadelphia and later with Zimbalist. In 1955 he joined the Boston SO, becoming leader in 1962, assistant conductor in 1971, and leading the orchestra's chamber ensembles; he left in 1984. He has given many solo performances with the Boston SO and other orchestras and has taught at Yale and Boston universities. He is one of the most accomplished American violinists of his time, with fine, resonant tone, impressive technique and exemplary musicianship. As a conductor he appeared with the Baltimore SO, 1981–3, then becoming artistic director of the Utah SO.

Sil'vestrov, Valentin Vasil'yevich (*b* Kiev, 30 Sept 1937). Soviet composer. He was a pupil of Lyatosyns'ky at the Kiev Conservatory (1958–64). Influenced at first by his teacher and by Shostakovich, he came in the early 1960s to use serialism, aleatory forms and other avant-garde techniques and in the 1970s to work with a plurality of styles, new and old. His works include symphonies, chamber music, piano pieces, songs, characterized by an individual, expressive lyricism.

Similar motion. In part-writing, the simultaneous melodic movement of two or more voices in the same direction.

Simile (It.). 'Like', 'similar': a word used to mean 'play as before' (used particularly if repeating the notation of intricate phrasing etc would clutter a score).

Simile aria [metaphor aria]. An aria in a Baroque opera, oratorio or cantata in which the singer compares his situation to some natural phenomenon or activity in the world at large, and the music provides appropriate illustration. The convention was no longer used by the end of the 18th century.

Simionato, Giulietta (*b* Forlì, 12 May 1910). Italian mezzo-soprano. She came into prominence singing at La Scala, where she made her début in 1936 and appeared regularly, 1946–66, in a large repertory including Rossini's Rosina and Cinderella, Charlotte (*Werther*) and Carmen. Her London début was in 1953, singing mezzo roles opposite Callas; her USA début was in 1954, and she sang at the Met from 1959. She retired in 1966. She had an agile coloratura mezzo, with a warm timbre; she was vivacious in comic roles, intense in serious ones.

Simon, Prosper-Charles (*b* Bordeaux, 27 Dec 1788; *d* Paris, 31 May 1866). French organist. His talent for improvisation was widely praised, particularly in connection with the Cavaillé-Coll organ at St Denis, Paris, where he was organist from 1840; he was nicknamed 'the Rossini of the organ'.

Simon, Simon (*b* Les-Vaux-de-Cernay, ?c1735; *d* ?Versailles, after 1780). French composer. A pupil of Dauvergne, he was a gifted harpsichordist and became teacher to the French royal family. He published three volumes of harpsichord works (some with violin), uneven but interesting: his suites (1761) have French and Italian traits, while his later pieces (sonatas and concertos) are thoroughly italianate and *galant*.

Simon Boccanegra. Opera in a prologue and three acts by Verdi to a libretto by F.M. Piave and G. Montanelli after Gutiérrez (1857, Venice); Boito revised the libretto and Verdi composed a new second scene (1881, Milan).

Simoneau, Léopold (*b* Quebec, 3 May 1918). Canadian tenor. He studied in Montreal and New York, then went to Paris and made his Opéra-Comique début in 1949; he soon established a reputation as a Mozartean, singing at Aix-en-Provence, Glyndebourne, La Scala and the Met (1963), and admired for his smooth, lyrical tenor. He later taught in Montreal. In 1946 he married the soprano Pierrette Alarie.

Simon le Breton (*d* Cambrai, 12 Nov 1473). French composer and singer. He was at the Burgundian chapel by January 1431 until 1464, when he retired to a canonry he held at Cambrai Cathedral. He was a colleague of Binchois and Dufay. A three-voice rondeau and a Flemish song are probably his. He may possibly be identified with Simon de Insula (*fl* c1450–60), a composer possibly from Lille, although the latter's four-voice mass cycle is stylistically different from the other works.

Simonsen, Rudolph (Hermann) (*b* Copenhagen, 30 April 1889; *d* there, 28 March 1947). Danish composer. He was a pupil of Malling at the Copenhagen Conservatory (1907–9), where he began teaching in 1916 and was appointed director in 1931. His four symphonies and other works show an admiration for Nielsen; he was a professional pianist and published several books.

Simple interval. An interval of an octave or less (as opposed to a COMPOUND INTERVAL).

Simple Symphony. Work for string orchestra (or quartet), op.4, by Britten, put together in 1933 from music written in the mid-1920s.

Simple time. A musical metre of which the main beats are divisible by two (as opposed to compound time, where they are divisible by three). *See* TIME SIGNATURE.

Simplex (Lat.). 'Simple': term used in medieval theory to denote: (1) monophonic, as in 'simplices conductus'; (2) simple (i.e. not composite), as in 'simplex organum'; (3) unligatured, of note forms, especially in rhythmic modal theory; or (4) prime, unlengthened, of durational values, as in 'brevis simplex'.

Simpson, Christopher (*b* ?Westonby, c1605; *d* ?Holborn, 5 May–29 July 1669). English theorist, composer and viol player. A Catholic, he served the royalist cause in the Civil War and then the Bolles family at Scampton, Lincs. The most important English writer on music of his day, he published *The Division-Violist* (1659), a comprehensive, practical and highly successful viol tutor. His many works for viol solo and consort include suites, divisions and fantasias.

Simpson, Robert (Wilfred Levick) (*b* Leamington, 2 March 1921). English composer. A pupil of Howells (1942–6), he worked for the BBC (1951–80). His main achievement has been his cycles of nine symphonies and eight string quartets, both begun in 1951 and both displaying a dynamic tonality quite individual in its energy and purposefulness, encouraged more than influenced by his admiration for Beethoven, Bruckner and Nielsen (on whom he has published studies).

Simpson, Thomas (*b* Milton-next-Sittingbourne, bap. 1 April 1582; *d* ?after 1630). English composer. Like William Brade, he was an expatriate viol player and served the Heidelberg (*c*1610), Bückeburg (*c*1615–21) and Copenhagen (1622–5) courts. His three consort collections (1610–21, over 50 pieces by him) fuse English tradition with continental practice and greatly influenced north German instrumental music.

Simrock. German firm of music publishers. It was founded at Bonn in 1793 by Nicolaus Simrock (1751–1832). Among its important early publications were three of Haydn's London symphonies, Beethoven's Kreutzer Sonata op.47 (1805) and works by Weber, as well as reprints of Bach and Handel. Mendelssohn's *Songs without Words*, *St Paul* and *Elijah*, Schumann's Symphony no.3 and, from 1860, most of Brahms's opp.16–122 followed. Music by Dvořák, Bruch and Johann Strauss the younger has also appeared in the catalogue.

Sinatra, Frank [Francis Albert] (*b* Hoboken, NJ, 12 Dec 1915). American popular singer and film actor. While singing with Tommy Dorsey's band (1940–42) he was a celebrity among young people on a scale matched only by Benny Goodman before him and later by Presley and the Beatles. After leaving Dorsey he began a solo career. In the 1950s Nelson Riddle's orchestral arrangements were particularly successful in drawing out the many facets of Sinatra's musical personality. He represents the consummation of the tradition of the American popular singer.

Sinding, Christian (August) (*b* Kongsberg, 11 Jan 1856; *d* Oslo, 3 Dec 1941). Norwegian composer. A pupil of Jadassohn at the Leipzig Conservatory (1874–8), he spent much of his later life in Germany: he attached himself to German culture through the influence of Wagner and Strauss, though he is more obviously Grieg's heir in his many songs and lyrical piano pieces. A prolific composer, he enjoyed wide fame in his lifetime. His larger works include an opera, four symphonies (1890, 1904, 1920, 1936), a piano concerto, three violin concertos and chamber pieces. He is best known for *Rustle of Spring*.

Sinfonia (It.: 'symphony'). Term used from the late Renaissance to designate various kinds of piece (usually instrumental). At first it seems to have been analogous to the ensemble CANZONA. Some early 17th-century keyboard preludes were published as 'sinfonie', and after 1650 sinfonias began to appear at the beginnings of groups of dances. By 1700 'sinfonia' was used interchangeably with the equally ambiguous 'sonata'.

From the 16th century the term 'sinfonia' was applied to music used to introduce dramatic works or to cover the sound of changing scenery, and the canzona type persisted into the mid-17th century as the most common operatic overture. By 1700 the term was used mainly for the three-movement 'Italian' overture (fast–slow–fast/dance). During the 18th century it increasingly designated the concert symphony, as opposed to 'ouverture'. The term has been revived in the 20th century for works shorter, more Italianate or less earnest than 'symphony' is sometimes taken to imply (e.g. Britten's op.20, 1940, and Berio's Sinfonia, 1968).

Sinfonia antartica. Vaughan Williams's Symphony no.7 (1952), for soprano, women's chorus and orchestra.

Sinfonia concertante. *See* SYMPHONIE CONCERTANTE.

Sinfonia da requiem. Orchestral work, op.20, by Britten (1940).

Sinfonia espansiva. Sub-title of Nielsen's Symphony no.3 (1911), which includes soprano and baritone soloists.

Sinfonia semplice. Sub-title of Nielsen's Symphony no.6 (1924–5).

Sinfonie capricieuse. Berwald's Symphony no.2 in D (1842).

Sinfonie sérieuse. Berwald's Symphony no.1 in G minor (1842).

Sinfonie singulière. Berwald's Symphony no.3 in C (1845).

Sinfonietta. An orchestral piece on a smaller scale, or of more modest aims, than a symphony. The term was apparently coined in a French form by Rimsky-Korsakov (*Symphoniette sur des thèmes russes* op.31, *c*1880) and has been used by Reger, Prokofiev, Britten, Poulenc, Hindemith and others.

Singakademie. German choral society established in 1791, as the Berliner Singakademie, renamed in 1793. In the 19th century it presented mainly German works, including the first performance after Bach's death of the *St Matthew Passion* (1829, conducted by Mendelssohn). Since 1882 it has performed regularly with the Berlin PO.

Singer, Peter (Alkantara) [Josef Anton] (*b* Unterhäselgehr, 18 July 1810; *d* Salzburg, 25 Jan 1882). Austrian composer, organist and instrument maker. He was the most famous musical personality of his day in Salzburg, winning esteem as a prolific church music composer, organist and harmonium builder; his most celebrated keyboard instrument was the 'Pansymphonikum' (1845).

Singing. Although the art of singing belongs to the earliest forms of music-making, modern Western styles of singing are generally thought to go back only as far as the late 16th century. Accounts of singing earlier than that are few in number and difficult to interpret. Probably the high male voice was generally preferred (in many ecclesiastical contexts singing by women was forbidden), and in the Middle Ages the virtuoso cantor capable of brilliant singing played an important part in elaborating certain types of chant. By the 15th century, chant was probably performed in a tone – which now would be considered 'oriental' – of a rather nasal, perhaps harsh kind. The division of the voice into chest, throat and head registers was recognized as early as the 13th century; the head voice would now be described as falsetto. The rise of polyphony and the attendant expansion in compass led to a growing appreciation and use of different ranges of male voice, as seen particularly in the use of the bass and baritone compass in late 15th-century music.

Until the later 16th century, few singers seem to have been famous as soloists; the earliest singers whose names are known were the troubadours, trouvères and Minnesinger of the 11th to 13th centuries, working in a tradition where poet, composer and singer were usually the same person. The singer as interpreter of other people's music is virtually unknown until later. In the mid-16th century, treatises show a new emphasis on singing. Until this time, most secular music was suitable for male voices alone (including falsetto), but from the later 16th century female voices came increasingly into use – notably with the three ladies of Ferrara, whose virtuosity furthered the new vogue of writing for high, mostly female voices. The rise of monody in the late years of the century led to an increased interest in vocal elaboration and virtuosity, as described in Caccini's *Le nuove musiche* 1601/2. The style emphasized free delivery of the text and the expressive use of dynamics, exclamations and portamentos. This led to the development of recitative. At the same time, the rise of the castrato and the invention of opera affected the art of singing. The castrato voice answered the need of Counter-Reformation composers for expressive, high voices in church music, and castratos were used in the Catholic church for the next three centuries. In opera, sopranos and castratos became the most prized singers during the Baroque era, with their unsurpassed eloquence in the new, flowing *bel canto* ('beautiful singing') style which developed in Italian opera in the middle of the 17th century; they also proved by far the best exponents of the brilliant ornamentation and divisions of the late Baroque and early Classical styles. Italian singers (like Italian opera itself) dominated music-making across the whole of Europe with the solitary exception of France, where a plainer singing style, with greater emphasis on verbal diction and less on tonal beauty, prevailed, and where castrato voices were never fully accepted; the French favoured male parts sung by the special high tenor known as the *haute-contre*.

At the beginning of the Romantic era larger voices, of greater sensuous beauty, came to be preferred, to meet the demands of the bigger opera houses and concert halls being built as public opera and concert-giving increased. Singers developed new types of resonance and dramatic expression. Acting ability was increasingly cultivated in some opera houses, notably the Opéra-Comique, Paris. Meanwhile, another class of singer developed, specializing in the intimacy of expression required for the lied repertory in Germany and its equivalents elsewhere (particularly in Russia and France). Examples are Schubert's friend J.M. Vogl and Brahms's friend Julius Stockhausen.

New ways of using the voice increased with the development of 20th-century idioms, notably *Sprechgesang*, a stylized mode of expression halfway between singing and speaking; it is associated with the Second Viennese School, and especially Schoenberg's *Pierrot lunaire*, though others had used it earlier. Special effects such as whispering, choral recitation, humming, glissando and shouting have been used extensively in choral music, somewhat less so in solo song. The development of the microphone, and the consequent ability to reach a large audience while singing quietly, has led to further developments in vocal technique, notably crooning. Other developments consequent on 20th-century technology include synthesizing the human voice; Stockhausen's *Stimmung* and *Gesang der Jünglinge* are notable examples of the use of electronically manipulated human voices. Conventional singing has, however, continued in the 20th century, as opera houses have multiplied and the demand grown. The Wagner cult of the interwar years brought about an array of excellent Wagner interpreters; and the demand for and supply of interpreters of Italian opera have continued to run high. Notable specialists in other repertories include Shalyapin (music for a deep Russian bass), Maggie Teyte (French song) and Conchita Supervia (Spanish song). In recent years the male alto (countertenor) voice, largely abandoned except in English ecclesiastical music, underwent a revival, provoked chiefly by Alfred Deller; and there has been a trend towards the authentic performance, in matters of ornamentation, articulation and timbre, among interpreters of music up to Mozart's time. At the opposite extreme are the group of sopranos (such as Bethany Beardslee, Cathy Berberian and Jane Manning) who have specialized in singing avant-garde music and in perfecting its new techniques.

Non-Western and folk-singing embraces many techniques unknown in Western art music. These include such devices as yodelling, Japanese 'split-tone' methods and types of polyphonic singing (by one individual) used in South-east Asia.

Singspiel. A German play with music. The term was in use in the 16th century, but it is now most commonly applied to 18th- and early 19th-century light or comic operas with spoken dialogue, of which Mozart's *Die Entführung aus dem Serail* is a prime example. In *Fidelio* Beethoven made the genre serve a more serious subject. By the 1870s the Singspiel had merged with the operetta.

Sinigaglia, Leone (*b* Turin, 14 Aug 1868; *d* there, 16 May 1944). Italian composer. A pupil of Mandyczewski in Vienna from 1894, he also had lessons from Dvořák (1900–01). He returned to Turin and devoted himself to collecting folksongs and composing in a Dvořákian, folk-influenced style, most of his works being instrumental. He wrote little after World War I.

Sinisalo, Helmer-Rayner (*b* Zlatoust, 14 June 1920). Soviet composer. He studied with Peyko at the Moscow Conservatory (1952–4) and Voloshinov at the Leningrad Conservatory (1954–5) and was a flautist. His works include ballets and orchestral pieces, often on Karelian themes; his *Heroes of the Forest* (1949) was the first Karelian symphony.

Sink-a-pace. *See* CINQUE PAS.

Sinopoli, Giuseppe (*b* Venice, 2 Nov 1946). Italian conductor. He studied composition with Stockhausen and conducting with Swarowsky. He made his operatic conducting début in *Aida* (1978, Venice) and has appeared widely in the Italian repertory, often surprising audiences with his vivid and dramatic readings. He has conducted at Covent Garden and the Met; he was appointed principal conductor of the Philharmonia Orchestra in 1984 and made his début at Bayreuth in 1985.

Siqueira, José (de Lima) (*b* Conceição, 24 June 1907). Brazilian composer. He was a pupil of Silva and Braga at the National Music Institute in Rio de Janeiro, where in 1935 he began teaching. He was founder-director of the Brazilian SO (1940–48). In 1943 he turned to musical nationalism, of which he became a leading Brazilian proponent. In 1954 he went to Europe for further study, notably with Messiaen, and his style became more sophisticated. His works include ballets, concertos and choral music; some are based on his own 'Brazilian trimodal' and pentatonic systems, others on Afro-Brazilian ritual.

Sir John in Love. Opera in four acts by Vaughan Williams to his own libretto after Shakespeare's *The Merry Wives of Windsor* (1929, London).

Sirmen [née Lombardini], **Maddalena Laura** (*b* Venice, 1735; *d* after 1785). Italian violinist and composer. She studied with Tartini, latterly by correspondence; the first of these lessons (1760) was later published (1770). Until 1772 she toured as a virtuoso (sometimes with her husband, the violinist Lodovico Sirmen), enjoying particular success in Paris and London, and composed concertos and chamber works. An attempt at a singing career was less successful.

Sirventes. A Provençal troubadour poem to a borrowed melody, treating not love but politics, satire or the crusades.

Sistro. A series of small, mushroom-shaped tuned bells mounted on a frame; akin to the glockenspiel, it was invented in Italy in the late 17th century and is occasionally required in Italian scores, notably Rossini's *Il barbiere di Siviglia* (1816).

Sistrum. An ancient type of jingling rattle with a long handle; it was common in Egyptian worship, particularly in the cult of Isis. It survives in the ritual of the Ethiopian Coptic church.

Sitar. A large, long-necked, fretted lute, prominent in the classical music of India, Pakistan and Bangladesh. The name comes from the Persian, meaning 'three-stringed', in which form the instrument can trace its ancestry back to the 11th century. It took on the outline of its modern form during the late Mughal empire, in the 18th century, when it was used as a solo instrument in art music. It was also frequently played in a five-string version. The 19th century saw the addition of the two drone or 'punctuating' strings and the dozen or so sympathetic ones (running under the main strings and resonantly tuned by pegs along the fingerboard) which go to make up the modern concert sitar. This instrument, held diagonally on the right thigh, has 20 frets which are movable and thus allow various modal tunings.

Many sitars have a small second gourd resonator attached to the neck. The instrument is played with a small wire plectrum worn on the right index-finger. (For illustration, *see* LUTE.)

Sitsky, Larry (*b* Tientsin, 10 Sept 1934). Australian composer and pianist of Russian descent. An accomplished pianist when he arrived in Australia in 1951, he studied with Burston at the NSW State Conservatorium (1951–8) and with Petri at the San Francisco Conservatory (1959–61): his involvement with Busoni's music (as musicologist and recitalist) deeply influenced his own works, which employ avant-garde techniques to expressionist ends. They include the operas *Fall of the House of Usher* (1965) and *Lenz* (1972), songs, chamber and piano pieces, some using electronics and aleatory effects. He has taught at various Australian institutions.

Sivori, (Ernesto) Camillo (*b* Genoa, 25 Oct 1815; *d* there, 19 Feb 1894). Italian violinist and composer. He was a protégé of Paganini, whose repertory he mastered but whose performing style he imbued with more sweetness of tone, gracefulness and delicacy. He toured throughout Europe and the Americas, becoming renowned as the most exciting violinist after Paganini. Of his compositions, the 12 Etudes-caprices op.25 for unaccompanied violin (1867) are noteworthy.

Six, Les. French group of composers: Auric, Durey, Honegger, Milhaud, Poulenc and Tailleferre. They gave concerts together from 1917, influenced by Satie and by Cocteau's anti-Romantic aesthetic, but in the early 1920s went separate ways.

Six-four chord. A three-note chord consisting of a bass note with a 6th and 4th above it, indicated in thoroughbass by a figure '6' above a '4'. It is the second inversion of a triad.

Sixteen foot. Term used of organ stops, and by extension other instruments, to indicate that they are pitched an octave below 'normal' (eight foot) pitch.

Sixteenth-note. American term for semiquaver; a note half the value of an eighth-note, or quaver, and double the value of a 32nd-note, or demisemiquaver. *See* NOTE VALUES.

Sixth. The INTERVAL between two notes five diatonic scale degrees apart (e.g. C–A, E♭–C); it is the interval produced when the 3rd is inverted at the octave. An octave less a minor 3rd is a major 6th; an octave less a major 3rd is a minor 6th.

Sixth chord. A three-note chord consisting of a bass note with a 6th and a 3rd above it; it is the first inversion of a triad. *See also* ADDED SIXTH CHORD; AUGMENTED SIXTH CHORD; and NEAPOLITAN SIXTH.

Sixty-fourth note. American term for hemidemisemiquaver; a note half the value of a 32nd-note, or demisemiquaver. *See* NOTE VALUES.

Sjögren, (Johan Gustaf) Emil (*b* Stockholm, 16 June 1853; *d* there, 1 March 1918). Swedish composer. He studied in Stockholm and Berlin, and is remembered principally for his songs (*c*200), many still in the Swedish repertory; a large number, both strophic and through-composed, are *Stimmungs-*

lieder, depicting a single mood, while others, notably the Jacobsen songs op.22 (1887) and the Li-Tai-Po songs (1911), are progressive in harmony and declamation.

Ska [bluebeat]. A style of urban popular music and dance originating in Jamaica in the late 1950s. It was the dominant indigenous popular music style there until supplanted in the mid-1960s by rock steady, a forerunner of reggae. It achieved fleeting acceptance in North America and Britain.

Skalkottas, Niko(lao)s (*b* Halkis, 21 March 1904; *d* Athens, 20 Sept 1949). Greek composer. He studied as a violinist at the Athens Conservatory and as a composer in Berlin with Juon, Kahn, Jarnach (1925–7), Weill (1928–9) and Schoenberg (1927–31). In 1933 he returned to Athens, where he worked as a back-desk violinist. His Berlin works are relatively compact and high-spirited, being almost exclusively instrumental and following the neo-classicism of his teachers (in 1927 his music became atonal, but not yet serial). But the bulk of his music dates from 1935–45, when the genres remained traditional but the forms were greatly expanded to contain a deep complexity of serial thematic working: major works of this period include the Third Piano Concerto (1939), the Fourth Quartet (1940) and the overture *The Return of Odysseus* (1943); he wrote several concertos, chamber and vocal music. He also produced tonal works, including a collection of 36 Greek Dances for orchestra (1936).

Skiffle. A style of popular music; the term originally referred to the entertainment at black rent parties in the USA in the 1930s. It was revived by white musicians in the 1950s and played at clubs and coffee houses in the USA, Britain and Germany. Skiffle bands often included acoustic guitar, harmonica, jug, washtub bass, washboard and drums, which would play a simple three- or four-chord accompaniment to the vocal part.

Skilton, Charles Sanford (*b* Northampton, MA, 16 Aug 1868; *d* Lawrence, KS, 12 March 1941). American composer. He studied at Yale and Berlin and taught at Salem and in New Jersey before becoming professor at Kansas University in 1903. He investigated American Indian music, which he saw as a new compositional source, and incorporated tribal melodies and folklore into his own works, such as his opera *Kalopin* (1927).

Skinner, James Scott (*b* Banchory Ternan, 5 Aug 1843; *d* Aberdeen, 17 March 1927); Scottish violinist, composer and dancing-teacher. He wrote over 700 violin works, mostly in Scottish style, of which *The Laird o' Drumblair* is his finest strathspey; *The Bonnie Lass o' Bon Accord* is his best-known air.

Skowroneck, (Franz Hermann) Martin (*b* Berlin-Spandau, 21 Dec 1926). German harpsichord maker. Self-taught, he built his first harpsichord in 1953. He has concentrated on re-creating instruments of Italian design and in the early (Ruckers) and late (Dulcken) Flemish tradition.

Skramstad, Hans (*b* Totan, bap. 26 Dec 1797; *d* Bergen, 15 June 1839). Norwegian composer. In form and harmonic language his four sets of varia-

tions for piano stand out as the first true Romantic Norwegian music.

Škroup, František Jan (*b* Osice, 3 June 1801; *d* Rotterdam, 7 Feb 1862). Bohemian composer and conductor. He devoted most of his energy to creating a Czech national opera, composing and singing in *The Tinker* (1826), the successful if naive first Czech opera. Later he worked as Kapellmeister at the Estates Theatre, Prague (1837–57). His incidental music to *Shoemakers' Fair* (1834) includes a song incorporated after 1918 into the Czech national anthem and he compiled an anthology of patriotic songs *A Garland of Patriotic Songs* (6 vols., 1835–9, 1844). His brother Jan Nepomuk (1811–92), choirmaster at St Vitus's Cathedral, Prague, composed sacred works, songs and incidental music.

Skrowaczewski, Stanisław (*b* Lwów, 3 Oct 1923). American conductor. He studied in Lwów, Kraków and Paris, and held posts with orchestras in Wrocław, Katowice and Kraków before becoming conductor of the Warsaw National PO (1956–9). He made his USA début in Cleveland in 1958 and was conductor of the Minneapolis (Minnesota) SO, 1960–79, and the Hallé Orchestra from 1984. He has appeared at the Met and Vienna Staatsoper (*Fidelio*, 1964) and is admired for the precision, vigour and elegance of his direction.

Skryabin [Scriabin], **Alexander Nikolayevich** (*b* Moscow, 6 Jan 1872; *d* there, 27 April 1915). Russian composer. He was a fellow pupil of Rakhmaninov's in Zverev's class from 1884 and at the Moscow Conservatory (1888–92), where his teachers were Taneyev, Arensky and Safonov. From 1894 his career as a pianist was managed by Belyayev, who arranged his European tours and also published his works: at this stage they were almost exclusively for solo piano, and deeply influenced by Chopin (most are preludes and mazurkas), though in the late 1890s he began to write for orchestra. In 1903 he left Russia and his family to live in western Europe for six years with a young female admirer, and his musical style became more intensely personal, developing a profusion of decoration in harmony becalmed by unresolved dominant chords or whole-tone elements. The major works of this period include the *Divine Poem* and again numerous piano pieces.

In 1905 he encountered Madame Blavatsky's theosophy, which soon ousted the enthusiasm for Nietschean superhumanism that had underlain the immediately preceding works. The static and ecstatic tendencies in his music were encouraged, being expressed notably in the *Poem of Ecstasy* and *Prometheus*, the latter intended to be performed with a play of coloured light. Still more ambitious were the plans for the *Mysterium*, a quasi-religious act which would have united all the arts, and for the composition of which the exclusively piano works of 1910–15 were intended to be preparatory, this journey into mystical hysteria going along with a voyage beyond tonality to a floating dissonance often based on the 'mystic chord' (C–F♯–B♭–E–A–D).

Orchestral music Pf Conc., f♯ (1896); Sym. no.1, E, with chorus (1900); Sym. no.2, c (1901); Sym. no.3, 'Divine Poem' (1904); Poem of Ecstasy (1908); Prometheus (1910)

Piano music 10 sonatas (1892, 1897, 1898, 1903, 1907, 1911, 1911, 1913, 1913, 1913); *c*80 preludes; nocturnes, waltzes, mazurkas, impromptus, poems, pieces

Skuherský, František Zdeněk (Xavier Alois) (*b* Opočno, 31 July 1830; *d* České Budějovice, 19 Aug 1892). Bohemian composer and theorist. As director of the Prague Organ School (from 1866) he taught J.B. Foerster and Janáček, also working as a choirmaster and advocating the church music reform. He produced the first systematic theory of composition in Czech (1880–84) and in his progressive view of harmony anticipated the ideas of Hostinský, Janáček and Hába.

Slancio, Con (It.). With dash, with impetus.

Slatkin, Leonard (*b* Los Angeles, 1 Sept 1944). American conductor, son of the violinist Felix Slatkin (1915–63). He studied at the Juilliard School and made his début in 1966. In 1968 he joined the St Louis SO, holding various posts and becoming music director in 1979 (after a period with the New Orleans Philharmonic SO); he has also conducted in Europe. His structural grasp and orchestral command have been applied to a wide repertory, including American music. His compositions include two string quartets and *The Raven* (after Poe, 1971) for narrator and orchestra.

Slavenski [Štolcer], **Josip** (*b* Čakovec, 11 May 1896; *d* Belgrade, 30 Nov 1955). Yugoslav composer. He was a pupil of Kodály and Siklós at the Budapest Academy (1913–16) and of Novák at the Prague Conservatory (1921–3). From 1924 he worked in Belgrade as a teacher and composer, the first Yugoslav of the 20th century to make an international reputation. He used Balkan folk music but also had modernist and mystical concerns, his works including the choral orchestral *Religiophonia* (1934), orchestral pieces, four string quartets and other chamber music, piano pieces and folksong arrangements.

Slavík, Josef (*b* Jince, 26 March 1806; *d* Budapest, 30 May 1833). Czech violinist and composer. At the Prague Conservatory he studied the violin with B.V. Pixis. The first modern Czech violinist to achieve an international reputation, he triumphed in Vienna, receiving encouragement from Schubert, Paganini and Chopin. His few surviving works, notably the Violin Concerto in F♯ minor (1823), show his interest in an expressive virtuoso style.

Slavonic Dances. Two sets of dances by Dvořák for piano duet (1878, 1886), often heard in their orchestral versions.

Slavonic Rhapsodies. Three orchestral works by Dvořák (1878).

Sleeping Beauty, The [Spyashchaya krasavitsa]. Ballet in a prologue and three acts by Tchaikovsky to a libretto by M. Petipa and I. Vsevolozhsky after Perrault (1890, St Petersburg).

Slendro. One of the two tuning systems used by GAMELAN ensembles in Java, a pentatonic tuning made up of intervals equivalent to large major 2nds and small minor 3rds, sometimes in combination. *See* INDONESIAN MUSIC.

Slentando (It.). Becoming slower.

Slezak, Leo (*b* Šumperk, 18 Aug 1873; *d* Egern am Tegernsee, 1 June 1946). Austrian-Czech tenor. His début was as Lohengrin (1896, Bern); in 1901 he was called to Vienna by Mahler and had a long and brilliant career there, in the main Wagner and Verdi roles, ending in 1933. He sang Othello at Covent Garden and the Met in 1909, remaining at the Met for four seasons. He was noted for his warm and brilliant tone and was an expressive singer of lieder. The tale of the tenor in *Lohengrin* asking 'What time is the next swan?' originates with him.

Slide. (1) An ornament consisting of a short run of two accessory notes, either upward or downward by step, to the main note. In rising form it is sometimes called 'elevation', in descending, 'double backfall' (it may be indicated by two commas). Purcell called it a 'slur', a translation of the French *coulé*.

(2) Term in string playing for a method of changing position (*see* SHIFT); it is effected by moving a finger already on the string to within a short distance of a new note to be taken by another finger. The effect is normally of a portamento.

(3) The telescopic joint of a SLIDE TRUMPET or a TROMBONE. Some wind instruments and organ pipes possess tuning-slides, which adjust the pitch by shortening or lengthening the sounding tube.

Slide trumpet. A natural trumpet fitted with a slide mechanism whereby the instrument's length could be altered while it was being played, filling in gaps in the harmonic series. The fundamental was between C and F. It was used on the European mainland during the Renaissance and Baroque periods. An English version, the 'flat trumpet', pitched in C, was built in the 17th century; Purcell wrote for it. In the early 19th century in England a new design was invented which used a spring to return the slide to its original position; the instrument was in F, with crooks. The advent of valved trumpets and cornets rendered it obsolete.

Slit-drum. A hollowed-out piece of wood used for musical or signalling purposes. They are found in most cultures and range from the oriental woodblock to the giant slit-drums of Oceania, some standing up to 5 metres tall.

Slobodskaya, Oda (*b* Vilnius, 10 Dec 1888; *d* London, 29 July 1970). Russian soprano. She studied in St Petersburg and made her début there in 1919 as Tchaikovsky's Lisa. She sang widely in the Russian repertory and from 1922 appeared in the West. From 1932 she sang in London, in Wagner, Delius and Musorgsky. After settling in England she was a frequent broadcaster and became the foremost interpreter there of Russian song of her time.

Slonimsky, Nicolas (*b* St Petersburg, 27 April 1894). American composer and writer on music. He studied at the St Petersburg Conservatory and in the USA and taught at the Eastman School of Music (1923–5). He conducted the Boston CO (1927–34) and the Harvard University Orchestra (1927–30); in the 1930s and 1940s he conducted in Europe and in the USA, becoming known for his first performances of composers of the Americas. He is best known for his editing of major music reference works: *Thompson's International Cyclopedia of Music and Musicians* (from 1946), *Baker's Biographical Dictionary* (from 1958); his work is noted for its whimsical turn of mind, also evident in his *Lexicon of Musical Invective*.

Slonimsky, Sergey Mikhaylovich (*b* Leningrad, 12 Aug 1932). Soviet composer, nephew of Nicolas. He was a pupil of Yevlakhov at the Leningrad Conservatory (1950–55), where he began teaching in 1959. His works of the early 1960s use a variety of modernisms (he was one of the first Soviet composers to use 12-note serial techniques) but the later operas are less adventurous; his opera *Mary Stuart* was given at the Edinburgh Festival (1986).

Slur. A curved line extended over a number of notes to indicate their grouping; the term is also applied to the effect thus obtained. With string instruments, it signifies that the notes should be taken within one stroke of the bow; with wind instruments, that they should be played in one breath without separate articulation; and with keyboard instruments, a legato touch (not releasing one note until the next is sounded) is called for. In vocal music, slurs are normally used to show which notes are to be sung to a single syllable. Some composers (and particularly editors) provide slurs too long to allow a single bow or a single breath, and these have to be interpreted as indicating larger-scale phrasing. When a slur is shown with staccato dots or other indications on the notes beneath it, a specific bowing or articulation technique will be called for. *See* ARTICULATION and PHRASE.

A curved line joining two notes of the same pitch is a TIE.

Smalley, Roger (*b* Swinton, 26 July 1943). English composer and pianist. He was a pupil of Fricker and White at the RCM (1961–5), of Goehr at Morley College (1962) and of Stockhausen in Cologne (1965–6). Works of 1965–7 are expressionist transformations of Tudor music close to Davies, but during the next decade he was powerfully influenced by Stockhausen: with others he formed the live electronic ensemble Intermodulation (1970–76), which played Stockhausen's music and his own; he also drew on the technique of *Mantra* in his large-scale *Accord* for two pianos (1975). But out of this came an interest in long-range tonal process, developed in works written since he took an appointment at the University of Western Australia in 1976 (String Quartet, 1979; Piano Concerto, 1985). He is an accomplished pianist; his essays show him a highly perceptive critic.

Smareglia, Antonio (*b* Pola, 5 May 1854; *d* Grado, 15 April 1929). Italian composer. He studied with Faccio at the Milan Conservatory (1873–7), becoming attached to Boito and the *Scapigliatura*, a literary reform movement. With a passion for Wagner he devoted himself to opera, composing ten (one destroyed) between 1879 and 1914. *Il vassallo di Szigeth* (1889) and *Cornil Schut* (1893) show dramatic energy and *Oceàna* (1903) striking symphonic writing, but the best is perhaps *Nozze istriane* (1895), with its rustic setting and tamed *verismo* style, reflecting Mascagni's *Cavalleria rus-*

ticana. Unjustly neglected by the public, he owed his survival to the patronage of Toscanini, the Tartini Conservatory at Trieste and the industrialist Carlo Sai.

Smart. English family of musicians. The most celebrated member was Sir George (1776–1867), a conductor, organist and singing teacher. His efficiency, meticulous knowledge of performing traditions and personal associations with Haydn, Beethoven, Weber and Mendelssohn made him one of the most well-respected music directors of his day. He conducted the English premières of Beethoven's Ninth Symphony and Mendelssohn's *St Paul* and presided at numerous London orchestral concerts (1813–44), provincial festivals (1823–40) and court musical events. His nephew Henry Thomas (1813–79), a largely self-taught organist and composer, was known for his expertise in organ construction and his voluminous organ and service music (including the popular hymn tune *Regent Square*) and attractive partsongs.

Smetáček, Václav (*b* Brno, 30 Sept 1906; *d* Prague, 18 Feb 1986). Czech conductor and oboist. He studied in Prague and in 1928 founded the Prague Wind Quintet, remaining a member for 27 years. From 1934 he conducted choirs and orchestras, notably the Czech PO, and first visited England in 1938. He was heard in a wide range of Slavonic works and conducted opera in Buenos Aires, Berlin and Milan. He taught at the Prague Conservatory, 1945–66.

Smetana, Bedřich [Friedrich] (*b* Litomyšl, 2 March 1824; *d* Prague, 12 May 1884). Czech composer. He took music lessons from his father, a keen violinist, and from several local teachers. In his teens he attended the Academic Gymnasium in Prague, but neglected school work to attend concerts (including some by Liszt, with whom he became friendly) and to write string quartets for friends, until his father sent him to the Premonstratensian Gymnasium at Plzeň. At first he earned a precarious living as a teacher in Prague until, in January 1884, he was appointed resident piano teacher to Count Leopold Thun's family, which provided him with the means to study harmony, counterpoint and composition with Josef Proksch. When he failed in an attempt to launch a career as a concert pianist in 1847, Smetana decided to found a school of music in Prague. This showed little profit, but he was able to earn something by teaching privately and by playing regularly to the deposed Emperor Ferdinand, and in 1849 he was able to marry Kateřina Kolářová, whom he had known since his Plzeň days.

Smetana's financial situation improved little in the years that followed, and political uncertainty and domestic tragedy only added to his unrest: three of his four daughters died between 1854 and 1856. When he heard there was an opening for a piano teacher at Göteborg he jumped at the chance. In Sweden his prospects improved, and he was in demand as a pianist, teacher and conductor. Inspired by Liszt's example, he composed his first symphonic poems. His wife's health forced him to return to Bohemia with her in 1859, but she died at

Dresden on the way home. After two further summers in Göteborg, between which he found a second wife in Bettina Ferdinandová, Smetana felt the need to return permanently to Prague in order to play an active role in the reawakening of Czech culture that followed the Austrian defeat by Napoleon III at Magenta and Soferino.

He was disappointed to find himself no more successful in Prague than he had been before. It was not until his first opera, *The Brandenburgers in Bohemia*, was enthusiastically received in January 1866 that his prospects there improved. His second, *The Bartered Bride*, was speedily put into production and soon found favour, though (as with his other operas) foreign performances long remained rarities. As principal conductor of the Provisional Theatre, 1866–74, Smetana added 42 operas to the repertory, including his own *Dalibor* (on a heroic national theme) and *The Two Widows*. *Dalibor* and *Libuše* (performed at the opening of the National Theatre in Prague in 1881) are Smetana's two most nationalistic operas; when completing the latter he also planned a vast orchestral monument to his nation which became the cycle of symphonic poems entitled *Má vlast* ('My fatherland'), including the evocative and stirring *Vltava*, a picture of the river that flows through Prague.

In 1874 there appeared the first signs of the syphilis that was to result in Smetana's deafness. The String Quartet *From my Life* (1876) suggests in its last movement the piercing whistling that haunted his every evening, making work almost impossible. He somehow managed to complete two more operas, a second string quartet and several other works, but by 1883 his mental equilibrium was seriously disturbed. In April 1884 he was taken to the Prague lunatic asylum, where he died the following month.

Smetana was the first major nationalist composer of Bohemia. He gave his people a new musical identity and self-confidence by his technical assurance and originality in handling national subjects. In his operas and symphonic poems he drew on his country's legends, history, characters, scenery and ideas, presenting them with a freshness and colour which owe little to indigenous folksong but much to a highly original and essentially dramatic musical style.

Operas The Brandenburgers in Bohemia (1866); The Bartered Bride (1866, rev. 1870); Dalibor (1868); Libuše (1872, perf. 1881); The Two Widows (1874); The Kiss (1876); The Secret (1878); The Devil's Wall (1882)
Orchestral music Jubel-Ouvertüre (1849, rev. 1883); Triumph-Symphonie (1854, rev. 1881); Má vlast: Vysehrad (c1872–4), Vltava (1874), Šárka (1875), From Bohemia's Woods and Fields (1875), Tábor (1878), Blaník (1879)
Other works Pf Trio, g (1855, rev. 1857); Str Qt no.1, e, 'From my Life' (1876); Str Qt no.2, d (1883); From the Homeland, vn, pf (1880); songs, choral works, pf music

Smetana Quartet. Czech string quartet, led by Milan Škampa. It was formed in 1945 and first travelled abroad in 1950, making its London and New York débuts in 1955 and 1957. Its repertory is based on the classics and Slavonic works, and it per-

forms from memory with a unity of ensemble deriving from great attention to dynamic and expressive detail.

Smethergell, William (*b* London, bap. 6 Jan 1751; *d* c1800). English composer. He was a church organist and a violinist. His output includes seven keyboard concertos, 12 overtures, chamber and keyboard pieces (some for beginners) and songs.

Smith, Bessie (*b* Chattanooga, TN, 15 April 1894; *d* Clarksdale, MS, 26 Sept 1937). American blues singer. She performed in touring minstrel shows and cabarets before her first recording, *Down-hearted Blues* (1923), and worked with important jazz instrumentalists including Louis Armstrong. The greatest vaudeville blues singer, she brought the emotional intensity, personal involvement and expression of blues singing into the jazz repertory with unexcelled artistry.

Smith, Cyril (James) (*b* Middlesborough, 11 Aug 1909; *d* London, 2 Aug 1974). English pianist. He studied at the RCM, where he taught. He was admired for his interpretation of the concerto repertory and for his duet playing with his wife, Phyllis Sellick; many works were written for them.

Smith, 'Father' (Bernard) (*b* c1630; *d* London, 1708). Organ builder and organist. Probably trained near Halle, he worked in the Netherlands; he is first noted in England in 1667, when he tuned the organs at Westminster Abbey. His first new organ in England was for the Sheldonian Theatre, Oxford (1670–71); by 1671 he was 'the King's organ maker', by 1676 organist at St Margaret's, Westminster, and by 1695 keeper of the king's organs, building instruments at Windsor and Whitehall. Among his most important were those for the Temple Church, London (1682–8; a contract won in acrimonious rivalry with Renatus Harris), Durham Cathedral (1684), St Paul's Cathedral (1695–6) and St Mary the Great (1698) and Trinity College, Cambridge (1708; surviving pipes and case). In common with current practice, Smith's organs were normally single-manual, of five to ten stops, with divided sharps and no pedals; they were noted for their sweetness and brilliance.

Smith, John Christopher [Schmidt, Johann Christoph] (*b* Ansbach, 1712; *d* Bath, 3 Oct 1795). English composer. He was the son of Johann Christoph Schmidt (John Christopher Smith) (*d* 1763), Handel's principal copyist and later his amanuensis. He had a few lessons from Handel and Pepusch but studied mostly with Thomas Roseingrave. His first opera was the Italian-style *Ulysses* (1733); later ones included two written for Garrick and based on Shakespeare – *The Fairies* (1755), after *A Midsummer Night's Dream*, and *The Tempest* (1756) – and a successful afterpiece, *The Enchanter* (1760). Several others remained unperformed. In 1759–68 he directed the annual performances of *Messiah* at the Foundling Hospital, where he was organist. Of his own oratorios, mostly written in the 1760s, *Paradise Lost* (1760) was the greatest success; three later ones were largely adaptations of Handel. Among his other works are five volumes of harpsichord music (1732–63) and a funeral service (1772) for the dowager Princess of Wales, who was his harpsichord pupil. He retired to Bath in the 1770s.

Smith, John Stafford (*b* Gloucester, bap. 30 March 1750; *d* London, 21 Sept 1836). English music antiquarian and composer. A pupil of Boyce, he sang in the Chapel Royal and at Westminster Abbey and was Master of the Chapel Royal Children, 1805–17. He won early success as a glee composer and also wrote church music, songs etc; one of his convivial songs, *To Anacreon in Heaven*, became the American national anthem, *The Star-Spangled Banner*. He did pioneering work in collecting, studying and editing early music; his *Musica Antiqua* (1812), including works from the 12th century onwards, was a landmark in English music studies.

Smith, Leland C(layton) (*b* Oakland, 6 Aug 1925). American composer. A pupil of Milhaud at Mills College, Sessions at Berkeley and Messiaen in Paris (1948–9), he has taught at the universities of Chicago (1952–8) and Stanford (since 1958). Ge has carried out leading research into computer programming for composition and music printing. His works use serial methods and computer sound synthesis.

Smith, (Joseph) Leo(pold) (*b* Birmingham, 26 Nov 1881; *d* Toronto, 18 April 1952). Canadian composer and cellist. He studied at the Royal Manchester College of Music and emigrated in 1910 to teach the cello at the Toronto Conservatory; he was also professor at Toronto University (1938–50). His works use Canadian folk melodies but retain an English spirit. His textbooks have been much used.

Smith, Robert (*b* c1648; *d* ?Sept 1675). English composer. Trained as a chorister in the Chapel Royal, he became a prominent composer of sacred music, theatre songs and dialogues and instrumental pieces. He was a musician-in-ordinary to the king from 1673. Another Robert Smith (1689–1768) was a mathematician at Cambridge who worked on acoustics, particularly temperaments, and published *Harmonics, or the Philosophy of Musical Sounds* (1748).

Smith, Theodore (*b* c1740; *d* 1810). English or (probably) Ferman composer. He worked mainly in London, where he wrote an overture and songs for the masque *Alfred* (1773). From 1774 he lived mainly by teaching; later he was also organist at Ebury Chapel. He was probably in Berlin c1780. Besides songs, he composed 12 keyboard concertos, quartets and trio sonatas, c40 keyboard sonatas (some with violin or flute) and over 20 keyboard duets.

Smith Brindle, Reginald (*b* Bamber Bridge, 5 Jan 1917). English composer. He studied at Bangor and in Italy with Pizzetti and Dallapiccola. In 1970 he was appointed professor at the University of Surrey. His works, subject to a range of avant-garde influences, include much for guitar and for percussion. His style has constantly changed but there is strong individuality in his music. He has written books on compositional techniques.

Smithsonian Institution. Part of the Museum of American History, Washington, DC, with a large collection of musical instruments which is used in concerts sponsored by the Institution; some are in the Hall of Musical Instruments (cap. 300) or Baird Auditorium (cap. 850) at the American Museum of Natural History.

Smorzando (It.). Dimming, fading away.

Smyth, Dame Ethel (Mary) (*b* Marylebone, 22 April 1858; *d* Woking, 9 May 1944). English composer. She trained in Leipzig, where she met Brahms and other leading composers. It was in Germany, too, that she had her first operatic successes, with *Fantasio* (1898), *Der Wald* (1902) and especially *The Wreckers* (1906, the chief representative of English *verismo*); other relatively early works include the large-scale Mass in D (1891), harking back to Beethoven. Her identification with the cause of women's suffrage was musically affirmed by her *March of the Women* (1911). Later works include the comedy *The Boatswain's Mate* (1916), two one-act operas, the Concerto for Violin and Horn (1927) and the choral symphony *The Prison* (1930). Her colourful, forceful personality is wittily conveyed in her writings, which include several volumes of autobiography.

Snare drum. A DRUM with strings stretched across its lower head (for illustration, *see* PERCUSSION INSTRUMENTS).

Snel, Joseph François (*b* Brussels, 30 July 1793; *d* Koekelberg, 10 March 1861). Belgian violinist, conductor and composer. He studied at the Paris Conservatoire, returning to Brussels as a teacher and conductor (at the Théâtre de la Monnaie, 1831–4) and composing ballets, music for wind band and a noteworthy Requiem.

Snetzler, John (*b* Schaffhausen, bap. 6 April 1710; *d* Schaffhausen, 28 Sept 1785). English organ builder of Swiss origin. In London from c1742, he built organs for the Moravian Brethren, notably at Fulneck (1748), and for St Margaret's, King's Lynn (1754). Among his most important later instruments were those for Buckingham House (1760, 1763), Peterhouse, Cambridge (1765), and Beverley Minister (1769). Apart from introducing European stops, he was noted for skilful voicing and elegant, imaginative casework.

Snow Maiden, The [Snegurochka]. Opera in a prologue and four acts by Rimsky-Korsakov to his own libretto after Ostrovsky (1882, St Petersburg).

Soave (It.). Mild, gentle.

Sob. A technique used in lute playing to produce a sob-like deadening of the tone; it is obtained by lightening the finger pressure on the string immediately after it is struck.

Sobinov, Leonid Vital'yevich (*b* Yaroslavl, 7 June 1872; *d* Riga, 14 Oct 1934). Russian tenor. He sang at the Bol'shoy from 1897; later appearances were at La Scala, Monte Carlo and Berlin and throughout Russia. His poetic approach and attractive stage presence made him popular in the Russian repertory and as Gounod's Faust and Romeo, Alfredo and Lohengrin.

Sobolewski, Fryderyk Edward (*b* Kołobrzeg, 1 Oct 1808; *d* St Louis, 17 May 1872). Polish conductor. He studied in Dresden with Weber and in Berlin with Zelter, working in Królewiec and Bremen before moving to Milwaukee and St Louis, where he directed the Philharmonic Association Orchestra

(1860–66). He composed operas, oratorios and orchestral music, esteemed by Schumann.

Society for Private Musical Performances. See VEREIN FÜR MUSIKALISCHE PRIVATAUFFÜHRUNGEN.

Society for the Promotion of New Music. British organization founded in 1942 (as the Committee for the Promotion of New Music). Young composers' works are discussed and played and many premières have been given (not all British).

Sociology of music. The study of the relationship between music and society. It is concerned with the function of music in society and the ways in which society influences the development of music. Music sociologists study such matters as patronage, direct and indirect, and its relationship to composition, and the ways in which music both reflects society and influences it. All kinds of music, popular and traditional as well as art music, fall within the scope of the discipline.

The formal study of musical sociology, though anticipated much earlier, dates back to the beginning of the 20th century (for example in Hermann Abert's studies of the relationship of the medieval church to popular music). Its most influential practitioner in the early 20th century was Max Weber (1864–1920), who, in *Die rationalen und soziologischen Grundlagen der Musik* (1921), discusses the relationship between social structures and technical aspects of Western music. Present-day musical sociology divides into three principal schools. One, empiricist or positivist, is concerned chiefly with the context and function of music within society, dealing with musical life and the music market and the relationship of different social groups to different types of music. Secondly, there is the school of Hegelian historical idealism, represented above all in the work of Theodor W. Adorno (1903–69), who developed a theory of the 'musical standard', according to which the most advanced music of a culture represents both the society itself and an aesthetic depiction of that society; it stresses the progressive character of music as a social indicator and draws social inferences from the nature of popular music. Thirdly, Marxism, or historical materialism, represented above all by the work of Hanns Eisler (1898–1962), sees changes in music as the result of changes in its economic and social role, and argues 'that each new musical style does not arise from an aesthetically new viewpoint, and thus does not represent a revolution in material, but that the alteration of the material is forcibly determined by historically necessary alteration of the function of music in society in general' (*Musik und Politik*, 1973). Recent thinking in the sociology of music has tended to explain individual works less according to their meaning or historical situation than in terms of social function (as the basis for the production and consumption of music) and social effect.

Socrate. Symphonic drama in three parts by Satie, a setting for voice or voices and piano or chamber orchestra of texts by Plato translated by V. Cousin (1918).

Söderman, Johan August (*b* Stockholm, 17 July 1832; *d* there, 10 Feb 1876). Swedish composer. After studying in Stockholm, he held theatre posts, writing and arranging music for the stage, but he made his most important contribution in epigrammatically concentrated works, especially ballads (*Tannhäuser, Die verlassene Mühle*, 1856–7) and songs, including those in the collection *Heidenröslein* (1856/7); in this and in his style he has much in common with Grieg.

Söderström(-Olow), (Anna) Elisabeth (*b* Stockholm, 7 May 1927). Swedish soprano. She sang Mozart's Bastienne at Drottningholm in 1947 and in 1950 joined the Swedish Royal Opera. She visited Covent Garden with the company in 1960 and has returned to London as Mozart's Countess and Fiordiligi and Mélisande. She has sung at Glyndebourne since 1957 in Strauss, Henze, Mozart and Tchaikovsky. Her Met début, in 1959, was as Susanna. Her musical intelligence and natural stage manner serve particularly well in Janáček's operas.

Soggetto (It.). A fugue SUBJECT, particularly one of the old 'ricercare' type (e.g. Bach, '48', ii, 9).

Soggetto cavato. Term coined by Zarlino to denote the special class of thematic subjects for polyphonic compositions that were derived from a phrase associated with them by matching the vowels of the words to the corresponding vowels of the Guidonian solmization syllables (*ut re mi fa sol la*). The earliest and most famous example of a 'soggetto cavato dalle parole' (literally, a 'subject carved out of the words') is that of Josquin's *Missa Hercules dux Ferrarie*, the vowels of which yield the subject *re ut re ut re fa mi re*, corresponding to the syllables 'Her-cu-les Dux Fer-ra-ri-e'.

Sogner, Pasquale (*b* Naples, 1793; *d* there, 28 Dec 1842). Italian composer. In 1809–35 he presented several comic operas (most with his own librettos) in Naples and other Italian cities. He was also a pianist and composed piano works and other instrumental pieces. His father Tommaso (1762–after 1821), a *maestro di cappella* and teacher in Livorno, composed operas, oratorios and church music, but only sonatas for keyboard and violin survive.

Sogno di Scipione, Il. Serenata written by Mozart in 1771–2 for the Prince-Archbishop of Salzburg, an allegorical work in one act to a libretto by Metastasio; it was long supposed to have been composed for the installation of Hieronymus von Colloredo but is now known to have been written in his predecessor's lifetime.

Sohal, Naresh (Kumar) (*b* Harsipind, Punjab, 18 Sept 1939). Indian composer. In 1962 he went to London, where his *Asht Prahar* drew him to public notice (1970). He studied quarter-tones and used them in some ensuing works (*Thyan I*, cello and chamber orchestra, 1974); but although he has set poems by Tagore (1970, 1977) and used Indian titles, his music is in line with current Western concerns, as in *The Wanderer* (1982), a setting of a poem about Man and a hostile universe, which uses aleatory features.

Soir (et la tempête), Le. Haydn's Symphony no.8 in G (?1761), the last of a group of three: no.6 is 'Le matin' and no.7 'Le midi'.

Soirées musicales. Collection of songs and duets by

Rossini (1835) of which Britten orchestrated five; the rest were orchestrated by Respighi for his ballet *La boutique fantasque*.

Solage (*fl* 1370–90). French composer. He was probably connected with the French court in the 1380s; three of his ballades contain references to the royal family. Though these show characteristics of the Ars Subtilior, his other songs – particularly his four-voice ballades and virelai – are close in style to Machaut.

Soldaten, Die. Opera in four acts by B.A. Zimmermann to his own libretto after Lenz (1960).

Soldier's Tale, The. Theatre piece in two parts by Stravinsky, 'to be read, played and danced', to a French text by C.F. Ramuz after a Russian folktale (1918, Lausanne).

Soler (Ramos), Antonio (Francisco Javier José) (*b* Olot, Gerona, bap. 3 Dec 1729; *d* El Escorial, 20 Dec 1783). Catalan composer and organist. He first worked as *maestro de capilla* at Lérida. In 1752 he joined the Jeronymite monastery at El Escorial, becoming *maestro de capilla* in 1757; he also spent time in Madrid, studying with Domenico Scarlatti. He was keyboard instructor to Prince Gabriel and an authority on organ building.

Soler's best known works are his 120 keyboard sonatas. Like Scarlatti's, they demand a virtuoso technique, but they are suitable for the piano and vary more widely in form than Scarlatti's; many later ones have three or four movements. Phrases of irregular length are typical. His other instrumental music includes six quintets for organ and strings (1776), concertos' for two organs and solo organ pieces. He also wrote over 300 vocal works (Latin church music, villancicos etc) and an important treatise on modulation, *Llave de la modulación* (1762).

Solesmes. A Benedictine abbey in France, between Le Mans and Angers, the centre of the Gregorian chant revival since its reestablishment in 1833. The community has undertaken a study and restoration of the Roman liturgy and of Gregorian chant, resulting in a series of scholarly publications; some of their liturgical books have been declared the official books of the Roman Catholic Church. Their performing practice is known for its free interpretation of chant rhythm.

Sol-fa. *See* TONIC SOL-FA.

Solfeggio (It.; Fr. *solfège*). Term originally referring to the singing of scales, intervals and melodic exercises to solmization syllables; it was later extended to include textless vocal exercises to develop agile singing. This became a basis of the curriculum. Many collections of *solfeggi* or *solfèges* were published in the 19th and early 20th centuries for singing instruction.

Solié, Jean-Pierre (*b* Nîmes, 1755; *d* Paris, 6 Aug 1812). French composer and tenor, later baritone. Initially a teacher of singing and the guitar, he devoted himself to singing from 1778 and in 1782 went to Paris, where from 1787 he was very successful at the Comédie-Italienne, now as a baritone. He composed over 30 stage works, mostly *opéras comiques*.

Sollberger, Harvey (Dene) (*b* Cedar Rapids, IA, 11 May 1938). American composer and flautist. He was a pupil of Beeson and Luening at Columbia (1960–64), where he founded the Group for Contemporary Music in 1962 and taught, 1964–74, then moving to the Manhattan School of Music. A virtuoso flautist, he has explored new performing techniques. His own works, many for flute, are concerned with problems of live performance; his works of the 1970s and 1980s sometimes use cyclic processes derived from non-Western processes.

Solmization. The use of syllables in association with pitches as a mnemonic device for indicating melodic intervals. Many such systems exist in world musical cultures, to serve as aids in the oral transmission of music and to assist teaching and memorization.

The principal solmization system of Western music dates from the early 11th century and is traditionally associated with Guido of Arezzo (*c*1000) although it is not mentioned in his extant writings. In this system, the syllables *ut, re, mi, fa, sol* and *la* are assigned to three different series of pitches, beginning on C, G (with a B natural) and F (with a B flat), to form sets of six notes or 'hexachords'. These are traditionally illustrated by drawings on a hand (the 'Guidonian hand'). In each hexachord, the interval *mi–fa* is a semitone. With the superimposition of these hexachords across the compass, from *G* to *e''*, each note had a name (such as 'C fa ut') which in most cases identified it uniquely.

In adding solmization syllables to chant, the chant would be placed in the appropriate hexachord and this helped singers to know when semitones could be sung rather than tones. The hexachord could be changed if the chant's range exceeded that of a single hexachord. Later, the hexachord system was expanded to admit additional notes.

The Guidonian system of solmization, besides being the basis for much early theory, was the prototype of many later systems, of which the best known is Tonic Sol-fa. The Guidonian syllable names were adopted in many languages to identify notes in preference to the letters of the alphabet favoured in English (*see* PITCH NAMES).

Solo (It.). 'Alone': term that identifies, in a score, a passage that needs to be brought out, or is to be played by one performer alone (rather than doubled by others), or shows which portions in a concerto are dominated by the soloist. The term is also used for a piece played by a single performer or, in the Baroque period, a single instrument with continuo accompaniment. The term 'solo sonata' may carry either of those meanings.

Solomon [Cutner, Solomon] (*b* London, 9 Aug 1902; *d* there, 22 Feb 1988). English pianist. He played Tchaikovsky's First Concerto in London at the age of ten but soon retired for further study. His American début was in 1926 and in 1939 he gave the première of Bliss's Concerto at the New York World Fair. His performances of Mozart and Romantic music were admired for their sensibility and unforced virtuosity; in 1965 his career was ended by a stroke.

Solomon. Oratorio by Handel to a biblical text by an unknown author, possibly Morell (1749, London).

Boyce wrote a serenata of the same name to words by E. Moore after the *Song of Solomon* (1742, London).

Solo organ. The manual of an organ, usually the fourth, given to strong solo stops (flutes, strings and reeds) not normally intended to blend into the chorus.

Solo sonata. Late Baroque term (sometimes simply as 'solo') for a sonata for a single instrument, most commonly violin, and continuo. The title was less often used for unaccompanied works, like Bach's for violin. The archetypal works are Corelli's 12 solo sonatas op.5 (1700).

Solov'yov, Nikolay Feopemptovich (*b* Petrozavodsk, 9 May 1846; *d* Petrograd, 27 Dec 1916). Russian composer and critic. He taught theory and composition at the St Petersburg Conservatory, having some success as a dramatic and choral composer, but he was known mainly for his reactionary criticism for St Petersburg journals.

Solov'yov-Sedoy, Vasily Pavlovich (*b* St Petersburg, 25 April 1907; *d* there, 2 Dec 1979). Soviet composer. He was influenced from childhood by folk music and trained at the Leningrad Conservatory (1931–6). He wrote hundreds of popular songs, those of the war years winning him widespread popularity (he toured the front with his own theatre group). He also wrote operettas, orchestral works and much incidental music.

Solti, Sir Georg (*b* Budapest, 21 Oct 1912). British conductor of Hungarian birth. His teachers included Bartók, Kodály and Dohnányi. In 1938 he conducted at Budapest Opera but had to leave Hungary the following year. Musical directorships at Munich Opera (1946–52) and Frankfurt (1952–61) were followed by ten years at Covent Garden. Standards of orchestral playing in particular were improved during his tenure. In 1969 he became musical director of the Chicago SO, arguably making it the finest orchestra in the world. Solti's big, decisive, exciting conducting style has been heard in many recordings, notably his historic *Ring* and the symphonies of Elgar and Mahler.

Sombrero de tres picos, El. *See* THREE-CORNERED HAT, THE.

Somers, Harry (Stuart) (*b* Toronto, 11 Sept 1925). Canadian composer. He was a pupil of Weinzweig at the Toronto Conservatory (1942–9) and of Milhaud in Paris (1949–50), working in the 1960s as a broadcaster and in music education. His works, covering all genres, have used a variety of styles and techniques, most of them brought together in his opera *Louis Riel* (1967), his most important achievement. Since the 1960s he has been chiefly concerned with new vocal techniques.

Somervell, Sir Arthur (*b* Windermere, 5 June 1863; *d* London, 2 May 1937). English composer. He studied with Stanford at Cambridge, at the Berlin Musikhochschule (1883–5), at the RCM (1885–7) and with Parry. As a composer he is best known for his five song cycles; he also wrote sacred music and orchestral pieces in a Germanic Romantic style. But his greatest achievement was as a pioneer in music education, helping establish music in schools and composing educational works, including operettas.

Somis, Giovanni Battista (*b* Turin, 25 Dec 1686; *d* there, 14 Aug 1763). Italian violinist and composer. He played in the ducal chapel at Turin and became soloist and leader there in 1707 after studying with Corelli in Rome. He was noted for his majestic bowstroke and had a powerful influence in France as well as Italy; among his pupils were Pugnani and Leclair. His works, mostly for violin, include three-movement solo and trio sonatas which combine elements of the church and chamber types. He also wrote virtuoso violin concertos. His brother Lorenzo (1688–1775), also a violinist and teacher in Turin, composed sonatas and concertos.

Sommeil (Fr.: 'sleep'). A slumber scene, found in French stage works of the 17th and 18th centuries. Typically, it is composed of a prelude in slow duple metre for flutes and strings followed by a vocal trio sometimes involving classical deities of sleep such as Morpheus. Lully introduced the *sommeil* in *Les amants magnifiques* (1670); there are examples in Destouches's *Issé* and Rameau's *Dardanus*. The *sommeil* is found also in cantatas, oratorios and instrumental music.

Sommer, Vladimír (*b* Dolní Jiřetín, 28 Feb 1921). Czech composer. He was a pupil of Bořkovec at the Prague Academy (1946–50) and from 1960 lecturer at Prague University. He was much involved with socialist development, conducting, teaching, arranging folksongs and writing popular songs. But he turned to instrumental music, developing a rich, individual style of direct emotional expression, related to those of Shostakovich and Prokofiev. His works include string quartets and symphonies.

Sonata. A piece of music, almost invariably instrumental and usually in several movements, for a soloist or a small ensemble.

In the late 16th century numerous terms were used for instrumental pieces, one of which was 'sonata', indicating something played as opposed to something sung ('cantata'). Until *c*1650 it was used interchangeably with 'canzona'. Around 1600 Giovanni Gabrieli popularized a type of sonata for two or more instrumental groups, but he also pointed to the future meaning of the word in his *Sonata per tre violini* (1615). In the early phase the forms are single-movement or multi-sectional, in the manner of the canzona. The single-movement sonata survived later in the era in such byways as G.C. Arresti's anthology of 18 *Sonate de organo* (*c*1700) and the keyboard sonatas (or 'toccatas') of Seixas, but by the time of Corelli (1653–1713) the sonata usually consisted of a number of separate movements.

Corelli was largely responsible for establishing the slow–fast–slow–fast order of movements in the SONATA DA CHIESA ('church sonata'). He used it in most of his trio sonatas opp.1 and 3, but added a fifth movement in his solo church sonatas op.5. The order of movements in the SONATA DA CAMERA ('chamber sonata') was less standardized, but many examples follow the order of the four main dances of the Baroque suite: allemande, courante, sarabande, gigue. More often the *chiesa* and *camera* types cross or even fuse, as in the earliest published sonatas of Telemann and Vivaldi.

In the late Baroque there is greater standardization both of the cycle and of individual movements, whether in the more conservative, motivic styles like Bach's, which still lead to fugal types of form, or in the more progressive, homophonic ones of composers like Tartini or Leclair, which lead to the newer rondo, the ternary *ABA* form and similar sectional, integrated designs.

As far as instruments are concerned, the main Baroque type was the trio sonata, especially that for two violins and continuo. In addition to those of Corelli, Handel and Bach, the 22 sonatas of Purcell are outstanding among the trio type (though the cello part is sometimes independent of the continuo). After 1700 the 'solo' sonata, for one melody instrument and bass, became more popular; violin, flute, oboe and cello were the most favoured instruments. More exceptional were sonatas for unaccompanied solo instruments, such as Biber's and Bach's for violin, Handel's for harpsichord and Bach's for organ.

A significant starting-point for the Classical period (*c*1735–*c*1820) is the sudden flowering of the solo keyboard sonata with D. Scarlatti, Alberti and C.P.E. Bach. As the clavichord and harpsichord were superseded by the piano, the keyboard sonata continued to rank high in the works of Haydn, Clementi, Mozart and Beethoven. Just as numerous, but of less artistic and historical importance, were the 'accompanied sonatas' for keyboard, usually with violin (sometimes optional). Only towards the end of the period, in the mature violin sonatas of Mozart and Beethoven, and in the latter's cello sonatas, are string and keyboard instruments treated as equals.

There is no consistent trend in the number and order of movements. The three-movement sequence, fast–slow–fast, predominates; a fourth is often present, but its character and placing vary. The so-called 'Italian plan' in two movements, usually both fast or one fast and one moderate, occurs in about half the sonatas of the main Italian composers from Alberti to Boccherini, and the single-movement keyboard sonatas of the three notable pre-Classical composers in Iberia – Seixas, Scarlatti and Soler – are often paired by key in the source MSS.

The first movement of Classical sonatas is most often in SONATA FORM. The slow movement may also approximate to sonata form, though usually with less development and a more simple phrase structure; other common forms include *ABA* or *AB* designs, rondos, variations and free fantasias. Among forms used for inner and final movements are the minuet or scherzo, the rondo or sonata-rondo and variations.

The sonatas of the Romantic period (*c*1790–*c*1915) exemplify the rich variety of national and personal styles that characterize that era. As far as structure and basic approach are concerned, they fall into two categories. To the first belong the sonatas of Schubert, Weber, Chopin, Schumann, Brahms, Grieg, Fauré and Franck, which expand the Classical three- or four-movement form but do not break with it. While rarely achieving the logic or fluent rhythmic organization of the high Classical masterworks, they often sought a more positive organization of the cycle of movements. The 'basic motif' in Brahms's Violin

Sonata op.78 and the 'cyclical procedures' in Franck's Violin Sonata represent conscious methods of tying the movements together. Among sonatas in the smaller second category are those based on a programme, like Liszt's *Après une lecture de Dante, fantasia quasi sonata*, or those which experiment with structure, such as the same composer's single-movement Piano Sonata in B minor.

While traditional sonata structures have served the expressive purposes of many 20th-century composers, including Prokofiev and Shostakovich, the distinctiveness of the genre has during this time all but disappeared. The title no longer necessarily implies a work in several movements, one or more of them in sonata form, for piano alone or with another instrument. The break with tradition is evident both in those sonatas by Bartók, Stravinsky, Poulenc and Hindemith which look back to a much earlier age and in the piano sonatas of Barraqué and Boulez, which have no links of form or genre with any previous sonatas.

Sonata da camera (It.). 'Chamber sonata': an instrumental work of the Baroque period, in three or more stylized dance movements (sometimes with a prefatory movement), scored for one or more melody instruments and continuo. Corelli's opp.2 and 4 contain typical examples. Sometimes such terms as 'trattenimenti' or 'allettamenti da camera' were used. After *c*1700 the genre overlapped increasingly with the sonata da chiesa and the title survived alone to describe the church or the fused type, such titles as partita, suite or *ordre* serving to describe collections of dance movements.

Sonata da chiesa (It.). 'Church sonata': an instrumental work of the Baroque period, usually in four movements, and scored for one or more melody instruments and continuo. Corelli's opp.1 and 3 were largely responsible for establishing the slow–fast–slow–fast order of movements, in which the second is typically a fugal Allegro and the third (in a related key) and fourth are binary forms that may resemble the sarabande and giga. (The third may be no more than a short, modulatory transition.) This type and the dance-based chamber sonata (*sonata da camera*) tended to merge after *c*1700.

Sonata form. The main form of the group embodying the 'sonata principle', the most important principle of musical structure from the Classical period to the 20th century: that material first stated in a complementary key be restated in the home key. Sonata form applies to a single movement, most often part of a multi-movement work such as a sonata, symphony or string quartet; independent movements, e.g. an overture or tone poem, may also be in sonata form. The structure may be considered an expansion of the binary form familiar in Baroque dances, but other genres, including the aria and the concerto, also impinged on its development.

A typical sonata-form movement consists of a two-part tonal structure, articulated in three main sections. The first section ('exposition') divides into a 'first group' in the tonic and, after transitional material, a 'second group' in another key (usually the dominant in major movements, the relative major in minor ones), often with a codetta to round the section off. Both groups may include a number of different themes. In 18th-century music the exposition is almost always directed to be repeated.

The second part of the structure comprises the remaining two sections, the 'development' and 'recapitulation'. The first usually develops material from the exposition in a variety of ways, moving through a number of keys. Compared with the exposition, this section is usually one of considerable tonal instability and of rhythmic and melodic tension. It also prepares the structural climax, the 'double return' to the main theme and to the tonic key which begins the recapitulation. This final section restates the themes of the exposition, usually in the same order; the second group is now heard in the tonic (possibly tonic major if the movement is minor), and there may be temporary excursions to other keys. Before 1780 the second part (development and recapitulation) was usually directed to be repeated. After that date this repetition became increasingly rare; the finale of Beethoven's 'Appassionata' Sonata furnishes a late example.

To the above outline of sonata form may be added a slow introduction and a coda. The primary function of the introduction is to strike a more serious or grander tone and to establish a larger scale of motion than would be possible by the Allegro alone. A coda usually restates the main theme, and most codas include some emphasis on the subdominant, especially if none has occurred in the recapitulation.

The 19th century brought many changes of emphasis: a concentration on contrasting first and second themes rather than on the tonal duality of the exposition; a tendency to avoid exact repetition; and a greatly expanded system of tonal relationships. A sense of strain between structure and content is often manifest, either in an academic approach to the form, as a mould rather than a process, or in the search for new methods of organization, e.g. thematic transformation (Berlioz, *Symphonie fantastique*; Schumann, Symphony no.4), or a freer approach (e.g. Liszt, Sonata in B minor; Schumann, Fantasie op.17; Chopin, Ballade in G minor). Sonata form has nevertheless served for some of the most ambitious and impressive tonal music of the 20th century by composers as different as Strauss and Hindemith, Elgar and Britten, Prokofiev and Shostakovich, and has even shaped movements (e.g. in Schoenberg's String Quartets nos.3 and 4) in which tonal centres as such have ceased to exist.

Sonata-rondo. A form with features of both SONATA FORM and RONDO.

Sonate facile. Name given by its earliest publishers to Mozart's Piano Sonata in C K545; Mozart himself described it as 'für Anfänger' ('for beginners').

Sonatina. A short, easy or otherwise 'light' sonata. The sonatina flourished in the late Classical era (examples include Schubert's D384–5 and 408) and has been revived in the 20th century by Ravel, Busoni and others.

Sondheim, Stephen (Joshua) (*b* New York, 22 March 1930). American composer and lyricist. His early interest in the musical was encouraged by Oscar Hammerstein II, a family friend. He studied compo-

sition with Milton Babbitt. It was as a lyricist that he first attained success, in Bernstein's *West Side Story* (1957) and Styne's *Gypsy* (1959). He went on to write words and music for a succession of Broadway musicals, beginning with *A Funny Thing Happened on the Way to the Forum* (1962), and including *A Little Night Music* (1972), *Pacific Overtures* (1976) and *Sweeney Todd* (1979). He is acknowledged as the finest theatre lyricist of his time and, by many, as the finest composer of musical plays; his work has brought new coherence and depth to the musical.

Sonetti di Petrarca, Tre. Three songs by Liszt for voice and piano (1839) later transcribed for piano and included in Book 2 of *Années de pèlerinage*.

Song. A piece of music, usually short and self contained, for voice or voices, accompanied or unaccompanied, sacred or secular. In some modern usage, the term implies secular music for one voice.

A large repertory of song existed in ancient Greece and Rome, but little survives, largely Greek of the Hellenistic period. Any links between Christian and ancient Greek song are probably tenuous. Ancient Jewish song is represented by psalm texts and there may be links between Jewish and Christian practice in psalm singing. Some medieval chant may have been influenced by popular song, but the evidence of surviving melodies is useless for reconstructing it.

The first notated song melodies since antiquity survive from the 9th century. Gregorian chant does not attempt to 'express' the text (a much later concept) and the style of word-setting, one or several notes to a syllable, was determined largely by liturgical considerations. The most melismatic settings occur in the chants following the reading of lessons, which are in a sense 'meditative'. Some non-liturgical Latin song survives in 10th- and 11th-century MSS, and a larger repertory is associated with the goliards (wandering scholars and clerics) of the 12th century. The contemporary CONDUCTUS repertory consists of strophic songs generally with Latin texts.

Few vernacular secular lyrics survive from before 1100, but from the next centuries there are numerous examples in the rich flowering of monophonic song among the TROUBADOURS and TROUVÈRES in France and in the German MINNESANG (and later MEISTERGESANG) repertory. There is some uncertainty about the rhythmic interpretation of this music and the inclusion of instruments. After 1300 French composers set mainly such forms as the BALLADE, RONDEAU and VIRELAI, which became almost exclusively polyphonic. A comparable polyphonic repertory existed in 14th-century Italy, with the BALLATA, CACCIA and MADRIGAL. Monophonic song became less important in art music after c1450, but the old forms with their imagery of courtly love remained popular in the polyphonic songs of French and Netherlands composers as late as the 16th century, when they disappeared in favour of the CHANSON and the Italian FROTTOLA and MADRIGAL. The principal German type was the three- or four-voice TENORLIED, which flourished c1450–c1550. In England, the strophic CAROL remained popular into the 16th century. The desire of some 16th-century madrigal composers to 'imitate' the text, often by illustrating individual words, was carried further in the Italian MONODY of the early Baroque, in which expressive vocal lines are supported by relatively static basses and simple chords on a lute or other instrument. While songwriting in Italy after *c*1630 was largely diverted into the ARIA, which had its place within more extended forms such as CANTATA and SERENATA and in theatrical and church music, the Italian style influenced the German continuo lied as cultivated by Albert, Krieger and Erlebach, and the English lute AIR of Dowland and declamatory songs of Henry Lawes and Purcell; it had less influence on the French forms, the AIR DE COUR and the later types of AIR, but reasserted itself in the French cantata at the turn of the century.

In the 18th century a new genre of song arose in France, the *romance* (a term that in Italy and Spain had long signified a ballad-type song); here it implied an unaffected, sentimental song, sometimes archaistic in character. But the most important developments were in Germany where, by the end of the century, the influence of folksong and hymnody was felt in a simple type of art song, typically with piano, which reached its apogee with Haydn and Mozart and which led, via lesser composers like Zelter and Zumsteeg, to the rich harvest of the 19th-century German LIED.

A far-reaching division occurred in the early 19th-century song repertory between a large 'popular' category (recreational song for a mass middle-class market, song for edifying the lower and poorer classes, folksong etc) and a smaller 'serious' type which started primarily with Schubert. Some later lied composers, notably Schumann, extended the rhapsodic element; others, such as Mendelssohn and Brahms, were concerned to perfect the musical shape or, like Wolf, to concentrate their attention on declamation and inner meaning.

German influence predominated in the serious art song of Bohemia (Tomášek, Smetana, Dvořák etc), the Netherlands and Scandinavia (Grieg). In France Schubert's songs contributed to the rise of the MÉLODIE, the French counterpart to the lied, brought to perfection by Fauré, Duparc and Debussy. In Russia a national style was cultivated by the Russian Five, especially Musorgsky, and combined with German and French traditions in the songs of Tchaikovsky and Rakhmaninov.

German and French influences, both from the 19th century and from Schoenberg and Satie's followers, have remained central in European 20th-century art song. Traditions were subject to far-reaching experimentation, including the use of SPRECHGESANG for the voice and ad hoc chamber ensembles for the accompaniment; Schoenberg's *Pierrot lunaire* (1912) uses both. At the same time, new song repertories have developed along more traditional lines in several countries, often stimulated by the recovery of folk music or by the presence of outstanding vocal composers. Both these factors have helped to shape the English-language song repertory as represented in Britain by Vaughan Williams, Finzi, Britten and others, and in the USA, where more popular influences have affected the work of such men as Ives, Thomson and Copland.

Song cycle. A group of individually complete songs, unified by a narrative thread or by some common descriptive or expressive theme. As generally understood, the song cycle is a 19th-century form; its development may be traced from Beethoven's *An die ferne Geliebte* (1816) through a line that includes Schubert's *Die schöne Müllerin* and *Winterreise*, Schumann's *Dichterliebe* and *Frauenliebe und -leben*, Mahler's *Lieder eines fahrenden Gesellen*, *Kindertotenlieder* and *Das Lied von der Erde* and Schoenberg's *Pierrot lunaire*. Notable song cycles from outside Germany include those of Fauré, Musorgsky, Dvořák, Debussy, Tippett and Britten.

Song form. English equivalent of the German 'liedform', applied to music, instrumental as well as vocal, in BINARY FORM or (particularly) TERNARY FORM.

Song of Destiny. Choral work by Brahms (op.54, 1871), setting of a poem by Hölderlin.

Song of the Earth, The. [Das Lied von der Erde]. Song cycle (symphony) by Mahler (1909), settings for tenor and alto or baritone soloists and orchestra of six poems (with his own additions) from Hans Bethge's *Die chinesische Flöte*.

Song of the Flea. Song by Musorgsky (1879), a setting for voice and piano of Mephistopheles' song in Goethe's *Faust*.

Song of the High Hills, A. Work by Delius for soprano, tenor, orchestra and (wordless) chorus (1911).

Songs and Dances of Death [Pesni i plyaski smerti]. Song cycle by Musorgsky (1877), settings for voice and piano of four poems by Golenishchev-Gutuzov.

Songs of a Wayfarer. *See* LIEDER EINES FAHRENDEN GESELLEN.

Songs of Travel. Song cycle by Vaughan Williams (1904), settings for voice and piano of nine poems by Robert Louis Stevenson.

Songster. A black American musician of the post-Reconstruction era who performed a wide variety of ballads, dance-tunes, reels and minstrel songs, singing to his own banjo or guitar accompaniment. Songsters were sometimes accompanied by 'musicianers', or non-singing string players.

Songs without Words. *See* LIEDER OHNE WORTE.

Song without words (Ger. *Lied ohne Worte*). A short piano piece of a lyrical nature. The term was invented by Mendelssohn and used for 48 pieces he composed between 1829 and 1845. Tchaikovsky also used the title (op.2 no.3 and op.40 no.6).

Sonnambula, La. Opera in two acts by Bellini to a libretto by Romani (1831, Milan).

Sonneck, Oscar G(eorge) T(heodore) (*b* Lafayette, NJ, 6 Oct 1873; *d* New York, 30 Oct 1928). American musicologist. He studied in Germany and returned to the USA with the aim of studying music there in the manner of German musicologists. He applied this first to American musical life before 1800, later to bibliographical topics. In 1902 he became head of the new music division of the Library of Congress, where he developed an extensive collection. In 1917 he resigned and became director of the publications at G. Schirmer, whose *Musical Quarterly* he had edited since its first issue (1915); subsequently he became vice-president. His books on early American music, his scheme of music classification (1904) and his work on early opera librettos remain outstanding.

Sonnleithner [Sonnleitner]. Austrian family of musicians and writers. The most celebrated members were Joseph (1766–1835), an archivist and librettist who managed the Theater an der Wien and helped found the Gesellschaft der Musikfreunde, and his nephew Leopold von Sonnleithner (1797–1873), a barrister and great friend of Schubert, who was largely responsible for the publication of Schubert's *Erlkönig*.

Sontag [Sonntag], **Henriette** (Gertrud Walpurgis) (*b* Koblenz, 3 Jan 1806; *d* Mexico City, 17 June 1854). German soprano. Despite a long interruption in her career (1830–49), owing to her husband's diplomatic position, she was one of the most consistently successful and popular sopranos of her day, possessing great beauty, a lively and attractive voice and natural charm. She created the title role of Weber's *Euryanthe* (1823) and sang in the premières of Beethoven's Ninth Symphony and *Missa solemnis* (1824), excelling in light and brilliant parts by Rossini, Bellini, Mozart and Donizetti.

Sophie Elisabeth, Duchess of Brunswick-Lüneburg (*b* Güstrow, 20 Aug 1613; *d* Lüchow, 12 July 1676). German composer. She was the wife of Duke August the Younger of Brunswick-Wolfenbüttel and a leading musical figure at his court (at Brunswick and from 1644 at Wolfenbüttel). Her composition teacher and music adviser was Schütz, who became senior Kapellmeister in 1655. She composed many sacred songs and several secular and theatrical works.

Sopra (It.). 'Above': a word used in piano music to indicate in passages for crossed hands which hand should be above the other. *See also* COME SOPRA.

Sopranino (It.). Diminutive of soprano; term applied to the highest pitched instrument in certain families, including the clarinet, the recorder and the saxophone.

Soprano (It.). The highest female voice, normally of the range *c'–a''*. The term is also used for a boy treble voice (or for a castrato of the same range). Until the early 16th century, the female voice was little used in art music as it was not considered proper for ladies to sing or for gentlemen to make music in ladies' presence. The soprano voice, accordingly, did not come into prominence until the mid-16th century (e.g. in Cipriano de Rore's madrigals of the 1540s). Later in the century, at Ferrara, female singing was particularly developed and this helped provoke the composition of many madrigals exploiting the beauty of high voices. In Catholic church music, however, the prohibition on women's voices meant that high parts were sung by castratos or falsettists.

Women sopranos found an important place in opera, as early as Monteverdi's *Arianna* (1608). They were well suited to the *bel canto* melodies of late 17th-century Italian opera and to the florid music of the late Baroque period; and most of the solo parts in the numerous Italian chamber cantatas of the middle and late Baroque period were written for soprano voice. In the early 18th century, agility, beauty of tone and the ability to ornament an aria were the chief qualities demanded of a soprano, but later composers

came to appreciate differences among soprano voices that had also to do with timbre and characterization, as Mozart's soprano roles demonstrate.

This trend developed further in the 19th century as seen in the differences between the soprano roles of such composers as Rossini, Bellini, Beethoven and Weber. The roles of Bellini and Donizetti formed the basis for the careers of many famous sopranos, such as Pasta and Grisi, but non-Italians too, such as Schröder-Devrient and Sontag. Voices needed to be more powerful for the larger opera houses and concert halls of this period, and still more so for the great Wagner roles, to be sung with great dramatic force often against a large orchestra. The first Brünnhilde was Amalie Materna (1845–1918); more recent Wagner sopranos have included Kirsten Flagstad and Birgit Nilsson. Verdi too came increasingly to demand a powerful, dramatic soprano, for such works as *Aida* and *Otello* (Desdemona), as opposed to the lighter, more lyrical soprano capable of florid singing which had served for *La traviata* (Violetta) or *Rigoletto* (Gilda).

Some modern sopranos, notably Maria Callas, have shown themselves to be equally at home in all Italian music from Bellini to Verdi and Puccini; others, such as Joan Sutherland, sing primarily the earlier 19th-century repertory and go back to the florid music of the 18th. Recent developments in soprano singing include the coming of the avant-garde specialist, with perfect pitch and extraordinary agility, and the growth of the period specialist who uses lighter tone and a fluent command of florid writing, and little or no vibrato, to sing music of the 17th and 18th centuries in authentic style.

'Soprano' is often used to qualify other terms. The soprano clef is one with the sign for middle C on the lowest line of the staff. For some instruments, such as the clarinet, 'soprano' signifies the standard member of a family. In the recorder family, the basic member is the alto and the soprano (in American usage; British is descant) refers to the next highest instrument. The soprano cornet is pitched in Eb, a 4th above the standard instrument. The soprano saxophone is normally pitched in Bb, sounding a major 2nd below written pitch. *See also* SOPRANINO.

Sor, (Joseph) Fernando (Macari) (*b* Barcelona, bap. 14 Feb 1778; *d* Paris, 10 July 1839). Spanish composer and guitarist. After leaving Spain he lived in Paris (1813–15 and from 1826) and London (1815–26) and visited Russia (1823). He was a famous concert performer and wrote over 60 guitar works (sonatas, studies, variations etc) and an important method (1830). His guitar music is notable for its part-writing. He was also admired for his songs and eight ballets (1821–8); other works include an opera (1797) and chamber and keyboard pieces.

Sorabji, Kaikhosru Shapurji [Leon Dudley] (*b* Chingford, 14 Aug 1892). English composer of Spanish-Sicilian-Parsi parentage. Largely self-taught, he became known in the 1920s for luxuriant and polyphonic piano works in a style relatable to Szymanowski and Busoni, and sometimes of enormous duration: the *Opus clavicembalisticum* (1930) plays for nearly three hours. But soon after writing it he withdrew from public activity and placed an embargo on his music, though he continued to compose immense piano and symphonic works, many incorporating Eastern influences. Only in 1976 did he allow performances to recommence. He was a biting critic of flashing wit, who often praised composers who only later became fashionable; his two books contain many of those essays.

Sorcerer, The. Operetta by Sullivan to a libretto by Gilbert (1877, London).

Sorcerer's Apprentice, The [L'apprenti sorcier]. Symphonic scherzo by Dukas (1897) after a poem by Goethe.

Sordino (It.). Mute; the instruction 'con sordino', often found in string music, means 'with mute'.

Sordun. A double-reed instrument of the late 16th century and early 17th. It had a cylindrical bore that doubled back on itself, and was made in several sizes, including Gross Bass (lowest note *F*), Bass (*B*♭ or *c*), Tenor/Alto (*e*♭) and Cantus (*b*♭). There were 12 finger-holes and sometimes two controlled by keys. The instrument was said to sound like the crumhorn.

Sorge, Georg Andreas (*b* Mellenbach, 21 March 1703; *d* Lobenstein, 4 April 1778). German composer. He was court and civic organist at Lobenstein from 19 and became famous as a writer and keyboard composer. An authority on organ building, he wrote chiefly on tuning and temperament; he also published major treatises on composition (1745–7) and improvisation (1767), which have a forward-looking emphasis on harmony.

Soriano, Francesco (*b* Soriano, 1548–9; *d* Rome, 1621). Italian composer. A pupil of Zoilo and possibly Palestrina, he was *maestro di cappella* of S Luigi dei Francesi, Rome (*c*1580), the Mantuan court (1581–6), then at the three leading Rome churches – S Maria Maggiore (1587–99, 1601–3), St John Lateran (1599–1601) and the Cappella Giulia (1603–20). A distinguished, versatile and progressive composer, and a master of the polychoral style, he published motets (1597, 1616), masses (1609), a Passion (1619) and madrigals (4 bks, 1581–1602). In 1612 he completed Palestrina's revision of the chant books.

Sorochintsy Fair [Sorochinskaya yarmarka]. Opera in three acts by Musorgsky to his own libretto after Gogol, written 1874–80; it was completed and orchestrated by Lyadov, V.G. Karatigin and others (1913, Moscow). Other completions were made by Cui, Tcherepnin and Shebalin.

Sosarme. Opera in three acts by Handel to a libretto after Salvi (1732, London).

Sospetto, Il. Vivaldi's Violin Concerto in C minor RV199.

Sostenente piano. Term used for several attempts, none of them established, to make a strung keyboard instrument capable of producing a sustained sound. Various methods were used: endless bows, often in the form of a rosined wheel, which have been explored from the 16th century to the present day (C.P.E. Bach composed a sonata for a *Bogenclavier* of 1754); compressed air, producing essentially an aeolian harp controlled from a keyboard; transmitted vibrations, using a rod to sound the strings as opposed

to direct friction (as in the harmonichord, for which Weber composed an Adagio and Rondo with orchestra, J115); rapid repetition of the hammers (as in the *piano trémolophone* of Philippe de Girard, 1842, with two keyboards, one exclusively for tremolando notes); a hammer striking the string which then set free vibrating reeds in motion (e.g. the *piano scandé* of 1853, which also had pedals to swell the tone); and the use of electricity, which provided the means for making the first wholly successful sostenente pianos, notably, in the 1960s, the so-called 'electric piano' where the sound can be sustained at will.

Sostenuto (It.). Sustained.

Sotin, Hans (*b* Dortmund, 10 Sept 1939). German bass. He studied in Dortmund and in 1964 joined the Hamburg Opera, where he soon took the main bass roles, including Wotan. Singing Sarastro, he made his Glyndebourne début in 1970 and his Met début in 1972; he has appeared at Bayreuth as Wotan, the Vienna Staatsoper (début King Mark, 1973), Covent Garden (Hunding, 1974) and La Scala (Ochs, 1976). He is also a notable recitalist and brings weight and gravity to the oratorio repertory.

Soto de Langa, Francisco (*b* Langa, 1534; *d* Rome, 25 Sept 1619). Spanish composer and editor. He sang in the papal chapel in Rome (1562–1611, *maestro di cappella* from 1590), at the S Filippo Neri oratory (1566–75), where he became famous for his singing of *laude spirituali*, and at S Giacomo degli Spagnoli (1611–19). He edited several important volumes of *laude* (1583–98), which include some composed by him; other *laude* of his are in anthologies (1599, 1600).

Sotto (It.). 'Below', e.g. *sotto voce*, an indication that a passage is to be played in an undertone, i.e. without emphasis.

Soubrette (Fr.). 'Servant girl': a stock character of 18th-century French theatre, the clever servant girl who comments on the behaviour of the ladies and gentlemen of the household and may become involved in their intrigues. In opera, the term normally applies to secondary characters, such as Despina (*Così fan tutte*) and Adele (*Die Fledermaus*), but can extend to such a role as Susanna, a central figure in *Le nozze di Figaro*. A voice so described is usually mezzo-soprano or soprano, light and fluent in delivery.

Soul music. A style of popular music composed, performed and recorded chiefly by black Americans from the early 1960s. It should convey the performer's strongly felt emotions and perceptions and evoke similar ones in the listener. It thus involves impassioned, dramatic and animated modes of vocal expression, with such devices as sighs, sobs, falsetto, melismas, spoken or chanted interpolations, shouting delivery or rasping tone.

Soundboard. The thin sheet of wood coupled to the strings of a piano, harpsichord, clavichord or the like that serves to make the sound of the strings more audible and helps to form the instrument's characteristic sound.

Soundbox. The hollow body of a string instrument, which serves as a RESONATOR.

Soundhole. An opening, such as the f-holes in a violin or the circular holes of guitars and zithers, designed to increase the volume and enhance the instrument's tone quality.

Soundpost. A small wooden pillar fixed inside a string instrument, particularly one of the viol or violin families, vertically connecting its back and its belly and thus not only easing the pressure on the bridge but also distributing the vibrations of the strings over the instrument's body.

Sound recording. The recording of sound is accomplished by representing, in some form susceptible of reproduction, the minute rapid fluctuations in air pressure that constitute sound. The first step was taken in 1857 by a Frenchman, Léon Scott, who found a means of representing soundwaves on a surface; but it was Thomas Edison, in 1877, who first made a recording (of 'Mary had a little lamb') that could be replayed, on his 'phonograph', essentially a grooved cylinder covered with tinfoil and rotated by a crank, connected by a sharp metal point to a speaking tube so that the point indented the foil in response to the vibrations. Its course could later be retraced by the metal point in order that they be reproduced. Flat discs were launched by Emil Berliner in 1896; this had the advantage of readier manufacture in quantity by production from a 'master' and ousted the cylinder by the 1920s. Recordings were acoustical (i.e. mechanical) in basis until the mid-1920s, when electrical recording was developed. A wider range of frequencies and dynamics could be impressed on the record, using electrical cutter heads. Discs were made of shellac, normally black; the standard 12-inch (30 cm) disc normally took 4 to $4\frac{1}{2}$ minutes of music on each side, the ten-inch (25 cm) 3 to $3\frac{1}{2}$; most record companies adopted a standard speed of 78 rpm. The information cut on to each disc was in lateral rather than the original 'hill-and-dale' form, so that the needle followed a horizontal pattern rather than riding vertically.

In the late 1940s, the brittle, easily scratched and noisy shellac disc was replaced by softer, more flexible vinylite, capable of much finer grooves. These, revolving at $33\frac{1}{3}$ rpm (45 rpm for the small 7-inch, 18 cm, 'single' generally used for popular music or short pieces), could take up to 20 or 25 minutes of music per 12-inch side (more recently, well over 30 minutes without loss of quality). Stereophonic records were introduced in 1957, involving the engraving on the disc of two sets of information in different planes and transmitting them to two distinct amplifying and reproduction systems; this gives an effect of spatial reproduction instead of compressing the original sound into a single source. A four-channel ('quadraphonic') system was also evolved but proved not to be susceptible of commercial development. The rise of the LP (long-playing) record was much assisted by the development of magnetic tape for recording, which meant that, with careful editing, long stretches of music could be assembled from several 'takes' to produce 'perfect' performances. In 1979 this sytem was further improved by the application of digital (instead of the existing analogue) systems to recording and editing; its basis is the use of computerized systems for the instant storage of the wave-form and its reconversion into sound. Digital systems were applied to the playback process when, in 1983, the CD (compact disc) was made available: here a metal disc, 4.7 inches in diameter, and capable of storing more than an hour's music, is inscribed with a microscopic pattern of dots in spiral form, in a binary code, which is read by a laser beam of infra-red light that converts the musical information into sound. This not only permits much longer stretches of music to be heard at a single, continuous sitting (well over an hour), but also allows the listener to select any track or movement instantaneously and provides a much clearer and more faithful sound reproduction with no accompanying noise.

Sound sculpture. A sculpture or construction that creates sound, not always of a musical nature, by means of its own internal mechanism, or when it is activated by environmental elements such as wind, water or sunlight, or when it is manipulated. There was a flourish of activity in sound sculpture in the early 20th century when the futurists constructed noise instruments. Environmental sound performances harnessing industrial noise began after World War I, and from the 1930s musicians like Harry Partch, I.A. Mackenzie and the Baschet brothers began experimenting with new instruments and sound-producing constructions. Mechanical systems, electric motors, electronic circuitry and vibratory mechanisms were used, along with the elements, to activate sound sculptures. John Cage and Earle Brown are among the composers who have used sculptures as percussion instruments, and since 1960 outdoor sculptures that produce musical sounds have been designed by many Western musicians and artists.

Soundtable. *See* BELLY.

Souris, André (*b* Marchienne-au-Pont, 10 July 1890; *d* Paris, 12 Feb 1970). Belgian composer. He studied at the Brussels Conservatory (1911–18) and with Gilson and worked in Belgium as a teacher and conductor. Before 1923 he wrote Debussian songs, but then turned in the direction of Les Six, until in 1928 he began to work with found materials and styles. After World War II he wrote comparatively little but became a notable cinema composer; he published many editions of 17th- and 18th-century music. One of the leaders of Belgian musical life, he wrote numerous articles.

Sousa, John Philip (*b* Washington, DC, 6 Nov 1854; *d* Reading, PA, 6 March 1932). American composer, conductor and writer, known as the 'March King'. He was an apprentice in the US Marine Band, then played the violin in theatre orchestras before turning to conducting. In 1892 he formed the popular Sousa's Band (which continued until 1931). Sousa had great impact on American musical tastes and achieved worldwide fame; the sousaphone, made to his specifications, was named after him. He was best known as a composer of marches, including *The Washington Post* (1889) and *The Stars and Stripes Forever* (1897), which have a vigorous melodic line. Sousa wrote much vocal music: his operettas, e.g. *El* *capitan* (1895), had considerable success. He was also famous for his band arrangements.

Sousaphone. A form of bass tuba designed by J.P. Sousa for use in his marching bands. It is helical in shape and encircles the player, resting on the left shoulder and passing under the right arm with the large flaring bell pointing forward above the player's head. Sousaphones have three or four valves and are made in E♭ and B♭. They were first made in 1898; in the earliest models, the bell pointed upwards.

Souster, Tim(othy Andrew James) (*b* Bletchley, 29 Jan 1943). English composer. He studied at Oxford but was most stimulated by Stockhausen's courses at Darmstadt in 1964; he was assistant to Stockhausen in Cologne (1971–3). He was associated with Smalley in the live electronic ensemble Intermodulation and later his own group OdB and has written mostly for instrumental–electronic combinations; many of his works and writings reflect his interest in rock music.

Souterliedekens (Dutch). 'Little psalter songs': the term was used by the Antwerp printer Symon Cock for his edition of rhymed Dutch psalms published in 1540 (which went into over 30 editions). Most of the melodies are Dutch folksongs.

South American music. *See* LATIN AMERICAN MUSIC.

South Bank Centre. Arts complex in London on the south bank of the Thames, on the site of the Festival of Britain (1951). It includes the Royal Festival Hall (1951, cap. 2895), used mainly for concerts by leading British and other international orchestras; Queen Elizabeth Hall (opened 1967, cap. 1094), used for chamber orchestras and choirs, recitals and films; and the Purcell Room (opened 1967, cap. 368).

Southern Cathedrals Festival (UK). Annual (summer) festival established in 1904. It takes place in turn in Chichester, Salisbury and Winchester, with the cathedral choirs as chief participants.

Souzay, Gérard (Marcel) (*b* Angers, 8 Dec 1920). French baritone. He studied at the Paris Conservatoire and with Bernac, giving his first recital in 1945. His New York début in 1950 was followed by several world tours; he performed with velvety tone and sensitive articulation in the French song repertory and also won praise for his mastery of the German lied. His opera début was as Monteverdi's Orpheus at the New York City Center (1960) and in 1965 he sang Mozart's Count at the Met.

Sowerby, Leo (*b* Grand Rapids, MI, 1 May 1895; *d* Port Clinton, OH, 7 July 1968). American composer and church musician. Trained in Chicago and Italy, he taught at the American Conservatory in Chicago (1925–62) and was organist and choirmaster at St James's Cathedral (1927–62). His output includes five symphonies and two organ concertos as well as much music for the Anglican liturgy. His *Canticle of the Sun* (1944) won a Pulitzer Prize.

Sowiński, Wojciech [Albert] (*b* Łukaszówka, 1805 [?1803]; *d* Paris, 5 [?2] March 1880). Polish writer on music, composer and pianist. He studied the piano with Czerny in Vienna. His most important work was a dictionary of *c*1000 early and modern Polish

musicians, first issued in Paris in French (1857).

Spagna. A 15th-century Italian *bassadanza* tune, widely used as a *cantus firmus* in the 16th century and early 17th. Some 280 polyphonic settings are known.

Spagnoletta. A late 16th-century Italian dance whose harmonic scheme was used in the 17th century, mostly in triple metre, for dances, songs and instrumental variations. There are two versions by Farnaby in the Fitzwilliam Virginal Book.

Spangenberg, Johann (*b* Hardegsen, 29 March 1484; *d* Eisleben, 13 June 1550). German composer and theorist. He studied in Erfurt and established a new Lateinschule in Nordhausen. A devoted follower of Luther, he wrote a student music textbook (1533) and an important liturgical songbook (1545). His son, Cyriac (1528–1604), continued his work, publishing a hymnbook (1568).

Spangler, Johann Georg (Joseph) (*b* Vienna, 22 March 1752; *d* there, 2 Nov 1802). Austrian tenor and composer. He sang at three Viennese churches and was choirmaster at St Michael's from 1794, succeeding his father, the tenor Johann Michael Spangler (*c*1721–1794). He was a leading Viennese church composer in the high Classical style; some of his sacred works were widely popular. His sister Maria Magdalena (1750–94), a soprano, sang in Haydn's operas at Eszterháza, 1768–76; his brother Ignaz (1757–1811) was a tenor and composer in Vienna.

Spanisches Liederbuch. Collection of songs by Wolf, settings for voice and piano of 44 Spanish poems translated by Paul von Heyse and Emanuel Geibel (1852).

Spanish Caprice [Capriccio espagnole]. Orchestral work, op.34, by Rimsky-Korsakov (1887).

Spartacus [Spartak]. Ballet in four acts by Khachaturian to a scenario by Volkov (1956, Leningrad).

Spasm band. An ensemble similar to a washboard band, formed by black Americans around New Orleans in the early 20th century. It was a model for jug bands and skiffle bands in the folksong revival of the 1950s and 1960s.

Spataro, Giovanni (*b* Bologna, ?1458; *d* there, 17 Jan 1541). Italian theorist and composer. He entered the choir of S Petronio, Bologna (1505), and later (1512) became *maestro di canto*. He studied theory with Ramos de Pareia and in his writings distinguished the *stile antico* and *stile nuovo*, praising Josquin; he took part in a polemical war with the more traditional Gaffurius, advocating tempered intervals rather than Pythagorean tuning. Only six motets and one *lauda* by him are extant, though he is known to have composed much more.

Spatzenmesse (Ger.: 'Sparrow Mass'). Mozart's Mass in C K220/196*b* (1776).

Spaur. Mozart's Mass in C K258.

Spechtshart, Hugo (*b* Reutlingen, *c*1285; *d* 1359–60). German theorist, teacher and priest, based in his home town throughout his life. His pedagogical *Flores musicae modis cantus Gregoriani* of 1332 enjoyed lasting influence; revised in 1342 and published in 1488, it treats solmization, modes, intervals and the monochord; he also wrote a work dealing with flagellant songs.

Species counterpart. An approach to strict counterpoint, i.e. the addition of contrapuntal voices to a given melodic line (*cantus firmus*), that proceeds methodically from simple to complex combinations of voices. The system was formulated by Fux in 1725. The five types ('species') are: note against note; two or three notes against each note in the *cantus firmus*; four notes against each note in the *cantus firmus*; note against note, but syncopated; a florid line against the *cantus firmus* (a combination of the other species with occasional notes of smaller value).

Specification. Term used by organ theorists to denote a list of the speaking stops, accessories and compass of an organ. To an organ builder, it would imply a complete technical description.

Spectre's Bride, The [Svatební košile]. Dramatic cantata by Dvořák to a text by Erben (1885, Plzeň). Novák set the same text as his op.48 (1913).

Speer, Daniel (*b* Breslau, 2 July 1636; *d* Göppingen, 5 Oct 1707). German composer and theorist. He worked in Stuttgart, Tübingen and elsewhere before becoming a teacher at the Lateinschule, Göppingen, in 1673. After a period of imprisonment (for his political views) he returned there in 1694 and later became Kantor. His wide musical experience is reflected in his textbook *Grund-richtiger Unterricht der musicalischen Kunst* (1687, rev. 1697), which gives valuable information on contemporary musical conditions and practices and contains many instrumental pieces. As a composer he led a trend towards simpler sacred works, and his book of chorales arranged for two voices and continuo (1692) was the first of its kind. His output also includes quodlibets and various writings.

Spem in alium numquam habui. 40-part motet by Tallis for eight five-voice choirs.

Spendiaryan, Alexander Afanasii (*b* Kakhovka, 1 Nov 1871; *d* Erevan, 7 May 1928). Armenian composer. A pupil of Rimsky-Korsakov in St Petersburg (1896–1900), he worked as a conductor, and wrote an opera (*Almast*, 1928), orchestral pieces etc which, in their synthesis of folk music and the Russian tradition, laid the foundations of an Armenian nationalist style.

Sperger, Johannes (?Matthias) (*b* Valtice, 23 March 1750; *d* Ludwigslust, 13 May 1812). German double bass player and composer. He studied under Albrechtsberger in Vienna, then served at Bratislava (1779–83) and at the Erdődy court at Fidisch (1783–6). Finally he entered the Ludwigslust court Kapelle, in 1789; he also made concert tours. A prolific composer as well as a leading performer, he wrote 18 double bass concertos, numerous other instrumental works and various vocal pieces.

Sperontes [Scholze, Johann Sigismund] (*b* Lobendau, nr. Liegnitz, 20 March 1705; *d* Leipzig, 28 Sept 1750). German poet and musical anthologist. He wrote plays and Singspiel texts for Leipzig in the 1740s. His main work was *Singende Muse an der Pleisse* (1736–45), a collection of strophic German songs with unpretentious texts on everyday topics and simple *galant* music (mostly borrowed). It was extremely popular and began a new era of German songwriting, culminating in the 19th-century lied.

Spervogel (Ger.: 'sparrow'). Name applied to three German poets of the 12th–13th centuries who wrote *Sprüche*. Älterer Spervogel (*fl c* 1150–80) was an itinerant poet of the central Rhineland; his 28 poems show him as a pioneer of the courtly Minnesang. Spervogel (*fl c* 1200) is named as writer of 23 formally identical *Spruch* stanzas, one of them with a melody, similar to those of the Ältere Spervogel without his religious viewpoint. Der junge Spervogel (*fl* 13th century) is thought to have written a small number of *Sprüche*.

Speuy, Henderick (Joostzoon) (*b* Brielle, *c* 1575; *d* Dordrecht, 1 Oct 1625). Netherlands composer and organist. A much respected organist, he served at the Grote Kerk and Augustijnen Kerk, Dordrecht, from 1595. His *De psalmen Davids* (1610), a book of bicinia, was the earliest printed Netherlands keyboard music.

Spianato (It.). Smoothed out, level, even.

Spiccato (It.). In modern string playing, a term sometimes synonymous with the bouncing stroke SAUTILLÉ, but also used for a controlled thrown-and-lifted stroke; before 1750 'spiccato' and 'staccato' were often used as equivalents, both meaning 'detached' or 'separated' as opposed to legato.

Spiegelman, Joel (Warren) (*b* Buffalo, 23 Jan 1933). American composer. Trained at Yale, Buffalo and Brandeis, and in Paris with Boulanger (1956–7), he has taught at various institutions. His music of the 1950s and early 1960s was in a Stravinskyan neo-classical style, but later works have used electronics and other techniques. He toured widely as a harpsichordist, latterly as a pianist, and has conducted.

Spieloper. A type of German 19th-century comic opera with spoken dialogue. Examples include Lortzing's *Zar und Zimmermann* and Flotow's *Martha*. The term has also been used, in exactly an opposite sense, for an all-sung opera as opposed to one (a *Sprechoper*) with spoken dialogue.

Spies, Claudio (*b* Santiago, 26 March 1925). American composer of Chilean origin. A pupil of Boulanger and of Fine and Piston at Harvard, he has taught at Swarthmore (1958–70) and Princeton (from 1970). He has written notably on Schoenberg and serial Stravinsky. His works are mostly for small forces.

Spies, Leo (*b* Moscow, 4 June 1899; *d* Ahrenshoop an der Ostsee, 1 May 1965). German composer. He was educated in Moscow, where he encountered the music of Skryabin and Prokofiev, and in Dresden and Berlin. He worked in Germany as a theatre conductor and teacher and wrote in most concert genres, influenced by the Russian Romantics and by Janáček. In the 1920s he joined the circle round Eisler and worked with the workers' choral movement; latterly he has written for young people.

Spiess, Meinrad (*b* Honsolgen, 24 Aug 1683; *d* Irsee, 12 June 1761). German composer and theorist. A priest at the Benedictine Abbey of Irsee, he became music director in 1712. His works include several sacred collections, instrumental pieces, and an influential treatise on writing church music (1745).

Spike fiddle. A type of string instrument in which the neck passes through the sound chest to protrude as a spike at the lower end; the strings are attached to it.

The instrument is known in many parts of the Middle East and Central and South-east Asia.

Spinet. A small domestic keyboard instrument of the harpsichord family. It is usually defined as having strings running diagonally from left to right as opposed to directly away from the player (as in a normal harpsichord) or transversely (as in a virginal). There is normally one keyboard and a single set of strings and jacks; variation in tone colour is rare. Apart from a few small, German rectangular instruments from the late 16th century, the earliest surviving spinets are early 17th-century Italian. They are often made in uneven five- or six-sided shapes with the keyboard on the longest side. The wing-shaped 'bentside' or 'wing of mutton' spinet, also an Italian invention, achieved its greatest popularity in England, where it replaced the rectangular virginal to become the normal domestic keyboard instrument in the late 17th century. (For illustration, see KEYBOARD INSTRUMENTS.)

Spinner, Leopold (*b* Lwów, 26 April 1906; *d* London, 12 Aug 1980). Austrian composer. He was a pupil in Vienna of Pisk (1926–30) and Webern (1935–8), to whose music his own is affiliated: his small output of orchestral, chamber and vocal music shows a refined gift and fastidious construction. From 1938 he lived in England.

Spinto (It.). Term for a lyric voice, usually soprano or tenor, that can sound powerful and incisive at dramatic climaxes; the full expression is 'lirico spinto'. The term is also used for roles that require such voices.

Spiritoso (It.). Spirited, lively; also *con spirito*, 'with vivacity'.

Spiritual. A type of folksong that originated in American revivalist activity between 1740 and the end of the 19th century. The term is derived from 'spiritual songs', a designation used in early publications to distinguish the texts from the metrical psalms and hymns in traditional church use.

Black spirituals constitute one of the largest surviving bodies of American folksong and are probably the best known. They are principally associated with the Afro-American churches of the Deep South. Mid-19th-century reports indicate that the tunes were sung in unison and abounded in 'slides from one note to another, and turns and cadences not in articulated notes'. There is disagreement as to whether there are significant African elements in the songs and whether they were the innovation of black slaves or adaptations of white sources. Black spirituals were first brought to an international audience from 1871 by the Jubilee Singers of Fisk University, Nashville, Tennessee; interest was awakened in the form as a concert item. However, as they grew in popularity with a general audience, their appeal waned in black churches and they lost ground to GOSPEL music.

The white spiritual is a less well-known, but important category. It embraces the subtypes of religious ballad, folk hymn (associated with the 18th-century Separatist Baptist movement) and camp-meeting spiritual (associated with 19th-century revivalism): all have close associations with secular folksong.

Spisak, Michał (*b* Dąbrowa Górnicza, 14 Sept 1914; *d* Paris, 29 Jan 1965). Polish composer. He was a pupil of Sikorski in Warsaw (1935–7), then of Boulanger in Paris, where he remained. He was among the most outstanding Polish composers of his generation. Deeply influenced by Stravinsky's neoclassicism, he wrote mostly instrumental music, with an assured technique and an extraordinary feeling for orchestral colour.

Spitta, Julius August Philipp (*b* Wechold, 7 Dec 1841; *d* Berlin, 13 April 1894). German music historian. A lifelong friend of Brahms and a leading figure in later 19th-century musical scholarship, he is remembered particularly for his epoch-making study of Bach (1873–80), emphasizing historical context. He was a co-founder of the *Vierteljahrsschrift für Musikwissenschaft* (1885) and from 1875 professor at Berlin University.

Spivakowsky, Tossy (*b* Odessa, 4 Feb 1907). American violinist. He studied in Berlin where he made his début in 1917 and toured, 1920–33, before going first to Australia and (in 1940) to the USA, where he has pursued an active career. He gave the American première of Bartók's Violin Concerto no.2 (1943) and has a wide repertory including much contemporary music. He taught at the Juilliard School from 1974. His new bowing techniques have aroused controversy.

Spofforth, Reginald (*b* Southwell, 1768–70; *d* Kensington, 8 Sept 1827). English composer. From the 1790s he was a teacher and organist in London, and for a time chorus master at Covent Garden Theatre. He was a leading composer of glees (notably *Hail, smiling morn*, 1810) and also wrote songs and duets.

Spohr, Louis [Ludwig] (*b* Brunswick, 5 April 1784; *d* Kassel, 22 Oct 1859). German composer, violinist and conductor. He gained his first important experience as a chamber musician at the Brunswick court, soon becoming a virtuoso violinist and touring throughout Germany; his playing was influenced particularly by his admiration for Rode. As Konzertmeister in Gotha (1805–12) he took up conducting (with a baton) and had some of his own works performed but was most successful as a touring artist (1807–21) with his wife, the harpist Dorette Scheidler. Operatic conducting posts at Vienna (1813–15) and Frankfurt (1817–19) coincided with significant bursts of composing activity, yielding chamber music and the successful operas *Faust* (1813) and *Zemire und Azor* (1819). He settled down as Kapellmeister at Kassel in 1822, where the premières of *Jessonda* (1823; his greatest operatic success), the oratorio *Die letzten Dinge* (1826) and the Symphony no.4 (1832) were major achievements; here too he contributed to the cultivation of interest in both Bach and Wagner. A favourite in England, he received international honours and became Generalmusikdirektor at Kassel (1847), but by the 1850s he was an aging, middle-class representative of a rather sober tradition, and after his death his works were largely forgotten.

Spohr's early Romantic origins and his devotion to Mozart largely determined his style, with its careful craftsmanship and adherence to classical forms but also its freely expressive elements (much chromaticism and a fondness for the elegiac). Among his instrumental works (15 violin and ten other concertos, ten symphonies, virtuoso solo works, scores of chamber works, including a series of double quartets), the four clarinet concertos, the string quartets, the Violin Concerto no.8 ('In the form of a vocal scene') and the Octet and Nonet for wind and strings are noteworthy. His operas anticipate Wagner in being through-composed and in their use of leitmotif.

Dramatic music Faust (1813); Zemire und Azor (1819); Jessonda (1823); 7 others; incidental music for 3 plays
Orchestral music 10 syms. (incl. no.6, 'Historical', no.9, 'Seasons'; 1 inc.); 3 ovs.; 15 vn concs.; 4 cl concs.; double concs.; Qt conc. (1845); Other virtuoso solo works
Chamber music Nonet, F, fl, ob, cl, bn, hn, vn, va, vc, db (1813); Octet, E, cl, 2hn, vn, 2va, vc, db (1814); 4 double str qts; Septet, fl, cl, hn, bn, vn, vc, pf (1853); Str Sextet, C (1848); 7 str qnts; Pf qnt, D (1845); 36 str qts; virtuoso vn pieces with str trio; str duos; works with pf; 6 sonatas, vn, harp; solo works, incl. Violin-Schule (1831)
Vocal music 4 oratorios incl. Die letzten Dinge (1826); other sacred works; secular choruses, partsongs; over 90 songs

Spoleto Festival [Festival of Two Worlds] (Italy). Annual (summer) event, founded (1958) by Menotti to promote young artists in opera, plays and concerts. An American branch, an annual (spring) festival, was established in Charleston, SC, in 1977. Events (up to 140) include opera, concerts, jazz, country music and dance.

Sponsus, Play of. A play of the late 11th century on the theme of the wise and foolish virgins (*Matthew* xxv. 1–13), from St Martial, remarkable for its early use of vernacular words and non-liturgical melodies, four of which suffice for the whole play.

Spontini, Gaspare (Luigi Pacifico) (*b* Maiolati, 14 Nov 1774; *d* there, 24 Jan 1851). Italian composer and conductor. During his early career (1796–1802) he produced operas for Rome, Venice, Florence, Naples and Palermo with little success. Only in Paris (from 1803) and under the patronage of Joséphine did he gain public attention, notably with the triumphant première of his Gluckian *tragédie lyrique La vestale* (1807). *Fernand Cortez*, a spectacular historical pageant meant to glorify Napoleon, failed in its first version (1809) but won a place in the repertory when revised (1817). For two years (1810–12) he was an effective director of the Théâtre-Italien, though problems created by his proud and truculent personality led to his dismissal. His last *tragédie lyrique* for the Opéra, *Olimpie* (1819), was a colossal failure. In Berlin (1820–42) as Generalmusikdirektor, he was supported only by the king and came into conflict with Weber, while his complex and grandiose works were outpaced by the newer styles of Rossini and his arch rival Meyerbeer. His most important German opera was the last, *Agnes von Hohenstaufen* (1837), moving away from solo numbers to massive ensembles and a more continuous construction. His style in general however was a synthesis of newer French and Italian elements implanted into the traditional French framework, with triumphal processions, temple rituals and oath-swearings; a large part is played in his operas by calculated musical *coups de théâtre*.

Dramatic music La vestale (1807); Fernand Cortez (1809, rev. 1817); Olimpie (1819), rev. as Olympia (1821); Nurmahal (1822); Agnes von Hohenstaufen (1837); c10 others; 2 stage works; contributions to other composers' works
Vocal music occasional choral works; sacred pieces; songs, duets
Instrumental music orch pieces; marches for military band; pf music

Spontone, Bartolomeo (*b* Bologna, bap. 22 Aug 1530; *d* Treviso, ?1592). Italian composer. He was *maestro di cappella* at S Petronio, Bologna (1577–83), S Maria Maggiore, Bergamo (1584–6), and Verona (1586–8) and Treviso cathedrals (1591–2). He was an accomplished composer of madrigals (4 bks, 1558–83) and masses (1588). His brother Alessandro (1549–c1590) composed madrigals. Ludovico (1555–c1608), also Bolognese, a composer of madrigals and motets, may have been a member of the same family.

Sporck, Count **Franz Anton** (*b* Lysá nad Labem, 9 March 1662; *d* there, 30 March 1738). Bohemian nobleman and patron. He maintained an orchestra and from 1724 a Venetian opera troupe. By introducing the French hunting-horn (*cor de chasse*) in the 1680s he played a major role in establishing the Austro-Bohemian horn tradition.

Sprechgesang, Sprechstimme (Ger.). 'Speech-song', 'speech-voice': term for a type of vocal enunciation between speech and song. It was probably first used by Humperdinck (1897) but was exploited particularly by Schoenberg, who wrote (preface to *Pierrot lunaire*) that it should 'give the pitch exactly but then immediately leave it in a fall or rise; the performer should ensure that Sprechgesang resembles neither natural speech nor true singing'. It is notated in various ways, most often with a cross through the stem of the note or forming its head – or, in Berg's 'half-sung Sprechgesang' in his operas, with a stroke through the note's stem.

Sprezzatura (It.). Term used in early 17th-century Italy for expressiveness and freedom of tempo in monodic music. Caccini was the first to apply it musically (1600), indicating that it stood for a natural manner of performance, negligent of regular rhythm and true singing.

Springer. Term for an ornament akin to a changing note, as shown in the example below. It was sometimes called the 'acute' or 'sigh' (Fr. *accent, aspiration, plainte*; Ger. *Nachschlag*).

Spring Sonata. Nickname of Beethoven's Violin Sonata in F op.24 (1801).

Spring Symphony. Schumann's Symphony no.1 in B♭ (1841).

Spring Symphony, A. Choral work, op.44, by Britten, settings of English poems for soloists, boys' choir, chorus and orchestra (1949).

Spruch. Term for two categories of medieval poetry. The verbal *Spruch*, written for spoken delivery, is normally in rhyming couplets and of didactic content; the lyric *Spruch*, a form of Middle High German song, together with the Minnelied and the *Leich*, is a more extended form built on repetition. Contemporary usage did not distinguish between Minnelied and *Spruch*, confusingly, particularly as the later *Spruch* tended to adopt bar form, the basic form of the Minnelied. The difference is seen primarily on the basis of content and performance: the *Spruch*, addressed to a wider public, is didactic, the Minnelied is an intimate love-song.

Musically, the *Spruch* tends more towards recitation. The didactic genre goes back to the earliest tradition of the German lyric, and becomes more widespread in the 12th century; it may have been influenced by the Provençal sirventes. The earliest extant examples are connected with the Älterer Spervogel, but it was Walther von der Vogelweide who established it as a recognized genre in the courtly tradition. After him the tradition declined; Frauenlob's 300 *Sprüche* mark the end of the Minnesinger *Spruch* but at the same time his works herald the later Meistersinger tradition.

Squarcialupi Codex. Italian MS of the early 15th century. It consists of 216 folios containing 354 pieces, mainly ballatas and madrigals, of the period 1340–1415, by Landini (146 pieces) and others. Possibly all written by one scribe, it is arranged chronologically by composer, with a portrait of each. It once belonged to the Squarcialupi family, passed to the Medicis and then to the Biblioteca Medicea Laurenziana, Florence.

Square. English musical term of the 15th and 16th centuries for the bottom part of a 14th-century polyphonic composition which is used in a later composition.

Square dance. A dance performed by sets of four couples facing one another in a square. It evolved in the USA from popular ballroom dances of French origin such as the quadrille. The sequence of movements is sung or chanted by a 'caller' to the accompaniment of a piano, fiddle, guitar, banjo, double bass, accordion or wind instrument, or combination of these. The music is usually borrowed from popular Anglo-American songs in duple metre.

Square pianoforte. A piano in a horizontal rectangular case, a direct descendant of the clavichord and the most common domestic keyboard instrument for most of the 19th century. It was the principal vehicle for the development of the pianoforte in Germany in the mid-18th century. (For illustration, *see* KEYBOARD INSTRUMENTS.)

Staatskapelle (Ger.). 'State chapel': a state music establishment (*see* CHAPEL), normally developed from a court organization, such as the orchestra known as the Dresden Staatskapelle.

Staatsoper (Ger.). 'State opera': a national opera house or opera company, such as the Vienna Staatsoper, which developed from the earlier Vienna court opera (*Hofoper*).

Stabat mater (Lat.: 'His mother stood'). A 13th-century poem of uncertain authorship taken into the Roman liturgy as a sequence in the late 15th century, removed by the Council of Trent (1543–63) but revived in 1727 for use on the Feast of the Seven

Dolours (15 September). It is also used as an Office hymn on the Friday after Passion Sunday. There are polyphonic settings by Palestrina, Lassus and D. Scarlatti. In the 18th century it was often set for soloists, with or without chorus, and orchestra; composers include Pergolesi and Haydn. Among later settings those of Rossini, Dvořák, Verdi and Poulenc are well known.

Stabile, Annibale (*b* Naples, *c*1535; *d* Rome, April 1595). Italian composer. A pupil of Palestrina in Rome, he was at the Polish court before 1575, then *maestro di cappella* at St John Lateran, Rome (1575–8), the Collegio Germanico (1578–90) and S Maria Maggiore (1591–4). He published sacred works (4 bks, 1585–92) and madrigals (3 bks, 1572–85), notable for their lyrical style and supple rhythms. His younger brother Pompeo was also a composer.

Stabile, Mariano (*b* Palermo, 12 May 1888; *d* Milan, 11 Jan 1968). Italian baritone. He sang at Palermo from 1911 but wider recognition came only in 1921 when he appeared as Falstaff at La Scala under Toscanini. He repeated the role on his Covent Garden début (1926) and was successful at Glyndebourne, 1936–9, as Mozart's Figaro and Malatesta (*Don Pasquale*). He was known for dramatically exuberant, clearly enunciated interpretations.

Stabinger, Mathias (*b c*1750; *d* Venice, *c*1815). Composer and conductor. He was a flautist and clarinettist in France, then presented stage works in Italy (*c*1777–1780); in 1785–99 he was a theatre orchestra director in Moscow, composing many successful ballets and operas (some in Russian), and was involved in educating serfs in the arts. He also wrote duos, quartets and other chamber music.

Stabreim (Ger.). Alliteration: device used in German literature, and extensively by Wagner in his operas (particularly the *Ring*) 'to bring [his row of words] to the feeling's understanding in an easier and more sensuous form'.

Staccato (It.). 'Detached': of a note in performance, separated from its neighbours by a perceptible silence of articulation and given a certain emphasis, not quite MARCATO but the opposite of LEGATO. Staccato is notated with a dot, a vertical dash or a wedge.

Stade, Frederica von. *See* VON STADE, FREDERICA.

Staden, Johann (*b* Nuremberg, bap. 2 July 1581; *d* there, bur. 15 Nov 1634). German composer and organist. His first post was as organist to the Bayreuth court (in 1605–10 at Kulmbach). By 1611 he had returned to Nuremberg where in 1616 he became organist at the Spitalkirche and then at St Lorenz. From 1618 he was organist of St Sebald, the foremost musical post in the city. In his later years he was the city's leading musician and established the so-called Nuremberg school; a teacher–pupil tradition runs from him and his pupil Kindermann to Johann Krieger and Pachelbel. Besides Sigmund Theophil, his sons included Adam Staden (1614–59), a composer and poet.

A distinguished and versatile composer, Staden was significant as one of Germany's first exponents of the concertato style (both choral and solo) and the continuo, which he combined with traditional German features. *Harmoniae sacrae* (1616) contains some of the earliest sacred concertos in Germany. His most expressive work is the sacred collection *Kirchen-Music* (1625–6), which also includes a treatise on continuo. In his *c*150 songs (sacred and secular) and *c*200 dances, symphonias, sonatas etc he was much influenced by Hans Leo Hassler; his instrumental music was among the most important in the Germany of his time.

Staden, Sigmund Theophil (*b* Kulmbach, bap. 6 Nov 1607; *d* Nuremberg, bur. 30 July 1655). German composer and instrumentalist, son of Johann. He studied with his father and with the instrumentalist Jakob Paumann. By 1627 he was a city instrumentalist in Nuremberg, and from 1634 he was organist at St Lorenz. He was also active as a conductor, notably in a historical concert of 1643. Though a lesser composer than his father, he is important for his *Seelewig* (1644), the first extant Singspiel; it is modelled on the school dramas of the 16th and 17th centuries but includes recitatives. He also wrote other dramatic pieces, incidental music for oratorio-like religious plays, instrumental music (mostly lost) and sacred and secular songs. These last are mainly in a simple, conservative style, but his collection *Seelen-Music* (1644–8) was popular long after his death. Also successful was his musical manual for schools (1636).

Stadler, Anton (Paul) (*b* Bruck an der Leitha, 28 June 1753; *d* Vienna, 15 June 1812). Austrian clarinettist and basset-horn player. He was a clarinettist at the imperial court in Vienna with his brother Johann (1755–1804). He invented a downward extension to the clarinet; it was for this 'basset clarinet' that Mozart (a close friend) wrote his Clarinet Quintet and Clarinet Concerto. Stadler composed a number of clarinet and basset-horn pieces and devised a new plan for musical education.

Stadler, Abbé Maximilian [Johann Karl Dominik] (*b* Melk, 4 Aug 1748; *d* Vienna, 8 Nov 1833). Austrian composer. Ordained at Melk Abbey in 1772, he held ecclesiastical posts in Austria, in 1796 settling in Vienna where he became prominent in musical life and a respected composer. He was music adviser to Mozart's widow Constanze, completed (among other works) a number of Mozart's fragments and sketches and wrote articles defending the authenticity of his Requiem. Vocal music (Latin and German sacred works, stage music, cantatas, songs etc) predominates in his own output; he also wrote some instrumental pieces and made arrangements and editions of other composers' works. Notable among his writings is the first known history of music in Austria (MS, *c*1816–25).

Stadlmayr, Johann (*b* ?Freising, *c*1575; *d* Innsbruck, 12 July 1648). German composer. By 1603 he was a musician at the Salzburg court, where he became vice-Kapellmeister and then (in 1604) Kapellmeister. In 1607–18 he was Kapellmeister to Archduke Maximilian II at Innsbruck; remaining in the town afterwards, he was re-employed by his successor, Leopold V, in 1624. He was a renowned and prolific composer of Catholic church music, including masses, Magnificats, psalms etc. The earlier of his works continue 16th-century traditions of polyphony and Venetian-style chordal writing. His later music, beginning with his 1628 cycle of hymns for the church year, has more varied scorings (often with solo voices and added instruments) and makes increasing use of the modern concertato style.

Stadtpfeifer (Ger). 'Town piper': professional musician employed by civic authorities. The term has been used in German-speaking countries since the late 14th century, when it was applied to minstrels employed for a specific occasion or paid by the event. Written contracts began in the 15th century, together with more fixed salaries. Duties included playing at official celebrations, festival parades, royal visits, civic weddings and baptisms and other church occasions, and training apprentices; in return they had the exclusive privilege of providing music in the city limits, and several other more practical perquisites. Social position and income ranged widely from town to town. In smaller towns they might hold another job at the same time, but in larger, more important ones a completely musical career could be followed. Even so, a move from city to court musician meant a rise in social position. The all-round *Stadtpfeifer* was eventually supplanted with the rise of the specialist towards the end of the 18th century. Training was by apprenticeship – the *Stadtpfeifer* generally had to master a large number of wind and string instruments – and posts were secured by audition unless passed on through family connections, as in the Bach family, who held posts as Thuringian town musicians for generations. Other Baroque composers like Telemann and Quantz were trained in this environment.

Staempfli, Edward (*b* Berne, 1 Feb 1908). Swiss composer. A pupil of Jarnach and Maler in Cologne (1929–30) and of Dukas in Paris, where he was based until the war, he later returned to Switzerland, but moved to Germany in 1951. Influenced by impressionism and neo-classicism in Paris, he later embraced serial procedures. His large output includes symphonies and concertos, quartets, oratorios, cantatas and piano music. He often appeared as a conductor or pianist.

Staes, Ferdinand(-Philippe-Joseph) (*b* Brussels, bap. 16 Dec 1746; *d* there, 23 March 1809). South Netherlands composer. An esteemed performer, he worked as a harpsichordist and organist in Brussels and wrote keyboard works with instrumental accompaniment.

Staff [stave]. A set of lines on, between, above and below which notes of music are written. A five-line staff has been the most widely used type since early 13th-century north French MSS containing polyphony; a four-line staff has been used for plainchant since the 12th century and a six-line one was used by some early theorists and scribes. Except for plainsong, the five-line staff became standardized during the 17th century. *See also* CLEF, LEGER LINE, NOTATION and TABLATURE.

Staggins, Nicholas (*d* Windsor, 13 June 1700). English composer. He served at court as a violinist from 1670 and as a flautist from 1673, and was Master of the King's Musick from 1674. In 1684 he became the first professor of music at Cambridge. He composed music for a masque, several odes, songs and instrumental pieces.

Stainer, Jacob (*b* Absam, Tyrol, ?1617; *d* there, late Oct or early Nov 1683). Austrian violin maker. Apprenticed to a German maker in Italy, he perfected an earlier German style in his violins, which during his lifetime and for 150 years were esteemed above those of the Cremona masters. Surviving examples, 1638–82, have a relatively broad lower back, wood and varnish of the best quality, superb craftsmanship and silvery tone. He also made alto and tenor viols, cellos and double basses.

Stainer, Sir John (*b* London, 6 June 1840; *d* Verona, 31 March 1901). English organist, scholar and composer. After appointments at St Michael's College, Tenbury, and Oxford University he became organist at St Paul's Cathedral (1872–88), reforming the musical service there, increasing the number of musicians and expanding the repertory. He soon became a pre-eminent church musician, scholar and composer, helping found the Musical Association, and becoming professor at Oxford University. He was knighted in 1888. As a scholar he made valuable editions of music before Palestrina and Tallis (*Early Bodleian Music*, 1901). His services and anthems were fashionable during his lifetime and his hymn tunes are still used; his oratorio *The Crucifixion* (1887) is one of his best-known works.

Stainer & Bell. English music publishing firm. Founded in 1907 as an outlet for British compositions, it originally issued works by Stanford, Vaughan Williams and Bantock, subsequently undertaking scholarly series of early English music (edited by E.H. Fellowes, then Thurston Dart), including from 1951 the Musica Britannica series for the Royal Musical Association.

Stamitz, Anton (Thadäus Johann Nepomuk) (*b* Havlíčkův Brod, 27 Nov 1750; *d* Paris or Versailles, 1789–1809). Bohemian composer, son of Johann Stamitz. He joined the Mannheim court orchestra in 1764, and in 1770 went to Paris with his brother Carl. Remaining there after Carl left, he was successful as violin and viola player, composer and teacher (notably of Rodolphe Kreutzer). In 1782–9 he served at the French court. He wrote principally concertos, quartets and duos.

Stamitz, Carl (Philipp) (*b* Mannheim, bap. 8 May 1745; *d* Jena, 9 Nov 1801). German composer, son of Johann Stamitz. He was trained at Mannheim by his father and others, and joined the court orchestra in 1762. In 1770 he went to Paris, where, as a violinist, viola and viola d'amore player, he gave concerts with his brother Anton and was for a time composer and conductor for the Duke of Noailles. From the 1770s he travelled as a virtuoso, performing in cities including Vienna, London and The Hague. He was briefly concert director in Kassel (1789–90). Latterly his fame declined; in 1795 he became Kapellmeister and teacher at Jena University.

Stamitz was one of the most prolific Mannheim orchestral composers, writing more than 50 symphonies, 38 *symphonies concertantes* and 60 concertos. He also composed much chamber music, two stage works and other vocal pieces. Notable for its leisurely lyricism, his music combines Mannheim conventions with foreign features such as an Italian three-movement pattern in symphonies and a frequent use of rondos (popular in France) in finales.

Stamitz, Johann (Wenzel Anton) (*b* Havlíčkův Brod, bap. 30 June 1717; *d* Mannheim, ?27 March, 1757). Bohemian composer. One of a family of musicians, he was engaged by the Mannheim court in *c*1741, becoming first violinist in 1743, Konzertmeister in 1745–6 and director of instrumental music in 1750. In 1754–5 he visited Paris, where his music was very successful. Under him the Mannheim orchestra became the most renowned ensemble of the time throughout Europe (*see* MANNHEIM SCHOOL).

One of the foremost early Classical symphonists, Stamitz wrote over 50 symphonies, ten orchestral trios, numerous concertos (most for violin), many chamber works and a few sacred pieces. Especially imaginative and distinguished are his symphonies and orchestral trios, which were the first symphonic works consistently (though not always) in four movements, including a minuet and trio. Stamitz was important for transferring and adapting the Italian overture style to the symphony. He added more wind parts to the usual ensemble (strings, sometimes with two horns), often giving them a distinctive role; he used striking dynamic effects (notably the crescendo); and he introduced contrasting thematic material in many first movements. He strongly influenced other Mannheim composers.

Orchestral music over 50 syms.; 10 orch trios; over 25 concs., incl. 14 for vn, 11 for fl, 1 for cl; dances
Chamber music 14 trios; 8 vn sonatas; vn solo works
Vocal music Mass, D (1755); 4 sacred works; 2 secular vocal works

Stamping tube. An idiophone consisting of a tube of wood, which may be hollow (often bamboo), and is stamped on the ground or against another object. They are known in East Asia and Africa and are particularly important in South America, the Caribbean and the Pacific.

Stanchinsky, Alexey Vladimirovich (*b* Vladimir govt., 1888; *d* Crimea, 6 Oct 1914). Russian composer. He studied at the Moscow Conservatory. His few surviving works are all for solo piano. The early ones show a kind of improvisatory musical impressionism but that gave way to a more objective approach and obsessive formalism, touched with dry humour. He became something of a cult figure before his premature death.

Ständchen. The German equivalent of SERENADE.

Standford, Patric [Gledhill, John Patrick Standford] (*b* Barnsley, 5 Feb 1939). English composer. He was a pupil of Rubbra at the GSM, where he began teaching in 1967. His works include orchestral pieces and sacred music (*Christus-Requiem*, 1972).

Standfuss, J(?ohann) C. (*d* after *c*1759). German composer. He composed three influential Singspiels, the first of which was *Der Teufel ist los* (1752, Leipzig), based on Charles Coffey's ballad opera *The Devil to Pay*; it is often considered the earliest such work in Germany.

Standley (*fl c*1450). Composer, presumed to be English on grounds of his name, musical style and the MS context of his works. Two three-voice mass cycles and two motets are ascribed to him and reveal him as belonging to the generation of Frye and Bedyngham.

Stanesby. English woodwind instrument makers. Thomas Stanesby (i) (*c*1668–1734) started his business in London in 1691; his surviving instruments include nine recorders, five oboes and a bassoon. His son Thomas (ii) (1692–1754) was apprenticed to him in 1706, then set up his own workshop in the Temple Exchange; he made numerous transverse flutes (some of ivory), recorders, oboes (including the tenor oboe), bassoons and double bassoons. With Bressan, the Stanesbys made most of the finest English Baroque wind instruments (later examples showing simplified classical exteriors) and enjoyed a European reputation.

Stanford, Sir Charles Villiers (*b* Dublin, 30 Sept 1852; *d* London, 29 March 1924). British composer. He was educated at Cambridge (1880–84), where he was appointed organist of Trinity College in 1873 and professor in 1887; from 1883 he also taught at the RCM (his own education had been completed under Reinecke in Leipzig, 1874–5, and Kiel in Berlin, 1876). A demanding and highly influential teacher, he also demanded much of himself in living up to the great tradition, though the weight of academic responsibility could be leavened by his Irish heritage of folksong and mysticism and by his keen feeling for English words. Yet, apart from his Anglican cathedral music, little of his large output (nearly 200 opus numbers) has remained in performance. His works include ten operas (notably *Shamus O'Brien*, 1896; *Much Ado about Nothing*, 1901; and *The Travelling Companion*, given posthumously, 1926), a quantity of choral music and songs (his Bb Service of 1879 is still used, and some of his sensitive partsongs are remembered, particularly *The Blue Bird*), seven symphonies and other orchestral scores (Clarinet Concerto, 1902, and a series of Irish Rhapsodies), eight string quartets, and organ and piano music.

Stanley, John (*b* London, 17 Jan 1712; *d* there, 19 May 1786). English composer. Blind from childhood, he studied with Reading and Greene and was a church organist from the 1720s. In 1734 he became organist to the Inner Temple, London; his playing was so greatly admired that, when he held three organist's posts, a trail of people would follow him from church to church to hear him. He was also a violinist, teacher and director of concerts (especially oratorio). From 1779 he was Master of the King's Band, composing a number of court odes. His output reflects the move from the Handelian Baroque to the *galant* style. Works such as his six string concertos (1742) and three sets of organ voluntaries (1748–54) are traditional in idiom, while his six keyboard concertos (1775) and other late works use simpler forms and textures. Among his other works are 19 English cantatas, three oratorios

(modelled on Handel's), several stage works, anthems, songs and flute sonatas.

Starer, Robert (*b* Vienna, 8 Jan 1924). American composer of Austrian origin. He studied at the Jerusalem Conservatory and the Juilliard School (1947–9). He remained in New York, eventually becoming professor at Brooklyn College (1963). He has composed in most genres, his music characterized by direct expression, chromaticism, modality and driving rhythms. His settings of Hebrew texts have won praise.

Starker, Janos (*b* Budapest, 5 July 1924). American cellist. He made his solo début when he was 11 but left Hungary after the war and settled in the USA, becoming principal of the Met Opera Orchestra, 1949–53, and then the Chicago SO. In 1958 he became professor at Indiana University, Bloomington. His expressive tone and intellectual grasp are best displayed in Bach's solo suites and Dvořák's Concerto.

Starzer, Joseph (?**Franz**) (*b* 1726/7; *d* Vienna, 22 April 1787). Austrian composer, violinist and administrator. He joined the Burgtheater orchestra in Vienna, *c*1752. In 1758–9 he went to the Russian imperial court where he became composer of ballet music and concert director. Returning to Vienna in 1768, he composed ballets for Noverre and Angiolini, was an official of the Tonkünstler-Sozietät (from 1771) and directed Baron van Swieten's concerts (Mozart succeeded him in the latter post), for which he arranged works by Handel.

Starzer was especially esteemed for his ballets, which number over 30. They are well written to follow the stage action, often departing from customary dance forms, and some have unusual scorings. Among his other works are symphonies and concertos, over 20 string quartets (notable for their counterpoint) and other chamber pieces; his few vocal works include an oratorio (1778) and a Singspiel.

Stasov, Vladimir Vasil'yevich (*b* St Petersburg, 14 Jan 1824; *d* there, 23 Oct 1906). Russian critic. He worked as a civil servant and librarian, by 1856 becoming the belligerent champion of the young Balakirev and his circle, coining their nickname 'Mighty Handful' in 1867. He was a passionate lover of Russian legend, literature and the heroic past and played a leading role in the inception of Rimsky-Korsakov's *Sadko*, Musorgsky's *Khovanshchina* and Borodin's *Prince Igor*. Among his writings on music are biographies of Musorgsky (1881) and Borodin (1889) and an extended essay on recent Russian music (1883).

Šťastný. Czech family of musicians. Jan Šťastný (*d c*1799) was an oboist in Prague. His sons Bernard (*c*1760–*c*1835) and Jan (*c*1764–after 1826) were cellists and pedagogues; Bernard served in Prague, Jan at courts in Germany and probably also visited Paris and London. He was a prolific composer of cello sonatas, duos etc.

Staudt, Johann Bernhard (*b* Wiener Neustadt, 23 Oct 1654; *d* Vienna, 6/7 Nov 1712). Austrian composer. He was *regens chori* at the Jesuit monastic house in Vienna from 1684 and taught music at the

Jesuit college. Besides church music, he wrote music for 39 secular and sacred school plays (most by J.B. Adolph) staged on ceremonial occasions; they include choruses, arias, songs, recitatives and ritornellos.

Steber, Eleanor (*b* Wheeling, wv, 17 July 1916). American soprano. She studied in Boston and in New York, and made her début at the Met as Sophie (*Rosenkavalier*) in 1940. She was a leading soprano there until 1963, singing in a large repertory but admired above all in Mozart; she also sang Violetta, the Marschallin, Eva and Marie (*Wozzeck*) and created Barber's Vanessa. An admired recitalist, she was noted for her warm voice and broad, musical phrasing. Later she taught at the Juilliard School.

Steel band. An ensemble of tuned percussion instruments made from pans or oildrums, with a few rhythm instruments. They first developed in Trinidad in the 1930s and 1940s as bands for carnival processions, but their use has spread to Europe and particularly Britain where they are used in music education and exist in large numbers as amateur or semi-professional bands.

There are three categories of pan: tenor, for tuneplaying with a range of two octaves upwards from *c'* or one and a half from *f*; rhythm, an octave from *c*; and bass, three to five notes in the octave from *C*. However, pitch, tuning, note layout and nomenclature are not standardized. The pans are hit with rubberheaded sticks and may be hung round the player's neck or mounted on stands.

Steel guitar. *See* HAWAIIAN GUITAR.

Stefani, Andrea (*fl* Florence, *c*1400). Italian composer. He wrote two ballate and one Petrarchan madrigal as well as some three-voice *laude* (now lost). In 1399 he served as singer in the processions of the Bianchi Gesuati in Florence. He used both the Florentine technique of writing for two voices and the three-voice French manner.

Stefani, Jan (*b* Prague, 1746; *d* Warsaw, 24 Feb 1829). Polish composer. After a period in Vienna, he became violinist and conductor of the royal orchestra in Warsaw in 1779 and cathedral Kapellmeister. He wrote nine Polish operas (1787–1808), other vocal works and instrumental music. His use of the polonaise was influential.

Stefano, Giuseppe di. *See* DI STEFANO, GIUSEPPE.

Steffan, Joseph Anton. *See* ŠTĚPÁN, JOSEF ANTONÍN.

Steffani, Agostino (*b* Castelfranco, 25 July 1654; *d* Frankfurt, 12 Feb 1728). Italian composer and diplomat. In 1667–88 he served at the Munich court; after studying in Rome (1672–4) he became court organist and in 1681 (the year of his first opera) director of chamber music. He next moved to the Duke of Hanover's court, where he became Kapellmeister, but he grew increasingly active in diplomatic affairs and spent some time in Vienna and Brussels involved in negotiation. After entering the service of the Elector Palatine at Düsseldorf in 1703, he virtually gave up music; he had three operas staged, but only one was certainly new. He returned to Hanover in 1709 as Apostolic Vicar in northern Germany. In 1727 he became president of the Academy of Vocal Music in London, for which he composed.

Steffani's principal works are his *c*70 chamber duets for two voices and continuo, which represent an important stage in Italian secular music between Carissimi and Handel. They have up to six movements and feature perfect formal balance, supple melody and elegant counterpoint; Handel was much influenced by them. Many duets appear in his 18 dramatic works, which also have French features. His six full-length Hanover operas (1689–95) influenced opera development in northern Germany. Among his other works are psalms, motets and solo cantatas.

Steffens, Johann (*b* Itzehoe, *c*1560; *d* Lüneburg, *c* summer 1616). German composer. From 1593 he was organist of the Johanniskirche, Lüneburg, where he remained for 20 years. He wrote German madrigals and dance-songs (2 bks, 1599, 1619), influenced by Hassler, as well as miscellaneous sacred and instrumental pieces.

Stegmann, Carl David (*b* Staucha, 1751; *d* Bonn, 27 May 1826). German composer. Active mainly in northern Germany, he presented his first stage works in Königsberg and Danzig. He was in Hamburg, 1778–83, then worked in various centres including Frankfurt, where his Singspiel *Heinrich der Löwe* was given in 1792; he then returned to Hamburg. Besides Singspiels and operas, he wrote music for plays, instrumental works and keyboard arrangements of music by Mozart and others.

Steibelt, Daniel (*b* Berlin, 22 Oct 1765; *d* St Petersburg, 20 Sept 1823). German composer and pianist. Until 1810 he was based in Paris, with excursions to Germany and London for concert appearances and productions of his operas and ballets. He also composed much piano music, including the celebrated Third Concerto (1799), the finale of which introduces an imitation of a storm, and the 50 studies of the *Etude* op.78, his most enduring work. From 1810 he was director of the French Opera at St Petersburg (succeeding Boieldieu), where he composed stage works, notably *Cendrillon* (1810), and performed his Eighth Piano Concerto (with choral finale). Though he was a capable composer with a superficially brilliant playing technique, most of his music seems doomed to oblivion; reports of his vain, reckless and even dishonest character – he sold old works as new – have further undercut his reputation.

Steigleder, Johann Ulrich (*b* Schwäbisch Hall, 22 March 1593; *d* Stuttgart, 10 Oct 1635). German organist and composer. After serving at the Stephanskirche, Lindau, he was organist of the abbey church, Stuttgart, from 1617 and also ducal organist from 1627. In his keyboard collection *Ricercar tabulatura* (1624) he adopted five-line musical notation in place of the traditional lettering, as did Scheidt (also in 1624, *Tabulatura nova*); his ricercars are markedly instrumental in character and show the influence of English virginal style. His principal other work is a set of 40 keyboard variations on the chorale *Vater unser* (1627). His father Adam Steigleder (1561–1633) and his grandfather Utz Steigleder (*d* 1581) were also organists and composers.

Stein, Johann (Georg) Andreas (*b* Heidelsheim, 6 May 1728; *d* Augsburg, 29 Feb 1792). German keyboard instrument maker. He settled in Augsburg in 1750 and built his masterpiece, the organ of the Barfüsserkirche (1755–7). His experiments with action and register resulted in four types of combination instrument (including the 'Poli-Toni-Clavichordium', 1769, and the 'Melodika', 1772). He is best known for the innovatory escapement and damper mechanisms of his pianos (praised by Mozart): he used individually hinged and spring-loaded escapement levers to keep the hammers from jamming against the strings, and flexible shock-absorbers on the wooden *Kapseln*. From 1794 his daughter Nannette carried on the business with her husband J.A. STREICHER in Vienna; his son Matthäus Andreas established his own firm, André Stein, in Vienna in 1802.

Steinbach, Fritz (*b* Grünsfeld, 17 June 1855; *d* Munich, 13 Aug 1916). German conductor. Associated chiefly with the Meiningen and (from 1903) Cologne orchestras, he was well known for his Brahms interpretations. His brother Emil (1849–1919), also a conductor, gave the first public performance of Wagner's *Siegfried Idyll* (1877).

Steinberg, (Carl) Michael (Alfred) (*b* Wrocław, 4 Oct 1928). American music critic. He studied at Princeton and taught music history at the Manhattan School of Music, becoming critic of the *Boston Globe* while teaching at various colleges and universities. He became director of publications with the Boston SO in 1976 and in 1979 artistic adviser and publications director to the San Francisco SO. His wide sympathies, scholarly knowledge and lively style make him one of the most esteemed writers in the USA.

Steinberg, William (Hans) (*b* Cologne, 1 Aug 1899; *d* New York, 16 May 1978). American conductor. He was Klemperer's assistant at Cologne and after working in Prague was musical director at Frankfurt from 1929, conducting the première of Schoenberg's *Von heute auf morgen* there (1930). He left Germany at the rise of the Nazis and in 1936 co-founded the Palestine Orchestra (later Israel PO). From 1938 he worked in the USA, notably as music director of the Pittsburgh SO (1952–76). He was at his best in late Romantic music.

Steiner, Max(imilian Raoul Walter) (*b* Vienna, 10 May 1888; *d* Hollywood, 28 Dec 1971). American composer of Austrian origin. He conducted musical comedy in Europe and elsewhere and in 1914 worked on Broadway. He moved to Hollywood in 1929 and became a leading film composer.

Steinitz, (Charles) Paul (Joseph) (*b* Chichester, 25 Aug 1909; *d* Oxted, 22 April 1988). British conductor. He studied at the RAM and in 1947 founded the (South) London Bach Society. His performances of Bach's works at St Bartholomew-the-Great (where he was organist, 1949–61) pioneered smaller-scale, German-language Bach performance in England. Steinitz was also a champion of 20th-century music. He taught at the RAM and at Goldsmiths' College, London University, 1948–76.

Steinkopf, Otto (*b* Stolberg, 28 June 1904; *d* Celle, 17 Feb 1980). German woodwind instrument maker. He was the first 20th-century maker to reproduce many Renaissance and Baroque woodwind instruments, including crumhorns, kortholts, rackets, dulcians, shawms, cornetts and Baroque bassoons and oboes.

Steinmeyer, G.F. German firm of organ builders. It was established at Oettingen in 1847 by Georg Friedrich Steinmeyer (1819–1901); over 700 organs were built (chiefly with cone valve chests and mechanical actions), including the cathedral organs of Bamberg and Munich. In 1928 his son Friedrich Johannes (1857–1928) built for Passau Cathedral what was then the largest church organ in the world, with five manuals and 208 stops. His son Hans (1889–1970) and grandson Fritz (*b* 1918) continued the tradition, changing from tubular pneumatic action (1890) to tracker action (1945). Notable examples of their work are the organs in St Michaelis, Hamburg (1960), the Meistersingerhalle at Nuremberg (1963), the Hall of Congress, Augsburg (1972), and the church of the Holy Spirit, Heidelberg (1980).

Steinway. American firm of piano makers. It was established in New York in 1853 by Heinrich Engelhard Steinway (Steinweg) (1797–1871). Its success was based initially on overstrung, iron-framed instruments – square pianos from 1855, grands from 1859 and uprights from 1863; in the first decade annual production reached 2000. Steinway's eldest son C.F. Theodor (Theodore) (1825–89) advanced technological and design innovations still further, giving the player control over a tone of unprecedented volume and richness; his brother William (1836–96) consolidated the firm's commercial position (with marathon virtuoso tours and exhibition appearances, endorsements from Berlioz, Wagner and Liszt, European court patronage etc). A Hamburg branch opened in 1880. Steinway pianos have continued to dominate concert platforms since World War II.

Steirische Herbstfestival (Austria). Annual (autumn) festival in Graz, established in 1968. It includes concerts, symposia, jazz and much contemporary music.

Stelle, Officium (Lat.: 'ceremony of the star'). Title in medieval MSS, and adopted by modern scholars, for Latin church plays of the 11th–13th centuries on the visit of the Magi. Some 14 or 15 texts with music survive. Characteristically, the play opens with a threefold chant on a Lauds antiphon, and includes antiphons, responsories, hymns and processional chants. They are varied and complex and follow no strict or chronological pattern.

Stenhammar, (Karl) Wilhelm (Eugen) (*b* Stockholm, 7 Feb 1871; *d* there, 20 Nov 1927). Swedish composer. Brought up in a cultivated and musical family, he composed from childhood and had little formal training. His earlier music is in a late Romantic style showing influences from Wagner, Liszt and Brahms, but from 1910 he moved towards a more classical manner, stimulated by contrapuntal studies and a profound concern with Beethoven. Much of his music has a Nordic colour, though he did not use folk material. His works include two symphonies (1903, 1915), two piano concertos, a Serenade (1913), cantatas (*Sången*, 1921), six string quartets (1894–1916) and songs. An admired pianist, he was also conductor of the Göteborgs Orkesterförening (1906–22), making the city a musical rival to Stockholm.

Štěpán [Steffan], Josef Antonín (*b* Kopidlno, bap. 14 March 1726; *d* Vienna, 12 April 1797). Czech composer. A pupil of Wagenseil in Vienna, he became known as a gifted composer and brilliant harpsichordist. He was also a famous teacher and for a time a keyboard master at the Viennese court.

Štěpán is most important for his keyboard music, including sonatas, divertimentos, capriccios and variations. It shows development from an italianate idiom to a Viennese Classical style; his sonatas of the late 1770s, conceived for the piano, are notable for structural ingenuity, fantasia effects and programmatic elements. He also used original formal schemes in his *c*40 keyboard concertos, which are dominated by the soloist. His other compositions include symphonies, chamber works and vocal pieces. His lied collections (1778–82) were the first of their kind published in Vienna.

Stephan, Rudi (*b* Worms, 29 July 1887; *d* nr. Tarnopol, 29 Sept 1915). German composer. He studied in Frankfurt and Munich. His instrumental works of 1911–13, all called *Musik für...*, were seen as belonging to a new classical movement for pure, absolute music. His 16 songs (1914) recall Wolf while his only opera (*Die ersten Menschen*, 1914) looks back to Beethoven and Gluck.

Stephănescu, George (*b* Bucharest, 13 Dec 1843; *d* there, 25 April 1925). Romanian composer. He studied at the Bucharest Conservatory (1864–7) and the Paris Conservatoire (1867–71) and returned to Bucharest to become an outstanding singing teacher at the conservatory (1872–1904). He also composed operas, the first Romanian symphony (1869), liturgical and chamber music, wrote criticism and translated librettos. He was perhaps the greatest Romanian musician before Enescu.

Stephanie, (Johann) Gottlieb (*b* Breslau, 19 Feb 1741; *d* Vienna, 23 Jan 1800). Austrian dramatist and actor. He became director of the National-Singspiel in Vienna in 1779 and wrote both plays and librettos. Among the latter are those for Mozart's *Die Entführung aus dem Serail* (1782) and *Der Schauspieldirektor* (1786).

Stephens, Catherine (*b* London, 18 Sept 1794; *d* there, 22 Feb 1882). English soprano and actress. Praised by Hazlitt, Hunt and Macready, she made her name in English operas and adaptations of foreign works, including the first performances in English of *Don Giovanni* (Covent Garden, 1817) and *Le nozze di Figaro* (1819).

Steppes of Central Asia. *See* IN THE STEPPES OF CENTRAL ASIA.

Sterkel, Johann Franz Xaver (*b* Würzburg, 3 Dec 1750; *d* there, 12 Oct 1817). German composer. At first an organist in Neumünster, he was ordained priest in 1774. He moved to Mainz and became court chaplain, but toured Italy as a pianist, 1779–82. In 1793–7 he was court Kapellmeister at Mainz; when the chapel was disbanded he went to Würzburg, Regensburg and later Aschaffenburg, where he served the Grand Duke of Frankfurt, 1810–14. A prolific and successful composer he wrote mostly instrumental music, including symphonies and concertos, chamber works with keyboard solo, piano sonatas and piano duets. Many of the sonatas have a lyricism and loose-knit structure pointing towards Schubert. Among his vocal works are an Italian opera (1782, Naples), Italian arias, songs and ensembles and German lieder. His works as well as his distinctive playing style (which impressed Beethoven in 1791) contributed to the development of a pianistic idiom.

Stern, Isaac (*b* Kremenets, 21 July 1920). American violinist. After study with Persinger and Binder he made his recital début in 1935. His European début was in 1948 and from 1960 he played in a trio with Leonard Rose and Eugene Istomin. Recognized as one of the world's foremost violinists, he is admired for his vital, expressive performances, with warm tone and impeccable style; he has given premières of works by Bernstein, Schuman and Maxwell Davies.

Stern, Leo(pold Lawrence) (*b* Brighton, 5 April 1862; *d* London, 10 Sept 1904). English cellist. He studied at the RAM and in Leipzig and gave the première of Dvořák's Cello Concerto (London, 1896).

Sternberg, Erich Walter (*b* Berlin, 31 May 1891; *d* Tel-Aviv, 15 Dec 1974). Israeli composer of German origin. A pupil of Leichtentritt, he settled in Palestine in 1932 and taught at the Tel-Aviv Conservatory; he helped form the Palestine (later Israel) PO. He wrote largely vocal music, often on biblical or Jewish subjects, in a late Romantic style.

Steuermann, Edward (*b* Sambor, 18 June 1892; *d* New York, 11 Nov 1964). American pianist and composer of Polish birth. He studied with Busoni and Schoenberg and took part in the first performance of *Pierrot lunaire* (1912), thereafter being closely associated with the Second Viennese School. He emigrated to the USA in 1938; his Beethoven recitals in New York were admired for their structural clarity. From 1952 he taught at the Juilliard School.

Stevens, Bernard (George) (*b* London, 2 March 1916; *d* there, 2 Jan 1983). English composer. He was a pupil of Dent and Rootham at Cambridge (1934–7) and of Morris and Jacob at the RCM (1937–40), where he began teaching in 1948. His works include orchestral pieces (*A Symphony of Liberation*, 1945), cantatas and chamber music in a refined tonal style.

Stevens, Denis (William) (*b* High Wycombe, 2 March 1922). English musicologist. He studied at Oxford, was a violinist and violist in the Philharmonia Orchestra and then (1949–54) a BBC programme planner and producer, working principally on early music. He taught at several universities in the USA, including Columbia (1965–74) and the University of California at Santa Barbara. He was founder and director of the Accademia Monteverdiana, a chamber ensemble specializing in early music, and has made many records and published several critical editions. Among his books are studies of Tudor church music (1955), the history of song (1960) and Monteverdi (1977, 1980).

Stevens, Halsey (*b* Scott, NY, 3 Dec 1908). American composer and musicologist. He studied in Syracuse and California and from 1948 taught at the University of Southern California. He has lectured widely on modern music; his writings include a study of Bartók (1953). A prolific composer, he has won many awards and commissions. His music is characterized by its vigorous rhythm, firm tonal centres, supple melodic contours and command of timbre; *Symphonic Dances* (1958) and the Clarinet Concerto (1969) are notable works.

Stevens, Richard John Samuel (*b* London, 27 March 1757; *d* there, 23 Sept 1837). English composer. He worked mainly as an organist (from 1796 at the Charterhouse) and in 1801 became Gresham Professor of Music in London. His *c*50 glees are among the finest of their time and show the influence of instrumental music (especially Haydn's); some use Shakespeare texts. He also wrote church music, an opera and an oratorio, songs and keyboard pieces, and left a lively, informative set of MS memoirs.

Stevens, Risë (*b* New York, 11 June 1913). American mezzo-soprano. She studied at the Juilliard School and with Gutheil-Schoder, singing in Prague and Vienna. Her Met début was as Thomas's Mignon (1938); she was with the company for 23 seasons, notably singing Carmen, Octavian (the role of her Paris Opéra début, 1949) and Gluck's Orpheus. She felt that Wagner and Verdi were unsuited to her warm, lyrical, well-controlled mezzo.

Stevenson, Robert M(urrell) (*b* Melrose, NM, 3 July 1916). American musicologist. He studied at the University of Texas, the Juilliard School, Yale, Rochester, Harvard, Princeton Theological Seminary and Oxford. He taught at the University of California at Los Angeles from 1949 to 1987. His chief interest has been Latin American music, in which his research has been extensive and outstanding; he has also contributed to the history of Spanish and American music, notably Afro-American and that of the Protestant church. His numerous publications reveal an impressive command of bibliographical tools and literature. In 1978 he became founder-editor of the *Inter-American Music Review*.

Stevenson, Ronald (*b* Blackburn, 6 March 1928). Scottish composer. He studied at the Royal Manchester College and in Rome and since 1952 has lived in Scotland as a pianist and composer. His output is mostly of piano music, orchestral pieces and songs, the variety and intensity of his music suggesting his enthusiasm for Busoni; he draws on elements of many musical cultures, including Scottish, and advocates 'world music'. As a pianist he is admired for his intellectual breadth.

Sticcado-pastrole. A percussion instrument of the late 18th century consisting of glass rods struck with knobbed sticks and producing 'very soft music indeed'; they were made by George Smart (*d c*1805) in London.

Stich, Johann Wenzel. *See* PUNTO, GIOVANNI.

Sticheron. Term used in the Greek Orthodox Church for the hymn sung after psalm verses.

Stich-Randall, Teresa (*b* West Hartford, CT, 24 Dec 1927). American soprano. She made her début in Thomson's *The Mother of us All* (1947) and sang Nannetta in Toscanini's 1950 *Falstaff* recording. In Europe she was admired as a Mozart interpreter for her performances in Aix-en-Provence, Vienna and elsewhere. She sang Gilda in Chicago (1955) and made her Met début as Fiordiligi (1961). Her pure, sweet, sharply defined voice has also been admired in Bach and Handel.

Stiedry, Fritz (*b* Vienna, 11 Oct 1883; *d* Zurich, 8 Aug 1968). American conductor. He studied at the Vienna Academy of Music and worked at Dresden, Prague and elsewhere, becoming principal conductor at the Berlin Staatsoper (1914–23), then the Vienna Volksoper (1924–5) and the Berlin Städtische Oper (1928–33). He had to leave Germany and worked in Russia until 1937, then in the USA, where he conducted at Chicago, then at the Met (1948–60), notably in Mozart, Verdi and Wagner.

Stiffelio. Opera in three acts by Verdi to a libretto by Piave after *Le pasteur* by Emile Souvestre and Eugène Bourgeois (1850, Trieste); it was unsuccessful and Verdi revised it as AROLDO.

Stignani, Ebe (*b* Naples, 10 July 1904; *d* Imola, 5 Oct 1974). Italian mezzo-soprano. She sang at La Scala from 1926, appearing with distinction in the Italian repertory and as Saint-Saëns's Delilah and Gluck's Orpheus. At Covent Garden (1937–57) she sang Verdi and Bellini with dramatic intensity and rich tone.

Stile antico (It.). 'Old style': term for the archaic style, imitating Palestrina, used in music written after 1600. It was often used for church music by composers from Monteverdi to D. Scarlatti. It also influenced Classical and even Romantic composers of church music, including Rossini and Verdi.

Stile concitato (It.). 'Agitated style': term used by Monteverdi to denote one of the three styles of music named by Greek philosophers (agitated, soft, moderate). It is characterized by rapid repeated notes and used notably in *Il combattimento di Tancredi e Clorinda* (1624) and in the collection *Madrigali guerrieri et amorosi* (1638).

Stile rappresentativo (It.). 'Representational style': term for the theatrical solo vocal style of early 17th-century dramatic pieces set completely to music.

Still, William Grant (*b* Woodville, MS, 11 May 1895; *d* Los Angeles, 3 Dec 1978). American composer. He studied at the Oberlin Conservatory and with Varèse. He became best known for nationalist works, in a tonal Romantic style, often using black and other American folk idioms. His *Afro-American Symphony* (1930) was the first by a black American to be played by a leading orchestra, and he was the first black American to have an opera staged by an important company. His output also includes five symphonies and other orchestral scores, choral pieces, piano music and songs.

Stimme (Ger.). 'Voice', 'part': term for a vocal or

instrumental part in a composition, or the paper on which it is written. It can also mean an organ stop or the soundpost of a string instrument.

Stimmung (Ger.). (1) Mood; *Stimmungsmusik* is 'background music' or 'mood music'.

(2) Tuning.

(3) Work for two sopranos, mezzo-soprano, tenor, baritone and bass by Stockhausen (1968).

Stivori, Francesco (*b* Venice, *c*1550; *d* probably Graz, 1605). Italian composer. He was an organist at Montagna, near Padua (1579–1601), and at the Graz court (1602–5). An influential composer of the Venetian school, who helped introduce multiple choir music into Austria, he published motets (6 bks, 1579–1601), madrigals (7 bks, 1583–1605) and instrumental works (3 bks, 1589–99).

Stobaeus, Johann (*b* Graudez, 6 July 1580; *d* Königsberg, 11 Sept 1646). German composer. He studied with Johannes Eccard and served under him as a bass in the Königsberg Kapelle from 1602. In 1603–26 he held a post at Kneiphof, then becoming Kapellmeister to the Königsberg court. Heinrich Albert was one of his pupils. One of the city's leading composers, he used a conservative style in his music, which includes chorale-based motets, Magnificats, simple, easily performable Protestant hymns, chorales and festal songs, and many occasional works; the latter were especially influential. He also edited chorale arrangements by Eccard.

Stock-and-horn. An obsolete 18th-century pastoral reedpipe, like the melody pipe of a bagpipe but with a single reed. It was apparently played in the southern half of Scotland.

Stockhausen, Julius (Christian) (*b* Paris, 22 July 1826; *d* Frankfurt, 22 Sept 1906). German baritone of Alsatian descent. He studied in Paris, where his teachers included Cramer. He conducted at Hamburg (1863–7) and taught at his own singing school in Frankfurt (from 1880). Though a distinguished opera and oratorio singer (he sang in the première of Brahms's *German Requiem*, 1868), it was as an interpreter of lieder that he made the strongest impression, helping popularize the songs of Schubert and Schumann – he gave the public première of *Die schöne Müllerin* in 1856 – and inspiring his friend Brahms to write the *Magelone Lieder*.

Stockhausen, Karlheinz (*b* Burg Mödrath, 22 Aug 1928). German composer. He studied with Martin at the Cologne Musikhochschule (1947–51), but the decisive stimulus came from his encounter with Messiaen's *Mode de valeurs* at Darmstadt in 1951. There he saw possibilities of long-range serial process which he pursued in *Kreuzspiel* (1951) and *Kontra-Punkte* (1952), both for piano-based ensemble.

The latter piece was written during a period of study with Messiaen in Paris, and while there he made a first essay in electronic music. On returning to Cologne he continued this activity, notably in *Gesang der Jünglinge* for vocal and synthesized sounds on tape (1956). At the same time, he pursued the ramifications of serial instrumental music in a cycle of 11 piano pieces (1956), in *Zeit-*

masse for wind quintet (1956) and in *Gruppen* for three orchestras (1957). In all these scores he began working with large groups of notes rather than with the isolated points that the avant garde had inherited from Webern and Messiaen. He also concerned himself with abstract processes and discoursed on these in a series of articles and in his teaching at Darmstadt, where he first lectured in 1953: his influence extended over a whole generation of European composers, including such contemporaries as Boulez and Berio. That influence depended not only on his theoretical rigour and personal charisma but also on the conviction and drama in his music.

In 1958 he made his first visit to the USA, and around this time his music became more relaxed, both in its density of events and in its notational exactitude. This was partly a result of Cage's influence; partly it came from the experience of electronic music, which suggested a different way of hearing, tuning in to sound events rather than expecting them to be items in some pattern. Hence the comparatively leisurely pace of *Carré* for four choral-orchestral groups (1960), *Kontakte* for piano, percussion and tape (1960) and *Momente* for soprano, choir and instruments (1964, extended 1972). Then the habit of working with sound as a substance led to a period of virtual concentration on electronic pieces, many of them written for the performing group with whom Stockhausen toured: *Mikrophonie I* (1964), *Prozession* (1967), *Kurzwellen* (1968), *Aus den sieben Tagen* (1968), these gradually relinquishing notation to the point where the last work consists only of prose poems designed to stimulate intuitive music-making. There were also, however, major works composed on tape: *Telemusik* (1966), created during a revelatory visit to Japan, and *Hymnen* (1967), both using recordings from around the world.

The return to a more conventional medium came abruptly in *Mantra* for two pianos and electronics (1970), an hour-long, fully notated work based on transformations of a melodic theme. Nearly all Stockhausen's subsequent works have been similarly thematic, though not at all symphonic, since his style remains fundamentally heterophonic rather than harmonic. At the same time, the latent drama in his music has become explicit. *Trans* (1971) requires the orchestra to be bathed in violet light and seen through a veil; *Inori* (1974) has one or two mimes executing hieratic attitudes in synchrony with the orchestra; and *Sirius* (1977) is a ceremonial for four costumed musicians and synthesized tape. Since then all Stockhausen's works have been parts of *Licht*, intended to be a heptalogy for performance on the evenings of a week: so far *Donnerstag* (1980) *Samstag* (1984) and *Montag* (1988) have been completed.

Operas Licht (1977–): Donnerstag (1980), Samstag (1984), Montag (1988)

Orchestral music Gruppen (1957); Stop (1965); Fresco (1969); Inori (1974); Jubiläum (1977)

Chamber music Kreuzspiel (1951); Kontra-Punkte (1952); Zeitmasse (1956); Refrain (1959); Adieu (1966); Für Dr K

(1969); Sternklang (1971); Ylem (1972); Herbstmusik (1974); Musik im Bauch (1975)

Solo instrumental music Klavierstücke I–IV (1953), V–X (1955), XI (1956); Zyklus, perc (1959); Harlekin, cl (1975); Amour, cl (1976); In Freundschaft (1977)

Instruments with tape Kontakte (1960); Trans (1971); *with electronic transformation* Mikrophonie I (1964), II (1965); Mixtur (1964); Solo (1966); Prozession (1967); Mantra (1970); *with short-wave receivers* Kurzwellen (1968); Spiral (1969); Pole (1970); Expo (1970)

Vocal music Stimmung (1968); Atmen gibt das Leben (1974); *with instruments* Carré (1960); Momente (1964); Sirius (1977)

Tape music Elektronische Studie I (1953), II (1954); Gesang der Jünglinge (1956); Telemusik (1966); Hymnen (1967)

Unspecified forces Plus-Minus (1963); Aus den sieben Tagen (1968); Für kommende Zeiten (1970); Alphabet für Liège (1972); Tierkreis (1975)

Stoessel, Albert (Frederic) (*b* St Louis, 11 Oct 1894; *d* New York, 12 May 1943). American violinist, conductor and composer. He trained at the Berlin Musikhochschule and became a violinist in the USA. He worked in New York as a conductor and teacher. At the Juilliard Graduate School (from 1927) he organized the premières of several American operas. His orchestral works have been widely played.

Stojanović, Petar (*b* Budapest, 6 Sept 1877; *d* Belgrade, 11 Sept 1957). Yugoslav composer. A pupil of Hubay at the Budapest Conservatory and of Fuchs and Heuberger at the Vienna Conservatory, he moved in 1925 to Belgrade to teach and compose. His works, in a late Romantic style, include operas, orchestral scores (seven violin concertos) and chamber music.

Stojowski, Zygmunt (Denis Antoni) (*b* Strzelce, 14 May 1870; *d* New York, 6 Nov 1946). Polish composer and pianist. He was a pupil of Żeleński in Kraków and Diémer and Delibes in Paris. In 1906 he went to the USA to teach and compose, his works including virtuoso piano and orchestral pieces in a late Romantic style. He wrote extensively on piano teaching.

Stoker, Richard (*b* Castleford, 8 Nov 1938). English composer. He was a pupil of Berkeley at the RAM (1958–62), where he was appointed a professor in 1963, and of Boulanger in Paris. His works include much chamber music in a strict tonal but serially orientated style.

Stokowski, Leopold (Anthony) (*b* London, 18 April 1882; *d* Nether Wallop, 13 Sept 1977). American conductor of British birth and Polish parentage. He studied at the RCM. His conducting début (1908, Paris) led to an appointment with the Cincinnati SO. He conducted the Philadelphia Orchestra, 1912–38, taking it to the forefront of American ensembles through his vivid direction and giving early performances of music by Rakhmaninov, Varèse and Stravinsky. From 1938 he led an independent career, forming several orchestras and returning to Europe in 1951. He became a controversial figure through his orchestral transcriptions of Bach and others and his revised instrumentation of established classics. An interest in acoustics led him to seek improved tonal quality through unconventional platform arrangements.

Stolle, Philipp (*b* Radeburg, 1614; *d* Halle, 4 Oct 1675). German composer. A colleague of Schütz's, he worked at Dresden and Copenhagen as singer and theorbist; later he was at Halle, where he successfully wrote operas and songs.

Stoltz, Rosine [Noël, Victoire] (*b* Paris, 13 Feb 1815; *d* there, 28 July 1903). French mezzo-soprano. With a fine voice and magnificent stage presence she created (besides several Halévy roles) Ascanio in Berlioz's *Benvenuto Cellini* (1838) and Léonore in Donizetti's *La favorite* (1840).

Stoltzer, Thomas (*b* Schweidnitz, *c* 1480–85; *d* nr. Znaim, early 1526). German composer. He became *magister capellae* at the Hungarian court in Ofen in 1522. After Finck and Hofhaimer he was the most important early 16th-century German composer. *c* 50 works by him survive (masses, motets, hymns and partsongs), all dating from after 1530. His greatest works were his 14 Latin and four German psalm motets: the latter, for five- to seven-part choir, are among the first large-scale vernacular sacred pieces, successfully uniting German features with the style of Josquin. Other works include 39 hymns (published 1542), ten lieder and a cycle of eight five-part instrumental fantasias.

Stolz, Robert (Elisabeth) (*b* Graz, 25 Aug 1880; *d* Berlin, 27 June 1975). Austrian composer and conductor. He was a pupil of Fuchs at the Vienna Conservatory and Humperdinck in Berlin; he lived in Vienna (1907–24), where he wrote songs and operettas, in Berlin (1924–40), where he worked for cabaret and cinema, in the USA (1940–46), where he continued his film work, and again in Vienna. He first enjoyed international popularity with the song *Hallo, du süsse Klingelfee* (1919) and the operetta *Der Tanz ins Glück* (1920).

Stolz [Stolzová], **Teresa** [Teresina] (*b* Kostelec nad Labem, 5 June 1834; *d* Milan, 23 Aug 1902). Bohemian soprano. A leading interpreter of later Verdi – she was the first Italian Aida (1874) and the first soprano in the Requiem (1874) – she was the Verdian dramatic soprano par excellence, powerful, passionate in utterance but dignified in manner and secure in tone and control.

Stolze, Gerhard (*b* Dresden, 1 Oct 1926; *d* Garmisch-Partenkirchen, 11 March 1979). German tenor. He studied in Dresden and Berlin, and sang in those cities and from 1951 at Bayreuth; he was a noted interpreter of Mime and of 20th-century roles.

Stölzel, Gottfried Heinrich (*b* Grünstädtel, Erzgebirge, 13 Jan 1690; *d* Gotha, 27 Nov 1749). German composer. He taught in Breslau from 1710; after presenting his first stage work there (1711–12) and others in Naumburg and Gera, he went to Italy (1713–15) and then Prague. By 1718 he was Kapellmeister at the Gera court, and from 1719 at the court of Saxe-Gotha. He gained a wide reputation as a composer (his music was valued by Bach, among others), teacher and theorist.

Stölzel's output combines traditional Baroque features with more progressive traits. It includes stage works and oratorios (some to his own librettos), numerous masses, over 700 sacred cantatas and *c* 100 secular, and many concertos, trio sonatas and keyboard pieces. Among his writings are treatises on canon (1725) and recitative.

Stone Flower, The [Kamenny tsvetok]. Ballet in a prologue and three acts by Prokofiev to a libretto by M. Mendelson and Lavrosky (1954, Moscow).

Stone Guest, The [Kamennïy gost]. Opera in three acts by Dargomïzhsky, a setting of Pushkin's play (1860s); Rimsky-Korsakov orchestrated it and Cui wrote an overture (1872, St Petersburg).

Stop. Term for the holes of a wind instrument or the key used to block them; also the registers of an organ or harpsichord or the knob drawn to control them.

Stopped flute ensemble. An ensemble, of a kind found throughout Africa, based on sets of end-blown flutes closed (i.e. stopped) at their distal ends by natural nodes or movable tuning plugs. They are mostly single-note flutes, blown by one man while dancing, accompanied by drumming and singing. They have been termed 'reed-pipes', but may be made of materials other than reeds; ensembles of panpipes could also be included in the term.

Stopped notes. On string instruments, notes sounded with the string pressed hard to the fingerboard as opposed to those produced by the full length of the string. On the horn, some notes outside the harmonic series can be obtained by closing the bell to a greater or lesser degree with the bunched fingers of the right hand; a stopped note is also obtained by completely occluding the bell and attacking the note sharply.

Stopped pipe. In organ building, a flue pipe in which the end remote from the mouth is closed by a movable stopper or airtight cap. This provides a means of tuning. In general, any tube that communicates freely with the ambient air at one end and is completely closed at the other. Examples include the clarinet and such folk instruments as end-blown flutes.

Stopping. *See* STOPPED NOTES.

Storace, Bernardo (*fl* late 17th century). Italian composer. He probably came from northern Italy; in 1664 he was *vice-maestro di cappella* to the senate of Messina, Sicily. His keyboard collection (1664), containing many variations on passamezzos and several other bass patterns as well as passacaglias of highly original structure, toccatas and ricercares, is an important link between the music of Frescobaldi and of Pasquini.

Storace, Nancy [Ann Selina] (*b* London, 27 Oct 1765; *d* there, 24 Aug 1817). English soprano, sister of Stephen Storace. She began her operatic career in Italy but moved in 1783 to Vienna, where she married the English composer J.A. Fisher. Highly successful in comic operas there, she created the role of Susanna in Mozart's *Le nozze di Figaro* (1786). Later she sang in her brother's works in London and toured Europe with the tenor John Braham, with whom she lived until 1816.

Storace, Stephen (John Seymour) (*b* London, 4 April 1762; *d* there, 19 March 1796). English composer. The son of Stephen Storace (*c*1725–*c*1781), an Italian double bass player in London, he was trained in Naples. In 1785–6 he presented two Italian operas in Vienna (notably *Gli equivoci*, after

Shakespeare) and may have studied with Mozart, who was a friend of the family (the tenor Michael Kelly was another associate). Returning to London, he composed another Italian opera and in 1788 began a successful series of 15 English dialogue operas. Among these are the afterpiece *No Song, No Supper* (1790) and the full-length opera *The Pirates* (1792), his English masterpiece. All contain borrowed material; some resemble works by Shield, but Storace's insistence that the singers continue to act while singing was new to England. His other works include an all-sung English opera (1792), a ballet (1793), canzonets, arias and instrumental pieces.

Störl, Johann Georg Christian (*b* Kirchberg an der Jagst, 14 Aug 1675; *d* Stuttgart, 26 July 1719). German composer. A pupil of Pachelbel, he held posts as organist (1699) at the Stuttgart court and, after two years in Vienna and Italy, Kapellmeister (1703); he also became Stiftskirche organist (1707). His output includes sacred cantatas, psalms and sonatas for cornett and three trombones.

Stout, Alan B(urrage) (*b* Baltimore, 26 Nov 1932). American composer. He was a pupil of Cowell, Riegger and Holmboe (a year at Copenhagen University, 1954–5, inclined him towards Scandinavian culture) and began teaching at Northwestern University in 1963. He has written numerous sacred works and orchestral, chamber and piano music, synthesizing traditional and experimental techniques.

Stoyanov, Vesselin (*b* Shumen, 20 April 1902; *d* Sofia, 29 June 1969). Bulgarian composer. A pupil of Schmidt in Vienna, he taught at the Sofia Academy from 1937, becoming its director. He was a reflective composer whose works are distinguished by classical, formal logic, monumental scale, expressiveness and rich orchestration; they include three operas, symphonies, piano concertos and chamber music.

Strada del Pò, Anna Maria (*b* ?Bergamo; *fl* 1720–40). Italian soprano. She began her career in Venice and Naples and in 1729–37 worked in London as Handel's leading soprano, creating more roles for him than any other singer, including the title roles in *Partenope* (1730), *Deborah* (1733) and *Alcina* (1735). She alone remained loyal to Handel when his other singers moved to a rival company. Her voice, carefully coached by Handel, had both a large compass and a wide expressive range even if her personal charms were limited ('she was usually called the *Pig*', Burney wrote).

Stradella, Alessandro (*b* Rome, 1 Oct 1644; *d* Genoa, 25 Feb 1682). Italian composer. He spent most of his career in Rome, where he lived independently but composed many works to commissions from Queen Christina of Sweden, the Colonna family and others. Most of his stage works there were prologues and intermezzos, notably for operas by Cavalli and Cesti revived at the new Tordinona Theatre in 1671–2. His life included many scandals and amorous adventures. He left Rome in 1677 after a dispute, and went by way of Venice and Turin (escaping an attempt on his life) to Genoa (1678). His only comic opera, *Il Trespolo tutore*, was given there in c1677; later he presented several other operas, including *Il Corispero*. He was killed there in 1682, again a consequence of an amorous intrigue.

Stradella was one of the leading composers in Italy in his day and one of the most versatile. His music was widely admired, even as far afield as England. Most of it is clearly tonal, and counterpoint features prominently. His vocal output includes c30 stage works, several oratorios and Latin church works and some 200 cantatas (most for solo voice). In his operas the orchestra consists of two violin parts and continuo, but some other works, such as the oratorio *S Giovanni Battista* (1675, Rome), follow the Roman principal of concerto grosso instrumentation. There is a clear differentiation between aria and recitative (which sometimes includes arioso writing), but their succession is still fluid; various aria forms are used. Stradella's 27 surviving instrumental works are mostly of the *sonata da chiesa* type. The scoring and textures of a *Sonata di viole* of his make it the earliest known concerto grosso; it was apparently a model for Corelli's concertos op.6.

Stradivari, Antonio (*b* ?Cremona, 1644; *d* there, 18 Dec 1737). Italian violin maker. Since the end of the 18th century he has been regarded as the greatest. He learnt his craft from Nicolo Amati, making his first violin in 1666 and, until 1680, plucked instruments (probably harps, lutes, mandolins and guitars). From 1680 to 1690 his work moved away from Amati's and his fame spread beyond Cremona; in the 1690s he worked on a new, longer design and adopted more robust features – wider purfling, bolder soundholes, stronger arching. (Though two of his sons worked with him from this time, they seem to have had no independent careers.) By c1715 his instruments reached a peak of perfection both visually (his varnish took on the well-known orange brown colour) and tonally; outstanding examples include the 'Betts' (1704), the 'Alard' (1715) and the 'Messiah' (1716) violins, as well as the 20 or so surviving smaller cellos of this period, noted for their extraordinary sound quality. His instruments are unsurpassed; c650 survive, many used by the world's leading players. Though his style had always been copied, imitations proliferated in the 19th century.

Straeten, Edmond vander [Vanderstraeten, Edmond] (*b* Oudenaarde, 3 Dec 1826; *d* there, 25 Nov 1895). Belgian writer on music. He studied in Brussels with Fétis. Apart from his work as a music critic (*Le nord*) and librarian (Bibliothèque Royale), he wrote extensively on Netherlands music, musical institutions and musicians in the Low Countries, Italy, Spain and France, making his chief contribution in *La musique aux Pays-Bas avant le XIXe siècle* (1867–88). He should not be confused with the German cellist, writer and composer Edmund S. J. van der Straeten (1855–1934).

Strambotto. A form of Italian poetry, also known as *ottava rima* or *rispetto*, in which each stanza had eight 11-syllable lines. Types include the *strambotto toscano* (rhyme scheme *ababab cc*), often set to music in the 15th and 16th centuries, and the *strambotto siciliano* (*ababab*), common to early 17th-century monodies (*arie siciliane*).

Straniera, La. Opera in two acts by Bellini to a libretto by Romani (1829, Milan).

Strascinando (It.). Dragging, i.e. heavily slurred.

Straszny dwór. *See* HAUNTED MANOR, THE.

Stratas, Teresa (*b* Toronto, 26 May 1938). Canadian soprano. She studied in Toronto and made her début as Mimì in 1958 (the role of her Covent Garden début, 1961). She sang at the Met from 1959, in such roles as Micaela (*Carmen*), Mařenka (*Bartered Bride*), Desdemona, Mélisande and Lulu (which she sang in the Paris Opéra complete première, 1979). She is admired for her lyrical *spinto* voice and her keen stage sense.

Strathspey. A Scottish REEL of slower tempo which originated c1750. The music, in common time (crotchet = 160–68 or slower), is characterized by a dotted rhythm.

Strattner, Georg Christoph (*b* Gols, c1644; *d* Weimar, bur. 11 April 1704). German composer. He was a chorister under his cousin Samuel Friedrich Capricornus. In 1666–82 he was Kapellmeister at the Baden-Durlach court, and then at the Barfüsserkirche, Frankfurt, in 1682–92. After a year as a tenor at Weimar he became court vice-Kapellmeister there in 1695; from 1697 he was also director of the opera house. A prolific composer, he especially wrote cantatas (most to biblical texts) and hymns (notably in his edition of Joachim Neander's hymn collection). He also left some ballets and other dramatic works and songs.

Straus, Oscar (*b* Vienna, 6 March 1870; *d* Bad Ischl, 11 Jan 1954). Austrian composer. A pupil of Bruch in Berlin, he worked as a provincial theatre conductor before winning success as a composer of over 40 Viennese operettas; these include *Ein Walzertraum* (1907), *The Chocolate Soldier* (1908), *Der letzte Walzer* (1920). He also wrote film scores and cabaret songs and toured internationally conducting his works.

Strauss. Austrian family of dance musicians and composers, who gave the Viennese waltz its classic expression. Johann (i) (*b* Vienna, 14 March 1804; *d* there, 25 Sept 1849), a violinist in Josef Lanner's dance orchestra, formed a band in 1825 which became famous for its open-air concerts with his original dance music and paraphrases on the symphonic and operatic music of the day, all performed with exquisite precision. He took the band on European tours from 1833, creating a sensation with the fire and finesse of his conducting, violin in hand. His music, its Austrian folk flavour refined by a characteristic rhythmic piquancy (cross-rhythms, syncopations, pauses and rests), includes over 150 sets of waltzes, besides galops, quadrilles (which he introduced to Vienna), marches (notably the Radetzky-Marsch op.228), polkas and potpourris.

He had three sons who were composer-conductors. Johann (ii) (*b* Vienna, 25 Oct 1825; *d* there, 3 June 1899), also a violinist and the most eminent member of the family, directed his own orchestra, 1844–9, in rivalry with his father's; after 1849 the two Strauss bands were merged into one. Vienna's imperial-royal music director for balls, 1863–71, and Austria's best-known ambassador (the 'king of the waltz'), he was acclaimed by swarms of admirers, especially on European tours, 1856–86, and in the USA (1872). In form, his waltzes resemble his father's – slow introduction, five waltzes and coda – but the sections are longer and more organic; the melodies, often inspired, are wide and sweeping, the harmonic and orchestral details richer and more subtle, even Wagnerian in places. Among his most celebrated waltz masterpieces, dating from the 1860s and early 1870s, are *Accellerationen* op.234, *Wiener Bonbons* op.307, *An die schönen, blauen Donau* ('The Blue Danube') op.314, *Wein, Weib und Gesang* op.333 and *Wiener Blut* op.354. Of his 17 operettas, the sparkling *Die Fledermaus* (1874) and the colourful *Die Zigeunerbaron* (1885) deservedly claim a central place in the repertory.

His brother Josef (1827–70), unlike Johann (ii) a melancholy introvert, shared the direction of the family orchestra in the 1850s and 1860s, and composed waltzes in a more serious, Romantic vein, as well as polkas, quadrilles and marches. Their younger brother Eduard (1835–1916), Vienna's imperial-royal music director for balls, 1872–1901, became the best conductor of the family and was much sought after by orchestras throughout Europe.

Strauss, Christoph (*b* ?Vienna, *c*1575–80; *d* Vienna, mid-June 1631). Austrian composer. He served the Habsburg court from 1594, becoming organist at the court church by 1601 and later serving briefly as director of court music. From at least 1626 he was musical director at St Stephen's Cathedral, Vienna. One of the leading Austrian composers of his day, his 36 motets (1613) and 16 masses (1631) include both modern textures (with contrasting vocal and instrumental groups) and polyphony.

Strauss, Richard (Georg) (*b* Munich, 11 June 1864; *d* Garmisch-Partenkirchen, 8 Sept 1949). German composer. His father, a professional horn player, gave him a musical grounding exclusively in the classics, and he composed copiously from the age of six. He went briefly to university, but had no formal tuition in composition. He had several works given in Munich, including a symphony, when he was 17, and the next year a wind serenade in Dresden and a violin concerto in Vienna. At 20, a second symphony was given in New York and he conducted the Meiningen Orchestra in a suite for wind. In 1885 he became conductor of that orchestra, but soon left and visited Italy. He had been influenced by Lisztian and Wagnerian thinking; one result was *Aus Italien*, which caused controversy on its première in 1887. By then Strauss was a junior conductor at the Munich Opera. Other tone poems followed: *Macbeth*, *Don Juan* and *Tod und Verklärung* come from the late 1880s. It is *Don Juan* that, with its orchestral brilliance, its formal command and its vivid evocation of passionate ardour (he was in love with the singer Pauline von Ahna, his future wife), shows his maturity and indeed virtuosity as a composer. With its première, at Weimar (he had moved to a post at the opera house there), he was recognized as the leading progressive composer in Germany. He was ill during 1891–3 but wrote his first opera, *Guntram*, which was a modest success but a failure later in Munich. His conducting

career developed; he directed many major operas, including Wagner at Bayreuth, and returned to Munich in 1896 as chief conductor at the opera. To the late 1890s belong the witty and colourful *Till Eulenspiegel*, a portrait of a disrespectful rogue with whom Strauss clearly had a good deal of sympathy, the graphic yet also poetic and psychologically subtle *Don Quixote* (cast respectively in rondo and variation forms) and *Ein Heldenleben*, 'a hero's life', where Strauss himself is the hero and his adversaries the music critics. There is more autobiography in the *Symphonia domestica* of 1903; he conducted its première during his first visit to the USA, in 1904.

Strauss was now moving towards opera. His *Feuersnot* was given in 1901; in 1904 *Salome* was begun, after Wilde's play. It was given at Dresden the next year. Regarded as blasphemous and salacious, it ran into censorship trouble but was given at 50 opera houses in the next two years. This and *Elektra* (given in 1909) follow up the tone poems in their evocation of atmosphere and their thematic structure; both deal with female obsessions of a disordered, macabre kind, with violent climaxes involving gruesome deaths and impassioned dancing, with elements of abnormal sexuality and corruption, exploiting the female voice pressed to dramatic extremes.

Strauss did not pursue that path. After the violence and dissonance of the previous operas, and their harsh psychological realism, Strauss and his librettist Hofmannsthal turned to period comedy, set in the Vienna of Maria Theresa, for *Der Rosenkavalier*; the score is no less rich in inner detail, but it is applied to the evocation of tenderness, nostalgia and humour, helped by sentimental Viennese waltzes. Again the female voice – but this time its radiance and warmth – is exploited, in the three great roles of the Marschallin, Octavian and Sophie. It was given at Dresden in 1911 with huge success and was soon produced in numerous other opera houses. Strauss followed it with *Ariadne auf Naxos*, at first linked with a Molière play, later revised as prologue (behind the scenes at a private theatre) and opera, mixing *commedia dell'arte* and classical tragedy to a delicate, chamber orchestral accompaniment. The two versions were given in 1912 and (in Vienna) 1916.

Strauss had been conducting in Berlin, the court and opera orchestras, since 1908; in 1919 he took up a post as joint director of the Vienna Staatsoper, where his latest collaboration with Hofmannsthal, *Die Frau ohne Schatten*, was given that year: a work embodying much symbolism and psychology, opulently but finely scored, and regarded by some as one of Strauss's noblest achievements. His busy, international conducting career continued in the inter-war years; there were visits to North and South America as well as to most parts of Europe in the 1920s, which also saw the premières of two more operas, both at Dresden, the autobiographical, domestic comedy *Intermezzo* and *Die ägyptische Helena*. His last Hofmannsthal opera, *Arabella*, an appealing re-creation of some of the atmosphere of *Rosenkavalier*, followed in 1933. Of his remaining operas, *Capriccio* (1942), a 'conversation-piece' in a single act set in the 18th century and dealing with the amorous and artistic rivalries of a poet and a musician, is the most successful, with its witty, graceful, serene score.

During the 1930s Strauss, seeking a smooth and quiet life, had allowed himself to accept – without facing up to their full import – the circumstances created in Germany by the Nazis. For a time he was head of the State Music Bureau and he once obligingly conducted at Bayreuth when Toscanini had withdrawn. But he was frustrated at being unable to work with his Jewish librettist, Stefan Zweig (Hofmannsthal had been part-Jewish), and he protected his Jewish daughter-in-law; during the war years, when he mainly lived in Vienna, he and the Nazi authorities lived in no more than mutual toleration. When Germany was defeated, and her opera houses destroyed, Strauss wrote an intense lament, *Metamorphosen*, for 23 solo strings; this is one of several products of a golden 'Indian summer', which include an oboe concerto and the Four Last Songs, works in a ripe, mellow idiom, executed with a grace worthy of his beloved Mozart. He died in his Garmisch home in 1949.

Operas Guntram (1894); Feuersnot (1901); Salome (1905); Elektra (1909); Der Rosenkavalier (1911); Ariadne auf Naxos (1912, rev. 1916); Die Frau ohne Schatten (1919); Intermezzo (1924); Die ägyptische Helena (1928); Arabella (1933); Die schweigsame Frau (1935); Friedenstag (1938); Daphne (1938); Die Liebe der Danae (1940, perf. 1952); Capriccio (1942)
Instrumental music Aus Italien (1886); Don Juan (1888); Macbeth (1888); Tod und Verklärung (1889); Till Eulenspiegels lustige Streiche (1895); Also sprach Zarathustra (1896); Ein Heldenleben (1898); Don Quixote, vc, orch (1897); Symphonia domestica (1903); Eine Alpensinfonie (1915); Metamorphosen, strs (1945); 2 hn concs. (1883, 1942); Ob Conc. (1945); c50 other works; 15 chamber works; 30 pf works
Vocal music 8 choral works with orchestra; c30 unacc. choral works; nearly 200 songs, including Frühling, September, Beim Schlafengehen, Im Abendrot ['Four Last Songs'] (1948)

Stravaganza, La. Title of Vivaldi's 12 concertos op.4 (c1712–13).

Stravinsky, Fyodor Ignat'yevich (b Noviy Dvor, 20 June 1843; d St Petersburg, 4 Dec 1902). Russian bass of Polish descent, father of Igor Stravinsky. As principal bass at the Mariinsky Theatre, St Petersburg (from 1876), he was especially successful in Russian opera, being noted for his portrayals of Holofernes in Serov's *Judith*, the miller in Dargomïzhsky's *Rusalka* and Varlaam in *Boris Godunov*; he sang in the premières of several Tchaikovsky operas.

Stravinsky, Igor (Fyodorovich) (b Lomonosov, 17 June 1882; d New York, 6 April 1971). Russian composer, later of French (1934) and American (1945) nationality. The son of a leading bass at the Mariinsky Theatre in St Petersburg, he studied with Rimsky-Korsakov (1902–8), who was an influence on his early music, though so were Tchaikovsky, Borodin, Glazunov and (from 1907–8) Debussy and Dukas. This colourful mixture of sources lies behind *The Firebird* (1910), commissioned by Dyagilev for his Ballets Russes. Stravinsky went with the company to Paris in 1910 and spent much of his time in France from then onwards, continuing his associa-

tion with Dyagilev in *Petrushka* (1911) and *The Rite of Spring* (1913).

These scores show an extraordinary development. Both use folktunes, but not in any symphonic manner: Stravinsky's forms are additive rather than symphonic, created from placing blocks of material together without disguising the joins. The binding energy is much more rhythmic than harmonic, and the driving pulsations of *The Rite* marked a crucial change in the nature of Western music. Stravinsky, however, left it to others to use that change in the most obvious manner. He himself, after completing his Chinese opera *The Nightingale*, turned aside from large resources to concentrate on chamber forces and the piano.

Partly this was a result of World War I, which disrupted the activities of the Ballets Russes and caused Stravinsky to seek refuge in Switzerland. He was not to return to Russia until 1962, though his works of 1914–18 are almost exclusively concerned with Russian folk tales and songs: they include the choral ballet *Les noces* ('The Wedding'), the smaller sung and danced fable *Renard*, a short play doubly formalized with spoken narration and instrumental music (*The Soldier's Tale*) and several groups of songs. In *The Wedding*, where block form is geared to highly mechanical rhythm to give an objective ceremonial effect, it took him some while to find an appropriately objective instrumentation; he eventually set it with pianos and percussion. Meanwhile, for the revived Ballets Russes, he produced a startling transformation of 18th-century Italian music (ascribed to Pergolesi) in *Pulcinella* (1920), which opened the way to a long period of 'neo-classicism', or re-exploring past forms, styles and gestures with the irony of non-developmental material being placed in developmental moulds. The Symphonies of Wind Instruments, an apotheosis of the wartime 'Russian' style, was thus followed by the short number-opera *Mavra*, the Octet for wind, and three works he wrote to help him earn his living as a pianist: the Piano Concerto, the Sonata and the Serenade in A.

During this period of the early 1920s he avoided string instruments because of their expressive nuances, preferring the clear articulation of wind, percussion, piano and even pianola. But he returned to the full orchestra to achieve the starkly presented Handel-Verdi imagery of the opera-oratorio *Oedipus rex*, and then wrote for strings alone in *Apollon musagète* (1928), the last of his works to be presented by Dyagilev. All this while he was living in France, and *Apollon*, with its Lullian echoes, suggests an identification with French classicism which also marks the *Duo concertant* for violin and piano and the stage work on which he collaborated with Gide: *Perséphone*, a classical rite of spring. However, his Russianness remained deep. He orchestrated pieces by Tchaikovsky, now established as his chosen ancestor, to make the ballet *Le baiser de la fée*, and in 1926 he rejoined the Orthodox Church. The Symphony of Psalms was the first major work in which his ritual music engaged with the Christian tradition.

The other important works of the 1930s, apart from *Perséphone*, are all instrumental, and include the Violin Concerto, the Concerto for two pianos, the post-Brandenburg 'Dumbarton Oaks' Concerto and the Symphony in C, which disrupts diatonic normality on its home ground. It was during the composition of this work, in 1939, that Stravinsky moved to the USA, followed by Vera Sudeikina, whom he had loved since 1921 and who was to be his second wife (his first wife and his mother had both died earlier the same year). In 1940 they settled in Hollywood, which was henceforth their home. Various film projects ensued, though all foundered, perhaps inevitably: the Hollywood cinema of the period demanded grand continuity; Stravinsky's patterned discontinuities were much better suited to dancing. He had a more suitable collaborator in Balanchine, with whom he had worked since *Apollon*, and for whom in America he composed *Orpheus* and *Agon*. Meanwhile music intended for films went into orchestral pieces, including the Symphony in Three Movements (1945).

The later 1940s were devoted to *The Rake's Progress*, a parable using the conventions of Mozart's mature comedies and composed to a libretto by Auden and Kallman. Early in its composition, in 1948, Stravinsky met Robert Craft, who soon became a member of his household and whose enthusiasm for Schoenberg and Webern (as well as Stravinsky) probably helped make possible the gradual achievement of a highly personal serial style after *The Rake*. The process was completed in 1953 during the composition of the brilliant, tightly patterned *Agon*, though most of the serial works are religious or commemorative, being sacred cantatas (*Canticum sacrum, Threni, Requiem Canticles*) or elegies (*In memoriam Dylan Thomas, Elegy for J.F.K.*). All these were written after Stravinsky's 70th birthday, and he continued to compose into his mid-80s, also conducting concerts and making many gramophone records of his music. During this period, too, he and Craft published several volumes of conversations.

Operas The Nightingale (1914); Mavra (1922); Oedipus rex, opera-oratorio (1927); The Rake's Progress (1951)
Miscellaneous dramatic music The Soldier's Tale (1918); Renard (1922); The Flood (1962)
Ballets The Firebird (1910); Petrushka (1911); The Rite of Spring (1913); Song of the Nightingale (1919); Pulcinella (1920); The Wedding (1923); Apollon musagète (1928); Le baiser de la fée (1928); Perséphone (1934); Jeu de cartes (1937); Circus Polka (1942); Scènes de ballet (1944); Orpheus (1948); Agon (1957)
Orchestral music Sym., E♭ (1907); Fireworks (1908); Syms. of Wind Insts (1920); Pf Conc., pf, wind, timp, dbs (1924); Capriccio, pf, orch (1929); Vn Conc., D (1931); Conc. 'Dumbarton Oaks' (1938); Sym., C (1940); Danses concertantes (1942); Circus Polka (1942); 4 Norwegian Moods (1942); Ode (1943); Sym. in 3 movts (1945); Ebony Conc. (1945); Conc., D, str (1946); Movements, pf, orch (1959); Variations (1964)
Choral music The King of the Stars (1912); Sym. of Psalms (1930); Babel (1944); Mass (1948); Cantata (1952); Canticum sacrum (1955); Threni (1958); A Sermon, a Narrative and a Prayer (1961); The Dove Descending (1962); Introitus (1965); Requiem Canticles (1966)
Solo vocal music Two Bal'mont Poems (1911); Three Japanese Lyrics (1913); Pribaoutki (1914); Berceuses du chat (1916); 3 Shakespeare Songs (1953); In memoriam Dylan Thomas (1954); Abraham and Isaac (1963); Elegy for J.F.K. (1964); The Owl and the Pussy-Cat (1966)
Chamber music 3 Pieces, str qt (1914); 3 Pieces, cl (1919); Concertino, str qt (1920); Octet (1923); Duo concertant (1932); Septet (1953); Epitaphium, fl, cl, harp (1959)
Piano music 4 Studies (1908); Piano-Rag-Music (1919); Sonata (1924); Serenade, A (1925); Conc., 2 pf (1935); Sonata, 2 pf (1944)

Street cries. Calls of street vendors involving a melodic motif have often been used in music, chiefly in the QUODLIBET. Well-known English examples are fantasias for voices and instruments by Weelkes, Orlando Gibbons and Deering.

Streich, Rita (*b* Barnaul, 18 Dec 1920; *d* Vienna, 20 March 1987). German soprano. A pupil of Domgraf-Fassbänder, Ivogün and Berger, she made her début as Zerbinetta (1943, Aussig) and sang at the Berlin Staatsoper, 1946–51, in such roles as Blonde, Gilda and Olympia; in 1951 she moved to the Berlin Städtische Oper and the Vienna Staatsoper in 1953. She was a noted Queen of Night, and made her American début as Sophie (1957, San Francisco). In the 1960s and 1970s she was chiefly admired as a sensitive lieder singer.

Streicher. Austrian firm of piano makers. It was founded in 1802 in Vienna by Nannette (Maria Anna) Stein Streicher (1769–1833), who had learnt from her father J.A. STEIN. The most eminent firm in Vienna, having contacts with Beethoven and Hummel, it perfected the Viennese action; after the mid-19th century (the firm ceased in 1896) it built more Anglo-German and English actions. Surviving Streicher grands are beautifully veneered and usually have four pedals.

Streicher, Theodor (*b* Vienna, 7 June 1874; *d* Wetzelsdorf, 28 May 1940). Austrian composer, born into the family of piano makers. His 30 *Wunderhorn* songs (1903) brought him wide acclaim as Wolf's successor in German song, but later lieder were less regarded.

Strepitoso (It.). Noisy, loud.

Strepponi, Giuseppina [Clelia Maria Josepha] (*b* Lodi, 8 Sept 1815; *d* Sant'Agata, 14 Nov 1897). Italian soprano, second wife of Verdi. Although her stage career was brief (1834–46) and limited largely to Italy, she aroused special admiration as Donizetti's Lucia, Bianca in Mercadante's *Il giuramento* and most of Bellini's heroines, being praised for her smooth, limpid voice, excellent technique and deep feeling. Donizetti wrote his *Adelia* (1841) for her and she created the role of Abigaille in Verdi's *Nabucco* (1842). From 1846 she taught singing in Paris.

Stretto. (1) In fugue, the introduction of two or more subject entries in close succession (e.g. Bach, *Das wohltemperierte Clavier*, i, no.1, bars 7–8). A 'stretto maestrale' involves all the voices in a fugue (Bach, ibid, i, no.22, bars 67–71). 'False stretto' occurs when at least one voice does not complete the subject (Bach, ibid, ii, no.5, bars 27–9; alto incomplete).

(2) The term is sometimes used, alternatively with *stretta*, to indicate a faster tempo at a point of climax, particularly in an operatic finale.

Strich (Ger.). 'Stroke', 'line': in bowing *Aufstrich* is upbow, *Niederstrich* downbow. A *Taktstrich* is a bar-line.

Strict counterpoint. The rigorous application of the principles of consonance and dissonance, and of part-writing in the fitting of a polyphonic voice or voices to a given melodic line (*cantus firmus*). INVERTIBLE COUNTERPOINT and SPECIES COUNTERPOINT are strict, as opposed to FREE COUNTERPOINT.

Stride. A solo jazz piano style that arose after 1910 in Harlem, New York, largely derived from ragtime, adapting ragtime's left-hand patterns to form the distinctive 'stride bass'. The style generally called for fast tempos, use of the piano's full range and many pianistic devices.

Striggio, Alessandro (*b* Mantua, *c*1540; *d* there, 29 Feb 1592). Italian composer. A Mantuan nobleman and principal composer at the Medici court in Florence from the 1560s, he was in charge of music there and composed *intermedi* for state occasions. In 1567 he was a political emissary to the English court and he also had contacts with the Munich court. In 1584 he visited Ferrara, then went to the Gonzaga court in Mantua as a musician. A leading composer of *intermedi* and other stage music (now lost), he was also a fine madrigalist (7 bks, 1558–97) and wrote sacred music; his success is shown by the many anthologies and foreign MSS that contain his works. He was also famous as a player of the *lirone* and the viol.

His son, also Alessandro (*b* Mantua, *c*1573; *d* Venice, *c*15 June 1630), a Mantuan diplomat, wrote opera librettos, notably for the *Orfeo* (1607) of Monteverdi, of whom he was a friend and correspondent.

String. A length of any material (commonly gut, silk, wire or plastic) that can produce a musical sound when stretched and then excited (by bowing, plucking, striking etc).

Various factors influence the sound produced by a vibrating string. If it, or the air in contact with it, is damped, the upper harmonics are reduced and the pattern of sound decay is affected. The stiffness of the string increases the sharpness of the harmonics with relation to the fundamental ('inharmonicity'); the greater this is, the more the sound approaches that of a bell. Any inequality of thickness or straightness in a string will cause a distortion of the harmonic series and may introduce beats into the sound.

The material chosen for strings depends on the required pitch and tone. Bass strings must have their mass increased to produce a drop in frequency if they are not to be of impractical length, so they are thicker, and often overspun with wire. The more powerful the tone the stronger the strings must be; thus piano strings are much heavier in size and material than, for example, violin ones.

String drum. A friction drum in the form of a cylindrical vessel with one end open and the other closed with a membrane. A length of resined cord is passed through a hole, pulled tight and rubbed with a coarse glove, the drum membrane acting as a resonator. The end of the string may be loosely attached to a wooden handle, forming a whirled fric-

tion drum. The instrument, also called 'lion's roar', is known in Europe, China and India.

Stringendo (It.). 'Drawing tight', 'squeezing': a direction to perform with more tension, therefore faster.

String [stringed] instruments. Instruments sounded by the vibration of strings; their organological name is 'chordophones'. They fall into several groups: the zither types (including those with resonators, such as the dulcimer and the piano); the lute and lyre types (including the guitar and such 'bowed lutes' as the violin and the viol); and harp types. String instruments are set in vibration by striking, plucking or bowing the strings. The term 'strings' is often used collectively for the group of violin (and viol) family instruments that form the basis of the Western orchestra, normally two groups of violins, with violas, cellos and double basses.

For further information see under the names of individual instruments; for illustration, *see* VIOLIN, LUTE and EARLY MUSIC.

String quartet. A composition for four solo string instruments, usually two violins, viola and cello. The genre was not firmly established until the time of Haydn, though its origin may be located in various late Baroque compositions. With Haydn's op.9 (1769–70) a four-movement scheme was established, along with a generally well-distributed four-part texture. In his op.33 quartets (1781), which introduce the scherzo into the genre, Haydn achieved a new clarity of structure and balance of texture (though brilliant writing for the first violin always remained part of his style). In his op.76 a new experimentalism appears, with features anticipating Beethoven.

No contemporary except Mozart reached the level sustained by Haydn in the medium, but many other composers, among them Vanhal, Boccherini (some 100 quartets each) and Ordonez (over 30), made quartet writing a major preoccupation. Mozart's quartets were influenced by the Milanese style of G.B. Sammartini's with their 'singing allegros' dominated by the first violin, and it was not until he wrote the set dedicated to Haydn (1782–5) that Mozart attained a fully integrated quartet style. Italian composers, including Cambini and Boccherini, developed a more lyrical style, often with virtuoso first-violin writing. This style was taken up in France by Gossec, Viotti and others and in Germany by Spohr. It is not to be confused with that of the QUATUOR CONCERTANT, in which all the instruments share the interest.

Vienna remained an important centre for the quartet in the first quarter of the 19th century and nourished the most important developments in the medium. Beethoven's op.18 quartets are written largely within the framework of an established convention, but no.1 in F already hints at the expansion of scale that marks the Razumovsky Quartets op.59 as belonging to the post-'Eroica' period. With op.59 counterpoint assumes a new dramatic purpose, and the slow movements of the middle-period quartets are scored with an ear for richly sonorous and elaborated textures. The late quartets show still more contrapuntal interest and textural variety; the range of Beethoven's imagination outdistances that of his contemporaries in every respect, and individual quartets may encompass both deep seriousness and lighthearted gaiety without incongruity.

The early Romantics, among whom Schubert and Mendelssohn were outstanding quartet writers, took the middle-period rather than the late quartets of Beethoven as their starting-point. They also borrowed features (including the tremolo, much used in Schubert's three masterpieces of 1824–6) from orchestral and piano writing; pianistic figurations play an even larger part in Schumann's quartets. Many lesser composers in Germany chose to follow Spohr's example, writing variations on popular airs, potpourris and *quatuors brillants*. In France few composers escaped the tyranny of the *quatuor brillant*, though the quartets of M.A. Guénin and Cherubini rise above the average; Berlioz (like such other 'progressive' composers as Liszt and Wagner) wrote no quartets. Italy had little to offer before Verdi's E minor Quartet of 1873.

The string quartet seemed to present few possibilities to late 19th-century composers preoccupied with the grandiose conceptions of the symphony and symphonic poem; Smetana's E minor Quartet 'From my Life' (1876) is a rare instance of a programmatic quartet. The genre found stronger adherents among composers such as Brahms and Reger, who continued in the Classical tradition, but it also attracted the attention of Dvořák and of the Russian nationalist school. Both Borodin and Tchaikovsky introduced folktunes into their quartets.

The revival of chamber music in France owed a good deal to Franck, whose D major Quartet (1889) uses cyclic methods. It has been followed by the quartets of Debussy and Ravel (also with cyclic elements), Fauré, Milhaud and others. The medium has absorbed the various neo-classical, atonal, serial, nationalist and other idioms of the 20th century, and explored a wide variety of experimental textures, but few important composers have made the genre central to their output. An exception, perhaps, is Bartók, whose six quartets have been widely recognized as the true successors of Beethoven's late quartets in the sense that they extend the expressive range of the medium and have been enormously influential. The 15 of Shostakovich also represent a significant contribution to the form. Most other composers of international repute have been content to write a few or even isolated examples. Among the best known are those of Bloch, Ives, Hindemith, Schoenberg, Webern, Berg, Britten, Tippett, Lutosławski and Carter.

String quintet. A composition for five string instruments. The early history of the quintet for two violins, two violas and cello is similar to that of the string quartet, though the repertory is smaller. Outstanding are the mature quintets of Mozart, which realize fully the textural richness and variety of which the medium is capable. The quintets of Beethoven and Mendelssohn are not among their finest chamber works; and in the later 19th century only

Brahms's two are on a high level. Martinů and Milhaud are among the few 20th-century composers to have used the medium.

The quintet for two violins, one viola and two cellos has also been extensively cultivated. Its chief exponent in the 18th century was Boccherini, who composed over 100, and the repertory includes one towering masterpiece, Schubert's Quintet in C D956. Of the few works in which a double bass replaces the second cello, the best-known is Dvořák's op.77.

String trio. A composition for three string instruments, either two violins and a cello or violin, viola and cello. The former combination was an outgrowth of the Baroque trio sonata, and in such trios by Haydn, Boccherini, Dittersdorf and others it is often uncertain whether or not a continuo instrument was still envisaged. Orchestral performance was often permissible as well. After *c*1770 the trio for violin, viola and cello began to take precedence. Haydn may have been the first to use this combination, soon followed by Simon Le Duc, Boccherini and Giardini. The same period saw the development of the *trio concertant* (*see* QUATUOR CONCERTANT), of which Mozart's Divertimento K563 is a supreme example. The string trios of Beethoven and Schubert complete the most valuable part of the Classical repertory.

The slender nature of the medium seems to have been unattractive to later 19th-century composers, one of the few rewarding examples being Dvořák's Terzetto for the rather unusual combination of two violins and viola. Among 20th-century trios for the conventional combination, those of Webern and Schoenberg are particularly admired.

Strobel, Valentin (*b* Halle, bap. 18 Oct 1611; *d* Strasbourg, after 1669). German composer and lutenist. His main court posts were at Darmstadt (from 1629) and at Strasbourg (1634–8), where he remained later. In his playing he used the new French arpeggiated style; he wrote lute music and a few vocal pieces. His father, Valentin (*c*1575/80–1640), was also a lutenist and composer.

Stroe, Aurel (*b* Bucharest, 5 May 1932). Romanian composer. A pupil of Andricu at the Bucharest Conservatory (1951–6), where he began teaching in 1962, he also studied at Darmstadt (1966–9). His music, in several genres, uses avant-garde techniques; one of his aims is to create a complex work uniting visual and musical forms with technological resources (e.g. in the cycle of eight orchestral pieces *Démarche musicale*, 1971).

Strogers, Nicholas (*fl* 1560–75). English composer. He was parish clerk at St Dunstan in the West, London (1564–75), and in charge of music there. His compositions, which include service music, consort music and consort songs, show a pleasing melodic gift; particularly appealing is *A doleful deadly pang*, with its D major coda to the repeated 'I die' of the text. His Short Service was widely copied.

Stroh violin. A type of violin developed by Augustus Stroh (1828–1914), *c*1900, for early recording studios. It consisted of a narrow piece of wood incorporating a fingerboard; a metal horn attached to a flexible membrane was mounted by the bridge, helping to amplify and direct the string sound which in conventional instruments was too soft and diffuse to record well. A single-string variant, the Phono-fiddle, was introduced in 1904.

Stromentato. Short for *recitativo stromentato*, i.e. RECITATIVE accompanied by instruments (normally the orchestra).

Strong, George Templeton (*b* New York, 26 May 1856; *d* Geneva, 27 June 1948). American composer. A pupil of Jadassohn in Leipzig from 1879, he lived in Wiesbaden and visited Weimar, and became associated with Liszt's circle. He taught in the USA, 1891–2, but in 1892 settled in Switzerland, composing in a style influenced by Raff, Liszt and Tchaikovsky. His works include three programmatic symphonies, symphonic poems, songs and piano pieces.

Strophic variations. Term for a structure used in early 17th-century Italian vocal music in which the melody of the first strophe is varied in subsequent strophes while the bass remains essentially the same. Strophic variations are found in opera (e.g. 'Possente spirto' in Act 3 of Monteverdi's *Orfeo*), in solo songs and duets and in the early CANTATA.

Strozzi, Barbara (*b* Venice, 6 Aug 1619; *d* ?Venice, after 1663). Italian composer and singer, adopted daughter of Giulio Strozzi. She was a pupil of Cavalli and a leading singer in Venice. Her works, among them madrigals (some to texts by Fiulio Strozzi), cantatas and ariettas, reflect Cavalli's influence. Bantatas such as *Lagrime mie* (1659) show a sure handling of form as well as numerous imaginative touches.

Strozzi, Giulio (*b* Venice, 1583; *d* there, 31 March 1652). Italian librettist. He was one of the poets involved in the creation of Venetian opera. Among his librettos are *La finta pazza Licori* (set by Monteverdi, 1627), *La finta pazza* (Sacrati, 1641) and *Veremonda* (Cavalli, 1652). A number of his smaller-scale texts were also set by Venetian composers. Barbara Strozzi was his adopted daughter; the composer and Camerata member Piero Strozzi (*c*1550–1610), an amateur musician who fostered new music through the Camerata, was a relative of his.

Strozzi, Gregorio (*b* S Severino, *c*1615; *d* ?Naples, after 1687). Italian composer. He worked as organist and chaplain in Amalfi and Naples. His *Capricci da sonare*, probably an early work (but published in 1687), contains 29 keyboard pieces, covering almost every form found in keyboard music at the time: contrapuntal capriccios, ricercars and sonatas, virtuoso toccatas, dance pieces, variations and an intabulated madrigal. He also wrote some sacred music and instructional pieces.

Structuralism. A mode of 20th-century thinking that sees human phenomena as 'structures' rather than elements; it seeks to uncover the laws governing their relationships. Music, as so concerned with relationships between ideas, lends itself to structuralist analysis (or 'semiology of music').

Structures sonores. Generic name for the instruments and sound sculptures invented since 1952 by Bernard and François Baschet, many of them on the principle of the NAIL VIOLIN. It has also been used as the name of two ensembles who perform on the instruments. The Baschets' system of mechanical transmission produces strong vibrations which create a sustained resonance for several seconds after the activation of the sound-source has ceased. Best known are the *orgues de cristal*, in which glass rods are stroked by wet fingers, and which are used in the soundtrack of the film *The Dream of the Wild Horses* (1960).

Strungk, Nicolaus Adam (*b* Brunswick, bap. 15 Nov 1640; *d* Dresden, 23 Sept 1700). German composer. He first worked as a court violinist at Wolfenbüttel and at Celle, and in 1661–5 was at the Viennese court. After a period at Hanover, he was director of music to the cathedral and city of Hamburg, 1678–92, where he had several operas staged. He returned to Hanover as court composer and organist (1682–6); in 1685 he visited Italy. In 1688 he became vice-Kapellmeister and chamber organist at Dresden, and in 1692 Kapellmeister. Later he presented at least eight operas in Leipzig. Of his 18 or more operas, the Hamburg works *Esther* (1680) and *Semiramis* (1681) were especially successful. He also wrote sacred and instrumental music and songs. His father, Delphin Strungk (*c*1600–1694), was a composer and organist at Brunswick.

Strunk, (William) Oliver (*b* Ithaca, NY, 22 March 1901; *d* Grottaferrata, 24 Feb 1980). American musicologist. He studied at Cornell University (1917–19) and after studies in composition returned as a musicology student of Kinkeldey (1926–7). After a year at Berlin University he joined the staff of the Library of Congress (1928) and in 1934 became head of its music department. From 1937 to 1966 he taught at Princeton. Strunk was a founder of American musicology and one of its most influential practitioners. His publications cover Byzantine music, the Italian Ars Nova, 15th-century English polyphony, the 16th-century motet, Palestrina, Haydn's style and Verdi's operas. His best-known work is *Source Readings in Music History* (1950), a critical anthology of writings.

Strutz, Thomas (*b* Stargard, *c*1621; *d* Danzig, bur. 5 Oct 1678). German composer. Active in Danzig, he was organist at Holy Trinity from 1642 and at St Mary's from 1668. He aimed to reform the liturgy by the use of simpler, more accessible music, and mainly wrote sacred works for small forces – simple sacred songs, dramatic dialogues, small concertos and oratorio Passions. His oratorio Passion of 1664 is similar to Schütz's *Die sieben Worte*.

Stuart, Leslie (*b* Southport, 15 March 1864; *d* Richmond, Surrey, 27 March 1928). English composer. He wrote well-known music-hall songs (*Lily of Laguna*, 1898) and musical comedies (*Florodora*, 1899).

Stück (Ger.). 'Piece'; hence *Klavierstück*, piano piece; *Fantasiestück*, fantasy piece.

Stuck, Jean-Baptiste (*b* 1680; *d* Paris, 8 Dec 1755). Italian composer and cellist. From 1705 he worked in Paris, where the Prince of Carignan and the Duke of Orléans were his patrons. His solo performances helped to popularize the cello in France. His finest works are 20 French solo and duet cantatas (1706–14), the later ones fusing Italian and French styles. He also composed three French operas, an Italian opera (1715, Livorno) and sacred music, *airs* etc.

Stuckenschmidt, H(ans) H(einz) (*b* Strasbourg, 1 Nov 190*r*). German critic and musicologist. He studied privately and was self-taught in music theory and history. He first worked as a freelance composer and writer, concerned particularly with new music, in various cities, notably Prague. But in the 1930s and 1940s he was banned from journalistic activity. In 1946 he became director of new music at RIAS, Berlin, and critic of the *Neue Zeitung* (1947). Subsequently he taught at the Technical University, Berlin, and was Berlin music correspondent for several leading newspapers. A sound judge and indefatigable supporter of contemporary music, he gave early recognition to Schoenberg and Stravinsky in particular; the former, of whom he has written a comprehensive biography, is central in his many books and essays.

Study (Fr. *étude*). An instrumental piece designed primarily to exploit and perfect a particular facet of performing technique. Before 1800 a variety of terms was used for didactic pieces, but the early 19th century brought a flood of teaching material aimed at the amateur and budding professional: the studies of Cramer, the earlier parts of Clementi's *Gradus ad Parnassum*, Moscheles's *Studien* op.70 and the many collections of Czerny. The origins of the concert study, intended as much for public performance as for private instruction, can be traced to Liszt's *Etude en 12 exercises* (*c*1827), revised as the *Grandes études* (1839) and again as the *Etudes d'éxécution transcendante* (1852). Meanwhile Chopin had revealed the poetic possibility of the study in his opp.10 and 25, each including 12 pieces. Piano studies in sets of 12 were also published by Alkan (two sets, covering all 24 keys) and Debussy. Studies for many other instruments have been written in the 19th and 20th centuries, and the word 'study' (or its equivalents in other languages) has been used in the titles of numerous orchestral works, including Stravinsky's *Quatre études pour orchestre* (1929) and Rawsthorne's *Symphonic Studies* (1939).

Sturgeon, N(?icholas) (*d* 31 May–8 June 1454). English composer. In addition to serving in the Chapel Royal, 1413–52, he held canonries (notably at Windsor and St Paul's) and other posts. His seven surviving compositions are in the second layer of the Old Hall MS, in score or parts (though these do not differ greatly in style). He does not appear to have used plainchant in his mass movements, but only in his one extant motet possibly, like a related motet by Damett, composed for the Agincourt victory celebrations.

Sturm und Drang (Ger.). 'Storm and stress': a movement in German letters, reflected in the other arts, that reached its highpoint in the 1770s. Its aim was to frighten, to stun, to overcome with emotion; it emphasized an anti-rational, subjective approach to the arts. The young Goethe was the leading figure. In music, 'Sturm und Drang' tendencies are found in Gluck's *Don Juan* ballet (1761) and the Furies scene in his *Orfeo ed Euridice* (1762), in the melodramas of Georg Benda (1774–5) and in such Mozart works as *Idomeneo* (1781) and *Don Giovanni* (1787). The impassioned, minor-key symphonies composed by Haydn and others *c*1770 may also be seen as a 'Sturm und Drang' phenomenon.

Sturzenegger, Richard (*b* Zurich, 18 Dec 1905; *d* Berne, 24 Oct 1976). Swiss composer and cellist. He was a pupil of Boulanger and Casals in Paris. From 1935 he worked in Berne as a cellist (including in the Berne Quartet), teacher and composer, becoming director of the Berne Conservatory in 1963. His output includes four cello concertos, choral and chamber works in a tonal style.

Stutschewsky, Joachim (*b* Romny, 7 Feb 1891; *d* Tel-Aviv, 14 Nov 1982). Israeli composer of Ukrainian origin. Trained at the Leipzig Conservatory, he was the cellist of the Kolisch Quartet, a soloist, composer, teacher and writer. He moved in 1938 to Palestine, where he became a respected musical figure. His works, in most non-dramatic genres, pointed the way towards a national style based on Jewish folk music. His writings include the influential *Die Kunst des Cellospiels* (1929–38).

Stuttgart Opera. German company, formerly the Württemberg court opera. In the 18th century and in the 20th it helped make the town an important musical centre. It has a large repertory; its many premières have included *Ariadne auf Naxos* (1912) conducted by Strauss and works by Hindemith and Orff.

Style brisé (Fr.). 'Broken style': term for a broken, arpeggiated texture in keyboard music; it has been used to characterize the transference to the harpsichord of lute figuration, particularly in mid-17th-century French music.

Subdominant. The fourth step or degree of the major or minor scale, so called because it lies as much below the tonic as the dominant lies above the tonic, i.e. a 5th (not because it lies a step below the dominant).

Subito (It.). Suddenly, immediately.

Subject. A theme on which a composition is based. In FUGUE the term may refer to the main theme in general, or it may distinguish its initial form from that of the ANSWER that follows. In SONATA FORM the term is used for each of the two principal themes or groups of themes in the exposition.

The term 'subject group' is often used for each of the two sections that make up the exposition of a movement in sonata form, implying several musical ideas defined by function rather than their nature as themes.

Submediant. The sixth step or degree of the major or minor scale, so called because it lies as much below the tonic as the mediant lies above the tonic (i.e. a 3rd).

Subotnick, Morton (*b* Los Angeles, 14 April 1933). American composer. A pupil of Milhaud and Kirchner at Denver University and Mills College, he has taught at various institutions, since 1969 at the California Institute of the Arts. He has composed mostly electronic music realized on Buchla synthesizers and in computer studios. His works include *Silver Apples of the Moon* (1967); with *Two Life Histories* (1977) he started a series of 'ghost' works for orchestra, ensemble, voices and tape.

Subtonic. The seventh scale degree in a harmonic context; in a melodic context it is called the leading note.

Suchoň, Eugen (*b* Pezinok, 25 Sept 1908). Slovak composer. A pupil of Kafenda at the Bratislava Academy and of Novák at the Prague Conservatory (1931–3), he returned to teach in Bratislava at the academy (from 1933) and university (1959–74). He composed at first in a nationalist style and then, from the 1950s, in a modally inflected serial manner. His works include operas (*The Whirlpool*, 1949; *Svätopluk*, 1959), orchestral and choral music and folksong arrangements.

Suchý, František (*b* Březové Hory u Příbrami, 21 April 1891; *d* Prague, 13 June 1973). Czech composer. He was a pupil of Horník and Stecker at the Prague Conservatory (1913–14) and attended Nikisch's conducting classes. His music is direct and simple, influenced by the folk music of his native mining region. He wrote on a range of subjects.

Another František Suchý (1902–77), unrelated, was a pupil of Kvapil and Novák, a leading oboist who taught at the Brno Conservatory, and composer of four symphonies etc in a neo-classical style.

Sudrophone. A group of valved brass instruments, of soprano to contrabass pitch, invented by the Parisian maker François Sudre and patented in 1892. Acoustically they resembled the saxhorns, but the shape was different as the main tube was doubled back on itself, giving a vertical appearance. Sudrophones included a device, based on a movable silk membrane, to modify the tone at the player's will.

Sugár, Rezső (*b* Budapest, 9 Oct 1919). Hungarian composer. He was a pupil of Kodály at the Budapest Academy (1937–42), where he began teaching in 1968. His works, in many genres, show influences from Bartók and Honegger, the latter particularly in his oratorio *Heroic Song* (1951) and cantata *Kelemen the Mason* (1958).

Suggia, Guilhermina (*b* Oporto, 27 June 1888; *d* there, 31 July 1950). Portuguese cellist. She studied in Leipzig, then lived and worked with Casals, 1906–12. She later went to England, where her warm and graceful playing was much admired.

Suite. An ordered set of instrumental pieces meant to be performed at a single sitting; in the Baroque period, an instrumental genre consisting of several movements in the same key, some or all of them based on the forms and styles of dance music (other terms for the Baroque groups of dances include PARTITA, OVERTURE, ORDRE and SONATA DA CAMERA).

The practice of pairing dances goes back at least to the 14th century, but the earliest known groups called 'suite' are *suyttes de bransles* by Estienne du Tertre (1557). These, however, constitute the raw material for a dance sequence rather than a sequence that would actually be played. Most dance groups from the 1540s to the end of the century are pairs, a pavan or passamezzo with a galliard or saltarello. The impulse towards suite-like groupings seems to have emanated from England at the turn of the century, with William Brade and Giovanni Coprario, but the first publication of suite-like groupings as uniformly constituted composite works was Peuerl's *Newe Padouan, Intrada, Däntz und Galliarda* (1611), where the title's four dances recur in ten 'suites' united by key and thematic material. Schein's *Banchetto musicale* (1617) contains 20 sequences of *paduana, gagliarda, courente, allmande* and *tripla,* similarly unified.

The development of the 'classical' suite, consisting of allemande, courante, sarabande and gigue in that order (A–C–S–G), took place in two stages. The initiative for the A–C–S group probably lay with the Parisian lutenists or the dancing-masters of the French court; the first such groups that can be firmly dated occur in the *Tablature de mandore de la composition du Sieur Chancy* (1629). The gigue enjoyed only scattered acceptance when it began to appear in suite formations after 1650, and at first it rarely assumed its classical position at the end. Froberger left only one authentic A–C–S–G suite; his usual structure of A–G–C–S was altered by his first publishers in 1697–8, by which time the norm had been set for German composers by Buxtehude, Böhm and Kuhnau. In England the suite with gigue was exceptional (the gigue does not appear in Purcell's suites, for example), and in France during Louis XIV's reign it was common in viol and harpsichord suites to follow the A–C–S–G group with other dances. Features of the French harpsichord suite of L. Couperin, D'Angelbert and others include the PRÉLUDE NON MESURÉE and the tendency to bring together existing pieces (sometimes by a different composer). There are only five more or less classical suites among François Couperin's 27 *ordres* – in nos. 1, 2, 3, 5 and 8, each consisting of five to ten pieces. The others include programmatically linked groups and miscellanies.

The French also used the ensemble and orchestral suite, the latter often composed of pieces from diverse sources (especially Lully's operas and ballets). Many began with an overture, and the 'overture-suite' was enthusiastically taken up by Germans, including J.S. Kusser, J.C.F. Fischer and Georg Muffat. Telemann claimed to have composed no fewer than 200, but Bach's four orchestral suites and Handel's Water Music and Music for the Royal Fireworks show the genre at its best.

In their other suites both Bach and Handel usually followed the pattern prelude–A–C–S–X–G (where X is one or more extra dances or dance pairs). Handel's keyboard suites, numbering about 22, are mostly compiled from pieces which already existed. Bach showed more interest in the genre, with six cello suites, three partitas for solo violin and sets of six English suites, French suites and partitas for harpsichord. Bach uses the suite as a building-block in a larger whole, arranging each one to do something different – or the same thing in a different way – so that the set is a kind of thesaurus of the suite for that particular medium.

After 1750 the sonata, symphony and concerto began to fill the suite's functions. To write a suite became an archaic exercise, as with Mozart's K399/385i and the much later suites à l'antique of Ravel, Debussy, Strauss, Hindemith and Schoenberg. In the 19th century the title 'suite' was increasingly used either for an orchestral selection from a larger work (especially a ballet or opera) or for a sequence of pieces loosely connected by a descriptive programme (e.g. Holst's The Planets) or by an exotic or nationalistic one (as in some of the suites of Grieg, Sibelius, Tchaikovsky and Rimsky-Korsakov). Independence from dance forms means that the genre can be said to encompass works to which the title 'suite' was not given, including Schumann's piano cycles, Schoenberg's Five Orchestral Pieces and Stockhausen's Momente.

Suite bergamasque. Piano work by Debussy (1890).

Suivez (Fr.). 'Follow': an indication that the next movement or section should follow without a break, or a direction that the accompanying parts should follow a soloist whose part is moving independently of the prescribed rhythm or tempo.

Suk, Josef (i) (b Křečovice, 4 Jan 1874; d Benešov, 29 May 1935). Czech composer and violinist. He studied at the Prague Conservatory, 1885–92, where he was Dvořák's favourite pupil, and in 1898 married his daughter. Dvořák was, too, the dominant influence on his early music, as in the Serenade for strings (1892) and the Fairy Tale suite (1900); later, most notably in the vast symphony Asrael (1906) – written under the impact of the deaths of his wife and his father-in-law – he developed a more personal style comparable with Mahler's in structural mastery and emotional force. He drew little on folk music. Other works include two published quartets (he was second violinist in the Czech Quartet for most of his life and played in over 4000 concerts), piano pieces (Things Lived and Dreamed, 1909) and a group of symphonic poems, A Summer's Tale (1909), The Ripening (1917) and the choral-orchestral Epilog (1929). From 1922 he directed a master class in composition at the Prague Conservatory.

Suk, Josef (ii) (b Prague, 8 Aug 1929). Czech violinist, grandson of Josef Suk (i) and great-grandson of Dvořák. He studied in Prague, making his début in 1940. In 1952 he formed the Suk Trio, with Josef Chuchro (cello) and Jan Panenka (piano). Wide appearances with the Czech PO in 1959 were followed in 1964 by his London début. His playing is admired for its unobtrusive lyric expressiveness.

Suling. Bamboo ring flute of Indonesia, Malaysia and the southern Philippines.

Sullivan, Sir Arthur (Seymour) (b London, 13 May 1842; d there, 22 Nov 1900). English composer. A Chapel Royal chorister, he became a pupil of Sterndale Bennett at the RAM (1856) and studied at the Leipzig Conservatory (1858–61). The promise shown by his incidental music for The Tempest (1861) and other early concert works led to festival commissions and conducting posts, which he complemented with work as organist, teacher and song

and hymn tune writer; from 1866, he also dabbled in comic opera. His increasing success in this last field – with C.F. Burnand in Cox and Box and then W.S. Gilbert in Trial by Jury – culminated in the formation by Richard D'Oyly Carte of a company expressly for the performance of Gilbert and Sullivan works. With HMS Pinafore the collaborators became an institution. Their works, produced at the Savoy Theatre from 1881 (the most popular 'Savoy Operas' were The Mikado and The Gondoliers), won a favour with English-speaking audiences that has never waned. Sullivan was knighted in 1883 and continued to conduct, notably the Leeds Festival and the Philharmonic Society concerts, but his serious ouput dwindled. A breach with Gilbert (1890), recurring ill-health and the relative failure of his last works clouded his final years.

Sullivan was essentially an eclectic, drawing on elements from opera, ballads, choral and church music, by composers from Handel to Bizet. Some lack of emotional depth and an unsure grasp of large-scale structure have limited the success of his more serious music (Golden Legend, Ivanhoe). It was in Gilbert's satirical subjects and witty verses that his talents found their happiest, most graceful and consistent inspiration, underpinned as they are by a highly professional compositional technique. Here his inventive melodies fit perfectly the sense and accentuation of the words, while lively choruses underscore traits of particular groups (male and female) and deft instrumentation points up character. His clever parodies of serious music and use of 'tune combination' increase the fun.

Dramatic music Cox and Box (1866); Trial by Jury (1875); The Sorcerer (1877); HMS Pinafore (1878); The Pirates of Penzance (1879); Patience (1881); Iolanthe (1882); Princess Ida (1884); The Mikado (1885); Ruddigore (1887); The Yeomen of the Guard (1888); The Gondoliers (1889); Ivanhoe (1891); 11 others; incidental music to 7 plays; 2 ballets

Orchestral and chamber music 'Irish' Sym., E (1866); In memoriam, ov. (1866); Vc Conc., D (1866); Overture di ballo (1870); choral works with orch, incl. The Golden Legend, cantata (1886); 2 oratorios; 9 chamber pieces

Church music service music, anthems; over 50 hymn tunes, including St Gertrude ('Onward, Christian soldiers')

Songs c20 partsongs; over 80 songs, duets, trios, including cycle, The Window (1871); The Lost Chord (1877)

Sul ponticello (It.). 'On the bridge': instruction in string playing to bow close to the bridge, producing a thin, nasal, glassy sound. Rossini particularly used it.

Sul tasto (It.). 'On the fingerboard': instruction in string playing to bow near or over the fingerboard, resulting in a bland, flute-like tone.

Sulzer, Salomon (b Hohenems, 30 March 1804; d Vienna, 17 Jan 1890). Austrian cantor and composer. As Obercantor in Vienna from 1826 to 1881 he raised standards of composition and performance in the synagogue and produced Schir Zion (1838–40, 1865–6), an organized, model repertory of synagogue music set for cantor and four-part male choir; his baritone-tenor voice was much admired.

Sumer is icumen in [Summer Canon]. A singularly elaborate specimen of the rota, composed c1250, probably in Reading. The piece is also related to the motet, because the round is supported by a texted *pes*, the two halves of which are combined with each other by means of voice-exchange. Detailed instructions as to performance are found in the source. Its importance lies not only with its potential as the earliest example of a six-voice piece, but also because it displays most of the quintessential facets of 13th-century English polyphony.

Summer Night on the River. Orchestral work by Delius (1911), the second of his Two Pieces for Small Orchestra (the other is *On Hearing the First Cuckoo in Spring*).

Sunless [Bez solntsa]. Song cycle by Musorgsky (1874), settings for voice and piano of six poems by Golenishchev-Kutuzov.

Sun Quartets. Title given to Haydn's op.20 string quartets (1772) after the title-page design of their first edition (1774).

Sunrise. Haydn's String Quartet in B♭ op.76 no.4, so called because of the rising and glowing music for the first violin with which it opens.

Sun-treader. Orchestral work by Ruggles (1931).

Suor Angelica. Opera in one act by Puccini to a libretto by G. Forzano; it is the second of *Il trittico*, the other operas being *Il tabarro* and *Gianni Schicchi* (1918, New York).

Superius (Lat.). Term used particularly in the 16th century, with the advent of music publishing, for the highest voice part in a polyphonic composition.

Supertonic. The second step or degree of the major or minor scale, so called because it lies a step above the tonic.

Supervia, Conchita (*b* Barcelona, 9 Dec 1895; *d* London, 30 March 1936). Spanish mezzo-soprano. She sang Octavian in Rome in 1911; during the 1920s she was known in Spain and Italy in the French repertory. From 1925 her rich, flexible voice and vivacious stage presence made her outstanding as Rossini's heroines. She appeared at Covent Garden in 1934-5.

Supičić, Ivo (*b* Zagreb, 18 July 1928). Yugoslav musicologist. He studied in Zagreb and Paris, and in 1964 began to teach at the Zagreb Academy of Music. In 1967-8 he was a visiting Fellow at Harvard University. He is editor of the *International Review of the Aesthetics and Sociology of Music* and a leading scholar of musical sociology.

Suppé [Suppè], **Franz (von)** [Francesco Ezechiele Ermenegildo Cavaliere Suppé Demelli] (*b* Split, 18 April 1819; *d* Vienna, 21 May 1895). Austrian composer and conductor of Belgian descent. In Vienna he became Kapellmeister at the Theater in der Josefstadt (1840), Theater an der Wien (1845), Kaitheater (1862) and Carltheater (1865). He wrote a string of effective stage scores, from overtures (*Poet and Peasant, Light Cavalry*) and incidental music to genuine Viennese operettas, opera parodies and even operas, some of which survive as viable theatre works. Among the most popular were the farce *Gervinus* (1849) and the operettas *Flotte Bursche* (1863), *Fatinitza* (1876) and above all *Boccaccio* (1879). At its best his music is light and fluent, elegant and immediately appealing.

Supposition. (1) The concept, proposed by Rameau, that chords of the 9th and 11th, among others, arise from a 7th chord by placing a 'supposed' bass one or two 3rds below the FUNDAMENTAL BASS (e.g. in the chord *f-a-c'-e'-g'-b'* the fundamental bass is *c'* and the 'supposed' bass is *f*).

(2) The imagining of a different clef sign, or the existing one differently placed, in a piece of music, thus enabling a player to transpose music that he is playing.

Surinach, Carlos (*b* Barcelona, 4 March 1915). American composer of Spanish origin. He studied in Barcelona and Germany and moved to the USA in 1951. He has won particular acclaim as a composer of dance scores.

Surprise Symphony. Nickname of Haydn's Symphony no.94 in G (1791), so called because of a sudden loud drumbeat in the slow movement.

Survivor from Warsaw, A. Schoenberg's op.46, a setting for narrator, male chorus and orchestra of his own text (1948, Albuquerque).

Susanna. Oratorio by Handel to a libretto after the *Apocrypha* (1749, London).

Susanna's Secret [Il segreto di Susanna]. Opera in one act by Wolf-Ferrari to a libretto by E. Golisciani (1909, Munich).

Susato, Tylman (*b* ?*c*1500; *d* ?Antwerp, 1561-4). Music publisher and composer active in Antwerp. A town player until 1549 and a composer of *chansons*, Flemish songs, motets and dance music, he worked as a music publisher (1543-61), establishing the first important music press in the Low Countries. He issued 25 books of *chansons* (mostly anthologies, with music by Josquin, Gombert and Lassus), three of masses, 19 of motets and 11 *Musyck boexken*, a pioneering series of Flemish songs and *Souterliedekens*, or metrical Dutch psalm settings intended for home use. He was succeeded by his son Jacques (*d* 1564).

Suspension. In part-writing, a dissonance configuration in which the dissonant or non-harmonic note is tied over from the previous chord (where it occurs in the same part) and resolves by step, usually downwards.

Susskind, (Jan) Walter (*b* Prague, 1 May 1918; *d* Berkeley, 25 March 1980). British conductor. He studied with Suk and Hába and later with Szell. He conducted in Prague (début in *La traviata*, 1934) but left in 1938 for England, where he played the piano in the Czech Trio, becoming conductor of the Scottish (National) Orchestra, 1946-52. He conducted the Victoria SO in Melbourne, the Toronto SO (1956-65; he founded the NYO of Canada in 1958) and the St Louis SO (1968-75). His sound musicianship was supported by an eagerness in exploring the orchestral repertory.

Süssmayr, Franz Xaver (*b* Schwanenstadt, 1766; *d* Vienna, 17 Sept 1803). Austrian composer. He was active until 1787 as a singer, violinist and organist at the monastery in Kremsmünster and had several stage works performed there. After settling in Vienna as a music teacher in 1788, he became a pupil and friend of Mozart, who employed him as a composer and occasionally a collaborator; after Mozart's death, Süssmayr completed his Requiem. Later he studied with Salieri and in 1794 became Kapellmeister of the German Opera at the National Theatre in Vienna. The most popular of his over 20 stage works were *Der Spiegel von Arkadien* (1794), a Singspiel in the tradition of *Die Zauberflöte*, and a ballet *Il noce de Benevento* (1802). He also wrote sacred music, secular cantatas and instrumental works.

Sustaining pedal. Name for the piano pedal on the right. When it is depressed it raises the dampers from all the strings, allowing them to vibrate freely in sympathy with any notes being played.

Suter, Hermann (*b* Kaiserstuhl, 28 April 1870; *d* Basle, 22 June 1926). Swiss conductor and composer. Trained at the Stuttgart and Leipzig conservatories, he worked in Zurich (1892–1902) and then in Basle as a conductor, teacher and composer. His music shows a Swiss variety of late Romanticism; it includes choral music (notably the oratorio *Le laudi di S Francesco d'Assisi*, 1925, which brought him international recognition), a symphony, a violin concerto and three string quartets.

Suter, Robert (*b* St Gall, 39 Jan 1919). Swiss composer. He was a pupil of Geiser and teacher at the Berne Conservatory (1945–50), then at the Basle Academy. His music shows a highly controlled contrapuntal style influenced by Bartók and, harmonically, by the pre-serial music of the Second Viennese School, though in the 1960s there came a loosening with the introduction of avant-garde techniques. Many of his works are cantatas and chamber pieces; among the best known are the *Musikalisches Tagebuch* (1946–50).

Sutermeister, Heinrich (*b* Feuerthalen, 12 Aug 1910). Swiss composer. He was a pupil of Courvoisier and Orff at the Munich Musikhochschule (1932–4). In the 1940s he achieved international renown as an opera composer, using a bold style influenced by Verdi and Orff (*Romeo und Julia*, 1939; *Die Zauberinsel*, 1942; *Raskolnikoff*, 1948), though he has also written concertos and popular choral works.

Sutherland, Dame Joan (*b* Sydney, 7 Nov 1926). Austrilian soprano. After early tuition in Sydney, where she made her stage début in 1951, she studied at the RCM. Her Covent Garden début was in 1952 but recognition did not come until 1959 when she sang Donizetti's Lucia, the role of her début (1961) at the Met, where she remains a favourite. Under the guidance of her husband, Richard Bonynge, she specialized in the *bel canto* repertory, singing with brilliant tone and perfectly played coloratura, especially in Bellini and Donizetti. She is also successful in French opera and as Handel's Alcina and Cleopatra. Since 1965 she has often returned to Australia.

Sutherland, Margaret (Ada) (*b* Adelaide, 20 Nov 1897). Australian composer. She studied with Bax in London, and in Vienna (1923–5), and from 1935 was active in Australia as a pianist, teacher and composer, contributing greatly to musical life and championing the work of other Australian composers. She was one of the first Australian composers

to write in an idiom comparable with that of her generation in Europe. She was influenced by Bax but also Bartók, Hindemith and French neo-classicism but she integrated these into a personal idiom. Her works cover many genres and include the tone poem *Haunted Hills* (1950) and the opera *The Young Kabbarli* (1965).

Suzuki, Shin'ichi (*b* Nagoya, 18 Oct 1898). Japanese educationalist and violin teacher, creator of the Suzuki method. His father Masakichi Suzuki (1859–1944) was a maker of shamisen and later of violins; he made them by hand but mechanized production and created the largest violin-making firm in Japan. Shin'ichi studied the violin under a pupil of Joachim and in Berlin; he established the Suzuki Quartet with three of his brothers, and founded the Tokyo String Orchestra. He developed his educational method in the 1930s, basing it on his understanding of the learning process in young children. He believed that any child could develop a high standard of ability by adapting external stimuli. In 1948 he organized his first, experimental class of 40 students; in 1950 he developed an institution for teaching violin playing according to his method. This involved working with children of 3 or 4, learning a fixed repertory (usually of pieces by 18th- and 19th-century composers) in order of difficulty; instruction is by ear and by rote, involving listening, much repetition and active parental participation. Technique and musicianship are strongly emphasized. The method was used first on the violin, but has been extended to other string instruments, the piano and wind instruments. It has enjoyed outstanding success, not only in Japan but also in the USA and Europe, and has met with wide but not universal approval from traditional music teachers.

Svanholm, Set (Karl Viktor) (*b* Västerås, 2 Sept 1904; *d* Saltsjö-Duvnäs, 4 Oct 1964). Swedish tenor. After an early career as an organist he studied singing with John Forsell and made his début in 1930 as a baritone. His tenor début was in 1936 and he was soon in demand as Othello and especially in Wagner. At Covent Garden (1948–57) he was admired for his intelligence and musicianship, often appearing with Flagstad.

Sveinbjörnsson, Sveinbjörn (*b* nr. Reykjavík, 28 June 1847; *d* Copenhagen, 23 Feb 1927). Icelandic composer and pianist. He studied in Copenhagen and with Reinecke in Leipzig, and taught the piano in Edinburgh. A refined, lyrical composer showing Danish influence, he wrote chiefly songs and choral pieces but also piano works paraphrasing Icelandic folksongs (*Idyl, Vikivaki*). His hymn for the 1000th anniversary (1874) of the Norse settlement in Iceland became the Icelandic national anthem.

Svendsen, Johan (Severin) (*b* Oslo, 30 Sept 1840; *d* Copenhagen, 14 June 1911). Norwegian composer and conductor. He began his career as a violin virtuoso but in 1865, while at the Leipzig Conservatory, his interest shifted to composition. Among his early works, the String Octet op.3, Symphony no.1 op.4 (considered strongly national by Grieg) and String Quintet op.5 were particularly well received. After a time in Paris and at Bayreuth, where he was close to Wagner, he conducted the Christiania Music Society concerts (1872–7) and composed his most notable works, including the orchestral legend *Zorahayda* op.11, the fantasy *Romeo og Julie* op.18, the Symphony no.2 op.15 and three Norwegian Rhapsodies opp.17, 19 and 21. He wrote his last important work, the popular Romance for violin and orchestra op.26, in 1881. From 1883 he was conductor at the Royal Opera, Copenhagen, where he enjoyed a commanding position in the city's musical life. Though contributing to the culmination of national Romanticism in Norway, Svendsen's style was marked by a natural mastery of the orchestra and of large classical forms. His two symphonies are the earliest by a Norwegian to have won an audience in Norway and to have remained in the repertory.

Svetlanov, Evgeny (Fyodorovich) (*b* Moscow, 6 Sept 1928). Soviet conductor. After graduating from the Moscow Conservatory he conducted at the Bol'shoy from 1955. In 1965 he became principal conductor of the USSR State SO, giving a large repertory of classical and Soviet music including in particular symphonies by Tchaikovsky and Myaskovsky, with sensitive attention to detail and a firm command of structure. He has many times appeared in the West.

Sviridov, Georgy Vasilevich (*b* Fatezh, 16 Dec 1915). Soviet composer. He was a pupil of Shostakovich at the Leningrad Conservatory (1936–41) and began his career as a pianist, becoming active in the composers' union. His works include choral pieces and songs, often based on agit-prop texts and folksongs; his combination of a personal style with ethnic elements has produced results of strong and direct appeal to Soviet audiences.

Swan Lake [Lebedinoye ozero]. Ballet in four acts by Tchaikovsky to a libretto by V. Begichev and V. Heltser (1877, Moscow).

Swan of Tuonela, The [Tuonelan joutsen]. Symphonic legend, op.22 no.3, by Sibelius (1893).

Swanson, Howard (*b* Atlanta, 18 Aug 1907; *d* New York, 12 Nov 1978). American composer. He studied at the Cleveland Institute and with Boulanger in Paris (1938). His works, in a lyrical, neo-classical style influenced by black folk music, include symphonies, *Night Music* (1950), chamber music and songs.

Swarowsky, Hans (*b* Budapest, 16 Sept 1899; *d* Salzburg, 10 Sept 1975). Austrian conductor. Schoenberg and Strauss were among his teachers. He held opera appointments before the war and in 1957 became permanent conductor at the Vienna Staatsoper and principal conductor of the Scottish National Orchestra. He was often heard in Mahler, Berg and Webern. Abbado and Mehta were among his pupils.

Swayne, Giles (*b* Stevenage, 30 June 1946). English composer. He studied at Cambridge and the RAM and with Messiaen from 1976. He gained some success with the orchestral pieces *Orlando's Music* (1974) and *Pentecost Music* (1977); wider recognition came with *Cry*, for 28 solo amplified voices (1978) and an 18th-century pastiche, the opera *Le nozze di Cherubino* (1984).

Sweelinck, Jan Pieterszoon (*b* Deventer, ?May 1562; *d* Amsterdam, 16 Oct 1621). Netherlands composer. He studied with his father, organist of the Oude Kerk, Amsterdam, succeeding him in or before 1580. He remained in this post all his life, with a few excursions to inspect new organs in other cities. Among the most influential and sought-after teachers of his time, he included Germans among his pupils, notably Scheidt, Jacob Praetorius and Scheidemann. He wrote over 250 vocal works, including a complete French psalter (1604–21), motets (1619), *chansons* (1594, 1612) and Italian madrigals (1612). But he is best known for his *c*70 keyboard works, which include monumental fugal fantasias, concise toccatas and well-ordered variation sets. He perfected forms derived from, among others, the English virginalists and greatly influenced 17th-century north German keyboard music, becoming one of the leading composers of his day. His son Dirck (1591–1652), who succeeded him at the Oude Kerk in 1621, edited a popular song collection (1644) and also composed songs and keyboard music.

Sacred vocal music 153 psalms; canticles; 39 motets
Secular vocal music 33 chansons; 19 madrigals; canons
Instrumental music over 20 sets of variations, kbd; *c*40 other kbd works, incl. toccatas, fantasias, echo fantasias; lute pieces

Swell. A device for the graduation of volume in keyboard instruments. The Swell organ is a department of an organ whose chest or pipes are enclosed in a box, one side of which has a shutter that may be opened and closed with a foot lever. A stop or half stop, or even several departments may be enclosed in this way. Two swell devices, operated by pedals, were developed for the harpsichord in England in the latter half of the 18th century: the 'nag's head', which opens a hinged section of the lid, and the 'Venetian', which works on the principle of the Venetian blind. The disadvantage is that the tone of the instrument is muffled.

Swert, Jules de (*b* Louvain, 15 Aug 1843; *d* Ostend, 24 Feb 1891). Belgian cellist. He studied at the Brussels Conservatory. In 1876 Wagner entrusted him with the formation of the orchestra at Bayreuth. From 1888 he was professor at the conservatories in Ghent and Bruges.

Swieten, Gottfried (Bernhard) Baron van (*b* Leiden, 29 Oct 1733; *d* Vienna, 29 March 1803). Dutch-born musical patron. A resident of Vienna, he trained as a diplomat; his main posting was to Berlin (1770–77), where he developed a taste for the music of Handel and J.S. and C.P.E. Bach. Returning to Vienna as Prefect of the Imperial Library, he became a champion of these composers. He led a group of the nobility which sponsored private performances of oratorios, notably Handel's *Messiah* (arranged by Mozart) and Haydn's *The Creation* (1798) and *The Seasons* (1801) (both to librettos compiled by van Swieten). He was also a minor composer.

Swing. A style of jazz and a related style of popular music. Originating *c*1930 when New Orleans jazz was in decline, it was characterized by a greater emphasis on solo improvisation, larger ensembles (notably the 'big bands'), a repertory largely of Tin Pan Alley songs and more equal weight given to the four beats of the bar.

SWV. Abbreviation that identifies works by Schütz by their number in the *Schütz-Werke-Verzeichnis*, ed. W. Bittinger and W. Breig (1960, 1979).

Sydney Opera House. Australian theatre and concert hall complex, opened in 1973. The concert hall (cap. 2700) and opera theatre (cap. 1500) are used mainly by national companies.

Sydney Symphony Orchestra. Australian orchestra formed in 1934 by the Australian Broadcasting Commission; in 1936–46 it was also known as the ABC SO.

Syllabic style. In plainchant, the setting of text mainly with one note per syllable, whether as a recitation tone or a fully developed melody (e.g. of a Credo). It is contrasted with neumatic or group style (mainly two to four notes per syllable) and melismatic style (characterized by florid groups of notes sung to each syllable).

Sylphides, Les. Ballet in one act to music by Chopin (1907, St Petersburg); it was originally called *Chopiniana*.

Sylvia. Ballet in three acts by Delibes to a scenario by J. Barbier and Mérante (1876, Paris).

Sympathetic strings. In string instruments, strings that are not played but sound 'in sympathy' with the same note (or one of its partials) emanating from another string, giving an added resonance. They are found, for example, in the viola d'amore and the sitar and sometimes in the high register of the piano, when they are known as ALIQUOT strings.

Symphonia. (1) Term for consonance in late Greek and medieval theory.

(2) Medieval term for various instruments, particularly those capable of playing two or more notes simultaneously. It has been applied to instruments of the bagpipe and hurdy-gurdy types, as well as keyboard instruments.

(3) 17th-century term for an orchestral piece, usually an introduction to a larger work. *See* SINFONIA and SYMPHONY.

Symphonia domestica. Orchestral work, op.53, by Richard Strauss (1903).

Symphonic band [concert band]. American term for an ensemble of wind instruments, with some percussion and occasionally double basses; it corresponds closely to the European MILITARY BAND.

Symphonic Dances. Orchestral work, op.45, by Rakhmaninov (1940).

Symphonic Metamorphosis on Themes of Carl Maria von Weber. Orchestral work by Hindemith (1943).

Symphonic poem. An orchestral form in which a poem or programme provides a narrative or illustrative basis. Its origins can be seen in the *Egmont*, *Coriolan* and third *Leonore* overtures of Beethoven, with their more or less explicit enactment of dramatic events. The concert overtures of Berlioz and Mendelssohn may be considered direct prototypes of the Lisztian symphonic poem, the earliest of which, *Ce qu'on entend sur la montagne*, is based on a poem by Hugo. This was the first of Liszt's 12 such works (1848–58).

The symphonic poem was taken up in Bohemia and Russia as a vehicle for nationalist ideas. In 1857 Smetana embarked on a group of symphonic poems, on literary subjects, clearly influenced by Liszt, but his *Má vlast* ('My Country') is on episodes and ideas from Czech history. It was succeeded by a profusion of symphonic poems by his younger compatriots, including Dvořák and Suk. In Russia, Glinka's *Kamarinskaya* (1848) was a prototype for the symphonic poems of Balakirev, Musorgsky and Borodin on national subjects. Tchaikovsky, by contrast, chose literary material for his *Romeo and Juliet*, *Francesca da Rimini* and *Hamlet*.

Franck had written an orchestral piece on Hugo's *Ce qu'on entend sur la montagne* before Liszt, but the genre came to life in France in the 1870s, supported by the new Société Nationale. Saint-Saëns's examples, including *Le rouet d'Omphale* and *Danse macabre*, were followed by d'Indy's and Duparc's and in 1876 Franck returned to the symphonic poem with *Les Eolides* and later added *Le chasseur maudit* and *Les Djinns*. Among French symphonic poems Dukas's *L'apprenti-sorcier* is a brilliant example of the narrative type.

Richard Strauss, who preferred the term 'Tondichtung' ('tone poem'), contributed a unique body of great works to the repertory in his early career, including *Don Juan*, *Till Eulenspiegel*, *Also sprach Zarathustra* and *Don Quixote*. In them he drew on his virtuosity as an orchestrator, his mastery of chromatic and diatonic harmony and his abundant skill in the transformation of themes and interweaving them in elaborate counterpoint.

Sibelius was perhaps the last composer to contribute significantly to the repertory of the symphonic poem. Its decline in the 20th century may be attributed to the rejection of Romantic ideas and their replacement by notions of the abstraction and independence of music.

Symphonie concertante (Fr.; It. *sinfonia concertante*). A concert genre of the late 18th and early 19th centuries for solo instruments (usually two, three or four) and orchestra. It is closer to concerto than symphony, but resembles the Classical divertimento forms in its lighthearted character. Major keys and melodic variety are characteristic. About half the known examples are in two movements, the rest mainly in three.

From *c*1770 to 1790 the genre was primarily Parisian, its composers including Gossec, Pleyel and Cambini. They satisfied a taste for virtuoso display, colourful sonorities and a pleasing melodic line. Mannheim composers, notably Cannabich and Carl Stamitz, also contributed to the early flowering of the symphonie concertante, and its popularity spread. In London J.C. Bach and in Vienna Wagenseil, Vanhal and Dittersdorf were among the active composers. Boccherini was one of the relatively few Italian contributors. Outstanding examples of the genre are Mozart's for violin and viola (1779) and Haydn's for oboe, bassoon, violin and cello (1792). After 1830 the symphonie concertante virtually disappeared. Some 20th-century composers have revived the term for works of a symphonic rather than concerto-like character with one solo instrument, including Szymanowski, Walton (both piano), Jongen (organ) and Enescu (cello). Hilding Rosenberg and Frank Martin have used the term in its original sense.

Symphonie espagnole. Lalo's op.21 (1874) for violin and orchestra.

Symphonie fantastique (Episode de la vie d'un artiste). Symphony, op.14, by Berlioz (1830).

Symphonie funèbre et triomphale, Grande. *See* GRANDE SYMPHONIE FUNÈBRE ET TRIOMPHALE.

Symphonie liturgique. Honegger's Symphony no.3 (1946).

Symphonie sur un chant montagnard français. Work for piano and orchestra by d'Indy (1886).

Symphony. An extended work for orchestra, usually in three or four movements. It is traditionally regarded as the central form of orchestral composition. In the 17th century the term was used in other senses: for concerted motets (e.g. Schütz's *Symphoniae sacrae*), for introductory movements to operas etc (*see* OVERTURE), for instrumental introductions and sections within arias and ensembles, and for ensemble pieces which might be classified as sonatas or concertos (*see* SINFONIA).

Features of the Classical symphony may be traced to the Italian overture of the late 17th century in three movements (fast–slow–fast). With Italian opera composers such as Leo, Pergolesi, Galuppi and Jommelli, the movements became longer and more developed. G.B. Sammartini was among the first Italians to write concert symphonies; composers of the next generation, including Boccherini and Pugnani, inherited his essentially lyrical approach, but Italian composers were not generally interested in the richer, more developed style favoured in Austria and Germany.

Many composers of the new symphony were active in London, Paris, north Germany and elsewhere, but the main centres were Vienna and Mannheim. About 1735 the Viennese symphony, drawing on the opera overture and chamber music, began to establish an independent course, notably in the works of Monn and Wagenseil. They and their younger contemporaries, Gassmann and Ordonez, continued to prefer three-movement form, but with four prolific, gifted composers – Hofmann, Dittersdorf, Vanhal and Michael Haydn – the four-movement symphony, with minuet and trio preceding the finale, became the norm. Their works represent the highest achievements in the Viennese Classical symphony apart from Haydn and Mozart. At Mannheim, where the electoral court assembled a concentration of talent, the virtuosity and discipline of the court orchestra led to new developments in orchestral style, particularly ones involving the striking use of dynamics and the stylized use of melodic figures. J.W.A. Stamitz provided the model and the motivation; his 'army of generals' included such names as F.X. Richter, Holzbauer, Antonín Fils and, among the next generation, Toeschi, Cannabich, Eichner, Beck and Stamitz's son Carl.

The achievements of Haydn and Mozart place them far above any of these local groupings. Haydn's appointment at the Esterházy court in 1761 required a steady production of symphonies: he responded with many fine examples, often building whole expositions on a single thematic idea and exploiting the unexpected. His supreme achievements began with six symphonies written for Paris in 1785, with their new heights of ingenuity, humour and unpretentious intellectuality; the last symphonies (nos.93–104), written for London, exceed even these in breadth of conception, melodic appeal and magisterial command.

As a child, Mozart met Italian-style symphonies through his friendship with J.C. Bach; his Austro-German background added harmonic depth, textural interest, subtlety of phrasing and orchestral virtuosity. In his early symphonies these and other influences appear. In his symphonies after 1773, one or other occasionally predominates (Parisian in no.31, Mannheim style and Italian form in no.32 etc), but stylistic conflicts and imbalances are resolved in symphonies which show increasing enlargement of scale and complexity of development and texture, leading to the remarkable depth and originality of his final masterpieces in the form, nos.38–41.

Whatever the view of his contemporaries, the early 19th-century symphony is now typified by Beethoven. While his first two symphonies shared a development from Haydn's, no.3 was a departure: its four movements were on an unprecedentedly large scale, and its dedication to Napoleon (later erased) proclaimed that its grandeur and power celebrated personal courage and the unconquerable human spirit. The later symphonies work out in fresh terms the same type of struggle, and all end in triumph, for example in the brilliant C major finale of no.5 in C minor. No.9, the Choral Symphony, is a solitary masterpiece, bringing together two projects that had long been in the composer's mind, a gigantic symphony in D minor and a choral setting of Schiller's *Ode to Joy*. Beethoven's achievements were such that the merits of Schubert's more lyrical ones were long overlooked, even those of the expansive yet often closely argued 'Great C major'; while those of later composers tended to be judged by how they matched up to Beethoven's. The more conservative Romantics, notably Mendelssohn, Schumann and Brahms, remained broadly faithful to the Classical conception of the symphony even if they sometimes changed the number and order of its movements or sought new ways of unifying them, as Schumann did in his cyclic treatment in no.4. There is some 'programmatic' tendency, but it is rarely pursued by Mendelssohn beyond titles that evoke a source of the music's inspiration ('Scottish', 'Italian') or by Schumann beyond general atmosphere ('Spring', 'Rhenish' – in which one unorthodox movement is specifically evocative of Cologne Cathedral). Brahms rejected even such mood painting, but nevertheless made far-reaching innovations within the standard four-movement pattern. There are motivic links within and between movements and elaborately worked contrapuntal textures, adding strength to his sonata-form structures. The finale of his fourth and last symphony, however, is cast in his own version of the Baroque passacaglia form. In the first three, he substituted a lyrical, intermezzo-like movement in moderate tempo for the Beethovenian scherzo. Another composer who may be classed as a conservative Romantic was Tchaikovsky, who adhered to the traditional forms even though his material was not always susceptible to the organic unity on which they depend. Several symphonies, notably no.4, involve the cyclic recall of themes; this may be connected with the programmatic content that he is believed to have followed and which no doubt (his programmes were not generally disclosed) governs the unorthodox use of a slow, despairing finale to his last symphony, no.6 ('Pathetic'). At several points in his symphonies, notably no.4, he used Russian folk melodies but he did not, like the more overtly nationalist composers, adapt his style to accommodate a folk idiom.

While many of the more radical Romantics found a congenial outlet for their ideas and aspirations in the SYMPHONIC POEM, there were some for whom the symphony was a challenge. In the *Symphonie fantastique* and *Harold en Italie* Berlioz sought to unite the Beethoven conception of the symphony with his own penchant for descriptive, literary-inspired music by means of a recurrent *idée fixe*. His example was followed by Liszt's pupil d'Indy in the *Symphonie sur un chant montagnard français*. Lalo's Symphony and Saint-Saëns's Third also show Liszt's influence in their style and the use of thematic transformation, and Franck's D minor Symphony, although non-programmatic, goes further in that direction.

Although some nationalist composers, including Borodin and Balakirev in Russia and Dvořák in Bohemia, felt close enough to the centre of a tradition to contribute to the genre, by the end of the 19th century it had become largely a bastion of the orthodox. Only Bruckner succeeded in creating a new model, basing his symphonies first on Beethoven's Ninth and secondly on a Wagnerian expansiveness and (to some degree) style and orchestration. He extended the sonata-form tradition in some of his first movements to involve three rather than two thematic and tonal groups; wrote long and deeply contemplative adagios, often capped by a huge orchestral climax, and scherzos which often have a demoniacal drive contrasted with lyrical middle sections; and he extended finales, often again with three tonal areas, sometimes incorporating chorale-like material and (from no.3 onwards) ending with a recall of the symphony's opening theme.

The period 1901–18, during which Mahler, Sibelius, Elgar and (though his greatest symphonies came later) Nielsen were active, brought the Romantic symphony to its fullest maturity and to its end. The sense of an end is strongly present in the music of both Mahler and Elgar, and, although Sibelius's structural innovations (culminating in the single-movement Seventh Symphony of 1924) seemed to point a way forward, changes in the artistic climate and in the language of music after 1918 threatened to undermine the concept of the symphony. Avant-garde composers either did not write them or wrote symphonies in which received standards were deliberately outraged.

Composers closer to the 19th-century tradition, and particularly those whose music has retained links with tonality, have continued to write symphonies in the traditional mould (for example Ives, Honegger, Roussel, Prokofiev, Myaskovsky, Henze, Martinů, Vaughan Williams, Simpson, Tippett, Sessions, Harris and Vagn Holmboe). But among 20th-century composers of international stature, perhaps only Shostakovich, whose symphonies range from the political manifesto (nos.2 and 3), the heroic and sometimes programmatic (nos.7 and 10–12) to the bitterly ironic (nos.13 and 14), has found in the symphony a natural vehicle for his most challenging and original music.

Symphony in Three Movements. Orchestral work by Stravinsky (1945).

Symphony of a Thousand. Nickname of Mahler's Symphony no.8 in E♭ (1906), so called because of the enormous vocal and orchestral forces it requires.

Symphony of Psalms. Choral work by Stravinsky, a setting for chorus and orchestra of a Latin text from Psalms xxxviii, xxxix and cl (1930, Brussels).

Syncopation. The regular shifting of each beat in a measured pattern by the same amount ahead of or behind its normal position in that pattern. *See also* CROSS-RHYTHM.

Synthesizer. An electronic instrument capable of generating and processing a wide variety of sounds. Available models differ considerably in their capabilities, manner of operation, size and appearance, though with most the output must be passed through an external amplifier and loudspeakers to be heard as sound. Synthesizers are customarily divided on the basis of their methods of sound production into analogue and digital types. In principle, an analogue synthesizer uses continuously varying voltages to model soundwaves internally, whereas a digital synthesizer uses discrete units of information.

The forerunners of the synthesizer as it is now understood were unique programmable composition machines such as the RCA Electronic Music Synthesizer, Mark II (1958). The first true analogue synthesizers, the Moog, Buchla and Synket of 1964, were orientated towards use in electronic music studios and were assemblies of individual devices that could be interconnected by patchcords (cables with a plug at each end). Their extensive use of the principle of voltage control enabled complex interaction between the devices and permitted the creation of sounds whose properties – pitch, envelope, amplitude, timbre, reverberation, modulation etc – could be controlled automatically. Such synthesizers were essentially monophonic, and the patchcord system meant that setting up new voicings could be very time-consuming.

The 1970s saw the production of new synthesizers designed as performance instruments. These were generally smaller, with fewer component devices than their studio-orientated counterparts, and it was easier to set up voicings. Polyphonic synthesizers became available from c1975.

The first commercially manufactured digital synthesizer was the Synclavier (1976). A digital synthesizer is a polyphonic instrument based on a microprocessor; it is thus in essence a modified computer, offering the benefits of programmability, large memory and detailed and accurate control over the dimensions of sound and timing of events.

Syracuse Symphony Orchestra. American orchestra formed in 1961 with Karl Kritz as conductor; orchestras with the same name had been formed from 1890. Its home is the Crouse-Hinds Concert Theater (cap. 2117). Activities include regular concerts in other towns in NY and youth concerts. Syracuse University Oratorio Society (formed 1975) performs with it.

Syrinx. Greek term for PANPIPES. Greek panpipes were originally made from cane, later of wood, clay or bronze. The syrinx, in Greek and Roman iconography, had from five to 13 short pipes. Debussy composed a work for solo flute called *Syrinx* (1913).

System. Two or more staves, usually joined by a brace at the left-hand end, which present the whole of the musical texture for any one line of music on the page.

Systems music. *See* MINIMALISM.

Szabelski, Bolesław (*b* Radoryż, 3 Cec 1896; *d* Katowice, 27 Aug 1979). Polish composer. A pupil of Szymanowski and Statkowski at the Warsaw Conservatory, he taught at the Katowice Conservatory (1929–39, 1954–67). He played an important part in Polish music in using pre-Classical forms (e.g. the Toccata, 1938). After 1958, with the orchestral piece *Sonety*, he also used novel techniques. His works include five symphonies (1926–68) and two string quartets.

Szabó, Ferenc (*b* Budapest, 27 Dec 1902; *d* there, 4 Nov 1969). Hungarian composer. He was a pupil of Weiner, Siklós and Kodály (1921–6). A member of the communist party from 1927, he was obliged to withdraw to the USSR (1932–44), then returned to teach at the Budapest Academy (1945–67). His works include much choral music (including *Song of the Wolves*, 1930), chamber and orchestral pieces and film scores.

Szabolcsi, Bence (*b* Budapest, 2 Aug 1899; *d* there, 21 Jan 1973). Hungarian musicologist. He studied at Budapest University, Leipzig University and the Budapest Academy of Music. Ge worked in publishing and criticism, and from 1945 was professor at the Budapest Academy. A prolific scholar, he worked on a wide range of topics, among them monody, Mozart, Jewish music, Bartók, Hungarian art and folk music and the nature of melody, and was a leading figure in the growth of musical studies.

Szałowski, Antoni (*b* Warsaw, 21 April 1907; *d* Paris, 21 March 1973). Polish composer. He was a pupil of Sikorski at the Warsaw Conservatory and of Boulanger in Paris (1931–6), where he remained. An outstanding representative of the interwar Paris school, he composed in an elegant Franco-Polish neo-classical style, mostly orchestral (Overture, 1939) and chamber pieces.

Szamotuł, Wacław z (*b* Szamotuły, c1524, *d* ?Pińczów, probably 1560). Polish composer. He lived in Lithuania (1545–7), then became composer to the Polish court. From 1555 until his death he served the Calvinist Duke Mikołaj Radziwiłł in Lithuania. A poet and many-sided Renaissance figure, he wrote sacred polyphonic works which mark a highpoint in Polish *a cappella* music.

Székely, Endre (*b* Budapest, 6 April 1912). Hungarian composer. He was a pupil of Siklós at the Budapest Academy and played a leading role in Hungarian musical life as administrator and journal editor. His earlier works are mostly choral, developing from the Kodály school to socialist realism, but since the mid-1950s he has written chamber and orchestral pieces using techniques from Bartók and the Second Viennese School. Latterly his style broadened (e.g. in *Musica notturna* (1968) for chamber ensemble).

Szelényi, István (*b* Zólyom, 8 Aug 1904; *d* Budapest, 31 Jan 1972). Hungarian composer. He studied with Kodály at the Budapest Academy, where he later taught (1956–72). As a pianist he introduced works by Schoenberg and Hindemith to Hungary in the 1920s, and his own inter-war works were constructivist. Later he came under the influence of Kodály and Liszt (one of his research interests), returning to his earlier style in his last years.

Szeligowski, Tadeusz (*b* Lwów, 15 Sept 1896; *d* Poznań, 10 Jan 1963). Polish composer. A pupil of Wallek-Walewski in Kraków and of Boulanger in Paris (1929–31), he returned to Poland to teach. He composed in most genres, including opera, in a highly eclectic style, drawing on contemporary French music, medieval music, Polish folklore etc.

Szell, George (*b* Budapest, 7 June 1897; *d* Cleveland, 29 July 1970). American conductor. After study in Vienna he conducted at the Berlin Staatsoper from 1915; later appointments were at Strasbourg, Darmstadt and Prague. His American début was in 1931 and he settled in the USA in 1939. From 1946 to 1970 he was musical director of the Cleveland Orchestra, developing a superb ensemble that embodied his strict notions of discipline in producing an orchestral sound with the clarity and balance of chamber music. He toured with that orchestra and also became closely associated with the Amsterdam Concertgebouw Orchestra and the Salzburg Festival.

Szervánszky, Endre (*b* Budatétény, 1 Jan 1911; *d* Budapest, 25 June 1977). Hungarian composer. He studied with Siklós at the Budapest Academy (1931–6), where he began teaching in 1948. His earlier music was influenced by Kodály and Bartók, the latter remaining a presence during his development through the highly expressive Concerto for Orchestra (1954) and the tightly motivic Second Quartet (1957) to the serialism of the Six Orchestral Pieces (1959), which marked a significant point in Hungarian music and enjoyed enormous success. Later works include choral, orchestral and chamber pieces.

Szeryng, Henryk (*b* Warsaw, 22 Sept 1918; *d* Kassel, 3 March 1988). Mexican violinist. After study with Flesch he made his solo début in 1933, then studied further with Nadia Boulanger. War service on behalf of the Polish government, and entertaining Allied troops, was followed by a move to Mexico. He resumed his concert career in 1954 and his versatility, elegance and technical command were quickly recognized. He formed a recording partnership with Artur Rubinstein.

Szigeti, Joseph (*b* Budapest, 5 Sept 1892; *d* Lucerne, 19 Feb 1973). American violinist. He made his début in Berlin in 1905 and appeared regularly in London from 1907. He was often associated with contemporary music, giving the first performances of works by Prokofiev, Bloch, Bartók and Martin. He settled in the USA in 1940 but returned to Europe in 1960. His technique was not flawless but he convinced by the force of his musical personality.

Szirmai, Albert (*b* Budapest, 2 July 1880; *d* New York, 15 Jan 1967). American composer of Hungarian origin. A pupil of Koessler at the Budapest Academy, he wrote 19 successful operettas. From 1926 he lived in New York as musical director for Chappell.

Szokolay, Sándor (*b* Kúnágota, 30 March 1931). Hungarian composer. He studied with Szabó and Farkas at the Budapest Academy. His main works are expressionist operas (*Blood Wedding*, 1964; *Hamlet*, 1968; *Sámson*, 1973).

Szymanowska [née Wołowska], **Maria Agata** (*b* Warsaw, 14 Dec 1789; *d* St Petersburg, 24 July 1831). Polish pianist and composer. From 1815 to 1828 she gave acclaimed concerts throughout Europe before settling in St Petersburg, where she taught and mixed with the artistic élite. Her piano works, particularly the early Romantic studies, nocturnes and dance miniatures, occupy an important position in the history of Polish music before Chopin.

Szymanowski, Karol (Maciej) (*b* Tymoszówka, 6 Oct 1882; *d* Lausanne, 29 March 1937). Polish composer. He was born into an artistic family of the Polish landed gentry and began his musical education with his father. At 13, in Vienna, he was powerfully impressed by hearing Wagner for the first time. He then had formal tuition from Zawirski and

Noskowski in Warsaw (1901–4), and during the next decade began to make an international reputation for music in the German tradition, relating to Wagner, Strauss and Reger: the main works of this period include the Symphony no.2 (1910), Piano Sonata no.2 (1911) and the opera *Hagith* (1913).

During these years he visited Italy, Sicily and north Africa; he also encountered *Pelléas, The Firebird* and *Petrushka*, and all these enriching influences were remembered in his abundant output of 1914–17, when he was confined by the war to Russia. Works of this period are typically classical or oriental in inspiration, and ornately figured in a manner relating to Skryabin or Debussy. They include the choral Symphony no.3 (1916), Violin Concerto no.1 (1916), *Myths* for violin and piano (1915) and the piano triptychs *Metopes* (1915) and *Masques* (1916). He then used this new, highly sensuous language to tackle the theme of *The Bacchae* in his opera *King Roger* (1926), set in the orientalized Norman kingdom of Sicily.

In 1919 he settled in Warsaw, now the capital of an independent Poland; and he began while completing *King Roger* to compose in a nationalist style, drawing on folk music in his choral orchestral *Stabat mater* (1926), ballet *Harnasie* (1935) and other works. He accepted the directorship of the Warsaw Conservatory (1927–32), but his last years were dogged by ill health, and he wrote nothing after his Violin Concerto no.2 (1933) and a pair of piano mazurkas, adding to a set of 20 dating from 1924–5. Other works include two quartets, songs, folksong arrangements and cantatas.

Operas Hagith (1922); King Roger (1926)
Ballet Harnasie (1935)
Orchestral music Concert Ov. (1905); 4 syms. (1909, 1910, 1916, 1932); 2 vn concs. (1916, 1933)
Vocal music Love-songs of Hafiz, orch (1914); Songs of a Fairy-tale Princess, orch (1933); choruses, solo songs
Choral music Stabat mater (1926); Veni Creator (1930); Litany to the Virgin Mary (1933)
Chamber music 2 str qts (1917, 1927), 6 works for vn, pf
Piano music 3 sonatas (1904, 1911, 1917); Metopes (1915); Masques (1916)

T

Tabachnik, Michel (*b* Geneva, 10 Nov 1942). Swiss composer and conductor. He studied in Geneva, and with Boulez, whose assistant he became (1971) and who has influenced his works. As a conductor he has specialized in the 20th-century repertory and given several Xenakis premières. His *Mondes* for two orchestras (1972) recalls Stockhausen.

Tabarro, Il [The Cloak]. Opera in one act by Puccini to a libretto by Adami after Didier Gold's *La houppelande*; it is the first of *Il trittico*, the other operas being *Suor Angelica* and *Gianni Schicchi* (1918, New York).

Tablā. A pair of small, hand-played kettledrums, treble and bass, found in north and central India, Pakistan and Bangladesh. Dating from the end of the 18th century and originally associated with dance, the *tablā* are the principal drums of modern classical music in the subcontinent and their repertory has developed many highly complex and varied forms, combining the influences of Hindu and Muslim cultures. The smaller, right-hand drum is a slightly tapering cone, wooden, *c*1 cm thick; the larger, left-hand one is a roughly hemispherical bowl, straightened at the top, of copper and chrome or of traditional terracotta.

Tablature. A notational system that uses letters, numbers or other signs rather than staff notation. The basic principle of tablature is that the player is told, by letters or figures placed on a staff, how to produce the sound of the required pitch from his instrument. A further indication shows the duration of each note. The most important tablature systems are those for keyboard (mainly organ) and lute. Most keyboard music of the late Middle Ages and the early Renaissance is notated in tablature, using letters and note stems with flags. Early examples present the top part in staff notation. This German system continued in occasional use into the 18th century. There also existed Spanish systems, in the mid-16th century, using numerals.

For the lute and other plucked instruments, tablature systems serve an obvious purpose. There exist several different systems, some using numerals and some using letters, but they all follow the same basic principle in that they tell the player which string he should stop and at which fret he should stop it. The cumbersome German system uses all the letters of the alphabet; French tablatures use letters, repeating the pattern on each string (i.e. 'a' indicates an open string, 'b' stopping at the first fret etc). Spanish and Italian tablatures use numerals in the same sense; in Spanish and French tablatures, the lowest line of the 'staff' corresponds to the string or course lowest in pitch, but in Italian it corresponds to the highest.

For the guitar, tablatures originally followed the system used for the lute in France, Italy or Spain. In 1606 an alphabetical tablature system was devised whereby each letter stands for a particular chord. Tablatures have been used for most plucked instruments, such as the chitarrone, the mandolin and the theorbo, using the French system or the Italian. Among bowed instruments, the one for which tablature was chiefly used was the lyra viol (or viola bastarda). In recent years tablatures have been designed for such instruments as the ukulele and the accordion. They have also been used for wind instruments to indicate to the player which finger-holes should be covered. Strictly speaking, systems such as those used for the notation of harmony and Braille notation rank as tablatures. So does Tonic Sol-fa, which is a form of solmization.

Table. *See* BELLY.

Table-book. A manuscript or printed book of the 16th century or the 17th, in which the vocal or instrumental parts of an ensemble composition are displayed so that the performers can read theirs while seated round a table. It is an extension of the choir-book system used earlier. The table-book format was used for French *chansons*, lute duets and songs for the lute.

Table entertainment. A British species of performance, usually consisting of a mixture of narration and singing delivered by an individual seated at a table facing the audience. It probably originated in the mid-18th century. Charles Dibdin gave such entertainments in London between 1789 and 1809. The performances of Joyce Grenfell and others may be seen as a modern survival.

Tabor. A small side-drum, with snares; *see* PIPE AND TABOR and SIDE DRUM.

Tacchinardi-Persiani, Fanny (*b* Rome, 4 Oct 1812; *d* Neuilly-sur-Seine, 3 May 1867). Italian soprano. A pupil of her father the tenor Nicola Tacchinardi

(1772–1859) and wife of the composer Giuseppe Persiani, she was a distinguished interpreter of Bellini and Donizetti, creating the title role of *Lucia di Lammermoor* (1835). Her voice was small and delicate but sweet, her technique impeccable and her ethereal presence perfectly suited to roles of the early Romantic 'amorosa angelicata'.

Tacet (Lat.). 'He is silent': an indication that a performer is silent for a considerable time; *tacet al fine* shows that the performer is not required for the rest of the piece.

Tactus. Term for a beat, i.e. a unit of time measured by a hand movement, used in the 15th and 16th centuries. In theory, each *tactus* (representing a downward and an upward motion of the hand) stood for a semibreve in normal tempo, and was approximately equal to the pulse of a man breathing normally (between 60 and 70 times per minute). The term is also used at this period for an improvisatory piece played on the organ and for a fret on a lute or clavichord.

Taddei, Giuseppe (*b* Genoa, 26 June 1916). Italian baritone. He studied in Rome and sang there regularly, 1936–42, his roles including Alberich and Verdi's Germont. He sang at the Vienna Staatsoper, 1946–8, then resumed his Italian career, singing at La Scala and elsewhere in such roles as Pizarro, Sachs and the Dutchman; later he turned to Mozart, as Papageno and Figaro. His dramatic versatility and his firm, warm voice were heard at Covent Garden in the 1960s as Macbeth, Rigoletto and Scarpia; he also sang in the USA.

Tadolini [née Savonariʃ, **Eugenia** (*b* Forlì, 1809; *d* Naples, ?). Italian soprano. She appeared in the premières of Donizetti's *Linda di Chamounix* (1842) and *Maria di Rohan* (1843) and was one of the first sopranos to take up Verdi's cause, singing Elvira in *Ernani* (1844) and Odabella in *Attila* (1846) and creating the title role of *Alzira* (1845). Her husband Giovanni (?1789–1872) was a composer, conductor and singing teacher.

Tafelmusik (Ger.). 'Table music': term used since the 16th century for music for feasts and banquets. The best-known examples are Telemann's three sets of *Musique de table* (1733).

Taffanel, (Claude) Paul (*b* Bordeaux, 16 Sept 1844; *d* Paris, 22 Nov 1908). French flautist. He studied with Dorus. For his influence at the Opéra, the Société des Concerts du Conservatoire and the Société des Instruments à Vent, and as professor at the Conservatoire (from 1893), he may be regarded father of the modern French school of flute playing.

Tag, Christian Gotthilf (*b* Beierfeld, 2 April 1735; *d* Niederzwönitz, 19 July 1811). German composer. He was Kantor in Hohenstein-Ernstthal, 1775–1808, and had a high reputation as Kantor and organist. His sacred music (including over 100 cantatas) has Baroque features, while his lieder keyboard pieces show the influence of Hiller and the Berlin school. His nephew Christian Traugott Tag (1777–1839), also a composer, became Kantor and director of music in Glauchau.

Tagliapietra, Gino (*b* Ljubljana, 30 May 1887; *d* Venice, 8 Aug 1954). Italian composer. He studied with Busoni, the dominant influence on his output largely of piano music. He also taught in Venice at the Liceo Musicale (1906–40).

Tagliavini, Ferruccio (*b* Reggio Emilia, 14 Aug 1913). Italian tenor. He studied in Parma and in Florence where he made his début in 1938 as Rodolfo. He sang at the Met between 1947 and 1962, and also at Covent Garden. Essentially a *tenore di grazia*, he excelled in Bellini and Donizetti.

Tagliavini, Luigi Ferdinando (*b* Bologna, 7 Oct 1929). Italian organist and musicologist. He studied at the conservatories of Bologna and Paris and the University of Padua and taught the organ in Bologna, Bolzano and Parma, and music history at Bologna and Fribourg. He has been a pioneer in organ restoration and his performances of older music combine his musicology and practical musicianship to produce lively and authentic interpretations.

Taglietti, Giulio (*b* Brescia, *c*1660; *d* there, 1718). Italian composer. A violin teacher in Brescia, he published 13 collections (1695–1715) of concertos, sonatas, instrumental arias etc. His concertos have more in common with the concerto grosso than with the solo type. He was probably the brother of the composer and trumpet marine player Luigi Taglietti (1668–1715), who also wrote instrumental music.

Tahourdin, Peter Richard (*b* Bramdean, Hants., 27 Aug 1928). English composer. He has taught electronic music in Australia since 1965 (from 1973 at Melbourne University Conservatory).

Taille (Fr.). 'Tenor': term used in French music for a middle part of tenor pitch, in a composition. By the mid-16th century it implied a tenor voice, but it was more commonly used to signify an instrumental part with a tenor function. Bach used it for an oboe at tenor pitch; French Baroque composers used it for chorus tenors. In a string ensemble it can imply a viola part.

Tailleferre, Germaine (*b* Parc-St-Maur, 19 April 1892; *d* Paris, 7 Nov 1983). French composer. Trained at the Paris Conservatoire, she became a member of Les Six. She wrote in most genres with neo-classical fluency, her style showing a graceful spontaneity and tender humour. Notable are the Violin Sonata no.1 (1924), the ballet *Marchand d'oiseaux* (1923) and the sparkling orchestral *Ouverture* (1932).

Tailpiece. The piece of wood or metal to which the strings are attached at the lower end of a string instrument.

Tajčević, Marko (*b* Osijek, 29 Jan 1900; *d* Belgrade, 19 July 1984). Yugoslav composer. He studied in Zagreb, Prague and Vienna (with Marx). He taught, conducted and was a critic in Zagreb and was a professor at the Belgrade Academy (1945–66). He was an outstanding representative of the Yugoslav national school and concentrated on elegant piano and choral miniatures; his *Seven Balkan Dances* (1927) became a classic. He wrote several theory books.

Takács, Jenö (*b* Siegendorf, 25 Sept 1902). Austrian composer of Hungarian origin. A pupil of Gál and Marx in Vienna, where he was in contact with the Schoenberg school, he has taught widely, in Cairo, Manila (from where he made ethnomusicological expeditions) and Cincinnati as well as Europe; he toured as a pianist and conductor in his own works.

He used Hungarian and other folk music in a contemporary tonal style in works in many genres.

Takemitsu, Tōru (*b* Tokyo, 8 Oct 1930). Japanese composer. He was a pupil of Kiyose from 1948. Influenced by Webern, Debussy and Messiaen, he has reflected what is most oriental in these composers: a concern with timbre and elegant sound and with the precision of the moment rather than with pattern and development. His music often gives the impression of spatial experience and of materials evolving freely of their own accord; silence is fully organized. Some of his works use Japanese instruments, but most are for Western orchestral and chamber media. Among the best known are *Requiem* for strings (1957), *November Steps* for *biwa*, *shakuhachi* and orchestra (1967) and *A Flock Descends into the Pentagonal Garden* (1977).

Takt (Ger.). Metre or time, as in *Dreivierteltakt* (3/4 time), *im Takt* (in strict tempo) etc; or bar (measure), as in *Taktstrich* (bar-line).

Taktakishvili, Otar Vasil'yevich (*b* Tbilisi, 27 July 1924). Soviet composer. He studied with Barkhudaryan at the Tbilisi Conservatory, where he taught from 1947; in 1965 he was appointed Georgian minister of culture. His main works are operas and oratorios on Georgian subjects, often using folk materials; the trilogy of one-act operas *Three Stories* (1967) marked a new development in the Georgian musical theatre.

Tal, Josef (*b* Pinne, 18 Sept 1910). Israeli composer of German origin. He studied with Hindemith and others at the Berlin Musikhochschule and moved to Palestine in 1934; in 1950 he began teaching at the Hebrew University, where in 1961 he founded an electronic studio. His works often use biblical and Jewish subjects, but in a vigorous, dramatic 12-note style that reflects his central European origins. His output includes operas (*Ashmedai*, 1971; *Massada 967*, 1973) three symphonies and several concertos (including three for piano and tape), cantatas and chamber music.

Tala. Indian term, often translated as 'rhythm'; it is a fixed and cyclically repeated time-span for music, articulated into segments by beats of the hand or of a percussion instrument.

Talea (Lat.). Medieval term usually understood to denote a freely invented rhythmic pattern, several statements of which constitute the note values of the tenor of an isorhythmic motet (or at least its first section). Medieval writers differed as to the term's exact meaning, and the distinction between 'tenor' and 'color' (generally understood today to indicate a melodic rather than a rhythmic pattern) was less clear.

Tale of Tsar Saltan, The [Skazka o Tsare Saltane]. Opera in a prologue and four acts by Rimsky-Korsakov to a libretto by Bel'sky after Pushkin (1901, St Petersburg).

Tales from the Vienna Woods. Waltz, op.325, by Johann Strauss (ii) (1868).

Tales of Hoffmann, The. *See* CONTES D'HOFFMANN, LES.

Talich, Václav (*b* Kroměříž, 28 May 1883; *d* Beroun, 16 March 1961). Czech conductor and violinist. After study at the Prague Conservatory he was briefly leader of the Berlin PO. From 1906 he worked in Prague and in 1919 became chief conductor of the Czech PO, with which he toured widely; from 1935 he was also head of opera at the National Theatre. He brought Janáček's operas into the repertory and was noted for his interpretation of Smetana, Dvořák and Suk.

Talking drum. Obsolescent term for a drum beaten so as to imitate recognizable features of a text, such as syllabic tone, stress and quantity, and phrase or sentence intonation; such drums are used for signalling and musical performance in parts of Africa.

Tallis, Thomas (*b c*1505; *d* Greenwich, 23 Nov 1585). English composer. He was organist of the Benedictine Priory of Dover in 1532, then probably organist at St Mary-at-Hill, London (1537–8). About 1538 he moved to Waltham Abbey where, at the dissolution (1540), he was a senior lay clerk. In 1541–2 he was a lay clerk at Canterbury Cathedral, and in 1543 became a Gentleman of the Chapel Royal; he remained in the royal household until his death, acting as organist, though he was not so designated until after 1570. In 1575 Elizabeth I granted him a licence, with Byrd, to print and publish music, as a result of which the *Cantiones sacrae*, an anthology of Latin motets by both composers, appeared later that year.

His earliest surviving works are probably three votive antiphons (*Salve intemerata virgo*, *Ave rosa sine spinis* and *Ave Dei patris filia*) in the traditional structure common up to *c*1530: division into two halves, with sections in reduced and full textures. Other early works include the Magnificat and another votive antiphon, *Sancte Deus*, both for men's voices. Two of his most sumptuous works, the six-voice antiphon *Gaude gloriosa Dei mater* and the seven-voice Mass '*Puer natus est nobis*', date from Mary Tudor's brief reign (1553–8), the former featuring musical imagery and melismatic writing, the latter expert handling of current techniques of structural imitation and choral antiphony. He also composed six Latin responsories and seven Office hymns for the Sarum rite and large-scale Latin psalm motets early in Elizabeth's reign. The 40-voice motet, *Spem in alium*, an astonishing technical achievement, may have been composed in 1573.

Tallis was one of the first to write for the new Anglican liturgy of 1547–53. Much of this music, including *If ye love me* and *Hear the voice and prayer*, is in four parts with clear syllabic word-setting and represents the prototype of the early English anthem. His Dorian Service is in a similar style. Among his Elizabethan vernacular music are nine four-voice psalm tunes (1567) and various English adaptations of Latin motets (e.g. *Absterge Domine*); the Latin Lamentations and the paired five-voice Magnificat and *Nunc dimittis* also date from this period. His instrumental works include keyboard arrangements of four partsongs and many *cantus firmus* settings and a small but distinguished contribution to the repertory of consort music which includes two fine In Nomines. Tallis's early music is relatively undistinguished, with neither Taverner's mastery of the festal style nor Tye's modernisms. But much of his later work is among the finest in Europe, ranging from the artless perfection of his short anthems to the restrained pathos of the Lamentations.

Tallis Scholars. English vocal ensemble, founded in 1978 by Peter Phillips (*b* 1953); they specialize in Renaissance music, particularly Josquin and English composers, singing two voices to a part.

Talma, Louise (*b* Arcachon, 31 Oct 1906). American composer. She studied at the New York Institute of Musical Art and with Boulanger and has taught at Hunter College. Until 1952 her music was neoclassical, but later works combine tonal and serial elements. Her output includes the opera *The Alcestiad* (1962), choral, vocal and chamber music.

Talvela, Martti (Olavi) (*b* Hiitola, 4 Feb 1935). Finnish bass. He studied at Lahti and in Stockholm, where he made his opera début in 1961 as Sparafucile (*Rigoletto*); in 1962 he joined the Deutsche Oper, Berlin, and sang at Bayreuth. His large, deep voice and impressive stage presence have served him well in Musorgsky (he sang Boris Godunov at the Met in 1974), Verdi and Wagner; he has also recorded songs by Sibelius and Kilpinen.

Tamagno, Francesco (*b* Turin, 28 Dec 1850; *d* Varese, 31 Aug 1905). Italian tenor. His heroic voice, with its trumpet-like top notes, was heard to best advantage in Verdi roles, especially Othello, which he created (1887), Riccardo (*Un ballo in maschera*), Don Carlos and Radames (*Aida*). A forceful actor, he brought great vocal and dramatic excitement to all his performances.

Tamberlik, Enrico (*b* Rome, 16 March 1820; *d* Paris, 13 March 1889). Italian tenor. His robust voice was marked by a fast vibrato, but his musicianship and handsome, exciting stage presence made him a superb interpreter of Beethoven's Florestan (*Fidelio*), Rossini's Othello and Verdi's Manrico (*Il trovatore*).

Tambourin. (1) An 18th-century French character piece, supposedly based on a Provençal folkdance accompanied by pipe and tabor. It is usually in a lively 2/4 metre, with a repeated bass note simulating a drum. There are examples in Rameau's operas and ballets.

(2) A double-headed drum of Provence with a long cylindrical body and a single snare on the upper head, known since the 15th century. It is usually struck with a single drumstick, using simple rhythmic sequences and played with a three-holed pipe (*galoubet*); it is *c*70 cm deep and 35 cm wide.

Tambourin de Béarn [tambourin à cordes]. A dulcimer, used primarily in southern France as a rhythmic bass accompaniment to the pipe. Popular during the Renaissance for dancing, it became fashionable at the French court in the 18th century. It has six gut strings stretched across a wooden resonator *c*90 cm long and is played with a three-holed pipe (*galoubet*).

Tambourine. A small single-headed FRAME DRUM, consisting of a shallow wooden ring, usually hung with jingles, covered on one side with parchment, calfskin or plastic (for illustration, *see* PERCUSSION INSTRUMENTS). It can be played in a variety of ways: the head struck with the palm, knuckles or closed fist; held aloft and shaken, for a tremolo effect; rolled

with the thumb, for a quiet tremolo; the rim struck with drumsticks; and other effects called for by composers, such as dropping it on the floor (as in Stravinsky's *Petrushka*) or flicking the jingles (as in Walton's *Façade*).

The tambourine has a long ancestry and seems to have been found in most parts of the world from ancient times. The Egyptians used it for mourning, the Israelites for mirth; in the pre-Islamic Middle East it was used for both. It became popular throughout Europe during the Middle Ages, and though usually associated with wandering showmen it rose to the ranks of court ensembles (Henry VIII had four in his band of 79 musicians). Gluck and Mozart both wrote for it and by the early 19th century it was established in the orchestra as the need arose for special effects of a Spanish or gypsy character.

Tambura. Term for a long-necked lute of south-east Europe, related to the *tambūrā* of the Indian subcontinent and the *ṭanbūr* of the Middle East and Central Asia.

Tamburini, Antonio (*b* Faenza, 28 March 1800; *d* Nice, 8 Nov 1876). Italian baritone. In Paris and London he was successful as an interpreter of Mozart, Rossini, Bellini and Donizetti, creating the parts of Ernesto in Bellini's *Il pirata* (1827), Valdeburgo in *La straniera* (1829), Sir Richard Forth in *I puritani* (1835) and Israele in Donizetti's *Marino Faliero* (1835). His extreme popularity in London is attested by the 'Tamburini riots' of 1840.

Tamerlano. Opera in three acts by Handel to a libretto by Haym after Piovene (1724, London).

Tampon. A double-headed drumstick used for playing rolls on the bass drum.

Tam-tam. Term, of Malay origin, for the unpitched GONG used in Western orchestras.

Tancredi. Opera ('melodramma eroico') in two acts by Rossini to a libretto by Rossi after Tasso and Voltaire (1813, Venice).

Taneyev, Sergey Ivanovich (*b* Vladimir-na-Klyaz'me, 25 Nov 1856; *d* Dyud'kovo, 19 June 1915). Russian composer. At the Moscow Conservatory he studied with Nikolay Rubinstein (piano) and Tchaikovsky (composition), whose friend he became, giving the première of Tchaikovsky's First Piano Concerto (1875) and succeeding him as teacher at the conservatory (1878). He eventually became director (1885–9) though it was as a teacher that he had the greater influence (his pupils included Skryabin, Rakhmaninov and Glier). An eclectic and conservative at heart, he was early drawn to the music of Bach and the Renaissance contrapuntists; these studies, allied to his diligence in formal planning, gave him a compositional skill unsurpassed by his Russian contemporaries. His most successful works are the large-scale instrumental pieces, particularly the fluent sonata structures, as in the C minor Symphony (1898) and the First String Quintet (1901), where his craftsmanship and contrapuntalism lend uncommon precision and polish to the musical argument. But his unoriginality and rejection of the indigenous Russian tradition resulted in conventional melodies and wooden musical characterization, for example in his ambitious opera *The Oresteia* (1887–94). Apart from the important chamber works (six string quartets, three quintets), Taneyev wrote choruses and many songs (some in Esperanto); his last work, the cantata *At the Reading of a Psalm* (1915), was acclaimed and considered by some his masterpiece. He wrote books on counterpoint and on canon.

His uncle Alexander Sergeyevich Taneyev (1850–1918), by profession a civil servant, was a pupil of Rimsky-Korsakov and composed operas, chamber and piano music and orchestral works including three symphonies.

Tangent. The brass blade at the back of a CLAVICHORD key which strikes the string when the front of the key is depressed. The term was earlier sometimes used for a jack.

Tangent piano. A keyboard instrument whose strings are struck by slips of wood like harpsichord jacks rather than by hammers, as in the piano. Various designs were tried from the early 18th century onwards, but the most successful were made by Späth and Schmahl after 1790. These look like grand pianos of the period, although their action is less complicated and their sound, to judge from surviving examples, is very beautiful.

Tanglewood. Estate near Lenox, MA, the site of a music school, Tanglewood (formerly Berkshire) Music Center (founded 1940) and of the Music Shed (1938, cap. 6000). The annual (summer) Tanglewood Music Festival (formerly Berkshire Music Festival, 1937) includes chamber concerts, jazz, folk and contemporary music and concerts by the Boston SO and Boston Pops Orchestra.

Tango. A Latin American song and dance genre. Formerly the term had a differing significance according to region and country, but it primarily designates the most popular urban dance of Argentina which became internationally popular in the 1910s. Up to *c*1915 it was normally in 2/4 time, then often in 4/4 or 4/8; after 1955 it became rhythmically more complex.

Tannhäuser (und der Sängerkrieg auf Wartburg). Opera in three acts by Wagner to his own libretto (1845, Dresden).

Tannhäuser, Der (*b c*1205; *d c*1270). German Minnesinger of noble Bavarian birth. His six *Leiche* and ten lieder reveal a life of adventurous travel, including participation in the fifth crusade (1228–33). His verse, particularly in his dance-songs, shows Neidhart von Reuental's influence. Although he was included by the Meistersinger as one of the 12 *alte Meister*, it is not clear which surviving melodies can firmly be attributed to him.

Tansman, Alexandre (*b* Lodz, 12 June 1897; *d* Paris, 15 Nov 1986). French composer and pianist of Polish origin. He studied with Rytel and in 1919 moved to Paris, where he came under the influence of Ravel, Milhaud and Stravinsky. He made his first tour as a pianist in 1927 with the Boston SO, later touring internationally as a pianist and conductor. During World War II he lived in the USA, returning to France in 1946. His large output covers most genres in a fluent variety of styles, though with a French neo-classical slant.

Tans'ur [Tansur], **William** (*b* Dunchurch, 1700, bap. 6 Nov 1706; *d* St Neots, 7 Oct 1783). English psalmodist and theorist. He taught in various parts of England, settling in St Neots. His several psalm collections contain metrical psalms, hymns and anthems, chiefly his own; one volume, *The Royal Melody Compleat* (1754–5), was later published in America. He was a successful exponent of the elaborate hymn tunes of the time, and influenced practices in country churches.

Tanto (It.). 'So much', e.g. *allegro ma non tanto* ('*allegro*, but not so much', i.e. slower than *allegro*).

Tap dance. A stage dance in which rhythmic patterns are sounded by the toes and heels (to which metal plates or 'taps' are fitted) striking the floor. It developed in the 19th century from such dances as the jig and clog dance. A related dance is the 'soft shoe', performed without taps on the shoes.

Tapiola. Tone poem, op.112, by Sibelius (1926).

Tapissier, Johannes (*b c*1370; *d* by Aug 1410). French composer and pedagogue; his real name was Jean de Noyers. One of the principal French poet-musicians of his day, he was in the service of Philip the Bold, Duke of Burgundy, by 1391 and he travelled widely with the court. Choirboys were trained at his 'escole de chant' in Paris. His extant works comprise a Credo and Sanctus for three voices and a four-voice isorhythmic motet lamenting the Great Schism.

Tapray, Jean-François (*b* Gray, Haute Saône, 1738; *d* Fontainebleau, *c*1819). French composer. He was organist of Besançon Cathedral, 1763–8, then moved to Paris, where besides performing and composing he became a famous keyboard teacher. In 1776–86 he was *maître de clavecin* and organist at the Ecole Royal Militaire. His works include concertos, *symphonies concertantes*, chamber music and many keyboard pieces: he was one of the first in France to write specifically for the piano.

Tār [t'ar]. Plucked lute of the RABĀB family, with a membrane as a soundtable, found in Iran and the Caucasus. It is used in popular urban entertainments, but is associated more with art music. It should not be confused with the *ṭār*, a circular frame drum of the Arab world.

Tarantella. A folkdance of southern Italy. Like the tarantula, its name is derived from the town of Taranto, but the legend that the dance was a cure for the spider's toxic bite is discredited. It is performed by a couple to a regularly phrased tune in 3/8 or 6/8 which alternates between major and minor and gradually increases in speed. The tarantella was revived as a concert piece in the 19th century by Chopin, Liszt and others.

Ṭăranu, Cornel (*b* Cluj, 20 June 1934). Romanian composer. He was a pupil of Toduță at the Cluj Conservatory (1951–7), where he immediately joined the staff; he also studied in Paris (1966–7) and at Darmstadt. His works combine folk and avant-garde influences and include the opera *Don Giovanni's Secret* (1970).

Taras Bulba. Rhapsody for orchestra by Janáček after Gogol (1918).

Tarchi, Angelo (*b* Naples, *c*1760; *d* Paris, 19 Aug

1814). Italian composer. Trained in Naples, he presented his first comic operas there, 1778–80. He then composed mostly for theatres in Rome, Florence and Milan, achieving great popularity; from 1785 most of his operas were *serie*. He was music director and composer at the King's Theatre, London, 1787–9. After a less productive period in Italy, he had seven *opéras comiques* staged in Paris, 1798–1802, with limited success. He worked finally as a singing teacher. A striking feature of his *c*50 operas is their grateful vocal writing; he also composed sacred works.

Tarditi, Orazio (*b* Rome, 1602; *d* Forlì, 18 Jan 1677). Italian composer and organist. He travelled widely, holding organist's posts at Arezzo Cathedral (1624–8), Murano and Volterra, and later serving as cathedral *maestro di cappella* at Forlì (1639), Jesi (1644–5) and Faenza (1647–70). His many sacred collections comprise concertato and solo motets, small and large concertato masses and psalm settings; following the trend of the time, his later works mostly use intimate scorings. He also composed some madrigals, canzonets, arias etc.

Tarditi, Paolo (*b* late 16th century; *d* after 1649). Italian composer. Working in Rome, he was first an organist and later *maestro di cappella*, notably at S Maria Maggiore (1629–40) and the church of the Madonna dei Monti (from 1649). He wrote motets, psalms etc; his 1620 collection contains some of the earliest music by a Roman composer with obbligato instrumental parts.

Tardos, Béla (*b* Budapest, 21 June 1910; *d* there, 18 Nov 1966). Hungarian composer. He studied with Kodály at the Budapest Academy (1932–7). His works include cantatas (*At the Outskirts of the City*, 1944, 1958), songs and functional music as well as three quartets.

Tárogató. A woodwind instrument with a reed, usually associated with Hungarian music. The ancient *tárogató* is a variant of the Eastern oboe and comes with or without finger-holes, straight or curved, ending in a bell; the double reed, with a disc to support the lips, produces a harsh, shrieking tone. The modern instrument consists of a straight wooden body with a conical bore and a clarinet (single-reed) mouthpiece. The keywork is like the modern oboe's and its tone, dark and penetrating, resembles the english horn's. Mahler and Hans Richter directed its use for the shepherd's tune in Act 3 of *Tristan und Isolde*.

Tarp, Svend-Erik (*b* Thisted, 6 Aug 1908). Danish composer. A pupil of Jeppesen at the Copenhagen Conservatory, he taught in the 1930s and 1940s, but became involved in administrative work. He composed in a French-orientated neo-classical style, concentrating on works for smaller ensembles and on piano music, but he has also written symphonies etc and is an admired film-music composer.

Tárrega (y Eixea), Francisco (*b* Villarreal, Castellón, 21 Nov 1852; *d* Barcelona, 15 Dec 1909). Spanish guitarist and composer. Hailed as 'the Sarasate of the guitar', he prepared the way for the rebirth of the guitar in the 20th century, giving concerts, teaching and composing for the instrument

(78 original works, 120 transcriptions), notably *Recuerdos de la Alhambra, Capricho árabe* and *Danza mora*.

Tartini, Giuseppe (*b* Pirano, 8 April 1692; *d* Padua, 26 Feb 1770). Italian composer and violinist. After abandoning plans for a monastic career he studied in Assisi (probably with Černohorský) and by 1714 had joined the orchestra at Ancona. He later spent time in Venice and Padua, where he settled in 1721 as principal violinist at the basilica of S Antonio. He worked there until 1765 except for a period in Prague (1723–6). Besides performing with success, he founded in 1727–8 a 'school' of violin instruction; his many pupils included J.G. Graun, Nardini and Naumann.

Tartini was one of the foremost Italian instrumental composers, writing over 400 works: these include violin concertos and sonatas (many with virtuoso solo parts), trio sonatas and sonatas for string ensemble. Most have three movements, ordered slow–fast–fast (sonatas) or fast–slow–fast (concertos). His later works in particular approach Classical structures and display *galant* features, including regular four-bar melodic phrases. Elaborate cadence formulae are especially characteristic. He also composed some sacred music. Noteworthy among his writings are a work on violin playing and ornamentation, *Traité des agréments de la musique* – published only in 1771 but thought to have been written earlier (L. Mozart, in 1756, is thought to have borrowed from it, but it may be the other way round) – and two treatises on the acoustical foundations of harmony (1754, 1767), in which his discovery of the DIFFERENCE TONE phenomenon is discussed.

*Orchestral music c*135 vn concs.; other concertos
Chamber music 4 sinfonie and sonatas, strs, bc; *c*40 trio sonatas; *c*135 sonatas, vn, bc, incl. 'Devil's Trill', g; L'arte del arco, variations (*c*1747); *c*30 sonatas, single movts, vn solo
Vocal music sacred pieces

Taskin, Pascal (Joseph) (*b* Theux, 1723; *d* Paris, 1793). French harpsichord maker. A senior workman in the Blanchet workshop in Paris, he succeeded to the firm's management on the death of François Etienne Blanchet (ii) in 1766, also becoming 'facteur des clavessins du Roi'. He was a fine and innovatory workman, from the 1760s popularizing the use in one register of soft buff leather plectra instead of quills and perfecting a system of knee levers for changing registers (1768). He rebuilt and enlarged Ruckers harpsichords, bringing the Blanchet workshop to its greatest prosperity. Piano making increased from the late 1770s.

Tasso, Torquato (*b* Sorrento, 11 March 1544; *d* Rome, 25 April 1595). Italian poet. He was long connected with the Este court at Ferrara. The technical perfection of his verse attracted countless madrigalists and monodists, especially his pastoral *Aminta* and above all his famous epic *Gerusalemme liberata*, a prime source for opera composers in the 17th century and later – it tells the story of Rinaldo and Armida, and was set by (among others) M. Rossi, Lully, Handel, Gluck, Haydn and Dvořák.

Tastar, tastar de corde (It.). 'Testing of the strings': a 16th-century term for a preludial style of lute writing designed to test the tuning and to set the mode for the pieces that followed.

Tasto. The key of a keyboard instrument, or the fingerboard of a bowed string instrument. The phrase 'tasto solo' was used by composers to instruct the keyboard player of a continuo part to play the bass notes alone, without chords above.

Tasto solo (It.). 'Single key': a phrase instructing the keyboard player of a continuo part to play the bass note(s) alone, without chords above.

Tate, Jeffrey (*b* Farnham, 28 April 1943). English conductor. He studied at Cambridge and qualified as a doctor, then worked at Covent Garden (1970–77), Bayreuth, Cologne Opera and from 1979 at the Met; his début was at Goteborg (*Carmen*, 1978), and he first conducted at the Met in 1980 (*Lulu*) and Covent Garden in 1982 (*Zauberflöte*). He has held posts as music director at Cologne and as guest conductor at Geneva and (from 1986) Covent Garden; he became principal conductor of the ECO in 1985. His musical sympathies are wide but he is specially admired for his insights in Mozart.

Tate, Phyllis (Margaret) (*b* Gerrards Cross, 6 April 1911; *d* London, 29 May 1987). English composer, she studied with Farjeon at the RAM (1928–32). Her works are relatively few and usually for small forces, in an English neo-classical style; they include the opera *The Lodger* (1960) and much educational music.

Tátrai Quartet. Hungarian string quartet, led by Vilmos Tátrai. It was formed in 1946, won the Bartók competition in 1948 and toured widely from 1952, playing the central Classical and Romantic repertory and new Hungarian works specially written for them. They have recorded complete Beethoven and Bartók cycles.

Tatum, Art (*b* Toledo, OH, 13 Oct 1909; *d* Los Angeles, 4 Nov 1956). American jazz pianist. He played in nightclubs and on radio before going to New York in 1932 and made many recordings. He worked with bands and his own trio but usually appeared as a soloist in clubs. His technical abilities, lightness of touch and control of the instrument's range were unprecedented; he had an unerring sense of rhythm and swing, a seemingly unlimited capacity to expand and enrich a melody and a profound grasp of substitute harmonies.

Tauber, Richard (*b* Linz, 16 May 1891; *d* London, 8 Jan 1948). Austrian tenor, naturalized British. He sang at Dresden from 1913, soon becoming popular throughout Germany and Austria in operas by Mozart and Strauss. From the 1920s he was widely successful in operetta, notably Lehár's *Das Land des Lächelns*. His voice showed the strain of repeated engagements but he was admired as Mozart's Ottavio when he returned to Covent Garden in 1947.

Tausig, Carl [Karol] (*b* Warsaw, 4 Nov 1841; *d* Leipzig, 17 July 1871). Polish pianist. He was the most gifted and famous of the first generation of Liszt pupils, with an impulsive, impassioned style of playing and an infallible technique in a repertory from Scarlatti to Liszt. He toured continually, composed a few pieces for solo piano and transcribed many more before dying of typhoid at the age of 29.

Tavener, John (Kenneth) (*b* London, 28 Jan 1944). English composer. He studied with Berkeley and Lumsdaine at the RAM (1961–5). Most of his music is explicitly religious, influenced by late Stravinsky but containing strong, bold images from a variety of other sources; his biblical cantata *The Whale* (1966) enjoyed a vogue. An early leaning towards Catholic devotion reached a consummation in the Crucifixion meditation *Ultimos ritos* (1972) and the opera *Thérèse* (1979). In 1976 he converted to the Russian Orthodox faith, composing in a simpler, luminous style (*Liturgy of St John Chrysostom* for unaccompanied chorus, 1978).

Taverner. Opera in two acts by Peter Maxwell Davies to his own libretto (1972, London).

Taverner, John (*b* south Lincs., *c*1490; *d* Boston, 18 Oct 1545). English composer. The earliest unequivocal references to him occur in 1524–5, when he was a lay clerk at the collegiate church of Tatershall. In 1526 he accepted the post of instructor of the choristers at Cardinal College (now Christ Church), Oxford, and *c*1530 became a lay clerk (and probably instructor of the choristers) at the parish church of St Botolph, Boston. By 1537 he had retired from full-time employment as a church musician. Although he was embroiled in an outbreak of Lutheran heresy at Cardinal College (in 1528) there is no evidence, contrary to popular opinion, that his views were seriously in conflict with Catholicism or that he ceased composing on leaving Oxford.

Most of his extant works, which include eight masses, three Magnificats, numerous motets and votive antiphons and a few consort pieces and fragmentary secular partsongs, probably date from the 1520s. The three six-voice masses use *cantus firmi*, sectional structure, huge spans of melisma and skilful counterpoint; of the smaller-scale masses 'Western Wynde' is based on a secular tune and in a less expansive, more Lutheran style. Characteristic of his writing is the development of a melodic or rhythmic fragment in imitation or canon or as an ostinato figure. The Magnificats are large-scale, florid works in the English tradition, also using *cantus firmi*. Two of his antiphons, however, *Mater Christi sanctissima* and *Christe Jesu, pastor bone*, clearly show Josquin's influence. His four-voice In Nomine, the prototype of this English genre, is simply a transcription of the 'In nomine Domine' section of his *Missa 'Gloria tibi Trinitas'*.

Taverner was pre-eminent among English musicians of his day: he enriched and transformed the English florid style by drawing on its best qualities, as well as on some continental techniques, and produced simpler works of great poise and refinement.

Sacred music 8 masses, incl. Missa 'Gloria tibi Trinitas', 6vv; 'Western Wynde', 4 vv; 3 Magnificats; over 20 motets; works adapted to English translations
Secular music partsongs; instrumental pieces

Taverner Choir. English early music choir, founded in 1973 (also Taverner Orchestra). *See* PARROTT, ANDREW.

Taylor, (Joseph) Deems (*b* New York, 22 Dec 1885; *d* there, 3 July 1966). American composer. He worked as a music critic and broadcaster in New York. His music, like his writing, is often witty but is now forgotten; it includes *The King's Henchman* (1927) and *Peter Ibbetsen* (1931), both given at the Met.

Taylor, Franklin (*b* Birmingham, 5 Feb 1843; *d* London, 19 March 1919). English pianist and teacher. He studied at the Leipzig Conservatory, where his teachers included Moscheles, and worked under Clara Schumann in Paris. He was well regarded as a professor at the RCM (from 1882), publishing several useful methods and collections of studies.

Taylor, Rayner (*b* London, 1747; *d* Philadelphia, 17 Aug 1825). American composer. He was a Chapel Royal choirboy in London and sang at Handel's funeral; he became an organist and teacher in Chelmsford, and had works performed in London theatres, also being associated with the pleasure gardens. He left England in 1792 and became organist of St Peter's, Philadelphia (1795–1813), and composed for the theatre. He wrote anthems, glees and small-scale piano music but is chiefly notable for his theatre music, including a lively opera *The Aethiop* (1814, Philadelphia).

Tchaikovsky, André. *See* TCHAIKOWSKY, ANDRÉ.

Tchaikovsky, Pyotr Il'yich (*b* Kamsko-Votkinsk, 7 May 1840; *d* St Petersburg, 6 Nov 1893). Russian composer. His father was a mine inspector. He started piano studies at five and soon showed remarkable gifts; his childhood was also affected by an abnormal sensitivity. At ten he was sent to the School of Jurisprudence at St Petersburg, where the family lived for some time. His parting from his mother was painful; further, she died when he was 14 – an event that may have stimulated him to compose. At 19 he took a post at the Ministry of Justice, where he remained for four years despite a long journey to western Europe and increasing involvement in music. In 1863 he entered the Conservatory, also undertaking private teaching. Three years later he moved to Moscow with a professorship of harmony at the new conservatory. Little of his music so far had pleased the conservative musical establishment or the more nationalist group, but his First Symphony had a good public reception when heard in Moscow in 1868.

Rather less successful was his first opera, *The Voyevoda*, given at the Bol'shoy in Moscow in 1869; Tchaikovsky later abandoned it and re-used material from it in his next, *The Oprichnik*. A severe critic was Balakirev, who suggested that he wrote a work on *Romeo and Juliet*: this was the Fantasy-Overture, several times rewritten to meet Balakirev's criticisms; Tchaikovsky's tendency to juxtapose blocks of material rather than provide organic transitions serves better in this programmatic piece than in a symphony as each theme stands for a character in the drama. Its expressive, well-defined themes and their vigorous treatment produced the first of his works in the regular repertory.

The Oprichnik won some success at St Petersburg in 1874, by when Tchaikovsky had won acclaim with his Second Symphony (which incorporates Ukrainian folktunes); he had also composed two string quartets (the first the source of the famous Andante cantabile), most of his next opera, *Vakula the Smith*, and of his First Piano Concerto, where contrasts of the heroic and the lyrical, between soloist and orchestra, clearly fired him. Originally intended for Nikolay Rubinstein, the head of Moscow Conservatory, who had much encouraged Tchaikovsky, it was dedicated to Hans von Bülow (who gave its première, in Boston) when Rubinstein rejected it as ill-composed and unplayable (he later recanted and became a distinguished interpreter of it). In 1875 came the carefully written Third Symphony and *Swan Lake*, commissioned by Moscow Opera. The next year a journey west took in *Carmen* in Paris, a cure at Vichy and the first complete *Ring* at Bayreuth; although deeply depressed when he reached home – he could not accept his homosexuality – he wrote the fantasia *Francesca da Rimini* and (an escape into the 18th century) the *Rococo Variations* for cello and orchestra. *Vakula*, which had won a competition, had its première that autumn. At the end of the year he was contacted by a wealthy widow, Nadezhda von Meck, who admired his music and was eager to give him financial security; they corresponded intimately for 14 years but never met.

Tchaikovsky, however, saw marriage as a possible solution to his sexual problems; and when contacted by a young woman who admired his music he offered (after first rejecting her) immediate marriage. It was a disaster: he escaped from her almost at once, in a state of nervous collapse, attempted suicide and went abroad. This was however the time of two of his greatest works, the Fourth Symphony and *Eugene Onegin*. The symphony embodies a 'fate' motif that recurs at various points, clarifying the structure; the first movement is one of Tchaikovsky's most individual with its hesitant, melancholy waltz-like main theme and its ingenious and appealing combination of this with the secondary ideas; there is a lyrical, intermezzo-like second movement and an ingenious third in which pizzicato strings play a main role, while the finale is impassioned if loose and melodramatic, with a folk theme pressed into service as second subject. *Eugene Onegin*, after Pushkin, tells of a girl's rejected approach to a man who fascinates her (the parallel with Tchaikovsky's situation is obvious) and his later remorse: the heroine Tatyana is warmly and appealingly drawn, and Onegin's hauteur is deftly conveyed too, all against a rural Russian setting which incorporates spectacular ball scenes, an ironic background to the private tragedies. The brilliant Violin Concerto also comes from the late 1870s.

The period 1878–84, however, represents a creative trough. He resigned from the conservatory and, tortured by his sexuality, could produce no music of real emotional force (the Piano Trio, written on Rubinstein's death, is a single exception). He spent some time abroad. But in 1884, stimulated by Balakirev, he produced his *Manfred* symphony, after Byron. He continued to travel widely, and conduct; and he was much honoured. In 1888 the Fifth Symphony, similar in plan to the Fourth (though the motto theme is heard in each movement), was finished; a note of hysteria in the finale was recognized by Tchaikovsky himself. The next three years saw the composition of two ballets, the finely characterized *Sleeping Beauty* and the more decorative *Nutcracker*, and the opera *The Queen of Spades*, with its ingenious atmospheric use of Rococo music (it is set in Catherine the Great's Russia) within a work of high emotional tension. Its theatrical qualities ensured its success when given at St Petersburg in late 1890. The next year Tchaikovsky visited the USA; in 1892 he heard Mahler conduct *Eugene Onegin* at Hamburg. In 1893 he worked on his Sixth Symphony, to a plan – the first movement was to be concerned with activity and passion; the second, love; the third, disappointment; and the finale, death. It is a profoundly pessimistic work, formally unorthodox, with the finale haunted by descending melodic ideas clothed in anguished harmonies. It was performed on 28 October. He died nine days later: traditionally, and officially, of cholera, but recently verbal evidence has been put forward that he underwent a 'trial' from a court of honour from his old school regarding his sexual behaviour and it was decreed that he commit suicide. Which version is true must remain uncertain.

Dramatic music The Voyevoda (1869); The Oprichnik (1874); Vakula the Smith (1876); Eugene Onegin (1879); The Maid of Orleans (1881); Mazeppa (1884); The Sorceress (1887); The Queen of Spades (1890); ballets: Swan Lake (1877); The Sleeping Beauty (1890); The Nutcracker (1892); incidental music
Orchestral music Sym. no.1, g, 'Winter Daydreams' (1866, rev. 1874); Sym. no.2, c, 'Little Russian' (1872, rev. 1880); Sym. no.3, D, 'Polish' (1875); Sym. no.4, f (1878); Sym. no.5, e (1888); Sym. no.6, b, 'Pathétique' (1893); Manfred, sym. (1885); Romeo and Juliet, fantasy ov. (1870, rev. 1880); Francesca da Rimini, sym. fantasia (1876); 1812, ov. (1880); Hamlet, fantasy ov. (1888); Pf Conc. no.1, b♭ (1875); Pf Conc. no.2, G (1880); Pf Conc. no.3, E♭ (1893); Vn Conc., D (1878); Variations on a Rococo Theme, vc, orch, A (1876); Serenade, strs (1880); over 20 other works
Chamber and keyboard music 3 str qts (1871, 1874, 1877); Pf Trio, a (1882); Souvenir de Florence, str sextet (1890); 12 other chamber works; Pf Sonata, G (1879); over 100 other pf pieces
Vocal music c30 choral works, incl. sacred pieces, secular cantatas; over 100 songs and duets

Tchaikowsky, André (*b* Warsaw, 1 Nov 1935; *d* Oxford, 26 June 1982). British pianist. After escaping from Poland to Paris in World War II, he returned to study at Łódz; he studied at the Paris Conservatoire, in Warsaw and under Boulanger and Askenase. He made his American début in 1957 and his London début the next year, settling in England. A spirited and responsive musician, he had a wide repertory and was also valued as a composer; his works include a String Quartet (1967), a Piano Concerto (1971) and song cycles.

Tcherepnin, Alexander (Nikolayevich) (*b* St Petersburg, 21 Jan 1899; *d* Paris, 29 Sept 1977). American composer of Russian origin. His father Nikolay Nikolayevich (1873–1945) was a pupil of Rimsky-Korsakov who wrote ballets for Dyagilev (*Le pavillon d'Armide*, 1908) and settled in Paris in 1921. Alexander completed his studies there and became associated with Martinů and Beck, experi-

menting with new scales in a Franco-Russian neo-classical style (including one sometimes known by his name: C–D♭–E♭–E♮–F–G–A♭–A♮–B–C). In 1934–7 he travelled in the Far East, which brought about additions to his range of materials. In 1950 he settled in the USA. His large output, spirited in style and cosmopolitan in manner, includes ballets, four symphonies (1927–57), six piano concertos (1919–65), chamber and keyboard music. His sons Sege (*b* 1941) and Ivan (*b* 1943) are also composers.

Tear, Robert (*b* Barry, 8 March 1939). Welsh tenor. He studied at Cambridge and joined the St Paul's Cathedral Choir. He sang with the English Opera Group, notably as Quint in *The Turn of the Screw*; Pears's roles suited his voice well. He created Dov in Tippett's *Knot Garden* (1970) at Covent Garden, where his other roles have included Lensky. He sang Monteverdi's Nero with the Netherlands Opera and Loge at the Paris Opéra (1976). He is much admired for the clarity, precision and taste of his singing, which serves well in lieder and Bach's Passions.

Teatro alla Scala. See SCALA, LA.

Teatro Colón. Theatre in Buenos Aires (1857–88, reopened 1908), staging opera seasons with international performers.

Teatro La Fenice. See FENICE, LA.

Teatro Olimpico. Theatre in Vicenza, Italy. It has fixed scenery and was built by Palladio in 1579 for the Accademia Olimpica (founded 1555). Operas suitable for its stage are given there each autumn.

Teatro San Carlo. See SAN CARLO.

Teatro San Cassiano. See SAN CASSIANO.

Tebaldi, Renata (*b* Pesaro, 1 Feb 1922). Italian soprano. She sang in Italy from 1944 (La Scala, 1946–54); in 1950 she appeared as Desdemona at Covent Garden and in 1955 made her début at the Met. She was admired for the unforced, natural beauty of her voice in such roles as Violetta and Tosca.

Techelmann, Franz Matthias (*b* Dvorce na Mor, *c*1649; *d* Vienna, 26 Feb 1714). Austrian composer. He worked in Vienna from 1678 as an organist and is noted for his keyboard suites in the Froberger tradition.

Tedesca (It.). Term for German dances since the 15th century. It was sometimes used for the allemande, and by Beethoven for music in the style of a *deutscher Tanz*. See GERMAN DANCE.

Te Deum. A chant in praise of God sung at the end of Matins on Sundays and feast days, and also as a processional chant and song of thanksgiving. Polyphonic settings are rare before the 16th century, from when there are settings by Taverner, Sheppard, Anerio, Lassus and Handl. A new tradition of festive settings was inaugurated in the Baroque era by Benevoli, Lully and others, and continued in the 18th century by Michael and Joseph Haydn. Among later settings, those by Berlioz, Bruckner, Dvořák, Verdi and Kodály are particularly striking.

The *Te Deum* in English occupies a regular place in the Anglican SERVICE. Festal settings begin with Purcell's (1694) and continue with those of Handel, Sullivan, Parry, Stanford and Walton. Luther's version, *Herr Gott dich loben wir*, based on the Gregorian melody, was set six times by Michael Praetorius; organ settings include those of Scheidt, Buxtehude and Bach.

Teitelbaum, Richard (Lowe) (*b* New York, 19 May 1939). American composer. He studied at Yale and with Nono and Petrassi in Italy, where he was a founder member of Musica Elettronica Viva. In 1970 he returned to North America to teach, compose and perform but spent time in Japan. Most of his works are for ensembles of conventional and electronic instruments.

Te Kanawa, Dame Kiri (*b* Gisbourne, 6 March 1944). New Zealand soprano. She studied at the London Opera Centre. Her first major role was as Mozart's Countess, at Covent Garden in 1971. She made her American début, at San Francisco, the following year and in 1974 sang Desdemona with great success at the Met. In operas by Mozart, Strauss and Puccini she has been admired for her fresh, full voice and dignified stage bearing.

Telemann, Georg Philipp (*b* Magdeburg, 14 March 1681; *d* Hamburg, 25 June 1767). German composer. He was one of the most prolific composers ever. At ten he could play four instruments and had written arias, motets and instrumental works. His parents discouraged musical studies, but he gravitated back to them. At Leipzig University he founded a collegium musicum; at 21 he became musical director of the Leipzig Opera; at 23 he took on a post as church organist. The next year he moved to Žary, as court Kapellmeister, where he wrote French-style dance suites, sometimes tinged by local Polish and Moravian folk music, and cantatas. In 1708 he went in the same capacity to the Eisenach court and in 1712 to Frankfurt as city music director. As Kapellmeister of a church there, he wrote at least five cantata cycles and works for civic occasions, while his duties as director of a collegium musicum drew from him instrumental works and oratorios.

He was offered various other positions, but moved only in 1721, when he was invited to Hamburg as director of music at the five main churches and Kantor at the Johanneum. Here he had to write two cantatas each Sunday, with extra ones for special church and civic occasions, as well as an annual Passion, oratorio and serenata. In his spare time he directed a collegium musicum and wrote for the opera house; the city councillors waived their objections to the latter when he indicated that he would otherwise accept an invitation to Leipzig. He directed the Hamburg Opera from 1722 until its closure in 1738. In 1737 he paid a visit to Paris, appearing at court and the Concert Spirituel. From 1740 he devoted more time to musical theory, but from 1755 he turned to the oratorio. He published much of his music, notably a set of 72 cantatas and the three sets of *Musique de table* (1733), his best-known works, each including a concerto, a suite and several chamber pieces. He was eager to foster the spread of music and active in publishing several didactic works, for example on figured bass and ornamentation. He was by far the most famous composer in Germany; in a contemporary dictionary he is assigned four times as much space as J.S. Bach.

Telemann composed in all the forms and styles current in his day; he wrote Italian-style concertos and sonatas, French-style overture-suites and quartets, German fugues, cantatas, Passions and songs. Some of his chamber works, for example the quartets in the *Musique de table*, are in a conversational, dialogue-like manner that is lucid in texture and elegant in diction. Whatever style he used, Telemann's music is easily recognizable as his own, with its clear periodic structure, its clarity and its ready fluency. Though four years senior to Bach and Handel, he used an idiom more forward-looking than theirs and in several genres can be seen as a forerunner of the Classical style.

His grandson Georg Michael (1748–1831) was a Kantor and teacher at the cathedral school in Riga; his output includes church and organ works and writings on music.

*Sacred vocal music c*1700 church cantatas; 27 Passions and Passion oratorios; 6 oratorios, incl. Der Tag des Gerichts (1762); 17 masses; 2 Magnificats; *c*30 psalms; 16 motets; sacred songs, duets, canons; occasional cantatas, oratorios
Secular vocal music 9 operas, incl. *Der geduldige Socrates* (1721), *Pimpinone*, intermezzo (1725); music for other composers' operas; occasional serenades, cantatas; *c*50 solo cantatas; over 100 songs
*Orchestral music c*120 ovs.; 4 syms.; 2 divertimentos; 47 concs. for solo inst; *c*50 other concs
Chamber music 36 solo fantasias; duos; *c*100 vn sonatas, fl sonatas; over 100 trio sonatas; over 50 qts, qnts; lute pieces
Keyboard music fugues, chorale preludes; suites, fantasias, minuets

Telephone, The. Opera in one act by Menotti to his own libretto (1947, New York).

Telharmonium [dynamophone]. An electromechanical keyboard instrument developed in the USA by Thaddeus Cahill in the 1890s. It used the tone-wheel principle to generate sounds. Three models were built (1900, 1906, 1911). The second version, weighing nearly 200 tons, was used to transmit daily concerts over the telephone network in New York City. The third version was even larger. A commercial failure, it was not used after 1914.

Tel jour, telle nuit. Song cycle by Poulenc (1937), settings for voice and piano of nine poems by Paul Eluard.

Tellefsen, Thomas (Dyke Acland) (*b* Trondheim, 26 Nov 1823; *d* Paris, 16 Oct 1874). Norwegian pianist and composer. He was taught by Chopin, who became a friend, and was especially admired as a Chopin interpreter, soon becoming one of the outstanding pianists of his time. Besides two piano concertos and chamber music he composed 16 mazurkas.

Temperament. A tuning of a scale in which most or all of the concords are made slightly impure in order that none or few are distastefully so. Equal temperament, in which the octave is divided into 12 uniform semitones, is the standard Western temperament today except among specialists in early music.

Temperaments are necessary mainly because the concords of triadic music – octaves, 5ths and 3rds – are in many cases incommensurate in their pure forms. Thus three pure major 3rds fall short of a pure octave by about one-fifth of a whole tone; four pure minor 3rds exceed an octave by half as much again; the circle of pure 5ths does not quite cumulate in a perfect unison; and the major 2nd produced by subtracting a pure minor 3rd from a pure 4th is about 11% smaller than that produced by subtracting a pure 4th from a pure 5th.

The earliest temperament known to have been used in Western music was Pythagorean, with most of the 5ths pure. Mean-tone temperaments, with pure (or very nearly pure) major 3rds, succeeded during the Renaissance and early Baroque period. Irregular or 'circulating' temperaments were, however, advocated by some Renaissance and Baroque theorists and were recommended by some writers of the time, in the late 18th century especially, for the particular character they gave to each key (advocates included Tartini and Bach's pupil Kirnberger). This in turn was succeeded, as music became increasingly chromatic and ranged wider in key, by equal temperament. Equal temperament had been advocated by theorists as far back as the 16th century, and came increasingly to prevail during the 18th and 19th. It is uncertain whether Bach had equal temperament in mind when writing his *Well-Tempered Clavier*; but this was the system recommended by Rameau (1737) and C.P.E. Bach (1762). This system is, necessarily, the one universally used today for recent and contemporary music, though specialists in early music endeavour to use historically correct temperaments – as is necessary if the music is to sound as it did at the time and place when and where it was composed.

Tempest. Beethoven's Piano Sonata in D minor op.31 no.2 (1802), so called because of its tempestuous character.

Tempesta di mare, La (It.: 'storm at sea'). Title given to two programmatic concertos by Vivaldi: for violin in E♭ op.8 no.5 RV253, and for flute in F op.10 no.1 RV433 (in different versions RV98 and 570).

Temple block. *See* WOODBLOCK.

Tempo. The 'time' of a musical composition, hence the speed of its performance. Tempo may be specified by a composer in terms of metrical units per unit of time; this may be measured by a metronome or, before the invention of the metronome, by a pendulum, a man's heartbeat or some other means. Tempo has been more generally indicated since the late Baroque period by the use of one of the standard Italian tempo indications, such as *allegro, andante, adagio* etc (some of which may suggest a piece's mood as well as its speed). Still earlier, before the use of Italian tempo indications, the time signatures used in proportional notation gave some indication of speed. Other clues as to a piece's intended tempo may come from its relation to the speeds of dances on which it might be modelled.

Tempo and expression marks. Verbal and other directions to performers are found in musical scores from the 16th century, but are rare until the 17th. By the late 17th century, the basic Italian tempo directions as well as dynamic instructions were established and internationally understood. Probably the earliest extensive listing of them is in Sébastien de Brossard's *Dictionaire* (1703). Their Italian origin reflects the domination of Italian music in Europe in the period 1600–1750, when tempo and expression marks developed into a system. But marks in English and German are known in early music, and in France a comprehensive system of French-language directions developed in the early 18th century. Some German composers of the 19th century favoured their own language, as have many composers of other nationalities at various times, but the standard Italian terms have prevailed through the strength of usage and tradition. Further, 'musicians' Italian' does not always correspond to the language itself in that musical meanings are sometimes only loosely related to literal ones and many terms are not normal Italian (*andantino, glissando*).

Other factors besides tempo instructions may affect the speed at which a piece should be taken. In early music, the time signature or mensuration sign was significant; at all periods, the choice of note values is significant. There has also been a general understanding, at some periods, of a 'tempo giusto' or normal speed – a concept related to the Renaissance *tactus* and sometimes measured in terms of the heartbeat or of walking or breathing. Other factors may include the relationship of music to an established dance tempo and the text content of a piece. Since the early 19th century composers have been able to use the METRONOME as a precise measurement of tempo, but many have been reluctant to do so because of its rigidity, which could be taken to suggest that tempo was unalterable in the course of a piece and that the right tempo was unrelated to external circumstances of performance (like the acoustic of the room in which a piece was to be heard).

A number of conventions for the use of tempo and expression marks in music are established: that tempo and similar instructions are printed at the top of each movement, commonly in bold, roman type; that dynamics are notated below each staff, separately for each performer or voice, in bold italic type, using the traditional letter abbreviations (*see* DYNAMICS); that marks of expression (including modifications of dynamic or tempo marks) are printed in normal italic type; and that technical instructions are printed in roman type ('con sordino' etc).

Tempo giusto (It.). 'Just time', 'strict time': either the abstract concept of a 'correct' tempo for a piece, or a tempo designation indicating a speed that the style demands, or a direction to return to strict tempo after a deviation.

Tempo ordinario (It.). 'Common time': either the Italian for 4/4 (common time), or a designation for a tempo that requires no further description.

Tempo primo (It.). 'First pace': an indication that, after a change of tempo, the opening pace of a piece is to be resumed. It is often notated 'Tempo I'.

Tempora mutantur (Lat.: 'times change'). Title, probably authentic, of Haydn's Symphony no.64 in A (*c*1775).

Tenaglia [Tanaglia], **Antonio Francesco** (*b* Florence, *c*1616–20; *d* Rome, after 1661). Italian composer, keyboard player and lutenist. He spent most of his career in Rome, where his patrons included Cardinal Antonio Barberini (from 1644). After a period abroad he was active from 1654 as a keyboard virtuoso and lutenist, and at some point he was organist of St John Lateran. With Carissimi, Luigi Rossi (whom he emulated) and others, he was a leading composer of solo cantatas. Over 60 by him survive; they are notable for their intense and varied expression and their interplay between the vocal and continuo lines. He also had two operas performed (1656, 1661) and wrote several vocal duets and trios.

Tender Land, The. Opera in two acts by Copland to a libretto by H. Everett and E. Johns (1954, New York).

Tendre, tendrement (Fr.). Tender, tenderly.

Tenducci, Giusto Ferdinando (*b* Siena, *c*1735; *d* Genoa, 25 Jan 1790). Italian castrato soprano and composer. An opera singer in England from 1758, he was associated with J.C. Bach, whose arrangements of Scotch songs for him created a vogue for this genre. Mozart, another friend, later wrote an aria for him in Paris (1778; it is lost). He presented several (unsuccessful) operas in Dublin and wrote songs, airs and a singing tutor.

Tenebrae (Lat.: 'darkness'). Name for the combined Offices of Matins and Lauds on the Thursday, Friday and Saturday of Holy Week; the name is connected with the extinguishing of candles. The musically significant portions are the first three of the nine Matins lessons, from the LAMENTATIONS of Jeremiah and the responsories that follow (*see* RESPONSORY). Composers of Tenebrae music (apart from the Lamentations) include Gesualdo, Handl, Lassus, Morales, Palestrina and Victoria.

Teneramente (It.). Tenderly.

Tenney, James (Carl) (*b* Silver City, NM, 10 Aug 1934). American composer and pianist. He was a pupil and associate of various musicians, including Partch and Varèse; he also performed with Reich and Glass in the late 1960s, since when he has taught in California and Toronto. Many of his works use computer and other electronic means, on which he has done pioneering theoretical work. As a pianist and conductor he is associated with Ives.

Tennstedt, Klaus (*b* Merseburg, 6 June 1926). German conductor. He studied at the Leipzig Conservatory and held posts in Halle and Dresden and as conductor of the Schwerin State Orchestra (1962–71). He conducted in Sweden from 1971 and the next year became Generalmusikdirektor of the Kiel Opera. He appeared in North America in 1974 and made his London début in 1976. In 1979 he was appointed chief conductor of the Norddeutscher Rundfunk SO, Hamburg, and chief guest conductor of the Minnesota Orchestra (1979–82); he was appointed musical director of the LPO in 1983. Though an experienced opera conductor (he made his Met début in *Fidelio*, 1983), he is admired chiefly for his breadth of grasp and strength of feeling in the symphonic repertory, especially in Beethoven and Mahler.

Tenor. Term, from the Latin *tenere* ('to hold'), originally meaning a sustaining part or possibly one that 'held up' a contrapuntal structure; through a series of derivations it has also come to mean a high male voice.

In the Middle Ages and Renaissance, polyphonic pieces were usually based on a *cantus firmus* or given melody, which was normally assigned to the tenor part. With the development of polyphony in the late Middle Ages and early Renaissance, the tenor part was supplemented by one or two contratenor ('against tenor') parts; the tenor tended to assume a range apt to a high male voice and the term came to be understood as descriptive of a vocal range.

The tenor remained the most important solo voice during the 16th century and part of the 17th. It was used not only in sacred music but also secular, where much early monody was designed for it. Giulio Caccini, the pioneer monodist, was himself a tenor. Monteverdi's Orpheus was sung by a tenor (Francesco Rasi), but with the rise of the castrato the tenor was relegated to secondary status except in France, where the very high tenor or *haute-contre* (equivalent to the English countertenor) was cultivated. While in Passion music the tenor retained the traditional role of narrator, in the opera house he was rarely assigned anything more than a comic or character part (an old man, a confidant, a schemer, even in travesty as an elderly nurse).

By the 1720s, however, heroic roles were occasionally assigned to tenors and by the Classical period tenors often assumed hero-lover roles. In the early 19th century a more powerful and dramatic type of tenor voice was developed, with the operas of Rossini, Bellini and Donizetti; such types as the *tenore robusto* (a powerful, baritone-like voice) and the *tenore di forza* (more lyrical but capable of powerful climaxes) came into use, while in Germany the *Heldentenor* (heroic tenor) was being developed for such roles as Tristan and Siegfried in the *Ring*. The lyric tenor persisted in French opera. A type also used in the late 19th century was the *tenor altino* (or *tenore-contraltino*) which extends into the treble region in true head tone (i.e. not in falsetto). The light 'tenorino' was also popular, though more in the salon than in the opera house.

Caruso, with his incomparable recordings from the beginning of the century, set a standard for tenors of the 20th century, which has been maintained in the Italian repertory by Martinelli, Gigli and more recently Domingo and Pavarotti; other outstanding tenors of this century include Melchior, in the heroic Wagner roles, Björling, for his purity and refinement in the Italian repertory, Pears, whose special style and artistry generated a new repertory, mainly from Britten, and Vickers, widely regarded as the leading interpreter of many heroic roles.

The term 'tenor' is sometimes used adjectivally for a member of a family of instruments whose pitch roughly corresponds to the tenor voice. TENOR VIOLIN (or simply 'tenor') usually means viola, occasionally a small cello; 'tenoroon' is a contraction of 'tenor bassoon'; and the term is also used for particular sizes of viol, recorder, saxophone and tuba. The tenor trombone is the basic type. The tenor clef shows middle C on the fourth line of the staff.

Tenor C. Term for *c*, an octave below Middle C.

Tenor cor. A valved brass instrument, distinct from the TENOR HORN, dating from the 1860s. It is circular, like the horn, and pitched in F but of only half the horn in F's tube length. The higher harmonic series and the wider conical bore and mouthpiece make it much easier to play than the real horn, and it has been used as a substitute, particularly in military bands. But improved teaching of the modern German orchestral horn and its improved facility and power have rendered the tenor cor largely obsolete.

Tenor horn. A valved brass instrument of alto pitch, often referred to as the E♭ horn. It is an essential component of brass bands, which normally contain three. Historically it is the modern form of the E♭ alto saxhorn, also termed 'tenor'. The brass band instrument in B♭ known as 'baritone' in England and the USA is called 'Tenorhorn' in Germany, where the tenor horn is known as 'Althorn'.

Tenorlied. The principal type of German polyphonic lied during the period *c*1450–*c*1550. It consists of a pre-existing lied melody set as a *cantus firmus*, or tenor, accompanied by two or three contrapuntal parts. ('Tenor' does not mean the tenor voice, though from *c*1500 the existing melody was usually assigned to the tenor in four-part settings.)

Tenor mass. A setting of the Ordinary of the Roman Catholic Mass in which the same borrowed material appears as a *cantus firmus* in the tenor of each section. There are examples by Dunstable, Ockeghem and Josquin.

Tenoroon. A small BASSOON in F, now obsolete, pitched a 5th above the standard instrument.

Tenor saxophone. A SAXOPHONE in B♭ (or C), sounding a major 9th (or octave) lower than written.

Tenor tuba. A TUBA in B♭, often called a EUPHONIUM.

Tenor violin. Term for a string instrument, most often a viola or small cello. In its earliest uses, in the 16th century, 'tenor violin' referred to a three-string viola tuned *c–g–d'*; later, it sometimes meant an instrument resembling a small cello with a tuning between the modern cello and viola (in 5ths from *F* or *G*) which died out after the mid-17th century. But the most common meaning was a *c*-tuned viola larger than normal, as distinct from the 'alto' viola. These were used as the alto and tenor parts of a four-part string ensemble until after 1700.

Tenso [tenson]. A debate between two or more troubadours or trouvères in the form of a poem in which the participants expressed their own opinions on a chosen topic. This is supposed to have distinguished it from the *partimen* where the participants took sides only for the sake of discussion, although the distinction was not always observed in practice.

Tenuto (It.). 'Held': an instruction normally applied to single notes or groups of notes that can denote holding them to their full length or completely interrupting the metre.

Ternary form. A tripartite musical form, *ABA*. The recurrence of *A* may be modified by ornamentation or development (*ABA'*). The *da capo* aria and the minuet and trio are examples, and ternary structures are also found in the slow movements of many Clas-sical sonatas, symphonies and concertos and among 19th-century piano pieces such as Mendelssohn's *Lieder ohne Worte* and Chopin's waltzes and nocturnes.

Ternina, Milka (*b* Doljnji, 19 Dec 1863; *d* Zagreb, 18 May 1941). Croatian soprano. She made her début at Zagreb in 1882, then sang at Leipzig (Elisabeth in *Tannhäuser*) and in 1890 joined the Munich company, singing Beethoven's Leonore. Her Covent Garden début, in 1898, was as Isolde; she later appeared as Brünnhilde, and the next year sang Kundry at Bayreuth. She sang the same roles at Boston (1896) and appeared at the Met as Elisabeth; she also sang Tosca there (as she had at its London première, 1900) and Kundry. She retired in 1906. She was noted for her large, warm voice and her fine dramatic gifts.

Terradellas, Domingo Miguel Bernabé (*b* Barcelona, bap. 13 Feb 1713; *d* Rome, 20 May 1751). Spanish composer. Trained in Naples, he achieved his first major success with the opera *Merope* (1743; Rome). He also worked at the Spanish church in Rome, 1743–5. In 1746–7 he presented three stage works in London. In all he composed ten *opere serie*, three other stage works, two oratorios and much church music, using a vigorous italianate style notable for its vigour and strong contrasts. His operas were among the first to use wind instruments in accompanied recitative.

Terrasse, Claude (Antoine) (*b* Grande-Lemps, 27 Jan 1867; *d* Paris, 30 June 1923). French composer. His notable contribution (*c*28 operettas, most given in Paris) to the renaissance of *opéra bouffe* includes the successful *Le sire de Vergy* (1903) and *Le mariage de Télémaque* (1910).

Terry, Charles Sanford (*b* Newport Pagnell, 24 Oct 1864; *d* Westerton of Pitfodels, 5 Nov 1936). English historian and Bach scholar. He taught history at Newcastle upon Tyne and later became professor at Aberdeen. He worked on Bach from about 1915, was excellent at collecting and organizing information and published many books on his life and work, including a detailed and readable biography. He should not be confused with his contemporary Sir Richard Runciman Terry (1865–1938), first organist of Westminster Cathedral (1901–24) and scholar and reviver of English Catholic church music, especially of the 16th century.

Tertiary [tertian] **harmony.** Term for a harmonic system based on the interval of a 3rd (as in the major–minor tonal system, as opposed to medieval QUARTAL HARMONY.

Tertis, Lionel (*b* West Hartlepool, 29 Dec 1876; *d* London, 22 Feb 1975). English viola player. He studied in Leipzig and at the RAM. After playing as principal in the Queen's Hall and Beecham orchestras (from 1900), he appeared widely as a soloist, doing much to overcome the public want of interest in the viola as a solo instrument. He performed with power and depth of tone – using a large viola of his own design – in a repertory that included many British works written for him and numerous of his own transcriptions.

Terzakis, Dimitri (*b* Athens, 12 March 1938). Greek

composer. He was a pupil of Papaioannou at the Hellenic Conservatory (1959–64) and of Zimmermann and Eimert at the Cologne Musikhochschule (1965–9); since 1974 he has taught in Düsseldorf. His works have used Byzantine elements, particularly microtones (e.g. in *Ikos* for chorus, 1968).

Terzet. 18th-century term for a composition for three voices, with or without accompaniment. Dvořák's Terzetto op.74 exemplifies a rare use of the term for instrumental music.

Tessarini, Carlo (*b* Rimini *c*1690; *d* ?Amsterdam, after 15 Dec 1766). Italian composer. After several years in Venice he was a violinist at Urbino Cathedral (probably from *c*1733), also playing at other centres including Brno, Rome and probably Paris, finally settling in the Netherlands. His output includes over 20 sets of solo and trio sonatas, concertos and sinfonias (mostly for strings), often dance-like in character and technically demanding, and showing Vivaldi's influence. He also wrote a violin method (1741).

Tessier, Charles (*fl c*1600). French composer. A lutenist in Henri IV's service, he wrote two books of *airs* (1597, 1604), mainly strophic and suitable for several voices or solo voice and lute. He had connections with the Essex family in England. He may have been related to Guillaume Tessier, a Breton composer who in 1582 published a book of airs dedicated to Elizabeth I.

Tessitura (It.). Term used to describe the part of a vocal (or instrumental) compass in which a piece of music predominantly lies. The tessitura of a piece is concerned with the part of the range most used, not by its extremes.

Testi, Flavio (*b* Florence, 4 Jan 1923). Italian composer. He studied at the Turin Conservatory and taught at the Padua and Milan conservatories. His works include operas, cantatas and orchestral music in an eloquent, almost atonal style. His writings include two music history books.

Testo (It.). 'Text': term used for the narrative, and for the role of the narrator, in Italian oratorio and Passion settings of the 17th century; also occasionally for the narrator in secular dramatic works (such as Monteverdi's *Il combattimento di Tancredi e Clorinda*, 1624). The *testo* part is normally set as recitative with continuo; it is usually sung by one soloist or occasionally by a group.

Tetrachord. A series of four notes, contained within the limits of a perfect 4th. In ancient Greek theory it serves as a basis for melodic construction, in much the same way as the HEXACHORD functions in modal music and the major and minor scales in tonal music. They fall into three types: the diatonic, semitone–tone–tone; the chromatic, semitone–semitone–minor 3rd; the enharmonic, quarter-tone–quarter-tone–major 3rd. In medieval theory the form tone–semitone–tone was common.

Tetrazzini, Luisa (*b* Florence, 29 June 1871; *d* Milan, 28 April 1940). Italian soprano. She appeared from 1890 in Italy, largely in the coloratura repertory, and also sang in Latin America. Her London and New York débuts as Violetta were in 1907 and 1908. She dazzled opera audiences with her brilliant coloratura and shapely line. After World War I she sang mainly as a concert artist.

Teutsche. Corruption of *Deutsche*; see GERMAN DANCE.

Texture. A term used when referring to the vertical aspect of a musical structure, usually with regard to the way individual parts or voices are put together; it may be described as polyphonic, homophonic etc. The term can also be used of a melodic part, in reference to its shape, its level of activity etc.

Teyber. Austrian family of musicians. Matthäus (*c*1711–1785) was a violinist at the Viennese court and a friend of the Mozart family. Four of his children won distinction as musicians. Elisabeth (1744–1816), a soprano, became a successful opera singer in Italy. Anton (1756–1822) was a composer, pianist, organist and cellist, touring in Italy and elsewhere. He worked at the Dresden court, 1787–91, then became Viennese court composer in 1793; he wrote a melodrama (1779, Vienna), oratorios, church music, lieder, symphonies, and chamber and keyboard works. Franz (1758–1810) toured as conductor and composer to Schikaneder's troupe, writing Singspiels and incidental music. He settled in Vienna in 1798, becoming organist at St Stephen's Cathedral in 1809 and court organist in 1819; his other works include sacred pieces, songs and instrumental works. Therese (1760–1830), a popular soprano in operas and Singspiels in Vienna, created Blonde in Mozart's *Die Entführung aus dem Serail* (1782).

Teyte, Dame Maggie (*b* Wolverhampton, 17 April 1888; *d* London, 26 May 1976). English soprano. She studied in London and with Jean de Reszke. Her first major role was as Mélisande, for which she was coached by Debussy. She soon appeared in England, notably with the Beecham Opera Company, and from 1911 sang widely in the USA; her Mimi was particularly admired. From 1937 she made many fine recordings of French songs, performing with remarkably pure tone.

Thaïs. Opera in three acts by Massenet to a libretto by Gallet after A. France (1894, Paris).

Thalben-Ball, Sir George (Thomas) (*b* Sydney, 18 June 1896; *d* London, 18 Jan 1987). British organist and composer of Australian birth. He studied at the RCM, becoming a fellow of the RCO in 1902. He was organist of the Temple Church, London, from 1923 and appointed Birmingham University Organist in 1949. His interpretations were exuberant, romantic and highly influential. Until 1970 he was a music adviser to the BBC.

Thalberg, Sigismond (Fortuné François) (*b* Pâquis, 8 Jan 1812; *d* Posillipo, 27 April 1871). German or Austrian pianist and composer. He studied the piano with Hummel in Vienna (and theory with Sechter) and later with Moscheles in London. He began an international career in 1830; in the 1850s he went as far as Brazil and the USA. With Liszt (his rival for a time), he was the greatest virtuoso pianist of the period, admired for both his brilliant technique and expressive, singing style. He mostly played his own music, which includes many fantasias and variations on opera arias, studies and nocturnes. He also wrote a few other instrumental works, two operas, songs and a piano method.

Thayer, Alexander Wheelock (*b* South Natick, MA, 22 Oct 1817; *d* Trieste, 15 July 1897). American writer. He studied at Harvard. In 1849 he went abroad to study German and prepare a corrected translation of Schindler's biography of Beethoven; but he immediately began work on a Beethoven biography of his own. Three volumes of a German edition appeared (1866–79) but he completed the work only as far as 1816. Other scholars, using his notes, supplied the last two volumes. His exhaustive search for source material and objective presentation established a new standard for musical biography; his *Life of Beethoven* is still definitive in its 1964 revision by Elliot Forbes, incorporating new biographical knowledge, excluding information and reorganized to conform to Thayer's manner of presentation. He contributed to several periodicals and reference works (among them *Grove 1*).

Theater an der Wien. Theatre in Vienna, opened in 1801. *Fidelio*, Beethoven symphonies and concertos and operettas by Strauss and others were first performed there. Its seasons include operettas and musicals and Vienna Festival events.

Théâtre National de l'Opéra. *See* OPÉRA.

Théâtres de la Foire. Theatres erected at the Parisian fairs of St Germain and St Laurent in the 17th and 18th centuries. They were important as sites for the *comédie en vaudevilles*, out of which grew the *opéra comique*.

Theile, Johann (*b* Naumburg, 29 July 1646; *d* there, 24 June 1724). German composer and theorist. He was a pupil of Schütz. After a period in Lübeck, he became Kapellmeister at the Gottorf court in 1673, following his patron to Hamburg in 1675. Later he was Kapellmeister at Wolfenbüttel, 1685–91, and served at Merseburg, 1691–4. He also taught throughout his career.

Theile was most important for his sacred works (34 survive). His St Matthew Passion (1673) was one of the first Passions to include arias commenting on the story, and some of his motets are progressive in structure with a series of short movements. Counterpoint is prominent in his music; most of his masses are in the *stile antico*. He also wrote three operas (1678–81, Hamburg), secular vocal music, instrumental pieces, and six counterpoint treatises. His *Musikalisches Kunst-Buch* contains pieces illustrating various contrapuntal techniques and may have given Bach the idea of writing *The Art of Fugue*.

Theinred of Dover (*fl* 12th century). English theorist, probably identifiable with the monk Tenredus. His treatise (*De legitimis ordinibus pentachordorum et tetrachordorum*), a pedagogical manual, is a comprehensive and meticulously detailed account of proportions, intervals, species and ratios and includes a description of hexachord transposition.

Thematic catalogue. An index to a group of musical compositions incorporating citations of their opening notes, principal melodic features or both. They may be guides to a composer's output, inventories of a library's or individual's collection, advertisements by publishers or copyists, or guides to a repertory. The best-known composer catalogue is Köchel's, of Mozart's works (1862, several subsequent editions); other scholarly thematic catalogues of composers are those of Bach (Schmieder), Beethoven (Kinsky), Schubert (Deutsch), Haydn (Hoboken) and Handel (Baselt).

Theme. The musical material on which part or all of a work is based; usually the term implies a recognizable melody. 'Theme' and 'subject' are sometimes used interchangeably but 'theme' implies a certain completeness that distinguishes it from the shorter MOTIF. A theme may be used to identify a work and may be the melody on which a set of variations is based.

Theodora. Oratorio by Handel to a text by Morell (1750, London).

Theodorakis, Mikis (*b* Khios, 29 July 1925). Greek composer. He was early influenced by Byzantine music and Cretan folk music. He studied at Paris Conservatoire from 1954 and returned to Greece in 1959 when he issued a manifesto attacking the Greek musical establishment. He was imprisoned for his revolutionary doctrines when Greece was under right-wing rule, but released in response to worldwide demand in 1970. He has composed oratorios, ballets and film music (notably for *Zorba the Greek*), mainly based on Greek subject matter.

Theorbo. A large member of the lute family, first developed in Italy around the end of the 16th century. It has one set of fretted strings, tuned like those of a lute, and another of longer, unstopped bass strings forming a diatonic scale; each set has its own pegbox. There are 13 or 14 courses. It was used as a solo instrument but more frequently as an accompanying one in the 17th and early 18th centuries and was much used as a continuo instrument in large ensembles. Some authorities regarded it as identical with the CHITARRONE.

Theremin [aetherphon, termenvoks]. A monophonic electronic instrument developed in the USSR by Lev Termen and first demonstrated by him in 1920. It operates on the principle of heterodyning two radio frequency oscillators and is customarily played by moving the hands to and fro in mid-air before two antennae, one controlling pitch, the other volume. There are also versions with a keyboard or a fingerboard.

Theresienmesse. Haydn's Mass no.12 in B♭ (1799), a reference to the consort of Emperor Francis II of Austria.

Thésée. *Tragédie lyrique* in a prologue and five acts by Lully to a libretto by P. Quinault (1675, Saint Germain en Laye).

Thibaud, Jacques (*b* Bordeaux, 27 Sept 1880; *d* Mont Cemet, 1 Sept 1953). French violinist. He studied at the Paris Conservatoire, graduating in 1896. After an early career as soloist with the Concerts Colonne he toured widely in Europe and made his American début in 1903. In the 1920s and 30s he formed a trio partnership with Casals and Cortot, making notable recordings of Schubert and Beethoven. His playing was distinguished by purity of tone and warmth of expression. In 1943 he founded a competition for violinists and pianists with Marguerite Long.

Thibaut IV (b Troyes, 30 May 1201; d Pamplona, 7 July 1253). French trouvère, Count of Champagne and Brie, King of Navarre. He was one of the most important northern trouvères, with a larger surviving output of poetry and music than any other. He was crowned King of Navarre in May 1234; he headed a crusade in 1239 and made a pilgrimage to Rome in 1248. As a poet-composer he was prolific and versatile, his output including pastoral, courtly and crusade songs and jeux-partis as well as religious works including a lai, a serventois and *chansons* to the Virgin. He exploited a wide variety of strophic structures in his poetry; most of his melodies are in bar form and display great originality in shaping and some use mensural rhythm. He should not be confused with the early 13th-century trouvère Thibaut de Blaison, of Pocitou, known for 11 poems, with music.

Thibouville. French family of instrument makers. The best-known member is Jérôme Thibouville-Lamy (1833–after 1905) who, recognizing the importance of mass-production and lower-priced instruments, founded a firm in 1865. At its height it had three factories, one for brass instruments at Grenelle, which introduced C trumpets c1880 and four-valve trumpets from 1905; one for woodwind at La Couture, opened by Martin Thibouville in 1820 (later operating as Thibouville Frères; noted for its clarinets and oboes); and one for strings at Mirecourt, where a trade school was opened in 1890. The brass factory closed in 1961, but the firm continues in London, selling instrument accessories.

Thielo, Carl August (b Copenhagen, 7 Feb 1707; d Høsterkøb, 2 Dec 1763). Danish composer, theatre director and writer. Of German descent, he studied with J.G. Walther in Weimar and became a music teacher and organist in Copenhagen. In 1746 he established a Danish theatre there, arranging and writing music for various stage works. He also wrote songs, musical instruction books in Danish and German and a musical magazine (1756).

Thierry. French family of organ builders. The most celebrated members were Pierre (1604–65) who, besides working under Louis Couperin's supervision at St Gervais, built the St Germain-des-Prés organ (1661, his masterpiece) and succeeded Desenclos as 'facteur du Roi' in 1664; and his son Alexandre (1646/7–99), whose work includes the organs of St Louis-des-Invalides (1679–87) and St Eustache (1681–9), Paris.

Thieving Magpie, The [La gazza ladra]. Opera in two acts by Rossini to a libretto by Gherardini after d'Aubigny and Caigniez (1817, Milan).

Third. The INTERVAL between two notes two diatonic scale degrees apart (e.g. C–E, E♭–G); it is the interval formed when a perfect 5th is divided into two consonant intervals to make a triad. A 3rd made up of two whole tones is a major 3rd; one made up of a tone and a diatonic semitone is a minor 3rd.

Third stream. Term coined by Gunther Schuller in the late 1950s for music which, through improvisation or written composition or both, synthesizes the characteristics and techniques of contemporary Western art music and types of ethnic music. It was originally used for a style that had existed for some years and that attempted to fuse elements of jazz and Western art music.

Thirty-second note. American term for demisemiquaver; a note half the value of a 16th-note, or semiquaver, and double the value of a 64th-note, or hemidemisemiquaver. See NOTE VALUES.

Thomas, (Charles Louis) Ambroise (b Metz, 5 Aug 1811; d Paris, 12 Feb 1896). French opera composer. He studied with Le Sueur at the Paris Conservatoire, winning the Prix de Rome in 1832. He then devoted himself to writing for the stage. Though his early *opéras comiques* marked a modest improvement on Auber's in melodic invention, sentiment and delicacy of orchestration, they followed contemporary taste in their dependence on virtuoso coloratura soprano roles and in the absurdity of their librettos; *Le caïd* (1849) and *Le songe d'une nuit d'été* (1850) were successful, leading to a professorship at the Conservatoire (1856). Thomas won still higher acclaim with the sentimental *Mignon* (1866) and *Hamlet* (1868), in emulation of Gounod's *Faust* and *Romeo et Juliette* respectively. Despite their conventionality, these works contain effective vocal characterization and appealing atmospheric writing. *Mignon* received over 1000 performances at the Opéra-Comique between 1866 and 1894, becoming one of the most successful operas in history. His critical and popular reputation clinched, Thomas succeeded Auber as director of the Conservatoire (1871), instituting reforms while remaining essentially conservative. He was troubled by the growing influence of Wagner and showed little sympathy for the work of younger French composers (except Massenet). His reputation, once comparable with Verdi's, was eclipsed within a few years of his greatest triumphs.

Thomas, Arthur Goring (b Ratton Park, 20 Nov 1850; d London, 20 March 1892). English composer. He was in Paris at a formative period, and French influence can be heard in most of his compositions. In London he studied with Sullivan and Prout at the RAM, and later with Bruch. He composed graceful and elegant if not dramatically powerful operas and choral works. The English recitatives and some single lyrical numbers in his operas *Esmeralda* (1883) and *Nadeshda* (1885) contain his best music.

Thomas, Christian Gottfried (b Wehrsdorf, 2 Feb 1748; d Leipzig, 12 Sept 1806). German composer, writer and publisher. At first a horn player, he became a prominent figure in Leipzig musical life: he founded a music copying business and MS storehouse in 1776 and in 1778–81 published his plans for them, including a control procedure and an ingenious subscription scheme. He also organized concerts in Leipzig and other cities. His short-lived music periodical (1798) discusses these, as well as his own sacred and secular vocal works, several of which are on an ambitious scale.

Thomas, John [Pencerdd, Gwalia] (b Ogmore, 1 March 1826; d London, 19 March 1913). Welsh harpist and composer. He was harpist to Queen Victoria (1871), professor at the RCM and GSM and a popular lecturer on Welsh national music. He composed mainly choral music and harp studies.

Thomas, Kurt (George Hugo) (*b* Tönning, 25 May 1904; *d* Bad Deynhausen, 31 March 1973). German choral conductor and composer. He studied in Leipzig, taught in several cities and becoming director of the Thomaskantoren and Thomasschule in Leipzig (1955–61). He then left for Cologne and Frankfurt. He played a significant part in the renewal of Protestant church music in Germany and had a high reputation as a choir trainer and conductor; his *Lehrbuch der Chorleitung* (1948) has remained essential.

Thomas, Mansel (Treharne) (*b* Tylorstown, 12 June 1909; *d* Abergavenny, 8 Jan 1986). Welsh composer. A pupil of Dale at the RAM (1925–30), he worked as a conductor and as BBC head of music in Wales (1950–65). His works are mostly choral, in a diatonic style; his songs *Four Prayers from the Gaelic* (1962) attracted attention.

Thomas, Michael Tilson (*b* Los Angeles, 21 Dec 1944). American conductor. He studied in Los Angeles; his first post was as assistant conductor of the Boston SO, 1969. He was music director of the Buffalo PO, 1971–9, and directed young people's concerts with the New York PO, 1971–6. He was a principal guest conductor with the Los Angeles PO, 1981–5, and was appointed conductor of the LSO from 1988. He has recorded both as pianist and conductor and is notable for his wide musical and intellectual interests and his sympathetic and vigorous conducting of a wide repertory.

Thomas, Theodore (Christian Friedrich) (*b* Esens, 11 Oct 1835; *d* Chicago, 4 Jan 1905). American conductor. He studied the violin as a child in Germany and went with his family to New York in 1845 where he became known as a violinist. He began conducting in 1859, directing numerous concerts, some with his own orchestra. He held appointments in Philadelphia and Cincinnati and was conductor of the New York PO, 1877–91; later he worked in Chicago. He did much to popularize European music in the USA with his prodigious energy and organization, giving concerts for mass audiences, children and working men throughout the country.

Thomaskirche. Church in Leipzig; it was for long the centre of the city's musical life. Its most famous music director was J.S. Bach (1723–50).

Thompson, Randall (*b* New York, 21 April 1899; *d* Boston, 9 July 1984). American composer. Trained at Harvard and with Bloch, he taught at various institutions before returning to Harvard (1948–65). His music is in a diatonic style; he is best known for his choral music, three symphonies (1929, 1931, 1949), two string quartets (1941, 1967) and the symphonic fantasy *A Trip to Nahanti* (1954).

Thomson, George (*b* Limekilns, 4 March 1757; *d* Leith, 18 Feb 1851). Scottish folksong editor and publisher. Between 1791 and 1841 he devoted his spare time to publishing what he hoped would be an important collection of folksongs of the British Isles arranged for voice and instruments (mostly piano trio) by the greatest living European composers. Hundreds of settings, by Haydn (187), Pleyel, Kozeluch, Beethoven (126), Weber, Hummel and Bishop, appeared; present-day taste sees some stylistic conflict, however, between genuine folksong and Viennese Classical harmony.

Thomson, Virgil (Garnett) (*b* Kansas City, MO 25 Nov 1896). American composer. He was educated at Harvard (1919–23), though spent a year (1921–2) in Paris, where he had lessons with Boulanger and met Cocteau, Satie and Les Six; from 1925 to 1940 he was again in Paris. Stravinsky became an important influence. Also crucial was his meeting Gertrude Stein (1926), with whom he collaborated on two operas, *Four Saints in Three Acts* (1934) and *The Mother of us all* (1947). In 1940 he returned to New York and became critic of the *Herald Tribune* for 14 years, his lively wit, keen ear and elegant writing establishing him as one of the sharpest critics in the USA. Later works include a third opera, *Lord Byron* (1972), and much else in many genres especially song. He produced a highly original body of diverse music rooted in American speech rhythms and hymnbook harmony, controlled by exquisite sensibilities. The greatest influence on him was Satie's music.

Operas Four Saints in Three Acts (1934); The Mother of us all (1947); Lord Byron (1972)
Ballets Filling Station (1938); Parson Weems and the Cherry Tree (1975)
Film scores The Plow that Broke the Plains (1936); The River (1937); Louisiana Story (1948)
Orchestral music Sym. on a Hymn Tune (1928); Sym. no.2 (1931); Sym. no.3 (1972); Vc Conc. (1950)
Choral music Missa pro defunctis (1960)
Solo vocal music Five Songs from William Blake (1951)
Chamber music Sonata da chiesa (1926); Vn Sonata (1930); 2 str qts (1931, 1932)

Thorborg, Kerstin (*b* Venjan, 19 May 1896; *d* Falun, 12 April 1970). Swedish mezzo-soprano. She was a member of the Royal Theatre, Stockholm (1924–30). From 1935 she sang at Salzburg and Vienna. In the late 1930s at Covent Garden she was admired in the Wagnerian repertory and she sang at the Met, 1936–50. Her recording of *Das Lied von der Erde* (1936) gained wide circulation.

Thoroughbass. *See* CONTINUO.

Thorpe Davie, Cedric (*b* London, 30 May 1913; *d* Dalry, 18 Jan 1983). Scottish composer. A pupil of Morris, Vaughan Williams and Jacob at the RCM, of Kodály in Budapest and of Kilpinen in Helsinki, he taught at the Royal Scottish Academy of Music (1936–45) and St Andrews University (1945–78). His works include incidental scores, orchestral and choral pieces, often on Scottish subjects and latterly for young people and amateurs.

Thrane, Waldemar (*b* Oslo, 8 Oct 1790; *d* there, 30 Dec 1828). Norwegian composer, violinist and conductor. He studied in Copenhagen, Oslo, and in Paris with Baillot, Reicha and Habeneck. He wrote the first Norwegian opera, *Fjeldeventyret* (1824), which in its use of folk idioms has a strong national flavour.

Three Choirs Festival (UK). Annual (summer) festival established *c*1715. It is based in turn around Gloucester, Hereford and Worcester cathedrals, with concerts by their choirs; events include orchestral and chamber concerts in other venues. From the

19th century it has given premières of British works (notably Elgar and Vaughan Williams).

Three-cornered Hat, The [El sombrero de tres picos]. Ballet in one act by Falla to a scenario by Martinez Sierra after Alarcon (1917, Madrid).

Threepenny Opera, The [Die Dreigroschenoper]. Opera in a prologue and eight scenes by Weill to a libretto by Brecht and E. Hauptmann after Gay's *The Beggar's Opera* (1928, Berlin).

Three Places in New England. Orchestral work by Ives, also known as the First Orchestral Set (or *A New England Symphony*) (*c*1912): its movements are *The Saint-Gaudens in Boston Common, Putnam's Camp* and *The Housatonic at Stockbridge*.

Threni: id est Lamentationes Jeremiae prophetae. Choral work by Stravinsky to a biblical text (1958, Venice).

Threnody. A poem, or its musical setting, expressing grief for the dead; a lament. It has also been used for instrumental compositions, such as Penderecki's *Threnody for the Victims of Hiroshima*.

Through-composed. Term, from the German *durchkomponiert*, for settings of songs in which the music for each stanza is different.

Thuille, Ludwig (*b* Bolzano, Tyrol, 30 Nov 1861; *d* Munich, 5 Feb 1907). Austrian composer of Savoyard ancestry. A leading musical figure in Munich, he was a choral conductor and professor of theory and composition at the Königliche Musikschule. Innately conservative but influenced by Alexander Ritter, he won distinction as a composer of chamber music, notably the Sextet op.6 (1889) for piano and wind and the Piano Quintet op.20 (1901); his successful whimsical opera *Lobetanz* (1896), combines his gift for structural clarity with ingratiating melodic invention.

Thunder machine. An instrument used to produce an imitation of thunder. It may be a revolving drum filled with hard balls, pebbles flung against a metal surface or (customary today) a large suspended metal sheet that is shaken.

Thurston, Frederick (John) (*b* Lichfield, 21 Sept 1901; *d* London, 12 Dec 1953). English clarinettist. He studied at the RCM and played in several orchestras, becoming principal clarinet of the new BBC SO, 1930–46. Thereafter he concentrated on chamber music, playing many new works, some dedicated to him. He was admired for his firm, clear tone and polished technique. He taught at the RCM, where his pupils included Thea King, whom he married.

Thybo, Leif (*b* Holsterbro, 12 June 1922). Danish composer and organist. He studied in Copenhagen at the conservatory (1940–44) and university (1945–8), at both of which he has taught, also serving as a church organist. In his music, covering most genres, he has sought new kinds of tonality under the influence of Stravinsky, Bartók and Britten; among his organ pieces are two concertos (1952, 1956).

Tibbett, Lawrence (*b* Bakersfield, CA, 16 Nov 1896; *d* New York, 15 July 1960). American baritone. After an early career as an actor he made his Met début in 1923, taking leading Italian roles over 27

seasons, giving fervent performances in the basic repertory and in several premières. He sang successfully on Broadway in the 1950s.

Tibia. Ancient Roman wind instrument, similar to the Greek AULOS, consisting of two pipes, sometimes with bell extensions to increase the volume. It was used by the Etruscans and Romans in religious ceremonies and rituals, was prominent in Roman literature and played an important part in the theatre.

Tiburtino, Giuliano (*b c*1510; *d* Rome, 16 Dec 1569). Italian instrumentalist and composer. An accomplished violone player, he spent most of his life in the papal employ. The bulk of his music, instrumental and sacred vocal, was published in two collections (Venice, 1549).

Tichatschek, Joseph (Aloys) (*b* Teplice, 11 July 1807; *d* Blasewitz, 18 Jan 1886). Bohemian tenor. Associated chiefly with the Dresden Court Opera (from 1838), he was renowned for the beauty and brilliance of his voice. His repertory included the principal tenor parts of *Idomeneo*, *Die Zauberflöte, I Capuleti e i Montecchi* and *La muette de Portici*, but he was also the prototype of the Wagner *Heldentenor*, creating the title roles of *Rienzi* (1842) and *Tannhäuser* (1845).

Tie. A curved line between two notes of the same pitch indicating that they should be performed as a single note with their combined values. It is particularly used to connect notes separated by a bar-line, and enables a note value of five or seven units, which cannot be expressed in a single symbol, to be shown. Occasionally a tie may imply a gentle repetition of the second note.

Tieffenbrucker [Dieffopruchar, Dieffoprukhar, Dubrocard, Duiffoprugcar]. German family of string instrument makers. They were from Tieffenbruck, Bavaria. One branch, of which Gaspar the elder (1514–71) was the most famous member, settled in Lyons, specializing in viols and other bowed instruments. The larger branch became established chiefly in Venice and Padua, making mainly lutes; Magno the younger (*fl* 1589–1621) and Leonardo the elder (*fl* early 16th century) are notable members.

Tiefland. Opera in a prologue and two acts by d'Albert to a libretto by Rudolph Lothar after Guimerà (1903, Prague).

Tielke, Joachim (*b* Königsberg, 14 Oct 1641; *d* Hamburg, 19 Sept 1719). German string instrument maker. He worked in Hamburg. Among his nearly 100 surviving instruments are lutes, guitars, citterns, violins and especially viols, often lavishly decorated and very fine musically.

Tiento (Sp.: 'touch'). Term used in the 16th and 17th centuries for Spanish and Portuguese equivalents of the ricercare, often interchangeably with *fantasia*. The earliest examples seem to have been written to enable the performer to try out his instrument. Composers of *tientos* include Luis de Milán (for vihuela), Cabezón and Cabanilles (for organ).

Tierce. An organ stop, a mutation at $1\frac{3}{5}'$ pitch, sounding two octaves and a major 3rd above the main note. It was popular in French organs of the 17th–

18th centuries, where a Double Tierce, at $3\frac{1}{5}'$ pitch (one octave and a major 3rd above the main note), was also used.

Tierce de Picardie [Picardy 3rd]. The raised third degree of the tonic chord at the end of a movement or composition in a minor mode; it gives the ending a greater sense of 'finality'. It was commonly used in the 16th century and throughout the Baroque era.

Tiersot, (Jean-Baptiste Elisée) Julien (*b* Bourg-en-Bresse, 5 July 1857; *d* Paris, 10 Aug 1936). French musicologist and folklorist. A pupil of Massenet (composition) and Franck (organ) at the Paris Conservatoire, he became head of the library there, president of the Société Française de Musicologie and active on behalf of early and contemporary music; meanwhile he wrote books on French Revolutionary music, on music in Molière's comedies and on Rousseau. His chief importance lies in his work as a folklorist, especially in the classic collection *Mélodies populaires des provinces de France* (10 vols., 1888–1928).

Tiessen, Heinz (*b* Königsberg, 10 April 1887; *d* Berlin, 29 Nov 1971). German composer and critic. He studied in Berlin at the Stern Conservatory and privately with Klatte; he also came under Strauss's influence. In the 1920s he became associated with expressionism and a committed advocate of new music, though he also composed traditionally. His music was censured in 1933, but he remained in Berlin, teaching. His output includes orchestral pieces, chamber and piano music (some quoting birdsongs, the subject of one of his writings), many songs, musical plays and film scores.

Tietjens, Therese (Carolina Johanna Alexandra) (*b* Hamburg, 17 July 1831; *d* London, 3 Oct 1877). German soprano. She was most closely associated with the title role of Donizetti's *Lucrezia Borgia*; she also portrayed Norma, Medea, Donna Anna and Leonore (*Fidelio*) with a vocal power and authoritative stage presence that made her the successor to Pasta, Malibran and Grisi.

Tigranyan, Armen Tigran (*b* Leninakan, 26 Dec 1879; *d* Tbilisi, 10 Feb 1950). Armenian composer. He was a pupil of Klenovsky and Ekmalyan in Tbilisi. His *Anush* (1912) provided the foundations for Armenian opera; his use of the chorus was developed in *David-Bek* (1950).

Tigranyan, Nikoghayos Fadeyi (*b* Leninakan, 31 Aug 1856; *d* Erevan, 17 Feb 1951). Armenian composer. He studied at the Vienna Institute for the Blind (1873–80) and with Rimsky-Korsakov at the St Petersburg Conservatory. He collected Armenian folk music, which he used in arrangements (many for piano) and original compositions, and was the first composer to translate such music into orchestral terms.

Till Eulenspiegels lustige Streiche. Tone poem by Richard Strauss (1895).

Tilson Thomas, Michael. *See* THOMAS, MICHAEL TILSON.

Timbales. A pair of single-headed, metal-shelled tunable cylindrical drums, most often used in Latin American dance orchestras but also in modern orchestral music and rhythm ensembles.

Timbre. (1) Term describing the tonal quality of a sound; a clarinet and an oboe sounding the same note are said to produce different 'timbres'. *See* ACOUSTICS.

(2) Term of late 18th-century origin applied by scholars to pre-existing *opéra comique* songs, 16th- and 17th-century *chansons* and in a special sense to medieval monophony. In the French popular song it served to identify the tune to accompany a new text adapted to a well-known melody, usually in the form of a tag from the refrain or opening lines of the original poem. It is closely associated with large 19th-century anthologies of *airs*, *chansons* and vaudeville songs. It is also sometimes used to characterize standard melodic themes, phrases or figures in medieval monophony that recur in different compositions and are underlaid with different words.

Time signature. A sign or signs placed at the beginning of a composition, after the clef and key signature, or in the course of a composition, to indicate the metre of the ensuing music. In modern usage, two figures are usually given, one above the other: the lower indicates the unit of measurement, relative to the semibreve; the upper indicates the number of such units in each bar. Thus a signature of 3/2 indicates that there are three minims (or half-notes) in each bar; 12/8 indicates that there are 12 quavers (eighth-notes). Where the upper figure is divisible by three, the music is in compound time, i.e. the units represented by the lower figure are grouped in threes. 12/8 thus means not only that there are 12 quavers to a bar but that these 12 form four groups each of three quavers. Some signatures are given in a form akin to the letter C; this, popularly understood to stand for 'common time' and representing 4/4, is a survivor of the broken circle of the mensuration system. With a vertical stroke, ¢, this sign normally represents 2/2. *See also* NOTATION.

The table opposite shows the principal time signatures used in modern notation.

Timpani (Fr. *timbales*; Ger. *Pauken*). Kettledrums: the most important orchestral percussion instruments, used by all major composers since the 18th century, partly because they can be tuned to precise pitches. Their pitch can be altered during performance to any note within the range of up to an octave and a 6th between the standard number of three drums. Tuning is effected by tightening the drumhead either with hand-screws, or (as with modern 'machine' drums) with a single master-screw, rotating bowls or, most commonly, pedals. The heads are made of calfskin or plastic; the large, deep bowls are usually copper or fibreglass (for illustration, *see* PERCUSSION INSTRUMENTS). Timpani are played with a pair of drumsticks, in a wide variety of shapes and textures according to the effects demanded by the composer.

The kettledrum dates from antiquity, when it was made from tree-trunks, clay or tortoise-shells. During the 13th century the use of a pair was adopted in Europe from the East for martial occasions. Larger versions infiltrated from Arabia in the 15th century, became established as cavalry kettledrums and were absorbed into the orchestra by the 17th century. By

TABLE 1

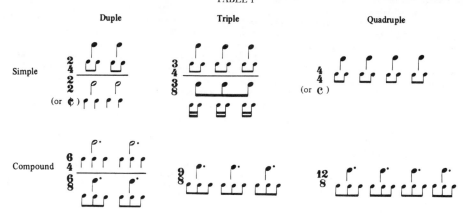

then their tuning was standardized to the tonic and dominant of the key of the piece, and they were usually treated as transposing instruments, notated as *c* and *G*.

Lully was one of the first composers to use them in the orchestra; Bach used them with the brass and full choir; Handel wrote elaborate parts for them. By the late 18th century, tuning had progressed from exclusively the tonic and dominant to other intervals (Salieri and Beethoven used a diminished 5th); several composers used three, four and even up to eight timpani for special effect. Haydn, who himself played the timpani, used seven changes of tuning in *The Creation*. Hard sticks were generally used at this period. Improved construction and tuning methods in the 19th century led to increased exploitation, and to larger numbers being used (Berlioz's *Te Deum* is scored for 16). Late Romantic composers made heavy demands on them, and when the machine drum (the development of which began in the 1820s) became highly sophisticated in the 20th century many effects such as glissandos and fast chromatic passages became possible. Bartók in particular exploited timpani in his Music for Strings, Percussion and Celesta and Sonata for Two Pianos and Percussion. Several concertos and a number of sonatas for timpani have been written this century.

Tinctoris, Johannes (*b* Braine l'Alleud, *c*1435; *d*?1511). Franco-Flemish theorist and composer. He may have been a singer at Cambrai Cathedral (under Dufay) in 1460. He was instructor of the choirboys at Orléans Cathedral in 1463. In *c*1472 he taught at the court of King Ferdinand I of Naples and in 1487 was commissioned by him to recruit singers from the French king, Charles VIII, and King Maximilian.

He was one of the most important music theorists of his time, whose writings provide information on the performing practice and notation of Renaissance music. Of his 12 surviving treatises, only two were published in his lifetime and only two can be dated precisely, though most seem to have been written during the 1470s. The most important, *Terminorum musicae deffinitorium*, contains 299 definitions of

terms relating to *musica plana* and *musica mensurabilis* and is the oldest printed music dictionary. The others cover such topics as the powers attributed to music, mensural notation, solmization and mutation, singing and composition. Apart from some anonymous music examples in the treatises, he is known to have composed five masses, a setting of the Lamentations and a few motets and *chansons*.

Tinel, Edgar (Pierre Joseph) (*b* Sinaai, 27 March 1854; *d* Brussels, 28 Oct 1912). Belgian composer. He was a pupil of Gevaert at the Brussels Conservatory, where he was appointed professor in 1896; in 1910 he became *maître de chapelle* to the king. His works include sacred choral music (e.g. two *Te Deum* settings), songs and piano pieces.

Tin Pan Alley. Nickname for the popular song-writing and sheet-music publishing industry centred in New York from the 1890s to the 1940s.

Tiomkin, Dimitri (*b* St Petersburg, 10 May 1894; *d* London, 11 Nov 1979). American composer of Russian origin. He was a pupil of Glazunov in St Petersburg and of Busoni in Berlin. In 1929 he moved to Hollywood, where he became a successful composer of film music, notably *High Noon* (1952), *Dial M for Murder* (1954) and *The Guns of Navarone* (1961).

Tippett, Sir Michael (Kemp) (*b* London, 2 Jan 1905). English composer. He studied with C. Wood and Kitson at the RCM (1923–8), then settled in Oxted, Surrey, where he taught, conducted a choir and began to compose. However, dissatisfaction with his technique led him to take further lessons with Morris (1930–32), and he published nothing until he was into his mid-30s. By then he was conducting at Morley College, of which he became music director in 1940; there he performed his oratorio *A Child of our Time* (1941), which uses a story of Nazi atrocity but draws no simple moral from it, concluding rather that we must recognize within ourselves both good and evil. Earlier works, like the String Quartet no.1 and the Concerto for double string orchestra, had married Stravinskian neo-classicism with a bounding rhythm that came from the English madrigal, but the oratorio added to these a Baroque concept of form and black spirituals to replace the chorales of a Protestant Passion. It also made clear Tippett's willingness to exert himself in the public world, which he did again as a conscientious objector in 1943 in accepting imprisonment rather than conscription.

A Child of our Time seems further to have released creative energy that went into a series of works – two more quartets, the cantata for tenor and piano *Boyhood's End* and the Symphony no.1 – leading to the composition of the opera *The Midsummer Marriage* in the years 1946–52. This, at once a pastoral, a modern morality and a mystery play of psychic growth, called for a further extension of resources: luminous static harmony, orchestral brilliance, a bold command of large spans of time, and a lively variety of rhythm in the largely danced middle act. The message is again that of the oratorio: before marriage the central characters must each accept the wedding within their personalities of intellect and carnality. The theme relates to *The Magic Flute*, and Tippett's sources for his own libretto also include Shaw, Yeats and Eliot.

The opera's musical exuberance spilt over into succeeding works, including the Fantasia concertante on a Theme of Corelli for strings and the Piano Concerto, but then through the Symphony no.2 (1957) came a clearing and hardening of style towards the vivid block forms and declamatory vocal style of the opera *King Priam*, composed in 1958–61, which concerns the problem of free will. Once more an opera had its offshoots; notably in the Piano Sonata no.2 and the Concerto for Orchestra, with its distinct gestures and circular formal schemes, but followed by a new, ecstatic continuity in the cantata *The Vision of St Augustine* (1965). Here the baritone's central narrative is subverted by huge choral parentheses, representing the density of thought and feeling embracing the simple account of the circumstances leading up to the vision. In his opera *The Knot Garden* (1970) he concentrates on the emotional substance of clashes of personality and their outcome. His unusually candid if stylized presentation of raw human relationships and of the need to make a success of the seemingly incompatible ones produce a score of lapidary compression, notable for its metallic sonorities, its use of a 12-note theme (though not serial technique) to represent fractured relationships and its revival of blues and boogie-woogie in a manner analogous to his use of spirituals in *A Child of our Time*.

Symphony no.3 continues to explore the seemingly inexhaustible flow of invention stimulated by the 'light' and the 'shadow'; the abstract musical argument of the first part is answered by the overtly human involvement of the second, where blues again express a basic human predicament and Beethoven's music provides archetypal gestures. The range of reference is wider in the opera *The Ice Break*, where again the blues stand for human warmth in a time of uncertainty but where the composer alludes to diverse strands of high and popular culture in a work that depicts and transfigures clashes of age, race and milieu. Again, the opera is composed of fragmentary scenes in which arche-

typal characters confront one another, but now in a context of global discord; the musical style is even more jaggedly kaleidoscopic, as it is also in the Fourth Symphony, which abandons the vocal solution of the Third but finds in purely musical development a metaphor of physical birth, growth and dissolution. Other late works include the full-length oratorio *The Mask of Time* (1982), a grand restatement of Tippett's musical and philosophical concerns, as well as a Concerto for string trio and orchestra.

Operas The Midsummer Marriage (1955); King Priam (1962); The Knot Garden (1970); The Ice Break (1977)
Incidental music The Tempest (1962)
Choral music A Child of our Time (1941); Crown of the Year (1958); Magnificat and Nunc dimittis (1961); The Vision of St Augustine (1965); The Shires Suite (1970); The Mask of Time (1982); motets, madrigals, folksong arrs.
Orchestral music Conc. for double str orch (1939); Fantasia on a Theme of Handel, pf, orch (1941); 4 syms. (1945, 1957, 1972, 1977); Little Music, str (1946); Suite, D (1948); Fantasia concertante on a Theme of Corelli, str (1953); Divertimento on Sellinger's Round (1954); Pf Conc. (1955); Conc. for Orch (1963); Conc. vn, va, vc (1979); Festal Brass with Blues, brass band (1983)
Solo vocal music Boyhood's End (1943); The Heart's Assurance (1951); Music for Words Perhaps (1960); Songs for Achilles (1961); Songs for Ariel (1962); Songs for Dov (1970)
Chamber music 4 str qts (1935, 1942, 1973, 1979); Sonata, 4 hn (1955); Wolf Trap Fanfare, 6 brass (1980)
Piano music 4 sonatas (1938, 1962, 1973, 1984)

Tirade (Fr.). Term for an ornament (It. *tirata*) consisting of a scale-like passage passing between two notes in a melodic line; see the examples below, from Leopold Mozart's *Versuch einer gründliche Violinschule* (1756).

Tirana. A dance-song, probably Andalusian in origin, popular in Spain in 1780–90 as the finale of the *tonadilla*; it was usually in a fast 6/8 time with syncopation. Although banned for its increasing licentiousness, it survived into the late 19th century.

Tiranna, La. Boccherini's String Quartet in G op.44 no.4, G223.

Tishchenko, Boris Ivanovich (*b* Leningrad, 23 March 1939). Soviet composer. He studied at the Leningrad Conservatory and with Shostakovich (1962–5). He is an outstanding representative of a generation that reinvigorated Russian music in the 1960s. His richly inventive works include symphonies, concertos, string quartets, piano sonatas, and children's stage pieces.

Titan. Mahler's Symphony no.1 in D (1888); it was originally called simply Symphonic Poem.

Titelouze, Jehan (*b* St Omer, 1562–3; *d* Rouen, 24 Oct 1633). French composer. He was organist at St Jean, Rouen, from 1585 and at the cathedral from 1588 until his death; he also acted as an organ consultant. The first significant French composer of organ music, he published polyphonic organ versets based on plainsong (2 bks, 1623, 1626), to be played in alternation with the choir during services. In two-staff notation (not tablature), they are austere and relatively conservative.

Toccata. A keyboard piece, often free in form, intended primarily for 'touching' the keyboard, i.e. for displaying dexterity. The term has also been applied to pieces for other instruments (e.g. the opening fanfare of Monteverdi's *Orfeo*).

The toccata had antecedents in the prelude and ricercare. The earliest printed toccatas are those of Bertoldo (1591) and Diruta (*Il transilvano*, 1593, including some by A. and G. Gabrieli). Most are in a chordal style with brilliant runs. Merulo's (1598 and 1604) are more sectional, fugal and chordal passages alternating with brilliant passage-work. In Frescobaldi's toccatas the contrasts are more violent and the passage-work more complex; his second book (1627) includes two lengthy toccatas for the Elevation. His followers include M. Rossi, Pasquini and Zipoli, and his style was transmitted to Austria by Froberger, who to some extent incorporated in his toccatas the principle of the variation canzona or capriccio. The Austrian and south German tradition was continued by such composers as Kerll and Georg Muffat.

In the Netherlands, Sweelinck took A. and G. Gabrieli as models for his toccatas, whose chief characteristic is rhythmic regularity. His successors include Scheidt, Scheidemann and later Reincken and Buxtehude, with whom the toccata became a large-scale work in which rhapsodic and fugal sections alternated.

In Italy A. Scarlatti's multi-sectional harpsichord toccatas were a departure, incorporating fugue, recitative and variations. They influenced Handel's keyboard style and also Bach's in such works as the Chromatic Fantasia and Fugue. Bach's harpsichord toccatas are large-scale works of individual design, incorporating fugal movements. His organ toccatas are either works in which the toccata and fugal elements are closely linked, as with Buxtehude, or independent movements preceding a fugue (e.g. BWV540). The justification for the title here is the largely continuous semiquaver movement, a feature of the modern toccata, in which rhapsodic and fugal elements are largely abandoned. Among the best-known examples for piano are those of Schumann (op.7), Debussy (in *Pour le piano*), Ravel (in *Le tombeau de Couperin*) and Prokofiev (op.11).

Toch, Ernst (*b* Vienna, 7 Dec 1887; *d* Santa Monica, 1 Oct 1964). Austrian composer; naturalized American. Self-taught, he had a notable teaching career in Mannheim (1913–29), Berlin (1929–32) and the USA, where he settled in 1934 (naturalized 1940). In Berlin he took part in modernist activities

(*Gesprochene Musik* for speaking chorus, 1930), but most of his music is neo-classical, tonal and in traditional forms. He was primarily a chamber-music composer: his output includes 13 string quartets (the first five are lost); he also wrote seven symphonies (1950–64), piano concertos, vocal and piano pieces and film scores. His strong personal philosophy and its relationship to music is expressed in several of his writings.

Toda, Kunio (*b* Tokyo, 11 Aug 1915). Japanese composer. A pupil of Moroi and influenced by Leibowitz's writings, he began using 12-note methods in the 1950s. His works cover many genres including opera; he has also taught and written books, notably on Russian music.

Tod Jesu, Der. Passion oratorio by C.H. Graun to a libretto by C.W. Ramler after Princess Amalia of Prussia (1755, Berlin); it enjoyed unique popularity in late 18th-century Germany.

Tod und das Mädchen, Der. *See* DEATH AND THE MAIDEN.

Tod und Verklärung [Death and Transfiguration]. Tone poem by Richard Strauss (1889).

Toduţă, Sigismund (*b* Simeria, 30 May 1908). Romanian composer. He studied at the Cluj Conservatory (where he returned to teach in 1946) and in Rome (1936–8) with Pizzetti and Casella. As mentor to a group of younger composers, he established Cluj as the second musical centre in Romania. His works, combining neo-classical and folk elements in an individual way, include symphonies, concertos and choral pieces (*The Ewe Lamb*, 1958).

Toebosch, Louis (*b* Maastricht, 18 March 1916). Dutch composer. He studied at the Liège Conservatory, was organist and choirmaster at the church of the Sacrament in Breda (1940–65), conductor of the Tilburg SO (1946–52) and director of the Brabant Conservatory (from 1965). His works include sacred choral and organ pieces.

Toeschi, Carl Joseph (*b* Ludwigsburg, bap. 11 Nov 1731; *d* Munich, 12 April 1788). German composer. A pupil of J. Stamitz and Fils, he became Konzertmeister of the Mannheim orchestra in 1759 and music director of the electoral cabinet in 1774. In 1778 he followed the court to Munich. Especially popular in Paris, he was one of the foremost second-generation Mannheim composers, writing *c*200 instrumental works (symphonies, concertos, flute quartets etc) and *c*30 ballets. His style combines Mannheim, Italian and French features.

His father Alessandro (before 1700–1758) was a violinist and composer at Mannheim, Konzertmeister by 1742 and director of instrumental church music from *c*1750. His brother Johann Christoph (1735–1800), also a violinist and composer, became Konzertmeister at Mannheim in 1774 and music director at Munich in 1793; he too composed ballets and instrumental works. Johann Christoph's son Karl Theodor (1768–1843) served at Munich and wrote mostly instrumental music.

Togni, Camillo (*b* Gussago, 18 Oct 1922). Italian composer. He studied with Casella in Siena and Rome (1939–42) and at Darmstadt (1951–7). He was the first Italian to break with pre-war neo-classicism and in the 1950s developed a post-Webernian style, which he has used chiefly in vocal and instrumental chamber music.

Tokyo Quartet. Japanese string quartet, led by Koichiro Harada. It was founded in 1969. Three of its members studied at the Juilliard School. It plays with great precision in a repertory that includes, along with the classics, Bartók and contemporary Japanese works.

Tolbecque. Belgian family of musicians who settled in France. The most celebrated members were Jean-Baptiste-Joseph (1797–1869), a conductor and composer of dance music, and his nephew Auguste (1830–1919), a cellist and instrument maker who restored and wrote about early string instruments.

Tollis de la Roca, Matheo (*b* c1710; *d* Mexico City, 5–18 Sept 1781). Mexican composer. He arrived in Mexico, presumably from Spain, in 1756 and was appointed to the staff of the cathedral, holding various posts including chief organist (1761) and interim *maestro de capilla* (1771) although he was criticized for 'slothful composing'. He was a fine keyboard player and reorganized the cathedral music archive; his works include four masses, a requiem and 14 motets.

Tollius, Jan (*b* Amersfoort, *c*1550; *d* ?Copenhagen, after 1603). Netherlands composer. He was a *kapelmeester* in Amersfoort and went to Italy in the 1570s. From 1601 he sang in the Danish royal chapel. His motets (4 bks, 1590–97) and madrigals (1597) foreshadow the early Baroque style.

Tomadini, Jacopo (*b* Cividale del Friuli, 24 Aug 1820; *d* there, 21 Jan 1883). Italian composer. He was esteemed as a composer and reformer of church music, producing over 300 sacred works, notably the cantata *La risurrezione del Cristo* (1864) in the Haydn tradition.

Tomášek, Václav Jan Křtitel [Tomaschek, Wenzel Johann] (*b* Skuteč, 17 April 1774; *d* Prague, 3 April 1850). Bohemian composer and teacher. Largely self-taught and remaining outside the musical establishment of Prague, he nevertheless enjoyed a considerable reputation as a music teacher, first among noble families and from 1824 at his own school, where his young disciples included Dreyschock, Hanslick and the composers J.V. Voříšek and J.B. Kittl. As a composer he was a figure of the Classical–Romantic transition, his symphonies and early keyboard sonatas following Mozart's model, the piano works and songs from *c*1810 setting a trend of Romantic lyricism. His pioneering eclogues, rhapsodies and dithyrambs for piano and his 41 Goethe settings of 1815 (opp.53–61), for example, foreshadow Schubert. The Czech songs are less successful. For their shrewd observations on the musical personalities of his time his memoirs, published in *Libussa* (1845–50), make lively reading.

Tomasi, Henri (*b* Marseilles, 17 Aug 1901; *d* Paris, 13 Jan 1971). French composer. He was a pupil of Vidal and Caussade at the Paris Conservatoire. His music is direct in feeling, highly coloured, rich in contrast and brilliantly orchestrated. He established his reputation with stage works (*L'Atlantide, Miguel de Mañara*) but also wrote numerous concertos in-cluding one for guitar (1967).

Tomasini, Alois Luigi (*b* Pesaro, 22 June 1741; *d* Eisenstadt, 25 April 1808). Italian violinist and composer. He served at the Esterházy court and after studying in Italy (1759) became first violinist, later Konzertmeister; he both played under and studied with Haydn, and appeared as a soloist. He wrote mainly chamber music, including over 20 string quartets and baryton pieces.

His sons Anton (1775–1824) and Alois (1779–1858) also played in the Esterházy orchestra; Anton became its director in 1818.

Tombeau (Fr.: 'tomb'). An instrumental piece or group of pieces commemorating someone's death. The term was originally literary; it was first used for music by Ennemond Gaultier in a *tombeau* for the lutenist Mesengau (*d* 1638). There are examples for lute by other members of the Gaultier family, and *tombeaux* were also written for guitar (by Robert de Visée), viola da gamba (by Marais) and harpsichord (by L. Couperin, D'Anglebert, Froberger and others). F. Couperin's *apothéoses* of Lully and Corelli continued the *tombeau* tradition, but the name itself was discarded and rare in the 18th century. It has been revived by 20th-century French composers following Ravel's *Le tombeau de Couperin* (1917).

Tombeau de Couperin, Le. Piano suite by Ravel (1917), later orchestrated (1919).

Tom Jones. Opera in three acts by Philidor to a libretto by Poinsinet after Fielding (1765. Paris).

Tomkins, Thomas (*b* St Davids, 1572; *d* Martin Hussingtree, bur. 9 June 1656). Welsh composer. From a musical family, he claimed Byrd as his teacher. He divided his time between Worcester Cathedral (organist from 1596) and London, becoming a Gentleman in Ordinary of the Chapel Royal by 1620, assistant organist from 1621 and senior organist from 1625; that year he wrote music for Charles I's coronation. He left Worcester in 1654. A prolific and respected successor of Byrd, he composed church music, including over 100 anthems (*Musica Deo sacra*, 1668), madrigals (1622, among them *When David heard*, a moving, polyphonic setting of a powerful text), over 50 keyboard pieces and a few highly original fantasias, pavans and galliards for viol consort. His half-brothers John, Giles and Robert and his son Nathaniel were also musicians.

Tommasini, Vincenzo (*b* Rome, 17 Sept 1878; *d* there, 23 Dec 1950). Italian composer. He was a pupil of Bruch in Berlin, but his early music is Debussian. He arranged Scarlatti sonatas for the Dyagilev ballet *Le donne di buon umore* (1916) which was his only international popular success. Later works, in many genres, showed neo-classical tendencies, the best having an aristocratic distinction.

Tom-tom. Name applied to certain African and Eastern drums, but more generally to the woodenshelled, cylindrical rod-tensioned drums used in Western rhythm bands (for illustration, *see* PERCUSSION INSTRUMENTS). They are usually doubleheaded, and frequently played with side-drum sticks, especially in jazz bands, of which they are an essential component. Composers to have written for them include Stravinsky (*Agon*) and Cage (*She is Asleep*).

Ton (Ger.; pl. *Töne*). Term used in medieval and Renaissance German literature for a verse form (including the entire metrical and poetic scheme of the stanza) and its melody. Several poems could be written to the same *Ton*, particularly from the 14th century onwards. Among the Meistersinger it was common to write poems on a received *Ton*, usually by another Meister; Hans Sachs (1494–1576) wrote *c*4300 Meisterlieder in only about 275 *Töne*, of which he composed 13 himself.

Tonada (Sp.). 'Song': term for any Spanish melody. In the 17th century *tonada* (or *tono*) referred to a short secular or sacred solo song. In Chile and Argentina *tonada* denotes a love song (or duet).

Tonadilla. Originally a solo song appended to Spanish theatrical interludes; later a short stage piece in its own right. By 1750 it was a one-act satirical or political sketch for one to five characters, exploiting national dances and folk-type melodies. It developed into a broadly humorous entertainment, often with a romantic element. The main composers were Luis Misón, Esteve y Grimau, Blas de Laserna and Jacinto Valledor. By 1810 the *tonadilla* was in decline and soon gave way to the ZARZUELA.

Tonal, real. *See* REAL, TONAL.

Tonality. Term to denote the series of relationships between pitches in which one particular pitch, the 'tonic', is central. The term is most usually applied to the system used in Western art music from the 17th century to the 20th. In this system music is said to be in a particular key, or to have a particular tonality, when the pitches predominantly used form a major or minor scale; the key is that of the tonic or the final of that scale and is major or minor according to the pitches of the notes that the scale comprehends. 'Tonality' takes in the word 'key' but also has wider implications, especially concerning the functional association of other notes and chords with the tonic. The word is also sometimes used to embrace the modes and to describe groups of notes linked by consonants in a heirarchy.

The word 'tonality' is used in various compounds: atonality means non-tonality, and is applied to music with no key centre (Schoenberg used 'pantonality', all-tonality, in a similar sense); bitonality applies to music where two notes (and polytonality to music where more than two notes) exercise a tonal pull comparable with that of the tonic in tonal music.

Tonary [tonal]. Liturgical book of the Western church in which the antiphons of the Office and the Mass, also the responsories and other chants, are classified according to the eight psalm tones of Gregorian chant. Tonaries are theoretically self-contained but were often copied in other liturgical books and collections of musical treatises. Their terminology, of Byzantine origin, laid the foundations for the vocabulary of modal theory. The earliest surviving tonary, of the late 8th century, is from St Riquier.

Tondichtung (Ger.). Tone poem; *see* SYMPHONIC POEM.

Tone. Term used in several different senses. As an interval, it is the equivalent to a major 2nd, or the sum of two semitones (*see* INTERVAL).

The term is also used to describe a musical sound; an oboe may be said to have a 'reedy' tone, or a violinist's playing may be described as 'silvery in tone'. In acoustical parlance, 'tone' is used for a steady sound. In American usage, it may signify pitch or pitch-class (the equivalent of the English 'note').

In PLAINCHANT, 'tone' denotes a recitation formula.

Tone cluster. *See* CLUSTER.

Tonelli, Antonio (*b* Carpi, 19 Aug 1686; *d* there, 25 Dec 1765). Italian cellist and composer. Trained in Bologna, he served in Parma, Finale Emilia, Alassio and elsewhere, and visited Denmark. From 1746 he lived mainly in Carpi (*maestro di cappella* at the cathedral, 1755). He wrote an opera (1731), oratorios and other sacred pieces, but is of interest for his famed eccentricity (he wanted to marry a pupil 62 years younger than himself), his treatise on teaching music to young children and the insights offered by his writings on 18th-century performance (notably a continuo realization of Corelli's op.5).

Tone poem. *See* SYMPHONIC POEM.

Tonguing. In playing mouth-blown wind instruments, the technique by which detached notes, or the first notes of phrases, are articulated. With reed instruments this is done by placing the tip of the tongue lightly against the reed and drawing it back while blowing; in the flute or cup-mouthpiece instruments the tongue is placed against the palate behind the upper teeth. The movement is similar to that used in forming the letter *t*. When tempos are too fast for the player to maintain repeated *t* strokes, double or triple tonguing is used: the tip and back of the tongue are used alternately forming *t* and *k* consonants (double, *t–k*, *t–k* etc; triple, *t–k–t*, *t–k–t* etc). Modern composers sometimes call for FLUTTER-TONGUING.

Tonic. In the major–minor tonal system, the main note of a key (its key note), after which the key is named; the name of the scale-step or degree of that note; the triad built on that note.

Tonic accent. The emphasis that may be given to a note on account of its higher pitch.

Tonicization. In harmony, the treatment of some other scale degree than that of the key note as a tonic.

Tonic Sol-fa. A form of musical notation and a system of teaching sight-singing which depends on it; both were designed by John Curwen in mid-19th-century England. Curwen based his system on a treatise by Sarah Glover, which used a system similar to that of SOLMIZATION. Curwen's system used the syllables *doh, ray, mi, fah, soh, lah* and *te* for the notes of a rising major scale (each abbreviated to its initial letter in actual notation); chromatic degrees are noted by changing the vowel (the sharpened subdominant is *fe*, the flattened leading note *ta*), and a system of printed punctuation marks indicates rhythm. The system has a 'movable *doh*' where, at a modulation, a new tonic is named *doh*. The *doh* is defined at the beginning of a piece, or the *lah* if it is in a minor key (in which case an extra syllable, *bah*, is used for the sharpened 6th).

The Tonic Sol-fa system was extensively used in 19th-century England and remains popular in many parts of the world; Curwen founded a Tonic Sol-fa College in London in 1869, which still exists. Often the initial letters of the system are used as a teaching aid without the rest of the system. Though not a substitute (as was once proposed) for staff notation, Tonic Sol-fa remains a valuable aid for those who cannot read staff notation and for the learning of it. A modified version was adopted by Kodály for use in Hungarian schools and it remains widely used for educational purposes.

Tonus. Latin term that can mean a church mode (e.g. *primus tonus*), a plainchant recitation formula (e.g. *tonus lectionum*) or a whole tone (the interval of a major 2nd).

Tonus peregrinus (Lat.: 'wandering tone'). The late medieval name for an 'irregular' psalm tone. Its tenor, or recitation tone, changes in pitch after the mediation; its name comes either from this or from its use for the 'Pilgrim's Psalm', Psalm cxiii.

To October [Oktyabryu]. Shostakovich's Symphony no.2 (1927), with a choral setting of a text by A. Bezïmensky in the finale.

Töpfer, Johann Gottlob (*b* Niederrossla, 4 Dec 1791; *d* Weimar, 8 June 1870). German organist. A close associate of Liszt, in Weimar, he was one of the most important authorities on organ building and wrote the influential *Lehrbuch der Orgelbaukunst* (4 vols., 1855).

Toradze, David Alexandrovich (*b* Tbilisi, 14 April 1922, *d* there, 7 Nov 1983). Soviet composer. He was a pupil of Glier at the Moscow Conservatory and has taught at the Tbilisi Conservatory since 1952. His works include operas (*Bride of the North*, 1958), ballets, two symphonies and songs in a strongly epic and pictorial Georgian nationalist style.

Torchi, Luigi (*b* Mondano, 7 Nov 1858; *d* Bologna, 18 Sept 1920). Italian musicologist. He wrote an influential study of Wagner (1890) and, as editor of the *Revista musicale italiana* (1894–1904), notable essays on Italian instrumental music.

Torelli, Gasparo (*b* Borgo S Sepolcro; *d* ?Padua, in or after 1613). Italian composer. He was active in Padua by 1593. Canzonettas (3 bks, 1593–1608) and madrigals (1598, some to his own texts) by him survive as well as his best-known work *I fidi amanti* (1600), a *favola pastorale* for four voices in madrigalian dialogue style.

Torelli, Giuseppe (*b* Verona, 22 April 1658; *d* Bologna, 8 Feb 1709). Italian composer. He studied with Perti in Bologna and in 1686 joined the S Petronio orchestra as a violinist; he also played the viola and tenor viol there, but his reputation was as a violin virtuoso. In 1696–9 he was at the Ansbach court, briefly as *maestro di concerto*. He then went to Vienna before returning to Bologna, where he was a S Petronio violinist again from 1701.

Torelli composed some 150 instrumental works and contributed significantly to the development of the concerto grosso and solo concerto. His first four printed collections (1686–8) are all of chamber music, but they show experimental steps towards concerto scoring and ritornello form. These features are more pronounced in his many pieces (entitled variously 'sinfonia', 'concerto' and 'sonata') for trumpet and strings, mostly written for S Petronio before 1696. In later works Torelli arrived at a mature concerto style: his last collection (1709) consists of three-movement concerti grossi and solo violin concertos, with clearcut ritornello forms and relatively simple textures. He also wrote an oratorio and a few other vocal works.

Toronto Mendelssohn Choir. Canadian choir founded in 1894. It first toured the USA in 1905 and from 1918 gave seasons in Toronto with leading American orchestras. It has performed with the Toronto SO since 1935.

Toronto Symphony Orchestra. Canadian orchestra. The original Toronto SO was founded in 1906 by Frank Welsman and disbanded in 1914. In 1926 the New SO (founded by Kunits in 1923) acquired the charter and assets of Welsman's orchestra, becoming the Toronto SO. Its conductors have included Susskind, Ozawa, Ančerl and Andrew Davis.

Torrejón y Velasco, Tomás de (*b* ?Villarrobledo, bap. 23 Dec 1644; *d* Lima, 23 April 1728). Peruvian composer of Spanish birth. He went to Peru in 1667 when his employer was appointed viceroy there. He held administrative (non-musical) posts until 1676 when he became *maestro de capilla* of Lima Cathedral. He was admired for his villancicos, some of them polychoral; he also wrote liturgical music (notably vespers for Charles II) and an opera *La púrpura de la rosa* (after Calderón) celebrating Philip V's 18th birthday in 1701; it is the earliest surviving opera from the New World.

Torres y Martínez Bravo, Joseph de (*b* ?Madrid, *c*1665; *d* there, 3 June 1738). Spanish composer. He became principal organist of the Madrid royal chapel *c*1697 and *maestro de capilla c*1718. Most of his *c*170 works are liturgical; he at first used the traditional Spanish style, then adopted French and (later) Italian features, becoming one of the earliest in Spain to use a modern style. He wrote two musical treatises which he published himself along with other music books.

Torri, Pietro (*b* Peschiera, *c*1650; *d* Munich, 6 July 1737). Italian composer. He was *maestro di cappella* at the Bayreuth court, leaving in 1684 to travel in Italy; he joined the Munich court in 1689 and spent some of the ensuing years in Brussels and elsewhere because of political events. He wrote *c*20 operas (mostly after 1715, when the court returned to Munich) as well as many oratorios and other dramatic works; their manner is basically Venetian, with some influence of A. Scarlatti and (from his Brussels years) Lully – there is French-style declamation, ballet and instrumentation in his late works. His vocal chamber music, cantatas and especially duets, was well known and much admired.

Tortelier, Paul (*b* Paris, 21 March 1914). French cellist. After study at the Paris Conservatoire he made his début in 1931 with the Concerts Lamoureux. His British and American débuts were in 1947 and 1955. He is a noted exponent of Bach's cello suites, and brings to the Romantic repertory poetic phrasing and tender expression. Among his compositions are two cello concertos. His daughter Maria de la Pau (*b* 1950) is a pianist and his son Yan Pascal Tortelier (*b* 1947) a conductor and violinist.

Tosca. Opera in three acts by Puccini to a libretto by Giacosa and Illica after Sardou (1900, Rome).

Toscanini, Arturo (*b* Parma, 25 March 1867; *d* New York, 16 Jan 1957). Italian conductor. After study at the Parma Conservatory his early career was as a cellist. His conducting début was in Rio de Janeiro, at the age of 19, with *Aida*. On his return to Italy he worked at Turin, where he gave the première of *La bohème* (1896) and championed Wagner. As music director at La Scala from 1898 he was concerned to present opera as an integrated dramatic art. He was artistic director of the Met, 1908–15, giving the première of *La fanciulla del West* (1910). During the 1920s his career was again centred on La Scala and he toured in Europe and North America with the house's orchestra. A successful career at Bayreuth and Salzburg was halted by the rise of the Nazis. In 1936 he conducted the inaugural concert of the Palestine SO in Tel-Aviv and he gave memorable concerts with the BBC SO in London, 1935–9. He was principal conductor of the combined Philharmonic and Symphony orchestras of New York, his performances being notable for their clarity, precision and intensity. In 1937 he conducted the newly formed orchestra of the NBC, with which he remained until his final concert in 1954, and made most of his recordings. He gave dynamic, superbly disciplined performances of Brahms, Verdi and Beethoven; respect for the composer's intentions was at the centre of his art.

Tosi, Pier Francesco (*b* Cesena, *c*1653; *d* Faenza, 1732). Italian writer on music and singer. One of the most admired castratos of his day, he performed in many cities, taught singing in London for a time and was also a diplomat. He wrote a few vocal works and an important singing treatise, *Opinioni de'cantori antichi e moderni* (1723), which reflects the *bel canto* practice of the late 17th century and the first two decades of the 18th. It was translated into many languages, including English (by J.E. Galliard as *Observations on the Florid Song*, 1742).

Tosi's father, Giuseppe Felice Tosi (*fl* 1677–93), who held posts as an organist and *maestro di cappella* in Bologna and Ferrara, was a composer of operas, oratorios and other vocal pieces.

Tosti, Sir (Francesco) Paolo (*b* Ortano sul Mare, 9 April 1846; *d* Rome, 2 Dec 1916). Italian composer and singing teacher. He settled in England in 1880 and became singing teacher to the royal family (knighted 1908); the songs *Forever*, *Goodbye*, *At Vespers*, *Amore* and *That Day* were among his successes.

Tost Quartets. 12 string quartets by Haydn: op.54 nos.1–3, op.55 nos.1–3, op.64 nos.1–6 (1788–90), dedicated to the Viennese violinist Johann Tost.

Totentanz. Work for piano and orchestra by Liszt (1849), and variations on the *Dies irae* plainchant.

Tote Stadt, Die. Opera in three acts by Korngold to a libretto by 'Paul Schott' (the composer and his father) after Rodenbach's *Bruges la morte* (1920, Hamburg and Cologne).

Touch. Term used to describe, in keyboard instruments, the amount of force required to depress a key and/or the distance that a key travels; in performance, it refers to the manner of striking the keys. The relationship of a player's touch to tone on the piano is a matter that has been much disputed; in fact the pianist can control only the volume of individual sounds but with control of touch can give the illusion of varying the tone by means of sensitive balance and articulation.

The word 'touch' was used in the 16th and 17th centuries to refer to drawing sound from an instrument, in the sense that *toccata* means 'a touching'.

Tourdion. A lively 16th-century dance in triple metre, resembling the galliard. The music usually consists of two or three repeated eight-bar strains. The earliest surviving examples are printed as afterdances to the *bassedanses* in a collection of 1530.

Tourel, Jennie (*b* Vitebsk, 22 June ?1900; *d* New York, 23 Nov 1973). American mezzo-soprano. She left Russia in 1918, settling in Paris, where she sang at the Opéra Russe and in 1933 the Opéra Comique (Carmen, Charlotte in *Werther*). She made her Met début as Thomas's Mignon in 1937, also singing as Rosina and Carmen. Her career was primarily in recital and concert; in French music she was unrivalled, and she also sang the Italian coloratura mezzo repertory and Bernstein's music. She was admired for her versatility, her sensitivity to nuance and colour and her elegant style.

Tournemire, Charles (Arnould) (*b* Bordeaux, 22 Jan 1870; *d* Arcachon, 4 Nov 1939). French composer and organist. He was a pupil of Widor at the Paris Conservatoire and of Franck, whose place as organist at Ste Clotilde he inherited in 1898; from 1919 he also taught at the Conservatoire. His works include operas, oratorios and eight symphonies (1900–24), often on religious and esoteric subjects. But he is remembered for the monumental *L'orgue mystique* (1932), 51 organ masses using plainsong melodies appropriate to a particular Sunday, for the liturgical year, in a mystical style between Franck and Messiaen.

Tourney. Music for or preceding a tournament. The genre was cultivated particularly in the 17th century at the courts of northern Italy and at Paris, Munich and Vienna, often to celebrate a wedding or birthday; it was in effect an equestrian ballet preceded by short scenes. The music (little of which survives) consisted of recitatives, arias and choruses for the introduction and similar scenes, and music for the ballet or 'contest'. The subject, allegorical, classical, mythological or fantastic, symbolized the dispute over the merits of the contestants. Among composers who wrote for tourneys were Peri, Monteverdi, Lully, Steffani, J.H. Schmelzer and J.C. Kerll.

Touront, Johannes (*fl* ?Bohemia, *c*1450–80). Composer probably active in Bohemia. Most of his music – masses, motets and other liturgical settings – belong in style to the later 15th century. His skill is best seen in his four-voice mass setting based on a *cantus firmus* which appears in various voices.

Tours Festival (France). *See* Fêtes musicales en
Touraine.

Tourte. French family of bow makers. (?Louis)
Tourte, called Tourte *père* (*fl* Paris, *c*1740–80), was
a skilful workman whose bows, in variety of length
and design of head and frog, show the evolution of
the transitional bow; his elder son, known only as
Tourte *l'aîné* (*fl c*1765–*c*1800), appears to have
created an even more heterogeneous output. The
younger son, François Tourte (1747–1835), is by far
the most famous member of the family. Regarded as
the 'Stradivari of the bow' for the extraordinary
beauty and superb playing qualities of his bows, he
established (*c*1786) the standard 'modern' type of
bow (a few details apart). Synthesizing the work of
many predecessors he fixed the length of the
bowstick and of free hair, the balance point and the
form of nut and frog, with unsurpassed craftsmanship.

Tovey, Sir Donald (Francis) (*b* Eton, 17 July 1875;
d Edinburgh, 10 July 1940). English music scholar,
composer and pianist. He was educated, musically
and generally, by Sophie Weisse, who trained him as
a pianist, and began to compose at the age of eight.
He went on to study classics at Oxford. At first he
pursued composition (he had works performed in
Berlin and Vienna) and the piano (he played with
Joachim's quartet), but in 1914 he was appointed to
the Reid Chair of Music at Edinburgh University.
It was for the Reid Orchestra, which he founded in
1917, that the extensive series of programme notes
were written which subsequently achieved a more
permanent form as *Essays in Musical Analysis*
(1935–9). These, distinguished by many penetrating insights, did much to create new standards in
English writing about music; their reverence for the
classics of German music from Bach to Brahms now
seems excessive, but at their best they are magnificent products of a broadly stocked mind of acute
sensibility and rare insight.

Tower, Joan (*b* New Rochelle, NY, 6 Sept 1938).
American composer. She was a pupil of Luening
and others at Columbia and in 1969 was founder-
pianist of the Da Capo Chamber Players. Her
music, vividly evocative and strongly rhythmic, is
chiefly instrumental and acknowledges influences
from Beethoven and Stravinsky (e.g. in *Pet-
roushskates* for ensemble, 1980).

Tower music. *See* Turmmusik.

Toy. An unpretentious piece for lute or virginal. More
than 50 survive in English sources for the period
*c*1590–*c*1660, including some for lute by Dowland
and for keyboard by Bull, Gibbons and Tomkins.

Toy Symphony. A Symphony in C using toy instruments, long attributed to Haydn, now thought to
have been composed or arranged by Leopold
Mozart; others who may have been involved with it
are Michael Haydn and Edmund Angerer. Various
composers have also written symphonies with toy
instruments.

Tozzi, Antonio (*b* Bologna, *c*1736; *d* there, after
1812). Italian composer. A pupil of Padre Martini,
he presented his first operas in Italy and Brunswick.
He became court Kapellmeister at Munich in 1774

but in 1776 went to Spain as conductor of an Italian
opera company; he worked mostly in Barcelona. Besides 20 Italian operas he composed oratorios and
sacred works.

Tozzi, Giorgio (*b* Chicago, 8 Jan 1923). American
bass. He made his début on Broadway in 1948, in
Britten's *The Rape of Lucretia*, and sang in Italy
from 1950, making his début at La Scala in 1953.
From 1955 he was successful at the Met in operas by
Mozart, Gounod, Wagner and Verdi. Later he was
admired in films and musical comedy and as a concert singer.

Trabaci, Giovanni Maria (*b* Irsina, *c*1575; *d* Naples,
31 Dec 1647). Italian composer and organist. After
serving for a time as organist at the Oratorio dei
Filippini, Naples, he became organist of the Naples
royal chapel in 1601 and its *maestro di cappella* in
1614. A versatile, prolific composer, he is most
noted for his keyboard works, which comprise over
160 ricercares, canzonas, toccatas etc; in their chromaticism, thematic transformations and sectional
discontinuity they foreshadow Frescobaldi. He also
wrote *c*170 sacred vocal works (including four Passions, 1635) and 60 secular.

Tracker action. The traditional key mechanism of
the organ, in which the key is directly connected to
the pallet or valve by a system of thin, flexible strips,
usually of wood (called 'trackers').

Tract. Chant of the liturgy of the Proper of the
Roman Mass, occurring before the gospel on days of
penitence. Dating from the 9th century or earlier, it
has no set place in the liturgy but is sung mainly
before and during Lent and on the four Ember
Saturdays. It usually replaces the alleluia and sometimes the gradual. Its text is usually from the
psalms. Sung with no refrain, it is an example of
direct psalmody (without addition, repetition or
antiphony).

Traetta, Tommaso (Michele Francesco Saverio)
(*b* Bitonto, 30 March 1727; *d* Venice, 6 April 1779).
Italian composer. He studied with Porpora and Durante in Naples and had his first operas staged there
and in Rome and Venice. In 1758–65 he was *maestro
di cappella* to the court at Parma, where he began to
adopt features of French *tragédie lyrique* in his
operas; the works of Jommelli and (later) Gluck
were also influential. *Ippolito ed Aricia* (1759),
which borrows from Rameau's *Hippolyte et Aricie*,
was an early success among these 'reform' operas.
Notable among those for other theatres were *So-
fonisba* (1762, Mannheim) and *Ifigenia in Tauride*
(1763, Vienna). After three years as director of the
Ospedaletto conservatory in Venice, he became
music director of the Russian court chapel in St
Petersburg, 1768–75; his finest work there was *Antigone* (1772). He later went to London and elsewhere,
and presented his last two operas in Venice.

Traetta's reform operas show a powerful dramatic
sense and melodic gift. They generally feature classical subject matter, large scene complexes, more
orchestral music and accompanied recitative than
was usual, and dramatic choruses. His output also
includes some more conventional serious operas and
several comic ones (*c*40 stage works in all), pieces for

pasticcios, sacred music, songs and a few instrumental works.

Tragédie lyrique. The name given to serious French opera of the 17th and 18th centuries, as exemplified in the works of Lully, Campra and Rameau.

Tragic Overture [Tragische-ouvertüre]. Concert overture, op.81, by Brahms (1880).

Tragic Symphony. Schubert's own title for his Symphony no.4 in C minor (1816).

Tranquillo (It.). Quiet.

Transcendental Studies after Paganini. Piano works by Liszt, transcriptions of six of Paganini's violin caprices (1838); they were revised in 1851 as *Grandes études de Paganini*.

Transcription. Term for a written copy of a musical work involving some change. It may be a change of medium (thus meaning the same as 'arrangement'); or it may mean that its notation has been changed (e.g. from tablature to staff) or its layout (e.g. from parts to score). The term may also include the writing down of music from a live or recorded performance, or its transference from sound to some graphic form by electronic or mechanical means.

Transfiguration de notre Seigneur Jésus-Christ, La. Choral work by Messiaen to biblical and liturgical texts (1969).

Transfigured Night. *See* VERKLÄRTE NACHT.

Transformation, Thematic. The process of modifying a theme so that in a new context it is different and yet manifestly made of the same elements. Dance pairs of the 17th century provide notable early examples, and Bach subjects the 'royal theme' to thematic transformation in the *Musical Offering*; but the process belongs above all to the 19th century, when it became a favourite method of achieving cohesion both within and between the movements of a work and at the same time imparting different meanings to a musical idea. Berlioz based his *Symphonie fantastique* (1830) on a theme that undergoes transformation in the light of the 'programme' of the work; Liszt and Franck were among many later composers who made extensive use of similar methods, as was Wagner in his treatment of the LEITMOTIF, combining, adapting and altering motifs to reflect the dramatic action.

Transition. A passage which leads from one well-defined section of a piece to another, for instance the 'bridge passage' between the first and second subjects in sonata form. Modulation is usually involved.

Transposing instruments. Instruments whose music is not notated at its sounding pitch but transposed up or down by a specific interval. Transposition is reckoned relative to the pitch C, so that an instrument 'in F' sounds F when C is notated. The intention is to maintain the same fingering etc among instruments of a similar kind but of different pitch.

In the woodwind, an example is the english horn, pitched a 5th below the oboe (in C). The same fingering for both instruments will produce sounds a 5th lower in the english horn; its music is therefore notated a 5th above sounding pitch so that the player can read it with the same fingering. This principle applies to virtually all types of clarinet, the

alto flute and piccolo, the double bassoon and the saxophones. With brass instruments, the notes of their harmonic series have traditionally been written in the key of C whatever the pitch of the instrument. Typical transposing brass are the horn in F and E♭ and the trumpet in B♭, A and D. Among the few transposing string instruments the most common is the double bass, whose music is written an octave above sounding pitch.

Transposing keyboard. A keyboard that enables the player to have music sound in a different key from that in which it is written. In most early versions, the keyboard slides sideways under the jacks or hammers; a later type used a false keyboard that could be moved laterally over the real one. Both require extra strings or pipes at either end of the instrument to avoid loss of range when the keyboard is shifted. This facility was commonly used in the 18th century, on harpsichords and organs and occasionally in the 19th on pianos.

Transposition. The notation or performance of music at a pitch different from that in which it was originally conceived, by raising or lowering all the notes by the same interval.

Transverse flute. Term used for the side-blown flute until about the middle of the 18th century, to distinguish it from the end-blown recorder.

Trapp, Max (*b* Berlin, 1 Nov 1887; *d* there, 31 May 1971). German composer. He studied with Juon and Dohnányi at the Berlin Musikhochschule (1905–11), teaching there from 1920 and later at the conservatory. His works, at first in a late Romantic style, but later neo-classical, include seven symphonies and a Concerto for orchestra (1935).

Trap set. *See* DRUM SET.

Traquenard (Fr.). A late 17th-century dance found in ballets by Erlebach, J.C.F. Fischer, Kusser, Georg Muffat and others. It is rhythmically and structurally identical with the gavotte.

Traubel, Helen (*b* St Louis, 20 June 1889; *d* Santa Monica, CA, 28 July 1972). American soprano. She made her concert début in 1923 and appeared at the Met in 1937. From 1941 she succeeded Flagstad in the Wagnerian repertory, singing Brünnhilde, Kundry and Isolde with vocal grandeur and expressive warmth. She left the Met in 1953 to pursue a career in films and television.

Trauer (Ger.: 'funeral'). Haydn's Symphony no.44 in E minor ('Trauersinfonie', *c*1770); Bach's Cantata no.198, *Lass, Fürstin, lass noch einen Strahl*.

Träumerei [Reverie]. Piano piece by Schumann, no.7 of his *Kinderszenen* (1838).

Trautonium. A monophonic electronic instrument whose name is derived from that of its inventor, Friedrich Trautwein (1888–1956). It was first exhibited in Berlin in 1930 and has been used by Hindemith (who wrote a concertino for it), Strauss and Egk. It has a fingerboard of resistance wire, stretched over a metal rail, coupled to an oscillator; on pressing the wire to the rail the performer completes the circuit and the oscillator is amplified and heard through a loudspeaker. The position of the finger determines the pitch. It has a range of three octaves, which can be transposed; the timbre can be varied by additional button-operated circuits and the volume is controlled by a pedal.

Travenol, Louis-Antoine (*b* Paris, 1698 or 1708; *d* there, 1783). French composer and writer. After serving at the Lorraine court he became an orchestral violinist in Paris (by 1739). He composed violin sonatas, orchestral pieces and a vaudeville but was best known for his disputes with illustrious figures; his writings include two polemical pamphlets directed against Rousseau (1753, 1754) and an attack on Mondonville (1758), as well as a history of the Opéra (1753).

Travers, John (*b* ?Windsor, *c*1703; *d* London, June 1758). English organist and composer. He was apprenticed to Greene and became a friend of Pepusch. As an organist he served lastly at the Chapel Royal (from 1737). His works include church music, canzonets and canons as well as a book of organ voluntaries.

Traverso, traversière (It., Fr.). TRANSVERSE FLUTE.

Travesty, travesti. Terms for an operatic role in which a singer impersonates the opposite sex, in particular a BREECHES PART.

Traviata, La. Opera in three acts by Verdi to a libretto by Piave after Dumas fils's *La dame aux camélias* (1853, Venice).

Treble. A high voice, especially of a boy or girl. From the Latin *triplus*, it referred in the 14th and 15th centuries to the top voice of a three-part composition or the second highest part in a four-part one. It is also used to qualify other terms, such as clef (the 'treble clef' is the G clef), recorder or viol.

Trebor (*fl* 1390–1410). French composer. He was associated with the southern courts of Foix and Aragon and may be identifiable with the musician 'Trebol' in the service of Martin I of Aragon in 1409. Six works attributed to him in a late 14th-century Chantilly MS have unusual features, such as irregular poetic lines.

Tre corde [tutte le corde] (It.). 'Three strings': in piano music, a direction to release the left (UNA CORDA or 'soft') pedal.

Tregian, Francis (*b* 1574; *d* London, 1619). English musician. A Catholic, educated and employed on the Continent, he is known for the three music anthologies (including the Fitzwilliam Virginal Book) he compiled while imprisoned in London for recusancy (1609–19); they contain over 2000 early 17th-century English and Italian vocal and instrumental works, a few by him.

Treiber, Johann Philipp (*b* Arnstadt, 26 Feb 1675; *d* Jena, 9 Aug 1727). German composer and theorist. He probably collaborated with his father, Johann Friedrich (1642–1719), on an 'operetta' (1705, Arnstadt) once attributed to Bach, then working in Arnstadt; he also wrote a throughbass manual (1702). Later he was a professor of law in Erfurt. Johann Friedrich, a schoolmaster and writer, composed mostly sacred pieces.

Tremblay, Gilles (Léonce) (*b* Arvida, 6 Sept 1932). Canadian composer. He studied at Montreal with Champagne and at the Paris Conservatoire with Messiaen, Loriod and Martenot, working in the Groupe de Recherches Musicales; later he studied with Boulez and Pousseur. He returned to Canada and taught at Montreal Conservatory. His music, much concerned with sonority, uses wind and percussion instruments particularly, as well as electronics (he plays the ondes martenot). He often uses rarefied textures, with mosaic forms and sections sharply contrasted in pitch, dynamic and intensity; some works have aleatory elements. His works always embody an element of poetic symbolism, notably the three entitled *Champs* (*II: Souffles* and *III: Vers*, 1969), *Solstices* (1971, for up to four groups of six solo instruments) and *Compostelle I* (1978, for 18 instruments).

Tremolo (It.). 'Trembling', 'quivering': the rapid reiteration of a note or chord without regard to measured time values. It was used as an ornament in the 17th and 18th centuries, particularly in early 17th-century Italian vocal music where lightly reiterated impulses are used to highly expressive effect (the TRILLO). The effect is much used in orchestral music, for sustained, emphatic tutti passages or to create an agitated effect.

Tremulant. An accessory stop on the organ creating a tremulous effect. Tremulants have been used since *c*1500. Some are based on a sprung valve, which causes the wind to be admitted in uneven pulses; others create blocks in the flow of wind.

Trent Codices. A collection of six MSS of music of the period 1400–75. They were discovered by F.X. Haberl in Trent Cathedral library and were taken to Vienna for study and editing by a team of scholars under Guido Adler, and returned to Trent in 1918; two years later a seventh was discovered. The six MSS contain 1585 compositions (the seventh, mainly a duplicate, adds a further 65). The two earliest (of 265 and 264 folios) were copied *c*1435–50 in northern Italy, Piedmont, north-east France and the Savoy-Basle region; the remaining five (of 465, 382, 422, 425 and 259 folios) were copied in Trent, 1445–65. The repertory, largely of sacred music, includes works by the leading Franco-Flemish composers of the time (above all Dufay, also Binchois, Busnois, Brassart and many others), a few French, Italian and German composers, and several English (Dunstable, Power, Benet and others).

Trepak. A Russian dance of Cossack origin in animated 2/4 time. There is one in Tchaikovsky's *Nutcracker* suite.

Treu [Fedele], **Daniel Gottlob** (*b* Stuttgart, 1695; *d* Breslau, 7 Aug 1749). German composer. After studying with Vivaldi in Venice, he was Kapellmeister to an Italian opera company in Breslau (1725–7), where four of his operas were given, then served noble families in Prague, Vienna and Silesia. He was a prolific composer but only a little church music and a serenata survive.

Triad. A chord consisting of three notes which can be arranged to form two superimposed 3rds. If the lower 3rd is major and the upper 3rd minor, the triad is said to be major (C–E–G); if the lower 3rd is minor and the upper major it is a minor triad (C–E♭–G). If both 3rds are major it is augmented (C–E–G♯); if both are minor, diminished (C–E♭–G♭).

Trial by Jury. Operetta ('dramatic cantata') in one act by Sullivan to a libretto by Gilbert (1875, London).

Triana, Juan de (*fl* 1478–83). Spanish composer. A prebend of Seville from *c*1478, he was master of the choristers at Toledo Cathedral in 1483. 20 of his compositions, which include five sacred pieces and numerous secular songs, appear in the Cancionero Musical de la Colombina.

Triangle. A percussion instrument consisting of a steel rod bent into the form of a triangle, with one angle left open (for illustration, *see* PERCUSSION INSTRUMENTS). It is normally suspended and struck with a steel beater (or a drumstick), producing a high, silvery sound of indeterminate pitch. Dating from ancient times, it was used in the Middle Ages and Renaissance for religious purposes as well as in secular music. It was used in the orchestra by the end of the 18th century (Mozart, Haydn and Beethoven all wrote for it), in military and janissary-related music, but in the 19th century its varied uses included the tremolo (e.g. Wagner's *Die Meistersinger*) and even the solo (Liszt's E♭ Piano Concerto).

Tricarico, Giuseppe (*b* Gallipoli, 25 June 1623; *d* there, 14 Nov 1697). Italian composer. He worked first in Rome and in the 1650s he was a *maestro di cappella* in Ferrara. Moving to Vienna, he became *maestro di cappella* to the Dowager Empress Eleonora, *c*1660–1663, and helped establish elements of Italian style. After this he taught in Gallipoli, near Lecce. His works include operas and oratorios, church music and secular vocal pieces.

Tricinium. In modern usage, a three-part vocal or instrumental composition of the Renaissance or early Baroque. Some 16th-century Lutheran editors used the term particularly for didactic pieces.

Tricklir, Jean Balthasar (*b* Dijon, 1750; *d* Dresden, 29 Nov 1813). French cellist and composer. Trained at Mannheim, he made several concert tours and from 1783 served at the Dresden court. He wrote cello concertos and sonatas and two theoretical treatises.

Tricotet (Fr.). Term used in the 16th and 17th centuries for various tunes and dances in France and England, so called because the feet moved as fast as the hands in knitting. Two particular melodies, characterized by three-bar phrases, were known by the term. An example appears in Rameau's harpsichord suites of 1728.

Triebensee, Josef (*b* Wittingau, 21 Nov 1772; *d* Prague, 22 April 1846). Bohemian composer. He was a frequent oboe soloist in Vienna and first oboist and Kapellmeister to Prince Liechtenstein's wind band, 1794–1809. Later he was a theatre composer in Brno and in 1816–36 director of the Prague Opera. His large output includes music and arrangements for wind band, 12 comic operas, some smaller vocal pieces and orchestral and chamber works.

Triébert. French family of woodwind instrument makers active in Paris (1810–81). Their work may be said to have established the definitive characteristics of the French-style oboe as we know it.

Trigōnon. A common name for the Greco-Roman HARP, taken from the word meaning triangle.

Trill. An ornament consisting of a more or less rapid alternation of a note with the note a tone or semitone above it. The trill (or shake) may begin on the upper note or the main note, partly depending on whether its function is more melodic or harmonic; in the Baroque and early Classical periods, where it is largely harmonic, trills were commonly but not invariably begun on the upper note. Many trills end with a turn or with a note anticipating the final note. Ex.1 shows a lute trill as written out by Bernhard

Ex. 1

Schmid (1607); ex.2, from Leopold Mozart's *Violinschule* (1756), shows two ways of performing a

Ex. 2

cadential trill; ex.3, from Chopin's Bolero op.19, shows his notation of trills (*a* and *c*) and their realization, one starting on the main note (*b*) and the other on the upper (*d*).

Ex. 3

For short types of trill, *see* PRALLTRILLER and MORDENT. The TRILLO is not a trill in the modern sense.

Trillo (It.). An ornament, a form of vocal tremolo used particularly in early 17th-century Italian music.

Trimble, Lester (Albert) (*b* Bangor, WI, 29 Aug 1923). American composer. He studied with Lopatnikoff at Carnegie-Mellon University and with Milhaud and Honegger in Paris and has worked as a critic and teacher (from 1971 at the Juilliard School). His works, in many genres, show his concern with thematic unity (e.g. the Symphony no.2, 1968, based on a single theme); latterly he has used newer techniques and written for the harpsichord (Concerto, 1978).

Trinity College of Music. Conservatory founded in London in 1872 as a college of church music; it was incorporated as Trinity College, London, in 1875 and renamed in 1904. All branches of music have been taught since 1876, when the college founded a professorship at London University.

Trio. A piece of music for three players or singers. Common types are the PIANO TRIO and the STRING TRIO; *see also* TERZET, TRICINIUM and TRIO SONATA. The word was often used in the 18th century for pieces in three voices or parts – such as the organ sonatas or sinfonias (or three-part inventions) of Bach – even if performed by only one player.

From the 17th century onwards the second of two alternating dances was called a 'trio', whether or not it was in three parts; the usage probably derived from the contrasting sections for two oboes and bassoon used in dances in Lully's operas. This use of the term is most familiar from the minuet (or scherzo) and trio of Classical and later composers.

Trionfi. Trilogy of stage works by Orff (*Carmina burana, Catulli carmina, Trionfi d'Afrodite*; 1953, Salzburg).

Trinofo dell'onore, Il. Opera by A. Scarlatti (1718, Naples).

Trionfo del Tempo e del Disinganno, Il. Oratorio by Handel to a text by B. Pamphili (?1707, Rome); it includes the earliest piece for solo organ and orchestra. Handel later adapted it radically as *Il Trionfo del Tempo e della Verità* (1737, London); it is also related to his *The Triumph of Time and Truth* (1757, London).

Trionfo di Afrodite. Scenic concerto by Orff to medieval Latin lyrics (1953, Milan), the third part of the trilogy *Trionfi*.

Trionfo di Camilla, Il. Opera by Giovanni Bononcini (1696, Naples); it was given as *Camilla* in English in London, 1706.

Trionfo di Dori, Il. Anthology of madrigals published by Gardane of Venice in 1592; each madrigal ends with the refrain 'Viva la bella Dori'. It provided the model for Morley's THE TRIUMPHES OF ORIANA.

Trio sonata. A sonata for two melody instruments and continuo. It was the central instrumental form of the Baroque period and reached its height with the four sets by Corelli (opp.1–4, 1681–94). The commonest instrumentation was for two violins and continuo. See SONATA.

Triplet. A group of three notes to be performed in the time of two of the same kind or in the time of any number of another kind. They are indicated by a figure *3*, usually under a slur; the same notation may be used to signify any triple-rhythm figure (such as a two-beat note followed by a one-beat note).

Triple tonguing. See TONGUING.

Triplum, triplex (Lat.). 'Triple'; terms used in medieval theory to denote: (1) three-voice polyphony (e.g. 'organum triplum'); (2) the third voice of a polyphonic work, an independent voice composed against a tenor and duplum (it was used in the 13th and 14th centuries in organum and the motet, and in the 15th was replaced by such terms as 'cantus' or 'superius', though the English 'treble' persisted; (3) diminution or augmentation by a factor of three ('proportio tripla') in mensural notation; and (4) the name 'triplex', for the highest of three partbooks of a set in the 16th and 17th centuries.

'Tristan' chord. The first chord in Wagner's *Tristan und Isolde*, *f–b–d#'–g#'*. The name has been used for any four-note chord constructed with the same intervals (sometimes called a 'half-diminished 7th chord' in American usage); its harmonic significance in Wagner's opera has led it to be viewed as the basis of a 'crisis' in Romantic harmony.

Tristan Schalmei. A double-reed woodwind instrument, of conical bore with six finger-holes, with characteristics of the MUSETTE and SHAWM, designed by Heckel for the shepherd's rustic pipe in Act 3 of Wagner's *Tristan und Isolde*. The HOLZTROMPETE, however, probably had the sound closest to Wagner's idea (the *tárogató* and english horn have also been used); the Tristan Schalmei is now obsolete.

Tristan und Isolde. Opera in three acts by Wagner to his own libretto (1865, Munich).

Tritone. The interval equal to the sum of three whole tones, i.e. an augmented 4th; it is exactly half an octave. Its instability led it to be nicknamed 'diabolus in musica' in the Renaissance. That instability has been exploited in the extension and suspension of tonality.

Tritonius, Petrus [Treybenreif, Peter] (*b* Bolzano, *c*1465; *d* ?Hall, *c*1525). Austrian composer. A humanist scholar, he probably studied at Vienna and Ingolstadt universities and later held various teaching posts. With Celtis's guidance he composed four-voice settings of Horatian odes in note-against-note style, strictly observing the classical metres and quantities. They were published in 1507. His *Hymnarius* (1524), the oldest-known printed Catholic hymnbook, contains the texts of 131 hymns with blank staves on which the melodies could be written.

Trittico, Il. Triple bill of operas by Puccini: IL TABARRO, SUOR ANGELICA and GIANNI SCHICCHI (1918, New York).

Trittico botticelliano. Orchestral work by Respighi (1927).

Tritto, Giacomo (Domenico Mario Antonio Pasquale Giuseppe) (*b* Altamura, 2 April 1733; *d* Naples, 16/17 Sept 1824). Italian composer and teacher. He studied and then taught at the Turchini conservatory in Naples, becoming *primo maestro* in 1799; from 1806 he was a *maestro* of the new Collegio Reale di Musica, and he was also *maestro* of the royal chamber from 1804 and the royal chapel and chamber from 1816. He composed over 40 operas, 1780–1810; many were comic works for Naples, but latterly he concentrated on *opera seria*. He also wrote church music and two didactic works.

Triumphes of Oriana, The. Anthology of madrigals assembled probably in the late 1590s by Thomas Morley and published in 1601 as an entertainment to honour Queen Elizabeth I. 23 composers are represented in the collection, which is modelled on the Italian anthology *Il trionfo di Dori* (1592); each madrigal ends with a refrain in praise of 'Oriana' (the queen), 'Long live fair Oriana'.

Triumphlied. Choral work, op.55, by Brahms (1871), to a text from *Revelation*, xix.

Triumph of Time, The. Orchestral work by Birtwistle (1972).

Triumph of Time and Truth, The. Oratorio by Handel (1757), related to his IL TRIONFO DEL TEMPO E DEL DISINGANNO.

Troiano, Massimo (*b* in or nr. Naples; *d* after 1570). Italian composer. He sang in the Munich Hofkapelle under Lassus from at least 1568 to 1570 and composed *canzoni alla napolitana* (4 bks, 1567–9), setting his own texts. His published account of Duke Wilhelm V's wedding celebrations (1568) vividly describes music at the Bavarian court.

Troilus and Cressida. Opera in three acts by Walton to a libretto by Christopher Hassall after Chaucer etc (not Shakespeare) (1954, London).

Trojan, Václav (*b* Plzeň, 24 April 1907; *d* Prague, 5 July 1983). Czech composer. He was a pupil of Suk, Novák and Hába at the Prague Conservatory and is best known for his scores for animated films. He also wrote *The Roundabout*, an opera for children.

Trojans, The [Les troyens]. Opera in five acts by Berlioz to his own libretto after Virgil. In order to have it staged he divided it into two: Acts 1 and 2 became *La prise de Troie* and Acts 3 to 5, with a new prelude, became *Les troyens à Carthage*; the latter was performed in Paris in 1863, the whole work in Karlsruhe in 1890.

Trojan Turnovský, Jan (*b* Turnov, *c*1550; *d* in or after 1595). Czech composer. A Utraquist priest in Sepekovice (1581) and Netvořice (1595) and an important composer, he wrote music for the Czech literary brotherhoods, including arrangements of Czech sacred songs and polyphonic liturgical works; only a few survive.

Tromba (It.). TRUMPET.

Tromba da tirarsi (It.). SLIDE TRUMPET.

Tromba marina (It.). MARINE TRUMPET.

Trombetti, Ascanio (*b* Bologna, bap. 27 Nov 1544; *d* there, 20–21 Sept 1590). Italian composer. He played the cornett in Bologna from the 1560s and was *maestro di cappella* of S Giovanni in Monte (1583–9); he died at the hands of an outraged husband. His publications include madrigals, graceful and often florid (4 bks, 1573–87), and motets (1589). His brother Girolamo (1557–1624) was also a wind player and composer.

Trombly, Preston (Andrew) (*b* Hartford, CT, 30 Dec 1945). American composer. He was a pupil of Whittenberg at the University of Connecticut and of Arel and Davidovsky at Yale. He has taught at various institutions and since the early 1980s become increasingly active as a clarinettist and saxophonist. His works, mostly for ensembles, often with tape, reveal a brilliant sense of instrumental colour.

Tromboncino, Bartolomeo (*b* in or near Verona, *c*1470; *d* in or near Venice, *c*1535). Italian composer. He spent most of his life in the Marquis of Mantua's service, though his career there was stormy (in 1499 he killed his wife after finding her with her lover). He was in Ferrara (1502–8), in Lucrezia Borgia's service, and may have stayed there until 1521, when he was living in Venice. One of the most prolific and gifted frottola composers in the early 16th century, he wrote over 170 in various forms. By 1507 he was setting serious, madrigalian texts, an innovatory step, but his importance waned in later years. His textures tend towards non-imitative polyphony rather than the simple homorhythmic style of many frottolas. His extant sacred works – a motet, a setting of the Lamentations and 17 *laude* – are basically homorhythmic with contrasting sections of non-imitative polyphony.

Trombone (Old Eng. sackbut; Ger. *Posaune*). A brass instrument with a cup-shaped mouthpiece and a tube whose bore is cylindrical for two-thirds of its length before expanding into a bell (for illustration, *see* BRASS INSTRUMENTS). The most common form has a telescopic slide for varying the length of the tube. The slide technique involves seven positions that lower the pitch of the harmonic series progressively by semitones, the 1st (highest) with the slide fully retracted, the 7th (lowest) with it fully extended. The fundamental on the standard B♭ tenor trombone, in 1st position, is *B♭*, in the 7th *E′*. The higher fundamental (or 'pedal') notes can be played and have sometimes been used for special effect (as in Berlioz's *Grande messe des morts*).

The trombone is built in various sizes, though the B♭ or tenor has always been the most typical. The tenor-bass, or B♭/F, dating from 1839, is also commonly used and has an extension that takes it down to C, the lowest note in classical trombone parts. The surviving form of bass trombone in G (another, in F, disappeared by the 20th century) still appears in British brass bands, and contrabass trombones exist with extensions down to B♭″. Alto trombones were used from the 16th to the 18th centuries but declined when the tenor, which covers most of their range, became established in the orchestra. The soprano, an octave above the tenor, appeared in the 17th century but has never been widely used. Valve trombones were developed in the 19th century and were popular until the turn of the 20th, but have intonation problems and a less sensitive legato than the slide instrument.

The trombone or sackbut first appeared in the 15th century and was well established by the 16th. It was a regular member of town and court bands, and was especially espoused by Schütz and G. Gabrieli in their church music. It could play with a technical agility comparable with the cornett or violin. During the century it was often used in sacred music for doubling the choir, and it was established in the orchestra by the end of the century; it was long associated with the ecclesiastical or supernatural (e.g. the cemetery scene in Mozart's *Don Giovanni*). It was traditionally used in groups of three, originally alto-tenor-bass, now two tenors and bass. Berlioz used it in a wide range of contexts, but it was mostly used for adding volume and brilliance or playing themes that should cut through the rest of the orchestra. The 20th century brought the first use of glissando (Schoenberg's *Pelleas und Melisande*); its avant-garde possibilities have been explored by Vinko Globokar. The instrument has been popular with jazz and dance musicians, such as Tommy Dorsey and Glenn Miller; it has long had a place in military and brass bands for its firm, well-defined tone.

Tromlitz, Johann Georg (*b* Reinsdorf, 8 Nov 1725; *d* Leipzig, 4 Feb 1805). German flautist. Initially a performer, he was among the first to design flutes with additional keys; he also planned a keyless chromatic flute. His output includes flute treatises and a few compositions.

Trommelbass (Ger.). 'Drum bass': term for a bass

part consisting of steady repeated notes (usually quavers), used much in the middle of the 18th century to give animation to the music.

Trope. A piece of music, in the Middle Ages, complementary to plainchant. It may take the form of an introduction to a Gregorian chant, or a series of such introductions, one for the chant as a whole and others for its sections. It could also be a series of interpolations in a chant, consisting of music with or without words; further it may mean a substitute for a chant, conveying the same meaning as the chant and occupying the same liturgical position. Adding a trope to a chant is called 'troping'.

The practice of troping is almost as old as the development of the chants the tropes complement. The SEQUENCE can be regarded as an early example of the troping of the jubilus of the alleluia (though it subsequently enjoyed an independent existence, not generally found with tropes). Central to introductory tropes is the text of the liturgical chant that is being introduced: a trope would highlight aspects of the text, often making it more dramatic, and at the same time it served as an invitation to join in the main chant. In the trope MSS of the 10th and 11th centuries, there are introductory tropes for the introit, offertory and communion, and also for chants other than those of the Mass Proper (for example the Gloria). Tropes for the introit work their text around that of the introit itself and its presentation of the theme for the liturgy of the day; it may form a simple introduction or be a dialogue (an important example of this is the Easter *Quem queritis*, which contributed to the development of liturgical drama). The idea of dialogue is inherent to the trope: it was generally sung by the cantor, the choir responding with the actual introit. Trope texts are often made up of phrases borrowed from the Bible, like those of many Gregorian chants. Introit tropes show a wide range of styles. There are a few examples of Kyrie tropes, though more commonly these melismatic melodies are set syllabically with Latin prosulae. The short phrases of the Gloria, however, allow for troping at various points, notably at 'Laus tua Deus'; the Gloria trope *Spiritus et alme* became very popular from the 13th century onwards. In the Sanctus, which is already preceded by the Preface, introductory tropes are rare and troping usually begins after the first word. Tropes are found for the Agnus Dei.

While all these tropes serve the function of interpreting the liturgical texts, melismatic tropes – purely musical melismas inserted into existing works – clearly had a different purpose. The practice may go back to the 9th century, although they are commonly found in MSS only from the 12th. They appear most often in connection with Office responsories in the final section of the chant that returns as a refrain after the verse. The term 'substitute trope' is used for liturgical texts that have been paraphrased and set to music; in the troped office, texts are included that are not normally troped elsewhere, such as the Creed or the epistle.

The term 'troper' is used for an MS containing a significant number of tropes; a troper from a particular church is usually dependent on the same church's gradual for its musical and textual qualities.

Troppo (It.). 'Too much', e.g. *allegro non troppo* ('lively, not too much so').

Troubadours, trouvères. Lyric poets or poet-musicians of France in the 12th and 13th centuries. Poets working in the south of France, writing in Provençal (*langue d'oc*), are generally termed troubadours; those of the north, writing in French (*langue d'oïl*), are called trouvères.

The first centre of troubadour song seems to have been Poitiers; it eventually extended from Bordeaux to northern Italy and included Catalonia. The earliest lives of the troubadours are the *vidas*, compiled in the 13th and 14th centuries, which have lent a romantic air to the troubadour; this is only gradually being dispelled, to reveal a well-educated and highly-sophisticated verse-technician, whose music and poetry combined in the service of the courtly ideal of love. Troubadours were often of high social standing (like Guillaume IX of Aquitaine, generally described as the first of the troubadours) from the nobility, but they could come from any social background as long as they conformed to courtly ideals and could appreciate and acquire the refinement that went with courtly love.

No single theory as to the genesis of the troubadour lyric has won general acceptance; the principal hypotheses centre on backgrounds ranging from Arabic, Celtic, Cathar and liturgical to fuedal-social, classical Latin, goliardic and folkloristic. Troubadour songs can be best classified by genre – the poets themselves were intensely conscious of everything to do with form and style. The main topic of troubadour poetry is love in its various aspects, and it was the need to express them as succinctly as possible that led to the establishment of genres, distinguished less by form than by content or implied situation.

The principal genres are: *canso* (courtly love-song), *dansa* (mock-popular song based on a dance form), *descort* (discordant in verse form or feeling), *escondig* (a lover's apologia), *gap* (a challenge), *pastorela* (an amorous encounter between a knight and a shepherdess), *planh* (a lament), *sirventes* (a satirical poem devised to a borrowed melody), *tenso*, *partimen* and *joc-partit* (songs of debate) and *vers* (an early term used by troubadours). Most troubadour songs are strophic, based on stanzaic patterns repeated throughout the song to the melody of the first verse in widely ranging schemes, always devised with a great awareness of technical accomplishment.

The French of the trouvères was not standardized but rather a collection of related, regional languages from Champagne, Picardy, Normandy and England. The tradition is close to (but not necessarily derived from) that of the troubadours, and parallels exist, including the fact that it is essentially courtly poetry celebrating love, or *fine amour*, in a refined mode of expression. Even more than with the troubadours, the trouvères' art was often quickly channelled into literary groups or *puys* (that at Arras is the best documented). The genres resemble closely those of the troubadours, though some (like the *sirventes*) dropped out while others, especially the *jeu-parti* (*joc-partit*), acquired new popularity. The *chanson d'amour* relates to the *canso*, and the *lai* to the *descort*, but genres unique to the trouvère tradition include the *chanson avec refrains*, in which the strophic repetition is broken into by the insertion of refrains (courtly tags with tunes), and the *chanson de toile* (weaving-song, old French *chanson d'histoire*), a courtly, mock-popular song like the *pastorela*. There are also religious songs in the trouvère repertory. The trouvères were always ready to devise variations within set and accepted traditions.

The verse of the troubadours and the trouvères was inextricably linked to its performance through music. Unfortunately music survives for only *c*282 of more than 2500 troubadour poems, though most of the *c*2100 trouvère poems do have music; here the same text often survives with several different melodies, making authorship uncertain. In both traditions the relationship between text and music remained flexible until the late 13th century; a melody for a poem could be replaced, or homage to an admired poem and melody could be paid by imitating the poem's structure while retaining the original melody (resulting in numerous contrafacta). Variants are a feature of the transmission of troubadour and trouvère melodies, by contrast with the relative stability of contemporary liturgical chant. Oral versus written transmission is a factor, but does not provide the complete solution. These melodies use a much greater modal variety and flexibility than their liturgical counterparts, some displaying the equivalent of modulation. Formally, the melodies also reflect the variety of poetic form, although these texts normally receive strophic setting (exceptions are the *lai* and *descort*). Troubadour and especially trouvère musical forms may be modified with refrain structures (in the *chansons avec refrains* each stanza has a different refrain). The *formes fixes* (rondeau, virelai and ballade) appear toward the end of the period but were never central to either tradition.

Only a small proportion of the two repertories survive in any form of mensural notation, making rhythmic interpretation particularly problematic. A few later examples are notated in modal rhythm, but its application to the bulk of the repertory nearly always results in conflict between poetic and musical stresses. A flexible, declamatory mode of performance has been suggested by scholars, ensuring a perfect fit between text and melody, but this would assume, contrary to other evidence, that the musical organization was totally subservient to poetic law.

Trout, The [Die Forelle]. Song by Schubert (D550, 1821), a setting for voice and piano of a poem by Schubart; Schubert used the theme for variations in his Piano Quintet in A (D667), the 'Trout' Quintet (1819).

Trovatore, Il [The Troubadour]. Opera in four parts by Verdi to a libretto by Cammarano (and L.E. Bardare) after A. Garcia Gutiérrez (1853, Rome).

Troyanos, Tatiana (*b* New York, 12 Sept 1938). American mezzo-soprano. She studied at the Juilliard School and made her début in the New York première of Britten's *Midsummer Night's Dream* (1963, City Opera); her roles also included Cherubino and Carmen. She sang at Hamburg regularly from 1965, also appearing at the principal festivals, singing Octavian at Salzburg, Covent Garden and at her Met début (1976). She is noted for her warm yet firmly focussed voice of wide range and her intensity as an actress.

Troyens, Les. *See* TROJANS, THE.

Truman, Ernest Edwin Phillip (*b* Weston-super-Mare, 1870; *d* Darlinghurst, NSW, 6 Oct 1948). Australian organist and composer of British birth. He studied in Leipzig and became well known as a city organist in Sydney from 1909, giving *c*3000 public recitals of over 20,000 individual pieces. His most successful composition was *Pied Piper*, a 'cantata grotesque'.

Trump. *See* JEW'S HARP.

Trumpet. A brass, lip-vibrated wind instrument. In its modern form it has a tube of 130 cm (for the B♭ instrument) with a narrow cylindrical bore widening to a conical flared bell, a cup-shaped mouthpiece and three valves (for illustration, *see* BRASS INSTRUMENTS). Its range normally extends from *e* to *d'''*; jazz trumpeters may play to *bb''''* or higher. Notes of the harmonic series are obtained by overblowing and intermediate ones by use of the valves; any note not naturally in tune can be adjusted by lip technique. The most common forms in orchestras today are in C (non-transposing) and B♭ (transposing). Others include the bass trumpet, which goes down to *F♯*, and smaller trumpets in D or E♭ and high A or B♭.

In its earliest form (ancient Egyptian, Assyrian and Hebrew), the trumpet was short, straight and made in one piece, of wood, bronze or silver. The Greeks and Romans also had trumpet-like instruments. During the Middle Ages the instrument was played by vagrants, but trumpeters later found posts as town musicians; by the Renaissance they had considerable importance in court functions. The tessitura rose; only up to the 4th partial was used *c*1300, but up to the 13th by the 16th century. In the 15th century the tube was lengthened and looped back in a more compact arrangement than the older straight form. In the 17th century the trumpet came to be used in 'art music'; its large repertory includes sonatas and concertos by Bolognese composers, sonatas by Biber from the Kroměříž court, demanding high parts in Viennese court operas, obbligatos by Purcell and Handel in London, and ringing high parts in sacred works for the court of Louis XIV. Bach used the trumpet for high parts in his festive church music and wrote for trumpet along with recorder, oboe and violin in Brandenburg Concerto no.2. The high 'clarino' register was less used in the Classical period, however, when the trumpet's main role was the reinforcing of orchestral tuttis.

The natural trumpet was prevalent until the development of valves, though slide trumpets had existed since the 15th century (and continued into the 19th), and in the 18th century other attempts to gain the complete chromatic scale included keyed trumpets (for which Haydn and Hummel wrote their concertos) and trumpets in which chromatic notes were available by hand stopping. In the 1820s the valve trumpet was introduced, with the advantages of greater chromatic facility and homogeneity of tone.

Berlioz and Rossini were among the first to call for this instrument. Most early valve trumpets were made in F or G; later the smaller B♭ and C models prevailed for their superior flexibility. A high D trumpet (called 'Bach trumpet') was made for use in Baroque works (half the length of the trumpet in D of Bach's time). In the 19th century there were many improvements in manufacture, to make intonation more exact and to refine technical detail. During the 20th there has been a move towards larger bores. Some of the developments in trumpet technique have come from jazz, including the upwards extension of range, glissandos, flutter-tonguing, 'smears', 'rips' and the use of new mutes (e.g. 'cup', 'wa-wa', and 'plunger') in addition to the traditional straight variety. Such techniques have been absorbed into contemporary orchestral playing.

Trumpet marine (It. *tromba marina*). A bowed monochord with a vibrating bridge, in use from the 15th century to the mid-18th. In its most popular form it was *c*2 metres long and consisted of a hollow wooden resonator with a solid neck and a peg for tuning. The single string passed over the bridge, which had a free foot and was awkward to adjust. The instrument could sound all the pitches of the harmonic series up to the 16th partial and had a trumpet-like, brittle timbre. Lully and A. Scarlatti are among the few composers to write for it.

Trythall, (Harry) Gil(bert) (*b* Knoxville, 28 Oct 1930). American composer. Trained at the University of Tennessee and Cornell, he was appointed professor at West Virginia University in 1975. He has composed for instrumental and electronic media in an eclectic style. His brother Richard Akre (*b* 1939), a pianist and composer, studied at Princeton and has taught mostly in Rome since 1966. He is a noted exponent of complex modern scores and his own works show a clever mix of traditional and topical styles.

Tsar Saltan, The Tale of. *See* TALE OF TSAR SALTAN, THE.

Tsar's Bride, The [Tsarskaya nevesta]. Opera in four acts by Rimsky-Korsakov to a libretto after L.A. Mey's play, with a scene by I.F. Tyumenev (1899, Moscow).

Tsintsadze, Sulkhan Fyodorovich (*b* Gori, 23 Aug 1925). Soviet composer. A pupil of Bogatïryov at the Moscow Conservatory, he has taught at the Tbilisi Conservatory. He was first acclaimed for his chamber music, especially his eight string quartets in the Prokofiev–Shostakovich tradition. Other works include operas, ballets (notably *The Demon*), symphonies and two cello concertos, mass songs and film scores.

Tuba. A wide-bored valved instrument used as a bass or contrabass member of the band or orchestral brass section. It is a type rather than a specific instrument, comprising the euphonium, the sousaphone, the lower saxhorn and others as well as instruments called simply 'tuba' (a category to which the WAGNER TUBA does not wholly belong). Its wide conical bore, wide bell and deep cup-shaped mouthpiece give it a smooth, rich tone more like the horn than the trumpet or trombone and help in sounding the lowest notes of its harmonic series. Most tubas are elliptical in shape with the bell pointing upright; in some models, designed for marching or recording, the bell faces forward or is tilted. Usually tubas have four valves; to improve intonation, some have five or six. (For illustration, *see* BRASS INSTRUMENTS.)

Tubas in use today include the tenor in B♭ with four valves (described as 'euphonium' when used in brass bands) and a range from *E'* to *bb'* or higher; bass tubas in F and E♭; and contrabass tubas in C and B♭ (sometimes called CC and BB♭). The bass tuba in E♭, with a full bore and four valves (sometimes called EE♭), is the type most used in English orchestras; the contrabass in C has become standard in the USA, Germany and several other countries. In France the most popular is a small tuba in 8'C with six valves, with a four-octave range; this is reflected in the high tuba parts written by French composers. The extremes of range normally required in orchestral tuba music are *A''* and *ab'*.

A latecomer to the brass section, the tuba was developed in the 1820s and 1830s. The prototype, pitched in F, had five valves and could be played down to the fundamental notes. It was soon modified and improved, and came to supersede the ophicleide during the century as bass to the brass section. Wagner used it extensively (notably for the dragon's music in the *Ring*); Mahler, Strauss and others continued to exploit its solo possibilities within the orchestra. Several concertos were written for it in the 20th century, notably Vaughan Williams's in F minor; Hindemith wrote a sonata with piano. The tuba has been much taken up by jazz musicians and avant-garde composers, and players are required to use a wide variety of effects and timbres.

The word tuba also referred to an ancient Roman instrument, a straight cylinder usually of bronze or brass, between 1.2 and 1.5 m long. Its use was primarily military and ceremonial.

Tuba curva [corva]. A crude wind instrument, created during the French Revolution and first heard publicly at Voltaire's reburial on 11 July 1791. No authentic specimen survives. Probably of brass alloy, it had a mouthpiece but was otherwise an unbroken tube, *c*2.5 metres long, curved into a 'G' shape; there were no finger-holes. It was used in choruses and instrumental pieces during the Revolution, last in 1807; composers who used it include Gossec and Méhul.

Tubbs. English family of bow makers. They include Thomas (*fl c*1790–*c*1830), his son William (*fl c*1825) and his grandson James (1835–1919). James, who worked first for W.E. Hill and from the 1870s on his own, was a distinguished craftsman. He is said to have made 5000 bows for violin, viola and cello, the best having a broad but delicate head, with narrow chamfer, a plain silver button and face, rectangular frog and mounted with gold and ebony.

Tubin, Eduard (*b* Kallaste, 18 June 1905; *d* Stockholm, 17 Nov 1982). Estonian composer. He was a pupil of Eller at the Tartu Academy (1924–30); in 1944 he moved to Sweden. His music often combines propulsive rhythm with expansive melody, orchestrated in an expressive manner; he wrote ten symphonies (1934–73).

Tubular bells. A set of tuned metal tubes, used for bell effects in the orchestra and on the operatic stage. They hang in a frame and are struck at the top end with a rawhide mallet. Their compass is normally *c″–f‴*. (For illustration, see PERCUSSION INSTRUMENTS.)

Tuček. Bohemian family of musicians. The most celebrated members were Jan (*c*1743–83), a composer who in the 1760s brought the provincial tradition of Czech Singspiel into professional theatres in Prague, and his son Vincenc (1773–1821 or later), a singer and Kapellmeister to the Leopoldstädter-theater in Vienna, who composed popular but ephemeral stage works.

Tuck, tucket. Term used from the 14th century to the 18th for a signal or a flourish on trumpets or drums.

Tucker, Richard (*b* Brooklyn, 28 Aug 1913; *d* Kalamazoo, 8 Jan 1975). American tenor. From 1945 his career centred on the Met, where he sang 30 leading roles. He made his European début at the Verona Arena in 1947 as Enzo to Callas's Gioconda. His fervour and vocal security made him almost unequalled in the projection of italianate passions but his acting, though energetic, was unsubtle.

Tuckwell, Barry (Emmanuel) (*b* Melbourne, 5 March 1931). British horn player. He played in orchestras at 15 and studied at the Sydney Conservatorium; in 1950 he went to Britain and was principal horn of the LSO, 1955–68. Since then he has mainly played solo and chamber music. Works have been written for him by Musgrave, Hamilton and others. An authoritative player, with sturdy tone yet sensitive control, he has recorded Mozart's concertos and other standard repertory.

Tudor, David (Eugene) (*b* Philadelphia, 20 Jan 1926). American pianist and composer. A pupil of Wolpe, he has worked with Cage from *c*1950, giving many first performances of works by him and Stockhausen and becoming associated with the Merce Cunningham Dance Company. During the mid-1960s he began independent work as a composer, showing interest in the construction of electronic equipment and mixed-media performances. His works include *Rainforest I–IV* (1968–73). He has taught in New York and California.

Tudway, Thomas (*b c*1650; *d* Cambridge, 23 Nov 1726). English composer. Trained as a chorister in the Chapel Royal, he was organist of King's College, Cambridge, from 1670, and until 1680 was also Master of the Choristers there. Later he also became university organist, organist of Pembroke College and (in 1705) professor of music. In 1714–20 he transcribed a large collection of cathedral music for Robert, Lord Harley, including earlier music (notably by Thomas Tomkins) as well as contemporary works; 19 are his own. In style he was a successor to the school of John Blow. His output comprises *c*20 anthems (most of them occasional), several services and other church works, an Ode for Queen Anne and a few songs and catches.

Tůma, František Ignác Antonín (*b* Kostelec nad Orlicí, 2 Oct 1704; *d* Vienna, 30 Jan 1774). Czech composer. He studied with Fux in Vienna and was composer and Kapellmeister to Count Kinsky by 1731. After serving as Kapellmeister to the dowager empress, 1741–50, he remained in Vienna as a composer and viola da gamba and theorbo player. His output of over 50 sacred works and chamber and orchestral sonatas, sinfonias etc belongs mainly to the late Baroque, with contrapuntal textures predominant. Several masses are in *a cappella* style, reflecting Fux's influence.

Tunder, Franz (*b* Bannesdorf, 1614; *d* Lübeck, 5 Nov 1667). German composer and organist. After serving as court organist at Gottorf, he was organist from 1641 at the Marienkirche, Lübeck, where he also organized evening concerts (*Abendmusiken*). One of the most original and inventive German composers of his day, he laid the foundations for the future development of the north German school of composition that centred on Buxtehude, his successor at Lübeck and his son-in-law. Most of his 32 surviving works reflect Italian influences, and his Latin sacred settings (ensemble works and solo motets) are notable for their expressive harmonies. His chorale cantatas were the first in the line of development that culminated in the work of Bach. Chorale arrangements predominate among his surviving organ pieces.

Tuning. The adjustment of the pitch of an instrument, or the sets of pitches to which its elements (strings, pipes etc) may be tuned. Wind instruments are tuned in an ensemble by adjusting the length of tubing, by means of tuning slides in brass instruments or elements within the tube (between the joint or where the reed is attached) in woodwind; such adjustments may put the instrument slightly out of tune with itself. String instruments are normally tuned by adjustment of the tension or sometimes the sounding length of each string. Keyboard instruments are normally tuned by setting one note (often *a* or *c′*) then tuning the central octave through a network of consonant intervals; the tuning is then extended to the other octaves. The tuner normally listens for beats among the overtones of the two notes he is tuning to secure an exact adjustment.

Tuning fork. A metal device for establishing pitch. When struck, its two prongs vibrate and produce a note which, though faint if the fork is held in the air, becomes louder if its stem is pressed on a wooden surface. Invented in 1711 for musical purposes, it was also developed for scientific use in the 19th century.

Turandot. Opera in three acts by Puccini to a libretto by Adami and R. Simoni after Gozzi; it was completed by Alfano (1926, Milan).

Turangalîla-Symphonie. Orchestral work by Messiaen (1948).

Turba (Lat.). 'Crowd': term used for the passages in a Passion sung by a crowd or group (e.g. the disciples, the Jews or the soldiers).

Turca, Alla (It.). 'In the Turkish style': title given to the Rondo of Mozart's Piano Sonata in A K331/300*i* (and appropriate to other works of the kind) because of its imitations of 'Turkish' or JANISSARY MUSIC.

Turchi, Guido (*b* Rome, 10 Nov 1916). Italian composer. He studied with Pizzetti in Rome, where from 1941 he taught at the conservatory. In 1970 he became director of the Accademia di S Cecilia. He is also a music critic and essayist. His works include the opera *Il buon soldato Svejk* (1962), orchestral, vocal and chamber pieces, drawing circumspectly on mid-century masters (Hindemith, Bartók, Petrassi).

Turco in Italia, Il. Opera in two acts by Rossini to a libretto by Romani (1814, Milan).

Tureck, Rosalyn (*b* Chicago, 14 Dec 1914). American pianist. She studied at the Juilliard School and made her recital début in 1936; soon she specialized in Bach's keyboard music, playing with clarity of line and sharply defined rhythms if also a certain deliberation. She made her European début in 1947 and from 1956 appeared as a conductor of Bach's orchestral works.

Turina, Joaquín (*b* Seville, 9 Dec 1882; *d* Madrid, 14 Jan 1949). Spanish composer. Trained in Seville, Madrid and Paris (at the Schola Cantorum), he was associated with Falla, with whom he returned to Spain in 1914; he remained there, working as a teacher, critic and composer. His Schola experience gave him a command of the grand scale, moderated by Sevillian grace and wit. His works include operas, orchestral works (he was the only leading Spaniard of his generation to compose a symphony), chamber music, guitar music, songs and numerous piano pieces, including many colourful and effective character and genre pieces as well as some larger-scale works.

Turini, Francesco (*b* Prague, *c*1589; *d* Brescia, 1656). Italian composer and organist. He was court organist at Prague from the age of 12 and studied in Italy. After serving in Venice, by 1720 he had become cathedral organist at Brescia, where he was highly esteemed. His three books of madrigals (1621–9), scored with two violin parts, are among the earliest vocal chamber works in the concertato style; the first book also contains some of the earliest trio sonatas. He also wrote solo motets and other sacred works. His father Gregorio (*c*1560–*c*1600) was a singer and cornett player in the Prague Hofkapelle from 1582, who published motets (1589), German secular songs (1590) and Italian canzonettas (1597).

Türk, Daniel Gottlob (*b* Claussnitz, 10 Aug 1750; *d* Halle, 26 Aug 1813). German theorist and composer. He studied with Bach's pupil Homilius and with Hiller. In 1774 he went to Halle as a Kantor; he became music director at the university in 1779, organist and musical director of the Marktkirche in 1787 and professor of music in 1808. He also directed concerts and stage works, leading a revival of the city's musical life.

Renowned as a scholarly teacher, Türk wrote several treatises; most notable are his *Clavierschule* (1789), the last keyboard textbook before the era of the piano, and his *Kurze Anweisung zum Generalbassspielen* (1791). Keyboard works, including 48 sonatas and many shorter pieces, are central to his musical output; he also wrote cantatas, lieder and an opera (1783).

Turkish crescent [jingling johnny; Chinese pavilion]. A percussion stick in the form of an ornamental standard with a conical pavilion at the top, surmounted by a Muslim crescent and hung with bells and jingles. It is held vertically and shaken. Mainly a military band instrument, it was used by Berlioz in his *Grande symphonie funèbre et triomphale* (1840).

Turkish music. *See* JANISSARY MUSIC.

Turmmusik (Ger.). 'Tower music': music played from the tower of a church or town hall, normally on wind instruments. The practice was common in Germany from the late 16th century to the early 18th, the repertory consisting of harmonized chorales and occasionally more extended pieces.

Turn. An ornament consisting essentially of four notes: the note above the main note, the main note, the note below and the main note again. In some circumstances the main note may be sounded initially, as in ex.1 (Purcell, 1696). Ex.2 (Couperin,

Ex. 1

Ex. 2

1713) shows a more normal turn (or *doublé*, Fr.). The turn can be inverted, so that its main figure rises rather than falls, as ex.3 (Marpurg, 1750)

Ex. 3

shows; the inversion may be signified by a vertical line through the normal turn sign. Sometimes the turn sign is shown on its side; authorities differ as to whether this means a normal or an inverted turn. The speed at which it is executed depends on the

Ex. 4

Adagio　Moderato　Presto

tempo, as ex.4 (C.P.E. Bach, 1753) indicates. Normally, if a note in the turn is inflected (as compared with the key signature) a flat, sharp or natural will be placed above or below the sign as appropriate. A popular use of a turn was between two notes, particularly in a rising figure or one in dotted rhythm;

Ex. 5

ex.5 shows typical cases. The Italian term for turn is *gruppetto* (occasionally *groppo, circolo mezzo*); the

Ex. 6

German term is *Doppelschlag*. Unlike most other Baroque and Classical ornaments, the turn remained current as an expressive device in Romantic music; Wagner (ex.6) was particularly fond of it.

Turnage, Mark-Anthony [R.] (*b* Essex, 10 June 1960). English composer. He studied at the RCM, with Oliver Knussen and John Lambert. He gained wide attention with his first orchestral score *Night Dances* (1981) which won the Guinness Prize and revealed the eclectic nature of his style, drawing on a wide range of early 20th-century sources and the inflections of jazz and blues harmonies. An even wider stylistic net informs *On All Fours* for 13 instruments (1986), in which Baroque dance forms, refracted through the model of Stravinsky's *Agon*, provide the rhythmic impulsion. He attracted wide attention with his opera *Greek* (1988, Munich).

Turner, Dame Eva (*b* Oldham, 10 March 1892). English soprano. She studied at the RAM and made her début with the Carl Rosa Opera in 1916, remaining until 1924. At La Scala she sang from 1924, notably as Aida and Leonora in *Il trovatore*. In 1926 she sang Turandot for the first time, the role with which she was particularly identified. She appeared at Covent Garden until 1948 in major dramatic roles, notably Wagner and Verdi. From 1959 she taught at the RAM.

Turner, William (*b* Oxford, 1651; *d* London, 13 Jan 1740). English composer and singer. Trained as a chorister at the Chapel Royal, he returned there as a countertenor in 1669 after a time as master of the choristers at Lincoln Cathedral. He also sang in the King's Private Musick from 1672, and later at St Paul's Cathedral and Westminster Abbey. He wrote mainly church music, including over 40 anthems. These range from his early unaccompanied pieces to his later, Italian-influenced works with instrumental ritornellos. Among his other works are three services, four odes, a cantata, many songs and a few pieces for stage productions.

A William Turner was active in London in the early 18th century, composer of two masques (1716–17) and incidental music for Lincoln's Inn Theatre as well as recorder sonatas, and writer of two theoretical works; it is uncertain whether this is the composer noted above or another man. A William Turner from Wales wrote in 1697 a book discussing hymn singing and instrumental practices.

Turnhout, Gérard de (*b* Turnhout, *c*1520; *d* Madrid, 15 Sept 1580). Flemish composer. He served Antwerp Cathedral as music master (1562) and *maître de chant* (1563) of the Confrérie de la Vierge and from 1572 was *maestro de capilla* at the Madrid court. He published 40 sacred and secular works (1569). Jan-Jacob van Turnhout (*c*1545–after 1618), *maître de chapelle* at the Brussels court by 1586, was probably his brother; he published madrigals (1589) and motets (1594).

Turn of the Screw, The. Chamber opera in a prologue and two acts by Britten to a libretto by Myfanwy Piper after Henry James (1954, Venice).

Turnovský, Martin (*b* Prague, 29 Sept 1928). Czech conductor. He studied in Prague under Ančerl and made his début in 1952. He held posts with the Brno State PO (1960), the Plzeň RO (1963) and the Dresden Staatskapelle (1967); in 1968 he made his American début with the Cleveland Orchestra. He was music director of Norwegian Opera, 1975–80.

He is a sympathetic conductor of the Classical repertory and Czech music, notably Martinů.

Türrschmidt [Durrschmied], Carl (*b* Wallerstein, 24 Feb 1753; *d* Berlin, 1 Nov 1797). German horn player. The son of a Wallerstein horn player, he became the most celebrated *cor basse* virtuoso of his day, regularly performing with Johann Palsa. The two served at the Berlin royal court, 1786–92.

Tutti (It.). 'All'; the opposite of *soli* or solo. More loosely, it is used to denote a passage for full orchestra, or even the sound of a full orchestra.

Tveitt, (Nils) Geirr (*b* Kvam, 19 Oct 1908; *d* Oslo, 1 Feb 1981). Norwegian composer and pianist. He studied at the Leipzig Conservatory and in Vienna and Paris. His often rhythmic, dynamic music derives from Norwegian folk music and he wrote two concertos for the Hardanger fiddle. He was heard as the soloist in his six piano concertos.

Twardowski, Romuald (*b* Vilnius, 17 June 1930). Polish composer. He studied with Woytowicz at the Warsaw Conservatory and Boulanger in Paris. His works include dramatic, choral and orchestral music affiliated to the modern Polish school; *Antifone* for three instrumental groups (1961) and *Trittico fiorentino* for ensemble (1966) are typical.

Twelfth. The INTERVAL of a compound 5th, i.e. the sum of an octave and a 5th.

Twelve-note music. Music constructed according to the principle, enunciated by Hauer and Schoenberg independently in the early 1920s, of 12-note composition. According to the Schoenbergian principle, the 12 notes of the equal-tempered scale are arranged in a particular order, forming a series or row that serves as the basis of the composition. In Schoenberg's 'Method of Composing with Twelve Notes Which are Related Only to One Another', the note-row may be used in its original form, or inverted, or retrograde, or retrograde inverted; in each of these forms it may be transposed to any pitch (each note-row may thus have 48 possible forms). All the music of the composition is constructed from this basic material; any note may be repeated, but the order must be maintained. Octave transpositions are permitted. Notes may occur in any voice and may be used chordally as well as melodically.

Later developments of 12-note theory introduced the idea of using six-, four- or three-note segments of a row as compositional elements (*see* COMBINATORIALITY). As originally designed by Schoenberg, the method was intended to preclude tonality, though later composers, notably Berg, found ways of using the technique in a tonal context – as indeed did Schoenberg himself. *See also* SERIALISM.

Twilight of the Gods. *See* GÖTTERDÄMMERUNG.

Twist. A rock dance of the 1960s, the first of the rock dance-songs. Originally danced to a song of the same name, it is in a fast, pounding, evenly stressed 4/4 metre; the partners dance without contact, rotating their hips.

Two-step. Fast ballroom dance originating in the USA in the late 1880s; it was popular in America and Europe until replaced by the one-step and foxtrot in the early 1910s.

Two Widows, The [Dve vdovy]. Opera in two acts by

Smetana to a libretto by Emanuel Züngel after P.J.F. Mallefille (definitive version, 1878, Prague).

Tye, Christopher (*b c*1505; *d*?1572). English composer. In 1536 he took the MusB at Cambridge and in March 1537 became a lay clerk at King's College. He probably began his adult musical career after 1525 and there is no evidence to connect him with various other Tyes who were at King's College, 1508–45. By Michaelmas 1543 he was *Magister choristarum* at Ely Cathedral and in 1545 proceeded MusD at Cambridge. In 1548 he was awarded the Oxford DMus degree and was introduced to the court in the late 1540s. In 1561 he resigned his Ely post in favour of the rich living of Doddington-cum-Marche in the Isle of Ely.

Of his 22 extant Latin works (of which only 11 are complete) the Jesus-antiphon *Ave caput Christi* may date from *c*1530–35, and the five-voice mass in the Peterhouse Partbooks and the *Mass 'Western Wind'* may also date from before 1540. The Latin psalm settings *Omnes gentes, plaudite* and *Cantate Domino* and the fine six-voice *Mass 'Euge bone'*, with their accomplished use of continental motet techniques, must date from Mary Tudor's reign. The 15 extant English anthems probably date from Edward VI's reign, while his *The Actes of the Apostles* (1553), for didactic and recreational use, features metrical texts and simple, four-square four-voice music. He composed much consort music, including over 20 individual, five-voice In Nomines. A composer of great talent who mastered the latest continental techniques in the 1530s, he used certain types of imitative procedures repeatedly, with the result that much of his music has a routine quality.

Church music 3 masses, incl. Mass 'Euge bone', Mass 'Western Wind'; *c*18 Latin works; 15 English anthems; other English settings
*Instrumental music c*30 consort works

Tympanum. Ancient hand drum, much used in Greece and Rome in association with the orgiastic cults of Dionysus and Cybele.

Tyrolienne. A fast triple-metre dance and song type, a modified form of *ländler*. The name was first used in English to refer to fashionable ballet music of the early 19th century; the best-known example is the chorus 'A nos chants viens mêler tes pas' in Rossini's *Guillaume Tell*.

Tzigane (Fr.). 'Gypsy': term for a piece supposedly influenced by gypsy music. Ravel used the title for a rhapsody for violin and piano (1924).

U

Uccelli, Gli [The Birds]. Suite for small orchestra by Respighi (1927).

Uccellini, Marco (*b c*1603; *d* Forlimpopuli, 10 Sept 1680). Italian composer. He became head of instrumental music at the Modena court in 1641 and *maestro di cappella* at Modena Cathedral in 1647. From 1665 he was court *maestro di cappella* at Parma. He composed instrumental music, stage works and vocal pieces; his solo and ensemble sonatas (1639–49) are notable for their thematic unity, chromaticism and advanced violin technique.

'Ūd. Short-necked, plucked lute of the Arab world, the direct ancestor of the European lute, whose name derives from *al-'ūd* ('the lute'). Its history is uncertain; it is first mentioned in 9th- and 10th-century texts but was known in the Arabian peninsula at least two centuries earlier. The number of strings has varied from two to seven; the five-course *'ūd* is the most common and popular among modern performers. It is played with a plectrum or by plucking the strings with both hands.

Udbye, Martin Andreas (*b* Trondheim, 18 June 1820; *d* there, 10 Jan 1889). Norwegian composer. He studied in Leipzig and became an organist in Trondheim. He composed operas (including *The Peacemaker*, 1858), choral and orchestral works, chamber and organ music in a German early Romantic style and was one of the most gifted Norwegian composers of his time.

Uffenbach, Johann Friedrich Armand von (*b* Frankfurt am Main, 6 May 1687; *d* there, 10 April 1769). German amateur musician. After extensive travels, he held an administrative post in Frankfurt and organized concerts there. His travel journals provide much important and fascinating information about musical life in the many centres he visited, in England, France, Germany and Italy.

Uhl, Alfred (*b* Vienna, 5 June 1909). Austrian composer. A pupil of Schmidt, he began teaching at the Vienna Musikhochschule in 1945. His output, in a fluent neo-classical style, includes much chamber music often featuring wind (notably the clarinet); his concertante pieces have been widely successful.

Uilleann pipe. *See* UNION PIPE and BAGPIPE.

Ukulele [ukelele]. A small four-string guitar from Hawaii, where it was taken in the late 19th century by immigrants from Madeira. Its small size, low cost and light weight, combined with a simple tuning (usually $a'-d'-f\sharp'-b'$) and an undemanding technique, contributed to its wide adoption in the USA as a portable instrument for accompanying popular songs.

Ulenberg, Kaspar (*b* Lippstadt, 1549; *d* Cologne, 16 Feb 1617). German composer. A Lutheran pastor in Lippstadt, then a Catholic priest, mainly in Cologne, he published a Catholic psalter (1582) which remained popular well into the 18th century; he may have composed its 80 tunes.

Ullmann, Viktor (*b* Prague, 1 Jan 1898; *d* ?Auschwitz, ?1944). Austro-Hungarian composer. A pupil of Schoenberg and Hába, he spent most of his life in Prague, until his arrest in 1942. He wrote the opera *Der Kaiser von Atlantis* at Terezín before being transferred to Auschwitz; other works include songs, three string quartets, seven piano sonatas and orchestral pieces.

Ulster Orchestra. Northern Irish orchestra formed in Belfast in 1966 with Maurice Miles as conductor; it gives concerts in the city, provincial towns and in schools.

Umlauf, Ignaz (*b* Vienna, 1746; *d* Meidling, 8 June 1796). Austrian composer. He was an orchestral viola player in Vienna and presented his first Singspiel *c*1772. In 1778 he became Kapellmeister to the new 'German National Singspiel', writing the first work of the venture, *Die Bergknappen*. Notable among his other Singspiels was *Die schöne Schusterin* (1779). By 1782 he was also deputy Kapellmeister of the Italian court opera. He was the most successful Viennese Singspiel composer before Dittersdorf; his works show a real but slender gift for melody, dramatic timing and characterization. He also wrote some sacred and instrumental music.

His son Michael (1781–1842), a court violinist in Vienna and a theatre Kapellmeister by 1815, assisted Beethoven as conductor, notably at the première of the Ninth Symphony (1824); he composed successful ballets, three Singspiels and sacred pieces.

Umstatt, Joseph (*b* Vienna, 5 Feb 1711; *d* Bamberg, 24 May 1762). Austrian composer. After a period as musical director to Count Brühl in Dresden, he became Kapellmeister and court composer to the Prince-Bishop of Bamberg (1752). His works include masses and other sacred pieces and many symphonies, concertos and sonatas. Like those of his Viennese contemporaries they show the gradual change from Baroque to Classical style, with embryonic sonata forms and, in the concertos, extended, virtuoso solo episodes.

Una corda (It.: 'one string'). Term for the left (or 'soft') pedal of the piano, or direction for its use. Depressing the pedal involves shifting the action sideways so that the hammers strike only two (or in earlier pianos, one) of the three treble strings, and only one of the two upper bass strings (while still striking the single lower bass strings). Some composers, notably Beethoven, distinguished between 'una corda' and 'due corde'. On an upright piano, the left pedal moves the hammers closer to the strings, softening the stroke and reducing the volume; it does not alter the timbre as the true 'una corda' pedal does. The earliest known pedal of this kind is on a piano of 1726.

Unanswered Question, The. Work for small orchestra by Ives (1906), one of Two Contemplations (the other is *Central Park in the Dark*).

Unfinished Symphony. Schubert's Symphony no.8 in B minor (1822), of which only two movements are complete.

Unger, Karoline (*b* Székesfehérvár, 28 Oct 1803; *d* Florence, 23 March 1877). Austrian contralto. After singing in the premières of Beethoven's *Missa solemnis* (partial) and Ninth Symphony (Vienna, 1824) she had her greatest triumphs on the Italian stage; Donizetti wrote *Parisina* and *Belisario* for her, Bellini *La straniera* and Pacini *Niobe*.

Union [uilleann] pipe. An Irish bellows-blown BAG-PIPE, known from the 18th century, also called uilleann (Gaelic: 'elbow') pipe.

Unison. The 'interval' between two notes identical in pitch; the simultaneous execution of one polyphonic part by more than one performer or performing group, either at identical pitch or at the octave ('in unison').

Universal Edition. Music publishing firm, founded in Vienna in 1901. Originally intended simply to make the Austrian music trade independent of German firms, it soon established a pre-eminent reputation in modern music, making contracts with Bartók (1908), Mahler and Schoenberg (1909), Webern, Zemlinsky and Berg (1910), Janáček (1917), Krenek (1921), Milhaud (1922), Weill (1924) and Martinů (1926). The same bias is reflected in its catalogues of the 1950s and 1960s, including works by Berio, Birtwistle, Boulez, Ligeti, Stockhausen and Takemitsu, though the firm has also published the important historical series Denkmäler der Tonkunst in Österreich (1919–42), complete editions of Monteverdi and Gabrieli and the Wiener Urtext Edition (from 1972). Among its noteworthy periodicals are *Musikblätter des Anbruch* (1919–38), *Die Reihe* (1955–62) and the *Haydn Yearbook* (1962–75).

Upbeat [anacrusis]. The impulse in a measured rhythm that precedes and anticipates the DOWNBEAT, the first and strongest of such impulses.

Upright pianoforte. A piano with the strings ar-

ranged in a vertical plane. The earliest models were in a 'pyramid' shape or in the 'giraffe' design, in which the strings rise perpendicularly from the piano and are enclosed in a curved, harp-shaped case. The familiar modern upright piano was developed by John Isaac Hawkins of Philadelphia at the beginning of the last century. The 'tape-check' action, the basis of modern upright actions, was patented by Robert Wornum of London in 1842; he was also responsible for the first experiments in 'cottage pianos', low-case instruments later further developed with the use of diagonal stringing. (For illustration, *see* KEYBOARD INSTRUMENTS.)

Urbani, Valentino (*fl* 1690–1719). Italian alto castrato. After working in Italy and Berlin he became the first castrato to sing regularly in London (1707–17), where he appeared in Italian operas by Handel and others, creating Eustazio (*Rinaldo*) and Aegaeus (*Teseo*).

Urio, Francesco Antonio (*b* Milan, ?1631/2; *d* there, 1719 or later). Italian composer. A Franciscan friar, he held *maestro di cappella* posts in Spoleto, Urbino, Assisi, Genoa, Rome, Venice and Milan. He composed oratorios and other sacred music; Handel borrowed from his *Te Deum* in four works (including *Israel in Egypt* and the Dettingen *Te Deum*).

Urreda, Johannes (*fl* late 15th century). Composer, possibly Flemish, active in Spain. A singer in the Duke of Alva's chapel (1476–7), he became master of King Ferdinand V's chapel and was with the court in several Spanish cities. He was internationally known and esteemed as a composer, his works appearing not only in Spanish, but also in French and Italian MSS and publications. Among his few extant sacred works his four-voice hymn *Pange lingua* was widely known and quoted by later composers. *Nunca fue pena mayor* was the most popular of his three surviving three-voice *canciones*. His specifically Spanish musical and poetic themes combined with Franco–Burgundian features results in an unusual contrast between style and content in his works and emphasizes his ambiguous historical position.

Ursuleac, Viorica (*b* Chernovtsy, 26 March 1894; *d* Ehrwald, 22 Oct 1985). Romanian soprano. After study in Vienna she sang at the Vienna Volksoper and the Frankfurt Opera. During the 1930s she appeared at the Vienna Staatsoper and in Berlin and Munich. She and her husband, Clemens Krauss, were close friends of Strauss; she created Arabella (1933) and the Countess in *Capriccio* (1942) and sang in all 506 performances of 12 Strauss roles.

Urtext (Ger.). 'Original text': term applied to a modern printed edition of earlier music in which the aim is to present an exact text without editorial additions or alterations.

Usandizaga, José María (*b* San Sebastián, 31 March 1887; *d* there, 5 Oct 1915). Spanish composer. Trained in Paris at the Schola Cantorum (1901–6), he helped lay the foundations of Basque music, and had particular success with his stage works, notably *High in the Mountains* (1911) and *Las golondrinas* (1914).

Usiglio, Emilio (*b* Parma, 8–18 Jan 1841; *d* Milan, 7/8 July 1910). Italian conductor and composer. He was well known as a conductor, directing Boito's revised

Mefistofele (1875) and the Italian premières of Thomas's *Hamlet* (1876) and Bizet's *Carmen* (1879); of his six operas (all comedies) only *Le educande di Sorrento* (1868) achieved success.

Usmanbaş, Ilhan (*b* Istanbul, 28 Sept 1921). Turkish composer. He was a pupil of Alnar at the Ankara State Conservatory, where he joined the staff, and studied in the USA with Dallapiccola. He is the main Turkish advocate of 20th-century techniques, his small output being chiefly instrumental music.

Uspensky, Viktor Alexandrovich (*b* Kaluga, 31 Aug 1879; *d* Tashkent, 9 Oct 1949). Soviet composer and ethnomusicologist. He was a pupil of Lyadov at the St Petersburg Conservatory (1908–13) and in 1918 was co-founder of the Tashkent Conservatory. He has studied Uzbek music and folk instruments and used central Asian materials in his orchestral, vocal and piano pieces etc.

Usper [Sponga], Francesco (*b* Parenzo, Istria, before 1570; *d* Venice, early 1641). Italian composer. A pupil of Andrea Gabrieli, he was organist (1596–1607) and then chaplain of the confraternity of S Giovanni Evangelista, Venice, and by 1614 also organist at S Salvatore. He wrote mainly madrigals and church music. His instrumental works (sinfonias, canzonas, etc) show a sensitivity to form unusual for their time. His nephew Gabriel Usper (*fl* 1609–23) was also a composer and organist.

Ussachevsky, Vladimir (Alexis) (*b* Hailar, Manchuria, 3 Nov 1911). American composer. He arrived in the USA in 1931 and studied at the Eastman School, then moved to Columbia, first as a student and later as lecturer. In 1951, with Luening, he began composing electronic pieces (*Of Wood and Brass*, 1965), notable for their flexible and skilful treatment of sound sources; but he has also produced choral music in a style indebted to his Russian Orthodox heritage.

Ustvol'skaya, Galina Ivanovna (*b* Petrograd, 17 June 1919). Soviet composer. She was a pupil of Shostakovich at the Leningrad Conservatory (1939–47), where she remained as a teacher. She developed an independent style, her works including symphonies, piano sonatas and choral works.

Utah Symphony Orchestra. American orchestra formed in 1940 in Salt Lake City as the Utah State SO; it became fully professional in 1946 and was renamed. Maurice Abravanel conducted, 1947–79. Its home is Symphony Hall (opened 1979, cap. 2800). Activities include performances with Utah Opera Company and Ballet West. It sponsors the Gina Bachauer International Piano Competition and visiting orchestras.

Utendal, Alexander (*b c*1530–40; *d* Innsbruck, 7 May 1581). Netherlands composer. He served the Habsburgs, working at Prague (1564) and Innsbruck (1566), where he was vice-Kapellmeister. His music – motets (3 bks, 1571–7), penitential psalms (1570), masses (1573), responsories (1586) and German and French songs (1574) – is often richly scored and chromatic and sometimes polychoral.

Utopia Limited. Operetta by Sullivan to a libretto by Gilbert (1893, London).

Utrecht Te Deum and Jubilate. Liturgical settings by Handel composed to celebrate the Peace of Utrecht (1713, London).

Utrenia. Choral work by Penderecki after the Russian Orthodox liturgy; its two parts are 'The Laying in the Tomb' (1970, Altenberg) and 'The Resurrection' (1971, Münster).

Uttini, Francesco Antonio Baldassare (*b* Bologna, 1723; *d* Stockholm, 25 Oct 1795). Italian composer. A pupil of Padre Martini, he presented three operas in Italy before 1752–3, when he became conductor and composer to the touring Mingotti troupe. After producing works in Copenhagen and Hamburg, he settled in 1755 in Stockholm, where he became Master of the King's Music in 1767. His 13 operas there included Italian, French and Swedish works; *Thetis och Pelée* (1773) was the first grand opera in Swedish. He also composed other vocal music and several instrumental works.

V

Vaccai, Nicola (*b* Tolentino, 15 March 1790; *d* Pesaro, 5/6 Aug 1848). Italian composer and teacher. He studied in Naples under Paisiello. In spite of his hopes and hard work, only two of his 17 operas – *Zadig ed Astartea* (Naples, 1825) and his masterpiece *Giuletta e Romeo* (Milan, 1825) – won success, largely for their delicate, Rossinian style; the penultimate scene of *Giuletta* was even interpolated by Malibran into Bellini's later *I Capuleti e i Montecchi*. From 1838 to 1844 Vaccai was *censore* at the Milan Conservatory, instituting reforms and enlarging the repertory to include the German classics. He also composed sacred works and many songs. But he left his chief mark as a singing teacher; his *Metodo pratico di canto italiano per camera* (1832) is an excellent primer and valuable for the study of 19th-century performing practice.

Vachon, Pierre (*b* Arles, June 1731; *d* Berlin, 7 Oct 1803). French composer. A soloist in Paris from the 1750s, he became first violinist in the Prince of Conti's orchestra in 1761. After some ten years in London he went to Germany and was leader of the royal orchestra at Berlin by 1786. He was one of the first French composers of string quartets, writing 30 or more (*c*1773 onwards); some are notable for their relatively independent part-writing. He also composed other instrumental and stage works.

Vačkář, Dalibor Cyril (*b* Korčula, 19 Sept 1906). Czech composer and writer. He studied with Šín and Suk at the Prague Conservatory (1923–31), was a violinist in the Prague RO (1934–45) and a journalist. He has composed in most genres, serious and light, showing skilful instrumentation in his many film scores.

His father Václav (1881–1954) composed chiefly light orchestral pieces, conducted, wrote for Czech music journals and was active in music education. Dalibor's son Tomáš (1945–63) was also a promising composer.

Vadé, Jean-Joseph (*b* Ham, Picardy, 17 Jan 1719; *d* Paris, 4 July 1757). French poet and composer. A tax collector, he wrote over 20 *opéras comiques*, mostly for the Paris fair theatres, 1752–7. Besides vaudeville melodies, they contain airs by Vadé himself and were popular for their realistic tone and earthy humour. Notable among his librettos is that for Dauvergne's influential *Les troqueurs* (1753,

Paris), modelled on *opera buffa*.

Vaet, Jacobus (*b* Courtrai or Harelbeke, *c*1529; *d* Vienna, 8 Jan 1567). Flemish composer. He studied at Louvain from 1547 and was singing in the Vienna Hofkapelle by 1550. From at least 1554 until his death he was Archduke (later Emperor) Maximilian's Kapellmeister. A prolific and respected composer, influenced by Gombert and, later, by Lassus, he wrote motets (2 bks, 1562), nine masses, *c*24 other sacred works and a few *chansons*.

Vagner, Genrikh Matusovich (*b* Zhirardov, 2 July 1922). Soviet composer. He studied at the conservatories in Warsaw and in Minsk, where he remained as a teacher. His works include ballets (notably *The False Bride*, 1958), orchestral pieces and numerous songs, at first traditional but later including Stravinskian and Bartókian elements.

Vaillant, Jehan (*fl* ?1360–90). French composer. He may have been the Johannes Valentis in service at the papal chapel at Avignon, 1352–61, or one of the functionaries of this name at the Duke of Berry's court. The style of his five works, despite individual features, suggests a younger contemporary of Machaut.

Valderrábano, Enríquez de (*fl* mid-16th century). Spanish composer and vihuelist. He served Francisco de Zúñiga, 4th Count of Miranda. His *Libro de música de vihuela, intitulado Silva de sirenas* (1547) contains a rich, varied repertory divided into seven 'books'. Among its contents are transcriptions for voice and vihuela of motets and secular music by internationally known composers (including Josquin, Morales, Willaert and Arcadelt), music for two vihuelas, fantasias, pavans and 'sonetos'.

Valen, (Olav) Fartein (*b* Stavanger, 25 Aug 1887; *d* Haugesund, 14 Dec 1952). Norwegian composer. A pupil of Elling at the Copenhagen Conservatory and of Bruch at the Berlin Musikhochschule (1909–11), he remained in Berlin until 1916, then returned to Norway. Until 1924 he lived in Valevåg and worked at developing a personal 12-note style, richly polyphonic but also clear and lyrical. From 1924 to 1938 he was a librarian and teacher in Oslo; he retired to Valevåg. His works include four symphonies (1939, 1944, 1946, 1949) and other orchestral pieces, choral music, songs, a few chamber pieces and piano music. His violin concerto (1940) is a landmark in Norwegian music; almost a symphonic poem, it has a coda built on the chorale *Jesu meine Zuversicht*.

Valente, Antonio (*fl* 1565–80). Italian composer. Blind from childhood, he was organist at S Angelo a Nilo, Naples (1565–80). His influential keyboard volume of 1576 was an early contribution to the Neapolitan keyboard school; it contains ricercares, variations, dances etc. He also wrote organ versets (1580).

Valentine, Robert (*b* Leicester, *c*1680; *d c*1735). English flautist and composer. He lived in Rome for over 20 years, returning to England in 1731. A successful composer, he had 15 sets of sonatas and other chamber works published, most for one or two recorders and bass.

The Valentine family played a leading role in Leicester's musical life. Prominent among its other members was John (1730–91), possibly Robert's nephew, who composed instrumental pieces for amateurs and several vocal works.

Valentini, Giovanni (*b* Venice, 1582/3; *d* Vienna, 29/30 April 1649). Italian composer, keyboard player and poet. A renowned player, he was organist at the Polish court before going to the Habsburg court at Graz in 1614. After the court moved to Vienna in 1619 he became imperial court organist and later Kapellmeister (by 1626). His conservative Venetian style had a lasting influence there, his many sacred works for the court including a Mass, *Magnificat* and *Jubilate Deo* for seven choirs (1621). Some of his works are in the *stile antico*. He also left secular vocal and instrumental pieces (some more modern and experimental in idiom), texts for setting to music and other writings.

Valentini, Giuseppe (*b* Florence, *c*1680; *d* ? Paris, after 1759). Italian composer. He was violinist to Prince Ruspoli in Rome until 1713, and later probably served the Prince of Caserta. He wrote some oratorios and cantatas but is chiefly noted for his unusually adventurous sonatas, concertos etc. His sonatas show the influence of Corelli (who may have taught him) but the concertos are more Venetian in style. He often used remote keys, abrupt harmonic shifts and high positions on the violin.

Valentini, Pier Francesco (*b* Rome, *c*1570; *d* there, 1654). Italian composer and theorist. An amateur musician, he was considered one of the most learned Roman contrapuntists of his day. His large output includes motets, complex canons (one for 96 or more voices) and other sacred pieces, and many canzonettas, arias etc. He wrote on many aspects of music theory and proposed a system of 24 modes instead of the traditional 12. He was also a poet.

Valeri, Gaetano (*b* Padua, 21 Sept 1760; *d* there, 13 April 1822). Italian composer. He was organist at two Padua churches and in 1785–1803 the cathedral (*maestro di cappella*, 1805). His works are mostly sacred, many of them scored with large orchestra and/or organ. He also wrote over 40 organ sonatas, among the last Italian works in the genre, other instrumental pieces and two stage works.

Valesi, Fulgenzio (*b* Parma, ?*c*1565; *d* ?after 1614). Italian composer and printer. He was a Cistercian

monk and lived in Rome (1593–1600), where the printing privilege he held for chant books involved him in much litigation; from 1600 he seems to have embarked on a life of adventure. A book of *napolitane* (1587) and one of canons (1611) by him survive.

Valiha. A zither-type instrument used in Madagascar; one of the oldest Malagasy instruments, it has become the symbol of cultural unity in the island. Made from bamboo, wood or raffia, it has ten to 19 strings, usually of metal. It was originally played at sacred rituals by the aristocracy but is now mainly a secular instrument.

Valkyrie, The. *See* WALKÜRE, DIE.

Vallée d'Obermann. Piano piece by Liszt, no.6 of Book 1 of *Années de pèlerinage*.

Vallet, Nicolas (*b* ?Corbény, *c*1583; *d* ?Amsterdam, after 1642). Netherlands lutenist and composer. Active in Amsterdam, he was a leading figure in Netherlands lute music at the time of Sweelinck. His lute pieces, mostly written in 1614–20, take full advantage of the lute's resources; he also composed other instrumental pieces and some vocal works.

Vallin, Ninon (*b* Montalieu-Vercieu, 8 Sept 1886; *d* Lyons, 22 Nov 1961). French soprano. After study at the Lyons Conservatory she soon won Debussy's admiration and sang in the first performances of *Le martyre de Saint Sébastien* (1911) and the *Trois poèmes de Mallarmé* (1914). She sang at the Paris Opéra-Comique (1912–16) and the Opéra (début 1920, as Thaïs) and was successful in Buenos Aires for over 20 years. She was a distinguished interpreter of the songs of Fauré, Chausson and Hahn.

Vallotti, Francesco Antonio (*b* Vercelli, 11 June 1697; *d* Padua, 19 Jan 1780). Italian composer and theorist. A Franciscan priest, he lived in Padua from 1721 and probably studied with F.A. Calegari. He became third organist at the basilica of S Antonio in 1723 and *maestro di cappella* in 1730; the leader of the famous orchestra there was Tartini. Vallotti composed many sacred works for up to eight voice parts, often using organ and strings; his works in a strict contrapuntal idiom combining Renaissance techniques with tonal harmony won him a wide and lasting reputation. Notable among his writings is *Della scienza teorica e pratica della moderna musica* (i, 1779; ii–iv, MS), which contains both practical guidance and technical explanations. His theories were related to Calegari's and Tartini's. He devised a valuable system of unequal temperament for keyboard tuning.

Valls, Francisco (*b* Barcelona, 1665; *d* there, 2 Feb 1747). Spanish composer. After work at Mataró and Gerona he became *maestro de capilla* of S María del Mar, Barcelona, and assistant at Barcelona Cathedral (1696); he was titular *maestro* of the cathedral, 1709–40. Widely famous as a composer, he wrote many Latin sacred works and villancicos. A long controversy raged over an unprepared 9th chord in his *Missa 'Scala aretina'* (1702).

Valois. Rulers of France, 1328–1589, and patrons of music. Many members of the family were keenly interested in music and some were performers; all maintained royal chapels with professional singers and organists and employed instrumentalists for entertainment. The kings of the direct Valois lineage (which ended with the death of Charles VIII in 1498) employed such leading musicians as Vitry, Machaut, Ockeghem and Compère. Under the later Valois-related kings, notably François I (ruled 1515–47), the musical organization was greatly expanded. His musicians included Mouton and Sermisy; Arcadelt and Janequin were among those of his son Henri II (1547–59).

Valse (Fr.). WALTZ. The *valse à deux temps*, popular in the mid-19th century, is not in fact in duple time but in 3/4, with a sideways slide on the first two beats of the bar and a gliding turn on the third. For the *valse boston, see* BOSTON.

Valse, La. Orchestral work ('poème choréographique') by Ravel (1920).

Valses nobles et sentimentales. Piano work by Ravel (1911), orchestrated in 1912.

Valse triste. Sibelius's op.44 (1904), a waltz for strings written as part of the incidental music for Järnefelt's *Kuolema*; Sibelius orchestrated it and arranged it for piano.

Valve. A mechanical device for altering the basic tube length of a brass instrument while it is being played, thus extending the instrument's range from the harmonic series to more or all the notes of the chromatic scale. The mechanism was invented *c*1814 by Heinrich Stölzel, a German horn player whose intention was to avoid the then obligatory encumbrance of a full set of crooks for all keys. He went into partnership with Friedrich Blühmel and together they patented the first valve. Three types are in use today: the piston valve, in which a sprung piston works up and down in a casing (the down position diverting the windway through supplementary tubing); the rotary valve, introduced in 1853 and based on the principle of the stop-cock in which a turn of the rotor (activated by a sprung lever) diverts the air passage through the valve slide; and, the rarest category, the double piston or Vienna action, in which two pistons are simultaneously depressed by one lever thus diverting the windway from one to the other via the valve slide.

On most brass instruments, the first valve lowers the fundamental by two semitones, the second by one and the third by three. Compensation is generally needed when they are used in combination (as the length required to lower the pitch by a given amount is not absolute but proportionate to the length of tube on which it is acting); an automatic system for this was devised by D.J. Blaikley in 1874, or additional valves could be fitted. Valves are also used to raise pitch, by cutting off a length of tube, or (particularly on the horn) to change the key of an instrument, usually by a 4th.

Vamp. A verb meaning to extemporize the simple accompaniment to a vocal or instrumental solo. In popular music the instruction 'vamp till ready' indicates that a simple short passage is to be repeated by the accompanist until the soloist is ready to begin.

Vampyr, Der. Opera in two acts by Marschner to a libretto by W.A. Wohlbrück after Nodier, Carmouche and de Jouffroy (1828, Leipzig).

Vancouver Symphony Orchestra. Canadian orchestra founded in 1931. In its early years it was conducted by guest conductors (including Beecham and Klemperer); subsequently Irwin Hoffman and Kazuyoshi Akiyama are among those to have been appointed permanently. The orchestra claims to have more subscribers than any other in North America, where it was the first to present programmes devoted exclusively to 20th-century music.

Vančura, Arnošt (*b* Vamberk, *c*1750; *d* St Petersburg, ?1801). Czech composer. He served at the Imperial Theatres in St Petersburg, 1786–97, and was also a pianist. His works include a Russian opera (1787), three 'national' symphonies using folk melodies (1798) and keyboard pieces.

Van den Gheyn. Flemish family of bellfounders. They worked in Mechlin until *c*1695, later branches of the family working in St Trond, Tirlemont and Louvain. The most celebrated member was Matthias van den Gheyn (1721–85), a composer, organist and carillonneur in Louvain, whose carillon compositions are now part of the repertory.

Vanderhagen, Amand (Jean François Joseph) (*b* Antwerp, 1753; *d* Paris, July 1822). South Netherlands clarinettist. He settled in Paris, where he wrote *Méthode nouvelle et raisonnée pour la clarinette* (1785), the first tutor for the new instrument.

Vandini, Antonio (*b* Bologna, *c*1690; *d* ?Padua, after 1771). Italian cellist. From 1721 he was first cellist at the basilica of S Antonio, Padua, returning after a period in Prague (1723–6). He often performed with Tartini, who was both a friend and a musical influence. He composed cello sonatas and concertos.

Vanhal [Vanhall, Wanhal], Johann Baptist (*b* Nové Nechanice, 12 May 1739; *d* Vienna, 20 Aug 1813). Czech composer. His first posts were as organist and choirmaster; he was also a violinist and cellist. In *c*1761 he went to Vienna, where he studied with Dittersdorf and became famous as a composer and teacher (Pleyel was among his pupils). He travelled in Italy, 1769–71; after an illness he returned to Vienna *c*1780 and worked as one of the first independent musicians.

A prolific and popular composer, graceful and accomplished, Vanhal wrote over 700 instrumental works. Until the mid-1780s most were symphonies, concertos and chamber works (especially string quartets and trios), but later he turned to lighter pieces (many for keyboard). His early symphonies are important for their distinct sonata structures in the outer movements. His output also includes two operas, many sacred works and songs.

Vanni-Marcoux [Marcoux, Jean Emile Diogène] (*b* Turin, 12 June 1877; *d* Paris, 22 Oct 1962). French baritone and bass. He sang in Italy from 1894. At Covent Garden (1905–12) he was successful in a variety of roles, including Rossini's Don Basilio and Debussy's Arkel. From 1908 he sang in the Paris Opéra, making his début as Gounod's Mephistopheles. His American début was at Chicago, in 1913, as Scarpia. He was a splendid actor as well as an accomplished singer.

Van Rooy, Anton(ius Maria Josephus) (*b* Rotterdam, 1 Jan 1870; *d* Munich, 28 Nov 1932). Dutch bass-baritone. After study with Julius Stockhausen he appeared at Bayreuth from 1897, quickly becoming recognized as the leading interpreter of such roles as Wotan and Sachs, noble in tone and style. He sang at Covent Garden, 1898–1913, and at the Met, 1898–1903; his assumption of Amfortas in the unauthorized *Parsifal* of 1903 led to his being banned at Bayreuth.

Van Vactor, David (*b* Plymouth, IN, 8 May 1906). American composer. Trained as a composer and flautist in the USA, Vienna and Paris, he played in the Chicago SO (1931–43) and taught at the University of Tennessee (1947–76), also conducting the Knoxville SO (1947–72). His works include symphonies, sacred cantatas and chamber music.

Vaquedano, José de (*b* Galicia; *d* Santiago de Compostela, 17 Feb 1711). Spanish composer. He was *maestro de capilla* at a Madrid monastery and then at the cathedral at Santiago de Compostela (1681–1710). One of the finest Spanish composers of his time, he wrote many villancicos and other sacred works, most of them polychoral.

Vaqueras, Bertrandus (*b* c1450; *d* ?Rome, by 3 May 1507). Singer and composer. He was a priest in the diocese of Cavaillon, France, and from 1483 was a singer in the papal chapel. His extant works comprise two masses, two Credos, three motets and a *chanson*. Except for the inferior Credos, his music is worthy of interest though not in the first rank.

Varady, Julia (*b* Oradea, 1 Sept 1941). Romanian soprano. She studied in Bucharest and appeared with Cluj State Opera; later she sang in Italy and West Germany, joining the Munich Opera in 1972–3, where she was admired for her Mozart roles, such as Elvira (as in her Met début, 1978) and Vitellia, as well as Verdi (both Leonoras, Violetta) and Puccini (Butterfly, Liù). She is noted for her emotional power and serenity of line. She is married to Dietrich Fischer-Dieskau.

Varèse, Edgard [Edgar] (**Victor Achille Charles**) (*b* Paris, 22 Dec 1883; *d* New York, 6 Nov 1965). American composer of French origin. He studied with d'Indy at the Schola Cantorum (1903–5) and Widor at the Paris Conservatoire (1905–7), then moved to Berlin, where he met Strauss and Busoni. In 1913 he returned to Paris, but in 1915 he emigrated to New York; nearly all his compositions disappeared at this stage, with the exception of a single published song and an orchestral score, *Bourgogne* (1908), which he took with him but destroyed towards the end of his life. His creative output therefore effectively begins with *Amériques* for large orchestra (1921), which, for all its echoes of Debussy and of Stravinsky's early ballets, sets out to discover new worlds of sound: fiercely dissonant chords, rhythmically complex polyphonies for percussion and/or wind, forms in continuous evolution with no large-scale recurrence.

In 1921 he and Carlos Salzedo founded the International Composers' Guild, who gave the first performances of several of his works for small ensemble, these prominently featuring wind and percussion, and presenting the innovations of *Amériques* in pure, compact form: *Hyperprism* (1923), *Octandre* (1923) and *Intégrales* (1925). *Arcana* (1927), which returns

to the large orchestra and extended form with perfected technique, brought this most productive period to an end.

There followed a long stay in Paris (1928–33), during which he wrote *Ionisation* for percussion orchestra (1931), the first European work to dispense almost entirely with pitched sounds, which enter only in the coda. He also took an interest in the electronic instruments being developed (he had been calling for electronic means since his arrival in the USA), and wrote for two theremins or ondes martenot in *Ecuatorial* for bass, brass, keyboards and percussion (1934). The flute solo *Density 21.5* (1936) was then his last completed work for nearly two decades.

During this time he taught sporadically and also made plans for *Espace*, which was to have involved simultaneous radio broadcasts from around the globe; an *Etude pour Espace* for chorus, pianos and percussion was performed in 1947. Then, with electronic music at last a real possibility owing to the development of the tape recorder, he produced *Déserts* for wind, percussion and tape (1954) and a *Poème électronique* (1957–8), devised to be diffused in the Philips pavilion at the Brussels Exposition of 1958. His last years were devoted to projects on themes of night and death, including the unfinished *Nocturnal* for voices and chamber orchestra (1961).

Surviving works Un grand sommeil noir, 1v, pf (1906); Amériques, orch (1921); Offrandes, S, small orch (1921); Hyperprism, 9 wind, 7 perc (1923); Octandre, 7 wind, db (1923); Intégrales, 11 wind, 4 perc (1925); Arcana, orch (1927); Ionisation, 13 perc (1931); Ecuatorial, B, ens (1934); Density 21.5, fl (1936); Etude pour Espace, chorus, 2 pf, perc (1947); Déserts, 14 wind, pf, 5 perc, tape (1954); La procession de Vergès, tape (1955); Poème électronique, tape (1958); Nocturnal, S, B chorus, small orch (1961)

Varesi, Felice (*b* Calais, 1813; *d* Milan, 13 March 1889). Italian baritone. A prototype of the dramatic baritone that evolved from the operas of Donizetti and of early- and middle-period Verdi, he was powerful in the title roles of *Macbeth* (1847) and above all *Rigoletto* (1851), creating both. His Giorgio Germont in the première of *La traviata* (1853) was less successful.

Variations. A form in which successive statements of a theme are altered or presented in altered settings. In the 18th and 19th centuries the theme was usually stated first, followed by a number of variations – hence the expression 'theme and variations'.

In the 16th century, dances were much used as frameworks for instrumental variations. The art reached a high stage of development in 16th-century Spain in works for vihuela and keyboard by Cabezón and others. The English virginalists late in the century, notably Bull, Farnaby, Gibbons and Byrd, also excelled and influenced continental composers, especially Sweelinck and Scheidt.

In 17th-century Italy, Frescobaldi, continuing to write traditional framework-variations such as the romanesca and folia, tended to place the framework notes on strong beats, changing the framework into a repeating scheme. Later (e.g. with Pasquini) variation of the melody became more important, a trend continued in the variations of G.B. Martini, Platti, Alberti and above all J.C. Bach. The insertion of a minor variation in a major set began to appear about this time.

In north and central Germany chorale variations were developed in the 17th century, first by Sweelinck and Scheidt and then by Weckmann and Tunder, who varied each verse of organ chorales, often with motifs related to the text. Free variations became characteristic of north German usage, leading to the chorale fantasia as perfected by Buxtehude. By contrast, in south Germany, with Pachelbel, strict forms were preferred and the final variation of a set is often a fugue. J.S. Bach used nearly all types: passacaglia and chaconne in works for organ and solo violin; grounds in several vocal movements, including the 'Crucifixus' of the Mass in B minor; chorale partitas for organ in the style of Böhm and Buxtehude; and canonic variations for organ on *Vom Himmel hoch*. The Goldberg Variations represent the highest artistic development of the bass-framework variations.

C.P.E. Bach and Haydn continued to cultivate the thoroughbass type, but from *c*1770 melodic variations predominate in their works and those of others. Haydn wrote few independent sets, but included variation movements in several chamber and orchestral works, often varying two themes alternately (e.g. the second movements of Symphonies nos.53 and 63, and the variations in F minor for piano). Sometimes he combined variations with rondo or ternary form. Mozart's independent sets of variations for piano, akin to his improvisations, were popular in his lifetime and well into the 19th century. He also used variation form in divertimentos, serenades and concertos, occasionally in string quartets and piano sonatas, but never in a symphony. Nearly all are of the melodic type with fixed harmony. The penultimate Adagio variation (usually highly embellished), a contrasting minor-key variation and a fast final variation (often in 6/8 metre) are features. In his earliest variations he echoed Baroque practice by repeating the theme at the end, but later he composed expanded final variations.

A climactic final variation, in effect a developmental coda, is a feature of most of Beethoven's sets. His early ones are mainly based on songs and popular operatic melodies. Between 1800 and 1812 he often used variations within a larger form (e.g. in the finale of the 'Eroica' Symphony and in the slow movements of the Fifth and Seventh Symphonies, the Piano Trio op.97 and the 'Appassionata' Sonata op.57); from 1818 variations became the spiritual centrepiece of several important works, including string quartets, the piano sonatas and the Ninth Symphony. The Diabelli Variations represent a microcosm of late Beethoven variation style and technique.

Variations of the early 19th century fall into two groups: 'formal variations' of the Viennese Classical type and 'character variations' determined by the new ideals and imagery of Romanticism. The first category is represented by Hummel, Cramer and Spohr, the second by Weber, Schumann and Mendelssohn. Schubert used both types; Chopin and Liszt brought high virtuosity to their character variations. The greatest master of variations in the late 19th century was Brahms. His Handel Variations for piano represent the metrically strict continuous variation type with final fugue; the bass is the sustaining element, as in the finales of the Fourth Symphony and the St Antony Variations. The Paganini Variations are examples of the Romantic virtuoso type as a series of 'studies for piano'. Brahms also combined variations with other forms.

During the late 19th century and early 20th fantasia variations, incorporating free material, took precedence. Examples include Tchaikovsky's Variations on a Rococo Theme for cello and orchestra, the Symphonic Variations of Dvořák and Franck, and Strauss's *Don Quixote*. Elgar's Enigma Variations, while containing programmatic elements, are more conventional in form, but the most important representative of older traditions is Reger. He and Brahms influenced Schoenberg, Berg and Webern. Schoenberg acknowledged Brahmsian precedents in his Variations op.31 for orchestra. Webern's treatment of variations deserves special study, and subsequent composers, including Dallapiccola and Nono, have used the variational possibilities offered by serialism. Among non-serial composers, Hindemith and Britten have made conspicuous use of variation techniques.

Variations on America. Organ work by Ives (?1891), arranged for orchestra by William Schuman and for concert band by Schuman and W. Rhoads.

Variations on a Theme of Frank Bridge. Britten's op.10 for string orchestra (1937).

Varnay, Astrid (Ibolyka Maria) (*b* Stockholm, 25 April 1918). American soprano. Her family, who were from the opera world, emigrated to the USA in 1920; she studied there and made her Met début in 1941 singing Sieglinde and Brünnhilde, going on to other Wagner roles. She sang Italian roles in Mexico City, 1948, the year of her Covent Garden début as Brünnhilde, which she followed with Isolde. She sang at Bayreuth, 1951–68, and appeared much in Germany in these years. Later she sang mezzo roles such as Strauss's Herodias and Clytemnestra. Her intense, passionate singing made her an outstanding Wagnerian.

Varney, Louis (*b* New Orleans, 30 May 1844; *d* Paris, 20 Aug 1908). French composer. Though he was a well-known, prolific operetta composer, only *Les mousquetaires au couvent* (1880) has remained in the repertory.

Varsovienne. A dance originating in France during the 1850s: it was a genteel version of the mazurka, incorporating elements of the waltz.

Varviso, Silvio (*b* Zurich, 26 Feb 1924). Swiss conductor. He studied in Zurich and Vienna. He was principal conductor of the Basle Opera (1950–62) and conducted opera in Berlin and Paris from 1958. His American début was in 1959 at the San Francisco Opera. In 1962 he conducted at Glyndebourne and Covent Garden. In the early 1980s he was music director at the Paris Opéra. He is noted for his elegant, lively style in Rossini, Bellini and Donizetti and clarity and expressive character in Mozart, Wagner and Strauss.

Varvoglis, Mario (*b* Brussels, 22 Dec 1885; *d* Athens, 31 July 1967). Greek composer. From 1902 to 1920 he was in Paris, where he studied with d'Indy and others. He then taught at the Athens and Hellenic conservatories and wrote articles and criticism. His music, in many genres, is generally in a conservative style more akin to Franck, d'Indy and Fauré than to the impressionists.

Vásáry, Tamás (*b* Debrecen, 11 Aug 1933). Swiss pianist. He studied in Budapest and was much influenced by Kodály; his career was already under way when he left Hungary in 1956. He made a highly successful series of débuts (Vienna, New York, London) in 1960–61, showing himself a sensitive yet powerful Liszt interpreter and a delicate and poetic Chopin pianist. He made his conducting début in 1971 and was musical director of the Northern Sinfonia (1979–82).

Vasconcellos, Joaquim (António da Fonseca) de (*b* Oporto, 10 Feb 1849; *d* there, 2 March 1936). Portuguese lexicographer. He is noted for his early, comprehensive dictionary *Os musicos portuguezes: biographia-bibliographia* (1870).

Vasilenko, Sergey Nikiforovich (*b* Moscow, 30 March 1872; *d* there, 11 March 1956). Soviet composer. He was a pupil of Taneyev and Ippolitov-Ivanov at the Moscow Conservatory (1895–1901), where he taught composition (1906–56). His earlier music shows enthusiasm for folk music, Old Believer song and symbolist poetry; after 1910 he was attracted to central Asian folk music (as in the ballet *Iosif the Beautiful*, 1925). He wrote operas (including *The Snowstorm*, 1938, the first Uzbek one) and musical comedies, five symphonies (1904–47), concertos, songs and chamber music; he was a masterly orchestrator.

Vásquez, Juan (*b* Badajoz, *c*1510; *d* ?Seville, *c*1560). Spanish composer. He held posts at the cathedrals in Badajoz (1530–39, 1545–50) and Palencia (1539). His only sacred music, the monumental *Agenda defunctorum* (1566), for four voices, shows his skills as a contrapuntist and his mastery of sonorities. He achieved greatest fame with his secular music, especially the 93 villancicos with their simple counterpoint, careful text declamation, charm and variety. He also published guitar and vihuela music.

Vaudeville. In the 17th and 18th centuries, a satirical or epigrammatic French poem or song; since then, a theatrical entertainment similar to modern musical comedy or variety shows.

The term arose from the cohesion and confusion of two genres. The *vau de vire*, a popular, satirical song, took its name from its place of origin in Normandy. The *voix de ville*, a courtly Parisian song, was current in the 16th century. By the early 17th century 'vaudeville' was used for both, but in Louis XIV's reign it came to mean a satirical song about political or court events. The *comédie en vaudevilles* – comedy using vaudeville tunes with new texts – enjoyed a vogue in the late 17th century and the early

18th before being superseded by *opéra comique*. The *vaudeville final*, however, in which the main characters assemble to sing a few verses to a vaudeville melody, survived. Its influence is present in Mozart's *Die Entführung aus dem Serail*, Verdi's *Falstaff* and Stravinsky's *The Rake's Progress*. In the 19th century the vaudeville absorbed more popular elements and by 1890 was patterned after the English music hall.

Vaughan, Denis (Edward) (*b* Melbourne, 6 June 1926). Australian conductor and organist. He studied the organ in Melbourne, London and Paris. In 1953 he became assistant to Beecham at the RPO, also forming the Beecham Choral Society. He later conducted opera in Germany and Adelaide (musical director, South Australia State Opera, 1981–4) and was widely heard as a keyboard player. He has worked towards the establishment of accurate texts of Verdi and Puccini's operas and on concert-hall acoustics.

Vaughan, Sarah (Lois) [Sassy] (*b* Newark, NJ, 27 March 1924). American jazz and popular singer. She established a lasting reputation as a jazz singer in the mid-1940s when she worked with such bop musicians as Dizzy Gillespie and Charlie Parker. Most of her career has been involved with commercial popular music to which she brought high artistry.

Vaughan Thomas, David (*b* Ystalyfera, 15 March 1873; *d* Johannesburg, 15 Sept 1934). Welsh composer. He studied with Joseph Parry and at Oxford, then worked as a teacher, adjudicator and lecturer. As a composer he is best known for his choral music and songs setting Welsh texts.

Vaughan Williams, Ralph (*b* Down Ampney, 12 Oct 1872; *d* London, 26 Aug 1958). English composer. He studied with Parry, Wood and Stanford at the RCM and Cambridge, then had further lessons with Bruch in Berlin (1897) and Ravel in Paris (1908). It was only after this that he began to write with sureness in larger forms, even though some songs had had success in the early years of the century. That success, and the ensuing maturity, depended very much on his work with folksong, which he had begun to collect in 1903; this opened the way to the lyrical freshness of the Housman cycle *On Wenlock Edge* and to the modally inflected tonality of the symphonic cycle that began with *A Sea Symphony*. But he learnt the same lessons in studying earlier English music in his task as editor of the *English Hymnal* (1906) – work which bore fruit in his Fantasia on a Theme by Tallis for strings, whose majestic unrelated consonances provided a new sound and a new way into large-scale form. The sound, with its sense of natural objects seen in a transfigured light, placed Vaughan Williams in a powerfully English visionary tradition, and made very plausible his association of his music with Blake (in the ballet *Job*) and Bunyan (in the opera *The Pilgrim's Progress*). Meanwhile the new command of form made possible a first orchestral symphony, *A London Symphony*, where characterful detail is worked into the scheme. A first opera, *Hugh the Drover*, made direct use of folksongs, which Vaughan Williams normally did not do in orchestral works.

His study of folksong, however, certainly facilitated the pastoral tone of *The Lark Ascending*, for violin and orchestra, and then of the *Pastoral Symphony*. At the beginning of the 1920s there followed a group of religious works continuing the visionary manner: the unaccompanied Mass in G minor, the Revelation oratorio *Sancta civitas* and the 'pastoral episode' *The Shepherds of the Delectable Mountains*, later incorporated in *The Pilgrim's Progress*. But if the glowing serenity of pastoral and vision were to remain central during the decades of work on that magnum opus, works of the later 1920s show a widening of scope, towards the comedy of the operas *Sir John in Love* (after *The Merry Wives of Windsor*) and *The Poisoned Kiss*, and towards the angularity of Satan's music in *Job* and of the Fourth Symphony. The quite different Fifth Symphony has more connection with *The Pilgrim's Progress*, and was the central work of a period that also included the cantata *Dona nobis pacem*, the opulent *Serenade to Music* for 16 singers and orchestra, and the A minor string quartet, the finest of Vaughan Williams's rather few chamber works.

A final period opened with the desolate, pessimistic Sixth Symphony, after which Vaughan Williams found a focus in the natural world for such bleakness when he was asked to write the music for the film *Scott of the Antarctic*: out of that world came his Seventh Symphony, the *Sinfonia antartica*, whose pitched percussion colouring he used more ebulliently in the Eighth Symphony, the Ninth returning to the contemplative world of *The Pilgrim's Progress*.

Operas Hugh the Drover (1914, perf. 1924); The Shepherds of the Delectable Mountains (1921); Sir John in Love (1929); The Poisoned Kiss (1929, perf. 1937); Riders to the Sea (1932, perf. 1937); The Pilgrim's Progress (1951)
Ballet Job (1931)
Symphonies A Sea Sym., with vv (no.1, 1909); A London Sym. (no.2, 1913); Pastoral Sym. (no.3, 1921); no.4, f (1934); no.5, D (1943); no.6, e, (1947); Sinfonia antartica, with vv (no.7, 1952); no.8, d (1955); no.9, e (1956–7)
Other orchestral music The Wasps, ov. (1909); Fantasia on a Theme by Thomas Tallis, str (1910); The Lark Ascending, vn, orch (1914); English Folk Song Suite, band (1923); Toccata marziale, band (1924); Flos campi, va, SATB (1925); Conc. accademico, vn (1925); Pf Conc., C (1931); Suite, va, small orch (1934); 5 variants of Dives and Lazarus, str, harps (1939); Ob Conc., a (1944); Tuba Conc., f (1954)
Vocal-orchestral music Sancta civitas (1925); Five Tudor Portraits (1935); Dona nobis pacem (1936); Serenade to Music (1938); An Oxford Elegy (1949); Hodie (1954)
Smaller choral Mass, g (1921); many motets, partsongs, folksong arrs., carols, hymns
Songs On Wenlock Edge (1909); 10 Blake songs (1957); folksong arrs.
Chamber music Str Qt, a (1944); Vn Sonata (1954)

Vautor, Thomas (*fl* 1600–20). English composer. He served George Villiers, Duke of Buckingham, at Brooksby, Leics., from 1600, and took the Oxford BMus in 1616. His extant madrigal book (1619–20) ranges widely and includes well-known pieces (*Weepe, mine eyes*; *Sweet Suffolke owle*), some with viol accompaniment.

Vaynberg, Moyssey Samuilovich (*b* Warsaw, 8 Dec 1919). Soviet composer of Polish origin. A pupil of Zolotaryov at the Minsk Conservatory (1939–41), he settled in Moscow in 1943. He has written in most genres (including ten symphonies) in an intense style alternating between driving vitality and lyric introspection; his harmony is essentially tonal.

Vecchi, Orazio (Tiberio) (*b* Modena, bap. 6 Dec 1550; *d* there, 19 Feb 1605). Italian composer. A priest, he was *maestro di cappella* at the cathedrals of Salò (1581–4), Modena (1584–6) and Reggio Emilia (1586), then went to Correggio, before returning to Modena as *maestro* in 1593 (court *maestro* from 1598). A pioneer of dramatic music, he provided a link between the madrigal and early opera. His *L'Amfiparnaso* (1597), a madrigal-comedy in 13 scenes for *commedia dell'arte* characters, combines madrigalian dialogue with light entertainment music. He also wrote other large-scale secular works (1590–1604), canzonettas (6 bks, 1580–97), madrigals (1583, 1589) and sacred works (5 bks, 1587–1607).

He should not be confused with the Milanese composer Orfeo Vecchi (*c*1550–1604), who wrote *c*24 books of sacred music (1588–1609).

Vécsey, Jenő (*b* Felsőcéce, 19 July 1909; *d* Budapest, 18 Sept 1966). Hungarian composer and musicologist. He was a pupil of Kodály at the Budapest Academy and studied in Vienna. He worked in Budapest as a music librarian, edited classical and 19th-century Hungarian works and composed orchestral and chamber pieces.

Vega, Aurelio de la (*b* Havana, 28 Nov 1925). American composer of Cuban origin. He was a pupil of Frederick Kramer (1942–6) and in Los Angeles of Toch (1947–9). He then went back to Cuba, returning to California in 1959 and working there as a teacher. His music, in many genres including tape pieces, has developed from a Szymanowskian post-impressionism to a use of diverse avant-garde techniques, all of it expressive, forceful and carefully structured; since 1974 many of his works have included visual elements.

Veggio, Claudio Maria (*b* Piacenza, *fl c*1528–44). Italian composer. The quantity of keyboard and sacred music by him in MSS at Castell'Arquato suggests that he was organist there. His *Madrigali a quattro voci* (1540) was dedicated to his patron, Count Federico Anguissola of Piacenza. His keyboard music, which includes eight ricercares and several arrangements, is idiomatic, featuring alternate contrapuntal and figurative sections, parallel 3rds in the left hand and extensive florid passages.

Végh Quartet. Hungarian string quartet led by Sándor Végh. It was founded in 1940; since 1946, when it left Hungary, the ensemble has performed with distinction a repertory that includes complete cycles of the quartets of Bartók and Beethoven.

Veichtner, Franz Adam (*b* Regensburg, 10 Feb 1741; *d* Kalnciems, 3 March 1822). German violinist and composer. He was Konzertmeister to the Courland court at Jelgava 1765–95, and later served at St Petersburg. His output includes three Singspiels, other vocal works, *c*60 symphonies and violin music.

Veit, Václav Jindřich (*b* Řepnice, 19 Jan 1806; *d* Litoměřice, 16 Feb 1864). Bohemian composer. A lawyer by profession, he had a high reputation as a pianist. He was a pioneer of Romanticism in Czech music, producing chamber music in the style of Onslow and Spohr, Czech songs and patriotic choruses and a notable Symphony in E minor (1859).

Vejvanovský, Pavel Josef (*b* Hukvaldy or Hlučin, *c*1633 or *c*1639; *d* Kroměříž, bur. 24 Sept 1693). Moravian composer, trumpeter and music copyist. He worked at Kroměříž from 1661 and in 1664 became principal trumpeter and Kapellmeister to the Prince-Bishop of Olomouc there. He also directed the choir at St Mořice and was important as a copyist. His output includes numerous masses, motets, litanies etc and many sonatas and other instrumental pieces, variously scored. In both vocal and instrumental music he made considerable (and sometimes adventurous) use of the trumpet and other brass instruments; he was apparently influenced by J.H. Schmelzer, with whom he may have studied. His sacred music is notable for its homophonic vocal writing, which anticipates 18th-century style. Many of his works show the influence of Moravian folk music.

Velluti, Giovanni Battista (*b* Corridonia, 28 Jan 1781; *d* Venice, 22 Jan 1861). Italian male soprano. The last of the great castrato singers, he was unrivalled in Europe for most of his career. Among his favourite roles were Arsace in Rossini's *Aureliano in Palmira* (1813) and Armando in Meyerbeer's *Il crociato in Egitto* (1824), both of which he created.

Veloce (It.). Swift, rapid, quick.

Velut, Gilet [Egidius] (*fl* early 15th century). French composer. He may have served in the papal choir, 1420–41. The style of his eight extant compositions indicates the early 15th century; some of his works, however, notably his three ballades, display French late 14th-century style.

Venegas de Henestrosa, Luis (*b c*1510; *d c*1557 or later). Spanish composer. He seems to have spent his life in Toledo, where he worked, not necessarily in a musical capacity, as a priest. His *Libro de cifra nueva* (1557), intended primarily for keyboard, contains arrangements of fantasias, tientos and settings of hymns and other plainchant melodies, with arrangements of vocal music, variations and a keyboard duet based on a Crequillon *chanson*.

Venetian Games [Gry weneckie]. Work for chamber orchestra by Lutosławski (1961).

Venetian swell. A device invented by BURKAT SHUDI in 1769 for varying the volume on the harpsichord, using louvred wooden shutters (on the principle of the Venetian blind) to adjust the volume. A similar mechanism was later adopted for the organ; *see* SWELL.

Veneziano, Gaetano (*b* Bisceglie, Bari, 1656; *d* Naples, 15 July 1716). Italian composer. A pupil of Provenzale, he was organist at the Naples court chapel from 1678 and *maestro di cappella*, 1704–7. He was also first *maestro di cappella* of the S Maria di Loreto conservatory. His output includes oratorios, Passions and over 100 other sacred works, from sim-

ple hymn settings to elaborate polychoral masses and motets.

His son Giovanni (1683–1742) was organist at the Naples court chapel, 1704–7, returning there in 1735; from 1716 he was second *maestro* at the Loreto. Of his several vocal works, the three comic operas (1714–15) are early examples of the Neapolitan dialect type.

Venice Conservatory [Conservatorio Nazionale di Musica 'Benedetto Marcello']. Conservatory founded in 1877, one of the leading Italian music colleges.

Veni Creator Spiritus (Lat.: 'Come Creator Spirit'). A hymn in the Roman rite sung at Whitsuntide and at other solemnities. It first appears in a 10th-century MS; its melody has served as the basis for many masses, including a six-voice one by Palestrina. Mahler set the words in his Eighth Symphony.

Veni Sancte Spiritus (Lat.: 'Come Holy Ghost'). The sequence for Pentecost, one of four retained by the Council of Trent (1543–63); it was set by Dufay, Josquin, Palestrina, Lassus and others.

Venite (Lat.: 'Come'). In the Roman rite, the opening chant of Matins, properly *Venite exultemus Domino*; in the Anglican liturgy, the first canticle of Matins.

Vento, Ivo de (*b c*1543–5; *d* Munich, 1575). ?Flemish composer. A choirboy in the Munich Hofkapelle (1556–9), he studied the organ in Venice from 1560, probably under Merulo, and became an organist at the Munich court. He published nearly 100 motets (4 bks, 1569–74); his German songs (7 bks, 1569–75) influenced later composers (Lechner, Hassler) and long remained popular.

Vento, Mattia (*b* Naples, 1735; *d* London, 22 Nov 1776). Italian composer. Trained in Naples, he presented his first three operas in Italy. In 1763 he settled in England, where he became a popular composer and taught the harpsichord. He had six Italian operas staged in London and contributed to Italian and English pasticcios. His other works include songs and instrumental pieces, notably 11 sets of keyboard sonatas (most with violin), 1764–76. Simple and graceful melodies are a feature of his style.

Ventura, Angelo Benedetto (*b c*1781; *d* 1856). Inventor, composer and teacher. In London from at least 1813, he created and marketed eight harp-lute-guitar hybrids, for which he gave lessons and composed simple pieces. His most important invention was the 'Harp Ventura' (1828), a 17- to 19-string, easily modulated harp-lute.

Venturi del Nibbio, Stefano (*fl* 1592–1600). Italian composer. He was in Venice in 1592 but by 1594 had moved to Florence. Though in touch with progressive circles, he was essentially a polyphonist and wrote almost exclusively ensemble madrigals (5 bks, 1592–8); two were reprinted in London with new English texts.

Venturini, Francesco (*b* ?Brussels, *c*1675; *d* Hanover, 18 April 1745). German composer and violinist. He served at the Hanoverian court, becoming Konzertmeister in 1713 and later Kapellmeister. His 12 orchestral suites (*c*1714) are richly scored; each has a substantial first movement and a series of shorter movements, mostly dances.

Venus and Adonis. Opera in a prologue and three acts by Blow to a libretto by an unknown author (*c*1684, London).

Vêpres siciliennes, Les. *See* SICILIAN VESPERS, THE.

Veprik, Alexander Moiseyevich (*b* Balta, 23 June 1899; *d* Moscow, 13 Oct 1958). Soviet composer. He studied with Myaskovsky at the Moscow Conservatory (1921–3), where he remained to teach until 1943; under Stalin he was imprisoned. His works, in many genres, represent the Russian Jewish school in their emotional, ornamental style.

Veracini, Francesco (*b* Florence, 1 Feb 1690; *d* there, 31 Oct 1768). Italian composer and violinist. He studied with his uncle, the composer and violinist Antonio Veracini (1659–1733), G.M. Casini and others. For the next ten years he was mostly abroad: he stayed in London (1714) and Düsseldorf (1715) and later served at the Dresden court (1717–22). While in Florence, 1723–33, he composed and performed mainly religious music, but on later visits to London (1733–8, 1741–5) he had four operas staged. He had an outstanding reputation as a violinist and continued to perform in old age; he became *maestro di cappella* at S Pancrazio, Florence, in 1755 and succeeded his uncle at S Michele in 1758.

Veracini's compositions reflect his independent and eclectic outlook. The earliest of his *c*60 violin sonatas (1716) are in a very progressive *galant* style, but he later developed an elaborate contrapuntal idiom, notably in the.12 *Sonate accademiche* (1744) and in his revisions of Corelli's op.5 sonatas. He also wrote concertos (some influenced by Vivaldi), a treatise and some vocal music, including operas, oratorios, cantatas and songs.

Verbunkos. An 18th-century Hungarian dance, deriving from the method of enlisting recruits. It has a slow introductory section (*lassu*) alternating with a quick one (*friss*), usually followed by a coda-like, ornamented appendix (*figura*), a trio-like middle section (*disz*) and sometimes a second trio. Its rhythmic vitality derives from the brilliant performing style of gypsy violinists. Liszt drew inspiration from *verbunkos* music for his Hungarian Rhapsodies; it was also used by Beethoven, Schubert, Brahms, Ravel, Bartók and Kodály.

Vercoe, Barry (Lloyd) (*b* Wellington, 24 July 1937). New Zealand composer. A pupil of Finney at the University of Michigan, he remained in the USA, working on computer music at Princeton and, since 1971, MIT. He is best known for developing several computer music languages.

Verdelot, Philippe (*b* Verdelot, ?1470–80; *d* before 1552). French composer. Little is known of his earlier career; later he held posts in Florence (1523–7) and Rome. He wrote *c*58 motets and two masses, which fall into three stylistic groups. His early style features conjunct melodic progressions, melismas, narrow-range and short, closed phrases (e.g. *Sancta Maria sucurre miseris* and *Gaudeamus omnes in Domino*) and may date from the 1510s. After a 'middle' period (*c*1520–25), in which he produced a more declamatory style (e.g. *Ad Dominum cum tribularer*), his mature phase evolved: such motets as *Congregati*

sunt and *Letamini in Domino*, from the late 1520s, have fewer melismas, longer note values and a unity of text and music. Some of his many madrigals date from the 1520s, making him one of the earliest madrigalists. Their style varies from chordal, mostly syllabic four-voice settings to highly imitative ones. Like his motets, his madrigals were widely known throughout the 16th century. The surprisingly few *chansons*, and their retrospective musical traits nearer to Josquin and Mouton than to the Parisian *chanson*, seem to confirm his early departure from France.

Verdi, Giuseppe (Fortunino Francesco) (*b* Roncole, 9/10 Oct 1813; *d* Milan, 27 Jan 1901). Italian composer. He was born into a family of small landowners and taverners. When he was seven he was helping the local church organist; at 12 he was studying with the organist at the main church in nearby Busseto, whose assistant he became in 1829. He already had several compositions to his credit. In 1832 he was sent to Milan, but was refused a place at the conservatory and studied with Vincenzo Lavigna, composer and former La Scala musician. He might have taken a post as organist at Monza in 1835, but returned to Busseto where he was passed over as *maestro di cappella* but became town music master in 1836 and married Margherita Barezzi, his patron's daughter (their two children died in infancy).

Verdi had begun an opera, and tried to arrange a performance in Parma or Milan; he was unsuccessful but had some songs published and decided to settle in Milan in 1839 where his *Oberto* was accepted at La Scala and further operas commissioned. It was well received but his next, *Un giorno di regno*, failed totally; and his wife died during its composition. Verdi nearly gave up, but was fired by the libretto of *Nabucco* and in 1842 saw its successful production, which carried his reputation across Italy, Europe and the New World over the next five years. It was followed by another opera also with marked political overtones, *I lombardi alla prima crociata*, again well received. Verdi's gift for stirring melody and tragic and heroic situations struck a chord in an Italy struggling for freedom and unity, causes with which he was sympathetic; but much opera of this period has political themes and the involvement of Verdi's operas in politics is easily exaggerated.

The period Verdi later called his 'years in the galleys' now began, with a long and demanding series of operas to compose and (usually) direct, in the main Italian centres and abroad: they include *Ernani*, *Macbeth*, *Luisa Miller* and eight others in 1844–50, in Paris and London as well as Rome, Milan, Naples, Venice, Florence and Trieste (with a pause in 1846 when his health gave way). Features of these works include strong, sombre stories, a vigorous, almost crude orchestral style that gradually grew fuller and richer, forceful vocal writing including broad lines in 9/8 and 12/8 metre and above all a seriousness in his determination to convey the full force of the drama. His models included late Rossini, Mercadante and Donizetti. He took great care over the choice of topics and about the detailed planning of his librettos. He established his basic vocal types early, in *Ernani*: the vigorous, determined baritone, the ardent, courageous but sometimes despairing tenor, the severe bass; among the women there is more variation.

The 'galley years' have their climax in the three great, popular operas of 1851–3. First among them is *Rigoletto*, produced in Venice (after trouble with the censors, a recurring theme in Verdi) and a huge success, as its richly varied and unprecedentedly dramatic music amply justifies. No less successful, in Rome, was the more direct *Il trovatore*, at the beginning of 1853; but six weeks later *La traviata*, the most personal and intimate of Verdi's operas, was a failure in Venice – though with some revisions it was favourably received the following year at a different Venetian theatre. With the dark drama of the one, the heroics of the second and the grace and pathos of the third, Verdi had shown how extraordinarily wide was his expressive range.

Later in 1853 he went – with Giuseppina Strepponi, the soprano with whom he had been living for several years, and whom he was to marry in 1859 – to Paris, to prepare *Les vêpres siciliennes* for the Opéra, where it was given in 1855 with modest success. Verdi remained there for a time to defend his rights in face of the piracies of the Théâtre des Italiens and to deal with translations of some of his operas. The next new one was the sombre *Simon Boccanegra*, a drama about love and politics in medieval Genoa, given in Venice. Plans for *Un ballo in maschera*, about the assassination of a Swedish king, in Naples were called off because of the censors and it was given instead in Rome (1859). Verdi was involved himself in political activity at this time, as representative of Busseto (where he lived) in the provincial parliament; later, pressed by Cavour, he was elected to the national parliament, and ultimately he was a senator. In 1862 *La forza del destino* had its première at St Petersburg. A revised *Macbeth* was given in Paris in 1865, but his most important work for the French capital was *Don Carlos*, a grand opera after Schiller in which personal dramas of love, comradeship and liberty are set against the persecutions of the Inquisition and the Spanish monarchy. It was given in 1867 and several times revised for later, Italian revivals.

Verdi returned to Italy, to live at Genoa. In 1870 he began work on *Aida*, given at Cairo Opera House at the end of 1871 to mark the opening of the Suez Canal (Verdi was not present): again in the grand opera tradition, and more taut in structure than *Don Carlos*. Verdi was ready to give up opera; his works of 1873 are a string quartet and the vivid, appealing Requiem in honour of the poet Manzoni, given in 1874–5, in Milan (S Marco and La Scala, aptly), Paris, London and Vienna. In 1879 the composer-poet Boito and the publisher Ricordi prevailed upon Verdi to write another opera, *Otello*; Verdi, working slowly and much occupied with revisions of earlier operas, completed it only in 1886. This, his most powerful tragic work, a study in evil and jealousy, had its première in Milan in 1887; it is notable for the increasing richness of allusive detail in the orchestral writing and the approach to a more continuous musical texture, though Verdi, with his faith in the expressive force of the human voice, did not abandon the 'set piece' (aria, duet etc) even if he integrated it more fully into its context – above all in his next opera. This was another Shakespeare work, *Falstaff*, on which he embarked two years later – his first comedy since the beginning of his career, with a score whose wit and lightness betray the hand of a serene master, was given in 1893. That was his last opera; still to come was a set of *Quattro pezzi sacri* (although Verdi was a non-believer). He spent his last years in Milan, rich, authoritarian but charitable, much visited, revered and honoured. He died at the beginning of 1901; 28,000 people lined the streets for his funeral.

Operas Oberto, Conte di San Bonifacio (1839); Un giorno di regno (1840); Nabucco (1842); I lombardi alla prima crociata (1843); Ernani (1844); I due Foscari (1844); Giovanni d'Arco (1845); Alzira (1845); Attila (1846); Macbeth (1847); I masnadieri (1847); Jérusalem (1847); Il corsaro (1848); La battaglia di Legnano (1849); Luisa Miller (1849); Stiffelio (1850); Rigoletto (1851); Il trovatore (1853); La traviata (1853); Les vêpres siciliennes (1855); Simon Boccanegra (1857); Aroldo (1857); Un ballo in maschera (1859); La forza del destino (1862); Don Carlos (1867); Aida (1871); Otello (1887); Falstaff (1893)
Vocal music Requiem (1874); Quatro pezzi sacri (1898); 7 other choral works; songs, trios
Instrumental music Str Qt, e (1873); pf pieces

Verdonck, Cornelis (*b* Turnhout, 1563; *d* Antwerp, 5 July 1625). Flemish composer. He studied under Cornet in Antwerp (1581), sang in the royal chapel in Madrid (1572–80, 1584–98) and was back in Antwerp by 1599. His works include *chansons* (1599) and madrigals (1603) which show skill and refinement.

Verein für Chorgesang. Choir founded by Schumann in Dresden in 1848. It gave the first performance (1849) of part of his *Szenen aus Goethes 'Faust'*; it was later renamed, then became part of the Philharmonic Choir.

Verein für Musikalische Privataufführungen. Society founded by Schoenberg in Vienna in 1918 to help narrow the gap between the contemporary composer and the public. It presented properly rehearsed performances of modern works to a genuinely interested membership (programmes were not divulged in advance). In the three years before inflation forced it to cease, it gave 353 performances of 154 works, including music by Reger, Debussy, Bartók, Schoenberg and Berg.

Veress, Sándor (*b* Cluj-Napoca, 1 Feb 1907). Swiss composer of Hungarian origin. A pupil of Bartók and Kodály at the Budapest Academy, he was involved during the 1930s in folksong work with Lajtha and Bartók; in 1949 he settled in Berne, teaching at the conservatory and university. He is an outstanding representative of the Hungarian generation after Bartók: he used 12-note technique in the 1950s, though with Bartók's clarity and inquisitiveness remaining. His many works cover most genres, with emphasis on orchestral, choral and piano music. Notable are the Violin Concerto (1939) and *Hommage à Paul Klee* (1952). His numerous writings include many on Bartók and several on music education.

Veretti, Antonio (*b* Verona, 20 Feb 1900; *d* Rome, 13 July 1978). Italian composer. A pupil of Alfano at the Bologna Conservatory, he taught at and directed various institutions (including the Florence Conservatory, 1956–70). His works at first followed Alfano and Pizzetti, then approached neo-classicism and serialism.

Verhulst, Johannes (Josephus Hermanus) (*b* The Hague, 19 March 1816; *d* there, 17 Jan 1891). Dutch composer and conductor. He became a close friend of Schumann in Leipzig, where he conducted programmes of progressive music. Holding conducting posts in Rotterdam, The Hague and Amsterdam, he virtually controlled Dutch musical life until 1886. His compositions, strongly influenced by Schumann and Mendelssohn, include choral works, songs, overtures and piano pieces.

Verikivsky, Mykhaylo (*b* Kremenets, 20 Nov 1896; *d* Kiev, 14 June 1962). Ukrainian composer and conductor. A pupil of Yavorsky at the Kiev Conservatory, where he taught from 1946, he conducted operas at Kiev (1926–8) and Khar'kov (1928–35). His works include ballets, oratorios, orchestral music and songs in a nationalist style; his *Pan Kanyovsky* was the first Ukrainian ballet.

Verismo (It.). 'Realism': term for the Italian version of the late 19th-century naturalist movement of which Zola was the dominant literary figure. It is associated with operas that deal with the unpleasant realities of life, introducing characters from the lower social strata, poverty, passion and brutality. Mascagni's *Cavalleria rusticana* (1889) was an early and influential example; others include Leoncavallo's *Pagliacci* and Puccini's *La bohème*.

Verklärte Nacht [Transfigured Night]. Schoenberg's op.4 for two violins, two violas and two cellos, (1899) after a poem by Richard Dehmel; Schoenberg arranged it for string orchestra (1917).

Vermeulen, Mathijs (*b* Helmond, 8 Feb 1888; *d* Laren, 26 July 1967). Dutch composer and writer on music. He was an influential critic, and wrote seven symphonies, chamber music and songs in a chromatic, introspective style.

Verocai, Giovanni (*b* Venice, *c*1700; *d* Brunswick, ?13 Dec 1745). Italian composer. He worked in Breslau, 1727–9, and then joined the Dresden court orchestra, also playing in Warsaw. He was at the Russian court, 1731–8; lastly he became Kapellmeister and opera director at Brunswick, where he composed some 12 operas. His other works include instrumental pieces and a cantata.

Verona Festival (Italy). Annual (summer) festival established in 1913; open-air performances of opera are given in the Roman arena (built 1AD, cap. 25 000).

Véronique. Opera in three acts by Messager to a libretto by Vanloo and Duval (1898, Paris).

Verrett, Shirley (*b* New Orleans, 31 May 1931). American mezzo-soprano. She studied in Los Angeles and at the Juilliard School. Her opera début was as Britten's Lucretia (1957). From 1959 she

sang in Europe, notably as Carmen, the role of her La Scala (1966) and Met (1968) débuts. At Covent Garden she has sung Verdi and Gluck. Her rich voice, even over more than two octaves, allows her to sing such soprano roles as Norma and Lady Macbeth.

Vers. Term used by troubadours to describe a lyric poem of five to ten stanzas followed by one or two *tornadas* (curtailed dedicatory stanzas). It is hard to distinguish it from the *canso*, but it seems to have been used for the earliest troubadour songs.

Verset. *See* ORGAN VERSET.

Versicle. In Christian liturgies, a short text (often said by celebrant or deacon) followed by an answer or 'response' (from congregation or choir).

Vers mesurés (Fr.). 'Measured verses': a type written in the late 16th century, by Jean-Antoine de Baïf and his followers, in an attempt to apply the quantitative principles of Greek and Latin poetry to French. With his musical associates, Courville, Maudit, Costeley and Le Jeune, he devised a technique for setting *vers mesurés* (or *vers mesurés à l'antique*) to music. In *musique mesurée* each long (accented) syllable was set to a minim and each short (unaccented) one to a crotchet. The result was homophonic texture, in irregular rhythmic groupings, with occasional, brief melismas. Many collections of neo-classic verse set to *musique mesurée* appeared in the 1570s and 1580s and even into the 17th century; Baïf's influence is still evident in French opera recitative of the late 17th century.

Verstovsky, Alexey Nikolayevich (*b* Seliverstovo, 1 March 1799; *d* Moscow, 17 Nov 1862). Russian composer. In St Petersburg his teachers included Field. From 1825 he was inspector (from 1842 director) of all the Moscow theatres, playing a leading part in their management until 1860. He composed solo songs (sentimental romances, pseudo-folksongs and narrative ballads) and operas with spoken dialogue, notably *Pan Twardowski* (1828; the first Russian romantic Singspiel, strongly influenced by Weber's *Der Freischütz*) and *Askold's Grave* (1835), his only real success and the first Russian opera performed in the USA (New York, 1869). With their elements of evil magic, scenes from everyday life and stock vocal types his operas are glorified Russian vaudevilles.

Verticalization. The simultaneous statement, in TWELVE-NOTE MUSIC, of two or more adjacent members of a note-row.

Vespers. The seventh service of the Divine Office, traditionally performed at twilight. It begins with the versicle and response *Deus in adjutorium* followed, in the Roman use, by five psalms (chosen according to the day or feast). A responsory may follow, then a versicle, antiphon, the Magnificat, prayers and *Benedicamus Domino*. On some feasts two Vespers services are sung. The music at Vespers increased during the Middle Ages, possibly as the length of processions increased. Responsories began to be set polyphonically in the Notre Dame repertory. A large-scale setting by Monteverdi dates from 1610.

Vesque von Püttlingen, Johann (*b* Opole, 23 July 1803; *d* Vienna, 30 Oct 1883). Austrian composer. He was taught by Sechter and Moscheles and was perhaps the most significant Austrian song composer between Schubert and Wolf (*c*300 settings); they show his scrupulous respect for the texts and penetrating sense of literary irony, satire and symbolism.

Vessel flute. A wind instrument in which the body of the pipe is globular or vessel-shaped rather than tubular. The best-known example is the OCARINA. Vessel flutes date back to ancient Egypt, where, made from a gourd or a hollowed coconut, they were regarded as possessing magic powers. Most have finger-holes; the action of opening them raises the pitch.

Vestale, La. Opera in three acts by Spontini to a libretto by Jouy (1807, Paris).

Vestris. French family of dancers and musicians of Italian origin. The most celebrated members were Gaetano (1729–1808), a dancer and choreographer who, as *premier danseur* at the Paris Opéra (1751–81) and at court, contributed to the reform of the ballet; and his granddaughter-in-law Lucia Elizabeth [née Bartolozzi] (1797–1856), a favourite contralto and actress at Drury Lane Theatre, London, from 1820. She sang in the English premières of many Rossini operas, created the role of Fatima in Weber's *Oberon* (1826) and had great influence as a manager of the Olympic (1831–8), Covent Garden (1839–42) and Lyceum (1847–55) theatres.

Viadana, Lodovico (*b* Viadana, *c*1560; *d* Gualtieri, 2 May 1627). Italian composer. A minorite friar and possibly a pupil of Porta, he had connections with Padua and Rome and was *maestro di cappella* of the cathedrals of Mantua (at least 1594–7), Concordia (1608–9) and Fano (1610–12). In 1623 he left Viadana for Busseto, then went to Gualtieri. An influential teacher and prolific composer, he ranks high among his contemporaries for the freshness, fluency and expressive quality of his music. He wrote mainly sacred vocal works (23 bks extant, 1588–1619) and is best known for his successful 100 *concerti ecclesiastici* for one to four voices (1602), the earliest sacred vocal publication with a continuo bass part. His secular works comprise canzonettas (1590, 1594) and instrumental ensemble works (1610).

Vianna da Motta, José (*b* S Tomé, 22 April 1868; *d* Lisbon, 31 May 1948). Portuguese pianist. He studied in Lisbon and Berlin and later under Liszt and Bülow. He toured widely from 1902 in Europe and South America and was director of the Lisbon Conservatory, 1919–38, as well as conducting there. He was a friend of Busoni and an authoritative interpreter of Bach and Beethoven, and did much to raise musical levels in Portugal.

Viardot (-García), (Michelle Ferdinande) Pauline (*b* Paris, 18 July 1821; *d* there, 18 May 1910). French mezzo-soprano of Spanish origin. The younger daughter of Manuel García (and the sister of Maria Malibran), she won immense success in highly dramatic parts, notably as Fidès in the première of Meyerbeer's *Le prophète* (1849) and in the title role of Gluck's *Orfeo* (ed. Berlioz, 1859). She also gave the first performance of Brahms's Alto Rhapsody, and was the dedicatee of works by Schumann, Saint-Saëns and Fauré. She was close to writers including Turgenev, and from 1843 a princi-

pal channel through which Russian music reached the West. Among her own compositions are operettas (*Cendrillon*, 1904) and songs.

Vibraphone. Percussion instrument with metal bars, arranged keyboard-fashion. Its distinctive tone is produced by electrically powered resonating tubes placed under the bars and containing a rotating vane which can be switched on to add a pulsating effect. The instrument is usually mounted on a metal frame, at the base of which there is a sustaining pedal. It generally has a three-octave compass (f–f''') and is played with soft beaters.

Since its development in the USA in the early 1920s it has become common in dance and jazz bands and plays an increasingly important part in contemporary music, particularly for small ensembles. It was first used in orchestral music by Milhaud in *L'annonce faite 'à Marie* (1933), by Ravel in the orchestrated versions of his *Don Quichotte* songs and by Berg in *Lulu*.

Vibrato (It.). A fluctuation of pitch (less often, intensity) on a single note in performance, especially by string players and singers. Vibrato was known as early as the 16th century. In string playing, it is produced by rocking the finger stopping the string (an earlier technique consisted of rocking one finger while allowing a second to touch the string lightly). Until the 19th century vibrato was considered primarily an ornament, although some authorities (notably Geminiani) advocated its near-constant use. It came into constant use only in the 19th century along with the need for a bigger, richer tone. Similar factors affect vibrato in wind playing (known by 1707) and in singing.

Vicentino, Nicola (*b* Vicenza, 1511; *d* Milan, *c*1576). Italian composer and theorist. He may have been a pupil of Willaert in Venice and later served Ippolitto III, in Ferrara, Rome and Siena. By 1563 he was *maestro di cappella* at Vicenza Cathedral. In 1551 he debated with Lusitano the interpretation of chromatic genera, his own theories forming part of his treatise, *L'antica musica ridotta alla moderna prattica* (1555). He helped to free theory from its adherence to the ecclesiastical modes and experimented with harmony. He contributed towards the development of the 17th-century *seconda prattica* and to the equal temperament of more modern times. His extant works include two volumes of five-voice madrigals, a book of five-voice motets and a handful of works surviving only in MS.

Vickers, Jon (athan Stewart) (*b* Prince Albert, 29 Oct 1926). Canadian tenor. He studied in Toronto, where he made his début as the Duke in *Rigoletto*. He joined the Covent Garden company in 1957, making his début as Riccardo in *Un ballo in maschera*; he went on to Don José, Aeneas (*Les troyens*) and Verdi's Radamès and Don Carlos. He made his Bayreuth début in 1958 as Siegmund, returning as Parsifal in 1964. His Met début was as Canio (*Pagliacci*) in 1960; other notable roles there and in London include Florestan (the role of his La Scala début, 1960), Othello, Peter Grimes, Samson (both Saint-Saëns and Handel) and Tristan. With his ringing tone, fine enunciation and phrasing and passionate involvement in his roles, he is one of the great heroic tenors of his time.

Victimae paschali laudes (Lat.: 'praises to the paschal victim'). The sequence for Easter, one of the four retained by the Council of Trent (1543–63); it was set by Busnois, Josquin, Lassus, Palestrina, Victoria, Byrd and others. The text is ascribed to Wipo (*d c*1048).

Victoria, Tomás Luis de (*b* Avila, 1548; *d* Madrid, 20 Aug 1611). Spanish composer. He was a choirboy at Avila Cathedral; when his voice broke he was sent to the Jesuit Collegio Germanico, Rome (*c*1565), where he may have studied under Palestrina. He was a singer and organist at S Maria di Monserrato (1569–at least 1574) and from 1571 to 1576–7 he taught at the Collegio Germanico (*maestro* from 1575). He became a priest and joined the Oratory of S Filippo Neri. In the 1580s he returned to Spain as chaplain to Philip II's sister the Dowager Empress Maria, at the Descalzas Reales convent, Madrid, from 1587 until her death in 1603; he remained there as organist until his death, apart from a visit to Rome (1592–5), when he attended Palestrina's funeral.

The greatest Spanish Renaissance composer, and among the greatest in Europe in his day, he wrote exclusively Latin sacred music. Most was printed in his lifetime; in 1600 a sumptuous collection of 32 of his most popular masses, Magnificats, psalms and motets appeared in Madrid. Though his output ranged widely through the liturgy, he is chiefly remembered for his masses and motets, which include well-known pieces (*Missa Ave regina caelorum, Missa pro victoria, O magnum mysterium, O quam gloriosum, O vos omnes*). Like Palestrina, he wrote in a serious, devotional style, often responding emotionally to the texts with dramatic word-painting. Some of his more poignant pieces are characterized by a religious, almost mystical fervour.

*Sacred vocal music c*20 masses; Officium defunctorum (1605); 18 Magnificats; music for Holy Week (2 Passions, Lamentations, responsories etc) (1585); *c*50 motets; over 30 hymns; 13 antiphons; 8 psalms; 3 sequences; litany

Victory, Gerard (*b* Dublin, 24 Dec 1921). Irish composer. Educated at Dublin University, he joined Irish radio in 1948 and has written fluently in several genres in various styles; his operas include *Chatterton* (1970).

Vida breve, La. Opera in two acts by Falla to a libretto by Carlos Fernández Shaw (1913, Nice).

Vidal, Paul Antonin (*b* Toulouse, 16 June 1863; *d* Paris, 9 April 1931). French conductor, teacher and composer. A pupil at the Paris Conservatoire and friend of Debussy, he directed performances at the Paris Opéra (from 1894) and at the Opéra-Comique (1914–19) but is particularly remembered as a fine teacher sympathetic to new ideas. Among his most successful compositions were the ballet *La maladetta* (1893) and the light opera *Eros* (1892).

Vidal, Peire (*fl c*1175–1210). Provençal troubadour. A restless wanderer, he served a large number of southern monarchs, and also supported Richard Coeur-de-lion, supposedly accompanying him as far as Cyprus on the third crusade (1193–4). His *c*50

extant poems (of which 12 survive with music) reveal his technical ease and power and an original approach to traditional themes.

Vidu, Ion (*b* Mînerău, 17 Dec 1863; *d* Lugoj, 7 Feb 1931). Romanian composer and choral conductor. Trained at the Iaşi Conservatory (1890–91), he made Lugoj a noted Romanian choral music centre and collected folksongs. His collection of choruses *Severina* (1899) enjoyed enormous success and his later works (all choral) were admired for their intense patriotism.

Vielle (à roue) (Fr.). HURDY-GURDY. For the *vielle organisée, see* LIRA ORGANIZZATA.

Vienna Boys Choir. Austrian choir school, probably established in the 15th century; it is part of the Hofmusikkapelle, Vienna's oldest musical institution. Its four choirs make foreign tours annually, perform with the Vienna Staatsoper and make recordings and broadcasts; their wide repertory includes comic opera and folksong.

Vienna Festival (Austria). Annual (summer) festival established in 1951; it coincides in alternate years with festivals organized by the Gesellschaft der Musikfreunde and Konzerthausgesellschaft. It includes opera, concerts and ballet.

Vienna Philharmonic Orchestra [Wiener Philharmoniker]. Austrian orchestra established in 1842; regular seasons were given from 1860. It performs in the Grosser Musikvereinssaal (opened 1870, cap. *c*1950) and is also the Vienna Staatsoper orchestra. It has been among the world's finest since its foundation, one of its greatest periods being under Hans Richter (1875–98); subsequent conductors have included Mahler, Furtwängler and Abbado. Activities include subscription concerts, performances at Salzburg Festival (from 1925) and foreign visits.

Vienna Staatsoper. The principal Austrian opera company and its theatre. Originally the Hofoper (court opera), its traditions go back to the 17th century. In the 18th, it used the Burgtheater (where several Mozart operas had their premières, 1782–90) and then the Kärntnertortheater (where Beethoven's *Fidelio* was given in 1814 and Weber's *Euryanthe* had its première in 1823). A new house was built in 1869; it was rebuilt in 1955 (cap. *c*2200). One of its greatest periods was under Mahler (1897–1907); another was under R. Strauss and F. Schalk (1919–24), and there were fruitful periods under Krauss (1929–34), Walter (1936–8) and Böhm (1943–5, 1955–6). Karajan (1956–64) introduced more opera in its original language and gave many 20th-century works; more recent conductors have included Maazel and Abbado. The orchestra is the Vienna PO.

Vienna Symphony Orchestra [Wiener Symphoniker]. Austrian orchestra founded in 1900 as the Wiener Concert-Vereinorchester, twice renamed after amalgamations. It is administered by the Gesellschaft der Musikfreunde and other groups, including Austrian radio, and became the Viennese municipal orchestra in 1938. Chief conductors have included Sawallisch, Krips and Giulini.

Vienna Volksoper. *See* VOLKSOPER.

Viennese Classical school. Term for the group of composers who worked in Vienna in the late 18th century and the early 19th. It is usually applied in particular to Haydn, Mozart and Beethoven; but it can be extended to include others active in or around Vienna at the time (e.g. Gluck, Dittersdorf), or to take in Schubert, or even to stand for the music of an entire era, roughly the half-century from 1770.

Vie parisienne, La. Opera in four acts by Offenbach to a libretto by Meilhac and Halévy (1866, Paris).

Vierdanck, Johann (*b c*1605; *d* Stralsund, bur. 1 April 1646). German composer. Trained by Schütz at the Dresden court, he was an instrumentalist there (1630–31) and briefly at Güstrow. From 1635 he was organist of the Marienkirche, Stralsund. His main works are two volumes of sacred concertos (1641, 1643), influenced by Schütz, and two instrumental collections (1637, 1641); the second of the latter includes some of the earliest violin duets without continuo and some concerto-like pieces.

Vier ernste Gesänge. *See* FOUR SERIOUS SONGS.

Vier letzte Lieder. *See* FOUR LAST SONGS.

Vierne, Louis (*b* Poitiers, 8 Oct 1970; *d* Paris, 2 June 1937). French organist and composer. He was a pupil of Franck and Widor, whom he succeeded as organist at St Sulpice and the Conservatoire. In 1900 he moved to Notre Dame, where he died at the organ. His works include six organ symphonies (1899–1930) and chamber and piano music and songs.

Vieru, Anatol (*b* Iaşi, 8 June 1926). Romanian composer. A pupil of Khachaturian at the Moscow Conservatory (1951–4), he began teaching at the Bucharest Conservatory in 1955. His works, in most genres, have combined folk and avant-garde elements; they include *Steps of Silence* for string quartet and percussion (1966).

Vieuxtemps, Henry (*b* Verviers, 17 Feb 1820; *d* Mustapha, 6 June 1881). Belgian violinist and composer. He studied the violin with Bériot and composition with Sechter and Reicha, from 1834 receiving praise throughout Europe for his virtuosity and compositional skill. He was particularly successful in Russia (1846–51) and America but spent his last years teaching at the Brussels Conservatory, where Ysaÿe was among his pupils. Apart from brilliant short violin pieces he wrote seven concertos; by setting an enriched (but not Paganinian) solo part in a modern symphonic framework he rejuvenated the grand French violin concerto, at the same time introducing original form, especially no.4 in D minor (*c*1850), praised lavishly by Berlioz. Of his two brothers, Lucien (1828–1901) was a respected piano teacher in Brussels and Ernest (1832–96) a solo cellist in London and Manchester.

Viganò, Salvatore (*b* Naples, 25 March 1769; *d* Milan, 10 Aug 1821). Italian choreographer, dancer and composer. His father Onorato (1739–1811) was one of the best-known choreographers in Italy and a dancer and impresario, active mainly in Venice and Rome. Salvatore studied composition with Boccherini (his uncle) and wrote music for some of his father's and his own ballets besides appearing as a dancer. An inspired but controversial choreographer, he spent several years in Vienna where he choreographed Beethoven's *Creatures of Prometheus*; from 1811 he worked at La Scala, Milan, where he produced an important series of dramatic ballets. Many other members of the Viganò family were dancers and musicians.

Vihuela. A plucked string instrument of the viol family which flourished in Spain in the 15th and 16th centuries. Originally the word was applied to all string instruments and distinguished according to the method of performance: *vihuela de pendola* (with a plectrum), *vihuela de arco* (with a bow) and *vihuela de mano* (with the hand). By the 16th century the term 'vihuela' usually referred to the *vihuela de mano* (or *vihuela comun*). It was played like a guitar, which it resembled although larger, and had six or seven courses (each paired in unison), generally tuned as in a lute. The first printed music is in a teaching manual by Luis de Milán (1536); the instrument reached the height of its development at Charles V's court, where it had a prominent role in secular and private music-making. In the 17th century it was superseded by the guitar.

Village Romeo and Juliet, A [Romeo und Julia auf dem Dorfe]. Opera in a prologue and three acts by Delius to a libretto by C.F. Keary after Gottfried Keller (1907, Berlin). Delius added the orchestral intermezzo *The Walk to the Paradise Garden* (1910).

Villa-Lobos, Heitor (*b* Rio de Janeiro, 5 March 1887; *d* there, 17 Nov 1959). Brazilian composer. His father taught him to play the cello and in his teens he performed with popular musicians in the city. He then travelled widely, returning to Rio in his mid-20s for a few formal lessons. From 1923 to 1930 he was in Paris, where he wrote several works in his *Chôros* series, giving Brazilian impressions a luxuriant scoring: Messiaen and others were impressed. He returned to Brazil, where he did valuable work in reforming musical education. In 1945 he founded the Brazilian Academy of Music in Rio de Janeiro. Also during this period he produced the cycle of nine *Bachianas brasileiras* for diverse combinations (1930–45), marrying the spirit of Brazilian folk music with that of Bach; the two for eight cellos (one with soprano) have been especially successful. His gigantic output includes operas, 12 symphonies (1916–57), 17 string quartets (1915–57), numerous songs and much piano music.

Villancico. Spanish musical and poetic form consisting of several stanzas (*coplas*) linked by a refrain (*estribillo*). Originally derived from a medieval dance lyric and associated with rustic or popular themes, it was cultivated in the late 15th and 16th centuries. More than 300 appear in the famous Cancionero Musical de Palacio (*c*1490–1520), in three or four parts, with a melody in the top voice and a simple contrapuntal style. In the 16th century all voices shared in text and melody through imitation, as in the Italian madrigal; religious themes gained in importance and the genre entered the liturgy.

In the 17th century the religious villancico became more popular while the secular form was largely displaced by the ROMANCE. From 1700 the villancico was affected by the Italian cantata style, and the dramatic effects became increasingly theatrical. Villancicos with vernacular texts were prohibited in the churches in 1765 but remained popular in both Spain and Latin America into the 19th century. Since then 'villancico' has meant simply 'Christmas carol'.

Villanella [villanesca]. A light vocal form, popular in Italy and elsewhere from the 1530s to the early 17th century. It first appeared in Naples, apparently developing from the late frottola. Features are a simple, largely homophonic texture with the tune (sometimes borrowed) usually in the top voice and regular, declamatory rhythms with some syncopation. Different types are distinguished by their social function or their texts; they include the VILLOTTA, the MASCHERATA, the GIUSTINIANA, the GREGHESCA and the MORESCA.

The beginning of the villanella is marked by an edition of anonymous *Canzone villanesche alla napolitana* (1537), followed by similar volumes; the songs are for three voices, mainly homophonic with frequent consecutive 5ths. The form spread from Naples, especially to Venice, where it was taken up by Willaert and others as a more sophisticated, strophic song. Lassus's villanellas (1555, 1581), some of them parodistic, retain the simple homophony and lively rhythms of the early Neapolitan type and are among the most attractive light pieces of the century. In the 1570s the madrigal's influence was felt in words and music. The villanella, however, retained its strophic form, so word-painting is rare. It appeared in 'madrigal comedies', where its role of caricature contrasts with the serious pieces.

Villanelle (Fr.). Rustic song: a 16th-century term for pastoral verses, of which examples were set by Arcadelt, Certon and others. The term was also used for instrumental and vocal pieces by Telemann, Berlioz, Chabrier and Dukas.

Villano. A sung dance popular in Spain and Italy in the 16th and 17th centuries. The music is built on the recurring harmonic pattern I–IV–I–V–I, with various discant melodies.

Villar, Rogelio del (*b* León, 13 Nov 1875; *d* Madrid, 4 Nov 1937). Spanish composer and musicologist. From 1919 to 1936 he taught at the Madrid Conservatory. He used Leónese folk music in his three string quartets and songs, whose lyricism earned him the title 'the Spanish Grieg'. His many writings show him a conservative nationalist.

Villi, Le. Opera in one act by Puccini to a libretto by F. Fontana (1884, Milan); Puccini made a two-act version (1884, Turin).

Villiers, P(?ierre) de (*fl* 1532–*c*1550). French composer. He may have lived at Lyons in the late 1530s and been a music teacher at the Collège de la Trinité there. His interest in counterpoint is demonstrated by *Elle est m'amye*, a canonic *chanson*, and his single mass setting. His five motets are pervasively imitative and his numerous courtly *chansons* are more akin to the Flemish style than to the homophonic Parisian *chanson*.

Villoteau, Guillaume André (*b* Bellême, 6 Sept 1759; *d* Tours, 27 April 1839). French writer on music. After an expedition to Egypt (1798–1800) he wrote several works on music in Middle Eastern countries, collectively published (1846). He is also known for his (conservative) theories on the relationship between music and language, found in *Recherches sur l'analogie . . . langage* (1807).

Villotta. A type of Italian popular music, closely related to the VILLANELLA, which flourished *c*1520–*c*1545. It differs from the villanella in its folk origin and in its avoidance of parody. The villotta has four 11-syllable lines and a nonsense refrain; it was normally for four voices, sometimes using folktunes. After 1545 such villottas disappeared, but the term persisted for north Italian variants of the villanella.

Vīṇā. Term for many different forms of string instruments in south Asia. The name has been used for nearly 3000 years and referred variously to varieties of lute, to the musical bow, to early harps, to medieval zithers and to bowed instruments. The modern word denotes several plucked lutes used in Indian classical music, including the Hindustani *bīṇ* and especially the Sarasvatī *vīṇā*, the large, long-necked lute with four main strings and three side strings, the principal instrument of south Indian classical music.

Vinaccesi, Benedetto (*b* Brescia, ?1670; *d* Venice, ?1719). Italian composer. He served first near Mantua, then in Brescia. From 1704 he was second organist of St Mark's, Venice; he was perhaps also *maestro di cappella* of the Poveri Derelitti orphanage. He composed several successful stage works and oratorios, many motets for two and three voices, and two sets of trio sonatas: the earlier set, of 1687, is notable for its inclusion of minuets.

Vinay, Ramón (*b* Chillán, 31 Aug 1912). Chilean baritone, later tenor, of French-Italian descent. He studied in Mexico City, making his début as Alphonse in *La favorite* (1931), going on to Verdi and Puccini; his tenor début in Mexico City was 1943 as Don José. He sang at the Met from 1946, his roles including Tristan (also at Bayreuth), Samson and Othello, which he sang under Toscanini and at La Scala (1947), Covent Garden (1955) and Paris (1958). In 1962 he resumed baritone roles. He was noted for his full tone, intelligence and musicianship.

Vincenet, Johannes (*b c*1400; *d c*1479). French composer. He was apparently contemporary with Dufay and possibly sang in the papal chapel in the 1420s. He was in Naples by *c*1466; his four secular works (including a Spanish villancico) are in a book copied there in the 1470s. Four masses, based on pre-existing material and including an early parody mass (his Mass *O gloriosa regina* is based on all three voices of Touront's motet), are attributed to him.

Vincenti, Giacomo (*d* Venice, 1619). Italian bookseller and music printer. He first printed in partnership (1583–6) with Amadino. From 1586 his own production included music of most of the principal north Italian composers of the day, including Marenzio and Banchieri; he printed Artusi's attacks on Monteverdi (1600, 1603, 1608) and reprinted Caccini's *L'Euridice* and *Le nuove musiche* (1615). His son Alessandro (*fl* 1619–67) was particularly active, issuing among other important works the first editions of Monteverdi's eight and ninth books of madrigals (1638, 1651) and Frescobaldi's *Canzoni* and *Fiori musicali* (1635) as well as theory books. The firm's surviving trade lists are of special historical interest.

Vincentius, Caspar (*b* St Omer, *c*1580; *d* Würzburg, 1624). Flemish composer. He was civic organist of Speyer in *c*1602–1615, and after a period in Worms became organist of Würzburg Cathedral in 1618. He edited the first three volumes (1611–13) of the motet collection *Promptuarium musicum* with Abraham Schadaeus and compiled the fourth (1617) himself; the motets include 25 of his own, which are mainly conservative in style.

Vinci, Leonardo (*b* Strongoli, *c*1690; *d* Naples, 27/8 May 1730). Italian composer. In 1725 he became *provicemaestro* of the royal chapel in Naples. He was also *maestro di cappella* at the conservatory Poveri di Gesù Cristo (where he had studied); Pergolesi was one of his pupils.

Vinci composed mostly dramatic works. Among the earliest were 11 *commedie musicali* in Neapolitan dialect (1719–24). In 1722 he began a successful series of over 20 *opere serie*, most for Naples, Rome or Venice. The last, *Artaserse* (1730, Rome), was especially popular. These operas were the first to break clearly with the Baroque style of A. Scarlatti's era and had a strong influence. They are notable for their simple, graceful melodies, thematic contrasts and other pre-Classical features. Vinci's other works include a serenata, an oratorio, chamber cantatas and a few instrumental pieces.

Vinci, Pietro (*b* Nicosia, *c*1535; *d* there or Piazza Armerina, *c*15 June 1584). Italian composer. From *c*1560 he taught in Naples. He was *maestro di cappella* of S Maria Maggiore, Bergamo (1568–80), and had close connections with Milan. He returned to Sicily in 1581, possibly to become *maestro di cappella* of Nicosia Cathedral. The founder of the Sicilian polyphonic school and a prolific composer, he was highly rated in his day; Antonio Il Verso was among his pupils. He wrote over 250 madrigals (10 bks extant, 1561–84), generally in a reserved expressive style and reminiscent of Rore, showing great polyphonic mastery. He also published masses (1575, 1581), motets (8 bks, 1558–91) and instrumental works (1560).

Viñes, Ricardo (*b* Lerida, 5 Feb 1875; *d* Barcelona, 29 April 1943). Spanish (Catalan) pianist. He studied in Barcelona and moved to Paris in 1887, becoming associated with contemporary music and giving premières of works by Ravel and Debussy and the French premières of Spanish and Russian music. His most famous pupil was Poulenc.

Vingt regards sur l'enfant Jésus. Piano work by Messiaen (1944), 20 pieces each with a title.

Viol. A bowed string instrument with frets, usually held vertically on the lap when played or, in larger sizes, between the legs (hence the name 'viola da gamba', literally 'leg-viol'). It appeared in Europe (probably first in Spain, from North Africa), in the late 15th century and subsequently became one of the most popular Renaissance and Baroque instruments, much used in ensemble music. During its

history the viol was made in many different sizes: *pardessus* (high treble), treble, alto, small tenor, tenor, bass and violone (contrabass). Only the treble, tenor and bass viols were regular members of the consort. (For illustration, *see* EARLY MUSIC.)

In spite of much early variability a standard shape for the viol emerged in the 16th century. The instrument has broad ribs, sloping shoulders and a flat fretted neck. Most viols have six strings (though the French Baroque solo bass viol had seven strings and the *pardessus* five); the three principal tunings are: *d*–*g*–*c'*–*e'*–*a'*–*d''* (treble), *G*–*c*–*f*–*a*–*d'*–*g'* (tenor) and (*A'*–)*D*–*G*–*c*–*e*–*a*–*d'* (bass). The bow, usually slightly convex, is held in an underhand grip and the player's fingers govern the tension of the horse-hair.

The viol seems to have had its origins in attempts to fuse the principles of the bowed rebec to large plucked instruments such as the vihuela in Spain in the second half of the 15th century. Its early history is difficult to establish because of the generic use of the word 'viol' for any bowed instrument. It seems, however, that sets or 'consorts' of vertically held viols were found at courts as well as in homes from the early 16th century. The earliest printed collections of music for viol consort are the two editions of Gerle's *Musica teusch* (1532, 1546), containing transcriptions of German and French vocal music. By *c*1540 Henry VIII had engaged a complete consort of Italian players. This royal patronage may have inspired an English school of performance and composition which, fuelled by remarkable composers such as Byrd, Jenkins, William Lawes and finally Purcell, continued to thrive long after the viol had been superseded by the violin on the Continent. The French school of viol playing did not share the English penchant for consort music, preferring to explore the bass viol as a solo virtuoso instrument. 'Pièces de viole' (for viol and continuo), duets for two viols, and trio sonatas for violin, viol and continuo were written by composers such as François Couperin, Boismortier and the renowned bass viol virtuoso Marin Marais. In Germany the viol was much used in solo and chamber music, in Vienna and also in the north (including the Low Countries); it was used by Schütz in his sacred music, by Buxtehude in his cantatas and in sonatas and trio sonatas with violin by the viol virtuoso Johann Schenck. J.S. Bach wrote three sonatas with harpsichord and often used the viol as an obbligato instrument in sacred works. In the next generation, it was much used by Telemann and C.P.E. Bach in chamber music; the last great German viol player was C.F. Abel, whose main career was in England. The 20th century has seen a resurgence of interest in the viol for the authentic performance of early music.

Viola. Bowed four-string instrument, an alto version of the violin, which it closely resembles (for illustration, *see* VIOLIN). The strings are tuned *c*–*g*–*d'*–*a'*, a 5th lower than the violin's; the tone, though less assertive than the violin's, is more than its equal in richness and warmth. Although the viola was firmly established as a member of the new violin family as early as 1535 it was not called 'viola' since the term had a variety of applications referring either to specific instruments or generically to any string instrument, plucked or bowed. By the 18th century the viola was normally designated by the term *viola di brazzo* (from *viola da braccio*, an early form of violin, and the source of the word *Bratsche* by which the viola is known in modern Germany). From the 17th century the viola was the vital middle instrument in string ensembles; there were often two or three, fulfilling both alto and tenor roles and built in sizes to match. In French five-part string groups the three middle parts were played on violas.

The 18th century saw a standardization of string ensembles both in orchestras and in chamber music groups, in which the violas were fewer in number and more specific in their role than the violins. Mozart, in his use of the instrument in chamber music – his string quartets and two-viola quintets – and in his Sinfonia Concertante for violin and viola, did much to develop its potential. The 19th century saw considerable exploration of the viola's possibilities in orchestral music, particularly by Berlioz, whose *Harold in Italy* is a thinly disguised viola concerto, Tchaikovsky, Brahms and Wagner. In the 20th, concertos have been written for it by Hindemith, Bartók and Walton among others.

Viola bastarda. An Italian 16th- and early 17th-century term for a small bass viol, the continental equivalent of the English DIVISION VIOL.

Viola da braccio. Generic term of the 16th and 17th centuries for any bowed string instrument played on the arm, normally a member of the violin family; later it came to apply mainly to the viola.

Viola da gamba. Italian term for the VIOL (literally 'leg-viol'), to distinguish it from the 'arm-viol', the *viola da braccio*.

Viola d'amore. A kind of viola popular during the late 17th and 18th centuries. It is the size of a viola but with many of a viol's characteristics, including a flat back, sloping shoulders and a carved head. There are usually 14 strings, seven bowed (normal tuning *A–d–a–d'–f♯'–a'–d''*) and the rest sympathetic, tuned to the same notes. Its sound is particularly soft and sweet and it has been used, especially in music of highly emotional content, by many composers, notably by J.S. Bach, in cantatas and the *St John Passion*, Telemann in his 1716 Passion *Der sterbende Jesus*, Charpentier in *Louise* and Janáček, who used it as a motto instrument for the eponymous heroine in *Katya Kabanova* (1921).

Viola di bordone (It.). BARYTON.

Viola di fagotto (It.). A bowed string instrument with the tuning and range of a cello, but played on the arm like a viola. Some of its strings were overspun with copper wire in such a way that it produced a buzzing sound, like a bassoon (*fagotto*).

Viola pomposa (It.). A bowed string instrument with five strings, played on the arm; the tuning was *c* (or *d*)–*g–d'–a'–e''*. It was used between 1725 and 1770.

Violetta (It.). Term of the 17th and 18th centuries for the viola; earlier it sometimes meant a small, three-string instrument, probably a violin. The *violetta marina* had sympathetic strings; Handel used it in *Orlando* (1733).

Violin. The soprano member of the family of string instruments that includes the viola and the cello; one of the most versatile and durable instruments in the history of music. Its capacity for sustained tone is remarkable and scarcely another instrument can match its range of expression and intensity. It can play all the chromatic semitones (and even microtones) over a four-octave range, and is capable of playing chords. This versatility is reflected in its repertory; it has been used as a soloist, accompanied and unaccompanied, and has been essential to all chamber and orchestral music for over three centuries.

In spite of its apparent simplicity, the modern violin is composed of over 70 separate parts. The body is a hollow box consisting of arched top and back plates joined by 'ribs' over which they protrude. The top plate (or 'belly') contains two f-holes and is surmounted by a tailpiece that anchors the strings, and an unfretted fingerboard which extends beneath them along the neck to the pegbox; this is crowned by an ornamental scroll by which the violin was originally suspended. The strings themselves run from the tailpiece over a carefully fitted bridge of maple, and are carried over the fingerboard to an ebony (or ivory) nut and secured to the pegs, which regulate their tension and bring them to their proper pitches, *g–d'–a'–e''*. These strings were originally made of gut; modern violinists prefer gut strings wound with metal wire, although the thinner E-string is often made of steel. When a bow sets the strings in motion the vibrations are transmitted to the belly and the back via the bridge and an internal soundpost, thus amplifying the sound; the f-holes form a secondary acoustical system and add considerably to the total resonance.

Although it was preceded by a three-string model, the four-string violin was already familiar as early as 1550. The instrument was an amalgam of the rebec, the Renaissance fiddle and the *lira da braccio* (a developed form of fiddle). It had two main functions, the doubling of vocal music and playing for dancing. Both these uses placed the violin lower down the social scale than the viol, and neither required printed music; the former was played from the vocal part, the latter from memory. By the 17th century, composers were making more demands on the instrument, particularly in opera, sonatas and concertos. The Italian school of makers, which had begun in the mid-16th century with Andrea Amati in Cremona and Gasparo da Salò in Brescia, kept abreast of these demands by dint of constant emendation and improvement. Violin making enjoyed its most illustrious century from 1650 to 1750 with the work of the Austrian Jacob Stainer, the Cremonese Nicolo Amati and his pupils Giuseppe Guarneri and Antonio Stradivari. The work of the last two is characterized by much flatter shape and was more suitable for the modernization necessary to ensure the power required for the larger concert halls and orchestras of the 19th century. A bow with the weight, length and power for such an instrument was developed in Paris in the late 18th century by François Tourte.

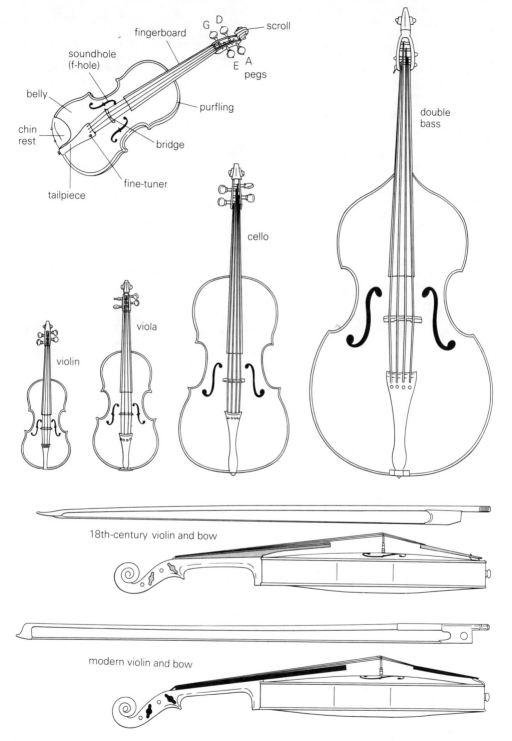

fingerboard

G D

scroll

soundhole
(f-hole)

E A
pegs

belly

purfling

double
bass

chin
rest

bridge

fine-tuner

tailpiece

cello

viola

violin

18th-century violin and bow

modern violin and bow

The violin family

In spite of minor changes, such as the invention of the chin rest (by Spohr, c1820), the violin's form and technique were standardized by 1800. This is reflected in the fact that most modern virtuosos play an old Italian violin with a Tourte-type bow. The instrument is normally modernized, however, with internal reinforcement, a higher bridge and the neck more sharply angled to the body to allow for higher string tension; there is also a longer fingerboard to permit playing at higher pitch. For playing Baroque and Classical music, players now often prefer to use an instrument in original condition, with a pre-Tourte bow, so as to approximate more closely to the tone and articulation of the instrument for which composers wrote.

There has been no significant development of the violin since the 18th century in spite of attempts to improve body shape, the materials from which the instrument is made and its acoustical structure. Violins have been mass produced for educational use for nearly two centuries, not only in the traditional centres such as Mirecourt in France and Mittenwald in Germany, but also in the USA and particularly Japan.

The normal tone of the violin is obtained by passing the bow smoothly over the strings, agitating them and causing them to send vibrations through the bridge to the belly and, through the soundpost, to the back. A great variety of bowstrokes is available, to enable the player to produce notes of many degrees of smoothness or detachment. Other special effects are possible, such as pizzicato (plucking the strings), tremolo (agitating the bow very rapidly back and forth across the strings), col legno (using the wooden back of the bow to produce a clattering effect), sul ponticello (playing close to the bridge, producing a glassy tone) and sul tasto (playing close to the fingerboard and producing a bland tone). By angling the bow so that it plays two strings, two-note chords can be obtained; on impact, across the strings, chords of three and even four notes may be obtained but they cannot be held because of the angle at which the strings lie. The player can move his left hand up the neck to different 'positions', making a different selection of notes available as the music demands. Most modern players use vibrato on all but the quickest notes. Harmonics can be produced by lightly touching a string rather than pressing it firmly to the fingerboard; these are gentle, flute-like sounds. The first few natural harmonics of each open string are easily obtained, and 'artificial harmonics' – when the player stops the string and touches at a point equivalent to a note a 4th higher than the one he is stopping – can be produced, two octaves higher than the stopped note.

The violin has an enormous repertory, from sonatas (for one or two instruments) with continuo accompaniment in the Baroque period to the sonata with piano from the late 18th century onwards, and the entire repertory of chamber music, where the violin plays the leading role in such genres as the piano trio and the string quartet. There is a large concerto repertory, from the Baroque period (represented by Bach, Vivaldi and Tartini), through the Classical (Mozart, Viotti, Beethoven, Spohr) to the Romantic (Mendelssohn, Brahms, Bruch, Tchaikovsky, as well as a host of lighter pieces by such composers as Lalo and Saint-Saëns) and the 20th century (concertos by Bartók, Berg, Stravinsky and Schoenberg). Virtuoso composers (e.g. Paganini and Wieniawski) wrote works designed to exhibit a high level of technical brilliance.

Violino piccolo. A small violin of the 17th and 18th centuries; its strings are tuned a 4th higher than the ordinary violin.

Violoncello. The bass instrument of the violin family, often abbreviated 'cello' (for illustration, *see* VIOLIN). It originated in the early 16th century as a member of the family called 'viole da braccio'. The earliest source (1529) refers to a bass violin with three strings, tuned $F–c–g$. Later instruments added a fourth tuned to Bb thus completing the sequence of 5ths taken from the tuning of the violin. This tuning remained in use into the late 17th century but was found not to be ideal for ensemble playing and the present-day tuning ($C–G–d–a$, an octave below the viola's) was adopted.

The instrument's size fluctuated considerably during the 16th and 17th centuries; most models were considerably larger than the modern standard size, fixed by Stradivari c1710. Further experiments in the 18th century led to the invention of the 'violoncello piccolo' (a small instrument used by Bach in his Leipzig cantatas) and a five-string violoncello (for which Bach wrote a suite). The violoncello was played held between the knees until the use of the endpin or spike, known in the late 18th century but not universally used until the late 19th, brought increased security and resonance.

During the 18th century, the cello outgrew its Baroque role as primarily a continuo instrument, with the rise of a number of virtuoso players; of these, the most distinguished was Boccherini, who wrote cello sonatas and concertos as well as a great quantity of chamber music involving high and demanding cello parts. Haydn wrote concertos for the cello, of which two survive, Beethoven a triple concerto with violin and piano. He also wrote the earliest important cello sonatas, a lead followed by Mendelssohn, Chopin and Brahms among Romantic composers. Unaccompanied cello music was written by Bach, in his six suites; this medium did not find further favour until the 20th century, with Reger and Kodály. The Romantic repertory of cello concertos consists of three important works, by Schumann, Dvořák and Elgar; more recent composers to have produced works for cello and orchestra include Prokofiev, Shostakovich and Britten.

Violoncello piccolo (It.). 'Little violoncello': a small cello used in the early 18th century, called for in several of Bach's cantatas.

Violone. In modern terminology, the double bass viol, the direct ancestor of the double bass. Historically, however, the word is notoriously imprecise, embracing a variety of meanings: any viol, a large viol (particularly a low-pitched viola da gamba) and even (in some Italian sources) a bass violin or a violoncello.

Violons du Roi (Fr.). 'Violins of the king': title of the royal string band (violins; 1st, 2nd and 3rd violas; and bass violins) of Louis XIV. The '24 Violons du Roi' played for ballets, ceremonies and large-scale events, the 'Petits Violons', 21 players in 1702, for smaller ones and private entertainment. Under Lully they attained new standards of ensemble discipline and represented a landmark in the development of the orchestra.

Viotti, Giovanni Battista (*b* Fontanetto da Po, 12 May 1755; *d* London, 3 March 1824). Italian violinist and composer. A pupil of Pugnani, he served at the Turin court, 1775–80, then went on a concert tour (initially with Pugnani). After great success in Paris (1782–3) he served at Versailles. In 1788 he founded a new opera house, the Théâtre de Monsieur (from 1791, Théâtre Feydeau). Moving to London, he turned again to performance and was orchestral leader and director at the King's Theatre, 1797–8. He returned to London after several years' exile, but seldom played in public. In 1819–21 he was director of the Paris Opéra.

Viotti was the most influential violinist of his time and the last great representative of the Italian tradition deriving from Corelli, with whom Pugnani's teacher G.B. Somis studied. He is considered the founder of the 'modern' (19th-century) French violin school; the power and full tone of his playing affected Kreutzer, Rode (one of his pupils) and many others. Foremost in his output are his 29 violin concertos, which balance virtuosity and drama with lyricism and expression and show a development from the *galant* style towards Romanticism; the last ten (*c*1792–*c*1805) are the most imaginative in form and texture. Composers influenced by them include Beethoven and Spohr. Viotti also wrote string quartets and trios, violin duos and sonatas, and a few piano pieces and arias.

Virchi, Paolo (*b* Brescia, *c*1550; *d* Mantua, May 1610). Italian composer. He was an organist in Brescia by 1574, then served the courts of Ferrara (*c*1580–98) and Mantua. He is known for his cittern book (1574), containing ricercares and arrangements, and for his madrigals (3 bks, 1584–91).

Virdung, Sebastian (*b* Amberg, 19/20 Jan *c*1465; *d*?). German theorist and composer. He studied at Heidelberg University and held various court and cathedral posts in Heidelberg, Stuttgart, Konstanz and Basle. He is best known for his treatise *Musica getutscht* (Basle, 1511), the oldest printed manual on musical instruments; in the form of a dialogue, it attempts a classification of instruments and discusses notation. It was highly regarded in its day. He composed a hymn and four four-voice songs.

Virelai. One of the three fixed forms (with the ballade and the rondeau) that dominated French song and poetry in the 14th and 15th centuries. Its musical structure is *ABBA* (disregarding subtleties of rhyme and metre in the text). It may be descended from 11th-century Arabic song-types; or its source (and that of courtly song in general) may be the musico–literary patterns of the liturgy. 'Virelai' comes from Old French *virer* ('to turn', 'to twist'), confirming its dance origins, at least in France. The distinction between the early virelai and the ballade lies in the refrain, which in the virelai is normally several lines long and occupies the entire first musical section, whereas in the ballade the refrain is commonly only one line and appears at the close of the second. By the 14th century it was established with the following features: a refrain several lines long (*A*); two sets of matching text (*BB*); repetition of the refrain (*A*). In the 14th century metrical patterns became more complex. The virelai's principal topic is courtly love; the 'realistic virelai' often portrayed love with imagery from the hunt or the battle, which encouraged musical painting. The virelai was cultivated less than the ballade and rondeau; Machaut set 33 virelais, only eight of them polyphonically.

Virginal. A small type of harpsichord, with one set of strings and jacks and one keyboard. The term was used in England until well into the 17th century to denote any quilled keyboard instrument. There is however an accepted specific definition: a virginal is an instrument whose strings run parallel to the keyboard, as opposed to diagonally (as in the spinet) or directly away from the player (as in the harpsichord). The term was first used *c*1460 in a treatise describing it as 'having the shape of a clavichord and metal strings making the sound of a harpsichord'. This rectangular form was the earliest of many. Italian virginals showed a particularly wide variety of harp-shaped or polygonal designs with the keyboard protruding from the main body of the instrument. Flemish models had a keyboard built into the instrument, either centred in one of the long sides or to the left (in which case the virginal was termed a 'spinett') or to the right (called a 'MUSELAR'). English virginals followed the Flemish design. The double virginal, in which two keyboards are superimposed and played separately or coupled, is also a Flemish development. (For illustration, *see* KEYBOARD INSTRUMENTS.)

Virtuoso. A musician of exceptional technical skill. Its early Italian application to music could imply a skilful theorist or composer as well as a performer. The term was used widely by Italian musicians of all kinds in northern Europe. In the late 18th century it came to mean a musician who pursued a solo career but in the 19th it was increasingly applied to performers of outstanding brilliance, notably Liszt and Paganini. Suspicion of technical skill, as opposed to other kinds of musical gift, have sometimes led to the term's being used pejoratively.

Visée, Robert de (*b* late 17th century; *d* early 18th century). French guitarist and composer. He was a guitarist at the French court from *c*1680, playing at the bedside of Louis XIV and in chamber music and later teaching the king. He was also a theorbo and viol player and a singer. With Francesco Corbetta he was the foremost guitar composer of the French Baroque. He wrote two collections of suites and other pieces for five-course guitar (1682, 1686), which fully exploit the instrument, and a book of lute and theorbo music (1716).

Vïshnegradsky, Ivan Alexandrovich (*b* St Petersburg, 14 May 1893; *d* Paris, 29 Sept 1979). Russian composer. A pupil of Sokolov and disciple of Skryabin, he moved to Paris after the Revolution and produced much quarter-tone music; from 1936 he used two differently tuned instruments for ultra-chromatic compositions. He also created projects for his music to be accompanied by coloured lighting.

Vishnevskaya, Galina (Pavlovna) (*b* Leningrad, 25 Oct 1926). Russian soprano. She made her début in operetta (1944) and in 1952 joined the Bol'shoy; her repertory included Tchaikovsky's Tatyana and Lisa and roles in operas by Shebalin and Prokofiev. Her polished technique and strong dramatic talent were admired in her Met (1961) and Covent Garden (1962) débuts, both as Aida. She has been associated with the music of Britten and Shostakovich, giving several first performances, and is often heard with Rostropovich, whom she married in 1955.

Vision of St Augustine, The. Choral work by Tippett to texts from St Augustine's *Confessions* and the Bible (1965).

Visions de l'amen. Suite for two pianos by Messiaen (1943).

Visions fugitives [Mimoletnosti]. Prokofiev's op.22, 20 pieces for piano (1917).

Visitatio sepulchri (Lat.). Name for the largest single category of medieval Latin church plays ('Visit to the sepulchre'); it is based on the dialogue *Quem queritis* but is distinguished from it by its placing at the end of Easter Matins, after the third responsory, by its numerous accretions of chants and laments, and by dramatic amplification as an acted representation of the Resurrection story with impersonation and (sometimes) costuming. There are three types: (1) a dialogue between the Marys and the angel in which the sequence *Victimae paschali* is added; (2) in which the apostles Peter and John appear; and (3) in which Christ also appears.

Visit of the Old Lady, The. *See* BESUCH DER ALTEN DAME, DER.

Vitali, Filippo (*b* Florence, *c*1590; *d* ?Florence, after 1 April 1653). Italian composer. He served as a priest in Rome (from 1631) and became a singer in the papal choir in 1633; he was *maestro di cappella* in Florence (1624) and Bergamo (1648–9). His main work is a cycle of 34 hymns for the church year (1636), in the late Renaissance polyphonic style. He also used the modern style, in sacred pieces, solo and ensemble secular songs and three stage works – of which *Aretusa* (1620), influenced by Peri and Caccini, was the first opera staged in Rome.

Vitali, Giovanni Battista (*b* Bologna, 18 Feb 1632; *d* there, 12 Oct 1692). Italian composer. A pupil of Cazzati, he became a singer and a player of the violincino (an early form of cello) at S Petronio, Bologna, in 1658, and *maestro di cappella* of S Rosario in 1673. In 1674 he went to the Este court in Modena as a *vice-maestro di cappella*, serving briefly (1684–6) as full *maestro*.

Vitali was an influential composer of instrumental music, publishing 12 sets in all, and was important for his work in establishing the Baroque ensemble sonata, especially the trio sonata. In both the *sonata da chiesa* and the *sonata da camera* he created a more unified style and used counterpoint more consis-

tently than earlier composers. He was among the first to include the French bourrée and minuet in the *sonata da camera*. His instrumental works also include *Artificii musicali* (1689), a pedagogical collection of contrapuntal pieces. Besides these he wrote a number of oratorios, cantatas etc.

Several other members of Vitali's family were musicians at the Este court. The most distinguished was the composer and violinist Tomaso Antonio Vitali (1663–1745), who became leader of the orchestra. He wrote trio sonatas and other instrumental music. The chaconne long attributed to him is probably not authentic.

Vitásek, Jan (Matyáš Nepomuk) August (*b* Hořín, 22 Feb 1770; *d* Prague, 7 Dec 1839). Bohemian composer. He studied with Dušek and Kozeluch in Prague and came to know Mozart, of whose music he was a renowned interpreter. He became choirmaster of St Vitus's Cathedral (1814–39) and composed much church music. His piano pieces show Dušek's influence but his songs are original: among the first 19th-century settings of Czech texts, they paved the way for the nationalistic revival.

Vite, vitement (Fr.). Fast, quickly.

Vītols, Jāzeps (*b* Valmiera, 26 July 1863; *d* Lübeck, 24 April 1948). Latvian composer. He was a pupil of Rimsky-Korsakov at the St Petersburg Conservatory, where he returned to teach (1901–18); Prokofiev was among his pupils. He moved to Riga and dominated the musical life of independent Latvia, conducting the Opera from 1918 and founding the Latvian Conservatory (1919). He composed the first Latvian symphony (1888), string quartet (1899) and piano sonata (1885) and wrote songs and choruses.

Vitry, Philippe de (*b* Paris, 31 Oct 1291; *d* there, 9 June 1361). French theorist, poet and composer. He studied at the Sorbonne and held numerous prebends, but his main sphere of activity was the French court, where he was secretary and adviser to Charles IV, Philippe VI and Jean II, and known as a leading intellectual. He undertook many diplomatic missions, some to the papal court in Avignon. In 1351 he became Bishop of Meaux. In his capacity as a musician, for which he received many tributes, he wrote a famous and authoritative treatise, *Ars nova* (*c*1322–3), and composed motets and other music. The most original part of *Ars nova* is the last ten chapters, on mensural rhythm and notation. Vitry presented normative formulations of new concepts of rhythm and notation; the two main features are the minim (half-note, for which he established the notational symbol) and imperfect mensuration (the division of note-values into twos as well as threes at every level). Much of his creative and literary output is lost, but he probably wrote the fine poetic texts of his surviving motets. The earliest of them were inserted into the ROMAN DE FAUVEL, where some of the monophonic contributions may also be Vitry's. His original approach established a hierarchic concept of the voices, in which the sustained tenor had a clearly defined structural foundation. He combined a slow-moving, patterned tenor with a superstructure of two faster moving voices, allowing increased melodic and contrapuntal flexibility. Each composition is an entity with a specific structural and poetic indivduality. Of the 12 motets that can be ascribed to Vitry, none has a *chanson* tenor, and only one has French texts. His structural use of isorhythm in the expanded motet clearly influenced Machaut.

Vittadini, Franco (*b* Pavia, 9 April 1884; *d* there, 30 Nov 1948). Italian composer. He studied at the Milan Conservatory and spent most of his life in Pavia, teaching and composing operas and church music. He had international success with the picturesque, atmospheric opera *Anima allegra* (1921).

Vitzthumb, Ignaz (*b* Baden, nr. Vienna, 20 July 1720; *d* Brussels, 23 March 1816). South Netherlands composer. He was first violinist and tenor in Brussels, and directed military bands. He worked at the Brussels Grand Theatre from 1769, and was joint director from 1772, winning fame for his productions; after working in Ghent, 1779–81, he returned to the theatre in 1785. He was *maître de musique* of the royal chapel, 1786–91. His output includes stage and sacred works, symphonies and wind-band music.

Vivace (It.). Vivacious, flourishing, full of life; in music up to *c*1750–1800 it often indicates only a moderate tempo.

Vivaldi, Antonio (Lucio) (*b* Venice, 4 March 1678; *d* Vienna, 28 July 1741). Italian composer. He was the son of a professional violinist who played at St Mark's and may have been involved in operatic management. Vivaldi was trained for the priesthood and ordained in 1703 but soon after his ordination ceased to say Mass; he claimed this was because of his unsure health (he is known to have suffered from chest complaints, possibly asthma or angina). In 1703 he was appointed *maestro di violino* at the Ospedale della Pietà, one of the Venetian girls' orphanages; he remained there until 1709, and held the post again, 1711–16; he then became *maestro de' concerti*. Later, when he was away from Venice, he retained his connection with the Pietà (at one period he sent two concertos by post each month). He became *maestro di cappella*, 1735–8; even after then he supplied concertos and directed performances on special occasions.

Vivaldi's reputation had begun to grow with his first publications: trio sonatas (probably 1703–5), violin sonatas (1709) and especially his 12 concertos *L'estro armonico* op.3 (1711). These, containing some of his finest concertos, were issued in Amsterdam and widely circulated in northern Europe; this prompted visiting musicians to seek him out in Venice and in some cases commission works from him (notably for the Dresden court). Bach transcribed five op.3 concertos for keyboard, and many German composers imitated his style. He published two further sets of sonatas and seven more of concertos, including *La stravaganza* op.4 (*c*1712), *Il cimento dell' armonia e dell' inventione* (*c*1725, including 'The Four Seasons') and *La cetra* (1727). It is in the concerto that Vivaldi's chief importance lies. He was the first composer to use ritornello form regularly in fast movements, and his use of it became a model; the same is true of his three-movement plan (fast–

slow–fast). His methods of securing greater thematic unity were widely copied, especially the integration of solo and ritornello material; his vigorous rhythmic patterns, his violinistic figuration and his use of sequence were also much imitated. Of his *c*550 concertos, *c*350 are for solo instrument (more than 230 for violin); there are *c*40 double concertos, more than 30 for multiple soloists and nearly 60 for orchestra without solo, while more than 20 are chamber concertos for a small group of solo instruments without orchestra (the 'tutti' element is provided by the instruments all playing together). Vivaldi was an enterprising orchestrator, writing several concertos for unusual combinations like viola d'amore and lute, or for ensembles including chalumeaux, clarinets, horns and other rarities. There are also many solo concertos for bassoon, cello, oboe and flute. Some of his concertos are programmatic, for example 'La tempesta di mare' (the title of three concertos). Into this category also fall 'The Four Seasons', with their representation of seasonal activities and conditions accommodated within a standard ritornello form – these are described in the appended sonnets, which he may have written himself.

Vivaldi was also much engaged in vocal music. He wrote a quantity of sacred works, chiefly for the Pietà girls, using a vigorous style in which the influence of the concerto is often marked. He was also involved in opera and spent much time travelling to promote his works. His earliest known opera was given in Vicenza in 1713; later he worked at theatres in Venice, Mantua (1718–20), Rome (probably 1723–5), possibly Vienna and Prague (around 1730), Ferrara (1737), Amsterdam (1738) and possibly Vienna during his last visit. He was by most accounts a difficult man; in 1738 he was forbidden entry to Ferrara ostensibly because of his refusal to say Mass and his relationship with the singer Anna Giraud, a pupil of his with whom he travelled. More than 20 of his operas survive; those that have been revived include music of vitality and imagination as well as more routine items. But Vivaldi's importance lies above all in his concertos, for their boldness and originality and for their central place in the history of concerto form.

Orchestral music over 230 vn concs., incl. 'Four Seasons', op.8 nos. 1–4 (*c*1725); *c*120 other solo concs. (bn, vc, ob, fl, rec etc); *c*40 double concs.; ensemble concs.; ripieno concs. and sinfonias; 4 concs. for double orch
*Chamber music c*40 vn sonatas; 9 vc sonatas; *c*10 fl sonatas; 27 trio sonatas; 22 chamber concs.
Sacred vocal music Gloria, D; Magnificat, g; psalms, hymns, motets etc; Juditha triumphans (oratorio, 1716)
*Secular vocal music c*20 operas, incl. Teuzzone (1719), Tito Manlio (1720), Giustino (1724), Orlando (1727), La fida ninfa (1732), Griselda (1735); 3 serenatas; *c*40 solo cantatas

Vivanco, Sebastián de (*b* Avila, *c*1551; *d* Salamanca, 26 Oct 1622). Spanish composer. He was *maestro di capilla* of the cathedrals of Lerida (until 1576), Segovia, Avila (1588–1602) and Salamanca, where he was also university music professor. A leading composer of his age, erudite and harmonically bold, he published masses (1608), Magnificats (1607) and motets (1610).

Vives, Amadeo (*b* Collbató, 18 Nov 1871; *d* Madrid, 1 Dec 1932). Spanish composer. A pupil of Pedrell, he wrote mostly operas, operettas and zarzuelas of which *Doña Francisquita* (1923) is considered his masterpiece.

Viviani, Giovanni Buonaventura (*b* Florence, 15 July 1638; *d* ?Pistoia, Dec 1692 or later). Italian composer. He was a violinist at the court of Innsbruck and in 1672–6 was music director there. Later he returned to Italy; he directed an opera troupe in Naples between 1678 and 1682, was *maestro di cappella* to the Prince of Bisignano in 1686 and at Pistoia Cathedral, 1687–92. His works include operas (given in Venice and Naples), oratorios, solo cantatas (similar to Cesti's), other vocal pieces and instrumental music. His cousin Antonio Maria Viviani (?1625–*c*1685) was an organist, singer and composer.

Vivo (It.). Alive, vigorous.

Vlach Quartet. Czech string quartet, led by Josef Vlach. Founded in 1951, it takes much of its character from its leader (also a guest conductor with the Czech PO). Its repertory ranges from Tartini to Janáček, performed with great technical assurance and interpretative feeling.

Vlad, Roman (*b* Cernăuţi, 29 Dec 1919). Italian composer and writer of Romanian origin. He moved to Rome in 1938 and studied with Casella and in 1968 was appointed professor at the Perugia Conservatory. His works cover many genres, and show from the *Studi dodecafonici* (1943) an attachment to 12-note serialism extended after 1960 with new techniques (e.g. aleatory writing, electronics). His many writings are mostly on modern music and include a book on Stravinsky (1958).

Vladigerov, Pancho (*b* Zurich, 13 March 1899; *d* Sofia, 8 Sept 1978). Bulgarian composer. A pupil of Khristov in Sofia and Juon in Berlin, he worked for Reinhardt in Berlin as pianist, conductor and composer (1921–32), then returned to teach at the Sofia Academy (until 1972). His output, in many genres, shows an exuberant, colourful use of Western classical traditions together with Bulgarian folk music.

Vlijmen, Jan van (*b* Rotterdam, 11 Oct 1935). Dutch composer. A pupil of Van Baaren at the Utrecht Conservatory, he has taught at the Conservatory of The Hague since 1967. His earlier works were influenced by Berg, but then elements of the Darmstadt avant garde entered his music. Most of his pieces are for one or more instrumental ensembles; he became internationally known for *Construzione* (1960) for two pianos, then *Gruppi* for four ensembles (1962).

Vocalion. A type of REED ORGAN, developed by James Baillie Hamilton in England in the 1880s in an attempt to combine the sounds of free reeds and strings. It produces a smoother, more powerful sound than the average reed organ and was popular in small churches in the late 19th century and early 20th.

Vocalise (Fr.). A textless vocal exercise or concert piece, sung to one or more vowels. Since the mid-18th century, singing teachers have used vocal music without words as exercises, and in the early 19th teachers began to publish solfeggios and exercises for wordless voice and accompaniment. A number of vocalise-style compositions have been written, including a sonatina with piano by Spohr, pieces by Fauré, Ravel, Rakhmaninov, Medtner, Giordano and Respighi; there is a concerto for soprano and orchestra by Glier. Choral 'vocalisation' has been used by several composers, including Debussy (*Sirènes*) and Holst (*The Planets*). In jazz, 'vocalese' refers to a vocal arrangement of an instrumental number.

Voces intimae. Sub-title of Sibelius's String Quartet in D minor op.56 (1909).

Vogel, (Johannes) Emil (Eduard Bernhard) (*b* Wriezen an der Oder, 21 Jan 1859; *d* Nikolassee, 18 June 1908). German musicologist. He studied in Berlin and is remembered for his work on 16th- and early 17th-century Italian music, especially his pioneering bibliography of printed secular music (1892).

Vogel, Johann Christoph (*b* Nuremberg, bap. 18 March 1756; *d* Paris, 28 June 1788). German composer. A horn player in Paris, he composed two operas showing a promising dramatic gift; the first, *La toison d'or* (1786), was much influenced by Gluck. He also wrote an oratorio and various instrumental works. His grandson Charles-Louis-Adolphe (1808–92) composed chamber music, songs and romances, and stage works including four *opéras comiques*.

Vogel, Wladimir (Rudolfovich) (*b* Moscow, 29 Feb 1896; *d* Zurich, 19 June 1984). Swiss composer of German-Russian parentage. Brought up in Russia, and influenced by Skryabin, he travelled in 1918 to Berlin, where he was a pupil of Tiessen and Busoni, but where he also came in contact with the expressionist movement. He made a speciality of the use of speech, begun in his *Drei Sprechlieder* for bass and piano (1922) and continued most notably in the oratorio *Thyl Claes* (1945), written after his move to Switzerland in 1933 and after his adoption of 12-note methods in his Violin Concerto (1937). Later works include more large-scale choral pieces and orchestral scores.

Vogelweide, Walther von der. *See* WALTHER VON DER VOGELWEIDE.

Vogl, Heinrich (*b* Munich, 15 Jan 1845; *d* there, 21 April 1900). German tenor. With his powerful voice and legendary stamina he excelled in the Wagnerian roles of Loge (*Das Rheingold*) and Siegmund (*Die Walküre*), both of which he created, and of Siegfried (*Siegfried*, *Götterdämmerung*) and Tristan. He composed an opera, *Der Fremdling* (1899), and songs. His wife, the soprano Therese Vogl (1845–1921), was Sieglinde in the first *Die Walküre* (1870).

Vogl, Johann Michael (*b* Ennsdorf, 10 Aug 1768; *d* Vienna, 19 Nov 1840). Austrian baritone. A valued member of the Vienna Hofoper (1795–1822), he excelled as Orestes (*Iphigénie en Tauride*), winning the admiration of Schubert who became his close friend and accompanist; he sang *Erlkönig* in public in 1821 and received the dedication of three Schubert songs.

Vogler, [Abbé] Georg Joseph (*b* Pleichach, 15 June 1749; *d* Darmstadt, 6 May 1814). German theorist and composer. He joined the Mannheim court and was chaplain by 1772. After studies in Italy with Vallotti and others he returned as vice-Kapellmeister (1775) and founded a conservatory, Mannheim Tonschule. He remained when the court moved to Munich in 1778 but rejoined it as first Kapellmeister in 1784. Later he was Kapellmeister at Stockholm, 1786–97, and at Darmstadt, 1807–14. He influenced many younger composers (notably Weber and Meyerbeer) through his teaching and travelled widely to perform (his improvisation was especially admired) and to study (and use) 'exotic' melodies.

As a theorist Vogler developed an approach to harmony that anticipated trends of the Romantic period; his important first treatise was *Tonwissenschaft und Tonsetzkunst* (1776). Among his other books are didactic works and writings on organ reform. His music, including sacred works, stage and other vocal works and instrumental pieces, uses colourful instrumentation and progressive harmony, reflecting his theories and experiments.

Voice. *See* SINGING; *see also* ALTO, BARITONE, BASS, CONTRALTO, COUNTERTENOR, SOPRANO and TENOR. The word is also used to denote a strand in a polyphonic texture, whether instrumental or vocal; thus a 'fugue in four voices', 'a three-voice texture'. *See also* VOICING.

Voice-exchange. A medieval polyphonic technique in which two voices of equal range exchange in alternation (it might better be called phrase-exchange). Easily achieved in two-part counterpoint, it was widely practised in the 12th century; it also often appears in Notre Dame polyphony and was much used by English composers in the 13th-century rondellus. With the expansion of the two-voice framework beyond an octave and the consequent gradual separation of the voices after 1300, voice-exchange fell into disuse.

Voice-leading. Term preferred in American usage for PART-WRITING.

Voicing. The means by which the timbre, attack, loudness etc of the pipes or strings of keyboard instruments and some non-keyboard wind instruments are given their desired quality and uniformity. In the organ, voicing concerns the amount of wind issuing from a flue or the thickness and curvature of the reed tongue. In harpsichords and other quilled instruments, voicing involves adjusting the quill to arrive at an even touch and tone. The voicing of pianos involves altering the hardness of the sub-surface felt of the hammers.

Voix de ville. *See* VAUDEVILLE.

Voix humaine, La. Monodrama for soprano and orchestra ('tragédie lyrique') in one act by Poulenc to a text by Cocteau.

Voix sombrée (Fr.). 'Darkened voice': a technique of voice production, made famous by the tenor Gilbert Duprez in the 1830s, who held his larynx at a low level even at high pitch to achieve a sombre tone.

Volbach, Fritz (*b* Wipperfürth, 17 Dec 1861; *d* Wiesbaden, 30 Nov 1940). German conductor and composer. Trained at the Königliches Institut für Kirchenmusik in Berlin, where he began teaching in 1887, he became professor at the University of Münster (1918–30). As conductor and scholar he was devoted to Handel, founding the first German Handel festival in Mainz. His own works include a Brucknerian symphony, choral and instrumental pieces.

Volkmann, (Friedrich) Robert (*b* Lommatzsch, 6 April 1815; *d* Budapest, 29 Oct 1883). German composer. He studied in Freiberg and Leipzig. A prominent figure in Budapest musical life (from 1875 teaching at the Hungarian National Music Academy), he wrote instrumental works showing the influence of Mendelssohn and Schumann; chief among them are the String Serenade no.3, the Cello Concerto, the Overture to *Richard III* and the Bb minor Piano Trio.

Volkonsky, Andrey Mikhaylovich (*b* Geneva, 14 Feb 1933). Soviet composer. He was a pupil of Boulanger in Paris (1945–7) and of Shaporin at the Moscow Conservatory (1950–54). Always strained, his relations with the authorities became more awkward after his first serial piece, *Musica stricta* for piano (1956), and later works – like *Les plaintes de Chtchaza* for soprano and quintet (1961), in a style deriving from Stravinsky and Boulez – have received little attention, his official activities being restricted to playing the harpsichord and composing for films. He was acknowledged as the leader of the Soviet musical avant garde. He left the USSR in 1973.

Volksoper. Opera company and theatre in Vienna. The theatre opened in 1898 (cap. 1710); the company was established in 1903 (renamed Städtische Volksoper, 1938). It presents standard repertory in German as well as musicals and operetta.

Volta (It.). (1) 'Turn': a court dance of Provençal origin popular from *c*1550 to 1650, characterized by three-quarter turns. These are executed partly with a high jump by each partner, partly by the gentleman lifting the lady high into the air. The music is in triple time but is commonly notated with six crotchets in a bar.

(2) 'Time': the indications 'prima volta' and 'seconda volta' instruct the performer that the bars so marked are to be played only the first or the second time through a piece.

Volti subito (It.). 'Turn [the page] immediately'.

Volumier, Jean Baptiste (*b* ?Spain, *c*1670; *d* Dresden, 7 Oct 1728). Flemish violinist and composer. Until 1708 he was Konzertmeister and dancing-master at the electoral court in Berlin. He then moved to Dresden, where as court Konzertmeister from 1709 he improved the orchestra's playing. He composed violin music and many ballets and was a friend of Bach's.

Voluntary. A composed or improvised piece, usually for organ in the context of a church service. 16th- and 17th-century English composers used the term interchangeably with 'verse' or 'fancy', and Byrd, Weelkes and Tomkins wrote voluntaries in a fugal style. Greene established the form of a slow introduction followed by an Allegro in fugal or concerto style, and most 18th-century composers, including Stanley and the elder John Alcock, used this structure. The form's continuous history ended with the Bach-inspired works of Samuel Wesley, but many voluntaries for use before or after divine service have been composed since.

Vomáčka, Boleslav (*b* Mladá Boleslav, 28 June 1887; *d* Prague, 1 March 1965). Czech composer. He studied with Novák (1909–10) at the Prague Conservatory. Between the wars he was in the vanguard of Czech music, using folksong in songs and choral pieces and bold dissonance in his compact instrumental works; the opera *The Watersprite* (1937) is noteworthy. But later works are extremely simple. He was a critic and influential on Bohemian musical life.

Von heute auf morgen. Opera in one act by Schoenberg to a libretto by Max Blonda (Gertrud Schoenberg) (1930, Frankfurt).

Von Stade, Frederica (*b* Somerville, NJ, 1 June 1945). American mezzo-soprano. She studied in New York and in 1970 made her début at the Met, where her roles have included Rosina (*Barber of Seville*) and Zerlina (*Don Giovanni*); at Santa Fe she has sung Mélisande. She has been particularly admired as Cherubino (Paris Opéra and Glyndebourne, 1973) and Octavian, and has sung in several new works and revivals of early ones. Her firm, well-formed tone and sense of phrasing serve her well as a recitalist.

Voormolen, Alexander (Nicholas) (*b* Rotterdam, 3 March 1895; *d* The Hague, 12 Nov 1980). Dutch composer. A pupil of Wagenaar in Utrecht and of Ravel and Roussel in Paris, he returned to Holland in 1923 and worked as a critic and librarian. His works comprise orchestral scores (including the *Baron Hop* suites), chamber music and songs, in a neo-classical style.

Voříšek, Jan Václav (*b* Vamberk, 11 May 1791; *d* Vienna, 19 Nov 1825). Bohemian composer. His disciplined study with Tomášek in Prague and his enthusiasm for Beethoven's works led him to pursue a musical career in Vienna, where he was a successful conductor, piano soloist and accompanist; by 1818 he was conductor of the Gesellschaft der Musikfreunde and by 1823 principal court organist. His compositions, chiefly church works and keyboard pieces, reflect his assimilation of contrapuntal technique and his early Romantic expressiveness. Among the most individual are the Piano Sonata op.20, the Mass in B♭, the song *An Sie* from op.21, the Violin Sonata op.5 and the Symphony op.24.

Vorlová, Sláva (*b* Náchod, 15 March 1894; *d* Prague, 24 Aug 1973). Czech composer. She was a private pupil of Novák and later of Řídký, under whom she graduated from the Prague Conservatory in 1948. Her work represents a restrained development of the Novák school in an output including operas, orchestral pieces and jazz songs.

Vorschlag (Ger.). APPOGGIATURA.

Vorspiel (Ger). 'Prelude', especially (from Wagner's *Lohengrin*, 1846–8 onwards) one closely linked to an operatic act. The term is used also of preludes in general, e.g. *Choralvorspiel*, denoting a chorale prelude. (In its derivation from *vorspielen*, the word can also mean 'performance'.)

Vox humana. Name for organ stops that aim to imitate the human voice and produce a thinnish tone at 8′ pitch with an undulating effect. Some used mistuned octave pipes; some are mixtures or mutation stops; and some used specially devised methods.

Voyevoda, The. Opera in three acts by Tchaikovsky to a libretto by Ostrovsky and the composer (1869, Moscow); Tchaikovsky destroyed it and it was reconstructed by Pavel Lamm.

Vuataz, Roger (*b* Geneva, 4 Jan 1898). Swiss organist and composer. An influential figure in Geneva musical life as organist, conductor, teacher and radio music director, he wrote several oratorios as well as orchestral and keyboard music, coloured by the music of Bach and the austere tradition of the Protestant psalm.

Vuillaume, Jean-Baptiste (*b* Mirecourt, 7 Oct 1798; *d* Paris, 19 March 1875). French violin maker and dealer. He established a workshop in Paris in 1828 and became the pioneer of imitation, producing impressive copies (not fakes) of the best Italian makes. By 1850 his was one of the leading shops in Europe; he supervised the making of over 2000 high-quality instruments, nearly all bearing his own label. His innovations with bows, including the 'self-rehairing bow', were less successful.

Vulpius, Melchior (*b* Wasungen, *c*1570; *d* Weimar, bur. 7 Aug 1615). German composer. He was a schoolteacher in Schleusingen (1589–96) and Weimar (1596–1615), where he was also Kantor. He was the most important composer of Protestant hymn tunes in Germany in his day and one of the most productive and popular. Some 400 survive (1604–14); with the tune in the top voice, they have a marked tonal feeling and a close relationship between the text and the music. Nearly 200 motets (1602–10), a *St Matthew Passion* (1613) and occasional works by him also survive.

Vuota, vuoto (It.). 'Empty', 'void': either an instruction in string music that a note is to be played on an open (empty) string, or a general pause (empty bars).

Vycpálek, Ladislav (*b* Prague, 23 Feb 1882; *d* there, 9 Jan 1969). Czech composer. A pupil of Novák (1908–12), he worked in the library of Prague University; he was also active in the Czech Academy and the National Theatre. He wrote mostly vocal works and a luminous and dissonant polyphonic style, including the *Cantata of the Last Things of Man* (1920–22) and *Czech Requiem* (1940), and was recognized as the leading Czech composer after the deaths of Novák and Foerster.

W

W, Wq. Abbreviation for Wotquenne, used to identify works by C.P.E. Bach in Alfred Wotquenne's thematic catalogue (1905).

Waart, Edo de. *See* DE WAART, EDO.

Wachsmann, Klaus P(hilipp) (*b* Berlin, 8 March 1907; *d* Tisbury, 17 July 1984). British ethnomusicologist of German birth. He studied at Berlin with Blume, Schering, Hornbostel and Sachs (1930–32). In London he studied African languages, then worked in Uganda, becoming curator of the Uganda Museum, Kampala (1948). Later he taught at the Institute of Ethnomusicology, University of California at Los Angeles, and at Northwestern University, Evanston, Illinois. He was president of the International Folk Music Council in 1973. His research was mainly on the tribal music of Uganda and African instruments; but he was also an influential thinker on the methods and ethics of ethnomusicology and writing the musical history of non-literate cultures.

Waelrant, Hubert (*b* 1516–17; *d* Antwerp, 19 Nov 1595). Flemish composer and music editor. From at least 1544–5 he was a singer at Antwerp Cathedral and taught music. With the printer Jean de Laet he issued 16 volumes of music (1554–66) by various composers, including himself. He was an innovator among mid-16th-century Flemish composers, and his style bridges the gap between that of Gombert and the mature Lassus. His works include motets (1556), psalms, madrigals and *chansons* (1558) and *napolitane* (1565); many are in a serious yet forward-looking style, characterized by careful attention to the relationship between text and music, with some striking word-painting.

Wagenaar, Bernard (*b* Arnhem, 18 July 1894; *d* York, ME, 19 May 1971). American composer. He was a pupil of his father, Johan (1862–1941), also a composer, at Utrecht University. In 1920 he moved to New York, where he taught at the Juilliard School (1925–68) and wrote orchestral and chamber pieces, a chamber opera (*Pieces of 8*, 1944), and vocal music in a neo-classical style.

Wagenaar, Johan (*b* Utrecht, 1 Nov 1862; *d* The Hague, 17 June 1941). Dutch composer. A pupil of Richard Hol, whom he succeeded as teacher and cathedral organist in Utrecht, he was later director of the Conservatory of The Hague (1919–37). His works, in an individual style drawing on Berlioz and Strauss, show remarkable powers of orchestration (overtures, *Cyrano de Bergerac*, 1905; *De getemde feeks*, 1909).

Wagenseil, Georg Christoph (*b* Vienna, 29 Jan 1715; *d* there, 1 March 1777). Austrian composer. A favoured pupil of Fux, the Viennese imperial court Kapellmeister, he was court composer from 1739; he was also organist to Empress Elisabeth Christine (1741–50) and keyboard master to the imperial archduchesses. Except for two visits to Italy he travelled little, but he won widespread fame through his instrumental works. He was also renowned as a keyboard virtuoso and teacher (notably of J.B. Schenk, who taught Beethoven).

Wagenseil was a central figure among mid-18th-century composers. He wrote 15 stage works, much sacred and other vocal music, and several hundred instrumental works (mostly in three movements), among them symphonies, concertos (chiefly for harpsichord), string trios, other chamber pieces, and keyboard divertimentos, sonatas and suites. His earliest works are late Baroque in style (the masses reflect Fux's influence), but those of after *c*1750 make increasing use of the *galant* idiom, and the later symphonies approach Classical sonata-form techniques. His stage works, composed mostly in 1745–50, include large unified scene-complexes which point towards Gluck's operatic reform.

Wagenseil, Johann Christoph (*b* Nuremberg, 26 Nov 1633; *d* Altdorf, 9 Oct 1708). German scholar. His writings include the first treatise on the mastersingers of Nuremberg (1697), used by Wagner as the basis of his opera *Die Meistersinger* (1868).

Wagner, Johanna (*b* Seelze, 13 Oct 1826; *d* Würzburg, 16 Oct 1894). German soprano, adopted daughter of Richard Wagner's elder brother, Albert. She created Elisabeth in *Tannhäuser* (1845) and, while at the Court Opera, Berlin (1850–61), took over Fidès in *Le prophète* from Viardot. She also appeared in London (1856) and later Bayreuth, winning praise especially for her acting and her magnificent stage presence.

Wagner, Peter (Josef) (*b* Kürenz, 19 Aug 1865; *d* Fribourg, 17 Oct 1931). German musicologist. He studied in Trier and Berlin and taught at Fribourg from 1893. In 1927 he was elected first president of the IMS. His central work, *Einführung in die gregor-ianischen Melodien* (1895–1921), is the first comprehensive survey of medieval chant based on modern musicological research methods. He also published important studies on medieval Spanish chant.

Wagner, (Wilhelm) Richard (*b* Leipzig, 22 May 1813; *d* Venice, 13 Feb 1883). German composer. He was the son either of the police actuary Friedrich Wagner, who died soon after his birth, or of his mother's friend the painter, actor and poet Ludwig Geyer, whom she married in August 1814. He went to school in Dresden and then Leipzig; at 15 he wrote a play, at 16 his first compositions. In 1831 he went to Leipzig University, also studying music with the Thomaskantor, C.T. Weinlig; a symphony was written and successfully performed in 1832. In 1833 he became chorus master at the Würzburg theatre and wrote the text and music of his first opera, *Die Feen*; this remained unheard, but his next, *Das Liebesverbot*, written in 1833, was staged in 1836. By then he had made his début as an opera conductor with a small company which however went bankrupt soon after performing his opera. He married the singer Minna Planer in 1836 and went with her to Königsberg where he became musical director at the theatre, but he soon left and took a similar post in Riga where he began his next opera, *Rienzi*, and did much conducting, especially of Beethoven.

In 1839 they slipped away from creditors in Riga, by ship to London and then to Paris, where he was befriended by Meyerbeer and did hack-work for publishers and theatres. He also worked on the text and music of an opera on the 'Flying Dutchman' legend; but in 1842 *Rienzi*, a large-scale opera with a political theme set in imperial Rome, was accepted for Dresden and Wagner went there for its highly successful première. Its theme reflects something of Wagner's own politics (he was involved in the semi-revolutionary, intellectual 'Young Germany' movement). *Die fliegende Holländer* ('The Flying Dutchman'), given the next year, was less well received, though a much tauter musical drama, beginning to move away from the 'number opera' tradition and strong in its evocation of atmosphere, especially the supernatural and the raging seas (inspired by the stormy trip from Riga). Wagner was now appointed joint Kapellmeister at the Dresden court.

The theme of redemption through a woman's love, in the *Dutchman*, recurs in Wagner's operas (and perhaps his life). In 1845 *Tannhäuser* was completed and performed and *Lohengrin* begun. In both Wagner moves towards a more continuous texture with semi-melodic narrative and a supporting orchestral fabric helping convey its sense. In 1848 he was caught up in the revolutionary fervour and the next year fled to Weimar (where Liszt helped him) and then Switzerland (there was also a spell in France); politically suspect, he was unable to enter Germany for 11 years. In Zurich, he wrote in 1850–51 his ferociously anti-semitic *Jewishness in Music* (some of it an attack on Meyerbeer) and his basic statement on musical theatre, *Opera and Drama*; he also began sketching the text and music of a series of operas on the Nordic and Germanic sagas. By 1853 the text for this four-night cycle (to be *The Nibelung's Ring*) was written, printed and read to friends – who included a generous patron, Otto Wesendonck, and his wife Mathilde, who loved him, wrote poems that he set, and inspired *Tristan und Isolde* – conceived in 1854 and completed five years later, by which time more than half of *The Ring* was written. In 1855 he conducted in London; tension with Minna led to his going to Paris in 1858–9. 1860 saw them both in Paris, where the next year he revived *Tannhäuser* in revised form for French taste, but it was literally shouted down, partly for political reasons. In 1862 he was allowed freely into Germany; that year he and the ill and childless Minna parted (she died in 1866). In 1863 he gave concerts in Vienna, Russia etc; the next year King Ludwig II invited him to settle in Bavaria, near Munich, discharging his debts and providing him with money.

Wagner did not stay long in Bavaria, because of opposition at Ludwig's court, especially when it was known that he was having an affair with Cosima, the wife of the conductor Hans von Bülow (she was Liszt's daughter); Bülow (who condoned it) directed the *Tristan* première in 1865. Here Wagner, in depicting every shade of sexual love, developed a style richer and more chromatic than anyone had previously attempted, using dissonance and its urge for resolution in a continuing pattern to build up tension and a sense of profound yearning; Act 2 is virtually a continuous love duet, touching every emotion from the tenderest to the most passionately erotic. Before returning to the *Ring*, Wagner wrote, during the mid-1860s, *The Mastersingers of Nuremberg*: this is in a quite different vein, a comedy set in 16th-century Nuremberg, in which a noble poet-musician wins, through his victory in a music contest – a victory over pedants who stick to the foolish old rules – the hand of his beloved, fame and riches. (The analogy with Wagner's view of himself is obvious.) The music is less chromatic than that of *Tristan*, warm and good-humoured, often contrapuntal; unlike the mythological figures of his other operas the characters here have real humanity.

The opera was given, under Bülow, in 1868; Wagner had been living at Tribschen, near Lucerne, since 1866, and that year Cosima formally joined him; they had two children when in 1870 they married. The first two *Ring* operas, *Das Rheingold* and *Die Walküre*, were given in Munich, on Ludwig's insistence, in 1869 and 1870; Wagner however was anxious to have a special festival opera house for the complete cycle and spent much energy trying to raise money for it. Eventually, when he had almost despaired, Ludwig came to the rescue and in 1874 – the year the fourth opera, *Götterdämmerung*, was finished – provided the necessary support. The house was built at Bayreuth, designed by Wagner as the home for his concept of the *Gesamtkunstwerk* ('total art work' – an alliance of music, poetry, the visual arts, dance etc). The first festival, an artistic triumph but a financial disaster – was held there in

1876, when the complete *Ring* was given. The *Ring* is about 18 hours' music, held together by an immensely detailed network of themes, or leitmotifs, each of which has some allusive meaning: a character, a concept, an object etc. They change and develop as the ideas within the opera develop. They are heard in the orchestra, not merely as 'labels' but carrying the action, sometimes informing the listener of connections of ideas or the thoughts of those on the stage. There are no 'numbers' in the *Ring*; the musical texture is made up of narrative and dialogue, in which the orchestra partakes. The work is not merely a story about gods, humans and dwarfs but embodies reflections on every aspect of the human condition. It has been interpreted as socialist, fascist, Jungian, prophetic, as a parable about industrial society, and much more.

In 1877 Wagner conducted in London, hoping to recoup Bayreuth losses; later in the year he began a new opera, *Parsifal*. He continued his musical and polemic writings, concentrating on 'racial purity'. He spent most of 1880 in Italy. *Parsifal*, a sacred festival drama, again treating redemption but through the acts of communion and renunciation on the stage, was given at the Bayreuth Festival in 1882. He went to Venice for the winter, and died there in February of the heart trouble that had been with him for some years. His body was returned by gondola and train for burial at Bayreuth. Wagner did more than any other composer to change music, and indeed to change art and thinking about it. His life and his music arouse passions like no other composer's. His works are hated as much as they are worshipped; but no-one denies their greatness.

Dramatic music Die Feen (1833, perf. 1888); Das Liebesverbot (1836); Rienzi (1842); Der fliegende Holländer (1843); Tannhäuser (1845); Lohengrin (1850); Tristan und Isolde (1865); Die Meistersinger von Nürnberg (1868); Der Ring des Nibelungen (1876): Das Rheingold (1869), Die Walküre (1870), Siegfried (1876), Götterdämmerung (1876); Parsifal (1882); incidental music
Orchestral music Sym., C (1832); Siegfried Idyll (1870); ovs., marches
Piano music 3 sonatas; Fantasia (1831); other pieces
Vocal music Das Liebesmahl der Apostel, biblical scene (1843); other choral pieces; 5 songs to texts by Mathilde Wesendonck (1858); songs, arias

Wagner, Siegfried (Helferich Richard) (*b* Tribschen, 6 June 1869; *d* Bayreuth, 4 Aug 1930). German composer and conductor, son of Richard Wagner. It was on his birth that his father composed the *Siegfried Idyll*. Two of his operas once had success, but he is now remembered for the Bayreuth Festival productions of his father's works, 1906–30, in which he introduced new styles of presentation. His sons Wieland (1917–66) and Wolfgang (*b* 1919) followed him in innovative production and stage design. In 1951 they revived the Bayreuth festivals with starkly modern, symbolist productions, Wieland in particular using bare settings, reduced stage movement, strong characterization and emphatic lighting, suggestive in some cases (the 1965 *Ring*) of highly political interpretations. Wolfgang, sole director of the festival from 1966, has used some romantic and semi-naturalistic elements; he won

praise for his 1970 *Ring*, set on a tilted disc, and his colourful *Mastersingers of Nuremberg* (1973). With Wolfgang's encouragement, Bayreuth has remained a workshop for modern opera directors and designers.

Wagner-Régeny, Rudolf (*b* Szász-Régen, 28 Aug 1903; *d* E. Berlin, 18 Sept 1969). German composer of Romanian origin. He went to Germany in 1919, and from 1920 studied in Berlin with Schreker and others. At first influenced by Les Six, he drew nearer Weill in his operas *Der Günstling* (1935), *Die Bürger von Calais* (1939) and *Johanna Balk* (1941), which at the same time lost him official support. He resurfaced as a composer in the early 1950s, teaching in Rostock and East Berlin and writing in a 12-note style until his return to tonality in the biblical cantatas and songs of his last years. He was an accomplished pianist and clavichordist.

Wagner tuba. A kind of tuba devised by Wagner for the *Ring* and intended to bridge the gap between the horns and trombones. It differs from the horn in that the conical bore increases steadily throughout the whole length, culminating in a long bell which rises obliquely from the body of the instrument, which is played resting in the player's lap. Wagner directed for a set of these instruments to be played by an extra quartet of horn players who alternate between the two instruments as the music requires. The quartet consists of two tenor tubas in B♭ (compass $E♭–f''$) and two bass tubas in F ($B♭'–a'$). Its sombre, dignified sound has attracted many later composers to the Wagner tuba, notably Bruckner, Strauss and Stravinsky, who used it in *The Firebird* and *The Rite of Spring*.

Wainwright. English family of musicians. John Wainwright (1723–68) was an organist and composer in Manchester, who wrote hymn tunes and other church music. Two of his sons became organists. Robert (1748–82) played at the Manchester Collegiate Church (later the Cathedral) in 1768–75 and then at St Peter's, Liverpool; his works include an oratorio and church and chamber music, notably a set of piano quintets influenced by J.C. Bach. Richard (1757–1835) also worked at St Peter's and composed hymns, songs and glees. Another son, William (*d* 1797), was a singer and double bass player in Manchester.

Wait. A town or household watchman, who used a horn or a shawm; also the shawm itself (sometimes called 'wayte-pipe') or its player. The term came to apply to a civic minstrel (equivalent to the German *Stadtpfeifer*; town waits, who at first often played three shawms and a slide trumpet or sackbut, were widely employed by the late 15th century, mainly to attend on ceremonial occasions though they were also licensed to provide music in the streets at night. During the 16th century their talents became more diverse and they played a variety of instruments. Minstrelsy of this kind gradually died out in the 18th century. The term is also used for Christmas singers, after the civic minstrels who sang and played Christmas songs seasonally in the streets. *See* MINSTRELS; GUILDS; and STADTPFEIFER.

Walcha, Helmut (*b* Leipzig, 27 Oct 1907). German

organist. He studied in Leipzig, making his début there in 1924. Blind from the age of 16, he has toured widely, performing Bach in a cool style marked by contrapuntal clarity; he has recorded all Bach's organ music. He has held posts as organist and teacher in Frankfurt. In 1929 he became organist at the Frankfurt Friedenskirche and in 1933 professor at the Music Institute.

Walcker. German family of organ builders. Founded in 1780 in Cannstadt by Johann Eberhard Walcker, the firm was moved to Ludwigsburg in 1820 by his son Eberhard Friedrich (1794–1872), who built organs for the Paulskirche, Frankfurt (1829–33), Ulm Minster (1841–56) and the Festival Hall, Boston (1863). The company built important instruments for Riga Cathedral (from 1881), the Gewandhaus, Leipzig (1884), and St Stephen's Cathedral, Vienna (1886); electro-pneumatic action was introduced in 1899. The founder's great-grandson Oscar (1869–1948) oversaw work on the 'Praetorius' organ, Freiburg University (1921), among other instruments; since 1948 c3200 organs have been built under Oscar's grandson Werner Walcker-Mayer (b 1923), among them those for Zagreb Concert Hall and the Mozarteum, Salzburg.

Waldis, Burkhard (b Allendorf an der Werra, c1490; d Abterode, c1557). German Protestant poet and hymn writer. A Franciscan monk in Riga, he became a Protestant and travelled widely. Widely recognized as a poet, he provided many hymns for the new church and translated the psalter into metric verse; he used Minnesang verse structures and provided them with original melodies.

Waldscenen. Schumann's op.82 (1849), nine piano pieces.

Waldstein Sonata. Beethoven's Piano Sonata no.21 in C op.53 (1803–4), dedicated to Count Ferdinand von Waldstein.

Waldteufel [Lévy], (Charles) Emile (b Strasbourg, 9 Dec 1837; d Paris, 12 Feb 1915). French composer and pianist. Active chiefly as a society musician, he enjoyed international acclaim during the 1870s and 1880s for his (c300) waltzes, polkas and galops; the waltz *Manolo* (1874) and *The Skaters' Waltz* (1882) were among his most successful.

Walking bass. Term used of a bass line in Baroque music (particularly Italian) that moves steadily and continuously in note values contrasting with those in the upper part or parts. In jazz, it refers to a line played pizzicato on a double bass in regular crotchets in 4/4 metre, the notes usually moving by step; it may also refer to the repeating piano left-hand broken-octave patterns in boogie-woogie.

Walk to the Paradise Garden, The. Orchestral intermezzo by Delius, added (1910) to his opera *A Village Romeo and Juliet*.

Walküre, Die [The Valkyrie]. Music drama in three acts by Wagner to his own libretto (1870, Munich), the second of the cycle DER RING DES NIBELUNGEN.

Wallace, (William) Vincent (b Waterford, 11 March 1812; d Château de Haget, 12 Oct 1865). Irish composer. He made his early reputation as a pianist and violinist, first in Dublin and then in Sydney (1836–8), Valparaiso, Chile (and other Latin American cities), New Orleans (1841), Philadelphia (1842), Boston and New York (1843), Germany, the Netherlands and finally London (1845). With the librettist Edward Fitzball he produced the immensely popular English opera *Maritana* (Drury Lane, 1845), rivalled only by Balfe's *Bohemian Girl* (1843); of his five subsequent operas only *Lurline* (1847; Covent Garden, 1860) approached its success. The vigour and spontaneity of Wallace's best works derived from foreign influences little known in England, for example the exotic Spanish and gypsy harmonic colouring in *Maritana* (later used by Bizet in *Carmen*). They are also remarkable for their sustained dramatic interest, genuine emotion and careful use of a 'big tune'.

Waller, Fats [Thomas Wright] (b New York, 21 May 1904; d Kansas City, MO, 15 Dec 1943). American jazz pianist, organist, singer, bandleader and composer. In his brief, extraordinarily active career he made nearly 500 discs and many piano rolls and composed c400 works, including such successful songs as *Honeysuckle Rose* (c1928) and *Ain't Misbehavin'* (1929). His outrageously funny performances brought him a wide following but overshadowed his serious talents.

Walliser, Christoph Thomas (b Strasbourg, 17 April 1568; d there, 26 April 1648). Alsatian composer. After studying in many European cities, he returned to Strasbourg to teach music at the Protestant Gymnasium (1598–1634), also serving the Thomaskirche (from 1600) and the cathedral (from 1606). A leading musical figure in Strasbourg, he published mainly chorale-based motets and theatrical works, more modern and italianate (1602–41).

Wally, La. Opera in four acts by Catalani to a libretto by Illica after W. von Hillern (1892, Milan).

Walmisley, Thomas Attwood (b London, 21 Jan 1814; d Hastings, 17 Jan 1856). English composer and organist, son of the glee composer Thomas Forbes Walmisley (1783–1866). He studied composition with his godfather Thomas Attwood, becoming organist of both Trinity and St John's Colleges, Cambridge (1833), and succeeding Clarke-Whitfeld as professor of music (1836). His lectures, skill as an organist and choir trainer and his devoted leadership of amateur musical circles were a major contribution to Cambridge musical life. As a composer he revitalized, with S.S. Wesley, English cathedral music, notably with his classical Evening Service in D minor (probably 1855), considered his masterpiece; he also wrote attractive songs and madrigals.

Walsh, John (b c1665; d London, 13 March 1736). English music seller, publisher and instrument maker. From 1695 to c1730 he published music, often with John Hare, on a scale previously unknown in England; besides works by English composers he printed much popular continental music (including Corelli's sonatas), often pirated from Dutch editions. He was an excellent businessman, advertising widely and using plates economically; quick to adopt new methods (subscription issues, free copies) and to imitate the innovations of others, he remained pre-eminent in England, attracting Handel's *Rinaldo* (1711), by which he made a great profit. His son John (1709–66) developed the firm's relationship with Handel from *c*1730, publishing all his later works.

Walter, Bruno (*b* Berlin, 15 Sept 1876; *d* Beverly Hills, 17 Feb 1962). German conductor. He studied at the Stern Conservatory, Berlin. After appointments at Cologne, Hamburg and Breslau he joined Mahler at the Vienna Court Opera in 1901, visiting Covent Garden in 1910. After Mahler's death he conducted the première of *Das Lied von der Erde* and the Ninth Symphony. He was musical director of the Munich Opera, 1913–22, and gave there the première of Pfitzner's *Palestrina* (1917). He visited the USA from 1923 and returned to Covent Garden, 1924–31. In 1925 he began a long association with the Salzburg Festival. He became director of the Gewandhaus concerts at Leipzig in 1929 but with the rise of the Nazis pursued a career in Austria and with the Concertgebouw Orchestra. In 1939 he was obliged to settle in the USA, conducting the Los Angeles SO, the New York PO and at the Met, 1941–57. From 1947 he returned to Europe, notably at the first Edinburgh Festival and in Salzburg, Vienna and Munich. He was best known for his mellow, deeply considered and often intensely expressive performances of Mozart, Mahler and Strauss.

Walter, Johann (*b* Kahla, 1496; *d* Torgau, 25 March 1570). German composer. He studied at Leipzig University and sang in the Elector of Saxony's Hofkapelle (1521–5). He spent time in Torgau and also directed the Dresden Hofkapelle (1548–54). A strict Lutheran, he is important for his *Geystliches gesangk Buchleyn* (1524), which made an early use of the German Tenorlied, and for his organization of music in several towns and residences in Saxony. Luther wrote the preface to his hymn book, which was widely used. His other compositions include more ambitious works for four to seven voices, eight four-voice Magnificats and two Passions. His son Johann (1527–78) composed a hymn, a motet and a *Te Deum*.

Walter of Châtillon (*b* Lille, *c*1135; *d* ?Amiens, *c*1190). French poet and scholar. He was head of a school in Laon and a canon of Reims, then in the 1160s, entered the service of Henry II of England; he studied canon law in Bologna and possibly Rome. From *c*1176 he was in Reims and later in Amiens. He wrote many rhythmic poems, eight of which survive with music, including monophonic and polyphonic settings in the Notre Dame conductus collections. It is not clear whether the music is his.

Waltershausen, Hermann Wolfgang (Sartorius) Freiherr von (*b* Göttingen, 12 Oct 1882; *d* Munich, 13 Aug 1954). German composer. He was a pupil of Thuille in Munich, where he taught at the academy (1920–33). His works include Romantic operas and orchestral pieces; his opera *Oberst Chabert* (1912), which received international attention, was an early adaptation of *verismo* to German opera. His many writings concentrate on opera.

Walther, Johann Gottfried (*b* Erfurt, 18 Sept 1684; *d* Weimar, 23 March 1748). German composer and lexicographer. He first worked as organist at St Tho-

mas's, Erfurt. In 1703–7 he made a study tour, meeting musicians including the theorist Andreas Werckmeister; he then became organist of St Peter and St Paul, Weimar, and music teacher of Prince Johann Ernst. His cousin J.S. Bach, who worked at the court, 1708–17, became a close friend. Walther joined the court orchestra in 1721 but never reached a higher position. In 1732 he published his *Musicalisches Lexicon*, the first major music dictionary in German; it includes both musical terms and biographies of musicians, drawing on Walther's own theoretical treatise (1708) and many other works. As a composer he wrote some 90 sacred vocal works (now mostly lost), over 100 chorale preludes for organ and other instrumental and keyboard music. His chorale preludes are especially fine: they display most of the chorale variation techniques developed by German composers from Pachelbel to Bach but are nevertheless highly personal in style.

Walther, Johann Jakob (*b* Witterda, *c*1650; *d* Mainz, 2 Nov 1717). German violinist and composer. He served at the Dresden court from 1674, and by 1684 had moved to the court at Mainz. He wrote two volumes of virtuoso violin music, scherzi with continuo accompaniment (1676) and *Hortulus chelicus* (1688); they are notable for their programmatic elements, and (like Biber's works) feature polyphonic writing, multiple stopping and high positions. Walther was later called the Paganini of his century.

Walther von der Vogelweide (*b c*1170; *d* ?Würzburg, *c*1230). German Minnesinger. He probably came from Franconia or Austria; he was at the Viennese court *c*1190 and came across Reinmar von Hagenau, whose work was first a model, later a source of rivalry. From 1198 he wandered to various European courts, making his name for a new, politically trenchant kind of *Spruch*, which achieved a recognized place in cultural courtly life. By 1212–13 when he entered the Emperor Otto IV's service, he had also freed the Minnelied from its restricted style and content and transformed it into a genuine, universally valid lovesong. After the Battle of Bouvines (1214) he sided with Friedrich of Sicily (later Friedrich II), who *c*1420 granted him a fief in the Würzburg area. His poetry represents the culmination of the German medieval lyric. He was considered the leading poet and musician among his colleagues. He perfected the content and form of the Minnelied and the *Spruch*; his style is characterized by highly original metaphors. Unfortunately, of all his works – one *Leich*, 86 lieder and some 140 *Spruch* strophes – only one complete melody survives; other melodies transmitted with his poems are almost certainly spurious.

Walton, Sir William (Turner) (*b* Oldham, 29 March 1902; *d* Ischia, 8 March 1983). English composer. He was educated at Oxford, and was a member of the Sitwells' circle from the beginning of the 1920s. His first important work was *Façade*, setting poems by Edith Sitwell for reciter and sextet and evidently modelled on *Pierrot lunaire* while looking more to Les Six in its wit and jazziness. The next works again showed Parisian connections: with Stravinsky and Honegger in the overture *Portsmouth Point*, with Prokofiev in the Viola Concerto. Then, without losing the vividness of his harmony and orchestration, he responded to the English Handelian tradition in *Belshazzar's Feast* and to Sibelius in his First Symphony, though here Elgar too is invoked, as in much of his later music. The Violin Concerto (1939) confirmed this homecoming.

The next decade was comparatively unproductive, except in film music (*Henry V*, *Hamlet*). At the end of it he married and moved to Ischia, where all his later works were composed. These include the opera *Troilus and Cressida*, found theatrically effective if conservative in approach when given at Covent Garden in 1954, and his one-act opera *The Bear*, a parodistic Chekhovian extravaganza, given at Aldeburgh in 1967. Among the late orchestral works are a Cello Concerto, cooler and more serene than the earlier concertos, a Second Symphony and miscellaneous pieces including a finely-worked set of Hindemith Variations, which shows an improvisatory character typical of his late music.

Operas Troilus and Cressida (1954); The Bear (1967)
Ballet The Quest (1943)
Orchestral music Portsmouth Point (1925); Siesta (1926); Sinfonia concertante (1927); Va Conc. (1929); 2 syms. (1935, 1960); Vn Conc. (1939); Scapino (1940); The Wise Virgins (1940); Johannesburg Festival Ov. (1956); Vc Conc. (1956); Partita (1957); Variations on a Theme by Hindemith (1963); Capriccio burlesco (1968); Improvisations on an Impromptu of Benjamin Britten (1969)
Choral music with orchestra Belshazzar's Feast (1931); In Honour of the City of London (1937); Coronation Te Deum (1953)
Choral music with organ The Twelve (1965); Missa brevis (1966)
Vocal music Façade (1922); A Song for the Lord Mayor's Table (1962)
Chamber music Str Qt (1947); Vn Sonata (1949)
Film music The First of the Few (1942); Went the Day Well? (1942); Henry V (1944); Hamlet (1947); Richard III (1955); The Battle of Britain (1969)

Waltz (Fr. *valse*; Ger. *Walzer*). The most popular ballroom dance of the 19th century. Its origins are obscure, but are bound up with the history of other triple-time dances, the *Deutsche* (German dance) and *ländler* of the late 18th century. The waltz increased in popularity in the early 19th century despite objections to it on medical grounds (the speed at which the dancers whirled around the room) and on moral grounds (partners held each other in close embrace).

Hummel was an early piano virtuoso to compose waltzes, and Beethoven's Diabelli Variations were on a simple waltz tune; but Schubert was the first major composer to produce music specifically described as waltzes. Weber's piano rondo, *Aufforderung zum Tanze* (1819), foreshadowed the form later adopted by major dance composers: a sequence of waltzes with a formal introduction and a coda referring to themes heard earlier. This form was established in the 1830s by Joseph Lanner and the elder Johann Strauss, and from then the waltz was particularly associated with Vienna, although it was popular throughout Europe.

With Strauss's sons, Johann and Josef, during the 1860s the waltz reached its peak as dance form, musical composition and symbol of a gay, elegant age. With Josef's death in 1870 and Johann's turn to operetta, the two major exponents of the waltz were lost to it. Their place was taken by minor composers, but some of the best waltzes of the late 19th century are found in the operettas of Lehár, Offenbach, Suppé and Messager. The waltz featured prominently in ballet and in such operas as Tchaikovsky's *Eugene Onegin*, Puccini's *La bohème* and, especially, Richard Strauss's *Der Rosenkavalier*. Stylized waltzes are to be found in instrumental and orchestral works. Some of the most original are those for piano by Chopin, Brahms's *Liebeslieder Walzer* for voices and piano duet, the third movement of Tchaikovsky's Fifth Symphony and the *Valse triste* of Sibelius. The waltz era is effectively summed up in the *Valses nobles et sentimentales* (1911) and the choreographic poem *La valse* (1918) of Ravel.

Waltz, Gustavus (*fl* 1732–59). English bass of German birth. Active mainly in London, he sang in Handel's operas and oratorios, creating a number of roles (including Saul); he also appeared in English theatre pieces by Lampe, Arne and others. He was supposedly once Handel's cook.

Wanderer Fantasia. Nickname of Schubert's Fantasia in C for piano D760 (1822), so called because the Adagio is a set of variations on a passage from his song *Der Wanderer* D489.

Wand of Youth, The. Two orchestral suites by Elgar, opp.1a and 11b, arranged 1907–1908 from earlier material.

Wanhal, Johann Baptist. *See* VANHAL, JOHANN BAPTIST.

Wannenmacher [Vannius], **Johannes** (*b* ?Neuenburg am Rhein, *c*1485; *d* Berne, spr. 1551). Swiss choirmaster and composer. He held posts at Berne and Fribourg. His 26 extant compositions in all the vocal genres of the age place him among the most important Swiss composers of the Reformation.

War and Peace [Voyna i mir]. Opera in five acts and an epigraph by Prokofiev to his own libretto after Tolstoy (concert performance 1944, Moscow).

Ward, John (*b* Canterbury, bap. 8 Sept 1571; *d* by 31 Aug 1638). English composer. A chorister at Canterbury Cathedral, he moved to London to join the Exchequer and was household musician to the influential Fanshawe family. By 1636 he was living in Essex. He composed madrigals in a serious vein (1613), fantasias and In Nomines for viol consort, services and over 20 anthems.

Warlock, Peter [Heseltine, Philip (Arnold)] (*b* London, 30 Oct 1894; *d* there, 17 Dec 1930). English composer. He was self-taught, though in contact with Delius from 1910, and was a friend of Van Dieren, Moeran and Lambert. Under his original name of Heseltine he wrote on music and edited English works of the Elizabethan era. As Warlock he produced a large output of songs, some dark, desolate and bleakly intense (*The Curlew* for tenor and sextet, 1922), others rumbustious, amorous or charming, but all informed by an exceptional sensitivity to words and high technical skill. He also wrote choral music and a few instrumental pieces (notably *Capriol Suite* for strings, 1926, based on 16th-century dances).

Warren, Leonard (*b* New York, 21 April 1911; *d* there, 4 March 1960). American baritone. After study in Italy he made his Met début in 1938, remaining until his death as the foremost local exponent of the baritone roles of Verdi and Puccini. He also sang in Latin America and at La Scala (début 1953). Possessor of a large, smooth voice, he died on the Met stage during *La forza del destino*.

War Requiem. Choral work by Britten, settings of nine poems by Wilfred Owen interpolated into the Requiem Mass (1962, Coventry).

Warsaw Autumn Festival (Poland). Annual festival of contemporary music established in 1956; as well as presenting much new east European music, it promotes the music of leading Polish composers, notably Lutosławski and Penderecki.

Warsaw Philharmonic Orchestra. *See* NATIONAL PHILHARMONIC ORCHESTRA.

Washboard. A corrugated board which is scraped; it is popular as a rhythm instrument, particularly in Afro-American music. Washboards were frequently used to accompany blues singers and enjoyed a brief vogue in the 1950s in 'skiffle'.

Washington Opera. Company formed in 1956 as the Opera Society of Washington, DC, to present unfamiliar works at low cost; it achieved an international reputation. It was renamed in 1971, when it moved to the Opera House at Kennedy Center. In the 1980s, under Martin Feinstein, its repertory and seasons were expanded and guest conductors were engaged. Casts are mainly American.

Wasielewski, Wilhelm Joseph von (*b* Grossleesen, 17 June 1822; *d* Sondershausen, 13 Dec 1896). German violinist, conductor and writer on music. He was one of the first pupils at the Leipzig Conservatory, where his teachers were Mendelssohn, Hauptmann and David. In Düsseldorf (where he was close to the Schumanns), Bonn, Dresden and Sondershausen, he performed and wrote. He produced the first definitive biography of Schumann (1858) and valuable books on early music and instruments.

Wasps, The. Incidental music by Vaughan Williams for tenor and baritone soloists, male chorus and orchestra for Aristophanes' play (1909, Cambridge).

Wassenaer, Count Unico Wilhelm van (*b* Twickel, 2 Nov 1692; *d* The Hague, 9 Nov 1766). Dutch composer. He studied at Leiden and took possession of his family estate in 1717, when he also embarked on the Grand Tour; later he held administrative posts and was United Provinces ambassador abroad. He was a keen musical amateur and composer, and the *Concerti armonici*, published anonymously in 1740 and long attributed to Pergolesi, Ricciotti, Chelleri, Birkenstock and others, are now known to be his composition. They are written in a somewhat conservative, south Italian style, with several fugal movements and rich seven-part scoring. Wassenaer's autograph of the concertos survives, along with a motet *Laudate Dominum*.

Water Carrier, The. *See* DEUX JOURNÉES, LES.

Water-drum. A percussion instrument making use of the acoustic properties of water. They are of two sorts, consisting either of a hollow drum filled with a variable amount of water (popular among North and South American Indians) or of a hollow vessel, often a gourd, floating in water within a larger container (as in Africa and New Guinea).

Water Music. A collection of music by Handel, supposed to have been written to restore himself to favour with George I after his (also supposed) truancy from the Hanoverian court (where George had been elector). The traditional story does not quite hold water, but there is evidence that Handel composed for a royal water party on the Thames in 1717. The *Water Music* consists of three groups of pieces, one in F major (in which horns are prominent), one in D major (using trumpets) and one in G (major and minor) of a more chamber-music character: possibly this last was used to entertain the king over supper while the others were actually played on the river.

Water organ. An organ blown and sounded automatically by air compressed directly by water, for example by a waterfall or a stream. Because they play without human intervention they have been associated, since ancient Greek times, with magic and mystery. They were often built into secret grottoes in ornamental gardens. In the 16th and 17th centuries they were familiar playthings in princes' palaces. As they became increasingly ornate the vogue passed; none survives. (It is distinct from the HYDRAULIS.)

Watson, Thomas (*b* London, *c* 1557; *d* there, bur. 26 Sept 1592). English poet. His *Italian Madrigalls Englished* (1590), an anthology of Italian madrigals (mostly by Marenzio) for which he wrote new English texts, greatly advanced the popularity of the Italian madrigal in England.

Watts, Helen (Josephine) (*b* Milford Haven, 7 Dec 1927). Welsh contralto. She made her début in Bach at a 1955 Prom, and her chief reputation was in oratorio; from 1959 she sang in opera, notably by Handel, Britten (Lucretia, 1964) and Tippett (Sosotris, Covent Garden, 1968); her American début was in *Kindertotenlieder* at Carnegie Hall (1970). Her warm and intelligent singing and her attentiveness to words make her a distinguished interpreter of lieder and 20th-century song.

Wat Tyler. Opera by Alan Bush to a libretto by Nancy Bush (concert performance, 1951, London; staged 1953, Leipzig).

Waxman, Franz (*b* Chorzow, Poland, 24 Dec 1906; *d* Los Angeles, 24 Feb 1967). American composer and conductor. He studied in Berlin and played in cafés and a jazz orchestra; he was involved in supplying music for films but left in 1933, going to Paris and then to the USA. He worked at MGM and Warner Bros and wrote scores for over 140 films, and was also active as a conductor. Among the films for which he supplied music are *Sunset Boulevard* (1950), *Peyton Place* and *The Spirit of St Louis* (both 1957); he also wrote two choral works (1959, 1965) of Jewish inspiration.

Wayes. Title used *c* 1600 for short didactic contrapuntal pieces in two or three parts on a *cantus firmus*.

Webbe, Samuel (*b* ?London, 1740; *d* London, 25 May 1816). English composer. He was active as a composer from the 1760s, became organist at the Portuguese and Sardinian chapels in London in 1776 and was an influential teacher. Recognized as the finest glee composer, he won 27 Catch Club prizes, 1766–92, and became the club's secretary in 1794. He wrote over 100 glees of which the best known was *Glorious Apollo* (1787). Notable for their lyrical melodies, they range from simple three-part homophony in strophic or rondo form to elaborate pieces in several movements, some with finely worked counterpoint. Webbe also wrote songs, cantatas etc, a large amount of Roman Catholic church music (mainly simple in style), some English anthems and psalm tunes, keyboard pieces and three singing tutors.

His son Samuel (*c*1770–1843) was an organist and composer in Liverpool and London; he wrote glees, songs, church music and piano pieces.

Webber, Andrew Lloyd. *See* LLOYD WEBBER, ANDREW.

Weber. German family of musicians. The most celebrated members were Fridolin (1733–79), a singer and violinist at Mannheim; his brother Franz Anton (1734–1812), a composer, violinist, Kapellmeister at Eutin and travelling theatrical manager, the father of CARL MARIA VON WEBER; and his daughters Josepha (1758/9–1819), the dramatic soprano for whom Mozart wrote the Queen of Night role in *Die Zauberflöte*, Aloysia (1759/61–1839), also a soprano, for whom Mozart wrote concert arias, and Constanze (1762–1842), who married Mozart. Carl Maria had two half-brothers, Fridolin (1761–1833), a violinist in the Esterházy orchestra, and Edmund (1766–1828), a minor composer active at Würzburg, Berne and Lübeck.

Weber, Bedřich [Friedrich] **Diviš** [Dionys] (*b* Velichov, 9 Oct 1766; *d* Prague, 25 Dec 1842). Bohemian composer and teacher. He studied in Prague (with the Abbé Vogler) and was much influenced by Mozart. Most of his compositions are light dance pieces in a conservative style. He is remembered for his influence over music education in the Czech lands: he was the first director of the Prague Conservatory (from 1811) and (from 1839) director of the Organ School.

Weber, Ben (William Jennings Bryan) (*b* St Louis, 23 July 1916; *d* New York, 16 June 1979). American composer. Largely self-taught, he worked at first as a copyist and came to be recognized only in the 1950s. His music, much of it 12-note, is marked by its virtuoso Romantic style and its vocal quality; it includes much chamber music, for a wide range of combinations, orchestral music (including concertos for violin and piano), piano music and songs.

Weber, Bernhard Anselm (*b* Mannheim, 18 April 1764; *d* Berlin, 23 March 1821). German conductor, composer and pianist. He toured throughout Europe but worked chiefly at Berlin, becoming first musical director of the Nationaltheater (1796–1820), where his Gluck productions were particularly successful. Among his compositions, the incidental music to Schiller's *Wilhelm Tell* (1804) is best known.

Weber, Carl Maria (Friedrich Ernst) von (*b* Eutin, ?18 Nov 1786; *d* London, 5 June 1826). German composer. He studied in Salzburg (with Michael Haydn), Munich (J.N. Kalcher) and Vienna (Abbé Vogler), becoming Kapellmeister at Breslau (1804) and working for a time at Württemberg (1806) and Stuttgart (1807). With help from Franz Danzi, intellectual stimulation from his friends Gänsbacher, Meyer-

beer, Gottfried Weber and Alexander von Dusch and the encouragement of concert and operatic successes in Munich (especially *Abu Hassan*), Prague and Berlin, he settled down as opera director in Prague (1813–16). There he systematically reorganized the theatre's operations and built up the nucleus of a German company, concentrating on works, mostly French, that offered an example for the development of a German operatic tradition. But his searching reforms (extending to scenery, lighting, orchestral seating, rehearsal schedules and salaries) led to resentment. Not until his appointment as Royal Saxon Kapellmeister at Dresden (1817) and the unprecedented triumph of *Der Freischütz* (1821) in Berlin and throughout Germany did his championship of a true German opera win popular support. Official opposition continued, both from the Italian opera establishment in Dresden and from Spontini in Berlin; Weber answered critics with the grand heroic opera *Euryanthe* (1823, Vienna). His rapidly deteriorating health and his concern to provide for his family induced him to accept the invitation to write an English opera for London; he produced *Oberon* at Covent Garden in April 1826. Despite an enthusiastic English reception and every care for his health, this last journey hastened his decline; he died from tuberculosis, at 39.

Weber's Romantic leanings can be seen in the novel emotional flavour of his music and its relevance to emergent German nationalism, his delicate receptivity to nature and to literary and pictorial impressions, his parallel activities as critic, virtuoso pianist and Kapellmeister, his dedication to the evolution of a new kind of opera uniting all the arts and above all his wish to communicate feeling. His role as a father-figure of musical Romanticism was acknowledged by those who succeeded him in the movement, from Berlioz and Wagner to Debussy and Mahler. His melodic and harmonic style is rooted in classical principles, but as he matured he experimented with chromaticism (the diminished 7th chord was a particular favourite). He also was among the subtlest of orchestrators, writing for unusual but dramatically apt and vivid instrumental combinations (clarinet and horn, muted and unmuted strings etc). All his most successful music, including the songs and concertos, is to some degree dramatically inspired.

Weber won his widest audience with *Freischütz*, outwardly a Singspiel celebrating German folklore and country life, using an idiom touched by German folksong. Through his skilful use of motifs and his careful harmonic, visual and instrumental designs – notably for the Wolf's Glen scene, the outstanding example in music of the early Romantic treatment of the sinister and the supernatural – he gave this work a new creative status. *Euryanthe*, despite a weak libretto, makes a further advance in the unity of harmonic and formal structures, moving towards continuous, freely composed opera. In *Oberon* Weber reverted to separate numbers to suit English taste, yet the work retains his characteristically subtle motivic handling and depiction of both natural and supernatural elements. Of his other works, some of the German songs, the colouristic *Konzertstück* for piano and orchestra, the dramatic clarinet and bassoon concertos and the virtuoso *Grand duo concertant* for clarinet and piano deserve special mention.

Dramatic music Abu Hassan (1811); Der Freischütz (1821); Die drei Pintos (1821, perf. 1888); Euryanthe (1823); Oberon (1826); incidental music for Turandot (1809), Heinrich IV (1818), Preciosa (1820) and other plays; scenas, songs, romances, 5 concert arias
Choral music 3 masses; Agnus Dei; 6 secular cantatas, incl. Kampf und Sieg (1815); acc. choral works; 24 unacc. canons, male-voice choruses, partsongs
Vocal music c80 songs, incl. gui songs, Italian canzonettas, Scottish folksong arrs.; Leyer und Schwert collection, i–ii (1814); Die Temperamente beim Verluste der Geliebten (1816); 6 duets
Orchestral music 2 syms.; Pf Conc. no.1, C (1810); Pf Conc. no.2, E♭ (1812); Konzertstück, f, pf (1821); Cl Conc. no.1, f (1811); Cl Conc. no.2, E♭ (1811); Cl Concertino, E♭ (1811); Bn Conc., F (1811); Horn Concertino, e (1815); ovs., marches
Chamber music Pf Qt, B♭ (1809); Cl Qnt, B♭ (1815); Grand duo concertant, cl, pf (1815); 4 pf sonatas; Aufforderung zum Tanze, pf (1819); pf duets, variations
Writings poetry, concert notices, articles on new operas; Tonkünstlers Leben, novel (1819), inc.

Weber, Georg (*b* Dahlen, *c*1610; *d* after 1653). German composer. A singer, poet and clergyman, he was a member of the school of songwriters centred on Königsberg and Danzig. He was important for his songs with instruments. He is not to be confused with Georg Weber (*c*1540–1599), a composer of Protestant church music in Weissenfels and Naumburg.

Weber, (Jacob) Gottfried (*b* Freinsheim, 1 March 1779; *d* Kreuznach, 21 Sept 1839). German theorist and writer on music. A lawyer by profession and a self-taught musical theorist, he set out in the *Versuch einer geordneten Theorie der Tonsetzkunst* (Mainz, 1817–21), a theory of harmony with important pedagogical applications. He also contributed to several journals, notably *Cäcilia*, which he founded and edited (1824–39).

Weber, Ludwig (*b* Vienna, 29 July 1899; *d* there, 9 Dec 1974). Austrian bass. After his début at the Vienna Volksoper (1920) he sang at Elberfeld, Düsseldorf and Cologne. From 1933 he was the leading bass at the Bavarian Staatsoper, Munich, creating Holsteiner in Strauss's *Friedenstag* (1938). He was successful at Covent Garden between 1936 and 1950, and from 1951 his Marke, Hagen and Gurnemanz set a standard at Bayreuth.

Webern, Anton (Friedrich Wilhelm von) (*b* Vienna, 3 Dec 1883; *d* Mittersill, 15 Sept 1945). Austrian composer. He studied at Vienna University under Adler (1902–6), taking the doctorate for work on Isaac; in composition he was one of Schoenberg's first pupils (1904–8), along with Berg. Like Berg, he developed rapidly under Schoenberg's guidance, achieving a fusion of Brahms, Reger and tonal Schoenberg in his orchestral Passacaglia, already highly characteristic in its modest dynamic level and its brevity. But he was closer than Berg in following Schoenberg into atonality, even choosing verses by the same poet, George, to take

the step in songs of 1908–9. His other step was into a conducting career, which he began with modest provincial engagements before World War I.

After the war he settled close to Schoenberg in Mödling and took charge of the Vienna Workers' Symphony Concerts (1922–34). Meanwhile he had continued his atonal style, mostly in songs: the relatively few instrumental pieces of 1909–14 had grown ever shorter, ostensibly because of the lack of any means of formal extension in a language without key or theme. However, the songs of 1910–25 show a reintroduction of traditional formal patterns even before the arrival of serialism (especially canonic patterns, no doubt stimulated, as was the instrumentation of many of these songs, by *Pierrot lunaire*), to the extent that the eventual adoption of the 12-note method in the Three Traditional Rhymes (1925) seems almost incidental, making little change to a musical style that was already systematized by strict counterpoint.

However, Webern soon recognized that the 12-note principle sanctioned a severity and virtuosity of polyphony that he could compare with that of the Renaissance masters he had studied. Unlike Schoenberg, he never again sought to compose in any other way. Rather, the highly controlled, pure style of his Symphony appears to have represented an ideal which later works could only repeat, showing different facets. His use of the series as a source of similar motifs, especially in instrumental works, merely emphasizes the almost geometrical perfection of this music, for which he found literary stimulus in Goethe and, more nearly, in the poetry of his friend and neighbour Hildegard Jone, whose words he set exclusively during his last dozen years. With Schoenberg gone, Berg dead and himself deprived of his posts, Webern saw Jone as one of his few allies during World War II. He was shot in error by a soldier after the end of hostilities, leaving a total acknowledged output of about three hours' duration.

Orchestral music Passacaglia (1908); 6 Pieces (1909); Five Pieces, small orch (1913); Sym. (1928); Conc., fl, ob, cl, hn, tpt, trbn, vn, va, pf (1934); Variations (1940)
Choral music Entflieht auf leichten Kähnen (1908); 2 Songs (1926); Das Augenlicht (1935); 2 cantatas (1939, 1943)
Chamber and piano music 5 Movts, str qt (1909); 4 Pieces, vn, pf (1910); 6 Bagatelles, str qt (1913); 3 Little Pieces, vc, pf (1914); Str Trio (1927); Qt, cl, t sax, vn, pf (1930); Variations, pf (1936); Str Qt (1938)
Songs 10 George songs (1909); 2 Rilke Songs with octet (1910); 4 Songs (1917); 4 Songs with orch (1918); 6 Trakl Songs, cl, b cl, vn, vc (1919); 5 Sacred Songs, S, fl, cl/b cl, tpt, vn/va, harp (1922); 5 Latin Canons, cl, b cl (1924); 3 Traditional Rhymes, cl, b cl, vn/va (1925); 3 Songs, cl, gui (1925); 6 Jone songs (1934)

Weckerlin, Jean-Baptiste (Théodore) (*b* Guebwiller, 9 Nov 1821; *d* Trottberg, 20 May 1910). French folklorist, bibliographer and composer. As librarian of the Paris Conservatoire (1876–1909) he doubled its holdings, enriching it particularly with rare collections of French folksong. Apart from his sensitive editions of early folk music, his best-known book is *La chanson populaire* (1886).

Weckmann, Matthias (*b* Niederorla, 1619 or earlier; *d* Hamburg, 24 Feb 1674). German composer and organist. A favoured pupil of Schütz at the Dresden court, he became organist of the electoral chapel in 1637 after studying in Hamburg. In 1642-7 he was organist (under Schütz) at the court chapel in Nyköbing, Denmark; he then returned to his Dresden post. From 1655 he was organist at the Jacobikirche, Hamburg; he founded a collegium musicum in 1660.

Weckmann wrote sacred music (with instruments), chamber music and keyboard pieces; many of his works are now lost, while others have been wrongly attributed to him. Instead of following the general trend of his time towards simpler textures and clearer forms, he developed elements of Schütz's earlier works such as expressive word-setting and strong dissonances and used intricate counterpoint. His son Jacob Weckmann (1643-80) was an organist and probably a composer.

We Come to the River. Opera ('actions for music') in 11 scenes by Henze to a libretto by Edward Bond (1976, London).

Wedding, The. See NOCES, LES.

Wedge Fugue. Nickname of J.S. Bach's Fugue in E minor for organ BWV548 (1731), so called because its subject proceeds in increasing intervals.

Weelkes, Thomas (*b* ?Elsted, ? bap. 25 Oct 1576; *d* London, bur. 1 Dec 1623). English composer. He was organist at Winchester College (1598-*c*1602) and then Chichester Cathedral. He took the Oxford BMus in 1602 and may have been a member of the Chapel Royal. After his temporary dismissal from Chichester for drunkenness (1617), he spent time in London. A leading church composer and gifted madrigalist, he produced ten services, over 35 anthems, nearly 100 madrigals (4 bks, 1597-1608) and a little consort music. His best works are noted for their brilliant counterpoint and inventive textual imagery; they include the well-known sacred madrigal *When David heard, As Vesta was, from Latmos Hill descending* (in *The Triumphes of Oriana*, 1601), *Thule, the period of cosmographie* and the remarkable *O care thou wilt dispatch mee.*

Weerbeke, Gaspar van (*b* Oudenaarde, *c*1445; *d* after 1517). Netherlands composer. Early in the 1470s he arrived at the Sforza court, Milan, and in winter 1480-81 became a singer in the papal choir in Rome, where he remained for eight years. After a period of service to the Sforzas, and (from 1495-7) with the court choir of Philip the Fair, in 1500 he returned to the papal choir. His eight surviving Mass Ordinaries are mostly based on pre-existing material, and all use imitation sparingly. The 18 motets of his two mass cycles are largely homophonic and organized by the structure of the text, which is delivered syllabically. His early Milan motets are influenced by the Italians, but others blend the Netherlands motet style with that of Italian popular sacred music. He also composed a Magnificat and Lamentations.

Wegelius, Martin (*b* Helsinki, 10 Nov 1846; *d* there, 22 March 1906). Finnish educationist. A pioneer in Finnish music education, he founded and directed the Helsinki Music College (now the Sibelius Academy) in 1882, his pupils including Sibelius and Palmgren. He also wrote theory textbooks.

Weigl, Joseph (*b* Eisenstadt, 28 March 1766; *d* Vienna, 3 Feb 1846). Austrian composer. A son of the cellist Joseph (Franz) Weigl (1740-1820), who played under Haydn at the Esterházy court before becoming famous in Vienna, he was a pupil of Albrechtsberger; he had contact with Mozart and conducted his operas in Vienna. By 1790 he was deputy Kapellmeister at the court theatre and in 1792 he became Kapellmeister and composer. Up to 1823 he composed over 40 Italian operas, German operas and ballets, most of them for 9 Vienna; later he wrote mainly sacred music. In 1827-38 he was court vice-Kapellmeister. His dramatic works are based on the Viennese Classical tradition, but those after 1800 move towards more emotional and domestic subject matter and more Romantic orchestral colours. The highly successful Singspiel *Die Schweizerfamilie* (1809, after *The Swiss Family Robinson*) is the prototype of a German lyrical folk opera. Weigl also composed cantatas, lieder and instrumental pieces.

His brother Thaddäus (1776-1844) conducted at the court theatre and composed stage works; he was also a publisher.

Weigl, Karl (*b* Vienna, 6 Feb 1881; *d* New York, 11 Aug 1949). Austrian composer, later naturalized American. A pupil of Zemlinsky and Adler, he was assistant to Mahler at the Vienna Hofoper, 1904-6. He taught at the New Vienna Conservatory from 1918 and at the university from 1930, then moved to the USA in 1938 and taught at various institutions. He enjoyed a considerable reputation in Vienna and wrote numerous lieder in the Wolf-Mahler tradition; he also wrote six symphonies (1908-47) and eight string quartets (1903-49).

Weill, Kurt (Julian) (*b* Dessau, 2 March 1900; *d* New York, 3 April 1950). German composer, American citizen from 1943. He was a pupil of Humperdinck, Busoni and Jarnach in Berlin (1918-23); their teaching informed his early music, including the choral *Recordare* (1923) and the Concerto for violin and wind (1924), the latter also influenced by Stravinsky. But the deeper influence of Stravinsky, coupled with an increased consciousness of music as a social force, led Weill to a rediscovery in the mid-1920s of tonal and vernacular elements, notably from jazz, in his cantata *Der neue Orpheus* and one-act stage piece *Royal Palace*, written between two collaborations with the expressionist playwright Georg Kaiser: *Der Protagonist* and *Der Zar lässt sich photographieren.* In 1926 he married the singer Lotte Lenya, who was to be the finest interpreter of his music.

His next collaborator was Brecht, with whom he worked on *The Threepenny Opera* (1928), *The Rise and Fall of the City of Mahagonny* (1929) and *Happy End* (1929), all of which use the corrupted, enfeebled diatonicism of commercial music as a weapon of social criticism, though paradoxically they have beome the epitome of the pre-war culture they sought to despise. Yet this is done within the context of a new harmonic consistency and focus. These works have also drawn attention from the theatre works in which Weill developed without Brecht during the early 1930s, *Die Bürgschaft* and *Der Silbersee* (with Kaiser again).

In 1933 he left Germany for Paris, where he worked with Brecht again on the sung ballet *The Seven Deadly Sins*. Then in 1935 he moved to the USA, where he cut loose from the European art-music tradition and devoted himself wholeheartedly to composing for the Broadway stage, intentionally subordinating aesthetic criteria to pragmatic and populist ones. Yet these works are still informed by his cultivated sense of character and theatrical form.

Dramatic music Der Protagonist (1926); Royal Palace (1927); Der Zar lässt sich photographieren (1928); Die Dreigroschenoper (1928); Aufstieg und Fall der Stadt Mahagonny (1929); Happy End (1929); Der Jasager, school opera (1930); Die Bürgschaft (1932); Der Silbersee (1933); Die sieben Todsünden, sung ballet (1933); Johnny Johnson, fable (1936); Knickerbocker Holiday, operetta (1938); Railroads on Parade, pageant (1939); Lady in the Dark, musical play (1941); One Touch of Venus, musical comedy (1943); Street Scene, Broadway opera (1947); Down in the Valley, college opera (1948); Love Life, vaudeville (1948); Lost in the Stars, musical tragedy (1949); film, theatre and radio music

Orchestral music Sym. no.1 (1921); Divertimento (1922); Sinfonia sacra (1922); Conc., vn, wind (1924); Sym. no.2 (1933)

Vocal music Recordare, chorus (1923); Der neue Orpheus, S, vn, orch (1925); Vom Tod im Wald, B, wind (1927); Das Berliner Requiem, T, Bar, B, chorus (1928); Der Lindberghflug, T, Bar, chorus (1929); Kiddush, T, chorus (1949); songs

Chamber music 2 str qts (1919, 1923); Vc Sonata (1920)

Wein, Der. Concert aria for soprano and orchestra by Berg to words by Baudelaire, translated by George (1929).

Weinberg, Henry (*b* Philadelphia, 7 June 1931). American composer. A pupil of Rochberg, Sessions, Dallapiccola and Babbitt, he was appointed to Queens College in 1966 and has worked particularly with rhythmic structuring, high sonorities and fluctuating textures.

Weinberger, Jaromír (*b* Prague, 8 Jan 1896; *d* St Petersburg, FL, 8 Aug 1967). Czech-American composer. He was a pupil of Křička and Hoffmeister in Prague and of Reger in Leipzig. His outstanding success was with *Shvanda the Bagpiper* (1927, Prague), a brilliant and colourful folk opera. In the 1930s he wrote three more operas, then fled to the USA, where he wrote orchestral and religious works using folk music.

Weiner, Leó (*b* Budapest, 16 April 1885; *d* there, 13 Sept 1960). Hungarian composer. He studied with Koessler at the Budapest Academy (1901–6), where he began teaching in 1908. While sharing the nationalist concerns of Bartók and Kodály, he remained essentially within the German Romantic tradition and wrote mostly instrumental music (five orchestral divertimentos, two violin concertos, three string quartets, piano music).

Weingartner, (Paul) Felix, Edler von Münzberg (*b* Zara, 2 June 1863; *d* Winterthur, 7 May 1942). Austrian conductor and composer. He studied in Graz and Leipzig and after an early career at Gdańsk, Mannheim and Hamburg became court Kapellmeister of the Berlin Opera and director of the royal orchestral concerts (1891). He was director at the Vienna Court Opera, 1908–11, and conductor of the Vienna Philharmonic concerts until 1927. He conducted in London from 1898, becoming associated with the Royal Philharmonic Society and the LSO. His American career, from 1905, centred in New York and Boston. After World War I his European career was confined largely to Basle and Vienna. He was considered one of the most eminent classical conductors of his day, performing Beethoven and Schubert with a clear beat and precise tempos. His compositions include seven symphonies (1899–1937) and several operas widely performed in Austria and Germany.

Weinzweig, John (Jacob) (*b* Toronto, 11 March 1913). Canadian composer. He studied at Toronto University (1934–7) and the Eastman School, where he became acquainted with Stravinsky, Schoenberg and Berg: his First Piano Suite (1939) contains the earliest Canadian 12-note music. In the 1940s he wrote much music for Canadian radio, but his activities have been mainly in teaching and administration on behalf of Canadian music. His output consists mostly of concertante pieces (Violin Concerto, 1954), chamber music and songs.

Weir, Gillian (Constance) (*b* Martinborough, NZ, 17 Jan 1941). British organist. She studied with Downes, Heiller and Alain and made her Festival Hall début in 1965. She has toured widely in Europe and the USA and is a notable interpreter not only of Bach but also of 20th-century music, particularly Messiaen, to which her virtuosity, acute perception and sense of style suit her well.

Weir, Judith (*b* Aberdeen, 11 May 1954). Scottish composer. After study with Tavener she worked on computer music at MIT (1973) and studied with Holloway at Cambridge. She gained attention for her instrumental pieces (*The Art of Touching the Keyboard* for piano, 1983); her opera *A Night at the Chinese Opera* (1987) was widely acclaimed for its characterization, evocative orchestration and flowing vocal lines.

Weis, Flemming (*b* Copenhagen, 15 April 1898; *d* there, 30 Sept 1981). Danish composer. Trained at the Copenhagen Conservatory (1916–20) and the Leipzig Musikhochschule (1920–23, with Graener), he was organist at the Annakirke in Copenhagen (1929–68) and contributed significantly to Danish musical life. He wrote two symphonies (1943, 1948), chamber and choral music in a post-Nielsen style.

Weisgall, Hugo (David) (*b* Eibenschütz, Czechoslovakia, 13 Oct 1912). American composer of central European origin. His father, a cantor, took the family to the USA in 1920, and he studied at the Peabody Conservatory, the Curtis Institute and intermittently with Sessions (1932–41). He has taught at various institutions (including the Juilliard School, 1957–70) and vigorously promoted American music as a conductor. He is one of America's most important composers of operas and large-scale song cycles. Their literary merit, original vocal style and attention to musical and dramatic detail make them significant contributions to the genre. The operas are in a broad-spanned, eclectic style that has incorporated 12-note elements since the late 1950s (*The Stronger*, 1952; *Six Characters in Search of an Author*, 1956; *Athaliah*, 1964).

Weismann, Julius (*b* Freiburg, 26 Dec 1879; *d* Singen am Hohentweil, 22 Dec 1950). German composer. A pupil of Rheinberger, von Herzogenberg and Thuille, he worked in Munich and Freiburg as a conductor, teacher and composer. His operas, notably *Leonce und Lena* (1924), were successful between the wars; he also wrote copiously in other genres.

Weiss, Adolph (*b* Baltimore, 12 Sept 1891; *d* Van Nuys, CA, 21 Feb 1971). American composer. He studied with Schoenberg in Berlin (1925–6) and was one of the first to introduce 12-note techniques in the USA, composing mostly chamber, orchestral and piano music.

Weiss, Silvius Leopold (*b* Breslau, 12 Oct 1686; *d* Dresden, 16 Oct 1750). German lutenist and composer. He served in Breslau, then spent 1708–14 in Italy where he worked with the Scarlattis in Rome. By 1717 he had joined the Saxon court chapel at Dresden. He performed in cities including London, Vienna and Leipzig (where he met Bach in 1739). He was both the greatest of all lutenists and the most prolific of solo lute composers, writing nearly 600 pieces. Most are grouped in dance suites (often starting with an unbarred prelude); they are mainly late Baroque in style, but later works show more *galant* features. He also wrote sonatas and concertos for lute with other instruments.

His father Johann Jacob (*c*1662–1754) was a lutenist (at the Palatine court, from 1720 at Mannheim), as were two of his brothers. Johann Sigismund (after 1690–1737) served at the Palatine court, becoming director of instrumental music by 1732, and wrote mostly lute music (concertos, sonatas etc). Johann Adolf Faustinus (1741–1814) worked at the Dresden court from 1763 and travelled widely; he composed many pieces for lute (by then old-fashioned) and some for the more popular guitar.

Weisse, Christian Felix (*b* Annaberg, 28 Jan 1726; *d* Leipzig, 16 Dec 1804). German poet. He wrote Singspiel librettos for a company in Leipzig. The earliest, including *Der Teufel ist los* (set by J. Standfuss, 1752), were based on English ballad operas, but from the 1760s he took *opéra comique* as his model and introduced more opportunities for songs; Hiller's settings were highly successful. His lyric poetry was set by Mozart, among others.

Weissensee, Friedrich (*b* Schwerstedt, *c*1560; *d* Altenweddingen, 1622). German composer. He taught at Gebesee and Magdeburg and from 1602 was a clergyman at Altenweddingen. A leading German Protestant church composer, he published Latin and German motets in a Venetian-influenced style for multiple choirs with instruments (*Opus melicum*, 1602), and occasional works.

Weldon, John (*b* Chichester, 19 Jan 1676; *d* London, 7 May 1736). English composer and organist. A pupil of Purcell, he was organist of New College, Oxford, 1694–1702, and then St Bride's, Fleet Street, London. He became Chapel Royal organist in 1708 and second composer in 1715; from 1714 he

was also organist at St Martin-in-the-Fields. His stage works include the masque *The Judgment of Paris* (1701) and *The Tempest* (*c*1712; perhaps the setting attributed to Purcell); he also composed an ode, songs and duets, over 30 anthems and a few instrumental pieces. Varied melodic expression and unusual formal designs are features of his writing.

Welin, Karl-Erik (*b* Genarp, 31 May 1934). Swedish composer. He studied at the Stockholm Musikhögskolan. As an organist he is internationally known as a performer of avant-garde music and for unconventional performances of the Baroque repertory. His works range over many styles, emphasizing the dramatic and destructive.

Welitsch, Ljuba (*b* Borissovo, 10 July 1913). Austrian soprano of Bulgarian birth. After study in Vienna she made her début at Sofia (1936). She sang in Graz, Hamburg and Munich and in 1946 joined the Vienna Opera. Her finest role was Salome, which she performed with passion and vocal purity, and which she sang at Covent Garden (1947) and at her Met début (1949). Her rise to international fame was meteoric but insufficient care of her remarkable voice denied her continuing success.

Weller, Walter (*b* Vienna, 30 Nov 1939). Austrian conductor and violinist. He studied in Vienna and played in the Vienna PO from 1956. In 1958 he founded the Weller Quartet, which has made many recordings of the Viennese Classics and 20th-century music, distinguished by an expansive, romantic style and polished tone. Weller led the Vienna PO and the Staatsoper Orchestra, 1961–9. He made his conducting début in 1966 and has held posts in Duisburg (1971), with the Royal Liverpool PO (1977) and the RPO (1979).

Wellesz, Egon (Joseph) (*b* Vienna, 21 Oct 1885; *d* Oxford, 9 Nov 1974). Austrian composer and musicologist. He was a pupil of Schoenberg and Adler like his close friend Webern. Unlike Webern, though, he continued to pursue both creative and scholarly activities, before and after his move to England in 1938, where he lectured at Oxford from 1943. He did important, far-reaching work on Venetian opera, Viennese Baroque music and Byzantine chant, especially notation and hymnography; his compositions cover many genres and extend from a Schoenbergian style towards Bruckner (especially in the nine symphonies 1945–71, his major works in England), Bartók (in his chamber music, which includes a fine octet, 1949, a Clarinet Quintet, 1959, nine string quartets, 1912–66) or Strauss (in the operas, notably *Alkestis*, 1924, *Die Bakchantinnen*, 1931, and *Incognita*, 1951).

Wellington's Victory. *See* BATTLE SYMPHONY.

Well-tempered Clavier. Term used to signify a keyboard tuning suitable for all 24 keys. It does not denote any specific system of temperament, nor does it necessarily mean equal temperament. Bach used the title for his first (1722) book of preludes and fugues in each of the major and minor keys; it is now habitually applied to both books of this collection, the '48'.

Welsh National Opera. Company founded in 1946 and based in Cardiff, where it gives four seasons annually; it also tours in Wales and England. Its reputation was built mainly on its chorus and its productions of Verdi; recent and new works have been added to the repertory. It is noted for its progressive productions. Its orchestra, the Welsh Philharmonia, was formed in 1970, and became known as the Orchestra of the Welsh National Opera in 1979.

Wendling, Johann Baptist (*b* Rappoltsweiler, 17 June 1723; *d* Munich, 27 Nov 1797). German flautist and composer. He served at the Mannheim court, moving with it to Munich in 1778. One of the best flautists of his day, he toured widely (in 1778 he performed with Mozart in Paris) and composed flute concertos, quartets, trios etc.

His wife, Dorothea (1736–1811), was a singer; she created Ilia in Mozart's *Idomeneo* (1781). His brother Franz (1729–86) was a violinist at Mannheim and Munich; Franz's wife, Elisabeth Augusta (1746–86), created Electra in *Idomeneo*. Johann's daughter Elisabeth Augusta (1752–94) also became a singer; Mozart wrote two *ariettes* for her. His nephew Karl (1750–1834), a violinist, became a conductor at the Mannheim National Theatre.

Went [Wendt], Johann (Nepomuk) (*b* Divice, 27 June 1745; *d* Vienna, 3 July 1801). Bohemian oboist and composer. After serving as an english horn player, he became second oboist in the emperor's wind band in Vienna in 1782. He transcribed over 40 stage works (including five Mozart operas) and wrote music for wind band and other ensembles.

Wenzinger, August (*b* Basle, 14 Nov 1905). Swiss viola da gamba player and conductor. He studied at the Basle Conservatory and in Cologne. In 1933 he was a founder of the Schola Cantorum Basiliensis, directing many period-style performances and teaching there. At Herrenhausen (Hanover), 1958–66, he conducted stylish, authentic performances of Baroque operas.

Werckmeister, Andreas (*b* Benneckenstein, 30 Nov 1645; *d* Halberstadt, 26 Oct 1706). German theorist and organist. He held a series of posts in Hasselfelde, at the Quedlinburg court and (from 1696) at Halberstadt. Although he lived only in Thuringia, he had a wide influence through his many writings, which reflect his conservative view of music as a gift from God and a mathematical science. He was a celebrated organist and organ examiner, and devised a temperament system for keyboard instruments which moves towards equal temperament. He was also a composer.

Werder, Felix (*b* Berlin, 22 Feb 1922). Australian composer of German origin. He was brought up in Berlin and England (1934–41) before his move to Australia, where he has worked as a critic and composer. His works, in many genres, draw on a wide range of 20th-century techniques and include operas and concertos.

Werkprinzip (Ger.: 'department principle'). Term used to describe the building of organs in which each 'department' or *Werk* (i.e. a keyboard with its chest) has a separate structure. Almost all organs before *c*1700 followed this principle.

Werle, Lars Johan (*b* Gävle, 23 June 1926). Swedish composer. A pupil of Moberg and Bäck, he is noted for his dramatically innovatory operas (including

Dream about Thérèse, 1964; *Tintomara*, 1973).

Werner, Gregor Joseph (*b* Ybbs an der Donau, 28 Jan 1693; *d* Eisenstadt, 3 March 1766). Austrian composer. After a period as organist of Melk Abbey he moved to Vienna. He was Kapellmeister at the Esterházy court in Eisenstadt from 1728 and brought the Kapelle to a high standard. After Haydn took over in 1761, he remained Oberhofkapellmeister, responsible for sacred music, but resented the younger composer. Among his many sacred works are oratorios, masses and antiphons in a Neapolitan idiom, contrapuntal *a cappella* masses and Christmas pieces containing folksong-like themes. He also wrote secular cantatas and instrumental music, including symphonies, trio sonatas and a *Musicalischer Instrumental-Calender* (1748), which uses representational effects.

Wernick, Richard (*b* Boston, 19 Jan 1934). American composer. He studied at Brandeis and Mills College (under Kirchner). In 1968 he joined the faculty at the University of Pennsylvania. His works, in a dramatic, eclectic style, include ballets, chamber and choral music. *Visions of Wonder and Terror* (1977) for mezzo-soprano and orchestra won a Pulitzer Prize.

Werrecore, Matthias Hermann (*b* ? Vercore/Warcoing, *d* after 1574). ? Flemish composer. He was *maestro di cappella* at Milan Cathedral. In addition to his famous four-voice *Bataglia taliana* (1525), celebrating the defeat of France at the Battle of Pavia, he wrote at least six motets and other pieces.

Wert, Giaches de (*b* ? Weert, 1535; *d* Mantua, 6 May 1596). Flemish composer. He first served at minor Italian courts and was *maestro di cappella* at the Gonzaga family's new ducal chapel of S Barbara, Mantua, from at least 1565 until 1592. In 1580, partly through his affair with the singer Tarquinia Molza, he became involved with poets and musicians at the Este court at Ferrara. His madrigals and other secular vocal works (*c*230, in 16 bks, 1558–1608) and sacred pieces (over 150, in 3 bks, 1566–81, and MSS) show his great contrapuntal mastery. A versatile composer, he was sensitive to contemporary styles; his later works reflect progressive ideas at Ferrara, and his declamatory style and expressive intensity greatly influenced his successors at Mantua, notably Monteverdi.

Werther. Opera in four acts by Massenet to a libretto by Blau, Milliet and Hartmann after Goethe (1892, Vienna).

Wesendonck Songs. Five songs by Wagner (1858), settings for voice and piano of poems by Mathilde Wesendonck.

Wesley. English family of religious leaders and musicians. John (1703–91), an Anglican clergyman and the founder of Methodism, spent much of his life travelling and preaching, supervising and inspiring his followers. His belief in the great power of music over men's hearts led him to compile tune books and hymn collections (1737, 1742, 1761 and 1780) in which popular or operatic songs in the fashionable *galant* style were adapted to religious words, a measure that not only won converts but ensured the superiority of Methodist congregational singing.

His brother Charles (1707–88), the celebrated hymn writer, had two musical sons, Charles (*b* Bristol, 11 Dec 1757; *d* London 23 May 1834), a minor composer and organist whose works include organ concertos and string quartets, and Samuel (*b* Bristol, 24 Feb 1766; *d* London, 11 Oct 1837), one of the most gifted of his day. Lacking a permanent salaried post, Samuel lectured, took pupils, played in concerts and held appointments as organist or conductor, also composing much church music, Latin (he was briefly Roman Catholic) and Anglican, and an important group of instrumental works in Classical style. Among his best pieces are the motet *Confitebor tibi Domine* (1799), the Piano Sonata in D minor, the four organ concertos and the remarkable Symphony in Bb (1802) and Concert Overture in E (*c*1834). He was the central figure in the early revival of Bach's music in England (from 1808).

Samuel's illegitimate son Samuel Sebastian (*b* London, 14 Aug 1810; *d* Gloucester, 19 April 1876), also a renowned organist, was the greatest composer in the English cathedral tradition between Purcell and Stanford. Despite his abrasive personality and outspoken views on the defects of cathedral music conditions, he held appointments at Hereford, Exeter, Winchester and Gloucester Cathedrals and Leeds Parish Church, concentrating his creative effort on service music (notably the monumental Service in E, 1841–5), imaginative anthems (*Wash me throughly, Thou wilt keep him, Ascribe unto the Lord, Blessed be the God and Father, Let us lift up our heart, The wilderness*) and devotional hymn tunes (especially *Aurelia*, 'The church's one foundation').

Westenholz, Carl August Friedrich (*b* Lauenburg, July 1736; *d* Ludwigslust, 24 Jan 1789). German tenor, composer and conductor. A singer at the Mecklenburg-Schwerin court, he became Konzertmeister and director of the Kapelle (at Ludwigslust) in 1767 and Kapellmeister in 1770. His principal works are German sacred cantatas; he also wrote an oratorio, other sacred music, vocal works for court occasions and a few instrumental pieces.

His first wife, Barbara Lucietta Fricemelica (1725–76), was an Italian soprano; his second, Sophia Maria (1759–1838), was a distinguished singer and pianist, and composer of songs and piano pieces. Among his children were an illegitimate son, Friedrich Carl (1756–1802), a cellist and organist; Friedrich (1778–1840), an oboist and composer of *symphonies concertantes*, songs and piano music; and Carl Ludwig Cornelius (1788–1854), a violinist, pianist and composer.

Westergaard, Peter (Talbot) (*b* Champaign, IL, 28 May 1931). American composer. A pupil of Piston at Harvard (1951–3), Milhaud at the Paris Conservatoire (1953–4), Sessions at Princeton (1954–6) and Fortner in Germany (1956–8), he has taught at Columbia (1958–66) and Princeton (from 1968). He has a predilection for clarity, projecting intricate musical ideas in uncluttered, unhurried, effortless-sounding surfaces. His operas include *Mr and Mrs Discobbolos* (1966); he has written chamber music.

Western Wynde. English song of the 16th century,

used as a *cantus firmus* by Taverner, Tye and others.

Westhoff, Johann Paul von (*b* Dresden, 1656; *d* Weimar, bur. 17 April 1705). German composer and violinist. One of the leading German virtuoso violinists of his day, he served at the Dresden court (1674–97) and later at Weimar. He is remembered for his unaccompanied violin music, a suite (1683, the earliest multi-movement work for solo violin) and a set of partitas (1696) involving imaginative polyphonic writing.

Westminster Choir College. School of music in Princeton, NJ. It was founded in 1926 in Ohio, for the training of church choirmasters, by J.F. Williamson, who in 1920 had formed a choir at Westminster Church, Dayton. It has influenced American choral music through performances, recordings, broadcasts and publications.

Westrup, Sir Jack Allan (*b* London, 26 July 1904; *d* Headley, 21 April 1975). English music scholar. He studied at Oxford and worked as teacher, conductor and critic, holding professorships at Birmingham University, 1944–7, and Oxford, 1947–71. He was head of the *New Oxford History of Music* from 1947 and editor of *Music & Letters* from 1959. His interests ranged from the Middle Ages to the 20th century, but most of his work was on 17th-century English music. He had a keen interest in historical method and was much concerned with the relationship of scholarship and practical music-making. He prepared many editions and while at Oxford revived a number of unfamiliar operas. He also composed in a variety of media.

West Side Story. Musical by Bernstein to a libretto by Sondheim after Laurents (1957, Washington, DC).

Wetzler, Hermann (Hans) (*b* Frankfurt, 8 Sept 1870; *d* New York, 29 May 1943). American conductor and composer. Born to American parents, he was brought up in the USA but returned to Frankfurt, studying at the Hoch Conservatory with Clara Schumann among others; he spent much of his career in Germany as an opera conductor. His works include an opera and orchestral pieces in Straussian style.

Wexford Festival (Eire). Annual (autumn) festival established in 1951. Three operas, usually unfamiliar, are performed in an 18th-century theatre; chamber concerts are also given.

Weyse, Christoph Ernst Friedrich (*b* Altona, 5 March 1774; *d* Copenhagen, 8 Oct 1842). Danish composer of German extraction. From 1789 he was in Copenhagen, becoming distinguished as a pianist and church organist; from 1816 he was professor at the university and from 1819 court composer, producing cantatas, Singspiels and songs and enjoying undisputed eminence. Among his most important works are the innovatory *Allegri di bravura* for piano op.51 (1796), the fine if traditional ensembles in his sacred cantatas and above all the songs, particularly the famous spiritual ones to texts by Ingemann (1837–8).

Whale, The. Dramatic cantata by Tavener to his own text compiled from *Collins' Encyclopedia* and the Vulgate (1968, London).

Where the Wild Things Are. Opera in one act by Oliver Knussen to a libretto by Maurice Sendak (1980, Brussels).

Whettam, Graham (Dudley) (*b* Swindon, 7 Sept 1927). English composer. Mainly self-taught, he has written in many media, producing vividly scored, exuberant orchestral music showing affinities with Bartók. Among his works are four symphonies, three string quartets and other chamber music.

Whip. A percussion instrument formed by two pieces of wood hinged at the base and slapped together. It is often used in orchestral music, notably by Mahler, Britten and Ravel, who opened his Piano Concerto in G with a whip crack.

Whistle. A short, high-pitched flute, either without finger-holes or with no more than one. The addition of a captive pellet or pea gives the familiar sound of the referee's whistle. Whistles of all sorts are known to all cultures from prehistoric times to the present.

White, John (*b* Berlin, 5 April 1936). English composer. He studied with Lutyens and at the RCM (1954–7). His first works were influenced by Messiaen, but that influence then extended towards Cage and towards such Romantic eccentrics as Alkan, Busoni, Liszt and Reger. His works include numerous piano sonatas as well as commercial music. *Machine for tuba and cello* (1968) lasts over four hours.

White, Maude Valérie (*b* Dieppe, 23 June 1855; *d* London, 2 Nov 1937). English composer. A pupil of Macfarren at the RAM (1876–9) and Fuchs in Vienna (1883), she wrote *c*200 songs to English, German and French texts.

White, Robert (*b c*1538; *d* London, Nov 1574). English composer. In 1553 he was in London; he then attended Trinity College, Cambridge (1555–62, MusB 1560). He was Master of the Choristers at the cathedrals of Ely (1562–6) and Chester (by 1567) and at Westminster Abbey (from 1570). His works include two fine sets of Lamentations, psalm motets and other Latin liturgical works, as well as anthems. His six viol fantasias are among the earliest known in England.

Whitehill, Clarence (Eugene) (*b* Marengo, 5 Nov 1871; *d* New York, 19 Dec 1932). American baritone and bass-baritone. After study in Paris he made his début in Brussels (1898). He sang widely in Europe, creating the title role in Delius's *Koanga* at Elberfeld (1904). He was often heard in Wagner at Bayreuth and Covent Garden. At the Met his pure phrasing and dignified style were admired from 1909 until his death.

Whiteman, Paul (*b* Denver, 28 March 1890; *d* Doylestown, PA, 29 Dec 1967). American bandleader. He was at first a viola player in the Denver SO and the San Francisco SO; in 1919 he founded his first band, and he toured widely with a large band from the 1920s to the 1940s. His first concert (1924, New York) included the première of *Rhapsody in Blue* with Gershwin at the piano. He appeared in numerous films and employed leading jazz musicians in his band, but regarded jazz devices as only one of many resources, moving away from jazz orthodoxy on to a more individual path, in particular in orchestral invention.

Whithorne, Emerson (*b* Cleveland, 6 Sept 1884; *d* Lyme, CT, 25 March 1958). American composer. He studied with Fuchs and the piano with Leschetizky and Schnabel. He lived in London (1907–15) before returning to the USA. His works include two symphonies and other orchestral pieces, songs and piano music, in a tonal style tinged with impressionism and ethnic elements.

Whittaker, William G(illies) (*b* Newcastle upon Tyne, 23 July 1876; *d* Orkney Isles, 5 July 1944). English music scholar. He studied at Durham University, where he taught, 1898–1929, and was noted for his conducting of Bach. He was professor at Glasgow University, 1929–38, and principal of the Royal Scottish Academy of Music, 1929–41. His writings include a substantial book on Bach's cantatas (1959); he was also a prolific composer and arranger.

Whole-note. American term for a semibreve; a note half the value of a breve, or double whole-note, and double the value of a half-note, or minim. *See* NOTE VALUES.

Whole tone. The INTERVAL equal to the sum of two semitones, i.e. a major 2nd.

Whole-tone scale. A scale that divides the octave into six equal-tempered whole tones: C–D–E–F♯–G♯–A♯(=B♭)–C or its sole transposition, D♭–E♭–F–G–A–B–C♯(=D♭). As all the intervals between adjacent degrees are the same, the scale is tonally unstable and it lacks the fundamental harmonic and melodic relationships of major–minor tonality (it has no dominant or leading note). It has therefore provided a means of suspending tonality, a characteristic exploited particularly by the French impressionists, notably Debussy.

Whytbroke, William (*fl* 1520–50). English composer. He may have been the 'Whitbroke' who was chaplain of Cardinal College, Oxford, in 1529–30 and later (1531–5) at St Paul's Cathedral, London. His music is in the florid pre-Reformation style, essentially non-imitative and with long, ornate phrases. His large-scale Mass *Apon the Square* features vigorous writing and phrases of *cantus firmi* moving freely from voice to voice. He also wrote a votive antiphon, a four-voice In Nomine and two English pieces dating from the reign of Edward VI.

Whyte, Ian (*b* Dunfermline, 13 Aug 1901; *d* Glasgow, 27 March 1961). Scottish conductor and composer. A pupil of Stanford and Vaughan Williams at the RCM, he was head of BBC music in Scotland (1931–45) and an enterprising conductor of the BBC Scottish Orchestra (1945–60). His large output, influenced by Scottish themes and folk music, includes the ballet *Donald of the Burthens* (1951).

Whythorne, Thomas (*b* Ilminster, 1528; *d* London, *c*31 July 1596). English composer. After studies at Oxford, he was a music tutor and visited Italy. By 1555 he was music master to the Archbishop of Canterbury (Parker), 1571–5. His *Songes* (1571) for several voices were the first single-composer secular collection published in England; a book of duets (1590) also survives. His autobiography (*c*1576) provides valuable information on musical life in early Elizabethan England.

Widerkehr, Jacques(-Christian-Michel) (*b* Strasbourg, 18 April 1759; *d* Paris, April 1823). Alsatian composer. He made his living in Paris as a teacher, cellist and composer. The most popular of his many instrumental works were his melodious *symphonies concertantes* for several wind instruments. He also composed symphonies, chamber works (mainly for amateurs) and a few vocal pieces.

Widmann, Erasmus (*b* Schwäbisch Hall, bap. 15 Sept 1572; *d* Rothenburg ob der Tauber, 31 Oct 1634). German composer and organist. A player of various instruments, he worked as an organist at Eisenerz, Styria, and then at Graz before becoming Kantor at Schwäbisch Hall in 1598–9. In 1602–13 he was at the Hohenlohe court at Weikersheim, then at Rothenburg ob der Tauber. He was active as a teacher and was also a poet. A versatile and prolific composer, Widmann wrote mainly in a late Renaissance polyphonic style, but sometimes used modern features such as homophonic or antiphonal textures. His output includes secular songs (on a wide range of subjects), German and Latin sacred works, instrumental canzonas and dances and a treatise.

Widmer, Ernst (*b* Aarau, 25 April 1927). Brazilian composer of Swiss birth. A pupil of Burkhard at the Zurich Conservatory, he went to Bahia in 1956 to work as a teacher, and has composed in various styles, influenced by mid-century masters and by the avant garde.

Widor, Charles-Marie(-Jean-Albert) (*b* Lyons, 21 Feb 1844; *d* Paris, 12 March 1937). French organist, composer and teacher. He studied in Brussels with Fétis (composition) and J.N. Lemmens (organ). He was organist at St Sulpice, Paris, for over 60 years (1870–1934) and professor of organ (1890) and composition (1896) at the Conservatoire, his pupils including Louis Vierne, Albert Schweitzer, Marcel Dupré, Honegger and Milhaud. As a performer he is remembered for his rhythmic precision and traditional interpretations of Bach, whose music he often used in teaching. Though he composed prolifically in many genres, he is best known for his organ music, most of it secular and conceived to make full use of the elaborate resources of the grandiose contemporary instruments, notably those of Cavaillé-Coll. He created the organ symphony, a decorative, powerful multi-movement piece that treats the organ as a kind of self-contained orchestra, using a wide variety of heavy technical demands. From the ten he composed (1876–1900), the most famous movements are the 'Marche pontificale' of the First and the Toccata of the Fifth.

Wiechowicz, Stanisław (*b* Kroszyce, 27 Nov 1893; *d* Kraków, 12 May 1963). Polish composer. Trained in Kraków, Dresden, St Petersburg and Paris, he taught at the conservatories of Poznań and Kraków. He wrote in a brilliant, highly accomplished style based on folk music, most of his works being choral.

Wieck, (Johann Gottlob) Friedrich (*b* Pretzsch, 18 Aug 1785; *d* Loschwitz, 6 Oct 1873). German music teacher, father of Clara Schumann. A largely self-taught musician, he settled in Leipzig, giving piano lessons and opening a piano factory and music lending library. His methods, derived from Logier but illustrated in his *Klavier und Gesang* (1853), emphasized concurrent instruction in theory, harmony and playing. His students included Bülow and Schumann, but his most successful pupil was his daughter Clara (1819–96); deep concern for her career may have been behind his near-fanatic opposition to her marriage to Schumann.

Wiegenlied (Ger.). 'Cradle song', equivalent of the English lullaby.

Wieland, Christoph Martin (*b* Oberholzheim, 5 Sept 1733; *d* Weimar, 20 Jan 1813). German poet. Active at Weimar from 1772, he became one of the most prominent German writers. His most important libretto was for Schweitzer's *Alkeste* (1773, Weimar); stories from his collection *Dschinnistan* (1786–9) were used in operas, including *Die Zauberflöte*. Also influential in music was his *Oberon* (1780), on which Weber's opera was based.

Wielhorski, Count Michal (*b* St Petersburg, 11 Nov 1788; *d* Moscow, 10 Oct 1856). Russian composer and patron. With his brother Mateusz (1794–1866) he did much to promote concerts of contemporary Western music (notably by Beethoven, Liszt, Berlioz and Schumann) in Russia.

Wiener Festwochen. *See* VIENNA FESTIVAL.

Wieniawski, Henryk [Henri] (*b* Lublin, 10 July 1835; *d* Moscow, 31 March 1880). Polish violinist and composer. After studying at the Paris Conservatoire he embarked on the career of a travelling virtuoso, giving concerts in Russia, Germany, Paris and London. At the bidding of Anton Rubinstein he settled in St Petersburg (1860–72) and exerted a decisive influence on the growth of the Russian violin school. Meanwhile he composed his best works, including the demanding *Etudes-caprices* op.18, the *Polonaise brillante* op.21 and his masterpiece, the Second Violin Concerto in D minor op.22. Further world travels, notably to the USA and Russia, and a period as violin professor at the Brussels Conservatory (1875–7) contributed to the breakdown of his health. One of the most important violinists of the generation after Paganini, he was known for the emotional quality of his tone. As a composer he combined the technical advances of Paganini with Romantic imagination and Slavonic colouring, showing Polish nationalism in his mazurkas and polonaises. His brother Józef (1837–1912) was an accomplished pianist who taught in Moscow, Warsaw and Brussels; their nephew Adam (1879–1950) was a director of the Chopin Music School in Warsaw.

Wigglesworth, Frank (*b* Boston, 3 March 1918). American composer. A pupil of Luening and Cowell at Columbia and of Varèse, he has taught at various institutions (including the City University of New York) and composed in a lucid contrapuntal style of European orientation. His works include stage pieces, masses, orchestral, chamber and vocal music. *Three Portraits for Strings* (1970) demonstrates his brilliant orchestral command.

Wigmore Hall. London concert hall (cap. 550), originally the Bechstein Hall (opened 1901, renamed 1917). Many musicians make their London debuts there. It is also used for recitals by established British musicians and visitors from abroad.

Wikmanson, Johan (*b* Stockholm, 28 Dec 1753; *d* there, 10 Jan 1800). Swedish composer. He was organist of the Dutch Reformed Church in Stockholm, 1772–81, and then of the Storkyrkan Cathedral. Influenced by his teachers Abbé Vogler and J.M. Kraus, and by Haydn and C.P.E. Bach, he composed keyboard pieces, three string quartets (1801), *c*30 lieder etc.

Wilbye, John (*b* Diss, bap. 7 March 1574; *d* Colchester, Sept–Nov 1638). English composer. He served the Kytson family at Hengrave Hall, near Bury St Edmunds, from at least 1598 until Lady Kytson's death in 1628, then moved to Colchester to serve her daughter. He was one of the first English madrigalists: his madrigals (*c*60 in 2 bks, 1598, 1609) range from light canzonets in Morley's style to larger-scale serious sonnets of great intensity; they include some of the most refined and superbly crafted of all English madrigals (e.g. *Adew, sweet Amarillis, Sweet hony sucking bees, Draw on sweet night*). He had a gift for matching textual mood perfectly with music, using pictorial imagery, and for varying textures and sonorities for expressive purposes. A few of his sacred vocal and instrumental pieces also survive.

*Secular music c*60 madrigals incl. Adew, sweet Amarillis, Draw on sweet night; inst pieces
Sacred music 2 anthems; 2 Latin pieces

Wild, Earl (*b* Pittsburgh, 26 Nov 1915). American pianist and composer. Egon Petri was among his teachers. He made his début with Toscanani and the NBC SO in 1942, soon becoming known in the late Romantic repertory (he revived concertos by Scharwenka and Paderewski). He made his London début in 1973. With a prodigious technique, he is a leading exponent of Liszt and Gershwin.

Wildberger, Jacques (*b* Basle, 3 Jan 1922). Swiss composer. A pupil of Vogel, influenced also by Boulez, he began teaching at the Basle Academy in 1966 and has written orchestral, solo instrumental and, notably, vocal pieces.

Wilder, Philip van [de] (*b* ?Flanders, *c*1500; *d* London, 24 Feb 1553). Flemish lutenist and composer. One of Henry VIII's most favoured and highly paid musicians, he may have entered the king's service as early as 1520. From 1525 he is frequently mentioned in court records, principally as a lute teacher, and in 1550 he became a man of property. He was esteemed for his lute playing but only one lute piece by him, an attractive four-voice fantasia, survives. Of his sacred vocal music, the five-voice motet *Aspice Domine* is a fine example of the expressive, richly textured, freely imitative Netherlands style. Over 30 *chansons* by him survive, some of them expanded and elaborated versions of music by other composers; others are arranged as instrumental solos or scored for voice and lute.

Wilder, (Jérôme-Albert-)Victor (van) (*b* Wetteren, 21 Aug 1835; *d* Paris, 8 Sept 1892). Belgian music critic, translator and writer. A passionate Wagnerian, he wrote for Paris journals, translated at least 500 German or Italian opera texts and wrote librettos.

Wilderer, Johann Hugo von (*b* Bavaria, 1670–71; *d* Mannheim, bur. 7 June 1724). German composer. He studied with Legrenzi in Venice and worked as court organist at St Andreas, Düsseldorf. By 1696 he was court vice-Kapellmeister. He moved with the Kapelle to Heidelberg and then Mannheim (1720), where he was joint music director. His output reflects the musical prestige and cosmopolitanism of these courts. His ten operas, mostly written at Düsseldorf, combine a Venetian style with French features and include colourful scorings. He also composed oratorios, cantatas, motets etc.

Wildgans, Friedrich (*b* Vienna, 5 June 1913; *d* Mödling, 7 Nov 1965). Austrian composer. A pupil of Marx and excluded from public office under the Nazis, he taught at the Vienna Academy from 1945. He composed in a style influenced by Stravinsky, Hindemith and Milhaud, using 12-note elements in a functional harmony. His large output includes much for his own instrument, the clarinet; his writings are on 20th-century music and include a book on Webern (1966).

Wildschütz, Der. Opera in three acts by Lortzing to his own libretto after Kotzebue's *Der Rehbock* (1842, Leipzig).

Wilhelmj, August (Emil Daniel Ferdinand Viktor) (*b* Usingen, 21 Sept 1845; *d* London, 22 Jan 1908). German violinist. He studied at the Leipzig Conservatory and in 1865 began a series of concert tours. His career encompassed orchestral leadership (he was Konzertmeister at the Bayreuth Festival in 1876) and teaching (violin professor at the GSM, London, from 1894). He was one of the greatest violinists of his day, noted for his technique, tone and poise.

Wilkinson, Marc (*b* Paris, 27 July 1929). Australian composer. He was a pupil of Messiaen in Paris and Varèse in New York. His work has been mostly for the London theatre and for films.

Wilkinson, Robert (*b c*1450; *d* ?Eton, 1515 or later). English composer. A lay clerk at Eton (1496–1515) and master of the choristers there in 1500, he contributed nine pieces to the Eton Choirbook. His nine-voice *Salve regina* is one of the finest pieces in that collection.

Willaert, Adrian (*b* Bruges/Roulaers, *c*1490; *d* Venice, 17 Dec 1562). Flemish composer. After studying law in Paris and music under Mouton, he was a singer in the service of Cardinal Ippolito I d'Este in 1515. In 1517 he accompanied Ippolito from Ferrara to Hungary, and in 1520 he transferred to the service of Duke Alfonso. In 1527 he was appointed *maestro di cappella* of St Mark's, Venice, where he remained for the rest of his life. He was one of the most influential teachers of his time, presiding over one of the major musical establishments of the period. Among his pupils were Rore, A. Gabrieli, Porta and Zarlino.

A prolific composer, he was one of the most versatile figures between the death of Josquin and the full maturity of Lassus and Palestrina. His output includes works in almost all genres of sacred music, French *chansons*, Italian madrigals and instrumental music.

His eight masses, mostly early works, are indebted to earlier composers, especially Josquin and Mouton. The six-voice *Missa 'Mente tota'*, for example, is based on a motet by Josquin. In 1542 he published 23 polyphonic settings of hymns, followed, in 1550, by a more important and influential collection of polyphonic psalms for double chorus. His greatest and most enduring works are his numerous motets. About 173 of these survive and many were published during his lifetime. The four-voice ones embrace a wide range of liturgical categories, from antiphon and respond to settings of the Mass Proper, and the early ones exhibit a range of contrapuntal techniques. The five-voice ones are often addressed to patrons or celebrate contemporary events. Nearly all of the six-voice motets are late works which feature canonic structure, the abandonment of *cantus firmi* in favour of a pure contrapuntal-harmonic structure, excellent declamation and shifts in sonority.

His numerous *chansons* range in style from canonic four-voice works to works in a freer, more flexible manner, but he does not seem to have contributed to the outpouring of Parisian *chansons* during the 1520s and 1530s. He published his first madrigals in 1536 and belonged to the first generation of madrigalists, having a special relation to Verdelot. His madrigals cover the genre's range of expression; those of the *Musica nova* (1559) virtually originate the sonnet cycle as a large-scale vocal composition, in which the madrigal adopts the serious modes of expression previously reserved for the motet.

Sacred music 8 masses; over 50 hymns, psalms; over 170 motets
Secular music c60 chansons; over 70 madrigals and other Italian settings; ricercares

Willan, (James) Healey (*b* London, 12 Oct 1880; *d* Toronto, 16 Feb 1968). Canadian composer and church musician. Trained as an organist, he went to Toronto in 1913 and taught at the conservatory and university, and was precentor of St Mary Magdalene. He became a leading figure in Canadian music. His works include much choral and organ music, imbued with Renaissance and plainsong influences and frequently performed in North America, as well as two symphonies and other orchestral scores in a late Romantic manner. His influence as a teacher was far-reaching.

Willcocks, Sir David (Valentine) (*b* Newquay, 30 Dec 1919). English conductor and organist. He was a chorister at Westminster Abbey, then studied at the RCM and King's College, Cambridge, where he was organist, 1957–74 (after appointments at Salisbury and Worcester Cathedrals); he made many recordings with the King's chapel choir. He was conductor of the London Bach Choir from 1960, directing annual performances of the *St Matthew Passion*. In 1974 he was appointed director of the RCM; he retired in 1984.

Will Forster's Virginal Book. English MS of keyboard music, consisting of 236 folios containing some 80 pieces by Bull, Byrd, Morley and others and some sacred pieces. It is now in the British Library, London.

Williams, Alberto (*b* Buenos Aires, 23 Nov 1862; *d* there, 17 June 1952). Argentinian composer. He studied at the Paris Conservatoire, returning in 1889 to Buenos Aires, where he had a decisive influence on Argentinian music education (at his own conservatory, 1893–1941) and worked as a conductor and composer. His works include nine symphonies (1907–39), most of them influenced as much by international as nationalist trends.

Williams, Grace (Mary) (*b* Barry, 19 Feb 1906; *d* there, 10 Feb 1977). Welsh composer. A pupil of Vaughan Williams and Jacob at the RCM, and of Wellesz in Vienna, she wrote mostly orchestral and choral music, influenced by Vaughan Williams and Elgar until the mid-1950s, when her writing became more individual. She is best known for her orchestral *Fantasy on Welsh Nursery Tunes* (1940) and *Sea Sketches* (1944).

Williams, John (Christopher) (*b* Melbourne, 24 April 1942). Australian guitarist. His family settled in England in 1952 and he played publicly in 1955; after study with Segovia he made a formal début in 1958. He has taught the guitar at the RCM (1960–73) and at the RNCM (1973). Many composers have written for him. He has toured widely and is interested in combining the guitar with electronics and drawing on popular and non-Western idioms; he founded a rock group, Sky.

Williams, Ralph Vaughan. *See* VAUGHAN WILLIAMS, RALPH.

Williamson, Malcolm (Benjamin Graham Christopher) (*b* Sydney, 21 Nov 1931). Australian composer. He studied with Goossens in Sydney and Lutyens in London, where he has spent most of his time since 1950. His earlier works lean either towards Messiaen and sometimes Boulez, or towards a Stravinsky–Poulenc kind of neo-classicism. Partly under Britten's influence, this dichotomy was resolved in his operas *Our Man in Havana* (1963) and *English Eccentrics* (1964). Later works include more operas, choral works (*Mass of Christ the King*, 1978), symphonies and concertos. In 1975 he was appointed Master of the Queen's Music.

Williamson, T(homas) G(eorge) (*b* London, 1758–9; *d* Paris, Oct 1817). English composer and music publisher. He became a music publisher after army service in India. His works includes sonatas, 'original Hindostanee airs' and other pieces for piano, songs to translated Indian texts and many writings.

William Tell [Guillaume Tell]. Opera in four acts by Rossini to a libretto by Jovy and H.-L.-F.Bis and others after Schiller (1829, Paris).

Willis, Henry (*b* London, 27 April 1821; *d* London, 11 Feb 1901). English organ builder. He was established in London from c1848. Though for most of his career he preferred tracker action, his engineering skill led to improvements based on pneumatic principle (e.g. thumb pistons for controlling groups of stops, 1851; use of tubular pneumatic action to allow the spatial division of large organs), which won favour with concert organists and architects. Tonally his organs were idiosyncratic, showing affinities with contemporary French organ building (brilliant reed stops) but also a characteristic variety of orchestral and accompanimental voices. His consoles were well built and simply laid out; from 1851 he often installed the concave, radiating 'Wesley-Willis' pedal-board. Among his most important organs were those for the Royal Albert Hall (1871) and St Paul's Cathedral (1872) in London and the cathedrals of Salisbury (1877), Truro (1887), Hereford (1893) and Lincoln (1898).

Wilson, James (*b* London, 27 Sept 1922). Irish composer of English origin. A pupil of Rowley in London, he moved to Eire in 1948. He has worked with Bartókian complex metres in operas (*Twelfth Night*, 1969), choral works, concertos and chamber music.

Wilson, John (*b* Faversham, 5 April 1595; *d* Westminster, 22 Feb 1674). English composer and lutenist. He joined the King's Musick as a lutenist and singer in 1635 and later moved with the court to Oxford, where he was professor of music at the University, 1656–61. He became a Gentleman of the Chapel Royal in 1662. Foremost in his output are his many songs, which range from tuneful ballads to serious declamatory settings; some were written for plays. He also composed psalms and lute pieces.

Wilson, Richard (Edward) (*b* Cleveland, 15 May 1941). American composer. He studied at Harvard and Rutgers and in 1966 began teaching at Vassar College. His works include string quartets, concertos and vocal pieces in a freely atonal but consonant style, of colourful harmony and expressive melody.

Wilson, Thomas (Brendan) (*b* Trinidad, CO, 10 Oct 1927). Scottish composer. He studied at Glasgow University, where he began teaching in 1957. His works, in a style of cosmopolitan modernism, include operas, orchestral and chamber pieces and sacred choral music; among them are *Touchstone* for orchestra (1967) and the opera *The Confessions of a Justified Sinner* (1976).

Winchester Festival (UK). *See* SOUTHERN CATHEDRALS FESTIVAL.

Winchester Troper. English MS dating from *c*996–*c*1050, by far the earliest known collection of polyphony. From Winchester, it contains, in 198 parchment folios, 174 organa, written by three scribes in English neume notation. It is now at Corpus Christi College, Cambridge.

Wind-band Mass. *See* HARMONIEMESSE.

Wind-cap instruments. Wind instruments on which the reed, usually double, is encased in a rigid cap; they include the crumhorn, the cornamusa and various bagpipe chanters.

Windgassen, Wolfgang (*b* Andemasse, 26 June 1914; *d* Stuttgart, 8 Sept 1974). German tenor. He studied in Stuttgart and sang with the Opera there, 1945–72, at first in the Italian repertory. From 1951 to 1970 he sang at Bayreuth, becoming the leading postwar *Heldentenor*. He sang Tristan and Siegfried at Covent Garden, 1955–66, with no great power but keen intelligence. After his retirement he produced a number of operas.

Wind machine. An instrument used to reproduce the sound of the wind. The commonest form consists of a barrel framework covered with cloth which rubs against it as the barrel is rotated with a handle. It can be heard in Strauss's *Don Quixote* and Ravel's *Daphnis et Chloé*.

Wind quintet. A composition for five wind instruments, normally flute, oboe, clarinet, bassoon and horn; also the ensemble that plays such a piece. The repertory belongs mainly to the 19th and 20th centuries and includes works by Reicha, Danzi, Nielsen, Milhaud, Hindemith, Schoenberg and Henze.

Windsperger, Lothar (*b* Ampfing, 22 Oct 1885; *d* Frankfurt, 29/30 May 1935). German composer. A pupil of Rheinberger and others at the Munich Academy, he worked for Schott for whom he compiled *Das Buch der Motive* (*c*1921), a standard source for identifying Wagner's leitmotifs. He wrote orchestral, chamber and choral pieces in a late Romantic style; some of his small piano pieces show a moderate modernism.

Winkelmann [Winckelmann], Hermann (*b* Brunswick, 8 March 1849; *d* Vienna, 18 Jan 1912). German tenor. A leading tenor of the first generation of Wagner singers, he created the role of Parsifal at Bayreuth (1882) and became the first Tristan in Vienna (1883).

Winner, Septimus (*b* Philadelphia, 11 May 1827; *d* there, 22 Nov 1902). American composer and publisher. He was largely self-educated but played several instruments and as a young man became active with his brother Joseph (1837–1918) as a music publisher. He wrote and published many simple instrumental pieces, made *c*1500 arrangements and issued cheap elementary instruction books. He is best known for his enormously successful popular songs (issued under the pseudonym Alice Hawthorne); his *Listen to the Mocking Bird* (1855) sold more than 20 million copies.

Winter, Peter [von] (*b* Mannheim, bap. 28 Aug 1754; *d* Munich, 17 Oct 1825). German composer. He was a violinist in the Mannheim court orchestra from a young age and became its director after the court moved to Munich in 1778, also conducting *opéras comiques*. He composed his first stage work in the same year. He became vice-Kapellmeister in 1787 and Kapellmeister in 1798. From the 1790s he presented operas in other cities, achieving his first major success with *Das unterbrochene Opferfest* (1796, Vienna). Later he composed mainly church music and taught singing; he was ennobled in 1814.

Winter composed over 40 stage works. The earliest are melodramas modelled on G. Benda's and dramatic ballets of the Noverre type. The operas, reflecting various influences, include examples of *opera seria* and *buffa*, *tragédie lyrique*, Singspiel and works following Mozart – notably *Das Labyrinth* (1798, Vienna), a sequel to *Die Zauberflöte* – and Gluck. They have a fine cantabile style, learnt from Salieri; the later works herald early Romantic opera in their large scene-complexes, chromaticism and varied instrumentation. Among Winter's other works are cantatas, lieder, instrumental pieces and a singing method (1825).

Winter Dreams. Sub-title of Tchaikovsky's Symphony no.1 in G minor (1866).

Winterfeld, Carl Georg Vivigens von (*b* Berlin, 28 Jan 1784; *d* there, 19 Feb 1852). German musicologist. He is remembered for his *Johannes Gabrieli und sein Zeitalter* (1834) and for his studies of

Lutheran church music.

Winternitz, Emanuel (*b* Vienna, 4 Aug 1898; *d* New York, 22 Aug 1983). American musicologist of Austrian birth. He studied law in Vienna and taught at Hamburg. After studies in music and instruments he went to the USA, where he taught at the Fogg Museum, Harvard University (1938–41), then worked in the instrument collection at the Metropolitan Museum, New York (curator, 1949–73). He worked on the history of instruments, instruments as and in works of art and musical iconography.

Winterreise. Song cycle by Schubert (D911, 1827), settings for voice and piano of 24 poems by Wilhelm Müller.

Winter Words. Song cycle, op.52, by Britten (1953), settings for soprano or tenor and piano of eight poems by Thomas Hardy.

Wiora, Walter (*b* Katowice, 30 Dec 1907). German musicologist. He studied in Berlin and at Freiburg, teaching at Freiburg (from 1946), Kiel (from 1958) and Saarbrücken (1946–72). He worked in many areas: folk music, aesthetics and the concept of music, periods and countries, genres (especially the lied) and species of music and composers (Josquin, Brahms). He tried to bring together systematic and historical musicology and to give a universal perspective to music history, relating folk and art music and abandoning European centrality.

Wirén, Dag (Ivar) (*b* Striberg, 15 Oct 1905; *d* Danderyd, 19 April 1986). Swedish composer. He was a pupil of Ellberg at the Stockholm Conservatory (1926–31) and of Sabeneyev in Paris (1932–4), where he became a neo-classicist (Serenade for strings, 1937). Later works include symphonies, chamber and piano pieces and light music.

Wise, Michael (*b* ?Salisbury, *c*1647; *d* there, 24 Aug 1687). English composer. He was organist and instructor of the choristers at Salisbury Cathedral from 1668, but often neglected his duties there after becoming a Gentleman of the Chapel Royal (where he had sung as a boy) in 1676. Shortly before he was killed (by a nightwatchman) in 1687 he had been appointed Master of the Choristers at St Paul's Cathedral. He composed mainly services and verse anthems with organ, which feature many melodic solos and ensembles for treble voices and show unusual qualities of pathos and expression.

Wishart, Peter (Charles Arthur) (*b* Crowborough, 25 June 1921; *d* Frome, 14 Aug 1984). English composer. A pupil of Boulanger in Paris (1947–8), he taught at the GSM and Birmingham and Reading universities and wrote neo-classical operas (*The Clandestine Marriage*, 1971), as well as orchestral and chamber pieces and much church music. His scores possess a strong, individual lyricism.

Witches' Minuet. Nickname of the third movement of Haydn's String Quartet in D minor op.76 no.2, derived from its driving nature and its harsh textures (canonic, in open octaves).

Witt, Christian Friedrich (*b* Altenburg, *c*1660; *d* Altenburg or Gotha, 13 April 1716). German composer and keyboard player. Trained in Nuremberg, he became chamber organist at the Gotha court in 1686 and Kapellmeister in 1713. He was esteemed as a keyboard player and a teacher. His vocal output comprises many church cantatas (in an old-fashioned style), some occasional pieces and *Psalmodia sacra* (1715), one of the most important hymnals of the period, which contains both new and borrowed tunes. Among his instrumental works are ensemble suites in the French style, Italianate sonatas and many keyboard works, including a passacaglia which was once attributed to Bach.

Witt, Franz Xaver (*b* Walderbach, 9 Feb 1834; *d* Landshut, 2 Dec 1888). German church musician and composer. A leader in the Cecilian movement, he wrote books, articles, music and two journals to spread the idea of German Roman Catholic church music reform, ultimately founding the Allgemeiner Deutscher Cäcilien-Verein at Bamberg (1869) and the Scuola Gregoriana in Rome (1880).

Wittgenstein, Paul (*b* Vienna, 5 Nov 1887; *d* Manhasset, Long Island, 3 March 1961). Austrian pianist. He made his début in Vienna in 1913 but the next year lost his right arm in the war. He soon acquired considerable virtuosity with his left hand and commissioned works from Schmidt, Strauss, Prokofiev, Ravel and Britten. He settled in New York in 1939, becoming an American citizen in 1946.

Wizlâv III von Rügen (*b* 1265–8; *d* Barth, nr. Stralsund, 8 Nov 1325). German Minnesinger. Prince of Pomerania and Rügen from 1302, and from a Slavonic royal family, he was one of the few noblemen to write and set not only Minnelieder but, like the wandering poets, *Sprüche*. Of his 14 Minnelieder and 13 *Sprüche*, 17 survive with melodies which, like his poetry, exhibit an independently artistic and highly developed formal sense.

Woelfl, Joseph. *See* WÖLFL, JOSEPH.

Woldemar, Michel (*b* Orléans, 17 June 1750; *d* Clermont-Ferrand, 19 Dec 1815). French composer. A pupil of Lolli, he was a violin teacher in Paris, director of a dramatic troupe and finally *maître de chapelle* of Clermont-Ferrand Cathedral. His works include violin concertos, duos and studies, a violin method (1798) and a musical shorthand method (1800). He also invented a 'violon-alto' with five strings.

Wolf. Term used for two unpleasing sound effects that may occur in performance. On keyboard instruments tuned in certain systems, the interval Eb–Ab has to be represented by Eb–G#, which may be unpleasantly ill-tuned (the chord is supposed to resemble the howling of a wolf). In some instruments, a faulty note due to an irregularity in resonance is called a 'wolf note'; it is found on many string instruments (usually, on a cello, around *e* or *f*) and on certain horns and bassoons.

Wolf, Ernst Wilhelm (*b* Grossen Behringen, bap. 25 Feb 1735; *d* Weimar, 29–30 Nov 1792). German composer. He studied in Jena, where he directed and composed for the collegium musicum. After periods in Leipzig and Naumburg, he joined the Weimar court as music tutor to Anna Amalia's sons. He stayed there, becoming Kapellmeister in 1772. As a composer he strove to create new modes of expression, and became widely known. His *c*20

Singspiels and other operas, written for Weimar and elsewhere, have a sensitive melodic style, sometimes with folk elements. He also wrote numerous sacred and secular vocal works, orchestral, chamber and keyboard works and books on music. His wife was the singer and harpsichordist Maria Carolina Benda (1742–1820); he was related to J.F. Reichardt.

Wolf, Hugo (Filipp Jakob) (*b* Slovenj Gradec, 13 March 1860; *d* Vienna, 22 Feb 1903). Austrian composer. He played the violin, piano and organ as a child and studied briefly at the Vienna Conservatory (1875–7, meeting his idol Wagner) but, lacking discipline and direction, he had to rely on friends and cultured benefactors for help and introductions. His first important works, the songs of 1877–8, arose from the effects of his sexual initiation and first romantic attachment. Some are bright, others agonized, reflecting his depression and illness from a syphilitic infection. Though in 1880 this cloud seemed to abate, a pattern of cyclic mood swing and sporadic creativity was already established. Holidays, studies of Wagner and radiant song settings alternated with personal estrangements and a dark, dramatic strain in his music. For three years (1884–6), he wrote trenchant musical criticism for the *Wiener Salonblatt*, siding with Wagner and against Brahms, meanwhile working on *Penthesilea* (1883–5) and the D minor Quartet (1878–84) and beginning a secret love affair with Melanie Köchert. Compositional mastery and a sense of purpose came only in the late 1880s, when he turned from subjectivity to imaginative literature as a stimulus. In 1888 Eichendorff's poetry and in particular Mörike's inspired a sudden flowering of song music that in profusion and variety matched Schubert and Schumann. His acclaimed public performances won new converts, and in February 1889 he finished the 51 songs of the Goethe songbook, in April 1890 the 44 Spanish songs. Publication and critical recognition turned his thoughts to opera but from 1891 physical exhaustion and depressive phases stemmed the flow of original music. In 1895 he composed his only completed opera, *Der Corregidor*, but it was unsuccessful; in 1897 he composed his last songs and had the mental breakdown that led to his terminal illness.

Wolf's strength was the compression of large-scale forms and ideas – the essences of grand opera, tone poem and dramatic symphony – into song. Combining expressive techniques in the piano part with an independent vocal line, and using an array of rhythmic and harmonic devices to depict textual imagery, illustrate mood and create musical structure, he continued and extended the lied tradition of Schubert and Schumann. Yet he was original in his conception of the songbook as the larger dramatic form; each one seems to have been planned in advance to represent a poet or source. Folk music, nature studies, humourous songs and ballads peopled by soldiers, sailors, students or musicians recur in the German settings, while religious or erotic themes dominate the Spanish and Italian songbooks.

Songs 245 published settings, incl. 53 of Mörike (1889), 20 of Eichendorff (1889), 51 of Goethe (1890), 44 in Spanisches Liederbuch (1891), 46 in Italienisches Liederbuch, i (1892), ii (1896); 103 unpublished or posthumously published settings

Dramatic music Der Corregidor, opera (1896); Das Fest auf Solhaug, incidental music (1891)

Choral music Christnacht, solo vv, mixed vv, orch (1886–9); 3 other acc. works; 12 unacc. choruses, mixed/male vv

Instrumental music Penthesilea, sym. poem (1883–5); Str Qt, d (1878–84); Intermezzo, E♭, str qt (1886); Serenade (Italienische Serenade), G, str qt (1892); pf variations, character-pieces

Wolf, Johannes (*b* Berlin, 17 April 1869; *d* Munich, 25 May 1947). German musicologist. He studied in Berlin and Leipzig and was professor in Berlin from 1907. He worked at the Prussian State Library from 1915 and was director of the music collections, 1927–34. A pioneer in source studies, he wrote two standard works on notation: *Handbuch der Notationskunde* (1913–19) and *Geschichte der Mensuralnotation von 1250 bis 1460* (1925–9). He also worked on the Ars Nova, music theory and Protestant church music and edited the works of Obrecht and others. His achievements lay behind the huge growth in medieval and Renaissance music studies over the last half-century.

Wolfenbüttel MSS. *See* MAGNUS LIBER.

Wolff, Albert (Louis) (*b* Paris, 19 Jan 1884; *d* there, 20 Feb 1970). French conductor. He studied at the Paris Conservatoire and in 1906 joined the Opéra-Comique as répétiteur, becoming musical director in 1921 and director-general in 1945. He conducted the French repertory at the Met and Buenos Aires opera houses. He was a dedicated exponent of the French music of his time, giving premières of works by Milhaud, Roussel and Poulenc among others.

Wolff, Christian (*b* Nice, 8 March 1934). American composer of French origin. He arrived in the USA in 1941 and associated with Cage in the early 1950s while studying classics at Harvard; he remained there as a teacher until 1970, when he was appointed professor of classics and music at Dartmouth College. His early compositions (*c*1950–57) are fully notated, and make much use of silence; in his next phase (to 1964) more choice is allowed to the performers. From the mid-1960s his works explore ways of giving freedom to the performer in 'parliamentary participation', allowing them to mould the music, latterly in an explicitly political programme of liberation (e.g. in *Changing the System*, 1973).

Wolff, Christoph (*b* Solingen, 29 May 1940). German-American musicologist. He studied in Berlin and Erlangen and has taught at Erlangen, Toronto, Columbia University and (from 1976) at Harvard. He has worked on early keyboard music and Mozart but is chiefly noted for his research on the style and chronology of Bach's music.

Wolff, Hellmuth Christian (*b* Zurich, 23 May 1906). German musicologist and composer. He studied in Berlin and Kiel and taught at Leipzig (1954–71). His numerous publications concentrate on the history of opera (particularly Baroque opera); his interest in the visual aspects of music led him to several studies of iconography, including a pictorial history of opera (1968).

Wolf-Ferrari, Ermanno (*b* Venice, 12 Jan 1876; *d* there, 21 Jan 1948). Italian composer of Bavarian-Italian parentage. He was a pupil of Rheinberger at the Munich Academy (1892–5) and spent most of his life near Munich or Salzburg, though with regular visits to Venice. Many of his operas were first performed in Germany, including his three semi-pastiches of 18th-century Venetian comedy (*Le donne curiose*, 1902–3; *Il quattro rusteghi*, 1906; *Il segreto di Susanna*, 1909). In *I gioielli della Madonna* (1911) he essayed post-Mascagni *verismo*, but later works return to Goldonian comedy. He also wrote orchestral, choral and chamber music.

Wölfl [Wölffl], Joseph (*b* Salzburg, 24 Dec 1773; *d* London, 21 May 1812). Austrian pianist and composer. Trained as a chorister by Leopold Mozart and Michael Haydn at Salzburg Cathedral, he taught music in Warsaw and won recognition as a pianist in Vienna and on tour (1795–1801), his skill at improvisation being compared with Beethoven's or C.P.E. Bach's. From 1805 he was acclaimed in England as a virtuoso and favourite composer. Some of his early piano sonatas, notably those of op.6 (1798), reflect Clementi; he also wrote two symphonies, seven piano concertos and much highly regarded chamber music. The later works, including the flute sonatas op.35, show his talent for meeting English amateurs' needs.

Wolfram von Eschenbach (*fl* 1170–1220). German poet who, on the basis of his epic *Parzival* (?*c*1200), is ranked as probably the greatest medieval German poet. He was named as one of the 12 'old Masters' by the Meistersinger, but no music survives for his seven extant lyric poems. Two melodies (from later Meistersinger MSS) are associated with him; that for his fragmentary epic *Titurel* (after *c*1217), is important as one of the few known examples of a melody appropriate for epic singing.

Wolf Trap Farm Park for the Performing Arts. National park near Washington, DC, opened in 1971, the only one of its kind in the USA. It includes the Filene Center (amphitheatre, cap. *c*6900) and a concert hall (cap. 350) in the Barns at Wolf Trap (opened 1982). Annual (summer) festival events include concerts, ballet and musical theatre; the Wolf Trap Opera Company (a summer training course) presents operas with established soloists.

Wolpe, Stefan (*b* Berlin, 25 Aug 1902; *d* New York, 4 April 1972). American composer of German origin and Russian-Viennese parentage. He studied with Juon and Schreker at the Berlin Musikhochschule (1919–24) and also benefited from contact with Busoni and from attending lectures at the Bauhaus. Up to 1933 he gave himself to the cause of radical socialism and wrote populist songs while using an atonal style for larger works. In March 1933 he fled to Vienna, where he had orchestration lessons from Webern. The next year he reached Palestine and wrote Hebrew songs influenced by local folk music, while subjecting his atonal style to rigorous discipline. In 1938 he moved to the USA, where he taught and continued to explore ways of achieving dynamism in an athematic, atonal style: the breakthrough came in *Enactments* for three pianos (1953),

followed by a succession of almost exclusively instrumental compositions of similar abstracted energy and determination. He had a substantial impact on some younger New York composers.

WoO. Abbreviation for 'Werke ohne Opuszahl' (works without opus number); it is used in identifying items by composers only some of whose works bear opus numbers, in particular Beethoven, following the numeration in the thematic catalogue by G. Kinsky and H. Halm (1955).

Wood, Charles (*b* Armagh, 15 June 1866; *d* Cambridge, 12 July 1926). Irish composer. He was a pupil of Stanford at the RCM (1883–7), where he taught from 1888; he taught at Cambridge from 1897 (professor, 1924). His output includes choral and theatre music, but he is chiefly remembered for his music for the church, organ preludes, anthems and morning and evening services.

Wood, Haydn (*b* Slaithwaite, 25 March 1882; *d* London, 11 March 1959). English composer. He trained at the RCM and in Brussels as a violinist. He made his name writing sentimental ballads (*Roses of Picardy*, 1916) but he also composed orchestral and chamber pieces.

Wood, Sir Henry J(oseph) (*b* London, 3 March 1869; *d* Hitchin, 19 Aug 1944). English conductor. After study at the RAM his early career was with minor opera companies. In 1895 he inaugurated the Queen's Hall Promenade Concerts remaining in charge until 1940. This series, later at the Albert Hall, was his greatest achievement. He helped to improve the orchestral repertory in London and gave early British performances of works by Schoenberg, Mahler, Bartók and Sibelius. Much of his career was spent in the provinces, directing choral societies in Norwich and Sheffield and raising orchestral standards. He fostered young talent and for 20 years worked with the students' orchestra at the RAM.

Wood, Hugh (*b* Parbold, 27 June 1932). English composer. A pupil of Hamilton and Seiber, he has taught at various institutions, notably Morley College (1958–67) and Cambridge (from 1976). He has composed within an essentially post-Schoenberg style broadened by influences from Messiaen and Gerhard. His works include concertos, string quartets and songs; among the best known is *Scenes from Comus* for soprano, tenor and orchestra (1965).

Woodblock. A percussion instrument, consisting of a hollow piece of wood, often with one or more slits for added resonance. The orchestral version is small and rectangular and related to the oriental temple block. It entered the West through early jazz and ragtime and soon acquired cylindrical and spherical form; woodblocks are often grouped in a series of four or five of varying pitch. (For illustration, *see* PERCUSSION INSTRUMENTS.)

Woodcock, Robert (*b* ?late 17th century; *d* by 1734). English composer and recorder player. His main work was a set of 12 concertos with solo parts for various wind instruments (1727–30), which achieved some popularity.

Wooden Prince, The [A fából faragot királfi]. Ballet in one act by Bartók to a scenario by Béla Balázs

(1917, Budapest).

Woodward, Roger (*b* Sydney, 20 Dec 1942). Australian pianist. He studied in Sydney and moved to Europe to study in London and Warsaw, remaining in Poland, 1965–71. His Warsaw and London débuts were in 1967, and he played widely, in Australasia, the Far East and the USA as well as Europe, sometimes presenting marathon programmes. He has helped found contemporary concert series in England and Australia. His powerful virtuoso technique and controversial style are heard in the traditional repertory (Bach, Beethoven, Chopin) and in avant-garde music; Penderecki, Meale and Brouwer are among those who have written music for him.

Woodwind instruments. Term for wind instruments (aerophones) whose air-column is set in vibration either by the impinging of a stream of air on an edge or by a reed. They may be made of wood, ebonite, metal (including brass, in the case of the saxophone), ivory or other substances. Different notes are obtained by the covering or uncovering of finger-holes, to vary the length of the vibrating tube; instruments can also be overblown (i.e. made to vibrate in sections, producing a higher note), normally by an octave or an octave and a 5th, depending upon the physical properties of the tube.

The principal instruments sounded by the player's directing his breath at an edge are the flute type, both end-blown (such as the RECORDER) and side-blown (such as the FLUTE itself). Instruments sounded by a double reed (two blades of cane bound together) include the OBOE and the BASSOON; among those sounded by a single reed beating against the mouthpiece of the instrument are the CLARINET and the SAXOPHONE. Among earlier reed instruments is the CRUMHORN, in which the reed does not come into contact with the player's lips; it falls within the category known as WIND-CAP INSTRUMENTS. The main woodwind instruments used in the modern orchestra are the flute (in several sizes, including the small piccolo and the large alto flute), the oboe (and the larger english horn), the clarinet (made in several sizes, notably the alto basset-horn and the bass clarinet) and the bassoon (and the double-bassoon, pitched an octave lower): see illustration, p. 838.

Worcester Festival (UK). *See* THREE CHOIRS FESTIVAL.

Worcester fragments. A repertory of more than 100 anonymous polyphonic compositions of *c*1225–1330, in 59 MS leaves in a fragmentary condition at Worcester Cathedral. Worcester may have been a major and influential centre of polyphonic composition. The repertory, which has interesting notational features, falls into five main groups. The earliest pieces are mostly two-voice settings of sequences, largely note-against-note. About three-fifths of the repertory, from *c*1270, consists of rondelli, motets on a *pes*, motets on a *cantus firmus* and troped chant settings, all to Latin (mostly Marian) texts; they confirm the loose distinction between conductus and motet in England and reveal the English predilection for homogeneity of style and the major mode. The next group (*c*1280–90) uses the same genres; but the two surviving, from *c*1295–

1315 and *c*1330, show more use of four voices, the increasing rarity of rondelli and the emergence of the three main types of English 14th-century polyphony – cantilenas, chant settings without textual tropes in the upper parts, and motets (especially *cantus firmus* ones).

Worcester Music Festival (USA). Annual (autumn) concert series founded in 1858 in Worcester, MA. Oratorios were given at early festivals, contemporary works from 1897. The Philadelphia Orchestra has appeared regularly, and in concerts with the Worcester Chorus.

Word-painting. The musical depiction in a vocal work of the meaning of a word or phrase, e.g. an ascending passage for 'exalted', a dissonance for 'pain'. Word-painting was a standard device in the 16th-century madrigal and was much used by composers up to and including Bach and Handel. Thereafter it became decidedly old-fashioned and only a few later composers (e.g. Haydn, *The Creation*; Brahms, *German Requiem*) were able to use it convincingly.

Wordsworth, William (Brocklesby) (*b* London, 17 Dec 1908; *d* Kingussie, 10 March 1988). English composer. He was a pupil of Tovey in Edinburgh (1934–6). His works, in a thoughtful and unspectacular diatonic style, include symphonies, concertos, string quartets and songs.

Worgan, John (*b* London, 1724; *d* there, 24 Aug 1790). English composer. A much-admired organist, he worked at several London churches and at Vauxhall Gardens, where he had numerous songs performed. He also composed oratorios, cantatas, anthems etc and keyboard works, in a conservative, late Baroque style. His brother James (1715–53) was a London organist and song composer, and his son Thomas Danvers (1774–1832) a composer and theorist. His grandson George (1802–88) was also a composer.

Work. American family of musicians. John Wesley Work (1873–1925) was a conductor, composer and tenor, who studied music at Fisk University in his native Nashville; he became a leading authority on black American music and conducted the Jubilee Singers. His wife Agnes Haines (1876–1927) was a fine contralto. His brother Frederick J. Work (1880–1942) was a composer and scholar who taught in the South and published several studies of black American folk music. John Wesley's son of the same name (1901–67) studied music at Columbia and Yale universities and taught at Fisk from 1933, conducting the Jubilee Singers; he was a prolific composer, of orchestral and other instrumental music, but chiefly of choral folksong arrangements based on black folk music, on which he was a noted authority.

Work, Henry Clay (*b* Middletown, CT, 1 Oct 1832; *d* Hartford, CT, 8 June 1884. American composer. A printer by profession, he was largely self-taught in music. His first songs appeared in the 1850s; more than half his output was written by 1866, the remainder during creative periods in the mid-1870s and in his very last years. He helped develop the verse–chorus form of popular song; best known

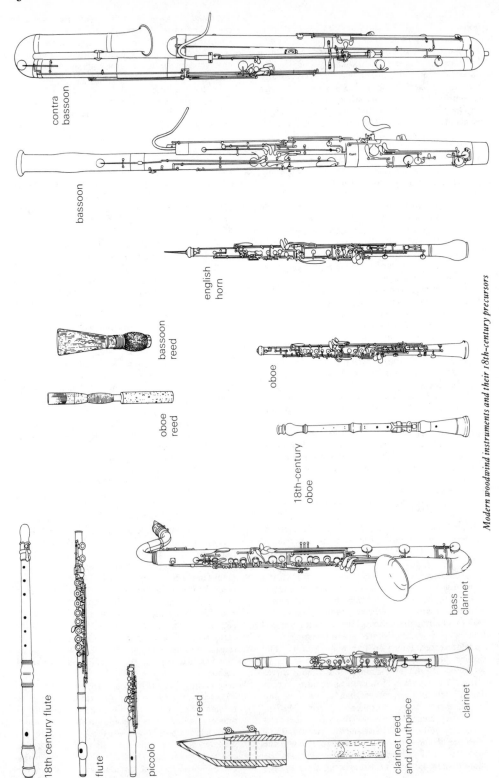

contra bassoon

bassoon

english horn

bassoon reed

oboe

oboe reed

18th-century oboe

18th century flute

flute

piccolo

reed

clarinet reed and mouthpiece

bass clarinet

clarinet

Modern woodwind instruments and their 18th-century precursors

among his songs are *Marching through Georgia* (1865) and *Grand-father's Clock* (1876). Many are dialect songs from minstrel shows, celebrating emancipation.

Worshipful Company of Musicians. English organization based in London. It grew from the London Fellowship of Minstrels guild (1500) and in 1604 gained control over music-making in and around London. Later it aimed to promote all aspects of music. It awards scholarships and prizes.

Woschitka, Franz Xaver (*b* Vienna, 1728; *d* Munich, 3 Nov 1796). Austrian composer and cellist. He served at the Schwerin court and from 1766 at Munich. An esteemed composer, he wrote viola da gamba and cello works and other instrumental music.

Woytowicz, Bolesław (*b* Dunajowce, 5 Dec 1899; *d* Katowice, 11 July 1980). Polish composer. He trained as a concert pianist, then studied composition with Boulanger in Paris (1929–32). He taught at the conservatories of Katowice (from 1945) and Kraków (from 1963). His comparatively small output of orchestral pieces, cantatas, songs, piano and chamber music assimilates new techniques but reveals formal control and emotional power.

Wozzeck. Opera in three acts by Berg to his own libretto after Büchner (1925, Berlin).

Wranitzky, Anton (*b* Nová Říše, 13 June 1761; *d* Vienna, 6 Aug 1820). Czech composer, violinist and music teacher, brother of Paul Wranitzky. In the 1780s he was a choirmaster in Vienna, where he studied with Mozart, Haydn and Albrechtsberger. He was Konzertmeister of Prince Lobkowitz's orchestra by 1790, Kapellmeister from 1797; later he was orchestral director of the Vienna court theatres (1807) and the Theater an der Wien (1814). A renowned composer, performer and teacher, he was a founder of the Vienna violin school; he wrote a violin method (1804), numerous violin concertos, many other instrumental works and a few vocal pieces.

Wranitzky, Paul (*b* Nová Říše, 30 Dec 1756; *d* Vienna, 26 Sept 1808). Czech composer. He was choirmaster at the theological seminary in Vienna and later probably studied with Kraus and Haydn. He became music director to Count Johann Esterházy *c*1785 and head orchestra director of the Viennese court theatres *c*1790. Both Haydn and Beethoven liked him as conductor of their works. Of his *c*20 operas, ballets etc the best known was his early Singspiel *Oberon* (1789) which influenced *Die Zauberflöte*. Foremost in his instrumental output are *c*50 symphonies and numerous chamber works; they include cantabile slow movements and have folklike elements in the minuets and rondos. He also composed concertos, divertimentos etc and a few vocal and keyboard pieces.

Wreckers, The. Opera in three acts by Ethel Smyth to a libretto by Brewster (1906, Leipzig).

Wright, Maurice (Willis) (*b* Front Royal, VA, 17 Oct 1949). American composer. He studied at Duke University and Columbia and in 1980 joined the faculty at Temple University. His earlier works are 12-note, but in 1978 he began using a more lyrical tonal style. His large output includes chamber, choral and electronic music.

Wroński, Adam (*b* Kraków, 1850 or 1851; *d* Krynica, 17 Dec 1915). Polish violinist, conductor and composer. He was an influential conductor in Krynica, Kraków, Kolomiya and Lwów. A prolific composer of light dance music, including waltzes in Viennese style, he was nicknamed 'the Strauss of Poland'.

Wüllner, Franz (*b* Münster, 28 Jan 1832; *d* Braunfels, 7 Sept 1902). German conductor and composer. He is chiefly remembered as conductor of the Munich court opera, where the premières of Wagner's *Das Rheingold* (1869) and *Die Walküre* (1870) were among his successes, and as director of the Dresden and Cologne conservatories. His son Ludwig (1858–1938) was well known as a singer and reciter.

Wunderhorn, Des Knaben. *See* KNABEN WUNDERHORN, DES.

Wunderlich, Fritz (*b* Kusel, 26 Sept 1930; *d* Heidelberg, 17 Sept 1966). German tenor. He studied in Freiburg and from 1955 appeared at the Stuttgart Opera, later singing with the Frankfurt and Munich companies and at Vienna. During his short career he was the leading tenor in Germany, with a well-formed voice, clear and firm of timbre. His singing of Mozart was internationally admired.

Wuorinen, Charles (*b* New York, 9 June 1938). American composer. He studied with Luening, Beeson and Ussachevsky at Columbia University, where he later taught (1964–71) before joining the faculty at the Manhattan School. His large varied output is mostly instrumental (he has written many concertos). It uses serialism and often deploys highly contrasting speeds as a means of shaping structure. He is a virtuoso pianist and conductor, and with Harvey Sollberger founded the influential Group for Contemporary Music (1962).

Wurlitzer. American firm of instrument makers and dealers. Started in Cincinnati in 1853 by Franz Rudolph Wurlitzer (1831–1914), it was directed successively by his three sons until 1941, when it moved to Chicago. From importing musical instruments it turned in the 1880s to marketing automated instruments, including disc-changer machines and coin-operated pianos; the 'Mighty Wurlitzer' theatre organ was introduced in 1910, followed by the successful coin-operated phonograph, or juke-box (1934–74). In 1909 the company began making harps; they were far more durable than European prototypes, and from 1924 to the 1930s eight acclaimed models were available. The firm's violin department, independently directed by Rembert Wurlitzer (1904–63) from 1949, became a leading international centre for rare string instruments. Among Wurlitzer's electronic instruments, beginning with electric reed organs in 1947, the most important have been the fully electronic organs, especially the two-manual-and-pedals 'spinet' type (from 1971 with synthesizer features) for domestic use.

Württemberg Sonatas. C.P.E. Bach's six keyboard sonatas W49 (1744), so called because of their dedication to the Duke of Württemberg.

Wycombe, W. de (*fl*?late 13th century). English composer. He was precentor and scribe at the priory of Leominster in Herefordshire in the later 1270s.

Some of his settings survive in the Worcester fragments. He wrote polyphonic alleluias; most are no longer extant though there is a list of them in the source of the famous Summer Canon. They are four-section settings; the second and fourth set, the solo portions of the respond and verse, each preceded by a free introductory polyphonic trope.

Wyk, Arnold(us Christian Vlok) van (*b* nr. Calvinia, 26 April 1916; *d* Bellville, Cape, 27 May 1983). South African composer. A pupil of Holland at the RAM, he taught at the universities of Cape Town (1949–60) and Stellenbosch (from 1961). His works include orchestral pieces, chamber music and songs in an essentially tonal style.

Wylde, John (*fl* 1425–50). English editor and copyist. He was either precentor or *Informator choristarum* of the monastery of the Holy Cross at Waltham and compiled, edited and copied (but did not write) music treatises. His manuscript (now in the British Library) seems to be a retrospective collection by a working choirmaster and is interesting for its discant treatises in Middle English and for its account of faburden.

Wyner, Yehudi (*b* Calgary, 1 June 1929). American composer. He studied at the Juilliard School, Yale and Harvard, and in Rome; his teachers included Hindemith and Piston. In 1963 he joined the faculty of the Yale School of Music. His earlier works show neo-classical influence; in later ones (for example the *Concert Duo* for Violin and Piano, 1957, the *Friday Evening Service*, 1963, or *Fragments from Antiquity*, 1981) a wider expressive range is found. He is married to the soprano Susan Davenny (*b* 1945), who made her New York début in 1972, her opera début in 1977 (New York City Opera, Poppaea) and her Met début in 1981; she has given many premières.

Wynne, David [Thomas, David Wynne] (*b* Penderyn, 2 June 1900; *d* Pencoed, 23 March 1983). Welsh composer. He studied at University College, Cardiff (1925–8), and began composing seriously only in 1944, at first in a neo-classical style, but from 1955 with increasing chromaticism. His works consist mostly of chamber and vocal music.

Wyttenbach, Jürg (*b* Berne, 2 Dec 1935). Swiss composer and pianist. A pupil of Veress at the Berne Conservatory, he began teaching at the Basle Academy in 1967 and has been influenced by Boulez, Huber and Holliger in his compositions (*Drei Sätze* for oboe, harp and piano, 1963).

X

Xenakis, Iannis (*b* Braïla, 29 May 1922). French composer of Greek parentage and Romanian birth. In 1932 his family returned to Greece, and he was educated on Spetsai and at the Athens Polytechnic, where he studied engineering. In 1947 he arrived in Paris, where he became a member of Le Corbusier's architectural team, producing his first musical work, *Metastasis*, only in 1954, based on the design for the surfaces of the Philips pavilion to be built for the Brussels Exposition of 1958. This, with its divided strings and mass effects, had an enormous influence; but in ensuing works he moved on to find mathematical and computer means of handling large numbers of events, drawing on (for example) Gaussian distribution (*ST/10*, *Atrées*), Markovian chains (*Analogiques*) and game theory (*Duel, Stratégie*). Other interests were in electronic music (*Bohor*, 1962), ancient Greek drama (used in several settings) and instrumental virtuosity (*Herma* for piano, 1964; *Nomos alpha* for cello, 1966). His later output, chiefly of orchestral and instrumental pieces, is large, many works from the mid-1970s onwards striking back from modernist complexity to ostinatos and modes suggestive of folk music.

Ballets Kraanerg (1968); Antikhthon (1971)
Orchestral music Metastasis (1954); Pithoprakta (1956); Achoripsis (1957); Duel (1959); Syrmos (1959); Stratégie (1962); ST/48 (1962); Akrata (1965); Terretektorh (1966); Polytope (1967); Nomos gamma (1968); Synaphaï (1969); Eridanos (1973); Erikhthon (1974); Empreintes (1975); Jonchaies (1977); Pour les baleines (1982); Shar (1983); Lichens (1984); Thallein (1985)
Choral music Polla ta dhina (1962); Hiketides (1964); Nuits (1968); Cendrées (1974); Anémoessa (1979); Nekuia (1981); Pour la paix (1982); Chant des soleils (1983)
Chamber music Analogique A, 9 str (1958); ST/4, str qt (1962); ST/10, ens (1962); Morsima-Amorsima, ens (1962); Amorsima-Morsima, ens (1962); Atrées, ens (1962); Eonta, 5 brass, pf (1964); Anaktoria, ens (1969); Aroura, 12 str (1971); Phlegra, ens (1975); Epeï, ens (1976); Windungen, 12 vc (1976); Ikhoor, vn, va, vc (1978); Palimpsest, ens (1979); Khall Perr, brass, perc (1983); Tetras, str qt (1983);

*c*25 works for 1–3 insts (1964–84), incl. Herma, pf (1964)
Vocal music N'shima (1975); Anakthos (1977); Ais (1980)

Xylophone. A percussion instrument consisting of a number of wooden bars of graduated length (for illustration, *see* PERCUSSION INSTRUMENTS). It is found in the folk music of many cultures. Its origins are unclear; its ancestry has been variously ascribed to Asia and Africa. The earliest written reference comes from Mali in the 14th century. African instruments range from primitive free-key xylophones, mounted over the players' thighs or laid over pits, to sophisticated models with fixed keys with or without resonators and suspended from frames. African slaves took the instrument to South and Central America where it is known as the 'marimba' and plays an important part in folk music. In Java and Bali a form of xylophone with keys resting on cloth and placed over a wooden trough is commonly associated with the gamelan ensemble.

The modern orchestral xylophone derives from the European instrument used by itinerant virtuosos in the 19th century. Its bars are arranged like a piano keyboard, suspended from cords passing through them, and mounted over tube resonators corresponding to their pitch. The compass is either four octaves from c' or three and a half from f' or g'. Saint-Saëns used the xylophone to represent the rattling of bones in his *Danse macabre* and in *Le carnaval des animaux*; Puccini used it to add oriental flavour to *Madama Butterfly* (1904) and *Turandot* (1926). It was first used non-representationally by Mahler in his Sixth Symphony (1903–4).

Xylorimba. A xylophone with an extended compass which includes the bottom notes of the MARIMBA; the normal compass is five octaves, $C–c'''$.

Xyndas, Spyridon (*b* Corfu, ?1812; *d* Athens, 12 Nov 1896). Greek composer. His clever and popular opera *The Parliamentary Candidate* (1867) was the first composed to a Greek libretto.

Y

Yamada, Kōsaku (*b* Tokyo, 9 June 1886; *d* there, 29 Dec 1965). Japanese composer. A pupil of Bruch and Wolf at the Berlin Musikhochschule, he conducted the first concert by a Japanese Western orchestra, in 1915. He produced a large output of operas, symphonic poems, choral music and songs, in a German Romantic style with Japanese inflections, laying the foundations for modern Japanese music in the European tradition.

Yamaha. The brand name of musical instruments (and also of motorcycles, sports articles etc) manufactured by Nippon Gakki, Hamamatsu, Japan. Founded in 1887 by Torakusu Yamaha (1851–1916), the company was named Nippon Gakki Co. in 1897, developing diversified interests. Its first upright piano was produced in 1900 and its first grand in 1950; later models achieved a considerable reputation in Europe and the USA. Wind-instrument manufacture began in 1965; with the merger in 1970 of Yamaha and Nikkan (brand name of the Japan Band Instrument Co. of Nippon Kangakki), the firm runs possibly the largest brass instrument factory in the world, making trumpets, cornets, flugelhorns, trombones, horns, euphoniums, tubas, clarinets, flutes, piccolos and saxophones. Since 1958 Yamaha has produced over 100 models of electronic instruments, including synthesizers and digital electronic pianos; in 1976 it became the first instrument manufacturer to develop its own large-scale integration chips.

Yamash'ta, Stomu (*b* Kyoto, 15 March 1947). Japanese percussionist and composer. He studied in Kyoto and in 1961 joined the Kyoto PO and the Osaka PO as percussionist, making his solo début in Milhaud's concerto (1963). He then studied in the USA, played jazz and appeared as a soloist. His *Fox*, for dancer, percussionist and tape, was televised in 1968; his virtuosity drew a new work, *Prison Song*, from Henze (1971) and several from Takemitsu and others. His own works (e.g. *Keep in Lane* and *The Man from the East*) draw on oriental, pop and avant-garde music systems.

Yampol'sky, Abram Il'ich (*b* Dnepropetrovsk, 11 Oct 1890; *d* Moscow, 17 Aug 1950). Soviet violinist. He studied in St Petersburg and in 1922 became director of orchestral and violin classes (later professor) of the Moscow Conservatory. He was the director, 1922–36, of the first Soviet conductorless orchestra. A founder of the modern Soviet violin school, he enriched Auer's principles and had many distinguished pupils.

Yansons, Arvid (*b* Liepaya, 1914; *d* Manchester, 21 Nov 1984). Latvian conductor. He studied the violin and made his conducting début in Riga in 1944. He later became principal conductor of the Leningrad PO and was chief guest conductor of the Hallé Orchestra from 1965. He was admired for his conducting of Mahler and his energetic performances of Russian music. His son Mariss Jansons (*b* Riga, 14 Jan 1943) is also a conductor, and in 1979 was appointed music director of the Oslo PO.

Yardumian, Richard (*b* Philadelphia, 5 April 1917; *d* Bryn Athan, PA, 15 Aug 1985). American composer. As a child he became familiar with his ancestral Armenian folk music but studied formally only from 1939. Influences on his works include Appalachian ballads and the techniques of Debussy and (later) medieval and Renaissance modality and polyphony. He devised a system giving rise to homophonic free chromaticism, as heard in his Violin Concerto (1949). His other works include two symphonies, an oratorio, sacred works, chamber and keyboard music.

Yehudi Menuhin Festival of Music (Switzerland). Annual (summer) event in Gstaad, established in 1956; concerts are given by members of the Menuhin family and others.

Yeomen of the Guard, The. Operetta by Sullivan to a libretto by Gilbert (1888, London).

Yepes, Narciso (*b* Lorca, 14 Nov 1927). Spanish guitarist. He studied in Valencia and made his début in Madrid in 1947 in Rodrigo's *Concierto de Aranjuez*, which he also recorded. He studied further in Paris and toured widely; a specialist in Spanish and Baroque music, he plays on a ten-string guitar of his own design. He has composed music for several films.

Yodel (Ger. *jodeln*). To sing or call using a rapid alternation of vocal register. Yodelling is performed in mountainous regions (notably the European Alps) and among the forest-dwelling pygmy peoples of Africa.

Yonge, Nicholas (*b* ?Lewes; *d* London, bur. 23 Oct 1619). English music editor. A singer at St Paul's Cathedral, London (1594–1618), he edited two anthologies of over 80 Italian madrigals with new English texts (*Musica transalpina*, 1588, 1597), which greatly influenced the spread of the Italian madrigal in England.

York Festivals (UK). Festivals were held annually in York Minster, 1791–1803, then occasionally to 1835. A summer festival established in 1951 (triennial; quadrennial from 1973) includes the York mystery plays and concerts. The annual (summer) Early Music Festival established in 1977 includes concerts by international artists in historic buildings.

Young, La Monte (Thornton) (*b* Bern, ID, 14 Oct 1935). American composer. A pupil of Leonard Stein (1955–6) and Richard Maxfield (1960–61), he also attended the 1959 Darmstadt courses, where he encountered Cage. His earlier works had been Webernian, but in 1960–61 he turned to minimalist music-theatre, and in 1962 began working with repetitive drone-based music in just intonation, performed in conjunction with light shows by his wife, the artist Marian Zazeela. Much of his activity since 1975 has been devoted to *The Well-tuned Piano*, a semi-improvisatory piece for piano tuned in just intonation. In 1971 he became director of the Kirana Center for Indian Classical Music.

Young, Lester (Willis) [Pres; Prez] (*b* Woodville, MS, 27 Aug 1909; *d* New York, 15 March 1959). American jazz tenor saxophonist. He played in various bands but his most important association was with Count Basie's (1934–44 with interruptions). After a traumatic period in the army (1944–5) he worked mostly freelance with small ensembles. Unlike previous saxophonists, he used a light tone, almost without vibrato, concentrating on clarity and understatement. The most original jazz improviser between Louis Armstrong and Charlie Parker, he had a lasting influence on later jazz musicians.

Young, William (*d* Innsbruck, 23 April 1662). English composer and viol player. He was in the service of Archduke Ferdinand Karl at Innsbruck by 1652, when he visited Italy with him. A renowned performer, he helped to popularize on the continent the English manner of playing the viol lyra-way. His music is mostly for viol; it includes fantasies in the English style and sonatas and dances reflecting German and Italian influences.

Young Person's Guide to the Orchestra, The. Orchestral work, op.34, by Britten, written for a film (1946); it is a set of variations on a theme by Purcell, often performed with a narrator.

Ysaÿe, Eugène(-Auguste) (*b* Liège, 16 July 1858; *d* Brussels, 12 May 1931). Belgian violinist, conductor and composer. He studied under Wieniawski at Brussels and Vieuxtemps at Paris, forming close ties with Franck, Chausson, d'Indy, Fauré, Saint-Saëns and Debussy. As professor at the Brussels Conservatory (1887–99) he initiated the Concerts Ysaÿe, appearing as violinist and conductor in contemporary French and Belgian music, meanwhile becoming renowned throughout Europe and in the USA (conductor of the Cincinnati SO, 1918–22); the shift to a conducting career was necessitated by his increasingly unsteady bowing arm. Idolized by a generation of violinists for his intense but poetic playing, he also composed with expertise in a post-Romantic style, notably for the violin (Six Sonatas op.27, eight concertos, *Poème élégiaque, Caprice ... Saint-Saëns*). His brother Théophile (1865–1918) was a well-known pianist who composed orchestral works, piano pieces and songs.

Yuasa, Jōji (*b* Kōriyama, 12 Aug 1929). Japanese composer. He is self-taught, though he associated with Takemitsu in the 1950s. His works cover many genres, instrumental, vocal and electronic (*Comet Ikeya*, 1966; *Love and Asura*, 1967), and he was one of the first Japanese composers to take an interest in *musique concrète*.

Yun, Isang (*b* Tongyong, 17 Sept 1917). German composer of Korean origin. Trained in Osaka and Tokyo, he taught in Korea, then continued his studies at the Paris Conservatoire (1956–7) and Berlin Musikhochschule (1958–9), also attending the Darmstadt courses. Most of his subsequent career has been spent in Germany. His music fuses avant-garde and Far Eastern thought: many of his works exploit instrumental virtuosity, in solo or concertante contexts, but he has also written Taoist operas (*Sim Tjong*, 1972).

Z

Z. Abbreviation for Zimmerman, used to identify works by Purcell by their numbering in Franklin B. Zimmerman's thematic catalogue (1963).

Zabaleta, Nicanor (*b* San Sebastián, 7 Jan 1907). Basque harpist. He studied at the Madrid Conservatory and in Paris, where he made his début in 1925. He is known in a wide repertory and has done much to promote the harp as a solo instrument. Ginastera, Milhaud, Piston and Villa-Lobos are among those who have written concertos for him.

Zacar. A name associated in various forms with two, possibly three, musicians of late 14th- and early 15th-century Italy, notably Antonio Zachara of Teramo and Nicola Zacharie of Brindisi (a singer in Florence and then in the papal chapel, 1420–24, 1434). Antonio Zachara's secular works were popular enough to be used in mass parodies and keyboard arrangements. Some of Nicola's motets are associated with the papal chapel; his works are generally more complex, with canon and isorhythmic techniques.

Zacconi, Lodovico (*b* Pesaro, 11 June 1555; *d* Fiorenzuola di Focara, 23 March 1627). Italian theorist. From 1575 a priest at Pesaro, he studied in Venice (1577–83), notably under A. Gabrieli. He sang in the court chapel in Graz (1584–90) and in the Munich Hofkapelle under Lassus (1590–96) before returning to Pesaro. His *Prattica di musica* (2 pts, 1592, 1622) is a comprehensive treatise for singers of figured chant; it misinterprets some earlier theorists, but is a valuable source on performing practice.

Zach, Jan (*b* Čelákovice, Bohemia, bap. 13 Nov 1699; *d* Ellwangen, 24 May 1773). Czech composer. He worked first as a violinist and organist in Prague churches. Leaving Bohemia, he became Kapellmeister at the Mainz court in 1745 but was dismissed in 1756. Afterwards he visited many courts and monasteries and spent time in Italy. His large output is varied in mood and reflects a transition from late Baroque style to pre-Classical; it includes masses, other sacred pieces, sinfonias and partitas (some in three movements), concertos, and chamber and keyboard music.

Zacher, Gerd (*b* Meppen, 6 July 1929). German organist and composer. He studied in Detmold and Hamburg and at Darmstadt, where he was influenced by Messiaen. He has held posts as cantor and organist in Santiago, Chile (1954), and Hamburg (1957) before becoming head of the institute of Evangelical church music at Essen. He has done much to promote the revival of the organ as a medium for avant-garde composers, extending the instrument's range of effects; he has written music for his own instrument and choral music for the church.

Zacher, Johann Michael (*b* Vienna, bap. 6 Aug 1651; *d* there, 30 Sept 1712). Austrian composer. He was Kapellmeister of St Stephen's Cathedral, Vienna, from 1679 until his death, and an imperial court musician from 1698. In 1705 he became court Kapellmeister (his successor was J.J. Fux). His output includes several Jesuit dramas and other stage works and many sacred pieces, some of them on a large scale.

Zachow, Friedrich Wilhelm (*b* Leipzig, bap. 14 Nov 1663; *d* Halle, 7 Aug 1712). German composer and organist. From 1684 until his death he was organist of the Marienkirche, Halle, where he also directed musical performances. He became an eminent teacher, numbering Handel among his pupils.

Zachow's main works are *c*100 church cantatas (about a third survive). These range from pieces with pure Bible texts in the tradition of the sacred concerto to the madrigalian cantata of the Bach period, and use a broad variety of musical forms. Foremost among his organ music are over 40 chorale-based fugues, preludes etc which show him as an important predecessor of J.S. Bach. He also composed other keyboard pieces and a few Latin sacred works.

Zadok the Priest. The best-known of the four coronation anthems written by Handel for the coronation of George II at Westminster Abbey in 1727; it has been sung at every British coronation since.

Zador, Eugene [Zádor, Jenő] (*b* Bátaszék, 5 Nov 1894; *d* Hollywood, 4 April 1977). American composer of Hungarian origin. A pupil of Reger in Leipzig (1912–14), he taught in Vienna and Budapest, then left Hungary in 1939 and settled in Hollywood as a film composer; he also produced numerous operas and orchestral pieces.

Zagreb Festival of Contemporary Music (Yugoslavia). Biennial (summer) festival founded in 1961;

events include opera, concerts and ballet.

Zahn, Johannes (*b* Eschenbach, 1 Aug 1817; *d* Neudettelslau, 17 Feb 1895). German music scholar. His most important work was the six-volume *Melodien der deutschen evangelischen Kirchenlieder* (1889–93), a compendium of almost 9000 melodies.

Zaide. Title given to an unfinished, untitled opera in two acts by Mozart to a libretto by Schachtner after F.J. Sebastiani's *Das Serail* (1779, Salzburg).

Zaïs. *Pastorale héroïque* in a prologue and four acts by Rameau to a libretto by Cahusac (1748, Paris).

Zajal. A Spanish strophic song with refrain. The word, of Arabic origin (Sp. *zéjel*), goes back at least to the 12th century. The *zajal* may have served as a model for early Iberian and European refrain songs; or it may have been modelled on an earlier European form. It provides evidence of an early type of traditional or troubadour-type song. The oldest surviving settings, in the 13th-century *Cantigas de Santa María*, are mostly in a form akin to the virelai.

Zajc, Ivan (*b* Rijeka, 3 Aug 1832; *d* Zagreb, 16 Dec 1914). Croatian composer. He was the most important figure in Croatian music from 1870, when he settled in Zagreb as director of the opera, conductor, teacher, organizer and composer, until his retirement in 1908. He favoured strong dramatic effect in his music (1202 opus numbers, chiefly stage works, vocal and instrumental pieces, choral music, songs and orchestral works), allied to Italianate rather than nationalistic melody. His most important opera is the historical tragedy *Nikola Šubić Zrinjski* (1876).

Zampa, ou La fiancée de marbre. Opera in three acts by Hérold to a libretto by Mélesville (1831, Paris).

Zampogna (It.). BAGPIPE.

Zander, Johan David (*b* 1753; *d* Stockholm, 21 Feb 1796). Swedish composer. He played in the Swedish court orchestra (from 1788, deputy Konzertmeister) and was a frequent soloist in Stockholm. From 1784 he was also a theatre music director. He composed several Swedish comic operas and other stage works, instrumental pieces and songs.

Zandonai, Riccardo (*b* Sacco di Rovereto, 30 May 1883; *d* Pesaro, 5 June 1944). Italian composer. He was a pupil of Mascagni in Pesaro (1898–1901), where he later taught. He followed the tradition of his teacher and Puccini in his operas, notably *Conchita* (1911), *Francesca da Rimini* (1914, his most admired work) and *Giulietta e Romeo* (1922), with piquant harmony and orchestration, sometimes using archaic touches to atmospheric effect, and much vigorous orchestral rhetoric, even if emotion is sometimes overstated. There is some harmonic exploration in *I cavalieri di Ekebù* (1925) but his later operas move to a simpler, more contemplative manner. He wrote instrumental music, notably a *Concerto andaluso* for cello (1934).

Zanella, Amilcare (*b* Monticelli d'Ongina, 26 Sept 1873; *d* Pesaro, 9 Jan 1949). Italian composer. He was a pupil of Bottesini and others at the Parma Conservatory, which he directed (1903–5) before becoming director of the Liceo Musicale, Pesaro

(1905–40). His early works are freakish, some unbarred; later he became more conformist.

Zangius, Nikolaus (*b* Mark Brandenburg, *c*1570; *d* Berlin, *c*1618). German composer. He worked at Iburg, (1597), Danzig (1599–1602) and Prague (1602–5, 1610–12) before becoming Kapellmeister to the Elector of Brandenburg in Berlin. In his secular ensemble songs (6 bks, 1594–1620) he adapted the Italian villanella style to German usage; sacred works (3 bks, 1602–11) and occasional pieces also survive.

Zannetti, Francesco (*b* Volterra, 28 March 1737; *d* Perugia, 31 Jan 1788). Italian composer. As a child he mastered the violin and other instruments; he became *maestro di cappella* at Volterra at 17 and at Perugia Cathedral in 1760. His output includes operas, sacred music, songs and many *galant* chamber works.

Zarębski, Juliusz (*b* Zhitomir, 28 Feb 1854; *d* there, 15 Sept 1885). Polish composer and pianist. He studied in Vienna and St Petersburg and for a year (1874) with Liszt, whose favourite pupil he became. He was the most original Polish composer of the second half of the 19th century, writing piano works that in their rich colour, advanced harmony, enterprising rhythm and exploitation of the keyboard extend the techniques of Liszt and Chopin. His finest work is his Piano Quintet op.34 (1885).

Zaremba, Nikolay Ivanovich (*b* Vitebsk govt., 15 June 1821; *d* St Petersburg, 8 Sept 1879). Russian teacher. He succeeded Anton Rubinstein as director (a notoriously conservative one) of the St Petersburg Conservatory (1867–71), his pupils including Tchaikovsky and the critics Laroche and Solov'yov. His brother Vladislav (1833–1902) and his son Sigismund (1861–1915) were musicians, working respectively in Kiev (on Ukrainian folksong) and Voronezh.

Zarlino, Gioseffo (*b* Chioggia, ?31 Jan 1517; *d* Venice, 4 Feb 1590). Italian theorist and composer. He was educated by the Franciscans and became a priest. At Chioggia Cathedral he was a singer (1536) and organist (1539–40) before moving to Venice (1541), where he studied under Willaert. From 1565 he was *maestro di cappella* of St Mark's; his pupils included Merulo, Diruta and Artusi. In 1558 he published *Le istitutioni harmoniche*, a landmark in the history of music theory; it aims to unite speculative theories based on ancient sources with modern compositional practices. The rules for practical counterpoint (deriving from Willaert) influenced many later generations of composers; those relating to tuning and temperament proved less reliable. He also composed *c*40 motets (2 bks, 1549, 1566); a dozen or so madrigals also survive.

Zart (Ger.). Delicate, tender, sensitive, subdued.

Zarth, Georg (*b* Hochtann, 8 April 1708; *d* ?Mannheim, after 1778). Bohemian composer and violinist. Trained in Vienna, he worked with F. Benda at several courts; from 1734 they served crown prince Frederick, following him to Berlin on his accession as king (Frederick the Great) in 1740. Zarth moved to the Mannheim court in 1757–8. He composed sonatas, trios, concertos etc.

Zar und Zimmermann [Tsar and Carpenter]. Opera in three acts by Lortzing to his own libretto after a play by A.H.J. Mélesville, J.T. Merle and E. Cantiran de Boirie (1837, Leipzig).

Zarzuela. A Spanish musical dramatic form with spoken dialogue. The name comes from Philip IV's hunting-seat near El Pardo, rebuilt in 1634 to put on spectacles of the type given at other royal centres. A play in the new theatre was called 'fiesta de la Zarzuela': though the name referred merely to locale, the word 'zarzuela' came to be adopted for a distinct genre. The remaining music (mainly by Hidalgo) suggests that the zarzuela was then predominantly Italianate, with recitative, arias, duets, four-part choruses and dances with popular songs between the acts.

Development came to a halt with the Bourbons' advent in 1700, but the zarzuela was briefly revived in the 1760s and 1770s by the dramatist Ramón de la Cruz with Rodriguez de Hita and other composers; on the death of de la Cruz the zarzuela was swamped by Italian opera and by the public's craze for the TONADILLA. Only in the 1840s, after the success of the one-act *El novio y el concierto* (1839) by the Italian composer Basilio Basili, did the zarzuela become a popular entertainment, partly spoken, partly sung, with a distinct national character. Popular airs and dances were an ingredient, audience participation was encouraged and plots ranged from farce to tragedy. The main architect of this new revival was Barbieri, who wrote over 70 zarzuelas. Other composers include Gaztambide, Arrieta, Chapi and Bretón. A deterioration in the early 20th century towards the revue sketch was for a time countered by a handful of talented musicians, among them Vives, Serrano, Guridi, Usandizager and Torroba and others of the next generation.

Zauberflöte, Die. *See* MAGIC FLUTE, THE.

Zauberharfe, Der [The Magic Harp]. Melodrama in three acts by Schubert to words by Hofmann (1820, Vienna); the overture is now generally but incorrectly known as Overture to *Rosamunde*.

Zavrtal. Czech family of military musicians. The most celebrated members were Václav Hugo (1821–99), a bandmaster at Milan, Vienna and Trieste and theatre conductor at Barcelona, Treviso and Modena, who was in close touch with Mozart's son Carl between 1848 and 1859; and his son Ladislao (1849–1942), a conductor and band instructor active in Glasgow from 1872, who composed six operas, notably *Una notte a Firenze* (Prague, 1872–3).

Zedda, Alberto (*b* Milan, 2 Jan 1928). Italian conductor and musicologist. He studied in Milan, made his début there in 1956 and taught in Cincinnati. He then conducted at the Deutsche Oper, Berlin, and New York City Opera. His critical edition of the *Barber of Seville* (1969) aims to restore Rossini's original; he made his Covent Garden début conducting it in 1975. Zedda is co-editor of the New Rossini Edition.

Zeitmasze. Work by Stockhausen for flute, oboe, english horn, clarinet and bassoon (1956).

Zelenka, Jan Dismas (*b* Lounovice, 16 Oct 1679; *d* Dresden, 22 Dec 1745). Czech composer. After serving Count Hartig in Prague, he became a double

bass player in the royal orchestra at Dresden in 1710. He studied with Fux in Vienna and Lotti in Venice, 1715–16; from 1719 he remained in Dresden, except for a visit to Prague in 1723. Having gradually taken over the duties of the ailing Kapellmeister, Heinichen, he was made only church music composer (1735); Hasse was the new Kapellmeister. He composed mainly sacred works, among them three oratorios, 12 masses, and many other pieces; his output also includes a festival opera (1723, Prague), six chamber sonatas for oboes (*c*1715) and other instrumental pieces. His music, like that of Bach (whom he knew), is notable for its adventurousness, its contrapuntal mastery and its harmonic invention.

Żeleński, Władysław (*b* Grodkowice, 6 July 1837; *d* Kraków, 23 Jan 1921). Polish composer. Apart from his cantatas and nearly 100 solo songs, he wrote four operas, becoming the foremost representative of Polish dramatic music after Moniuszko.

Zellbell, Ferdinand (*b* Stockholm, 3 Sept 1719; *d* there, 21 April 1780). Swedish composer. A pupil of Telemann, he was *hovkapellmäster* of St Nicholas's Church in Stockholm from 1750 and organist from 1753, and a leading figure in the city's musical life. He wrote an opera (1758, St Petersburg), cantatas, arias etc and various instrumental pieces. His father, Ferdinand (1689–1765), preceded him as organist at St Nicholas's and served in the Swedish royal chapel; he composed mostly instrumental music.

Zeller, Carl (Johann Adam) (*b* St Peter in der Au, 19 June 1842; *d* Baden, 17 Aug 1898). Austrian composer. He achieved his greatest success with the operetta *Der Vogelhändler* (1891), which revived the fortunes of Viennese operetta during the 1890s.

Zelter, Carl Friedrich (*b* Berlin, 11 Dec 1758; *d* there, 15 May 1832). German composer. Trained as a mason, he was a violinist from the 1770s. He became a highly influential figure in Berlin's musical life, notably as director (from 1800) of the Singakademie, which he made one of the leading choral organizations of its kind; he particularly promoted Bach's music. He established the *Liedertafel* (a men's singing society) in 1809 and an institute of church music in 1822, and was also a prominent teacher (Mendelssohn was one of his pupils). Foremost among his works are his 200 lieder, some of which have texts by his friend Goethe, who approved his settings above all. In some he used more varied forms, advanced harmonies and expressive accompaniments than were normal, approaching Schubert's style and strongly influencing other Berlin composers. He also wrote secular and sacred choral works, keyboard pieces and essays and letters on music.

Zémire et Azore. Opera in four acts by Grétry to a libretto by Marmontel after M. Le Prince de Beaumont's *La belle et la bête* (1771, Fontainebleau). Tozzi, Spohr and Garcia have also written operas on the same subject.

Zemlinsky, Alexander (von) (*b* Vienna, 14 Oct 1871; *d* Larchmont, NY, 15 March 1942). Austrian composer. He was a pupil of Fuchs at the Vienna Conservatory (1890–92). In 1895 he became a close friend of Schoenberg's; he also had encouragement from Mahler, who presented his opera *Es war einmal* at the

Hofoper in 1900. His orchestral fantasy *Die Seejungfrau* dates from these years. By this time he was working as a theatre conductor in Vienna; his later appointments were at the German theatre in Prague (1911–27) and the Kroll Opera in Berlin (1927–31). In 1933 he fled to Vienna, and then in 1938 to the USA. From the same background as Schoenberg, and similarly influenced by Mahler and Strauss, he developed an impassioned style in such works as his Second Quartet (1914), one-act operas *Eine florentinische Tragödie* (1917) and *Der Zwerg* (1922), and Lyric Symphony (1923). Later works, including the opera *Der Kreidekreis* (1932), the Sinfonietta (1934) and the Fourth Quartet (1936), are influenced more by Weill and German neo-classicism.

Zenatello, Giovanni (*b* Verona, 22 Feb 1876; *d* New York, 11 Feb 1949). Italian tenor. He sang in Italy from 1898, creating Pinkerton at La Scala in 1904. He sang Verdi's Riccardo at Covent Garden in 1905 and from 1907 his career was centred on the USA, particularly Boston and Chicago. His best roles were Don José, Radamès and Othello, which he sang with a warm, resonant timbre.

Zeno, Apostolo (*b* Venice, 11 Dec 1668; *d* there, 11 Nov 1750). Italian librettist. He was a leading figure in Venetian literary life and served, 1718–29, at the imperial court in Vienna, where he was succeeded by Metastasio. He wrote over 40 serious opera librettos (some in collaboration with Pietro Pariati), 1695–1734, and 17 oratorio librettos, 1719–37; most of those for Vienna were set by Caldara. Like others of the day, his librettos are closer to classical models than those of the previous generation; Metastasio's reforms built on this trend. In addition, Zeno's characters are more fully developed than was usual. He also left biographies and scholarly works.

Zheng [cheng]. A Chinese zither known since antiquity. In its standard modern form it has 16 strings, each with a small bridge, which are plucked with the fingernails of the right hand.

Ziani, Marc'Antonio (*b* Venice, *c*1653; *d* Vienna, 22 Jan 1715). Italian composer, nephew of Pietro Andrea Ziani. He was strongly influenced by his uncle. His first two stage works were adaptations (1674, 1676) for Venice of operas by Cesti and Draghi. Presenting over 20 of his own works there in 1679–1700, he became a leading composer of Venetian opera. He also served the Duke of Mantua and from 1686 was *maestro di cappella* at S Barbara, Mantua. In 1700 he went to Vienna as imperial vice-Hofkapellmeister; he won a high reputation and became Hofkapellmeister in 1712. Besides *c*20 more operas, he wrote 12 oratorios and *sepolcri* and many other sacred works.

Typical of Viennese court music, Ziani's works show a proficient technique and are often contrapuntal; many of his sacred works are in the *stile antico*. They also feature carefully rounded forms, motivic links and imaginative instrumental writing. The operas are notable for their effective characterization.

Ziani, Pietro Andrea (*b* Venice, ?before 21 Dec 1616; *d* Naples, 12 Feb 1684). Italian composer and organist. He was organist at S Salvatore, Venice, and was active as an opera composer from 1654. He was *maestro di cappella* at S Maria Maggiore, Bergamo,

1657–9; in 1662 he became vice-Kapellmeister to the Dowager Empress Eleonora in Vienna, where like Cesti he was a leading champion of opera. In 1669–77 he served as first organist of St Mark's, Venice, succeeding Cavalli. He then became honorary court organist in Naples, and in 1680 *maestro di cappella*.

Ziani's *c*20 operas reflect the trend towards the use of purely musical forms and have strong comic elements. He also wrote several oratorios (notable for their counterpoint), sacred and secular vocal music and sonatas.

Zichy, Count Géza (*b* Sztára, 23 July 1849; *d* Budapest, 15 Jan 1924). Hungarian pianist and composer. Despite losing his right arm at 14, he became a celebrated virtuoso and was a pupil and friend of Liszt. He was intendant of the Royal Hungarian Opera, 1891–4 (precipitating Mahler's resignation), and director of the National Conservatory, 1895–1918. He wrote piano works, notable for their use of left-hand techniques, choral and instrumental music, and five operas including three on the life of Rákóczy (Mahler refused to stage one of his operas in Vienna).

Ziegler, Christiane Mariane von (*b* Leipzig, bap. 30 June 1695; *d* Frankfurt an der Oder, 1 May 1760). German poet and cantata librettist. She published several collections of verse and other writings in 1728–39. Bach composed nine church cantatas (BWV103, 108, 87, 128, 183, 74, 68, 175, 176) to her librettos.

Ziegler, Johann Gotthilf (*b* Leubnitz, 25 March 1688; *d* Halle, 15 Sept 1747). German composer. He was a child prodigy and later studied with Bach (1715) and others. He became assistant organist at the Ulrichskirche, Halle, in 1716, and *director musices* and organist in 1718; he was also famous as a teacher. A leading Halle composer, he wrote many cantatas, other sacred works and three treatises. His nephew Christian Gottlieb (1702–after 1760) was a composer, theorist and organist in Quedlinburg.

Ziehrer, C(arl) M(ichael) (*b* Vienna, 2 May 1843; *d* there, 14 Nov 1922). Austrian composer. He was one of the finest Austrian march composers and chief Viennese rival to the Strausses as a dance composer. He also wrote operettas, notably *Die Landstreicher* (1899).

Zieleński, Mikołaj (*fl* 1611). Polish composer. He served at Łowicz as organist and director of music to the Archbishop of Gniezno, primate of Poland. The leading Polish composer of his time, he wrote two sacred collections (1611), each containing a cycle for the church year. His *Offertoria* comprises 56 monumental polychoral compositions, while the 57 pieces of his *Communiones* include the earliest Polish monodies and concertatos, some more traditional motets and three fantasias, the earliest Polish works specifically for instrumental ensemble. His music is typical of the age of transition from Renaissance to Baroque styles.

Zigeunerbaron, Der [The Gypsy Baron]. Operetta in three acts by Johann Strauss (ii) to a libretto by Ignaz Schnitzer after M. Jókai's libretto on his story *Saffi* (1885, Vienna).

Zigeunerlieder. Brahms's op.103 (1887), settings for four-part chorus and piano of traditional Hungarian texts adapted by Hugo Conrat.

Zillig, Winfried (Petrus Ignatius) (*b* Würzburg, 1 April 1905; *d* Hamburg, 18 Dec 1963). German composer. A pupil of Schoenberg in Vienna and Berlin (1925–8), he then worked as a conductor, mostly in Germany. He wrote 12-note works of all kinds in a style close to Berg. He also made a performing version of Schoenberg's *Die Jakobsleiter.*

Ziloti, Alexander Il'yich (*b* nr. Kharkov, 9 Oct 1863; *d* New York, 8 Dec 1945). Ukrainian pianist and conductor. At the Moscow Conservatory his teachers included Rubinstein and Tchaikovsky. He quickly became recognized as a leading east European pianist and after further study with Liszt toured in the West. He conducted in Moscow and St Petersburg in the early years of the century but in 1922 moved to New York, teaching at the Juilliard School, 1924–42.

Zimbalist, Efrem (Alexandrovich) (*b* Rostov-on-Don, 21 April 1889; *d* Reno, 22 Feb 1985). American violinist. He studied with Auer at the St Petersburg Conservatory. His Berlin and London débuts were in 1907. After his American début at Boston in 1911 he settled in the USA, teaching at the Curtis Institute (1928–68) and performing until 1949. His penetrating interpretations were noble and fine-grained, avoiding virtuoso exhibitionism.

Zimbelstern. A toy stop for organs, common in northern Europe from the 16th century to the 18th, consisting of a revolving star to whose wind-blown driving wheel a set of bells was attached.

Zimmermann, Anton (*b c?*1741; *d* Bratislava, 16 Oct 1781). Austrian composer. A violinist and organist, he was active in Bratislava by 1772 and in 1776 became Kapellmeister and court composer to Count Joseph Batthyany; the court orchestra reached a high standard under his direction. His compositions include many symphonies and other orchestral pieces, melodramas, and sacred works. At least two of his symphonies have been confused with Haydn's.

Zimmermann, Bernd Alois (*b* Bliesheim, 20 March 1918; *d* Königsdorf, 10 Aug 1970). German composer. He encountered the music of Stravinsky and Milhaud while serving in the army, and in 1942 was able to return to studies, with Lemacher and Jarnach; he also attended the courses given by Fortner and Leibowitz at Darmstadt, 1948–50, and most of his published works date from after this period. From 1957 he taught at the Cologne Musikhochschule. At first he brought together Stravinskian neoclassicism and 12-note technique, but in the mid-1950s he passed through extreme Webernism to a style rich in allusions and quotations, expressing an aesthetic of 'pluralism'. His main works of this kind include the opera *Die Soldaten* (1960) and the *Requiem für einen jungen Dichter* (1969); later his style became sparer. His output includes concertos (*Dialoge* for two pianos, 1960) and other orchestral scores and chamber music, these instrumental works often cast as imaginary ballets. His writings throw light on the state of composition in his day.

Zimmermann, Pierre-Joseph-Guillaume (*b* Paris, ?19 March 1785; *d* there, 29 Oct 1853). French pianist, teacher and composer. At the Paris Conservatoire he studied with Boieldieu and Cherubini. He was one of the most influential French keyboard teachers of his time, his pupils including Franck, Alkan, Louis Lacombe and Marmontel.

Zimmermann, Udo (*b* Dresden, 6 Oct 1943). German composer. He was a chorister in the Dresden Kreuzchor, studied there and under Kochan in Berlin, and worked as producer with the Dresden Staatsoper. His works, which have a strong dramatic element and are noted for clarity of structure and the occasional use of serial and aleatory techniques, include four operas, orchestral works (*Dramatic Impression on the Death of J.F. Kennedy*, solo cello, 1963; Timpani Concerto, 1965; *Choreographien nach Degas*, 1972; *Sinfonia come un grande lamento*, 1977) as well as chamber music and songs (including settings of Neruda).

Zinck, Hardenack Otto Conrad (*b* Husum, 2 July 1746; *d* Copenhagen, 15 Feb 1832). German composer and instrumentalist. After studying with C.P.E. Bach in Hamburg, he was a flautist at the Ludwigslust court, 1777–87. He then went to Copenhagen as accompanist in the court chapel, worked as an organist and teacher, and in 1800 founded a Singakademie. Much influenced by C.P.E. Bach, he composed German and Danish sacred music, cantatas and lieder, a Danish Singspiel (1790), six keyboard sonatas (1783) and other instrumental pieces. His brother Bendix Friedrich (1743–1801) was a violinist and keyboard player who served at Ludwigslust and toured; he too studied with C.P.E. Bach and wrote symphonies and sacred music.

Zingarelli, Niccolò Antonio (*b* Naples, 4 April 1752; *d* Torre del Greco, 5 May 1837). Italian composer and teacher. Between 1785 and 1804 he was known as a composer of *opera seria*, most of his works being based on mythological subjects calling for noble, heroic expression; his best-known opera, *Giulietta e Romeo* (1796), was a favourite vehicle for Maria Malibran until *c*1830. His secular cantatas show a similarly refined if conservative style. From 1804 he was a church composer (at St Peter's, Rome, then Naples Cathedral) and from 1813 a teacher and administrator of the Naples Conservatory, where his most famous pupils included Mercadante, Michael Costa and Bellini. Though his prolific and wide-ranging output of church music was functional and most of his instrumental music meant for teaching, certain works stand out for their musical interest, including the *Missa classica di requia*, the *Christus e miserere alla Palestrina* (1826) and the one-movement symphonies (*c*1815–*c*1835).

Zingarese, Alla (It.). In gypsy style.

Zink (Ger.). CORNETT.

Zinzendorf, Nikolaus Ludwig von (*b* Dresden, 26 May 1700; *d* Herrnhut, 7 May 1760). German Lutheran Pietist, founder in 1722 of the Renewed Moravian Church. The Moravian Church began among Moravian refugees on his estate in Upper Lusatia. A bishop of the church from 1727, he encouraged the use of music in services and wrote some 2000 Moravian hymns, many of which were sung to German chorale tunes.

Zipoli, Domenico (*b* Prato, 16/17 Oct 1688; *d* Santa Catalina, Argentina, 2 Jan 1726). Italian organist and composer. He studied in Italy with Alessandro Scarlatti, Bernardo Pasquini and others, and had two oratorios performed in Rome, where he became organist of the Jesuit church in 1715. In 1716 he published his collection *Sonate d'intavolatura*, which was widely popular for its charming, tuneful style; it contains both organ and harpsichord pieces. Recruited by the Jesuits for work in the New World, he went to Córdoba in 1717 and studied for the priesthood (but died before ordination). His masses, motets etc were much in demand in South America.

Zirler, Stephan (*b* Rohr, *c*1518; *d* Heidelberg, 1568). German composer. He worked and studied in Heidelberg, where he became an official at the Palatine court. His extant works comprise 23 German songs on tenor *cantus firmi*, popular in their day, and a four-voice motet.

Zirra, Alexandru (*b* Roman, 14 July 1883; *d* Sibiu, 23 March 1946). Romanian composer. A pupil of Gatti at the Milan Conservatory (1905–11), he taught at Iaşi and Cernăuţi, establishing a reputation as a remarkable teacher. His works include nationalist operas and symphonic poems.

Zither. In its original and most familiar sense the word refers to a group of Alpine folk and popular instruments. They consist of a box mounted with fretted melody strings and open strings; they were developed from rural instruments in the 1830s. The most familiar form is the Salzburg model in the shape of a rectangle with a semi-circular projection and resonating holes cut into its body. It has five melody strings fingered with the left hand and plucked with a plectrum attached to the right thumb.

The term 'zither' is also used generically to denote any instrument consisting of a resonator and a detachable body of strings. The term excludes all harps, lutes and lyres but encompasses a large variety of string instruments of all cultures, including dulcimers, harpsichords and pianos.

Znamenniy. A type of Russian liturgical chant, in use from the Middle Ages to the Baroque era; the term derives from the Russian word for neume.

Zoilo, Annibale (*b* Rome, *c*1537; *d* Loreto, 1592). Italian composer. He was choirmaster of S Luigi dei Francesi (1561–6) and St John Lateran (1567–70), Rome, and sang in the Sistine Chapel choir (1570–77), before serving at Todi Cathedral (1581–4) and the Santa Casa, Loreto (1584–92). In 1577–8 he worked with Palestrina revising Roman chant books. His masses, motets etc and madrigals (1563) are in the Palestrinian style. His son Cesare (1584–after 1622), a *maestro di cappella* in Rome, composed madrigals and motets.

Zöllner, Heinrich (*b* Leipzig, 4 July 1854; *d* Freiburg, 8 May 1941). German conductor and composer. He studied at the Leipzig Conservatory and from 1885 taught at the Cologne Conservatory; he conducted male choral societies in Germany and the

USA and the Flemish Opera in Antwerp (1907–14). A prolific composer, he wrote ten operas, notably *Die versunkene Glocke* (1899), choral and orchestral works and male choruses. His father Carl Friedrich (1800–1860) was the leading figure of the popular male-chorus movement in mid-19th-century Germany.

Zoppa, Alla (It.: 'halting', 'limping'). Term applied to a rhythm in which the second quaver in a bar of 2/4 time is accentuated, typical of some Hungarian dances and of American ragtime.

Zoras, Leonidas (*b* Sparta, 23 Feb 1905). Greek composer and conductor. He studied in Athens and Berlin, conducted the Greek National State Opera (1948–58) and in Berlin (1958–68) and became director of the Athens National Conservatory in 1968. His early works show a Ravelian treatment of folk material but later ones are more atonal; they include many songs.

Zoroastre. *Tragédie en musique* in five acts by Rameau to a libretto by Cahusac (1749, Paris).

Zuccari, Carlo (*b* Casalmaggiore, 10 Nov 1704; *d* there, 3 May 1792). Italian violinist and composer. He worked from 1741 in Milan, where he played under G.B. Sammartini. About 1760 he was in London, where he published 12 violin adagios in plain and ornamented versions (as *The True Method of Playing an Adagio*); later he returned to Italy. He also composed violin sonatas and concertos.

Zucchini, Gregorio (*b* Brescia, *c*1550; *d c*1616). Italian composer. He was a monk in Venice and also spent time in Rome. He composed many sacred works which gained him renown abroad. His first collection (1602), of polychoral motets and masses, shows him as one of the most important and skilful emulators of Giovanni Gabrieli; his other works are mainly for four to seven voices and in the traditional *stile antico*.

Zukerman, Pinchas (*b* Tel-Aviv, 16 July 1948). Israeli violinist. On Stern's recommendation he entered the Juilliard School, New York, and in 1967 was joint winner of the Leventritt Competition. His New York and London débuts were in 1969. He is admired for his expressive phrasing and brilliant technique, often heard in partnership with Barenboim and Perlman. He has conducted since 1971.

Zumaya, Manuel de (*b* Mexico, *c*1678; *d* Oaxaca, March–May 1756). Mexican composer. He studied in Mexico City under Salazar and Ydíaquez and by 1708 was an organist at the cathedral. His three-act opera *Partenope* was given in 1711, the earliest known full opera produced in North America. He became *maestro de capilla* at Mexico City Cathedral in 1715, moving to Oaxaca in 1739. His works include sacred music and villancico-cantatas, noted for their florid Italian style and graceful writing.

Zumpe, Hermann (*b* Oppach, 9 April 1850; *d* Munich, 4 Sept 1903). German conductor and composer. He travelled widely and held important positions in Stuttgart, Schwerin and Munich. He was highly regarded as a Wagner conductor, comparable with Richter, Mottl and Levi, first appearing in Bayreuth in 1872. His operas show Wagner's influence.

Zumpe, Johannes (*fl* 1735–83). English harpsichord and piano maker of German origin. He emigrated to London after the Seven Years War and worked briefly for Shudi before setting up his own shop in 1761 (until 1783). Though he made a few harpsichords and guitars, he is best known for his square pianos. The earliest surviving one (1766) resembles a clavichord and exemplifies the 'English single action'. Normally the soundboards are small and the scaling of the lower strings restricted; the hammers are light and the dynamic range not great. In 1768, on his own Zumpe square, J.C. Bach gave the first solo piano performance in England.

Zumsteeg, Johann Rudolf (*b* Sachsenflur, 10 Jan 1760; *d* Stuttgart, 27 Jan 1802). German composer. Trained at the Stuttgart court, he became solo cellist there in 1781 and in 1793 court Konzertmeister. Foremost in his output are his *c*300 lieder and ballads, which, midway between the Berlin school and Schubert (whom they strongly influenced), are notable for their interpretative word-setting and adventurous harmonies. Many are simple lyrical settings in strophic form, while some of the ballads are long, sectional dramatic pieces using recitative and descriptive accompaniments. Among his 12 operas, Singspiels etc, the earliest show Jommelli's influence; the later stage works, notably the duodrama *Tamira* (1788, Stuttgart), use melodrama technique, following G. Benda's *Ariadne*. Zumsteeg also composed incidental music, choral works and instrumental pieces.

Zupko, Ramon (*b* Pittsburgh, 14 Nov 1932). American composer. He was at the Juilliard School and in Vienna and later studied electronic music at Columbia and in Utrecht. In 1971 he joined the faculty at Western Michigan University, Kalamazoo. His works include mixed-media, orchestral, chamber and electronic pieces, often in response to literary images.

Zūrnā. Folk oboe of the Arab world, in the form of a conical wooden tube played with a double reed. Its tone is powerful and strident.

Zweers, Bernard (*b* Amsterdam, 18 May 1854; *d* there, 9 Dec 1924). Dutch composer. He studied in Leipzig and became professor at the Amsterdam Conservatory (1895–1922). He cultivated a personal, selfconsciously Dutch musical style, notably in the folklike melodies and thick chordal writing of his third Symphony, *Aan mijn vaderland* (1890).

Zwick, Johannes (*b* Konstanz, *c*1496; *d* Bischofszell, 23 Oct 1542). Swiss hymn writer. He studied in Bologna and Siena and taught at Basle University. A follower of Luther, he wrote 23 hymn texts, most set to well-known tunes; seven of the melodies may have been composed by Zwick himself.

Zwilich, Ellen Taaffe (*b* Miami, 30 April 1939). American composer. She was a pupil of Carter and Sessions at the Juilliard School. Her works include two symphonies, a piano concerto and chamber music, characterized by long melodic lines, compelling rhythms and fine instrumentation, especially for strings. She was the first woman to receive a Pulitzer Prize (for Symphony no.1, 1983).

Zwillingsbrüder, Die [The Twin Brothers]. Singspiel in one act by Schubert to a libretto by G.E. Hoffmann (1820, Vienna).

Zwingli, Ulrich (*b* Wildhaus, 1 Jan 1484; *d* Cappel, 11 Oct 1531). Swiss humanist and church reformer. He studied in Basle, Berne and Vienna and worked in Zurich. Of all the 16th-century reformers he was the most musically gifted and yet the most antagonistic towards the use of music in public worship. Under the influence of his radical vernacular liturgy of 1525, ritual and ceremony were reduced to a minimum and music was excluded. Three complete song settings by him survive and he is said to have composed a four-voice Cappel song, *Herr, nun heb den Wagen selb* (only the melody survives).

Zwyssig, Alberik (**Johann Josef Maria**) (*b* Bauen, 17 Nov 1808; *d* Mehrerau, 19 Nov 1854). Swiss composer. A Cistercian monk, he wrote *c*80 pieces, chiefly sacred choral works and simple songs; his popular 'Swiss psalm' *Trittst im Morgenrot daher* (1841) became the Swiss national anthem.

Żywny, Wojciech [**Adalbert**] (*b* Bohemia, 13 May 1756; *d* Warsaw, 21 Feb 1842). Polish piano teacher of Bohemian origin. His most famous pupil was Chopin, whom he taught from 1816 to 1822.